The Laser Video Disc Companion

Updated Edition

A guide to <u>the</u> high-end delivery system for home video.

by Douglas Pratt

New York Zoetrope

The
Laser Video Disc
Companion
Updated Edition

Library of Congress Catalog Card Number: 91-67114

ISBN 0-918432-89-8

New York Zoetrope
838 Broadway
New York NY 10003

The text of this book is set in Times Roman, Helevtica Bold, and Bodoni Poster.
The QuarkXPress files were output by Southern California PrintCorp.
Printed and bound by Edwards Brothers Incorporated.

Production and design: David Henry

Printed in the United States of America
First Printing: January 1992

5 4 3 2 1

Table of Contents

for Loretta

Introduction

WHAT IT MEANS TO OWN A MOVIE

In the same spirit with which Hollywood epics about ancient Egypt mingled styles of apparel or cultural rites historically separated by hundreds of years, so, too, will future generations look at the Twentieth Century and miss the nuances. The sixty years it took to go from Kitty Hawk to the moon will seem like an instant. School children will get the order of development wrong on tests. They will grow up, go to Hollywood, and get the order wrong there, as well.

Visual entertainment, during the same eons that man remained flightless, was limited to live human beings acting out fantasies for all who would pause to watch. Then, suddenly, the retention and exposition of these fantasies became possible through technology, first in silent black-and-white, then with sound in black-and-white and then with sound in color. In the home, sound was first, but in a generation it, too, was followed by black-and-white, and then color images.

Movies offer the ability to replay a dream at will; to trust the reliability of characters who will always do the same thing in the same way; to share in the heroism, the voyeurism, the terror and the comedy; and to learn through repeated exposure. They let you participate from a safe distance, and it should not be discounted that the best movies are artistic, giving one the complex fulfillment which art instills. A well-made film can provide the discovery of patterns in existence and the interpretation of the intangible through a language involving both sight and sound.

Even the wealthiest individuals cannot buy what doesn't exist. Thus it was, even a year before the advent of home video, that a movie 'fan' could only dream of owning a favorite film, or spend hundreds of dollars for a used 35mm print and suffer the efforts of cranking the thing through a bulky projection system. Technology, however, is the arch rival of inflation. Today, the same fan can own dozens of movies for what one movie used to cost. Tomorrow, the days when movies couldn't be owned by the masses and when unseen authority figures provided the only choices for entertainment on television will be as forgotten as the 15-stop cross country flight.

Since the advent of home video, it is difficult to imagine how one got along without it. A disorganized committee stood between the artist and the viewer, dictating show times, commercial slots, or the company one had to keep during the viewing. By watching a movie you are consigning a certain percentage of your senses, your emotions, and your mind to a calculated set of manipulations. The more freedom you have to choose what those manipulations will be, the better you can tailor the stimuli to suit your feelings.

It is the laser video disc which offers the most freedom of all, because it delivers the purest quality of picture and sound. You are not only free to choose what you wish to watch and when you wish to watch it, you are free of the barriers which impede the realism of the entertainment. A disc presentation captivates your complete attention because it offers no impurities as distractions. Laser discs are the first true step to 'virtual reality,' bringing the theatrical experience not only into your living room, but into your head.

To understand what it means to own a movie, or any audio visual program, the initial thrill of ownership must be discarded.The joy in knowing that one can spend an afternoon moving through the *Psycho* shower scene frame by frame; that one can, if suffering from a bout of sleeplessness, watch *Return of the Pink Panther* or *Autumn Sonata* in the dead of night; and that one can play *The Road Warrior* over and over and over again if one wishes; all these joys will eventually subside. The movie will still be on your shelf, waiting to be played again.

The best place to search for what it means to own a movie is in the examination of what it means to buy a movie. If you had only enough money to make a single purchase would you choose *Plan Nine from Outer Space* or *Out of Africa*? How closely related are value and quality? There are titles one would pay a hundred dollars for without thinking twice, and other titles for which one would hesitate to pay five dollars.

One buys a movie with the intention of watching it, but how many times? Collectors with large bank accounts can afford to purchase many movies and simply wait for the mood or the impulse to watch a title. They may never watch every movie they own. Impoverished collectors face a different dilemma. They may have made a sizable investment in titles and yet still be unable to match their every mood. On certain nights they might pore over and over their collection, searching for anything they have not watched numerous times before, and end up turning to broadcast television instead.

After establishing a collection, interesting situations develop. Some movies are best seen only once. Others, twice. Others, a few times, and others, many times over. The pleasure one can elicit from each movie under each condition is an end in itself. You might buy a film you have never seen before, watch it once very late at night, and then put it away forever, but recall the night and the movie fondly. Or you might watch a movie so often that snippets of dialog become a regular part of your vocabulary.

Pleasure can follow a bell curve. The way in which a movie is constructed can prevent you from fully appreciating it the first time through. After several viewings you comprehend the themes the filmmakers were intending to communicate. And after several more, the flaws in the construction or the themes become evident and your enthusiasm subsides.

In films which are plotted and edited tightly enough to withstand many viewings, it is often the minor roles which, when multiplied, become the major focus of the entertainment. Eli Wallach in *The Good, The Bad, and The Ugly*, Michael Pare in *The Warriors*, Edith Evans in *Tom Jones,* and Milo O'Shea in *Barbarella* are just a few examples of roles which are not the central focus of the plot but end up becoming the essential part of the entertainment and the primary cause for revisitation.

Environmental conditions can have a lot to do with the enjoyment of a feature. *Thank God It's Friday* is only pleasurable when viewed on a Friday night in a crowded urban movie house. It is simplistic and uninvolving in a quiet room. On the other hand, *Spies Like Us*, *Legend*, and other shows which seem pretentious in a theater are whittled down to size on a small TV screen. And even the most wretched horror film can have certain appeal once the clock moves past the stroke of twelve.

Mediocrity is the condition least amenable to ownership. Really bad movies can be just as enjoyable as really good ones, but movies which are neither good nor bad have nothing going for them.

Unlike pinned butterflies or comic books which have never felt a human fingerprint, a decent collection of audio visual programs — movies, concert performances, short or experimental works, documentaries — is supposed to be used, and sometimes used again and again. This is where the other advantage of the laser video disc format, durability, becomes essential.

To own a movie is to obtain the potential for satisfying a complex, and sometimes even contrary, state of emotions. When collecting movies, it is best to attune yourself to the different moods you want to satisfy. It is also good, so long as your wallet can stand it, to trust your instincts. If you have an unaccountable desire to purchase a title, your subconscious is trying to tell you something. So purchase the title.

A HISTORY OF THE VIDEO DISC

The video disc has been around as long as television itself. John Logie Baird created the first 'Phonovision' in Great Britain in 1927, which could replicate a picture with 30 lines of resolution — comparable to what one sees upon waking up after having consumed an ill-advised quantity of hard spirits.

The need to record and broadcast pictures without interim processing resurfaced in the 1950s as an adjunct to commercial television. The first 'instant replay' machines used in sports broadcasts were disc based, but video tape technology soon advanced to become the more practical video recording medium.

Lasers were also developed in the 1950s, as improved knowledge of particle physics led to the practical manipulation of lightwaves. A beam of light could be focused and maintain a focus when sent through a gaseous bombardment which regulated and ordered otherwise randomly traveling photons. When a light is focused by a crystal or a lens, it can maintain a more or less organized path for a couple of hundred yards (such as in a drive-in theater). Light which has been amplified to a laser can bounce off the moon and return to earth without diffusion.

The early video disc machines utilized a stylus to record and playback platters of different consistencies. In the 1970s, Philips, a Netherlands-based electronics company, and MCA, an American-based entertainment conglomerate, both developed video disc systems which would utilize a laser beam in the place of a stylus. The system, on which they quickly decided to collaborate, would eventually become the first commercial laser application.

Television is broadcast using the same basic technology as radio. Radio waves are, essentially, particle waves like light, which lack the characteristics required to be reflected by the human eye but have other properties, such as width and vibration rates, which can be maintained for great distances.

If a property such as the height of the wave is used as a constant, then the other properties can be coded by a sender and decoded by a receiver. (One of the loveliest visual interpretations of this process can be seen on side two of Walt Disney Home Video's *Tron.* A ship docking at a port passes through a 'wall' which strips it of all decorative accoutrements, leaving just the skeleton or the 'raw structure' of information.)

The picture on a television tube is a simple series of tiny dots flashing by at a rapid rate so that the eye only registers the image the dots have formed. Inside the television, the dots are sent to the screen in an order and nature based upon the variations contained in the coded electronic signal the TV set has received and generated. The sound also comes along for the ride.

On a laser video disc, microscopic 'pits' of varying lengths imbedded in the disc are measured by a laser beam. The measurements are interpreted photoelectronically to reproduce both the sound and the picture in a television set, as if the laser had actually been an antenna receiving wave signals.

Initially, enough information was stored on a disc to deliver an analog picture signal and two independent analog audio signals. Later, two additional digital audio signals were added to the information stored on the pits without disturbing the other data, so that 'digital sound' as well as 'analog sound' could be played back from a disc.

MCA and Philips were very excited. MCA, in particular, had visions of marketing its 11,000 title library at mid-'70s prices of $1.99 to $9.99. But consumers weren't excited. By December of 1978, when the first consumer video disc player, from (North American Philips) Magnavox, placed a cautious toe in the retail market (in Atlanta, initially), video cassette recorders had already established a touch which would eventually become an iron grip on the home video consumer.

The marketing fallacy to which the MCA/Philips 'DiscoVision' producers succumbed is easy enough to understand. They liked movies. The people they worked with liked movies. Therefore, they thought everybody in America and the free world liked movies enough that they would want to own movies. Even the movie companies thought this and were pulled into the video tape rental market kicking and screaming all the way. Prerecorded video discs are and will probably remain cheaper to produce than prerecorded video tapes on a unit basis, but the ability to record off of broadcast television, combined with the easy availability of tape rentals, made the video cassette recorder (VCR) the perfect multipurpose video machine (add a camera and you had instant home movies).

All was not lost, however. The bright silver-plattered video disc offered a better picture (with 350 to 400 lines of resolution) and better sound than video cassettes. Movie enthusiasts lined up overnight to buy the first laser video disc players. That created a core group which had to be expanded if the laser video disc was to survive. So who should come to the rescue, but video cassettes!

It was not the dream world initially envisioned by the DiscoVision trustees, but cassette players increased the general enthusiasm and appreciation for the movies. As the VCR penetration expanded, so, too, did a film consciousness. Cinematic experiments such as *Eraserhead,* which a few years previously had been known to only a handful of midnight screening patrons, suddenly became topics for conversation at the office and in the school yard. As this new-found thrill for the movies proliferated, a steady percentage of those exposed found themselves wanting more. Hence the appeal of the laser video disc, which eventually came to be sold as the 'compact disc' of video products. (The analogy is not 100% accurate, since, unlike the digital CD, the picture information encoded on the laser disc is still analog-based. But it gets the idea across.)

Throughout its first decade, quality of presentation was the primary selling point of the laser video disc and a major thorn in the sides of the companies doing the selling. The picture is unequivocally better than video tape and always has been. The discs offered stereo sound almost from their inception and continue to stay one step ahead of tape in that realm as well. But the manner in which discs were manufactured, especially during the first production efforts, left them susceptible to defect rates as high as 50% before they got out of the factory door.

To make a disc, a videotape master, struck from an original negative or print of a movie, is interpreted by a machine which transcribes the image and audio information into the pit format and then 'burns' the pits on a disc-sized sheet of photosensitive material. That sheet is then used as a molding from which another master, or 'stamper,' is created to be placed in a press and used for the mass production of the actual discs. In the pressing process, the clear plastic disc is imbedded with the pits from the stamper. That side of the disc is then covered with a reflective aluminum coating and glued to a companion sheet which would, if everything worked out properly, contain the second half of the movie. Thus, one video disc is actually two discs, glued back to back.

Obviously, until quality control measures had a thorough shakedown, there were many points in the process where the pits could be corrupted. The first discs were priced below manufacturing costs to begin with, so one can imagine the havoc which was raised by the defect rates. Many of the early DiscoVision titles became collector's items not so much because of their basic scarcity, but because fewer of the copies which did exist could play flawlessly.

The defect rate subsided, but so did the quantity of disc releases. In concentrating upon 'maintaining' the initial DiscoVision catalog, few new releases were forthcoming. The whole endeavor would probably have died a welcome death had it not been for the intrusion of two corporate institutions with opposing motivations and cultural orientations — Pioneer Electronics and IBM.

IBM actually entered and exited the video disc market very quickly and prudently, but its visitation was enough to orient the one aspect of the market which has never stopped making money: non-commercial discs. The ability of a laser disc to reproduce a single still frame or to present random segments upon request expands its applications beyond the realm of 'linear entertainment.'

The educational potentials, particularly when the player is linked to a micro processor, created a demand which, unlike home video, no other medium could satisfy. Very early on, General Motors bought 10,000 video disc players for distribution to dealerships, with the purpose of providing both training and product promotional materials in a simplified and consistent manner. Today, the United States Government purchases and uses more laser video disc products than anybody else. To familiarize a steady influx of personnel with the complicated mechanisms required to operate sophisticated weaponry, the interactive video disc has become an irreplaceable part of the military training process. The demand for video disc products by corporations and institutions subsidized the home video market during a critical incubation period.

The first Magnavox laser disc player did not work. It was not calibrated to read the discs correctly. But, like the first explorers who wandered all over the Western Hemisphere thinking they were in India, someone eventually got it right. In this case it was the Japanese company, Pioneer Electronics. Like Columbus, Balboa, and Magellan all rolled into one, Pioneer built a decent low-defect-rate pressing plant (in Japan), constructed a series of machines which not only worked but continually pushed to provide consumers with the most technologically advanced playback options available, and nudged the product image out of the mass market doldrums and into the 'high end' consumer winds.

At a critical point Pioneer was also helped by a fad, the coin-operated interactive video game. Games such as *Dragon's Lair* and *Space Ace* utilized animation on a video disc which followed story paths determined by a player's joystick movement. Demand grew so high that Pioneer used both industrial and consumer players to construct the game machinery, but as soon as the popularity wore out, the company went back to making consumer and industrial players without excessive retooling.

IBM, not wishing to become entangled in consumer-oriented projects such as Th*e Touch of Love...Massage,* divested.
Gas lasers were replaced by solid state lasers. The compact disc was developed, digital sound was added to laser video discs, and Pioneer introduced a machine which could play both video discs and CDs. Philips, bolstered by the success of compact discs, manufactured functional video disc players and went on to create a machine which plays all laser-read audio and video formats. Soon, every home electronics company big enough to build a toaster had a laser disc player in its product line. Consumers who already owned two VCRs and wanted to know why the their TV picture wasn't as sharp as the set hooked up a laser player at the local electronics store finally began to take serious notice.

America and Japan have a broadcast color standard, NTSC, which is incompatible with the multitude of other incompatible video formats around the world. Philips produces some discs in Europe, particularly in the PAL format, but the market is moribund because of a lack of international support. (PAL discs, when played on unmodified NTSC units, provide a black-and-white picture without sound. Later European units have been built which play both NTSC and PAL discs on PAL monitors.) Discs produced in Japan, however, play on American TVs, and vice versa.

The Japanese, who have as foreign a culture to Americans as one will find without leaving the planet, developed an affinity for singing into machines at bars, following video-based prompts. This was no *Dragon's Lair* fad, it has become as ingrained in the Japanese social venue as preparing kindergarteners for college exams. The application, however, is ideally suited for the random access and limited wear of the video disc. While VCRs are well established in Japan — they make most of them, after all — there is not a strong rental market, and laser video discs are firmly established as a home video entertainment product, whether it is to watch movies or to follow the bouncing ball.

Pioneer bought the DiscoVision disc pressing plant in America, cleaned it up, and, depending upon fluctuating economies, appears to maintain a profitability by using one market to support another, wherever the action is hot. 3M, Sony, and others opened disc pressing plants and began manufacturing consumer discs.

A decade after the first consumer player appeared, the market is healthy, the technology is still exciting, and, because of many random factors beyond their control, motion picture fanatics can own and play movies whenever they want.

CAV and CLV

A program can be 'encoded' on a disc in two different ways.

One method assigns a single video frame to every revolution of the disc, despite the difference in length between an 'inside' and an 'outside' revolution. Since the timing of the disc revolution is the same for an entire side, the format is called the Constant Angular Velocity format, or CAV. CAV is also known as 'Standard Play' and 'Full Feature Format' because of the frame manipulation abilities inherent in its design.

Although the laser follows a spiral path (on all discs, the playback begins in the center and advances out, toward the rim), every frame begins and ends in the same area on the CAV disc, so it is just as easy for the laser to read the same information again and again as it is to advance to the next frame. The primary disadvantage of CAV is that it can only hold 30 minutes of program ('54,000 frames' at 30 frames a second) on a side. Since most feature films run longer than an hour, they require more than one disc when pressed in CAV.

The rate of disc revolution within a player is governed by the beginning and ending of a frame. The motor spinning the disc constantly adjusts itself so that the requisite 30 frames a second is achieved. Since pressing 90-minute movies on two discs proved uneconomical, a second format was developed which kept all frames on the disc to a minimum necessary length. The motor automatically slows down the RPM as more frames are included in each revolution, particularly in the outer reaches of the disc.

This format is called the Constant Linear Velocity format, or CLV. Its sacrifice is that the frames are no longer lined up in a manner conducive to easy manipulation. Replaying a single frame is impossible except under the artificial conditions provided by later-generation high-end players which 'store' a random frame in 'memory' and then play it back. (At best, near the beginning, sophisticated players can grab one out every two frames; near the outer edge of a disc the draw is closer to one out of four. This is not to say, however, that the capability to breakdown and manipulate an important sequence on any laser disc is not terrific fun.) But the CLV format, which is also known as 'Extended Play,' holds an hour of program on each side and can thus contain the average feature film on a single platter.

Some disc producers are cognizant of the advantages in putting programs in CAV. If they are unwilling to take the financial risk of formatting an entire program in CAV, they may, if the running time arithmetic works out, format one side of a disc in CLV mode and the second side in CAV. Unfortunately, this practice is more often an exception than a rule.

It is the CAV Standard Play features which make the laser video technology more than simply a mechanism for playing movies. Each one of the 54,000 frames on one side of a disc can be played back on a TV set or monitor as a single, clear image. Discs have been produced, replicating museum photo collections, which hold more than 100,000 photos on two sides.

The 30 'frames' which comprise a second of a video image actually consist of 60 venetian blind style striped half-frames which, when flashed alternately, blend together to make full frames. Each 'half' frame makes up half a revolution on a CAV disc. When a still frame is played, the two halves of the single image are flashing 60 times a second. But, if the disc has been improperly mastered, each of the halves can belong to a different frame, giving the still a jittery effect wherever movement was captured. Since movies are usually filmed at 24 frames a second, there are six extra scattered duplicate frames which, if not divvied out correctly, will cause the still image to flicker. Many CAV discs are mastered correctly, but it is less expensive to master them leaving unsteady still frames, usually two out of every five. The images are not completely wrecked, but the CAV advantage is compromised when this occurs.

Every CAV frame is encoded with a unique 'frame number.' Thus, each and every frame can be called forth in the span of a couple seconds. 'Random Access' to any part of the disc can be employed in a variety of ways: In educational material to send a user to different parts of a disc depending upon a 'right' or 'wrong' answer; in games or adventure stories in which the user chooses the path the hero should follow; in archival material such as the museum collection mentioned above, where any photo, usually listed in an 'on disc' index, can be called forth at will; or, in analyzing a movie, so that individual scenes or frames can be called and studied.

Every CLV frame is encoded with an hour, minute, and (on most discs) second marker. The hour marker is only used to identify a side and is not employed consistently. All but the oldest laser players can search on the minute marker, which places the viewer approximately where the viewer wishes to be when calling up a scene. Many players can also search on the second marker, providing a more accurate landing spot. Players also have a 'repeat' option which allows one to constantly replay a passage in a disc or mark a point on the disc, like a book mark, as a place to return after advancing to investigate other passages.

Still, whether one is searching by frame on a CAV disc or by time on a CLV disc, memorizing or noting exactly where one wishes to land on a disc can be taxing. Therefore, both CAV and CLV discs can be encoded with 'Chapter' markers, which are assigned by the disc producer to significant scenes or segments on a disc. 'Chapter Search' brings the viewer to the beginning of the chapter. Although a disc can be segmented into as many as 79 'Chapters,' few are provided with more than a dozen or so. That is preferable, however, to the status of most discs, which are given no 'Chapters' at all. Since the chapters are usually delineated on the jacket cover accompanying the disc, they provide a quick and easy method of locating one's favorite scenes, provided the disc producer has correctly anticipated what one's favorite scenes are going to be. To facilitate an ability on later-generation players to 'program' chapter play in any order the viewer wishes, the end of a significant passage ought to have a chapter marker, but this occurs rarely. Some disc producers have become quite adept, not only in encoding chapters, but in providing curt mnemonic descriptions of the chapter contents in the jacket copy.

In addition to still frames and random access, CAV enables a user to manipulate the speed and direction of the playback. Slow motion can be adjusted to flip past a single frame a full second at a time or simply to run at half normal speed. Some players have the ability to play at just a fraction off normal speed, which is ideal if you want to examine the nuances of a scene without distorting the action. Frames can also be played at multiple speeds in reverse order, causing the action on the screen to move backwards. The audio is automatically suppressed during any manipulation and no consumer player has ever been given the option to override the suppression, although there are machines which play sound while showing a succession of still frames.

Slow motion and 'still step' freeze frame can enable one to 'deconstruct' stunts or gags in a movie (for example, you can watch stunt people 'not' hit one another), but such manipulation can also be utilized for educational purposes. Folding origami or playing a musical instrument, for example, can be demonstrated and studied best when the student has the option to slow down, stop, or back up the action. Several innovative

CAV discs have actually been designed to be used as scientific experiments. Since the timing of any action pictured on a disc can be broken down to exactly a thirtieth of a second, the speed and distance in which objects travel relative to their size or other stated conditions can be measured precisely.

A CAV disc can also be played at 'fast speed' which is three times the normal speed. Although it is only every third frame which is sampled, the effect causes an optical illusion which makes the picture look hyper realistic. This can be especially satisfying when watching very old black-and-white movies, because the people and places within have not been viewed with such clarity or sharpness since the day they were filmed. 'Fast' can also be used to observe camera movement or movement within the frame in a more composite manner, revealing designs which would be obscured during the distractions of regular play. 'Fast' functions in reverse as well, to predictable but nonetheless satisfying results, particularly when elephants or explosions are involved.

Another option available on CAV discs is the 'Stop' function. When a 'Stop' command is encoded at the beginning of a frame, the player automatically shifts into still frame mode and does not advance until the user intervenes by activating 'Play' or one of the other motion instructions. (In an annoying semantic trend, many disc producers use the term 'Chapter Stop,' which ought to indicate the coordinated placement of a 'Stop' and a chapter marker, as a generic term for all chapter encoding.) 'Stop' is an effective method on interactive discs to combine still frame and motion sequences. Without it, the still frame segments pass by so quickly that a user would have to be faster with the 'Still Step' button than Gary Cooper in *High Noon* to hit the right frame.

Other common play manipulation functions, besides the ones listed above, are 'Pause' and 'Scan' (and 'Eject,' which terminates playback). 'Scan' provides the ability to persue an entire disc side in about a minute's time, going in either direction. In CAV one can apprehend a fairly coherent picture of the disc contents being scanned, but in CLV the picture is distorted, except on the players using frame memory storage and playback, and the 'Scan' operation must often be interrupted for normal play if one wants to arrive at a specific location.

'Pause,' in CAV and CLV, ceases the disc output while holding onto the location so that 'Play' will resume from the same point on the disc where the 'Pause' was activated. In CLV, it is often a good idea to get out of 'Pause' by tapping the reverse direction 'Scan' button before returning to 'Play,' so that one can be assured of not missing a key line of dialog or significant frame. If one intends to interrupt play for any great length of time, however, it is always smarter to take note of one's frame or time position and stop playing the disc altogether than it is to leave the disc in 'Pause' mode. These machines don't last forever. Later model players will 'remember' where play left off provided the disc is not ejected.

Finally, it is worth noting that most programs, and, specifically, movies, require more than one side of a disc. This means that, at some point during the program, your concentration will be interrupted as you stop to flip the disc over. (Machines which 'play both sides' of a disc still have a lengthy pause as the side play changes.) In the case of a CAV disc, a viewer has to change sides several times, a situation which some find so annoying that the advantages of CAV do not outweigh the hassle. The interruption has, however, provided a serendipitous advantage in making a viewer consciously aware of a movie's structure. When filmmakers block out a script or plan a film, they are often meticulous about a film's pacing and rate of dramatic exposition. Since disc producers usually break a two-sided disc program as near to the middle as possible, the scene which (good) filmmakers intend to use as the principle shift in the drama, by placing it in the center of the movie, is unintentionally drawn to attention. Whether it is a hero's discovery of something or of love, a murder or an elaborate chase, or the first trouble which leads to an eventual downfall, the telltale scene will often occur either immediately before or immediately after the break between the first and second side. Since you can't help but notice the break, you cannot help but become aware of what the filmmakers believe to be the most significant moment in the unfolding of the film's theme. It is an inadvertent educational advantage to discs which, once you start taking note of it, you will find difficult to ignore.

LASER VIDEO DISC SOUND

There is a sequence in *Alien* where the heroine is studying a computer terminal, alone, in a compartment on a space ship. Suddenly, a character standing behind her speaks. The audience is startled, but the heroine is not. Critics complained about the continuity of the scene, but if one watches and *listens* to the movie on laser video disc, there is no failure in continuity. Moments before the second character speaks, you can hear the gentle "whoosh" of the compartment doors opening and closing. You can't hear it in a theater unless you are sitting directly beneath a speaker, but you can hear it if you have a decent sound system, a little privacy, and a laser video disc player.

No one should own a laser video disc player without hooking it up to a stereo. It is not simply that characters in a movie will speak from the left when they are standing on the left or that helicopters and trains will actually seem to pass through your living room if the film is stereophonic. When you watch a program in stereo, each of your ears hears a different amount of the same thing and your mind responds by believing, just a little tiny bit, that it is hearing reality and not the TV. This sharpens your concentration and opens your emotional responsiveness to the material. You see the movie better and you think about the movie better and, usually, you like the movie better because you are listening to a better sound.

Not all movies can or should be played at the same volumes. Very old movies or movies made on a small budget in a foreign country naturally have rough soundtracks. Even these films, however, can sound better when played on a stereo system and it is rare that a movie sounds so bad that it requires the limitations of a TV speaker to suppress its distortions.

From the beginning, the audio capabilities of the laser video disc have exceeded those of the other consumer formats. At first, laser discs were the only way one could play back a movie in stereo at home, making the home video experience a little more like visiting a theater and a little less like watching TV. As stereo in other video formats emerged, CX-encoding signals were included on discs to compensate for the minor imperfections in reading and playing back the audio signal. As stereo in other video formats improved, an additional digital code was squeezed onto the disc which could provide the equivalent of Compact Disc quality sound.

Usually a soundtrack, even an aged monaural soundtrack, will sound cleaner with CX-encoding. As do all noise suppression schemes, it compromises the accuracy of the sound re-creation, particularly in the lower ranges, but it provides a more dependable and, usually, more listenable sound by suppressing the distraction of other inevitable imperfections. With many players, however, there is no opportunity for comparison, because the CX-encoding is switched on automatically and can not be overridden by the listener. Like fluoridation in the water supply, many disc owners would prefer to decide for themselves whether they want or do not want to listen to a noise-suppressed soundtrack. As more and more discs have been digitally encoded, CX-encoding has become less of an issue.

The implementation of digital sound on laser video discs was a significant event. In terms of marketing, it aligned the technology with the highly successful compact disc. In terms of quality, it improved the losses in the upper ranges of the analog signal and, if the source material was equally pure, provided hiss and crackle-free sound.

All digital players retain the option to toggle between digital and analog, but it is rare that an analog track will contain a fidelity or an attitude which is not available on the digital track. Engineering difficulties prevented the first digital discs from containing more than 55 minutes of program on a side. Until this problem was overcome, disc producers usually opted to release a 110-120 minute film without digital encoding.

With older movies, which are given a stereophonic digital soundtrack when released on laser disc, sound technologies have probably improved so much since they first played in theaters that, since revival houses have lousy sound systems, the film has *never* sounded as good as it does on a good home audio system. And if a film company has restored an older monaural soundtrack through digital processing, encoding the disc digitally prevents the step of moving the sound back to analog.

Occasionally, analog and digital discs are released with 'electronically rechanneled stereo sound.' In these programs the sound is sampled and certain types of noises are separated between the two channels so that the illusion of stereo is accomplished. At best, an original mono soundtrack which is released in stereo has a strong fidelity and a clean playback, with, perhaps, a full-sounding musical score. At its worst, the sound simply drops out of one speaker to pretend that the source of the sound is coming from the other side of the screen.

To play even more tricks on the mind's ears, many discs are encoded with Dolby Surround Sound (or similar) matrix codes. Surround processors are enjoyable devices that can be manipulated, through phase shifting, to give any soundtrack the illusion of dimensionality. When a stereo film is encoded for surround, however, specific noises are routed to the rear speakers and the result is a joy to behold. More so than even picture quality, it is probably the spectacular nature of a well produced surround audio track that is a laser video disc's strongest selling point.

A CLV laser disc has the potential to provide eight hours of monaural audio sound in accompaniment with two hours of picture. This is because the left and right channel analog audio signal and digital signals are all encoded separately on the disc. When one channel is played and the other is not, you *only* hear the one channel.

The most popular utilization of dual audio has been to put the soundtrack of a film on one audio channel and then provide a lecture about the movie on another. The viewer can listen to the movie or, at the flick of a switch, listen to a lecture which discusses how the movie was made. Other uses of dual audio have included providing English and foreign language soundtracks for the same movie, the isolation of a film's musical score or sound effects track, alternate explanations of an artwork or mechanism depicted on the screen, and the ability to turn Jane Fonda on or off without disrupting the music and the exercising.

WHAT IS AVAILABLE ON LASER VIDEO DISC

Most movies are made or supported by corporations. Since corporations employ a great many people, when one person leaves or is fired, the person who fills the position must adapt, for the most part, to the methods or the 'culture' which has already been established in the office. Even if, over time, there is a complete turnover of personnel, the 'culture' remains, and those who join are indoctrinated. Thus it is that movies from various companies have always had a consistent 'feel' to them. People who see many movies can easily distinguish an MGM film from a Warner Brothers, Paramount, or Columbia Pictures movie. Even people who don't see movies that often know when they are watching a Walt Disney film.

The three companies which have shown the most wholehearted support for the laser video format are Pioneer LDCA, Image Entertainment, and The Voyager Company.

Pioneer LDCA is the software arm of Pioneer and markets several of its own disc labels. One, 'Pioneer Artists,' concentrates on music programs, from rock and pop to ballet, opera, and jazz. The 'Pioneer Special Interests' label promotes innovative experimental filmmaking and educational programs, most of which are originated in Japan but are redesigned for American viewers. Pioneer's 'Official Import' label brings specific Japanese titles directly onto the American market without any change in packaging save for an 'Official Import' sticker on the shrink wrap.

In that Pioneer also owns a disc manufacturing plant, the company makes and even distributes discs for a number of other disc companies, a relationship which can sometimes be confusing to outsiders.

Image Entertainment is solely and wholeheartedly a laser video disc company. The Los Angeles based firm does nothing but market laser video discs. Although Image serves occasionally as a distributor for other disc producers, its primary business strategy is to obtain the rights to titles from other home video companies and then release the titles on an Image label. To fill the gaps between blockbusters, Image releases small quantities of a great number of titles, and it is safe to say that any random individual pulled off the street would be enamored with at least one or two titles in Image's catalog — if not *The Bells of St. Mary's*, then *Best Buns on the Beach*. Image's 'CinemaDisc Collection' label is devoted to releasing foreign language films, and there are more subtitled movies in Image's catalog than in the catalogs of all the other disc companies combined. The same is true of silent films. Although you have to read the fine print to identify their involvement, the X-rated adult discs are also handled by Image. Since Image does not own a disc manufacturing plant, it must contract out to have the discs pressed, the economics of which are often reflected in its sticker prices.

Laser discs are high end video software products, and The Voyager Company produces the high end of the high end. Their discs are exquisitely designed and produced. Voyager's film releases are usually licensed from other home video companies and issued on the highly regarded 'Criterion Collection' label. Not only are the titles remastered exclusively for Voyager's presentation, but the discs often contain extraneous material concerning the production of the film, and are packed with different features or opportunities to utilize the CAV format. Voyager also goes to great lengths to obtain the best source material available to transfer films onto disc. The expenses which go into producing the discs are again reflected in the sticker price. In addition to creating collector's editions of such classics as *King Kong* and *2001: A Space Odyssey* Voyager also releases educational and experimental programs, many designed specifically for laser disc.

About forty different companies have tried releasing programs on laser video disc. Fewer release discs on a regular monthly basis.

Each of the major home video companies has, at one time or another, unduly frustrated the laser disc market, yet each has also, at one time or another, been highly innovative in the design and manner of its releases. You can often tell, in fact, when someone who loves discs achieves a position of power in one of these establishments, as there is a sudden flood of long awaited releases and quality productions.

MGM/UA Home Video, Warner Home Video, Walt Disney/Touchstone Video, RCA/Columbia Pictures Home Video, CBS/Fox Home Video, MCA Home Video, and Paramount Home Video tend to control the most highly desired titles. Consumers have generally found MGM/UA and Warner to offer the highest quality at a low price. After a slow start, MGM/UA became especially sensitive to making its catalog available and has been including short films and other special features with its titles. MCA is probably the most systematic, releasing a small but steady mix of recent and classic titles each month. The latter is usually part of its popular 'Encore Edition' collection and often contains special features. CBS/Fox has been innovative in presenting blockbuster films mastered specifically for laser disc and including special features with their titles, but their release schedule has been erratic and their prices tend to be on the upside. Walt Disney is as aggressive at dropping titles from its catalog as it is in bringing out replacements, but has been consistent in bringing out its classic cartoon feature films in both CLV and CAV format.

The trend with all the major home video companies has been to improve the product and make it more specifically designed for the laser disc market. In this regard, Republic Home Video has also entered the fray, with a number of classic and public domain titles, including motion picture serials, which it is treating as the other companies treat their biggest hits.

Philips, which owns a pressing plant in Europe, has, like Pioneer, concentrated on music titles, using its subsidiary, Polygram, and the various off-shoots, Deutsche Gramaphon, London, and others to release operas, classical recitals, jazz concerts and rock.

The Denver based Lumivision has a small but steady output and a loyal following. They tend to release minor foreign films, educational programs, or impressionistic musical efforts. Home Vision, in New Jersey, concentrates on imported Jazz titles and educational films dealing with the Arts. LVA Film Classics releases public domain material.

The quality of the material coming from the video companies which do not have motion picture industry parents varies depending upon the quality of their sources. Vestron Video, Nelson Home Entertainment, Karl-Lorimar, Pacific Arts, and HBO Video have released discs which make full use of the medium and discs which are an embarrassment to keep in one's library. Other companies, such as NFL Home Video and Coliseum Home Video, have released some product on disc and then failed to follow up with subsequent releases. Shifts in licensing arrangements will sometimes cause a title to be released several different times by several different companies, increasing the chances that one, at least, will produce the film properly on disc.

Because of the quality of a laser video disc's sound reproduction, an extensive selection of music-oriented programs have been produced. Following the maturation of the 'music video,' which happened at the same time that the video disc itself came of age, the images accompanying the music evolved into much more than simply shots of musicians performing their craft. Drawing on the concepts of avant-garde cinema, the best music videos provide a visual equivalent to the poetry of the lyrics and the rhythm and melody of the music. These were ideally suited for the audio and visual abilities of a laser video disc. And with an equal vengeance, bad music video appeared, with silly narratives and what essentially was the visual equivalent to lousy music.

Rock and pop concert programs can vary in quality depending upon the energy and charisma of the performer or the ability of the director to make something out of loud and energetic nothings.

Several marketing variations were introduced largely to attract pop music fans to the laser video disc format. The '8-inch' disc holds about 20 minutes a side of CLV material (and a little less in CAV). While it could be used for anything, it has been marketed exclusively as a music video format. It is normally less expensive than a '12-inch' disc, and does not contain as much 'filler' material.

The CD-Video or 'CDV' is a genuine CD disc, cast in gold instead of silver coloring. The disc contains one music video with three or four audio-only cuts and requires a special player or combination player for playback.

Opera is particularly well represented on laser disc, and well suited to the flexibility of the home video environment. Although the earliest opera releases did not utilize subtitles, the presence of an onscreen English translation to the lyrics is nowadays standard.

Ballets which have not been choreographed for video lose much of their impact when they appear on a television because the choreography is compromised on the cropped screen. It is surprising that more home video renditions of Broadway and off-Broadway stage productions are not available. One would think that with all the effort which goes into producing them, a simple videotaped record of a stage show would almost be a matter of course. Instead, very few are available, making those which are that much more worth having.

The laser disc is also an ideal children's home video delivery system. Peanut butter, maple syrup, or just about any greasy contaminant can be removed from the disc as easily as it was applied. Since discs do not have to be rewound, a child can watch the same program a number of times without soliciting an adult's assistance. Indeed, most laser disc players are so easy to operate that a child will usually master its basic functions before he is capable of speaking a complete and coherent sentence.

Because of licensing discrepancies, there are many American movies which are available in Japan but not in the United States, just as there are many American films, and even one or two Japanese pictures, which are available in the US, but not in Japan. A healthy import business has built up on both sides of the Pacific in reaction to these unbalances. At times, Japanese currency has been favorably valued in relation to American currency and at other times it has been unfavorably valued, but in either case, if a Clint Eastwood fan wants a title which the American distributor has refused to release in the United States, a stiff yen is not going to stand in the way.

American movies released in Japan on laser disc are in English. The only exceptions to this have been a few Walt Disney cartoons, which were dubbed into Japanese specifically to discourage import to America. In the early days, there was a practice with monaural films of providing the English language dialog on one audio track and dubbed Japanese on the second, but today most American movies released in Japan have Japanese subtitles. Occasionally the subtitles are set vertically, on the far right, but most of the time they are spread across the bottom of the screen. You get used to them after a while. The only situations in which they truly interfere are with films where heavy dialog scenes are shot with innovative or otherwise significant cinematography, so that the slightest blemish is distracting. Many non-English language films are also available in Japan, but these are in their original language with Japanese subtitles, a combination which will be alienating to all but the most enthusiastic English-speaking collectors. Japanese movies are also available and, of course, they have no subtitles at all. Neither do the many Japanese animation features, but these are tempting to American animation collectors anyway, because of the sophistication and scope of the cartoons.

The selection of music discs is even more extensive in Japan than in America. The Japanese do not use subtitles for song lyrics, so it would be impossible to tell, other than the Interpol copyright warning, that a disc depicting an American rock group was not from the US. Often a printed sheet of lyrics can be found in the jacket sleeve and it, too, will be in English. The Japanese also have many 'mood discs' or 'image music' discs. On these, mediocre musicians play uninteresting (but often superbly recorded) music while uninteresting (but crystal sharp) images of nature, cities, or models cavort on the screen.

The great and mostly unfulfilled promise of the laser video disc is the potential for interactivity which the dual audio channels and CAV functions provide. 'Interactive' programs are rare, and few fully realize the potential of the medium. Some companies have created material expressly for laser video disc. Other than Voyager's efforts, the best have been from Optical Data Corporation, which has utilized material from NASA and other sources to create educational discs for both the consumer and the institutional markets. A single one of these discs can be used by several different people for different types of learning activities and explorations.

'Game' discs in which frame search queries lead one through differing strings of narratives or 'right' and 'wrong' question and answer exercises are less successful. After moving through the disc once or twice, the tendency is to put it away and never touch it again.

Discs which have been produced for the educational market are usually more expensive than consumer discs, but the program material is sometimes rich and innovative. In these, the ability to stop motion at specific points is intrinsic to the utilization of the motion sequences. Instead of telling you which frame to access, you choose to follow cross references and paths of learning on your own. Also available are still photo collections containing hundreds of thousands of pictures of airplanes, plants, fabrics, musicians, cattle ranches, planets, and moons, to name just a few. Dual audio can be used to provide 'two sides' to one story or to give a simplified and a detailed explanation to the same visual sequences. Many educational discs are also provided with PC links to prompt and control the random access features.

Ideally, an interactive disc should make you want to grab the disc player remote control and never let go of it. On every frame there should be a multiple dimension of options and every option should provide a different revelation about the material observed. Theoretically, you ought to be able to watch a CAV disc and discover things no one else has found, because the combination of commands you use for the discovery will be unique.

HOW DO YOU FIT A RECTANGULAR PICTURE ONTO AN ALMOST SQUARE SCREEN?

The symbiotic relationship between television and the movies makes the two formats act like homicidal rivals who are joined at the hip. At first, all movies were composed with the same, nearly square aspect ratio of about 1.33:1. When television was invented, it was natural that the screen would be given the same dimensions. And when the popularity of television began to threaten motion pictures, the laws of natural selection led to stretching the projection dimensions of movies to provide a wider field of view and a more enveloping viewing experience.

But what to do when it came time, inevitably, to project these movies on the TV? The most popular method is known as 'pan and scan,' where a technician, who, most probably, is privy to nothing beyond the obvious or literal intentions of the filmmakers, centers the image upon the most 'significant' portion of the screen and 'crops' everything else. This usually means that the technician must move or pan the image across what originally was a stationary shot in order to keep up with shifting points of interest.

Cropping inevitably causes closeups in places where a director did not intend that a character be examined closely. In a stereo film, a character standing and speaking at the far left will be centered on the screen. Screen composition is a tremendously important component in the art of filmmaking. Whether it is a balance of images, an inclusion of objects or characters, or simply the utilization of blank space, widescreen movies were, for a long time, composed for the widescreen only.

Another option, which is occasionally employed, although its results are even more disastrous than scanning and cropping, is to 'squeeze' the image, elongating the dimension vertically to bring in more horizontally. This makes the cast members look gaunt and everything else look terribly silly.

The alternative to squeezing or scanning and cropping images is to show the film on television in its original aspect ratio, with black space at the top and bottom of the television screen to compensate for the difference in proportion. This is known as 'letterboxing,' for want of a better term, since the image usually has the same dimensions as a British letter-box slot.

On a letterboxed image, the film director's full, original screen composition can be viewed without subversion. On a small television screen it can only be viewed as a generalized image, since details are only half normal size. With some monitors a 'shimmer' appears when the compact image contains more detail than the monitor's resolution capabilities can accommodate. It is worth noting, however, that viewers who are initially alienated by the letterboxed image usually become addicted to it by and by. Exposure to letterboxing makes the viewer aware of how much of an original film is missing on a cropped presentation, and soon it is the missing picture information and not the black bands which becomes the most irritating to a viewer. Some consumers have found that by covering the bands with a dark cloth, particularly on a large projection screen, the letterboxing is less distracting.

(The aspect ratios of width to height provided in this book are intended to be used as a generalized reference, since the actual figure will vary from one monitor to the next. Most monitors display less picture information on all four sides than is delivered to them from a laser player.)

When home video became a major source of income for motion picture companies, the rules changed again. Before home video, movies were composed for the wide motion picture screen exclusively, but after home video, movies had to be composed 'TV safe.' A movie director is still allowed to create rectangularly significant pictures, but more often than not he is obliged to set up his shots so that the image will also have coherency when squared. The irony here is that the better the director, the better the alternative video version will be.

Hence, while it is vital that every widescreen movie from the Fifties, Sixties, and Seventies be letterboxed, contemporary widescreen films are less dogmatically rectangular and must be judged on an individual basis. Often, the original source material will have the same dimension as a TV screen, and will be 'matted,' or covered over, to achieve the director's intended aspect ratio. Sometimes, when the matting is slight, the 'standard' non-matted video presentation will actually contain more (and usually irrelevant) picture information. Damaged source material may also cause disc producers to present letterboxed movies in unpredictable aspect ratios, following a desire to mask the most frayed edges. In other situations, the picture information contained on the source material is so important that the image will be 'windowboxed,' with black borders appearing on all four sides of the image. Therefore, although there are several distinctive types of widescreen film processes, such as Cinemascope and Panavision, the size of the aspect ratio on a disc will not necessarily be consistent from one film to the next, even when the source material used the same widescreen process.

Some disc companies provide movies exclusively as scanned and cropped full screen presentations (there are also one or two squeezed presentations still on the market). Other disc companies provide movies exclusively as letterboxed presentations, which alienates viewers who haven't become addicted to watching movies on their TV with black bands at the top and bottom of their viewing screen. (It is a myth that you need a large monitor to enjoy letterboxing, however, since the impact of a film director's original screen compositions is still quite accessible on even very small screens.)

To satisfy the most viewers, when it is economically feasible, the trend is to present on disc two versions of a film, the scanned and cropped version and the letterboxed version. As viewers have grown up with great affection for some movies seeing them only on the TV in cropped format, it is a legitimate practice. However, if the first or second time you watch a movie letterboxed and it turns you off, try it a couple more times anyway. Since a widescreen movie was designed to provide the most entertainment to you in a widescreen format, you are cheating yourself when you don't view it that way.

ON THE QUALITY OF LASER VIDEO DISCS

When you attend a season's worth of performances at one of New York City's major ballet companies, a funny thing happens. For a long time afterward, you cannot attend a performance of a regional ballet company and feel satisfaction. All you see are the mistakes the dancers are making. This has nothing to do with being a snob. It is simply that when you've felt the thrill of seeing dancers move to music in perfect athletic unison, then that thrill is what you search for when you return. An emotional response is partially inhibited by every error which occurs. If you haven't been exposed to perfection, then the level of emotion which you achieve when viewing imperfection is satisfying to you; it is better than nothing at all. But once you have had a stronger emotional response, the failure to achieve that level the next time means that the difference between the two levels will be filled by a negative emotion, frustration; nothing at all would probably be better.

It is this two-edged emotional sword which has cleared the path to success for the laser video disc and, at the same time, almost cut it off at the knees.

When you view a movie, poor quality is like electrical resistance and the laser video disc is, next to building a 70mm theater in your basement, the closest thing to super conductivity in home entertainment. Mediocre films provide the best example. If there were a movie which you saw in a theater and did not dislike, you may watch it on video cassette and wonder what it was you saw in it. Watch the same film on video disc and suddenly you will remember. Your subconscious is as much a movie critic as anybody. It sees indistinct images or hears limited audio playback and it begins to dismiss the input. The sharper picture and improved sound from a video disc increases concentration. You appreciate the movie more, because the medium is no longer rubbing you the wrong way.

But even though all laser video discs are an improvement, some turned out to be more of an improvement than others.

In the beginning there were severe quality control problems. The discs were not being produced in a 'clean room' environment and so dust and other contaminants were sealed into the pits, causing speckles or 'snow' to disrupt the picture. Similar flaws would impede the laser's ability to follow the correct path of pits, causing the picture to 'lock' and often prevent the disc from playing through a full side. Entire production runs of DiscoVision titles would be released and then recalled because of severe errors. While this situation did create collector's items out of the few DiscoVision titles which actually fell into consumers' hands, it did not endear those who were patiently waiting for more than three titles to play on their $600 machines.

(In some cases, the DiscoVision producers would take what they thought had been 'bad' runs and glue them to the back of odd-sided discs, discs which needed only 1, 3, or 5 sides to hold a program. Although these 'dead sides' were coated with a solution to inhibit playback, collectors discovered that the solution could be buffed off with the help of a little rubbing alcohol and that the 'unused' side contained all sorts of rare or unusual program material. Today, dead sides contain a brief, generic message suggesting that the other side would make for more interesting play.)

By the time Pioneer obtained the DiscoVision plant, the discs were in much better condition. Pioneer had a laser disc production plant in operation in Japan, and used it in part to supplement production for the American market. The Japanese plant had been built with stronger quality control standards and the discs manufactured there had a cleaner, clearer picture. But once exposed to the improved quality, most consumers reacted negatively when a purchase failed to match the standards set by the best discs.

The solution to this problem was to improve the video disc players themselves. Circuitry and mechanical features were added so that the laser could read warped discs or ignore obvious faults imbedded in the pressing. This cleared up problems such as 'crosstalk' (where, on CLV discs, the laser reads not only the frame it ought to be reading, but adds information from an adjacent track) and increased the clarity of the image. A satisfactory clean room environment was also established and, finally, the differences between Japanese-pressed discs and American-pressed discs narrowed.

Because many titles are remanufactured after their initial press run sells out, there is no way to tell today whether a disc sitting in a rack is going to be in good shape or not. Sometimes there is no way to tell after you have bought the disc, either. Just as disc quality began to settle on a consistent plateau, it was discovered that the metallic reflective base in the pits would oxidize rapidly if the acrylic coating had not been applied correctly. Discs which played perfectly well when purchased would, six months later, not play at all.

Since most dealers and all manufacturers willingly replace defective discs, this problem was little more than an inconvenience to the consumer, but it raised some questions about the reliability of the medium and was unaffectionately referred to as 'laser rot.' All discs oxidize eventually, including CDs, but that could take eons and no one really knows what the life span of a properly manufactured laser video disc is.

Sensible handling and storage of discs is a wise precaution to insure that a disc program will look and sound as nice on its hundredth play as it did on its first. The surface of the disc should never be handled. If it is smeared it can be cleaned with a damp cloth. Discs should be stored vertically, away from heat or other disruptive influences. (Dust can sometimes collect on the lens of a player, causing some discs to skip. The lens is usually reasonably accessible and can be wiped off with a Q-tip.)

The recommendation which some disc companies provide to 'flatten' a warped disc is generally useless. A disc which is purchased warped can be flattened for playback, but it is an awkward process and not worth the trouble. On the other hand, a disc which has been warped from improper storage conditions will return to its original shape if allowed to stand freely for a month or two.

If the physical condition of the disc were the only point of failure, perfection could easily be obtained. But in order to make a good disc, the source material has to be in good condition. If the producers of the laser disc are unknowledgeable, they may think that video disc owners have the same tolerance levels as video cassette owners.

The source material for a program can sometimes have severely faded color, many scratches and splices, or be missing important footage. If the source for a film comes from a print which was used for television, it may be trimmed to fit certain timeslots. It might also be trimmed simply to fit onto a video cassette. Sometimes it may be just a few frames of film, but it will be enough to set the blood of movie collectors boiling, such as the loss of the 'James Bond will return in *Goldfinger*' message from the end of *From Russia with Love.*

Since CLV discs have an absolute time limit of an hour (and twelve seconds) a side, some disc producers attempt to find ways to cheat and squeeze movies which run a few minutes over two hours onto a two-hour disc. This practice, called 'time-compression,' involves removing a frame or two from various portions of the film so that, collectively, minutes could be trimmed without harming the continuity. Guided by their subconscious, which could quite clearly discern the difference, viewers rebelled. The practice was eventually abandoned, except for special instances, involving silly older titles, where its use is clearly publicized, and most titles which were originally released on a single platter have been reissued without compression.

Video cassette consumers may prefer to watch foreign films which have been dubbed in English, but laser video disc owners most certainly do not. There is some interest in repeating the Japanese experiment, of putting the English language dialog on one audio track and the original language dialog on the other, but after a flurry of initial protests involving dubbed discs without alternate soundtracks, most 'foreign' films have been released with subtitles. Subtitles allow you to hear the original soundtrack, but they prevent you from understanding background conversations or incidental dialog.

Most laser discs come in cardboard jackets, which are indistinguishable from the jackets of record LPs. The jackets are wrapped in a tight saran which ought to be taken off the day they arrive at the store and, at the very least, should be removed upon purchase. Discs which need two platters are sometimes released in 'gatefold' jackets which contain two sleeves joined together at the spine. Other discs come in boxes, like opera LPs, and these are often accompanied by fancy booklet inserts and hefty list prices, though the luxury of the package as a whole can be elegantly pleasing.

The best jacket covers use either the original advertising artwork or big, scrumptious stills. The 'innerspread' of a gatefold jacket can support a wonderful array of artwork. Text essays or other information about the program can also be integrated on a well-designed jacket. When legitimate effort has gone into their composition, these essays can often add an appreciation to the program material. Chapter listings ought to be mandatory when a disc has been encoded with chapter markers, but that is not always the case. Most companies include the running time on the back of the jacket, a piece of information which one cares very little about when one is attending a movie theater, but one can find quite useful when scheduling entertainment at home. Within the jacket, one or more discs are contained in paper or wax plastic sleeves.

The best laser video discs are not always derived from the best films. Interactive and educational discs are constructed with extra care and usually rank among the finest looking and most intriguing programs. Movies have been transferred to disc with masters generated from original nitrate negatives, which were tracked down by the video disc producers specifically to achieve the finest picture and sound available. A movie's trailer may be included at the end of the disc, demonstrating how audiences were first taught to approach the film. If the disc has been produced in CAV, advertising and promotional photos are sometimes included on still frames, as are essays describing the movie's production history or storyboards and original shooting scripts. Added footage can be included and, with the utilization of chapter markers, alternate cuts of controversial films can share the same side and allow the viewer to choose which version is superior.

ABOUT THIS BOOK

The reviews which follow cover a hefty selection of domestic and imported laser video discs, most of which were released between 1984 and 1990, incorporating some material which was published in a previous edition of this book. The condition of the pressing which was viewed is usually not mentioned, because there is no assurance that the copy you purchase comes from the same batch. The quality of the transfer is discussed, as is the condition of the sound, et cetera, but certain assumptions are made. If the picture or sound qualities are discussed without extensive detail, it can be assumed that these attributes fall within a certain understood standard and that no surprises await you when you slice open the shrink wrap. Some technical details left out of the review are provided in the appendices at the end. A basic familiarity with the most popular movies is also presumed.

Discs are in CLV format except where noted. The indication of the presence of CX-encoding has been dropped, since it is no longer a relevant guide to the quality of a disc's soundtrack, having been superseded by digital encoding and by the passage of time. The presence or lack of CX is still indicated in reviews where the information is deemed relevant. As a general rule of thumb, discs produced after 1987 have higher and more reliable standards of quality than those produced before, and they are getting better all the time.

Titles have been taken from the jacket spine in most cases. The title of a disc is not always specific, particularly with classical music discs. Although typographical errors on the jackets have been ignored, in some instances the disc producers deliberately add verbiage to a film's title, such as with *Alfred Hitchcock's Rebecca*, and these must be referenced as the producers have intended.

Disc prices vary widely and are beyond the scope this publication. Some of the discs which are reviewed have gone 'out of print,' but since the discs themselves, supposedly, remain is good shape, the reviews can function as a guide for collectors who wish to trade with others or obtain 'previously owned' used discs.

Nothing made by human beings is perfect and laser video discs aren't either. The product is a terrific improvement over other home video formats and, because of its quality, it can stimulate the spirits of film lovers, music lovers, and those searching for a knowledge of the world around them. The popcorn is optional.

A-HA – HUNTING HIGH AND LOW
(see **THE DREAM ACADEMY**)

ABBOTT & COSTELLO MEET FRANKENSTEIN
The first 'cult' hit in the laser disc market, the DiscoVision version of *Abbott & Costello Meet Frankenstein*, is highly sought after, in part, because only a few hundred copies were issued, but also because it is the type of classic film that disc owners want to have. MCA, beset by a gaggle of collectors desperate for any dusty copy which might still be lying around, reissued the film as an Encore Edition release.

The picture source material is fairly grainy and the sound shows its age. Side two is in CAV format, thus enabling one to freeze frame or slow speed the Wolfman metamorphosis and Dracula changing to and from an animated bat. The side also contains an original theatrical trailer. The movie is short and it is packed with ideas and monsters. Unlike many other cinematic attempts by the comedy duo, there are no slow spots or extended routines here which upset the pace.

THE ABOMINABLE DR. PHIBES/ DOCTOR PHIBES RISES AGAIN
Although *The Abominable Dr. Phibes/Doctor Phibes Rises Again* has been released as a 'Double Disc Set,' the package has four sides and each movie appears on its own platter. We would assume that unless one is a die-hard Joseph Cotten fan, wanting either movie is the same as wanting both.

The picture transfer on 'The Abominable Dr. Phibes' is gorgeous. The bright, poison candy colors in Phibes' laboratory are perfectly and solidly preserved, and one looks as forward to seeing what colors are going to show up next as one looks forward to see how the next murder is going to be committed. 'Dr. Phibes Rises Again' is passable, but in sharing the disc with the first film, the picture quality is a letdown. The edges are soft and the darker scenes are murky. The monaural sound is at the mercy of the original, tacky soundtrack.

The movies, which star Vincent Price and a collection of British character actors, are horror comedies, which shift between mild slapstick and gruesome torture/murders. Cotten appears in the first film as the victim who gets away, although the main hero in both programs is a police detective, cheerfully played by Peter Jeffrey. The first film has a tighter script, but the second movie has the best murder: an unflinching, down-the-pants scorpion attack which ought to be a crowd pleaser at your next Halloween party.

ABOUT LAST NIGHT
Since it was adapted from a stage play, *About Last Night* has a tight script and witty, practiced dialog. The story concerns late-'70s courtship rituals and mating practices. The picture is a bit on the grainy side. The stereo surround separations apply primarily to the pop music soundtrack and a few rumbles from Chicago's elevated mass transit trains.

ABOVE THE LAW
For once the exaggerated publicity surrounding the debut of an action oriented performer is well deserved. *Above the Law* is a bread-and-butter Warner film, and the lead, Steven Seagal, is the perfect Warner star. He's a cross between Christopher Lambert and Robert De Niro, a martial arts expert who is still entertaining when he is bound hand and foot. Only the music seems to be in stereo. The picture, though clear, is a bit on the orange side, particularly where flesh is involved. The plot is a typically scatter-brained tale about the CIA, Chicago gangsters, and drugs. Seagal, however, is completely comfortable sorting through it, and we can't wait to see what he does next.

ABSOLUTE BEGINNERS
ABSOLUTE BEGINNERS (Import)
The Japanese version of *Absolute Beginners* is in letterboxed format, with Japanese subtitles appearing beneath the picture, and the domestic release is a standard full screen version. We expected that the cropped version of the film would be a disaster, but it is not. Although the musical numbers are severely harmed by the lack of a wide screen, the dramatic interludes don't seem as empty, and so the flow of the film improves. The incredible *mise en scène* which opens the movie is just mildly harmed by the thinner picture, since it is the lack of cuts and not the width of the screen which gives the impression that the filmmakers have performed the impossible.

The picture quality on both discs is the same. The movie is quite colorful and this is conveyed by the discs, but the print has speckles and a few scratches and one can only imagine how colorful it might have been had a fresher source been employed. The sound is clean, but it hasn't much atmosphere, although that may be a shortcoming of the recording. There is a full, split-second dropout late on side one of the domestic disc.

Absolute Beginners is a depiction of a make-believe London in the late fifties, where everyone dances in step and sings in tune. The story begins as a *La Dolce Vita* on a beautifully elaborate street set meant to represent late-'50s London. Abandoning style for content, however, the show ends with a race war. We would have preferred a spectacular dance number.

ABSOLUTION
Anthony Shaffer wrote the script for *Absolution*, a 1978 effort starring Richard Burton and directed by Anthony Page, which languished on the shelf until the economics of home video thankfully retrieved it.

Burton, whose performance is marvelously engaging, portrays a priest at a Catholic boys' school who is tormented and eventually drawn into murder by lies spoken to him in confession. The plot has some good twists, so that one will wish to watch the movie twice at the very least (there is one brief shot, however, of a hand picking up a rock, which we would take exception to, since it misleads the emotions of the mystery).

The picture looks softer and older than a recent release, but it is not damaged in any way. The sound crackles a little if turned up too high. There are some nice folk songs on the soundtrack.

THE ABYSS
With a picture as sharp as *Patton* and a soundtrack as powerful as *Robocop*, *The Abyss* makes a terrific disc. The underwater adventure fantasy presents many video transfer problems – deep sea activities which have a great many details and little illumination, intensely lit panels and warning lights, weird luminescent purple creatures – but all come across the disc more accurately and sharply than in all but the most concerned theatrical presentations.

The Abyss was not a widescreen movie. However, the disc has an aspect ratio of about 1.85:1 and the picture composition looks correct, with no significant details lost on any of the four sides. The strength of the disc, however, is not so much in the image design as the image content. Some scenes were filmed grainy and look grainy, but the precision in focus and color detail from the opening 20th Century Fox logo to the (endless) end credit scroll is exhilarating.

The digital surround sound knocked objects off our shelf which we had thought were tied down. The basses boom. Alan Silvestri's tongue depressor musical score can be subject to easy ridicule, but it comes through the disc so clearly defined and with such sweeping fullness that it sets a standard for other clichés to copy rather than sounding like one itself. And then there are the many wonderful sound effects in between the booms and the music – creaking pipes, sonar pings, and especially a perfectly pitched chain ratchet which the bad guy drags on incessantly after he has gone mad. You don't hear the sounds on the disc, you feel them.

For those who know nothing of the movie, the narrative is best left to be discovered. The film has action, but is refreshingly free of violence. It has a villain, but is refreshingly free of evil. It has special visual effects, but they are only employed at a point where technology could no longer suffice. The movie also has no ending and no fish, but the latter will bother the viewer far more than the former will.

CBS/Fox has issued the disc in a gatefold jacket. There is a short 'Making of' film added to the end, which takes nothing away from the impact of the film itself. Making *The Abyss* was an adventure all of its own. Water was pumped into an unfinished power plant cooling tower and much of the movie was filmed 'on location' in a huge makeshift pool. Special aquatic apparatus designed specifically for the film are demonstrated, and the actors are shown gamely tolerating the physical demands of the production. Whatever hardship they endured, they can have their revenge now, because the director, James Cameron, has a giggle-inducing underwater interview which, thanks to the disc, he will be trying to live down forever.

ACADEMY OF ANCIENT MUSIC – MESSIAH
BEETHOVEN'S NINTH SYMPHONY (Import)
The movement to perform and record music using the instruments of the period in which the music was written is admirable, but the concept is not always successful, as one can see and hear on *The Academy of Ancient Music – Messiah*. It is not the instruments which will disappoint the unprepared, but the size of the choir. The group, from the Westminster Abbey Choir, is considerably smaller than the groups one usually associates with the piece. Their rendition is uplifting but not fulfilling.

Technically, the disc is in perfect condition. The performance is in English and there are chapter markers to denote each movement. We generally like to see closeups in shows of this nature, but there are not enough establishing shots to tell you how a performer is situated in relation to his peers.

On the Japanese release of *Beethoven's Ninth Symphony*, which was done live in Prague, the camera focuses not only on those who are performing, but those who are waiting to perform as well. When the choir finally joins in at the end, the effect is thrilling, because you know they've been standing there for close to an hour, waiting their turn. In *Messiah*, the different movements were filmed separately and there is no audience except for the viewer. The presentation is meant to imitate the way it would have sounded in Handel's era, but that spirit is interrupted by the cut and paste construction. In Handel's day, you played it through once for the King and either he stood up because the music moved him or he didn't.

THE ACCIDENTAL TOURIST

Warner has purposefully letterboxed *The Accidental Tourist*. The aspect ratio is 2:1 and manages to impart the original picture compositions without hesitation. It is difficult to imagine how the film, which is so precariously comical that it relies on every piece of output to formulate humor, could survive as a scanned and cropped feature. Characters and objects consistently appear at the far edges of the screen to neutralize eye contact, and the dialog is often intended to avoid direct attention, to sneak up on the viewer. Those who have only seen *Tourist* in cropped video are probably mystified as to what all the excitement was about.

The Accidental Tourist is a glib tale about a travel writer overcoming the death of his son, a tragedy which has also caused his marriage to disintegrate. The film is not perfect. The scenes relating to the writer's work don't seem to go anywhere, and some situations are too conveniently absurd. However, the characters in the film are deliberately eccentric, so that the narrative can avoid the stereotypical responses which a standard drama would create for such a set of circumstances. The hero, played by William Hurt, is in a perpetual fog, and yet runs his life rather successfully by radar. The women, Geena Davis, Kathleen Turner, and Amy Wright, have magnified quirks to hide their basic similarities (and their performances are all marvelous). The film is comical because of the calm way in which the personalities come into contact with one another. In real life the tension would explode. In the movie, it just tickles the viewer a little and gives the hero a bad back.

The picture is grainy in scenes involving strong autumnal lighting, and the copy we viewed opened with a little speckling. On the whole, however, the transfer is acceptable. The volume is set a little lower than on most discs, but when raised it presents no other problems. The movie runs a minute over two hours and is spread evenly across three sides in CLV with chapter encoding.

THE ACCUSED

A rape occurs at the beginning of *The Accused*, but it is not seen until a flashback during the courtroom climax, from which we would infer that the filmmakers are capitalizing on the same sort of titillation their movie condemns. The script is engaging, concentrating not upon the rapists, who are sent to jail early on, but on obtaining convictions against the barroom spectators who encouraged the rapists to continue. Jodie Foster's performance is utterly convincing, though the press, badgering her when she won awards for the film about the violence which has shadowed her personal life, apparently learned nothing from it. Both the picture and the sound are in good shape, though the image does look a little soft in the darker scenes.

ACROBATS OF GOD (see **THE ROYAL BALLET – SWAN LAKE**)

ACTION JACKSON

We were looking forward to *Action Jackson*, a decently-budgeted action film with a primarily black cast and ad art which imitated the James Bond pictures. By and large we were not disappointed. The plot has a host of inconsistencies, but what exploitation film does not?

The picture is grainy throughout most of the first half, and the lack of a widescreen is inhibiting during the stunts. Carl Weathers stars. The bass and stereo effects are enjoyable, and one of the final gag lines, concerning the demise of the villain, elicited from our jaded demeanor an unrestrained guffaw.

ADAM – GISELLE – FRACCI – BRUHN

Real running water and real horses are used in *Adam – Giselle – Fracci – Bruhn* to assist in transporting the experience of 'Giselle' away from the stage. True, these segments are mostly inserts and most of the program was filmed in a studio, but the camera, sometimes handheld, is often shoulder to shoulder with the dancers.

Recorded in 1969, the picture is a little pale in color. The ADD sound has no distinctive advantages or disadvantages. The music, performed by the Orchestra of the Berlin Opera, was not recorded in tandem with the dancing, but since the program has been blocked for the cameras and edited to the music, this is not a problem. The dancing of Carla Fracci, who portrays Giselle, is excellent, and the other dancers, Erik Bruhn, Bruce Marks, and Toni Lander, are also effective. The chorus is performed by the American Ballet Theatre.

The ballet retains what some would consider to be too much pantomime. This is advantageous to the filmmakers, however, because when the pantomime is going on, they can get as close to the dancers as they wish without significantly disrupting the choreography. The natural flow of the film between close shots and long shots disguises the still awkward and exploratory shifts between acting and dancing that the ballet possesses.

The disc has been intelligently chapter encoded (some last as little as 34 seconds) and the brake between side one and side two comes at the change between the first and second act. An informative but inelegant essay, written in 1987, is printed on a jacket insert in English and French.

ADAM'S RIB

It is only incidental to the entertainment that *Adam's Rib* fully manages to avoid any of the clichés of movie sex battles – it would probably still be funny if it hadn't – but it is that aspect which has kept the film fresh.

The disc has CX-encoding without automatic tripping, but it sounds best with the CX off. The print is so nice looking that one is riveted not only by the closeups and the sets, but by the throwaway location shots showing New York in the late forties. The black and white source looks as new and sharp as Katharine Hepburn's cheekbones. There is no question that the quality of the image increases one's concentration and enjoyment. You don't want to blink while the disc is running.

This is the film where Tracy and Hepburn portray husband and wife and prosecuting attorney and defense attorney. There are a pair of hysterical appearances by Judy Holliday and Jean Hagen, and, even when not deliberately comical, the byplay between the two leads is still so intricate as to be humorous and captivating. The weird ending, which a slightly exaggerated essay on the back of the jacket avoids mentioning, that has Tracy crying directly into the camera, is unsettling, but it provides just the right tone for the conclusion because it makes the viewer take the whole film seriously, despite its farcical aspects.

The CLV disc has 17 chapter markers. A lengthy, original theatrical trailer appears at the end. A lot of work seems to have gone into creating the trailer to hide what the film is really about.

ADRIADNE AUF NAXOS

The clever Richard Strauss opera, *Adriadne auf Naxos*, is presented by The Metropolitan Opera on a Deutsche Grammophon release. Both Jessye Norman and Kathleen Battle appear, which makes for some spectacular singing sequences on side three, along with Tatiana Troyanos and James King. The picture transfer looks acceptable, with some scrumptious closeups (one can really analyze the shifts in the singers' facial muscles as they change from one note to the next) and long shots which look slightly soft, but undistorted. The staging is reasonably compact. However, the video presentation still seems inept from time to time, as camera angles are sometimes chosen which leave out important stage activity.

The stereo sound is a perfect match for Norman's and Battle's vocal artistry. Free of distortion, the audio captures every inflection. The disc is presented in a box jacket and is accompanied by an insert which contains a very good essay about the opera in English and entirely different discourse in French. The opera itself is in German, with English subtitles.

The opera opens on a group of performers who are under pressure to put on a show. After that prolog, the show itself is presented, a wild mix of Grecian heroic tragedy and French romantic farce. (Strauss' music is also a daring and slightly flighty mixture of styles which can be quite appealing if one has become restless with the norm.) The prolog is presented on side one, and the opera on sides two and three, with the break between the latter two coming at an ideal moment. After the prolog on side one, however, there is a fifteen minute documentary about the rehearsal for the performance. Of course, watching the documentary, a suspiciously jovial depiction of James Levine working with Norman and Battle, is optional – you can proceed with the opera instead – but it does whet a viewer's appetite for what is to come and sharpen an awareness of key passages.

ADVENTURES IN BABYSITTING
One of the more enjoyable teen romps, *Adventures in Babysitting*, finds a lot of comedy in doing clichés one better, and places its protagonists in threatening situations without amplifying a viewer's anxieties. The disc is a bit on the grainy side, which exaggerates the already weak matte shots, and causes colors to run. The sound is digitally encoded stereo with surround effects, but it rarely calls attention to itself. There is a final gag after the end credit scroll.

THE ADVENTURES OF BARON MUNCHAUSEN
The Adventures of Baron Munchausen was not a widescreen production and is presented on disc without matting or letterboxing. The digital surround sound is well rounded and very enjoyable. Most of the time the picture looks great. When the film offers severe challenges, however, the transfer can't quite live up to them. There are a number of scenes lit heavily in red. Many of them do not look grainy, but a few look terribly so. A sequence near the beginning which appeared washed out on theatrical prints looks even more washed out on the disc.

The have-it-both-ways ending doesn't even seem to follow the illogical logic of the rest of the film, but getting there is great fun. The movie, an enormously budgeted effort that could never hope to earn back its expenses, is yet another gift to laser owners, who get to purchase it for about .000001 of its original cost. The special effects are grand. The film is filled with fairly literal flights of fancy – men riding cannonballs, people falling off the moon and cushioned in their drop to earth by the hot air from a volcano – and the narrative keeps plodding along, if only to generate more fantasy. It seems that Terry Gilliam will never make a film as perfect as his *Time Bandits* because he has become more interested in his visuals than in his characters, but we are quite happy to watch him continue to try.

THE ADVENTURES OF BUCKAROO BANZAI
The Adventures of Buckaroo Banzai has a potential cult appeal because the more often it is watched the more jokes one is going to pick up. Unfortunately, director W.D. Richter's mastery of film technique is not as innovative as his sense of comedy. The movie ought to come at you from every angle, just as the jokes do. Instead, the clutter looks messy without a coordinating idea and the actors are under-utilized except for John Lithgow, who portrays a mad Italian scientist. His hair looks like a bundle of exclamation points. The disc is appealing even though the movie fails. Projects like this don't get financed too often and are thus endearingly rare. They fill a void where most people believe a void should remain. Although the image is cropped, the picture transfer is workable and the soundtrack is fun.

THE ADVENTURES OF CAPTAIN MARVEL
The twelve episode serial, *The Adventures of Captain Marvel*, runs 216 minutes and fits on four sides with only one of the episodes interrupted by a side break. The first (introductory) episode lasts about a half hour, while the others run between fifteen and twenty minutes. Republic has marked each episode with a separate chapter code. A trailer for the whole program appears at the beginning.

A serial is like an emotional disorder. One moment everything looks hopelessly bleak, then an obvious solution is provided and you wonder what it was you were worried about, and then something else happens and things look hopelessly bleak once more. (And only the bad guys have the leisure to be introspective.) With *Captain Marvel*, the ups and downs are physical as well as mental. The special effects are amazing – except when they are silly, but that is fun, too – as the superhero leaps off of buildings and cliffs to collar crooks in the same way that an owl nabs a field mouse. The film, which encompasses the hero's origin, has him battling The Scorpion to protect the components of a weapon that have been distributed among a group of eventual victims. The action is constant, and even when the disc is viewed in one sitting, the situations never become boring or repetitive.

The transfer is good. The black and white source material has no significant flaws and the image has only a mild softness to impart its age. The digital monaural sound has an unusually strong bass and no more than an occasional distortion.

THE ADVENTURES OF ELIZA FRASER
Based upon a true incident, *The Adventures of Eliza Fraser* is about the young wife of an aging, indignant sea captain. On their final trip to England, after stopping at a penal colony on the Australian coast, their boat shipwrecks and they end up living for a while with aborigines before returning to civilization. The story, which has the complexity of a pop novel, includes several subplots involving the penal colony. These all converge in a series of deadpan conclusions in which every character eventually gets what he or she deserves.

The transfer is a disappointment but the charming musical score, like the film's funniest sequences, will linger when the disc is over.

THE ADVENTURES OF MARK TWAIN
Will Vinton's 'Claymation' process is known for Oscar-winning shorts and raisin commercials, but *The Adventures of Mark Twain* is his first feature length film. It is a clever enfolding of a dozen or so Twain tales using a 'trip to Halley's comet' as a linking device for the different stories, even though they are quite capable of standing by themselves. While the plot veers close to the dangerous shoals of education several times, it manages for the most part to keep an even, entertaining keel, despite having almost every comment Twain makes be an actual Twain quote ("A cauliflower is just a cabbage with a college education.")

The animation, as anyone who has been exposed to it is well aware, is fantastic. Objects grow out of objects and move about with an uncanny smoothness. The disc is very colorful and makes an unusual addition to one's visual library. The tale which elicits the most attention from the animators is Twain's 'The Diary of Adam and Eve.' It is not surprising that they should identify with this, since they themselves are creating life from clay.

THE ADVENTURES OF ROBIN HOOD
(Voyager CLV)
THE ADVENTURES OF ROBIN HOOD
(Voyager CAV)
THE ADVENTURES OF ROBIN HOOD
(CBS/Fox)
The Adventures of Robin Hood was the fifteenth film to be made in Technicolor and the colors on the Criterion Collection disc are so playfully resplendent that it is advisable to lock your remote control in the closet before you start the movie. Otherwise, the temptation to freeze and gawk is just too strong to resist.

And who would want to interrupt such a marvelous movie, especially if it has been a while since one's last screening? The familiarity of the characters (and the actors filling the roles), the pacing (for one thing, Robin's meeting with Friar Tuck is pared to a single halfstream crossing), the stunts, the believable romance, and the reliable (if historically questionable) pitting of good against evil are all factors in the entertainment. *The Adventures of Robin Hood* may be a textbook example of the reliability of proven formulas, but one wishes only that more movies had been as successful.

The colors on the disc are wonderful, particularly where the costumes are involved and most particularly of all where Olivia de Havilland's costumes are involved. There is a closeup of her as she pauses to eavesdrop while descending a staircase in a shot that is made up entirely of whites, silvers and greys (except her red lips!) Cloth drapes around her face like a silken frame. The color is so accurate that the texture of each material touching her flesh is communicated to the viewer. You'll want to run to your closet and grab the remote. The picture transfer on the CLV version is slightly brighter and more pleasing than the CAV presentation.

The discs have two brief errors which are worth mentioning only to prevent unneeded surprises. The picture goes out of focus briefly in chapter 10 on the beginning of side two and the volume drops out of a speech by Claude Rains in chapter 24 on side three. The sound was transferred from a '35 nitrate optical negative.' Recorded in 1938, it is a bit on the tinny side, but ought to conform to the expectations of most viewers. The analog component on both discs has alternate material on the second audio track, a talk by industry historian Rudy Behlmer. The analog sound is CX-encoded without automatic tripping and has significantly less noise when the CX is activated.

Although of little use beyond a single run-through, Behlmer's comments on Robin Hood cover both the legend (though he fails to note the similarity between Robin's first meeting with Little John and Arthur's first run-in with Lancelot) and a knowledgeable summary of the movie's production history. Behlmer manages to answer just about every question one may have about the film or about Robin Hood, and he avoids the pitfalls of other Criterion narrators by letting the action speak for itself except when screen illusions are involved.

The CAV 'Supplementary Section' includes a lengthy and varied amount of behind-the-scenes footage and an early rerelease trailer. The best part, however, is a gathering of front pages and covers from the printed tales of Robin Hood, some nearly 150 years old. More than 250 still images are utilized, showing book illustrations, glimpses of texts, published songs about Robin Hood, and press material from several Robin Hood movies.

The Adventures of Robin Hood has appeared previously on disc, via CBS/Fox, in CLV. That transfer, done some time earlier, is in pretty bad shape. The colors are vivid, but they are not correct (in the staircase shot, de Havilland is surrounded by egg green) and the image is often too dark around the edges. In addition, the volume levels on the sound are set too low.

THE ADVENTURES OF SHERLOCK HOLMES/SHERLOCK HOLMES AND THE VOICE OF TERROR

The CBS/Fox two-for-the-price-of-one-and-a-half release of *The Adventures of Sherlock Holmes/Sherlock Holmes and the Voice of Terror* is good fun. Except for the reel changes, the black and white prints are in good condition and have nice, sharply defined lines. The sound is substantially cleaner than the analog track and sounds okay.

Side one has the first movie. Side two has the end of the first movie and, marked with a chapter, the beginning of the second. Side three has the end of the second movie. The chapter listing on the back of the jacket for *Adventures/Terror* is incorrect, since the first movie is marked with chapter '0' (not '1') and the second movie with chapter '1' (not '2').

The use of the double bill is especially strong in this pairing because 'Voice of Terror' is not especially good, and is more entertaining as a dessert (it is only an hour long) after the main feature. 'Adventures,' in which Professor Moriarty tries to throw Holmes off the trail while committing the 'crime of the century,' is both elaborate and engaging. Even though the script has more than a few holes, it has many memorable and even haunting scenes. We can't say what some of them are without giving too much away (a statue loses its head), but there is one which is quite basic and quite wonderful, where Holmes, holding a lamp, tramps through the evening mist looking for clues.

In 'Voice of Terror,' Holmes is fighting Nazis, and however fiendish they may be, the era is wrong. The curious aspect to this film is the final speech which Rathbone gives. He warns that a 'wind is coming from the East,' and it is almost as if the scriptwriters were hedging their bets, in case England actually got invaded or lost the war (the film was made in 1942).

THE ADVENTURES OF THE AMERICAN RABBIT

A feature length cartoon about a rabbit with super powers, *The Adventures of the American Rabbit* was withdrawn from the market shortly after release. The animation was done in Japan, but the voices will be familiar to those who watch Saturday morning TV. The cartoon has many animal inspired characters, who appear to live anthropomorphically in genuine US locations. The plot opens with the Rabbit's origins and then pits him against an evil genius who wins one or two small battles, but loses the war. Some sequences are comical, but the animation on the whole is limited and not very inspiring. The transfer is competent but not thorough and some strong colors look a little grainy. The disc has a few chapter markers and passable digital monaural sound. Side two is in CAV. Due to the nature of the animation some still frames quiver and some are duplicated.

THE ADVENTURES OF THE LITTLE PRINCE (see ROBIN HOOD)

AEROSMITH: LIVE TEXXAS JAM '78

The sound quality of *Aerosmith: Live Texxas Jam '78* is deadening. The stereo sound seemed flat to the point of not being stereo at all, and lacks a decent dynamic range. The program is a depiction of a decade-old outdoor concert in the Cotton Bowl and is definitely for fans only. The program cuts between the group playing at night to fans gathering for the concert during the daytime, a combination which inhibits the viewer from obtaining a sense of the atmosphere surrounding the evening concert. The program is an hour long and the disc has only one side. The picture is mildly grainy.

AFFAIR IN TRINIDAD

Affair in Trinidad looks very clean. The black and white image is consistently crisp and blemish free. The sound is also in good shape.

The movie, a romantic intrigue, is probably a conscious reworking of *Notorious*, though it was intended to rekindle the fires lit by *Gilda*. The film stars Rita Hayworth and Glenn Ford. Set in the Caribbean, it opens with the discovery of a dead body and then follows the police inspector to the victim's widow, who is performing a rambunctiously provocative song and dance act at a local night club. The plot is never quite as good as it is during those first ten minutes, but the movie is enjoyable and is well served by the disc.

AFRICA SCREAMS

What Voyager did for *Citizen Kane* and *The Magnificent Ambersons*, Image has done for *Africa Screams*.

Africa Screams? Yes, *Africa Screams*, an Abbott and Costello picture which is the epitome of every silly jungle comedy ever made. There are men in ape suits, rear-projected lions, and rubber crocodiles. There are even cannibals, who don't notice the lean Abbott because they can't take their eyes off of the plump Costello.

Image, under the direction of Bob Furmanek who had also provided materials to MCA for their Abbott & Costello discs, has mastered the disc from an original nitrate negative, provided an essay mixing text and production stills to describe how the film was made, included outtake scenes where the actors flub their lines or play practical jokes on one another, and added reams of promotional stills, presskit material, and lobby artwork. The film is 79 minutes long. Side one is in CLV and side two, which contains the special features, is in CAV.

The disc might make graduate-level film students chew off the ends of their pencils, but avid movie collectors will take delight in the irreverent style and rude mechanical humor of the film and will value the care with which it has been transferred to the silver platter.

Yes, the cannibals turn white when they see a gigantic ape, but no other gag is racially malicious (although some of the ad art is) and most of the material is so archaic that a youngster will not feel his or her heritage is threatened by the proceedings. The film also features Frank Buck, heavyweight champion Max Baer, Shemp Howard, Hillary Brooke, and Joe Besser. The jacket cover, which depicts the original lobby art, looks atrocious, but don't pass it by. The movie is every bit as bad as the cover implies, and the disc brings it all back, alive.

AFTER HOURS

A beguiling paranoia, which *After Hours* substitutes for charm, can be very effective the first time through, but false and manipulative on subsequent viewings. The travails of a young man who goes out for an evening and is detained from returning home through progressive sets of circumstances could be a gigantic trick which is being played upon him for the sake of conceptual art, or it could just be coincidence. The monaural sound is excellent and the picture is fine.

AGAINST ALL FLAGS

Against All Flags is inconsistent in appearance (one reel is noticeably grainy), but it looks good over all. In additon to the film, the disc sports a collection of more than 140 production stills at the end of side two. Side one is in CLV, but side two is in CAV and the movie has a marvelous sword fight at its resolution. The colors are incredible in this sequence, especially when the disc is run in slow motion. The camera is stationary, so the people move while the planks and ropes on the ship deck stay perfectly still. The background looks so crisp that it gives the illusion of real time, and makes the actors appear surreal. (Unfortunately, on early copies of the disc, every other still frame jitters. MCA corrected the problem on subsequent pressings, but never recalled the originals.) The production stills on side two, which include some advertising material and a few storyboard drawings, are a trip, particularly the one in which the director, George Sherman, is showing Errol Flynn and Maureen O'Hara how to kiss.

The monaural sound shouldn't bother anyone. Flynn portrays a British officer who goes undercover to bust some pirates. He's up to his normal tricks, and the best closeups give his face a wonderful texture. Most appealing, however, is O'Hara, who plays a pirate until Flynn melts her sword.

AGAINST ALL ODDS

Despite long passages in which very little occurs, *Against All Odds* is an involving mystery story. The hero (Jeff Bridges) is offered an unusually large sum to locate a woman (Rachel Ward) in Mexico. Instead of reporting back, he becomes involved with her.

Eventually there is a murder and by the end several more individuals meet with violence. The title song, which was a hit video/trailer, sounds particularly sharp on the disc's stereo audio track. The picture is a bit grainy but viable. Lanie Kazan has a small part as a secretary in a law office and almost steals the whole movie because she, unlike the others, refuses to slow down.

AGATHA CHRISTIE'S PARTNERS IN CRIME – THE SECRET ADVERSARY
AGATHA CHRISTIE'S THE AMBASSADOR'S BOOTS/THE MAN IN THE MIST
AGATHA CHRISTIE'S THE SUNNINGDALE MYSTERY/THE CLERGYMAN'S DAUGHTER

For those who are unfamiliar with the *Agatha Christie's Partners in Crime* series, it is set in England between the Wars and concerns a dashing young couple, Tuppence and Tommy Beresford (Francesca Annis and James Warwick), who run a detective agency. The episodes are charmingly romantic and often quite funny. Annis brings an especial amount of wit and humor to her role. With Christie's influence, her character is just as likely to achieve the solution to the crime as Warwick's is, and whenever the two take lodgings away from the city during an investigation they often put things off to try out the accommodations. It is always important to approach Christie's work in the right frame of mind. If you expect plot twists you are likely to be disappointed, but if you revel in the atmosphere of mystery, in an appreciation of the set-up rather than the solution, then you will have a wonderful time.

Pacific Arts released a single offering from the series, *Agatha Christie's Partners in Crime – The Secret Adversary*, which was very grainy and had a weak monaural soundtrack. Ever want to flip to the end of a detective story to find out who done it? To have *The Secret Adversary* on home video is to be confronted with an even stronger temptation. It is revealed early on that the viewer has actually seen the criminal mastermind whose identity is otherwise not revealed until the end, some ninety minutes later. The temptation to scan back and see who it is will separate the pure of heart from those who cheat at solitaire.

Somewhat later, Image and Pacific Arts began releasing single hour episodes as double bills, two to a disc. The video tape source material looks much fresher, and the sound is also cleaned up. It seems to be symptomatic of the series that the outdoor shots are fuzzier than the indoor scenes, but when the lighting is right the image looks fantastic.

In 'Ambassador's Boots' on *Agatha Christie's The Ambassador's Boots/The Man in the Mist* a diplomat's valise is swapped and then just as mysteriously returned. Don't miss the moment near the end when Tuppence, with too much aplomb, borrows a knife from a police inspector and slices his hand in the process. It is a wonderful throwaway gag. 'Man in the Mist' is a nicely constructed story about a famous actress who is murdered in her room and the limited number of suspects who had access to her. The episode also gets a good deal of mileage out of a disguise which adorns Tommy as the piece opens up. He is dressed as a Catholic priest.

'The Clergyman's Daughter' actually appears on side one of *Agatha Christie's The Sunningdale Mystery/The Clergyman's Daughter*. The Beresfords visit a haunted mansion in disguise to find out who is trying to scare the owner away, and why. They solve 'The Sunningdale Mystery' without ever coming into contact with the participants, piecing it together from newspaper accounts (which are acted out in flashback) and then visiting the scene of the crime to discover a crucial piece of evidence.

AGNES OF GOD

A 'mystery' once signified a religious rite, so you can see what scenarist John Pielmeier is up to with *Agnes of God*, even though it doesn't work. His desire to begin with a conventional mystery and then switch to an ancient one fails because the former lacks wit and the latter is too agnostic. There aren't enough closeups of Jane Fonda, either, so you don't share her discoveries or get misled in the ways that her character does. Norman Jewison did a great job directing *A Soldier's Story*, but he thought he was making the same movie here, with nuns. The picture transfer is unexceptional and mildly grainy.

THE AGONY AND THE ECSTASY

The movie about Michelangelo's painting of the Sistine Chapel, *Agony and the Ecstasy*, has been released by CBS/Fox as a 'Special Wide Screen Edition' disc. Like painting one's living room, the drama tends to come in three forms – choosing the right color (or design), disastrous drips (twice the Pope comes that close to getting splattered), and exhaustion. (Will it ever be completed?) The problem with the movie is that while Michelangelo is a more famous person, Pope Julius II had a more dramatic life. The intention is to draw parallels between the Pope's coaxing of the artist and a sculptor's 'release' of a figure from marble.

The movie, which stars Charlton Heston and Rex Harrison as painter and Pope, is rendered tolerable by the disc presentation. The source material is imperfect, and early reels tend to have mildly faded colors. The latter half of the movie looks better and the focus is consistently sharp. Overall, the colors and details are strong enough to hold a viewer's attention. The image has been letterboxed with an aspect ratio of about 2.1:1. A twelve minute 'prolog' created for the film, which focuses on Michelangelo's sculpting career, is also in widescreen, an ideal framing for the works that are depicted. Both prolog and film have digital stereo surround sound. Surround effects are limited to the musical score, but the dialog is often separated to the left or right channels, which can be fun. The soundtrack is in fairly good condition.

AIDA – TEATRO ALLA SCALA
AIDA ARENA DI VERONA

Adolescent boys are advised to turn straight to side two on *Aida – Teatro alla Scala*, for it opens with the 'Dance of the Moorish Slaves,' and they are decadently topless. You can bet no one tried to win a charity raffle to appear as an extra in that scene.

This is the second version of Giuseppe Verdi's Egyptian tragedy to be released by Pioneer. One of Pioneer's very first operatic discs was *Aida Arena di Verona*. The La Scala production is a 1986 effort which stars Luciano Pavarotti, Maria Chiara, Ghena Dimitrova and Juan Pons. The 1981 Verona production also featured Chiara in the title role, with Fiorenza Cossotto, Nicola Martinucci, and Giuseppe Scandola supporting. Set outside in the huge Arena di Verona, the earlier production is quite a spectacle, with a cast of hundreds. The La Scala staging, however, is also impressively elaborate, and has more going for it than just naked slaves.

The *La Scala* disc is digitally encoded, with the analog track having a noticeable gain in hiss over the digital track. *Verona* has CX-encoding with manual tripping and is noisier, but as far as the actual recording goes, the *Verona* soundtrack is in several ways superior to the *La Scala* recording. Of course, Martinucci's singing cannot compete with Pavarotti's, but Chiara has more energy in the earlier effort, and the sound in the outdoor arena is crisper than the unaccountably flat acoustics on the *La Scala* disc. The scale of the Verona staging is intimidating, though in the third act, when the camera can just settle on the two or three leads, the result is captivating. The direction on the *La Scala* video still can't get everything in, but over the length of the show it succeeds in not distracting a viewer's attention from the singing.

As for the picture, the quality of the *La Scala* transfer is a disappointment and is fairly grainy, making it only slightly better than the often out-of-focus *Verona* effort. Both discs have chapter markers for the same music highlights, and are broken to four sides, matching the opera's four acts. *Verona* runs 154 minutes and *La Scala* is 6 minutes longer. The opera is sung in Italian and *La Scala* has English subtitles while *Verona* does not. The plot synopsis for the *Verona* disc, however, is superior to the *La Scala* effort (the *La Scala* synopsis contains a typographical error; either a line or a sentence has been left out of Act III) and the type in the enclosed libretto is more appealing, though *La Scala*'s libretto also includes a few nice stills.

AIRPORT

"You'll kill yourself for nothing if you explode that bomb!" is the most memorable line of dialog we have ever heard in a movie trailer or movie commercial. Part of its impact comes from Dean Martin's overly sober delivery and poor syntax, but most of its strength lies in the ten words themselves; it is an instant cliffhanger; you'll sit patiently through more than half the movie waiting for the sentence and the scene, and to see what follows.

The line is heard twice on *Airport*. It is in the movie, and it is on the trailer which appears after the movie is ended. The disc opens to a black screen and the sounds of a crowded, impatient airport terminal. Then the orchestra strikes up Alfred Newman's theme and the screen opens to the hectic pandemonium of the central concourse, as the title of the film looms forward to fill the entire screen, "*AIRPORT*." You know you are in for a ride.

As a movie, *Airport* is easy to dismiss, but as home video, it is not. The cockpit scenes and the split screen sequences are letterboxed. The rest of the movie is not, but the one shot which is truly harmed by scanning and cropping – a priest crosses himself and then slaps a hysterical aisle mate – does appear in widescreen on the letterboxed trailer. The print is flawless and the color sparkles. The stereo mix is grand, with the music shifting to alternate channels whenever the briefcase bomb is near. The digital track has slightly less hiss than the analog track and the movie comes from an era when sound recording was less sophisticated, but from the opening blank screen murmur to the closing jet engine whine, the sound mix is as cute as Helen Hayes's dimples and as solid as Burt Lancaster's jaw.

Side three of the 137-minute film is in CAV. Every still frame creates a perfect picture. Fast speed increases the purity of the image, particularly where models have been used for the planes. Slow motion lets one savor the expressions of the stars as they 'act.' Martin never could act, but to appreciate how hard he is trying here, as if it were his 'big chance' or 'comeback,' is to understand that great movies don't always have to be technically or poetically accurate to succeed. All they need is a little chutzpa.

AIRPORT '77

Jack Lemmon has a nervous personality even when relaxed, so you can imagine what it is like when he tries to tell the passengers of a 747 which has submerged in the Bermuda Triangle in *Airport '77* that they should not panic. They start screaming. He plays the captain, and there are more stars than we care to list portraying passengers and members of the crew. If you start out by watching the trailer at the end of the disc, then you will be in the proper mood for the movie itself. The plane must have crashed into the hypotenuse of the Bermuda Triangle, since the movie is essentially a sum of many squares.

The picture and sound on the disc will not cause one to grab for an oxygen mask. The sound seems best suited for the little single speaker which is imbedded on most television sets. The picture is in acceptable condition, but MCA has been known to try harder. The trailer has its own chapter marker and strains to squeeze as much excitement as there is in the movie into its brief sales pitch.

The film has one other passage which will be of interest to laser video disc owners. There is a blatant and silly plug of MCA's DiscoVision system at minute 19 on side one. The actress loading the disc in the player gets her dirty fingers all over the surface of the platter and has trouble (!) putting the hole onto the spindle. The disc turns out to be a 'hello' message recorded by the plane's owner and, apparently, intended to be played in only one place at only one time, a utilization totally unrelated to mass produced entertainment. With such marketing wonders at the helm, it is no wonder the whole laser disc home video concept almost ended up in the Bermuda Triangle with the plane and the movie.

AIRSHOW

As there are a number of airshow discs available and *Airshow* is simply more of the same. The hour long program depicts different flying teams, including the Blue Angels, Snowbirds, Patouille de France, and Frecce Tricolori, performing precision flying routines while the soundtrack alternates between jet sounds and bland Japanese pop music. The video transfer is exquisite, as it usually is in such programs, and the digital stereo surround does what it is supposed to do.

AL JARREAU IN LONDON

The advantages of digital sound are readily apparent on *Al Jarreau in London*. The disc is considered to have one of the best audio transfers of all. Jarreau's careful, off-balance phrasing comes through sharply on the analog track, but in digital it sears through the music. Included on the program are such hits as 'We're in This Love Together,' 'Our Love,' and Jarreau's version of 'Take Five.' The picture is grainy and blurs considerably when the camera catches a spotlight. The effect occasionally gives Jarreau an aura, but with his talent, he deserves one.

ALABAMA – GREATEST VIDEO HITS

The nine music videos included on *Alabama – Greatest Video Hits* are all straightforward but unconvincing when strung together, because a different model is used in each effort, so the blonde to whom the lead singer has been declaring his devotion is replaced, in the next number, by a brunette. The one-sided CLV disc is 37 minutes long. The picture and sound are fine.

THE ALAMO

John Wayne's meticulously designed and executed tribute to the siege of the Alamo has been given a 'Deluxe Letter-Box Edition' treatment by MGM/UA. The disc, which has an aspect ratio of about 2.1:1 and a nice stereo surround soundtrack, gives viewers the best opportunity on home video to appreciate Wayne's accomplishment.

The Alamo is both problematic and magnificent. Wayne shifts comfortably between telling the story and demonstrating that the emotional strength of the characters was the strength that created our country and our liberties. It has to be viewed in widescreen to be taken seriously, because it is only when one can fully view William Clothier's cinematography that one understands the depth of Wayne's commitment to the project. Other artists – many other artists – may have assisted him in the production, but the movie is clearly his. *The Alamo* is unique, damnable, and glorious.

The film scores of Dimitri Tiomkin are often too literal. Instead of prickling a viewer's subliminal responses to a scene, his music often emphasizes the obvious, becoming the aural equivalent of a large white arrow. Wayne's direction, however, is also straightforward, so much so that in several scenes he nearly drops the illusion of drama to address the viewer directly. In this context, Tiomkin's music is effective, because he can't possibly over-emphasize what is already being played to the hilt. The disc's audio and the musical score go together very well. The entr'acte, instead of simply rehashing the overture, is a swelling, choral interpretation of the traditional 'Eyes of Texas,' and the chills it gives you is representative of the impact the movie can have.

The disc's running time is 172 minutes. It is squeezed into three sides, with the intermission placed in the middle of side two. The break between side two and three occurs about a minute after a natural fade-to-black. This is the generally accepted theatrical version of the film and the most complete version available. Some twenty minutes from Wayne's initial final cut is gone, most of it *Donovan's Reef*-style drinking scenes and an intolerable birthday party for a character played by Wayne's granddaughter. A few key scenes involving Richard Widmark were also removed, but the film is sufficiently coherent as it stands.

The color transfer is okay. The image looks a little pale, but the color schemes are all dusty yellows and browns, so it is often difficult to gauge. The picture is sharply focussed and free of any distracting glitches. The sound is very directional and lots of fun. Listen for the drum marchers sequence – it's a knockout.

ALAMO BAY

Unless you have a particular fondness for Ed Harris, Amy Madigan or Ho Nguyen, it is doubtful that you will want to watch *Alamo Bay* more than once, if at all. The screenplay is of film-student quality, with every scene advancing only a single idea. The story, about Vietnamese immigrants upsetting the way of life on the gulf coast of Texas, romanticizes the racial problems in a situation which has actually been caused by economics, thus perpetuating the very bigotry they wish to condemn.

The sound is an example of how good monaural discs can be even if they haven't been CX-encoded. The picture is a little grainy.

ALAN QUARTERMAIN AND THE LOST CITY OF GOLD

(see **KING SOLOMON'S MINES**)

ALCHEMY DIRE STRAITS LIVE

Text on the cover of *Alchemy Dire Straits Live* states, "It contains no re-recording or overdubs of any kind." The volume levels and levels of clarity among the instruments and various performers swing wildly, and however much Dire Straits could use a little roughing up, a noisy live concert, in which the group tends to stretch each number out, is not the answer.

The stereo sound is at the mercy of the concert recording. The picture quality is at the mercy of the stage lighting and most of it is poor. There is a constant halo of fuzz around any of the musicians lucky enough to receive illumination. The disc is an hour and a half long, but only hard Dire fans should consider it.

ALEXANDER NEVSKY

It is difficult to maintain a straight face watching Sergei Eisenstein's *Alexander Nevsky*. The cinematography is breathtaking and the editing is doctrinal, but the nickelodeon-level acting is immensely silly and Sergei Prokofiev's over-rated original musical score is outlandishly inappropriate. Some viewers have complained about the quality of the disc but we find nothing wrong with the transfer when it is compared to other non-Hollywood efforts from the thirties. The print has a few scratches and a white line running through it for a while, but it looks passable. The digitally encoded monaural sound has a limited dynamic range, but the theaters *Alexander Nevsky* was intended for weren't exactly wired for Dolby. The movie is a sound film, though most of the dialog and sound effects are post-synchronized. The English subtitles use a mockheroic syntax, often beginning sentences with verbs. Prokofiev's score is typical of an independent genius's input. It is totally out of synch with the film's mood. The music provides carnival style flippancies during the most melodramatic plot turns.

The film tells of a Russian prince who organizes a line of defense to repel Teutonic interlopers. It is set in the thirteenth century but serves as a reminder that the Germans often enjoyed dropping in on their eastern neighbors. Eisenstein instructs the actors to exaggerate their characters. It looks sloppy and can easily inspire a giggle, especially since it is in conflict with the carefully composed visuals. The screen composition is designed, like a musical score, to explore and repeat motifs of textures.

The disc is still a strong candidate for one's home video collection, however. Not only is the cinematography compelling, but there is a battle scene which lasts a full half hour and is definitive in its execution. Like most action adventure movies, *Alexander Nevsky* has its flaws, but in the excitement of the moment, faults are the least of a viewer's concerns.

ALFRED HITCHCOCK PRESENTS

Four episodes which Alfred Hitchcock himself directed for his original television series make an unexpected and pleasing addition to one's Hitchcock collection on *Alfred Hitchcock Presents*. 'Banquo's Chair' is superbly preserved and presented with a bright, fresh picture and heightened sound. The other three, 'Lamb to the Slaughter,' 'The Case of Mr. Pelham,' and 'Back for Christmas,' are more on par with what one sees and hears on late-night TV. All are black-and-white and have monaural sound.

'Lamb for the Slaughter' is a concise mixture of all of Hitchcock's favorite themes. A woman murders her husband with a leg of lamb, cooks it, and serves it to the investigating detectives. Hitchcock's interest is also clearly perked by the domestic tensions in 'Back for Christmas.' The series was famous for Hitchcock's opening and closing remarks. The most often quoted of these, a rapid fire series of puns comparing Hollywood to a jungle, can be seen bookending 'Banquo's Chair.' It alone would have made the disc worthwhile.

ALFRED HITCHCOCK PRESENTS

(Import)

Although they certainly are not in the same class as the originals, the four episodes on the Japanese disc, *Alfred Hitchcock Presents*, which are the same four that were broadcast in the pilot for the 1985 revival of the series, are all entertaining and engaging and feature colorized renditions of the actual Hitchcock introductions. The broadcast was in stereo, but the disc is monaural and has not been CX-encoded. It has subtitles. The picture is in such excellent condition that an episode which takes place in the neon-lit environs of a Las Vegas hotel has no difficulty exhibiting sharply focused details no matter what shifts occur in the lighting schemes.

The first episode stars Ned Beatty as a man who is mistaken for a serial killer by a lynch mob. The second is about a wager involving a fancy car, a cigarette lighter, and the little finger on a left hand. It stars John Huston, Steve Bauer, and Melanie Griffith. Tippi Hedron appears in a brief scene with Melanie, which is a treat, and Kim Novak also shows up with a surprise. The third episode is about a child walking around with a loaded gun, and you bite your tongue every time she pulls the trigger. The finale is a straightforward nurse-trapped-with-a-nurse-killer-during-a-storm scream-generator which accomplishes exactly what it sets out to accomplish.

ALFRED HITCHCOCK'S REBECCA
ALFRED HITCHCOCK'S REBECCA

(CAV)

The Voyager CAV 'Criterion Collection' release of *Alfred Hitchcock's Rebecca* has an audio lecture on a second soundtrack, and side six is in CLV and contains three and three quarter hours of audio material. Additionally, there is an extended still frame section. A CLV release retains the lecture but none of the other special features.

We have never seen a bad copy of *Rebecca*. Voyager's presentation, taken from a '35 mm fine grain composite master print' looks very sharp and finely detailed. There are sections which are weaker. The source material goes soft and mildly grainy, or markings such as scratches appear, but the overall impression is a positive one. When the CAV triple speed function is employed, particularly in the opening view of Manderley, the quality of the image is captivating.

There are no differences in picture quality between the CLV and CAV versions. The sound, from a '35 mm optical negative soundtrack' is strong, though as is explained in the supporting materials sound editing was not one of the film's stronger points. The audio lecture is by Leonard J. Leff, whose book about Hitchcock and David Selznick, *Hitchcock and Selznick* qualifies him as the most informed source on the subject. Leff's talk is padded somewhat with descriptions of what is readily viewable on the screen, but his scene-for-scene knowledge of how the film was put together is informative, and he is forever filling in the viewer not only with how many takes were needed to accomplish a specific shot, but why they were needed. A larger view of the film's impact, both on the public and on the artists involved, would have been appreciated, but every other aspect of the movie is thoroughly covered.

Rebecca is not exactly a title we have longed to manipulate in CAV. Other than the aforementioned twiddling with the faster speeds, there are not many applications which can be considered useful. Since David Selznick commandeered the editing from Hitchcock, most of the shots last so long that there is no reason to freeze them longer. The still frame section placed at the end of side five after the film is ended includes some of the famous 'Selznick memos,' a few production notes, some good publicity stills, a thorough advertising display, and some other odds and ends.

Each of the four audio tracks is used independently on the CLV side six. Two of them contain radio programs. Orson Welles' Campbell Playhouse rendition, made shortly after Daphne du Maurier's novel became a bestseller, has appeared previously, on Voyager's *Theatre of the Imagination* disc. A version from Lux Radio Theater, which traditionally involved condensed representations of popular films, is specifically adapted from the movie and features Ronald Coleman, Hitchcock and Selznick's first choice for the role, as Maxim de Winter. It is clear from his reading that he would have made a stronger presence in the part and perhaps, if such a thing is possible, increased the appeal of the film. Welles' version was thrown together in a week's time and, though it was a 'ratings hit,' has little to offer in the way of artistic merits. The latter is also in weak physical shape.

Several interviews are to be found on another one of the audio tracks. Due to the nature of the source material the track has extreme swings in volume and is best heard from an output unit which can be controlled by a remote control. Actual recordings which were transcribed in the *Hitchcock/Truffaut* book embellish the printed words with Hitchcock's enunciations, pauses, and other considerations. Truffaut's questions are supplied by a translator. Unfortunately, the segment only deals with *Rebecca* and a few spin-offs. One wishes that the entire session could be put out in some audio format, such as a multiple audio track laser disc. Telephone interviews Leff conducted with Joan Fontaine and Judith Anderson while researching his book follow. The pieces have a wonderful feeling of nervous spontaneity – if you could call up an elderly movie star, what would you ask – and jovial cooperation.

The most pleasing part of the disc is the collection of screen tests on side six. They are accompanied by the last audio track. Loretta Young, Vivien Leigh, Margaret Sullavan, and Anne Baxter go through extensive tryouts, but it is clear that the quivering inflections in Fontaine's voice are superior to the attempted mannerisms in the others. The incongruity of Leigh's presence, which was done as a favor to Laurence Olivier, is probably the high point. Rounding out the side is silent footage from the Oscar ceremony, narrated by Leff, and an early re-release trailer.

ALICE ADAMS

Very little of Katharine Hepburn's performance in *Alice Adams* is believable these days, but it is more the fault of the script than of the actress. Her personality is too exaggerated to accommodate what is otherwise a slight domestic tale about a woman who longs for economic status and a good-looking boyfriend. She gets both, which also seems disappointingly contrived.

The black-and-white picture is soft and has a few speckles, but it is not so bad as to prevent those who are inclined from obtaining the disc. The sound is of standard quality.

ALICE COOPER TRASHES THE WORLD

"Lines form on my face and hands," croaks the singer, Alice Cooper, near the opening of *Alice Cooper Trashes the World.* A few moments later when he reaches the refrain, "I'm eighteen," his voice now completely bereft of verve, the viewer's immediate thoughts will be something to the nature of, 'We're talking Martian years here, right Alice?'

The 90-minute program is a fairly accurate

record of the same basic stage concert Cooper has been putting on now for at least two generations of eighteen-year-olds. It isn't so much a rock concert as it is a misogynist's musical comedy. Not even Bruce Botnick, who is listed in the credits as having tinkered with the sound, can save Cooper's vocals. The picture is somewhat grainy, but passable. The program was recorded in Birmingham, Alabama.

ALICE COOPER VIDEO TRASH

The 8-inch *Alice Cooper Video Trash* contains no surprises. The three cuts, 'Poison,' 'House of Fire,' and 'Bed of Nails' are all conceptual videos full of lingerie, leather, and leers. Cooper may be getting a little old for this stuff, but he's consistent, at least. The picture transfer is satisfactory.

ALIEN FROM L.A.

The misleading title, *Alien from L.A.*, does its film a disservice, as does the ad art which is recreated on the jacket cover. The film has problems, but it is a contemporary remake of *Journey to the Center of the Earth*, and those who enjoy variations on Jules Verne's Saknussen saga have no way of knowing that they might be attracted to the story, just as those who love movies about men falling in love with spacewomen have no way of knowing that *Alien from L.A.* isn't one of those.

The film has a decent budget and some impressive matte artwork. Its principal fault is that the heroine, played by model-with-limited-acting-experience Kathy Ireland, is whiny and ineffectual, making it tough for the viewer to identify with her. While searching for her father she stumbles down a pit and discovers a huge underground civilization which has no contact with the outside world. It is a rough, Mad Maxish place, but she manages to make a few friends and save her father. The plot has more holes than the caverns, but the pace is decent and the action is enjoyable. The film is no undiscovered gem, but it is an apple which has been labelled as an orange and deserves a more clear-minded promotion.

Underground, many scenes are bathed in brown or blue light. The disc manages the lighting effect properly about half the time, and dissolves into a blurry fuzz the other half. The Ultra-Stereo sound has some decent surround effects, but overall the sound seems a little harsh.

ALIEN NATION

The stereo surround sound on *Alien Nation* is terrific. The movie has obvious science fiction elements, but it is a basic cop/buddy picture, not a science fiction film. There are no special hardware effects, only gunshots and car chases. The sound mix is a big production, however, and it has been fully realized in the disc transfer. The picture also looks good, and the disc will make yet another excellent demonstration album.

The film succeeds despite a number of flaws. Its premise concerns the near future, after several hundred thousand aliens, from an abandoned space ship, have integrated with the rest of society on Earth. One human cop, one alien cop, alien drugs, alien drug lord, etc. The editors or the director often miss the right reaction shot, and the director makes the human cop act less intelligently than an adult normally would act. The script has the linear development of a decent TV episode, but the violence, the sound effects and the cast are all big-budget quality, and the investment pays off, at least so far as the disc is concerned.

ALIENS
ALIEN

Along with releasing *Aliens*, CBS/Fox repressed *Alien*, squeezing the latter, a 116 minute film, onto a single platter when formerly it required three sides. The catalog number is the same for the reissued *Alien* as it was for the initial Magnetic Video label release, but the newer iteration not only has CX-encoding where the older one did not, it also has slightly stronger colors, and, inevitably, a cleaner pressing.

The *Alien* transfer is not as accomplished as the *Aliens* transfer. Except for the scenes which are bathed in red or blue light, the picture quality on *Aliens* is exceptional. The darker scenes do not go fuzzy and they do not add colors where colors do not belong, the way the reissue of *Alien* still does.

There is no excuse for not releasing *Aliens* with digital sound, but CBS/Fox didn't. *Aliens* is best remembered for its thunderous finale, which, to really bring it off, requires woofers the size of refrigerators. The stereo mix on *Alien* is much more subtle and complex (although the transfer is a little noisier). Action which occurs offscreen is sometimes denoted by the soundtrack alone. Turn the volume up and you can hear the eggs get excited when John Hurt stumbles into the incubator.

ALIENS, MONSTERS, DRAGONS & ME – THE FANTASY FILM WORLD OF RAY HARRYHAUSEN (Import)

The documentary, *Aliens, Monsters, Dragons & Me – The Fantasy Film World of Ray Harryhausen*, is available on disc in Japan in English (narrated by Gary Owen) with Japanese subtitles, and is in CAV. The 46-minute program was a promotional effort for *Clash of the Titans*, but excerpts from nearly every Harryhausen effort are shown, as are valuable glimpses of the movies he made as a teenager and the demo reels he put together when he was first looking for work. Absolutely no material is included showing Harryhausen manipulating models or demonstrating the process of making films. Harryhausen is interviewed and discusses his techniques, but the thrust of the program is career accomplishments, not mechanics.

ALL ABOUT EVE

A mild graininess throughout *All About Eve* undercut our confidence in the picture. The print is clean and complete. It is only lacking in strong contrasts, which, when combined with the grainy image, makes the picture slightly pale.

All About Eve, however, is so diverting that most viewers will be happy enough just to have and watch the disc. The cleverly scripted plot has everything from catchy one-liners to elaborate, fully realized, offstage subplots. It gives both Bette Davis and George Sanders a chance to revel in their own public images, and they both do so with great vigor. The cast is so good, in fact, that the film's continuity becomes its weakest attribute. The performances make such a strong impression that when closeups or alternate camera angles are used, the viewer is immediately aware of the changes in stances, positions or expressions.

The digital and the analog soundtracks on the disc are very different, and matters of taste will guide each viewer individually in choosing one over the other. The digital sound is almost noiseless, but it is subdued and a bit bland. The analog sound is full of background hiss and crackles, but it is also sharper and more alive, making it easier to feel the dialog as it is delivered.

The three-sided disc is in CLV. A busy but interesting still has been chosen for the jacket cover. The jacket also says the disc is in stereo, but that is a mistake.

ALL DOGS GO TO HEAVEN
ALL DOGS GO TO HEAVEN (CAV)

In that the strongest asset of Don Bluth's misguided *All Dogs Go to Heaven* is its artwork, the CAV version of the 85-minute animated feature is the better buy. The narrative has clearly been truncated, making it confusing and even more unappealing than, apparently, it was initially intended. The voices chosen for the characters are all terribly ill-conceived, particularly Burt Reynolds, whose weak and indistinctive line readings as the hero put the viewer to sleep long before his character reaches that state. The morals and dramatic conceptualizations of the film are also odd, but the artwork is heavenly – richly colored, imaginatively landscaped, and decisively rendered. The sharpness of the image is inconsistent, but that looks suspiciously like a fault in the source, a result of the panic trimming. The picture and sound quality of both the CLV and CAV versions is identical. Individual still frames look crisp on the CAV disc, but triple speed is best for increasing the vividness of the artwork. Since the soundtrack is useless anyway (although it is in digitally encoded stereo surround, only the music is enhanced and the music is uninteresting), watching the whole movie in triple speed is probably the best way to appreciate what inspiration it has.

ALL OF ME

Steve Martin's performance in *All of Me* is loaded with complicated contortions as he pretends to be two different people sharing one body. You can watch different parts of him each time you see the film and laugh at what he does with a single limb. The monaural sound has not been CX-encoded and the more one concentrates on what is being said, the more flaws one becomes aware of. Fortunately the movie survives these indignities.

ALL QUIET ON THE WESTERN FRONT

The mixture of boot camp, battle scenes, and 'incidents' which was perfected in *All Quiet on the Western Front* puts the film in synch with contemporary audiences. The dramatic rhythm inevitably bogs down in one or two places, but the movie still works. The battle scenes are wild and exciting. The movie depicts the business and the sadness of war. It seems to get the proportion of the amount of time a soldier spends fighting and the amount of time a soldier spends waiting just right. You feel the movie's messages instead of consciously noting them.

MCA has released the 1930 Oscar winner

on disc with restored footage. The picture condition varies. Sometimes it is in excellent shape and other times it shows its age. The added footage is especially worn, but the value of its presence outweighs the flaws of its condition.

The film runs 130 minutes, but the narrative shifts in subject often enough to never become tiresome. The story is about a German soldier during World War I and how the war affects him and his companions. MCA has included a trailer from a re-release of the film and has encoded side three in CAV. The trailer is interesting only in that it attempts to emphasize non-existent romantic subplots, to the point of showing a scene where a brother and sister embrace without delineating their relationship. The action still frames do not jiggle, but the age of the print inhibits significant utilization of the CAV functions.

Physically, the quality of the sound is comparable to rural telephone service during a thunderstorm. Conceptually, the sound is brilliant. Particularly the constant roar of cannon fire, which you become so accustomed to hearing that when it stops, you feel the same eerie silence the characters feel. It is best heard through a TV set instead of a hi-fi, unless you want listen to the sounds of the recording equipment. Set properly, however, the sound is an impressive component of the film. The final gunshot startled us.

ALL THE BEST, STEVE ALLEN
Charlton Heston appears in the strongest skit on *All the Best, Steve Allen*, a 45-minute collection of clips from Allen's late fifties television variety/talk show. Heston, in total deadpan, portrays an actor who is incapable of completing a simple western barroom scene. It is amusing, as is an impersonation Johnny Carson does of Jack Benny, but most of the pieces are silly or trite, and if this is all the best, sitting through the show every night must have been a mind numbing experience.

The picture has the blurry grain which is typical of old TV clips, and the sound is monaural and tinny. Image has provided chapter markers in all the appropriate places.

ALL THE KING'S MEN
Based on Robert Penn Warren's novel, this 1949 black-and-white film examines the rise and apparently inevitable assassination of Louisiana's Depression-era governor, Huey Long.

The movie is too busy with sweaty close-ups to get a handle on the conflict between humanitarian accomplishments and misuse of public office. Only the performances of Mercedes McCambridge, who is gloriously earthy even in the still on the back of the jacket, and Broderick Crawford, who seems to understand the dilemmas better than the director does, make the show worthwhile.

RCA/Columbia, which released the disc, should pay closer attention to both the transfer and the jacket copy. The front jacket cover says that McCambridge's Oscar was for 'Best Supporting Actor.' No editorial comments, please.

ALL-STAR SWING FESTIVAL
The concert performance featured in *All-Star Swing Festival* will be of interest to fans only. The picture is 15 years old and looks it. The sound is in stereo, but the separations are a bit extreme. The trumpets sit behind the trombones in Count Basie's Orchestra, for example, but their sound comes out of the right speaker while the trombones come out of the left. There are some nice moments, such as Ella Fitzgerald singing 'Body and Soul' and The Benny Goodman Quartet. The low point comes when Doc Severinsen, who also acts as emcee, plays a 'tribute' to Louis Armstrong. It is sort of like hearing Debbie Boone do a tribute to Maria Callas.

ALLEGHENY UPRISING
Although the boxoffice has never been kind to America's formative years, the stories are often intriguing, because it was a time when Indian tribes actually aligned themselves with foreign powers rather than going it alone. In traditional westerns, before an enlightenment wound down the genre, Indians were roving bands of terrorists allied only with corrupt officials or criminals. But in the earliest frontier days, they were terrorists who were allied with the Establishment, and a far thornier set of moral positions was involved. Thus in *Allegheny Uprising*, the political alignments are not unlike those depicted in films, such as *Miami Vice II*, of the present day drug industry. The good guys are trapped between a criminal class which is inflicting violence upon them and an economic establishment which finds it profitable to sustain the criminals.

John Wayne is a little sleepy as the hero, but the 80 minute film, in which George Sanders makes a terrifically snotty villain, is fast paced and entertaining. You have to make allowances for the depiction of women and for other, similar indiscretions, but the populist message is fascinating. The government is the enemy. No wonder audiences prefered the less unnerving 'lawless' West of a century later.

The picture transfer is fine. The print doesn't look perfect, but it never becomes irritating. The sound is also passable. Side two runs less than a half hour, but is in CLV.

ALLEGRO NON TROPPO
The Italian, self-declared 'Fantasia' parody, *Allegro non Troppo*, is generally humorous, quite colorful, and at least somewhat thought provoking.

The movie uses a dubbed live action skit to link the six major cartoons and numerous short, animated black out gags. The live action skit, limited slapstick involving an orchestra performance, is in black and white with a faint wash which changes hue from scene to scene. The footage is difficult to view or tolerate. The cartoons are set to well known short orchestral pieces, 'The Bolero,' 'Prelude to Afternoon of a Fawn,' etc., and it is only during these passages that the digitally encoded sound is in stereo surround. The animation, which depicts the effects of progress, aging and evolution, is imaginative, and has been transferred to disc without significant problems. Side two, which contains the most elaborate montages, is in CAV, with two unsteady still frames out of every five. The disc is chapter encoded and there is some mild nudity.

ALLMAN BROTHERS BAND – BROTHERS ON THE ROAD
The Allman Brothers Band begin their open-air concert in Gainesville, Florida, depicted in *The Allman Brothers Band – Brothers on the Road*, with a lengthy instrumental – hardly the way to arouse a crowd already sleepy from the afternoon sun. Were the disc to have covered that concert alone, it would have been pretty dreary.

But squeezed onto the program along with the Gainesville concert is a far more exuberant effort in the Capitol Theater of Passaic, New Jersey, a lazy midnight session of strumming in a Florida hotel room and a carefully conceived studio 'jam,' which is so accurately reconstructed on the laser disc that it seems as if they are playing in the next room.

ALL'S FAIR
Sally Kellerman and George Segal give juvenile, unconvincing performances in a worthless comedy called *All's Fair*. The film is about a group of wives who challenge their husbands in weekend war games, but the plot is so witless, it doesn't even live up to that premise. The only amusement comes from Lou Ferrigno, whose speech impediment is used, in good humor, as a parody of Arnold Schwarzenegger's accent. The picture quality of the disc is below average, as every solid color has a liquid center, but the Ultra-Stereo sound is well executed, for what it is worth.

ALOHA SUMMER
Set in Hawaii in 1959, *Aloha Summer* is a genuine attempt to make a surfing movie. It is lightly serious, about a group of young men from different backgrounds who become friends while visiting Oahu one summer. There are extended surfing sequences and kendo sequences (one of the boys is from Japan), forays into Hawaiian culture, romance, bigotry, and a couple of brawls.

The disc has monaural sound and no chapter markers, but the best part of the program is the collection of nostalgic songs included on the soundtrack, which stand apart from the rest of the audio track. The picture looks good and the many lovely scenery shots are effectively delivered. One in particular, of blue water, blue sky, and the boys wearing blue shirts, seemed to exemplify the ability of the disc to keep every shade and hue separate.

ALPINE FIRE
Alpine Fire ('Hohenfeuer'), is an interesting, if melodramatic, drama about a family living on a steep hillside in the Swiss Alps, removed from the rest of civilization. There are two adolescent children, one of whom is deaf, and their isolation eventually leads to incest and other passions. The film's value, however, is in its depiction of life at a forty-five degree angle. It is so good at showing the details of day-to-day Alpine farming that it doesn't really need the big traumas to succeed. The quotation on the cover of the jacket, however, "One of the century's most beautiful films!" is stretching things a bit.

The film is in German with big yellow subtitles. The picture is a little hazy and has one or two blotches, but it is passable. The picturesque scenery makes up for the low-budget film stock. The monaural sound is largely irrelevant except for an occasional cow bell, and the musical score is uninspired.

ALVIN RIDES AGAIN
(see **RAW COURAGE**)

ALWAYS
A Henry Jaglom film about a couple who spend one last weekend together before finalizing their divorce, *Always* appears initially as if it will be pasted together with platitudes. But as one gets to know the characters their humor and lightweight philosophical talk is no more troubling than it would be coming from one's friends. Filmed entirely in somebody's house and backyard, the production values are at survival-only levels and these are reflected on the disc. The surprising thing about films like this is how many times you can end up watching them. It's like having the same group of people over for a weekend. No matter how bothersome they are, a few days after they've gone you start thinking about inviting them again.

ALWAYS
With every Steven Spielberg film comes a collection of astonishments. Jacket cover critic quotations not withstanding, *Always* is not one of Spielberg's best films, but even though the scenes with Audrey Hepburn and the scenes with Brad Johnson don't work for most viewers, the aerial sequences are gripping. As a disc, then, *Always* is wonderful. With a bright, mildly rectangular picture, and a fully directional stereo surround soundtrack, the flying footage is spectacular and every bit as impressive on video as it was in a theater. There is also John Goodman, whose humor is less alienating than Hepburn's ethereal hostess bit. The rest of the narrative is good enough to string it along and perhaps even the most curmudgeonly viewers will, for a moment anyway, be touched. The film, which stars Richard Dreyfuss and Holly Hunter and involves fire fighters and the afterlife, is about love and grief, a subject which usually is given a smaller percentage of screen time in hardware spectacles. Here that doesn't happen, but the laser disc can accommodate both those with the patience for romance and those without.

The picture is a touch too orange/pink, but that is its only shortcoming. Side three, which contains the climactic rescue sequence, is in CAV with perfect still frames.

AMADEUS
A lengthy essay on the back of the jacket of *Amadeus* turns out to be a complete plot synopsis. The picture is grainy, the colors have no richness. The sound quality is passable. The 158-minute film has been spread across four sides of two discs. The breaks between sides all occur in the middle of conversations, but this is not as awkward as it first appears. Succeeding scenes are bridged by Mozart's music, and the only way to avoid a disturbance of the musical continuity is to break where there is no music.

Amadeus is not true biography. You would barely have a sense that Mozart wrote more than a half-dozen operas. Its intention, and what it succeeds well at, is to be musical criticism. The sources of Mozart's inspiration and the power of his work are dissected in an entertaining manner. The more often we see the disc, the more the stage presentation, which was an amazing accomplishment (imagine the movie, performed 'live'), fades from our memory. The movie provides a lively introduction to the music and life of Mozart. It also provides an adequate sampling of Mozart's music for those who feel like being entertained, but cannot settle on a single work for their entertainment.

AMAZING GRACE AND CHUCK
Fables which are made into movies, relying entirely upon the script and acting to be a success, try one's patience even when they succeed. *Amazing Grace and Chuck*, the story about an adolescent Little League pitcher who begins a successful movement to eliminate ICBMs, is intermittently entertaining and embarrassing. When the movie works, it can be moving, but because of its limitations, reality continually intrudes upon one's consciousness to dismiss the proceedings. There aren't enough distractions. The picture has an acceptable transfer. The stereo sound is limited in effect, but is also passable.

AMAZON WOMEN ON THE MOON
In case you haven't heard, there is a skit in the comedy feature, *Amazon Women on the Moon*, in which a group of 'video pirates' find a treasure trove of video products. As they slobber over the cassettes and make plans to defy the FBI warning, one thick-headed lackey tries to bring his captain's attention to the video discs in the pile. "What good are they," the other hands pipe in, "You can't record on them." Ha ha.

The 85-minute MCA release is a collection of comedy sketches, strung together by the clever title piece, a parody of Fifties sci-fi films. The program is inevitably weaker in total impact than one would hope, although there is a take off on *The Invisible Man* which is uproarious. Side two, which includes a blackout inspired by Russ Meyer, is in CAV. Each of the 23 segments has its own chapter marker. The transfer is spotless and the CX-encoded monaural sound is decent.

THE AMBUSHERS
The third Dean Martin-as-Matt Helm movie, *The Ambushers*, is the only one available on disc. Several of the episodes, like this one, dealt with flying saucers and took place in Acapulco, so the only way to differentiate *The Ambushers* is to note that it is the one in which women kill bad guys with guns disguised as brassieres.

RCA/Columbia has done a nice job transferring the Sixties styled film to disc. The colors are as bright and gauche as ever and the flat monaural sound, although not CX-encoded, is strong and not badly distorted. The teaser for 'The Wrecking Crew' is still tacked on to the end.

The sexist gags, Martin's horrible double-takes, and the ridiculously contrived special effects all work fine when they are supported by a sharp picture and fresh color. At last we could see what attracted us to these movies in our adolescence. It wasn't just the girls traipsing around Las Brisas in their bikinis, it was the celebration of tacky glamor. If you identified with James Bond, you had to know your wines. If you identified with Matt Helm, all you had to do was drink and not fall down.

AMERICAN ANTHEM
About 18 months before the story in *American Anthem* begins, the hero (Mitch Gaylord) had his arm broken by his unemployed father in a fight, so he turned down a college athletic scholarship. In an early scene to establish his character, the camera pans about his room and ends up focusing on his trophies. They are covered by more cobwebs than Miss Havisham's candelabra. We didn't stop laughing until well into side two.

The jacket copy claims that the disc has digital sound, but in reality it does not. The stereo track has little going for it, but the sound is superior to the grainy picture. There are two promotional videos on the disc after the movie is finished, one by John Parr and one by Andy Taylor. We give the whole thing a perfect zero.

AMERICAN BALLET THEATRE IN SAN FRANCISCO
American Ballet Theatre in San Francisco, features a mixture of classical and modern musical pieces performed live on a stage with a minimum of setting and costume. The CX-encoded sound is clear enough that you can hear the feet of the dancers plop and tap upon the stage floor.

Directed for 'videogram and television' by Brian Large, the point of view is rarely at odds with what a member of the audience would see. The camera seldom has less than the full figure of a dancer in view.

The program features five different pieces. Pioneer has been very liberal with chapter markers (18), although a few more, particularly on side two, would have been desirable. Included are a standard Paul Taylor piece set to the music of Handel called 'Airs' ; Antony Tudor's depiction of infidelity set to the music of Ernest Chausson, 'Jardin Aux Lilas,' which has the strongest plot and the most set decorations; the third act pas de deux from 'Swan Lake,' 'The Black Swan,' starring Cynthia Gregory and Fernando Bujones, and choreographed by Marious Petipa; the balcony *pas de deux* from Prokofiev's 'Romeo and Juliet' listlessly interpreted by Kenneth MacMillan but danced well by Natalia Makarova and Kevin McKenzie; and the enjoyably elaborate 'Great Galloping Gottschalk' with music by Louis Gottschalk and choreography by Lynne Talor-Corbett.

AMERICAN BALLET THEATER LIVE AT THE MET
Instead of the monstrous 90-minute spectacles on most ballet discs, *American Ballet Theater Live at the Met* contains four separate ballets, each lasting a sensible 20 minutes or so. The disc gives a much better impression of what a normal evening at the ballet is like.

'Les Sylphides,' the first ballet, is probably included to lend the program respectability, but it is a sleepy piece and Michel Fokine's choreography is too spread out to work well on a TV screen. Mikhail Baryshnikov stars, and his dancing is predictably spectacular, but his performance is missing an edge, as if he didn't know that he should be going all out for the cameras. 'Sylvia,' has more spark to it and warms one up for side two. And side two is what makes this disc worthwhile. The first dance, 'Triad,' performed to the bright, fastidious music of Serge Prokofiev, involves a limited number of dancers and so it fits well on a small screen. Following that, Cynthia Gregory and Fernando Bujones appear in 'Paquita,' and they *are* up for the camera, improvising and showing off whenever they can slip something in.

The CX-encoded stereo sound is excellent. The picture is above average, but not perfect. Near the end, the dancers all have faint ghosts. Close to two dozen chapter markers have been included.

AMERICAN FLYERS

With *American Flyers* Steve Tesich returns to bicycle racing, but he's forced to throw in a subplot about an incurable movie disease to make the thing work. There are glimmers of wit and the director, John Badham, doesn't do a bad job with the film's second half (that is, the big race), but film audiences understandably stayed away and home video consumers, with the possible exception of bicycle racing and incurable disease enthusiasts, are likely to do the same. The picture and sound are fine.

THE AMERICAN FRIEND

The transfer of *The American Friend* to disc is excellent. The movie was not made with quality film stock, but the picture on the disc is crisp and unblemished. The colors, however depressing, are accurate. A faint black band lingers at the bottom of the screen throughout the film, but it is not enough to qualify as 'letterboxing.' The sound is also impressive. It is monaural (partially in German with English subtitles and partially in English), but the digitally encoded soundtrack has strength and gives the program the ambience of a theatrical presentation.

When the film was released theatrically, critics seemed to wish it was a new kind of dark thriller (there are even some quotations to that effect on the back of the gatefold jacket). The story, based upon a book by Patricia Highsmith, is about a family man who is tricked into performing a pair of contract murders. Wim Wenders appears to give his actors very little direction, which, among other things, slows the pace of the film. At times the cast, principally Dennis Hopper and Bruno Ganz, finds the right mix of comedy and realism and does a good job, but in other stretches the lack of guidance makes the material come across as pretentious. The movie was not a breakthrough thriller, but it is self-consciously amusing and suitably newwavish entertainment.

The three-sided CLV disc also includes a 20-minute interview with Dennis Hopper, 'Art, Acting, & The Suicide Chair.' The interview, produced by Image exclusively for the disc (although originally intended to accompany 'Colors,' it fits perfectly, if not better, with *American Friend*), is superb. The director/interviewer, George Hickenlooper, not only asks well-researched, intelligent questions, he coaxes fascinating answers and comments out of Hopper.

AMERICAN GOTHIC

American Gothic concerns a group of young adults stranded on an island in the Northwest which is inhabited by a strange elderly couple. The narrative is adeptly paced, but predictable and a little sick, even for a cheap horror movie. Rod Steiger, who seems to be enjoying himself, and Yvonne De Carlo star. The picture is grainy and mildly worn down. The sound is adequate.

AN AMERICAN IN PARIS
AN AMERICAN IN PARIS (Remastered)

How could MGM/UA do what they did to *An American in Paris* the first time they released it? Not only was the print faded and hazy, but the picture was out of focus and the sound was tone deaf. That release was deplorable, but MGM/UA's subsequent version is flawless.

The reissued *American in Paris* is in vivid Technicolor, best exemplified, if any random frame weren't enough, by the perfume shop scene, in which each colored bottle is a bright, jeweled beacon. At that point you could care less about Gene Kelly and Leslie Caron. Color is one of director Vincent Minnelli's strongest tools, and throughout the film every object, costume and backdrop has a hue all of its own.

The flesh tones appear too orange in the opening scenes, but by the end the problem disappears. Overall, the picture looks fantastic. The sound is a little soft, as if someone had been working too hard to clean it up, but it has no significant distortion and the Gershwin music sounds great. MGM/UA has chapter encoded the song numbers only, but the final ballet has six markers.

Critical backlash has been so long-standing and dogmatic on *An American in Paris* that it is about time somebody found something good to say about the film again. There was a brief moment when people thought this was the future of dance, and that is probably what those who bad-mouth the film are still reacting against. The movie has so many experimental sequences, however, that the concluding twenty-minute ballet, when it finally comes, is an integrated crescendo which merges perfectly with all that has gone on before. In keeping with its own premise, the narrative is no more than a few romantic sketches, which are subsequently filled in through other media. The humor in Alan Lerner's script is often extremely dry, but the performers don't have to veer too far from their own personalities. *An American in Paris* is simply a series of movie musical styled impressions and if it can achieve an underdog status, so much the better, since people will come to it only looking for, and finding, a good time.

AMERICAN NINJA 2

Those who enjoy escapist action pictures should not miss *American Ninja 2*. The movie has inventive fights and stunts which occur at regularly timed intervals, and enough of a plot to hold one's attention in between. The film is about a mad scientific plot to take over the world, kidnapped Marines, and billion-dollar drug deals. It is not so farfetched as to require strenuous suspension of disbelief, and in the end the Marines come to the rescue. The hero is played by Michael Dudikoff, who is not the greatest actor that ever lived, but catches arrows and poison darts with his bare hand, something Laurence Olivier would be hard-pressed to accomplish.

Except for a vague, vertical white line running through the picture on side two, the image is bright and colorful. The sound is done in Ultra Stereo, which sends the swish of the Ninja swords circling around one's video room.

AN AMERICAN TAIL

MCA released *An American Tail* as a CAV collector's package without going through the normal process of issuing the title as a standard release first. The three-sided disc contains such added features as a still frame text essay, production photos, and a theatrical trailer.

The picture is sharp and colorful. The digital sound has less hiss than the analog sound and the analog sound has hardly any to begin with. The sounds are very sharply defined, and many of the stereo effects are pleasing.

Rarely have we had as much pleasure watching an animated CAV disc at quarter speed. Usually, the leaps in cel progression will appear jerky, or will lack any movement at all. With *Tail*, the CAV slow motion functions allow you to observe the mechanics of the animation – which cels are moving, which part is permanent background – without spoiling the illusion which the animation is creating. The function also allows one to observe the cartoon's limitations. In the text essay which is contained on still frame at the end, the filmmakers are proud of the number of moving elements in their work. They have a right to be, but rarely is an element in a peripheral area of the screen given mobility. Even in the late Disney cartoons, objects, etc., away from the center of attention would be animated, giving a viewer the impression that more was going on than could be observed. By holding the movement to the center of attention, the filmmakers miss an opportunity to provide the appearance that they have accomplished more. You can also catch frame-by-frame inconsistencies, such as the whiskers disappearing and the reappearing on one of the younger mice in a dance scene.

The 81-minute movie comes in a gatefold jacket. The inner spread contains yet another essay on the film's production, slightly less informative and more promotional than the text contained on the disc. The songs have their own chapter markers, but none of the significant action scenes are so encoded.

The story of immigrant mice, coming to infest America, is, perhaps, an inadvertent evocation of age-old resentments, but every decent cartoon has a dark undercurrent. The essay also points out that the filmmakers went to great effort to make their period evocations of New York City as accurate as possible. If that is the case, however, why is the sun rising in the west? What can you expect, though, in a world where mice talk.

AMERICAN VISIONS ARCADIA
AMERICAN VISIONS GREAT SMOKEY MOUNTAINS
AMERICAN VISIONS OLYMPIC

Although it is a bit difficult to determine the content from the jacket notations, the three *American Visions* discs, subtitled 'Portraits of the National Parks,' each run a half hour on a single side, in CAV. Depicting a single park, each disc has sporadic narration which splits evenly between being factual and being impressionistic (example of the latter: "Thoughts of long-forgotten Indian feasts drift by, in the whisper of a breeze.") Behind the narration there are environmental sounds and a musical score, by Jackson Berkey. The narration is present on the analog track only, however. The digital track contains just the environmental sounds and background music.

The picture quality on the discs is meticulously clear (the sound isn't bad, either). No people appear in the images, which shift from still photos to lyrical video taped motion footage with relaxed ease. As informational sources, the discs, *Arcadia*, *Great Smokey Mountains*, and *Olympic*, are of limited use, but as a spotless window on the peacefulness and beauty of each park, the programs can bring a touch of respite to the most hectic living room.

AN AMERICAN WEREWOLF IN LONDON (MCA)
AN AMERICAN WEREWOLF IN LONDON (Image)

We have always been happy with our copy of the MCA release of *An American Werewolf in London*, but Image, which has picked up the title through Vestron, decided that the movie was good enough to release again, and so they have. Image's version of the monaural film is digitally encoded, and has less hiss than MCA's, which was not even CX-encoded. The picture on the Image version is darker, which adds to the colors, but loses details in the shadows.

The fewer jokes there are in a John Landis movie, the funnier it is, and *An American Werewolf in London* is outlandishly humorous. Griffin Dunne's performance, Jenny Agutter's smile, and the peak-a-boo effect shots make the movie difficult to dislike. As with all of Landis's films, the movie works better on a TV than it does in a theater, though not so much so that one should buy it twice.

Both discs have been encoded with chapter markers. MCA's chapters highlight the gore and are listed on the back of the jacket. Image's mark the pop songs on the soundtrack ('Moondance,' 'Bad Moon Rising,' and umpteen versions of 'Blue Moon'), and are not listed on the back of the jacket. Image is also lazy with the running time, declaring it to be, 'Approximately 90 Minutes,' while MCA more accurately clocks it at 98.

AMITYVILLE 3-D

On the jacket in big giant letters, it says, '*Amityville 3-D*.' In little tiny letters underneath, it says, 'Home video version – not in 3-D.' This kind of marketing is difficult to understand. If a person has eyesight problems, why would he be interested in 3-D?

Despite the numerable sharp objects poking at the center of the screen, there is no raunchy gruesomeness of the sort necessary if a film like this is going to please. One scene, where the mother sees her just-drowned daughter walking up the stairs sopping wet, has a chill to it but, other than that, this is the series about the house with the flies in the attic and the hole in the cellar. Well, flies aren't scary and the hole never lives up to its promise. The picture and sound are passable.

AMSTERDAMNED

The director of *Amsterdamned*, Richard Haas, was also responsible for the silly concoction about man-eating elevators, *The Lift*. Rumor has it that the dubbed version of *Amsterdamned* is also close to intolerable, but the disc is the original Dutch language version, with English subtitles, which works fairly well.

The story is about someone or something which lurks in the canals of Amsterdam and preys randomly upon nighttime strollers. A resourceful cop tracks down the predator. There is a spectacular speedboat chase and a number of tense moments. The ending is a little overdone, but by then most viewers will be too exhausted to feel critical.

The picture and sound transfers are super. All of the evening scenes and murky water scenes make it onto the screen without the slightest distortion, and in the bright daylight the colors look solid. The sound has mild stereo surround encoding, and is especially effective during the motorboat chase. The disc has plenty of chapter markers and the subtitles have plenty of off-color language. The picture has slight black bands at the top and bottom of the screen, enough to create a rectangular image on most picture tubes, but not enough to qualify as a 'letterbox' or 'wide screen' image as the jacket cover claims. No matter, enough is shown to get the job done.

AMY GRANT – FIND A WAY

Amy Grant's Christianity is sort of a secret vice, which she will share only after you have fallen for her. That feeling only comes across in one of the five videos collected on the 20-minute 8-inch, *Amy Grant – Find a Way*.

She does a determined, chaste striptease, as she sings 'Don't Run Away,' that is more erotic than any of the contrived poses most rock stars show themselves off with. Unfortunately, a mindset hides her best angles from viewers in the other four videos, 'Find a Way,' 'Wise Up,' 'Angels,' and 'It's Not a Song.' All are visually stimulating, but they keep Grant at a distance and the Siren's Song side of her is suppressed.

Grant's numbers are not engineered with the same standards that the more sinful rock stars are accorded. In a couple of songs there seem to be a lot of dropouts in the mid-range and zero ambience, making her voice sound like it has been constructed artificially.

ANATOMY OF A MURDER

Directors often shape the stars of their films in their own images (see Jack Nicholson in *The Shining*). In the black-and-white courtroom drama, *Anatomy of a Murder*, Otto Preminger does it twice. Jimmy Stewart's hair is often hidden by a hat or slicked down to the skull with oil (he also chomps on a cigar) and Joseph Welch is seen marching up a staircase with a royal gait and a cane.

The disc runs to three sides. The print looks good but the sound is not CX-encoded. Preminger was often sloppy with details – what Army is it that is not involved when a Lieutenant is charged with murder? – but few directors have been as successful at creating lasting entertainment.

ANCHORS AWEIGH

The MGM/UA disc of *Anchors Aweigh* shows off the film's candy store Technicolor designs admirably. The two and a half hour film is a musical without any truly memorable songs, and it has not aged well, although several individual sequences are spectacular, especially the complete Gene Kelly and Jerry the Mouse interlude. Frank Sinatra and Kathryn Grayson appear (the film was a box office hit, capitalizing on Sinatra's appeal with the nation's youngsters – the last era of cultural gentility), as does Dean Stockwell, in one of his child roles. There is a mental tendency to pencil in a mustache as you watch him.

The print has some shifts in quality, but it is generally quite good and the disc sports a fleet of bright colors. The strongest hues, however, have a tendency to blur. The sound is passable. The songs have been chapter encoded, but musical sequences which do not have lyrics have not been marked.

AND GOD CREATED WOMAN
AND GOD CREATED WOMAN (Remake)

The first time Cinemascope was used to show a naked woman stretching from one side of the screen to the other was in Roger Vadim's 1957 French soap opera, *And God Created Woman*, starring Brigitte Bardot. Movies have never been the same since. A dubbed, cropped and scanned version of the film was released by Vestron. Bardot is chopped in half, but at least the scandalous shot lasts long enough so that both halves of it can be shown sequentially.

Those who find minor flaws in the transfers of films to disc to be annoying would be aghast at the condition of the print in this older effort. The colors are so faded and so pumped up for the video transfer that objects and people look like cutouts pasted against a blank backdrop. The sound is also a horror. Even when played through a cheap TV sound system, the audio is warped and distorted. Needless to say, it is monaural and not CX-encoded. The awful dubbing, with French accents and bad English ("I'm willing to offer whatever it's worth. Suppose we say six millions."), makes matters even worse.

But if you can tolerate all of that, the movie, and even the disc, is a lot of fun. Bardot stars with Jean-Louis Trintignant. Both are very young, and yet both are true stars who can captivate a viewer not so much by finding the emotional truth in a character but by imposing their personalities and their emotions on their sections of the screen. They command the viewer's attention even when their voices are replaced, and the story, about a marriage of convenience which matures into real love, is all that they need to keep their actions legitimate.

Not having enjoyed a boxoffice success in a while, Vadim decided to make another movie called *And God Created Woman*, thirty years after making the first one. He moved the locale from St. Tropez to Sante Fe, New Mexico, and changed most, but not all, of the plot specifics. He retained, however, the central theme – a marriage of convenience which blossoms into romance – and he preserved the soapy essence of the narrative.

The film breaks no new ground and it does not bother, cinematically, to explore Vadim's past experiments. Rebecca De Mornay and Vincent Spano will never be the subjects of 'The Films of ...' books, but what they lack in star power they compensate with acting lessons. The one performance in the film which is on par with the entertainment of the original is that of Frank Langella, who has the Curt Jurgens role and hams it up as much or even more than Jurgens did.

The picture is in good shape and the stereo sound has a number of nice separation effects. Like the first film, the movie is fun – to emphasize that the marriage is not true, for example, there is a shot of De Mornay eating

'Almost Home' cookies – but it lacks the emotional weight of the original (nobody tries to murder anybody) and, despite 'added footage for home video' of grappling couples, it lacks the sensationalism.

ANDREA CHENIER TEATRO ALLA SCALA

The *Teatro Alla Scala* production of Umberto Giordano's *Andrea Chenier* is in Italian and has English subtitles. An English/Italian libretto is also included. The 123 minute program is stretched to four sides. The digitally encoded stereo sound is effective and the picture is clear. The story is about a poet caught up in the French Revolution. He ends up going to the guillotine because he falls in love with a woman from the right side of the tracks. Enough of the complex staging is on display so that home video audiences can become almost as excited about the artistic feats as the audience at La Scala does.

ANDREW DICE CLAY LIVE! THE DICE MAN COMETH

The foul-mouthed Andrew Dice Clay performs for 40 minutes in front of a live and unnervingly sympathetic audience in *Andrew Dice Clay Live! The Dice Man Cometh.* We must admit that after a few minutes we were laughing right along with them, but there is bound to be at least something on the program which will be offensive to every viewer. The sociology of his rap can actually be fascinating, because comedians can be condemned for how they act in society, but not for how they reflect it.

The camera seems a little too eager to cut to the audience member who is laughing the most uproariously at Clay's latest punchline, but the picture transfer, from a video tape source, is very crisp and clean. The stereo sound is also sharp. The disc has chapter markers for the different phases in his routine. There is also an opening and closing skit to stretch out the show – which still fits on a single sided CLV disc – but it is limp compared to Clay's stage act.

ANDREW WYETH: THE HELGA PICTURES

Some may find the price of *Andrew Wyeth: The Helga Pictures* to be intimidating. The disc has been released by Videodisc Publishing, Inc., the company which also released the expensive *National Gallery of Art*. In both cases it is necessary to ignore the price when judging the discs. The *Wyeth* disc is excellent, but it is a short program and the budgetary criteria for adding it to one's collection will vary from collector to collector.

Charlton Heston gives a 36 minute lecture about Wyeth's 'Helga' cycle and how it came to pass. His talk encompasses many aspects of the artistic process – the major themes represented in the paintings, Wyeth's background, technical details of the media Wyeth employed – but skirts over the scandal which the paintings caused when they were introduced to the public. Heston's talk is an excellent introduction to the whole subject, but by no means the last word.

Heston speaks while standing in locations on Wyeth's property in Chadds Ford, Pennsylvania, but his surroundings are never directly related to the paintings. When the camera is on Heston and not an insert, one tends to follow his eyes as they read the teleprompter. They're the only things which are moving. The inserts show the major paintings as well as a liberal number of influencing paintings from other artists, and a few detail shots. The extensive nudity in the paintings is not without erotic appeal, despite the educational tone of the lecture.

The disc is in CAV and Heston's narrative is split evenly between the two sides. After it is over, 237 paintings, drawings and sketches are presented in still frame, each followed by a title card. Actually, there are only two dozen major works represented in the segment, but the many studies leading to each piece involve the viewer in the artistic process. You will need a large television screen for some of the incidental pencil sketches, but all have been rendered in perfect clarity on still frame, retaining not only minute details, but a sense of texture as well. The CAV functions can also be used to 'flip' through the collection at varying speeds. Heston's jaw quivers in still frame mode, but the paintings are rock solid.

An insert accompanying the disc provides more information about Wyeth, and also presents a complete frame number index, not only of the works represented in the final segment, but of the many paintings inserted in the lecture.

As for Wyeth's paintings, they have an intense emptiness indicative of a creator who doesn't get out very much. Even without Heston's cheerleading, though, it is easy to recognize that they are a significant accomplishment, deliberately reinforced with contemporary folklore and destined to take a permanent place in American art history. Are they any good? Is the disc worth the bucks? Each beholder will have to allow his or her own eyes to decide.

ANDROID

Although it is inconsistent, *Android* keeps moving at an entertaining pace and never dwells on a single concept for too long. Basically, the story is about several groups of humans and androids on a remote space station who, through different sets of motivations, end up wanting to murder each other. Most of them do.

Side two is in CAV. The picture is a little aged and pale, but the feature was independently financed and it is doubtful that a better print exists.

ANDY WARHOL'S BAD

Andy Warhol's Bad has been given a very nice transfer, strengthening its potential for repeat viewings. The picture is solid and has no markings. Although the movie was filmed on a low budget, it is clear that the color transfer is fresh and accurate. The sound is also fine. The movie, which treads slightly on John Waters territory, is about a Queens woman who runs a hit squad as if it were a neighborhood service. The film is mildly humorous as social commentary, but contains some scenes of semi-graphic violence directed against dogs and babies, limiting its general appeal. The cast includes Carroll Baker, Susan Tyrrell and Perry King. Unlike some of the other movies which Warhol lent his name to, the acting is enjoyable and does not make a viewer restless.

ANDY WARHOL'S DRACULA
(see **BLOOD FOR DRACULA**)

ANDY WARHOL'S FRANKENSTEIN
(see **FLESH FOR FRANKENSTEIN**)

ANGEL AND THE BADMAN (Disc Factory)
ANGEL AND THE BADMAN (Republic)
ANGEL AND THE BADMAN (Image)

One of the most proliferate of the public domain titles is *Angel and the Badman*. Every minor home video company seems to have a version out, indicating not only that the title has a basic appeal, but that there must be a lot of collectors' prints floating around. Only Republic has the original negative, however, and Republic's release is the logical source to turn to should one desire the film on disc. An early release, by The Disc Factory, is in very bad condition and is pretty useless. Image released the title with chapter markers and a more sensible side break than Republic thought to choose. The Republic release, however, is clearly superior in picture and sound quality, so much so that the other existing versions are difficult to tolerate in comparison. The Republic presentation still looks a little ragged, and the grey scale seems to be limited. The image is sharply focussed, however. The whites are bright and the blacks are deep. The monaural sound is also sharp, and admirably free of distortion.

John Wayne portrays a vagabond who hooks up with a family of Quakers and is eventually convinced that a life of peace is more promising than a life of gun-slinging and cattle-rustling. Gail Russel, as a young Quaker girl, finds it impossible to pretend that she believes in passivity. Her natural inclination, which shows through her every expression, is to molest Wayne as soon as she gets him alone.

ANGEL HEART

An excellent interview with the director, Alan Parker, has been included in a jacket insert with *Angel Heart*. Not only does Parker identify the ten seconds which had to be left out of the theatrical version (encouraging many people to wait for the home video release), but he gives an excellent description of how to work with actors in general and Mickey Rourke and Robert De Niro in particular. Unfortunately, no amount of words will compensate for the movie itself, a potentially intriguing tale about a private detective hired by the Devil to find a man who reneged on his contract. The ending is legitimate, but the flashbacks which are supposed to prepare the viewer for the conclusion are overworked and ineptly presented. The movie has no soul, and its mechanics are creaky.

The picture is faintly grainy and seems a little pale. The digital surround sound has some entertaining quirks. There are about a dozen chapter markers on the disc, but it was never clear to us what the encoding was marking.

ANGEL III THE FINAL CHAPTER

Now let's see. Angel's mom abandoned her when she was 12, and when she returns to LA after rising above her profession of necessity to become a successful photographer, she says she hasn't seen her mother in 14 years. That makes her 26. But the mother says Angel has a sister, born after the abandonment. So how come the actress playing the sister looks older than the actress playing Angel? (They're both on the jacket cover, make your own comparisons.) No time for an answer, because Mom is murdered and Angel must go where others fear to tread to save her sister and extract her revenge in *Angel III The Final Chapter*. Fortunately, the TV with a heart of AU is there to help her, though he/she is now driving an ice cream truck and isn't good for much. To catch the killers, Angel descends to the worlds of prostitution, pornography, white slavery, and topless cocktail waitresses, but she remains chaste throughout. No wonder she never caught VD.

The picture is okay, but the lighting is very poor. If the shadows of the equipment are not crossing the viewing area, then the glare of the arc lamps is. The sound is passable.

ANGELS DIE HARD

Although the coming attractions trailer for *Angels Die Hard*, tacked onto the end of *Toy Soldiers*, was energetic and kinky, the actual film is dull and inept. (Ever find the lighting of a film amusing? Check out the shiny foreheads and stark wall shadows here.)

Angels is a motorcycle movie, a genre which never really established itself but was a loveable staple for some time on the drive-in circuit. Bikers are portrayed as violent outlaws who have codes and standards of their own making and are strongly adverse to figures of authority. Thus, one of the songs in the soundtrack of *Angels Die Hard* is called 'People Have a Tendency to Be Free.' Another song, 'The Man Who Kills the Ants,' is about a man who kills ants and is played right before a solitary Angel runs off the road and dies. The significance of this is left to the viewer.

ANGELS OVER BROADWAY

An extremely attractive jacket cover graces *Angels Over Broadway*. The print looks immaculate (a break near the opening of side one and some vertical lines near the opening of side two notwithstanding) and sustains sharp, rich contrasts from beginning to end. The sound, although monaural and not CX-encoded, has a strength one normally associates with more recent theatrical releases.

Ben Hecht, who normally stayed on the pencil side of such productions, chose to direct his own script about a pair of money-hungry club hoppers (Douglas Fairbanks, Jr. and Rita Hayworth) who try to fleece a crooked card game. The story has the odd, off-balance meanderings one associates with modern plays and would not warrant attention were it not for the beautiful job which has been done putting it on disc.

ANGUISH

The place to see *Anguish* is in a movie theater, but it is too late for that now. If you have to watch it on disc, be sure to invite several perfect strangers to watch it with you, for effect. The poor picture quality, monaural sound, and bad acting are all explained within the film not too long after it begins. Hang in there. The movie makes clever use of stereo and mono sound, and a lot of other things as well. The one which pleased us the most was an odd-looking eye chart.

Anguish is an enjoyable, single-gag horror movie. It contains some gruesome murders and many victims lose their eyeballs, but it is all in good fun. The picture, when all is said and done, is still a little pale. The sound also crackles sometimes, but it is effective.

ANIMAL BEHAVIOR

Karen Allen, Holly Hunter, Armand Assante and a chimpanzee star in *Animal Behavior*, an unintelligent romantic comedy set on a college campus in the Southwest. The plot summary on the back of the disc jacket leaves nothing out, for those who wish further details. The Ultra-Stereo surround sound is passable, as is the picture transfer.

ANIMAL CRACKERS

The master used for *Animal Crackers*, the Marx Brothers film, is full of scratches and blurs, but the movie itself was made with the most minimal production values imaginable. What sometimes looks like a break in the film is actually bad editing to begin with. In transferring what was essentially a stage vehicle to the screen, the camera remains static throughout the whole movie and the volume levels go up and down as people move nearer to or further away from the mikes.

Because of the presence of the Marx Brothers, the condition of the movie is irrelevant. It is legitimately entertaining and only slightly more erratic than their best pictures.

ANIMAL FARM

The *Animal Farm* master comes from a fresh, 35mm source. Its colors look brand new and certainly not 30 years old. The fable also seems as fresh today as it was when Stalin was having Trotsky assassinated. It applies to what has been happening to mankind since the beginning of time. Some of the darker scenes could, perhaps, have been lightened a bit, but such suggestions are only encouraged because the picture is so vivid to begin with. As for acquiring the cartoon as a family investment, we would recommend it only for households where the rule is benignly autocratic. If harsher conditions exist, then the disc could only serve to stir dissension.

ANIMAL FOLLIES

Hanna-Barbera cartoons featuring a number of different characters can be found on *Animal Follies*. Only Snagglepuss (with his memorable "Exit, stage left" line), who is presented in two shorts at the very end, makes the disc worth consideration. Coherent excerpts from an episodic sequential cartoon, 'Ruff'n Ready,' are cleverly spread throughout the program. There are two shorts each of 'Yippee, Yappee and Yahooey,' 'Touche Turtle' (more inventive than the others), and 'Augie Doggie and Doggie Daddy.'

The image quality varies depending upon the cartoon, with the older efforts looking soft (and colored only nominally), while the later efforts look nice. The sound also shifts in clarity and is best left with minimal amplification.

THE ANIMATED ADVENTURES OF GENE RODDENBERRY'S STAR TREK

The *Animated Adventures of Gene Roddenberry's Star Trek* contains all 22 episodes from the Saturday morning cartoon series' two-year run. Although two episodes of the half hour program appear on each side of a platter, the disc set has not been chapter encoded. (The second episode always begins at 24:36.)

The box contains six platters with a total of eleven sides. The episodes are listed on the back of the box in order, but the side contents can only be determined by counting them down or reading the platter labels. The episodes are numbered 1 through 23, with the absence of episode 12, which does not show up in reference books on the series, either. Each side opens with close to a minute of Paramount logos, and every episode contains the full opening and closing credits. The box is too flimsy to hold six platters and should be grasped firmly after the seal is broken. We found that the application of packing tape to the cover and one of the box's edges improved its stability. However, the package design is especially awkward for access by young children, who might otherwise be attracted to the title.

The sound is monaural and is worth amplifying mildly since one of the show's biggest selling points is the presence of the voices of all the principal cast members. The background is hissy, though. The animation is often stilted, and the characters, even Spock, are not distinctively drawn. Intriguingly, DeForest Kelly's voice has the strongest sense of presence.

The picture looks quite sharp, with only strong reds and oranges appearing unstable. The limited animation expenditure can be telling, since the disc is so sharp that you can see wrinkles and dust on the original shooting materials. Fortunately, the programs are strongly scripted, so that the addition of the voices and a few imaginative images were all that were required for success.

A good example of what the series has to offer can be found in an episode written by the science fiction novelist, Larry Niven, called 'The Slaver Weapon.' The piece discards the conventions of the program (the Enterprise and Captain Kirk are never seen) and uses Spock and two minor characters, isolating their resources and pitting them against a group of furry, cat-like antagonists in a conflict over the possession of a powerful weapon. Niven's plot, however, is only a device to generate the kind of situations and characterizations that make science fiction such a unique and stimulating form of literature. A sour looking alien enters the room. "The lean bedraggled one is a reader of minds," whispers Spock. "I've heard all the Khzinti telepaths are unhappy neurotics," answers Uhuru. At every turn, Niven is jabbing the viewer with imaginative spears of fantasy. The pleasure of the episode is not in its resolution, but in its execution, and in the many rapid-fire concepts Niven manages to discharge.

Other highlights in the package include the first episode, a well thought out 'sequel' entitled 'More Trouble with Tribbles'; equally satisfying sequels to 'Shore Leave' ('Once Upon a Planet') and 'Mudd's Women' ('Mudd's Passion'); a cleverly scripted quest adventure with imaginative characters including a bug who is an expert lock picker, 'The Jihad'; an amusing piece in which the Enterprise crew starts shrinking in size and must operate the ship by jumping on buttons, 'The Terratin Incident'; a feminist effort called 'The Lorelei Signal'; a complicated tale in which Kirk and Spock are turned into mermen, 'The Ambergris Element'; an enjoyable story about Spock going back in time to meet himself as a youngster, 'Yesteryear'; a story which may have inspired the script for *Alien*, 'Beyond the Farthest Star'; and a cute effort, 'The Practical Joker,' in which the Enterprise gets its own personality and, among other things, writes 'Kirk is a jerk' on the back of the Captain's uniform while it is in the laundry.

Walter Koenig's voice and character never appear in the episodes, but Koenig did contribute 'The Infinite Vulcan,' a pedestrian effort compared to the others, but tellingly better than many of the live action episodes.

There is not a single offering in the collection which doesn't have some positive attributes, and most are quite entertaining.

ANITA BAKER ONE NIGHT OF RAPTURE

Anita Baker performs a concert running a little under an hour at the Constitution Hall in Washington DC on *Anita Baker One Night of Rapture*. Concert segments, which appear in sepia and white on the single sided disc, are separated by a full-color interview and documentary scenes of Baker preparing her stage equipment for the concert. The picture transfer is fine, although the sepia takes some getting used to. The sound is excellent.

Baker has an alert off-stage personality and comes across, appealingly, as someone who is not going to be tripped up by fame and fortune. She claims her music is out of the mainstream, though after going platinum that is a little difficult to support. Rather, she has come across a niche – blending gospel into light jazz instead of rock or progressive jazz – that no other female performer ever quite filled. Her music is okay, but the sedate manner of the audience is indicative of the quietness in her passion. It is less evocative of rapture than of stretching one's arms.

ANNA

An easygoing retread of *All About Eve*, *Anna* uses Czechoslovakian refugees in New York City as its milieu. The ending, in which the heroine has a nervous breakdown, is false, and the dialog is too 'natural' to be witty or engaging. The most comical sequences involve a very bad stage production for which the title character is an understudy. Much of the movie, however, seems more like an exercise than an accomplishment. The sound was recorded inexpensively. The picture is passable only because the movie has not set very high goals.

ANNA PAVLOV (Import)

The Japanese disc, *Anna Pavlov*, is a joint Soviet-Western production which is presented in English with Japanese subtitles hanging discretely on the far right of the screen. Intended as a biography of Pavlov, the film has a mixed international cast, including James Fox as the narrator/lover and Galina Beliaeva in the title role.

The dance scenes in the 138-minute film are good, but the story drags on and on and the shots are poorly composed. The sound is also fluttery and undependable. Boredom sets in quickly. Instead of being a tribute to Eastern culture, the disc reminds one of a shelf in a Soviet grocery, proudly offering a single, bent can of preserves.

ANNIE
ANNIE (Letterboxed)

Although you can hardly tell it from the jacket cover, RCA/Columbia has released a letterboxed version of the musical, Annie. The picture has an aspect ratio of about 2.3:1. The screen composition gives the film a fighting chance for holding your attention, something the former scanned and cropped version was too belligerent to pull off.

The movie is something of a clunker, but in the rectangular images the characters are balanced with space or with other characters, and the irritating nature of the presentation is softened. On the scanned and cropped version there are enormous closeups and no balance at all, and the result – a cascade of rust-colored curls surrounding two bulging eyes – can be frightening. Not only is the negative impact of the film softened by the letterboxing, but the choreography is also improved. The big dance numbers look better organized, and convey the spectacle that the filmmakers were attempting to achieve.

The color scheme of the film is grungy. Even when the orphans are left behind the set designers still seem to have a thing for browns and faded oranges. No matter how good the color transfer is, the disc will never look overly pleasing. Judging from the fleshtones, the colors appear to be in good shape, though there is a mild paleness to them.

The stereo surround sound is cleaner and brighter than the analog sound on the earlier *Annie* release. The disc jacket has a chapter listing, but the disc, which runs a little over two hours and is spread to three sides, is not chapter encoded.

ANNIE HALL (CBS/Fox)
ANNIE HALL (MGM/UA)

The CBS/Fox version of *Annie Hall* contains a curiosity – the opening credits appear against a blue background instead of the signature black background which appears correctly on the MGM/UA version. On the whole, however, the CBS/Fox transfer is passable, if one has a copy which is free of speckles added during the manufacturing process. The MGM/UA disc looks sharper, but, like the CBS/Fox, remains grainy in a number of scenes involving problematic lighting effects. The monaural sound on the MGM/UA disc is analog with CX-encoding, an improvement over the noisy CBS/Fox version.

At the time when *Annie Hall* was released theatrically, it was an important step for film comedies. Both Woody Allen and Mel Brooks had been making theme comedies – a funny western, a funny science fiction movie, etc. – and from that perspective Allen's *Annie Hall* truly seemed like a breakaway film, a comedy with emotional and analytical depth. In fact it was, though for all its cleverness it no longer seems like such a remarkable accomplishment. It is about adults who are incapable of maintaining long-term romantic relationships. In the case of the title character, she doesn't appear to be interested in more than going through the motions, a weakness which seems to be more a lack of sympathy on the part of the character's creator than a realistic and complete personality portrait. It is the side gags, which Allen gradually abandoned in his subsequent films, that give the movie its spirit, and the movie was successful because the gags were not the core of the film.

ANOTHER COUNTRY

The formative years of the British traitor, Guy Burgess, are examined in *Another Country*. The story centers on politics and homosexuality in an elite preparatory school. The young men cuddle with each other and coo about what a terrific job Stalin is doing. There is a falseness about the whole project that makes the disc, which has been transferred with a cropped screen and a number of speckles, seem tedious. When the spy, at the end, claims that the only thing he really misses is cricket, it is the story's one effective poignancy. The politics within the boys school is fascinating, but you don't for a moment believe that these events began, nurtured, or fixated his desire to betray his country just as you can't believe that in the entire school there isn't at least one youngster suffering from acne.

ANSEL ADAMS: PHOTOGRAPHER

An hour-long interview with the late photographer, Ansel Adams, provides many insights to the nature of photography as an art form on the single sided *Ansel Adams: Photographer*. As a young man, Adams studied to be a concert pianist (he plays a piece at one point during the interview), and the parallels which he draws between photography and music are intriguing. He suggests that a negative is like a musical score, and that the photographer then interprets the negative in his darkroom, the way a musician interprets the music on the stage. Remaining true to this philosophy, he has preserved his original negatives so that artists in the future can reinterpret his work as new darkroom techniques are developed.

The documentary material is in color, though the easy, relaxed closeups of Adams' prints fill the screen with black and white. The picture quality is mildly grainy but passable. The monaural sound is digitally encoded, with standard clarity.

THE APARTMENT

MGM/UA presents its 'Deluxe Letter-Box Edition' of Billy Wilder's romantic comedy, *The Apartment*, with a rousing aspect ratio of 2.4:1. Those who believe that fully letterboxed images are troublesome may complain, but since the film is in black and white, the details ought to appear sharp enough to be viewed without difficulty on a small screen. In fact, a small screen presentation may be preferable to a larger one, since there are occasional problems with the picture quality which remain manageable when the image is compact but become distracting when it is magnified. Specifically, there are segments when the contrasts look washed-out and portions of the screen appear too grainy. The problem seems to be most pronounced during the first third of the film.

The Apartment is about an insurance company employee who works his way up the corporate ladder by loaning his apartment to his bosses as a trysting nest, until the situation impacts his own love life. Fred MacMurray gives an enjoyable performance as the villainous boss, and Shirley MacLaine is charming. Jack Lemmon's performance as the hero, however, is probably the most interesting. It is difficult to like either him or his character in the film, but that appears to be intentional, and an unease about his personality makes the film not only more interesting, but more repeatable.

The digital monaural track is almost completely free of noise, but the analog track is not. The letterboxing is thrilling. It is clear that the screen composition recreates the original image to the absolute limit. Although the film is designed much like a stage play, it is often important to view two sides of a room or office simultaneously, to watch what each character is up to. There is also the sense of cramped spaces which, ironically, you would lose if the image were cropped so that you could not see the walls.

APHRODITE

The credits are in French, as is a brief text prolog, but *Aphrodite* has been dubbed into English. The film is a softcore erotic exercise with a couple of hardcore images mixed into the montage. The narrative, based upon a French novel, concerns political and romantic intrigue at a mansion in the spring before World War I. The picture has many black speckles and looks a bit worn down, but the colors are probably as fresh as they appeared on the original source. Because of the dubbing, the sound is awkward, but the musical score, a mixture of classical pieces and Mediterranean strains, is nice. Capucine appears, likely without knowledge of what is going on in the inserts.

THE APPALOOSA

Our mother had the hots for Marlon Brando and she dragged us to *The Appaloosa* when we were little. We thought it was the worst movie we had ever seen, an excruciating tale about a man trying to get his horse back. When the disc appeared, however, our curiosity was perked. It had been a long time since we suffered through the original 99 minutes watching it, and the photo on the jacket cover of Brando decked out in his sombrero and his poncho looked intriguing. Besides, we appreciate good movies better after seeing how bad other movies are.

This time through we did not find the film to be excruciating, but, despite Brando, it is as bad as we remembered. With many more hours of film viewing under our belt, we realized what the problem is. The director, Sidney Furie, often fails to convey key information in the action scenes so, particularly at the end, you don't know what is happening until well after it happens. Shots which would show retributions, or explain how a character got from point A to point B are absent. If you didn't know the clichés, you would have no idea what was going on. Instead of establishing shots which show a character's surroundings, there are huge closeups of the character's rotting teeth, like a mountain range in summer, filling the screen.

The other problem with the movie is that everybody is supposed to be speaking Spanish, but of course, they're speaking English since it is an American film. Every once in a while, however, the characters break into real Spanish. Does this mean they're actually speaking English? The supporting cast is largely Hispanic. Brando portrays an American who was raised with a Mexican family. When he decides to chase after the bandits who took his horse, he rubs coffee grounds on his face so he can pass through Sonora unnoticed. He doesn't fool anyone, but when he is captured and dragged before the chief bandito, who does it turn out to be? John Saxon – they probably had to use an entire urn on him.

The transfer isn't bad. In some of the scenes the color looks totally washed out, but that's just Furie being consistent in artistic quality. The sound isn't bad, either. If you find yourself wishing you could hang the jacket cover on the wall, then you probably won't mind the film. Spare your little ones, however. They won't understand.

APPOINTMENT WITH DEATH

The cast of *Appointment with Death*, an Agatha Christie mystery with Angela Lansbury as Miss Marple, includes Lauren Bacall, Carrie Fisher and Haley Mills, and all are delightful. The script has class but the movie was directed by Michael Winner, who comes very close to wrecking it. The musical score for the period (thirties) film is so jarring that it alienates one's concentration, and the editing has a slapped-together look to it. Individual scenes are poorly conceived, with the actors not just left to their own devices, but often given, clearly, the wrong emotional interpretations and wrong activities to perform. In the end, the movie is no better than a Christie story itself, worth watching once, but only worth watching again if so much time has passed that one has forgotten the resolution until its denouement is obvious.

The picture transfer is vivid. It is helpful, also, that most of the movie takes place in the bright sun. The sound is monaural, but with the music and everything it is best confined to a low volume. The disc also has a good selection of chapter markers.

APPRENTICE TO MURDER

The jacket cover of *Apprentice to Murder* is terribly misleading and the scene depicted in the artwork never appears in the disc. The movie is an interesting study, 'inspired by a true story,' of a man practicing holistic medicine in the backwoods of Pennsylvania during the Depression. His skills are eventually superseded by a psychosis, and the events leading up to a tragedy caused by his madness are seen through the eyes of a young assistant. The film and the disc have a rustic look, and the evocation of place is the movie's strongest attribute. The monaural sound is digitally encoded and is indicative of a limited production budget.

APRIL FOOL'S DAY

By now the entire free world has heard about the ending of *April Fool's Day*, a jokey take-off on *Friday the 13th*. There are a lot of amusing sound effects in the digitally encoded release, a surround encoded zipper, an overabundance of birds and crickets, and weird background noises. The music is heavily directional and sometimes comes out of only one channel. A great deal of effort clearly went into the technical details. In fact, we would be tempted to say that the movie will eventually be recognized as one of the greatest sound films ever made...but it isn't April 1st yet.

ARENA BRAINS – A FILM BY ROBERT LONGO

The performance artist/comic/whatever, Robert Longo, is featured on a super-perfectly produced disc, *Arena Brains – A Film by Robert Longo*. The 34 minute program, which uses various Electra artists for barely audible background music, is a collection of sophomore-level sketches separated by some fancy video editing. The sketch characters, in various situations, question the standard material values of our society, but have little to offer in alternative. The sound, however, has an extensive range and is almost completely clean. The picture is of post-Windex quality. If only Longo had something truly meaningful to say, the medium would have delivered his message with great impact.

ARETHA FRANKLIN THE QUEEN OF SOUL

A good hour-long documentary about Aretha Franklin, *Aretha Franklin The Queen of Soul*, features interviews with Franklin and people who have worked with her, along with film clips spanning her musical career. Its emphasis is on an analysis of her rise in the pop field, particularly early on as she made the important shift from singing Gospel to singing soul. The documentary is so cleverly constructed, however, that biographical bits from Franklin's private life continually slip into the narrative, as if by accident. The portrait is thorough, and its only real drawback is that few of the songs are allowed to play from beginning to end. The program should have been twice as long, to accommodate that.

Many of the film clips are old, but even the material recorded especially for the documentary looks a little fuzzy on the disc. The digital sound is stereophonic, which is pumped a little during the music, but not detrimentally.

ARGERICH/FREIRE

The cameras are set up all around the pianos in *Argerich/Freire* to watch the hands of the two performers from both sides. A 60-minute concert program, Nelson Freire performs a Debussy piece and two numbers by Chopin before he is joined by Martha Argerich for Rachimaninoff's 'Suite No. 2 Op. 17' and Ravel's 'Waltz.' Freire gives a competent performance, but he hasn't got the ability to transcend the music with interpretation. In tandem with Argerich for the Ravel work, however, the music finally comes alive. Although the two are never closer than ten feet and rarely glance at one another, their synchronization has an element of eroticism. Pioneer has promoted the disc as a CAV title, but it is in CLV on both sides.

ARIA

Aria is a collection of music videos, made by well-known filmmakers and set to arias from various operas. Like regular music videos, the visual narrative often has little to do with the lyric. The best segments come from Jean-Luc Godard, who proves he is not over the hill by creating a stunning ballet of musclemen and naked cleaning women; Ken Russell, who has a good handle on the genre and is actually able to tell a story while supplying the film with its most dynamic visuals; and a 'can't lose' comedy piece by Julien Temple starring Buck Henry, Anita Morris and Beverly D'Angelo. The other segments are also appealing, if not on the first viewing then on subsequent viewings, and all have healthy amounts of nudity and obscure purposes. There are, unfortunately, no chapter markers, and no listing of the segments on the jacket cover (you have to read the credit scroll to get it all). The picture quality is below average. The image is grainy and fuzzy. The music never has the clarity it is capable of achieving.

ARMAGEDDON (Import)
Modern Japanese fantasy often seems to have the specter of nuclear holocaust looming behind it. One of the most haunting shots in *Armageddon* is a closeup of a tape cassette deck quietly spinning, while the volume level lights pulsate in a glowing red.

The story shifts between three levels of fantasy. In the lowest, there is practically no fantasy at all as the hero, who is a bit of a snobbish wimp, has crushes, talks to his friends, and suffers from adolescent low self-esteem. On the highest level, the forces of good and the forces of evil have a wild blue-and-red ray battle for eternity and existence. The middle level, which the story should not wander from as much as it does, has the kid acquiring his own point-your-finger-and-a-blue-ray-comes-out powers. The appeal of the disc is in its unrestricted, zigzagging mixture of fantasy and realism.

The stereo surround sound is good. The music track draws from Bach, Mozart, and other sources. At 131 minutes, the show is a little long to take in with one sitting, what with the Japanese dialog and all, but the story is easy enough to follow. The picture has some trouble with severe, fiery reds, but is otherwise impressive.

ARMED AND DANGEROUS
About 50% of the budget for *Armed and Dangerous* appears to have been allocated for destroying automobiles. John Candy portrays a security guard who uncovers an organized theft ring and, after a suitable amount of destruction and embarrassment, brings the guilty to justice. Tito Puente shows up in a nightclub scene and does 'Oye Como Va,' which is about the best surprise the film has to offer. The rest is fairly standard, but is not badly executed. The picture is a little fuzzy and the sound is passable.

ARMED RESPONSE
Too much violence and too much bad acting reduces *Armed Response* to a rubble. We enjoy watching death and destruction as much as the next person, but when a character cuts off his finger and there is a closeup of the stub, before the minute marker on side one has even changed from 1 to 2, you can tell this isn't a movie for a romantic evening. Lee Van Cleef portrays David Carradine's father, but they are thrown in with a cast which has difficulty with line memorization, let alone emotional projection. The disc has a blurry picture and monaural sound which is not CX-encoded. It isn't any fun because, all the way through, you keep thinking about the finger.

AROUND THE WORLD IN EIGHTY DAYS
Great trepidation normally accompanies the laser disc release of a movie such as *Around the World in 80 Days*. Will the loss of the widescreen image spoil the entertainment? Will the prolog still be there? Will the intermission and exit music be retained? And will the movie be as good as one fondly remembers?

The disc's stereo is wonderful, with so many alternate sound levels that you will go dizzy just listening to the movie. Since the sound recording is from the mid-fifties, it is not perfect, but few viewers will be displeased with it, especially if they are relaxed and having a good time. There is a major sound dropout half way through side two on both the analog and digital tracks, and some milder dropouts scattered through the remainder of the film.

The intermission occurs 11 minutes into side three on the 179-minute, four-sided disc. Both the intermission and exit music are retained, accompanied by title cards. There are six to eight chapter markers on each side of the disc. The picture is well preserved and colorful, but in the darker scenes, points of light tend to be accompanied by red or blue ghosts.

The movie was made in a wider aspect ratio than is being presented on disc. This is made particularly obvious during the prolog, which begins in a box and then bursts stereophonically to the edges at a key moment. The director, however, was not as accomplished at utilizing the wide aspect ratios as other filmmakers have been, and so the movie is not significantly harmed by the cropping. There are some deliberate widescreen travelog-type shots which lose their impact, and a few minor gags, such as when Passepartout thanks Buddha for the apple, but the plot and the main characters and cameos are all in the center. We still feel that the movie should be shown with its edges left on, but the image presentation is bearable.

The movie, despite its carefully plotted, serial inspired source, is essentially a travelog. The pauses to soak up the culture at each new point of arrival often last longer than the incidents which advance the narrative. The source material is also missing a few scenes that may be restored in future versions.

ART AWARENESS COLLECTION FROM THE NATIONAL GALLERY OF ART (see **THE NATIONAL GALLERY OF ART**)

ART BLAKEY AND THE JAZZ MESSENGERS
Art Blakey and the Jazz Messengers is part of 'The Jazz Life 7(b5)' series. The program, a single set that runs just a little over an hour (the disc is CLV throughout), can make your whole living space feel like a jazz club. The shots shift from closeups to super closeups (the screen, for example, can be filled with three fingers pumping trumpet keys). The stereo sound is immediate and perfectly distributed (even Blakey's drums are separated vividly). The set is a good one, too. At the time, Blakey's 'Messengers' included both Wynton and Branford Marsalis, along with Charles Fambrough, Billy Pierce and Donald Brown. The Marsalises had yet to succumb to commerciality and they play raw, exciting, and alert improvisations. The picture, from a video tape source, is a little soft, but not enough to harm the entertainment.

ART FILM GALLERY 1 MATISSE
(Import)
Art Film Gallery 1 Matisse is a French film which runs an hour, in CAV, and is loaded with both art and data, much of it in potentially interactive form. The picture quality is excellent, primarily from a video tape source, and a color bar chart is included in many individual shots, for reference. The disc is digitally encoded, but that doesn't help much. There is only Japanese dialog on the digital track, while the analog track has Japanese on one audio channel and the original French narration on the other.

The evolution of the artistry of Pierre Matisse, from painting impressionistic landscapes at the beginning of the century to his cutting and pasting colored shapes in the forties, is documented chronologically on the disc. Thirty works are depicted in detail and are identified, with frame reference numbers, on an insert which comes in the jacket sleeve. The locales that Matisse inhabited are visited. Rare footage of the painter at work, in slow motion, can be examined on a frame-by-frame basis to observe his instinctive hand and brush movements. There are also twenty studies of a reclining nude, presented in a dissolve montage which leads to the painting, 'Nu Rose.' Manipulating the speed of the montage can reveal different aspects to the development of the composition.

ART PEPPER – NOTES FROM A JAZZ SURVIVOR (Import)
Art Pepper – Notes from a Jazz Survivor has a fairly steady CX-encoded stereo music soundtrack, but the music is overlayed with an hour-long interview (in English, with Japanese subtitles). Pepper talks about his music and his days as a criminal and how happy he is with his wife, who is also interviewed, but mostly he talks about his addiction to heroin. Near the end he pulls up his shirt to show the camera where doctors have removed a portion of his belly. This is not a disc one would put on at a dinner party.

Pepper's saxophone playing seems to have the perfect mixture of precision and inspiration. How can a person who had discarded so much of his humanity produce such lovely, innocent music?

THE ASPHALT JUNGLE
There is a cute publicity still on the cover of *The Asphalt Jungle* showing Sterling Hayden being pawed by both Jean Hagan and Marilyn Monroe. In the film itself, Hayden and Monroe have no scenes together.

The disc is in CLV and has no special features except chapter markers. The black-and-white picture in *Jungle* is not stunning, but it is in excellent condition and shouldn't disappoint anyone. The sound is not CX-encoded.

The older we get the more we begin to appreciate the films of John Huston. Not only did he avoid repeating himself, he has always shown a respect for his source material which few other directors ever demonstrated. The opening of *Asphalt Jungle* is wonderful. Taught, tough, and entangling, it ticks off the events leading to a jewel robbery without glamor (despite Monroe, who is captivating) or Hollywood interference. Hollywood does make an imposition on the ending, especially with an hysterical 'Rosencrantz and Guildenstern are dead' announcement concerning a corrupt policeman, but by then the movie is already over. Its pleasure is not in its resolution but in its unfolding.

THE ASSASSIN
Steve Railsback stars in *The Assassin*, a passable action film about CIA agents protecting a senator in Latin America. The Americans seem oblivious to the fact that they are guests in a foreign country, but the movie has enough sex and violence to hold one's attention, and there is surprising stunt fall onto the roof of an automobile. The picture is grainy, but the Ultra-Stereo surround sound is fun.

ASSASSINATION
Image took special care to note on the jacket cover of *Assassination* that side two is in Standard Play, and they broke the playing time of the 88-minute film up so that side two would run under 30 minutes. But they neglected one important detail. They mastered side two in CLV.

So what's to miss? Well, there are some good stunts involving a speed boat and a jetski, some nice portraits of Charles Bronson and Jill Ireland pretending to be tense, a few gunfights, and Michael Ansara getting shoved out of a glass elevator. All this in 30 minutes almost prevents the movie from becoming boring.

Yet, if it is late at night, and you're looking for mindless entertainment which has an unaggressive stereo score and a bright, flawless picture, there are worse movies one could watch. And it has been a long time since we've seen Michael Ansara.

ASYLUM
The British horror anthology film, *Asylum*, is a cute concoction from the early seventies, starring such cinematic treasures as Barbara Parkins, Robert Powell, Peter Cushing, Herbert Lom, Britt Ekland, and Charlotte Rampling. The screenplay was penned by Robert Bloch. The linking device is a psychiatrist interviewing four mental patients in a hospital for the insane. Each has a gruesome story to tell. The musical score over-uses 'Night on Bald Mountain' in a very entertaining way, and the whole film has a kind of lurid innocence, always cutting away when it is time to chop or slash a victim. The quality of the source material is fair. It looks faded, but intact. The sound is a little fuzzy. The jacket art is misleading and will cause potential fans to overlook the disc.

AT CLOSE RANGE
The sound drops out of the right channel for nearly a minute at the end of side one on *At Close Range*. There is a hum at the very opening and the usual amount of background noise whenever the music calms down enough to reveal it.

Sean Penn and Christopher Penn portray brothers who idolize their father, a successful burglar. The father eventually assassinates one of them and comes close to doing in the other one. The look of the film is inconsistent and the director does not try enough visual tricks to encourage repeated study, but the performances are wonderful, no matter what the critics say, and any appeal the movie has comes from the Penns and their instinctively grandstanding style. *At Close Range* is based on a true story, but it is doubtful that the individuals involved sported anything like the haircuts the actors and actresses portraying them possess.

ATLANTIC STARR – AS THE BAND TURNS...THE VIDEO
Three music videos are featured on the 16 minute CLV 8-inch, *Atlantic Starr – As the Band Turns...The Video*. The sound is a little rough and the picture is grainy in the darker scenes, but the flaws are minor. 'Secret Lovers' is an awkward mixture of concert footage and confused scenes depicting the joys of infidelity. 'Freak-a-ristic' is a spirited party and dance number. The last, 'If Your Heart Isn't in It,' is the best. The singers watch their music video performances in a screening room with different emotions from those depicted on the screen.

AU REVOIR LES ENFANTS
A typical Louis Malle scene can be found in *Au Revoir les Enfants*. A group of Nazi soldiers are dining in a restaurant. French collaborationist officers come in and begin to make trouble for an elderly Jewish man who is sitting at another table. Much to the relief of the heroes, who are also dining in the restaurant, the Nazi soldiers tell the French collaborationists to get lost. Malle, the director, can often be counted upon to approach an idea with a fresh point of view, and his movies are usually very entertaining as a result.

Au Revoir les Enfants is about a young Jewish boy who is riding out the War in a Catholic boarding school. It is in French and has yellow English subtitles which are easy to read but seem inadequate to the task of capturing the overlapping playground conversations. The disc is mildly stereophonic, with surround codes generally reserved for air raids. The picture is a bit too orange, but most viewers will find the delivery to be fully acceptable. Image has included an excellent interview with Malle on a jacket insert, which will add significantly to a viewer's appreciation of the film.

Malle works very hard to avoid being cute in his schoolyard scenes, and the result has the sort of blandness which is typical of real life. The two boys who are supposed to be close friends fight often and feel resentment toward one another. The emotional trump played at the end is intended to support the weak narrative preceding it, but not every viewer will find Malle's light construction sufficient to support multiple viewings.

AUDUBON SOCIETY'S VIDEOGUIDE TO THE BIRDS OF NORTH AMERICA: 1
What could have been an innovative utilization of interactivity on laser disc is, instead, a modestly successful linear program. *Audubon Society's VideoGuide to the Birds of North America: 1* is a video cassette program which has been adapted to laser disc Extended Play. Obviously, the program would be more effective in the CAV format than it is in CLV. Equally disappointing, however, is the failure to take advantage of the independent audio channels. The narrator is usually speaking at the same time the birds are, and there is no way to listen to one without the other. As a field guide, the program is an interesting step beyond the well-thumbed picture books of the past. If the great cormorant and double-crested cormorant are shown with stills, the olivaceous cormorant is shown in motion to give one an idea of how the others would look.

The 90-minute disc has 126 chapter markers, detailed on the back of the jacket for easy reference. Some of the older nature photography is faded and blurry while many deliberately planned shots are video crisp.

AUNTIE MAME
The monaural sound on *Auntie Mame* is best when amplified, but the lack of stereo does seem to cramp the title character's style a little. Fortunately she is not cramped when it comes to the picture image, which has been letterboxed with an aspect ratio of about 2.3:1. The image is constantly composed in rectangular groupings. If there aren't people or amusing objects on the far edges of the screen, there is at least an appropriate splotch of color. The picture transfer is beautiful.

The way in which the film remains bound to the trappings of a stage work – single sets, identifiable scene changes, even the use of a spotlight in the place of an iris – is interesting because it also transcends staginess at all the right moments. The editing is effective and the camera angles are well chosen. The presentation is never an awkward adaptation of another medium. It is, instead, a gung-ho springboard.

The two-and-a-half-hour movie is about a woman, memorably embodied by Rosalind Russell, who has a Bohemian attitude and a Rivolian lifestyle. The dialog is witty and mildly risqué, and the narrative spans two decades. The characters, although they are intended to verge on the absurd, are too dated in their quirks to fully satisfy today's viewer, but the movie is sufficiently free-spirited to remain enjoyable.

AUTUMN SONATA
THE MAGICIAN
SAWDUST AND TINSEL
FANNY AND ALEXANDER
Nobody likes dubbed movies, but experience tells us that subtitles are not always a more satisfactory alternative. Movies often have more than one character talking at a time. Subtitles tell you what is being said in the foreground, but dubbing lets you hear the background as well. There are several Ingmar Bergman films available on disc which provide good examples of the different challenges encountered when presenting foreign films on home video and how they are surmounted.

In *Autumn Sonata* Ingrid Bergman portrays a concert pianist visiting her daughter for a weekend. The daughter, played by Liv Ullmann, shares a house with her husband, a minister. A sister, who is suffering from a degenerative disease, lives in the house as well; a situation the mother is unaware of before her arrival.

Most of the film consists of closeups on Bergman or Ullmann as they converse and argue. Each has done her own dubbing, so that even though the words do not match the lip movements in the tight shots, it is rarely distracting. Furthermore, the reaction shot is often shown instead of the talking shot, so that while one character is speaking, we are watching the other. Despite the poor condition of the transfer and pressing, we are pleased with the disc. Whether you will want it for your collection depends upon your concepts of entertainment.

Two of Ingmar Bergman's early black-and-white films are available through Embassy. One often thinks of Bergman films as being dour and bleak, but there are quaint touches of frivolity in both movies.

The Magician is dubbed, and here the process hurts ones enjoyment of the film. The cadence of the original Swedish is gone and the dialog is poorly mixed with the sound effects. A magician and his troupe visit a large house where they play some particularly nasty tricks on their host and his overbearing guests. You can view the house as representing man's soul if you wish, or you can just get wrapped up in watching the plot twist and turn.

Sawdust and Tinsel is subtitled, and the advantage of listening to the original dialogue supersedes the distraction of reading what is being said. The only problem is that the plot is weak and not as entertaining as *The Magician*.

Sawdust and Tinsel (also known as 'The Naked Night') is about humiliation. The owner of a traveling circus is rejected by his wife, his mistress, and eventually his audience, as he tries to raise funds. You can view the circus as representing man's soul if you wish, or you can find enjoyment in watching the characters cheat on one another. There is one classically Bergman image that ought to be reproduced more often: a closeup of a gun being pointed at the head of a clown. A metaphor for Sweden's tax laws, perhaps?

Fanny and Alexander was given very special treatment. One audio track has the original Swedish dialog, and subtitles printed on the screen. The second audio track has the dubbed version of the dialog, so that if you choose, you can turn on the English and suppress the Swedish. The subtitles remain, regardless. We watched side one in Swedish, appreciating the rhythm of the dialog and the richness of the voices.

We started to watch side two in English but we could only take about fifteen minutes of it before switching back. The voices on the original language track are full and exist in an atmosphere. The voices on the English track sound as if they are being spoken in an empty room, which, in fact, is where they were recorded. The idea behind dual languages is that you'll watch the English version so that you know what is going on and then switch over to the original language. But subtitles work the same way.

The youngster, Alexander, attends a Christmas party at his grandmother's mansion. Soon afterwards, he and his sister, Fanny, are thrust into a colder world when his father dies and his mother marries a sourpuss minister. They eventually escape (the movie's one faulty sequence – not enough information is given to the audience to appreciate how they brought it off) and the family is reunited. For once, Bergman seems less worried about mankind's soul and more interested in sharing the warmer parts of his own spirit.

AUTUMN WHISPERS...WINTER DREAMS

Fifty minutes of seasonal Colorado scenery set to music which sounds like the instrumental passages in an Anne Murray song can be had on *Autumn Whispers...Winter Dreams*. The video tape source is in poor condition, constantly afflicted by colored horizontal lines. The disc is in digitally encoded surround, and the picture transfer is probably too good, highlighting the faults of the source.

THE AWAKENING (Import)

One of the best mummy movies, *The Awakening*, is available on disc in Japan. The movie is in English with Japanese subtitles. The stereo effects are engaging, although the soundtrack has a fair amount of hiss. The colors are rich and the print does not have too many scratches. In some places the colors run together, but generally, the image is satisfying. The musical score by Claude Bolling is exceptional.

The film is a modernized version of 'Jewel of the Seven Stars,' and stars Charlton Heston, Susannah York, and Stephanie Zimbalist. Like most mummy movies, it is a simple tale of possession. The spirit of an evil ("I am sure of one thing though, there was a royal child whose name was erased years after its birth."), ancient Egyptian queen is released from her tomb on the day an archaeologist's child is born. Eighteen years and several not-so-mysterious deaths later...

The Awakening has one purpose and executes it perfectly. The story itself may have dramatic flaws – the queen wins – but it is everything a mummy movie ought to be, with real Egyptian locations, a few gruesome murders, and a marvelous, eye-rolling performance by Zimbalist as the possessed daughter. Every once in a while you're in the mood for this kind of stuff, and the disc can be sitting there, awaiting excavation from one's shelf.

THE AWFUL TRUTH

Irene Dunne is so funny in *The Awful Truth* because she isn't trying to be. The show is humorous enough as it is. She entertains you like a hostess instead of an actress, poised and remaining the center of attention no matter what is going on around her. The print has a few scratches and the sound is full of snaps and crackles. The story, about a couple who have to go through a divorce to realize they want each other, is based on a stage play and much of the risqué dialog is retained. This adds to Dunne's allure and prevents the film, which is half a century old, from seeming out of date.

B.B. KING: LIVE AT NICK'S (see THE JAZZ LIFE 7(b5): CHICO HAMILTON)

B.B. KING LIVE IN AFRICA
B.B. KING & FRIENDS "A NIGHT OF RED HOT BLUES"

We can't choose between *B.B. King Live in Africa* and *B.B. King & Friends "A Night of Red Hot Blues,"* so we guess you'll just have to get both. Both have very good picture transfers and vivid digitally encoded stereo sound.

The two programs complement one another nicely. The focus of the 45-minute concert in *Live in Africa* is King himself. The camera, which is responsible for some luscious closeups, rarely leaves him out of view, and his backup band rarely does more than maintain the beat. The whole focus is on King and his guitar, and it is a rousing, dynamic session.

Red Hot Blues was an hour-long cable television special which is loaded with guest stars, including Patti LaBelle, Gladys Knight, Etta James, Chaka Khan, Paul Butterfield, Dr. John, and others. King does play his guitar, but he also spends a lot of time performing master of ceremonies duties. Were it not for the *Live in Africa* disc, a viewer might feel the jam session on *Red Hot Blues* was disorganized and jumpy. But when the two discs are paired together, in either order, each can act as a super encore set to the other.

B.C. HOLIDAY HAPPENINGS

The popular comic strip, B.C., has been transferred to animation with mixed success in *B.C. Holiday Happenings*. Side one, 'B.C. The First Thanksgiving,' has amusing drawings but a thin plot which presents only one gag at a time. 'B.C. A Special Christmas' is more inventive. Comedians Bob and Ray do some of the voices and the story – two unscrupulous characters decide to 'invent Christmas' to make a fast buck – works in some great puns (the two agree that the creature delivering the gifts should have "sanitary claws") and fairly complex morals. The sound and picture are acceptable.

BABES IN ARMS

The formula Mickey Rooney/Judy Garland picture, *Babes in Arms*, directed by Busby Berkeley, has none of the spectacle he is normally associated with and the grand finale is more of a 'pffft' than a bang. The songs, including several one normally attributes to *Singin' in the Rain*, are not distinctive and the one big production number is an embarrassing minstrel tribute in blackface.

The print is sharp, speckled only at the reel change points. The music suffers from its own sources and is not CX-encoded.

BABES ON BROADWAY
ZIEGFELD GIRL

Although the movie, *Babes on Broadway*, is of mixed quality, the MGM/UA disc is a winner all the way. Busby Berkeley directed the film, which stars Judy Garland and Mickey Rooney. Garland's combination of youthful optimism and vulnerability was rarely so unrestrained. Her romantic scenes with Rooney are beautifully acted and her ability to induce a crush extends far beyond the limitations of time or space. Hence, even though only half of the musical numbers have zing, and even though the movie goes on for more than two hours, *Babes on Broadway* is worth sitting through, especially in the comfort of home.

The disc, however, has even more to offer. Not only does it open with a trailer for *Ziegfeld Girl*, it also contains the famous ten minute short film featuring Garland and Deanna Durbin, 'Every Sunday.' Although 'Sunday,' about a band concert in a park, was intended to promote Durbin, it was Garland's presence that turned the heads of MGM's executives, starting her on her career.

The picture transfer of *Babes on Broadway* looks very good. The source material has almost no blemishes and delivers a solid black-and-white image which is clear and sharp. The sound has no significant flaws. The musical, in which Rooney plays a young performer who cynically uses a needy children's program to gain the attention of a Broadway producer, includes a blackface number that stops just short of becoming annoying and also features Rooney doing a Carmen Miranda number in drag.

You can bet the latter is not among the excerpts used in the trailer for *Babes on Broadway*, which appears at the opening of MGM/UA's *Ziegfeld Girl*. Girl also runs over two hours (both discs come in gatefold jackets), but since the soapy plot has more narrative paths and fewer digressions, it seems to move more quickly than Broadway. Garland appears, though slightly outside of her normal typecasting. The center of the movie, however, is Lana Turner, as an elevator girl who loses her principles and eventually everything else when she's thrust into the glamor spotlight.

The source material is not as distinct as *Babes on Broadway*. The volume is set a little lower than normal and has to be pushed. MGM/UA has also included an enjoyable promotional film with the trailer at the beginning of the disc, 'We Must Have Music.' Made in 1941 and including a Garland number which was dropped from *Girl*, the short purports to demonstrate how MGM's music department is leading the fight against Fascism (or Communism – we couldn't really tell) by making music which 'the free peoples of the world' can enjoy. The short also contains, among other things, a wonderful alphabetized but untitled montage of MGM's stars.

BABETTE'S FEAST

The tale of *Babette's Feast*, the award winning Danish film, suggests that any remote corner of the world can be the center of the universe, and by extension it suggests that every life has a supreme importance. Told in Danish, with bright yellow English subtitles (which can be bothersome and insufficient simultaneously), the story is about two sisters who inherit a French maid and, in the film's second half, a meal the maid prepares one night for a special occasion. The first half of the film invests in the characters and background details at the expense of a limp and zigzagging narrative, but that is all simply a setup for the 'Feast,' which is so beautifully executed and fulfillingly comical that a viewer's patience is rewarded many times over.

The film stock is not of Hollywood or even Parisian quality, so there is a certain amount of grain which the picture can never shake. The picture is sharp and often so clear that it rescues even the flaws in lighting and photography caused by the filmmakers themselves. In addition, the stereo surround is of Hollywood quality. The music and sound effects are as elaborate and subtle as the Feast itself, and the mix even differentiates dialog from the voice-over narration.

BABY BOOM

Most of *Baby Boom* provided us with anxiety instead of laughs. Only in the movies can a savvy and talented businesswoman be made to look like such an idiot. Fortunately, Diane Keaton is a talented actress, so she breezes through the embarrassing material as brazenly as if she were a circus clown, and then seizes on the intermittent portions of the script which are genuinely funny and enjoyable, and provides these sequences with a relaxed, classy understanding of their comic potential. The film has undergone an uninteresting but acceptable transfer to disc. The music track and some of the sound effects are in stereo. The twins who play the toddler are bright and talented, and it is easy to go gaga over them, but on multiple viewings, you can start to spot when each one is used. Their personalities are different, as is the flavor of their gaze.

BABY...SECRET OF THE LOST LEGEND

The soundtrack is one of the best aspects to *Baby...Secret of the Lost Legend*. There is a wonderful Jerry Goldsmith score which is allowed to flourish like jungle overgrowth in order to hide other deficiencies in the film. There are some nice gunshots and animal sounds, too, and there is Patrick McGoohan's voice, which has a rich, articulate vibration, well-suited for loud, stereophonic playback. The picture is probably in too good a condition, since the special effects would be more convincing if the film were blurry or full of scratches. The move, about the discovery of a dinosaur family in contemporary Africa, has an enjoyable plot, some humorous cross-cultural gags, and real African locations. The dinosaurs aren't convincing, but the acting is, and that is enough to carry an undemanding viewer along.

BABY, THE RAIN MUST FALL

Horton Foote's plays have as much liveliness as the Texas landscape where most of them are set – flat, dusty, and unvaried as far as the eye can see. The early sixties Steve McQueen film, *Baby, the Rain Must Fall* (no comma in the film's title card, but in every instance on the disc jacket), is based upon a Foote play. A viewer approaching the film can still have a good time provided it is understood that not much is going to happen. On the plus side there is McQueen, Lee Remick, Don Murray, Elmer Bernstein's souped-up score, Lazlo Kovak's gorgeous black-and-white cinematography, and the shower-perfect title song.

The picture usually looks okay. There are some scenes which appear too grainy and there is an occasional scratch. The oddest incident occurs near the end of side one, when the image appears to slip above the bottom edge of the frame for a few seconds.

The plot is about a man suffering from manic depression in a town where the cure is jail instead of therapy. He's out long enough to see his wife and, for the first time, his daughter, to play a few rockabilly gigs at a local tavern, and to witness the death of his crotchety guardian who was responsible for his neurosis in the first place. Then it's back to the slammer. The problem with the film is that the focus is supposed to be on Remick's character, but McQueen has such a powerful screen presence that her character becomes a secondary interest whenever he enters the scene.

The sound on the disc is digital monaural and is good enough to press the volume for the musical numbers (in which McQueen is awkwardly dubbed) if you don't mind a little fuzz. The disc has chapter markers, but Image has allowed several songs to slip by unmarked.

BABYFACE: TENDER LOVER THE VIDEOS

Three music videos are presented on the 8-inch *Babyface: Tender Lover The Videos*. The singer, Babyface, uses very attractive backup dancers in his videos, so there is little reason to pay attention to him. The first two, 'It's No Crime,' and 'Tender Lover,' are shot in an abandoned industrial site – hardly a first – and are adequately produced. The finale, 'Whip Appeal,' although tamer than its title implies, is a memorable exercise in music-star indulgences, depicting an audience of women going wild over his cute cheeks. The picture is mildly grainy throughout. The sound is fine and even has a touch of surround here and there.

THE BABYSITTER

William Shatner makes a grand theatrical entrance near the beginning of *The Babysitter*, delivering his first line ("Tara, eat your vitamins, all of them. Do it now.") in mid-stride and then pausing as if he expected applause for having appeared. The whole cast, including Patty Duke-Astin and Stephanie Zimbalist, is full of misplaced energy, and they give the best dinner theater performances they have in them. The film is typical short story material, about a housekeeper (Zimbalist) who starts manipulating her employers. Murder is involved and the movie gets creepy near the end, if you can stop giggling at Shatner's fractured inflections long enough to get into it.

The picture transfer is acceptable, though the program has a TV movie look to it. The sound is monaural and has not been CX-encoded. The musical score, which sounds as if it were recorded off-key, comes out the worst.

BACHDISC

The two-sided CAV *Bachdisc* analyzes the life and talent of the great composer, Johann Sebastian Bach. Side one has digitally encoded sound, but side two does not, for no apparent reason. The analog tracks are CX-encoded without automatic tripping, but the difference between the digital track, the analog track with the CX on and the analog track with the CX off is minimal. Except for some crosstalk which can be heard when silent passages are turned up full blast, the sound is pure. Each side contains a different work by the video artist, Juan Downey. One was made in 1986 and one in 1988, but both have the vivid sharpness of fresh video, and both have a problem with unsteady frames when movement is manipulated with the CAV functions.

Side one, the 1988 program entitled, 'Fugue #24 in B minor,' is excellent. The fugue is played 14 times in the chapter encoded sequence. First normally while viewing the fingering on a keyboard, then to a music scroll, then to a keyboard and music scroll together, then the three parts shown in split screen on three separate keyboards with single hands, then just the 'Soprano and Alto' using the split screen, then the 'Alto and Bass,' then 'Soprano and Bass,' after which the three are played separately to a music scroll again, which is then followed by an upside-down view of the keyboardist accompanied by an electronically inverted score, to be followed by the keyboardist shown in reverse and slow motion while the score, once again, is artificially manipulated. The side ends with a table of contents which is accompanied once more by the full, normal score. Fingering on the keyboard (of a Hubbard harpsicord) is shown from every conceivable angle. Our only complaint concerns the scrolling score. The notes often do not appear until they are played, preventing the viewer from anticipating the fingering.

The documentary on side two, 'J.S. Bach: His Life and Work,' is less satisfying, because the egos of the filmmakers are in direct conflict with the grandeur of their subject. Scenes from the areas in Germany where Bach lived and worked are displayed on the screen while a narrator provides facts about the composer's life and music. The face of the narrator, however, is often incorporated, through electronic video techniques, with the documentary images. The effect is grotesque and demeaning. The chronology of Bach's career is deliberately shuffled, making the scope of the information untrustworthy, and there is an analytical emphasis on emotion instead of emotional insight. The filmmakers speculate upon Bach's feelings, but rarely demonstrate how those feelings, if they were true, were transposed upon his music.

THE BACHELOR AND THE BOBBY-SOXER

A major but harmless error on *The Bachelor and the Bobby-Soxer* will pass by a few viewers before they've realized something is amiss. There is about two minutes of footage on side two which is repeated, but it occurs during a montage of competitive sporting events at a picnic, and it is easy to assume that the repeated footage is simply a representation of more activities. Otherwise, the black and white print has a few splices and scratches, but it looks sharp and is fairly satisfying. The monaural sound is a little fuzzy, but passable.

The film stars Cary Grant, an adolescent Shirley Temple, and Myrna Loy. It has the sort of make-believe plot – about a judge ordering the hero to date her sister – which can be good fun if you are in the right mood. The performances are all quite good. Temple is funny, Loy is constrained but charming, and Grant is given material which allows him to use his sophisticated demeanor and still generate laughs. It is Rudy Vallee, however, whose performance makes the movie a special treat. Vallee's experiences in Hollywood are usually seen as secondary to his singing career, but there are many reasons to give his filmography a good, critical look. In *Soxer* he delivers his lines with a comical rhythm which is as unique as it is humorous, and fits perfectly with the film's extensive use of overlapping dialog. He livens up his part so much that you look forward to seeing him even though you want his character to fail.

BACHELOR MOTHER

The 1939 black-and-white *Bachelor Mother*, starring Ginger Rogers and David Niven, is superbly photographed. Unlike the practice in most movies, the filmmakers dare to have Rogers act and change expressions during her closeups. The source material Image has used is in decent shape, with no major problems. The sound is also passable. The 83-minute disc is in CLV.

Bachelor Mother can be contrasted to recent 'baby boom' efforts on a structural level – the baby is rarely emphasized, and Rogers' character has no difficulty with becoming an instant mother – but it has many laughs and charms which transcend its era. The comedy comes not so much from the embarrassment Rogers suffers being mistaken for an unwed mother, but in the timing of the editing and the manner of the performers. Sometimes their expressions are so amusing it would not matter what they were talking about, but other times the dialog is appropriately inspired, such as when the bejowled Charles Coburn utters in blustering and mistaken pride, "Why, he looks exactly like me!" (What baby doesn't?)

BACK TO BATAAN

Better than some, but not as good as others, *Back to Bataan* is a run-of-the-mill John Wayne World War II film. As with most of Wayne's war films, the theater of operations is the Pacific, in this case the resistance movement on the Philippines. Anthony Quinn also stars, as a Filipino guerrilla leader. The sound is passable. The black-and-white print has a few speckles, but the picture looks okay overall. The many night scenes, effectively lit, survive without distortion. Viewers today will grow impatient with the heavy-handed patriotism, though we find it hard to believe that viewers at the time had not had their fill of it, either. Quinn is a good foil for Wayne and their scenes together are enjoyable. The action scenes are also good, except for an annoying tendency of the filmmakers to shake the camera every time a shell goes off, regardless of range.

BACK TO SCHOOL

From the opening sepia montage of burgeoning Tall and Fat Man stores to Rodney Dangerfield's enthusiastic recitation of 'Do Not Go Gentle into That Good Night,' *Back to School* has a lot of class. The movie is not just an amalgam of Dangerfield-in-the-classroom jokes. It is a caring and enjoyable tale about filial ties and living life to the fullest, and it is as cleverly constructed as a villanelle.

The disc, however, is from HBO, and they have no respect for the medium. The jacket art runs down the middle of the cover with wide, blank margins, as if it were a flattened video cassette box. On the back, they even call the disc a 'video cassette.' Hey, we'd like to see them try to rewind it. The movie is in stereo. Big deal. The sound comes out of both speakers. The picture is grainy. How grainy? When we turned the disc over, a camel fell out...

BACK TO THE BEACH

If you enjoy parties where no one drinks, you'll probably like *Back to the Beach*, the late Eighties update to the old Sixties 'Beach' films. On the other hand, if you enjoy parties where everyone gets totally stoned, you'll probably like it even more. The movie's Ultra Stereo is digitally encoded and contains almost as many cute separations as the plot itself. The picture is a little on the hazy side, but it could very well be smog since the film takes place in Los Angeles.

The story is a put-on, with Frankie Avalon and Annette Funicello portraying abstract interpretations of their own images. The movie succeeds by never straying from its premise, so the viewer only has to accept one set of rules. There are many cameo appearances. It is interesting that Tony Dow turned out to be better looking than Jerry Mathers, since he always seemed like such a jerk. The best bit part, however, belongs to Don Adams, who says all of his most famous lines in digitally encoded stereo. They never sounded better, proving that there's still life in his gags, and in the old gang.

BACK TO THE FUTURE

From the opening credit sequence to the closing Whoosh!, the sound on *Back to the Future* is almost as much fun as the script. Although analog bound, the soundtrack is clean and is in good condition. The picture does not lose any significant elements in transference to a smaller screen. To be sure, there are jokes on the peripheral edges which drop from view, but the essence of the movie is retained and you don't feel frustrated watching it. The image transfer looks crisp.

Be sure to check out the name of the shopping mall at the beginning and end of the film.

BACK TO THE FUTURE PART II
BACK TO THE FUTURE PART II

('Letterboxed')

The non-special effects parts of *Back to the Future Part II* were shot flat, with the intention of being projected on a theater screen with the top and bottom masked, as the image appears in the matted Letterboxed version. Hence, in scenes where the screen composition can be easily calibrated – the date readout on the car panel or the shot through Christopher Lloyd's binoculars – the image appears to be exactly the same width on both the Letterboxed version and the standard version. However, the special effects shots were made with a wider aspect ratio and appear on the source material with hard mattes already imbedded on the top and bottom of the film. It is on these sequences that MCA had to scan and crop the standard version. For example, when Michael J. Fox's character first meets the older Biff and his grandson, the standard version shows only the duplicated images of Thomas Wilson, while the Letterboxed version is able to include Fox in the shot. Otherwise, the standard version has more confident colors and a crisper image, and provides more satifying viewing.

The stereo surround sound has many directional stereo effects but fewer surround effects or gut level kicks. The sound quality is the same on both disc versions. The digital soundtrack is clean, and some of the more lightly applied sound effects are good fun.

The film has been subject to a number of critical pendulum swings. At first it was hailed as the energized roller-coaster ride that it is. Then, as audiences who came looking for romance were confronted instead by time travel paradoxes and deteriorating sanity, the film was reassessed as being dry and mechanical. It is best to approach *Part II* as a joyride, the sort of film which may not stimulate a viewer's heart, but certainly sets it to pounding. There are definitely aspects of laziness to the script – jokes which haven't been fully considered, simple-minded characterizations, subplots which have no life outside of the narrative – but at the same time the movie has a spirit of exploration and daring, in the application of the special effects and in the choice of exposition, which few films have ever managed to achieve.

BACKFIRE
A young, well-to-do Vietnam vet is having some severe and realistic flashbacks. He turns catatonic, and his wife gains control of his estate, but then odd things begin to happen to her, as well. *Backfire*, which stars Karen Allen and Keith Carradine, takes a while to get started and cheats here and there, but the plot is clever enough to be worth a bowl of popcorn or two. The picture transfer is okay, though the film stock is inexpensive. The Ultra-Stereo sound mix is uninteresting. The story is set in the Pacific Northwest.

BACKSTAGE AT THE KIROV
The participants in *Backstage at the Kirov*, although they go about their daily routines, tend to modify their activities for the camera. You often get the sense that while they are supposed to act as if it is not there, they are very aware of the camera's presence. The film breaks down the confines of realism further when it shifts from a depiction of what is going on immediately before the curtain is drawn to following the dancers, with the camera, right onto the middle of the stage (you almost expect the POV to say 'Whoops' and go running back). The effect, however, is very pleasing, and strengthens the viewer's involvement with the proceedings. Much of Act II from 'Swan Lake' is presented, though in a mildly segmented fashion, as the dancers are shown rehearsing as well as performing. As an informational source, the film gives only a cursory look at what it is like to be employed by the Kirov, but as a celebration of 'the dancer's life' it is an effective and enjoyable film.

The movie, which has a film source and was released theatrically in the US, is mildly grainy and also suffers from a mild loss of color. The sound has a touch of stereo here and there, and is in good condition under the circumstances. Side two of the 80-minute disc is in CAV, but every still frame is unsteady.

THE BAD AND THE BEAUTIFUL
We have always disliked the central thesis supported by the point of view in *The Bad and the Beautiful*, that career achievements are more important than interpersonal relationships. It sours what is otherwise a juicy tale about Hollywood, full of inside jokes and barely veiled references to real personalities. The level of detail with which the filmmakers attack their subject is so rich, however, that the disc is worth considering. The film is a great candidate for repeat viewings.

Contrary to the misleading running time notation on the back of the jacket, the movie is actually 118 minutes long, and breaks comfortably at the halfway point. The black-and-white print is almost spotless, the cinematography is gorgeous, and the contrast levels on the disc are almost perfect. There is one day for night shot which should have been given individualized attention, but otherwise the image is free of distraction. The sound is CX-encoded monaural and the volume may be set a little lower than on other soundtracks, but not enough to create a problem.

BAD DREAMS
The classy black and white ad campaign for the color horror film, *Bad Dreams*, is recreated on the cover of the disc. The movie is deserving of its artwork. It is by no means a masterpiece, but it is efficiently executed, true to its own logic, and contains a satisfying number of thrills. It is also admirable in that the protagonists are only vaguely sympathetic. The plot concerns a woman who awakens from a coma after witnessing a mass murder a number of years earlier, and the torments she must suffer. The sound is stereophonic and is digitally encoded. The sound transfer is good – the bass has a decent rumble – but the many terrific rock numbers on the soundtrack ('I Had Too Much to Dream Last Night') have not been marked by chapters. The picture quality is disappointing. Although the source material is fresh, the image is blurry at times and speckles and white lines appear in several places.

BADGE OF THE ASSASSIN
A well constructed teleplay, *Badge of the Assassin*, is about a district attorney building a murder case against a group of black radicals in the late sixties. The colors look worn down and the sound is average in quality, but the cast – including James Woods as the D.A., Yaphet Kotto and Alex Rocco as detectives, and Rae Dawn Chong and Pam Grier as witnesses – is wonderful, and the narrative is a pleasing mixture of procedural and courtroom dramatics. The film also draws a clear philosophical line on the limits of social protest which is easier to accept in hindsight than, perhaps, it was in the era depicted.

BAILOUT
Bail Out is a lightweight action comedy starring David Hasselhoff and Linda Blair, about bounty hunters who must rescue a kidnapped heiress so she will not miss a court date. There are a sufficient number of car chases, explosions, and gags to pass the time, but such time could just as easily be spent elsewhere. The picture is a little soft, but bright, and the surround sound has a usable number of separation effects.

BAJA OKLAHOMA
The multi-talented Lesley Ann Warren appears in *Baja Oklahoma*, and she is the difference between enjoying and not enjoying the film. She portrays a barmaid and would-be C&W songwriter in a small Midwestern town. The bar is an unusually lively, brightly lit, social gathering place, but that is just one of the film's many incongruities. If you stick with it, you can watch Warren demonstrate a great depth of ability and sensitivity, which comes to a cumulation in the film's last (and best) scene. Her work in that sequence justifies the whole movie.

The music numbers are chapter marked, and the digital stereo sound is most effective during the songs. The picture generally looks fine, but degenerates in one or two places to the condition exemplified in the color stills on the jacket. The plot summary on the jacket also contains a typographical error, but we'll make things fun and not say what it is.

BALL OF FIRE
STELLA DALLAS
The sound on *Ball of Fire* is riddled with scratches and not suitable for amplification. The black-and-white picture is clean, but some scenes look more faded than others.

Ball of Fire has been categorized as a 'Snow White and the Seven Dwarfs' for adults. It is a satisfying comedy about a gangster's girl friend (Barbara Stanwyck) who hides from the police by staying with a group of professors, one being Gary Cooper. At one point, Cooper's character enters a dark room and begins talking, not realizing that Stanwyck is there. Indeed, all we see of her is the barest flicker of light around her eyes. Thanks to cinematographer Gregg Toland, when it is said that Stanwyck's character looks attractive in the sunlight, it is not left to the imagination. Toland's influence on the look of American films cannot be underestimated. It is an added treat that these discs offer a thorough representation of his work.

Barbara Stanwyck also stars as *Stella Dallas*, a woman of low breeding and poor aesthetic taste who wants the best for her daughter. In the beginning of the movie, Stanwyck looks too alert and you can't believe her character would really become that dumb. On side two, after she commits *faux pas* upon *faux pas*, Stella's personality finally suppresses Stanwyck's class and the story starts to work. The ending, where she stands outside in the rain to watch, through a window, her daughter's wedding, is one of those grand conceptual moments that make people love the movies. The soundtrack has more than the usual amount of hiss and buzz.

THE BALLAD OF CABLE HOGUE
One of Sam Peckinpah's nicer movies, *The Ballad of Cable Hogue*, has made it onto laser disc in good condition. The quality of the picture is as good as the stills on the back of the jacket. The film, which takes place in a desert, has a strong, brownish color scheme, and if the print were at all faded, the different shades of wood, leather, and dirt would all run together. They don't.

Jason Robards portrays a man who discovers a waterhole near a stagecoach route and sets up shop selling water to thirsty passengers. Robards is generally an engaging actor, but he is even more attractive than usual playing Hogue. A balance of lightness and earthiness allows him to hover above the story without weighing it down in pathos or floating away in impishness. The plot is supposed to be symbolic of the American Dream and of the end of the Wild West, but it isn't pushy, not even in the end when Hogue is run over by a car. His death is lamentable only because Robards brought him so thoroughly to life.

The sound is in excellent condition. There are many pleasing effects and a nice Jerry Goldsmith score, but it is also worthwhile pumping through one's sound system just for the pleasure of savoring Robards's voice.

BALLET ESPANOL – CARMEN DE YASUKO NAGAMINE (see **THE ROYAL BALLET – SWAN LAKE**)

BAMBI (CLV)
BAMBI (CAV)
We still can't get over the idea that *Bambi* is actually available for home video. What an incredible thrill! A movie which everyone assumed was tantamount to gold reserves is suddenly as accessible as one's own wallet. And what an inspiration it is to view! The animation is as thick and luscious as the forest it is depicting. The humor, the melodrama, and the science create a sort of pleasure which is just about the closest technology can

come to the joys of walking in the woods.

Walt Disney has released two laser disc versions, one in CLV and one in CAV. The picture quality of the two versions is interchangeable. The source material after having undergone major theatrical reissues every seven years or so for close to the last fifty, has many speckles and more than a few soft edges. If you watch much in the way of older animation you learn to cope with such imperfections (*Pinocchio* has segments which were in much the same condition), but some viewers may be distracted.

The digitally encoded sound is stereophonic, something Disney did a while ago for the theatrical runs. It is very directional, and we found the specific effects to be quite entertaining. Unlike *The Lady and the Tramp*, there is no distortion when the film is played through a monaural audio unit. The sound is old, however, and an occasional musical note sounds wobbly.

The CAV disc has 14 chapters, fairly decent considering that the film only runs 68 minutes. The side breaks on the CAV disc are evenly distributed, but occur at ideal moments. The CLV disc has no chapters and the side break is placed at nearly the exact center of the film and interrupts a gag. The advantages to the CAV version exceed the capabilities of CLV still frame playback. In fast motion, the opening shot of the forest has tremendous depth, and the forest fire is a molten spray. In slow motion, the tricks of the animators can be best analyzed – how the swirling leaves that indicate the start of fall are executed on two levels to impart distance, and how the rhythm in the seemingly random movements of the forest creatures are carefully coordinated with each other (and with the music). In still frame, there are the elaborate drawings of the deers themselves. Of particular interest are the comprehensive series of postures given to Faline when she bounds around Bambi the first time she meets him. Every frame contains a different naturalist's pose.

If you ever want to pop a kid's balloon, just show him *Bambi* and watch his expression when Bambi's mother gets killed. At some point children have got to learn that life isn't all Flower and Thumper, even in the make-believe world of TV. *Bambi* is a learning experience for youngsters, a cruel one, but eventually everyone is exposed to grief, so the sooner the emotions to facilitate it are in place, the better. In that respect, *Bambi* is as velvety a hammer as there could be, though one wonders if its other message – that men don't do housework – is being absorbed with equal subversion.

BANANARAMA THE GREATEST HITS COLLECTION

Nine music videos from the all-girl dance rock group, Bananarama, are available on *Bananarama The Greatest Hits Collection*. The single sided CLV disc runs 38 minutes. The first cut is actually a medley of five earlier Bananarama music videos – a medley of both music and images – and, contrary to the listing on the back of the jacket, it has just a single chapter marker. The picture and sound transfers are good.

The videos lack narratives but are rich in choreographed flamboyance. The group's interpretation of 'Venus' on video more than makes up for the way they homogenized the song. Music videos for female rock groups have it easy, because the visuals can exploit them instead of others. That none of the three women will tolerate exploitation makes the videos all the more tense, fetishistic, and repeatably enjoyable.

THE BAND IS BACK

The members of The Band never leave their positions on the stage, but the string of resurrected hits which they pretty much play with their eyes closed draws great rounds of applause from the audience. These guys were supposed to be retired. Instead of collecting Social Security, they went up to Canada on tour and one of their concerts has been captured on *The Band is Back*. The picture on the disc is grainy and every time colored stage lights are activated, the images melt and fog. The music is clear, but since the recording is a concert mix it remains unremarkable. The Band plays their best known songs – fortunately they have enough for an hour set – and look as though they have a better time on stage than in the rest home.

BAND OF THE HAND

An updated version of 'The Mod Squad,' *Band of the Hand* unfolds suspiciously like a TV pilot. The Miami-based Michael Mann production looks terrific on disc and the soundtrack is more subtle than one would expect from a brat pack action picture.

The plot leaves much to be desired. It might make great television, but it is a lousy movie and the title sounds like something out of a Danny Kaye routine ('the Band of the Hand is the clan with the tan...').

THE BAND WAGON

The colors in *The Band Wagon* are super, so bright and vivid that in the Central Park dance scene Fred Astaire and Cyd Charisse, dressed in white against a green grass and indigo sky background, appear to be dancing in 3D, whirling in front of the TV screen rather than on it. Viewers should be warned, however, that the print also has a flaw, a vertical blue band which makes several appearances on a couple of reels and shows up twice during the big 'Girl Hunt' number. The sound is okay for its age, but some listeners are apt to be put off by the volume dropouts used to suppress the noise in silent passages.

The musical, highly respected by some, is a weaker effort by those involved, although anything written by Betty Comden and Adolf Green has a reliable amount of humor to it. The score, unfortunately, has no strong numbers except for 'That's Entertainment,' and Charisse and Astaire, even when they step off the screen and into your living room, are barely sympathetic to each other. The movie, at least, is colorful. If you get the disc be sure to watch for the moment when Charisse takes off an olive raincoat to reveal a red sequined dress. Your whole picture tube will pop.

THE BANK DICK

One of the most marvelously vulgar titles for a movie ever to sneak past the watchdogs of public decency is W. C. Fields' *The Bank Dick*. The movie is scattered with other double entendres too, all vague enough so that Fields could march by the censors with thumb pointedly attached to bulbous nose (there is even just cause to snicker at his initials).

Side two of the 72-minute movie has been pressed in CAV. There is an automobile chase and specifically there is a stunt involving a half-dozen ditch diggers bending over just as the cars pass above them. Watching the gag in slow motion will give you a good sense of how stunt men earn their pay. The print is in very good condition. Although the dialog sounds in some places as though it was recorded underwater, the CX-encoded soundtrack preserves the film's audio probably as best as is possible.

BARBARA A PANTIN (Import)

On the Japanese disc *Barbara A Pantin*, she sings 25 songs in a 100-minute concert, blurting out phrase after phrase with a modulated sing-song voice that never lets up. Her songs are in French, subtitled in Japanese, and come out clearly in CX-encoded stereo. She looks tough and often only her face is lit by the spot light. Most of her songs are about heartbreak, sadness, and love. She apparently knows her subject well.

THE BARBARIANS

An old fashioned Italian muscle movie with up-to-date gore, *The Barbarians* opens with a terrific, extended action scene, and possesses, on the whole, a pleasant balance of humor and sword stunts. The picture has too much orange in it, but the quality of the image is not bad enough to spoil the film. The stereo sound is too much fun to warrant complaints. There is even a dragon, but don't get your hopes too high. The movie was such a low budget effort that one of the 'virgins' has a very prominent caesarean scar below her tassels.

BARBARY COAST

"Women are like frogs. You can never tell which way they're going to jump," says Edward G. Robinson halfway through Howard Hawks' *Barbary Coast*. Robinson portrays an effete gambling boss (he wears jewelry on his left ear) during San Francisco's lawless Gold Rush era. Miriam Hopkins is the object of his amphibic simile and Joel McCrae is a poetry-minded prospector vying for her affections. As in every script written by Ben Hecht and Charles MacArthur, the press plays a key role in the plot. The picture does not look bad, but the sound has a few rough moments and a speckle or two are noticeable during the night scenes.

BARBRA STREISAND – A HAPPENING IN CENTRAL PARK

Barbra Streisand's third television special, *Barbra Streisand – A Happening in Central Park*, filmed in 1967, has been released on a single-sided disc. It is quite a treat, combining the spontaneous thrill of a live event (Streisand, in one of her monologs, performs that curious New York-bred semantical error of swapping 'subscription' for 'prescription') with the gloss of a primetime production.

Pioneer has included an apology on the jacket cover for the age of the master, but they needn't have bothered. It looks terrific. The digitally encoded sound is not in stereo, but it has a brassy range and is admirably recorded.

Except for a pair of numbers from *Funny*

Girl, and 'Happy Days Are Here Again,' the songs are not as familiar as her material has been elsewhere, but it is refreshing to hear her sing show tunes without apologizing or acting like she is at some artistic precipice. The disc is the sort of program fans relish – a chance to see their star in an environment or performance which is at variance with the established norm.

BARBRA STREISAND – ONE VOICE

Barbra Streisand has the kind of voice which can sound better in a bug-infested 'live' environment than in an audio-climate-controlled studio. Thus, *Barbra Streisand – One Voice*, where she gives a concert in her 'backyard,' sounds terrific. It is digitally encoded, although even the analog track sounds nearly spotless. Streisand proves that she doesn't need loops (well, not as many) to achieve vocal control, as she manages the slides at the end of 'Evergreen' just fine.

The concert is a benefit for ending nuclear proliferation. The picture is spotless and vivid, and the evening performance is lit perfectly for video. The shots of the audience remind one of the Oscars (Look – there's Kurt and Goldie!), but none of the interruptions, or Streisand's mildly obscure patter concerning exactly what it is she wants to help, get in the way of the music. The pauses frame and enhance each song.

Despite the title, Robin Williams warms up the audience beforehand, and Barry Gibb appears for two numbers. The program is 65 minutes long and split evenly between the two sides. There are chapter markers for every song.

BARBRA STREISAND "PUTTING IT TOGETHER" THE MAKING OF THE BROADWAY ALBUM

CBS/Fox has eschewed its normal bars and stripes to make the front of *Barbra Streisand "Putting It Together" The Making of The Broadway Album* look exactly like the LP. Streisand's comments about how no one wanted her to make this album sound suspiciously like a Madison Avenue counter-sell. The embarrassingly simplified lyrics Stephen Sondheim added to 'Send in the Clowns' for her seem intended to market the subject matter to a younger but upwardly mobile crowd.

The disc is in digital and sounds even better than the CD with the improved surround. The picture isn't bad either, and there are chapter markers. The full thrusts of some songs are felt in tantalizing snippets, but enough complete numbers are presented (about five) to give the impression that the album is incredible.

BARFLY

The picture and sound transfer on *Barfly* are excellent. The movie, a contrived 'comedy' about alcholics, is not.

THE BARKLEYS OF BROADWAY

Fred Astaire and Ginger Rogers made a number of black and white films together at RKO in the mid-thirties. A decade later, they reunited at MGM for a final film, in color, called *The Barkleys of Broadway*. Critics and effete opinion makers tend to look down upon the movie, considering it to be but a pale reminder of the pair's former glories, but anyone who sees the movie without worrying about its history is bound to like it, because it is marvelous fun. The Technicolor is gorgeous, and Astaire and Rogers appear to pick up on the sympathy they show for one another as if only weeks instead of years had passed since their previous collaboration. The script, by Betty Comden and Adolph Green, uses a typical and reliable Comden and Green plot device. The heroine is tempted away from musical comedy by the luster of doing serious drama, but is saved, after a little scheming, by the hero. *Barkleys of Broadway* is a tremendously romantic film. The two main characters are married, and the familiarity between them provides the perfect ingredient to kindle the Astaire/Rogers magic. They are maturely at ease with one another not just when they are singing and dancing, but when they are doing their comedy or romantic scenes.

The disc is an exhilarating, but not perfect, transfer. Some scenes are exquisite. On the Scottish stage number, for example, the colors in the film are toned down for the fake stage set, and transfer flawlessly onto the disc presentation. At the end, the background view from the window of the Barkleys' Sutton Place apartment is so captivating that one forgets to watch the actors. There are other moments, however, where the color becomes too intense, too dark, or too lacking in contrast. It is not enough to ruin the disc by any matter, it just prevents one from doing more than a few cartwheels over it.

The disc is poorly chapter encoded, with the most memorable dance number, because it involves no singing, left unmarked. Because of the era of the recording, the sound is clear, but a little dull. This is especially noticeable during Oscar Levant's atrocious piano solos, because it makes them sound even more awful than they already are. What did he do, anyway, practice with glue on his keyboard?

BARRY GIBB NOW VOYAGER (Import)

Barry Gibb Now Voyager is a Japanese release in English with Japanese subtitles, featuring nine music videos linked together by a quasi-dramatic dream sequence starring Gibb and an uncredited Ralph Richardson. The sound is spectacular in an amateurish sort of way and the clarity is captivating. When a car goes off a bridge the sound of water splashing to the left seems to match the angle of the splash perfectly. The next challenge for sound producers will be to hide the overlays and edits which are becoming so obvious on laser disc as to be distracting.

The picture has a greenish tint. The disc is 80 minutes long and ends before one tires of it.

BARRY LYNDON

Barry Lyndon is not the sort of movie one should watch on the fly, even if one is trying to kill the requisite 185 minutes. Given the concentration it deserves, however, the film becomes a rich and memorable portrait of life before the advent of household appliances. At first glance, the director, Stanley Kubrick, appears to paint visions of how dull and purposeless existence can be. The elaborate manners by which the characters in *Barry Lyndon* conduct themselves fuses with Kubrick's staid and lethargic tableaux. When some movies advance too slowly, your mind wanders beyond the screen. It is Kubrick's elaborate attention to detail which prevents you from leaving the film. As the hero's fortunes wax and wane you feel the emotions of his surroundings and understand how life was conducted in the era depicted. The movie gets better the more times you watch it, because a familiarity with the plot causes your attentions to wander, and the details you discover continually reinforce the veracity of Kubrick's vision. It is worthwhile, too, because the longer you stay with the characters, the more you are privy to the feelings beneath the manners.

The monaural sound is in excellent condition. It is so well reproduced that the musicians playing the film's soundtrack can occasionally be heard shuffling their sheet music. The picture is a touch grainy, but this aspect is generally disguised by the antique appearance of the sets and characters. The break between side two and side three should properly occur at the break in the film between 'Part I' and 'Part II', but it does not.

BARRY MANILOW THE CONCERT AT BLENHEIM PALACE

Barry Manilow performs before an audience of 40,000 people and who knows how many country animals at a concert on the grounds of a palace in rural England in *Barry Manilow The Concert at Blenheim Palace*. Whether the hedgehogs returned to their burrows whistling 'Mandy' is hard to say, but the audience clearly digs every move Manilow makes.

The disc is 90 minutes long and both the sound reproduction and the picture transfer are superior to their sources. Manilow can be seen clearly, in well lit, tight closeups, and he has only a slight red shadow following him around. The best, raw moment comes when he invites a young lady from the audience to sing 'Can't Smile Without You' in duet. The thrill she feels passes, if only momentarily, to the viewer.

BASIC SPANISH BY VIDEO
BASIC FRENCH BY VIDEO

Basic Spanish by Video is 70 minutes long and provides a vocabulary of about 1000 words. The images show moving pictures of different subjects (i.e., 'At the Beach,' 'Drinks and Food'). Subject words are printed in both Spanish and English over the pictures, while the word is pronounced in Spanish (only) on the audio track. Additional words and phrases are then presented on black screen/white text title cards, which are also narrated in Spanish. The picture quality is awful, and the male and female models look as though they regularly earn spare cash doing something else, but it is surprising how much you can start to soak up in 70 minutes.

Not only is the original picture quality poor, but the transfer also leaves much to be desired. At many times, white horizontal lines float through the picture. The sound is best kept to one's TV speakers. There are 53 chapter markers, but it is sometimes difficult to find a specific word from the chapter descriptions.

Basic French by Video is a little better organized than *Basic Spanish*. Although the jacket cover says the disc is 70 minutes long, it actually runs on for 88. The images used are the same ones which were used for

Spanish (well almost – on the French disc, a picture of a flute is shown for the word 'clarinet'), but they are organized differently, and flow from idea to idea a little more smoothly. The format is the same, with French and English text appearing superimposed on the pictures and on title cards, as the words are repeated in French on the audio. The transfer is better, although the image still looks like it was filmed through a dirty lens, and there are a couple of typos in the English text. Both discs are in CLV. *Basic French* opens with an on-screen chapter listing, but the chapters are interior to the program and differ from the chapter encoding on the disc itself.

BAT 21

There is a tendency to eyeball the running time during *Bat 21*, because it always looks as though the downed intelligence officer, played by Gene Hackman, is just about to get saved, but since you know it isn't time for the movie to end, then you know something is going to get messed up, and something always does. Danny Glover portrays the pilot who tries to guide him to safety from the air. The film is based on the actual experiences of an officer who was downed in Vietnam, and some aspects of the film, as well as Hackman's fine performance, have a ring of authenticity. The movie also has plenty of hardware and explosions, all done in glorious digital stereo surround. The big finale, however, is staged too dramatically and is out of synch with much of the story. The film has a few things to say about military service and about the Vietnam War, but it is a minor contribution to the burgeoning genre.

The disc has a good looking picture, great sound, and chapter encoding. The many night scenes manage to evoke fleshtones without distortion, and the sunrises never blur.

BATMAN

The Adam West *Batman*, which is subtitled 'The Movie' on the disc's jacket cover, is enduring in an empty-headed sort of way. Although it lacks the feverish pace of the TV show, it is a movie which is difficult to stop watching once you have started, and is a natural for video collectors. In accordance with this, CBS/Fox has included pressbook clips and lobby cards at the end of the disc. The disc is in CLV, but the stills are presented ten seconds at a time, with detail shots also last ing ten seconds each.

The colors in the movie are disappointingly bland, though otherwise the transfer looks sharp. The sound is good fun and worth amplifying. The movie has some wonderfully funny scenes, such as Batman's attempt to dispose of a bomb on a crowded pier, but longer stretches of plot drag a bit while the mechanics are put into place. One less conspicuous comical touch is the freedom with which the filmmakers mix exteriors from Los Angeles and New York to create Gotham City. Concerning a diabolical robbery, the film features four of the primary villains from the TV series, but it is Burgess Meredith, as The Penguin, who manages to steal the movie along with everything else.

BATMAN

We are blissfully unfamiliar with the quality of the *Batman* video cassette, though we have heard it gives watching the film at a drive-in before the sun has set a run for its money. On disc, however, the darkest scenes are as clear, colorful and distinctive as the Joker's countenance. We would still recommend drawing the blinds, but that is only so one can better savor the wonderful visual experience which the movie provides.

The movie is presented on the disc in matted format, with an aspect ratio of about 1.66:1. The running time extends slightly over two hours, so the disc is spread to three sides. The break between side one and two is great. It cuts off after a maniacal laugh which seems to hang in the air even after the disc has ejected. The incredible artistic detail which was part of the theatrical experience is compromised on a small screen, but other aspects of the movie improve, such as the presence of Kim Basinger. She no longer seems dwarfed by everything that is going on around her.

While detail in the cityscape may be obscured, details in the darkness are not. The disc delivers shadings and shadows accurately, and in the bright light the most intense colors remain solid. The picture quality is not perfect. In the dark area which creates the matting, a mild graininess can be observed, which, we assume, carries over into the picture. The flaw is not sufficient to impact the entertainment, however. The film's finale – the fight in the belfry – is so shrouded in dimness that the image could easily be led astray. The disc's picture remains stable and delivers the excitement without distraction.

The digital stereo surround sound is also forcefully and accurately presented. You can make out the lyrics to the Prince songs and feel the thunder as the Bat Plane rips across Gotham City's shopping concourse. It doesn't take long for Danny Elfman's woozy score to start vibrating inside you, either. Warner has encoded 31 chapters on the disc.

BATTLE OF ALGIERS

Gilo Pontecorvo's engrossing, systematic account of the *Battle of Algiers* runs 122 minutes (though some reference books list its running time at 118) and is spread to three sides on the disc. The finale is in CAV with two unsteady still frames out of every five. The picture quality is no better or worse than a standard theatrical print. The movie, which the producers felt compelled to preface with a statement that no newsreel footage was used in its construction, is so realistically tattered that it has always been difficult to tell where art ended and maintenance began. It is in black-and-white and tends to go soft on focus and heavy on scratches in some places. There are also a couple of splices. A number of our friends have expressed disappointment that the title was not letterboxed. The film is in French and has white English subtitles. The sound is as messy as the print, sometimes falling out of synch.

Battle of Algiers depicts the establishment of a terrorist group by an indigenous populace and its subsequent dismantling by colonial authorities. Set in French Algeria in the late fifties, the film concentrates on the process – how the terrorists organize themselves, how the military uses terror to destroy them – and leaves moralizing to the viewer. The movie is history with good editing. The more public the scenes, the more incredible it is that they have been staged, since every moment in the movie that is not an intimate two person conversation looks like it was compiled by news cameras. The manner in which it is compiled, with each step clearly defined and quickly executed, makes *Battle of Algiers* a thrilling action movie. The unique nature of the staging and subject matter makes the film a masterpiece.

*BATTERIES NOT INCLUDED

The lighting and camera work in **Batteries Not Included* have an intensely realistic sheen. The stereo sound editing is also intense, and far more elaborate that what one finds on most major film productions. Added to this is an increased level of attention when it comes to transferring a film to laser disc. The image on the disc is gorgeous, and the sound, which has been digitally encoded, is a delight. Many passages will be ideal for showing off your surround system to skeptical listeners.

The film, unfortunately, has a built-in concept that hurts it on the word-of-mouth circuit. It is about miniature flying saucers which help the residents of a condemned tenement. The problem is that these are not really flying saucers, they are miniature robots shaped like flying saucers, for if they are populated with beings, one is as aware of the crew as one would be aware of the cells which populate one's own body. To enjoy the film you have to approach it expecting a faerie tale about high-tech elves.

BATTLESHIP POTEMKIN

The *Battleship Potemkin* disc contains a 'restored' version of Sergei Eisenstein's classic black and white silent film, constructed in Moscow in the mid-seventies. The title cards inserted to advance the story are new, but they are in Russian, with English subtitles superimposed on the screen. Frames have been doubled to suppress the jerky speeded up motion most silent films have, but the effect makes the movie almost appear like it is being run in slow motion. The sequence of monatage also seems to have a different order than on some theatrical prints.

Image has listed the chapters incorrectly on the back of the disc jacket. Side two of the 74-minute film is in CAV, but time prevents the Odessa Steps sequence from being included. It comes at the end of side one.

Because of the frame doubling, the two unsteady still frames out of every five on the CAV side are sometimes not unsteady. The music, a collection of pieces by Dimitri Shostakovich, is monaural and a little scratchy, but it is ideally suited to the film and adds to the drama. There is no mistaking the age of the source material, but the print is in fine shape and does not inhibit the film's pleasures. We wonder, however, if the original movie had quite as many title card inserts as this version does.

Battleship Potemkin is exciting and contains at least three climaxes. The film is full of beautifully photographed moments, from the sailors hanging in their hammocks in the beginning, to the battleship slicing the frame at the end. Eisenstein's staging, his sense of drama, his affection for humanity and his feeling for the texture of surfaces make a viewer as pleased to view an individual shot as to see which shot is next. The film, about mutiny and revolution, is a grand accomplishment and a worthy addition to any viewer's library.

THE BAY BOY

Keifer Sutherland's debut film, *The Bay Boy*, is a coming of age story which clearly and calmly shows the hero making the key decisions that will define his adult life. There is a murder in the plot, but it is irrelevant to the point of the film and has been included just to move the center of the story along a little quicker. Sutherland is awkward in some of his scenes with adults, but he shines when he is among his peers. The movie is set on Nova Scotia in the mid-thirties. It is a relaxed and warm look at first romances, mixed with the tragedies that life springs on people.

The transfer is fine, although the colors of the film seem inspired by the almost constantly overcast sky in the outdoor scenes. The sound has no special problems. The musical score, a rare effort by Claude Bolling, is valuable but somewhat out of place.

BEACH BLANKET BINGO
(see **MUSCLE BEACH PARTY**)

THE BEACH BOYS – AN AMERICAN BAND

If someone were coming to interview you as part of a documentary on you and your family, wouldn't you at least put on a nice shirt and comb your hair for the camera? Brian Wilson, on *The Beach Boys – An American Band*, conducts an interview, which is used throughout the documentary, from his bed with the covers pulled up to his neck.

We used to wonder why talented artists could be extremely creative in their youth and then lose it as they got older. As the documentary makes clear, the answer is hardly mysterious. Drugs. Of all the rock groups around it is most difficult to picture those healthy, clean looking Beach Boys polluting themselves with chemicals.

The disc is in CX-encoded stereo, although some of the song clips are monaural. The picture looks a little rough when older black-and-white or video footage is used. The documentary is 100 minutes long, but it is in chronological order so that the first part of side one covers the glory days and after that it is one long slide to Dennis Wilson's drowning accident. All the hits get played on side one, as well. Unlike other documentaries we have reviewed, every song here gets full play without annoying interruptions.

BEACHES

One of the pleasures of home video is that it allows you to enjoy movies like *Beaches* without feeling guilty about it. The Bette Midler/Barbara Hershey friends-for-life drama is superficial and tacky (right down to the pun in the film's title), but that has been the essence of Midler's style for a long time. The performances are good (Lainie Kazan is marvelous as Midler's mother) and the music is nice (Midler portrays a singer). The sequences which are intended to be humorous are legitimately humorous, and it doesn't matter if the sequences intended to be dramatic aren't as compelling. In the comfort of one's home, it is okay to schlepp.

The disc runs a few minutes over two hours and is spread evenly to three sides. The jacket cover design is simple, but effective. The picture tends to become grainy when strong colors are involved and leaves the fleshtones looking on the pink side. The stereo surround sound has occasional separation effects, but only the music gets a real boost from it.

BEANY AND CECIL VOLUME I

The witty and memorable Bob Clampett cartoon series, *Beany and Cecil*, finally arrived on disc with *Beany and Cecil Volume I*. The animation is a low budget effort, but the imagination of the artists compensates for the restricted movements, and the dialog is completely unbound. The adventures of the young boy, Beany, and his sea serpent pal, Cecil, was used by Clampett as a guise to sneak in many adult subjects and puns. If cartoons are seen as somehow restricting the intellectual development of children, then work such as *Beany and Cecil* is clearly an exception. The constant verbal barrage is a stimulant to both the imagination and to vocabulary and language skills. It is the best kind of teaching because children have no idea they are being taught (or what, as is the case with some of the puns, such as the South Sea island visited in one cartoon, 'No Bikini Atoll').

The colors appear moderately pale, but were subdued when presented originally. There are six cartoons on the disc, each running a little over five minutes (the running time is 40 minutes, not an hour as is mistakenly stated on the back of the jacket). Our favorite offering on the disc was 'Wildman of Wildsville,' in which the heroes seek out a beatnik artist (he lives on 'the Hungry I-land'). The backgrounds take on the designs of a number of modernist paintings. Other offerings include 'Cecil Meets the Singing Dinasor' (sic.), which includes a number performed by Dinah Shore; a classic of sorts, 'The Spots Off a Leopard,' which contains a wild array of spot puns; 'Little Ace from Outer Space,' a Cape Canaveral parody; 'Invasion of Earth by Robots,' a flying saucer encounter; and 'Super-Cecil.'

THE BEAR

We hesitate to recommend *The Bear* without reservation only because the structure of the film may be alienating or plain dull to some viewers. It is a fictional wilderness film which has no smarmy narrator with a make-believe country accent telling you what is happening. Directed by Jean-Jacques Annaud, the movie is most reminiscent of Annaud's *Quest for Fire*, and has much the same tone and setting. Those who are open to the basic concept – a competently stylized depiction of a young bear and an older bear surviving in the wild – however, should welcome the disc with a great big hug.

The picture transfer is beautiful and the surround sound is even better. It is letterboxed with an aspect ratio of about 2.3:1. The framing is eloquent, and effectively captures the relationship between the animals and their environment. In many scenes the color transfer is sharply detailed, and even the most complex night sequences are replicated without difficulty. The sound quality is often similar to the outdoor pieces on surround demonstration discs. The ambience is so precise that you can feel the presence of danger even before the wooly heroes display an indication that they are aware of it.

THE BEAST MUST DIE

Looking like something the cat dragged in, *The Beast Must Die* is still an enjoyable werewolf disc. The 1973 film is unique in that a black performer, Calvin Lockhart, is cast as the hero in a role which is relatively free from stereotype (though the filmmakers tend to photograph him in a somewhat lurid fashion). Lockhart portrays a millionaire who invites several people to his estate, having obtained evidence that one of them may be a werewolf. The movie is presented in an enjoyably carnival-like manner. As a prelude to the finale, the narrative comes to a halt and a question mark flashes on the screen, as the viewer is asked to guess which one of the suspects is hiding the hormone imbalance.

The source material looks old. It has scratches, jiggles, and faded colors. The monaural sound is no better and is plagued in passages by a background hum.

THE BEAT

An overly artistic, dopey movie about modern delinquents, *The Beat* looks and sounds terrific on disc. The film is an embarrassing concoction about a slightly batty kid who touches the hearts of the neighborhood toughs. The setting is impoverished East Coast urban and the time is the present, but the planet cannot possibly be Earth. The movie has been constructed, however, with every cinematographer's trick and every sound editor's twiddle imaginable, and the transfer captures it all without distortion.

BEAT STREET (see BREAKIN')

BEAT THE DEVIL

Humphrey Bogart once claimed that anyone who appreciated *Beat the Devil* was a 'phony.' Well, you can count us in as phonies, because we love the film. Back before there were discs, we always made a special effort to catch it when the movie played on the late show, though certainly the mere fact that it appeared so often on the late show ought to provide some sort of proof of its worthiness. The movie was written by John Huston and Truman Capote, rather on the fly, apparently, and was directed by Huston. It stars Bogart, Robert Morley, Peter Lorre, Gina Lollobrigida, Jennifer Jones and a half-dozen other character actors, all of whom can inspire laughter merely by holding their breath. The plot, such as it is, sends the group toward an East African colony they never quite reach. It is the interaction between the characters, and Capote's subversive dialog, which makes the film so engaging, and funnier every time you watch it.

The black-and-white print looks quite sharp, but has a good share of scratches and a couple of invisible, but nevertheless disruptive, splices. The monaural sound is noisy, and the higher pitched voices have a tendency to break into hiss. The transfer is clear enough that you can differentiate dialog which was recorded during the filming from dialog which was dubbed in later, and an awareness of the latter raises the level of intrigue about the methods by which the film was constructed.

THE BEATLES – MAGICAL MYSTERY TOUR

Do you realize that kids today can get up and dance to a song that was a hit before their mother was born and 'Your Mother Should Know' can be that song?

When it first appeared on the art house circuit, the 50-minute 1967 television film made by the Beatles, *Magical Mystery Tour*, seemed vital. Whether one was searching for further clues pointing to evidence of Paul's demise, or just relieved that there existed more footage of the foursome up to their Lesteresque antics, the film seemed like an important addition which the original British television audiences had stupidly misunderstood. Looking back upon it now, it is apparent that British television audiences were actually prescient. Since the advent of video compilations, even KISS's home movies are better organized than these.

The jacket cover of *The Beatles – Magical Mystery Tour* looks like the album, which is a nice touch. The songs in the film were used for one side of the American album release. Although friends insist to us that the music sounds better on the video disc than it does on the CD, we find, in direct comparison, that the CD audio is brighter and more detailed. However, the songs sound good on the digitally encoded video disc, especially if you haven't heard them in a while. The other sound components are badly recorded, and the picture is a strain. The disc has chapters encoded for the songs.

The program is for fans who know what they are getting into. Others will be better off flipping through the pages of the booklet which came with the LP in a fast, animated manner.

BEAUTY AND THE BEAST

Jean Cocteau's *Beauty and the Beast* is a stunningly lyrical motion picture which anyone who is enamored of film and fantasy will want to have for their library. Cocteau was not just a film director. He was an artist who wrote stories and stage dramas, designed scenery for theater, dabbled in every craft from plate design to wall hangings and making movies gave him an opportunity to apply all of these skills on a single medium. Watching a film by Cocteau is like floating through a dream. The images soothe your anxieties and the narrative aggravates them. Between the reel changes, which are a little jerky, the picture on the Embassy release is decent. The black-and-white contrasts are rich and the film's deliberate haze never gets out of control. The movie is subtitled, but Cocteau's opening essay is irreverently replaced with one written in English.

The differences between obsessive love and deep spiritual love are explored on a level that even children, at least those who are not scared to death by the faces in the walls and on the pots, will understand. Cocteau accomplished numerous special effects that have never been successfully imitated.

BEAUTY AND THE BEAST
(see **FAERIE TALE THEATRE**)

BECKET

The lively performances of Peter O'Toole and Richard Burton in *Becket* are best appreciated in the presence of a large audience. The humor and wit in their delivery is often so precise that you need a big group of people to collaborate on catching all the facets. Still, the disc is an impressive accomplishment. It is letterboxed, with an aspect ratio of about 2.3:1, making it far more acceptable than the version which usually shows up on television. Then there is the digital stereo sound, which not only has many directional dialog sequences (as well as O'Toole gargling), but adds considerable oomph to the otherwise sleepy church processional scenes. The age of the recording impacts its consistency, but the soundtrack is enjoyable and worth amplifying.

The picture transfer is good. It is difficult to come across a really pristine copy of the film, and parts of the presentation look slightly pale or oddly shaded, but other segments are lovely, particularly the outdoor scenes, and the overall impression is satisfying. The source material is also a little tattered at the reel changes. The 148 minute film is spread to three sides, but the side breaks seem ill-chosen.

The movie is based upon a historical play by Jean Anouilh which has finely honed dialog and a few anachronistic metaphors (the characters speak of 'well-oiled' machines long before such items existed). It tells of the relationship between Thomas à Becket and King Henry II of England, using, as most historical plays do, a few pertinent facts to construct a drama that has meaning both on a human level and on a more encompassing scale. The dialog verges on the poetic, and it can sound outright silly if mishandled or if analyzed too closely, but when left to the gifts of artists such as those who collaborated on the film, the drama captures the finer senses in one's imagination.

BEDROOM EYES II

Bedroom Eyes II is a murder thriller with plenty of twists which will keep one – well, not guessing, exactly, but attentive – right up to the end. Wings Hauser stars as a successful stock broker with marital and *Fatal Attraction* -type problems. Linda Blair, looking more and more like Annette Funicello, also appears. The inclusion of scenes involving the hero's business successes effectively adds to the 'stake' the viewer has in seeing that he stays alive.

The picture is fuzzy, but the sound is okay. An enjoyable theatrical trailer for the film, which squeezes every last piece of excitement out of it, plays after the end credit scroll.

BEDROOM WINDOW

Elizabeth McGovern doesn't appear in *Bedroom Window* until the film is well underway, but the movie doesn't seem to be going anywhere until she arrives and takes charge. Her glow is unaffected by her maturity, but her increased confidence is magnetic. Steve Guttenberg, who is the center of attention early on when he is sharing scenes with Isabelle Huppert, disappears into the woodwork when he's paired with McGovern. *Bedroom Window* is a thriller, the plot of which is best left undiscussed for those who haven't seen the film. For those who have seen the film we have just one question – doesn't the killer recognize the address from the first time? Except for that one discrepancy the story is tight and very entertaining.

The film is monaural and is not CX-encoded. The sound isn't bad if you play it through the speaker on your TV. The picture quality is passable. Much of the movie takes place at night, but the image is not distorted.

BEETHOVEN – DEBUSSY – LISZT – THE 80TH BIRTHDAY RECITAL – ARRAU

The eighty-year-old Chilean pianist, Cluadio Arrau, floats over the keyboard in a live concert at Avery Fisher Hall in New York on *Beethoven – Debussy – Liszt – The 80th Birthday Recital – Arrau*. The sound is free of all but a faint background hiss. The applause and coughing are stereophonic, but only one mike seems to be covering Arrau's piano.

Arrau performs five numbers during the 83-minute concert, Beethoven's 'Waldstein' and 'Appassionata' Sonatas, Debussy's 'Reflets dans l'Eau,' and Liszt's 'Les Jeux d'Eaux a la Villa d'Este' and 'Ballade No. 2.' He plays them effortlessly. The camera stays on Arrau. He is clearly illuminated, but surrounded by blackness, which is transferred to the disc without distortion. The camera angles seem to be a bit arbitrary, but the emphasis is on the audio portion of the program. The video is just an extra.

BEETHOVEN: SYMPHONIES NOS. 3 & 7

Two of Beethoven's symphonies which have appeared previously on disc have been combined for the first time on *Beethoven: Symphonies Nos. 3 & 7*, performed by the Vienna Philharmonic with Leonard Bernstein conducting. One symphony appears on each side of the CLV disc, and is presented by the orchestra before a live audience in a Viennese concert hall. While Bernstein's presentation of 'Symphony No. 3' lacks the precision and insight found on *Beethoven – Symphony No. 3 – Bruggen*, his rendition of 'Symphony No. 7' is inspired and more satisfying than the Carlos Kleiber interpretation.

The stereo mix is a little too wild at times, particularly during 'Symphony No. 7,' and both recordings have some background hiss. The picture quality on 'Symphony No. 3' is solid, but a little faded. 'Symphony No. 7' is grainier and less confident. The film editor who compiled the programs must have worked overtime to make sure that every instrument making a significant contribution was included, visually, while the contribution was being made.

BEETHOVEN – SYMPHONIES NOS. 4 & 7 – CARLOS KLEIBER

Beethoven's 'Fourth' and 'Seventh' symphonies are presented in reverse chronological order on Beethoven – Symphonies Nos. 4 & 7 – Carlos Kleiber. This is appropriate, however, since the 'Seventh,' which is on side one, was a highly experimental piece while the 'Fourth' was a cumulative and stabilizing effort. Kleiber conducts the Concertgebouw Orchestra of Amsterdam in a live performance of the two symphonies. The picture is bright and clear, and matches the quality of the sound. The placement of the cameras in the Concertgebouw hall, however, is limited. The cameras appear to have been set up to record the 'Fourth Symphony,' which is generally well covered. The essence of the 'Seventh Symphony,' however, always seems out of reach. The disc makes nice listening, but it is difficult to really concentrate on watching it, because the portion of the orchestration which is commanding the attention of one's ears is often at odds with the images chosen for one's eyes.

BEETHOVEN: SYMPHONIES NOS. 5 & 6
Leonard Bernstein and the Vienna Philharmonic perform before a live audience on *Beethoven: Symphonies Nos. 5 & 6* (the '"Leonore" Overture' appears on side one with 'Symphony No. 5'). Each work was recorded at a separate time in 1978/79 at the Vienna Concert Hall, but the disc is edited as if the program were presented on a single evening. The age and environment of the recording works against it. All the pieces are in stereo, but only 'Symphony No. 6' has any real dimension. The picture quality is also a little old. You get to know all the camera angles by the time the first movement of the first work is finished, and only Bernstein's personality keeps you from turning away. Again, the 'Sixth Symphony,' which is by itself on side two, is the most effective and entertaining offering. The expression Bernstein gives, in a tight close up, when a piccolo comes on a little too strong during the fourth movement, is priceless. The disc has chapter markers for every movement. The jacket contains an insert which features introductory remarks not really relative to Beethoven, by Bernstein, and a brief, generalized essay on Beethoven, with only a passing mention of the two featured symphonies, by Constantin Floros.

BEETHOVEN – SYMPHONY NO. 3 – BRUGGEN
Beethoven – Symphony No. 3 – Bruggen was recorded in late 1987 by the Orchestra of the 18th Century in Amsterdam. The picture is crisp and the sound is marvelous. The background noise can't even be called hiss, it is more like a faint fuzz. The music is beautifully recorded. Ironically, 'original instruments,' the musical devices from previous centuries which are used by the orchestra, probably benefit more from high-tech digital recording than do the present-day instruments of a regular orchestra. The older instruments tend not to blend as blandly into the sound of the orchestra as a whole, and with digital encoding, each quirk is preserved. The rendition presented of Beethoven's 'Symphony No. 3' is dry and almost tart. An analog recording would take away its sting, and even the analog track on the disc is not as bright as the digital track.

BEETHOVEN: SYMPHONY NO. 9
Others may picture Malcolm McDowell beating up derelicts or Bruce Willis running across broken glass in his bare feet, but the first movement of Ludwig Beethoven's '9th Symphony' reminds us of sailing on the water, the second movement of being caught in a storm, the third movement of having been washed ashore, and the final movement of strolling, resuscitated, on the beach in the warmth of the sun. No work of art better broaches, and at the same time epitomizes, the shoreline division between humanity and divinity. In an essay on an insert sheet accompanying *Beethoven: Symphony No. 9*, Mary Wittall states that some musicians have sought to 'preserve' Beethoven's music by discouraging it from being played so much. That, however, would be a denial of the egalitarian spirit inherent in the work. Somewhere, someone is hearing it for the first time, or wants to and finds fulfillment in hearing it again, and they have as much a right to it as the musician who has heard it every day.

The concert on the disc is played by the Vienna Philharmonic and conducted by Leonard Bernstein. Bernstein slam-dances as he conducts, but he brings both tension and energy to the orchestra and chorus, and draws a fine performance out of them. The film, however, is grainy, and the camera angles are unimaginative. We'd rather see the man waiting to hit his kettle drums at the beginning of the second movement. They'd rather show the drumsticks hitting the drums and then move on to the next highlighted instrument.

The sound is adequate, particularly since the performance is live. The division in sides comes between the second and third movements. The jacket insert also contains a translation of Schiller's poem, 'Ode to Joy,' and three weird paragraphs of comment by Bernstein.

BEETHOVEN – SYMPHONY NO. 9
(see **VERDI – AIDA**)

BEETHOVEN'S NEPHEW
The oxymoronic tag lines on the cover of *Beethoven's Nephew*, "In the tradition of *Amadeus*. A film by Paul Morrissey," say it all. If you can imagine *Amadeus* directed by Paul Morrissey, then you can imagine *Beethoven's Nephew*, a film in which every cast member has a different accent and all have dilated retinas. The plot concerns the famous composer's efforts to maintain guardianship and dominance over his nephew, who became his sole heir. The movie gives just enough history to make one want to know what really happened, but it will not send anyone running to put on Beethoven records. According to the movie there wasn't a single person in all of Vienna during the early nineteenth century who possessed even one redeeming personality trait. The movie is Beethoven without the music, and it is played too straight to be camp, so it goes sour instead.

The sound is flat. An annoying black bar hovers at the bottom of the screen. The picture quality looks decent, but after a while, you start to long for an *Amadeus*-style haze.

BEETHOVEN'S NINTH SYMPHONY
(see **THE ACADEMY OF ANCIENT MUSIC – MESSIAH**)

BEETLEJUICE
Beetlejuice is in gorgeous condition. The picture is bright and the colors are sharp. Objects and faces look so immediate that a viewer, at personal risk, can get very wrapped up in what is going on in the film. The sound is also terrific. It is digitally encoded and provides an audio equivalent of the playful visuals. The lower ranges have a good boom to them, and the upper ranges can tickle the back of one's neck. Unlike the conditions in a crowded, boisterous movie theater, the sound delivery is so clear that one will have no problem catching Michael Keaton's slurry, vulgar dialog.

The movie is about two people who must come to terms with death – their own. The disc has fifteen chapter markers, but there is actually something hysterical, gross, or witty happening about every thirty seconds. One effect we admire is the way the name of the title character is continually misspelled and mispronounced. The spelling even varies between the disc jacket cover and the film's title card. *Beetlejuice* postulates that the afterlife is even screwier than real life, but only ends up proving that movies can be the craziest escape of all.

BEING THERE (Warner)
BEING THERE (CBS/Fox)
Warner has released *Being There*, which was previously available through CBS/Fox. Warner's picture transfer is a considerable improvement over the CBS/Fox effort. Caleb Deschanel's cinematography has many soft brown tones. CBS/Fox was unable to coax color out of it, but Warner does. The picture is still a little grainy in some shots, but the focus is usually sharp and the transfer is very good considering the age and awkwardness of the source material. Warner has also provided chapter markers and digital sound for the monaural title, two more improvements upon the previous release.

Being There is a film which one tends to watch only between long separations of time. Although it has many fine qualities, including very touching performances by both Melvyn Douglas and Peter Sellers, it is essentially a one-gag show (about a man brought up in a virtual cocoon whose reactions when he steps into the world are misinterpreted, by those around him, as profound actions), and the concept stays with the viewer afterward. There seems to be no need to go back and see it again, but it is nice to know that the Warner disc is out there, should the desire arise.

THE BELIEVERS
We hope that *The Believers* isn't the only kind of assignment John Schlesinger is going to pull from now on. He just isn't right for it, and the movie, which ought to be a slight horror confection, goes down like a thick dramatic soup and just sits there. It is about voodoo and human sacrifice. The last twenty minutes are reasonably suspenseful, but Schlesinger, instead of trying to scare or thrill an audience, tries to make them feel what the hero is feeling. Nausea.

The music is in stereo, but nothing else is. The transfer of both the picture and sound is adequate.

BELL, BOOK & CANDLE
The source material for *Bell, Book & Candle* looks fresh, with only a few errant marks on it, but the colors are dull. With a movie such as *Bell, Book & Candle*, because the script is not very good, the film succeeds or fails on looks (the monaural sound is digitally encoded and is passable) alone. The closeups of Kim Novak and the cat have to be magical, because the screenwriters never found an alternate expression for their powers. With James Stewart badly miscast and Jack Lemmon given nothing but a few street lamps to work with, the film must mesmerize the viewer cinematically, and if the picture quality is poor it cannot. The colors are dull and so is the disc.

BELLE DE JOUR (Import)
Luis Buñuel's quizzical *Belle de Jour* is available only on import, in French with Japanese subtitles. In *Belle de Jour*, scenes depicting a woman's imagination are interspersed with 'normal' scenes. This is done in such a way that it is impossible to tell where the former ends and the latter begins, but on the subtitled prints shown in America, the subtitles for the 'dream' scenes are in italics. The trick with the movie is that it may all be a dream, so the italics are pretty useless. Fortunately, whatever the Japanese equivalent of italics is, it is not employed. The transfer is good and the colors are bright and lively. The sound is what one would expect from a sixties foreign film.

BELLS ARE RINGING
An unnecessary echo pops up near the end of side one on both the digital and analog tracks in *Bells Are Ringing*. It is evidence that MGM's sound enhancements, most of which have been praiseworthy, occasionally go awry. Other than that, the sound is acceptable. It does not have the normal stereo mix, but the music sounds terrific.

Bells Are Ringing, which was directed by Vincent Minnelli, stars Judy Holliday and Dean Martin, but its success can really be attributed to the writers Betty Comden and Adolf Green. No one else has ever achieved the mixture of literate parody and boisterous good will which these two manage to concoct time and time again. The picture is cropped and loses Minnelli's most colorful touches. The whole film looks a little more drab on disc than it actually is.

THE BELLS OF ST. MARY'S
Although the notation, 'Mastered from the Original Film Negative,' appears on the jacket cover of *The Bells of St. Mary's*, the black and white picture looks soft and does not have the attributes one usually associates with early generation source material. The presentation is alright, but it is not exceptional, and there are a few splices. The sound is more impressive. It is distorted in places, but it also has a good level of detail, and is especially effective in musical passages.

The three-sided disc comes in a gatefold jacket. The innerspread contains essays about the film and the filmmakers, and contains replications of original promotional materials. *Bells*, which stars Bing Crosby and Ingrid Bergman, is the sequel to *Going My Way*. The narrative is nearly a duplicate of the first film. The priest arrives with a secret mandate which he does not reveal to the staff. There are mixed-up kids who get straightened out, a marriage in need of counselling, and a stubborn staff member who is putty in the priest's hands. Although the two movies are really too long to show together, they might be quite enjoyable on successive nights. In *Bells*, the recipe may not be as fresh the second time around, but as holiday leftovers it still makes a fine meal.

THE BELLY OF AN ARCHITECT
(Import)
Peter Greenaway's *The Belly of an Architect*, has been released on disc in Japan. Brian Dennehy gives a superb, understated performance as a dying architect working in Rome on a museum architectural exhibition. The film lasts from the moment of conception to the moment of birth of the architect's child, though in between his marriage crumbles, his career collapses and his rationality deteriorates. *Architect* also has its elements of paranoia, as well as an exploration of the art of Rome and dialog which sometimes suggests Michael Cimino writing for PBS. Dennehy is a rare performer, a heavyset actor who has previously avoided stereotypical 'overweight' parts. His belly is the subject of a great deal of attention in *Architect*, but he manages to slip past the typecasting by appearing confident and even proud about his figure and appearance. The part is well written (it is the artsy stuff which Greenaway tends to overdo – the last shot, of a body lying on the roof of a car, is a howler) and Dennehy improves on it.

The picture is heavily laden with a grain and several instances of nudity are covered by the Japanese censors with localized blurs. The digitally encoded stereo surround sound is indistinctive. The film is in English with Japanese subtitles, but there are a couple of significant passages which are in Italian and not translated to English.

BEN SIDRAN – ON THE LIVE SIDE
Ben Sidran likes to lecture his audience as he plays. Nothing esoteric. He talks about the history of jazz music and about his own experiences. Actually, he's singing, but it comes across more like talking in key.

The one sided *Ben Sidran – On the Live Side* originated in St. Paul in a large auditorium. The lighting is shaded, but very clear on the disc, which has a strong picture. When Sidran is lit by a blue spotlight, the shadow of the lid on his piano passes across his hands and across the keyboard.

The stereo separations are not coordinated with the picture, so that a musician standing on the right is heard playing on the left speaker. The quality of the sound is very good, however, and unhindered by the live environment.

Appearing with Sidran is Steve Miller, who has gone from acid rock to glitter rock and now to jazz. He has closely cropped hair and is dressed like a businessman, so you would never suppose his past was that risqué, until he plays his guitar. He energizes Sidran's music much more so than Phil Woods (saxophone) or Billy Peterson (bass), and the lectures pretty much stop when he appears on the stage.

BEN-HUR
BEN-HUR (letterboxed)
MGM/UA's Deluxe Letter-Box Edition of *Ben-Hur* has the most severe aspect ratio of any letterboxed disc. The aspect ratio measures about 2.7:1. Some viewers find that the decreased height is not accommodating, particularly on a small screen TV, but others will find that no matter what the size of the image is, the return to the film's original screen compositions are essential and thrilling. Even the closeups, which are full on the cropped version, and merely centered in rectangular air on the letterboxed version, are more attractive on the latter. The details, although smaller, are more precise, more realistic.

William Wyler directed *Ben-Hur* and Robert Surtees was the cinematographer. Neither appears to have a special passion for MGM's 'Camera 65' widescreen process, and the cropped version makes tolerable television entertainment. Since literally half the original picture is missing, however, shots of two people continually turn into shots of one person, as if MGM/UA could have released a second cropped disc with different footage and even a different cast. Important objects are often placed at the center of the screen, so that while Wyler rarely utilizes the full width, he often uses its symmetry, and that disappears in the cropping as well.

When an image is cropped, it is also blown up in size, and so cropped and scanned discs often have blurry, indistinct pictures. The color on MGM/UA's first *Ben-Hur* is strained anyway, so intense that no solid hue is able to stay within its boundaries. The letterboxed version fixes everything. It shows all the actors in a scene simultaneously, it shows the expensive sets and backdrops in their entirety, and it condenses the image to provide a sharply focused picture. This, combined with the added care and knowledge which has gone into transferring the color makes the presentation unconditionally superior to the earlier version. Once you watch any part of it, there is no turning back.

The color is far more consistent than it has ever been before. The sound is also improved on the letterboxed release. Those who think the movie peters out after the chariot race are going to be in for a surprise when the final thunderstorm starts to roar. It is best to have your dishes nailed down. The earlier disc was CX-encoded, but with or without digital encoding, the new version is much improved. One example of this occurs near the beginning, when the tiles slip. On the first disc, the clink is muffled. On the new disc, the effect is as sharp and precise as a bell tone.

Ben-Hur is the type of movie one watches once in a long while, but finds satisfaction from the experience. Individual scenes are well scripted, and some of the secondary acting – particularly Hugh Griffith's sheik – are repeatedly entertaining. The big set pieces – the sea battle and especially the chariot race (which works fantastically on the disc) – are great fun. The story, about the fall and rise of a rich Jewish merchant whose destiny is tempered by the appearance and widely documented fate of Jesus Christ, has surprisingly few goals. There is no romance, there is only lip service given to Christ's teaching, and a threat to the hero's life, near the end, is forgotten. The filmmakers concentrate too much on just working their way through the plot. The movie succeeds, however, because the plot is so big, the setting is so big, and the pretensions are so grand. The letterboxed disc is a fitting tribute to the film.

BEN-HUR A TALE OF THE CHRIST
We haven't had as much fun in quite a while as we had watching the silent version of *Ben-Hur A Tale of the Christ*. What action! What spectacle! What rapture! The film is only two and a half hours long, yet it seems to encompass even more than William Wyler's grandiose remake. The sets are huge, the extras are endless, and the special effects are remarkable. The story moves along at a decent clip, and is subject to no more than a few silent film archaisms (the lepers, for example, are noticeably unleprous). The ending still fizzles out for the sake of a Higher

Purpose, but somehow the movie makers toss an earthquake into the golgotha and generate a little Old Testament destruction in the process.

The print is entertaining in another way, because you never know when it is going to break into glorious two-strip Technicolor. The color sequences are scrumptious, and regularly re-charge the pace of the film. A stereophonic musical score, designed expressly for the film and performed by the London Philharmonic Orchestra, fits the movie perfectly and can be turned up loud without distracting one from the visual proceedings.

Except for a handful of shots, movement in the film looks natural. The black-and-white scenes are pleasantly tinted to match the mood of the drama. On top of the softness which comes from the age of the production, the disc does seem slightly grainy in places, but it is not enough to disrupt a viewer's concentration.

BENATAR

'Love Is a Battlefield' is anthem material and the music video, which has been tacked on to the end (after the credits, even) of *Benatar*, does the song a disservice by confining the story line to runaways and prostitution. The majority of the disc is a Pat Benatar concert. The picture is often speckled and the cameras stay so far away that not a single shot can qualify as a close up. The sound is poorly mixed, with the guitars drowning the vocals. You can even hear the input from Benatar's singing being jacked up and the guitars being suppressed, but she has a terrific stage presence. Her music is fast, loud, serious, and mostly devoid of clichés. Benatar herself is confident, attractive, and clearly intelligent. If she hadn't become a rock star she would have made a great CEO.

BENJAMIN BRITTEN – WAR REQUIEM – WRITTEN AND DIRECTED BY DEREK JARMIN

A collection of images filmed and compiled by Derek Jarmin and edited to an impressive recording of Benjamin Britten's *War Requiem*, opens with a poem read by Laurence Olivier and includes footage of Olivier portraying an elderly wheelchair-bound soldier being attended by a nurse. Britten's work was inspired by the poems of Wilfred Owen, a young writer who died near the end of World War I. Glimmers of a narrative depicting Owen's childhood and war experiences give the visual portion of the program its unity, although there are also lengthy, typical Jarminian excursions, and a good deal of documentary footage depicting the horrors of war.

The spine of the disc reads *Benjamin Britten – War Requiem – Written and Directed by Derek Jarmin*. The sound has been remastered from a recording Britten himself conducted at Kingsway Hall in London in 1963, with the London Symphony orchestra and soloists Galina Vishnevskaya, Peter Pears, and Dietrich Fischer-Dieskau. The restoration is superb and the soundtrack captures both the power and drama of Britten's music. Chapter markers note the beginnings of significant passages. Jarmin's images vary in type and quality, but the picture transfer is properly executed. A slight black band appears at the bottom of the screen. Jarmin's editing is in synch with Britten's themes, and the rhythm of the images attunes the viewer to the music's components.

BENJI THE HUNTED

At 89 minutes, *Benji the Hunted* is twice as long it should be. The plot has Benji lost in the woods, protecting several mountain lion cubs and attempting to find a suitable guardian for them. All of this is very cute, but to sustain the feature film running time, many of Benji's activities and many of the plot machinations are repeated. Adults will recognize the repetitions, and kids will just react to the length and lack of variety.

The disc is in stereo, but that means the nerve-wracking musical score, inserted to compensate for the lack of dialog, never disappears. The picture has too much contrast but is otherwise in good condition, and the Pacific Northwest scenery is pretty.

A BERENSTEIN BEARS COLLECTION

A good example of why adults stop watching cartoons, *A Berenstein Bears Collection* will try the patience of any viewer old enough to realize that bears don't really talk. While the backgrounds, done in water colors, are pretty, the foreground characters are blandly constructed and have personalities to match. Worse still, the dialog is in verse, often missing scansion, but rhyming with tedious regularity. Anthropomorphism at its lowest ebb, side one is about Thanksgiving and is entitled 'The Berenstein Bears Meet Big Paw.' Side two is 'The Berenstein Bears' Christmas Tree.' It is recommended that you obtain the disc only for the children of relatives or acquaintances against whom you hold a grudge.

BERLIN

The first two music videos on *Berlin* are not remarkable, but the remaining three ('Dancing in Berlin,' 'Sex,' and 'Now It's My Turn') are interesting and worthwhile. The lead singer is sort of a second-rate Deborah Harry, but the group has a strong beat, an intelligent lyricist, and a creative recording style.

The disc is in CAV. The soundtrack was unusually clean and noiseless, but did have an occasional difficulty in carrying the higher pitched instruments. It was not enough to spoil the fun.

BERLIN BLUES

An uncredited contemporary remake of 'The Blue Angel,' *Berlin Blues* concerns an East German orchestra conductor who defects when he falls in love with a low-life cabaret singer. Julia Migenes is fetching as his object of desire, but the film is slow-paced and has the temerity to conclude with a quasi-happy ending. The songs are by Lalo Schiffrin and Mark Mueller and they are embarrassingly bad, particularly with Migenes' brick-like phrasing. The English dialog usually matches the lip movements of the performers, but often with a visible delay. The picture is fresh looking, but a few scenes are grainy. The sound is passable.

BERNSTEIN: WEST SIDE STORY – THE MAKING OF THE RECORDING

In the same way that the *Barbra Streisand "Putting It Together" The Making of the Broadway Album* was an improvement over the album itself, because it broke up the too-perfect numbers and gave the whole production an edge, so too is *Bernstein: West Side Story – The Making of the Recording*, a more satisfying and pleasurable experience than listening to the album. Not only is there more tension, because you never know if the take is going to be good or bad, but the interruptions and the brief interviews undercut the monotony of listening to opera singers sing pop songs (it is like listening to good singers sing children's songs). The repetition of other passages, as the singers go through several takes before their efforts meet with Bernstein's approval, is also enjoyable, because the songs come out a little rougher and because you can hear the same piece sung with slight differences each time.

The documentary even has a villain, though through no fault of his own. Poor Jose Carreras has been cast as Tony in a vocal work where accent is as critical as pitch, and his inability to not sound Hispanic is a frustration not only to him, but to Bernstein and to everyone else that the camera happens to glance upon. To be sure, Carreras rises above this inconsistency for the critical portions of the score, and his voice soars, but the other singers do all that as well, and still get the accent right. He knows he is out of place, and the tension adds enormously to the drama of the documentary. It may not work on the album, but makes great video.

In contrast, Kiri Te Kanawa and Bernstein can't stop sending Valentines to one another through the interviews. Their enthusiasm is well deserved, however, and side two opens with Te Kanawa recording 'Somewhere.' It gave us goose bumps. (Marilyn Horne sang the song on the album, since technically it is not supposed to be coming from an on-stage character.)

The actual recording sessions, even the bad takes, sound terrific. The film was shot in 16mm with poor lighting which makes everything look yellow, brown and grainy. The disc is 90 minutes long and has plenty of chapter markers. An essay on a jacket insert was written by the documentary's director, but embellishes only slightly what is already in evidence on his film.

BERT RIGBY, YOU'RE A FOOL

If you like musicals a lot, don't miss *Bert Rigby, You're a Fool*. The film has pacing problems (it seems to last much longer than its 90-minute running time), but as a chapter encoded laser disc it is marvelous. The film was directed by Carl Reiner, whose interesting directoral career – and numerous box office hits – has largely been ignored by critics. Reiner's principal fault really isn't a fault at all, but his films suffer from it nevertheless. He is too fastidious, too anxious to make his narratives logical and complete. He is capable of producing brilliantly comical sequences, but he often links the sequences too carefully – a director who was more impulsive might leave gaps in the plot, but would not leave an audience feeling edgy and restless.

The parts of *Bert Rigby* which are good – the song and dance numbers – are so good that the laser disc is worth acquiring simply for the pleasure of chapter skipping to them again and again. The movie stars Robert Lindsay as an English coal miner who longs to become a star. You first see him singing 'The Continental' as he is coming out of the coal mine, and if that isn't enough to win you over right there, a little later on he does a two-minute summary of the movie, *Singin' in the Rain*, that will have you cheering in your living room. We had to replay the sequence three times before we could go on with the movie. There is also a lovely tribute to an Astaire/Rodgers dance, in which Lindsay's partner is, gracefully, very pregnant.

The disc has stereo surround sound. The sound editing is not elaborate, but the music is pleasantly enhanced. The picture quality is fine, with no significant flaws. Although the Panavision image is mildly cropped, the essence of the film appears to be preserved.

BEST BUNS ON THE BEACH (see THE WORLD WET T-SHIRT FINALS)

BEST DEFENSE
Panic must have set in on the producers of the Dudley Moore movie, *Best Defense*, when they realized their commercial prospects were limited. Instead of punting, they designed a twenty-minute epilog. It is broken up and scattered through the whole show and stars Eddie Murphy. While the result was insulting to movie patrons who expected to see Murphy and Moore together on screen (the two never are), the Paramount disc is actually mildly amusing and nice, though not enthralling, entertainment. The picture is a little soft and the sound is fine.

Moore portrays an aerospace engineer who saves his company by acquiring an innovative design for a guidance gyroscope. Murphy portrays the commander of a tank on a training run in the Middle East two years after the Moore episode. The tank must rely on the gyroscope to survive a border skirmish. Whoever heard of a defense item going from design to production in only two years?

THE BEST OF BLONDIE
The one-sided *The Best of Blondie* follows the program material of the similarly-titled LP fairly closely, but contains several extra numbers. The picture varies with the age of the clips and for the most part looks lusciously sharp. The monaural sound is workable. Most of the videos are restricted to performance environments. The best exception is 'The Tide is High' which shows large goldfish swimming outside the windows of a loft in lower Manhattan while Deborah Harry sings about waiting in line for the man she loves, who turns out to be Darth Vader.

THE BEST OF CHEVY CHASE
The hour-long, single-sided *The Best of Chevy Chase* is a collection of choice skits from the first couple years of ''Saturday Night Live.' It features one of our favorite pieces of editing, 'The Claudine Longet Invitational,' in which downhill skiers are seen wiping out to the sound of gunshots and the announcement that they have been "accidentally shot by Claudine Longet." Amazingly, even Chase's Gerald Ford imitation retains much of it humor. People may forget why his telling the real Ron Nesson, "I beg your pardon," was so funny, but the slapstick pratfalls are timeless and Chase's suave demeanor is still relatively unique.

The disc hasn't got chapter markers, but the picture and sound are gorgeous. Most of the video segments are brighter and clearer than when they were broadcast. The skit in which Chase and Richard Pryor call each other racially bigoted names is the only segment which looks less than perfectly preserved, but its inclusion is both historically and comically imperative. The sound is too good, and one will have to keep one's volume down to prevent the flaws in the original recording from distracting one's attention.

THE BEST OF COMIC RELIEF III
Another installment in the annual all-star comedy charity event, *The Best of Comic Relief III* contains close to two hours of the best known stand-up comics, but the individual sets are short and some performers don't get their steam up in time. There are some funny segments, a couple of gross scenes, and a number of dull stretches where the jokes don't work. One joke, from Steven Wright's set: "A friend of mine has an answering machine on his car phone. The message is, 'Hi. I'm home right now...'"

The picture transfer, from a video tape source, is vivid, with only the most intensely illuminated colors looking unstable. The stereo sound is also fresh and distinct.

Billy Crystal, Whoopi Goldberg and Robin Williams host the event, and have a terrific opening song and dance number. For some reason, Goldberg's participation is downplayed. Both Crystal and Williams have monologs which can be numbered among the best and funniest pieces on the disc (Williams' interpretation of the animals telling God that the hole in the ozone is man's fault is hysterical). Goldberg, however, never appears alone and never does anything but intros.

THE BEST OF ELVIS COSTELLO AND THE ATTRACTIONS
Seventy minutes of Elvis Costello music, 22 songs, are featured on the two-sided CLV disc from *The Best of Elvis Costello and The Attractions*. The disc is all performance videos, without interruption, and makes a decent LP even without the video. Although no mention is made on the jacket cover, the disc is digitally encoded and is in stereo. Every song has a chapter marker and there is a listing on the back of the jacket.

The picture quality varies from clip to clip. Some are sharp and others are grainy and have runny colors. Most of the videos are little more than performance sequences in unusual locales, though with Elvis Costello, nothing is ever completely normal. Two exceptional pieces are the animated 'Accidents Will Happen,' and a montage of old movies, 'Watching the Detectives.' Costello's music is energetic and catchy, and his only fault has always seemed to be his prolific talent. He does so much that the public never settled on one thing to make him a big star.

THE BEST OF MARY HARTMAN, MARY HARTMAN, VOLUME I
THE BEST OF MARY HARTMAN, MARY HARTMAN, VOLUME II
Basking in the early success of his first TV series, Alfred Hitchcock once told an interviewer, "Where I expected to find in TV a generalized simplicity because of the enormous range in the age of the audience, I discovered that I was able to use many more offbeat stories with unhappy endings than I had ever been able to use in the movies. The children love them."

Hitchcock was right, there is a lot an artist can do on American television that can not be attempted or funded in the cinema or even on the stage.

Norman Lear's 'Mary Hartman, Mary Hartman' is as good an example as any, and since *The Best of Mary Hartman, Mary Hartman, Volume I* and *Volume II* are available on disc, it is possible to get a sense of what some of the outer boundaries of entertainment really look like. Three episodes have been included on each disc and the 70-minute CLV programs run 35 minutes a side.

Episode 1, Episode 45, and Episode 325 are contained on Volume I. Episode 1 provides something of an introduction and 43 contains what many consider to be the show's most humorous sequence, a man passing out and drowning face-down in a bowl of chicken soup.

Volume II contains three sequential episodes. Specifically, episodes 2, 3, and 4. Watching them in order, and after Episode 1 on the *Volume I* disc, a viewer can get a better sense of the show's style and comic depth. It is satisfying, but leaves one wishing for more.

The fact that *Mary Hartman* has been released on disc and shows like 'The Jeffersons' or 'Happy Days' probably never will points to the divergence between mainstream home video and mainstream broadcast television. It is the difference between choosing what you want to watch and watching whatever is on.

THE BEST OF SPIKE JONES VOL. ONE
We once went to a recital of avant-garde music at Carnegie Hall and one of the performers thought he was being innovative by doing the same thing with horns, bells, and cap guns that Spike Jones did 30 to 40 years earlier.

Paramount has provided an opportunity to see the original by releasing *The Best of Spike Jones Vol. One*, which contains excerpts from the 'Spike Jones' TV show. The skits range from textbook examples of vaudeville slapstick to strained and pushy anarchy. Jones sometimes becomes so busy directing traffic that he forgets his clown persona and doesn't even bother to smile for the camera. The disc gives one a chance to see the hoary underside of television's 'Golden Era,' and the vulgar pandemonium which set the true tone for most of what followed.

There are 16 chapter markers on the single-sided disc. The black-and-white kinescope looks as good as can be expected. Paramount has misleadingly placed stills on the back of the jacket which have nothing to do with the program material.

THE BEST OF SPIKE JONES, VOL. TWO
The second compilation of sketches from the old 'Spike Jones' TV show, *The Best of Spike Jones, Vol. Two*, is a much stronger package than *Vol. One*. The pieces are tighter and fit together with less repetition. Much of it is entertaining or funny. Two men in chicken suits cluck their way through a chorus of

'Holiday for Strings.' An Arab sultan croons to a maiden, "Take my hand, I'm a stranger in paradise..." He steps back, and suddenly she is holding a disconnected hand.

The program runs 53 minutes on one side of the disc and is in kinescoped black and white. The picture is generally sharp and not unusually distorted. It is doubtful anyone would really want it to be clearer than it is. The humor is vulgar, but it is adeptly presened.

THE BEST OF THE CUTTING EDGE VOLUME I AND II

The purpose of 'The Cutting Edge,' an MTV program which is represented on a Music Disc' from Rhino and Image as *The Best of the Cutting Edge Volume I and II*, is to introduce struggling musicians who have rejected mainstream pop formats. The program has musical sequences, but its main concern is to profile the musicians, with interviews and video tours of their creative environments. This would all be terrific, except that the interviews are often edited into the middle of the music, so that the viewer is rarely treated to a number from the beginning to the end. It is as if the producers didn't believe in or trust the music, most of which sounds raw and exciting, and attempt instead to extract entertainment by subtly allowing the musicians, who haven't got much experience when it comes to dealing with the media, to make fools of themselves.

Two hour-long programs, with opening and closing credits, are contained on the disc. There are chapter markers but no listing. The stereo sound is more often mono and the picture is intentionally rough looking. Acts include R.E.M, X, Tom Waits, Squeeze, The Alarm, and others. There is also a memorable story told in one of the interviews about Gene Vincent's final concert.

BEST OF THE FESTIVAL OF ANIMATION

Best of the Festival of Animation is entirely CAV. Linking six short films (the Oscar winning 'Closed Mondays' is not included) and two behind-the-scenes snippets is a running take-off on the 'sneak previews' format.

The best of the films is 'Dinosaur.' Pretending to expand from the imagination of a child, the elaborate work creates an antediluvian scenario which could easily support a feature film. Two other of the short films are worth noting. Vinton tells the story of the earth's development – from the Big Bang to the evolution of man – in a purely scientific fashion in 'Legacy,' and then tells the alternate version in an adaptation of Genesis called 'The Creation.' Our guess is that when you are creating men out of clay, you can pretty much do what you want.

The still frames shiver in two out of every five, spoiling some of the potential for utilizing the CAV functions effectively. The program is monaural, and the sound quality on the short films varies from one to the next. The picture quality is generally acceptable. The biggest temptation for using the still step function is an interlude showing the creation of a Claymation figure, filmed using stop-action photography. The animators begin with a wire frame, and then pack clay around it in a rough approximation of human tissue, with clay clothing added separately. To keep the figure true to life, they even include, buried in the appropriate location under mounds of clay flesh, a little red heart.

THE BEST OF THE LITTLE RASCALS

Republic has collected six Little Rascals shorts on a single disc entitled *The Best of the Little Rascals*. The shorts are spread three to a side, marked with chapters, and arranged chronologically. The quality of the black and white featurettes is not bad, though the earliest ones look creaky. The digital monaural sound is scratchy but coherent.

The arrangement of the shorts reveals that the earliest ones, which are the most enjoyable in the collection, relied primarily upon slapstick gags, while the later ones are more elaborately scripted and slower paced. The films are amazing, with close to a dozen kids performing gags and routines while appearing completely oblivious to their craft. The pieces include 'Hi! Neighbor,' about a rivalry involving rideable toy fire engines; 'First Roundup,' about sleeping outside; 'Divot Diggers,' about golf course caddies, including a chimp; 'Second Childhood,' about an old lady who needs to cut loose; 'Glove Taps,' about a boxing match with a bully; and 'Hearts Are Thumps,' about a Valentine's lunch which has been spiked with soap.

THE BEST OF THE WWF VOL. 1
HULKAMANIA
WRESTLEMANIA
WRESTLING'S – BLOOPERS, BLEEPS AND BODYSLAMS

We recall when we were much younger being fascinated by the wrestling shows on television, usually on the schedule of the local independent TV station with a picture quality which was only acceptable if you lived next door to the broadcast antennae. We also remember wondering how such moves as slamming one's knee on the floor next to an opponent's ear could cause the opponent so much pain, especially since it did not seem to harm our younger sibling in the slightest. We are wiser now.

Coliseum has opted to put one side of the less-than-90-minute programs in CAV. (One disc's time is listed as '93 minutes,' but a group of coming attractions common to the other discs has been dropped to squeeze it in the 90-minute slot.) The picture quality is usually sharp, although wrestlers frozen in midair with CAV tend to appear as fuzzy blobs. The sound is not CX-encoded, but maintains a dull mono clarity.

The Best of the WWF Vol. 1 and *Hulkamania* feature numerous wrestling matches, some 'edited' to speed things up. The editing on *WWF Vol. 1* was more disorienting than on the *Hulkamania* disc, but the latter has some slow moving 'interviews,' including one lengthy piece which eats up valuable CAV space. The antics of the interviewers and announcers are either stupid or amusingly stupid depending upon your frame of mind, but wrestling and intellectual discourse get along about as well as Andre the Giant and Big John Studd.

The 120-minute *Wrestlemania* is entirely CLV, but it has the best picture, best sound, and best program (a Madison Square Garden extravaganza) of all the discs. None of the matches are edited, so the continuity is never disrupted.

The one carnival rip-off in the bunch is *Wrestling's – Bloopers, Bleeps and Bodyslams*. There is one bleep, no bloopers, and only a token collection of bodyslams, most culled from the other videos. The disc also has very little wrestling and is primarily excerpts from an excruciatingly tedious 'talk show' featuring various wrestling stars. It ends with a cream pie fight, and you know how much fun that can be.

THE BEST OF TIMES

The charming Robin Williams/Kurt Russell movie, *The Best of Times*, is about coming to terms with one's thirties. The sound is a weak monaural and picks up an unintentional echo for a couple of minutes on side one. The colors are slightly faded, but it was the film's intention to make the small town where the heroes live look dull. The performance of Robin Williams is anything but dull. From his perfectly spoken opening monologue, to an hysterical scene where he attempts to watch a ball game on TV during a romantic dinner, to the upbeat finale, his comedy plays mumble-typeg to his acting. He never flinches.

BEST SELLER

The chance to see two talented actors play off one another in a pair of meaty roles is the reason to obtain *Best Seller*. Brian Dennehy and James Woods portray an author and a psychotic killer who team together to unmask a crooked business leader. Their verbal and emotional dancing carries the whole movie, providing an excuse for the illogical and unrealistic aspects of the plot.

The film has undergone a nice transfer to disc. With the exception of some blotches which appear in a night driving scene, the darker portions of the screen are always free of impurities. In brighter scenes, the colors look solid and are sharply defined. The digitally encoded monaural sound is not bad, particularly during a sequence involving a public address system near the end.

THE BEST YEARS OF OUR LIVES
(see **THE LITTLE FOXES**)

BETRAYED

The ambitiously contrived *Betrayed* is about a female FBI agent who practically marries a white supremacist involved in an assassination conspiracy. The stereo film is presented in analog, and is stretched evenly to three sides. The picture is mildly grainy, but passable. If the viewer allows the filmmakers their numerous dramatic liberties, or if the viewer has an affection for the star, Debra Winger, then the movie will be enjoyable. It is long, though, so repeat viewings will require more of a commitment than most casual viewers are willing to make.

BETTE MIDLER – ART OR BUST

The sound on *Bette Midler – Art or Bust*, an 80-minute collection of concert footage, has an unusually low volume level. There are a few glimpses of colorful video effects playing up to the '*Art*' motif, but most of the stage show is a celebration of the gauche. Midler does a couple of numbers dressed in a mermaid outfit while sitting in a wheelchair which is decorated with a seaside theme. You cringe at the thought of what her apartment must look like.

She settles down near the end of side two to sing some nice blues numbers. Clips from Midler's earliest public appearances are also included on the disc.

BETTY BLUE
The surprise opening of *Betty Blue*, after the credits are done, leaves a glow of good feeling which lasts almost for the whole movie. It looks like one of those amateur X-rated videos, only filmed by professionals. The eroticism is idealized, but not in the way most movie sex scenes are. It is a picture of what happens when everything clicks, and that nothing else in the movie or in the relationship of the characters ever quite lives up to that first moment is the point of the film.

The director, Jean-Jacques Beineix, knows about such things. He, too, clicked at the very beginning, making one perfect movie at the start of his career, *Diva*, and never equalled that accomplishment in subsequent attempts. *Betty Blue*, in French with readable English subtitles, comes the closest. It is lightly comical, sexy, and has a narrative which keeps moving even though the plot has nowhere to go. After two hours of watching the romantic couple playing house at the beach, in the city and in the country, however, the *Cuckoo's Nest* finale is a head shaker.

The disc is CLV throughout. Side one was fine on the copy we viewed. Side two was grainy, pale, and had faint white vertical lines in several scenes. Side three fell somewhere between the first two. The digital stereo sound is nice, but rarely aggressive.

BETTY BOOP: 50TH ANNIVERSARY SPECIAL COLLECTOR'S EDITION
The most Freudian of all the old cartoons, the Max and Dave Fleischer Betty Boop shorts, have been compiled in an excellent anthology, *Betty Boop: 50th Anniversary Special Collector's Edition*. The source material comes from prints made for television, but the 13 black-and-white featurettes are in very good shape. They don't sparkle, but they don't look tattered, either. The sound is passable, with no more than one or two mild shifts in volume and the expected amount of background noise. Unfortunately, and contrary to the listing on the jacket cover, the disc has not been chapter encoded.

The cartoons were made in the early thirties, before the censors put a stop to such scenes as Betty being lassoed by a ringmaster's whip and the whip hitching up her skirt to give a flash of her lingerie ('Boop-Oop-a-Doop'). Did someone say these cartoons were for children? The best are loaded with the kind of imagery that starts haunting people's dreams once puberty sets in – objects growing larger and then being lopped off, bodies squeezing through holes and encountering horrors, a chase where everything moves but the pursued. In cartoons such as these, when a rooster is depicted in a boxing match with a cat ('Morning, Noon and Night'), the figurative meaning is as deliberate as the literal. It is what makes the entertainment so compelling.

Several of the cartoons contain nasty caricatures of black figures, including one, 'I'll Be Glad When You're Dead You Rascal You,' in which Louis Armstrong's image dissolves into that of a cartoon cannibal. The inclusion of these pieces are justified within the context of the anthology, though viewers who are angered by them had best avoid the disc.

BEVERLY HILLS BODYSNATCHERS
A cheap but occasionally amusing farce about mobsters, corpses and zombies, *Beverly Hills Bodysnatchers* is stupid, but that is not always a barrier to laughter. Curiously, the film's veteran actors – Frank Gorshin and the like – ham it up too much, while the young newcomers, playing two innocents who are stuck with summer jobs at a mortuary, give funnier, more relaxed performances. The picture transfer is very sharp. The Ultra-Stereo sound is heavily directional and more than adequate to the material.

BEVERLY HILLS COP
The gunfight at the end will have your neighbors calling the police but, other than that, the digital sound on *Beverly Hills Cop* is not exceptional. The picture is a little grainy, particularly when the characters are not standing in the bright Beverly Hills sun.

Eddie Murphy's performance is so intertwined with the script that unraveling the two becomes difficult (they ended up nominating the *script* for an Oscar). Murphy does have clear flashes of brilliance, particularly in the Detroit police station at the beginning. From there on, though, Murphy is too enamored with his own humor and he really falls out of character, because anyone who is that pleased with his own jokes would also be excited about the progress he was making in solving the mystery, even if he were hiding that excitement by acting cool. Murphy doesn't bother, and judging by the film's popularity, he didn't have to.

BEVERLY HILLS COP II
Like a second ice cream cone, *Beverly Hills Cop II* isn't as good as the first, but it doesn't matter. It is similar enough to lengthen the pleasure until one is filled. The first film was directed for comedy, this one has been directed for glitz, the assumption being that by now, one laughs automatically whenever Eddie Murphy grins. Needless to say, the mystery portion of the plot is resolved by a series of outrageous coincidences, but they pass so quickly and with such flash that one's initiative to complain just melts in the southern California sun.

The disc looks great, in part because of the bright sunshine and in part because the camera never lingers on anything long enough for the flaws to register. The sound is also good. The disc has been digitally encoded, and the sound editing in the film is the one component which really does seem like it came from Beverly Hills.

BEVERLY HILLS MADAM
Like the ladies themselves, *Beverly Hills Madam* is gussied up with a stereo soundtrack and a PG-13 rating, but it is nothing more than a telefilm. It stars Faye Dunaway and a bunch of Robin Givens types, all of whom toil in their bubble baths and fancy hotel suites, dreaming of the day that a john will turn into Prince Charming and sweep them away. There is something incongruous, or at the very least, unsympathetic, about a brokenhearted call girl crying into her mink, but that is the gist of it, so if you like soap operas and can tolerate television broadcast standards, you probably won't kick it off your set.

The musical score is by Lalo Schifrin, and, with the exception of one glaring dip, doesn't sound bad with digital encoding and the stereophonic mix. A few sound effects are also directional. The picture transfer is spotless but dull.

THE BICYCLE THIEF
The Italian classic about poverty and desperation, *The Bicycle Thief* has an ending that makes you want to throw your shoe at your television set. The disc has English subtitles which rarely distract from the picture. The sound is naturally in rough shape, and it wouldn't be *The Bicycle Thief* if it didn't have scratches and splices. It was the intention of the filmmakers to have their work look impoverished as much as it was a necessity. There is nothing in the presentation of the film on the disc, no matter how ratty it may seem, which will interfere with a viewer's emotional responses to the movie.

The film continues to encourage positive emotions (disgust with the ending, though endemic even on multiple viewings, is only fleeting) for two reasons. The first is simple. The filmmakers, in telling the tale of a man who loses his chance to earn a living when his bicycle is stolen, never lose sight of the real story, the man's relationship with his young son. That is a universal plot construction which can transcend historical modifications. The other reason for the film's artistic success is more complicated. The hero's dilemma is contrived – there must be a dozen options for him if he would just get his act together – but you can't help thinking as you watch the film that while this exact set of circumstances may not be true, there must be dozens of situations which are almost as similar – of adults trying their hardest but failing to cure their poverty or save their families. The movie is not an allegory and it is not even a parable, but it exposes the viewer to the emotions of despair and puts one in touch, if only momentarily, with the heartache of the world.

BIG
The body switching movie with class, *Big*, has been released on disc by CBS/Fox. Reds tend to be grainy and blurry, and other strong colors also look a little unstable. The transfer is adequate, but not outstanding. The sound is satisfactory and there are a decent number of chapter markers.

The filmmakers were careful not to exploit their gimmick – a young boy wakes up one morning twenty years older than he is supposed to be – and so the movie holds up well to multiple viewings. In fact, the movie is even better the second time around, when the viewer is no longer distracted by the plot. The first time through, one can become very impatient with the scene in which Tom Hanks and Robert Loggia dance on a floor length keyboard. On subsequent viewings, it is the soul of the movie.

BIG BANDS AT DISNEYLAND – CAB CALLOWAY AND HIS ORCHESTRA WITH CHRIS CALLOWAY
BIG BANDS AT DISNEYLAND – WOODY HERMAN AND THE YOUNG THUNDERING HERD
BIG BANDS AT DISNEYLAND – LIONEL HAMPTON AND HIS BIG BAND

Part of the serendipity when visiting Disneyland is discovering their evening musical programs. Three such concerts have been released on discs as a collection of *Big Bands at Disneyland.* The audience at these shows, for the most part, did not come that day to see Lionel Hampton or Cab Calloway or Woody Herman; they came to see Disneyland. Unlike filmed concerts before paying audiences at jazz clubs, there is a genuine feeling of discovery here which comes out in the applause and the enthusiasm of those clustered around the stage watching the bands perform. When the camera scans the eyes of the audience you can see the life-has-its-special-moments feeling in every face. The bands seem to respond to the joy as well, and all three discs are a pleasure to watch.

Our own tastes gravitate toward *Cab Calloway and his Orchestra with Chris Calloway* as the best of the three. Unlike the other two discs, many of the songs Calloway performs here are well known and there are more vocals, too.

The programs have been shot on video tape and the clarity is captured on disc in a transfer which is almost distortion-free. The sound is CX-encoded stereo. Every show fits on one side of a CLV disc. Peter Marshall acts as host and interrupts the performance to interview and give a short, informative history of each band leader. We would have preferred they kept playing.

Woody Herman and the Young Thundering Herd is a little more laid back than *Lionel Hampton and his Big Band.* Both bands are versatile and provide an opportunity for a large number of musicians to have their moments in the spotlight. They also make for two pleasing hours of big band sound.

THE BIG BLUE

A boxoffice smash in Europe, *The Big Blue* was understandably a flop in America, where people speak English. Not that the dialog is bad, but it reinforces the all too obvious plot, about two men who have to find themselves by diving into deep water without scuba gear.

The sound, which has not been carefully transferred, tends to run together some as a result, although the music score, by Bill Conti, has some nice touches. The picture is generally reliable although the image has been cropped and intense colors tend to blur slightly. The opening is in black and white and the shift to color is stunning.

The first thirty minutes of the film are brilliant (so much so that those with money to sink might want to get the disc anyway), and so open-ended that it is disheartening the script writers chose the paths they did to complete the story. It begins as a macho scuba film, zipping across the globe from the Aegean to a frozen lake in the Peruvian Andes and quickly delineating the two main characters, more childhood rivals than friends. Roseanne Arquette is the love interest. But, instead of presenting a tale of international intrigue or a modern mythological odyssey, the movie becomes a sports film, with the two protagonists competing in a diving competition. The winner talks to dolphins, which is probably what turned on the Europeans, but no matter how deep the hero descends, the spiritualism remains shallow.

BIG BUSINESS

The inevitably hysterical *Big Business,* with Bette Midler and Lily Tomlin as swapped twins, is in good condition. The picture is brightly lit and colorful, although intense hues tend to look slightly unstable and the fleshtones seem too orange in some places. The stereo sound is subdued but problem free. We wished the film had gone on for another hour, there were so many permutations the writers never got to, but what is there is wonderful.

BIG BROTHER AND THE HOLDING COMPANY BALL AND CHAIN

The black-and-white 36-minute *Big Brother and the Holding Company Ball and Chain* was made before Janis Joplin became the center of attention, so her vocals tend to be but one pathway in the group's meandering search for the blues. Each number is separated by an interview with the band members, many of whom are so spaced out (though not Joplin) that they not only forget who Big Brother was (though they remember that the character came from *1984*), but seriously suggest that young people should run away from home, recommending San Francisco as a destination. Joplin is always fascinating, but only die-hard fans will want to sample the disc. Other than being an old black and white video tape recording, the picture looks okay. The monaural sound, however, tends to take long dips in volume which may or may not be unwelcome.

BIG CITY COMEDY

Big City Comedy, which runs under an hour, is a collection of blackout sketches from a Toronto-based TV show starring Billy Crystal, John Candy, Martin Mull, Tim Kazurinsky, and others. Margaret Trudeau also appears and blows the four or five lines she struggles to deliver. The picture is poor. It is only because the comedians have become popular that the collection has been compiled.

BIG COUNTRY

Only in Scotland could a bagpipe band interrupt the middle of a rock concert (albeit at the stroke of twelve on New Year's Eve) and be cheered by the toughs in the audience. But hey, where else in the world would everybody know the words to 'Auld Lang Syne.' Big Country, a Scotch rock group which wears torn plaid shirts and plays vaguely folk-inspired rock and roll, is featured in a live New Year's Eve concert on *Big Country.* The picture is a bit grainy but well lit, and the group isn't very active on stage so the cameras have time to capture it all. The stereo sound has a weaker bass on the analog track. The show runs 70 minutes and side two comes in under a half hour, but is in CLV.

THE BIG EASY

One of Hollywood's favorite evil minorities is Cajuns, so it is a relief that *The Big Easy* casts them in a somewhat kinder light than many other Louisiana-based thrillers have. Oh, they still steal, cheat, lie in French, and dance in the backyard, but here they do so with a conscience. The film, about gangland killings and police corruption in New Orleans, has a strong romantic subplot and was a hit on the date circuit. Its potential for repeat viewing is questionable, but it is definitely entertaining the first time through. Everything down to the jacket cover is a little too orange and a little too pink, but the print is bright and no harm is done. The sound is CX-encoded monaural ('Mono Dolby,' it says on the jacket cover) and only fluctuates at insignificant moments.

THE BIG HEAT

Keep an eye on small objects in the films of Fritz Lang. Every prop inevitably has a meaning which exceeds its utilitarian function. In *The Big Heat,* widely considered to be Lang's best American film, Glenn Ford portrays a cop investigating a suicide. Everyone the cop comes into contact with meets with disaster. Even at home, he attempts to place a block on his little girl's makeshift building and causes the entire thing to tumble. A few moments later his home life is destroyed when his wife is murdered, and the fallen blocks take on an added significance.

The nice-looking print has only one major splice and hardly any speckles. The sound has no significant problems. The plot has a couple of contrivances, but the film is a legitimate classic, a hard-boiled (literally, based on one of the movie's most notorious sequences) crime picture with fast-paced action and memorable characters. The break Image has chosen to separate side one from side two is better than if the film were allowed to run without interruption.

THE BIG RED ONE

The producers of Sam Fuller's ambitious, autobiographical story of World War II, *The Big Red One* ran out of money before the film could be properly finished, but the movement of characters is covered sufficiently by the voice-over narration, and the confusing sequences depicting North Africa are long forgotten by D-Day. The transfer to disc is excellent. The film was originally made in stereo, and it is a shame that CBS/Fox has used a monaural track for the CX-encoded disc. Even unfinished, however, the movie is one of the best World War II dramas ever put together. Fuller's straightforward film style is ideally suited for home video and he covers himself well. The inexpensive action scenes are better disguised on a small screen than on a large.

BIG SHOTS

Whoever came up with the marketing strategy for *Big Shots* (the movie; the disc properly repeats the film's ad campaign on the jacket cover) ought to be thrown in jail. The story is a multiple hanky tearjerker, about a young boy who loses his father and then comes to terms with his grief by helping a friend and the friend's old man reunite. After sampling the preview cards, an ad campaign should have been developed around the emotional aspects of the film. One of those silhouette drawings should have been utilized in the posters to emphasize the story's poignancy and warmth. Instead, the ads used a photo of the two eleven-year-old leads, dressed like pimps, and the tag line reads, "They stole a Mercedes with a body in the trunk." You could be more successful selling bicycles to Eskimos.

The picture quality varies in levels of graininess, but is generally acceptable. Some of the sound effects are stereophonic, as is the unmemorable music score. The sound quality is okay. The film runs about 90 minutes. Side one uses up almost two thirds of that, yet the break between the two sides is unusually abrupt.

BIG TOP PEE-WEE
Although not as brilliantly conceived as *Pee-Wee's Big Adventure*, *Big Top Pee-Wee*, directed by Randal Kleiser, has a number of fine attributes. It successfully creates an imaginary world (Pee-Wee's farm, where a circus is transported one night in a big wind) and tickles the viewer with it. The strongest component is Danny Elfman's marvelous score, which is both dreamy and comical, continually working to keep the viewer in the right frame of mind. Less consistently, Herman's humor is inspired. It is Jerry Lewis' baby antics gone adolescent in a more jaded era.

The picture is acceptable. It looks very nice most of the time and only a little fuzzy in its weakest moments. The stereo surround mix is weak and sporadic.

THE BIG TOWN
We know the perfect system for winning at dice, or any game of chance: Become a character who wins all the time in a dumb movie. That is what happens to Matt Dillon's character in *The Big Town*, an ineptly written neon and dice effort. The picture quality is passable and the digital sound, though not in stereo, gives life to a few choice oldies (the movie supposedly takes place in 1957, in Chicago). The break between the two sides comes in the middle of a scene. The impetus to turn the disc over in a rush, however, is minimal.

THE BIG TREES
The jacket cover on the 1952 Technicolor film, *The Big Trees*, states that the disc is 89 minutes long, but with 55 minutes on side one and 20 minutes on side two, 14 minutes got lost somewhere. It is thus rendered nearly useless. A dam appears out of nowhere. So does a baby. Kirk Douglas portrays an unscrupulous lumber man who ends up joining a religious cult in the redwood forests of northern California. Some things never change.

BIG TROUBLE
The John Cassavetes comedy starring Alan Arkin and Peter Falk, *Big Trouble*, had limited theatrical exposure. Consequently, it received fairly good play on home video. It begins as a take-off on *Double Indemnity* and then twists into a farce about a pair of characters who are desperate enough to do anything for money. Many scenes would be funnier if one were watching in a crowded theater, but the second side is clever and amusing. The picture looks grainy and suffers from a reddish tint, a problem which carries over onto the jacket stills.

BIG TROUBLE IN LITTLE CHINA
A comic book for *Big Trouble in Little China* must have looked terrific. The movie is nothing more than a series of storyboards depicting visions of fantasy and, for the sake of action, martial arts. To provide some comedy, and to give a link which the audience can identify with, Kurt Russell appears as a truck driver with an inflated sense of self-importance. He journeys to the bowels of the Earth beneath San Francisco, battling demons and sorcerers, in order to retrieve his truck. He also assists in the rescue of a group of kidnapped ladies and, in retrospect, this rescue should have taken a backseat to saving the truck.

The movie was filmed in Panavision, but it loses very little on disc by appearing scanned and cropped. If anything, the compositions are tighter. The picture on the disc is grainy, and the colors lose some of their 'Made in Hong Kong' brightness. The sound, which is as overbearing as the special effects, is in CX-encoded stereo and is too loud to contain any subtle errors.

BIG WEDNESDAY (Import)
Big Wednesday was made by John Milius, but it is a lovely, gentle movie and not at all like the he-man epics he usually churns out. He takes John Ford-type western sentiments and transfers them to a story about surfers in the '60s. It holds up especially well against the mindless coming-of-age movies which are distributed today, and the surfing footage is gripping. Since people do not talk while they surf, we found ourselves noticing the Japanese subtitles only sporadically. The film loses something on a small screen, and the picture transfer is a little weak.

BIGGLES
Time travel fanciers are to be alerted to *Biggles*, a feature film which nevertheless has the scent of a television pilot. The script is marvelous, about a frozen food executive who finds himself bouncing between the present and World War I at unexpected moments. Despite some nice aerial footage, however, the direction, the acting, and the musical score leave much to be desired. There are too many neutral camera angles, and the film steadfastly refuses to impart a sense of wonder.

The stereo sound is good, although it gives too much emphasis to the European rock score, by a group called Stanislas. The picture is clear, to no advantage.

BILL AND TED'S EXCELLENT ADVENTURE
The picture transfer of the engagingly irreverent time travel farce, *Bill and Ted's Excellent Adventure*, is a little soft and the stereo surround is not distinctive.

Two high-school kids use a time machine to kidnap historical personages for a history class presentation. The young stars are directed to act in broad comical strokes, stretching each colloquialism to the limit of meaning and enunciation. The movie is padded to make ninety minutes, but the bare bones of it are marvelously witty and there are a few amusing gags in unexpected places (approaching Socrates, Bill and Ted read up on their man: "'The only true wisdom consists of knowing that you know nothing.'" "That's us, dude." "Oh. Yeah."). The film is unarguably silly, but it is funny enough to redeem its many indiscretions.

BILL COSBY, HIMSELF
Bill Cosby's earliest material was about his own childhood and his later routines dealt with his life as an adolescent and the earlier stages of adulthood. Now his act is all about his own family, his wife and children, and the material seems especially rich.

Bill Cosby, Himself, is one of those rare stand-up comedy performances that one could actually contemplate watching more than once. Cosby, who sits on a chair in the middle of an otherwise bare stage, acts out incidents from his family life, imitating every member in turn. Filmed before he began work on his hit television series, the performance is also unique in that next to nothing in it is offensive (although he does have a disturbingly humorous bit at the beginning about alcohol and drug use). The disc is poorly produced. When the screen isn't filled with his face, the colored background lights blur like a bad video effect. Even with disappointing sound and numerous speckles, though, the disc is worth watching. It is like having Bill Cosby on a chair in your living room.

BILL VIOLA SELECTED WORKS
BILL VIOLA – I DO NOT KNOW WHAT IT IS I AM LIKE
As people go through that slow dissolve from childhood to adulthood, they tend, at least consciously, to forget what it means to be at play. If you watch a toddler playing, you can see that the actions are dedicated entirely to learning how the world functions and what the limits are to self-knowing. The four video pieces collected on *Bill Viola Selected Works* are playful. The artist is playing with the technology, just as you played with your laser video disc machine the first day you hooked it up. What the artist learns from such play – that is, the texture of sight, the meaning of vision or time, et cetera – becomes the subject of a great many essays and the focal point of discussion concerning the work. But when you are holding the disc in your hand at the store, reading the text on the back of the jacket and maybe even rolling your eyes at phrases like, "Both are about the limits of perception, one on the microscale, the other on the macroscale," it is important to remember that the 'Works' are born of play.

Viola is an accomplished artist and a skilled technician; he is so adept at his play that he can communicate the lessons he has learned without saying a word. There are three short pieces on side one (each with its own chapter marker). Because of the complexity in scope and detail there are more surprises on subsequent viewings and, the more you watch the pieces, the more you start to think about what you have seen.

The audio consists largely of monotonal buzzing and a few environmental sounds. It seems like cheating that the disc is in CAV. The images are strongest when presented exactly as Viola originally presented them, and little is gained from re-manipulating the material. Since the pieces were created on videotape, there is an occasional stray line of interference which comes from the source and not the disc.

A somewhat bossy, booklet-sized essay by

Gene Youngblood is included with the disc. The best part concentrates on how Viola shot each piece, although, like using the CAV controls, reading it compromises your experience of the work. Most praiseworthy of all, Youngblood uses specific disc frame numbers as reference points in his discussion. He also gives a brief biography of Viola and it is revealed that, at a key point in his career, Viola landed what has to be one of the most enviable jobs in existence, "artist-in-residence at the Sony Corporation's Atsugi laboratory." Sort of like being a toy tester for Mattel.

When you split the shrink wrap and open *Bill Viola – I Do Not Know What It Is I Am Like*, the jacket cover turns into a two foot wide photo of an owl's face. *Selected Works* was a free-spirited effort in which Viola playfully experimented with video technology. In *I Do Not Know What It Is I Am Like*, Bill Viola goes to the zoo. This piece, which is 88 minutes long (on three sides, in CAV), has its lighthearted moments, some of which can only be discovered by using still step. But it also has a more elaborate and organized purpose, so that the five fairly disparate chapters do blend in meaning after the disc is over.

The disc has a CX-encoded stereo soundtrack, and while this largely consists of whatever noises were happening during the shoot, the stereo is impressive. At one point there is a thunderstorm, and it feels cool and refreshing just listening to it. In some situations the coordination of frame alignments are such that a still frame will have a flickering picture, but in general the disc looks very good.

Like going to the zoo, the disc is both relaxing and educational. The zoo material, in which Viola sets himself up in an aviary and has his camera look into the eyes of various birds, takes up only one of the five chapters, but it is in this segment that you can peer into the soul of the work.

One of the chapters takes place outdoors, capturing the thunderstorm, showing carcasses being picked by scavenger insects, and observing a group of sleepy American buffalo. One uncompromising shot, which shows a buffalo urinating, ought to delight any nine-year-olds who wander into the room and wonder what the hell is on the television set.

The finale shows a group of Hindu men from the Fiji Islands sticking themselves with acupuncture-styled needles and walking on coals. At first a viewer may feel defensive toward the segment, but that is only from fear that the celebrants might not stop escalating the severity of their self-inflicted pain. In that this sequence is followed by a magnificent backwards helicopter shot, all is forgiven. The temptation to contemplate the parallels Viola is making supersedes distaste for the subject matter.

The inside of the jacket cover has two essays. On the left, there is a typically well-intentioned but awkward attempt to explain what Viola is up to. Reading it is optional. But on the right, there is an essay by Viola himself, and it is wonderful. It manages to encapsulate the entire program, to jump wildly from one concept to the next, and to present so many ideas about the work that you can't help but seize one or two concepts to A) decide that is what *I Do Not Know What It Is I Am Like* is *actually* about, and B) make some important discovery about existence which no one but yourself, and maybe Bill Viola, ever thought of before.

BILLY CRYSTAL – A COMIC'S LINE
Billy Crystal doesn't have an hour's worth of material for *Billy Crystal – A Comic's Line*, and while he stretches things out with some creative skits, his routines seem unpracticed, as if he didn't know from experience what works and what doesn't. The picture is fuzzy and the sound is fair.

BILLY CRYSTAL – DON'T GET ME STARTED
Side one of *Billy Crystal – Don't Get Me Started* is a miniature version of *This Is Spinal Tap*, featuring much of the same crew. The sequence is not as clever, but it is an inspired piece of video. The disc is an hour long and is in CX-encoded stereo. You never know when the picture is *supposed* to be bad, but the quality of the transfer appears presentable. Side two is a brief performance in front of a live audience.

BILLY JOEL: EYE OF THE STORM
The rapid-fire imagery in Billy Joel's recent videos can be deconstructed on *Billy Joel: Eye of the Storm*, a 25-minute CAV release. The disc includes Joel's hits, 'The Downeaster "Alexa",' 'We Didn't Start the Fire,' and 'Leningrad.' The picture and sound transfers are very good.

Because of the video tape source, movement in some of the still frames is unsteady, but the character blocking is such that even this produces interesting effects – two people will be solidly formed while the third is a complete blur. Joel's lyrics and 'causes' are terribly simplistic, but his music is nicely varied, as are the approaches in his different videos, and the disc has much to offer. Contrary to the notation on the jacket cover, however, no interview with Joel appears after the program is over.

BILLY JOEL – THE VIDEO ALBUM VOLUME I
BILLY JOEL – THE VIDEO ALBUM VOLUME II
Ten of Billy Joel's better videos have been included on the 48-minute digital disc, *Billy Joel – The Video Album Volume I.* The best one, 'Pressure,' is an amusing depiction of the dreams which are usually triggered by a physiological difficulty developing when one has had too much liquid before falling asleep. Ostensibly, the piece is about the pressures of song writing, but since it was directed by Russell Mulcahy, the other interpretation is totally valid. The only question would be if Joel is in on the joke or not.

The quality of the picture depends upon the age of the clip. The sound is consistently superb. There are chapter stops for each of the numbers, though they are not marked on the cover. The jacket is impossible to read anyway, but, with gold flake on Romanoff red, it looks classy.

Although it has 'Uptown Girl' and 'For the Longest Time,' *Billy Joel – The Video Album Volume II* is a little more desperate for material than was *Volume I.* There are several straight performance videos and a couple of flip-side narrative pieces. The picture quality is more consistent than was the compilation on the first disc.

BILLY ROSE'S JUMBO
The presentation of *Billy Rose's Jumbo* is colorful and impressive. The disc is a Deluxe Letter-Box Edition and has an aspect ratio of about 2.2:1. The image compositions are constantly rectangular and benefit fully from being presented correctly on the screen. Without letterboxing, the entire visual impact of the movie would be lost, and it would also be difficult to make out the pachyderms. The stereo surround sound has many old fashioned separations and is good fun. There is a mild softness in the dialog track but its effect is not significant.

The disc comes in a gatefold jacket which has rather boring artwork. Side three runs under a half hour but is in CLV. The picture is consistently sharp and the fleshtones always look accurate.

With the letterboxing in place, the movie is much more bearable on home video than it is in a theater. For example, the anti-climactic musical number finale, which has too great an emphasis on clowns to come at the end, is easier to sit through or avoid in the home environment. The musical contains some top level Rodgers and Hart numbers, and is about the adventures of a near-bankrupt circus. The spectacle, in all of its letterboxed glory, is enlivening, and the movie leaps comfortably from circus acts to songs to what plot there is. The performers are also a joy. Jimmy Durante and Martha Raye can clown quite effectively without any makeup at all. Doris Day, of whom disastrous things were predicted, has turned out to have great staying power in her film roles, and is an ideal vocalist for the songs of Rodgers and Hart. Last but not least there is Stephen Boyd, whose presence is such an embarrassment (the opposite of an ideal vocalist for the songs of Rodgers and Hart, not that he's singing, but he still has to do the lead-ins) that it becomes pleasurable watching how bad and elephantine he can be. A good actor, in such a wishy-washy part, would never have stood out so well behind Durante.

BILOXI BLUES
The image composition in *Biloxi Blues* is efficient but uninteresting. The film, written by Neil Simon and directed by Mike Nichols, is a sequel to *Brighton Beach Memoirs*, but it is only a sequel in that the same wisecracking hero appears in both films. *Brighton* contained an amusing collection of family characters and, as a disc, sported an excellent digital monaural soundtrack. *Biloxi* contains a less amusing collection of barracks characters and sports an average, well-produced digital stereo soundtrack. The picture quality is fine.

The ad campaign duplicated on the jacket cover has little to do with the film, which has one memorable interlude with a prostitute, one lightly romantic sequence, and is otherwise taken up with cracks about army food, army discipline and the pains of decent exercise. The hero keeps a journal in both films in which he records his true feelings and emotions, but there is an unspoken dark cloud which hangs over the whole effort – he's going to grow up to be Neil Simon.

BIO SCI VIDEO DISC
Videodiscovery, a Seattle firm which publishes *Videodiscs for Science & Industry*, designed and priced the *Bio Sci Video Disc*

for the educational market. The disc contains more than 6000 biology-oriented photographs. There is no audio.

Utilizing only 20,000 frames, it is a shame that the material can't be widely distributed with a more inexpensive price tag. The first portion of the disc includes several segments of moving pictures and drawings to examine the chemistry of cell division. It is difficult to follow without the added resources available in an educational environment. The photos which comprise the remainder of the disc need no more support than the two or three word notes provided in the accompanying frame index. Only one still frame in the group quivered. According to the notes, these 6,000 were culled from 400,000 images. Nearly all are arresting.

There is a strong preference of the flora and fauna of the Pacific Northwest, from slugs and flying termites in the vertebrate section to the Seattle skyline and a can of Olympia beer in a section on 'Human Effects.' Living things from all around the world are included, though, and some, such as the snout beetle, look like they came from a different planet.

The colors are exciting, all the more so because they are natural. A shell creature looks as if he has been sprayed by graffiti artists. Other photos are more dramatic. A human hand holds an elephant embryo, three inches long, which has all the features of an adult.

The best photograph is of a horsefly larvae stretched upon wood and half covering a tarnished penny which has been provided for scale. Numerous shades of brown match the coloring of the larvae and the dark copper of the penny. Lincoln, peering out over the larvae's mid-section, adds just the right touch of humor.

BIRD

Whenever Clint Eastwood wants to be artistic he closes the aperture on the camera. Sometimes it seems to be the only trick he knows. His two-and-a-half-hour portrait of jazz saxophonist Charlie Parker, *Bird*, has been released on a three-sided disc. Virtually every shot in the beginning of the film, where the look is intended to set the tone for the movie, is ridiculously dark. The narrative, full of flashbacks within flashbacks, is confusing and uninspired. The script fails to offer an explanation for the development of Parker's musical talent and fails to provide any insight on how his compositions were constructed. The script's one success, musically, is to capture the atmosphere of the postwar bebop milieu. Fortunately, that, and the superficial tale of Parker's rise and fall, is enough to make an entertaining laser disc, particularly because of the well-publicized sound editing.

Eastwood does have one inspired shot, and it is ideal for showing off the disc: At an audition for saxophonists, the camera dollies backward past more than a dozen musicians, each warming up on his instrument. One's viewing room gradually fills with the sound of unrestrained saxophones. The sound throughout is terrific. It is not just the music. There are rainstorms and other precisely executed effects. Parker's own solos were isolated artificially from his original recordings and added as a front to a contemporary backup band – you can hear the slight flatness of Parker's recording in comparison to the stereophonic backup, but it is still an impressive and functional accomplishment. It beats the impossible task of trying to imitate his style.

There are shots and intensely luminous images which appear much too grainy, but there are other problematic situations – all the darkness caused by Eastwood's retentive aperture – which remain undistorted. On the other hand, Warner's chapter encoding is not as thorough as it could have been, and fails to help one sort through the flashbacks or find the saxophone audition shot (it is in Chapter 2 on side 1, at minute 18).

THE BIRD WITH THE CRYSTAL PLUMAGE

Dario Argento's witty murder thriller, *The Bird with the Crystal Plumage,* is letterboxed with an aspect ratio of about 2.2:1. The movie was made in Italy and the film stock is none too glossy. The picture is a little soft, but the colors are reasonably strong. Contrary to the jacket cover, the movie is in English and has no subtitles. The dialog matches the lip movements, but was post-synchronized so that the actors seem to be dubbed even when they are not. The digital monaural sound does boast of a classic Ennio Morricone score, but is best routed through one's TV speakers. The plot has so many twists that you can watch the film several times without remembering who the villain is. Framing the action is a wonderful utilization of bird-and-cage imagery, which is made even more distinctive by the letterboxing.

THE BIRDS

Alfred Hitchcock used images of birds to represent parents harassing their children from his first sound film, 'Blackmail,' clear up through *Psycho* (where the condition of Norman's birds is quite similar to the condition of Norman's mother).

In *The Birds*, Hitchcock and screenwriter Evan Hunter blended an awkward romance, in which several adults must come to terms with parental relationships, and a wild environmental horror story. By emphasizing scenes in which the birds attack innocent school children, Hitchcock gives the romantic subplot a universal appeal. The threat of parental interference in a romantic relationship is depicted subtly on the human level and graphically in the scenes where birds are shown pecking at the heads of children.

The picture is nice. The monaural track was so well produced that it will come out of a good sound system with more dimensionality than most stereo recordings. Although the film is 119 minutes long, it runs to three sides. When it concludes on side three, MCA has thrown in not one, not two, but *six* trailers for different (and previously released) Alfred Hitchcock films. We don't know why each trailer didn't make it onto its own film, but we're glad to have them all in one spot.

The first trailer, naturally, is for *The Birds*. Hitchcock gives an entire lecture on the 'loving' relationship between man and fowl. The trailer for *Rope* contains an entire scene which takes place before the real movie begins. If the circumstances surrounding the presentation of *Rope* as an editless feature are to be remembered, then this scene, which has a couple of cuts and takes place in Central Park, is quite significant. The trailer for *The Man Who Knew Too Much* opens with an hysterical cheap shot at Doris Day, whose deliberate off-key singing at the tense finale is fobbed off as the best she has to offer. The trailer for *Rear Window* is not the original trailer, but the promotion used for the 1962 re-release. It contains much of the original trailer, however, including an important and carefully edited sequence in which Hitchcock demonstrates the classic Russian concept of film editing. By mixing shots of Jimmy Stewart with various subjects which Stewart is supposedly observing, he imposes emotion upon Stewart's nonexistent 'performance.' The last trailer is Hitchcock's classic tour of Norman Bates's house, motel, and bathrooms. The importance of bathrooms in Hitchcock's stream of thought cannot be underemphasized.

The trailers are in a rougher condition than the film. No one knew they were supposed to be preserved for posterity when they were made.

BIRDY

William Wharton's *Birdy*, brought to the screen by Alan Parker, is the story of a boy whose neurotic obsession with birds is turned into a full-fledged psychosis after a stint in Vietnam. It could have become an instant classic, but Parker's literal rendition will not endear anyone to the story the way a mystical or over-blown production might have. The movie ought to be bloated with images, references, and allusions to birds and flight. When you pick the disc up, feathers ought to fall out of the jacket. Parker captures the emotions of a nervous breakdown, but he doesn't give the audience any escape from it. The story's ending is perfect, but few viewers are going to want to stay with it till the end. The picture and sound are fine.

THE BISHOP'S WIFE

Cary Grant portrays an angel who helps an overworked bishop, David Niven, largely by romancing his pretty wife, played by Loretta Young, in *The Bishop's Wife*. The most charming aspect of the film is the amount of comedy Elsa Lanchester, who portrays a maid, packs into the few moments she is on the screen.

The principals barely understand the confused logic which is intended to render their predicaments charming. The film's soundtrack has been remixed for stereo. The most unsettling moment is when Grant plays a harp and it is very clear, from the angle, that his are not the hands working the strings. For cinematographer Gregg Toland, as for almost everyone else involved, the movie was not a shining accomplishment.

BIZET'S CARMEN

We had great difficulty getting through the three-sided disc of the Francesco Rosi film, *Bizet's Carmen*. When side one was finished, instead of turning the disc over, we just let it play again, and again. When we finally played side two, the same thing happened – we let it start back up instead of going on to side three. We wonder if we will ever have the discipline to watch the disc in a linear fashion. When the ability to command an encore resides in the touch of a button, you get spoiled quickly.

The movie is a marvelous thrill and the opera embraces today's moralities with the passion of a new lover. The music, bits and pieces of which everybody has heard practically from birth, sounds fresh and invigorated. Rosi keeps the decor as simple as the Spanish countryside where the story takes place, so that Bizet's opera can unfold without interference. (The film is in French with English subtitles which we feel could have been a little more poetic.)

The disc is in CX-encoded stereo, but it has a fair amount of hiss. Whether the characters are outdoors or inside, they all sing with the same studio echo. At times, the sound balances take the movie into account – when a scene is observed by someone from a distance, the music is muted – and other times there seems to be no spatial relation between the people on the screen and the singing on the soundtrack. In the climax on side three, the sound continuity broke on two occasions. The left and right channels are switched on an early reel as well. The picture is sharp and the colors are fresh, as were the scratches which appeared on the print every once in a while. After the finale, one of Carmen's famous arias is replayed for the credit roll. The credits finish fairly quickly, but the aria is allowed to play through to a blank screen. We obviously weren't the only ones who wanted an encore.

BLACK AND WHITE IN COLOR

Jean-Jacques Annaud, who later went on to make *Quest for Fire* and *The Name of the Rose*, got his start directing *Black and White in Color*, which surprised many people by winning an Oscar for Best Foreign Film. It is an efficient little movie, about a French fort miles from nowhere in the African jungle and the half-dozen French citizens who declare war on a neighboring German encampment when they learn of the outbreak of World War I. Much of it is comical, as the French attempt to motivate the local natives into joining the fight, and the comedy has a fairly easy target in the bigoted racism practiced by most of the colonials. The film also provides a lesson in management strategies, and this aspect is what makes the piece moderately intriguing.

The print has marks all over it, but the color is not faded and the image is usually sharp. The monaural sound is digitally encoded and is in no worse shape than what one would expect. The film is primarily in French, and the disc retains the original subtitles, which occasionally run off the edges of the screen.

BLACK CAESAR

Larry Cohen wrote and directed the 1973 exploitation effort, *Black Caesar*. Cohen's work shows great promise, though instead of maturing, he just kept on making movies similar to this one. *Caesar* has Cohen's loopy pacing and his disregard for pulling convincing performances out of his cast. It also has a solid, intelligent plot and plenty of action. Cohen, however, works against himself. He creates fascinating characters and then lets his actors mess them up. He conceives witty and elaborate action scenes and then tries to film them without investing enough of the budget to let the sequences pay back.

The print is not perfect. Side two starts out with a vertical line running through the middle of the picture and there are scattered speckles at regular intervals. The colors, however, look as fresh as the first day the movie appeared in drive-ins. The digitally encoded monaural soundtrack includes a score by James Brown and, "Music Edited for Home Video." The film's sound editing, however, is weak (a passing airplane accidentally drowns out one dialog passage) and the disc only serves to emphasize its faults.

The story, which is summarized incorrectly on the back of the jacket, is about the rise and fall of a black mobster, played by Fred Williamson. It contains coarse racial language which was the rage during the fading sixties but today sounds as inept as the outfits and hairstyles look. A still from a different Williamson film is used on the jacket cover. Somebody else didn't like his outfit or hairstyle, either.

BLACK MOON RISING

A good old-fashioned caper movie, *Black Moon Rising* even has one of Lalo Schifrin's tweaky jazz scores that he likes to pass off as thriller music. For those who like to see mistakes in the jacket copy, there's a good one here. The text goes on and on about a valuable "computer disk" which the hero (Tommy Lee Jones) hides in an experimental automobile. In the film, the object is quite clearly a computer tape cassette, and is referred to as such. While not a milestone in cinema, *Black Moon Rising* is an entertaining feature which invites multiple viewings. The picture is mildly grainy.

BLACK NARCISSUS

Most assuredly assisted by the quality of the film itself, Voyager's Criterion Collection edition of Michael Powell and Emeric Pressburger's *Black Narcissus* is breathtaking, heart-stopping, and mesmerizing. The picture retains every shading, every tinted filter and every flicker of light that the filmmakers intended to present. It is a magnificent bouquet of images, outdoor and indoor, natural and man-made, veritable and imaginary. The disc meets each challenge, whether it is a red wash, darkness illuminated only in blue, an intricately detailed matte painting, or several such effects, combined.

The film is about a poorly managed group of Anglican nuns who attempt to establish a convent in an abandoned cliffside seraglio high in the Himalayas. Much is made of the tension between the steamy amoral valley and the cold, aesthete precipice looming above it, but the movie has a rhythmic set of emotional conflicts which are imbedded deeply by the masterful style of the filmmakers and so the most obvious themes never slip out of control. The film isn't just about the difficulties in working for an employer who measures profits in moral souls, it is about the different ways to reconcile the beauty of existence and the horror of life.

The CLV disc has a dual audio soundtrack and has not been CX-encoded. The film's soundtrack has a natural amount of hiss (it was made in 1947) and the volume is a bit low, but the sound quality does not hinder the entertainment. On the second audio track, Martin Scorcese and the film's director, Powell, provide loosely synchronized commentary (the audio quality of their voices is excellent, incidentally). Scorcese's hyperactive input is a bit daft, but his thoughts provide the perfect supplement to Powell's sleepy-voiced anecdotes, and the presentation (edited from a real conversation into a lecture) is a far richer enhancement to one's appreciation of the film than a straight scholarly talk would have been.

Black Narcissus was filmed entirely in the British Isles and mostly on soundstages, but one never loses the feeling that the locations are Asian, even when the paintings outside the windows look obvious. It is a movie about burning desires, ambiguous memories, and political failures. Yet its true power is its own fantasy, that it is a creation which has escaped the bounds of its creators. This is revealed in Powell's final anecdote on the disc, ostensibly concerning the way he created the film's concluding rainstorm, which inadvertently describes the exotic pleasures of making movies in England: "These splendid raindrops are all being done by me with a teacup on a wonderful, large tropical leaf I found, and then the local fire brigade takes over."

BLACK ORPHEUS
BLACK ORPHEUS (CAV)

Even worn down copies of *Black Orpheus* are colorful, so you can imagine what a carnival the print used in the Criterion releases is. The CAV disc looks a bit sharper than the CLV presentation, but both are gorgeous. Even the long, strained view of Rio's harbor after nightfall is as clear as one's own eyes could achieve on a misty evening.

Although the myth of Orpheus – which is detailed on the inside of the jacket cover – has many episodes, the one which captures the imagination is the dilemma Orpheus finds himself in when he is informed that he may only be with his deceased wife if he does not look at her. It is a succinct presentation of the impossible balance one must achieve between accepting fate and holding onto memory.

The movie, which is discussed with pleasant precision in a second essay on the back of the jacket, transports the myth to the Rio de Janeiro Carnival and the squatters (abject poverty is a topic for some other film, not this one) who live in the hills above the city. *Black Orpheus* often receives derision from highbrow critics, but the world would be a poorer place were it not for movies like this. The director, Marcel Camus, knew full well that he was stretching the limits of acceptable myth-making, but as time recedes, so does the audacity of his accomplishment.

Anton Carlos Jobim did the music and a couple of the tunes were eventually adopted as American pop standards. The monaural sound is analog bound on the CAV disc but digitally encoded on the CLV presentation, though there is little difference between the two. The sound was transferred with the same care which governed the picture transfer. The movie was made in 1959 and is in Brazilian Portuguese with English subtitles.

BLACK RAIN
BLACK RAIN (Letterboxed)

Paramount has released two versions of Ridley Scott's *Black Rain*, a full screen standard rendition and a letterboxed rendition which has a challenging aspect ratio of about 2.4:1. The movie was filmed in a process known as 'Super 35,' creating, initially, a non-widescreen image which is then masked at the top and bottom for theatrical screenings. *Black Rain* played in theaters as a legitimately widescreen film, but a comparison of the letterboxed and non-letterboxed disc images will quickly reveal that while the letterboxing adds a little bit of image to the left and the right, the standard version adds as much to the top and the bottom as is lost by the mild trimming on the sides.

Collectors who want the film as it was shown in the theaters should obtain the letterboxed version, but those who are uncomfortable with letterboxing will not be missing anything by obtaining the standard version.

Both versions appear to have been carefully and artfully composed. In some shots, an additional light or object will appear on the very edge of the screen on the letterboxed version. The viewer is also aware, however, that the top and bottom cropping is very tight on the letterboxed picture, and there are a number of shots where the composition on the standard version is more pleasing. One example occurs in the police headquarters scene at the end of the film. The face of one of the investigators is completely cut off on the letterboxed version, but looms eerily at the bottom of the screen on the standard version, adding another witness to the heroes' atonement. None of the action scenes are harmed by the mild cropping on the standard version, and the background atmosphere is only shifted from the sides to the top.

One of the flaws a viewer usually sees in comparing letterboxed and standard images is a graininess when the center of the picture is blown up on a non-letterboxed image. With Super 35, however, this is not the case, and the standard version is just as sharp and glossy as the letterboxed version. *Black Rain* is a problematic video transfer. It is filled with moody colors, Scott's over-enthusiastic smoke machines, and a dozen other slick visual effects that can easily be spoiled on the journey from film to video. Paramount has done an excellent job transferring the movie. Only a handful of shots fail to look as crisp or as colorful on the discs as they did in the theater. The intensity and solidity of the image also varies somewhat between the two versions, but it is on a scene-by-scene basis and it cannot be said that one version has a better color transfer than the other.

The stereo surround soundtrack is the same for both discs and it is a good one, full of impressionistic music and well-timed sound effects. The movie has rightfully been accused of pandering to 'Remember Pearl Harbor' sentiments, but it is first and foremost an action film, the sort which works well on disc, and it is difficult to remain righteous towards it once the plot starts hopping. The views of Osaka, which make the city look more futuristic than LA in *Blade Runner*, are as captivating as they are falsely represented. There is also one wonderful scene which stops the movie dead, in which Andy Garcia gets up in a crowded nightclub and starts singing 'What'd I Say.' It is Scott's little message to the viewer to stop being so uptight and just enjoy what is going on.

THE BLACK ROOM

A Universalish, gothical tale of terror, *The Black Room*, has been released by RCA/Columbia and Image. The 1935 film stars Boris Karloff, who has a dual role as a good and a bad twin, fated by prophecy to do one another in. Although you have to give the hour and ten minute film a half hour to get started, the plot has some great hooks, the performances are marvelously campy, and the movie is good fun.

The black and white print has a frozen frame splice and a number of scratches, but the condition of the picture never interferes with the entertainment. The sound is also a bit noisy, and is best kept at manageable volume levels. Side two is in CAV, with two unsteady still frames out of every five.

THE BLACK STALLION (CBS/Fox)
THE BLACK STALLION (MGM/UA)

Carroll Ballard's lopsided but enthralling *The Black Stallion* was reissued by MGM/UA after previously being available from CBS/Fox. We prefer the color quality on the old version. MGM/UA's is so dark in places as to spoil some of the film's magic. However, the MGM/UA disc is less grainy than the earlier effort, and the digitally encoded surround sound on the newer disc is exceptional, particularly during the opening sequences when the low pitched hum of the ship's engines – completely missing on the CBS/Fox version which is not even CX-encoded – is ever-present.

The beginning of the movie is so beautifully conceived and executed that it would be difficult for any narrative to live up to it, and after multiple viewings, the film does seem to come close. The movie has three acts. In the opening, a boy on a ship makes friends with a horse and is then saved by the animal when the ship sinks. Ballard captures not only a sense of adventure and excitement, but meticulously evokes small details, such as the rocking of the ship, which are so powerful that hours later you can still feel the effects of them. In the second act the boy learns to ride the horse on a deserted coastline and is then saved by a passing trawler. The segment is worthy of the first sequence and holds one's curiosity. Ballard cleverly avoids cliches by sending the camera underwater during significant emotional interactions. The last act, however, takes up half the movie, and is set in the boy's home town. To purge the grief that his adventures have caused him, he is obsessed with teaching the horse to race and with winning an important match. On first viewing, this segment completely upsets the mood established in the first half of the film. On subsequent viewings, adequately prepared, it does not. It is almost as sparse in dialog as the first sequences are. Mickey Rooney appears as a retired horse trainer and Teri Garr appears as the boy's mother in this segment. Through no fault of theirs, the casting drags down these characters instead of advancing them. Having opened with breathtaking splendor, the movie then pauses too long and never gets back its wind.

BLACK WIDOW

Debra Winger portrays an investigator following a woman, played by Theresa Russell, who may be murdering her rich husbands in *Black Widow*. The movie is enjoyable, and works because it is more than just a mystery. It is a humorously perverse examination of the career/family choices women must make in their twenties and thirties. Both the sound and the picture are acceptable, but not exceptional.

BLACULA

For a film which is only 15 years old, the racially-oriented jokes in *Blacula* are surprisingly dated. The movie is self-conscious of its blackness and it tries to be hip about race, but like the wide collars and long sideburns on the actors, some of its components have gone out of style. The film, however, can be effective if you accept its premise and production values.

The picture is in excellent condition. There is a darkroom scene which maintains its amber lighting without going all fuzzy the way similar scenes in many classier features have done. The sound is ridiculous, but that comes with the territory. The transfer, however, is marred by foggy vertical bars which plague the image throughout most of the disc.

BLADE RUNNER (Voyager CLV)
BLADE RUNNER (Voyager CAV)
BLADE RUNNER (Embassy)

When you are introduced to an adult character in the beginning of a movie you naturally presume the character has had a full life leading up to the first moment you see him, but what if that wasn't the case? This was the premise of *Blade Runner* before the film's producers chickened out. Harrison Ford's character, Deckard, was to have been revealed at the end to be a robot, and the first shot of him, it would probably have been implied later on, was actually his first experience in the world, although, because of implanted memories, he wouldn't realize it himself. Had that plot twist not been corrupted, the film could have been a truly great cinematic work, because, among other things, it would have ignited a philosophical self-examination strong enough to support the dense special effects and intense actions sequences. Characters in movies really don't have pasts, and really do enter into existence in the first shot they appear.

The movie, as it was actually produced, was a failure in film houses, but was a hit, and has achieved a cult following, under the relaxed standards of home video. This is ironic, since it means that most who profess to enjoy the movie have only seen about half of it, as is represented on a dark and blurry, scanned and cropped Embassy release. It is not even the standard home video version, since it lacks several seconds of violence which had been excluded from the US theatrical release – contrary to the reproduction of the video cassette copy on the jacket cover.

Voyager, however, transferred and released the film properly, letterboxing it with an aspect ratio of about 2.5:1. The source material which Voyger used received director Ridley Scott's blessing as the official, final, intended version. It contains the snippets of eye- and nose-gouging violence left out of the Embassy disc, and retains the condescending narration and the why-doesn't-everybody-move-there trip-to-the-north ending. The print is so sharp that you can make out the minute details in the models and matte paintings on the edges of the screen composition. The print is also so luscious that there is a tendency to stop the picture every 1000 frames or so (on the CAV version) and just gawk.

The disc has been digitally encoded and

almost as soon as the images start hitting you, the sound starts hitting you as well. (The analog track is noisier and not quite as impressive.) The Vangelis score sounds as if it is playing inside your head instead of outside, and the sound effects seem to be coming from everywhere. Each component is almost perfectly defined, with clear, rounded tones.

A supplementary section on the CAV disc includes an excellent still frame scrapbook that contains a set of notes, detailing everything that is right and wrong about the film (such as the fate of the mysterious sixth android); many of the original conceptual drawings by Syd Mead, accompanied by explanations about evolution of the drawings to the completed sets and vehicles; an excellent *Blade Runner* Bibliography; and a silly little trivia test (which can encourage you to concentrate on the film's details).

The CLV version has no special features and the picture is a little less sharp than on the CAV disc.

Why is the film so popular on home video? At its best, *Blade Runner* is poetry, an evocation of the future and some of the philosophical problems spurred by technology, set in a languid, repetitive, moody meter. It provides many futurist concepts, but not so many that a viewer is drowned in them. You can't see or hear everything no matter how many times you watch it. There are just too many details to savor. It is drenched in action and special effects, but, more importantly, it drips with style, and viewers, desperate for anything which is unique and imaginative, lap it up.

BLAKES 7 (Import)
BLAKES 7 I (Import)
Essentially, if you like the *Star Trek* television series, you will like *Blakes 7*. It is recorded primarily in video (some model effects are filmed) with sets and effects which are a little more elaborate than the average 'Dr. Who' episode, but lean by Hollywood standards. The picture quality of the two discs varies from shot to shot. Some retain the vivid immediacy of fresh video tape while others have turned copper green and have become quite blurry. On the whole, however, the picture is tolerable. The monaural sound is not CX-encoded and is best left at a reasonable volume. There is a horrid opening theme song which sounds like Chopin's 'Polonaise' being played while descending a hillside.

The show, however, is superbly scripted, and that is certainly half the battle when it comes to science fiction. Both discs cram three 40-minute 'hour time slot' episodes onto a single platter. (The side breaks work out okay, and the side break on the second disc is actually inspired.)

The first disc, *Blakes 7 I*, is the complete pilot, showing how a band of renegades meets, obtains a special space cruiser, and starts to wreak havoc with the totalitarian Federation. There is a good narrative twist every 5 minutes for the entire 120. The renegades don't all like one another, which adds another level of tension, because one never knows how close to the surface betrayal is lurking. Since the material involves the origination of the characters, the disc is the stronger of the two and the most advisable purchase if one wishes to sample the series.

The second disc has three episodes which are more independently structured but are linked by a common theme, as a specific villain, assigned to track and destroy the rebels, is introduced in the first episode on the disc and appears to be relieved of his duties by the end of the third. One of the episodes on the second disc uses the same concept as the *Star Trek* episode 'The Savage Curtain.' (The presentation of teleportation appears to be more deliberately derivative of *Star Trek*, though the function has its own clever delimiter – to transport, a character must be wearing a special bracelet which always seems to come off in fights.) All three episodes involve cat-and-mouse type trickery, set on a galactic scale.

On the whole, there is less philosophy than the best *Star Trek* offerings, but the pace and the plotting make the episodes very addicting. Even if you put one of the *Blakes 7* discs on pause to take care of something, there is a tendency to run back quickly after you've dealt with the interruption.

BLAME IT ON RIO
A congenial and amusing farce, *Blame It on Rio* makes good use out of its exotic locale to embellish the story of a mid-life crisis victim (Michael Caine) who has a brief fling with his best friend's teenage daughter. The nudity is more memorable than the humor, but the mixture is balanced so as to entertain rather than offend. The picture is bright. The one fault with the disc is the flat monaural sound.

BLAZE
Too often films based on contemporary history are contrived efforts, bent out of narrative shape by the force of real events. Even Paul Newman found his way into one such turkey, *Fat Man and Little Boy*, so nothing quite prepared us for the charm of his performance in *Blaze*, a precious little film about the governor of Louisiana, Earl Long, and the exotic dancer, Blaze Starr. The movie manages to provide substance, depicting Long's political maneuverings and drawing parallels from these maneuverings to the entire American political system in the forties and fifties, while using Long's more absurd activities to keep a viewer attentive and entertained.

The picture transfer looks fine and manages several difficult lighting tricks without difficulty. The stereo surround is also good and has a number of well chosen surround effects. Be sure to leave the disc on to the very end of the credits, by the way, as there is a brief radio interview with the real Earl Long slipped in at the end.

BLIND DATE
Blake Edwards is daring in a different manner from the way in which other film directors might be daring. He follows all the rules of establishment filmmaking to produce hit movies, but he also pokes around in the loopholes. He has had strings of flops, in which he failed to coordinate the comedy, the story, and his own style, but in *Blind Date* everything came together. There are even two musical numbers, so thoroughly blended with the storyline that you barely notice the movie pausing for them.

Blind Date would be more elegant on a larger screen, but the disc is a pleasure to watch. His confidence in how the comedy will affect the audience allows him to use many sight gags without drawing undue attention to them. Although the humor is base, it is being presented in a way which doesn't insult your intelligence.

The quality of the picture on the disc is acceptable. The sound, which is in stereo, is also quite nice. When a car weaves through traffic, squealing tires shift from the right channel to the left channel and then back again. One gag is even relegated to the soundtrack. A character is told to shoot a dog which has been the cause of a few problems. In the middle of pandemonium on the screen, a gunshot can be heard in the right speaker, although nothing else is ever made of it.

The movie itself is something of a classic in situation comedy. A man is set up on a blind date with but one caveat, his date should not be allowed to drink. One could do just about anything with the premise and generate a few laughs, but the performances of the many television stars in the cast and the self-control of the director accomplish more. The laughs continue, and even increase, on multiple viewings.

BLINDSIDE
An enjoyable set of plot twists makes up for some other deficiencies in *Blindside*. The script includes a few characterizations which are too simplistic to be believable, but the basic plot is nicely executed, and the viewer has to really concentrate to piece everything together. Harvey Keitel stars as a reclusive motel/apartment manager who begins tracking some nasty goings-on with a building surveillance system. Soon he must determine how much of the activities are real and how much are simply being put on for his benefit. His character is well developed, so that although his personality is basically unappealing, by the end of the film the viewer will respect his intelligence.

The transfer is passable. Strong reds and browns look grainy, and the image is usually a little soft. The sound is a little scratchy.

BLISS
Don't be tempted by the Magritte-inspired artwork on the jacket cover of *Bliss*. The film, which won awards in Australia, is an experience which is at odds with its title. The script was partially written by the author of the book upon which the movie was based, and that always spells trouble. It is structured, slightly, like a folk tale, though it deals with an advertising executive who has a nervous breakdown after nearly dying of a heart attack and who eventually abandons the rat race for a quiet life in the woods. There are absurd incidents, and a few gross effects (he imagines waking up during his own heart surgery), but because of the inept use of voice-over narration and the budget limitations which cause the filmmakers to be overly dependent upon editing to achieve the effects, *Bliss* can't shake giving the impression that it is just jerking the viewer around. It never becomes serious enough to be magical. The picture transfer is satisfactory and the sound isn't bad.

THE BLOB (Fifties)
THE BLOB (Eighties)
It doesn't belong on the same shelf as *The Magnificent Ambersons*, but the Voyager Criterion Collection release of *The Blob* can certainly hold its own against the likes of *The Seventh Seal*, a film it fails to imitate even

slightly but nevertheless places in a proper perspective. The two would make a great double bill.

The Blob is about a ravenous globule from outer space which gets larger every time it eats a person. As for the film's merits, we defer to the excellent essay on the back of the jacket cover, written by Michael Dare. Witty and forthright, even if you don't buy the disc you should pause in a video emporium long enough to read Dare's remarks.

The disc is in CLV – darn – and even though it runs under 90 minutes the ending, with its drippy, blink-quick special effects, has been left in extended play. Voyager has letterboxed the goo-gobbling epic at about 1.7:1, which changes very little from the full screen image one sees in the trailer at the end of the disc. There are a few shots where it is clear that the letterboxing was absolutely necessary, especially one where a doorway and the Blob separate a nurse from a doctor, but most of the shots don't look any different.

The DeLuxe color print which is used is in nice condition, though it is never quite as good as the gorgeous still on the jacket cover. Voyager clearly did not take the time with *The Blob* that they took with *2001*, but the disc still looks and sounds better than most contemporary releases. Major faults include blurs surrounding intense colors, a couple of splices and dialog hiccups, and a mild fuzziness whenever darkness descends. On the positive side, the skin tones look perfect, the movie never looked this good on television or at the drive-in, and the digitally encoded monaural sound is almost (in a scene involving car horns and sirens) stereophonic. The analog track, which is CX-encoded without automatic tripping, is far more subdued than the digital track and may be unsatisfactory to some listeners.

There are two theatrical trailers at the end of the disc. One for the first *Blob*, and one for the recent remake. It is a marvelous effect, pulling the viewer back into the reality of the eighties.

And where would we be without the eighties? Image has released the terrific remake of *The Blob* on laser disc. If you let your kids watch the older one, be sure to hustle them out of the room before putting on the new one. The new *Blob* is as entertaining as the older one, if not more so. It is both witty and scary, cleverly scripted, and has enough gruesome special effects to make you think twice about eating jello.

The disc is in excellent condition. There is virtually nothing wrong with either the picture or the digitally encoded Ultra-Stereo sound. The program also has as many chapter markers as the Criterion *Blob* does, though there is no listing of them on the jacket.

We wonder if, thirty years from now, the nervewracking special effects on the new *Blob* will look as phony and be as easy to dismiss as the giggle-inducing special effects on the old Blob. If that is the case, then what will state-of-the-art special effects be like? Will our hearts be able to take it?? Where will it all end???

BLONDES VS. BRUNETTES TEXAS STRIP-OFF
TOPLESS DANCING TEXAS STYLE

Both *Blondes vs. Brunettes Texas Strip-Off* and *Topless Dancing Texas Style* have stereo sound, and *Strip-Off* features the addition of surround codes. What this means, however, is that the beat of the disco music is more diffuse, since virtually everything else comes out of the middle. The two discs are hour-long CLV programs which were filmed at the same Vegas-style money vacuum in Houston, a topless night club called 'Rick's Cabaret.'

On both discs the picture is blurry enough to make the makeup on the ladies appear smeared. *Blondes* features a series of paired women performing stripteases on a runway in the main lounge. A lengthy portion of *Topless Dancing* is filmed in the 'VIP' room, where women 'dance' for individual customers. The latter contains a significant amount of carefully disguised repeat footage and takes the concept of the tease to an extreme. We hope the customers are on expense accounts, because they spend more than the price of the discs and get as much or less in return.

BLOOD FEAST

The quality of the print looked and sounded so good on Hollywood Home Theater's *Blood Feast* that we thought it was a take-off on early-sixties horror pictures instead of the real thing. The bright, basic colors are preserved unusually well for a cheap independent feature made over twenty years ago.

Only two factors give the origins of *Blood Feast* away. One, the gore just isn't up to the standards of contemporary gruesomeness (though some primitive 'splattering' does occur near the end). Two, the acting is just so bad that the best actors in the world could never imitate the lack of abilities displayed by the cast.

The actors and actresses are constantly reading their lines from pieces of paper hidden on counters or in their hands or, when an excuse can be found, from the script itself in the guise of a report or phone book. At one point a policeman is interrogating a victim whose face is bandaged and he reads his questions off her left cheek. Who's going to know, right? The disc, although beautifully produced, has some value as camp, but few thrills.

BLOOD FOR DRACULA (ANDY WARHOL'S DRACULA) (Import)

Carlo Rimbaldi, before he became famous, did the slasher effects on *Blood for Dracula*, a film which was several years ahead of its time in terms of sex and gore, and was released domestically as *Andy Warhol's Dracula* since Warhol was listed as the producer in the credits. The film is available on disc in Japan, with slight letterboxing (a thin black line at the top and bottom of the screen) and video generated masking of the genital areas by the Japanese censors. The disc is in English with Japanese subtitles on the bottom of the picture.

How can actors and actress who read their lines so poorly do the neck biting thing so well? Perhaps it is in their blood. In this rendition, the Count comes to Italy in search of virgins and winds up at an estate where Joe Dallesandro, playing a gardener, is always one daughter ahead of him. Dracula vomits if the blood isn't pure, and one of the most engaging shots is a bathtub-point-of-view depiction of his reaction after slurping the eldest daughter. No one in the movie has the same accent, even members of the same family, but they all talk in the same way, reading from the little pieces of paper taped just out of camera range.

The genital masking actually contributes to the camp, though it is sure to infuriate hard core fans. The picture is in excellent condition and the sound is without major problems.

BLOOD SIMPLE

Surely the most entertaining movie about adultery to appear in some time, *Blood Simple* revels in sweat and seedy lust. It is a comedy of sorts. The husband, played by Dan Hedaya, looks like Richard Nixon and deserves everything that happens to him. The wife and her lover mistake each other's intentions almost from the beginning and the errors lead to bloodshed.

The film is directed with a tacky, overly artistic style, and reminds one of a tavern with too much decoration. The picture has a slight graininess, but this is only noticeable because much of the movie takes place at night. It is apparently too much to ask to see the entire screen, but the opening shot is hurt by even minor cropping. The film's sound is monaural, but it was conceived better than many stereo soundtracks are and the CX-encoded disc captures the full, often subliminal, effects.

Blood Simple purposely takes place in Texas so that the heat and the emptiness will further excuse the sins of the characters. Watching the disc is more fun than being bad, because the characters do it much better than a normal viewer could ever hope to.

BLOOD WEDDING
EL AMOR BRUJO

The first and last installments in Carlos Saura and Antonio Gades' dance trilogy, *Blood Wedding* and *El Amor Brujo*, are available as part of Image's CinemaDisc Collection and join *Carmen*, which was released earlier as a standard Image offering.

How we envy those who have never seen the films before and can now watch them in order in a single afternoon! The movies comprise the best type of series – each is very different, yet Gades' choreography is constant. The same basic cast appears in each film as well, and while the actors and actresses portray different characters, their archetypes are always the same, so that a viewer has the same emotions toward each performer throughout the trilogy. *Blood Wedding* is a realistic record of a dance group which is seen briefly preparing makeup and costumes, and then shown performing a full dress rehearsal of a flamenco rendering of Federico Lorca's 'Blood Wedding.' *Carmen* merged the rehearsals of a dance interpretation of 'Carmen' with a drama among the dancers which paralleled the plot. *El Amor Brujo* is entirely fantasy, introduced on a soundstage to comfort viewers who are put off by *One from the Heart*-style pretensions. It tells a story of love, violence, and ghosts, partially in dance. The characters break into step the way they would break into song in a standard musical, but with Gades' choreography, it is movement and not lyrics which advance the narrative. The films are in Spanish with English subtitles.

Brujo was made in stereo, but appeared theatrically in the United States as a monaural film. Image has obtained a stereo audio track for the digitally encoded disc, and although the separations are limited, the fidelity is impressive. At the reel changes there are pops and crackles (this isn't Hollywood), but the music and the sound effects have real thrust. *Blood Wedding*, which also has digital encoding, is monaural and sort of pales in comparison to the *Brujo* sound, but it is the movie which ought to be watched first anyway, and the transfer is adequate. The quality of the color on the two discs matches that of the audio. There is nothing wrong with the print of *Wedding*, but it is not very stimulating. The print for *Brujo* is richer and livelier. Both transfers make the images appear slightly blurry.

Both discs are chapter encoded. *Blood Wedding* has a listing of the chapters on the back of the jacket (a rarity these days) and is in CAV on side two. With two unsteady still frames out of every five it is difficult to analyze the dance steps too closely, but manipulating the flow of the choreography can be intriguing.

BLOODHOUNDS OF BROADWAY
RCA/Columbia has delivered *Bloodhounds of Broadway* in a Special Theatrical Presentation Format, but the black bands at the top and bottom of the screen are so slight as to be inconsequential. The movie itself is a mixture of deliberately hazy photography and something a little sharper, and so is the disc. The fleshtones, when not affected by moody nightclub lights, look accurate enough. The movie is monaural, but the sound, though it lacks punch, is nice.

The movie, with some reservations, is a delight. Based upon Damon Runyon stories, it is a deliberately playful depiction of the lives of several characters during a single evening in the Roaring Twenties, with the dogs of the title tracking one of the characters through a number of Manhattan nightspots. The cast includes Madonna, Matt Dillon, Randy Quaid, Rutger Hauer, Julie Hagerty, and Anita Morris. Madonna's one musical number and half-dozen principal scenes will be sufficiently satisfying for her fans. The whole cast gives passable performances, but only Jennifer Grey is able to rise completely to the material's potential.

BLOODSPORT
Fans of martial arts movies don't care about acting, or even if the lip movements match the dialog, and they won't want to miss *Bloodsport*, which has lousy acting, synchronous dialog, and lots of great fights. The plot is little more than a distraction to pace the fighting sequences in a tournament the hero has entered. The picture is as sharp as the hero's karate kick. The digitally encoded Ultra-Stereo sound has some hiss, but the mix is well done, and gives the movie gloss. A number of chapter markers are encoded. Jean-Claude Van Damme's one romantic scene is a howler, as he tries to kiss the heroine with his teeth, but in the ring he is anything but awkward.

BLOWUP (Voyager)
BLOWUP (MGM/UA)
The centerspreads of the gatefold jackets in the Voyager Criterion Collection have often disappointed us, so we were surprised when we opened *Blowup* and found the artwork, although completely in keeping with the style of the other disc jackets, to be an absolutely perfect expression of the film – three of the blown up black and white photos, set against the background of the park's painted green grass.

The disc is in CAV and runs to four sides. The color transfer, from 'MGM's 35mm interpositive, a negative image reversal print struck from the original negative,' is captivating, and contributes enormously to the atmosphere of the film. The scenes in the park, with an overcast, midday light, are more beguiling and creepy than they have ever seemed on faded prints, or even on MGM/UA's recent CLV version. The MGM/UA disc would normally seem like a fine transfer, but set against the Criterion disc, it looks grainy and over-ripe.

We apologize for the following, but there is a discrepancy in the Criterion *Blowup*, and it involves Vanessa Redgrave's breasts. Now this may sound juvenile, but one of the film's subjects is fashion photography, and a prurient interest in the uninhibited lifestyle of the hero is a contributing factor in the decision to purchase the disc by many consumers. It was, in fact, an emphasis of the original advertising campaign for the film itself. Anyway, an insert provided with the Criterion disc states that the aspect ratio of the letterboxed program is 1.85:1. When Redgrave first removes her shirt, there is a brief glimpse of her right breast which is cropped out of the scanned, full TV screen MGM/UA CLV version, but several shots later, when Redgrave first turns to peck David Hemmings, there is a full frontal view of her chest on the MGM/UA disc which is almost entirely lopped off the bottom of the picture on the Criterion presentation.

Otherwise, the combination of the letterboxing and CAV is quite thrilling. Much of the movie is designed with photographically-styled image compositions, and it is difficult to watch the disc without succumbing to the temptation of manipulating the images. At the end of the disc, Voyager has included three items: An early theatrical trailer (brilliantly conceived as the scroll of a photographer's camera, it also contains some nudity), the Julio Cortazar short story, 'Blow-Up,' which was the inspiration for the film, and a collection of production stills which are presented in real time to a replay of one of the film's jazz numbers.

The sound is monaural and has no CX-encoding. It is fine, but cannot be raised beyond a certain volume without distortion taking over. MGM/UA's version does have CX-encoding, but the effect is about the same. On the back of the disc jacket is an uninteresting essay which fails to deal with some of the film's central quandaries, such as whether the hero isn't imagining everything. There is also a chapter listing which gets one of the best quotes in the film wrong. It says, "Nepal is full of antiques," when the actual line goes, "Nepal is all antiques," 'Nepal,' and 'all' rhyming too perfectly.

There are two particular revelations in Cortazar's short story. The story is a bit convoluted and does not involve a murder per se, only some other nasty goings on. The first revelation is in its location. The story is set in Paris, and one realizes, looking at the film, that other than the rock concert scene, the film is more Parisian than it is British. Not even in the swinging sixties would you ever have seen mimes in London. The other change is in the character of the narrator. He screams when he realizes the horror he is viewing in the photographs. Director Michelangelo Antonioni has Hemmings remain cool and quiet, distancing the viewer from the film, and, as time passes, the film from any cinematic pantheon.

BLUE CITY
Most of *Blue City* takes place in the bright Florida sun, but even the night scenes look sharp and clear. The movie, based on a book by Ross MacDonald, advances with a series of expertly crafted twists and turns. It is about a young man seeking to avenge his father's murder in the midst of a corrupt Sun Belt community. The piece has everything one requires of a brief thriller. The picture is okay. The sound is monaural and CX-encoded, with music by Ry Cooder.

BLUE COLLAR
When *Blue Collar* first opened in movie theaters, it had the gloss of a brand new car. Now it looks like it has been parked in the alley too long. The print is grainy and noticeably aged. Yaphet Kotto has an olive green complexion through most of the film. The sound is in passable shape. The Jack Nitzsche/Ry Cooder 'I'm a Man' score sounds better the louder the volume is increased.

The movie is a pessimistic fantasy about three workers in an automobile assembly line who burgle their union. The filmmakers tend to convey their message with the subtlety of a pneumatic drill, but if you hold onto the disc long enough, the story may seem relevant again as soon as the next Depression starts. Richard Pryor is the star, but Kotto has the best time and looms larger as the real central character in multiple viewings. The trailer is included at the end of the disc. If you watch it first you won't have to bother with the movie, since it summarizes the entire film from the first shot to the last.

THE BLUE MAX
CBS/Fox has done a glorious job transferring *The Blue Max* to disc as part of their Special Wide Screen Edition series. The movie, however, is not for viewers who demand that characters act with consistent logic or that performers act at all. For those who are happy enough watching two and a half hours of bi-plane and tri-plane dogfights, George Peppard modeling German uniforms (and pronouncing 'general' with a hard 'g'), impressively budgeted widescreen battle scenes, and the bare, anamorphic torso of Ursula Andress, *The Blue Max* is an enjoyable treat.

The picture has been letterboxed at an aspect ratio of about 2.3:1. Everything about the movie which is good – the hardware, the action, and the sex – is best seen in its full width. Everything about the movie which is bad – the acting, the emotions, and the plot – would be all that was left if the image had been cropped. The source material is gorgeous. There is some red shifting in a few scenes and a mild paleness on a few reels, but the picture is sharply focussed and richly detailed – often the only saving grace during an interior scene.

The stereo surround sound is also great fun. As the camera dollies past a taxiing airplane, the sound shifts from left to right and then from front to back. The soundtrack has a level of hiss and crackles which one normally associates with older recordings, but who can hear it during the dogfights? The musical score was written by Jerry Goldsmith, combining a soaring melody for the aerial sequences and a militaristic march for the ground scenes. A couple minutes of closing and opening Intermission music provides a pause in the middle of side two. The disc comes in a gatefold jacket which also contains a satisfying collection of background tidbits. A listing of the chapter markers can be found on the innerspread.

The Blue Max, directed by John Guillermin, is about a German infantry soldier who joins the air corps and feels intimidated by the largely aristocratic crew of pilots. He compensates by aggressively seeking to down enough enemy aircraft and earn the medal identified by the film's title. The plot details are a series of annoying unlikelihoods, but the cast, which also includes James Mason and Jeremy Kemp, do add a touch of glamor to the proceedings, if nothing else. Even with Andress's polio vaccination scar in full view, the film is more palatable than the World War I air battle movies which try too hard to be serious. We enjoy the movie for all the wrong reasons, but we enjoyed the disc for all the right ones.

BLUE STEEL

The conclusion of *Blue Steel* gets awfully ridiculous, though that does not necessarily spoil the fun. The plot has many similarities to *Dirty Harry*, as it is about a psychotic killer who just can't seem to get arrested without having his rights infringed upon in the process. Jamie Lee Curtis is the frustrated cop trying to pin the rap on him and the twist here is that they were dating for a while. In the end though, he keeps coming back for another bullet wound, like Michael Myers, and by the time she blows him away it is hard to believe in the film's validity. The stereo surround sound is boisterous, and the sound editors have a special affection for passing automobiles. The picture is sharp and flawless.

BLUE SUEDE SHOES – A ROCKABILLY SESSION WITH CARL PERKINS AND FRIENDS

George Harrison, Ringo Starr, and Eric Clapton are just a few of the talented performers appearing with Carl Perkins on a marvelous 55-minute disc, *Blue Suede Shoes – A Rockabilly Session with Carl Perkins and Friends*. The videotaped performance looks nice and clear, and although it is apparent that the engineers recording the sound mix didn't get to rehearse much, the digital sound on the disc is a decent representation of the original. The program features 16 numbers, all marked by chapters and all basic, fresh, and pure rock and roll. The guest stars come on and off the stage to perform with Perkins, and then everybody reappears for an ensemble romp through 'Blue Suede Shoes.' The disc is interactive CLV, because you would have to be chained down and gagged to not sing along.

BLUE VELVET
BLUE VELVET (Letterboxed)
BLUE VELVET (Import)

Blue Velvet was initially released in America by Karl-Lorimar with a scanned and cropped image, but, later on, Warner absorbed the Karl-Lorimar titles and reissued the *Velvet* with a letterboxed image which has an aspect ratio of about 2.3:1. There is an inept Japanese import which has milder letterboxing, censored nudity, and a poor picture transfer. The picture on the original Karl-Lorimar version was also poorly executed, and both renditions are irrelevant in light of the Warner version.

The picture on the Warner disc is mildly grainy, likely a result of the source material, originally a Dino De Laurentiis property, changing bankrupted hands so often. None of the flaws, however, harm the impact of the disc's image. The letterboxed picture does more than simply rescue the film from cropping, it lets the objects within the picture composition breathe. The space surrounding a character is very important within the film – where he can run, what he can see that someone else cannot – and it is simply a pleasure to look at the way some designs have been grouped together – chairs, curtains, and lamp shades are deliberately placed to stimulate portions of the screen.

The improvement of the picture quality is also gratifying. Laura Dern's initial emergence from the darkness is breathtaking. The complicated lighting effects, which seem to deliberately alternate between hyper-realism and misty impressionism, never become confused or out of control. The stereo sound supports the film's wonderfully quirky sound editing.

Blue Velvet is a masterpiece. Instead of presenting academic symbols for sexual tension and disparity, every component of the film is set up to make a viewer feel sexual conflict. When the screenwriter/director David Lynch puts the apartment where the young man has his liaisons on the seventh floor of a building which never visibly has more than six floors, it is not a mistake. Although the location of houses and streets are often discussed in detail, it is no failure on the part of the viewer that the real relationship between one location and the next is indistinct. Lynch is artistically imitating the way in which the sexual drive becomes separated from rational thought. He is not imposing a metaphor on anyone. The viewer, distracted by the drugs and corruption plot, cannot pay attention to that kind of detail. So it is felt instead of noted.

Some reserved observers may question the need for experiencing the emotions which the film kindles. The point is that the emotions are there anyway, hidden or in the open. *Blue Velvet* has got to be one of the best movies about the final stages of growing up that we know of. It challenges the viewer to admit that secret thoughts are present in everyone. Unlike other films, it is about the way people really do slip into adulthood, not with any great test of strength, but with a series of diminishing mistakes and improved attention spans. It is also a very strong comedy about life in America, and it often dares you to laugh. Lynch was a sculptor. Where most artists turn ideas into forms, he has succeeded in creating forms out of ideas, and they hold together long after the disc is over.

BLUES ALIVE

Side one of *Blues Alive* looks pretty good, but the picture on side two is so grainy the expressions on the faces of the musicians are barely discernible. The disc sounds much better than it looks. It is a terrific record of a rare concert event, and the opportunity to hear John Mayall's British blues/rock work as back-up to folk blues artists such as Albert King, Sippie Wallace, and Junior Wells puts nearly all the pop music played during the last 25 years in correct perspective.

THE BLUES BROTHERS

MCA's re-release of *The Blues Brothers* has a nice picture transfer, digital stereo surround sound, chapter encoding, all those car crashes and Steven Spielberg on side three in CAV, and a theatrical trailer which pretty much gives you all the other big gags in CAV, too. It is the R-rated version, for language. Like most of John Landis' films, the movie plays much better on home video than it does in the theaters. Although it has its dry stretches, there are also moments of terrific comedy and many memorable scenes, including Aretha Franklin's number, the Ray Charles jokes, the country/western bar set, all those car crashes again, and a nun who doesn't need legs.

BOB & CAROL & TED & ALICE

The beginning of *Bob & Carol & Ted & Alice* demonstrates that although the film may be dated, it is still relevant and humorous. The movie opens to a gauche rendition of the 'Hallelujah Chorus' from Handel's 'Messiah.' The age of the recording, as it has been transcribed onto the digitally encoded audio track, makes it sound even worse, and magnifies its true purpose. Critics at the time complained that the use of the piece, even for ironic effect, was cliched. But they apparently missed the point. The director, Paul Mazursky, was not employing 'The Messiah' to laugh at the thought that his characters had found the ultimate answer to life, he was employing a rotten version of it, set to a pop beat, to show that his characters, if they followed the pop trends, were *never* going to find the answer. The humor, largely unseen at the time, is in how awful the music sounds, and in how awful the presumptions of the characters sound, as well.

There is a single chapter encoded on side two for the concluding pop song, 'What the World Needs Now.' The film was made in Eastmancolor and looks reasonably fresh, though with that ungainly film stock it is sometimes difficult to tell. There are scratches and speckles, but, like the themes of the film itself, the print is surprisingly well preserved.

The film's subject, often forgotten in the concentration upon the cumulating scene which inspired the famous advertising still, concerns the compromises one must make with honesty to maintain a relationship or inner stability. It is told in reverse, as the characters forever get themselves into trouble by attempting to be too honest. One of the more unfortunate legacies of the sixties was the employment of psychoanalytic techniques in situations, such as the day to day life of perfectly healthy people, which do not require analysis. If nobody today confronted you with their 'feelings,' or questioned yours, then *Bob & Carol & Ted & Alice* would probably be irrelevant. But we still hear that babble often enough to find not only pleasure, but wisdom, in the film.

BOB DYLAN – DON'T LOOK BACK

If it weren't for home video, *Bob Dylan – Don't Look Back* would still be languishing on a shelf somewhere. Removed from distribution for quite a while, you couldn't have seen the film in the seventies if you had wanted to. It is a black-and-white documentary about a 1965 Dylan tour in England. You don't hear any numbers from beginning to end, but D.A. Pennebaker's work is an impressive accomplishment. He shows exactly enough concert material to give the viewer an essence of Dylan's performance style, and he also manages to capture a realistic portrait of life backstage. There is a sequence with Dylan's managers negotiating over the telephone which must have brought horror to the parties on the other end when they finally saw the film.

The disc is monaural, but it is CX-encoded and doesn't sound any worse than a basement tape. The original film was hopelessly dark and grainy and has been preserved in that condition.

BOB LE FLAMBEUR (BOB THE GAMBLER)

Bob le Flambeur is an entertaining tale about a doomed casino heist, but it is also an affectionate tribute to old French gangster movies. It is beautifully photographed, uses lurid lettering for the credit sequence, and has a jazzy, hard-bitten musical score. The film is ideal for high-fidelity playback, because the sound recording captures the style of the fifties without an accompanying hiss.

The picture is spotless and no evidence of distortion shows up in the darker areas of the screen. The film is in French with detailed but readable white English subtitles.

BOBBY McFERRIN – SPONTANEOUS INVENTIONS

Bobby McFerrin is like an improvisational comedian, except that he tells songs instead of jokes. When he is not wandering down the aisles with his cordless microphone, he sits on a stool and turns his voice into just about every jazz instrument you can think of. The sound and the picture are perfect. The replay potential of *Bobby McFerrin – Spontaneous Inventions*, however, is weakened by stunts such as having the audience do 'Itsy Bitsy Spider.' The first time it's cute, but on subsequent viewings one may start grabbing for the scan command.

BOBBY SHORT AND FRIENDS (LIVE AT THE CARLYLE)

We always wanted to go and see Bobby Short at the Carlyle Hotel, where he has played the piano nightly for umpteen years, but after sitting through *Bobby Short and Friends (Live at The Carlyle)*, we are glad we didn't. He does have an effective act, but he sounds as though he could use a vacation. His best number, 'I Can't Get Started,' is a fresh interpretation of a forgotten classic, but moments like that are few and far between. Jack Lemmon joins him for one number and Lucie Arnaz for another.

The disc does not have chapter stops, but it does have digital sound. The recording can't seem to capture the ambience of the lounge and is not totally without hiss. The disc costs as much as the cover charge for two and a round of drinks, but you don't have to get dressed up to watch it.

BODY AND SOUL GOLDEN BOY

Two classic black and white boxing movies are available through Image. *Body and Soul* is a Republic Pictures title and *Golden Boy* is from RCA/Columbia Pictures. Both prints look as though they've gone the full fifteen rounds, with the source material for *Body and Soul* looking especially beat (the jacket cover has one of those reverse disclaimers, "Mastered from the original film negative," but the program ends with a British Review Board title card). Despite splices, the contrast levels and clarity on both discs are decent, and most viewers will be able to tolerate the flaws. The digital sound on both discs fluctuates a bit. Again, *Body and Soul* is the worst offender, sporting a bad hum near the beginning and shifting volume levels at the end. Both discs have chapter markers.

Body and Soul is the generic boxing film, about a first-generation American fighter who works his way to the top only to be told by his manager that it is his turn to take a fall. The film may be clichéd by default, but individual scenes are engrossing and the narrative remains enjoyable even when you know what is going to happen every step of the way.

John Garfield is the boxer, Lilli Palmer is his girlfriend with an accent which the screenwriters try to explain at one point (she grew up in a number of European cities) and then contradict elsewhere (her father worked in a pharmacy), and William Conrad is outstandingly wicked as the manager – what a shame he did not become a full-fledged star earlier in his career. The musical score is exceptional, as well.

The big fight scene in *Golden Boy* doesn't come until the very end, but it is incredible, and no wonder William Holden looks completely different in his subsequent films. The two boxers/actors just wail away at one another.

The script, by four writers attempting to cinematize Clifford Odets, is an awkward mess, in which some passages of dialog are marvelous but many character motivations and plot twists come out of nowhere (well, the left, since this is Odets). Lee J. Cobb and Adolph Menjou are woefully miscast as the boxer's father and manager. The former is supposed to be a cuddly, boisterous Italian and the latter a slick boxing promoter. Since the boxer isn't being asked to throw the fight, there's a dramatic hole at the end, which may be why the boxing gets so vicious, but Holden's scenes with Barbara Stanwyck are enchanting.

BODY DOUBLE

Brian De Palma's films are often criticized for their violence but that is really all many of them have been good for. We like watching violence on our television set. The thrill we feel as the blood sprays every which way is probably the same thrill early man felt as he pounded his neighbor on the head with a club. So long as none of it gets on our carpet, we're willing to sit though all sorts of maiming and destruction.

In *Body Double* there is this scene where a woman is dispatched by a man with an electric drill. Sounds exploitive? Sure, on paper, but it is actually a very clever scene. When the murderer first approaches the woman and attempts to thrust with the drill, it comes out of the electrical socket and stops! As the struggle continues, the camera shifts downstairs where the hero is trying to get past a vicious dog to save her. The drill pops through the ceiling and blood comes pouring with it. The only graphic vision is in the viewer's own imagination. The stereo surround sound is great and the picture is okay.

Long before there were movies there were folk tales and daydreams which contained just as much violence. Even though our abilities to depict the imagination have improved technologically we will never be free of childish or animal-like impulses. Imaginations will continue to run wild. So long as people can continue to share fantasies, they can come closer together, not further apart, and be safer still.

THE BODY SNATCHER

The print they dug up for *The Body Snatcher* is immaculate. The film is almost too serious to be fun. It is about the complications which arise when a doctor hires a grave robber to keep a medical school supplied with cadavers. The film is well-crafted and disturbing and the disc will be satisfying for those who do not need to have their horrors graphically portrayed.

THE BOHEMIAN GIRL/THE MUSIC BOX SAPS AT SEA/OLIVER THE EIGHTH SONS OF THE DESERT/BLOTTO

Three of 3M's Collectible Classics Laurel and Hardy discs provide examples of how satisfying and unsatisfying the series has been. *Sons of the Desert/Blotto* is CX-encoded with automatic tripping. *The Bohemian Girl/The Music Box* and *Saps at Sea/Oliver the Eighth* are also CX-encoded, but do not have automatic tripping. The source material does have scratches, blurs, and a few breaks here and there. With some exceptions, the movies were hardly made with preservation in mind.

The Bohemian Girl/The Music Box is an excellent double bill. 'Girl' is one of several operettas which was peripherally adapted to serve as a Laurel and Hardy feature. Playing gypsy pickpockets, they intrude just as the songs are beginning to wear out their welcome and vice versa. 'Music Box,' of course, is a witty classic in which the two manage to destroy an entire house while trying to deliver a piano.

Both features on *Saps at Sea/Oliver the Eighth* (the only disc in which each show appears on a single side; on most, the second feature is a short, with its own chapter marker, filling in the runover on side two) are well directed and consistently amusing. The first has an elaborately funny opening. Oliver starts going bananas after working too long as a horn tester. In 'Oliver the Eighth,' Hardy becomes engaged to a woman who has murdered her last seven husbands, all of whom were named 'Oliver.'

Sons of the Desert/Blotto is for hardcore fans. Both stories deal with henpecked husbands attempting to sneak away from their wives. Television advanced this genre so far that these attempts at domestic comedy seem undeveloped and crude.

BOLERO

The sound on *Bolero* is fair and the picture has speckles. No great loss though, *Bolero* isn't good enough to be stupid. Directed by John Derek and starring Bo Derek, the shots are usually too dark, they usually last too long, they are placed and organized incorrectly so that one never can tell where characters are located in a set or scene, and the cast has not been directed so much as handed the script and told to bite their lips. If you've ever seen someone tell a joke to a group of people who remained dead silent when the punch line came, you'll know what the humor in *Bolero* is like. We'd recommend the disc as a non-prescription sedative, but even then it is a bit difficult to swallow.

THE BOLSHOI BALLET – DIVERTISSEMENTS

Pioneer has chosen to release a program called 'The Bolshoi Ballet in the Park' (at Battersea in London) on a disc entitled *The Bolshoi Ballet Live – Divertissements*. We have no idea why they lacked the nerve to use the original title, but the disc itself is nothing to shy away from. Even those with limited budgets should strongly consider purchasing the disc. Those who regularly obtain ballet discs or who have extra cash on hand should not hesitate to grab it.

The three-part program takes place in a tent pavilion. The acoustics are wonderfully light and airy, with the wooden stage and the canvas providing just the right amount of substance to the sounds (unlike outdoor concerts, nothing evaporates too quickly). This has been transferred to disc with digital encoding, and while the analog track has some hiss on it, the digital track is clear and silky.

The program is a live sampler of the Bolshoi's repertoire; a succinct and stunning display of the best they have to offer. It opens with a complete rendition of 'Les Sylphides,' choreographed with exquisite simplicity by Michel Fokine and danced very nicely by Natalia Bessmertnova, Lyudmila Semenyaka, and Nina Semizorova.

On side two, the second act of 'Spartacus' is performed. While the complete ballet is available elsewhere, the second act is the high point, and taken out of the context of the rest of the ballet, it is even more riveting. Erek Moukhamedov reprises the title role, and his athletics are glorious.

The final side is a series of short pieces, the 'Divertissements' of the borrowed title. Some of these dances are from other Bolshoi Ballet discs, including *Sleeping Beauty* and *The Golden Age*, but here they are performed without sets or elaborate costumes, by the Bolshoi's best dancers (including Moukhamedov again). The result is one show stopper after another.

The picture quality is less satisfying. 'Sylphides' has a copperish tint and 'Spartacus' is too red. The cameras, however, usually encompass the entire stage, keeping the disruption of the choreography to a minimum (the one thing they don't seem to cover is entrances, dancers continually appear out of nowhere).

THE BOLSHOI BALLET – SPARTACUS THE KIROV BALLET – GISELLE

The Bolshoi Ballet – Spartacus, suffers the fate common to most ballet discs. The editing, switching from one camera to the next, often seems to happen just before a viewer can settle on the ideas the choreography is attempting to represent.

The ballet *Spartacus* is a pleasing spectacle. Aram Khachaturian's score is varied and symphonic. The lead dancer, Erek Moukhamedov, is quite an athletic crowd-pleaser and is welcome to defect any time he wishes. The Spartacus legend is retold as a grudge match between the leader of the slave revolt and the Roman general who once owned him.

The 129-minute show is spread over three sides so that each side is an 'act.' Fine, but what an opportunity is missed by not putting a portion of Moukhamedov's performance in CAV. The sound is excellent, but the picture is what one would expect from Russian television.

Like *Spartacus*, the picture on *The Kirov Ballet – Giselle* is a bit grainy and awkwardly filmed. *Giselle* is not a very complicated ballet, however, and so with the exception of a few key moments which would require a wide screen to get in everything properly, the essential choreography is captured.

BON JOVI – BREAKOUT!

We do not ask much of heavy metal rock groups, simply that they acknowledge that women are human beings and that they learn how to play more than one note before they start making music videos. On the 8-inch *Bon Jovi – Breakout*! the gender play is teasing but respectful and the group's music is energetic. Who knows, perhaps hardcore heavy metal fans think these guys are wimps.

The disc has 28 minutes of music on two sides, 18 minutes on one and 10 on the other. The videos mix plots and interesting visuals into a nice jumble. The picture is a bit grainy. The sound on discs like this doesn't count.

BON JOVI NEW JERSEY THE VIDEOS

Some of the videos available on *Bon Jovi New Jersey The Videos* have been included elsewhere. The best one, however, 'Living in Sin,' appears for the first time. Until the cop-out ending, the black and white piece is a well executed depiction of young romance which evokes both longing and carefree abandon. 'Sin' aside, the videos follow a specific format, depicting the rock group performing in concerts, carefully edited with non-live footage to enhance the impact of the group's abilities. The band members appear between each number as well, in an amusingly loose interview which was apparently made immediately before a performance. Although the disc is primarily for fans, those who enjoy a decent rock beat and admire talented entertainers will not be disappointed.

The program runs 45 minutes, not an hour as is listed on the jacket cover. The freshest video material looks perfect, but the blurrier music videos are either conceptually foggy or generational pass-me-downs. The sound is loud and clear.

BON JOVI – SLIPPERY WHEN WET

The 40-minute *Bon Jovi – Slippery When Wet – The Videos* is a single-sided disc which is, digitally mixed and mastered. It contains six songs – Bon Jovi's music videos are all concert oriented – and extensive interview or home movie footage between each number. The band members may all be professional musicians, but they are like your worst relatives when it comes to mugging in front of a camera. The picture quality on the disc is passable.

THE BOOST

If you want to relax, don't put on *The Boost*. The characters don't start taking drugs until the 40-minute mark, but they are hyperactive from the first frame, and the movie's only accomplishment is to be real enough that you get hyper along with them. The film induces ulcers. An unpleasant tale, starring fun couple James Woods and Sean Young, *The Boost* traces the success, addiction, and failure of an individual who had it coming from day one. John Williams' guitar work is the only exceptional aspect to the stereo surround sound, which otherwise lacks energy. The picture is a little hazy, and the movie, along with all its other faults, isn't all that pretty.

BORIS GUDUNOV – THE BOLSHOI OPERA

Mussorgsky's elaborate operatic interpretation of Pushkin's 'Boris Godunov,' subsequently cleaned up by the Maxwell Perkins of Russian music, Nikolai Rimsky-Korsakov, is available on laser disc through Pioneer Artists from the only group who could probably do the work justice, *Boris Godunov – The Bolshoi Opera*. It is in their blood, and the sets and costumes look like heirlooms.

Mussorgsky's music is skinned from Russian folk tunes and wrapped in multiple layers around Pushkin's prose. It is wintry and full of stormy basses, which blast out of the digitally encoded soundtrack like the air from a window which has loosened in the night. (The analog track is less clear.)

The opera is long, as the story is faithful to the spirit of Pushkin, who used tragedy and other devices to bring his readers closer to his characters. In any other opera a character such as Godunov would be unredeemably evil, but here his morality seems irrelevant, and the torture upon his conscience is endless. Evgeny Nesterenko portrays Godunov, Vladislav Paivko portrays Grigory and Tamara Sinyavskaya is Marina. None of the singing is spectacular in the live production, but the cast is competent and they have the confidence of heritage to back them up.

The picture quality starts out fine, but deteriorates as the evening progresses. By the end it is noticeably fuzzy, and many of the golds and reds blend together. The opera is in Russian and has English subtitles, punctuated by commas which often look more like periods. The four-sided disc is side-separated at breaks between acts or scenes. The still on the inside jacket spread is beautiful. A libretto has been included with the disc and we were annoyed to discover that only the English translation and not the original Russian lyrics were present within.

BORN FREE

The story of the pet lion who must be reintroduced to the wild, *Born Free*, has held up very well under the passage of years. The only aspect of the film which has dated it is the problematic portrayal of blacks in what is, after all, Kenya. The two servants are often used for comic effect, and the natives are remote and alien. Nevertheless, the film is a fascinating accomplishment, with trained lions achieving virtually every dramatic and scripted action expected of them. There is just enough story to avoid the barriers that a documentary can impose upon a viewer's involvement with the characters. We recall when we were younger being quite tickled by the habit of the married couple (childless, apparently) who use one set of pajamas between the two of them – she the tops and he the bottoms. It was one of the first glimpses we had of the potential for married life which really sunk in. The movie, without leaving the confines of the family film format, succeeds in presenting the maturation of the lion as a metaphor of the inevitable separation between human parents and their children, allowing a viewer to feel both sides. Like John Barry's ubiquitous title song, the film has resonance.

The transfer looks okay. The locations are dusty, but the color only seems a bit faded. The sound may not have all the power that it should, but there are some decent, full-throated roars.

BORN IN EAST L.A.

The critics who found fault with the religious overtones in Cheech Marin's enjoyable *Born in East L.A.* were being too picky. Anybody who writes and directs their own film is, in essence, acting as God to the characters on the screen, and so if he wishes to appear to them that way as well, it is his choice. Marin has a marvelous premise to work with (an American of Hispanic descent leaves his wallet home one day and is deported to Mexico) and even though he can't come up with enough comical adventures in Tijuana to support the film's running time, the ending is perfect. He deserves to be as proud of it as he appears.

The picture is cropped, but only a handful of shots are harmed by it. The image is extremely sharp, and the colors look perfect. The analog sound is monaural and has been CX-encoded. The music track is stronger than similar efforts in many stereophonic programs.

Side two of *Born in East L.A.* is in CAV. No major artistic insight can be gained by manipulating the images, but we felt compelled to slow a few scenes down, to savor the faces of the performers. Finally, it is worth noting the intriguing value of one scene in which Cheech attempts to teach 'Twist and Shout' to a group of Mexican musicians and they insist that it is 'La Bamba.' There is a lot of valuable musical criticism available solely through the medium of film comedy, if you stop to think about it, and this is one of the clearest examples of how effortlessly complex ideas can be communicated when humor is the mode of communication.

BORN ON THE FOURTH OF JULY
BORN ON THE FOURTH OF JULY

(Letterboxed)

A movie like Oliver Stone's *Platoon* is entertaining because it pushes you to a certain level of emotional intensity and never lets up. Stone's *Born on the Fourth of July*, however, is a biographical drama (about Vietnam veteran/activist Ron Kovic) and the emotions are more scattered. Except for the single viewing to satisfy one's curiosity, it is difficult to think of the movie as entertainment. The film is intent upon rubbing a viewer's nose in the unseemly aspects of war, veterans' hospitals, and paraplegia. It is efficiently educational and artistic, but its rewards are minimal. To top things off, the star, Tom Cruise, gives a sporadic and mostly pedestrian performance. He transcends the material in only a handful of scenes and is bound by it most everywhere else. In marked contrast, Willem Dafoe appears all too briefly in one segment and is so fully captivating that you wish the story would follow his character instead of Cruise's.

There is both a standard version and a letterboxed version, the latter sporting a tight aspect ratio that measures about 2.5:1. Those who dislike letterboxing or long for full screen closeups of Tom Cruise will find the standard version to be satisfactory. A comparison of any randomly chosen scene, however, will reveal how badly cropped the standard version is and how essential the letterboxing is for recreating the film's original screen compositions. On the letterboxed version, almost every shot is carefully balanced and filled with details which enhance the meaning and importance of a scene. The film will have such a tenuous hold on most viewers anyway that seeing the image as it was intended could very well make the difference between liking the movie and not liking it.

The picture quality is very good. The film has many difficult filter effects and all have been rendered superbly. The standard version is naturally a bit blurrier than the compact letterboxed version. The sound is fine, though the stereo mix is not exceptional and the dialog levels often seem a touch too low. On both discs side three is in CAV. The still frames are steady, though the utility of Standard Play on the title seems limited.

BORN YESTERDAY

The black and white print of *Born Yesterday* has shiny, deep blacks and no significant scratches or markings. The picture is slightly grainy from time to time, but those who obtain the disc will find the image tolerable. The monaural sound has not been CX-encoded, but is otherwise in good condition.

The movie is a little dated, and nasty in its depiction of ignorance. The timing between Judy Holiday and Broderick Crawford, however, will never erode. Although Holiday tries, she never establishes the same rapport with the always self-righteous William Holden. We wonder if the movie would be fresher today if Holden and Crawford had switched roles. If you collect good movies, you can pass this one by, but if you collect great movie moments, then the scenes with Crawford and Holiday shouting at each other are a must.

THE BOSTONIANS

Based upon a novel by Henry James, *The Bostonians* is a love story absolutely without passion. Those familiar with Henry James will recognize the style which James Ivory and Ruth Prawer Jhabvala have faithfully transferred to the screen. Endless conversations, chaste lovers who can be parted from each other for months and then pick right back up as if nothing had happened, characters gaining and losing power over others inch by subtle inch; it is all there, but except for Linda Hunt, virtually none of it is interesting.

The filmmakers took exceptional care to capture the feeling of an era, but the realism only emphasizes how boring life must have been back then.

BOUND FOR GLORY
A VISION SHARED A TRIBUTE TO WOODY GUTHRIE AND LEADBELLY

We thought we'd be smart and create a double bill by watching A *Vision Shared A Tribute to Woody Guthrie and Leadbelly* before watching the *Bound for Glory*. The problem is that *Tribute* tells all the real stories, making it easier to spot the dramatizations and falsities in *Bound for Glory*. For example, one of Guthrie's acquaintances in *Tribute* explains that 'Union Maid' was written on request because most other union songs were male oriented and there was a desire for a song with which women could identify. In *Bound for Glory*, Guthrie, played by David Carradine, is seen writing the song in haste for the sake of a union meeting, as if it were just another brotherhood and organizing anthem.

Carradine's remarkable performance is *Bound for Glory*'s one saving grace. The movie wasn't in stereo and never really gives Guthrie's music the attention it deserves. The film pokes in and around Tom Joad country, depicting Guthrie's life from the point that he first visited California to the point that he left for New York City. After listening to the stories told in *Tribute*, few of the experiences concocted by the screenwriters seem legitimate. Most are too pat and avoid the complexities of real life. It wasn't just the subject matter that caused the film to fail financially, it was a sense that there should be more to the story than there is.

The award-winning cinematography is especially mangled on the disc, but it points up a few conceptual problems. The deliberately fuzzy edges and faded colors in the film look phony when the source material is truly fuzzy and faded. The movie has two famous camera shots. A breathtaking matte shot of a dust storm descending upon a Texas town, which appears intact on the disc, and a how'd-they-do-that combination crane shot and hand-held stroll through a migrant worker's encampment. The latter, however, is over-praised, because all the extras insist on glancing at the camera (the younger ones even smirk as it passes) and too many can be seen with un-migrant-like clean hair.

The sound does not impart a theatrical fidelity. It is Carradine's performance which makes the disc worth considering. He survives the transition from *Tribute* without missing a beat, capturing not only the mannerisms and attitude of Guthrie, but the voice as well. Emotionally, he is at the mercy of the script, but in two and a half hours there is enough substance for Carradine to remain sympathetic, despite a barrage of stoic torments.

Tribute is a sort of two-for-one documentary, looking at the life and art of both Guthrie and Leadbelly. It is 78 minutes long (side two is in CAV) and can only give an overview of each singer's life, but at least one gets a taste of the biography and the artistic accomplishments of both musicians. The picture has no flaws to speak of, and the chapters are listed on the back of the jacket. Many contemporary performers are shown playing Guthrie's or Leadbelly's songs, in digitally encoded stereo which has the fullness one longs for on *Bound for Glory*. The disc ends with a composite performance of 'This Land is Your Land.'

BOXCAR BERTHA

After listening to Martin Scorsese's talk on *Taxi Driver*, his strategies in his first major commercial effort, *Boxcar Bertha*, suddenly become very clear. His use of jump cutting and other New Wave tricks leap out at you, as does his attempt to blend the devices with film techniques from the Thirties, but he is not experimenting. Each effect is applied with a definite purpose, to enhance a viewer's feeling or understanding of a character. The style, which Scorsese has gradually refined over the years, is both raw and promising in *Bertha*, and it sets the film apart from the standard Roger Corman/American International Pictures productions. The necessities of a drive-in attraction are also there – terrific sex, chases, a violent finale which is so similar to *Taxi Driver* you have to wonder if Schrader was familiar with it – but Scorsese squeezes intelligence into every exploitable crack.

The picture is in decent shape, when one takes the nature of the low budget production into account. The sound is acceptable. The Depression-era period film, about a group of union activists who are coerced into becoming outlaws, stars Barbara Hershey and David Carradine.

A BOY AND HIS DOG

The first batch of *A Boy and His Dog* contained an annoying whirring sound which lasted for close to twenty minutes near the beginning of side one. The discs were recalled, but be wary if you purchase the CX-encoded disc that you have not acquired one of the faulty copies.

There has never been a print of *A Boy and His Dog* which does not look as ragged as the two heroes, primarily because the film was made on a small budget. The movie is 89 minutes long and has been pressed in CLV. The jacket cover has the original advertising art on the front.

Don Johnson plays the boy. His voice sounds like the Don Johnson everyone is familiar with, but his appearance is very different. He is much younger and gangly. Tim McIntire, we were surprised to learn, does the voice of the dog, and his Wellesian vocal control adds a multitude of nuances to the dog's expressions. The story takes place in a 'Mad Max' setting, although the last third is sidetracked to an underground city intended to mock middle America. It would have been better off staying with its initial premise, but the infamous final scene, which is just as pleasing on multiple viewings as it is the first time through, makes the whole show worthwhile.

THE BOY WHO COULD FLY

The Spielbergish *The Boy Who Could Fly*, written and directed by Nick Castle, tries to toe the thin line between fantasy and a depiction of neurosis, as such disparate films as *The NeverEnding Story* and *Picnic at Hanging Rock* have done, but at the end it cans the psychology stuff and just goes with the narrative freedom of the cinema and special effects. The results are sure to drive some people crazy, and be a pleasant surprise to others.

The disc jacket cover claims the program is in stereo, but you could have fooled us. The picture is a little over saturated, but not too much is wrong with it.

THE BOY WHO LEFT HOME TO FIND OUT ABOUT THE SHIVERS

(see **FAERIE TALE THEATRE**)

BOYFRIENDS AND GIRLFRIENDS

Eric Rohmer's delightful *Boyfriends and Girlfriends* (it is actually called 'L'Ami de Mon Amie,' or 'The Friends of My Friends'– as in 'the friends of my friends are my friends') looks gorgeous. The film was made with inexpensive film stock which lacks gloss, but it is a recent movie, with bright colors and accurate fleshtones. The monaural soundtrack is marvelously atmospheric and can support extensive amplification, which is best for obtaining its full effect. The film is in French and has yellow English subtitles which seem adequate.

Until a key moment near the end, *Boyfriends and Girlfriends* takes place in a world without cars. It is set in a campus-like mall and planned community called Cergy Pontoise, which is a healthy train ride outside of Paris. Although there are cars in the distance and the characters refer to their own autos at times, Rohmer appears to deliberately avoid street scenes. The characters are seen on the mall, in their homes, or at a park surrounding a lake. He creates an atmosphere that almost has a fairy tale feeling to it.

The narrative concerns two young women who are in the process of settling into relationships. Rohmer asks a lot from his cast, placing them in very awkward situations and having them stutter and shift uneasily as they would in true social situations. The acting is at times off-putting, but, once the narrative gets going, the performances gather a real strength in conveying the emotions of the characters to the viewer. The film is a romance, and although it is very much like real life, it has an odd setting and a happy ending, making it a wonderful escape from the kind of real life most viewers are burdened with.

THE BOYS IN COMPANY C

One of the first Vietnam war movies, *The Boys in Company C* has withstood the release of subsequent and more adeptly philosophical Vietnam films without losing its basic impact. Like so many war films, the first third of the script takes place in boot camp. It is worth noting that the drill sergeant role remains one of the most rousing and indulgent parts an actor can land. The movie embraces all of the basic clichés and ends with a symbolic soccer game in which the American officers order their team to lose to the South Vietnamese team, even though the Americans could easily beat them on their own (for the sake of the film's entertainment, the Americans win anyway). The most intriguing aspect of the script is the precedent it sets by making the American officers the enemy. Although there are a number of action sequences, not a single VC is seen up close in the film.

The picture is a little washed out, but is in acceptable condition. The sound is interesting for the elaborate background noises on the soundtrack which would have been impressive if the movie had been stereophonic. The image is cropped, significantly damaging the dramatic impact of a couple of scenes. The film runs 126 minutes and side three, which lasts less than a half hour, remains in CLV. There are a few chapter markers.

THE BOYS IN THE BAND

To use the film's own overly focussed vernacular, CBS/Fox has produced another *tres gauche* jacket cover, this time to house *The Boys in the Band*. The unflattering photograph on the front of the jacket looks beset with algae. The disc itself is in much better condition. The picture is sharp and the print looks fresh, with no significant flaws. The sound volumes fluctuate mildly during the second half, but background sound effects and music are stereophonic, and the presentation is surprisingly classy. There are also chapter markers. The film, about a small evening's gathering of gay men, manages to remain reasonably sharp and amusing, despite the passage of time and that trying anathema of modern drama, the psychological party game, which takes up most of the second act. The disc jacket may belong in the closet, but the disc itself can be comfortably brought out for view.

THE BOYS NEXT DOOR

After beginning with a quick sketch of personality traits common among real mass murders, the emphasis being that they are unassuming and appear or act like 'normal people,' *The Boys Next Door* proceeds to introduce two young men who are so obnoxious and socially outcast that they were probably voted 'Most Likely to Become Mass Murderers' by their high school class.

The disc has a digital soundtrack which is cleaner than the analog track, but the aural advantages are limited. The picture is of standard quality, with a little grain in the darker scenes.

The film is actually an excuse to share the fantasy, to follow the boys on a trip to LA and stand right behind them as they mash heads. There are two prevalent theories about this. One says that these types of programs provide a release for aggressive emotions, while the other says that such displays of violence encourage the real thing. We subscribe to the first theory, but who knows what goes on next door.

BOYS NIGHT OUT

A contest to see who can eat a banana in the most erotic fashion is typical of the material to be found on *Boys Night Out*. The hour long CLV strip program comes from a video tape source and has bright colors, but the image is consistently soft and blurry. The monaural sound is poorly recorded. The show features close to a dozen acts, most of which are embellished with some sort of gimmick.

THE BOYS OF SUMMER

An oral history of the Brooklyn Dodgers which was made expressly for home video, *The Boys of Summer* is a lovely program, containing interviews with and about the core group of players who carried the team into respectability from 1947 until they were moved to LA in 1958. Our favorite reminiscence came from Carl Erskine, who tells how his father once got so involved in explaining the dynamics of a curveball that a cabinet full of china was destroyed. The Dodgers, of course, were the first team to include black players, and the pressures which this policy created are fascinating and inspiring.

BRADDOCK: MISSING IN ACTION III

Braddock: Missing in Action III is more consciously scripted than most Chuck Norris movies. The plot sends his Vietnam vet character, Braddock, back to retrieve a wife and child he didn't know he had. It moves almost too logically from one point to the next, diminishing any surprises in the fighting or the chases. The break between side one and side two, however, is a well chosen cliffhanger.

The volume levels on the analog track are often louder than on the digital track, but both have a disappointing murkiness which takes some of the fun out of the film. The night scenes don't have a confident look to them, and it is not until the end, where the chase and the explosions take place in the bright sunlight, that the disc starts to shape up. By then it is too late.

BRADY'S ESCAPE

John Savage portrays an American flyer shot down over Hungary during a World War II bombing run. His presence is not enough, however, to save *Brady's Escape* from the bargain bin. Having dropped into the midst of Nazi-hating Hungarian ranchers, Brady learns Hungarian, teaches a Hungarian kid English, trains a horse, and helps with the roundups.

The end credit roll reveals a crew which is almost entirely Hungarian. Filmed on location, the scenery is interesting and is reproduced on disc with all the fog-greyed colors in tact. The sound, on the other hand, is wimpy.

BRAHMS: PIANO CONCERTOS NOS. 1 & 2

The magnificent piano concertos of Johannes Brahms are available on *Brahms: Piano Concertos Nos. 1 & 2*. Presented by the Vienna Philharmonic, with Leonard Bernstein conducting and Krystian Zimerman on the piano, the music – always bright and always challenging – has been given a fine, sophisticated interpretation by the musicians. The sound on the disc is effective in bringing out full, rounded tones from the orchestra (the acoustics in the hall help) and compensate for the inevitable hiss which accompanies the live recording. The disc has chapters encoded for every movement (the concertos are split one to a side) and a decent pair of essays can be found on a jacket insert, which explain Brahms' efforts on the works. The picture, unfortunately, is noticeably grainy throughout, inhibiting one's visual concentration.

BRAHMS – SYMPHONY NO. 1 – WEBER – EURYANTHE: OUVERTURE

Filmed in Carnagie Hall, volume 6 of the 'Arturo Toscanini Collection,' *Brahms – Symphony No. 1 – Weber – Euryanthe: Ouverture* is a winning program all the way through. The cameras aren't always pointing where you want them to point, but the angles are varied and the images are consistently watchable. The recording is clear and yet is clearly in synch with the performers. Brahms is probably the least appreciated of all the great composers, but Toscanini's presentation – halfway between traditional and reinterpretive, according to the jacket notes – is supremely friendly without sacrificing the music's essential seriousness. It works exactly as Toscanini intended it to, and is probably the best introduction to Brahms an exploring listener could hope to discover.

BRAHMS: VIOLIN CONCERTO/ DOUBLE CONCERTO

Brahms: Violin Concerto/Double Concerto is a fun disc. Leonard Bernstein conducts the two works, 'Concerto for Violin and Orchestra in D Major, op. 77' and 'Concerto for Violin, Violoncello and Orchestra in A minor, op. 102,' (one per side) live, with the Vienna Philharmonic and soloists Gidon Kremer and Mischa Maisky. Brahms is like a blackjack dealer who shuffles the cards after every hand. His music is always surprising and yet steadfastly mature. He uses unexpected twists to challenge a listener's complacency; familiarity with his strategies broaden one's awareness of the world and the enigmatic patterns of life. The performance of these two concertos makes an excellent subject for a film, because the parts for the soloists are thoroughly integrated with the parts for the orchestra. The contrast on the stage is exciting, as the individuals give way to the group voice and then reclaim the floor. There is even a primitive looking zoom at one point as the cellist (Maisky) breaks into a cumulative passage.

The incongruity of the picture and the sound on the disc will be disturbing at first. The image is grainy and looks aged. The sound is so clear that it is hard to believe it was recorded at the same time, although a close observation of the soloists indicates that it was (there is a curiosity, the shadow of a sound boom waves across Kremer's head on the closeups, but the boom is nowhere to be seen on the long shots). The recording is excellent, and the visuals, even Bernstein, are so enjoyable they enhance the pleasure of the music.

BRAINSTORM (Import)

Originally intended to show off Douglas Trumbull's Showscan system, compromises led to *Brainstorm* being filmed in regular 70mm instead. When the film's point of view is omniscient, the screen size is the normal 1:1.66, but when a character places the machine on his head which allows him to experience prerecorded thoughts, the screen expands to 1:2.5. The disc is faithful to this formula. The normal scenes are shown in a box which sits in the center of the screen and the sides shoot to the edges only when the wide screen material appears.

Of course, the larger the screen, the more fun this is, but at least a record of Trumbull's intentions now exists. The picture is clear and nearly flawless. Some of the night sequences could have been lightened a bit, but the picture quality equals that of the best American discs.

The sound is in stereo throughout, but the intensity of the surround changes when the screen widens. The digital track is a little noisy, but not enough to be a point of contention.

The disc, a 'Collector's Item' series offering, is in CAV. We used the CAV functions a few times, particularly to replay a couple of the show-off sequences – a roller coaster ride and a jump off a highway – at different breathtaking speeds. The choices for chapter markers are clearly those of another culture. The roller coaster doesn't get one, but the credit roll memorial, "For Natalie," does.

BRANDED

The picture on *Branded*, an Alan Ladd western, shifts between sharp and fuzzy. When the image looks good the colors are rich and the presentation is pleasing. When the image looks soft, one's attention can start to wander. The sound is aged but passable. Ladd portrays a gunfighter who masquerades as the long lost son of a wealthy rancher and then has a change of heart when he meets the rancher's daughter. The action is minimal, but Ladd's character has a touch of moral ambiguity and the script moves things along at a satisfying pace.

BRANFORD MARSALIS STEEP

Interviews which separate the numbers in *Branford Marsalis Steep* are set at a lower volume than the music. It is a good thing, though, because the interviews are less disruptive to the flow of the program if one doesn't pay as close attention to them. Most involve well known personalities, such as Spike Lee, Danny DeVito and Sting, singing Marsalis' praises. This is fine, but not very informative.

The musical passages are clips from concerts in a number of different locales, but the digitally encoded stereo sound is consistently clear and fresh. Marsalis' quartet is recorded in a very directional manner, so that listeners can really get a concert-style feeling that the band is spread out before them. The program is 90 minutes long. The picture is grainy.

BRASS

A failed television pilot featuring Carroll O'Conner as a chief of detectives in New York City, *Brass*, nevertheless makes a fine feature program. The episode, designed for a two hour time slot, weaves three separate narratives together as the detective chief divides his time between major cases and administrative problems.

The color scheme is almost black and white, and looks pale. Some of that is conceptual, however, because the transfer is spotless, and the fleshtones are undistorted. The monaural sound is acceptable.

Brass uses a lot of real locations and real addresses, and has a no-nonsense feel to it (the paint is peeling in every office). O'Conner is engaging and it is a shame the program was recognized as being commercially unviable before the producers had a chance to sink more money into it and generate a few more memorable episodes.

BRASS TARGET

The robbery of many millions of dollars in gold and the death of General Patton are not enough to make *Brass Target* even moderately interesting. The large cast emphasizes the producer's lack of trust in the script. Only

Patrick McGoohan is enjoyable and he gets knocked off by 0:35.

For a mono disc, the sound quality is quite good and the picture is very sharp. It's just the movie that is dull.

BRAVO COMPANY – TOUR OF DUTY
(see **TOUR OF DUTY**)

BRAZIL
MCA has released the standard 131-minute version of *Brazil* with digital stereo surround sound. The colors are as perfect as your television allows. The quality of the sound lets one raise the volume high enough to catch many subtle, comical sound effects. The film's mixture of odd fantasy and social nightmare is an acquired taste, but it is a fascinating spectacle and is effectively delivered on disc.

BREAK EVERY RULE STARRING TINA TURNER
One of the formats used in several Tina Turner music videos was a mock stage show where she pretended to perform in front of a live audience. Now she has done a whole concert that way, entitled *Break Every Rule* starring Tina Turner . The audience consists of attractive models, of both sexes, pretending that her performance is sending them into a state of orgiastic euphoria. If we had been there, we'd probably have felt the same way. The set allows Turner to appear both dominant and intimate with her audience, and lets her get her moves just right on multiple takes. She sacrifices the sincerity and spontaneity of a truly live event, but she's been doing that for quite some time with her make up and her clothing anyway, so it is a natural progression.

The disc is an enjoyable hour of music and the sound is passable. Turner's recordings are rarely state-of-the-art efforts, but neither are her fans. The picture quality, since it was filmed under a controlled environment, is very good.

BREAKHEART PASS
For a cozy night with hot chocolate and marshmallows, you can't find much better entertainment than *Breakheart Pass*, a Charles Bronson movie with an Alistair MacLean script about nasty doings on a steam train which is chugging its way to a snowbound fort. Sure, the workmanship is a little shoddy (the footprints in the snow change from shot to shot; a car loaded with soldiers is seen breaking up on a cliff empty) and the plot doesn't make much sense, but the classic MacLean hooks are all in place, and to pace the plot twists there are all those gorgeous shots of the train puffing over snow-caked trestles. The film has an entertaining cast, including Jill Ireland, Ben Johnson, Charles Durning and Ed Lauter. To boot, it was probably the last movie in the world to use Indians as bad guys, and they chortle as they attack the train, just like in the old days.

The original advertising art is retained for the jacket cover and it looks great. The picture transfer is very good, though the cinematography is not as elegant as it could have been. Night scenes and snowy outdoor scenes survive without distortion. The sound is in acceptable condition. Jerry Goldsmith's standard western riffs can be heard on the soundtrack, which is most impressive during the opening credit sequence as the rhythm of the steam engine becomes a deliberate part of the musical score.

BREAKIN'
BEAT STREET
Why was *Breakin'* a hit and *Beat Street* a failure in the theaters? For one thing, *Beat Street* had to be filmed in the New York winter to be released to the summer market and its look – all cold and indoors – does not impart the sense of freedom songs of the street life are supposed to celebrate. *Breakin'* was filmed in Los Angeles, where seasons are irrelevant.

The sound on both discs is terrific, with *Beat Street* having maybe a bit stronger and more interesting mix. The picture is also sharp on both discs.

In the early summer of 1979, the Sugarhill Gang performed at a concert/dance in Brooklyn and a couple of weeks later you could not walk through Times Square on a Friday night without hearing 'Rapper's Delight' – which hadn't even been released by a real record company – booming from one or sometimes several portable cassette players. Listening to the words, it was possible to discern the folk tale/oral history roots of the art form, with the aa bb cc rhymes and the steady, pulsing meter. The best raps were also complex stories with food/sex imagery and questions of honor and duty. There was really no difference between these narratives and *Beowulf.*

Both *Beat Street* and *Breakin'* have sensational dance sequences. *Beat Street* also features lessons on despoiling public property with graffiti. *Beat Street* is worth watching. *Breakin'* is worth owning.

BREAKING IN
Bill Forsyth's *Breaking In* stars Burt Reynolds and is about a burglar who takes on an apprentice. The film is a lighthearted character study, less concerned about the heists than about the personalities of the two burglars. Not much happens, but the film is entertaining and even repeatable because Forsyth balances the characters and the humor without overplaying any one facet of the script. The picture is mildly grainy and mildly faded, with some reels looking a bit worn and other looking fine. The sound has a stereo musical score and a few surround sound effects. It, too, is light but effective.

BREAKOUT
The contribution of *Breakout* to the history of motion pictures was in the marketing rather than the artistic category. The Charles Bronson film, released in 1975, was the first to take advantage of the burgeoning multiplex theater craze, and to open at a large number of theaters at one time, supported by widespread television advertising. This is how virtually all major films are presented today. Hence, the movie's title has resonance which goes beyond its subject matter. The boxoffice success of *Breakout* signalled the opening of a new era in the way audiences learned about movies and were attracted to them.

The picture is mildly faded and has at least one splice, but looks passable. The sound is frustratingly flat, putting a damper on the enthusiastic Jerry Goldsmith music score.

Bronson's character is hired to extract a man from a Mexican prison, a job which he eventually completes, with the assistance of a helicopter. The script follows a set formula very closely. There are so many sex scenes, so many action sequences, and so many special effects, all paced to prevent a viewer's attention from wandering. It works, but if you've only seen the movie on broadcast TV, watch out for a rather shocking splatter effect near the end.

BREWSTER'S MILLIONS
A half dozen supporting players make *Brewster's Millions* so enjoyable that the main plot, which has Richard Pryor spending 30 million dollars, is easy to take. Pryor seems to be losing his touch. The director, Walter Hill, covers for him with a strong sense of what will and will not work with the farfetched premise. The transfer is very good but the stereo surround sound is not too interesting.

BRIAN'S SONG
The made-for-television athletics tearjerker, *Brian's Song*, has a pale color scheme and, except for some cleverly filmed football stadium sequences, a low budget look, though the source material has been transferred to disc without further impediments. The monaural sound, with Michel Legrand's irritating score, presents no significant problems. Side two of the 74-minute disc is in CAV, with two unsteady still frames out of every five.

Based on a true story, the film, which stars James Caan, Jack Warden, and an almost unrecognizable Billy Dee Williams, is about the friendship between two professional football players and the tragedy of a terminal illness. The script moves smoothly and is not affected by the lack of commercial interruptions, though the brief running time brings the basic teleplay structure into clear view. The above-television-level performances by the stars are what make the film so enduringly appealing.

THE BRIDE
QUADROPHENIA
Jennifer Beals is in traction at the opening of *The Bride* and you assume it is from the backflips she was doing in *Flashdance*. Sting unwraps her bandages and declares that she will be a modern woman. She hisses at him.

The disc is grainy, but not unduly so. The sound is in Dolby Surround and effective as far as that goes. Franc Roddam once made a very nice movie about coming of age in the early '60s, *Quadrophenia* (the picture and sound transfers to disc, however, were awful), and he showed a good sense for knowing how an audience feels about the characters on the screen. *The Bride* splits into two plots and you can see how Roddam gravitates toward the better story – a 'Mice and Men' adventure involving Frankenstein's monster and a dwarf – than toward the scenes involving the two stars who do nothing but envy each other's wardrobes. The movie is mostly boring, so that you're muttering 'O Sting, where is thy death?' long before it actually occurs.

THE BRIDE OF FRANKENSTEIN
Despite its age, *The Bride of Frankenstein* is blushingly clear of deterioration and the CX-

encoded sound is as clean as could be expected. Since the movie runs but 75 minutes, side two of the MCA Home Video Encore Edition release is in CAV. The pressing is sharp and flawless.

Bride is the sequel to the original *Frankenstein*. The first thing one notices when they are played in order is that, after the Lac Leman opening, women are in the mob chasing the monster. In *Frankenstein*, the mob was exclusively male. The shift is intriguing. Did the director think no one would notice?

A BRIDGE TOO FAR

The smaller your video screen, the more you will enjoy MGM/UA's Deluxe Letter-Box Edition release of the star-studded World War II movie, *A Bridge Too Far*. The picture has an aspect ratio of about 2.25:1, and if the viewing area is small enough, the television antennas on the rooftops beyond the Arnheim Bridge no longer jut annoyingly into the proceedings. You no longer worry that the parachutes, which at times fill the screen like clusters of jellyfish in the sky, are going to get caught on them.

The picture transfer on the disc is okay. There are sequences where the image is weak, looking grainy or a bit washed out, but there are other sequences which look terrific. The letterboxing is a necessity because the movie's two strongest assets, its cast and its battle sequences, would be excised without it. Who wants to look at Ryan O'Neal, even when he's talking, if Sean Connery is in the same shot? Subtitles for the German and Dutch dialog appear beneath the image.

There isn't much in the way of surround effects, but the directional stereo separations are quite active. Some of the dialog is a bit low in volume, but the many explosions, gun shots, and tank engines make up for it. The 178-minute film has been fit onto three sides and an entr'acte appears in the middle of side two.

Since *Bridge* tells the story of a poorly conceived and partially unsuccessful military campaign, it lacks a unifying spirit of patriotic enthusiasm, and since it was directed by Richard Attenborough, it is a bit clunky even in the best sequences. However, it is still a big-budgeted World War II action picture, with stars from Elliot Gould to Robert Redford showing up right when they are sorely needed. If they can get around the TV antennas then so can the viewer.

BRIDGES AT TOKO-RI

One of Paramount's rah-rah Armed Services recruitment efforts from the fifties, *Bridges at Toko-Ri*, bears many similarities to *Strategic Air Command*. The colors look very good, the plot is a dull pastiche of incidents with no real drama until the final third, and the CX-encoded monaural sound has inconsistencies in volume. Since the film was not a widescreen effort, cropping is not a problem. Highpoints include a nude bathing scene with Grace Kelly and all that hardware which the Navy provided, gratis, under the assumption that young men in the audience would run right out of the theater and sign up to work on an aircraft carrier and take baths with Grace. In demonstration of the film's sloppy dramatic construction, much is made in a scene about the entrance of a carrier into a Japanese harbor without the assistance of tugboats. Yet, when the carrier leaves, to the bittersweet beckoning of a now fully clothed Grace, there are tugboats in clear view, helping it out. Paramount had such little faith in the material that an apprentice copywriter was assigned to do the jacket text, producing more entertainment than the film itself: "Also starring Grace Kelly as his loving, luminescent wife." Just what we always wanted – a glow-in-the-dark spouse.

BRIGADOON
BRIGADOON (Remastered)
BRIGADOON (Letterboxed)

MGM/UA released three versions of *Brigadoon*. The first reissue of the title has the same catalog number as MGM/UA's initial release, but the film was transferred from a new master, with digital sound and a few more chapter markers. Later, MGM/UA released a Deluxe Letter-Box Edition of the film.

The film was made with Ansco color instead of the more reliable Technicolor, and there is just so much which can be done with it. Since costumes and art direction seem to constitute one half of the appeal of a Vincente Minnelli film, even the best transfer will seem dry and sleepy. Having logged that consideration, let us say that the color transfer on the letterboxed disc is lovely, and that the color scheme of the movie, in its own way, is haunting. The digital stereo sound, though affected by the age of the recording, is terrific. The picture on the earliest release was too dark, and the analog sound was less accomplished, but the second cropped release is closer in picture and sound quality to the letterboxed version.

The presentation of the film in letterboxed format makes a significant improvement over the scanned version. In practically every shot the movie gains magic and lyricism from the added picture information on the sides of the screen. The choreography is enhanced the most, but of nearly the same importance are the soundstage sets, some of which contain amazingly illusionary vistas that are completely lost when the edges are dropped. Minnelli's careful balancing of colors is restored by the letterboxing, and Van Johnson gets more screen time, which adds to the impact of his role and brings more sense to his character.

We like *Brigadoon*. It is not a great movie, but it is a nice one. However, whenever we sit through it, we can't stop our mind from wandering, and imagining a comedy skit, 'Brigadoon II: The Following Week,' where a succession of crazier and crazier characters wander into the village as each day progresses. The movie is just ineffectual enough that you can daydream without missing anything important and still enjoy the songs.

BRIGHT LIGHTS, BIG CITY

The main character in *Bright Lights, Big City* is played by Michael J. Fox. He doesn't embarrass himself in the role, though he is shown taking drugs and living an undisciplined existence. The movie is passable entertainment on the strength of Fox's modifying influence – almost any other actor would have gone too far over the edge and ruined the whole thing. (The character is never punished for his drug use.) The movie is glamorous and a bit silly, narrated in the second person, and contains an hysterical gem of a walk-on by John Houseman.

The disc's finest component is the digital stereo sound, though that is silly too since the music is so separated stereophonically that it is like two different scores, one playing on each speaker. The picture is a little blurry and has a few white speckles. The break between side one and side two occurs about thirty seconds after a natural, title card pause.

BRIGHTON BEACH MEMOIRS

The sound on *Brighton Beach Memoirs* is impressive. Although the film is not in stereo, the sound is more realistic and immediate than many stereo soundtracks. Every detail is captured and reproduced with precision — the cracks in Judith Ivey's voice when she screams, the music, footsteps, and the dishes in the sink. On side two there is a rollerskate hockey game which escapes the confines of one's audio video equipment. Since the sounds which have been engineered with such great care are not the sounds one normally associates with showing off a sound system, the disc can make for an entertaining demonstration. Blythe Danner rattling the pots is not Tom Cruise taking off from an aircraft carrier, but the results are equally sophisticated and Danner's activities are a lot more surprising.

The picture quality is in good condition and the movie is hard to dislike, although it may just have been that the quality of the sound made us more amenable to the material. Neil Simon's mildly autobiographical story is a predictable mixture of memory and cliché, but it is well intentioned and contains a witty collection of one-liners.

BRINGING UP BABY/SYLVIA SCARLET (Import)
SYLVIA SCARLET

Numerous double features of old RKO titles have been released in Japan. They are presented in the disc packaging as a real double feature, with the second platter holding the second movie, marked with 'Side Three' and 'Side Four,' and the running time on the jacket represents the combined running times of the two films. The title pairings match common revival house combinations.

We managed to get a hold of *Bringing Up Baby/Sylvia Scarlet*. Of course, in the privacy of your own home, you don't have to watch the two movies together, but in keeping with the spirit of the packaging, that was what we did.

And it helped us tolerate *Sylvia Scarlet*, a film which usually has us running for the exits after thirty minutes or so. 'Bringing Up Baby' is an entertaining screwball comedy with odd but amusing performances by Katharine Hepburn and Cary Grant. Delightful innuendo and double entendres are generated when Hepburn's wildcat, 'Baby,' gets loose and when Grant, a paleontologist, loses his 'bone.' *Scarlet* is more like an Ingmar Bergman movie, about the foibles and angst of a travelling performance troupe, and although it features Grant and Hepburn (it was made two years before 'Baby,' and both stars receive lower billing than Edmund Gwenn), neither are terribly appealing. When tacked onto the tail end of 'Baby,' however, the program has more to offer, because when the first film ends you still haven't gotten enough of the two stars, and it isn't until the end of the second show that you feel satiated.

Each of the four sides has about four chapter markers. Neither movie is CX-encoded. The black and white prints are not of archival quality. 'Baby' looks the best. It has rich, bright contrasts, but also sports a few scratches and splices. *Scarlet* is more blurry and has its own scratches. After the first ten minutes or so, we hardly noticed the Japanese subtitles on either movie. *Scarlet* is also available domestically with a picture and sound transfer which is no better than the Japanese effort.

BRITNY FOX: YEAR OF THE FOX

The heavy metal group, Britny Fox, is represented by four music videos and a bit of commentary on *Britny Fox: Year of the Fox*. The disc runs less than a half-hour and is in CAV, with two unsteady still frames out of every five. The picture quality is fairly good and the still function creates a number of worthy profiles for fans. The best clip is 'Girlschool,' an amusing video about a classroom which is liberated by rock 'n roll. Both the songs and the interludes are chapter encoded. The stereo sound has a decent bass and is reasonably clear.

BROADCAST NEWS

The digital soundtrack on *Broadcast News* is much cleaner than the analog soundtrack. Early press runs of the disc were extensively flawed, so beware if you come across a copy which has been sitting around for a while. The picture transfer is reasonably decent.

Broadcast News is a film which is difficult to categorize, other than to say it involves people who work for a network news program and that it is funny. The characters are insecure in an exaggerated sort of way, and television news (which provides an excellent supplement to printed news) is predictably criticized for its lack of depth and detail. The component which comes under the strongest attack is the news anchorman, whose responsibility is actually that of a master of ceremonies, but who has come to represent, in terms of income, the pinnacle of American journalism. We don't really see what's wrong, but we enjoyed the movie, anyway. The ending has come under vehement criticism for being evasive and lacking in crescendo, but it seems in keeping with the flow of the film, since the movie is more enjoyable for its scenes than for its narrative.

BROADWAY MELODY OF 1940

To say that *Broadway Melody of 1940* is one of the better Fred Astaire movies is to say that it is outstanding, because even his run-of-the-mill films are worthy accomplishments. He stars with Eleanor Powell, who makes a sympathetic partner for him and is no slouch as a dancer herself. The plot is simple, concerning mistaken identities and the chance to achieve stardom in a Broadway show, but it moves at a brisk pace and gives just the right amount of breathing room between dance numbers. There is also a cute specialty act involving a juggler.

The black and white picture is in fine condition throughout and the sound has no significant problems. There are also plenty of chapter markers and plenty of sequences worth marking. The music is by Cole Porter.

BRONCO BILLY

Clint Eastwood's direction is mechanically competent but often lacks the kind of artistic vision needed to give viewers a sense of consistency and a reason to pay attention. In *Bronco Billy*, however, Eastwood stumbled onto an appealing concept that he could focus on, and he really seems to be directing the film from more than a page of script at a time. *Billy* belongs in the 'madcap heiress romantic comedy' genre, though it could also be classified in the more European 'tribulations-of-small-time-travelling-show-people' category. Perhaps it can't be classified at all, for it is a unique and genuinely pleasing film. Eastwood's shortcomings as a director actually work to his advantage in *Billy*, because a more enthusiastic helmsman would not have wanted to trust that the script already contains the necessary elements for success. The same goes for Sondra Locke, who plays the heiress. Her simplified emotions and body movements are more in keeping with film acting styles of the thirties, but what the heck – who doesn't like movies from the thirties? The artificial stereo effects are bothersome and the picture is a little fuzzy.

BRONSKI BEAT – THE FIRST CHAPTER (Import)

The 8-inch Japanese release, *Bronski Beat – The First Chapter* has a terrific picture although the four numbers have been split two to a side so that the first side runs nine minutes and the second, ten. You barely get settled in before it is time to flip the disc over. The songs featured on the program are 'Smalltown Boy,' 'Why?,' 'It Ain't Necessarily So' (yes, the Gershwin song), and a medley of 'Love to Love You Baby,' 'I Feel Love,' and 'Johnnie Remember Me.' The videos tend to march to a different drummer and are free of clichés. A lyric sheet, in English, is included with the disc.

BRONSON DEATH WISH 4: THE CRACKDOWN

The plot of *Bronson Death Wish 4: The Crackdown* is tighter than its predecessors and the direction, from J. Lee Thompson, is also improved, but the movie has an inferiority complex. The film looks cheap and awkward, as if everyone expects the *Death Wish* movies to live up to their patronym in quality as well as body counts. The picture is often grainy and the colors blend together too readily. The stereo sound is digitally encoded, but it is uninteresting except for the fine jazz score.

THE BROOD

Of David Cronenberg's earlier films, *The Brood* is essentially the strongest. It has the best combination of narrative and gruesome horror. The special effects are frightening, but the inventions aren't overused, and are only employed to move the story forward.

The film was made on a small budget and lacks polish, but other than a few scratches, the picture has accurate if yellowish colors and a sharp focus. The sound is lightweight, but has no noticeable flaws.

The story revolves around a woman committed to an unusual psychiatric institution run by a shady doctor. The woman's husband and daughter are terrorized by creatures reacting to the woman's mood swings. Cronenberg's filmmaking style is accomplished, even with his limited production finances, and however silly the movie may seem in retrospect, the sense of discovery guiding the viewer through the heat of it makes no allowances for needless contemplation.

BRUCE SPRINGSTEEN/VIDEO ANTHOLOGY/1978-88

The disadvantage is that there aren't any other Bruce Springsteen laser discs, but the advantage is that *Bruce Springsteen/Video Anthology/1978-88*, packs a decade's worth of high points into a single 100-minute program. Like Springsteen's own physique, there's not an ounce of fat on the entire disc. The program is a collection of 19 (chapter encoded) music videos. Some are simple concert performances while others have been directed by Brian De Palma and John Sayles. Presented chronologically, the earliest segments are a little grainy, but the recent material is spotless. Except for his acoustical stuff, Springsteen's music is the sort which survives tiny AM automobile speakers without losing its essence, so there is little the disc could do to harm it. In fact, the digitally encoded stereo sounds terrific.

BRUCKNER – SYMPHONY NO.7

George Solti conducts the Chicago Symphony Orchestra in London's grand Royal Albert Hall on *Bruckner – Symphony No.7*. A six-minute interview with Solti precedes the concert. He tells of how he came to appreciate the modest works of Anton Bruckner, and how he approaches Bruckner's music. The music is divided in half on the disc, the first two movements appearing on side one and the second two movements on side two. Solti seems excited about the performance and conducts with an earnest intensity. The picture quality is fair, with the plush red velvet seats in Albert Hall being subject to a slight blurring effect. The sound makes good use of the hall's acoustics. A jacket insert accompanying the disc contains an essay which reiterates much of what Solti has to say in the interview.

BRYAN ADAMS – RECKLESS

The CLV *Bryan Adams – Reckless* is only 26 minutes long. Most of the six music videos are quasi-concert performances. The opening number, 'This Time,' is the most elaborate concept video, a standard search-for-the-girl-in-the-demolished-building piece filmed without flair in black-and-white.

BUCK PRIVATES

The Bud Abbott and Lou Costello comedy, *Buck Privates*, improves significantly when given the MCA 'Encore Edition' treatment. At 84 minutes, the disc is CLV on side one and CAV on side two. After the film is concluded, the original theatrical trailer appears, followed by nine lobby cards and 100 promotional stills. The disc also has chapter markers for each of the musical numbers.

The print has a few scratches and breaks but is in good, bright condition over all. Highlights include a scene featuring Costello and Shemp Howard, which is usually dropped when the film is broadcast on local television, and the Andrews Sisters singing 'I'll Be with You in Apple Blossom Time' and 'Boogie

Woogie Bugle Boy.' The CAV provides an excellent opportunity to observe phony movie punches, especially during a comical boxing match. There are also a few explosions and a couple of elaborate dance routines to run backwards and forwards.

To have the advertising materials on the same disc as the film itself is cake and icing for motion picture enthusiasts. The still collection is rich with portraits of the leads and setups which are not seen in the show.

THE BUDDY HOLLY STORY

The picture on *The Buddy Holly Story* has an orange/pink tint. A slight, vertical white line is present on part of the first side, as well, but the source actually looks as though it is in good condition, or it was before they turned it into a disc. The analog sound is also imperfect, but the film's stereo mix is excellent.

Holly's music has achieved a sort of 'Ur' status in the annals of rock and roll. Gary Busey plays Holly in the film and sings the songs with the same primal immediacy which the original recordings possessed. The story is curiously vacant of insight, which may be why the film ended up being a boxoffice failure. Almost every other aspect of the movie, however, is, like the spirit of the music, near perfection.

BUFFET FROID

The front jacket cover for *Buffet Froid* implies that the movie is a thriller, but it was directed by Bertrand Blier, whose films are not so easily categorized. Starring Gerard Depardieu, Bernard Blier, and Jean Carmet, the film is a collection of absurd incidents, many involving murder. It is not a very good movie, though it improves a little on multiple viewings, after one is prepared for the illogical narrative and frivolous emotions. Blier has given the film a very elegant look and the look is sustained on the disc, which has a nice picture transfer. The image appears both solid and fresh. The digitally encoded monaural sound is fine, and the movie is in French with yellow English subtitles that still get lost in bright white backgrounds.

BUGS BUNNY CLASSICS

Yosemite Sam, train robber, stands square in the tracks, guns drawn, as a locomotive speeds toward him. The engine, with no signs of stopping, comes closer, and closer, until it passes right over the top of Sam, who is as short as he is ornery. He turns after it passes, slightly perplexed, places his revolvers in his holsters, and runs to his horse to try again. This is but a sample of the many pleasures to be found on *Bugs Bunny Classics*, a new two-sided MGM/UA release which contains 14 cartoons from the forties, all of them dandies. Only one, 'Hare-Raising Hare,' has appeared on disc previously. All show Bugs in high form and extract steady humor from his antagonistic co-stars.

The opening cartoon, 'The Heckling Hare,' is a classic depiction of Bugs frustrating a hunting dog. He also frustrates an Indian in a similar piece, 'A Feather in His Hare.' Another dog appears in 'Hare Force,' annoyed at Bugs for sharing his spot by a fire in an old lady's house. It is not as good as the others (and looks blurrier). Bugs battles a group of street dogs in 'A Hare Grows in Manhattan,' however, with great comical success. A close approximation of Edward G. Robinson, along with that of Peter Lorre, show up in 'Racketeer Rabbit,' battling Bugs for the use of an abandoned house. Another high point is 'Acrobatty Bunny,' in which Bugs frustrates a circus lion. Yosemite Sam appears as described above in 'Hare Trigger,' and also weighs in as a pirate in 'Buccaneer Bunny,' which is equally entertaining, and in 'Bugs Bunny Rides Again,' another western-themed effort that is weaker than the others. 'Haredevil Hare' sends Bugs to the moon where he prevents the Martian with the brush on his helmet from bombing Earth. Bugs makes Elmer think he is sick and seeing spots in 'Hare Tonic,' and frustrates Elmer's attempt to catch the Easter Bunny in 'Easter Yeggs.'

The individual transfers look okay, though none look stunning. Yosemite's red hair has a mild halo, as do some other strong colors, and it also changes hue from shot to shot. There are mild shifts in volume levels among the individual cartoons. MGM/UA has chapter encoded the disc, but a mix-up on the jacket cover lists the cartoon which opens side two as being on the end of side one.

BUGS! & ELMER! DAFFY! & PORKY!

A treasure trove of old Warner cartoons has been made available on discs from MGM/UA. The original Technicolor and Cinecolor prints look spotless and have been transferred to disc without distortion, though on some cartoons intense reds appear mildly unstable. A few gags are lost to top and side edge trimmings. Every cartoon is chapter marked and the sound presents no problems beyond the expected, age-generated scratchiness.

The Bugs Bunny in the seven shorts on side one of *Bugs! & Elmer!* is not the Bugs Bunny most viewers know and love. His features are hard, and he lacks resourcefulness, even to the point where he is beaten in a race by a tortoise in two cartoons, 'Tortoise Wins by a Hare' and 'Rabbit Transit.' He fares better in 'Baseball Bugs,' single-handedly defeating a tough opposing ball team, but ends in a draw against the Three Bears in 'Bugs Bunny and the Three Bears,' against a buzzard in 'Bugs Bunny Gets the Boid,' against an unstoppable hunting dog in 'Hare Ribbin',' and against an amusingly macho monkey in 'Gorilla My Dreams.' In some of these, you can see the cartoonists were experimenting with characters under consideration for stardom, but the versatility of the Bugs Bunny character remains consistent, even in his earliest manifestations.

The Elmer Fudd cartoons on side two are more varied and funnier. Many are actually Bugs Bunny or Daffy Duck cartoons in which Elmer has a principal role. In the most amusing cartoon on the disc, 'The Hare Brained Hypnotist,' Elmer the hunter tries to hypnotize Bugs, but his plans backfire. Bugs also appears in 'The Wabbit Who Came to Supper,' 'The Wacky Wabbit,' and 'Elmer's Candid Camera,' while Daffy appears in 'What Makes Daffy Duck?' and 'A Pest in the House.' In 'Goodnight, Elmer,' Fudd battles a candle which won't let him sleep.

The cartoons on *Daffy! & Porky!* are a little shorter, and so eight are featured per side. Daffy's character has remained more stable over the years than that of the other characters, and the collection on side one is the most pleasing on both discs. Included are 'Slightly Daffy,' in which Daffy and Porky hold down a fort against an Indian attack; an imaginative and surreal 'Book Revue' which adapts puns and comic sketches from the titles of famous books; 'Daffy Duck in Hollywood,' filled with insider gags; 'The Great Piggy Bank Robbery,' in which Daffy becomes 'Duck Twacy'; the mildly racist 'Mexican Joyride'; 'The Upstanding Sitter,' in which Daffy baby-sits a baby punk; 'Daffy Duck and Egghead,' an early manifestation of the Daffy and Elmer Fudd characters; and 'Yankee Doodle Daffy,' in which Daffy is a would-be performer pestering Porky the talent agent.

Porky originated as part of a 'Little Rascals' take off, and one of those cartoons, 'I Haven't Got a Hat!' opens side two of the disc. There is then a digression, 'I Love to Singa,' an amusing lampoon of 'The Jazz Singer' with owls, but no Porky. Porky gets to practice baby-sitting in 'Brother Brat,' attempts to discourage an overly eager would-be pet in 'Little Orphan Airedale,' and battles a family of cats for possession of a house in 'Kitty Kornered.' 'Daffy Doodles' is a classic in which Porky, as a cop, attempts to capture Daffy, a vandal who is drawing mustaches on every face in the city. The opening of 'Baby Bottleneck,' is hysterical. The stork goes on strike, causing babies to be delivered to the wrong parents. Porky and Daffy then attempt to take over the business. The final cartoon, 'My Favorite Duck,' appeared with less intense colors on *Bugs Bunny Superstar*.

One final note: While the Warner cartoon factory traditionally played Daffy Duck/Donald Duck to Walt Disney's Bugs Bunny/Mickey Mouse in terms of status, there was one aspect in which Warner will always be decidedly superior – incidental music. While Disney's characters were forever stuck whistling 'Zip-A-Dee-Doo-Dah,' Warner's characters can be heard humming everything from 'We're in the Money' to the theme from *Now Voyager*.

BUGS AND DAFFY: THE WARTIME CARTOONS

Eleven Warner cartoons from 1943 and 1944 appear on *Bugs and Daffy: The Wartime Cartoons*. Leonard Maltin introduces some of the cartoons but never remains on the screen for too long. MGM/UA has provided a listing of chapters on the back of the jacket, but the disc itself has not been chapter encoded. The picture transfer is very nice, and though Maltin sometimes looks a little blurry, all of the cartoons are sharp and colorful. The sound has no significant problems.

The cartoons are surprisingly watchable for so era-specific a subject, and even young children will enjoy them. Only the first one, 'The Weakly Reporter,' is a generic War Bonds rally. Bugs Bunny meets Hermann Goering in the Black Forest ("I knew I should have turned left at Albuquerque.") in 'Herr Meets Hare,' but Goering is just one more buffoon for Bugs to exasperate. Bugs also appears in an amusing takeoff, 'Little Red Riding Rabbit,' in which Little Red Riding Hood has a noticeable bust and a loud mouth, in 'Super Rabbit,' which pits him, empowered by super carrots, against a bloodthirsty Texas rancher, and in 'Falling Hare,' in which Bugs comes up on the short end of a battle against a gremlin. The gremlins take over in 'Russian Rhapsody,' the most elaborate and strongest cartoon on the disc. Adolf Hitler himself is the villain, flying a bombing run to Moscow which is foiled by a lively soviet of miniature troublemakers.

Daffy Duck can be seen trying to avoid the inescapable draft in 'Draftee Daffy' (he even tries to hide in Hell, to no avail), trying to avoid a female spy in 'Plane Daffy,' and battling the enemy in his own immitigable fashion in 'Daffy the Commando.' (There is a touch of nudity in this latter cartoon, on the far right, at 42:53.) Animation in the latter is particularly strong.

Rounding out the disc are a Porky Pig effort about chickens falling for roosters who have pop singer similarities, 'Swooner Crooner,' and an early Sylvester manifestation, 'Fifth Column Mouse,' in which a group of mice learn the hard way the folly of capitulating to the cat's demands.

BUGS BUNNY SUPERSTAR
The feature film, *Bugs Bunny Superstar*, was partly responsible for rekindling interest in the Warner Looney Tunes/Merrie Melodies cartoons. Not that they had faded from the public consciousness, but general interest in Bugs Bunny, Daffy Duck, and the gang had stalled in the early seventies, and might have diminished further if this film had not appeared. Instead, the ball started rolling again, and today, new, theatrical-quality cartoon shorts are being produced, using the characters and the surviving artists.

The film, a sole representative of MGM/UA's Cartoon Moviestars series, presents most of nine cartoons, linked with documentary material about the Warner cartoon factory narrated by Orson Welles. One may feel impatient with the fill material on first viewing, when one is anxious to view the cartoons, but on subsequent viewings the footage is surprisingly repeatable. The first pair of cartoons are in a weak condition. The sound, which is CX-encoded monaural on the disc, sputters furiously. The subsequent cartoons, however, are in a lot better shape, and pose little problem for the viewer. On all, the color lacks the immediacy which the well-preserved Disney shorts possess, and the lines are a little soft, but joy in the program material overcomes any resistance to their presentation. It is good enough.

The disc has not been given chapter markers. The nine cartoons are 'What's Cookin', Doc?,' 'A Wild Hare,' 'I Taw a Putty Tat,' 'Walky Talky Hawky,' 'The Old Grey Hare,' 'My Favorite Duck.' and 'Hair Raising Hare.' As can be garnered from the titles, the programs feature not only Bugs and his nemesis, Elmer Fudd, but Daffy Duck and Porky Pig, Sylvester and Tweetie, and Foghorn Leghorn.

BUJONES – IN HIS IMAGE
(see **FONTEYN & NUREYEV: THE PERFECT PARTNERSHIP**)

BULL DURHAM
The first two-thirds of *Bull Durham* is fantastic and although by the time of the seventh-inning stretch the story is basically finished, the mop up operation doesn't stop the movie from being a winner. It is rare that a film about baseball actually plays as baseball literature or the best color commentary, and rarer still that it can do so and still appeal to a wide audience. *Durham* is amazingly innovative, with a gutsy, voice-over stream-of-consciousness which not only tells one what the players are thinking on the mound or at the plate, but really, accurately sounds like the voice in one's head during such moments. The non-sex parts of the plot use the standard coach-takes-raw-talent-and-grows-while-processing-it genre, but disguises it by changing the coach into just another player. As for the sex, well everyone knows you're suppose to think about baseball...and *Bull Durham* is home video that was designed with rainouts in mind.

The disc looks great, with no major problems and nothing to distract one from the joys of the film itself. The stereo is generally saved for the music soundtrack and the always impressive ballpark PA echoes, and poses no problems. The disc has a healthy number of chapter markers but it would need many more to capture every highlight.

BULLETPROOF
"Gary Busey is *Bulletproof*," claims the opening title card, as well as the jacket cover. Maybe so, but the plot is full of holes. *Bulletproof* will please viewers who enjoy gun battles, but the script deserves some sort of prize for reaching a previously uncharted peak in stupidity. We still can't believe it, but the story is about a Latin American and Arab terrorist camp, supported by the Russians, which is located a few miles south of the Texas border, in northern Mexico. That's just the start. The US army has a new high-tech tank loaded with special equipment which, unlike the Sergeant York in real life, actually works. So, the military deliberately transports the tank across the Mexican border so the terrorist group can capture it, because one of the officers assigned to the transportation unit is female and was once romantically involved with Busey's character. The reason, apparently, is to coax Busey into coming out of retirement so he can wipe out the camp. Did we miss anything? Oh yes, the head terrorist is a Libyan who takes an immediate liking to the heroine, particularly after she bites him and calls him all sorts of bad names. To show his respect, he treats her to a romantic candlelight dinner before he rapes her. Ah, the movies truly are bulletproof if they can get away with stuff like this.

The disc is in reasonably decent shape. It is doubtful those compelled to obtain it will mind the minor blur which appears in the most intense colors or the slightly yellowed look which the skin tones sometimes develop. The Ultra Stereo sound has a few surround effects and gets the job done.

BULLIES
The concept has become so stale and predictable that movies like *Bullies* aren't even fun anymore. The MCA release is about a family who terrorizes a small town until a newcomer stands up to them, gets the living daylights beat out of him for the effort, and then justifiably homicides them all in return. It was filmed in Canada, so the scenery is pretty and the film stock is cheap. The sound is passable. One of these days, maybe they'll make a movie where the bullies win.

BULLITT
Bullitt takes place over a Mother's Day weekend. We first saw the movie during adolescence and responded to it more fanatically than we ever had to any other film, though it was not until 15 years later and a passing knowledge of Freud that we discovered why.

The action scenes are spectacular – the movie won an Oscar for editing – but it is the relationship Bullitt (Steve McQueen) maintains between the father figure (Robert Vaughn, who actually threatens to castrate him at one point) and the mother figure (Jacqueline Bisset) which clearly cements a young viewer's identification with the rebellious hero. Bisset, portraying Bullitt's girlfriend, is so safely sequestered from the other men in the film that she never shares a scene with anyone but McQueen.

Warners has done a beautiful job restoring the film. The picture has a slight graininess which one can associate with its age, but the colors are exact and no other blemishes appear. The sound is ideal. The reprocessing enhances the vividness of the sound effects and every instrument performing Lalo Schifrin's score. There are only a few separations – sirens crossing from left to right and that sort of thing – but the whole movie has a heightened thrust which it never had before, even in theaters.

This is most effective in the great car chase sequence, and one quickly realizes that another reason why the chase has never been equalled lies in the sounds being used for the car engines, points of friction, and aerodynamics. Much of what the director, Peter Yates, is trying to pass off as linear sequencing is actually the same take from three different cameras (watch for the green VW). The chase provides a free-flying thrill, a feeling that movies, like dreams, can do anything.

THE 'BURBS
The sound editing during the opening ten minutes of *The 'Burbs* is superb, and throughout the film Jerry Goldsmith's jokey score is enlivened by the quality of the audio mix.

The film's title is too broad and somewhat misleading, since the story is about a group of neighbors wondering what is going on in one of the houses on their cul-de-sac. Because the film was directed by Joe Dante it has a number of inspired comic touches (two grown men whine like six-year-olds when the wife of a third won't let him join them) and a weird, or at times even harsh, point of view. Tom Hanks stars, but the most enjoyable performances are registered by Corey Feldman, who functions rather amusingly as an audience surrogate, and Carrie Fisher, because one rarely sees her draped so in normalcy. The film is more mainstream than any of the advertising had implied and is one of Dante's least challenging but most amiable efforts.

BURGLAR
Lesley Ann Warren almost steals *Burglar* from Whoopi Goldberg, although we could live without one of the scenes they do together, a dentist and patient bit which adds nothing new to vaudevillian tradition. The movie is great fun. Goldberg portrays a burglar who witnesses a murder while she is rifling an apartment. The story is tight enough to get by, and there is a super streets-of-San Francisco car chase. The disc looks sharp and

has an excellent stereo soundtrack. Warner has failed to include chapter markers, but has otherwise pulled off an admirable job.

BURKE AND WILLS

Nothing overly cinematic happens in *Burke and Wills*, despite the many dream sequences (parched explorers thinking their loved ones are near) and potentially scenic vistas. The film is a dramatization of the first successful effort by European Australians to cross their continent from south to north, braving the uninhabitable, endless stretch of ancient seabed.

Perhaps it is the loss of the widescreen, or the limited conflict created by the constraints of the material, but not enough happens in *Burke and Wills* to encourage multiple viewings. One run through of the 141-minute film provides all of the historical and anthropological (Victorian era Australians as a subject) information one could possibly require. Repeating the journey a second time is probably not something even Mr. Burke or Mr. Wills would have wanted to do. (They couldn't anyway. They both die.)

The disc has a severely grainy picture. Although a little on the tinny side, the stereo separations are inventive and the soundtrack is the most entertaining component of the film.

BURNING SECRET

We were surprised to discover that we enjoyed *Burning Secret*, a film starring Faye Dunaway and Klaus Maria Brandauer which was preceded by so much adverse publicity that it had all the earmarks of a stinker. It isn't. The narrative, based on a short story by Stefan Zweig, is told through the eyes of a young boy, who witnesses his mother's infidelity when the two visit an Austrian spa (not Vienna as the largely erroneous jacket copy suggests). The reported tension between Dunaway and Brandauer works perfectly on the screen, creating an atmosphere of furtive nervousness which is not the least inappropriate for the situation. The film is not by any means brilliant, but it is a competent and admirable accomplishment which should please those who like snowy Continental dramas with elegant settings.

The disc is also a decent accomplishment. The picture has a minimum of grain despite a number of problematic lighting conditions, and the film itself has a richly polished look. Surround effects are limited to the music, but the score is lovely. Composed by Hans Zimmer, it is a rip-off of Ennio Morricone's work right down to the pan flutes. Scholars, however, can argue about its derivations – the music envelops one's viewing area and creates a relaxed mood, allowing the story to unfold in an aura of peaceful accommodation.

THE BURNS AND ALLEN SHOW – VOLUME 1

Others will say Catherine Deneuve, or Diana Rigg, or Vanna White. To our way of thinking though, if we were asked to choose the 'ideal' or 'perfect woman,' it would be Gracie Allen. Gracie is both independent and loving and she is more calculating than crazy, having insulated herself from the inanities of contemporary society without losing her freedom.

RCA/Columbia's *The Burns and Allen Show – Volume 1*, not only contains the original episodes (two episodes on a single-sided disc), it also has the original BF Goodrich commercials. With an hysterical emphasis on phony and even falsified science, the tire and floor tile commercials are almost as amusing as the shows themselves.

RCA/Columbia has not provided chapter markers and has not CX-encoded the disc, which, of course, is in black-and-white. The jacket cover contains no information on the history of the episodes and even merges the cast listing instead of providing the credits for each show separately.

The initial episode features Sheldon Leonard as a gangster who comes to the Burns household to eliminate George, but quickly finds himself in an apron, drying dishes for Gracie. ("You dry them now," she tells him, "I'll wash them later.") In the second show, Gracie talks herself into believing that she and George were not married by a legitimate justice of the peace and George must enlist the help of Jack Benny to convince her otherwise.

BUS STOP

The Cinemascope picture in *Bus Stop* is hopelessly cropped, but at least vestiges of the original Technicolor colors are still accessible. The sound is passable.

Bus Stop is a play, about a rodeo contestant who falls for a bar girl. You have to be able to tolerate Don Murray, Arthur O'Connell and the plays of William Inge to get through it, but ultimately it is a nice little love story and the star, Marilyn Monroe, is captivating. She wears a skimpy green cocktail outfit through most of act I which would stand out even without the support of Technicolor green. It is an eye-popper.

BUSTER

In *Buster*, Phil Collins plays a train robber who has difficulty spending his earnings. Julie Walters portrays his overly domestic middle-class wife. The British based film isn't funny enough to be a comedy, but it is too inconsequential to be anything else. Collins hasn't the talent to turn the film into a charmer, but it is doubtful that even a more accomplished actor could have pulled it off, since not even Walters has much to offer. The film is rated R, although there is little evidence on the disc as to why this is. The picture transfer is spotless. The surround effects are limited to the musical score.

BUSTER KEATON A HARD ACT TO FOLLOW

The three-part, three-hour documentary, *Buster Keaton A Hard Act to Follow*, comes in a gatefold jacket which uses a single gorgeous still photo, bled to all four sides, on the innerspread. The documentary tracks Keaton's life and artistic accomplishments. The first program takes him from the beginning of his life to the height of his popularity. The second details his subsequent successes and failures as he slid back into obscurity. The third episode covers the resurgence of his popularity in the late part of his life. The show uses both familiar and unfamiliar footage and features a decent amount of interview footage with Keaton himself. The picture transfer is very good and the Carl Davis score, though monaural, backs up the narration effectively on the digitally encoded soundtrack.

The most pleasing moments on the disc are the pieces viewers do not normally come upon, whether it is Keaton's early two-reelers or his television commercials from the fifties. There is a clip from a piece he did for 'Candid Camera' which is hysterical. Heavy details from his personal life are beyond the scope of the program, but the overview of Keaton's ups and downs and the essential aspects of his art are entertainingly presented. While a viewer may feel apprehensive about obtaining the disc as a substitute for the films themselves, the collection of Keaton's best stunts and creations quickly wins one over. Having the material in one place can provide more thrills than the combined offerings of a dozen of today's multiplexes.

BUY & CELL

Since the movie couldn't possibly have been intended to be shown in theaters, the sharp picture and 'Ultra-Stereo' sound of *Buy & Cell* must have been meant for laser disc presentation. The surround sound may be a bit pushy, but it makes good use of a disc's capabilities (in an opening gag, a bullet careens off every object in your viewing room). The film is a satire on prison films, and includes a mildly amusing social message by showing how the hardened criminals refuse to stoop to white-collar crime when they start up an investment company from behind bars. Robert Carradine does his nerd bit as the hero, an unjustly jailed broker. Malcolm McDowell is the villain, a tiresome role for him. Ben Vereen and Michael Winslow (the *Police Academy* sound effects guy) also appear. The disc has no chapter markers.

BYE BYE BIRDIE

Paul Lynde's performance as the father of a girl (teenaged Ann-Margret) who gets to kiss a rock star in *Bye Bye Birdie* is one of the best, or most typical, performances he ever gave. His timing and the way he chews on every syllable is delightful and it is the one aspect of the film which will remain consistent through the ages.

Filmed in Panavision, a few of the dance numbers, such as they are, get lost without the edges. The stereo, limited but fun, has been CX-encoded. The print has a few scratches and there is trouble with some of the solid color backgrounds. Janet Leigh and Dick Van Dyke are the nominal stars and Ed Sullivan, playing himself, has a lengthy bit part.

BYE BYE BRAZIL

Some of the joy has physically faded from *Bye Bye Brazil*. The colors on the source material do not look fresh, and the picture even looks a bit battered in places. The film remains satisfying, but the extra sparkle it once had to offer is gone. The Brazilian movie is in Portuguese with white English subtitles. The sound is satisfactory.

The story is about a travelling show which is trying to compete with television in the Brazilian hinterlands. The characters are comical but sympathetic, the view of Brazilian culture is fresh and intriguing, the sex is terrific, and the movie has a happy ending. It is a memorable show, and is worth watching on disc, dull colors and all.

C.H.U.D.
John Heard is one of our favorite actors but he is not the least bit interesting in *C.H.U.D.* The movie is about mutants living underneath Manhattan. Were you to come across it late at night on the television, you would probably not turn it off. It is competently made and perhaps a bit dull because it isn't as outrageous as it could be. The disc is 86 minutes long, but is in CLV all the way through. The colors are a little blurry and the sound is stale.

CABIN IN THE SKY
Vincent Minnelli's joy filled *Cabin in the Sky* is a rarity – a musical with an all Black cast which is not a revue and which has survived the passage of years to remain relatively popular and innocent. The stereotypes are workable and not embarrassing. The singing and dancing are wonderful, and, most importantly, the narrative has both humor and momentum. The analog sound has no significant problems and the black and white source material is in fine shape. The image is clean and the contrast levels are decent. Although the picture isn't stunning, it is certainly satisfying.

The story is something of a parable about temptation and consequences, involving the Devil's agents, but it is well integrated with the song and dance interludes. *Cabin in the Sky* has the weight of all that it represents bearing down on it, and that can get in the way of some viewers being able to relax with the film, but it is so lighthearted, so enjoyable, and so bursting with talent that concern for its historical or social attributes can just float away. The movie is good fun, and in the long run that is the most enduring requirement for its earning continued respect.

CAGE
Lou Ferrigno portrays a Vietnam vet who was shot in the head in *Cage*. His character, suffering from a mild mental handicap because of the wound, is tricked into entering an illicit wrestling contest. The narrative is contrived and racial stereotypes abound, but there are an adequate number of fight scenes to satisfy action fans. The picture is bright and clear, and the stereo surround sound is passable, though not elaborately edited.

THE CAINE MUTINY
One might be inclined to expect that Humphrey Bogart, who got his start playing bad guys, would overdo it as Captain Queeg in *The Caine Mutiny*, which has been released on disc with a fresh-looking print and acceptable monaural sound. He appears to enjoy his Nixonian rambling, however, and his relaxed paranoia puts the whole movie at ease. The story is about a group of executive officers who wrest the minesweeper, Caine, from their severely troubled captain and save the endangered ship during a storm. There is also a subplot about a boy learning to say no to his mother and some beautiful location footage from Yosemite National Park.

CALIGULA
Bob Guccione saw to it that a lot of Italian carpenters, athletic nineteen-year-olds, and bored British actors had food on their table by taking over a large Roman soundstage and employing them all in an effort to film something which was conceived as the story of Caligula, a famous Roman emperor who by all reports had even lower moral standards than Mr. Guccione.

Caligula, thankfully the R-rated version because anything which knocks minutes off of it is a blessing, stars Malcolm McDowell, who looks like a kicked puppy. If a group of people are watching the disc together, holding a contest – such as seeing who can spot the most polio vaccinations – might help to pass the time. The film is of strongest interest, of course, to twelve- and thirteen-year-old boys, and while restricting their access to it is advisable, if it is in the house, they will sniff it out.

You can bet the transfer and sound are of low quality, but if you are really lucky you will get a copy that skips and then, at least, you can return it, or, better still, toss it away.

CALIGULA (X-rated)
The thing which strikes one the most about the X-rated version of *Caligula* is that it has enough material for a year's worth of magazine layouts. All these youngsters, sacrificing hygiene for a day's pay and a few grapes. The frenetic Penthouse production combines endless scenes of mindless sex with endless scenes of mindless, Gibbonish dialog. Latin is more exciting and urn fragments are more erotic. The sex scenes are a mixture of hardcore and limpcore, giving the film an aura of elaborateness which most X-rated movies dispense with. Far be it from us to wish that one side of the three-sided, 143-minute, CLV disc had been formatted in CAV instead.

The disc comes in a gatefold jacket with an unimaginative inner spread. The monaural sound is digitally encoded and the transfer is stable, although the source material was obviously belabored. The picture is usually in focus when one wishes it wasn't and not in focus when one wishes it was.

CALL ME
The plot of *Call Me* concerns a woman in Brooklyn Heights who is being stalked by criminals and pestered by obscene phone messages. The script is not tight – a major character is not properly introduced – but in other ways it is very complex. The filmmakers have academic backgrounds and use techniques, such as 360-degree indoor pans, which one rarely sees in schlock films. The picture has weak colors but no serious flaws. The sound is in stereo with few separation effects.

CAMEO
The woman on the jacket cover of *Cameo* is not a member of the group and has only been put on the jacket to sell copies of the disc. The collection is in CAV and contains seven cuts which sound better than they look. There are two poorly conceived music videos which cannot work up any extended flow of images, three studio videos performed on a bright white set with a few props (catching a hand controlling a bowling ball which looks as though it is rolling itself is one of the advantages of CAV), and two older performance cuts. The group's taste in apparel is atrocious, the low point being their open-chested polar bear vests and sky blue tights that flair at the thighs.

Cameo's music, however, is excellent. Their style is funk, a loose and diversified collection of sounds which are tempered by a strong dance beat. In the best number, 'Talkin' Out the Side of Your Neck,' the parallel and conflicting lines of voices and instruments seem to build a scaffolding of music around your head. How can people with such poor taste in clothing make such wonderful music? It is one of the great mysteries of the rock era.

CAMILO SESTO – MADRID CON AMOR
Camilo Sesto is a Spanish vocalist who has a stage show that would not be out of place in a Vegas nightclub. His songs on *Camilo Sesto — Madrid Con Amor* are all Spanish, and vary in tempo. His voice is not overly melodic, but he takes command of the music when he sings. When one cannot understand the words, the expressions and poses of a performer tend to appear exaggerated, and Sesto has a grey, triangular tongue which spends an unpleasant amount of time on the wrong side of his teeth. His energy is contagious, however, and by the end of the disc there is a good possibility that you will be humming his numbers to yourself whether you know Spanish or not.

The sound and the picture are immaculate. The concert recording has a nice atmosphere and a strong stereo mix. The picture is so clear we could see smudges on our TV screen. The program is poorly edited, full of jump cuts which are generally uncoordinated to the music. The 54-minute disc has twelve chapter markings, although one of the numbers represented by a chapter is a medley of six songs.

CAN-CAN
CBS/Fox has letterboxed the dance numbers in the Todd-AO filmed *Can-Can* with an aspect ratio of about 1.9:1 and annoying orange borders. The rest of the film is scanned and cropped. The real news, however, is the fabulous digital stereo surround, which sounds just like an old-fashioned downtown movie theater. With overture and entr'acte music, the songs, the orchestra, the echoey voices and the slapping, stamping sound effects, the disc is as much fun as the dance.

The 133-minute musical, set in 'Belle Epoque' Paris, has a trifling story about a shady lawyer and a goody-goody judge vying for the affections of a cabaret owner. The songs, however, are by Cole Porter, and Cole Porter musicals are never more than lightly humorous, atmospheric excuses to present the music, anyway. The film stars Frank Sinatra, Shirley MacLaine, Louis Jordan, and Maurice Chevalier.

The disc is spread to three sides and the entr'acte occurs at the end of side two. The images which have not been letterboxed are rarely harmed by the cropping, while the Hermes Pan choreography is well served by the wider image. The colors are a little on the pale side, but generally satisfying considering the age of the film. The focus is sharp.

CAN'T BUY ME LOVE
Can't Buy Me Love never leaves the confines of its genre, but it is one of the better high school comedies, managing to be both amusing and thoughtful without compromising its characterizations. The story is about a nerdy

boy who helps a popular girl out of a monetary jam and demands the right to squire her for a couple of weeks in return, enough to establish his own popularity. The plot has no surprises, but the script is consistently funny, and the cast is appealing.

The film was shot in Tucson, and the picture transfer looks okay, avoiding instability in all but the most intense colors. The sound is monaural and has not been CX-encoded, but the oversight is not sufficient to taint the entertainment.

CANTELOUBE: CHANTS D'AUVERGNE

Kiri Te Kanawa sings a number of French folk songs orchestrated by Marie-Joseph Canteloube de Malaret on *Canteloube: Chants d'Auvergne*. The songs, performed in rural French dialect, have a Broadway musical bounce to them and the single-sided, 50-minute disc makes a decent, catchy audio program. A libretto, in the dialect and in English, is provided on a jacket insert. The disc has a well rounded sound with almost no impurities. Te Kanawa is accompanied by the English Chamber Orchestra.

The video program is uninspiring. A few token inserts of Te Kanawa are provided, but most of images are of the French countryside. The music, particularly the way it has been orchestrated, ought to be illustrated by mud, bitter cold, and barren suffering, in counterpoint. Instead, the pictures show an eternal spring. Except for one brief demonstration of a carver practicing his craft, the video is useless and not worth turning on.

CANYON CONSORT – THE PAUL WINTER CONSORT IN THE GRAND CANYON

Paul Winter's music is improvisational and minimal; one instrument's sound or one harmony at a time, separated with a good breath or two from the next. It is pleasing music, but it works better filling the small crevices on one's emotional precipice; it is not thick enough or expansive enough to plug the major faults.

Winter's method of operation is to record his music in unusual locales, discovering both inspirational and acoustical anomalies in his makeshift studio environments. Most of the recording on *Canyon Consort* took place in pitstops on a raft journey down the Colorado River, through the Grand Canyon.

The recording equipment was portable, so it was not state-of-the-art. Amidst the constant buzz of the river and the echo of the music, you can hear a certain amount of hiss. The picture, although clear, also has a rugged quality to it. Narration and dialog separate the musical efforts in the hour program, but the shifts are not upsetting.

CANYON DREAMS

The single-sided 40-minute digital disc *Canyon Dreams* features the music of Tangerine Dream and images of the Grand Canyon. The functional utility of discs such as this is to provide background stimulation while one's principal attentions are elsewhere. You can sit and concentrate on the disc once or twice, but it is designed to be atmospheric filler, something you never tire of looking at so long as you don't look at it too much.

The sound was digitally mastered and if there is any hiss on the digital track at all, it is very slight. The analog track is also clean, though the difference between the two is usually easy to detect. The picture is occasionally grainy, depending upon how much available light was present during the filming. The images depict the Grand Canyon from above and below, not comprehensively, but with an adequate variety of viewpoints. The most stunning is a view of the canyon in silhouette, by star light. Tangerine Dream's music is neither challenging nor totally invisible. The program has been divided into six chapters, as indicated on the jacket cover, but the disc has no chapter markers.

THE CAPTAIN'S PARADISE (see **KIND HEARTS AND CORONETS/THE CAPTAIN'S PARADISE**)

CARAVAN OF COURAGE – AN EWOK ADVENTURE (Import)
EWOKS: THE BATTLE FOR ENDOR

The made-for-television spin-off from the Lucas factory, 'The Ewok Adventure,' is available on disc in Japan with the title, *Caravan of Courage – An Ewok Adventure*, although the movie itself has the original title card. The program is in English with Japanese subtitles and is in CX-encoded stereo. The picture and sound are passable.

Ewok is no *Return of the Jedi*, but it isn't any worse than *Krull* or the many low-budgeted movies trying to pass for science fiction. The furry creatures of the title do not move their lips when they talk, but the special effects are impressive for a TV offering. The story is about two children who, with the help of the noisy but tight-lipped Ewoks, save their parents from a gargantuan ogre who acts suspiciously like a Wookie. The disc is more suitable for small children, provided they can hack the scary monsters.

As a sequel, *Ewoks: The Battle for Endor* is a bummer, because most of the characters from the earlier *Ewoks* movie are immediately killed off. As a free-standing film, however, it has some attractions, such as an impressive array of stop-motion special effects. There are monsters, ray guns, and other fantasy elements, all of which are executed with as much realism as a viewer would find in a true feature film. The second act is a yawner, but the opening is exciting and the ending will please any viewer who thrives on action, special effects, and Ewoks.

The picture transfer has a minor glitch or two but essentially looks as good as the original broadcast. The stereo sound is wimpy, with separations reserved primarily for the Sigfriedish musical score. When the rocketship passes overhead at the end, the sound does not follow.

THE CARDINAL

Image, obtaining the rights to *The Cardinal* from Hal Roach Studios, has made a special effort in transferring the Otto Preminger ecclesiastical soap opera to laser disc. The presentation incorporates both an overture and entr'acte music, stretching the three-hour disc to four sides. The picture has been decently letterboxed with an aspect ratio of about 2:1, and the source material is in excellent condition. Fleshtones may appear a bit pale, but the decorations look super. The transfer is gorgeous.

Now we are not going to try to convince anyone that *The Cardinal* is a great movie. It is too big, however, not to have some aspects worthy of praise, and if the viewer can suppress a natural prejudice against the hokey depiction of serious religious activity, a good time can be had. At its worst, the plot uses a white male protagonist to bear witness against the treatment of blacks in the American South and the treatment of Jews under the Nazis. But that is what is so much fun – one movie, and you get both persecutions, along with many other tests of conscience and faith, all sanitized and homogenized in the best Hollywood tradition. And everywhere the title character (Tom Tryon's one great, failed grab at stardom) goes, some famous actor or actress pops up to suffer and chew the scenery. Burgess Meredith, Ossie Davis, Romy Schneider, Carol Lynley twice (!), Raf Vallone and Dorothy Gish. No matter how tiny the church or small the hamlet – there they are. On a solidly positive note, John Huston also appears in an early turn as an actor, and with only a handful of scenes steals the movie from everybody – as an archbishop who never wastes a moment in expression or action. He bullies the whole film.

With the letterboxing, you will have no trouble catching the shadow of the camera, which is almost Otto Preminger's trademark. It shows up at least twice. The cinematography, by Leon Shamroy, is passionless but elaborate, and it must be seen in its original aspect ratio. The entire screen is always being utilized, and cropping the edges, as it usually appears on broadcast TV, takes away some of the fun. (In some scenes the top of the picture quivers, but it is only momentary and is not distracting.)

The sound recording was made in the early sixties and suffers from the crackle and hiss endemic to the era. With that, however, come all those terrific left and right field separations – voices so far away from center you turn to see who is there. The music score was done by Jerome Moross, who doesn't even try to prevent it from sounding like one of his westerns. With Tom Tryon as the star, why should he?

The Cardinal does not even hold up that well to repeat viewings. It is the sort of film one only watches when Easter falls in March. Seen too often, the narrative can become very stale. That shouldn't stop one from getting the disc, however. It is yet another epic film which has been given an elegant rendering on disc, another chance to achieve the effects of a movie theater for a whole afternoon without leaving your home.

CARIBE

Filmed in the jungles and Mayan ruins of Belize, *Caribe* is a simple-minded thriller about a black-market weapons deal gone bad and a law enforcement agent with no visible supervision. The film has a standard number of second rate stunts and explosions, and one surprisingly gory bit involving a ritual sacrifice. It is neither more nor less entertaining than other films of its ilk.

The disc has undergone a decent transfer. Although much of the film takes place at night and is poorly lit, graininess is negligible and the colors look accurate. The sound is monaural, but has some life to it and is well edited. Side one is in CAV, with two unsteady frames out of every five, although the biggest stunts occur during the final thirty minutes.

CARLIN ON CAMPUS

George Carlin makes a few funny faces and does some pantomime in *Carlin on Campus*, but being able to see him doesn't seem worth the added expense. The disc looks and sounds terrific. Despite some quick animated interludes and an interesting set of unused props on the stage, his hour of jokes is visually stiff. In fact, when one turns off the pictures and just listens, the humor flows more smoothly.

CARLY SIMON LIVE FROM MARTHA'S VINEYARD

If you are searching for tranquility, you will find it in *Carly Simon Live from Martha's Vineyard*. The program depicts a June evening in the harbor of Gay's Head on Martha's Vineyard. Simon performs with a makeshift band before a small gathering of locals. Behind her in the harbor, boats come and go. A steady breeze billows through her chemise and her hair. During the hour long concert, the solstice sun sets ever so gradually, casting a warm glow on her right cheek and illuminating the hills beyond the harbor. Even a heavy metal band would seem peaceful in that setting, but Simon, whose stage mannerisms are quite accomplished, adds an extra touch of class. Watching the disc will make a viewer feel both relaxed and luxurious.

The audio is heavily redubbed, which makes the music sound terrific, but subtracts a little from the atmosphere, though once in a while you can still hear a buoy dinging in the harbor. Simon's set covers the high points in her career without succumbing to a stream of greatest hits.

The picture, from a film source, looks fine. The program opens with a brief profile/interview which might have been better placed on side two so the concert would not be interrupted by the side change. As it stands, the final three numbers have been placed on the second side, in CAV, with two unsteady still frames out of every five.

CARMEN

After Francesco Rosi's wonderful *Bizet's Carmen*, it is difficult to settle for a sedate stage version, even one as honorable as the Metropolitan Opera presentation, *Carmen*. The rhythmic editing of Rosi's film, something most music critics were oblivious to, disappears in a taped stage presentation where the video director, in this case the ubiquitous Brian Large, seems frantic just trying to keep up with the action.

The Met production, filmed in early 1987, is a basic and almost introductory interpretation of the opera. The first act is especially weak, but the stage production and Large's approach is more clearheaded when the population on the stage decreases. Samuel Ramey is particularly good as Escamillo, and after his appearance, the performances of both José Carreras and Agnes Baltsa sharpen considerably. Leona Mitchell appears as Micaela. The program is in French with English subtitles.

The opera has been squeezed onto three sides, necessitating a side break after act III has begun, though the platter change interrupts spoken dialog and not music. The disc comes in a box jacket and has been extensively chapter encoded. An insert containing a chapter coordinated plot synopsis and a history of the story (including a detailed recap of Prosper Merimee's novel) and the opera's creation is provided.

The recording is kinder to the orchestra than to the singers, once again especially during the first act, but the disc audio transfer is spotless. The picture quality is also above average, though the drab staging makes few aspects of the program pleasing, except, perhaps, Baltsa's inviting décolletage.

CARMEN
CARMEN (Import)

The films of Carlos Saura have often seemed annoyingly introspective or superficially mystical. *Carmen* is a celebration of itself, and the ambiguous ending is part of the fun. A single movie doesn't have to be the answer for everything. The beauty of Saura's film is that it establishes its rules quickly and then accomplishes all that it sets out to accomplish. Every time we see this show, it gets better. The glances and smirks among the actors and actresses playing the parts of the dancers (who are rehearsing a flamenco interpretation of *Carmen* set mostly to Bizet's music) never seem false or self-conscious.

The American release is, in every way except one, superior to the Japanese. (The running time on the Japanese disc is listed as 101 minutes. On the American disc, it is listed as 99 minutes. However, both discs play a full 102 minutes.)

To begin with, Image's American release is CX-encoded and the Japanese release is not. The film is monaural and is supposed to sound a little rough, but with CX-encoding, it is much easier on the ears. The picture on the Image version is significantly brighter and in sharper focus. The Image disc is in Spanish and has English subtitles. The Japanese disc is in Spanish with Japanese subtitles hanging discretely on the right. The picture, like the sound, is still a little rough.

Still, there is a reason to obtain the Japanese disc. Image uses the American ad art for their jacket covers, whereas the Japanese disc uses the poster art which promoted the film in the rest of the world. The American photo is more erotic, but the pose of the two main characters in the international artwork leaps out at you. Besides, have you ever seen 'Carmen' spelled in Japanese? It has a dagger in it.

CARMEN MCCRAE LIVE

Carmen McCrae sings for 80 minutes on *Carmen McCrae Live*. Her set ranges from popular numbers, such as 'Evergreen' and 'But Not for Me,' to less well-known Latin and jazz pieces. She stands in front of a small back-up band and sings to an auditorium of undetermined size. She varies the types of songs that she sings – a slow one, a fast one, another slow one – without changing her manner of delivery all that much. Her vocals are careful and smooth, and her performance is enhanced significantly by the quality of the recording. The image, mostly closeups of McCrae, doesn't change much over the hour and a half, but it seems to match the essence of her concert. The picture and sound are beautiful.

CAROLS FOR CHRISTMAS ST. EDMUNDSBURY CATHEDRAL

The lovely *Carols for Christmas St. Edmundsbury Cathedral* will be nice to play for visitors before a big dinner or as a quiet evening's nightcap before retiring on Christmas Eve.

Twenty-four carols are sung by The Royal College of Music Chamber Choir, an attractive group of singers whose voices, in digital, are as pure as an undisturbed cover of snow. Leisurely edited into shots of the choir are pictures of works from The Metropolitan Museum of Art. Caroline Kennedy is listed in the credits as the coordinating producer. The artwork is not intended to be studied on the CLV disc, but there are detail shots and lengthy visual meditations on most of the pieces (an insert provides the title, artist, etc.) The footage of the choir is not as sharp as it could be, but the art images are flawless, as is the sound. The disc is a pleasing Christmas ornament which one can expect to pull out traditionally, year after year.

THE CARPENTERS – YESTERDAY ONCE MORE

A sense of morbid curiosity will hang over your first viewing of *The Carpenters – Yesterday Once More*. You watch Karen Carpenter's face, always glowing and happy, vary from slightly plump in the older sequences to mildly gaunt in the later pictures and cringe with the knowledge of what is going to happen. The 56-minute CLV disc sounds lovely and is worth playing on one's stereo system without the addition of images. The disc has 14 numbers, most of them familiar, and includes a few non-Carpenter classics such as 'Beechwood 4-5789.' It is a pleasant program and has been extremely popular.

THE CARS – HEARTBEAT CITY

The manner in which women are portrayed in music videos is a direct measure of the intelligence level of those who conceive the clips. Thus it is an extra pleasure to watch the forty minutes worth of videos on *The Cars – Heartbeat City*. Although each video has a different director and a different look, the women interacting with the band members of The Cars are treated as participants, not objects, and everyone is clearly having a good time.

The Cars are one of the few major groups who survived the transition from punk to new wave to vid wave. They have a clean, hesitant sound with a strong electronic beat. Their lyrics are intelligent and their videos all the more so, with lots of special effects and distinctive imagery. The last cut is a miniature documentary on the making of the first cut. The sound on the disc is above average, but the picture is speckled and fuzzy.

CARTOON CLASSICS: HERE'S MICKEY!/HERE'S PLUTO!
CARTOON CLASSICS: HERE'S DONALD!/HERE'S GOOFY!
CARTOON CLASSICS: SILLY SYMPHONIES/STARRING SILLY SYMPHONIES: ANIMALS TWO BY TWO

The Walt Disney *Cartoon Classics* series combines two features designed for another video format onto a single side of a single CLV disc. Each feature contains brief linking material and three cartoons, so each disc has six cartoons. There are chapter markers on the discs for the start of each feature and for the individual cartoons. The sound is monaural without CX-encoding, but it isn't bad and is worth playing with amplification.

The picture quality of the cartoons varies between good and excellent. One of the best is 'Orphan's Benefit' on *Here's Mickey!/Here's Pluto!* The colors are vivid and the detail is very precise. Another cartoon, 'Mickey's Garden,' is a wonderfully complex and hallucinogenic battle between Mickey and a forest of bugs, making the disc, which also includes 'Mickey's Birthday Party,' 'Mail Dog,' 'Pantry Pirate,' and 'Springtime for Pluto,' one of the most desirable collections. The cartoons span 1935 to 1947, and can give one a real feeling for the progression of style during Disney's best decades.

One cartoon on *Here's Donald!/Here's Goofy!*, 'For Whom the Bulls Toil,' contains an overly negative stereotyped depiction of Mexicans. 'Lion Down,' an elaborate tale about a mountain lion who wakes up to find that Goofy has transported his tree to a city penthouse, is the most entertaining. 'Wide Open Spaces,' in which Donald tries to sleep outdoors, 'Donald's Ostrich,' 'Crazy with the Heat,' showing Donald and Goofy in the desert, and 'A Knight for a Day,' with Goofy demonstrating medieval jousting, also appear.

Two collections of less familiar characters, both of cartoons from the mid-Thirties, appear on *Cartoon Classics: Silly Symphonies/Starring Silly Symphonies: Animals Two by Two*. Within, one pair of characters appears twice, a tortoise and a hare who race in 'The Tortoise and the Hare,' and box in 'Toby Tortoise Returns.' The best cartoon is a sequel to 'The Three Little Pigs' entitled, 'Three Little Wolves.' It also is the nicest looking. The elaborate, bare-bottomed 'Water Babies' appears as well, along with 'Father Noah's Ark' and 'Peculiar Penguins.'

CARTOON CLASSICS: MICKEY & THE GANG/NUTS ABOUT CHIP 'N' DALE

Six cartoons are featured on *Cartoon Classics: Mickey & The Gang/Nuts About Chip 'N' Dale*. Two of the first three, 'Boat Builders' and 'Moose Hunters,' star Mickey, Goofy, and Donald, a combination which always inspired elaborate inventiveness on the part of the Disney animators. As is usually the case, the gags have more variety than those in a single character cartoon. The third offering, 'Canine Caddy,' depicting Mickey in a round of golf with Pluto serving as caddy, also appeared on the DiscoVision compilation, *On Vacation with Mickey Mouse*. One of the Chip 'N' Dale cartoons, 'Two Chips and a Miss' also appeared in a DiscoVision offering, *The Adventures of Chip 'N' Dale*. About a rivalry between the two chipmunks over a cabaret singer, the narrative on the 1951 cartoon is weak, supplemented partially by a musical number, and has no definitive conclusion. 'Food for Feudin'' and 'Trailer Horn,' which were made two years earlier, are stronger. In the former, the chipmunks attempt to retrieve their acorn supply from Pluto's doghouse. In the latter, they take pleasure picking on Donald Duck at a campsite setting.

Strong colors on the Mickey cartoons have a mild graininess and the prints are a little paler than average, though the focus is sharp. The Chip 'N' Dale cartoons are in better shape, though none of the cartoons have the kind of stunning imagery which the best Disney transfers have offered. The sound is monaural with CX-encoding. The Chip 'N' Dale soundtracks are fine, but there is an audio flutter during a couple of the Mickey cartoons.

CARTOON CLASSICS: STARRING MICKEY & MINNIE/STARRING CHIP 'N' DALE

One of the best compilations of Walt Disney cartoon shorts is *Cartoon Classics: Starring Mickey & Minnie/Starring Chip 'N' Dale*. The single-sided CLV disc is a combination of two video anthologies. It contains a total of six cartoons, each of which is marked with a chapter. The strength of the soundtrack varies from one featurette to the next, but remains within the limits of acceptability. The picture transfer also does the cartoons justice.

Although the Chip 'N' Dale shorts were produced in the fifties and pale in comparison to the three classic Minnie & Mickey cartoons which precede them, the collection is one of the strongest Chip 'N' Dale presentations we have seen. In 'Working for Peanuts,' the two chipmunks discover the advantages of living near a zoo, much to the consternation of the zookeeper, Donald Duck. 'Donald Applecore' features their 'applecore' routine and a number of standard gags. 'Dragon Around,' in which the two mistake a steam shovel (operated by you know who) for a dragon, is conceptually the strongest Chip 'N' Dale cartoon there was. It is both imaginative and amusing.

'The Little Whirlwind,' which opens the disc, is an interesting exercise in which Mickey attempts to tame a miniature tornado. The second two cartoons are classics. 'Hawaiian Holiday' includes Donald, Pluto and Goofy along with Mickey and Minnie, in beach-oriented skits. The cartoon contains 30 seconds of footage involving Goofy and his surf board not found on the version which appears in the DiscoVision anthology, *On Vacation with Mickey Mouse*.

The last cartoon in the first collection is a certifiable classic, 'The Brave Little Tailor.' The irony of the Little Tailor's 'seven in one blow' brag is appropriate – the artwork is so rich that more effort must have gone into 'The Brave Little Tailor' than into all of the Chip 'N' Dale cartoons, combined. The detail, the complex movements, and the elaborate backgrounds are fascinating, and even if the other shorts on the disc had not been as worthy as they turned out to be, the disc would still be worth owning for that one masterpiece.

CARTOON CLASSICS VOLUME 13: SILLY SYMPHONIES – FANCIFUL FABLES
CARTOON CLASSICS VOLUME 14: SILLY SYMPHONIES – ANIMAL TALES

Four of the six Disney featurettes available on *Cartoon Classics Volume 13: Silly Symphonies – Fanciful Fables* that are in color seem brownish, but it is difficult to tell if this is due to fading or if they were composed that way. The sound is weak on the older cartoons, but the disc is CX-encoded and one can't expect miracles. The disc does not have chapter markers.

'The Merry Dwarfs' is a black-and-white exercise of little consequence. 'Playful Pan' is a horrifying depiction of a forest fire (the trees scream and die as the fire dances over them). 'Babes in the Woods' is an equally creepy rendition of 'Hansel and Gretel.' The witch turns Hansel into a hairy spider. 'Father Noah's Ark' has no surprises, but 'The Goddess of Spring' is about a beautiful maiden who is abducted by the Devil and forced into marriage. The famous compromise they work out has her staying below ground for half a year and above for the other half. If children need anything these days, it is more cartoons about Hell. The last segment, 'Little Hiawatha,' is a truly rare accomplishment. It manages to be cuddly and cute without making one ill from an overdose of sugar. The Longfellow opening helps.

The cartoons on *Cartoon Classics Volume 14: Silly Symphonies – Animal Tales* are less satisfying. The first two black-and-white cartoons, 'Monkey Melodies' and 'The Spider and the Fly,' are suitably elaborate. The colorful 'Cock O' the Walk' is a bouncy barnyard 'Carioca.' But 'Peculiar Penguins,' 'More Kitten,' and 'Elmer Elephant,' despite their Technicolor presentations, are standard quality shorts of no special interest. Like *Fanciful Fables*, the disc is CX-encoded and lacks chapter markers. The back of the jacket reads, "Sophisticated viewers and knowledgeable animation lovers will marvel at these skillfully created animated shorts." If that's the case, why did Disney drop the credits from each cartoon?

CARTOON FESTIVAL II
(see **LIMITED GOLD EDITION II CARTOON CLASSICS DISNEY DREAM FACTORY: 1933-1938**)

CASABLANCA (Voyager)
CASABLANCA (MGM/UA)
CASABLANCA (CBS/Fox)

Voyager's Criterion Collection CAV version of *Casablanca*, transferred from a '35mm nitrate archival fine-grain master archival negative,' is gorgeous. MGM/UA released a decent transfer of *Casablanca* on a CLV disc which was a significant improvement over the grainy and crackly CBS/Fox video presentation. Those who do not plan on obtaining the Criterion version should avoid screening the disc, however, because once you see it, there is no turning back. Where MGM/UA's disc has soft lines and indistinct shades, Voyager's has pinpoint sharpness and careful, detailed gradation. The disc provides a picture that looks closer to projected film than to projected video.

The sound, too, is great. On the digital track every sound comes out with solid confidence and only a hint of hiss to show the film's true age. The analog sound is split into two audio tracks to facilitate a lecture, and has optional CX-encoding. Voyager's chapter encoding, however, is inadequate, failing to mark many of the familiar and memorable passages within the movie.

The film looks and sounds so good that it will rekindle the film's pleasures for those who have burned themselves out memorizing dialog or humming 'As Time Goes By.' The clarity of the presentation brings out the background details in the elaborate nightclub scenes, enriching the locale's atmosphere and heightening a viewer's concentration. Often with a movie which has been subject to numerous repeated screenings, a viewer will see the film so many times that a poor presentation will leave an uneasy and disatisfied feeling. The flaws of the presentation will subconsciously be mistaken for flaws within the movie itself. If that has happened to you lately with *Casablanca*, it is time to watch the Criterion version and rediscover how much fun the film can be.

Voyager has also included the usual array of supplementary material. Ron Haver's written essay, appearing on the gatefold jacket cover, discusses specifically how *Casablanca* copped its Oscars, and is different from his audio essay, which covers the gestation of the script and the film's production history. Haver's talk, blissfully free of interpretative comments, provides a complete understanding of how *Casablanca* came to be, and the disc is only reticent in analyzing, or at least touching upon, how the film's popularity, since its Oscar win, has expanded.

In the still frame section after the film is ended, a synopsis of the play, 'Everybody Comes to Rick's,' is included (it is quite similar to the film), along with the movie's budget (Conrad Veidt got $25,000, Claude Rains got $22,000, and Dooley Wilson got $3500), censor adjustments (which can be for the better – it was the censors who demanded that Ilsa believe her husband to be dead when she has her affair with Rick in Paris, making her far more sympathetic), and editing notes which are supplemented, without much success, by excerpts from the film (a simple notation of frame and side references would have been satisfactory). The usual roundup of publicity stills and production photos are also included, as is an original theatrical trailer which, in retrospect, didn't have to try very hard to succeed.

Voyager has also included a few esoteric additions. There is a synopsis for a proposed sequel which, understandably, never got past the first reader. There is newsreel footage of the city of Casablanca during the War, reinforcing everyone's knowledge that the real city and the movie city are in two entirely different worlds. About twenty minutes of excerpts from the 'Lux Radio Hour' interpretation of the film are split awkwardly onto two of the audio tracks. The radio show has major stars reading the dialog (Alan Ladd, Hedy Lamarr), but the rehearsal time was clearly minimal and the utility of the material is miniscule. There is also a clip from the colorized version of *Casablanca* and we wish this segment had been expanded. Although the sequence looks more like a succession of the hand-colored lobby cards, depicted in the still frame collection, than like a real color film, the colorized version of *Casablanca* was given a great deal of attention and is worth a respectable analysis. It was colorized to imitate an early Technicolor production, and within the beige interiors of Rick's in the excerpt shown on the disc, there are brightly colored objects scattered about, deliberately intended to show off the joys that color can bring to a screen composition, and to evoke the era of film when such joys were a real discovery.

The beautifully edited, marvelously scripted, wittily acted film is always enjoyable to hear and see. There are many different reasons for this, but one is its feeling of oasis and respite. The war is very much a part of the plot, but it is happening somewhere else. Watching *Casablanca*, one feels the same escape from the pressures of life which the characters, most of them waiting to go elsewhere, are experiencing. The ending pulls one gently back into reality, concluding with a bittersweet ambiguity which becomes amplified only after the television is switched off.

CASANOVA (Import)

An adaptation of *Casanova* scripted by George MacDonald Fraser, which appeared on TV in the United States but was released theatrically in Europe, has been released on disc in Japan. Michel Le Grand wrote the intermittent music, Simon Langton directed the production, and the title role is portrayed by Richard Chamberlain. There is also a veritable polyglot of beautiful women, including Hanna Schygulla, Ornella Muti, Sylvia Kristel, and Faye Dunaway.

The three-sided disc has nice colors but a consistently grainy picture. The monaural sound is CX-encoded, but flat. Japanese subtitles appear on the picture, but one is rarely aware of them. The film is only interesting when Casanova is in prison, because he has a specific goal – to get out. Once out, Fraser never finds a motivation for Casanova's actions, and Chamberlain seems happier in solitary confinement than in powdered wigs.

CASANOVA'S BIG NIGHT

In some passages *Casanova's Big Night* the picture is slightly grainy, but the Technicolor print is gorgeous. The sound contains no flaws beyond an occasional flutter.

The movie is one of Bob Hope's tightest. There are hardly any slow passages and no extended gags which fail to sustain a comical premise. The plot, in which Hope learns what it means to be a gentleman when he imitates Casanova for the sake of 10,000 ducats, moves with speed and wit. The movie is a costume comedy and a showcase for Hope's clowning. It does not require great effort or concentration on the part of the viewer, but its rewards are substantial, nonetheless.

CASEY KASEM'S ROCK 'N ROLL GOLDMINE: THE BRITISH INVASION
CASEY KASEM'S ROCK 'N ROLL GOLDMINE: THE SAN FRANCISCO SOUND

Two collections in the rewarding *Casey Kasem's Rock 'n Roll Goldmine* run a little over a half hour in length each. Kasem introduces every number, interrupting the flow of the music. The clips, however, are often rare and compelling, and the monaural sound is excellent. Although the visual material is by nature in rough shape, it has been transferred to disc without further distortion. Most of the clips are in black and white, and those in color are about one step away. The discs are chapter encoded, but no chapter listing is provided and the songs are listed on the jacket out of sequence and incompletely.

The British Invasion is terrific. Among the groups appearing on the disc are The Kinks doing 'You Really Got Me,' The Animals doing a thrillingly moody 'We Got to Get Out of This Place,' Peter and Gordon doing 'World Without Love', Gerry and the Pacemakers doing 'How Do You Do It?,' and even Joe Cocker, doing 'Delta Lady.' Electric guitar fans won't want to miss The Yardbirds performing 'Heart Full of Soul,' but the best piece on the disc comes from The Troggs, doing 'Wild Thing' in a subway station. It is a rousing combination of humor and freedom, and will leave one appreciating the makeshift group, perhaps for the first time.

Less satisfying is *The San Francisco Sound*. The program has interviews with Jerry Garcia and Joe McDonald which are interesting but take up space that could be used for music. A Janis Joplin segment ('Ball and Chain') is naturally riveting, and it is enjoyable to see The Grateful Dead ('Truckin'') and Van Morrison ('Domino'), but with Santana ('Jingo'), Country Joe McDonald ('Fixing to Die Rag') and Steve Miller ('Living in the USA') filling out the disc, more seems to be missing than is included. 'Living in the USA' belongs to the seventies, anyway.

CASEY KASEM'S ROCK 'N ROLL GOLDMINE: THE SOUL YEARS

Casey Kasem's Rock 'N Roll Goldmine: The Soul Years features nine black artists from the sixties, captured on rare TV or concert appearances (including Otis Redding singing 'Try a Little Tenderness' a few hours before he died in a plane crash). When the artists aren't lip synching, the orignal recordings accompany the footage.

The disc has chapter encoding for each of the numbers. A few interviews are also scattered through the program, but it is, as the title implies, a cultural goldmine. The selections do more than provide a sampling of black artists during the glory days of the vinyl industry, they present a comprehensive portrait of what Soul Music in the 1960s was. Both the sound and the picture quality of the clips, however, is less impressive than it was on *The Sixties*, implying that the clips were even harder to come by.

CASEY KASEM'S: THE SIXTIES

Casey Kasem's: The Sixties is actually a collection of original performance clips by 8 of the biggest rock sensations of the late 1960s. The material is fabulous. The Jefferson Airplane's 'White Rabbit' is dubbed in over a performance of the song on a rug and tie-dyed stage which looks like every basement apartment you ever visited in 1972. Jim Morrison sings 'People Are Strange' directly to the camera, with intriguing vocal inflections. Steppenwolf performs 'Magic Carpet Ride' on an early music video which loses none of its appeal from looking horribly fuzzy and faded. The Who smash up their instruments at the end of a TV set performance of 'My Generation.' Jimi Hendrix licks his guitar on 'Purple Haze' and also participates in the only interview we have ever seen of him where he could actually recognize where he is and what time of day it was. Janis Joplin spews out 'Try' before a live audience and the audience puts as much energy into the song as Joplin does. The most exciting clip, however, is a live performance of 'Sunshine of Your Love,' by Cream. For some reason the beginning of it is clipped off, but that only makes the intense, frantic remainder look all the more rare and valuable. To round out the show, there is an interview with the Beatles on Dutch television and a different version of 'She Loves You,' run over black-and-white footage of mobbing fans.

The disc probably could not sound better than it does. The same with the picture transfer, which preserves the scraps of sixties culture for future generations to observe and marvel. Our only complaint with the disc is that it lacks chapter markers. Because of the Beatle material the disc had to be withdrawn from the market place shortly after release and so it is a collector's item.

CASINO ROYALE

We first got turned on to *Casino Royale* when a TV station in LA played it every night for a week. The movie, a gigantic, big-budgeted mess with five directors, three credited screenwriters, and a dozen stars, disappointed everyone who was expecting at least some kind of cash-in on the James Bond craze (*Royale* was Ian Fleming's first Bond novel and had been sold before the series became popular). Expectations having faded and the years having passed, the film emerges as the quintessential sixties comedy. It is wacky, irreverent, disjointed, psychedelic, and it gets funnier each time you watch it.

RCA/Columbia has released the same version which played on TV, with more than half the screen cropped. One misses many gags this way (near the end the viewer sees girls running around in gold, but not the artist who is painting them).

The sound is not in stereo and not CX-encoded, but it comes across clearly. Dusty Springfield's languid rendition of 'The Look of Love' never sounded better, and the opening Herb Alpert theme bounces around the room. The picture looks great, preserving all the odd things they did with colors in the sixties so that future generations can study and wonder. The movie is 130 minutes long, but nobody considered putting the slapstick ending (where Woody Allen, as 'Dr. Noah,' swallows an atomic bomb pill) in CAV. We can't really get angry though, we've waited too long just to own our own copy and someday we're going to play it every night for a week.

CASSANDRA

All the elements of a Dario Argento-style murder mystery are present in *Cassandra*, an Australian thriller. The movie will be frustrating to some viewers, but those who enjoy a few decent stabbings and the way in which every consecutive prime suspect is knocked off will be delighted. The stereo soundtrack is decent except for the scattered moments on both sides when the volume burps. The picture is alternately bright and a little grainy depending upon the time of day in which the action is taking place.

CASUAL SEX?

Under the guise of being topical, *Casual Sex?* is actually a feminist comedy which only pays lip service to the 'safe sex' quandary. It is daring, in a way, for it retains its experimental theater beginnings, such as having the two leads talk directly to the camera, and it is blatant in its feminism. The plot sends the two heroines to an exercise resort. The male characters they meet are horribly stereotyped, while the women, except a villainous blonde, have well-rounded and complex personalities. The leads, Lea Thompson and Victoria Jackson, are quite appealing, and Mary Gross has an hysterically giddy scene in which she demonstrates to the others her method for achieving orgasms. The picture is mildly grainy, but passable. The sound makes a good impression.

CASUALTIES OF WAR

The stereo surround sound on *Casualties of War* is incredible. The sound editing is so elaborate and so powerful that it puts all but a handful of other films to shame. The surround is truly used as a third channel, not obnoxiously but appropriately, taking on its share of the sound effects (there's a fantastic helicopter flyby, and loads of explosions) and enveloping the viewer in the movie's atmosphere. When played back in mono, Ennio Morricone's musical score seems overly floral and out of place, but in three dimensions, pieces of the instrumentation are divvied out and counter-balanced. The music not only becomes legitimate, it becomes a key device for prodding viewer's emotions. If you are at all partial to the title, the sound transfer makes it worth acquiring.

The cast and subject matter of *Casualties of War* scares many viewers away, though that is their own loss. Directed by Brian DePalma with his usual technical virtuoso style, the film is about a soldier in Vietnam who refuses to join in when his platoon kidnaps and rapes a peasant girl during a reconnaissance mission. Michael J. Fox and Sean Penn, who are both very right for their roles, star. It is obvious that the film is about moral choices in an amoral world, but it is also about the odd combination of chance and fortitude which separate heroes from villains.

The color transfer is very good. The focus is sharp, and the drenched intensity of the colors is clearly a deliberate effect chosen during the transfer process. Of course, for disc owners, the movie is also a spectacular pyrotechnical display. The disc has been letterboxed in what RCA/Columbia identifies as the 'Theatrical Presentation Format,' with an aspect ratio of about 2.3:1. The screen composition looks legitimate. DePalma's careful designs add not just tension but complete phobias to the film's emotional mood, making the letterboxed image a significant contributor to the constant environmental vulnerabilities of the characters.

CAT ON A HOT TIN ROOF

Cat on a Hot Tin Roof doesn't look as nice as it did when it was broadcast on television in 1981. The colors look ripened and there are fewer sharp edges. Much of the opening act is in mumbled dialect. You can hear the emotion, but there is a temptation to watch the disc with the text in your lap. This is the version with Tommy Lee Jones and Jessica Lange as Brick and Maggie, and with Rip Torn as Big Daddy. Kim Stanley, playing Big Momma, gives the strongest performance.

CAT PEOPLE
CURSE OF THE CAT PEOPLE

Although both *Cat People* and *Curse of the Cat People* run less than 90 minutes, neither disc is in partial CAV. Side two of *Curse* is just 29 minutes long, but it has been left in extended play. *Cat People* is clawed in a couple of places and it has a glitch on side two at the 15 minute point, but the print is sharp and you can see small details clearly. *Curse* has an unfortunate hum which is annoying in quiet moments, but despite the subtleties in the soundtracks on both films (was that a growl, or the wind?) these are not the sort of discs one should be playing too loud anyway.

If you've ever tried to stay up late to watch these movies, you would know that *Cat People* keeps you wide awake while *Curse* puts you right out. The former is an adult thriller about a woman who may or may not turn into a panther when emotionally stimulated. The latter, which features the same cast, is about a little girl with an imaginary friend (the 'cat woman' from the first film). Both films rely on mood and atmosphere to convey the horrors of sexual anxiety. In *Cat People* the fur really flies, but in *Curse* the filmmakers were just licking their thumbs.

CAT'S EYE

The CX-encoded stereo track on the fantasy anthology *Cat's Eye* sounds a little muted until you get to the last episode. An early episode where Robert Hays is goaded onto the ledge of a building by Kenneth McMillan ought to have the wind whipping around your ears, but you barely hear it even though it's blowing his hair sideways. Only the concluding segment, where the walls of Drew Barrymore's room are creaking with wicked intentions, does the stereo become an effective addition to the entertainment. The picture quality is decent.

A special note ought to be made about the first episode. James Woods portrays a smoker who is terrorized into breaking his habit by a group called Quitters, Inc. When he tries to sneak a puff, the group abducts his wife and tortures her with electrical shocks. The concept is farfetched, but the physical stress which his family goes through is really inconsequential compared to the emotional stress they would go through if he developed a terminal illness because of his inability to stop smoking. It is a neat little parable, and the message it carries should not be taken lightly.

CATCH A RISING STAR'S 10TH ANNIVERSARY

Pat Benatar performs two straight rock numbers on the comedy disc, *Catch A Rising Star's 10th Anniversary*. At least her set is entertaining. David Brenner, Richard Belzer, Gabe Kaplan, and Billy Crystal fill out space on the disc. The picture is clear, having been recorded as a special for HBO. The best part of the show has probably been cut out. Andy Kaufman begins his familiar spiel and is interrupted by a man in the audience. After a while they start arguing, and the man admits he is a plant, hired by Kaufman to disrupt the show. But just as things really start getting weird and off-color, there is a jarring cut, the man is gone, and Kaufman is preparing his Elvis imitation. Apparently, the fellow was one rising star who didn't get caught.

CATTLE QUEEN OF MONTANA

A curious thing happened to all of Ronald Reagan's movies after he was elected President: Nothing.

Given the situation as a hypothesis, one would certainly predict that 'Bedtime for Bonzo' would be one of the most familiar films in America. Instead, there was a mass sublimation, perhaps a refusal to come to terms with how the man earned his living before he entered politics. For those who are not afraid to face the facts, however, there is *Cattle Queen of Montana*, starring Reagan and Barbara Stanwyck.

Stanwyck portrays a woman whose hopes for starting a cattle ranch are destroyed by marauding Indians. Reagan portrays a sharpshooter (he lights a match at twenty paces) who joins with the bad guys but is too polite when Stanwyck is around to really be a villain.

The editing and Allan Dwan's direction are so disorienting that you never know where any of the characters are standing in relation to one another. This adds a subtle prudence to the opening – you don't know if Reagan can actually see Stanwyck while she is bathing – but gets ridiculous when the principal form of plot advancement is to have one character hide and listen to what the others are saying.

CAVEGIRL

Cavegirl is about a nerdy anthropology student who falls into a time warp, awaking 25,000 years before the beginnings of civilization. Suddenly, with the aid of his roll-on deodorant, he has no trouble meeting girls. The movie is full of jokes about things like nose picking and passing wind. It has a certain Neanderthal wit and club-wielding delicacy. The disc is well produced even if the movie was not.

CELEBRATING BIRD: THE TRIUMPH OF CHARLIE PARKER

The sound on *Celebrating Bird: The Triumph of Charlie Parker* is monaural, but it is well produced and has been digitally encoded. The disc has plenty of music, but it is actually a documentary, with talking heads, voice-over narration, and rare black-and-white footage of many jazz greats from the forties and fifties. The disc also has chapter markers, but not enough of them to cover every song.

The documentary is best at evoking the milieu of the be-bob age. Despite interviews with associates, the portion of Parker's personality which did not involve a saxophone remains mostly hidden. In all the photographs he is quiet and demure, though he looks cheerful. His drug use is treated tactfully, and his music is presented without undue analysis.

CELLAR DWELLER

A comic book artist brings a monster from Hell to life in *Cellar Dweller*, a short (78 minutes, with extensive credit rolls), reasonably intelligent, single-location horror film. The sound is sporadic in effect but the picture looks okay. Side two is in CAV, and slowing down the model and prosthetic work is interesting, even with two unsteady still frames out of every five.

CERTAIN FURY

What most cheap action movies expend on car chases, *Certain Fury* expends on art direction. The sets are so elaborate that every new location encourages a round of snickers. There is a courtroom with chairs all over the place, a sewer system with ducts, corridors, pipes, and water all over the place, an abandoned factory/opium den with candles all over the place, and garbage, all over the place. The garbage is particularly amusing, because it is in almost every shot of every scene. It is an effective visual representation of the entire movie.

Tatum O'Neal and Irene Cara portray fugitives from the law and the weight of the movie rests on their shoulders. They fall down immediately. Neither one can read a line of dialog without making it sound like reading a line of dialog. Between them and all the clutter, the movie rolls along, and if it is very late at night, it could be enjoyable. The picture and sound are acceptable.

THE CHAIN REACTION

Radioactive waste bubbling into the local water table in *The Chain Reaction* forces a corporation to use Nazi-like tactics to keep the contamination a secret. A couple spending a weekend at a cabin meet with some unplanned surprises as a result. All the characters are adults, but their actions bear only a remote likeness to the things real people do in tense situations. The hero puts a golf club sock on the tip of his rifle near the beginning of the film, anticipating the script's need for it, later. That's fine, but the cabin is a hundred dirt-road miles from the nearest golf course, so what are the clubs doing there in the first place? The picture is soft and the sound is adequate.

CHAKA KHAN – THIS IS MY NIGHT
CHAKA KHAN

Chaka Khan – This Is My Night looks as good as it sounds and it sounds great. Ostensibly a concert disc, the camera work and editing are so elaborate that each cut could be mistaken for a concept video. At 52 minutes the show captures and holds one's attention from beginning to end. Kahn, laboring under an umbrella of red hair, works the crowd while calmly switching from jazz vocals to pop hits. The separation and ambience on the digital track is amazing. You can pick out conversations in the audience during the breaks. When Khan attempts the normally disastrous have-the-audience-sing-the-chorus, you can hear them carry the tune.

You get less than a third of the program material from the 12-inch *Chaka Khan – This Is My Night* on the 8-inch, *Chaka Khan*, and it isn't even in digital. The picture quality isn't as good, either. The three cuts, 'I Feel For You,' 'Tell Me Something Good,' and 'Through the Fire,' represent the best parts of the other disc, but this is a case of less not being more.

CHANCES ARE

A marvelously romantic comedy which uses reincarnation to fuel its narrative drive, *Chances Are* manipulates the fantasy elements nicely, using no more unreal occurrences than necessary to score its points. The performances, particularly from Cybill Shepherd and Robert Downey, Jr., also lend credibility to the sequence of events. The romance is intoxicating and the humor is a pleasant bonus. The picture quality of the disc is less commendable, though in most sequences it gets by. At its worst the image is grainy and somewhat pale. The sound is in digital stereo surround, with a limited number of separation effects. Share the disc with someone you wish to seduce.

CHAPLIN LOST AND FOUND: KEYSTONE
CHAPLIN LOST AND FOUND: ESSANAY I
CHAPLIN LOST AND FOUND: ESSANAY II
CHAPLIN LOST AND FOUND: MUTUAL I
CHAPLIN LOST AND FOUND: MUTUAL II
CHAPLIN LOST AND FOUND: MUTUAL III

The collections of Charlie Chaplin's short films in the *Chaplin Lost and Found* series are less comprehensive and less pristine the further one moves back into time, but the entire series is still a worthwhile investment.

A little background is in order. Charlie Chaplin was born into relatively comfortable means, but lost everything and was forced onto the streets when his father died and his mother became ill. Because of his parent's show business connections he eventually found a job in a stage company, and during a tour of the US, he was spotted by Mack Sennett, who ran the Keystone Studios. Chaplin worked for Sennett in 1914, and such was the nature of the movie business back then, before television and before feature-length films, that he appeared in 35 featurettes over the course of the year. By the end of 1914 he had refined his screen persona and was a big star, so he signed up, for more money, with ESSANAY Studios, and made fifteen more films over the next year and a half (several legitimate films were put together later by ESSANAY with outtakes). He then moved to Mutual Studios, for an even larger sum, to make 12 featurettes in the following 18 months, before signing up to an astronomical contract with First National, founding United Artists, and focussing on feature length efforts that would soon take a year or more of production time to put together.

Chaplin's first film for Sennett, the first official 'movie' he ever appeared in, 'Making a Living,' is included on the single-sided CLV disc *Chaplin Lost and Found: Keystone*. Chaplin's debut is inauspicious. He looks like Cantiflas, with a droopy mustache and beady eyes. He is the star of the film, but little of what one sees in his later work, except the ballet-like control over his movement and over his interaction with the other performers, is in evidence. The print is in such a condition that, were the movie anything other than Chaplin's debut, it would be considered unwatchable (we have seen a better copy). It was the next film he made, which is not included on the disc, that he shortened the mustache and enlarged the seat of his pants. What is included on the disc, although it is not mentioned on the back of the jacket and is not encoded with a separate chapter marker, is the film considered to be Chaplin's first directorial effort (though the responsibilities were shared with Mabel Normand), 'Caught in a Cabaret.' For the record, since the jacket covers contain the other release dates, the film premiered April 27, 1914. The print appears to have come from a later source. It has more title cards than the other Keystone films, containing many bad puns and one minor plot change. It was the habit of the company to stretch its profits with its Chaplin material. The final shot from 'The Tramp' has also been tacked on. The remaining three shorts, 'Mabel's Busy Day,' 'The Masquerader,' and 'The Rounders,' provide good examples of how Chaplin's confidence and resourcefulness grew over the course of the year. Since each vignette was only eleven minutes long, it was often put together without a script – just a few ideas and a week in front of the cameras. The shorts give a viewer a glimpse at how talented the other famous comics, Mabel Normand and Fatty Arbuckle, were, and how smoothly Chaplin, who began directing or co-directing steadily after 'Cabaret,' matched their comic talents with his.

The shorts on the *Keystone* disc are all heavily scratched and rarely of good contrast. All of the *Chaplin* discs are digitally encoded. Some shorts have older music tracks accompanying them, while others have scores which were clearly recorded more recently. In some circumstances, the film has actually been cropped on the left so that an audio track could be added on the source material. In any case, it is best to employ the audio of the discs sparingly, just enough to kill the silence. With all the Chaplin shorts, even the primitive *Keystone* efforts, we found that the more often we watched them, the funnier they became, with no sign of our reaching a level of satiation any time in the near future.

Eight of Chaplin's ESSANAY featurettes appear on *ESSANAY I* and *ESSANAY II*. On each disc side one is in CAV and side two is in CLV. Even with two unsteady still frames in every five, the CAV is wonderful, especially when one has an opportunity to run Chaplin in slow motion. His movements are so precise and so elaborate that you wonder if he isn't thinking twice as fast as everyone else.

The CAV featurette on *ESSANAY I* is 'His New Job,' Chaplin's appropriately titled first effort for his new sponsor. The narrative is awkward but there are a number of instances which provide the opportunity to catch him in action, stealing a cigarette, slipping under someone's legs, or sneaking a poke at a neighbor. On side two is the film we wish had been on side one, 'The Champion.' Although the print is apparently missing an opening sketch about feeding a hot dog to a bulldog, the movie is a marvelously amusing comedy about boxing, with an elaborately staged championship finale. Following 'The Champion' is a seminal work in Chaplin's career, 'The Tramp.' Unlike a bum, Chaplin's tramp has known better days, and one can clearly see how events in his own life went into solidifying the character. Although he had been utilizing variations of the character for more than a year, it was in 'The Tramp,' that he clearly found the character's essence – resourceful and lucky in the short run, but unable to change his fortune; he saves the day but doesn't get the girl. As in 'Masquerade,' on the Keystone disc, Chaplin dresses in drag during the course of 'A Woman,' the final short on *ESSANAY I*. Fortunately, Chaplin is never satisfied with a single gag or concept, and the movie, while not as involving as 'Champion' or 'Tramp,' has its moments.

Two films are in CAV on *ESSANAY II*, 'By the Sea' and 'The Bank.' 'By the Sea' is badly damaged in several places. Both films offer opportunities to slow down Chaplin's physical dexterity, and in 'The Bank' a viewer can discover how Chaplin accomplishes a trick involving a robber's gun. 'By the Sea' has a limited narrative and does little more than provide an excuse for Chaplin to explore his comedy in a beach setting. 'The Bank' has more plot and plenty of slapstick. In CLV on side two are two elaborate efforts, 'Shanghaied' and 'A Night at the Show.' In 'Shanghaied' the Tramp is kidnapped and forced to work on a freighter. There are some good gags about cooking and seasickness. For 'A Night in the Show' Chaplin has two roles, as a rowdy balcony patron and as a soused swell in the front row. There is no plot, but as the acts on the stage progress, the movie gets funnier and funnier, especially when the snake charmer loses her very live props.

The dozen films which Chaplin made at Mutual Studios in 1916 and 1917 are most indicative of his artistic transition. For some reason, Media and Image have chosen to release the films in essentially reverse order. *Mutual I* contains the last four films, 'Easy Street,' 'The Cure,' 'The Immigrant,' and 'The Adventurer.' *Mutual II* contains three films from the middle, 'The Count,' 'The Vagabond,' and 'Behind the Screen,' and one of the earliest, 'The Fireman.'

'Fireman' and 'Count' are good examples of the slapstick format, with Chaplin's character, more unsympathetic than he would later become, causing a balletic ruckus whenever he waddles into a room. 'Vagabond' is indicative of his later work, combining inventive physical comedy and a narrative which concludes with the rich girl that the tramp had saved from the Gypsies almost driving off without him. The best of all, however, is a film which should not be missed, 'Behind the Scenes.' It is a movie about making movies (Chaplin portrays a stagehand's beleaguered assistant) and has as many 'in' jokes (some of which never age – the director dresses casually and sports a beard and dark glasses) as it does slapstick (there is a terrific bit involving a trapdoor which Chaplin is supposed to release when he hears a gunshot). 'Scenes' is entertaining and full of vitality, and it is the perfect place to start if you are apprehensive about the concept.

The narratives are significantly developed and the comedy is trimmed down to essentials in the four films on *Mutual I*. (The picture, throughout the disc, seems to be set too far to the right.) There are some hysterical moments – Chaplin drops a big glob of ice cream down the back of a matron in 'Adventurer,' and you can just feel it as it spreads and melts – and some good acrobatics (some so simple that any decent contemporary comic ought to be stealing from it). In each film, however, the hero's character is clearly defined, and the frantic free-for-all which had dominated his work just 18 months earlier had given way to a calculated and controlled focus that was to become the discipline with which Chaplin would later create some of the world's greatest and most lasting comedy.

The last volume of the films Chaplin made at Mutual Studios, *Mutual III*, rounds out the *Chaplin Lost and Found* collection. The four films on this CLV disc are in remarkably good condition. The characters move at near-normal speed, the contrast levels are comparable to a contemporary effort, and the inevitable scratches are kept to a minimum. Although this is the last Mutual collection, it contains earlier efforts from Chaplin's stint at the studio, including the first film Chaplin made there, 'The Floorwalker.' All four emphasize comedy over narrative, but they are tightly constructed and systematically generate laughter. 'Floorwalker' makes use of an elaborate set, including an (at the time seldom seen) escalator. Chaplin was apparently the first person to run up one without getting anywhere. 'The Rink' begins with the standard but amusing gags involving high jinks among restaurant employees. In the second half, however, Chaplin dons roller skates, and demonstrates a spectacular adeptness (he'd used them on the stage) at keeping his balance in the face of adversity. 'The Pawnshop' is another standard Chaplin effort with his character employed in a second hand store. The best movie on the disc, however, and one of Chaplin's funniest efforts, is 'One A.M.' It opens (the outdoor sequence is tinted in blue) with Chaplin, inebriated, having difficulty exiting from a cab. When Chaplin finally frees himself and approaches his house, the movie cuts to an establishing shot showing the glorious array of obstacles (a tiger skin rug, a stuffed gorilla, a large pendulum, etc.) that he will have to cope with if he manages to get in. It is hysterical in the anticipation, and Chaplin, being Chaplin, fulfills its promise.

CHARADE (Import)

Some movies are perfect, not because they are exceptionally well made, but because the positive elements within them are so strong that it is useless to find fault with the details. The deftly plotted thriller, *Charade*, is witty and suspenseful, so much so that it remains enjoyable even after you have every red herring memorized. It stars Audrey Hepburn and Cary Grant, and one would be hard pressed two name two individuals who better personify glamour, elegance, or perfection. To top it off, the film takes place in the Cary Grant and Audrey Hepburn of cities, Paris, and the locations adeptly merge an exotic romanticism with a metropolitan excitement.

The disc has Japanese subtitles running across the picture and the monaural sound, which has some worthy effects, has not been CX-encoded. The picture does not sparkle, but it does not look worse for wear, either.

THE CHARGE OF THE LIGHT BRIGADE

According to the 1936 *The Charge of the Light Brigade*, the suicidal charge won the Crimean War for the British. This would be like suggesting that Custer won the battle of Little Big Horn, but when Errol Flynn is involved it is time to take your boots off, put your history books away, and get the popcorn out.

Directed by the inevitably dependable Michael Curtiz, most of *Brigade* takes place in India and features the political intrigues of an Islamic leader unhappy with British rule. Considering its age, the presentation is acceptable. The monaural sound is interesting in that the gunshots don't sound like normal movie gunshots. They sound more like arrows.

CHARIOTS OF THE GODS?

"The longitude which runs through the center of the Pyramid of Cheops divides the continents and oceans into two equal halves." That is just one of the stunning imaginary facts spewed out in *Chariots of the Gods?*, the hit 1970 fictional documentary film. The digital monaural sound is so accurate that you can hear the shifts in tone as the producers attempted to cram as much narration as they could onto the images. Accurately transferred or not, the sound is irritatingly wimpy and tortuous upon the ears. Perhaps the filmmakers felt that pain would help distract viewers from the (mysterious, ancient) mounds of bovine excreta being heaped upon them. The picture quality isn't any better, and the source material has plenty of scratches and splices to supplement its, by necessity, blurred imagery.

CHARLIE CHAN AT THE WAX MUSEUM/CHARLIE CHAN IN RIO

If you can make it through lines such as, "Pretty girl like lap dog – sometimes go mad," without putting a brick through your television set, then you will probably enjoy the CBS/Fox double bill, *Charlie Chan at the Wax Museum/Charlie Chan in Rio*. The films are only a couple minutes more than an hour long each, yet they have twice as many plot twists and red herrings as the average TV mystery. Sidney Toler is the supposedly 'Oriental' hero, though, as with most ethnically defamatory performances, if you just pretend he's from another planet, you can enjoy the programs without feeling guilty of collaboration.

Contrary to the chapter listing on the back of the jacket, Chapter 6 marks the beginning of the second film on side two. The first movie is so enjoyable and is over so quickly that a viewer naturally wants to follow up immediately with the other one, to extend the pleasure. All three sides are in CLV.

Both films were made on about three soundstage sets. In 'Wax Museum,' a radio broadcast from the museum is interrupted when one of the participants is murdered in an unexpected fashion. In 'Rio,' a woman with a violent past is dispatched just as she is preparing to elope. In both films there is a large herd of suspects which Chan must keep corralled until he collects enough clues to brand the guilty party.

The transfers are very good. Both prints are free of markings and have sharp black and white images. The sound has no significant faults, but is set at a lower than average volume level, which must be compensated for on one's own audio system. The jacket is designed for a single platter, so copies kept in tight quarters may become damaged.

THE CHASE

Although it was a flop when it came out, *The Chase* has endured on late night and weekend television. As the opening credits reveal, the movie is cropped, but it works very well on television and makes for good home video. The closeups of Marlon Brando, Jane Fonda, Robert Redford, Robert Duvall, James Fox, Angie Dickinson and others fill the narrowed screen. You're encouraged to ogle. Lillian Hellman's literate script is hokey, but it's intelligently hokey so that you oogle attentively as the plot unfolds.

The picture is a little heavy on orange glows, but it is sharp and bright. John Barry's closing overture plays through to a blank screen after the film is over.

CHECKING DOLBY SURROUND

(Import)

Those wishing to demonstrate the advantages of their laser video disc and Surround sound systems might wish to consider the relatively inexpensive (by import standards) 26 minute CAV import, *Checking Dolby Surround*.

The image on the disc is perfect, and the digitally encoded surround sound is perfect, too. The program is divided into three segments. The first is a graphic and noise arrangement which enables you to verify that all five speakers in your audio system are functioning correctly. The instructions for capturing the subtleties and tuning your system accordingly are in Japanese and therefore not much help, but the basic idea is accessible to all.

The second segment features a series of Steadycam video adventures – following a turtle down the center of a shopping mall, floating through a park full of noisy people practicing their noisy hobbies, riding mass transit – which put the viewer in the middle of a clamorous, giddy world of sound and images.

The last segment contains footage of the Blue Angels roaring every which way, followed by footage of a pounding ocean surf. In the Blue Angel piece, the jets roar across your head and when the planes veer away from one another, the sound follows. The surf is supposed to calm you down after all that excitement, and it is here that the disc contains its most startling image, a view of the sun setting on the water which has the appearance of rippling, liquid gold.

The CAV still frames aren't any good, but the disc is a nice way to demonstrate the general superiority of laser playback and the justification for cramming your room with audio equipment.

CHECKING OUT

A movie which is even more idiotic than it looks, *Checking Out* is a comedy about a man, played by Jeff Daniels, who becomes obsessed with death after his best friend suffers a fatal heart attack. Why do filmmakers think this stuff is funny? Not only does the premise make the viewer feel uncomfortable, but the script's digressions are as dopey and pointless as the main plot. One or two gags may be effective, but life is too short to wade through the rest of the material on their behalf. For what it is worth, the picture is only mildly grainy and the sound has a few well chosen stereo surround effects.

CHEECH & CHONG'S THE CORSICAN BROTHERS

Even by the relaxed standards of their drug films, *Cheech & Chong's The Corsican Brothers* is not funny. Because of the 90-minute length, it is inevitable that one or two of the jokes are amusing, but what you have to sit through to hear them is alternately embarrassing and boring. Even the central gag – that when one brother is hit, the other brother feels it – is forgotten at key moments. Neither of the two comics has the energy required to do physical comedy, anyway.

Following the laws of inverse proportion, the stereo sound is excellent and the picture isn't bad, either.

THE CHEERLEADERS

The early seventies softcore effort, *The Cheerleaders*, was initially rated 'X' but was cut to an 'R.' The disc is the 'R' version. Although the jacket says the running time is 84 minutes, the disc actually lasts only 76. The movie is of unimportant historical value. Today teen sex comedies are all over the place, but when *The Cheerleaders* first appeared, believe it or not, care or not, no one had ever turned athletic cheers into lewd suggestions on the big screen before. The source material is faded and peppered with scratches. The digital sound is a limp monaural and side two is in CAV.

CHERRY 2000

An above-average low-budget science fiction/action picture, *Cherry 2000*, is about a man who hires a guide to take him into a forbidden zone so that he may retrieve a duplicate of his damaged android courtesan. The guide is played by Melanie Griffith. The stunts are superior, the script is occasionally thoughtful, and the ending, though inevitable, is fully satisfying. It is an enjoyable, popcorn-friendly disc. The sound is digitally encoded stereo and is in decent shape. The picture quality is also okay.

CHICAGO 17

Chicago 17 has only two music videos, 'You're the Inspiration' and 'Hard Habit to Break.' They are similar in style and suppress narrative to emphasize attractive pictorials of the band and various women. The album's audio program follows the videos, accompanied by a still of the jacket cover.

CHILDREN OF A LESSER GOD

The print transfer of *Children of a Lesser God* is exquisite. The flesh tones are exact and the black portions of the screen stay black. The 119-minute film has been spread to three sides, probably to avoid breaking the film up in the middle of the school show dance scene. Although the disc is three sides long, it hasn't been digitally encoded. The sound is acceptable, but the violin theme which lingers in the background is fuzzy.

Children of a Lesser God, starring William Hurt and Marlee Matlin, is about a man with normal faculties who falls in love with a deaf woman. The subject allows one to see aspects to emotion which are normally obscured in clutter. Both characters are obstinate and a little short-sighted, but if one overcomes the temptation to outguess them, the film has a pleasing warmth which is fully communicated on the disc.

CHILDREN SHOULDN'T PLAY WITH DEAD THINGS (Import)

The cheap and inept 1972 horror effort, *Children Shouldn't Play with Dead Things*, manages to give a hint of the talent the director, identified as Benjamin Clark but in reality Bob Clark, would later exhibit with greater confidence. This beginner's effort has been released on disc in Japan and we are reporting it because some people seem to be willing to buy any movie where the dead obtain mobility and feast on the living. The sound reproduction is so accurate that you can hear the cameras whirring and the actors blowing their lines. The ending is tame by today's standards but at least the insipid cast get what is coming to them. The movie has a lot of talking and there are a lot of subtitles.

CHILD'S PLAY
The big budget special effects in *Child's Play* are a relief after the endless low-budget efforts coming from elsewhere. The picture is in good condition and the stereo surround sound is energetic. The movie, about a killer who reincarnates himself in a child's doll, has its bad points – for example, a woman leaps out of a police car and goes running straight to the apartment of a murdered voodoo priest even though she has never been in the neighborhood before, much less the apartment building – and its good points. It is reasonably exciting, reasonably entertaining, and reasonably glossy. The director, Tom Holland, makes it all look so easy, as if such things happened every day. They seem to, though, if you watch enough discs.

CHINA GIRL
Everybody in *China Girl* wears black, except the hero and the heroine, who wear white. Too much yin and not enough yang. The story is an uncredited adaptation of William Shakespeare's *West Side Story*, pitting a Chinese youth gang against an Italian youth gang and providing a pair of star-crossed lovers who only want to go somewhere and dance. There are some stylish camera angles, and all those black outfits, but the movie is as simple-minded as a fortune cookie and as emotional as a pizza.

The digital track is cleaner than the analog track. The picture and the sound quality are as good as *Year of the Dragon*, a film which *China Girl* also resembles in all the wrong ways.

THE CHIPMUNK ADVENTURE
The 76 minute *The Chipmunk Adventure* is in CLV on side one and CAV with two shaky still frames out of every five on side two. If you haven't seen the cartoon, you should know that the Chipmunks do not look like chipmunks and, in fact, it is difficult to say what they look like since they are not exactly little boys, either. To appeal to a wider constituency, there are also three little girl Chipmunks, called the Chipettes, who receive equal coverage in the story, in which all six are duped into going for a race around the world in order to smuggle diamonds. Parents should be warned that one character, although evil, glamorizes cigarette smoking.

The picture transfer is vivid. The digitally encoded stereo sound is very good and embellishes the incidental music effectively. The songs, marked by chapter codes, are mostly original and not the 45-to-78 renditions of famous tunes which first established the Chipmunks in the imaginations of an older generation.

CHOOSE ME
Choose Me is terrifically sexy even though the cast keeps their clothing on because the characters are all a little crazy and when they talk about being with one another their vulnerability is a turn-on. A case could probably be made for the suggestion that the three main female characters represent one person with a split personality, as do the two male characters, but the easiest way to enjoy the movie is to accept the story as it is presented. A man released from a mental hospital walks into a bar and starts asking women to marry him. One finally does. The picture is a bit blurry and grainy, but not severely. Side two seems to start out a little louder than side one. The music disc is by Teddy Pendergrass.

A CHORUS LINE THE MOVIE
If it weren't for home video, *A Chorus Line The Movie* would not exist. The project shuffled around for ten years in search of a workable screen concept. Technology advanced and home video money became so abundant that finally a workable concept was no longer a necessary financing factor.

The show was recorded digitally and has been pressed in digital surround sound. Even though the sound editing is no better than the script, the sheer perfection of replication is quite impressive. At times it is even scary, because the cropped screen drops characters who speak on the far left before the scan reaches that side. The picture looks almost as sharp as it sounds, and there are 20 chapter markers. The 118-minute film is spread to three sides.

CHRISTMAS AT RIPON CATHEDRAL
If you miss the snow or long for hot crumpets baking in the oven, put on *Christmas at Ripon Cathedral*. An hour-long concert set in one of England's oldest churches, the program has a nice mixture of materials, making it one of the best holiday themed discs available. For one thing, the Huddersfield Choral Society, which is the centerpiece of the presentation, is as comfortable doing 'Have Yourself a Merry Little Christmas' as they are with 'For Unto Us a Child Is Born.' The Champion Black Dyke Mills Band, a relaxed and pleasantly indulgent group, contributes a couple of instrumental pieces, including a touch of Prokofiev which doesn't seem out of place in the slightest. Finally, there are readings of Christmas prose, a wonderful ornamental touch which provides an ideal break between the musical passages.

The picture comes from a video tape source and is passable, though the red gowns of the choral group often look fuzzy. The sound is competent, but the recording is not elaborate enough to capture the full thrust of the grandest ensemble numbers.

A CHRISTMAS CAROL
The black-and-white 1951 version of *A Christmas Carol*, with Alistar Sim as Scrooge (the film was originally titled 'Scrooge'), is not a release which is knowledgeable of the requirements of laser video disc presentation, and the smaller the television set you watch it on, the better.

The 16mm source has several severe splices, numerous scratches, and is often vaguely unfocussed. The sound has dropouts and other distortions, and is best left unamplified. The only really nice thing we can say about the disc presentation is that the jacket cover uses the original advertising artwork. It may be a little misleading, because it is in color, but it is a marvelously screwy ad ("Fred thought she was worth being disinherited for...and so will you!") and increases the value of the disc.

A CHRISTMAS STORY
The first time we saw *A Christmas Story* everyone watching the film was laughing, but none were laughing harder than the eight- and nine-year-olds in the audience. The laser disc has become a holiday favorite of ours, and we drag it out every Christmas Eve to brighten our spirits and put us to bed with a smile.

Set in the snowy days approaching a '40s Christmas, all viewers will respond to the mixture of dreamy nostalgia and outrageous pranks. There is a department store Santa scene which must be the ultimate of its kind.

Some of the humor is subtle, such as the grotesque meals the mother is forever preparing, and will only catch your attention after several viewings. The transfer is nothing spectacular, but the presentation is more than adequate and it is a jolly way to celebrate the holidays.

CHRISTMASTIDE
For some reason the 51-minute *Christmastide*, with Jessye Norman, has been split to two sides. The soundtrack has some hiss, and even a crackle or two, but every instrument and every voice is remarkably well-defined. 'Christmastide,' arranged by Donald Fraser, is a medley of carols, some familiar to everyone and some familiar only to die-hard choral group fans. A jacket insert provides the lyrics. Norman is supported by the American Boychoir, the Ely Cathedral Choristers, the Vocal Arts Chorus, and the Bournemouth Symphony Orchestra. The program was recorded in Ely Cathedral, although the visuals rarely move away from the singers. Norman is so over-lit that her dental work and upper palate are in full view during the closeups. The picture quality is okay, however, and the disc will be a good way to bring peace to the often frantic holidays.

CHUD II
Satire gives way to slapstick comedy in *CHUD II*, a zombie movie which has very little to do with its predecessor. The comedy is broad, as Gerrit Graham, playing a back-from-the-dead government experiment, wanders around a rural community infecting the populace. The humor is intermittent, but the filmmakers seem to be enjoying themselves, which helps relax the guard of the viewer. The Ultra-Stereo sound has a limited number of surround effects. The picture is okay. Side two runs under a half hour, in CLV.

A CHUMP AT OXFORD/MEN O'WAR
Like the other 3M Laurel and Hardy releases, *A Chump at Oxford/Men O'War* has two features on one disc. *Chump* is a little longer than an hour, so it runs on all of side one and part of side two, followed by *Men* which is identified by a chapter marker. *Chump* is actually a series of shorter films loosely linked together. After suffering through unemployment, the boys foil a bank robbery and win a scholarship to Oxford. The still on the back of the jacket is from another movie.

In *Men O'War* the two are sailors on leave to spend a day in the park. They end up in an amusing fracas on a hired rowboat. The source material is acceptable, but not exceptional and the print for *Men* isn't in as good shape as the print for *Chump*.

CINDERELLA
We hope that a forthcoming stroke of midnight will not change the beautiful CBS/Fox *Cinderella* into something more pedestrian. The transfer of the 1964 taped television special is lovely. Although a bar passes through the picture in a couple of places and a skip occurs at one point, the color and sharpness of the image is excellent and unquestionably superior to the wicked stepsisters of Beta and VHS, in whom it is doubtful the program even fits.

This was one of Rodgers and Hammerstein's last efforts together. An 'introduced' Lesley Ann Warren plays Cinderella. Walter Pidgeon gives the best performance, as the king, and Ginger Rogers is surprisingly ineffective as the queen. The show was taped in a TV studio, with minimal set decorations, moderately memorable costumes, and real horses. It is 82 minutes long and has not been given chapter markers.

CINDERELLA (CLV)
CINDERELLA (CAV)
The CAV version of the Disney release, *Cinderella*, was mastered from source material a generation further away from the original than was the CLV version. The difference is stunning. The CAV version looks very good, with the same picture quality which graced the other Disney 'Classic' releases. The picture quality of the CLV version, however, is so much better than the CAV that you don't even have to put the two on side-by-side monitors to recognize the improvement. Where bright solid colors, particularly reds and blues, still retain a faint instability on the CAV disc, as they did on the other Disney discs, the colors are rock solid on the CLV, and their intensity is tempered to blend better with the surrounding colors. The superior picture causes the same phenomena which we have noted so often in the past: The CLV disc, because it looks better, is more entertaining.

Both discs have been digitally encoded, and on both the analog track is noisier, but again the CLV disc seems to have an edge over the CAV. The differences are less pronounced, but sounds on the CLV disc have more confidence, and a fainter background hiss. The soundtrack, which was jerry-rigged into stereo a few years earlier for a theatrical release, has more positive than negative attributes. The exercise cleaned up the sound, but there are mildly nagging shifts of volume levels in the dialog. Only the CAV release has chapter markers (15 of them; the film is 76 minutes long) and its side breaks are well chosen. On the CLV disc, however, side two begins with a too emotional scene, and should have been started earlier, to give preparation, or later, after the melodrama has subsided.

Every still frame is jitter-free on the CAV disc. All the standard play functions can be enjoyably employed to manipulate the cartoon. Those wishing to study the technique of the film will find the many experiments in lighting and shadows to be fascinating. Using the slow motion or still step, one can monitor the increases and decreases in greys and browns as the characters move from daylight to darkness.

The release of *Cinderella* on home video, because of the tradition behind it, signifies, more than any other home video release, a momentous shift in the concept of commercial entertainment. It is an acknowledgement that movies have become material possessions; that they can no longer be withheld from the viewer's gaze when the theater closes or the station signs off at midnight.

CINDERELLA – TALES FROM THE GYPSY ROAD
Four music videos and two live concert sequences get stretched into an hour program on *Cinderella – Tales from the Gypsy Road*. The single-sided disc contains extensive interviews between each number. The interviews are enjoyable and the songs are good (the group plays a light heavy metal), but the disc can't really be used for music without extensive chapter programming. The picture transfer is okay, and the videos look sharp. The sound is fine.

CITIZEN KANE
Voyager's *Citizen Kane* laser disc is the 'Citizen Kane' of laser discs. Like the movie, the disc is the ultimate in boyish look-what-I-can-do technological enthusiasm. Originally released in CAV format on three platters, it was clear that Voyager wanted to utilize the laser disc format in every way possible.

Written by Herman Mankiewicz, photographed by Gregg Toland, scored by Bernard Herrmann, and edited by Robert Wise, the guiding force behind *Citizen Kane* was Orson Welles, who directed the film and also portrayed the title character. The film is structured as a biography of a rich newspaper publisher – patterned after events in the life of William Randolph Hearst – but what has earned it such praise as "the greatest sound film ever made" is the way it was constructed. Every scene and sequence is rich in technique and wit. Welles brought his experience in the stage and in radio to movie-making in a way that expanded, rather than limited, what could be done with film.

The movie was chosen as Voyager's premiere release in it's Criterion Collection series, and it expanded the concept of what could be done with discs. Among the added material are stills from the production, notes on appreciating the picture, and a genuine trailer for the movie, containing a few revelations of its own. Several scenes dropped from early drafts of the screenplay are described, including one which remarkably anticipates the Patty Hearst affair. Also tacked onto the disc is a five-minute, sped-up version of the entire film, the utility of which is beyond our understanding.

A later CLV version did not contain any of the supplementary material. Although not in stereo, the echoes, the whispers, the screams, and the music all come through with delightful exuberance on the Voyager discs. The image transfer is gloriously sharp and rich.

Image also released a version of the title, with an alternate audio lecture by Paul Mandell. The picture quality of the Image disc is not as good as the Voyager transfer, and looks grainy. The soundtrack is also less distinctive.

Any film scholar worth his weight could probably talk for a whole semester on *Citizen Kane*, but Mandell's work is a mistake. *Kane* upsets the lecture format anyway, because it opens with barrage of images and tricks, forcing Mandell to tick them off and wait 15 minutes before he can get around to introducing the film. His most disastrous suggestion comes at the very end, when he implies that Welles's career was wrecked by a Hearst blacklist. The world would be a much different place if the only obstacle to artistic creation was a lack of proper funding. That paradox, Mandell should have recognized, is one of the main lessons of *Citizen Kane*.

CLAIRE'S KNEE
The print used for *Claire's Knee* has a massive flurry of scratches in its opening moments, but then calms down, though the Nestor Almendros cinematography looks paler than it should. The subtitles are pale yellow. The disc never looks faded, but the film doesn't look fresh, either.

Fortunately, Eric Rohmer's movie will never age. It is about a diplomat, but he doesn't really look like a diplomat since he has a beard and hair which is about an inch too long. The flaws in his character are gradually revealed during the course of the film, as he spends his summer arranging for the sale of his vacation house and taking a passing interest in his neighbor's daughters. As his immaturity becomes more apparent, one's respect for his character diminishes, but an understanding of his humanity replaces the respect. The less you like him, the closer you get to him.

The sound is surprisingly good. In particular, there are some tennis racquets which sound more like tennis racquets than most movie tennis racquets do. The film is not a great masterpiece, but it is enjoyable. It is an excellent example of narrative and emotional efficiency, an efficiency which is too naturalistic to be duplicated in the United States. How could you sell touching a girl's knee as a 'high concept?'

THE CLAN OF THE CAVE BEAR
Jean Auel's books are crammed full of excitement, but the movie which was based on *The Clan of the Cave Bear* discards all of it to telescope the bare essentials of the plot in a short 100 minutes. Auel's best scenes took place on the steppes, describing the richness of the earth, the crafting of weapons and the thrill of a hunt. Most of the movie takes place in a cave.

That Daryl Hannah would reach the first zenith of her stardom just as the film was being cast is surely one of the most fortuitous strokes of picture-making in a long time. In the scenes where the camera stays on her for longer than ten seconds a cut, the movie is truly energized.

The disc is free of the normal flaws. The picture, however, looks smoky. Even the brightest daylight shots seem a bit dark. The sound is better. Before there were cars and refrigerators and ticking clocks there were only crows and the wind. You hear the silence.

CLARA'S HEART
The picture transfer on *Clara's Heart* is spotless and the stereo surround sound is clear and precise. Whoopi Goldberg is cast as a West Indian woman hired as a housekeeper and nanny by a couple who are splitting up. Her scenes are captivating and her accent is great fun, but the movie is a disappointment. There isn't a single character whose psychol-

ogy surprises you, and there isn't a single plot turn you can't anticipate well in advance.

CLASH OF THE TITANS
CLASH OF THE TITANS (Import)

The colors on the 1981 film, *Clash of the Titans,* are full and sharp on both the domestic release and the CAV import. The disc is not in widescreen format, so subtitles are plastered along the bottom of the picture on the Japanese offering. Little information is lost on the sides of the screen and when Ray Harryhausen's models are in action, there is no dialog which needs to be translated. The sound is fine.

The film was an attempt to merge Harryhausen's special effects with some big-name stars, complaints having come from Harryhausen's other efforts that the acting was so pathetic. It didn't help. The pleasures which the film has to offer remain mechanical, and the drawbacks remain emotional.

CLASS OF NUKE 'EM HIGH (Import)

Much of the same cast and production crew who put their all into *The Toxic Avenger* were also responsible for *Class of Nuke 'Em High,* which is available in Japan. Even the green slime which causes all the trouble in *Avenger* reappears, this time turning a group of honor students into degenerate punks. The film is tighter than *Avenger* and, for all of the gruesome effects, easier to stomach.

Japanese catalogs listed the title as being in widescreen format, but it is not. Virtually nothing is lost, however, with the picture filling the screen, and the Japanese subtitles are rarely troublesome. The transfer is excellent and the monaural sound, though not CX-encoded, is fine. There is even 'exit music' after the end credit scroll, though it seems most audiences would have run for the doors before then. The disc also has chapter markers, so you can find your favorite severed limbs in a hurry.

CLEAN AND SOBER

Warner released *Clean and Sober* in what the company is calling 'matted-screen format,' an image which is mildly letterboxed at about 1.66:1. The image is intended to closely represent the theatrical presentation of the film, although the width of the screen composition is identical to other video presentations of the title.

Clean and Sober runs a couple of minutes over two hours and is spread to three sides. The picture seems consistently hazy, but the colors look accurate and the image is sharply focussed. The sound is digitally encoded stereo. It is an average transfer with a little noise in the background and a few clever separation effects scattered through the show. Warner has also provided thorough chapter encoding and a listing of the chapters on the back of the jacket.

Clean and Sober is a comedy. Not the kind you laugh at, but a comedy nonetheless. It is about a man who enters a detoxification program to hide from the police and – punchline – detoxifies in spite of himself. It is good to know that Michael Keaton, who stars, can include restraint among his many fine talents. One shudders to think what many other actors would have done with the part. Even his vomiting scene is subdued. He knows that he's going to be on the screen a lot and that he doesn't have to exhaust himself to make an impression. It is because he treats the part so soberly that he is able to play up the irony of his character's situation, thereby saving the movie from going off the deep end.

CLEOPATRA

Fanciers of women's breasts will enjoy Cecil B. DeMille's *Cleopatra,* a film which lives for décolletage. Claudette Colbert portrays the scheming queen. She protects her country by throwing herself into the arms of the Roman leaders who come to conquer her land. It works twice. Colbert's performance is captivating because she acts like both a sex-pot and a true leader. She's intelligent, driven, and attracted to the power of the Ceasars. And, oh, those outfits! Egypt is a dry and hot country, very much like Southern California from the looks of the film, and the women apparently stay cool by wearing mesh and wires instead of cloth. The handmaidens fill the screen with flesh, but it is difficult to take your eyes off of Colbert, who really seems enjoy sunbathing for the sake of art.

The black-and-white print is not one of MCA's better preservation efforts, but it has no serious flaws. The sound is also past its salad days, but perhaps the film is more bearable with the airs of antiquity. Much of 100-minute soap epic plays like *Dune*, all highlights and no flesh outside of the handmaidens. It is not until one gets into the languid scenes which the scriptwriters wrote themselves that the dialog stops feeling static and the movie really seems to move. The most famous scene is semiliterally the heart of the movie, Cleopatra's seduction of Mark Antony, which ends in a classic reverse dolly shot, moving away from their bed on the Queen's barge to reveal the gentle stroking of the oars and the steady, intoxicating beat of the coxswain's drums.

After the film is over MCA has included two rerelease trailers marked by a single chapter code. Both intend to capitalize on another DeMille effort, *Samson and Delilah.* DeMille introduces and narrates the first, while a generic narrator does the second. Both are terrific, and adequate cause for those who do not enjoy women's breasts to consider getting the disc.

THE CLIMB

Movies about mountain climbing are always more entertaining than one anticipates, because it is hard to believe that dramatists will be able to create a useful narrative to accompany the physical stunts even though they wouldn't have tried if they didn't think they could pull it off. The innocuous artwork on the jacket cover of *The Climb* is not exactly going to encourage impulse purchases. The movie, a Canadian television production, deserves better, because it is a compelling and intelligent work.

The Climb is a chronicle of a German assault upon a Himalayan peak during the early fifties. It is a true story, drawn largely from the diary of the man who makes it to the top, and derives its power from the contrast between the disarray of the team's leadership and the determination of the individual climbers. The film's only drawbacks are an unsuccessful but necessary substitution of the Canadian Rockies for the Himalayas, and occasional dramatic confusion as the climbers move back and forth between their interim campsites.

The picture transfer is above average in quality. The combination of the snow, the dark mountain shadows, and other unusual lighting features never becomes a problem. The sound is limited from a production standpoint, but has no significant faults.

CLOAK AND DAGGER

Most run-of-the-mill suspense films start out great and then end awkwardly. *Cloak and Dagger* has a terrific ending, but the beginning is not successful. The show is about a boy with an active fantasy life who gets involved with an espionage plot and a real murder. The filmmakers chose to visualize the child's fantasies, so when the real action starts occurring the viewer is hesitant in cheering the boy along for fear that the dangers will turn out to be imaginary. Henry Thomas plays the boy and Dabney Coleman has fun with a dual role as the boy's father and as the boy's make-believe hero/playmate. The sound and picture are of good quality and the stereo is utilized cleverly.

CLOSELY WATCHED TRAINS

The Czechoslovakian Oscar winner, *Closely Watched Trains,* is about a boy working at a railroad station and coming of age during World War II. The black and white film has one unusually memorable scene, involving a rubber stamp, and a lighthearted mood which is undercut, deliberately, by a sad ending. Prints of the film have always looked a little bedraggled, so with that in mind, the transfer is okay. The monaural sound has digital encoding, for what it is worth. The English subtitles are white and are lost in the image on more than one occasion.

CLUB PARADISE

Jimmy Cliff is in *Club Paradise* and he may not have the comic instincts of Robin Williams, Peter O'Toole, or Adolph Caesar, who also appear in the film, but he has a pleasant personality and provides a nice musical score. Cliff and Williams portray the owners of a second rate resort who are being pressured to sell out. They don't, but it is enjoyable watching the story unfold, listening to the music, and laughing at the sparse moments of inspired humor. The disc has digital sound, all the better to hear the music and the careful and amusing diction of Williams, O'Toole and Caesar. The picture is bright and free of error. One can't say the same about the script, but standards tend to relax in the tropics, anyway.

CLUE

Nobody is ever going to watch *Clue* three times through to experience the different endings separately. We didn't. We were surprised to discover that the endings are almost intended to be seen sequentially, and they are the funniest when viewed in that manner. The standard denouement in the first ending disintegrates into near anarchy in the last ending, and the activities in the subsequent finales comment humorously on the activities in the preceeding installments. Each ending has been marked with a chapter marker, but there is no demarcation other than the chapter display to warn you that the first ending has begun. The picture and sound are passable.

COBRA
A cobra is a fairly dumb animal with an inflated head, so the appellation is appropriate to the star of *Cobra*, Sylvester Stallone. He portrays a shoot-first-and-don't-ask-any-questions-after cop who is battling a fitness and cutlery cult in LA. The cult keeps healthy doing jumping jacks with axes and gets into trouble when new members have difficulty picking up the exercise. The movie was a big hit in countries where English and basic concepts of democracy are unfamiliar, but it flopped here.

The disc is in surround. The telephones and gunshots sound like your own. The picture is a little grainy in the night scenes.

THE COCA-COLA KID
For some reason the makers of *The Coca-Cola Kid* don't admit the script is based on short stories by Frank Moorhouse until the fine print in the end credit role (on the other hand, they go out of their way to deny association with the Coca-Cola Bottling Co). The start is promising. The movie looks like it is going to be a high-pitched attack on corporate ways and means when a brilliant but eccentric young executive is sent to the Australian Coke headquarters to boost sales. Instead, he makes friends with a mouse in his hotel room, the bellboy assumes he works for the CIA, and the movie becomes more improbable and less funny by the minute. The picture is soft and the sound is a bit harsh.

COCKTAIL
Here is the secret to the successful *Cocktail*: It's a musical. Notice how that aspect was carefully concealed by the film's marketers. If they had said it was a musical, no one would have gone. Instead they pretended it was a flashy, lightweight bartender tale – with ads that made the script sound like a bad soap opera – and let the dozen major songs on the soundtrack and the elaborate, unlikely choreography sell the film subconsciously to audiences. Do you want to see Tom Cruise defy his girlfriend's rich father or do you want to see him dance with Bryan Brown? The ads sold the first, and audiences bought the second.

Intense colors and interior backgrounds tend to look grainy, but the image is sharp. The sound editing does not really catch the din of a crowded bar, but then verisimilitude is not one of the film's strong points. The songs come through okay. It's the kind of disc which is best played loud. Anything which helps numb a viewer's brain helps the movie.

COCOON
COCOON THE RETURN
Who wants to see a sequel to *Cocoon*? The story in the first film (about a contrived collection of elderly characters who are rejuvenated by mysterious alien objects) was resolute, and the movie was manipulative and uninspiring. The picture and sound transfers were first-rate, but film's production values were glossy and bland.

About the only nice thing we have to say about the sequel is that it obviously generated nice paychecks (assuming they were prescient enough to take their pay up front) to a group of performers who deserve the money, not for *Cocoon The Return*, but for the endless hours of pleasure they have collectively provided elsewhere. The sequel itself is useless. It has no tension, no confident humor, and no sense of discovery – the attributes which rescued the first film from being a total waste of time.

The disc, then, has little to offer. The picture is passable, although intense colors, even intense pastels, tend to blur. The sound has an active stereo surround mix.

CODE NAME: EMERALD
The 95-minute *Code Name: Emerald* could have used another 30 minutes. The plot, which is based on a World War II espionage novel, has many twists and turns. In the movie, most of them happen offstage. Ed Harris portrays a double agent who is sent into Nazi-occupied Paris to prevent a captured American officer from giving away D-Day. The movie was filmed in a muddy gauze and is never quite in focus. The sound is passable.

CODE OF SILENCE
We read somewhere that parents find Chuck Norris's movies to make reliable home video rentals because they never contain any sex. Shootings, beatings, knifings, explosions, and car crashes, yes. But no sex. *Code of Silence* has all of the above and no sex, also. No wonder Norris never seems to unwind.

The plot has an elaborate subplot which always promises to merge with the central story, but never does. Norris portrays a cop attempting to quell a Chicago mob war and, in the subplot, to prevent an incompetent fellow officer from returning to duty. The program, however, is by no means the worst effort Norris has ever participated in and the ending, in which he single handedly wipes out an entire brigade of bad guys, has a certain heroic charm to it.

The picture is much too light and often a little sloppy. The sound doesn't have any severe flaws. If you watch the disc, don't miss the small talk in the art gallery scene. Without sex, only comments such as, "Colors," "There's such a richness, it's, I don't know," "I love the snowflake," "Natural light," "Have you seen this?" "I really like your new stuff a lot, especially the 'Dead Dog' series, it's great," can keep you going between beatings.

COFFY
The picture quality of *Coffy* is much better than the still frames on the back of the jacket, but the image is consistently grainy. The digitally encoded sound is monaural and not very accomplished. There are chapter markers for the several awful songs on the soundtrack ("Coffy is the color,/Coffy is the color,/Coffy is the color of your skin,/Coffy is the world you live in./Coffy is the color,/Coffy is the color...").

The narrative concerns a nurse who turns into a vigilante after her sister dabbles in drugs. Pam Grier stars. There is a substantial amount of sex which, exploitative or not, has a touch of humor and feeling to it. Grier is marvelous but, maddeningly, the only thing her role in *Coffy* accomplished was to make her the first choice when mainstream movie producers wanted to cast the sort of stereotyped part she had so adeptly appeared to have risen above, i.e., the crazed, addicted hooker in *Fort Apache, The Bronx*.

COLD FEET
Tom McGuane and Jim Harrison wrote the screenplay for *Cold Feet*, a delightful black comedy. Tom Waits, Sally Kirkland (wearing vinyl jumpsuits two sizes too small), and Keith Carradine portray three unscrupulous crooks who are driven by compulsion to act out their true natures no matter how much trouble they get into by doing so.

Specifically, the plot is about a horse who has emeralds surgically implanted inside him (just exactly where is deliberately never made clear). That is just an excuse, however, for the characters to double-cross one another and chase each other from Arizona to Montana. The movie's humor is clownish, which may cause proper viewers to raise their noses, but if you just want to put your legs up and have a down and dirty good time, *Cold Feet* will do it for you. The picture transfer is fine, as is the sound.

COLLABORATION – GEORGE KAWAGUCHI MEETS SHELLEY MANNE (see **THE JAZZ LIFE VOL. 1**)

THE COLLECTOR
Although *The Collector*, the story of a young man who kidnaps a woman and keeps her confined in his cellar, uses a standard situation, the purpose of the drama is more to illuminate psychology than to provide a viewer with mundanely erotic thrills. Hence the opening title card, 'William Wyler's The Collector' is a little presumptuous, because even though Wyler and the scriptwriters did an excellent job adapting what was essentially a compilation of alternating interior monologues, the work is John Fowles' and no one else's, *auteur* theory or no *auteur* theory.

The colors are somewhat pale, but otherwise the picture and sound are fine. There is some amount of panning and scanning, but it is only obvious in a couple of sequences. The narrative is infinitely re-watchable, despite the essentially two-person cast, because of the finely hewn touches which Fowles provided. The score and its orchestration, by Maurice Jarre, uses many of the same instruments and chords as his *Doctor Zhivago* score, but it never seems out of place. Instead, it flits irreverently about the edges of the drama, like the butterfly motif, reflecting upon the randomness of all human interaction.

COLOR ME BARBRA
(see **MY NAME IS BARBRA**)

THE COLOR OF MONEY
There is a problem with the soundtrack of *The Color of Money*. The volume levels for the rock music soundtrack are significantly higher than the volume levels for the dialog. So you either blast yourself out of your video room or you come near straining to hear what is going on. The sound is digitally encoded and it has quite a kick. The picture has a faint blur in some lighting situations, but in general it looks as sharp as it sounds. The 119-minute Touchstone release requires three sides. It is well constructed and worth watching many times, provided your neighbors don't mind.

THE COLOR PURPLE
THE COLOR PURPLE (CLV)
One summer, a couple of years before the Steven Spielberg movie of *The Color Purple*

came out, every twelve year old girl on the subway in New York could be observed clutching a copy of Alice Walker's novel. Those who thrive on Spielberg's suspense and fantasy efforts may have found *Purple* to be a little too prissy, but there is an adolescent spirit which the movie speaks to in a voice as clear as the snakes and bugs of the Indiana Jones pictures. *The Color Purple* manipulates the emotions of familial happiness and self-discovery in the same way that *Jaws* manipulates fear and *Close Encounters* manipulates wonder. It is the purity of those emotions which drives some people crazy and others back to the film again and again.

There are no discernible differences in picture or sound quality in the CLV and CAV versions. The image is slightly letterboxed. The transfer of the film to disc was a complicated task and has been accomplished without major errors. Every scene seems to require a different set of colors and illuminations, and the disc manages each transition without hesitation. The colors, including the purples, are clear and bright. When the focus is supposed to be sharp the picture is exact, but when the image is supposed to be hazy, it becomes, in places, slightly too hazy. The sound recording was of superior quality and is well preserved on the disc. The differences between the digital and analog tracks are subtle, with the digital track providing more complete control over the individual sound definitions.

Different movies take to the Standard Play manipulations of CAV in different ways. Some offer the most rewards when run at triple speed; others are best savored by freezing individual frames. Fast speed and still frames provided us with fleeting pleasures as we watched the disc, but in slow motion, the film gained in visual and emotional strength. It goes without saying that the actors and actresses remain in character even when their smallest mannerisms are revealed. The slower motion increases an understanding of their intentions and their immediate feelings. The images are consistently striking and involving, so that a child running in a yard, behind a couple who are fighting, balances the emotions of the scene. Many say that Spielberg provided too much balance, but in slow motion a viewer has the time to take in both ideas independently, to experience good and bad feelings in one shot.

The way in which the 154-minute film has been broken across six sides on the CAV disc is revealing. First, it is important to point out that Warners has made every break at a perfect moment, so that the opening scene on each side has a renewed vigor. Unlike the three-sided CLV disc, which made it difficult to apprehend the film's structure, the six sides of the CAV edition make things very clear. The lesbian kiss (euphemistically identified on the jacket's chapter guide; both discs have 29 chapters) and the initial confrontation of Margaret Avery's character (also named Avery) with her father occur in the exact middle of the film. The last side contains not only the heroine's establishment of her own independent life and her reunion with her children, but it also features the reconciliation between Avery and her father, and further elaborations on the significance of the color purple.

The color purple is the color of bruises, the color of passion, and the color of the sort of prose Spielberg is often accused of creating on film. The first time we saw the movie we thought it was the ultimate emotional roller coaster ride, but those feeling have not lasted through multiple viewings. We haven't tired of the film, however, since its subtler charms – the humor, the photography, the performances – grow in stature as the deliberate heart tuggings diminish.

COLORS

Those who were afraid to enter a movie theater to see *Colors* can now obtain it for viewing in the safety of their home. The film is more about cops than about gangs, but they bump into one another enough to make everyone nervous. The casting of Sean Penn and Robert Duvall as two cops from different generations is inspired – we wish we could have seen what it was like on the set. The film could have used a more 'vérité' point of view, and we could have done without the epilog, but Duvall and Penn fill their roles so ideally that everything fits into place behind them. The movie is also rich in habit-forming street lingo.

The 127-minute CLV presentation includes 'new footage' not seen in theaters. The disc's stereo surround sound is terrific. The mix is superb, and it has made it onto disc with barely a whisper of background noise. The picture is mostly in good condition, though there are passages with mild imperfections.

COMBAT! 1 (Import)
COMBAT! 2 (Import)
COMBAT! 3 (Import)
COMBAT! 4 (Import)
COMBAT! 5 (Import)
COMBAT! 6 (Import)
COMBAT! 7 (Import)
COMBAT! 8 (Import)
COMBAT! 9 (Import)
COMBAT! 10 (Import)
COMBAT! 11 (Import)
COMBAT! 12 (Import)

Were it not for the grisly demise of actor Vic Morrow, the old television series *Combat!* would probably have not found its way onto laser disc in Japan. The releases, while appealing, perhaps, to a morbid fascination on the part of Japanese consumers, are nonetheless fortuitous, because *Combat!* is a unique and well executed television series. The individual episodes are often well scripted and directed. Morrow is marvelous, and many popular television personalities, such as Telly Savalas and Bill Bixby, pop up in guest parts.

Morrow's character, Sergeant Saunders, is beautifully developed. Although younger than many of his peers, Saunders is a natural leader and an instinctive judge of other men. He is earnest, takes no pleasure in war, and makes quick, confident decisions. No matter how well the character has been written, however, it is Morrow, with the curls of baby fat still in his cheeks and his beleaguered, war-weary grin, who brings these features to the fore. During pauses in the action he will often stop and light up a cigarette (there are a lot of cigarettes in this show). He has such command of the screen that these supposedly calming moments – just Morrow in closeup, smoking – are emotional peaks. In contrast, the series also starred Rick Jason as Lieutenant Hanley. Jason is a walking transparency, and the episodes in which Morrow does not appear must utilize strong guest stars to compensate.

The scripts were generally written short and then padded with gun battles. So many gun battles! If you think the TV shows of today are violent, you should check out a couple of these. There isn't much blood, but the shooting is almost incessant. (So long as you keep telling yourself that these are Nazis being killed, the itchy-trigger killings and the repeated utilization of the word 'Krauts' should not be disturbing.)

The scripts, however, are generally very good. The plots involve tests of endurance or character under the stress of war. The use of California wine country locations for Europe, although not fully convincing, is effective in widening the scope of the settings, preventing the episodes from seeming confined by soundstage sets. The only false note which runs consistently through the shows is the spanking new roof sported by every abandoned 'French' barn or farmhouse the troop comes across. Either it is an error in judgement or the show's researchers discovered that some French roofer made out like a bandit during the War. In general, the production budgets look proportionately larger than many of today's television programs and the show is never at a loss for explosions.

The music, by Leonard Rosenman, comes in two flavors. Endless variations of 'When Johnny Comes Marching Home,' for the good guys, and endless variations of 'Deucheland, Deucheland Uber Alles,' for the bad guys. In fact, you can always tell when a sniper is lurking, because the Nazi theme often kicks in before the bad guys actually appear.

Combat! 1 contains a Morrow episode, 'The Gun,' and a Jason episode, 'Anniversary.' In 'The Gun,' Saunders must motivate a group of soldiers to haul a German howitzer over a mile of rough terrain so that it can be used to destroy a strategically-placed bunker. The script has one unfortunate flaw. After dragging the gun up a hillside, it slips and falls back down. At this point one or two quick scenes should have been inserted showing the soldiers hauling it up again. Instead, there is just a cut to the other side of the hill, the second attempt apparently having been successful. Otherwise, the episode is one of the best. Telly Savalas appears with Jason in 'Anniversary.' He portrays a French Resistance fighter (love that accent!) who is suffering from hallucinations over the loss of his family and is killing Allied and Axis soldiers indiscriminately. The hallucinations are well executed.

Jason appears only briefly in 'Conflict' on *Combat! 3*, as both that episode and 'The Losers' belong to Morrow. In 'The Losers,' Saunders must commandeer a group of soldiers being held for court-martial to help him blow up a bridge. One of the soldiers is Bill Bixby, and the episode is a miniature lesson on the art of management and motivation. 'Conflict' is a weaker entry. Two soldiers in Saunders' unit are feuding due to a lack of sleep, but must work together at the end to save their company.

Both 'A Child's Game' and 'The Chapel at Able-Five' on *Combat! 4* are Morrow episodes, although Jason also appears in the latter. In 'Child's Game' Saunders' unit must wrestle with their collective conscience when they lay siege to a farmhouse held by teenaged soldiers. 'Chapel,' which guest-stars Fritz Weaver, is a juicy episode. Saunders is blinded by a mine and tricked into helping a wounded Nazi soldier return to German lines. Such plot convolutions are the essence of great TV entertainment.

'The Brothers' on *Combat! 5* is a Jason episode which guest stars Fernando Lamas and Sal Mineo. The two portray French Resistance fighters (with wild accents) who have alternate difficulties dealing with the fears of war. The story is unimaginative, but Mineo's presence enhances its value for collectors. Although Jason is listed in the credits and appears first on the intro, he never actually appears in 'Ollie Joe.' Robert Walker stars as the title character, a young, overly gung-ho soldier who idolizes Saunders. Walker's performance is unnerving, making the episode intriguing and entertaining. Claude Akins also appears.

Collectors wishing to obtain a single disc which epitomizes the best of the series should consider acquiring *Combat! 6*. The first episode, 'The Outsider,' guest starring Jason Evers, is a Jason episode which is typical of the standard series format. It is about a soldier who is distrustful of the other members in his unit, and how he learns, perhaps too late, the value of trust and comradeship. The other episode, 'Head Count,' is terrific. Saunders and four other soldiers must move a group of German prisoners, who outnumber them about five to one, across a battle zone. The show is clever and exciting, and there is a great plot twist at the very end which will make the viewer want to go back quickly and watch the program a second time.

Morrow is featured in both episodes on *Combat! 2*. In 'The Letter,' Sgt. Saunders becomes overly protective of a new squad member who reminds Saunders of his younger brother. Morrow's performance is hindered by a number of dramatic closeups which no actor could survive, but the action scenes are good and the supporting characters are well drawn.

A young Tom Skerritt appears in the second episode, 'The Gantlet,' as a chickenhearted sergeant who leaves Saunders in the lurch more than once when the two, who have been captured, attempt to return to their own lines. The episode also has a lurid hallucination sequence, caused when Saunders is given an injection of morphine. The plot has more than the usual amount of padding and too many unlikelihoods. Both episodes look grainy and 'Letter' is unusually faded in comparison to the series norm.

Both episodes in *Combat! 7* are legitimate artistic explorations, though the accomplishments are limited by the series format. James Franciscus appears with Morrow in 'Decision,' about a demolitions specialist whose true vocation is medicine. The plot has similarities to many other episodes, but events happen unexpectedly and Franciscus is a powerhouse compared to the supporting players who normally appear.

Morrow directed the second episode on *Combat! 7*, 'Gulliver,' and flexes his pull by dispensing with many format requirements. There are fewer gunfights than in any of the other episodes, and the show ends, powerfully, without a resolute conclusion. Although none of the episodes are overly patriotic, this one makes a particular point of showing that 'War' is the real enemy. Morrow appears just briefly at the beginning. The rest of the episode is about Little John, a regular series character portrayed by the large-framed Dick Peadbody, who is held captive by a band of scavenging children left orphaned by Allied and Axis bombing raids.

Robert Duvall has a guest role playing a German medic in 'Cry for Help' on *Combat! 8*. He speaks German, French, and accented English for the part, in which he is captured by the platoon and must examine the conflict between his loyalty to his country and his loyalty to his vocation. Duvall's presence makes the Rick Jason episode worthwhile, and unlike Skerritt, Duvall's maturity and talent are clearly evident in his performance.

Jason and Morrow are often highly entertaining in the scenes they have together, as is the case in 'Encounter,' the other episode on *Combat! 8*. It is rare, even in a long-running television series, to see two actors project the silent communication of their characters so clearly and accurately. Morrow is wonderful, saying more with a knowing shrug or a grimace than a paragraph of dialog could ever accomplish. The episode is about an estranged father and son who, through a set of believable circumstances, reconcile while under a siege in an abandoned farmhouse. The script says more about the nature of authority and respect in the few scenes involving Jason and Morrow, however, than in any involving the guest stars.

In 'Gadjo' on *Combat 9!*, Ricardo Montalban guest stars as the leader of some French Gypsies who have a personal grudge against a German officer that Saunders' patrol has captured. Montalban's acting is awful, but that is not to be confused with the dull performances that most guest stars deliver. Every accented emotion is supported with wild hand movements, and only a tight bandana prevents him from furrowing his brow whenever he pretends to think. The episode is good fun and the director uses a number of unusual point of view camera angles to take everything in. A soldier whose presence appears to cause bad luck joins the platoon in 'Jonah,' a Jason episode on side two. The show has no exceptional aspects, but it is entertaining and well constructed. 'Gadjo' is a little more pale than other episodes, and 'Jonah' has some very grainy night scenes.

Both Dan Duryea and Dennis Hopper show up in 'A Little Jazz,' on *Combat! 10*. They portray members of a USO band caught near the front without an escort. The band members speak jazz lingo and are a group of eccentrics, making it difficult for Saunders to protect them from the Germans. The episode is simple but nicely executed, and Hopper's performance, though minor, is memorable. The second episode, 'Entombed,' is a Rick Jason effort about a group of soldiers from all factions – American, German, and French Resistance – who are trapped in a mine cave-in and must work together to free themselves. The script is entertaining but the performances are a bit wooden. Both episodes have good transfers and look very nice.

The first episode in *Combat! 11*, 'Nightmare on the Red Ball Run,' is a simplified reworking of *The Wages of Fear* – the soldiers must transport two trucks loaded with explosives to the front lines – but for an hour television episode the application is both legitimate and marvelous fun. Vic Morrow appears briefly at the beginning, but the episode features the regular cast members, Jack Hogan and Dick Peabody, as 'Kirby' and 'Little John,' along with a guest star appearance by Claude Akins. The picture transfer looks good, with the colors appearing distorted in only a few opening night shots.

The flipside of *Combat! 11*, 'The Bankroll,' is more padded with gunfights and has a weaker premise. It is a Rick Jason episode although the focus is again primarily on the Hogan character, Kirby. His morality is questioned when his actions during a battle appear to be dictated by the presence of a soldier who owes him a large amount of money. The picture transfer is very good.

Combat! 12 has star power. One episode, 'The Masquers,' guest stars Nick Adams. Neither Jason nor Morrow appear in the program, which features Hogan again. The plot is an amusing contrivance in which German infiltrators pretend to be Allied soldiers and no one knows who is a good guy and who is a bad guy. If you are unfamiliar with the series and do not recognize Hogan, then the program is even more enjoyable, as he is as much a suspect as any of the others. The picture transfer is okay.

Robert Duvall and Claudine Longet appear in the second episode on the disc, 'The Partisan.' Duvall has a poor French accent, but there turns out to be a logical reason for this, so as an actor he is excused. Longet is a blind peasant woman. To say more would spoil things, but the program, a Morrow episode, is enjoyable. The print has a few scratches and is a little paler than normal.

COMBAT ACADEMY

Keith Gordon gives an engaging performance as an anti-social prankster sent to military school in *Combat Academy*. Gordon has an enticingly dark side, which is just what a mindless comedy like *Combat Academy* needs to stay interesting. Some passages are strained, but the narrative is never interrupted for long. The picture looks inexpensive, but has no further problems. The sound is also passable.

THE COMEDY OF TERRORS/THE OBLONG BOX

A satisfying double bill of Vincent Price films, *The Comedy of Terrors/The Oblong Box* looks good except for some mild speckling at the end of side two on the three-sided disc. The monaural sound is above average in quality on both films.

Although 'Comedy of Terrors' is scanned and cropped, the transfer is otherwise very satisfying. The Pathecolor colors are bright and enjoyable, matching the comical mood of the film. 'Terrors' is a good movie for slumming English teachers, since many of the characters quote heavily from Shakespeare as they run about trying to do one another in. Price portrays an undertaker who attempts to boost his business in the same manner that glass installers who secretly break windows boost theirs. Peter Lorre is delightful as his assistant, and the film also features enjoyable performances from Boris Karloff and Basil Rathbone.

The picture on 'The Oblong Box' is murkier, but it matches the tone of the film and after the initial shift is overcome, the viewer hardly notices the image's shortcomings. In contrast to 'Terrors,' 'Box' is a serious horror film, but it deals with the same subject – murder victims who do not stay dead. Both movies are set in period, both achieve a unique atmosphere, and both make effective use of Price's talents. Yet there is enough contrast between them that, as often happens with the double-bill discs, the two movies are stronger when paired together than they would have been if they had been released separately.

COMEDY VIDEOS
Although the 13 cuts listed on the jacket of *Comedy Videos* may look tempting, few are truly worthwhile. The Oscar winning 'Sundae in New York' is included (in full aspect), as is Mel Brooks's 'Hitler Rap' (a promotion for *To Be or Not To Be* which contains all new material) and Julie Brown's amusing 'The Homecoming Queen's Got a Gun.' John Candy can be seen in a wicked but dry take-off on *The Last Waltz*. The shorts tend toward concept (such as Franken and Davis pretending to be the Rolling Stones) and lack guffaw. Most are blurry or grainy and although one or two might be in stereo, the disc isn't even CX-encoded.

THE COMIC
The Comic is a veiled biography of Buster Keaton which stars Dick Van Dyke. When Van Dyke is doing the comedy routines, the film is very pleasing, but as his character sinks into obstinacy and obscurity, the film and Van Dyke sink right along with him. The movie is a painful experience, all the more so because parts of it are so pleasurable.

The transfer is superb. Except for one instance involving an intense red which looks blurry, the colors are fresh and sharp. The disc has digital monaural sound, but since the only good parts of the film are in pantomime the audio may be best left off.

COMIC RELIEF
A full two hours of standup routines can be found on the two-sided *Comic Relief*. The program features innumerable comedians, all the way from Henny Youngman and Steve Allen to Bob Goldthwait and Al Yankovic, performing at a benefit to assist 'The Homeless.' It is a decent selection of mainstream comedy, and provides an opportunity to see Billy Crystal, Robin Williams and Whoopi Goldberg work together, though only Williams seems up for it.

The transfer looks good and the monaural, digitally encoded sound is okay. The disc also has a chapter encoded for every act. None of the segments (the program is identified as a 'Best of') wear out their welcome, but the repeat potential is questionable. They're all funny, but they're not that funny.

COMING SOON (Import)
The Japanese disc release, *Coming Soon*, has 50 or so theatrical trailers on a single disc, all in CAV. This was a rare occasion where the Japanese subtitles truly bothered us, because the whole screen is used to transmit information and the subtitles inevitably interfered with a word or two.

Unobtrusively narrated by Jamie Lee Curtis, the emphasis is on Universal's old horror and fantasy films. Also included is some beautiful-looking footage from 'Abbott & Costello Meet the Mummy' and the two meeting Dr. Jekyll and Mr. Hyde. A trailer for *Abbott and Costello Meet Frankenstein* is a bit worse for wear. Other fairly complete trailers which appear are *King Kong Vs. Godzilla*, *This Island Earth*, 'Monster on Campus,' and 'Curucu, Beast of the Amazon.'

At the very end of the show, there is a rush of film logos which hardly qualify as trailers, although each one gets its own chapter marker (the disc has 67 all told). After the disc has ended, there is a Japanese-dialog trailer for John Carpenter's *The Thing*, which includes such tempting still-step segments as the blood bouncing out of the dish, the dog kennel, and the head sliding off the table.

COMING TO AMERICA
The story of an African prince who moves incognito to New York for the purpose of finding a bride, *Coming to America* never gets sidetracked with extended gags that have nothing to do with the plot. There are digressions in which Eddie Murphy and his co-star, Arsenio Hall, fill cameo rolls with elaborate makeup, but these sequences are briskly paced, and some are especially funny. The movie has some good laughs (exaggerations of the African setting and costumes are hysterical), a running time which lasts long enough (116 minutes) that a viewer won't feel shortchanged, and, at the very core, a nice, sweet, uncynical romance. Bonding it together is the theme of black Pride, reinforced by the cameos, which suggests that no matter what the exterior or the desperate circumstances, the dignity and worth within individuals should never be underestimated.

The picture generally looks so fresh that most viewers will be pleased with it, although the disc does have problems with intense reds, which, unfortunately, are a color motif within the film. A couple of speckles also appear and trimming the edge of the picture for the TV screen drops most of the 'Wednesday' off of director John Landis' signature 'See you next Wednesday' line. On the other hand, everyone should be pleased with the sound, which received the attention befitting a princely star vehicle and has been transferred to the digitally encoded stereo disc without a crackle. Many of the stereo and surround effects are great fun.

COMMANDO
If you live close to a military establishment or any sort of secured area you should probably avoid purchasing *Commando*. The finale raises such a ruckus that you are likely to look up afterward and see a National Guard unit clustered at your living room window, arms drawn and pointed at your laser disc player. The stereo soundtrack is enthusiastic, although it would have been even better had it been encoded digitally. The picture is satisfactory, but the colors wobble a little.

Arnold Schwarzenegger's character is called 'Matrix,' although one is sorely tempted to refer to the muscle-bound star as 'Spreadsheet.' The director doesn't cover the action correctly so the editor had a difficult time making key moments coherent, but the plot moves so quickly you even accept that Rae Dawn Chong knows what sort of gasoline old seaplanes use because she's taking flying lessons.

COMMUNION
Those who take their UFOs seriously and those who do not will both want to check out the very creepy *Communion*. The film stars Christopher Walken and Lindsay Crouse and is about a man who does not know if he is going mad or if weird creatures have been sticking needles in him and his family whenever they visit their summer cabin. Much of the film is set in a psychiatrist's office, and the narrative has a beguiling blend of real and unreal situations. The movie does not have a typical pace or plot construction, but it is unnerving nevertheless.

The picture looks glossy in some places and inexpensively grainy in others. The transfer appears to be an accurate rendition of the source material. The soundtrack has stereo surround effects, but the sound is fuzzy and not effectively delivered.

THE COMPANY OF WOLVES
A text-conscious adaptation of 'Little Red Riding Hood,' *The Company of Wolves* is crammed with images and moody subplots which encourage or even demand multiple viewings. In honor of its source, the movie is bloody as all get out, with dog heads popping out of people's faces and decapitated heads flying across the screen. There isn't a shot in the film that doesn't have some slimy acknowledgment of how icky secret thoughts or nightmares can be. The story is about the dreams of a girl suffering from the onset of puberty, which contain stories or dreams of their own, all wound around the 'Red Riding Hood' fable.

The movie's nicely thought out stereo sound comes through well on the disc, as does the quality of the picture. Angela Lansbury plays the grandmother. In the end her head gets smashed like a coconut.

THE COMPLEAT AL
So much of *The Compleat Al* is not funny that it will be a waste of time for most viewers. The show, by rock comedian 'Weird Al' Yankovic, includes several clever gimmick videos and long stretches of filler linking the videos together. The music videos are noticeably cleaner than the specially produced material. The picture is generally good when not being deliberately bad. Yankovic has had the most success with direct parodies, such as 'Eat It' and 'Like a Surgeon.' It was inevitable that someone would do this and it might as well be Weird Al.

COMPROMISING POSITIONS
The sound and the picture in *Compromising Positions* aren't as attractive as the script and the performers. The cast, including Susan Sarandon, Raul Julia, and Judith Ivey, are all pumped up and have a great time zooming through the story, a murder thriller. The heroine can't stop thinking about the mystery, and the enjoyment comes from her own delight when she realizes she has deduced more than the detectives working on the case. The film is also comical, suggesting that the suburbs are a hotbed of kinky adultery. A radical notion perhaps, but part of the fun in mysteries like this is discovering that *everyone* has something to hide.

COMPUTER MAGIC: A JOURNEY INTO THE WORLD OF COMPUTER IMAGERY

A sales film which somehow garnered an Oscar nomination for Best Documentary, *Computer Magic: A Journey into the World of Computer Imagery*, has been released as a two-sided CAV disc. Many of the clips have appeared elsewhere on disc, either domestically or on import, but the program does provide a reasonable summary of how commercials and network logos are put together, although it is always from a what-we-can-do-for-a-client point of view. The animated pieces are separated by demonstrations of how a few key works were put together (including the *Amazing Stories* intro), while the narrative acts as a relay passing from one effects house to the next, allowing each to twirl a barely veiled promotional pitch. The CAV still frames provide many clear images but also a number of foggy ones. The sound has a limited amount of stereophonic background music. The disc has been thoroughly chapter encoded, though it is unfortunate that no listing has been provided.

THE CONFORMIST

Bernardo Bertolucci's multi-layered drama, *The Conformist*, is reproduced on disc with permanent scratches, merging colors, lost hues, indistinct sound, noise, and dubbed dialog. Set in the late '30s, the story, by Alberto Moravia, is about a man who uses his honeymoon in Paris to assist in the assassination of an anti-facist. Everything that the characters say and do can be seen as a metaphor for Italian politics and Italian society under Mussolini.

The visuals are cramped considerably by the confines of the TV screen. Set to Georges Delerue's anxious score, the camera turns at odd angles to intrude on characters in private moments and then draws far back, engulfing them in architecture. The characters are Italian and the original film was in Italian although the principals, who are French, had their dialog dubbed. When they are in Paris, incidental French is spoken, but when dubbed in English, everything is dubbed in English. There is an amusing scene where a minor character is talking to himself in a Parisian park and an old woman passes, chastising him for talking in Italian to French birds. On the dubbed disc, the woman accuses him of screaming at the birds and complains that they do not talk to foreigners. The joke is lost.

A CONNECTICUT YANKEE IN KING ARTHUR'S COURT

The Technicolor print used for the Bing Crosby *A Connecticut Yankee in King Arthur's Court* is in beautiful shape and the monaural title has been encoded with digital sound, which removes a whole layer of hiss from the soundtrack. The film, however, is a trifle. The script impulsively leaps from one concept to the next, the songs aren't that memorable, and Crosby lacks a foil to cross witticisms with, something he needs like he needs a microphone if he is to succeed. Even if you like the movie, though, you may come away from the disc remembering the colors instead of the characters.

CONSUMING PASSIONS

The jacket cover for *Consuming Passions* claims that the disc has digital stereo surround encoding, and for the first few minutes we wondered what was going on, because the sound was timid and flat. Then, however, the hero steps inside the chocolate factory, and all of a sudden one's viewing room comes alive with blubs, glugs, blurps, and bips. It will make a great demo disc, particularly if you can get your friends to sit long enough for the build-up. The picture quality also looks good, with sharp colors and limited distortions.

The film originates from a stage play written by Monty Python alumni and concerns the good fortunes of a chocolate company when human corpses are accidentally added to the formula. It's what you'd expect, yet none of it is quite as pleasing as that first step inside the factory.

CONTEMPT

Jean-Luc Godard's *Contempt* is a masterpiece. Like a heavy cream sauce, it may seem to go slowly while you're taking it in, but it stays with you for a long time afterwards.

The story behind *Contempt*, briefly, is as follows. Most of Godard's films are uncommercial and are made with budgets which account for their boxoffice potential. With *Contempt*, however, Godard got backing from some major Hollywood wanna-be's and, in a spirit deliberately reflected by the film's title, proceeded, with a bigger budget, to make the same kind of uncommercial film he was making before.

Uncommercial, but not sloppy – the film has, in fact, a stronger narrative than most Godard efforts. It is about a script doctor (Michel Piccoli) called in by an uncouth producer (Jack Palance) to do rewrites for a film Fritz Lang (the real one) is making about Odysseus. The visit causes tension between the writer and his girlfriend (Brigitte Bardot), which leads to their breakup. The levels of meaning will strike the viewer immediately, as when a camera is pointed directly at the audience in the opening shot. An imagined rift between Penelope and Odysseus is at the forefront of the writer's concerns since he is experiencing a similar domestic discord. The writer is doing the job because he is being well paid, just as Godard was, and when he speaks of using the money for his apartment, is he also speaking of funding the film's lengthy and central 'apartment' scene? The blatant humor aimed at Palance's character turns to irony when directed at the writer's artistic problems, then to melancholy when directed at his love life. The story, however, can accommodate the scope of these resonances.

There is a wistfully throbbing score by Georges Delerue, exquisite cinematography by Raoul Coutard, and an incredible cliffside villa location used in the movie's finale. The original widescreen image has been cropped (Cinemascope, Lang says in the film, at least partially tongue-in-cheek, "wasn't meant for human beings, just for snakes and funerals.") but the presentation is functional. The color transfer is very good, becoming grainy only where there is an intense concentration of a single hue. The film is mostly in French and has bright yellow subtitles which are easily readable. The monaural sound is fine.

CONVOY (Import)

The Japanese release of Sam Peckinpah's *Convoy* is a little grainy and it is not in any kind of widescreen format. The dialog appears in Japanese subtitles on the bottom of the screen and the lyrics to the C.W. McCall pop hit appear vertically on the right when snippets of it are played.

Peckinpah's 18-wheel romp through the Southwest was not one of his best films, but his control over the action sequences makes the movie more entertaining than many more competent thrillers. Like McCall's song, the story is meant to be something of a comedy about a truck driver (Kris Kristofferson) who almost by accident finds himself leading an interstate rebellion against law enforcement harassment. The movie was an excuse to demolish a few big rigs and the stunts make the disc worthwhile.

"COOGAN'S BLUFF"

Clint Eastwood's first cop movie, *"Coogan's Bluff"*, was made in the late sixties, when monaural sound was especially tinny and even the most psychedelic of colors looked pale. The transfer preserves it all. The most intense colors are slightly unstable, and a couple of speckles appear, but the picture is acceptable. At the end of side two, there is a mint original theatrical trailer which is even more fun than the movie itself.

The film, directed by Don Siegel, was made in the era when it was difficult to distinguish a Universal film from a Universal television feature. Except for a few strategic, theatrical-sized scenes, the set decorations and camera setups look fast and cheap, indistinguishable from the television series, 'McCloud,' which the film would eventually inspire.

The plot concerns an Arizona detective sent to New York City on an extradition assignment which runs into complications. Eastwood looks very young, and his character paws every woman he meets. The fish-out-of-water gags are limited, but Siegel can be depended upon to keep a film moving at a decent pace. The music, which grates, is by Lalo Schifrin, and includes a song which is a front-running candidate for all-time badness, 'The Pigeon-Toed Orange Peel.' It is played in its entirety during a predictably frumpy discotheque scene.

COOKIE

Cookie was directed by Susan Seidelman, who can be relied upon to produce fresh, clever stories (*Desperately Seeking Susan*) and witty characters (*Making Mr. Right*). The movie features wonderful performances by Emily Lloyd, Peter Falk and Dianne Wiest. The script has some nice twists and is consistently funny. Falk portrays a mob figure looking to retire and Lloyd is his illegitimate daughter. The two characters are so much alike that they make an efficient team despite their filial bickering. The disc looks terrific and the stereo surround sound is bright and engaging.

COOL HAND LUKE
COOL HAND LUKE (remastered)

The opening credit sequence on Warner's remastered *Cool Hand Luke* is letterboxed, but the rest of the movie is scanned and cropped. The transfer is still an improvement over Warner's earlier effort, which had a squeezed credit sequence, analog sound, and pale colors. The colors on the newer release look very accurate, and the picture, cropping aside, is pleasing. The digital monaural sound is still a product of its age, but it is acceptable for a twenty-year-old recording. The new disc has chapter markers and different side breaks from the old disc, though they don't seem to work any better.

The film, which stars Paul Newman and George Kennedy and also features early appearances by Harry Dean Stanton, Dennis Hopper, and Anthony Zerbe, is an inconsistent work. It almost seems to have been written for black characters and then cast white, though there is no harm in that. It is mostly an excuse to show off Newman's charm, with Kennedy as the audience stand-in, and the movie seems to stop dead when Newman stops posing and starts acting. Some of the drama and the character motivation are lost with the cropping, but the movie no longer seems like the rebellion against authority that it once did. If *Cool Hand Luke* has a message, it fails to communicate it.

COP

An enjoyable police procedural starring James Woods, *Cop* eventually becomes too coincidental for its own good, and there is a character, an owner of a feminist book store, who practically melts the instant Woods steps into her parlor, but the spirit of a good, fast-paced thriller is there if you aren't too demanding. The sound is okay. The picture is a little pink, but it looks alright. Woods is also tolerable, and when he is crunching clues and spewing out conjectures, he is particularly well used.

CORTEGE OF EAGLES (see THE ROYAL BALLET – SWAN LAKE)

THE COTTON CLUB

The big-budgeted *The Cotton Club*, directed by Francis Coppola, has so many central characters that it has no central character. The scattered subplots come and go like so many musical numbers. The sound is wonderful – the sound in all of Coppola's films is wonderful – but a drama about Harlem gangsters in the '20s and '30s has to have some dramatic feeling to it.

We recall the colors of the film were quite distinctive the week it opened in the theaters. The color on the disc has a green/yellow wash which blends the flesh with the decor of the nightclubs and makes the movie look more aged than it is.

When Pioneer marketed its first digital machine, the company gave away copies of *The Cotton Club* with every player purchased. The thrill of digitally encoded rainstorms, gun shots, and tap shoes is hardly going to convince anyone that the movie is good, but the effects are enjoyable when sampled randomly. So the movie ends up being the first $30 million demo disc.

THE COUCH TRIP

Michael Ritchie's amusing *The Couch Trip* has received an above-average transfer. The picture has a bright gloss and never succumbs to weakness in darkly lit scenes. The monaural sound is clear enough that you can follow all the conversations during the many instances of overlapping dialog. The story, about a mental patient who, while impersonating a psychiatrist, achieves widespread popularity through a radio talk show, is tightly scripted and intelligently cast. Dan Ackroyd stars.

COUNTERFORCE

A poorly edited action picture which stars such luminaries as Isaac Hayes and Andrew Stevens, *Counterforce*, is about an elite fighting unit which is protecting a deposed Arab leader. The Ultra-Stereo surround sound is okay, but the movie is too disjointed and stretched out to be entertaining. The picture quality is tolerable.

COUNTRY (see THE RIVER)

THE COURIER

Dublin is the setting of *The Courier*, an Irish production about a young man working for a messenger service who disrupts the activities of a drug kingpin. The film stock 'by Fuji Ireland' is as bleak as an overcast bog. The sound is only fair, and there is a bothersome flutter in the dialog on the second side. The second half is more engaging than the first, if one can make it that far.

THE COURT JESTER (see THE SECRET LIFE OF WALTER MITTY)

THE COURT-MARTIAL OF BILLY MITCHELL

The print used as source material for *The Court-Martial of Billy Mitchell* is the disc's weakest point. It is faded and has a number of splices. The original Cinemascope image, however, has been letterboxed with an aspect ratio of about 2.2:1, and the film's original theatrical trailer (which twists the movie inside out to make it look better than it is) has been placed at the beginning. Republic has failed to use chapter markers, so those not wishing to sit through the trailer must scan past it, but since the trailer deliberately obscures the sequence and essence of the narrative, one's entertainment is not spoiled by watching it.

The monaural sound is digitally encoded and is in passable condition. The picture varies in quality and is never faded too badly, but the standards for such presentations have been climbing and in that context it is a disappointment. The side break is more awkward than necessary. The film was directed by Otto Preminger, and although there is evidence that his passion for the material is lacking, his use of the widescreen image is always significant. His body of work is among those most often obliterated by scanning and cropping, and for this reason the letterboxing is important.

The film stars Gary Cooper, whose performance improves as the story progresses. He portrays an army officer during the '20s who becomes frustrated at the lack of progress in the technological development of air warfare during peace time. When budget and initiative constraints lead to needless tragedy, the officer takes his case to the press and then must face a tribunal for having violated codes of obedience. The courtroom shenanigans are fun, and the 1955 movie, based on an actual incident, has historical value (both as an examination of the twenties and the fifties). In depicting a hero, however, whose own personality flaws, such as an impatience with following procedures, lead to his downfall, the movie hasn't much of a chance at winning over a great number of viewers. Too much like the hero, the *The Court-Martial of Billy Mitchell* is doomed before it starts.

COUSIN, COUSINE
COUSINS

Near the beginning of *Cousin, Cousine* a family is driving to a wedding reception and the father tells his children that they must behave when they arrive because, "It is a solemn occasion." The film then cuts immediately to the bride, guzzling a full pitcher of beer. In *Cousins*, the father says nothing and the film shows the family pulling up to the reception hall before cutting to the activities inside, including a shot of the bride guzzling beer from a pitcher. Thus are the differences between the original film and its American remake defined.

Cousin, Cousine was no great classic, but it was an entertaining romance which broke the barriers boxoffices usually construct around foreign language films because the emotions of the characters had a universal appeal. *Cousins*, which stars Ted Danson and a very Bergmanish Isabelle Rossellini, follows the plot – about in-laws who have a serious affair after their spouses have a fling – fairly closely, but it often seems to miss the point of the first film. There are some humorous moments, and the son of Danson's character is an amusing improvement over his counterpart in the original, but so often the texture of humor in the secondary characters is passed by. The first film's funniest line, a threat which the heroine levels at her husband after she returns from a romantic weekend with her lover, doesn't make it to the second film, either. The makers of *Cousins* copied the plot of *Cousin, Cousine*, but they didn't really study the movie.

The approach may not be able to work in any case, as is evident in the transfigured title. *Cousin, Cousine* is by necessity an intimate French film, made with a small crew and communicating a relaxed style which puts the viewer at ease. *Cousins* is a Hollywood production, filmed in Vancouver BC by the numbers, and it can't shake its formal atmosphere. The transfer of the latter is fairly good. Although fleshtones sometimes seem a touch too pink, there are a number of tricky lighting effects which survive without distortion. The stereo surround sound is passable, but separation effects are very limited. The sound on the former is monaural and is at the mercy of the film's production standards, though the musical score is catchy. The film has English subtitles which are easy to follow. The picture is accurate, though again the source material is not in the same class as the American production.

THE COVERED WAGON

A silent epic about the settling of the West, *The Covered Wagon* has a grand scale and an antique look which lends authenticity to its depiction of an even earlier era. The film, after all, was made when people who referred to 'the forties' still meant the 1840s. It was also made when filmmakers had no qualms about pushing a live horse off a cliff.

In many shots, the covered wagons stretch

for a mile or more into the vanishing point. The story follows a wagon train from Missouri to Oregon, with the usual sappy subplots built in to make the viewer care about the characters as they struggle against diversity. The second half is more entertaining than the first, but only those who are predisposed to the material should consider obtaining it, as the style and narrative are not distinctive enough to create converts.

The musical score is by Gaylord Carter. Carter's Wurlitzer organ is delivered in stereo, with the organ's different sounds routed to different speakers. The music is pleasant and unobtrusive. Many – but not all – of the original title cards are employed. The picture quality looks fine for a silent black-and-white movie, though the tone is always a little soft. The movements of the characters seem a bit jumpy, but not to the point of distraction. The disc runs 98 minutes.

CRACK HOUSE

The sex and the violence in *Crack House* are contemporary, but the morality comes straight from the fifties. The heroine's boyfriend is thrown in jail for his involvement in a gang altercation after his cousin is murdered. Two days later she's hooked on crack and by the end of the week she's Jim Brown's slave. The movie is hopelessly clichéd and the characters are all stereotypes. The harder the film tries to be hip, the sillier it gets. Still, those who enjoy Los Angeles gang wars may have a good time. The picture transfer is mildly grainy but passable. The analog Ultra-Stereo surround sound has only a handful of separation effects.

THE CRAWLING EYE

Side one of *The Crawling Eye* is in CLV and side two is in CAV. The breakup is perfect, because absolutely nothing happens on side one which is worth using Standard Play functions on. *Eye* is a late-fifties black-and-white bug-eye-monster movie. It takes place in the Alps (!), of which there is substantial location footage, and stars Forrest Tucker (!!), who is so relaxed that he never bothers to tell his colleagues that huge crawling eye monsters are attacking them when he is the first to see one. It's okay – they're really only puppets and you can see the strings pumping back and forth, particularly when you play the disc in slow motion.

The print is above average for its age and budget. The sound levels drop severely during a critical scene on side two, but that just makes you move closer to the edge of your seat.

CRAZY MOON

Keifer Sutherland portrays a wealthy, misunderstood eccentric in the Nelson release, *Crazy Moon.* He meets a hearing impaired woman, attractively portrayed by Vanessa Vaughn, and they fall in love. The script is not elaborate, nor is it very real, but amidst all the contrivances there is a moment or two of genuine romance.

The fleshtones are much too orange, and the sound is sometimes quite scratchy. Side two opens with the Nelson logo, which is a little disconcerting. The film, however, has one other component which potential owners might be interested in. The music soundtrack is made up almost entirely of thirties hits, superbly mastered, and the songs are played extensively even though the setting is present-day Montreal.

CREATOR

Creator was directed by Ivan Passer and contains a touch of science fiction, though it is a very light and inconsequential touch which has virtually nothing to do with the central narrative, other than the symbolism it provides. The central narrative is about two couples falling in love: one represented by Peter O'Toole and Mariel Hemingway, and the other by Vincent Spano and Virginia Madsen. O'Toole is a brilliant research scientist and Spano is his graduate assistant. That is all one really needs to know, because the mechanics of the plot are less important than the characters and the performances. We found ourselves replaying a number of individual scenes several times over, and were so happy with them that we really didn't care how the movie started or ended. There is a wonderful beach house seduction scene involving Spano and Madsen, a terrific turn by O'Toole as he goes before a grant committee to get his funding renewed, and a hysterical put-down rendered by Hemingway when another professor comes on to her. Those scenes, and a few others, are what the movie is really about, and where its pleasures are to be had.

The fleshtones are pale but the picture is passable. The digitally encoded monaural sound hasn't much to offer, and there is a bad scratching noise at the very end.

CREATURE

Creature is an *Alien* rip-off with legitimate special effects and a wonderful music score. Because of the cropped screen and a lack of originality, there is nothing in the movie to make you scream, but the tension remains fairly consistent.

The print has marks on it in places, but looks okay. The sound has an excess amount of hiss near the beginning, but most of the movie is so full of sound effects that additional noise is unnoticeable.

THE CREEPING FLESH

The Creeping Flesh is one of the many simple but enjoyable Peter Cushing/Christopher Lee horror films. Cushing is the hero in this one (they seemed to take turns), portraying a Victorian-era scientist whose experiments on a fossilized skeleton lead to murder and other horrors. The film's candy-bright colors are a little dull in the source material, but the picture is otherwise in good shape and has no serious flaws. The sound is also passable. *Flesh* may disappoint viewers who expect too much from it, but it is an ideal title to include in a double feature, a warm-up exercise in terror which the stern-hearted will find to be good, gruesome fun.

CREEPSHOW 2

The original *Creepshow* (which is available in Japan, but not in America) was a collection of three short narratives with an animated framing device. *Creepshow 2* follows the same format, and the three stories are arranged so that the plotiest is first and the scariest is last, aptly building momentum. The best interlude, however, is the middle story, about four teenagers trapped in a raft on a lake by a large black blob. If you liked the first feature, you will probably appreciate this one as well. Both the picture and sound are passable.

CRIME STORY THE COMPLETE WORKS (Import)
CRIME STORY

Did you ever see an episode of *Crime Story* on television? Did the program make any sense to you at all? Catching an occasional episode, we could never make head or tails of it, but the show, produced by Michael Mann, always seemed classy and intelligent, so when a collection of the first 20 episodes was released in Japan as a single boxed set we decided the investment would be worthwhile. The package, which weighs around 8 pounds, is handsomely designed and gives you a rush when you hold it. It contains 11 platters – the 96-minute pilot episode (which is available domestically) and 19 subsequent 47-minute episodes which comprise the first season and a half.

Thanks to this import release, disc owners can now discover what heretofore only the producers of the show, a handful of industry people, and energetic home taping enthusiasts knew. Viewed as a single entity, *Crime Story The Complete Works* is an incredible dramatic and literary accomplishment. We watched all 16 hours within a 30-hour time frame and just as it was almost impossible to watch the show broken up a week at a time (or worse), it is almost necessary to watch the disc in as close to a continuous play-through as possible. Personality ticks in characters, minute plot details and motivations for actions are planted episodes in advance of blossoming. The sort of things which are the first to fade from memory are the things which give the program so much class – even viewers who watched the show as it was broadcast missed its thoroughness and resonance.

Crime Story is the tale of two people. A Chicago cop, played by Dennis Farina, who is later assigned to a federal task force to fight organized crime, and a criminal, played by Anthony Denison, who always manages to elude the cop's grasp as he works his way up the ranks of organized illegalities. (The Oedipal symbolism in the names of the actors is such a marvelous touch it is a shame that it is not deliberate.) Set in the sixties, the show is a *roman a clef* about the development of Las Vegas and an expose of organizational corruption on the part of the US justice system. Without intentionally meaning harm, the bureaucratic arms of the Justice Department often end up strangling one another as the criminals slip through their grasp.

Fewer than a third of the episodes have enough subplots or 'normal' script elements to function independently of the others. An obvious theme which runs through the series is that the criminals live more materially rewarding lives than do the cops, although spiritually, the private lives of both are in equal shambles. As the criminals work harder to legitimize their operations, the cops escalate desperate and questionable measures to ensnare them. One beautiful touch on the part of the scriptwriters is that, while the viewer is privy to the strategies of both sides, neither the cops nor the criminals have more than the faintest idea what the other is up to.

The program is not a soap opera and not a normal television show. It is closest in format to the mini-series, a novel-length drama presented in components with a clearly accessible beginning, middle and end. Although the final episode is open ended to facilitate the second season, the episode is nevertheless resolute, and it is a marvelously comical and satisfying conclusion (it is also beautifully constructed as an episode, opening in a bomb shelter and ending in the Nevada desert during an atomic test).

For the record, the individual episodes are presented as follows: The unnamed pilot episode, 'Final Transmission,' 'Shadow Dancer,' 'St. Louis Book of Blues,' 'The War,' 'Abrams for the Defense,' 'Pursuit of a Wanted Felon,' 'Old Friends, Dead Ends,' 'Justice Hits the Skids,' 'For Love or Money,' 'Hide and Go Thief,' 'Strange Bedfellows,' 'Fatal Crossroads,' 'Torello on Trial,' 'The Kingdom of Money,' 'The Battle of Las Vegas,' 'The Survivor,' 'The Pinnacle,' 'Top of the World,' and 'Ground Zero.' Except for the pilot, each episode is confined to a single side of a platter. Introductory and concluding credit sequences usually appear after every three episodes (although the theme song, Del Shannon's 'Runaway,' is the one television theme song we would never get tired of hearing). Those who cannot manage a marathon viewing are advised that a comfortable break can be taken between 'Torello on Trial' and 'The Kingdom of Money.' If another break is necessary, we would recommend stopping between 'The War' and 'Abrams for the Defense,' but don't let it go for more than a day or two, or you'll have to start over. The pilot episode was also released domestically as a single two-sided disc.

The program is in English with Japanese subtitles which are rarely intrusive. The transfer is on par with the domestic *Crime Story* disc, which is not great praise. The picture is mildly grainy throughout, and the sound, originally broadcast in stereo, is presented in CX-encoded monaural. There are a number of audio dropouts. Each episode has a number of chapter markers, but the listing of them is only available in Japanese. Although the production values of *Crime Story* are more sophisticated than those of most TV efforts, budget restraints cause a few errors to slip through. The most obvious occurs when an elderly actor is reciting a lengthy monolog and grips are holding cue cards clearly reflected in the glass behind him.

CRIMES AND MISDEMEANORS

More and more, Woody Allen's characters all seem to speak with the same voice, and his feel for what people do to relax is almost anachronistic. Nevertheless, *Crimes and Misdemeanors* is a movie which not only entertains, but forces a viewer to pay attention to its moral arguments.

Sven Nykvist's cinematography is beholden to Allen's passion for near colorless browns and tans. However, the transfer handles even the most difficult lighting and color problems without difficulty. The sound is sophisticated enough to require amplification.

The elaborate story follows two central characters. One, an eye doctor played by Martin Landau, has problems with his mistress. The other, a filmmaker played by Allen, allows his aesthetic sense to impede his career. The heart of the film, however, is in a few brief clips of a documentary the filmmaker is putting together about a philosopher, modeled after Primo Levi. The snippets of the philosopher's conversations are so refreshingly dense that the entire movie is buoyed by the character's words. You suddenly realize how rare it is to come across an English-speaking film character who is demonstratively well-read.

CRIMES OF PASSION
CRIMES OF PASSION ('Unrated Version')

The first pressing of both *Crimes of Passion* and *Crimes of Passion* ('Unrated Version') were in extremely bad condition. A subsequent run of the 'Unrated Version' was much cleaner, but the 'rated' version has never been reissued.

Ken Russell can usually be counted on to test the limits of silliness in adult films and you'll probably end up giggling at *Crimes of Passion* instead of getting turned on by it, especially if you watch it more than once. The chief laugh inducer is Tony Perkins, who eyes the heroine with lust and fondles a razor-edged vibrator that he picked up God knows where. The heroine, played by Kathleen Turner, is not any more serious. By day she works as a clothing designer and by night she dons a blond wig and turns tricks in a cheap hotel room for honorariums and thrills. No pimps, venereal diseases, sleep, or other aspects of the real world intrude on this fantasy playland. The 'Unrated Version' contains six extra minutes of slobbering lust. A trailer for *Heart of the Stag* appears on the 'rated' version.

CRIMES OF THE HEART

The colors in *Crimes of the Heart* are rich and varied, though the image seems a little unstable. The sound is luscious, although we would prefer to hear Georges Delerue's score under rougher conditions. He sounds better that way. The movie is yet another Broadway play which obtains its forward motion by revealing, a little at a time, pieces of dramatic information. Such jigsaw exposition is acceptable in mysteries, but with regular drama it is often too manipulative to be effective. The artifice is too cute.

Crimes of the Heart is not the worst of its ilk, however, and the performances are engaging. The story is about three sisters who reunite to sort out their lives after one of them has shot her husband. The three stars, Diane Keaton, Jessica Lange, and Sissy Spacek, are typecast in their parts, and work up their strongest repartees when they are screaming at each other. The best performance in the film is given by Tess Harper, who abandons her normal sweet persona to portray the nasty neighbor/cousin. It is as if she had spent her entire career just waiting to do something lowdown, and finally got her chance.

CRIMINAL LAW

The script and the editing of *Criminal Law* give you information only on a strict, need-to-know basis. The film, then, keeps you alert not only because it is a thriller but because you have to catch every word to understand what is going on. The show is not perfect, but it is a very enjoyable concoction about a young lawyer who gets his client acquitted of a murder charge and then has second thoughts about his responsibility for having done so. Gary Oldman stars, and his performance is a pleasurable mix of slick confidence and awkward perspiration. The casting of Kevin Bacon, as the lawyer's client, is a bit more obvious, but Bacon also brings some surprises to his role.

The picture transfer is fine, with no significant faults. There are no show-off sequences, but the sound mix is decent and the disc's audio is impressive.

THE CRIMSON PIRATE

Since *The Crimson Pirate* is good-natured, enjoyable entertainment which has no enemies outside of the 18th century Spanish nobility, it can be recommended to anyone who likes laser discs. The transfer is spectacular. The side break is poor, but other than that, the disc is terrific.

The Technicolor print is gorgeous. In some ways the movie is designed to show off Technicolor's capabilities. Every time a character appears in a green costume the movie disappears. You are so awestruck by the rich texture and color you forget to pay attention to the proceedings. The color never lets the movie down. Even the night and underwater scenes contain consistent hues and moments of playful brilliance. The sky is always a deep azure.

A distinctive amount of noise is removed from the soundtrack when digital playback is activated. The film was made in 1952 and it is monaural. The cannon fire has no particular boom, but the sound is consistent and adequate.

As indicated by the ubiquitous oboe in the musical score, *The Crimson Pirate* has many clownish and farcical interludes, although the story is always presented as if it were a matter of life and death. The editing has a few flaws and one major character's murder is presented so obliquely that the viewer is surprised when the other characters refer to it. But the adventure and excitement which does appear on the screen is joyous. The image of Burt Lancaster using the rigging of his ship as a trapeze is one a viewer will remember and it represents the spirit of the entire film. The movie is a free-swinging thrill in an unlikely setting, but it carries you along wherever it goes.

CRITICAL CONDITION

The source material provided for the uninspired Richard Pryor movie, *Critical Condition*, is in excellent condition. Much of the movie takes place during a blackout and is in partial darkness, yet the shadows are rich and unblemished. The sound is strong and does nothing to hinder the disc.

The film was directed by Michael Apted, who once made some very classy movies, although that part of his career starts to fade from memory about one minute into this picture. To be fair, the plot has enough components – Richard Pryor is a patient at a mental institution who escapes and pretends to be a doctor at an associated hospital during the aforementioned blackout – that it may someday be considered an antic classic. But it also has an air of desperation. Pryor has always been willing to say or do almost anything to be funny, but the difference between then and now is that then he was funny.

CRITTERS
A variety of modest but well-executed special effects enlivens *Critters*, an otherwise run-of-the-mill effort about carnivorous aliens terrorizing a farm. The farm wins. The picture has a pinkish tint to it. The images, however, are sharp. The sound is okay and there is a surprise on the audio track after the end credit scroll, but in keeping with the rest of the film, it isn't really much of a surprise.

CRITTERS 2
The formula which made the original *Critters* reasonably enjoyable works again in *Critters 2*. Cheap but sharp special effects, a sense of humor, and a few gory thrills put the viewer in just the right mood for a tale about a small town, ravenous creatures hatching from eggs, and alien bounty hunters who come to the rescue. To guage the level of the humor: The bounty hunters can assume any form they wish, and one, upon observing a girlie magazine foldout, turns into a naked starlet with a large staple imbedded over her navel.

The picture is faded in places and is grainy, but the effect shots aren't as harmed by the flaws as are the filler conversation sequences. The analog Ultra Stereo surround sound is fun and shows a number of directorial touches. The side break is arbitrary, but it doesn't seem to matter.

CROCODILE DUNDEE
THE GOLDEN CHILD
Two of Paramount's biggest theatrical hits showed up in video stores on laser disc on the same day. *Crocodile Dundee* and *The Golden Child* are similar in several respects. The discs both have digital stereo sound and both run a little over ninety minutes. *Child* is more entertaining in the relaxed atmosphere of home presentation than it was in the theater, while *Dundee* is better suited for a wide theatrical screen and cheering urban audience.

The stereo on *The Golden Child* is magnificent. It has a raised consciousness and clearly benefits from the budgetary advantages afforded an assured hit. Every effect has a complete bouquet of resonance. *Crocodile Dundee* (the quotation marks don't appear on the jacket spine) is also in stereo, but it is a modestly budgeted Australian effort and the limitations are apparent, particularly on the analog track.

The picture on *The Golden Child* is also clearer. There is a slight grain in evidence in the darkest scenes in *Child*, but the flaw is fleeting. On *Dundee*, even the sunlit scenes are grainy, and much of the program is accompanied by a faint haze.

Eddie Murphy's reaction to the supernatural events he encounters in *The Golden Child* is easier to enjoy under the relaxed standards of home video and the anticipation which comes with multiple viewings. Our one complaint about the film is that no one involved was bright enough to have Murphy pull some moves on the demon at the end which he demonstrated on the basketball court in the beginning.

The classiest aspect to *Crocodile Dundee* was its widescreen presentation, and now that is gone. The movie is still funny and still romantic, but it isn't as cohesive with the sides snipped off. Not only do you lose the vistas, you lose the local color, both Australian and American.

"CROCODILE" DUNDEE II
The original *Crocodile Dundee* film did not work very well on disc. *"Crocodile" Dundee II* fares much better on the small screen. The script has a standard but reliable drug lord bad guy, who provides the story with a focus that the first movie, a romance, did not have. The show is still childish, but it is more dependable. The picture on the disc looks fairly decent. The sound has several showoff passages and, like the rest of the movie, is predictable but well executed.

CROMWELL
Richard Harris portrays Cromwell in *Cromwell* and Alec Guinness portrays the ill-fated Charles I. The contrast in their abilities is immediately apparent. Harris rarely moves his eyeballs, much less his arms, legs, or facial muscles, unless he moves them all at once in order to make a point. Cromwell is portrayed in the movie as having provided England with the foundations of real democracy. That's fair, it's only a movie, but one's sympathy falls with Guinness because the conflicts in his character's heart are more accessible.

The disc plays for 139 minutes in CLV. It opens in cropped screen, spreads to wide screen for the credits, back to cropped screen for the movie, and then wide again for the last shot. Only the strongest colors appear blurry. The costumes in the film won an Oscar, but the buttons on many of Harris's shirts look suspiciously less like mother-of-pearl than like mother-of-plastic.

CROSS COUNTRY
The acting in *Cross Country*, a monaural disc with a bland picture, is so bad that the star, Richard Beymer, can't manage his first onscreen line of dialog. He is supposed to ask a mechanic if a car's engine is in order – "Any problems, Mitch?" – and he draws out "Any..." while he desperately tries to remember what comes next. It is impossible to figure out what *Cross Country* is about by reading the notes on the jacket. They say it is the first part of a trilogy, but we hope they don't really mean it. "A chronicle of forming and ending – sometimes murderously – complex relationships; relationships of inevitable tension and relentless passion that have edged out into the fast lane." Even the copy writer can't act.

CROSS OF IRON (Import)
Sam Peckinpah's final masterpiece, the German-vs.-Russian-World-War-II action picture, *Cross of Iron*, is available in Japan. It is not in widescreen, and, being monaural, it has not been CX-encoded. Subtitles clutter the lower portion of the image, but people rarely speak when they are getting shot or blown up, so the titles do not interfere too much with the stunts.

The film is about death. War, for the characters, is a disorganized mess of mud and gunshots. It does not matter that the protagonists are German. Peckinpah goes through the cliché of making it clear that everybody in his movie hates the Nazis, but he really doesn't have to since there aren't any characters one can feel sympathy for, nor is it a requirement for admiring the film.

CROSSFIRE
Crossfire is an engaging murder thriller in which Robert Young, as a cop, attempts to outwit Robert Ryan, the murderer. In sidebar roles are Gloria Grahame, doing her fallen-woman-with-longing bit, and Robert Mitchum. Mitchum gets second billing after Young even though his character does nothing but stand on the sidelines somewhat angelically. As is reiterated in every plot summary, anti-Semitism is the motivation for the murder. The director, Edward Dmytryk, rushes through the preaching as fast as he can in order to get onto the real business of the film, the search for the criminal. It's over in 85 minutes, but everything else in life gets put on hold while it is on.

The transfer is fine. Side one looks much better than side two, which has a few splices and scratches. There is a mild hum in the background on the soundtrack, which shouldn't be amplified too greatly in any case. Side one, though, looks gorgeous, and it wins you over to the film well enough that side two can't spoil things.

CROSSING DELANCEY
The contemporary ethnic romance, *Crossing Delancey*, about a bookstore clerk with pretensions and a pickle merchant with none, has been transferred to disc without a single discernible flaw. The flesh tones are perfect, the details are sharp, and the darker corners of the screen have no impurities. The stereo sound is bright and, when the musical score is involved (many of the songs are by The Roches), scrumptious.

Crossing Delancey was directed by Joan Micklin Silver, who has never made a bad film, but has never been handed a big-budget project, either. *Delancey* has a number of marvelous scenes, though the material is stretched out to make the 97-minute running time. The movie is a cute trifle which is embellished by the quality of the disc presentation. All discs should be so good.

CROSSROADS
The RCA/Columbia release of *Crossroads* is a real disappointment. The movie is wonderful – the only reason it failed in the theaters is that the plot is impossible to summarize in twenty-five words or less. Since it was directed by Walter Hill, the production values are first-rate, but somewhere in the course of the transfer, the picture has picked up an overbearing orange hue.

The movie is about the blues, a pact with the devil, and growing up on the road. The music all sounds too much like Ry Cooder, but you accept it because it comes out so great in stereo.

CRY BABY
In what one would have to term a questionable career move, TV teen heartthrob Johnny Depp makes his motion picture top billing debut in a John Waters film, *Cry Baby*, a slick musical very similar to the *Grease* films, but loaded with Waters' inevitable camp touches. Either Depp is being made fun of, or he's in on the joke, but neither will boost his appeal with the core audience that he ought to be cultivating. As for the film, it contains some nice imitation-fifties numbers, and the pleasing artificiality that good musicals can get away with supporting.

The picture is exceedingly crisp and bright. The stereo surround sound is also clear, and the separations in the musical numbers are enjoyable. Side two, which contains a few stunts and the end credit scroll that tells you who everybody was, is in CAV.

CRY FREEDOM

The drama in *Cry Freedom* is about as exciting as MacNeil/Lehrer on location. The litany of each position is presented, and it is great if you are showing the disc to a seventh grade social studies class but hardly the sort of material to settle into the couch with. There are some good qualities about the disc. The digitally encoded sound is fantastic, and the performances are all engaging. But the movie is like going for a ride with your parents. They drive too slow, take no chances, and never turn or stop where you want them to.

One wishes that the material presented on Steven Biko (played to perfection by Denzel Washington) in the film were just outtakes, and that another movie was waiting in the wings which really showed how his own consciousness was raised and the drama of his rebellion. *Cry Freedom*, however, concentrates instead on a 40-year-old South African newspaper editor who discovers – stop the presses! – that his government is corrupt. The filmmakers are too stodgy and too literal to provide the tale with any sense of inspiration. The 'Sun City' video did it better and faster.

The two-and-a-half-hour disc is spread to three sides. The picture quality varies between good and very good. The sound has a we're-going-for-the-Oscar road-show resonance and is the only reason, unless we get a job someday teaching the seventh grade, why we would ever play the disc again.

A CRY IN THE DARK

No mystery exists in *A Cry in the Dark*, the Australian film starring Meryl Streep as a woman wrongfully accused of murder when a wild animal makes off with her baby during a camping trip. The appeal of the drama is in the painful process by which the family first loses their child and then, thanks to a competitive press and an apparently faulty judicial system, their dignity. The film is a great rental item because it is definitely worth seeing once. Ownership and multiple viewings, however, will be up to individual tastes.

The first part of the film looks overly grainy and blurs whenever a bright light appears. The second half stabilizes somewhat, but the picture remains soft throughout. It is best to keep the bass down, because there are some rumbles on the musical score which will leave cracks in the walls. The sound is well executed, as is Warner's dependable chapter encoding.

CRYSTAL VISTA
ILLUMINATION BY KEN JENKINS
NATURAL LIGHT: WINDANCE

LumiVision has released a trio of Visual Music discs, each lasting a half hour on single-sided CAV discs. The work featured is not on par with the best experimental video but it is generally colorful and relaxing. Because of the nature of the source material, not every still frame provides a clear image. All three discs, however, have decent picture transfers, clean digital stereo sound, and chapter encoding. The disc jackets provide informative supporting text.

Watching *Crystal Vista* is like coming to in a yoga store. New Age-style paintings – realist visions of angels, pyramids, and other ethereal subjects rendered in colors usually reserved for Christmas tree ornaments – are manipulated with video art effects as the one-pulsating-note-at-a-time music of Iasos lingers on the audio. The garishness of the images is subverted by the video effects and the disc is a bit silly, but likeable.

Slightly fuzzier but less assertive, *Illumination by Ken Jenkins*, contains a series of symmetrically mutating colors. The most impressive segment is the finale, a breathtaking (but nevertheless relaxing) sequence of vivid kaleidoscope patterns. There is a surprise on side two – a brief sequence which is even more elaborate and kaleidoscopic than the ending of side one. It stands alone, lasting just seven and a half minutes. The music is nondescript.

Combining shots of Mother Nature with instrumental music has been a popular video programming nook. *Natural Light: Windance* is one of the better efforts because the camera never lingers very long on any one image or subject. Although the music, which is more orchestral than the other discs though still predominantly electronic, is light and peaceful, the pictures, without seeming rushed, shift at a fast clip, changing from flowers to snow to sunsets to streams to branches and so on. The images are a bit soft, but the picture quality is fine.

THE CURE IN ORANGE
THE CURE STARING IN THE SEA – THE IMAGES

Two complementary discs have been released with material from the British rock group, The Cure. *The Cure in Orange* is an excellent, 113-minute concert program filmed at an outdoor amphitheater in the Cote d'Azure. *The Cure Staring at the Sea – The Images* is an 82-minute collection of music videos and home movie filler (identified as 'Conversation' on the jacket cover, but containing no spoken words).

The picture on *Orange* is mildly letterboxed and the transfer, from 35mm film, is excellent. The stage has been lit for filming, but even in the darkest corners, the image remains free of impurities. *Staring at the Sea* is a compilation of many sources, some barely clear enough to distinguish objects and faces, and others as sharp and vivid as the *Orange* material. The Cure in a studio, however, is quite different from The Cure on stage. The video numbers each have a distinctive sound, with clear vocals and separate tracks for each instrument. In concert, the sounds tend to blend together and the songs sound more like one another. The concert is actually a more flattering presentation of the group than are the videos, however, and is always engaging, despite its length and the lack of an exact coordination between the visuals and the sound. *Staring at the Sea* does have one component, though, which may widen its popularity beyond devoted Cure fans. The music video, 'Jumping Someone Else's Train,' features a time lapse trip on the front of an express train, creating a run from London to Brighton in 2 minutes and 47 seconds. Didn't it take Nicholas Nickelby two weeks to get there?

CURFEW

A mindless exploitation film, *Curfew*, about two prison escapees on a murder and torture spree, is mildly grainy but passable and the sound is standard. The actresses in the film playing high school coeds look old enough to have grandchildren, and some of the blunt instruments used in the murders tend to bend on contact, but that is the least of the film's problems. Lack of originality and tedium loom larger as grounds for avoiding the title.

THE CURSE

The Curse is a well executed meteor-on-the-farm tale. There is a misleading prolog which has little to do with the film itself and leaves the viewer expecting an ending that never comes, and – something we have never seen before in a legitimate film – a major character disappears from the plot without explanation at an important point early on, never to be seen or heard from again. But to its credit, the film has a nice, icky performance by Claude Akins, a satisfactory amount of suspense, gross moments, and a good stereophonic soundtrack. The sound has low-budget hiss, but digital encoding assures a basic, quality delivery of the effects. The picture, which was shot with Fuji film, becomes hopelessly grainy whenever the lights go down.

CURSE OF THE CAT PEOPLE
(see **CAT PEOPLE**)

CURSE OF THE DEMON

The running time on *Curse of the Demon*, is 94 minutes and not the 81 minutes printed on the jacket cover. The movie is in very good condition for an older, British black and white effort. The monaural sound is stabilized with digital encoding. The blacks are rich, the whites shine, and the greys are distinctive.

The film is a good occult mystery story, directed by Jacques Tourneur, of the is-it-real-or-is-it-a-hoax variety. It is clear from the pace of the film that Tourneur intended to keep the viewer in the dark at the end, and this would have made the film compelling and enigmatic. But Val Lewton was not involved, and Tournier's new producers insisted that the occult elements be brought into the light. It makes for an impressive but silly ending, and robs the film of a chance at immortality. Since the ending is no longer ambiguous, the viewer does not feel compelled to search the movie again for clues, but the disc can still be considered as repeatable entertainment, to be put on whenever a heavy fog rolls in.

CUTTER'S WAY

A Hamlet-ish murder mystery with a strong cult following, *Cutter's Way*, directed by Ivan Passer, is about a collection of losers who identify a murderer and then can't decide upon a judicial course of action. The two heroes, played by Jeff Bridges and John Heard, have a number of amusing lines, and Heard's comical performance as a war veteran who is missing an arm, a leg, and an eye is the stuff legends are made of. Unlike many cult films, however, the plot and the characters become less witty and charming on repeated viewings, and the film has no alternate rewards to fill the gap. The film is thoughtful, but its morals are as quickly digested as its one-liners.

Passer uses a lot of browns and these often tend to appear grainy, though most of the time the picture is presentable. The sound is monaural and has no significant attributes.

CYBORG

A post-apocalypse martial arts effort, *Cyborg* should satisfy action fans who are tolerant of illogical narrative steps. It is the sort of movie in which a momentarily painful bullet wound to the shoulder heals in ten minutes and fails to leave a scar.

The transfer is quite good, which contributes significantly to the disc's entertainment value. The Ultra-Stereo surround sound is appropriately torrential. The picture has a slightly soft focus, but is otherwise error-free and the flesh tones are refreshingly accurate.

CYCLONE

Heather Thomas's agent managed to get her name billed above the title in *Cyclone*, and if she ever becomes more famous than she is – which is unlikely – the disc will become valuable camp. There is normally nothing funny about electroshock torture, but when the bad guys apply it to her thighs to get her to tell them where the secret power device for her super motorcycle is located, the camera is placed such that the most significant portions of her anatomy lunge into the lens like jellyfish thrown by a current. The script, surprisingly, is very good. It is only the acting and the direction which are atrocious.

The print, with the exception of one or two fuzzy spots, is bright and clean. Stick with it for the full 89 CLV minutes, since the macho fistfight Thomas has with Ashley Ferrare at the end is the best part of the show, a hurricane of deliberately missed punches and grimacing afterthoughts.

CYNDI LAUPER IN PARIS

The thinking man's Madonna, Cyndi Lauper, finally appears on an American disc in *Cyndi Lauper in Paris*. Rick Derringer is on stage with her for the full 90-minute set and appears to have a good time not being the center of attention. Lauper, with her Lina Lamont voice and her anti-fetish outfits, is a joy to watch and to hear. Her live performance is not as melodic as her studio work, but there are some interesting stereo separations, and she sings 'Money Changes Everything' with unusual verve, as if she had been reminded recently of its lesson. The image is somewhat at the mercy of the stage lighting, but color, not sharpness, is affected. Any problems with either the picture or the sound are part of the source and not the transfer, which is well executed.

CYRANO DE BERGERAC
CYRANO DE BERGERAC

Certainly one of the most wonderful stage dramas ever composed is Edmond Rostand's *Cyrano de Bergerac*. Rostand creates the dramatic equivalent of the crane shot, beginning on a wide expanse of personalities and then moving in on one specific character, whose heroic and tragic nature has a magnetic appeal. Two versions are available on disc, the black-and-white Jose Ferrer film, considered definitive in its day, and a fine Royal Shakespeare Company production, from a translation by Anthony Burgess and starring Derek Jacobi.

For sheer emotional impact, the Ferrer film is preferable, although for fidelity to the source the RSC production is obviously the wiser choice. Neither transfer is outstanding. The black-and-white source material for the Ferrer movie has a number of splices and many splotches and speckles. The image is also soft. The RSC production is in color, from a video tape source which looks a bit worn down. Since the traditional RSC costume and set colors are always variations on ragged browns, the aged chroma on the source material is not as harmful as the mild blurriness which robs details from the expressions of the cast members in group shots. The monaural sound on both discs is manageable.

Ferrer's studied performance is thrilling, though a viewer does get hints that his magic would begin to stand out like a false nose if the movie were not such a truncated version of the play. The film's editing magnifies the best parts of his performance, but there is no harm in that. He captures your attention and affection early on, and holds it to his heart until the end.

The RSC production is filmed on a soundstage, though it is clearly adapted from a regular stage production. In contrast to the Ferrer movie, the editing is awkward and the players do not significantly modify their performance for the camera – they still play to the whole house instead of to the single eye. The program is a full hour longer than the Ferrer movie (it runs to four sides, while the Ferrer effort is contained on a single platter). Although Burgess plays one or two tricks with which we are not completely happy, the presentation is a legitimate rendering of Rostand's work, and the disc is a gratifying record of the production. Jacobi is as harmed by the camera angles and editing, however, as Ferrer was helped. What you get are hints of a captivating stage performance, made more dull and more obscure by the attention the camera angles are providing.

D.A.R.Y.L

The stereo track on *D.A.R.Y.L.* is the type which is a lot of fun on disc. The Marvin Hamlisch Broadway overture score sounds out of place, but the jet engines and the chirping birds enhance the entertainment measurably. The story is about an android child created by the government and accidentally placed with unsuspecting foster parents. The second part concerns the child's escape from military types, but after the lengthy emotional build-up in the beginning, the director underplays every clutch situation. The climax is neutralized and uninspiring. The picture looks good.

D.O.A.

Several splices upset the rhythm to the exciting conclusion of the original *D.O.A.*. The source material has other splices as well, along with scratches and similar markings here and there. The black and white picture is sharp, but it is never outstanding. It will depend upon the viewer as to whether these flaws defeat the film's pleasures. The movie has a breakneck pace and is enjoyable under almost any condition, be it a fuzzy midnight broadcast or a less-than-pristine laser disc. Side two is in CAV with two unsteady still frames out of every five. The digitally encoded monaural sound is a little scratchy and Dimitri Tiomkin's less-than-subtle score is an embarrassment.

The movie stars Edmond O'Brien, filling his role in such a way that you constantly picture what it would have been like if Bogart were playing the part. For those unfamiliar with the classics, this is the movie where a man is subjected to a fatal dose of radiation poisoning and compulsively searches for his murderer before he succumbs to its delayed effects. The pace, the plot twists, and the frantic search for 'truth' are lively fun, and the film manages to be metaphysical – why do we die? – without imposing a philosophy.

D.O.A.

The remake, *D.O.A.*, is anything but. The disc has a sharp picture transfer and a great digital stereo surround audio track. The gunshots and falling bodies are loud, the drips are intense, and there isn't a single speckle in the nighttime tar pit scene. The movie is also lively. It is a thriller in an academic setting, with the well-known plot device, of the terminally ill hero attempting to discover who has poisoned him, providing sufficient movement to touch upon several other crimes, romance, and contemplative pauses about life, passion, and mediocrity. Dennis Quaid stars. The film is an enjoyable escape, and the disc, because of the transfer, increases the entertainment.

DA

The film adaptation of the stage play, *Da*, utilizes the same narrative trick as its source, allowing a character who has arrived to attend his father's funeral carry on conversations with both his father and his own, younger self. These conversations lead to flashbacks which tell the story, such as it is. The device encourages inattention, since it is quickly obvious that nothing shattering is going to occur. The film was made on location in Ireland and uses the scenery well. There are also a handful of scenes which are legitimately touching or memorable – one in particular about a dog that almost drowns – but there is not enough to sustain intensity, and one can watch the disc in random segments and get as much out of it as watching it straight through. The picture quality is passable, but soft. The stereo effects are sporadic.

DAD

Not until *Dad* is three-quarters over does it start sounding like a film and stop sounding like something made for TV. The movie is based upon the novel by William Wharton, whose forte is a psychoanalytical exploration of his characters, and when the scriptwriter/director, Gary David Goldberg, starts taking advantage of it, the film's morals finally become interesting. The performances, by Jack Lemmon, Ted Danson, and Olympia Dukakis, are good, but most of the story concerns a man struggling through the final phases of his relationship with his father, and none of it appears to have the weight to bear a feature film. Whether a viewer can stick it out or not will be up to individual tastes. There is no great plot twist at the end, merely a solidifying of theme and intelligence which goes beyond the scope of the standard generational drama. The disc has a very crisp picture, which contributes noticeably to the intensity of the performances. The subject matter is not one which supports an interesting audio mix.

DAFFY! & PORKY!
(see BUGS! & ELMER!)

DAFFY DUCK'S MOVIE: FANTASTIC ISLAND
The 1983 quasi-compilation feature, *Daffy Duck's Movie: Fantastic Island*, contains moderately trimmed versions of ten classic cartoons, along with a linking device which spoofs 'Fantasy Island.' One of our favorite shorts is included among the ten, in which the big dog, Spike, and the little dog, Chester, mistake an escaped panther for Sylvester the cat, but the other sequences, however enjoyable, are not among the most famous episodes.

The transfer of cartoons to disc is usually dependable, because the images are basic and lacking in complexity. *Daffy* generally looks good, although bright solid colors regularly look fuzzy in the center. The sound is monaural and not CX-encoded, but it sounds no worse than it does when broadcast on Saturday morning.

DAFFY DUCK'S QUACKBUSTERS
Most of *Daffy Duck's Quackbusters* is new material, but it is not the vacant and weak animation which was used as connective material in *Daffy Duck's Movie: Fantastic Island.* To lift a phrase from the jacket copy, the 79-minute film is seamless. Only four older Warner cartoons are incorporated, along with a couple of new ones and pieces of a few others. The premise has Daffy running a *Ghostbusters*-type agency, and all of the cartoons are horror-themed. A viewer should not strenuously attempt to separate what was originally a short feature from the new material (although Warner has obligingly provided chapter markers), because it is best simply to relax and enjoy the disc as a whole. The new stuff is elaborately colored (although background movement is still more stiff than the older pieces) and the gags are on par with the classic routines, or perhaps even a bit more sophisticated.

Older cartoons seen in full include 'Transylvania 6-5000,' in which Bugs wreaks havoc on a vampire by repeating a couple of harmless magic words; 'Hyde and Go Tweet,' in which Tweetie consumes some of Mr. Hyde's formula and is soon chasing Sylvester; 'Claws for Alarm,' one of the series of cartoons in which Sylvester must save an unsuspecting Porky Pig from a group of murderous mice, this time in a western ghost town; and part of a surreal classic, 'Punch Trunk,' about a realistic elephant the size of a football. 'The Duxorcist,' a new Daffy Duck short which was made in 1987, is closer in style to the thirties cartoons than the fifties cartoons, with adult gags and topical humor. It was the first cartoon short to be made in a long time, and has the pent-up creativity of many artists finally letting loose. 'Night of the Living Duck,' another recent effort, is similar, though less intense.

The picture quality on the disc is fine, and the monaural sound, which is digitally encoded, is lively. The sound on the disc is so good, however, that the shifts in the character voices from old to new are often distinctive, and may be disconcerting. The disc is in CLV.

DAKOTA
Lou Diamond Phillips plays the title character in *Dakota*, a film about a drifter who takes a job on a horse ranch in Texas (it was filmed in Roanoke and McKinney). The movie has the feel of an Afterschool Special, as Dakota restores an antique automobile, touches the heart of the trainer's daughter without pawing the flesh around it, and helps a little boy with one leg to climb a mountain. There are even more subplots than that, and the show only runs 95 minutes, but the pacing is laborious and the disc seems to last forever. The picture and sound have no flaws to speak of.

DAMIEN – OMEN II
Every once in a while filmmakers try to apply Hollywood production values to cheap exploitation subjects, and although the results are inevitably disappointing, the effort is usually impressive enough to generate a sort of cult appeal. *Damien – Omen II* is not a good film, but the stars in the cast (William Holden and Lee Grant), Jerry Goldsmith's 'Black Mass' score, and the elaborately executed murders make it watchable in an idiot-proof sort of way. As for the plot, we still can't figure out what Damien is going to do with the world once he takes it over and how it could be any worse off than it already is.

CBS/Fox has released the film as a Special Wide-Screen Edition with an aspect ratio of about 2.2:1. The film is monaural, and the digitally encoded sound has a slight dullness to it. The color scheme of the film is somber and the disc can't provide a picture quality which wasn't in the original film to begin with, but the image is acceptable. The letterboxing helps the title significantly in that it is another touch of class which the movie doesn't deserve. CBS/Fox has also provided the trailers for the other two *Omen* films at the end.

DAMN THE DEFIANT!
RCA/Columbia and Image have released a scanned and cropped version of the Cinemascope title, *Damn the Defiant!*. This is likely to be the version viewers who have come upon the film by way of broadcast television are used to, and it works if you can tolerate Alec Guinness turning to the edge of the screen and giving orders to your goldfish or whatever is to the left of the TV set. The picture also loses its sharpness from having been blown up for the scan, and has a haze which changes in intensity from one shot to the next. The colors are not ideal, but seem tolerable for the package. The sound is also passable.

The 1962 film is a captivating mix of yardarm adventure and below-deck power struggles. It is set during the Napoleonic Wars and concerns the British Navy's modernization of personnel relations, as the officers aboard the ship face more danger from their own crew than from the enemy. Atypically, Guinness lacks the screen presence required for his role, but that may be partially the fault of the cropping. Viewers who are tempted to string up or lash those responsible for the disc had best simply avoid it, but those who are tolerant of mild indiscretions and like sea stories may have a good time with the title.

DAMN YANKEES
Warner has managed to bring *Damn Yankees* to disc without selling out to the devil. The movie was not a widescreen effort and it was not stereophonic. The disc is matted in places, as when the musical numbers employ split-screens or other such devices, but for the most part it is a standard full screen presentation which loses nothing it its translation to video. The colors look terrific. Some sequences appear soft or foggy, but that is a consequence of the original film production and not of the transfer. The monaural sound is digitally encoded and is quite good for its age. There is just enough hiss to make the voices sound fresh and immediate. The music also sounds solid and is free of distortion.

It is a great challenge to keep one's eyes glued to Tab Hunter during his scenes with Gwen Verdon. Verdon is magnetic, and when she's on the screen everything else could be cropped and it would hardly matter. She obviously captivated the film's editors in the same way, because if you watch the first scene she has with Hunter and if you can tear your eyes away from her, you can see Hunter break character and suppress a chuckle at one point.

We wish the whole movie had that sort of appeal, but its pleasures are sporadic. It can be enjoyable on an initial viewing, but its stage-bound construction retains the rests designed to give the major players a break during the show, and these passages wear quickly after multiple viewings. It is also the sort of musical where the lyrics are better than the tunes and the dancing is better than the choreography.

DANCE, GIRL, DANCE
Dorothy Arzner was virtually the only female director in America before the seventies to earn her position without beginning as a performer. Her movies followed the conventions, but as scholars later discovered, Arzner was undercutting the status quo at the same time she appeared to be adhering to it. For example, at the end of *Dance, Girl, Dance*, the heroine, Maureen O'Hara, is paired with the 'good' male lead, played by Ralph Bellamy. Bellamy's character, who runs an elite dance company, has provided the heroine with professional independence, but their personal relationship, on close examination, remains ambiguous. Adding to the ambiguity is the fact that Bellamy, whose entire career was spent never getting the girl, is cast in the role. Arzner's touches are subtle – they had to be for an establishment film in the forties – but her style gives her movies a lasting power by avoiding the inevitable Hollywood triteness which burdened all but the most special films of the era.

The picture transfer is very good. The print has no flaws, and its pristine appearance adds to the film's entertainment. The sound is fine.

Lucille Ball portrays O'Hara's roommate and rival, a pragmatic burlesque dancer. The film can be enjoyed for its surface pleasures – there are some terrific musical numbers, and Ball and O'Hara provide rich emotional contrasts. However, one doesn't have to be writing a graduate thesis to see that the movie is also about the corporeal and cerebral conflict within every woman's soul, and to get chills when the rivals lose their cool and start fighting on stage, to the delight of an auditorium of cheering and jeering males.

DANCE OF DARKNESS BY EDIN VELEZ

The Japanese avant-garde dance form, 'Ankokuh Butoh' (roughly, 'Dance of Darkness'), is mime two centuries from now. Butoh is a dance of abstract movement and images where the performers look like they have stepped out of the torture chambers in *Dune*, a dance in which, for example, the dancer makes his tongue look and act like a slug emerging from his mouth, and a dance that transposes the spiritual crippling of nuclear war onto the limbs and poetic movements of the dancers. Voyager has released an hour long documentary about butoh entitled *Dance of Darkness by Edin Velez*.

This is one of the few discs where we would recommend a thorough study of the jacket notes before viewing the program. The jacket essays provide an understandable introduction (the program itself just sort of dives into the middle of everything) and lend credence to the subject matter. The introductory essay on the back of the jacket is easy to follow and the chapter notations are superb.

The show, which introduces some of the main proponents of the art and also presents a healthy selection of performance sequences, is refreshingly different from anything else that is on disc and is delightfully weird. Often using several sections of the screen to display different pieces of visual information, Velez profiles the dancers and some of the theoretical basis for the dance. The program was recorded on video tape and the transfer is excellent. The digitally encoded sound is stereophonic, and the only substantial complaint we have about the disc is that the analog track is brighter and is preferable to the digital track.

DANCE OF THE DAMNED

Most of the vampire-themed *Dance of the Damned* is a two-character, single-set effort. The film was made on a low budget, so the picture is grainy and monochromatic by nature and the sound is weak.

A stripper with suicidal longings is picked up by a vampire who needs a hit, but they get to talking and decide to spend the night together first. There is nudity, some well-chosen low budget special effects, and even a bit of humor. There is also the expected bad acting and pretentious dialog (the vampire keeps asking her what the sun is like – she says she doesn't know because she works nights). Side two is in CAV, with two unsteady still frames out of every five. The filmmakers don't know how to end the script, so they freeze-frame without making the final decision. On the whole, however, we've seen worse.

DANCE WITH A STRANGER

Based on a true story, *Dance With a Stranger* is about the events leading up to the murder of a cad race car driver by a wronged woman. The story takes place in 1954, and they were able to budget enough to re-create some of the old formula racing cars. But because reality looms heavily over the project, characters and plots take unwieldy lurches and turns the way they do in life. The purse-string British production had a weak picture to begin with, but the disc presentation seems unusually grainy. The sound is a muddy monaural and no help at all in clarifying the heavily accented dialog.

DANCERS

Our heart leaped when the opening credit scroll on *Dancers* finished and the picture began. The transfer is stunning. The colors are so vivid and the image is so crisp that the presentation looks more like projected film than like video.

We always look forward to seeing the films of Herbert Ross. Although he is categorized as a mainstream director, his work is often daring and innovative – so much so that it defies one's concepts of risk or innovation. Wishing to make a movie of the ballet, 'Giselle,' but prudently realizing that such a project wouldn't have a ghost of a chance, Ross and Mikhail Baryshnikov have made a movie about dancers making a movie of 'Giselle,' and they've also concocted a subplot which, to a point, shadows the plot of the ballet. This is enough, particularly under the relaxed constraints of home video, to provide feeling, critical insight, and selective highlights, while maintaining a coherent and inviting narrative. They get away with making a movie about 'Giselle' and only doing the parts of 'Giselle' that they really like.

The sound is clean, particularly when dialog and music are not combined, and, because of its clarity, the music recording enhances one's appreciation of the piece. The disc has chapter markers and the end credits are letterboxed. There is some mild scanning and panning, causing us to notice one jitter as the screen image attempted to follow Baryshnikov leaping back and forth across the stage. The interruption was momentary, but it may be the disc's only significant flaw.

DANGEROUS LIAISONS

We get tongue-tied trying to repeat the plot of *Dangerous Liaisons* to friends. It is a period costume drama about sneaky aristocrats who have nothing better to do than compromise virtue and indulge in intrigues. It is the he-does-this-to-her-because-she-wanted-the-other-one-to-embarrass-him stuff that becomes so confusing so quickly you need to talk in color codes to keep everyone straight. It is better just to see the drama for yourself and absorb as much as you can. The film, starring Glenn Close and John Malkovich, is marvelously entertaining. Few characters in drama are more enjoyable to watch than wily degenerates trying to get one up on each other. The script has been honed by endless adaptations and onstage tryouts. The film is beautifully directed by Stephen Frears with static screen compositions serving only to bundle and charge the energy of the characters within.

The image is in matted format, with a slight black band at the top and the bottom of the screen. Even though the rectangularization is slight, and even though the edges could probably have been extended a bit further, the effect is superb in the way it captures the meticulously composed shots. The color transfer is also decent. Many scenes use complex or delicate lighting in an attempt to approximate the true illumination available in 18th century chateaux, and the disc conveys each scene accurately.

The picture is not the disc's only advantage. *Dangerous Liaisons* also has an excellent stereo surround track. Harpsichords, footfalls, peacocks – the movie actually has a more aggressive soundtrack than many contemporary action features, and the disc recreates each effect with panache.

DARIO ARGENTO'S WORLD OF HORROR

Many of the innovative approaches the Italian movie director, Dario Argento, uses to enhance his films are discussed in *Dario Argento's World of Horror*. The Italian interviews are translated into English, though the English subtitles are loaded with typos. The 70-minute film has a slapdash picture quality (the fault of the source, not the transfer – many of the film clips also look second-rate) and workmanlike digital monaural sound. The jacket cover is grotesque and best kept out of sight. Side two is in CAV, with the rate of unsteady and blurry still frames dependent upon the source material. The documentary covers nearly all of Argento's films, and whets one's appetite for those which have been subject to a limited availability.

DARK BEFORE DAWN

A serious movie which is so devoid of technique that it verges on parody, *Dark Before Dawn*, is good, at least, for a chuckle or two. The story is a thriller about – we're not kidding – farm price supports. It is earnest to the point of repetition, explaining how agri-business is manipulating the marketplace and causing the small farmer financial ruin. The film is an amalgam of every bad intrigue movie you've ever seen, set in an absurd venue. Most of the roles were apparently filled by locals, who don't get to practice conversation all that much, let alone have a chance to learn how to repeat dialog convincingly. The camera is all over the place, hiding the bad guy so that the viewer doesn't learn his identity until the three guesses are exhausted, shaking in imitation of the farmer that is running his auto into a tree trunk, and swinging frantically to point at the actor doing the talking during a two person *tête-à-tête*. The picture transfer is passable, but the original film often looks soft or mis-colored (Did we mention that the filmmakers use filters which make the sky look purple at midday?) and the digital monaural sound lets you hear every ill-chosen word, loud and clear.

THE DARK CRYSTAL

Jim Henson was actively involved in the compilation and transfer of *The Dark Crystal*. It is clear from the disc program that Henson understood the unique nature and advantages of laser video, and he has left a wonderful gift for disc collectors. *The Dark Crystal* is admittedly not a fully entertaining film. It is, however, a unique creation, and as such, when supported by the quality transfer and additional materials which Henson and Image have provided, it becomes a satisfying disc. The movie has no human characters and was made entirely with human-sized models and puppets. The narrative concerns a quest thrust upon a young elf-like hero. He must first determine what his quest is and then venture into an evil castle to fulfill it. When the puppet work is especially elaborate and the activity on the screen is busy, the movie is stimulating and enjoyable. The design used for the hero, however, is unattractive and dull, and the narrative matches the inflexibility inherent in the characters. With five years and many millions of dollars having gone into the production, however, the film is a valid fantasy which still has much to offer a viewer's imagination.

The picture transfer on the disc is a better presentation of the film than most theatrical presentations were. Most theaters projected the film with too much luminance, heightening the colors and the artificiality of the production. With Henson's close supervision, the colors on the disc are precisely the colors which he and co-director Frank Oz intended. Each shot achieves an almost breathtaking similarity to Brian Froud's storybook illustrations that served as the film's conceptual design. The picture has been letterboxed, with an aspect ratio of about 2:1. The image is also mildly grainy, and may be more satisfying on a smaller viewing screen than on a larger projection system.

The movie has stereo surround sound, but the separation effects are relegated primarily to the Trevor Jones score. The music is noticeably improved when spread out among one's speakers.

The disc comes in a gatefold jacket. The film is contained on a single platter and an hour-long 'making of' movie, 'The World of The Dark Crystal,' appears on the single-sided second platter. If one is at all familiar with the movie, then it is best to watch the documentary first, as a warm-up. The program is loaded with demonstrations of the mechanics which went into creating the characters and their environment. The manner in which the personalities of the creators were filtered into the screen characters, although not specifically demonstrated, can often be easily ascertained. The picture is in much poorer condition than the feature and the program is monaural. In addition, after the film has ended on side two, there is a theatrical teaser and two theatrical trailers, as well as a funeral sequence which was cut from the final print. Notations provide the exact location where the sequence was to have been included. The entire disc has been given 86 chapters, all of which are effectively identified on the innerspread.

DARK PASSAGE

The first couple of reels in the black-and-white *Dark Passage* are tinted blue. The tinting disappears without any logical relationship to the story, so one has to assume that CBS/Fox got stuck with a mishmash print. The picture is often speckled or fuzzy, even when it isn't blue.

The movie is really only half a Humphrey Bogart picture. He does a lot of voice-over on side one, and his character is present most of the time, but you actually don't get to see his face until side two. The plot has some admirable twists and turns and Agnes Moorehead, as the villainess, has three wonderfully showy scenes. Lauren Bacall also stars. The production is kind of crazy and the disc is kind of crazy, but it can be entertaining if one's standards are relaxed.

DARK TOWER

Barcelona is the setting for *Dark Tower*, a haunted office building movie which has a couple of decent thrills along with the standard man-eating elevator buffoonery. Michael Moriarty, at his most distracted, and Jenny Agutter, whose idea of serious acting is to not move her rear molars when she speaks, star. The color transfer is reasonably decent for a movie where the dialog doesn't always match the lip movements, and the picture, other than a mild graininess, is acceptable. The sound has bad dubbing, but there is a promising musical score by Stacy Widelitz.

DARK VICTORY

Dark Victory is the classic terminal illness movie, in which Bette Davis's character has one of those Hollywood diseases that renders its victims both eloquent and graceful, right up to the final fatal moment. We all should die so well. This disc has a bad side break, right in the middle of a conversation. The black-and-white print has some speckles, but the picture generally leaves a good impression and the sound is alright. Humphrey Bogart (with an Irish accent) and Ronald Reagan (not very convincing as a playboy inebriate) have supporting roles.

DARLING (Voyager)
DARLING (Nelson)

The director of *Darling*, John Schlesinger, speaking on the alternate audio track on side one of the Voyager Criterion Collection release, says that he thinks the film is dated and that it is not very good, which surely must have pleased Voyager's marketing department to no end. No wonder only one of the three sides of the CLV disc has Schlesinger's commentary. His remarks are pasted together to make a continuous lecture, but the recording was obviously made during a screening, and he makes references to scenes other than the scene being shown on the disc, with no more of an identifying comment than the word 'this.'

Schlesinger should not be so glum, however, for *Darling* has lasting qualities which make it more than simply a leading trendsetter of the mid-sixties and an English language *La Dolce Vita*. (The story, vaguely comical, concerns a young model beset by equal amounts of boredom and success.) The three stars, Julie Christie, Laurence Harvey, and Dirk Bogarde, give excellent performances, but more importantly they are true movie stars, and so the material need not be wholly valid to succeed. For example, the scene which embarrasses Schlesinger the most, in which a group of characters strip themselves literally and psychologically, allows Harvey and Christie to exaggerate their emotions without leaving their characters. Viewers, especially today, are watching the movie because of the cast, not because of what the film has to say about society, and are pleased when the cast takes risks.

The black-and-white picture transfer is impeccable. The film is monaural and the disc has no CX-encoding, but there is nothing significantly wrong with the sound. A quote-the-critics trailer appears after the film is ended. Negative comments and indistinct commentary aside, Schlesinger's talk is highly informative and valuable in providing an understanding of how the film came to be structured as it was.

Darling is also available in CLV through Nelson. The running time of the Nelson disc is 5 minutes shorter than the running time of the Criterion disc. The picture is also inferior. The Criterion disc is sharper and has a better level of contrast – dark smudges around the names in the opening credits on the Nelson disc are absent on the Criterion presentation. The Nelson disc has only two things going for it. One, the sound is CX-encoded and comes across more clearly than the Criterion version. Two, the jacket, though not gatefold, has better cover art.

The disc is shorter because Nelson is using a 'censored' print which has been doctored in at least four places. A brief but powerful pair of suggestive shots, showing Harvey going down on Christie and her reaction, have been excised. A lengthy Parisian sequence concerning a voyeuristic exhibition, which precedes the strip scene and introduces all of the Parisian characters, is completely gone, and scattered shots within the strip scene, emphasizing transvestism, have been removed. Finally, a nude scene so fleeting that it is impossible to see anything anyway has been chopped up so that the viewer won't even think something could have been seen. The impact is obvious; it is like watching the movie on broadcast television.

THE DARYL HALL & JOHN OATES VIDEO COLLECTION: SEVEN BIG ONES

The picture on the first cut of *The Daryl Hall & John Oates Video Collection: Seven Big Ones* is grainy, but the remainder of the double-sided CLV 8-inch is much sharper. Although they have registered their ampersanded names as a trademark, Oates appears to be getting the short end of the deal. Hall dominates the seven music videos on the disc to the point where he often leans to the left or right to stay between the camera and Oates. Many of their hits are here and all of the videos are effective. One, 'Adult Education,' is excellent, combining lyrics about adolescent romance with visuals of a pagan ceremony which is almost as weird as a senior prom.

DATE WITH AN ANGEL

The picture on *Date with an Angel* is severely grainy, but the movie isn't worth solidifying. The film, about an angel who hurts her wing on a satellite on her way to Earth and convalesces in the care of a man about to be married, is so dumb that a list of its virtues could fit on the head of a pin. The disc does have an impressive stereo surround soundtrack, but that is hardly enough to redeem it.

A DATE WITH JUDY

Although a little soft, the source material used for *A Date with Judy* looks scrumptious. The film is in Technicolor, and it is often difficult to take one's eyes off the wardrobes long enough to watch the performers. It always amazes us how 'real' clothing looks on good Technicolor prints. The vivid colors bring out the texture of the fabric.

The movie stars Jane Powell as an earnest high school girl wavering between two men, and Elizabeth Taylor as a spoiled, rich rival. Carmen Miranda also appears as a dance instructor and singer. The film runs close to two hours, but is lighthearted and insubstantial. The sound has no significant problems.

DAVID AND LISA

If you want to see how movie music can sometimes wreck a scene, there is a good example in *David and Lisa*. David and Lisa are schizophrenic youngsters staying at a special hospital. David hates being touched and

Lisa, in a moment of vindictiveness over an imagined slight, threatens to touch him. Instead of the scene being dead silent, the music attempts to build up the tension, but it telescopes what will happen, because the finale to the tune occurs several beats before Lisa drops her threat.

The picture and sound are okay. The break between side one and side two has been sloppily placed in the middle of an important scene. The movie was once considered daring because of its subject material, but time has passed it by.

DAVID BOWIE

In CAV mode, 8-inch discs can handle 15 minutes a side, which is maybe three or four music videos. This isn't so bad. Most rock artists only *have* three or four music videos that are worth keeping.

David Bowie only has two, and they are both included (along with a third) on the *David Bowie* disc. 'Let's Dance' was a milestone in the short history of rock video. It expanded the scope of what could be told visually in the course of a song and raised the standards (and budgets) of music videos to follow. The song was also Bowie's first big hit in almost a decade. The second cut, 'China Girl,' is wilder and closer to Bowie's norm. The presentation is playful and there is an erotic display of flesh at the end as Bowie and his oriental paramour cavort in the surf.

DAVID BOWIE – JAZZIN' FOR BLUE JEAN

The only advantage to *David Bowie – Jazzin' for Blue Jean* is its CAV format. Okay, but the one song on the disc lasts only a few minutes and the rest is an amateurish story about a wimp (Bowie) trying to impress a girl by taking her to a concert featuring a rock star named 'Screaming Lord Byron' (also played by Bowie). It is obvious that Bowie would like to establish a career in film, but do his fans have to pay for his screen tests?

The transfer is beautiful. The sound is sharp and the picture is nearly perfect. Use of still-frame during the 'Jazzin' for Blue Jean' number is particularly effective. Not only are the images clear, they are far more interesting without motion or sound.

DAVID BOWIE: LOVE YOU TILL TUESDAY

A music video-style compilation which David Bowie filmed in 1969, before he was famous, *David Bowie: Love You Till Tuesday* looks a little pale but is generally well-preserved. The soundtrack is in stereo. Not much of it is separated, but the sound is bright and immediate.

The 30-minute film is comprised of nine 'singing heads' numbers fairly similar in format, with no connective sequences. Only one song, 'Space Oddity,' carried over to Bowie's later career. The CLV disc is valuable, however, not only as a collection of baby pictures for fans, but for the sixties nostalgia inherent in Bowie's fashion and music. The further away from the sixties we get, the more amazed we are that we lived through the decade without noticing anything was wrong.

DAVID BOWIE: THE GLASS SPIDER TOUR

An aimlessly elaborate stageshow highlights the lack of direction which has plagued David Bowie's whole career in *David Bowie: The Glass Spider Tour*. The disc is, at least, one of the more thorough and better-produced David Bowie discs. In presenting some 20 chapter-marked numbers during a live concert performance, the disc reveals that Bowie has really never had anywhere to go. There is so much activity on the stage that the songs seem like afterthoughts.

The picture, though filmed with a soft focus, is brightly lit and well transferred. The digitally encoded stereo sound is also clean and bright. Bowie sings his older numbers with the same blandness that he shouts his more recent hits, and they all start to sound alike. Appearing with Bowie for most of the concert is the briefly famous guitarist, Peter Frampton. Bowie's music has always concentrated on following trends, and the 103-minute concert reveals that he has been using the same song over and over, just dressed differently to suit succeeding fashions.

DAVID COPPERFIELD

The source material for *David Copperfield* looks as if it was found in an orphanage. Often blurry, sometimes marked, and rarely problem-free, the quality of the picture is an impediment to concentrating on the film or enjoying it. The sound is more consistent, but elderly.

The film, which was directed by George Cukor, runs into the problem that any cinematic adaptation of a long novel encounters, namely a lack of balance between the pace of the plot and the depth of emotion. Although many of the scenes feel like summarizations, the movie still runs 12 minutes over two hours and takes up three sides. One significant plus is the presence of W.C. Fields in the secondary role of Micawber. This was one of his rare forays into mainstream dramatic acting, and the utilization of him is ideal. The turning point of the whole film, however, is Copperfield's walk from London to Dover. It is the one sequence in which Cukor really invests some time and its success carries the remainder of the movie. It is a shame one can't say the same thing about the disc.

DAVID SANBORN – LOVE & HAPPINESS

For those who like to watch their jazz while they listen to it there is *David Sanborn – Love & Happiness*. The program is in black-and-white and is stylishly tailored to suit the music. The image often appears as if the film had slipped out of its sprocket on the projector, but it appears this way at just the right times in conjunction to shifts in the tempo. Sanborn plays the saxophone, and since the cameras are generally set up below the stage, they are often pointing at his neck. His throat pulsates as he blows into the sax, and it seems as if he is singing through it.

When the beat of the music quickens, the imagery becomes dramatic. For a piece called 'Smile', the editing and the images are playful. The musicians react emotionally to their efforts. Ostensibly a live performance, the 37-minute set is almost too impressive to be real. The sound is impressive. The disc sounds so immediate that you might wonder if your speakers are not hard-wired to the studio. The disc is so enjoyable that we didn't mind that it was only 37 minutes long. We just played it over and over.

DAVIDSBUNDLERTANZE – NEW YORK CITY BALLET

George Ballanchine's choreography for Robert Schumann's music on *Davidsbundlertanze – New York City Ballet* includes the placement of a piano on the stage with the dancers. The piano, which is the sole source of music for the 18 short pieces which comprise the ballet, is not just an obstacle – it is a deliberate, black weight which counterbalances the lightly costumed dancers wherever they move on the stage. But on video programs of ballets, television directors always seem to think that the first row is superior to the First Circle, and so the piano is treated as a visual annoyance and is avoided in favor of the dancer's faces. This is preposterous, and the result hardly deserves to retain Ballanchine's name on the jacket cover, but laser disc owners are so starved for decent ballet programs that they will undoubtedly welcome the Pioneer Artists release with open arms. The portion of the choreography which does make it onto the screen is enchanting.

The single-sided disc runs 43 minutes. The program is not performed in front of an audience, but it has all the other qualities of a live presentation. The digitally encoded sound is excellent and gives the piano a full, expressive resonance. The picture, if faintly hazy, is beautiful. There are only 10 chapters encoded for the 18 pieces, however, and that rather sums up the presentation – you're privy to about half of what is going on.

DAWN OF THE DEAD

George Romero's zombie epic, *Dawn of the Dead*, was made with inexpensive film stock, but the picture could have been brighter and fresher than it is. Viewers tend to have a wider range of tolerance with films of this nature, however, and the presentation is passable. The digitally encoded monaural sound is efficient but uninteresting. Since the film runs beyond the two hour mark, side three is in CAV with two unsteady still frames out of every five. There is a zombie massacre at the end, but the most interesting effect we deconstructed was the ricochet of a bullet off a wall. This is the uncut version.

The more often we see *Dawn of the Dead* the more brilliant it seems. Since it contains oodles of grotesque makeup and mutilation effects, some viewers understandably will not have the patience for it. However, it may be the best merger of a daydream and a nightmare anyone has ever achieved, and viewers who tolerate or live for grotesque thrills should not pass it by. The movie's most daring aspect is not its special effects but its length. At 127 minutes, it deliberately takes its excruciating time showing the process the characters must go through to protect themselves (the movie is about four people who attempt to hold out in a shopping mall after zombies begin to take over the world – the events are communicated in a low-key style which adds considerably to the viewer's acceptance of the narrative). It is an elaborate satire on middle-class life and shopping habits, it is a thriller, and it is a low-budget spectacle. Most importantly, however, the running time allows the movie to not only play the nightmare through, it gives the viewer a full chance to soak up the daydream (having the run of the mall) as well.

THE DAY AFTER
The day after *The Day After* was shown on network television everyone came to work or to school with carefully rehearsed opinions to offer their colleagues and friends. The broadcast was a shared event, turning America into the 'global village' Marshall McLuhan talked about before home video isolated viewers from the tribal circle.

Emotionally powerful to the point of being upsetting to some, *The Day After* works on moods and responses which are too little massaged for our own good. Opening to the gushy monaural strains of the worst type of ABC Event music, characters and situations are established quickly. (The sound is not CX-encoded. The picture is accurate but bland.) Everyone loves everyone, yet for some reason the Russians and the Americans are fighting each other on the East German border. There are no mean characters. No neighbors mad at each other. No rudeness, even when mobs are scrambling for groceries.

John Cullum slowly emerges as the center of the film's spirit. When his character dies, in a manner which is just as arbitrary as the nuclear attack, it echoes the earlier deaths and is deeply disheartening. The understanding of what such a war would do to life doesn't come right away, and that is the point the movie is trying to make.

When we first bought our laser disc player and hooked it up in a sweaty fury to play a disc, we watched the revolving webs and spreading fan of the MCA DiscoVision logo and realized that, for the first time, we were watching something on television that no one was going to interrupt with a special bulletin, no matter how important that bulletin might be. And even today, when we have finished watching a disc, we always switch back to network television before we turn off the set. To make sure the global village is still there.

DAY OF THE DEAD
The print used for George Romero's unambitious sequel, *Day of the Dead*, has a few scratches, but the presentation is not distracting. The mixed feelings of secured enclosure and insecure surroundings which Romero creates in *Day* are different from the daydream/nightmare atmosphere which he created in his first two films. The disappointment is that he has not taken the large thematic leap he seemed to be promising. Instead, it's just more gruesome zombies, wandering around like tourists who left their maps in the motel. One also wonders what people who are trying to cope with real tragedies think about movies like this.

THE DAY OF THE TRIFFIDS
What if everybody in the world but you were blind? That is the premise in the engaging, old-fashioned science fiction effort, *The Day of the Triffids*, which has been letterboxed, with an aspect ratio of about 2.25:1. The film tries very hard to conquer an epic story with a modest budget, and it is surprisingly effective up to a point. It lacks the intelligence of the novel, but so does every other science fiction film.

The monaural sound has no significant problems. After the movie is ended there is an enjoyable theatrical trailer which recaps the film's best thrills.

The source material used for the picture transfer is a little worn down. The colors are green/brownish and nothing is shiny. The Cinemascope movie takes advantage of the wider screen inconsistently, but the letterboxing enables the viewer to catch the occasional shot which is disrupted when one sees the movie on broadcast television. Triffids are large man-eating plants which do not run very fast and, hence, can only defeat a man if he is blinded. Near the finale there is a shot of a forest of Triffids attacking a hacienda, and the image has an evocative sweep which could not be replicated with cropping. The film follows two sets of characters who never interact, as the few people in the world who can still see after mysterious lights have blinded everyone else try to find a way to stop the encroaching plant monsters. The color transfer isn't bad, just a little dull, and, time having passed and special effects having advanced, one can say the same about the film.

THE DAY THE EARTH STOOD STILL
Robert Wise's *The Day the Earth Stood Still* has a nice transfer which should satisfy most viewers, although there are several curiosities to it. The black-and-white picture is usually near-perfect, with only a scratch or two to show its age. In one place, however, the print looks overexposed. In a couple of other segments, the picture seems to let down its guard and turn a bit fuzzy.

The sound will probably drive perfectionists batty, but it is a lot of fun. It has been remixed for stereo and is strengthened considerably by the digital encoding. Bernard Herrmann was responsible for the daring and innovative musical score. Rather than utilizing a single note for the vibrating bass associated with the landing of the flying saucer, Herrmann alternates between several notes, creating a melodic rumble which puts *Close Encounters* to shame. The music, which has received most of the attention in the stereo remix, comes across a little louder than the rest of the audio track. The payoff is in the bass, which never could have shaken audiences in the fifties the way it can today.

Wise began as a film editor, and *The Day the Earth Stood Still* lives and breathes through the art of montage. In the newsreel-styled passages showing the world stricken with entropy, in the fear generated as the robot approaches the heroine, and in every other memorable scene, it is the pace and sensibility of the cuts which prevent the film from being just another fifties flying saucer hoot. The movie works just fine today. It states its premise, and then backs off on the special effects to present science fiction in ideas instead of images. The film also has a message, and one can only pray that someday it will become antiquated.

THE DEAD
We read somewhere that high school and college kids rent videos to cheat on their reading assignments in literature classes. While that practice might lead a student to academic doom with something like 'Sweet Bird of Youth,' a work such as John Huston's film of the James Joyce short story, *The Dead*, can do wonders to enhance one's understanding of the material. Joyce's work is considered the first 'modern' short story, a popular art form which had not been in existence for very long prior to his improvement upon it. The old style of short story existed to provide the reader with a quick thrill or two, usually executed at the story's end. The style which is preferred today – by the intelligentsia, not necessarily by the majority of people who read – simply provides a slice of life, one where characters are presented subtly but vividly and insignificant events are structured so that the reader will ponder them long after the story is ended.

However obscure today's short fiction may be, Joyce's work, as exemplified in Huston's film, is rich in humanity and philosophy. The film is enchanting, provided that one is prepared for it. The disc is also lovely. The jacket is embossed with gold lettering and is a pleasure to hold in one's hands. The transfer is very good, although the film itself was grainy and some of the grain survives. It doesn't look nearly as bad as it did on the big screen. The stereo sound is digitally encoded and brings a warmth to the easy but accomplished sound editing and to Alex North's brief but memorable score.

The break between side one and two is in the perfect spot, at the end of the dinner party which comprises most of the film, and the second side of the 86-minute disc is in CAV. There are two unsteady still frames out of every five, and what one would actually do with CAV here is hard to fathom, but it is a nice touch that adds to one's confidence about the disc.

The story concerns a dinner party in Dublin, shortly after Christmas just after the turn of the century. It ends, like Joyce's most famous novel, with a long soliloquy which touches only partially upon what has gone on before. The movie, however, is a marvelous, intelligent, cozy experience. If you put it on during a winter's night, you can almost feel like you are mixing with the dinner guests, listening to their conversations and enjoying their company. A friend once told us that there had never been a good 'great film' which had a short story as its source. *The Dead* is at least one exception to that rule.

DEAD AIM
Ed Marinaro has been cast against type as a smart, sexy police detective in *Dead Aim*, about a series of topless dancer murders in Atlanta. The plot is best not examined too closely and the ending is exactly the same as that of *Lethal Weapon II* ("I have diplomatic immunity!" "Ka-pow!"), but everything is coherent and moves at a decent pace. The picture is hazy but free of grain. The sound is unimpressive and only a little bit of the musical score is stereophonic.

DEAD-BANG
Fans of action films will want to obtain the cheap *Dead-Bang*. The movie was directed by John Frankenheimer and it is a typical Frankenheimer effort – a stylistic tour de force shackled with a blatant disregard for common sense. The plot, about a detective tracking a murderer through several western states, has a number of unlikelihoods, but who has time to stop and think about them? Unlike a few other thrillers, it uses a white supremacist group for villains but does not get bogged down in paranoia. The disc also looks and sounds terrific. The picture suffers from a mild cropping, but is otherwise flaw-

less. The flesh tones look perfect and dark scenes have no elements of distortion.

The sound is even better. Don Johnson's character lives in an apartment under a flight pattern, and you will think the planes have started going over your own living space during the scenes there. The musical score is also admirably separated, creating a full, three-dimensional orchestration.

DEAD CALM

Warner has released a wide screen edition of the marvelous boat-in-the-middle-of-the-ocean thriller, *Dead Calm*. The picture has an aspect ratio of about 2:1. The image is still trimmed a bit on each side (the binocular views are not completely round). After a short prolog, the film has only three characters, and camera angles are probably the most important component in holding the viewer's attention. Most of the shots combine two elements, whether it is a foreground and a background or an object on the left and an object on the right, and the elements inevitably ignite. A scanned and cropped version of the film would either be dead or calm (or adca) and would lose too much of the tension and excitement.

The picture transfer looks very good. A slight halo can sometimes be seen around intense reds, but otherwise the picture is steady and solid. There are some views of the starlit sky at night which are quite captivating, and the combination of sails and blue water inevitably provides some appealing scenery. The sound is even better. The sound editing is full of creaks and drips, and makes full use of the back channel. There is also a heavy reverberation which kicks in just as your stomach is already starting to tighten.

The movie is good fun, the sort where you have a tendency to shout advice to the characters. Warner's reliable chapter encoding is in place and the listing on the back of the jacket is a model of discretion, identifying the scene without giving away the plot. We see no need to give the plot away either, except to mention that the violence isn't bad by today's standards and that the script loses its logic at only one point, when a woman incapacitates a man who has just tried to murder her. All she does is tie him up. She could have at least broken his kneecaps or something – that is what we were screaming at her to do.

DEAD END

The print that Embassy dusted off for *Dead End* is gorgeous. The black-and-white picture is virtually flawless and the contrasts are rich and distinct. The movie was based on a stage play and takes place on a single, complicated set. Were it not for the presence of Joel McCrea and Humphrey Bogart, the show would have made a good musical. Photographed by Gregg Toland, the lighting and the controlled environment make the disc look like a live broadcast. This was the movie which introduced the Dead End Kids. The story has something to do with pulling oneself out of the slums in a virtuous fashion. McCrea does and Bogart does not. It is a fun movie and the plot isn't nearly as important to one's enjoyment as watching Toland bob around that set for an hour and a half.

DEAD HEAT

We suspect that a fairly accurate 'Horror Pleasure Index' can be derived by dividing the number of gross effects in a film by its production budget. Cheap, disgusting movies are often great fun. Expensive, disgusting movies are usually just disgusting, and *Dead Heat* pretty much falls into the latter category. The film, starring Treat Williams and Joe Piscopo, is about murdered cops who are regenerated as functional zombies long enough to hunt down the men who killed them. The concept has some potential, but the movie's emotions are all wrong and the film is never sufficiently outrageous. It has too many cosmetics and is too ungainly, like a walking corpse.

Side one is in CAV, but the two shaky still frames out of every five prevent one from appreciating the special effects. The picture and sound are passable, and there are some enjoyable digital stereo effects.

DEAD MAN OUT

Dead Man Out is quite an interesting drama about the relationship between a death row inmate and his psychiatrist. The film has the feel of a stage drama because of its confined locations and limited cast, but it also has a strong feeling of authenticity. Danny Glover is the doctor and Ruben Blades is his patient. The script avoids the normal dramatic psychology tricks, such as the revelation of symbols, and instead dives right to the heart of what good therapy provides, namely, helping the patient deal with immediate problems. The entertainment comes from trying to determine when the characters are being sincere to one another and when they are not.

The picture is soft but acceptable. The stereo sound is effective, as there is always a background din of voices and slamming doors. Side two is in CAV with perfect still frames, providing the viewer with a chance to examine the craft of two fine actors on a microscopic level.

DEAD OF NIGHT

Although the ventriloquist tale tends to dominate critical discussions of *Dead of Night*, the film's clever structure allows even the weakest of the sketches to be effective, because there is less of a need to balance the impact of each story. The black and white source material is scratchy and ragged, but the edges are sharp and the contrasts are rich. The sound matches the condition of the picture. The volume is set a bit low, so it must be amplified some, but raising it too much brings out a great deal of background noise. The chapter encoding goes beyond simply marking the installments and is effective. On multiple screenings of this well-known British anthology, about a group of people enigmatically gathered at a country house and swapping stories of terror, it is the linking tale in *Dead of Night* which becomes the most haunting, with a circular construction that calls one back for another and another view.

DEAD POETS SOCIETY

We stopped caring about *Dead Poets Society* when the boy committed suicide. Here is a movie in which the central figurehead, an English teacher portrayed by Robin Williams, admonishes his students to avoid cliché and seek out the path not taken by others, and all the while the script is following every cliché available. The film is also Peter Weir's most flagrant attempt yet to turn America into Australia.

The picture transfer is very good. Most sequences are sharply focused and accurately colored. The stereo surround does not have much to offer in separation effects, but you may have to suppress the urge to stand and gather your books together whenever the school bells ring.

DEAD OF WINTER

The disc to watch when one is comfortably settled in for a blizzard, *Dead of Winter* is an enjoyable movie under any atmospheric conditions, but it has that special combination of mystery and environment which encourages an extra level of concentration when synchronized with the weather outside. The plot of the film is dependent upon the snowstorm to keep the heroine trapped in a menacing house and victimized by a screwed-up blackmail scheme. There the acting takes over, as the cast, including Mary Steenburgen and Roddy McDowall, enthusiastically gnashes its way through greed, fear, and bent morals.

The picture is often grainy or mildly blurry. In error, the FBI warning appears for a flash at the end of side one. The sound is in analog stereo and has some scattered problems, including a dropout in the left channel at one point. The movie's sound mix, however, is very nice. A couple of thumps made us stop the disc and leave to assure ourselves that the front door was locked. The music is also eerie, with individual instruments sometimes floating out of a single channel. And then there is the constant roar of the storm, whistling through the rafters. It might be a good movie to watch during a hot summer evening, after all.

DEAD OR ALIVE: RIP IT UP LIVE

The Dead or Alive stage act is a cross between Boy George and a Chippendale's show, replete with bare-bottomed backup singers. The group appears in *Dead or Alive: Rip It Up Live*. The program combines two live shows filmed in Japan, cutting back and forth from shot to shot. The group performs the same set in both shows, but wears different outfits. The music has a mushy live sound to it, and the group is more into posing than composing anyway. The picture is grainy but sufficiently detailed and, unlike the days of Elvis and Ed Sullivan, the program director is not above holding onto shots which show neither faces nor fingering. The disc lasts 50 minutes and is chapter encoded, with the euphemistic song titles listed on the back of the jacket.

THE DEAD POOL

The Clint Eastwood-as-Dirty Harry effort, *The Dead Pool*, is not a very good movie. The main clues for tracking down the killer are discovered off-screen and then announced. There is no actor or actress of stature in the cast to get Eastwood's adrenaline running. And there isn't a single gag line to incorporate into the national vocabulary. On the other hand, there is Eastwood shooting his Magnum every time things seem to be getting slow. The film is brief, running just 91 minutes, and can fit comfortably into a Dirty Harry marathon.

The picture is sharply focussed and accurately colored, but a faint grain appears from time to time, and the darker scenes are troubled in places by a faint haze.

DEAD RECKONING
No one filled the role of the hero in hard-boiled thrillers better than Humphrey Bogart. His detective films are established classics, but it is in some of his second-tier movies that his value becomes truly apparent. He looks tough enough to handle unsolicited trouble and wise enough to get himself out of a fix. You know that he knows he has edges on all the odds.

Dead Reckoning is perfect in its own way, with only the ingenue, Lizabeth Scott, lacking the strength to pull her weight. The drama is quite a load, too, and must be narrated in great chunks in a silly voice-over by Bogart who supposedly is telling most of the story to a paratrooper priest. Ahem, but the movie is better than it sounds. It has many plot twists and fulfills every expectation, if you approach it with your eyes open.

You may, however, wish to look the other way when it comes to the quality of the picture and sound transfer on the disc. The print is no worse than what one sees on broadcast television, but it has many scratches and other age-generated impurities. We assume the shots which are out of focus were part of the original film. The sound is monaural, not CX-encoded, and best played over one's TV speakers.

DEAD RINGERS
The film that David Cronenberg's *Dead Ringers* reminds us the most of is the underrated *I'm Dancing As Fast As I Can*, which was about a couple who attempt to pull themselves out of drug addiction by locking themselves up in their apartment. In Cronenberg's *Ringers* the same thing happens, but it is embellished with Cronenberg's dark and weird outlook on existence. The film may not be appealing, but it is difficult to forget once you have seen it and the disc is perversely attractive.

Image has done an excellent job transferring the title to disc. The picture not only retains every tricky lighting effect, but it also preserves the smallest details without distortion. The stereo surround has no problems, and the disc has been thoroughly chapter-encoded. An extensive and intelligent interview with Cronenberg is included on a jacket insert which comes with the disc.

Dead Ringers is about identical twin gynecologists who tend to collaborate too closely on all aspects of their professional and private lives. It is a technological tour de force and features an expectedly clever performance by Jeremy Irons. Cronenberg creates many tensions – between the twins, between the doctors and their patients, and between normality and madness. He never gives the viewer a release, but he makes the atmosphere so thick that one's desire to escape it is dulled. It is a disc which you want to smash and throw away after you've seen it, but begin to contemplate watching again after a day or so has passed.

DEADLINE
Although it lacks the sophistication and neutrality of 'Circle of Deceit,' *Deadline* is an excellent film about the anarchy in Lebanon. Taking the point of view of a naive American journalist, played by Christopher Walken, who is manipulated by several different factions of Christians and Muslims, it presents an ever fascinating view of a land where murder and destruction have become an accepted form of social aggression. The plot skates on thin ice at the end, when it places the journalist in one of the camps where refugees suffered from a horrible massacre at the hands of the Christian Phalangists, and has him witness a group of Palestinian children cheering at the anticipation of engaging their enemy. The film tries to suggest that certain Palestinian factions themselves encouraged the massacre to create a martyrdom. Reality, however, is never as simple as that.

Deadline has a rough newsreel look to it, which is becoming something of a cliché in foreign correspondent movies, but is still good way to keep the budget under control. The transfer can be judged as being very good when the quality of the source material is taken into consideration. The picture may not look glossy, but it doesn't look worn down, either. The monaural soundtrack is free from any significant flaws, and the analog track is almost indistinguishable from the digital track.

THE DEADLY COMPANIONS
Sam Peckinpah's first feature film, *The Deadly Companions*, is an impressive work, with a strong narrative and a complex moral atmosphere. It stars Brian Keith and Maureen O'Hara, and features Chill Wills as a gratifyingly greasy villain. The plot has a number of well-crafted details, but essentially concerns four people who dislike each other and must journey across hostile territory together.

The original Panavision image is cropped, and the color quality leaves much to be desired. There are also a few tatters, though the focus is generally sharp. The sound is passable and the musical score, by Marlin Skyles, is oddly compelling, a good match for the worthiness of the film itself.

DEADLY DREAMS
The low-budget murder thriller, *Deadly Dreams*, is not true to its own logic, but it does have a couple of nice twists, however telescoped they may be, and an attractive cast. The story concerns a young man who is tormented while he is awake by figures from his nightmares. The digital sound is 'stereo enhanced,' but don't expect much. The picture, which was made with second-rate film stock to begin with, is grainy and blurry.

DEADLY FRIEND
The big moments in *Deadly Friend* are well-directed, but all the filler scenes are sloppy. The actors are self-conscious when they haven't got a major task to perform, and it doesn't help when the shadow of the sound boom is jiggling in their faces. The movie is about a boy who logically and scientifically turns his deceased girlfriend into a murderous zombie. Happens every day, at least in Wes Craven movies. The picture is grainy, but the analog stereo isn't too bad. Craven knows how to keep his audience nervous, but he should learn how to calm down his cast.

DEADLY ILLUSION
Billy Dee Williams appears in *Deadly Illusion*, in which his character is caught in a series of murders and frame-ups. Williams solves all of this by shooting everybody, which is efficient in a Gordian knot sort of way, but lacks an appropriate finesse. The film has two directors, William Tannen and Larry Cohen, and Cohen's idiosyncratic flourishes continually undercut the tension. The picture is sharp. The sound was recorded in Ultra-Stereo and, when the filmmakers remember to utilize it, it is fun.

DEADLY POSSESSION
The word 'Hitchcockian' is applied with far too great an abandon these days, but there is no more efficient means with which to communicate the pleasures that *Deadly Possession* has to offer. The Australian film was made with a low-grade film stock which looks grainy and muddy. The transfer appears to deliver it without further harm. The digitally encoded monaural sound is also at the mercy of the original recording, and is too fuzzy to play at an increased volume.

No matter, the movie is a terrific murder thriller which will have you screaming by the climax no matter how murky the image appears on your monitor. The music department of a small college is the setting, and passages from operas and choral works are carefully employed to enhance the drama. The film is also feminist in the best sense. All of the major characters are female. Men, when they appear, remain on the periphery. One of the most amusing aspects of the script is that a man who initially appears to be the hero is wrongfully identified as the murderer when he is seen leaning over the first body. He is caught quickly and disappears from the movie while his ex-wife sets out to solve the crime. The filmmakers have no high sense of cinematic style, but they have the essentials down and remain in firm control of the viewer's emotions from beginning to end. Many movies try to create a taut mixture of mystery and suspense, but *Deadly Possession* is one of the few which succeeds.

DEATH BEFORE DISHONOR
Scenes of Marines finishing their basic training are casually intercut with scenes of Arab terrorists going through training of their own in the opening of *Death Before Dishonor*. Nothing else in the film, however, has quite the same elegance, and the film is cheapened by a consistent, bigoted presentation of Arabs as venal barbarians. The one exception, a character who helps the Marines locate their kidnapped commander, turns out to be an Israeli in disguise.

The picture quality is generally good. The sound recording, although processed in Ultra-Stereo, is flawed, making a few passages of dialog difficult to follow.

DEATH OF A SALESMAN
We studied *Death of a Salesman* in college. We saw it on the stage. We saw it on TV. We just got finished watching the disc. We still don't understand it. What does the play have to say about the human condition that makes it so special? It has too little poetry and too much pessimism to work as an entertainment. It is interesting to watch Dustin Hoffman work his craft, but after two and a quarter

hours, Willy Loman overstays his welcome. The presentation is a special soundstage rendition of a Broadway revival which was telecast on network TV. The picture and sound are indistinguishable from the quality of the broadcast presentation.

DEATH OF AN ANGEL

Another case of the jacket cover/ad art misleading potential purchasers can be found on *Death of an Angel*. The tag line reads, "Two desperate characters. One deadly sin." Those who are looking for a sleazy exploitation film are going to be disappointed, and those who might truly be attracted to the Sundance Institute production are likely to pass it by or goggle and then pass it by. (The jacket cover still is from a brief dream sequence.)

In reality, *Death of an Angel* is an honest-to-goodness contemporary allegory about two priests, one of them female, and a Cross which bleeds on cue. Those who roll their eyes at such matters are advised to avoid it, but to those who find satisfaction in religious-themed films, the disc is recommended. The narrative is intelligent and challenging, and although the ending is inevitable, it is the movie's center – the arguments about faith and calling – which gives the film a true cumulation of emotion.

The transfer, unfortunately, is only of average quality. The digital sound is monaural and unnoteworthy. The picture is mildly grainy.

DEATH ON THE NILE
EVIL UNDER THE SUN

Since *Death on the Nile* was the first serious Agatha Christie movie to be made after *Murder on the Orient Express*, the filmmakers were still trying hard to get the movie right. It has a super cast, with Bette Davis, Angela Lansbury, Mia Farrow, and David Niven, to mention only a few, and a decent production budget which shows through on the screen. Peter Ustinov portrays Hercule Poirot. The director, John Guillerman, was probably not the best choice to corral the performers effectively, but he does manage several fine touches. The first closeup of Ustinov is followed immediately by a cut to the face of the Sphinx. If the viewer can summon an appreciation for the Christie format – which is less an appreciation for plot twists than it is for distinctive characters and threatening moods – then *Nile* will materialize as one of the best. Farrow's performance is exquisite and will continue to gain stature over the course of time.

The highlight of the digital monaural soundtrack is Nino Rota's unforgettable score, set to the tempo of the pleasure ship chugging up the river and swooning with murderous melodic heat. The picture transfer is fine. The colors look good, but the focus is soft here and there in a way that goes beyond Jack Cardiff's gauzy cinematography. The source material also sports numerous scratches and speckles. Although the movie was not a widescreen effort, even the slightest cropping harms a number of shots and takes its toll on the film's star parade. Side three, the parlor denouement, is in CAV, with perfect still frames.

By the time of *Evil Under the Sun*, unfortunately, the budget had contracted. The movie, another Ustinov-as-Poirot effort, sports Diana Rigg and the always dependable Maggie Smith – who is also in *Nile* – but after that the stellar aspects of the film dwindle, and some of the fun goes with it. There are fewer arched eyebrows, fewer preludes to foul play, and fewer moments of fun. The movie is still enjoyable for the basics, but other than a duet with Rigg and Smith singing 'You're the Top,' it has nothing special to offer.

The picture transfer is a little soft, and the colors lack the deep rich shine which the film, set on a Mediterranean isle, initially displayed. The transfer does not hurt the entertainment, however. The sound is okay. The producers had the great idea to use Cole Porter tunes for the score, but they just play three or four of Porter's best known efforts over and over again, diminishing the music's charm.

DEATH ROW GAMESHOW

The sound is flat and the picture looks cheap, and even though side two is in CAV and contains two trailers, the parodic *Death Row Gameshow* is a total waste of time.

DEATH TRAP THE BIOLOGY OF CARNIVOROUS PLANTS

The education-market-oriented Videodiscovery's only consumer market offering, *Death Trap The Biology of Carnivorous Plants*, also titled 'The Death Trap Videodisc,' is an hour-long CLV disc which contains a marvelous nature program about plants which digest bugs. The program is fascinating and ranks with the best consumer nature programs, to which it is similar in style. After a somewhat lurid introduction, various carnivorous plants are shown in action while the narrator explains what is known about the metabolism, evolutionary heritage, and ecological niche of the plant on view. The photography is excellent, as one incredible microscopic or time-shifted or plain lucky shot after another shows the plants in action, capturing and digesting insects. One of the many intriguing pieces of information the disc provides: The Venus flytrap works like a mine, and has a half dozen hair-sized triggers on its surface. The victim must hit two triggers, or one trigger twice, within twenty seconds to spring the trap, a safety device which cuts down the digestion of random pieces of dust. The mechanism which causes the trap to close is also clearly explained. The disc is thoroughly chapter-encoded and has institutional-quality sound.

DEATH WATCH

Sometimes science fiction can get by on the power of suggestion. *Death Watch*, a low-tech fantasy about society in an indistinct future, is entertaining because it keeps moving and always stays a step ahead of predictability.

The talented Swiss director, Bertrand Tavernier, makes no attempt to disguise his Glasgow locations or embellish them with fabulous decor. Dialog is used to present Tavernier's concepts. Through conversation it is established that death by natural causes is rare. A woman (Romy Schneider) becomes a celebrity because she is dying at a relatively young age. A television executive (Harry Dean Stanton) tricks her into signing a contract for exclusive coverage of her last days and then allows her to think she has given him the slip. Harvey Keitel, whose eyes (we are told) have been replaced by cameras, befriends her and her final experiences are broadcast surreptitiously. Even though the audience has to do most of the paddling, one's attention never drifts.

The Embassy release is riddled with scratches and has a weak soundtrack, but the movie was probably filmed and produced that way.

DEATH WISH 3

Death Wish 3 is more of the same for the series, with Charles Bronson drooping his shoulders and sulking until he is forced into action. The sound is monaural but contemporary. The picture should not be examined too closely because the director didn't care about the edges of the screen and they often belie what is happening in the center. The reproduction is a bit blurry, but not enough to make counting the bodies difficult.

DEATHSTALKER

A chorus on the soundtrack of *Deathstalker* goes, "Ah oh, oh ah," whenever something significant happens. The show is supposed to be about swordsmen and wizards, but it is mostly about nice looking women and the lack of undergarments in the Middle Ages. The picture is cheap and blurry and the sound is monaural. At eighty minutes, the story is over before the plot can be explained.

As is mentioned on the disc's jacket cover (the artwork of which has nothing to do with the film), one of the stars of *Deathstalker* is Barbie Benton. Her acting is so bad that she can't even hold a serious expression for an entire take. It is obvious that reading dialog is beyond the range of her talents. Although she appears in a substantial amount of *Deathstalker*'s footage, the filmmakers were forced to pare her spoken lines down to the following, which we have transcribed in chronological order and in entirety: "Where's mine?" "Please, no, please, somebody pro..." "Stop him, please. Stop him, please." "Please stop him." "Please stop, please." "Oh my lord, this is very uncomfortable." "It's cold." "I'm Princess Codille." "No!" "My..."

DEATHSTALKER II
DEATHSTALKER III

Deathstalker II was filmed in 1986, and *Deathstalker III: The Warriors from Hell* was filmed in 1988. Each movie has a different cast and production crew, and is a continuation of the first *Deathstalker* in spirit rather than plot.

Deathstalker II is the better of the two discs, and should probably be watched after *Deathstalker III* if one is indulging in the inevitable double or triple bill (its ending is also the most resolute). The production will never be mistaken for a large budget effort, but it has a glossy, vivid picture which only serves to make the sets and special effects look all the more chintzy. It is also a bit ragged, but has been transferred to disc without degradation.

Although the action is constant, the plot is quickly forgotten, something about a princess who needs Deathstalker's help to overthrow an evil, sexy clone. Side two is in CAV, with two unsteady still frames out of every five, but plenty of fights, disrobings and phony special effects to deconstruct. The end credit scroll – in CAV, remember – is run over a collection of bloopers, adding significantly to the value of the title.

Deathstalker III has a more coherent plot, as the hero takes on a quest to join three parts of a gem and reveal a jeweled city. The film, however, was made with a grainy film stock, making it look pale and foggy. Although the movie runs less than 90 minutes, it is CLV throughout. Both films have monaural sound which is set slightly lower in volume than average.

DEBAJO DEL MUNDO

An uncomplicated but engrossing tale about a Jewish family in rural Poland hiding from the Nazis, *Debajo del Mundo*, is an Argentine production which was made in Czechoslovakia. The cast speaks Spanish, which is translated to yellow English subtitles. After the initial adjustment is made, the language oddity is not bothersome. The film is intelligently scripted and paced, inviting multiple viewings. Because of the intense subject, the emotions in the film are detached, but the concentration on minor details and the neutral camera angles does not inhibit a viewer from being moved by the story.

The picture and sound transfers are well done. The print is fresh and the colors look accurate, although intense hues are unstable and there are a few grainy passages. A handful of chapters have been encoded on the disc. The sound is monaural and is worth running through the hi-fi. The family in the film hides in a series of underground hollows and bunkers which they have built for themselves, and the thumping from above when they are in danger of being discovered is unnerving.

DEBUSSY/RAVEL

Herbert von Karajan appears on *Debussy/Ravel* with the Berliner Philharmoniker. There is an audience, and the camera angles follow the music standard manner. The program features 'La Mer,' 'Prelude a l'Apres-Midi d'un Faune,' and 'Daphnes et Chloe.' The latter two are unexceptional, though certainly competent. Karajan's approach to 'La Mer' is more interesting. He achieves forceful crescendos without relying on his percussion section the way most conductors do when tackling the piece. The stereo sound has the ambience of an older recording, and seems removed atmospherically from the images, but it gives the music a monaural-like solidity with a stereophonic flourish.

THE DECEIVERS

Nicholas Meyer's intriguing period drama, *The Deceivers*, has a below-average picture transfer. The image is consistently fuzzy, and bright colors, especially strong reds, often bleed into the surroundings. The picture is so weak that a viewer is likely to be distracted, especially during the first half hour. The movie has a tense script and eventually takes control of one's attentions but enjoying the disc is harder than it could have been. The sound is much better than the picture. There are some cute, low bass rumblings associated with elephant footsteps which are fun.

The film is about a British territorial governor in India during the early nineteenth century who goes undercover to investigate an organization of murderous thieves traditionally known as 'Thuggees.' Although based upon a true story, the script has elements of fantasy, and it is not the straight costumed detective drama it seems to promise at first. Some viewers may find the philosophical and spiritual aspects of the story to be rewarding. In any case, the setting is a pleasant change from the standard film thriller.

THE DECLINE OF WESTERN CIVILZATION

Punk music had the same effect upon rock and roll as Borgia Italy had upon Western culture, pulling it violently and brilliantly out of the Dark Ages. Hence the documentary about punk music in Los Angeles in early 1980, *The Decline of Western Civilization*, is misnamed. Sure, both the music and the musicians are rough, but they prevented the eighties from being defined by the medieval likes of Duran Duran. No pain, no gain.

Anyway, the documentary is quite enjoyable. It focuses on seven bands playing the club scene in LA, covering not only the band sessions, but the way the musicians live and think. It is well researched, so that any comment in an interview is covered, in irony or in confirmation, by alternative footage. The interviews are funny, too. In one anecdote, a singer tells how she and her brother found a dead painter in their backyard. They took pictures with the stiff before calling an ambulance. Well, to hear her tell it, it's funny.

Since the source material is a documentary about seedy bars, the picture quality is as aesthetically pleasing as a Sex Pistols jacket cover. The digitally encoded monaural sound seems muffled, as would be one's own hearing after an hour of this stuff live. Many of the songs are supported with English subtitles, for those who are not fluent in punk.

DEEPSTAR SIX

Deepstar Six is a good old-fashioned monster movie, about a ravenous something-or-other attacking an elaborate sea-floor missile complex. The director, Sean Cunningham, who was responsible for the original *Friday the 13th*, has a firm understanding of how a thriller should work (he lifts the best scream from a similar shot in *Friday the 13th*, but even though you expect it, you still jump). The cast of unknowns he has assembled are all refreshingly competent. On a large screen, or even a multiplex screen, the phony underwater models were probably a turn-off, but on the TV they are no problem. The film has R-rated gore during the final 20 minutes, and it could have gotten by without it, because Cunningham's clear-headed execution of the formula is sufficiently entertaining.

The picture quality is terrific. Computer monitor displays, panel lights, and fake underwater photography all look as crisp as the brightest lit scenes. The digital surround sound is good fun, although the audio is slightly out of synch with the picture. It lacks the sophistication or purity of a big budget effort, but with all those hatch doors and water leaks, the audio can't lose. Neither can a viewer, if you dive into the disc with the right frame of mind.

DEF LEPPARD – HISTORIA

Def Leppard is a great group to play on your car stereo as you are driving speedily down a freeway. One shouldn't attempt to watch the disc, *Def Leppard – Historia*, under those conditions, however, because the videos are as much fun as the music and require a viewer's full concentration. *Historia* is a compilation of 18 music videos, each introduced by an informative title card explaining the circumstances under which the video was produced. The title cards flip by too quickly to read without the help of some remote control functions, but that shouldn't be a problem. The group's videos are competently produced and have been popular more because of their efficiency than because of any innovative features. The back of the jacket lists the songs in order, but the chapter markers on the disc restart at zero on side two, and an extra video appears after the credit scroll is finished. Intense colors are blurry and the older videos look a little worn down, but the picture is acceptable. The sound seems to pack all the bass it needs to be effective.

DEFENSE OF THE REALM

The plot of *Defense of the Realm* is fictional, but it has is just enough basis in actual events to play like a British version of *All the President's Men*. There are marvelous performances by Britain's newest generation of character actors, especially Denholm Elliott and Ian Bannen, and feelings of nervewracking paranoia are evoked as a reporter, played by Gabriel Byrne, uncovers unexpected motives while investigating a Cabinet level sex scandal.

The soundtrack is reasonably clean and the slightly foggy picture is usually camouflaged by the film's atmosphere. Only one brief scene in a darkroom gives away the disc's true weaknesses, when there is a complete inability to recreate the illumination of the safety lamp. The flaws, however, are limited, and the film has a great potential for repeated viewing, as the reporter tracks down his leads and the character actors do their stuff. The final credit scroll, which is written in "British," is also a nice treat.

DEJA VIEW

Deja View is inappropriately titled, for although ten of the eleven songs on the disc are classic tunes from the Sixties, the videos accompanying them are brand new productions. And what productions! Terri Garr in a sequence about a magician directed by Bob Balaban to The Zombies' 'She's Not There'; Procol Harum 'A Whiter Shade of Pale' directed by Paul Hogan and featuring Harry Dean Stanton; Michael Pare portraying an escaped convict who wants to return to his baby and, surprise, her mother, in 'The Letter'; or Sly Stone and faces, faces, and more faces flashing by to 'Everyday People.' No cut and paste jobs here. There is an elaborate translation of 'American Pie,' examples of how 'It's My Party' would look in other lands, and the cast from 'St. Elsewhere' acting out 'Good Lovin'.' The 53-minute disc has chapter markers and is digitally encoded.

THE DELTA FORCE

Image has released the *The Delta Force* in partial CAV. There is a mistake on the back of the jacket; "Side 1 & 2 Standard Play, Side 3 Extended Play." Really, the first two sides are in Extended Play (CLV) and the boisterous finale is in full feature format Standard Play (CAV).

The film is an unabashedly patriotic treatment of recent events in the Middle East which follows history very closely up to a point and then shows how every hostage crisis would be solved if life were like the movies. Not only does it star Chuck Norris and Lee Marvin, but it has a wonderful cast of classy bit players including Joey Bishop, Lainie Kazan, Bo Svenson, Susan Strasberg, and Hanna Schygulla.

DEMONS

"Those screams sound real." "Come on, it's the Dolby System." Not on this disc it isn't. A compatriot of Dario Argento, Lamberto Bava, directed *Demons*, which has been released on disc by Image. Argento produced the film and contributed to the script, which concerns patrons trapped in a movie theater by frothing zombies. The line about the Dolby System is a favorite for fanatics, and the Dolby logo appears in the end credit scroll, but Image spoils everything by giving us the movie in monaural. Lousy monaural, for that matter.

The movie is best seen in a theater anyway, preferably in a strange town where all the other patrons mutter and hiss. Both the digital and analog tracks are free of major distortions (there is an abrupt dropout at one point, but it is well-timed to the action and adds an extra shock). While the basic sound effects have some atmosphere, the dialog and the heavy metal score sound flat.

Image has done a good job transferring the picture, but the picture isn't much to speak of. Lighting effects are used to bathe the screen in orange, blue, or red, and, amazingly, the disc presents these effects without losing control. There is no getting around the limited budget the filmmakers had to work with, however, so the quality of the picture does little to pull you into the film.

DEMONSTONE

The ad art on the jacket cover of *Demonstone* is misleading and sells the movie to the wrong viewer. The film, though it has occult trappings, stars Jan-Michael Vincent and is an action picture about Marines stationed in the present day Philippines. R. Lee Ermey, often typecast in military roles, is especially effective as a major who is investigating a mass murder that may or may not have been caused by an American serviceman. The film is like many other cheap Southeast Asia action films, and the picture and monaural sound are commensurate, but the performances are enjoyable, and with the demon stuff thrown in, there is a little something for everyone.

DENNIS DE YOUNG – THREE PIECE SUITE

Two embarrassing narrative-styled music videos, 'Desert Moon' and 'Don't Wait for Heroes,' open the 8-inch *Dennis De Young – Three Piece Suite*. The third, 'Call Me,' abandons narrative and is a strong improvement over the first pair, but the CLV disc ends at that point. The picture and sound are satisfactory. De Young has a voice which is a shade too pleasant and an acting ability which is best served in situations where he need do no more than pretend to play the guitar and sing.

DER FLIEGENDE HOLLANDER

An untraditional staging of Richard Wagner's *Der Fliegende Hollander* ('The Flying Dutchman'). The Unitel Production was filmed at Bayreuth under conditions similar to the Philips 'Ring Cycle,' with the opera recorded in real time onstage, without an audience. Conceived by Harry Kupfer, the massive sets are moved and changed while the singers remain in view. It is impressive, even on a small TV screen, because the scale is so readily apparent. Kupfer's modifications to the presentation include keeping Senta, played by Lisbeth Balslev, in sight throughout the action, often having her observe from above on a scaffolding. Since the opera is only an advisable purchase for those who are already familiar with the work (an early Wagner composition which is lovely, but not as clearly delineated as his later efforts), Kupfer's explorations are tolerable. His staging does force the performers to act as well as to sing, and his emphasis on the drama helps the disc to succeed as a video program.

The picture quality is passable, hampered more by the toneless stage lighting than by any flaws in the transfer. The image is a little soft, but the most elaborate moments are communicated effectively. The opera is sung in German and is presented with English subtitles. The stereo sound is clear and well-balanced.

Blaslev's performance is excellent, in both acting and singing, and Simon Estes, in the title role, also makes a strong impression. The other cast members, including Matti Salminen, Robert Schunk, and Anny Schlemm, do a good job as well.

The three-sided disc comes in a box jacket, accompanied by an insert which contains a chapter summary and two informative essays, one about the opera and one about Kupfer's production. The side breaks are well-chosen, but still upset the flow of the program.

DER ROSENKAVALIER

Although it is improper to take notice when a female singer is cast as a male character in an opera, John Schlesinger deliberately teases his audience with the substitution in the Royal Opera performance of *Der Rosenkavalier*. As the curtain rises, Anne Howells, portraying the young impetuous cavalier, Octavian, is standing with her bare back to the audience. She waits until the last possible moment before pulling a chemise over her head and turning around. When, after a few opening bars, she embraces Kiri te Kanawa and nibbles on her shoulder, the opera achieves an erotic subtext which would be buried in bland normality if a man were playing the part.

The Richard Strauss opera is a difficult work to present on stage without succumbing to the temptation of doing it as slapstick. The plot is a farce, but the music is too complex for that sort of frivolity; it doesn't have enough self-contained songs. Strauss never ends the musical themes he establishes. Instead, he lets his motifs dwindle into others, the way the lovers' hearts are superseded by new-found amours, the way that youth is superseded by age, and the way that the lustful first step of the waltz is inevitably followed by the melancholy of the second and third steps.

The disc has English subtitles. The sound is very good when the singers are not overpowered by the orchestra. Schlesinger did not direct the videotaping, but the use of closeups and the consistently correct placement of the camera indicates that he must have provided a little advice, at the very least. The program is 198 minutes long, on four sides, with about seven chapters per side.

DER ROSENKAVALIER

The orchestra sounds great on *Der Rosenkavalier*, but the singers aren't miked as well and lose a little in the transition. The three-hour performance is live, by the Bavarian State Opera staged by Otto Schenk and conducted by Carlos Kleiber. The opera is in German with English subtitles. It has been transferred well, but the voices moves in and out of focus and lack the perfection found on other live recordings.

The production, starring Gwyneth Jones, Brigitte Fassbaender, Lucia Popp, and Manfred Jungwirth, has some inventive and satisfying moments. Except for shots of the orchestra, which look green, the picture quality is decent and the cameras get so close to the performers that one often forgets the performance is live. The opera, however, is overwrought, and no production can really alleviate its basic problems. There is a good essay by Werner Burkhardt, which comes in a jacket insert (along with a plot synopsis generated by the chapter markings), extensively detailing the creation of the work, but Burkhardt's arguments remain unconvincing. If the work is a comedy, it is too big and too slow. If it is not a comedy, it is too frivolous. The music, with a few exceptions, seems drawn out and forced. Burkhardt does provide one description, however, which places Strauss' music in its best light: "The period between the *fin de siècle* and the outbreak of the First World War appeared to harbor a wish once more, perhaps for the last time, to stem a process of decay with the integrating power of harmony." That is exactly what one hears in the waltz, 'Ohne mich, ohne mich jeder Tag dir so bang,' an unravelled knot of melody which holds a listener with pattern instead of bindings.

DESERT BLOOM

Not to be confused with *Desert Hearts*, another Nevada-based nostalgia piece, *Desert Bloom* is about a 14-year-old girl living in Las Vegas with her sisters, mother, divorcee aunt, and alcoholic stepfather in 1950. The stepfather (Jon Voight) provides most of the drama, being kind or cruel to his family depending upon his state of mind and level of intoxication. The title refers to a flower growing in an unlikely place, to the girl coming of age, and to the atomic bomb, the testing of which becomes the historical focal point for the story. Voight's drunk is too incoherent to pull on the viewer's emotions the way his character is able to pull at the family. Thus, the movie is dreary and cannot draw enough joy from its environment to blossom.

THE DESERT FOX

It was daring in 1951 to produce a WWII movie in which the hero is a German general, Field Marshal Erwin Rommel, but age reveals how backwards the filmmakers who put together *The Desert Fox* had to bend to make their subject palatable. It runs only 89 minutes (with extensive documentary battle footage, though very few real action sequences) and completely ignores Rommel's successes in the African desert (which would have made a great 20-minute opening these days), beginning, instead, when things started going badly for him and for Germany, and then concentrating, during the remainder of the film, on his growing doubts about the competency of Hitler.

James Mason does an excellent job portraying the title character, merely by surviving with a script which is so awkwardly and sensitively composed that no line of dialog, even the ones which are clearly verbatim transcriptions, sounds true or natural. Mason forces believability into his part, and after 89 minutes you feel exhausted for him. The structure of the film, unfortunately, is beyond his control, and with time having mellowed the movie's shock value, its other benefits, except as raw history, are limited.

The disc looks especially crisp. The print has some wear marks, even outside of the documentary footage, but the edges always look sharp and the contrasts look rich. The monaural sound is also impressive, particularly when big guns are involved.

DESERT HEARTS

Desert Hearts is about a woman staying at a ranch near Reno, waiting out a divorce. She falls in love with the ranch owner's daughter. Parts of the story are fairly contrived, with the good characters being obnoxiously good and the bad characters being obnoxiously bad, but the performances are strong and side two is very erotic. The picture is a little soft and the sound is no more than functional, but, because of the eroticism, portions of the disc are highly repeatable.

DESPERATE HOURS

The original VistaVision image on William Wyler's *Desperate Hours* is not too compromised by the video presentation. The cinematography is very good, although the black-and-white picture is grainy at times. The sound is more scratchy than average.

The movie is very enjoyable. Humphrey Bogart, in a late bad guy role, portrays a convict who holds a family hostage until the family finally outwits him. The script is a clever mixture of mind games and explosive tension, and Wyler is adept at coaxing a maximum of entertainment out of the situation.

DESPERATELY SEEKING SUSAN

The clever and cheerful *Desperately Seeking Susan* was released by Thorn/EMI/HBO Video, a company with a short and unimpressive history of disc transfers. Although the movie has a rock score, it is not in stereo and no one felt it was necessary to have the disc CX-encoded.

Although the jacket cover screams, "The Madonna Movie," *Susan* is actually a witty farce about amnesia and mistaken identity in which Madonna plays a minor (but important) part. The director, Susan Seidelman, never gets overly caught up in what the characters say or do and so when there are lapses in the logic of events – and there are many – you aren't worried. In the place of narrative forcefulness, there are some terrific gags and a wonderful cast of characters who talk about each other so much that by the end of the movie you feel they're all your friends, even the bad guy.

DESTINATION MOON

The spectacular, Technicolor space-tech effort, *Destination Moon*, may have enthralled audiences in its day, for it was conceived a decade before the first manned space flight, but it hasn't any extended dramatic conflict and can only be considered a curiosity now.

The authenticity is impressive, even if it does come from a time when people still thought that radioactivity was our friend. The filmmakers start out with a plot that hints of spies, sabotage, and a clear anticipation of SDI ("The first country that can use the moon for the launching of missiles will control the Earth. That, gentlemen, is the most important military fact of this century." Even though the missiles would take two days to get here?), but the rocketship takes off before side one is over, and that puts an end to the plot. The most fascinating assumption that most early science fiction movies make, and this one makes it, too, is that spaceflight would be a restricted access event, the way it ended up being in Russia. If there is a moment which summarizes the entire film, however, it is the crew's first encounter with zero gravity. A crew member removes his seat belt and it goes 'thunk' the minute he drops it. He then starts to float.

The disc is not CX-encoded. A sticker which has been placed on the shrink wrap explains why. The color remains consistent and reasonably accurate, and the print is only ragged near the reel changes. A Woody Woodpecker cartoon is inserted during the beginning of the film to explain the course the rocketship will take.

DESTROYER

A movie company making a film in an abandoned prison is stalked by a former inmate who still lives in its bowels in *Destroyer*. Tony Perkins portrays the director and Lyle Alzado is the murderer. The sound was recorded in Ultra-Stereo, so we don't know why the jacket cover says 'Stereo Enhanced.' The audio on the digitally encoded disc has strength, and the picture is only grainy in few scenes. Other than a few 'in' movie jokes, however, the program has little to offer.

DETOUR

Most movies are harmed when the source print is in really bad shape, but *Detour* seems to thrive on it. The black-and-white source material is fuzzy, scratchy, and has splices that drop pieces of dialog. Yet the film is so deliberately nihilistic that it is easy to take in the flaws without losing the mood – *Detour* is about people who *want* to be dragged through the dirt. The 69-minute cult classic, directed by Edgar Ulmer, is superbly plotted, about a man hitchhiking across the country whose life is destroyed when a strong-willed woman crosses his path. Tom Neal stars, but it is Ann Savage who dominates the film, achieving a magnetic screen appeal by going against every movie star glamor rule. Side two is in CAV with perfect still frames. The sound is still in rough shape even when it is synched up.

THE DEVIL AND DANIEL WEBSTER

Not only is *The Devil and Daniel Webster* not CX-encoded, the print also looks a little worse for wear. Ragged or not, however, the movie (which was actually called 'Daniel and the Devil' and, before that, 'All That Money Can Buy') is based on a wonderful Stephen Vincent Benet story capturing the spirit of a modern folk tale. A farmer who is getting beat up by life sells his soul to the Devil for wealth and good living. As the time for retribution approaches, the farmer asks the famous politician, Daniel Webster, to help him break the contract. Walter Huston's presence as the Devil is so marvelously textured that you can almost feel his breath and gristle on your own cheeks. As Webster, Edward Arnold does not make much of an impression until side two, but when he declares that he would "fight a thousand Devils to save a New Hampshire man," you realize that the build-up is calculated. If you had to convince a jury of the worst traitors and murderers in American history, including Benedict Arnold and Captain Kidd, that a man who has sold his soul to the Devil ought to have a second chance, what would you say? Put on *The Devil and Daniel Webster* and find out.

DEVIL IN THE FLESH

The complete, X-rated version of Marco Bellochio's *Devil in the Flesh* has been released on disc. The picture transfer looks strong. The colors are accurate and only bright oranges and reds seem mildly fuzzy. The sound is less impressive. There are crackles and pops scattered through the soundtrack and from time to time the voices seem out of synch with the lip movements. The film is in Italian and has yellow English subtitles which are discreet and well-executed.

The movie has only one X-rated scene – the rest could easily be shown on PBS, at least late at night. The story is about a young man who has an affair with a young woman while the woman's fiancé is in jail awaiting sentencing. The woman is a little nuts and the young man's motives, beyond his initial curiosity, are obscured. The dialog is laden with classical, philosophical, and political quotations, which are intended to balance the sex, but the whole thing has an adolescent's presumptuousness to it, and succeeds more because of the attractiveness of the two stars, Maruschka Detmers and Federico Pitzalis, who both look great in the nude, than it does because of any intelligence associated with the script.

THE DEVIL'S RAIN

The opening credit sequence on *The Devil's Rain* is not letterboxed, but the rest of the film is, with an aspect ratio of 2.2:1. The transfer is gorgeous, though why Image has gone through this much trouble for a film which has no redeeming attributes is beyond us.

Lack of redemption is one of the few discernible themes of the film itself, which is primarily about a group of people, made of paraffin and led by a goat, who melt when their oracle is smashed. The film was pointless, and never achieved the status which its publicity over the extensive makeup effects for the final meltdown hoped to inspire. It is too disjointed and boring to sustain one's attention until the finale.

One of the film's few enjoyable aspects is the collection of bad actors it has assembled. There is John Travolta, with a single line of dialog, whose entrance as one of the paraffin people is typically confused – if he's a zombie, why are his reflexes so quick when he fights? There is William Shatner, who begins to deteriorate, with those mid-sentence pauses, an hour before he is even turned into paraffin. And then there is Eddie Albert, who never gets turned to paraffin at all, but who reads his lines with the urgency of someone going over a grocery list (our favorite part is his offhanded declaration, "These're, these're written in blood, these signatures.") Ernest Borgnine plays the goat. We suppose the publicity people never really had a chance, since they were trying to convince potential viewers that it was a big deal to make Borgnine look ugly and potential viewers quickly wrote it off as Hollywood's easiest makeup trick.

But the disc is beautiful. The fleshtones and paraffin tones and chamois tones are perfect. Borgnine's red robes remain stable. The image is sharply focussed and the print is free of any contaminants. The sound is mildly stereophonic. The mix is a jumble which is representative of the movie's other production values, but the disc recreates it faithfully. The jacket cover claims that the film is rated R, but the tag at the end of the film on the disc says PG.

DIAL M FOR MURDER (Import)

It was *Dial M for Murder* to which Hitchcock was referring when he said, "A murder without gleaming scissors is like asparagus without hollandaise sauce." Released on disc in Japan, the print is a bit worn and faded. We barely noticed the subtitles, which is surprising for an adaptation of a dialogue-bound stage play. One reason perhaps is that the movie was originally made in 3D, so the center of concentration is higher when the screen is flat. Hitchcock found that he had to compose his shots differently, putting innocuous clutter in the foreground. As a result, one tends not to look at the bottom of the screen. If you have only seen *Dial M* on broadcast television then you are in for a startling surprise. There are a couple of gruesome seconds present on the disc that inevitably get lopped off by the censors elsewhere, which is like having hollandaise sauce without the asparagus.

DIAMOND HEAD

The dopey 1962 film, *Diamond Head*, is based upon a dopey book about miscegenation. The topic is less relevant than when the film was made, but the plot will seem even more mystifying on the disc because the skin tone of every character in the movie is an orange pink. The sound is fair. Charlton Heston plays a strong-willed (hence a double meaning for the title of the Hawaiian-based story) estate owner who badgers his family and his workers from beginning to end. The credit sequence is in widescreen, but after that, everything is cropped. There are a couple of deaths and a few love affairs to give the soap opera-styled narrative some momentum, but the way to enjoy it is to sit back, ignore the the blurry colors, and soak up all the bad acting.

DIAMONDS ARE FOREVER (CBS/Fox)
DIAMONDS ARE FOREVER (MGM/UA)

We suspect that the script for *Diamonds Are Forever* was written generically, before Sean Connery was nailed down for the lead. He misbehaves, slapping Jill St. John for no urgent reason, and calling her a "stupid twit." The movie, however, can be refreshing, because the average viewer has usually memorized less of it than of the other Connery Bonds, and there are some truly witty touches. We particularly enjoy Connery's entrance on the gaming floor of a Las Vegas casino. He's dressed in a white evening jacket while everyone around him is wearing Nevada casuals. It must also be remembered that while the car chases may seem lame by today's standards, they were pre-Hal Needham efforts and impressive for their time.

The image has an aspect ratio of about 2.21:1, and the color transfer is perfect. There are one or two shots near the beginning which are exceedingly grainy, but it appears to be a production problem with the film, because the rest of the program is sharp and completely free of distortion. The monaural sound is digitally encoded and features a pleasant John Barry score.

The movie runs 5 minutes over two hours and the disc comes in a gatefold jacket. Side three is in CAV, so a viewer can toy with the final shoot out, with helicopters, aboard a deep sea oil rig. The film's theatrical trailer, which seems oddly coy about Connery's return as Bond, also appears on side three, so that the best moments of the film can also be manipulated with standard play functions. The trailer is letterboxed, but has a darker picture than the feature.

CBS/Fox released a scanned and cropped version of the film earlier. The action sequences are more difficult to follow when the movie isn't shown in wide screen, and the image was very grainy.

DIANE SHURE AND THE COUNT BASIE ORCHESTRA

The picture is less than perfect on *Diane Shure and the Count Basie Orchestra*, which is surprising since the program, although 'live,' was recorded in a controlled studio environment. The image is slightly grainy. The digitally encoded sound, fortunately, is unharmed (the analog track has less definition, but still sounds excellent). We would have preferred that Shure be miked better, her voice separated more from the orchestra. She paces herself in any case, and saves her best efforts for the final numbers. There are twelve songs and two band numbers on the single sided disc. Shure's choices for material, including 'I Loves You Porgy' and 'Climbing Higher Mountains,' are subtle. Her vocals are clearer than water, however, and one is encouraged to wish that she would sell out and bring some class to the commercial pop market.

THE DIARY OF A CHAMBERMAID

The 1964 Luis Buñuel film staring Jeanne Moreau, *The Diary of a Chambermaid*, is in French with yellow English subtitles which are occasionally distracting. The opening credit sequence is letterboxed, but the rest of the movie is not, to its detriment.

The movie is a masterful exercise in cinematic narrative, free of the trickery which pervades many of Buñuel's other films. In 1964 it was probably considered racy, but by today's standards its level of innuendo is scant and almost chaste. This removes a layer of distraction, so that one can see the movie simply as a story being told – about a woman working as a maid in a country estate – with exquisite style and humor. The cropping of the picture's sides is harmful, because Buñuel is always using the whole image, not only to advance the plot, but to 'frame' it in irony and wry comment. The black and white picture is free of speckles, sharply focused, and has reliable contrast levels.

The sound represents the older monaural soundtrack as well as can be expected. The narrative includes a murder, but the pleasure one receives from the film does not come from anticipating what will happen next, it comes from continually recognizing what is happening. Like the maid in the film, the viewer is constantly confronted by the contrast between the airs the characters are putting on and their truer natures. For the maid it is a life-threatening situation; for the viewer, it is pure fun.

THE DIARY OF ANNE FRANK

For the first time since the film's initial big-city theatrical run in 1959, *The Diary of Anne Frank* is presented with its full 183-minute running time, by CBS/Fox exclusively on disc. The film is spread to four sides, with an intermission and entr'acte dividing the two platters (there is also an overture), and comes in a gatefold jacket as one of CBS/Fox's Special Wide Screen Edition offerings. Side four is in CAV.

Based upon a stage adaptation of Anne Frank's writings, the film was directed by George Stevens when he was at his peak as a stylist and literary interpreter. It is beautifully composed, and fully dependent upon the widescreen image to convey all of its emotional and textual details. The black and white picture is crisply transferred and retains an aspect ratio of about 2.3:1. There are a scattering of markings and similarly brief flaws, but none are significant enough to disrupt the program. The CAV encoding on side four allows one to examine Stevens' technique on a frame-by-frame basis.

The sound mix is fantastic and comes across well on the digital stereo surround channels. Every creak could give the family away, and every creak reverberates with a chilling persistence. The soundtrack also contains some of the faults of the recording's age, particularly a roughness when the music or dialog reaches a full pitch.

The complexity of meaning, which Frank's autobiographical journal from the time her family spent hiding in an attic from the Nazis, is well known. Stevens touches upon the essence of the diary, although the era in which the film was made prevented the most graphic passages from being realized on the screen. The film is highly repeatable, since you know how the story is going to end before you start. Perhaps not enough years have passed yet to think of Frank's diary as entertainment, but that is certainly what the movie is – three hours of characters getting on each other's nerves and learning about themselves in the process. The performances are a bit predictable but still satisfying, and in such an ensemble piece it can be as fulfilling to watch the background as it is to concentrate upon the foreground.

By restoring the footage in so pristine a

condition, CBS/Fox has retrieved a classic film from near-oblivion. Other versions of the movie run anywhere from fifteen minutes to a half an hour less (or even shorter when broadcast television time slots are involved). *The Diary of Anne Frank* is about tension in cramped spaces, and the added footage stretches and swells that tension, increasing the emotional impact of the film by whole-number exponents.

DICK CLARK'S BEST OF BANDSTAND

We never expected *Dick Clark's Best of Bandstand* to excite us as much as it did. The 47-minute program is a collection of performances on 'American Bandstand' by a choice selection of early rock and roll pop stars. The black-and-white kinescope video is wonderfully clear and full of terrific closeups. More importantly, though, Clark scrounged up the original recordings and remastered them, so that the songs sound better than they ever have before. The disc is analog and has no chapter markers.

Since the performers only lip-synch their recordings, they concentrate on how they look and over do it in all the right ways. Highlights include The Big Bopper rolling his eyes as he talks to the telephone in 'Chantilly Lace,' Sam Cooke grinning his way through 'You Send Me,' Jerry Lee Lewis igniting the keyboard and the audience with 'Great Balls of Fire,' and rare footage of Buddy Holly doing 'Peggy Sue.'

DICK CLARK'S BEST OF BANDSTAND: THE SUPERSTARS

Dick Clark's Best of Bandstand: The Superstars is almost as much fun as the first disc was. Clark has collected kinescopes of lip-synched performances by ten rock and roll stars from the late fifties and early sixties (and in the case of the Jackson Five, 1970). The music has been remastered digitally from the original recordings, and once again, Vestron has failed to encode the disc with digital sound. Nor have they provided chapter markers.

The 44-minute, one-sided disc has some precious moments. The Supremes, dressed in ski lodge furs, thrust their arms out like traffic cops for an appreciative mountain resort audience, while doing 'Stop in the Name of Love' and 'Baby Love.' Connie Francis moves through an incredibly camp rendition of 'Who's Sorry Now,' which she sings while assisting a clown in applying makeup. And Roy Orbison rolls his w's in 'Pretty Woman.'

The picture is black-and-white (except for the Jacksons, who are in color). The sound was remastered and transferred in stereo. The separations are awkward in places, with too much of the sound shifted too far to the left. Clark interviews the performers at the introductions of the songs, which are mostly clips from 'American Bandstand.' The intros are fine and do not interfere with the flow of the program, so you will not be tempted to scan through them until you have played the disc at least a dozen times.

DIE EHE DER MARIA BRAUN (THE MARRIAGE OF MARIA BRAUN)

(see **A YEAR OF THE QUIET SUN**)

DIE FLEDERMAUS

Die Fledermaus was the *Saturday Night Fever* of its time. Johann Strauss, at the height of his popularity, could pack an auditorium as easily as the Bee Gees, with attendance figures on outdoor concerts occasionally passing into six digits. The waltz, like disco music a century later, brought young couples close together in a risqué but socially acceptable manner and became a rage from which Western civilization has never completely recovered. What better epitome of the relationship between men and women than three beats to four quarters: Having their own desires and their own pleasures and yet uniting, sublimely, every fourth measure.

The disc release of *Die Fledermaus* was recorded at London's Royal Opera House on New Year's Eve, 1983. *Die Fledermaus* is often used for galas and other special occasions because it is short and has a natural break in the second act (a party where there is entertainment) which provides an opportunity for guest stars to appear and sing a number or two, unrelated to Strauss, without spoiling the atmosphere of the production. It is also a fun piece, about people running around in bat costumes.

The show runs 175 minutes. The interlude in the second act features Charles Aznavour singing 'She' and a pair of dotty British performers mugging their way through 'Three Little Maids from School.'

Conducted without much daring, but with competence, by Placido Domingo, the opera stars Kiri te Kanawa, Hermann Prey, Hildegarde Heichele, and Benjamin Luxon. The sound and the picture on the disc are sparkling clean and the voices are picked up with remarkable clarity for a live performance. There are no subtitles, so a libretto has been provided. A good portion of the dialog is in English, but the singing and other key conversations are in German.

DIE FLEDERMAUS

In this presentation, *Die Fledermaus* is performed by the Bavarian State Opera, with Eberhard Wachter, Pamela Coburn, Brigitte Fassbaender, and (particularly effective as Adele) Janet Perry, in front of a live audience. There are no problems with the clarity of the singing, which is uniformly excellent and, on the recording, in perfect balance with the orchestra. The stereo separation is also superb. The picture quality is faintly grainy but quite acceptable.

The operetta is in German, but it has English subtitles throughout (except for one off-color limerick). The staging, conducted by Carlos Kleiber (who has so much confidence in the music's familiarity that he sometimes stops conducting and just lets the orchestra play) and directed by Otto Schenk, is so full of theatrical pleasantries and gags that the camera, which is often intimately placed despite the live setting, can't keep track of them all. The dialog is as funny as the music is memorable, and the two-and-a-half-hour production, which is not ground to a halt by any interruption during the banquet scene, would not be out of place as a contemporary Broadway musical.

DIE HARD

Wow! *Die Hard*, the movie that Twentieth Century Fox promoted with precedent-setting 'theater experience' advertising to entice audiences away from their video systems, has been released on laser disc by CBS/Fox in a format which can rival all but the best theatrical presentations. More importantly, the exclusive Special Wide Screen Edition, unavailable in any other video format, is the premiere title in an entire line of quality laser disc releases from the CBS/Fox library. The company has even designed a wonderful variation on their standard logo to open the program on the disc, which creates a high level of excitement before the movie begins.

The film has been letterboxed at about 2.2:1 and provides the same screen composition one would have observed in a movie theater. The sound is digitally encoded surround and will probably sound better than the theatrical experience. The audio track is superbly transferred, and creates the sort of precise sounds which are lost in a cavernous auditorium. On cue, however, the sub channels explode, so if you intend to watch the disc, nail down your houseplants and china.

The disc's weakest component is the picture, which exhibits a faint graininess as well as imperfect reds and oranges. It is too bad CBS/Fox did not take the necessary care to achieve the same precision in the quality of the image that is achieved in the screen design and the sound. Strengthened by the letterboxing, however, the picture is compact enough to survive these minor inconsistencies, and once the movie is underway an awareness of such flaws evaporates. The movie is too exciting.

Contrary to its advertising, *Die Hard* probably works better as a home video program anyway. The special effects look more realistic on a smaller screen, and the general improbability of the narrative is easier to accept. The plot, about a cop who foils a hostage crisis in a large skyscraper, has several marvelous Alistair MacLean-style hooks, and the more often one is exposed to them, the deeper they sink. Those who have seen it only once previously, for example, will delight in the prophetic dialog which opens the film.

Although the screen composition rarely makes use of symmetrical designs or symbolic counterpoints, the wide screen effect provides many more details than a cropped picture could exhibit. When the hero is wandering around an empty floor in the building, it is important to see the emptiness and feel his exposure. When the villains are going about their tasks, it is important to see all of them, to get the feel for how well organized they are. And since the film's pyrotechnics fill the entire screen anyway, lessening the expanse of the explosions would lessen the impact the explosions make upon the viewer.

The disc comes in a gatefold jacket, giving the CBS/Fox art department an opportunity to celebrate the film's imagery and their new commitment to quality laser disc presentations. Chapters have been encoded, but are not listed in the expanded jacket text.

DIE ZAUBERFLOTE

For those who are tired of watching *The Magic Flute* in Swedish, there is a more stagebound version, *Die Zauberflote*. The production was taped live at the Bayerische Staatsoper in Munich. Directed by August Everding, the program is long enough, at 160 minutes (on four sides) that it does succeed in a number of scenes. On the whole, however, it is a big production with only a little magic and will be of interest to few, other than dedicated fans.

Although it was made in 1983, the picture has a mild blur, increasing a viewer's edginess with the program. The stereo sound is okay and the singers are in good balance with the orchestra. Few of the singers are better than average in their parts, however. Edita Gruberova is disappointing as the Queen of the Night and Francisco Arazia is competent but un-moving as Prince Tamino. The only two performers to stand out are Wolfgang Brendel, who sings Papageno well even though he doesn't look the part, and Kurt Moll, who makes an effectively authoritative Sarastro. Lucia Popp plays Pamina.

Each of the two acts appears on a separate platter. The side breaks on the platters are awkward but necessary. The opera is sung in German and there are English subtitles. On the essay which is included on an insert in the box jacket, Everding, after complaining that the delights of *The Magic Flute* often elude those staging the work, proceeds to explain, "The stage direction for the opening actually pictures a craggy landscape overgrown with trees...But I prefer an almost bare stage." Those seeking an introduction to Mozart's work are advised to stick with the Ingmar Bergman film, Swedish and all.

DIM SUM

The quotation on the jacket cover of *Dim Sum*, which compares the film to *Terms of Endearment*, is misleading and unfair, because *Terms of Endearment* was a long, drawn-out tale about dying of cancer and *Dim Sum* is a short and tart snapshot of life in which nobody dies or even comes close to it. Although the film was made with a limited budget, the picture transfer is admirable, and makes the already enjoyable feature even more of a pleasure to watch. Digital encoding adds stability to the monaural sound.

The 88-minute film, which is partially in Cantonese with English subtitles, and partially in English, is about the generational differences in a contemporary family living in San Francisco's Chinese community. The filmmakers are masterful at the art of montage, and this allows them to get away with the film's central conceit – the truly dramatic tremors in the lives of the characters all happen offscreen, and the viewer only experiences the aftershocks. The acting is so compellingly realistic that the viewer will feel like a neighbor, listening in. Yet as the film is pieced together, image by image and incident by incident, a complete, slightly humorous, slightly poignant view, not only of the characters, but of the American immigrant experience, fully materializes. *Dim Sum* is ideal for home ownership because, if you will pardon us for saying so, an hour after you've finished watching it, you want to watch it again.

DINNER AT EIGHT
GRAND HOTEL

Dinner at Eight, the story of the invitees to an upper-crust dinner party and how their lives are affected by the Depression, is depressing without relief. Many people remember the film fondly because the last 30 seconds or so are truly clever, but the rest of the show is stagey, stiff, and unflattering. There are a couple of breaks in the print on side one.

Compare *Dinner at Eight* to *Grand Hotel* and you will see the difference between a filmed stage play and a real movie. Even though many members of the cast appear in both movies, they are more glamorous and appealing in *Grand Hotel*. The camera in *Hotel* flows through the lobby and down the hallways, peering in on this life and that. There is overlapping dialogue, camera shots looking straight down, and Greta Garbo. Splices are in evidence on side one.

DIPLOMANIACS

A worthy companion piece to *Duck Soup*, the Wheeler and Woolsey comedy, *Diplomaniacs*, contains a number of amusingly absurd routines. The two are hired by an Indian tribe as ambassadors to a peace conference in Geneva. After a bomb explodes the whole conference turns blackface to sing a musical number. The spirit of anarchy exceeds the spirit of stupidity, however, and you can't help but to laugh at pieces of the film no matter how dumb you think the whole of it is. Hugh Herbert, incidentally, is liberated from his normal typecasting to appear as a Chinese spy, and he is hysterical no matter how innocuous his lines are ("It says in the 'Book of the Rabbit,' 'How much ocean can one man drink?'")

The black-and-white picture transfer is very good. There are no more than a few scratches and the blacks are solid and shiny. The focus is also reasonably sharp. The sound is fine for its age (1933). The movie runs a little over an hour and close to half of it, on side two, is in CAV with two unsteady still frames out of every five.

THE DIRT BIKE KID

The print used for *The Dirt Bike Kid* is colorful and spotless. The quality, however, is wasted on a feature which properly belongs in the children's bins. It is about a boy who befriends a magical dirt bike and saves a hot dog stand from a nasty banker.

DIRTY DANCING

An informal survey at the office where we used to pass our time revealed that women liked *Dirty Dancing* very much, whereas men disliked it, sometimes vehemently. To this latter reaction we would respond with a macho non-committal and slink away, lest it be discovered that we were not of the same opinion. In the privacy of this paragraph, however, we are happy to report that we think *Dirty Dancing* is absolutely great.

And so is the disc. *Dancing* is digitally encoded and deserves to be. The analog sound has a level of noise which the digital sound completely disposes of. The music soundtrack is a mixture of favorite oldies and energetic filler (not much else is actually stereophonic), and without the digital encoding it all blends together. The picture has some grain to it but is unencumbered by any further contaminants.

Dirty Dancing is about the sin of mixing with another social class on a summer vacation, and how every once in a while a special relationship can develop from a rendezvous. The cast has a great time, because the roles they play are archetypical but believable. They can fulfill romantic and filial fantasies (and Jerry Orbach's embodiment of the girl's father is just as appealing as Patrick Swayze's embodiment of her lover) without stepping out of character. The movie dances with the viewer. It is sexually provocative without providing an explicit, graphic payoff. Which is probably why some of our friends found it so frustrating. They're the ones who are always in a hurry.

DIRTY DANCING IN CONCERT

Dirty Dancing in Concert depicts a live concert at the Greek Theater in LA by headliners who could never have filled the place without the 'Dirty Dancing' concept, a dancing chorus performing scenes from the film in pantomime while the singers are belting out numbers from the soundtrack. The result is slick, but a little on the bland side. The performers, Bill Medley, Eric Carmen, Merry Clayton, and The Contours, seem restricted by the stage show and rarely let loose. The dancing is pleasant, but not exceptional, and the choreography starts to look repetitive well before the 90-minute running time is over. The disc is in good shape. The picture has a fresh video tape source and no significant flaws. The stereo sound tends to feel overly canned for a live presentation, but it gets the job done.

THE DIRTY DOZEN

Directed by Robert Aldrich, *The Dirty Dozen* is a two-and-a-half-hour war/adventure film with a large cast ranging from such forgotten icons as Trini Lopez and Clint Walker to the more lasting presences of Lee Marvin, Ernest Borgnine, Charles Bronson, Jim Brown, John Cassevetes, George Kennedy, Telly Savalas, and Donald Sutherland. Marvin, in the central role as the officer assigned to take twelve men condemned to death and turn them into a crack commando squad, is flamboyant and effective. Borgnine, Cassevetes, Kennedy, and Savalas overplay their parts while Bronson and Brown underplay their's. Sutherland, in a small role, adds some flair without chewing up the screen.

The MGM/UA disc is terrific. The color is far more genuine than the stills on the jacket lead one to expect and the stereo is separated in the old-fashioned way with sounds coming from the left and right in coordination with the action. The only thing missing is the widescreen.

DIRTY HARRY
DIRTY HARRY(Digital)

Warner re-issued the Clint Eastwood film, *Dirty Harry*, with a scrumptious jacket cover, chapter encoding, and digitally encoded 'reprocessed for stereo' sound. In contrast to the earlier release the opening credit sequence is squeezed, but the movie is cropped from there on. The colors are victimized by the bland film stock being used in the early seventies, but the image is sharper and less dark than the older disc. The picture looks fine in the daylight but grainy at night. The stereo sound is a bit silly, mashing some of the incidental dialog, but the sound processing does seem to enhance Lalo Schifrin's score which, perhaps because it is now a relic of its era, we appreciated for the first time.

DIRTY ROTTEN SCOUNDRELS

The pairing of Steve Martin and Michael Caine as two con artists attempting to one up each other on the French Riviera in *Dirty Rotten Scoundrels* is an inspired mixture of urbanity and cynical humor. The witty script is ideal entertainment for those who find refreshment in farce, and will appeal to the generation which finds Martin's standard roles to be juvenile or annoying, without alienating his regular fans.

The picture is lovely, depicting evening harbor lights with no more blur than the cinematographer originally intended. The jaunty musical score is effective in stereo surround, but the dialog is less distinct and a slight manipulation may be required to achieve a decent balance between the two. The 110-minute disc, which one will wish were much longer, has chapter encoding.

THE DISCREET CHARM OF THE BOURGEOISE
THE PHANTOM OF LIBERTY
THE MILKY WAY

Before there was *Nightmare on Elm Street*, there was Luis Buñuel. Though his films rarely contain sequences which send a viewer diving under the seat, the divisions within, between dreams and reality, are usually missing. His movies do not encourage complacency. Three films from the final decade of Buñuel's long career, are part of Image's CinemaDisc Collection. They are in French, and have English subtitles which are cast in readable yellow. The transfers probably passed through too many hands, because the prints are not completely fresh, but the picture also has problems stemming from the stamping and pressing. Bright colors have indistinct boundaries, and darker scenes are inundated with faint bands and increased grain. Digital encoding takes away a portion of the noise on the monaural soundtrack, but enough is left over to discourage high volume play. The films have been made available on disc in no worse condition than what one sees in revival houses, but they aren't in much better shape than that, either.

One of Buñuel's most dream-like efforts, *The Discreet Charm of the Bourgeoise*, follows a half dozen characters who never quite seem to sit down to dinner. In a dream, one can rarely concentrate upon a goal long enough to accomplish it, and that is what happens in the film, as distraction after distraction turns the plot inside out. To make matters worse, there are acknowledged dream sequences too, the problem being that you are never quite sure when they end.

Buñuel's talent, however, is not just manifested in the development and execution of clever scripts. He is a director who, by the time *Bourgeoise* was made, had developed an enormous familiarity with the language of film. His camera angles, his editing, his use of sound, and the performances he elicits from his casts are not only confident, they are pleasurable and utterly manipulative, so that a viewer is massaged even while emotions are being irritated.

The Phantom of Liberty is more obviously intended to simulate fantasy. It is an amusing adaptation of 'La Ronde,' which always moves on to the next story just as you are really getting interested in the story at hand (and never comes back). The film's construction provided a good excuse to employ many well-known French actors, so that their sudden disappearances (two characters will be walking, and the camera will follow the one the viewer doesn't know instead of the one the viewer does know) all the more frustrating – and fun. A litany of sexual taboos are included as well, though once again the tease is always followed by a total shift in attention. The film is successful because Buñuel's style is so commanding that you accept anything he puts in front of you.

One of our favorite Buñuel efforts, and the best film in this group (it also has the best looking print, although there is still room for improvement), is *The Milky Way*. The narrative has the structure of a pilgrimage (and what a shame Image did not put a map of the route, through southern France and northern Spain, on the back of the jacket), set, ostensibly, in contemporary times, but subject to leaps across centuries in a manner few besides Buñuel can accomplish successfully. The film is about religion and principally about Catholicism. The script draws dialog extensively from classical writings on theological arguments and tales of miracles. (The subtitles pass by quickly in places – thank goodness for remote control.) By placing these stories and arguments in the mouths of unlikely sources, Buñuel spans two millennia of Western thought and culture. (In one of the best scenes, a maître d' explains Christ's Divinity to waiters and busboys, providing marvelously witty, if sarcastic, satire on Church hierarchies.) To give Buñuel the benefit of the doubt, he is not using the words of the Church to damn the Church. Rather, he is exploring the metamorphosis of religious belief to create a context whereby that belief can be properly and legitimately understood. The film is very amusing (there is also a dry, dry look at Jesus himself, which will be hysterical to some and bland, rather than offensive, to others) and it is uplifting because it serves as a reminder that any chosen belief has more layers of meaning, emotion, and resonance than a single sentence in an argument or a conversation could possibly represent.

DISCURSIONS

The two-sided CAV disc, *Discursions*, is a filmed record of sixteen different graduate thesis projects in video (primarily disc) design by the Architectural Machine Group at MIT. Most of the projects represent the practical future in optical disc applications and the demonstrations are captivating. Although not regularly available in stores, the disc can be obtained through mail order.

A consumer player and personal computer will not be enough to run such applications, but their potential is clear. *Discursions* is *about* laser discs, and these projects are entertaining because the machine one is using to watch them is the star of the show. One demonstration is a video 'book' of an automobile repair manual. The image is in the upper corner and the text wraps around it. By touching any portion of the text, the video is advanced to that part of the repair procedure. Other touch commands enlarge the demonstrations to a full screen or play them forward and backward at optional speeds.

Another disc system given substantial coverage in *Discursions* is the 'Interactive Movie Map' of Aspen, Colorado. This disc system, as it is presented, allows a viewer to choose, from a map or an aerial view, any roadway in Aspen which looks interesting. Whisking down the mountain resort's streets at a chosen speed (and season), the viewer turns left or right and sees exactly what one would see if one were to go to the trouble of traveling there. When an intriguing building is spotted, the user can enter it and learn its history and function from the inhabitants. About the only thing the viewer can't do is peek into the bathroom.

Approximately 150 stills of artwork by Pablo Picasso are contained on the disc, as is a section of stills examining modern American architecture. The 150 stills are not enough to give one a sense of Picasso's career, and many of the still images in *Discursions* are blurry.

Also of interest are several image manipulation projects. In one, a computer takes a photograph of a human face and renders it in caricature which can be stretched, fattened, or aged at the artist's whim. Another turns a dancer into a stick figure whose movement marries physiology to mathematics.

At the very end is a collection of photographs taken by members of the Architectural Machine Group. Surprisingly entertaining, this collection of baby pictures, graduate school get-togethers, economy vacations, and Bostonian erratum is more fascinating than one would expect, partially because you can flip through the photos at whatever speed is comfortable and partially because some very intelligent people took the snapshots.

DISNEY'S CHIP 'N' DALE RESCUE RANGERS: CRIMEBUSTERS/DOUBLE TROUBLE

The cartoon series, *Disney's Chip 'N' Dale Rescue Rangers*, a combination of 'The Rescuers' and the Chip 'N' Dale characters (who have been given more distinctively separate personalities), is a very high quality production. As a disc which combines two video cassette programs, *Crimebusters/Double Trouble* has plenty to offer. Specifically, both episodes on 'Double Trouble' are wonderful. In the first, 'Dale Beside Himself,' an alien who can assume any form tricks Dale into leaving on a spaceship and then takes Dale's place with the Rangers, so well that no one wants the real Dale back. In 'Flash, The Wonder Dog,' Dale's television hero is kidnapped and he is crushed when the Rangers save the dog, only to discover that the dog is a wimp and that a stunt double does all his heroic athletics on the show. The dog is drawn very realistically, and both episodes are extremely witty. The offerings on 'Crimebusters' are weaker, but the artwork remains inventive and the picture transfer is satisfying and bright. The sound is pushy and is best kept subdued.

DISNEY'S DUCKTALES: ACCIDENTAL ADVENTURERS/SEAFAIRING SAILORS

Donald Duck appears in both episodes on the 'Seafaring Sailors' side of *Disney's DuckTales: Accidental Adventurers/Seafaring Sailors*, one of the more enjoyable *DuckTales* discs. In 'Sphinx for the Memories' Donald is kidnapped by a sect who believe him to be the reincarnation of an ancient Egyptian-type god. Scrooge and his nephews must rescue him and cope with mummies, camels, etc., in the process. 'All Ducks on Deck' is a weaker episode, as too many (however enjoyable) side gags detract from the central narrative, which involves the theft of an invisible jet plane from the aircraft carrier.

A cute 'Tarzan' take off is the subject of 'Jungle Duck' on 'Accidental Adventurers.' The second episode, 'Maid of the Myth,' is wonderful. It opens with Mrs. Beakly, Scrooge's housekeeper, singing Brünnhilde in 'Die Walkure,' (well, she's going 'la lala la'). Real Vikings, who speak with chuckle-inducing Scandinavian accents, land in town on a pillage and end up kidnapping her. The episode is witty and imaginative, and makes good use of both the regular characters and the program's format.

Accidental Adventurers/Seafaring Sailors has digital monaural sound. Except for one volume drop, the sound is clean and efficient. The picture transfer looks good, and the exciting color design is very pleasing.

DISNEY'S DUCKTALES: FEARLESS FORTUNE HUNTER/MASKED MARAUDERS

As is standard on these collections, four episodes of *DuckTales* were combined into two home video programs and then released on a single, two-sided CLV disc, *Disney's DuckTales: Fearless Fortune Hunter/Masked Marauders*. The colors are fabulous. Economics prevents shadings or subtleties unless the entire screen is swathed in a shadow, but the hues are vivid and intense. The disc's principal fault, in fact, is that the most intense colors tend to destabilize. The narratives incorporate a substantial amount of science fiction with fantasy, and are designed for a wide age range.

The audio is a somewhat noisy monaural, with CX-encoding. Each episode runs about 20 minutes and is chapter marked. 'Fearless Fortune Hunter' contains two 'adventure' stories, 'Earth Quack' and 'Masters of the Djinni.' 'Masked Marauders' contains two 'heist' stories, 'Send in the Clones' and 'Time Teasers.' The latter features one of our favorite fantasy gimmicks, a watch which freezes time for the beholder. The stories, which revolve around the wealthy, brogue-speaking Scrooge McDuck and his three nephews, Huey, Dewey, and Louie, are creative, and are a treat for the imagination as well as the eyes. A feast, no. A nutritious meal, maybe not. But a treat, nevertheless.

DISNEY'S DUCKTALES: LOST WORLD WANDERERS/DUCK TO THE FUTURE
DISNEY'S DUCKTALES: DAREDEVIL DUCKS/HIGH-FLYING HERO

A couple of the episodes on *Disney's DuckTales: Lost World Wanderers/Duck to the Future* are especially amusing. In 'Dinosaur Ducks' Uncle Scrooge and his nephews visit a 'lost world' plateau, replete with dinosaurs and cavemen, the latter busily manufacturing wheels. The vistas are particularly lovely, and the cavemen (or, rather, caveducks) are good for some basic slapstick. In 'The Curse of Castle McDuck,' Scrooge and his nephews investigate a haunted Scottish castle. The episode opens with a captivating train ride through the highlands, though on the whole it is a lesser effort. The character who usually espouses the most repeatable dialog, Magica de Spell, appears in 'Duck to the Future,' in which Scrooge sees what life would be like 40 years hence if he allowed her to steal his most prized possession. A basic lesson on totalitarian capitalism is brought home along with some amusing twists on the paths of maturity among the regular characters. 'Sir Gyro de Gearloose' is also an enjoyable episode involving time travel, as the tinkerer, Gyro, and Scrooge's nephews travel back to the time of King Arthur. There is a portly dragon who is quite funny and several nice variations on the normal Arthurian clichés.

The collection on *Daredevil Ducks/High-Flying Hero* is weaker, though the best episode, 'Home Sweet Homer,' is a gem. In it, Scrooge and his nephews become involved with characters from Greek mythology. There are several monsters and some hauntingly peaceful 'Golden Age' settings. Donald Duck also makes one of his occasional cameo appearances and is treated, as usual, with great disrespect. In 'Daredevil Ducks' the Beagle Boys use a transportation device to steal Scrooge's money. Launchpad McQuack is duped into robbing banks when he thinks he is making a movie in 'Hero for Hire.' McQuack also appears in 'Launchpad's Civil War,' an odd but mildly comical tale about Civil War centenarians hiding in a cave because they are ashamed of a military defeat.

The discs are monaural and not CX-encoded, but the sound presentation is strong and worth amplifying. The picture quality is often fabulous. Although the animation suffers from the standard limitations one associates with the current market, the colors (and, for that matter, the lighting) are incredibly vivid and often unique. The most intense colors remain stable, as well, and there appear to be no noticeable image problems with either of the newest releases, save for a slight instability in some of the strongest colors.

DISNEY'S SING-ALONG SONGS THE BARE NECESSITIES/YOU CAN FLY

The single-sided *Disney's Sing-Along Songs The Bare Necessity/You Can Fly* is monaural and has not been CX-encoded. The picture transfer is passable but not stunning, and every sequence has a chapter marker. The disc combines two home video programs. 'Bare Necessities' contains 'You Are a Human Animal,' 'Cinderella, Cinderella,' the *Old Yeller* title song, 'Figaro and Cleo' from a cartoon short which used the *Pinocchio* characters, the Winnie-the-Pooh theme, 'The Ugly Bug Ball' from 'Summer Magic' and sequences from *Dumbo*, 'The Jungle Book,' and 'The Aristocats.' 'You Can Fly' has more numbers from *Dumbo* (the crows), *Winnie the Pooh*, and 'Jungle Book,' along with songs from *Peter Pan*, *Pinocchio*, and *The Lady and the Tramp*. Also featured are 'The Beautiful Briny' sequence from *Bedknobs and Broomsticks*, the 'Step in Time' dance number from *Mary Poppins*, and 'The Merrily Song' from 'The Adventures of Ichabod and Mr. Toad.'

DISNEY'S SING-ALONG SONGS: ZIP-A-DEE-DOO-DAH/HEIGH-HO

The methods by which the Walt Disney organization stretches its product, creating programs which consist mostly of excerpts from other programs, usually turns us off to the material. Disney's *Sing-Along Songs: Zip-A-Dee-Doo-Dah/Heigh-Ho*, a one-sided CLV disc, is better than most, however, because it generally sticks to complete song numbers. 'Bibbidi-Bobbidi-Boo,' 'Whistle While You Work,' 'Heigh-Ho,' and 'The Dwarf's Yodel Song' are included, as are 'Following the Leader,' 'The Siamese Cat Song,' and others. As an added extra, the opening to 'The Mickey Mouse Club,' 'Zorro,' and scenes from 'Davey Crocket' are featured, as are two Disney theme park plugs, 'It's a Small World' and 'Yo Ho.' Sometimes, the sequence is not exactly the same as it originally appeared. For 'Give a Little Whistle,' the visuals cut away to clips of other Disney characters whistling. 'Casey Junior' is a compilation of *Dumbo* and 'Casey Jones'.

The lyrics to the songs are superimposed upon the images in a sporadic fashion. Sometimes they get in the way and sometimes they don't. The introductory material is in stereo while most of the songs are not. The excerpts are not strong in picture quality but are enough to give one a decent sense of the art and talent which went into making the various cartoons.

DISORDERLIES

The Fat Boys ought to be taking lessons. Their music videos were disappointing because they didn't seem to be living up to their true comic potential. *Disorderlies*, their first feature film, is something of an improvement. It is directed by Michael Schultz, who doesn't always film the gags from the funniest angle, but there are glimmers of humor and potential. The disc has an efficient soundtrack and a clear picture. Warner failed to see the necessity for encoding chapters on the disc and left the 87-minute feature in CLV.

DISORGANIZED CRIME

The amusing caper movie, *Disorganized Crime*, has a wonderful ensemble cast. Lou Diamond Phillips is the best-known name in the bunch, and he shows a flair for comedy which has been missing in some of his other roles, but his part and billing is no greater than the others. Ed O'Neill, Ruben Blades, and Fred Gwynne are especially delightful, and the lack of real star presence in the film is one of its strongest charms.

Crime is set in a small Montana town and concerns a group of bank robbers who, because of a series of circumstances, have no idea why they've been called there. The circumstances and coincidences then start to intensify. The disc's picture is a little intense, leading to some very rich colors but also to an occasional shot which is oversaturated and a fleshtone which is too pink. The surround sound is vivid and full of enjoyable – though not always realistic – effects.

DISTANT HARMONY: PAVAROTTI IN CHINA

The visit by Luciano Pavarotti to China in *Distant Harmony: Pavarotti in China* is far more satisfying and enjoyable than Isaac Stern's visit depicted in *From Mao to Mozart*. Unlike the condescending and snobbish Stern, Pavarotti appears to sincerely enjoy working and playing with his hosts. He tries their instruments, and even dresses up in their makeup to take a shot at Oriental opera. His enthusiasm rubs off on the viewer and the 85-minute film is a lot of fun.

Snatches of a full dress production of 'La Boheme' can be viewed, often from intriguing backstage camera angles. Pavarotti also performs a recital in a cavernous hall with ten thousand fans in attendance. The picture has a documentary look to it, but the transfer is okay. Side one is in CAV, with two unsteady still frames out of every five. The sound is stereophonic, but the recording is limited in scope. However, you can hear Pavarotti elsewhere while it is rare that you can catch him in as good a behavior as he is on this program. His trip provides the viewer with a true view of the best both cultures have to offer.

DISTANT THUNDER

The opening ten minutes of *Distant Thunder* is an action sequence set in Vietnam, and the rest is a drama, with touches of melodrama, about a veteran who prefers living in the wilderness to re-entering society. The disc has an impressive stereo surround track, and the opening action scenes are terrific for those who enjoy turning their viewing room into a war zone. The disc's picture is also in good shape, although strong reds are unstable and there is a mild graininess at times. The fleshtones look accurate.

The movie is set on the Olympic Peninsula in Washington State. John Lithgow's performance in the central role makes the film worth watching. He makes his character's touchy reconcilement with his teenage son so believable that the movie's contrived crises seem irrelevant. *Distant Thunder* is at odds with most target audiences because of its mix of subject material, but it is a disc which is worth viewing at least once, and certainly worth running through the amplifier.

DISTANT VOICES, STILL LIVES

Although *Distant Voices, Still Lives* is slightly letterboxed, Image hasn't bothered to identify it as such on the disc jacket, yet this is a case where the mild increase in rectangularization not only looks perfect, but feels perfect. There is certainly no indication that the heads and feet of characters are being truncated. Instead, the addition on the left and right edges contains clearly intended balances of design and screen composition, contributing significantly to the viewer's emotional response to the film.

The film itself is a remarkable accomplishment. From beginning to end it is played out in a stream-of-consciousness style, shifting in time and mood without ever seeming to anchor on any one scene or event. What eventually materializes is a three-decade portrait of a working class family in Liverpool. Some of the sequences are overly stylized – to conform to the film's design the children never fidget – but as it is unclear what in the narrative is memory and what is reality, even the most awkwardly blocked scenes are at least excusable.

In contrast to the full color stills on the jacket cover, the film is largely monochromatic, set in shades of brown which have been transferred with great care. The picture is free of impurities and is admirably executed. The stereo sound is weaker. Separation effects are rare, except during a couple of instances where sounds suddenly 'blurt' out. Image's choice for chapter locations is questionable, and there is no point in the 90-minute movie, even during the fades to black, that could comfortably accommodate a side break.

The weakest selling point of *Distant Voices, Still Lives* is that the life it depicts is ungodly dreary. The highlight is the a cappella renditions of pop tunes, which the characters break into now and then to amuse themselves (some are so memorable that the film could qualify as a musical), but it really appears that these are the high points of the characters' lives as well. The women end up hating their husbands. The husbands end up hating and hitting everything that comes in their way. Ultimately though, the style of the film, which is not a gimmick, is the ideal delivery mechanism for the subject material. The viewer sees bits and pieces of memory, merging together, going off on tangents and then coming back. By the time one realizes what is going on, one is as trapped as the characters are in living out their experiences and grasping for whatever small pleasures there are to be had during the course of it.

DIZZY GILLESPIE – LIVE AT CONCERTS BY THE SEA
(see **THE JAZZ LIFE VOL.1**)

DO THE RIGHT THING

"Wake up!" someone says at the beginning of every Spike Lee movie. Few American filmmakers are so adept at simultaneously teaching and entertaining in a dramatic format. *Do the Right Thing* is Lee's most accomplished and brilliant film to date. It is riveting entertainment, and it utilizes the art of movie making as fully as it has been utilized in any cinematic masterpiece. The movie is about a very hot day in a fairly poor neighborhood and it ends with violence. It is peopled, however, with a dozen vibrant characters, and the camera spends much of the time cruising up and down the street during the course of the day, peeking in on them. The shifts in style are radical but elegant, so that Lee's asides, when characters seem to be speaking more to the camera than to each other, work like musical bridges to facilitate a disguised quickening in the dramatic tempo.

Lee also demonstrates an adoration for language, something which few filmmakers have been interested in since the days of radio. His subject material, essentially the life and culture of black Americans, is a turn-off for many viewers, so much of a turn-off that these viewers will refuse to accept what the film has to teach about the realities of contemporary life. Since the narrative is partially about that refusal, in another context, those who feel uncomfortable watching *Do the Right Thing* are inevitably reacting to their own emotional reflections.

Unfortunately, the carefully scaled tones and subtleties of color in Ernest Dickerson's cinematography are transformed into a gooey blur of oranges and browns, all of which look grainy. The surround sound does not have the impact it ought to provide, and separation effects are limited.

DOCTOR PHIBES RISES AGAIN (see **THE ABOMINABLE DR. PHIBES/ DOCTOR PHIBES RISES AGAIN**)

DOCTOR ZHIVAGO
DOCTOR ZHIVAGO (Letterboxed)

The Deluxe Letter-Box Edition of *Doctor Zhivago* was released at the same time as the letterboxed *Ben-Hur*, ushering in MGM/UA's inspired program of letterboxing classic films.

Although *Ben-Hur* is the greater spectacle, *Doctor Zhivago* is the better movie. Where *Ben-Hur* uses characters to conveniently view historical events, the characters in *Doctor Zhivago* represent the emotions of the events surrounding them. The woman, Lara, can be seen as the 'spirit' of Russia, and 'Revolution' enables her three or four lovers to vie for her soul. The symbols, however, never get out of hand, because the story is also a captivating romance which has the time to fully develop the personalities of the characters. The film is appealing both as a generational tale and as a tale of great adventure, one which spans the world's largest continent during one of its most turbulent eras. The seasons, the fear, the inspiration (the hero, Zhivago, is supposed to be Russia's William Carlos Williams), and the film's cinematic details hold the viewer in rapt attention.

The disc won us over before the overture was finished. Not only did the cornets seem to break free from the orchestra, but suddenly there was triangle which left the speakers altogether and leapt into the middle of the room. The audio track has some imperfections and even shifts into mono on one reel, but, the soundtrack is glorious. The more familiar one is with Maurice Jarre's score, the more goosebumps one will feel whenever it is cued. As for the quality of the picture, it is so close to being ideal that even when it is not, the difference is negligible. The disc is gorgeous, one of the best we have seen. Both the audio and the image quality are significantly improved over MGM/UA's first release of the title.

The letterboxing of *Doctor Zhivago* has an aspect ratio, about 2.25:1. The director, David Lean, deliberately uses the entire screen composition in every shot, and so much is lost when the sides are missing. Several examples are worth noting. First, we should mention that during the final shot of Lara in the cropped version, a poster of Stalin has completely disappeared – purged, as it were. Then there are the yellow flowers which are associated with Lara throughout the film and are always the first item to disappear when the image is cropped and scanned. A beautiful long shot of a steam train, chugging across the snow looks befuddled when the rear of the train is missing. Finally, there are the natural breaks which Lean uses to divide the image as characters are parting from one another – trees, poles, and columns. When the composition is narrow, the emotion of division is lost.

The movie's last shot, of a rainbow created by the mist of a dam's spillway, was much criticized in its day, perhaps deservedly though the film never claimed to be making a universal statement about the Soviet Union's moral status. With today's headlines, the shot seems more appropriate, and the central theme of Dr. Zhivago – that beneath both wicked and benign political machinations there are human beings struggling to make lives for themselves – may at last come to be recognized as a workable truth.

On the final frame, beneath the rainbow, are the words, Metro-Goldwyn-Mayer. Hence, for laser disc owners, does the rainbow represent not just the hope of the film's Soviet Union, it also represents the glowing promise of laser disc home video presentations – in its full, uncropped arc, the rainbow is a promise and a colorful, complete reality in one.

DODSWORTH
Walter Huston's performance in *Dodsworth*, portraying a retired industrialist travelling in Europe, conveys both the naïveté of an American on his first trip abroad and the sharpness of a man who has spent his entire life making executive decisions. The film, based upon a Sinclair Lewis story and directed by William Wyler, is mature in the best sense of the word. The disc's potential for repeated viewings is high because of the quality of the performances. The black-and-white picture is in fairly good condition, and the sound is okay.

THE DOGS OF WAR
Black bands randomly appear on *The Dogs of War* to widen the image slightly in a couple of scenes. The picture is solid and many night scenes run without distortion. The colors remain a little pale, but we vaguely recall that the film looked almost the same way the first day it was released in theaters. With stereo surround sound to support the action sequences, the presentation should not disappoint the film's fans.

The Dogs of War is a dry and methodical depiction of a mercenary force organized to depose an African dictator. Although the movie runs close to two hours, it seems much shorter because of the straight forward pace. Now that the film has had a couple of years to settle into our consciousness, its cheerless point of view seems less trendy. The disc is the perfect sort of entertainment if you're in the mood for a few explosions, but feel guilty about it.

DOJOJI TEMPLE/HOUSE OF FLAME – KIHACHIRO KAWAMOTO
(see **THE MAGIC BALLAD – TADANARI OKAMOTO**)

DOKKEN UNCHAIN THE NIGHT
The 45-minute, single-sided *Dokken Unchain the Night* is a compilation of music videos, separated by home movie footage. While the interim footage is rough, the videos are crystal clear and sound as strong as album recordings. Dokken's heavy metal music is melodic and the vocals communicate the song lyrics clearly. The videos, though never innovative, have attractive and compelling images, and the disc is decent, well-presented rock and roll.

DOLLARS
RCA/Columbia and Image Entertainment have released the Richard Brooks caper movie, '$,' with the cop-out title, *Dollars*. The film was made pretty much at the end of the caper era, but like most of Brooks' films, it has an edge to it, an exaggeration in format which sets it apart from others in the genre.

The disc runs a full two hours and, having been spread to three sides, comes in a gatefold jacket (the inner spread of the jacket contains an excellent interview with Brooks, although *Dollars* is never discussed). It has a muddy, dull picture. The sound also seems antiquated. Despite a musical score which includes a couple of Little Richard numbers, there is only one chapter marker, for a song at the end of the film.

The movie stars Warren Beatty and Goldie Hawn. They give period performances, both stumbling through the film like spaced-out hippies. The unusual aspect of the script is an extended chase sequence which takes up the final third of the picture. The actual ending seems like an afterthought. Still, the film is entertaining for those who enjoy the players (Gert Frobe also appears) or the concept, and withstands multiple viewings without taxing one's mental or emotional facilities.

DOLLS
On a dark and stormy night, a couple too long without rest to continue their journey seek refuge in an imposing mansion inhabited by a mysterious elderly couple and untold numbers of inanimate playthings which whisper and giggle in the shadows. That is as thrilling as *Dolls* gets. The filmmakers are trying for a balance between mock-serious humor and real screams, but miscalculations with the cast result in their not achieving either effect.

The picture is mildly hazy but the sound, originally processed in Ultra-Stereo, is digitally encoded and is one of the film's most satisfying components. Although side two is less than 30 minutes in length, it has been left in CLV. In the end credit scroll, the filmmakers thank the Brothers Grimm. We highly doubt that, if the brothers were around today, they would return the salutation.

DOMINICK & EUGENE
People mistrust movies such as *Dominick & Eugene*, and often with good reason. Even when the films mean well, viewers are forced to look at an aspect of life which they may prefer not to see. Dominick, played by Tim Hulce, had an accident as a child and is slow-witted as a result, although he is competent enough to work as a garbage collector, putting his brother Eugene, played by Ray Liotta, through med school. The dramatic payoffs are held for the very end. There are revelations about the past and a misguided but heroic act which is an effective tear generator. The film is relaxed, mildly comical, and innocently earnest, but it is conceivable that viewers may not wish to stick it out. Hulce's career, however, continues to be fascinating. He fills every role so completely he seems to have no personality of his own, an heir-apparent to Peter Sellers and Alec Guinness.

Both the picture and the stereo surround have no significant flaws and the disc has a healthy number of chapter markers. The film is set in Pittsburgh.

DOMINO
If you've ever been to the movies much in Europe you may have come across a type of film which rarely shows up in the US. It is photographed and edited like a perfume commercial, has a narrative that delves into eroticism, and is so outrageously pretentious that even when the dialog is in another language you know the film is witless. Well, one such movie has slipped past Customs: *Domino*, starring Brigitte Nielsen. The color transfer is very good, but the image has minor speckling from time to time. The digitally encoded sound is monaural. The musical score, which includes a couple of Billy Holiday tunes, is set higher in volume than the dialog.

The Italian production is in English, but you soon wish that it weren't. ("Ah, you've got a great smile. It flits across your face like a fresh wind across the evening sky." Say what?) The film is virtually abstract in design, making the narrative, limited as it is, irrelevant. For the record, Nielsen portrays a famous personality who suffers from romantic ennui and is taunted by crank phone calls. Her loft and the places she visits are barely disguised stage sets, but every camera angle and every shot is glossy and sumptuous. If you own a clothing store you might wish to play the disc in a continuous repeat mode on the store monitor, but we can think of no other use for it.

DON CARLO
(see **LUCIA DI LAMMERMOOR**)

DON JOHNSON HEARTBEAT
The 65-minute LP promotion, *Don Johnson Heartbeat*, features every song from Johnson's album, set to an elaborate but repetitive video about a photographer shooting both a war in Latin America and a fashion spread in an LA barrio. Lots of women are in it, and some R-rated groping and licking has been tacked on to one of the final numbers.

The sound is digitally encoded and often makes you cringe because you can clearly hear the lyrics ("Back on the street, Baby I'm downbeat, you know it's you I seek, in every girl I meet." Scansion! Rhyme! Metaphor! He commits every poetic vice imaginable.) and his nuts-and-bolts voice. Technically the sound processing is excellent, but it leaves Johnson with no excuses, if he cared. The picture is also video crisp and there are chapter markers for the songs, although the jacket cover provides no guide to them.

DONA FLOR AND HER TWO HUSBANDS
An unfortunate picture and sound transfer prevents *Dona Flor and Her Two Husbands* from being as charming as it can be. The picture is pale, the colors faded, and there are scratches. The film had carnival colors and luscious sex scenes. The disc has dull colors and the sweat during the sex no longer glistens. The viewer tends to have less stake in the characters because the whole film has less appeal. The sound is also weak, spoiling the high notes in some of the incidental songs. The movie is in Brazilian Portuguese, and has white English subtitles which often blend into the image.

The film is based upon a novel by Jorge Amado and set in Amado's Bahia. Dona Flor's first husband is a scoundrel who succumbs from hard living. Her second husband is a pharmacist whose life is orderly and staid. As she settles into her second marriage she begins to long for the passion of her first, so much so that the ghost of her first husband materializes and refuses to go away again. The plot is a common one, ideal for romantic comedy and a symbolic division of the needs in a marriage. Seen under the right conditions, *Dona Flor and Her Two Husbands* adds a tropical earthiness to the mix, presenting in a rather satisfying fashion thesis that before you can have spirit, you have to have body. Don't look to the disc, however, to provide such conditions.

DONOVAN'S BRAIN

The black-and-white *Donovan's Brain*, about a brain kept alive in a glowing fish tank, has a Robert Ludlum-style plot twist concerning large sums of money which sustains a viewer's interest past the why-don't-they-just-tip-the-table-over incredulities. Nancy Davis appears. The print is spotless, which is also fun, and the digitally encoded monaural sound has no problems. Side two is in CAV with two unsteady still frames out of every five.

DON'T MESS WITH MY SISTER!

A semblance of entertaining drama is visible in *Don't Mess with My Sister!* The filmmakers don't have enough story to justify their 85-minute running time, and every scene is padded with repetitive or unnecessary footage. However, the blue-collar characters are made realistic by the amateurish but talented cast, and the story, about marriage and infidelity, has the right blend of humor and truth. There is a murder, but it is incidental to the plot and handled tactfully. The film takes a rather dim view of both sexes, but it is also a tribute to the capacity in people to redeem themselves and to forgive.

The movie was made with cheap film stock and has a rusty look, but the transfer seems adequate. The monaural soundtrack takes an almost deliberate joy in its fidelity to background noise, hiss, and every other kink in the audio environment. It is not out of place.

DOOBIE BROTHERS: LISTEN TO THE MUSIC

A 70-minute profile of the rock group, The Doobie Brothers, entitled *Doobie Brothers: Listen to the Music*, chronicles the band's successes and ever-changing personnel. Musical numbers, comprised from clips, are separated by interviews. The band members have a few personality quirks and the usual rock star vocational ailments, but the tale is a reasonably interesting look at the concept of a rock group as an institution independent of its musicians. (There are no actual 'Doobie' brothers, it was a joke which stuck.)

Some songs are interrupted by talking and others are not. The recordings are mostly stereophonic but often differ from the standard versions, providing a fresh viewpoint to the group's accomplishments. The sound isn't vivid, but it is passable. The picture quality varies depending upon the source material, but is always a little on the dull side.

THE DOORS – DANCE ON FIRE

A retrospective collection of songs, *The Doors – Dance on Fire*, is an excellent, well-produced disc with clean, noiseless sound and a sharp, distortion-free picture. The concept is also free of distraction. It presents ten complete songs and two 'spoken songs,' introduced by brief readings from Jim Morrison's poetry. The visuals include concert and performance footage which has been coordinated to the music, candid shots, and conceptual videos which make no bones about having been constructed a decade after the fact.

The disc chapter markers do not catch the intros for the song clips and sometimes miss the opening chords. Some of the numbers are the most familiar recordings and contain the same dropouts and other sound errors which by now seem indigenous to the songs. 'Light My Fire' is a monaural television performance but it is not out of place because 'Light My Fire' is one of those songs that is *too* familiar and thus the variation is welcome.

By the end of the disc, one will have a good sense of the personalities that went into The Doors and the music that came out. All this is achieved without a single interview or analysis, or, except for the end credit sequence, word of information. This is how musical retrospectives ought to be done.

THE DOORS LIVE AT THE HOLLYWOOD BOWL

Rough recordings of concert performances by great rock groups are inviting, because one has heard the standard studio performance so often that any variation is welcome, even if it is imperfect. Take The Doors, in *The Doors Live at the Hollywood Bowl*, for example. Even when they do something innocuous, like taking a repeat a couple of extra times, it is exciting, as if they are answering a variation you had formed in your own imagination.

The concert, a 1968 effort, looks like it was rather excruciating for those in attendance. The lead singer and lyricist, Jim Morrison, has to be the worst poet since Alfred Lord Tennyson. He is the personification of youthful lust, however, and his performance has a Byronic intensity. For those at the Bowl, to whom he must have appeared as no more than an illuminated dot, his lyrics command too much attention and restlessness ensues. But with the closeups on home video, he is excused. It is as if he is *performing*, portraying a brooding, impatient young man who believes his words. He's the Heathcliff of rock.

The sound has been resurrected by experts in digital processing. It is officially in stereo, but the effects are limited and a bit artificial. The sound is well done, considering that no one knew about the popularity of home video when it was recorded, but the acoustics at the Bowl just sort of drift away into nothing.

The picture is always clear and interesting. The Doors don't do much except to play their instruments and sing. Time, however, has turned this lack of stage exhibitionism into a minimalist masterpiece. CAV on side two allows one to capture Morrison's two major forays away from the microphone, and both are a lot of fun to repeat in slow motion. Special mention ought to be made of Morrison's partner and keyboard player, Ray Manzarek. His ability to anticipate Morrison's spaced-out pauses and sudden screams is fascinating. It has to be extrasensory, because the fluctuations are different here than in other live recordings from the same tour.

THE DOORS LIVE IN EUROPE 1968

A seedy, black and white film of Jim Morrison performing on a stage, presumably in front of an audience, somewhere in Europe with The Doors makes for a captivating disc program, *The Doors Live in Europe 1968*. The show has been padded with informative reminiscences to stretch the material. Most of the non-concert footage is bunched in the front of the program, so that the main part runs uninterrupted. Image has marked both the songs and the interludes with chapters and provided a listing on the back of the disc. It is the raw view of Morrison, performing in a state which can neither be classified as conscious nor unconscious, that makes the disc so riveting.

The soundtrack is superb. Although it is in mono, it comes across cleanly and vividly, always in coordination with the movements of the musicians. The picture is voyeuristically blurry, but the transfer is obviously well executed.

DORF ON GOLF

Tim Conway, standing in holes with shoes on his knees to make him look short, provides a half hour of cartoonish slapstick in *Dorf on Golf*. The show, a parody of golf instructional programs, has a laugh track and is not, on the whole, all that funny, though some may find it entertaining simply because of its utter stupidity. The program has been a monstrous hit on video cassette. The picture has a videotape source and looks very sharp. The sound has a few stereo effects and has no difficulties.

DOUBLE INDEMNITY

The black-and-white source used for *Double Indemnity* has no marks on it, but the picture is a little foggy. The movie is a marvelously involving concoction, since the hero, played by Fred MacMurray, seems just normal and dumb enough to become involved in a murder. What is missing from the film, though, is real sex and violence, the kind which would give the viewer the same commitments that the hero has. The sound is fine for a WWII-era monaural film. There are two terrific color stills on the back of the jacket, including one which makes Edward G. Robinson look improbably skinny. On the disc itself, an original theatrical trailer has been included at the end, and it has a good, punchy sell.

DOWN AMONG THE "Z" MEN

Collectors should be familiar with the 'Goon Squad' comedy, *Down Among the "Z" Men* (pronounced 'Zed Men'), before obtaining the disc, for as precious as the movie may be it is also an incomprehensible mess most of the time. The story, such as there is, involves a plot to steal a formula from a scientist who is visiting a military base. The Goon Squad humor ranges from some very witty puns to people trying to be funny by speaking loud, all almost intrinsically disorganized. Needless to say, the black-and-white source material is of tentative quality at best, and the sound is no help when it comes to deciphering the heavily accented dialog. Side two is in CAV with perfect still frames and includes the movie's highlight (for us, anyway), Peter Sellers doing an unnervingly precise imitation of an American.

DOWN AND OUT IN BEVERLY HILLS

Down and Out in Beverly Hills was based on a charming but obscure French play, and subsequent film, about a derelict who is saved from drowning and ends up as a permanent house guest of the fellow who saved him. Paul Mazursky's project was doomed from the start except, like the characters it depicts, it turned out to be not so bad after all. The film's success is a surprise because it is rare to see such good taste demonstrated by mass opinion.

The transfer looks great. The skin tones are maybe a half-shade too pink in places, but otherwise the picture is sharp and clear.

DR. JEKYLL AND MR. HYDE

Although *Dr. Jekyll and Mr. Hyde* is not the best literary adaptation ever to come out of Metro-Goldwyn-Mayer, it has that MGM formula of combining famous stars with plum roles which could generate excitement in the most arcane situations. Spencer Tracy is too much of a good guy and Robert Louis Stevenson's Dr. Jekyll is not, having given himself over to immorality long before his exterior gives him away. Ingrid Bergman's barmaid, however, is provocatively drawn and exquisitely displayed.

The black-and-white print used for the disc is in excellent shape and the sound, although it has not been CX-encoded, is fine.

DR. NO (CBS/Fox)
DR. NO (MGM/UA)
FROM RUSSIA WITH LOVE (CBS/Fox)
FROM RUSSIA WITH LOVE (MGM/UA)
GOLDFINGER (CBS/Fox)
GOLDFINGER (MGM/UA)

Can you believe that when *From Russia with Love* was first released in theaters, it was criticized as being too derivative of *North by Northwest*? The popularity of the James Bond films has since exceeded such trivialities, to the extent that, since has remastered and CX-encoded the first three titles, *Dr. No*, *Russia*, and *Goldfinger*, we have been inundated with queries as to whether collectors should replace their older non-CX CBS/Fox discs (which have decidedly superior jacket art). The quick answer is don't bother, they're not improved enough. There are differences worth noting, however.

In one instance, *Dr. No*, the CBS/Fox version is actually better looking than MGM/UA's effort. The colors on the Fox disc are richer, and there is a tendency on the MGM/UA release for the image to go soft. The only change in the sound is the presence of the CX, and that does not provide a significant enhancement, since the soundtrack is fairly old and noisy in any case.

The film would be far less tolerable if it were not the first episode in what is now the most extensive action and adventure saga motion pictures have produced. Sean Connery's accent still has a heavy Scotch brogue, and his acting is too leery to be suave or worldly. He drinks heavily, smokes like crazy, and practically rapes every woman he meets. Worst of all, he treats the impossibly stereotyped black fisherman and part-time CIA operative, Quarrel (John Kitzmiller), as a second-class being. At one point he tells Quarell to, "Fetch my shoes," as he himself goes traipsing into the woods with Ursula Andress.

There are at least three shots in the film where you can see the camera crew, and unnatural light reflections are present in almost every scene. What made *Dr. No* spellbinding when it was first released, however, and what makes it still entertaining twenty-five years later, is the pacing. The new wave editing of the late sixties was still generally unknown, but the style of the Bond films presaged its coming into fashion. *Dr. No* is a movie which refuses to slow down, and that is, perhaps, why you don't notice the reflections of the camera crew until you've watched the film a hundred times.

The MGM/UA release of *From Russia with Love* is, like the CBS/Fox version, still missing the 'James Bond will return in 'Goldfinger'' tab at the end, so it still rates an 'unacceptable' in our final tally. The source, however, is superior to the CBS/Fox release. The source material, which has splices and marks in different places than the splices and marks on the CBS/Fox print, is crisper and richer in color. The sound is significantly better as well, and out of all three MGM/UA releases, the sound on *Russia* was the fullest and most satisfying. And MGM/UA does let the song finish before they bring in their logo at the end.

Russia is indeed the most Hitchcockian film in the series, exemplified by the choice sequence where the NATO spies use the sewers to get a peak at the Russians. The film is consciously symmetrical and, perhaps, the most deliberately thematic (it was also one of Ian Fleming's strongest novels). Everybody in the film spies on everybody else, and one person's choices almost always turn out to be someone else's gambits. The plot moves even faster than in *Dr. No*, and you have to watch the movie many times or use the reverse scan button and listen very carefully to figure out why the heroes, after stealing a Russian code machine in Istanbul, decide to take the hot contraband to London by riding on a train through Eastern Europe.

The first time we watched *Goldfinger* on the CBS/Fox disc we were disappointed. Although we were vaguely aware that the picture was faded and fuzzy, we thought the problem was in the film itself, that it was just too far-fetched and disjointed to withstand the test of time. Thus we were surprised at the pleasure we received from the MGM/UA version. Although it is not pristine, the picture quality is much better, and we didn't have to fight as much to pay attention to the entertainment. We did take notice that the editing is excellent, the best in the whole series, and that unlike its imitators, little superfluous information is supplied. You *have* to pay attention to follow what is going on.

Unfortunately, MGM/UA has left off the opening note in the intro music, just as CBS/Fox did. Hence, the definitive version has yet to be released. But if, like us, you were disappointed with the movie when you bought the CBS/Fox release, you might want to take a chance with the MGM/UA offering, especially if it was the joy of having seen the film in a theater which made you put your money down in the first place.

THE DR. SEUSS VIDEO FESTIVAL

The collaboration of Dr. Seuss and Chuck Jones is enough to make the palate of the smallest and largest cartoon fan salivate. Jones's direction, all clutter and flair, shows off Seuss's material with wit and great care.

MGM/UA's *The Dr. Seuss Video Festival* is broken in two; 'How the Grinch Stole Christmas' and 'Horton Hears a Who!' Even though the disc is a whole lot of fun, the spoilers at MGM/UA put everything on side one. No chapter markers are used and what is even worse, if you watch them on the Fourth of July, the seasonal 'Grinch' still comes on first.

The sound is weak and the songs are poor, but the drawings and stories leave you wishing for more. The 'Grinch' is a despicable Scrooge-like creature. 'Horton,' elephant, is one of the great altruistic heroes in kiddie lit'rature. Jones's animation is brisk and inventive. We recommend the disc, with plenty of incentive.

DRACULA (1931) – THE RESTORED VERSION

Life has been retrieved from the dead with *Dracula (1931) – The Restored Version*. The film previously looked and sounded so ragged (in the old DiscoVision release, for example) that portions reminded one more of a silent film than of a sound era production. With great care, restorers returned to the original elements and transfused a vivid image and improved soundtrack to a new master. The sound is so strong now that it does not lose its reflection in the CX-encoding, and the black and white image provides a new illumination to the sets, costumes, and closeups. No new footage has been added, but the original material has miraculously re-composed.

Side two is in CAV, and also contains an early rerelease trailer and more than 250 publicity stills. The still collection, compiled from two private collections, provides the best opportunity to view the film from new angles. There are no behind-the-scenes views of the director or crew working with the cast, but there are several poses staged from scenes which are not present in the film, and many more which have been shot at a different time and different angle.

Dracula may be old and dated, but it can easily withstand many viewings, and is destined to be around for an eternity. It is also so short (75 minutes) that it is over before one tires of it. That is another advantage to the still collection, which helps one stretch the entertainment. It can take as long to flip through the photos as it does to watch the movie.

DRAGNET

The comedy, *Dragnet*, which stars Dan Ackroyd and Tom Hanks, has a reasonably nice transfer, although the stereo surround sound was not digitally enocoded and lacks oomph.

DRAGONSLAYER (Import)
DRAGONSLAYER

The print which was used for the letterboxed *Dragonslayer* available on import (it was later withdrawn and is now a collector's item) looks like it has been used for several other purposes as well. It is scratched and speckled in a number of places, and occasionally sports a blue band across the bottom of the image. Still, the image quality is no worse than the domestic Paramount release and the color accuracy often looks a little better. The film has many processed shots and a lot of dark, shadowy scenes. At its worst the scenes are grainy and take on artificial hues, but, at its best, the fleshtones look accurate and the focus is crisp.

The picture has an aspect ratio of about 2.1:1. It is set almost as high as is possible on the screen, with Japanese subtitles appearing beneath the image. The spectacular special effects are greatly improved by the letterboxing – you get to see more of the dragon, and every extra scale is a thrill. The screen composition during the non-special effect sequences is also improved though it is of less consequence. The sound is digitally encoded stereo surround. The Paramount disc had manual CX-encoding, but the film's soundtrack is so well mixed that it still worked quite nicely. The improvements offered by the digitally encoded audio will be negligible for most listeners.

The dragon's den scene has long been one of our favorite demonstration sequences. It has great, booming basses (plus absolute silence the moment before the dragon exhales his flame), a super mixture of model and live special effects, and a miniature drama of its own, as the boy trying to escape and/or kill the dragon must cope with an engaging set of surprises along the way. The ending of the scene is a cheat – it just cuts to later on with hero miraculously still in one unfried piece and the dragon off doing something else. The film as a whole is entertaining if you accept its premises and its casting, neither of which is all that accommodating. The story is set in the Dark Ages and concerns a wizard's apprentice who volunteers to assist a kingdom terrorized by a dragon.

DREAM A LITTLE DREAM

A small but gregarious fantasy, *Dream a Little Dream* looks terribly grainy and speckled, and the chapter markers are not coordinated to either the hit singles or the dream sequences (a character, at one point, essentially challenges you to return to an earlier scene before going forward, yet you have to scan to find it). The only thing the disc has going in its favor is an impressive, surround soundtrack, and, of course, the movie itself.

Dream is another entry in the body substitution genre, closest in spirit to *Peggy Sue Got Married*. The filmmakers err in anticipating their audience. The style of the film is designed for younger viewers, with dialog segments interrupted at regular intervals by sequences half intended to stand alone as music videos. The music is loud and sometimes obnoxious, and the story slows down to a crawl when it plays. The dream sequences, however, are superbly executed and encourage instant replays. The enigmatically romantic plot is about an elderly couple, played by Jason Robards and Piper Laurie, who must discover the truth in their love when they are transmuted to the bodies of Corey Feldman and Meredith Salenger. Hence, although the movie is populated with younger stars, it is best appreciated, loud music and teen antic interludes aside, by those with more mature sensibilities and experiences.

THE DREAM ACADEMY
A-HA – HUNTING HIGH AND LOW

Dream Academy has a unique sound. How many rock groups using an oboe can you name? The group's songs don't quite become the epics they seem to want to make them, but the music is multi-layered and not too superfluous.

The disc, *The Dream Academy*, contains three music videos, followed by an audio-only program which is accompanied, visually, by a photo of the jacket cover and textual identification of the song being played. One song represented by a video, 'Please, Please, Please Let Me Get What I Want,' is not repeated on the album portion, but 'Life in a Northern Town' and 'The Love Parade' are. The videos are well executed and good examples of the genre. The picture is a little grainy, which is a shame because the colors in all three videos are complex and need as accurate a re-creation as possible.

Another disc that presents several music videos followed by an audio-only program, *A-Ha – Hunting High and Low*, is worth looking into. One video, 'Take on Me,' is a highly respected piece of sketch animation, depicting a girl who is pulled into a comic book. The members of A-Ha, despite their high, whiny voices, make good rock and roll and the album is a pleasure.

DREAM MACHINE AN ANTHOLOGY OF COMPUTER GRAPHICS

The two-sided CAV disc, *Dream Machine An Anthology of Computer Graphics* is a comprehensive collection of current computer design and animation capabilities, supported by 102 chapter markers. An unseen narrator describes different types of graphic systems and utilizations, with some superficial explanations concerning which buttons were pushed to create what effects. The product of the different graphics houses and systems are displayed, usually with the creator identified on a superimposed title which can occasionally interfere with the graphic. An undistinguished electronic musical score is also present.

The manipulations of color and aspect are fascinating. Animated characters look as realistic as clay puppets, and it won't take much more to move from clay to flesh. The disc features a view from the deck of an aircraft carrier which could easily be mistaken for the real thing. A portrait of a vase and an apple also looks like a photograph, until the color and texture of the shapes change to marble, to glass, to pastel.

Because of the way the program was filmed, some still frames wiggle and some do not. It varies from piece to piece. The picture quality is quite good, and the colors in some of the segments have probably never appeared on your television set before.

The sound is constructed in dual audio, so the narration or the music can be suppressed. The narration increases in volume and fidelity when isolated. Even when played without the narration, the music never sounds as if it completely inhabits one's speakers, but after listening to the narration once, for the record, it will be preferable to play the disc as a lengthy music video.

DREAM MACHINE VOLUME TWO: COMPUTER DREAMS

There are some stunning graphics on *Dream Machine Volume Two: Computer Dreams*. The two-sided CAV disc is a documentary about computer graphics, but the narration is isolated on one audio channel on the analog track, and is not present at all on the digital track. This may be disconcerting when viewers first spin up the disc.

Although footage of artists at work is included, the bulk of the program is a display of the end results. Many of the sequences are excerpts, which is frustrating, but there is so much and it is so fascinating that a viewer hasn't got time to lament that which is missing.

The collection largely represents work done in 1988. Some of the compositions are startlingly realistic, while others are intriguingly abstract. The transfer is excellent, and a majority of the pieces have perfect still frames. Among the best: A view of a bicycle shop which could easily be a real photograph, a cartoon about a desk lamp and his father called Luxo Jr., and an advertisement for Sunbeam's 'Expressmeals' which shows other kitchen appliances disturbed over the arrival of the Sunbeam unit. There is also a primitive attempt to put Humphrey Bogart and Marilyn Monroe in the same room.

The disc features 174 different sequences and 56 chapter markers. The narration, delivered by Amanda Pays, is modestly informative, as is the essay on the back of the disc jacket. From the looks of the pieces presented on the disc, computer animation is just about at the point where, if someone develops a script with a decent story, the next phase of motion pictures will truly be underway.

THE DREAM TEAM

The cast of *The Dream Team*, Michael Keaton, Christopher Lloyd, Peter Boyle, and Stephen Furst, play so well together that they are funny even when the dialog isn't. The film, about four mental patients on an unplanned furlough in Manhattan, has all the comedy a viewer needs for a good time. The script, which uses a murder as the plot activator, keeps things moving and is just serious enough to hold the other elements in balance. The four actors have such sharp timing you don't know which one to watch in the group shots.

The fleshtones are a shade too orange and some solid colors look mildly grainy, but the focus is sharp. The surround sound is not elaborate and has less to offer. The thunder during a rainstorm, for example, sounds phony.

DRESSED TO KILL
SHERLOCK HOLMES AND THE SECRET WEAPON

The old Basil Rathbone/Nigel Bruce Sherlock Holmes film, *Dressed to Kill*, is a good example of 3M's efforts to reproduce older favorites on laser video disc. The 35mm print has a few scratches but it makes a clearly focused picture with nice contrasts. The sound is a little less tinny than the quality of the typical Saturday morning television broadcast. The movie itself is great. At one point the clever villainess leads Holmes into a trap by using his own curiosity against him. You can't ask for more from movies than the expression on Rathbone's face when Holmes realizes he has been foolish.

Sherlock Holmes and the Secret Weapon has him fighting Nazis, which is admirable, but a bit un-Victorian. This disc does not have automatic CX tripping. When turned on manually, the noise level seemed to drop without affecting the volumes, so the disc is probably CX-encoded. The print has some splices but not enough to upset anything.

DRIVING MISS DAISY

Warner has issued the Oscar winner, *Driving Miss Daisy*, in a stylishly white, single platter gatefold jacket. On the innerspread is a brief essay about *Miss Daisy* by Alfred Uhry, the author of the screenplay and the stage work upon which the screenplay was based. He speaks about how the work was shifted from a rather bare stage to the real locations used in the film, some of which were houses and towns he knew from his own childhood, and he concludes by praising the laser disc for preserving this vision of his past for his children and grandchildren.

The picture transfer is very nice. Some of the camera work in the film is purposefully dreamy and a bit on the hazy side, but the disc never throws the continuity out of balance when it shifts from sharp to artistic fuzz. The image, which is no wider than the standard video cassette release, has been slightly matted at the top and bottom to recreate the intended theatrical presentation. The framing always looks precisely balanced and is never a distraction. Although stereo surround effects are understandably limited, the sound has no significant flaws.

The film, though somewhat trifling, is pleasant and engaging. About the relationship between an elderly woman and her black chauffeur in the South after World War II, the filmmakers wisely avoid any obvious commentary that would undercut the film's reasonably light mood. The tension inherent in the situation – not only the dramatic situation, but in the cast members acting out their roles – is plain enough that it needs no further attention drawn to it to be effective or to support the superficial aspects of the plot. Like the characters themselves, the film is much wiser than it first appears, and, as Uhry suggests, with the disc, one can take the time to discover its wisdom.

DRUGSTORE COWBOY

About a quartet of drug addicts who somehow manage to stay ahead of the law while they cop pharmaceuticals, *Drugstore Cowboy*, however technically adept and however competently acted, is pathetic. The film has humor and drama, but it is not entertaining, and by the time William Burroughs is trotted out to pontificate on the joys of addiction it gets positively stupid. The movie's colors are dull, and the disc's picture is soft and fuzzy. The Ultra-Stereo sound is inconsistent in effect.

DRUMS ALONG THE MOHAWK

John Ford's wonderful *Drums Along the Mohawk* is nominally about early pioneers holding down the edges of the frontier during the Revolutionary War. There is even a decent stockade attack sequence during the final half hour. Two things, however, are quickly apparent. One is that most of the movie is taken up with how the pioneers lived and interacted with one another. The second is that the characters are as representative of 'America' as they are of real people. Thus Ford can leap from communicating the joys of having a child to evoking the pride of creating a republic at something close to light speed, and with almost the same sort of thrill.

The film stars Henry Fonda and Claudette Colbert. The Technicolor picture is richly detailed, although the colors often look too brown and there are a few tatters. The sound is fine in the first half, but takes on more distortion in the second half.

DTV GOLDEN OLDIES

The Walt Disney organization reminds us of a bar which waters down its liquor. We spotted footage of Donald Duck getting hit in the head with rubber tipped arrows three times on *DTV Golden Oldies*. After sitting through that one, we just didn't have the heart to watch the other two, *DTV Pop & Rock* and *DTV Rock Rhythm & Blues*.

The DTV concept – setting cartoons to songs in a music video format – is a good way to fill in the spaces on Disney's cable channel. Releasing them as a unique product is a cheat.

The *Golden Oldies* disc has a few good songs – Lena Horne's 'Stormy Weather' is one – and some which would better qualify as 'Leaden Oldies,' such as Annette Funicello's 'Tall Paul.' In every case the material was more inspiring in its original context.

DUCK SOUP

The balletic movements of Groucho, Harpo, and Chico Marx can be slowed down to a step-by-step still frame progression or sped up to a slow, comical glide on side two of *Duck Soup*. The 70-minute feature is in CLV on side one and CAV on side two. It has a pair of chapter markers denoting the two major musical numbers. The rarely seen theatrical trailer is also included on side two. The print starts out roughly but shapes up after the first fifteen minutes or so. The sound is fairly clear.

Running the famous 'mirror scene' in slow motion, wherein Harpo, dressed as Groucho, tries to keep up with ever more complicated challenges of imitation, you can catch more humorous details than can be apprehended at full speed. CAV proves that their talent is ingrained and obviously hereditary.

DUCK'S UNLIMITED'S VIDEOGUIDE TO WATERFOWL AND GAME BIRDS

The CLV *Ducks Unlimited's Videoguide to Waterfowl and Game Birds* began as a video cassette program, so except for the extensive and well-indexed chapter markers, the advantages of the video disc are not utilized. The program, for example, runs 75 minutes, but is in CLV throughout, and the bird calls are not on a separate audio channel from the narration. The picture and sound quality are both a little rough, but the job gets done and the condition of the disc should not bother anyone.

The scope of the coverage, 'Waterfowl and Game Birds,' is specific enough that a great amount of detail can be provided for every species. The sounds of the birds are heard, motion picture and still photos of each are provided, and computer-generated drawings analyze the flight patterns and wing movements of virtually all the birds. The narration concentrates on assisting the viewer in recognizing each bird and telling one apart from the other. Habitat areas and unusual idiosyncrasies are also noted. The disc is ideal for bird lovers, bird hunters, or those who want to know what is nesting by their backyard pond.

DUDES

Three young men dressed in punk regalia are driving from New York to Los Angeles when they run afoul of some good ol' meanies in the Southwest, and end up chasing the bad guys into Montana to extract revenge for a murder. It happens all the time in home video, with different characters and locales but the same basic 90 minutes of catch up and show-down. One variation in *Dudes* is that the heroes have dreams and totems to guide them, but the more the movie tries to be different, the more it isn't. The picture transfer is good and the stereo sound is also decent. There are a number of chapter-marked rock songs on the soundtrack.

DUNE

Nothing is wrong with *Dune* that another 90 minutes or so of movie wouldn't have fixed. At 137 minutes, there just isn't enough time to tell the story and so, especially in the latter half, the plot goes boom boom boom to push everything through. Directed by David Lynch, *Dune* is good when it comes to atmosphere and ideas and weak in plot, cast, and special effects. Cropping to a small portion of the original picture (after the credit sequence tantalizingly shows the amount one could be viewing) deflates many of the visual effects. The picture is mildly grainy and the sound is subdued.

Dune is about a young man who is destined to lead the hidden population of a waterless planet to revolution against a galactic empire. How he succeeds is dependent so much upon the internal logic of the fantasy that if any one aspect were left out, the whole story would slide. Lynch manages to include everything by relying heavily on voice-over narration and by eliminating any casual dalliances on image or thought. He has achieved a unique look for the sets and has included enough snippets of Frank Herbert's attitudes to keep a viewer concentrating.

THE DUNGEONMASTER

No less than seven directors are listed in the credits of *The Dungeonmaster*. The movie is a valiant attempt to do something slightly different with the genre. The guiding plot has a satanic figure whisk away a computer wizard and his fiancée to the netherworld where the two are submitted to various challenges. Each of the challenges was directed by a different person, but none amounts to more than showing off a few special effects. The best known of the seven, David Allen, has included an accomplished piece of stop-action model work in his segment. Except when scenes are bathed in red light, the picture exhibits no particular flaws.

DURAN DURAN
DURAN DURAN – DANCING ON THE VALENTINE

One of the best collections of music videos from a single group is contained on the 12-inch disc, *Duran Duran*. The 55-minute program is in CAV and spread to two sides. The eleven cuts include what is, perhaps, the seminal music video, 'Rio,' along with such goodies as 'Hungry Like the Wolf' and 'Girls on Film.' The picture is perfect and the sound is very good.

The material on the Duran Duran 8-inch, *Duran Duran – Dancing on the Valentine* supplements the 12-inch. Two of the cuts are unremarkable. 'Union of the Snake,' however, is an exciting video with a catchy tune and a carefully conceived progression of images involving lizard people, desert warfare, and Hell.

DURAN DURAN – SING BLUE SILVER

The digital concert disc, *Duran Duran – Sing Blue Silver*, is well produced. The picture, which is very sharp, is in wide screen (except for the concert material), with informational text occasionally flashing in the black band across the bottom. Unfortunately, the group only plays four complete songs during the 84-minute show, with bits of other numbers thrown in. Most of the disc is taken up by backstage and day-off shots of Duran Duran on tour. They visit the FBI, go boating, drive through the snow, and look seriously concerned when the stage equipment is faulty. If they'd sung a little more and talked a little less, the disc would have been worthwhile.

E.T. THE EXTRA-TERRESTRIAL
E.T. THE EXTRA-TERRESTRIAL (CAV)

The deservedly popular *E.T. The Extra-Terrestrial* has not been well-served as a disc. The single-platter CLV release has a particularly grainy picture, especially during the opening night scenes. The image is improved on the CAV 'Collector's Edition,' but on that disc the audio channels are reversed. The film's sound editing is very sophisticated, and the one saving grace for the CAV disc is that the separations are more impressionistic than directional. The channels on the CLV disc are correct.

On both discs, The image is presented in an aspect ratio of about 1.85:1. There are many incidences of foreground and background objects on opposite sides of the screen deliberately composed to give a feeling of depth – in fact, we know of few films where the cinematography has seemed as purposefully three dimensional – and the viewer would lose not only the effect but the involvement it encourages if the image had been scanned.

The film may not seem to have much to offer as a CAV title, but Allen Daviau's exceptional cinematography benefits significantly from the disc's perfect still frames. The CAV version also several supplementary features including a pre-release theatrical trailer is cleverly constructed to show what happens without showing what happens and a collection of publicity department releases which, since they are accurately dated, chronicle the phenomenal popularity of the film. A few production photos are also included and are adeptly identified.

E.T. The Extra-Terrestrial is magnificent, as virtually anyone without an axe to grind will freely admit. When the disc is finished, you either want to play it again or play *Close Encounters* to keep the fix going. The plot draws inspirations from the New Testament and from 'Peter Pan' (or, as those with an axe to grind are wont to suggest, it draws parallels *between* the New Testament and 'Peter Pan'). The story, regardless of its religious overtones, is truly profound, as the boy first approaches the creature as a pet and then gradually comes to understand that the being is his equal, eventually understanding it so well that his commitment becomes a passion.

EADWEARD MUYBRIDGE: MOTION STUDIES

The single-sided CAV disc, *Eadweard Muybridge: Motion Studies* is subtitled, 'by James Sheldon,' who produced the Voyager release in coordination with a museum exhibition he also organized. Muybridge designed a sort of rapid-fire device which 'snapped' (to use a contemporary term for a much more elaborate process) an array of cameras in quick succession, capturing a dozen or so images of an object in motion. It did not take Muybridge long to realize that the popular toys of the day, which utilize an optical illusion involving a small carousel to animate silhouettes and drawings, could animate his photos just as easily. The primary display of his efforts, however, remained the publication of the sequential photographs.

Muybridge's primary interest was in the physiology of humans and horses. Educators and others should be warned up front that the program contains extensive nudity, something the jacket cover fails to emphasize. Included among Muybridge's studies are many sequences involving young children participating in innocent activities which, because of their state of undress, could create controversy in certain academic situations, particularly in today's moral climate.

The disc contains three main sections and an addendum. The audio tracks are silent except for one of the analog tracks during the first segment, on which a lecture that was once given by Muybridge is read by a narrator as a number of the studies are presented at a speed which makes them comprehensible in 'play' format. In the second section, many more studies are presented on a frame-per-frame basis. The most effective method of viewing these is with the utilization of the slow speed playback options. The third section contains replications of many more sequential displays, but they are shown in still frame as they were originally published (i.e., twelve or more photos squeezed onto a single frame). To view these effectively a large screen TV or projection system is needed. The addendum contains photos of Muybridge's apparatus and other supporting materials. There is also a carousel demonstration, and a similar demo after the disc's credits are over. The majority of Muybridge's studies depict the movement of horses and the basic activities of humans. But, as a side bar, he also recorded a number of other firsts. He was the first to capture a slapstick gag, showing a man butt his head against a donkey. He was the first to use special effects, throwing explosives at chickens. He was also the first to record motion simultaneously from two different angles, and he seems to have known instinctively what those angles ought to be.

THE EAGLE

Rudolph Valentino stepped slightly out of form to portray a Robin Hood-style bandit in the silent adventure comedy, *The Eagle*. The film never amounts to much of a swashbuckler or much of a romance, and is more significant historically than as entertainment. Valentino is talented and has a good camera presence, but the production fails to make effective use of him. The restoration is passable, though some sequences appear tattered or fuzzy. The stereo Carl Davis score is nondescript. The title cards are new and the disc opens with an informative but poorly narrated introduction.

AN EARLY FROST

The only reason that the made-for-television AIDS drama, *An Early Frost*, remains emotionally convincing is that the cast pulls out everything they have to present it without embarrassment. There is a tendency among the characters to present positions rather than to react with the subtle fears and angers of real human feelings. The actors stand their ground, however, and deliver their lines with heartfelt sincerity. If the cast had been any less talented than Gena Rowlands, Ben Gazzarra, and Sylvia Sydney, the movie would not have been good enough to release on disc. The picture is a little orange, but the transfer is acceptable.

EARTH GIRLS ARE EASY

While *Earth Girls Are Easy* has poorly conceived scenes and badly stereotyped characters, it is also a satisfying blend of genuine stop-the-narrative musical numbers, crazy special effects, and astute comical performances. Geena Davis and Jeff Goldblum star. She is sunbathing one day when he crash lands in her pool. It's in LA, so no one notices that he's odd.

The partially animated credit sequence is letterboxed, but the rest of the movie is scanned and cropped, which severely impacts many of the amusing reaction shots. The color transfer is okay. The surround sound delivers the songs effectively, but the sound effects are uninteresting.

EARTH VS. THE FLYING SAUCERS

The layout of stills on the back jacket cover of *Earth vs. The Flying Saucers* is quite striking. The Ray Harryhausen effort looks good on disc. There is however, a formatting flaw. As you may be aware, the ending is a spectacular sequence depicting a battle over Washington DC, with crashing saucers knocking down monuments and generally causing almost as much destruction as the British did in 1812. The beginning of the 83-minute film, which has some special effects, has been formatted in CAV (with two shaky still frames in every five), but the grand finale is in CLV.

The black-and-white film has been given a nice transfer. The picture is usually quite sharp and the contrasts are rich, though we wonder if some of the night sequences couldn't have been a bit lighter. The scratchy monaural sound is digitally encoded and sounds just fine. The film, though no great accomplishment, is entertaining, perhaps more so than usual because of the disc presentation.

EARTHQUAKE

We got tired of watching *Earthquake* a long time ago, but we never get tired of listening to it. Since most people do not have speakers the size of refrigerators, they probably will not be disappointed that the digital disc is only surround encoded and not Sensesurround encoded. It is enough to have a decent set of woofers and let it rip. Patient neighbors and understanding family members help as well.

The movie is dumb but people watch it anyway, dumbfounded at the silly shake-the-camera effects and the ridiculous melodramatic subplots. (There is no plot, only subplots.) The film's one bright idea is to show movie theater patrons watching a movie when the quake first hits. It is a shame they didn't come up with a home video version showing the actors watching TV.

The picture quality is below average. It looks grainy and muddy. The film runs 3 minutes over two hours and so it has been spread to three sides, allowing MCA to do side three in CAV. Not only do you get the dam break, but, because the trailer is also included, you get just about every decent special effect in the movie, along with many of the lousy ones. The trailer is also in widescreen and has its share of rumbles.

EAST OF EDEN

The 'Reprocessed for Stereo' sound on *East of Eden*, despite numerous dropouts, has real atmosphere to it. *East of Eden* is always one of the titles which get dragged out when the glories of widescreen are being discussed. The director, Elia Kazan, was not an innovator with the widescreen medium, but he did use the techniques masterfully and so any presentation, such as this disc, which does not show the complete frame, loses important physical and emotional balances. The colors in the film intentionally emphasize the browns and yellows of the Salinas/Monterey landscape, but there may be a little freshness missing from the print which was used.

Jo Van Fleet won an Oscar for her performance as the estranged mother, but anyone who wants proof of James Dean's abilities as an actor has only to flip to the scene where he asks her for a loan in her office. Usually, actors from the old school, such as Van Fleet, leave the Dean-type method actors mumbling for air, but here Van Fleet's theatrics look grossly artificial when they are bounced off of the emotional aura Dean establishes and maintains around his character.

THE EASTER BUNNY IS COMING TO TOWN

A 50-minute animated program using stop-action models, *The Easter Bunny Is Coming to Town*, is narrated by Fred Astaire. The sound is tinny, and the picture looks a little worn, but the presentation is acceptable. Although the story purports to explain a number of Easter traditions, in a non-theological sort of way, it also draws extensively from 'The Little Engine that Could.' The animation is limited but workable, and the children we associate with seemed to enjoy it.

EASTER PARADE

The picture transfer of *Easter Parade* is gorgeous. The flesh tones are so vivid and the colors of the costumes are so bright that the musical numbers seem to leap out of the screen. We wish only that we could say the same of the sound which, although it has been digitally encoded, is muffled to the point of annoyance. The songs do not suffer as badly as the dialog, but if MGM/UA is claiming that the sound is "digitally enhanced for stereo," they would have been better off leaving it alone. The film is best thought of as a revue and the less one pays attention to the plot, the more one will enjoy it. Fred Astaire, Judy Garland, and Ann Miller look terrific on the disc, and that is all most viewers require to be entertained.

EAT TO THE BEAT – BLONDIE (Import)

Eat to the Beat – Blondie was an early experiment in music video. The disc's weakness is that too many of the songs do not seem to deserve the attention they receive in this format. The strongest conceptual video clip is 'Victor,' a wonderful vision of madness in an urban wilderness where Debbie Harry spends about three minutes screaming straight into the camera.

The disc is in CAV and is split to side one and two in tandem with the LP.

ECHO PARK

Sometimes reading the fine print in the credits can be more fun than watching the movie. Paramount's quirky *Echo Park* turns out to have been financed by an Austrian consortium and is thus protected under Austrian, rather than American, copyright laws. Don't bother searching for loopholes, however, because the movie isn't worth pirating or plagiarizing. The show is about several young adults living in an unfashionable LA neighborhood and coping with life's realities. It tries as hard to be poignant as it tries, for tax purposes, to be Austrian, but it is only moderately successful at either endeavor. The picture and sound are tolerable.

ECHOES OF ELLINGTON, VOL. 1

Everybody is always doing Ellington, but *Echoes of Ellington, Vol. 1* really seems to get it right. The program's mix of performers is what makes the show so satisfying. The set shifts between ensemble pieces and solos, saving Dianne Reeve's vocals for the very end, when you're no longer expecting her. Appearing with Reeves are Randy Brecker, Tom Scott, Robben Ford, and Bill Evans. The deliberate shifts in emphasis from keyboard to sax to trumpet and to the vocals provides a survey of approaches to Ellington's work, while the discipline of the hour concert format imposes continuity. The picture and sound are very good.

ECLIPSE (see L'ECLISSE)

EDDIE AND THE CRUISERS
EDDIE AND THE CRUISERS II: EDDIE LIVES

One film which we hoped we'd never see a sequel to was *Eddie and the Cruisers*. The original movie was so satisfying and resolute that belaboring the concept seems pointless. They've done it anyway and the result isn't bad, but it confirms our initial impression. *Eddie and the Cruisers* is one of those films. For an early release, the transfer was not bad. The analog stereo sound is reasonably clean and the picture, though mildly soft and grainy, has fresh colors. The songs in the film were wonderful – you could really believe that they were hits, and the intelligent evocation of the band's musical maturation provided a solid background for the plot, told in flashback, about the band's demise and the mysterious death of the lead singer.

Eddie and the Cruisers II: Eddie Lives has the singer biding time anonymously in Montreal – a nice, Glenn Gouldish touch, though that probably isn't why it was filmed there – a number of years later. The IVE Image release shows how far basic disc production has come. The sound is digital stereo surround and is stronger and clearer than the earlier disc, even though the earlier film had better sound editing. The picture transfer is solid and unblemished, although the film's images are unremarkable. The disc is also chapter encoded.

Feeling pressure from a renewed interest in his music, Eddie gets the itch and puts a band together. Michael Pare's performance is notable. Although he doesn't do the vocals for the songs, his voice even seems changed in the dialog, and one has no trouble assuming that years have passed for him between the two films. The script for the sequel is not as tight as the first effort, and its pleasures are scattered instead of continuous. The music still sounds good, but if you are looking to relive the first movie, instead of turning to the sequel, it makes more sense to play the first one again.

EDDIE MONEY: PICTURES OF MONEY (THE FIRST TEN YEARS)

A 50-minute collection of Eddie Money videos, *Eddie Money: Pictures of Money (The First Ten Years)*, contains 14 numbers which amount to a 'greatest hits' collection. Even the oldest videos look sharp, and the sound is strong. The videos are of standard design and often feature women who have some kind of relationship with the singer. Money's music has never been daring enough for our tastes, but the program, which has no interruptions or distractions, shows him in his best light.

EDDIE MURPHY RAW

The things Eddie Murphy has to say about male and female relationships, while exaggerated in the manner of all standup comedy, are so true that he's almost a walking sociological primer, with jokes. The 90-minute edited stage show, *Eddie Murphy Raw*, is much stronger than Murphy's earlier standup effort, *Delirious*. Without straying far from the one theme which, for the lack of a better word, one might identify as 'love,' Murphy induces a steady flow of laughter and holds a viewer's attention throughout. He never goes onto an unsuccessful tangent and he never gets desperate. His picture of the chemical and financial needs of men and women may not be pretty, but it is more accurate than many would be willing to admit, particularly if one accepts his voice as it is presented on the program, that of a fictional character trying to figure the world out. The picture on the disc is grainy. The digitally encoded sound is clear.

EDGE OF SANITY

Tony Perkins goes through his usual pop-eyed dithering in *Edge of Sanity*, a film which gives no credit acknowledgement to Robert Louis Stevenson, but takes the 'Dr. Jekyll and Mr. Hyde' characters and pushes them a step further by turning Hyde, with his medical knowledge, into Saucy Jack. It is a fairly lurid exercise, but it has been composed with a confident sense of visual style (up to, but not including, Perkins' make up). Every shot is carefully color coordinated, mostly in Victorian reds and browns which the disc handles quite well. Much of the film takes place in nocturnal shadows, and these, too, survive without distortion. There is graininess in a shot or two, but it is minimal.

The surround sound is also elaborately executed. Whether you will be impressed by it depends upon what you think about rainstorms in which the surround pitter is distractingly different from the front channel patter. As for the movie – uncut, if it makes any difference – the visual exuberance holds ones attention until it becomes clear that Perkins' Hyde is more prepossessing than Perkins' Jekyll, and far less interesting.

THE EGG AND I

The couple played by Fred MacMurray and Claudette Colbert in *The Egg and I* have a very strange marriage. They don't consult each other on anything. He buys two farms without telling her. She has a baby without telling him. The film will make feminists, and anyone else in possession of a little common sense, cringe. The men dictate and the women follow orders and it is supposed to be oh so funny when they don't follow the orders exactly. Well, sometimes it is, but that's just because it's hard to get mad at old movies.

The Egg and I is also the film which introduced the world to Ma and Pa Kettle, and if that doesn't mean anything to you, then the future has arrived. The black and white print looks very nice. It has deep, rich tones and a sharp focus. The monaural sound is okay. A trailer for a re-release of the movie appears on side two with its own chapter marker. It is a wonderfully typical trailer with boisterous graphics and enthusiastic voice-over narration, worth collecting even if the film is not.

81/2 (see **LA DOLCE VITA**)

EIGHT MEN OUT

In the involving John Sayles film about the 1919 World Series gambling scandal, *Eight Men Out*, the root cause of corruption among the players is corruption among their employers, and even if the individuals were not as angelic as the filmmakes them out to be, the gist of the situation is probably captured accurately.

The sound is clean, but not elaborate. The disc has chapter markers and runs a full two hours, with the time codes on the sides running clear up to 59:59. The picture has many browns and other faded color schemes, and the disc maintains them without letting the colors shift or go fuzzy.

Many of the performances in the film are engaging, yet no one character or actor is emphasized. Sayles shifts smoothly between the details of the crime and the personalities of those involved. While the subject may hold the possibilities for many discussions and explorations, Sayles' team approach is most interested in giving an introductory overview – a summary of the events, the people, and the times.

8 MILLION WAYS TO DIE

Although *8 Million Ways to Die* gets off to a very promising start, it disintegrates without accomplishing anything. You can almost smell Jeff Bridges' performance as an alcoholic ex-detective who is hired to protect a nervous hooker. It is the most involving aspect of the movie, but every time his character sobers up, the plot becomes confused and incoherent. The picture has a strong orange tint in places. Otherwise, it is in good condition.

18 AGAIN

Another 'switching bodies' movie, *18 Again*, is actually one of the better offerings in the genre, though the world would not have been a poorer place if it had never appeared. George Burns manages to deviate slightly from his normal screen personality, which is a notable accomplishment, but he remains conveniently in a coma for most of the film while Charlie Schlatter, portraying his grandson-turned-alter-ego, does all the work. The sound is passable and the picture transfer is above average.

THE EIGHTH VAN CLIBURN INTERNATIONAL PIANO COMPETITION

That the same sheet music on the same piano can be played in an infinite number of ways without deviating from the written score is one of the most difficult concepts to communicate to those who have no direct experience with manipulating the instrument. *The Eighth Van Cliburn International Piano Competition*, actually a film entitled 'Here to Make Music,' comes a long way in explaining just how these differences can be manifested. The film is a documentary about the 1989 competition. It briskly follows the experiences of the different competitors and is thorough enough that a camera is almost always pointing at the right face at the right time. The musical passages on the disc are abridged, but there is still a lot of piano playing, filmed in closeup, and the variety in approaches which the young competitors use is the primary focus of the program.

After the documentary is ended, the 110-minute disc includes three longer musical sequences, one each from the three finalists. It is an important addition to the disc which increases its viability as a music title. The stereo sound is effectively employed, and the picture is vivid.

84 CHARRING CROSS ROAD

84 Charring Cross Road is for the little old lady in all of us. As a novel, it is a collection 'letters' between an American woman and a London bookseller. As a movie it is the same thing. The narration of the letters is read in voice-over while the film depicts, with some added dialog, the lives of the characters, living through three decades on two continents and never meeting. It is as exciting as a tea biscuit, but it is also as perfectly designed. Nothing happens, the attempts by the filmmakers to evoke the post-War period in London and New York are only partially successful, and significant gaps remain in an understanding of the psychology of the characters. Yet, what is presented is affectionate and good-willed, and one can't help feeling friendly towards it. Both the picture quality and the sound are okay.

'84 24 HEURES DU MANS MERCEDES BENZ 100 YEARS 1886-1986

The 24-hour road race at Le Mans (1984) has been consolidated onto *'84 24 Heures du Mans*. Impressions of the race captured with different photographic styles and angles are accompanied by nondescript pop instrumentals. Occasionally the sounds of the race itself are heard, in stereo, but the CAV disc would not be good for much were it not for a single, thrilling segment, where the camera is placed next to the helmet of a driver as he takes one of the vehicles out for a spin. At the end of the disc the race standings are posted, in English, on still frame. A map of the course, also in English, is printed on an insert.

THE EIGER SANCTION

The popularity of the first best seller from the author, 'Trevanian,' *The Eiger Sanction*, probably surprised him as much as anybody. The book itself is full of little jokes – men walking into lamp posts, characters with sophomorically suggestive names – and is the sort of effort no one would take seriously. Although the script for the film, which Clint Eastwood directed, cleaned up the worst of it and made the whole project more serious than it was intended to be, much of the humor remains. It is awful. Jokes so universally demeaning it is a wonder there is anyone left to laugh at them. Yet the movie is admirable, primarily because of the fantastic climbing scenes, which are superbly integrated with the inserts. Eastwood starts out nervous, as if he didn't understand off-color jokes, but by the end of the movie he discovers his character's persona, a wise-cracking, above-the-fray, tough guy. The film is not the work of a lazy star. He grows in it, as if the conditioning his character goes through worked on him, as well.

The colors have the same, cheap Universal look which they had the day the movie came out. The transfer is excellent even if the film stock doesn't deserve it. The sound is even better. Although the program is monaural, the sound has been digitally encoded. This prevents deterioration and calls attention to a rare pre-*Jaws* score by John Williams.

The film runs ten minutes over two hours and side three has been done in CAV. This is where the most dramatic climbing scenes can be found, and still frame manipulation produces perfect images. You can even see the reflection of the camera crew in the shiny hats the climbers wear. The trailer for the film is also included, and has its own chapter stop on side three. The trailer is letterboxed.

EL AMOR BRUJO
(see **BLOOD WEDDING**)

EL DORADO

We knew about westerns from the moment we were old enough to keep our head steady while the television was on, but we didn't develop a heart-pounding, Cupid's arrow infatuation for the genre until we happened to see Howard Hawks' *El Dorado* in the late sixties on the bottom half of a Saturday matinée double bill. This was long before we knew who Hawks was, or cared, but the film seized us instantly in conceptual terms – this was a *western* – while at the same time it entertained the daylights out of us. We could really see how the western genre format created the situations and the rules, so that all the filmmakers had to do was plug the characters in and keep the plot moving to create entertainment. And boy, with Leigh Brackett writing the script and John Wayne, Robert Mitchum, James Caan, Christopher George, and Ed Asner, to mention just a few, acting in it, did they get plot and characters!

We offer these personal reminiscences in order to bear witness for *El Dorado*. The picture transfer is precious. Since the movie was not a widescreen effort there is no compromise in the image presentation to prevent the viewer from appreciating the film. The colors are gorgeous and the fleshtones are perfect. The set designers occasionally plant brightly colored fabric or objects in the back of a set, and whatever function the items are providing (they tend to liven up longer conversations) is fully realized on the disc presentation. The image sharpness is a little on the soft side. The disc is digitally encoded monaural, but the audio is extremely vivid – better than all but the most sophisticated monaural sound transfers – and has terrific atmosphere. You can hear the dialog overdubs, but the jingle in John Wayne's spurs are also ever-present.

The film runs six minutes over two hours and Paramount could have found more logical side breaks than the ones they have utilized, but that is the nearest the disc comes to imperfection. *El Dorado* has vague similarities to Hawks' more highly respected 'Rio Bravo' and is often dismissed by critics because of this. There are enough mythological archetypes in the film to pass the initial rungs of serious analysis, and too few universal themes to make it much further. But *El Dorado* is a perfect movie, not because it lacks flaws, but because it is able to supersede them. In prioritizing the gathering and pacing of the talent, Hawks created a film which is not just great fun, but one which teaches you, by example, how to relax and enjoy not just westerns, but every movie you see.

ELECTRA GLIDE IN BLUE

Electra Glide in Blue which scandalized pre-MTV critics with its (tame by today's standards) stylized visuals, has little to offer today's viewers as a scanned and cropped title. The opening and closing sequences on the disc are squeezed and the remainder is cropped, removing much of the film's impact. All that is left is the weakly executed narrative about an Arizona motorcycle cop (Robert Blake) whose career ambitions are sparked when a murder occurs on his beat. The film's ending is a deliberate twist on *Easy Rider*, a movie the film wanted desperately to be better than. In terms of style, *Easy Rider* was king, but *Electra Glide in Blue* begat kings.

The disc's picture is generally grainy, although the many daylight outdoor sequences survive without difficulty. The film's sound was stereophonic, but the sound editing is not elaborate and the music is overproduced. So was the ad campaign, appropriately resurrected on the jacket cover, which mystified a lot more potential viewers than it attracted.

ELECTRIC BOOGALOO BREAKIN' 2

Anyone who thinks that they don't make musicals the way they used to is advised to check out *Electric Boogaloo Breakin' 2*. Oh sure, the music is loud (the stereo on the disc is terrific) and you can't always understand the lyrics, and if Mickey Rooney and Judy Garland were doing their thing today this probably wouldn't be it, but the plot and spirit is the same and the film is as popular with young people today as other musicals were in another time. To save a community center from being torn down, the kids put on a show. The plot seems so universally appealing you wonder why it hasn't been discovered in Sumerian texts.

ELECTRIC DREAMS

The stereo on *Electric Dreams* is full of fun little beeps and tones, popping out every which way. The picture, a bit on the blurry side, is less satisfying. The story never had a target audience. Since it is about an architect who falls in love with the woman living in the apartment above him, children did not identify with it. Since the architect's home computer suddenly develops a consciousness, unlimited power, and a crush on the same woman, adults found it difficult to accept. We found the fantasy to be uninspiring and the humor intermittent.

THE ELECTRIC V. THOMAS WILBRANDT

One of the most impressive conceptual videos we have seen, *The Electric V. Thomas Wilbrandt*, is subtitled 'the four seasons variations.' The picture transfer is perfect, and the disc has a strong potential as a demonstration piece.

Wilbrandt uses Antonio Vivaldi's 'The Four Seasons' as his foundation, conducting the Philharmonia Orchestra. The orchestral rendition, however, is continually interrupted by digressions involving sound effects and synthesizers. The disc's stereo sound packs a wallop – the volume is set higher than average. If you heard Wilbrandt's rendition of 'Seasons' without seeing his images you would probably dismiss it as trite, a failed attempt to breathe technological vitality into an over used musical piece. The images, however, are stunning. Wilbrandt is so successful at turning the video into part of his orchestration that is unfair to judge the music without it.

The images not only change to the rhythm of the music, they follow, in repetition and variation, the music's patterns. Recognizable objects are fleeting. Many appear just long enough to register an association with the appropriate season (the disc runs 90 minutes with 'Spring' and 'Summer' on side one and 'Autumn' and 'Winter' on side two). Like Vivaldi's music, Wilbrandt's emphasis on the seasons is more emotional than physical. He uses an incredible array of video manipulation techniques to change and twist the images. At times the screen divides so that different portions can be synchronized with different instruments or melody lines. Like the music again, a single image is often reconstituted in a number of different ways. Wilbrandt creates new images for some passages, but there are also patterns and ideas which he deliberately repeats throughout the program. The disc is simply a barrage of colorful video effects tightly coordinated with music, but for 90 minutes it is a tour de force performance which is utterly captivating.

ELEKTRA – RICHARD STRAUSS

Pioneer has released the Metropolitan Opera production of *Elektra – Richard Strauss* in a sleeve jacket instead of a box. Accompanying the disc is a nice booklet containing a libretto, a decent essay about the opera's composition, and a plot synopsis with cross-references to the chapter encoding. The production was video taped in 1980 and the picture has a mildly worn appearance, although the images are still vivid.

The presentation differs from the London release, *Richard Strauss Electra*, in that it is a live event. The singers aren't miked consistently and are at the mercy of mishaps. To appreciate the opera, the London version is preferable, but fans will be interested in the Met version for several reasons. It stars Birgit Nilsson, who is past her prime for singing the part, but still displays the sort of command which enables stars to hold onto their audiences even as their abilities decline. Leonie Rysanek, Mignon Dunn and Donald McIntyre also appear. The digitally encoded sound has been accurately transferred. The recording is truly live, and is of more value as a record of the afternoon (it was a matinée) than as a recording of music.

The single-act production is difficult to break apart for side changes. Pioneer has done a better job than London in that regard, but the optimal point has yet to be found. The Met staging is simple but effective and maintains a mood conducive to the experimental abstractness of Strauss' work.

ELENI

Steve Tesich took a marvelously cinematic true story about a man's search for his mother's murderer and turned it into an empty, literal screenplay. Although *Eleni* was directed by the normally reliable Peter Yates, the first half is almost embarrassingly lacking in subtlety. The filmmakers have tried so hard to tell what really happened during the Greek Civil War that they have forgotten the cardinal rule about letting audiences figure things out for themselves. The CX-encoded stereo is nice, but the picture is grainy.

ELMER GANTRY

Elmer Gantry is based upon a famous novel which on one hand caused an uproar for muckraking revivalism but on the other hand did not go far enough in exposing the hypocrisy of the religion business. In the movie, starring Burt Lancaster and Jean Simmons, the real issues are beyond the scope of the characters, and out of reach for the filmmakers. The intention of the novel was to examine a peculiarly American institution to try and discover why it was accepted and why it was American. The shove-it-down-your-throat direction of Richard Brooks makes it difficult to digest. Glaring closeups and seedy goings on mislead the viewer and when it turns out that none of the characters are really bad, the dramatic plot twists unravel with a fizzle.

The flesh tones look as genuine as they would in fresh photographs. The sound is monaural and limited, but the print for the 1960 film looks good all the way through its two-and-a-half-hour running time.

ELTON JOHN – BREAKING HEARTS TOUR

A 54-minute concert in a large outdoor sports stadium is depicted in *Elton John – Breaking Hearts Tour* and includes many split screen effects along with plenty of decent closeups. Because it takes place during the day, the stage lights do not wash out the other colors and only a token amount of graininess is visible. The sound is of concert quality, blending the performers together to make audio stew.

ELTON JOHN LIVE IN AUSTRALIA

Side one of *Elton John Live in Australia* is aptly identified as 'Elton and Band,' while side two is called 'Elton and Orchestra.' The two may be separated by microns of aluminum and glue, but they are worlds apart in tolerability. The 'Band' section is a cacophonous live recording of Elton doing his umpteen hits for the umpteenth time. He's done it so often that he lies on the stage and reaches over his head to play his piano without missing a note. Some may think that is talent, but it looks like boredom to us.

On side two, however, Elton is accompanied by the Melbourne Symphony Orchestra and, since he rarely performs with 90-odd instruments backing him up, he takes more interest in his material. He also gets to do songs which he needs a full orchestra to do properly ('Sixty Years On,' etc.) and the sound recording, while not of studio quality, is sweeping and great fun.

The picture is acceptable. The stage production isn't lit for video and so the clarity varies depending upon the color of the lighting. The sound is digitally encoded. The analog track is not quite as consistent as the digital track, but it is usually sharp. According to the jacket cover, the show includes numbers which haven't appeared on other video renditions of John's Australian gig.

ELVIRA MADIGAN

The carefully photographed *Elvira Madigan* has been released by LumiVision in Swedish with small white English subtitles. The image has slight black bands at the top and bottom of the screen, but not enough to add to the image. The picture transfer is good. The lyrically hazy images look neither faded nor distorted. The colors are precise and the skin tones are perfect. LumiVision has fooled with the sound, turning it into processed stereo though the effect can easily be suppressed by isolating an audio channel. The film has the sort of vacant soundtrack (annoying Mozart score and all) where it really doesn't make much of a difference.

Some people like *Elvira Madigan* a lot, and they should obtain the disc forthwith. Others will think it hopelessly silly, and they are advised to obtain something else. The movie, based upon a real incident, depicts a pair of young lovers who abandon their responsibilities (the young man even goes AWOL) to walk through the fields and hold hands. It is like a 90-minute Clairol commercial. Even when the woman has exhausted her last coin and must eat berries and leaves to stave off hunger, she apparently has plenty of shampoo, for every strand of her silken blond hair is as fresh as the spring greenery she is munching upon. The film is respected because it is so extreme in its style, and the disc presents it well, but it is not for cynics or those who long for strategically placed cow droppings.

ELIVRA MISTRESS OF THE DARK

The surprisingly entertaining concoction, *Elvira Mistress of the Dark* stars the television hostess, Elvira. Both the picture and the sound are in good condition. The separation effects are sporadic, but the sound is free of major impurities. The colors are fresh and the night scenes are not distorted. The disc is also chapter encoded, without a guide.

Elvira's performance is no different than it would be during the introduction of a latenight movie on a local TV channel, but the script is witty and accommodating. The plot seems to anticipate viewer rejection and consistently mixes things around just enough to keep one's interest perked. The only cerebral effort required of the viewer is the interpretation of the many double entendres. Elvira plays 'Elvira,' herself, fired from the late show intro gig and ending up in a small Massachusetts town to collect an inheritance. There is also some well-executed special effects work.

ELVIS '56

Every concert and television appearance Elvis Presley made in 1956 is chronicled on *Elvis '56*. Presley's half dozen television performances are shown in total, the performances which catapulted him from a 'regional curiosity' to a national superstar in just 12 months. Wherever recorded sound exists but motion pictures do not, still photos are used to depict recording sessions, tours, and private moments. The year is presented on a month by month basis, as the narrator, Levon Helm, explains the entertainment industry politics and social atmosphere which Elvis shook, rattled, and rolled his way through.

The picture and sound on the disc are excellent. We were surprised that so many kinescoped television performances are available, but they look and sound terrific. The actual performance is always used on the soundtrack, so one hears different versions of several hits, but in all cases the recordings have been digitally remastered and the disc is digitally encoded. The result is a clear monaural sound which hasn't been heard since the day the recordings were made. The program is a full 60 minutes long and is relegated to a single side.

ELVIS – HIS 1968 COMEBACK SPECIAL
ELVIS – ALOHA FROM HAWAII

The picture on *Elvis – His 1968 Comeback Special* is so sharp that background reds, which normally blur out on discs with this kind of TV lighting, remain distinct no matter how dark the surrounding area becomes. The CX-encoded soundtrack has been electronically re-channelled for stereo.

Elvis, in this situation, is still skinny, and his songs have real energy. There are a few production numbers, reminiscent of *Jailhouse Rock*, only in color. There is a Gospel and a 'Gotta Dance'-type sequence, both over-choreographed but quite entertaining. Most of the program, however, features Elvis and a small backup group on a tiny stage, surrounded on four sides by an audience of enthusiastic, older fans. Elvis acts like a punk and he is enjoying himself. The feeling is contagious.

The importance of the *1968* disc is clear when one sees *Elvis – Aloha From Hawaii*, which was recorded just five years later. Elvis is in a large auditorium. He stands in the center of the stage and sings his songs slowly. When he wants to move to the edge to accept a lai from an adoring fan, he walks. His calm voice renders such tunes as 'What Now My Love' and 'I'm So Lonesome I Could Cry' beautifully, but when he tries to do 'Blue Suede Shoes' or 'Hound Dog,' he no longer has the spirit.

The picture is excellent. The genuine stereo is sporadic and not as effective here as the retouched sound was on the *1968* disc. The presentation also suffers from an overabundance of editing, an apparent attempt to compensate for the lack of movement on the stage.

ELVIS MEMORIES

Elvis Memories is a 48-minute hour TV show featuring interviews with people who knew Elvis and rare film clips from concerts, press conferences, and a wedding. Some of the material strains one's definition of relevancy. Elvis's dentist is interviewed ("He was always appreciative of anything you had done for him..."), as is his cook ("Vegetables – he liked stringed beans, creamed potatoes, sauerkraut..."). But as the individuals who knew him reminisce about his later years, they provide a real insight on his generosity and on the correct perspective with which one should view his career and his life. He himself is spaced-out and guarded in a couple of interviews, but very forthright and thoughtful in a couple others, particularly when he talks about the roots of his own music.

The clips are fairly ragged, but that is to be expected. There is more talking than singing and few numbers are played to their entirety, but for some people, anything about Elvis is worth collecting.

ELVIS ON TOUR

The 1972 effort, *Elvis on Tour*, shows Elvis before his figure ballooned and his manner declined, but the spark that one usually senses when a performer ignites an audience is gone. It is hard to understand why the audience is so ecstatic except that this is Elvis and he is singing and smiling and handing out scarves.

Part of the problem here is the film itself. Most of it is in widescreen format, but the picture is split in half or in thirds, a trick documentary filmmakers use when they have many hours of wonderful footage they wish to squeeze into a presentably brief frame of time.

Despite the border on the top and bottom of the screen, portions of the side panels are still clipped off, distorting the intended imagery. Glimpses of genuine excitement – at one point Elvis practices karate on the stage – speed by while the poor quality of the concert sound (in CX-encoded stereo) and the disorganized feel of the stage show prevent any real build-up of enthusiasm. The best parts of the film were made in a recording studio where the sound is better and there are fewer distractions. The high point is Elvis' rendition of 'Proud Mary.' He gives the song a little energy without being obnoxious, and makes the words sound like real poetry, as if he were actually lyricising about his own past. The same technique, however, fails miserably with 'I've Never Been to Spain.' He takes the nonsense lyrics and the bad rhymes too seriously.

ELVIS: ONE NIGHT WITH YOU

One of the strongest segments in the multiple part *Elvis – His 1986 Comeback Special* had Elvis and four other musicians playing acoustical guitars and singing to an intimate audience cuddled around a small square stage. Those segments represented the highlights of that session, but with Elvis being so popular it was decided that a larger portion of the concert, close to an hour's worth, could sustain an independent release.

Elvis: One Night with You is a single-sided disc. The picture is as clear as the image was in *Comeback Special*, and the stereo sound is digitally encoded. The stereo qualities are limited and the recording has some rough spots, but the value of the material excuses its shortcomings.

Elvis sings 14 numbers (each marked with a chapter), but some songs are repeated two or three times. He is relaxed and chatty, particularly in the beginning as he warms up both his audience and himself. The program is professionally edited and the footage which made it onto the *Comeback Special* is indiscernible, visually, from the material which did not. Elvis looks great, sounds terrific, and is captured right at the point of transition, where he still enjoys singing 'Lawdy Miss Clawdy' and is not quite ready to put his heart and soul into 'Memories.'

ELVIS: THE GREAT PERFORMANCES VOLUME ONE: CENTER STAGE
ELVIS: THE GREAT PERFORMANCES VOLUME TWO: THE MAN AND HIS MUSIC

The two discs, *Elvis: The Great Performances Volume One: Center Stage* and *Elvis: The Great Performances Volume Two: The Man and His Music*, are separate programs because they are too similar to be combined. Both span Elvis Presley's entire career and mix rare film clips with standard selections from his movies and television specials. The genuinely rare footage is amazing – shots of Elvis cavorting with Buddy Holly, shots from his stint in the army, shots at a roadside rest stop, shots of him cavorting with Liberace in his first Las Vegas appearance, the earliest motion footage of him known to exist, his first screen test, etc. One gets the feeling, however, that by simply dropping a clip from *Elvis His Comeback Special* or *Jailhouse Rock*, the most satisfying material could all have been squeezed onto one show. The narration also seems too cooperative with the Elvis Estate, and brushes past some of Elvis' thornier career decisions.

Despite the descriptive jacket text, there is really no thematic difference between the two programs. We found that *Volume One* held our attention a little better, but maybe it was because we watched it first. The picture and sound transfers are fine. The picture and sound quality of the program itself is more problematic. Although the movie clips look fairly good, the *Comeback Special* and *Hawaii* excerpts look inferior to the original versions available on disc. The sound seems weak on the lower end and is not as impressive as other Elvis documentaries have been. There are some stereo separations, but they are most often employed to fade out the music and fade in the narration. Buena Vista has chapter encoded the discs and provided decent listings on the jacket covers, but the chapters are usually placed well before the start of a song.

EMERALD FOREST

The surround effects on *Emerald Forest* sound terrific, but the picture looks as though jungle rot has set in. Speckles flicker through the night scenes like fireflies and the colors in the day scenes blend together in a blur, like camouflage.

Emerald Forest does not have the lyrical intensity of John Boorman's *Deliverance*, but it is a good story, like a tale told around a campfire. A young boy wanders away from his father at an Amazonian dam site and is kidnapped/adopted by an indigenous aboriginal tribe who call themselves 'The Invisible People.' The father does not find the boy until years and nuptials have gone by, but the boy must eventually call on his past for assistance in battling a rival tribe ('The Fierce People') and civilization.

EMERSON, LAKE & PALMER PICTURES AT AN EXHIBITION

Emerson, Lake & Palmer's useless rendition of Mussorgsky's 'Pictures at an Exhibition' is presented in a single 42-minute concert performance on *Emerson, Lake & Palmer Pictures at an Exhibition*.

Unless you used to make out while the LP was on and are searching to reclaim your lost youth, the disc will have little to offer. The very concept of three overaged men in tight pants crunching out Mussorgsky rock 'n roll on electronic instruments is giggle-inducing. The program itself is amusingly inept. The video director is constantly shooting the band members from the wrong angle, obscuring their activities, and cutting to something important just as it is ending. Then there are some silly video effects which appear just when you wonder how more stupid the show could become.

The picture comes from a video tape source and is passable but not pristine. The image is soft, and strong colors tend to blur. The sound is gross in a live, unengineered sort of way. The stereo does provide a full range of tones, from cat-frightening trebles to dish-breaking basses, but only the drummer seems to be in pitch.

THE EMISSARY

A South African film, *The Emissary*, pretends to be about American and Russian spies, though why they are running around Cape Town is never completely explained. Few of the Americans have convincing accents and a gratuitous curse is directed at the one black cast member. That's South Africa, for you. The plot concerns the blackmailing of a diplomat's wife. The mechanics are elaborate, but there are no surprise turns and very few interesting action sequences. The picture is decent, but the stereo-enhanced sound remained monaural so far as we could tell.

THE EMPEROR AND THE NIGHTINGALE (see PECOS BILL)

EMPIRE OF THE SUN
EMPIRE OF THE SUN/THE CHINA ODYSSEY

Steven Spielberg's splendid World War II adventure, *Empire of the Sun*, was released in two different manifestations. Fans who are carefree with their laser disc budgets may wish to purchase both versions, because each has something unique to offer. *Empire of the Sun/The China Odyssey* is a four-sided CLV disc which comes in an attractive gatefold jacket. The 153-minute film is contained on the first three sides and 'China Odyssey,' a 50-minute documentary about the filming of *Empire*, appears on side four. The alternate offering, *Empire of the Sun*, is a six-sided CAV disc which comes in the most poorly designed slip jacket we have ever seen. As soon as it is opened, the discs will never properly fit inside it again. The CAV disc does not include the documentary. Why would one want the second package, particularly when many consider the CAV format to be obsolete? The CLV disc looks terrific, but sub-consciously throughout and consciously often enough, the CAV disc looks better. Noticeable advantages to the CAV presentation include more observable details within shadows, sharper lines and edges, and less blur around strong reds or oranges.

Both discs are digitally encoded, both have the same chapter markers (and side breaks – with one side on the CLV disc equalling one platter on the CAV), and both are letterboxed. The difference in audio tracks between the two discs is negligible. From the opening boy's choir, to the explosions, the crowds, and the creaking silence of loneliness, the stereo editing is so much better than in most movies that any subsequent disc you may decide to run, even the following day, will seem inadequate.

The CAV disc has two unsteady frames out of every five. The uses of the CAV functions are obvious, as Spielberg's command of his craft invites analysis on a frame-by-frame basis.

'China Odyssey' has undergone a decent transfer, though it did not receive the same attentiveness that *Empire* enjoyed. The documentary is narrated by Martin Sheen, though an interview with J.G. Ballard, the author of the book upon which the movie was based, is also used extensively in voice-over. The program provides important historical data for those who are unfamiliar with the circumstances the film is depicting, particularly the complicated status of Shanghai's 'International Settlement' before Pearl Harbor. There is also plenty of footage of Spielberg doing his thing. The documentary has one substantial misrepresentation however – it vaguely implies that the entire film, rather than simply the downtown Shanghai sequences, was filmed in China – and this makes the relaxed and cheerful labor-of-love work atmosphere circumspect. The documentary, however, will assist the viewer in comprehending the themes that Ballard and Spielberg wanted to convey, the themes of bonding, separation and maturity.

A few decades from now people will no longer have axes to grind and will appreciate the movies of Steven Spielberg for what they are – brilliant, moving, astoundingly adept entertainment. *Empire of the Sun* is the perfect boy's adventure. Watch it when you are young, and you will wish you could be the hero in the film. Watch it when you are old, and you will wish the hero was your own child. We don't understand why our friends argue that the movie fails because only one character is fully developed, or the last third is slow, or the film is derivative of other movies. Set in an exotic locale and filled with continuous tension, the movie elaborately depicts an internment camp and the modifications to everyday living which internment created, and then concludes with three emotional crescendos – an air raid, the atom bomb, and a reunion. That most films cannot manage the emotional impact of any one of these sequences is hardly the point. *Empire of the Sun* is so abundant in feeling, excitement and adventure that Warner's ill-fitting CAV jacket may be an appropriate representation of the disc after all. It is bursting with entertainment.

THE EMPIRE STRIKES BACK
(see **STAR WARS**)

ENCYCLOPEDIA OF ANIMALS VOLUME 1 MAMMALS 1
ENCYCLOPEDIA OF ANIMALS VOLUME 2 MAMMALS 2
ENCYCLOPEDIA OF ANIMALS VOLUME 3 MAMMALS 3
ENCYCLOPEDIA OF ANIMALS VOLUME 4 BIRDS 1
ENCYCLOPEDIA OF ANIMALS VOLUME 5 BIRDS 2
ENCYCLOPEDIA OF ANIMALS VOLUME 6 REPTILES AND AMPHIBIANS
ENCYCLOPEDIA OF ANIMALS VOLUME 7 INSECTS AND SPIDERS
ENCYCLOPEDIA OF ANIMALS VOLUME 8 FISH AND I NVERTEBRATES

Each *Encyclopedia of Animals* disc is supplemented by a text booklet which provides an excellent introduction to the video material. For *Volume 6 Reptiles and Amphibians*, introductory text discusses the attributes of both the reptile and amphibian classes, and then describes each order in detail. Following the introduction, there is a listing of each family within each order, along with vital statistics such as distribution, egg-laying habits, size, etc. At least one species from each family is represented on the disc, and sometimes several species appear. The text provides more vital statistics for the represented specie, as well as the chapter marker where the video material can be found. The booklets also contain suggestions for further reading and suggestions for further viewing. In the latter category, for example, the listing on *Reptiles and Amphibians* includes the *National Geographic Video – Realm of the Alligator*.

The video segments vary in length but average 45 seconds each. The two-sided CAV *Reptiles and Amphibians*, for example, has 70 chapter markers. The segments, while displaying specific species, show different functions, so that one segment might be about egg laying, while another concentrates on feeding. Each disc also contains a brief still step section in front of each side, which summarizes the chapters, provides location/distribution maps and gives a representation of the size of various species in relation to a human.

Narration is limited to one audio track on the disc so that, when suppressed, only environmental sounds or the sounds made by the creatures themselves can be heard. Some of this material is obviously dubbed, but it is still effective. The narration, by Barry Cooper, doesn't try to cover everything, and would be a little frustrating if the material in the booklet were not also available. Like all encyclopedias, the discs don't so much encompass knowledge as they do summarize it, and provide the pathways for further research.

The star of *Reptiles and Amphibians* is the tuatara, a reptile which is in an order by itself, can only be found on some islands off New Zealand. The creature makes of a habit of keeping a bird as a roommate, has no male genitalia, lives to be 120 years old, and has probably survived since the age of the dinosaurs. There must be a message there somewhere. Other highlights include a chameleon with a suction pump tongue which it spits out a full body length to grab a nearby insect, a Nietzschean march to the sea by a group of baby turtles as they are picked off by predators until only a hardy few remain, and a parrot snake, which, except for its cute little beady eyes, looks exactly like a tree vine.

The chapters may vary in terms of video source material, but the standard of quality is decent. Slow motion photography and even X-ray photography are used to depict different activities. Pioneer's admirable warning, "Some segments will not provide a complete still picture," is present on every disc, but it is hardly necessary, since we never came across a segment which did not give us satisfaction on a frame by frame basis. The sound is more problematic, as hums, hisses, and other distortions come and go with each animal. The dual audio disc is not CX-encoded.

The first time we put on *Encyclopedia of Animals Volume 4 Birds 1* (it is subtitled 'Ostriches Penguins Birds of Prey Cranes and Others'), we left the narration off. Along with everything else, it makes a nice environmental disc and a viewer can become very caught up in the calls of the different species. After listening to everything from pelicans to eagles, one realizes the turkey's 'gobble, gobble, gobble,' has an unmatched timbre and nobility.

The text booklet for *Birds 1* goes into great detail about wings, bills, feathers, etc., noting, among other things, that the bone marrow in an embryo is reabsorbed after its work is done, so that the skeleton remains hollow and light.

The disc's subdivisions are similar to those of *Reptiles and Amphibians*. The disc has 111 chapters and follows a format which is also similar to the other disc, so that some birds are seen eating, others hunting, and others taking care of their young. You get a sense from the disc, particularly when the narration is turned off, of how artistically birds use the air. They dip and soar and land and take off with a quick flutter or a slight bend this way and that.

A brief survey of the history of science will reveal that its process is usually divided into two sequential activities, classification and research. The only point at which research becomes truly valuable is after the classifications are completed and understood. Classification is the essence of the *Encyclopedia of Animals* discs. While it took naturalists hundreds of years and strained the limits of Latin, it is now all there, on 8 discs, for anyone to browse and observe in the comfort of their own home.

Volume 1 Mammals 1 has the subtitle, 'Carnivores and Sea Mammals,' and covers cats, dogs, bears, badgers, seals, whales, and the like. As with the previous discs, at least one species from each family (the sub-grouping of an order) is represented.

We were disappointed with only one aspect of the disc. As with the other *Encyclopedia* efforts, *Mammals 1* has dual audio, so the narration can appear on one track and sound effects can be isolated on the other. Unfortunately, the sound effects are just that – wind blowing, crickets chirping, and not a lion's roar nor a whale's song to be heard.

Other than that, the disc is another impressive effort in compiling the world's fauna onto laser disc. Again, as with the other discs, the accompanying booklet adds immeasurably to the value of the package. The disc itself has 72 chapters. The best sequences include one of the better slow-motion depictions of running cheetahs we have seen, the contours of their bodies looking like those of athletes in heavy training, and narwhals jousting with each other using their huge singular tusks. CAV features provide a closer examination of inspired, mammalian activities, such as the way in which a sea otter lazily places a rock on his tummy and smacks a clam shell against it, all the while doing a back float and catching some sun.

Volume 2 Mammals 2 covers herbivores. The disc covers elephants, hippos, zebras, giraffes, deer, buffalo, oxen, rodents, rabbits, and an unclassifiable curiosity, the elephant shrew. Among the more interesting footage is a depiction of the normally docile hippopotamus in a fierce territorial battle, an aardvark who manages to free himself from the jaws of a lion, and a hamster who refuses to let a polecat remain in his burrow. The program is informative and does a good job showing how herbivorous mammals fit into the earth's ecology.

Volume 3 Mammals 3 is subheaded 'Primates and Others,' the 'others' generally being bats, moles, and marsupials. Man is not included in the primate segment save for a brief mention in the text of the accompanying booklet. The material covering gorillas, chimpanzees, macaques and the like is fairly common. They are seen creating tools and passing culture along to their young. More interesting are the intriguing-looking tamarins of Brazil, and the manner in which monkeys with very long tails and monkeys with no tails at all have both adapted to life in the trees – what was it that caused one species' tail to disappear and the other's to elongate, when both appear to perform the same acrobatic feats?

The highlight of the disc is rare footage from the 1930s of the now (presumed) extinct Tasmanian wolf, a marsupial with strong canine features. The disc also provides delicious views of vampire bats feeding on unsuspecting livestock and shows how a mole digs through the earth. An explanation for the sloth's lethargy is also provided – the animal eats food of so little nutritional value that its body must conserve its metabolism. Those who live on junk food should take note.

Although the disc has dual-audio tracks, specific animal sounds are rarely included. Moles don't make much noise, anyway. The footage, which comes from many sources, generally looks aged, making the CAV functions more difficult to utilize effectively.

Dual-audio is far more useful on *Volume 5 Birds 2*, since a healthy number of actual calls make it onto the soundtrack. Eliminating the narrator in favor of the birds themselves can be a pleasure. *Birds 2* is subheaded 'Plovers – Woodpeckers – Passaerines and Others.' To be more specific, it covers gulls, terns, pigeons, parrots, cockatoos, owls, hummingbirds, cuckoos, wrens, sparrows, finches, bowerbirds, birds of paradise, the crow, and the jay.

Although varied, the footage is in fairly good shape, and the CAV functions can be useful in analyzing flight or freezing a lyrebird in full plumage. As the disc progresses through different species, it also shows different functions, from building a nest to catching food, so that the concept of life as a bird is communicated along with the fabulous variety of styles which that life can take on.

The coverage of fishes on *Volume 8* is particularly lackluster. A viewer fails to get a real sense of how a fish operates, and spawning is the only activity which is given more than a cursory illustration. Conversely, the coverage of invertebrates is highly comprehensive and informative. Did you know that a Portuguese man-of-war is actually made up of a dozen different animals, each performing a different function? The disc adeptly depicts evolutionary progress from the singular amoeba to the complex jellyfishes, anemones and worms. The creature which we found to be the most intriguing, however, was a sea slug which not only eats poisonous anemones, but collects and uses the poison for its own protection.

The coverage of insects on *Volume 7* is also enjoyable. Knowing that they can't even come close to cataloging every variety, the producers of the disc have opted instead for the most entertaining material. There is a depiction of a dragonfly hovering which has been filmed in slow motion so that with the CAV functions the exact movement of his wings can be plotted (the dragonfly's ancestors were the first creatures capable of flight).

After viewing the material, you will probably never wish to eat a fig again, knowing that both the fig wasp and the parasitic wasp, which feeds on the fig wasp, live inside. The former is actually a necessity for the fig's reproduction. Other revelations include the intriguing suggestion that ants practice both agriculture – collecting leaves in order to cultivate fungus – and domestication – keeping a small bug corralled so it will ward off predators and generate a form of honey for the ant colony. Also presented are the many adaptations spiders have developed to utilize their silk. Some spiders construct nets which they drop over their prey. Others lasso their prey and hog tie it, and some even construct 'bolas' to rope in their next meal.

END OF THE LINE

If the sight of a railroad train gives you a special little thrill, you might be interested in *End of the Line*, a warmhearted but inconsistent comedy. The movie has a loving attitude toward everything from railyards and dilapidated stations to diesel locomotives and model electric sets. The film is timidly conceived, so there are not as many trains in the movie as there is an affection for trains, but the appeal is deliberate.

End of the Line has a surprisingly large cast for an obscure film. Mary Steenburgen, Bob Balaban, Kevin Bacon, Holly Hunter, Rita Jenrette, Wilford Brimley, Levon Helm, Barbara Barrie, and Clint Howard all appear. Maybe they all liked trains, too. Some of the stereo sound is fun, such as the hum inside the cab when the diesel engine is cruising. The picture quality is a little better than average, but the cinematography is a little worse. The story concerns the closing of a freight yard in a small Arkansas town. Two disgruntled workers hijack an engine and take it to Chicago to confront the rail company executives. Unfortunately, the film maintains an HO scale, as the scriptwriters were unable to establish a link between working on the railroad and the human condition.

ENEMIES, A LOVE STORY

We wish more Isaac Singer stories would get made into movies. They always provide a fresh point of view, often transporting a folktale to a modern setting, and introduce a collection of characters one is unlikely to meet anywhere else in fiction. *Enemies, A Love Story*, directed by Paul Mazursky, is a Singer story, and it has just a touch of fable to it, presenting a situation which is so unlikely that it has to be make-believe, yet seems so ordinary that one remains attentive to its lessons.

A description of the plot belittles the film, because it places undue emphasis on the story's mechanics, but, for the sake of memory, *Enemies* is about a writer who, in one form or another, is married to three women. It is set in New York shortly after World War II, and evokes the period nicely. Ron Silver, Angelica Huston, Lena Olin and Margaret Sophie Stein star. The movie uses the awkward predicaments caused by the writer's infidelities to advance the plot, but the reactions of the characters are never predictable. The viewer soon realizes that while the elements of farce may be present, as is a symbolic attempt split and compartmentalize the concept of marriage, the movie is really an attempt to isolate the values of life which are permanent from those which are fleeting.

The film has an intentionally nostalgic look, but the picture is badly colored, grainy, and cropped. The image also jiggles occasionally. The stereo surround sound is a little better, although the potential for a dynamic audio channel is limited.

ENEMY MINE

Before they even fired the first director, *Enemy Mine* was marketed incorrectly. That's what happens when filmmakers think they have such a great plot twist they've got to keep it a secret. You end up hearing about the baby in the reviews or word of mouth, but you don't hear that he grows up, gets captured by some bad guys, and then gets rescued. The movie may be kind of silly, but it is not as stodgy as it sounded when the publicity department was keeping the lid on the plot.

The picture on the disc is passable, but the sound mix is uninteresting.

ENERGY TRANSFORMATION USING THE BICYCLE

Some educational discs are suitable, in one way or another, to teach first-graders through college undergraduates. In *Energy Transformation Using the Bicycle*, however, the instruction and exploration are for calculus and physics students only.

Although *Energy Transformation* is intended to be used with a computer-controlled disc player, it can be understood and is perfectly effective when operated through manual control. Accompanying the disc is an 'Instructor's Guide' and workbook which contain the minimum amount of information needed to conduct a lesson on one's own.

The disc program is a thorough deconstruction of the forces at work which enable bicycles to move, "with less energy expended than almost any other form of transportation by humans or animals." Four different types of bicycles are pedaled down inclines and past distance posts under different types of set conditions. By using the still frame advance, the user can time or count the revolutions of both the wheel and the chain on each bicycle. The application of certain physical formulas can then be employed to demonstrate the bicycle's efficiency.

The disc features a clear CAV picture and institutional dual-channel sound.

THE ENFORCER

One of our favorite 'second tier' Humphrey Bogart films is *The Enforcer.* The film is fast-paced and lasts less than 90 minutes. The picture transfer is very good. The black and white image is very sharp, with rich, shiny blacks and carefully scaled greys. The source has no more than a handful of scratches or other markings, and its quality enhances one's attentiveness and pleasure. The soundtrack is generally acceptable, although the volume drops a bit low on one or two reels. The disc opens with an original theatrical trailer, and the disc jacket includes a shot of an original poster.

Bogart plays a D.A. following leads to build a case against a man running a murder-for-hire operation. Much of the film is told in flashback and flashback-within-flashback. The disc's crisp picture does wonders with the faces of the many character actors who show up in the film – Zero Mostel even had a pre-blacklist part – and increases the sweaty, dark, and intense mood that the filmmakers wanted to create. The film also has several inventive action scenes. Bogart's character has no life outside of his job and the movie has no far-reaching philosophies to impart, but if you're looking to kill a little time, you could do worse than hiring *The Enforcer.*

THE ENFORCER

Tyne Daly got her start in *The Enforcer.* Her performance is memorable, as it is difficult to differentiate the breathless eagerness of her character from the big break she's getting as an actress. The film's only gimmick, however, was to give Clint Eastwood's Dirty Harry a female partner. Unlike *Magnum Force*, which always seems to be taking place in the bright sunshine, much of *The Enforcer* is overcast, and so the picture on the disc comes out a little duller. It is a sloppy film, and the print has scratches in a couple of places. The reprocessed-for-stereo sound is awkward. The voices of characters standing to the left are thrown to the netherworlds of one's bookshelf.

EPHEMERAL FILMS
(see **TO NEW HORIZONS: EPHEMERAL FILMS 1931-1945)**

ERASERHEAD

Ostensibly, *Eraserhead* is the story of a man living in an icky apartment and caring for a noisy thing/baby which looks like a cross between ET and a leech. The fantastic apparitions which bob onto the screen whenever the man turns his head can be written off as part of the man's own imagination or can be accepted as really occurring. Viewer's choice. The point is that director, David Lynch, has sculptured these visions with precision. Even if a viewer rejects them in disgust, the effect is successful.

The disc originally suffered from severe manufacturing problems. The monaural sound is fairly scratchy. The film is in black-and-white and not all the shadings of grey can be discerned on a television. This is a film which ought to be presented in as best condition as possible to facilitate concentration. For those who pine for something out of the ordinary, *Eraserhead* is definitely worth acquiring. The opportunity to see a dream and then see it again is too rare to pass by.

ERIC CLAPTON AND FRIENDS

There are some good closeups of Eric Clapton's guitar playing in *Eric Clapton and Friends*, and some of Phil Collins on drums, but the image is softer. When the stage lights go red, so does the rest of the screen.

Collins' 'In the Air Tonight' is, surprisingly, the most captivating number in the set, despite competent renditions of 'White Room,' 'Layla,' and several other hits. The digitally encoded sound is acceptable but not exceptional. The disc is encoded with chapters which match the songs, identified without associated chapter numbers, on the back of the disc – except for 'Badge,' which makes an unlisted encore appearance at the end.

ERIC CLAPTON – LIVE NOW

Too much gloss spoils Eric Clapton, so it is just as well that *Eric Clapton – Live Now* has a grainy and fuzzy picture. The live recording is limited in range, and this, too, adds to Clapton's mystique. You feel as though you ought to be in a shack, or the backseat of a car, when you listen to his music, and a frayed laser disc matches those moods. The stage is not lit for video, but Clapton doesn't move around much, so the camera has no trouble focusing on his guitar playing.

ERIC CLAPTON – THE CREAM OF ERIC CLAPTON

A nice collection of video clips tracks Eric Clapton's performances from his early days with The Yardbirds to recent duets with Tina Turner *Eric Clapton – The Cream of Eric Clapton*. Eighteen songs are featured on the 75-minute disc, which contains no interruptions between numbers. The sound is genuine – monaural on some of the earlier pieces, stereo with surround applause on the later ones – and is quite vivid, although the performances are not as satisfying as the standard recordings. The clips vary in quality depending upon their age, but all remain mildly blurry. Those searching for closeups of Clapton's fingering, however, will not be disappointed.

ETERNAL EVIL

Eternal Evil lasts 85 minutes. It opens with a viewer-point-of-view astral projection, but it was raining the day the filmmakers leased the helicopter, so this is the first astral projection in the history of the cosmos to have streaks. After that, the movie gets better. The script is a variation on *The Hunger*, but it holds a viewer's attention and the hero's astral trips are diverting. The picture is blurry and the sound, weak-willed.

EUGENE ONEGIN
THE QUEEN OF SPADES

Two of Peter Tchaikovsky's best-known operas, *Eugene Onegin* and *The Queen of Spades*, made into films in Russia in the late fifties, have been released on disc by Corinth Video and Image. Each disc runs a little over 100 minutes and comes on a single platter. Both have flawed but generally satisfying picture transfers, at least when one takes into account the conditions under which the original productions were created. Both are in color, which looks soft, but genuine. Both have scratches, and passages involving very bad splices. On both there are white English subtitles which sometimes get lost in the background. The subtitles are sporadic, and often fail to fill in more than a summary of the lyric. The sound is monaural and is a product of its era, though we found moderate amplification to be satisfying. The singing, which is effective but never masterful, was originally dubbed, and the credits list both the actor and the singer for each character. There are hardly any sound effects or other embellishments. Both movies use some outdoor sequences but were made primarily in studio soundstages.

The two discs make a worthwhile double bill, but it is important that the *Queen of Spades* be watched first. In every way except chronology, *Onegin* is a more mature and accomplished work. Even the characters experience a more mature form of love and a more sophisticated moral conflict. Tchaikovsky's music for *Onegin* is superb, and in comparison *Spades* is less inspiring. The films reflect these differences as well.

The *Queen of Spades* movie has few inspired visual moments beyond some typical Russian closeups, and the ending, which has great cinematic potential, is rushed and slapdash, as if the filmmakers had one day to do the last ten minutes. *Onegin*, on the other hand, is consistently interesting to look at, even though the production is clearly under the same budgetary restraints as *Spades*. It is as if the increased complexity of Tchaikovsky's music motivated the filmmakers to increase the complexity of their camera angles. When viewed together, however, each film enhances the other's strengths. The movies are no replacement for a full-fledged operatic production, but they both have much to offer.

EUROPE THE FINAL COUNTDOWN WORLD TOUR

The picture is a little blurry on *Europe The Final Countdown World Tour*, but the stage lighting is accommodating to video and the show is bright and colorful. The stereo sound is consistently clear and the pliant metal band puts on a decent, hour long show.

EURYTHMICS – LIVE

The Eurythmics play a 90-minute concert on *Eurythmics – Live*. Except for a few impenetrable inserts, the concert is presented simply, but it is adeptly filmed and well lit. The use of film instead of videotape creates a slightly pale image, but it is made to look stylish and cannot be considered a flaw. Even the faint haze in the picture feels like part of the concept. The digitally encoded sound is decent, though it is a concert recording and hasn't the purity of the group's studio efforts. The disc has chapter markers for every number and Annie Lennox sings one of the songs in her underwear, which ought to attract a few extra fans to the disc.

AN EVENING WITH KIRI TE KANAWA

If Hollywood had seen Warren Mitchell perform excerpts from 'My Fair Lady' with Kiri Te Kanawa at the Royal Albert Hall, he'd be one of the hottest character actors working today. Mitchell's performance can be viewed on the two-sided *An Evening with Kiri Te Kanawa*. A depiction of what apparently was a single evening's concert, the disc is a combination of two BBC concert programs, each lasting close to an hour and containing both opening and closing credits. The picture quality has no significant flaws and the sound is free from noise. The sound mix from the orchestra could have used a stronger hand, however, as the trombones tend to bleat a little too independently on the right.

On side one Te Kanawa sings a few choice arias, from 'The Marriage of Figaro,' 'The Magic Flute,' 'Louise,' and so on. The London Symphony Orchestra, conducted by John Mauceri, also performs a Mozart overture and a suite of orchestral music from 'Carmen.' The acoustics in the cavernous hall work well for Te Kanawa, though her song selections are not daring and her performance is adequate rather than spellbinding.

The 'My Fair Lady' suite, on side two, also lasts an hour. Kanawa's performance is again passable. She has more polish and less emotion than Marni Nixon or Julie Andrews, and that was the concept behind the project to begin with. Jeremy Irons appears with her to perform the Henry Higgins numbers and he is either very nervous or lax in study because most of the time he reads and sings his lines without any real feeling for the words.

Mitchell, however, gives a definitive version of both 'With a Little Bit of Luck' and 'I'm Getting Married in the Morning,' stepping completely into character while remaining in tuxedo and tie. The audience goes wild – the only time they do in both programs – and deservedly so, because every inflection of every syllable not only has the right emotion and pitch, it is also matched by the appropriate permutation of his visage. For example, to look sneaky while singing the line, 'Wit' a little bit, wit' a little bit,' he hides his upper lip inside his mouth, covering it with his mustache while maintaining a grin, lowers his voice to an articulate mumble, and glances surreptitiously from side to side. The disc is worth acquiring for that one passage alone.

AN EVENING WITH PAUL ANKA

The sound on *An Evening with Paul Anka* has noise which was probably picked up during the live recording. The picture is fairly decent when Anka is bathed in white stage light, but the view gets blurry when red or blue mood lights take over the set. When Anka moves too quickly, a ghost image follows him.

We found his performance enthusiastic but bland. Even though he wrote 'My Way,' he doesn't accomplish the phrasing as well as Sid Vicious, let alone Frank Sinatra. In fact, an audience member comes up to sing a couple of bars, and even *he* does it with more feeling.

EVERY TIME WE SAY GOODBYE

Tom Hanks looks a little lost in *Every Time We Say Goodbye*. He plays an American RAF pilot, stationed in Jerusalem in 1942, who falls for a local girl. There is also a subplot involving another couple. The movie is a regional, locally financed effort – a production genre which transcends plots with a common set of attributes, such as the filmmakers feeling they have to provide a curt explanation of their culture, the utilization of the cheapest film stock and recording equipment available, and one American star eating up half their budget but justifying all of theirfinancing. Hanks can be an effective actor, and he even does some good work here when he actively mixes anger and romance, but he never conveys a sense of being war weary. The lousy photography has been transferred accurately and the poor sound has not been CX-encoded.

EVERY WHICH WAY BUT LOOSE
The curiously popular sequel to *Any Which Way You Can*, *Every Which Way but Loose*, provides a cogent argument in support of those who question the quality of mass tastes. The film, a pugilistic road comedy, is dopey. Since none of the scriptwriters are humorously inclined, and few of the cast members are true comedians, it is not all that funny, either. After a couple of viewings, the silliest passages can be anticipated and the tolerability level, thanks to the presence of Clint Eastwood and the orangutan, rises a little bit. Why anyone could possibly want to see the movie more than once is another matter. The artificial stereo sound is tolerable. Strong colors are slightly unstable and fleshtones look a bit too orange.

EVERYBODY'S ALL-AMERICAN
The makeup in *Everybody's All-American* is amazing. The things Dennis Quaid allowed Dick Smith to do to his appearance are startling – and a bit risky for someone trying to establish himself as a romantic superstar. The lasting image one has when the film is over (and it is worth noting that the end credit scroll tries very hard to compensate for this by rerunning earlier footage) is not the bedroom scenes but Quaid's bloated, messy face.

The film, which also stars Jessica Lange and Timothy Hutton (both of whom go through equally interesting, but far more flattering metamorphoses), is about a college football hero who is unable to adjust to a civilian life. The plot spans twenty five years and the script is adept at showing how relationships can blossom and change over time. The performances are all terrific and the movie, although much of the second act is an emotional downslide, is romantic and entertaining.

The picture transfer is generally passable, although flesh tones tend to look a bit on the pink side. The digitally encoded stereo sound is marvelous and the mix even throws some dialog to the surround track, a wonderfully eerie effect which is not used as often as it should be. Has the director, Taylor Hackford, ever made a film which ran under two hours? This one comes in at seven minutes above and is spread evenly to three sides.

EVIL DEAD (Import)
One of the hoariest gross-out films to come from a culture which is forever trying to outdo itself has become available on laser disc only by leaving the country and then coming back again through import. *Evil Dead*, a Japanese release, was made in the backwoods of Tennessee on a minuscule budget, but the terror sequences work as well or better than bigger-budgeted horror thrillers because the effects have been applied to an H.P. Lovecraft-type story about possession and demons. It is so unnerving that if you show the disc to guests, you would be well advised to make them sign releases first, absolving you of responsibility for their mental well-being.

The Japanese subtitles appear on the sides rather than at the bottom of the picture, switching from the left to the right somewhat randomly. The film looks cheap, of course, but the soundtrack contains many subtle demonic mutterings which were inaudible in a theatrical environment.

EVIL DEAD 2
The most gross/scary movie we know is *Evil Dead*. The sequel, *Evil Dead 2*, a return to the evil forest of possessed souls is more flagrantly amusing than the first effort was, it still is not the sort of disc one ought to keep in the summer cabin.

The movie, which has an especially clever ending, has many special effects and clearly enjoyed a budget exponentially larger than its predecessor. But while the first *Evil Dead* had but one purpose – frighten the viewer to the point of exhaustion – number *2* is a satire of the genre and a tease. The picture exhibits grain and fog, but the result is not inconsistent with the mood of the film. Although the sound is not CX-encoded, we were generally too nervous or horror stricken to pay much attention to its technical aspects. Much of the dialog is obviously dubbed in after the fact, but even this aspect ends up to be consistent with what happens to the characters, who start speaking in tongues as soon as you turn your back on them.

THE EVIL THAT MEN DO
Charles Bronson stars in *The Evil That Men Do*, a competent action picture directed by J. Lee Thompson. It is about a hit man who decides to rub out a torturer as a favor to the torture victims. The methodical way he closes in on the bad guy and the political overtones incorporated into the subject matter give the show a legitimacy which Bronson films often lack. The sound is monaural and not CX-encoded, but the mix is accomplished and worth routing through the hi-fi.

EVIL UNDER THE SUN
(see **DEATH ON THE NILE**)

THE EVOLUTIONARY SPIRAL WITH MUSIC BY WEATHER REPORT
The Evolutionary Spiral with Music by Weather Report is poorly transferred, from source material which appears a bit over used, and the sound lacks the clarity which the group, Weather Report, deserves. However, the 15-minute program, which features three chapter-encoded numbers, is pleasing and easy to tolerate. The visuals, vaguely providing an ideogrammatic history of astronomy, tolerate to some extent the graininess and imperfection of the image, since who is to know what true wild, spiraling colors were intended. The well-known fusion jazz group sounds like it is reading its music off of meteorological maps, but the result is that the disc can play through several times before you recognize a passage, and many more times before you tire of it.

EWOKS: THE BATTLE FOR ENDOR
(see **CARAVAN OF COURAGE – AN EWOK ADVENTURE**)

EXCALIBUR
The plot of *Excalibur* has the structure of a legend – episodic, meandering, sometimes fantastic and sometimes menial. It was compelling enough to be a hit movie, and is especially compelling now that it has been released on disc. The movie probably worked so well because, except for the quest of the Holy Grail segment, which could be written off as an hallucinogenic indulgence, the film concentrates the moral lessons of friendship, loyalty, etc. The director, John Boorman, has a mature love for the material. He just tells the story as if he had heard it somewhere else and was repeating the parts he liked the best.

The transfer is gorgeous, and the quality of the disc increases one's enjoyment of the film, because there are no impediments to involving the viewer. The film was made with a slight haze, which effectively transports one to the Dark Ages. On the disc you can see the haze, but you can also see through it, to the sharp focus and precise colors of the original film. The digital monaural sound is excellent, and creates a dimensional atmosphere without ever deviating from the central channel.

EXILE: LIVE IN CONCERT!
Only a handful of shots look grainy on *Exile: Live in Concert!* and most of the time each band member is lit brightly and vividly. The stereo sound is also energetic and captures the thrill of the concert without losing the music to distortion. The band is as much a rock group as a country group and their audience is young and boisterous. The concert lasts an hour.

THE EXORCIST
THE EXORCIST (Remastered)
The first theatrical release of *The Exorcist* was in monaural, but for an early reissue of the film, the director, William Friedkin, supervised a stereo re-mix of the soundtrack, and that is the version which appears on Warner's re-release. The old disc was monaural (it was also time-compressed onto a single platter) and the difference in sound quality and excitement between the two is startling. The analog sound on the old disc just sits there. The digital sound on the new release is everywhere, and there is no escaping the thrills it provides. When the girl, Regan, played by Linda Blair, develops a fit of possession, it sounds as if someone has started up a chainsaw. The sound has left and right directional elements, but uses the rear channel only for enhancing the loudest noises. The recording is old, and is heavily manipulated, so it is not as clean as the best contemporary soundtracks. But when Captain Howdy or Pizzuzzu or whoever starts raising hell, the sound grabs you as effectively as Regan grabs the psychiatrist.

The picture is also improved. The film still looks aged. There are speckles here and there, and the colors are soft, but the fleshtones look accurate, at least when they are supposed to, and the presentation is no longer alienating. The film was not a widescreen effort, and the essential part of the image is always on view.

Side three of the disc, from the point when

Max von Sydow reappears, is in CAV. Oh boy. There is her tongue in slow motion. There are subliminal flashes that can be frozen and analyzed. There is the levitation sped up to three times normal speed (watch Miller and Sydow move in unison), and there is the pea soup, which is best taken care of using reverse play. The head turning sequence we will leave to you.

It has been difficult to enjoy *The Exorcist* on home video in the past. We always thought it was because the film became dull after multiple viewings, but that is not the case at all, it was the transfer which was dull. Warner's new rendition will bring back the unnerving sense of excitement you felt the very first time you saw the movie.

EXOTIC PLANTS: A VIDEODISC COMPENDIUM

Priced for the educational market *Exotic Plants: A Videodisc Compendium* is an 8-inch disc contains nearly 4000 still frames displaying some 2000 photographs of exotic plants. Excepting a handful of photos where bright reds or pinks fill the screen, the quality of the still collection is well exhibited on laser disc. Subtle or wispy decorations of color on billowing petals are freely distinctive.

The pictures are initially grouped in alphabetical order by family. Most are then repeated in an alphabetical grouping by genus. Shorter groupings, such as habitat, common names, et cetera, also replay many of the stills. A user's guide of more than 100 pages provides the classification and occasional miscellaneous information about every plant depicted.

'Why Plants Flower,' a time lapse piece, is quite informative. A flower is shown in infrared – which is how a bee would see it – to reveal what appears to be a landing pattern guide from petal to pollen. Another segment, filmed at normal speed, shows a bee bobbing around a flower. Utilizing the CAV functions to examine the bee's routine was especially intriguing. The film has narration on one audio track and guitar music on the other.

THE EXPENDABLES

Only die-hard Vietnam genre fans will want *The Expendables*, a low-budget action picture. The image is pale and blurry. The sound is monaural and has almost no upper range, though it hardly seems to matter since much of the time the filmmakers neglect to put in sound effects. The plot, stuffed with clichés, concerns a squad of misfits who coerce long enough to chase after an escaped VC colonel. There is not a single scene in the entire film which has even an iota of realism to it, and even the gunfire is laughably phony. Nobody ever gets hit until it is time for them to get hit.

EXPERIMENT IN TERROR

The black-and-white print used for *Experiment in Terror* has no more than a few speckles. The contrast looks a bit soft, but few viewers should have any problems with it. The sound is also acceptable and there is a pre-commercialized Henry Mancini score.

Blake Edwards directed the Glenn Ford and Lee Remick film, about a woman who is the victim of an extortion plot. Ford plays an FBI man, back in the days before the Bureau had a tarnished image, and his efficiency and politeness almost induces a giggle now and then. The plot, however, always hooks us when we see it on TV, and the disc is no exception in that regard. Remick's character receives her first threat, cleverly manages to contact Ford, and the wheels are set in motion. There is no surprise ending, but by the time one gets to the conclusion the dramatic payoffs have already been profitable. Side three on the 123-minute disc runs under a half hour, but is in CLV.

EXPLORERS

The first pressing of *Explorers* did not contain a digitally encoded soundtrack, contrary to what appeared on the jacket cover. The 107-minute program was recalled and remastered, but copies of the first run may still be sitting in the bins here and there. No matter, the CX-encoded stereo on *Explorers* is excellent. The picture on this Special Home Video Version (with footage both added and subtracted) is pretty sharp as well.

The story is excellent science fiction, getting right to the heart of the conflict between the beautiful divinity of existence and the crazy randomness of culture. The spectacular visit to the alien's spacecraft is hurt considerably by cropping and reduction to a small screen. The aliens, who have implanted the diagrams for a workable space shuttle in the heads of some kids, revel in the peripatetic clutter they've captured on the television frequencies. If we ever do meet a civilization from another solar system, their aesthetics will probably be as absurd as ours are, which is the one insight the science fiction films from the '40s and '50s have over the ones from today. Dante's message is that only Earth has a Mr. Ed. He's wrong, but he tells his tale very well.

EXTREME PREJUDICE
DOUBLE BORDER (EXTREME PREJUDICE import)

Whenever the characters in *Extreme Prejudice* stand in the shadows you can't see their faces – the contrasts are too high – but otherwise the transfer is quite good. There are no distortions in the picture and nothing to interfere with one's enjoyment of the disc. The import version is mildly letterboxed and the domestic version is not, but the domestic version has a better picture transfer. The import is grainy and the colors are faded. The stereo sound is digitally encoded and in that the Japanese version is distinctly superior – the great scene near the end when 200 guns are cocked in unison doesn't quite have the same kick on the domestic disc. Once again, however, the American version is adequate and shouldn't disappoint anyone.

John Milius contributed to the script and he appears to have a thing for stories about men who have set up their own private empires. Walter Hill directed the film, and he has a thing for not explaining character motivations to his audience. Hence, Hill's movies are usually more entertaining on subsequent viewings, because it takes an initial runthrough to figure out what is going on. *Prejudice*, about a Texas Ranger, played by Nick Nolte, who finds himself in the middle of a treacherous drug battle, has all the action and witty macho posturing one needs for a slow afternoon, and when everything is over it doesn't matter if the characters were motivated or not – most of them are dead.

EXTREMITIES

Farrah Fawcett performed the same part on the stage that she now has on the screen in *Extremities*. The movie, by using tense close-ups for key moments of the drama, removes some of the attention from her, but you get the feeling that she is still acting even when you can only see her feet or her arm. The story, about a rape victim who manages to repel and hog tie her assailant, avoids the severe gratuitousness of properties like *Last House on the Left*, but it is single-threaded and has no subplots. The disc is 89 minutes long and once the idea is put forward – will the victim pass judgement on her attacker? – few variations of approach are offered. The picture and sound are acceptable.

THE EYE HEARS THE EAR SEES

The Eye Hears The Ear Sees contains enough excerpts from Norman McLaren's short films (a few are shown in full) to stand on its own as a collector's item.

The program was made in 1989, but the film stock used for the interviews with McLaren is worn down and makes the show look much older. The full scope of McLaren's career is covered and his methodologies are demonstrated, so that the viewer can see how his most well-known films and film styles were created. Among the shorts given extensive attention are 'Neighbors,' 'Hen Hop,' 'Fiddle-De-Dee,' 'La Poulette Grise,' 'Blinkity Blank,' 'Spheres,' 'Mosaic,' 'Striations,' and the lovely 'Pas de Deux.' Samples of the works by artists who influenced McLaren, Emil Cohl and Len Lye, are also provided.

The picture quality is at the mercy of the original production materials, but McLaren's films come through okay. The sound is also a little rough, due to the nature of the source. We shall refrain from developing an extensive essay to the theme of 'Norman McLaren is to Canada as Tex Avery is to the United States,' although the thought does present itself on more than one occasion during the course of the documentary. McLaren's artistry and inventiveness are undeniable, but so is the suspicion that he may never have gotten away with the career he has had if he had been forced to operate in a more competitive environment.

EYE OF THE DRAGON (Import)

Eye of the Dragon is a Chinese martial arts film dubbed (without a second audio track) in Japanese. It was also the first full-fledged, full-length feature film to be released on laser disc in 3-D. Packed in the jacket with the disc are two cardboard glasses with red cellophane for the left eye and blue cellophane for the right.

We darkened the lights in our living room, upped the contrast a bit on our TV, held the glasses to our eyes, and started the disc. After a lengthy and incomprehensible series of written, onscreen, Japanese instructions for adjusting one's TV set, the movie began, opening on a furious fight involving a dozen people and an equal number of wooden poles. The poles quickly provided proof of the 3-D effect as various assailants thrust and swung at one another. Suddenly, a man standing in the back took a pole and threw it like a javelin, straight at the screen. We swear that we screamed and dove for the floor.

The story, as best as we could make out, is about treachery in a provincial fief where a lord attempts to regain his rightful place in a palace by usurping an imposter with the assistance of a ragged group of outcasts. Dialog in movies like this is irrelevant anyway, and certainly if the concept of the disc appeals to you, you should not let the language barrier be an impediment. As an added treat, the film is letterboxed.

It took us an hour or so of fiddling and adjusting to get our TV to obtain the full, astonishing impact of the effects. We also found that the show looked the best when we combined *both* glasses. When we finally got this combination working, we were surprised to find that the movie was in color. Only bright, basic colors were discernible and subtleties in hue were out of the question, but it was all there.

The picture is in pretty bad shape. Side one of the copy we viewed was in a constant state of speckling throughout, and the print on both sides had breaks and scratches. The monaural sound was lackluster.

EYE OF THE NEEDLE (Import)

The wonderful adaptation of the Ken Follett story, *Eye of the Needle*, is available in Japan. The picture takes up the whole screen and is awash with Japanese subtitles. The print is a little ripe and has a scratch here and there, although other parts of it look very nice.

The plot is a mindless best-selling thriller which has no unusual plot twists and telescopes its ending almost from the opening scenes. But the movie, directed by Richard Marquand and scored by Miklos Rozsa, is an elegant, classically-styled exposition of story, character, eroticism, and conflict. The first three-quarters of the film, which takes place during World War II, is about a Nazi spy attempting to sneak out of England. The last quarter, in which the spy meets the heroine and has an affair with her, is timed and played so carefully that the emotions surprise viewers who have been lulled into expecting nothing but action. Movies like this are usually inept when bedrooms are involved, but Marquand shows the same discreet care for lovemaking that he shows for murder. The ending is so exciting you even stop eating popcorn until it is over.

EYES OF FIRE

Eyes of Fire, takes place in pre-Revolutionary War America, 1750 to be exact, in the wilderness. The film's premise is a confrontation with the occult, and it is a pleasing concept, because it merges a modern-day American horror genre with memories of 'Sleepy Hollow' and 'Young Goodman Brown.'

The film has a cheap look to it, but this helps a viewer's mind stay in period, the way a glossy, expensive movie (such as *Revolution*) often does not. The transfer looks excellent, under the circumstances. The sound is monaural and has not been CX-encoded. It is a little noisy.

Most of the actors and actresses speak with legitimate Scotch-Irish accents, and the Indians sound as if they're really talking Shawnee. The dialog never seems out of place and has moments of real wit ("Why in Heaven's, man, are we bringing all these ducks?") The ending could have been thought out a little more clearly, but in general the script, about a group of settlers trapped in a valley controlled by the Devil, is effective. The disc is creepy, and the perfect choice if you ever set your player up at a campfire.

THE EYES WITHOUT A FACE

A wonderfully macabre black-and-white French horror film, *The Eyes Without a Face* is about a doctor who kidnaps young women and removes the skin from their faces, attempting to graft the tissue onto his disfigured daughter. Although a little too languorously moody, the movie is as enjoyable as any other black-and-white horror film and is especially entertaining when viewed with a spirited group of friends. The picture is soft but appears to be in acceptable condition. The image is very slightly letterboxed – it may not even show up on some monitors – and English subtitles, which are easy to follow, appear on the picture. The sound is a little weak, but it features a rare fifties score by Maurice Jarre which he later adapted as a sub-motif in *Doctor Zhivago*.

EYEWITNESS

The first batch of *Eyewitness* discs suffered from extensive manufacturing flaws, so be wary. The transfer is also weak. The picutre is grainy and has indistinct boundaries between colors. The digitally encoded soundtrack is also bad. It has almost no upper range, and the analog track is only slightly better. But, as far as we are concerned, the movie isn't any good anyway, so the quality of the presentation is almost irrelevant. The film's only attractive feature is the appeal of its two leads, William Hurt and Sigourney Weaver, who were still edging their way up stardom's ladder when the movie was made. The script, which is awful, hinges on a coincidence so elaborate and so silly that even on secondary viewings, when you know it is coming and you shouldn't care about it any more, it still seems so stupid that the murder thriller could have had the greatest transfer and pressing in the world and it still wouldn't have made a worthwhile disc.

F FOR FAKE (Import)

The last film directed by Orson Welles to receive a general theatrical release was a documentary about the writer Clifford Irving and the art forger Elmyr de Hory. It was entitled *F for Fake* and is available, in English, on disc in Japan. Although one is apt to categorize the movie as a minor effort by Welles, it is still a compelling film and quite effective as home video. The movie is a rare sort of documentary, one which we could easily watch many, many times. The reason for this is quite simple. Welles not only filmed it, he narrates it.

For those who are unfamiliar with the characters, a quick summary is worthwhile. Clifford Irving wrote a book about Elmyr de Hory, suggesting that many works of art in museums around the world which have been attributed to major talents were actually produced by de Hory. After the publication of that book, Irving went on to write an autobiography of Howard Hughes, which was quickly revealed to be a hoax.

Piecing together home movies (which Welles, as a certified member of the jet set, made at de Hory's Riviera villa), newsreel footage, and other odd scraps, *F for Fake* calls into question the extent of de Hory's accomplishments (though it is likely that he did move a number of works through a few unscrupulous art dealers) and postulates on de Hory's involvement (forging signatures? mastermind?) in the Howard Hughes affair.

The material is just interesting enough to be worthy of a documentary presentation, and that is all Welles needs to put on a grand performance. He uses his most manipulative voice, not the Jehovah intonations which one is normally familiar with, selling wine before its time and the like, but his radio voice, which, through unnatural pauses and changes in pitch, pulls your whole head into the speaker with him. The makeshift visuals cannot be dismissed, either, as there will often be a clever transition between one piece of film and the next. Like the work of Picasso and the other artists discussed in the film, the movie may have the look of having been thrown together, but it was guided by the instincts and strengths of a master.

Owing to the nature of the source material, the picture on the disc looks rough. The sound is in reasonable condition and there is a music score by Michel Legrand.

F.I.S.T.

Although Norman Jewison's film about the rise of a fictional Teamster's Union, *F.I.S.T.*, starring Sylvester Stallone, is fairly ridiculous, it does have a couple aspects which make repeated viewings, at least separated by long periods of time, enjoyable. There are a number of supporting roles, including those of Tony Lo Bianco, Brian Dennehy, and Rod Steiger, which contain the sort of inspirations that performances in other Jewison films have been noted for. Despite the many unlikelihoods, the plot's overall impact leaves a viewer with a true historical sense of how the Mob and the Teamsters Union became perpetually entwined. Finally, the film is two and a half hours long and the story spans several decades, so you feel like you've sat through something when it is over, no matter how silly Stallone looks with greying temples.

The film was made when epics could still be monaural, so the sound is flat and, except for one or two sound effects which stand out, uninteresting. The picture transfer is passable, although the image becomes grainier as the disc progresses. An interview with Jewison is included on a jacket insert. The piece is good, although it wisely concentrates on Jewison's overall career and tiptoes through *F.I.S.T.* ("Somehow I failed. Maybe it was the casting.") briefly at the end.

F/X

The popular and cleverly scripted suspense film, *F/X*, has a slightly grainy picture, but not unduly so. The sound is stereophonic and has many realistic effects. Despite a gratuitous car chase, the movie is consistently entertaining, with the acting being as much fun as the plot and action.

THE FABULOUS BAKER BOYS

So much attention has been paid to Michelle Pfeiffer that it is worth taking a moment to praise Beau Bridges' performance in *The Fabulous Baker Boys*. He has the most thankless role, as the stodgy, unsexy, less talented, balding older brother, and it is the best thing he's ever done. There is an unstated rapport between him and his brother, Jeff, and however uncomfortable his character makes you feel, you can't take your eyes off of him, at least when Pfeiffer isn't wearing too fetching an outfit. As for Pfeiffer, she sings her own songs and makes her character serious and funny at the same time. The whole movie, which is about two piano players and a singer struggling through the cocktail lounge circuit in Seattle, is a delight, a romance which also has interesting things to say about adults growing up.

The disc is less delightful. On the positive side, the digital surround sound is clean, and the score is super. The sound has full, rounded tones, and the separations split the two pianos effectively. The picture transfer, however, is a disappointment. The image is grainy and the colors look muddy.

THE FABULOUS FLEISCHER FOLIO – VOLUME ONE

Walt Disney released *The Fabulous Fleischer Folio – Volume One*, a collection of six lush color cartoons by the Fleischer brothers, Max and Dave. The Fleischers were responsible for several famous cartoon characters and the promotion for this disc has down-played the fact the these six cartoons do not contain those characters. Fortunately, the cartoons included are rich with another aspect which the Fleischers were noted for – intentionally Freudian imagery where dislocation, castration, and phallic symbols are the rules rather than the exceptions.

Take 'Small Fry,' for example, a cartoon about a young fish who skips school to hang out at a pool hall and become a member of the hall's fraternal organization. Put through the initiation rites, the young fish is scared out of his wits and goes screaming home to his mother. Kids hate cartoons like this; it is only when one is old enough to understand the perverseness of what is happening that the features take on a cultish attractiveness.

Of the other cartoons on the disc, the best is a detailed exposition of an ant colony under attack by an anteater, 'Ants in the Plants.' The collection also contains a travelog of California, 'The Golden State,' which includes a karaoke sing-along of 'California, Here I Come.'

THE FABULOUS FLEISCHER FOLIO – VOLUME TWO

Volume Two of *The Fabulous Fleischer Folio* is a continuation of the collection in *Volume One*. These cartoons are not for children – at least we could not stand them when we were younger – but the quality of the artwork and the inventive images are beyond the reach of today's animators.

'Hawaiian Birds,' for example, is about adultery, despair, bondage, suicide, and heartbreak. Don't worry, it has a happy ending. 'Greedy Humpty Dumpty' is a mixture of Mother Goose, Babel, Icarus, and Fleischer. 'All's Fair at the Fair,' one of the few cartoons in the collection which kids might like, is about a wildly art-deco world exhibition where anything is possible. 'Snubbed by a Snob' is a story about a horse and a donkey which has a racial undercurrent. 'Base Brawl' is a clever animalization of a baseball game (If mice were to play against elephants, who do you think would win?), but it is interrupted by a karaoke rendition of a popular seventh inning stretch tune. The last cartoon, 'Somewhere in Dreamland,' is a gooey peek into the fevered dreams of two starving children.

The color on several of the shorts is faded or blurred, but this encourages one to be thankful that the cartoons were rescued from oblivion.

FAERIE TALE THEATRE:
BEAUTY AND THE BEAST
JACK AND THE BEANSTALK
RAPUNZEL
THE NIGHTINGALE
THE TALE OF THE FROG PRINCE
PINOCCHIO
GOLDILOCKS AND THE THREE BEARS
THE PRINCESS AND THE PEA
HANSEL AND GRETEL
THUMBELINA
SLEEPING BEAUTY
LITTLE RED RIDING HOOD
THE BOY WHO LEFT HOME TO FIND OUT ABOUT THE SHIVERS
SNOW WHITE
RUMPELSTILTSKIN

Shelley Duvall capitalized on the ability of low cost video productions made for cable TV to be profitable, especially since the subsequent video releases for children would be as likely to be sold as to be rented. Her concept – to film well known fairy tales in video for these markets and convince prominent entertainers (Mick Jagger, Robin Williams, et cetera) that it would be fun to appear therein – was met with the usual executive skepticism. As with the heroes of her stories, perseverance paid off and Duvall has become the Sister Grimm of the video era.

Fifteen of Shelley Duvall's *Faerie Tale Theatre* collection are available from CBS/Fox. Most are 45 minutes long, none take up more than one side of a disc. The transfers are uniformly sharp and the monaural sound is adequate. But there the similarities end. No two have quite the same style and since different groups of talented people were behind each production, the quality changes from one show to the next. The best were made by the most accomplished directors (Ivan Passer, Lamont Johnson, Roger Vadim), but variety is an important concept in the series – out of the fifteen, every viewer is going to find at least a few they can respond to.

One of the best is surely Roger Vadim's rendition of *Beauty and the Beast*. It pales when compared to Jean Cocteau's classic film interpretation and, in fact, draws some of its most haunting moments (human arms extend from the walls of the Beast's hallways, holding lamps) directly from Cocteau's vision. Ten-year-olds are not going to quibble. Susan Sarandon stars.

Our favorite offering is Lamont Johnson's *Jack and the Beanstalk*. The special effects are terrific, especially when Jack (Dennis Christopher) and the giant's wife (Jean Stapleton) appear to be in the same kitchen even though she's three times his size. Elliot Gould is the giant and his reading of "Fee fi fo fum," is exquisite. Jerri Hall appears in a surprise cameo which won't be revealed here.

Rapunzel is nearly perfect. Shelley Duvall stars in this one in a double role as Rapunzel and Rapunzel's mother. Jeff Bridges also doubles as Rapunzel's father and the handsome prince. Gena Rowlands is the witch.

An incredible amount of talent went into making *The Nightingale*, but it lives up to expectations. The script was written by Joan Micklin Silver and directed by Ivan Passer. The production stars not only Mick Jagger, but Barbara Hershey, Bud Cort, Edward James Olmos, Keye Luke, and Mako.

Teri Garr has a good time in *The Tale of the Frog Prince* as a spoiled princess who revels in her own self-importance. Directed by Eric Idle, the frog is performed by Robin Williams with his usual antic inventiveness.

Few children will respond to *Pinocchio* as the jokes and the subject matter are crafted with adults in mind. The whole cast speaks in Chico Marx Italian and the story is narrated by Don Novelo in his Father Guido Sarducci getup. Carl Reiner portrays a puppet maker who wishes for a son and a pre-Pee Wee Paul Reubens is the puppet come to life.

Few adults will tolerate *Goldilocks and the Three Bears*. Small children may respond to the simplicity and bareness of the narrative but the older one is the more unbearable it will be.

Tatum O'Neal is Goldilocks in that she is wearing a blond wig and called by that name. John Lithgow and Carole King are her distracted parents. Hoyt Axton is a park ranger and Alex Karras is Papa Bear. The latter two bring some humor to their roles, but the someone's-been-eating-my-porridge/sitting-in-my-chair/sleeping-in-my-bed bit comes halfway through the show and the rest is padding.

Tom Conti and Liza Minnelli star in *The Princess and the Pea*. Tim Kazurinski portrays a jester whose buffoonery holds the piece together. Beatrice Straight and Nancy Allen, as the principal villains, provide an energetic threat to the well-being of the other characters.

Hansel and Gretel starts off well, with Joan Collins as the wicked stepmother trying to off woodsman Paul Dooley's children so he will make babies with her instead. The second half of the show is weaker. The witch, even with her desire to fatten and cook small children, isn't nearly as evil a character as the stepmother.

The episodic structure of *Thumbelina* prevents one from responding to any character other than the heroine. Adults may feel frustrated because the segments of her adventures are largely disconnected and Carrie Fisher, as Thumbelina, is too gracious to bring much tension to her predicaments.

Sleeping Beauty is a Russian fairy tale, and it should have been played very straight. Instead, it is presented as a burlesque, as if no one really had confidence in the material or in the attractiveness of Christopher Reeve (handsome prince) and Bernadette Peters (sleeping beauty).

A very literal re-creation of *Little Red Riding Hood* provides some wonderful surprise plot twists guaranteed to gross out anyone over the age of five. It takes time to get there, though, and while Malcolm McDowell's cockney wolf is gluttonous enough, the usually dependable Mary Steenburgen just does not seem as naïve as Little Red Riding Hood ought to be to get suckered into talking with a long-tailed stranger.

Peter MacNicol is so American in *The Boy Who Left Home to Find Out about the Shivers* that you can't really believe it is a close adaptation of a fairy tale. It is nearer in genre to the the Three Stooges/Abbott & Costello in a haunted house cartoons, with malevolent skeletons and malicious battle axes. The premise, that MacNicol is impervious to fear and keeps a straight, bored face while assorted ghouls molest him, is good for more than a few chuckles, and the cast includes some classy performances by Christopher Lee, David Warner, and a demented Frank Zappa.

The mirror in *Snow White* is portrayed by Vincent Price and you can be sure that no one has ever played a piece of furniture with such polish. Vanessa Redgrave (evil stepmother), Elizabeth McGovern (S.W.), Price, and Michael Preston (the huntsman) give wonderful performances, but Rex Smith (yet another handsome prince) and the dwarves lower the standards. The dwarves never click as an ensemble and their lines aren't funny enough. When Redgrave and Price are mugging each other, *Snow White* is sublime entertainment.

Finally, there is *Rumpelstiltskin.* It is said that good editing should not draw attention to itself, but the editing in this production is breathtaking. Want to see straw turn into gold? No special effects are required here, just a few choice camera angles. Script calls for the queen to be alone with the villainous midget when she wins her baby back? No problem, the reaction shots of Shelley Duvall (as the miller's daughter who has become queen) and Herve Villechaize (as Rumpelstiltskin) are so carefully selected and timed that the presence of more characters (the cast also includes Paul Dooley, Bud Cort, and Ned Beatty) would be distracting.

FAHRENHEIT 451

From the opening credits, which are spoken, to the the closing montage of recitations, François Truffaut's English language *Fahrenheit 451* is an intellectually stimulating film for those who want to give their minds a rest. Based on Ray Bradbury's novella about a society where firemen burn books every day, the movie teases the viewer with glimpses of favorite titles and quotations from favorite passages. Truffaut's scenes are staged with broad, impulsive expressions of shallow thoughts and emotions. One piece of Truffaut's (limited budget, but memorable) vision of the future which pleased us was the presence of widescreen televisions in every home. Even the little portable TVs have decent aspect ratios.

Although they did not take Truffaut's hint about widescreen, MCA has done a good job transferring the film to disc. The fire engine reds look solid and nothing appears faded, although the movie is twenty years old.

Bernard Herrmann's score imitates the same quick, wide brushstrokes which Truffaut used to set the appearance and pace of the movie.

It is difficult to imagine someone making a better film version of Bradbury's work than what Truffaut has done. The story mistakes the pleasures of collecting books for the pleasures of reading, but it is satisfying home video material and suitable for many repeated viewings. Now that there are discs, who needs books, anyway?

FAIRPORT CONVENTION – IT ALL COMES 'ROUND AGAIN

The program almost seems like a put-on. Fairport Convention, a rock band with an affinity for Celtic folk songs and a history which makes the group appear like a cross between Spinal Tap and Menudo, is profiled on *Fairport Convention – It All Comes 'Round Again.* The band has its own convention every year in rural England, where members and former members join and play for a burgeoning audience of Celtic rock lovers.

The disc features one of these concerts, interspersed with lengthy interviews and documentary footage that journal the group's development. Like the diaries of Samuel Pepys, the subject is less important than the microcosm of an era it inadvertently reflects. Their hairstyles run the gamut, the severest substance abusers die, and the least talented band members carry on as more accomplished musicians come and go.

The sound (stereo for the concert, mono in the clips of earlier concerts and most of the interviews) is in good shape, and the music sounds excellent. The picture is acceptable. Chapter markers identify the musical numbers and are listed on the back of the jacket.

FAITH GEORGE MICHAEL

Five George Michael music videos, chained together with an interview, have been released on *Faith George Michael.* In the interview Michael sits on a stool, speaking calmly about his career and attempting to be as self-effacing as possible. The constant use of reverse angle head shots, however, tends to distant one's attention from the content of his conversation.

The picture is faintly grainy but passable. The disc runs a little over a half hour and is in CLV. Michael's music is delicately mixed and his vocals are restrained. The videos, 'I Want Your Sex' ('uncensored'), 'Faith,' 'Father Figure,' 'One More Try,' and 'Monkey,' are elaborately but conservatively produced. The imagery, even all the garter belts and skin, never intrudes upon the impact of the music.

THE FALCON AND THE SNOWMAN

It is hard to imagine someone wanting to watch *The Falcon and the Snowman* more than once. The stereo mix is nicely done and adequately transferred to disc, but the picture is grainy and pedestrian. The movie was based upon a true story about a pair of aimless buddies who end up selling secrets to the Russians largely out of the lack of respect they have for themselves. The film stars Timothy Hutton and Sean Penn. Neither their performances nor the script adequately explains why they did it or what it was like. The movie has no tension, no grand moments, and no focus beyond relating the facts of the story.

FALSTAFF – CHIMES AT MIDNIGHT

(Import)

No one wrote better plays than William Shakespeare or made better movies than Orson Welles, and, fortunately, they are two stars who keep their motion perfectly in one sphere. *Falstaff – Chimes at Midnight* was the last significant film to be directed by Welles and released theatrically while he was alive. At the time of its release it seemed a little embarrassing, because Welles's backers had run out of money. But as time advances, the film's strengths become more apparent.

Falstaff is available in Japan. It is mildly letterboxed, with many bothersome Japanese subtitles strung vertically, on the right, often reducing the full portion of aspect ratio which had been saved by the letterboxing. It is CX-encoded monaural, with a lovely, guttural bass and a fuzzy higher range which has been victimized by the post-dubbing and obviously lengthy relooping. The picture, notorious jumps and freezes on the original negative aside, flickered occasionally and contained a light graininess.

The movie was supposedly adapted from Shakespeare's 'Henry IV, Part I,' 'Henry IV, Part II,' 'Henry V,' and 'The Merry Wives of Windsor.' This has been stated elsewhere and is even printed on the jacket. In reality, the movie is 'Henry IV, Parts I' and 'II' with a snippet of 'Henry V' at the end. We've never been able to identify material from 'Wives' and doubt there are any lines to be found in the completed film. The movie is 116 minutes long (stretched to three sides, the third is in CLV although it lasts less than a half hour), so it is clear that Welles paired the two 'Henry's' to fit, but he has retained the essential emotions, lessons, and ambitions of the plays.

The story is a classic by any standard, about a frivolous prince who matures when the responsibilities of leadership are pressed upon him. Welles's command of filmmaking is more expansive than Falstaff's two-yard girth. He coaxes a bewitching performance out of Keith Baxter, who portrays Prince Hal and provides a rare amount of feeling to the title role which he himself filled.

When the subtitles aren't in the way, the widescreen is captivating. It is a true masterpiece and one of a handful of titles which those who love film would go to any length to obtain.

FAME

FAME (Digital)

MGM/UA's first release of *Fame* had a dark, muddy picture and analog sound. The source material for the digital reissue has the same scratches, but the transfer has brightened the image and cleaned up the worst of it. The surround sound is also sharper, though the mix still fails to live up to its potential (the title song sounded better as a single). In addition, MGM/UA has put the three-sided disc in a gatefold jacket, chosen better side breaks, provided more chapter markers than even a stage mother could hope for, and added a trailer to the end which, although it is in monaural, has a punch which the film itself is missing.

In that *Fame* is about a 'Performing Arts' High School, it is a veritable compendium of performing arts movie clichés. It manages to include the basic clichés about struggling dancers, struggling comics, struggling musicians, struggling singers, struggling actresses, struggling songwriters, and those struggling with their sexual identity. The clichés prevent the film from achieving greatness, but they also prevent the film from achieving obscurity, as the movie is an easy, mindless experience which a viewer can dip into and out of at any point, always knowing immediately what the score is.

THE FAMILY

The picture in Ettore Scola's *The Family* is grainy and hazy from beginning to end, and the edges of the screen often look washed out. The monaural sound is passable, but the chapter markers flicker. The film is in Italian and has yellow English subtitles.

None of the disc's faults, however, was a strong enough impediment to prevent us from loving the film. *The Family* takes place in one location, a single, full-floor apartment in Rome, over the course of eighty years. It depicts the five generations who live there through the eyes and observations of one character. Although cast members portray multiple parts (their shifts in personality are sometimes quite witty), the script doesn't go overboard with coincidences or disasters. The scope of the film enables one to grasp what eighty years of life is like, and it increases one's appreciation of one's own ancestors.

There is a recurring shot which is used to denote passages of time within the movie, where the camera dollies down the main hallway of the apartment. The entire film is constructed in the same way – one life is followed, and the lives of others are only shown as they intersect it. The beauty of the film is that from those intersections, a viewer's imagination can extrapolate what the lives of the other characters are like, what the lives of the people they meet are like, and on until one understands all of humanity, without ever leaving the apartment.

FAMILY PLOT

There were several points in his career where Alfred Hitchcock thought he was making his last movie, so that one can't give too much credence to the finality of *Family Plot*. It is worth mentioning, however, that the film is more good-natured than any he had made in a long time. He also appears to have adapted a few of the sets from his earlier films – notably the shipping magnate's office, which looks as though it came straight from *Vertigo*, and Mrs. Rainbird's study, which has interesting similarities to the main set in *Rope*.

The movie is superbly made, with cuts and plot twists which will have one totally captivated on the first viewing, and editing, performances, and camera angles which will keep one attentive many viewings later. The economy with which the automatic garage door is introduced in the beginning, for example, gives its use later on the precise comical and dramatic impact. The film is about a pair of would-be hustlers who unwittingly cross paths with a pair of serious kidnappers. Although it supposedly takes place in one city, the scenes involving the first couple were filmed in Los Angeles and the scenes involving the kidnappers were done in San Francisco. The effect is a perfect disorientation of locale, so that you have to meet the film on its own terms.

The transfer is decent. An attempt to give the Los Angeles footage a dusty, weary look, and to give the San Francisco scenes a sharper gloss was less successful, and so the movie has always had kind of a worn down appearance. There is nothing much to do with the CAV functions on side three, but it is always enjoyable and instructive to watch a Hitchcock movie in slow motion. The sound is reasonably pleasing. The score by John Williams, who was on his best behavior, helps considerably.

After the 121-minute film there are two trailers and more than 50 production and publicity stills. The black-and-white stills, which are marked by a chapter stop, encapsulate the film's visual pleasures and present posed, but interesting, behind-the-scene views. Both trailers are marked by a single chapter notation. Each has its amusing moments, but together they demonstrate that Hitchcock was unquestionably past his prime, as far as his cute trailers went. Historically they are valuable since it was the last time one was to see him doing his thing.

FANDANGO (Import)

Every Japanese catalog we have says that *Fandango* is in widescreen format, but, unfortunately, the disc is not. In three different scenes a small black band appears at the bottom of the screen to widen the image slightly, but that is it.

From a standpoint of craft, the movie is quite impressive, and it plays well on a television screen. It is the story of five college kids driving across the desert for one last fling before they get drafted, get married,or whatever, in the early seventies. It is a comedy, but the director pays attention to the bugs and lizards of the desert and will often come up with an astonishing camera angle or stunt which gives the film more depth than the typical youth comedy can muster. It is so self-assured that it is a pleasure to view and it is funny without being obnoxious.

The print used for the disc is a little dirty, with unnecessary scratches and speckles popping up at regular intervals. The sound is in better shape, and nine pop numbers from the seventies which appear on the soundtrack have their own chapter markers. The disc is in English with Japanese subtitles.

FANNY AND ALEXANDER

(See **AUTUMN SONATA**)

THE FANTASY FILM WORLDS OF GEORGE PAL

To begin with, the first half-hour of *The Fantasy Film Worlds of George Pal* concentrates on his 'Puppetoons,' and it is just enough of a sampling to communicate the sense of magic which his animated figures inspired without becoming tiresome. The remaining hour looks at the major feature films which Pal produced and directed. *When Worlds Collide* is given a short shrift and 'The Power' isn't even mentioned, but films such as *Destination Moon*, *The War of the Worlds*, *The Time Machine*, and 'The Wonderful World of the Brothers Grimm' are depicted with extensive film clips and enriched with interviews covering background information and production history.

The clips are in decent condition, although the sound quality varies a bit. The documentary is an excellent supplement to the films of George Pal which are on laser disc. It also provides the rare clips of Pal's early animation efforts and a promotional sequence in which he miniaturizes Ed Sullivan. The program ends with the charming moral that concludes 'The Seven Faces of Dr. Lao,' which, paraphrased, suggests that if you want real magic, grab a handful of earth and examine it closely. With this disc, however, you don't even have to get yourself dirty.

FAR FROM HOME

Drew Barrymore is rapidly becoming the Linda Blair of her generation. Already looking a bit pudgy, she stars in *Far from Home*, a concoction about a girl and her father stranded in a Nevada town, because the town has no gasoline, and stumbling over a couple of gruesome murders. Although it is supposed to be a secret, you can spot the murderer as soon as he is introduced. Barrymore has a wet t-shirt scene and prances around in a bikini for a while, but it is enough to indicate that she has a whole career of exploitation films ahead of her. Anyone interested in a pool on when she will make her first women's prison feature?

The print has a number of splices, but they are so adeptly covered you may think you have blinked instead. The picture is a little soft, but adequate for the material. The sound is monaural, but well mixed, and is worth amplifying.

FAR FROM THE MADDING CROWD

Directed by John Schlesinger, *Far from the Madding Crowd* is based upon a novel by Thomas Hardy. In contrast to D.H. Lawrence, Hardy doesn't hit you over the head with symbolism. In the beginning of the film, for example, a dog goes mad and forces a herd of sheep to leap off a cliff. The incident is intrinsic to the narrative and only later does one realize that it also foreshadows the suicidal urges to which passion leads the central characters. The plot is about a woman, played by Julie Christie, who inherits a large farm, and her relationship with three men from different social backgrounds, portrayed by Alan Bates, Peter Finch, and Terence Stamp. The drama explores the different ways in which love can manifest itself and also paints an inspired portrait of rural life in Victorian England.

The movie runs 169 minutes, but the disc has been expanded to four sides so that the intermission break can separate the platters. The digital stereo surround sound is good. There are a few hiccoughs, but no flaws which distract the viewer after the age of the film is taken into account. Richard Rodney Bennet's musical score is one of our favorites. Bennet blends real folk music with orchestral flourishes and modernistic dissonance, capturing not only the romantic structure of the drama, but also the deterioration of that romance in the context of industrialization.

The cinematography, by Nicholas Roeg, is, with one conceptual exception, gorgeous. The exception is the closeups of Christie, which are often in gauze though it is exceedingly clear from the shots which are not that she looks perfectly fetching without it. The shots are disorienting on the disc because the picture looks perfect except when it looks blurry. The colors are deliberately yellowish. The fleshtones are inconsistent in some sequences, but rich enough to indicate that for the most part the transfer is accurate. Roeg will also allow the sun to catch the camera lens and flash a glare across the image, but the error is deliberate. Like a flaw in a diamond, he gives the image a touch of imperfection in order to give the look of the film some character.

The film has many memorable, captivating sequences arising out of seemingly ordinary or mundane events. It is difficult to communicate the thrill to be found in scenes about protecting haystacks from fire and from a raging storm, much less the scene involving a group of sheep dying from intestinal gas, but Schlesinger's artistry makes the dramatic incidents seem vital. He uses the lengthy running time to develop the characters fully, so that one cares as much for the villain, Stamp, as for the heroine. There is a fencing demonstration which turns into a seduction and a Christmas party which ends in a tragedy. The scenery is gorgeous and the stars are gorgeous. Thus, the letterboxed image, which has a thrilling aspect ratio of about 2.4:1, is an absolute necessity.

A FAREWELL TO ARMS

A Farewell to Arms, has a sharp picture, but the print is full of breaks and splices. None of the dialog appears to be lost in the breaks, so one's concentration is distracted only briefly. The sound is noticeably aged.

Whoever cast the film was a genius. Gary Cooper removes from the Hemingway hero the one flaw a Hemingway hero usually has – too much intelligence to be talking in such short sentences. Pairing him with Helen Hayes was another coup, because she can convey intelligence and passion without uttering a word. All the director has to do is cut to a pillar illuminated by lightning and you know exactly what is happening.

FAREWELL TO THE KING

John Milius' *Farewell to the King*, comes close to being a terrific movie, but somewhere it fizzles. Viewers who thrive on adventure may still be entertained, but others will feel impatient. Like much of Milius' work, *Farewell to the King* has a breathtaking opening and a stimulating, intelligent, satisfying finale, but the middle is flat and confused.

The movie takes place in Borneo during World War II. An AWOL soldier paws his way inland and joins a tribe of natives, eventually becoming their chief. He cannot escape the war, however, and as the fighting draws near, the British enlist his help, for a price, to harass the Japanese. The film tends to digress, though, and the narrative becomes impeded by the jungle.

The photography is gorgeous and the disc looks quite good. A number of exotic filters are used, taking advantage of the almost constantly overcast sky to paint moods upon the heavens. The disc manages every trick, including an extensive cloudy night battle, without slipping into distortion. The digital stereo surround sound is impressive as well.

FAST FOOD

The owners of a struggling restaurant slip an aphrodisiac into the barbecue sauce on their hamburgers in *Fast Food*, a film of limited amusement or value. Traci Lords appears in a few brief scenes. The disc has a passable picture and soundtrack.

FAST FORWARD

Although *Fast Forward* has the format of a kids-trying-to-make-it-to-the-big-talent-show musical, it generates more anxiety than it relieves. The ending is upbeat, but the trials which the kids are submitted to on their way to show biz glory leave one uncomfortable. Part of the problem is the lack of personality or talent among any of the cast members.

The movie was directed by Sidney Poitier. The stereo sound is clean, but unremarkable, and the picture is fresh, but uninteresting.

FAT MAN AND LITTLE BOY

The story of the creation of the atomic bomb has been done about a half-dozen times, and television usually does it better than the movies do, since the subject is best suited for an unrushed and talky format. The theatrical feature starring Paul Newman, *Fat Man and Little Boy*, is poorly conceived and disappointing. Although it hits the major scientific, philosophical, and historical factoids, it also spends a lot of energy on the Hollywoodish love lives of the different scientists. Newman can't really be blamed for the weak way in which the script presents his character, but only one actor, John Cussak, is able to rise above the material, and he has the most poorly written part of all, that of the token minor scientist/witness.

Vilmos Zsigmond's cinematography has been scanned and cropped. When orange and brownish tones are excessivley utilized the picture destabilizes a little, but it is basically in good shape. The sound is only entertaining when the loudspeakers in the movie are turned on. There is also a musical score by Ennio Morricone, but it is too derivative of his other works.

FATAL ATTRACTION

Although the popular venereal thriller, *Fatal Attraction*, is more violent (and humorous) emotionally than physically, it appeals to anyone who ever went on more than one date. Paramount has released the 120-minute film on a single platter, with digital encoding. The stereo mix in the film is finely detailed, and this is rendered to near perfection on the digital soundtrack. (The analog track is almost as good.) The picture, unfortunately, is grainy, especially in the darker portions of the screen. The quality of the acting in the film is truly wonderful, but there is, perhaps, one lesson that the plot imparts which has not been as widely publicized as the movie's central conceit: Living in the city may be dangerous, but living in the suburbs is worse.

FATAL BEAUTY

In *Fatal Beauty*, Whoopi Goldberg portrays a cop who seeks out trouble. The film was intentionally a female Eddie Murphy experiment, and it fails because she doesn't do Eddie Murphy-type comedy. You can even feel her contempt for the sex-related one liners she has to throw out at the beginning. The movie gets better as it goes along, and there is even a scene where Goldberg does a lengthy, imagination-capturing monolog, but the plot is a contrivance and it is set in a contrived world. It would probably have been better if she had just sat at a microphone and told the whole story herself.

The picture is clear enough to bring the sound boom shadows into sharp focus. The colors have a nice gloss, with a minimal amount of bleeding. The stereo sound is analog only, though it is probably just as well. The sound recording takes in too much of the surrounding atmosphere – despite the proximity of the boom – and is inconsistent in strength. There is also a music soundtrack which periodically blasts out of nowhere and then disappears again. We suspect it is there just to keep viewers awake.

FATAL VISION

Without the intrusion of commercials, the TV miniseries, *Fatal Vision*, still runs a marathon 192 minutes, not counting the time it takes to turn the discs over. Almost every minute, however, is great TV. The disc is so systematic in its structure that, by the time the three-plus hours are over, you have a real sense of the ten years it took to accumulate and organize the evidence which was needed to convict the Green Beret doctor of murdering his family. It is a good mystery and, unlike feature films, it can pick up some slack as it unravels. The picture and sound quality is on par with a standard television film.

FATHER

Istvan Szabo's *Father* is a Hungarian movie about a baby boomer who can barely remember his father, killed shortly after the end of the war. The political overtones are obvious, yet lightly applied. The movie shifts between scenes of the boy growing up and fantasy scenes in which the boy imagines what his father was like. The movie does not make the one feel guilty about one's relationship with one's parents, even though the content inspires a flood of memories. *Father* is delightful and its lessons are entertaining.

Made with grainy black and white stock, the picture inevitably looks ragged. The disc's image, however, seems to have an extra level of softness and can be uncomfortably fuzzy at times. There are pale yellow subtitles which are easy to read. The monaural sound is in better shape and there is a catchy musical score.

FATHER'S LITTLE DIVIDEND

The transfer of *Father's Little Dividend*, which comes from a '1951 35mm safety fine grain composite master,' has just a couple of splices and otherwise looks very nice. The black and white picture is sharp and the grey levels have a satisfactory level of detail. The sound is less consistent, but workable.

A friend who began watching the disc with us got up after twenty minutes and declared, "Nothing happens in this movie, does it?" In a way our friend is correct. Like the first effort to which *Father's Little Dividend* is a sequel, 'Father of the Bride,' the script is all surface incidents. The first film managed to cumulate, through incidental details, a spirit of love and coming of age that gave the entertainment substance. *Dividend*, however, never quite builds the same head of steam. It is calculated enough that there are inevitably a few touching moments between Spencer Tracy and Elizabeth Taylor, but the film's title is unfortunately a lot more accurate an assessment of its content than was intended.

FEAR

For a comparison between advertising art and reality, look at the front and the back of the jacket of *Fear*, which stars Frank Stallone. The still on the back is what he really looks like. The still on the front, from no scene in the movie, must have taken hours or days to compose, making him look as much like his brother as possible. His performance is enjoyable, but he gets knocked off about halfway through the film. In fact, all of the interesting characters – hardened criminals who escape from a bus transporting them to a penitentiary – die early on, and the viewer is left with a few wimpy, desperate cons, and the wimpy, desperate family they hold hostage. The film starts out with some promise, but never follows through, so the only entertainment comes from watching the cigarettes change sizes in the closeups. The sound on the disc, although monaural, has a good kick. The picture turns grainy in the dark but is fine when there is enough light.

FELLINI SATYRICON

In *Fellini Satyricon* the director/conceptualist, Federico Fellini, follows the text of 'The Satyricon,' by Petronius, fairly closely. The story is actually a few middle chapters of a much longer narrative, the beginning and ending of which, apparently, are lost to the dust of ages (it is not an unfinished work, as is claimed in the skittish jacket notes, and has a definite sense of direction, although the film ends, deliberately, in mid-sentence, in honor of the fragmentary source). Although Fellini follows the text more admirably than one, not having read it, would have supposed, he botches practically every scene, missing the satire, the eroticism, and the impatience of the characters who seem confounded by life in Nero's Rome. In a thoroughly entertaining and surprising hour film which has been included on the disc, 'Ciao, Federico!,' a BBC documentary by Gideon Bachman, about the making of *Satyricon*, Fellini is observed being hopelessly ill-prepared for many of the scenes he is filming. He counts on his cast to compensate for his lack of organization, and then he bullies them when they inevitably fail. So what compels a viewer to see the film more than once? Fellini has taken a not especially good, but genuinely classical novel and turned it into a not especially good, but genuinely Felliniesque film, and in doing so he has created a back door to Antiquity. Fellini and Petronius (who was Nero's 'Arbiter of Elegance,' sort of a 'fashion advisor') are Italian soul mates, and to be exposed to *Fellini Satyricon* is to be exposed to the satisfying concept that people have been going off the deep end for centuries.

Like the acting, the cinematography in *Fellini Satyricon* is awful. If it's not too much smoke, it's lights glaring back at you or it's a shot which is so clear and so well lit that you can see the location is an unreal studio set. The picture quality on the disc, however, is superb. The image is letterboxed with an aspect ratio of about 2.2:1 and has been obtained from the 'best available 35mm negative,' which has a couple of splices, some speckles, and a couple feet of faded color, but is otherwise scrumptious. Fellini muffs the camera setups when it comes to discovering the dramatic essence of a scene, but when it comes to showing off his wild set designs and costumes, he's right on top of it. Hence this is a dream disc to have in CAV, which is how Voyager has released it (the 149-minute movie is on five sides; the hour long 'Ciao, Federico!' is in CLV on side 6). Apart from the many apparitions of decadence, we caught an intriguing effect utilizing the Still Step command. A character looks up at the evening sky and for two frames the sky is blank. On the third it fills with starlight.

The sound is monaural and has not been CX-encoded. It is as scratchy as any Italian film made in the late sixties. The film is dubbed in Italian (the actors came from everywhere and Fellini's color films almost always have the dialog looped in later) and has English subtitles which appear below the letterboxed image on the laser disc. The subtitles have been taken from the film's dialogue continuity script. This is inadequate. While the central dialog is covered well enough, incidental conversation is not. There are lengthy passages in which only background dialog and sound effects are heard, but not a single subtitle appears.

The documentary is in 16mm and naturally looks a little rough, but it is impossible to turn off once you start watching it. One high point is a visit to the set by Sharon Tate and Roman Polanski. Most of it though, captures Fellini cursing his actors, his actresses, his crew, and the people making the documentary. Included on side five of the disc, after the movie is ended, is the original theatrical trailer, and a short excerpt from the dining scene in the Petronius text. We recommend watching the trailer before starting the film, because it sets you in the right frame of mind and fools you into thinking the movie is more exciting than it is. About the tag line for the film, by the way, though it has always been one of our favorites – "Rome. Before Christ. After Fellini." *Satyricon* takes place in AD 60.

FELLINI'S CASANOVA (DiscoVision)
FELLINI'S CASANOVA (Import)

In *Fellini's Casanova* Donald Sutherland portrays the famous Casanova in his waning days, as he travels from a bubonic Venice to a syphilitic London and a tubercular Germany, all without ever leaving the soundstages of Rome. The dialog is all post-synched and there's no telling what was actually spoken on the sets while all this was going on. The DiscoVision version is mostly in English. The Japanese version is in Italian and German, with Japanese subtitles plastered on the picture.

The most compelling aspect of *Casanova* (as it has been with all of Fellini's films since he lost his understanding of a need for plot) is Nina Rota's lovely music. It is Rota's most mature and complex score, teetering between cacophonous anarchy and intricate harmony. Midway, there is even a ten-minute, two-person-plus-chorus opera about a wimpy moth and a perverted butterfly which alone makes the discs worthwhile. The sound on the DiscoVision disc is typically full of crackle and hiss. The sound on the Japanese release is not CX-encoded either, but it is very clean and serves the music well.

Because of the differences in the picture and dubbing, it is almost necessary to own both discs. The widescreen version is an absolute necessity to apprehend Fellini's vision and talent. Masks and faces which mock the camera in the opening carnival scene are missing from the American disc, as is the recurring motif of shadows in the upper left corner of many other scenes. But the erotic ceramic tiles and occasional glimpses of flesh have been censored with gauze on the Japanese disc and in this case the CAV functions are advantageous.

THE FEMALE IMPERSONATOR PAGEANT

The photography in *The Female Impersonator Pageant* is as out of focus as the stills on the jacket cover. Much of the proceedings is taken up by a fashion show in which the announcers all but tell the prices of the outfits and how to place an order. After these commercials are finished, each of the 10 finalists performs an image impersonation of a famous female personality. In effect, you see the same act ten times over if you last that long. The whole thing was taped in some hotel in Houston and yes, the winner cries.

FERRIS BUELLER'S DAY OFF

The wonderfully irreverent *Ferris Bueller's Day Off* has a sharp-looking print transfer and digitally encoded sound. It is not in widescreen format, which spoils the Art Institute of Chicago interlude and a few other choice moments, but it is in perfect condition otherwise, and is an ideal disc for truants, or those who simply wish they could be.

Bueller, portrayed by Matthew Broderick, is a modern day cross between Tom Sawyer and Huckleberry Finn. He can talk his way in and out of anything and even talks to the camera numerous times, conning the viewer just as he is conning everyone else. The director, John Hughes, should forget about making dramas, for which he has less sensitivity, and just stick to comedies. The movie is an energetic and free spirited amusement in which everyone gets what is coming to them and Ferris Bueller gets away with it all.

The colors on the disc are perfect all the way through. Don't turn it off until it is really over, because there is a surprise at the end.

FIDDLER ON THE ROOF

Letterboxed, *Fiddler on the Roof* obtains its most assured balance between the intimacy of home video and the bravado of a widescreen presentation. The movie is a depiction of a Russian Jewish community near the turn of the century, and it is serious about evoking the simplicity and poverty to be found there. As a big, roadshow spectacular, the texture of the setting and the significance of the characters are over-magnified. On TV with scanning and cropping, as it appeared previously on laser disc from CBS/Fox, the rhythm, the design, and the atmosphere of the musical are obliterated. The MGM/UA Deluxe Letter-Box Edition, then, with an aspect ratio of about 2.1:1, is the ideal compromise and the best way to see the film.

The movie runs three hours and is presented on four sides in a gatefold jacket, with the intermission opening the second platter. The picture transfer is quite good. Some night and indoor sequences look weak, but most of the movie is bright, accurately colored, and spotless. The soundtrack does not have much in the way of surround effects, but the digital stereo sound carries the music well at high or low volume settings.

An impressive theatrical trailer for the film, which captures all of its best moments, is included at the end of side four, but if it had been put on side one there almost wouldn't be a reason to watch any of the other sides. The structure is a big problem. All of the best-known songs and the strongest song-and-dance sequences appear in the first act, making the last hour, depicting a pogrom, a long, unstoppable let down. Home video provides some relief, because after a viewer has seen the movie once, and is prepared, the ending can be appreciated and even respected during repeat viewings. In that sense, the trailer is ideally placed, because it gives you one last shot of the fun the film has to offer, and leaves you wanting to watch it again.

FIELD OF DREAMS

The critics who called *Field of Dreams* a yuppie male fantasy, or the critics who had anything bad to say about it at all, are the ones who can't see the ball players in the field. The film is beautifully composed, letting the viewer relive the past, appreciate the present, and dream about the future, all in one harmonic emotion.

The sharp but cropped picture has a lot of carefully lit night shots which survive the transfer without a blemish. Unfortunately, the stereo audio channels are reversed.

There is one sequence in *Field of Dreams*, a meeting about banning books, which is necessary to the plot, but poorly researched and staged. Otherwise, the movie is beautifully crafted, standing far enough away from the characters so that their passions never seem exaggerated, but hugging them at all the right moments, so that the viewer continues to care about their concerns. The story is about a corn farmer, Kevin Costner, who is compelled by voices to build a genuine baseball field where he ought to be growing corn. Like all the really good ghost stories, psychology and fantasy are so closely entwined that they become a single entity.

Ultimately, the movie is like playing baseball past twilight. If you stop to think too much about it, you realize you can't see the ball and you quit. But if you're really into the game, you just go on playing and playing.

FIELD OF HONOR (CHAMP D'HONNEUR)

The Franco-Prussian War is the setting for *Field of Honor (Champ D'Honneur)*. After some initial markings, the picture transfer is reasonably nice and the sound is fine. The film is in French with pale yellow English subtitles, though dialog is generally sparse. The mildly symbolic narrative begins as a tale about a young farm boy who joins the army. After a disastrous battle he is separated from his regiment and makes friends with an orphaned Flemish child. In the film's second half, the narrative shifts its focus to the child, who eventually finds his way to the young soldier's home. As stimulating as the plot may seem, however, the movie is not terribly cinematic. There are endless shots of characters walking down long roads and similar sorts of padding. Side two is in CAV with all movement appearing blurry in still frame.

52 PICK-UP

John Frankenheimer is a great director, but he usually picks the worst scripts imaginable. *52 Pick-up* is an exception, because the story is by Elmore Leonard. It is about normal people, and since they are being portrayed by the stars Ann-Margret and Roy Scheider, it takes a good portion of the movie for the viewer to realize that they are normal people, and that the blackmail plot being directed against them is the sort of sloppy, ill-conceived conspiracy which usually only occurs in life and not in the movies. The credits claim that *52 Pick-up* is stereo, but we were never able to detect sounds deviating from the central channel.

FIGHT FOR US

The adeptly constructed *Fight for Us* was made clandestinely in the Philippines and has a neo-realistic, rag tag look. The picture may seem a bit worn, but it is clear that the transfer has done no additional harm. The sound is passable, as well.

Fight for Us is in Spanish and has English subtitles. Based on actual events, the film depicts the abuses instigated by over-zealous vigilante groups who have the tacit backing of a government anxious to suppress discord and maintain order.

FINAL CHAPTER – WALKING TALL
(see **WALKING TALL**)

THE FINAL CONFICT

The demons responsible for bad laser discs have worked overtime on *The Final Conflict*, the finale to the 'Omen' series, which has been released by CBS/Fox as a Special Wide Screen Edition offering. The picture transfer is fuzzy, pale and grainy. The disc is letterboxed, with an aspect ratio of 2.2:1. The mind boggles. If it is this fuzzy letterboxed, what does it look like scanned and cropped? At the end, CBS/Fox has tried to make the package a little special by including a pair of trailers for the other *Omen* films. The digitally encoded surround sound is demure, with only Jerry Goldsmith's frustratingly accomplished score sounding at all stereophonic. Early copies also suffered from widespread manufacturing flaws.

At least it couldn't have happened to a more deserving film. The series, which was never strong on logic to begin with, reaches a pinnacle of how-could-adults-have-created-this-mess ludicrousness. Does Damien, the Devil incarnate, want to rule the world or destroy it? Or does he want to destroy the world and then rule it, anticipating that the administrative headaches would be fewer? The film can be appreciated only for the giggles it induces. There is Rossano Brazzi, whose accent seems magnified for the occasion. He portrays a priest who wants to stop Damien from killing all the new born 'bebees.' Our favorite, though, is Don Gordon, who taps his forehead as if he were realizing he could have had a V-8 and then informs his boss that his wife had gone into labor that afternoon, asking for the rest of the evening off.

THE FINAL COUNTDOWN

Though cropped, the picture on *The Final Countdown* looks terrific and even the many scenes filmed with strong orange or red lighting remain stable. The sound alternates between monaural and stereophonic sources – it was no easy task putting together a decent version of the film – and e result is workable if not satisfying.

The quality of the presentation enhances the film's entertainment value considerably. The story, about an atomic aircraft carrier which slips through a time warp to find itself sitting between the Japanese fleet and Pearl Harbor in early December of 1941, is more suitable for the tolerance levels of home video than for film theaters. The pre-*Top Gun* presentation has its share of glossy high-tech sights and sounds, and would be severely compromised if the disc had come up short on spit and polish. The film cleverly combines extensive carrier operations footage with wishful fantasy. Some of the stars, such as Kirk Douglas, remain too dry in their potentially juicy roles, but Charles Durning, who really understands how to not take the concept seriously, milks his part for all it is worth. No matter how frustrating it may seem, incidentally, the story's ending is well chosen. It lights a fire under the viewer's own imagination, a fire which is fanned by the disc.

A FINE MESS

Although the title alludes to Laurel and Hardy, *A Fine Mess* is closer in spirit to Abbott and Costello. One wonders how many script revisions the movie must have gone through, so that the cumulative piano-up-the-stairs scene which was originally its *raison d'etre* now occurs off stage and without so much as a bead of sweat on the brows of the two comics, Ted Danson and Howie Mandel, who are up to other business and can't be bothered. The RCA/Columbia disc is monaural and not CX-encoded, although the movie itself has an obnoxiously loud and ill-fitting score. The picture is unblemished, but the careers of everyone involved are not.

FINE YOUNG CANNIBALS – LIVE AT THE PARAMOUNT

Seattle's venerable Paramount Theater is the setting for *Fine Young Cannibals – Live at the Paramount*. The show lasts just over an hour and is spread to two sides in CLV. Each number is treated as an individual video in terms of style and visual execution, though the program forms a complete live concert. The vocals and horns aren't given enough volume in the recording, but otherwise the digital stereo sound is fine. The picture is flawless. FYC's music has an island beat and an intelligent pop sound which could potentially attract a wide range of fans. The disc provides an excellent demonstration of their talent.

FIRE & ICE

Fire & Ice has some spectacular skiing sequences and a spectacularly stupid narrative to link them together. The film is almost entirely dubbed, with narration by John Denver. John Eaves portrays a daydreamer who follows Suzy Chaffee from New York to Aspen. Every time he catches sight of her, he imagines they are doing some crazy sort of thing together, with skis or kites or streamers or windsurfers or you name it. Since both Eaves and Chaffee are champion skiers, they do their own athletics, but one wishes someone had found stunt doubles to do their acting for them.

The dichotomy continues on the picture itself. The ski sequences look fantastic – bright, sharp, and richly detailed. The story part looks as if it was made with film picked up in a drug store. The end credit scroll, containing highlights from the film, is letterboxed. The sound is in stereo to support music video styled segments, with bands such as Alan Parsons Project providing the score. The music is acceptable, but the dubbed dialog is barely mono compatible and sound effects are almost non-existent.

The movie is only 80 minutes in length, but the narrative makes it harder to tolerate than if the filmmakers had just pieced together the skiing stuff. Some say the world will end in fire, some say in ice. We say if this movie had gone on for ten more minutes, that would have done it.

FIRE AND ICE

The fire which once burned from the hands of movie animators has chilled in the past three decades so that figures no longer move with any sort of fluidity and everything except the central figure is frozen solid. For a while, Ralph Bakshi solved the problem by tackling subjects which weren't normally addressed by animators. When that failed, he took one of his occasional stabs at sword and sorcery, hoping to capitalize on the involvement of fantasy artist Frank Frazetta. If the animation in *Fire and Ice* looked half as good as Frazetta's ad (jacket cover) art, it wouldn't have played to so many empty theaters.

The disc is in stereo. The music is recorded appropriately, but the sound effects seem as limited as the sketchy drawings. The print is in good condition, at least, but there is also a fairly blatant racial division between the civilized good guys and the animalistic bad guys which discourages us from ever wishing to watch the film again.

THE FIRESIGN THEATRE – HOT SHORTS

We recommend that you watch side two of *The Firesign Theatre – Hot Shorts* before watching side one. The disc is a collection of nine different adventure serials from the 1940s done up *What's Up Tiger Lily?* style. The first two 'Shorts' on side one are a bit vulgar and can give one the wrong impression. The serial episodes are uncredited, so it is difficult to identify them all, but Flash Gordon, Commander Cody, and Spy Smasher are among the characters who are given new voices and lines by The Firesign Theatre comedy troop. The serials, of course, were infinitely humorous *without* superimposed craziness, but these excerpts, combined with the twisted logic that is the group's trademark, caused us to laugh aloud several times.

FIRESTARTER

The monaural and grainy looking *Firestarter* is, nonetheless, one of the better adaptations of a Stephen King work. Drew Barrymore portrays a young girl who can create fires psychically and, along with her father, is being pursued by a nasty government agency. King's primary theme in almost all of his work is the parallel nature of supernatural horror and sexual maladjustment. The girl's separation from her father and the attention she gets from a bevy of adult suitors who want to analyze her powers make an ideal counterpoint to the exposition of those powers.

FIREWALKER

The sound quality and stereo mix on *Firewalker* are excellent. The picture has scratches in a couple of places and looks blurry here and there, but the problem is with the movie itself, which was filmed without a completed script and edited without complete cover shots. The story, about jewels in jungle ruins, is enjoyable enough, but the first half hour makes no sense at all, and whenever something exciting happens it is inevitably shown at the least exciting angle. The film will only be of interest to small children or hard core Chuck Norris fans.

FIRST BLOOD
FIRST BLOOD (Import)

To its advantage, the Japanese release of *First Blood* was in widescreen. To its disadvantage, it was grainy and had a few scratches (not to mention subtitles). Thorn/EMI/HBO Video released *First Blood* in the US. It is not in widescreen. There are no scratches, but if the print is any less grainy or blurry than the Japanese print, we would be surprised. Without the wide screen, one notices a couple of things: The action isn't as interesting and Stallone's They-spit-on-me-when-I-came-back-from-'Nam speech is more embarrassing. The sound is no better or worse than its Japanese counterpart. We remain convinced that the best thing about this movie is Jerry Goldsmith's multiple warhead score, but we realize we are in a minority.

FIRST BORN

Usually, realistic movies about families breaking up or going through stress are no fun to watch and audiences don't want to see them. In the case of *First Born*, however, the realism shouldn't scare one away, because the director, Michael Apted, is an excellent craftsman and he's made a very entertaining drama about a young man who has to deal with his mother's new boyfriend.

The back of the disc's jacket cover says absolutely nothing about drugs or cocaine. This is as it should be, for although the original publicity for the Paramount release turned people off by suggesting that the mother (Teri Garr) was a dope fiend, the drugs are a minor plot device and insignificant to the true impact of the story.

A special word should be put in for Sarah Jessica Parker, who portrays the eldest son's girlfriend. She is so unlike the type of woman who is normally cast in such parts and so exactly like a real teenage girl that it is a joy to watch every frame she is in.

The sound on the disc is strong, but since it was not made in stereo, it has not been CX-encoded. The picture looks grainy and fuzzy, giving Apted's visuals an extra degree of lusciousness they do not need.

FIRST NAME: CARMEN

Jean-Luc Godard forged an entire and highly respected directorial career around his inability to make a true movie. His films, as the jacket copy on the back of *First Name: Carmen* the disc takes pains to explain, are accessible – you just have to get onto his wavelength. By accepting his indulgences, the viewer is treated both to his wry sense of humor and his refreshing intelligence.

What narrative there is takes off vaguely from the standard 'Carmen' story, as a bank guard falls in love with a bank robber, tagging along with her during the getaway. The narrative, however is constantly interrupted and deliberately coy, incorporating pleasures as varied as a string quartet playing Beethoven and Godard himself in a hospital bed, goosing nurses.

The transfer is quite good. Investors are willing to fork out only so much to let Godard do his thing, so the film naturally looks a little rough, but the colors are fresh and the focus is sharp. The sound editing is superb, a daring mishmash of overlapping effects, dialog, and even musical scores. The monaural sound is a little noisy, but acceptable. Side two, which contains extensive nudity, is in CAV, with two unsteady still frames out of every five.

A FISH CALLED WANDA

You need the chain reaction of a large audience to get the most out of *A Fish Called Wanda* the first time you see it, but that is no reason not to buy the laser disc and invite a lot of friends over. Furthermore, the dishonor-among-thieves comedy is suitable for multiple viewings because most of the humor comes from the performances of the stars instead of from witty one-liners. Our only complaint about the film – they worked on it for four years and yet they couldn't design a shot to show the guy flattened in the wet cement?

The disc is in fairly good condition. The picture transfer is fine, with no discernable flaws. The sound is efficient but unremarkable. The program also has a few encoded chapter markers, although no listing is provided for them. Although the video cassette Schwepps commercial doesn't appear on the disc, there is a gamey theatrical trailer at the end. Capturing many of the film's highlights, the trailer is an easy way to enjoy the movie if you only have two minutes to watch the disc.

THE FISHERMAN AND HIS WIFE
(see **PECOS BILL**)

FIST FIGHTER

There is a cute dog in *Fist Fighter* who puts his paws over his eyes whenever his master starts boxing. Fortunately, the dog gets shot soon after the beginning of side two. The film, made in Mexico but set in Peru, is about an itinerant American fighter searching for revenge. It is the sort of movie where the hero's hair remains blow dried even after he has spent days in the cramped solitary confinement cell of a Peruvian prison. The picture transfer looks adequate, though the image is soft and the colors tend to favor shades of yellow. The Ultra-Stereo surround sound is loud, and has intermittent separation effects.

A FISTFUL OF DOLLARS
A FISTFUL OF DOLLARS (Letterboxed)

Almost as important as the letterboxing on MGM/UA's Deluxe Letter-Box Edition of *A Fistful of Dollars* is the restoration of three to four minutes of footage which was missing from the CBS/Fox release. There still is no scene showing Baxter's son being captured, but the whole escape involving the barrel is no longer a cryptic mixture of voice-over and sound effects. Every shot which belongs in the scene is there, and suddenly one can clearly see not only how Clint Eastwood's character escapes, but the pain he must endure to do so.

The Techniscope film is presented with an aspect ratio of about 2.4:1, and it is greatly improved by the additional width. The monaural sound, which has been digitally encoded on the MGM/UA disc, is much cleaner than the CBS/Fox presentation, though it is still a bit on the rough side. It quickly becomes apparent that Ennio Morricone's precedent setting score is carefully coordinated with the widescreen images. The horns, in particular, are utilized to fill empty portions of the screen, and gain a tremendous emotional power in the process. Every shot on the letterboxed version has a stronger, clearer and more satisfying composition than on the CBS/Fox scanned and cropped version, with the exception, perhaps, of a couple closeups.

In direct comparison, the colors on the MGM/UA version are paler than those on the CBS/Fox rendition, but the difference is deceptive. The CBS/Fox picture is oversaturated and excessively contrasted, while the MGM/UA image is smooth and accurately detailed. Ideally, the fleshtones ought be somewhere between these two versions, but it is so exciting to see a presentation of *A Fistful of Dollars* which doesn't look as if it was found in an alley in Rome that viewers will not mind such minor drawbacks.

FIVE EASY PIECES

The presentation of *Five Easy Pieces* is not pristine, but most viewers will find it to be acceptable. Voyager's greatest error is to place their Videoscope logo on the jacket cover, because no more than a sliver of matting appears at the top and bottom of the screen. Even though the movie was made at a time when low-budget productions were the industry rage, the source material is a little pale and a little ragged. One brief sequence has hair-thin vertical white lines running through it. In some places the fleshtones verge on an orange tint. There are also sequences which look super – a close up of Susan Anspach, for example, in which every nuance of her hair and complexion appears to be rendered precisely – but on the whole, the presentation is not out of the ordinary. We also found the sound required some adjusting to achieve clear, listenable tones.

The title of the film refers to both the five country/western songs and the five classical music passages that appear on the soundtrack during the course of the narrative. The film, about an itinerant oil field hand who comes from a prominent family of musicians, strikes a nerve in most viewers because it speaks to the desire for a different lifestyle, whether it is the wish for the luxury that appears to come with a prominent position or the freedom that appears to come with a lowly one. The concept is so powerful that the film's flagrantly humorous passages, particularly the scenes with the hitchhikers which seem to have been included to lighten the film's mood, don't feel contrived or cheap. *Five Easy Pieces* is about a man in his twenties, played by an overly mannered Jack Nicholson, whose youth was so ordered that it will take a very long time for him to stop fighting its shadows. The hero is a no-good jerk, yet the viewer feels sympathy for him without feeling superior. Since the movie makers both mock and revere popular and classical music, and the lifestyles the music evokes, the viewer has nowhere else to turn. Viewers see the film differently, depending upon their own backgrounds or age, but it is a consistently pleasing work which is good for a number of repeat screenings over time. It is one of those movies you can grow with.

THE FIVE PENNIES (Import)

The Danny Kaye film, *The Five Pennies*, is one of those maudlin efforts which, once you come across it on TV or something, is difficult to turn off or turn away from. Although not CX-encoded, the sound isn't bad, and the picture is in good condition, faltering only during the strong red lighting in some of the night club scenes. The Japanese subtitles are not bothersome.

Kaye portrays the coronet player, Red Nichols, who abandons a successful career when his daughter becomes ill. Louis Armstrong is in the movie, and so is Barbara Bel Geddes. In all the wrong ways the film is a classic, and it is certainly ideal home video material.

THE FLAME AND THE ARROW

"In the twelfth century – all Northern Italy lay wretched under the armies of the German emperor Frederick Barbarossa..." If a movie executive saw that on the first page of a script today, eyes and heads would roll.

Fortunately, the movie is already in the can, so it is too late to stop it. Twelfth century Italy may not get coverage in the pages of *Spin*, but *The Flame and the Arrow* is the type of movie laser disc collectors go crazy for. It has everything. Burt Lancaster doing somersaults and flips, swordplay, galloping horses, evil deeds, Max Steiner's music, and romance: Lancaster pauses in the middle of a frantic battle to plant a kiss on a kitchen maid.

The sound is solid and typical of a late forties effort. The day-for-night transfer is poor and a couple of other sequences are weak but in most of the movie the Technicolor hues are distinctive and gratifying. Just as they don't make movies like this any more, they don't use these colors, either.

THE FLAMINGO KID

Matt Dillon proves his versatility in *The Flamingo Kid* as he portrays a bright, enthusiastic boy from Brooklyn who lands a summer job in a private beach club in the early '60s. The songs chosen to grace the music soundtrack are ideal. For example, several tunes by The Drifters are used while the one song you would expect to hear, 'Under the Boardwalk,' is not. A slightly indistinct haze in the transfer adds to the nostalgic feeling of the film without doing any great harm to the presentation.

FLASHPOINT

The quotations from critics which have been affixed to the jacket cover of *Flashpoint* do not praise the movie. Instead, the blurbs, in awkward and fragmented English, reveal the film's ending, that the money, which the border patrolmen (Kris Kristofferson and Treat Williams) have unearthed, was a payment for the Kennedy assassination. If one keeps in mind that those who play their trump cards on the first pass do not have strong hands, one will obtain a fair assessment of the entire film by simply picking up the jacket cover and reading the front and back of it.

Since most of the story takes place in the bright Texas sun, the picture is strong. The film features a score by Tangerine Dream which contributes successfully to an atmosphere of tension.

FLESH AND BLOOD

When the action in *Flesh and Blood* slows down, the viewer will notice the excessively grainy picture and indistinct color edges, but in point of fact the action rarely slows down. The film takes place in Renaissance Europe but involves characters who still haven't shaken off the Dark Ages. The contemporary dialog, in an English that usually matches the lips of the actors, has a mildly anachronistic tone which doesn't always sustain the mood of the film. The romantic aspect of the plot is very adult (the heroine doesn't love either of the two protagonists, but is strongly attracted to both of them anyway) and satisfying. The violence keeps the plot moving and the characters honest.

The Paul Verhoeven film (identified as 'Flesh + Blood' everywhere but the jacket spine), stars Rutger Hauer. Verhoeven and Hauer have made better films together, but this one has a rainy Saturday afternoon sort of appeal to it. It runs 126 minutes, but is CLV throughout. It comes in a gatefold jacket with an attractive inner cover. The disc is digitally encoded stereo. The sound quality is passable, although the film itself lacks a Hollywood gloss on the technical level.

FLESH FOR FRANKENSTEIN (ANDY WARHOL'S FRANKENSTEIN) (Import)

Andy Warhol's Frankenstein (which Warhol had nothing to do with with beyond lending his name to the title) was known overseas as *Flesh for Frankenstein*, which is how the Japanese laser disc release is titled. The disc offers the best and the worst of a Japanese release. It is in widescreen, and the subtitles appear below the picture, but the male and female genitals, of which there are many, are covered with annoying flesh-colored blurs.

Since the movie was originally in 3-D, entrails, knives, and dead bodies all get flung at the camera. The film is a mixture of camp and gore. The acting is about level with an elementary school play, but the meat-market guts are fun and there are a couple of terrific decapitations. The monaural CX-encoded sound is a little noisy. The 2-D print looks fairly fresh, so you can easily make out the colors of the different organs.

FLETCH

Fletch is the type of mystery story we enjoy very much. Parts of the script are clever, such as the way Fletch (Chevy Chase) pays off his alimony with murder contract money and the way a sweepstakes offering pops up twice in the course of the story. The plot ends up not being very complicated, but getting there is all the fun. The music, an imitation of the *Beverly Hills Cop* soundtrack, has a good strong beat. The print and sound are sharp.

FLETCH LIVES

Until the script has to settle down and concentrate on solving the mystery, *Fletch Lives* is fairly funny. There are some good one-liners in the beginning and a dream sequence, unlike the dream sequences in the first film, which works quite well (it includes some amusing animation). After all that, we were quite happy to sit back and enjoy everything else, even if it followed a mildly downhill course. Chevy Chase repeats his role as a reporter who uses disguises while digging up stories about corruption and scandal. In *Fletch Lives* he inherits a dilapidated Southern mansion and soon finds himself in the middle of a development conflict, involving an amusement park called Bible Land. The possibilities for satire are left largely unrealized, however, during a climatic chase sequence through the amusements.

The picture is sharp and the colors look accurate. The musical score, although something of a waste of time, takes command of one's entire viewing area. The sound effects are marvelous. For various and sundry reasons, a lot of metal gets crunched during the course of the film, and crunched metal has never sounded as vivid on a disc as it does here.

THE FLIGHT OF THE NAVIGATOR

The reason *Flight of the Navigator* failed at the theaters is that it is made up of two different concepts which don't work in the retelling. The first part of the movie is straight out of 'The Twilight Zone,' with a boy waking up from a fall in the woods to discover his family and the rest of the world have aged eight years. The second half of the story has the boy zipping through the air in a gravity-defying flying saucer. Surprisingly, although the flight scenes seem repetitive and stretched to meet the film's 89-minute running time, this is the segment which stays with you long after the movie is over. It manages to make the wildest day dreams quite believable.

The disc has an impressive analog stereo soundtrack. The picture looks good, but it is slightly grainy in a couple of spots.

THE FLIGHT OF THE PHOENIX

Because *The Flight of the Phoenix* takes place in the desert, it already has a dusty, faded color scheme. The copy released on disc does not look worse for wear and survives the cropping from a wider screen by gaining in claustrophobia what it looses in bully force. The sound is shrill from the quality and practices which were common when the movie was made, and has been transferred to disc accurately.

The two and a half hour story about a group of men who build an airplane to rescue themselves from the Sahara is good, repeatable entertainment. As the film progresses and the characters become weaker, the actors shrivel and blister convincingly. Hardy Kruger, who portrays the designer of the rescue plane, allows his passion to slip out for only the briefest moments. Jimmy Stewart, as the pilot of the downed aircraft which stranded the group, starts to shake more and more as the events progress, and then rekindles his inner strength when it is needed.

THE FLINSTONES (see YOGI BEAR)

FLOATING WEEDS

Yasujiro Ozu's *Floating Weeds*, is in color and the screen compositions are incredible. Minutely balanced Mondrian squares seem to seize hold of every camera angle. On one hand the set designs are so delicately complex that you wonder how the filmmakers had any time left to tell a story, and yet on the other hand the story flows so freely you wonder if the images aren't just chance occurrences.

In the same way that a painter can take an ordinary flower and, by interpreting it on canvas, make it unique, so, too, does Ozu take situations out of everyday life and turn them into portraits of life's essence. Usually Ozu's films depict urban or suburban households. *Floating Weeds*, however, is about the visit of an acting troupe to a small town, and Ozu appears interested in adding the variable of transience to his standard domestic exploration. The leader of the troupe has a mistress and an illegitimate son in the town, and a jealous companion in the troupe. The others are bored. The film is systematic in working its way through these melodramas, but it does so in a relaxed and unhurried manner.

The transfer is gorgeous. Some of the strongest colors blur a little, but none appear faded or worn down. Annoying grey bands are sometimes used to highlight the white English subtitles, but otherwise the image is spotless. Ozu's sound editing is almost as complex and mannered as his cinematography (if you get the disc, you might want to listen to it sometime with the picture turned off) and is worth amplifying despite an occasional scratch. The film runs a few seconds under two hours and has been fit onto a single platter, with a couple of dozen frames from the end of side one repeated at the beginning of side two.

FLORIDA STRAITS

We can't imagine watching *Florida Straits* more than once or twice in the course of our life, but it isn't a bad film. Raul Julia and Fred Ward give enjoyable performances and the plot is a get-the-gold-out-of-Cuba adventure which never slows down. The sound, or at least the music and the jungle insects, is in stereo and is enjoyable. The picture quality is acceptable, though some of the darker scenes seem a bit blurry. There is one impressive location, an abandoned power plant, which the filmmakers clearly and deservedly take delight in using. But the limits of their imagination are also present. Near the beginning of the film there is a card game and, despite the movie's title, the winner and the loser have a full house.

FLOWERS IN THE ATTIC

If you suppress your expectations and can get through the opening twenty minutes, you may find *Flowers in the Attic* to be a stimulating and enjoyable movie. It is only an hour and a half long, and so it cannot compete with its source, but when the plot finally puts the kids in the attic and presents alternatives for their escape, it's got you. Even the excessively poor acting demonstrated by the youngsters ceases to be a problem when they've got a real conflict to act out.

The picture quality is quite poor. The image is often grainy, and contributes to an urge to dismiss the program before it really gets under way. The monaural sound, despite its digital encoding, is not much better.

THE FLY

No one infuses quite as much intelligence with gross-out horror as does the director, David Cronenberg. When the eccentric hero in Cronenberg's remake of *The Fly*, who accidentally mixes his genetic pool with a fly's, starts mouthing his ideas and his theories, they are really worth listening to even though he is a nut. Later, when he's well on the road to insectivity, he starts quoting Kafka. If only an allusion like that was common enough to be a cliche. In so many other effect and guts movies, you wonder if anyone even knows how to read.

The stereo mix is tremendous. The music and the sounds come from all over the place, but the standard levels of background noise are there as well, since it has not been digitally encoded. The picture transfer looks fine when enough lighting fills a scene, but as soon as the locale darkens, the fidelity is weakened.

THE FLY II

Although the film has plenty of grotesque special effects, one still gets the feeling that *The Fly II* should have been raunchier than it is. Instead of hiring Chris Walas, who did the makeup on *The Fly* remake, to direct, the producers should have found the sickest, most deranged movie director they could get their hands on. Walas' film is not bad. It is involving and moves at a well-balanced pace, with enough thrills that the repeat potential is viable. But it is also a safe movie, never too surprising or exploratory, and it is just a shame that, with the opportunity to do mischief (after the hero starts mutating, his girlfriend doesn't even kiss him), the filmmakers chose to keep to a formula.

The disc has a terrific digital stereo surround soundtrack and a slightly soft but workable picture. Eric Stolz stars as the son of the character in the first movie, trying to rebuild his father's equipment before the dormant genetic codes inside of him become active.

THE FLY/RETURN OF THE FLY

Scanning and cropping prevents one from spotting the claw of the fly when it is first revealed. The horror classic is part of a cropped Cinemascope double bill, *The Fly/Return of the Fly* .

The first film is in color and has stereo surround sound. The second film is monaural and is black and white. The break between the two is marked with Chapter 9 on side two of the three sided package. The color on the first film is mildly washed out, but rich enough to satisfy most viewers. The sound mix is dumb in a fun sort of way – when the disintegrator/ integrator machine is turned on, the sound effect begins with a noisy hum and then shifts to a loud mashing noise set at peak volume. The sound on the sequel is a real letdown, not because there is anything wrong with it but because, after you've had a taste of the first, the standard monaural effects aren't good any more. The black and white picture on the second film shifts in and out of focus and looks a little muddy.

The films go well together because the first is designed to leave the viewer both satisfied and hungering for more. James Clavell wrote the screenplay of the first film, and it is worthwhile to note one aspect in which the sequel, which Clavell had nothing to do with, lets down its predecessor. In the first film, a scientist, who has a loving family, experiments on a matter transportation unit and mixes up his own molecules with those of a fly. Part of him is left on the small fly, which escapes. His larger half is able to communicate with his wife and urges her to capture the insect, so the two beings can be re-run through the machine and unmixed. The wife anxiously attempts to capture the fly, and enlists her son in the task, who approaches it, as any child would, as a game. The chilling way in which the son is oblivious to the horror as he tries to cooperate with the crazy adults is one of the film's most lasting and unsettling emotional coups. Well, in the sequel, the son grows up, recreates his father's experiments, and is himself transmorgified almost exactly in the same manner that his father was. Even though 'Return' was a lesser effort intended only to capitalize on the first, it is a disappointment that somehow, the realization that he is now on the other end of the game could not have been communicated or elaborated upon.

THE FLYING LEATHERNECKS

A typical VidAmerica Classic Series release, *Flying Leathernecks*, is riddled with flaws. At first the colors look good. But then, at the reel change, the colors practically disappeared. As it turned out, the quality of the print varies from reel to reel, some looking okay and others pretty bad. The movie was an episodic do-as-you're-told effort by Nicholas Ray for Howard Hughes. It usually runs 102 minutes. The jacket cover says the movie runs 102 minutes. The disc runs 92 minutes. One reel, apparently, disappeared altogether.

FOLK CITY

The 25th Anniversary Concert for the nightclub, Folk City, is anything but nostalgic as it appears *Folk City*. The all-star performances are terrific and the music is surprisingly vital, reinforcing the concept that real folk music never ages. The concert, which was recorded on video tape and is presented on the disc with a clean picture and solid blacks, took place on a pier and featured 15 well known singers, from Joan Baez to the punk-folk Violent Femmes.

The music is topical and good fun (Tom Paxton, singing to the tune of 'Ghostriders in the Sky': "All the salad bars were empty, all the quiche Lorraine was gone/I heard the yuppies crying as they vanished in the dawn..."), and the brief interviews between the numbers put everything in perspective without disrupting the flow of the program.

The stereo sound is adeptly recorded, capturing both the live atmosphere (a cruise ship at a nearby dock blasts its horn at one point) and the rich singing voices. The 83-minute program has chapters which are listed on the back of the jacket cover.

FOLLIES IN CONCERT

A documentary of the all-star performance, *Follies in Concert*, is not a replacement for the audio recording, but it is does provide a number of visuals which will delight fans. The 90-minute program covers the entire effort, so that the first half of the disc concerns rehearsals and the actual concert is abridged to about 40 minutes. The picture is a grainy 16mm effort and the sound recording, even for the concert sequences, is not as pure as the CD.

The disc reflects the limitations in the film. We would have preferred to see more concert and less rehearsal, but the material is genuinely interesting and the concert is by itself on side two if one loses patience with the opening part. The disc is also chapter encoded, adequately for the rehearsal segment, but inadequately for the concert.

'Follies,' with music and lyrics by Stephen Sondheim, is about a reunion of chorus girls and uses a number of different song styles to represent the fates of the different characters. As a concert recital, backed by the New York Philharmonic, it is pleasing, because the stars have been chosen to suit the songs and each has an opportunity to shine brilliantly. Although singers such as Barbara Cook and Erie Mills dominate the pleasures of the album, Carol Burnett and Elaine Stritch steal the show when the audio is combined with the visuals. Good singing is one thing, but good singing with convincing emotion is something only film or video can capture.

FONTEYN & NUREYEV: THE PERFECT PARTNERSHIP
BUJONES – IN HIS IMAGE

A welcome assessment of the intertwined careers of Margot Fonteyn and Rudolph Nureyev is presented in *Fonteyn & Nureyev: The Perfect Partnership*. It begins by focussing upon Fonteyn, who had the ultimate in a second wind. An established star and one of the world's premiere ballerinas, she was entering what appeared to be the final stage of her career – fewer performances and more benefits – when a pairing with the young defector, Nureyev, catapulted her achievements to even greater heights. Nureyev's ability and drive forced her to re-examine her priorities and to improve her own skills. In turn, she gave Nureyev instant access to the pinnacles of success and was one of the few dancing partners good enough to reflect his talents. For a while they achieved perpetual artistic motion, each drawing the same amount of energy from the other to accelerate.

The documentary scrapes together clips from early BBC broadcasts and even bootlegged 8mm movies to show both performers during all the major phases in their careers. Aspects of the two's personal lives are also touched upon, and narrative covers the downs as well as the ups. Most of the footage is aged, and that which is in color is usually soft in appearance. The interviews are clear (the reminiscences from those who worked with the pair provide the program's strongest insights) but the music is employed more as a reference to the dancing than as a collaboration with the dancers. The major excerpts include pieces from 'Le Corsair,' 'Les Sylphides,' 'Marguerite and Armand,' 'Romeo and Juliet,' and a Martha Graham work, 'Lucifer.' The disc runs 90 minutes.

Bujones – In His Image, is an hour-long program which is both better and not as good as *Fonteyn & Nureyev*. As a documentary, the show is lacking in substance and style. The description of Fernando Bujones' rise to fame is unsystematic and shallow. Bujones is interviewed extensively, but he lacks an ability to project an appealing personality on camera. The profile of Bujones' private life is stagey and uncomfortable (in contrast, the moderately warts-and-all presentation of Fonteyn and Nureyev increases a viewer's sympathy for them). Few of Bujones' dancing partners are identified during the segments in which they appear and the descriptions of his talent are rarely more than platitudes.

The dancing, however, is fantastic – even better than the *Fonteyn & Nureyev* clips. Bujones benefits from having come to his own in the age of video. Whereas the *Fonteyn & Nureyev* program had to utilize whatever visual material could be scraped together, it is clear that the Bujones pieces have been culled from vast collections of taped performances. No matter, the end result, which includes Bujones performing in 'Giselle,' 'Raymonda,' 'Swan Lake,' 'Don Quixote,' 'Le Corsaire,' 'La Sylphide,' and Maurice Bejart's 'Seven Greek Dances,' is one breathtaking exhibition after another. His athleticism and stamina are showcased, but the artistry of his precision is also clearly evidenced.

The clips are all mildly blurry. The quality of the image, however, rarely impacts the effect of dancing scenes. The music, although ratty at times, feels legitimate.

FOOD FOR THE GODS PART 2

Except for the general premise, *Food of the Gods Part 2* has nothing to do with the first 'Food of the Gods' film, but that is probably in its favor. It is a hokey but fun movie about big nasty rats on a college campus. The movie has a sense of humor, and the cheap special effects collude with one's intelligence instead of insulting it. The picture is in very good condition, which adds to the film's respectability. The monaural sound also has some strength. The movie runs under 90 minutes, but remains in CLV. There are enough scenes of gore to warrant the film's R rating.

FOOTLIGHT PARADE

Footlight Parade is the best of all the Warner Brothers Busby Berkeley musicals for one reason – James Cagney. The formula for these musicals is always great fun – the wild production numbers, the singable songs, Ruby Keeler's monstrously awkward performances – but inserting Cagney gives the movie moxie it could never achieve on its own. Not only is Cagney comfortable doing the dance numbers, he's at ease with the silly let's-put-on-a-show-in-24-hours plot convolutions, and he controls your attitude toward the movie with the same confidence that his character controls those around him. The two effects are inseparable, actually.

The movie is a joy. Not only does it conclude with three spectacular production numbers, but it is filled with saucy, pre-Code dialog, a script which has more linear movement than most, and an unusual subject, the creation of live prologs to introduce motion picture screenings.

Every time *Footlight Parade* appears on broadcast television an important news wire display which opens the film is cropped off the top of the screen. Not so on the disc, which MGM/UA has wisely manipulated so that the viewer can see everything the characters are reading. The print looks its age, but no worse than that. The disc opens with a wonderfully deteriorated cartoon about insects, set to the 'Honeymoon Hotel' number. It is in color, sort of, and has a naughty, inventive, Fleischerish tone. After the cartoon, a trailer for 'Dames' appears, which contains highlights from five different Berkeley spectacles. The CX-encoded analog monaural sound is soft but reasonably clean.

FOOTSTEPS OF GIANTS
A 45-minute documentary on America's space program, from the flight of Friendship 7 to the Challenger disaster, *Footsteps of Giants*, has been released in CLV. The film jumps around chronologically and seems to reach a crescendo every five minutes. It is apparently an attempt to keep the spirit up – emphasizing the positive results of the space program so far and assuring the viewer that what happened to the Challenger was an unfortunate but momentary setback in the inevitability of space exploration. The documentary footage contains little, other than the Challenger break up, which has not appeared elsewhere on disc.

The transfer is okay. The older the NASA footage, the weaker the quality, but the talking heads (including some refreshingly philosophical comments from James Oberg and from Norman Mailer) are all sharp. The sound is also adequate.

FOR ALL MANKIND
FOR ALL MANKIND (CAV)
The US space program and Apollo lunar missions have been extensively covered on laser video disc, but anyone with an interest in the subject will want to acquire *For All Mankind*, as will anyone searching for new frontiers to demonstrate their audio-video systems.

From over two thousand hours of 16mm NASA footage shot by the Apollo astronauts, filmmaker Al Reinert selected 78 minutes which capture the essence of a voyage from the earth to the moon and back again. The images were carefully transferred to 35mm and were combined with audio excerpts from extensive interviews with the Apollo astronauts, fabulous sound effects, and a typical, though well-crafted Brian Eno musical score.

For All Mankind is a science non-fiction movie. Footage and sounds from all the Apollo flights are deliberately merged into a single impressionistic journey. The astronaut commentary varies in subject matter, shifting from key technical details to generalized personal experiences and thoughts. The film is composed to give the viewer the same sense which the astronauts themselves had leaving the embryo of Earth – not all the dials and the endless checklists, but the shifts in gravity and the receding horizons. One of the astronauts mentions the cliché about the insignificance of earth, but the quality of the film is so strong that the world we live on, described at one point as being the size of a marble, looks more like a rare blue gem, cast alone in the sands of nothingness.

The disc is a blast. It has digital stereo surround sound which will knock visitors out of their chairs. When one of the astronauts says, "It feels just like it sounds," only the restrictions of your audio system will prevent you from understanding exactly what he means. The picture quality often possesses the inherent grain caused by the original manipulation of the 16mm source material, but it is impeccably transferred, and when the source is pure the disc image is pure. Some of the film looks so vivid it seems fake.

Voyager has released the disc in both CLV and CAV formats. There is no significant difference in picture or sound between the two formats. The CLV disc has none of the special features found on the CAV disc detailed below, but it does have an interesting commercial for other Voyager programs.

In addition to giving the viewer interactive access to the film, the CAV disc has a fourth side which contains a collection of odds and ends concerning the Apollo program. The audio track on the fourth side is split into three parts to contain an hour-long interview with astronaut Alan Bean and a half hour of miscellaneous event recordings. Bean is specifically talking about paintings he has made, which can be seen in still frame at one point on the side, but the real function of the interview is to listen to his moon experiences, using each painting as a jumping-off point. Excerpts from 'A Trip to the Moon,' 'Die Frau im Mond,' and *Rocketship X-M* are also included on the side, as are about 500 still photos from the Apollo project and minor material depicting the world press coverage of the first moon landing.

A bundle of stills – the same stills – appears on each side of the disc, after a picture stop marks the end of the film. An insufficient attempt to identify the speakers in the film's narration also appears at the end of each side. The utility or sensibility of these items is questionable.

The best feature of the CAV disc is an excellent conference interview with Reinert which runs during the movie on an alternate analog audio track. Reinert may be a bit too mystical in his overview – he sites the life experiences of the astronauts since they retired as evidence that the moon trip affected them deeply, and while there is no doubt that it did, it has been our experience that all retired military men are a bit batty – but he has fascinating things to say about what the space program achieved, what he went through during the ten years it took him to put the film together, and what a trip to the moon was like. He also provides the essential facts for those who are unfamiliar or only partially familiar with the Apollo program.

For All Mankind demonstrates clearly that while pure scientific knowledge is enhanced by visits to outer space, so are Man's philosophies and self-awareness. The film gives the journey the feeling of a Hollywood adventure, but it also demonstrates how enriching the rewards from the journey have been, not just to the men involved, not just to the United States, but to every person living, dead, or yet to be born, whoever paused in the night to gaze at the sky.

FOR ME AND MY GAL
The wonderful, inspiring ending of Gene Kelly and Judy Garland movie, *For Me and My Gal*, leaves a viewer feeling good about the entire film. The black-and-white musical is about a pair of WWI-era vaudeville performers who continue to put off getting married. MGM/UA has enthusiastically chapter encoded the disc, so that in a medley montage, every song has its own marker. The print is in good shape, and even where the source is damaged it has been repaired to hide the flaw. The sound is fine.

FOR KEEPS
There are a handful of deftly written (and acted) scenes in *For Keeps*, especially one which borders on black comedy – an argument at a Thanksgiving dinner as to whether a pregnancy should end in abortion or adoption. The rest of the film, however, is unimaginative and uneventful, so that neither the cute little infants which take turns standing in as Molly Ringwald's surprise package, or Ringwald herself, can save the material. The disc is only for those who are totally committed to having it.

The disc has chapters for several baby-oriented pop songs on the soundtrack. The digital sound is in stereo, but it is not a first-rate mix, and has no outstanding features. The analog track is even less stimulating. The picture quality is no better than acceptable, as the colors take on a life of their own at times.

FOR YOUR EYES ONLY (CBS/Fox)
FOR YOUR EYES ONLY (MGM/UA)
There are plenty of reasons to obtain the MGM/UA Deluxe Letter-Box Edition of *For Your Eyes Only* if you are a James Bond fan, but there are also some compelling reasons for not discarding the CBS/Fox version. The transfer of *For Your Eyes Only* by CBS/Fox was exceptional in its day, though it looks both cloudy and grainy when compared to the MGM/UA letterboxed version.

Except for a couple of night scenes which take on a little grain, and a sequence bathed in orange-red light, the picture on the MGM/UA disc is smooth and glossy. The fleshtones are ideal and the underwater footage is completely undistorted.

The image has an aspect ratio of about 2.2:1, providing a clear and coherent view of the many action sequences. The action is harder to follow on the cropped and scanned CBS/Fox disc, though some key moments are more exciting when magnified on the cropped image.

The MGM/UA disc has digitally encoded stereo surround sound. The sound on the CBS/Fox disc is analog CX-encoded stereo surround. Although it is noisier, the sound delivery is significantly better on the CBS/Fox disc than on MGM/UA's effort. Sound effects which are buried on the MGM/UA soundtrack are fully and distinctly amplified on the CBS/Fox version. The most telling comparison can be found in the nerve-wracking climb of the monastery cliff in the finale. When the bad guy kicks James Bond off the edge and the stunt man falls thirty feet or so until he is arrested by his safety rope, there is a loud crunch when the rope takes hold on the CBS/Fox disc and virtually no sound at all on the MGM/UA offering.

For Your Eyes Only was a calculated effort on the part of the James Bond producers to change the formula slightly, increasing the number of action sequences and decreasing the dialog and witticisms needed to bridge them. The result is not all that successful. Although the film is captivating the first time through – it hardly allows you to catch your breath between stunts – the repeat viewing potential is limited, because the illogical plot turns and empty dramatics become more pronounced as the film becomes more familiar.

For Your Eyes Only had what it takes for a terrific trailer however, perhaps the best in the series, and that can be found on side three of the MGM/UA disc, conveniently in CAV so that all of the highlights, and not just the monastery sequence, can be manipulated.

FORBIDDEN GAMES
The audio on *Forbidden Games* has two tracks, one in the original French language

and one in English. The one in English gives the movie the feel of a martial arts flick. It is horrible, and the only possible application we could see for it would be if someone wanted to share the film with a person who was too young to read subtitles.

The French soundtrack isn't all that easy going either, since, like most foreign films from the fifties, it is in a little rough shape. The sound, which is not CX-encoded, has hums, crackling, hiss, and a host of other noises, and both the music and the dialog crack up in the higher frequencies. But all that is to be expected. The print is really no better. It is complete, but is often marked with scars and scratches. The subtitles have been redone for video and are in a slightly obnoxious shade of yellow, which takes a while getting used to.

The movie is a favorite of many people and has a strong emotional impact on the first viewing, although repeat viewings are more mellow. It is about a five-year-old girl, orphaned at the start of World War II, who spends some time with a family on a farm she wanders into. Much has been said, rightly, about the film's power in expressing the impact of war, death, and childhood. Less often mentioned, however, is that the movie is also a cute little parable of the way in which women manipulate men, and even has vague parallels, from the title on down, with the story of the Garden of Eden.

FORBIDDEN PLANET (MGM/UA)
FORBIDDEN PLANET (Voyager)

Anybody who is enthusiastic enough to obtain *Forbidden Planet* for their laser disc collection is going to want to own the CAV Criterion Collection version. In a supplementary section after the film is ended, clips from scenes which were dropped during the final editing and preview process are available to the general public for the very first time. The screen image is letterboxed at 2.3:1, wide enough so the viewer can see Robby zap the monkey. The picture, though still shackled by the deflated capabilities of the original Eastmancolor source, is clean of defects and sharply focussed. The picture is significantly improved over MGM/UA's scanned and cropped CLV version.

The movie epitomizes all which was right and wrong with science fiction films before the art of special motion picture effects had advanced to the point of adult believability. (Only ten years separate *Forbidden Planet* from *2001: A Space Odyssey*, but the difference seems as great as the lifetimes it took to go from Kitty Hawk to Apollo.) In the wrong category, the film's ambience is soundstage-bound, the repartee among the crew on the spacecraft is vaudevillian, and more time is spent trying to amaze the audience than trying to tell the story. But, in the right category, MGM contributed its art and costume design muscle to create the ultimate fifties science fiction trip. Since the movie makers couldn't disguise the artifice, they did the next best thing. They made the critical effects sequences so creative and awe-inspiring that the imagination is captivated whether or not a viewer believes in what comes before or after. Finally, the screenwriters had the inspiration to use one of William Shakespeare's most ambivalent and thought-provoking plays, 'The Tempest,' as their source material. The ending avoids becoming a dime-store Freudian interpretation of Shakespeare's work because of the scope of the fantasy. The Calibanish 'Id' monster is not the result of a father's lust for his daughter, it is the unleashed fury of an entire, dead *civilization*, one which wanted immortality and got eternal damnation instead.

The sound on the disc is digitally encoded stereo, from a 2-track stereo Dolby-encoded magnetic soundtrack. The analog track is CX-encoded without automatic tripping, and is significantly cleaner when the CX is activated. Although the soundtrack is not as elaborate as other epics, the innovative electronic musical score is especially effective when the volume is raised. Much has been written about the music, by Louis and Bebe Barron, but it is worth noting that it seems to be locked into the pulse of the film. Every detail worth appreciating in the film's visuals is echoed in the eerie, furtive score.

Those who are prone to purchase the film in the first place will undoubtedly have sequences they wish to manipulate with the CAV functions. The disc comes in a gatefold jacket with thumbnail biographical sketches of the major contributing artists gracing the innerspread. Along with the cut footage, the supplementary section contains a variety of stills and text essays about the movie's production. The material gives a satisfactory overview of how *Forbidden Planet* came into being. Among the most significant revelations in the added material is why the tiger attacks when he does. It is the sort of thing which would not have been removed if the movie hadn't been made in the fifties.

FORCE OF EVIL

Abraham Polonsky's fascinating and intense drama, *Force of Evil*, has been released on laser disc by Republic. Contrary to the jacket cover, a theatrical trailer has not been included with the film, but otherwise the disc transfer is superb. The black and white print is razor sharp, and the strongest blacks and whites gleam with a shiny gloss. The sound is very clean.

The only film which Polonsky directed before he was blacklisted, *Force of Evil* is a brief but complex tale about two brothers involved in a mob takeover of the numbers racket in New York City. The project is doomed from the beginning, but the stormy relationship between the two brothers complicates things further. John Garfield stars. The film is unusual and striking. Visually it is very rewarding, which is why the excellent transfer makes the $30 disc so valuable, but the atmosphere and the interaction between the characters are also exceptionally entertaining. The narrative is bleak, but the narrative pace is upbeat, and the combination is explosive.

FOREVER LULU

Hanna Schygulla, Deborah Harry, and Annie Golden all appear in *Forever Lulu*. Unfortunately, casting them was the only creative inspiration the filmmakers had, and the movie looks as if more than half of its budget went to Schygulla's salary. The script is closer to a first draft than a final draft, and the film's 86-minute running time becomes intolerably long as a result. The picture transfer is good. The digitally encoded sound is passable, but the stereo sound mix in the film is as dreary as its other elements. Side two is in CAV, with two shakey still frames out of every five, and includes a visit to an S&M establishment and a lengthy scene involving Schygulla and a bath of bubbles.

The plot casts Schygulla as a would-be author who strikes it rich from the publicity generated when she stumbles into a drug deal. Harry, as Lulu, has an index card's worth of dialog and just strolls though the set once in a while, for effect. Golden shows some promise as the author's best friend, but her presence is wasted by the ineptness of the film. Schygulla, whose entire career developed because she never understood, or never looked as though she understood, her director's jokes, has no grasp for the comic elements of her part, and looks even more lost than her character is supposed to be.

FORT APACHE (VidAmerica)
FORT APACHE (Image)

Although other VidAmerica transfers were scandalously inadequate, the transfer of John Ford's *Fort Apache* was quite good. However, the film has been released again anyway, by Image. The source material for the two discs are different – the scratches are in different places – and on just picture alone the VidAmerica offering is superior to the Image effort. The picture is sharper, brighter, and has fewer splices. However, Image's release is still quite nice looking and has a number of other advantages. The disc has digital monaural sound as well, while VidAmerica's version wasn't even CX-encoded. It also has chapter markers and side three, with the climatic Indian battle, is in CAV, with two unsteady still frames out of every five.

This was a transitional picture for Ford. Indians were just beginning to become heroically noble in his vision of the west. *Fort Apache* 's 127 minutes amounts to 120 minutes of 'life on the Fort' vignettes and seven minutes of action. Commercially, it was a risky venture which Ford could only undertake after having scored several popular successes. The story – nominally about a Colonel (Henry Fonda) trying to turn an assignment at a dusty outpost into a career advancement – has a Shakespearean construction where subplots about the enlisted men at the fort take up as much screen time as the politics of their superiors. On multiple viewings the material not central to the main plot becomes tiresome, while the plot itself becomes more gripping and exciting. John Wayne also stars.

45/85: AMERICA AND THE WORLD SINCE WORLD WAR II VOLUME I: 1945-1952
45/85: AMERICA AND THE WORLD SINCE WORLD WAR II VOLUME II: 1953-1960
45/85: AMERICA AND THE WORLD SINCE WORLD WAR II VOLUME III: 1961-1975
45/85: AMERICA AND THE WORLD SINCE WORLD WAR II VOLUME IV: 1976-1985

ABC broadcast *45/85: America and the World Since World War II* on one evening, but Vestron broke the documentary into four discs, *Volume I: 1945-1952*, *Volume II: 1953-1960*, *Volume III: 1961-1975*, and *Volume*

IV: 1976-1985. Each disc is one-sided, CLV, and not CX-encoded. Although the jacket covers state the programs run, "Approx. 60 Minutes," the actual running time is a television-style hour of 50 minutes.

On the whole, this ABC special is for people who don't read. Misconceptions are perpetuated (They claim Korea was 'the first war America did not win,' as do most people who stopped studying the War of 1812 in grade school.) and intrinsic events, from the formation of the United Nations to the conviction of Spiro Agnew, pass without a mention. Commentary is limited to suggestions of cause and effect, and many of these will be questionable depending upon one's political point of view.

Volume I includes some rare color footage of Winston Churchill and Harry Truman, but this sort of serendipity is not a hallmark of the series. In *Volume IV*, there is a documentary editor's dream, as interviews with Nixon, Ford, Carter, and Reagan are spliced together to create a discussion of the show's themes. Something must be wrong, however, because Nixon comes across as the most thoughtful of the four.

If you want a summary of what every disc contains, the back of the jackets will tell you almost everything. Don't trust the front of the jackets, though, as they display stills of subject material which is never broached on screen.

42ND STREET (CBS/Fox)
42ND STREET (MGM/UA)

MGM/UA's *42nd Street* goes into your player a disc, but it comes out a star. It opens with a naughty (but amusing) black and white cartoon, 'Shuffle Off to Buffalo,' which seems to have something to do with making babies – we're not sure what, but storks are involved – and a variety of ethnic singers. Then there is a gaudy trailer for *Goldiggers of 1933*, a really fascinating look at how the film was sold to audiences at the height of the Depression. Finally, there is the bawdy, sporty feature film, one of those rare hit parade accomplishments that brought nearly a half-dozen actors and actresses, as well as a choreographer/director, to stardom.

The black and white source material is anything but young and healthy. CBS/Fox released a *42nd Street* disc several years earlier. Although both versions have their share of scratches and worn edges, the CBS/Fox transfer is substantially darker than MGM/UA's, losing many details to the shadows. MGM/UA's version allows viewers to see much more of the costumes, the set designs, and even the expressions on the faces of the characters. It is also interesting to note that the CBS/Fox disc is cropped slightly at the top of the screen, while the MGM/UA presentation is cropped, by about the same amount, at the bottom. The CBS/Fox disc was not CX-encoded and MGM/UA's analog presentation is, though the differences between the two audio tracks are less distinctive than the differences in picture.

Busby Berkeley did not direct the movie, but he was responsible for the creative musical numbers. 42nd Street is certainly one of the best of the Warner musicals which Berkeley was involved with. Since it was the first, it is not as polished as some of the later efforts, but it has the relaxed advantage of not having to top what had gone on before. And then there is Ruby Keeler's amazing performance. Was she really as inept as her character? There seems to be no dividing line between the actress on the stage and the actress on the screen. Ask her for perky enthusiasm and she gives you all she's got. Ask her for pensive concern and she gets completely confused. She's the only actress with fat, leaden feet who ever tap danced her way to the top.

THE 400 BLOWS

Francois Truffaut's *The 400 Blows* is an intimate look at the maturation of a young Parisian delinquent. Black-and-white images convey the texture of the boy's surroundings – the stone walls, chain fences, and cramped apartments.

The subtitled print is in good condition considering the era and budget under which it was produced, but it does have a number of scratches. Although there are moments on the second side where one channel will drop out for an instant, the sound, which is CX-encoded monaural, is especially good. Through the quality of the disc, as blasphemous as it may sound, the famous freeze-frame ending becomes more powerful on television than it ever was in a theater.

THE FOURTH MAN

Paul Verhoeven's *The Fourth Man* which has a number of erotic scenes involving several different persuasions, is a silly, inconsistent contrivance about a man struggling to understand his psychic visions. The color, accurately transferred, is dull and the digitally encoded monaural sound is just as flat. There is a slight black band, usually at the bottom of the screen, which increases or decreases from shot to shot. The subtitles are white, and are lost in a few camera angles involving the hood of a white automobile. The man visits a woman who has had three former husbands, all of whom met with tragedy. One died in the air, one on land, and one in the water. What will happen to the hero? Who cares – as far as the plot is concerned, the movie had exhausted its themes even before he was introduced.

THE FOURTH PROTOCOL

When you watch a spy thriller which has been adapted from a bestseller, you expect to feel nervous. You can also expect disappointment in the ending, not because it will be inept, but simply because the plots usually stretch the nervous tension for so long that anything short of a musical chorus with dancing bears and trapeze artists will feel like a letdown. The point when watching a movie such as *The Fourth Protocol* is not to expect that everything will make sense or mean something but that it will all be fun – if that is what teeth grinding excitement is – while it lasts.

Image's jacket cover contains the original advertising artwork, which completely misrepresents a key facet of the plot concerning the setting on a clock and also presents the false impression that Michael Caine and Pierce Brosnan are partners instead of antagonists. To make up for it though, Image has included a marvelously droll publicity photo on the back, with Caine, Brosnan, and Joanna Cassidy in full costume and all clearly wishing they were anywhere else. The narrative concerns a plot to explode a nuclear bomb on an American airbase in England.

The digital track is excellent, much better than the analog track. The picture is often grainy. The opening and closing credits are very nicely letterboxed, but the rest of the movie is cropped, scanned, and sometimes even squeezed. Michael Caine hasn't looked this thin since 'Alfie.'

FRAME UP 14 CONTRE 1

The potential for creating enjoyable games by combining a laser video disc program with the memory and search control of a personal computer has barely been realized and is beyond the reach of standard consumer player configurations in any case. Sometimes, however, it is enjoyable to sample an innovative experiment, even if one's player is not hooked up to a PC. Watching an intentionally interactive disc in a linear fashion is like walking behind a stage set, but it can also be as stimulating. You see how the artists have constructed things and what they intended to accomplish. Then you contemplate how you might have done it.

A significant interactive program which was developed in France, *Frame Up 14 Contre 1*, is available in NTSC format (and English, it has been dubbed) from Imedia International Inc. A computer diskette comes with the disc. A professional video disc player and RS-232 cable are required to run the disc properly from a PC, but the essential design of *Frame Up* is accessible to anyone with a remote control in their hand.

The narrative, which is in color, concerns a boy who awakens in a department store after closing and must finagle his way past the locked doors. The store is not empty, as the cleaning staff, security staff, and some thieves are all going about their business. The narrative has a limited number of decision points – about a half dozen – and is set so that one should choose the least likely answer in order to win (the decision point searches cannot be activated without a PC).

A major segment of the disc, however, is taken up not by the color narrative, but by black and white images representing the store's ten security cameras. It is this material, which one would piece together with a PC or a sophisticated program/frame search device, that can keep one busy for hours, attempting to follow a character from one security camera image to the next. You can build a literal bargain-basement *Anderson Tapes* drama out of the material.

The sound is monaural and not CX-encoded, but it is vivid. The picture is bright, and although the CAV still frames cause moving figures to blur, one suspects that may have been deliberate. There is some nudity, so teachers are advised to scan the disc carefully before hooking it up in the classroom, even though the PC controls offer an ability to censor the sequence.

FRANCESCA DA RIMINI

The most admirable component of the 'Live at the Met' offering, *Francesca da Rimini*, is the gorgeous libretto booklet they have included with the disc. It contains some wonderful photographs from the Met's first production of the opera in 1916, along with the lyrics in Italian and English (the disc itself has English subtitles), a plot synopsis which is keyed to the chapter markers, and an excellent essay about the opera. This is the kind of textual enhancement which every laser disc ought to have, and it is greatly appreciated.

The opera is 155 minutes long and runs across four sides so that every act can have a side of its own. The picture quality and sound quality are admirable.

The production stars Renata Scotto, Placido Domingo, and Cornell MacNeil. They are predictably superb, as is most of the cast. The opera, by Riccardo Zandonai, concerns lovers in 14th century Italy whose fate echoes the legend of Camelot. It is a work more satisfying to opera companies than to audiences, since it allows for some interesting sets and costumes while not straining the talents of anyone involved. The Met effort is totally engrossing, but it is not the sort of property which one tries to catch every performance of in a season, and it is not the type of disc which one is going to play more than once or twice a year.

FRANCK – SIBELIUS – DEBUSSY – ROSSINI

'William Tell,' which epitomizes the tenuous intersection between classical music and commercial public broadcasting, is the rousing finale on volume 8 of the 'Arturo Toscanini Collection,' *Franck – Sibelius – Debussy – Rossini*. The program opens with Franck's 'Redemption: Symphonic Interlude,' and then proceeds with 'En Saga' by Sibelius and 'Nocturnes' by Debussy. Toscanini's handling of the Franck piece is unexceptional, but 'Nocturnes' and 'En Saga' are astounding. He coaxes such incredible precision from each musician in the orchestra that it really does seem as if it is he who is playing all the instruments. The recording will stand up against any contemporary effort, and despite the monaural presentation the music is marvelously dimensional. Toscanini lets loose a little to have fun with the Rossini number, but it is worth turning way up, even if the volume causes some unnatural distortion. It may be that Toscanini designed his presentation of the piece with its scratchy ubiquity in mind.

The video presentation of volume 8 is not impressive. The camera stays on Toscanini a majority of the time, and rarely looks at the musicians beyond the first row. The kinescopes are often very blurry and have a severely limited number of scaled greys.

FRANK CAPRA'S "IT'S A WONDERFUL LIFE"

(see **IT'S A WONDEFUL LIFE**)

FRANK CAPRA'S MEET JOHN DOE

The print used for *Frank Capra's Meet John Doe* is thought to be the best surviving print of the film. It has speckles and a few hiccups, and the transfer has softened the edges a little, but when one considers the condition of most of the existing copies of the movie, it looks marvelous. The quality of the image never inhibits one's enjoyment of the film.

The sound is okay, too. It is CX-encoded without automatic tripping. Sometimes the music sounds like it is coming from a warped record, but never for more than a moment. The disc has been encoded with 20 chapters, and the jacket cover contains a superb mixture of original advertising art and informed background information. Side three of the disc is in CAV, with two unsteady frames out of every five. The cast is truly marvelous, and the temptation to freeze Gary Cooper, Barbara Stanwyck or even the bad guy, Edward Arnold, and stretch the pleasure of their performances, is all too tempting.

The film runs 123 minutes (not 132, as some reference books mistakenly list it). If one is only familiar with the film through broadcast television, one may never have truly seen the whole movie, since it is often pared down even when filling a two and a half hour time slot. The thing is, for the movie to work for a viewer, it has to be shown at full length. Capra's sense of film rhythm is so perfect that when any sequence is left out, the show is thrown out of balance. It is best to view the movie more than once if you have never seen it before, because the first time through is such an emotionally draining experience that one is apt to respond to the plot on too personal a level.

FRANK SINATRA PORTRAIT OF AN ALBUM
FRANK SINATRA IN JAPAN (Import)

MGM/UA's *Frank Sinatra Portrait of an Album* is a depiction of the recording sessions which contributed to Sinatra's LP, 'L.A. Is My Lady.' The cuts are interspersed with interviews, but the songs are played in full. There are no chapter markers. A small amount of hiss is evident on the digital soundtrack. The picture is a little blurry, too, but no more so than the average release. In fact, we would probably have been even more enthused about this disc had we not come across one which was even better, *Frank Sinatra in Japan*.

No recording can ever impart the complete effects of Sinatra's control over his voice and phrasing of songs which can be heard in a live performance. The sound waves have to roll through the moisture in the air and lap against your ears before you truly understand what is meant by 'liquid delivery.' The digitally encoded Japanese laser disc, *Frank Sinatra in Japan*, however, is probably the closest any recording will ever achieve in imitating the experience of a Sinatra concert. This is a full 18-number 76-minute concert, recorded digitally at Tokyo's cavernous Budokan Hall.

The picture quality on the disc is also near perfection, and every song has a chapter marker. No subtitles appear. Sinatra mentions the composer and arranger of each number, but beyond that and occasional stage patter, he sings without interruption. This is the sort of disc which gets people to buy players.

FRANKENSTEIN GENERAL HOSPITAL

A vaudeville of less-than-amusing doctor jokes keep one's eyes open during *Frankenstein General Hospital*, but little more. The film has the audacity to claim it is 'based on the novel "Frankenstein" by Mary Wollstonecraft Shelley,' but owes more to Mel Brooks – the hero, Mark Blankfield, even looks and acts like Gene Wilder – and to the excesses of puberty. The picture is bright and in good shape. The monaural sound is digitally encoded and deliberately loud.

FRANKENSTEIN MEETS THE WOLF MAN

The buzz-saw electronic sounds when a doctor tries to revitalize the Frankenstein monster and the Wolf Man with 'negative pole' electricity is the best part of *Frankenstein Meets the Wolf Man*, but the amassed villagers, who shout, "Ahhhhh! The monster! The monster!" are almost as much fun. Bela Lugosi is Frank and Lon Chaney, Jr. is Wolf. They have some terrific times together before drowning in a flood. The script jumps around some and you can see the shadow of the sound boom early on the first side, but basically the MCA Home Video Encore Edition release is another low-class movie which has been given a high-class treatment worth savoring.

The sound is CX-encoded and side two of the 73-minute presentation is in CAV. Upon completion of the movie there is a trailer for an early theatrical re-release. The trailer disappointed us since it can't seem to get too excited about its product, despite the bulging typography and exclamation points. After the trailer, there is a still file, with 37 original promotional photos and lobby cards. It is an excellent disc for Halloween parties or whenever you have made too much popcorn.

FRANKENSTEIN – THE RESTORED VERSION

A more accurate description of the restored footage in *Frankenstein – The Restored Version* would be 'restored inches.' With the exception of showing the monster toss the girl into the lake like a bag of mulch, the missing material consists of three lunges and a blasphemous invocation of the Deity. The running time listed for the film, in fact, is the same as the old DiscoVision (non-restored) version, 71 minutes. Side two is in CAV, with many of the dramatic highlights from side one replayed to fill out the disc and give viewers an opportunity to further utilize CAV. (The break between side one and two occurs as the townspeople gather for the final chase.) Also included on side two is the theatrical trailer for an early re-release of the film and advertising materials, in still frame, from the collection of Forest J. Ackerman. The movie is old, and so the print is a little worn down. The sound is CX-encoded.

We like to play the trailer before we watch the movie, but we could not bring it up with chapter search until we figured out that it was not at chapter 1 on side two, as it is listed on the jacket, but at chapter 6. The chapter markers on the first side denote the scenes where material has been restored.

Not only is the story a classic (the credits list the novel as having been written by "Mrs. Percy B. Shelley," a chauvinistic appellation which probably has her mother turning over in her grave), but it is filmed with an angular expressionistic style which is well suited for frozen-frame appreciation. Two things we noticed this time through: Colin Clive tossing dirt in the face of a statue of Death as he robs his first grave, and the tumors on Dr. Frankenstein's father's neck, which are similar to the monster's bolts and add more irony to the man's desire for a grandson.

FRANKIE GOES TO HOLLYWOOD – FROM A WASTELAND TO AN ARTIFICIAL PARADISE
Normally if the same song appeared twice on a disc which only boasts of four songs we would be annoyed, but when it comes to *Frankie Goes to Hollywood – From a Wasteland to an Artificial Paradise* we're willing to make an exception. The music video which opens the one-sided CAV 12-inch disc, 'Relax,' is a notorious romp through a den of inequity which has been censored by the BBC, MTV, and all other decent, law abiding acronyms. The group made another music video with it and put that one at the end of the disc. The other two videos, 'Welcome to the Pleasure Dome' and '2 Tribes,' are also pretty wild, but the overriding factor here is that the quality of the videos, like Frankie's music, is superior to the normal, staid, and uncensored rock and roll effort. They let loose, but they do it with style. Unfortunately, the CAV still frames are blurry.

FRANTIC
The ending of *Frantic* is a little contrived – the ruthless bad guys start acting stupid and unruthless – but endings aren't as important in thrillers as the thrills. The excitement is more mental than physical. There aren't too many car chases or similar stunts, but the feelings of helplessness and elation are still present. It could have been more exciting, more unexpected, or more ambiguous, but *Frantic* is still 120 minutes of exotic, escapist fun. It is a good thriller, and successfully transfers the hero's anxieties to the viewer in an entertaining way.

The picture quality is unusually grainy and a little heavy in oranges. The disc has chapter markers. Only the music seems to be in stereo. Ennio Morricone's score, however, is used extensively, and contributes significantly to the entertainment.

FREAKS
MGM/UA put the soundtrack to *Freaks* in digital. It is the original 1932 recording which MGM has processed digitally through their Videophonic Sound video transfer procedure. The dialog is still difficult to follow, in part because of the primitive recording equipment used when the film was made and in part because of the thick accents of some of the players.

Freaks is a flagrantly sensationalized cult feature about lust and revenge among circus employees who are handicapped with birth defects. The black-and-white picture is unmistakably old, but the images are clear enough to get the point across. The film is 67 minutes long. Best moment: The pleasure in a Siamese twin's expression as her sister kisses a lover. We're just glad the disc isn't in CAV, because we'd probably be tempted to use it.

FREDDIE HUBBARD LIVE AT THE VILLAGE VANGUARD
If you want to turn your living room into a jazz joint, put on *Freddie Hubbard Live at the Village Vanguard* and light a dozen cigarettes. The digitally encoded sound is so real your neighbors will believe you have mastered the trumpet. The picture is excellent, too, if you get around to turning it on.

In the minus column, the disc is 58 minutes long and is split evenly into two short sides. There are also interviews with the musicians and with the venerable owner of the Vanguard, Max Gordon. The talking does not spoil the mood as much as one would expect it to.

Hubbard plays the trumpet, Ron Carter is on bass, Cedar Walton is at the piano and Lenny White does the drums. The visuals give you a chance to watch them playing at a very close range without dispelling the sense that they are playing in a public place. The clarity of phrasing is enhanced by the recording and by its presentation on disc. All the more reason why it should have been longer – couldn't they have recorded both the early and the late set?

FREEDOM BEAT
The outdoor concert put on by Artists Against Apartheid in *Freedom Beat* takes place in London and includes many groups which American audiences may not be familiar with. The music generally has an African motif and survives the live recording environment without difficulties. One of the performers, Princess, is especially attractive, but all, including Style Council, Sade, Sting, Elvis Costello (singing 'Don't Let Me Be Misunderstood') and others, give personable, entertaining presentations. The disc lasts 70 minutes and each artist performs only one number, but they gather together at the end for a couple of group anthems, 'Free Nelson Mandela,' and 'Biko.' The picture quality is fairly decent, even after the sun sets. Contrary to the jacket cover, side two is not in CAV.

FREEWAY
A roving sniper spills blood on the major arteries of Los Angeles in *Freeway*. The picture is grainy, especially in the dark, and the monaural digitally encoded sound has little going for it. The script, while it contains some witty radio talk show repartee, is lacking in logic and intelligence. Real rush hours are more exciting.

FRENZY
FRENZY (DiscoVision)
We react differently to the rape and murder scene in Hitchcock's *Frenzy* every time we see the movie. The scene is not simply a casual thrill included by the scriptwriter, Anthony Schaffer, to build tension. Hitchcock had been searching for a filmable property which depicted a rape and murder for twenty years (he almost made one with Audrey Hepburn in the late fifties – the storyboards are still available). As much as he was titillating audiences, he was also living out a misogynistic fantasy of his own by directing the scene. During the sequence, the camera takes the assailant's point of view and never stops staring at the face of the victim as she is strangled. The purpose of movies is to give one's fantasies a harmless release, and everyone has fantasies they would never act out in real life. Sometimes we react to the character and are excited by the scene. But other times we react to the actress, Barbara Leigh-Hunt, and are disgusted, not by what the scene arouses in our own emotional depths, but because it is so blatantly pandering to such feelings. It was as if, after years of making legitimately violent pictures because he was creating art, Hitchcock decided to sneak in some real violence using his reputation as an artist to cover himself.

The movie, about a serial killer and an innocent man accused of the killer's crimes, was filmed in London, the first time Hitchcock had made a movie there in a very long time. The principal advantage to making the movie in England was the collection of wonderful British character actors Hitchcock managed to obtain for his cast. The performances make the film almost inexhaustibly repeatable.

Frenzy was previously available on the old DiscoVision label. The subsequent standard release is a disappointment. Strong reds refuse to stay within boundaries and all solid bright colors look faintly unsteady. The contrast is bright, an improvement over the DiscoVision version, but the flesh tones do not look as accurate as they did on the older disc. (A warning, however, to those wishing to collect the DiscoVision version: Every frame on side five was imbedded with a stop command.) The sound is muted. The dialog is clear enough, but background noises and the musical score are too subdued, and nothing pierces one's viewing room the way the sound would in a theater. To conclude the disc, there is a marvelous theatrical trailer in which Hitchcock is seen shopping for ties.

FRESH HORSES
Although *Fresh Horses* has a bad attitude about women, alternately distrusting them or patronizing them, the star power in the film is so electric that it is easy to just enjoy the show and ignore its chauvinism. You have to like the stars of course, and some people still cringe at Molly Ringwald and Andrew McCarthy, though in the future that will be less of a problem. The script is based on a play, but it is opened way up, so it doesn't feel stagey, and it retains just enough of the sort of unpredictable dialog which plays do better than movies to stay fresh without becoming weird. The story is about a young college student who breaks off an engagement when he meets a farm girl of deliberately ambiguous maturity. The narrative isn't pushy, but even when the story doesn't seem to be going anywhere you don't feel impatient with it.

You may feel a little impatient with the disc, however. The picture is too grainy and often too orange. The stereo surround sound is extra hissy. It was difficult to tell if the separations were living up to their potential, because the hiss discouraged us from raising the volume too greatly.

FRIDAY THE 13TH PART V – A NEW BEGINNING
There are enough *Friday the 13th* movies on disc to hold a dusk-to-dawn *Friday the 13th* slumber party. Nothing in this series will ever equal the classic scream-inducing cut which came at the end of the first film, but that was enough to stimulate the success of every blood drenched sequel. *Friday the 13th Part V – A New Beginning* offers more of the same.

The transfer to disc is good, but the monaural sound and flat photography are almost not worth the effort. If the discs ever are shown at a slumber party, it will have to be in reverse order to keep everyone awake.

FRIDAY THE 13th PART VI JASON LIVES
The even-numbered sequels to *Friday the 13th* have so far been more satisfying than the odd-numbered sequels. A case in point is *Friday the 13th Part VI Jason Lives*. Where Part V was sloppy in its mix of slapstick comedy and gruesome murders, *Part VI* had us laughing and screaming in regularly timed intervals. The jokes are more sophisticated (one of the children at the summer camp is reading Sartre's 'No Exit') and the blood is more fleeting, allowing the imagination to fill what in the past would have been a gory closeup. The tension is just as strong and we don't think we have had as much fun watching a *13th* since the very first episode.

The stereo mix is wonderful and at every excuse, like when someone steps on a twig, the bass gives out a whompf which will knock you out of your pajamas. *Part VI* is nocturnal, as is the series and its audience, but none of the darker scenes exhibited picture imperfections of any significance.

FRIDAY THE 13TH PART VII – THE NEW BLOOD
Now there is a *Friday the 13th* for every day of the week! Contrary to the logo on the jacket cover, *Friday the 13th Part VII – The New Blood* has not been digitally encoded. The silly but enjoyable Ultra-Stereo sound mix, however, is still the film's best feature. The picture is a little too orange, though the night scenes have been transferred without a smudge and look fine. A new plot twist pits Jason against a girl with telekinesis, giving her the ability to oppose him while staying out of axe range.

FRIDAY THE 13TH PART VIII – JASON TAKES MANHATTAN
As you surely have heard by now, Jason doesn't hit New York proper until the last twenty minutes of *Friday the 13th Part VIII – Jason Takes Manhattan*. Still, while some movies may follow a formula, this one revels in it, and it can be entertaining if one is in the proper state of mind. The picture is a little grainy and the Ultra-Stereo sound is a little scratchy, but if your standards are that high you're not going to be watching the disc anyway.

FRIENDLY PERSUASION
Saddled with decrepit jacket art, *Friendly Persuasion* is an overly Hollywood-ized depiction of a cute, loveable Quaker family trying to get through the Civil War without shooting anybody. A few sequences are thoughtful and pleasing, but most of it is contrived and juvenile. The print used for the transfer is wildly inconsistent. At times, portions are so grainy that its looks as if bugs are crawling on a character's forehead. In other places the skin tones are too orange or the colors are flat. The sound is passable but not elaborate. The film is very well edited (see the carnival sequence), which may be one of the reasons why it is remembered more fondly than it deserves to be. It runs over two hours and is spread to three sides. Along with Gary Cooper and Dorothy McGuire, Tony Perkins stars, and it is interesting to note that he was hunching his shoulders and drooping his head well before *Psycho*.

FRIGHT NIGHT
Vampire movies never seem to die. The genre always manages to attract fresh blood. The nice thing about *Fright Night* is the lack of procrastination. Right off the top, the kid sees that a vampire has moved next door and the vampire sees the kid and each knows that the other knows. The rest of the movie is a collection of clever twists and turns as the vampire and the kid try to outwit one another.

Some of the stereo separations are playful, but the balance doesn't distract your attention. With the exception of a few special effects, you'll be too involved with the story to notice any blurry images.

FRIGHT NIGHT
What we liked about the first *Fright Night* film was that it leapt straight into the central narrative without the teasing preliminary tricks that most horror movies use to pad their running times. *Fright Night: Part II* is more run-of-the-mill. While the vampire movie eventually becomes entertaining and the special effects eventually amount to something, you have to give the story a good forty minutes to really get going. Those first forty minutes are also when the disc looks the worst. It starts out very grainy, but improves to just grainy as the film progresses. The Ultra-Stereo sound has a few surround effects. The soundtrack is generally subdued, and a powerful amplifier is required to coax the stereo mix into the open.

FROG
There are many other films around which take much longer and expend much more energy to provide the exact same payoff which *Frog* – a Shelley Duvall cable TV effort – provides, but the piece is no great classic. It is an hour-long contemporary fable about a frog who sings 'That's Amore' and a science student who learns that girls are more fun than reptiles. The picture quality is average or maybe a little below, as there is a fair amount of grain. The digital sound is stereophonic, but the mix is commensurate with the budget for the rest of the program and the only available miracles are the ones which take place in the story itself.

FROM BEYOND
Although *From Beyond* only runs 85 minutes, Vestron released it in CLV. The movie is perfect home video material if you are partial to sex, gore, and thrills. It is also fairly intelligent, having been based upon an H.P. Lovecraft story. The plot lies beyond the realm of summarization, but suffice to say that it is a brief and well-told tale about a monster from the other side who attempts to possess human souls via the pineal gland. Never mind.

The print looks a little faded in the beginning and the sound has been done in Ultra-Stereo, which is sort of the K-Mart of sound processing. The mix is thorough, but higher pitched noises are forever going fuzzy and who knows where the bass went. No matter, the movie is over too quickly to be anything other than entertaining and delightfully gross.

FROM HERE TO ETERNITY
The sound on the analog release of *From Here to Eternity* is so bad in places that we could hear the distortion, a raspy echo, even after we became disgusted and switched the audio from our stereo system to our television set. It is apparently a fault in the transfer, because it happens in the same places on every copy of the disc which has been reported to us, and it always starts or stops at the reel change marks.

The print isn't all that great, either, which is a shame because the title is a highly commendable home video property. Even after thirty years, the emotional swells and dips remain captivating. The thrilling ending, where the Japanese attack on Pearl Harbor negates all plot convolutions preceding it, can still give one goosebumps.

FROM MAO TO MOZART
The award winning documentary about violinist Isaac Stern's 1979 visit to China, *From Mao to Mozart*, has been released with digitally encoded stereo sound. The musical passages are stereophonic. They do not have the clarity of a concert recording, but achieve a resonance which surpasses the abilities of a monaural recording. The picture quality varies depending upon what sort of camera was used for a sequence, and the movie looks like a documentary. Contrary to the label, side two of the disc is in CAV, but with two jiggling still frames out of every five, it is difficult to focus on fingering.

Although any film spending as much time as this one does depicting Stern teaching others the art of the violin is valuable, there is a condescending tone running through the program which takes away from its charm. True, in 1979 China was still new, and the documentary includes a chilling, eyewitness account of the insanity which raged during the xenophobic Cultural Revolution less than a decade earlier. But from a moment early on when Stern dismisses a suggestion that Western music was fueled by the Industrial Age (he states, incorrectly, that Mozart's genius would have flowered in any era) to the absence of any desire on Stern's part to pick up one of the interesting Chinese string instruments, the point of view is one way and one way only. Stern tells a young pupil that, "Music is not black and white. It is every color and some that even painters don't have." Well so is life and so is China, but not here.

FROM RUSSIA WITH LOVE
(see **DR. NO**)

FROM STAR WARS TO JEDI – THE MAKING OF A SAGA (Import)
A PBS documentary called *From Star Wars to Jedi – The Making of a Saga*, directed by Richard Schickel, has been released on disc in Japan. It is primarily a promotional film for *Return of the Jedi*. Scenes which are broken apart in detail include Jabba's den, the monster eating the pig guard, the sand barge set, the forest chase, and the Ewok battle. Schickel also interviews George Lucas extensively, providing some insight on how the story and the characters took their final forms.

The CLV disc is in CX-encoded monaural. The sound is all right, but the footage from the *Star Wars* films looks as though it was recorded off a TV set. Japanese subtitles sometimes fill much of the lower portion of the screen.

FROM THE EARTH TO THE MOON

All talk and almost no special effects, *From the Earth to the Moon* is a fifties science fiction film that is too dated to be of any value today. Joseph Cotten, who ought to have been good, is ineffective as the hero, an armaments industrialist who, as Jules Verne so accurately prophesied, realizes that during peace time he's got to retool for space. The nice-looking source material displays some of its original Technicolor grandeur. It has a number of splotches, scratches, and other markings, but the richness of the colors makes a worthy tradeoff. The jacket cover, utilizing original advertising materials, is also very nice. The sound is dull.

FROM THE HIP

Bob Clark depicts yuppie lawyers in *From the Hip* the same way he depicted adolescents in *Porky's* and pre-adolescents in *A Christmas Story*, as good natured, outrageous pranksters who want to do what is best for the world and for themselves, not necessarily in that order. The movie is a riot, with a courtroom argument over the appropriateness of an off-color word which had us laughing harder than anything we have seen since, well, *Porky's* and *A Christmas Story*. Clark's talents exceed vulgar amusement, however, as he coaxes a marvelously creepy performance out of the usually overbearing John Hurt and gives the star, Judd Nelson, the chance to display a wide range of emotions and moods.

The sound is digitally encoded. It is monaural, and sounds harsh when the volume is raised beyond standard levels. The picture is also grainy, but half the time our eyes were so blurry from the tears of laughter that it didn't make a difference what the screen looked like.

THE FRONT

The fine Martin Ritt film, *The Front*, stars Woody Allen and is about blacklisted show business professionals in the fifties. Although monaural, the digitally encoded sound does wonders with the Frank Sinatra rendition of 'Young at Heart' which opens and closes the film. The movie had a pale, institutional color scheme to begin with, so the picture is not too appetizing, but the transfer looks competent. Along with Allen, Zero Mostel turns in a fabulously grungy performance as a comic who is losing his grasp on his career.

THE FUGITIVE 1 (Import)
THE FUGITIVE 2 (Import)
THE FUGITIVE 3 (Import)
THE FUGITIVE 4 (Import)
THE FUGITIVE 5 (Import)
THE FUGITIVE 6 (Import)

Sometimes an actor lands just one role in his life that fits him. For David Janssen, it was the television series, *The Fugitive*. In most theatrical films and other television appearance, Janssen usually appeared ill-at-ease, fumbling his emotions or seeming miscast even when he was typecast. In *The Fugitive*, however, it was like he was rolling sevens in every episode. Portraying a man convicted of murdering his wife and avoiding the police while he searches for the true killer, he conveys a subdued desperation and intelligence (the character, Richard Kimble, is a doctor) in every scene of every episode. His performance opens a vulnerability in the viewer, increasing a receptivity to the specific drama in each show.

Eleven episodes from the mid-sixties serie have already been released in Japan. (Curiously, the pilot/introduction program is not included in the collection.) The sound on each disc is analog monaural without CX-encoding. The memorable Quinn Martin Production 'act' structure is preserved with the chapter markers.

In general, the episodes, which are all in color, have lovely transfers. The outdoor shots look grainier and weaker than the indoor/soundstage shots, but the best looks as good as the best color film transfers from the era.

The transfer of 'A Clean and Quiet Town,' on *The Fugitive 1*, is especially nice, and the episode is exceptional. Kimble stumbles into a small town which is controlled by mobsters, one of whom turns out to be his wife's murderer, the fabled 'one-armed man.' The episode, directed by Mark Rydell, stretches reality just enough to suggest a totalitarian society comfortably adapted to a Middle America framework without turning into fantasy. The second episode, 'Death Is the Door Prize,' features Howard Da Silva, Ossie Davis, and Kevin O'Neal. Kimble witnesses a shooting, but is unwilling to step forward and testify about the sequence of events. The setting is cleverly confined to a hotel/convention center, which Kimble cannot leave without being spotted.

On *The Fugitive 2* there is an enjoyable episode, 'Second Sight,' in which Kimble is temporarily blinded by a chemical explosion. He goes right past the one-armed man and doesn't know it! It is an enjoyable dramatic exaggeration which twists the standard series format effectively. The other episode, '10,000 Pieces of Silver,' is a weaker effort, combining several half-ideas and not developing any of them. Kimble is working on a ranch and befriends the rancher's daughter, who has a moderate mental handicap. There is another escaped murderer in the area trying to avoid the police, and a hefty reward for Kimble has just been published in the paper, bringing out the greedy nature of a few locals. The episode is typical, but has nothing special to offer.

Bruce Dern, his eyeballs half out of their sockets, is the leader of a motorcycle gang in 'The Devil's Disciples,' on *The Fugitive 3*. Kimble is taken prisoner by the gang for reasons which are not entirely clear, but uses psychology to create a wedge among the gang's leaders. The second episode, 'The Evil that Men Do,' is particularly strong, as Kimble uncovers a plot to murder his archnemesis, Inspector Gerard, and, good egg that he is, races across the country to save the poor man. James Daly guest stars.

Charles Bronson and Anne Francis appear in 'The One that Got Away,' on *The Fugitive 4*, providing enough star power that it hardly matters what the plot is about. A woman charters a boat to see her husband who is hiding in Mexico after having embezzled a large sum of money. Bronson is a government agent posing as the boat's captain, and Kimble just happens to be working as a deck hand. The episode is good fun, but the audio is below average and some of the conversation is fuzzy. Although somewhat less attractive, the stars in 'There Goes the Ball Game' make that episode worthwhile as well. Martin Balsam portrays a rich publisher whose daughter has been kidnapped. Vincent Gardenia is the local police chief, and Kimble is the only witness to the kidnapping.

Black actors are prominently featured in both episodes on *The Fugitive 5*. Percy Rodriguez portrays a Montana sheriff in 'Passage to Helena.' He is transporting Kimble and another criminal across thinly populated countryside when a series of occurrences place the three on foot in the wild. The episode is a no-nonsense exercise which is quite satisfying. We wish we could say the same for 'Dossier on a Diplomat,' in which an African ambassador, played by Ivan Dixon, grants Kimble sanctuary at his embassy. Unfortunately, the character motivation is vague and the plot takes one awkward turn after another.

The thrilling two-part conclusion to the series, 'The Judgement,' is featured on *The Fugitive 6*. Gerard sets a trap for Kimble using the one-armed man as bait, but then begins to wonder which of the two is really the criminal. There are several surprises, and the program culminates in one of the all-time classic fistfights, atop a high tower. The show is especially rewarding if the viewer has been exposed to some of the other episodes shortly beforehand, and it has a satisfying sense of resolution, something which is getting to be rarer and rarer in Hollywood these days.

FULL METAL JACKET

The 117-minute *Full Metal Jacket* must be seen at least twice, and the second viewing seems much shorter than the first, because the plot avoids following normal narrative conventions. The first half (which runs 45 minutes, and so part of the second half also appears on side one of the disc) is a tightly constructed short story, about boot camp. The second half is an aimless collection of incidents witnessed by the central character from the boot camp story and taking place during the Tet Offensive in Vietnam. A viewer's anticipation, on the first viewing, is hopelessly befuddled. It is not a coincidence that America's political approach to the war had a similar structure.

The transfer of Stanley Kubrick's film to the disc is superb. The film's sound is monaural – a radical approach these days – but digital encoding strengthens the mix and delivers it in a nearly pure form. Much of the first half is comprised of single voices, shouting sequentially. The second half, again, is far more complex, and could easily have collapsed into a mash of war noises if Warner's transfer had been less attentive. The picture transfer is also outstanding. Kubrick's lighting is incredibly complicated. The first half ends in blue light, the second half ends in orange light and darkness. The disc manages every lighting effect correctly, and captures all the subtle changes, not only from scene to scene, but within the shadows on the same image.

The film was not made in a wide aspect ratio, but two of the most memorable effects from the movie are lost with the trimming of the sides. The first is the dizzying crane shot as soldiers at the boot camp scale a tall, wooden, climbing obstacle. Without the edges, the viewer does not feel the vertigo which the soldiers feel. The second is the sunset that comes at the finale, as the soldiers are attempting to quell a sniper. The effect in the film was incredible, as if Kubrick had the same command over the sun which he had over the rest of his performers. Without the edges, an awareness of that light source is diminished, and it is presumed by the viewer that the orange glow is coming from incidental firelight. Warner has also failed to encode the disc with chapter markers, a curiosity since so many less deserving films are packed full of them.

As a filmmaker, Kubrick challenges the feelings of his viewers by erasing easy emotions from his dramas. He demands that subjects be seen from previously unexamined angles, and that mankind be given the same examination in his films which individuals, 'characters,' are given in the films of others.

FULL MOON IN BLUE WATER
The final third of *Full Moon in Blue Water* is fairly amusing. The characters are gathered in a crisis situation and their true natures are revealed. The first two thirds of the film, however, are dull and repetitive. So, if for some reason you obtain the disc, stick with it. The picture is a little grainy, but the monaural sound has a decent hi-fi fullness. The story is structured suspiciously like a stage play, although it is not credited as such. Gene Hackman portrays the owner of a boondock tavern who is mourning over his missing wife. Teri Garr is a local who wants to snap him out of it. Garr's performance is typically charming, and Hackman has some inspired moments.

FUN AND FANCY FREE (Import)
The Japanese Walt Disney disc, *Fun and Fancy Free*, has two 30-minute cartoons strung together with intros by Jiminy Cricket. The first, narrated by Dinah Shore, is called 'Bongo,' about a circus bear who escapes to the woods and learns that bears have an unusual way of demonstrating their affections. The second is a retelling of 'Jack and the Beanstalk' with Mickey Mouse, Donald Duck, and Goofy. Narrated by Edgar Bergen, the sequence also mixes a substantial amount of live footage featuring Bergen, who is telling the story to three wooden dummies.

The disc is bilingual, with Japanese on one audio track and English on the other. The cartoons look scratchy in places, but the colors still vibrate with the Disney glow.

FUNERAL IN BERLIN
Michael Caine's second Harry Palmer movie, *Funeral in Berlin*, is primarily entertaining because of the plot and because of Caine. The movie would have been more pleasing if Paramount had letterboxed it, but it gets by, just as it does when one catches it on late night TV.

The film pretends to be about Cold War intrigue, as Palmer is sent to Berlin to arrange an escape from the East. Like all the best in the genre, however, the Russians really aren't bad, the British really aren't good, and other agents are in the middle, with goals of their own. It is rewarding to see Caine in a self-effacing role which lets him be witty without being irresponsible.

The musical score, by Konrad Elfers, is enjoyable, with canny echoes of Kurt Weill giving it momentum. The sound is on par for its age. Along with being cropped, the picture is a little pale, but the condition of the image is tolerable.

FUNLAND
The ad art sells the amusement park comedy rated PG-13, *Funland*, as a thriller, and the central character is clown ventriloquist with a split personality who is amusingly creepy, but the murders are held to a minimum and the emphasis is on satire instead of gore. There are a number of offensive stereotypes and the humor is often desperate, but the film has its moments. The picture is usually blurry, too dark, and badly colored. The sound has a minimal number of stereo effects and a lot of background noise.

FUNNY FACE
Fred Astaire portrays a Richard Avedon-type photographer in *Funny Face*, but the movie also stars Audrey Hepburn and it is her charm which the viewer will remember. She does her own singing – Gershwin tunes, including ''S Wonderful' – and dancing, too, but it is her acting, such as when she is posing for the photographer and he asks her to look sad, which will hook one onto the film. The print has a few scratches and the back of the soundtrack emits an occasional hum. The 1950 stereotypes are compensated by fascinating location shots in New York and Paris from the same era.

FUNNY FARM
George Roy Hill directed *Funny Farm*, but it appears he could never decide whether to present the star, Chevy Chase, as a real character, or just as Chevy Chase. The movie, about city folks who move to the country, has a great third act and a few amusing gags, but it is inconsistent.

The flesh tones appear too orange, especially in the beginning, and the focus is a little fuzzy throughout. Only Elmer Bernstein's score and a few sound effects are in stereo. The digital soundtrack is alright, but Bernstein's music is a sad reminder of the way movie music used to sound – it is full of sweeping flourish, for about five seconds.

FUNNY LADY
Where *Funny Girl* went through laborious out-of-town tryouts, rewrites, touch-ups after it opened, constant rehearsals, and many performances before it became a movie, *Lady* was produced from scratch with its star often not showing up until the last moment. Added to that is the fact that everybody, even Fanny Brice, mellows out a bit when they get older. The energy is missing. The contrast between the Billy Rose songs, which sound great, and the new numbers, which sound strained, is also noticeable.

THE FURTHER ADVENTURES OF TENNESSEE BUCK
Because the film takes great pains to avoid mistakes, *The Further Adventures of Tennessee Buck* is vaguely entertaining. One can imagine, in desperate situations, being comforted by it. The movie spans time. It has extensive Sri Lankan locations, a contemporary low-budget Ultra Stereo soundtrack, the latest in naked women, and up to the minute violence, but it also has old fashioned racially demeaning head hunters and a creaking plot which does little more than send hero into the jungle and then have him try to get back out. The disc production is not lacking in acceptability, only maturity.

FUTURE HUNTERS
What is one to think about a movie in which characters run across what is supposed to be solid concrete and the soundtrack effect is clearly footsteps on fresh plywood? *Future Hunters* is ambitious, we'll give it that. It moves in location from the future to the present and from California to Hong Kong to uncharted jungles in the Philippines. Although the leads are American, Bruce Li appears in the Hong Kong sequence for an extended martial arts interlude, and many cast members have dubbed voices. The sound recording is often pathetic and the picture isn't much better. After the film has been running for ten minutes, the credits suddenly appear. For a moment we thought the whole movie was over, but no such luck.

G-MEN VS. THE BLACK DRAGON
At the end of one of the chapters in *G-Men Vs. The Black Dragon*, a Republic serial, the hero is seen tumbling out of the window of a tall building during a scuffle with a bad guy. At the beginning of the next chapter the scene is replayed, only this time he grabs a fire hose on his way out. Scanning back to check it out, you can clearly see that he has nothing in his hand as he drops the first time. The cheaters – and to think that the story is about the protection of American values!

Anyway, the 15 episode serial, which runs close to four hours (or more, according to the jacket), is fit on a four sided disc. The first episode runs about twenty-five minutes, while the subsequent chapters clock in at fifteen apiece. None of the side breaks interrupt a chapter. Each episode begins and ends with credits, and each has been given a disc chapter marker.

Potential collectors should be warned that *G-Men* was made in 1942. Characters of Asian decent are, with one exception, cast in the film as the enemy, in no uncertain terms. They are often referred to with language which is frowned upon these days for good reason. Viewers who would feel uncomfortable or offended by this should avoid the disc.

G-Men is loaded with action, so impregnated with it that the emotional highpoints of the show are the rare occasions when the hero, Rex Bennett, played by Rod Cameron, gets to speak a line of dialog which is contemplative and not activity-oriented. Sometimes he goes for chapters without a breather. He has at least one fist fight per chapter as well, and he must be a mass of bruises by the end of the day, because he doesn't always win. He is lucky though. How many people do you know, if trapped in an experimental robot plane loaded with explosives, would be fortunate enough to find a parachute stowed on board?

The picture quality is not quite as good as *The Adventures of Captain Marvel*, but after the initial episodes, which are especially foggy, the clarity of the image improves. The sound has no serious problems, though if you watch too many of the chapters without a break, the 'next crescendo, next crescendo, next crescendo' music can start to get to you.

Republic has included a theatrical trailer which contains clips that are not in the film.

Nevertheless, the action in *G-Men* is non-stop and the plot is episodic but not tiresome. The cliff hangers are manipulative (the heroine even gets chained to a board approaching a power saw) and not always pure, but the program is fun. The film's stated theme is the fight for democratic values, but the real lesson one learns from the show is to always jump off something before it crashes.

GABE KAPLAN AS GROUCHO

When Gabe Kaplan would do a Groucho imitation while playing another character it was all right, because the imitation's shortcomings could be seen as the character's shortcomings, and not Kaplan's. With Kaplan's presumptuous one-man show, *Gabe Kaplan as Groucho*, Kaplan's shortcomings are his alone. The stage performance, filmed in 1982, is maudlin and contrived, with Kaplan providing a poor substitute for the real thing.

That said, the show is surprisingly not tiresome. Constructed as a 90-minute biographical sketch, the narrative gives a satisfying summary of the major events in the lives of the Marx Brothers, particularly for viewers who never got around to reading any books on the subject. The jokes from each career move are also presented, of course, and one never has to wait too long for Kaplan to get to one ("You see Harpo would sneak into Grandma's room when she wasn't there and practice on the harp. He never had a lesson. He was a natural. He learned to play the harp totally by ear. Now if you think it's easy running your ear over those steel strings you've got another think coming."). An actor playing Chico and an actress portraying a number of incidental figures also appear.

The live presentation has no severe picture problems although the blue background is consistently grainy. The sound is said to be in stereo, though effects are limited and some of the applause has an annoying electronic twang. There are a few chapter markers and there is a two-minute musical entr'acte at the end of side one. Don't wait through it, just turn the disc over.

GABY – A TRUE STORY

Is *Gaby – A True Story* entertaining? To be sure it is inspirational, since the title character, afflicted with cerebal palsy, overcomes the ignorance of her environment to graduate from college, and it has plenty of narrative manipulations during its 115-minute running time. Obviously it is well acted, but the lack of subtlety in any of the characters removes real challenge from the performances of the cast. The filmmakers deliberately keep their distance. At first, the effect is justifiable, since the viewer is meant to become familiar with Gaby's human qualities before the severity of her handicap sinks in. But as the story moves along, the point of view remains with Gaby's nurse/companion, who interprets Gaby's words and reads Gaby's messages aloud. At the very end, the character (who types on an electric typewriter with her toes) finally speaks for herself, via subtitles which represent her typing. At that point you realize what has been missing – Gaby. The movie is not entertaining, because it cops out. The filmmakers, although they depict prejudice against the handicapped, reinforce the prejudice by keeping their subject alienated from the full gaze of the camera.

The picture is quite hazy. The sound is digitally encoded monaural, but it is very good and often has the illusion of being in stereo. There is also an effective score by Maurice Jarre.

THE GADD GANG LIVE ON DIGITAL VIDEO

The picture and sound on *The Gadd Gang Live on Digital Video* are beautiful. The image has a heightened graininess that is more a matter of style than of error. The Gang are five musicians, playing at a small jazz club, and the cameras enthusiastically capture the fingering and expressions of each band member, often in a sequence which cannot be anticipated. The band plays jazz renditions of popular songs, such as 'Whiter Shade of Pale' and 'My Girl.' Although hardly at the forefront of musical experimentation and discovery, the hour-long set (the disc is single-sided) is pleasing and allows each musician an opportunity to display his craft.

GALLAGHER – THE MADDEST
GALLAGHER – STUCK IN THE SIXTIES
GALLAGHER – SOME UNCENSORED EVENING

The transfers on *Gallagher – The Maddest* and *Gallagher – Stuck in the Sixties* look about standard, with an occasional line of interference floating through the picture. Gallagher has nothing particularly funny to say about the sixties and has difficulty molding his routines to fit his theme. *The Maddest* is better. He shows off a very polished act with a good deal of improvisation and some terrific props. His audience is in a large auditorium and he shouts to them, the way street comics have to shout to their audiences in New York. As the trend in sophisticated comedy is towards low-voiced, practically interior monologues, his public address delivery is energizing.

Gallagher – Some Uncensored Evening, is a better transfer and it captures Gallagher earlier in his career. His routines and jokes are fresher and he's working a more intimate audience. Gallagher's trademark routine is to spray the front rows of his audience with pieces of food. Instead of getting annoyed, the fans seem to eat it up.

GAMERA/GAMERA VS. GUIRON

The English language dialog in the orignal 'Gamera,' part of *Gamera/Gamera Vs. Guiron*, is fairly amusing: "It must be coated with anti-electric wave paint, sir," goes one technologically informed soldier. Better still is the following exchange between a US Air Force commander and his helpful assistant. The commander has just been handed an SOS message: "Hmmm. Huge turtles. Sixty meters. What's going on around here?" His assistant replies, "I don't know, sir. It looks like a huge turtle made its appearance."

The black-and-white image is scanned, and alternates between fuzzy and functional. The film, in which the giant turtle first makes its appearance, shows Gamera wreaking havoc upon the Japanese infrastructure, but hedges its bets by demonstrating that the turtle has a soft spot for children and by not killing him off at the end.

The dubbing is probably more ridiculous on 'Gamera Vs. Guiron' than on any other dubbed film we have ever seen, but that is not necessarily a bad thing. The speakers take weird pauses between words and have no synchronization with the lip movements of the cast. The little boys sound like twenty-year old women speaking with high-pitched voices, and the women all sound like a distracted Roseanne Barr. The picture is in moderately faded color and is cropped or occasionally squeezed. The humor generated by the poor dubbing, coupled with the imaginative setting (two young boys ride a flying saucer to another planet, where Gamera must protect them from a monster with a curved blade for a nose and from two evil alien women) makes the movie the most appealing of all the Gamera films released on disc in America.

For adults, anyway. The disc is being sold as family entertainment, but that is somewhat dubious. Not only do the monsters amputate the limbs of one another, blood aspraying, but the two evil female aliens lock the kids in cages and shave off their heads after announcing, "While they are sleeping we'll eat their brains raw." Fortunately, the giant turtle makes its appearance just as the drill is about to open the little boy's skull, but not before the idea is transmitted in a manner that every four-year-old will be sure to comprehend, if not imitate upon a younger sister.

The second film starts on side two at chapter four. At the end of side three, there are some home video trailers for the other Gamera films. The sound on both movies is tolerable.

GAMERA VS. BARUGON (Import)

Gamera Vs Barugon is entirely in Japanese and it is in color. Barugon is a cross between a gila monster, a rhinoceros, and a 10-story apartment complex. He is unearthed by a group of inept gangsters and one of the film's faults is that there is a half-hour stretch on side one where no monsters appear at all. When Gamera finally steps in to prevent Barugon from further lowering property values and raising insurance rates, the conflict has a universal appeal. No, we can't solve the world's problems with giant turtles, but then the world's problems aren't being caused by giant gila monsters. The comfort is in knowing that if they were, we could.

GAMERA VS GAOS/GAMERA VS ZIGRA

Both movies on *Gamera VS Gaos/Gamera VS Zigra* are pretty bad. Gaos is a huge bat-like monster who emits a yellow beam that slices anything it hits. The film's one unique feature is the few gags involving cars, helicopters, airplanes, etc., that get sliced. Zigra is a large crown-like spaceship in the first half of the latter feature, and a nasty metallic monster fish in the second. The characters in the second movie are a bit more personable and the action has a better pace. The color picture transfer is also a little stronger in the second, though both features tend to look soft. The scanning and cropping is especially noticeable on 'Zigra,' and the panning often reveals an elegance in the original widescreen image which is totally missing from the video presentation. The sound is fair.

THE GAP BAND – VIDEO TRAIN

If you enjoy playing with CAV then you'll

probably be interested in obtaining the 8-inch, *The Gap Band – Video Train*. The two-sided 23-minute Standard Play disc has five music videos, two of which are ideally suited for CAV applications. The first is a breakdance display called 'Party Train' and the second is a superior time lapse painting of Los Angeles called 'Jam the Motha.' While the transfer is a bit disappointing, the opportunity to manipulate the images is a real treat.

THE GARDEN OF THE FINZI-CONTINIS

Scratches and blurry colors prevent *The Garden of the Finzi-Continis* from being compared favorably to regular feature film releases. The sound, similarly, is awkward and unkempt, but with digital encoding you can still push the volume a little. It will sound no worse than your local monaural theater.

Image has chosen to retain the print's original English subtitles (the film is in Italian, though some of the players are dubbed). The lettering is a bright white, and washes out when set against a light background.

The story of the disintegration of the Jewish community in an Italian town during the initial phases of World War II is told as a romance, and the priorities in the lives of the characters mutate as slowly as the seasons. Few directors have Vittorio De Sica's ability to take everyday events and give them a legitimately universal resonance. His presentation of Dominique Sanda's character, for example, changes what was, on paper, a stereotypical princess, into a passionate human being, one who suffers anguish over her own capriciousness. In the end she is the last and strongest blossom, still standing at the onset of winter. Why he has used a French actress to represent Italy is beyond us, but the emotional impact of her situation, with the help of the digitally encoded music, will stay within one's reach long after the movie has finished.

GARDENS OF STONE

The better your stereo system is, the more worthwhile it will be to obtain Francis Coppola's *Gardens of Stone*. Not that the film has undergone any great effort in transference to disc. It is a standard transfer, neither inspiring nor significantly bad, with a slightly yellow picture and analog sound (the boom even appears in one scene). The sound editing in a Coppola picture is usually a work of art, however, and *Gardens of Stone* is no exception. There are layers upon layers of sound effects. Atmosphere sounds, gadget sounds, background conversations, and incidental music. There is also the power of the main audio track, with clarity in the dialog, subtlety in Carmine Coppola's dirgey score, and kick in the rifle salutes.

Gardens of Stone is about the soldiers assigned to Arlington Cemetery during the height of the Vietnam War. The plot does not have a strong or tense center, but it is a drama with a potential for repeated viewing because the resourceful cast, including James Caan, James Earl Jones, Dean Stockwell, and Angelica Huston, makes for pleasant and engaging company. The film is somber, but stimulating.

GARY SHANDLING SHOW 25th ANNIVERSARY SPECIAL

The Gary Shandling Show 25th Anniversary Special is an hour long take-off on the Anniversary program the 'Tonight Show' does every year. Since the 'Tonight Show' itself is conducted with tongue partially in cheek, the satire never becomes too biting, but it has its moments. The black-and-white segments depict make-believe 'early' shows, one featuring 'Mr. Ed' who has a mouth which would make Wilbur blush. In a brilliant stroke, the real Donny Osmond is hauled out for some good-natured ribbing. The picture and CX-encoded stereo sound are good, with the 'older' clips suffering from some manufactured but convincing wear and tear.

GASLIGHT

The print for *Gaslight* is in good condition. The modulations in Joseph Cotten's voice are such a pleasure that his presence would be reason enough to acquire the disc. *Gaslight* also features one of Ingrid Bergman's most famous roles – though virtually any actress could shine in the part – as a woman whose husband (Charles Boyer) has married her under false pretenses. It is a mystery, replete with London fog, and Cotten is the police inspector who saves the day.

THE GATE

Most definitely not a disc to watch while you are babysitting, *The Gate* is about some youngsters who uncover a passageway to Hell in their backyard while Mom and Dad are away for the weekend. The set-up takes a while, so that the best special effects and the scariest moments are all on side two, but the rest of the film is unassuming, and, in its own way, charming. It is not a great horror film, but you never get the urge to turn it off, either.

The transfer is fairly ragged, so that even the CX-encoded stereo sound will be a problem on decent playback equipment. It runs less than 90 minutes and is in CLV all the way through.

THE GAUNTLET

The nice looking picture in *The Gauntlet* is hampered only be a slight graininess in the darker scenes. The film must be seen more than a single time, because Clint Eastwood's character is a confused combination of his normal tough-guy persona and a complete loser, and it takes a couple of viewings to sort things out. Eastwood plays a Phoenix cop sent to Nevada to return with a witness who is supposed to testify at a racketeering trial. The cop's boss, however, is crooked, and the trip back to Phoenix becomes increasingly dangerous. The finale, in which a bus is demolished by gunfire, is far-fetched, but that, too, is more swallowable when you know it is coming. The music is in stereo and the sound is in good condition.

THE GENERAL

The greatest choo-choo train movie ever made, Buster Keaton's *The General*, has been transferred to disc using gorgeous nitrate source material. The presentation is fantastic and the movie is a timeless joy, an absolutely necessary and welcome inclusion to any home video collection.

The black and white picture has the smooth, solid grey tones which only well preserved nitrate stock can deliver. The image looks so fresh it is nearly impossible to believe that the film is closer in years to the Civil War than it is to us. There is an occasional spot or two, but they are so fleeting as to be irrelevant. The picture is also extremely crisp. Details are not only clear in closeups, but are easily discernible in the longest wide-angle shots. The speed of the film has also been adjusted correctly, so that none of the movements look jittery or unnatural. The film was already a pleasure to watch, but the disc presentation makes the experience even more enjoyable and rewarding.

There is a digitally stereo musical score arranged and composed by Carl Davis, who has done the music on a number of silent programs. The sound is fine and the score utilizes a few of traditional tunes. It is worth amplifying, but it is also unassuming and not distracting to the film. Although the film runs less than 80 minutes, Image has sadly left the disc in CLV.

Owning *The General* is worthwhile because the movie is so much fun. Keaton portrays an engineer in the Confederacy (this is one of the few films in which viewers can feel no qualms that the hero is a Confederate, since politics and race relations have nothing to do with the story) whose train is stolen by spies. He chases them across enemy lines, retrieves the train, and is then chased himself as he races back to warn his side of an impending attack. There are digressions, and he rescues his girl along the way. It is the romance that solidifies the film, which would otherwise be nothing more than a series of spectacular stunts and gags involving several magnificent old (really old) locomotives. The wit of the film was in doing the romance on the run, mixing little incidents which bring the two closer together with the wild acrobatics that momentarily send them off in different directions.

GENTLEMAN JIM

The photograph of Errol Flynn on the cover of *Gentleman Jim* shows him with his pencil-thin mustache, but he is clean-shaven in the movie and it may take a while before you spot him. The film, directed by Raoul Walsh, is gentle and robust. The first ring fight Flynn (as James J. Corbett) participates in is conducted at almost a whisper. The sound on the disc is strong for a 1942 film. The black-and-white print has its share of scratches and other markings, but the contrasts are clear and the images distinct.

Depicting the era when the Irish were the ethnic minority grasping at the boxing ring to lift themselves into society, the movie manages to show a protagonist with many personality flaws and yet maintains an upbeat feeling as he rises to the top. It is Ward Bond's portrayal of John L. Sullivan, however, which stays with you long after the movie is ended and Flynn's presence has faded away. The emergence of modern boxing is used as a symbol for the assimilation of an ethnic class. The symbol is effective because of Corbett's failings. Sullivan, the proud Bunyanesque beer-drinking brawler, is the real hero.

GENTLEMEN PREFER BLONDES

The grotesque 'gimme, gimme, gimme,' of Madonna's 'Material Girl' video is all the more disgusting when it can be compared to the musical number it was imitating, Marilyn Monroe's teasing 'Diamonds Are a Girl's Best Friend' in *Gentlemen Prefer Blondes*. It was as if Madonna didn't realize she was taking the grasshopper position to Marilyn Monroe's ant.

The film is a musical which was initially done on the stage with Carol Channing, and it is intriguing to see Monroe fall into Channing's personality for the musical numbers, but reassert herself with a twinge of bitterness in the straight comedy between the songs. The story is about two gold diggers aboard an ocean liner and also stars Jane Russell, whose performance is almost as fascinating as Monroe's.

The print has a blue line running down it from time to time and a few scratches, but the colors, except for shots lit with red lights, are as sharp and tight as Monroe and Russell's outfits. The sound is a little hissy. In spite of the songs, it is best not to turn the volume up too high.

GEORGE CARLIN – PLAYING WITH YOUR HEAD

George Carlin has a fuzzy halo around his own head throughout *George Carlin – Playing With Your Head.* The one-sided disc is a depiction of a Carlin performance, introduced and ended by a black-and-white video narrative which makes no sense at all. Carlin's material is mostly new and mostly not humorous. He makes jokes about the handicapped. The sound is in stereo, like Carlin is funny.

GEORGE GERSHWIN REMEMBERED

Ever come home from a day at the art museum with a burning desire to break out the easel? The same feeling occurs after *George Gershwin Remembered* is finished. You want to run to the nearest piano and start to tinker.

The 90-minute BBC/PBS documentary about the life of Gershwin is monaural, but has a decent fidelity and digital sound. The picture combines color with black and white footage, but the disc sometimes adds a level of graininess to the images. The documentary is quite good, providing a biography of Gershwin, including interviews with people who knew him intimately, and giving a scholarly undergraduate analysis of the basic components in his composition style. Home movies capture some rare moments from behind the scenes, while extensive clips from popular films show how Gershwin's music was put to use.

GEORGE JONES THE LIVING LEGEND IN CONCERT

George Jones The Living Legend in Concert is an hour-long program which was filmed in Ft. Lauderdale. Jones is an overly polished performer who has been singing his songs for so long that, in a live environment, he tends to throw in little vocal jokes now and then to keep his interest up. The best segment on the disc, however, is a medley of several of his hits, perhaps because he's too busy trying to blend them together to mess with them any other way. Jones has the sort of country-western style which turns some segments of the population completely off, such as when he sings, "She's my rock, and I'm not going to throw her away...," but fans will obviously be pleased to see that the program material on discs has expanded far enough to include him.

When the concert lighting is plain, the picture is good, but whenever colored lighting is used, the image goes blurry. The stereo sound is okay for a concert recording. The songs are listed on the back of the jacket in order and the disc is chapter encoded.

GEORGY GIRL

Georgy Girl is just as amusing and charming now as it was when it was first released theatrically. The comedy concerns two roommates, a reserved and slightly frumpy homebody, the title character played by Lynn Redgrave, and an uninhibited rail-skinny ingratiate, played by Charlotte Rampling. Rampling is hysterical, especially after her character has a baby she wants nothing to do with. Redgrave's performance is also notable. She achieves an instant rapport with the audience, and her smile is as catchy as the title song. The print is tolerable, as is the sound.

GERRY MULLIGAN – LIVE AT ERIC
(see **THE JAZZ LIFE VOL. 1**)

GETZ/COLE: HARVEST JAZZ

Richie Cole appears on side one of *Getz/Cole: Harvest Jazz* and Stan Getz appears in CAV on side two. The picture and digitally encoded stereo sound are Windex-level clear. Both musicians interrupt their own playing with inserts in which they provide elementary explanations of their craft. Movement jitters on every CAV still frame, but the many closeups give one an opportunity to study Getz's fingering and panache.

GHOST CHASE

Only youngsters will be able to tolerate *Ghost Chase*, a blurry and grainy inheritance comedy. The picture is often dark and murky. The sound is 'enhanced' stereo and is serviceable if one raises the volume a little. The plot concerns two young filmmakers and a ghost who takes possession of a puppet model the filmmakers have built. The movie is barely tolerable, and watching it on disc is less so.

GHOST TOWN

Several genres are successfully combined in *Ghost Town*, a haunted western. A county sheriff searching for a woman who abandoned her car in the middle of a deserted highway stumbles upon a wild-west town which has yet to make its peace with eternity. Most of the special effects are achieved with editing, and the makeup is straight schlock, but if you can't decide between watching a cheap horror movie and watching a silly western, then *Ghost Town* is a satisfying compromise.

The picture looks inexpensive, but fresh. The Ultra-Stereo sound has a number of dropouts and is not as good as Ultra-Stereo can sometimes be. Side two is in CAV with two unsteady frames out of every five. There are a couple of trick gunshot explosions worth examining.

GHOSTBUSTERS
GHOSTBUSTERS (CAV)

The RCA/Columbia cropped CLV release of *Ghostbusters* was rushed to video stores with a grainy and blurry transfer which was most unsatisfying. The one decent aspect to the disc is the terrific bass track which will knock the plants off your neighbor's shelves with poltergeistial exuberance.

The only input we can add to what everyone already knows about the movie is to point out the emphasis of the linkage between the ghosts and food. The script, by stars Dan Ackroyd and Harold Ramis, zeros in on an association between the phantoms and junk food and won't let go of it. The movie suggests that demons are waiting for you in refrigerators and pantry shelves everywhere.

The print, sound, and scanning are the same on the Special Standard Play Edition of *Ghostbusters* as on the CLV version. The transfer, however, is an improvement over its hastily-issued counterpart.

The people who will want a CAV copy of *Ghostbusters* are the same people who like to pick apart Mallomars. The model work is actually more interesting when sped to the hyper-realistic thrice-normal speed. We found ourselves freezing parts of the movie that had nothing to do with special effects at all – the newspaper headlines, for example, which turn out to be superimposed over real issues, and a series of concentric circles on a map in the mayor's office supposedly depicting the incidents of spectral hi-jinks which have emanated from the Ghostbusters headquarters. The flag marking the center is very close to one of John Belushi's old lower Manhattan haunts.

GHOSTBUSTERS (Voyager CLV)
GHOSTBUSTERS (Voyager CAV)
GHOSTBUSTERS (RCA/Columbia Letterboxed)

Voyager has released CLV and CAV 'Criterion Collection' presentations of *Ghostbusters*, letterboxed with an aspect ratio of a little more than 2:1. Letterboxed, *Ghostbusters* is a different movie. Along with destroying the original screen composition, scanning and cropping a widescreen film imposes a new editing rhythm. In *Ghostbusters* the scanning on the original RCA/Columbia release telegraphed every major gag, and lost more than a few minor ones. On the Criterion release, the humor is more subtle, and is more accommodating to multiple viewings. The impressive special effects can also be seen in their entirety.

Although the source material still looks grainy in some early scenes, Voyager has made the fleshtones look like real fleshtones and prevented the image from disintegrating during the most complex special effects shots. The best moments look spectacular. The sound has been digitally encoded and packs a strong punch.

Upon close examination, there are slight but distinctive differences between the CLV and CAV pictures. The CAV version has a more confident image, but the colors are pale. The CLV version is grainier, but is also more colorful. Choosing one over the other, however, will be more a matter of preference than of quality.

The CLV release has chapter markers and two original theatrical trailers. The CAV release contains, in a supplementary section, two brief scenes which were dropped from the final cut of the film, as well as a split screen comparison of several sequences before and after the special effects were added, enjoyable excerpts from a 'Making of Ghostbusters' film, storyboard excerpts, and the complete screenplay which includes scenes and jokes dropped or changed in the completed film (and, in one case, moved to the sequel). Details are also provided on how the special effects were created, although much of the text is drawn from a book about the film's production. The CAV disc also has the trailers (though the green tags, which were on the CLV trailers, have been removed for some reason), and ends with an unidentified series of takes showing an elderly actress screaming. Voyager unfortunately missed a strong marketing opportunity by not including the popular 'Ghostbusters' music video.

The CAV disc has an experimental format. Supplementary material is included at the end of each of the four sides separated by an imbedded stop. On the first three sides, the material refers specifically to the portion of the program contained on the side. The concept works fairly well because one can refer from the film to the text or motion excerpts without having to change sides or exchange platters. All of the text material, however, is repeated again on side four.

After analyzing the supplementary material closely, we have decided that the junk food motif which runs throughout the film was a subliminal artistic effect, a recurring apparition which was never consciously intended by the filmmakers. A friend once called *Ghostbusters* a *Raiders of the Lost Ark* in Manhattan, and that is an apt description of the film's initial appeal. Repeat viewings, however, depend upon hidden linkages, such as the junk food, and on the wonderful cast. In a perverse way, the scanned and cropped version magnified the movie's strongest asset, by isolating the performances with vulgar closeups. With the letterboxed rendition, however, you can watch the actors who are not speaking along with the actor who is, and the entertainment, as well as the comedy, is multiplied many times over.

RCA/Columbia subsequently released a CLV letterboxed version with a picture and sound transfer which are identical to the Voyager efforts. The Voyager discs list an incorrect running time on the jacket cover, while RCA/Columbia lists the correct time, 105 minutes. The disc has not chapter encoding.

GHOSTBUSTERS II

Ghostbusters II, about a possessed painting kidnapping a baby, isn't very funny on the first viewing, and holds even fewer surprises on subsequent viewings – on the first film, the humor in the personalities of the three principals tends to grow the more often you watch them. But, the hit sequel did provide enough special effects and basic gags to get by, and all have been included on the disc.

The picture is slightly matted. The presentation generally looks good. There is still a slight red shifting and a mild pinkishness to some of the fleshtones, but the night scenes are undistorted and viewers interested enough in obtaining the film will likely be satisfied with the way it looks. Everyone will be satisfied with the way it sounds. The disc has digital stereo surround sound, and the effects are adequately deployed.

Among the film's main disappointments we would highlight the shift and short changing in the personalities of the minor characters, particularly those portrayed by Annie Potts and Rick Moranis. The biggest disappointment, however, comes right near the beginning of the film and seems to epitomize exactly what is wrong with it. In the first movie, one of the best lines was Sigourney Weaver's analysis of Bill Murray's character, "You don't seem like a scientist. You're more like a game show host." In the opening of the new movie, he is a talk show host. It is supposed to show how low his character has stooped, but it only shows how low the writers, two of the movie's stars, were willing to bend to steal from the first film.

GHOULIES II

Ghoulies II, about rubber puppets who terrorize a carnival, is predictable and sleepy. The picture and sound transfers are quite good.

GIACOMO PUCCINI – LA BOHEME – HERBERT VON KARAJAN

An intriguing aspect to *Giacomo Puccini – La Boheme – Herbert von Karajan* is that the 1967 program was directed by Franco Zeffirelli, who also directed the Pioneer Artists 'Live at the Met' production in 1982. Zeffirelli carried many pieces of business from the earlier effort, and refined other ideas as the years passed. The earlier production has no audience, and since the voices are dubbed over the action the performers can be a little more physical than they are on the Met stage. Zeffirelli's experience clearly shows in the latter effort, however, and there is less of a difference between the two productions than one would expect.

The disc comes on a single platter, with acts one and two on the first side and three and four on the second. The sound is very clear, though the performers pale in comparison to the Met's all star cast. Adriana Martino makes the strongest impression, as Musetta, but Mirella Freni and Gianni Raimondi, as Mimi and Rodolfo, are no better than average. The chorus and orchestra are also from La Scala.

The image has scratches and a little graininess, but is in acceptable condition for a twenty year old recording. The English subtitles are an improvement over the Met subtitles and are genuinely poetic. The disc also has chapter markers. A six page insert provides an extensive plot synopsis coordinated to the chapter markings, and an excellent essay on the history of the opera.

GIANT

The Warner disc release is the best way to enjoy the *Giant* outside of a theater. The sound on the disc has been reprocessed for stereo and what this amounts to is a strong, but erratic, monaural audio track. Depending upon the sensitivity of one's equipment, a viewer will hear crackles, hisses, surges, flutters, and pops scattered throughout the 203-minute presentation. The most embarrassing moment comes when a horse is silhouetted on the screen in a long shot but sounds as though it is standing immediately behind the left speaker.

The art direction on *Giant* is as perfect as art direction on a film could be. Everyone remembers the mansion sitting in the middle of absolutely nowhere. Add to that, the huge painting in Hudson's den, the interior of another mansion which allows Hudson to draw up behind Taylor as she stands in a wedding party, the windmills and oil gushers. A movie about Texas which calls itself *Giant* has to have this stuff.

The break between side two and three does not come at the normal intermission, but the break between side three and four is lovely. A three-minute overture has been included at the very end, accompanied by a blank screen. The jacket cover, on the other hand, is grotesque.

GIDGET

Gidget is one of those great, unlikely titles which are fun to acquire just for the surprise it will cause when others examine your library ("You've got *Gidget*?!"). There are speckles here and there, color which was probably processed wrong to begin with, and the movie was in Cinemascope so the edges are lost. The sound will remind one of portable record players and transistor radios, but who would want it any other way?

Sandra Dee, shock of shocks, gives an excellent performance as a girl who matures physically and emotionally during her seventeenth summer, most of which she spends at a beach hanging out with surf bums. The awful back projection shots lead one to believe that she did not even try surfing to prepare herself for the role, but her spontaneity and romantic fluctuations are genuinely charming. Can you afford not to have this disc for parties?

GIFT OF THE WHALES

A 25-minute primer about whales, *Gift of the Whales*, was shot in video tape and looks nice and glossy on the CAV disc. The whales are generally seen from afar, but the many seascapes and sunsets compensate somewhat for the lack of extensive close contact with the subject. What is known about whales is discussed in very generalized terms by a 'whale scientist' who bumps into three indigenous American children, recently pumped with whale lore by their grandfather, on a beach in Neah Bay, Washington. Only youngsters will have patience for the program, and even they may feel antsy with its Earth Mother wholesomeness. The CAV still frames tend to blur slightly when movement is involved. The stereo sound is acceptable.

GIGI

GIGI (Letterboxed)

The disc is beautiful, but letterboxing and a gorgeous transfer do not make *Gigi* any better than before. The movie has too many narrative gaps where not much happens, and there is not much to look at while nothing is going on. Vincent Minnelli directed the Alan Jay Lerner and Frederick Loewe musical, which somehow managed to garner a number of Oscars, more out of sentiment than merit. Louis Jourdan, who has a major part, not only looks ill-at-ease, he transmits the feeling to the viewer. And who needs Eva Gabor – what a shame Hermione Gingold didn't play both sisters! Maurice Chevalier's pedophilial opening number is less unnerving when excerpted as a clip. The final twenty minutes of the turn-of-the-century Parisian romance are enjoyable, and Chevalier redeems himself with 'I'm Glad I'm Not Young Anymore,' but the other musical numbers are too few and the gorgeous sets aren't utilized effectively. If anything, the MGM/UA cropped version of *Gigi* makes you think you're missing something, while the new MGM/UA Deluxe Letter-Box Edition makes it painfully clear that you are not.

The screen composition has an aspect ratio of about 2.1:1 and is shifted a little to the right. The picture is very sharp and the colors look fresh. The swans floating behind Jourdan as he realizes Gigi is no longer an ugly duckling are blindingly white, and the coming-of-age red wallpaper in Gigi's aunt's apartment remains pleasantly stable. The print has a couple of splices which occur during the center of the film. The stereo sound is clean, but seems a little subdued. Neither the voices nor the orchestral passages have the sort of sharpness that might have been retained if the soundtrack were allowed its hiss. The songs have chapter markers.

GILDA

The reel change points are all fairly messy, with splices and scratches, but the rest of *Gilda* looks pretty good. The black and white 1946 Rita Hayworth vehicle has been released by RCA/Columbia. The image is sharp and often contains rich contrasts. The sound is not CX-encoded, but if the volume is kept at a sensible level there is no major interference.

The movie is all personality and star power, and it is grand entertainment. Hayworth and Glen Ford portray expatriates in Argentina who have such a deep love that they're always throwing rocks at each other. She marries somebody else. He marries her and then ignores her. It takes 110 minutes for them to realize that the underlying basis for their hostility is desire. It is obvious to audiences much sooner.

GIRL CRAZY

It seems that at every reel change on *Girl Crazy* there is a flurry of speckles or other markings. On some reels the the black-and-white picture looks soft, as well. The movie, however, is one of the more enjoyable Judy Garland and Mickey Rooney collaborations, and MGM/UA has included two other treats in the package, an original theatrical trailer and a delightfully weird and wild Pete Smith short. The short, 'Studio Visit,' is a compilation of several intriguing sketches, a straight comedy piece about a movie set, a musical number featuring Lena Horne which was dropped from *Cabin in the Sky*, a quick documentary about the bead and the three nutshells trick (in which, by filming from beneath a glass table, it is shown how the bead is palmed from the obvious nutshell and slipped into a different one), and an acrobatic act involving a young girl in which it ultimately does not matter whether or not hidden wires are being employed to keep the girl steady because the posing she does with her partner just gets more and more outrageous.

The sound on *Girl Crazy* is acceptable, and the disc has a good selection of chapter markers. The narrative has a Southwestern college setting and the music is by the Gershwins. The finale, supervised by Busby Berkeley and set to 'I've Got Rhythm,' merits special attention. Berkeley is best known for the inventive scale of his productions, but he got his start organizing marching drills for the Army, and it is his sense of visual rhythm that, combined with Gershwin's Bachian swing number, creates a piece of cinema as mathematical as it is musical and imaginative.

GIRLFRIEND FROM HELL

Dana Ashbrook stars in *Girlfriend from Hell*, a relatively useless movie except for the scenes in which he appears. The disc has a mildly grainy picture and a fun 'Ultra-Stereo' surround soundtrack. A demon possesses the body of a wallflower who is at a party on a blind date, turning her into a vixen and the party into a nightmare. Ashbrook is chasing the demon but stops to romance one of the other women at the party. The imaginatively written digressions are better than the central plot and Ashbrook has wonderful potential, not only for grabbing the camera whenever it points in his direction, but for reading innocuous lines without tripping over them.

GIRLS JUST WANT TO HAVE FUN

Sarah Jessica Parker stars in *Girls Just Want to Have Fun*, and while her performance is not totally consistent, her personality and intuition bring life to a tired format. Cyndi Lauper has absolutely nothing to do with the film (Ed Lauter is a feature player. Maybe the marketing people were hoping that some percent of the population would misread his name.) The title song, rendered by a different vocalist, is played along with a few other hits during the course of this gotta-win-the-dance-contest plot. The songs have chapter markers. The disc is in CX-encoded stereo, but what that means is that a sound effect is sometimes thrown to the far left or right.

GIRLS OF ROCK AND ROLL

From Playboy Video and CBS/Fox comes *Girls of Rock and Roll*. Included are a dozen music videos, some of which are surprisingly entertaining. Although a couple of the girls drop the sort of non sequiturs which have endeared us to employees of the Playboy organization in the past ("I think women groups today are very popular just because women in general today are popular."), most are good, struggling rock performers picking up a few extra bucks by cavorting in the nude while they sing their songs.

The transfer is poor. Interference is in evidence through most of the disc. The sound is CX-encoded stereo, but not very imaginative.

GIULIETTA DEGLI SPIRITI (JULIET OF THE SPIRITS) (Import)

Fredrico Fellini's initial and scrumptiously dotty foray into Technicolor, *Giulietta degli Spiriti* (*Juliet of the Spirits*), has been released on disc in Japan. The 3-sided, 136-minute disc is in Italian, with Japanese subtitles on the picture (the film's sound is obviously post-synchronized, since Fellini made multiple language versions, but this is the soundtrack one would consider the original). A tiny black band appears at the top and bottom of the picture, giving it a rectangular form, but since characters are still cut off on the edges, the picture could have been a little wider than it is. The print also has a couple of splices and a thin white line running vertically through the image for one or two reels. The colors, however, are fresh and vivid.

Hats, parasols, boas, flowers, feathers, cosmetics, stained glass – if it has impressive color, Fellini found a way to include it in the movie. Even that most colorful of drinks, sangria, is given significant attention. He also made use of light and shadows, not just dramatically, but to vary the shadings of a single-colored entity, such as the green lawn.

Although laser discs didn't exist when Fellini made the film (1964), *Giulietta* is a perfect laser program. The irrelevant story, about a woman whose fantasies are seizing control of her consciousness as her age accumulates and her marriage crumbles, can try one's patience in an art house theater with hard seats, but has just enough idiosyncrasies to hold one's attentions in the comfort of home video. From there, the quality of the disc presentation takes over. True, the disc would be slightly more enjoyable if one could understand what the characters are saying, but having it this way is infinitely superior to not having it at all.

The film was a transitional work for Fellini, his first movie after making a movie (*8 1/2*) about a man who didn't know what to make his next movie about. It was a watershed effort, however, for his collaborative composer, Nina Rota, perhaps because Fellini's weakening discipline allowed Rota's talents to reign free. The soundtrack is Rota's richest effort save for his operas, and another pleasure of the disc is to catch the handful of passages which are not contained on the soundtrack LP.

GIVE MY REGARDS TO BROAD STREET

You never believe that a movie like *Give My Regards to Broad Street* is as bad as everyone says it is until you sit through the thing yourself. As an excuse for Paul McCartney to perform a bunch of his songs, it is bound to attract some attention. Ringo can also be seen wandering through the picture. It was probably a mistake for McCartney to have included so many of the older Beatles numbers next to his newer material since it only serves to emphasize what a better lyricist John Lennon was. The disc has no chapter markers. It is CX-encoded and the transfer is far better than the original material deserves. The movie's photography is often pale or washed out. If there was once a script, it looks as though someone must have dropped it on the floor and not cared about the order of the pages when picking it up. The quality of the stereo will please fans, but the music reverberates with too great a clarity while the dialog is unintelligible, even when it can be heard.

Apart from McCartney's singing, the only pleasure in the movie is a brief, amusing glimpse of Britain's Elstree Studios. Many great films were made there and this is not one of them.

THE GLADIATOR

The Gladiator is an overly preachy telefilm about vigilantes and drunk drivers. Despite the extensive driving sequences and an almost uncredited cameo appearance by Linda Thorson, the film is a waste of time, and will encourage more drinking than it discourages. Interestingly, a few stunt inserts were video taped, while the rest of the movie was filmed. Most of the disc looks grainy. The digital monaural sound is not noteworthy.

GLAMOUR THROUGH YOUR LENS

Three scantily clad models are photographed at a shoot on the grounds of a mansion, *Glamour Through Your Lens* a program which tells you the dos and don'ts of photographing centerfold models. The advantages of makeup, filters and lighting techniques are explained, but there is about five minutes of hard information in the hour-long program. The picture is sharp enough to support the filter demonstrations. The background music is in stereo. The most important tip: Get the model to think she is involved in the creative process. How? By saying, "Oh, I like that, yes, more of that, yes," etc.

THE GLASS MENAGERIE

Being a memory play, *The Glass Menagerie* is dimly lighted, sentimental, and not realistic. The Tennessee Williams play is limited in plot, but rich in characterization. On paper it hardly makes sense, but when actresses and actors embody the characters, the whole effort comes magically to life. Paul Newman's interpretation, which stars Joanne Woodward, John Malkovich, Karen Allen, and James Naughton, has a few problems, but these are sufficiently transparent to let the beauty of the Williams poetry and the emotional complexities of the characters shine through. The 134 minute film has been released on a three-sided CLV disc. The picture transfer is average, with grain and even a speckle or two contributing to what already was an overly orange image.

In memory everything seems to happen to music. That is why the score sounds nothing like the tinny Victrola from which it is supposedly emanating. The monaural sound is CX-encoded and you have to turn the volume very high to overcome Malkovich's mumbling. We weren't bothered so much by the disc's sound, though, as we were by the sound in the film itself. If there is one thing a person in a dingy apartment hears, it is the sounds of the neighboring dingy apartments, yet the feeling one gets from the film is that this is the only apartment in the whole dingy building. Williams provides the excuse, saying that he's presenting memories and not reality, but it doesn't synch up with Newman's otherwise realistic approach, so realistic that the last line no longer makes sense. And although most of the fragrant, lyrical dialog remains, the cuts which have been made are mystifying. Did the producers really think that no one would understand the references to Guernica?

GLEAMING THE CUBE

The balance between plot and skateboard stunts in *Gleaming the Cube* almost works. The story, which involves several murders, has just a few too many loose ends, and while some of the stunts are spectacular, there are also a few too many shots of the hero hotdogging as he ponders life. The film is passable entertainment if one is partial to skateboarding or if one's standards are not too strict. The disc has a faint blur at times, though the colors appear accurate. The sound is unremarkable. There is a momentary volume surge on side one.

GLEN AND RANDA

For those unfamiliar with Jim McBride's post-apocalypse hippy movie, *Glen and Randa*, which stars Steven Curry and Shelley Plimpton, it was filmed in a national forest and a few junkyards, and depicts a young man and a young woman who are two generations beyond The Big One. No *Mad Max* rough stuff, here. Everyone simply scrounges for cans, commenting with ironic ignorance on the remnants of civilization. Even after all these years, the movie is still mildly appealing, but it is one long toke and not for viewers who want material thrills.

The movie was produced with stock which looked like leftovers itself, so the picture is speckled and scratched, but all things considered the colors look quite nice and the image is sharp. The sound has a lot of noise and is best left at low volume. The film has extensive nudity.

THE GLENN MILLER STORY

The soundtrack of *The Glenn Miller Story* is a little noisy, the picture is a little grainy, and the print has periodic color flaws in the center of the screen. The disc still looks and sounds better than most releases, and it has chapter markers for all the big numbers. The sound is recently remastered in stereo surround. The mix is conservative, but truly stereophonic.

Recently uncovered records indicate that Miller's plane was downed by a freak chance of fate while flying below Allied bombers who were releasing their payload before landing after an aborted bombing run. In the movie Jimmy Stewart just takes off into the fog and that's it. Except for a tune performed by Louis Armstrong, all the songs and all the chapter markers come on side two. Stewart and June Allyson are left to fill the gaps. As young lovers they are somewhat out of place but after a decade passes, their romance becomes the heart of the movie. One nice touch – when Stewart kisses Allyson he holds her chin lightly with his fingers, the same way he holds his trombone slide.

GLORIA ESTEFAN AND MIAMI SOUND MACHINE HOMECOMING CONCERT

When Gloria Estefan sings in Spanish her entire act soars, but when she goes back to English her balloon loses a little air. We shouldn't complain though, since if it were not for her English language hits, we wouldn't get to see and hear her doing her Spanish numbers. *Gloria Estefan and Miami Sound Machine Homecoming Concert* was filmed live in Miami. The auditorium and the lack of a studio controlled production removes much of the dance beat from her music, but there is still enough left to encourage the crowd to form one huge conga line.

The 80-minute program is in CLV. The picture quality is fine, although strong-colored stage lighting tends to go blurry. The stereo sound is terrific, tempered only by the problems in the recording mentioned above. Estefan's act is commendable. The stage show is simple, but direct. Feminists might find the dynamics of the relationship she has with her all-male band to be intriguing, since even though she is the star, the limitations on her movements and actions appear clearly defined, framed by the men around her. Nevertheless, she maintains a hold over the audience through her own exhilarating willpower, and the disc is all Estefan's show.

GLORY

What a terrific movie *Glory* is – it not only has exciting battle scenes and a drama to support the action, it also has historical consequence. The drama, about a black regiment fighting in the Civil War, is flawed in the way that it avoids complexity in characterizations and conflicts, but it has so many lofty goals that most viewers will be quick to excuse these shortcomings. If in the script the characters are sketchily conceived, on screen they are divinely embodied by the wonderful cast. The motivation behind each character's activity may not be clear, but it is readily apparent that each has a soul, and there is a feeling of gratitude in being able to spend time with the group. This feeling extends to Matthew Broderick as well, whose ungainly top billing carries an oddly accurate and positive resonance to his character.

The disc has mild letterboxing, with an aspect ratio which measures about 1.85:1. The image looks accurately composed with the letterboxing, and the picture is more often properly framed by the band at the top of the screen than it is truncated by it. The colors sometimes appear too orange, but the film's cinematography is beautiful, and the image is crisp. The surround sound is also fine, especially during the battle scenes, but the filmmakers tend to cheat with voiceover narrative to avoid recreating the sounds of the regiment's camp, and James Horner's score is both too low-key and too lofty.

THE GO-BETWEEN (Import)

Joseph Losey's *The Go-Between*, with a screenplay by Harold Pinter and a haunting score by Michel LeGrand, has been released on disc in Japan. The picture is faintly pink and not consistently fresh. The sound is monaural and has not been CX-encoded. The film's sound editing is quite good, and is harmed a little by the transfer to disc. The film is in English with Japanese subtitles.

The story concerns a boy who is spending the summer with his wealthy cousins in rural, Edwardian England. One of his cousins is having a liaison with a local farmer, and his involvement as the courier of their missives unduly affects the rest of his life. Pinter's spare but poignant dialog, and Losey's willingness to let the story unfold through the eyes of the boy, creates an entertainment which is ideal for repeated viewing, since the essential portion of the drama happens only on the edges of the scenes. Like the boy, you catch no more than glimpses of what is going on. And, like the boy, who is reminiscing about the episode in the film's epilog and framing device, you play the disc over and over again, not only searching for more details, but to re-live the nostalgic moments of a fading summer.

GO JOHNNY GO

Go Johnny Go (the film is usually identified as 'Go, Johnny Go!'), is a marvelously bad rock and roll movie from 1959 starring Alan Freed, Chuck Berry, Jackie Wilson, and a clutter of lesser talents. The sound, hopelessly monaural like most fifties recordings, is CX-encoded. The print is so fresh that you can see the poorly executed optical processing during every dissolve. The story is about two orphans who meet at a recording studio, cut a record, send it to Freed, and become famous, the week before Christmas. No, Berry isn't one of the orphans. He hangs out with Freed and does three rousing numbers. At every excuse a rock and roll song is played or performed. Some of them are good, but most of them are so bad they are better.

GOD TOLD ME TO

The script for *God Told Me To* is crammed with good ideas and the cast, headed by Tony Lo Bianco, is admirable. The writer/director, Larry Cohen, however, tends to film on the cheap, and his style has an alienating effect. The camera setups are dull, the film stock is bland, and the backgrounds are makeshift. *God* is one of Cohen's better efforts, about a string of mass murderers who all claim to be following Divine guidance, and a police detective with a cloudy past, but it ought to be creepier and more thrilling than it is.

The picture is an accurate transfer and is fairly sharp, though the natural wear and original condition of the source material is telling. It was never too colorful and still is not. The sound is also an accurate transfer from an inept and harsh source.

THE GODDESS

RCA/Columbia has provided a nice-looking black-and-white print of *The Goddess*, Paddy Chayefsky's bossy interpretation of the life of Marilyn Monroe, in which the lack of a mother's love is revealed to be the blame for it all. It is paced very much like a stage play and all the good stuff seems to happen offstage. The acting is engaging, particularly Kim Stanley. The music is by Virgil Thompson, of all people. The sound transfer is fine, but it is difficult to say whether the score is brilliant and ingeniously subtle or just simple-minded and straightforward. The movie, on the other hand, is easier to call.

GODLEY & CREME – HISTORY MIX

Godley & Creme – History Mix runs for 18 minutes and, frustratingly, has no chapter markers. The two musicians did behind-the-camera work on many well-known music videos, and the visuals on the title cut combine excerpts from a number of them. The best number, however, is 'Cry,' which is performed to a steady portrait of an ever-changing face. Their music is surprisingly sharp, with a decent beat, and the disc encourages a viewer to remain attentive.

THE GODS MUST BE CRAZY

Few films have leveraged shoddy production standards as successfully as *The Gods Must Be Crazy*. The title can be said to apply to the filmmakers themselves, who have pieced together faded, poorly-focused snippets of film, pasted on a soundtrack with only a passing attempt at synchronization, and then pawned the whole endeavor off as being deliberately out of kilter. Those who dote upon perfection may cringe or be bored, but most viewers will be won over on the second side when the hero, an errant Bushman returning a Coke bottle, assists in rescuing a group of school children from terrorists.

There is some legitimate question as to whether or not profits from the film contribute to the support of apartheid, if only in a roundabout way. Claims that the subject material is racially slanderous, however, are clearly unfounded.

GODZILLA FANTASIA (Import)

We know you don't want to hear about it but if we can sit through the 90-minute disc, you can sit through the review. We're talking about *Godzilla Fantasia*. Yes, 'Godzilla,' as in Japanese monster movies, and 'Fantasia,' as in a program with images moving to symphonic music. Monstrous images. Rubber monstrous images. The import disc has no dialog. It contains the highlights from many Japanese monster and science fiction movies, most of them in letterbox format. The music, performed by a full orchestra, is comprised of monster movie scores. Most of it is nondescript, but even the blandest music has a little zing. The images are chosen so that Godzilla pounds on Mothra's egg, etc., to the beat of the music.

In general the anthology will allow a scene to play for a while before shifting to another. The quality ofthe picture is comparable to most monster discs. The prints aren't pristine and the black and white movies look a little run down, but the colors are bright and the focus is sharp. The sequences have been chosen with some care and represent the real highlights of the genre. There are no chapter markers. At the very least, the disc is a good way to keep adolescents and preadolescents happy. Well, we enjoyed it.

GODZILLA 1985

The post-cycle *Godzilla 1985* is a serious Godzilla film in that the great fanged lizard is not battling Mothra or trading body slams with Baragun but is instead leading a one monster protest against atomic proliferation. More power to him, except that he chooses to vent his rage against a non-nuclear armed nation, Japan, and can thus do little there except to kick in a couple of cooling towers.

Even if more monster movies were available in America on laser disc, *Godzilla 1985* would still be worth obtaining. The action is well paced and the effects show the confidence gained from thirty years of smashing skyscrapers. The sound is CX-encoded and is supposed to be in stereo. The dubbing is also pretty bad, but that is part of the fun.

GODZILLA VS. GIGAN/GODZILLA VS. MECHAGODZILLA

We love the jacket cover for *Godzilla Vs. Gigan/Godzilla Vs. Mechagodzilla*. Especially the tongue-in-cheek line at the bottom, "All New! Never Before Seen on Videodisc!" Now, the movies themselves are widescreen features (and are available letterboxed in Japan) which are presented on the disc in scanned and cropped format, and dubbed, of course. Cropping makes many of the action sequences difficult to follow – not an easy task considering how mindless the films are – but this is the format most viewers will be familiar with, and perhaps even feel a nostalgic affection for, since the movies are more commonly seen on broadcast television than in the local bijous.

On both features, the picture quality is passable, though the actual source material for *Mechagodzilla* is exceptional. In general, strong colors tend to blur, and there are a few splices, but the colors look new and the faults aren't too bothersome. The sound is monaural, and adequate to the requirements of the disc. 'Mechagodzilla' begins at chapter 4 on side two.

Still, even within the loose strictures of the Japanese monster genre, these two are pretty bad. We had fun watching them, but it is best to leave some space between and not try to tackle both back to back.

In *Godzilla Vs. Gigan*, aliens disguised as humans bring Gigan (a mechanical looking lizard with a buzz saw in his stomach) and Ghidrah (the three-headed dragon) to destroy the Earth, or at least suburban Tokyo, and lure Godzilla into a deathtrap. Thanks to some quick-thinking humans and the tenacity of the gigantic lizard hero, the Earth survives. The film takes a very long time to establish its premise (only the last twenty minutes, or so, are decently entertaining) and the action scenes, at least in cropped form, are not among the most memorable. For that matter, the dubbing isn't as campy as it can sometimes be, either. The picture is soft throughout, a problem which is aggravated by the magnification of the cropped image.

Godzilla Vs. Mechagodzilla has virtually the same plot, but the narrative details are sharper and the film is basically the more enjoyable of the two. The print has a few scratches, and the disc causes some color blurring, particularly in a lengthy scene involving strong red lighting and steam, but the colors and fleshtones are outstanding, and the image is sharply focussed. Cropping spoils the reaction shots when Godzilla first confronts his mechanical nemesis. Godzilla also tends to bleed profusely when struck, something else we don't recall seeing in the days of late night monster marathons on TV.

GODZILLA VS. THE SMOG MONSTER/MONSTER FROM A PREHISTORIC PLANET

From beginning to end, 'Godzilla Vs. the Smog Monster' is noticeably squeezed. The actors not only look thinner, but their faces curve in an odd manner, and the sun is inevitably oval whenever there is a shot of it. The viewer's patience may be tried by this, but then the film is so relentlessly silly that one is not likely to be purchasing it unless already prepared for the dark underside of cultural exchange. The movie appears on *Godzilla Vs. the Smog Monster/Monster from a Prehistoric Planet*, which will surely tempt those who have abandoned better judgement.

The transfer of 'Smog Monster,' squeezing aside, is alright. The colors are passable and the dubbing even provides the songs with English lyrics ("You've got to make your own best choice, you know what it's worth, to save the Earth, raise your voice..."). Made in 1971, the film came out after the Godzilla series had exhausted itself, but just as the era of psychedelia was reaching the ancillary markets. The movie is filled with Japanese hippies taking hallucinagens, wearing clothing designed by people who took hallucinagens, and thinking that peace and songs, rather than Godzilla, can stop the monster which has risen from polluted sludge. The movie has animated sequences, really bad special effects, and every other attribute which makes it as idiotic as it is watchable, whether one is using hallucinagens or no.

Although not squeezed, 'Monster from a Prehistoric Planet,' which begins at chapter 4 on side 2, is so stupefyingly cropped that the last title card says, "HE EN." The color transfer is murky and the dubbing – which was actually pretty decent on 'Smog Monster' – is distractingly obvious. The plot is a standard one, with adventurers bringing a gargantuan hatchling back to civilization not realizing that the hatchling's parents, displeased, are close behind. Some of the miniatures are nice.

Both films have monaural sound which is at the mercy of the other production values. Still, Godzilla's cry, when amplified sufficiently, can have a rousing effect on one's neighbors.

GOING MY WAY

Nothing on the jacket or the label indicates that side three of *Going My Way* is in CAV, but it is. MCA has also included a trailer, placed some rare, color stills on the jacket cover, and put chapter markers on all the songs. The trailer is in fact for the post-Oscar re-release, but we were happy to see it anyway.

The last scene showing the old priest embracing his even older mother, which thanks to CAV can be broken down to frame-by-frame analysis, is, emotionally, a movie in itself. The rapport between Bing Crosby and Barry Fitzgerald is indulgent, but no one would expect any less. The movie harks to the days when the worst crime a priest could be involved in was the theft of a turkey. Life was easier to swallow then.

Although the sound is CX-encoded, it is subdued and you have to strain at times to understand Fitzgerald's patter. The black-and-white transfer is fine.

GOING UNDERCOVER

The plot of *Going Undercover* relies upon that often-used device, the inept private eye hired with the anticipation that he will mess things up. Chris Lemmon stars as the detective, assigned to keep an eye on a young woman travelling in Europe. Lea Thompson is attractive as the object of his surveillance, but the movie, despite some moderately budgeted action stunts, never finds its voice. It is not funny enough to be a comedy and not serious enough to be anything else. The surround sound has some thrust to it, though the quality of the recording is inconsistent. The picture is acceptable. The movie was filmed in Los Angeles and Copenhagen.

THE GOLD AND THE GLORY

A splashy Australian sports film, *The Gold and the Glory*, looks and sounds great, but doesn't amount to much. The movie is pushy, with loads of telephoto slow-motion shots and an almost constant stereo surround musical score by Bill Conti (*Rocky* -ish, but without memorable hooks). The story is about two brothers who enter a fancy Australian marathon competition, and their stressful relationship with their father, who had failed to win the event twenty years earlier. The picture transfer is good, though there are speckles in a couple of places.

GOLD DIGGERS OF 1933

Of all the actresses who appeared in the Warner Brothers Busby Berkeley movies, Joan Blondell was not only the most attractive, but she always got the best lines. Her most satisfying effort was probably *Gold Diggers of 1933*, in which she plays a roommate who bamboozles her best friend's future brother-in-law when the latter comes to town to stop the marriage. At the beginning and the end the film is also a stage musical, but the entire center of the movie is given over to the romantic comedy, making it a little less popular than the cream of the Warner musicals, though that only means that it should not be one's introduction to the series. The musical numbers are marvelous and one, 'Pettin' in the Park,' is extremely risqué. The women are also constantly running around in their lingerie, something they would be unable to do again for another thirty years. Blondell sang and danced well enough, but she also had a wonderful set of facial expressions and a perfect sense of comic timing. Ginger Rogers, though usually miscast, always seems like a block of wood when the two are in the same shot.

MGM/UA has released *Gold Diggers* on disc, and, like their other Warner musical releases, the program is more than just the movie. It opens with what appears to be a British trailer for *42nd Street*. The trailer is fascinating, as the narrator essentially gives a 'lecture' about the film while the American-style graphics continually assault his reserved intonations. Then there is a black-and-white cartoon, called 'We're in the Money.' Although appropriate to the program (the movie wittily opens with that number, which is then interrupted when marshals come to foreclose the show), it is not exceptionally creative or memorable.

THE GOLDEN AGE – THE BOLSHOI BALLET

Unlike other Soviet long-form productions, *The Golden Age – The Bolshoi Ballet* is always engaging and stimulating. The music, by Dmitri Shostakovich, is varied and involving. The three principal dancers, Natalia Bessmertnova, Gediminas Taranda, and, especially, Erek Moukhamedov, are spectacular, and the normally sedate, someone-is-watching-us Bolshoi audience goes understandably wild over some of their moves. The ballet has just enough narrative to provide choreographical excuses without sacrificing dance for plot. Yuri Grigorovich's choreography is as flexible as Shostakovich's music, and provides a variety of exceptional images. The dancing illustrates the score without distracting from it.

If the production were less accomplished, the disc would still be worth playing, for the music alone. The plot of *Golden Age* concerns flappers and Bolsheviks, as the carefree heroine must choose between the slick, effete gangster and the earthy, masculine fisherman. The second side opens with a full orchestra and ballet troop interpretation of 'Tea for Two,' which is lyrical and sweeping.

The analog sound is noisier than the digital sound. As with most Soviet productions, the picture is a little less perfect than American and British recordings, but not so much as to spoil the entertainment. The camera work is frustrating, since you are either too far away to see the dancers or too close to see the full choreography. The editor tries, by showing the full stage and then the closeup whenever a move is repeated, but you always feel as if there is something you're not seeing.

GOLDEN BOY (see BODY AND SOUL)

GOLDEN EARRING – LIVE FROM THE TWILIGHT ZONE

The opening of *Golden Earring – Live from the Twilight Zone* is a sharp looking video skit about spies or something, but the concert which follows is a grainy 16mm job in washy yellow. Similarly, the CX-encoded stereo sound on the Pioneer Artists release is clever on the opening cut, but as dull as the concert itself for the remainder of the program. Golden Earring is a Dutch rock band responsible for 'Radar Love' and several other undistinguished hits. The guitarists play their instruments phonetically and the drummer seems to concentrate most on not hitting himself in the head.

THE GOLDEN CHILD (see CROCODILE DUNDEE)

THE GOLDEN VOYAGE OF SINBAD

We had to get up several times during the beginning of *The Golden Voyage of Sinbad* to lower the volume. The disc is monaural and the sound is easily distorted. This is the fault of the film, not the disc, but it is a shame that Miklos Rozsa's score sounds like it is coming from a tin can tied to a string. The music is especially witty – Rozsa steals a little from Respighi in the 'Fountain of Destiny' sequence, for example – and it ought to have a pulse which matches the adventure of the story.

There are scratches and smudges at the reel change points and the colors, which were tentative when the film was brand new, travel beyond their boundaries. The movie was the last to come from animation expert Ray Harryhausen in which plot is more important than model work.

GOLDFINGER (see FROM RUSSIA WITH LOVE)

GOLDILOCKS AND THE THREE BEARS (see FAERIE TALE THEATRE)

GONE WITH THE WIND
50TH ANNIVERSARY GONE WITH THE WIND

The first MGM/UA release of *Gone with the Wind* was often a globby mass of reds or a dark blur of vague figures, but the title was been restored to its original Technicolor glory with MGM/UA's reissue, *50th Anniversary Gone with the Wind*. In scene after scene the colors are fantastic, a revelation, with distinctive shadings and shifts of color (many not red at all), and clearly detailed objects, costumes and faces. The images give the story a believable diorama, since the muck which prevented a viewer from fully accepting the characters and their fates has finally been eliminated. The awful bleeding sunsets, which seemed to stop the movie dead at all the key moments, have completely disappeared. Instead the beauty, created by combining the suggestion of a setting sun with lights and paints and Technicolor, enhances the dialog in the same way that artfully applied makeup enhances a pretty face.

The disc comes complete with an overture and entr'acte, more than 100 chapter markers, and takes a whole evening to watch. The earlier release had a processed stereo soundtrack, with analog encoding, but the remake eschewed that effort in favor of the original monaural track, which has been digitally encoded. It is fine.

The appeal of *Gone with the Wind* rests with the conniving, selfish personalities of Scarlett O'Hara and Rhett Butler. Tragedy is passed by in the best novel-into-film manner, and the Civil War, while it is genuinely felt, barely intrudes upon the proceedings (and the racism inherent in any story glorifying the South's efforts during these times is soft-pedaled so well that even today there are only a few embarrassing moments). What you are treated to instead is Vivien Leigh's Scarlett and her performance is so involving that you want her to succeed in every scheme she concocts. Poor Leslie Howard and Olivia de Havilland must portray Ashley Wilkes and Melanie Hamilton and no matter how convincing they are, Ashley and Melanie are too naive to earn admiration. Making Melanie a little snooty and Ashley a little lecherous would have enlivened the ménage and made them more realistic. No one wants Melanie to be happy, anyway.

GOOD-BYE MY LADY

William Wellman's *Good-Bye My Lady* is set in *Yearling* country. The black and white film is dominated by Walter Brennan, giving a better-than-usual performance as a backwoods character who lives with his young nephew, Brandon De Wilde, in a small cabin. The appearance of an unusual stray dog and how the dog's presence matures the two of them is the focus of the central narrative. Wellman's sense of craft makes the film compellingly watchable. William Clothier's photography is well-served by Warner's careful picture transfer. There are no memorable flaws and the image is often striking. The sound is also acceptable.

GOOD MORNING, BABYLON

The sound editing on the films of Paolo and Vittorio Taviani is always inventive, and *Good Morning, Babylon* is no exception. So much happens on the soundtrack, in fact, that we were surprised to examine the back of the jacket cover after the film was over and realize that the sound was not in stereo. The effects are more dimensional than in many stereo films. The disc is digitally encoded and the digital track is more defined than the analog.

The picture transfer is also a fine accomplishment and maintain the color, brightness, and contrast of the original film.

The film is about the weakening links between pride of craft and responsibility to family. The plot follows the fate of two brothers who immigrate to America and end up in Hollywood, designing sets for D.W. Griffith. Like the history of cinema itself, the story starts to deteriorate after 'Intolerance' is finished, and the ending can leave one in a state of lingering melancholy. It builds one up with the joys of making movies and then makes one fall farther and harder with the onslaught of World War I.

GOOD MORNING, VIETNAM

Since *Good Morning, Vietnam* runs a minute over two hours, it is spread to three CLV sides. The picture is passable, but looks a little soft. The digitally encoded stereo sound is also in decent shape, although the analog track is weaker and the film's soundtrack lacks atmosphere. No chapter markers have been provided for the many pop songs, unfortunately.

We have never enjoyed the films of Barry Levison, so we were quite surprised at how marvelous *Good Morning, Vietnam* is. The movie never falters from its goal, which is to put the comedy of Robin Williams into a believable context. There are no distractions and no mushy subplots – just a romance where the hero never gets to first base (he's too busy pitching) and the lessons/meanings/horrors of Vietnam, done lightly but sufficiently. Unlike the war, we wished the movie would never end.

THE GOOD MOTHER

Leonard Nimoy's *The Good Mother* is an interesting failure, one which is worth viewing even though the lessons it provides center on Nimoy's errors instead of the film's subject matter. The stereo surround sound is quite good, and the film's sound editing is its best feature. It is thorough, yet subtle. The disc's picture has a few problems. Although the colors are bright, fleshtones tend to appear unstable, even when other objects look solid. There are some pretty night scenes on a lake which transfer well, but a number of indoor scenes look less confident.

The film is almost nothing like the description provided by film critics, who tended to emphasize an incident that occurs off stage and is a minor factor in the custody battle which takes up the film's second act. Based on a novel by Sue Miller, the story is a generational exploration of womanhood, and what a woman's responsibilities are to herself and to her family. Freudians could have a field day with the interviews Nimoy gave around the time the film came out, in which he stated that the film was "about loss." You-know-what envy is certainly an integral part of the tale, but whatever emotion Nimoy felt the film should have, he failed to communicate it to his audience. He is frustratingly neutral in his approach to the characters. It is as if one of the standoffish male characters in the film had directed it. The movie fears emotion, to the point where Diane Keaton's big screaming scene looks as though it is being filmed from a hidden camera. Enough material is presented to hint at Miller's intentions, and the film is interesting as a study of how Nimoy skewered them.

GOOD NEWS

The good news is *Good News* has been given a nice transfer to disc. The bad news is insignificant – Peter Lawford's red sweater looks fuzzy and other intense colors to overflow the edges of objects. The skin tones, however, look exact, and the brightly colored costumes and decorations look wonderful. The sound is okay. There are chapter markers for all the songs.

Good News has been called the *Grease* of its time, and the comparison is fairly accurate. It is a musical about life on campus in a previous era (twenty years earlier than when the film was made, in both cases). The movie was immensely popular, and Lawford pretty much coasted off its success for the rest of his career. The lack of a strong cast – June Allyson co-starred – has prevented the movie from showing up in revival situations as often as other MGM musicals do, but, like *Grease*, it is great fun. The college setting allows the screenwriters, Betty Comden and Adolph Green, to utilize their unique brand of literate humor, and it is their contributions which prevent the inevitably silly romance from seeming overly sophomoric.

THE GOOD, THE BAD, AND THE UGLY

The more often we watch Sergio Leone's *The Good, the Bad and the Ugly*, the more we love Eli Wallach's performance, particularly the way he keeps crossing himself every time there is violence. Clint Eastwood and Lee Van Cleef remain locked in their archetypes, and are only bearable because the film is so beautifully photographed that you're too busy taking in the view to notice the deficiencies in their parts. Wallach, however, saves the movie, ingratiating himself to the viewer as successfully as he fails to ingratiate those around him in the film. He not only makes the Civil War epic tolerable, he makes it worth savoring.

MGM/UA has released the title as a Deluxe Letter-Box Edition offering. Leone's camera angles being what they are, we wonder how we were able to tolerate the CBS/Fox cropped version even once, now that we have seen MGM/UA's rendition. It looks great, with the Techniscope image providing an aspect ratio of approximately 2.3:1. The colors in the film are deliberately dusty, but the average print, and the CBS/Fox disc, look much worse than this one. Flesh and a few other objects still come across on the pale side, however, and the print also has a couple of splices.

The digital monaural sound is good once you get used to it. The gun and cannon fire have a real kick to them. Most of the voices are post synchronized, which can be disconcerting, and there are electronic twangs associated with certain sound effects which are part of the movie's original sound editing.

Before the film begins, MGM/UA has included an original theatrical trailer which is quite amusing, as it misidentifies which actor is playing the Bad and which is the Ugly. In the extended opening of the film, where the labels identifying the three characters, in script, are written upon the screen at key points, the words are in Italian, but trust us, you won't mind. The disc comes in a gatefold jacket and has no chapter markers.

GOODBYE NEW YORK

Julie Hagerty, best known as the stewardess in *Airplane!*, stars in *Goodbye New York*. The film was written, produced and directed by a guy named Amos Kollek, who also stars and gave himself the most sympathetic role in the story. The production standards are barely up to that of a travelog and watching the film on disc will make you think you have a bad cold – the picture looks foggy and the sound is stuffy. Hagerty's character quits her job, leaves her unfaithful husband, and decides to go to Paris. She falls asleep on the plane and wakes up in Tel Aviv. She lives on a kibbutz for a while and learns the value of hard work, meets Kollek and learns the value of sincerity, and struggles for 90 minutes to hide her embarrassment about being in a bad movie. If you feel any sympathy for her, avoid the disc.

THE GOODBYE PEOPLE

Lord save us from playwrights who direct film adaptations of their own plays. Herb Gardner is the culprit behind *The Goodbye People*. Essentially a three-character play which takes place on the beach at Coney Island, the movie drags around in the sand for 104 excruciating minutes. The manipulative construction is so obvious that you don't for a minute think these are characters and not actors. The director can't discern the uncinematic nature of his carefully composed dialogue. The disc is just as bad. The sound is monaural, the picture is fuzzy, and the jacket cover is plain ugly.

THE GOONIES

When we saw *The Goonies* in the theater, we enjoyed it very much, but there was a ten-year-old boy sitting in front of us in abreactive catharsis for the entire 114 minutes. The film is for kids, but it is constructed with such a strong knowledge of what kids will get off on that an adult, by dropping inhibitions and enjoying the silly thing, can touch the long lost feelings of childhood. We have a friend who complains that, "all they do is scream through the whole movie." A favorite Spielberg motif and a certification of boisterous energy, screaming helps circulate the blood.

Since much of the footage takes place underground, a fair amount of graininess is in evidence on the transfer. The stereo mix is well suited to home video. Not only does the music fill one's viewing room, but the sound effects seem to be perfectly matrixed to the action. You can scream along with the cast and no one will notice.

GORGO

The mass destruction in the finale of the 1961 British monster movie, *Gorgo*, is in CAV with two unsteady still frames out of every five. The quality of the picture throughout the film changes from shot to shot. The movie is in color, though underwater photography and many night scenes reduce the amount of footage in which color plays an appreciable role. On the whole, the presentation is murky. The sound is weak and has a couple of volume drop outs.

Gorgo is about a prehistoric-type behemoth captured off the Irish coast and brought to a London circus, with predictably disastrous results. The film has the standard number of shoddy and passable special effects, but is entertaining because it moves quickly (the running time is only 76 minutes) and has no romantic subplot to bog things down. The movie also functions as a cautionary and somewhat prophetic political allegory, condemning the British presence in Northern Ireland.

THE GORGON

A terrific Hammer film from 1964, *The Gorgon* transposes the legend of Medusa, a gorgon, to a turn-of-the-century European village. The print, although not mint, is in acceptable condition. There is a splice, and in other spots the picture freezes for a split second, but the Eastmancolor has faded only slightly and scratches show up only at the reel changes. The sound is also a little scratchy.

The component which gave the British-made Hammer films so much class was the acting. While certainly not on the level of the Royal Shakespeare Company, the performers, even in the bit parts, are far more competent than their counterparts in American low-budget efforts. As usual, Peter Cushing and Christopher Lee star, with Lee playing the good guy and Cushing, with the larger role, playing the bad guy. The end of the disc, which has all the special effects (they don't last long), is in CAV, with two unsteady still frames out of every five. The disc is a lot of fun, and it is the sort where a few flaws are not enough to spoil the entertainment.

GORILLAS IN THE MIST

There is something noticeably un-movie-ish about *Gorillas in the Mist*, the Dian Fossey bio starring Sigourney Weaver. Although the gorilla scenes are quite a technical accomplishment, the normally dependable director, Michael Apted, fails to sustain a sense of wonder or adventure. The excitement of scientific discovery is unrealized, and the battle against the poachers is so undefined that the end title cards, which claim that poaching has dropped off, are curiously vague. Weaver should have been playing a female Kurtz in a sort of National Geographic 'Heart of Darkness.' Instead, she never escapes her own over-the-title billing or the film's singular biographical concept. With too much violence to be a family film, the movie is like the proverbial 500-pound gorilla who sits anywhere. It has no real direction.

The stereo surround sound is enjoyable, and the musical score is by Maurice Jarre. Side three is in CAV with steady still frames. The picture throughout the disc, however, is too grainy, and some viewers may find it difficult to tolerate.

THE GOSPEL ACCORDING TO AL GREEN

An interesting, filmed documentary of soul singer turned preacher, Al Green, *The Gospel According to Al Green*, is mildly blurry and somewhat run down, but the subject has enough energy to make up for it. The sound is rarely stereophonic and sometimes fairly noisy. There are chapter markers but no listing.

Green is interviewed and profiled in the 90-minute documentary. He talks about being 'born again' and about the time a woman poured hot grits on him then killed herself, and also shares the standard tales about writing hits and being a star. Green, however, is crafty, and slips a number of moral tales into his experiences. His comments are intelligent and are not offensive, and his preaching is as easy to take as his love songs.

GOTCHA

The jacket cover of *Gotcha*, looks provocative, but the movie is good, old-fashioned fun. It has a typical boy-meets-girl-who-tricks-him-into-helping-her-smuggle-microfilm-across-the-border-and-they-fall-in-love-later plot, and even that gets stretched pretty thin. As the hero, though, Anthony Edwards always seems to maintain the right tone of nervousness, and the scene where he tries to tell his parents what happened to him on vacation is inspired.

One wishes that all monaural discs could sound as good as this one does. The picture looks a little grainy however, and the colors, often surprisingly well chosen, seem a bit ripe. A speckle or two was also in evidence, particularly during a bedroom scene that left the screen totally dark for an unusual length of time.

GOTHIC

Ken Russell's *Gothic*, about Lord Byron and Percy Shelley, may bring despair to the hearts of scholars and bricks to their hands, but we, being not scholars but enthusiasts, take delight in his outrageous visual expressions. In reality, Percy Shelley, Mary Shelley, and Mary's half sister, Claire Clairemont, met Byron and John Polidori at Lake Geneva. The results of their stay had a great impact on English literature – Byron's best poetry was written then (probably encouraged by Shelley), Mary formulated 'Frankenstein,' (also encouraged by Shelley), and even Polidori pitched in with the first manifestation of a contemporary vampire fable. Claire might have slept with all of them.

Since it depicts but one evening in their lives, it runs a scant 87 minutes, but is CLV throughout which, considering the overly clever editing, is a shame. The picture is fresh, but has a stray horizontal line flitting through it at times. The sound is CX-encoded stereo and is a bit on the noisy side, although the sound effects are quite elaborate and worth distorting with volume. Thomas Dolby did the musical score and which slips easily from baroque sounds to rock.

The movie is about the evening when much of this creativity appears to have been sparked. They have a very wild time taking drugs – primitive drugs at that – and seeing their fantasies Russellized before their eyes. In the end, the film comes closest to capturing the critical essence of 'Frankenstein,' which is the most elaborate tome ever written about the horrors and emotional exhaustion of procreation. You know Russell – fetuses dressed in baby clothes and nipples which turn into eyelids. Every time you turn over the disc, Byron, Shelley, et. al. will probably turn over in their graves.

GRACE JONES: STATE OF GRACE

The God-understandably-broke-the-mold-after-this-one singer, Grace Jones, appears in *Grace Jones: State of Grace*. The single-sided disc features eleven chapter marked numbers, a mixture of performance sequences and pornographic music videos. Jones' music is more innovative in rhythm than it is in melody, but seeing her is far more entertaining than simply listening to her records and staring at her provocative album jacket covers. Unfortunately, the transfer is not exemplary. The picture is often grainy and faded, and the sound lacks a decent dynamic range.

THE GRADUATE (Voyager CLV)
THE GRADUATE (Voyager CAV)
THE GRADUATE (Magnetic Video)

The colors are on Voyager's Criterion Collection renditions of *The Graduate* are so sharp that you can actually follow the rack focus when Howard Suber talks about it on the audio commentary channel. The print is also presented in letterboxed format with an aspect ratio of about 2:1, and since screen composition is integral to the messages and feelings the movie makers want to convey, the disc fulfills a requirement for the film's presentation which home video has heretofore ignored. The CLV presentation has a slightly crisper picture than the CAV version, but both are excellent.

The discs have three audio tracks. On the digital track, the film's sound includes the Simon and Garfunkle songs remixed for stereo. On one of the analog tracks, the soundtrack plays in its original monaural, while on the other analog track, Suber gives his talk about the movie. The monaural soundtrack is dull and not worth utilizing if your equipment can process the digital encoding. One is used to hearing the songs in stereo, not mono, and the enhanced effect is not distracting. The digital sound is also cleaner than the analog.

Suber's avuncular talk is nice, although we can't imagine listening to it more than once or twice. He speaks with an intimate voice, providing a sort of private monolog for the viewer. Occasionally his comments are obtuse, but his conversational tone keeps the atmosphere friendly, as if he knew you were going to discard two thirds of what he has to say. He concentrates on a critical interpretation of the film – why Benjamin's mother and Mrs. Robinson always wear black and white outfits, etc. – but he is also adept at naming the lenses used in various zooms.

The CAV is further enhanced by a scrapbook of still frames and other errata which appears on side four after the movie is ended. The best segments include pieces of the producer's original notebook, excerpts from unused screenplay drafts, the actual auditions of several unknown actors and actresses, and of Katharine Ross, interviews and reviews about the film, an elaborate collection of behind the scene still photos, and a quirky video tribute to the movie.

The Graduate is a film that most people may feel they have already seen enough times. It is fun, but its messages seem obvious and the comedy can become repetitive after a few viewings. The Criterion Collection rendering, however, changes the movie and removes any social or era-bound stigma associated with it. The picture is so crisp that a viewer's concentration will not be hindered by disc-bound distractions. Nowhere is this more evident than in the last shot, of Dustin Hoffman and Ross sitting in the back of the bus. The picture is so vivid, it is as if they are sitting in front of you. You can almost look inside their heads and share the emotional thought processes which their characters are going through. And with the widescreen, nothing prevents you from feeling both of them at once.

The film was released initially on the Magnetic Video label with a grainy, faded picture. A cropped presentation is also available through Nelson.

GRAND HOTEL
(see **DINNER AT EIGHT**)

GRAND ILLUSION
The advantages of having a humanist film such as *Grand Illusion* in CAV eludes us. It could be that after multiple, multiple viewings, manipulations which could provide insight to the points of view will manifest themselves. For the most part, however, the technique of the director, Jean Renoir, is all-encompassing. What can be added if the picture is frozen, slowed, or accelerated? Even subtleties in the performances of the actors are accessible at normal speed, because Renoir instinctively captures and reveals their souls in every shot. The Criterion Collection release, is spread to four sides. The disc has chapter markers and a second audio track lecture by Peter Cowie.

The French movie is a tale about the camaraderie among POWs during World War I. It was made in the thirties and confiscated during the Second World War. The film had always been highly praised as an evocation of pacifism. It was a decade after World War II had ended that a copy of the 114-minute version was retrieved and restored, the discovery providing the impetus for the film's elevated position as a cinematic classic.

The print, then, is a little rough, but the transfer is excellent, and the picture is clear and crisp. The sound clear, if antique. Fresh subtitles appear on the picture. They are comprehensive (for some reason, even the dialog which is in English is reiterated) and perhaps a little more distracting than the old faded and inconsistent subtitles would have been.

Cowie provides important information about the film's production and history, but he also spends an inordinate amount of time describing what one is watching on the screen. His introduction to the second appearance of Erich von Stroheim is confusing, since it fails to take von Stroheim's first appearance into account.

Since the film's power is in its humanity, you have to get to know the characters through a couple of viewings before the strengths of the work become fully apparent. The movie will be an acquired taste in any case, but one hopes that more than just those who are familiar with the film will consider obtaining the disc.

THE GRAPES OF WRATH
Alright, thanks to CBS/Fox, disc owners can at last point to their collections as the place, uh-hem, where *The Grapes of Wrath* is stored. John Ford's classic film has almost exceeded in respect the John Steinbeck novel upon which it was based. This is partially due to Henry Fonda's magnificent portrayal of Tom Joad, taking Steinbeck's high-minded dialog and really delivering it as a common man would think and speak it (and to Ford's direction – for example, he wouldn't let Fonda rehearse the famous last scene). The film's success, however, is also due to the cinematography of Gregg Toland. Toland handled the cinematography for the first films of both Orson Welles and Busby Berkeley, and his influence upon the emotional resonance of the movies he shot cannot be underestimated. Had Ford worked with a less daring photographer, the movie's subject matter would have overwhelmed a viewer's sensitivities. Toland, with his silhouettes and odd angles, keeps a viewer tingling. The story at hand and its universal message are both easier to accept.

We cannot recall seeing a black and white print of *The Grapes of Wrath* which looks any better than the one CBS/Fox has employed for the disc. Whenever there is any amount of darkness in the composition, however, the darkness looks grainy, sometimes extremely grainy, and Toland's accomplishments are obscured by the print. The digital monaural track is cleaner than the analog track.

GRAVEYARD SHIFT
The nocturnal vampire in *Graveyard Shift* works as a cab driver, thirsting on an occasional female passenger. Although he's been around many centuries, things start coming to a fore as the movie opens. His victims dress up in leather and begin attracting and murdering foolish men.

The film is stylized, reminding one of *The Hunger* except that it is less vacant. It has impressive camera angles and almost continuous sex, which ought to give the disc a basic constituency. The continuity, however, often hangs by threads, and the movie was clearly made with a limited budget and cheap film stock. Most of it, inevitably, takes place at night, but the picture has almost no real blacks. Instead there are reds and greens swirling in the darkness. The monaural sound is digitally encoded, and the analog track is fuzzier, but the soundtrack's appeal – the volume is raised when something important happens – is strictly visceral.

GREAT BALLS OF FIRE
Great Balls of Fire looks and sounds terrific. The color is glossy and bright. The digitally encoded stereo surround sound is energetic and free-wheeling. The movie, directed by Jim McBride and starring Dennis Quaid, depicts the brief flameout at the beginning/peak of Jerry Lee Lewis's career, from the time he cut his first hit, to the time, not much later, when he sank from popularity after marrying a very young cousin. The romance is the center of the film, and the movie glosses it over just a little too much. Perhaps no one can actually fathom Lewis' motivations, but the filmmakers don't really give it a decent try. Success stories are always fun, however, and the up lasts much longer than the down in terms of running time.

THE GREAT MCGINTY
Quick! What is thirty-seven and thirty-seven? Sixty-four? The wonderful writer/director, Preston Sturges, and the wonderful character actor, William Demarest, will have you believing it, for a few seconds at least, in *The Great McGinty*, one of Sturges' witty verbal romps. The film, about a crooked politician whose meteoritic career is cut short when he tries to go straight, is a pleasurable sashay through the morals and values of America's political system. Don't worry, it is also a romance, one of the subtlest ever executed.

The film is in black and white and looks great except near the reel changes. The sound is also passable. Side two was done in CAV, and every other still frame jitters. An original theatrical trailer has been included at the end of the disc. The trailer is valuable from a historical viewpoint, even though it is lackluster. It manages to include clips from every significant and amusing scene in the film, yet it still seems to miss the soul of the movie. Sturges' films can't be described anyway, they have to be seen, and heard.

GREAT NATIONAL PARKS YOSEMITE/GRAND CANYON/ YELLOWSTONE
Three separate hour-long documentaries, each about a popular American National Park, have been released on a three sided CLV disc entitled *Great National Parks Yosemite/ Grand Canyon/Yellowstone*. Each documentary opens with logos and ends with a credit scroll, as though it were independent of the others.

The documentaries are very similar in construction, but the parks are different enough to make each program unique. The shows avoid the controversies surrounding the public use of the parks and the ecological planning by the park administrators, but otherwise provide thorough and informative material to the viewer. Although it is best not to watch all three in one sitting, the programs are entertaining, educational, and even slip in some humor by catching the best park ranger monologues ("These mules are going in that canyon today because you want to go, not because they want to go. They've been there.").

Footage of the parks was not obtained during a single weekend's filming. All four seasons are depicted at each location, and a knowledge of the best vistas guides even the most casual shot setups. The transfer tends to make the strongest colors blur at the edges, but the impact of the scenery is unhindered.

A decent listing of the chapter markers can be found on the inner spread of the gatefold jacket. Background music on the digitally encoded disc is stereophonic. The score is effective, but utilitarian.

A geography professor once pointed out to us that only the most worthless, unusable land is set aside for a national park. Fortunately for everyone, nature's investment in these lands has been more uninhibited. The documentaries go into great detail about how the land was sculpted over the eons and how man has adjusted to living with majesty. The disc is a must for anyone who plans to visit the parks and a fair alternative for those planning to stay at home.

THE GREAT OUTDOORS

The lack of urban amenities is the subject of *The Great Outdoors*. The disc has a good-looking picture and well-executed digital stereo sound.

The film, however, is a failure. The inability of Dan Ackroyd to create a realistic personality which can mesh with the other performers inhibits a viewer's acceptance of the material. The scenes involving John Candy in which Ackroyd is not present have potential, but whenever Ackroyd appears, emotional involvement with the characters disappears. The end credits are letterboxed and there is a mindless gag when the credits are over. In the middle of the movie, however, there is one marvelous pun: as Candy and Ackroyd use brooms to try to swat a flying mammal that has invaded their cabin, one of the other characters shouts, "Keep your eye on the bat!"

THE GREAT QUAKE OF '89

ABC News' Interactive Special Report, *The Great Quake of '89* is a good souvenir for laser disc owners who live in San Francisco and Santa Cruz, for news junkies, and for those who are attracted to educational programs in general. The footage from the October, 1989 earthquake in the San Francisco area, not all of it familiar, is stunning. Some of it is horrifying, though the disc producers manage a balance between reporting death and regarding privacy which nightly newscasts are often unable to maintain.

The CAV disc has two parts. Side one covers the actual quake, with chapters devoted to footage of the quake, the scene at the World Series in Candlestick Park, snippets which capture the gist of the earliest TV reports, The Bay Bridge, Highway 880, the Marina district, Santa Cruz, and what the following day was like. On side two the program expands to subjects ranging from the Richter Scale to building design, and contains footage of the rubble from other recent earthquakes, as well as an excellent description, with real film of the aftermath, of the 1906 San Francisco quake.

Diane Sawyer hosts the program, though other ABC personalities also make appearances. The picture transfer is excellent. The nature of the footage prevents every still frame from being steady, but many are and it is clear that great care went into placing the material on the disc.

Although the documentary provides almost everything a viewer could expect from it, the interactive features of the disc are lackluster and could have used a great deal more brainstorming. An imbedded stop has been placed between each chapter, though why anyone wouldn't simply watch the program straight through is difficult to understand. A few still frames are also scattered about the stops, but they have clearly been generated by an organization which is used to putting text on a screen for five seconds at a time.

THE GREAT WALDO PEPPER

Although unmentioned on the jacket cover and lacking a chapter marker of its own, the trailer for *The Great Waldo Pepper* appears in letterboxed format at the very end of the disc. Even though the film itself is scanned and cropped, the scenes which you really would have wanted to see in widescreen are all repeated in the trailer. We got so excited we almost watched the whole movie again.

Pepper is a fairly daring film. Not only because of the life-threatening stunts, but because of the bleak and uninspiring content of the plot. The film's most dramatic moment is an honest-to-goodness soliloquy, where a character describes, in evocative detail, a dogfight which took place over France in World War I. The story takes place after the war is over and is about barnstorming pilots trying to make a living by showing off. Robert Redford, who stars, never stays in a situation long enough to make a strong impression, and the film is one of his weaker efforts.

The print doesn't always appear as fresh as it should for its age. The jacket cover says that this is the 'Home Video Version' and the running time, at 109 minutes, is a minute longer than the standard 108.

A GREAT WALL

Although *A Great Wall* was made with equipment and materials which lack the quality of mainstream Hollywood productions, the effort and care which has gone into the transfer is so evident that it will increase a viewer's respect and appreciation for the film. The picture quality is superb, and never falters. The digitally encoded sound is probably too good, since it picks up the hum of the recording equipment and every other impurity which found its way onto the original soundtrack, but so long as the volume is held to sensible levels, it is not detrimental.

There is a black and white still on the jacket cover, but the film is in color, and is partially in English and partially in Mandarin with English subtitles. The story concerns an executive who brings his family to Peking for an extended visit with his sister. It is a gently amusing city mouse/country mouse tale with resonances on every political and social level imaginable. The acting skills of the cast are often tentative, and the cinematography has a utilitarian look, but the disc forces the viewer to take the film seriously. The reward is that the limitations of *A Great Wall* are greatly diminished, while the positive attributes are magnified.

GREED

A brief prolog introduces Erich von Stroheim's *Greed*. It is probably unnecessary, since the film works fine without one knowing that three to five hours were removed from it without the director's consent. However, the history is nice, the tantalizing behind-the-camera views are thrilling, and the film is important enough to deserve extra attention. MGM/UA has released the two-and-a-quarter-hour epic about a very neurotic marriage on disc. It is a silent film and the efficient Carl Davis background score is stereophonic. The transfer contains footage which looks incredibly fresh and vivid, as well as footage which looks inevitably aged and worn. The characters move smoothly and the title cards are easy to read.

Greed is misleadingly titled, because it is not a depiction of the cold-hearted, calculating sort of greed which oil companies or corrupt politicians practice. Instead, it is about two people too unstable to be married to each other. The man needs guidance and understanding. The woman, who is so obsessed with saving money that she breaks the spirit of their lives socking it away, needs a partner with a stronger sense of self. The plot, then, is about a couple who begin promisingly and dwindle into desperation, but the movie has further goals and is highly respected because of the manner in which von Stroheim executes them. Because the woman so meticulously refuses to allow the marriage to absorb income, the film becomes a portrait of the ugliness of life which money hides. It strips away a veil on one of the nastier aspects of humanity and demonstrates how dependent humans are upon economics. Also brilliant is the film's setting. It begins in the Sierra Nevadas, moves to San Francisco and ends in Death Valley. Deliberately, even in its truncated form, *Greed* is superimposed on California, as von Stroheim draws damning parallels between the emotional state of avarice and the Golden State where he himself is laboring for art.

GREEN ICE

The emeralds in *Green Ice* are a lovely sapphire blue. Fleshtones look a bit on the orange side, and the picture is grainy. The sound is in stereo which has no surround effects and has a musical score that tries too hard. The disc opens with a lengthy theatrical trailer for *On Golden Pond*. There are a couple of spectacular stunts in the film itself, but the plot, about an emerald heist, is too contrived and padded to be satisfying, and the leads, Ryan O'Neal and Anne Archer, are at a loss when the script deserts them. Their outfits look great, though.

GREENPEACE NON-TOXIC VIDEO HITS

When an anthology such as *Greenpeace Non-Toxic Video Hits* features different recording artists, the video clips are usually conceived and directed by different people as well.

Therefore, the collection is more diverse and interesting. Unfortunately, the disc has a grainy picture and no chapter markers.

There are 15 videos on the disc. A George Harrison song is included, but Harrison is not seen. Some of the performers appearing, including Heaven 17, Thomas Dolby, Tears for Fears, and Depeche Mode, have made a career out of intelligent rock and it makes sense that these would be the stars bright enough to contribute their talents to a worthy cause. Proceeds from sales of the disc go to painting fur seals green or something so that seal hunters will stop crushing their brains with cricket bats.

GREMLINS

The sound effects on *Gremlins* are marvelous. Voices hang in mid-air. Noises and vicious giggles come from so far on the left and the right that for a moment you think the creatures have jumped off the screen and are really running around your video room. Switch the digital audio off and the CX-encoded stereo turns the disc into normal entertainment. Switch it back on and the whole room comes alive again.

The picture is a little on the grainy side. The essence of the film is its clutter and so the loss of even 5% of the screen with cropping means missing many of the gags, especially on multiple viewings. The director, Joe Dante, included many allusions to other cultural and film icons, like 'The Time Machine' and the theater marquee with the working titles for *E.T.* But our favorite reference is the lengthy inclusion of 'Hemo the Magnificent' in the biology class scenes. It is actually the Bell System documentaries, and specifically 'Hemo,' that stands at the base of motion picture consciousness for any school child who grew up in America during the '50s, '60s and '70s. You didn't just see it once, you saw it again and again, semester after semester, year after year. *Gremlins* is funny because Dante knows who he is talking to and what he wants to say. Those who think the movie was created to sell toys are missing the point. This is a comic nightmare aimed and sprayed at the plastic toy generation.

GREY FOX

The sound on *Grey Fox* is so accurate that you can sometimes hear the changes in atmosphere when the dialogue is post-dubbed. The print which was used for transfer is nearly flawless. There is even a nice little freeze-frame to help preserve the mood at the end of side one.

Grey Fox is about an elderly train robber pulling off a couple of jobs near the turn of the century. Richard Farnsworth portrays the bandit with perhaps a touch too much wisdom. The movie is filled with images of fog-bound forests, misty winter mornings, and lanky, earnest steam engine trains.

GREYSTOKE: THE LEGEND OF TARZAN, LORD OF THE APES

Greystoke: The Legend of Tarzan, Lord of the Apes is not the ultimate 'Tarzan' movie, but it is a good one. It is serious enough and brief enough to capture one's imagination. Hugh Hudson's film is a luscious, straight-faced, realistic attempt to dissect the parallels between Victorian society and life in the jungle. There is a pleasing amount of footage devoted to the political structure within the ape society and some terrific Victorian lust once Tarzan and Jane finally let down their hair.

Greystoke was filmed with great concentration on the quality of the look and the sound, and this care also went into the video transfer although the earliest copies of the disc were littered with pressing impurities. The surround is enjoyable, and not just because of the jungle noises. The clarity with which one can discern the tinkling of the wine glasses during the dining scenes in Scotland is breathtaking.

GRIEG/CHOPIN/SAINT-SAËNS: PIANO CONCERTOS

There is a restless elegance in the manner of Arthur Rubinstein on *Grieg/Chopin/Saint-Saëns: Piano Concertos* (the disc is called 'Rubinstein in Concert' everywhere but the jacket spine). The program is a valuable preservation of Rubinstein's technique and attitude. He appears with the London Symphony Orchestra, conducted by Andre Previn, at Fairfield Hall in Croydon, England. No audience is present, however, and the hall is used as a studio with acoustics which have room to breathe. Rubenstein is patient with Previn and with the orchestra, but there is a hint of condescension in his pauses. The film, however, reveals the consummate perfection of his playing. His fingers strike the keys with a mechanical precision while his hands flow across the keyboard with a natural grace.

The sound is excellent. The picture quality is also very good. A jacket insert contains two essays on a single page. One is a basic biography of Rubenstein and the other is a quick sketch of the origins of the three pieces he plays, Grieg's 'Piano Concerto in A Minor,' Chopin's 'Piano Concerto No. 2 in F Minor,' and Saint-Saëns' 'Piano Concerto No. 2 in G Minor.' The first movement of the Chopin piece appears on side one, and the remainder of it appears on side two. The disc producers have neglected to give the first movement a chapter marker, although there is a listing for it on the back of the jacket.

GROSS ANATOMY

A med school *Paper Chase*, *Gross Anatomy* stars Matthew Modine. In contrast to the film's trailer, which has appeared on several other Touchstone discs, the movie is not dominated by comedy. It is fairly straightforward, with some scenes so poorly written that not even Modine can rescue them while others are strong enough that one will likely recall them for a long time after the film is over. The picture on the disc is acceptable, but the sound is unremarkable.

GROTESQUE

Linda Blair's character in *Grotesque*, is awakened from her slumber in a mountain cabin by some nasty punks who proceed to murder her best friend and her parents. Still clad in her pajamas, Blair escapes, and is chased by one of the punks through the snow, all night long and into the following morning. Worried that her toes will get cold? Don't fret. From the looks of it, she went to bed wearing twenty pairs of socks.

The 80-minute film, a combination of over- and under-acting styles, is primarily a story of revenge and funny-looking masks. Surprisingly, Blair doesn't make it to side two alive, and Tab Hunter must pick up the slack. There is a lot of slack.

Although the film stock used by the producers is not of prime quality, the picture transfer is good, with no significant flaws. The sound is of limited interest. Side two is in CAV with two unsteady still frames out of every five and no practical application other than taking a good look at Blair's fat feet.

GROUND ZERO

A dandy Australian conspiracy thriller, *Ground Zero*, is about a cameraman whose research into his father's murder is both encouraged and discouraged by various governments, government agencies, and other interested parties. The murder was motivated by evidence the father had collected concerning a cover-up of errors in desert atomic bomb tests during the fifties. There are a few paranoid, nerve-wracking sequences, and a satisfying depth of drama as the cameraman's search causes him to examine his memories of his father and his relationship with his own son. The multi-layered ending is perfectly constructed, though we found we had to replay it with one of the audio channels suppressed to hear everything. The sound is digitally encoded stereo surround and contains several show-off moments. The picture transfer looks good, and there are a number of chapter markers.

GRP ALL-STARS LIVE FROM THE RECORD PLANT

So many of the discs released on the Pioneer Signature label are of such high quality that it becomes difficult to find the superlatives when a truly exceptional program is issued. Such is the case with *GRP All-Stars Live from the Record Plant.* The 50-minute concert is a 'best of the best' collaboration featuring the major performers from G.R.P. Records. The picture, naturally, is perfect. The sound is even better. A faint hiss is in evidence, but unobtrusive, and the recording has an exquisite atmosphere.

Included are Lee Ritenour, Dave Grusin, Larry Williams, Carlos Vega, Abraham Laboriel, and Phil Perry. What makes the disc worth acquiring, however, is the presence of Diane Schuur and Dave Valentin. Schuur has fantastic vocal control which will inhabit and dominate the furthest reaches of one's sound system. Valentin has a riveting number called 'Awakening' in which he utilizes several primitive-styled instruments. We only wish that the show could be longer than 50 minutes, even if the performers just did the whole thing over again on side two.

THE GUESS WHO – TOGETHER AGAIN

The Guess Who wrote all those songs that you used to hear on the radio in between the songs that you turned on the radio to hear.

So, Guess Who had a comeback concert which is now available on disc. It is called *The Guess Who – Together Again* and is a 59-minute one-sided offering with fairly decent sound and a grainy picture. The concert, a celebration of Pop mediocrity, opens with a rendition of 'Shaking All Over' which barely wiggles and goes down hill from there. All the hits get played, so you'll never have to get another Guess Who disc if you get this one.

GUESS WHO'S COMING TO DINNER
The significance of *Guess Who's Coming to Dinner* is twofold. First, the film single-handedly changed miscegenation from a metaphor of lust to a metaphor of social harmony within our popular culture. The second point of significance is that Spencer Tracy was dying when he worked on the film. The producers could not even get the standard insurance policy to cover his presence. The cast spent long hours waiting on the set while Tracy gathered enough strength to do a scene. The spirit of camaraderie within the cast, inspired by both these factors, is what keeps the movie alive today. Tracy, Katharine Hepburn, and Sidney Poitier all give the sort of inviting, spellbinding performances that can keep one coming back to watch the material again and again.

The color schemes and film stock throughout the picture are, by design, pale, and that's how the RCA/Columbia release looks.

GULLIVER'S TRAVELS (LVA)
GULLIVER'S TRAVELS (Image)
GULLIVER'S TRAVELS (Republic)
The animated Fleischer brothers full-length feature cartoon, *Gulliver's Travels*, is a public domain title which has been released on disc several times. The earilest release, by Vestron, is out of print. The three versions still available are fairly similar in quality. The Republic presentation has the palest colors, but the edges are sharp and details within the image are clear. The Image release has stronger, more saturated colors than the LVA version, but it is also darker, and tends to let shadows blend together. The LVA presentation is probably the best compromise among the three. Although all are presentable, none seem to capture the cartoon's full potential.

Both the Image and Republic discs have digitally encoded monaural sound, while LVA's disc is analog. The volume on Repbulic's presentation is set a little lower than the other two. LVA put side one of the disc in CAV, with perfect still frames and Image put side two in CAV, with two unsteady still frames out of every five. Both are chapter encoded. Republic left the disc in CLV with no chapter codes and has used a very poorly chosen side break.

Image and Republic present just the film. LVA's disc includes an original theatrical trailer and a cartoon short, 'It's a Hap-Hap-Happy Day,' featuring the film's central character, an impish night herald named Gabby. LVA's disc jacket displays three original theatrical posters, including a gorgeous six-sheet, and an excellent essay about the film's production.

Like so much of the Fleischer product, the film itself is problematic. The Fleischers seem to have an affinity for the colors one normally associates with old vegetables, and their fantasies are closer to the mind's eye of the grizzled old men who shuffle around a public park instead of to the children playing on the swings. Nevertheless, the *Gulliver's Travels* is a magnificent effort, full of techniques of animation which would be impossible to duplicate with today's economics. It is humorous, musical, fantastic, and, once you get used to it, repeatedly enjoyable.

GUN FURY
The objects which got thrown at the camera for the 3D version of *Gun Fury* make you jump out of your seat even in 2D. Despite a dizzying point-of-view shot which opens the movie from the driver's seat of a stagecoach, the actors really don't start throwing things until the end. When they do, be prepared to duck.

The Technicolor print which RCA/Columbia has used is faded in some spots, but very bright in others. The quality of the color matches the stills on the back of the jacket, so you can judge for yourself before you buy. The print slips and bends in a couple of places, but the presentation, on the whole, is satisfying. The sound is 1D monaural, not CX-encoded, but it isn't any worse than one would expect.

THE GUNFIGHTERS
A failed television pilot, *The Gunfighters*, features George Kennedy as a guest-star bad guy. It is a western so riddled with clichés that very little of it seems original or interesting. The central narrative depicts two brothers and a cousin who turn to crime when an evil landowner destroys their ranch, but eventually gain the good graces of the territorial governor and, at fade out, become roving marshalls. The picture is bright and decently colored, but the freshness of the image is curiously off-putting. The transfer is also inconsistent, since there are stretches which look faded or grainy, and there is even a splice at one point. The sound is acceptable.

GUNG HO
In between megahits, Ron Howard directed an innocuous little comedy called *Gung Ho*, about a Japanese company which takes over an American auto plant. The picture is grainy, but the stereo soundtrack is better than average. The movie stars Michael Keaton, who is a resourceful and spirited comedian. There are one or two scenes which are hysterical, at least the first time through.

GUNGA DIN
The influence of *Gunga Din* on movies such as *Conan* or *Raiders of the Lost Ark* cannot be underestimated. The story is about a trio of British soldiers in Victorian India who have a run-in with a murderous cult of religious nationalists. The action is constant and spectacular. The screenplay was written by a famous pair of former newspaper reporters, Charles MacArthur and Ben Hecht, and it is interesting to see how high points in the script hinge on breakdowns or successes in communication. Rudyard Kipling even appears as a character in the end, a correspondent who provides the film's conscience by reading the end of his poem over Gunga Din's grave, notwithstanding that the story had little to do with Kipling's lyric narrative. Cary Grant and Douglas Fairbanks, Jr. star, with Sam Jaffe in the title role. The print used for the master is a rough at the reel change points, and is a bit washed out from beginning to end. The sound also shows its age.

THE GUNRUNNER
The Gunrunner is one of those movies which would never have shown up on video if the star appearing in it hadn't afterwards become famous for other work. The star in this case is Kevin Costner, but the film is not your usual low budget beginner's effort. It is poorly produced – there are jump cuts which suggest errors in camera angle coverage and characters who audibly move in and out of microphone range – but it is a period work about Montreal in the twenties and the plot is an elaborate concoction about warring gangsters, the Socialist movement, and family commitments. It may also have vague similarities to the actual founding of the Seagrams empire. Anyway, Costner, although mildly impatient with the production, is appealing and competent. His part, as the title character, is extensive, and though he remains superficial he projects enough sympathy that a viewer is willing to see him through each scheme. The picture quality is hampered by the original budget, but suffers from little further deterioration. The monaural sound, when not victimized by poor recording levels, is passable and the lightly jazzy musical score is especially clear.

GUYS AND DOLLS
GUYS AND DOLLS (Digital)
If you wish to see an example of the power and magic an actor can achieve, few better examples are available than Marlon Brando's work in *Guys and Dolls*. The script is so intentionally artificial that it would seem juvenile even when performed by high school students. Brando's total understanding of what he is in and total control over what he is doing legitimates the entire production. His every move and every syllable may communicate an I-can-even-make-junk-like-this-look-good smugness, but the play is so contrived that he can get away with it. He's not just filling the role of a character, he's holding onto the hearts and minds of an audience, making them stay with the show, and making them enjoy it.

CBS/Fox reissued *Guys and Dolls* with a partially letterboxed image and digitally encoded sound. To identify the new *Guys and Dolls* from the old *Guys and Dolls*, you must turn the jacket over and look at the back. The new version has UPC bars and the Digital Sound logo in the band containing the screen credits. The old version just has the credits.

The aspect ratio measures 1.7:1 (the measure may vary slightly, depending upon one's monitor). This is by no means the original proportions of the Cinemascope print, but it is a significant improvement over the scanned and cropped version released initially. You may not see the edges, but you do see the principal cast members in the same shot, and no longer feel like you've got a seat behind a column while you're watching the disc. The quality of the picture itself is also improved.

Although the digital and analog tracks sound quite similar, the sound has been improved. Some listeners may find the older version more enjoyable, since it is noisier and more vivid, the way an LP can be. The new track is much cleaner and a little calmer, but more background sounds can be distinguished. On both discs, the audio channels appear to be separated correctly, although there is one moment on both when a voice comes from the left even though the character is off screen on the right. It appears to be an error within the film itself.

Like the sound, some viewers may prefer the color transfer of the older disc, which, although much sloppier and dirtier, errors on the side of intensity. On some reels, the image on the new disc looks perfect, but on others, however clean it may appear, it also looks a little pale.

The three-sided disc has no chapter markers. A useful listing of the musical numbers on the back of the jacket has an improperly titled heading, 'Chapter Stops,' but lists the minute markers for the beginning of each song.

H.M.S. PINAFORE
(see **YEOMAN OF THE GUARD**)

HAIL MARY
Except for two or three very brief passages of dialog that mix off-color words with references to theological figures, there is nothing in *Hail Mary* that any church leader in his right mind would ban or even bother with. It was lucky to have generated indignation, because that was its only path to black ink. The film, which Jean-Luc Godard made in the mid-eighties, is confused and taciturn, apparently concerning a young woman who claims to be pregnant. The film's one strength lies in its discussion of theological issues, to which, banning be damned, it takes a liberal but pro-Church viewpoint. Coupled with the movie, however, as it was in most theatrical venues, is a 25-minute film by Anne-Marie Mieville, 'The Book of Mary,' about a precocious girl, near puberty, who is shuttling between her separated parents. The piece is excellent, equal to and evocative of Godard's best works, yet unique in its strength of characterization and humanity.

'Book' opens the disc and has the same screen credit typeface as *Hail Mary*, which begins at chapter four. Both films are similar in appearance and tend toward dark blue tones which seem just a little bit too dark on the disc. The transfer is adequate, as is the monaural sound. The films are in French with white English subtitles that are easy to follow.

HAIRSPRAY
When *Hairspray* is not self-conscious it is a fairly entertaining film, but like the villainess within the movie, as soon as the show starts to draw attention to its own appearance it is a turn-off. The movie, a comedy, is about a television dance program, a beauty contest, and racial integration during the early sixties. The music and the choreography are enjoyable and the Ultra-Stereo sound is satisfactory. The picture goes a little soft in places, but not badly enough to distract from the entertainment.

HALF MOON STREET
Half Moon Street is only a block long. It is situated near the center of London. One end opens onto a major thoroughfare and the other end provides a camouflaged entrance to a quieter residential street. On the busy corner there are offices for Middle Eastern airlines and other establishments which have window stencilings in Arabic script. On the quieter end, around sunset, you can catch glimpses of hookers, identified as 'escorts' in *Half Moon Street*, waiting to be picked up by their scheduled 'dates.' The street is also the address of Algernon's apartment in the opening act of 'The Importance of Being Earnest.'

The print used for the disc looks as if it is one generation too far removed from the original and is grainy in places. The sound is monaural, but it has been CX-encoded and is not bad.

Sigourney Weaver portrays a Ph.D. working in London who starts turning tricks on the side to supplement her scholarly income. Like most Ph.D.s, she is atrociously naïve, and soon falls into a plot to discredit a prominent politician (Michael Caine) who is trying to bring peace to the Middle East. He has the spot for the Nobel Prize already picked out on his mantle. She apparently wants to study petrodollars from all imaginable angles. In the end, you still don't know which one is really earnest.

HALLOWEEN
When *Halloween* first came out, one reviewer went so far as to compare it to *Meet Me in St. Louis*. The appeal of the mayhem in the film is secondary to the manner in which it captures the atmosphere of a Halloween. The late October light, the scattered leaves and the ubiquitous jack-o'-lanterns transport the viewer into a chilly, dark, suburban Halloween night where a psychopathic killer might just be stalking in the shadows.

The disc is disappointing. The director, John Carpenter, used a lot of oranges and dark browns and now everything looks even more orange. The disc's worst flaw is that the screen picture is squeezed, making Jamie Lee Curtis's jaw look more skeletal than it already is. The picture is also more blurry than the average disc presentation and higher pitched sounds have more than average distortion. Sitting near the front in a theater, viewing *Halloween* on a widescreen, one never knew from which side the killer was going to emerge. That thrill is gone, but in its place is the quickening in one's heart when one realizes the faint, circular image behind the heroine's shoulder is in fact the face of the killer.

HALLOWEEN 4 – THE RETURN OF MICHAEL MYERS
When last seen, Michael Myers was fried to a crisp, but what's a charred epidermis to a sequel potent horror film fiend? *Halloween 4 – The Return of Michael Myers* pays lip service to the conclusion of *Halloween 2*, and gives Michael a decade to recover, though as soon as he's up, he's back at it again. The narrative for Halloween 4 is admirably efficient and moves quickly and logically from one situation to the next without cheating the viewer. The gore and the sex are PG-ish, though the film still has an R rating. Even more so than anticipated, however, the ending is flagrantly open-ended.

The Ultra-Stereo surround sound is wonderful. The picture is grainy in places, but the many night shots, like Michael himself, survive without significant distortion.

HAMBURGER
An opening montage of real hamburger places and real hamburgers lifts one's hopes for *Hamburger*, which is identified in the screen credits as 'Hamburger, The Motion Picture.' But not only is nothing else in the movie as well done as the opening footage, nothing else in the movie is worth watching at all. The film is about a group of young adults attending a fast food management school. None of the jokes are funny. There are racial slurs which are passed off as humor. And the movie goes grinding on for 90 minutes before it has the decency to roll the final credits.

The picture and sound are decent. The sound has CX-encoding without automatic tripping, but who is going to care enough to turn it on?

HAMBURGER HILL
Problems which one might have had with *Hamburger Hill* cease to be problems with the presentation of the film on disc. The movie seems relentless and confusing, like its subject matter, and is short on drama, as opposed to action. In home video, however, the confusion and even the relentlessness is easier to deal with, and the little dramas, as each soldier tries to survive, supersede the need for a larger conflict. On laser disc, the quality of the picture and sound heightens what is good about the film and diminishes what is bad.

The digital stereo sound is superb, with the digital track providing clearer separations than the analog track. When thinking back, after the disc is over, the only image one has in one's head is a color; a muddy olive green. The picture transfer is nearly perfect.

The 'Hamburger Hill' episode was one of the Army's biggest publicity efforts during the whole Vietnam conflict, an attempt to Americanize a supposedly strategic point, so as to glamorize its capture. Such ulterior motives are absent in the film, which deals only with the soldiers on the front line, who must respond to their idiotic orders. Were the filmmakers unaware of the cynicism behind the battle orders, and did they succumb to the same hook, so they could use the title? No matter, because the movie gets the point across anyway. Even if the Army's intentions had been totally honorable, the waste of men was still pointless and the film's microcosm-for-the-whole-war presentation is still justifiable.

HAMLET
Words, words, and words have been written about the meaning and the structure of Shakespeare's 'Hamlet,' but has anyone ever examined it as an entertainment? Here is a play which is an encyclopedia of philosophy, a founding treatise on existentionalism, and a detailed guide to the ambiguous execution of power, all formed with words which give the drama the same beauty that stars give the night sky, and yet somewhere in the second act you take a deep breath, let go of all your defenses, and just start enjoying the thing. Perhaps it is the richness of the personalities in the characters, perhaps it is the becalmed plot billowed by a slight, but corrupt breeze, or perhaps it is just the pure intelligence which realizes that an entertainment need not be confined to a single or narrow set of subjects. 'Hamlet' may be the first 'modern' play, but in its breadth of examining life and existence it still has no equal. Today's dramas are arcane in comparison.

Laurence Olivier's post-War interpretation (in which most of the references to war have been excised) won the Oscar for Best Picture. He directed the film and starred in it, and brought a rather embarrassing, overly Freudian interpretation to the most significant scenes. The soundstage sets are as bare as real castles, and Olivier's mashing is amplified by the empty echoes. He lets the other actors off the hook, not pushing them hard enough, while he himself comes across as if he had been doing 'Oedipus Rex' on alternating nights in repertory. Except for the cuts to models which imply movement about the castle, the film is not very cinematic. Half the shots don't work; they show the actors at the wrong moments and angles, and they convey no sense of the court or of any real life beyond the stage. Added to that, the shadow of the sound boom makes more appearances than the ghost of Hamlet's father.

On the big screen these faults are magnified. On home video, they are better contained, so that the passages which are effective (the scenes where Olivier isn't trying so hard) leave a stronger impression than those which are not. Paramount has released *Hamlet* on laser disc. It is 155 minutes long and runs through three sides (and, alas, lacks chapter markers). The monaural sound is CX-encoded, but it is still rough going and best kept to a sensible volume. The surviving prints are not sweet, but the black and white copy which Paramount has utilized, and which opens with the British Board of Film Censors Certification card, is generally satisfying. There are scratches, dots, and blurry segments, but even when the picture is pure you can see that Olivier's concern for the medium was secondary to his concern for the material. Yours should be as well. This is the only version of 'Hamlet' available on laser, and the play's the thing, not the disc.

HAMMERED: THE BEST OF SLEDGE

We didn't watch 'Sledge Hammer!' too often, but every time we caught an episode we ended up in hysterics. The short-lived cop spoof has been resurrected in *Hammered: The Best of Sledge*. The disc contains four half-hour programs, two to a side, each complete with opening and end credits. A single chapter marker is used to flag the beginning of each episode.

The picture is marvelous. Most of the time it looks brighter than a broadcast image. One of the episodes, 'Under the Gun,' appears to be a pilot (Hammer's partner is introduced), and some backgrounds on it are slightly grainy, but that is the only flaw in the compilation. The monaural sound is solid and provides reverberation to Sledge's trigger-happy gunfire.

The TV comedy was a take off on *Dirty Harry* and 'Hunter.' It wasn't as funny as *Police Squad!*, but it managed to last longer, so perhaps there is a lesson in that. The four episodes on the disc all have amusing moments and a number of throw-away gags. In 'Wild About Hammer,' for example, Hammer enters the house of a woman he knows to be a psychotic killer and who had attempted to seduce him. For just a brief moment, and without attention called to it, 'Misty' plays in the background. A more obvious lampoon can be found in 'Witless,' in which Hammer leaves town when a murder contract is taken out on him, and is sheltered by an Amish-type family. The best gag in that episode is the cinematography, which is deliberately blurry in an exaggeration of the whiter-than-white *Witness* look. In 'All Shook Up' a serial killer is murdering Elvis impersonators. David Rasche, as Hammer, doesn't quite match Leslie Nielson's 'Tribute to Judy' in *More! Police Squad!*, but he has some good lip curls, and there is a police line-up scene which is hysterical.

HANDEL – SCHUBERT – SCHUMANN – NORMAN – PARSONS

Although the jacket cover of the Jessye Norman recital, *Handel – Schubert – Schumann – Norman – Parsons* lists the running time as 58 minutes, it actually runs over 70 minutes and is split to two sides on the CLV disc. There are two basic camera angles covering the program, a close up and a long shot. Norman sings traditional songs, as well as pieces by Handel, Schumann, Schubert, Brahms, and Richard Strauss, accompanied by Geoffrey Parsons on the piano. The sound presents her voice without distortion and gives the piano a dimensional presence. The picture image has no discernable flaws. The concert was recorded live at the Hohenems Festival in Austria. A short but informative essay concerning Norman's song choices and singing strategies is included on a jacket insert along with a multi-lingual libretto.

HANGMEN ALSO DIE! (Import)

Believe it or not, the films of Fritz Lang are under-appreciated, particularly many of the thrillers he made during the forties and fifties. Dismissed when they were released as hack work from a fading talent, the subtleties in perspective and the adeptness in cinematic style are only now becoming apparent. One Lang film, almost totally forgotten despite the fact that it represented scriptwriter Bertolt Brecht's sole Hollywood effort, is *Hangmen Also Die!* The disc is available in Japan.

We would not recommend the film to the unprepared. To enjoy it, you have to be able to accept Walter Brennan as a college professor, complete with goatee, representing the film's intellectual conscience. But then again, maybe you don't. The plot is about the Nazi occupation of Czechoslovakia and a less-than-thorough Gestapo search for a nationalist assassin. (Although the patriotism is deliberately heavy-handed, or, more accurately, thick, the specific plot machinations are clever.) The essence of the film, however, is in its Hollywood underpinnings. Despite the steady cut aways to scenic shots of Prague, the film was shot on the same cobblestone streets one sees in *Frankenstein*. The filmmakers are undercutting 'it can't happen here' attitudes by making Prague seem as American as possible. No one can say we don't hold Walter Brennan in the same respect that other countries hold their college professors. In the best Brechtian sense, the movie itself becomes part of its internal message.

Those who find a transfer to be unacceptable if it contains a single splice or speckle are advised to avoid the disc, because the black and white print contains many. It has a curious provenance, as well. The film is in English (and some German), with Japanese subtitles, but the source material is French, so the credits are in French, and every insert of a letter, telegram or Nazi proclamation is also in French (and the soundtrack goes dead during the inserts). The monaural sound is not CX-encoded. The running time of the movie is listed in various publications as being anywhere from 10 to 20 minutes over two hours, but the disc fits on a single platter and clocks in at a full 120. There are some significant gaps in the narrative logic (we never learn if Brennan's character lives or dies), but enough is left to make for a coherent, rousing and bizarre couple of hours. Those who are onto Brecht's or Lang's wavelengths will find the film to be teasingly subversive, and would-be Walter Brennan impersonators will not be able to leave the dialog alone.

HANK WILLIAMS JR.: A STAR SPANGLED COUNTRY PARTY

Hank Williams Jr.: A Star Spangled Country Party is a one-sided CLV depiction of a concert aboard the aircraft carrier Constellation. The picture is sharp, usually unaffected by the stage lighting, and includes a lot of close-ups. The sound is fine. The disc's worst flaw is a lack of chapter markers.

Waylon Jennings appears with Williams, as does Jessi Colter, Earl Thomas Conley, and Gus Hardin. The stage patter between the songs is entertaining, because Williams is able to elicit fevered applause with the mildest comment or aside. The best moment occurs when he presents the commander of the Constellation with a tour jacket.

HANNA-BARBERA PRESENTS TOP ROCK (Import)

We disliked the *DTV* series from Walt Disney, where clips from various Disney cartoons were compiled and set to popular songs. Hanna-Barbera has a similar set of discs, called 'HBTV,' available in Japan. We liked these discs better for two reasons. The songs on them really are popular songs, without any Annette Funicello filler. And we don't feel as though we are being deprived by not seeing the source from which the clips are pulled. After all, the roller skate dancing episode of 'The Flinstones' isn't exactly *Bambi*.

One 'HBTV' disc we managed to get our hands on is called *Hanna-Barbera Presents Top Rock*. The animation includes clips from 'Yogi Bear,' 'The Flinstones,' 'The Jetsons,' 'Quickdraw McGraw,' 'Scooby Doo,' 'Alice in Wonderland,' 'Gulliver's Travels,' and some esoteric efforts which we did not recognize. No dialog is heard. The songs featured are Lionel Richie 'All Night Long,' Ray Parker, Jr. 'Ghostbusters' (to 'Scooby Doo,' naturally), Bee Gees 'Stayin' Alive,' The Police 'Every Breath You Take,' Roman Holliday 'Don't Try to Stop It,' Rockwell 'Somebody's Watching Me,' Hall & Oates 'You Make My Dreams,' Huey Lewis & the News 'You Crack Me Up,' Stevie Wonder 'Whereabouts,' and Aretha Franklin 'Freeway of Love.'

The picture is a little on the blurry side. Although the sound is in digital, the songs are recordings of recordings and have no special depth to them. The CLV disc is 32 minutes long.

HANNAH AND HER SISTERS

Most of *Hannah and Her Sisters* takes place indoors or at night, and the fluorescent lighting makes everything look a little orange. The edges are soft and the darker scenes are indistinct. The CX-encoded disc is monaural.

Woody Allen's script contains a much more elaborate mixture of drama and comedy than he had attempted in his earlier films, and it works very well. The movie has one hysterical scene which ought to become a staple in acting classes everywhere, about a childless couple who ask their best friends to assist them with artificial insemination. The performance which anchors the film for us, however, is that of Max von Sydow. His presentation of character is so perfectly detailed that you feel his every emotion and know where his every thought comes from.

HANNA'S WAR

The 150-minute *Hanna's War* tells the story of an Israeli immigrant who returns to her native Hungary during World War II as a British commando and is promptly captured and imprisoned, later to be executed just a few weeks before the war ends. The diretor, Menahem Golan, has a competent style. He coaxes a superior performance out of Donald Pleasance, who portrays a Hungarian security officer, and prevents the film from grinding to a halt even though the entire second half is set in the prison. Maruschka Detmers, as the heroine, survives the lengthy attention given to her without embarrassing herself. She is quite good in the all too brief commando section, but can't quite achieve the charisma needed to remain spellbinding during the torture scenes.

The disc, unfortunately, does not present *Hanna's War* in a flattering manner. The anamorphic movie has been awkwardly scanned, cropped, and squeezed. The overly thin locomotive on the jacket cover sets the theme for the entire disc. On top of that, the picture is grainy. The sound is better, but the sound editing is unremarkable and the musical score is a hodgepodge of ideas and emotions. The break between side two and side three is also poorly chosen, needlessly interrupting a carefully paced sequence.

THE HANOI HILTON

The intensely patriotic *The Hanoi Hilton* is daring not because of its viewpoint, but because it is a downer, without action or even much in the way of camera movement to stimulate a viewer. Lengthy segments of the movie consist of stationary shots of one to four characters, ending in blackout. Under home video, which is the market the film was truly targeted for, the experience is less strenuous, but one can still become restless watching the American POWs resist alternating sessions of torture, boredom, and visits from Jane Fonda. It is interesting that the film is not much different from the type which Costa-Gavras was making a decade earlier, but it has received the opposite sort of press. It lacks the flair of inspired technique, but then leftists seem to be better at creating stylized art, while those on the right are more adept at crude entertainment.

The Ultra-Stereo is stood in good stead by digital encoding – the rats sound as if they are everywhere. The left channel is out for the opening minute, but no other flaws appear, and the analog track is nearly as clean as the digital, though it is less precise. The picture is accurately transferred, although the color schemes of a POW compound are not stimulating. The film runs a few minutes over two hours and is spread to three sides.

HANOVER STREET

In *Hanover Street* Harrison Ford is a WWII bomber pilot who falls in love with a woman (Lesley-Anne Down) and later finds himself behind enemy lines with the woman's husband (Christopher Plummer). However, the movie is also an essay on love, told in broad, bold strokes by the director, Peter Hyams. The film can offer a romantic experience to any viewer who is willing to sit back and not examine details too closely.

Unfortunately, even a cursory examination will reveal problems with the disc. The film was originally in stereo but the disc is monaural with a slight phase shift. The film was originally widescreen but the disc is scanned and cropped. The film was originally bright looking and impressively photographed but the disc is over-saturated, orangish, and too dark in places.

HANS CHRISTIAN ANDERSON

(see **THE SECRET LIFE OF WALTER MITTY**)

HANSEL AND GRETEL

The stereo sounds wonderful on the Metropolitan Opera production of *Hansel and Gretel*, with little background noise and clear, sharp tones. The opera is presented in English and conducted with youthful enthusiasm by Thomas Fulton. It makes a better impression than its original broadcast did because of the fidelity the laser disc medium can convey. Engelbert Humperdinck's music has no sustained ideas, but it is pretty and unobtrusive. The show is meant to be a holiday spectacle, with forest fairies flying all over the place, a gingerbread house which comes alive, and a slimy witch. The picture is a bit grainy in places.

HANSEL AND GRETEL

(see **FAERIE TALE THEATRE**)

HARD TO HANDLE: BOB DYLAN WITH TOM PETTY AND THE HEARTBREAKERS

Gillian Armstrong, the Australian film director, put together the hour concert film *Hard to Handle: Bob Dylan with Tom Petty and the Heartbreakers*. Working only with stage lighting and the cramped positioning inherent in a live performance, Armstrong captures Dylan's image with clarity. The picture quality is sharp and is not distorted by the colored lights and minimal illumination. The sound, which has been digitally encoded, is also impressive. The vocals are terribly rough, because of the live recording, but the instruments are distinctly separated and sound remarkably clear.

Since every number ends with a blackout, it is difficult to tell how continuous the material actually is. Dylan's performance clearly improves as the disc progresses and he enunciates his vowels much more regularly on side two than on side one. There are ten songs from a mixture of Dylan eras. Each has a chapter marker, but the number is not noted on the jacket cover.

THE HARD BODY WORKOUT

Brief glimpses of the girls working out on exercise equipment are followed by standard topless-dancing stage routines in *The Hard Body Workout*. The 53-minute program takes place in Rick's Cabaret in Houston and, like the other programs set there, it has a dishonest feel to it (the women who talk about their exercising read prepared scripts, sometimes phonetically). The picture is improved over previous efforts, however, and manufacturing problems which have plagued such titles in the past appear to be under control. The picture, from a video tape source, is bright and colorful. The monaural sound is uneventful.

A HARD DAY'S NIGHT (Voyager CLV)
A HARD DAY'S NIGHT (Voyager CAV)
A HARD DAY'S NIGHT (MPI)

A chapter marker has been placed at the true beginning of *A Hard Day's Night* on both the CLV and CAV Voyager versions. This allows the viewer to start at the true beginning of the film, and not mess with the 'I'll Cry Instead' song and still photo prolog which was tacked on for the Dolby-ized 1982 theatrical reissue. United Artists, thinking they had a fleetingly popular property, readily gave up the long-term rights when the film was first released. The distributor who obtained the rights thought that the film had to be 'changed' in order to retain its popularity. Who is going to complain about the addition of another Beatles song, right? We wouldn't mind if it came at the end, but the beginning ought to have been left alone. The version which Criterion has released on disc is this new official version, with the prolog, the song passages remixed in stereo, and the Dolby logo sneaked into the credits. What this means is that the movie's original opening – a fresh, cold water rush of pop music – has turned to a lukewarm trickle. To surprise your friends with the true, joyous effect, you have to be fast on the draw with the chapter search command.

The print used for the Criterion release does not have the 'reach out and touch them' clarity which other Criterion releases have, but it looks very good. The CLV presentation is noticeably sharper than the CAV version. Both versions, however, are much better than the one put out by MPI a few years earlier.

The digital track is cleaner than the analog track. True purists might have a problem with listening to the songs in stereo while the rest of the movie is monaural, but we found the effect to be pleasing, as it was on Criterion's version of *Help!*.

Voyager has included three special features on side four of the CAV disc. The first, a theatrical trailer for the 1982 rerelease, is less valuable than a 1964 trailer might have been, although it appears to retain much of the same structure. The second feature is an interview with the film's director, Richard Lester which, when combined with the useful jacket notes provides a good sense of the film's origins. The last feature is a complete presentation of Lester's rough and experimental 'The Running Standing Jumping Film.' The print is in a primeval state, so blurred that you can barely make out Peter Sellers or Spike Mulligan, but we've never seen a copy which wasn't. Having the short on a CAV disc is more than a special treat. At the loss of a few sound effects, the ideal conditions for watching the film is to run it at triple speed.

After a number of viewings of *A Hard Day's Night* one can begin to see how the movie was designed to accommodate the limited acting talents of the cast, and how much more at ease Ringo and John were at performing in front of the camera than George or Paul. The songs, vivid or not, still sound great.

HARD TO KILL
The plot of *Hard to Kill*, about a cop who comes out of a seven-year coma to avenge his wife's murder, is fairly ridiculous, but the movie features Steven Seagal, the martial arts star who can act, and he carries the film just as he carried *Above the Law*. The gunfights and bone crunchings are satisfying and the plot is just valid enough to support such activities. The stereo surround effects aren't bad and the picture is sharp.

HARDBODIES 2
James Karen has been in more than his share of really awful movies, and you can add *Hardbodies 2* to the list. He portrays an inept film producer. The show is about a movie company filming a romance on a Greek island which has topless beaches. You get to see both the movie and the movie within the movie and it is a toss-up as to which one is stupider. The picture is unblemished and the sound is free of CX-encoding.

HAREM
The numbingly stupid *Harem* opens with a shot of the Statue of Liberty covered in scaffolding. Get it? Nastassja Kinski is a Wall Street stock trader who is kidnapped and taken to Morocco, where she is put up in the harem of an Arab prince, played by Ben Kingsley. *Nothing else happens*. There is an attempt in the script to execute a piece of ironic drama at the end, but it is so inept that it is easily the most humorous part of the whole film. The one other comical moment: When the eunuch is cleaning the prince's den, he puts a record on the prince's stereo. An opera. 'Abduction from the Seraglio.' But think about, if you were a eunuch, wouldn't that be your favorite opera?

The stereo is very good, accounting for more than a few amusing touches of its own, such as a seagull cry which first signifies that Kinski's boat ride is more than she had bargained for (she'd paid $5, but Kingsley never gives it back, even after they are friends). As usual, the desert locations look great on disc, but even the indoor shots are sharp. It is only the movie which is duller than the blunt edge of a sword.

HARLEM NIGHTS
HARLEM NIGHTS (Letterboxed)
Except for a pronounced streak of misogyny, Eddie Murphy's *Harlem Nights* is enjoyable. Murphy's humor is inspired, and he allows his supporting players the latitude and attention they need to please an audience. The one disappointment in the cast is Richard Pryor. He was once one of the most promising actors working in film, but his talent was instinctive and he literally burned it out. If he had half the spirit of Redd Foxx or Della Reese, his role would have allowed both him and the movie to become twice as funny. Fortunately, Pryor is only one cog, and the film works just fine even when he doesn't. We doubt that the 'MF' word was used as widely in the thirties as it is used in this film, but then we doubt everything else about the setting and story as well. It doesn't matter. The movie has humorous moments. It has a plot which lacks depth but manages to stay on course from start to finish. It is slick, and the cast is good fun.

Paramount has released two versions of *Harlem Nights*, a full-screen standard version and a letterboxed edition. In contrast to *Black Rain*, there is not an iota of additional picture on the sides of the image. The letterboxing has been used only to mask the top and the bottom of the screen in order to provide a presentation of the film that is truer to the theatrical release. It has an aspect ratio of about 1.85:1. On the standard version the top of the screen is usually filled with empty, soundstage-accommodating walls and high ceilings, and there is usually nothing of significance at the bottom, either.

The choice would be entirely one of personal preference, except that the picture transfer is slightly better on the standard version. On both discs, the image is very shiny and glossy – the movie is very pleasing to look at – but many shots on the letterboxed version are murkier when compared directly to the standard version. The picture isn't quite as sharp, and the colors are faintly duller. The stereo surround sound is the same on both releases, and it is very satisfying. Both discs also have chapter encoding.

HARRY AND THE HENDERSONS
As the bubblegum packages for *Harry and the Hendersons* languished on the counter of our local deli long after the film disappeared from the theaters, we began to feel sorry for the movie. Surely some starry-eyed youngster would spend his hard-earned nickels and dimes for a stick of pink, chewable tar and a few slimy cardboard squares imprinted with blurred images of Harry and his adopted family. But no, they just sat there in their pathetic green wrappers until finally, one day, the whole box of them disappeared.

We wish the disc, which is not edible, a better fate. *Harry* has a wonderfully understated but thrilling closing shot, a nice ending, and a funny beginning. It is only the middle which drags, in part because Harry is not there and in part because the movie makers didn't come up with the spectacular sorts of stunts which movies like this are supposed to have to pass the time.

It opens with a marvelous surround stroll through a Pacific Northwest forest, but once the movie gets back to the city, the sound is all grunts and heavy 'oomphs.' The audio track is well-produced. The picture also looks good, which is to be expected, since no one wore the negative out making copies for extra bookings.

HARVEY
The black-and-white image on *Harvey* is a little soft in places, but otherwise it is spotless, and the contrasts are rich. The sound is also clean and well-preserved. The program opens with a five-minute talk by Jimmy Stewart played over a montage of publicity photos and footage from the film run in slow motion. The disc closes with an interesting original theatrical teaser which fails to communicate the film's essence. The disc is also chapter encoded. Intriguingly, the film –a popular favorite about a man whose best friend is a large invisible rabbit –retains much of the risque innuendo from its origins on the stage, making it a darker portrait of Man's brighter side than one would assess at first glance.

THE HARVEY GIRLS
The best way to see *The Harvey Girls* is on a big, big screen. The movie is not a widescreen film, but it just seems to work better when the locomotives are larger than you are. We don't want to discourage those with small televisions from obtaining the disc, however, because the western-themed musical is one of the most likeable and least taxing of all MGM's factory efforts. Along with Judy Garland and an Oscar winning song ('On the Atchison, Topeka, and the Sante Fe') which, for once, is central to the film's structure, the movie features the far too rarely seen Ray Bolger, along with Cyd Charisse, Angela Lansbury, Marjorie Main, Chill Wills, a female saloon brawl, romance, singing, dancing, and some decent action sequences. What more does one need? The disc looks terrific, in the best MGM rhinestone fashion. The volume is a little low and has to be pushed some but the sound is acceptable. There are plenty of chapter markers.

HAUNTED HONEYMOON
Attempting to rekindle the success he'd had in the genre parodies of Mel Brooks, Gene Wilder directed several comedies himself which made fun of popular film styles and categories. The problem was that he could never figure out what to do with a cliché beyond repeating it, and that was his problem in *Haunted Honeymoon*.

The disc has a typical HBO grainy picture, although the picture of the film itself attempts to be scrumptious and sometimes succeeds. The stereo is more consistent, but is not remarkable enough to save the disc.

Wilder moves though the mechanics of a haunted house comedy, but since he is making fun of haunted house comedies, the punchlines come in the wrong places. The film runs a brief 88 minutes and looks as though it has been trimmed considerably. At least one character disappears between side one and side two, never to be heard from again. Movies like this can be a total mess and still be entertaining, but they require a loyalty which *Haunted Honeymoon* continually undercuts. Wilder not only got the clichés wrong, he even blew the mistakes.

HAUNTED SUMMER
We wouldn't want to impose *Haunted Summer* upon anyone else although we thoroughly enjoyed the film. Based upon the same incident which inspired Ken Russell's *Gothic* – a summer spent on Lake Geneva by Percy Shelley, Mary Shelley, and Lord Byron – *Summer*, directed by Ivan Passer, has higher-minded goals than *Gothic*, though it still is sexy and delirious (*Haunted Summer* is to *Gothic* what People Magazine is to the National Enquirer).

The subject could make an interesting drama – Percy Shelley was a far better poet, perhaps the greatest metaphorist in the English language, but Byron was far more popular and successful in his time. The personalities in the entourage are fascinating; a structure which consciously drew from their writings could have great resonance; and an exploration of the creativity that occurred at the lake that summer (ostensibly a group of spoiled brats out for a summer frolic, taking advantage of the post-Napoleonic poverty in

Europe), which had such lasting results (it can even be seen today on supermarket shelves, with Frankenberry cereal) should be all that a movie needs to succeed. Yet it doesn't, just as *Gothic* didn't, probably because the filmmakers who approach the subject are so intent upon diving into the assignations and amours that they back off on the poetry, which at the very heart is what made the incident so important.

Passer makes a serious attempt to be literate. There are numerous references to the times and backgrounds of the writers. There is one marvelous scene in which the two poets have a contest, taking turns at improvising a poem, and Shelley leaves Byron in the dust, but who besides dedicated English lit nerds is going to get excited over something like that? Passer does not include a scene showing the poets meeting for the first time, and uses sepia and brown tones in great excess, though the disc handles the colors well. He does a commendable job filming around Lake Geneva, and even at Chillon, without allowing roadways and utility poles to intrude on the shots. The image on the disc, however, is cropped, cutting into the balances Passer created.

The picture is a little soft, but otherwise the transfer looks fine. The volume is set a little low, but the sound effects are great and the music, by Christopher Young with supplements by Josef Haydn, is exceptional. The film stars Eric Stoltz, Laura Dern, Alice Krige, and Philip Anglim.

THE HAUNTING

In *The Haunting*, losing even the slightest edge of the picture to cropping adversely affects the presentation. The black-and-white print MGM/UA used for the release also looks a little worn out. Why couldn't they pay the same attention to quality with this feature that they do with their precious Technicolor musicals?

This is one of the only movies ever made which can scare the daylights out of you through the power of suggestion alone. That is why the quality of the picture is so important. The clearer the presentation, the more you concentrate and the scarier it becomes. The sound is monaural and is not CX-encoded. Cleaning up the hiss a little might also have improved the impact of the film.

HAWAII
HAWAIIAN PARADISE

In George Roy Hill's 1966 film *Hawaii*, the hero, played by Max von Sydow, is a relentless pain in the neck, but there are so few movies which can be said to have an appreciable scope and spectacle that one clings to each like a cherished idol. MGM/UA has done such a beautiful job transferring *Hawaii* to a Deluxe Letter-Box Edition laser disc that it is impossible to say that the movie was not made yesterday. The picture is as fresh as the island greenery and as clear as the Polynesian sea.

The film is an epic in structure, though not in emotional impact. However, viewing the disc does take up a good portion of the afternoon, and there is entrance, exit, and entr'acte music to put one in the right frame of mind. The film is about missionaries who settle in Hawaii in the early nineteenth century. The scriptwriters seem to abhor the thought that the story could actually offer spiritual rewards, and use James Michener's tale to condemn colonialism with the same numbing righteousness that the hero uses to convert the indigenous population. Julie Andrews stars with von Sydow, but her part is so poorly written that except for a childbirth scene she never has anything to do.

The show lost 20 minutes after its initial theatrical presentation, and MGM/UA has meticulously restored the original cut. The film has no gaps and plays without feeling rushed. It would take more than added scenes to fix the movie, but the new version improves the film's integrity. The disc's exclusive letterboxing, which has an aspect ratio of about 2.3:1, gives the viewer an opportunity to soak up the scenery and the various native delights. The sound has been digitally enhanced for stereo surround. It is Elmer Bernstein's wave-on-the-shore score which is the sole beneficiary of the enhancement, but that is sufficient reason to boost the volume. The film is spread to four sides with the intermission separating the two platters. The disc comes in a gatefold jacket and has tons of chapter markers. An original theatrical trailer, which doesn't sell the movie very well but doesn't lie about it either, appears after the walkout music.

If you really want to make a day of it, or just want to soak up as much escapism as you can, we recommend preceding *Hawaii* with LumiVision's 90-minute *Hawaiian Paradise*, a Reader's Digest documentary. The program provides a full historical profile that supports Michener's fictions just as he intended. With a thoroughness which is the hallmark of most of the Reader's Digest offerings, each of the major islands in the Hawaiian chain is depicted and discussed. Hawaii's major industries, sight seeing points, cultural artifacts, and other relevant aspects are covered clearly and efficiently. The picture is often grainy and stereo effects are limited to the predictable background score, but the program is both interesting and satisfying, and by the end of the day you'll probably be booking your flight.

HAWK THE SLAYER

The Dark Ages action film *Hawk the Slayer*, has gore, a pronounced fantasy bent, and cheap production values. There is a charismatic (though, played by John Terry, not convincingly so) hero, a dark villain with a chip on his shoulder, a group of good humored sub-heroes each of whom has a speciality, and a narrative which substitutes going from one place to another for a plot. The 1980 film is murky and fuzzy, and must have given drive-in movie viewers fits. The picture is often blurry and the sound is flat.

HAWKIN'S BREED

Much of *Hawkin's Breed* is given to voiceover narration in order to avoid the difficulties of sound recording on site. The soundtrack is probably an accurate recreation of the film's original audio track, but the sound fluctuates wildly and rarely makes for pleasant listening. The picture on the modestly-budgeted production also has a basic haze to it, and the colors lack confidence.

The narrative is set in the Appalachians in the early nineteenth century, and the film strives for accuracy in recreating the life styles and concerns of the backwoods characters fighting with each other and with the elements. The characters have to walk when their horses get stolen, and their horses are always getting stolen. The violence is uncomfortably realistic and the film is too pragmatic to be entertaining, but watching it communicates on an emotional level how glad we all are that the nineteenth century is behind us. Peter Fonda stars.

HAYDN – CELLO CONCERTOS – ROSTROPOVICH

Mstislav Rostropovich simultaneously conducts the Academy of St. Martin-in-the-Fields and plays the lead cello in *Haydn – Cello Concertos – Rostropovich*. The concert is performed privately in Henry Wood Hall in London. The room absorbs too much resonance, but the presentation of Haydn's 'Cello Concerto No. 1' and 'No. 2' still has a lot going for it, and should please most listeners. The sound has an ADD code and is free of distortion. The picture is a little grainy, but captures Rostropovich and his accompanists from every angle, including a number of ankle-level point-of-view shots. A jacket insert contains essays on both Rostropovich's career and Haydn's gestation of the concertos.

HAYDN – DIE SCHOPFUNG – BERNSTEIN

A two-hour recording of Joseph Haydn's 'The Creation' is available in an impressive box jacket which bears the title *Haydn – Die Schopfung – Bernstein*. Leonard Bernstein conducts the Bavarian Radio Chorus and Symphony Orchestra with the soloists Judith Blegen, Thomas Moser, Kurt Moll, Lucia Popp, and Kurt Ollmann. The work is sung in German and has no subtitles, but a four-language libretto is provided on an insert, along with an uninteresting essay about the creation of 'The Creation.'

The work is staged and recorded in the Basilica of Ottobeuren in Bavaria. There is a faint background hiss present, probably due to the location recording, but the audio is clean and the disc's soundtrack is impressive. The acoustics are full, but airy. The hall has very little echo, but it doesn't eat up the sound either, so that Haydn's deliberately forceful opening chords linger with just the right balance between, well, Earth and Heaven.

Performing before a somewhat sedate audience, the musicians, under Bernstein, still seem to have their adrenaline going. Musically, the presentation is excellent. Of the singers, Kurt Moll stands out in the part of Raphael, his modulated, peaceful voice seeming both contemporary and yet completely compatible with Haydn's intentions.

The picture on the disc is bright and in sharp focus. Some of the colors bleed, but that appears to be more a fault of the source material than of the transfer. At times the image is extremely vivid, and at other times it is a little messy.

The director keeps the cameras pointed at the action, which lessens the human drama inevitably present in such a large-scale production. One example: In Raphael's 'No. 22 Aria' on side two, Haydn uses contra-bassoons, briefly, while telling of God's bringing animals ('beasts') onto the Earth. The camera cuts to the contra-bassoon players for the split second that the spotlight is their's, and then cuts away, never to return. With two hours to work with, we wouldn't have minded seeing more footage of them preparing for their short-lived moment of glory.

HE MAN AND THE MASTERS OF THE UNIVERSE VIDEODISC, VOLUME II

The state of the art in popular animation is well represented on *He Man and the Masters of the Universe Videodisc, Volume II*. The four twenty-minute cartoons on the disc represent four separate episodes of the Saturday morning TV series. Although the animation is limited, the action is rapid and constant. He Man, with his Elliot Ness voice and his personable sidekicks, reacts to the constantly threatening schemes of an inept but resilient group of bad guys. Careful use of logic and intelligence make the stories partially interesting, but the constraints of Saturday morning standards and practices drain the life from them. The picture is mildy grainy.

HEAD
NEW LOOK MAGAZINE, VOL. 1

Our dictionary has 28 entries for the word 'head' and it seems as though Bob Rafelson and Jack Nicholson intended to invoke at least that many interpretations with their movie, *Head*, the feature-length film starring The Monkees. 'The Monkees' TV show was meant to cash in on *Help!* (as opposed to *A Hard Day's Night*) in such a way that licensing rights would not be involved. *Head*, however, which appeared near the end of the Monkees' first wave of popularity, is a darker, more philosophical work than either of the Beatles movies. The script and the production values border on the edge of student filmmaking, but there is a coherency in the blackout skits which are indicative of the quality Rafelson would bring to his later work. The color print is a bit faded and the sound is a flat, flat mono (and not CX-encoded).

If you ever get a chance, don't miss Bob Rafelson's 10-minute short film on the otherwise forgettable but rare laser video disc, *New Look Magazine, Vol. 1*. It is an amusing and subtle work which becomes funnier – and wilder – every time you play it. *Head* is the same way. At one point, for example, the four boys are presented as dandruff in Victor Mature's oily hair. Many movies like *Head* fail so miserably that you can't last halfway through side one. With an open mind, a little patience, and a soft spot for nostalgia, you'll want to play *Head* several times over.

HEART

The rock group Heart lost its relevancy with the advent of New Wave, and then regained it when music videos became the rage. With two female leads sporting jungles of hair, their videos cause severe cardiological palpitations. Pioneer Artists released an 8-inch CLV disc called *Heart* which has four videos, 'What About Love?,' 'Never,' 'These Dreams,' and 'Nothin' at All.' The concluding video was filmed on the blurry side, but the rest look clear and all sound fine. The music is forgettable, but the group is not.

HEART OF DIXIE

Ally Sheedy portrays a Southern belle who goes through a consciousness-raising experience in the late fifties in *Heart of Dixie*. The jacket art is interesting in how it misleads the potential viewer, for the scenes of racial strife depicted do not actually occur until very near the end of the film. Most of the movie is a nostalgic look at sororities back before women went to college to learn a profession. We're not going to say that the anti-segregation scenes are just an excuse for the other, but if you added up all the footage that was depicting pre-Civil Rights Act Southern life as a luxurious dream and all the footage that was depicting the realities of racial inequality you would have one very large number and one very small one.

The picture transfer is fine. The stereo surround effects are limited mostly to the musical score, which includes a few choice oldies.

HEART OF MIDNIGHT

The misleading ad artwork on *Heart of Midnight* is provocative, but the film isn't. The is-she-crazy-or-is-there-a-bad-guy story, which uses too many contrivances to be a legitimate puzzle, concerns a woman who inherits a night club undergoing renovations. The place remains empty throughout the film, but someone or something is inside, spooking the heroine. The film is also loaded with psychological symbolism, as the many cubbyholes in the night club are meant to represent different parts of the heroine's psyche, and the resolution supposedly solves not only the mystery but her neurosis as well.

The digital sound is okay, but the stereo surround effects are limited to the music. The picture has some weak moments which were probably filmed incorrectly, but looks fine when the lighting is bright.

HEARTBREAK HOTEL

The script for *Heartbreak Hotel* left us cold. The story is about a boy, hoping to cheer up his mom, who kidnaps Elvis Presley during a 1972 concert tour. It is a self-proclaimed fable, but nothing in it rings true and it fails to build a momentum of charm.

The surround sound is okay, as the music mixes real Elvis tunes, which sound great, with David Keith's impersonation, which is different enough to get by. The picture is mildly grainy, particularly when strong reds are involved. Tuesday Weld is the mom.

THE HEARTBREAK KID

The Heartbreak Kid is unpredictable only in that it is so predictable you can't believe the plot would actually move in the ways that it does. A man meets a woman, marries her, meets another woman on his honeymoon, divorces the first and marries the second. He even matures from the experience. Had the filmmakers reversed the situation a little, to have Cybill Shepherd portray Charles Grodin's first wife, and to have him discover that there is more to love than good looks and athletic ability, it might have had a lasting moral. But with Shepherd portraying the second wife, the viewer is left anticipating what will happen on the second honeymoon. The script doesn't even mention that there is a second honeymoon.

The print has scratches and a worn appearance. The CX-encoded monaural sound is tinny, as one would expect from the era in which the movie was made.

HEARTBREAK RIDGE

We can't really say that we prefer to watch Clint Eastwood *acting* as opposed to shooting people or beating them up, but it is sometimes a welcome change of pace. Most of *Heartbreak Ridge* is fort-and-barracks bound, with interludes of stationary action, such as fights, spaced just far enough a part to keep a restless, thrill-addicted audience satisfied. The plot goes through some somersaults to have Eastwood give his men basic training after they should already have had it. There is a certain monotony to Eastwood's personality in the film. He doesn't cry, or laugh too much, or appear all that sensitive, but in his own way he is acting, holding a viewer's attention through force of character alone. The Grenada invasion interlude at the end is a sort of reward to the viewer for being so patient with him.

The most praiseworthy component of the disc is the presence of chapter markers, 27 of them in the 130-minute film. They are also adequately described on the back of the jacket. The print is new and fairly reliable, but at times, even in the bright daylight sequences, the image has background patterns, faint speckles, and other impurities. The sound has been digitally encoded. Special attention was paid to the gunshots, as a distinction between the discharges of different rifles is discussed in the dialog. With the verisimilitude of digital playback, you can master the differences from the safety of your own living room.

HEARTBURN

Meryl Streep's performance in *Heartburn* is fantastic, but the movie isn't entertaining. If there is any reason for obtaining the movie at all, it is to watch her practice her craft.

The show is billed as a comedy but it looks as though adultery just isn't funny any more. Streep's character lacks a sense of humor and most of the laughter is squashed. The cinematographer, Nestor Almendros, is economic in his visual approach, giving the film what could be mistaken for a washed-out look if one didn't know better. The soundtrack is not in stereo, but it exhibits no flaws unless one counts the 12-second loop of music which Carly Simon wrote.

HEARTCOCKTAIL (Import)

We were intrigued by the thought of obtaining an 8-inch selection of excerpts from the Japanese cartoon, *Heartcocktail*, but we should have known better. The animated figures rarely move, and act out romantic dramas by looking distraught while voice-over narration (in Japanese) does all the work. There is also a dull cocktail-type musical score. The disc is digital, to no effect, and seems endless at 19 minutes.

HEARTLAND REGGAE

The 90-minute *Heartland Reggae* is monaural and sounds like a decent bootleg record. The format mixes grainy footage from several concerts featuring reggae stars with commentary on Rastafarian beliefs and Jamaican politics. The hardcore nature of the presentation is both its strength and its weakness. It is serious, but you've got to be serious to like it. The most impressive of the singers is Judy Mowatt, who provides a female slant on what one realizes is a very male-dominated music genre.

HEAT
The sparks in the plot of *Heat* are spread too far apart to ignite. Burt Reynolds portrays a person who lives in Las Vegas and beats people up. Sometimes he gets paid for it and sometimes he does it for free. He is poor at keeping a budget, so he must continue practicing violence even though he would prefer to move to Venice. He has posters of Venice in his office. And a map of Italy, with the location of Venice marked prominently in felt-tip pen. Although he's rocking on a gondola by himself in the last shot, practically ready to break into a chorus of 'O Sole Mio,' there is an hysterical epilog preceding the finale in which all the good guys who one had assumed were killed turn out to be all right after all. The sound is acceptable. The picture is also in decent shape. Only the movie is a mess.

HEAT OF DESIRE
The plot twists in *Heat of Desire* are not fully justified until the end of the film, a point which some viewers may not wish to wait for. The movie is about a woman who randomly selects a man, seduces him, and eventually falls for him while using him to con money out of an important politician. The story is told, however, from the man's point of view. It is in French with English subtitles, and seems pretentious at times. ("Being an intellectual, I was surprised the more she gave the more I wanted.")

Although the jacket cover has a steamy nude shot of the woman, the sex in the film is limited to glimpses of nudity and post-coital repose. The plot turns out to be mildly clever, but the movie is stylistically dull, and will turn off more viewers than it turns on, as will the disc. The colors are somewhat faded and were drab to begin with. The print also has a number of speckles. The sound is passable.

HEATHERS
The sleeper hit, *Heathers*, is so well executed that it rises above its genre and will appeal to viewers who would normally not give high school comedies a second thought. It is most reminiscent of the cult classic, 'Pretty Poison,' and is constructed with deliberate digs at the established clichés and expectations of the high school comedy format, so that at the same time the heroine is rebelling against her peers, so too are the filmmakers. The surprise twist in the script is that it turns out to be logical after a viewer is convinced the story has gone wacko. In the best black comedy tradition, the film is about suicide, murder, and similar amusements. The dialog is marvelous, and the movie will appeal to any viewer who can tolerate straying from the norm. The picture is extremely sharp, and has no flaws. The sound is digitally encoded monaural, but worth running through the hi-fi.

HEAVEN
Diane Keaton's documentary, *Heaven*, is an absorbing collection of opinions on the subject of afterlife. The 88-minute program is a combination of interviews and film clips. The clips are marvelous, ranging from *Metropolis* to Sunday morning talks shows from the fifties. The interviews are intelligently conceived. The subjects are placed in odd-looking furniture and lit with expressionistic shadows, so that the program staves off the feeling that these are just people talking. What Keaton's film manages to impart is not so much a consensus on the make-up of the Eternal ("The walls are made of jasper."), but a demonstration that the range of human emotions is wider and deeper than the sky on a sunny day. How people deal with the concept of death, it could be suggested, is a fair litmus test for how they approach life, and the film brings forth the realization that no two are exactly alike.

The jacket claims that the digitally encoded sound is stereophonic, but that would be limited to a handful of music tracks at the most. The sound is to some extent at the mercy of the film clips, but it always seems to crackle a little bit. The picture quality shouldn't upset anyone. Side two is in CAV, with two unsteady still frames out of every five. We found the standard play features most helpful in reading the lengthy attributions in the credit scroll.

Keaton's film lacks any investigation into the history of the concept of Heaven, or how the concept is approached in other cultures, though America alone seems diverse enough. There is one questionable juxtaposition, where a clip of Fred Astaire and Ginger Rogers is followed by a demeaning look at a 'Black' Heaven, but most viewers will only find the film offensive if they have difficulty confronting the subject of death itself. We enjoyed the disc, but we are in no hurry to find out if any of it is true or not.

HEAVEN CAN WAIT
Contrary to the notation on the back of the jacket cover, it is not just the analog track on Ernst Lubitsch's *Heaven Can Wait* which has had the music and sound effects separated from the rest of the soundtrack. The digital track has also been split. Whether one is listening to the analog or digital track then, it is necessary to isolate the single audio channel that contains the film's complete soundtrack to hear the movie properly, and to isolate the other track when one wishes to take advantage of the special audio feature. Playing both tracks, as the jacket notation indicates, results in an unsatisfying distortion.

The film, which has nothing to do with Warren Beatty's adaptation of *Here Comes Mr. Jordan*, has no fantasy elements outside of a bookending narrative device that has the lead character, played by Don Ameche, telling his life story to the Devil, assuming that his sins have relegated his afterlife to the Inferno. The actual plot, constructed with a stagey device that sets successive scenes on the hero's successive birthdays, is a frivolous but charming tale about a wealthy man growing up during the beginning of the century. The strength of the performances, by Ameche, Gene Tierney, Charles Coburn, and others, gives the film an enduring quality; although one can never remember it being about much after it is over, it is habitually watchable whenever one stumbles across it on broadcast TV.

The source material has a few stretches which are not perfect, but it gives the impression, overall, as having more color than several other movies combined. The soundtrack is also acceptable, although it would have been preferable that the separated audio programs be left exclusively on the analog track. The isolation of the music and sound effects not only enhances one's awareness of Alfred Newman's score, it also increases one's appreciation of Lubitsch's film techniques. Lubitsch's silent film experience, telling the story with pictures alone, is revealed for the viewer by the removal of the dialog overlay. When the comical character, Albert, reappears on side two, the camera pans wildly to encompass the reaction of the other characters to his entrance. Using the pan instead of an edit enhances the comedy, because it tells the viewer that not even the filmmakers are taking Albert seriously.

HEAVEN CAN WAIT
(see **HERE COMES MR. JORDAN**)

HEIDI/THE POOR LITTLE RICH GIRL
CBS/Fox has loaded the Shirley Temple double feature, *Heidi/The Poor Little Rich Girl*, with chapter markers, even though it requires the user to seek out Chapter 7 on side two for the beginning of the second film. This wouldn't be a problem except the jacket cover claims that 'Rich Girl' begins at Chapter 2. The chapter codes, incidentally, and even the time markers near the beginning of the disc, tend to fluctuate wildly in places.

'The Poor Little Rich Girl' is in pretty decent shape. The black-and-white print has no major flaws and the digitally encoded sound, enhanced with stereo during the musical numbers, isn't bad. The film is a lesser Temple vehicle, in which the moppet is misplaced in Manhattan and becomes a radio star before being reunited with her rich dad, all in about a week. The pedophilia is unusually pronounced, making Temple especially charming.

'Heidi' is a stronger film, but may present something of a strain to some viewers. The film is heavily tinted in brownish orange, having been mastered from the original sepiatone print. The sepiatone would be quite acceptable, giving the film a woodsy, Old World feel, but the tinting and the pressing don't get along too well. Every speckle is magnified, and the stronger-toned backgrounds are constantly unstable. The sound is also weaker, and the volume is set lower than on the second film. Most viewers will find that the narrative, expertly directed by Alan Dwan, compensates for the difficulties in the presentation, but it is best to know what you are getting into.

HELEN L. ALLEN TEXTILE COLLECTION
The most effective utilization of interactivity for educational purposes which we have seen employed on laser disc is a combination of narrative and photo archive. A good example can be found on *Helen L. Allen Textile Collection*, a one-sided CAV disc released by the University of Wisconsin, School of Family Resources and Consumer Sciences.

Not only does the disc contain 20,000 stills depicting close to 10,000 pieces of fabric in the Allen Collection, it also contains a brief history of how Allen gathered the materials and a tour of a specific museum exhibit involving a few choice items. The disc is intended to provide scope, not interpretation, and with the help of two hefty frame catalogs (together they are more than an inch thick), that is the sort of educational value it offers.

We could not fathom the criteria for organizing the frames, but the second catalogue provides cross-references by technique, by type, by era, and by country, so that with a little frame manipulation you can follow a design or a concept around the Pacific rim and see what each succeeding culture has done with it.

Every piece depicted is followed by one or more closeup detail shots. A scale and color bar are in every photo, so that the relative size of each object can be easily assessed. Allen's emphasis was on knots, stitches, and weaves. Hence, textiles as opposed to fashions, though the latter is certainly in evidence amidst the fragments of old cloth and endless selections of lace. The most interesting pieces are those which look as though they were actually used at some point, such as a Yugoslavian tablecloth with intricate stitching covered by food stains and ancient strips of Coptic religious garments which have been through a thousand years of dust and prayer.

Despite the many closeups, it is difficult to get a good feel for the weave of the threads. You have to touch such objects before you can truly understand them. But the impact of the designs and the intentions of the various contributing artisans are usually quite clear. Not a single still quivers, and slight variations in dyes and inks are easy enough to spot. It impresses us that a heretofore obscure museum collection can be so readily accessible because of the laser disc.

HELL COMES TO FROGTOWN

The provocatively titled *Hell Comes to Frogtown* is a marvel of low-budget efficiency. The script is nearly perfect – about a vagabond hired by the government to impregnate women living in the 'Forbidden Zone.' Yes, its the post-apocalypse again, a low-budget movie maker's dream when it comes to using abandoned buildings and not caring what is in the background. The title characters, possessing varying degrees of makeup, also inhabit the Zone. A confrontation is inevitable, and boy, can the bad guys jump.

Frogtown stars the wrestler, Roddy Piper, and Sandahl Bergman. The movie is something of a home video cult hit, and deservedly so. Piper's fight scenes are good, but an actor with more verbal skills might have made the material even wittier. The directors, R.J. Kizer and Donald Jackson, have done an excellent job, and clearly get the most out of their budget in every scene. The sound is weak. The picture transfer is accurate. The film runs less than 90 minutes but is presented in CLV.

HELLBOUND: HELLRAISER II

Be wary of the first sequel to a successful low budget horror film. It is inevitably disappointing. Such is the case with *Hellbound: Hellraiser II*, a lethargically paced and uninspired sequel to the witty and enjoyable *Hellraiser*. Except for the final third of the film, which takes place in an effects laden, labyrinthine inferno, the pace of the editing is excruciatingly slow and padded with superfluous footage. The narrative is so pointless it is an insult to the first movie, and none of the effects, however elaborate, are chilling enough to make the unrated label which is plastered on the jacket cover anything more than a carnival sham.

The picture is grainy in places but the transfer is adequate. The stereo surround sound is in decent shape, but the sound editing, like everything else in the picture, has no direction. The disc has plenty of chapter markers.

HELLHOLE

Doctor: "You have amnesia, Susan." Patient: "I just don't understand why I'm here." In *Hellhole*, a softcore terror concoction, the heroine loses more than just her vocabulary. As a guest at a sanatorium/insane asylum/women's prison, Judy Landers has so much trouble remembering her lines that it is just as well her character suffers from an absence of memory. The sound is weak and the picture is only fair. The plot lurches from one threatening or sexy situation to the next, but there is no attempt to match the beginning to the end or to provide any sort of consistent story line. The film's high point ends up being a brawl which bare-chested Edy Williams has with another inmate as ten stark-naked women look on and cheer. People have been known to buy discs for less.

HELLO AGAIN

Frank Perry once made serious, adult dramas, but he has now been reduced to doing *Hello Again*. The disc has an excellent picture and digital sound transfer. The movie, however, places its talented cast in such an awkward situation that you have to ignore the plot to take pleasure in their performances. There used to be only a handful of movies about individuals returning in the afterlife to assist their loved ones, and they were special, personal films. Now, unfortunately, the plot device is regularly and less-interestingly employed. It's no fun coming back from the dead anymore.

HELLRAISER

Hellraiser is not just another horror movie, it is the horror movie you long for. It has everything. Sex, romance, gore, special effects, gruesome looking things (there is creature which is half human, half scorpion), first-rate storyboarding and editing, irony (the biggest scream comes from the inopportune appearance of a statue of Jesus), a coherent, even clever plot with a beginning, middle and satisfactory ending, and stereo sound. Both the analog and digital soundtracks are very clean and free of everything but horror, in its most indefensible form. The picture is excellent as well. The transfer comes from a clean source and looks as fresh as a newly minted print. The story has echoes of the legend of Pandora, but if you are at all partial to depictions of Man's darker fears, grab the disc immediately and break open the seal. That which is inside has been designed to make your life a little less dull.

HELLO MARY LOU: PROM NIGHT II

The director of *Hello Mary Lou: Prom Night II*, Bruce Pittman, has a good command of the genre. In the film's best moment, the heroine is swallowed by a blackboard. The cast is appealing and the plot, a tale of possession among prom queens, is amusing. The digital stereo sound is thorough and workmanlike. The colors are bright, but the darker the hallway the more pointillist the image.

HELP!
HELP! (CAV)

Bob Furmanek has done an excellent service for laser disc movie collectors. He provided a wonderful still file collection for *Buck Privates*. He supplied Image with a gorgeous negative, stills, out-takes, and a production history for *Africa Screams*. And he has supplied Criterion with some terrific Beatles memorabilia to close out side four of the Special Edition CAV digital release of *Help!*.

The print used for the CAV release is the same as the CLV release. Although colorful, it has a few faded spots, lots of very tiny speckles in places, and the same cheap look which the theatrical release had, but that is to be expected. The disc was pressed by Pioneer, in America.

The sound has been processed with such care that there are no noticeable differences between the digital and analog tracks. The songs are in stereo and some of the sound effects seem to have been boosted although *Help!* is basically a monaural film. Because of Richard Lester's dynamic camera angles, half the time the Beatles are positioned on the screen in the way that the music is separated and half the time they are not.

Except for reading a vague attempt at a throwaway gag which is stenciled on a box of TNT, and catching a clever pun concerning electrical measurement, we hadn't much use for the CAV functions on the film itself. The film has been transferred correctly, so that each still frame is motionless.

The main reason to consider investing in the more expensive Special Edition, however, is to obtain Furmanek's exclusive '*Help!* Scrapbook,' which is not available on the CLV disc. This section contains the original theatrical trailer (which includes scenes left out of the completed film), silent footage of the film set and of the world premiere, stills, posters, sheet music, record jackets, radio ads (on audio during the silent footage), and an open interview, originally designed for disc jockeys, which you can utilize to fake-out friends and surprise family members by reading the prompts on the screen and pretending to talk to the Beatles. The many still photos, some of which are introduced by text describing the production history of the film, are the most impressive portion of the scrapbook. There are a couple of hundred, but the one which made the strongest impression on us was a lovely color shot of John relaxing peacefully in a field, unmenaced by a tank looming behind him.

HENRY V (Import)

Laurence Olivier made *Henry V* during World War II as a patriotic booster for struggling England, the message being that if they took Normandy once, they can take it again. The disc is a Japanese release, in English with Japanese subtitles. The print has fresh colors, but also a few speckles and a couple of splices. The splices damage the poetry.

Shakespeare's *Henry V* can be used as an anti-war tract or as a rousing glorification of dying for one's homeland. You can quickly see why other men are willing to follow him into battle and yet also see that Henry doesn't completely understand why he is trying to conquer France. The battle scenes are spectacular. The play has been pared down a bit, but the disc still runs two and a quarter hours.

HER ALIBI

Except for the wonderful musical score from Georges Delerue and a perfectly timed performance from William Daniels, there isn't much to like about the Tom Selleck movie, *Her Alibi*. Most Selleck movies tend to be similar in temperament – he can't seem to take his persona seriously enough and often makes his characters too flawed or comical. The movie is a basic mystery comedy, about a writer who falls for a woman involved in a murder. It was directed by Bruce Beresford, who usually can be relied upon to inject a dark undercurrent, but none is forthcoming. Instead the film turns nearly to slapstick, and the hero's brushes with danger never feel threatening. However, the romantic touches are handled well, and every time the movie really starts to slow down, Daniels appears with a brilliantly delivered remark or wince. It is passable entertainment which could have been improved upon.

The colors look accurate and the image is rarely grainy. The stereo surround sound has some luster and a nice bounce.

HERCULES

Hercules, starring Arnold Schwarzenegger, released by The Disc Factory, is one of the worst laser discs in existence. Filmed in 1969, the show is not really a movie in the sense that it was seriously intended for theatrical exhibition. Films like this are on shelves everywhere. Would-be producers get together a bank roll – this one must have been *at least* $2000 – and everyone involved tries to make something which they can put on their résumé with the confidence that no one reading the résumé will have actually seen the stupid picture. On the shelf this one would have remained, too, were it not that Schwarzenegger – whose voice is dubbed – is now a hot name. It is impossible to differentiate the quality of the transfer from the pathetic quality of the original production. If you can make it past Schwarzenegger wrestling with someone in a poorly-stitched bear suit, you'll be doing better than us.

HERCULES UNCHAINED

Hercules Unchained, starring Steve Reeves, is an Italian gladiator movie from 1959 (the direct sequel to Reeves's *Hercules*), filmed in Eastmancolor and 'Dyaliscope.' The scope is gone, but the gloriously silly colors almost have the smell of new paint. The disc presentation turns bad monaural dubbing into an engaging display of obvious sound effects and shifting ambience. Unless your speakers are situated immediately behind your video monitor you will find the nonsynchronization to be disorienting. We wouldn't have it any other way.

The stills on the back of the jacket cover are from a different movie. *Hercules Unchained* has the legend of strength returning to Thebes just in time to see Oedipus trip over his robes and fall into Hades. Boring passages outnumber exciting moments, especially since Reeves seems to remind one more than anything else of an accountant who has found something seriously wrong with the books. Still, when Sylvia Lopez grabs him at the knee and won't let go, you will realize that this laser disc has captured the stuff rainy day movies are made of.

HERE COMES MR. JORDAN
HEAVEN CAN WAIT

With the release of *Here Comes Mr. Jordan* disc owners can analyze the maturation of public taste by watching a double bill of that film and Warren Beatty's remake, *Heaven Can Wait*. Both movies are based upon a stage play. Beatty and his collaborators made several significant improvements while not varying all that much from the original script. Unlike some pairings of remakes and originals, *Jordan* and *Heaven* play well together, provided they are shown in chronological sequence.

The first film establishes the basic concept – an athelete's soul and consciousness are pulled out of his body by mistake and must be placed in another vessel because the body is cremated before the mistake is caught – but fails to take complete advantage of the situations which the gimmick has to offer. The subplots which Beatty cast and enhanced so perfectly are given only token attention in the first film. The makers of *Here Comes Mr. Jordan* presumed that the public would be so intrigued by the central plot device that nothing else would matter.

Beatty's movie would never have survived if it had been so singular in its execution. Audiences are more sophisticated and to placate contemporary viewers, the roles of the two schemers attempting to murder the man whose body the athelete's soul has entered were wisely magnified. Charles Grodin and Dyan Cannon, in the parts which were played by virtual non-entities in the first film, are hysterical, and if you haven't seen the movie for a while, there is a tendency to laugh aloud at their timing, as if you were seeing it for the first time.

Beatty also cleans up the murder investigation, making it less embarrassing. His only failure is to follow the logic which moves the hero's saxophone from place to place. It is a device which works very well in the first film, and by abandoning it (his character carries it almost as an afterthought) as a plot motivator, he weakens the finale.

The *Jordan* transfer is fairly ragged. There are splices, blotches, and scratches throughout the slightly blurry print. The disc is monaural and has not been CX-encoded. *Heaven* was released twice. The first time it appeared, on the DiscoVision label, it represented a significant change in marketing strategy on the part of laser disc producers. Although CLV discs had appeared previously, *Heaven Can Wait* was the first to appear after it had been decided that all feature films would be formatted in Extended Play. In essence, it was the first 'modern' disc. The quality of both the picture and sound was fairly weak, and Paramount later reissued the title on its own label, sharpening the transfer. Although still a little soft by today's standards, the colors look decent and the presentation isn't bad.

One final comparison should be noted. The stars in both films do their jobs well, but whether it is Robert Montgomery or Warren Beatty, Edward Everett Horton or Buck Henry, James Gleason or Jack Warden, it is clear that any talented performer, with the script and with adept direction, could have pleased audiences in a particular part. James Mason has the Jordan role in *Heaven Can Wait*, however, and although his performance is faultless, comparing the two movies reveals the uniqueness of Claude Rains. Rains is one of a very limited number of stars whose presence made a real difference. Some theories of acting claim that the performer must totally absorb the part, but Rains filled a variety of parts, believably, without sacrificing an aspect of his personality – a self-wisdom. Even on a small TV he is larger than life, an irreplaceable, reappearing symbol of mankind's better, more urbane instincts.

HERO AND THE TERROR

Even though the title is appropriate, the Chuck Norris film *Hero and the Terror* should probably have been called something else. It is about a cop and a serial killer, but the title suggests something raw or supernatural while the movie emphasizes character and process. The script is leisurely paced, but Norris remains entertaining between the action sequences. The picture looks decent. The Ultra-Stereo sound is a little bloated. A few chapter markers are encoded.

HEROLD/HERTEL – LA FILLE MAL GARDEE – KOSLOVA – BASLER BALLET

We hope that those whose only exposure to *La Fille Mal Gardée* was the Pioneer *Royal Ballet* presentation will not think the piece itself is not worth viewing because Philips has released an excellent interpretation on *Herold/Hertel – La Fille Mal Gardée – Koslova – Basler Ballet.* The Unitel production was video taped on a soundstage and, apparently, not in real time. Although the set design and blocking remains similar to a stage presentation, the cameras are free to roam and to crowd the dancers. We have often voiced our reservations about choreography which has been designed for the stage being presented on a video screen, but the program overcomes the difficulties as well as one could hope. Little of the essential dancing has been left out. The picture quality is very good. Strong reds and browns blur slightly and the edges are a little soft, but the image is generally bright and clear.

The stereo sound has very little hiss. The music, sharply performed by the Vienna Symphony, was recorded separately from the dancers, although the sounds from the dancers, such as footfalls, are retained.

Gardee is traditionally a ballet of mime instead of athletics. Heinz Spoerli's brilliant choreography, however, brings in many dance elements without sacrificing the essential pantomime. Martin Schlapfer, as Alain, has a spectacular solo in Chapter 10 on side one. The lead, Valentina Kozlova, is never given as showy a moment, but her performance is as enthralling as she shifts comfortably between performing with her hands and with her feet. Chris Jensen, Otto Ris and dancers from the Basler Ballet also appear.

HEY BABU RIBA

The opening credits for *Hey Babu Riba* are slightly matted, while the rest of the movie is not. This tends to bother some viewers more than it bothers us, at least in this case, since the picture composition never seems so deliberate as to be compromised by the slight loss on the sides. The color transfer is also less than perfect, and this, too, will frustrate some viewers more than others. The picture is a little soft, and the colors lose a lot of shine. The transfer is accurate, but it is at least one generation too removed from the original to be inspiring. The sound has an odd twang during some sound effects and is generally dullish. The Yugoslavian film is in Sebro-Croatian with yellow English subtitles which function effectively.

Hey Babu Riba tells, within a clever flashback, the story of a young woman and her four male companions coming of age in post-war Yugoslavia. On this level the tale is pleasant but contains no unusual or memorable sequences which set it apart from other movies about European teenagers. However, the film is also a political allegory, in which the girl is the spirit of Yugoslavia and her four companions are the spirits of the various sub-nationalities uniting in good faith to create a nation. On this level, the movie is both unique and compelling, because the viewer can grab almost any incident or detail within the film and make a symbol out of it.

THE HIDDEN

A top-notch horror thriller, *The Hidden*, opens up with a devil-may-care car chase and never slows down. There are only a couple of scenes involving gross special effects. The rest of the movie is terror by insinuation. The plot is expertly crafted and totally logical, so that you half anticipate each minor twist and yet are fully surprised by the major turns. As a plus, the film stars Kyle MacLachlan, who chalks up one more unusual role for his intriguing career by appearing as another very weird FBI agent.

The disc has been expertly transferred. The print is always sharp and only a few night scenes look even mildly grainy. The sound is monaural and the digital and analog tracks are nearly identical in quality. Except for some crackling at the reel changes, the soundtrack is clean.

THE HIDDEN FORTRESS

Back in the seventies when we first saw *The Hidden Fortress*, it was the habit of revival house managers to 'introduce' their feature film. At the screening we attended, the manager began by insisting that *Fortress* was an enjoyable movie, but apologized because no swordplay occurs until the second half. This is no way to approach a wonderful adventure story. The three or four swordfights are but a minor component of the entertainment.

Those anticipating a samurai epic will be looking at the wrong things on the screen and be getting excited at the wrong moments when they watch *The Hidden Fortress*. When Toshiro Mifune leaps on a horse and chases a pair of soldiers, sword raised high in the air, it is an inspiring moment, but most of the excitement comes from watching the characters react to their environment. Can they make it up a steep hill of gravel? How will they carry a heavy load of gold without their horses? It is a trait in many Japanese movies to have the characters be so closely tied to the nuances of nature. This is partially out of necessity, since gravel is easier to budget than special effects, but the Japanese have demonstrated a consistent tradition of turning necessities into art forms, and no one does it better than the movie's director, Akira Kurosawa. The adventure in *The Hidden Fortress* is as compelling as the best-scripted Hollywood adventures. The culture guiding the film and depicted within the film may be foreign, but the sense of chase, of discovery, of treasure, of danger, and of wit is part of a universal language which is freely communicated to a beguiled viewer with any background.

The 139-minute black and white feature is available on five sides in CAV format and comes in a box. The 'Tohoscope' print has been transferred in letterboxed format, with the English subtitles for the Japanese language film appearing in the black band beneath the picture. The advantages of obtaining any movie on disc in original aspect are well established, but it should be noted that the Kurosawa often utilizes the extreme edges of the screen and some important details are still lost to cropping. The print has no scratches or other inconsistencies and is in very good condition. The sound is fine.

HIDE AND GO SHRIEK

Teenagers sneak into a furniture store one night to have a party and 'try all the beds.' Little do they know that a psychopathic murderer has decided to join in the fun. *Hide and Go Shriek* is no better and not much worse than any of the others, though the psychopath's motivation reeks of negative gay stereotyping.

The jacket cover claims that the disc contains footage too shocking for the theatrical release. It must have really been boring before. There is one marvelous decapitation, and not a moment too soon, but there are too many shots of the same teenagers, tiptoing through the shadows, giggling, and then screaming when they bump into mannequins. What are mannequins doing in a furniture store? Don't ask.

Since the lights are off, everything outside of the center of the screen is grainy. The sound is a little weak.

HIGH AND LOW

Akira Kurosawa's *High and Low* is letterboxed. The letterboxing is sufficient to fit the English subtitles beneath the widescreen image, but it is not wide enough to include actors standing on the far edges of the screen. Unfortunately, as we noted in *The Hidden Fortress*, that is where Kurosawa often likes to place people. This is bothersome during the first hour, and unnoticeable thereafter. The film is black and white. The opening credits are in English, but the rest of the movie is Japanese. The contrast is sometimes too light, but the print is in excellent shape. The monaural sound is digitally encoded. Since the film was made in Japan in 1963 there is a fair amount of hiss, but the digital track is not as raspy as the analog track.

The movie is super. It is a contemporary thriller and partially a police procedural, but in the hands of Kurosawa it also becomes a semester's lesson on the frailty of Japan's social structure and the unsolvable moral dilemmas posed by chance occurrences. It is beautifully constructed. The first hour is almost like a stage play and takes place on a single set with a limited number of characters. Then, as the hero's stature deteriorates, the movie opens up in a way which would be impossible to recreate on a stage. That is the key to the film's power – Kurosawa has taken an Ed McBain novel ('King's Ransom') and filmed it as if he were doing another one of his Shakespeare adaptations. Shakespeare used to do the same thing himself.

HIGH NOON
HIGH NOON (CAV)

The western, *High Noon,* is due for a pendulum swing. Long the butt of serious critical consideration, the film nevertheless continues to stand tall on repeated viewings, and it's minimalist construction is worth a hard look. The movie has many basic elements, but the questions it asks about violence, marriage, masculinity, etc., are complex, and it never provides clear answers. The viewer is both entertained and provoked to think, a combination which is more rare than one would expect, even among the Criterion titles.

The added features which come with Voyager's CAV presentation include the original (pre-Oscar) theatrical trailer, the original short story on which the film is credited as being based upon, screenwriter Carl Foreman's notes on the backgrounds of the characters and locations, production and promotional stills, and storyboard sketches. All of that is on side three, after the movie is ended.

The print is beautiful, but, like the hero of the film, the picture has a few scars and scratches. The CAV version is slightly sharper than the CLV version. The CAV disc is in analog only, while the the CLV version is digitally encoded. Not even digital encoding, however, can rescue the weakest parts of the soundtrack, particularly the musical score.

Both discs contain an alternate audio track lecture by Howard Suber, who has a pleasant voice and concentrates on the representations of archetypes and myths within the execution of the story. For *High Noon*, this is the academic equivalent of shooting a barn door at ten paces, but Suber's presentation is thorough and informative. The best thing Suber does is to point out the passages when CAV utilities can be advantageously employed.

Suber, in talking about the appeal of the 'outsider' archetype in myths, never mentions an important facet. The audience identifies with Gary Cooper's character. Throughout the whole 80 minutes, as you watch it, you tell yourself that you would stand by him, even though none of the regular people in the movie are willing to.

HIGH SOCIETY

Along with Grace Kelly, *High Society* also stars Bing Crosby and Frank Sinatra, which would be like having a movie today with Mick Jagger and Michael Jackson. Crosby portrays the former husband who returns to win back the heart of his ex-wife on the eve of her wedding. The show is a musical version of an even funnier play, *The Philadelphia Story*, and loses some of its humor to squeeze in a few Cole Porter songs.

The entertaining disc has been released on MGM/UA with a reasonably fresh print. The sound is rich in a quaint sort of way, but unlike the original theatrical release, it is not in stereo. Neither has it been CX-encoded.

HIGH SPIRITS

Peter O'Toole's performance during the first ten minutes of *High Spirits*, mostly a telephone monolog, is hysterical, but the movie is all downhill from there. O'Toole even disappears for large stretches of time after the first half hour. The film's initial premise is promising. The bankrupt owner of a decrepit castle/hotel decides to capitalize on the establishment's state of disrepair by promoting it as a haunted house. This upsets the ghosts who actually do haunt the place. Unfortunately, the movie, although it has some impressive minor special effects, gorgeous sets, and a big-budget gloss, is as unorganized and silly as any haunted house comedy which comes to mind, and is especially disappointing since it starts out so well. (The film was reportedly chopped apart by the producers.) The disc gives the movie its best shot. The picture is classy and the stereo surround sound has luster.

HIGHER AND HIGHER

Frank Sinatra plays himself in *Higher and Higher*, and the filmmakers bluff his entrance twice before they actually produce him. The 1943 black-and-white musical has a few scratches and a couple of splices, but provides a solid, shiny image most of the time. The sound has no significant problems when the age of the property is taken into account. The disc's most bothersome error is its chapter encoding, which is set to major scene shifts and ignores the musical numbers.

Victor Borge, portraying a character named Victor, and Jack Haley also appear. The narrative concerns the servants in a Fifth Avenue mansion plotting to prevent their employer from going bankrupt by fobbing off a scullery maid as a society debutante and getting her married to money. Sinatra plays a next-door neighbor and has no real function except to break up the action and sing. Some of the songs are integrated with the plot, but the film is kind of an oddball effort and would be of little interest if Sinatra didn't sound so good.

THE HIGHEST HONOR

An Australian film, *The Highest Honor* ends up being about a group of captured Australian commandos in World War II who are waiting to have their heads lopped off, bushido style. Based much too closely on facts, the disc begins as a war adventure film and then shifts into an interesting drama about the 'friendships' between the imprisoned commandos and their Japanese captors. The ending, though, is such a drawn-out downer – the prisoners go through three choruses of 'Waltzing Matilda' the night before the execution – that it cannot be recommended to anyone except manic depressives. The disc is in stereo and has a crisp picture, but it isn't any fun.

HIGHPOINT

The balance between humor and suspense in *Highpoint* is way, way off. Richard Harris stars as an unemployed sophisticate who becomes involved with a rich family, a CIA plot, and organized crime. There are some brisk action sequences and a couple of amusing one-liners, but the script edges too far into the realm of farce and none of what happens is believable. The final fight between Harris and Christopher Plummer on top of the pointy tower in Toronto is cleverly done, but most viewers will end up scanning to get to it. The less one sees of the beginning and the middle, the better.

THE HILL (see **TOUR OF DUTY**)

THE HILLS HAVE EYES

Wes Craven's *The Hills Have Eyes* is a basic stranded-in-the-broken-camper thriller. The bad guys are gross and too many good guys die for the film to be any fun, but it set a precedent, long since surpassed, for grotesque activities, and some people still find it collectible. The disc has the expected number of splices and scratches, and strong reds tend to blur. The sound is on par with the print.

HISTOIRES EXTRAORDINAIRES

(Import)

None of the three episodes in the anthology 'Spirits of the Dead' are in English on the disc released in Japan under the film's original title, *Histoires Extraordinaires*. The program is in letterboxed format, and is in French, with Japanese subtitles appearing on the picture. The sound is monaural and it is a bit fuzzy. Despite a few scratches, the colors are only a little worn and the picture is clear. Since the movie is 121 minutes long, each of the three tales, loosely adapted from Edgar Allen Poe, appears on a different side.

The first of the three, directed by Roger Vadim, is so often bad-mouthed by those discussing the movie that we have inevitably acquired a great affection for it, like one would with the runt of a litter. It stars Jane Fonda and Peter Fonda, or, rather, it stars Jane Fonda and has Peter in a couple of scenes before he may or may not turn into a horse who then draws Jane inexorably to her death. Sounds like Poe, right? The events take place in medieval times or in the 1960s. With Vadim there really isn't any difference. Fonda rides the horse naked (though not so much as to encourage any Japanese censorship), takes a bath with a parlor maid, and wears *haute couture* medieval leather outfits. Revival houses have been known to drop the segment entirely, but they are missing the point. The piece establishes a bemused and irreverent mood, cleansing the palate, as it were, for the quality of the following two efforts.

Louis Malle's 'William Wilson' is about a mean-spirited man whose bad deeds are interrupted by a spoilsport Doppelgänger. Alain Delon has most of both parts, and Brigitte Bardot shows up with jet black hair. It is a forthright parable, told with such economy that one need not comprehend a word of the dialogue to understand exactly what is happening.

If the silly Vadim episode represents cinema at its lowest capability and the tight storytelling of the Malle episode represents cinema at its most efficient narrative execution, then Frederico Fellini's 'Toby Dammit' represents cinema at its most transcendent. The piece opens with an airplane landing at an airport near Rome which, with a simple, grotesque red wash on the film, equates the descent into Rome with a descent into Hell. Terence Stamp portrays the title character, an inebriated movie star who, after milling with the demons and lost souls of Rome's café society, goes on a sports car joyride which ends with his decapitation.

The disc reveals the magic in Fellini's wand. The dialogue, for example, is in French. The program survives perfectly well if one does not understand it, yet, as a component, the drunken discussions Stamp has with those he slobbers over are sorely missed. The music with its schizophrenic tempo, the phony sets and absurd costumes, and the balanced montage of facial closeups and medium length point-of-view shots can each survive as art and entertainment without the other parts. Fellini stirs it all together, concocting demons, and not even the Japanese subtitles can upset the brew.

HISTORY IS MADE AT NIGHT

History Is Made at Night bobs between being a screwball comedy and a tragic adultery and murder drama without ever settling into one groove or the other, despite a happy ending. Jean Arthur portrays the wife of a shipping magnate (played by Colin 'Dr. Frankenstein' Clive) who is pushed by her suspicious husband into an affair with a French waiter, Charles Boyer. The movie works better on subsequent viewings because, once you know where it is going, you are not thrown off by the emotional twists and turns. Both the sound and the black-and-white picture are in rough shape.

THE HIT

The literature accompanying *The Hit* leads one to believe that the movie is something special. "A rollicking black comedy," says one of the quotes on the jacket cover. "A hallucinatory fairy tale," says another. The only hallucinating comes from whomever made up those quotes. A hit man, John Hurt, kidnaps his mark, Terence Stamp, with the purpose of taking him to Paris to be killed in front of the man who took out the contract. Instead, after the requisite 97 minutes, Hurt shoots him at the border and then is killed himself by stupidly marching through the main street of a town where a witness is waiting to identify him. Stamp's performance has some humor to it, but rollicking it isn't. The disc is not CX-encoded, but part of the music soundtrack is performed by Eric Clapton.

HIT LIST

Jan-Michael Vincent portrays an ex-Marine – or something like that – who lives across the street from an FBI safe house and accidentally becomes the target of a mob attack in *Hit List*. Vincent is a little quiet, but Rip Torn and Leo Rossi are good fun as the principal mobsters. The film uses an interesting array of camera angles and has some exciting stunt work, including a cringe-inducing ride on the top of a van through a garage with a low ceiling.

The Ultra-Stereo surround sound has elaborate separations and is quite satisfying. We wish we could say the same for the picture, but it is often too yellow, and fairly grainy. The film is rated R for violence.

HIT THE DECK

When MGM/UA made the decision to letterbox a number of their widescreen films, the transfer of *Hit the Deck* to video had almost been completed. The last reel – about four minutes, containing the 'Hallelujah' number which was excerpted in *That's Entertainment* – had not been processed yet, so quick thinking enabled the finale to be letterboxed. MGM/UA was still learning the ropes, so the ending has an aspect ratio of about 1.8:1, while the opening credits, which are also letterboxed, measure about 2.2:1, but the effect makes a rousing conclusion to what is already an enjoyable program.

The musical, which stars Jane Powell, Ann Miller, Debbie Reynolds and a trio of less permanently stellar male performers, is about sailors on leave in San Francisco and the trouble they get into following their hearts. Individual scenes are wittily scripted (Alan King shows up in an amusing bit part as an MP), the dancing is dazzling, and the music is pleasing.

The stereo effects are scattered – sometimes even the music is lacking in separations – but the feeling that one is watching a classic movie of the sort which is not made anymore remains. The picture transfer is good. There are a few scratches here and there, but the colors are bright and the details are sharp. Due to an error in the manufacturing of the disc, it has no chapter markers although a listing of where they were intended to go can be found on the back of the jacket.

THE HITCHER

The spooky road thriller about a boy who gives a lift to a serial killer, *The Hitcher*, has received a problematic transfer to disc. An excellent example of what is both right and wrong with the disc happens at the exact beginning. The sound volume is set too high and is unusually harsh, but the first activity in the film is the striking of a match in the absolute darkness and the sound and the flare cause you to jump out of your seat. Later on, the picture becomes extremely grainy in certain scenes, but rather than causing a distraction, the fuzzy, indistinct picture adds to the tension.

The film is also problematic. The script takes a horrible turn near the end by killing off the boy's romantic interest. Since the movie is entertainment and not art, we can't understand why the screenwriter did that. By spoiling the film's potential as a super date movie (the rest of it is very well done and quite exciting), the twist probably lost the producers millions of box office – and even home video – dollars.

THE HITCHHIKER VOLUME 1
THE HITCHHIKER VOLUME 2
THE HITCHHIKER VOLUME 3
THE HITCHHIKER VOLUME 4

A cable television anthology series of half hour thrillers made in Canada, *The Hitchhiker* is being released in groups of cassettish threes. The difference between The Hitchhiker episodes and episodes in other television shows is the amount of nudity and passionate groping which is incorporated into each plot. The programs feature well known American stars on the Barry Bostwick/Tom Skerritt level, most of whom look totally bored with what they are doing and probably took the gigs just to have a shot at the sex scenes. The episodes are only moderately clever. While one never becomes impatient with them, few are memorable, either.

The discs are monaural and have been digitally encoded, with the sound editing providing odd leaps between vivid immediacy and detached multiple generation recordings. It works better on a television speaker than on a hi-fi.

The image quality is generally disappointing. The source material is fresh, but soft, and obviously passed through too many transfers before reaching disc. Two episodes are featured on side one in CLV, and one episode, usually the strongest, appears on side two in CAV with two jittery still frames out of every five. Our preference in the presentation of television episodes on disc is to sit through the full intro at the beginning of each episode. On The Hitchhiker collections, however, the full introduction only appears at the beginning of the disc, although each episode ends with a complete credit scroll.

The three episodes on *Volume 1* all have a common theme, retribution. In their respective programs, Gary Busey, Karen Black and Harry Hamlin portray characters who have done harm in the past and are beset with guilt in the guise of very real demons. The Busey piece, in which he is a radio evangelist, is the strongest, giving an interesting variation to the Prodigal Son parable. The Hamlin piece, however, rightly appears in CAV on side three, and there is an excellent opportunity to see how the filmmakers managed to show a live snake bursting out of his shoulder.

The jacket cover for *Volume 2* contains a rather embarrassing error. On both the front and the back, the copy promotes an episode directed by Paul Verhoeven which in fact is not contained on the disc. A reasonably engaging episode directed by Phillip Noyce, 'Man of Her Dreams,' takes its place on side three, and is about a woman whose daydreams anticipate the actions of a serial killer. Noyce also directed another episode on the disc, 'Night Shift,' in which Margot Kidder portrays a nursing home staff member who steals jewelry from the wrong patients. Darren McGavin also appears. Also on the disc is an episode directed by Roger Vadim about a writer, played by Susan Anspach, whose homecoming brings old crimes to light. Each episode has promise, but bumps into the time limit before delivering.

Volume 3 features Bostwick, William Dafoe, and Emmett Walsh in a predictable tale of suspicious suicides entitled 'Ghostwriter,' Skerritt as a fairly dense-headed haunted convent investigator in 'True Believer,' and Stephen Collins, in the strongest episode, as a high school photography teacher who literally becomes trapped in the dreams of one of his students.

Although ultimately plagued by the time limitations which almost all half-hour dramatic works must suffer, *Volume 4* has the best three episodes in the series. One stars Robert Vaughn as a plastic surgeon who parties too late one night before an important operation. Michael O'Keefe gives an unnerving performance in an episode about a young man who befriends a very nasty dog. In CAV, Greg Henry portrays a pickup artist who becomes the victim of every paranoid's fantasy. This would certainly be the disc to sample if you only wanted to try one *Hitchhiker*, and it may encourage you to pick up the others.

HOBSON'S CHOICE

One of the advantages with David Lean's older films is that they remain intact on one's television screen. *Hobson's Choice* has beautiful black-and-white source material and looks lovely. The sound is of standard quality for an early-'50s British film. There are actually two stories within *Hobson's Choice*, neither one strong enough to support a whole movie which is why they twist around each other and end up forming a partnership. The worst one can say about the film is that it is a tad too clever and sweet.

THE HOLCROFT COVENANT

Ten minutes into *The Holcroft Covenant* you won't be able to turn it off. The film, which stars Michael Caine, is adapted from a bestseller by Robert Ludlum, a writer who has mastered the art of the addictive plot. The story, of which the less is said the better, twists and twists and twists until you are never really sure who is a good guy and who is a bad guy. If by the end, the whole effort seems a little far fetched, that can be excused, because getting there was the point. Ludlum stories have logical conclusions, but the climax is always at the beginning.

The picture is bright, but gives way to a mild distortion in some of the night shots. The sound is stereophonic, but it is in analog and is accompanied by a fairly steady and pronounced hiss. The disc opens with trailers for two other video programs, and no chapter encoding has been provided to avoid them.

HOLIDAY

The stills on the jacket cover of *Holiday* are well chosen, and the print is also fairly nice. The volume is set a little lower than normal. The movie stars Cary Grant and Katharine Hepburn. They are rich and romantically entangled and don't we wish we all were. Another character in the film, played by Doris Nolan, goes through an unlikely personality change for the last third of the story. The plot requires it so that Hepburn and Grant can get together, but one wonders if things couldn't have been handled with a bit more subtlety. Nevertheless, the movie is airy and leaves one imagining what life would be like living in a house which had elevators.

HOLIDAY INN

Holiday Inn makes regular yearly appearances on local TV stations, but never with disc-quality sound or chapter markers, and rarely with a print which looks as nice as the one used for the disc. For those who have been too busy shopping every year to pay attention, the movie stars Fred Astaire and Bing Crosby and has a fairly amusing plot as the two vie for the affections of a young female performer. Stretching the running time to almost two hours are the numerous Irving Berlin songs, including the perennial 'White Christmas.' Astaire has a terrific dance number with firecrackers and Crosby sings 'Easter Parade,' 'Happy Holidays,' and other seasonal tunes, every one of which has its own chapter marker. With the exception of an embarrassing blackface number celebrating Abraham Lincoln the wrong way, the show is a lot of fun.

HOLLYWOOD ON TRIAL

The condition of the source material is weak for *Hollywood on Trial*, a documentary about the era of blacklisting in the motion picture industry. Not only are the old kinescope and newsreel prints severely grainy, but interview footage made expressly for the film is faded to nearly a complete loss of color. The sound has some variances in volume, though the condition is manageable. The 90-minute disc has no chapter markers.

The appeal of the title, then, is in program content alone. The documentary manages fairly well to maintain a neutral viewpoint. Most of the spokespeople for the industry make arcane arguments, but many of blacklist victims have difficulty substantiating their motivations.

The documentary spends a lot of time on the experiences of the original 'Hollywood Ten' and then expands in a more general manner to cover the reverberations and extensive blacklisting which followed when the Ten failed to win their case. Among the best footage is a clip from an Emmy Awards ceremony in which a scriptwriter, at the end of his acceptance speech, announces to the audience that he was the victim of blacklisting. A behind-the-scenes look at the filming of *The Front* is also interesting, and there is an almost scary interview with Ronald Reagan, who explains why the blacklist – the existence of which is continually denied by industry officials – was important and beneficial for Hollywood.

HOLLYWOOD OUT-TAKES AND RARE FOOTAGE

The footage on the 82-minute *Hollywood Out-takes and Rare Footage* is by its very nature scratchy and difficult to hear. This sort of compilation is inevitably disappointing when set against one's imagination. Anticipating the stars in their off-guard moments, one still expects them to behave as stars.

The collection includes seldom-seen shorts of a promotional nature – Bette Davis for GE, Joan Crawford for Motherhood, Mickey Rooney and Judy Garland for the March of Dimes, et cetera. The two major set pieces are the 1939 Oscars (in which Hattie McDaniel's win for Best Supporting Actress looks truly significant) and the macabre opening night festivities for the 1954 *A Star Is Born*. Separating these is the expected editing floor footage of various celebrities mucking up their lines and then cursing. Also featured is a silent, home movie of Marilyn Monroe at a party and a costume fitting for Humphrey Bogart and Lauren Bacall. Bogart's presence is one of the few which seem vital. About the only repeatable material – a segment one would want to watch more than once – is a rehearsed radio broadcast, captured on film, with Bob Hope and Lana Turner doing their stuff for the USO. The other clips will satiate one's curiosity long before the 82 minutes have expired.

HOLLYWOOD SHUFFLE

Robert Townsend has his cake and eats it too with *Hollywood Shuffle*. The film is about the comical fantasies of an aspiring black actor, and the fantasies give Townsend – pardon the expression – carte blanche to make fun of racial stereotypes. Townsend, however, is too nice, and so his humor is more apt to provoke bemused smiles in the place of guffaws. Still, the comedy is probably more compelling in a crowded urban theater than it would be at an empty rural emporium, not to mention one's living room.

The volume level on the sound is set too high, but for a low-budget film the stereo is decent and the sound is digitally encoded. The picture is also acceptable. The best sequence, an elongated, black-and-white take-off of detective films, is in letterboxed format. *Shuffle* is only 81 minutes long, and a portion of that is an endless credit scroll. Side two is in CAV format with two unsteady still frames out of every five.

HOMBRE

The picture is so sharp on the CBS/Fox Special Wide Screen Edition release of *Hombre* that some of the widescreen picture compositions look almost three dimensional. The film is set in the dusty Southwest and was filmed with color by Deluxe, but the transfer appears to be about as accurate as could be deemed possible. There is certainly nothing in the picture transfer, which has an aspect ratio of about 2:1, which would discourage a collector from obtaining the disc. The monaural sound is fine, though the film's sound editing is indistinct.

The Martin Ritt film was written by Elmore Leonard and stars Paul Newman. The movie is engaging although its linking themes about prejudice and class differences have little influence upon the narrative, which actually concerns fallout from a stage holdup.

HOME IS WHERE THE HART IS

A talented comedy which shows promise even when the gags don't work, *Home Is Where the Hart Is* was released briefly and then withdrawn because of legal difficulties. Since it seems unlikely that much effort will be made to re-release it it could possibly become a collector's item someday. Only a couple of hundred copies made it to the marketplace.

The movie, a Canadian production set in the US, is about two elderly twins chasing after their wealthy, centenarian father. He has been kidnapped by an inept golddigger who starts breaking things whenever anyone questions her word. The film has every type of comedy imaginable, from verbal word play and clever sight gags to physical slapstick and black humor. The cast does an almost textbook job of playing their roles as straight and subdued as possible. Leslie Nielson even pops up as a sheriff, and has a surprisingly substantial role that seems to be modeled on his *Police Squad!* character.

The film stock looks inexpensive, but the picture transfer is very good. The image is sharp and the colors are stable. The sound is monaural, but it has a strong punch and should definitely be amplified.

To give just one example of how well the humor in *Home Is Where the Hart Is* is underplayed: A character is looking out his second story window while talking on the telephone and observes a blind person walking down a street near an open manhole. The conversation on the telephone is important to the plot and the camera cuts away to an interior shot, but then cuts back to the view of the street before the blind person could possibly have had enough time to walk out of sight. Yet, he is nowhere to be seen and the camera lingers nervously on the manhole for a moment before cutting back to the interior, while the character talking on the phone stops concentrating, momentarily, on his conversation. End of gag.

HOMEBOY

In *Homeboy*, Mickey Rourke is a punch-drunk fighter who wobbles and mumbles his way from one fight to the next. There is a silly subplot involving Christopher Walken and a jewel heist, and the finale is an elaborately intercut climax to two stories that turn out to have nothing to do with each other. The fight scenes are okay, but Walken should start looking at people when he talks to them.

The transfer is fine, but the picture has dour colors and a mild haze. The stereo surround sound has only limited effects and lacks the clarity to support Rourke's mumbling. Eric Clapton contributed to the efficient musical score. The film was made in Asbury Park, New Jersey.

HONEY, I SHRUNK THE KIDS

The Roger Rabbit cartoon 'Tummy Trouble,' which opens *Honey, I Shrunk the Kids*, is every bit as wild, frantic and violent as the cartoon that opens *Who Framed Roger Rabbit*. The intense reds tend to bleed and look unstable, but other details are as sharp as the hypodermics flying at Roger. The cartoon has a surprise ending and leaves you panting for the relative calmness of the film to follow. Disney has not chapter encoded the disc.

The picture and sound in *Honey, I Shrunk the Kids* is satisfying. Although the movie is effects laden, it was made under stern budget constraints. Some of the special effects are reminiscent of the old Disney formula films, and the disc can do nothing to help them. Others, however, have the power of modern technology backing them up, and these look very pleasing, such as the shot when the camera moves without interruption from the big world to the small world. The stereo surround sound is competent but unmemorable. The most frustrating aspect of the film is James Horner's musical score, since instead of writing his own tunes he seems intent upon lifting reams from Nino Rota. It gives the film a circusy atmosphere and it sounds great in stereo, but it is unacknowledged and wrongheaded.

The movie, however, is a delight, as the boxoffice has confirmed. There are no glaring compromises in delivering the film's image to home video, and the adventure and comedy aspects make the movie highly repeatable entertainment. It is worth noting that the movie was a success because the filmmakers concentrated upon the basics. Every character, even the 'ant,' has a clearly defined and sympathetic personality, and the interaction between the characters is as full of magic as any of the special effects.

HONKEYTONK MAN

Clint Eastwood's I'll-make-another-Dirty-Harry-if-you-let-me-direct-this-first exercise, *Honkytonk Man*, is more accessible. The film runs a couple of minutes over two hours, and is about a boy and his uncle making their way from Oklahoma to a Nashville singing contract during the Depression. Now press screening rooms across America must have gagged trying to stifle the giggles when Eastwood croons, "When I sing about you, Every note seems to be right on key...," but the film is undemanding and enjoyable. Although Eastwood's character dies of tuberculosis at the end, the show is surprisingly upbeat. The normally instinctive Warner Brothers advertising department must have written the movie off in advance, because the artwork is both misleading and uninviting. Eastwood will never be mistaken for Martin Ritt, but *Honkytonk Man* has a number of enjoyable episodes and deserves more respect than it received. The artificial stereo sound is tolerable. Strong colors are slightly unstable and fleshtones look a bit too orange.

HOOSIERS (HBO)
HOOSIERS (Image)
A well-edited movie can drive you crazy on home video. You keep stopping it to replay sequences and ferret out the emotions which the filmmakers are deliberately holding back. *Hoosiers* is such a film, a compelling, enjoyable yarn about a high school basketball team of limited manpower whipped into a championship unit by a gung ho coach (Gene Hackman). Like the coach's own game plan, the movie doesn't let you peak too soon. It's fun, but exasperating.

HBO released the disc initially. The picture was fuzzy and the analog stereo sound was unaccomplished. Image re-released the title with an improved picture transfer and digital sound. There is still a faint grain to the image, but the colors are vivid and the picture is free of distortion.

The digital encoding cleans up the background noise present on the HBO disc, but the stereo effects still never seem to break free. The film, by the way, is just as exciting and just as inspiring on multiple viewings as it is on the first viewing.

HOPE AND GLORY
The picture is too orange and the sound is too scratchy, but *Hope and Glory* is too entertaining to be seriously affected by the disc's drawbacks. The film is an autobiographical look at London during the start of World War II seen through the eyes of a child. The movie catches the odd pieces of activity and conversation which a child remembers but cannot make sense of. The acting is wonderful, especially the performance of Sarah Miles as the mother who is both frustrated and liberated by the war. *Hope and Glory* has much to offer both adults and children, and repeated viewings will help one fit more pieces together.

HOPPITY GOES TO TOWN
A jinx which has plagued the Max Fleischer feature *Hoppity Goes to Town* – it opened theatrically on the weekend Pearl Harbor was attacked and has never been as widely disseminated as Fleischer's *Gulliver's Travels* – is finally broken by a gorgeous disc release from Republic. While the animation may not be at the level of the finest classic Walt Disney pictures, it is certainly as good as any Disney or Don Bluth effort.

The jacket cover states that the disc has been digitally mastered from an original film negative. The image is sharp and spotless, and the colors are much richer than the fuzzy publicity stills on the back of the jacket. In some areas, particularly the backgrounds, the animation is more elaborate and dimensional than anything done today. The hues are delicate and could easily blend into mush if the source material had been at all worn down. What's more, and it is very unusual for a feature cartoon from the early forties, there is hardly a scratch, speckle or splice to be seen.

The sound is also in good shape. It is relatively free of noise, though splices which are present are often heard rather than seen. The program runs 85 minutes and is split exactly in half, without regard to scene content. Republic missed the opportunity to put one of the sides in CAV, and also deserves chiding for spelling the side numbers instead of using numerals on the label, since this is obviously a children's program.

The narrative concerns a group of bugs living in a rundown garden who must find a new home when the property is leveled for a skyscraper. There are good bugs and bad bugs and a few brief and tolerable songs. None of the characters are too appealing, and the hero is a nitwit, but the storyboards are clever enough to sustain an interest in the narrative from beginning to end. The 'bug view' visions of the human world are especially well executed, and the occasional reverse angle views of the bugs scurrying like real vermin are challenging.

There are all too few full-length animated feature films in the world of any worth at all, and even fewer made with the classic animation techniques that are no longer economically viable. *Hoppity Goes to Town* is one of a handful, and the pristine disc is a welcome confirmation of its status.

HOROWITZ IN MOSCOW
If the rest of Vladimir Horowitz has become diminutive over the passage of time, his hands certainly have not. They float above the keyboard masterfully in *Horowitz in Moscow* and it is all the more amazing when one observes the frail mechanism which is guiding them. Horowitz can still pound away at a piece by Scriabin or Rachmaninoff with the same luster which a young prodigy might have, and the only difference is that he used to hang out with the composers. He may be performing entirely by rote, but he is alert to the atmosphere of the hall (which has wonderful, solid wood acoustics) and plies his music to suit his audience.

The disc is digitally encoded and runs over 40 minutes on each side. Horowitz moves through a fairly standard repertoire, stretching from Mozart to Chopin. The sound does not have the fresh silence of a studio recorded CD, but it is so clear that you can hear the squeak of the foot pedals. The picture is exceptionally sharp. The primary camera at the back of the stage provides closeups of his hands from the left. Unfortunately, the depth of field is limited and consequently only the hand playing the bass clef is in focus. The hand playing the melody is usually a blur.

HOROWITZ PLAYS MOZART
A recording session by Vladimir Horowitz, with Carlo Maria Giulini conducting the La Scala Orchestra, of Mozart's 'Piano Concerto No. 23 in A major,' is the subject of a documentary film by Albert Maysles, *Horowitz Plays Mozart*.

The work by Maysles makes similar programs look amateurish in comparison. The editing always provides the most important visuals for every sequence, so that when a passage is complicated, the camera is showing Horowitz' fingering, but when things calm down it is looking elsewhere.

The film is 50 minutes long and was recorded in analog, although the music recording was done digitally. The 16mm picture is grainy. The session, one of several in reality, has a single bad take, during the third movement. Between every movement, however, the film includes interviews and other recording studio activity. Some of what Horowitz has to say, which is also supported in an essay provided on a jacket insert, is quite educational about Mozart's intentions and the way to approach Mozart's music. His demonstration is even more valuable, though a few more errors and interruptions might have helped to show the viewer what the artists are striving for.

HORROR PLANET
An adept and inexpensive *Alien* rip-off, *Horror Planet*, depicts an archaeological station which stumbles across some odd crystals on a supposedly deserted planet. The crew has an equal number of men and women, and they act like real people as they try to cope with a sequence of disastrous events. Ultimately, the film cannot live up to its promise, but viewers who enjoy such efforts will appreciate how close it comes. The source material is a little rickety, but the transfer is okay. The colors aren't too worn down, although the image does have a used look to it and a number of scratches. The monaural sound is in keeping with the rest of the production and is acceptable.

HORSE FEATHERS
Due to the short running time, a good chunk of the hour long Marx Brothers college romp, *Horse Feathers*, including the manic football game and Groucho's amusing rowboat sequence, is in CAV on side two. The film, however, is not one of the group's better efforts and is so anarchic that it can seem long even at 67 minutes. It is best sampled a small piece at a time.

The opening credit sequence is beautifully transferred, providing the entire, crisp film image within a mild on-screen frame. The black and white print used for the rest of the film is okay, but looks soft in places and a couple of sequences are damaged by splices and breaks which affect the dialog. The sound is generally passable, but dips in volume in a couple of instances. The musical numbers have been marked with chapter codes.

HORSE'S MOUTH/TUNES OF GLORY
TUNES OF GLORY
THE HORSE'S MOUTH
Voyager initially took two Alec Guinness movies and put them together as a 'double bill' double-disc set, *Horse's Mouth/Tunes of Glory*. It was a brilliant stroke, for while each of the films has its merits, the presence of Guinness in both enlarges the appeal of the disc. You were not just paying double to get two good movies. You were also getting the 'concept' which originally made them popular. They are best viewed like a real double bill, because the more you watch Guinness in a sitting, the better and better he becomes.

Unfortunately, when it came time to re-release the set, Voyager broke them up and released them as separate discs.

There are no subtitles, but the first ten minutes of *Tunes of Glory* will likely remind you of the first time you were assigned to read a Robert Burns poem. The movie is about a Scottish major who has worked his way up through the ranks as one of the boys and the conflict which ensues when a new colonel is assigned to his regiment. The motivations of the characters and the emotional interplays are far more dense than anything one sees today on the screen or on the stage. Every time you think you have a firm understanding of a character's personality, something totally logical occurs which completely changes that assessment. There is no action beyond the tensions which simmer in the power plays within the regiment, but there is music in Guinness's brogue and flair in his bright orange hair.

The source material is grainy and never achieves the gloss of the still on the jacket cover. The picture on the older Voyager version is slightly better than the newer disc, but the print is so close to being borderline that every slight degradation brings it nearer to failure. The sound is naturally rough, though we have finally seen the movie enough times now that we're starting to understand the nearly impenetrable Scottish dialog.

The one advantage to obtaining the disc is a brief interview with the director, Ronald Neame, which appears after the film is ended and was not included on the earlier release. In the clip, Neame talks extensively about Guinness's talent, lamenting with some amusement that it is difficult editing Guinness's scenes because of the desire to watch his performance even when he is not speaking. Hearing that makes watching a Guinness movie quite difficult, because Neame is right – Guinness is always up to something, and you stop paying attention to the plot for the joy of watching him practice his craft.

The principal improvement created by having broken up the pair, however, is that there is now no excuse not to obtain *The Horse's Mouth.* The film is funny the first time you see it, funnier the second, and hysterical every time after that. The movie is a delight, with Guinness portraying a smelly bohemian painter who can't help but fluster every individual he comes into contact with.

The picture is also slightly poorer than the earlier presentation, but the source material is strong, so the movie is not harmed much by the difference. There is still a substantial amount of grain in the image, though, owing to the age and budget of the source material. The sound is only slightly better than *Tunes*, until one scene, involving a bulldozer, which manages to achieve a contemporary rumble, as if it always had the potential but chose not to utilize it until just then.

After the disc is ended there is a collection of clips from several other Guinness films, the inclusion of which was of limited value on the double bill disc and is nothing but a tease on this one. *The Horse's Mouth*, however, is the sort which can become one's favorite of all, and even if it doesn't, it is still worth whipping out when one hasn't smiled in a while.

HOSTILE TAKEOVER

One clever idea is the basis for *Hostile Takeover* : A man, played by David Warner, holds several others hostage in an office building. He makes no demands, other than to threaten violence if the police attempt to interfere. Unfortunately, the filmmakers have no more idea why he is doing what he is doing than anyone else does, and the movie's ending is perfunctory. The picture looks too green and the sound is set too low. The film's production values are limited as well.

HOT PURSUIT

The last fifteen minutes of *Hot Pursuit* are marvelous, but it sure takes a long time to get there. Most of the film, in which a young man attempts to catch up with his girlfriend's family vacationing in the Caribbean and is constantly delayed, strenuously fails to be either funny or charming. The disc is suitable for multiple viewings because once you know where everything is leading it is easier to take, but getting through it the first time is a challenge.

The picture is often grainy in scenes which take place after dark, and sometimes portions of the image are blurry. The footage which was recorded in the bright tropical sun is sharper and colorful, but over all the quality is average. The Ultra-Stereo separations are fun, and the digital track is sharper and stronger than the analog track. The disc has one other nice touch. The break between side one and two is perfect. Side two opens with a boat under sail in the bright daylight, while side one had closed on the same sailboat, drifting in the moonlight.

HOT ROCK VIDEOS – VOLUME 1

The Eurythmics's 'Sweet Dreams' music video which opens the two-sided CLV 8-inch, *Hot Rock Videos – Volume 1*, also appeared on the *Eurythmics* disc. 'Dreams,' however, is one of the best cuts on the disc, along with Lou Reed's involving 'I Love You, Suzanne' and The Alan Parsons Project animated gem, 'Don't Answer Me.' The dregs are represented as well, with Jefferson Starship's 'No Way Out' and Rick Springfield's 'I've Done Everything for You.' The Kinks' 'Come Dancing' and Icicle Works' 'Whisper to a Scream' fill out the disc. The picture and sound all leave something to be desired.

HOT ROCK VIDEOS – VOLUME 2

Lou Reed appears to be an artist who really doesn't believe in his own talent. He wastes himself on things like 'My Red Joystick' (which appears on side two of *Hot Rock Videos – Volume 2*), a mildly comical number with obvious and dopey double entendres. The video is combined with two other gimmicky pieces, 'Rappin' Rodney,' which loses its welcome much faster than one would anticipate, and a pair of mediocre dancers twirling and acting youthful to a recording of Elvis Presley's 'Blue Suede Shoes.' Side one of the CLV 8-inch compilation disc from Pioneer Artists also contains two wasted efforts, Meatloaf's 'Modern Girl' and Jefferson Starship's 'Layin' It on the Line,' so that the only decent video on the whole disc is Thompson Twins' 'Hold Me Now.' The picture is grainy throughout. The sound is alright on 'Shoes' and 'Hold Me Now,' but is less satisfying on the other cuts.

A HOT SUMMER'S NIGHT WITH DONNA

Donna Summer's stage show, on view in *A Hot Summer's Night with Donna*, is quite an act, with sets and costumes and elaborate choreography. It is a seamless production of a single concert performed in an outdoor theater in California.

She opens wearing a white and black sequin outfit that appears to be glued to her clavicle. She sings 'MacArthur Park' and, after the first chorus, starts acting out the words with her hands. Her happiness is infectious. Two outfits later she is dancing in circles, on one foot, in the audience, and side one isn't half over. A while after that she stops the pace to talk about the Lord, a brief, soft, but unfortunate intrusion. In *Elvis on Tour*, Presley handled things better, by singing a couple of religious songs without stopping to explain his motivations to his fans. Her message comes across better when she is singing and smiling.

The interruptions are momentary. 'Romeo,' the number she does in the audience, is the best part of the show, but her energy and her desire to please carries on to the end. Dara and Mary Bernard provide backup vocals and prove to be amusing foils in a couple of skits. The sound quality is good enough and the picture is especially crisp. There are chapter markers so that you can play 'Romeo' over and over again without leaving your seat.

HOT TO TROT

Sometimes you're in the mood for a really stupid talking-horse movie, and if you haven't got the DiscoVision version of *Francis, The Talking Mule*, who wasn't a horse anyway, then all there is on disc is *Hot to Trot.* Warner had so much faith in this title that they didn't even give it chapter markers, but they just don't understand that in a certain state of exhaustion only a talking-horse movie will do.

The stereo mix is not afraid to take chances – what has it got to lose – and the disc delivers the audio with a solid confidence. The picture is less satisfying. On some reels, the flesh tones become very pink and solid colors begin to destabilize. Other reels look better.

The deliberately irritating comic who talks as if someone were continually kicking him between the legs, Bob Goldthwait, stars. John Candy provides the voice for the horse. The script veers this way and that, nibbling on comic ideas but then turning elsewhere before a direction can be truly established. If you're in the mood, you don't mind, and if you're not in the mood, you're not going to put the disc on in the first place.

HOTEL COLONIAL

The volume levels on *Hotel Colonial* swing wildly. The music on the analog stereo soundtrack is too loud, but the dialog is often difficult to hear. The picture is mildly grainy.

A man flies to Colombia to identify his brother's body, supposedly a suicide. Simple ballistics indicate otherwise, however, and the body turns out to be someone else's. Soon he is venturing into the jungle trying to find the truth. The film, which stars John Savage and Robert Duvall, is padded with extensive travelog-style footage, but the scenery is more interesting than the story.

THE HOUND OF THE BASKERVILLES/ SHERLOCK HOLMES FACES DEATH

The best of the CBS/Fox 'Sherlock Holmes Double Bill' combos, *The Hound of the Baskervilles/Sherlock Holmes Faces Death*, pairs the first and most well known of the Basil Rathbone Holmes features with one of the better of the later, Universal Rathbone offerings. As an added treat, a rare ten-minute talk by Sir Arthur Conan Doyle appears after the second feature is ended. The elderly author, with a hound of his own at foot, talks about the popularity of the Holmes stories and about his fascination with Shirley MacLaine-style mysticism. It is a very early sound film recording, and it is a unique, time-tunnel view of an even earlier era. With the many permutations of Sherlock Holmes that have manifested over the years, the film clip helps reorient one to the original essence of the character.

And speaking of character, the print of 'Baskervilles' is the one which was used for the film's reissue in the mid-seventies, with the restored closing line, "Oh Watson, the needle!" The prints for both movies look and sound fine. There are age marks on the films, but the focus remains sharp and the contrasts are adequate. The two films and the interview fit comfortably on three sides, with the second film beginning in the middle of side two. Each program has a separate chapter marker.

The only fault of 'Baskervilles' is that, due to the requirements of the plot, Holmes must drop from sight for an extended length of time as the story unfolds. Nigel Bruce, being not quite the nincompoop he would later become, prevents the movie from grinding to a halt in Rathbone's absence. It is also worth noting that while many of the films had drawing room-type excitements, 'Baskervilles' has several legitimate action sequences, not to mention a very real and nasty looking dog. 'Death' is a shorter exercise, set in a mansion which doubles as a convalescence home to increase the number of suspects at hand. When Holmes solves a puzzle leading to treasure in the mansion, he finds a fresh corpse and must flush out the murderer. There are fewer opportunities to revel in the atmosphere of mystery or enjoy Rathbone's Holmesian quirks, but, as the second half of a double bill, the movie stretches out one's pleasures without taxing one's patience.

HOUSE
HOUSE II

A split-level cello and violin theme is the first thing you see or hear in *House*. The music sets the mood and fortunately the script is up to it. The story is about an author, played by William Katt, who moves into a haunted house to purge his own psychological demons. The inexpensive looking monsters who visit him are just as scary as expensive monsters would have been. The plot even has a satisfying ending, something normally lacking in movies like this. It would be advisable to wait a long time between viewings, but the nervous energy, which is created by the cello, the violins, and unexpected peek-a-boo's, makes the disc worth keeping around.

House II (which has the subheading, 'The Second Story') is also a comedy, but with different aspirations. The house is presented as having become 'unstuck in time,' and the plot has a pair of normal guys trying to deal with dinosaurs, Aztecs, and gunslingers as they attempt to retrieve a crystal skull. The film doesn't completely work, but once again the presentation is so oblivious to its faults that its spirit grows on you. The left channel drops out momentarily at one point, but otherwise the picture and sound are fine.

HOUSE OF GAMES

The playwright and scenarist, David Mamet, wrote and directed *House of Games*. The film would make a very good radio play. The narrative is entirely verbal, as Mamet displays no more than a rudimentary sense of how to tell a story with images. The plot, however, has its pleasures. It is about a woman, played by a somewhat rusty Lindsay Crouse, who joins in with a group of confidence artists. The viewer will inevitably be one or more steps ahead of the characters (that's one of the faults of Mamet's approach, unlike his confidence men he provides no visual distractions to take the viewer's mind off the plot developments), but when the story starts to twist it creates and projects a real emotion, an intense anxiety which is both impossible to shake and, since it is only a movie, gratifying.

Since Mamet's visual sense is limited, the picture quality is mundane, though the transfer appears to be problem free. The sound is monaural and is also subject to production blemishes created by the filmmakers and preserved with accuracy.

THE HOUSE ON CARROLL STREET

The period setting and mild-mannered violence in *The House on Carroll Street* are deliberately intended to evoke another era in style as well as content. Featuring a wide-eyed blond heroine (played by Kelly McGillis) with a deliberately Nancy Drewish demeanor (though she's also a leftist radical – one of the film's more amusing touches) and an earnest young FBI man (played by Jeff Daniels), the viewer is supposed to revel in the atmosphere it creates, and be charmed by its relative innocence. The plot has too few mystery-type twists to succeed in capturing one's imagination on a sustained basis, but the movie has some nice sequences (a beautifully photographed and executed finale in an amazingly period-looking Grand Central Station) and essentially has less going against it than going for it. The sound is monaural, with a Georges Delerue score, and is in good shape. The picture also looks okay, with no significant improprieties.

HOUSE ON HAUNTED HILL/ATTACK OF THE 50 FOOT WOMAN

In an inspired move, CBS/Fox has compiled a double bill using two movies which have virtually nothing to do with one another, *House on Haunted Hill/Attack of the 50 Foot Woman*. Both would be too stupid to consider purchasing individually, but as a combined piece of entertainment the package makes a carefree way to spend a rainy afternoon.

Contrary to the listing on the back of the jacket cover, the chapter markers on the three-sided disc start over at zero on each side, requiring a great deal of subtraction to be useful. 'Woman' begins with Chapter 3 on side two. Neither print is free of speckles or marks, but no flaw is so exaggerated as to spoil either of the films and friends who should know claim this is the best condition in which either film has appeared in several decades. The sound survives amplification.

The only thing common about the two movies is that they are black and white exploitation films from the fifties. 'House on Haunted Hill' is a legitimately entertaining William Castle effort, about a group of people trapped in a house with apparent ghosts and murderers. There are a couple of good screams, not nearly enough plot twists, and a basic horror-film atmosphere which all but the most straightlaced viewers cannot help but appreciate.

It is more difficult to sing the praises of 'Attack of the 50 Foot Woman' and remain in key. Fortunately the film runs only a few minutes over an hour, so that it can remain stupid without slipping into tedium. The special effects are awful – double exposures in which the backgrounds can clearly be seen through the superimposed gigantess. The production designers must have used a sliding scale to design her, because she changes size in every shot. Before contact with a superimposed UFO made her big she was a rich lady living off Route 66 in the California desert with 'The Star of India' diamond on a 25-cent chain around her neck and a husband who wanted to put her away but keep the diamond. She finally puts her foot down. Anyway, the appeal of the film is the brief, brief moment that the viewer allows his own imagination to wander, before leveling judgement upon the proceedings, and watching it after 'Haunted Hill' is like having marshmallows after hot dogs.

HOUSE PARTY

The double standard which prevents white people from making movies like *House Party* but lets black people make movies like *House Party* is to be praised if it means that movies like *House Party* get made. The film is a riot, and along with many other humors, it wallows happily in the comedy of racial stereotypes (desperate to be bailed out of jail, the hero tells his friend on the phone to bring the money using 'Japanese people time'), a form of amusement which has been suppressed for so long it inevitably breaks loose every once in a while. The most important aspect of the movie, however, is the confident sense of visual style that the director, Reginald Hudlin, integrates with a comfortable feel for guiding groups of performers. The movie has so much going on in almost every shot that you don't have time to laugh at it all on the first viewing.

The glossy picture looks flawless and the stereo surround sound, though more subdued than other aspects of the film, is great.

The plot concerns a high school student who sneaks out of his home to attend a party at a friend's house. The story, however, is fairly non-generational, as the movie uses the setting not to revel in teenage antics, but to explore with satire the unique aspects of the black middle class experience. Ironically, *House Party* stands as a significant brace in fortifying the very social situations it is lampooning. With the constraints against blacks crumbling, America is obtaining a second voice, and, more and more, the voice reaches forward in good spirit instead of turning back with despair.

HOUSEBOAT

The print which Paramount dredged up for *Houseboat* is so well preserved that you can clearly see the ill chosen makeup on the faces of the actors and actresses. Sophia Loren's cheeks are a veritable palette of pinks and tans. The worst application, however, is on the children. They probably shouldn't have had any coloring at all. Instead, their cheeks are heightened with dark brown, while their lips are insufficiently contrasted, giving them a fading pallor which inadvertently matches their performances.

The print has one vertical, hair-sized flaw, midway on side two, but is otherwise in mint condition. The transfer, however, has added a haziness to the picture, so that it looks like a slightly foggy morning on a bright summer's day. The sound is fairly strong, although there were moments on side two when the left channel dropped out.

The movie itself is such an embarrassment than it can be appealing if you are in the proper frame of mind. Cary Grant has no rapport whatsoever with the trio who are pretending to be his estranged children. It goes beyond acting. He is so self-conscious in their presence that you can see him doing little bits of business – glances, nervous movements with his hands – to try and stay in character. Around Loren, on the other hand, he is his suave, normal self, adeptly swinging between klutzy slapstick pratfalls and an otherwise refined, confident manner.

THE HOUSEKEEPER

Rita Tushingham portrays a dyslexic in *The Housekeeper* who becomes annoyed when anyone discovers she can't read. Homicidally annoyed. The movie has some interesting and creepy interludes, but the characters are all slightly artificial, inhibiting the viewer from completely accepting or enjoying what takes place. The transfer is very good, as is the digitally encoded stereo sound.

HOW I WON THE WAR

As Richard Lester explains during an interview which appears on a printed insert accompanying *How I Won the War*, copies of the film which were made for the original American theatrical release contained a grievous error, turning sequences which were supposed to have been tinted into pure black and white. The disc presents the film correctly, therefore providing an iota of logic to the characters who show up on the color sequences suddenly painted in bright hues.

How I Won the War was one of Lester's more difficult comedies from the sixties. It requires patience, as well as a deft ear for the exaggerated British dialog. The plot vaguely follows a platoon which is sent behind enemy lines in the Sahara to build a cricket court at an oasis, but veers into take-offs on the nostalgia for both World War II and World War I, always taking pains to point out that war tends to be a little messier than memories admit. John Lennon appears in the film more as a mascot than an actor.

Recognizing that *How I Won the War* has its faults, it is still an elaborate work which will be of interest to a number of collectors. With this in mind, it is worth reporting that Image's transfer is not only superb, but, because of the restoration of the tinted sequences – first time in America, and all – it is significant. The picture still has a cheap, tattered sixties look to it, but it is clear that the colors are fresh and that one would be hard pressed to produce something better. The monaural sound also has some fullness to it, though we suspect some of the dialog is deliberately incomprehensible.

HOW THE LEOPARD GOT HIS SPOTS (see **PECOS BILL**)

HOW THE RHINOCEROUS GOT HIS SKIN AND HOW THE CAMEL GOT HIS HUMP (see **PECOS BILL**)

HOW THE WEST WAS WON

Perfectly straight logs bend as they pass through the Cinerama screen division on MGM/UA's *How the West Was Won*. That's okay, because the logs bent when you saw it in the theater, but what isn't okay for us, and for a growing number of consumers, is the lack of a wide screen. The blurry line which marks the two edges where the images joined on the original Cinerama presentation provide an excellent orientation to where the center of the screen *ought* to be and how the picture is being scanned to include what someone unconnected with the original production feels is the most important part of the composition. Instead of a row of cannons going off one after another, one sees two waves of blasts, as if the first shot were simply being repeated (a complete cut from the left screen to the right). The peril in the final fight on a flatcar full of logs is indecipherable when one can't see how precariously the logs are swinging.

West had three directors and there is occasional critical debate over who did the best job, but any child can tell you it was the assistant directors; the second unit crews filming the spectacular stunts and action sequences.

Digital encoding preserves the sound with a far greater fidelity than has been paid to the picture. The classiest aspect of the movie, in fact, is probably the use of traditional folk songs from the era as the central motif of the music score. The old-fashioned stereo mix sends the voices of the characters on the far left and right to the relative audio positions. The scanning upsets the balance here as well, because when the picture shifts to show a person talking, the person is moved to the center of the television screen while his voice remains in the prairie on the left.

The 165-minute feature is spread to four sides so the intermission can break the first disc from the second. Blurry Cinerama lines and cropping aside, the quality of the picture is up to MGM's normal standards of preservation, although there are scratches in a couple of places.

HOW TO GET AHEAD IN ADVERTISING

The play on words in the title, *How to Get Ahead in Advertising*, refers to a grotesque face which appears in a boil on the shoulder of an advertising executive who is cracking up. The comedy was directed by Bruce Robinson, who was also responsible for *Withnail and I*. Both films are excruciating experiences which can only be termed entertainment in the loosest sense of the word. *Advertising* is also a didactic bore, raving about the supposed evil of mass marketing. An interesting portrayal of insanity is the script's only redeeming feature, but the context prevents the viewer from relaxing and appreciating it. The picture and sound transfers are good. The picture is uniformly sharp and the surround sound makes effective use of the stereo mix.

HOW TO MARRY A MILLIONAIRE

An overture to *How to Marry a Millionaire*, performed on screen by the Twentieth Century Fox Orchestra and conducted by Alfred Newman, opens the disc. Text on the back of the jacket explains what the orchestra is doing there – the film was the second to be made in Cinemascope. The text then goes on to discuss the glories of the widescreen process, but, sadly, the disc itself is yet another crop and scan job. The colors, at least, are beautiful.

Millionaire stars Marilyn Monroe, Lauren Bacall and Betty Grable. Seeing it in tandem with the similarly entertaining *Gentlemen Prefer Blondes* may leave one with the impression that all good-looking women want men with money. The sound is in Cinemascope even though the picture isn't, and it is wonderful. The separations are so wide Bacall sometimes sounds as if she is talking from the next room.

HOW TO SUCCEED IN BUSINESS WITHOUT REALLY TRYING

The spunky white-collar satire, *How to Succeed in Business without Really Trying*, is eminently re-watchable as a scanned and cropped feature on late night TV, and it is even more fun as a gorgeous Deluxe Letter-Box Edition disc from MGM/UA. The musical exaggerates reality, showing executives singing, dancing, and snipping at each other like little children, yet it catches the real spirit of what working in an office is like. It is a refreshing mixture of comedy, music, and social commentary which hasn't dated in the slightest and looks as if it never will.

The songs are catchy when heard as singles, but they are staged with such wit that they become even more compelling and repeatable on the screen. The choreography is terrific – it isn't just dancing, it is taking the activities in an office environment and imbuing them with synchronicity and rhythm. The image on the disc has been given an aspect ratio of about 2:1 and the choreography is freed by the widened image, as are the comical effects of Robert Morse's double takes, and the intriguing set decorations.

The disc runs a couple of minutes over two hours and is spread to three sides. There are chapter markers for the musical numbers. The picture transfer looks flawless, although some footage from the original theatrical presentation may be missing. The colors have a slight paleness that appears to be inherent in the source material, but the red carpeting and wallpaper remains stable and the fleshtones are cool and clear. The monaural sound is a little dull.

HOWARD THE DUCK

Howard the Duck ought to have done to Cleveland what *Rocky* did to Philadelphia. The essence of the comic strip is a mad clash between the fantastic and the real, with Howard, a Cleveland-based, cigar-chomping duck who has no trouble getting dates, embodying both sides and inevitably finding himself in the middle of the conflict. When the characters leave Cleveland for their chase through the countryside, they abandon any possibility of giving an audience something to identify with.

The sound is quite good and the movie contains many moments of stereophonic playfulness. The picture looks sharp. The property would probably fare best as a television series, but the chances of that happening in this universe, thanks to the film, are now about as good as getting down off an elephant.

HOWIE MANDEL'S NORTH AMERICAN WATUSI TOUR
JAY LENO: THE AMERICAN DREAM

Neither Howie Mandel nor Jay Leno accomplish much on *Howie Mandel's North American Watusi Tour* and *Jay Leno: The American Dream*. It is a toss up as to which disc is worse.

Mandel stands on a stage for 50 minutes goofing on his audience and acting silly. The sound is in stereo and it isn't bad, if you like being surrounded by lukewarm laughter. Same with the picture.

Leno has a stand-up routine which also involves making fun of his audience, but his 50-minute program also features some David Letterman-type patronization segments in which Leno visits factories, bingo parlors, restaurants, and school rooms to ask real people for their definition of 'The American Dream.' The sound on these segments is noisier than the stand-up material and the picture is grainier. Leno is not as obnoxious as Mandel, but he isn't as inspired, either.

THE HOWLING
THE HOWLING III
THE HOWLING IV
HOWLING V THE REBIRTH

About the same time that *Dracula* and *The Mummy* (via *The Awakening*) were being updated, so, too, was *The Wolfman* given a contemporary re-working with *The Howling*. The film, directed by Joe Dante, had the usual graphic gore, great sex scenes, and several good screams. It was released on disc by Embassy and had a terrific jacket cover, monaural sound without CX-encoding, and a picture transfer which is much too dark and grainy by today's standards. Still, it is an enjoyable disc which can withstand a few multiple viewings.

Howling III is an Australian production, directed by Philippe Mora, and is about a group of marsupial werewolves patterned after the extinct Tasmanian wolf. There is a full marsupial birth, with the little eraser-shaped pup crawling up his mother's hairy belly and into her pouch. There is at least one decent thrill and plenty of blood, but there is also an extended epilog which takes a long time to go nowhere, and other loose ends which never amount to much.

The transfer is good. The sound has plenty of directional sound effects and little distortion. Most of it was filmed in the bright outdoor sun, providing a stable and bother-free picture.

The plot of *Howling IV* is a simplified retelling of the first film. A woman and her husband move into a mountain cabin for a therapeutic break from the city. Area residents act strange and nervous around newcomers. The woman begins to hear howling in the night and the husband becomes involved with a local vixen. It takes a while to become interesting, but eventually we were locking our windows, turning on all the lights, and holding onto pillows for protection.

Howling IV is not even as classy a production as *Howling III*. The digitally encoded sound is monaural, often way out of synch, and subject to occasional crosstalk. The picture is mildly grainy and comes from an inferior film stock. But at least the filmmakers know enough to end the movie while the viewer is still nerve-wracked. We have yet to let go of the pillow.

Howling V The Rebirth, which draws from *The Beast Must Die*, is set in a Hungarian castle, in which a typical collection of glamorous strangers find themselves invited for a mysterious weekend. The film is full of POV shots on characters saying, "Oh, it's just you...Arrghh!" but contains no more than 30 seconds of werewolf footage, spread out among a number of murders. The film is poorly acted and not the least bit frightening, but it does have a few positive attributes, particularly the stereo surround sound. The sound, legitimate Dolby, swells and growls much better than it has any right to, so if you get the disc, turn it up. The picture is mildly grainy.

THE HUBLEY STUDIO'S THE AGES OF HUMANKIND

Walt Disney has gone sort of overboard plastering warnings on the jacket cover of *The Hubley Studio's The Ages of Humankind*, claiming the program material is for, "mature, adult audiences." We watched the entire 53-minute disc without blinking and we didn't see anything. True, one is more likely to come across the disc's five animated shorts in school rather than on television, but surely Disney could have come up with a different way to warn parents that this isn't Mickey Mouse, particularly since a young friend of our acquaintance was spellbound by the final cartoon. We'll explain in a moment.

The sound is a little rough. The quality of the picture varies depending upon the age of the short. Each piece has its own chapter marker. The first, 'The Tender Game,' is the vaguest, a depiction of romance among stick figures which is set to an Ella Fitzgerald/Oscar Peterson number. The second, 'Dig,' is an excellent summary of geological and archeological basics, explained by a talking rock with Jack Warden's voice. It has an 'approved by the NEA' tag on the end credits. 'WOW' is an impressionistic survey of the experiences women have had throughout history. 'People, People, People' is a quick and witty summary of civilization in North America over a 20,000 year span. The last cartoon, 'Cockaboody,' features the common, but nevertheless charming gimmick of recording the conversations of children and then setting the recordings to animation. Our friend, who, admittedly, had become a bit restless somewhere around the history of women's enslavement, stopped dead in his tracks when he heard the children talking and sat, transfixed to the screen, for the remainder of the disc. In our book that constitutes a far more reliable seal of approval than anything the NEA could come up with.

HUCKLEBERRY HOUND AND FRIENDS (see **YOGI BEAR**)

HUEY LEWIS AND THE NEWS – THE HEART OF ROCK 'N' ROLL

The 53-minute concert, *Huey Lewis and the News –The Heart of Rock 'N' Roll* was recorded in San Francisco's Kabuki Theater. The concert is lit for video and the picture looks very sharp except when the camera lenses are deliberately gauzy. The sound is a concert-type mix, but it is digitally clear and satisfying. Lewis's music is more pep rally than rock. He is too clean to actually perspire, but he tries to work up a sweat and his performance is diligent. The audience looks pleased.

HUEY LEWIS AND THE NEWS VIDEO HITS

The timings for the cuts contained in *Huey Lewis and the News Video Hits* are listed on the back of the jacket down to the microsecond. Why CBS/Fox listed it like that is beyond us, though sassy cuteness seems to be an intrinsic part of Lewis's personality. The disc covers much of the same material the live disc does, but this time the numbers are music videos. In general, the group sounds better than they look and their video conceptions are as uninspired as their stage performance. Some of the numbers are just outtakes and still photos slipped underneath a song to fill out the program. The collection runs about 45 minutes – who counts microseconds? – and will only be of interest to fans and news hounds.

HULKAMANIA
(see **THE BEST OF THE WWF VOL. 1**)

HUMPERDINCK: HANSEL UND GRETEL

A lively and magical presentation of *Humperdinck: Hansel und Gretel* begins in an Old World opera house as an imaginary production being observed by a crowd of sedate and earnest children. In front of them, Sir Georg Solti conducts the Vienna Philharmonic in the extended overture, and the scene looks like something out of a Chris Van Allsberg book. Then, as the action begins, the camera moves onto to the stage and the setting moves into a soundstage environment, freed from the constraints of the theater. Later, there are video effects and animated sequences. It is a pleasing rendering of the opera, nicely sung by Brigitte Fassbaender, Edita Gruberova, Hermann Prey, Helga Dernesch, and Sena Jurinac.

The digital sound, which is not always in perfect synchronization with the singers' lips, is very good. There is no running time listed on the jacket, but the program, in German with English subtitles, runs 107 minutes. The picture is both grainy and a little blurry. Included with the jacket is an excellent history of the opera, a chapter listing, and a plot synopsis which is also cross-referenced to the chapters.

THE HUNCHBACK OF NOTRE DAME
THE HUNCHBACK OF NOTRE DAME (Digital)

Image reissued its original release of *The Hunchback of Notre Dame* with digital encoding and chapter markers. The picture was slighty improved as well, but the picture transfer was very good to begin with and the improvement is insignificant. The film, which stars Charles Laughton, is an exciting classic with amazing set designs.

Both versions contain an alternate audio track lecture by Paul Mandell. Mandell sometimes succumbs to describing the action on the screen – pointless unless a viewer's head is turned. The lecture tracks have a distinct hum in the background. The volume levels vary wildly and sometimes drop so low that Mandell cannot be heard. The digital track, which has no lecture, still has a tendency to suffer from volume swings. Mandell's lecture is useful, but we wish there could have been more of it. A good, two-hour talk could probably break down everything one would need to know about how the movie was constructed, why it was made, and what the significant images contribute to the film's spiritual core. Instead, Mandell lays on the trivia and, for long stretches of time, does not talk at all.

THE HUNGER
THE HUNGER (Import)

A brief three years separates the theatrical release of *The Hunger* and its arrival in the Japanese MGM/UA Collector's Item Series, so the quality of the print is not a problem as it has been on some of the older titles in the series. Rich vampires, crumbling corpses, and piano music, all done up to look like an ad for perfume. The import is in CAV, is digitally encoded, and is letterboxed (with Japanese subtitles beneath the picture). This combination still makes us want to nibble no matter what sort of bait is on the hook.

Digital encoding improves the quality of the sound considerably by cleaning up the playback. The American release was not even CX-encoded and side two contained a hum in the left channel which encouraged one to run the right audio track by itself (the film is monaural). The colors on the American transfer are weak. In direct comparison, the picture is too dark on the American version and too light on the Japanese.

There are many subliminal insert shots which last for less than a second and these are suitable for freezing when the CAV functions are activated. All the Standard Play activities imaginable, however, are not going to assist the viewer in understanding the plot.

HUNK

A variation of 'Faust,' *Hunk* is a well-constructed little film which, within the confines of its marketing requirements, is witty and enjoyable. A nerdy computer programmer gives up his soul for a 'three month trial run' in exchange for wealth and popularity. James Coco plays the Devil with a fiendish only-veteran-in-the-cast indulgence. The picture on the disc is in good condition, but the sound is problematic. Only the music and scattered sound effects are actually in stereo. The dialog is poorly recorded in some scenes, and often sounds fuzzy.

THE HUNT FOR RED OCTOBER
THE HUNT FOR RED OCTOBER (Letterboxed)

Those who labor at white-collar occupations will have a special affection for *The Hunt for Red October*, a movie about a man who makes such a sharp impression during a briefing to senior officials at a crisis meeting that 40 hours later he is on a Russian submarine helping the captain sneak the craft past the Soviet navy. Oh, the movie has torpedo fights and similar pieces of excitement, but nothing quite matches the high it achieves showing people sitting in chairs and doing their jobs well.

A scanned and cropped version and a letterboxed edition are both available. The cropped version is truly cropped, with no additional material added to the top or bottom of the image and plenty missing from the sides. The letterboxed version has an aspect ratio of about 2.35:1. The end credits are squeezed, but the screen composition is generally an accurate rendition of the theatrical presentation, and is in one aspect improved –the subtitles for the incidental Russian appear beneath the image.

The cropped rendition is also a fine presentation of the film. The essential components of the narrative and atmosphere are conveyed. The most severe negative impact occurs with the underwater scenes, in which the rhythm of the images is upset by the magnification created by the cropping –vessels approaching from the distance on the letterboxed picture are given a false immediacy on the cropped picture. Otherwise, the cropping appears to remove only minor details and a mild sense of location.

The letterboxed edition comes in a gatefold jacket which has a beautiful innerspread containing three big color stills. Unfortunately, the picture transfer on the letterboxed version has a slight increase in grain over the standard version. The movie, set underwater and in dimly lit submarine compartments, is fairly grainy to begin with (especially in the second half). In scenes where the letterboxed disc seems to lose control of the grain, the scanned and cropped version retains a sense of solidity. The colors are a little more stable and brighter, and the image is a little less hazy.

The stereo surround sound is identical on both presentations. The separations are not outstanding, but they are still good fun, particularly with all the undersea noises.

The film stars Alec Baldwin, who is super, and Sean Connery, who gets the job done but is less appealing, and contains a terrific team of supporting actors. Our favorite is Joss Ackland, as the Soviet ambassador who squirms in his seat as he lies to the national security advisor. John McTiernan's direction is also inspired, achieving a pace which is steady but unrushed, pulling the viewer further into the story with every pulse. The film, which is a bright adaptation of a novel that had seemed impossible to coerce into a theatrical time frame, is a terrific adventure with limited violence and a good sense of realism.

HUNTER

Steve McQueen spent his entire career playing out adolescent fantasies. This added extra poignancy to the final shot in his final film, *Hunter*, where, for the first time in any of his movies, his character fathers a child and, holding it, realizes the responsibilities of adulthood. The acceptance in McQueen's expression is the cumulative moment of his onscreen personas.

The movie is a mildly comical portrayal of a bounty hunter. The picture and sound transfers are passable.

HUNTER'S BLOOD

If you collect *Deliverance* imitations, *Hunter's Blood* is not the least competent film ever made, but there are a few amusing faux pas, such as the way that the hunters who are running for their lives still have time to lie down on the sticks and leaves to catch some shut-eye, even though they had plenty of sleep the night before. The picture is on the blurry side and the sound is dull.

THE HURRICANE

The approaching storm hangs over events in John Ford's *The Hurricane* like a stalking deity. You have a stronger sense of the moral choices the characters are making and you have a stronger sense of their faith because you know that pretty soon the wind is going to whip through and wipe it all away. The lighting and photography is impressive on the black-and-white film and it has been transposed well to disc.

HYPER SAPIENS: PEOPLE FROM ANOTHER STAR

A scanned and cropped science fiction film for kids, *Hyper Sapiens: People from Another Star*, is about two adolescent human-looking aliens who stowaway on an Earth probe and then meet a teenage Wyoming boy riding a dirt bike. The picture transfer is sharp looking and the surround sound is adequate. The filmmakers compromise their work by creating a furry pet for the two aliens which is not in keeping with the quality of the other special effects. The film's opening and closing are interesting, but the center is void of adult stimulation.

I AM THE LAW

One of Edward G. Robinson's best 'good guy' roles can be found in *I Am the Law*. Robinson portrays a naïve law professor who is hired as a special prosecutor by corrupt officials wishing to manipulate an investigation into their wrongdoings. Contrary to his usual persona, there is not a wicked bone in his body, but his flaccid befuddlement and angelic temperament make his eventual success all the more satisfying. The movie runs a brisk 83 minutes, lacks even a rudimentary feeling for actual judicial process, and is loads of fun.

The black-and-white picture has rich contrasts and is generally satisfying. The focus is a little soft in some sequences, and there are both splices and speckles scattered through the print, but nothing which will stop a viewer from wanting to see what happens next. The sound has no significant problems.

I CLOWNS (Import)

The colorful Fellini effort, *I Clowns* ('Clowns'), is available in Japan. Since much of it is given to the depiction of circus clowns and their routines, it is more accessible than most non-English language discs. The Japanese subtitles, unfortunately, appear vertically, at the right of the screen. This is more distracting than subtitles at the bottom, since your eyes scan there whenever there is a cut.

The image is not letterboxed, but it is in excellent condition and, for a Fellini movie, that is always a treat, since he seems to think with his eyes. The film is a quasi-documentary. The marvelous three-ring antics are interspersed with scenes of Fellini and his crew interviewing famous clowns or the families of famous clowns. A relaxed sense of entertainment – at one point the whole crew appears to exit from the back seat of a cab – is present throughout the program and Fellini establishes just the right balance between journalistic inquiry and free-spirited comedy.

The 91-minute disc is monaural and has

been CX-encoded. The sound is limited in scope, but it is well represented by the disc presentation.

I CONFESS (Import)
Many critics treat Alfred Hitchcock's 1953 film, *I Confess*, as a lesser effort, and the movie was not very successful at the box office. The story is about a priest (Montgomery Clift) who hears the confession of a murderer. As the plot twists, the priest is accused of the crime and cannot defend himself without breaking the sanctity of the confessional. We feel this is one of Hitchcock's strongest accomplishments, a movie that is about real moral choices and an exploration of what it means to have and use a conscience.

Released in Japan on laser disc, the lower part of the screen is often riddled with Japanese subtitles (there isn't much action). The sound is monaural and suffers from crackles and periodic pops. The print looks worn as if it were several generations away from its source.

Filmed in Quebec City, a location which deserves the attention of Hollywood far more than it has received to date, Hitchcock uses the Catholicism of the entire town to weigh upon the choices the characters must make.

I COULD GO ON SINGING
The MGM/UA Deluxe Letter-Box Edition transfer of *I Could Go on Singing* is lovely. The print is in excellent shape. The colors are rich and detailed, and the widescreen picture is presented with an aspect ratio of 2.25:1, capturing some beautiful lighting compositions and a breathtaking helicopter tour over London. The disc has a bevy of chapter markers and when the film is over there are two original theatrical trailers, one for the American release and one for the British release, where the film was called 'The Empty Stage.' Both are letterboxed and contain a shot not seen in the film. The monaural sound is unremarkable but the transfer presents no problems.

I Could Go on Singing was Judy Garland's final film. The story is about a singing star who attempts to forge a link with a son she had given up in pursuit of her career. Garland's performance is incredible. She modulates her voice in her dramatic scenes as if she were interrupting herself. The plot has long stretches of inactivity, including a problematic opening scene in which two characters must argue at length over issues which, for dramatic purposes, cannot be fully revealed until later in the film. Garland's magnetic appeal, however, enables the movie to overcome its deficiencies, and the quality of the disc allows one's appreciation of both Garland and the film to soar.

I LOMBARDI
Since *I Lombardi* was taped at La Scala for Italian television, it has no subtitles. The three-sided 128-minute disc has been released with CX-encoded stereo analog sound. A libretto has been provided in Italian and English with succinct act synopses to let you in on what is happening.

The stage design is limited and uses black space to fill the gaps between large rocks or curtains. Within the black space one can see the flaws of the disc, such as squiggles, colored speckles, and pulsing lines. The colors of the costumes and the lighting have a tendency to bleed.

Lombardi was one of Giuseppe Verdi's earlier efforts. It is rarely revived, and listening to it is sort of like coming across a Beatles song which never made it onto an album. The music is familiar but different, and one's concentration is heightened by the discovery of new angles in Verdi's musical constructions. The plot is about the crusades and, near the end, Verdi toys with giving the Christians ecclesiastical melodies, and the Moslems more oriental-type sounds. It is not a masterpiece. It is a variation on other masterpieces by the master himself.

I LOVE LUCY VOLUME 1
I LOVE LUCY VOLUME 2
I LOVE LUCY VOLUME 3
I LOVE LUCY VOLUME 4
What a wonderful performer Lucille Ball is! In the first episode presented on *I Love Lucy Volume 1*, 'Lucy Does a TV Commercial,' Lucy is practicing a sales pitch so that she can appear on television in a commercial. The product has a strong alcohol content and every time she does a run through she takes a little swig and gets a little more drunk. Even though the sequence is edited, one can't help but admire how carefully the stages of her inebriation are delineated. In every episode there are usually several sequences where she takes a simple but amusing premise and, solely through her own talent, realizes it to perfection.

Four half-hour episodes are presented on each *I Love Lucy* disc, two to a side (each side represents a video cassette collection) with chapter markers. The black and white prints are nice and clear, and the monaural sound is fine.

The other episodes on *Volume 1* also contain situations which are designed to let Ball improvise. In 'Lucy's Italian Movie' she ends up in a wine vat, stomping grapes in her bare feet, and from her expression the viewer can picture every grape that squeezes and breaks between her toes. In an often excerpted sequence from 'Job Switching,' Lucy is on an assembly line in a candy factory, trying to wrap chocolates in pace with the conveyer belt. The final episode on the disc, 'Fashion Show,' has her exhibiting a tweed jacket ensemble over a painful sunburn at a charity fashion event.

The episodes on *Volume 2* are of a different nature, but both collections are ultimately so hysterical and so enjoyable that it is impossible to recommend one disc over the other. The first side of *Volume 2* is set in Hollywood. One of the episodes, 'Lucy Meets Harpo Marx,' need not be described except to note that there is a mirror scene. The other, however, is even funnier. Entitled 'L.A. at Last!,' it features William Holden, playing himself. In a scene set in a restaurant, Holden's ability to keep a straight face during an onslaught of Lucy's uninhibited star-gazing intensifies the comedy tremendously. It makes one wonder how funny the show could have been if the regular cast members supporting Ball had been more talented.

Desi Arnaz, however, is shown in his best light on side two of *Volume 2* in episodes which deal with each end of Lucy's pregnancy, 'Lucy is Enceinte' and 'Lucy Goes to the Hospital.' Only the most hardened and world-weary of viewers will still have a dry eye at the end of the first episode, as Lucy is frustrated in attempting to announce to Ricky that she is pregnant and finally manages to get the news to him while he is performing. The scene is so wonderful somebody should steal it. The second episode could have been done a thousand different ways. It is predictable, but nonetheless funny for being so, and it focuses on Arnaz rather than Ball, having him arrive at the hospital straight from a club act and still in costume.

'Lucy and Bob Hope,' on *Volume 3*, doesn't have to be inspired to be funny. The episode has a baseball subplot, and as soon as Lucy sticks the chewing tobacco in her mouth the viewer becomes oblivious to all else. 'Lucy and Superman' is even funnier, as Lucy invites George Reeves to her son's birthday party and then attempts a last-minute substitution when she thinks he is not going to show up. The episode's closing line is one of the most memorable in the whole series. The highlight of 'Pioneer Women' is Lucy's battle with an ever-rising lump of bread dough. In 'The Camping Trip,' Lucy plays a trick on Ricky and only pretends to be roughing it during an outdoor weekend. The episode has a nice moral and is pleasantly romantic. The picture transfer on the disc is a little softer than the other offerings.

The funniest episode on *Volume 4* is 'The Handcuffs,' in which Lucy and Ricky are joined at the wrist the day before an important event. In 'The Ballet' Lucy practices a dance routine and a vaudeville comedy routine and then gets the two confused. Both 'The Courtroom' and 'Never Do Business with Friends' concern conflicts which arise between Lucy and Ricky and their best friends, Fred and Ethel, over the condition of some major appliances, a TV set in 'Courtroom' and a washing machine in 'Business.'

I, MADMAN
Not even special effects can get the script writers of *I, Madman* out of the corner they've written themselves into at the end. The film is a super horror thriller up to the last 30 seconds, when it becomes clear that no final twist is going to wrap up the loose ends. The disc has an enjoyable Ultra-Stereo surround soundtrack, with adept atmospheric separations. The movie was filmed with brown tones, but the picture transfer is crisp and commendable. The plot is about a woman who discovers that a series of murders parallel those in a book she is reading. Passages from the book are played out on the screen, and then the two worlds begin to merge. There are some nice stop-motion model effects for a monster in the fantasy sequences, but the effort which went into it should have gone into coming up with an explanation for everything else. As it stands, stupidity, rather than madness, becomes the guiding force.

I MARRIED A WITCH
The print used for *I Married a Witch* is in poor condition and the sound has a noisy hum. Footage is apparently missing, as well. Although *Bell, Book, and Candle* is the true precedent for sitcoms such as 'Bewitched,' René Claire's *Witch* was an early attempt to offer romance between natural and supernatu-

ral characters. The plot seems to generate more tension than it manages to relieve, but the film is remarkably risqué for a 1942 venture and satisfying up to a point.

I NEVER SANG FOR MY FATHER
The fleshtones on *I Never Sang for My Father* are excessively orange-pink. Otherwise, the picture and sound are bearable, though the false hues can be distracting when one is attempting to concentrate on the drama. The film, which features two good performances by Melvyn Douglas and Gene Hackman, is an oft-told tale about father and son reconciliations. Hackman and Douglas save the film from seeming so close to life that you're not escaping anything by watching it. They are both eloquent, and can focus the faults of their characters without getting lost in the haphazard mess of life that less experienced performers might mistake for the essence of truth.

I SPIT ON YOUR GRAVE (VidAmerica)
I SPIT ON YOUR GRAVE (Image)
The improved picture transfer in the VidAmerica and Image release of *I Spit on Your Grave* is surprising. The colors and the image sharpness are significantly upgraded from the old Vestron version. The digital monaural sound is still a mess. The film, which has an acknowledged cult following, gives off more bad karma than good in its graphic depiction of a gang rape and the subsequent murders of the perpetrators. Image's jacket copy is also fixed up, as the Vestron jacket, transposing the original ad copy, got the number of murders wrong.

I VITELLONI
Federico Fellini's *I Vitelloni* was made in Italy in the early fifties, so one can't expect it to look new, but we have definitely seen better looking prints than the one that made it to disc. The picture is continually pock-marked, ragged, and blurry. The sound is also a little fuzzy, though its condition is more excusable. The film is in Italian and has large white subtitles which sometimes run off both sides of the screen at once.

Those who only know Fellini from his crazy color films may not realize that he once was a film director of great promise. In few sequences is this more clear than the opening of *I Vitelloni*, which begins all spread out, during a small town summer carnival and beauty contest, and then compacts, with the help of a rainstorm and a rush indoors, so that the winner of the contest is almost suffocating and the viewer, so it seems, is led into her sudden claustrophobia. She faints. It turns out she's pregnant.

The plot is commonly perceived to be about a group of young men, living in the town, who do not do much with their lives. In reality it is about one couple, the girl and her shotgunned husband. The husband's friends, the other men, have stories of their own, but the film never settles on them for very long. The more bitter and realistic the romance becomes, the more romantic it feels.

Nina Rota's score, though it is not helped by the digital encoding, is worth mentioning. His melody is a theme that he did not use as repeatedly as many of his other compositions, and it matches the idleness of the characters perfectly. The theme veers this way and that but never quite reaches the point that it seems to be heading towards.

I WALKED WITH A ZOMBIE
The atmospheric voodoo drama from Val Lewton and Jacques Tourneur, *I Walked with a Zombie*, pleases some fans immensely, while others find the movie to be insubstantial and trifling. The film runs only a little bit over an hour and tells the story of a nurse who becomes involved with a Caribbean plantation owner while tending to his 'walking comatose' wife. The plantation owner's family has a couple other gothic skeletons locked away, and the local farmhands perform strange rituals after the sun goes down.

The black and white print has a couple of splices, but is in pretty good shape, and the sound is stable.

I WAS A TEENAGE ZOMBIE
The dialog on *I Was a Teenage Zombie* sounds like it was recorded on a portable cassette player using cheap tape. No matter. It may take five or ten minutes to adjust your ears to what the characters are saying, but that is part of the film's aesthetic. It is a punk horror movie. A cheap, barely coagulated effort which you have to stay with clear into side two before the comedy – a return from the dead somewhat in the spirit of *American Werewolf in London* – starts to click. The actors warm up to it, too.The stiffer their characters become, the more their performances loosen up.

The release, billed as the original uncut version, is CX-encoded monaural, although that is giving the sound more credit than it deserves. The picture is also wanting, but the transfer has clearly not interfered with bringing the original 16mm source material to the screen in all of its abject splendor.

I WANNA HOLD YOUR HAND
The Beatles appear only peripherally in *I Wanna Hold Your Hand*, but they are the catalyst for the action. The movie, about a group of resourceful kids trying to meet their heroes, is hysterical, even after a dozen viewings. It features early performances by Bobby DiCicco, Nancy Allen, Wendie Jo Sperber and others, and few of them have ever been as fresh and as funny as they are here. It was witty and refreshing when it first came out and it is still witty and refreshing now that it is on disc. And you can't beat the music on the soundtrack.

The transfer has a few flaws. Strong colors tend to blur and, although the picture looks fresh, there are a few speckles and even a scratch. The monaural sound is okay, but it doesn't grab one the way it did in a theater. The disc is chapter encoded, but perhaps even more importantly, the listing of the chapters on the back of the jacket is a model of how such listings ought to be composed. Whoever writes them at Warner must memorize the films before starting, because every significant highlight is mentioned.

ICE PIRATES
Some people wince at the thought of slapstick in science fiction, and those people should avoid *The Ice Pirates*. The film is a clutter of ideas and bits which don't work and lousy special effects, but it manages to come up with one good joke just often enough to keep you from pressing the eject button on your player. Robots have been around a long time, but movie makers are only beginning to realize their true entertainment potential. Here a robot who is too chicken to fight vomits up oil and bolts in the face of danger. Hysterical? Maybe not, but it is not a dead end, either. The disc transfer and sound are of standard quality.

ICE STATION ZEBRA
Patrick McGoohan performs the same duty in *Ice Station Zebra* which Richard Burton performed in *Where Eagles Dare*. He reads the long monolog that explains the plot with such a brandy-flavored voice that you can't help becoming intoxicated, not only by his every word, but by the plot he is describing. The movie has just enough action, just enough engaging performances (Ernest Borgnine as a Russian!), and just enough plot to keep one entertained. If the sea swells on a small screen can not send a viewer swooning the way they did when the Super Panavision film was first released in Cinerama, there are still plenty of other pleasures to be had with the program, especially with MGM/UA's neat Deluxe Letter-Box Edition.

Due to flaws on the source material, the aspect ratio measures about 2.3:1, a little more confined than the original theatrical presentation, but wide enough so that no more than a wing or two of a Russian jet really gets lost. The screen compositions are entertainingly composed, and standard cropping would severely harm the power which each shot is intended to convey. Not artistic power – the closest thing to art which the movie achieves is its fairly literal symbolic depiction of the Cold War – but entertainment power, showing the viewer the whole submarine as it dodges ice ridges, showing the full cramped cabin as it fills with gushing water, showing the action played out upon a wider stage than a standard presentation could possibly offer.

If there were flaws on the source material, they have been successfully hidden. The picture transfer is wonderful. The colors are crisp and stimulating, and the focus is precise. The sound, with one exception, is also great fun. The exception is a ten-minute reel on side one, beginning at minute 28, in which the sound becomes badly fuzzy and remote. Otherwise, the surround effects are super, particularly for a sixties film, and Michel Legrand's score, taking its cues from bow crests and sonar pings, has a pleasing dimensionality, complete with a full overture, entr'acte and exit music.

ICEMAN
A synopsis of *Iceman* alienates potential viewers because so many awful movies in the past have dealt with the same subject. Researchers discover a man who has been frozen in the Arctic for 40,000 years. At first they have no expectation of reviving him, but when they thaw out the body and attempt to perform a biopsy, the vital signs start to tick.

The scientists have a huge greenhouse, which looks like the atrium in a large shopping center, in the middle of their snowbound research station. An anthropologist (Timothy Hutton) convinces the others that the iceman (John Lone) should be let loose in the atrium and studied.

Lone is so totally convincing as the primitive that you forget he is an actor. In one scene, where the two perform a 'duet' of 'Heart of Gold,' the effect is so precious you wish it had been released as a single.

The quality of the picture and the CX-encoded stereo surround is superb. *Iceman* is entertaining and it never insults your intelligence. Instead, the film adds to it.

THE IDOLMAKER

Ray Sharkey has fun with his role as a man who turns young nobodies into rock and roll stars in *The Idolmaker*. His delivery is rapid and energetic, but you are always aware that his character is thinking and analyzing, with ideas and plans which never surface in the dialogue.

The film does not fall into any popular genres. It is too conservative to be a rock and roll movie but too boisterous to be a musical. *The Idolmaker* is entertaining because it has a fresh angle. The picture and, especially, the stereo sound are impressive.

IDOMENEO

Mozart's first complete opera, *Idomeneo*, is seen as his one acknowledgment of the traditional operatic forms which he would soon turn upside down with his more popular and famous works. The plot is based upon a Greek myth and the characters are archetypes first and human only by default. The music, which had been considered a lesser accomplishment, took on a complexity and subtlety which could only be appreciated after several generations of familiarity with his work.

The 'Live at the Met' production of *Idomeneo* is an example of how uncomfortable some people still are with the material. The costumes are late-18th century and the set looks like something out of a Vermeer sketch. The story is supposed to take place on Crete, shortly after the Trojan War. The music should be enough to counterpoint the activities on the stage, and the singers ought to be walking around like Steve Reeves. Instead, they are hidden in milkmaid and minuet costumes, and Mozart's careful ironies are replaced by production designer Jean-Pierre Ponnelle's bad ideas.

No one buys operas for their stories and costumes. The music is digitally encoded, though it seems to have an analog master. There are clear differences in noise levels between the analog and digital tracks and aside from silly glitches like having Luciano Pavarotti's voice come from the left speaker when he is standing on the right, the digital track is admirable. If too many instruments sound stuck together, it must be remembered that this is a live performance and the jacket notes are adamant in emphasizing that no alternate recording sources were used. The picture is too grainy, but this is only noticeable when one is close to the screen. The subtitles are discrete and sufficient. The performances by Pavarotti, Hildegard Behrens, and Fredrica von Stade are super and James Levine's conducting is dependably thorough. Behrens seems particularly energized by the presence of an audience.

IF....

The sixties gave us Peter Max posters, Nehru collars, and an eclectic style of filmmaking which lasted just about as long as smoking bananas before giving way to the more consistent realism of the seventies. Of this brief foray in jump cuts, mixed film stocks, and unsubtle symbolism, only an incense burner's worth of movies have withstood the changing times. One essential sixties film is *If....*

Derived from the French classic, 'Zero for Conduct,' and from the boyhood memories of the filmmakers, the script is about a ghastly upper-class British boarding school. The school is hopelessly ritualized with questionable sexual hierarchies and unscholastic educational practices.

Characters talk seriously about horoscopes and exchange lines of dialogue such as, "Violence and revolution are the only pure acts." Scenes of fantasy edge in on the proceedings (hence, the title). The hero, Malcolm McDowell, is rebellious and scruffy. The villains, students who have inherited the privileges to bully others, are prissy and unscrupulous. The director, Lindsay Anderson, had substantial stage experience and brings the rhythm of a fast-clipped drama to the dialog. The symbolism is diverse enough to prevent one from being overwhelmed in the obvious. The use of fantasy allows the script to take several surprise turns.

A case of expenses dictating style (was hippy clothing any different?), part of the film is in color and part is in black-and-white. The disc retains the speckles which undoubtedly reside upon the original negative. Despite continued catalog listings to the contrary, the disc is not CX-encoded and is not in stereo.

Different versions of the film are shown in revival houses around the country, some containing one or two scenes of frontal nudity while other copies have substituted frames which are less revealing. Paramount has chosen to release the prudish version, apparently not realizing that times and standards have changed.

IL BARBIERE DI SIVIGLIA THE BARBER OF SEVILLE – GLYNDEBOURNE FESTIVAL OPERA

The Glyndebourne Opera house is small, and *Il barbiere di Siviglia The Barber of Seville – Glyndebourne Festival Opera* is ideally suited for video. The whole stage can be framed on the screen and you can still make out the expressions on the faces of the performers. The closeups are so intimate that the production looks more like it was done on a soundstage than in a live auditorium. The lighting is superb, and even in 'stage' darkness, details and colors are incredibly clear.

The woman appearing as Rosina (Maria Ewing) may not have a vocal control to match the world's foremost divas, but she has the most incredibly licentious mouth, and so moves a viewer's spirit in other ways. All the performers – Ewing, John Rawnsley as Figaro, Max-René Cosotti as Count d'Almavina, and Claudio Desderi as Bartoli – are adequate singers, and give vigorous, engaging performances. The production demonstrates that Rossini is much better served when his works are not over-produced (or too-perfectly sung). The staging is breezy, festive, and wonderful fun.

The disc's most stunning component, however, is the digitally encoded sound. From the very beginning, as the conductor, Sylvain Cambreling, strode toward the podium and the echo of his steps reverberated through our room, we were held in awe by the quality of the sound recording and presentation (the analog track is only slightly less perfect). The supreme moment also comes early on the disc, during Figaro's entrance aria. In the middle of it, Rawnsley throws out a whistle which bounces off both walls and the ceiling.

Each of the opera's three scenes (two in the first act and one in the second) is on a separate side. Unencumbered by curtain calls or other distractions, the 156-minute program moves briskly. A bulky, bilingual libretto is included in the packaging. *Barber* is presented in Italian, with English subtitles, providing an opportunity to further demonstrate the production's charm and humor. When Figaro reads Rosina's letter to the Count, the two men are kept on the left side of the screen. On the right, the subtitles start to scroll upward, line by line, until the entire missive is completed.

IL TRITTICO – TEATRO ALLA SCALA

Bernard Herrmann lifted the melody from Giacomo Puccini's 'Gianni Schicchi,' the third opera in *Il Trittico – Teatro Alla Scala*, to use as one of the principal themes in *Vertigo*, further proof that Puccini was born 50 years before the world really needed him. *Trittico* is a collection of three short operas which are conveniently separated one to a side on the disc. Puccini is at his best when he doesn't have to produce motif-related filler material, so the short format of the three pieces, which also include 'Il Tabarro' and 'Suor Angelica,' is an excellent demonstration of his best abilities. The La Scala production does no harm to the music, either.

A different cast appears in each opera. Juan Pons has the title role in 'Gianni Schicchi' and Rosalind Plowright has the title role in 'Suor Angelica.' Piero Cappuccilli, Nicola Martinucci and Sylvia Sass form the tragic lover's triangle in 'Il Tabarro.' All sing superbly, although the live recording tends to favor the orchestra and leave the singers slightly out of balance. The sound has no significant problems other than those caused by the source material.

The picture is a little soft, and the limited camera angles used to record the production are frustrating. The 'Tabarro' set is fantastic, but no one shot ever savors the design, and you have to look around things to see it. The depth of field is also poor throughout the program.

Subtitles are provided to accompany the Italian lyrics, and a full Italian/English libretto comes with the disc. The disc has chapter markers. Each opera ends with a credit scroll and lengthy curtain calls.

I'LL CRY TOMORROW

No matter how turgid you find *I'll Cry Tomorrow*, the biography of Lillian Roth which stars Susan Hayward, do not miss the MGM/UA disc. Borrow it or rent it, at least. After the film – which runs two hours and details Roth's slide into alcoholism and subsequent recovery – is ended, MGM/UA has included a Warner Brothers Vitaphone featurette, 'The Story Conference,' which stars Roth herself. Since the short runs 20 minutes, it is rarely seen. It is sort of a Warner musical in miniature, the highlight of which is an amusing take-off on 'Honeymoon Hotel,' entitled 'Alimony Hotel' ("I told the judge he slapped me, and how he used to yell; at that, that man was better than the Alimony Hotel."). Hayward may be a more elaborate actress, but it is clear from the piece that Roth had a powerful charisma. MGM/UA has also thrown in the original theatrical trailer for *Tomorrow*, which screams about the degradations on view in the film with big block letters and carefully manipulated film clips.

The movie itself is more valuable as camp than as any sort of cinematic accomplishment. It is a typical star-as-victim tale of mean husbands and encouraging bartenders. Hayward's performance is all chaser, but she does have one marvelous double take when she first sees Eddie Albert which is worth sitting through the whole movie just to catch in the right frame of mind. The black-and-white picture transfer is fine and the picture looks very clean. The monaural sound supports Alex North's musical score and Hayward's songs without distortion. The condition of 'Story Conference' is naturally more rough.

ILLUMINATION BY KEN JENKINS
(see **CRYSTAL VISTA**)

ILSA HAREM KEEPER OF THE OIL SHEIKS
Ilsa Harem Keeper of the Oil Sheiks is a tad more subdued than the other two Ilsa films, but it retains a distasteful emphasis upon mutilation and other unpleasant activities. The transfer is also a little better than other Ilsa offerings. Although there are still markings on the print, the colors appear to be close to original and the lip movements match the dialog. The sound is passable. As for the narrative, the title is self-explanatory.

ILSA THE WICKED WARDEN
ILSA SHE WOLF OF THE SS
The 'Ilsa' movies are vile concoctions. Some viewers find them stimulating, while others believe them to be a complete turnoff. Sex in the programs is not explicit. The poor production values and bad acting contribute to the films' reputation as camp entertainment, but the narratives focus on violence against women, which is close to explicit and tends to negate the incidental pleasures that the films have to offer. Potential owners should be familiar with the material beforehand.

Ilsa The Wicked Warden is set in an unidentified Latin American women's mental hospital, in which the patients are flagrantly maltreated. A heroine has herself committed in order to find a loved one and expose the institution's corruption. Things don't go well.

The dialog is rarely synchronized with the lip movements of the characters. The print is no more or less faded and mangled than a typical theatrical presentation of the film. The camerawork itself is sometimes out of focus, so for all we know the print, which is yellowed and consistently soft, may be pristine. Fans will likely not care. The disc has monaural sound, which is on par with the picture quality, and a few chapter markers.

Ilsa She Wolf of the SS is set in a small concentration camp and deals with grotesque medical experiments. The dialog is in synch with the lip movements and the sound has only a couple volume dropouts. The source material is less ragged than *Warden*, but the picture is still on the pale side. The chapter markers flicker.

IMAGE DISC
Image Premastering Services of Mendota Heights MN has issued *The Image Disc*, a one-sided CAV program that is partially a commercial for and demonstration of the materials Image Premastering can deliver, but it is also a legitimately educational and entertaining work, full of peripatetic fun.

The core of the disc is a collection of approximately 20,000 still frames. 3000 demonstrate the use of a laser disc as an artist's portfolio, showcasing the work of a dozen or so midwestern artists and photographers. Some of this material is erotic and would not be recommended for classroom use without pre-screening.

Slide shows presenting useful hints for determining the difference between a healthy cow and an unhealthy one, or for mating hogs, seem only to straddle the new medium and not utilize the advantages of laser. Shorter chapters cover displays of arrowheads and Nigerian textiles.

The best sections in the disc are a 4000-still collection on Minnesota native Americans and a 7000-snapshot spread exploring the genealogy of an average middle-class family.

The Indian material is taken from the Minnesota Historical Archives. Most of the photos and clippings are from the turn of the century to WWII. The best is a collection depicting one 'John Smith,' hobbling about at 125 years of age and looking as if he's enjoyed every day of it. More legible captions accompanying these photos would have increased their value, but one can learn a lot just browsing through them.

The genealogical collection follows several families through different fortunes and technologies as they converge to become the well-adjusted contemporary nuclear unit. Along with enjoying some very precious photographs (a boy in a band uniform standing in an overgrown yard with his fist buried in his French horn) you learn a couple of significant things. The first is that death (the obituaries) does not negate the fullness of the life that preceeded it, even when the person who dies is very young. The second is that people have the same personalities from the moment they are born. The kids whose faces shine, even in the oldest worn photographs, become vivacious and socially wealthy adults. The kids who hide from the camera or have sour expressions either fade totally from view or continue to have the same sour expressions when their grandchildren are jumping on them.

IMAGES OF ANTIQUITY
An 'amateur' video disc called *Images of Antiquity* has been compiled by Rev. Joseph L. Ponessa. The single-sided disc is in CAV. Although Ponessa's motivation came from hobby interests instead of business interests, the design of the program compares favorably to the best interactive educational programs we have seen. His utilization of chapter encoding is inspired, and the variety of material contained on the disc is a joy.

Excluding an extensive on-disc index, the program contains three segments: A 'still file' containg a few hundred slides of ancient monuments from Europe and the Middle East, meticulously organized in chronological sequence, is followed by two videotaped sequences, a narrated tour of the Jerusalem Wall and its gates, and a conceptual look at the bridges of Rome accompanied by a reading of Thomas Macaulay's narrative poem, 'Horatius at the Bridge.'

In the still file section, Ponessa has cleverly employed chapter encoding to assist the viewer in understanding not only the eras which generated the monuments, but the flow of history itself. The pictures are present day photographs of the remains of the various civilizations which flourished on the edges of the Mediterranean Sea. The first 30 chapters are coordinated with the thirty Egyptian dynasties and the first 2500 years of recorded history. Although not all the dynasties are represented with photographs, every era gets at least a chapter and a title card. When photos of obelisks, temples, and other architecturally oriented creations are included, they are also preceded by identifying title cards. Chapters 31 through 39 are associated with the first nine centuries of Western civilization, with an emphasis on Roman architecture, although a few Mayan ruins can be seen as well.

The still section is 600 frames long, including the title cards. The photographs were not taken with specific comparative lessons in mind, but the basics will be obvious to any student. The stone-by-stone simplicity of the earliest Egyptian works are followed by grander and more complex designs. The Roman arch makes an appearance, and within a few hundred years it is being employed by the dozens to support double-decker aqueducts. And 3000 years after the Egyptians, the Mayans can be seen starting their pyramidical versions of blocks on blocks all over again. The disc also contains an index which sorts the still frames by type and by location. The only major design flaw is that the index appears between the two motion sequences instead of at the end of the program, where it could have been marked with an imbedded stop. A map of Western Europe, showing a couple dozen site locations, has been provided on a jacket insert.

The Jerusalem Wall segment is a model of simple, clearheaded documentary filmmaking. It takes the viewer on a counter-clockwise trip around the Wall. The narrator discusses the names and functions of the few gates which allow passage to Old Jerusalem, and includes other Wall-related trivia where appropriate. The camera angles are not always distinctive and the narration is not always concise, but the purpose of the segment is clear and its execution is simple enough to be successful.

Our favorite part of the disc, however, and the part which gives the academic material a soul, is the 'Bridges of Rome' piece. The mildly unsteady views of Roman bridges begin without contemporary intrusions. The narrator starts her reading of the poem by bumping the microphone and the viewer immediately recognizes the amateur nature of the recording. As the poem progresses, one realizes that it, too, is no great accomplishment, being a florid, early-Victorian ballad about overly heroic Romans defending their city from invaders, taking a stand at a bridge not unlike the bridges one is viewing. Then, at the point when these realizations set in, the camera moves up a little to let the people, cars and the trappings of modern-day Rome mix with the antiquity of the bridges.

The duality is beautiful – there is the lasting perfection of simple architectural forms, compromised by the imperfection of the modern world, and there is the idealized vision of the past, compromised by the poet and the narrator. Yet true beauty is to be found in reality, not idealism, and so it is the modern day viewpoint which is truly moving – the bridges, trod upon by hundreds of years of grimy civilization, never actually existed in pastoral, Pax Romana settings. The poem and its reading are wonderful, because they remind one where the real values and joys of life are to be found. The disc represents that same feeling. It isn't slick or thoroughly professional, but its strength comes from the most perfectly constructed and lasting foundation of all, the human heart.

IMAGINE: JOHN LENNON

Sound engineers continue to out-do themselves resurrecting older recordings. The music on *Imagine: John Lennon* sounds incredibly crisp no matter how obscure or ancient the source material. Even the press conferences are in stereo. The documentary film covers familiar ground, but it is a story most people never get tired of hearing – the creation and break-up of The Beatles. The film, which was released theatrically, not only excels in its soundtrack, the picture quality is also impressive.

Most of the songs are played from beginning to end, making the interviews less disruptive than similar sequences have been in other documentaries. Both the picture and sound on the disc do the film justice. Warner has provided a great number of chapter markers and has included a thorough chapter content summary on the back of the jacket, so even if there are songs which should have had chapter markers but don't, the jacket cover still shows how to find them.

IMAGINE THE SOUND

A jazz disc which makes all other jazz discs seem like Raffi concerts, *Imagine the Sound*, has been released by Voyager. The film, made in the early eighties, profiles several musicians, including Paul Bley, Bill Dixon, Archie Shepp, and Cecil Taylor, and examines the shift in the art form that paralleled the change in performing venues over the last couple of decades, from dungeon cafes to lofts. Some of the musicians have become so abstract that their work is more performance art – a catchall that artists of many different persuasions drop into when they push things too far – than jazz.

Nevertheless, the program, which is mostly music, is both fascinating and satisfying. A few subdued interviews, scattered between the numbers, help the viewer understand how the musicians comprehend their music, without interrupting the flow of the presentation. The sound is digitally encoded monaural, but it was captured in single takes and sounds more alive than many stereophonic efforts. What is lost from the lack of a sophisticated recording is more than gained back by the vitality of the performances. The movie was shot in 16mm and is quite grainy, but that seems to go with the territory.

IMPULSE

Asking the viewer to believe more than the normal share of impossible things for a single day, *Impulse* is a silly movie about a town which goes crazy because its milk is poisoned. The print is scratchy in places, and unremarkable. The plot is inconsistent, pointless, and uninspired. Unless they had a grudge against the Dairy Association, it is difficult to believe anyone would actually put up money to have the film made. Decisions like that are usually born from something a little stronger than milk.

IMPULSE

Sondra Locke's *Impulse* is an enjoyable thriller about a cop (Theresa Russell) sitting on $900,000 and wondering whether she should turn it in or not. It is sexy (she's in Vice and has ambiguous feelings about playing the decoy), romantic (she has to choose between the money and the guy), and has a sufficient number of flashy action scenes to support the moral quandaries. The plot is not totally logical, but few thrillers are, and unlike many, the story gives the viewer a chance to think.

The picture is glossy and solid, and the stereo surround sound is fine.

IN COUNTRY
JACKNIFE

Based upon a Bobby Ann Mason novel, *In Country* is one of the few Vietnam veteran dramas that doesn't ask you to feel sorry for its characters. The veterans are actually peripheral to the central character, a young girl, played by Emily Lloyd, whose father was killed in combat before she was born. Her persistent questions to her uncle, a vet nicely underplayed by Bruce Willis, about her father and about Vietnam, are closely tied to her acceptance of the responsibilities of adulthood. Set in 1989, the film can also be seen as a reading of contemporary attitudes toward the war and its aftermath. The individual dramatic sequences, which also involve day-to-day events in the girl's life, are pleasantly compelling.

The picture transfer is excellent. The colors are solid and elaborate lighting effects survive without distortion. The sound is also well produced.

Don't watch *Jacknife* after *In Country*, or all you will think about is how awful the picture looks. The colors are pale throughout and the image is fuzzy in places, but it would not be so noticeable if *In Country* wasn't so sharp. The stereo 'surround' sound has few separations and almost no surround effects.

The film is based upon a stage play, so characters leave the frame 'to get some beer' and other characters have important conversations while they are gone. At its best, the movie is an enjoyable romance between a garage mechanic, winningly played by Robert De Niro, and a biology teacher, played with equal charm by Kathy Baker. De Niro's character is a Vietnam vet, as is the brother of Baker's character, and it is a shame some other device couldn't have been used to get the two together, because the film becomes maudlin and soggy whenever the subject of the war and its aftereffects comes up.

THE IN CROWD

Sometimes you want to add a movie to your disc collection not because the movie is any good, but because it contains one perfectly constructed scene, a single scene which is worth, as it once was said, the price of admission. *The In Crowd* is a good example of a useless film which nevertheless makes a tempting purchase. The movie is about a Bandstand-type television show and a young man who manages to become a regular dancer on the program. The plot is a mess, taking place in 1965 after enthusiasm for dance programs had subsided and presenting characters who are so narrowly focussed that they have less interesting personalities than the real dancers on such shows. The movie is also lacking in all but rudimentary choreography. It does have a nice rock and roll score. The sound is in good shape and the picture quality is fine.

The sole spellbinding scene is marked by the second chapter on side two, though one should watch the whole disc up to that point at least once to understand what is going on. The moment is an unexpected tearjerker. It has depth because the script is so inept that the viewer is as surprised by what the hero does as are the other characters. We can't say more without spoiling things, but poignant, rich, optimistic emotion is so rare that 2 1/2 minutes of it is a treasure.

IN LIKE FLINT

If you yearn for a Flint film, *In Like Flint* is definitely the film to choose. Not only is the color transfer a little stronger than *Our Man Flint*, but the film itself is tighter and less dated. Oh, it is still silly, but it is not as frivolous, and benefits in its production budget from the success of the first feature. The disc has been letterboxed with an aspect ratio of about 2.5:1. Although most of the film would be perfectly understandable in cropped format, the widescreen image allows the viewer an opportunity to absorb more of the film's inventive art design. Lee J. Cobb once again shines as Flint's boss, but James Coburn is also sharper in the title role, more attuned to what works comically and what doesn't. The only disappointment is Jerry Goldsmith's score, which is less innovative than his first Flint effort. The monaural sound is fine. A trailer for *Our Man Flint* appears after the film is ended.

IN THE HEAT OF THE NIGHT

Though it seemed like a topical film when it was first released *In the Heat of the Night* has held up remarkably well over the passage of years. Credit can go to the scriptwriter, Stirling Silliphant, and the director, Norman Jewison, but also to Sidney Poitier, whose portrayal of a yuppie black homicide detective stuck in a small Mississippi town for want of a train connection is, in the lingo of the time, 'right on.' He is not 'perfect' or a 'superman' as those complaining about the portrayal of blacks in films, particularly during that era, claimed in backhanded criticism. His character is tight, someone – like the character Edward James Olmos plays in *Miami Vice* – who had to work extra hard to achieve what comes easy to those with other social backgrounds, and his meticulousness and paranoia almost cause him to blow the case.

In the Heat of the Night may not have deserved the Oscar, but it is a wonderful movie with great repeated viewing potential. The filmmakers were prescient enough to create a work which is not chained to an era or a social argument. It is about the timeless resentments between the rich and the poor, and it is twisted so the resentments can be revealed at unexpected turns.

The picture quality deteriorates as the film progresses. At its best it almost looks new and at its worst it looks like a drive-in screening on a foggy night. The audio is a little scratchy, but gets the job done. Ray Charles sings the title song.

IN THE MOOD

In the Mood opens with a terrific big band stereophonic blast of 'In the Mood.' The film is a rare achievement, a comedy based upon a true incident. It concerns a fifteen-year-old who becomes involved with a succession of older women and whose exploits have the bad luck of occurring during a slow news period for the nation's press in early 1944. He was dubbed 'The Woo-Woo Kid.'

The picture quality and the sound quality on the disc are both very nice. The movie is extremely nice, with barely enough sex to pull a PG-13 rating. The dialog is often witty and the improbability of the events is always overshadowed by the reality of their historical basis, truth being stranger than fiction and all. Although the filmmakers present the young man as winning the hearts of his lady friends through innocence and charm alone, there is an early scene which does not really strike one as significant until after the disc is ended. The stated purpose of the scene is to show how weird the boy's parents are, but when the kid makes marks on a doorway to see how tall he has grown, his father makes him clean the marking off by licking it.

INCIDENT AT CHANNEL Q

We dislike half-baked narratives designed to string pre-existing music videos together. *Incident at Channel Q* features heavy metal rock videos, presented by a video jockey at a TV station under siege by anti-heavy metal protestors. The videos are transfers of transfers, so they all look fuzzy and worn down. The sound is also a copy of a copy. Unlike the picture, the distortion is not flagrant.

Heavy metal music videos are not the type which show lovers running toward one another slow motion in a field of daffodils. The mixture here is fairly good, with most of the pieces providing either an effective evocation of a fantasy world or an enjoyably wanton disregard of decorum. The producers are pretending that the program is a feature film, and have even put an 'R' rating on the jacket cover, but it won't fool anyone.

THE INCREDIBLE HULK – VOL. 1

Three episodes from the 1982 cartoon series, 'The Incredible Hulk,' have been compiled on *The Incredible Hulk – Vol. 1*. Some of the narration is by Stan Lee himself. The first two episodes, 'Origins of the Hulk' and 'Enter the She-Hulk,' provide an updated explanation of the Hulk's beginnings and a twist which demonstrates that raging ids are not confined to one gender. The third, 'Bruce Banner Unmasked,' sits by itself on side two and is in CAV. It concerns Hulk's battle against an evil mastermind called 'The Puppet Master.' The CAV provides two shaky still frames for every three steady ones. Despite the fact that the Hulk is green, the colors are not that interesting.

THE INCREDIBLE HULK RETURNS

The 93-minute 'two-hour' television feature, *The Incredible Hulk Returns*, is actually a spin-off pilot for another Marvel comic character, Thor. Although he understandably never earned his own series, the wisecracking Thor character, played by Eric Kramer, provides a cheerful contrast to the single-minded Hulk, played by Lou Ferrigno, and his dour human alter ego, played by Bill Bixby. The editing is jumpy and awkward, and the acting is equally strained, but once all the characters are introduced and the action begins, the program provides a certain amount of dopey fun.

The disc has chapter markers for all the commercial breaks and also utilizes an appropriate black-out to separate side one from side two. After the standard Hulk intro, the music shifts into stereo. The sound is over-bearing and sometimes distorted, although it seems to match the show's other production values. The picture is sharp, but the most intense colors appear grainy.

THE INCREDIBLE MR. LIMPET

The jacket for the partially animated World War II comedy starring Don Knotts, *The Incredible Mr. Limpet*, is a joy. The movie, however, fails to sustain one's interest. Because of Knotts' presence, it is more visually stimulating before he turns into a fish. The picture is nice and the sound is fine.

THE INCREDIBLE STORYDISC

The story goes that there were a limited number of copies of *The Incredible Storydisc* pressed and that no more will ever be made. What may make the disc even rarer is the number of copies which are similar to the one we viewed. The endings on both sides skipped and would not play through, in effect, ending the disc prematurely. This obvious flaw aside, the disc looked and sounded excellent. It is a collection of well-known stories (including '20,000 Leagues Under the Sea,' 'The Snow Queen,' 'The Night before Christmas,' and five others) rendered in animation specifically designed for laser disc, or, at least, modified for CAV interactive use. It has been filmed at 30 frames a second, so there are no quivers during freeze frames (though precious little moves from one frame to the next). Stereo and dual channel sound are also utilized. On one cartoon, the left and right channels have been switched accidentally. Several of the cartoons are given dual channel sound to tell two tales with one set of drawings. The second tale is usually kind of flaky, but it is a nice touch.

Getting the most out of the CAV format, every cartoon has a still-step activity section at its end. The activities range from games involving drawings which have been 'hidden' on single frames of the cartoons to some limp riddles which seem to go on forever. The best idea offered is a detailed explanation on how kids can record their own dialogue for the cartoons on a cassette and then play what they have recorded through their stereo while the cartoon is running.

INDIANA JONES AND THE LAST CRUSADE
INDIANA JONES AND THE LAST CRUSADE (Letterboxed)

The letterboxed *Indiana Jones and the Last Crusade* has an aspect ratio of about 2.2:1. The picture is less saturated than the cropped version – the faces don't look as orange. Sometimes when a letterboxed version and a full monitor version are compared, the blown up image on the latter will look fuzzy, but that rarely happens on the cropped *Indiana Jones* disc.

The stereo surround soundtrack is the same on both discs. The dialog volume levels are not equal with the music and sound effects. The viewer has to concentrate a little harder to fully absorb a conversation, particularly when other noisy things are going on, and especially if one's audio system lacks the ability to manipulate surround volume levels.

Even though the basic transfer doesn't look as sharp, however, we enjoyed the scanned and cropped version of *Indiana Jones and the Last Crusade* more than we enjoyed the letterboxed version, and will likely turn to it when we feel like watching the movie again. The movie is wonderful fun – the boxoffice receipts can attest to that – and is clearly the creation of filmmakers who have far more imagination and cinematic instinct than most. But it also is a bit lazy in its construction. The film's perfect climax occurs at the end of side two on the discs – with Sean Connery quoting Charlemagne to Harrison Ford, and the third act is just an uninspired grind.

The opening credit sequence is both squeezed and cropped on the cropped disc and it truly looks ridiculous. From there on, however, there are only a handful of shots which are improved by the letterboxing, and many more which are improved by the magnification of the composition's center and the loss of its sides. Even in the rare instance where two characters are placed so far apart that one of them must be dropped, the film is sometimes improved. We mentioned an inherent softness in the presentation of the dialog. The conversation in which Jones describes his father as, "The one the students hope they don't get," is presented as a two shot on the letterboxed disc and with Harrison Ford talking into empty space on the cropped disc. The distraction of the other character on the letterboxed image, however, is just enough to spoil your concentration on the gag, while in the cropped version the focus is on Ford only, and it is easier to pay attention to what he is saying.

INDIANA JONES AND THE TEMPLE OF DOOM
INDIANA JONES AND THE TEMPLE OF DOOM (CAV)

Paramount, the first company to release a digitally encoded laser disc in America, was also the first domestic company to release a digitally encoded CAV feature film, *Indiana Jones and the Temple of Doom*, along with a CLV version. The CLV release was spread to three sides, but the CAV runs only one further. The break between side three and four on the CAV disc interrupts an action scene. The other two breaks occur at natural pauses.

Some scenes seem slightly sharper on the CAV disc, although most were impossible to differentiate. The quality of the sound is also indistinguishable between the two releases. There are no quiet passages and in all the softer dramatic moments, John Williams's score keeps playing and playing. The film's sound production is an elaborate effort which is well served by the digital encoding. When the raft falls into the river, waves are suddenly splashing everywhere around you. And when the arrows are shot across the gorge, they seem to travel through your living room to get there.

The utility of having the disc in CAV will probably be questionable to many. We prefer the format whenever we have a choice but, honestly, could not derive as much pleasure from the CAV functions on *Indiana Jones* as we can from other Standard Play discs.

The story is not a cynical manipulation as some would suggest, but rather a revelry in the adventure format. When the movie first came out there was some crazy talk about its being 'too violent.' Perhaps, on the first viewing, it is 'too exciting.' After that, it is too much fun to criticize. It wasn't until we'd watched the disc several times that we truly appreciated the last shot, where the boy, Short Round, puts his hands over his eyes before Jones and the heroine smooch.

INDIGO GIRLS LIVE AT THE UPTOWN LOUNGE

Two female folk singers from Athens, Georgia, who call themselves the Indigo Girls do an hour-long concert in their home town on *Indigo Girls Live at the Uptown Lounge*. The program, which also contains interview material spliced between some of the numbers, seems designed to sell the pair to a wider audience, and tends to homogenize their personalities and their appeal in the process. Their music, however, is super – raw, energetic, and heartening.

The picture in the source material is conceptually grainy and the disc maintains the image. The sound turns what is clearly a live recording into studio quality playback. Side two is in CAV with two unsteady still frames out of every five. Chapters are listed on the back of the jacket.

THE INFORMER

The black-and-white picture on *The Informer* looks old and sports both soft edges and speckles. Parts of the movie have the feel of a silent film, however, so unless one has seen a copy in better condition, which we have not, the presentation is adequate. The sound is best kept at a reasonable volume, but the accented dialog is always understandable.

Directed by John Ford, the story is about a man too dumb to take the money and run. The film is an excellent exploration of moral viewpoints and it is also reasonably entertaining, if you can tolerate the hero's excruciating stupidity. Victor McLaglen's basic character would later show up in minor roles in other Ford films. The essence of *The Informer*, then, is that a secondary character can never rise above his station, which is why his flaws and the movie's shortcomings are so closely entwined.

INGMAR BERGMAN'S THE MAGIC FLUTE

The sound systems in art houses are about as good as the worst radio you own, so the quality of the stereo on *Ingmar Bergman's The Magic Flute* is a real surprise. The disc is digitally encoded. The sound does not have the absolute perfection of the latest recordings, but it is clear, reasonably consistent, and absent of distortion. There is a level of background noise, some unintentional reverberation, and a handful of dropouts, but the recording is sure to please even the most stringent audio/video purists. Too much artistry is involved.

Mozart's eclectic opera never leaves the confines of the stage in Bergman's production, but, with editing, the world it depicts is limitless. There are reasons why nobody ever wrote a great opera in Swedish – any attempt would probably turn into a drawn-out dirge. Even Abba sings in English. Predictably, Bergman is turned on by the somber aspects of Mozart's fanciful masterpiece. Staging it in Swedish makes one long for the lightheartedness of the original German, if such a situation is possible.

Which is not to say that the movie is not positively wonderful and excellently suited for home video. Bergman's approach is intimate and caring. You can hear the patterns in the music and, despite their Scandinavian incarnation, the wordplay in the lyrics. The use of stage artifices are balanced properly so as to excuse the manner of the production without calling attention to it. The story, in which good turns out to be evil and evil turns out to be good but the pure at heart remain pure, is kept close at hand except for a couple of passages where Bergman acknowledges that Mozart could not restrain his compositional urges.

Since the 134-minute show was originally made for Swedish TV and since Bergman always seems to buy all of his film in Sweden, the picture is not as searing as on other discs. The chapter markers run a sensible 1 to 20, but are listed on the back of the jacket as 1 to 8, 1 to 7, and 1 to 5. Finding a favorite aria will involve some quick arithmetic.

INHERIT THE WIND

Spencer Tracy, Frederic March, and Gene Kelly star in *Inherit the Wind*. It is based on the Scopes 'monkey' trial, but filmed by people who still had the McCarthy era fresh in their heads. Tracy, as the Clarence Darrow character, has the easiest role and is thus the least interesting. March, except for his too well-shaven bald pate, is superb as the William Jennings Bryant character, bringing more sympathy to him than even the director seems to want to allow. Kelly, who was an awful actor outside of musical comedy, does a good turn as a cynical reporter and only falters at the very end, when he starts twisting his lip around, listening to Tracy lecture him.

The black-and-white print is never flawed enough to distract one from the proceedings. The sound is harsh, but that is from the film, not the disc.

The filmmakers miss the central ironic point of *Inherit the Wind* – that the jury returned the correct verdict. The man on trial had broken a law on the books of the state by teaching evolution in a public school. The higher courts decide if the law is just or not.

INNERSPACE

The director of *Innerspace*, Joe Dante, is a screen pack rat. The movie was too weird to be a hit, but that is what saves it from being a waste of time. The premise – a miniaturized one-man sub is injected into an unsuspecting nebbish – keeps the plot moving, but it isn't even the focus of most of the gags. The asides and the extraneous jokes (an extended bit involving an Italian cowboy, in particular) make an audience feel uncomfortable in a theater. They start wondering what they paid their money to see. But when the film is purchased and the intention is to view it a number of times, the viewer knows the entertainment is going to be a little queer.

The best component is Jerry Goldsmith's score, not only for the quality of the music, which is as studiously odd as the film itself, but for the way it has been laid down on the stereo soundtrack and transferred to the digitally encoded disc. None of the sound effects or dialog tracks escape the confines of the recording as smoothly as the music does. The picture is matted. The image has a few scattered inconsistencies, but most of the time the picture looks bright and sharp. The three-sided 120-minute disc is chapter encoded.

AN INNOCENT MAN

Peter Yates directed *An Innocent Man*, an effective prison film starring Tom Selleck. The disc has a decent-looking picture and uninteresting stereo surround sound (some of the crowded prison sounds are good). F. Murray Abraham gives a wonderful performance as a lifer who befriends Selleck, and Selleck himself is less wooden than normal.

INSIGNIFICANCE

Nicholas Roeg's *Insignificance* is adapted from a stage play based upon a spurious and embellished piece of gossip linking Marilyn Monroe with Albert Einstein. Enhanced visuals widen the material beyond the boundaries of the stage and make the film appropriate for home video. It is an idiosyncratic feature which will turn off more viewers than it will turn on, but the movie works better than it would seem to on paper, and manages to communicate its ideas without trivializing them. The most important concept presented, which uses the Jewish Einstein character as a focal point, is a comparison of the incendiary practices of the Nazis with the bombing of Hiroshima and Nagasaki. Most of the action takes place in a hotel suite. The characters talk about fame, love, relativity, and other concepts.

When the jazz score is not playing the sound is mildly hissy. The monaural sound has been CX-encoded. The picture is a little grainy. The side break comes at an awkward moment, but it would have been difficult to divide the 110-minute film anywhere else and still keep it to one platter.

Roeg has a frustrating film style which often seems to border on amateurism, despite the number of movies he has made. He is not afraid to take chances and he does not always win. The movie fails more often than it succeeds, but with home video, even the minor victories are significant.

INTERACTIVE CATALOG 1

50,000 historical photographs from the George Eastman House museum are contained on *Interactive Catalog 1*. The photographs were transferred directly from negatives to a video tape master and from the master to the disc. Any cropping or contrast enhancements which the photographer might have performed during the printing process has not been replicated, so in this sense the collection is somewhat raw. No more than a dozen of the stills quiver. The complete picture, edges and all, appears on the the screen, and so the size of the photo varies depending upon the proportions of the negative. Those which match the proportions of a TV screen look the best, but even the tall, narrow pictures which take up just a third of the screen have sufficient detail to be engrossing.

The works of Bassano, Matthew Brady, Anne Brigman, John C. Browne, Francis Bruguiere, Alvin Langdon Coburn, S. Fisher Corlies, Edwin Emerson, Ch. Chusseau Flaviens, Lejaren A. Hiller, Lewis Hine, Osa & Martin Johnson, Gertrude Kasebier, Nathan Lazarnick, William Mortensen, Nickolas Muray, Scott & Van Altena, Aaron Siskind, Josef Suded, Katherine Week Ward, and Edward Weston are represented, although it is difficult to tell where one ends and the next begins without the crib sheet which is provided with the disc (no information is provided on the subject matter of the photos). Within a specific photographer's collection, the photographs follow vague sequential patterns, but two prints depicting the same subject from the same angle are as likely to appear a 100 frames apart as they are to appear one after the other. The disc has been architected for interactive use, where certain stills are separated or combined to facilitate anticipated search patterns.

The random subject matter of the photographs take on a narrative resonance which could only be accomplished through the scope of the project. The disc begins with depictions of Italian military men of leisure at a camp or fort of some sort during the turn of the century. There is then a shift to views of several European cities in the same era. Views of the European countryside follow, as do photos of Egypt, Africa, the Far East, and America. The majority of the disc is pre-World War I, although there is an excellent examination of the construction of the Empire State Building and a portrait gallery of movie stars from the late thirties and early forties. Other memorable sequences include the aftermath of a flood, a Victorian-era visit to the Sphinx, life in a pre-technological Dutch countryside, paperboys in Washington DC, still lifes of shoes, a 1912 road rally across a good portion of America, scenes of New York in winter which have often been anthologized in other collections, more than 400 'Valentines' with superimposed moons illuminating amorous couples intended for use as lantern slides to promote romantic sheet music, and some intriguingly chaste photos of nudes. The disc ends with a rousing and extensive African safari (nearly 8,000 frames) run by Osa and Martin Johnson, a fascinating and spunky couple who seem treat the jungle as if it were a large backyard on their estate (see *National Geographic – Cameramen Who Dared*).

Almost every photograph has something going for it, and the quality becomes numbing if too many are observed in a single sitting. Our favorite photograph was of two thoroughly dressed Victorian ladies hanging from cables which comprise a crude, Indiana Jones-type thrill ride at a carnival of some sort (frame 3920). Another picture which gave us pleasure was of an old-fashioned train engineer, replete with hat, gloves and bushy mustache, hanging his head out of the side of his cabin to see what is ahead (frame 14144).

INTERMEZZO
JUNE NIGHT
SWEDENHIELMS

Three black-and-white films that Ingrid Bergman made in Sweden in the late thirties, including the one which brought her to the attention of American film producers, have been released separately on laser discs from Lumivision. The packaging is nice, with the design of the disc jackets looking somewhat similar, but each having a distinctly different color scheme.

The films, *Intermezzo*, *June Night*, and *Swedenhielms* each run under 90 minutes, and all three discs are in CAV on side two, though movement is consistently blurry on the still frames. The black and white picture transfers are generally quite good (*Swedenhielms* is a little more worn down than the other two). There is an errant splice here and there, but vivid contrasts and sharply focussed images are the rule. The digitally encoded sound is a bit more troublesome, but that can be gotten around. The films have been given reprocessed stereo soundtracks which we found to be considerably annoying – especially when run through a monaural TV speaker. Even when a stereo amplifier is used, the 'twang' is distracting. We solved the problem, however, by suppressing one of the audio channels – it doesn't matter which one. When manipulated thus, the artificial stereo disappears, but the sound remains strong and confident (there is a brief sound dropout on the digital track near the end of *Swedenhielms*). The films are in Swedish and have white English subtitles which are backed by shading in white areas, making them legible at all times. The discs are also chapter encoded, and listings appear on the back of the jackets.

The American *Intermezzo* took the best parts of the Swedish and then improved on the rest – even Bergman's phony piano playing is much better in the second film. Though 20 minutes longer, the Swedish version is not as slick or as good as the American version. Bergman, however, looks much younger and the two discs are worth comparing simply for the opportunity of watching her blossom. The plot is nearly the same, as are some of the sets and outfits. It is easy to see why the film catapulted her to America, because her presence is so strong that the movie is energized when she's in a scene and flaccid when she is not (except for the ending, which is an obvious but effective heartstring-puller and the only sequence in which the remake, by trying to be too elegant, is inferior to the original).

June Night was made a couple of years later, when Bergman had achieved a screen personality that she would maintain in most of her films, a cross between a fallen woman and your big sister. She portrays a single girl with a scandal in her past who moves to the city and whose presence upsets the romances of her new friends. The script is all build-up, so that what in most films would be introductory scenes are in *June Night* the core of the film. The story also ends just as it starts to get interesting.

Swedenhielms, made in 1935, is *very* Swedish. It is a domestic comedy which does not translate well to another culture. The narrative in *June Night* has some legitimate appeal, but beyond the presence of Bergman in a supporting role, *Swedenhielms* is awful. It is about a spoiled family which has gone into debt and must count upon the father's winning of the Nobel Prize to stave off financial and social ruin. Not only are the presumptions of the plot fairly silly, but the story isn't told well. Bergman portrays the fiancée of one of the characters.

INTERMEZZO

As is implied by the title, *Intermezzo* is a brief work. The film runs 70 minutes, but the disc remains in CLV. The print is ragged at the reel change points but fairly solid during the interims.

The sound has not been CX-encoded which is ridiculous when the subject is so musically oriented. Even though the recording is old, it comes through clearly, like a 78. The sound recording is also responsible for the movie's most embarrassing moment: Ingrid Bergman and Leslie Howard have their backs to the camera as they speak sadly of deserting one another. Their images, however, are reflected in a store window and their lips move without synchronization to the dialog even though the plot mentions nothing about them being ventriloquists as well as musicians.

INTERNAL AFFAIRS

Richard Gere plays a bad guy in *Internal Affairs* and, no offense, the role appears well suited to his true personality. At first, the casting seems curious, as if Andy Garcia, who is a better actor and plays the hero, should have been given the more challenging part, but, as the coldness and venality of the villain are revealed, Gere gorges himself on every evil nuance and Garcia can barely keep up. The film, about the investigation of a bad cop in L.A., is pleasing while it is underway. The disc has a satisfactory picture transfer and an excellent surround soundtrack. The viewer, held by the conflict between the two characters and mesmerized by the disc's production values, will likely be enchanted by the presentation. After the show is over, however, the spell breaks. An awareness of the film's condescending attitude toward women, its unlikely depiction of police procedures, the poor staging of the few action scenes, and the basic lack of enough narrative substance to justify a two-hour film supersedes memories of the film's ability to entertain.

INTERNATIONAL HOUSE

Any disc which contains footage of George Burns and Gracie Allen is a precious commodity, but their presence is the only redeeming aspect to the otherwise forgettable International House. The film featured a number of stars, including W.C. Fields and Bela Lugosi, searching for humor where none is to be found (though Fields does have one good gag, using an opium pipe to smoke a cigar). Rudy Vallee and Cab Calloway have film-within-film musical numbers. The print is in remarkably good condition for an unimportant 1933 film and side two is in jiggle-free CAV. The movie's trailer, which makes it look more exciting than it is, has been included, although it is not marked by an automatic stop. Five chapters are also encoded, primarily to mark the musical numbers, such as they are, and the producers did not have the imagination to include the famous earthquake clip.

THE INTERNS
An early sixties soaper about rookie surgeons at a city hospital, *The Interns* is a mindless mix of characters and overly plotted situations. There is a birth sequence in which the dialog is so juvenile that it comes as a shock when they incongruously pull a real newborn baby out for the camera. The film's principal asset is its cast – Nick Adams, Telly Savalas with hair, Buddy Ebsen, Stephanie Powers, Cliff Robertson and others live up to the single-minded nature of the characters they are inhabiting. It is good fun watching them mash their lines. The picture is in black and white, and has no significant flaws. The sound has a lower-than-average volume level, but no problems which cannot be adjusted.

INTO THE FIRE
Although the film stock looks inexpensive and the lighting insufficient, the picture transfer of *Into the Fire* is very good, and several scenes are especially haunting. The sound is fine, although there is a flutter in the closing song. The script is clever and sexy. It concerns a murder plot and has a satisfying number of twists and betrayals. There are also some ghostly nightmares which have nothing to do with the story, but add significantly to a late-night viewer's nervousness.

INTO THE HOMELAND
An ex-undercover cop searching for his missing daughter infiltrates a white supremacy organization in *Into the Homeland.* The movie, which stars Powers Booth and C. Thomas Howell, runs a full two hours (though it makes it onto a single platter). It is clear the screenwriters did some research on their subject, but the bad guys just don't seem real. Perhaps the actors couldn't believe the dialog enough to deliver it convincingly. The story maintains an easy balance between social revelations and the drama at hand, but neither aspect is as focused as it ought to be. The picture quality on side one is good, but side two deteriorates a little. The jacket cover says that the film is in stereo, but it didn't seem that way to us, although the digitally encoded sound is otherwise acceptable.

INTO THIN AIR
Ron Howard was one of the executive producers on *Into Thin Air*, so his accomplishments are unduly splashed across the jacket cover. The movie is actually a Canadian effort with twinges of realism, about a boy who disappears while driving to college. The first half turned us off, because the last contact the family has with the boy is a collect phone call, and nobody bothers to trace the number after he disappears. Robert Prosky shows up on side two, however, as a private detective, and he picks up the whole film, especially when the detective and his wife decide to combine a Thanksgiving holiday with business.

The monaural sound is of average quality. The picture transfer is satisfactory, but the film's visual concepts are pedestrian. A red-tagged trailer for *Frankenstein General Hospital* appears after the film is ended.

INVADERS FROM MARS
The thinnest of black borders graces the top and bottom of the screen throughout *Invaders from Mars*. Ignoring the pasted-on twists at the end of the show, the story is *Invasion of the Body Snatchers* with a happy ending and a few more fireworks. The irony here is that the little boy's parents, before they lose their souls to the Martians, are too perfect. Mom burns the bacon and Dad drools coffee on his chin only after they become possessed.

The only severe problem with the movie is that the director, Tobe Hooper, has filmed almost every exciting moment from the wrong angle, so that you find out what would have caused you to gasp only after a skirmish is finished.

None of the red or orange lights which illuminate the alien craft cause a problem. The CX-encoded stereo has a few cute sound effects and a pretty musical score.

INVASION EARTH
Avoid *Invasion Earth*. The program mixes clips from old science fiction films with a fictional narrative link which has the feel of a midnight horror film intro on a local independent television station in a small city. It is nonsensical until the last ten minutes and quite tedious throughout. The transfer looks fine and the digital monaural sound is okay, but despite claims to the contrary on the jacket cover and label, side two, which is less than a half hour in length, is in CLV. No matter, because you won't want to watch it after suffering through side one.

INVASION OF THE BODY SNATCHERS
INVASION OF THE BODY SNATCHERS
(CAV)

Use of the freeze frame will be the most popular CAV application on Voyager's presentation of the 1956 *Invasion of the Body Snatchers*. The print is so crisp that you can't increase the clarity by running it at three times normal speed. But stopping the picture at regular intervals to savor the screen compositions of director Don Siegel and cinematographer Ellsworth Fredericks is a pleasure. No matter which frame you choose, it looks more like a photograph than part of a moving picture.

The image on the CAV disc is faintly sharper than the image on the CLV disc. The picture is presented in widescreen format with an aspect ratio of about 2:1. The movie was originally an exploitation feature and was filmed to accommodate both widescreen and standard projection. The sound on the CAV disc is analog only and has not been CX-encoded. The sound on the CLV disc is in digital and the analog track is CX-encoded. On both discs, the sound quality is credible and presents no significant problems.

The CAV disc carries the 80-minute feature on three sides. After the film's conclusion, the theatrical trailer, a printed interview with Siegel, and a widescreen/cropped screen demo round out side three. There are plenty of chapter markers encoded on the disc and the inside of the jacket cover contains amusing samples of the film's display advertising. The CLV disc has no special features.

A 'Professor of Film Studies,' Maurice Yacowar, gives a full-length talk on the alternate audio track of the CAV disc. It is heavier on interpretation than on production gossip, but the mere fact that the film's soundtrack is suppressed while Yacowar is speaking causes one to notice things in the picture which one would likely miss if one were concentrating on the story. Yacowar does try to draw a lame allusion to McCarthy's character's name, 'Bennell,' suggesting it be read as 'banal.' Later on, he points to Bennell's telephone exchange (!), 'Madison,' and suggests that it is utilized to hint that Bennell is 'mad.' We have an even lamer suggestion: McCarthy is employed in the film to represent his namesake in the Senate (of whom there is much discussion concerning the paranoid atmosphere the film evokes and what it is meant to represent) and Madison is tossed in as an allusion to said namesake's home town.

INVASION U.S.A.
Chuck Norris helped write the screenplay for *Invasion U.S.A.* and the plot – something about organized terrorists in Florida who cause so much trouble that people have to sneak to church – is vacant of sensibility, like Norris's acting.

The sound is both bad and wonderful, capturing with perfection the awful, flat diction of the actors and actresses who are even worse than Norris (an actor playing an Hispanic recites his Spanish phonetically, a woman playing a reporter waits a full breath every time someone speaks to her before she remembers the line she's supposed to reply). The picture is okay.

THE INVISIBLE KID
The first trick the invisible kid plays on his friend in *The Invisible Kid* is to lift the top bun on the friend's hamburger up and down and say, "Oh please sir, don't eat me!" It's all downhill from there. The plot machinations are elaborate, but the utilization of the invisibility gag generally is not, and the movie is only sporadically funny. The picture is grainy and the Ultra Stereo sound is weak. There is a gag after the end credits are finished, using a blooper take.

THE INVISIBLE MAN
A collection of 63 promotional photos are included on side two of *The Invisible Man*. The still photos primarily depict scenes from the movie, with few behind-the-scenes or candid shots, although there is a nice portrait photo of the young Claude Rains. It is a shame they couldn't also have thrown together a quick and dirty essay on how the special effects were accomplished, but the disc is an admirable production and a worthy addition to one's library. Side one is in CLV, side two is in CAV.

The black-and-white print is in good condition. The contrasts and shadings are often distinctive, and there are no more than a few blemishes on the negative. The sound is enhanced considerably with digital encoding, which seems to take ten years off the age of the picture.

For those who have not seen the film recently, the story is essentially constructed around the efforts of the police to capture the title character, who has become criminally psychotic as a side effect from the drugs he has taken to turn transparent. The movie is only 71 minutes long, and since it concentrates on the chase, the narrative does not feel as antiquated as other thirties horror films. The film's subtext, which is inevitably sublimated by the many other distractions, concerns the Invisible Man's various states of undress. When he cannot be seen, he is naked, and consciously or subconsciously, the viewer is left to fill in the blanks.

INVITATION TO A LITTLE "ORGEL MUSEUM" (Import)
For those who are searching for innovative applications of digital sound, we would recommend a Japanese disc which has an odd English title, *Invitation to a Little "Orgel Museum."*

The one-sided 50-minute digitally encoded disc is about music boxes. The soundtrack contains close to 40 music box tunes while the picture shows various music boxes and mechanical toys in operation. A substantial selection of outdoor Alpine footage is also included.

Both the picture and the sound are near perfection. Some of the music boxes tend toward cacophony, but for the ones which perform their function with clarity, every 'twing' floats above the listener's head with silky precision. The music ranges from Beethoven to Scott Joplin. It is appropriate that the boxes should be preserved on laser disc for in the age of the microchip these delicately crafted treasures seem as natural as wooden totems or earthen vases. One wonders how long it will be before today's hi-tech becomes tomorrow's museum exhibition.

INXS – IN SEARCH OF EXCELLENCE
An excess of interview material upsets the Polygram release, *INXS – In Search of Excellence.* Not only is there talking between each number, but the songs themselves are sometimes interrupted for chatter. Worse still, it isn't just the artists who speak. Everybody up to the prime minister of Australia chimes in to say what a great group INXS is. The songs, when played in full, are okay, but you have to sort through the disc to get to them. The program lasts a little over an hour and is not chapter encoded. The stereo sound is fine, as is the image.

IREZUMI (SPIRIT OF TATTOO)
The sound is out of synch during much of *Irezumi (Spirit of Tattoo).* As one's eyes are usually drawn to the English subtitles (the film is in Japanese), it is not always noticeable, but it can still be disorienting to a viewer's concentration. The monaural sound is otherwise passable. The picture has some mild inconsistencies – speckles, a flutter at one point, mildly pale colors, mild cropping – but these problems are less inhibiting.

The film is an austere concoction about a master tattooist, his apprentice, and a young woman whose lover has demanded that her back be decorated. Thus, the movie is about sexism, about craftsmanship, and about the oddball pleasures which are mixed into pain. It is also an exploration of cultural eroticism, and will therefore be very stimulating for some viewers and mystifyingly innocuous to others.

IRON EAGLE
After *Top Gun, Iron Eagle* looks like a puppet show. You can almost see the wires hanging from the models, and when the planes explode, they appear to do so from a stationary position. The cockpit displays look positively antique as well, but *Iron Eagle* does have one thing *Top Gun* lacked. A plot.

The story tells of a boy living on an Air Force Base and how he and his friends save his father, a pilot, who has been shot down in an unfriendly Mideast nation. The tale is far-fetched, but engaging.

The picture has a pinkish tint, but is in good condition. The sound is analog stereo. When the boy pushes his jet past Mach 1, the sonic boom is supposed to be the movie's crescendo. It's flat, and not even worth showing off to your friends.

IRON EAGLE II
Iron Eagle preceded *Top Gun,* but *Iron Eagle II* owes more to the latter than the former. The effects still look cheap, and the sound is Ultra-Stereo, but Iron Eagle II constantly imitates the style and thrust of *Top Gun.* The producers even hired a Tom Cruise look-alike, Mark Humphrey, to wear sunglasses and provide empty-headed grins. The moviemakers were smart enough to carry over only the Lou Gossett, Jr. character from the first film. In the sequel, a group of American military rejects are teamed with a group of Russian military rejects on a mission to blast away some Muslims. Higher powers want the mission to fail. Instead, the team buries their differences and rises to the occasion.

In coordination with the awkward-looking jacket cover, the picture is a bit grainy and the fleshtones are much too pink. The surround sound, however, is great fun.

IRON MAIDEN VIDEO PIECES
The 8-inch *Iron Maiden Video Pieces* utilizes portions of one's sound system normally left dormant. The first cut and the last cut are redeemed by the inclusion of extensive silent film footage. The middle cut, 'Flight of Icarus,' centers around a mysterious figure standing on a cliff, the figure's face obscured by a cave-like hood. To try and tell these folks that the legend of Icarus has nothing to do with Trolls or Middle Earth seems pointless. Hey, it all took place before 1960, right?

THE IRON TRIANGLE
An opening title card says that many of the plot details in *The Iron Triangle* were taken from the diary of a VC soldier. The film is evenly balanced, not in terms of ideology, but in depicting the strategies and internal troubles on both sides. Beau Bridges portrays an American officer who is briefly a prisoner of the VC soldier (Liem Whately). They do not become bosom buddies as was suggested in some of the film's advertising teasers, but they meet long enough to respect each other's honor. The picture and sound are in very good condition.

IRONWEED
The digitally encoded stereo sound on *Ironweed* is good. The sound effects are clear and full blooded. The music bumps into a ceiling in the higher ranges, but that is hardly noticeable. The analog stereo track, however, is weaker and sounds tinny. The channels, which are correct on the digital track, are reversed on the analog, making the presentation even more confusing. The picture is decrepit in places, much too grainy and sometimes too light. Some of the cinematography in the film is accomplished, but the disc is never pleasing to the eye. The first manufacturing run of the title was notoriously inept so beware if you obtain a copy which has been sitting around for a while.

At least this could not have happened to a more deserving movie. *Ironweed* is tortuous to watch, a marathon of unappealing characters talking, drinking, throwing up and dying. Believe it or not, the film is a comedy, but only in the most abstract sense, since it is not the slightest bit funny.

ISHTAR
When movies cost exorbitant amounts of money to make and do not, subsequently, make exaggerated returns on the investment, the merits of the movies themselves are often called into question. This is unfair to potential viewers, who will inevitably approach such films with the specter of failure looming in the pleasure centers of their brains. We approach such films differently. They are rare, since film studios are not conned more than once or twice a management team into spending $40 million on a single project. *Ishtar* may be an ugly little conglomeration of sand and digestive juices, but it is also a pearl.

From a stockholder's point of view, it is immediately obvious that the production should never have been okayed. But we're not stockholders. We own laser discs, and we are more than happy to add *Ishtar* to our collection. It is not worth $40 million, but it is worth the price of a disc.

Contrary to the essential word of mouth which has been spread about the picture, it is not another Dolly Parton and Sylvester Stallone musical. True, Warren Beatty and Dustin Hoffman sing awfully, but that is just a framing device to get them onto the desert and into trouble. The movie is not riotous. You laugh at the gags after they've passed, rather than in anticipation of punchlines. The humor is everywhere, both foreground and background, left and right, text and subtext. That is why the disc is a strong choice; the repeated viewing potential is compelling. People are not going to go running back the theater to pick up jokes they missed the first time through about men's sewing abilities ("Look at this thread, it's all sloppy and crooked. Shirra's brother must have sewed it in!"), but there is a strong desire to replay the disc, to discover new jokes and savor the ones you know. It is like a treasure hunt in a garden. You don't have to find what you're looking for to achieve peace of mind.

Forty million dollars for a movie and they can't CX-encode the disc. Oh well, at least they used modern recording equipment to make the monaural film. So long as you don't pump the volume too much, it is all right. The picture is no shimmering star in the jeweled sky either. The print has some marks on it in places, and the colors blur together in the shade. One may as well acquire the disc, however, since the stature of the film is inevitably going to rise. It can't, after all, sink much lower.

ISLAND
A silly, violent concoction about contemporary Caribbean buccaneers, *Island* is best suited for home video since ideal viewing conditions call for a large and relaxed gathering of inebriated revellers with strong stomachs. The digital track has more hiss than the analog tack, but it also has stronger, clearer

sounds. There are some nice moments as far as the soundtrack goes – a thunderstorm which doesn't drown out the sound of individual raindrops, an Ennio Morricone score where one can hear every contributing instrument as a distinctive sound component, and Michael Caine's mad, deafening slaughter of all the pirates aboard a Coast Guard cutter.

The picture is not grainy, we'll give it that much. It is not letterboxed, which is probably just as well since being stuck with half a screen means half the violence has been left out. The print is in good shape, but it does not sparkle.

MCA has included the original, desperate, theatrical trailer, and, like all bad movies with big budgets, it is fascinating, as the salesmanship repeatedly verges on flagrant mis-truth to sell the film's charms. Whoever pasted it together even tacked the only two explosions in the movie right next to each other, providing a double crescendo for the trailer's finale. It fooled no one.

ISLAND BREEZE

Windsurfing in the curl of a wave is like wearing a belt and suspenders, but when the surfer suddenly cuts back across the top of the wave and does an aerial loop, it is a wonder that he can keep his bathing suit on. This move and others are captured in CAV on *Island Breeze*. The two-sided disc, which carries the subheading, 'Robby Nash's Windsurfing Fantasy,' is a thorough pictorial of windsurfing on the beaches of Maui. A light jazz score accompanies most of the program, although sometimes the music stops and the microphone leaps onto the board to go along for the ride. One side two, Nash discusses windsurfing techniques in a superficial manner and demonstrates the basic tacks and jibes. The picture is sparkling clear. The sound is so realistic that you may find some seaweed on your carpet the morning after you play the disc.

THE ISLAND OF DR. MOREAU (Import)

The movie which started American International Pictures on the quick slide to oblivion, *The Island of Dr. Moreau*, is available on disc in Japan. The picture looks clear and you don't notice the subtitles at all. The sound is a flat monaural. AIP had been making money-producing cheap movies for two decades when the company changed its policy and embarked on an investment in big-budget features. The first was *Moreau*, the second was 'Meteor,' and that was the last anyone heard of AIP.

The story, an H.G. Wells tale, has philosophy and fantasy and had been made into a moderately entertaining movie once before. But this version simply doesn't work. The makeup isn't inspiring and there is no sense of discovery or horror as Dr. Moreau's experiments are revealed. The stars, Burt Lancaster and Michael York, would have been more effective had they exchanged roles.

IT CAME FROM BENEATH THE SEA

You can't really ask for more from monster movies than a quick rhythm and bad acting. In *It Came from Beneath the Sea* a five-legged octopus the size of a half-dozen cable cars attacks San Francisco. Kenneth Tobey portrays a randy naval commander who starts pawing a marine biologist (Faith Domergue from *This Island Earth*) as if he had five hands himself. Perhaps part of the film's continuing appeal is its unintentionally satirical look at America's attitude toward the military, scientists, technology, atomic power, and San Francisco during the 1950s. The disc, which has not been CX-encoded, has a '50s-era soundtrack, but it works well on a good sound system and you can hear things which would not be discernible on a TV broadcast. The black and white print is lovely, but some copies have a skip at minute 25 on side two.

IT SHOULD HAPPEN TO YOU

The black-and-white source material for *It Should Happen to You* is spotless, and the delineations of greys and blacks are carefully detailed. The digitally encoded monaural sound is also acceptable. The movie, which stars Judy Holliday, a very young Jack Lemmon, and Peter Lawford, is beloved by many. It is about a young woman whose fortunes change when she rents a large billboard with the last of her savings. We find that the script gets a little too preachy in the third act, but the performances are endearing and the movie is undeniably memorable. It was directed by George Cukor.

IT'S A GIFT

The 68-minute W.C. Fields movie, *It's a Gift*, is in nice condition, with some sequences looking very clear and none looking old or worn. The sound is consistently stable.

A few of Fields' juggling and sleight-of-hand gags are amusing, but most of the comedy in the movie comes from the supporting characters, such as a blind man with a destructive cane, the usual array of bratty kids, and a homely dog. The editing is particularly bad, cutting off dialog and awkwardly retaining the same camera angles to give the impression that the print has been massively spliced. The story has Fields moving his family from New Jersey to California, but the production is so inept it is obvious they never left California to begin with. Side two is in CAV, with two unsteady still frames out of every five.

IT'S A WONDERFUL LIFE (Republic)
IT'S A WONDERFUL LIFE (Voyager)
FRANK CAPRA'S "IT'S A WONDERFUL LIFE" (LVA)

It's a Wonderful Life is the only movie we can think of where evil is negated instead of defeated. It teaches a lesson which is so important and yet so often overlooked, that the best way to be rid an enemy is to discount the enemy's potency. The other lesson which the film teaches, put in simplistic terms, is the value of friendship. The joy which is shared at the movie's conclusion easily escapes the confines of a screen to embrace every viewer. *It's a Wonderful Life* has created its own community, and across the years, as people have seen it and felt it, life itself has become a bit more special.

The film is in the public domain, so anyone with access to a copy can release a disc. 3M issued a colorized version which we haven't the heart to see. Of the three black-and-white versions available, the best looking presentation is clearly the Republic release. Details which are lost in the dark on the Voyager and LVA discs are clearly visible on the Republic disc. To cite just one example, the close up of Jimmy Stewart at the end of the scene in which his character returns to his mother's house and she does not recognize him, has a powerful emotional impact on the Republic disc because you can see the tension and pain in his face. On Voyager's version, the right side of his face (screen left) is nearly erased by shadows, and the shot and the sequence seem less significant as a result.

Voyager's transfer is slightly sharper and superior to LVA's, though both presentations are workable. On all three discs the sound tends to be a bit indistinct and laden with background noise.

Republic's disc opens with a trailer, but has no chapter markers. Side three runs less than thirty minutes but is in CLV.

Voyager's Criterion Collection version is in CAV entirely, and has special features, filling six sides on three discs. It comes in a white box with red trim. There is also a lecture on the second audio track by Jeanine Basinger. Basinger has useful insights to share. Near the beginning, for example, she breaks down the dynamics of the dinner table scene between George and his father to provide the viewer with a real understanding of the skills utilized by the director, Frank Capra. She reveals the way Capra prevents the scene from being boring and how he conveys more information to his audience than is contained in the dialog. The CAV functions can be used to supplement her talk.

After the 130-minute movie is ended, on side 5, there are still-frame essays concerning the film's production and Capra's artistry, as well as a collection of advertising art and publicity photos (a trailer for an early theatrical rerelease is also included). Between the lecture and the essays, the disc provides an excellent basis for studying the picture. Obviously, you don't need any of it to appreciate the movie, but anyone who has been touched by *It's a Wonderful Life* is inevitably going to be curious about the film's power and magic. Capra himself is featured on side six, in a 1981 seminar appearance. He talks for a half-hour about working at Columbia Pictures and about the importance of character in film.

LVA has also provided a theatrical trailer and an interview with Capra. The trailer is the same re-release promotion which Criterion used. The first part of the interview is audio-only, and runs on the second audio track while the end of the film is playing. Capra discusses the various performers and technicians, how they came to be hired, and how they contributed to the production. When the fifteen-minute talk is finished, the second audio track reverts to the film's soundtrack for the conclusion of the movie. After the film, there is another fifteen-minute interview with Capra, who sits in a lawn chair in a back yard and reminisces on how the story was formulated and how the film was made. He attributes *Life*'s initial box office problems to the recession that followed World War II, noting that the whole film industry went through a slump then. It is insight like that which is lacking when one listens to second-hand lectures on the history of a film.

IT'S ALWAYS FAIR WEATHER

MGM/UA's Deluxe Letter-Box Edition release of *It's Always Fair Weather* is something of an acquired taste. The picture transfer has some mild inconsistencies – a paleness here and there, and an off-center framing in several sequences – but on the whole it looks sharp and gains much from the letterboxing. The same with the sound, which has only a few memorable surround effects and definitely reflects its age (1956), but it is stereophonic enough to keep one's toes tapping. The letterboxing, which has an aspect ratio of about 2.2:1, is vital to the choreography and the comedy. There are some wonderful dance sequences – including Gene Kelly's balletic roller-skating solo which seems cramped with the image cropped – and some intriguing split screen effects. It is the split screen sequences which are affected the most by the image's off-center look.

Although the story has a happy ending, it also has a strong sense of bitterness. The narrative concerns three army buddies who reunite after ten years, and their optimism at the conclusion of the film cannot erase the sense of waste and despair which has dogged them up to that point. It creates an odd mood, because the script and the song lyrics were written by Betty Comden and Adolf Green, who can always be counted upon to produce elaborately witty and topically humorous material. It may just be that in this case, their writing was so good that the negative emotions leave as lasting a mark upon the viewer as the positive emotions do.

IT'S HOWDY DOODY TIME: A 40-YEAR CELEBRATION

We have only vague, toddler-enshrouded memories of the original 'Howdy Doody Show,' but if the episodes were anywhere near as excruciating as *It's Howdy Doody Time: A 40-Year Celebration* then we finally understand why our parents speak so ill of the program. We must have driven them crazy insisting that it remain on during dinner.

The disc, which runs 110 minutes and seems three times as long, is a 40th anniversary special which was filmed in 1987. It is in color, from a videotape source, but the edges are consistently soft. The digitally encoded sound has stereo effects, generally marking applause which is supposedly coming from the clearly restless studio audience.

The special does contain a scattered collection of old black and white clips (extra are added for the video presentation, including a couple of bloopers which are practically the program's only tolerable moments), but the show is primarily an excuse for Buffalo Bob and his geriatric supporting players to run through their vaudeville routines again. The format could provide intriguing fodder for analysis of the show's subliminal and formative consumer messages, particularly since the program encouraged youngsters to emulate a puppet. The main prop in most of the gags is a seltzer bottle, and in real life a seltzer bottle is used for only one thing, to enhance alcoholic beverages. You need a few anyway to deal with the program, which also has an endless number of song interludes.

IT'S NOT EASY BEING ME

Both aspiring and aspirating comics appear on *It's Not Easy Being Me*, an hour-long summary of live performances at Dangerfield's cabaret in New York. The disc lacks chapter markers, an unfortunate error since one will wish to pass by some of the comics as quickly as possible. Dangerfield appears between each act in skits with a pre-famous Roseanne Barr, and there is enough of them to be enjoyable. One of the featured players is Robert Townsend and his set, too, is engaging, but a couple of the other entertainers just aren't funny and why the people in the audience are laughing at them is a mystery for social scientists of the future to ponder with amazement. The picture quality is quite good although there are only two or three camera setups. The digitally encoded sound, nominally in stereo, is also bright and clear.

IVAN THE TERRIBLE PART 1
IVAN THE TERRIBLE PART II

Although it is conceivable that a collector would obtain one of Sergei Eisenstein's magnificent final films, *Ivan the Terrible Part I* and *Ivan the Terrible Part II*, and not the other, it is unlikely. Both are legitimate classics of world cinema and both are entertaining.

The problems which we ticked off concerning *Alexander Nevsky* were eradicated by the time Eisenstein tackled *Ivan*. The sound is integrated, yet in no way diminishes the impact of the visual composition. Sergei Prokofiev's score is less flippant and more in harmony with the film's emotional impact. And the acting, although still melodramatic, is better integrated with the drama. The emotions of the characters are believable, or, in the case of the actor portraying a man who realizes he made the right decision in the nick of time, priceless.

Eisenstein planned and storyboarded the films for several years before going into production. The image compositions have a binding force, locking a viewer's gaze to the screen. It is disruptive even to read the sometimes illegible white subtitles, because isolating part of the screen takes away from its overall impact.

Part I is a patriotic portrayal of the consolidation efforts by the ruler who first united Russia. It is straightforward and upbeat, as Ivan directs battle efforts and begins cleansing his court of aristocrats. The disc runs 99 minutes and has no chapter markers. The picture transfer looks fine for a war-era non-American black-and-white film. The sound has less hiss on the digital channel than on the analog channel, but distortion is still ever-present, because of conditions during the original recording. Most viewers will expect this.

Part II was the inspiration for Francis Coppola's *Godfather Part II*, not only in title, but in the use of a sequel to present scenes from earlier as well as later events, and as an opportunity to explore established characters (it is clear from the structure of the film that, as is explained in the informative essays on the backs of the two jacket covers, a Part III was intended, though it never came to light). The patriotism subsides in *Part II*, replaced by the paranoia of maintaining a power base (needless to say, Stalin was not as happy with it as he was with *Part I*). Both the picture and the sound are in passable condition.

The disc runs less than 90 minutes and the second side is CAV. The film is in black and white, but has an extended (and well-preserved) color sequence which begins, perfectly, at the start of side two. Image has chosen, however, to let two out of every five frames flicker. Nevertheless, the presence of the CAV is still advantageous, since manipulating Eisenstein's imagery at unnatural speeds increases one's awareness of the supremacy of Eisenstein's talent.

I'VE HEARD THE MERMAIDS SINGING

The sound recording in *I've Heard the Mermaids Singing* is inadequate, making some of the dialog difficult to understand. Made in Toronto on a small budget, the movie is innovative in its mixture of film and videotape footage, but retains a low budget appearance. The picture is also a little blurry. The music soundtrack is stereophonic and the disc is analog with CX-encoding.

Mermaids is a charming contrivance about a young woman working as a receptionist in an art gallery. The star, Sheila McCarthy, has a unique face and personality which would make her a prime contender for a supporting role in almost any network television series. Including dream sequences, the CLV disc runs less than 90 minutes. The ending ties together the few loose ends the plot manages to generate. Viewers not put off by the obviousness of the film's intentions should find the disc quaint and entertaining.

J. EDGAR HOOVER

Treat Williams portrays *J. Edgar Hoover* from the start to the end of his career. The program relies primarily on documented incidents or best-guess speculations to summarize Hoover's accomplishments. It is almost like a stage production, encapsulating Hoover's life as a series of meetings with the weak and the powerful. Some material is presented which could lead to a psychoanalytic study of why Hoover saw communists lurking behind every unfamiliar tree, but the movie spans too long a time period to work up any interesting drama and is too bent upon accuracy to be entertaining. Williams makes the effort to become Hoover, but his makeup is often distracting and he never loosens up.

The picture is functional, but the colors are a bit dour and white speckles appear from time to time. The sound has a few stereo effects but is also a bit on the fuzzy side.

J. GEILS BAND

The 8-inch *J. Geils Band* contains one video which was featured on the 12-inch *Picture Music*, 'Freeze Frame.' The second cut, 'Angel in Blue,' ought to be a quiet ballad, but the screen is just as busy as in 'Freeze Frame' and the subject matter, Marilyn Monroe, seems far removed from the lyrics. The lyrics and the visuals of 'Centerfold' do match, but the display of rock stars drooling over scantily clad females is something most 8-inch discs have managed to avoid.

J.S. BACH – SIX BRANDENBURG CONCERTOS

If you are thinking of obtaining just one of the non-dramatic classical music programs, we strongly recommend *J.S. Bach – Six Brandenburg Concertos*. If you have already picked up several of the other titles, then there is even less cause to hesitate in adding this one to your collection. The picture is terrific, the sound is fantastic, and the music is sublime.

The concertos, performed by Concentus musicus Wien and conducted by Nikolaus Harnoncourt, were recorded in the main chamber of a private library in Vienna. The group uses original instruments and the combination of the delicate acoustics in the chamber and the digitally encoded sound captures every nuance in each one. The dozen or so musicians are positioned geometrically about the room and their distance from one another can also be felt in the soundtrack. When two women playing treble recorders are sent up to a balcony for a passage in Concerto No. 4, their music truly seems to waft above the other instruments. The quality of the sound on the disc is so good that you can turn the volume down to almost a whisper and still hear every component clearly.

The musicians are brightly lit and in sharp focus, which heightens a sense of immediacy in their performances. The editing does not always include the players one ought to be watching for a given passage, but the cameras are pointing at the faces of the musicians as much as at their fingers or the antique instruments. By the end of the 102-minute program the personality, as well as the musical ability, of every performer is intimately communicated to the viewer.

Some of J.S. Bach's work was so innovative that today it is cliched. The 'Brandenburg Concertos,' however, remain a subtle and moving accomplishment. They combine his wildly precise symmetrics with a relaxed exploration of sound varieties. This is why it is so important that they be heard with the instruments of Bach's era. No other composer has had his work so polluted by the industrial age – and how refreshing it is to experience these pieces unburdened by the grime of progress.

The disc comes with a jacket insert containing a fine essay on the source and the dynamics of each concerto. To fit the works onto a single disc, Concerto No. 1, No. 2, and No. 4 appear on side one, while Concerto No. 3, No. 5, and No. 6 appear on side two. The only fault the disc has is in the chapter listings on the back of the jacket, which do not coincide with the actual chapter encoding. Every disc should be so flawed.

JACK AND THE BEANSTALK
(see **FAERIE TALE THEATRE**)

JACK AND THE BEANSTALK

A successful combination of live action and animation, *Jack and the Beanstalk* is an hour-long television special from the mid-sixties starring Gene Kelly, with songs by Sammy Cahn and James Van Heusen. Although the special effects lack the sophistication of today's computer-guided media mixing, the technical accomplishments are nevertheless impressive, and Kelly's dancing with cartoon figures is as amazing as ever. Kelly portrays the bean salesman, who, in this version, accompanies young Jack up the beanstalk. The child actor portraying Jack can sing and dance, but he can't carry a line of dialog convincingly for the life of him, and his presence is the show's weakest attribute.

The colors seem a little aged on top of the degradation which is a natural part of the special effect process. The monaural sound is fine.

JACKNIFE
(see **IN COUNTRY**)

JACQUES TATI'S MR. HULOT'S HOLIDAY

Except for the sound effects, you lose none of the comedy running the Criterion Collection CAV rendition of *Jacques Tati's Mr. Hulot's Holiday* at three times normal speed. Conceivably, you could digest the entire film in a half hour. The print is in such lovely condition, however, that you may find yourself using the freeze-frame instead, to savor individual comic tableaux.

The three-sided disc has no added materials, but the rich tones of grey and bright blacks and whites enhance one's attentiveness to all that is going on in the film.

The print opens on a shot of a mediocre surf, obscured in part by an English script with a repetitive explanation that the film which one is about to see is a comedy, but that you have to be patient to enjoy it. Unless this was intended to be a put-on, it is condescending. Tati is one of those filmmakers who doesn't stop toying with a film after it is in the can. He apparently took nearly 20 minutes off of his initial cut very shortly after it was first released in 1953. The standard French version was 90 minutes long. The English language version, constructed and dubbed by Tati himself in the mid-fifties, was 86 minutes long. In the early sixties, the musical score was re-orchestrated in Rota-ish jazz. In 1977 there was a major and highly successful revival of Tati's films in Paris, and the Hulot which was shown had the newer music. The 1977 revival containing Tati's English dubbing, is the print Criterion has used for the disc. It, too, is 86 minutes long. It would have been nice if they had explained the provenance of their source material on the disc jacket, since we are guessing at some of the details. It is probable that this cut was the best looking source available, and the print is beautiful enough to justify its utilization. The dubbed English is not necessarily a bad thing, since the dialog is entirely incidental and background oriented, undeserving of the sort of attention subtitles would call to it, but containing just enough information to warrant translation. The sound has not been CX-encoded.

We have never liked the movie that much, but we like the disc a lot. The CAV manipulations allow one to spot comical intentions, obviously planned by Tati, which remain largely invisible at normal speed. In the grand finale, for example, Tati's character, M. Hulot, accidentally ignites a shed full of fireworks. The most obvious comedy occurs as he dodges the individual skyrockets. Less obvious, but still accessible, is the way in which the editing of the entire sequence is made to imitate a battle scene. But completely obscured by the pyrotechnical display is Tati's choreography. When the disc is operated at fast and slow motion, you can see that Tati has timed and edited the movements of his own body to match the seemingly random paths of the rockets.

JACK NICKLAUS SHOWS YOU THE GREATEST 18 HOLES OF MAJOR CHAMPIONSHIP GOLF

In *Jack Nicklaus Shows You the Greatest 18 Holes of Major Championship Golf,* Nicklaus, with Jack Whitaker, identifies the 18 ideal holes, from nine courses in the US and Great Britain, which would comprise his dream championship course. He visits most of the holes and discusses the strategy for playing each in a variety of winds and other complications. Footage from actual tournaments in which the holes proved to be the turning point is shown, often in split screen to depict the golfers who won or lost playing the hole.

The two-sided disc is in CAV. There are a number of opportunities to still step Nicklaus's swing. Intense colors look unstable, and the videotape source has an occasional line running through it. Side one is separated from side two in the middle of a shot. The sound is monaural and is digitally encoded, although the analog track has less distortion. There are plenty of chapter markers, and a scorecard has been included as a jacket insert, in case the viewer ever has an opportunity to visit the courses depicted.

JACK'S BACK

A strong command of narrative makes *Jack's Back* a highly entertaining disc, even though the picture and sound transfer are poor. The story, a murder mystery, has twists which even the most dedicated crime thriller fans will not anticipate. James Spader stars. The film is crisply edited and has an appealing cast. We only wish that the disc looked and sounded better than it does. The picture is particularly bad. It is almost constantly too grainy and too fuzzy, and contains a few speckles as well. The monaural sound seems rough in places. The flaws will not prevent a viewer from enjoying the film on the first run through, but the condition of the disc will discourage repeat viewings.

JAGGED EDGE

The main concern we had with *Jagged Edge* was its ability to sustain multiple viewings. Would it be worth watching again if you knew what happens? The answer is a qualified 'yes.' At least the disc presentation does not get in the way. There is a surround stereo soundtrack which is particularly effective at the moments when it is supposed to be, although it is a lazier mix outside of those moments. Glenn Close wears one red-orange outfit which the disc has a little trouble recreating. The story is as involving on subsequent viewings as it is the first time through. The ending, alas, lacks the realistic logic which holds the rest of the plot together.

The first time you see the film, it is through the eyes of the Close character. In subsequent viewings, it is through your own eyes. The performance of Jeff Bridges is far less frustrating when you know what is going to happen. But the conclusion is a contrivance. Why would the murderer, who has been very clever all the way through, re-establish a dangerous relationship after successfully avoiding detection? When a mystery is logical all the way to the end, you can watch it dozens of times and still enjoy the revelations. When it is untrue to its own rules, you start to feel cheated.

JAILHOUSE ROCK

Elvis Presley's third film was a widescreen black-and-white MGM feature that is considered one of his best. *Jailhouse Rock* was filmed in lousy mono and it has been transferred that way to disc. The cropped screen jerks back and forth to cover both sides of the wide picture. Elvis is charming, especially when he curls his lip. The movie is considered to be good because Elvis made a lot of other movies that were a lot worse.

JAKE SPEED

Watch out when movies are being sold as spoofs. It usually means that the filmmakers weren't trying hard enough to be real. There are some promising elements in *Jake Speed* but the story is one cop-out after another and not even the explosions are interesting. Even though it was filmed in Paris and Zimbabwe, the plot constantly undercuts any feeling of adventure. It spends too much time examining the genre and not enough just getting on with the story. The disc has a nice stereo soundtrack but a grainy picture.

THE JAM VIDEO SNAP!

One of the first punk/new wave bands to be picked up by a major label, The Jam, appears on *The Jam Video Snap!*. Unfortunately, the group's recording contract served as verification of their mediocrity – and of the beginning of the end for the movement in general – and their only real claim to fame was that they were probably the only rock group, ever, to use the word 'tantamount' in the lyrics of one of their songs (it is not included on the disc). Still, the beat and speed of the music is refreshing, even today.

The 47-minute disc contains 15 performance videos progressing chronologically over the course of five years, but not varying all that much either musically or visually. The disc is monaural. The older numbers sound flat and look ragged, although the later pieces achieve a brighter audio and video shine.

JAMES CLAVELL'S TAI-PAN

What a movie James Clavell's *Tai-Pan* would have made! The author had earned the leisure to write the book by directing films and had as much of a mind for the cinema as he had for the art of the novel, but it was always just a little too expensive to do justice to on the screen, and so the rights passed from hand to hand until they were finally grabbed by the privateer who knows not the meaning of the word 'justice' when it comes to the movies, Dino De Laurentiis.

James Clavell's Tai-Pan plays as though it has been adapted from a work of the stage, with every memorable piece of action and adventure, save the typhoon, excised. The print is dirty and the picture is moderately grainy, but the colors have their original tone. The stereo mix is enjoyable (lots of sound effects on the extreme edges), but there is extraneous noise in the left channel. Side three is 11 minutes long, in CLV.

Bryan Brown is an ideal choice as the hero, but he never gets a chance to be heroic. We had always heard that the idealism of youth is trampled as the years pass, but never believed it until we sat through the movie and realized we would never live to see a real motion-picture adaptation of *Tai-Pan*.

THE JAMES DEAN STORY

Made just two years after James Dean's fatal car accident, *The James Dean Story* is an oddly constructed but effective (if sanitized) documentary tracing the realization of Dean's talents and torments, and his rise to stardom in Hollywood. The black and white film, which Robert Altman was involved in making, interviews many of Dean's relatives and neighbors in Fairmount, Indiana, suggesting, incidentally, that there is a trove of valuable Dean memorabilia to be found in the town. The interviews have an odd tone because the film's unseen narrator, Martin Gabel, poses the questions although the answers have obviously been filmed and recorded beforehand. Even when the film is embarrassingly bad (whenever Dean's childhood home is pictured, an empty swing in front of the house is always moving, and the attempt to be straightforward and still remain obscure about his love life generates narrative somersaults), the you-are-there point of view effectively smooths the rough spots and provides a wealth of information. The strongest impression one comes away with is the differentiation between Dean's true intelligence and the vaguely consistent personality of the characters he played in his three principal films. In 1950 Dean was pledging a fraternity at UCLA and had yet to take his first drama class. In 1955 he was dead, and the film is effective in explaining how it all could have happened.

The movie has undergone a decent transfer. The black and white images (even the film clips are in black and white) always look sharp. The digitally encoded monaural sound is satisfactory. Side two is in CAV, with two shaky stills in every five but plenty of opportunities to freeze-frame Dean behind the scenes.

JANE FONDA'S NEW WORKOUT

Jane Fonda can do things with her body we haven't been able to do since we were nine years old. *Jane Fonda's New Workout* has the same format as her other exercise discs, although, for variety, the permutations of limb alignments and stresses become more complex with each succeeding disc.

There is no dual audio capability, but Fonda's commentary is limited. The stereo music has a strong dance beat and one of the women on Fonda's exercise team pretends to sing a song while working out. Not the sort of thing one should try at home.

The picture and the sound are in as good a condition as the performers. The disc is 90 minutes long, with a 35-minute program on side one and the same exercises, complicated to 55 killer minutes, on side two. We searched in vain for a lack of continuity in the sweat marks on the exercise togs. People can't really do this stuff without stopping, can they?

JANE FONDA'S PRIME TIME WORKOUT

If you have *Jane Fonda's Workout*, then getting *Jane Fonda's Prime Time Workout* would be like buying a second wrist watch. As with the first, the production values are excellent on the 52-minute program. The camera angles enable you to understand clearly how each exercise is performed, yet the look of the show is never utilitarian. There are chapter markers for particular sets of exercises and dual channel sound if you feel Fonda should be seen but not heard.

JANE FONDA'S WORKOUT

The CLV *Jane Fonda's Workout* has two exercise programs on it. Side one is a 35-minute set for starters, and side two is a 53-minute workout for those who thought side one was fun. To many it is boredom, not strain, that discourages a daily physical regimen. That is where the visual stimulation comes into play. The camera work displays the exercises adequately and the format holds your attention. The longer workout is subtly different from the shorter one, adding a few extra moves to each unit without seeming more impossible.

JANE FONDA'S WORKOUT CHALLENGE

Jane Fonda opens *Jane Fonda's Workout Challenge* by telling the viewer to stand with "the stomach pulled flat," and already we knew we were in trouble because we haven't been able to make it do that since Gerald Ford was president. In *Workout Challenge*, Fonda conducts most of the exercises in an empty studio. She has two helpers during the aerobics section, but otherwise it is one on one. She is more talkative on this disc, trying to tell jokes and convince her audience that the exercises are easy. The disc has dual channel sound. Fonda, appropriately, is heard on the left speaker.

The music is flat and consciously changes from disco to country/western to a can-can and other nondescript styles. The editing often cuts from one camera angle to the next on a change in movement. This could disorient a viewer frantically attempting to watch and do at the same time.

JANET JACKSON – CONTROL THE VIDEOS

The five videos collected on *Janet Jackson – Control The Videos*, are relaxed, entertaining, and colorful. Jackson is easygoing, yet full of energy, and the disc is the sort one is apt to leave on automatic play all afternoon. The colors on the disc look like a display of glossy cosmetics. The reds and blues have a rich sparkle which shine under the confidence of the laser playback. The first two numbers, 'What Have You Done for Me Lately' and 'Nasty,' are particularly colorful. The concluding number, 'Let's Wait Awhile,' is in black and white, but it is also impressive, and the photographic effects would be convoluted if the resolution were any less sharp. Jackson's singing is better when you're looking at her, because you can see she's having fun and it excuses a lot. The sound on the disc has no unusual flaws.

JANET JACKSON'S RHYTHM NATION 1814

The exciting half-hour Janet Jackson video production, *Janet Jackson's Rhythm Nation 1814*, has been released on disc by A&M. The extended concept video, which incorporates 4 songs and some incidental music, is a black and white extravaganza. Combining terrific choreography with a flurry of gorgeously photographed high-tech images, the piece has a slight narrative – about avoiding drugs – and a lot of punch. The music, in fact, is probably the project's weakest link. The songs are not as innovative or as rich as the choreography or the conceptualization deserve. Jackson's singing isn't strong, either, but her sense of presence is, and in the world of video, posing is more important than vocalizing.

The picture transfer is excellent. The image has matted letterboxing, with an aspect ratio of 1.66:1. The stereo sound also has plenty of thrust.

Rounding out the disc is a half-hour color documentary detailing the making of the video. We recommend not watching it immediately after the main feature, but saving it for another time instead, perhaps as a prelude to the second or third viewing of the primary work. It is thorough in its coverage and naturally gushy about Janet Jackson.

THE JANUARY MAN

The stereo surround sound on *The January Man*, is very pleasing. The sound effects are just standard atmospheric touches, but they are so well executed that you don't realize the noises are coming from the movie. The musical score, a competent Marvin Hamlisch effort, is also nicely separated.

The movie is a perfect example of how a film can be bad and still be legitimately fulfilling and entertaining. The script, about a disgraced police detective called back to outthink a serial killer, is silly and unpolished. The dialog is contrived, the character motivations are illogical or convenient, and there is a subplot, about political corruption, which is poorly developed. However, there are a collection of wonderful actors, including Kevin Kline, Mary Elizabeth Mastrantonio, Alan Rickman (as a good guy, for once), Danny Aiello, Susan Sarandon, and Rod Steiger, giving the material everything they can, and they pull it out. The scenes which are well written are extremely charming, and the scenes which would appear awkward or disjointed on paper still hold your attention because the cast members are embellishing the words with wit of their own. Only Harvey Keitel fails, and it is because he is miscast, as Kline's brother and police commissioner.

The picture is mildly grainy throughout the disc, but the colors look accurate and the cinematography is not accomplished enough to be disrupted by the flaws. The movie meanders for close to 90 minutes and then races to a quick and exciting conclusion, but you don't mind the meandering, because the cast is so much fun, and you don't mind the conclusion, except that it means the movie is over.

JAWS THE REVENGE

The editing is a textbook example of how not to cut a thriller, and the very thought that the dumbest fish in the sea has suddenly obtained a grasp of strategic planning strains one's patience, but the laser disc laws of inverse quality are at work once again: The movie may be difficult to swallow, but *Jaws The Revenge* is an appetizing disc.

In some places the picture quality is only very good, but for the most part it is fantastic. So clear, in fact, that you can tell when the actors are in a tub and not really out on an open sea. The shades of colors are vivid and feel absolutely correct. The picture is solid and never hesitant. It makes up for the bad editing.

Lorraine Gary portrays that most feared of all beings, the fighting-mad grandmother. Her performance is wonderful and it continually saves the movie from sinking. It is one of those rare situations where a person has landed a role not from matching a marketing analyst's concept of how the role should be filled, but because of an outside precedence. In this case that would be her steely presence in the first *Jaws* movie fifteen years earlier. She fit in then, but the movie has to fit around her now, and she raises the quality of the whole project. She makes up for the stupid intelligent shark.

The program runs less than ninety minutes, but the disc is CLV throughout. Scenes have been added for the home video version, but the continuity is never disrupted. The sound on the disc is a little fuzzy, but competent.

Michael Caine floats in and out of the film, but he has one line of dialog which is worth committing to memory. It just has to come in handy some day, especially if one identifies the source when repeating the quote: "The world would be a better place if more sons danced with their mothers." No, the disc is not for those who cringe at the sight of rubber teeth, but if for any reason you think you might be partial to the material, be advised that the quality of the disc should stimulate, and not hinder, your purchase.

JAY LENO: THE AMERICAN DREAM
(see **HOWIE MANDEL'S NORTH AMERICAN WATUSI TOUR**)

THE JAZZ LIFE 7(b5): CHICO HAMILTON
THE JAZZ LIFE 7(b5): JOHNNY GRIFFIN
THE JAZZ LIFE 7(b5): MIKE MAINIERI
B.B. KING: LIVE AT NICK'S

Several jazz concerts have been released as one-sided CLV presentations on the Sony Video LP label. These shows take place in cramped night clubs where the cameras convey the intimacy shared by the performers and the audience. The discs are slightly blurry, and the sound is analog but passable. For all the camera angles and reverse camera angles, the stereo matrix remains fairly constant without ever seeming out of synch.

Drummer Chico Hamilton brings his band to the Village Vanguard in *The Jazz Life 7(b5): Chico Hamilton*. The vocals are not well-miked, but every contribution is picked up and the balance seems in keeping with the structure on stage, the vocalist (Kathlene Adaar) having been pushed far to one side. *The Jazz Life 7(b5): Johnny Griffin* is not in stereo, but it is the most pleasant of the discs. Griffin plays the tenor sax and indulges in a little incoherent stage patter between numbers. There are some terrific closeups of Mike Mainieri's vibraphone sticks in *The Jazz Life 7(b5): Mike Mainieri*. This is the appeal of the series. Along with getting numerous reaction shots from the Vanguard audience, the cameras are so close to the band that they can pick up the smallest aspects of technique and feeling.

Nick's of Dallas is a larger emporium, but it is probably as intimate a place in which a performer of B.B. King's stature is likely to appear. *B.B. King: Live at Nick's* has a better picture than the other discs, and the sound is consistent. King's voice has a limited range but an unlimited sense of rhythm and his vocals lock in on one's pulse. His guitar playing locks onto one's entire bio-rhythmic system. The concert is interspersed with interview segments, but these are too short to annoy and King has some amusing anecdotes to share, particularly one about how he came to sing the blues instead of gospel (he got better tips).

THE JAZZ LIFE VOL. 1 (Import)
THE JAZZ LIFE VOL. 3 (Import)
SONNY ROLLINS – FESTIVAL INTERNATIONAL DE JAZZ DE MONTREAL (Import)
WEATHER REPORT LIVE IN TOKYO – JAPAN DOMINO THEORY (Import)
GERRY MULLIGAN – LIVE AT ERIC (Import)
COLLABORATION – GEORGE KAWAGUCHI MEETS SHELLEY MANNE (Import)
DIZZY GILLESPIE – LIVE AT CONCERTS BY THE SEA (Import)

The Jazz Life series has been the most reliable collection of Japanese jazz discs we have viewed. On all of them, the sound has been dependably crisp and the picture exquisitely sharp. An added bonus is the use of CAV on the 60-minute sets, a feature musically inclined viewers will find particularly educational.

As a preservation of technique, or as a unique way to set a special mood, the discs are very effective. *Vol. 1* features Richard Cole on his alto saxophone. *Vol. 3* showcases Nat Adderley and his coronet. The acoustics in the tiny, personable Village Vanguard are easily overloaded and since the sound reproduction on the discs is extremely accurate, the quieter moments come across better than the full-tilt passages.

One can see putting these discs on during a party to import a little night life into the atmosphere. Other concert jazz discs are more difficult to justify. Sonny Rollins has some nice moments on the Japanese disc, *Sonny Rollins – Festival International de Jazz de Montreal*, standing on the edge of the stage playing his saxophone, but he is playing to a huge auditorium and intimacy, an important component in improvisation, is lost. The disc is in CLV and has a grainy look.

Weather Report Live in Tokyo – Japan Domino Theory is a Japanese disc of a group which often sounds more like it is warming up than actually playing. The band's sound is precise and disjointed and the music can only be appreciated if concentration is at a maximum. The camera angles are not as daring as the music calls for. The break between side one and side two occurs in the middle of a number instead of on a pause.

Intimacy does not always make for an entertaining disc. *Gerry Mulligan – Live at Eric* loses the advantages of appearing at a small club because one never sees the audience. The camera angles aren't as interesting as the *Jazz Life* discs and you really get tired of looking at the group. We found it was easier to appreciate drummer Billy Hart when we turned the picture off.

In *Collaboration – George Kawaguchi Meets Shelley Manne* there is no audience. The CAV disc depicts a studio recording of two big bands. The disc has all the atmosphere of a hospital waiting room. This may be how most music on records is produced, but it isn't a romantic sight, all the musicians wearing headphones, flanked by panels, with wires everywhere.

On CLV from Redondo Beach comes the Japanese disc, *Dizzy Gillespie – Live at*

Concerts by the Sea. The music is fast and loud, the atmosphere is warm, and right off you know you're in for a good time. Gillespie has a trumpet which looks like a bent paper clip. To play it, his cheeks swell like a blowfish and his fingers move rapidly while his hands remain perfectly still. Personality – what choices a musician makes – can be conveyed directly to an audience and can communicate feelings which really have nothing to do with music, and that is what this disc does.

JE TE VEUX

An extensive biography of Eric Satie and notes on each of the seven works featured on *Je Te Veux* can be found on an insert accompanying the official Pioneer import disc. Unfortunately, it is all in Japanese. The disc itself features people-less photographs of the French countryside, blending from one to the next at the rate of about five a minute, and the Satie pieces, performed by Jean-Joel Barbier on piano. The disc is digitally encoded, but it was recorded in analog and does not capture the piano sounds as clearly as a decent CD. The high notes tend to blend together. Barbier plays most of the pieces too quickly for our tastes, although the title song, which has always sounded like silent film music and is thus appropriately titled, comes across with a nice bounce. There is one impressive photograph of bottles aligned on a fence, but the rest of the images fade as quickly as they pass from view.

JEAN AUGUSTE DOMINIQUE INGRES/FERDINAND VICTOR EUGENE DELACROIX (Import)

Jean Auguste Dominique Ingres/Ferdinand Victor Eugene Delacroix is a single-sided, hour long CLV import offering which tours the museums of Europe to examine the principal works of the two painters. The narration, which would add significantly to the program, is in Japanese, and the background music is in stereo.

The picture quality is the disc's chief disappointment. It is consistently grainy and although the camera spends a good deal of time examining each painting in detail (there are 35 chapters and about as many paintings on the disc), the insufficient clarity of the image eliminates any value the disc might offer over a decent picture book.

Both Ingres and Delacroix are fascinating painters, and both delved excessively in contemporary-styled nudes long before such efforts were fashionable or even scandalous. The disc, however, is only a teaser, and would be insufficient in critical perspective even if one could understand the narration.

JEAN DE FLORETTE
MANON OF THE SPRING

Although the discs, like the theatrical films, have been released separately, *Jean de Florette* and *Manon of the Spring* are a single work, and one would be foolish, or poorer, for obtaining one without the other.

The two films make an elegant, satisfying work which lasts for four hours and possess an ending worthy of every minute leading up to it. The story is about farmers in rural France and the tragedy and duplicity surrounding the hidden existence of a natural well ('spring' refers to water, not the season). *Florette* tells of several misdeeds, and then *Manon*, which takes place ten years later, tells of the consequences. Although the plot spans several generations, the story is not an epic. The director, Claude Berri, has made a number of small, perfect little films, and these two conform to his scale although they combine to make something greater.

The surround soundtrack on both discs is marvelous, whether the setting is the noisy marketplace or the still, summer countryside. The analog track is also good, though it is not quite as sharp. The picture is in good condition. A few shots look too gauzy and some of the night shots seem pale, but the rest is fine. The credit sequences are letterboxed, but the movies, unfortunately, are scanned and cropped. As is prominently displayed on both jacket covers, the movies are in French with yellow English subtitles.

JEFFERSON STARSHIP

The Jefferson Starship (née Airplane) has been around for twenty years, making it older than most of the members in the audience of the concert featured on *Jefferson Starship*. Only one band member who was with the group when they recorded their first album in 1966 is with the present collection of musicians, but they play their two most famous hits, 'White Rabbit' and 'Somebody to Love,' and try to resurrect the spirit of a band which has seen better times.

Interspersed with the concert footage is a foolish skit about a pirate broadcasting station in outer space which is pretending to transmit the music to the viewer. Like the band's attempts at music video, the *Jefferson Starship* disc is ill-conceived, and one is tempted to label them with most severe curse of their day – they've become hopelessly square.

JERMAINE JACKSON – DYNAMITE VIDEOS

Here's an opportunity few will want to miss: A chance to own one of the all-time greatest bad music videos. Yes, it is available as part of the 31-minute two-sided 8-inch video disc with a somewhat muddy picture, *Jermaine Jackson – Dynamite Videos*.

The awful music video we are referring to is 'When the Rain Begins to Fall,' in which Jackson, having borrowed the family epaulets, portrays the leader of a gang of third world types decked out in dark leather. No, that's not funny, but the gang confronts a group of motorcycle-riding WASP types in white leather and with them, wearing silver underwear over her white pants, is Pia Zadora. They begin to sing 'When the Rain Begins to Fall' while their associates demonstrate to little ones all across the country how to have a race war. "And when the rain begins to fall, I'll be the sunshine of your life," Zadora and Jackson sing as the dark leather gang kicks the creases out of the white leather group. Poor Jermaine has to flatten out his voice to harmonize with screaming Pia and he has to pretend that he's attracted to her, though you can see, at the end, he is relieved when she leaves with the white guys.

JESSE JAMES
THE RETURN OF FRANK JAMES

If you want to see the difference between a bad color transfer and a good color transfer look at *Jesse James* and *The Return of Frank James*. The color in *Jesse James* is poor, all faded and greenish, and the image prevents the viewer from fully relaxing and enjoying the film. The Technicolor source for the sequel is rich and glossy. Some reels don't look quite as sharp as others, but the film, which is less compelling than the first, becomes more involving on disc because you don't want to take your eyes off of it. Both discs have digital monaural sound which has no major problems. They come in similar looking jackets, encouraging consumers to obtain them as a pair. *Return* has no special features, but CBS/Fox has provided a theatrical poster and a couple of production stills at the end of the first film.

Jesse James seems to have inspired both the narrative and the emotional structure of *Bonnie and Clyde*. The James brothers are cast as heros, robbing institutions but respecting the rights and property of individuals. It was a daring move which paid off at the box office in the late thirties. Although there are some exciting stunts in both films, one cringes at the maltreatment of the animals involved in the gags. Tyrone Power overplays Jesse, and Henry Fonda underplays Frank, but they balance each other nicely. Many cast members repeat their roles in the second film, which was directed, without much personality, by Fritz Lang. The movie is about Frank's vengeance against Jesse's murderers, but it only touches upon the real fascinating and dramatic aspect to Frank's life – he continually beat the rap and was never convicted of any crimes.

JESUS CHRIST SUPERSTAR

Beware of *Jesus Christ Superstar*. The disc was initially released with a monaural soundtrack, and although it was recalled and quickly reissued with the correct stereo tracks, copies of the first version may still be lurking about. The soundtrack has a little noise, but is generally pleasing.

The quality of the print is okay, although at times the edges of things are just soft enough to remind one of the movie's age. The picture is soft and a bit dusty looking. The film was originally made in TODD-AO 35, and it has been cropped. How much has it been cropped? There are only 8 disciples at the Last Supper.

The teenager inside of us has always resented *Jesus Christ Superstar*. It was one of the earliest signifiers of the move by record companies to reclaim and banalize rock music in the shift from the sixties to the seventies. Calling it a rock opera was an insult. Ian Anderson or Ginger Baker it wasn't, let alone Pete Townshend. But the adult inside of us has great respect for it. It was the first major hit by Weber and Rice, who today have become two of the premier forces in innovative musical theater. The movie is silly in that all musical drama is silly, particularly when sung in as exacting a language as English. Some of the rhymes are atrocious (fire/Messiah) and the shifts in vernacular are awkward ("What's the buzz?..."?) The emotions of music and dance are supposed to supplement the dramatic exposition while massaging the viewer. Some viewers stiffen and don't give it a chance, which is understandable, all things considered, but those who do are apt to pick out favorite chapters (23, but there should be twice that) and play them until the laser burns a hole through the disc.

The script looks like it was written after a major budget cut, positing a group of players in the middle of a desert to act out selected passages from the New Testament in song. The script does not cover the Resurrection, but the disc does, in a way, since it contains, at the end, the movie's trailer, which runs through high points from the various passages in the film with a minimum of supporting comment.

JETHRO TULL SLIPSTREAM
The hour-long collection of conceptually linked music videos and concert footage on *Jethro Tull Slipstream* looks grainy and sounds dull. The songs are mostly live recordings and whatever melody they once had is lost in the transcription. Even Ian Anderson's flute solos sound as if he is blowing across the top of a beer bottle. The conceptual footage is based on the Aqualung character, who has survived for twenty years now despite his apparent lack of any basic personal hygiene concerns. The picture is blurry and the program will be of interest to fans only, if the group has any left.

JETS AND CLASSICS
Jets and Classics contains a program which is similar in format to the *Rolling in the Sky* series, with glossy video shots of airplanes in action accompanied by impressionistic background music. Side one covers jet planes and side two looks at propeller planes. Among those lovingly depicted are a B-25, a Corsair, a P-51, F-16s, an F-14, and a rare view of the B-2 Stealth bomber not crashing.

The disc has been planned and executed with exquisite care. The picture quality is always bright and spotless, and the digitally encoded stereo sound is free of noise and full of body. The disc is in CAV, although the video tape source material causes blur in some of the still frames.

There is a nice selection of still photos at the end of each side, taken by the photographer Mark Meyer, who was also responsible for planning and executing the video images. An insert accompanying the disc details the still photos and includes essays about the video and sound components of the disc.

It is difficult, however, to determine what sort of viewer *Jets and Classics* has been designed for. Although most of the segments are musical, there are just enough jet noise interruptions to prevent the disc from serving as a relaxing musical program. There are not enough airplane noises, on the other hand, to satisfy those who feel impatient with the music. The disc's oddest segment is a collection of jet plane sounds which has been placed at the end of side one. Although they are introduced by an index and are marked separately with chapters, the sounds are played to a blank screen, which at least could have been given a text identification of the airplane making the noise, if not a picture.

THE JEWEL OF THE NILE
One of the best looking and sounding discs is unquestionably *The Jewel of the Nile*. Since most of the action takes place on the desert in the bright daylight, the picture rarely has an opportunity to falter. From the deliberately phony sunset in the opening scene to the firelit kiss at the end, the transfer handles every problem of light and darkness without distorting the image. Were it not for the scanning and cropping, the presentation would be on par with the best theatrical exhibitions.

You can hear what's been added in the studio and pasted onto the soundtrack and you can hear when the reverberators are passed off as real echoes, but you also get a complete flurry of sound effects from everywhere and every noise is the audio equivalent of a precious gem.

JEZEBEL (MGM/UA)
JEZEBEL (CBS/Fox)
As is explained in *The Making of Gone with the Wind*, *Jezebel* was 1) a sneak attack by Warner Brothers to capitalize on *GWTW*'s publicity and production delays, and 2) a two-hour Scarlett screen test for Davis, though it won her an Oscar anyway. The film is an enjoyable vehicle for Davis, as her character must pass through some extensive emotional and moral changes, all of which happen right before the viewer's eyes.

The black-and-white picture on the CBS/Fox disc has less contrasts than the MGM/UA disc, causing details to get lost in the darker and lighter portions of the screen, but the MGM/UA image is a bit grainier, perhaps a necessary compromise to obtain the detail. MGM/UA's monaural sound is CX-encoded, while CBS/Fox's is not, but we prefer the raw sound on the latter, which seems less manipulated and filtered. MGM/UA has blown the side change, which CBS/Fox properly placed five minutes later, when a reel change creates a natural fade to black.

JIMI HENDRIX JOHNNY B. GOODE
A 26-minute compilation of music videos set to the music of Jimi Hendrix has been released in CLV on *Jimi Hendrix Johnny B. Goode*. The digitally encoded sound is stereophonic, but in some instances that amounts to routing the vocals to one channel and the guitars to the other. There are 6 chapters, although one segment is actually a medley of a number of Hendrix tunes. One concept video and three performance videos all show Hendrix in action. Two other numbers cut between images of Hendrix and contemporary artists working on Hendrix-oriented imagery. The disc sounds okay and doesn't look bad.

JIMI HENDRIX LIVE AT MONTEREY
The independent documentary maker, D.A. Pennebaker, was smart enough to retain all the footage he took at the Monterey Pop Festival, and now it is beginning to pay off as he goes back and compiles the individual sets of each artist who performed there. *Jimi Hendrix Live at Monterey* (entitled 'Jimi Plays Monterey' on the program itself) runs 50 minutes, providing a brief but informative history of Hendrix's rise to fame as well as his half hour festival stage performance.

The picture was photographed under minimal lighting and other untried conditions, but the transfer from that point onward is very good and preserves all that Pennebaker initially recorded. The sound is more monaural than stereo and sounds a bit flat, but considering the conditions under which it was made, few viewers will find reason for complaint.

What other musician could so naturally integrate *feedback* with the rest of his harmonies? On audio his music sounds like an exploration so elaborate and uncharted that it will take years of repeated play to even initiate comprehension. Visually, Hendrix is even more amazing, because the parts of his body which have nothing to do with playing his guitar still appear to be contributing to the music rather than reacting to it. The excerpt of Hendrix's performance in *Monterey Pop* may have been the grand finale, but his entire stage show had the constant, total intensity of a moth trying to land on a lit wick.

JIMI PLAYS BERKELEY
The jacket cover says *Jimi Plays Berkeley* runs 55 minutes. The actual running time is 49 minutes, only 40 of which covers the concert Jimi Hendrix played at Berkeley on Memorial Day in 1970. The remainder consists of documentary footage capturing the tense and confrontational mood upon the campus at the time the concert was taking place. The picture is understandably hazy and never seems to cover Hendrix from the right angle. The brevity of the program, however, works in its favor, so that the blurry picture and the modestly stereophonic concert recording never become tiresome. The eight, highly improvisational numbers are marked with chapter encoding, a listing of which is provided on the back of the jacket.

JOAN OF ARC
Too much pomp and not enough circumstance mar *Joan of Arc*, the pious Ingrid Bergman vehicle. Bergman can usually be counted on to convey a sisterly-type warmth in her performances, but here she's less like a saint and more like a cold and lifeless icon. The story is no help, taking an excessively literal interpretation of the Joan of Arc legend and providing few details to support the headline events in Joan's life. To make matters worse, the original running time of the film was 145 minutes, but the single-plattered disc is only 100 minutes long. The color transfer is fair and the sound is average.

JOE COCKER – MAD DOGS AND ENGLISHMEN
Joe Cocker – Mad Dogs and Englishmen was a concert film made in the early seventies when it was *de rigueur* to present rock concert films in widescreen and then use double and triple shots to get the most from the mounds of available footage. The disc shows portions of the movie in full screen and then, when the screen splits, the aspect narrows (with a distracting blue border) to a third of the initial height.

The footage is worn and faded, but that is just how it looked the day the movie opened. Many chapter markers have been included. Be sure to leave the disc on all the way through the credits, as the Pioneer logo makes a pleasing curtain call.

JOE COOL LIVE
Joe Cool Live, a fusion band, is all-electronic and not very electrifying. The 90-minute set only comes alive when Sadao Watanabe joins the group with a saxophone for a couple of numbers. The pure, fresh sounds of the sax are quite a relief after a dull, steady onslaught of twangs and pings. We do have to say one

thing in the disc's favor. The picture transfer is stunning and the sound is excellent.

JOE JACKSON LIVE IN TOKYO

It is rare that a straight concert presentation will be of interest to those who are unfamiliar with the performer's music, but we would wholeheartedly recommend *Joe Jackson Live in Tokyo* to anyone. The digital stereo sound is outstanding. Not only does the bass pack a powerful wallop, but every instrument and vocal is superbly recorded and mixed, creating a sound which is clearly live, yet not the slightest bit compromised by the spontaneous environment. The moment you hear it, you want to turn the volume up.

The disc runs close to a full two hours and has chapter markers, although the listing of songs on the back is not numbered. The picture quality varies from very good to grainy depending upon the stage lighting.

Jackson, who tends to dress like M. Hulot, can be annoying at times when, through boredom or a lack of confidence, he fools around on stage instead of simply trusting his music. The disc is so long, however, that a viewer can dip in and out of it randomly and still obtain the pleasures it has to offer. It is a great disc for showing off one's audio system or, if things are slow, getting energized with some good, wound up rock 'n roll.

JOE JACKSON – THE BIG WORLD SESSIONS

It is difficult to categorize Joe Jackson's music. His songs have a slow rock tempo, but they are unlikely to be heard on any easy listening radio stations. The 8-inch, *Joe Jackson – The Big World Sessions*, is easier to categorize: It's a good disc.

The two-sided 33-minute CLV program depicts Jackson recording six songs in front of a live audience. As the jacket notes explain, this is a real recording session, without any overdubs, and it has a veracity which is fresh and exciting.

JOE VERSUS THE VOLCANO

Every shot in *Joe Versus the Volcano* is composed for and makes complete use of the rectangular Panavision screen. If the disc had not been letterboxed, with an aspect ratio of about 2.3:1, you would miss a third of the gags. If the cast members are not spread out in an even balance across the image, then curious objects or shades fill the edges, or the image simply soaks up a full panorama. The cinematography is gorgeous, and the color transfer is as sharp and as gratifying as the letterboxing. It is rare that one sees a film photographed as deliberately and as richly as *Joe Versus the Volcano*. The stereo surround sound is equally elaborate and powerful, and fully supported by the disc transfer.

The movie, however, is something else again. Written and directed by John Patrick Shanley, the film would not be out of place if it were found in the collected works of Terry Gilliam. It is a fantasy, reminiscent of both *Brazil* and *The Adventures of Baron Munchausen*, and the tone, which is always a bit reserved, may even be disturbing to some viewers. The first time you see it you half think that the events – concerning a young man who is given carte blanche if he will travel to the South Seas and leap into a volcano – are the dreams of a firefighter near death after rescuing some children (the clues are there), but the opening titles say, "Once upon a time," the closing titles say, "And they lived happily ever after," and everything between, taken at face value, is consistent in spirit. We have no idea how Shanley got the movie companies to pay for his fantasy, but the film is an instant cult attraction, off beat and indulgent, and the disc preserves it exquisitely.

JOHN COUGAR MELLENCAMP – AIN'T THAT AMERICA

A few interviews are scattered through *John Cougar Mellencamp – Ain't That America*. Neighbors from the town where Mellencamp grew up tell how he used to throw rocks at people and generally act as though he was on his way to reform school. Instead, he's making hundreds of thousands of dollars as a rock star, which just goes to show that there is no justice in the world.

Mellencamp has a sound that is perfect for digital encoding. He doesn't like the artificiality of the studio and he attacks his music with the same enthusiasm that he used to attack barn windows.

The opening video, 'Jack and Diane,' is the best and looks the sharpest. There are a few black-and-white videos which were not photographed or lit correctly, and other color numbers which look grainy. Mellencamp's attempt at an epic, 'Pink Houses,' which everyone usually thinks of as 'Ain't That America,' is a mixture of several styles and is pleasantly understated. The 55-minute CLV disc has been broken in two. This sets a majority of the interviews (and 'Pink Houses') off from the standard videos.

JOHN FITZGERALD KENNEDY

John Fitzgerald Kennedy, subtitled, 'A Celebration of His Life and Times,' runs close to three hours. The program is comprised of film clips and still images, with a narration that tags along. The result is similar to a biography made up entirely of photos and picture captions. When a picture isn't available, the subject isn't covered.

The quality of the footage, which includes many home movies, is impressive. Old color stock is squeezed for every last bit of chroma, and ancient black and white images look sharp and detailed. The sound bytes from different eras are also effectively restored, but Peter Thomas' narration has too much of a Casey Kasem pitch to take seriously. The disc is digitally encoded monaural.

Each side contains a separate program, with full opening and closing credits. There are 42 chapters altogether. Kennedy's life is covered in relative chronological sequence and is divided into the expected thirds – his early years, his Senate terms, and the presidency. The first program also covers Kennedy's heritage, and includes motion footage which, it is implied, depicts immigrants escaping Ireland's potato famine, in the 1850's. In a way, that sets the tone for the whole program.

The show is frank enough to depict Joseph Kennedy cavorting with Gloria Swanson, but it leaves out the famous clip of Marilyn Monroe singing, "Happy birthday, Mr. President." In some matters the program is informative, and in others it is not. When there is good footage available of a particular political fight, the history becomes especially entertaining. The only serious breach comes at the end. By accommodating its own format but not showing the Zapruder film, the program will mislead viewers who are unfamiliar with the details of Kennedy's death – he is seen stopping and shaking hands with supporters right before he is shot.

JOHN LENNON AND THE PLASTIC ONO BAND

Terrific footage from a 1969 concert has been compiled on *John Lennon and the Plastic Ono Band*. The hour-long program opens with a recent Yoko Ono interview and then cuts to footage filmed by D.A. Pennebaker at a rock'n' roll revival concert in Toronto. Bo Diddley, Jerry Lee Lewis, Chuck Berry, and Little Richard are each shown performing a number, followed by Lennon, Ono, and a makeshift band which included Eric Clapton, who play six songs and two of whatever it is Ono does (that's not nice, because we respect her music greatly, but her two numbers come at the end of the disc and seem to go on forever). Lennon has a full, washed, unclipped beard and very long hair, as was the style of the time, but for fans the material will seem fresh and vital. Considering the age of the footage, the quality of the color film is amazing, and the program is superbly edited. The sound is nominally in stereo although most of it seems to stay in the center and there is a certain amount of hiss.

JOHN LENNON – IMAGINE

Except for the Pioneer Artists Laser Disc logo on the very top, the front jacket cover to *John Lennon – Imagine* looks exactly the same as the LP. The disc is an excellent collector's item. It contains every number which is on the *Imagine* LP, plus a couple Yoko Ono pieces. Many of the images are only vaguely tied in to the music and lyrics, but the pieces which are closely linked, such as the political 'I Don't Wanna Be a Soldier, Mama,' the amusing 'How Do You Sleep?' and the indulgent 'Oh Yoko,' leave the strongest impression.

Filmed in 1971 without an emphasis on preservation, the picture is a bit tattered and amateurish in look. There is one beautiful, languid, circular helicopter shot as John and Yoko drive to a lake, board a rowboat, and cross to an island (to 'Jealous Guy'), but for the most part, there is a lot of home-movie-type shooting and cutting. The disc is CX-encoded but it contains a fair amount of noise. The power of the disc comes from the quality of the music in *Imagine* and the finite nature of the images.

JOHN LENNON – LIVE IN NEW YORK CITY
PAUL McCARTNEY & WINGS ROCKSHOW

It is an interesting exercise to compare *John Lennon – Live in New York City* with *Paul McCartney & Wings Rockshow*. The Lennon disc is digitally encoded, so naturally the sound is better. (The sound was digitally remastered from Lennon's last concert, a spur-of-the-moment show at Madison Square Garden in 1972 to raise money for some worthy cause.)

McCartney's show was part of an extravaganza tour, with lasers and thoroughly rehearsed production numbers. Lennon's only prop is a can of beer and his backup band is constantly making errors in the chord or rhythm shifts. Lennon himself forgets the words to one of his songs. Yet the McCartney disc is mostly boring and the Lennon disc is totally captivating. Why?

For one thing, there is spontaneity in Lennon's performance. He cuts a macho figure standing on the stage in his jeans, with his guitar. He gives the simultaneous impressions of being a seasoned professional and an improvising hobbyist.

The picture is surprisingly good considering that no one ever expected to put a show together like this, 14 years after the concert. The disc is wonderful, and it enables one to retrieve at least a small part of what was lost.

JOHN WAITE – NO BRAKES LIVE

Taking his life into his hands, John Waite leaps from the stage and plods through the crowd while singing a rock song through his cordless microphone. It is a testament to his popularity that he emerges unruffled and never misses a note, if in fact it is notes that the man is singing. *John Waite – No Brakes Live* is an hour-long concert disc. The picture is grainy, but the camera hovers very close to the performers and the whole stage is lit in white so that the act is easy to see and follow. The sound has a limited dynamic range and the recording mix is typical of a live performance. Those who are unfamiliar with Waite's work are advised to remain so.

JOHNNY BE GOOD

The jacket cover claims that *Johnny Be Good*, starring Anthony Michael Hall, includes 'new, sexually suggestive footage.' Note the use of the word, 'suggestive,' rather than 'explicit.' Virtually all of it could appear on broadcast television without a blip.

The film is not very good. Directed by Robert Downey, and co-starring Robert Downey, Jr., the story is a comedy about college football recruiting. It is poorly paced, badly organized, and not the least bit funny. The picture quality is decent, as is the sound. There are many chapter markers to encompass the soundtrack album score.

JOHNNY GOT HIS GUN

In 1971, when even remotely violent movies were seen as commenting upon the war in Vietnam, Dalton Trumbo made a film adaptation of his own anti-war novel about a soldier incapacitated during World War I, *Johnny Got His Gun*. The film is one of the most unmarketable titles ever brought to the screen, and it isn't entirely the fault of the concept. Trumbo was a fine scriptwriter, but he had no previous experience in film direction. The limbless soldier's memories and dreams are not cinematically stimulating or innovative, and so the film grinds from beginning to end as a test of a viewer's open-mindedness and tolerance. Those who purchase the title should be familiar with the film before they obtain it.

An excellent interview with Timothy Bottoms, which illuminates Trumbo's motivations, is included on a jacket insert. The movie combined black and white with color footage, but generally looks a little old and grainy. The sound is adequate.

JOHNNY GUITAR

Nicholas Ray's amusing mixture of pent-up passions and cowboy outfits, *Johnny Guitar* looks a little ripe, but since the delivery is stable and only a little blurry most viewers will find the presentation acceptable. The sound is okay. The disc also has chapter markers in all the right places.

Having seen the movie a number of times now, we have come to appreciate the performance of Mercedes McCambridge to the point of ignoring the rest of the cast whenever she is in a shot. The other performances are fine, and do justice to the overly analytical nature of the narrative, but McCambridge brings something extra to her role. She is on every moment, and, dwarfed by more than a dozen male actors who appear as her henchman, she continually jumps around to seize the center of attention. She gives her character vulnerability, tenacity, and bitterness, emotions which are no more than vaguely alluded to in the script. With the others, you have to guess what they are feeling.

JOHNNY HANDSOME

Johnny Handsome was directed by Walter Hill, whose rapt filmmaking style is quite effective on home video. *Handsome* has a number of impressively executed action scenes, but the story is as stupid as they come. Mickey Rourke portrays a convict whose face is misshapen from a form of Elephant Man disease. He's given an operation, which completely erases his deformity, and a parole. He proceeds immediately to seek vengeance against the couple who set him up, we guess because elephants never forget. They all kill each other in the end.

The picture transfer is okay. The picture has a moderate amount of gloss, and the many night sequences are delivered without distortion. Ry Cooder's musical score never shuts up, but it makes effective use of the stereo surround, as do the sophisticated gunshots. Image has included a good interview with Hill about the film on a jacket insert.

JOHNNY WINTER LIVE

Johnny Winter's famous mane of white hair remains hidden beneath a large, black, bathead hat, as do his eyes and everything down to the tip of his nose, throughout the 48-minute concert on *Johnny Winter Live*. The picture is grainy but the sound is clear. The stills on the jacket cover have nothing to do with the concert. Winter's music is a mixture of careless rock and thoughtful blues. He plays an adept 'Johnny B. Goode' and pretty much gives the audience what they want to hear. Rock stars who tell audiences that they wish they could play all night, however, ought to have sets which last longer than 48 minutes.

JOJO DANCER, YOUR LIFE IS CALLING

Richard Pryor's thematically autobiographical *Jojo Dancer, Your Life Is Calling* is another victimization-of-the-famous tale. Poor Jojo, written, directed and acted by Pryor, has no control over the fans who are lacing him with drugs and delusions of irresponsibility. The movie says nothing about the formation of a comic's or a dope addict's career. It is difficult to ascertain what the movie is trying to say, except, perhaps, that death is scary.

The disc is not a first-rate effort. The print has a few marks on it and looks a little aged. The sound is better, with several Motown classics coming through the stereo soundtrack with energetic clarity. One number, however, is used to drown out a montage of comedy routines which we would have preferred hearing. Pryor should have made a comedy. Instead, he's turned his life into a joke.

THE JOLSON STORY
JOLSON SINGS AGAIN

Al Jolson is thought to be the first pop star of this century and progenitor of a line which then traveled through Bing and Frank and Elvis and the Fab Four and on to Michael or Bruce or whoever. The whole concoction of *The Jolson Story* works because even though he's not acting in it, he's singing the songs, and the singing becomes the focal point of the action. Like Jolson, the movie is indefatigable, and it never gives up trying to please, even with its crazy, bittersweet ending.

We were surprised at how poor the RCA/Columbia transfer looked. The stills on the back of the jacket are gorgeous, and the movie was restored and stereo enhanced for a brief theatrical run about ten years before the disc was released. But the picture is faded and whole movie has an orange tint to it. At times, the characters have slight red and green halos around them. The sound has little distortion.

Like the plot, the crummy transfer on *Jolson Sings Again* picks up right where *The Jolson Story* left off. An orange haze often surrounds every piece of exposed flesh and the movie starts to look like it is about a singing creamsicle. The colors are over-ripe and the break between side one and side two occurs, for no reason other than laziness, in the middle of a conversation between two characters.

The sound has not been CX-encoded. It sounds worse on the dialog track than it does on the musical numbers since the latter were recorded with extra care, as is demonstrated in the movie itself.

If you've got *The Jolson Story*, you have to get *Jolson Sings Again*, although the combined show amounts to close to four hours of 'Mammy' and 'Swanee' (and the sublime 'Quarter to Nine'). That's fine by us, because the movie is more a celebration of Jolson's music than it is a critical examination of Jolson's life. The end of *Jolson Sings Again* is about the filming of *Jolson Story*, a tongue-in-cheek situation which the filmmakers pull off with great aplomb.

JONNY QUEST (see **YOGI BEAR**)

JONNY QUEST VOLUME 2

The format of *Jonny Quest Volume 2* is different from the first Jonny Quest disc. Whereas the first disc contained four episodes of the animated program, *Volume 2* is a single-sided CLV disc and contains just two. There is no added commentary, and the complete opening and closing credits for the program are shown at the beginning and end but not between the episodes.

The two episodes on the disc, 'Mystery of the Lizardmen' and 'The Curse of Anubis,' are more satisfying than the cartoons on the first disc. The animation has more depth of field and the colors are stronger. The picture transfer is good, and the monaural sound includes some nice echo effects. In 'Lizardmen,' Jonny stumbles across bad guys who are testing a laser in the Sargasso Sea. 'Anubis' is about a stolen Egyptian shrine and a mummy who stalks the thief. The cartoon series has some limitations. Although Jonny travels all around the world, there are never any women in the episodes, not even in the background atmosphere shots. And in the height of the Egyptian noonday sun, Jonny still runs around in his black turtleneck.

JOSEPH CAMPBELL & THE POWER OF THE MYTH WITH BILL MOYERS

Voyager has released so many intelligent, specialized video disc programs it is hard choosing superlatives to indicate that *Joseph Campbell & The Power of the Myth with Bill Moyers* is yet another exciting offering. The complete, six-part PBS series has been released on three platters in a box. It is CX-encoded monaural with a decent, journeyman soundtrack. The picture has a mild distortion to the darker parts of the screen but seems adequate. Voyager has done a superb job chapter encoding the disc – each hour episode has more than twenty markers – but they fail to associate numbers with the listing of the chapters on the back of the jacket, so the viewer must either count when one is needed, or scratch the numerals in.

Each episode is basically a conversation between Moyers and Campbell, with occasional illustrative inserts. The final episode is filmed in a different location from the previous five, and has the feel of a need by the producers to come up with a stronger conclusion. On the downside, Moyers is a PBS journalist through and through. Whenever he improvises from his prepared notes the blandness of his intellect is disheartening. On the upside, the twinkle in Joseph Campbell's eye as he makes what he thinks is an important point cannot be recreated in books or program transcripts. The purpose of the program was not to badger Campbell, but to obtain a summation of the lessons he has learned, and in that Moyers is successful. The six hours of talk is an excellent way to digest some very complex concepts, and its presentation in the video format assists greatly in focussing a viewer's attention. The disc or its excerpts are also a superb way to begin a conversation with a group of friends or students on anthropology or theology, providing a much stronger common ground to work from than a shared mimeographed text could provide.

Campbell uses an analysis of mythology to unify the world's religions. Paraphrased, his central concept could be interpreted as saying that atheists are the closest to God because they have no metaphor or 'mask' obscuring their understanding of metaphysical issues. Moyers never completely grasps this idea, but his stabs at it lead the conversation to Genesis, Churches, icons, computers, cave paintings, the need for stories, 'love,' human sacrifice, death, eternity (which is not endless time, but the absence of time), circles, the differences in myths caused by hunting and farming, motherhood, Epiphany, and dozens of other topics. The essential episode is the second one, 'The Message of the Myth,' in which Campbell best explains how the layers of narration and characterization can be removed from a tale to reveal its 'truth,' and how that is used to help those who hear the tale function in the world around them.

We only became annoyed with one point, in which Moyers attempts to lead Campbell into declaring that young people today have no rituals or discipline and are the poorer for it. Before Campbell can back out of it, Moyers changes the subject and editing does the rest. As for Campbell's ideas, our only quibble would be in his postulating that the commonalties between myths separated by great geographical distances are founded either in 'diffusion,' a shared ancestral myth, or 'separate development, a myth so strong to the heart of man that it developed exactly the same way in two different places. It would appear to us that the answer is not either/or, but both, that the strength of the concepts enabled the tales to wander the earth throug'h time without significant change. The tale is the hero and that it is human is Epiphany.

JOURNEY INTO FEAR

We have never seen a copy of *Journey into Fear* which could come anywhere near to the quality of the print used for the disc. Usually, the picture will look worn and tattered, and will serve as a reminder of how the film itself was constructed. The disc looks fantastic. The black and white source material has no more than a handful of inappropriate markings, and the contrasts and focus are razor sharp. When side one, which is in CAV, is run at triple speed, some of the scenes turn one's monitor into a window onto the past. The digitally encoded monaural sound is also impressive. Although the analog track contains some noise, the digital track is almost free of it, and the dialog and sound effects are bright and vivid.

Nominally directed by Norman Foster, *Journey into Fear* was guided by Orson Welles in the same way that *The Thing* was guided by Howard Hawks and *Poltergeist* by Steven Spielberg. The film is rich in Wellesian camera angles and character movement, unmatched in all but a half-dozen or so of Welles' other films. There are also more than a few innovative audio effects.

The one thing that you have to accept when watching *Journey into Fear* is that it only lasts 68 minutes. It is over before it really hits its stride, and it takes a couple of viewings to adjust to the film's structure. There is a voice-over narration and epilog which were clearly added on after the fact and are best ignored. The plot, based upon an Eric Ambler story, has nothing to say about the human condition, or other far-reaching themes of the sort that strengthened Welles' best work. It is just about a man, played by Joseph Cotten, who wants to avoid being murdered, primarily while he is on a small steamer in the Black Sea. The narrative structure has a dream-like feeling. The characters are, to the last, wonderful, and the performers – mostly Welles' Mercury Players group – are marvelous. The more familiar they become, over repeated viewings, the less the holes in the plot seem to matter and the more fun the movie becomes.

Image wisely chose to put the beginning, instead of the ending, in CAV. Although the last half-hour contains two great action sequences, it is the beginning which contains the most dynamic ensemble pieces and the most extensive dolly shots. The CAV is terrific fun, too, because at faster or slower speeds, the images take on new points of view. The disc is visual candy, and we can't get enough of it.

THE JOURNEY OF NATTY GANN

The stereo on *The Journey of Natty Gann* is quite enjoyable. The somewhat episodic story is about a girl who hikes and rides freight trains, during the Depression, to cross the country and join her father. Whether the sound effects involve the bustle of the city, the chugging steam engines and rattling rails, or the eerie quiet of an autumn forest, the disc captures and recreates each atmosphere. Added to this is an excellent musical score by James Horner. It not only sounds good, but it shifts in tempo and feeling to match each locale the heroine visits.

The picture on the disc is acceptable. The film would be more impressive if it weren't cropped. The movie might have been stronger if it had been trimmed by 5 or 6 minutes, but it is enough of a treat for one's senses that one's sensibilities readily follow.

JOURNEY TO THE CENTER OF THE EARTH

The perils of transferring a Cinemascope picture to home video screens are in evidence at the very opening of *Journey to the Center of the Earth*, as a rotating globe is made to look like an egg in order to squeeze the credits onto the square field of view. Cropping aside, the overall quality of the print is so good that the faded colors are easy to spot on the one inferior reel which is used on side two from minute 13 to minute 28.

Bernard Herrmann's music is well served by the stereo soundtrack, especially when it moves away from the pounding introductory organ bass for an exploratory harp score that seems to hang in midair. The film takes a long time getting started and is often pretty silly, but there are a couple of well executed action sequences.

JOURNEY TO THE 7TH PLANET/ANGRY RED PLANET

Both films in the 'Sci-Fi Double Bill,' *Journey to the 7th Planet/The Angry Red Planet*, depict a future where the transistor has yet to replace the vacuum tube. 'Angry Red Planet' is actually a reasonably good film, about a journey to Mars which ends in disaster. The movie is in color, and the disc transfer looks quite good. For the scenes on the Martian surface, however, the picture is slightly solarized and washed entirely with red (in reality, the way things would look on Venus), a clever visual trick which helps mask the cheap special effects. The heroine, Nora Hayden, acts reasonably intelligent and the narrative moves at a quick pace. Unless you asked for a lot more, you can't really ask for more.

'Journey' is a hokier effort, a cross between a typical *Star Trek* and 'Outer Limits' episode, about astronauts who land on Uranus (they pronounce it, 'you're on us') and are greeted with a number of curious hallucinations. It is best that the film is the first in the double bill. The image is blurry and the colors aren't as sharp as they are on 'Red Planet.' On both films, the sound is passable but the chapter encoding seems incomplete.

JOY OF LIVING
Although Lucille Ball has seventh billing on *Joy of Living*, Image has released the film, which stars Irene Dunne and Douglas Fairbanks, Jr., as a 'Lucille Ball Signature Collection' title. She has about four scenes and is not the center of attention in any of them. The movie is a romantic comedy about a Broadway star who is living too much of her life for others, and a man who finally sweeps her away. There are some long drunk scenes that don't work too well, but the cast, which also includes Guy Kibbee and the reliable Eric Blore, is talented, and the movie is moderately entertaining. The black-and-white print looks a little soft. There are a few Jerome Kern numbers sprinkled through the production, making one wish that the sound was mildly sharper than it is.

JPL PUBLIC INFORMATION ARCHIVE
(see **THE PLANETARY IMAGE VIDEODISC – VOLUME II**)

JUDGEMENT AT NUREMBERG
One of the earliest dramatic films to focus on the Jewish holocaust under the Nazis was Stanley Kramer's 1961 war crimes courtroom epic, *Judgement at Nuremberg*. Kramer displays far more sensitivity to the art of legal drama than he did in *Inherit the Wind*. He gives both sides an equal chance to win the sympathy of the viewer before revealing the stunning moral consequences which are hidden in plain view throughout the narrative.

The film is long, over three hours, and is mostly composed of talking heads, but that is what courtroom dramas are traditionally about, and the cast, including Spencer Tracy, Judy Garland, Richard Widmark, and Maximilian Schell, is up to the task. The film needs to be that long so that nothing is compromised. It can pull you all the way in, really get you involved in the judicial process and in the arguments.

The black-and-white print is in excellent condition. The sound is acceptable. There is both entrance and exit music, and plenty of chapter markers. Our only complaint is with the side breaks. The break between side one and side two interrupts not only a dramatic moment, but an important sequence of camera angles escalating the emotion of the scene. The break between side three and side four is also ill-chosen, and the free space at the end of the disc implies that more judicious interruptions could have been found.

JUDY'S FAVORITES
One of Judy Garland's last achievements was a quixotic television series which ran for less than a full season in the fall of 1963 (ironically, it was probably inspired by the ratings success of *Wizard of Oz*). The show was a variety hour, but Garland sometimes used it as a solitary performance showcase. Two of these concert hours have been released on laser disc by Image Entertainment. The jacket claims that the second side of *Judy's Favorites* is in stereo, but it is only some applause which has been rechanneled and even that is a little distracting. The sound is excellent, as is the black-and-white picture which is so sharp the instruments in the orchestra shine whenever the camera lights catch them. An annoying white line runs down the center of the picture for the first 20 minutes, but it disappears after that.

Garland's performance is invaluable. Her rendition of 'The Man That Got Away' is the most chillingly mature version she ever recorded (listen to her voice, at the end, follow the saxophone). Her tramp and clown getups are more jocular and less psychological than in other late performances. She sings a few songs which aren't part of her normal repertoire, such as 'Make Someone Happy' and 'When Johnny Comes Marching Home' and revitalizes 'favorites' like 'That's Entertainment' and 'On the Atchison, Topeka, and Santa Fe.' Throughout the 100-minute disc, she not only displays a full command of the studio stage, she also explores the intimacy of music on television. Her work was innovative, accomplished, and significant. CBS replaced her with a pair of game shows.

JULES AND JIM
Despite the nice transfer, *Jules and Jim* does not fare as well on disc as *400 Blows* does. Originally shot in 'Franscope,' which has a wider aspect ratio than one's television, the film loses much of the feeling the director, François Truffaut, had for his characters and for the distancing he placed between them and the rest of the world.

The black-and-white movie, about a double love affair among three friends which lasts years longer than it should have, is in French and has English subtitles which are often lost in the white chemises worn by the characters. The monaural sound is CX-encoded and adequately supports one of Georges Delerue's most haunting and deceptively calm scores.

What remains strongest about the film is the personality of the characters and their ever changing emotions. It is the sort of movie which ought to be seen multiple times if it is to be seen at all.

JULIA
The picture transfer on *Julia* is grainy and a little muddy. Douglas Slocombe's cinematography had a number of failed gauze shots, attempting, unevenly, to evoke memory, but the transfer's shortcomings have nothing to do with the film's own fuzziness. The colors on the disc are off a little. The opening shot of Lillian in the rowboat and the closing shot of Lillian in the rowboat should have the same bluish tones. The closing shot is close to accuracy, but the opening shot is too dark.

The analog stereo soundtrack is excellent. The stereo enhances Georges Delerue's score and enlivens a number of sound effects. The digital track, however, has an added layer of hiss which is distracting, and lacks any redeeming attributes which would make it preferable to the analog. The few chapter markers and accompanying descriptions ("Julia is killed.") are ridiculous.

As for the movie, the complicated interweaving of fact and fiction makes it difficult to judge on a value basis. Vanessa Redgrave's performance is tantalizing, and her saintly character – loving a child born from a rape, undaunted by physical pain – is a heroic role model to be honored and emulated. Jason Robards' Dashiel Hammett is also good fun. Jane Fonda's Lillian, however, is emptier and more inconsistent. At times she copies Myrna Loy's Nora Charles (especially during the opening night scene). At other times she exaggerates her character's obliviousness beyond sensibility – would a person who wrote as vicious and paranoid a play as 'The Children's Hour' really act so naïvely as to not follow simple instructions while smuggling money into Nazi Germany? The film has star appeal and gossip appeal, and the disc's soundtrack makes viewing it worthwhile, but sometimes you want to reach through the screen, reach through characters, reach through the words, reach through every layer of artistic endeavor, and strangle Lillian Hellman.

JULIA AND JULIA
Although it played in a few theaters, *Julia and Julia* was produced by Italian television with high definition video tape source material. It will remind one, in style, of an afternoon soap opera. The movie is a deliberately confusing puzzle about a woman whose mind is bearing the stress of remorse and guilt by playing tricks on her. It stars Kathleen Turner and Sting, and is performed in English (it was filmed in Trieste). Some viewers may find the format (it doesn't just have the texture of a soap opera, it has the acting, art direction, camera setups, and music of one as well) alienating, but if you can get through the first ten minutes or so, you'll probably be hooked for the rest of it. The picture quality of the disc lacks the crispness of some standard video tape recordings and looks like it has been transferred more times than necessary. It is in stereo, but the sound still reminded us more of daytime TV than of anything else.

JULIAN LENNON LIVE AT YOMIURI-LAND EAST, JAPAN 86 (Import)
The Japanese release, *Julian Lennon Live at Yomiuri-Land East, Japan 86*, is a full 54-minute concert. Lennon comes across as a performer 'in his own write,' and not just another pop celebrity with a version of 'Stand By Me.' He does 12 numbers, including 'It Won't Be Long,' and there is a little bit of jamming done to stretch the set out, but he puts on a satisfying show. He is a charismatic performer with a strong stage presence.

The concert takes place in an amphitheater on a bright August afternoon, so that the combination of sunlight, stage light, video recording equipment and laser disc playback produces a picture which is clearer than most window panes. The sound is digitally encoded and nicely mixed, although there would have been no harm if they had boosted Lennon's voice a little more than they have.

No subtitles appear on the disc. Like most Japanese music discs, a lyric sheet is provided on a jacket insert, in English.

JULIET OF THE SPIRITS
(see **GIULIETTA DEGLI SPIRITI**)

JULIO IGLESIAS IN SPAIN
Although *Julio Iglesias in Spain* depicts a live concert, every number is separated by interview material. Fortunately the disc is carefully chapter encoded and a listing is provided on the back of the jacket. The hour-long program, however, will be of interest to dedicated fans only, since the acoustics of the recordings are pale imitations of Iglesias' studio efforts. The stereo surround sound is adequately transferred. The picture is a little soft and often conceptually grainy.

JULIUS CAESAR
THE TRAGEDY OF ANTONY & CLEOPATRA

Jason Robards' first line in *Julius Caesar*, "A soothsayer bids you beware the ides of March," is so succinctly and dryly delivered it becomes instant proof that the film is a worthy endeavor and not just a star-studded exercise in haughty theatrics. Robard's full portrayal of Brutus has its good and bad points. At times he is too dry and flat, but at other times his delivery and manor are totally captivating, making a worthy counter-point to Charlton Heston's dunderheaded Marc Antony. John Gielgud is Caesar and is predictably regal, but the real surprise is Robert Vaughn, who appears very comfortable portraying Casca. Diana Rigg has one scene, as Portia.

The 1970 film, directed by Stuart Burge, is a worthwhile rendition of one of Shakespeare's very best plays. The film brings out the political aspects of the drama, the power struggles and secret positioning which each leader goes through to outmaneuver his peers. Woven throughout the drama are Shakespeare's assessments of man's endeavors. His lines are always spoken in character, but always have resonance which go beyond the necessities of conversation.

The disc is an honorable effort. It is letterboxed, with an aspect ratio of about 2:1, and the widescreen presentation assures the inclusion of all the major characters and activities when needs arise. The cinematography is not exceptional, but the wide image is constantly utilized, and the film would be very confusing without it. The source material is in rough shape in places, particularly during the first half-hour. There are splices, scratches, blurry colors, segments which, for a second or two, have a picture but no sound, and segments, the same length, which have sound but no picture. But the disc is an honorable effort. The cinematography itself is blurry in some shots, attempting, apparently, to evoke faded frescoes. The color and the sharpness, even after the condition of the image stabilizes, is never more than ordinary. The digital sound, lengthy dropouts aside, is strong enough to withstand amplification. And the disc is an honorable effort.

Shakespeare's *Julius Caesar* is a crowd pleaser. It has battle scenes, a tight plot, and a number of terrific one-liners. His sequel, *The Tragedy of Antony & Cleopatra*, also has spectacle and political intrigue, but it is a more challenging work, intended to ruminate not upon the glories of man's endeavors but upon the uncomfortable truths about marriage and middle age. It is a highly respected play, but requires shrewd and comprehensive artistic guidance to hold an audience for all of its three hours. The disc, which features a production that is more competent but in the same vein as *The Tempest*, lacks the ingredients needed it bring it off.

Lynn Redgrave is adept as Cleopatra, and Timothy Dalton, though weaker, makes a passable Antony. But Walter Koenig as Pompey? At first his stiff manor and nervous hand gestures provide comic relief, but after a while you stop taking the project seriously (Nichelle Nichols also appears, as one of Cleopatra's handmaidens, but her performance is workable). Confined to a single soundstage set with few decorations, the presentation wears out its welcome long before the play nears its conclusion.

Taken from a videotape source, the picture is mildly fuzzy but passable. The sound goes through an early shakedown, as it did on *The Tempest*, but is serviceable. The four-sided disc comes in a gatefold jacket. An elaborate plot synopsis, coordinated without enumeration to the chapter encoding, appears on the innerspread, though the effort is marred by a typographical error which repeats several lines of text.

JUMP THE BLUES AWAY

The Joe Walsh, Albert Collins, Etta James concert, *Jump the Blues Away*, is rousing and noisy. Walsh looks a little past his prime, but Collins is energized and James responds with enthusiasm. The numbers are short and the time limit on the show seems to hurry everyone along a bit, but there may be nothing wrong with that. Besides, the theme of the show is getting rid of the blues, not keeping them. The picture and sound are fine.

JUMPIN' JACK FLASH

The opening to *Jumpin' Jack Flash* has 20th Century Fox's stereophonic flourish and it is a disappointment that CBS/Fox has opted to leave the soundtrack in analog. There are many cute little separations and an energetic musical score, and the transfer short changes them. The picture is slightly grainy as well, but this is less bothersome than the sound, because it has less potential.

The movie is a classic execution of the comedian-playing-an-innocent-who-falls-in-with-spies genre, and is every bit as efficient as *They Got Me Covered*, etc.,in generating laughs and good feelings. Some of the situations in which Whoopi Goldberg's character finds herself are ridiculous, but they are also traditional slapstick-type gags, where reality is less important than the humorous effects of physical improbabilities.

Goldberg is provided with a wonderful cast of supporting actors, from Stephen Collins to Carol Kane, who help to balance the intensity of her own presence. When Goldberg has scenes with extras or a few of the actors who are not so talented, she tends to dominate the whole screen.

JUNE NIGHT (see **INTERMEZZO**)

JUNGLE BOOK

Alexander Korda's interpretation of Rudyard Kipling's *Jungle Book*, starring Sabu, was released by Embassy as part of its Children's Treasures series, although the abandonment of the baby in the jungle at the beginning may be disturbing to youngsters.

The lavishly photographed Technicolor film suffers from what are now archaic transfer-to-video methods. The picture has way too much contrast, the print has splices and even slips at one point, and the sound, not CX-encoded, is warped and scratchy. The movie, however, is so richly decorated that not even these faults can keep the disc from looking scrumptious.

The script must trivialize Kipling's work to maintain a human drama and circumvent the need for elaborate special effects. There are a few talking animals, and snakes operated by clearly delineated wires, but the plot concentrates on Mowgli's life in a village near the jungle, and the greed ignited by his knowledge of hidden treasure. The movie has a wide-eyed affection for adventure which contemporary films are often condemned for imitating. For that matter, it is impossible to imagine Sabu being a star today.

JUST A GIGOLO

Any movie with David Bowie in it seems to automatically obtain a cult following, and such is the logic for making *Just a Gigolo* available to disc fans. *Gigolo*, directed by David Hemmings, has difficulty finding its style and voice. The second half is less experimental and is better than the first half. Set in Berlin between the wars, the story is about a German ex-army officer, played by Bowie, who drifts through society in a somewhat numb state as politics and sex simmer and boil around him. Hemmings lacks the experience to coax a usable performance out of Bowie, but other performers pop up, including Kim Novak and an elderly Marlene Dietrich, to keep things interesting.

The movie was made on a low budget, but the source material doesn't help matters any. The picture is soft and the predominantly golden tones are often quite blurry. There are also scratches and other signs of wear. The sound is monaural, but on side one the audio seemed to be easier on the ears when isolated to a single channel. The film is in English, but the dialog does not always match the lip movements.

JUST ONE OF THE GUYS

The photo of Joyce Hyser holding the football helmets can be found in all the ads for *Just One of the Guys*, and it's on the jacket, but her character never goes near a football and doesn't so much as undo her shoelaces in the locker room. She does pretend to be of another gender, but only for two weeks and under predictable circumstances. With the exception of Billy Jacoby, who portrays the little brother and ingratiates himself the way little brothers are apt to do, the whole cast seems out of place. The picture is mildly grainy and the sound is unexceptional.

K-9

A movie can be perfect even when it is flawed, and so can a disc. *K-9* is a wonderful little action comedy that has indulgences which some viewers may not have the patience for. Jim Belushi portrays a narcotics detective who obtains a police dog to assist him as he goes after a kingpin. The script has contrivances, but each one advances the humor, if not the plot. Belushi's dialog is amusing. His performance has an appeal and a confidence which was missing in *Red Heat*. The dog also has his day.

The picture transfer is very good and has no significant discrepancies. The film's soundtrack, however, is flawed, and the problems show up clearly on the disc playback, though it doesn't spoil the fun in the slightest. There are passages which surge inappropriately, and a scene with echoes which is awkwardly executed – but none of that matters. The digital stereo surround sound is terrific. It is totally enveloping and as obnoxiously ingratiating as Belushi's cop and his slobbering buddy.

KAJAGOOGOO
The 8-inch, *Kajagoogoo*, is not quite as bad as the name implies, though neither is the group at the forefront of innovative musical style. 'Too Shy,' about a waitress who never seems quite able to get across the dance floor, is the best on the disc. It is not offensive, but it has no lasting qualities either. The picture and sound are okay.

KANDYLAND
Sandahl Bergman, who had a promising career before she was out-statuesqued by Brigitte Nielsen, portrays a stripper who dreams of being a ballet dancer in *Kandyland*. Surprisingly, Bergman, and the film's principal, Kim Evenson, give wonderful performances, particularly in the scenes they have together. Bergman does such a classy job, in fact, that her potentially ridiculous finale, a drugged-out, dying swan bit ending in a death leap from the roof of the Kandyland Club (as the pounding disco music gives way, oh so briefly, to strains of Tchaikovsky), is grand camp. Evenson portrays a novice stripper whose experiences provide her with maturity. The film has elements common to cheap exploitation films, but it also has touches of intelligence.

The sound was recorded in Ultra-Stereo and the mix has a few entertaining turns of its own. The picture is a little grainy and the neon lights have a faint blur.

KANSAS
What are movie viewers supposed to do with Andrew McCarthy and Matt Dillon now that they're here? Take *Kansas*, for example. Dillon is the bad guy and plays his role letter-perfect, as a bank robber on the run. McCarthy is the good guy, initially involved in the robbery, he subsequently saves a girl from drowning and is 'wanted' as a hero. He plays his role perfectly, too, with panache and the right touch of mystery. They look great, they're established stars, they both do good work, and yet the film is so empty when they're on the screen that the narrative momentum repeatedly collapses. It may partially be the director's fault, since he never uses a close up when a long shot will do, but that magical something called charisma eludes McCarthy and Dillon completely.

The disc has a slightly grainy picture, and uninteresting stereo surround. The musical score, though, by Pino Donaggio, sounds great, full of dramatic flourish which the film can't possibly equal.

KAOMA WORLD BEAT THE LAMBADA VIDEOS
The 8-inch disc, *Kaoma World Beat The Lambada Videos*, is all of 9 minutes long – 18 seconds for every letter in the disc's title. One cut is a conceptual video, set at a beach resort, and the other is a concert clip. Both are pleasant, but the disc is over before you really have time to relax. The picture transfer is fine and the videos are in CAV, with blurred movement in the still frames.

THE KARATE KID
The Karate Kid is a good movie when it is dealing with honest emotion and embarrassing when it has to make things up to move the plot along. The boy, played by Ralph Macchio, will suddenly do or say something very stupid so that his character will get into trouble. Part of the fault is Macchio's acting, because he doesn't convince the viewer that his character would, indeed, do such a thing, but part of the problem is the script which calls for him to do it so he can learn a lesson.

Pat Morita, portraying the handyman who teaches the boy martial arts, is perfect all the way through, superfluous to the fact that he seems to live in two different places and doesn't go to his job for weeks on end. When Morita is the center of attention, the movie soars. The film was a big hit because the intelligence which went into the scenes with Morita legitimized the plot's trumped-up conflicts. The picture is mildly grainy and the sound is passable.

THE KARATE KID PART II
How can you find fault with a film which gives as much attention to the intricacies of a Japanese tea ceremony as it does to each blow in the final duel-to-the-death fight? *The Karate Kid Part II* is an improvement over the first episode in that Ralph Macchio is more at ease with his character, and the conflict, although far more elaborate, is much less contrived. Since you get a complete and cogent summary of the first *Karate Kid* during the opening credit scroll, having this one disc takes care of owning both movies.

The picture has a slight orange tint. The stereo sound is well-mixed and executed. Bill Conti's music is also well served. His early work showed no promise whatsoever, but many of his later scores have been remarkable. In *Karate Kid Part II*, he is basically just repeating his music from the first film. The orchestration, like Macchio's performance, is both calmer and more confident.

THE KARATE KID PART III
Ralph Macchio is about a foot taller in *The Karate Kid Part III* than he is in the opening prolog which contains excerpts from the first film, even though the events of the movie are set only a few months later. Once again, the kid's girlfriend from the previous movie is conveniently dispensed with a line of dialog at the beginning. Once again the kid acts stupidly and seems to remember his lessons on an erratic basis. This time the plot becomes a little too farfetched, with a villain who is super-rich and equally mean, but the essential pleasures of the series, such as they are, can still be had.

The picture has a very slight matting, and the color transfer looks good in most shots. The stereo surround sound has little to offer.

KATE BUSH – THE SINGLE FILE (Import)
KATE BUSH LIVE AT HAMMERSMITH ODEON (Import)
Kate Bush sings as if someone had just dropped an ice cube down the back of her dress and she didn't want anyone to know. Two hour-long Kate Bush laser discs are available in Japan, *Kate Bush Live at Hammersmith Odeon* and *Kate Bush – The Single File*.

The Single File is supposedly a collection of music videos, though you have to get through about half the disc before the numbers become more than just Kate Bush standing in front of a gauzy lens in a weirdo outfit, singing. There is one satisfying video, 'Babooshka,' in which she dances with a bass fiddle, but, other than that, there aren't enough to fill a poor 8-inch, let alone a decent 12. On one, the recording is 'live' (there's clapping) while the video is of Bush alone in a room.

Live at the Hammersmith Odeon is even less satisfying, since she doesn't do 'Babooshka' (the discs share only three numbers) and there are no pieces which stand out. Bush has a microphone that is suspended in front of her mouth like an orthodontal retainer and generally goes through the same costume changes and exaggerated movements ('choreography') that she did on her videos.

KAZUMI WATANABE – SPICE OF LIFE
The title, *Kazumi Watanabe – Spice of Life*, is just what Watanabe's music is missing, the 'spice of life.' He plays MOR fusion jazz, and although the musicians get all sweaty (the disc is a record of a live performance) the music has no energy. The concert runs a little over an hour and although side two is only 28 minutes long, it is in CLV. The cameras get fairly close to the performers and stay there, so technique can be studied from the disc if nothing else. One or two segments present some alternate visuals, but these passages are exceptions to the format. The picture and sound are perfectly rendered and perfectly dull.

KEATON'S COP
Abe Vigoda plays a retired mobster who becomes a target in *Keaton's Cop* and Lee Majors plays the detective assigned to protect him. Don Rickles also appears for a little while. Vigoda and Rickles are enjoyable, but no one else in the movie can act, and the filmmakers are forever shooting away from the cast member who is talking, or even shooting the cast member from behind, and then filling in the dialog after the fact. As a result, the conversations are often out of synch and sound fuzzy. The sound effects are well executed and the Ultra-Stereo surround sound is worth amplifying. The picture is mildly blurry in places, but generally acceptable. The film is set in Galveston, but everyone talks like they're from New York.

KEETJE TIPPEL
Although there are erotic sequences in Paul Verhoeven's *Keetje Tippel* which brush against hardcore, the 1975 film has an old-fashioned, plotty narrative. It is a period film, about a woman pulling herself out of poverty in Amsterdam near the turn of the century. The movie is in Dutch and the colors have an inexpensive European cinema look to them and are somewhat faded. The focus is soft in places. The digital monaural sound is passable and the movie has a pleasant musical score.

KELLY'S HEROES
KELLY'S HEROES (Import)
The Japanese release of *Kelly's Heroes* is in letterboxed format (with Japanese subtitles appearing beneath the picture) and has digital sound. The colors are a little faded. The sky is never blue and a comparison of the appropriate scenes with the stills on the back of the jacket reveals that the brightest distinctions between hues and shades are gone. But more is gained than lost. The digital encoding

effectively captures and enhances the marvelous stereo soundtrack, with explosions, gunfire, tank engines, bells, and a rainstorm. The wide screen not only allows you to see more explosions and gunshots, it also enables you to catch several of the best visual gags, such as the showdown with the German tank or the double reaction shot of Clint Eastwood and Telly Savalas responding to Donald Sutherland's "positive waves," all of which are lost when the movie is scanned for TV.

The American MGM/UA release, in comparison, has stronger colors, but it is not letterboxed and even the analog sound on the Japanese disc is less noisy than the CX-encoded stereo sound on the American disc.

Kelly's Heroes has gained in stature since it was first released. Initially dismissed as a lame Clint Eastwood movie, with one of the worst theme songs ever written for a major film, the story is not just a World War II heist comedy. It is an intriguing examination of management styles. Eastwood portrays Kelly, a disillusioned soldier who was busted from the officer corps for following orders. Despite his lowered rank, he has no trouble motivating others to follow his lead. Savalas portrays a sergeant whose leadership style is more direct. Sutherland, as the spaced-out commander of a tank company, has an indirect style which is just as effective. The staff officers in the film are portrayed as powerless and unable to do more than claim accomplishments which are actually beyond their control. And the whole film cumulates when the heroes decide to *negotiate* with the Germans to get what they need. Not that there isn't plenty of mayhem and destruction before the negotiation starts.

The 146-minute film is suitable both for entertainment and study. It is contained on three sides, with an entr'acte opening side three of the Japanese disc. Most of the music matches the spirit of the film and is especially effective with digital encoding. But oh, that theme song, 'Burning Bridges.' Music by Lalo Schifrin and lyrics by Mike Curb. The same Mike Curb who went on to do to California politics what he did to poetry with this concoction. It is the sort of song which you only have to hear once and you will remember for the rest of your life. Fortunately, the pleasure the film provides is equally memorable.

KENNETH MACMILLAN'S ROMEO AND JULIET – THE ROYAL BALLET

Kenneth MacMillan choreographed a rather traditional-looking *Romeo and Juliet* to go with Sergei Prokofiev's score, which is anything but traditional. Prokofiev deliberately undercut the traditional formats with his hit and run themes, forcing most choreographers to interpret his music with modern concepts. But MacMillan, ever British, went right ahead and staged a regular *Romeo and Juliet*, with a ball, a balcony, a bedroom, a chapel, a market place, a crypt, and a cast of dozens.

The Orchestra of the Royal Opera House does a rousing, full-tilt rendition of Prokofiev's score. Audio distortion is minimal, although some of the higher pitched instruments get fuzzy in places. The stereo separations are a treat, and when Mercrutio and Tybalt fight, the sounds of their swords cross from left to right as they do.

The picture is not bad. The sets and costumes are all problematic shades of red, orange, gold, and maroon, yet the disc is only mildly blurry at the color interfaces. The 128-minute program is assigned to three sides and has 13 chapter markers, one for each scene. Alessandra Ferri is Juliet and Wayne Eagling is Romeo. Their efforts are inconsistent, but captivating during the most important passages. It isn't necessary that one watch the disc too closely anyway. Even though it is ballet, it is music most of all.

KENNY AND DOLLY – REAL LOVE

Kenny and Dolly – Real Love runs close to an hour and is contained on a single side. After some video-manipulated voiced-over openings, each star does a solo turn before the final duet. There is too little country-western material on laser disc to find fault with such an offering. The sound is digitally encoded. Filmed in Portland, Oregon on a circular runway in the center of an arena, the recording hasn't the purity of studio material, but most of the numbers have been heard so often that it is refreshing to have a different angle on them. The picture is perfectly fine and displays the stars to good advantage.

KENTUCKY KERNELS

Cable is responsible for the resurrection of Bert Wheeler and Robert Woolsey, two enormously popular comics from the early thirties whose films lacked the critical appeal and academic staying power of the more elite comedians. Buried in the clutter of the past, they were finally dusted off by Ted Turner and have attracted the sort of cult following which makes their films ideal for disc collecting, particularly when chapter encoding can prompt the viewer past the slower passages.

Kentucky Kernels is a family-feud spoof set in a very Southern California-ish Kentucky. The film was directed by George Stevens of all people, and boasts Noah Beery, Margaret Dumont, and Spanky McFarland among the supporting players. Now all we have to do is say something like, "Watch what happens when the horse drinks the moonshine," and you will get a fairly accurate idea of what the film is up to. There are never any gut-wrenching guffaws, but there is a steady stream of clowning. Wheeler and Woolsey are very adept at relaxing the viewer. They entertain not only by placing their characters in funny predicaments, but by half acknowledging that they are comics making a movie – telegraphing every gag so far in advance that it no longer matters when they get around to executing it. The humor is in the anticipation.

The black-and-white picture is a little washed out, but passable, as is the sound. The movie runs 75 minutes, but has been left in CLV.

THE KEY

Carol Reed's *The Key* is a black-and-white Cinemascope production which has been, except for the credit sequences, scanned and cropped. The scanning also causes the image to jiggle a bit. The cinematography is excellent, and the cropping robs a significant amount of the film's atmosphere. The basic quality of the source material looks good, but the transfer looks a little soft as well. Side three of the disc runs only twenty minutes, but the break between side two and three could not come at a worse time. It happens right in the middle of a Morse Code message.

We are surprised that *The Key* does not have a stronger cult following. The film is about British tug boats assigned to rescue crippled cargo ships during the early days of World War II, but it has a hint of the supernatural, and that is usually enough to inspire fanatical devotion. William Holden and Sophia Loren star (their presence as foreigners is logical in the script) and the film has a good mix of exciting naval action sequences and enigmatic romantic scenes. Perhaps if the whole movie were letterboxed, it would get the attention it deserves.

KID CREOLE AND THE COCONUTS LIVE IN CONCERT "AT THE RITZ" NEW YORK (Import)

Worth mentioning because the transfer, both video and sound, is spectacular, *Kid Creole and the Coconuts Live in Concert "At the Ritz" New York* is a Japanese release. The sound is so clear that the music almost seems as if it was recorded in a studio instead of in front of a bobbing mob.

Kid Creole is a band in a category unto itself, a cross between new wave, reggae, and aerobicise. Creole is an entertaining performer and his lyrics are catchy, but one's attention is inevitably drawn to the Coconuts, his slender female backup vocalists. They go through a complex set of synchronized calisthenics for close to an hour without missing a note. It is no wonder they are so skinny.

THE KID FROM BROOKLYN

Embassy outdid themselves with the gorgeous Technicolor print on *The Kid from Brooklyn*. Even the reel change marks are bright magenta. The film, starring Danny Kaye, was a rare color effort by the great cinematographer, Gregg Toland. It looks scrumptious on disc. To point out just one choice moment: Eve Arden is standing in a dimly lit room, wearing what is clearly a two-tone green dress. She flicks a light switch and her dress explodes in florescence.

This is one of Kaye's better efforts in that he does not digress from the plot for too long too often. It is about a milkman who is conned into thinking he can be a prizefighter. The songs are by Styne and Cahn.

KIDNAPPED

Two sisters are visiting a zoo and taking pictures. One is kidnapped. The other shouts and must duck to avoid gun fire. Realizing the situation is dangerous, does she pick up her camera and take pictures of the abductors? No, she goes running after them, screaming, camera swinging in her hand. Does the detective assigned to her case ask her for the film to see if, by chance, she'd taken a photo of the criminals earlier in the day? No, he asks her out to dinner. Since the detective has a pet monkey, which he leaves at home, unattended, is his house a complete mess when he comes home from a long day's work? No, it is immaculate, and the monkey's outfit is unsoiled. Is *Kidnapped,* which has a grainy picture and non-stereo stereo digital encoding, a really stupid disc? Yes.

THE KILLER ELITE

After Sam Peckinpah completed *The Killer Elite* it was edited by the producers to obtain a PG rating, a move which saved the film financially, but bankrupted its potential for long term annuity. Viewed once, the movie is both taut and mildly comical, an uneasy balance between satire and seriousness which manages enough thrills to keep a viewer happy. In multiple viewings, however, the satire begins to overwhelm everything else, and even though it is still one of the most violent PG movies this side of the *Temple of Doom*, the action is too brief to escape anticipation.

The disc has a running time of 124 minutes. The sound is digitally encoded monaural and has no severe problems although the sound editing is overloaded with effects, music, and noise. Except for occasional shots which look faded at the bottom of the screen, the picture is in decent shape. The disc has chapter markers and side three, which features the big shoot-out, is in CAV, with two unsteady still frames out of every five.

KILLER KLOWNS FROM OUTER SPACE

Perhaps *Killer Klowns from Outer Space* doesn't quite live up to the vision which the title inspires – the film's lighting and color quality, for example, isn't as glossy as one would hope – but the script is amusing enough to satisfy those who are attracted to it in the first place. The plot is just as the title says. Alien creatures, who bear the resemblance and mannerisms of circus clowns, land near a small town and collect its inhabitants in cotton candy cocoons. The filmmakers have enough gags and ideas to fill a one-ring circus and no more, but at its most inspired (the heroine, attempting to escape from her house, runs to the window, only to see the clowns outside holding a rescue net, eagerly waiting for her to jump) the movie is difficult to resist.

The picture is passable. The sound is mischievous and captivating, but there is a fault with one of the sound effect and dialog tracks on the film, which comes out fuzzy at key moments. The disc has a number of chapter markers. It opens with a trailer for *Sticky Fingers*, which makes that film look much more energetic than it is, and closes with a music video for the *Killer Klowns* title song, performed by The Dickies.

THE KILLERS (Import)

The 1966 Don Siegel film in which Ronald Reagan is cast as the main bad guy, *The Killers*, is available in Japan. Because Reagan made the movie so late in his acting career, his appearance is especially familiar, you recognize the creases.

The print used for the transfer is super. It has one or two splices, but the color is terrific and the image is sharp. It looks so good that the Japanese subtitles become bothersome. The sound is monaural, not CX-encoded, and is a little noisy.

The movie is also terrific. It is about a pair of assassins who try to solve the mystery of why they were hired to kill a man. The plot, which involves automobile racing, never slows down and the cast, including Lee Marvin, Angie Dickinson, John Cassavetes, Norman Fell and, in an especially amusing role as a high-strung murderer, Clu Gulager, is wonderful.

THE KILLING

The depthless essay on the back of the jacket for *The Killing* calls the plot, "fairly straightforward." In reality, and in a form which echoes the narrator's weaving metaphors, the plot continually hiccups in time. It jumps forward and backward and all over the place to build the exposition of a racetrack heist from an emotional/dramatic logic instead of a chronological logic. The film, Stanley Kubrick's first mainstream effort, is wonderful fun, and the shuffling of the narrative works just as it is supposed to, because a viewer can go nuts trying to guess what will appear next on the screen. And, after it is all over, the film ends on one of the most marvelous, self-depreciating lines of dialog the movies have ever generated.

The black-and-white contrasts are clear enough that you can see the shadow of either equipment or personnel being moved out of the way when Elisha Cook, Jr. crosses the room to a new toe mark. Minor technical errors like that aside, Kubrick's approach is as innovative in technique as it is in narrative. Long dolly shots through a cramped apartment. The same footage is utilized more than a single time in the editing. It is a shame the disc is only in CLV, especially since the 1956 film is just 84 minutes long.

We had difficulty ferreting out background dialog, which always seemed perfectly clear when heard in a theater, but it may just be that the more you concentrate on such things, the less your subconscious is willing to help out. The disc has plenty of chapter markers, and their denotation on the jacket cover assists in an understanding of the plot's structure.

A KILLING AFFAIR

A woman spends a couple of tense days with the man who murdered her no-good husband in *A Killing Affair*, an interesting if limited drama. It is set in West Virginia (though it was filmed in Georgia) during the forties. Peter Weller, with an accent, does a good job as the murderer. The film's own color scheme is extremely pale, but the disc transfer is accurate and adds no distortion to the presentation. The sound is okay. John Barry did the score.

THE KILLING FIELDS

Fortunately, the Warner release of *The Killing Fields* is in beautiful condition. Since the movie's budget was limited, the screen composition is well scaled to a television set. The CX-encoded stereo has a terrific mix.

The Killing Fields is a tense adventure film which makes the similarly-plotted *Year of Living Dangerously* feel like a cartoon in comparison. It is based on a true story and the verisimilitude is supposed to provide the message. The nature of life comes strongly into question when the political events within and outside of Cambodia lead to the slaughter of a great percentage of its populace. Even though *The Killing Fields* concentrates relentlessly on the excitement of escaping the slaughter, one gets a sense that the filmmakers wanted to tell people about what happened in Cambodia so the events would not be forgotten. They went about it in the right way, and since the movie has been so excellently preserved on disc, the record is permanent.

THE KILLING TIME

Beau Bridges is the only problem with an otherwise dandy murder thriller, *The Killing Time*. The less said about the plot the better, except that it cleverly winds several different characters around each other so tightly that they all eventually explode. Keifer Sutherland, Wayne Rogers, and Jon Don Baker give natty, inspired performances, but Bridges is supposed to be a James Cain-type hero, whose intellect is clouded by passion, and every time the camera comes straight onto his face you just can't believe it. He's too much of a cuddly frump.

The movie was filmed in various towns along the northern California coast, and has a nice, misty atmosphere. The picture transfer is decent, although the photography is occasionally out of focus. The monaural sound is digitally encoded and never calls attention to itself.

KILLPOINT

The title, *Killpoint*, is something of a misnomer, because the characters in the film dispatch one another the same way one would dynamite fish. The disc is a poorly transferred jumble of bad acting, uninspired violence, and unchoreographed martial arts. Leo Fong portrays a government agent investigating an armory theft. His performance is acceptable but the people playing his two bosses must have been brought in off the street. The confused plot ends are explained by these two as they talk to each other on the telephone by holding the receivers and reading cue cards. The bad guys shoot anything that moves and many things, such as a row of aerosol cans, which do not move at all. The bodies pile up, but so does the tedium.

KIND HEARTS AND CORONETS/THE CAPTAIN'S PARADISE
THE LAVENDER HILL MOB/THE MAN IN THE WHITE SUIT

Four black-and-white Alec Guinness films are available on two disc collections, *Kind Hearts and Coronets/The Captain's Paradise* and *The Lavender Hill Mob/ The Man in the White Suit*. Both sets come in gatefold jackets which contain the same essay on the innerspread, a nice summary of Guinness' rise to fame, by Jeff Schwager. *The Lavender Hill Mob/The Man in the White Suit* fits on three sides, with 'Suit' beginning at chapter four on side two. *Kind Hearts and Coronets/The Captain's Paradise*, runs to four sides and is separated a film to a platter.

None of the source material is any better than what one sees on TV or in the revival houses. 'Kind Hearts' is about the cleanest and sharpest. 'Suit' also looks sharp, but has a few more tatters. 'Captain's Paradise' has a much softer image that also has a few scratches. 'Mob' is the most difficult to assess. It is sharp, but the contrasts are so high that details in the white areas of the screen sometimes get lost and the image has a tentative feel to it. We recall seeing copies on broadcast TV which had a stronger and more detailed image, but they also tended to have more splices and scratches than this version. The monaural sound on all four films is passable.

We recommend, if you can afford it, watching all four in one sitting (though it is best if one reverses the order in *Mob/Suit* to watch 'Mob' as the finale). Even though there are a number of similarities among the films – all are set in narrative flashback, some characters actors appear repeatedly, all have ambiguous endings – watching them together never becomes tiresome the way some other marathons can become tiresome, even when one is overly familiar with all the films. Most people like 'Mob' the best, though our own favorite is 'Captain's Paradise.' 'Mob' is a heist film, a very early offering in the genre, and one which has some charming moments. Although it runs a scant 77 minutes, however, it is padded with chase scenes and is a bit too linear to provide resonance beyond its story line. 'Paradise,' on the other hand, is loaded with resonance. It is about a bigamist who maintains a different lifestyle with each of his two wives, commuting between them as the captain of a boat on the Gibraltar/Morocco run. Although interpretations of it may have shifted, the content has not been dated by the rise in feminist consciousness, since the emotional point of view remains understated throughout. Guinness, without the assistance of the cute sound effects that help him in the other films, adds to the movie's success by not gloating over his character's accomplishments.

'Kind Hearts' is a murder comedy in which Guinness has a secondary role as do all the victims. The script is very careful to maintain sympathy for the hero throughout his activities, and the episodic nature of the narrative makes the movie highly repeatable. 'Suit' is the weirdest of all the films, about a genius who sneaks into textile laboratories to develop a grotesque but stain-resistant fabric. The plot then illogically proposes that its development would threaten the textile industry. Only the efforts of the wonderful cast keep the viewer attentive.

THE KINDRED

Rod Steiger appears in *The Kindred*, long enough to slip and fall into a slimy pit. He acts, however, as if he never got W.C. Fields completely out of his system, and he is good for an arched eyebrow or two. The film is, as the quotes on the jacket cover assure potential buyers, gruesome. The puppet work is good and the plot, although lacking in literary merit, gets points for moving from beginning to end without any pauses. The low budget picture quality has been transferred accurately, with only a couple of splices. The monaural sound is without the benefit of CX-encoding, but is noisy enough to prevent one from nodding off during the proceedings.

KING CRIMSON LIVE IN JAPAN – THREE OF A PERFECT PAIR (Import)

The first disc to be encoded with digital sound was the Japanese release, *King Crimson Live in Japan – Three of a Perfect Pair*. The 90-minute concert disc will not meet everyone's tastes in entertainment. King Crimson is a group of musicians, including Robert Fripp, who take their music seriously. They have a very electronic, scholarly sound, and they just sort of grind and tweak away at one melodic idea or another.

KING DAVID

In a way it is a shame that the 114-minute *King David* was not done in digital, because the soundtrack is absolutely spectacular. As it is, the CX-encoded stereo sound is utterly noiseless and the mix harks back to the biblical epics of old. The picture is grainy and murky and spate with an occasional horizontal line. The sound, however, is so much fun that the film's tedious content doesn't start getting to you until well into side two.

Verily, the first part of the movie is actually enjoyable. The major fault is the presence of Richard Gere in the title role. Someone else, or perhaps merely the representation of David as a glowing orb, would have been more effective. What the movie lacks most, though, is eroticism. If this is not going to be a Basal Reader interpretation, then it ought to have some good, steamy sex. Instead, there's hardly even any kissing. Thankfully, the Lord, who ought to smite those responsible for the film's narrative collapse, has smiled upon the disc in the face of adversity. Get the disc, and as it starts to get boring, just start jacking up the sound.

KING KONG (Voyager)
KING KONG (Voyager CAV)
KING KONG (Image)

Voyager's *King Kong* had a much better picture transfer than what was usually broadcast on local television or shown in revival houses when it was first released. Since that time, further restoration efforts have produced even better presentations, but Voyager's version is still the best available on disc.

A CAV disc was released initially, followed, several years later, by a CLV rendition. The picture transfer is good, except for the famous 'censored' inserts which look more blurry than everything else. The 1933 sound has subtleties, especially in Max Steiner's score, which would have remained lost if less care had gone into transferring the film to disc. The CAV version has a slightly sharper image than the CLV version.

Both discs contain an alternate audio track lecture by Ronald Haver, which we found entertaining but a bit too enthusiastic. On side four of the CAV disc, after the film is ended, there is a still-step essay documenting the making of *Kong* and a marvelous stop-animation short about a man who shoots a baby dinosaur.

Image has also released a version of King Kong with an alternate audio track lecture, this time by Paul Mandell. The picture quality is not as good as Voyager's rendition and looks a little washed out. Like Haver, Mandell sometimes succumbs to describing the action on the screen – pointless unless a viewer's head is turned. The lecture track has a distinct hum in the background but the film's audio track is much cleaner. Mandell enjoys trivia and conveys many nuggets with which you can astound your friends (for example, Jim Thorpe is in one of the native panic scenes), while imparting a fair sense of how the film was put together.

The script and the special effects in *King Kong* are brilliant. The story has symmetry. In the very first scene, a producer goes into New York at night to search for a girl, as Kong will do at the end. Some people will say *King Kong* is about the horrors of the 1930 depression. Others prefer to examine the relationship between Wray and her three leading males. As much as anything though, *King Kong* is about movie making. It is about what a film producer will go through to give his audience a good time, from the rituals and anxieties on Skull Island to the opening night disaster in Manhattan. If there is one thing Haver's lecture manages to make clear, it is that the people who made *King Kong* loved what they were doing. The discs impart that same feeling.

KING KONG LIVES

The channels are reversed on the analog soundtrack of *King Kong Lives*, but on the digital soundtrack, the left and right separations are correct and match the images on the screen. The picture is a little grainy. The digital sound is cleaner, but the analog seems to have more detail. The movie opens with scenes from the first Dino De Laurentiis *Kong* picture, before shifting gears and becoming an American version of a Japanese monster movie. The same director even made both Kong films, but where the first was an attempt to invoke artistic allusion, the second is an intriguing adaptation of Japanese commercialism. Without the Japanese passion for miniaturization, however, the concept lacks its basic drive.

KING: MONTGOMERY TO MEMPHIS

The Reverend Martin Luther King, Jr. made a timely and lasting contribution to American society. The documentary *King: Montgomery to Memphis* makes it evident that if King had attempted to organize his non-violent resistance movement before there was television, the clarity and forcefulness of his argument, and the stupidity of the violence used against him, would not have been as evident to as great a number of people as was needed to support the changes he strived for. It is a useful argument against those who charge that television only encourages violence. Nevertheless, the courage it took to stand in the face of anger and not become angry, and the gift for speaking with intelligence, emotion, focus, and persuasiveness, made King a great man. His accomplishments will not fade as time passes.

The documentary is clever. It is meant to be a log of King's major speeches, but to give the film drama, footage of the speeches is interspersed with footage of the marches and the confrontations. It is never boring. King's most famous pronouncement, the 'I Had a Dream' speech, at the conclusion of side one, is shown not just in its entirety, but in its context as well, demonstrating, dramatically, what a truly momentous speech it was. The footage is generally quite ragged, as its historical importance at the time was underappreciated. Everything is in black and white and ranges from worn to blurry. The disc transfer itself is probably quite good, as the 1970 film was concentrating on content and not decoration. The sound preserves the recordings as well as can be expected.

KING OF HEARTS

Philippe De Broca, whose every movie is a cult classic of one sort or another, directed the charming and memorable World War I comedy, *King of Hearts*, in the mid-sixties. Voyager has released a nice-looking presentation of the color film, which has as perfect a closing shot as any movie could ever provide. The image has been letterboxed with an aspect ratio of about 2.1:1, and English subtitles appear beneath the picture. (A great deal of the movie has no dialog at all. Other parts of it, however, are in French, German, and even English. In one sequence, the hero, played by Alan Bates, reads a message in English which is superseded by a French voiceover, although the English can still be heard underneath, and subtitles are provided for the French. We have seen theatrical copies where more of the English dialog was dubbed over in a similar manner, but that is not the case here.)

The source material has a few mild flaws, both on the picture and on the soundtrack, but the colors look nice and the image is satisfying. The one exception is a poorly filtered day for night passage. Early copies were subject to manufacturing errors and lock or skip at the end of side one.

The film is universal in its appeal and a description of its contents is essentially irrelevant. We would like to make note of Georges Delerue's musical score, however. There is a sequence in which the central characters, inmates from a local asylum, explore and take over an abandoned town. The sequence is mainly free of dialog, but the music is worth many words. Each character has a different theme, and as the characters become bolder in the roles they assume, the music also builds, both in melody and flourish. There is also an off-tempo polka which strikes up at key moments and almost immediately dissolves into dissonance, again in reflection of the mental stability of the characters.

KING OF KINGS

The Samuel Bronston/Nicholas Ray Biblical epic from the early sixties, *King of Kings* has a steady mixture of action and theism. It is a significant accomplishment, because it gives the filmmakers sufficient tension to present key passages from the New Testament without alienating skeptical viewers. The presentation is not complex enough to give a truly adult interpretation of the moral conflicts inherent in the parables of the text, but it is a mature effort. The emphasis on Salome, Ray's instinctive use of spears, and Jeff Hunter's impossibly blue eyes are not a correct counterpoint for the Sermon on the Mount, but they are fun, and they encourage one's attention.

While the disc will satisfy those who have only seen the movie on TV, cropping hurts any Ray film and diminishes the impact of every significant scene in *King*. The colors are a little light and there are some marks on the print, but most viewers will find its physical condition acceptable. MGM/UA has included the entrance, intermission, and exit music, an admirable practice which deserves praise. In order to keep the movie on three sides, however, the intermission break occurs before the end of side two.

The analog sound is typical of an early sixties stereophonic recording. It crackles some, and there are variances in the volume levels during a few significant dialog passages.

KING SOLOMON'S MINES (Import) ALAN QUARTERMAIN AND THE LOST CITY OF GOLD (Import)

The Japanese release of the Richard Chamberlain effort *King Solomon's Mines* looks and sounds so good that it makes an otherwise stupid movie worth owning and watching. It is in widescreen (with Japanese subtitles underneath the picture) and only loses its crispness when the film itself is out of focus. The scenes which take place in the African sunlight are brilliantly colorful and clear to the smallest detail. Even the bad special effects are rousing. The classiest aspect of the movie is Jerry Goldsmith's non-stop mock adventure score, which swells and swells from every direction.

The sequel to *King Solomon's Mines* , *Alan Quartermain and the Lost City of Gold*, is also available in Japan. Like its predecessor it is in letterboxed format, with Japanese subtitles appearing beneath the screen. The picture quality is very good and the Ultra-Stereo sound is clear and effective. The film doesn't have any of the stunts which stopped one from blinking through most of *King Solomon's Mines*. The plot has the sort of wide-eyed adventure which one longs to treat children to, and the sort of wide-eyed violence which one tries to help them avoid. The letterboxed screen has limited advantages, but Sharon Stone has a complete circumnavigation of Chamberlain which would not be as amusing or appealing if it were cropped, and the special effects are easier to understand and appreciate when seen in their entirety.

THE KIROV BALLET – GISELLE (see **THE BOLSHOI BALLET – SPARTACUS**)

THE KIROV BALLET – SLEEPING BEAUTY (see **THE ROYAL BALLET – SWAN LAKE**)

THE KISS

A few good screams are elicited from *The Kiss* – it is surprising how many horror films have no screams at all – but the film is a bit empty in the lengthy passages leading up to these moments. The disc has a decent picture and some eerie whispers can be found on the soundtrack. The film, however, is over produced, and thus appears to promise more than it delivers. The story has a contemporary setting and concerns a young, exotic woman who visits the homey family of her late sister with the ulterior purpose of passing an internal demon to her niece. Mimi Kuzyk does a nice turn as the heroic neighbor lady, but the movie has 30 minutes of plot and 105 minutes of running time, and it is more talk than action.

KISS – ANIMALIZE LIVE UNCENSORED

The live Detroit concert on *KISS – Animalize Live Uncensored* appears to have been lit for video. The multi-colored lights and glitter come across the laser medium without distortion, like so many jewels. The pearls-before-swine quality continues with the disc's sound. The digital encoding assures that one will be hard pressed to discern atmospheric hiss, but then one has a difficult time discerning electrical guitars when the band really gets going. The members of KISS have forsaken their makeup, but this does not appear to have made them more shy. The 90-minute show is impressively captured and by the end you will certainly agree that the band has chosen an accurate name for themselves. When it comes to entertainment and music, they Keep It Simple and Stupid.

KISS – CRAZY NIGHTS

Three similar, workmanlike videos are available on the 13 minute 8-inch, *KISS – Crazy Nights*. All three, 'Turn on the Night,' 'Reason to Live,' and 'Crazy Crazy Nights,' blend phony and genuine concert footage with glimpses of attractive women. The picture and sound transfers are decent, but the disc will only be of interest to dedicated fans.

KISS – EXPOSED

KISS – Exposed has a carnival-styled 'Warning' on the front of the jacket cover: "Contains situations that will disgust some and titillate others." In reality, the program will do neither to anybody, but that, too, is part of the put-on. The disc, at least, is not a rip-off. It is a full 90 minutes long, containing 15 musical numbers and a phony 'life-style interview' narrative. The numbers include some the group's more notorious concept videos, and a mixture of rare and not-so-rare concert footage. There is one hysterically bad ballad, called 'Beth,' but otherwise the music is fast enough to stay ahead of judgement.

The sound on the disc is very good. Even the rare footage has clearly been re-engineered to the max. The picture is more than a decent number of generations away from the original material, but one really doesn't want to see these people any more clearly than one has to. That was why they used to wear make-up, right?

KISS ME KATE

The miracle it would take to get *Kiss Me Kate* presented on home video the way in which it was filmed, in 3D, remains in the realm of wishful thinking, but at least it has been released on disc with bright, fresh colors and digitally encoded sound.

The colorful emphasis on depth and perspective which was meant to bring out the 3D sometimes leaves empty areas in the middle of the TV screen, but detail and clarity compensate for the odd (and cropped) compositions. The plot, about the performance of a really bad Cole Porter musical based on 'Taming of the Shrew,' is ingenious in that the whole musical is included, along with a backstage musical comedy about the tempestuous romantic relationships between the principal players. The 'Shrew' part of the movie doesn't even begin until the opening of side two (the disc has three sides).

KISS OF THE SPIDER WOMAN

You have to be very clever to trick audiences into lining up for a film about torture and repression, which is why *Kiss of the Spider Woman* is so ambivalently flamboyant. That consumers would buy the movie for home video after having seen it in a theater shows how successful the director was at masking the film's intentions.

The disc re-creates the colors very well except in scenes which are bathed in red or orange light. The sound is not CX-encoded, but the monaural track is sophisticated.

KISS TOMORROW GOODBYE

Except for a poorly chosen side break which interrupts a key dramatic turning point, *Kiss Tomorrow Goodbye* is very nice. The black and white source material has only a couple of small glitches, and generally appears sharp. The sound has no major flaws, and

Republic opens the program with an original theatrical trailer. The movie is a fairly uncompromising tale about a crook, played by James Cagney, who is not smart enough to know when to stop. The script is a little weak, but the film's morality is progressive for its day (it was made in 1950) and Cagney is captivating.

KITARO THE LIGHT OF THE SPIRIT

The 48-minute single-sided *Kitaro The Light of the Spirit* is a beautiful collection of pretty video images depicting the play of light upon water and landscape. Little of it is spiritual, but much of it is soothing. The accompanying music is mushy jazz, including some wordless vocals. The transfer is scrumptious, but one wishes that the energy which goes into making discs like these so perfect could be directed toward worthier causes.

THE KITCHEN TOTO

The narrative of *The Kitchen Toto* is well constructed, making the disc play like a page turner. The break between side one and side two is especially compelling, so it is a good idea to hook up the answering machine and eliminate all other potential interruptions before viewing begins.

Some of the dialog is in a strong patois and is difficult to make out. The picture is disappointingly grainy and may distract some viewers.

Set in Kenya shortly before independence, the story is about a young boy working as a servant in the household of a white law enforcement official. The boy dies at the end, an emotional deflation which should not distract one from the events which precede his death, though this and several other aspects may be disturbing to young viewers. (Warner mistakenly bills the movie as a coming-of-age tale. How can it be a coming-of-age tale when the character coming of age dies before the movie is over?) The plot has a number of threats and complications, but even when the story takes a pause, the depiction of colonial Africa holds the viewer's attention. The filmmakers leave judgement of the characters to the prejudices of their audience. To give one example, the official has a young son who would be portrayed in most movies as a snotty monster. In *Kitchen Toto*, however, enough of his activities can be glimpsed to show that he is bored out of his wits living in what to him is the middle of nowhere. However contemptible his actions, we still felt a little sorry for him.

KITTIES PUPPIES (Import)

Every once in a while the Japanese come up with a really terrific idea. One was building a laser video disc player that works right. Another is pressing a laser video disc which contains nothing but a classical music soundtrack and two hours of frolicking puppies and kittens.

Kitties Puppies is a Japanese disc also known as 'The Vitamin Disc.' To those who own video retail outlets, we recommend that you obtain this disc and play it on the monitor in your window.

Side one is a pair of kittens exploring a room while their mother lies comfortably in the sun. Admittedly, our interest began to wane after about ten minutes. Other members of our household, however, became militant at even the slightest suggestion of turning the thing off. The high point: The two kittens begin to chase each other's tails as they run around a vase of roses.

Side two is a half dozen Collie puppies loose in a park. They are less cuddly than the kittens, but far more eager to approach and lick the camera lens.

Each session is just like spending an hour with the real creatures, except that they'll never grow up and they don't smell or make noises. If your children have been pestering you for a pet, perhaps this disc is the answer.

KNIGHTS OF THE ROUND TABLE

Knights of the Round Table looks a little rough near the reel changes, but is in better condition otherwise, with the Technicolor effects providing an entertaining boost to the complicated heraldry and colors of each knight. The film is an odd work. The script, a reasonably serious attempt to adapt Sir Thomas Mallory's 'Le Morte D'Arthur,' seems somewhat independent of a standard MGM production format, although the cast, the California locations, and the 'look' are pure factory. There are battles and sword fights, but the film is not a swashbuckler.

Although the colors are appealing, they still fall short of the best Technicolor transfers. The disc is stereophonic, but the stereo effects are limited and the sound, like the picture, is a little flat. The film was originally made in Cinemascope, and has been scanned and cropped for its video presentation.

KNOCK ON ANY DOOR

The credits for *Knock on Any Door* look fairly impressive – "Starring Humphrey Bogart," "Directed by Nicholas Ray" – until you see the prominently displayed, "Introducing John Derek as Nick Romano." If you thought Bo had difficulties mastering the basic requirements of her profession, wait until you see the man who taught her everything she knows demonstrate his talents.

Connoisseurs will appreciate Nicholas Ray's style of direction, but Derek, who portrays the film's central character, a street criminal from the days when even lowlifes wore suits and ties, is awful. He has an empty-headed grin which is becoming the Derek family trademark.

RCA/Columbia has done a fine job transferring *Knock on Any Door*, although the sound is predictably monaural and aged. The sets are particularly evocative and the black-and-white photography is haunting. Ray is one of those directors whose ability to make movies far exceeded his ability to choose which movies to make.

KNOWLEDGEDISC

You can pick up a fairly decent encyclopedia in a used-book store. It may list Lyndon Johnson as the current president, but it will have everything you would need to write a report on kelp or Manifest Destiny. It will also require several trips to lug the 20 or so volumes to the car or into your home. The *KnowledgeDisc* from Grolier can be held with two fingers. It costs about the same as a used set, which is much less than a brand new encyclopedia, and includes information as current as late 1984. It is all text, some 9,000,000 words, and covers just about every subject worth covering. The disc has no sound.

So much text appears on each frame of the one-sided CAV disc that your television screen must be in good adjustment or you will lose an edge or two. *KnowledgeDisc* goes out of its way, however, to be user-friendly. Every frame number is printed on the screen, and a scale close by gives a physical picture of how the current frame is positioned in relation to the beginning and end of a letter group. Next to the frame number and scale is the topic covered at the opening of the page, so even if you are scanning through the alphabet at a rapid rate, you have a clear assessment of where you are.

The front section of the disc is an index which lists every subject and frame number. Since we could not take the time to read every word on the disc, we spent an afternoon reading the entire index and then spent several subsequent evenings looking up topics of interest based upon the notes we had accumulated.

The *KnowledgeDisc* entries are short, but thorough. Like most encyclopedias, many people contributed articles and so the writing is inconsistent in quality and presentation. The coverage of the Sumerian legend, 'Gilgamesh,' for example, is longer, more intelligent, and more interesting in the entry, 'mythology' than in the entry, 'Gilgamesh.' An article on 'geographical linguistics' is superbly lucid and descriptive, while an article of equal length on 'anthropological linguistics' is confusing and slightly misleading. Sometimes, the writing is so awkward that teachers will never suspect plagiarism if a student copies it, such as this sentence from the entry on the carrot: "It is naturally a biennial, but it is grown as an annual for its sweet orange-colored fruit."

The entries for film directors are generally dry and dispassionate, while the entries for authors are often insightful and heartfelt. Important novels are given separate entries with ample plot and thumbnail analyses. Most of Shakespeare's plays are included, but here again, the entries for 'A Midsummer Night's Dream' and 'The Tempest' are thoughtful while 'Hamlet' is as confused as the title character.

Omissions are inevitable. Lawrence Durrell is included, but not his equally accomplished brother, Gerald. Grant Tinker appears, but Fred Silverman does not. Ursula LeGuin, Satyajit Ray, and Jean-Paul Belmondo are in, so where are Frank Herbert, Akira Kurosawa, and Toshiro Mifune? A fact sheet is provided at the end of every presidential entry, listing the cabinet members and other statistics related to a president's term, but it has been left off of the entry for Franklin Pierce. Literal errors which we came across included the listing of *Poltergeist* under Steven Spielberg's directorial credits and the suggestion that the sun passes through the constellation Libra from October 24 to November 22.

KnowledgeDisc is an adaptation of the 5-inch Personal Computer optical data disc, which has the same content and the same errors. The most exciting aspect to the PC disc is its ability to cross-reference any of the 9,000,000 words in a blink of the eye. That is beyond the capability of the video disc, but it is a tantalizing demonstration of what the future holds for information storage and retrieval.

KOOL & THE GANG – TONIGHT!
The digital sound on *Kool & the Gang – Tonight!* starts out with an oomph! and sounds great all the way through. For a live concert, the separation is remarkable and the harmonies usually lost in the din of a live set are re-created pleasurably.

Kool & the Gang have authored many pop classics and move through an 80-minute concert with confident ease. They act as though they didn't spend too much time practicing their synchronized dancing, which is gratifying, and they project immense amounts of energy without ever seeming to expend any of their own.

KOYAANISQATSI: LIFE OUT OF BALANCE (Pacific Arts)
KOYAANISQATSI: LIFE OUT OF BALANCE (Image)
When *Koyaanisqatsi: Life out of Balance* was first released by Pacific Arts, the disc appeared to be in almost perfect condition. Going back to look at it now will show how far quality has come, because it is grainy and bleeds wherever the light is strong. Image has used the same master for their release. Since the earlier disc was also digitally encoded, there is no need to replace it. Those seeking out the title for the first time, however, can rest assured that the other version is no better than the one they are obtaining. The picture isn't bad, it just isn't perfect.

Image has put side one in CAV, with two unsteady still frames out of every five. There are many possibilities, but simply scanning in CAV can be advantageous, revealing the sequential structure of the images. Image has also included chapter markers, though not enough on side two to suit us. The soundtrack is excellent.

The first third of the 80-minute feature is free of human presence. Desert vistas, forests, breaking waves, and empty plains stretch out upon the screen. The other two thirds are about civilization – cities, industries, and people. Special photography is used to enlarge, speed up, or slow down the size and pace of urban life. Accompanying the images is the music of Philip Glass. The electronic keyboard pieces take a single musical idea and repeat it mercilessly before going on to the next. With the addition of digital sound, one can hear the keyboard player shuffle his feet now and then. The music goes with the images the way very heavy cream goes with strawberries.

Having owned *Koyaanisqatsi* for some time now, we have found it to be an addictive little program. The fact that the progression of images has a deliberate theme is of little consequence – a viewer is inevitably going to be stimulated by the images. The rhythm and the patterns, however, tap an inner pulse, and once they lock on, they won't let go. *Koyaanisqatsi* has always been a disc in which the interruption to turn from side one to side two is a real bother.

KROKUS – THE VIDEO BLITZ
Members of the audience toss objects at Krokus during their concert, but apparently it is a show of affection. Getting knocked in the head or on the guitar doesn't seem to upset the group's rhythm, but it is doubtful that even tomatoes could throw them off. *Krokus – The Video Blitz* is a concert disc (perhaps their next will be 'The Concert Blitz' and be a collection of videos). The hard rock group looks good on stage and their performance has been filmed to impart a fair sense of action and excitement. Much of the picture being dark, flaws like crosstalk are a little more visible than normal. The sound is by nature loud and distorted.

KRONOS
The black-and-white fifties space invasion movie, *Kronos*, comes from a scratch-infested print which looks murky and slightly blurred on the screen. On side two, the picture skips and shakes at one point. Side two is also in CAV, with every three steady still frames followed by two flickering ones.

In the film, a large crankshaft and piston contraption lands on the coast of Mexico and starts thumping towards Los Angeles. It eats hydrogen bombs for breakfast and can only be stopped by something which turns energy into matter. Fortunately, scientists on the scene have just the thing in prototype and they blow the crankshaft to kingdom come.

KRUSH GROOVE
The digital track in *Krush Groove* has no bass or thrust. In 95 minutes 23 numbers are performed, but most of the songs can only be heard in bits and pieces. The plot and the mangled subplot, about success in the recording industry, are supposed to be true, but it seems unlikely. The picture transfer isn't all that great, either.

KYOTO VIVALDI "THE FOUR SEASONS"
The editing of imagery on *Kyoto Vivaldi "The Four Seasons"* is nothing short of superb. Static shots are mixed with moving shots, inanimate subjects are mixed with animate subjects, posed shots are mixed with candid shots, technology is mixed with nature, and each successive concept flows or repeats with the simple purity exemplified by Vivaldi's score. As if that weren't enough, the video is duplicated on both sides of the disc. On side one the pictures are accompanied by a standard, but decent, chamber orchestra rendition of 'Four Seasons.' On side two, the music is performed on traditional Japanese instruments, (which end up sounding like a collection of mandolins and lutes when playing Western compositions, but no matter). Careful observation will reveal that the material has actually been cut to fit the chamber orchestra version, and it is not advisable to watch both sides in quick succession. The overall effect, however, leaves the consumer feeling that two discs have been obtained for the price of one. (For some reason, the Western version ends with a Japanese credit scroll and the Japanese version ends with an English language credit scroll. Is this deliberate juxtapositioning, or simply a mix-up?)

The picture is nearly flawless, and the digitally encoded sound, which has less hiss than the analog track, is precisely defined. Chapter markers are encoded on each side for each season, but the identifiers do not coincide with what has been printed on the jacket.

L.A. BOUNTY
Sybil Danning wrote, produced, and stars in *L.A. Bounty*. The movie has something to do with a kidnapped mayoral candidate and an ex-policewoman seeking revenge for her partner's murder, but it is primarily a series of set-ups created to let Danning emerge from the fog or the shadows in a macho stance and shoot bad guys. Sometimes it is fun and sometimes it stretches the imagination a little too far. The film's Ultra-Stereo sound is a dud on the digital surround soundtrack. The gunshots have no life or zing. The transfer looks accurate, but the colors are generally dull and uninteresting.

LA BAMBA
In some movies a single scene will serve as the nucleus for the whole film. It will be a turning point for the viewer, the moment when any remaining defenses against enjoying the feature are abandoned, and it will often be the scene that the filmmakers themselves worked the hardest to design, perhaps even creating the rest of the film as an afterthought. In *La Bamba* it is 'La Bamba.' The whole movie is nice. It hasn't got any smarts, but it has personality, and it is one of those rare movies which can get by without action, humor, or drama – a musical. It tells the story of Ritchie Valens in pleasant, easy to digest pieces, and takes its time setting you up for the big scene. He's in New York. He hasn't appeared too often in front of a live audience. The artists who have preceded him on the stage have worked the audience into a frenzy. He goes on. The people in the audience settle into their seats and become unusually quiet. Oh no! Is he going to somnabulate them with 'Donna?' Every cut is perfect. When he starts rockin' with his guitar you want to run to your windows, throw them open, and sing in Spanish at the top of your lungs.

The picture is a little too orange but the focus is sharp. The sound is passable.

LA BOHEME
The extreme popularity of *La Boheme* is somewhat baffling. It is good, but it isn't that good, either musically or dramatically. If anything, Giacomo Puccini's score is more sophisticated than one would expect from an intensely popular work. Audiences fell in love with the the snow and the consumptive heroine and accepted the work with enthusiasm almost from its inception.

The 'Live at the Met' presentation is certainly *the* version to acquire. The production, mounted by Franco Zeffirelli, who also takes specific credit for the sets, is scrumptious. The snowbound set in act III brings an ovation from the audience as does a sunset over the rooftops of Paris in act IV.

Our only complaint is that the video coverage is not equal to Zeffirelli's vision. The cameras don't seem to have the correct lenses and you can tell from the real long shots that the closeups are missing more than they should. The picture is slightly grainy, but receives passing marks.

Since Puccini was not really one for having the entire orchestra play at the same time, the separations, aided by the digital technology, sound as good in performance as they do in a studio. The thrilling vocal performances of Teresa Stratas and Renata Scotto make the disc worth acquiring even if you do not own a television set.

LA CAGE AUX FOLLES 3

A poll we conducted of disc consumers showed that some consumers want foreign films with subtitles and some want dual audio tracks, but almost none could stand the thought of purchasing films unaccompanied by the original soundtrack. We thought the video companies had paid heed, but *La Cage Aux Folles 3* has voices from who knows where.

Not that *3* is any great classic, but intrinsic to the humor throughout the series has been Michel Serrault's perfectly timed squeaks and whinnies. Watching the disc, you see Serrault moving and you hear, eons later by the standards of eye/ear perception, a stunted attempt to speak with a high pitch. If someone had been clever, they would have tried using a woman's voice to replace Serrault's. As it stands, the only redeemable aspect to the comedy is gone, and there is no reason to purchase the disc.

LA CENERENTOLA

A character in *La Cenerentola* is dictating a proclamation to those standing around him. When he declares that his next statements are to be capitalized, the English subtitles supporting the Italian lyrics immediately shift into upper case. It is a perfect example of the intelligence which has gone into producing the disc, from the huge and superb essay which appears on a jacket insert, explaining everything anyone would ever want to know about the opera, to the digital stereo sound, which is as good as a studio recording, but follows the audio position of every character running about the stage.

The filmed program, directed by Jean-Pierre Ponnelle, appears to have been made on the stage and in the lobby at La Scala, although no audience is present and the camera set-ups are more similar to those of a soundstage production. Ponnelle's flexibility makes meticulous use of La Scala's huge sets, but provides appropriate cinematic effects, such as presenting the characters in silhouette during a cumulative sextet. The opera, by Giocchino Rossini, is immediately accessible because of Ponnelle's confidence in his presentation. The disc makes a good movie.

The picture quality is the disc's weakest component. The image is consistently grainy. On side three in chapter four, the picture even jiggles for a moment, and there are stray scratches every so often. The four sided, two and a half hour disc comes in a box jacket. The sides do not seem to be broken at really logical intervals, but the music is never interrupted. Along with the essay, which is in both English and French, the jacket insert contains an elaborate plot synopsis, linked directly to the chapter encoding.

The story of *La Ceneretolla* is 'Cinderella,' set as a farce (an 'opera bouffe') with the fantasy elements replaced by more down-to-earth machinations. Although the opera was written in a month, it is a lasting achievement, filled with Rossini's breakneck duets and melancholy arias. Frederica Von Stade has the title role, Francisco Araiza is the prince, Paolo Montarsolo is the step-father, and Claudio Desderi is the prince's valet, Dandini. All sing adequately and are assisted by the quality of the recording and the perfect pitch of Ponnelle's eye.

LA CHIENNE

The black-and-white image on Jean Renoir's *La Chienne* is soft, the picture jiggles in places, and the monaural sound is best subdued in favor of the subtitles (which are easy to read), but the presentation is adequate and the film's pleasures are accessible.

Chienne is probably the most typical Renoir film, a French-style tale about obsession and infidelity which is told with a bittersweet impishness. The pleasures of the first viewing, where one is never quite sure exactly what is going to happen next, give way, on multiple viewings, to an enjoyable cast of characters who are only humorous when you don't examine them closely. The narrative concerns a meek and hen-pecked clerk who takes a prostitute for a mistress. From that point, however, the story blossoms in so many different ways that to mention any plot point is to give it undue weight against the balance of the others. Renoir's film style is equally diffuse and devious, for whenever a shot comes along which seems too obvious or basic, there is inevitably a plot turn later on which turns one's view of the previous scene upside-down. The film is a classic and it is relatively fault proof, because if you don't like it the first time, you just have to watch again.

LA CLEMENZA DI TITO

Jean-Pierre Ponnelle may well be the greatest film director whose work never appeared in a theater. *La Clemenza di Tito* is further evidence of this, as many of the opera productions released by PolyGram have been. And for once, with *La Clemenza di Tito*, the quality of the disc lives up to the quality of the production.

The opera, as is thoroughly explained in an accompanying essay which appears, along with a chapter and plot synopsis, on an insert in the box jacket, was Mozart's last, commissioned on the fly to be part of a coronation festival. The plot concerns a Roman emperor who grants clemency to those who have mistakenly conspired against him. Its style, dictated by a pre-exisitng libretto which Mozart was working from with a minimum of changes, harks back to an earlier era, when characters in operas sang and acted independently of one another, describing their actions more often than doing them.

Ponnelle places the cast in the Baths at Caracalla, at the Arch of Titus in Rome, and at the Villa Adriana in Tivoli, and embraces the style of the opera by isolating the performers within the immense backdrops and intriguing acoustics of the ancient ruins. He uses his knowledge of the score to place zoom shots, jump cuts and long pans at punctuation points within the music. He gives the film a bare, isolated look, and then revs it up, just as Mozart was doing as he re-worked old composition and constuction styles with a new 'modernist' understanding of the format.

The film was made in 1980 and it is in beautiful condition. Sometimes the picture is so bright and sharp that the white subtitles hurt your eyes. The recitatives were recorded during the filming, while the important vocal work was done in a studio. The sound matches the quality of the picture. It is bright and sharply detailed. The only thing we can think to complain about the 135-minute disc is that the opening chapter marker begins at the silent credit scroll instead of the start of the overture.

James Levine conducts the Vienna Philharmonic and the Vienna State Opera Choir. Tatiana Troyanos, Carol Neblett, Anne Howells and Eric Tappy all give fine performances. The opera is not as immediately accessible as Mozart's other works are, and neither is Ponnelle's film. But since it is available on laser disc, a viewer can obtain it and watch it enough times so that it does become accessible. When that happens, the realization that Ponnelle captured and executed the essence of Mozart's beauty will start to sink in.

LA DOLCE VITA
8 1/2

Oddly, *La Dolce Vita* and *8 1/2* are rarely shown together in revival houses (both have long running times) although *8 1/2* is essentially a sequel to *La Dolce Vita*, using many of the same cast members and production personnel. If one is at all interested in obtaining one of the films, we highly recommend that both be purchased.

Image's presentation of *La Dolce Vita* is almost on the level of a Criterion offering. The jacket is gatefold, and contains an excellent thumbnail biography of Fellini. The picture has been letterboxed, at about 2:1, and the English language subtitles, including a few choice off-color remarks, appear beneath the image.

The black-and-white picture is sharp throughout the film, and digital encoding keeps the scratchy soundtrack manageable. The disc is chapter marked and although no listing of the chapters appears, the placement is informed, marking the clearly segmented episodes which comprise the film.

The improvement of the picture and sound quality on Voyager's *8 1/2* has more to do with the availability of source material than the adeptness of the transfer. The black and white image looks vivid, and is presented with mild letterboxing at about 1.7:1, with subtitles appearing on the picture.

8 1/2, which comes in a gatefold jacket, has been digitally encoded and adequately chapter marked. A theatrical trailer for the first general US release appears after the film is ended. (The monstrous trailer is a hysterical example of the way desperate distributors use sex to sell films. It is a shame, however, that Voyager doesn't take a few lessons for their jacket designs.)

It is worth noting that since both discs are digitally encoded, both offer an excellent opportunity to hear Nina Rota's sublime musical scores. In *8 1/2*, Rota's music is supplemented by an on-screen orchestra playing famous classical music passages, but it is nearly impossible to note when the classical music by the great masters ends and Rota's own effort takes over.

Although *La Dolce Vita* was viewed as being scandalously topical and stylishly nihilistic when it was first released theatrically, the strength of its humanistic components have withstood the test of time. The narrative follows a gossip reporter who mixes with the swells of Roman society during the course of several nights. The reporter's adventures are presented in clearly delineated segments (each one, for some reason, containing a staircase).

On multiple viewings, the strongest segment for us is the sequence involving the reporter's father, who looks up his son during a visit to the city, and proceeds to go club-hopping with him. The segment seems to offer proof that the movie is about real people, and situates the more flamboyant high-society characters in a proper perspective. A brief conversation the reporter has with a spotlight operator during the Virgin Mary segment serves the same purpose. Fellini maintains a surprisingly neutral view of his characters, causing audiences and opinion recorders to impose their own emotional values on the film. The movie is an epic of vacuity, and its lasting accomplishment is to show that even the vacuous have substance.

The narrative of *81/2* is paradoxical. *81/2* is a fictional film about the making of *81/2*. With the exception of a jokey short film, Fellini's previous production was *La Dolce Vita*. References to its impact upon his career and the rest of the movie world abound. *81/2* is Fellini's strongest stylistic effort. The visual conceptualizations are remarkable and the editing is faultless. The show is comical and its obscure structure is valid, though one of the great mysteries of artistic endeavor is why, after *81/2*, Fellini began making the very sort of films he was consciously criticizing and lampooning with it.

LA FILLE MAL GARDEE (see **THE ROYAL BALLET – SWAN LAKE**)

LA LECTRICE (THE READER)

One of the rarest film genres, the literate comedy, makes a happy appearance on laser disc with *La Lectrice (The Reader)*. The story, which is set inside a clever framing device, concerns a woman who places an ad offering her services as reader. The film shifts between her interaction with the various people who hire her and realizations of some of the passages she reads, with cast members filling multiple roles within the realizations. The film spends a pleasant amount of time wallowing in the language of fine literature, and it manages to get away with it because of the heroine's perky demeanor. The film is light fun, and it is one of the few comedies to take real advantage of a viewer's intelligence and love of knowledge without covering itself by the inclusion of more vulgar amusements.

The picture quality is reasonably decent. The colors look slightly pale and the edges are soft, but the production budget is as great a contributor as the transfer to the image's imperfections. The monaural sound has a mild phase shift that cannot be eliminated by isolating a channel. The soundtrack also has an increased level of noise which again can be attributed to the original production environment. The film is in French with bright yellow English subtitles. The dialog, among other things, contains many poetic amusements – strings of similar-sounding words, mild puns, etc. – the spirit of which cannot be translated, but viewers who do not speak French will still be able to catch many of the gags. After all, in poetry, sound is of equal importance to semantics.

LA RONDE (Import)

Roger Vadim's remake of *La Ronde* is available in French with Japanese subtitles, so not too many collectors will be interested, but it is worth noting that the disc is letterboxed (with the subtitles on the picture). The color is aged but not faded and the transfer is grainy. The sound is not CX-encoded. The story follows one lover to the next to the next until the woman who appeared at the beginning reappears to conclude the circle. Among the more well-known performers to appear are Jane Fonda, Catherine Spaak, and Anna Karina. The couplings are so chaste that the Japanese never have an opportunity to employ their enthusiastic censorship.

LA STRADA

We toyed with the single audio tracks on the Criterion Collection release of *La Strada* for a couple of minutes before realizing that we were most satisfied listening to both at the same time. One track contains the original Italian soundtrack, with Giulietta Masina's voice and dubbing for Anthony Quinn and Richard Basehart. The other track contains the English dialog. Masina is dubbed, but Quinn, and presumably Basehart (it barely sounds like him, but he was young), provide their own voices. The result, when you listen to both mono tracks simultaneously, is an electronically reprocessed stereo. Nina Rota's score is enriched tremendously, and sound effects, such as crickets and barking dogs, rarely show up on both tracks in the same place. Not to belabor the point, but in crowd scenes, the English dialog is easy to follow, and, except for long speeches, the English and the Italian rarely coincide; one either precedes or follows the other. Of the two tracks, the English track is actually the better. The Italian track has fewer sound effects (or music cues, for that matter) and is adversely affected by a hum on a couple of reels. English subtitles appear in support of the Italian dialog.

The print looks like it has been on the road a while itself. The disc may or may not have been made from the best source material available, but it has scratches, marks, and other neo-realistic contaminants. The contrast levels are rich, however, and anyone who is used to seeing the film will not find the problems to be distracting. The disc has 12 chapter markers and is not CX-encoded.

La Strada is a relaxed, unassuming tale about an itinerant strong man and his simple-minded assistant. It can be read symbolically, allegorically, etc., but it doesn't have to be since the story is strong enough to stand on its own. The director, Fredrico Fellini, creates and displays his characters so clearly that their every thought and motive is accessible to the viewer. For the film's 90 minutes, you are on their road instead of your own.

LA TRAVIATA (see **OTELLO**)

LABYRINTH

Not until the very end of a nearly endless credit scroll in *Labyrinth* is acknowledgment given to Maurice Sendak. We went back to the film's theatrical pre-release publicity and were surprised to find no mention that the opening plot device and strongest image, of a fat-cheeked baby surrounded by goblins, is lifted directly from Sendak's 'Outside Over There.'

The movie had a humongous budget and fell at the boxoffice with a great thud. Still, like many ambitious cinematic failures, *Labyrinth* is a good disc. The sound is cluttered, but is kept fairly clean by the digital playback. Embassy has included 14 chapter markers.

David Bowie portrays the villain and he has several musical numbers which stop the film dead. The story, which follows a girl's tribulations as she journeys through a deceptive, labyrinthine world to retrieve her baby brother from the goblins, doesn't really pick up until the second side. A cumulative scene based upon an optical illusion by M.C. Escher is spectacular. The only real problem with the movie is that the scriptwriters, once they got to the maze, didn't know where they wanted to go.

THE LACEMAKER

Voyager has magnified the attributes of a minor French film, *The Lacemaker*, by releasing it as a Criterion Collection title. The film has just enough emotional ambiguity so that it may someday become the classic Dan Peary's excellent essay on the back of the jacket claims it is, but it could just as easily remain as anonymous as its central character. The picture looks sharper than it did in its initial US theatrical release, and the adept transfer increases the film's pleasures.

The story is about a young girl who doesn't talk much. While on holiday with a friend, she meets a young man and they eventually move in together. When they split up, she has a nervous breakdown. The film is a little presumptuous when it comes to hiding aspects of the personalities of the characters from the viewer. What one assumes is style on the part of the director, Claude Goretta, depicting the quiet moments and pauses between conversations in the lives of the characters, turns out to be the substance instead. Isabelle Huppert stars, and the film's strongest selling point is the familiarity and affection one feels for her during the course of the narrative.

The picture has a mild black band at the top and the bottom of the screen, and white English subtitles appear on the image. Since the conversations are sparse, the subtitles are easy to follow. The sound is fine.

THE LADIES MAN

The Ladies Man is a good example of the pure Jerry Lewis style. The Technicolor film, which has been given a luscious transfer, has essentially one set, the interior of a huge mansion which is a boarding house for aspiring actresses. Lewis portrays a befuddled young man who obtains a job at the house. Lewis' film techniques are captivating (the set is several stories high and the camera swings up and down at will) as often as they are inept (the editing continuity is atrocious), just as Lewis can be funny as often as he appears silly or desperate. There is no real plot, just random incidents and gags. The film is best appreciated by isolating the gags which are funny and playing them over and over. After a couple dozen repeats, the stuff which didn't seem funny at first will probably start to induce giggles as well. The sound is fine.

LADY AND THE TRAMP (CAV)
LADY AND THE TRAMP (CLV)

For some people, romance was defined in the movies by the way Bette Davis accepted Paul Henreid's cigarette, or the way Ryan O'Neal and Ali McGraw studied together. But for us, the penultimate moment of romance in the movies is when the Tramp and the Lady share a plate of spaghetti by candlelight in the back of Tony's Restaurant. So what if they're dogs. Tony and his cook are making a fuss over them, they are confident and enjoying themselves, and the evening is still young. (They end up sleeping together!)

Walt Disney has released two versions of *Lady and the Tramp*, one in CAV and one in CLV. Both are stereo and have been digitally encoded. The CAV disc has 16 chapter markers, while the CLV has none.

Although the movie is only 75 minutes long, the CLV disc is in CLV on both sides. There is no perceptible difference in picture or sound quality between the CAV and CLV discs. Both look great. The cozy, early-1900 setting is evoked with bright, spring colors which transfer very well to disc. The drawings are bold and plain, but realistic. Unlike *Pinocchio*, rapid movement in *Lady and the Tramp* is not accompanied by impressionistic streaks (when examined in CAV). The Disney studio was making many profit margin compromises, but the traditions of quality and simple storyboard know-how endured. From Lady's Rita Hayworth hairdo to the Tramp's heroic battle with the rat, the animation is vivid and satisfying.

The CAV functions enhance one's viewing and analysis in several different ways. Along with the still frames, which have been accomplished without quivering, the three times normal speed function provides the most opportunities. As the dogs converse, you can watch their diaphragms flutter.

The analog track has a slightly stronger level of noise than the digital track. The stereo has an enhancement which makes the movie sound like it is playing in a cavernous picture house. This effect may not have much to do with what is on the screen, and even sounds distorted on monaural TV speaker playback, but it provides a wonderful feeling, reminiscent of candy counters and velvet upholstery. Sort of like the date at Tony's.

LADY BEWARE

A woman who designs department store window displays is stalked by a man turned on by the erotic content of the displays in *Lady Beware*, the hottest movie to be filmed in Pittsburgh since *Flashdance*. *Lady* stars Diane Lane, who has been subliminally provoking audiences since she was eleven. The movie is entertaining and true to its internal logic, making multiple viewings a real possibility.

The night scenes are overly grainy, but the rest of the footage is all right. The sound is in stereo, but effects are limited to the music and a few threatening footsteps. The disc also has chapter markers.

THE LADY EVE (see VERTIGO)

THE LADY FROM SHANGHAI

The dialog has the rhythm of free verse, the cinematography is lit like an old master painting, and the story is about murder, adultery, and sweaty San Francisco lawyers. *The Lady from Shanghai* is a masterpiece of filmmaking, but then nearly every movie Orson Welles made is a masterpiece. RCA/Columbia released *The Lady from Shanghai* on disc using a bright black-and-white print and a reliable soundtrack.

Drawing from theater and radio as well as filmmaking, Welles packs each shot with gimmicks and tricks which comment on the story. If a character is seen through a distorted lens, the character's thoughts are equally distorted. If dialog or background noises distract from the proceedings, the hero is being distracted and confused by the cluttered morality surrounding him. And if voices modulate so much that no one would ever talk like that in real life, a lie is being spun.

Rita Hayworth portrays the temptress who suckers an unemployed sailor, Welles, into a conspiracy of deceit and homicide. Most of the plot, upon close examination, is far-fetched or unlikely, but the show moves so rapidly and is so rich in imagery and theatrics that it doesn't matter.

There are a pair of jumps in the film, but it must be realized that one will rarely, if ever, see a theatrical copy of the movie which is in as good a condition as this. On side two, the sound becomes very weak during the jail scene and then flips wildly to the right speaker before settling down in the courtroom scene which follows. Again, the non-CX-encoded 1948 recording is about as accomplished as one could hope for. Ultimately, it would be preferable to be able to see the entire screen since every pixel here is precious.

LADY IN WHITE

After twenty minutes of overly lyrical build up, *Lady in White* finally appears to get down to business. A boy, locked in a closet at his school, sees the ghost of a murdered girl and is almost killed himself. The mystery, with supernatural embellishments, then proceeds to unfold at same loopy pace with which it opened.

The picture is often too grainy but is otherwise acceptable. The stereo sound is passable, but the soundtrack lacks inventiveness. The analog track is noisier than the digital track.

The movie is klutzy, but it gets the job done. It claims to take place in 1962, and opens on a Friday, which is said to be Halloween, although anyone with a perpetual calendar handy could tell you that Halloween came on a Wednesday that year. Still, *Lady in White* offers an adequate number of chills and some interesting special effects, which is all one can really ask of a ghost story, even if one wishes for more.

LADY JANE

Everything we know about English history we learned from the movies. That's the way it is these days. No longer can children gather around an elder who reads them passages from 'A Child's History of England.' There isn't any time any more. From *Lady Jane* we learned that one of Henry VIII's most significant acts was to redistribute the lands, seized from the Catholic Church, amongst his loyal nobles. Thus could Lord Byron, several hundred years later, conduct wild bacchanals in an abandoned abbey on his father's estate, downing wine, it is said, from the skull of an abbot. The pieces all come together if you are alert.

Which you may not be by the end of *Lady Jane*. It is a well-groomed disc, with a mostly stable digital soundtrack and a mostly unblemished picture. The photography is gauzed (and occasionally, if the gauze is removed at the wrong moment, you get thrown back into the twentieth century) and grainy. Were it not for the last third of the movie, which drags on intolerably, repeating itself every step of the way, the disc could be highly recommended. The story is a surprisingly appealing and romantic portrayal of a young lady who sort of ruled England for nine days and who certainly established the precedent that encouraged Elizabeth to usurp Mary. It kind of takes the wind out of 'The Prince and the Pauper,' however.

THE LADY VANISHES
THE 39 STEPS
THE THIRD MAN

The effort which went into finding the sources for *The Lady Vanishes*, *The 39 Steps*, and *The Third Man*, places those involved with the Criterion Collection discs near the forefront of the movement to preserve old motion pictures. All three discs are in CLV format and none utilize any special disc functions beyond chapter markers and CX-encoding, but all have clearly been struck from the best sources available.

The most exciting effort is *The Lady Vanishes*. If you have ever seen this film in a revival house you may well have witnessed an amusing phenomenon. Shortly after the film begins, a sort of 'musical chairs' erupts in the audience as viewers quickly realize they must find seats closer to the speakers if they are to hear the dialogue or anything quieter than the gunshots and train whistles. Those viewing the film for the first time on disc may think that it looks like any other movie, but that is the point. For the first time in decades, it does.

Lady was directed by Alfred Hitchcock. It mixes a genre which he is less remembered for – the comic foibles of British tourists – with one which left a more lasting impression – the spy thriller. Since much of the story is invested in characterization, it is a good prospect for home viewing. Hitchcock had only a wisp of a story to work with, but his confidence is what carries the movie along.

The video master for *Lady* was taken directly from a negative, but the last known nitrate negative of Hitchcock's *The 39 Steps* crumbled into oblivion before Voyager could get ahold of it. Thus, Voyager had to use a PAL master taken from a fine-grain print made from a negative that no longer exists. Still, the occasional scratches and generational loss makes the disc one of the least satisfying in the Criterion line.

Steps, one of Hitchcock's most popular films, is about a man wrongly accused of a crime. He must avoid the law and entrap the real criminals. Multiple viewings will reveal holes in the fabric of the plot but the performances of Robert Donat and Madeleine Carroll (and, in a small, memorable part, Peggy Ashcroft) hold the movie together. The scenes where Donat and Carroll have been handcuffed and go from hating one another to loving each other can be viewed many times. The movie's final shot, in fact, is one of Hitchcock's many acerbic comments on the institution of marriage, zeroing in on the couple and the handcuffs.

The quality of *The Third Man* is thrilling. When seen on a projection TV, the display is indistinguishable from a motion picture projection. Here again, a fine grain print made from an original negative was used for the master. The higher ranges on some of the dialogue seemed to go a little flat, but the famous theme music sounds as good on the disc as it does on the *The World of Anton Karas and Harry Lime* record album.

The movie is absolutely a necessary purchase for any home video library and this is obviously going to be the best presentation of it for some time to come. Watching *The Third Man* more than once is like going to a play on successive nights. Each time you see it, different aspects of the characters are revealed, as if the actors were actually modifying their roles every time through.

Directed by Carol Reed and starring Joseph Cotten, Trevor Howard, Orson Welles, and (Alida) Valli, the film is about corruption in post-war Vienna. Reed could afford to film the movie in a flamboyant and expressionistic style because the Graham Greene script kept the obvious emotions understated to the point of banal realism.

The result is a mistake-free masterpiece of adult feelings. It will make you fall in love with Vienna, with the zither, with bent camera angles, with the English language and its accents, with the movies, and now, thanks to Voyager, with laser discs.

THE LADY VANISHES

The nadir of Cybill Shepherd's career was a record album too accurately titled *Cybill Shepherd Does It to Cole Porter*. Shortly after that, she appeared in a remake of Alfred Hitchcock's *The Lady Vanishes*, scripted by George Axelrod (who tightens up the ending somewhat, but otherwise follows the first film closely) and directed by Anthony Page. It also starred Elliot Gould, whose career was in its fading days, and Angela Lansbury, who was as far away from a hit television series as Shepherd was. So no one paid attention to the movie and it closed the week after it opened just about everywhere. It is, however, a sharp, well-executed remake of a fun film, and Shepherd, seen in today's context of her abilities, is marvelous. She's bright, energetic, sly, and hysterically self-possessed. The part, as the passenger on a train who seems to be the only one to notice that another passenger has disappeared, is perfect for her aggressive presence. She works well with Gould, too, and never allows her character to become mean towards him as the dialog and the earlier film would have her become. There are those who would say, 'Why remake a classic?' but the reason here is obvious. Shepherd hadn't been born when the first version was made.

We wish that the disc were in better condition than it is. It is passable, but the print looks a little worn down and has its share of speckles. The sound, in digitally encoded monaural, is better, and all the train effects are satisfying. The credit sequences are letterboxed, and one becomes painfully aware that the rest of the movie is not. Page uses the full screen in his compositions and it is always obvious that something has been obscured on either the left or the right.

LADYHAWKE

With digital stereo surround sound, *Ladyhawke* is transformed from a little drizzle of a movie to a thunderstorm of entertainment. There is no denying that the movie is bad. The story is not consistent with its own logic and parts were obviously cut to hold the running time to 121 minutes. The photography by the normally reliable Vittorio Storaro is well composed, but the lighting is bad and glare or double images are not uncommon. The electric sledgehammer music is less intelligent than the inept villains.

The story takes place in some kind of medieval town which looks like El Greco's Toledo. Michelle Pfeiffer and Rutger Hauer portray lovers who have been cursed by a wicked bishop. Pfeiffer's character is a hawk during daylight and Hauer's character becomes a wolf after dark. Matthew Broderick portrays a thief who helps the lovers break the curse.

The night scenes are either washed in blue grey if lit by 'moonlight' or washed in orange if lit by 'fire,' but the daylight scenes have the sharp glossy colors one associates with the laser medium at its best. The break between sides two and three comes at the wrong time, spoiling the tension of a scene.

The soundtrack is as inept as the rest of the movie. Every clang, clomp, and cry is overbearing and artificial. The result, however, turns a living room into a first-run film theater. The sounds of horseshoes on stone (going the wrong direction, but the error is momentary), metal sword on metal sword, and wind on forest branches are stunning.

LAGUNA HEAT

A cop leaves the LAPD under troublesome circumstances and returns to his hometown to become a detective in *Laguna Heat*. His first murder case involves his own past and he must search painful childhood memories for part of the solution. Although the film was made for cable TV, it is well directed (by Simon Langton) and never fails in maintaining the mood of a Sun Belt corruption thriller. The ending has an unexpected twist. Harry Hamlin stars, and his intensity, along with Langton's tight direction, makes the movie work even in scenes which have been weakly scripted. Because most of the film takes place in the bright Laguna sun, the picture quality is fine. The monaural sound has no significant problems.

THE LAIR OF THE WHITE WORM

The transfer of Ken Russell's feverishly slinky snake movie, *The Lair of the White Worm*, is impeccable. The colorful picture is preserved detail for kinky detail, and the surround sound is clean and efficient. Even Russell's most problematic screen compositions, the ones which are similar to the hallucination scenes in 'Altered States,' remain completely stable and sharply focussed. The sound editing is not elaborate, but it has one or two little surprises.

The movie is based upon a novel by Bram Stoker which follows the same formula of possession and earnest heroism that many of his stories utilized. Russell gives it a contemporary setting and mixes science, folklore, and sex in lively doses. Specifically, the plot concerns a mysterious woman who is searching for a sacrifice to offer a gigantic albino worm living in a cavern beneath the cellar of her mansion. There are two male and two female heroes who must stop her before one of their number becomes the sacrifice victim. With Russell at the helm, the plot description does not do justice to the movie, which constantly urges the viewer to remain alert and to think. Among the many odd and challenging images are scenes which tamper with standard religious symbols and may be offensive to some viewers. After a dose of normal horror films, however, *Lair of the White Worm* is as refreshing as the English countryside in which it is set. Russell proves that you don't have to be thirteen to take delight in the cinema of red dyes and rubber latex, and that you don't have to turn off the smart portion of your brain so that the dumb portion can have a good time.

LAMAZE METHOD: TECHNIQUES FOR CHILDBIRTH PREPARATION

The 45-minute CLV disc, *The Lamaze Method: Techniques for Childbirth Preparation*, is a video tape program hosted by Patty Duke Astin. It has been given four chapter markers although it ought to have sixteen if the interruptions in the narrative were truly respected.

A certified instructor guides 'Marlene and Mark' through techniques for relaxation, breathing, and 'expulsion' on a homey, rec room set. Patty Duke hovers about, seemingly unnoticed by the others, explaining the ins and outs of birth preparation. 'Relaxation,' which consists of lying on some pillows next to one's partner, is the most pleasant exercise to practice, and something which even couples not in the family way might enjoy.

The disc is intended to supplement birthing classes, and to this end, it is effective. Good intentions and the idealism of parents-to-be are usually not enough to suppress a natural human tendency for practicing all the exercises the first week, a few the second week, none by the end of the classes, and forgetting everything by the time the exercises must be put to use. Dropping the disc on, one or two evenings a week, is a pleasant and useful way to bide one's time in preparation for the Big Event. Its lessons will all be abandoned five minutes after the onset of labor, in any case.

L'AMOUR DES TROIS ORANGES THE LOVE OF THREE ORANGES

Sergei Prokofiev's wonderfully wacky opera about a prince who falls in love with an orange, *L'Amour des Trois Oranges The Love of Three Oranges*, is available in a performance by the Glyndebourne Festival Opera. Prokofiev's music has inspired many a film soundtrack. Rather than attacking one's music sensibilities head on, Prokofiev makes a series of guerilla raids. He wears down one's resistance to his apparent lack of structure, and his idiosyncratic melodies, mistaken by movie composers for 10-second cues, keep a listener alert and engaged.

The Glyndebourne interpretation, by Frank Corsaro and Maurice Sendak, makes use of the relatively small Glyndebourne stage by turning the show into a carnival of sorts, with jugglers and acrobats accompanying the singers. The bigger and crazier *Oranges* is, the better. With the restrictions of Glyndebourne's house and, for that matter, talent, the show is not the most entertaining rendition possible, but it is the only rendition available on disc and it is adequate.

The production was taped live, but transition scenes utilize video effects and it is unclear how these were presented to the audience. The stereo sound picks up every foot shuffle and prop drop. The music is perfectly recorded and presented, and the better one's audio system the better it will sound. The singers, however, are exposed by this clarity and could have benefitted from whatever is the audio equivalent of a paper lampshade.

The picture is less impressive than the sound and the image is soft. The opera is in French and has English subtitles. No plot synopsis appears on the disc jacket. There is a chapter listing, though we felt the chapter encoding could have been more extensive.

THE LAND BEFORE TIME
THE LAND BEFORE TIME (CAV)

The poster for *The Land Before Time*, which is recreated on the jacket cover of the CLV version, looked very promising, but the actual animation, and the movie itself, was a disappointment. The poster shows not only the young dinosaur heroes and the villain of the piece, it also shows a highly detailed Mesozoic background. The characters are in the movie, the background is not. The economics of today dictate that every vista cannot be hand painted to the smallest detail, but the animators, directed by Don Bluth, compromised too much and left out too much. There just isn't enough scenery to inspire a viewer's imagination. In comparison, *An American Tail*, which had its faults, was nevertheless a wonderland of inspired scenery, making for easy scene shifts and pleasant day dreaming.

The movie only runs an hour – the stated 69 minute running time includes 6 minutes of end credits. The narrative is straightforward and fairly simple, as the young heros, separated from their parents, avoid the bad dinosaur and journey to safety. The characters are engaging and many individual scenes are reasonably effective, but the elaborations and enhancements are limited.

MCA has released both a CLV version and a Special Collector's Edition CAV version. The picture and sound quality on both discs is the same, and overall the transfer is good. Strong red and blue washes have a mild blur, but when the animation is less impressionistic the image is sharp and colorful.

The digitally encoded sound is okay. Sound effects in animated features are usually limited and that is the case here, but a strong bass thumps around in a few places, and James Horner's symphonic suite makes full use of the surround.

The CLV disc is formatted in a lopsided manner, with side two containing just 15 minutes of the story. On the three-sided CAV disc the same break point is used, but it is more appropriate in relation to the first two sides. The CLV disc has no special features. The still frames on the CAV disc are accurately rendered, but because of the nature of the animation, some still frames are repeated. The CAV disc has a supplementary section which features a trailer, background notes, and promotional stills. The trailer and the stills are great, but the notes, which have a strong publicity-department flavor to them, are a disappointment.

LASSIE COME HOME

The pet-with-an-uncanny-sense-of-direction drama, *Lassie Come Home*, stars a young Roddy McDowell and an equally youthful Elizabeth Taylor. The Technicolor classic has been given a nice transfer, although the source material has its rough spots. The picture still looks a little too dark in places and some of the reds blur too much. At its best the fleshtones are ravishing and the strange location shots that are meant to pass for England look luscious. The monaural sound is acceptable. An original theatrical trailer, which emphasizes the popularity of the story's author, is included after the film is ended.

At the opening of the disc, however, there is a real treat, two Pete Smith shorts about Franklin Roosevelt's dog, Fala. The first, 'Fala,' is in black-and-white, and shows Fala's life in the White House. The second, 'Fala at Hyde Park,' is in color, which is nicely transferred. Although the programs are pleasing from an adult point of view for all the wrong reasons, the emphasis on the dog is so strong that children will be delighted with the shorts on a literal level, and will find the pair to be the perfect lead-in for Lassie. Ah, the good old days. Not only do we no longer fawn over our leaders like that, we don't even fawn over our pets that way any more.

THE LAST DAYS OF MAN ON EARTH

Although *The Last Days of Man on Earth* runs less than 75 minutes, Image has not even tried to put one of the sides in CAV, as each runs a little over a half hour. It is a shame, for no matter how silly one thinks the film is, the tacky special effects on the 1974 British cult science fiction title are worth deconstructing. Understanding that the film was made on the cheap, the picture transfer is very good. The colors are accurate and the focus is sharp. The sound is less successful at overcoming the limited production budget. The narrative concerns the son of a dead scientist who is asked by a consortium to recover some microfilmed formulas from his brother. Around him, civilization is collapsing. There are, however, a few caveats. One is that the viewer is always under the impression that this is not really the son of a famous scientist, but merely an actor (Jon Finch) running through colored sheets and playing with toy guns. Another is that, because they knew no one would take it seriously, the filmmakers opted to make the film a comedy. The humor is scattered, and often feels like an excuse, but as many viewers will be amused by the surprise gag ending, and by the movie, as will be infuriated by it.

THE LAST EMPEROR (Import)
THE LAST EMPEROR
THE LAST EMPEROR (CAV)

From Japan comes a disc release of *The Last Emperor* with a 219-minute running time, some 55 minutes longer than the version which won the Oscar for Best Picture. The major sequences which have been restored appear primarily in the center of the film, but camera shots and pieces of dialog have been added to almost every scene. The presentation on the Japanese disc indicates that the trimming had occurred for purely economic reasons, to reduce the running time so theaters could maintain a certain number of screenings per day.

Nelson released two versions of the standard theatrical presentation in America. One, a scanned and cropped CLV disc, had a poor color transfer and was pretty useless. The second, a letterboxed CAV version, with an aspect ratio of about 2.25:1, had an improved color transfer and is at least a tolerable presentation of the movie, though it is still grainy and mis-colored. The film has many fascinating visual details, and the CAV functions can be very useful for examining them better.

The Japanese long version is also letterboxed, at the same aspect ration as Nelson's effort, and is in CLV. The film is entirely in English, and Japanese subtitles appear beneath the image. An important scene involving newsreel footage of Japanese war atrocities has been trimmed a little. The sequence was also censored in the Japanese theatrical presentation.

The picture is set a little too dark, and also looks washed out in a few shots, but it is, without question, much better looking than the two American releases. The flesh tones finally look genuine. The colors are accurate and do not bleed. The focus is very sharp, and details which even appeared blurry on the CAV disc are perfectly defined on the Japanese release.

The sound is digitally encoded stereo. It is mildly noisy, but demonstrates no severe problems. Among many other things, the musical score is greatly enhanced by the longer presentation. The viewer has more time to become familiar with melody and instrumental motifs and how these passages are coordinated with the drama. In a direct comparison of the short and long versions, the removal of individual shots plays havoc with the score. The disc also has a number of chapter markers, often coordinated with the most significant new footage. It comes in a gatefold jacket which features a map, in Japanese, of the Forbidden City.

The Last Emperor is the story of the last Chinese Emperor, Pu Yi. Although he abdicated his throne when he was still a child, his position as a figurehead was maintained by various political factions, including, during World War II, the Japanese, until the Communists took control of the country. The story is structured in flashback. As Yi goes through his 're-education' in a Communist prison, he recalls the events in his life which have led to that point. The major scenes restored to the film add historical information or insight, explaining events more clearly to the viewer. The relationships Yi has with his servants and family are also expanded, so that one better understands his emotional isolation and pampering.

Details which those obtaining the disc can look forward to include: A 'flashback within a flashback' depicting an audition of wet nurses; a purely Bertoluccian vision of the empress and the first consort dancing to a violin rendition of 'Old Man River' (not acknowledged in the song credits, incidentally); the expansion of Peter O'Toole's role, which brings his careful syllabic enunciation into a more sympathetic light; a number of elaborations on the corruption among the eunuchs; enlightenment on the economic manipulations Japan imposed upon Manchuria, using opium to generate cash for the war; a theme which is repeated throughout the film, that all men are born good; and editing (which won an Oscar anyway) that flows luxuriously from image to image and idea to idea – even the re-education scenes contain moments of great beauty.

The greatest reward which the disc provides, however, is not in the individual additions, but in the overall effect. The film is no longer in a rush, and scenes which may have seemed pushed or overly dramatic in the shorter version are welcomed when more time and detail lead up to them. Most of the passages have become so completely integrated that we are no longer mystified as to why we disliked the film the first time we saw it. The director wasn't being deliberately obscure with the material, the distributor was.

LAST HOUSE ON THE LEFT

An unsettling aspect of the most severe exploitation films is that if one is not disgusted enough to stop watching, one is left wishing that the movie would show more than it does. *Last House on the Left* is a grainy X-rated attempt to share the feelings of rape and murder with viewers who are always free to turn it off. The original print looks and sounds as if it was done in Super-8, but the transfer is faithful. The jacket cover wrongly identifies Wes Craven's other film credits. What can you expect from a movie titled thus in which every dwelling significant to the plot is on the right of an approaching character?

THE LAST HURRAH

John Ford's funereal political comedy, *The Last Hurrah*, is available on disc from RCA/Columbia. The black and white print is in good condition and in focus. The sound is passable. The disc runs a couple of minutes over two hours and is split evenly onto three sides.

All films dealing with the American political system are weird. Perhaps the subject is too far beyond the limits of believability and logic to dramatize rationally. Ford's effort, a portrait of an aging Irish politician in an unidentified New England city, gives him an opportunity to explore his standard themes of kinship and social ceremony from a new angle. *The Last Hurrah* is not successful, however, because Ford didn't have the guts to confront the script's true message – that the petty corruption within a city's government was a necessary source of power for the poor to do battle with the wealthy. He whitewashes Spencer Tracy's character and blanches the film's potential in the process. Ford's heroes always confronted problematic situations by ignoring illusions and acting on truth, but in creating *The Last Hurrah*, he failed to follow the examples of the role models he himself created.

THE LAST OF THE BLUE DEVILS

For a grainy 16mm film, the color transfer on *The Last of the Blue Devils* looks good, and there are no more than a few scratches. The sound is monaural and is commensurate with the image quality. The documentary is about a gathering of jazz musicians who reminisce, eat, and play in a Kansas City ballroom. Relaxed and jovial, personalities such as Count Basie and Big Joe Turner pay little attention to the camera as they tell stories about the Kansas City music scene in the thirties and forties, and talk about the different career paths various musicians have taken. There are performance sequences and historical clips to vary the program's menu. Although the importance of the 1979 film has been deflated somewhat by the influx of video-based jazz documentaries, it is still a unique and engaging portrait of one of the finer aspects of American character.

THE LAST RADIO STATION

The made-for-video narrative, *The Last Radio Station*, is about a radio station which is closing down and has one last call-in show. It is all an excuse to play the songs, which include 'Never Can Say Goodbye,' 'Let's Get It On,' 'If I Were Your Woman,' 'Dancing in the Street' and others, but there is substantial dialog between each number which may inhibit using it for background entertainment. The program lasts 41 minutes.

LAST RITES

There is a good plot twist ten minutes before the end of *Last Rites* which goes a long way in excusing the story's worst shortcomings. Viewers, however, need not seek absolution for failing to make it that far. The film, even after the twist is digested, is still a silly, far-fetched concoction about a priest who protects a witness to a mob rub-out. Tom Berenger stars, and it is all he can do to not embarrass himself during the montage scene of the priest's daily activities – you know, performing baptisms, stopping to give last rites to an accident victim during a stroll, etc. The transfer is satisfactory but not exceptional, and the sound is uninteresting.

THE LAST STARFIGHTER
THE LAST STARFIGHTER (Import)

Well-produced laser discs can improve silly movies. A case in point is the Japanese Collector's Item Series letterboxed CAV release, *The Last Starfighter*.

Although the American disc looks and sounds fairly good, it is replicated with a scanned picture which shows only about half the screen. Not so with the Collector's Item release. Particularly improved by the widescreen is the wonderfully corny final scene, where the boy returns for his girlfriend and his neighbors learn that he has not just saved Earth, but the entire galaxy. The impact of seeing the neighbors grouped together, all wide-eyed and open-mouthed, is much stronger than seeing each neighbor individually, as one does on the domestic version. The Japanese subtitles appear beneath the image.

The digital sound on the Japanese disc is not much of an improvement over the analog stereo track on the American disc. The CAV features will be of interest to those who wish to dissect the computer-animated special effects. The CAV is also helpful in another scene. The boy's lizard co-pilot shows him a collection of photographs which flash by one per frame. Flipping through a frame at a time, you discover that the filmmakers have been lazy and repeat snapshots. Now that discs are here, those who make movies are going to have to start working harder.

THE LAST TEMPTATION OF CHRIST

The makers of *The Last Temptation of Christ* knew that the film would cause an uproar, yet even they could not anticipate the vehemence with which some reacted to the film's existence. The irony is that within the film, the most offensive passages are truly the Devil's work – scenes that are part of an hallucination which Satan presents to Christ during the Crucifixion. The film is intended to stimulate a viewer's thought about the teachings and foundation of Christianity. It has a structure which is surprisingly similar to *2001: A Space Odyssey* and is formulated as an argument or a set of debate points. As a movie, it also has images of violence, history, scenery, and exotic behavior, as well as a pleasing musical score and some entertaining performances by the cast members.

As a disc, it is less compelling. Although it was not a widescreen film, even a mild cropping disturbs the elegance of Scorsese's screen compositions. The disc transfer encounters problems achieving a decent looking picture, understandable considering the trouble home video companies often confront when dealing with any Martin Scorsese feature, but disappointing nonetheless. There are red halos around almost every illuminated object, and the flesh tones and interior shots look much too orange. A comparison of the still photograph on the back of the jacket with the same shot in the film, which comes near the end of side one, will demonstrate how much work remains to be done. The sound is a lot better. It is in digitally encoded stereo surround and provides separations which are both clear and clean.

For those who want to explore the metaphors of our culture, who want to think about the foundations of western civilization, who are brave enough to re-examine the basis for their own emotional stability, and who want, at least sometimes, to do more than just react viscerally to an action or comedy picture, *The Last Temptation of Christ* is a worthwhile film.

LATINO

James Karen portrays an inept general in *Latino*, sending his CIA-sponsored military advisors across the Honduran border to blow up a Nicaraguan farm cooperative grain silo. The picture swings from looking good to looking grainy and dark. The stereo sound, however, is worth considering. The gunshots and thunder have a real 'ooomph.'

LAURA

Exclusively on disc, CBS/Fox has released *Laura* with a brief segment of restored footage which had been cut during the initial theatrical release. The sequence, a montage with voiceover narration, gives greater detail to the, shall we say, unusual relationship between Waldo and Laura, depicting the columnist's obsession with choosing her hairdo, wardrobe, etc., and his remarking that others envied him because of her. The reason for having excised the footage from the 1944 film was a fear that the boys overseas would be disheartened to think that their sweethearts were now in the clutches of such layabouts. In any case, the sequence, which has been marked with a chapter, improves the film by giving greater detail to the otherwise fuzzy relationship the two seem to have, and it is very pertinent to the denouement of the mystery in both a real and a symbolic sense.

Laura, directed by Otto Preminger, can be seen multiple times without losing its appeal. Even after the basic and highly memorable plot twists are digested, the characters and the mood can beckon a viewer to nibble again. Much of the reason for this is Preminger's direction. The camera set-ups are elaborate, and although the story could function perfectly well as a talky radio drama, the visuals are so stimulating that you can't take your eye off the movie.

The picture transfer is a little messy. The black and white image is generally sharp and has nice contrasts, but it also looks speckled in places, and scratched. The left edge on several reels is noticeably worn. The sound is fine for its age, but should not be amplified too extensively.

LAURA BRANIGAN

The audience in Ceasar's Palace on *Laura Branigan* shouts encouragement and agreement as Branigan sings about being alone and being unhappy and having nervous breakdowns ('Gloria'). The sound on the 59-minute disc is almost too clear to have really been recorded live and there probably was substantial mixing after the fact. One inserted number, 'Self Control,' is a terrific video about night life.

THE LAVENDER HILL MOB
(see **KIND HEARTS AND CORONETS/ THE CAPTAIN'S PARADISE**)

L'AVVENTURA

With the Voyager Criterion Collection transfer of *L'Avventura*, the movie, which has long seemed a pointless exercise in contemporary despair, becomes the true work of art which enthusiasts have always claimed it to be. The picture is so sharp and clean that suddenly the nuances in every composed image leap out at you. The subtle shifts in mood and emotion which the director, Michaelangelo Antonioni, was in part attempting to map, stand in relief. The brisk precision by which one shot follows the next and one angle follows the next is what gives the movie its strength. Antonioni relies so much on the visual that the slightest blemish sets off a chain reaction of missed emotions. The balance between being profound and being trite is so delicate that a hair on a single frame could tip the scale. With the Criterion Collection presentation, intelligence wins.

For those who are unfamiliar with the work, the plot follows a woman who goes on a boat trip with her friend, her friend's boyfriend, and several others. They stop at an island, seemingly remote and barren. The woman's friend disappears, never to be seen again (the film's most famous and over-analyzed, but cute, indulgence). The woman and her friend's boyfriend look for her friend first in earnest and then, back on the mainland, less feverishly, as they become attracted to one another instead. The film ends after they have a falling-out and seem to reconcile.

Although the characters are well-to-do, the plot is no more complex nor simple than the events one might come across in real life. The cinematography, however, is so precise that every camera angle lets the viewer peer into the minds of the characters. Antonioni accomplishes this by placing his cast in front of carefully chosen backgrounds. The backgrounds reflect the emotional states of the characters and are perceived subconsciously – emotionally – by the viewer, creating a direct communication of feeling which is bypassing the viewer's cognizance. It was this aspect which so astonished viewers when the film was first shown (in 1960), that a movie could so effortlessly convey the psychology of an individual – it was as if movies had broken some barrier and gotten closer to the soul.

It is all there, in CAV. The picture has been mildly letterboxed at about 1.85:1. The film is in Italian with English subtitles which appear on the image. While Antonioni's visual compositions are complex and purposeful, his soundtrack is (as on many of his films) a tease. The digitgal monaural sound seems a bit light in volume, though that can be adjusted. It has no significant flaws.

The analog audio track contains a lecture by Gene Youngblood on one of the channels. Youngblood catalogs a set of insights, though, inevitably, as he takes the time to discuss, say, a reflection in a mirror, a significant shadow passes unnoted. He also tries to include information about the production, but his attention to this subject dissipates at about the same pace as the heroine's interest in her missing friend. At best, the talk will give the viewer an introduction to the work and an understanding of some of Antonioni's intentions.

The 143-minute film ends on side five. Side six contains a supplementary section. The theatrical trailer is presented, as are two appropriately chosen essays by Antonioni and still photos which trace logistics of the production.

LAW OF DESIRE

Pedro Almodovar's gay-themed *Law of Desire*, which is sort of a *Fatal Attraction*-style comedy, paints an amusing portrait of a self-centered film director and has several funny moments. Unlike Almodovar's other work which has appeared on disc, however, the film has little to offer viewers who are outside of its basic constituency. The color transfer is very good and makes an excellent showcase for Almodovar's uncanny sense of screen composition. After some initial shifts, the image settles in with a mildly letterboxed aspect ratio of about 1.85:1. The film is in Spanish with thin white English subtitles which are usually difficult to read. The sound is fine.

LAWRENCE OF ARABIA
(RCA/Columbia original)
LAWRENCE OF ARABIA
(RCA/Columbia restored)
LAWRENCE OF ARABIA (Voyager CLV)
LAWRENCE OF ARABIA (Voyager CAV)

So many times we watched *Lawrence of Arabia*, searching for the thrill that we felt the first time we saw it, and so many times, in the theater and on TV, something just wasn't right. The epic was there, the marvelous acting, the panorama (even cropped for TV), and the action, but it all seemed like shorthand, as if viewing it again was not an experience, but merely a pale reminder of the first viewing. The desert inevitably looked washed out, skin looked bleached and the big action sequences had no lasting power. The narrative, while seemingly intact, was known to be missing scenes, and these sequences took on a mystical notoriety, as if the film's philosophical essence had been stolen with them.

Then, fortunately within one lifetime, came home video, a new market for old movies. The cost justification for restoring the original *Lawrence of Arabia* could be found in the potential it could realize as a reissued video cassette. The motivating factor behind the restoration, however, was, next to getting to see it on a big screen, preserving and distributing the movie on laser video disc. And preserved it has been, to the point of overkill.

RCA/Columbia has released a CLV version of the restored Lawrence on two platters in a single sleeve jacket. Voyager released two Criterion Collection versions, a CLV version which comes in a gatefold jacket and a CAV version on 4 platters in a sturdy box jacket. All three come from the same video master which originated at Voyager. All have superb digitally encoded surround sound, a razor sharp image, and letterboxing with an aspect ratio of about 2.2:1. There is no difference in picture or sound quality on any of the three discs.

The restoration was more than simply the addition of a few scenes. The picture, accurately transferred on disc, looks brand new. It is a marvel of visual detail. Of course there are the sunsets and the exotic Arabian tents, but almost every shot has some breathtaking facet, whether it is the change in the sunburn on Peter O'Toole's face or the delicately shifting shades of sand. The old version has been available on RCA/Columbia for some time, and though it is of little use now except as a curiosity, comparing any random scene on that disc with one of the new versions will demonstrate how much of *Lawrence of Arabia* has been restored to every frame of the film.

The soundtrack is even more of an unexpected pleasure. The stereo separations are quite a treat. The strongest show-off sequence begins with O'Toole singing 'The Man Who Broke the Bank at Monte Carlo' with an echo and concludes with a bomb explosion on the far right and an airplane raid on the Arab encampment. Only a few shifts in tone, denoting the restored passages that required contemporary re-dubbing, are noticeable, and the dialog is so rich in these passages that the flaw is barely distracting. The older portion of the soundtrack has some noise, but not enough to spoil the higher sound peaks or any of the music (an overture, entr'acte, and walkout music are included, all played to a dark screen). The bass is fantastic.

The Criterion Collection edition has chapter markers and a supplementary section. Although spread to eight sides, the CAV version manages each side break with a minimum of disruption to Anne V. Coate's precise editing. (Only a handful of cuts in all of cinema are as effective as her first cut to the desert in *Lawrence*, shifting from O'Toole blowing out a match to the sun breaking on the horizon, with the tiniest sound overlap of O'Toole's breath.)

The back of the CAV jacket is sloppy. The essay contains two typographical errors and the chapter listing fails to note exactly where the side breaks occur. For example, if you were to look for the 'No prisoners!' scene, the jacket says that it can be found in chapter 34 on side 7. In fact, only a brief piece from the beginning of the scene is there, as most of it is to be found, still encoded as chapter 34, at the beginning of side 8. If we really wanted to quibble we would complain that on the CAV version, chapter 25, 'The attack on the train' Oscar clip, begins one frame too late, since the beginning is so brief and needs every split second. Voyager's CLV disc is also chapter encoded, but RCA/Columbia is not.

At the end of side eight of the CAV disc, there is about 10,000 frames of space left, but Voyager has only provided 60 or so production stills. The stills are adequately documented and contain some interesting views from the other side of the cameras.

Voyager's CLV disc has the same side breaks as the RCA/Columbia version. The two-platter set (the intermission occurs a number of minutes into side three) comes in a gatefold jacket with nice looking photos displayed on the innerspread. After the film is ended there is a brief supplementary section containing a five minute post-*Zhivago* promotional film depicting the Lawrence production, silent footage of a similar nature, a brief clip depicting the 1962 premiere, and a coda showing the premiere of the restored version in 1989. Voyager's CAV disc does not included these film clips.

Voyager has provided an informative jacket insert which details the major points of restoration. As for the restored scenes, they contain not philosophical expansions, but political elaborations. The overall effect, however, strengthens every aspect of the narrative. By enhancing the political detail, the other aspects of the script – the history lesson, the adventure, the use of the clean/dirty desert as a symbol of Man's nature, Lawrence's skewed psychology, etc., are all brought into proper balance. The old version had been pared down so much that it had lost its sense of purpose – it was still a great movie, but it sampled too many themes without seeming to resolve them. When it becomes clear, after the addition of 20 minutes of material almost entirely devoted to it, that the politics surrounding Lawrence's actions are the story's driving force, the other explorations can be seen as supporting that central theme. They need no more enhancement to be resolute, (this is especially true of Lawrence's personality quirks), and what in the old version had appeared to be simply a gag line, "On the whole, I wish I'd stayed in Tunbridge Wells," becomes, instead, the perfect and obvious ending to the film.

LE GRAND CHEMIN

The story of a young boy spending the summer away from his parents has been told dozens of times, but if the narrative is well-executed, the situation never becomes tiresome. *Le Grand Chemin* is lyrical and touching. The film is pleasant and the transfer does nothing to reduce its charms. The one variation which raises *Chemin* above others in the genre is that the nine-year-old's visit affects not only his own outlook on life, it affects his hosts with equal significance. The disc may only last 104 minutes, but by the end the viewer knows the characters as well as if they'd been around the entire summer. The colors are faintly pale in some places but are otherwise perfectly transferred. The film is in French with big white English subtitles which do not inhibit the entertainment. The sound is rough in a few places. The score consists of a single riff played over and over again. The music lingers in one's head after the disc is ended, but, then, so does the rest of the film.

LEAN ON ME

Morgan Freeman gives a terrific performance as the high school principal Joe Clark in *Lean on Me*. The script is an unenviable attempt to take real life and mold it into a movie and it only half succeeds, but Freeman takes it the rest of the way. Freeman's Clark is flawed, so wrapped up in the imposition of discipline at the school that he can't release the choke hold once he's achieved order. It is easy to play a hero – like Jim Belushi in *The Principal* – who comes out swinging and righting wrongs, but it takes a lot more gumption to portray a hero whose flaws are insurmountable and to make it not matter.

The picture is okay, though the boundaries between strong colors often tend to look soft. The digitally encoded stereo sound is transferred well enough, but the editing is weak. The music and assembly murmurs show up on the surround channel intermittently, and without a clear policy as to when the effect should or shouldn't be used. The recording of Freeman's voice is also questionable. His dialog is intelligible, but his timbre is light, even when he's using the megaphone.

L'ECLISSE (ECLIPSE) (Import)

Michelangelo Antonioni's *L'Eclisse* (*Eclipse*) is available in Japan, in French with Japanese subtitles. The black-and-white picture, which is mildly letterboxed, is super sharp and the sound, although in mono, is rich and quite clear. The subtitles appear on the picture.

Eclipse is considered to be inferior to *L'Avventura*, but the disc is equally, if not more, entertaining than its austere cousin. The subject matter is the same, a directionless young woman drifts in and out of an affair, but the scenes are given a comic thrust and Alain Delon has a convincing performance as a young stockbroker whose approach to seduction has not left adolescence. The girl in both films is played with a bit too much victimness by Monica Vitti. The last ten minutes of the movie is a visual montage of places and objects visited during the course of the story. This is a daring withdrawal, and coupled with the earlier explorations that Vitti and Delon go through as they get to know one another, Antonioni proves that he is an artist, at times an artist of astonishing ability.

LEGAL EAGLES

Debra Winger and Daryl Hannah in the same movie. Stay our beating heart! Winger couldn't be dressed or downplayed any more than she is, but the effect does nothing to hide the aura of her availability. To have them together in the same shots is like trying to decide between vanilla and strawberry ice cream. We'll take both.

Robert Redford is in the movie, too. It is called *Legal Eagles* and was reasonably popular but cost an enormous amount to make because of the stars and because of the spectacular special effects involving several fires. (Director Ivan Reitman, who also did *Ghostbusters*, appears to be something of a pyromaniac.) The film has also been badmouthed because everyone involved had the same agent. However, the movie is just enough of a mystery/comedy about murder and art fraud to retain a coherent plot and support repeated viewings. The jacket cover is a classic, to be hung next to *Shampoo* for symmetry. The film has an expensive surround soundtrack that does everything it ought to do in a living room. Critics tended to find the movie shallow and manufactured, but they don't understand star appeal.

LEGEND

LEGEND (Import)

The MCA release of Ridley Scott's *Legend* contains the American theatrical release, running 89 minutes and sporting a workmanlike electronic musical score by Tangerine Dream. However, the film was released theatrically in Europe with a longer running time and an elaborate orchestral score by Jerry Goldsmith. We have no idea what sort of theatrical version played in Japan, but the laser disc version of *Legend* released there is 90 minutes long and appears to be a pastiche of the American and European versions. It has the Goldsmith score and several important sequences which are missing from the American version. There is also some footage in the American version that has been dropped from the Japanese version for no distinct reason (particularly a conversation the heroine has with a wren), encouraging a viewer who has compared the two discs to imagine what a longer film might have contained.

MCA did a fine job transferring the American version to disc, but that version contained so many overdubs that the stereo surround soundtrack could not disguise its imperfections. It is still a lot of fun if you avoid the temptation to raise the volume too high, but those who are sensitive to audio clarity had best avoid it. The Japanese disc has the opposite problem. It is not loud enough, and no amount of pushing can coax a confident presence from it. Goldsmith's score is fantastic – leaping believably from choral passages to sweeping and moody orchestral turns to light instrumentals – but it doesn't seem to be balanced correctly against the dialog (which has dull tones) and the sound effects (which aren't as aggressive as on the American disc). The picture on the Japanese disc is also paler than the luscious MCA version. On both discs the film is scanned and cropped, and the Japanese disc has Japanese subtitles.

What seemed in the American version to be a misguided attempt to recreate a Victorian faerie story comes much closer to legitimacy on the Japanese disc. The improvements are epitomized by one scene, in which the heroine dances a long and languorous waltz with a mysterious figure before assuming the figure's garbs. Although the devil is viewed early on in the American version, his appearance is withheld on the Japanese disc until the end of this scene. Other significant additions include the heroine's singing to the unicorns in order to attract them at the beginning, a riddle which the hero must solve before he is accepted by the elf, and an extended conversation with the swamp witch. The heroine is identified as a princess on the Japanese version, and there is another character in the house she visits in the film's opening (you can spot him on the American disc after you know where to look). Among the shots dropped from the Japanese disc are a closeup of the unicorn's horn being sheared (and restored), and a longer take of the swamp witch's decapitation.

The movie, which must have cost a fortune to make, has always been reasonably entertaining if you weren't put off by its pretensions. The Japanese version eliminates much which is superfluous, from the opening text prolog to the early shots of the Devil and the

Tangerine Dream score. It reveals that Scott was probably on the mark in creating the type of world which had captured the imagination of the young right before movies were invented. All it really seems to need is another ten to fifteen minutes of atmospheric detail and a cleaned-up transfer. We hope that obtaining such a version someday will be more than just an idle daydream.

THE LEGEND OF HELL HOUSE

Although *The Legend of Hell House* comes from an era of less explicit blood and nudity, it can still rouse a viewer. The film, which stars Roddy McDowall, Pamela Franklin, Clive Revill, and Gayle Hunnicutt, is about a team sent to exorcise a haunted mansion, and is effectively atmospheric and somber. McDowall is particularly inspired, and it is odd that he is not considered a genre performer although he always has so much success in suspense and horror films. With a script by Richard Matheson, the story also employs a touch of science to justify its ghosts, one of the facets which Tenney clearly lifted for his feature.

The picture looks very worn and grainy, and although stereo was mistakenly imprinted on the jacket cover, the audio, which is a little weak, is digital monaural.

THE LEGEND OF SLEEPY HOLLOW

(see **PECOS BILL**)

LEGEND: THE BEST OF BOB MARLEY AND THE WAILERS

When Eric Clapton released his rendition of 'I Shot the Sheriff,' we thought it was the stupidest song we had ever heard, but several years later, when we finally heard it performed by its author, Bob Marley, it suddenly made perfect sense. It was Clapton's shower-stall rendition and not the song itself which was at fault. With Marley's reggae rhythm and vocals, 'Sheriff,' one of the songs on *Legend: The Best of Bob Marley and the Wailers*, takes on a political and social/economic strata and tension which is not evident when one reads the lyrics on a page. Marley's music and lyrics are fully ingrained, the way one imagines Italian opera to be to native speakers, and the lyrics, divorced from the music, lose half their meaning.

The single-sided disc is a collection of 13 video sequences, mostly in stereo. The jacket cover lists the songs as chapters, but the disc producers neglected to give the disc chapter encoding. Some of the numbers are in a concert format and some are lightly impressionistic music videos. The picture quality varies according to the age of the clip, some being very grainy and others being reasonably sharp. Separating most of the songs are excerpts from an interview with Marley, his patois rapidly diverging from true English but still readily understandable and almost as melodic as his songs.

L'ELISIR D'AMORE

The Metropolitan Opera video presentation of *L'Elisir D'Amore* was taped six years previous to appearing on disc. Hence, the color is ever so slightly faded and when the singers move too fast, faint ghosts follow them. Fortunately, time has done less harm to the sound recording and the digitally encoded disc, from Pioneer Artists, still looks and sounds better than most.

Gaetano Donizetti's opera is an easily accessible and whimsical look at love. It imparts the real feelings of romance and, at the same time, satirizes romantic excess. Luciano Pavarotti stars. His acting is limited but his singing abilities are boundless. Even his laughter and his asides are fluid.

The 132-minute program is resident on three sides. There are 24 chapter markers. The booklet has the complete libretto in Italian and English and an excellent essay about the history of the opera lifted directly from the performance program notes.

LEONARD PART 6

It was no great secret that *Leonard Part 6* was going to be a stinker, as the gossip columns had been whispering about it almost from its inception. This was one of those situations where too much money had been invested too quickly for any of the involved parties, in particular the producer and star, Bill Cosby, to back out. But what a stinker the movie is. In levels of awfulness, it is only surpassed by low-budget efforts such as *Plan Nine from Outer Space*. From the opening assassination, where a killer tuna, swimming furiously through a pipe leading to his target's swimming pool, stops to glance and giggle at a discarded copy of *Playboy* in the middle of the pipe – this is a tuna, mind you – to the end, where Cosby sits and smiles adoringly as his character's ex-wife playfully and endlessly piles a seven-course meal upon his head and shoulders, so that all that is left is food and his Cheshire grin, the movie is shamefully, pitifully, scandalously stupid. The disc, which runs under 90 minutes and is in CLV, has an average picture transfer and a tolerable stereo soundtrack.

LEONCAVALLO – PAGLIACCI – PRETRE

A soundstage production, *Leoncavallo – Pagliacci – Pretre* runs 70 minutes and is presented on a single disc, with the break between the two sides separating the opera's two acts. The program was directed by Franco Zeffirelli, conducted by Georges Pretre, and stars Teresa Stratas, Placido Domingo, and Juan Pons. The orchestra and chorus are from La Scala.

Zeffirelli has made a neat little movie. Leoncavallo's *Pagliacci* is a well-known Italian repertory item about clowns with messy domestic lives. The film has a confined and intimate feel, and moves from the backstage to the performance scenes with an involving believability. You can tell he didn't spend too much time blocking the thing, and there aren't enough closeups, but Zeffirelli accomplishes his main concept. Freed from a live audience, his camera becomes part of the crowd within the opera, one of the breathless observers who are powerless when life's dramas interrupt the comedy.

The sound is exceptional, although even the most careful appraisers will find themselves so mesmerized by the singing of Domingo and Stratas that it will be difficult to concentrate on the technical contributions. Suffice to say that the recording and replication does not get in the way. The picture is fair, and is often a little too murky. The heads of singers with brown or black hair blend into the darker backdrops. *Pagliacci* is in Italian and has English subtitles. A single sheet insert accompanies the disc, containing a plot synopsis and a history, which starts off with great promise and then meanders too much.

LES MISERABLES

Victor Hugo's *Les Miserables* has one of those wonderfully captivating plots which, as it turns and turns, tightens its grip on a viewer or reader both morally and viscerally. The most highly respected English language film version was produced by Darryl Zanuck in the mid-thirties, starring Frederick March and Charles Laughton. The film runs only 104 minutes and could have used a few more embellishments, since it is when the plot slows down a little in favor of characterization that a viewer's attention is massaged. In this respect, Charles Laughton, as the villain Javert, steals the movie, because he is able to squeeze so much personality into each brief appearance.

The black and white print has its share of scratches and weary edges, but few viewers will be disappointed. The sound withstands amplification without severe problems.

LES MISERABLES – STAGE BY STAGE

An hour long profile of the popular stage musical, entitled *Les Miserables – Stage by Stage* opens with a nose-thumb at the London critics who panned the show, something the producers appear to resent deeply since the subject comes up later as well. The disc is in stereo and one gets to hear the immediately addictive score while watching excerpts from the show depicted with swooping crane shots and other enthusiastic camera angles. The individuals who contributed to the conception and construction of the musical are interviewed, but none of the cast members are heard from. Excerpts from the Oslo production, sung in Norwegian, and the Budapest production, with Hungarian recitatives, are included, since the program is an attempt to promote every CD, stage production and eventual movie adaptation in existence. The picture tends to wash out in a single color and often looks grainy. The jacket cover lists chapters, but none are encoded.

LES PARAPLUIES DE CHERBOURG (THE UMBRELLAS OF CHERBOURG)

(Import)

The French filmmaker Jacques Demy has always been guilty of being overly clever. In 1964, he made a 'musical' where every line of dialog is sung to music by Michel Legrand. *Les Parapluies de Cherbourg* (*The Umbrellas of Cherbourg*) is in French with Japanese subtitles, but the dialog is so simple, and the story so easy to follow, that the language barrier is really not a problem. The picture, fortunately, retains its wide-screen format. The colors are fresh, but the master is scratched and has a couple of splices.

Catherine Deneuve and Nino Castelnuovo star as young lovers who are separated when the Castelnuovo's character is drafted. They never reunite. The dialog and the situations are banal, but one could make a case for the film by suggesting that this is deliberate – Demy wants to show that life is rich even in simplicity and that the dreams in a lover's memory are not as important as the realities of a relationship. The sound is in mono, but it is CX-encoded. *The Umbrellas of Cherbourg* was a *One from the Heart* ahead of its time. The problem is that for most viewers, that time still hasn't come.

LES PAUL & FRIENDS HE CHANGED THE MUSIC

Paul, whose guitar is rigged up to sound like an organ and who has accompanied Bing Crosby and Judy Garland among others, is joined by Eddie Van Halen, Steve Miller, The Stray Cats, Carly Simon, Rita Coolidge and more on *Les Paul & Friends He Changed the Music*, subtitled 'Live at the Brooklyn Academy of Music in New York.' Most of the performers do a single number, either with Paul or evoking his music. The stereo sound is fresh and very clear, which tends to bring the viewer closer to the performers. A smoke machine is rigged up to give the stage an overly atmospheric look, and the smoke adds to a mild softness and slight grain on the picture. The colored stage light effects aren't too distorted, and the presentation is acceptable. Due to the odd collection of stars, the music is different, making the program both unique and intriguing. The single-sided disc is an hour long.

LES TROYENS

The massive Metropolitan Opera production of Hector Berlioz's two-part *Les Troyens* has been released on disc as an equally massive three-disc boxed set. The show runs 253 minutes. However, the opera, which tells of the fall of Troy and the flight of Aeneas to Carthage, can be comfortably viewed in successive sessions. The first two sides hold act I. The last three sides contain act II, which has often been produced as a separate work.

Unlike the Met's *Idomeneo*, these Trojans look like Trojans. The staging, by Fabrizio Melano, is a bit too processional and empty, but the video production is magnificent. Video director Brian Large does not feel compelled to jump from angle to angle or to catch every singer all the time. He can take a lengthy pan across a chorus or do a five-minute slow zoom on Jessye Norman as she sings an emotional aria. At the beginning of side four there is an orchestral interlude which is made to be just as exciting as the opera's dramatic turns. The camera takes its time, viewing each musician's contribution and technique. Finally, as the piece builds to its conclusion, the attention turns to the conductor, James Levine, who by this time is pumping away as if he were playing every instrument himself.

Subtitles accompany the French lyrics, but no libretto has been included. The stereo recording is live and the verisimilitude more than compensates for the occasional glitches. The first act belongs to Jessye Norman and the second is dominated by Placido Domingo. Aside from the arias, the choral passages are particularly inspired. They are expansive, yet delicate.

LES UNS ET LES AUTRES (Import)

Claude LeLouch's *Les Uns et les autres* played for months in Montreal, two years in The Netherlands, and is probably still playing in the theater in Paris where it opened in 1981. It played in a modified form in New York for about three weeks under the title, 'Bolero' and never appeared on disc in America. The Japanese release is on the Herald Videogram label and runs for the original three hours and five minutes (One of the 'stars,' Fanny Ardent, appears for all of 30 seconds – LeLouch has an even longer cut designed to be broadcast on television).

If one thinks of the way movies are put together – the crane shots and dollies – as 'type,' then Claude LeLouch is the only director who makes his films in longhand. His love for the medium is in evidence on every shot, whether he's got the camera on his shoulder as he spins around his characters, or on the hood of an automobile dodging through Parisian traffic. He experiments and explores and discovers just as much through film as a Bresson or a Godard does and he is not afraid to tell a story, like a Hawks or a Hitchcock. But like the kid who turns in a handwritten thesis when everyone else has typed theirs, few take him seriously.

Only a third of the movie is in French – the rest is in English or involves musical sequences – but the story spans three generations of characters and the same actors and actresses play the generational roles, so you have to be on top of what is going on to know who is who and what is happening when. The story is not told in the familiar manner, either. Following the lives of a dozen major characters, the narrative touches only upon major incidents, like death or marriage, and upon the relationship between the characters, most of whom are musically talented, and their artistic skills. A narrator, speaking the credits at the beginning, announces that the story will be very banal and it is, if one is expecting to follow the life of a single character. Instead, it is celebrating humanity by glorifying only one part of that humanity and skimming the rest.

A 'We Are the World' type performance of Ravel's 'Bolero' with Maurice Bejart's choreography serves as a frame for the picture. Bejart's well-known interpretation, where one performer stands on a round table and dances his guts out for ten minutes while other dancers loiter around the table's edge, is shown in full. The movie opens on the dancer doing the piece, cuts to his mother performing to the same music 30 years earlier, and then winds its way back. The first hour (side one) is a flurry of dancing, music, marriages, and war. James Caan and Geraldine Chaplin appear as personalities during the big band era and then again as the couple's son and daughter.

The songs, written by Michel Legrand *and* Fancis Lai, are addictive in the best French pop manner. A few of the dance sequences are spectacular. Only when the scene shifts to a subplot which does not involve music does the movie get bogged down. The film is in stereo and has been CX-encoded (without automatic tripping). The picture is, unfortunately, cropped and the Japanese subtitles are all over the place – down the left side, down the right and across the bottom. The transfer is good, though, and the sound, for a French film, is excellent.

LESS THAN ZERO

We envy anyone who can write a bestseller and then trick Hollywood into buying it, so we did not have misgivings most reviewers had about the mangled film adaptation of the Bret Ellis novel, *Less than Zero*. Now we are not going to go and get ourselves into trouble by saying that it is a good film, but it is a legitimate film, and CBS/Fox has done a fine job transferring it to disc. The picture has problems with heavy red lighting, but is otherwise glossy and sharp. The sound is only analog, but the stereo mix is elaborate. There is an icy, bleached rock score which is particularly effective on the disc.

The best way to approach the movie is to treat it as high camp, but it can also be taken seriously. The story is about three kids from well-to-do families. They are friends, just out of high school, and are following different paths to adulthood. *Less than Zero* is not about adults, though. It is about the way eighteen-year-olds picture their adulthood in their heads, and that is what the cast acts out on the screen, to perfection. Here are teenagers who aren't yet a decade past puberty, and they're acting as suave and world-trodden as Rick and Ilsa and Victor Laszlo. We laughed until it dawned on us that we don't even have fantasies like that anymore.

LETHAL WEAPON

Style is what makes *Lethal Weapon* a great movie. The script is just another improbable action thriller, with a complicated and illogical plot about mean drug runners. The action scenes, however, have a crisp and furious impact; the director always supplies exactly enough information so that you know what is going on, but never any more than that, so you don't have time to think about it. Visually, the film is pleasing, not because of any fancy camera angles but because, even when there is no action, the director keeps showing you things. Although the disc is not letterboxed, the movie's images are still arresting. You feel that if you turned away, you'd miss something.

The casting was also an inspiration. Danny Glover is perfect as a hero – straight, bland, and tough. It is a relief seeing him on the screen in the place of the many flamboyant personalities which Hollywood would normally place in a role like that. Mel Gibson fulfills all the requirements for flamboyancy, yet it is clear his character is subsidiary to Glover's.

The picture quality is acceptable, although a few scenes on the original print seem to be a touch grainy. The sound works very well. The music has intensity, but never overpowers the dialog or special effects.

LETHAL WEAPON 2

Lethal Weapon 2 is letterboxed with an aspect ratio of about 2.3:1 and has a gorgeously crisp picture. The gold in the back of the car trunk has an incredible sparkle. The film's many night scenes, and even the underwater night scenes, are flawless, though a mild grain stops the transfer short of perfection.

The picture needs letterboxing not only to give the viewer the full impact of the stunts, but also to catch the comical expressions of the actors when they aren't repeating dialog. The film opens with its foot on the gas and never really lets up. Although the movie, which runs just under two hours, seems a bit long, we can't imagine leaving anything out of it. The stunts are gratuitous (when Mel Gibson's character jumps on the back of the tow truck, why doesn't he just wait until the suspect reaches his destination – he doesn't have to start a fistfight at 60 MPH) but they are creative enough to be excused. The disc also reveals that the bomb-in-the-toilet scene is the film's center and turning point, magnifying the importance of the relationship between the two central characters. The opening of side two also has an abrupt audio intro, which is interesting, but we cannot decide whether it is effective or a nuisance. The soundtrack is aggressive and will turn your viewing room into a battlezone without much effort.

LETHAL WOMAN

Rape victims inhabiting an island resort invite men there with the promise of an exotic weekend, and then torture and murder the foolish guests in *Lethal Woman*. The hero, a military intelligence agent investigating the deaths, romances one of the women to cure her and kills most of the others to cure them. The film has the requisite concentration of nudity and violence, but the narrative is reasonably sustaining.

The source material is ragged. The colors are faded and the picture is marked with scratches, dots, and large ugly smears. The sound is also quite noisy.

LET'S DANCE

Betty Hutton's singing tends to irritate one's ears, but if you can get past that hurdle, *Let's Dance* is an enjoyable feature. Hutton stars with Fred Astaire, whose character is a little more flawed and undependable than usual. She plays a war widow who wants to keep her son out of the grasp of her rich in-laws. Astaire plays her old song-and-dance partner, whom she happens to bump into at a fortuitous moment. The dance numbers are not among Astaire's best, but with Astaire that hardly matters. The color transfer is pleasing but not exceptional and the sound is passable.

THE LETTER

The opening scene of *The Letter*, where Bette Davis empties a revolver into her lover, carries the rest of the film. It is great fun watching the poor souls on the screen as their feelings are hurt and their lives are ruined, but the whole plot, as masterfully as it has been composed, simply unravels from the opening scene until it can unravel no further. The movie is brief, campy entertainment which is well suited for ownership and repeated viewing. The print has a burp on side two, but no more than a few scratches elsewhere. The sound has been CX-encoded, and the music sometimes comes close to breaking free from its monaural recording.

LETTER FROM AN UNKNOWN WOMAN (see **LOLA MONTES**)

LETTER TO BREZHNEV

Despite the terribly grainy picture, looped dialog, and just barely stereophonic sound, *Letter to Brezhnev* is nice. It was filmed entirely in Liverpool, which is a plus not only because of the locations but because of the accents, and was a low-budget enterprise which gets by on charm, spunk, and a solid, clever script. The dialects add to the film's personality, and the sound, although rough, is good enough that, if you concentrate, you can follow the colloquial dialog.

The story is about two working-class girls who meet a pair of Russian sailors one evening. It isn't until halfway through side two that the point of the story – one of the girls seriously considers moving to Russia and, in terms of her living conditions, the change wouldn't be that great – obtains emotional power, but the incidents which lead up to it are pleasant and not domineering the way American comedies about young love can often be.

LEVIATHAN

Set in an underwater mining station which is the size of a Marriott Hotel and twice as luxurious, *Levianthan* lacks elan. The underwater setting seems arbitrary and is not as effectively utilized as it was in Sean Cunningham's more basic but just as much fun *Deepstar Six*. The horror sequences are grotesque but disorganized. Still, the movie has all the basic features that make discs enjoyable: A huge budget, providing oodles of shiny control panel lights and computer screens. A good cast, featuring Peter Weller, Amanda Pays, Ernie Hudson, Richard Crenna, and, less effectively utilized, Daniel Stern. Digital surround sound that squeezes every last drop of terror out of the station's creaking infrastructure. A picture which could easily dissolve into a blur of grainy colors but, thanks to the disc transfer, does not (there is only a mild fuzz in some shots around the brightest illuminations). And an aspect ratio of about 2.2:1, which lets you see the whole monster, a very mean shrimp.

LICENCE TO KILL

The James Bond movies are getting to be like too much sex. Even when they're good, they're not great. *Licence to Kill*, which has been released as a Special Wide Screen Edition, is good home video. It is full of really spectacular stunts, lively action sequences, enjoyable sound effects (listen for the bullets hitting the tanker in the finale; they clang to the 'James Bond Theme'), and exotic lifestyles. Yet it is not vital. The screenwriters tend too often to resort to a narrative shorthand in bridging the major sequences, implying to the viewer that the plot is not wholly important. Timothy Dalton's much-heralded acting abilities are downright embarrassing at times. At best, he tends to blend in with his surroundings, but he never becomes a hero you can just mindlessly root for.

About half way through the three-sided disc, the picture transfer changes from being good to being very good. In the early scenes, the night sequences are grainy. Later on, they're solid. The whole romantic powerboat interlude is stunning on the disc, as if the filmmakers and disc producers had actually achieved a differentiation in shades of black. In daylight, as well, the fleshtones and focus seem to sharpen slightly in the second half.

The letterboxing has an aspect ratio of about 2.3:1. The trailer for the film, which is not letterboxed, appears at the end and allows the viewer to compare a cropped rendition with the letterboxed version, at least for split seconds. It is immediately apparent that while many of the stars' closeups are improved by the cropping – and that it might encourage viewers to care more about the characters – the action scenes, which are the real draw of the film, are simply paired down, inspiring less awe. The surround sound, like the picture, seems to become more interesting in the second half. Along with the *Licence to Kill* trailer, CBS/Fox has included a mildly letterboxed trailer for *The Living Daylights*.

LICENSE TO DRIVE

The plot of *License to Drive* follows the standard format of ever-increasing anxieties as a young hero sneaks out for an evening cruise in his grandfather's Cadillac. The gags are unoriginal, but amusing. The picture is spotless and the stereo surround sound, with the standard number of pop hits, is satisfactory.

THE LIFE AND DEATH OF COLONEL BLIMP

Colonel Blimp was a British political cartoon character who represented the sort of kneejerk conservatism one associates with older gentlemen in general and older military gentlemen in particular. 'Blimp' was a concept, not a person, and so the Michael Powell film, *The Life and Death of Colonel Blimp*, concerned an individual, a military man, who grew into (Life) and out of (Death) a Blimp stereotype. But, of course, kneejerk conservatives who are one's friends are cuddly old codgers and seemingly not kneejerk conservatives at all. The movie has a brief opening, where one is shown the main character, contemptibly, from afar, and then, a flashback to some forty years earlier follows the character's life so that at the end, when the scene is replayed from different camera angles, one's sympathies have totally reversed.

The Life and Death of Colonel Blimp has been released on laser disc by the Voyager as part of their Criterion Collection. The film is an inviting journey through the first half of the twentieth century in the British upper-class, told with the delicacy and lyricism which Powell and his collaborator, Emeric Pressburger, brought to all their best works.

The film was originally 163 minutes long and that is the running time of the disc. The movie, however, existed only in severed form in the United States until its reconstruction a few years ago, and so, previous to the release of the disc, exposure to its full range and impact was limited. The print which Voyager used looks marvelous. There are some soft edges and a few reels which seem weaker and grainier than others, but a viewer will be so captivated by the lighting and the photography and the sets and the costumes that an occasional blurry spot hardly seems to matter. The monaural sound has not been CX-encoded and is best kept at reasonable levels.

The disc has a second audio track on which Powell and Martin Scorsese alternate in providing commentary. They make a great team. Scorsese talks a mile a minute and leaps from his personal feelings to technical comments on the construction of shots and scenes. Powell, speaking slowly and sometimes with a slur, meanders from anecdotes about putting the film together to philosophizing about trivia such as the importance of Deborah Kerr's wardrobe. Especially her hats, for which he has a great fondness. ("That's a good hat, isn't it. It must be about two and a half feet across.") Their dialog provides a nice excuse to watch the disc without paying such close attention to it, and leaves one with the desire to play the movie again.

Roger Livesey, portraying the main character, gives one of those rare performances where one is fully convinced that the actor has truly aged and is not simply wearing obnoxious makeup. Kerr, who has three different parts, is more fortunate. She grows younger as the film progresses.

Scorsese's unmitigated enthusiasm for the film is clear indication of the appeal which *The Life and Death of Colonel Blimp* can hold for contemporary viewers. The style of the film and the vitality of the characters will never age. As a social history of a vanished era, it should become more valuable as the years pass, even if the title will make less and less sense (there should have been a short scene written which showed a political cartoonist being inspired by the hero to create the satirical image).

LIFEBOAT

What one first believes to be fog in the opening of Alfred Hitchcock's *Lifeboat*, turns out, as one watches for a while, to be a flaw on the image of the disc, a spotting which is present through most of the program. The flaw, a mark of deterioration, is slight, and since the picture was taken from nitrate source material it looks very sharp most of the time. But these days the spots are the only thing many viewers will see, and those with large screen monitors or those who are distracted by impurities had best avoid the disc. The sound is also inconsistent, with the volume changing in intensity on a couple of reels.

The movie has a simple and well known concept, but as entertainment it is highly repeatable. The cast, which includes Tallulah Bankhead, Hume Cronyn, Walter Slezak and William Bendix, is part of the reason for this, and Hitchcock's well thought-out handling of the script is the other part. As the characters adrift in the boat reveal themselves, Hitchcock fights against the tide, always including business or intriguing objects in his shots which pull a viewer's concentration away from the obvious dramatics. Being stranded in real life must be boring, but the movie never is, and surely some viewers will prefer having the disc to waiting for the late show.

LIFEFORCE

As a big budget space spectacle, *Lifeforce* was a bomb, but as a minor home video offering sitting shoulder to shoulder with the likes of Vestron's *The Mutilator* and *Wheels of Fire*, it holds its own. The movie is about vampires from outer space who wander around London stark naked and shrivel the life out of innocent bystanders. Movement from one plot point to the next is so painfully labored that it is hard to believe those responsible, including Tobe Hooper and Dan O'Bannon, have made other movies.

The worst special effects aren't as noticeable on the small screen and the better stuff becomes more enticing when, because of the cropping, you can't see it all. The picture is a bit grainy, particularly when scenes are bathed in extraterrestrial light, but the CX-encoded sound is forceful and the mix is kind of fun. Snippets of a score by Henry Mancini, of all people, waft through the blood and exploding zombies to impart at least a faint odor of redemption. The most clever aspect of the disc is the break between side one and side two, which occurs right in the middle of a blood-curdling scream.

THE LIFT

The further you get into *The Lift*, the more the dubbing in the Dutch-produced film begins to sound like something out of Woody Allen's *What's Up Tiger Lily?* With lines like, "You're wearing black underwear!" it starts to become difficult to take anything in the movie seriously. Since the movie is about a psycho elevator, it hasn't got a lot going for it to begin with, and it is fairly clear that the people who made it didn't have much on the top floor, either.

The photography tries very hard to be stylish – you have to do *something* to make an elevator look menacing – but there are often blue streaks when the camera catches the arc lamps wrong and at one point you can see the reflection of the whole film crew in a plate glass window. Truth to be told, however, all the cinematic shenanigans and giggle-inducing dubbing relaxed our guard so that we also screamed and jumped one or two times when the evil elevator attacked.

LIGHT OF DAY

The picture on *Light of Day* looks okay, although the movie is purposely decorated with industrial grime. The movie also feels much longer than its 107 minute running time, perhaps because, like the characters, it is never all that anxious to rise above its surroundings. The film stars Michael J. Fox and Joan Jett and is in stereo although they don't sing as much as they talk. The sound is a little noisy, but acceptable. Fox is great, holding the whole movie together with an authentic personality which is his character's and not his own. Jett is competent and has an easier part to play, since her character is something of an extremist. You find out after 18 minutes that they are portraying a brother and sister. They have a weekend band and a dying mother. Life is tough, and from the sound of their band, it is going to stay that way.

LIGHTNING OVER WATER

Lightning over Water is a film Nicholas Ray talked Wim Wenders into making to assuage the pain Ray was enduring, coping with terminal cancer. The film has so little artifice that technically it is a documentary, showing Ray and Wenders collaborating, brainstorming, and coping with each other's company.

The 90-minute CLV disc has digitally encoded monaural sound. The film's production values, however, were not the primary concern of the filmmakers, and both the sound and the picture strain one's patience. The transfer to disc, however, offers no further inhibition.

LIGHTYEARS

The animated *Lightyears* is a 78-minute feature which has the feel of a science fiction short story. Although the narrative spans a millennium, the plot doesn't have the scope or depth of a lengthy, complex work. Its pleasures are the pleasures which a science fiction short story has to offer, and its drawbacks are generally the irrelevant inevitabilities to be found by examining any work in the genre too closely.

This is the American Version of a film by Rene Laloux, who was also responsible for the similarly imaginative *Fantastic Planet*. Although the original screenplay was penned by Raphael Cruzel, adapted from a Jean-Pierre Andrevon novel, Isaac Asimov's name is plastered all over the ad copy of the American Version for having adapted a translation to facilitate dubbing by English speaking voices. The voices are also well known personalities, a waste of time (experienced cartoon voice talents would have done a much better job) except for Christopher Plummer's wonderful incarnation of a higher being who has second thoughts about his actions. Much of the conversations on the digitally encoded surround soundtrack are too soft in comparison to the sound effects – and the plot is complicated enough that the dialog is important. The viewer is left either being blasted away by the musical score (another American replacement, and boring) and the special effects, or straining to catch the intricate details that send the hero on his quest.

The print has a few marks on it, and solid, intense colors tend to appear blurry. Side two is in CAV, and due to the stilted nature of the animation there is a single unsteady still frame in about every four. The program is rated PG.

LIKE FATHER LIKE SON

The stereo surround effects on *Like Father Like Son* are good, particularly in the hospital emergency room scene, but the movie is more painful than giving birth. Both the picture and the sound transfer are quite good. The story, a role reversal exercise, is so embarrassingly bad that the artists involved all must have wished they were someone else when it was over. Lowest point: When the father, in the son's body, lectures his history class on details of American history which most people forget the moment they step out of school. There is no basis to believe his character is any different.

LILY IN LOVE

The script for *Lily in Love* is left begging for more production money and more attention. The basic idea is charming and clever. An actor, played by Christopher Plummer, disguises himself as a different actor to land a major role in his wife's film. But key scenes are missing, cumulative moments are not thought through, and lapses in logic are extensive. The impact of the final twist is lessened considerably by sloppy execution. Beyond casting the leads, setting part of the movie in photogenic Budapest, and providing the main story, the filmmakers do everything wrong. The picture is very grainy. The sound is monaural and not CX-encoded.

THE LILY TOMLIN SPECIAL – VOL. 1

A 42 minute hour television special starring Lily Tomlin, broadcast on CBS in 1973, has been released on disc with the title, *The Lily Tomlin Special – Vol. 1*. The program does not look 15 years old. The image is as fresh as if it had been taped last season and the digitally encoded sound is only inhibited by the flatness of its monaural recording. The program doesn't act like it is 15 years old, either. Although some of the filler material between the major skits is typical of television variety writing, the main pieces are unusually sophisticated. Some have barely a gag, but are brilliant little dramas.

The program isn't perfect, but parts of it are. Appearing with Tomlin are Alan Alda (who out-acts her in the best skit, about a separated couple bumping into one another at a restaurant) and Richard Pryor (who gives a devastatingly accurate portrayal of a junkie in the unnerving finale, a piece set in a diner).

LIMITED GOLD EDITION II CARTOON CLASSICS DISNEY DREAM FACTORY: 1933-1938
LIMITED GOLD EDITION II CARTOON CLASSICS HOW THE BEST WAS WON: 1933-1960
LIMITED GOLD EDITION II CARTOON CLASSICS AN OFFICER AND A DUCK
LIMITED GOLD EDITION II CARTOON CLASSICS DONALD'S BEE PICTURES
LIMITED GOLD EDITION II CARTOON CLASSICS LIFE WITH MICKEY
LIMITED GOLD EDITION II CARTOON CLASSICS FROM PLUTO WITH LOVE
LIMITED GOLD EDITION II CARTOON CLASSICS THE WORLD ACCORDING TO GOOFY
CARTOON FESTIVAL II (Import)

We have been put off by the way Disney has been releasing its 300-odd cartoon shorts to the home video/laser disc market. It certainly makes sense from their point of view, and young viewers won't give a whit, but someone trying to collect them all will have to bear the expense of many duplicated cartoon titles from one anthology set to the next in order to acquire a complete library. In the short history of laser discs, it is already possible to obtain 'Mickey and the Seal' or 'Mickey's Circus' on three different anthologies.

What has bothered us even more is that there doesn't appear to be an organized plan to release all or most of the cartoons. Our response to Paramount's intention to release every *Star Trek* episode was positive because they have a distinct plan which a fan can budget for and monitor.

The *Limited Gold Edition II Cartoon Classics* are by themselves a good starting place for those wishing to get a Disney sampler. There are no guarantees, however, that something better may come along. Each disc contains from five to seven cartoons and a short documentary linked to a specific subject. The running times on the jacket covers refer to the cartoons alone and not the documentary. The quality of the discs is consistent, although on cartoons where comparison to other discs was possible, such as 'Mickey's Circus,' the color on these looked slightly paler. Some of the original prints had scratches on them, and the sound is naturally tinny, but they look good and retain the spirit of the lovely Disney artwork.

The best of the seven discs is a collection of Silly Symphony cartoons, *The Disney Dream Factory: 1933-1938*. The first two, 'Old King Cole' and 'The Pied Piper,' are exercises in detail drawings comparable to the work of children's book illustrator, Anno. 'Merbabies' is about an underwater circus with fish taking the parts of the circus animals. It has probably not been circulated too widely since it was made, because the animators have taken great delight in giving the baby mermaids bare bottoms. Everyone will enjoy 'Three Blind Mouseketeers,' about a trio of sight-impaired, swashbuckling rodents who have no difficulty stealing cheese from a bloodthirsty cat. The other non-character oriented disc is *How the Best Was Won: 1933-1960*. Although the disc contains several classics, including the pacifistic masterpiece, 'Ferdinand the Bull,' and a 1960 effort about a tiny elephant, 'Goliath II,' some of the cartoons on it are tinged with racial gags.

The two Donald Duck discs are very specific in their orientation. *An Officer and a Duck* shows Disney's contribution to the war effort (though not the best contributions – maybe they are being saved for another collection). The one really clever cartoon here is 'The Vanishing Pirate' in which Donald discovers a can of invisible paint. *Donald's Bee Pictures* covers a series of conflicts between mean-spirited Donald and an insect with a needle-sharp stinger. The most amusing confrontation occurs on a precarious scaffolding in 'Window Cleaners.' One cartoon listed on the jacket, 'Bee at the Beach,' was accidentally replaced on the disc by a non-Bee cartoon about ants at a picnic, 'Tea for Two Hundred.'

Life with Mickey has a full stretch of Mickey Mouse cartoons from the early black-and-white '30s to the late, lush color '50s. One of the cartoons, despite an obvious cut, again utilizes racial humor. Another cartoon, 'Mickey's Polo Team,' has an interesting collection of Hollywood stars playing polo with the Disney cartoon menagerie. Another disc, *From Pluto with Love*, features Mickey's pet in a series of nose twisting adventures.

There have been a surprising number of Goofy discs released and in the *Limited Gold II* series, *The World According to Goofy* gives some reasons for this. Not only was Goofy used by the Disney people as a regular cartoon character – a cartoon on this disc, 'Baggage Buster,' about Goofy's attempt to load a magician's luggage onto a train is quite amusing – he was also used for serious and comical animated documentaries covering every subject imaginable. His attempts to fly a glider, bet a horse, and build a home are accompanied by 'how to' narration. Histories of sailing and dancing are also presented with the Goofy character appearing in every location and era. This is probably the best disc for shared family viewing.

One collection of Disney cartoons available in Japan which we managed to get a hold of was *Cartoon Festival II*. The two-sided CLV disc contains 10 cartoons, with chapter markers. The dialog is in English and there are no subtitles to be seen. At the end of the disc, there is a trailer for other cartoon collections and some of them, including the Three Little Pigs singing 'Who's Afraid of the Big Bad Wolf' (in *The Academy Award Review of Walt Disney Cartoons*), are in Japanese, while the regular Mickey Mouse type cartoons – *Cartoon Festival I* and *Cartoon Festival III* – are in English. The transfer is comparable to the US discs, but occasionally the prints look older and scratchier. For the record, *Festival II* contains 'Dragon Around,' 'Hook, Lion, and Sinker,' 'Sea Scouts,' 'Donald's Camera,' 'Clock Cleaners,' 'Mickey Down Under,' 'The Big Wash,' 'Cold Storage,' 'Chip 'n Dale,' and 'Pluto's Blue Note.'

LINDA RONDSTADT WITH NELSON RIDDLE AND HIS ORCHESTRA IN CONCERT WHAT'S NEW

When Linda Rondstadt's collaboration with Nelson Riddle was released as an LP it seemed like a one-joke concept. Despite songs by composers as varied as the Gershwins, Irving Berlin, and Gorden Jenkins, every cut had the same declarative style. While the album earned Rondstadt many new fans, it alienated more than a few of her earlier admirers.

The *Linda Rondstadt with Nelson Riddle and his Orchestra in Concert What's New* disc, then, came as something of a surprise. Naturally, for an hour's concert, Rondstadt had to find more material, but she expanded the range of songs and moods considerably, something which carried over into the subsequent LPs. Numbers like 'Kalamazoo' and the ubiquitous 'Mr. Sandman' provide the concert with counter-points the first album lacked. The fact that the event is live helps as well, giving the songs an edge which was missing in Rondstadt's icky-perfect studio recordings. She even has a fit of giggles during one song and has to start over when soap bubbles get blown in her face – a nice touch.

The picture is grainy during strong stage lighting effects, but is otherwise acceptable, and the sound is fine.

THE LION IN WINTER

The anachronistic dialog in *The Lion in Winter* continues to spoil the otherwise intriguing dramatics concerning Great Britain's formative years. The screenplay was written by James Goldman as adapted from his own stage play and so he can't let go of a witty line even if the laugh yanks one out of the drama. Peter O'Toole's performance is magnificent. He is able to pick up the character he played in *Beckett* just a couple of years earlier and add decades to his presence. Katharine Hepburn also appears, getting both the most amusing and most embarrassing lines.

The story is about Henry II bequeathing his crown to King John and Richard the Lionhearted. The characters would be just as interesting if they did not speak with the weight of history on their tongues.

The colors are good, but the print has a few scratches and is foggy at times. The screen is cropped, making the editing – particularly the many scenes which open on O'Toole shouting – more obtrusive than it already was.

LIONEL RICHIE – ALL NIGHT LONG

We were particularly disturbed by the opening cut of *Lionel Richie – All Night Long*. 'All Night Long,' directed by Bob Rafelson, is one of the best music videos there is. On the disc, the colors all run together. Worse still, there are speckles and blue streaks periodically flashing across the picture. The disc has four songs in six cuts (two songs are presented as music videos and again in concert footage). In contrast to the poor picture, the quality of the sound is superb.

LIONEL RICHIE – THE MAKING OF DANCING ON THE CEILING

Even if everyone involved took out sworn affidavits, we still can't believe that Lionel Richie didn't write the song 'Dancing on the Ceiling,' with the music video in mind. Yet, according to the chronology detailed on *Lionel Richie – The Making of Dancing on the Ceiling*, Richie wrote the song on impulse and only later did Stanley Donen, who had directed Fred Astaire's vertical parlor circumnavigation in *Royal Wedding*, offer to do Richie's video. Thus does the 33-minute CLV disc raise your appreciation of the music video, but only if you trust Richie's sincerity.

The picture quality of the music video, which is part of the documentary, is slightly inferior to the behind the scenes footage.

LIONHEART

Frank Schaffner directed *Lionheart*, and the best thing about it is that he dragged Jerry Goldsmith along to do the score. By necessity, the music gets used a lot to fill in the empty spaces, and having the disc is as good as having a soundtrack album. The picture has a faint haze around some colors, but in general it is too bright for its own good. Too many of the costumes for the Dark Age tale were cut from the same cloth, and the vividness of the image magnifies the artifice. The story is about kids avoiding a slave round-up, led by a young charismatic knight (Eric Stolz). There is a happy ending and a few enjoyable action sequences, but the movie hasn't enough thrills or charms to justify its existence, nor, music aside, does the disc.

LIQUID SKY

The colorful and turned-on new wave drug and flying saucer movie *Liquid Sky* is well served by disc. Although the feature was funded on a small budget and looks it, the colors are fresh and the print is in as good a condition as this sort of movie can be. The same with the CX-encoded sound, which is a very flat monaural but still has an effective punch.

The plot, something to do with a cheap flying saucer in search of opiate receptors, is a great excuse to let people do whatever they want in front of a camera. It is a bit padded in the middle, but the beginning and ending are brilliantly done, with images of punk makeup, illegal substances, neon, and sleaze jumping around to deliberately abusive dialog and a monotonous electronic beat. *Liquid Sky* is an exercise in unstructured theater which works almost as well in the wee hours on home video as it does at midnight in a crowded theater.

LITTLE DORRIT

A laser disc of truly Dickensian proportions, *Little Dorrit* runs nearly six hours and has been set upon 8 sides of 4 platters. The natural division between the first part, 'Nobody's Fault,' and the second part, 'Little Dorrit's Story' – each of which, by and large, appeared separately in theaters – is at sides four and five.

The most difficult point in the entire program at which to break off viewing, however, comes at the end of the first film, as there is a powerful narrative hook in the finale which will send one hurriedly to the next platter. The complete work is an admirable and captivating accomplishment. Although understandably made with a restrained budget, the craftsmanship is such that the movie never succumbs to the mass-produced demeanor or rushed execution of a television mini-series. It is, instead, a movie which has time to breathe, time to tell a great big yarn full of tangled characters, mysteries, and subversive social satire. Some of the film's best moments have nothing to do with its compulsive plotting. Instead, satisfactions come from an extended familiarity with the characters. When Derek Jacobi, who portrays the central character in the first film, smiles in pride as he surveys the establishment to which his character has just been made a partner, the feeling is infectious. Moments such as that are lost when movies have accelerated time tables.

The disc, which is packaged in a large and mildly loose fitting box, is accompanied by a 50-page booklet which contains lovely color stills, a complete cast and crew listing, quotes from the Charles Dickens novel upon which the movie is based, an introduction, and biographies of Dickens and Giuseppe Verdi. The essay on Verdi, whose music was used for the film's score, is in an odd tense and somewhat unintelligible, but the other pieces are worthwhile. Do not read the introduction if you have not seen the film, however, for it gives away many of the plot's secrets.

To speak of the differences between the first and second parts would also spoil some of the surprises that the movie has to offer. What can be said is that 'Little Dorrit's Story' is stronger in style than in narrative, and a viewer should be fresh for it, since it lacks some of the excitements which helped propel 'Nobody's Fault.' There is, for example, a sequence in the second part where the characters are idle, and their restlessness is transferred to the viewer just as all their previous emotions had been. Because of the style, incidentally, the side breaks may seem abrupt, though they do come at logical moments.

It is style, though, which makes *Little Dorrit* such a worthy accomplishment. One of the earliest scenes in the film places the hero in a house with limited furnishings which is lit only by candlelight, and the bareness of the illumination is striking. The film's images are either bleakly or softly colored. The picture is grainy at times, and a little tentative in focus, but it is accurate enough to do justice to the disc. There are inevitably a few speckles as well. The filmmakers use color and light to show both the fortunes and the psychologies of the characters, and it is the strength of the screen compositions which will inspire repeat play, or, at least, repeat sampling. The movie was not a widescreen effort and fits comfortably in the confines of a video image.

It is mostly the music which is stereophonic, though there are scattered directional sound effects. The most heavily accented dialog may be a bit difficult to follow. For effect, the music is louder than anything else, but since it is snippets of Verdi, one won't mind. The passages always seem to accent the drama perfectly. On the other hand, the filmmakers tend to compensate for their limited ability to shoot outdoors (due to the period setting) by exaggerating outdoor sounds, and the artificiality of their effort becomes distractingly clear because of the disc's fidelities.

Warner has also provided chapter encoding which would rival Dickens's own efforts in that regard. The movie depicts life on different social levels in early Nineteenth Century London. The satire is directed primarily at government bureaucracy. There is romance, surprising plot turns, and a wonderful array of characters. In the past there have been fantasies about books being replaced by electronic devices, and the disc, set elegantly upon one's bookshelf, would seem to bring such a future closer. The *Little Dorrit* disc does not replace the Dickens novel, but it deserves to stand at the book's side.

THE LITTLE FOXES
THE WESTERNER
THE BEST YEARS OF OUR LIVES
THE PRINCESS AND THE PIRATE

Embassy put out a series of classic films obtained from the Samuel Goldwyn collection and identified as 'Samuel Goldwyn Home Entertainment Presents.' In the first group released, almost every print looked exceptionally fresh. The sound, although dated, was adequately strong.

Four of the discs are films which were directed by William Wyler and photographed by Gregg Toland. Wyler coaxed good performances out of the leads in most of his films, but on the discs listed below, any stunning visuals which might catch your eye are Toland's doing.

The Little Foxes is a crafty play by Lillian Hellman that has one attention-getting scene, where a woman lets her husband die, which makes the whole drama worth sitting through. Played here by Bette Davis, Regina is an inspiring, witchy character who makes life miserable for her frail husband, well played by Herbert Marshall.

The print used in the Gary Cooper vehicle, *The Westerner*, has a few scratches, but nothing inhibits Toland's photography during an exciting fire-in-the-cornfield sequence. Of the many legends of the Old West to be transferred to the screen, Judge Roy Bean rarely fairs well, because of his immoral judicial pronouncements and his tedious infatuation with a picture of the actress, Lily Langtree. Walter Brennan portrays Bean, and Cooper portrays a drifter caught in the cattlemen/farmer conflict. A forced happy ending takes away any point the movie wants to make, and there isn't enough action for the film to work as a movie without a point.

The art direction in *The Best Years of Our Lives* is worth studying as an example of how to subvert the ordinary. The famous film is about three typical servicemen adjusting to civilian life at the end of WWII. The story balances between tedium and mawkishness and is redeemed by the performances of Myrna Loy, Dana Andrews, and others. The movie is well made, self-important, and goes on for three hours. (The jacket spine has misidentified the title as *The Best Years of Our Lives, Part I*, an unfortunate cross-pollination from the video cassette release.)

We would not mention that one of the characters in *The Best Years of Our Lives* has hooks in the place of his hands, except that the next Goldwyn film we watched, *The Princess and the Pirate*, makes fun of a character with a similar handicap, a pirate named The Hook. Bob Hope portrays a traveling performer who is kidnapped by The Hook, escapes with a Princess, and connives his way through numerous misadventures. At one point Hope hangs his hat and jacket on Hook's hook and inevitably he escapes when the hook gets caught in a bulkhead. The Technicolor print is beautiful, with bright, basic colors which haven't faded a day. Walter Brennan also appears (misidentified on the jacket cover) and is far more inspired in *Princess and the Pirate* than in his Oscar-winning performance in *The Westerner*. Many of Hope's topical one-liners will be beyond audiences in another twenty years, but his delivery is timeless. There is a surprise cameo at the end which ties the film up nicely, but you may have to explain to your kids why it is so funny.

THE LITTLE MERMAID
THE LITTLE MERMAID (CAV)
The Walt Disney animated cartoon *The Little Mermaid* has so much magic that you will find something new to be excited about every time you watch it. It is not just that the images are rich and satisfyingly detailed; even the angles of view are fresh and exciting, without seeming showy.

Disney has released two disc versions, a CLV and a CAV. There were problems with the first batch of CAV discs – two unsteady still frames out of every five, the audio channels reversed on the digital track – and they were recalled, although a few copies may still be floating around. The CLV disc is fine. The picture transfer looks identical on the two versions. The colors lack the luminescence of the theatrical presentation, but that is the only strong flaw. The focus is very sharp and even the brightest colors remain solid. The picture quality is sufficient to pull the viewer into the film's world.

The stereo surround sound is also impressive. There are directional effects, as well as an actively dimensional music score. The songs are great fun, though we will never figure out the psychology of the Oscar which was awarded to the jokey ditty, 'Under the Sea,' instead of to the more memorable and passionate 'Kiss the Girl.'

The film has a treasure chest of pleasures, too numerous to itemize. It shifts with ease between human characters and animal characters. It has violent scenes, such as the kitchen sequence, which could never have appeared in a Disney feature in the past, yet the humor is so deftly woven with the violence that the piece is one of the funniest in the film. It has romance, too. We can't remember the last time a cartoon movie ended on a shot of the hero and the heroine kissing, but we think it was probably during the Eisenhower Administration.

A LITTLE NIGHT MUSIC
Set in Sweden, Ingmar Bergman's 'Smiles of a Summer Night' had the atmosphere of a cool summer's evening in the northern latitudes. *A Little Night Music*, the film version of the musical adaptation of Bergman's movie, was set in Austria, and gained a sultry air in the transposition. The disc of *Night Music* has such a pale and destitute transfer that it will remind the viewer more than anything else of Winter. The underrated movie, which is astutely directed by Harold Prince, features wonderful performances by Elizabeth Taylor, Diana Rigg, and others, as well as one of the finest musical scores in modern theater. However, the picture has lost nearly all of its color and solidity, the digital monaural sound is noisy and fuzzy, and there are other, minor flaws scattered throughout the presentation. The only aspect to the film which the disc lives up to, in fact, is the movie's theme of aging and decay, as in 'Every Day a Little Death.'

LITTLE NIKITA
Don't approach *Little Nikita* expecting a logical or mature thriller. The movie is enjoyable, particularly as a vehicle to let Sidney Poitier, River Phoenix, and the many talented supporting players do their thing, but the plot doesn't remain true to its internal logic, let alone anything external. Briefly summarized, the story is about a renegade Russian agent who is murdering Russian moles in the San Diego area to extort ("Blackmail," one character says, incorrectly) money from the Soviets. Poitier is an FBI agent chasing the murderer and Phoenix is an all-American boy who doesn't know his parents are moles.

Some sequences are too orange and others are too soft, but the majority of the film looks sharp. The sound is in stereo surround, with the separation effects reserved for the musical score and minor atmospheric touches.

THE LITTLE PRINCE AND FRIENDS
Three medium length Will Vinton 'Claymation' efforts are available on *The Little Prince and Friends*. The treatment of Antonine de Saint-Exupéry's 'The Little Prince' is the least satisfying. The animation is limited (lips never move) and the narrative fails to get close to any of the characters. The piece appears on side one in CAV with an inconsistent measure of flickering and steady still frames. Vinton's interpretation of 'Rip Van Winkle' and Leo Tolstoy's 'Where Love Is, God Is,' titled 'Martin the Cobbler,' in CLV on side two, are more satisfying. He does not follow the 'Van Winkle' story as closely as we would have preferred, but the animation is extensive and elaborately detailed. The folkish 'Cobbler' story, which is narrated by Tolstoy's daughter (!), is enjoyable both for its narrative and artistic efforts.

The picture is fair, but the monaural sound is rife with flaws and best left at a low volume. The title was pulled from the market shortly after release and is a collector's item.

THE LITTLE PRINCESS
The colors on the print which 3M used for *The Little Princess* don't have that wax fruit look which well-preserved Technicolor prints can convey. The sound is typical of a 1939 production. Occasionally a dream sequence near the end of this film gets left off when local television stations want to fit the show into specific time slots, but this is the complete version. Shirley Temple portrays the daughter of a Captain who becomes MIA in the Boer War. Temple's curls battle constantly with her dimples for control of her cuteness. She has an effective dance step and a delivery which borders on the receiving end of ventriloquism. We assume that those obtaining the disc know what they are getting into and far be it for us to stand in the way.

LITTLE RED RIDING HOOD
(see **FAERIE TALE THEATRE**)

LITTLE SHOP OF HORRORS
Honest to goodness musicals don't show up much anymore, which is a shame since they usually are even more fun on home video than they are in the theater. *Little Shop of Horrors* is a wild, enjoyable, horticultural song fest; the kind of movie one finds impossible to believe somebody actually made, but is thankful that they did. There is a hairline mark on the negative which appears briefly, early on side two, but the picture has no problem with the many dark scenes or pale color schemes. The sound booms and squeaks all over the place, not only during the musical numbers, but during the many juicy sound effects. The disc has 14 chapters marking the film's catchy songs.

The big budget musical adaptation of a 1960 movie which had taken less than a week to make, about a man-eating plant, retains a breezy irreverence. Although the plant is from outer space, the movie is something it is hard to imagine could appear anywhere but Earth. No other planet could ever be as culturally scatterbrained.

LITTLE TREASURE
The music for *Little Treasure* is by Leo Kottke, but that is the only piece of class the movie has. Although it stars Margot Kidder and even has Burt Lancaster for a few minutes, the film is a talentless clutter of bad cinematic moments. The worst: Kidder is a stripper who has a wedding gown act and in the end her boyfriend marches across the stage with her in her costume as a symbolic recognition that they've decided to get hitched.

Although the sound is monaural and not CX-encoded, Kottke's guitar is rich and verges on stereo. The picture is fairly sharp.

LITTLE VERA
A story about a teenage girl feeling pressure from the desire to be independent and the necessity of living with her parents would not seem unusual, but *Little Vera* has attracted attention because it is a Soviet film. It contains some very mild and fleeting nudity, which is still a big deal in the land where people wear mittens over their gloves. There are a few details unique to the Russian experience, but for the most part Milos Forman did the same thing with *The Loves of a Blonde* twenty years earlier, before the Soviets sent in tanks to stop him.

The source material is a little grainy, but on par with most low budget foreign films. The picture has a slight matting at the top and bottom of the screen. The sound is bright and direct. LumiVision has digitally processed the soundtrack for stereo, but the result is not obnoxious and is in fact barely noticeable. The movie is in Russian and has white English subtitles which are lost to the background in a couple of instances.

LIVE AT THE VILLAGE VANGUARD
(see **WINDHAM HILL IN CONCERT**)

LIVING COLOUR: PRIMER
Five songs are featured on the half hour CLV disc, *Living Colour: Primer*, 'Middle Man,' 'Cult of Personality,' 'Funny Vibe,' 'Broken Hearts,' and 'Open Letter to a Landlord.' 'Hearts' is a live number and the rest are music videos with deliberately frantic, cluttered graphics. At one point in one of the videos the words 'guitar solo' flash onto the screen just as one kicks in.

Some of Living Colour's songs, which all have good funk rhythm, are strongly political, and 'Funny Vibe' takes a serious and uncomfortable look at racism. The videos have introductions which have not been given separate chapter encoding. The picture quality looks okay although some intense colors are a little blurry. The sound is fine.

THE LIVING DAYLIGHTS

The opening and closing title sequences of *The Living Daylights* are letterboxed and look very nice. The rest of the movie is panned and scanned, and when the pan is too speedy the picture flies out of focus. When the shot is stationary, however, the image is admirably sharp. The color washes in the opening credits are also handled with aplomb. The sound is a little troublesome. The stereo is entertaining, but it hasn't been digitally encoded, so it always seems to stop short of its potential. The disc has three sides, since the film runs 130 minutes (even then, the script has been trimmed a little). The script was written for a generic James Bond, a role eventually filled by Timothy Dalton, who tends to be a better actor when he is standing still than when he is moving. The film is a bit generic for the Bond series as well, but it is fun.

LOCK-UP

The Sylvester Stallone penitentiary movie *Lock-Up* is not very good. The script, about a mad warden (played by Donald Sutherland) who persecutes the hero, is farfetched. Stallone's character has no personality, and the action scenes are poorly edited (though other sequences are not). The movie is not an embarrassment, it is just boring and unbelievable. The film's art direction is understandably drab and institutional, but the picture transfer looks passable. The fleshtones are not precise, but they are usually close enough. The stereo surround sound has limited separation effects.

LOLA MONTES
LOLA MONTES (CAV)
LETTER FROM AN UNKNOWN WOMAN (Import)

The world Max Ophuls creates on the screen is a world your eye takes pleasure in dissecting. The rectangular screen image, which has been letterboxed on disc with an aspect ratio of about 2.1:1, is often broken by posts, swords, et cetera, into fifths or thirds. As a character walks in one direction, someone or something else will also be moving to maintain a compositional balance. Lola is seen on the far left of the screen and the man she will eventually marry is on the far right (her mother, trying to negotiate a different marriage for her, is in the middle). They glance at each other, but without the still frame CAV feature you could miss it because, even on a 19-inch TV, you still have to swing your eyes back and forth to see both players.

Lola begins and ends in a circus. The heroine, played by Martine Carol, is cashing in on her notoriety and the publicized affairs she has had with composers and kings. Her life is then depicted in a series of flashbacks integrated with the circus showcase. The cast, including Peter Ustinov (as the circus ringmaster) and Oscar Werner (as a young student), is appealing. Carol, who looks and acts more like a spinsterish Deborah Kerr than a royal seductress, suppresses all displays of emotion to short bursts and follows with long stretches of guarded determination. If the flashback scenes are approached as pieces of memory, then the fact that she is too old to depict herself as a child or that she accepts much of what happens to her without expression becomes understandable. Some say it is brilliant.

The film is French and subtitles appear beneath the screen. The movie is monaural and was made in 1955. There is a fair level of noise throughout, although the dialog is never distorted. The CLV disc has digital encoding and less hiss than the analog CAV disc.

The one other Max Ophuls film which is available on disc is a Japanese import, *Letter from an Unknown Woman*. Ophuls made the film in Hollywood, so it is in English, with Japanese subtitles. The black-and-white feature is better appreciated for its romantic story than for any dazzling cinematic feats, but almost every frame reveals the superiority of Ophuls' film sense. Louis Jourdan portrays a pianist who has an active social life and Joan Fontaine portrays the woman of the film's title, who has loved him since she was a young girl. The picture transfer is nice and the sound is acceptable.

LOLITA (Import)

The black-and-white picture is sharp, the monaural sound is crisp and the jacket cover is scrumptious. *Lolita*, a Japanese release (in English with Japanese subtitles), is Stanley Kubrick's 1962 adaptation of Vladimir Nabokov's tricky comedy. The movie opens with what must be one of the all-time perverse credit sequences and then goes to a marvelously funny prologue featuring Peter Sellers, with an obtuse American accent, before settling into the story of a gentleman (James Mason) whose infatuation with an underage temptress (Sue Lyon) leads him past the boundaries of decorum.

The story is all suggestion, even the parts that have nothing to do with sex. Nabokov knows how to present just enough so that the viewer's mind will fill the right blanks. His novel contained everything from word games and allusions (such as to the life of Lewis Carroll) to an almost romantic appreciation of America's quieter charms. Kubrick's control over the material is not as elaborate (Nabokov wrote the screenplay), but his pacing and manipulation is so adept that the 153-minute story whizzes by.

Best of all, there is Sellers, who becomes sort of a White Rabbit. His path crosses Mason's numerous times without an immediately apparent motive. With each encounter he has a more convoluted accent and a different story to tell. It may not be until the second or third time you watch the picture that you will start laughing uncontrollably at his staccato rendition of "Brewster, go and get some type A Kodachrome." When it happens, you will realize you have been indecently exposed to the deviations of three geniuses. Kubrick's eyes, Nabokov's ears, and Sellers' mouth will have you believing that evil is what makes life worth living.

THE LONE RANGER VOLUME 1

The spirited half hour television series from yesteryear, *The Lone Ranger*, appears on disc in a four episode collection, *The Lone Ranger Volume 1*. The episodes are in black and white and represent the early phase of the series, when many of the episodes were adapted from radio programs. The prosaic narration in the opening title sequence is also a holdover from the radio era. An inept insert begins each episode, featuring an almost incoherent Clayton Moore, but the programs play through uninterrupted, and with the full opening and closing credits.

Titles have also been provided for the episodes. Side one contains 'Message to Fort Apache,' about a cavalry officer who is accosted by bandits because he is carrying the names of conspirators who are to be arrested, and 'The Frightened Woman,' about a crooked deputy who masterminds a robbery and tries to scare off a witness. Side two features 'The Fugitive,' about a locksmith, on the lam for a crime he did not commit, who falls in with a band of lockbox robbers, and 'Ex-Marshall,' about a former lawman, with a past he would like to forget, who helps the Lone Ranger capture a holdup gang.

The quality of the source material is gorgeous. The prints are spotless and the grey scales are precise. The sound is scratchy and wobbly, but who can resist turning it up anyway, particularly during the opening credit sequence? There are chapter markers for each episode.

The programs contain egregious cuts between studio shots and outdoor shots, but the action, the characterizations, and the plots are efficient and lots of fun. The most awkward moment on the entire disc is when The Lone Ranger tries to tell Tonto why it is against the law to sell large quantities of guns to the Indians, but it is a *surprisingly* awkward sequence, as if Jay Silverheels, who plays Tonto, is uncomfortable with it, and it serves to emphasize how smoothly the rest of the material flows. The plots must be resolved in a TV half hour, but the dramatics are charming rather than corny and the mask helps a great deal when Moore has to recite aphorisms.

LONE RUNNER

If you are so burnt out from a hard day at the office that any sort of intelligent stimulation would be too taxing, then *Lone Runner* may be a suitable choice. The film is so mindlessly dumb that if you don't bother to expend the energy defending your sensibilities you can end up enjoying it.

Miles O'Keefe is the title character. He lives on a horse in the desert and never ages. When a young woman is kidnapped by Victorian era *Road Warrior* rejects, he saves her. Since the film is rated PG, he kills most of the kidnappers, but never kisses the heroine. Some of the voices are dubbed, there is a camel with comical expressions, and the second unit photography is often out of focus.

All of this has been transferred onto disc with a digital stereo surround soundtrack so silly it would make the camel grimace. You can bet it never played in a theater in stereo, if it played in a theater at all. The voices have a metallic sounding echo, indicating that the filmmakers have done as good a job with electronic phase as they have done with their sunny day for night shots. But like we said, you start enjoying it after a while.

Then there is the break between side one and side two. The heroine, exhausted because she has been walking in the desert sun for five minutes, loses her footing. She rolls and rolls and rolls down a sandy incline. End of side one. Turn the disc over. Start side two. She continues rolling.

Surprise, side two turns out to be in CAV, with two jittery still frames out of every five. Since the only sensible application for the CAV functions would be to run the fights in slow motion (though running at normal speed you can still see perfectly well that the actors are not hitting one another), the error in the transfer negates the utility of the feature. The picture is usually a little too brown and inevitably as grainy as the sands under the Lone Runner's horse's hooves. But we were sorry to see the disc end, if only because we were still waiting for O'Keefe to kiss either the heroine or the horse.

LONG DAY'S JOURNEY INTO NIGHT

The back jacket cover calls the enclosed production of Eugene O'Neill's *Long Day's Journey into Night* 'highly controversial.' That common euphemism is inappropriate nevertheless, for there is nothing controversial about the production whatsoever. It's lousy, pure and simple. The hook, however, is that O'Neill's play is not, and until the more respectable version comes along, this is a laser disc owner's only access to the work.

The disc has a gatefold jacket and runs eleven minutes under three hours. All of side one is marked as 'Chapter 1.' Side two begins as 'Chapter 0,' and then about halfway, when Act 2 begins, it changes to 'Chapter 1.' Side three has no chapter encoding.

The picture transfer looks okay, in part because it has been transferred from a video tape source. But the stage is so bare that when night falls and darkness creeps into the edges of the screen, impurities in the picture follow along. The sound is monaural, and has neither impediments nor ambience.

Performed on a ghastly under-decorated stage set, the production originated on Broadway and was recorded without an audience for PBS. Jack Lemmon, as the father, is the only performer to bring some magic to his role. The others flicker occasionally, except for Bethel Leslie, who portrays the mother as if she had just finished memorizing her lines and had yet to tackle the emotions of the role. You can grasp from watching the disc that O'Neill's work is a terrific exploration of four characters he knows very, very well, but except for Lemmon's efforts, the information comes to you by proxy.

LONG GONE

Long Gone is an enjoyable tale about minor league ball players. The made-for-cable film is set in the late Fifties in the Deep South and explores several issues – the effect a black player has on his teammates, the maturation of the team's player/manager, the maturation of a young rookie, etc. The sound is stereo and a number of Country/Western oldies can be heard on the soundtrack, emitting from natural sources within the film. The music is appropriately scratchy, though one may go running to check one's connections before recognition of this facet occurs. The picture quality looks good, and the disc has plenty of chapter markers.

THE LONG RIDERS

Walter Hill's enjoyably punchy rendition of the Jesse James gang legends, *The Long Riders*, has been well preserved. Hill made excellent use of the way sunlight streams through branches, cracks, and bullet holes, and the disc captures every glimmer with clarity. The film is not in stereo, but between the Ry Cooder score and all the gunshots, you'd think it was stereophonic. The sound is equal to the picture in quality.

The big gimmick in *Long Riders* is that brothers were cast as brothers, Stacy and James Keach as the Jameses, the Carradines as the Youngers, etc. One member of Hill's stock company, James Remar, shows up as an Indian who duels with David Carradine. With the exception of Pamela Reed and Christopher & Nicholas Guest, however, acting is not the movie's strong point. The script isn't designed to give the brothers opportunities to display fraternal empathy. It is an action film, an engaging one, and covers old ground with a contemporary style which never feels out of place.

THE LONG VOYAGE HOME

Directed by John Ford, photographed by Gregg Toland, and based upon a story by Eugene O'Neill, *The Long Voyage Home* is a black-and-white cinematic classic. John Wayne's name is plastered all over the jacket cover, but one of the beauties of the movie is that he only has a bit part. The plot concerns a cargo ship crossing the Atlantic in pre-convoy WWII. The ensemble cast drink, philosophize, and act rowdy, just as they do in every other Ford or O'Neill work. Wayne's enigmatic presence keeps the viewer alert and balances the excesses.

The picture quality starts off fair but has trouble with breaks and scratches at the reel change points. On side two, at minute 38, there is a startlingly bad stretch of film which looks as if it had been solarized. The sound is noisy in places but generally acceptable.

THE LONGEST DAY

There are some movies which defy the normal rules of filmmaking and get away with it. It would be easy to pick out the major conceptual flaws in *The Longest Day* but it would also be pointless, because the film works as entertainment and as history despite its shortcomings. It is based upon an oral-history journalistic effort, compiling as many different views and recollections of the D-Day invasion that the writer, Cornelius Ryan, could obtain. Filming such a work would seem tantamount to making a movie from the phone book, but the force of the event supersedes the players, and scattering a few Hollywood icons across the landscape appears to be all that is necessary to keep one's interest from flagging. In the skirmishes the filmmakers chose to highlight, the goals are clearly delineated so that even in the confusion of the battle the viewer understands the point of the action. The movie hitches its coalescence to the operation and succeeds with the day.

Letterboxing, at an aspect ratio of about 2.1:1, improves the detail in the action sequences, making the battles easier to follow, and gives the viewer a chance to spot more stars in a single shot. The black-and-white picture is in excellent condition. It has no blemishes and not even a hint of grain. The edges are sharp and the contrast levels are rich.

The surround is not elaborately employed, but the disc is worth amplifying. There are some deliberate separation effects – an airplane flyover during a John Wayne speech, for example – which are quite effective.

LOOK WHO'S LAUGHING

Look Who's Laughing is sort of a radio star version of *The Jetsons Meet the Flintstones* – specifically, Edgar Bergen and Charlie McCarthy (Lucille Ball has a secondary part as Bergen's assistant) meeting Fibber McGee and Molly. As is exemplified by the shot of Fibber McGee's closet meagerly disgorging its contents, much of *Look Who's Laughing* is best heard and not seen. Still, the film has a basic kind of appeal which reaches beyond nostalgia. At 78 minutes it is short, and the routines of the performers are not overly affected by the transition to a visual medium. That Ball would represent the next phase of comedy in American culture could not have been foreseen by the filmmakers, but as subdued as she is, after McCarthy she's the liveliest performer in the film and symbolic of where things were headed. She never lets down her reserve and watching the scene, one can't help thinking that Charlie McCarthy is to Edgar Bergen as Lucy is to Lucille Ball.

The black-and-white print has a few scattered markings and some shots look worn down, but it's generally sharp and free of significant flaws. The sound is in keeping with recordings of the era and is reasonably clear.

LOOK WHO'S TALKING

It is nice to see John Travolta in a role which doesn't tax his abilities. He plays a loveable lug in the mega-hit *Look Who's Talking*, his character refreshingly unencumbered by life's complexities. Like Travolta, the film can seem to do nothing wrong and the disc is in much the same condition. The fleshtones are a little orange, though much better than RCA/Columbia's past efforts, and the stereo surround sound has limited separation effects. The presentation is fine enough to communicate the film's pleasures. The movie is not so much clever as it is simply easy to get along with. It is Travolta, not the baby, who becomes the film's mascot. And, as a final note, although *Look Who's Talking* was directed by a female, Amy Heckerling, old sexual stereotypes apparently die hard. In the beginning there is a well-executed depiction of sperm rushing to inseminate an egg. Setting the theme for the comedy, the sperms are chattering like crazy as they make their way up the canal. The egg, however, remains silent and inanimate.

THE LORDS OF FLATBUSH

Before Henry Winkler's part was built up in 'Happy Days' and before anyone knew from *Rocky*, Winkler and Sylvester Stallone appeared with Perry King, Susan Blakely, Ray Sharkey, and other unknown actors and actresses in a cheaply made movie about growing up in Brooklyn, *The Lords of Flatbush*. The sound is actually too good, because you can hear every overlay, every patch, and every mistake the sound editors made. The picture, which the credit sequences reveal to be wider than the TV screen allows, is no more grainy or faded than the film was when it first came out.

There is one scene which is almost worth

the price of the entire disc. Sylvester Stallone (who is also listed in the credits as having contributed additional dialog), portrays a young man who is pressured into marrying his pregnant girlfriend. He is robbed of every last ounce of youth when he goes to a jewelry store with his fiancee and commits himself to purchase an expensive engagement band. The movie is not even episodic; it is a series of acting improvisations using a consistent set of characters.

LOST ANGELS
The plot of *Lost Angels* concerns a juvenile delinquent confined to a psychiatric institution. It is the film, however, which is schizophrenic. Donald Sutherland plays the boy's doctor. The scenes in which Sutherland appears are actually intelligent and watchable. The scenes in which Sutherland does not appear – and he doesn't show up until the film is a quarter over – are ridiculous and divorced from reality. The picture transfer is very good and the surround sound has no significant problems.

THE LOST BOYS
THE LOST BOYS (Letterboxed)
Most vampire movies serve as a metaphor to swooning passion, but *The Lost Boys* aligns the horror with teenage drug abuse, and the parallels match very neatly. It helps that the film is stylishly made and cleverly executed, because there would be no message if it were inept. The film is also humorous ("You're a vampire... wait till Mom finds out!"), an aspect which improves on multiple viewings.

Warner released the disc initially with a scanned and cropped image and then reissued it with a letterboxed picture that has an aspect ratio of about 1.9:1. A significant amount of picture information is returned to the sides with the letterboxing, framing characters with threatening objects and orienting the locations of things and people for the viewer. The action scenes are also easier to follow.

Much of the movie takes place under lighting conditions which are not harmful to a vampire's eyes, but the screen is only grainy (and sometimes it is noticeably so) when the filmmakers themselves are testing the limits of their emulsions. The reds and oranges are more stable on the letterboxed disc, which has a slightly sharper picture overall. The sound editing is superb, and both discs maintain clear definitions for every noise, even those in the upper or lower ranges.

LOST HORIZON
Whenever possible, we use the title on the spine of the jacket as the disc's official' title, so you can imagine the quandary we face designating *Lost Horizon*. RCA/Columbia, perhaps to acknowledge that the film contains extra, previously lost footage, has printed *Lost Horizons* on the spine (they call it *Lost Horizon* everywhere else).

The restored version contains as much as 22 minutes of material deleted after the initial theatrical run. We found the new version to be a worthy effort which we enjoyed immensely.

As with Warner's *A Star Is Born*, there are a few scattered minutes where the picture is missing and the dialog is played to still photos. The dialog track is complete, however, and it is clear that none of the footage should ever have been excised. If the still picture sections are any example, important changes in character, central to the mood of the whole film, were apparently the first to go.

The restored *Lost Horizon* is a great movie. It is not superbly directed, but it is an excellent adaptation of a rather silly novel. The film is given a chance to breathe, and to develop at the pace which was originally intended. To be sure, Shangri-La is still a Utopia where the white Europeans rule and the natives do all the hard work, smiling. But the emotions of the characters are easy to follow and feel, as the magic of cinema works its wonders.

The black-and-white picture is never stunning. The older, ragged footage blends well with the standard, better-preserved scenes. The sound is not CX-encoded, but remains consistently audible.

THE LOST PHARAOH: THE SEARCH FOR AKHENATEN
An interview with a little old lady who lives near a major Egyptian archaeological site is the highpoint of *The Lost Pharaoh: The Search for Akhenaten*. The woman, who is British, claims that she fell down a stairwell when she was three years old and was thought to be dead for a few hours. Shortly thereafter she happened across photos of the site in one of her father's magazines and she recognized the structures immediately from dreams she had been having. Be it true reincarnation or merely madness, she is of great assistance to the scientists working the area, helping them to determine how the buildings were once spread out and pinpointing the functions of items uncovered in the digs.

Lost Pharaoh is similar to the *National Geographic* programs, except that the scientists being interviewed are more nervous in front of the camera and editing is so lax that the viewer is treated to scenes of the locals hustling the graduate students. The tale which the program has to tell, however, is fascinating, and helps to clarify a significant turning point in ancient Egyptian history. Akhenaten was a radical liberal who so upset the powers that be that after his mysterious death an attempt was made to eradicate all memory of him. They don't find his tomb during the course of the program, they just uncover a few odds and ends, but the stories which are told while this is going on make the disc both educational and entertaining.

The picture and sound are adequate. There are no chapter markers. The program runs an hour and is presented in CLV on one side.

THE LOST SQUADRON
The filmmakers putting together *The Lost Squadron* began with the idea of showing some great flying stunts and then tried to build a movie around it. The script is weird, about a maniacal film director who wants to murder a stunt man, and the emotions of the film are discombobulated. The black and white effort is set after World War I, and stars Joel McCrea and Erich von Stroheim. The CLV disc runs less than 80 minutes. The source material has a number of scratches and a couple splices. It is not in great condition, but it is doubtful that anything nicer looking would have helped. More detrimentally, the sound is set very low and suffers from distortion when amplified.

THE LOST WEEKEND
These days you couldn't sell a movie about alcohol addiction if you gave away a free drink with every ticket, but *The Lost Weekend* won all the Oscars when it first came out and still elicits an unusual, anxious excitement. The characters all have a movie superficiality about them. The happy ending has an even more hollow ring to it than is intended. And the situation is uninteresting – the last thing someone wants to sit through is someone else's bender.

The reason for the film's popularity can probably be found in the abilities of Billy Wilder, who directed the film, and the co-scenarist, Charles Brackett. Just about any actor could have played Ray Milland's role with that team behind him and given a good performance. Wilder and Brackett pace the drama well, stay ahead of audience anticipations to some degree, and retain a fair amount of wit. They also prevent the hero from appearing like a raving lunatic. Basically, when Wilder and Brackett were in their prime, they could make just about any story work well on film.

The edges seem a bit soft, but the black and white print has no distinctive errors and looks fine. The sound is passable, but the music is a little creaky. After the film is ended, there is an original theatrical trailer. The sensationalist nature of the film's realism was the central selling point, though it is pretty tame by today's standards.

LOU REED: CONEY ISLAND BABY LIVE IN JERSEY
You may at first think the audience is booing Lou Reed on *Lou Reed: Coney Island Baby Live in Jersey*, but they are actually calling for him enthusiastically, and using his first name. The concert, which runs under an hour, is lit for video (though sometimes it is too monotonously red), and the cameras apparently had their run of the stage. The result looks impressive, and creates a comfortable and intimate showcase for Reed's music. The sound is digitally encoded stereo, and while it is undeniably live, his backup band is not overpowering. The program is nice, and refreshingly uncomplicated. Reed's music is stratified by the performance environment, creating a format which not only entertains, but presents the logic of his creative development. (The disc has twelve chapters, which are listed on the back of the jacket.)

THE LOUVRE (Import)
It opens like a soft-core porn flick and then looks like it is going to be a Parisian travelog, but it is actually a documentary about The Louvre contained on a four-sided two-disc set in CAV, from Japan. *The Louvre* has a beautiful, clear transfer. The volume levels are a little low, but the non-CX audio tracks are as clean as the picture. The disc almost doesn't have to be in CAV, because the camera is so patient in examining each piece of art. The narration is in Japanese, but the pictures speak for themselves.

Side one looks at ancient Egyptian and Middle Eastern sculpture. The camera glides around each piece, sometimes spending as much as 500 frames pointing at a single facet. The picture then cuts away to the land where the work originated. This can be misleading, for the lands which were teeming with life and vegetation when the sculptures were made are now dry and barren.

Works from the Greek to the Gothic period are shown on side two, but paintings are not exhibited until sides three and four. Demonstrations of art restoration are included along with shots of visitors in the Louvre yawning as they look at the exhibits. Unlike the segments on sculpture, there are almost no cutaways to show the origins of the paintings. In all, only a few hundred works of art are covered on the two-hour program, but they are covered so thoroughly that the disc is worthwhile for anyone who is interested in art on video.

LOUVRE 1 PAINTING, DRAWING
LOUVRE 2 SCULPTURE, OBJECTS D'ART
LOUVRE 3 ANTIQUITIES

The collections of the huge Louvre museum in Paris have been condensed onto three single-sided CAV video discs. The discs were produced in France, but are being released in America by Voyager. Stepping through the still frames can take longer than visiting the museum itself, but it is a lot easier on the feet. Each disc comes in a box which contains both the platter and a decent sized paperback catalog, although there is a danger that the book could provide a fulcrum which would snap the disc if pressure is accidentally applied to the box.

The discs have motion sequences which preface the still frame sections. These sequences profile a couple of dozen specific art works, and are narrated in English on one audio channel and in French on the second. The narration is limited to a few general points, but the inclusion of these segments is valuable, because, by example, they teach the viewer how to approach the other art works.

When used with the innovative computer programs that have been developed to support them, the discs are probably quite effective. As simple linear presentations, however, they are awkwardly designed and poorly chapter encoded. Specifically, stops are imbedded at the end of each motion sequence, a silly interruption since the viewer is most likely going to view all the motion sequences in one sitting. But at the end of the final motion sequence, where there ought to be an imbedded stop to prepare the viewer for the still frame collection, there is none – it just starts zipping by. The motion sequences are chapter encoded, but there are no chapters at all for any of the still frames, even though they are divided into logical arrangements which would be perfectly suited for chaptering. Instead, the viewer has to work out of the catalog and key in five digit frame numbers to arrive at a desired section.

The still frames, at least, are impressively composed. A picture of the complete work is presented, followed by a title card and then by a number of detail shots. There is an average of five detail shots per work, though some garner several dozen. It is the detail shots which make the discs worth their while, since the initial shot of a piece is often too general to impart the piece's essence to the viewer. For reasons imponderable, blank stills appear randomly through all three discs.

At first glance, *Louvre 1 Painting, Drawing* appears to be as valuable as the other two discs, *Louvre 2 Sculpture, Objects d'Art* and *Louvre 3 Antiquities*, combined. It contains about 1470 paintings and 1050 drawings. By way of comparison, Lawrence Gowing's 'Paintings in the Louvre,' published by Stewart, Tabori & Chang (New York) weighs 10 pounds, runs nearly 700 pages, contains none of the drawings and no more than about 800 paintings. 'Paintings in the Louvre' has 6 offerings from Francesco Guardi and 9 from Jean-Antoine Watteau, for example, while *Louvre 1* has 7 and 10 respectively. We did come across one painting which the book contains and the disc does not, 'Fantastic Landscape with Ruins' by Pierre Patel the Elder, but we doubt there are many, if any, others.

The disc is organized by schools of generalized nationalities, such as French and Italian, and within each school by artists in alphabetical order. The paintings and drawings collections are separate, so that some artists turn up in both. The works of a specific artist appear to be organized following the Louvre's own cataloging system, but the logic to it is not completely clear and is relatively unimportant. The viewer moving through the disc in a linear fashion loses the sense of development which a chronological organization by century can provide (that is how 'Paintings in the Louvre' is put together), but there is something to be said for the stimulation that can come from jumping around. At times you will see a painting which seems quite modern, such as Jean Cousin the Elder's deliberately erotic 'Eva Prima Pandora,' and be surprised in discovering when it was composed, in this case 1550.

Included in the motion sequences are looks at Leonardo da Vinci's 'Mona Lisa,' Titian's 'The Pastoral Concert,' Caravaggio's 'The Fortune Teller,' Rembrandt van Rijn's 'Bathsheba at Her Bath,' Jan Vermeer's 'The Lacemaker,' and Eugene Delacroix's 'Liberty Leading the People.'

The color transfer is inevitably problematic. Although 'Paintings in the Louvre' is a gorgeous book, close examination and comparison with the disc will reveal that the reds in the book are badly messed up. In comparing the book to the disc, the paintings on the disc often look too dark. One need only go so far as to compare Théodore Géricault's 'The Raft of the Medusa' in the opening motion sequence with the same painting in the still frame section to see how varied replication can be. The two representations look completely different and both versions, even with their elaborate closeups, fail to bring out the detail which a good printed photograph can provide.

Ultimately, as we studied a number of paintings on the disc and, with a magnifying glass, in the book, we found that each presentation gave us a different set of details and insights. The whole image of the painting was usually more distinctive in the book, but the disc's many detail shots of each work often revealed aspects which the book's resources could not come close to providing. It should also be noted that a painting's frame is never shown, and the image of the painting on the disc is mildly cropped, sometimes enough to obscure an important object or swath of color.

As anyone who has ever marched through its halls is undoubtedly aware, the Louvre's collection of paintings stops just as painting was starting to get really interesting, in the mid 1800s. The most modern painters represented are Eugene Delacroix and Camille Corot. The drawings collection, however, is another matter. Here there are some delightful and seldom seen efforts from Edgar Degas, Paul Cezanne, Paul Gaughin, and the underappreciated Camille Pissaro. There are also brief inclusions from Henri de Toulouse-Lautrec, George Seurat, Vincent Van Gogh, and even Victor Hugo. The drawings, which include water colors, pastels, charcoals, etc., begin with a fanciful proposal for a fountain in the shape of a huge elephant (by Jean-Antoine Alavoine) and are consistently freer in spirit and more exploratory in nature than the officious paintings. Together, in a single accessible unit, the paintings and drawings present a thrilling and incredibly thorough sampling of Western civilization and culture. The depth and scope of *Louvre 1* can overwhelm the viewer, and is certainly unequaled outside of the Louvre itself.

'Winged Victory' and 'Venus de Milo' both appear on *Louvre 3 Antiquities*, not *Louvre 2 Sculpture, Objects d'Art*, which confines itself to the First and primarily Second Millennium. When compared to *Louvre 1*, the offerings in *Louvre 2* may seem like a pittance, but there are still about 300 sculptures and 670 knickknacks, all of which can easily captivate a viewer's gaze for hours. The works, which come from Western Europe, are organized chronologically, with nationalities as a subdivision and, in the 'Objects' section, a further subdivision organizing types of objects, such as tapestries, jewelry, etc. The opening motion segments include looks at Michelangelo's 'The Slaves,' Pierre Puget's 'Milo of Crotona Devoured by a Lion,' Antonio Canova's 'Psyche Revived by Cupid's Kiss,' the Sceptre of Charles V, and Napoleon's Cameo Crown, designed by Martin Guillaume Biennais.

If painting undergoes changes when depicted by another medium, one can imagine what happens to sculpture. The photo of the ivory statuette 'Virgin and Child of Saint Chapelle' on the jacket cover has a completely different color from the same photo on the cover of the catalog, and is also different from the still photo within the disc (on the disc jacket box it is whitish, on the booklet it is pinkish, and on the disc it is yellowish). The detail pictures are not consistent in providing a reverse angle view of the statuary, and seem more arbitrarily chosen than the painting closeups.

Like the drawings in *Louvre 1*, the objects d'art in *Louvre 2* provide a pleasing and impish contrast to more stately sculptures. There are watches and ink stands and furniture and crowns. The items benefitting the most from the disc presentation are the elaborately gilded glass cups. Anything made of glass, actually, seems to quicken from the light aiding the photographer. Also impressive were the jewels, especially a captivating crimson piece cut in the form of a dragon, called the Coast of Brittany Ruby. Tapestries, although given many detail shots, are not effectively presented and should have been represented in at least one motion sequence.

There are fewer detail shots per item on *Louvre 3 Antiquities*, which is subtitled 'Near and Middle Eastern, Egyptian, Greek and Roman Antiquities.' The further back in time one travels, the more a mundane item becomes important, so discarded razors, combs, and spoons from Mesopotamia are afforded the same attention as a J.M. Turner masterpiece on *Louvre 1*. Some 381 works appear in the Near and Middle Eastern collection, 415 in the Egyptian, and 365 in the Greek and Roman section.

The first thing one notices studying Roman statues is how very much the Roman emperors look like the British character actors usually chosen to play them. Since the majority of works represented on the disc are either sculptures or objects d'art, and since some come from as late as the 19th Century, it is difficult to understand why this collection and the collection on *Louvre 2* weren't together. If we had to choose, we would say that *Louvre 3* is the stronger of the two. The works are more fascinating, more varied, and more representative of the development of western culture. As with the jacket cover on *Louvre 2*, the images on the jacket cover and the catalog of *Louvre 3*, 'Apollo of Piombino,' have different colors, and vary further from the still in the disc. Motion sequences for the Greek and Roman works have been placed after the still collection. The motion sequences include depictions of 'The Code of Hammurabi,' the Stele of Nefertiabet, 'Winged Victory,' and 'Venus de Milo.'

The appeal of antiquities, especially those produced during pre-Christian times, is in their proximity to the beholder. To stand in the presence of an early cuneiform tablet is to feel a physical link to the distant past. Except for small objects or outright statues, the disc cannot do justice to a lot of the Middle Eastern and Egyptian artifacts. The collection is also too small to give the viewer a real sense of cultural development across the dynasties. However, the selections are extensive enough to stimulate one's curiosity, and there are dozens of figurines and other objects which are more than just discarded household goods. Like the civilizations themselves, the Greek and Roman section pulls the disc together in a cumulative fashion, showing not only where the earlier art and craft techniques led, but the supreme execution of those same techniques.

One final note. Having spent several days pondering the many images which the discs have to offer, we became aware of a different angle on a profound change to humanity which has occurred in less than a hundred years – the obsolescence of the horse. Dogs, cats, and even children appear in these works of art from time to time, but the horse is everywhere. In drawings, his anatomy is studied as closely as man's, in sculpture and painting he is as indispensable as the sword or the cross. It is readily apparent that for centuries, horses were absolutely essential to man's well being. Where did they go?

LOVE AMONG THE RUINS

The utterly charming telefilm *Love Among the Ruins* stars Laurence Olivier and Katharine Hepburn, and was directed by George Cukor. The picture transfer is decent, although the haze in which Cukor and cinematographer Douglas Slocombe decided to shoot Hepburn is as annoying as it is unnecessary. The monaural sound is worth amplifying to magnify the voices of the two stars.

The film is about a barrister hired to defend a woman in a breach of promise suit uncomfortably similar to a jilting the barrister himself suffered at her hands many years earlier, although she claims not to remember the interlude. Olivier has rarely been as sweet or uncomplicated, and Hepburn gets to grandstand in a manner which she was rarely afforded in the later stages of her career. *Love Among the Ruins* is a work of pure Valentine, and the quality of one's own life is enhanced for having seen it.

THE LOVE GODDESSES

A few of the film clips on *The Love Goddesses* will probably never show up on disc as original films. The program, however, is of questionable value. It provides a brief summary of popular leading ladies over the first fifty years of film, but the narration lacks a sense of academic organization and fails to provide more than a few generalizations about the changing values of screen audiences and the actresses who capitalized on those changes. There is only one color clip, from 'It Started in Naples,' and the rest of the collection is in black and white. The disc is slightly letterboxed, which is an adequate representation of the documentary. However, most the clips depicted in the film were shot in the same aspect ratio as one's monitor, and were subsequently cropped to fit in the documentary in the first place. The sound is passable – the musical score is by Percy Faith – and the 90-minute disc has close to 60 chapter markers.

LOVE HAPPY

The amusing *Love Happy* is not a true Marx Brothers movie since Groucho's sequences are minimal and not integrated with the others, but there are enough comical moments to hold one's attention and a fairly spectacular conclusion involving a number of huge Times Square billboards. The story has something to do with valuable jewels and a musical in need of financing.

The black and white picture looks excellent. There are a few splices, scratches and a couple of sound dropouts, but the image has rich contrasts and shiny, solid blacks. The sound is acceptable and the 85-minute film is in CLV.

LOVE IS A MANY-SPLENDORED THING

Pure romance is rarely attempted any more. Movie makers usually have to find some other hook to attract audiences and make the romantic components a subplot to the action. It can be downright exciting then when a title such as the 1955 Cinemascope romance, *Love is a Many-Splendored Thing* is resurrected. Not only is it many-splendored, but love is the only thing this movie is about, especially on the cropped TV screen where you lose the panoramic vistas of Hong Kong. The colors in the movie look great (as does the jacket cover), although the print has more than its share of rough passages. The stereophonic sound is CX-encoded and is a bit subdued. William Holden portrays a reporter who is enamored of a Eurasian doctor, portrayed by Jennifer Jones. Both the plot and the score are pointedly reminiscent of 'Madame Butterfly.' The title song will stay with you for weeks afterward, since it gets played everywhere, as if it were number one on the charts in Hong Kong while they were filming the movie.

LOVE ME OR LEAVE ME

Although the sets and costumes of *Love Me or Leave Me* were designed with Technicolor in mind, the musical, starring James Cagney and Doris Day, was filmed in Eastmancolor and has a dullness which one associates with the imitator and not the standard bearer. Nevertheless, the movie has undergone a decent transfer to disc by MGM/UA. The original Cinemascope print has been scanned and cropped, but the effect is only debilitating in one or two instances. The image also has a graininess which we have come to associate with the blowing up of a Cinemascope picture to fill a TV screen, but otherwise it is sharply focussed and looks fine.

The film is a less-than-rosy look at the relationship between the singer Ruth Etting and her gangster patron, Marty Snyder. The movie still manages to gloss over life's nastier realities, but it seems to get the emotions right anyway, and that, after all, is the point of it. Day performs more than a dozen numbers, all of which have been marked by chapters on the three-sided, two-hour CLV disc. The stereo digital track has significantly less hiss than the analog track. For a 1955 recording, the sound is very good, and the songs sound as if they are coming from old hi-fi records, only without crackles.

LOVE WITH A PROPER STRANGER

The jacket for *Love with the Proper Stranger* is a collector's dream come true. It is adorned with a gorgeous color photograph (the film is in black and white) of the two stars, Natalie Wood and Steve McQueen, which looks so fresh and alive that not knowing any better one would suppose it had been taken expressly for the home video release.

The film is an enjoyable tale about a couple who fall in love the day they go looking for an abortionist. Wood's performance is outstanding, and McQueen's eternal adolescent routine fits his character perfectly. The black-and-white print is in decent shape, with a minimal number of flaws. The monaural sound, including a minor Elmer Bernstein score, has been digitally encoded, though there is no mistaking its age.

LOVES OF A BLONDE

Milos Forman's *Loves of a Blonde* is a very inexpensive black-and-white production, charming and inconsequential, about the romantic life of several women who work and live, really, in a shoe factory. The print is in acceptable condition and the monaural sound is okay. The movie is in Czechoslovakian with white English subtitles.

Forman's ability to take impossible material and turn it into a viable film by relying on the characters to tell the story is evident in *Blonde*. His humanist reputation was born partially from necessity, but his knack for telling a story with faces and showing the right face at the right time led him to larger budgets and great success in the West. Few of the flashier foreign directors have made the transition as smoothly, if at all. It is said that film is a universal language, but it would appear that the human face has an even greater, more accessible vocabulary.

LUCIA DI LAMMERMOOR
DON CARLO

The Metropolitan Opera presentation of Gaetano Donizetti's *Lucia Di Lammermoor* runs under two hours, but 15 minutes' worth are credits and applause, which stretches the show to two discs. Wisely, each of the three acts occupies a different side. Joan Sutherland is unnerving as the romantic lead, contorting wildly as she sings. Sutherland's voice is like honey laced with alcohol. Syrupy and intoxicating under the lax composition of the first act, her vocal control sweetens the best of Donizetti's invention with the kick that only a star performer can give. In act three she has an aria which amounts to a duet with a flute. The audience goes wild.

Derived from a Walter Scott novel, the story is about a pair of lovers who are doomed before their first kiss to suffer unhappiness, madness, and death through the decay and corruption of the Scottish nobility. As her lover, Alfredo Kraus has some rousing duets with Sutherland and earns his own rapturous applause near the end.

While subtitles allow one to follow the progress of the drama, the libretto provides much more detail and contains numerous chapter markers so that losing one's place is never a problem. Excellent notes on the history of the work are also included.

The presentation is not perfect. When the performers move about on the stage there is a slight but perceptible tendency in the sound to fade in and out. This particularly undercuts the authority of Paul Plishka's Raimondo, whose singing is already weak to begin with.

Guiseppe Verdi's *Don Carlo* is twice as long as *Lucia Di Lammermoor*, but the complexity and accomplishment of the work is exponential when compared to a Donizetti's. This is the sort of production at which the Metropolitan Opera excels – huge and serious. With a cast headed by Placido Domingo, there is no questioning the quality involved.

Andrew Porter's notes on the history of the opera are excellent and detail the goals Verdi was trying to achieve. The story is about Don Carlo's father, Phillip II, Spain's answer to the Borgias. Verdi manages to set a few arias and duets to essays on political theory and arguments about the separation of church and state. Great stuff. The narrative also involves a pair of lovers who are doomed before their first kiss to suffer unhappiness, madness, and death through the decay and corruption of the Spanish nobility.

Nicholai Ghlarvrov, as Phillip II, is nearly as arresting as Domingo. The cast also includes Mirella Freni as Elizabeth, the wife of Phillip II and object of Don Carlo's ill-fated affections, and Louis Quilico as Rodrigo. The sound recording is better on *Don Carlo*, perhaps because the singers move around less than they did in *Lucia Di Lammermoor*. The quality of the picture on both discs is excellent.

Nearly four hours long, *Don Carlo* can probably be viewed on consecutive evenings. Verdi's score is so complex that many viewings would be needed to link all the motifs from beginning to end. Just watching a scene a night can enliven one's week, raise one's spirit, and enrich one's mind.

LUDWIG (Import)

Originally filmed in Italian, *Ludwig* is letterboxed with an aspect ratio of about 2.2:1, with the Japanese subtitles appearing on the black space beneath the picture. The film is one of Luchino Visconti's duller efforts. It is over three hours long and turns completely on the conversations of the characters. Visually, Visconti's opulence is well served by the widescreen. The photography is stunning, and the care given to the look of the film – the ending is a perverse but haunting colorization of a scene near the end of F. W. Murnau's 'Sunrise' – clearly surpasses the care given to the dumb story about the mad king of Bavaria. The picture is unharmed by its height and greatly enhanced by its width.

LUST FOR LIFE

The colors at the beginning of Vincent Minnelli's *Lust for Life* are drab, but then, as Vincent Van Gogh (Kirk Douglas) develops his abilities as a painter, the world around him begins to brighten, first with a single object here or there, and finally, the entire landscape surrounding him. The film is about color and composition as much as it is about an emotionally unstable artist, and to view the movie under anything less than pristine conditions is to not see it at all.

Thus, MGM/UA has released *Lust for Life* the only way it can be released, as a Deluxe Letter-Box Edition. The disc runs just over two hours and comes in a gatefold jacket which has a super, original theatrical poster (which gives an utterly false impression of the film) on the innerspread. The side breaks are indiscriminate and interrupt dramatic scenes needlessly. The stereo sound comes from a four-track magnetic source, so there are no surround codes, but the sound effects, the directional dialog, and Miklos Rozsa's foggy but memorable score are grand. Early copies contained a flaw on the soundtrack, a startling 'pop' which occurs at about 23:20 on side two and those with sensitive audio equipment should be wary of it.

The image has been letterboxed with an aspect ratio of about 2.1:1 and it supports the director's intentions, not only spreading the characters apart, but documenting Van Gogh's painting and its sources. The picture transfer, which comes from 'an interpositive manufactured from the original camera negative,' is mildly inconsistent but generally satisfying. Some reels are grainy, some night scenes take on odd colored glares in what ought to be pure darkness and the color is a little pale in places. The film has so much color and so much to look at, however, that the disc's overall impact is positive. The fleshtones are sharply detailed, the set dressings shimmer, and the paintings set one's pulse pounding.

The paintings! There are museum exhibitions or other gatherings of talent of one type or another which, one realizes if one is lucky enough to observe them, will never happen again. No one today could ever assemble the original artwork that Minnelli assembled to shoot *Lust for Life*. Why did he bother? It is for the same reason that good filmmakers will use real jewelry or real gold. A viewer's conscious eye may not notice the difference, but the subconscious will. It is the incidental shots of the paintings and drawings of Van Gogh and other artists, leaning against a table leg on the floor, or squeezed together on a cluttered wall, that excite one's attention. Paintings represent the joining of a lust for material possessions with an understanding of the beauties of life. Now with laser discs, so do movies like this.

LUST IN THE DUST

Contrary to what the jacket cover says, *Lust in the Dust* is not CX-encoded. The stereo soundtrack is nice and the added noise shouldn't bother a viewer since the rest of the production values are raunchy, anyway.

The movie is a comic western. It has many double entendres and multiple-layered jokes, but little wit. Children may find the sillier aspects of the movie amusing. Since most of the sexual innuendo is too complex to catch, there would be little harm in letting kids watch it. Divine portrays a wandering cantina hostess who has half of a treasure map imprinted on her posterior (see *The Stranger and the Gunfighter*). Lainie Kazan has the other half and Tab Hunter puts them together. Because the CLV disc is only 85 minutes long, it never becomes tiresome. Cult movies like this one are what home video is all about, but avoid forcing it on your friends.

THE LUSTY MEN

Nicholas Ray's *The Lusty Men* has been given a nice looking picture transfer. The black-and-white image, enhanced by Ray's superior film sense, looks spotless and carefully scaled. The sound is less successful. The volume is too low to begin with, and drops even lower during one sequence.

That the movie is about rodeo riders should be of secondary consideration to potential viewers. Even the silly ending, in which doctors walk away from the hero so he can die from a punctured lung while talking to the heroine, is not enough to spoil the rich emotional subtext and taut storytelling. The film stars Robert Mitchum, Arthur Kennedy and Susan Hayward, and all three are terrific. The most memorable sequence, however, has nothing to do with rodeo riding or acting. In the beginning of the film, the hero visits the house where he grew up, which he has not seen in twenty years and is now owned by a stranger. His first action after walking onto the property is to dive beneath the house to retrieve some childhood treasures, a neat little piece of return-to-the-womb imagery which is both efficient and astute.

LUTHER VANDROSS: LIVE AT WEMBLY

Luther Vandross and his three backup singers stand on a circular stage in the center of Wembly Arena and perform for 86 minutes in *Luther Vandross: Live at Wembly*. The picture quality is good. The video tape source has no distortion and Vandross is well lit.

There are plenty of closeups and a good variety of camera angles. The stereo sound is clear, though the live environment takes a little polish off of Vandross' vocals. He has some amusing moments with two attractive female singers, but the format of the concert is limited and after a while the viewer is apt to listen without watching. Vandross' repertoire consists mostly of ballads and soul numbers, which he sings with a fresh exuberance. Side two is in CAV with movement blurred in all the still frames.

LUV
An awful play which was made into an even more awful movie, *Luv* makes for an awful disc. The movie, which stars Jack Lemmon, Peter Falk, and Elaine May, is laden with stage devices left over from the play, the most galling of which is a trap door in the middle of the foyer of a suburban house. The characters are stricken with unlikely idiosyncrasies designed solely to induce plot turns and stage laughs at key moments. It is a frightful work, and one can only be thankful that theater, or for that matter, cinema, did not embrace it as an innovative, focal model to be exalted and emulated. The picture is grainy and the source material is mildly faded, giving fleshtones an extra level of pink. The monaural sound is stronger, for what it is worth.

M
The print of *M* looks so sharply focused and clear that, even though it is full of breaks and scratches, collectors will find it acceptable. The dialog is in German and its quality also varies from reel to reel, but you can tell how fresh the print is by how sparkling the subtitles look. Another touch which pleased us was the break between side one and side two, which occurs at the perfect moment.

M, directed by Fritz Lang, has been accepted as a classic film for so long that it is a cliché to study it as such. It is an enticing, emotional movie. Lang's filmmaking techniques were often innovative and flashy, but the story, about a hunt for a child murderer, is told with remarkable economy. In the course of 100 minutes the effect of the murders is examined on every level of society, as is the ambiguity of justice. There are also 'M's' and objects (such as a Mickey Mouse) which start with 'M' all over the place. Yet it is the acting – Georg John's executive efficiency as the MacHeath-like crime boss and Peter Lorre's anxious compulsion as the molester – which will pull one back to the disc again and again.

MAC AND ME
There are more commercials in *Mac and Me* than in an afternoon of local television. A product logo is visible in every scene, if not every shot. The film must have made a profit before it played in a single theater. It better have, because it certainly didn't make one afterward.

The sort of children's film which makes adults cringe – justifiably – *Mac and Me* is about a family of beings sucked up from a moon of Saturn and deposited on Earth by an American-made space probe. The youngest alien is separated from his family when the probe is opened, and befriends a young boy who is confined to a wheelchair. The plot makes no significantly bad turns, it's just that when the alien becomes sick, he is revived with Coca-Cola – water doesn't work. Everybody not employed by the government appears to work at either McDonald's or Sears, and actively wears a uniform while lounging at home. The picture is in acceptable condition and the stereo surround sound is effective in a basic sort of way.

MACARONI
Jack Lemmon and Marcello Mastroianni star in *Macaroni*. Their performances are satisfying, but the movie, about two friends reunited in Naples 40 years after WWII, is inept and stereotyped. The timing and rhythm of the two principals save the show from being a total waste, but it is difficult to imagine who actually wants to buy things like this. The sound is awkward and the picture is a little pale.

MACARTHUR
Jerry Goldsmith's score for *MacArthur* is an intriguing variation of the fading horns and introspective march he used in *Patton*. The entire movie was designed to supplement *Patton* and provide one-half of an exhausting double bill on World War II commanders. The film fails because it holds too closely to the public record and does not embellish MacArthur's story with the slight touches of drama and motivation which would keep a viewer interested in the character. As a history lesson it is fine, required viewing for anyone studying WWII in the video age. But as a movie, it only has the music and Ed Flanders's incarnation of Harry Truman going for it.

The disc is digitally encoded, all the better to listen to the music. When Gregory Peck, as MacArthur, speaks into a public address system, the volume has a satisfying billow.

The picture, however, is quite disappointing. It is often grainy or blurry, and suffers from an occasional white speckle. None of the colors are faded, but the result is less excusable than it might have been if the movie had looked more worn down. As it is, parts of the transfer seem rather sloppy. Side three is in CAV. None of the frames jitter, but potential utilization of Standard Play seems limited. The trailer, which has been included at the end, makes the movie look more exciting than it is, but even its two minutes can strain one's patience.

MACBETH
Orson Welles's awkward production of *Macbeth* has received as good a transfer as is conceivably possible. The film's common running time of 86 minutes has been upped to its original 112, which solves the movie's most serious drawbacks, although many still abound. The soundtrack was recorded three ways, in British, British/American, and Scottish accents. As much of the Scottish brogue as possible has also been restored on the soundtrack of the disc, which is closer to Welles' original intentions than other versions have been, and again, the result smooths out the roughest passages.

The movie as it is presented on the disc works well from the point that Macduff leaves for England to the finale. The beginning, however, is still a mess. The rhythm of the play is completely off, and those unfamiliar with the text would have no idea what is going on. Welles filmed the movie at Republic, intending a sort of 'three penny opera' version for mass consumption. He took so many shortcuts, however, that the narrative is reduced to snippets of the most famous lines.

Anyone who has suffered through versions of this movie which looked bound from beginning to end in a dense fog will be amazed at how well the picture on the disc looks. Although the reel changes are announced by 'pops' and sudden shifts in tone, and although a number of shots look solarized, and although the entire film still maintains a mildly ragged appearance, it is not in as bad a shape as it has traditionally been presented. It is always in sharp focus, and some of the scenes are surprisingly bright and unblemished.

The sound is sufficiently stable to tolerate increases in volume on a viewer's audio system, a requirement which is unavailable in revival houses and necessary for a few of the weakly recorded dialog passages (the movie was made the way music videos are made, with the sound played on loudspeakers and the performers lip synching). The disc has a fair number of chapter markers.

The movie is so fragmented that no real interpretation of the play ever coagulates. As with all of Welles' films, however, there are a number of memorable moments. The complaints voiced by Lady Macduff are especially bitter, and provide a sharp counterpoint to Macduff's grief when he learns of her death. Banquo's killers are briefly but vividly drawn. The sleepwalking scene, which Welles fiddled with a bit, is more coherent than most presentations, and feels less like a dramatic digression meant to give Birnam Wood time to reach Dunsinane.

Mostly, the film is full of muted sounds and furies, signifying nothing. It is not advisable that those who are unfamiliar with the work obtain it, even if they are fans of Shakespeare or Welles. Those who are familiar with the movie, however, and can tolerate its lapses, will find the disc to be an admirable accomplishment.

MACBETH
The original theatrical release of Roman Polanski's *Macbeth* had the same dreary, faded colors which now dog the disc. The film is by no means hurt because it is in a mildly rough condition. *Macbeth* was intended, in part, to be the antithesis of Franco Zeffirelli's gushy *Romeo and Juliet*. It was also intended to evoke the murder of Sharon Tate and her companions.

The disc is hurt, however, by the loss of the Todd-AO widescreen. One of the most clever enhancements which Polanski and co-scriptwriter Kenneth Tynan provided was to embellish the part of the knight known as Ross. Not only does he become the 'third murderer' of Banquo, he also betrays Macduff's family and is the first to hail Macbeth, and, in due time, Malcolm, as king. But you will not see Ross hail Macbeth's crowning on the disc, because he has been cropped off the edge of the screen.

Polanski and Tynan added a few superior touches to the plot, such as a final blackout scene where the play's forgotten prince, Donalbain, is seen approaching the witches' encampment, but the screenplay subtracts much more than it adds. Although *Macbeth* was one of the shortest plays Shakespeare wrote, the movie is 140 minutes long. Even so, the poetry in the longer soliloquies and lengthier conversations has been excised. Without its poetic context, the film loses much of the play's cohesive rhythm.

MACK THE KNIFE
Although *Mack the Knife*, both the movie and the disc, has a number of imperfections, we would anticipate returning to it for repeat viewings many more times than we would

return to a more proper and perfect film. The RCA/Columbia disc never gives the viewer a chance to say no. Take for example, the digital sound logo emblazoned on the jacket. The disc itself is CX-encoded analog only, but Menahem Golan's movie has a boisterous Dolby Surround soundtrack, adequately transferred, which cannot be refused. The viewer may try to retreat upon seeing the absence of the digital indicator on the laser player, but the audio is enveloping and as soon as Kurt Weil's alluring music takes hold, giving in to it is the only available option.

Raul Julia received his first burst of stardom playing Mack the Knife on the stage. Golan's movie is a mixture of good ideas and ideas not thought through, and in places Julia gets buried by over-production. The essence of his definitive portrayal, a combination of total comfort with the dialog and songs mixed with an oozing sexuality, remains unfettered. As his character emerges more clearly in the second half of the program, he becomes both appealing and perversely sympathetic.

The film was not a widescreen effort, so the essential portions of it remain in view on the disc. While the choreography may not be elaborate and while it may be harmed by the slightest loss of the screen edges, it is well-timed and spirited. Made on soundstages, the movie is glossy and direct in the inevitable Golan manner. Fortunately the disc has a good command of the colors. Although the production design is heavy on beggar browns and red-light-district reds, the image remains sharp and clear. The two side breaks are ill-chosen and there are no chapter markers.

The film captures about two thirds of 'Threepenny Opera.' There are songs and ideas missing, or poorly realized ('Pirate Jenny' is a real disappointment), and the important curtain closing lines have also been dispensed with even though the soundtrack carries on over the end credits. The material is good enough, though, so that when Golan does think something through, the result is marvelous and makes the disc worthwhile. The lyrics, incidentally, are based mainly on an older and mildly prudish interpretation. The writers insist upon using 'two-by-four' for the German 'Bordell.' We wonder how many sailors using the translation as a guide have ended up, perplexed, in a lumber yard.

MACAO

Macao is a movie of intrigue which has no emotional or thematic depth but is nevertheless a great deal of fun. The picture looks terrific. It is spotless, and the greys and blacks are sharply defined. Side two is in CAV with two unsteady still frames out of every five, but at triple speed the image is incredibly vivid, creating mouthwatering portraits of Gloria Grahame, Robert Mitchum, and Jane Russell. Macao is a Portuguese Hong Kong nestled on the Chinese coast. It is the ideal setting for immoral and exotic goings on, and the soundstage-bound movie, about a gangster the police are trying to coax out of the city limits, is adept at evoking the type of adventure and light entertainment a viewer would expect from such enterprises. The sound is fine. Some of the dialog, involving barely veiled entendres, is quite enjoyable, but the high point is Russell singing the Mercer and Arlen song, 'One for My Baby,' in CAV.

MAD MAX
THE ROAD WARRIOR
MAD MAX BEYOND THUNDERDOME

In *Mad Max* every character except Max and his family is crippled in some way. By the end of the film, Max's family is dead and Max's leg is wrecked. In *The Road Warrior*, Max's leg is still bad, and he wears a metal brace. In *Mad Max Beyond Thunderdome* the brace and any trace of a limp have disappeared. But perhaps the most telling aspect of the sequel's failure to match the spirit of its predecessors is that the transference to home video is unhindered by the loss of the widescreen.

The first *Max* disc was released by Vestron and it was a speckled, blurry mess, adversely affected by the cropping. (The film is also dubbed, but rumor has it the original Australian dialog is not worth retrieving.) *Road Warrior* came out a little later from Warner and it wasn't much better. *Mad Max Beyond Thunderdome* has also been released by Warner. Although the disc has not been digitally encoded it sounds terrific. The picture is somewhat less satisfactory, but viewing it at home is no different than viewing it in a theater except for the matte shots at the very end. In the first two discs, you lose important information and wild thrills not having the full picture. In this one you don't miss a thing.

Road Warrior is a home video classic. The story has tight, mythical resonances, holding the right balance between action and emotion. *Thunderdome* had two directors, George Miller and George Oglivie, and the movie grinds to a halt during Oglivie's middle third. Miller, who did the previous two Max films, has a prodigious film style and his sequences, which open and close this movie, are grand. You can go fix yourself a sandwich during the film's middle section though, without bothering to turn off the disc. Along with Mel Gibson and Tina Turner, the movie stars Bruce Spence, who appeared in *Road Warrior* in a different role. Casting him here as a different character was the most ridiculous move the film's producers could make and, like the loss of the limp, it is more evidence that *Thunderdome* wasn't so much a sequel as a jump sideways.

MADAMA BUTTERFLY – TEATRO ALLA SCALA

The staging of *Madama Butterfly – Teatro alla Scala* is mildly modernist, with a minimum of distracting stage decorations and props. The production design and costumes, however, have the unmistakable elegance that is apparent in every La Scala effort, and the video program is filmed at intimate angles which reduce the emptiness one might have felt watching the show on the stage. It must be remembered, though, that emptiness is one of the undercurrents of the libretto.

Yasuko Hayashi sings Cio-cio-San, and while she is not 15, she is Japanese. Her performance is careful but commanding, and her singing, in the context of production, is wonderful. Her voice reminds one of the blossoms Butterfly scatters about her yard. The rest of the cast, including Hak-Nam Kim, Peter Dvorsky, and Giorgio Zancanaro, also give satisfying performances.

The transfer is very good. The sound recording is well balanced and has been transferred to disc with digital encoding (the analog track has more background hiss). The picture is never corrupted and never has the ghosts or other recording flaws which some European programs have. The 142-minute show is spread conveniently to three sides, one for each act. There are 19 chapter markers. The opera is subtitled, and an Italian/English libretto comes with the disc.

MADAME SOUSATZKA

The sound editing in *Madame Sousatzka* is dumb. The film is about a young piano prodigy whose talent is cultivated by an eccentric but enthusiastic teacher. The times in which stereo effects and surround effects are utilized in the movie seem almost arbitrary. Sometimes the music falls flat and other times it floats. In any case, the stereo is under-utilized, as if the director were uncomfortable with the technology.

Shirley MacLaine has the title role, and although the promotion for the film does a disservice by magnifying her part, she underplays it suitably and effectively. The other performances in the film are also admirable, making the movie and its musical interludes enjoyable.

Skin tones appear too orange, but otherwise the picture quality is acceptable. The film runs a minute over two hours, and MCA has put side three in CAV. The potential applications are limited, but every still frame is steady and the effort deserves praise.

MADE IN HEAVEN

Some viewers will inevitably like *Made in Heaven*, another obscure cult vehicle from the often intriguing film director Alan Rudolph. The movie, though, is too cloudy, and fails to deliver the emotional or romantic impact it appears to be promising. It is about angels who return to Earth to unite in the flesh, and Claude Lelouch did the whole thing far more effectively in 'And Now My Love' without ever resorting to the supernatural.

Rudolph has filmed the movie in kind of an overcast, glycerined haze, and it doesn't transfer to disc too well. The opening black and white sequence is particularly indistinct. The movie seems deliberately antipathetic to television.

The music on the soundtrack, including a couple of Neil Young tunes, is stereophonic, to little effect. The sound lacks the concentration Rudolph has utilized in other efforts. The disc jacket copy tries to be mysterious about Debra Winger's uncredited (and plain bothersome) presence, but it only serves to highlight the trick.

MADE IN USA

One of the worst excuses for a road movie, *Made in USA* is about two young men who steal cars to travel from Pennsylvania to California. Lori Singer, whose performance is practically the movie's only redeeming feature, portrays a slightly crazy stewardess that they pick up along the way. The sound is fair and the picture is fuzzy. The movie makes a point of commenting on various ecological problems, but a high-minded attitude toward the environment hardly seems to compensate for all the robbery and destruction in which the heroes so cheerfully indulge.

MADONNA
Watching Madonna sing 'Like a Virgin' is like seeing the Big Bad Wolf sing 'The Wiffenpoof Song.' She appears on an 8-inch disc, *Madonna*, in four fairly similar music videos that have slightly fuzzy pictures. In the first, 'Burning Up,' she rolls around in a parking lot. In 'Borderline,' which is probably the best of the four, she is rolling around on a rooftop. In 'Lucky Star' she rolls around on an empty white stage, and in 'Like a Virgin' she rolls around in a Venetian gondola. On the whole, she's got the rolling part down pretty good. It is the rocking she needs to work on.

MADONNA/CIAO ITALIA: LIVE FROM ITALY
The acoustics in the open air concert, *Madonna/Ciao Italia: Live from Italy*, leave much to be desired. Her voice is forced through so much amplification that the last remnants of melody, hardly a strong aspect to her singing in the first place, blurt indifferently from the digital stereo surround soundtrack. Her 100-minute act is full of busy choreography, and the picture quality of the disc is probably too good for the harsh lighting. It isn't rock 'n roll and it is barely music at all, but anyone who can fill an entire stadium by running around on a stage in nothing but underwear and shouting into a microphone is hardly encouraged to improve the artistic level of her act. Much of the footage, reportedly, comes from Japan and not Italy.

MADONNA LIVE – THE VIRGIN TOUR
Madonna and virgin. The words are synonymous, like 'black' and 'white' or 'termites' and 'ice cream.' Has anyone noticed that this woman cannot sing? In *Madonna Live – The Virgin Tour* the perfection of the digital sound only serves to emphasize the imperfection of the sounds emitted from the vocal cords of the mononymphet who is prancing around on stage in getups which make her look like she has just shoplifted two Cornish game hens. To be fair, this is a 'live' recording, and few artists can concentrate on being delicate in front of 10,000 or so screaming fans. Do they like her, though? At one point she asks the audience, "Will you marry me?" and they all shout back, "No!" (we swear). The picture on the disc is poor. It has troubles with the strong red and blue lighting and the show was badly filmed to begin with.

MADONNA – WHO'S THAT GIRL
(Import)
The 90-minute stage performance which Madonna puts on at an outdoor Tokyo stadium in *Madonna – Who's That Girl*, a 'Mitsubishi Special Live in Japan' available through import, is an elaborate spectacle. The stage has a running treadmill, a staircase, numerous pop-up figures, and is illustrated by a complex slide show. Madonna is flanked by decent dancers, and manages an hour and a half of real choreography without embarrassing herself. She performs pantomimes on the treadmill, constantly leaps up and down the stairs, and never stops moving. She also sings, although in the live environment that doesn't amount to much. The sound is thorough, but her voice misses the protection of studio engineering. She loses not only the high notes, but the middle notes as well, and is left with a sort of breathless, low pitched whine. But who watches the disc to hear her sing?

Throughout most of the show she wears a one-piece undergarment with tassels on the bust which will send Boy Scouts to bed dreaming of knots. There are no Japanese subtitles but a sheet containing the lyrics to her songs in both English and Japanese comes with the disc. The picture on the disc is efficient, but the image is at the mercy of the stage lighting. When the cameras are in the right place and the spots are turned up, you can see the creases on Madonna's face, but when things get dark, she gets blurry. Sometimes you wish she would remain blurry. At one point she sits on the stage facing the audience, spreads her legs just about as wide as they can be spread, and starts singing, 'Like a Virgin.' Who's that girl kidding?

THE MAGIC BALLAD – TADANARI OKAMOTO
DOJOJI TEMPLE/HOUSE OF FLAME – KIHACHIRO KAWAMOTO
Two of Pioneer's 'Animation Animation' releases focus on Japanese animators, *The Magic Ballad – Tadanari Okamoto* and *Dojoji Temple/House of Flame – Kihachiro Kawamoto*. (The latter is not identified as an 'Animation Animation' disc on the jacket cover, but is still part of the series.) The programs, which are collections of short films, are intended for dedicated animation enthusiasts and students. The Kawamoto disc is the more accessible of the two and may have a wider appeal, but both animators work primarily with puppets and similar figurines, and a strong feeling for the culture which has spawned them is needed to obtain the full pleasures the films have to offer.

Okamoto's art goes beyond simply animating stories. He attempts to find the right materials to illustrate his tales, so that both the images and the image textures contribute to the emotions of the story. He animates folk art to tell folk tales. Some of the pieces are deceptively simple, such as the use of yarn figures (reinforced with wire) to tell the story of a baby duck who runs away from home. Other works are more elaborate, and may incorporate a number of media. The folk tales, incidentally, are consistently sophisticated and contain complex moral messages.

The films on the Kawamoto disc are ghost stories and somber moral tales told with stunning and complex imagery. Kawamoto is so good at his craft that most viewers will immediately lose the inhibitions and alienation normally associated with animated puppets.

The pieces are excellent from a filmmaking point of view, and the presence of dolls instead of actors in the principle roles is almost secondary in importance. In an interview on the disc, Kawamoto, when asked what is the most important thing he has learned about his craft, answers with the full knowledge that what he is saying may sound simple but is actually quite profound, "A puppet can express different things from what a human can." Puppets are not people. As a filmmaker, he works in their world, and translates it to ours.

Both discs come in gatefold jackets and both contain a little under two hours worth of short films on four sides in CAV. The Okamoto disc has some stereo passages while the Kawamoto disc is entirely monaural. Neither is CX-encoded, but both are so carefully produced that they don't need it. Almost all of the dialog and narration is in Japanese and is accompanied by English subtitles, which diminishes the appeal of the discs to younger children.

Along with the short films, there are biographical photo still frames on each disc, along with interviews and 'Making of' sequences. The jackets also contain filmographies and other pertinent information. Utilization of the CAV functions is of great importance in breaking down the exact steps the animators went through to accomplish their magic.

THE MAGIC CHRISTIAN
If it weren't for the music *The Magic Christian* would be a total waste of time. The 1969 comedy, starring Peter Sellers and Ringo Starr, has the sort of narrative and attention span which one associates with substance abuse. The film is a mess. It isn't even nice. The plot is about a rich man who uses his wealth to demonstrate the corruption of others, but his targets are often innocent people who could really use the money. In any case, the episodes barely connect with each other and make little sense.

The picture is in good shape, though it has a standard late Sixties paleness. The sound recording is awful – flat, full of over-dubs, and as haphazard as the rest of the film. The monaural transfer, however, preserves the effort without further damage.

The music, mostly by the group Badfinger with heavy contributions from Paul McCartney, also sounds awful, in the sense that it isn't recorded any better than any other part of the film's soundtrack. It sounds wonderful, however, in the sense that it has a strongly nostalgic, late Sixties melody and beat. Every time a viewer is just about to give up on the film, the guitars kick in and convince one to hold out just a little longer.

MAGIC FLUTE (see **INGMAR BERGMAN'S MAGIC FLUTE**)

THE MAGICIAN
(see **AUTUMN SONATA**)

THE MAGNIFICENT AMBERSONS
One of Orson Welles's half-dozen cinematic masterpieces, *The Magnificent Ambersons*, has been released as a Criterion Collection title. The 88-minute film fits on three sides of the CAV presentation and contains a lecture about the movie on the alternate audio track. Side four contains an essay, with stills, about the film's production, two brief interview clips of Welles talking about the film, 164 storyboard illustrations which depict every major scene, the complete text of the original shooting script, excerpts from a silent film adaptation of *Ambersons* from 1925, and, after the Welles interview, the complete Mercury Theatre radio play adaptation starring Welles and Walter Huston. The radio drama runs close to an hour and is split onto both audio tracks, so that one must run side four through twice to hear the whole show.

The print was struck from "original nitrate material." The contrasts are rich and the detail, when one randomly freezes a still frame, is satisfyingly clear. The sound is CX-encoded, without automatic tripping, and it seems to be an accurate rendition of the original recording. Twenty-three chapter markers identify the film's best moments.

Robert Carringer's jacket notes give a more coherent summary of *Ambersons* than his rambling and disjointed 80-minute lecture. He takes an unusually literal approach to what is depicted on the screen and spends most of his time discussing the details of the production and where missing footage was once inserted.

Next to providing a medium for the film itself, the most significant accomplishment of the disc is the removal of the mystique associated with the film's production history. Welles did an initial cut which was clearly too long, but became involved in another project, out of the country, and could not supervise the paring and smoothing of the film's awkward edges. Enthusiastic RKO executives pressured those who were working on the film to throw out a good share of the baby with the bathwater. That material is apparently lost to eternity. Some of it, as depicted in rare still photos, storyboard drawings, and the shooting script, obviously does not belong. Repetitive scenes which emphasize the negative personalities of the major characters and the decline of the family fortune without advancing the story significantly ought to have been dropped. But there are also some tantalizing moments whose absence causes a great and painful longing. A scene in which an automobile is put 'to bed' for the night in a barn, a depiction of the Amberson grounds being torn up for a housing development, and visions of the steadily creeping soot and decay would have made the film stronger without harming its box office potential. The box office potential was pretty grim anyway, which is why several scenes, dialog intact, were re-shot by other directors to soften negative personality traits in the protagonists. After one is done with the disc, these scenes will stand out, but it should heighten one's appreciation of the film rather than diminish one's enjoyment of it. *Ambersons* remains a nostalgic, dramatically powerful tale and should ultimately be savored for what it is rather than rejected for what it is not.

MAGNUM FORCE

The opening and closing credits of *Magnum Force* are in letterboxed format and the picture throughout rarely looks less than crystal clear. Clint Eastwood's bull-in-a-china-shop attitude is also under control, since the script, although written by Michael Cimino and John Milius, gives his Harry character an intriguing glimmer of intelligence. When he talks to another character about Brazilian death squads, he sounds as if he actually had taken the time to read up on the subject.

The sound has been reprocessed for stereo and one would be hard pressed to discern that the original source had sounded differently. Lalo Schifrin's score, a hokey imitation of dinner club jazz, is freed from the confines of the screen, and reaches out to pull the viewer into the film. Watch out for the bullets.

MAHLER (Import)

"I don't want to imitate nature. I want to capture its very essence, so that, if all the birds and the beasts died tomorrow and the world became a desert, when people heard my music they would still know – feel – what nature was." Ken Russell's *Mahler*, one of the finest films about music ever made, is available on disc in Japan with digital stereo sound. The soundtrack still has hiss and crackles, and there is little difference between the digital and analog tracks, but the sound editing and the music are glorious. The picture quality is also decent, although it is clearly a couple of generations removed from the source; the colors are accurate, but the light sometimes gets fuzzy. The disc is in English, with Japanese subtitles which are rarely obtrusive.

The 111-minute film tells of Gustav Mahler's life in flashbacks and flashbacks-within-flashbacks as he has a reconciliation with his wife during a train ride shortly before his death. *Mahler* is no more a biography of Mahler, however, than *Amadeus* was a biography of Mozart. The film is about Mahler's music, and it has been storyboarded to his songs and symphonies, continually coaxing the viewer into approaching the most well known passages in his works from different points of view, to show the environment, the emotion, and the spirit which went into the music. Mahler is tough. His symphonies are not the kind of patter one puts on the hi-fi, low, during dinner parties. The movie works as an introduction or as an enlightenment, and it works because Russell has the guts to really takes risks with the images, to push them so far that you understand he is not providing the last word on the subject, he is only celebrating the majesty the music can inspire.

We once saw *Mahler* on PBS with the silly passage about Cosima Wagner cut out, and that was when we realized what a powerful film it is. The passage is pure Russell and easy ammunition for his detractors, since it depicts Mahler's career-inspired conversion from the Jewish faith to the Catholic faith in a tasteless, deliberately offensive burlesque. Although the scene is distracting, we did not feel it was out of place when we watched the disc. Russell is challenging the notion of religious bigotry by profaning religious symbols, and at the same time he is depicting a cynical, spiritual sell-out, the necessity of which ought to provoke the sort of anger that the scene provokes.

The soul of the film, however, is in the almost continual connections it provides between music and images or ideas. Walks in the woods, brass bands, the voice of a loved one or the death of a child all become as clear in the language of the music as they do in the language of images. After watching the film or the disc, you carry that language with you, increasing your understanding not only of Mahler's works, but of any music you might hear.

MAHLER: SYMPHONY NO. 2

Mahler: Symphony No. 2 is superbly filmed. Leonard Bernstein conducts the London Symphony Orchestra and Edinburgh Festival Chorus inside Ely Cathedral. The Mahler symphony, also known as the 'Resurrection Symphony,' is a peripatetic piece, and the cameras are placed to obtain closeups of every instrument that makes a significant contribution. The image is always in coordination with the music, and the performers you want to watch, when you hear a certain measure, are always the performers who are on view. This becomes especially evident when Shelia Armstrong sings the first soprano solo, in the third movement. It is the longest continuous shot in the program. The editors and director also make use of the location to focus on church icons at brief, appropriate and/or ironic (depending upon one's interpretation of Mahler's intentions) moments.

The picture quality is very good. The sound has a mild amount of makeshift recording hiss, but is passable. The acoustics of the Cathedral create airy, vibrant tones. Chapter markers note significant musical passages, and the disc breaks for a side change between the second and third movements.

MAID TO ORDER

Ally Sheedy has all the looks, spunk and talent of the young Ali McGraw, so you can imagine how positively awful *Maid to Order* is. The undigestible plot requires magic to take a spoiled rich girl and teach her how the other half lives, as a fairy godmother removes her from her own digs and forces her to find employment as a maid in a neighboring mansion. There are many musical numbers and many shots of Sheedy with a blank look on her face as the script attempts to impose humility, frustration, and even love upon her, all to no avail. With a running time of 90 minutes the film seems endless.

The disc and the movie deserve one another. The picture is consistently blurry and foggy, with strong colors tending to dominate the entire screen. The stereo sound is better off and the songs are chapter encoded.

MAJOR LEAGUE

The upbeat baseball comedy *Major League* has an acceptable picture. The surround mix is not as inspired as *Bull Durham*, but then, neither is the film. Written by the scenarist for *Slap Shot*, the narrative has much the same structure. The characterizations, however, are relatively original, and the mix of humor and pennant races is hard to beat.

MAKE MINE MUSIC (Import)

Although American hasn't been so lucky, a number of the original Walt Disney theatrical cartoon anthologies have been released on disc in Japan.

Each of the 10 chapters in *Make Mine Music* is a self-contained narrative, although some, like 'Blue Bayou' which has a stork flying through a blue swamp for several minutes, are pretty thin. The lyrics are supported by Japanese subtitles, but the incidental dialog within the cartoons are heard in Japanese on one audio track and English on the other. Unfortunately, the monaural music sounds better when both audio channels are turned on.

The two most well known cartoons are 'Casey at Bat' and 'Peter and the Wolf.' The latter has dual channel narration, so no subtitles spoil its splendor. Made during the last autumnal gasp of peaceful coexistence before the Cold War put a chill to the depiction of Soviet youth as heroic, the show teaches and entertains in a way few efforts do today. Our favorite segment, however, is a wildly funny and melodic tale called 'The Whale Who Wanted to Sing at the Met.' He does, sort of, and his costumes are even funnier than the hippopotamus ballerinas of 'Fantasia.'

MAKING MR. RIGHT

For a movie which opens with a woman absentmindedly shaving her legs while driving on a freeway, *Making Mr. Right* has a lot of class. So much class, in fact, that it does not deserve the compartmentalized advertising campaign it received, which made it out to be a sex-reversed *Mannequin*. Yes, the woman does become romantically involved with an android in a contemporary setting, but that is only an excuse. The movie is about characters – original, funny characters, and it has more of them than a half dozen other comedy hits combined.

The disc is appealing in all the right ways. The picture is fine. The stereo sound has a slight crackle, but is acceptable. The cast and the script are a perfect match and the film, despite first impressions, is the sort one can easily begin seeing on a steady basis.

MAKING OF GODZILLA (Import)

They say you can't judge a book by its cover, but when it comes to Japanese discs, that is pretty much the only feature we have to go on. We ordered what we thought would be a Japanese monster movie and received what turned out to be a CLV disc that has 26 Japanese monster movie *trailers* on side one and 'Making of *Godzilla* ' on side two.

The disc, which we will call *Making of Godzilla* since those are the only words in English on the jacket cover, is CX-encoded, monaural on side one and in stereo on side two. It is all in Japanese, except for the spurious washed-up American actor or two, mouthing inanities like, "I think Planet X is very short of water."

The trailers provide quite a 59-minute marathon. Aside from the first few black-and-white efforts (they are arranged chronologically), they are all in gorgeous color and in widescreen letterboxed 'Toho Scope.' The disc batters your senses with crazy monsters, smashed buildings, and high-pitched roars. Among the movies we recognized were (in Americanized titles) *Godzilla*, *Godzilla Vs. The Thing*, 'Mothra,' 'The Mysterions,' *King Kong Vs. Godzilla*, *Frankenstein Conquers the World*, and *Destroy All Monsters*. Curiously, the disc has no chapter markers, so calling up a favorite may take some practice.

The documentary on side two concerns the filming of what showed up in America as *Godzilla 1985*. Although the narration is in Japanese, the program is well-made and informative. When the filming of scenes from the movie are depicted, they are shown concurrently, so that you see how the monster was made to smash the building while also seeing how the actors are pretending to be shaken about. The documentary was made with video tape, so it has a sharply defined picture.

The disc is an enjoyable conversation piece and ideal for parties or video store window displays. Getting it was one of the better mistakes we've made.

MAKOTO OZONE – CRYSTAL LOVE

Except for some black-and-white shots of a girl wandering around someone's back yard, there are less than a dozen camera setups in the 54-minute digital jazz piece, *Makoto Ozone – Crystal Love*. Ozone's group consists of three musicians – Ozone on the piano, plus Gary Burton on vibraphone and Eddie Gomez on bass. The stationary shots of the musicians playing their music sometimes go on for more than six minutes. The music is legitimately pleasant and there is something to be said for the minimal support it receives from the visuals. The picture is grainy.

MALCOLM

Although the Australian heist comedy *Malcolm* is cheerful, the color scheme is oppressive. The title character is a befuddled genius who is befriended by an unsuccessful crook. The two eventually team up to pull off a perfect crime. The CLV disc is 86 minutes long. The sound is monaural and not CX-encoded.

MALONE

The ad art for *Malone*, which is repeated on the jacket cover of disc, is a travesty. It reinforces all of the negative images one has of Burt Reynolds, and provides no indication that the movie, a contemporary rendition of *Shane*, is neither mindless nor awkward.

The disc has a slightly grainy picture and uninteresting stereo sound, but it should not disappoint anyone who is partial to decent action films. And to see Reynolds suppressing a grin as he confronts the bad guy, played by Cliff Robertson, is to understand why there is no one else who could have approached the part from the right perspective.

THE MALTESE FALCON

CBS/Fox brought out *The Maltese Falcon* first, and several years later MGM/UA did. The two versions have the same source material – the splices and scratches are the same – but MGM/UA's transfer is much better. Not only is the picture sharper and cleaner, but it is framed better, without as much being cut off on top. The CBS/Fox disc has manual CX-encoding which is best left off. On the MGM/UA disc the CX is automatic.

The Maltese Falcon is a better film on television than it is in a movie theater, where large audiences tend to put Mary Astor in her place rather quickly. The pace is a joy and on TV the film's excesses are tamed by the smaller perspective. The plot does make perfect sense after you see the movie a dozen times, while the relationships between the characters continue to strengthen and develop. The director, John Huston, uses a number of visual tricks to enhance the links the characters have with one another. For example, don't miss the second reverse angle shot involving Peter Lorre, the umbrella handle, and Humphrey Bogart. Once you spot it, the movie will never seem the same.

THE MAMAS AND THE PAPAS STRAIGHT SHOOTER

The actual title of the program contained in *The Mamas and The Papas Straight Shooter* is 'The Story of John Phillips and The Mamas and The Papas Straight Shooter,' which describes the focus and slant of the material more accurately. The show is a documentary about Phillips and traces his entire career with rare film clips and liberal onscreen reminiscences from himself, his friends, and his ex-wives. Considering that Phillips was heavily involved in the program's production, it is reasonably fair minded and thorough. Only those who are looking for an in-depth profile of 'Mama' Cass Eliot will be disappointed, since, though her accomplishments are noted, she remains on the periphery.

The 81-minute program is in digitally encoded stereo, though the songs never seem to last long enough to take advantage of it. The clips look terrific, and one can tell the transfer is excellent because the material taped especially for the program is razor sharp. Side two is in CAV with steady and unsteady still frames dependent upon the source material.

MAN FACING SOUTHEAST

A hologram is constructed by splitting the beam of a laser. Part of the beam is reflected off the object being recorded and the other part is sent on a circuitous route avoiding the object. The beam which was reflected is then passed to a recording mechanism. Later, when another laser is split, one part is sent through the print made from the recording and the other part is reunited with it on the other side, creating a three dimensional projection. In the modern psychiatric theory championed by the French philosopher and psychiatrist, Jacques Lacan, the psychiatrist assumes the role of the 'Other' with the patient and a patient is cured when the 'Other' becomes a stable emotional entity without the psychiatrist, like the second beam which is split away and then returns. A whole mind has an imaginative part which is outside of itself, watching how the rest fits into place with the world. The nineteenth century philosopher, Hegel, used the same basic pattern to describe the relationship between God and man. Paraphrased, he suggested that God was the 'Other' and that 'Spirit' was that recompiled beam, creating a hologrammed soul. Current investigations on the sub-atomic level have led physicists to discover certain particles which act in unison for no apparent reason. This has led to the suggestion that they are linked together in another dimension, and that one is performing the role of the 'Other.'

We mention all of this to help you enjoy *Man Facing Southeast*, a film about a man who shows up in a mental hospital claiming to be a hologram sent from another planet, and who has a Christ-like charisma. The film is perfectly accessible without jumping into Lacanian or Hegelian theory, but the last shot, of a torn photograph (the 'Other' is missing), has more resonance when you understand through how many different philosophical and scientific disciplines the pattern of the hologram mechanism is starting to repeat itself. It may eventually be the unification theory which unifies all other unification theories and it is perfect, because it embraces exception.

The film is Brazilian, but the quality of the monaural sound recording is not bad, especially when heard with digital playback. The sound editing and fidelity is better than in many American productions. The picture has a static feel to it because of the film's budget, but the transfer is impeccable. The film is in Brazilian Portuguese, with English subtitles. The subtitles are yellow, and are a little distracting.

The movie could easily become a cult favorite. Its drawbacks include a non-American lack of squeamishness in showing pathology technicians dicing organs, and lengthy passages in which the director just points his camera and shoots the actors, using the dialog instead of the image to tell the story. But these are minor complaints. The film is stimulating, coy, and invitingly intelligent. It never embraces cliché or allows the viewer to settle on a single explanation of events. And last but not least, it rescues Beethoven's 'Ninth Symphony' from the damnation of *A Clockwork Orange*. Just exactly how that happens you will have to see for yourself.

THE MAN FROM SNOWY RIVER
RETURN TO SNOWY RIVER

The Man from Snowy River from CBS/Fox and *Return to Snowy River* from Walt Disney make a natural, thrilling double bill.

Although *The Man from Snowy River* is an older disc release, it stands up well in comparison to recent transfers. The night scenes have no distortion and only strongly illuminated wood tones have a mild graininess. The stereo surround sound is analog CX-encoded, and the sound editing is very impressive. The film is scanned and cropped, but that is the disc's only drawback.

Set in Australia, but retaining the genre format of an American western, the movie has adventure, action and romance in almost perfect amounts. The plot, based upon a ballad poem, has a great deal of background references which are used just to enhance the pasts of the characters, as if the film itself were a sequel. It tells the story of a boy who grew up in the mountains but must find work at a ranch in the valley when his father dies. There is a girl at the ranch, a wild horse on the periphery, and a gold mine back in the mountains. The script is a bit convoluted, but the viewer is bombarded with vistas and sounds and unexpected emotions. So much is happening at any one moment that no flaw, in the film or on the disc, is of the slightest importance.

Return to Snowy River is less elegant and more single minded than *Man from Snowy River*. The first half takes nearly an hour to set everything in place, and it seems to move slowly, especially when coming on the heels of the other film. The appearance of Brian Dennehy, in one of the two roles played by Kirk Douglas in *Man*, also takes some getting used to. The second half, however, reclaims the spirit of the series, and the climax is a perfect resolution to a conflict which began in the opening minutes of the first film.

The sound editing is as good as it was in *Man*, and the disc presentation of *Return* is even better, because it is digitally encoded and has a sharper, better defined bass. The picture, on the other hand, is a little more grainy, although it still looks quite nice. It, too, has been cropped.

MAN FROM UTAH & BLUE STEEL: JOHN WAYNE'S MOST WANTED WESTERNS
SAGEBRUSH TRAIL & RANDY RIDES ALONE: JOHN WAYNE'S MOST WANTED WESTERNS

Two sub-60-minute John Wayne westerns from the mid-Thirties have been put on disc, one to a side, in the wonderful *John Wayne's Most Wanted Western* series. Before there was television, many such features ran less than an hour and continuity was often not the first priority with the filmmakers. The movies all have the same cast (the leading lady changes, however) and use the same sets.

The embarrassing video marketing enhancement which has been added to the discs because, apparently, someone thought the double bills would be unsaleable without it, is a stereo music track. The substituted score only plays where the real music used to, but it sounds out of place with the otherwise raunchy soundtrack.

Part of the reason those movies are great is that they were very badly made. So bad that the filmmakers did not keep the camera stationary between takes. So bad that the shadow of the sound boom passes across the heroine at minute 15 in *Steel*. So bad that Wayne mounts a brown bull in *Utah* and is then seen riding a grey bull in the next cut. So bad that John Wayne's pancake makeup during his entrance in *Steel* makes him look like Lon Chaney in *Phantom of the Opera*.

Wayne is first seen in *The Man from Utah* riding a horse, playing a guitar, and – well, sort of – singing. He is enlisted to help clean up a crooked rodeo, from which there is a lot of extemporaneous footage to pad the plot.

Blue Steel is about a rancher who is terrorizing a supply wagon run so he can buy up all the land in the valley when the homesteaders leave and get the gold which is reportedly sitting just underneath the topsoil. Wayne plays a US Marshall. After crushing the rancher with a rock slide, he honest to goodness rides off hand in hand with the heroine into the sunset. Fist fights, quick draws, horse and wagon stunts, Yakima Canutt – what more can anyone ask from a movie?

In *Sagebrush Trail*, Wayne plays a fugitive from the law who, by outrageous coincidence, befriends the man who committed the crime Wayne was accused of, months and thousands of miles earlier. It takes the whole movie for them to figure out who is who and by then Wayne has also helped capture a whole gang of outlaws. The scriptwriters are able to utilize dialog with a remarkable economy. Is there room for Wayne in the gang? "Say, we need a new cook. The last one got hurt bad yesterday." In a rush to see a pretty girl, Wayne smacks his hand in some bacon grease and runs it through his hair. Nothing pleases women more than a man who smells like breakfast.

Wayne captures another band of outlaws who use the same hideout the first ones did in *Randy Rides Alone*. Here the criminal mastermind, who disguises himself in town as 'Matt the Mute,' chastises his sullen gang when they admit they were unable to steal $30,000: "And you call yourselves badmen!" *Randy* is actually the tightest and smoothest film of the bunch. It opens with Wayne walking into a cantina littered with dead bodies and ends with Mute Matt blowing up in a booby trap.

The prints are modestly ragged but always in passable condition. The sound is uneven, but has been CX-encoded.

A MAN IN LOVE

The actors in *A Man in Love* are better than the movie deserves. The film, about rich people who can't for the life of themselves maintain monogamous relationships, concerns a 'famous' actor who has an affair with an actress playing a minor part in the (really bad and pretentious – an impotent poet who kills himself) film he is making. Peter Coyote portrays the actor, Peter Riegert is his assistant, Jamie Lee Curtis is his estranged wife, and Greta Scacchi is the actress. They all have a strong presence and a confident ease with the dialog, so in places the film is engaging. The actor's spoiled seriousness is not appealing, however, and the actress's improbably mature detachment is unsympathetic (she turns out to be the 'hero' by retiring to write the 'story' which has just ended). The jacket cover hypes the film's erotic content, although the sequences are less involved than, say, *Don't Look Now*. The viewer is allowed a peek inside of Rome's Cinecitta Studios, but that turns out to be the movie's biggest thrill.

The disc has a below average picture transfer. The colors are fresh, but the image is terribly grainy in places. The opening and closing credits are letterboxed, but the rest of the film is cropped. The sound is stereophonic analog. It is passable, but the music, by Georges Delerue, is only a pale echo of his other scores.

THE MAN IN THE WHITE SUIT
(see **KIND HEARTS AND CORONETS/ THE CAPTAIN'S PARADISE**)

MAN OF LA MANCHA

Man of La Mancha has the sort of score you sing at the top of your lungs while riding a bicycle down a hill. So why cast Peter O'Toole as Cervantes/Don Quixote? He has a fine voice, but he is a consonant man and singing requires holding onto vowels, something he does not appear to have the patience for.

Had the movie makers attempted an intimate rendition of the show, they could have gotten away with the actors they used, but since they went with widescreen, they should have had singers with wide voices and expansive sets and costumes to match the delusional grandeur of it all.

The print is never faded, but it has marks and scratches and changes in contrast from one reel to the next. The print is also cropped and scanned, but the movie was so poorly directed that you don't lose much. The sound has a road show stereophonic mix. The most embarrassing aspect of the disc is the chapter markers. It looks like whoever did the markings plain fell asleep on side three, because there is just one change in chapters although several songs pass by both before and after.

MAN ON FIRE

Scott Glenn portrays a bodyguard in a mindless Italian production about the kidnapping of a millionaire's daughter, *Man on Fire*. The script is unbearably silly, with Glenn and the girl repeatedly comparing their own relationship to the portrait of companionship in 'Of Mice and Men.' Stylistically the film has a little more pizzazz, but since very little happens in the plot, the endlessly lyrical cinematography is clearly a stall for time.

The stereo surround sound is overly enthusiastic. The picture transfer is adequate and there are more chapter markers than there are significant sequences.

MAN ON THE MOON

Here's a great trivia question: What is the second thing Neil Armstrong said after he set foot on the moon? (Answer: "The surface is fine and powdery. I can kick it up loosely with my toe.") The hour-long documentary, *Man on the Moon*, consists primarily of footage from the original marathon news coverage of the Apollo 11 lunar mission. Film brought back from the flight and retrospective commentary by Walter Cronkite and Dan Rather are also included.

The program covers not only the details of the flight, but the excitement it generated, with normally cool anchor personnel becoming as tongue-tied as young schoolboys (the only woman to appear on the program is Mrs. Armstrong) when the Eagle begins its landing sequence. The documentary is an excellent depiction of the television coverage of the event, and therefore of the way in which most people initially absorbed the news. The basic technical aspects of the flight are recapitulated in a generalized, evening news sort of way. In keeping with the program's theme, Rather's hindsight summation is more interested in the engineering accomplishment than the scientific rewards.

CBS/Fox has put the disc in CAV format, with some unsteady still frames depending upon the source material of the footage. Although a fair amount of the images have never appeared on disc before, use of the CAV functions are limited. The sound is in good shape. Much of the earth-bound broadcast is in surprisingly decent condition, looking no worse and probably a bit better than it would have looked on televisions of the time. There are chapter markers, and a listing has been provided on the back of the jacket.

MAN OUTSIDE

Although the jacket cover makes *Man Outside* look like any other film which went straight from the editing room to home video without passing through movie theaters, the disc has many fine qualities. The opening credit montage is superb, and throughout the thriller, about a hermit wrongfully accused of abducting a child, the director, Mark Stouffer, demonstrates an above average command of the medium. He avoids clichés, uses clean, economic camera angles that actually make the film appear more expensive than it is (it was made in Arkansas), and helps the cast stay at ease with their roles. His script is also unusual in that it holds very close to an established formula, yet embellishes it efficiently, so that the themes of loneliness and entrapment recur in every character's predicament.

The disc has also undergone an above average transfer. The sound is stereophonic, and the mix is as adept as the film's other components. The picture is always sharply focussed and richly colored. Problematic sequences, such as visions of a fog hanging over a forest, reach the screen without distortion.

THE MAN WHO KNEW TOO MUCH

Alfred Hitchcock's first version of *The Man Who Knew Too Much* is available as a 3M Collectible Classic. Even when shown on Public Television, the first half hour or so is usually unintelligible because the sound is in such bad shape. On the disc the volume seems to have been pushed up a bit and the dialog is naturally indistinct, but for the first time we were effortlessly able to make out what the characters were talking about. Snobbish critics tend to prefer this 1934 version to Hitchcock's 1956 remake. In this one Hitchcock was still finding joy in the basics of filmmaking. There is a dissolve from St. Moritz to London at night which seems to say everything which needs to be said for the transition from tranquility to bustle. The film has more action than its successor but less psychological elegance.

THE MAN WHO KNEW TOO MUCH

Before color films were technically and economically feasible, Alfred Hitchcock would often share with interviewers his plans for making movies with more than black-and-white celluloid. "Suppose there's an incident in a film where one gangster wants to give another a signal," went his favorite example, "If he orders creme de menthe, a man is killed. If he orders port wine, he isn't. The contrasting colors of those drinks would tell the story." When color became possible, he kept to his word, often utilizing green as an indication that a character is starting to get into trouble and red when a character is overwhelmed by trouble and fate. If you think that the bus in the beginning of his remake of *Man Who Knew Too Much* is green purely by coincidence and in no way contrasts with the red London buses near the end, then you will be missing a whole level of humor which Hitchcock regularly made use of in all his films, his own in-jokes.

The movie is about an American couple (Jimmy Stewart and Doris Day) vacationing in Africa. Their son is kidnapped by international assassins. Day's performance often surprises viewers; not just her detractors, but those who are expecting her to do well, or those who have seen the movie before, can still be astonished by the sensitivity she conveys. The picture, while never faulty, is grainy and the sound could probably have been restored more carefully.

THE MAN WITH THE GOLDEN GUN
(CBS/Fox)
THE MAN WITH THE GOLDEN GUN
(MGM/UA)

The worst James Bond film, *The Man with the Golden Gun* was released by CBS/Fox as a time compressed monstrosity. MGM/UA released the movie properly, on three sides, but restoring the film's cadence does nothing to improve it. We recall at one point liking the movie, but we can't imagine why now. The script is dependent upon coincidences and absurdities in character. Roger Moore's Bond is a rude interloper who mistreats both women and children. Even Moneypenny dislikes him. Anyway, the color transfer on the MGM/UA disc is passable, and an improvement of the CBS/Fox rendition, although the film's colors are generally ugly. The source material has a number of scratches, and the digital monaural sound has no backbone, though it is improved over the analog CBS/Fox effort. For what it is worth, side three is in CAV and includes the theatrical trailer which has a crisper and better colored picture than the film itself.

THE MANCHURIAN CANDIDATE

John Frankenheimer is a wonderful director, but he has no story sense whatsoever. It is only when an excellent script is handed to him that he fashions a superb film. Fortunately, that was the case with *The Manchurian Candidate*. The film was instantly recognized as a brilliant work, but the story, about a left-wing slap face right-wing slap face left-wing plot to take over the US, included the assassination of a political candidate with a rifle, and eighteen months after it was released, the horror of the Kennedy assassination caused the critics, the public, and the film's producers to suppress the movie and its namesake assassin from their conscious memory. It has only been brought back now because the home video card was too tempting a play, and the film's fictions are now no more than vaguely historical.

The black-and-white print looks a little muddy, but is free of distinct flaws. It will not put anyone off, but it will not inspire viewers, either. The sound is also free of significant flaws. It is regrettable that the image is not letterboxed, since the dream sequence is the most effective when seen in its original aspect ratio.

The film runs 127 minutes and the CLV disc has three sides. Following the movie is an interview with Frank Sinatra, Frankenheimer, and screenwriter George Axelrod, which is more valuable for its assemblage of personalities than it is for any academic measure.

Only Frankenheimer would be silly enough to accept as a plot device that a group of soldiers have been brainwashed in three days (with 'drugs and hypnosis'), and that disaster is prevented because some of the soldiers 'remember' the incident. Yet that one piece of science fiction allows the story to exist, with its many layers of political and dramatic explorations. There is so much to the movie that has never been analyzed – the relationship between Sinatra's character and Laurence Harvey on the crisscrossed levels of class and rank, the use of images of Abraham Lincoln as more than just a prefiguring of the concluding violence – that its release is like the unearthing of a long buried scroll, a treasure which everyone gets an equal crack at. The film even contains a joke which is already on the point of becoming completely obscure, about Heinz Ketchup.

THE MAN WHO WOULD BE KING

If you've heard that CBS/Fox has included an alternate ending on *The Man Who Would Be King*, don't get too excited. The footage, which was used in the British theatrical release, is essentially a quick abridgement of the American ending and contains perhaps a second of material leading into a shot that appears on the American version. It is just as well that CBS/Fox makes mention of the addition nowhere on the jacket, though they ought to have provided a separate chapter marker for it. CBS/Fox has also made the side breaks on dissolves, repeating the disolve on both sides of the break.

The 129-minute film has been released as a 'Special Wide Screen Edition' title with an aspect ratio of about 2:1. Contrary to the notations on the jacket, the presentation is monaural. The digital sound is a little rough, though we do not recall the sound being any purer in its theatrical presentation. Likewise the picture, which has a dusty, washed out look most of the time. Although sections of the film look too fuzzy, most of the transfer seems to be a good approximation of the original. The letterboxing is wonderful, and brings all of the movie's glories into view.

There is one receding shot of an army strung out along a road which has not appeared in movies in a very long time. The image would by irrelevant if the viewer could not take the entire gathering of extras into a single view.

The Man Who Would Be King is a wonderful, spellbinding adventure film clear up to the ending, but even on multiple viewings the inevitability that the heroes will fail is still hard to take. Perhaps their fate is harder to accept because up until that point the movie has been so perfectly plotted that you expect the storytellers to pull one last, well planted surprise. They don't, but for those who love British India soldiering stories, and for those who get a kick out of Sean Connery and Michael Caine, the film has a crown which it will never lose.

MANHATTAN

"At the Producer's request, this film is presented in a full width 'letter box' format." Woody Allen's *Manhattan*, from MGM/UA, is not without speckles or scratches and characters on the edges may still be cut off depending upon how your monitor is adjusted, but the title was one of the first to be letterboxed and it was a gratifying effort.

At its best, *Manhattan* is an adept merge of comedy and disturbing emotions. The fancy widescreen black-and-white photography is used to trivialize the concerns of the characters, and this makes the sting more powerful when you realize they've been hurt. The story is about a writer who breaks off one affair to enter into another. At the same time, Allen tries to articulate why he likes New York City. His opening monolog, to Gershwin's 'Rhapsody in Blue,' is spellbinding.

So why, when he's gone through so much trouble to get the cinematography exactly right, does he not make the movie in stereo? On disc the sound comes through very well (much better than in *Love and Death*, for example, where the lovely Prokofiev excerpts are wrecked by the flat, scratchy sound), but it restrains the movie's potential. Allen is a great one for demonstrating that people sublimate their desires through contrary actions. By not allowing the sound to exhibit its full potential, perhaps he is doing the same thing.

THE MANHATTAN PROJECT

About a boy who builds a nuclear bomb, *The Manhattan Project*, has a little too much grain and the stereo surround sound seems a bit fuzzy, but these qualities are in keeping with the film itself. One of Image's superb director interviews, this time with Marshall Brickman, is included on an insert. The script is far fetched but the story is involving and fun once it gets started. The movie could have used some trimming and is not in the same class as *Wargames* or some other nuclear thrillers, but it is passable entertainment.

THE MANHATTAN TRANSFER – "VOCALEASE"

Despite their many accomplishments, the group depicted in *The Manhattan Transfer – "Vocalease"* has such an amateurish presence; they appear to be enjoying themselves too much.

The disc has five music videos amounting to 29 minutes of playing time. Each of the songs is based on an instrumental piece by a well known jazz musician, such as Dizzy Gillespie or Ray Charles, with lyrics added by Jon Hendricks. The first pair of cuts try too hard to entertain. One is a colorful but unoriginal attempt to make fun of prostitutes and pimps. The other is a black-and-white take-off on 'I Love Lucy' which doesn't get beyond the 'look what we can do' stage. The third number, however, is superb. In 'Another Night in Tunisia' the images are just abstract enough to counterpoint the music without distracting from it.

THE MANHATTAN TRANSFER – VOCALEASE LIVE 1986

The Manhattan Transfer – Vocalease Live 1986 runs 80 minutes. Nineteen chapter markers delineate the numbers performed by the group on stage at Tokyo's Nakano Sun Plaza Hall. The stage lights make the picture a bit too orange, but it is otherwise clear and sharp. The concert was digitally recorded and the stereo soundtrack has a minimum of noise.

MANHUNTER

A woman, alone in her house with her son, hears noises outside. She creeps into her living room to investigate the sounds. The camera moves parallel to her, and when she passes a divider, the viewer is treated to the luscious image of a tropical fish tank. It is a show-off shot, with the fish matching the outfits of almost everyone in the film, but it has meaning as well, because, at that moment, the woman, like the fish, is trapped in her container. The director is Michael Mann and the movie is *Manhunter*. Mann has this incredible ability to make form both lead and follow function, without going around in circles. In the spectacular finale, which is something of a plot contrivance so that the police can arrive in the 'nick of time,' the psychotic killer, who is about to do in his lover, ceremoniously, has put Iron Butterfly's 'Inna-Gadda-Da-Vida' on his stereo system. When the song, which is 20 minutes long, starts, the hero is still in an airplane. But through the magic of film editing, he is able to burst through the killer's living room window just as the guitar riff leaves the lengthy improvisational center and breaks back into the main theme. It is a stunning moment, and yet it all makes perfect sense, because if the psycho is the age his driver's license says he is, it is quite likely that he would still be playing that ridiculous song two decades after he first entered adolescence hearing it, and finding religion in it.

The disc is 120 minutes long and runs to three sides. It is a crime that digital encoding has not been employed, because the sound mix is fantastic and would have been well served. At several moments there are curious, single frame jumps, but these do not happen often enough to pose a problem.

The movie is terrific. The plot is so good that Michael Mann also stole it for an episode of 'Miami Vice.' In many ways it is a modern Sherlock Holmes story, with the detective using his brains to out-think the killer. It is not very violent, except for the final shootout, but you do not remember the movie as being cerebral after it is over. Mann has too much flash for that.

THE MANIAC AGE – YOJI KURI

An offering in Pioneer's 'Animation Animation' series, *The Maniac Age – Yoji Kuri* is 114 minutes long, in CAV on a double disc set. Despite the fact that every animated still frame which we froze was perfect, the jacket admirably caries a warning, "Due to source material used, some segments will not provide complete still pictures." The rest of the jacket copy is equally commendable. Although there is an awkwardly translated summary of Kuri's career on the back of the jacket, there is a much better one on the inside, accompanied by a complete filmography (though why couldn't they have asterisked the pieces included on the disc?) and detailed credit listings for the shorts which are featured.

Kuri's animation is like the interludes between Monty Python sketches, only weirder. There is a strong misogynistic streak running through his work, which may offend some, but his inspirations are diverse and intelligent.

Some of Kuri's earliest works represented on the disc are in black and white, but most are in color. All of them have been carefully transferred and the picture quality is excellent. The sound is monaural and has not been CX-encoded. Each of the shorts has a chapter marker. Three or four shorts appear on each side, interspersed with a video interview. Two still file collections also appear on the disc at the end of the odd numbered sides. The first is a snapshot album of Kuri's life and career. The second is a gallery of Kuri's paintings. The snapshots may be a little fuzzy, but the paintings look sharp enough to hang on the wall.

The best cartoon appears on side two. It is an animated contemplation of Hieronymus Bosch's 'Garden of Delights' called, 'The Midnight Parasites.' If Bosch's work was a depiction of Hell, then Kuri's animation is Hell on wheels. Worms crawling out of bodies, lizards swallowing people, hollow toads acting as carriages, and perverse renditions of normally private bodily functions: The images flow in a seamless nightmare of icky drawings. In one of the interviews Kuri explains that he intends his work to encourage viewers to think. This is an understatement, since watching 'Parasite' too many times could lead to institutionalization.

MANNEQUIN

The popular and enjoyable *Mannequin* actually makes use of two common daydream fantasies. One is fairly obvious, since the story is about a young man who falls in love with a department store mannequin that has come to life. But the second fantasy is equally effective, letting the hero and his enfleshed companion have the run of the store every night. They smooch in a tent, dance in the hi-fi department, and bundle themselves in furs. Escapism has rarely seemed so cozy.

The picture is sharp, and the many colors present in the various department store displays are vividly recreated. The stereo effects are not very subtle, and are often submerged in a wash of unnecessary rock music. The digital sound, however, does allow for a more effective management of amplification than analog playback can achieve.

MANON

(see **THE ROYAL BALLET – SWAN LAKE**)

MANON LESCAUT
Giacomo Puccini's crowd pleasing *Manon Lescaut* is performed by The Metropolitan Opera in a production directed by Gian Carlo Menotti. The three sided disc comes in a box and has the exemplary packaging common to all the Met discs. An enclosed booklet contains not only the Italian and English libretto, but an excellent essay by David Hamilton on why the plot is so screwed up (the original libretto had six writers).

The 1980 performance features fine performances by Placido Domingo and Renata Scotto. Scotto is particularly appealing, because her acting is as enjoyable as her singing. The picture quality, unfortunately, is aged. The picture has the green and brown tones of deteriorating video tape and shows distinct divisions in color only when the spotlights are illuminating a closeup.

Lescaut does possess one of Puccini's more tolerable scores. The digital sound, which comes exclusively from the live performance on 3/29/80, is in very good condition, and captures both the fullness of the music and the foot scuffs and late cues which can make live performances more stimulating than studio efforts. The analog track, however, is cloudier, and does not sound as sharp or as real.

MANON OF THE SPRING
(see **JEAN DE FLORETTE**)

THE MANY FACES OF BIRD
The Many Faces of Bird, subtitled 'The Music of Charlie Parker,' is an impressive and enjoyable tribute to Parker's art, featuring Richie Cole, Lee Konitz, Bobby McFerrin, James Moody and Bud Shank. McFerrin's vocal phrenetics are well suited to the program's format and provide a refreshing balance to the four saxophone players, who give fine but no more than vaguely evocative renditions of Parker's performances. The picture and sound are very good.

MARAT SADE
The value of *Marat Sade* as a film is derived from its significance as a stage work. The narrative depicts the inmates of an asylum, under the guidance of the Marquis de Sade, acting out the death of Jean-Paul Marat a few years after the assassination took place. There are constant asides to add commentary on the French Revolution and on the politics of poverty. The film takes the viewer where the members of the audience could not go, behind the bars. Even though the many closeups and angled shots of the film lose that aspect of the staging, the movie seeks to formulate the essence of the text and in this it succeeds. It is a record of an important play, and its value is greater than the sum of its cinematic attributes.

The source material, original production budget taken into account, looks reasonably good, though cropping tends to confine the image even further than the filmmakers intended. The sound has no significant problems.

MARIA CALLAS CONCERTS 1959, 1962
We dislike excerpts from operas because the songs, taken out of context, lose their supportive motifs. *The Maria Callas Concerts 1959, 1962* is an exception, however, since Callas herself becomes the context which binds the musical numbers together. The disc has two platters and comes in a dark box jacket. The three-hour program is derived from two concert appearances in Hamburg (in 1959 and 1962) which were recorded in black-and-white video on early Sixties sound equipment.

Callas stands in front of a German orchestra and sings an aria or two. She then disappears to rest her voice while the orchestra performs a famous overture. She reappears and the pattern is repeated. There appear to be only two camera setups. One is long distance to get in both Callas and the whole orchestra and the second is a closeup of Callas or, in her absence, the conductor. The primitive look and sound of the concerts, however, enhance the quality of the disc, because you really feel that you are watching and hearing something special.

She performs arias from 'La Vestale,' 'Macbeth,' 'The Barber of Seville,' 'Don Carlo,' 'Il Pirata,' 'Le Cid,' 'Carmen,' 'Ernani,' and 'Cenerentola.' The sound is CX-encoded monaural, but it has been produced with great care.

MARK TWAIN'S A CONNECTICUT YANKEE
The hour long dramatization of *Mark Twain's A Connecticut Yankee* classic fits onto a single side. It is geared for older children and achieves all of its special effects through editing. The program stars Richard Basehart (as Arthur, he seems to have the most fun), Roscoe Lee Browne (as Merlin, an excellent choice but he does nothing with the part), Tovah Felshuh, and Paul Rudd (as the Yankee, his accent changes from scene to scene).

The picture quality on the disc is bright and colorful, but the transfer does not appear to do justice to the original videotape recording, and images occasionally smear. The sound is not CX-encoded and is frustratingly uneven if unleashed outside of one's TV speaker. The disc is chapter encoded to set apart an introduction and epilog, presented by Bill Bixby. The program is more faithful to Twain's outlandish conceits than Bing Crosby was, but it cannot accomplish much in the hour format.

MARKED WOMAN
Marked Woman is a real fun movie. Bette Davis portrays a 'bar hostess' and Humphrey Bogart is a district attorney who wants to put away her boss. The transfer is fair. There are a couple of splices and parts of the print look a little faded. The sound also varies in intensity from time to time. The film has a speedy, crime drama clip, allowing Davis to spit out her lines as quickly as it suits her.

MARLENE
Maximilian Schell is not a professional interviewer and is unable to ferret much out of Marlene Dietrich in *Marlene*. An adept interviewer, instead of searching for secrets or insights, searches for subject matter (often lighting on it instinctively) which will cause the person being interviewed to relax and *talk*. The interviewer's job then becomes one of imposing discipline without interrupting the flow of memory, feeling, and information. Dietrich gets very annoyed at Schell for the ineptness of his queries and although he tries to pass it off as her being difficult, it is easy to side with her.

The movie, however, is much better than the interview. Contractually Schell was not allowed to film Dietrich, only to talk to her, so he makes a concerted effort to keep the visual material rolling while the interview is going on. Many clips from Dietrich's movies are utilized, but the selections never become monotonous; nor do they stand as a substitute for the films themselves. The disc is an effective supplement to Dietrich's movies and an enjoyable summary of Dietrich's career.

The picture transfer of the film to the disc is acceptable, understanding that miscellaneous footage within the film is inevitability going to be worn down or blurry. The break between side one and two could not have been chosen at a better moment, and the added pause enhances the film. The sound is in monaural. Although the jacket claims that the disc is CX-encoded, it is not. The sound recording has a portable feel to it, instead of a studio-type clarity, but under the given conditions one can appreciate the quality the laser playback allows in recreating the ambience and the limitations of Schell's tape unit.

MARNIE
The picture quality of *Marnie* is disappointing. The edges of the colors blur together, particularly on side one. The sound is acceptable so long as the volume is not pushed beyond reason.

One feature is definitely not a disappointment – the inclusion, on side three, of the theatrical trailer. Alfred Hitchcock's trailers are quite elaborate productions and his effort for this film has an air of desperation to it. The movie is much stronger on home video or in a revival house than it would have been as a first run feature, because the traits which Hitchcock tries to emphasize in the trailer – excitement, suspense, thrills – are what the initial audiences found to be lacking.

Marnie, which improves significantly with every viewing, is about frustration. It takes some practice to open oneself to these feelings without transferring them to one's opinion of the film. If you can maintain an emotional neutrality, then the apparent stiffness of the acting and intransigence of the characters suddenly disappear. One character describes a jungle flower which, upon closer examination, turns out to be a teeming array of insects. The image is applicable to the emotional states of the characters. They appear to be stable – even Marnie, who exhibits a strong willpower – but they are actually a bundle of fluctuating impulses.

Hitchcock reinforces the hidden instabilities with a heavy utilization of word play. There is the comparison of Marnie to a horse which pops up again and again in the film: She is described by another character as having 'good teeth' and at one point, in explaining to her mother why her voice is weak, says, "I'm still a little hoarse."

The point to all of this is that as you become alert to it, you begin to accept the sillier aspects of the story. You start listening to what the characters are saying and why they are saying what they say. The movie stops being a failed thriller with lousy special effects and becomes, instead, a two-hour fan dance where, straining and unblinking, the viewer tries to catch a glimpse of an exposed emotional truth.

THE MARRIAGE OF MARIA BRAUN
(see **A YEAR OF THE QUIET SUN**)

MARRIED TO THE MOB
A standard cop-falls-in-love-with-his-stake-out-subject romantic comedy, *Married to the Mob* was unaccountably a box office success. Except for the inspired performances by some of the cast members, particularly Dean Stockwell and Michelle Pfeiffer, and the lyrically filmed gun fights which are completely out of place in a comedy, the movie has nothing unusual going for it. It does tend to improve upon multiple viewings, however.

The picture is in decent shape with only the strongest colors turning blurry in the middle. The stereo sound is a little weak, but effective. There are a decent number of chapter markers, and the film has excerpts from outtakes during the credit scroll which answer a number of lingering questions about the order of events. One thing which bugged us right at the beginning, however – someone should have told the filmmakers that when members of the mob go out to eat at ceramic restaurants on Long Island they wear their suits over turtlenecks, not shirts and ties.

THE MARTIAN CHRONICLES
The fictional long form television mini-series, *The Martian Chronicles*, comes in a boxed set. The box is poorly constructed and should always be carried, after the shrink wrap has been removed, as if it contained a pizza. The program ran for three nights in two-hour time slots, which amounts to a little over 90 minutes of actual programming material a night. Each of the three 90 minute episodes comes on a separate platter, with logical side breaks and chapter markers for the points where a commercial would have been inserted. Each platter opens with the Image logo and the show's opening credit sequence, as if it were an independent disc. The first and second programs end with 'coming attractions' for the next episode. The second and third programs open with cumulative recap prologs.

The Martian Chronicles is based upon a book of short stories which Ray Bradbury ingeniously forged into a quasi-novel about the settlement of Mars and eventual abandonment of Earth. The mini-series, written by science fiction film veteran Richard Matheson, but directed by Michael Anderson, retains Bradbury's basic idea and a few variations (and simplifications) of some of his tales. A central character, pleasantly represented by Rock Hudson, is used as a common link through most of the stories. Other notable performers include Bernadette Peters, Christopher Connelly, Roddy McDowall, Darren McGavin, and Wolfgang Reichmann.

The production budget appears to have been stretched very thin. Although some of the art direction is imaginative, individual scenes often have a very blah look about them. The disc transfer is quite good, even though the source material and production environment is so inferior that the disc producers had to work hard just to keep things stable. The fleshtones always appear ready to dissolve or to flare, but always remain acceptably fleshlike. About a minute and a half of footage which was not broadcast originally – a night scene with Reichmann and Michael Anderson, Jr. – has been added to the second episode. The third episode is in the worst shape. There are speckles and dirt on the print, and the stronger colors look grainier than on the other platters. The sound is also flatter than the average mono feature (and the musical score is a strain).

The mini-series is one of the few formats where filmmakers can truly attempt a narrative with a novel-sized scope, real character development, and multi-layered thematics. Not every work, however, lives up to the ideal. Frankly, parts of *The Martian Chronicles* are plain ludicrous. The impact of all four and half hours, though, can leave a more positive impression. The stories are varied and are mostly entertaining (the Bernadette Peters sequence, for example, is far-fetched, but funny). When it is over, you don't think about the actor who couldn't take his eyes off the cue cards, or about the rocket ships that travel between Earth and Mars as if it were a week's trip – you think about Mars and about civilization and about all the things Bradbury wanted you to think about in the first place. He and Matheson were exploring the enigma of life by using fantasy to approach it from a different angle. As hard as Anderson and the demands of broadcast television try to force that angle back to normal, like the elusive Martians in the story itself, glimmers of intelligence keep peeking out from the cracks.

MARTIN
It appears that George Romero thinks a lot about his films before he makes them. Although the productions look inexpensive, there is a strong narrative drive which compels a viewer to keep watching, even when the gore gets heavy. *Martin* is Romero's variation on the vampire legend, set in Pittsburgh and concerning a young man who may or may not be mad but is certainly prone to murder and the drinking of blood from opened veins. The movie has a limited budget look and the feel of a loose production. The emotions which pull a viewer through it, however, are clearly deliberate and carefully constructed. Even the monotonous sequence which precedes the finale is probably intended to lull a viewer and lower defenses.

The movie looks cheap and grainy, although the source material for the disc seems a little more hazy than necessary. The sound is fine and includes an intriguing musical score by Donald Rubinstein.

MARTIN BRILEY – DANGEROUS MOMENTS
Three music videos are contained on the CAV 8-inch *Martin Briley – Dangerous Moments*. The first is about nuclear war, the second is about divorce and the third is about television evangelists. None are all too subtle and Briley, who wears a beret, plays his guitar and remains oblivious to the commotion around him. His music is not spellbinding, but it is re-created quite well on the disc. The picture is also sharp, but nothing on the program ever inspired us to manipulate the Standard Play features.

MARTY
The print used for *Marty* is full of speckles, breaks, freezes (which cover severe breaks), sound dropouts, and other impurities. Only the fact that the film is not cherished for its visual impact saves the disc from being a loser. The 1955 black-and-white monaural film has a couple of things going for it. First, the characters are so warm and amusing that they are tolerable company, at least for 89 minutes. Secondly, the manipulative script is funny and romantic, so that owning and watching the disc will be an easy way to kill time on a slow evening.

MARVIN GAYE
A fascinating hour-long profile, *Marvin Gaye* manages to convey the unsettled sense of purpose in Gaye's psychology while concentrating on his musical accomplishments. Mixing a few interviews with a great number of performance clips, the program is less disorganized than it first appears, tracing the many different musical styles which Gaye experimented with, trying to find the one that suited him best.

The many film clips vary in quality, but appear to have been adequately transferred. Songs rarely make it from beginning to end, which is the show's weakest attribute. One of Gaye's unusual successes was in the number of different duets he performed with female singers during his career, and these pairings are the highlight of the disc, along with Gaye's outstanding rendition of 'The Star Spangled Banner' at the 1983 NBA All-Star game. A useless medley of Gaye's songs performed by Ashford and Simpson is also included.

The stereo sound is distorted in places and the editing prevents the disc from being utilized as a greatest hits album, but many of the songs are in stereo and sound okay.

MARY OF SCOTLAND
John Ford's finest works were about the nobility of the common man, but when he dabbled in the common humanity of nobles such as in *Mary of Scotland* he was less successful. Katharine Hepburn stars in the title role, but even she has difficulty with the textbook-style dialog and the meaningless political intrigues which muck up her character's love life.

The black-and-white print has a couple of splices and looks a bit soft. The sound is set too low, and even when amplified the voices are sometimes distorted. There are plenty of chapter markers. The running time is a little over two hours, so the disc is spread to three sides. The third is in CAV, with two unsteady still frames out of every five and a slightly grainier image than the other two sides.

MARY POPPINS
MARY POPPINS (Import)
The picture quality of the letterboxed version of *Mary Poppins*, available as a Japanese import, is not as good as the scanned and cropped American Walt Disney release. The import doesn't look bad, but when compared to the domestic, the former clearly has more grain and less consistent color. Still, the 1.85:1 aspect ratio is wonderful, liberating the film from the prissy confines of the standard presentation. The opening credit sequence is freed from squeezing, the animated sequence gains significant detail on the edges, and the chimney sweep dance number, 'Step in Time,' no longer includes the arms and legs

of unseen dancers flaying about on the edges. Except for some closeups, the letterboxed picture composition is consistently more pleasing than the cropped image.

The sound on the import is digitally encoded stereo, but it is little improved over the CX-encoded analog stereo on the domestic disc, and in some cases the sound on the domestic version seems slightly better defined. The side breaks are clearly better on the domestic release (an earlier domestic release had bad side breaks and no CX), as the import randomly interrupts important scenes after the maximum of a side has been utilized. The import comes in a gatefold jacket and has Japanese subtitles set beneath the letterboxed image. Both the domestic and import discs are chapter encoded.

MASCAGNI – CAVALLERIA RUSTICANA

The lengthy instrumental passages in *Mascagni – Cavalleria Rusticana* give the director, Franco Zeffirelli, an opportunity to provide the film with a genuine cinematic feel. Not only does his camera explore the Sicilian village where the story takes place, but the pacing and style of the images are varied significantly, so that when the singing starts, the characters hardly seem locked to a specific room or square. *Cavalleria Rusticana* is a one-act tale of infidelity and betrayal (the history of which is described quite well in an accompanying insert) which lasts a brief and entertaining 70 minutes.

Mascagni's music is colorful and genuinely pleasing. The soundtrack was recorded by the Orchestra and Chorus of La Scala, conducted by Georges Pretre. There is no significant difference between the analog and digital tracks – both have a little extra noise – but the blending of the studio singing and location sound effects is quite good. The stars, Placido Domingo, Elena Obraztsova, Fedora Barbieri, Renato Bruson, and Axelle Gall, suit the camera as well as they suit the microphones.

The program was recorded in 1982, and the picture has a mildly grainy haze. The opera is sung in Italian and has English subtitles. No libretto is provided, and the plot summary which comes on the insert has some awkward grammar.

MASK

A depiction of the final year in the life of a young man suffering from a rare deformative disease, *Mask* is an acceptable pop entertainment gamble, but nothing happens in the story which can't be anticipated from its opening minutes. The director, Peter Bogdanovich, hurt his career by taking risks with the material he filmed. In *Mask*, however, Bogdanovich plays it so safe that he never steps off first base. The movie has emotions, but not emotional surprises and, for all its vaunted realism, very little insight.

The sound is not in stereo, but it has more dimensionality than many stereo releases we are familiar with. The picture is grainy in places, but above average overall. Cher and Eric Stoltz star.

THE MASK

3-D movies are like the effect themselves: their popularity is fleeting and they lack the foundation necessary for gaining widespread support and acceptance. Some viewers, however, are passionate about the concept and format, and the quality of laser disc playback will certainly add fire (in several directions) to their passion.

The Mask is an awful movie. As a theatrical experience, even a 3-D theatrical experience, it is a rip-off. There are only three 3-D sequences ("Put the mask on!"), totaling less than 15 minutes out of the 77-minute running time. There is the barest of a narrative, the worst fades-to-black we have ever seen (who can mess up a fade-to-black?), and acting which has so little dimension that you need more than glasses to tolerate the cast. However, as a disc, the movie is great fun, especially since you can repeat play the 3-D bits as long as your heart desires it or your eyes can stand it. The 3-D sequences are loaded with detail and retain their novelty well during multiple viewings.

The disc's packaging is wonderful. Image has used a gatefold jacket, placing the disc in one sleeve and four glasses in the other (you can order more glasses through your dealer). On the innerspread, there is a nice, thoughtfully composed essay about the history of 3-D movies, by Dennis Rood, and five groovy 3-D still photos. The print has a couple of splices, but the transfer looks sharp. The sound is also reasonably clean and efficient, though the film's own murky production standards leave their mark.

It remains to be seen whether color 3-D films can be effective on home video, but 3-D black-and-white movies, especially when presented on a high quality laser disc, work just fine. *The Mask* is in black-and-white. Rhino opens the program with a color 3-D sequence which is so bad it could potentially frustrate viewers and prevent them from enjoying the disc. The adjustments suggested during this sequence to achieve the 3-D effect don't work, anyway.

To get the best effects, wait for the first 3-D sequence in the film itself and then adjust your monitor to your satisfaction (don't worry about interrupting the flow of the narrative, there is none). We found that exaggerating red to the max on the color control and increasing the intensity of the hue control worked the best for us. It takes a few moments to adjust your eyes and mind to the effect – making partial 3-D movies like this one all the more frustrating – and something akin to meditation takes hold of you once you've got it. Within the image, you can focus your eyes on the background (assuming there is one – some of the sets are so cheap there's nothing behind the actors) or the foreground, and shift focus back and forth.

Now, this movie was produced by filmmakers who wildly adjust the key light on an actor in the middle of a normal one-shot, so why anyone trusted them with 3-D effects is imponderable. However, they use a buckshot technique, throwing everything they can at the camera, trying dozens of different perspective tricks in each sequence, and a good three quarters of it works just fine. The 3-D scenes are dream sequences caused when characters, "put the mask on!" thus freeing the filmmakers of any requirements involving logic or reference points. The best effects include a body falling through the air, a figure walking through a branchy grove, a woman with breasts which stick out like jello molds, arms flaying about, bodies materializing and de-materializing, fireballs, weird floating triangles, and wonderful rubber snakes.

To top things off, side two of the disc is in CAV, with no unsteady still frames. There is only one 3-D sequence on the side, but triple speed will enhance the vividness of the best effects, slow motion will reveal a clever, subliminal 3-D montage, and every still frame in the clip can be savored for all of its interactive glory.

THE MASKS OF DEATH

Have you ever noticed that American versions of the Sherlock Holmes stories are more British than the British versions? Americans tend to push the stereotypes to the hilt, while the British, as exemplified in *The Masks of Death,* remain, stereotypically, more understated. Peter Cushing portrays Holmes and John Mills is Watson in the 76-minute (CLV) 1984 program which has commercial break-styled blackouts at regular intervals. This is not the dream casting one would initially suppose. Cushing is actually portraying Holmes in retirement. He is aged and does not communicate an aggressive intelligence. Still, he fulfills his part better than Mills, who affects no attitude whatsoever as Watson. How is a viewer supposed to feel mystery, adventure, or burlesque if the viewer's surrogate shows no feelings at all? The script is potentially wonderful, with some good twists and a solid, exciting conclusion. But the editing lacks rhythm. Many scenes, which should enshroud one with the foggy chills of a good mystery, are frozen instead by icy chunks of flat dialog and neutral camera angles.

The quality of the sound transfer is standard. The musical score is poor and, as we intimated above, no one in the cast has much of a British accent. The picture is new looking and retains a decent amount of detail, but it has a red tint which it cannot shake.

MASQUE OF THE RED DEATH – THE PREMATURE BURIAL

Two Roger Corman films, *Masque of the Red Death – The Premature Burial* are available as a three-sided disc which comes in a single, gatefold jacket. The movies are from Corman's Edgar Allan Poe period, where he would take a title and sometimes a little more from Poe, add a star or two, and see who he could scare. 'Death' (88 minutes) encompasses all of side one and a portion of side two. 'Burial' (82 minutes) has its own chapter marker and begins on side two after 'Death' ends, before continuing on side three. Thanks to the Chapter Search function, there is no difficulty in watching the two films separately if one desires, but their appeal as a double bill is stronger, particularly in the case of 'Masque,' than their appeal as individual features.

The transfer is lovely, regardless of a splice or two. The colors are grand, especially the many candlesticks, which are all blue in 'Masque' and all red in 'Burial,' providing a link between the two films. Both movies were originally widescreen efforts. 'Masque' comes off the worst in this regard, since the image is often squeezed, but the distortion is not as upsetting as it would be in a more respectable picture. When Vincent Price looks taller and more gaunt, he simply looks more threatening. 'Burial,' has a gorgeously letterboxed credit sequence and then is panned and scanned. It is a sin, but the soul of the film is unblemished. The no-nonsense monaural sound is digitally encoded. A whirring can be heard behind the dialog on 'Burial' which is obviously part of the original recording. No harm is done if the volume is kept to sensible levels.

'Masque of the Red Death,' a slight effort about debauchery in a castle believed immune from the Plague, is cemented together only by Price's presence and recitation of the dialog. As an actor, his ability to convey motivation or emotion is limited, but his unrushed, serious, seductive delivery of every line makes the viewer believe his words to be more important than they are. Corman, with his handful of shock cuts, his love for exploring long, dark hallways, and his understanding of the need for balanced amounts of romance and gruesome effects, does the rest. The film may be a trifle, but it is over before you tire of it.

'Burial,' about a man with a fear of being buried alive who finds himself in an I-told-you-so situation, is a much better movie, and its position as the second part of the double bill is appropriate. Starring Ray Milland, the film has several nice screams and a few plot twists which make it worth viewing more than a single time. The disc is ideal for Halloween parties or as something you can take to your crypt when you want to be alone.

MASQUERADE

We always enjoy movies about rich people who try to kill each other, so we had a good time watching *Masquerade*. Others may be disappointed with the ending, or with the lack of a clearly defined 'story beneath the story' which mysteries are supposed to provide, but the movie has mansions, yachts, fast cars, sex, and corruption, and there isn't much more one can ask from life, at least for 90 minutes.

The disc is digitally encoded stereo, but we preferred the analog track, which we found to be more sharply defined. The picture transfer is passable.

MASS APPEAL

One of the popular forms of stage drama is to establish a unique situation and then peel away the layers of artifice draped upon the characters caught there. The end is supposed to reveal the 'truth,' usually involving psychological traumas and failures of spirit. This structure is nearly opposite of compositions such as *Hamlet* or *Macbeth*, where the inner desires of the principals are revealed immediately to the audience and a character's actions proceed to add – instead of remove – complexity. *Mass Appeal* does not work because you can see the playwright, Bill C. Davis, cranking out the secrets. It is enjoyable, however, to watch Jack Lemmon and Zeljko Ivanek engage in cerebral battles. Both give excellent performances and do the material more justice than it deserves.

The picture and sound are okay. Bill Conti's ecclesiastical score deserves a mention. The music – trumpets and violins pushing classical-like sounds just a little too hard – almost legitimizes the drama.

MASTERPIECES OF THE MET

The lectures which Philippe de Montebello gives on *Masterpieces of the Met* might make a few art scholars cringe, but it is an effective introduction to a number of artworks and should be pleasing to both novice and sophisticated viewers. A little bit of background and some technical information are provided for each piece, and symbolic interpretations are wisely kept to a minimum. Montebello himself is a bit difficult to take. He pronounces Van Gogh 'van go,' but he pronounces 'Renaissance' as if it began with an 'H.' At the end, however, he devotes most of his talk about a Rembrandt self-portrait to his own emotional responses to the piece. It is a daring and effective conclusion to the program, raising one's respect for the entire endeavor.

Thirty-one works, from all ages and areas of the globe, are given in-depth study. In moving from one piece to the next, the camera passes over and even pauses on a number of others. Montebello's talk is difficult to concentrate upon, not only because of his je-ne-sais-crois accent, but because of an insistent musical score, which intrudes whenever he stops speaking, suffocating one's alertness.

The picture, from a video tape source, is bright and precise. The cameras were brought into the museum and poke at the objects only from the angles available to the average museum patron. The stereo has no significant flaws. chapter markers are set for each of the thirty-one works, and an insert which accompanies the disc provides more information about them without reiterating what Montebello had to say. The program lasts about 90 minutes and side two is in CAV. At the end of the disc the thirty-one works are presented again in a still frame segment. Each is given a title card and a couple of detail shots.

MASTERS OF THE UNIVERSE

Unlike most premiere motion picture adaptations of cartoon source material, *Masters of the Universe* wastes no time trying to explain how the characters got their powers or what causes their eternal anxieties. Instead, the film starts out with a bang, a march, a thunderous order, and an evil whisper. It never stops. The program has been released by Warner and it is in beautiful condition, so even if you no longer play with the plastic figurines, you may still wish to consider the disc.

Dolph Lundgren, a short genetic distance from plastic figurineness himself, portrays the hero, He-Man. Although he is disappointingly oblivious to the large sword attached to his body, not to mention the beautiful women surrounding him, he makes effective use of the numerous ray guns at hand. The picture on the disc is so effective that Lundgren's chest remains golden bronze and never succumbs to bleeding oranges, despite the many special effects.

The plot is a loose adaptation of the quest for the Holy Grail, which the heroes eventually recover in Whittier, California. It is well paced and lasts for 106 minutes. A wider screen would probably have been better for presenting the action, as the cropping makes it difficult to effectively follow galactic conflict. The special effects are consistently excellent, as He-Man and his enemies joust on flying platforms above the streets of Whittier.

The soundtrack is marvelously silly. When He-Man is dumped into a wooded glen, the stereo suddenly comes alive with so much chirping that you would think he had landed in an aviary. The movie may be for the birds, but the disc is for anyone who likes to fly.

MATADOR

The sexuality in Pedro Almodovar's *Matador* is more serious than the other films of his which are available on disc. The movie has a touch of fantasy but is essentially a straightforward murder mystery buoyed by a very Spanish, thematic evocation of bullfighting. *Matador* is one of Almodovar's most impressive accomplishments because, stylistically, he integrates the patterns and strategies of the bullfight into his character blocking and camera movements. He gains such control of the concept that he is able to, at times, exaggerate it for comical touches without upsetting the dark Castilian overtones. Darkness and the comedy finally merge into a single conceptual entity at the film's end, when there is a deliberately symbolic but surprisingly well executed eclipse.

The picture has been slightly letterboxed, with an aspect ratio of about 1.66:1, and the movie is enhanced tremendously by the effect. White English subtitles appear on the picture. Strong reds – a major color motif in the film – have a tendency to blur and exceed their boundaries, but the source material looks fresh and the picture, on the whole, is stimulating. The sound is fine. *Matador*, incidentally, opens with a rape and several other adult occurrences, although most of the violence is relegated to the first twenty minutes or so.

MATEWAN

Although it was filmed on the cheap, *Matewan* could probably have received a better transfer than it has been given. The movie was made with lots of dark brown and lots of black, but whenever the picture gets at all dark it gets fuzzy, and the grainy image inhibits the flow of ideas. The movie is nicely scripted – a story about a coal miners' strike in the 1920s which is also about betrayal, courage, and liberty. The narrative is engrossing, and like the parables which the young preacher in the film tells his congregation, it can be mined for deeper meanings, but when a viewer's attention is distracted by the image, the Cause is damaged.

The three-sided disc is 131 minutes long. The sound is monaural. There is a steam whistle on a train which sounds more like a real steam whistle, more wet, than most movie steam whistles do. The sound quality on the disc is good, but like the picture, it often seems to fall short of perfection.

MAURICE

Although the jacket cover makes no mention of it, *Maurice* is stereophonic. The soundtrack, while it crackles a bit (the analog track is noisier, but sharper), is lovely. The voices have nice, rounded tones, and the musical score is wonderfully orchestral. Side one looks luscious, but as the film progresses, the image deteriorates and is often corrupted by speckles as well as grain. Early copies of the disc were subject to extreme manufacturing defects.

The 140-minute film has been given chapter markers, but the gatefold jacket contains no notation of them. The film, based upon an

E. M. Forster story about a stockbroker whose life is defined by the affairs he has with two other men, was made by the production team, James Ivory and Ismail Merchant, who put together *A Room with a View*, another Forster tale. It is true that the movie is not as stellar an accomplishment as *View* was, but then few films are. *Maurice* is surprisingly entertaining and, despite its running time, one never feels impatience with it. Ben Kingsley pops up in the second half with a marvelously witty cameo role. The film evokes its Edwardian, upper class setting with just enough humor to balance the lavish atmosphere, and just enough despair to balance the romanticism.

MAX HEADROOM 1 (Import)
MAX HEADROOM 2 (Import)
MAX HEADROOM 3 (Import)
MAX HEADROOM: THE ORIGINAL STORY

The first six episodes of the gratifyingly cerebral action television program, *Max Headroom*, have been released on disc in Japan.

The episodes have been released on three separate discs, *Max Headroom 1*, *Max Headroom 2*, and *Max Headroom 3*. The soundtracks are problematic. The music is stereophonic. Sound effects are relegated primarily to the right channel, and the principal dialog is restricted to the left channel. The digital sound is excellent, but the analog tracks are weaker. The image transfers are consistently well done. There is a softness to some of the edges, but as the source material switches (constantly) from video tape to film, the disc stays right with it, and you never feel uncomfortable watching it. The programs are in English and have Japanese subtitles which are discreetly shifted from the bottom to the side to keep them as inconspicuous as possible. Since there is so much text appearing on the screen via the program itself, you become oblivious to the extra characters rather quickly. Side two of each disc ends with trailers for five of the six episodes. The jacket cover designs are great.

Unlike films, which only have ninety minutes or so to create a universe, a television show about the future can take its time creating an alternate society. The world of *Max Headroom* may not be realistic, but it is valid, and after a couple of episodes, a viewer begins to recognize how rich the vision of the filmmakers is. A viewer will immediately recognize how rich the graphics in the program are. It is not just the title character, an errant computer program loose in the databanks of a major television network where his alter-ego is a street reporter, it is all the animation – graphs, maps, matrices, and even simple read outs – which continually appear on monitors or on the screen. The visual impact is so stunning that the filmmakers can get away with using a cheap street set now and then without spoiling the mood. The program not only looks like *Blade Runner*, it looks like it cost almost as much to make (and it has a better sense of hu-hu-humor humor).

Every episode manages to include derisive comments about television networks, political states, and advanced technology. There are also an unusual number of risque double entendres for a network program (albeit a last place one), but most are so sophisticated that there is a tendency to cheer when you hear them ("Very well," says the slick bad guy to the handsome hero when technical difficulties interrupt an interview, "Some other time, maybe, when your equipment is working...").

Max Headroom 1 contains both the strongest and the weakest episodes. The best is the pilot, 'Blipverts,' (The hour film upon which the pilot was derived is the version available domestically – see below.), which establishes all the characters and sets the whole series in motion. It is as exciting as it is complex when the reporter risks assassination to discover how his own network broadcasts may be murdering viewers. The weak episode, 'Rakers,' is still amply entertaining, about a deadly sport which combines motorized skateboards, jousting, and Freddy Kruger-style hand weapons. Although it tries to make a statement about violence on television, the plot is too contrived to support it, and the motivations of the characters are improbable.

Both 'Body Banks' and 'Security Systems,' on *Max Headroom 2*, are terrific fun. 'Body Banks,' about a wealthy financier who kidnaps vagabonds for the use of their organs to keep his mother alive, has a down-to-the-wire conclusion. 'Security Systems' gives Max a chance to romance another computer, which he does with his usual unique panache. There are some spectacular explosions in 'War' on *Max Headroom 3*, an episode which has a good balance between philosophy and action, as several TV networks vie for the rights to exclusive coverage of a terrorist's acts. The other episode on *3*, 'The Blanks,' promises a little more than it can deliver, but provides some interesting glimpses into the political structure governing the show's world and how it can be challenged.

The original hour-long drama which first appeared on British television, *Max Headroom: The Original Story*, was released on disc in the US. It is a TV show, but it is definitely a movie. The disc is ideal when you have to get a science fiction fix and you've only got an hour to be online. The visual style is aggressive and the narrative never bothers to pause and let you figure everything out. You can do that on multiple viewings. The single-sided disc is inexpensive, but it has more thrills per second than most major motion pictures. It should only be avoided by those who are more interested in the past than in the future. The picture and sound are good.

MAXIMUM OVERDRIVE

Stephen King wrote and directed *Maximum Overdrive*. He is conscientious about providing a logical explanation for the rebellion of the the driver-less big rig trucks against mankind. He compensates for his inexperience in manipulating suspense on the screen by utilizing plenty of gratuitous violence. He also has a sense of humor, and the movie would have been empty without it.

The film has an inexpensive look, but the disc handles the night scenes and darker sequences without any problems. The sound is CX-encoded stereo, although it is basically a mono movie with a few truck sounds and explosions branching out, and a music score by AC/DC.

MEAN SEASON
STREET SMART

Ethics in journalism is the subject of two entertaining discs, *Mean Season* and *Street Smart*. *Season* is about a reporter who becomes a serial killer's microphone to the public. The killer becomes agitated when the story makes the reporter famous. The film is a thriller. *Smart* is about a reporter who makes up a story about a pimp. A real pimp then finds it convenient to pretend he was the subject. Although serious in tone, the movie is a satire and is helped to no small extent by the witty performances of practically every actor and actress on the screen (except the star, Christopher Reeve). Although *Season* is predictable and comes up with no real insights or twists on the reporter's ethical position, it is exciting and enjoyable. Although *Smart* is sometimes awkwardly written, it is rarely predictable and adeptly manipulates the viewer's opinions. At first, the pimp seems like a sympathetic character, arrested for causing a death which was both accidental and justifiable. But as the movie unfolds, the pimp's true personality is gradually revealed, and the viewer is forced to reassess concepts of good and bad.

Both prints are slightly grainy. *Smart* is digitally encoded and is in stereo surround. The soundtrack is not sophisticated, but there is one cute, deliberately amplified effect involving a pair of scissors. *Season* is analog monaural, but the sound is fairly impressive. The soundtrack contains tricks and surprises, such as some toying with thunder and gunshots, and the film has a surprisingly tense and effective Lalo Schifrin score.

MEAN STREETS

The picture in *Mean Streets* has vague horizontal bars passing through it at one point, and the break between side one and two occurs in the middle of a romantic stroll down the beach. The pop songs on the music soundtrack come from real 45's and, thus, are naturally scratchy. The film was made back in the era of handheld cameras and unmodified interior lighting. Although the picture has always looked a bit rugged, it loses its impact on a TV screen. The cropping significantly decreases the feverish atmosphere of the film, making it less like an accentuated series of memories and more like an Italian-American soap opera.

MEATBALLS
MEATBALLS, PART 2

Entertainment is often a result of underestimated expectations. If you aren't expecting a movie like *Meatballs* or *Meatballs, Part 2* to be funny, then every third gag or so can actually set you to giggling. Of course, now that we've passed the word along, you will probably look for more in the discs than are actually there and be disappointed.

Meatballs, Part 2 is about kids in a summer camp, but it has nothing talentwise to do with the first *Meatballs* film. The first dealt with real emotions and featured an absolutely smashing performance by Bill Murray. In one fabulous sequence, he swings from being maturely sympathetic as he counsels a child who is intent on running away to being brazenly immature as he flirts with another camp counselor.

The second movie has no stars and features

a large group of teenagers well into their twenties, an alien, and the usual collections of pranks, chaste sex, and cross-lake rivalries. The alien, a stiff puppet with no facial movement, fits right in with the rest of the cast and has the funniest lines.

MEET JOHN DOE (see **FRANK CAPRA'S MEET JOHN DOE**)

MEET ME IN ST. LOUIS

Judy Garland's dress in the 'Trolley Song' scene of *Meet Me in St. Louis* is a different color in every version of the movie that we see. The color which we consider to be the most accurate is a rich velvet green. On the 'Special Gatefold Edition' from MGM/UA, her dress looks ink black, and only shows hints of green when the light catches it right. The picture transfer on the 'Technicolor Restoration' is good but not great. In many scenes the Technicolor source material brings out lovely details in the costumes and the sets, displaying the elaborate differences in shading that imbue both objects and flesh with the palpable texture that Technicolor is famous for. The jacket notes state that the disc was transferred after "A new interpositive was created by YCM Laboratories from MGM's original Nitrate Technicolor negatives." Some colors and some scenes, however, just look too dark. There are also segments of the film which have blotches, scratches, and similar markings, or look too soft, but these flaws are minor and do not detract from the impact of the program. Otherwise, the clarity and beauty of the picture transfer is satisfying.

The disc is digitally encoded and comes in a gatefold jacket, although only one sleeve is utilized. The monaural sound is passable and reasonably clean, but it has no particular thrust. The volume requires added amplification to be effective. Two supplementary pieces have been added at the end of the disc, a re-release theatrical trailer and a song which was cut from the film before release, played over black and white promotional stills. The song, 'Boys and Girls Like You and Me,' had a history of bouncing from musical to musical without ever making the final cut. MGM/UA had released the title previously, with a picture which is blurrier and much less compelling than their restoration effort.

MEGAZONE 23 PART II – PRESENT FOR YOU (Import)

Animation fans may be interested in a Japanese release, *Megazone 23 Part II – Present for You*, a science fiction cartoon which has been dubbed into English and given Japanese subtitles. The cartoon, which claims to be 'Original Video Animation,' was previously released in two volumes in Japanese. The English language release opens with a 12-minute summary of the first part and then presents *Part II* in its entirety.

The plot concerns the remains of Earth's civilization, floating in space in a huge craft which provides the inhabitants with the illusion that they have never left their home planet. The craft is controlled by a computer program which appears to the populace on television screens as a female pop star, the mood of her songs reflecting the needs and dangers of the colony. (Nice, huh?) The protagonists are an outlaw gang of motorcyclists and there is plenty of gory violence and even some sex (the hero uses his tongue when he kisses). The quality of the animation is standard – if it hasn't been rotoscoped, it looks like it anyway – but the beauty of science fiction cartoons is that they can always surprise you with a concept or a point of view which would be impossible to achieve with live action.

The stereo sound is not very elaborate. The transfer is okay, but the artwork has bad as well as good moments. One prevalence in Japanese animation which takes some getting used to is the utilization of brand name props. Members of the gang drink Primo and smoke Lucky Strikes. It makes their run-ins with metallic octopus aliens that much more fantastic.

THE MEIER CHRONICLES

An amusing spectacle is presented in *The Meier Chronicles*, in which 'experts' go at great lengths to marvel at photographs and motion footage of flying saucer models hanging from wires, and try their damndest to justify their conviction that the objects on view are not models hanging from wires ("The bobbing is due to the craft riding the waves of the Earth's magnetic surface, very much like that of a boat on the waves of an ocean."). If this sounds like fun, and we rather enjoyed parts of it, then you might well be interested in the superbly packaged disc.

The three-part program tells the story of Eduard Meier, an 'uneducated Swiss farmer,' the show explains in one of its many oxymoronic moments. Meier may be uneducated, but he speaks excellent English and named his children Gilgamesha, Atlantis, and Methusalem. He is also good buddies with the aliens, who have a direct line to his brain and ring him up whenever they feel a photo opportunity session coming on. It's an exclusive gig, however, because their Klingon – or whoever makes it – cloaking device is so sophisticated that they can show themselves to his field of view alone, while none of his neighbors are the wiser. But, and this is the part we love, *the aliens only let Meier take fuzzy pictures*. They are afraid, apparently, of the cultural shock they would cause if humans could actually read the 'Nuke the Whales' bumper sticker on the side of their saucer.

The four-sided disc, lasting a little over three hours, contains three distinctive sections which, because of their running times, tend to spill over from one side to the next. The first segment is a straight – and we use the term in a loose, curved space sense – documentary presented in English and produced by a Japanese and American crew. Collaborating with Meier (they never giggle while the microphone is on), the filmmakers present his story, going over his 'evidence' and how it was collected. For example, footage of a flying saucer model is shown being swung on a wire around some sort of tree. Then the crew hikes to the location where Meier says he shot the footage and look, with equal amounts of concern and amazement, at the spot where Meier claims the tree, which no longer exists, once stood.

On a technical level the documentary is poorly organized, making it difficult to understand who Meier is and what he has done, but the show is long enough that a viewer can eventually fill in the pieces. The second section is the most mind-numbing, an analysis of a metallic sample supposedly obtained from the aliens by Meier. The segment is presented in partial real time and we leave it to those who took metallurgy in college to tell us whether the 'expert' doing the magnification and electron microscope work, Marcel Vogel, is saying relevant things about what he has found in the sample. In the end it doesn't matter, since after the test was over and just as he was hopping into his car to rush the rock to NASA, Vogel put the sample in his pocket and it disappeared.

The last section, much of which is in CAV on side four, gives laser owners a chance themselves to manipulate Meier's 8mm masterpieces and decide if they can concur with 'Wally Gentleman, Director of Special Effects, National Film Board of Canada,' who is quoted on the jacket cover as saying that Meier, "Would have had to have a fleet of clever assistants," to achieve his images, something Gentleman assumes was, "outside his means." Yet there is the clip of the saucer 'taking off at nearly the speed of light' in which the ship is visible in one frame and not in the next. Because of the CAV still frame pulldown, severe movement is blurry while mild movement is not. Hence, a tree branch in the lower portion of the screen, which remains steady as the viewer ticks off the frames leading to the takeoff, suddenly blurs as it shifts position – at close to the speed of light? – in the same frame where the space ship disappears. In other words, Meier or one of his non-existent fleet of assistants ("Don't jiggle the camera, Gilgamesha!") shifted the view slightly when they stopped filming in order to remove the model.

The picture transfer is excellent, though the source material has its ups and downs. The monaural sound is often difficult to hear and must be excessively amplified. The disc comes in a terrific gatefold jacket which contains graphics that elaborate rather than draw from the program material.

MEIN KAMPF

In contrast to the jingoistic bombasticy of the *Victory at Sea* discs, the narration in *Mein Kampf* is sober and intelligent. The 1960 documentary presents ample evidence of the idiotic atrocities and the stupid, inhumane policies conducted by Adolf Hitler and his Nazi movement, and the script clearly states its moral that the rest of civilization is equally responsible for having allowed such horrors to occur, but the filmmakers know that in most cases the pictures speak for themselves.

One of the reasons *Mein Kampf* is so good is that the makers recognized their limitations. The German invasion and adventure in Poland is used as a detailed example of how the Nazis operated. Other major events of the war are summarized in a more brief fashion.

The first side of the disc depicts the rise of Adolf Hitler. The explanation of Weinmar politics is lucid and well organized. Not only are the political parties and their leaders identified, often with actual scratchy footage, but the forces behind the different parties are also explained.

As most of the disc utilizes historical footage, it is naturally grainy. One apparent error – the narrator claims that Hitler's right arm was paralyzed in the assassination attempt, yet from that point on it is his left arm which hangs useless at his side. There is a brief glimpse of Winston Churchill milling through the public during a political visit and the difference in atmosphere to Hitler's deathly cold charisma in a similar situation is striking. Shown only these two moments, one could easily tell who would win the war.

MEL BROOKS' SPACEBALLS
It is very gratifying that the jacket cover for *Mel Brooks' Spaceballs* says 'Spaceballs The Laserdisc,' although there is nothing special in terms of format which makes the disc a 'disc' and not just a movie. However, we have never seen a feature film which was so blatantly designed for home video consumption. Is Brooks not trying anymore or did he just run out of jokes? It is hard to say, but the movie really isn't funny. There is just enough concept in it, and in the gags, to encourage rental. You want to laugh at the thing, but ultimately, it just doesn't let you.

The sound is quite good. It is digitally encoded, and almost completely free of hiss. The picture isn't bad either, so the disc has got everything going for it except extended humor.

MEMORIES OF ME
Casting Alan King and Billy Crystal as father and son, in *Memories of Me*, was inspired. Not only are their appearances similar, but they legitimately represent two different generations of comedians. King doesn't show up in enough movies, anyway, so the film is worthwhile as an opportunity to watch him perform. The script, about a protracted reconcilement between the two, has some worthy sequences and some sequences which are more contrived. When the jokes work and the emotions are complex, the film is satisfying. When the jokes die and the emotional strategies are obvious, the film is boring.

The picture is weak, and strong colors also had a tendency to destabilize. The sound is passable and a listing of the chapters appears on the back of the jacket. CBS/Fox's normally reliable linear notes are limp, as is Georges Delerue's musical score. However, a theatrical teaser appears after the film is over, although it is not marked by a chapter and no mention of it appears on the jacket cover. The piece improves the disc, highlighting many of the good moments in the film and serving as a pleasant recap, especially since the film ends with a tragedy.

MEN DON'T LEAVE
The emotional payoff at the end of *Men Don't Leave* hardly compensates for the string of depressing events leading up to it. Jessica Lange portrays a mother who must cope after her husband is killed in an accident. The film is very well made and the disc has superb production values, including a crisp picture and an effective stereo surround soundtrack. The script, however, is dull and predictable, and clever surround effects are not going to improve it.

MEN WHO MADE THE MOVIES – ALFRED HITCHCOCK (Import)
One of the episodes from the Richard Schickel PBS series, *The Men Who Made the Movies*, has been issued on disc in Japan. *Alfred Hitchcock* has been put on two sides in CAV format, enabling one to still step and analyze Hitchcock's most notorious scenes. The clips from nine Hitchcock films are several generations away from their source. The color films are faded and the black-and-white ones have a blue tint. Scattered between the clips is a doting interview with Hitchcock in which he rambles through his repertoire of anecdotes without ruffling a line on his brow for thought. If you've never been exposed to Hitchcock's spiel before, then this part of the show may have something to offer, but otherwise, it is somewhat tedious. Other narration is provided by Cliff Robertson and all of it, along with the clip dialog, is supported by Japanese subtitles. The sound is of television documentary quality, so the richer Hitchcock soundtracks also lose their subtleties in the transfer.

The opportunity to obtain these sequences in CAV, however, will make this disc of interest to many Hitchcock fans. There is the Statue of Liberty scene from *Saboteur*, the full shower scene from *Psycho*, the attack on Bodega Bay by *The Birds*, the famous crane shot which goes down to the key held by Ingrid Bergman in *Notorious*, the awkward kitchen murder in *Torn Curtain*, the ugly rape in *Frenzy*, and the clever reverse dolly down the steps and out the door from that same film. Pieces of the crop duster sequence from *North by Northwest* are also shown, as are excerpts from *The Lodger* and *Shadow of a Doubt*. We would prefer that every one of these titles be readily available in CAV, but until that day comes, this disc will have to do.

THE MEN'S CLUB
It takes about a half hour to figure out what is going on in *The Men's Club* and about one minute after that to realize it's not working. The film stars seven major acting talents, Roy Scheider, David Dukes, Richard Jordan, Harvey Keitel, Frank Langella, Craig Wasson, and Treat Williams. The movie massacres them more efficiently than any little tailer. They form a coffee klatch to talk about how bad their wives treat them. Then they visit a whorehouse. Side one is the coffee klatch. Side two is the whorehouse. During the coffee klatch they decide to 'howl like dogs.' At that point we were howling ourselves. At the whorehouse, Harvey Keitel's character has a mock wedding with one of the prostitutes. By then we were throwing rice at the TV. The picture is blurry, but it looks like that is how it was filmed, perhaps so the shadow of the sound boom would remain out of focus.

MESMERIZED
Mesmerized retains its original title, 'My Letter to George' in the end credit scroll. Although the film stars Jodie Foster and John Lithgow, it was made on a small budget in New Zealand. It has a brownish look, but the focus is very sharp and the transfer seems about as accurate as the production will allow. The sound is monaural, but it has a fullness to it and is worth amplifying.

The narrative is about the circumstances motivating a woman to poison her husband. Loosely based upon real events, it takes place in the Nineteenth Century, and the stars are studious with their accents. The whole exercise would be dry and unrewarding if it weren't for Foster's eyes, which shine a bright light blue and captivate the viewer much more powerfully than in any of her previous films. Foster may already have a surplus of talent, but she apparently has a surplus of potential on top of it.

MESSENGER OF DEATH
The Charles Bronson film *Messenger of Death* is based on a legitimate crime thriller by Rex Burns, 'The Avenging Angel.' The picture is intermittently grainy and the Ultra-Stereo surround sound is too pushy. Bronson, who looks ill-at-ease taking notes, portrays a Denver-based newspaper reporter whose investigation of a multiple murder leads him to a Mormon cult, a family blood feud, a conspiracy to steal water rights, and other nasty activities. The plot twists just like a good crime story ought to, and is dotted with action at regular intervals. Bronson is Bronson, and even if he isn't convincing as a member of the Fourth Estate, it is doubtful anyone would tell him so to his face.

MERCEDES BENZ 100 YEARS 1886-1986
Mercedes Benz 100 Years 1886-1986 is in CAV and runs 53 minutes. It has only two excerpts of music, by Eddie Jobson, and is otherwise given over to the chugging and humming of the car engines and environmental sounds which are more realistic than the real thing. Side one depicts three present-day Mercedes models, tooling up and down an Autobahn. The camera and microphone move from inside the cars to outside, but lack sufficient curiosity to truly explore the design of the machine. At the end of the side, in English, there are statistics for each of the models printed on still frame.

Side two is a record of that ultimate in organized leisure, a road rally. Held in Germany, the four-day event lacks the bikini-clad excitement of the Pit at Le Mans. The soundtrack has no music. At the end of the side many of the cars are identified in still frames in English.

MERCENARY FIGHTERS
Boycott-conscious disc owners can afford to miss *Mercenary Fighters*, a South African production. The film, which has its share of gunfights and explosions, follows the Party line, showing immature, uncivilized Blacks fighting amongst themselves and portraying Whites as neutral, bemused bystanders who may be involved in a few battles but have no long reaching control over inter-tribal warfare. The disc has a solid picture, faded only by the poor contrasts. The monaural sound has a below average dynamic range.

METALICA $24.98 HOME VID CLIFF 'EM ALL!
Metalica $24.98 Home Vid Cliff 'Em All! is a deliberately junky-looking and sounding collection of concert clips which nevertheless sports such a sheen that even when the original image skips or jitters, the disc presentation looks perfect. The disc runs 90 minutes, utilizing bootleg home video camcorder footage and other stray shots to capture the heavy metal group at various concerts between 1983 and 1986. The color is faded, the image is more often blurry than not, and the sound lacks the power of a decent recording.

METROPOLIS

Fritz Lang's silent film classic, *Metropolis*, the story of a futuristic society where the ruling class and the working class are separated by technology and engineering, has been highly influential and universally admired. The disc comes from a contemporary re-release in which Giorgio Moroder has added a high-energy music score. The rock score whips one right into the middle of Lang's urban oligarchy. Even the silences, the pauses between the songs, are stunning.

Metropolis was a hugely expensive film, but Lang's sense of economy in film technique is what enables the movie to work today. Watch the editing the first time the lovers, Freder and Maria, move to embrace and kiss. Their approach and their embrace are opposite angle shots, an editing no-no which wrecks the continuity of a film by disorienting the viewer. But Lang's employment of it as a device to emphasize the feeling that the lovers are in their own world is immediate and completely effective.

Moroder did more than add music to the film. He located snippets of lost scenes, tinted different parts of the movie with different colored washes, and re-did the title cards, converting many to subtitles. It is this latter action which disappoints us the most (the sound can always be turned off). Of all the silent films we have ever seen, the *one* title card which burns in our brain is, "The False Maria!" and now it is gone in favor of Bonnie Tyler and "Here She Comes." It is like trading in an illustrated book of children's verse for a television set.

THE METROPOLITAN OPERA CENTENNIAL GALA

Both the sound and picture on *The Metropolitan Opera Centennial Gala* are extremely clear. The show lasts 233 minutes and has been edited from more than 8 hours of onstage celebration. The two discs come in a box like the other 'Live at the Met' discs and are accompanied by a valuable booklet giving a history of New York's Metropolitan Opera and details on the stars and the passages depicted on the disc.

Excerpts from operas are troublesome, because the music requires a context to be fully meaningful. The stars trot out on the stage in formal attire and sing one familiar aria or duet after the next. This would be dull, except that these are the most famous working opera singers in the world.

The performers, though they are not in costume, apparently must act in order to sing, and their expressions add some drama to the pieces. Subtitles are also provided for the songs and there are enough extra touches to make one believe that the disc is better than just a record album of the gala event.

MIAMI VICE

The picture on *Miami Vice* is crisp, the colors are bright and exact, and the sound is digitally encoded. Under the guidance of Michael Mann and others, the show brought broadcast television into the eighties. This is the pilot episode, which had too much crocodile and no Edward James Olmos. Except for the salsa and one Phil Collins song, the music soundtrack has been emasculated. This is because it would cost too much to obtain the rights to the rock songs which were in the original score, but the show definitely loses something when a two bit re-creation of 'Girls Just Want to Have Fun' lunges out in digital sound.

MIAMI VICE II – THE PRODIGAL SON

The opening episode for the second season of 'Miami Vice' had a better, more assured script than the pilot episode which opened the first season. It also had Edward James Olmos and no crocodile, but it is missing the concentrated stylization which made the first show worth watching a dozen times. The producers weren't selling a whole series with *Miami Vice II – The Prodigal Son*, they were just continuing it. No scene pulls one back for repeated viewings the way the 'All Night Long' sequence pulls one back to the first episode. The villains in *Prodigal Son* are more detached from the heroes and there is no interaction, just gunshots.

Both the picture and the sound are splendid. The color schemes used in the show are outstanding, and the laser medium conveys them well.

MICHAEL JACKSON MOONWALKER

The video oriented smorgasbord, *Michael Jackson Moonwalker*, contains a wide range of motion picture special effects, along with a study of Jackson's image over the years, a few coherent dance songs, spectacular choreography, intriguing audio effects, and a Pepsi commercial.

The stereo surround sound is appropriately over-produced, although Jackson's vocals on a number of songs appear to have been held to a lower-than-normal volume and are washed out by the beat. The picture is passable. In the extensive night scenes, the image tends to be a little grainy, and throughout the disc white speckles pop up once in a while.

The program runs 94 minutes, and the break between side one and side two separates a half-dozen short pieces from the main sequence, a model effects and live action effort. Among the short pieces is a Will Vinton Claymation segment which deftly merges animation with live figures, and a collage animation piece, filled with moving cutouts, set to Jackson's supermarket rag rag, 'Leave Me Alone.' The longer piece has a vaguely dramatic plot about a mastermind criminal running a drug addiction conspiracy, undone by a Go-Bot style metamorphic Jackson, who can change from rock star to *Star Wars* hardware at will. Like Jackson's music, the disc has a little something for everyone, modified so as not to turn off those who were looking for something else.

MICHAEL JACKSON THE LEGEND CONTINUES

Michael Jackson The Legend Continues is still an interesting program, particularly if one, watching the years and the hits fly by, has never really stopped to assess Jackson's career. Although the hour-long show is blatantly self-serving, it is difficult to argue with statements such as those made by Hermes Pan, comparing Jackson to Fred Astaire and Gene Kelly – if only success weren't discouraging him from performing more in the traditional venues! Every phase and accompanying hit is covered. There are plenty of choice film clips, interesting interviews, and chopped up singles. The picture quality varies but looks sharp when the material is recent. The music admirably ranges from monaural to stereo surround, depending upon the original recording, though it always remains a generation or two further from the original than one would have wished. The program is narrated by James Earl Jones.

MICHAEL JORDAN: COME FLY WITH ME

Michael Jordan: Come Fly with Me, a 40-minute profile of the Chicago Bulls forward, is the first non-fictional program concerning professional basketball to appear on disc in America. Few documentaries about sports are available on disc, and those that are issued usually sit on the shelves forever. Perhaps this one will be different because Jordan has a reputation for not sitting anywhere very long.

The program gives a brief biography of Jordan and shows footage from his high school and college games. It also surveys the career he has had in the pros, up to the All-Star game of 1988 where he was named MVP. The point of the video however, and it ought to be, is to show Jordan's moves. His turns are more complicated and organic than a ballet dancer's, but the purpose is the same – to create the illusion of flight. He must also out-think the anticipation of five opposing players, and the bulk of the disc shows him, in slow motion and at all angles imaginable, doing it again and again.

The single-sided CLV disc, which comes in an unusually bulky jacket, has a slightly blurry picture. Only the overbearing musical score is stereophonic. The disc also has a decent number of chapter markers.

MICHEL PETRUCCIANI LIVE AT THE VILLAGE VANGUARD

Michel Petrucciani's band consists of just three people. Himself, playing the piano, Palle Danielsson, playing bass, and Eliot Zigmond, lightly keeping time on the drums. The 53-minute set that they perform on *Michel Petrucciani Live at the Village Vanguard* (Jim Hall, with a guitar, joins them for one number) is a relaxing and quiet program. Although the camera gets very close to all the performers and is particularly adept at observing Petrucciani from several interesting and unusual angles, it is easy to play the disc without putting the TV on at all. The sound is perfect, the picture is perfect, and the atmosphere is perfect. It is the kind of perfection you can feel relaxed with.

MICK JAGGER RUNNING OUT OF LUCK

Dennis Hopper and Rae Dawn Chong appear in *Mick Jagger Running Out of Luck*. The 90-minute music video movie has enough class and enough sex to pass for a real feature film (it has even been given an R rating). There are eight or nine chapter-marked videos, filmed primarily in and around Rio, which advance a narrative depicting the tribulations of a lost rock star who is so far out in the sticks nobody recognizes him. The disc is digitally encoded and, except for a grid-textured background pattern which can be seen on the darker shots, the picture is perfect. The music videos are weird enough to stand on their own and yet logical enough to fit into the episodic story. One impressive sequence juxtaposes the architecture of a Brazilian prison with the architecture of a high class

Washington D.C. shopping mall. Jerri Hall is also featured, running around with spike heels and a whip, but that is Jagger's problem, not ours.

MICKEY KNOWS BEST/THE IMPORTANCE OF BEING DONALD (see **A TALE OF TWO CHIPMUNKS/THE UNSINKABLE DONALD DUCK**)

MICKI & MAUDE

For brief moments, *Micki & Maude* is funny without feeling labored. The print is new, but the color and composition of the movie are not inspired. About a bigamist, played by Dudley Moore, whose wives both become pregnant at the same time, the comedy ought to be a rollicking farce which moves so fast that you never have time to stop and think about what is happening. Instead it is slow and few of the gags work, relying on Moore's personality to fill the gaps left by the screen writers.

Ann Reinking, as a State Supreme Court judge who goes through a 180-degree change after conception, gives the movie its funniest and most touching moments. Amy Irving has the less believable role as a musician who becomes the second wife. The movie also has about three endings which shows that the filmmakers didn't really have a good script and were hoping that the concept and the cast would be enough. It wasn't.

MIDNIGHT COWBOY (see **RAIN MAN**)

MIDNIGHT CROSSING

That great triangular formula – money, adultery and murder – ignites once again in an enjoyable Sunbelt thriller, *Midnight Crossing*. Night scenes look fine, and the shots in the bright sun look more expensive than they are. The stereo sound is above average and worth playing at an increased volume.

Midnight Crossing is about the owner of a charter sailboat who is hired to retrieve money buried twenty years earlier on an island off Cuba. It has Faye Dunaway playing a blind woman, a number of good plot twists, and two terrific screams. The film's faults are insignificant – a little popcorn covers them right up – and anyone who doesn't enjoy the disc just doesn't know how to relax.

MIDNIGHT RUN

The director of *Midnight Run*, Martin Brest, was a prodigy who got himself into trouble making movies obsessed with death, and he didn't strike it rich until he played by the book with *Beverly Hills Cop*. He also plays it straight with *Midnight Run* and does a beautiful job with the fundamentals. The movie, a road picture, runs just over two hours, and could easily get bogged down at any interlude, but the pacing and the performances never let a viewer down. The movie is also a good opportunity to see Robert De Niro 'naked,' without the makeup or elaborate characterizations he usually uses to fig leaf his personality. De Niro portrays a bounty hunter taking a prisoner from New York to Los Angeles with every government and mob agency on his tail. The film is rated R entirely because of the off-color language, which is so witty that it rubs off all too easily.

The disc is a little disappointing. It has a crisp picture, but the flesh tones are slightly orange. The digitally encoded sound is okay, though the stereo is confined to the music and a few gun battles. The disc is three-sided, in CLV.

A MIDSUMMER NIGHT'S DREAM JIRI TRNKA

A near theatrical length animated puppet film appears on the Animation, Animation disc, *A Midsummer Night's Dream Jiri Trnka*, in letterboxed format with an aspect ratio of 2.3:1 and English subtitles, appearing beneath the image, for the Czechoslovakian narration. The film, 'A Midsummer Night's Dream,' runs into the third side of the four-sided CAV disc. Two shorter films, which are not letterboxed, round out the program.

Although Trnka works with puppets, the lighting and camera work in his films are comparable to presentations of the best filmmakers. It is actually one of the shorter films on the disc, 'The Song of the Prairie,' which shows Trnka at his best. The movie is a clichéd Western, about a bad guy, a good guy, a girl, and a stagecoach robbery. There is no dialog. While the height of the action is almost as exciting as the real thing, the humor takes unique advantage of the puppet format. The characters accomplish feats and double takes which only puppets could manage, while the camera angles and editing, by appearing legitimate, magnify the amusement.

The title piece is less accomplished in this regard. Although elegantly filmed, almost as if it were intended as test shots for blocking a live production, Trnka relies too much on the voice-over narration to advance the story. Parts of the movie are perfectly done, such as the 'Pyramus & Thisby' epilog, but long passages seem just to be logging puppet time for the sake of the sets and the plot. The widescreen will also cause some viewers frustration, even though the puppets are deliberately minimalist in their expressions. The scale is already small, and the even smaller image causes many details to become lost unless viewed on a large video screen. The last short on the disc, 'Two Frosts,' is dubbed in Irish-accented English, and depicts superimposed Casper-like winter spirits attempting to play tricks on rustic mortals. It is not as pleasurable as 'Prairie' or the best parts of 'Dream.'

The packaging is sloppy. The essays on the innerspread of the gatefold jacket, intended to inform one about Trnka and his work, are almost unintelligible, having been translated from Japanese with little concern for English syntax or punctuation.

The disc is analog monaural and has not been CX-encoded. The CAV still frames are jitter-free and are useful in analyzing the step-by-step placements of the animated characters. Even though 'Prairie' and 'Frosts' could have fit onto side four, part of 'Prairie' appears on side three after the end of 'Dream.'

MIGHTY JOE YOUNG
MIGHTY JOE YOUNG (Stereo)

Image released the enjoyable gorilla film *Mighty Joe Young* two times. The picture quality is preferable on the earlier disc, but the soundtrack is greatly improved on the second. Inflation being what it is, Joe is listed as being 10 feet tall on the jacket notes of the first disc, and 12 feet tall on the second.

The first presentation had no digital soundtrack and contained an alternate-audio track lecture, by Paul Mandell. Mandell knows a great deal about Ray Harryhausen's involvement with the film (too much really – one wonders if what Harryhausen has told him has been cross-checked) and is well informed about the movie's production history and aesthetics. Mandell's specialty is the historicai and mechanical perspective, not the critical. He points out every matte shot and explains the logistics involved as you are watching a scene, but is less adept at explaining *why* he likes something. The sound on the film's dialog channel has an unfortunate hum through most of the program. The movie soundtrack is suppressed on the lecture channel so that you will be most apt to turn the first audio track on and off between the gaps in Mandell's narrative.

The second release supersedes the older disc. The source material was the same for both transfers, as there is a splice at the same point in both versions. The new master is still an admirable effort, but the older disc has a much sharper and brighter picture, which makes the film all the more pleasing. The second disc has a poorer side break, which disrupts a dissolve, and uses a troublesome bright orange tint for the orphanage fire sequence.

The lecture has been dropped from the second release and the sound, which is digitally encoded, has been reprocessed for stereo surround. The film is given a more theatrical ambience by the audio improvements, and it is not disorienting to hear the original, scratchy soundtrack shift from one speaker to the next.

Mighty Joe Young is a classic movie and it makes for wonderful and repeatable home entertainment. One wishes filmmakers had utilized stop-motion techniques more often to show the ordinary, such as they do here, instead of the extraordinary. Whether Young is battling the cowboys in the beginning or saving the baby from the orphanage at the end, he is still an average gorilla and almost part of the real world. The transportation to fantasy is more deeply sublimated because the senses are not registering anything unusual. The pleasure slips past all your defenses.

THE MIGHTY QUINN

If you like the sounds of Jamaica – the music, the accents, and the atmosphere – then you should enjoy *The Mighty Quinn*. Its strongest asset is a stereo surround track which puts the viewer in the middle of the tropics. The sound is marvelous and the picture isn't bad. Although mildly grainy, the colors look accurate most of the time and the screen compositions are well framed.

The film stars Denzel Washington, who gives an attractive performance as a detective investigating a murder at a resort. Unfortunately, the story moves at an islands pace. The 90 minute film has 30 minutes of plot, 30 minutes of music, and 30 minutes of idle chatter. The music sounds so good, however, that with enough ganja you might not notice the flaws.

THE MIKADO
(see **YEOMAN OF THE GUARD**)

MIKHAIL BARYSHNIKOV'S DON QUIXOTE (see **THE ROYAL BALLET – SWAN LAKE**)

THE MILAGRO BEANFIELD WAR
Robert Redford's *The Milagro Beanfield War* is pleasant enough. Because of the many enjoyable characters (and character actors), it is an easygoing movie that still goes somewhere, and the repeat potential is strong. The film's biggest negative factor is the superficiality of some of the characters. There apparently wasn't enough time to show the private side of every player, since doing so would have made the movie meander even more.

The disc has an above average stereo mix, which is particularly strong on gun reports. The picture transfer is okay, but since Redford was trying to be winsome, too much gauze and haze were employed for our tastes. *The Milagro Beanfield War* is about an Hispanic American town rebelling against a real estate development, with a tiny bit of help from the local spirits.

MILDRED PIERCE (CBS/Fox)
MILDRED PIERCE (MGM/UA)
The picture on MGM/UA's *Mildred Pierce* has many scratches and a number of splices. The volume also seems to shift on a couple of reels. The black-and-white contrasts are rich, however, and most viewers will not be overly distracted by the markings. CBS/Fox released the title previously with a few less scratches, but it is darker and has a limited grey scale, erasing a number of minor details. MGM/UA has also included a bevy of chapter markers.

The film stars Joan Crawford and is based on a novel by James M. Cain. The plot is often paraphrased to focus on a single aspect of the story – a woman sacrificing her own happiness to help her ungrateful daughter – but its real emphasis is the standard Cain depiction of success, intrigue and passion in a seemingly commonplace vocational environment, in this case the restaurant business. Crawford is cool, but the production standards of the forties never could do Cain real justice, and much of the movie is spent telegraphing what can't be spelled out.

MILES FROM HOME
Bad socialist movies don't come much worse than *Miles from Home*, a timidly written on-the-lam drama redeemed only by some choice cameos by John Malkovich and Judith Ivey. Richard Gere and Kevin Anderson star as brothers who burn down their foreclosed farm and then remain steps ahead of the law by relying on the antiestablishment feelings of their fellow farmers. The script continually chooses the easy way out, even at the end, and offers no insight or variation that could help a viewer grasp a truth of the human condition. It is all headlines oriented.

The disc has an above average transfer. The picture suffers from a faint graininess, but looks accurately replicated and has no significant distortions. The sound editing in the film is simplistic, but the surround is effective when it is put to use.

THE MILKY WAY (LVA)
THE MILKY WAY (Image)
Both LVA and Image have released copies of the Harold Lloyd talkie, *The Milky Way*. The source material Image has used is a little cleaner and sharper than LVA's, but the LVA transfer has better framing and better contrast levels. The monaural film is digitally encoded on the Image disc and analog only on the LVA effort, and Image's audio is stronger and cleaner. LVA, however, has included a rare television interview with Lloyd. Although the picture is rough and the sound is under-amplified, the 15-minute piece is valuable not only in summarizing Lloyd's talent, but in giving the viewer a glimpse at the man behind the comic, who, middle-aged and semi-retired, seems at peace with his career and his art. He was promoting the theatrical release of the compilation film, 'The World of Harold Lloyd.'

Milky Way is an entertaining movie about a milkman who accidentally becomes a prize fighter. It was remade by Danny Kaye as *The Kid from Brooklyn*, but Lloyd's effort is a more relaxed and comical interpretation of the material. Lloyd mixes athletic amusements with an energetic verbal byplay. The cast is sharp, and Adolphe Menjou, who had no feeling for the role of a fight manager in *Golden Boy*, is wonderfully harried and devious here. There are a lot of silly gags, but there are an equal number of amusing antics.

THE MILKY WAY (see **THE DISCREET CHARM OF THE BOURGEOISE**

MILLENNIUM
Millennium is a time-travel tale, and the less said about the plot the better. We should note, however, that scenes in the beginning are replayed later on from a different point of view. The ending is kind of crazy, but the movie is real science fiction and the fantasy is so stimulating that the ending is unimportant. The movie was directed by Michael Anderson, and it is a distinct though not thorough improvement over his previous science fiction efforts, including *Logan's Run*. It stars Kris Kristofferson.

The picture is sharp and the source material looks fresh. There is a reasonably efficient stereo surround soundtrack.

MINDFIELD
The digital monaural sound on *Mindfield* is very poor – likely an accurate reflection of the film's own sound production – and the movie is confused and dumb. The sound is so dull that words in conversations just seem to fade into nothing, so it is difficult to concentrate upon what is going on. For all we know, however, the filmmakers planned it that way. This is an improbable story about CIA experiments on Canadian citizens to create assassins, and a cop (Michael Ironside), who is also one of the guinea pigs though he doesn't remember it. He also happens to bust up an extortion attempt which is also related to the CIA meddling. It gets even more ludicrous and ends in a stadium with every cop in the city, all of whom happened to be attending a nearby labor meeting, gunning down the bad guy. The picture is almost as dull as the sound.

MINGUS (CHARLIE MINGUS 1968)
A film crew who spent the day with Charlie Mingus as he was being kicked out of his living space by city marshalls captured a rare glimpse of an all too human artist succumbing to the pressures of daily life in *Mingus (Charlie Mingus 1968)*. A few performance clips and overlays are also scattered throughout the hour-long program, but even Mingus's most abstract chords seem tame when compared to the rambling monolog he delivers while showing the filmmakers his possessions and waiting for the outside forces to come and disrupt his life. His loft is littered with boxes and papers, and it is odd how his music, which is sublime in its pointed dissonance, can be so readily reflected in the random and unkempt mess of his off-stage environment. The black-and-white images are grainy and makeshift, but it is clear that the picture transfer is well executed, and the grain looks very sharp. The sound is so rough that it is oblivious to the distortions of amplification.

MIRACLE MILE
Miracle Mile is the closest anyone has come to imitating a decent 'Twilight Zone' episode. The less said about the specific plot the better, but we can say that you have to give it a half-hour to get started. Most of the movie takes place in real time, *High Noon*-style, and concerns two lovers who are continually separated during a crisis. The film will fill a viewer with anxiety, but it is a healthy, entertaining anxiety, the sort one feels peering over the edge of a cliff while a safety belt is firmly fastened to one's trunk.

The Ultra-Stereo surround sound mix leaves much to be desired, but the flatness of the audio is a problem with the source and not with the transfer. The picture is not exceptional, but it has no significant flaws other than some graininess during scenes illuminated with red or orange lighting.

MIRACLE ON 34TH STREET
The black-and-white print of *Miracle on 34th Street* is not in perfect condition, with speckles and scratches occasionally leaving the safety of the reel change points to invade other segments of the film. The sound is passable. The holiday classic is ineptly made, but the subject material overpowers all of its other attributes, and it was a sleeper success from the day of its initial release. The final courtroom scene needs to be excised by a third (the bit about the son of the prosecutor testifying, for example, could easily disappear) and the burgeoning romance between the lawyer and the little girl's mother seems to happen mostly off screen. But to touch a single frame would open one to accusations of humbuggery. It works the way it is, and plays like a happy accident, where mangled ideas and characters draw together and magically unmangle. Take Natalie Wood, for example. Her line reading is stiff and her precociousness ought to rub you the wrong way, but her face is relaxed and intuitive even when her voice is not, and her confidence is so regal that she becomes one of the few movie children you would really like to be friends with. It is clear that a miracle was at work when the film was put together, and its pleasures show no sign of abating now that the film is on disc.

MISCHIEF
The best movies about coming of age show the tension between young people of opposite genders who are trying to be friends. In the CBS/Fox release, *Mischief*, there is a gag

about mannequins which unintentionally depicts the bland personalities of the main characters. Some of the situations are erotic, but most of the movie is a dull, stereotyped look at teenage lust set, for no reason beyond the soundtrack score, in the 1950s.

THE MISFITS

Written by Arthur Miller and directed by John Huston, *The Misfits* represented the last complete screen appearance for both Marilyn Monroe and Clark Gable, as well as being nearly the last one for Montgomery Clift. The problems Huston encountered soliciting the performances he wanted from his cast have been widely publicized, and tend to distract critics from recognizing that Huston got the performances he wanted. Supported by Miller's insightful and poignant dialog, the acting, including efforts by Thelma Ritter and Eli Wallach, is spellbinding. Russell Metty's black-and-white cinematography is also captivating, and if Huston had to use long shots for Monroe in some passages, it was serendipitous, because they are the most memorable and striking shots in the film.

The narrative mixes together five characters, some who live in Reno and some who just happen to be passing through. Monroe portrays a divorcee and Gable is an itinerant cowboy. Although burnt out, both exude a sexual magnetism which makes today's yuppie stars seem frostbitten, and the current is further magnified by Alex North's dynamic score. One of the film's principal motifs is the use of animals as a representation of human desires, an effect which Huston employs with wonderful wit and restraint. The specific plot moves the characters from one place to the next (the film never feels like a play) as they become further removed from civilization and its spiritual trappings.

Although the source material is not in perfect condition, the picture transfer looks fine. Some shots are blurry for effect, but others look oddly smeared. Most of the time the picture is sharp and the contrasts are accurate. The digitally encoded monaural sound is good enough to support North's score with decent amplification. The disc runs a couple minutes over two hours and is spread to three sides, in CLV.

MISS FIRECRACKER

A tolerable Beth Henley play becomes a very entertaining movie, *Miss Firecracker*, thanks to a super performance by Mary Steenburgen and nearly as satisfying turns by Holly Hunter, Alfre Woodard, and Tim Robbins. The Fourth of July beauty contest in Yazoo, Mississippi, which inspires the title, is only a fuse that keeps the narrative popping. The central drama concerns the relationship between a young woman and her two cousins. Their emotional conflicts are realistically trite, but the script manages to be wacky enough to make realism seem amusing. Steenburgen, as a former beauty queen returning for the ceremonies, is so exquisitely smoothed over in her mannerisms that the bon mots imbedded in her dialog become comical land mines.

The picture looks excessively grainy. The colors are accurate but the most intense hues appear blurry. The stereo surround sound is adequate, but the mix is generally uninteresting.

MISS SADIE THOMPSON

The performance Rita Hayworth gives in *Miss Sadie Thompson* is amazing. Her own stellar persona is completely suppressed, and is replaced by a well constructed dramatic personality, a carefree woman with a dark past. The story, based upon a W. Somerset Maugham tale, takes place on a Pacific Island, where an influential figure interferes in the woman's travel plans after she makes friends with some local Marines. The drama has Maugham's sensible plot development and avoids steering characters in the most obvious directions. It is relaxed and lacks real momentum, but there is enough conflict to keep a viewer interested.

The picture is a little soft and lacks the Technicolor gusto of an original theatrical release. The source material is in acceptable condition for viewers who do not demand precision, and the colors are accomplished enough to give hints at how much better they might have been. The sound is a little rough as well, but has no problems which can't be anticipated by the film's age. The music and some of the higher pitched conversations tend to go fuzzy at peak moments. There are a number of songs in the film and Hayworth's lip syncing is often badly out of synch.

MISSING IN ACTION

The title, *Missing in Action*, fairly well describes Chuck Norris's career as an actor. He is moderately comfortable when running, jumping, hitting, and shooting, but so leadenly uncomfortable when trying to recite dialog that his personality completely disappears. The film is a cheap mess, from the lousy film stock and makeshift score to the Philippine locations which are supposed to represent Bangkok and Vietnam even though every sign you see is written in Spanish. The story has Norris, a recent POW/MIA, return to Vietnam as part of a US diplomatic negotiating party. He slips away from his hotel one night, murders a couple of citizens, and then takes off to organize a one-man rescue of some other MIAs. It works because it is too exploitive to stop and think about the issues. Unlike other famous non-actor actors, Norris doesn't care and he doesn't pretend.

The transfer captures the colors accurately. The sound is uninteresting, and an attempt to imitate *Apocalypse Now*'s one-side-of-your-room-to-the-other helicopter fly-by in monaural is a joke.

MISSING IN ACTION 2 THE BEGINNING

Recalling that *Missing in Action* began with Chuck Norris as a former MIA returning to Vietnam to negotiate the release of other MIAs, *Missing in Action 2 The Beginning* is intended to be the story of his first incarceration. As a basic escape picture, the movie has enough action to be entertaining and unlike the other *Missing* film, Norris is not asked to do more acting than he is capable of. Filmed with cheap stock, on St. Kitts, it is monaural and the sound levels in the movie were often all wrong. Every mistake has been preserved with wonderful fidelity.

MISSING PERSONS – SURRENDER YOUR HEART

The utility of the 8-inch disc is greatly evident provided the price remains reasonable. *Missing Persons – Surrender Your Heart* has three typical music videos and would certainly be the disc to acquire if you wanted just one example of what music videos are like. The disc does have a flaw imbedded in the transfer, which causes it to hiccup, but this should not temper enthusiasm for the otherwise well-produced disc.

It is the fourth number, 'Surrender Your Heart,' which is out of the ordinary. The song is nothing special, but the graphics have been done by Peter Max and are the most colorful five minutes you have ever seen on your television set. Bright basic colors, pastel swirls, squiggles, dots, squares, and a little beating red heart. You won't believe your television set is capable of reproducing colors such as these – until you see it. At ten dollars, anyone who owns a color television should buy this disc, just to show off.

THE MISSION
THE MISSION (Import)

Two versions of *The Mission* are available on disc. The American version has been released by Warner with digital sound and numerous chapter markers. The Japanese import version does not have chapter markers, but it does have digital encoding, includes the film's trailer, and is letterboxed. Contrary to expectations, however, the Warners release is unquestionably the better disc.

The primary reason for this will be apparent to anyone who compares the two transfers. Warner has done a superb job, not only in utilizing unspoiled source material, but in assuring a consistent and vivid quality of color. The color on the Japanese disc often looks too awash with a single hue, and occasionally falls victim to a noticeable green or red shift. If that weren't enough, the sound on the Warner release is also stronger and much better defined than the sound on the Japanese offering. The opening and closing kettle drums vibrate through your insides on the American disc; on the Japanese, they sound more like cymbals.

We normally prefer to see a film on video presented in its original aspect ratio. The cropping on the Warners disc does not improve the presentation, but it is not a detriment, either. There are only a handful of shots which convey more information in the widescreen than on the cropped screen, and with the lousy contrasts on the Japanese disc, more is lost in the dark than is added on the edges. About the only good thing we have to say concerning the Japanese disc is that we enjoyed the trailer.

Warner has done such a good job with the American release that the movie may find a few converts because of it. The film is imperfectly made, with scenes occasionally beginning too late or ending too early, but it has much to teach. The story is about the role which the Church played in the division of land between Portuguese and Spanish settlers on the Brazilian and Argentine frontier. Surprisingly, the Spanish preferred Portuguese rule, since the latter tolerated slavery. The Church hierarchy was forced to look the other way to protect their diminishing power in Europe, and the drama of the film comes from the only ones left to protest, the Jesuit missionaries. The concept of the Church as a 'nation' which exists inside but independently of other nations – much in the way that multinational corporations do today – has rarely been presented so clearly. If the movie seemed a little drawn out in a theater, it is more captivating in a home environment. Thanks to the disc, both the picture and the sound are stunning, and lower one's resistance to drama.

MISSION BATANGAS

The CX-encoding on the monaural *Mission Batangas* does not have automatic tripping. No matter, for it would take more than CX-encoding to disguise the poor production values which pasted this 1969 feature together. The sound magnifies how badly it was recorded in the first place, just as the pretty picture (the print obviously hasn't been used much in the last 16 years) makes the errors in the cinematography so easy to spot. The night scenes, for instance, look like they were filmed at noon.

Vera Miles and Dennis Weaver put in professional performances and the presence of Miles is probably the one pleasurable aspect to the film. Weaver portrays a pilot who contracts with Miles and a group of Philippine soldiers during the early days of WWII to transverse a jungle and fly out an airplane which will then be used to bomb a barge laden with gold. They are pursued by Japanese soldiers and stock war footage every step of the way. The drama has a decent pace to it, but the last shot of Miles superimposed in the sky as Weaver may or may not be crashing is a howler.

MISSION MANILA

The bad guy ties the heroine to a train track in *Mission Manila*, a supposedly serious action film about drug deals and betrayals in the Philippines. It is difficult to take anything seriously in the movie after the train track scene, but then the play acting leading up to it isn't all that easy to accept, either. The plot has twists but no turns. The picture is dark and blurry. The sound has limited separation effects and the dialog is often difficult to make out.

MISSISSIPPI BURNING

The cinematography in *Mississippi Burning* has a softness which could easily deteriorate during a video transfer, but the image on the disc is solid and commendable. The many difficult filter shots and night scenes are preserved without distortion of color. The digital surround sound is deliberately fuzzy, an intentional effect which prevents the viewer peaking before the two hour and seven minute drama is completed. Key pieces of dialog, however, are sometimes difficult to ascertain. The disc is presented on three sides, in CLV.

Much has been written to confirm the film's lack of historical – and by extension, moral – validity. However, the movie is also plain entertaining, and if the filmmakers are patronizing sensitive issues in order to achieve certain effects, it is their right to choose a point of view. The appeal of *Mississippi Burning* is in the procedural aspects of the investigation – into the disappearance of three civil rights advocates during the early sixties in the deep South – and the conflict in personality between the two primary investigators. The opportunity to watch Gene Hackman, unrushed, let out his character's personality a small piece at a time, is reason enough to see the film.

MOBY DICK

John Huston's *Moby Dick* is a good Cliff Notes-type summary of Herman Melville's plot and themes. The script was written by Ray Bradbury and it manages to present the story in a dramatic form, implying, but sacrificing, the thoroughness with which Melville approached his subject.

The opening line, "Call me Ishmael," ought to be a throwaway, as if it were the smallest, most unimportant sentence in the book. Instead, Richard Basehart booms it out as if he were reading Genesis to an auditorium. Gregory Peck, as Captain Ahab, looks too much like Abraham Lincoln, and we don't get to see his peg leg enough, but his obsession gradually becomes the moving force of the story.

The film is entertaining. It works just as well as a *Jaws* monster-type story than as a comparison of the moral conflicts in the soul and the drives which push men into sin. The disc is impressive. The sound is 1955 monaural, but the print is fresh and colorful. When 'The End' appears in that crazy typescript you may feel that the filmmakers still haven't decided on a direction or point of view.

THE MODERNS

In the opening cafe sequence of *The Moderns*, Mark Isham's soft, jazzy score plays as the camera moves through the milieu. Everything is stereophonic, and as the historical figures mingle with the fictional characters in the film, one becomes aware of the music and especially of the vibraphone, which almost exists separately from the other instruments. It is as if every tone the instrument sounds is denoting another larger-than-life manifestation.

Alan Rudolph's movie is full of nice touches like that. It never becomes the epic of Paris in the twenties that the opening seems to be promising, but it is still a cute little film, rich in atmosphere, romance, and art. Flesh is sometimes too orange, some of the darkest scenes look grainy, and other passages are not perfectly focussed, but most viewers will not be distracted by the imperfections. The stereo sound is great, and Rudolph's aggressive sound editing is a lot of fun. The 127-minute film comes on three sides and is in CLV.

MODEST MOUSSORSKY'S BORIS GODUNOV

Modest Moussorsky's Boris Godunov, another Russian film from the post-Stalinist cultural thaw, is an interesting and occasionally compelling film. It is in color, which looks both rich and archaic, although some reels are more faded than others. The opera is sung in Russian and the film has English subtitles.

Alexander Pirogov has the title role, but it is difficult to tell whether it is his own performance or the fifties monaural recording which makes him sound flat and unmelodious. The orchestral score also sounds tinny in places, but some of the supporting singers are quite good. The movie is not completely lacking in technique. There are some intriguing shots, particularly when the director moves heads or faces directly in front of the camera. Also unusually effective are the cuts between the soundstage shots and the outdoor scenes – the difference is so pronounced it is invigorating. The film presents the opera with some flourish, but it remains stagebound.

MON ONCLE (Embassy)
MON ONCLE (Voyager)

Embassy has a warning on the jacket cover about having used "the finest materials in the world" to master *Mon Oncle*, so you can bet the quality of the print is erratic. The color changes a little from reel to reel. Some parts have browned perceptively while others still retain the bright vegetable colors of the original. The sound is also pretty scratchy.

Using the same master, Voyager did a much beeter job. The Embassy version is horribly pale and misguided when compared to Voyager's effort. The fleshtones on the Voyager version are rich and genuine, and the toy-like colors in the film are vivid. The presentation increases the viewer's concentration and enjoyment, and provides improved aesthetic pleasures as well.

Voyager's disc has digitally encoded monaural sound, though the movie's recording environment prevents the audio from being amplified too greatly. Voyager has also left the exit music intact, which Embassy truncated as soon as the picture faded out. Voyager has done an admirable job chapter encoding the film's episodes, but the chapter descriptions and the jacket essay leave much to be desired.

The Jacques Tati film is almost a necessity for anyone who wants a decent disc library. It is a comedy about objects and characters, set in a suburban environment. You can spin the disc up, scan or chapter jump to any segment, and just watch Tati for ten or fifteen minutes to reclaim a proper perspective on the pressures of existence. Scientists have recently discovered that the structure of chaos may contain the meanings of existence (they have even given it its own constant, three point something), but Tati was onto it a long time ago. The screen is usually so crammed with jokes that you have to watch the disc several times just to get everything in. It is a shame that the edges are cropped. The dialog is in French with English subtitles, but little of it is important and none of it appears very often. The sound effects, on the other hand, are flagrantly amusing and should be savored, scratches and all.

MONA LISA

The script for *Mona Lisa* is a bare trifle, about an aging hood working as a driver and beard for a high class call girl. With Bob Hoskins portraying the driver, however, the movie is both fascinating and magnetic. Hoskins uses his whole body when he is acting – every limb seems to give insight to his character – but he never overplays his part. You can't stop watching him, but he doesn't block your view or distract from what is going on. As his character shifts from a comical awkwardness in the beginning to being efficiently heroic at the end, the emotional impact of his presence intensifies and is never sacrificed to his actions. You not only can tell what he is thinking, you can tell what he is feeling, and when his impulses conflict, you feel it yourself.

The disc has a decent looking picture and an acceptable soundtrack. As Hoskins wanders through London's red light district on errands, even the most intense crimson hues come across with no more than a mild grain. Image has included a jacket insert featuring an interview with the director, Neil Jordan.

THE MONEY PIT
In the spirit of the film itself, the audio channels on *The Money Pit* are reversed. The movie is about how everything can fall apart and it has a wonderful romantic moral, "If the foundation is okay...then everything else can be fixed." Too bad 'everything' didn't include making the sound of the train come from the left and go to the right, the way its image moves. The picture is also a little blurry.

But one cannot dismiss the disc so easily. The film was directed by Richard Benjamin, but the hand of executive producer Steven Spielberg is very obvious in the Rube Goldberg stunts and the elongated linear gags, such as when the bad wire in the kitchen catches on fire at the switch and travels methodically and inevitably to the television on the far counter. It is a movie which becomes more humorous the more times it is viewed. If you invite friends over, you can make a game out of the audio problem by seeing who can spot the most errors.

THE MONKEES
THE MONKEES VOLUME 2
Four episodes of the *Help!*-inspired half hour television series from the sixties, *The Monkees*, have been released on two single sided CLV discs. The show was created by Bob Rafelson, who directed both of the episodes on the first disc, *The Monkees*. Included are 'Monkee vs. Machine' (about a computer in a toy company) and 'Don't Look a Gift Horse in the Mouth' (about finding a home for a horse). Rafelson kept the pace moving so quickly that nothing registers for very long except the carefree and energetic nature of the show itself. James Frawley directed the two episodes on *The Monkees Volume 2*, 'Dance, Monkee, Dance' (about being stuck with lifetime dancing lessons) and 'Hitting the High Seas' (about a pirate ship, Michael Nesmith makes only a token appearance in the episode). Although still enjoyable, the pacing is more traditional on these episodes.

The gags are lighthearted, the locations are amazingly flexible for a half hour comedy series, and the pre-fabricated songs, many of which turned into hits, are inevitably refreshing, as is anything which reminds one of more innocent times.

The program was in color and all four episodes look great. The discs have a decent number of chapter markers. There is no enhancement to the monaural soundtrack, but it is certainly amplified in comparison to how it was first broadcast. In this respect, the first volume is stronger than the second.

THE MONKEES "HEART AND SOUL"
Appearing at the end of *The Monkees "Heart and Soul"* is a commercial for the cable channel, Nickelodeon, which is where the 37-minute profile from the group's 1987 revival tour was first shown. The program is a mixture of interviews, three recent music videos, two old Rice Krispies commercials, some performance footage from the tour, and a few other tidbits. The music videos are in good condition and are fairly entertaining. The interviews are more engaging than common sense says they ought to be, and the rest of the material is a waste of time for all but the most devoted fans. The picture quality is dependent upon the quality of the source material for each sequence, but is mostly a little tattered looking. The sound is monaural, but satisfying.

MONKEY BUSINESS
An original theatrical trailer for the Marx Brothers movie, *Monkey Business* appears at the end of the disc. The closer a trailer is to the original marketing and promotional concepts, the more valuable it is, not only in terms of film history but in understanding how a movie's popularity has sustained the passage of time. The trailer is ragged, but the movie was made in 1931, and the print used for the film isn't much better. The trailer is a thrill and its antiquity is the most attractive aspect to the entire disc.

Monkey Business was the third film the Marx Brothers made. In the first half, they appear as stowaways aboard an oceanliner. In the second half, which is in CAV, they attend a party given by a reformed gangster, and save his daughter from kidnappers. The plot, however, is not quinquevalent to the entertainment. Instead, there are riotous puns (much of the dialog is by S.J. Perelman), clever sight gags, and the usual barrage of insults. The insults, in fact, have aged much better than the puns, which just goes to show that the more mean the spirit, the more immortal the soul.

MONKEY BUSINESS
CBS/Fox has released the other *Monkey Business*, the Howard Hawks screwball comedy, as part of its 'Marilyn' series, even though Monroe has only a secondary role in the movie. The film, about a scientist and a simian who develop a short term youth serum, stars Cary Grant and Ginger Rogers. It is Rogers who actually steals the movie from Grant, the monkey, and everyone else, not only with her portrayal of an adolescent in an adult body, but also in her amusing interpretation of a prim and overly graceful adult. Monroe portrays a 'dumb secretary,' one who arrives on the job early because her boss had criticized her 'punctuation' the day before. The film gives several actors a chance to let loose and is full of witty one-liners. Monroe's presence has always seemed like a bonus, a minor component which brings the film all the more closer to perfection.

The transfer is pretty good. The monaural sound is analog, but it is CX-encoded and is quite strong. The black and white print usually looks quite sharp, and has no more than a few imperfections.

MONKEY SHINES
The monkey jumps out of nowhere too many times for our tastes in *Monkey Shines*, but since the anticipation threshold of each viewer is different, the director, George Romero, goes for every scream he thinks he can generate. He generates enough of them. The film, about a paraplegic with a trained but murder-prone simian assistant, is terrific fun. It is good, repeatable home video that will have the viewer jumping almost as many times as the monkey. Grain appears in some of the night scenes and scenes with intense red lights. Red shading also runs down the middle of the picture near the end, but generally the image looks good. The well-executed surround sound also contains a few surprises. Chapter markers have been encoded for the Peggy Lee numbers.

MONSTER FROM A PREHISTORIC PLANET (see **GODZILLA VS. THE SMOG MONSTER/MONSTER FROM A PREHISTORIC PLANET**)

THE MONSTER SQUAD
If the production budget for *The Monster Squad* had been $30 it would have been a great movie, but the addition of six zeroes to the end of that figure comes to naught. The movie has many fancy special effects, but none which enable it to overcome its cheap premise.

The opening and closing credits are letterboxed to a nice effect. That letterboxing, however, makes you more aware of the cropping and scanning in the rest of the film, which would be disjointed enough without it. (The movie runs under 90 minutes – but is in CLV on the disc – and characters waste no screen time whatsoever moving from one situation to the next.) The picture looks grainy, except for the opening and closing, where the letterboxing sharpens the focus. The sound is digitally encoded. The stereo track ate its share of the budgetary pie and belches accordingly.

Monster Squad is about a group of youngsters who do battle with infamous horror characters. It is a movie for kids, and is not without some humor (an overweight Squad-member slaps Dracula with his garlic bread sandwich to facilitate an escape), but it would probably have been more entertaining if they had made the movie and not just acted in it.

MONTAND INTERNATIONAL (Import)
Yves Montand has made such an impression as a weary man of the world in his film roles that it is disconcerting to see him grinning and clowning in his concert performances. *Montand International* is a Japanese disc, mostly in French with Japanese subtitles, showcasing Montand's stage performances in a variety of cities around the world. The filmmakers cut from audiences in Tokyo and Rio and New York for reaction shots to the same number, and while you can understand what it is they are trying to accomplish, they don't pull it off. The stereo sound captures his voice adequately, but his appeal is limited. When he starts doing his Charlie Chaplin imitation, you wonder if they would have ever let him up on the stage at all if he weren't Yves Montand. Better he should sit down, light a cigarette, and act a little more weary.

MONTEREY POP
All of the rock concert laser discs in your collection owe their existence to *Monterey Pop*. The event, the Monterey International Pop Festival, crystallized the maturation of rock and roll, and D.A. Pennebaker's documentary record of the event defined the way that modern rock and roll should be presented on film – not as a fad, but as an expression of society and social values.

The disc is in CLV, which is its one disappointing aspect since the 79-minute film could easily have lent its three closing acts, including Jimi Hendrix simulating you-know-what with his guitar, to a CAV side two.

One has only to look at the opening of side two, however, with the bright green lawn and the colorful fabrics wandering about it, to see what a beautiful transfer Voyager has done. The film was made in 16mm and is inherently grainy, but the colors on the disc are nearly perfect, and the grain is so sharply focussed that it looks more like a fancy visual effect than a basic flaw. Anyone who has seen the film knows that the photography, particularly of the groups which played after sunset, is primitive. Keeping that in mind, it is doubtful one could find a better delivery of the images than has been provided on the disc.

The sound is fantastic. The digitally encoded stereo gives the music a precision it lacked when it first played in film theaters. The analog audio track is CX-encoded without automatic tripping. The disc is unquestionably the best publicly accessible presentation of the concert's music. The fidelity is so crisp that it makes the songs, even the stupid ones, such as Simon and Garfunkle's '59th Street Bridge Rag' (mis-titled on the jacket cover), come alive.

Also worth noting is the superb documentation, mis-titling aside, which comes with the disc. The essay on the back of the jacket about the film and a program listing and essay about the groups playing the Festival, which comes on an insert, both written by Bruce Eder, are so thorough that even the most jaded rock and roll fan will find them informative.

The film is short, and over before one is really ready for it to end, but that may be why it works so well. It must have been disheartening to edit, since many hours of what was undoubtedly great footage had to be left out. The spirit, however, was retained. In moving quickly from one act to the next (there are 18 chapter markers), yet conveying a complete sense of the diversity of the audience between numbers, one is left not only with a view of what it was like to attend the Festival, but what it was like to see America's music industry usurped by a new generation.

MONTEVERDI L'ORFEO

If you constructed a graph using the X-axis to denote the passage of years and the Y-axis to denote some quantification of popularity, then the earliest opera to make a significant appearance on the graph would probably be Claudio Monteverdi's *L'Orfeo*. An essay inserted in *Monteverdi L'Orfeo*, even claims that *L'Orfeo* was the first 'opera.' Monteverdi's work is startlingly modern, and has been adapted for the screen by Jean-Pierre Ponnelle and the Zurich Monteverdi Ensemble under Nikolas Harnoncourt, with considerable flourish. Too much flourish, perhaps, since the elaborate staging within a staging within a staging (the story is acted out by players performing for an audience of nobles, themselves players performing for a make-believe contemporary audience) seems to be at odds with the simplicity of the original musical instruments. The program is in Italian and has English subtitles.

The picture on the disc has accurate colors, but it is grainy. The sound is much better, particularly during the choral passages. Ponnelle's editing is sometimes tied too closely to the music and not to the impact of the images themselves, but he obtains some gorgeous closeups. His interpretation distracts from the musical accomplishments of the Ensemble, but it effectively presents the opera as a narrative struggling to bind itself to music, and that, it can be said, is one of the many themes of the legend of Orpheus itself.

A MONTH IN THE COUNTRY

If you read the plot summary on the back of the jacket for *A Month in the Country*, you would think that the characters come out swinging: "The quiet of their rural haven erupts in conflict and confrontation that will forever change their lives..." In reality, there is no eruption, the drama just simmers a little. It is a British effort, an understated glimpse at a WWI veteran who restores a painting in a rural church one summer, and restores his own mental stability in the process. It is intelligent, and full of talking heads who forever avoid confronting real emotion. The film will appeal to studious viewers, and bore others.

The picture was filmed in a nostalgic haze and often looks so blurry it is a candidate for restoration itself. A speckle or two also show up near the end. The digital monaural sound is strained, but adequate.

MONTY PYTHON'S FLYING CIRCUS VOLUME ONE

The first Monty Python disc, *Monty Python's Flying Circus Volume One*, contains two early episodes from the second season of the series and one episode from the third season. Within are sketches about 'The Ministry of Silly Walks,' a naughty chemist, a Japanese film director masquerading as Visconti, the bureaucracy of gas companies, a crooked insurance agent, a restaurant in the middle of the jungle, people wearing funny costumes, and innumerable blackouts. The picture quality is a little faded and the sound is monaural television.

MONTY PYTHON'S FLYING CIRCUS VOLUME TWO

In keeping with their sometimes insane traditions, *Monty Python's Flying Circus Volume Two* retains the ninety minute video cassette running time by containing two episodes on side one and one episode on side two and none around the outer edge or inner rim, all in CLV and marked by chapter encoding so that side two, since it is only one episode, has only one chapter. At least it can be found quickly. In an improvement over past discs of this nature, the jacket notations actually state that the disc is a disc and do not mistake it for some inferior form of home entertainment. The sound is monaural, but it has been CX-encoded and is well preserved. No audience is present, but a live laugh track is, often laughing too hard at the wrong things. The picture has a ghost or two unassociated with the comedy but, like the sound, is in the sort of condition one would label as well preserved if one was speaking of British television shows from the 1970s in a normal tone of voice.

Volume Two contains Number 15 (Series 2, Episode 2) and Number 20 (Series 2, Episode 7) on side one and, Number 31 (Series 3, Episode 5) on side two. Since 31 has a different opening credit sequence from numbers 20 and 15, it can be deduced that these are two episodes from the second year of broadcast and one episode from the third.

The episodes have vaguely connective material, virtually impossible to describe, which renders each one identifiably different from the next. On *Two*, 15 contains a running gag about the Spanish Inquisition, 20 has pieces about Atilla the Hun and killer sheep, and in 31 every time a character in any skit talks on the phone, he or she is asked to report the size of his or her shoe. The blackout sketch which we found most amusing was a game show in which contestants attempt to summarize *Remembrance of Things Past* in fifteen seconds as a thermometer listing the titles of the seven books comprising the work charts their progress. There are also plenty of jokes about women's breasts. The episodes do not have to be watched in order and cannot be watched in order anyway since 16-19 and 21-30 are not on disc yet. It is best to watch a single episode, laugh heartily, and save another for another time. Unlike many cultural efforts from the 1970s, the skits have aged well and will still be funny tomorrow and the day after that.

MONTY PYTHON'S FLYING CIRCUS VOLUME THREE
MONTY PYTHON'S FLYING CIRCUS VOLUME FOUR

The three episodes collected on *Monty Python's Flying Circus Volume Three* are from 1970 and 1972, Episode 9, Series 2, Episode 2, Series 3, and Episode 12, Series 2. The back of the jacket has chapter identifications for each episode, but the disc is not chapter encoded. Although two episodes appear on side one and a single episode appears on side two, the disc is CLV throughout.

Volume Four is also in CLV and the jacket cover dispenses with identifying the specific episodes, though they seem to be mixture from two separate seasons. The disc has no chapter encoding, and the jacket has the words 'laser videodisc' stamped over the word 'videocassette' in a cheap attempt at humor.

On all the programs, the source material, although varying in quality, usually looks worn down, grainy, or, even at its best, soft. The sound is also limited in range and clarity. An annoying laugh track prevents one from hearing every funny line, even in the privacy of one's home.

We don't really know how to go about identifying the episodes for you, since the sketches are so scattered in subject matter that mentioning one will rarely spark a memory of the two on either side, so we have decided that a stream-of-consciousness scan will probably be the most ridiculous: *Volume Three* – First Episode: Australian outpost where everyone is named Bruce hiring a philosophy teacher interviewing a person who contradicts everything man wearing a false nose goes to plastic surgeon infantry marchers saying and doing funny things animated killer cars interlude inexpensive airlines detective satire turning into a satire of amateur performances by policemen. Second Episode: witty takeoff on Kon Tiki adventure using London suburbs talk show parody simplifying complicated things curing athletes foot with dynamite fish slapping dance Titanic crew trying to get on lifeboats Lulu and Ringo. Third Episode: 'Black Eagle' pirate movie parody Romanian translation book skit talk show parody asking Communist founders irrelevant questions making WWI movie artworks in museum come to life and go on strike asylum for overacting diner with spam in everything. *Volume Four* – First Episode: Tory women making men work faster and cleaning up arts stupid brain surgeons door-to-door mollusk lecturer expedition to lake in suburban basement. Second Episode: advertising campaign using gross concepts murder parody with concentration on train schedules filmmakers with tusks religion with hard sell how to keep from being seen 'yummy yummy yummy' in boxes. Third Episode: scaling Oxbridge Road cuts between suburban kitchen and boat in storm talk show parody on storage jars cheese shop without cheese Sam Peckinpah film of tennis party (bloody).

MOON OVER PARADOR

Richard Dreyfuss and Raul Julia star in *Moon over Parador*, about an actor cajoled into impersonating a deceased dictator. The timing between the two stars, who have worked together on the stage, contributes significantly to the comedy. The filmmakers take some wrong turns which probably turned off audiences, such as an extended gag that has the dictator hosting a televised aerobics program, although if you get a sandwich or scan past that segment, the rest of the movie is enjoyable.

The picture is grainy, too orange, and full of intense but unstable colors. The stereo surround sound has intermittent separation effects.

MOONRAKER (CBS/Fox)
MOONRAKER (MGM/UA)
OCTOPUSSY (CBS/Fox)
OCTOPUSSY (MGM/UA)

Two enjoyable Roger Moore James Bond movies, *Moonraker* and *Octopussy*, are available from MGM/UA as Deluxe Letter-Box Edition offerings. The films are impeccably transferred and amount to nearly four and a half hours of non-stop excitement and gorgeous, glossy fun. Both discs are introduced by neat theatrical trailers. Both have aspect ratios of 2.1:1, both come in gatefold jackets, and both are in CAV on side 3 with correct still frames. *Moonraker* appeared previously on disc in scanned and cropped format from CBS/Fox. *Octopussy* was also released cropped, simultaneously by CBS/Fox and MGM/UA. The first batches were notorious for having suffered from manufacturing defects.

The picture and digital sound on both discs are spectacular. The movies are young enough to have contemporary surround sound mixes, and the louder they are set the better. The picture is flawless on both films. A portion of the ending sequence in *Moonraker* is bathed in red light, which normally turns the whole image to a crimson fog, but on the new transfer the effect is stable.

Letterboxing improves both the stunt sequences and the art direction on both discs, and it takes some of the pressure off Roger Moore, who looks more at ease in medium shots (and is usually replaced in the long ones). On the cropped discs his face fills the screen in closeups and his jowls sag. On the letterboxed image he is usually centered in interesting surroundings, standing out only enough to remind you that he is there.

Consensus opinion would have it that neither movie is among the best of the Bonds, but with the quality presentation that MGM/UA has given them, the flaws are minimized and the pleasures are multiplied. Both movies function effectively as lighthearted cliffhangers and the quality of the presentations prevents one from becoming impatient with either title. We recommend them as a double bill.

We have always found *Moonraker* to possess a lasting freshness as a home video title, anyway. The fight in the precious glass exhibit, the concluding space battle, the opening free-fall fight and the many other elaborate location stunts are gags on a grand scale. The balance between imagination and humor is just right to keep the viewer attentive and in good temper. The narrative has no plot, but it doesn't need one. The itinerary works well enough as a linking device.

MGM/UA's one error with the disc is to short-change the CAV side by about 15 minutes. A number of special effects which occur at the end of side two could easily have been incorporated onto side three, and a more logical break point could have been chosen as well. Side 3 of *Octopussy* is more conscientiously filled.

George MacDonald Fraser had a hand in the *Octopussy* script and his fingerprints are all over the completed film. Who else would work things out so that Bond, of all heroes, is forced to dress as a circus clown? Who else would go to elaborate lengths just to get a female character to say, "That's my little Octopussy," supposedly in reference to a tattoo? And who else would make the heroine so morally ambiguous? If *Moonraker* is bereft of plot, *Octopussy* if full of it, and, between the spectacular stunts, repeat viewings can enhance one's appreciation of the Fraserisms lurking beneath the facade.

MOONSTRUCK

If you haven't got any neighbors or relatives who are like the characters in *Moonstruck*, then you may not think the movie is so funny, but we were clutching our stomach and rolling on the floor with laughter. The entertaining romance is presented in its best light by the disc, which has nearly perfect sound and a picture to match. Some reddish glows run a little bit, but in the many night scenes the dark sky is free of significant distortion and the only blur on the moon is what was put there by the filmmakers. The pop songs, the opera passages, and even the dialog sound so rich they are the audio equivalent of rum pastries. There is a little hiss on the digital track and a little more on the analog, but even the simplest background noises and sound effects are beautifully defined. The moon, incidentally, plays an important part in *Moonstruck*, and its role is emphasized by the disc, because side one ends at the conclusion of the moon's big scene, and you realize the scene was placed at the center and heart of the film.

MOONTRAP

Moontrap is not as good as you want it to be but it does have lofty goals for a low budget feature and manages to be moderately stimulating. The central narrative is about nasty things hiding on the moon and waiting for astronauts, but there is a lengthy lead-in (the moon segment doesn't begin until side two, although side one is very short) and another shift in locale for the conclusion. The numerous special effects are mostly unconvincing, but they are palatable. The fact that the movie makers were willing to try accounts for a lot of the film's appeal.

The picture is often foggy and is subject to odd color washes, but that appears to be a problem with the film's own production status and not with the transfer. The digitally encoded sound is monaural and is best left with limited amplification. The musical score is a strain.

Walter Koenig stars and his charisma compensates for his inability to act without strong direction. At several points during the movie skeletal remains are uncovered in the vacuum of outer space, although how they decomposed remains a mystery. On the other hand, there is a battle on the moon which is appropriately set in silence. It is a highpoint not only because of the fear created by not being able to hear the adversary, but also because the music gets turned off until it is over.

MORE! POLICE SQUAD!

"You are holding history in your hands. Because this videocassette, *More! Police Squad!*, contains the final three episodes of 'Police Squad!,' the hilarious TV cop show created by the outrageous team who brought you *Airplane!* and T*op Secret!*," says the back of the disc jacket. Cute, right? We thought we were holding a video disc. The jacket also shows stills from *Police Squad! Help Wanted*, and none from the disc enclosed.

Aired in the summer of '82, *Police Squad!* was a wonderful TV show because it didn't have a chance in the world of running more than six episodes and you knew it. Seeing all six at once, or at least the final three released on *More! Police Squad!*, may be something of an overdose, but the important thing is that they are available. The sound is loud and of television quality, although the incessant jazz score will surprise the viewer now and then. The picture is clean, but the prints look as if they'd been rescued from oblivion in the nick of time. Or is Nicholas with Newsweek now?

MORGAN STEWART'S COMING HOME

The picture quality on *Morgan Stewart's Coming Home* is passable, though the actors become too orange every once in a while. The sound is in stereo and has been CX-encoded, but it is not very interesting. The story is about a boy with rich parents and his attempts to break through their porcelain demeanor. It is a comedy, fairly artificial, but likeable.

MORGAN THE PIRATE

It may be cropped, it may be dubbed, it may look like an Italian biblical epic, but *Morgan the Pirate* is terrific fun. The film stars Steve Reeves as an Englishman mistreated by the Spanish governor of Panama, who escapes – well, it looks like the oar compartment of a slave galley, but then that can't be, can it – and starts plundering Spain's shipping lanes. Although filmed in widescreen, the action is perfectly understandable with the sides lopped off. All the viewer misses with the cropping is more of what is already on view. The color transfer is gorgeous, and the cast members all have great tans. The lip movements rarely match the dialog, but you're usually too busy staring at the tans to notice. There is an awful, Ravel-inspired score, by Franco Mannino, but that just adds to the lightheartedness of the proceedings.

THE MORNING AFTER

We had heard that *The Morning After* wasn't very good, so we were surprised to discover that it is just the opposite. It is a mystery which unfolds with all the right creases. The ending is much tighter than the endings of other popular contemporary murder mysteries, so what is the problem? Jane Fonda?

A scene near the end is lit with green neon, and the transfer holds the colors quite well, so that the objects and faces on the screen are cast in green light without merging with it. Some of the darker scenes, however, do not have the near-perfect black of the best discs.

MOROCCO

The pleasures of owning a classic, well executed film go beyond simply enjoying the story or spending time with the characters. *Morocco* was made by Joseph Von Sternberg and it is obsessively well made, down to the smallest detail. Movies don't need that kind of attention to succeed, and such attention does not even guarantee that the movie will be good (some of Sternberg's later films are awful), but it does assure that viewing such a film will not be a complete waste of time, and often, that multiple viewings will reveal new nuances. *Morocco*, about a cabaret singer who falls in love with a legionaire, would be totally unconvincing if the cabaret singer were not Marlene Dietrich and the legionaire were not Gary Cooper. She falls for him too quickly, but since it is Cooper, what woman wouldn't? Dietrich has such a mystique about her that when she so much as grabs Cooper's arm it is quite erotic, and it is no wonder that he falls for her. Thus their dialog, which is arch and silly, is no detriment to the sympathies they are conveying; they brought that with them in the marquee.

The source material is no better or worse than the copies shown on late night TV. There is one interruption in dialog on side one, and Cooper's hat is such a bright white that it often has a ghost around it, but for a 1930 film, it is in better condition than others have been. The picture is often a little blurry and the sound is rough, but you can hear the desert wind over the final credits, and the jacket cover is gorgeous.

THE MOSQUITO COAST

Harrison Ford was miscast as the distracted genius who transports his family to the jungles of Central America in *The Mosquito Coast*. His eyes are too sharp, and he never achieves the right balance between inspired brilliance and foggy brooding. The script also has a problem in that it tells a complete story on what amounts to two sides of the 119 minute disc and then meanders through a lengthy and destructive third act on side three. The filmmakers actually came closer to achieving a workable, entertaining movie than one would have thought possible, given the material. Like Ford's character, however, they inevitably fall short of their goal.

The disc creates an audio environment which encourages the viewer to swat at invisible bugs while the show is in progress. Jungle Surround. The disc's other attributes are average, with no glaring flaws or soaring technical achievements.

MOTEL HELL

A cult favorite which is more gruesome in suggestion than display, *Motel Hell* should nonetheless be sampled by the unwary before it is purchased. It is a black comedy about a rural businessman who runs a motel and murders wayward travelers, using their flesh to spice up his smoked sausages. The exposition falls a little closer to the *Texas Chainsaw Massacre* side of the continuum than the *Arsenic and Old Lace* side.

The print is worn out and grainy. The sound, surprisingly, is in digital. This enhances the music track, which has mixture of rock, country/western, and horror mood music, but does nothing for the dialog and special effects, which sound like they were recorded on cassette.

MOTELS

'Suddenly Last Summer,' on the 8-inch *Motels*, owes more to Frank Perry than Joseph Mankiewicz. The video is suitably dreamy and mysterious. The other number which really catches one's attention is 'Take the L' ("Take the L out of lover and it's over."), using split screens and several different stories to emphasize one theme. All four cuts are praiseworthy and the transfer is nice.

MOTHER

The classic Soviet silent film, *Mother*, is too basic for our tastes, lacking the artistic inspirations which make other silent films still seem so alive today. Others, however, find the familial and communal emotions and the undeniably superb editing to be sufficient for the film's canonization. They are probably right, but the movie just isn't fun.

The 84-minute CLV disc is similar in quality to the other Russian cinema classics on disc. The film speed is slowed to approximate real movement, though the result often exchanges the hyperactive activity of other silent films for a mildly sluggish kineticism. The title cards are in Russian with English subtitles which sometimes get washed out by the Russian lettering. The digitally encoded musical accompaniment is a little creaky.

MOTLEY CRUE – UNCENSORED

Interviews with the band members which separate the music videos on *Motley Crue – Uncensored* take up more running time on the 45-minute disc than the musical sequences. The interviews are interesting, and there are groupies all over the place if one is not interested in what the band members have to say, but the replay potential is diminished by the filler. The sound and picture transfers are superb, though some of the music videos, whether by design or after the fact, appear out of synch. The band members may wear lipstick during their performances, but they are normal, outlandishly rich kids off stage, and their music is both hard and sharp.

MOTOR FANTASY

No flaws are in evidence on *Motor Fantasy*, the Pioneer import which was the first laser disc to appear officially in the US sporting both digital encoding and a CAV format. Unfortunately, the disc's program is less appealing than its innovative design. Eight chapters feature eight contemporary automobiles, such as Lotus Esprit and Porche 911, cruising about on nondescript European roadways. At one point there are some cuts to a naked woman in an apartment – why, who knows – but other than that it is just the cars, all clean and shiny, coming down the road and driving past the camera and then coming down the road and driving past the camera again.

The music, by Yasunori Soryo, is mindless. The sound mix is quite pleasurable, however, and so the digital encoding is put to good use. You can only take so much of it though, before your attention starts to wander.

MOTORCYCLE CRASHES, VOL. 2

(Import)

The rider catches his breath and then pulls the visor on his helmet over his eyes. He lies down on the middle of the track near his motorcycle as other bikes whiz past him. There is a momentary, almost invisible pause, where both cycle and rider are at peace, and then, magnetically, they are drawn to one another. Somehow, the rider swings his legs to fit over the body of the cycle. Somehow the cycle, from its flying start, veers to the left and to the right until both rider and machine are balanced. They merge into the traffic gracefully and recede, facing the camera.

We thought we would kill a half hour one afternoon by watching a Japanese import we had picked up, *Motorcycle Crashes, Vol. 2*. Hey, we got it for the kids – you know. The CAV disc was dull, until it dawned on us to try playing some of it backwards. We ended up spending another half hour watching the entire disc in normal speed reverse. We couldn't get enough of it, observing the patterns of the crashes which, in forward motion, appeared to be a random jumble of chance occurrences, but, in reverse, took on a cosmologically determined sequence of events. We guess we will now have to move in reverse ourselves, and find *Vol. 1*.

MOTORHEAD – ANOTHER PERFECT DAY

Without any pretension or conceptual distractions, the heavy metal band, Motorhead, performs five energetic numbers on the one-sided CLV 8-inch, *Motorhead – Another Perfect Day*. The first song is live and the picture on it has a worn, live look to it, but the other four are performed in a studio and look clearer, if less spontaneous. At one point they sing, "You know the chase is better than the catch, you know," and you think, 'Hey, these guys know Keats,' but then you take a good, close look at the lead singer and you realize, 'Nah,' it is only a coincidence.

MOTOWN TIME CAPSULE: THE 60'S

Newsclips and cultural footage from the 1960s fill the screen during the 10 Motown oldies which are featured on *Motown Time Capsule: The 60's*. Since the disc is from Pioneer Artists, there are chapter markers for each of the songs. Each number represents a year, as do the accompanying black-and-white or faded color clips. Many of the clips are rarely seen and the mix of old commercials, desegregation sit-ins, and Kennedy family scenes create a great deal of nostalgia. The songs include 'I Can't Help Myself,' 'You Keep Me Hangin' On,' and 'For Once in My Life.'

MOTOWN TIME CAPSULE – THE 70'S

Picking up right where *The 60's* disc left off, *Motown Time Capsule – The 70's* features a second decade of brief film clips tied to a song a year. The film clips – resurrected bits of news footage, commercials, and cultural icons – are bound closely to the theme represented by the song, although they also manage to evoke the feeling of the year the song was a hit. Anyone who is old enough to buy the disc will have nostalgic twinges as the years and the music pass by. The songs, many of them in stereo, include 'War,' 'What's Going On,' 'Superstition,' 'Dancing Machine,' 'Boogie on Reggae Woman,' 'Love Hangover,' 'Easy,' 'You and I,' and 'Cruisin'.'

MOTOWN 25 – YESTERDAY-TODAY-FOREVER

The television special which celebrated Motown's 25th anniversary, *Motown 25 – Yesterday-Today-Forever*, is a great disc. The sound is so good that you can hear all the live production faults, such as when a volume level varies during a performer's solo.

You don't mind that you're only hearing snippets of all your favorite tunes, because the medleys are being performed by the original artists. Since the show is 130 minutes long, there is flexibility in the program material. It is a shame that no chapter markers have been provided. On the back of the jacket there is a 2" by 6" listing of all the songs in the order they occur. Some are from old film clips, but the balance between old and new doesn't exhaust you. The big moments – The Temptations/Four Tops 'battle,' Marvin Gaye, Smokey Robinson, Stevie Wonder, and Michael Jackson – are spectacular.

MOTOWN'S MUSTANG

The narrative of *Motown's Mustang*, a 43-minute 'movie' which features 11 Motown songs, follows the tribulations of a bright red Mustang convertible as it is passed from one owner to the next. The cyclical story has its ups and downs and the characters make only vague attempts to lip synch the songs, which include 'Money,' 'Psychedelic Shack,' 'Baby I Need Your Loving,' 'ABC,' and others. Although the sound on the disc is CX-encoded, early Motown is hardly famous for its stereophonic accomplishments.

MOULIN ROUGE (Import)

John Huston's biography of Henri Toulouse-Lautrec, *Moulin Rouge*, is available on laser disc in Japan. The sound is monaural, but passable. The picture is slightly dark, but the colors are rich and the print is in good shape. We rarely noticed the Japanese subtitles once the movie got underway. The film opens with a fabulous recreation of an evening at the Moulin Rouge, circa 1890. The sequence builds up so much momentum that it carries the rest of the movie, although on side two, when you realize that Huston is not going to repeat the effort, the entertainment becomes wistful.

The movie is successful in communicating the accomplishments of Lautrec's art, something which biographical dramas are sometimes at a loss to communicate. It is helped by the limitations of Lautrec's talent (which gets one to thinking that the best film biographies are not necessarily about the best artists), because the extent of his accomplishments and his sources are comprehendible to mortals. Had Lautrec been a better artist, he might not have taken the effort to produce the greatest theatrical posters the world has ever known. The movie is always positive about his art, generally negative about his emotional stability, and neutral to the upper and lower class societies which he straddled despite his limited stature.

MOUSERCISE

The 52-minute *Mousercise* program from Walt Disney is a bit exhausting, although the exercises are simple enough. The relentless, pushy format barely pauses from beginning to end. It is doubtful that children will actually follow it all the way through unless there is an older sister with strong organizational abilities in the household.

No chapter markers, no CX-encoding, no dual audio for the music, and no real way to stop between sets unless the young user is adept with the 'pause' button. The instructor, Kellyn Plasschaert, is adamant about pulse rates and avoiding strains by bending the wrong way or working too hard. The transfer is good and the show ends with a learnable dance routine, but the utility of the disc is questionable.

MOVING

The Richard Pryor effort, *Moving*, has no chapter markers, but there isn't much in it worth replaying. The sound has some kick and the picture is bright and clear, but Pryor's desperation has lost its humor. The film, about a family moving from New Jersey to Idaho, avoids any cultural commentary – when they get to Idaho it looks exactly like New Jersey. Some of the extraneous gags are amusing, but the movie doesn't go anywhere and it seems to last forever.

MOVING VIOLATIONS

As with most really stupid movies, parts of *Moving Violations* are very funny. The movie is about a group of errant drivers who must take a week-long driver's education course to retrieve their suspended licenses and impounded autos. The cop who busted them teaches the class and is trying to flunk them so he can profit on the impounded cars. The transfer is mediocre.

MOZART/BEETHOVEN: QUINTETS FOR PIANO & WIND

James Levine is featured on the piano in *Mozart/Beethoven: Quintets for Piano & Wind*, which was directed by Jean-Pierre Ponnelle. Appearing with him are Hansjorg Schellenberger on the oboe, Karl Leister on the clarinet, Gunter Hogner on the horn and Milan Turkovic on the bassoon. The program seems oriented more toward a conceptual presentation than a virtuoso performance. The music is good, but not exceptional, and Ponnelle's exploration of the quintet as they perform the pieces is as much a justification for the disc as is the audio.

The picture is slightly grainy, but the colors are okay. The sound has no significant problems. The single sided CLV disc presents the two pieces chronologically, though they might have been more effective if Beethoven's boisterous effort had come before Mozart's more sophisticated piece. An essay about the two works accompanies the disc on a jacket insert.

MOZART LE NOZZE DI FIGARO

Mozart Le Nozze Di Figaro ('The Marriage of Figaro') was filmed on a soundstage in 35mm and was directed by Jean-Pierre Ponnelle. The 184-minute opera is separated on disc to an act per side, and comes in a box jacket. Although no libretto is provided, an accompanying booklet (presented in English and French) provides an excellent history of the opera, a lengthy plot synopsis closely coordinated to the disc's many chapter markers, and a superb interview with Ponnelle, in which he discusses the freedom of exploration that he felt while directing the film. Some of his techniques are common, such as the use of the rhythm and melody of the opera to guide the editing and camera movements. Others are interesting experiments, such as the use of a matte so that Figaro can sing his fourth act aria about his disgust with women to himself. At its worst, Ponnelle's direction still rides the music to move the opera along. At its best, he adds humor and humanity by successfully pointing to the right face at the right phrase.

The film has a super cast, including Dietrich Fischer-Dieskau as the Count, Kiri Te Kanawa as the Countess, Mirella Freni as Susanna, and Hermann Prey as Figaro. The opera is sung in Italian and has English subtitles. The music is provided by the Vienna Philharmonic with Karl Bohm conducting. Many of the recitatives were recorded during the filming, while the songs were recorded beforehand. This enables the cast to concentrate upon their acting, and is an excellent compromise between the alienating effect of a fully pre-recorded soundtrack and a mistake ridden live performance. The sound is pressed to the limits by Te Kanawa's voice. Her opening aria at the beginning of Act Two is a stunner.

Figaro was made in 1976, and the image has some blur to it, particularly during the second and third acts. Overall the picture is acceptable, and some effects, such as the shadow which lifts from Freni's face as she steps out of the closet, are memorable. The stereo sound is mildly indistinctive, but functional.

Ponnelle and Bohm have made one or two minor cuts in the text to accommodate their staging, but the opera is fully realized. Generations have known it to be a delightful, uplifting experience, free of saccharin and full of salty humor. Ponnelle's accomplishment is to have provided a fresh viewpoint. By using the medium of film, he extracts new discoveries from the seemingly infinite potential of Mozart's work.

MOZART: PIANO CONCERTOS NOS. 19 & 23

Maurizio Pollini would have made a great quarterback. He's a team player. Unlike the precocious Arthur Rubinstein, whose collaboration with the London Symphony Orchestra on *Grieg/Chopin/Saint-Saens: Piano Concertos* was strained, Pollini, a brilliant, intelligent pianist, willingly adapts to the Vienna Philharmonic and conductor Karl Bohm on *Mozart: Piano Concertos Nos. 19 & 23*. He concentrates on fitting in, on adjusting his own emotions toward the piece to accommodate the mood of the orchestra. It is fascinating watching him, and it is obvious that he truly believes this is the best way to present the music, even if he is compromising his own fortissimo to achieve his goal.

The CLV disc runs less than an hour, but the two concertos are separated, one to a side. Chapter markers are provided for each movement. The performance was filmed in a Viennese salon in 1977. The image looks a little soft, but it is acceptable. The sound lacks clarity but should be of sufficient purity for most listeners. Except for a pointless, recurring long shot, which shows the whole orchestra but makes the musicians too small and dark, the video presentation is good. The camera angles emphasize fingering for the orchestra, but keep an ample eye on the faces of both Bohm and Pollini. There is also an excellent essay, in English and French, provided on a jacket insert, which explains what Mozart was up to with concertos in general and these two in particular.

MOZART: REQUIEM
VERDI: REQUIEM

Deutsche Grammophon has released interesting renditions of the two best known 'Requiems,' *Mozart: Requiem* and *Verdi: Requiem*. The two programs provide pertinent contrasts which go beyond their musical content, and they also make an appropriate musical double bill.

Mozart: Requiem is conducted by Leonard Bernstein and performed by the Bavarian Radio Chorus and Symphony Orchestra with soloists Marie McLaughlin, Maria Ewing, Jerry Hadley, and Cornelius Hauptman. The curious history of Mozart's work is thoroughly discussed in an essay which, accompanied by a libretto, appears on a jacket insert (the *Verdi* disc also contains a lengthy essay about Verdi's composition, along with the libretto which is nearly the same for both works). A number of different versions of Mozart's work exist, and the program features the edition conceived by Franz Beyer.

The sound is both clear and immediate. The picture transfer, from a video tape source, is also sharp and spotless. The orchestra performs in front of an audience which remains dead silent from start to finish. The singers are adequate and Bernstein's organization is forceful but even tempered. It is here, however, that comparisons to the second disc are appropriate.

Herbert von Karajan conducts *Verdi: Requiem* in front of the La Scala Orchestra with soloists Leontyne Price, Fiorenza Cossotto, Luciano Pavarotti, and Nicolai Ghiaurov. It is a 1967 recording – Pavarotti looks both very young and very nervous. Although the recording is older and clearly not as fresh as the *Mozart* disc, it is also clear that von Karajan's conducting, in this case at least, draws much more out of the work than Bernstein's does. Both the singers and the orchestra are more talented on the *Verdi* disc, but the precision and anticipation with which von Karajan guides the group through the piece is also more accomplished than Bernstein's effort.

Similarly, the video presentations of the two discs provide interesting contrasts. Humphrey Burton's direction of the *Mozart* program is standard for recent live programs. He mixes the shots well and follows the emphasis of the orchestration closely. The *Verdi* program was video taped at La Scala without an audience, directed by the noted French film director, Henri-Georges Clouzot. Although Clouzot's approach is seemingly analogous to Burton's, close examination will reveal that he often chooses the most interesting image over the most musically appropriate image. That is one of the reasons why the viewer becomes so aware of Pavarotti's nervousness, Clouzot finds it interesting, too. We would recommend, in fact, that one watch the *Verdi* disc at some time with the sound turned off, to see how Clouzot constructs the music with his images, and how his counterpoint adds so much to the disc that the tattered and blurry source material is just as pleasing as the slick, glossy *Mozart* effort.

MOZART: VIOLIN CONCERTOS NOS. 1-3 ETC.

Gidon Kremer appears with a judicious selection of the Vienna Philharmonic under Nikolaus Harnoncourt to perform *Mozart: Violin Concertos Nos. 1-3 Etc.*, the 'Etc.' being 'Sinfonia Concertante.' Each side ends with a credit scroll although all four pieces appear to have been filmed in the same locale by the same film crew. 'Sinfonia' and Concerto No. 1 appear on side one, and the other two concertos are on side two. The presentation is entirely adequate and provides a pleasant 102 minutes of Mozart, but Harnoncourt and Kremer seem to be more lively and interpretative on side two. Their rendition of 'Sinfonia Concertante,' in particular, is a bit sleepy and lacks personality.

The picture, from filmed source material, is a bit soft and a little faded. The films present closeups during solos and long shots during ensembles, a standard format which concentrates on technique rather than drama. The recording is pleasant, but not daring enough to cause any noticeable distortion. An insert accompanies the disc which presents an essay, in English, on Mozart's composition of the concertos, and another, different essay, in French, presumably on the same subject.

MOZART: VIOLIN CONCERTOS NOS. 4 & 5

A pale and grainy picture makes listening to *Mozart: Violin Concertos Nos. 4 & 5*, featuring Gidon Kremer and the Wiener Philharmoniker under Nikolaus Harnoncourt, preferable to watching it. The program, which was directed by Horant H. Hohlfeld, often uses odd and unbalanced camera angles that also distract from the flow of the music. Kremer's performance is memorable, and the sound is in good condition.

MR. BLANDINGS BUILDS HIS DREAM HOUSE

We have never completely accepted the strenuous domesticity forced on Cary Grant in *Mr. Blandings Builds His Dream House*. In Grant's good screwball comedies, he retained an innocence so that even when he was not presented as suave, the viewer could see that an embryonic suavity was lurking beneath his awkward demeanor. In *Blandings* he's a mature adult getting the shaft from every angle, and the viewer never gets to see Grant's persona wink, to let everyone know that things are all right. Myrna Loy fares no better, and the film really has something to offer only for those who are fans of Melvyn Douglas. He gets to sit on the side and kibitz, and the movie might have been better all around if he and Grant had switched roles.

The black-and-white print is in very good condition. There are only a handful of blemishes and just one noticeable splice. The image is smooth and sharply focussed. The sound is acceptable.

MR. DRUMS BUDDY RICH AND HIS BAND LIVE

An insert accompanies *Mr. Drums Buddy Rich and His Band Live* explaining how the set was recorded. It includes a diagram showing where every microphone was placed and describes in excellent detail the steps which brought the music from the instruments to the disc. The concert was recorded in a sound studio which was dressed up to look like a jazz joint, with people sitting at tables smoking and listening as Rich and his band move through their repertoire. With the exception of one microphone which has a buzz when it is turned up too high, the sound is flawless. Conversations in the audience sound as if they are coming from behind your back and the band seems to be everywhere.

Unfortunately, the producers chose to approach the visual recording in the same manner they approached the audio recording. There are cameras everywhere, including one stuck beneath Rich's Plexiglas drum stand taking in the view between the soles of his feet. Because of all the cameras, the editor feels compelled to jump from one angle to the next and the flow of a musical idea is rarely taken into account.

MR. HULOT'S HOLIDAY (see **JACQUES TATI'S MR. HULOT'S HOLIDAY**)

MR. LUCKY

The source material for *Mr. Lucky* has a number of speckles, but remains in acceptable condition. The digitally encoded monaural sound fluctuates some, especially near the reel breaks, but never gets out of hand. Cary Grant portrays a gambler who conceives a scheme for bilking a war relief charity event, but changes his mind when his heart is captured by one of the society debs running the charity. Grant's character is unusually negative, but his charm and smooth manner are not affected. His co-star, Laraine Day, can barely read her lines correctly, let alone achieve the proper emotion for them, but when she falls for Grant's character she's completely convincing since, after all, it is Cary Grant she's falling for.

MR. MISTER – WELCOME TO THE REAL WORLD

Mr. Mister – Welcome to the Real World has just two music videos. One of the two, however, 'Broken Wings,' is an excellent black-and-white rock-and-road video with a mysterious bird who follows the hero on his cross country drive. It has the correct mix of ambiguity and sensibility and the visuals complement the lyrics without interpreting them. The other video, 'Kyrie,' is less involving, depicting the band members performing the song. The album's audio program follows the videos, accompanied by a still of the jacket.

MR. & MRS. SMITH

The key to Alfred Hitchcock's *Mr. & Mrs. Smith* occurs in the opening credit sequence where, after a montage of increasingly specific location shots appear beneath the general credits, the words, "Directed by Alfred Hitchcock," are superimposed on a doorbell and nameplate which reads, "David Smith." Mr. Smith is played by Robert Montgomery, who is made to look very much like Hitchcock, or a romantic variation thereof. A reference is even made to his 'slanted forehead.' Mrs. Smith is played by Carole Lombard. When Hitchcock and his family first moved from England to the US, they rented Lombard's house in Los Angeles and Hitchcock developed a strong crush on her, one of the many unconsummated infatuations he was to have over the course of life and career. Hence the film, a marital comedy, is both a satiric jab at his own marriage and a twinkle-eyed valentine to Lombard. Watch for the scene where Montgomery is carrying the champagne bottle, and Lombard, the two glasses.

The transfer is admirable. The black-and-white print has rich contrasts and no blemishes. The sound is also okay, hindered only by noises which are natural for an older recording. Image has included chapter markers for major scenes, but we wish they had included an extra marker for the film's most brilliantly comical sequence, in which Montgomery attempts, face to the camera, to give himself a bloody nose. It is not only the funniest piece of business in Hitchcock's entire oeuvre, but Montgomery's execution of the scene ranks with the best efforts of Charlie Chaplin or Buster Keaton.

MR. NORTH

The Danny Huston film, *Mr. North*, which was scripted in part by John Huston, is very much like a typical John Huston effort, though for better or worse it is executed with a lighter touch. Like many of the elder Huston's films, it has literary underpinnings, and is based upon a Thorton Wilder story about a man drifting through a rich community (Newport, Rhode Island in the twenties) who improves the life of everyone he meets. There are several terrific performances, including those given by Angelica Huston, Lauren Bacall, David Warner, and especially Harry Dean Stanton, who portrays a part-time 'British' butler from Chicago. The film is whimsical, but a little too sedate to generate a strong following.

The Ultra-Stereo surround sound is limited mostly to the musical score and, except for a ballroom sequence, is generally unremarkable. The picture is grainy. An excellent interview with Danny Huston has been included on an insert with the disc.

MR. SKEFFINGTON

An odd mixture of comedy and melodrama, *Mr. Skeffington*, starring Bette Davis and Claude Rains, has been restored to its original running time of two and a half hours for its home video release. The CX-encoded monaural sound has a steady amount of background hiss and cannot be played too loudly, but the black-and-white picture looks almost new, and unlike some restoration efforts, there is no indication when the restored footage kicks in.

The film is exhausting, but there are worse ways to get worn down. Davis fans will surely be pleased with the disc. The plot is about one-sided marriages and immaturity, and also concerns the supposedly devastating effects of aging, which, in the film, are exaggerated to the point of camp.

MR. SMITH GOES TO WASHINGTON

About halfway through side two (at 0:34) of *Mr. Smith Goes to Washington* the film slips sideways a bit and is then readjusted as the picture rolls merrily along. The print at several other points is scratchy and faded, but the sound is acceptable. The story – Jimmy Stewart portrays a naïve senator whose inner strength topples political corruption – is so wonderful that excusing the disc's production flaws is very tempting.

The 130-minute feature contains sequences normally left out of the commercial broadcast version, including a clever montage which tells the history of the United States in a progression of Washington D.C. memorials. Claude Rains's rendition of a corrupt senator is such a satisfying performance that you almost wish the film were about his character instead of Stewart's. When Stewart babbles about how he has been assigned "Daniel Webster's desk," Rains's response is a whole lesson in social graces.

MS. 45

The nervy rape-revenge thriller, *Ms. 45*, has been given a super transfer to disc. The film is an exploitation feature which was made with a limited budget. The film stock looks cheap, but the cinematography is stylish, and the picture on the disc appears brand new. Except for a fleeting white speckle or two, the screen image is uncorrupted.

The sound on the disc has also been handled superbly. Once again, the monaural soundtrack recording is indicative of a low budget effort, but the digitally encoded disc delivers the audio with more clarity and depth than would have seemed possible. In addition, a theatrical trailer which is in as good a condition as the film itself has been included at the end of the disc.

Ms. 45 generated a cult following immediately upon its release in 1980. It is unusual in several respects, though it remains comfortably within the boundaries of its genre. The plot follows a woman who goes on a men-only killing spree after being raped two different times in one afternoon. With one exception, the protagonist never speaks, a dramatic innovation which forces the viewer to identify with her. The gore is rampant, but it sometimes takes on a feminist touch, such as when the heroine lugs parts of a victim around town in a shopping bag. If the viewer is tolerant of the genre then the show is highly recommended. It is not just another gory disc.

MTV CLOSET CLASSICS

The rock songs from the late '60s and early '70s compiled on *MTV Closet Classics* are accompanied by obscure, psychedelic styled telecast performances. Cream 'I Feel Free,' Moody Blues 'Nights in White Satin,' The Who 'Magic Bus,' Beach Boys 'Surfin' USA,' Steppenwolf 'Born to Be Wild,' Black Sabbath 'Paranoid,' T Rex 'You're My Love,' Free 'All Right Now,' Jimi Hendrix 'Wild Thing,' Yes 'All Good People,' Mungo Jerry 'In the Summertime,' The Byrds 'So You Want to Be a Rock and Roll Star,' Grateful Dead 'One More Saturday Night,' Santana 'Black Magic Woman,' and Ike & Tina Turner 'Proud Mary.'

Most of the clips are so overloaded with effects, poor camera angles, and deteriorated sharpness that seeing and appreciating the musicians is difficult. The sound, on the other hand, is much too fresh and often does not line up with a vocalist's lip movements.

THE MUMMY

The trailer for *The Mummy* gets you all primed for the movie while having nothing to do with the film. ("You'll feel the awful, creeping, crawling terror that stands your hair on end and brings a scream to your lips." "Ahaa!") The disc has CX-encoded sound and side two is in CAV. Included with the trailer at the end are 29 production stills and lobby cards.

The movie opens to the swooning theme from 'Swan Lake,' which isn't as crazy as it first seems since the story is about the complications of eternal love. *The Mummy* may not seem as exciting as the other Universal horror pictures on first view, but the performances are full of camp – such as Zita Johann who has a captivatingly slinky decolletage – and the plot has a fast pace.

The print is not pristine, but the movie is fairly old, so that is to be expected. The disc is better than the movie, and owning it is a lot of fun.

THE MUPPET MOVIE
THE MUPPETS TAKE MANHATTAN

The Muppet Movie had a lot of humor which was geared for adults and was a disc which the whole family could laugh at. *The Muppets Take Manhattan* doesn't try as hard to hold the attention of those over the age of seven. There are a few clever creations – a group of rats who make great waiters and a trio of frog ad executives that would probably get along just fine in the real world – but the songs and the attempts to be cute and the footage given over to Miss Piggy seem endless. Do kids really like these songs? Wouldn't they rather see the Muppets do funny things instead of singing?

The picture on *Muppet Movie* is fairly grainy and the sound is a little rough. *The Muppets Take Manhattan* is in stereo surround and looks a bit fuzzy. Cropping on *Manhattan* also hurts the entertainment.

MURPHY'S LAW

It takes seven minutes for the credits to finish appearing during the opening of *Murphy's Law* and once they are over, so is the suspense. The movie, directed by J. Lee Thompson, is a bit tighter than most Charles Bronson efforts, but still grinds to a halt whenever the stoic star opens his mouth. The show is strongest when Carrie Snodgress is on screen. She makes a delicious villain. The disc is CX-encoded and preserves what there is of the film's original condition.

MURPHY'S ROMANCE

James Garner has always been more effective on television than in the movies, so we usually look forward to seeing his latest films on the TV. *Murphy's Romance* is a fair example. We doubted the film's veracity early on, when a pair of characters throw away perfectly decent ice cream cones so they won't have to hold them for the next scene, but Garner gradually won us back over, even if the rest of the movie did not. His portrayal of a sixty-year-old widower aroused by the charms of a divorcee (Sally Field) half his age has a relaxed confidence.

The sound is monaural, but it supports the presentation fairly well, especially the Carole King/David Sanborn score. The picture looks like it was filmed blurry, but is not helped by the below average transfer.

MUSCLE BEACH PARTY
BEACH BLANKET BINGO

The colors look fresh in *Muscle Beach Party*, but the image is often grainy. The opening and closing credits are tantalizingly letterboxed, while the rest of the movie is poorly panned and scanned. But, you see, in movies like this, when a character speaks but does not appear on the screen because of inept panning and scanning, it simply adds to your enjoyment of the thing. When you go to the *Beach*, you leave class in the car.

Muscle Beach Party is a movie where Buddy Hackett cannot keep a straight face doing scenes with Don Rickles. It is a sequel to other Beach movies, and so Annette and Frankie Avalon comment knowingly and otherwise act as if they've been there before. It is also a movie which is unashamed to show its age, with lines such as, "I'm going to send you into orbit, with a blast off that will make Friendship 7 look like a wet firecracker!"

Peter Lorre also shows up, but he has no idea where he is. There ought to be an Eastern Teaching which could use these movies as an example of achieving perfection, the lesson being that if you want to live a perfect life, just lower your standards until you find goals you can achieve.

There is such a thing, however, as going in over your head. *Beach Blanket Bingo* is also available, but it is not as satisfying as *Muscle Beach*. It does contain a precious snippet of Buster Keaton go-go dancing, and a few Paul Lynde wisecracks which will never age, but on the whole the film is less vital than *Muscle Beach Party* and less memorable. It has some of the worst day for night sequences you will ever see, a mermaid, blurry sky-diving scenes, squeezed credits, and even worse panning and scanning than *Muscle Beach*. The sound is also awful.

THE MUSIC MAN

Because of the age of the recording there is a distinct level of background noise on the CX-encoded stereo soundtrack of *The Music Man*, but the swelling volume and the old fashioned left/right directional separations more than compensate. The songs sound much better than they do on the soundtrack LP; the voices are crisper and there is more atmosphere.

The restored picture is a worthy accomplishment. The colors look new. The disc even manages Robert Preston's bright red/orange uniform without adding more than a barely perceptible blur. The problem is the lack of a wide screen. The jokey introduction of Buddy Hackett's character, whose voice appears to be coming from the rear end of a horse, is lost when the horse can't be seen. The a cappella quartet which performs several numbers at different intervals appears as a trio or even worse at one point, a duet. Watching the movie at home is like looking at it in a theater through a rolled-up program.

MUTANT

Mutant is a lame zombie feature about a small town in which many of the inhabitants have disappeared. The town is so sleepy already that no one notices the individuals are missing. Enter a couple of city boys who stumble across bodies left and right and start to worry about the town's efficiency at law enforcement. The print looks a little old. The film is not scary or exciting and one will have to rely on the jacket cover explanation to understand what happened. Something to do with toxic waste.

MUTILATOR

Six college kids in a deserted beach condo during fall break: 1) Since when does a condo look like a single-unit dwelling miles from anywhere else? 2) What is a 'fall break'?

Four of them and one cop get mutilated: 1) Since *The Mutilator* is 84 minutes long, that is approximately one murder per 12 minutes. This would normally put the midnight pizza crowd to sleep except that the murders are as gruesome as the jacket cover (which also made for an awful movie poster) implies. Not scary – what's going to happen is telescoped every step of the way until a cute, macabre twist at the bloody finale. 2) Whoever wrote the jacket cover copy didn't see the movie.

We won't complain that Vestron left the movie in CLV and didn't CX-encode: 1) The production values of the film are so bad that when a light causes a glare on the camera lens, whoever was laying the music track gave the glare its own cue. 2) Vestron missed out on big sales by not putting side two in CAV, but it would have been blood money.

MUTINY ON THE BOUNTY
MUTINY ON THE BOUNTY (Letterboxed)

The Marlon Brando/Trevor Howard *Mutiny on the Bounty* runs a little over three hours. Brando, who comes off like the rock star Prince, is brilliant as Fletcher Christian, making his character entertaining, heroic, and a little mysterious. And the movie is artistic in the way that all large monuments are artistic, if they stick around long enough.

Letterboxed, *Mutiny on the Bounty* is a lovelier and more captivating film than it is scanned and cropped. The Deluxe Letter-Box Edition has an aspect ratio of about 2.35:1. The screen compositions are heavenly, especially when there is any combination of wooden sailing vessels and South Sea vistas. The action sequences have a stronger impact when the framing is proper, and a viewer has stronger emotional responses to the characters when they remain on the screen reacting to others. It is a better movie, letterboxed, because the precariously dramatic narrative is more valid when the participants in the drama remain in view. Besides, when you see *Mutiny on the Bounty* in widescreen you feel you're in Tahiti; when you see it cropped on the TV you feel you're in your living room.

The picture on the letterboxed version has also achieved other improvements which make the disc superior to the earlier version. The picture on the cropped version has a vague haze to it, and the colors usually miss the true thrill of original Technicolor. Although still too dark (there is no detail in the shadows) and too pale (sailors who have been in Tahiti for 9 months look like they just got off the plane), the reds on the letterboxed rendition are stable and the colors can serve, at least, as a guide to what the original Technicolor luster offered. There are a few splices on the letterboxed presentation, including an inopportune one which occurs during a hula, but they pass like jump cuts.

The cropped version has only analog stereo surround sound, with its old-fashioned stereo separations and processing, and can be rough going if one pays too close attention, but it can be fun, as well. The digitally encoded surround sound on the letterboxed disc tends to fluctuate in both force and range. The music also flutters at a couple of points. At its best, however, the surround effects are pleasing. The Intermission on both discs occurs at the break between the first and second platter, and both have an Overture and Entre'Acte music. On both discs the platter side breaks are poorly chosen, and on the cropped version artificial fades-to-black have been inserted. At the end of the letterboxed disc, there is a wonderful original theatrical trailer hailing the film's elaborate production logistics.

MY AMERICAN COUSIN

The red letters in the credit roll on the end of *My American Cousin* have red shadows, and the screen, when it is dark, has a light grid pattern, but the quality of the photography and lighting in the film is exceptional. The opening shot, of twilight on a lake in western Canada, is stunning, and throughout, you really can't take your eyes off the landscape to watch the story. The sound is monaural and contains many appealing sound effects.

The movie is about a young British Columbian girl whose older Californian cousin (male) comes to visit one summer. It takes place in the sixties and is intended to invoke nostalgia and depict the lost promise of youth which, on more than one occasion, is compared to the elusiveness of the stars in the night sky.

MY BEAUTIFUL LAUNDRETTE

My Beautiful Laundrette was a very inexpensive film, and so the picture isn't in quite the same shape that a big budgeted blockbuster would be. The movie is an unimposing portrait of a young Pakistani living in London and taking his first steps toward being a laundrette czar. It is in stereo. Few sounds wander far from the middle, but the bass has a nice pluck to it. Like the character in the film, the filmmakers clearly have bigger things in mind for the future.

MY CHAUFFEUR

The comedy in *My Chauffeur* is not all that bad. The cast is attractive and there are as many gags which work as there are gags which don't. The condition of the disc is less admirable. The monaural sound, not CX-encoded, is poorly recorded and hopelessly flat in execution. The picture has a worn, used look to it.

MY DARLING CLEMENTINE

The first couple of times we saw *My Darling Clementine* on the late show we watched the beginning, fell asleep in the middle, woke up at the end, and thought we had sat through one of the best films we had ever seen. Then we finally forced ourselves to stay awake through the middle third and realized that it was more than the time of day which was causing us to nod off. Nevertheless, we still have great admiration for the film, which was directed by John Ford, and are happy that CBS/Fox has released it on laser disc.

The movie, which stars Henry Fonda and Victor Mature, is Ford's interpretation of the 'Gunfight at O.K. Corral.' The black and white cinematography, by Joe MacDonald, is riveting even on a small black and white TV set, and the CBS/Fox transfer, though not exceptional, is sufficient to bring out the finer qualities of the image. Some scenes are grainy and there are a couple of scratches, but the long deep focus shots and the poignant silhouettes make the strongest impression. The sound is fine.

The beginning and ending of the movie concern the O.K. Corral story. Fonda plays Wyatt Earp, who becomes sheriff of Tombstone to avenge the murder of his brother. Walter Brennan is the bad guy and Mature is the consumptive 'Doc' Holiday. The middle of the film has the romantic *Clementine* subplot, and it is here that the church-social Fordisms stop the movie dead. In critical analysis the sequences are valid and clearly expand the scope of the drama, which would otherwise be a simple whodunit tale with a shootout conclusion. As entertainment, however, the script pulls in the reins on what could have been a galloping joy ride through one of the best legends of the Old West.

MY DEMON LOVER

By the three-minute marker on side one of *My Demon Lover* we wanted out. The movie opens with a woman walking down a street in Los Angeles but, surprise, it is supposed to be New York. She sees her boyfriend stealing her furniture and doesn't realize what is going on. We knew exactly what was happening. A movie was failing right before our eyes. We managed to get through most of it – the girl falls in love with a demon who turns out, whew, not to be the one doing the serial murders – but it was not a pleasant experience. The transfer is not pleasant, either. The picture is often orange or grainy and the noisy monaural sound is not CX-encoded.

MY DINNER WITH ANDRE

We know some people who become so annoyed at Andre Gregory in *My Dinner with Andre* that they can't stand the movie, but they just don't have a sense of humor. Louis Malle's English language talk-a-thon is a clever and innovative sketch of two people whose careers have caused them to over-examine life and become trapped in an endless number of mental paradoxes.

The film depicts a two-hour dinner conversation between two men at a restaurant. Both have theatrical backgrounds, and one, Andre, has travelled extensively. An excellent interview with Malle, which is contained on a jacket insert that comes with the disc, details the way in which the film was put together, and however haphazard the conversation on the screen may seem, one can spot its deliberate structure after a couple of viewings. (One of the more obvious touches is the way in which Andre's trip to the Sahara Desert is dismissed. The humor is so subtle that you may not start laughing until days have passed.)

Since home video provides a more comfortable viewing environment than a theater, those who find the movie difficult to sit through may have an easier time watching it from the sofa. On the other hand, in a large audience, more people are likely to pick up on the humor and begin giggling, sometimes uncontrollably, keying others to the nature of the entertainment. The disc is okay. The picture is mildly grainy, but the movie, after all, wasn't filmed in 70mm. The sound is monaural and the analog track is less noisy than the digital track.

MY FAIR LADY (see PYGMALION)

MY FAVORITE BRUNETTE

Bob Hope is such a beautiful actor that you can watch his best movies over and over again, long after you've memorized the plot and all the gags, just to savor his finesse. Image has released one of Hope's best black and white comedies, *My Favorite Brunette*, with digital monaural sound and side two in CAV. The source material they have used is somewhat ragged. There are stretches which look sharp, but more often the image is soft, containing many scratches and even a splice or two. The sound also contains a few indiscretions, though the flaws on the audio track are not distracting in the way that some of the weakest sections of the picture are. The analog track is superior to the digital track.

In *Brunette* Hope portrays a photographer masquerading as a private eye, who is hired in that capacity by the brunette, Dorothy Lamour, to guard a map, find an uncle, and generally get into trouble. The plot is eventually explained, but that is secondary to the situations Hope must face along the way – thinking he is at a resort and not a sanatorium, he plays golf with an inmate who uses an imaginary golf ball; not noticing a ring Peter Lorre frantically places in his view while, thinking he is alone, he searches a room for clues; and so on.

The CAV side has two unsteady still frames out of every five, but enough is in place to deconstruct the totality of his craft. The final confrontation, as five bad guys chase Hope around a hotel room, is a wonderful group piece, but it would seem stilted and slow if someone less talented than Hope were leading it. His body movements are balletic, and his center of gravity is always on the gag, preventing the attention of the viewer from wavering. When the gun goes off and Hope does a pratfall, his limbs may fly all over the place, but slow motion reveals that his head remains perfectly balanced and focussed on his adversaries.

MY LIFE AS A DOG

My Life As a Dog is a perky and touching coming-of-age tale. Although the characters are living in a slightly firmer economic environment, a small company town in Sweden, the need for the young hero to solidify his emotional and social skills are as vital as they were for the hero in *Sugar Cane Alley*. In comparing the two films, one might look at the hero in *Dog*, who flirts on more than one occasion with mimicking a canine to deal with the intense stress caused by the breakup of his family, as having the luxury of madness which the boy scraping for survival in the cane fields did not have. But in both cases, the protagonists are so young that, no matter what assistance they receive, the victories they make over their own psyches are heroic achievements. Above all, the two discs make an excellent double bill, and one should not be purchased without the other.

Dog is in Swedish and has made-for-video subtitles, which are yellow and sometimes eat up a good portion of the screen. The picture is generally fuzzy. The filmmakers may have intended a nostalgic, dreamy look, but on disc the picture is indistinct and bothersome. The sound has no severe problems. Lastly, the break between side one and side two is so well chosen that it is recommended the viewer take an extra break before starting up the second side. Savoring the pause will increase the flavor of the whole program.

MY MOM'S A WEREWOLF

My Mom's a Werewolf is one for the dogs. Susan Blakely stars as a suburban housewife seduced into lyncanthropy by John Saxon. The film tries to be a comedy, but neither the script nor the cast encourages the viewer to care about the characters. The picture is good and the monaural sound is worth amplifying.

MY NAME IS BARBRA
COLOR ME BARBRA

At an age when most people are getting their first real job or deciding which major to commit themselves to at college, Barbra Streisand was starring in a show on Broadway and making television specials in her spare time. CBS/Fox released the first two specials on two monaural CX-encoded discs, *My Name Is Barbra* and *Color Me Barbra*. Each is an hour long, separated into three thematic segments, and encoded with chapter markers for every song (although the markers are not listed on the jacket). There are almost 30 songs on each disc, but some last for no more than a phrase or two. Streisand also provides a nice introduction on both discs, talking about how the shows were put together. The first is in black-and-white and the second is in color. The picture quality on both is satisfying.

MY SCIENCE PROJECT

The jacket cover of *My Science Project* tries to tie it to *Ghostbusters*. The movie is teen oriented, not science fiction oriented, but so few movies are science fiction oriented that fans will often settle for drivel such as this. The disc's sound and picture are bright and clean. Except for the loss of the wider screen, the disc is as good as the theatrical presentation. The stereo mix is the movie's only redeeming feature. The dialog is peppered with stale phrases and the script is salted with spoiled ideas. The filmmakers apparently thought that just because they had a dinosaur on the screen for five minutes, they would have a hit movie.

MY STEPMOTHER IS AN ALIEN

A strong contender for the worst side break of all time would have to be the RCA/Columbia release of *My Stepmother Is an Alien*. It was clearly chosen with the soundtrack turned off, because although the image makes a clean cut from one location to the next, there is a sound overlap – nothing less than Bach's most famous fugue, and you get the first 5 notes or so on side one with the remainder thrusting forth at the opening of side two. It is ridiculous.

So is the movie, though as a rental item it is probably passable. Dan Aykroyd portrays a SETI scientist who attracts the ministrations of a bumbling but svelte alien, somewhat daringly portrayed by Kim Basinger. Much of the comedy falls flat and none of the special effects are interesting. The picture quality on the disc varies, but the colors often look a little washed out and a number of scenes appear grainy. The sound is in stereo, but the separations are limited and unimaginative.

MY YOUTH IN ARCADIA (Import)
SPACE CRUISER YAMATO – NEW VOYAGE (Import)
URUSEI YATSURA – ONLY YOU (Import)

A Japanese cartoon which is overly dependent upon the dialog to be entertaining for non-Japanese speakers, *My Youth in Arcadia* uses too little movement and far too much repetition to tell its story pleasurably. With emphasis on the maudlin, the show follows a group of pirates and their battles against authoritarian repressors on another planet. Several characters die, but they look exactly like the characters who survive, so despite the dreary music and the tears on the cheeks of their comrades, the viewer will be bored.

Briefer and far less mystifying is the Japanese release, *Space Cruiser Yamato – New Voyage*. Again the weighty violin score emphasizes a sorrowful conclusion and the space battles lack zest, but the story is shorter (95 minutes) and quite easy to follow.

A third Japanese animation release, *Urusei Yatsura – Only You,* is also known as 'Those Obnoxious Aliens.' The story is of two space girls who are in love with the same Earth boy. There are some nice fantasy images of alternate worlds and some teasingly bikini-level sex. Since the dialogue is in Japanese, subtleties within the story are difficult to follow, including the references to Japanese domestic social etiquette and mythology.

MYSTERIOUS ISLAND

The colors and the sound (though it is not in stereo or CX-encoded) are so distinct that the quality of the transfer adds to the entertainment of *Mysterious Island.* The opening refrains of Bernard Herrmann's spirited score accompany some incredibly colorful credits.

The excitement continues in the opening scenes. A fierce storm rages through a Southern prison camp near the end of the Civil War. A dozen different shades of dark blue and grey fill the screen. When the union soldiers escape in an observation balloon, you can even make out a faint rainbow formed by the arc lamps shining into the sprayed water. True, this is a technician's error, but in seeing it you know that this is as good a transfer as could be possible.

The soldiers are blown across North America and into the southern Pacific Ocean. Don't ask how. They are deposited upon an island inhabited by a sparse collection of Ray Harryhausen's giant beasts. Loosely based upon a novel by Jules Verne, the mysteriousness inevitably fades, but the story has a moral (the island's creator wishes to prevent the 'causes of war' by eliminating famine) and the pace is as sharp as the colors.

THE MYSTERY OF PICASSO

The Mystery of Picasso has a running time of 77 minutes, and yet both sides are in CLV. The program is an excellent home video property. A few critics had indicated their impatience at watching the movie in a screening room, but ownership allows one the leisure of studying the contents at a chosen pace. Because the images are so rich in artistic composition, sensory input can become overloaded if attempted in one sitting.

The film records the construction of a dozen or so canvases by Pablo Picasso. Most are in ink and are depicted in full screen on the TV, but the last few are done in oils on a Cinemascope canvas and are shown in letterbox.

The canvases are set up so that Picasso stands behind them to draw. The ink shows through and the camera is in front, seeing only the work in progress. At about the halfway point in the film, the filmmakers back up a little to show how they are creating their magic and to let Picasso, in his Bermuda shorts, expose some of himself to the camera.

The sound, European monaural jazz, is not CX-encoded. The conversations which the filmmakers have with Picasso are in French with English subtitles which are difficult to read.

MYSTIC PIZZA

It is easy to over-praise *Mystic Pizza,* a lightly applied depiction of three young women living in a foggy Connecticut seaport. Each becomes involved in a relationship which accelerates passage to adulthood. The movie undercuts the standard stereotypes, and doesn't try to shove jokes in as a substitution. Anyone who expects the earth to move while viewing it will be disappointed, but the story is good for a little tingle or two.

The flesh tones look too pink in some shots, but the picture quality is generally decent. The stereo surround sound is low key and supports a nice, unassuming musical score. The disc also has chapter markers.

NABUCCO ARENA DI VERONA

The Arena di Verona is not very accommodating to video presentation. In *Nabucco Arena di Verona*, for example, there is never a closeup shot of a singer's face which does not also include the singer's knees. The jacket is misleading in this sense, because the camera never gets as close as the photo on the cover suggests. The costumes the cast are wearing are designed to be seen from afar. Up close, even at knee's length, the gowns look like shower curtains and the hats look like pieces from a Parcheesi board. The transfer is six years older than the recording, and while the picture has a typical video brightness, it also has erratic squiggles, blurry spots,and other symptoms of middle age. And it should be noted that Guiseppe Verdi's opera, which is sung in Italian, has not been provided with subtitles.

But if the disc is somewhat stifling visually, it is a liberation for the ears. The program has been digitally encoded, and the acoustics in the Arena create an intimacy which defies the size of the stage. The sound may have its share of dropouts and hiss, but it sounds real, with every voice and instrument seeming to float right in front of you. The sublime moment comes at the end of Act III, when a huge chorus of Hebrew slaves line the edge of the stage and sing Verdi's soft and inspiring 'Va, pensiero.' The music is moving enough, but as the camera pans slowly across the faces of the chorus, and pans, and pans, the song is given a visual strength and depth which reinforces a viewer's emotional response.

The temptation to just keep replaying that one chapter is difficult to overcome. The 132-minute disc is spread across three sides, with Act II being interrupted by the break between side one and side two. There are sixteen chapter markings. A libretto, in Italian and English, comes with disc. Except for 'Va, pensiero,' which almost looks like it was filmed by a different director, the camera work is stodgy. When the Babylonian tower crashes in Act IV, the camera doesn't bother to follow the chunks of concrete.

NADINE

The bright colors in Robert Benton's *Nadine* are well preserved on the disc. The picture quality is quite good and, despite some hiss, the sound is vivid and satisfying. The film is a comedy thriller starring Jeff Bridges and Kim Basinger. For some reason it takes place in 1954, in Austin, Texas, and there are gaping holes in the plot, but the comedy is tight and the performances, including Rip Torn as the main bad guy, are wonderful.

NAKED EYES

'Always Something There to Remind Me' was already featured on Pioneer's 12-inch music video compilation, *Picture Music*, so its inclusion on the 8-inch *Naked Eyes* is a weak selling point. The other clips are uninstersting and the picture and sound are average.

THE NAKED GUN

We weren't impressed with *The Naked Gun* when we saw it in a theater, but it is much funnier on a small TV screen. The disc is beautifully produced. Although monaural, the sound is quite sharp. The picture quality is also bright and enjoyable, with no deterioration of either color or sharpness. The adjusted TV aspect ratio noticeably affects only one gag (it concerns some food placed on the top of a refrigerator) and it seems as if the film, which was based upon the enjoyable but short lived TV series, *Police Squad!*, was meant for video all along. To facilitate the running time, the gags are not as compacted as they were in the TV series, but there are plenty to keep one giggling after multiple viewings.

THE NAKED JUNGLE

Charlton Heston plays such a jerk in *The Naked Jungle* – he's a 34-year-old macho virgin – that a viewer tends to think ill of the movie afterward, although it is actually fairly enjoyable. Of course it is about ants attacking a jungle plantation, but the bulk of the movie is a romance between Heston's character and a mail order bride, played by Eleanor Parker. The balance is off – on most discs sour romances start to turn sweet by the time the side changes, but this one stays cold until the ants come at the very end – and the movie's negative emotions make a stronger impression than its positive emotions. The script, by the way, is very careful not to mention the ants until they actually appear, so if you obtain the disc, try to find a friend who has never heard of the movie, keep the jacket out of sight, and watch how much more enjoyable the film can be if the finale is a surprise.

The transfer is acceptable. The original Technicolor hues are much too pale, but the image never looks washed out. Since the movie was not anamorphic, the picture is not cropped to any significant extent. There is one splice and some other minor markings, but no flaws which are too distracting. The sound is a bit noisy and indistinctive.

THE NAKED KISS

Only Sam Fuller could make fun of handicapped children and get away with it. His films are energetic and inventive, aggressively courting a viewer's desire for adult stimulation. In *The Naked Kiss*, Fuller uses the handicapped kids as props, never openly ridiculing them, but utilizing the extremity of their situation to accentuate his humor. In the same way that some people chuckle when they are confronted by a life-threatening situation, Fuller combines comedy and drama in his thrillers. It isn't there for relief, it is there to intensify a viewer's nervousness. Part of the film's dialog uses some unrealistically exaggerated euphemisms, but the plot concerns some very real and base adult emotions. Fuller forces a viewer to surrender to his films by removing all the outside reference points. In other words, you give up criticizing or resisting the entertainment and just start going along for the ride, very early on.

The transfer is gorgeous. The image is presented with an aspect ratio of about 1.66:1, replicating the black and white cinematography of Stanley Cortez as closely as possible. The print is spotless, and its bright contrasts intensify a viewer's entrapment. Some sequences are so vivid they almost look three dimensional. The sound is fine.

The Naked Kiss is about a woman who attempts to overcome an immoral past. The more one has been exposed to standard cinematic narrative, the more one will appreciate and enjoy Fuller's sometimes radical approach. Hence, the more discs you have in your collection, the more this one belongs with them.

THE NAKED PREY

Paramount's anatomically incorrect *The Naked Prey* has a beautiful color transfer which cannot compensate for the cropping that the film has had to endure to be presented on disc. What good is its breathtaking panorama, its deftly managed action sequences, or its heroic sense of vulnerability if you can't see half the picture?

For the record, the analog monaural sound is impressive. The movie, about a white hunter being chased by tribal warriors (who have real personalities and even cry when their compatriots are killed) through the African jungle, is virtually dialog-less, and all the more captivating for its ability to tell a narrative entirely through images. Now, if only we could get to see the images.

THE NAME OF THE ROSE

By the time *The Name of the Rose* arrived on home video, its origins as a self-examining text about text, were as fleeting as the solution to the mystery of the murders in the abbey. The most impressive aspect of the disc is the stereo sound. The movie was filmed in parchment orange colors, which do not translate fluently on to video. Too much of the movie is dark and lit by firelight to escape errant speckles or a steady blur. But the sound, which is only in analog, has an atmosphere and a dimension which will turn the most cramped viewing quarters into a dank and airy cloister. Echoes are not simply an embellishment but central to the needs of the plot, and it is in the re-creation of the echoes that the disc excels.

The film is an entertainment and it is also a representation of the troubled marriage between the Church and the written word. It is about the early stirrings of the Reformation, which was doomed to failure until the invention of the printing press several centuries later.

A title card at the beginning declares that the movie is a 'palimpsest,' which is a document that has been copied and written over numerous times. The smug pride which caused that title card to appear is also a guide to the value of owning the disc. *The Name of the Rose*, as a CLV laser disc, may be simplified, cropped, and scanned, but it is faithful to the essence of its previous iteration. And to the echo of the original text.

NAPOLEON

Contrary to what the theatrics of Francis Coppola might lead you to believe, *Napoleon* did not appear out of nowhere. A version which was a solid four hours long and contained much of the closing triptych had long been a staple on the revival circuit. That version, however, contained a substantial amount of insert footage filmed by Abel Gance or his associates many years after the original silent production. The material was tedious and distracting. Those sections were fortunately dropped by Robert Harris in the restoration that Coppola presented at Radio City Music Hall and in the subsequent road show, with Coppola Sr. conducting a live orchestra. It is this restored version which was released on disc in an impressive boxed packet.

The disc is not a necessity, but it is a luxury of the first order. To begin with, the picture is flawless. At the very worst there are one or two fleeting blue lines zipping through a section of orange-tinted footage.

The silent French film is by nature fairly ragged in state. Carmine Coppola's four-hour suite often sounds as if it is about to break into Borodin or Prokofiev but, given the nature of the assignment, his accomplishment is palatable. The 235-minute film is contained on four CLV sides of two discs, with the intermission separating disc one from disc two. The last 30 minutes are letterboxed, displaying Gance's daring attempt to enlarge the viewing panorama for the inspirational finale.

A third disc, with one CAV side, contains 160 production stills, from both the original feature and the restoration effort, and replays of the sequences one would most like to manipulate in Standard full feature play.

The four-hour feature follows Napoleon from his first fight in the snow to the eve of his initial Italian campaign. The events would normally comprise the opening paragraph in a book about his accomplishments. An equal amount of time is given to re-creating the major events in the French Revolution and the Reign of Terror which followed. Danton and company are presented as a sequential group of poor managers and Napoleon is shown, in contrast, to be the ideal executive. He is also unrelievingly dour, which takes its toll somewhere around side three. As a movie, where you are supposed to cheer the hero and feel good about life, *Napoleon* is too impersonal. The disc, on the other hand, is thoroughly inviting. It is too unique and too well produced to ignore.

THE NARROW MARGIN

Richard Fleischer's high speed train thriller, *The Narrow Margin*, makes a terrific disc. The black and white transfer looks sharp and has no more than a few scattered speckles. The image is rich and pleasing to the eye.

The 1952 film is also pleasing. At 71 minutes it gets off to a fast start, does what it has to do, and ends before a viewer could possibly tire of it. Charles McGraw portrays a cop transporting a mob witness on the train from Chicago to Los Angeles. Marie Windsor, as his charge, is incredibly captivating, with a hard-bitten, world weary personality which is both tough and wistful. Fleischer has a great time lighting her bust from below, but this is a movie where that kind of effect can pass unquestioned. The whole cast gives marvelous performances, and the script, as if it weren't speeding along quickly enough already, has a couple of good twists right when you think things are settling down. The sound is in fine shape. Side two is in CAV, with perfect still frames.

NATASHA

The collection of solo and duet dance numbers featuring Natalia Makarova, *Natasha*, is a unique program. Makarova dances in eleven different pieces, several of which would be the highpoint of a normal evening's performance. Since there are only one or two people dancing, the camera captures almost everything. Along with the traditional ballet numbers, Makarova is seen in the Broadway musical, 'On Your Toes,' and in a seductive rendition of 'Begin the Beguine.' Her dancing is supple and leggy, and to see her pull out the stops for 66 minutes is quite a treat.

The audio is less than perfect. The pianos sound fuzzy. The picture has the bright, recorded-for-video clarity resident on most ballet discs.

Many choreographers are represented and particularly notable are dances designed by Roland Petit and by Maurice Bejart. The disc also offers a chance to compare Anthony Dowell's dancing in the 'Bedroom pas de deux' from 'Manon' to his performance on *Manon*, where he dances the same scene with Jennifer Penney.

NATIONAL AIR & SPACE MUSEUM ARCHIVAL VIDEODISC 1
NATIONAL AIR & SPACE MUSEUM ARCHIVAL VIDEODISC 2

If they were slides, they would stack as high as the Empire State Building. If every snapshot were three inches wide, they would stretch for ten miles. Instead, 200,000 photographs from the archives of the National Air and Space Museum have been transferred onto a pair of discs, *National Air & Space Museum Archival Video Disc 1* and *National Air & Space Museum Archival Video Disc 2*.

Organized alphabetically, the photographs are primarily black and white and cover all aspects of aviation. *Videodisc 1* is specifically about airplanes, listing so many makes and models that it only goes to the beginning of the W's. *Videodisc 2*, which is the disc to buy if you are tempted to get just one, finishes the alphabet (including the Wright Brother's work, which makes no appearance on the first disc) and then goes on to provide photos of everything from balloons to airports, including a 32,000-piece portrait collection of important contributors to achievements in flight.

The first disc is put together a little sloppily. The titles are inconsistent, some of the snapshots are upside down, and in one frame, hands can be seen holding the picture steady. The absence of color removes a level of detail from the pictures and makes one more aware of the limitations of video reproduction. On both discs, the images rarely fill the screen and are instead captured in their entirety – worn borders, old Scotch Tape marks, and all. The brochure photos are so prevalent that a viewer will quickly become blind to the style and see only what is different about each airplane. The neutrally candid photos are more captivating, even if they tell one less about the airplanes.

The oddities – the Miller Flying Platform, the McDonnell Goblin – provide more than simple amusement. While it is obvious today that the short, fat Goblin is an awful idea for a plane, someone had to try building it to make sure. You can see which ideas failed – multiple wings, multiple parallel cockpits, blunt noses – and which ideas continued to develop into the airplanes we have today.

A section on boomerangs and a section on kites actually belongs on the second disc, but has been squeezed onto the first, for variety. The most disappointing segment is the short spread (about 50 pictures) given to Lear jets. The Gossamer fuel-less vehicles are represented with only three stills.

The catalog which comes with the first disc identifies each aircraft (example: Sopwith Camel 39699-39776). There is no other accompanying literature, and further information must be obtained from other sources. This is where the second disc is so effective. For one thing, you can see what Mr. Sopwith looks like – and with his rounded cheeks and boyish expression he seems like the sort who would name his airplanes after animals. More importantly, the photographs on the second disc begin to place aircraft in a wider context of purpose and utility. The disc is an important addition for those who purchased the first and felt short changed by the restricted (if gargantuan) scope. For those who wish to purchase it alone, there is a reiteration of the airplane manufacturers that will adequately orient a viewer to the range of aeronautical invention.

The catalog for *Disc 2* is a mess, with the listing of the first frames pasted in the middle of the document. The disc, however, is a great improvement over the first in terms of production, with thorough title cards, a handy index at the end of each side, and every photograph right side up. The transfer was good on both discs, with only a half-dozen or so frames quivering.

Along with recapping the highlights of the first disc, *Disc 2* has so many other images. Balloons, airline schedules, logos, World War II 'nose' art, more photos of pressure gauges than you would ever wish to step through, airports, air bases, air museums, air shows, air photography, airline seats, ejection seats, parachutes, the Goodyear blimp, air mail postage stamps, an air cargo pictorial, air awards, the Edwardian dining facilities of the early passenger cruisers, and something called aerobic flying.

There is also a cute little art and literature section, with fantasy drawings (some in color), black-and-white stills from *2001*, 'My Favorite Martian,' et cetera, and depictions of flight in religion.

The "Aerospace Personalities" division is the most valuable aspect of the disc. You can construct biographies of Amelia Earhart (450 photos) and Charles Lindberg (420 photos) from what has been provided. Every American president of this century is represented, as are other world leaders who by chance strolled past an airplane. One of the nicest portraits is of Alexander Graham Bell. He has a bushy white beard and is standing in front of an early flying machine with a child sitting on a wing above Bell's shoulder. The child is wearing a leather helmet. Knowing what we do today, could any vision of the future be more naturalistic or more promising?

NATIONAL AIR & SPACE MUSEUM ARCHIVAL VIDEODISC 3

The *National Air & Space Museum Archival Videodisc 3* confirms that the scope of the NASM project is unparalleled and worthy of attention. The disc has 100,000 more photographs representing the Army Air Corps/US Air Force collection of World War II (side 1) and pre-1954 peacetime (side 2) pictures. Many of the photos are at least partially posed, but the disc as a whole takes on a human dimension which was only sporadic in the first two NASM discs. There are endless photos of aerial reconnaissance and endless more of people receiving medals (often taken from a stationary camera so when played at quarter speed they take on an odd realism) but the disc also has endless variety. Along with mechanics and aviators of all shapes and sizes, there are photos of gaskets and parachutes and wheels and war posters.

Some of the most interesting pictures include those showing black WWII pilots, a record of a rodeo held in Burma, and the war-weary civilians watching their fields turn into temporary landing strips. The high point of the disc is probably the hundreds of examples of 'Nose Art' painted on the sides of various B-17's. Most are typical of young men's day dreams, drawings of scantily clad women and titles such as 'Miss B. Haven' or 'Visibility Perfect.' But there is also one bomber which went by the name of 'Veni-Vidi-Vici' and another called 'Murder Inc.'

This is the best produced of the three discs. We only came across two photos which were upside down. As with the others, the entire snapshot is shown, pencil marks, wrinkly borders and all. On maybe ten percent of the pictures, typed or handwritten captions are readable. Each side of *Videodisc 3* has an index at the very end, an improvement to the booklets which accompanied the earlier releases.

The non-WWII material on side two is somewhat of a reiteration of the first discs. But the human element is on side two as well, whether it is the pilots sitting proudly in their cockpits or officers looking unrelaxed at their clubs. Our favorite photo needs no description beyond the typewritten caption which accompanies it: "Mrs. Lillian Janeway Alneter takes up hydroairplaning at Curtiss School Winter 1911-12."

NATIONAL AIR & SPACE MUSEUM ARCHIVAL VIDEODISC 4

The final Air Force Collection entry in the *National Air & Space Museum* series, *Archival Videodisc 4*, is a single sided disc which contains a wide scope of still frame images, including 6000 works of art – paintings, drawings, etc., commissioned or collected by the US Air Force.

Videodisc 4 contains a little bit of everything, and with 50,000 entries, that can be quite a lot. There seem to be fewer reams of medal ceremony photos than there were on the first disc (if you served in the Air Corps in WWII and had your picture taken, you're probably in there, somewhere), and fewer aerial photos of unidentified landscapes. There is a segment called 'Personalities' which features portrait photos of a number of Air Force dignitaries, as well as stray photos of important personages ranging from Franklin Roosevelt to Enrico Fermi. The disc also contains the museum's 'addendum' collection, consisting of loose photos that they have not cataloged with the main gatherings.

There are photos from every era of flight and pictures of planes, of air bases, and of anything to do with the US Air Force. There are photos of clouds, of maintenance procedures, of airplane parts, of an operation to drop hay for cattle stranded by a winter storm, and of company mascots. A collection of photos taken during USO tours in Korea includes a couple choice snapshots of Marilyn Monroe which we have not seen replicated elsewhere.

Many of the snapshots, especially those depicting people with airplanes, achieve eloquence if one stares at the compositions long enough, no matter how haphazardly the images were originally captured. Children and puppy dogs, however, will win photo popularity contests every time. One of our two favorite stills depicts three Eskimo children posing with mild curiosity for the camera, and the other depicts two Scottish Terriers standing on folded parachutes on the wing of a fighter plane, with the wing's guns adding just the right touch of reality to the image. Our favorite sequence is a group of photos from World War II entitled 'Women in Industry,' which depicts 'Rosie the Riveter' poses in a variety of situations. Although the photos are clearly publicity oriented, the women are genuine blue collar laborers, and there is something about their cheerfulness which sparks a deep feeling of patriotism.

It is the artwork segment, though, which endeared us to the disc. The images range from sketches that ended up in recruitment brochures to portraits which are hanging at the Air Force Academy in Colorado. Even the drawings which are the most pedestrian serve a function in the sequence, giving a viewer breathers between the more captivating pieces. With 6000 entries, there are inevitably works which will grab you and hold you, whether it is a jet fighter which has been given just the right gleam or a schizophrenic attempt to depict the essence of a mission in Vietnam.

NATIONAL AIR & SPACE MUSEUM ARCHVIAL VIDEODISC 5

A collection of 100,000 official NASA photographs can be found on the *National Air & Space Museum Archival Videodisc 5*. Other collections of NASA photographs have concentrated on planetary imagery, but *Archival Videodisc 5* spends a great deal of time on the ground, featuring snapshots of everything from the first monkey strapped into a capsule to a group of flight nurses posing under bed sheets. Views from space are given their due, however, as a collection of 40,000 photographs taken of Earth by astronauts aboard various shuttle missions rounds out side two.

The pictures are separated to black & white and color, and then ordered chronologically (through 1986). A number of the black and white photos are repeated with color. In accordance with the series format, the entire photograph appears, including its backing and whatever is sticking out underneath its edges. Along with photographs, the images feature speculative and memorial drawings, charts, and miscellaneous graphics.

A frame number index booklet is provided with the video disc which lists single word descriptions for groups of photographs, although more information can be obtained by writing addresses listed in the text. A copy of the index appears at the end of side one. At the end of side two there is a more impressive, sorted index designed to guide one through the 40,000 shuttle photographs, organized by subject (i.e., the country or continent in view).

The photographs from the early sixties are the most interesting and the least anthologized. Some of the color photographs are faded, but others are in excellent shape, such as the one in which John and Jackie Kennedy are greeting John Glenn and it is difficult to shift concentration from Jackie's bright red outfit. Also fascinating are the experimental aircraft which once commanded a decent portion of NASA's budget. There are numerous speculative drawings of nuclear engines as well as space station designs and early versions of what later became the Space Shuttle.

NATIONAL AIR & SPACE MUSEUM ARCHIVAL VIDEODISC 6

NASA's photos of the moon are collected on *Archival Videodisc 6*. About 80,000 images are included on the two-sided disc.

The photos include shots taken from both manned and unmanned missions, preparation activities, a biographical section on the Apollo astronauts, and a few Soviet images. Some sequential photos, when played back at quarter speed, create the illusion of movement. The bulk of the collection consists of quadrant by quadrant photos taken of the moon's surface, and many of these are cross-referenced to a collection of maps which identify prominent features.

The disc, however, is not one of the stronger National Air and Space Museum offerings. Much of the material has been anthologized elsewhere in a more accessible fashion. A number of the pictures are overexposed, and the color images are badly faded.

On the plus side, a printed index which accompanies the disc runs close to 200 pages and is the best organized and most informative of the *Archival* series. One only needs to obtain a decent Mercator map of the moon to utilize the disc fully and take advantage of the detailed, armchair exploration it can offer.

NATIONAL AUDUBON: GALAPAGOS

A superb, hour-long National Audubon Video nature program, 'Galapagos: My Fragile World,' has been released on disc with the title, *National Audubon: Galapagos*. Among other things, the disc puts *The Undersea World of Jacques Cousteau: Dragons of the Galapagos* to shame. Ostensibly a profile of the wildlife photographer, Tui De Roy, who grew up on the islands and has forged a remarkable career by photographing the fauna in her backyard, the program still manages to give a better sense of scope to the entire Galapagos ecosystem than any other documentary which has appeared on disc. The short pieces on the tortoises, iguanas, blue-footed boobies, and others are both memorable and informative vignettes which teach the viewer not only about the specific animal, but about the ways of the natural world.

The picture quality shifts between very good and excellent. There are some stunning shots, including the colors of the aforementioned boobies and a primordial vision of what are basically prehistoric tortoises, lumbering across a remote landscape. The sound is stereophonic, and for this type of program it is hard to imagine that the audio could be better than it is. Not only is the vaguely Ecuadorian background music stereophonic, but many of the animal and bird calls are as well, and all are clearly synched with the images.

THE NATIONAL GALLERY OF ART
THE ART AWARENESS COLLECTION FROM THE NATIONAL GALLERY OF ART (DiscoVision)

Value judgements are not easily applied to *The National Gallery of Art*. An important museum is thoroughly represented in a manner successful enough to make one believe that other collections will someday follow, but one can see improvements needed for similar projects in the future. 1645 frames depict various pieces in the museum's collection. Each is followed by a title card which provides the name of the work and the name of the artist, the name of the benefactor who gave the museum the work, the dates during which it was conceived, the medium used, and the size of the work, in inches.

Side one has a twenty-minute documentary on the history of the museum. Some nice newsreel footage of Washington D.C. in the '30s is shown as the narrator performs verbal somersaults to praise Andrew Mellon's philanthropy without dwelling much on how the man acquired the money to buy the paintings in the first place. Side two, after the stills, has a tour which gives no real sense as to how the museum is organized. The accompanying lecture is an adequate starting point to approach the history of Western art.

What the future holds for ventures like this is a rechannelling of how we look at and respond to art. The more carefully forthcoming collections are arranged and presented, the more important the disc medium will become.

One of the early DiscoVision titles was also derived from the same museum collection, *The Art Awareness Collection from the National Gallery of Art*. By itself the CAV disc was unremarkable, a collection of eight sixteen-millimeter films which one may very well have viewed in grade school. School children will certainly recognize the style, with a calm narrator and a sleepy camera bobbing gently over various paintings and assuring the viewer that even art has something to teach us.

In the context of *The National Gallery of Art* archival disc, however, the *Art Awareness* disc is advantageous in that it adds another hour's worth of informative lectures on the major works in the National Gallery's collection.

NATIONAL GEOGRAPHIC/AFRICA'S STOLEN RIVER

Africa's Stolen River is an amazing documentary about an area in Africa which goes through a major ecological change when a river dries up. We wish there were an accompanying 'Making of' feature, because the documentary, whether real or staged, contains so many unusual occurrences it would be a wonder even if it turned out the major players were people in elephant suits. The river in question, the Savuti in Botswana, appears and disappears over decades, likely spigotted by unseen seismic activity. The documentary, narrated by Richard Kiley but depicting no humans, captures a period of drying up, a disaster to the area which, clearly, the elephants, and perhaps some of the other, older mammals, can recall from thirty years earlier. They are seen scratching for existence, migrating, and even digging for water, as the normal social and territorial activities fall by the wayside. Many die. The footage must have taken hearts of steel to compile, but the result is an important contribution to the *National Geographic* library and to the tradition of nature films in general.

The sound is good and the picture is okay. A few sunsets look a bit blurry, but the night photography is solid.

NATIONAL GEOGRAPHIC/ AUSTRALIA'S ABORIGINES

We don't know enough about Australian Aborigines to tell when programs about them are insightful or when the programs are full of baloney, but all tend to verge a little too strongly upon the mystical aspects of the aboriginal beliefs, as if a translation were the only and proper way to convey their society to ours. *National Geographic – Australia's Aborigines* depicts a tribe which lives in a National Park, near Darwin in the Northern Territories. It is also a typical *National Geographic* ecological portrait, showing the wildlife and seasonal changes in the Park in great detail, with a token linking to the aboriginal legends involving the primary fauna.

The picture is soft and the sound is passable. The episode is all right, but we would have preferred more anthropology and less wide-eyed mysticism about the Dream Time.

NATIONAL GEOGRAPHIC/ CAMERAMEN WHO DARED

Gratifyingly free of flagrant self-promotion, *National Geographic/Cameramen Who Dared*, is a super documentary about the risks filmmakers expose themselves to for the sake of obtaining good footage. The program provides a history of risky filmmaking and includes more than a dozen profiles of cameramen placing themselves in unusual or life threatening situations. Nature photographers and war correspondents, men who deliberately tempt fate and men who never held a camera before, but happened to be in the right place at the right time, are depicted. All have contributed to what is known about the world and how we look at it in the twentieth century. One couple, Martin and Osa Johnson, who started the safari documentary fad, would make a terrific subject for a Hollywood adventure movie. Highlights in the program include going nose to nose with a great white shark and with a polar bear, a journey through labyrinthine ice formations beneath the waters surrounding Antarctica, scenes from the frontline in World War II and in Vietnam, hanging on vines with orangutans who try to untie the safety ropes, and a pirouette on the peak of Mt. Everest. The footage varies in quality depending upon its age, but the picture transfer is excellent and the sound is fine.

NATIONAL GEOGRAPHIC/ CREATURES OF THE MANGROVE

The mangroves in *Creatures of the Mangrove* are on an isolated island in a Borneo delta. The trees and mudflats are home to the monkeys that look like Jimmy Durante, fiddler crabs, fish called 'mudskippers' which spend a lot of time on land, 'archer fish' which can spit an ant off a branch at twenty paces, and the other bugs, reptiles, and assorted predators and prey. This type of program is one of the most enjoyable formats in the *National Geographic* series. With music and sound effects and occasional narration, the show is both informative and relaxing. People never appear on the screen. The richly textured sound is digitally encoded monaural. The picture is weaker than other *National Geographic* discs. The footage is grainier than usual, particularly during the night scenes.

NATIONAL GEOGRAPHIC/IN THE SHADOW OF VESUVIUS

The sound on *In the Shadow of Vesuvius* is weak, requiring a mild volume increase for playback. The picture has no significant flaws. *Vesuvius* is an informative documentary which manages to cover a variety of subjects concerning life around the Bay of Naples. The most fascinating information concerns the ruins of Pompeii, supported by elaborate graphics and recent archaeological finds. The second half of the program, depicting contemporary life in an earthquake prone area, is a bit more pedestrian (the program might have been stronger if the narrative segments had been reversed), but the letdown isn't enough to spoil the program's overall educational and entertainment values.

NATIONAL GEOGRAPHIC/LIVING TREASURES OF JAPAN

Viewers with an interest in crafts and folk art will not want to miss *National Geographic/ Living Treasures of Japan*, an excellent collection of profiles of about a dozen different artists. It has monaural sound which seems pretty clean and a passable picture.

Living Treasures takes a look at specific artists who are considered by the Japanese government to be the best in their field. They have been endowed with an official 'laureate' status, and spend their time practicing their art and training apprentices. A puppeteer, a Kabuki actor, a 90 year old woman who dyes cloth with indigo, a potter, a sword maker (the metal on the blade is folded over onto itself some 70,000 times), a bell maker, a doll maker, and a man who makes paper are among those featured. A brief history of each artist is provided by the narration, but the visuals concentrate upon the execution of the craft. Not only is each segment fascinating, but there is a tendency to avoid blinking for fear of missing an intriguing detail.

NATIONAL GEOGRAPHIC/LOVE THOSE TRAINS

National Geographic/Love Those Trains is not just about trains, it is about train nuts, people who prefer to ride on top of the box car instead of sitting comfortably in first class on the train from Guayaquil to Quito, people who spend their Saturdays cleaning grime out of the joints of a steam engine which goes nowhere, and people who meticulously build working replicas one eighth the size of the real thing and then make their passengers squeeze into modified box cars for a ride. The program, working from a rich resource, just dabbles in a few train related activities but still succeeds in fulfilling its established theme. In addition to the above, there is a depiction of the journey which a head of lettuce takes from a field in California to a salad in New York, a look at how twenty feet of snow is cleared from several miles of track, a parade for hobos held in Ohio, a disjointed history of the earliest steam engines and of building the Transcontinental railway, a trip on the Orient Express, and similar activities.

The sound is flat and disappointing, taking some of the thunder out of the steam whistles. James Whitmore's narration is also lackluster, and offers no tonalities which would impart a true enthusiasm for the subject. The interviews with the real enthusiasts can only compensate in part. The picture, from a film source, is a little grainy but passable.

NATIONAL GEOGRAPHIC/MYSTERIES OF MANKIND

Richard Kiley narrates *National Geographic/Mysteries of Mankind*, a decent anthropological update for those who have not been in school for a while. The program, which lasts a full hour, surveys the state of knowledge concerning man's origins. The most significant fossil discoveries are highlighted, as are the work done by scientists who study primates (there is fascinating footage of chimpanzees reacting to a realistic model of a leopard) and those who confine their explorations to the genetic maps in a test tube, where one day the genealogy of every species on earth may be accurately plotted. Speculation on what the earliest forms of man looked like and how they lived are also provided in an entertaining manner. The picture and sound are passable and the disc has more than a dozen chapter markers.

NAITONAL GEOGRAPHIC/RETURN TO EVEREST

Return to Everest profiles the later exploits of Sir Edmund Hillary, a man who quite literally peaked early in his career. Hillary spends a lot of time in Nepal doing penance, the program suggests, for having partially sparked the influx of tourism there (the National Geographic would be equally guilty on this account). He has assisted in the construction of more than a dozen school buildings, and in general has acted like a super-Peace Corps worker for the majority of his adulthood. We don't completely trust the portrait which the show creates – Hillary suffers from an altitude-sickness which induces symptoms similar to those of a stroke and while at times he seems completely alert, at other times his composure is similar to footage of the retired Muhammad Ali – but the segments of his life depicted are genuine, and the program also provides a good look at Nepal, as well as the ever-inspiring trail that leads to Everest. Although he appears throughout the program and can be heard talking to locals, Hillary is never interviewed on camera. The picture and sound transfers are fine. Richard Kiley narrates.

NATIONAL GEOGRAPHIC/THE RHINO WAR

The colors on *The Rhino War* are particularly rich and the sound, which includes the use of African folk music in the score, is very good. The disc has everything one could want to know about rhinoceroses and their sad decline. It dispels the myth that the animal's horn is sought after solely for sexual enhancement (it is mostly used for curing a variety of illnesses through Oriental folk medicine and in the manufacturing of handles for daggers) and details the difficulties involved in keeping the species alive in an uncontrolled environment. The program is quite interesting, and the rhinoceroses are cute if you look at them long enough.

NATIONAL GEOGRAPHIC/SEARCH FOR BATTLESHIP BISMARK

The construction of *National Geographic – Search for Battleship Bismark* is a little too obvious for our tastes, but the program still has its merits. A history of the German battleship's brief maiden voyage is juxtaposed with Robert Ballard's quest to find her remains. The cross cutting between the British searching for the enemy and Ballard searching for the rusty hulk is too blatant. It attempts to create symbolism where there is really none to be had. The individual tales, however, are worthwhile. The trip which the Bismark took, up to Iceland and then almost back to France, is clearly detailed, with rare battle footage and survivor interviews from both sides. Ballard's search is also a legitimate undertaking which is given its due. The picture and sound transfers are crisp.

NATIONAL GEOGRAPHIC/SEARCH FOR THE GREAT APES

Two half-hour presentations are combined into one program on *Search for the Great Apes*. The first part looks at a husband and wife scientific team in Borneo, studying orangutans. The second part is a profile of Dian Fossey, produced before the poachers got rough (a text epilog concludes the film).

The closing credits appear to apply only to the Fossey film, but both pieces are informative, particularly in showing how the scientists gather their data. The sound and picture transfer are okay, though the source material looks a bit old.

NATIONAL GEOGRAPHIC/THE SOVIET CIRCUS

The Soviet Circus would have been laughed off the drawing boards if it had been submitted to the same kind of scrutiny which the scientific *National Geographic* programs are subjected to. The show is a typical circus publicity puff piece, padded further by the government which is doing the exhaling. Don't get us wrong, we would love to watch an hour of circus acts, and we think a legitimate behind the scenes look at circus employees would also be interesting and could probably be objective and maintain a positive point of view. But the propaganda about how the workers are so happy and how all the children look forward from their first toddle to someday appearing in the ring is relentless. The few acts which are shown are entertaining, but they are not well photographed – the picture is generally blurry and grainy – and end all too quickly.

NATIONAL GEOGRAPHIC/STRANGE CREATURES OF THE NIGHT

An older program co-produced with David Wolper, *Strange Creatures of the Night*, offers a potpourri of limited-light nature photography. Among the most interesting sequences is the feasting of vampire bats on a herd of cattle and the depiction of a pack of hyenas who almost take down a baby rhinoceros. The picture and sound are a little more strained than most offerings – Leslie Nielsen narrates – but the material does not seem outdated and is varied enough to hold one's interest.

NATIONAL GEOGRAPHIC VIDEO – AFRICAN WILDLIFE

The narration in *African Wildlife* describes the seasonal cycle of wet and dry weather in northern Nambia, and how the wildlife adapts to deluges and heat waves. One of the most interesting creatures was a mother lion who surprised her cubs by presenting them with wounded game for a meal. The cubs had to figure out how to kill it before they could eat it. Like a teacher officiating a test, the mother sat swishing her tail in the sun and watched her pupils pass their exam. The picture and sound are fine.

NATIONAL GEOGRAPHIC VIDEO – AMONG THE WILD CHIMPANZEES

For those who fondly remember the first Jane Goodall program the National Geographic produced, there is a follow-up, and it has been released on laser disc as part of the *National Geographic Video* series. Entitled *Among the Wild Chimpanzees*, the 1984 effort tells the complete story (to date) of Goodall's studies. The first half includes the familiar footage (although it looks in much better condition than it ever did on the old 16mm prints we used to sit through) of her approach and initial findings. She sees the chimps turn sticks into tools to obtain termites and watches them pass culture from one generation to the next. The story then goes on, as tragedy after tragedy upsets the idyllic Eden which had been depicted in the first film. The apes get polio. They wage war upon each other. One becomes the chimpanzee version of a mass murderer, killing as many as 15 infants in her group over an extended period of time.

Despite these occurrences, the program remains intriguing and makes for excellent family viewing. Alexander Scourby's narration, however, simplifies much of the science being presented without acknowledging the simplifications. Chimpanzees are highly political animals, engaging in alliances and subterfuge which would make the Kremlin look like a contest for class president. Yet their activities, as depicted in the documentary, are never explained. Scourby often uses the excuse that 'we don't know why' the actions take place. Either Goodall hasn't done her homework, or the producers don't want to take the trouble to present complicated ideas and spoil all their 'Bedtime for Bonzo' shots.

The picture is a little faded, but as we mentioned above, it is in much better condition than we had expected. The sound is monaural and has not been CX-encoded.

NATIONAL GEOGRAPHIC VIDEO – ATOCHA: QUEST FOR TREASURE

Unlike the other *National Geographic Video* programs, which all try to be scientific and teach you something, *Atocha: Quest for Treasure* is more like the magazine itself. It tells the story of Mel Fisher, who spent 15 years trying to locate a sunken Spanish galleon and finally scored. The narrative is primarily a blue collar adventure story about Fisher and the persistence, conniving, and metal detectors he went through trying to find the galleon.

Narrated by Martin Sheen, *Atocha* has been one of the most popular titles in the series, probably because it shows 'normal' people doing adventurous things and because, unlike the treks down frozen northern rivers and the like, there is a payoff in the end. In Spanish gold.

NATIONAL GEOGRAPHIC VIDEO – AUSTRALIA'S IMPROBABLE ANIMALS

The narration provides in *National Geographic Video – Australia's Improbable Animals* insufficient and sometimes questionable information, and scattered between the nature photography segments are awkward scenes using actors to depict historical events. The nature photography is captivating.

The disc has a nice looking picture which extends to even the toughest night shots. The monaural sound, which includes an aboriginal music score but few animal sounds, is digitally encoded and free of problems.

NATIONAL GEOGRAPHIC VIDEO – BALLAD OF THE IRISH HORSES

The source material for *Ballad of the Irish Horses* is often grainy, but that is the disc's only major drawback. The music soundtrack is by The Chieftans, and though it hasn't got enough bass it still sounds great with digital encoding. The subject matter is refreshingly esoteric, as the hour long program tells one just about everything there is to know about the horses of Ireland.

When one thinks about horses at all, one usually thinks of them racing across wide open plains, so the story of how they came to adapt so well to a land of peatbogs and cobblestones is fascinating. The world's greatest race horses trace their ancestry to Ireland, as do many of the world's great riders. The show gives a history of the introduction of the horse to the island, then branches into the different sorts of horses and utilities or sports they are used for. Finally, although the program is about horses, it is also about the people of Ireland, and in particular it is about the individuals who have decided to cast their lives and vocations to be near the animals. Their rosy cheeks and their brogue provide a human connection which brings the viewer closer to nature than any of the misty shots of wild foals scampering across the paddock.

NATIONAL GEOGRAPHIC VIDEO – BORN OF FIRE

(see **NATIONAL GEOGRAPHIC VIDEO – SECRETS OF THE TITANIC**)

NATIONAL GEOGRAPHIC VIDEO – THE CREATURES OF THE NAMIB DESERT

The Creatures of the Namib Desert is a depiction of the ecosystem within a specific environment, in this case the Namib Desert of SouthWest Africa and Nambia. This is a desert which hugs the coastline and is actually beset by fog in the morning two months out of the year. The program is narrated by Burgess Meredith. The picture and sound are fine.

NATIONAL GEOGRAPHIC VIDEO – EGYPT: QUEST FOR ETERNITY

Egypt: Quest for Eternity is about the history of ancient Egypt and the efforts of recent archeologists to study and preserve historical sites. The narrator, Richard Basehart, leaps two thousand years in a single sentence at one point, but provides a decent sketch of the course of Egyptian civilization over six millennia. The jacket cover is misleading, since the golden treasures of King Tut have nothing to do with the program, which concentrates on hieroglyphics and architecture. Although the program was put together in 1982, the footage looks dusty and aged.

The narration leaves one with the impression that Ramses II, who was responsible for many of the monuments which still stand today, represented the pinnacle of Egyptian civilization. But it appears that the use of his name on certain contemporary products is rather misconstrued. According to Basehart, he had 125 children.

NATIONAL GEOGRAPHIC VIDEO – THE EXPLORERS: A CENTURY OF DISCOVERY

The National Geographic Society was a pet project of Alexander Graham Bell. The first Grosvenor to run the Society was Bell's son-in-law, and one can see an inventive hand extending through several generations, aggressively supporting adventurous scientific research and maintaining a consistently innovative reporting organ. This is the somewhat self-serving theme of *National Geographic Video – The Explorers: A Century of Discovery*, but it is a birthday celebration of the Society's centenary, and birthdays are supposed to be self-serving.

Much of the 90-minute program contains

rarely seen newsreel footage from the last Golden Age of terrestrial exploration. The later segements summarize recent programs and efforts, but even if you are overly familiar with the material, the presentation is still fresh. The disc will be fun for anyone who has ever enjoyed themselves flipping through an issue of the Society's magazine.

The program is narrated by E.G. Marshall. Although the disc is monaural, the orchestral musical score is grand. On the other hand, unlikely sound effects have been added to even the oldest silent documentary footage. The picture is acceptable. Side two is in CAV, though its emphasis is on recent expeditions and the CAV functions might have been better utilized on the older material. There are two unsteady still frames out of every five. There are also a great number of chapter markers, which is terrific, even if they haven't been identified on the back of the jacket.

NATIONAL GEOGRAPHIC VIDEO – GORILLA

Diane Fossey appears briefly in *National Geographic Video – Gorilla*, grieving over Digit, her lonesome gorilla friend who was murdered by poachers. Most of the *Gorilla* documentary, however, concentrates not on the rare wild gorillas, but on the life of gorillas in captivity. It is our loss that mankind has not been domesticating gorillas in social groups and teaching them sign language for the past 150 years. As it stands, they are only being culturized in isolated locations and it will be several generations before real interaction is possible. The disc just hints at this, but it does provide many videos of cute, anthropomorphic gorillas and interesting interviews with their devoted, often eccentric human supporters. One consumer caution: there is substantial footage of Koko, but nothing showing Koko playing with her kitten, as pictured on the jacket cover.

NATIONAL GEOGRAPHIC VIDEO – THE GREAT WHALES

(see **NATIONAL GEOGRAPHIC VIDEO – SECRETS OF THE TITANIC**)

NATIONAL GEOGRAPHIC VIDEO – THE GRIZZLIES

We were expecting *National Geographic Video – The Grizzlies* to be an older title, but we were surprised to find that it is an updated report compiled in 1987, and not the dart and collar epic we recalled from our grade school days. The producers couldn't resist retaining the classic footage from their older documentary in which a tranquilized bear wakes up too quickly and rampages through a scientific camp, but the emphasis on the new show is on the bears' deteriorating habitat. Man could never beat a grizzly in a fair fight, so for the past dozen decades he has been cheating, destroying the natural environment. Besides a few national parks, the only place not completely decimated yet is Alaska, and that is where most of *The Grizzlies* takes place. There is fascinating footage of the bears fishing and passing technique along to their young. The images and sound are relatively new, so the disc's audio and video components are in very good shape.

NATIONAL GEOGRAPHIC VIDEO – HIMALAYAN RIVER RUN

Himalayan River Run is similar in style and subject to *Iceland River Challenge*, but even though the program gets no closer to the daredevil adventurers than the other program did, it seems less impersonal. It may be that it is better edited, or it that Nepal is a more interesting place to visit than Iceland. In any case, the program is fairly entertaining, as the party hikes three miles into the air and then rides back down on little plastic boats. We'd rather sit at home and watch them do it on TV. The picture and sound are in good condition.

NATIONAL GEOGRAPHIC VIDEO – ICELAND RIVER CHALLENGE

The best National Geographic documentaries concentrate indirectly on the personalities attracted to adventure. The more times you watch the show, the more familiar you become with the central characters being interviewed or eaten by sharks, and as they become your friends, their experiences become more interesting. One of the faults with *Iceland River Challenge* is that you don't become intimate with the half-dozen masochists who try to tramp across a glacier and then kayak down a hundred miles of cataracts in northeastern Iceland. The picture and sound are okay.

NATIONAL GEOGRAPHIC VIDEO – THE INCREDIBLE HUMAN MACHINE

Unlike the other *National Geographic* discs, the picture and sound on *National Geographic Video – The Incredible Human Machine* are worn out. This is an older documentary, and includes scientific motion picture footage from a great variety of sources. It seems that clarity is far more important here than in any of the other episodes, and every double image or faded red removes a level of understanding and knowledge. Special photography is used to illustrate anatomical activities such as an eardrum transponding 'Yankee Doodle,' two heart cells beating in unison when they make contact, and the progress of an egg as it turns into an embryo.

NATIONAL GEOGRAPHIC VIDEO – THE INVISIBLE WORLD

One of the most popular *National Geographic* episodes is *The Invisible World*. The CLV disc is fascinating and quite entertaining. The program is about the photography of objects and events which can not be seen with the naked eye – everything from the ugly little bugs that live on your eyelashes to a bullet piercing a playing card. The construction of the program is such that it can cover a wide range of topics without abandoning the central subject. True, little is offered on how the physics and technology actually accomplish these incredible views, but the disc should hold both youngsters and adults spellbound. The transfer is decent. The picture is not always as glossy as it is on the two discs above, but it doesn't look bad. The digitally encoded sound is competent, though the special effect noises which accompany some of the images are poorly conceived.

NATIONAL GEOGRAPHIC VIDEO – JERUSALEM: WITHIN THESE WALLS

Christopher Plummer narrates *Jerusalem: Within These Walls*, an essay about the 'Old City' portion of Jerusalem. The documentary is similar to profiles in the National Geographic Magazine. It is not quite a travelog, yet it isn't science, either. A thumbnail history of Jerusalem is provided, and the four primary cultures which have survived there to present day receive the most attention. The material covers both archeology and weddings. It is a nice introduction to the locale and peoples, but by no means does it provide the last word on the subject.

The picture is in very good condition, and the sound, although it is monaural and not CX-encoded, is strong. Plummer's voice is soft and entertainingly inflected.

NATIONAL GEOGRAPHIC VIDEO – LAND OF THE TIGER

No humans appear in *Land of the Tiger*, but personalities abound. There are the monkeys and the butterflies and the crocodiles and the jungle buffalo and the kingfishers and the peacocks and, of course, the title cats. It has a sound mix which is better than most stereo productions. An off-camera narrator explains some of what is going on, but essentially the hour program looks at the passing seasons (rainy and dry) in two state-sized Indian wildlife preserves, through the eyes of the tiger. Family documentaries have come a long way since we were in grade school – there are scenes here of tigers spraying and copulating – but the biggest difference is in the sound quality and the full face closeups of all the wild jungle beasts. The disc is one of our favorites.

NATIONAL GEOGRAPHIC VIDEO – LIONS OF THE AFRICAN NIGHT

Lions of the African Night is an example of how rewarding and informative the National Geographic programs can be. Narrated by Richard Kiley, the format follows a reliable outline that other shows have also followed, depicting the ecology of a single area during the course of a set time period. A pride of lions is shown foraging and hunting for sustenance. At intervals, other creatures sharing their territory, from a tiny snake which gobbles centipedes larger than itself to a bull elephant, are also given attention. No humans appear in *Lions*, and the narration always answers plenty of a viewer's silent questions before moving on to the next subject.

The night photography varies in quality – some of it is even in black and white – but it is doubtful that a viewer could become dissatisfied with the results. The very use of lights to photograph at night, however, creates an unnatural environment for the subjects captured on film. Most of the images are fleeting. The digitally encoded sound is quite good, and pleasingly recreates the cries of the wild, recorded at the time of filming.

NATIONAL GEOGRAPHIC VIDEO – MAN-EATERS OF INDIA

The *National Geographic Video, Man-Eaters of India*, is not your normal *National Geographic Video*, though you would be hard pressed to discern this fact from the jacket cover art. The program is not a documentary. It is an 84-minute biographical drama jointly produced by National Geographic and the BBC.

Drawn from his own words, the program is a depiction of the later years in the life of a tiger hunter, James Corbett, as his awareness of civilization's encroachments on the tigers' habitat turns his energies toward the preservation, instead of the extinction, of the species. It has been done in grand BBC style. The actor portraying Corbett, Frederick Treves, has the accent, which has strong twinges of Hindi despite Corbett's ancestry, down perfect, and Treves never tries to make Corbett out to be more than the dull little fellow that he probably was. The drama, which was filmed on location, has been superbly merged with Geographic footage of the animals and their environment. It is the sort of program which, if one comes across it on PBS, one stops changing channels.

The picture is worn and grainy, but this works in the program's favor by keeping a parity with the aspirations of the film. It is a nice surprise, and one wishes that National Geographic would undertake more such artistic adventures.

NATIONAL GEOGRAPHIC VIDEO – MINIATURE MIRACLE: THE COMPUTER CHIP

There are some stunning computer graphic sequences and a few other intriguing scenes in *Miniature Miracle: The Computer Chip*, but the program, on a whole, is a disappointment. Although it pretends to be a history of computers and an analysis of potential microchip applications, the narrator never explains what a computer chip does or how it works. They seem to be taking the 'miracle' portion of the title literally.

NATIONAL GEOGRAPHIC VIDEO – POLAR BEAR ALERT

The material in *Polar Bear Alert* is padded to fill the full hour. There is about thirty minutes of good footage depicting the annual terrorization at Churchill, Manitoba by migrating polar bears. Interesting stuff, but the same information and scientific activities are presented two or even three times. The picture seems a bit old for a 1982 program, but it is not faded enough to impact the arctic vistas.

NATIONAL GEOGRAPHIC VIDEO – RAIN FOREST

All the creepy crawling things you would expect to find on the floor of a jungle take turns starring in *Rain Forest*. Filmed in Costa Rica, the program has a narrator, but no other humans appear until the very end when they start cutting down trees. The photographers have captured lizards, insects, frogs, and others in their natural environment, eating, escaping, and procreating. Among the highlights are a lizard who runs across the surface of water, a tadpole whose heart can be seen beating frantically as he flips himself to safety, a bug which is so skinny you wonder if he eats anything at all, and army ants, who build living bridges and even nests out of themselves, like a circus act with a cast of thousands.

Filmed in 1983, the picture is reasonably good and the sound, which mixes the narration with natural environment sounds and music, is not CX-encoded. If there is a lesson to be learned here, besides the fact that man is destroying this environment at the rate of "3000 acres an hour," it is that you should never, ever walk through a rain forest without wearing boots.

NATIONAL GEOGRAPHIC VIDEO – REALM OF THE ALLIGATOR

A beautiful, cocoa cream colored morning haze, drifting through Okefenokee Swamp in the opening shot of *National Geographic Video – Realm of the Alligator*, sets the tone for the entire disc. The episode is another of National Geographic's eco-system surveys. With little human intervention, most of the program leisurely depicts life in the swamp, as natural sounds and a subtle musical score fill the soundtrack. The sound is monaural and has not been CX-encoded, but it is hard to tell that it is not in stereo, since the animal and insect sounds seem to surround you.

The picture is also in excellent condition, and the nature photography is bright and immediate. The mood shots, scenic vistas of the swamp in unusual light, inserted to provide pauses in the narrative, are evocative and exquisite.

NATIONAL GEOGRAPHIC VIDEO – ROCKY MOUNTAIN BEAVER POND

Entitled 'The Beaver Pond' on the film itself, and running a scant 45 minutes, *National Geographic Video – Rocky Mountain Beaver Pond* is nevertheless fascinating. The beaver is essentially a huge, benign rat, and the program depicts not only the ecology supported by beaver ponds, but the intriguing dynamics within a beaver family. For example, beavers are apt to have litters before a previous litter has fully matured. When a dam breaks during a spring thaw, the father beaver – normally the chief engineer – stays at home to watch the babies while the mother and an elder brother leave to perform emergency repairs. The picture and sound are adequate and the program is narrated by Richard Kiley.

NATIONAL GEOGRAPHIC VIDEO – SAVE THE PANDA

The panda is a meat-eater who is too slow to catch anything, so it has found its niche eking out a nutritional pittance by gorging on acres of bamboo shoots. Its one fortunate evolutionary inheritance is a photogenicity which is superseded only by babies playing with puppies. *Save the Panda* documents efforts by the Chinese and some World Wildlife Foundation Americans to track, monitor, and artificially inseminate the poor creatures. Narrated by Richard Basehart, the show has only a few interviews with naturalists. Pictures of pandas abound, however, and it is that footage which will satisfy all but the blindest disc consumers.

NATIONAL GEOGRAPHIC VIDEO – THE SECRET LEOPARD

Although it runs only three quarters of an hour, *National Geographic Video – The Secret Leopard* is a satisfying study of a cat who would prefer to stay out of view. The show is not a full fledged ecological profile, but a sketch of two seasons in the life of a leopard mother and her three cubs. Noting that much of the wildlife on view gets nervous just when the wind shifts, the intimacy of the photography is amazing. No humans appear in the program, which is narrated by Richard Kiley. The picture and sound transfers are fine. And seen draped over her bulging muscles, the leopard's coat is a work of art more stunning and beautiful than any of Man's great masterpieces.

NATIONAL GEOGRAPHIC VIDEO – SECRETS OF THE TITANIC
NATIONAL GEOGRAPHIC VIDEO – BORN OF FIRE
NATIONAL GEOGRAPHIC VIDEO – THE GREAT WHALES

National Geographic Video – Secrets of the Titanic is an excellent documentary about the Titanic's voyage and the discovery, 75 years later, of its resting place. The program contains well-preserved footage and photos from the Titanic's launching and clear, bright video tape footage of its current state. Buried in the small print of the credits, however, is the disclaimer that some of the material is a recreation of actual events. One assumes that this refers to the scene depicting the initial discovery of the sunken vessel.

Throughout the one-sided disc, the man who led the discovery efforts, Dr. Robert Ballard, remains an enigma. He keeps his motivations and concerns to himself and even in the footage which one assumes is real, such as Ballard's triumphant return to the surface after his first exploration of the sunken hulk, he remains surprisingly unemotional. The disc is in stereo, or at least the music soundtrack is, and is narrated by Martin Sheen.

Ballard also shows up in *Born of Fire*, another *National Geographic Video*. He opens with a nice little talk about geological forces and the nature of life, and then becomes the show's representative scientist (the program is narrated by E. G. Marshall), flitting from one end of the world to the other to be shown geological anomalies.

The show is about ten years older than the disc. It lacks the crispness of the later *Geographic* episodes and has not been CX-encoded. It is worth watching once, but it is difficult to imagine a potential for much repeat use in a home environment since the material can be easily absorbed in one sitting. Extensive coverage of life on an island in the North Atlantic, which is being built up rapidly, from below, is probably the most dramatic and intriguing segment. Consumers who live near the San Andreas fault should probably avoid the disc lest they wish to be reminded, quite convincingly, that they ought to move somewhere else.

The Great Whales is about as old as *Fire*, but it is a much more satisfying disc. The scientists are open about their feelings when they have contact with the leviathan creatures, and by the end of the program the viewer is experiencing the same sense of awe.

NATIONAL GEOGRAPHIC VIDEO – THE SHARKS

The Sharks is a terrific disc which has great potential for repeated viewings, particularly by the younger and more bloodthirsty members of the household. You get to see sharks eating people and people eating sharks, and sharks of more shapes, sizes, or tempers than one would think possible. Yet what you really remember is not the sharks but the equally varied and curiously motivated shark scientists. Much of the footage is grainy, but that is to be expected.

NATIONAL GEOGRAPHIC VIDEO – SUPERLINERS: TWILIGHT OF AN ERA

A five day cruise aboard the QEII from England to New York is highlighted in *National Geographic Video – Superliners:*

Twilight of an Era. Intercut with the trip is a history of the biggest ocean liners in the Twentieth Century, and the competition which went on to be the fastest, classiest ship on the North Atlantic route. This is no travelog, since the QEII trip is drizzly and anything but glamorous, but the material is ideally suited for an hour's documentary and the details, from how the ships operate to what happened to them during World War II, are intriguing. Interviews with the QEII's staff are also enjoyable, since they are shown without the polish which a promotional film crew might impose. The picture is passable but never luxurious and the sound tends to vary in volume, especially during the interviews. The program is narrated by Alexander Scourby.

NATIONAL GEOGRAPHIC VIDEO – TROPICAL KINGDOM OF BELIZE
Like several other successful *National Geographic* discs, *Tropical Kingdom of Belize* displays and describes a single ecosystem, this time the tropical forests of Belize. No humans appear in the program. The narrator, E.G. Marshall, adds details to the wildlife footage shown on the screen. The picture quality is acceptable. The program includes everything from black fly larvae capturing microscopic food particles to a mountain lion feasting on an armadillo. You can learn how to eat a tarantula and watch bats earn their living by fishing. Along with Marshall's narration and a typical woodwind score, the sounds of the animals and the environment are represented on the disc. Although the disc is monaural and not CX-encoded, the environmental sounds are so realistic that they seem to be coming from all over the room. Thank goodness the creatures don't accompany them.

NATIONAL GEOGRAPHIC VIDEO – YUKON PASSAGE
Jimmy Stewart does the narration for *National Geographic Video – Yukon Passage*, and the greatest pleasure from the disc is the chance to listen to him chatter away for an hour about four fellows trekking by raft and sled across Alaska.

Yukon Passage has a bright, clear picture and an alive, unrestrained soundtrack. Since, after a while, the Yukon wilderness starts to look very repetitive, each of the four men opens up to the camera and talks about the philosophy of not working in an office.

NATIONAL GEOGRAPHIC – WHITE WOLF
National Geographic – White Wolf, narrated by Kiley as well, is about wolves who live so far north upon the Arctic tundra that they've never had contact with nor reason to fear human beings. Human scientists are depicted along with their subjects, as a pair of hardy researchers spend a summer camped out near a wolf den. The information they gather (and film) is valuable, though their inability to truly differentiate and characterize the individual dogs lessens the impact of the hunting and leisure scenes. The purpose of howling, which, after a couple of months without TV or AM radio the scientists become quite adept at imitating, is also investigated. The 50-minute program has passable picture and sound qualities.

NATIONAL GEOGRAPHIC – THE WILDS OF MADAGASCAR
The narration on *The Wilds of Madagascar* is too ecologically preachy, but the 50-minute program is fairly intriguing. Filmed by an apparently omniscient cameraman, the program depicts a naturalist's expedition to a remote plateau on Madagascar which contains a bevy of unique animal life. To reach the area, the scientists must climb mountains and raft through underground rapids. The animals they meet are fascinating and the trip is adventurous, but the narrator insists upon continually reminding the viewer of civilization's encroachments, a message which could just have easily been delivered once at the beginning or end of the program. The picture and sound transfer are fine, but the disc has flickering chapter markings and the image itself was subject to a couple of manufacturing flaws, causing it to appear unsteady in some instances.

NATIONAL LAMPOON'S ANIMAL HOUSE
MCA updates *National Lampoon's Animal House* from time to time. The most recent transfer has a picture that is in fairly good condition, but no real sprucing up is apparent. The darker scenes are grainy and the sound, even in digital, is noisy. A splice is still present in one of the parking scenes.

The movie remains a masterpiece of frantic, comical inspiration. It captured a generic phenomena which no movie had ever truly grasped before – macho comedy. John Belushi is more the film's mascot than its star. It is the slick repartee between Tim Matheson and Peter Riegert which enables the gross antics of Belushi and the many other comics to slide past your defenses. You may stop looking for characters taken out of National Lampoon's 'Yearbook,' searching for the 'See you next Wednesday,' or trying to catch every peripheral sight gag, but you never stop repeating the dialog. "Hey, come on, Flounder. You can't spend your whole life worrying about your mistakes. You screwed up. You trusted us."

NATIONAL LAMPOON'S EUROPEAN VACATION
Despite a brief flaw during the 30-minute mark on side two, *National Lampoon's European Vacation* looks and sounds okay. The picture is bright and colorful. The first *Vacation* movie was based on one of National Lampoon Magazine's wickedly knowing short stories, but this sequel was just a cash-in, and not a very funny one. If only the trailer, which was truly inspired, could have been tacked on to the end.

NATIONAL VELVET
The color in *National Velvet* comes and goes a little. The picture also seems blurry at times. When it looks good, however, it is a nice Technicolor transfer. The sound has a strength and fullness which is unusual for an older monaural feature. There are four original color stills on the jacket cover, and all of them look marvelous.

The 124-minute film is spread to three sides. Although the movie, which is always fun, belongs to Elizabeth Taylor and Mickey Rooney, it was Anne Revere, as Taylor's mother, who was justly awarded with an Oscar for her role. Her performance, as a former swimming star who has settled into the quiet life of a small town, is amazingly thorough and touching. Those with a sense of humor, however, might want to watch the film in tandem with *Who's Afraid of Virginia Woolf?* to see how the dreams of childhood can turn into the nightmares of adulthood.

NATIVE SON
Matt Dillon gives a marvelous, satirical performance in *Native Son*. He plays an earnest radical whose biggest thrill is to be on good terms with the impoverished. The film, ineptly directed and horribly edited, is just the opposite from Richard Wright's taut and exact prose. It is so boring that one's attention wanders in the middle of every scene and every conversation. The pacing is all wrong, and the lighting and camera angles are all wrong (and the vacant sets, with their bright, shiny 'grime' are ridiculous). If it weren't for Dillon or for the tension and irony in Wright's original story (the way everyone is more concerned by a victim's alleged rape than by her murder), the film would be totally worthless.

The transfer is decent and rarely grainy. The sound is monaural and has not been CX-encoded, but it isn't bad if the volume is kept down. The undisciplined musical score also provides some entertainment. The jacket cover reiterates the film's original, austere ad art, which, in keeping with the ineptness of the entire project, is a succinct lesson of how not to sell a movie (or target an audience). Sometimes a little sensationalism doesn't hurt.

NATURAL LIGHT: WINDANCE
(see **CRYSTAL VISTA**)

NAUGHTY MARRIETTA
(see **SAN FRANCISCO**)

NAZARETH LIVE
The hour-long program *Nazareth Live*, actually part of a series entitled 'Live in London,' captures the group on stage at the Camden Palace. Capturing the group is not difficult, since they do not do much on stage other than play their instruments and sing, and the show's producers use about three camera angles over and over again to cover them. The picture transfer is okay and the sound is fine. Nazareth has a solid rock sound with a strong beat, intriguingly raw vocals, and a good ol' boy flavor. They are competent but not overly exciting, and these attributes are emphasized by the disc.

NAZARIN
Directed by Luis Buñuel, *Nazarin* is as close to perfect as movies get, combining a real, complex analysis of social theology with an amusing, mildly episodic story about a priest who gets into loads of trouble while innocently attempting to follow the letter of his teachings. Unfortunately, the disc will try the patience of the most devoted viewer. The film was made on a miniscule budget in 1959, so one should not expect pristine material. The black-and-white print often looks damaged. We never found the presentation to be so off-putting that it spoiled the movie for us, but other viewers could easily find the smudges, scratches, wiggles, splices, and fuzzy focus to

be distracting. The sound is also rough, but it is generally limited to the dialog and the dialog is in Spanish, lowering its importance to English-speaking viewers. There are fresh yellow subtitles, which tend to rush by quickly whenever conversations get complicated.

NEAR DARK

The well-crafted vampire story *Near Dark*, like *The Lost Boys*, uses drug addiction rather than sex as its guiding metaphor. It is set in the Midwest, and tells the story of a young man who falls in with a group of nocturnal drifters, but who, with the help of his loving family, is able to extricate himself. Unlike so many other tales of this nature, the ending is satisfying and the script is resolute. The film is a talented accomplishment, with striking visual effects and a confident pace.

The disc also looks very nice, with no significant flaws in the picture. The Ultra Stereo sound is passable, but it is the film's least effective component.

NECROMANCER

A rape victim answers an ad for a 'revenge service' and unwittingly liberates a demon in *Necromancer*, a dull offering which fails utterly in living up to its title. The demon has red eyes on the jacket cover, but green eyes in the movie. The special effects are poor, it takes forever to get to a murder, nothing is scary, the picture is blurry, and the sound has limited separation effects.

NEIL DIAMOND I'M GLAD YOU'RE HERE WITH ME TONIGHT

"I may have a press conference today but I'm not sure. God I hope not. I don't think I can handle a press conference today. I don't have anything to say," laments Neil Diamond in *Neil Diamond I'm Glad You're Here with Me Tonight*, but he goes right on talking anyway. The 60-minute program was ten years old when it made it to disc and combines concert footage with interviews and concept videos. The sound was recorded in a controlled environment and then overlayed onto pictures of Diamond cavorting on a stage. There is enough music on the disc to satisfy fans and enough of Diamond's McKuenesque personality to keep everyone else pounding on the eject button.

NEIL DIAMOND'S GREATEST HITS LIVE

Neil Diamond appears at LA's Aquarius Theatre in *Neil Diamond Greatest Hits Live*, singing an hour's worth of hit songs before an overly dressed and overly appreciative audience. The best moments in his act are when a backup singer steps forward to do 'You Don't Bring Me Flowers' and when a guitarist in his band is spotlighted in 'Forever in Blue Jeans.' They're up, and the show energizes when the attention turns briefly to them.

Diamond sings fifteen hit songs from the various peaks in his career. After the end credits, a music video for a sixteenth number, 'This Time,' appears. The songs are chapter encoded. The stage show is brightly lit, though the background lighting is often a little unstable. The sound is passable.

NEIL YOUNG IN BERLIN

Although the jacket cover prominently displays the words, "Digital Sound," the first batch of *Neil Young in Berlin* did not have digtal encoding, although in later runs the omission was corrected. The picture quality is poor, but the cameras stay close to Young so his performance is all there on the screen. His ten numbers include some older hits and newer attempts. Having kept up with the times he does a couple of pieces using electronic distortions and updates the lyrics to his more famous songs. "Look at Mother Nature on the run, in the nineteen eigh-i-ties." People think they can get away with anything when they visit a foreign country.

NEIL YOUNG – SOLO TRANS

Neil Young – Solo Trans depicts a live concert emceed by a game show-type announcer. When performers get tired of their material they often start doing parodies of themselves. One would not expect the prolific Neil Young to fall into this trap, but he doesn't appear to know what more to create.

The CLV disc has 27 minutes of program on one side and 33 minutes on the other. The picture quality is only fair and for an hour show, Young only manages to sing 11 songs.

NELSON MANDELA – 70th BIRTHDAY TRIBUTE

Jessye Norman, Chubby Checker, and Stevie Wonder are just a few of the artists who appear on *Nelson Mandela – 70th Birthday Tribute*. It is the sort of show which sends a viewer down the street afterwards, fist in the air, chanting, "I ain't gonna play Sun City!" as if someone were actually going to ask you to. The two hour disc was recorded at Wembley Stadium in London. The daytime performances look great, but after the sun sets the image becomes grainy. The recording is not distorted by the stadium acoustics, and all the performers, including Sting, George Michael, Eric Clapton, Dire Straits, Peter Gabriel, the Eurhythmics, Al Green, Tracy Chapman, UB40, Whitney Houston, and others, are presented with clarity. A cameraman on the stage gets some terrific closeups of several different performers.

NEVADA SMITH
ONE-EYED JACKS

Henry Hathaway's pleasing *Nevada Smith* was one of the first films to apply the contemporary standards of sex and violence to an Old West setting. The film features a quiet but memorable performance by Steve McQueen in the title role and has an engaging narrative about a boy avenging the murder of his parents. Unfortunately, it is scanned and cropped, so much so that Karl Malden practically disappears from the opening scenes. The color transfer is decent, and the sound is okay.

Nevada Smith is usually paired with 'The Carpetbaggers' because the central character in the former was originally conceived as a secondary character in the latter. However, because of the revenge theme, the presence of Malden, and especially because of the strength in the leading role, *Smith* would also make an excellent double bill with Paramount's *One-Eyed Jacks*.

Jacks was directed by Marlon Brando who also stars as a bank robber seeking revenge against a partner, played by Malden. Brando's creation is highly respected, and with good reason. He sets most of the film in Monterey, and it is one of the few westerns which ever got away with taking place next to an ocean. The time he devotes to character and to action is so carefully integrated that the viewer is barely aware of the manipulation. *Smith* lasts 135 minutes and by the end you feel you've sat through an epic. *Jacks* is six minutes longer and at the end you wonder how the time passed so quickly. Brando seems willing to try things with his own character and with the others which some directors might shy away from – in the opening shot, for example, he's eating a banana while robbing a bank.

The movie was made in VistaVision. Little seems to have been cropped out of the presentation, and the disc has more problems with color, which looks a little blurry in the beginning and faded near the end, than with the framing. The focus also seems soft. The sound is fairly consistent.

NEVER A DULL MOMENT

The black-and-white picture looks good and the sound is fine on *Never a Dull Moment*. The movie, about a New York socialite, played by Irene Dunne, who marries a rancher, played by Fred MacMurray, is a comedy with the usual gags about burned biscuits. The performers, including a supporting cast that features Andy Devine, William Demarest, and a young Natalie Wood, are better than the material deserves, causing the film to shift between being pleasant and being an embarrassment.

NEVER GIVE A SUCKER AN EVEN BREAK

Even though *Never Give a Sucker an Even Break* may not be the funniest movie W.C. Fields made, it is probably the most intelligent. In the script Fields portrays himself, and much of the movie is given over to a materialization of his 'next film,' which is so wacky it could never be made, except that, because of this film's structure, it has. The result is both knowing and devious, an excuse to present some wild flights of fantasy and to stretch the limits of narrative decorum, something Fields was rarely respectful of in any case. MCA has included 88 production/publicity stills at the end of the disc, and there is evidence from the poses that several enticing scenes were left out of the 71-minute film, which is unfortunate, since the plot could accommodate virtually any indulgence.

The print is in very good condition. The sound has no significant distortions. Side two is in CAV, with every still frame providing a steady image. The movie is fun to manipulate with standard play. A matte shot which pastes a shear cliff onto a scenic mountain vista is easy to miss during normal play, but suddenly quite apparent when examined on a frame-by-frame basis. During the frantic and totally (but joyously) pointless concluding car chase, slow motion will reveal a shot where the film has been reversed, so that the stunt driver and the license plate of the car are, briefly, on the wrong side. On a disc like this, even a movie's mistakes are a pleasure.

NEVER TOO YOUNG TO DIE

The opening shot of *Never Too Young to Die* shows a city, presumably Los Angeles, at night. The second shot shows a dam in the bright sunshine. The third shot shows a wild, nocturnal orgy. How the daytime shot of the dam got in there, we don't know. Gene Simmons appears as a Lanie Kazan type and you can kiss off his acting abilities, as well. The hero is played by John Stamos, whose hair style changes length in every cut. Vanity, true to her name, is used by the movie as furniture. At one point the sound boom attacks her belly button.

The film is so bad there are breaks in the continuity where there isn't even any editing. The picture is often grainy. Simmons and a band of *Road Warrior* rejects try to irradiate the city water supply. They could probably have caused worse contamination by simply bathing in it.

THE NEVERENDING STORY

On first viewing, *The NeverEnding Story* may not appear to be worth much. It is too preachy and the creatures look like dashboard ornaments. Repeated viewings will not change the quality of the special effects, but the pristine 'reading is good' message starts to get more complicated. Why is the moral of the story – that humans should have more imagination – first presented by a devil character? Why is the child's imagination said to be released only when he screams out the name of his dead mother?

As a boy reads a book, the film flips from the boy to the fantasy story he is reading. The characters scream that the boy doesn't have imagination and at first you think, yes, this is an excellent anthem for school librarians. But what child does not have an imagination? Despite the movie's upbeat ending, there is just enough evidence to suggest that the boy is actually having a nervous breakdown.

The disc has a fairly nice picture and sound. The CX-encoded stereo track is especially playful. The loss of the wider screen helps to make the special effects more believable.

THE NEW ADVENTURES OF PIPPI LONGSTOCKING

At 100 minutes, *The New Adventures of Pippi Longstocking* is too long by 20 or so, but that is the film's only real failing. Otherwise it is an engaging children's show with a few catchy (perhaps too catchy) songs and some amusing stunts. For those who are unfamiliar with the character, a children's lit staple, Pippi is a precocious little girl with red braids who tends to defy authority and perform acrobatic feats which border upon the supernatural. The film concerns her experiences while she is waiting for her father to return from the sea, as certain townspeople want to send her to an orphanage and tear down the house she lives in.

The picture is in passable shape with only the most intense colors looking fuzzy. The stereo sound is passable, with only the music track exhibiting separation effects.

NEW ADVENTURES OF WINNIE THE POOH: NEWFOUND FRIENDS/GREAT HONEY POT ROBBERY

We often wake up blurry-eyed on Saturday morning and stumble downstairs to stare at whatever is on the television, only to be doused with a cartoon of such high quality and inventive flair that we are immediately jarred into alertness. A cartoon about monsters and the netherworld? No. A cartoon about reptiles with oriental martial skills? No. It is Walt Disney's *New Adventures of Winnie the Pooh*, episodes of which have been released on *Newfound Friends/Great Honey Pot Robbery*. The other Winnie the Pooh featurettes available on disc were theatrical efforts, and what is amazing is that the cartoon series diluted none of the concept's charm or artistic merit by pumping out episodes on a weekly basis. From Paul Winchel's voice of Tigger on down, the show retains the essential elements which made the first shorts so successful. The narratives are well developed, but non-exploitive. The backgrounds are elaborate and often include intriguing perspectives, while the foregrounds are always full of elaborate objects and smooth movement.

The disc contains two 45-minute video cassette programs, each placed on a side with complete opening and closing credits. Each collection contains three episodes. The disc is fully chapter encoded and has digital monaural sound which is worth amplifying (listen for the 'ping' when Tigger gets his stripes back in 'Stripes'). The colors look a touch too pale in places, but generally retain the rich pastels that set the series off from almost every other television cartoon. The plots for most of the episodes concern hurt feelings and misunderstandings, but they never turn maudlin and are a refreshing change from the standard good guy/bad guy polarization drive.

THE NEW CENTURIONS

The picture on *The New Centurions* has a level of graininess which goes beyond cinema verite. The film, based upon Joseph Wambaugh's life-is-messier-than-fiction novel, set a precedent which eventually led to 'Hill Street Blues' and other loopy, realistic police dramas. So, as the film is presented, it could have gotten away with a little grain, which might have given it a documentary feel, but when even the fade-to-blacks swirl with pinpoints of color, it is age and not art guiding the design. Along with an old and too grainy picture, the disc has an unremarkable monaural soundtrack.

In most films, a scene in an advancing narrative normally occurs within a few hours of the previous scene. In the clever *New Centurions* script, scenes regularly pick up weeks or even months after the preceding scene, so that the scope of Wambaugh's novel is condensed evenly. The movie was released at a time when Hollywood perceived the populace as perceiving cops with suspicion and resentment. The characters constantly spout excuses for the film's existence, and Stacy Keach, as the hero, seems unconvincingly single minded in his passion. Only one performer gets away with it. George C. Scott conveys the loneliness of his character, a retiring cop, so accurately that you can't help but feel for him, even when the filmmaking manipulations are obvious. His presence is the most memorable aspect of the film, the one argument for collecting it.

NEW EDITION – THE VIDEOSINGLES (Import)

New Edition is a group of youngsters who sound like the Jackson Family way back when. They have four very charming videos collected on a Japanese 8-inch disc, *New Edition – The Videosingles*. While the music has them singing mostly in harmony and backed up by a sophisticated band, the videos show them palling around with their girlfriends, breakdancing, and grinning for the camera as they wander around New York City. An hour of this stuff might be too much, but the 16-minute 8-inch provides exactly what an 8-inch disc is supposed to provide – the essence of a musical group at their best. The picture quality on 'Candy Girl' and 'Is This the End' is blurry, but 'Popcorn Love' and 'She Gives Me a Bang' are crisp. The lyrics to the songs are also included (in English) on a sheet in the sleeve.

THE NEW KIDS

Sean S. Cunningham, who directed the first *Friday the 13th* film, directed *The New Kids*. The movie is not a horror picture but a formula high school revenge number. Taking place in central Florida, the story is about an orphaned brother and sister who move to their uncle's home and have a series of run-ins with the class bullies in their new school. Since their late father was a military man, both brother and sister are skilled in the art of self-defense and so the conflict escalates as they fight back. The monaural sound is excellent, as is the quality of the picture transfer.

NEW LOOK MAGAZINE, VOL. 1
(see **HEAD**)

NEW VISUAL ARTISTS SERIES – TV FETISH (Import)

In one sense the six video works by Patrick Martin and Doobie Eylath, collected on the *New Visual Artists Series – TV Fetish* in Japan, are nothing more than glorified music videos. The music has a serious new wave tone which is coordinated closely with the rhythm of the visuals. But in another sense, the 29-minute CAV disc tests the limits of your television and your imagination.

Whether the image is a pulsating orange squiggle or a model strolling through an airport, it is manipulated in such a way as to make you think about the picture, daring you, perhaps, to categorize the image with what you already know about the world. At the same time, the ability of a television screen to present new colors, textures, and patterns discourages any break in concentration.

Both the stereo sound and the picture quality are excellent. The music, like the visuals, avoids settling on a single idea or theme. The lyrics are in English and no subtitles appear on the disc. The jacket inserts, which contain explanatory production notes, are in Japanese.

NEW YEAR'S CONCERT 1987 – WIENER PHILHARMONIKER – HERBERT VON KARAJAN
NEW YEAR'S EVE CONCERT 1988 – KISSIN – BERLINER PHILHAR MONIKER – HERBERT VON KARAJAN
NEW YEAR'S EVE CONCERT 1984 – A.S. MUTTER – BERLINER PHILHARMONIKER – HERBERT VON KARAJAN
ALL SOUL'S DAY CONCERT 1984 – BERLINER PHILHARMONIKER – HERBERT VON KARAJAN

The discs jackets alone on Sony's 'Herbert Von Karajan His Legacy for Home Video' are collectible, adorned with a faint holographic bust of Karajan and a work of abstract art by the painter, Peter Foeller. An essay on the inside sleeve of the pocket jacket describes the background of each recording, though the English translations on the essays are awkward. The chapter encoding is listed on the back of every jacket.

The picture transfers are spectacular. All programs were recorded on video tape which looked fresh and flawless. Flesh tones are perfect, details on the instruments are vivid, and blacks are pure without so much as a hint of distortion. The older recordings, from 1984, have a mild softness when compared to the more recent footage, but even these look impressive when compared to the average video taped concert disc.

The sound on the discs is superb. Even troublesome brass marches are replicated without difficulty. The stereo separations are active, but intelligent, and inflate the orchestra instead of segmenting it.

The camera angles on the musicians are also fairly consistent on the discs. There are some innovative depth of field shots and decent closeups of every soloist or lead instrument. Dissolves are used a bit too much for our taste, and there are no radical views, but we always found that the camera was pointing at what we wanted to look at. Other viewers may feel dissatisfied whenever the picture turns away from Karajan himself, but the scope of the series ought to satiate most fans.

Although the program is very similar to the fine *New Year's Concert in Vienna*, conducted by Karlos Kleiber, *New Year's Concert 1987 – Wiener Philharmoniker – Herbert von Karajan*, set in Vienna, is probably the most congenial and entertaining of the first four discs. The 90-minute concert of music by the Strauss family contains one highlight after another, and Karajan, though he is weak and has to support himself at times, becomes so relaxed and enthusiastic that by the end he is conducting the audience, which is clapping in rhythm to the 'Radetzky March.' During the concert, video presentations of the Spanish Riding School in Vienna and the Ballet of the Vienna State Opera were projected in the hall and replace the view of the musicians as the orchestra accompanies the images. The ballet choreography, by Gerlinde Dill, is unremarkable, but it is designed for video and is thus quite effective. The highpoint of the concert, however, is the appearance of Kathleen Battle, who sings 'Voices of Spring.' Her performance is outstanding and sobers one's appreciation of the undeniably festive endeavor.

We have become so used to watching octogenarians play the piano on home video that it comes as quite a shock to see the 17-year old Soviet prodigy, Yevgeny Kissin, attack the keyboard. His hands leap and dive all over the place and you half expect him to hit a passage so complicated that his fingers will become knotted together. He appears on *New Year's Eve Concert 1988 – Kissin – Berliner Philharmoniker – Herbert von Karajan* playing Tchaikovsky's Piano Concerto No. 1. The sound recording is also effective in delivering the orchestra with a full but airy thrust. As for Kissin, his performance is at times brilliant and at times inexperienced, but a video presentation of his abilities has definite advantages over a simple audio recording of his activities. The orchestra also performs Prokofiev's 'Symphony Classique.' Though well executed, it is just a warm-up.

Watching the musicians while listening to them is also important on *New Year's Eve Concert 1984 – A.S. Mutter – Berliner Philharmoniker – Herbert von Karajan*, featuring J.S. Bach's Violin Concerto No. 2 and 'Magnificat.' Karajan's interpretation of 'Magnificat' sounds too compartmentalized when heard alone on the audio. It is only when the viewer can watch the orchestra pass Bach's melodies back and forth that the production not only begins to make sense, but draws upon that extra touch of brilliance in both Bach and Karajan which cannot be documented in orchestration notations. Anne-Sophie Mutter is the violin soloist for Concerto No. 2, an all-strings work. Her performance is well executed but not exceptional. Instead of conducting, Karajan leads the group while playing the second harpsichord.

Finally, there is our favorite of the discs, *All Soul's Day Concert 1984 – Berliner Philharmoniker – Herbert von Karajan*, featuring 'Death and Transfiguration' and 'Metamorphoses' by Richard Strauss. The opening sentence of the jacket essay, referring to Strauss, gets it exactly wrong: "Who thinks, at the early age of twenty-five and as fit as a bean, of dying?" Everybody. Strauss' music is full of wonderful, virginal brooding and Karajan's presentation is a well-studied and complete performance of both works. This is one of the discs which has a slightly softer image, and of the four, the visuals are the most mundane, yet everything about the program is endearing. Karajan is not twenty-five, and he approaches Strauss' piece the same way that a teacher would edit a student's prize essay. He allowed Kissin his indulgences with Tchaikovsky, and let loose with the 'Pizzicato Polka' in the Vienna concert, but the essence of his art is the manner in which he corrals 'Death and Transfiguration,' demonstrating that although it is the composer and the musicians who are creating the music, it is the maestro who is conducting the breeding.

NEW YEAR'S EVE CONCERT IN VIENNA

A rousing *New Year's Concert in Vienna*, with music by the Strausses, is provided by the Vienna Philharmonic conducted by Carlos Kleiber. The mix of tunes is inspired, so that by the time the most well known pieces show up on the 95-minute program, even the most jaded Viennese fancier will be receptive to them. Kleiber's interpretations are a bit opinionated, but his intensity is one of the factors which makes the concert so involving.

The picture is crisp. The colors on the disc verge on over-saturation, and at times the fleshtones do look a little too orange, but generally the image appears brightly colored and matches the spirit of the music. The sound is also bright and clean. An insert containing a poorly translated essay about the traditional New Year's Concert is included with the disc.

The disc has chapter markers and the program's intermission serves as the side break point. Although there is applause between many of the numbers, it is enthusiastic, but not lengthy. The concert is adeptly filmed and edited. The show follows the standard format, observing the musicians highlighted by the orchestration, and always keeping a watchful eye on Kleiber. There is room for inventiveness, however, because at times just a single one of Kleiber's hands fills the screen.

NEW YORK, NEW YORK

The story was a downer, the sets were obviously fake, and the music was old-fashioned. Nobody wanted to see *New York, New York* and few critics had anything nice to say about it. But if they had dropped their preconceptions, they would have seen that the acting is arousing, the sets are evocative, and the music is smooth and sublime.

The CBS/Fox disc is the 163-minute version, with every musical number and drunken argument intact. Directed by Martin Scorsese, the story is about a saxophone player (Robert DeNiro) and a singer (Liza Minnelli) who manage to form the semblance of a loving relationship before success pushes them apart.

In the best sense, the musical numbers mirror and comment on the story. Liza Minnelli's thrilling 'The World Goes 'Round' comes immediately after a break of several years in the narrative. The restored portions of the 'Happy Endings' segment pull the viewer away from the story and ease the leap in time, preparing one for the unhappy coda which ends the picture.

The most evocative image, of a sailor and his date dancing beneath a lamppost, is badly trimmed by the cropping. Many scenes have strong red color schemes which the disc cannot handle as well as it ought to. The CX-encoded sound is not as spotless as it could be. This is annoying, but when you watch Liza Minnelli belt out the title song, such technicalities seem less important.

"NEW YORK, NEW YORK"

Collectors should exercise caution in obtaining the MGM/UA Deluxe Letter-Box Edition of *"New York, New York."* In some ways it is an exhilarating improvement over the CBS/Fox release, but the quality of the picture and sound may still frustrate those who are searching for perfection.

The most important improvement to the movie is in the presentation of the screen composition. The letterboxing is slight, with the image having an aspect ratio of 1.6:1. That is close to the proper, 'squared' image which the film, in part a tribute to old musicals, was originally supposed to be presented in. The CBS/Fox version, on the other hand, had cropped off not only the sides, but the top and the bottom of the picture. MGM/UA's transfer shows the complete, intended picture, and the movie's power is enhanced considerably. In one of the film's most memorable moments, a shot showing a sailor and a girl dancing in silence, both dancers remain onscreen for the entire sequence, restoring the music-like quality of their movements.

Transferring the picture image of *"New York, New York,"* however, presents a number of other problems. The scene designs are deliberately artificial and the lighting is complex. Still, CBS/Fox managed to coax a colorful image out of the film. Many scenes were grainy and fuzzy, but the gloss of the original theatrical presentation showed through. MGM/UA's picture is more hazy and not as colorful. Many scenes are almost as grainy as the CBS/Fox version, so the compromise of not pushing the color to gain a more solid image is not satisfying.

The digitally encoded soundtrack is also tiring. It is subdued, and suppresses some of the background noise, but it also puts a lid on the sound. The analog track may be rougher, but it is also more striking, and many listeners may prefer it. Both MGM/UA and CBS/Fox use a stereo enhanced soundtrack although the film was originally, and intentionally, monaural. The most obnoxious stereo effects, however, occur during the first 20 minutes, and for the most part, the separations are minimal.

MGM/UA has provided a great deal of chapter markers for the film – three have been used for the 'Happy Endings' sequence alone. CBS/Fox had less intelligent markings (they also left the quotation marks off the title on the jacket spine), but the side break choices on the older disc, particularly between sides two and three, are stronger.

The first half of *"New York, New York"* has the cadence of a comedy, and the vaguely improvised feeling of the dialog gets funnier and funnier the more one is exposed to it. The emotional downspin of the second half is obviously easier to tolerate when you know that it is coming, and the performances become stronger and less contrived the more one becomes accustomed to them. The film's strength may be too academic, which is why theater audiences weren't overly attracted to it, but the deliberate exploration of various old musical styles can be rewarding in multiple viewings, where analyzing the components of a movie comes naturally to a viewer.

NEW YORK STORIES

Each of the three *New York Stories* is relegated to a separate side of the three sided Touchstone release. The picture transfer is fine although the cinematography, by Nestor Almendros, Vittorio Storaro, and Sven Nykvist, contains challenging lighting and color problems, all of which the disc handles splendidly. The monaural sound is also in good shape, and each piece has a unique and enjoyable musical score.

Any of the segments is worth the price of the disc. The least appreciated of the three efforts, Francis Coppola's 'Life without Zoe,' is also the most sublime. Martin Scorsese's 'Life Lessons' is about a modern art painter whose relationship with his assistant is coming to an end. Nick Nolte and Rosanna Arquette star. The film is nearly perfectly made and captures the spirit of a short story so well that its only shortcomings are the shortcomings of the modern short story concept – a touch of life, a touch of emotion, a touch of an idea, and it is over. Woody Allen's segment, 'Oedipus Wrecks,' has the feel of one of Allen's magazine pieces. About a lawyer whose mother pesters him from the clouds above Manhattan, it has some hysterical scenes and is over as soon as it has exhausted the material's potential. But where Scorsese excited us and Allen made us laugh, only Coppola brought tears to our eyes. 'Zoe' is a children's fantasy about what it is like to be rich and to be a grownup while still being a child. The story depicts several adventures in the life of a young girl living in a Manhattan hotel while her parents are away on business. In the main adventure she returns a diamond earring to an Arabian princess. The film has just enough fantasy to excuse its excesses, and just enough fascination with pre-adolescent girls to tap a darker adult passion.

NEXT OF KIN

The skilled action director John Irvin was responsible for *Next of Kin*, a lively Patrick Swayze vehicle. The disc has a super digital stereo surround soundtrack. There is a train whistle sequence which you just want to stop and play over and over again. The directional effects are marvelous, with gunshots and arrows whizzing all over the place, and the audio reproduction is vivid. Jack Nitzsche's mixed genre score is well served. The picture transfer is also very good.

The story, to pare things down a bit, is about a conflict between mobsters and hillbillies. It is set in Chicago, and Swayze portrays a cop with close family ties to the hillbillies. The movie never completely lives up to its promise and the narrative takes a few too many liberties, but Irvin's ability to entertain rarely falters.

NEZMUSIC

A collection of seven Michael Nesmith music videos, many of which have already appeared on previous Nesmith discs, are available on *Nezmusic*. The single-sided CLV disc has chapter markers and opens with a commercial for another Michael Nesmith program. The picture quality is fair. All of the videos seem slightly hazy. The stereo sound varies from number to number, but shouldn't upset anyone. Nesmith appears to write some of his songs for video, as opposed to writing a song and then designing a video for it. A couple of the tunes are catchy, a couple are ridiculous, and a couple are bland. On the whole, it is best to come across Nesmith in an anthology of other artists, because he can become tiresome quickly.

NIAGARA

CBS/Fox has done a nice job transferring *Niagara*. The film, part visitor's bureau promo and part jealousy drama, was not made in a wide aspect ratio, so cropping is not a problem. The luster of the original Technicolor image is often recreated with stunning accuracy, and even when it is not, the effort is still commendable. The film is a bright postcard of shiny blues, rich greens, and deep reds with only the latter maintaining a mild blur. The monaural sound is okay if the volume isn't pushed.

The movie stars Marilyn Monroe, Joseph Cotten, and Jean Peters, but a key role is played by Casey Adams (as Peters' husband) and he is so embarrassingly bad that he drags the whole movie into the falls. The dialog is not particularly adept, but Monroe is luscious and Cotten's crooked stance is particularly memorable. A couple of murders occur, but the travelog material and Adams continually spoil the mood. The film was directed by Henry Hathaway.

NICHOLAS AND ALEXANDRA

About one third of the widescreen still which graces the jacket cover of *Nicholas and Alexandra* is actually visible when the scene plays. The movie was bad enough as it was, but adding this centrist's point of view only makes things worse. The print is also a little on the worn side. The film was made back when film producers had really crazy ideas about what would sell and what wouldn't. Of course, if *Doctor Zhivago* was a success, why not a big budget look at the fun couple who started it all?

A NIGHT AT THE OPERA
A NIGHT AT THE OPERA (CAV)

From the confetti lettering on the jacket cover to the home movies of Marx Brother memorabilia in the supplementary 'Video "Marxbook"' at the end of the disc, Voyager's CAV presentation of *A Night at the Opera* is a marvelous treat. The picture was transferred from a 35mm fine grain print which had been struck from an original 35mm negative (as is explained in an insert which comes with the disc; one wishes all the disc companies would include a citation of provenance with every title), and it is richly detailed. There are breaks, but they have been carefully mended so that dialog is not interrupted and the splices are as seamless as possible. The sound has not been CX-encoded, and there is a mild fluctuation in volume but, considering the age in the film, the condition of the soundtrack is no more severe than what one would expect. The picture quality of the CLV disc is identical, but the addition of digital sound on the CLV effort improves the audio presentation slightly.

Watching the Marx Brothers in slow or fast motion is almost as much fun as watching them at normal speed. Whether it is Chico's piano playing, Harpo's destructive urges toward private property, or just Groucho's raised eyebrows as he delivers a line, breaking the continuity of the film enhances, rather than destroys, their wit and their dexterity. The CAV still frames are perfect, and turn the disc into a collection of 150,000 Marx Brothers photos.

Night was their first film for MGM, a 'comeback' as is extensively explained in the disc's supporting materials. Whether one prefers it, with a subplot about a pair of opera singers whose careers are boosted with the benign yet chaotic assistance of the madcap trio, to their wilder, less structured films is irrelevant, it is still frantic, funny and inherently re-watchable. One moment, where Groucho makes a face at an 'Il Trovatore' gypsy woman, is so amusing that you can use the repeat function on your remote to play the sequence over and over, as you laugh harder and harder.

Leonard Maltin provides fairly useless running commentary on the second audio channel of the CAV disc. He starts out by saying he is not going to try to explain the significance of the Marx Brothers humor or analyze why they are funny and he doesn't. He just points out all the jokes. Maltin has some relevant information about the film's production history, but he also makes numerous statements which are purely speculative. His worst faux pas, however, is to not follow up on what would have been a fascinating piece of information. At one point, the brothers pretend to speak to one another in a foreign language. Maltin explains that the odd sounds are actually English played backwards, and he says that during the production of the video disc, the soundtrack was played backwards so the conversation could be heard. We waited in anticipation for Maltin to tell us what they are saying to one another, but he moves on to another subject, oblivious to the concept that actually running the audio backwards at that point on the second channel is what video discs are for.

One side four, after the 92-minute feature is ended, the 'Video "Marxbook"' kicks off with the three replacing MGM's Leo to introduce a trailer (with 'Marx Gratia Marxes' above them like a halo). In still frame there are advertising materials, publicity photos, and a brief text article about the film's first, and unsuccessful, sneak preview. Along with the early re-release trailer for *Night*, there is a strange trailer for 'The Big Store,' and Hollywood publicity footage of Groucho, Harpo, and Jackie Cooper racing go-carts. There is also a camcorder video tape of a fan's Marx Brother memorabilia collection, which is tastefully done and rounds out the disc nicely.

A NIGHT IN THE LIFE OF JIMMY REARDON

William Richert wrote the novel upon which *A Night in the Life of Jimmy Reardon* was based, then he wrote the screenplay, and then he directed the film. Somewhere along the line he started shorthanding his intentions, because the movie is an odd, directionless tale which works hard to avoid clichés, but has nothing to replace them with. It is anachronistic, taking place in 1962 but starring River Phoenix. *Reardon* is about a young man deciding what he should do with his life. He is proficient at romance and at ease in a ritzy Chicago suburb although his own family's fortune is less than modest. Nothing else happens. The disc is blurry and has an acceptable but uninventive soundtrack.

'NIGHT MOTHER

In *'night Mother*, the central character declares, at the beginning, that she will commit suicide, and at the end, she does. Unfortunately, the two-character film has nothing to say about humanity or life which is worth remembering. The script is so loaded with revelations about how awful the lives of its two characters are that it doesn't have time to suggest how one could cope with it, or to make one feel remorseful when the gun goes off.

The picture is nowhere near as clear as the stills on the back of the jacket and the interiors where the entire film takes place are all painted icky beige anyway, so there is little distinction between the walls and the flesh tones.

NIGHT OF THE CREEPS

Better than the title implies, *Night of the Creeps* will be great for dark and stormy nights. The story is about a sorority house infested with bugs from outer space. Humor and horror go steady throughout the film, and clichéd techniques, such as the simultaneous dolly and zoom, are repeated just often enough so that viewers can enjoy both the effect and the joke.

The picture is vivid and unblemished. The stereo sound is clean and the separations, like the camera work, are deliberately exaggerated. It is a lot of fun, and the screen writers have their trendy dialog down pat. The final shot, even though you know it is coming, is guaranteed to make you jump from your seat.

NIGHT OF THE GENERALS

Looking for a psychopathic murderer among a group of Nazi generals is sort of like searching for a cesspool in the middle of a garbage dump, but *Night of the Generals* is entertaining anyway. The disc is a reasonably good rendition of the 1966 film. The colors look faded in only a few places, the smaller screen hurts only a couple of scenes, and scratches and sound disturbances are kept to a minimum.

The story is cleverly plotted – it has to be, considering the material. Omar Sharif wanders about, lost without his mustache, looking for the murderer of a Polish prostitute, knowing only that the killer is a German general. Other things are happening as well, including a plot to kill Hitler, and, of course, World War II.

THE NIGHT OF THE HUNTER

It is appropriate that Charles Laughton's crazy *The Night of the Hunter* has been included in the Criterion Collection series, because Laughton's execution of the filmmaking craft is so arresting it hardly matters if the movie works for you or not. We can't stand the film, but we admire the disc and can anticipate watching it again when we're in a weird mood.

The CLV release has no special features except for chapter encoding. The black-and-white film is memorable for its stark cinematography, and the source material emphasizes the visual quality of the program. Even during the many times that part of the screen is completely black, no distortions appear in the darkness. The sound is no better or worse than one would expect for its age.

Like a bad Bible story, Laughton's effort has withstood the erosions of time. The first part of the plot is a contemporary thriller about a stepfather who wants to murder his new family for money. But that is not really the point of the movie, which wishes only to evoke such terrors and not swill in them. The second part is a medicinal allegory about God and Innocence, with Lillian Gish standing in for Him. This is the part which generates the deservedly adverse word-of-mouth, but it is also the inspiration for the film's meticulously pensive look. *Night of the Hunter* is the movie where Robert Mitchum's character has the words, 'LOVE' and 'HATE,' tattooed on his right and left knuckles. Someone should have marked the labels on side one and side two of the disc the same way.

NIGHT OF THE LIVING DEAD (Image)
NIGHT OF THE LIVING DEAD (3M)

Night of the Living Dead touches on one of man's most primary, subliminal fears: Neighbors dropping in unexpected for something to eat. Horror and humor both depend upon the unexpected and sometimes it is difficult to tell the two apart. In the sixties, when *Night of the Living Dead* was first released, parent groups were upset with the film's depiction of a child eating her father's arm and then stabbing her mother with a trowel. They were afraid children exposed to this sequence might get the wrong ideas.

Two companies have put out the movie on disc. When the Image release of *Night* is viewed head to head with the 3M release, some very interesting comparisons can be made. The Image version is CX-encoded and the 3M is not. The sound on the Image disc, however, has a very annoying hum which is noticeable when contrasted to the quieter 3M track. 3M's sound has the usual pulses and crackles associated with non-CX.

The differences in picture quality are fascinating. The picture coming from the Image disc is framed five to ten percent further to the left than the 3M presentation. In comparison, we found the 3M framing more satisfying, but we are not familiar enough with the film to tell if it is centered or hugging the right. The contrasts between black and white were sharper on the Image release. This generally made for a more dramatic picture, but 3M's washy print could sometimes present details which could not be discerned in the higher contrasts of the Image disc.

One category in which the Image disc is clearly superior: 3M's break between side one and side two comes at a very awkward moment whereas the break on the Image disc makes for a sensible pause.

The shocks have long since been surpassed by newer and more advanced methods of depicting mutilation to the human anatomy. If the movie has lost none of its appeal, it is only because it has a sense of humor. As the zombies wander about the yard and knock upon the door, the hero peers between a crack in the window shade and pretends not to be home. No, impressionable children should probably not be exposed to the work. They might start screaming the next time the doorbell rings.

NIGHT PATROL (see **RAW COURAGE**)

A NIGHT TO REMEMBER

The print for *A Night to Remember*, a black and white mystery comedy starring Loretta Young and Brian Aherne, has speckles and other splotches, but fans will probably not mind its condition. The sound also has a few crackles. The film was made in 1941, and has nothing to do with the movie made a few years later with the same title, about the sinking of the Titanic.

The performances are deliberately exaggerated and unnatural, a device intended to add to the comedy, which works about half the time. The two stars portray a jovial married couple who move into a small apartment house on the eve of a murder. The denouement is rushed, but getting to it is enjoyable enough. The film is also worth studying as a dead end in cinematic narrative technique, a process which has changed significantly over the years, though few seem to take note of it except to remark that 'they don't make 'em like they used to.' *Night to Remember* is a good example of why.

NIGHT ZOO

The Canadian production *Night Zoo* is in French with large yellow English subtitles. The film is tedious. It is mainly about a young man getting to know his dying father, but plot machinations concerning crooked cops and drug money have been stuffed into it to hold a viewer's interest. It doesn't help.

Contrary to the ad art, the film is not a stylistic accomplishment. It was inexpensively produced and has a cheap look, although the transfer does not do it any more harm. The stereo surround sound is a little better. Loud voices get fuzzy, but the background sounds have a nice dimensionality. The analog track has some hiss, but the digital track is very clean. *Night Zoo* also includes a few obscure scenes involving sexual interludes of more than one persuasion, but none of it is very flattering.

THE NIGHTINGALE
(see **FAERIE TALE THEATRE**)

A NIGHTMARE ON ELM STREET
Except for the final moments, *A Nightmare on Elm Street* will unnerve anyone who is old enough to watch it. The movie, directed by Wes Craven, is about a killer who is attacking teenagers in their dreams and how one young lady tries to stop him. Craven provides enough of a logical explanation for the story – that all the kids were once terrorized by a mass murderer – to let the horror rip loose without disturbing the movie's credibility.

The disc looks terrific. The monaural sound is as good as its source; it has no dimension or intricacy, but you pick up every whisper and squeak.

A NIGHTMARE ON ELM STREET 2
After getting scared out of our wits by *Nightmare on Elm Street*, we ran to the theater for more punishment the day *A Nightmare on Elm Street 2* opened. Boy, were we disappointed. Neither the sound nor the picture was all that great to begin with. There are a couple of sound dropouts on side two, but nothing is severely wrong with the presentation. It is the movie itself which is the ripoff.

A NIGHTMARE ON ELM STREET 3: DREAM WARRIORS
The picture on *A Nightmare on Elm Street 3: Dream Warriors* is grainy and too orange. The sound is strong, but none of the effects are interesting, and there is still a lot of noise. The movie is not scary, although it does have an array of special puppet and model effects which look as sharp as Freddy's kitchen helper fingernails. The real failure is that despite the film's premise – Freddy's victims, persecuted by realistic nightmares, band together to fight back in a collective dream – the heroes never coalesce into a group one can cheer for. These days, most viewers have started cheering for Freddy, anyway.

A NIGHTMARE ON ELM STREET 4: THE DREAM MASTER
America's dream date, Freddy Kruger, makes wisecracks and shreds teenagers in *A Nightmare on Elm Street 4: The Dream Master*. The series no longer attempts to surprise, only to reiterate, but *Dream Master* is fairly enjoyable. The wisecracks are funny and the teenagers are worth shredding. Earlier sequels seemed to be trying too hard at the impossible logic involved with shared dreams and mass hysteria. With *Part 4*, the series relaxes, and it is clear that Freddy will be coming back for more.

The image is not perfectly sharp, and some stronger colors tend to blur together. The volume is also set lower than it is on other stereo discs, and the analog track is brighter than the digital track. The disc opens with a trailer for *Kansas*, but a chapter marks the beginning of the film.

A NIGHTMARE ON ELM STREET 5: THE DREAM CHILD
Conceptually, *A Nightmare on Elm Street 5: The Dream Child* is the best of all the *Elm Street* sequels. It is easy to understand why the film was a disappointment at the boxoffice, because there is not a single scream inducing cut and because Freddy is given less personality, witty dialog, or screen time than in the earlier films. The special effects are incredibly elaborate, however, and some are quite gratifying. The script reminded us of those video arcade games where you need to spend ten dollars in quarters just to figure out what is going on. It is complicated, and to some extent the filmmakers are supplanting complications for substance, but for once the special effects, even the gross-est, cut-from-the-movie-and-restored-to-the-video special effects, do not seem gratuitous. The story is about a girl and her unborn child who match wits with Freddy and try to stop him from stealing the souls of the girl's friends. You have to be familiar with the series to understand what is happening, but that understanding will, in *5*, breed appreciation.

The picture transfer is very good. The stereo surround sound is engaging, but the volume is set low and has to be pushed a bit. Some of the dialog remains fuzzy in any case. After the film is ended, there is a promotional music video, featuring the group Whodini.

NIGHTSONGS
The 39-minute *nightsongs* contains six Duke Ellington numbers performed and improvised upon by Toshiyuki Honda, and accompanied by lifeless images of New York at night. The quality of the sound and the picture is admirable. The stereo mix is playful and Honda's interpretations of Ellington are adequately pleasant.

9 1/2 WEEKS
There is a low-pitched hum throughout *9 1/2 Weeks*. It is louder on the analog track but more distinct on the digital. The rock songs drown it out, except in the rare moments when the characters actually try to talk to one another. The picture quality is excellent.

The movie is about a pair of emotionally immature adults who meet and play games with blindfolds, food, and ice cubes for a couple of months until they get tired and want to go home. This is the European version which contained some scene that American preview audiences thought to be too alienating. At 117-minutes, the disc is 9 1/2 weeks too long. The notes on the jacket say that the film is a "story of a love affair that breaks every sexual taboo." Maybe some scene where they turn out to be brother and sister is still missing.

976-EVIL
Anybody who has longed to see Sandy Dennis eaten by cats will want to take a gander at *976-EVIL*. She portrays a repressive mother and one of the rewards for her son, who sells his soul to the devil over the telephone, is the chance to turn his mom into a Meow Mix special.

The movie, directed by Robert Englund, is a standard horror concoction, with plenty of blood and effects, but no frights. It has an analog Ultra-Stereo surround soundtrack with a few interesting separation effects and cheap but enjoyable sound editing (when the phones ring, the ring is mixed with an eerie, "Evil!"). The picture is grainy and often too orange. The jacket cover claims that this is the Special Laser-Disc Version which means that there is a little extra blood and gore, but it looks as fuzzy as all the rest.

1984
1984 (Import)
The American and Japanese releases of Michael Radford's intriguingly faithful adaptation of George Orwell's *1984* have some distinctive differences. The Japanese version has mild letteroxing with an aspect ratio of about 1.66:1, a slight squaring of the screen image which nevertheless increases the symmetry of the composition significantly.

The American disc opens with a dark screen while a Eurhythmics song plays on the soundtrack, while the Japanese disc opens with the movie itself (both discs end with another dark screen and Eurhythmics number). The musical score on the Japanese version, however, uses the controversial Eurhythmics instrumentals throughout the film, while the American version has a blander, orchestral score. The American version is more consistent with the tone and the concept of the film itself, but the Japanese version works better by presenting a subtle counterpoint to the images. Radford's film was made during April to June, 1984, in and around London, attempting to resurrect the environment of the novel as literally as possible. He is so intent upon being faithful to his source that the avant-garde score is a welcome relief from the intensity of Orwell's vision.

The film is monaural and the Japanese disc was not even CX-encoded. The American version is in digital and is considerably less noisy. The American version is also free of the annoying genital censorship in the Japanese release. The picture is deliberately mono-chromatic, but the Japanese still managed to coax more color out of it while maintaining the essential look. The American version, however, remains in keeping with the somber atmosphere which the film imparts.

George Orwell was terribly ill during the period when he composed *1984*. For all of the story's vaunted examination of life in a totalitarian or authoritarian or contemporary political state, the emotions of the work which really dig into you are the emotions of sickness. In putting together a home video library, or any sort of entertainment library, the object is to satisfy every mood you may ever have. You want to be able to go to your collection at any time and find something which can help you pass a couple of hours. If you are in a good mood, that is no problem. But if you are restless, depressed, or otherwise ill-disposed, you may find yourself attracted toward a program which parallels these feelings. That would be the advantage of owning *1984*. It is a metaphor of physical anxiety and can serve to cushion your tumble even when you are convinced that your state of being is far worse than anything they could come up with in Room 101.

1986 WORLD SERIES HIGHLIGHTS
RCA/Columbia's *1986 World Series Highlights* is in CAV and contains the highlights from each of NBC's seven World Series game broadcasts.

Since every significant play is replayed a

dozen times in slow motion, the Standard Play features do not come in as handy as one might expect. The still frames are a little blurry wherever rapid movement on the field is involved, and the faster speeds are upset by the abridged format of the program. One interesting manipulation which is worth toying with is reverse slow motion. Watching the emotions backwards allows you to spot exactly when a player realizes he has done something very right or very wrong.

The picture is as clear as it was during the game broadcasts, with the exception of an occasional line of interference from the videotape source. The sound is in stereo and it is wonderful. It turns one's living room into a baseball stadium and is especially effective when the Boston fans taunt Darryl Strawberry or when the New York fans launch into the spontaneous 'We Will Rock You.'

1900

One of the loveliest films we have ever seen is Bernardo Bertolucci's *1900*, but you'd have no way of knowing it from Paramount's faded and cropped laser disc release. Vittorio Storaro's luscious, classical cinematography is thoroughly desecrated by the crude and uncaring picture transfer. The film looked as glossy and elegant as any big budget Hollywood production. The disc looks like a cheap little import that was financed with government tax exemptions.

In fact, Paramount has never had much respect for the title. The company insisted upon excising more than an hour of footage from Bertolucci's final cut, as if audiences that would avoid a five hour film would flock to a four hour effort. The version released on disc is the one which played in the general American theatrical release. The three platter set, which is spread to five sides, comes in a box which cannot hold the platters vertically after the wrap is broken.

Paramount has not bothered to provide digital encoding. The monaural soundtrack is soft and indistinct. The film is in English, but the cast spoke several different languages, so there will inevitably be dubbing no matter which language the dialog is presented in.

The plot is about two half-brothers who witness the changes in Italy's political system over the course of the century. Although we have much to say about the film's dramatic content – it is long enough to be both brilliant and disappointing – after struggling through the disc we just don't have the heart.

1969

The problem with *1969* is that it seems like it was written then. The movie tries hard to recreate the times, at least one person's version of them, but does nothing to analyze the era with hindsight. The characters spout what are now academic arguments about Vietnam and the justifications for avoiding the draft, while spending the rest of the time aimlessly searching for romance and good highs.

The film stars Kiefer Sutherland and Robert Downey, Jr., with Bruce Dern in the thankless role as the patriotic father. The picture is a little soft and the digitally encoded stereo sound has only limited surround effects, but the musical score contains a number of pleasant oldies which you probably haven't bothered to obtain on CD.

THE NINETY-SIX: A CATTLE RANCH IN NORTHERN NEVADA

A study of life on a cattle ranch has been compiled on laser disc by the American Folklife Center. It isn't quite anthropology and it isn't sociology, either. *The Ninety-Six: A Cattle Ranch in Northern Nevada*, comes in a classy-looking box and is accompanied by a lovely booklet which has black-and-white photos and text describing the Paradise Valley Folklife Project. Most of the material served as an exhibition at the Smithsonian Institute.

Had the disc been produced with the same quality that went into the box and the booklet, it would have been stunning. Unfortunately, most of the film sequences are in 16mm and the sound is strained. The 3000 color slides and photos contained at the end of side one are far less interesting or moving than the two dozen black-and-white pictures printed in the booklet.

The Paradise Valley Folklife Project is an attempt to record the ways of life and business among cattle ranchers in northern Nevada, throwing in a little history to explain how things came to be the way they are. It is a very polite research project, with no analysis and little in the way of discovery.

Side one is in CAV. It contains a number of brief film clips describing the herding of cattle from summer pastures to winter lodgings, narrated by Les Stewart, owner of the Ninety-Six Ranch.

The still collection is at the end of side one. Each still is repeated twice, the second frame having been overlaid with a caption. This is a good method for describing stills on laser disc, since there is usually enough room to double everything. The best stills are the pictures borrowed from family archives, particularly the ones where you can watch a person grow through decades of faded snapshots. The slides taken by the researchers have no flair. Since so little else of the project really seems scientific, it is a shame they had to be so serious when it came to taking the still photos. Side one has also been encoded for interactive use through a keyboard hookup.

Side two is in CLV and contains longer film sequences of farming and ranching techniques. Films which Stewart took in the 1940s are included to show the changes technology has implemented. Stewart's home movies, which are actually rather elaborately produced, explain more about the tasks and processes than any of the films the researchers made. Side two also has two audio tracks. The first is the narrative to accompany the films, but the second is an unrelated collection of oral histories from the citizens of Paradise Valley, Nevada. The problem here is that only one microphone was used. You can hear the answers just fine, but you can't hear the questions.

The squeamish should be warned that there is a graphic depiction of how a calf is castrated near the end of side two. Stewart tells an amusing joke relating to this operation. The joke is explained in the annotation of the disc program contained in the booklet.

NINJA TURF

The transfer of *Ninja Turf* to disc is grainy, blurry, and chromatically indistinctive. The print which the disc comes from isn't any better, as the original film looks like it was made from leftover scraps of footage. The sound is equally awful – as is the acting, script, and editing. You might get some laughs at parties from the way the dubbed in dialog is delivered, but it will quickly become apparent that *Ninja Turf* is less entertaining than watching grass grow.

NINOTCHKA

In *Ninotchka*, director Ernst Lubitsch lets talky scenes go on and on, and yet they never become boring. Greta Garbo portrays a Russian envoy seduced by the inhibitions of capitalistic Paris. The role is an easy one. She need only maintain a straight face to be humorous. One wishes she had appeared in more comedies where taking her seriously was not a necessity. The sound is fine and the black-and-white print is nearly flawless.

THE NINTH CONFIGURATION

The Ninth Configuration was written, produced, and directed by William Peter Blatty, and we seem to recall that it was disowned by him as well, for a while, when cuts were made without his permission. The version which appears on the disc, however, is the full 115 minute version, and presumably has his blessing. For what it is worth.

Isn't it disturbing how neatly stories about madness and The New Testament go together? There's no argument one can put forth against either one which will stick. Blatty is on easy ground, and while his effort may have failed as a novel or as a movie, it succeeds most readily as home video, because it is just stimulating enough to keep your attention. The story ends up bypassing it's initial query – How did these soldiers, who are being kept at a special castle/asylum, become insane? – to deal with two characters, an astronaut who freaked out the day before his flight, and a doctor who may or may not be an insane killer or Christ or both.

Blatty has fun with the insane asylum and does just what you are supposed to do in insane asylum movies, keep the audience guessing as to what is real and what is a put-on. The technical aspects of the film, however, are definitely a put-on. The make up, particularly on Stacy Keach, is an embarrassment, and the shadow of the sound boom can often be seen floating across the shoulders and faces of the actors. The picture is cropped for the disc presentation and you are often aware of it. The monaural film is also a little old and grainy, though it isn't in too bad a shape. The analog track has less hiss, but less detail, than the digital track.

NO MAN OF HER OWN

The only film that Clark Gable and Carole Lombard appeared together in, *No Man of Her Own* is about a gambler whose life is reformed when he meets and marries a 'good' woman. The orignal film was trimmed to a breezy 81 minutes, so trimmed, in fact, that characters appear and disappear without introduction or good riddance. The print is beautiful. There is just enough of a story so that the charisma of the stars can be manipulated. Side two is in CAV. There is no action to manipulate, but there are the meandering closeups which become almost lyrical when run in slow motion. The sound is old, and contains noise which can be heard if the volume is pushed beyond standard levels. A collection of promotional stills and advertising art has been placed at the end of side two.

NO MAN'S LAND

Charlie Sheen has a forceful presence in *No Man's Land*. He portrays a rich, young car thief who is befriended by an undercover cop. The resolution of the story is as old as Pat Garret and Billy the Kid (or was it Brutus and Caesar?), but Sheen's performance is the factor which makes the story's morality contemporary and befitting of its title.

The digital sound is in stereo and recreates the purring combustion of a Porche (that's all he steals, Porches) with a driver's seat-like fidelity. The film takes place mostly at night or in dark garages, but the picture rarely looks strained. Our biggest complaint about the movie is that all of the scenes taking place inside the Sheen character's house were filmed in the kitchen, as if that was the only room the owners of the house allowed the filmmakers to use.

NO MERCY

Most of *No Mercy* takes place at night or in dark rooms and most of the disc has a grainy picture. Since the locale is New Orleans, however, the effect is more Vieux Carre than disruptive, and the movie, a pleasing mixture of action and romance, has its share of old fashioned charms. Richard Gere portrays a police detective who tracks down Kim Basinger because she witnessed his partner's murder. They can't stand each other, but right at the break between side one and side two on the disc (i.e., the exact middle of the film), their resolve softens. Gere and Basinger are too good looking to portray real people, which causes some viewers to dismiss the entertainment, but the contrast between glamor and grits shouldn't be a problem. Movies have a long tradition of showing characters who discover the best in themselves at times of crisis, and that is what stars personify.

The stereo surround sound is in better condition than the picture and contains effective renditions of birds, crickets and flies. Nothing out of the ordinary wavers from the middle, but the atmospheric touches are enjoyable.

NO RETREAT, NO SURRENDER

No Retreat, No Surrender is a martial arts film for children – well, older children. As in most martial arts films the hero gets beat up and then practices to become the best there is so he won't get beat up anymore. Only guess who trains him during his hour of desperation – the ghost of Bruce Lee. The story is presented in the cinematic equivalent of large type. Jean-Claude Van Damme appears at the end as a bad guy for the big final showdown, which is nicely choreographed and is presented in CAV (with two unsteady still frames for every five). The picture looks cheap and a bit grainy, and the sound is dull.

NO SMALL AFFAIR

The stated premise of *No Small Affair*, that it is about a 16-year-old boy chasing after a 22-year-old woman, does the movie a disservice. The film is a witty tale of two young people striving for success, in the spirit of *Sixteen Candles* and *Risky Business*. Directed by Jerry Schatzberg and filmed by Vilmos Zsigmond, *No Small Affair* is a class act all the way through. The stereo mix is excellent. The dialog is sharp ("I remember asking my mother once where babies came from and she told me one of the most outrageous, incredible stories that I'd ever heard...It turned out to be true."). Even the San Francisco locations are thoughtfully utilized. Although the transfer has added an extra level of fuzz to Zsigmond's photography, the disc is nearly perfect and, as entertainment, highly satisfying.

NO WAY OUT

No Way Out takes an almost Dickensian pleasure in utilizing coincidence. It is a suspense film, with plot twists and a murder, and while a half expected but nevertheless cute final twist supposedly excuses most of the other unlikely occurences, it really doesn't matter whether the story makes any sense or not. The characters are believable, and they're in trouble.

The quality of the disc, like the details of the plot, will not stand up well to close examination, but one generally becomes so excited watching the film as to pay no attention. The sound is in stereo, although it lacks real flourish. The picture is mildy blurry and grainy.

NOBODY'S FOOL

Beth Henley wrote *Nobody's Fool*, so it is full of deliberate idiosyncrasies which are charming on the stage and artificial on film. The movie does contain a consistently amusing and vicious portrait of a regional theater group, and it has a happy ending, but it is never completely convincing. Rosanna Arquette portrays a woman whose adulthood is a delayed reaction to life. The sound is sharp. The picture is generally bright and clear, but a couple of shots are grainy.

NORTH BY NORTHWEST
(Voyager CAV)
NORTH BY NORTHWEST
(Voyager CLV)
NORTH BY NORTHWEST (MGM/UA)
NORTH BY NORTHWEST (Import)

Voyager's Criterion Collection picture transfer of *North by Northwest* is gorgeous. Hitchcock begins the film in pale tones, and then seems to follow the ups and downs of the hero's romantic involvement with deeper and lighter colors. The affect upon the viewer is a growing infatuation with the look of the film as the movie progresses. Neither MGM/UA's version nor the import version came as close to replicating the colors so accurately, or providing as sharp and distinctive a picture. Neither had CX-encoding, either. Voyager's offering does, without automatic tripping. When activated, the volume levels drop precipitately. Although the sound is slightly cleaner, it is also duller, and we preferred leaving it off. The sound transfer is well done, and an insert comes with the disc which explains the history of the film's audio presentations.

The Japanese disc presented the final side of the 136-minute feature in CAV, but that was only a teaser. In full CAV, the viewer can read the headlines on newspapers (in which the word 'Northwest' is often featured), examine the lovely matte paintings, or just take more time watching the film. Scholars can catalog the objects and people appearing in the upper left corner of the screen, or can increase the speed of the film to better visualize the rhythm of camera movement and editing.

The Japanese disc also features the film's trailer, from an early sixties re-release. Voyager's supplementary material, concluding side five and filling side six, contains an original theatrical trailer in miserable condition, as well as a still photo section showing pressbook material, publicity stills, and behind-the-scenes photos. There is also a brief essay with photos explaining the movie's VistaVision film format, a thumbnail biography, again with pictures, of the composer, Bernard Herrmann, and a short, deliberately moody, black and white interview with Hitchcock, pretending to be commenting in real time upon a screening of the crop duster sequence.

As is explained on the CAV disc, VistaVision, which was originally Paramount's answer to Fox's CinemaScope, was intended for viewing without modification in any theater. Cropping the edges or the sides, depending upon the type of projector or screen being used, was expected. MGM/UA's release used the full television screen, showing much less of the sides of the image than the subsequent releases, but more of the top and the bottom of the screen than is seen anywhere else. The Japanese import went so far as to include a slim black band on the left and right of the screen to indicate that the complete width of the picture was being presented, and the image is wider than the Voyager version, but the height of the picture was diminished severely. Voyager's version is closest to what the director originally intended, though losing the decoration which is available on the extreme left and right of the import disc or extreme top and bottom on the first American disc, however proper, is disheartening. (Contrary to an error in the jacket insert which claims that the image is presented in 1.85:1, the letterboxing actually provides the correct ratio of 1.66:1.) At least one gets to see Martin Landau put the gun on the table and pick it up again, a piece of drama which the import presentation sliced away.

The disc's most exciting treat, however, is its inclusion of the original production storyboards. Storyboards of *North by Northwest*, particularly the crop duster sequence, are ubiquitous, but for the first time, two clips from the film are presented, in CAV, with the appropriate storyboard for each shot appearing in a box on the upper right. There is an immediate understanding of how much of the film Hitchcock planned in his head and how much he left to chance.

Voyager's CLV version has no supplementary material. The picture transfer is identical to the CAV version. Whereas the CAV disc was analog only, the CLV disc has the addition of digital sound. The audio track, however, has several flutters in it (Example: As Thornhill and his secretary pause at the newsstand.) which are not present on the CAV version.

NORTH TO ALASKA

North to Alaska has a sharp picture with colors that look mildly faded in some reels and not too faded in others. The stereo sound has some fluctuations. Not much more than the musical score is really in stereo, but voices tend to enter at different volume levels, and the sound generally has an unsteady ambience. The disc comes in a nice gatefold jacket, but one of the beautiful color stills on the back is from a different John Wayne movie and not this one. Early copies also suffered from widespread manufacturing problems.

The letterboxing is a treat. The scanned and cropped version has been playing on television for a very long time, and replaces frivolity with tension. When you are aware of what is going on around the characters, you tend to get on their wavelength better. The aspect ratio is about 2.2:1.

The film is based upon a stage play, unusual for a John Wayne movie, and there are lengthy segments where the characters remain in one location and talk their way through things. It becomes intriguing to watch Wayne work in this manner, and more intriguing still when he's paired with Stewart Granger, who has a completely different style of acting. The two don't really interact, but the pleasure when they are together on the screen is doubled because neither is overshadowed. The movie is a romantic comedy, set during the Alaskan Gold Rush, and it is worth sitting through all 123 minutes for the ending, which shouts charm at the top of its lungs and stays in tune while doing so.

NOTHING IN COMMON

With orange washes, blurry spots, speckles and vertical white lines, *Nothing in Common* has little in common with good video discs, except for the program material itself. When scenes take place in the bright sunshine, the picture is okay, but the quality is anything but consistent. The monaural sound is not CX-encoded and can't be pushed too much, either.

The movie, however, is a wonder. The comedy stretches much wider than the advertising art, which concentrates on Jackie Gleason and Tom Hanks, implies. While the scenes with Gleason and Eve Marie Saint, who appears as Hanks' mother, are amusing and poignant, it is the sharp portrayal of the modern ad agency where Hanks is employed which gives the movie its depth. One scene in particular, where an ad campaign is first presented to some potential clients, is so riveting it could almost be a two-minute drama on its own. The movie is definitely worth seeing, but the medium for viewing it is optional.

NOTORIOUS (Voyager CAV)
NOTORIOUS (Voyager CLV)
NOTORIOUS (Magnetic Video)

Voyager's Criterion Collection release of *Notorious* has an incredibly sharp picture, having been mastered from the original camera negative stored at the Museum of Modern Art. The blacks are ink solid and the whites are dazzling. Spread between those two extremes is a stunning array of grey shading, so fine that you can make out every strand of Ingrid Bergman's hair. The source material is also subject to a number of minor annoyances – speckles, particularly near the beginning, a couple of scratches, and fading which flares up from time to time on the far left. The picture certainly makes the old Magnetic Video version look like a hazy etching, but some viewers may need patience to become enamored with the Voyager disc. We found that although some of the markings were distracting (as, with the enhanced image, is Cary Grant's mole), it was the sharpness of the picture which lingered in our memory later, and reinforced the film's pleasures.

Voyager released two versions, a straight CLV rendition, and a CAV edition which contains a number of special features. The picture and sound transfers are identical. The soundtrack, transferred with the optical soundtrack from a 35mm fine grain element, is weak.

The combination of the crisp picture and the CAV triple speed play creates a hyper-vivid view of the cast, and puts the editing and camera angles into a wider perspective. In CAV slow motion, every scene becomes more tense and claustrophobic. The CAV edition contains a lecture on one of the analog audio tracks, and has about 15 minutes of excerpts from a 'Lux Radio Hour' rendition of the story crammed onto two audio tracks over the supplementary material.

Filling out the supplementary section is an original theatrical trailer, other brief promotional bites, a simplified explanation of rear-projection with clips from the film used as examples, production memos, excerpts from the story which inspired the film, a brief summary of scenes dropped at the last moment, and a collection of alternate endings which were under consideration. Among the memos are suggested changes emanating from the Hays office. One thing which has surprised us in the documentation contained on several Voyager titles is how the censor board seemed to improve scripts time and again, by suggesting ambiguities in scenes which have far greater resonance than the literal activities they were replacing.

Notorious, which was directed by Alfred Hitchcock, has been so thoroughly analyzed that most viewers are already aware of the film's principal thematic points, the most elaborate one exemplified by Bergman's wonderful line of dialog near the beginning, "The important drinking hasn't started yet." Rudy Behlmer's lecture, which is available on both Voyager discs, concentrates on the production history, and provides a general overview of the reasons why the film is so highly respected. He makes no mention of the obvious near-anagram in Grant's character name, Devlin, nor of the way in which no one seems to complete a trip up or down the notorious staircase until the very end. He also has a few pointless digressions, including an elaborate description of *Dead Men Don't Wear Plaid*, and perpetuates the bias against comedians in Hollywood by claiming, as others have, that Hitchcock is the most famous film director in the world. Charlie Chaplin is the most famous film director in the world. Hitchcock is number two.

NOVA/ALL AMERICAN BEAR

Nova/All American Bear intrudes on *National Geographic* territory, with mixed results. The program attempts to show a typical seasonal cycle in the life of an American brown bear. The narration, by Bill Mason, moves at a quick clip, but leaves information gaps at critical points. In comparison, the *National Geographic Video* programs tend to define the limits of what is going to be shown, so the viewer is not tempted to ask questions which can't be answered. It is an art which the makers of *All American Bear* have yet to master. On the positive side, the program gets into an excellent level of detail on the metabolism governing hibernation and presents the information clearly, with the help of computer graphics. The disc's picture quality is good and the sound is also okay, although some listeners may find Mason's voice to be mildly irritating.

NOVA: BACK TO CHERNOBYL

Back to Chernobyl contains very fresh looking footage and bright monaural sound. The program, made in 1989, is able to analyze the short and even medium term effects of the disaster. It leaves the impression that Three Mile Island and Chernobyl are the only two accidents which ever happened with nuclear power plants, but on its stated theme – a profile of the accident and the damage control – it is effective and informative.

The description of the accident itself is mind boggling. In essence, the crew deliberately initiated the meltdown as a test, not realizing that they passed the point of stopping the process almost immediately after they had begun. The filmmakers interview firemen and plant personnel who have so far survived, and assesses the impact the radiation has had on the surrounding areas. The filmmakers carry radioactivity meters and measure the levels in areas which they know are still hot, but they never point the devices at the potatoes in the Kiev market stalls.

NOVA: CITIES OF CORAL

Cities of Coral spends an hour poking around a reef off St. Croix and explaining what is to be found there. No humans appear in the program, which is narrated in a budgetary way by the episode's producer.

One intriguing specimen after another is examined and given just the right amount of attention to satisfy a casual viewer's curiosity. Interesting creatures include the puffer fish who inflates with spikes when another fish gobbles him, a ruffled slug who eats plants but stores the chloroforms to create its own solar energy cells, a three spot damsel fish who farms algae and keeps others away from its cultivations, and the parrot fish whose jaws are so strong that it bites the rocks (and leaves scar markings) along with the food attached, creating sand as it eats. The most fascinating segment is a time lapse sequence showing two corals 'fighting' for territory.

The disc has one of the nicer jacket covers in the series and has a strong digital monaural soundtrack. The picture is as clear as a fish tank. The underwater shots are soft to begin with, but most have been transferred without a significant addition of grain.

NOVA/EINSTEIN
NOVA/UFO'S: ARE WE ALONE?

An hour long biography of Albert Einstein, *Nova/Einstein* (called 'A. Einstein' on the program itself), is held to such a strict chronological order that it is done with theoretical physics before the disc is halfway finished. It is admirable that the program uses much of its running time to document and explain Einstein's social views, particularly since the physics material is also given a lucid, if succinct explanation. The disc is nicely transferred and the digitally encoded sound preserves Einstein's voice for the ages. The show contains photos or motion pictures of Einstein from every decade of his life. The high point of the newsreel footage is a tribute given in Einstein's presence by George Bernard Shaw. They have more in common than one would suppose at a glance.

"Einstein was one of them," says a character in *Close Encounters of the Third Kind*, a wonderful film which nevertheless gave far more credence to a wacky social phenomena than the subject deserves. The subject is UFOs, and 'Nova' has an anything-for-Nielsen-even-though-this-is-Public-TV show on UFOs entitled 'The Case of the UFOs,' which has been released on disc as *Nova/UFO's: Are We Alone?*. The show spends the first five to ten minutes going ooh and ahh over pictures of cigars and bowler hats which have been tossed in the air, and then the remaining 50 minutes is spent proving that the National Enquirer is not the reputable publication nobody thought it was. There is some legitimate science offered, including a demonstration that ionic charges are emitted when rock cracks under pressure (i.e., during seismic activity), but the show is limited to debunking three or four major incidents. The transfer is passable, but when people are deliberately trying to make flashlights on strings look extraterrestrial in 8mm, the result is not exactly crisp.

NOVA/ONE SMALL STEP

We weren't expecting much from *Nova/One Small Step*, about the US space program, and we were pleasantly surprised with the rewards the show had to offer. The program, which is more than ten years old, covers, in an hour, events from the initial failures at Vandenburg AFB to the Soyez linkup. The program is about the feats of engineers rather than astronauts, and depicts with frankness the political motivations and compromises which pushed and pulled America into space. Among the less anthologized footage are shots of failed launchings, and a terrific view of the astronauts in Gemini 7 waving to the astronauts in Gemini 8. The disc's picture looks a bit worn down, especially with *For All Mankind* still fresh in our minds. The monaural sound is okay.

NOVA/PREDICTABLE DISASTERS

After a typical *Nova*-ish lurid opening sequence involving a psychic, *Nova/Predictable Disaster*, turns into a fairly interesting overview of the science of predicting earthquakes. The program is more than ten years old, and much of the hard science information is outdated, but there are lengthy passages, dealing with structural engineering and making buildings safe, which are still quite relevant. As a primer on the subject, the show is acceptable.

The picture looks as old as the program is, and the wardrobes of the scientists prove that it is not only tectonic plates which have fault lines. The sound is unremarkable.

NOVA/SAVING THE SISTINE CHAPEL

For reasons so complex that the copy on the back of the jacket gets it completely wrong, art experts interviewed in *Nova/Saving the Sistine Chapel* condemn the efforts to scrub Michelangelo's magnificent frescoes. The gist of the argument, which starts to make sense as the documentary judiciously presents both sides of the issue, is that the restorers have removed imbedded grime which was actually placed on top of the artwork by the artist, intentionally darkening and enhancing the dimensionality of the paintings. The scrubbed paintings reveal "cartoon colors," unlike any other surviving Michelangelo work.

The disc, which has decent picture and sound, is one of the better *Nova* efforts. While concentrating on a specific topic, the documentary actually covers a wide range of subjects and manages to do so with intelligence. The Japanese have bought the film rights to the restoration itself, but Nova was able to cut a side deal which includes before and after footage, along with computer animated diagrams and summaries of the different scientific methods used to restore the paintings.

NOVA/UFO'S: ARE WE ALONE?

(see **NOVA/EINSTEIN**)

NOVA VIDEO LIBRARY: ANIMAL OLYMPIANS

If you can tolerate the endless stream of sports metaphors, the *Nova Video Library* episode, *Animal Olympians*, has many interesting moments. The documentary looks at the animals which excel at various physical activities – running, swimming, jumping, even shooting – and how the animals are designed to accomplish such feats. One intriguing segment shows a dog on an accelerating treadmill shifting distinctly from a walk to a trot to a canter to a gallop. Each speed is governed by a different coordination of the dog's four legs. Blandly narrated by Lee Remick, the program is so full of different animals and different information that there is bound to be something, or many things, of interest to everyone. The sound is passable, but the picture is consistently soft.

NOVA VIDEO LIBRARY: THE BERMUDA TRIANGLE

The 'Nova' program about the 'Bermuda Triangle,' *Nova Video Library: The Bermuda Triangle*, is similar in style to the episode about UFOs. The show spends about five minutes suggesting that there is a black hole in the middle of the Atlantic Ocean and then the next 55 proving that there is not. Whew. The program, which is entitled 'The Case of the Bermuda Triangle,' offers no significant scientific teaching, but it does contain one important lesson: Research is power. The main entertainment comes from watching the authors of the more outrageous books on the subject twist and duck as their answers are cross cut with the people they claim to be quoting or the documentation they are readily obfuscating.

The images vary in quality depending upon the age of the film clips. Substantial footage from a film, 'The Devil's Triangle,' is presented as the primary target to be discredited. The digitally encoded monaural sound also changes in quality depending upon how real they want the 'My God it's full of stars' radio messages to sound. An hour of it is a bit of overkill, but then proving that the Bermuda Triangle does not exist is not exactly difficult.

NOVA VIDEO LIBRARY: FAT CHANCE IN A THIN WORLD

No matter what your constitution, watching *Nova Video Library: Fat Chance in a Thin World*, will make you hungry. The scientists who are interviewed talk on and on about the psychology of eating, and you can't stop from thinking about your own psychology. Self-contemplation starts the automatic signals that send juices into your stomach and blinding, seductive, irrepressible 'Go Munch' signs in your brain.

The disc is very good. The transfer looks great, from fresh videotape, and the sound is bright and sharp. The program, from 1983, provides a thorough summary of the current theories concerning the way in which bodies maintain weight levels, and how, past a certain point, fighting it is almost useless, if not harmful. Mixing interviews, closeups of fat cells, footage from the most significant studies, and the expected candid shots of diet cheaters, the episode provides a surprising amount of technical information as well as a clear and well-balanced narrative. One concept communicated unequivocally is that any calorie which is not burned off, stays. Forever. Since the subject is one, like the weather, which is suitable for neutral conversations, it is conceivable that one would want to play the disc several times, to memorize passages. It is also a good disc to share with guests who refuse second helpings, or those who indulge in thirds.

NOVA VIDEO LIBRARY: HITLER'S SECRET WEAPON

An excellent *Nova Video Library* documentary about the development of the V-2 rocket, *Hitler's Secret Weapon* (subtitled, more sensibly, 'The V-2 Rocket at Peenemunde'), is made up of footage taken by the Germans during the development of the rocket and by interviews with several of the major figures involved, including Werner Von Braun and Walter Dornberger. The footage is old, but the transfer provides no further impedance to either the picture or the sound.

Weapon is thorough in its presentation of the chronology and political maneuverings which brought the development of the rocket into being. Major design milestones are also discussed. The show suffers only two minor deficiencies. When significant problems in the development of the design are mentioned, the show does not always explain how engineers eventually surmounted them. And statements by the rocket scientists, that they were really trying to explore outer space and were just tricking the military into funding their efforts, are repeated too many times to sound completely legitimate. The show never presses the issue.

NOVA VIDEO LIBRARY: THE SCIENCE OF MURDER

We had hoped that *Nova Video Library: The Science of Murder* would tell us a few high-tech ways to do in a neighbor or two, but no such luck. The 1981 program is partially an amusing tabloid-style ratings magnet and partially a superbly edited examination of the social and psychological causes of murder. The hoarier contributions include crime scenes re-created 'Current Affair'-style; an actual autopsy, in full unblinking closeup, performed on the victim of a drug-related execution; and the voice-over narrator, Andrew MacMillan, making close to a full breath pause between each syllable he speaks, in what can only be described as mock-calmness. On the plus side, there is an excellent interview with Ramsey Clark, who must be the nicest attorney general the United States ever had; a fascinating account by two criminals of their emotional state during the heat of their crimes; and the many facts and figures involving the identification of fingerprints, blood types (even identical twins have different blood, because of the different diseases they've been exposed to), and hair particles.

NOVA VIDEO LIBRARY: THE SECRET OF THE SEXES
The Secret of the Sexes is a can of worms, and at least some part of it is guaranteed to upset every viewer. The show looks at how parents consciously and unconsciously teach their children about the roles of gender. We are sure that the scientists being quoted have done gobs of research, but nothing they say is adequately substantiated on the program, and the studies which are shown in detail have no control groups. The episode is sensationalized and unscientific. The sound and picture transfers are passable.

NOVA VIDEO LIBRARY: THE SHAPE OF THINGS
Nova Video Library: The Shape of Things has an institutional-sounding audio track which makes the whole documentary feel worn down. The subject is potentially fascinating, and probably has not been studied enough by anyone. It is about the geometric patterns which are repeated again and again in nature, and what some of the sources for these patterns are. The concept is stimulating, but the program tends to be repetitive and unorganized. The visual material, from a wide variety of sources, is passable.

NOVA VIDEO LIBRARY: SIGNS OF THE APES, SONGS OF THE WHALES
Imagine that a storyteller could transmit a movie to a group of individuals clustered around him, without the assistance of technology. He could manipulate the movie at will, or in response to his audience, who would see and hear the narrative. Impossible for humans, but conceivable for the dolphin, whose primary sense organ and communication organ are one in the same. *Nova Video Library: Signs of the Apes, Songs of the Whales* is a fairly decent summarization of the major American research projects in animal communications with apes and sea mammals circa 1983. Anyone who owns a pet knows that most animals are more cognitively intelligent than scientists will credit them publicly. The program presents the main arguments for and against the recognition of language abilities in these animals, but, smartly, the program mostly lets the chimpanzees, gorillas, orangutans, dolphins, humpback whales, and even sea lions speak for themselves. Without succumbing to mysticism, the program presents enough facts to fuel the individual imagination of every viewer. It would be difficult to ask for more from an hour presentation.

The picture quality varies in accordance with the capabilities of the cameras used by the researchers. The image usually looks a little worn. The show has been narrated by Maureen Stapleton, whose voice is a little too quizzical for our tastes. The sound quality is average.

NOVA VIDEO LIBRARY: WHALE WATCH
A half dozen laser discs about whales are available – and that isn't including *Moby Dick* – but *Nova Video Library: Whale Watch* is one of the better efforts. The program provides a simple but thorough profile of the grey whale, which lives off the Pacific coast of North America. It includes graphic depictions of the whales mating (they do it in threes – two males and one female) and of the efficient slaughter developed on factory ships in the thirties. Also shown is the mechanics of their feeding, a fascinating process because the whale has a mouth the size of a Volkswagen and a throat which is smaller than an exhaust pipe. Although research scientists are depicted and interviewed, they don't intrude upon the subject the way they have done on other programs, and by the end you have a good feel for what is known about the grey whale and what there still is to wonder. The disc has a satisfactory picture and clear monaural sound.

NOVA/VISIONS OF THE DEEP
Nova/Visions of the Deep, subtitled 'The Underwater World of Al Giddings' on the program itself, leisurely shifts between depictions of how Giddings gets his best shots and some of the fabulous footage he has achieved. Included in the latter are eerie visions from beneath the ice pack in the Arctic, an amused look at some children in Tahiti who play with sharks, and daring eyeball-to-camera-lens views of creatures most people would be uncomfortable peering at from the safety of a portal. The underwater material is terrific, and there is enough extra information about Giddings and about the problems of filming underwater to keep the viewer attentive with narrative substance.

A few of the shots showing Giddings hunched over his moviola are hopelessly grainy, but the underwater sequences are gorgeous and are in perfect shape. Maybe the film gets the bends when it stays on the surface for too long. The transfer is good, and the sound is better than average.

NOVA: WAR FROM THE AIR
An intriguing argument against the effectiveness of bombing civilian populations during war time, *War from the Air* studies the major conflicts of the twentieth century and determines that aerial bombing has only been effective when employed against very specific military targets. The narration skims over Hiroshima, stating without sufficient proof that the Japanese cabinet was preparing to capitulate before the bombs were dropped, but provides strong evidence that attacks on Barcelona, London, Stalingrad, Dresden, Hanoi, etc., only served to unite the civilian population behind the resistance movement and war effort.

Made in 1975, *War from the Air* contains rare footage from the twenties and thirties (including Billy Mitchell's battleship demonstration, which the Japanese attended) and ends with a pre-detente nervousness about ICBM silos. The picture quality varies depending upon the footage, and the sound is passable. The program is narrated by Richard Kiley.

NOW THAT'S WHAT I CALL MUSIC VIDEO (Import)
A collection of music videos released in Japan, *Now That's What I Call Music Video* has thirteen cuts, but only three are worth viewing.

'That's All,' from Genesis, is the best one. The music is tight and the video concept – the band members play the song amid derelicts in an abandoned building – effectively counterpoints lead singer Phil Collins' personality. 'Working with Fire and Steel' by China Crisis is not as remarkable musically, but the video contains a lot of documentary footage from the early part of the century and it leaves a nice impression. Rock Steady Crew's 'Hey You' is a fast-paced break dancing number which most viewers will find invigorating.

The other ten videos, from groups such as UB40, Heaven 17, Simple Minds, and Orchestral Maneuvers in the Dark, are hardly inspiring. Two videos by Mike Oldfield are awful and something called 'Double Dutch' by Malcolm McLaren belongs on a different disc all together.

NOW VOYAGER (MGM/UA)
NOW VOYAGER (CBS/Fox)
Both CBS/Fox and MGM/UA released versions of *Now Voyager*, an entertaining Bette Davis film about a woman trying to come to terms with her overbearing mother. There are more similarities than there are differences between the two releases. The picture on both discs is sharp and the contrasts in the black-and-white photography are rich. The sound on both has a few pops and crackles, but Max Steiner's score will play over and over in your head, broken high notes and all, by the time the movie is done.

The scenes where Davis stands up to her mother's brow-beating are more fun than her romantic interludes with Paul Henreid, who portrays a lonely, married architect. However, both stories are necessary to build up the sympathy and pathos needed to carry the plot along. Time has taken its toll in one respect. This is the movie where Henreid is always lighting two cigarettes and then handing one to her and nowadays you are apt to cringe at the sight of it, because he always inhales to get them going.

THE NUTCRACKER SUITE (see **THE ROYAL BALLET – SWAN LAKE**)

NUTS
No, Barbra Streisand didn't deserve any awards for *Nuts*, but the movie is great fun. It is a tantalizing courtroom drama, about an insanity hearing, and every key part is played by an actor or actress so well established that it is impossible for any of them to become real characters. That, however, is part of the entertainment. The drama is too lightweight to deserve soul-searching performances. It is all mannerisms and teardrops at the right moment, and the cast are a bunch of old pros, enjoying their craft as much as their pay.

The surround effects are engaging. Unfortunately, the picture is a little hazy, and while some of this can be attributed to the cinematography, some of it is also the result of the transfer. The flaw, a mild blur around any direct or reflected light, is the disc's only drawback.

THE OBLONG BOX (see **COMEDY OF TERRORS/THE OBLONG BOX**)

THE OCTAGON
The sound is not stereophonic, the film stock is not high quality, and the plot makes no sense whatsoever, but *The Octagon*, starring Chuck Norris, has an unpredictable rhythm and many entertaining martial arts sequences.

The transfer is good, and the monaural sound, particularly the inexpensive jazz score, sounds fine. It will take us several more viewings to figure out just exactly what the story is about – it may have something to do with a terrorist/mercenary training center – but the dialog is so poorly written that it is great fun to absorb and ponder. When one character learns that a murder was committed by a group of 'Ninja,' he responds, "Ninja? Whew, talk about world class killers. Hey wait a minute. They've been outlawed for over three hundred years!" As if he just remembered he hadn't seem them around in a while.

OCTOBER
There has never been another film like Sergei Eisenstein's *October*. It is a cinematic restaging of a historic event (the Bolshevik revolution), presented like a news documentary. No one character appears for more than a few minutes, but the viewer is captured by the flow and drama of the events (thanks to Eisenstein's masterful style).

The disc presentation comes from a restored version of the movie which was put together, with incidental sound effects and a Dimitri Shostakovich musical score, shortly after Eisenstein died. Only some of the action has an artificial slowness caused by transferring a silent film to today's projections standards. Most of the movie looks realistic. The picture is in as good a condition as one can expect for a Russian silent film. The sound is digitally encoded monaural and the volume can be raised to an enjoyable level without significant distortion. White English subtitles appear over the white Russian print on the title cards, and are often next to impossible to read.

The film is exciting, and even if it were not aspiring to accurately render real occurrences it would still provide valuable lessons in the steps and half steps which lead to revolution. The most important component, however, is the cast. Even though characters are seen only briefly, the emotional manipulations are constant. The cliché that the film's hero is the proletariat is true in the most incredible way. Each actor and actress contributes a small but valuable part of his or her self, and when the film is ended it is the general events and not the individuals which the viewer remembers. The movie is more successfully communist than Communism itself.

OCTOPUSSY (see **MOONRAKER**)

ODD MAN OUT
Dramatically, *Odd Man Out* is one long, depressing slide, as a man wounded in a robbery is hunted down and killed by the police (though the plot is more interested in the people the fugitive meets than the fugitive himself). But stylistically, the movie has many artistic peaks, and so it becomes tolerable entertainment if one has tired of lighthearted frivolity. Carol Reed's direction, and everything he was famous for – shiny cobblestones, inflated shadows, etc. – keep the viewer questioning the assumptions of the characters.

The black-and-white print is in worse condition than the nice looking stills on the back of the jacket, but the images are rich and the flaws do not interfere with one's concentration. The sound is in the condition one would expect from the age and source of the film.

OF HUMAN BONDAGE
Bette Davis's lousy cockney accent makes one cringe through most of *Of Human Bondage*, but her big, "You're a cripple, cripple, cripple!" scene more than compensates. Released by 3M as a Collectible Classic, the movie stars Leslie Howard as an emotionally and physically disabled medical student infatuated with a waitress until she messes up his life one too many times. The 35mm print is ragged at the reel change points and fairly grainy throughout, giving London an extra layer of fog. The sound is commensurate with the age of the film and the quality of the print.

OFF BEAT
The jacket cover art of *Off Beat* gives an impression that the movie is a *Police Academy* styled comedy. In actuality, the film is a cute romantic comedy about a civilian who does a favor for a friend by pretending to be a cop, and then decides to continue the deception when he meets an eligible policewoman. The story has its share of cheap shots,but it also has a few choice cameo appearances – Harvey Keitel as a bank robber – and a nice helping of romance. The picture is grainy. The analog sound is monaural and has not been CX-encoded.

OFF LIMITS
The admirably scripted *Off Limits* is about military cops in Saigon looking for a serial killer. Unlike many murder mysteries, the detection process is cleverly logical, and the heroes, Willem Dafoe and Gregory Hines, make an appealing, no-nonsense duo. The disc has digital encoding, although not much more than the music seems to be in stereo. The picture transfer, with many troublesome night shots and neon bar scenes, looks steady and well-executed.

THE OFFICIAL STORY
The print used for *The Official Story* looks a bit ragged, which was how the film appeared in theaters. There are scratches, dreary colors, and a tinny monaural soundtrack. The movie is in Spanish with English subtitles. The film, despite its appearance, has great consequence. It is about a woman who realizes her adopted daughter was the child of political prisoners murdered by the desperate Argentine junta in the mid seventies. The film is tightly constructed, so that the woman and her family can easily be seen as representing the Argentine state, just as the classroom in which the woman teaches can be seen as the state's conscience. There is also a pointed view of a magician at a children's birthday party, pretending to torture a dove, and the real horror his act instills upon his young audience.

OH GOD! YOU DEVIL
The stereo and picture on *Oh God! You Devil* is perfectly acceptable, as is the comedy itself. Even Milton knew which one of the two made for better copy. George Burns stars in both title roles, primarily the second one. As Satan, he tempts a young musician with stardom and luxury. Burns's timing is often impeccable and he can make silly lines such as his hotel room exit, "If you want anything I'm in 666," sound hysterically witty. The limitations of a project like this are obvious, but the movie lives up to them.

O'KEEFE
An hour-long documentary that profiles the life of the artist Georgia O'Keefe, *O'Keefe* includes extensive interview footage with the elderly O'Keefe, photographs and home movies from the earlier portions of her life, and views of her artwork and environment. Although the disc lasts an hour, a piece of it is placed on side two so the second side could be rendered in CAV and include a still file section, recapping the paintings that were discussed in the film. Unfortunately, the actual still images of the paintings are mildly blurry and too far removed from the original works to have much utility. The sound has a documentary noisiness to it. An excellent jacket insert provides an organized chronology to both O'Keefe's life and the production of the film. The disc is thoroughly chapter encoded.

The program will give the viewer a reasonable overview of O'Keefe's life and will provide an introduction to her artwork. The filmmakers, however, tread lightly to avoid offending their subject and cancelling their project. There is little serious artistic criticism, and the details provided of O'Keefe's social and family life are so cleansed as to be nearly meaningless. The subject of sex comes up only once, in a discussion about her flower paintings, and O'Keefe, too quickly to sound sincere, pops up with a classic non-denial denial, "The people that see them that way, they were talking about their own self, not about me." They weren't talking about her, they were talking about the paintings, practically all of which – not just the flowers – are saturated with sexual imagery. It is the psychology of the paintings, more so than the innovative colors or literal subject matter, which place them in the exclusive pantheon of Twentieth Century painting, but some other program will have to cover that.

OKLAHOMA!
Folks will likely enjoy the CBS/Fox Special Wide Screen Edition release of *Oklahoma!* The transfer has a few minor deficiencies and a couple of conceptual problems, but the disc's positive attributes outweigh its drawbacks.
To begin with, the disc has a breathtaking aspect ratio of 2.4:1, so for once Agnes DeMille's choreography can be savored on the television without a loss of symmetry and visual rhythm. The colors bleed a little and look slightly pale, but the hues remain within an acceptable range and look accurate enough to avoid distracting the viewer. Dark reds also appear a little grainy.

The digitally encoded stereo surround sound bothered us a bit. The underused train whistle which opens the second scene is proof that the sound engineers who originally worked on the film did not have a true feel for the full potential of stereophonic entertainment. However, there seems to be a lid on the sonic range which goes beyond the age and manner of the sound recording. As hard as we pushed the volume we could never get the disc to give off sharp vocals or a theatrical airiness. The songs still sound fine, but they lack grandeur.

The movie itself, directed by Fred Zinnemann, is a bit deadly when it comes to camera angles anyway. The camera setups and editing don't flow from the soul of the music the way they do in the Robert Wise musicals. It is amazing how much less the camera moves without the panning and scanning (a version of which is also available on disc, from CBS/Fox).

The widescreen views are more beneficial than simply opening up the dance numbers, though. They give the movie simultaneous feelings of fun and importance. Zinnemann's rectangular compositions are deliberate, consciously incorporating the scenery beyond and around the characters. The furthest edges belong in the image, and any loss is significantly detrimental to Zinnemann's presentation of the piece.

Oklahoma! is not the most successful musical ever constructed on film. The title song, which was a last minute addition in the stage production, has never been properly fitted into the book and rightly belongs at the very end of the movie. Gordon MacRae sings well but lacks screen presence, a vacuum which is quickly filled by Rod Steiger. His intense mumbling may be silly, but he is one of the film's saving graces. The women, Shirley Jones, Gloria Grahame and Charlotte Greenwood, are stronger and bring enough energy to the movie to make it entertaining. (The movie was filmed twice, in Cinemascope and Todd-AO, and the performances in the Cinemascope version used for the disc are notoriously weary when compared to the Todd-AO rendition.)

If you're in the mood for the songs, for the dancing, or for carefully honed dialog full of jokes about male/female relationships, *Oklahoma!* will provide you with a good time. The letterboxing prevents any of the supporting players and any of the fun from being left out.

OLD GRINGO

The letterboxing on *Old Gringo* is mild, with an aspect ratio of about 1.85:1. The picture compositions look well framed, however, and the effect is pleasing. The picture transfer is a little grainy. The film production, though it has an expensive look, underwent a number of problems, and the end result sometimes appears tentative. The sound is fine, though separation effects are pretty much limited to the nice Lee Holdridge score.

The movie stars Jane Fonda and Gregory Peck. It is not a disaster, though it is hard to imagine viewing it more than a time or two in the course of one's life. Set in Mexico before World War I, it begins with a decent battle sequence as Mexican revolutionaries overrun a large hacienda. During the remainder of the film, however, the general who led the attack hangs out in the estate. Fonda portrays an American governess and Peck is a famous author whose career is behind him. The three interact, and while their conversations are interesting, it is difficult to remember what was said after the film is over. Little of it is profound or emotionally captivating. The movie was not planned out or edited clearly, and while the result does not seem dull, it is idle.

OLIVER!

The best of what is in *Oliver!* comes straight from Charles Dickens. The rest, including the musical numbers, doesn't quite make it. The disc, released by RCA/Columbia, is a disaster. The picture looks fresh and the colors are genuine, but there are a good share of scratches and a few jumps during the reel changes. Worst of all, the picture is backwards for a stretch, so that the 'Who Will Buy?' dance number is performed in reverse. The scanning removes much of the grand look of the original Panavision screen, but does not replace it with intimacy. The sound is CX-encoded stereo. The mix is nice, but there is hiss in the background.

OLIVER TWIST

David Lean's *Oliver Twist* is still the best filmed version there is. Dickens's story has one howling coincidence that cheapens an otherwise rich and complex tale about a young orphan who takes up with a band of equally young pickpockets led by an aging deviant. The farfetched plot turn which deposits Oliver in the house of his maternal grandfather is a lazy embarrassment that can cause one to take the story less seriously.

The boy playing Oliver, John Howard Davies, is toothy and beset by melancholy, just as one would imagine. Alec Guinness overcomes his poor makeup to give Fagin an air of false grace, zeroing in on the contrast to Oliver's bland and well-meaning guardian. Anthony Newley turns up in an early role as the Artful Dodger. There is clearly more to the relationship between Nancy and Bill and Fagin than was ever written down.

Being several decades old, the black-and-white print has a little wear, but Lean's visual sense is so powerful that the image on the disc is captivating. The sound is clear, but suffers, in a few passages, from enhanced static.

ON THE TOWN

Those who want to own *On the Town* will want the marvelous short feature that has been included with it on the digital reissue. The short, 'Mighty Manhattan, New York's Wonder City,' is a mind boggling view of New York City shortly after World War II. The narrator, using words we've never heard pronounced before, leaps up (well, halfway) and down the island to describe the different sites and neighborhoods. The featurette is not corny per se, but it accumulates a humor in the odd locales it chooses to emphasize and the strange and alien nature of the world it depicts. From there, it is no sweat to leap into *On the Town* itself, since the movie's make-believe New York seems no different from the documentary's.

The disc was initially released without the short or digital encoding. The re-release has no other special features, save for MGM/UA's extensive chapter encoding. The picture transfer on the earlier disc was fine, but the second effort does show a few improvements, brightening the image and making the colors and fleshtones a little more accurate. There is still a mild ghost which seems to dog the white sailor's uniforms, but that is the most serious imperfection. (The older disc was often subject to manufacturing flaws.) As with the first disc, the Empire State Building scene stands out in terms of image crispness and color quality. The digital monaural sound provides a more noticeable improvement over the older disc's noisy audio track.

Gene Kelley and Frank Sinatra are sailors on leave for 24 hours and trying to see as much of New York as they can before romance crowds their schedule. The movie itself is a delight, with witty dialog, memorable songs, and a surprisingly strong collection of dance numbers. Created by the musical comedy writing team of Adolf Green and Betty Comden, with music by Leonard Bernstein and choreography by Jerome Robbins, the film positively swamps you with flirtatious intelligence. One female character is a taxi driver, another is an anthropologist, and another is 'Miss Turnstiles.' By the time you've adjusted to one premise, the writers are off on the next.

ONCE BITTEN

Although *Once Bitten* has some of the trappings of a teen sex comedy, it also has some pleasingly absurd gags. It is a vampire movie, and it seems that there is always something redeeming about vampire movies. Here, after the sultry lady vampire has taken her first quart from the 'only 18-year-old virgin left in LA,' he is offered a glass of orange juice. The picture is terribly grainy. The sound is not CX-encoded although the film includes two self-contained music videos.

ONCE UPON A HONEYMOON

A lengthy and unfocussed comedy involving romance and intrigue during the Nazi takeover of Europe, *Once Upon a Honeymoon* stars Cary Grant and Ginger Rogers. Rogers portrays an American woman who unwittingly marries an upper echelon German agent. Grant portrays a radio commentator who falls in love with her.

The 1942 film is forced to deal with serious subjects, such as the implied Jewish pogrom, while attempting to maintain a lighthearted, romantic atmosphere. With a running time of just under two hours, enough plot turns take place to hold a viewer's interest, but it is an exhausting work which never settles on a mood or a goal.

The disc's source material is in a variety of conditions, with some of it looking quite good and some of it looking quite worn out. Taken as a whole, the picture quality is okay. The sound is mildly noisy, but passable.

ONCE UPON A TIME IN AMERICA

We bought the disc not having seen the film at all – trusting that the critics were wrong and that anything by Sergio Leone that runs for four hours has got to be magnificent. Please be aware: On our copy, the label which says "Side 3" is pasted on Side 4 and Side 4's label is on Side 3.

Sergio Leone's full 225-minute *Once Upon a Time in America* is a great film and, although it has been scanned and cropped, a worthwhile disc. The film has the scope and the design of a television mini-series, but it has the class of *The Godfather* or of Leone's other films. Using the structure of the immigrant-gangsters-become-rich-and-find-they-are-not-happy plot, the movie is a study of what children expect from life when they grow older and what people expected from America when they came here. Unlike other directors, Leone's adventures in philosophy are legitimate because his themes are understated and his use of violence is overstated. You are too busy ducking bullets to realize you're getting a sermon.

Robert DeNiro portrays a racketeer who has been pulled from anonymity to settle some old scores. As he goes through these motions, his mind naturally drifts back into time and with equal naturalness flits from one decade to the next as his memories are sparked. There is one of Leone's favorite trinkets – a watch – to emphasize how the characters (and the rest of us) are living on stolen time.

The picture has a speckle or two, but the colors are rich and the darker scenes are clear. The quality of the monaural sound is equal to the rest of the craftsmanship. One of the film's high points is a piece of business with Robert DeNiro stirring his coffee just slightly longer than he ought to. It is the noise of the spoon rubbing around the inside of the cup that gets on everyone's nerves.

ONCE UPON A TIME IN THE WEST

Sergio Leone advanced the levels of violence and adult themes in Westerns with his three Clint Eastwood movies. With *Once Upon a Time in the West*, he advanced the Western as a work of art. Until Leone, art in a Western consisted primarily of the landscape dwarfing man and the emotions of conflict. In *West*, the landscapes and the conflicts are a given, like horses and six-shooters. Languorous closeups of faces, beset with dust and flies, are Leone's primary medium for conveying the environment, the motives, and the spiritual presence of his characters.

Henry Fonda, Jason Robards, *and* Charles Bronson: What faces, what a rich opportunity! Once the initial plot is established, then the longer the camera points at one of these three, the more the lines in their faces tell us about their entire lives. Even Bronson's performance is convincing, as long as he holds a steady expression.

The plot, written by Leone, Bernardo Bertolucci, and Dario Argento, is about a greedy railroad man who wants to void a contract through unlawful means. The film has gone through numerous cuts and Paramount has provided what is generally considered to be the most complete version. Yet, about two-thirds of the way through, several scenes run very short, and a couple of viewings may be necessary to put all the details together.

The print has a few scratches. The color has always looked a bit washed out since most of the film takes place in either the bright sun or near total darkness, but it seems to have appeared on disc in as best a condition as exists.

The notoriously lengthy build-up to the first gun fight is shown in the correct aspect ratio to accommodate the credits. But right before the actual shooting starts, the credits finish and the screen fills up, knocking the edges off. If only they had waited another minute...

ONE CRAZY SUMMER

A genuinely absurdist spirit is present in *One Crazy Summer*. Although the movie has the structure of a typical teen summer vacation effort, the jokes are anything but typical. The show opens with an animated segment, which, incidentally, looks terrific on disc, and then proceeds with gags involving a high school commencement. The kids throw their hats up in the air and one of the hats comes back down, thump, killing somebody. The cartoon segments, present because the hero is an art student who likes to doodle, pop up several times, just as the regular movie is getting tedious. The jokes are either hysterical or so ridiculously stupid that the effect is the same. The best is a clever, inevitable gag involving a boy trapped in a Godzilla suit and an architect's model for a real estate development.

The picture, except for the cartoon segments, is slightly grainy.

ONE DAY IN THE LIFE OF IVAN DENISOVICH

We were sorry to see that the jacket cover of *One Day in the Life of Ivan Denisovich* did not use the original American ad art, which was taken from Sven Nykvist's inspired cinematography. Instead there is a drawing which encourages potential viewers to approach the film as a depressing allegory when it ought to be approached as the title and Nykvist's photography imply, as an alert view of a life at a given moment. One can compile lessons from the work later on – the movie is best enjoyed when it is taken at its most literal and immediate level.

The film depicts a day at a Soviet Gulag in the early fifties. The prisoners wake up in the dark, dress and have their morning meal, march to a construction site where they are laying brick and mortar under wintery conditions, march back, have their evening meal, stand to be counted, and retire.

The film has a very high repeat viewing potential because it is so simple and so well executed. On multiple viewings, different aspects and details attract a viewer's attention. Since the normal clichés of a prison film – the mano a mano with the commandant, the torture for trying to escape, any kind of action at all – are completely missing, the drama isn't weighted down by expectations that it will deliver more than what it promises. The movie was made in Norway, but stars Tom Courtenay and was recorded in English.

The print has speckles and smudges but the colors look genuine and the disc's flaws are not enough to distract from the entertainment. The sound is also passable.

ONE-EYED JACKS
(see **NEVADA SMITH**)

ONE FLEW OVER THE CUCKOO'S NEST

The monaural sound on *One Flew Over the Cuckoo's Nest* is very good. It is digitally encoded, with the digital track having less noise than the analog track. The picture, however, is often grainy, especially in the darker scenes, and the skin tones are consistently too pink. In a movie from a director whose emphasis has always been upon the human face this is almost a disaster. At best the poor color is a continuous distraction which disrupts the mood and intensity of the film.

The 133-minute disc has three sides, with the third side running under a half hour in CLV. The back of the jacket has a longer than normal essay about the film's production. We were surprised to see that both Danny DeVito and Christopher Lloyd are among the inmates. DeVito, who has since settled upon a single screen persona, is nearly unrecognizable.

The film has always seemed too obvious to us, with both the director and Jack Nicholson overplaying their parts. On the other hand, it is difficult to imagine the property being more successfully adapted to the movies than it was. It is hard to be academic around Nicholson anyway. He's always squirting water or worse at something.

ONE FROM THE HEART
ONE FROM THE HEART (Import)

When we first played our copy of RCA/Columbia's *One from the Heart*, we were overjoyed to have the film on disc, but we felt something was missing. There was one scene we thought we had seen in a theatrical screening which was not present on the disc, and there was a different emotional undertone to the whole show. Still, between the music, Francis Coppola's indulgences (the film's budget was comparable to the GNP of a lesser developed country), and the movie's essential romantic charm, we fell in love with the disc anyway, and played it often.

We paid no attention when *One from the Heart* was released in Japan, since it had no special features (the movie was filmed in an aspect ratio accommodating to video). But something kept gnawing at our subconscious and eventually we put the domestic disc on our player to check the running times of the two sides (this was before RCA/Columbia began putting that piece of useful information on the jacket) and then comparing that running time to the listing in the Japanese catalog. The result? Domestic release: 102 minutes. Japanese release: 107 minutes. Our own heart pounding, we sent away for the import.

Sure enough, the missing scenes and, more importantly, the missing undercurrents were restored. The majority of the missing five minutes is taken up by the following: A scene near the beginning reminiscent of 'The Gift of the Magi' where the two lovers (Frederic Forrest and Teri Garr) spend their money on inappropriate presents for one another; a conversation a little later where they discuss their plans and desires, which leads into an argument at the end of dinner that has been retained on the American disc; richer and more elaborate cross cutting when Forrest and Nastassia Kinski are making love in an abandoned auto and Garr and Raul Julia are doing the same in Julia's room; an extension of this the morning after, which opens with a stunning long shot of the junk yard; a comical bit on the roof of Julia's room before Forrest falls through the skylight; and an argument in the convertible after Forrest has abducted Garr, who remains topless despite wolf whistles from passing cars. Why these scenes were dropped from the American home video release we don't know, but they make the movie more erotic, more emotionally complex, and just more of a movie.

The American release was one of

RCA/Columbia's nicest picture and sound transfers. The CX-encoded stereo sound features Coppola's superb sound editing, and the picture is as bright and colorful as the neon lights of the Las Vegas locale (the film was actually shot in a studio, as an end title proudly proclaims). The Japanese disc has chapter markers, and the sound is as good as the American release. In some scenes, the color is not as strong as the American version, but most of the time you would have to run two discs side by side to notice any discrepancies. The Japanese disc also has Japanese subtitles.

We have heard many complaints about the point at which RCA/Columbia chose to split the American release between side one and two. It was probably done insensitively, since it happens at a reel change, but the effect has always been a plus for us and not a minus. At the end of side one, Garr and Julia are running down a hallway. At the beginning of side two, they burst out onto the streets of Vegas for a big dance number. The Japanese disc has a more logical break, occurring a few scenes earlier, but seeing combined what had been broken confirmed our suspicions – there is just enough of a true pause in the continuity so that the break on the American disc does not interrupt your concentration. It allows you to leave and return to the film without missing a beat.

ONE MAGIC CHRISTMAS

We would be satisfied playing *One Magic Christmas* every other Christmas or so. It has a standard goose-pimple-and-tears/back-from-the-dead plot and features Harry Dean Stanton, who looks more like Freddy Kruger than a Christmas angel, but that is part of the concept. The filmmakers realize the only way that they can succeed is if they hold the saccharine to the size of a Tic-Tac, and that's basically what they do.

The disc is in stereo, although more than one member of the cast is allowed to mumble to the point where it is difficult to catch the dialog without backing the disc up. The picture is in very good condition, even when a scene takes place at night. And if you get the disc, don't miss the stereo effects when Santa lands on the roof. If you're watching it on Christmas Eve, you may stop the disc and run outside to look for yourself.

ONE MILLION B.C.

The anachronistic classic *One Million B.C.*, stars Victor Mature, a bunch of elephants with bathroom rugs draped over their backs, and a bunch of lizards with fans glued on their spines. Despite breaks in the film and the sound (the screen goes completely blank at one point on side one), the print looks good and, considering the property, most collectors should be satisfied with the transfer. The jacket cover lists D.W. Griffith as a co-director (with Hal Roach), which was news to us, although the dawn of man would certainly have been an appropriate topic for him. The story is timeless: Only when people can build and hold more powerful weapons will there be true and everlasting peace. We keep on waiting for it to happen, and the spears keep on getting bigger.

ONE MORE SATURDAY NIGHT

An unusually grainy transfer hurts *One More Saturday Night*, but the movie isn't all that good anyway. It is a comedy, written by Franken and Davis, but all the best jokes, such as a witty take-off on *The Great Escape*, go on too long. The story has a potential for farce, since many of the characters end up in the same hotel, but inspiration is clearly missing. The soundtrack, which is in surround, is also noisy, but the rock score usually drowns out the problems.

ONE NIGHT WITH BLUE NOTE – VOLUME 1
ONE NIGHT WITH BLUE NOTE – VOLUME 2

One Night with Blue Note – Volume 1 is an hour-long presentation (split to two sides) of a concert performed in New York's creaky Town Hall auditorium by Herbie Hancock, Art Blakey, Freddie Hubbard, and others. The visuals are close clean views of the musicians playing their instruments. If we have any reservations about the disc, it is that most of the time they seem to be playing for the camera instead of for the Town Hall audience. This stimulates a different sort of adrenaline in their performances, but the point is hardly worth arguing. This is the way to see and hear jazz if you aren't within walking distance of Town Hall.

One Night with Blue Note – Volume 2 has a slightly blurrier picture than *Volume 1* and runs under 60 minutes. It features a multitude of famous performers, including Grover Washington, Jr., Woody Shaw, Charles Lloyd, and Jimmy Smith, in different combinations, playing a few famous jazz compositions before an unseen audience.

The beauty of this series is the ability it gives you to watch both a musician's technique and his emotional responses to the music. The camera compositions are knowledgeable and make watching the disc as pleasurable as listening to it. Side two is only 20 minutes long, but the disc ends with a piano solo by Cecil Taylor which is so exhausting it is impossible to imagine another number following it.

ONLY THE VALIANT

There are speckles and a scratch or two on *Only the Valiant* but the blacks are intense and the shadings are clearly defined. The picture transfer helps the viewer enjoy the movie – a western about a half dozen cavalry soldiers holding down an outpost – by sharpening the film's visual pleasures. The sound is a little scratchy, but passable. Republic opens the disc with the film's original theatrical trailer, a nice touch which enhances one's anticipation for the film without spoiling things. Gregory Peck stars.

OPERA DO MALANDRO

Lovers of musicals will want to consider obtaining the Brazilian film *Opera do Malandro*. The narrative, though original, is lifted in chunks from *Three Penny Opera*, as are many of the character names. It concerns a gangster involved with two women from different backgrounds. The music, by Chico Buarque, is extremely pleasant. The songs and choreography are often too brief, but many musical sequences are scattered through the film. Situations and characters shift freely from realistic settings to abstract groupings. The movie lacks the cohesive charm which made *The Umbrellas of Cherbourg* or *Black Orpheus* cult favorites, but it is a rare effort which is worth owning, particularly if one's collection already includes *Cherbourg* and *Orpheus*.

The disc is chapter encoded. English subtitles appear for both the dialog and the song lyrics, though they contain at least a couple of typographical errors. The picture quality leaves something to be desired. It is often too grainy, and the lack of a consistently shiny appearance is at odds with the intentions of the filmmakers. The sound, however, is stereophonic. It may not be Hollywood, but it will rival any old samba records you might still have laying around.

OPERATION PETTICOAT

There is a scene in Blake Edwards' *Operation Petticoat* where, through a series of comical incidents, a pig is posited in the lavatory of a submarine. Now if the movie were made today, or if it had been made by most anyone else, you would see the pig when an actor opens the lavatory door. But Edwards knows that is not necessary. He need only show Cary Grant's reaction and the viewer's imagination does the rest. Pairing Grant with one of his more witty imitators, Tony Curtis, was an inspired coup. The film is about the misadventures of a crippled submarine attempting to reach safety during the opening salvos of World War II. We found ourselves laughing at a number of silly gags in *Operation Petticoat*, and suspect that it is because there are even more comical manipulations in the editing and camera angles of which we are not consciously aware.

The source material is inconsistent. A few reels look more faded than others and some viewers may find the result spoils their entertainment. Speckles are kept to a minimum. The monaural sound is set a little low, but has no special problems.

OPPORTUNITY KNOCKS

The first name-above-the-title role for the comedian, Dana Carvey, *Opportunity Knocks* is a pleasant enough film once the introductions are out of the way. Carvey portrays a small time con-artist and burglar who falls into the lap of luxury when he is mistaken for a house sitter in a ritzy neighborhood. The opening sketches – antics to show what a con artist he is – are less appealing. The disc has an average looking picture and a passable but uninteresting stereo surround soundtrack. The movie has romance and a sufficient number of amusing moments to sustain one's attention, but this is an *Opportunity Knocks* which should be limited to a single transpiration.

OPTIONS

A likeable film which is both lightly absurd and lightly humorous, *Options* concerns a staid entertainment lawyer who ventures into the jungles of Africa to meet a reclusive, blue-blooded conservationist and option the rights to her life story. She tells him to get lost, but is kidnapped, and as he bumbles his way to saving her, they fall in love. The scene depicting their first kiss, in which they sing 'Do You Know the Way to San Jose?' to each other to stall for courage, is marvelous, and ideal for acting classes.

The picture is too orange and too grainy, but the film's sound production is very good and the surround soundtrack is super, especially when the musical score is involved. If you get the disc, pay attention to the opening credits, because there is a joke in the end which will be more effective if you've studied them and then are wondering what happened.

ORDEAL BY INNOCENCE

Ordeal by Innocence may not be perfect, but for those who don't ask for much more than fog and a couple of murders, it is nearly flawless. The one error the filmmakers commit is to reveal the murderer about 20 minutes before the protagonist discovers who it is. Of course, that won't matter for subsequent viewings.

To start off with, the movie has a persistent jazz score by Dave Brubeck which sounds terrific even though the disc is monaural and has not been CX-encoded. Next, there are the Turneresque morning fogs of Dartmouth, England, rendered with the clarity and color that only a laser disc can accomplish. If the picture is a tiny bit on the grainy side, it only adds to the mood. The cast, including Donald Sutherland, Christopher Plummer, and Faye Dunaway, arch their eyebrows at one another like true stars. Agatha Christie stories often stop dead when the plot must go over flashbacks, but the script writer here solved that problem by making the flashbacks a constant, feverish repetition of speculation. The hero can't stop thinking, can't stop trying to solve the mystery. His obsession and Brubeck's accompaniment will be as entertaining on the tenth viewing as on the first.

THE ORIGINAL FABULOUS ADVENTURES OF BARON MUNCHAUSEN (BARON PRASIL)

A 1961 Czechoslovakian film mixing many forms of animation and live action has been dusted off to capitalize on the popularity, or at least the awareness, of the Baron Munchausen character. The disc is entitled *The Original Fabulous Adventures of Baron Munchausen (Baron Prasil)*, but the real name of the movie, directed by Karl Zeman, is the part in the parentheses. It is dubbed in English, which isn't a problem since more dialog is heard in voiceover than in conversation.

The film is mostly in black and white or is tinted. There are some sequences where multiple tinting appears in a single frame, and a few shots which have the appearance of color. Segments with strong red tints tend to look the grainiest. The source material has a few splices and some other inconsistencies, but the film itself is something of a patchwork affair, so that most viewers will find the condition of the picture to be tolerable. The sound is accurately transferred, but the program's soundtrack, which also has its share of effects, is weak and rather scratchy.

The disc will surely please some viewers and frustrate others. Many different types of animation are used in the film, and some of the images are striking. The narrative includes a number of standard 'Munchausen' tales which are too complicated to describe at length. He and his entourage spend time inside a gigantic fish, take a trip or two to the moon, and become involved with intrigue in a Sultan's castle, among other things. The plot has no strong forward movement, making the movie more appealing to animation fans than to those who enjoy adventure stories. Often several different special effects will be combined in a shot, so that humans can be seen running past cut-out columns, as pen and ink birds circle in the air. The special effects are cheap but elaborate, and viewers who live for the magic that movies can provide will find the sleight of hand in Baron Prasil sustaining.

ORPHANS

Screen adaptations of not especially good stage plays can make horrendous viewing. The characters are all trapped in one room, saying weird things, and never break into a car chase to relieve the monotony of conversation. Sympathy with an audience is hindered by the barrier of the screen. The viewer is more apt to feel squirmy and impatient, and, with home video, the power to abandon the most annoying characters once and for all is tempting indeed.

Such is the case with *Orphans*. Were it not for the masterful presence of Albert Finney (he plays a gangster who hides in a house with two derelict brothers), the disc would be a total waste of time and as it is, only serious fans or gluttons for punishment are advised to sample it. The picture and digital monaural sound are both acceptable. The disc's strongest feature is the break between side one and two, which occurs at what obviously is the break between the first and second act. Due to a plot twist, the second act appears to open up in a change of venue, and for a few seconds you think you've got the wrong disc on.

THE OSTERMAN WEEKEND (Import)

Sam Peckinpah's final film, *The Osterman Weekend*, is available on disc in Japan. The print, although scratchless, seems a bit faded. There are Japanese subtitles to accompany the English dialog and minute flesh-colored masks covering genitals in a couple of instances.

A book such as *The Osterman Weekend* is not meant to be great literature. The writing is a series of truncated thoughts. The prose pulls you so quickly through a roller coaster plot that it is impossible to step back and see the illogical construction. Usually when movies get made from books like this they have to be shortened and, with the clutter cleared away, the holes in the plot are so obvious you wonder why you ever enjoyed the book so much. Peckinpah, however, gives the action scenes and CIA double-crosses his best short jabs. The film carries you along like a best seller. In the end, the conclusion does not negate the pleasure received from watching the story unfold. Peckinpah made a lot of bad movies, but he made great home video.

OTELLO
LA TRAVIATA

One would suppose that if film director Franco Zeffirelli combined the two genres he does the best, Shakespeare movies and opera movies, the result would be a sublime piece of work, but, sadly, that is not the case with *Otello*. The movie never becomes more than moving pictures set to music and singing. Many times the lip movements don't even match the voices. The recording is stereophonic to the hilt, but with virtually no sound effects or other distractions. Viewing the film is like watching the play while listening to the opera on a Walkman.

The movie is sung in Italian and has English subtitles, which are sparse at times. No chapter markers have been included. On close examination, the digital track appeared to have more noise on it than the analog track, without any compensating enhancements. The picture is slightly less satisfying. Not only are Zeffirelli's compositions listless, except for those he lifted from Orson Welles, but the transfer is grainy. The film is 123 minutes long and side three is in CAV. Whether it is because of the way the scenes are lit or because of the methods used for mastering the disc, side three is less grainy than the two CLV sides.

Zeffirelli's *La Traviata* transcended the boundaries of the stage to become a truly operatic film. The images became another component, balancing the vocals and the orchestra, and intensifying the entire experience. (The transfer to disc was excellent.) But *Otello* plays more like a 'Live at the Met' effort, despite the location filming in Venice and Crete. The production appears to have a lid on its budget, and the camera is always too far away, or, because of the editing, characters in a scene are so isolated it is difficult to tell how they fit with others. It is easy enough to sit back, listen to the music, and watch the actors walk through their enactment, but unlike the Shakespeare movies and unlike *Traviata*, Zeffirelli fails to communicate an unrepentant love for *Otello*.

OTELLO

Despite Herbert von Karajan's lack of experience as a film director, and despite the obviously smaller budget, Karajan's *Otello* is a more satisfying movie than Franco Zeffirelli's cinematic interpretation of the Giuseppe Verdi opera. Von Karajan also conducts the Berlin Opera effort. His staging, which has been filmed on multiple sets in a soundstage, carries the opera much better than Zeffirelli – who perhaps had too much money to spend – could do. The colors are bright and the camera is usually close to the principals, which makes sense since the dramatic aspects of the work are so strong. Even the modest performance by Jon Vickers in the title role and the more questionable effort by Peter Glossop as Iago (Mirella Freni is better as Desdemona) fails to harm the overall impact of the program, which presents Verdi's accomplishment lucidly, intelligently, and entertainingly.

The picture, except for some speckles near the end, and the sound are impeccable. The opera's four acts are broken up one to a side, with each running a little over 30 minutes. *Otello* comes in a box, and is accompanied by an insert which has an extensive essay on Verdi's creation of the opera and an elaborate plot synopsis coordinated with the chapter markers.

THE OTHER SIDE OF NASHVILLE

Much like MGM/UA's *The Compleat Beatles*, MGM/UA's *The Other Side of Nashville* is a documentary about the history of country music in which some terrific songs are continuously being interrupted by the damn narration. What good are the fiddle solos in Charlie Daniels' 'The Devil Went Down to Georgia' without the lyrics that tell you the Devil lost?

The quality of the narration is acceptable, per se. Various stars from different aspects of the Nashville music scene give introspective and analytical assessments of their own work and of the past and present state of country music. The stereo is fair and the picture is grainy. These weaknesses are excusable when historical footage is being used but imply cheap production values during the contemporary sequences. The scope of the entertainment will be wide enough to please most viewers, but it can only scratch the surface of the artistic pool and is limited to the 20 or so performers listed on the front of the jacket and the 36 numbers listed on the back. The high point is a duet with Bob Dylan and Johnny Cash. The narrator tantalizingly suggests there are two hours worth of material from the same session in a closet somewhere. One wishes it could be released no matter how poorly it was recorded.

OUR HOSPITALITY

The spectacular waterfall rescue in Buster Keaton's wonderful *Our Hospitality* can be examined in CAV on the Thames Video Image Silent Classics release. The still frames alternate a couple at a time between being steady and showing movement as a blur, but the magnificence of Keaton's timing can be examined on a microsecond level, or the glories of the scene can be enhanced by the vividness of double and triple speed.

The film has one other supremely memorable sequence, a re-creation of one of the first railroad trains, the Rocket. It is a comically stylized but loving depiction of an infant train which could be outrun by a dog, and the extended sequence, which is set early in the movie, wins one's heart to the film before the real plot has even started. The central narrative concerns a young man who unknowingly inherits a blood feud when he comes of age and returns to the town where he was born. There is a 'Romeo and Juliet' romance and many clever gags, but it is the two sequences identified above which bookend the movie's thrills and make it as valuable as any of today's big budget productions.

The disc has a pleasing, stereophonic score by Carl Davis. The picture transfer is good. The movements of the characters look natural, and the source material is clean. The title cards appear to be original.

OUR MAN FLINT

The inconsistencies of 'Color by DeLuxe' are on display in *Our Man Flint*. In place of the film's original bright, psychedelic colors are solid, sharp, paled substitutions. Cherry reds are replaced by rich brick, tans by anemia. Otherwise, the presentation is good fun. The letterboxed image has an aspect ratio of about 2.3:1, allowing one to soak up the wacky set designs and other silly goings on. The spy spoof plays better in the recesses of one's memory than it does on the screen, but if James Coburn's performance no longer seems inspired, Lee J. Cobb's (as his boss) hasn't lost a fraction of wit. The best aspect of the film, however, is Jerry Goldsmith's deliberately jokey score. The digital monaural soundtrack has age problems of its own – no high end and an occasional flutter – but the music sounds great if you don't amplify it too much. A theatrical trailer for *In Like Flint* is included at the end of the disc.

OUR RELATIONS/MURDER CASE

The last of the scheduled Laurel and Hardy features to be released as part of 3M's Collectible Classics, *Our Relations/Murder Case* ends the series on a high note. Literally, "Ahhhh!" as the boys fall off a pier, but also figuratively, because the films and the disc are among the best of the lot. *Relations*, in particular, is a witty comedy of errors as the pair unknowingly cross paths with their long lost twin brothers. 3M has found a nice looking print with a strong soundtrack and almost no scratches. *Murder Case* is an older short, and so it is a bit more ragged, but it was photographed by George Stevens and features a gorgeous cast of seedy bit players who meet at a decrepit house to determine who will inherit the 'Ebeneezer Laurel' estate.

OUT COLD

Yet another instance in which a really ugly jacket cover is probably scaring potential viewers away from a very pleasurable movie, *Out Cold* is much more captivating than the ad art makes it look. Starring Teri Garr and John Lithgow, it is about adultery and murder and the disposing of a couple of corpses, all executed with a subdued but gleeful sense of humor. Garr, whose character is nasty and calculating without redemption, is particularly enjoyable, since her role is so opposite from the sort she normally plays. The colors are on the pale side, but so are the set designs. Cropping does not seem to upset the narrative, and the stereo surround sound has a few effective touches.

OUT OF AFRICA

A Danish accent contains hints of a Scottish brogue but Meryl Streep's delivery in *Out of Africa*, which reportedly had them giggling in Copenhagen, is so dry it sounds as if she practiced her voice by watching Ingrid Bergman movies at slow speed. The film, with its IMAX style photography and digital sound, is effectively presented on disc. Even the John Barry score seems to have a lid on it in places. The plot, such as it is, has the elegance of a Gantt chart. It moves methodically, advancing one dramatic idea after another, but never really achieves feelings as moving as the pretty photography. Robert Redford's character, in whom the filmmakers supposedly have a significantly vested interest, dies off stage. One gets the feeling that the film has as much reason for existence as the European settlers had for planting themselves in Kenya in the first place.

OUT OF BOUNDS

The hero grabs the wrong suitcase. It has drugs instead of clothing. Someone close to him is murdered as the bad guys try to get the drugs back. The hero is blamed for the murder and must evade the police while tracking down the killer. He enlists the help of an innocent woman who doesn't believe him at first but is in love with him by the final curtain. Plug that plot with different actors, actresses, and chase scenes, and we could watch it again and again. Absolutely nothing original happens in *Out of Bounds*, but that hardly matters. It stars Anthony Michael Hall and Jenny Wright and takes place in Los Angeles. The stereo surround soundtrack has many rock songs, but is otherwise unimaginative. The picture is fine.

OUT OF THE DARK

A man in a clown mask is offing fantasy phone receptionists in *Out of the Dark*. The identity of the murderer is a contrived surprise, and the editing is a little too cute for its own good. However, the sex talk is fun and Paul Bartel was involved in the production. There is an uninteresting analog Ultra-Stereo soundtrack. The picture is a little fuzzy.

OUT OF THE DARKNESS

It is hard to believe that a police procedural about the 'Son of Sam' murders, *Out of the Darkness,* could be rendered so engrossingly, but it has. Martin Sheen portrays the detective who led the arrest, and the material is expanded to include events in the detective's private life, including the devastating (even for the viewer) death of his wife. The film is exceptionally well written and well acted, and is one of those rare instances where Hollywood and real life succeed in collaborating. The picture quality, unfortunately, is below average. The image is fuzzy, and the fleshtones are much too orange. The sound is fine.

THE OUTLAW

The jacket cover and all the reference books list *The Outlaw* as being 126 minutes long, but the 3M Collectible Classic disc runs 116 minutes. The movie is heavily padded, anyway, with lingering shots of walls and other decorations. It could stand to lose at least another 20 minutes.

The plot, which has a clever, final twist, concerns Doc Holliday, Pat Garrett and Billy the Kid. Garrett chases the other two, captures them, and tries to bring them back as Jane Russell tags along and tries to be tempestuous.

The print scraped together by 3M is blurry and even jams and breaks in one place. Howard Hughes had no control as a director and let the creative people around him get away with artistic excess. Hence, the editor and his shots of walls, Gregg Toland filming night scenes with tiny swatches of light, and Walter Huston, as Holliday, chewing up every scene he is in. There are a couple of good gun fights, but the action is limited. The movie relies on the the dialog to carry it along. It is intermittently entertaining and intermittently enjoyable.

THE OUTLAW JOSEY WALES

The best movie Clint Eastwood ever directed, *The Outlaw Josey Wales* is a gentle, violent film, unusually episodic and gradual in its unfolding. It is so well constructed that students could easily make a case for its representation of the Journey of the Mythic Hero, drawing upon Odysseus or even Orpheus for comparison. But more importantly, it is an engaging, witty movie, where action, drama, and humor are split into well-timed, self-propelled segments.

The disc looks good. The movie has sort of a washed out haze motif and too many shadows – Eastwood does not completely overcome his fondness for keeping the camera's aperture in one position regardless of light – but it is rare that the picture becomes noticeably grainy. Warner has electronically rechannelled the soundtrack for stereo, and the result is tolerable.

OUTRAGEOUS FORTUNE

There is a moment of poignant comedy in *Outrageous Fortune* when the two would-be actresses literally chase a spotlight to capture the attention of a helicopter at night. Most of the humor in the film, however, is more boisterous. Shelley Long and Bette Midler portray the actresses, rivals who become buddies as they chase the same boyfriend from New York to the New Mexican desert. The sript is enviably witty, as the two of them discover their true talents while saving the free world from nasty spies.

The stereo mix is quite nice, particularly during a scene involving a roomful of parrots. The picture is also in superior shape, as bright and colorful as Bette Midler's mouth. The disc has chapter markers.

OUTRAGEOUS STRIP REVIEW
(see **WET WATER T'S**)

THE OUTSIDERS
THE OUTSIDERS (Import)

For once we were not tempted to trade in our import copy for a domestic Warner release. The movie is Francis Coppola's *The Outsiders*. Warner has done a typically fine job with the title, digitally encoding it, maintaining the complicated color schemes, and letterboxing the opening titles and the final monolog. The Japanese version had analog sound, but the picture had the same color quality as the new release and the disc is letterboxed from beginning to end. To enjoy the movie, one must be treated to Coppola's complete vision, because the story is as agonizing as the drippy adolescents it depicts. The surreal lighting effects and intense camera placements give the concoction an epic feeling which almost excuses the exercise. Cropped and scanned, it is difficult to convince anyone that the movie is more than kids feeling sorry for themselves.

If the import is out of one's reach, however, there are other aspects to the domestic release which may make it worthwhile. Coppola's films always have excellent sound engineering, and *The Outsiders* is no exception. The higher one raises the volume, the more involved one becomes with the film, and the digital encoding facilitates amplification. And the movie has everybody in it. Ralph Macchio and Tom Cruise and Rob Lowe and Patrick Swayze and Emilio Estevez and Matt Dillon and C. Thomas Howell and Tom Waits and Leif Garrett and even Diane Lane. Where would movies be today if Coppola hadn't made this film?

OVER THE TOP

The confidence evident in the picture and sound quality of *Over the Top* disguises the precarious financial difficulties which the film subsequently caused its producers. The disc is best kept at arm's length. The picture is so bright and clear that one can read the fine print warning in the end title scroll against attempting to restage the movie's stunts in one's rec room. The sound is digitally encoded and is as clear as the picture. The music score by Giorgio Moroder sets the tone for the soundtrack. It is loud and busy.

The movie will fool no one. Sylvester Stallone arm wrestles with competitors whose biceps are three times the size of his, and he wins. Perhaps the movie should have been called 'Under the Table.' To make the film last longer than 20 minutes, there is a subplot in which Stallone's character reunites with his estranged son. After five minutes of it, you start hoping that he will tie the kid to the grill of his truck and drive sixty miles an hour into a swarm of gnats.

OVERBOARD

The filmmakers know that the premise of *Overboard* is an absurdity. The cast, specifically Goldie Hawn and Kurt Russell, enjoy themselves, and so will the viewer. A spoiled rich brat is stricken with amnesia and is abducted by a man who has a grudge against her, ostensibly to teach her a lesson; Cupid does the rest. If one can wade through the unlikely opening – so unlikely that a radio announcer in the small Oregon town where most of the action is supposedly taking place mispronounces "Oregon" – one can drift pleasantly through the remainder of it.

The picture quality is passable. The stereo effects on the analog release are limited, but the sound has no significant flaws.

THE OWL AND THE PUSSYCAT

An expletive has been dropped from *The Owl and the Pussycat*, an insult which Barbra Streisand hurls at a gang of toughs after a conversation with George Segal concerning refined vocabulary. A chase ensues, and the chase makes no sense whatsoever with the expletive missing. Yet another expletive, an eight letter barnyard expression, is left intact.

The movie is in rough shape. The monaural soundtrack, although digitally encoded, sounds as if it is coming out of a television speaker no matter how fancy the hi-fi system one tries to run it through. The colors have faded too much, the picture has gone soft, and everything is fuzzy. The disc has a few chapter markers on each side.

The Owl and the Pussycat is adapted from an excruciatingly bad play and only works as a film because Streisand is so energetically exact in her timing. The story is about two mismatched characters, a go-go dancer and a book store clerk, who fall for each other. It is a shame that the film does not end with the two characters in a rowboat, since it does end with them less than a few hundred yards from one, but a viewer is left with the impression that everybody involved in the film, except maybe Streisand, wanted to get it over with as quickly as possible.

THE OX-BOW INCIDENT

The transfer of *The Ox-Bow Incident* leaves several splices and a few other markings on the black-and-white image. The picture never has the impact of the excellent still chosen for the jacket cover and is often mildly grainy. On a more positive note, the dramatic finale on side two in CAV, and has included several nice selections of original promotional artwork in an addendum after the film is over. (Interestingly, the poster unfairly emphasizes a nearly non-existent romantic angle.) The sound is reasonably clear.

The movie is well known for being long on message and short on everything else. It has a western setting and is about an unjust lynching. Henry Fonda stars as the audience's point of view. If you are in a somber mood but don't mind a lot of talking, then it is easy to keep watching it, but the film inevitably simplifies the complexities of vigilante justice in order to drive home a few basic points. As with most message-heavy movies, the filmmakers made the mistake of deciding who was right and who was wrong before they started; in other words, they made the same mistake the characters make.

OXFORD BLUES

Rob Lowe portrays a kid who wants to go to Oxford because he idolizes their version of Princeton's Brooke Shields, played by Amanda Pays, in *Oxford Blues*. He just happens to be an accomplished sculler, even though he grew up in Las Vegas. It must require the same muscles you use playing one-armed bandits. The movie reeks from having been excised to a 98 minute running time, with some scenes being barely comprehensible as a result. It has an accomplished stereo mix, with many pleasing, off center sound effects. The picture is a little hazy.

OZZY OSBOURNE WICKED VIDEOS

Three harmless videos are contained on the 18-minute CAV disc, *Ozzy Osbourne Wicked Videos*. The picture is grainy throughout. The still frames jiggle consistently when the source material is videotape and two out of every five frames when the source is film. The sound is mildly stereophonic and does not do justice to the overly boisterous music. The three numbers are 'Miracle Man,' 'Crazy Babies,' and 'Crazy Train.' The most fun segment on the disc, however, is a lengthy introduction to 'Crazy Babies' containing amusing footage from behind the scenes that serves to humanize the band members.

P.K. AND THE KID

The jacket cover for *P.K. and the Kid* has the same pink graphics and Molly Ringwald, but *Pretty in Pink* it isn't. It is a previous-to-fame-and-glamor Ringwald effort, made before she was getting her hair done professionally or her dialog custom designed. The show does offer a chance to appreciate Ringwald's natural talent, since the lines which leave Paul le Mat, Alex Rocco and the other stars in the film stuttering and grunting don't seem to faze her in the slightest. The script, however, is preposterous. The stepfather of Ringwald's character consistently appears out of nowhere to chase her, and other characters start fights for no other reason than to provide the film with violence.

The daytime scenes look fine, but as soon as the picture gets dark, it gets grainy as well. This was probably the way it was filmed. The digital monaural sound is admirable, and the analog track is almost as good. The movie is also about arm wrestling, but it is worse than *Over the Top*, if such a thing is possible.

P.O.W. THE ESCAPE

Mako plays the commander of a POW camp in North Vietnam who wants to defect. The plot is even more unbelievable than that, but his presence is engaging. David Carradine plays the unimaginative hero (he ends up causing the death of more GIs than he rescues). Both the picture and sound are better than they deserve to be.

THE PACKAGE

The Package is a super mixture of action and intrigue, and it makes a terrific disc. The picture composition fits comfortably on the video screen and has a solid, clear image. The surround sound is also impressive. The movie stars Gene Hackman and Joanna Cassidy. It is a conspiracy thriller, with the hero acting as a potential monkey wrench that will clog machinations set to assassinate the leaders of the US and the USSR. There is a down-to-the-wire finish and plenty of tense moments leading to it, yet the narrative holds up, on a superficial level anyway, to logical inspection.

PAINT IT BLACK
If you like Alfred Hitchcock movies you will love the ending of *Paint It Black*, which was directed by Tim Hunter. Hunter goes so far as to use Bernard Herrmann's discarded musical score from *Torn Curtain* for key moments in the murder thriller, and the finale is a wonderful matte painting cliffside struggle. The film is not pure homage, however, as Hunter, who directed *River's Edge*, has his own sense for mixing the real with the absurd. The story is about an artist in Southern California whose career is furthered by a psychotic fan. It is kind of a mixture of *Strangers on a Train* and 'Buckets of Blood,' but it has a cult appeal all of its own. The picture is soft in places, but looks good overall and has no severe distractions. The stereo sound is okay. Separations are reserved primarily for the music, but there are a few key noises which take good advantage of the directional sound. The film is set in Santa Barbara.

THE PAINTED STALLION
Although not as sophisticated as several of Republic's best serials, *The Painted Stallion* is certainly one of the most enjoyable. With Ray 'Crash' Corrigan as the good guy, Duncan Renaldo as one of the bad guys, and heroes who have been given the names Jim Bowie, Davy Crockett, and 'Kit' Carson, the serial epitomizes everything that is wonderful about relaxing and watching the movies. The only thing it lacks is intelligence, but one can obtain that elsewhere.

The narrative has two major segments. In the first, a wagon train crosses the West to Santa Fe. In the second, an evil 'lieutenant governor' of Santa Fe attempts to prevent a US agent from completing a trade deal with Mexico. Throughout, a mysterious 'guardian' Indian, on a beautiful horse, fires whistling arrows to protect the good guys. The film has its flaws, but it has a satisfying collection of diverse action sequences and fulfills every nine-year old's fantasy about the Old West, at least it would if nine-year olds still had fantasies about the Old West.

The picture is often soft and shifts in quality from shot to shot. The sound has a manageable number of flutters and pops. Although side four runs only a half hour and could easily have held an extra chapter, none of the side breaks fall on chapter divisions. Contrary to the jacket cover, no theatrical trailer has been included.

PAINTING WITH LIGHT
Painting with Light is presented with a grey border completely surrounding the picture, so that nothing from the recorded image is lost. The program presents four established artists, each of whom has just been introduced to a sophisticated graphics technology, the 'Quantel Paint Box.' With the camera spending most of the time pointing at the computer screen, each artist adapts his craft to the technology. The end results are not as interesting as the process itself or each artist's ongoing off screen comments.

Contrary to the chapter listing on the back of the jacket, David Hockney appears by himself on side one, while Larry Rivers, Howard Hodgkins and Jennifer Bartlett appear on side two. Hodgkins' segment has extra chapter markers, dividing it in three parts. The Hodgkins segment, in which he is supposedly working on designs for a Stravinsky ballet, is the least satisfying. Hodgkins mumbles too much, and it is impossible to relate the expressionistic forms on the screen to the sets and costumes he claims to be designing. It would have been helpful if the program's producers had included photos of the realization of his designs. Hockney's chapter, in which he works his way through several electronic paintings, is the most elaborate and informative of the segments. Both Rivers and Bartlett begin by taking Polaroid photographs of their subjects, transferring the photos to the screen, and then set about modifying the images. Teachers should be warned, incidentally, that Rivers' segment contains some bemused comments about drug abuse.

The picture transfer is flawless. The monaural sound is also vivid, except for the Hodgkins segment. The 70-minute program is in CLV throughout. Films which depict major artists at work are always fascinating, especially when the artists are willing to share their thought processes with viewers. The computerized 'Paint Box' is just a gimmick to get them to expose themselves, but it works, so more power to it.

THE PAJAMA GAME
The narrative in *The Pajama Game* is all forward motion. The songs are satisfying or outright catchy ('Hernando's Hideaway') and the performers are pleasingly idiosyncratic. Most are so weird, in fact, that Doris Day's normality becomes captivating in their company. The story is about a management/labor conflict at a pajama factory, and that, too, is gratifying. About the only real problem we have with the movie is that the filmmakers went to the trouble of constructing a factory-sized soundstage set and then rarely take full advantage of it, usually treating it as if it were simply a bigger theatrical stage set. The image is sharp, the colors are terrific, and the sound is in fine shape.

PALE MOON – TENMEI & CARIOCA
An attempt to videocize Ansel Adams resulted in *Pale Moon – Tenmei & Carioca*. Delicate CAV video photography of Yosemite National Park by Tenmei Kanoh is accompanied by the light jazz sounds of Carioca. The music does not comment upon or assist in the understanding of the nature visuals. Instead, it trivializes them, making the clouds and the mists and the breezes look fluffier and lighter than they are. The transfer is lovely, but the sentiment is less than daring.

PALE RIDER
One witty reviewer pointed out that Clint Eastwood's *Pale Rider* is not so much a remake of George Stevens' *Shane* as it is an imitation of Stevens' 'The Greatest Story Ever Told.' Eastwood has been directing movies for more than a decade but no one yet has had the courage to tell him that the aperture is supposed to be widened when the camera is moved indoors. The transfer is only average and so whenever the screen darkens, little squiggles, bars, and flecks of light pop in and out of view. Eastwood portrays an enigmatic preacher who comes to the aid of an innocent group of homesteading gold farmers being pressured to abandon their land and claims by the owner of a large hydro-powered mining operation. The CX-encoded stereo sound is an added treat, however. When Eastwood blows up the mining operation with dynamite, the explosions have a beautiful, woodsy echo.

THE PALEFACE
The source material for *The Paleface* has a few scratches at the reel change points, but they are *colorful* scratches, and most of the time the picture looks brand new. The sound is also fresh. Accompanying the 91-minute show on the CLV disc is the movie's theatrical trailer.

Jane Russell, who can't act but has a nice sense of poise, teams with Hope to prevent bad guys from selling guns to Indians. The Indians are too eccentric to offend anyone. Hope *can* act. The cumulative scene in which he decides aloud to overcome his fear and save Russell pushes and pulls at your emotions as effectively as high drama. But don't worry, there's enough low comedy to satisfy one's baser needs.

THE PALM BEACH STORY
As William Demarest explains in the trailer for *The Palm Beach Story*, which appears when the film is over, the plot is about a married couple who separate over money troubles and then fall in love again. And as Demarest also explains, that has very little to do with the movie, which is really about all the crazy characters and situations they encounter on their upper class berth to reconciliation. Like the 'Ale and Quail Club,' a group of rowdy old men who destroy a train car by shooting crackers instead of quail. And like Rudy Vallee, whose musical training enables him to master the leaping dialog as if it were just another sliding scale.

Anyone who has never seen a Preston Sturges film is in for a real treat. Side two is in CAV, although that does not offer much until the final, trick camera shot. There is a stripe splitting off the left third of the picture, but you need a disc player to see it.

PALM SPRINGS WEEKEND
The color transfer on *Palm Springs Weekend* is so nice that you can see the inconsistencies in Troy Donahue's tan. Connie Stevens also stars, along with Stephanie Powers and Robert Conrad. The sixties teen vacation film is filled with adolescent antics from a more innocent age, but the sound is solid and the picture is attractive, making the disc a pleasant piece of nostalgia.

THE PAPER CHASE
The Paper Chase is memorable for only one facet, the presence of John Houseman, whose classroom lectures are so enlightening that the movie, about first year law students,

becomes immensely repeatable entertainment no matter how malodorous one's own memories of school may be.

The opening credit sequence is letterboxed, but the rest of the film is not. The picture is blurry, grainy, faded, and the pans jiggle. The sound is also fuzzy and unappealing.

PARADISE ALLEY

The Home Video Version of *Paradise Alley* has two extra minutes, but it hardly seems to matter, because if you can get past Sylvester Stallone singing the opening theme song, then you are committed enough to be strung along by the rest, regardless of what happens. Even when the truck loses its sides in a smash up and then miraculously regains its panels in the next shot. Even with dialog which doesn't get much better than, "'Ready, punk?' 'Hey, you know the word "punk" is a noun?'"

This was the first movie Sylvester Stallone directed, so the awful color and murky picture isn't the fault of the disc producers. The sound is subdued and uninteresting. The disc also contains the theatrical trailer, and you can bet the theme song is not sung there.

The story is about three brothers, who, in a symbolism so lacking in subtlety that even the character who said 'punk' was a noun would notice it, are representative of the three conditions of Man. One is 'smart,' one is 'strong', and one (Stallone – he also stars and wrote the script) is annoyingly obnoxious. Mind, Body, and either Soul or Bowel Movement, we haven't figured out which. They live in the slums of Hell's Kitchen during the post-War Depression of 1946. They talk and talk about pulling themselves out of poverty. What they don't realize is that all they have to do is walk a couple of blocks east and they'd be out of it. From the look of some of the long shots, they'd also be back in 1978.

PARAMEDICS

The humor is a little desperate in *Paramedics*. The genre by now is familiar, but the *Police Academy* films will seem literate and sophisticated in comparison to this. The picture is spotless and the sound, with surround effects, is better than one would expect.

Ray Walston appears in the film for about a minute, and Sally Kellerman, for some reason, dubs another actress's voice. We did laugh once or twice, but the ratio of gags which don't work to gags which do is horrendous, and one wonders why actors agree to participate in such shenanigans. Is money really that important?

PARAMOUNT COMEDY THEATER VOLUME 2 – DECENT EXPOSURES
PARAMOUNT COMEDY THEATER VOLUME THREE – HANGING PARTY
PARAMOUNT COMEDY THEATER VOLUME FOUR – DELIVERY MEN
PARAMOUNT COMEDY THEATER VOLUME 5 – CUTTING UP
WELL DEVELOPED

The *Paramount Comedy Theater* programs, filmed for video by Paramount, feature four or five comedians per disc and are hosted by a consistently amusing Howie Mandell. Taped live at a comedy club in Hermosa Beach, the picture quality is usually good but not great, with the strongest reds and magentas maintaining a slight blur.

The sound is stereo although often just one person is talking and the laughter rarely seems directional. The discs are analog and run a little over an hour in CLV. Since the routines are sequential on each disc, chapter markers ought to have been provided to separate the comics, but that was not the case.

Although there are amusing moments on each disc, some of the hours are more worthwhile than others. *Volume 2 – Decent Exposures* is particularly strong, with Marsha Warfield providing a steady stream of standard but amusing one-liners ('Why do dead people get to ride in such nice cars?') and Joe Alaskey doing elaborate impressions (the 'Star Trek' intro read by 'Woody Allen'). Doug Ferrari, who is less interesting but gets off a good round about winning a lottery and not leaving work, and Paul Feig, who tries but fails, also appear.

Bob Saget does a straight monolog on 'Paramount Comedy Theater Volume One,' *Well Developed* which is intermittently funny. Judy Carter mixes jokes with several magic tricks, most of which are successful. Bruce Mahler uses a couple of musical instruments and also employs a store-bought chicken as a puppet. The best of the four is Philip Wellford, who doesn't have too many funny jokes, but puts on quite a juggling act.

Volume Three – Hanging Party also has a strong line up. The energetic Susan Healy ("I have a boyfriend, but every once in a while, when I want a really nice meal, I start dating again.") covers a litany of topics and includes an amusing segment on sound effects made by women. Billy Riback ("A guy walks into the drugstore with a pentagram etched in the back of his head. Got a Mohawk in the front. The left side of his head is purple, the right side is green. He bought shampoo for 'Normal Hair.'") and Ritch Shydner ("I'm always amazed when Baptist ministers play rock albums *backwards* looking for Satanic messages. Why don't they try reading the album cover?") have lengthy sets which cover a wide range of subjects. Marty Hoffman makes use of his rotund figure to do a few unusual impressions and also has a number of off-color one liners. His funniest comment, however, comes as he is discussing 'Hands across America,' and he ponders what might have happened, "if a lightning bolt hit some guy in Montana." The best piece, however, is a short set by Mark McCollum, who mixes cartoon voices with contemporary ideas to come up with inspired bits such as a reggae song about Popeye: "Popeye don't smoke no ganja weed, Olive Oyl and spinach is all he needs...."

On *Volume Four – Delivery Men* Pat Hazell has an elaborate and entertaining set involving one liners and magic tricks. Luis Dinos ("I drink a lot of coffee. It's going to kill me. But when I'm dead, I'm going to be awake."), Jimmy Aleck ("Do you believe they're trying to ban aerosol cans? You got to feel sorry for policemen. They're trying to use this new roll-on Mace."), and Rick Overton ("I have a philosophy about working out. No pain – no pain.") do topical monologs, while Maurice La Marche mixes one liners with impressions. Some of the material is homophobic.

The series does not end on a strong note with *Volume 5 – Cutting Up*. Dale Gonyea has a routine involving a piano which rarely rises above weak word play. Lois Bromfield is energetic and inspired, but provides the best set on the disc only through the process of elimination. Teddy Bergeron faded from our memory so quickly we had to go back and watch him again to write this. His routine is primarily a series of weak one liners. ("I went out and bought her a Jaguar. You should have seen the look on her face when the damn thing jumped out of the box.") Worst of all was Louise Duart, who puts an automatic ceiling on her career by doing impressions of other second tier comedians. Her finale, an impression of George Burns talking on the phone to Gracie Allen in heaven, was excruciating.

Some final words. Many of the comics did jokes about salad bars, wood panelled station wagons (no wonder everyone buys vans these days), TV cartoons from twenty years ago, and turning thirty. They all talk about sex with a refreshing frankness, but not one of them did anything even vaguely political. And this was the generation that was going to change the world.

PARDON US/THE CHIMP

The Chimp portion of the Laurel and Hardy double bill from 3M, *Pardon Us/The Chimp*, is a fairly amusing short in which the pair inherit a gorilla-sized chimp from a bankrupt circus and then attempt to spend the night in a boarding house. *Pardon Us*, the longer of the two features, places the two in a prison setting. Their one escape has them hiding in blackface with a group of sharecroppers, a situation which some may find offensive although the gags for the most part are innocent or dated. Both prints have minor flaws and flickers with monaural sound which, due to its age, is strong enough to be understandable and not much more.

PARENTHOOD

The multi-generational comedy *Parenthood* has a consistently clear and unblemished picture and a fresh stereo surround soundtrack. The film runs a few minutes over two hours and is spread to three sides, in CLV. The movie is also a lot of fun. It could have been trimmed a little more – particularly Steve Martin's part – but shifts adeptly enough from one family member's problems to the next to stay humorous and good natured. The subplots all deal with parenting. Since the movie is as much about adult children and elderly parents as it is about toddlers and adolescents, it would seem that the baby boom angle is just a hook to pull the viewer in. The director, Ron Howard, can still be stodgy at times, tramping through the script without inspiration, but the best scenes in the movie are very funny and universal in appeal.

PARENTS

That sweet, good natured character actor, Bob Balaban, has directed one of the most grotesque films ever made. *Parents* is about cannibalism, but unlike the buffoonish *Motel Hell*, Balaban's effort is almost realistic enough to be true (for example, they have a logical access to fresh corpses). Seen mostly through the eyes of a child whose parents (played by Randy Quaid and Mary Beth Hurt) appear to be saving on their butcher bills, the movie is an intense comedy about psychological abuse which will repulse as many viewers as it pleases. The only reaction it will likely not instill is nonchalance.

The sound is supposedly in stereo surround, but very little of it comes off that way, and the dialog is often difficult to hear. The picture transfer has no particular flaws, although some intense colors quiver a little. Cropping tends to make some of the action difficult to follow. Side one is in CAV, with two unsteady still frames out of every five.

PARIS, TEXAS
The color transfer on *Paris, Texas* looks accurate, but the picture is grainy and soft, spoiling some of the impact of the film. Although it was not a widescreen movie, Robby Muller's cinematography is so vital that a slight extension of the sides to include it would seem an absolute necessity. However, CBS/Fox has chosen to leave it mildly cropped. The sound is fine. Side three is in CAV with perfect still frames, but is primarily an extended conversation between two seated characters. The CAV would have been more effective on the film's dynamic opening montage.

The film itself is an impressive accomplishment. It was directed by Wim Wenders and is set in Los Angeles and Texas. The story takes a deliberately long time to unfold, but every long take and every broken conversation increases the emotional impact when the viewer finally pieces together what has happened to the characters. Harry Dean Stanton gives an exceptional performance as the central character; it is unlike any of his other roles but unnervingly in step with his standard screen personality. Although *Paris, Texas* is long on conversations and short on activity, the 145-minute film can be involving and could be highly repeatable if it were presented correctly on disc. This time out, however, it wasn't.

PARSIFAL
The films of Hans-Jurgen Syberberg are monstrously indulgent epics which often go on for hours, full of unusual visual effects and vague, repetitive, false-literate narratives. What a fabulous inspiration, then, to have Syberberg film Richard Wagner's *Parsifal.* At four hours and fifteen minutes, the piece is a quickie by Syberbergian standards, and with the opera forced upon him as his text, his creativity can be concentrated on the one thing he does well – inventing dynamic images. From the other angle, the deal is also a good one. Musically, *Parsifal* is one of Wagner's most profound and satisfying works. Dramatically, however, it is notoriously slow going. The second act can be summarized in a couple of sentences, and yet takes more than an hour to execute. The work has always been popular as an audio entertainment, but requires the same sort of attendance commitment which a Syberberg film requires when presented live. The joining of Syberberg's visuals and Wagner's music, then, combines the best both artists have to offer.

Throughout the entire film, Syberberg uses an optical collage to decorate his soundstage sets. The viewer is never completely sure what or who is a real component of the shot and what has been added afterward. Puppets appear in the sky, rocks metamorphose before your eyes and characters pass through walls. The sets maintain semblances of how a normal 'Parsifal' stage might be configured, but symbolic statues and other odd objects inevitably loom from the corners. Nor is Syberberg content to simply mess with the backgrounds. Since the cast is lip-synching the singing anyway, two performers alternate appearances as Parsifal, one male and one female.

Image has done a beautiful job transferring the picture. With so many optical effects, one would think it inevitable that a color or a shadow might come out distorted, but the picture is sharp and blemish free for all four and a quarter hours. Some of the white English subtitles blend into the background, but the fault is minor. The side breaks seem well chosen, but except for one which occurs during a true intermission, all are inevitably awkward. The disc has chapter markers, but no guide or synopsis.

The sound is stereo surround, with the surround effects being limited to the more elaborate orchestral passages. There is a periodic flutter on the soundtrack, particularly on side two, and a few channel dropouts scattered through the presentation. On the other hand, if your speakers are sophisticated enough, you can hear the singers shuffling on their stools as they record the vocals. The music presentation is quite nice and, when free of the minor errors, quite satisfying. Reiner Goldberg sings Parsifal, Yvonne Minton sings Kundry, and Wolfgang Schone is Amfortas. With the luxury of working in the studio, they all give strong renderings to their parts. The Monte Carlo Philharmonic Orchestra and Prague Philharmonic Choir are also commendable. Actors usually appear completely lost in a Syberberg film, and some do here, though others bring enough of a sense of purpose to their part that they manage to transcend the artifice.

PART 2 – WALKING TALL
(see **WALKING TALL**)

PARTY INCORPORATED
Have you ever seen a movie where the set designer deliberately placed mirrors in sets to catch glimpses of the camera crew behind the actors? That is just one of the many self-mocking effects in *Party Incorporated*, an intentionally stupid movie which, no matter how hard we tried, we could not dislike. The film, which stars Marilyn Chambers, has no more than a trifle of a plot, but dopey gags about the making of the film deliberately and continually interrupt the proceedings. Highpoints include: Chambers out-of-lip-synch singing two of the worst songs you will ever hear; puns involving the diminutive form of 'Richard' which are so bad those who are so named would be advised to acquire and burn all copies of the movie; and the audacity of the director, Chuck Vincent, to take New Wave filmmaking techniques and apply them to the oldest hustle in entertainment – sex without sex. It is a party film, so aggressively and adolescently dumb that it is guaranteed to relax the guard of any viewer or group of viewers.

The disc is as outrageously awful as the film itself. Not only do intense colors appear to have the consistency of Jello, not only do the chapter markers flicker to the beat of the film's musical score, not only did the image contain the sort of interference we usually see on broadcast television the night of an electrical storm, but the CAV encoded side two on the copy we viewed began with an image one normally associates with security cameras and proceeded to play while displaying a single five digit frame number. Fortunately, this latter problem only lasted long enough to endear the disc to us all the more, and the rest of the side, beginning at about frame 3500, was fine.

PASCALI'S ISLAND
We don't know how effective repeat viewings of *Pascali's Island* may be, but the film is worth seeing at least once. The story is set on a Turkish island in the Aegean Sea shortly after the turn of the century, and concerns archaeological and political intrigues. The three stars, Ben Kingsley, Charles Dance, and Helen Mirren, give captivating performances (Mirren is particularly subtle). The mix of an exotic period locale with a plot which twists without sacrificing believability or intelligence makes the film a rarity in a market otherwise swelling with carbon copy features.

Although monaural, the sound is atmospheric and dimensional. The musical score has a suitably Levantine twang. The picture is a bit dark and grainy, but remains within the range of acceptability.

PASS THE AMMO
An attempt to rob the money room of a television evangelical program during broadcast hours leads to an on-air hostage crisis in *Pass the Ammo*. The 1987 film wants to be a comedy but it is better when it verges on real drama. It has a good share of pyrotechnics at the end and a clever final twist. The picture is grainy, but the digitally encoded stereo has some nice separations. Tim Curry appears as the preacher.

A PASSAGE TO INDIA
With the exception of scenes depicting brass bands, *A Passage to India* sounds terrific with the volume levels turned way, way up. The RCA/Columbia release has the expected amount of analog noise along with a subtle hum here and there in the beginning, but the film's soundtrack is superbly mixed and playing it loud is tantamount to bringing India into your video room.

The picture is only cropped a tiny bit, but when it comes to the films of David Lean, even the smallest loss is felt. The picture is vaguely grainy, but not severely enough to spoil either the night scenes or the rich detail. Using a foreign culture to represent sexual mystery is not an original concept, but it is difficult to accomplish without insulting the culture. Lean employs some of the most clichéd metaphors imaginable – monkeys representing animal lust, sea voyages representing death, changes in the weather keying changes in the plot, the cave as a representation of woman's anatomy – but his command of the narrative is so self-assured that the story appears mature and evenhanded.

Whether it is the smooth Maurice Jarre score, the haunting view of the moon over the Ganges or the exciting steam engine ride up to the caves, every viewer is going to find something on one of the three sides of *A Passage to India* that thrills the heart.

THE PASSION OF BEATRICE

Ron Carter is responsible for the musical score in *The Passion of Beatrice*, and although the drama takes place during the Hundred Years' War the music does not sound jarringly anachronistic. It is modern, but assists in sorting the emotions of the film and keeping the action in a proper perspective. The movie was directed by Bertrand Tavernier and is in French with small yellow English subtitles. The dialog is sparse and not difficult to follow.

The story is about a woman terrorized by her father who is himself beset by ennui following his return from the war. Bernard Pierre Donnadieu is excellent as the father, but Julie Delpy, as the title character, is overly mannered in typical French ingenue fashion and makes the film do what Carter's music had avoided – alienate the viewer. The plot also contains some vague allegorical references and will be of most interest to those who gorge on highbrow cuisine regardless of nutritional value.

The transfer is okay. The sound is monaural, but has been digitally encoded and is decently mixed (Tavernier also directed *Round Midnight*). The movie was made with inexpensive film stock, but does not suffer further in the transfer. Side three of the 133 minute disc runs less than a half hour and is in CLV.

PAT BENATAR – HIT VIDEOS

We like Pat Benatar's music a lot but we don't like her videos at all. 'Love is a Battlefield' appeared on the 12-inch disc, *Benatar*, and has also been included on the 8-inch, *Pat Benatar – Hit Videos*. The other three cuts on *Hit Videos*, 'Anxiety,' 'Lipstick Lies,' and 'Shadows of the Night,' are equally disappointing. The narratives are linear and the imagery is unimaginative. In a short documentary on side two of the disc, 'The Making of "Love Is a Battlefield,"' Benatar says that she doesn't want to get stuck in the rut of doing the same thing over and over. What she doesn't realize is that even though the subject of each video is different, the format, style, and mood is exactly the same from one to the next.

PAT BENATAR THE VISUAL MUSIC COLLECTION

In a direct comparison the music videos on *Pat Benatar – Hit Videos* look better than the same videos appearing on *Pat Benatar The Visual Music Collection*. The colors are stronger and the edges of things are sharper. The sound is a little better too, but the differences there are less noticeable.

Visual Music Collection is a 12-inch which contains 11 videos. The disc is not chapter encoded. The opening cut, 'You Better Run,' is captivating, and it takes several more before one realizes that it was the best in the collection. Benatar wears a simple black-and-white striped shirt, is impeccably made up and coiffed, and sings straight to the camera while her band plays behind her. We didn't blink until it was over.

PAT TRAVERS – JUST ANOTHER KILLER DAY

For an inexpensive one-sided CAV disc, *Pat Travers – Just Another Killer Day* has a lot going for it. The Pioneer Artists release has three music videos (a fourth number is played over the credits) linked with a story about Amazonian aliens. The videos vary in quality, some being blurrier than others. Characters from the story appear in the videos and the CAV can be utilized to explore the more interesting images. The outdoor scenes were filmed in Seattle.

PATHS OF GLORY

Stanley Kubrick's riveting study of motivation in war, *Paths of Glory*, has been given a super transfer on to disc. The black-and-white picture is flawless and the digitally encoded monaural sound is so clear that you can hear the drummers putting down their sticks when the music finishes at the end of the film.

The 87-minute movie, starring Kirk Douglas, is immensely repeatable entertainment. It takes place during the First World War and concerns the consequences of a failed assault. There is action and a basic trial and firing squad drama, but the moralities are fleeting and subtle. As a viewer ages, the villains in the film will change (there are no unblemished heroes), but a compelling fascination with the sequence of events and the emotions of the participants remains steadfast.

Paths of Glory is also gloriously cinematic, making the disc transfer all the more valuable. There are long, dizzying tracking shots through the trenches and tipsy camera angles which follow characters up staircases. The confusion of battle and the ordered world of the high command are both presented on a scale to show the characters overwhelmed by their surroundings.

THE PATRIOT

The Patriot would probably be fairly entertaining when observed under distracting conditions, but the amount of attention provided when it is shown on a TV is counter-productive. At one point, an actress's hair is wet *before* she dives into the water. Someone wasn't using the blow dryer enough between takes.

The picture hasn't many flaws, but the editing and the cinematography are both so bad that it doesn't make a difference. The story is about the theft of some atomic warheads which are stashed underwater, *Thunderball*-style. The hero is a bit dense, but so is the movie, so they go together.

PATTI LA BELLE – LOOK TO THE RAINBOW TOUR

Patti La Belle – Look to the Rainbow Tour is a two-sided concert disc. The picture is incredibly clear and loses next to nothing in transference to disc. It loses so little, in fact, that La Belle probably could have done with a little gauze on the lens for the extreme closeups. The sound recording is also accomplished, blending the immediacy of the concert environment with the separations of a good studio mix. The material will be of limited appeal to those who are not already her fans, but the quality of the disc may win her a few new ones.

PATTI ROCKS

Screenwriters fantasize about writing 'real dialog,' in which characters speak scatologically and discuss the subjects which people really discuss with their intimate friends. Then producers with money invest in the movie conditionally, and everything gets cleaned up. Until home video expanded potential incomes, the only forum for speaking frankly about bodily functions was Off-Broadway. By theatrical standards, *Patti Rocks* is still rather tame, but the blue dialog has caused quite an uproar and, should one own the disc, it is a good way to break the ice at a dull party.

The 86-minute CLV release has gone through an acceptable transfer. The music track is in stereo and the sound, cleaner on the digital track than on the analog, is solid. The picture may be faintly grainy in places, but one rarely notices it.

The plot is inconsequential to the situations it creates. Side one will bother some viewers, as the characters seem venal and talk about sexual acts in an insulting manner. But side two is utterly charming, if equally bawdy, and one realizes the lengthy build-up was necessary for the romantic punchlines which conclude the film.

PATTON

From the outsized Old Glory in the opening frame to the quixotic windmill in the closing frame, every scene and every shot of *Patton* has been reproduced magnificently on the Special Wide Screen Edition release. The presentation fully reveals the film's strengths, perhaps for the first time since its premiere. The former scanned and cropped version made the film seem workmanlike, overlong, and tiresome. Their new version makes the characters come alive, makes the history seem relevant, and turns the movie into the intelligently rewarding epic it was intended to be.

The picture transfer is incredibly bright and sharp. Every color looks accurate and is free of distortion. The skin tones are perfect, the skies are perfect, and red stripes in the flag are completely stable. The image has an aspect ratio of 2.25:1 (subtitles for the German dialog appear in the black beneath the picture) and fully encompasses the deliberately careful screen compositions of the 'Dimension-150' film. Not only do characters or objects which appear in the corners comment upon or anticipate the action (a soldier can be seen crying during a battle on the far left in a piece of throwaway staging which is not acknowledged but nevertheless foreshadows Patton's run-in with a battle fatigue victim), but even when the sides of the picture are free from clutter the wide composition has a purpose, pulling the viewer harder into the center of the screen.

The stereo surround sound is actively utilized throughout the movie. The separation effects are superbly executed, and the disc's volume levels prevent the battle scenes from sounding distorted.

The three-hour film is an amazing, gutsy accomplishment. To produce a big budget biography of an American general just as the anti-War movement was cresting in the early seventies took a lot of nerve. That *Patton* was accepted by audiences justified the intelligence with which it was constructed. Because of when the film was made, the script had to avoid moralizing, and it is the concentrated objectivity which gives the movie its lasting power. It is an effective portrait of three men – Patton, Omar Bradley, and the unseen but strongly felt Dwight Eisenhower – but it is also a portrait of the ways of war. Patton's fascination with reincarnation (which is beautifully echoed, especially on the disc with the help of the surround effects, by the horns in Jerry Goldsmith's score, playing their fading triplets) is cleverly deployed as a linking device to remind the viewer of the consistency of politics and warfare throughout history.

As a bonus, CBS/Fox has provided an epilog comprised of Movietonews reports which appears at the end of side three. Although one of the reports skimps on the details of Patton's auto accident, the newsreels are terrific and provide a nice splash of reality after three hours of Hollywood image making.

PATTY HEARST

Some people seek out mediocrity and others have mediocrity thrust upon them. Patty Hearst falls into the second category and many people feel that Paul Schrader's film, *Patty Hearst*, falls there as well. We would tend to disagree, though the dividing lines are slight. To his credit, Schrader has thought out the film carefully and given it a surprisingly stylistic thrust. The events depicted, however, are so absurd that the movie becomes, intentionally, a droll and almost wicked comedy. To this extent, Natasha Richardson's title performance is wonderful, particularly her ability to feign concentration in another intellect.

The narrative covers events from the point of the kidnapping to the end of the trial. Its interpretation of events seems believable and final. The difficult part is convincing potential viewers that they might want to watch a movie about Patty Hearst. The film itself reaffirms such reservations, but it does so with a stifled grin.

The transfer is okay, although the movie has low key colors and monaural sound. The audio hasn't much atmosphere, but it remains clear even when the dialog is muttered or whispered.

PAUL MAURIAT – CLASSICAL ELEGANCE

Paul Mauriat banalizes some of the world's finest music on *Paul Mauriat – Classical Elegance*. The disc was recorded digitally and is encoded digitally, so the sound is impressive, technically. But from the opening Bach fugue, which has a disco beat, to the 'Hungarian Dance,' by Brahms, 47 minutes later, Mauriat has his orchestra do to classical music what the people who make velvet paintings do to art.

Alternating with visuals of Mauriat's orchestra are images of a woman strolling through famous French castles. The picture has the typically clean import gloss to it. The woman is pretending to listen to Mauriat's music on a cassette player, but you know she really isn't. She's smiling too much.

PAUL McCARTNEY & WINGS ROCKSHOW (see JOHN LENNON – LIVE IN NEW YORK CITY)

PAUL MCCARTNEY – PUT IT THERE

Paul McCartney – Put It There lasts a little over an hour and features 22 tunes, most of them separated by interview material. The disc is chapter encoded, but the encoding and song order bear almost no relation to the listing on the back of the jacket, and the markers begin at the interviews instead of the songs. Most of the program is set in a recording studio, with some numbers filmed straight on and others, stylistically. McCartney mixes oldies with new material and gives a sharper presentation than he has in the past. Aging is finally stopping his voice from sounding so irritatingly mellifluous.

THE PAUL MCCARTNEY SPECIAL

Paul McCartney gives a newsworthy interview on *The Paul McCartney Special*, talking about the creative process and the breakup of the Beatles. The hour long program is vaguely intended to promote McCartney's album, 'Press to Play,' but contains rare film clips from throughout his career.

The picture looks stale and the monaural sound is flat and fuzzy. Although there is a tendency for the songs to get cut off before completing, fifteen numbers last long enough to make an impression. It is McCartney's words, not his music, however, which will attract fans to the disc. He is frank on a number of subjects and open to speculating and exploring the life choices he made.

PAUL McCARTNEY'S RUPERT AND THE FROG SONG ALSO LINDA McCARTNEY'S SEASIDE WOMAN/THE ORIENTAL NIGHTFISH

Animation fans will not want to miss the Pioneer Artists 8-inch, *Paul McCartney's Rupert and the Frog Song also Linda McCartney's Seaside Woman/The Oriental Nightfish*. The two-sided disc is in CAV. 'Rupert,' on side one, is the most complicated and fully realized of the three pieces. The colors are incredible (the stereo is terrific throughout the disc) and the drawings are very detailed although some of the still frames jiggle. The whole project has a Caldecottish look which goes beyond the scope of most contemporary cartoons. The CAV comes in for use at the end, because the dramatic high point is poorly storyboarded and you have to play it back step by step to see the king and queen frog escape the owl.

Side two offers a pair of animated shorts produced by Linda McCartney in 1977 and 1980. 'Seaside Woman' is a calypso ditty which is accompanied by elaborately colored cut-outs. The animation style matches the music which matches the subject (a little girl who lives on the beach with her parents) and it all has the zing of a cool tropical drink. 'Oriental Nightfish' uses metamorphic swirls to show figures turning into colors and shapes and back into figures again. It also is well done, but there is some nudity, so caution is advised if you are purchasing the disc for a favorite niece. Screen it first; you'll probably end up getting a second one for yourself.

THE PAWNBROKER

The picture quality on *The Pawnbroker* is impressive. The print has a few scratches, but the black-and-white image is especially sharp and glossy. The sound is passable, and the disc has been given a healthy number of chapter markers.

The story is about an embittered Holocaust survivor who runs a pawnshop in a black ghetto. His name is Nazerman and at the end he pokes his hand onto a receipt rod as atonement for his heartlessness. The symbolism is silly, but the jump cuts and the effective cinematography tend to hook a viewer into staying with the narrative until the very end. Rod Steiger effectively conveys the title character's personality, but perhaps he does so too well, because there is no mystery to the character and little motivation to tolerate his presence. One tends to excuse flaws in older films, however, and so the sixties-era *The Pawnbroker*, like a nasty looking object d'art, has now been around long enough to achieve respectability.

PECOS BILL
THE TAILOR OF GLOUCESTER
THE TALE OF MR. JEREMY FISHER AND THE TALE OF PETER RABBIT
THE EMPEROR AND THE NIGHTINGALE
THE LEGEND OF SLEEPY HOLLOW
HOW THE RHINOCEROS GOT HIS SKIN AND HOW THE CAMEL GOT HIS HUMP
HOW THE LEOPARD GOT HIS SPOTS
THUMBELINA
THE FISHERMAN AND HIS WIFE
THE THREE BILLY GOATS GRUFF AND THE THREE LITTLE PIGS

A group of picture book story videos, 'Rabbit Ears Storybook Classics' have been released by SVS and Image. The discs have impressive jacket covers, with the artwork spread to every edge. The transfers are impressive, too. The pictures are beautiful and the digitally encoded stereophonic soundtracks are vivid. Most of the discs are in CAV.

The animation is minimal, consisting primarily of dissolves and of cutout-sized figures traveling on simple vectors, but the artwork is comparable to the illustrations in children's books. The stories, each about a half hour in length, are narrated by well known personalities, and the scores also come from established musicians.

Such a format may sound uninteresting, but have you ever had a story read to you by Robin Williams? He narrates *Pecos Bill* the way cowboys ride bucking broncos. His ad-libs, his varieties of voices, and his vocal inflections leap and change from second to second. The drawings are also amusing and the program, which features a musical score by Ry Cooder, is entertaining. The disc is in CAV, with every still frame possessing a slight flicker.

Meryl Streep is a little more subdued than Williams, but is by no means monotonic in her reading of *The Tailor of Gloucester*. She affects different accents for the tailor, the industrious mice who assist him, and the cat who almost messes everything up. The music is by The Chieftains, and the CLV disc is almost worth acquiring for the stereophonic score alone.

The illustrations on *The Tale of Mr. Jeremy Fisher and The Tale of Peter Rabbit* are so elaborate that it is difficult to follow or appreciate them on a TV screen. Figures emerge from the background through subtle increases in density and shadings, and the image often fails to linger long enough for the full composition to sink in. The tales, which are separate, but animated by the same artist, are read by Meryl Streep. Her voice matches the sleepiness of the illustrations and the disc should not be one's first choice in exploring the series. The music, a piano score, is by Lyle Mays.

Mark Isham supplies his oriental themed musical experiments to the soundtrack of *The Emperor and the Nightingale*. The story is read by Glenn Close and the illustrations are brightly colored. Isham's score is elaborately recorded and separated. He also did the music on *Windham Hill Tibet*. Close's voice, however, is more subdued, and does not always capture the listener's imagination. The drawings are terrific, but they may have seemed to us a relief after suffering through *Peter Rabbit*.

Close also reads *The Legend of Sleepy Hollow*, an engaging tale which hits closer to home than *Emperor*. The illustrations, in Grant Woodish American gothic, are again bright and cleverly executed. The animation, though limited, is subject to some interesting variations involving silhouettes and cutouts. The music, by Tim Story, is appropriate but unremarkable.

Jack Nicholson's reading of the Rudyard Kipling 'Just So Stories,' *How the Rhinoceros Got His Skin and How the Camel Got His Hump*, will delight Nicholson's fans. He begins in a very detached manner, but as you are listening you start to realize that some of his vocal inflections are quite odd, and the dryly humorous effect sustains one's interest through both stories. Bobby McFerrin provides the score and Tom Raglin's illustrations are amusing.

Danny Glover reads *How the Leopard Got His Spots*, the Robert Louis Stevenson short story which, along the way, includes the tale of how the Ethiopian came to be Black, presumptively suggesting that his original skin color was White. Glover reads very well and the backup group, Ladysmith Black Mambazo, sounds lovely in stereo. The brightly colored illustrations are a bit difficult to follow, but the limited animation makes adept use of the camouflage theme. The images dissolve from trees and brush into animals as if the animals had been standing there all the while.

Nothing moves in the ink and watercolor illustrations of *Thumbelina*, but pans and dissolves keep a viewer reasonably attentive to the images. Kelly McGillis reads the well known Hans Christian Anderson story. Her voice is clear and strong, but the voices she does for some of the animals are a bit irritating. Mark Isham's score is supportive, but does not leave a strong impression.

Silhouetted cutouts by Diana Bryan move almost like puppets against a video controlled color background in *The Fisherman and His Wife*. Jodie Foster gives a rather sloppy reading of the story but the music, by Van Dyke Parks, is satisfying.

What a joy, then, it is to hear Holly Hunter read *The Three Billy Goats Gruff and The Three Little Pigs*. No syllable in either story is left unconsidered in her delivery, and the voices she comes up with for the characters are delightful. Just to hear her throat massage the 'u' in 'gruff' is enchanting. The music, by Art Lande, is purely background filler. The illustrations, by David Jorgensen, are competent and reasonably detailed. It is Hunter, however, who makes the story come alive.

PEE-WEE'S BIG ADVENTURE

Some kind of hum appears on the right channel during the fourth minute of *Pee-wee's Big Adventure* and it pops up a couple more times during the course of the program. It is a shame the movie wasn't given digital encoding. It's got the production values which transfer well to disc, particularly the cheery, solid colors and carnival soundtrack. The picture is a little grainy and doesn't carry the sunsets or fortune teller sequence effectively, but the stuff which takes place in the bright outdoors – most of the movie – is great.

Pee-wee's Big Adventure is hysterical. The reason lies with the young, prodigious director, Tim Burton, who will be a force to be reckoned with long after Herman is an answer to a trivia quiz. Burton gives Herman what Jerry Lewis never got – a tightly disciplined environment in which the comic can run rampant while the film stays on course. The only thing we want to find out is what happened to the boomerang bow tie.

PEE-WEE'S PLAYHOUSE FUN-O-RAMA
PEE-WEE'S PLAYHOUSE POTPOURRI
PEE-WEE'S PLAYHOUSE CHRISTMAS SPECIAL

For those who have never seen *Pee-wee's Playhouse* before, it is an amalgam of sophisticated stop-motion animation sequences, public domain cartoons, sappy documentaries, John Waters-type supporting players, and Pee-wee's own immitigably pubescent humor. It is as addictive as an off-color nursery rhyme and about as uplifting, but only those who never, ever did anything silly as a child will fail to comprehend the program's appeal.

Pee-wee's Playhouse Fun-O-Rama contains four episodes, split evenly on the two sides. Chapter markers identify all the commercial break points. The picture is bright and sharp, and although intense colors tend to destabilize a little, the variety of special visual effects survive the transfer admirably. The sound quality, however, is the disc's most impressive feature. Although the program is monaural, the digitally encoded audio track has a real kick to it.

The episodes were not originally titled, but have been given identifying names for the jacket cover, and the descriptive nature of the names may help viewers recall the specific program identified. In 'Luau for Two' Pee-wee wins a dinner for two at a Hawaiian restaurant and is disappointed when his friends suck up to him trying for the second diner spot. 'Ice Cream Soup,' 'Rainy Day,' and the invisibility-themed 'Now You See Me, Now You Don't' round out the disc.

Pee-wee's Playhouse Potpourri is a weaker collection. The episodes, nominally entitled 'Just Another Day,' 'Beauty Makeover,' 'Restaurant,' and 'Ants in Your Pants,' have no strong linking themes or exceptionally memorable sequences. The picture transfer is also not quite as glossy as the first group, though it still looks pretty good. As with the first *Playhouse* disc, the monaural sound is very good and definitely worth amplifying.

Although the basic format is followed, the 48-minute *Pee-wee's Playhouse Christmas Special* provides more variation than the repetitive episodes on *Potpourri*, and is quite amusing. There are a number of guest stars, including an uncredited appearance by Cher, and a more intense level of comic writing to backup Pee-wee's antics. The picture is fine and the stereo sound has some pleasing separation effects. The program is to regular television Christmas specials what gag Christmas songs are to traditional favorites, but for making merry and holiday cheer, a little of both never hurts.

PEGGY SUE GOT MARRIED

Peggy Sue Got Married is a sweet film about the good intentions each one of us has inside. The gauze which is supposed to give the film a nostalgic feel causes the colors to bleed together in the transfer, and the flesh tones are too pink, but the brightly painted automobiles look terrific and there is no problem in the picture quality which can interfere with one's concentration or enjoyment. The sound is monaural, but it bears the standards of quality one associates with Coppola.

Peggy Sue is about a woman who faints at her high school reunion and wakes up twenty years earlier, back in school. A sensible reason for the incident is provided at the end, concerning the only time travelling people can really do, looking through the tunnels of their own memories to see not incidents, but eras and feelings. The story is not a fantasy at all, just a foggy, jumbled memory of incidents and wishes.

It is exhausting watching the movie because it takes over your whole head, and most viewers will only want to daydream after it is over. It provides the kind of high very few movies can give, putting one in touch with the bittersweet peace of one's own cherished remembrances.

PENDULUM

Two suspects in a murder. One is the hero and the other is very, very bad, yet all the evidence seems to indicate that the hero commited the crime. Can he clear himself? That is the basic appeal of the enjoyable 1968 George Peppard film, *Pendulum*. The plot also contains condiments about the rights of suspects and takes place in Washington DC, which magnifies the issues aspect, but preaching never gets in the way of the story, which is well-executed. Adding to the film's appeal, Jean Seberg and Richard Kiley co-star. Seberg's performance is especially accurate and engrossing, and her presence adds significantly to the disc's value.

All movies made in 1968 seem to have bland color schemes, but the quality of the print is surprisingly good. Night scenes look a little grainy, and there are segments that are a bit worn down, but most of the film seems brand new. The sound is in acceptable condition and there are a good collection of chapter markers.

PENN AND TELLER GET KILLED

Directed by Arthur Penn, *Penn and Teller Get Killed* is an obtuse spin-off of 'Mickey One.' The fictional film stars the magician comedians, Penn and Teller, and by appearing as themselves, they make it look more egotistical than it really is. Teller, whose act requires muteness, has a strong movie personality and could conceivably fill an entertainment gap. But the film, in which the two stars invite the public to murder them and also play a number of practical jokes on each other, is an unbalanced conglomeration of ideas and is amusing only in short spurts. The disc has a sharp picture transfer, but the surround stereo has limited separation effects.

PENNIES FROM HEAVEN

The cinematography of Gordon Willis is extremely difficult to transfer onto any home video format. He uses oblique lighting and eccentric filters to create unique images which must be handled on a shot-by-shot basis during the transfer process if the integrity of his intentions is to be maintained. MGM/UA has done this successfully with *Pennies from Heaven*, the stimulating musical comedy directed by Herbert Ross and starring Steve Martin. No matter what the shift in hue or contrast, the disc stays with the film, and although intense, solid colors sometimes look jittery, the picture quality is very good.

Pennies is monaural and is analog only, but the sound recording is so impressive that many of the sound effects feel stereophonic. The disc also has a thorough collection of chapter markers.

This is the film where old recordings, such as Bing Crosby singing 'Did You Ever See a Dream Walking?,' are lip synched in numerous fantasy sequences by Martin and his co-stars, including Bernadette Peters and Jessica Harper. The Depression-era story is pointedly down-beat, and the movie is tough on multiple viewings, because the excitement of the inventive fantasies recedes as the pall of the narrative becomes more readily anticipated. Ultimately, though, the film is salvaged by Willis' photography, which is so rich and varied that the viewer is bonded to the film. The songs are also tireless.

PENTHOUSE LOVE STORIES

The single-sided, hour-long collection of erotic interludes, *Penthouse Video Love Stories*, is often blurry or gauzy. The stereo marking on the jacket refers to one or two rock songs on the soundtrack, as the rest is decidedly monaural. The disc is analog, and often accompanied by hums and other noise.

Chapter markers are provided for each of the twelve pieces. Some venture into the border area between hard softcore and soft hardcore and most lack dialog. There is one sequence, however, entitled 'Stripping in the Streets,' in which a man with a camera crew approaches a woman in a park in Santa Monica during mid-day and talks her into taking her clothing off. It is difficult to tell whether the piece is real or a put-on, but it doesn't matter, because it is superbly executed and seems real, which is the important thing. The woman's personality and uninhibited nature make the sequence free spirited and surprisingly nonexploitive.

PENTHOUSE VIDEO: ON THE WILD SIDE

A collection of erotic sequences without dialog are compiled in *Penthouse Video: On the Wild Side*, an hour-long CLV disc which is similar in content to *Penthouse Video Love Stories*. Although not listed on the jacket, the disc has ten chapters. Along with the vaguely plotted couplings, there are two segments of interest. A contrived view of the widely published still photos from Madonna's art school days, and a behind-the-scenes look at the filming of *Caligula*.

The source material is already past its prime and the transfer hasn't done anything to prevent it from looking worn and blurry. The digitally sound is fairly noisy, and the analog track is worse.

PEOPLE, PLACES, THINGS NO. 1 – FLIGHT OF THE DREAM TEAM

The subject of *People, Places, Things No. 1 – Flight of the Dream Team* is parachuting. The program is 30 minutes long, on a single-sided CAV disc. It has 10 chapters of skydiving stunts, a digitally encoded musical score and 500 still photos.

Some of the material is amazing. One segment shows close to a hundred skydivers linking together to form what looks like a gigantic, airborne drink coaster. They then shoot off in every direction to pull their ripcords. There is a woman alone in the air (if you forget that someone is filming her), performing ballet turns and spins in the ultimate of freedom and privacy. There are also the crazies, jumping off buildings and cliffs, or sharing parachutes. The CAV functions allow you to watch all the stunts in reverse, showing how parachutists can return to the plane if they forget something.

The disc has no narration and very little supplementary information to go with the images. The music score is bland, but it is cute, because it matches eras of blandness to the age of the footage – the older material is accompanied by a kind of psychedelic shuffle, while recent sequences have a New Wave bent. The sound transfer is very good, and the analog track is only slightly less defined than the digital track.

In motion sequences, two still frames out of every five jiggle when CAV functions are employed. This is mildly disrupting when a viewer wishes to slow the rate of descent. The picture looks terrific. The older footage is grainy, but that just makes it look more daring. The 'Dream Team' sequences are colorful and sharp.

The 500 still frames at the conclusion of the disc have no flaws, but that segment is the disc's one real disappointment. Most of the stills are just reiterations of the motion sequences, and where this section ought to be supplying the educational/background information in support of the rest of the program on the disc, it is instead an uninteresting repetition of what has already been seen.

PERFECT

Carly Simon has the right idea early on when she splashes tomato juice on John Travolta in *Perfect*. The movie could use a few hurled vegetables.

What does the disc have to offer? A very strong bass on side three (the movie goes on and on and on). An aerobics scene with Travolta and Jamie Lee Curtis in exercise outfits which will have you rushing to cover the eyes of all youngsters within view of the TV. The oft-used plot has Travolta, as a reporter, choosing between his conscience and his desire to get the story. The actresses – Curtis as the superstar instructor, Anne De Salvo as a press photographer, and Laraine Newman as a health club groupie – give excellent performances, but Travolta looks relieved when he finally dons his exercising togs and no longer has to pretend to be thinking.

THE PERFECT BODY CONTEST

Vestron and Image have released a single-sided, 58-minute disc entitled *The Perfect Body Contest*. The picture has a video tape source and looks sharp, but it seems a bit dark. The monaural sound may be digitally encoded, but the dynamic range is as limp as the MC's jokes. Ten chapters are encoded on the disc and are listed on the back of the jacket as follows: "1. Sugar Ray, 2. Lisa, 3. Lonnie, 4. Charlene, 5. Christy, 6. Becky, 7. Cindy, 8. Susie, 9. Jennifer, 10. Tabatha." Charlene wins. See, now you don't have to watch the disc.

PERFECT WITNESS

Brian Dennehy and Stockard Channing give super performances as coldhearted prosecutors who put the squeeze on an innocent witness (Aidan Quinn) in order to break open a racketeering case in *Perfect Witness*. The film is as much about manipulating people as it is about crime, but it has a nice final twist and if you can tolerate a few farfetched plot elements, the emotional payoffs are worthwhile. The picture is mildly grainy and there is a workable stereo surround soundtrack.

THE PERILS OF GWENDOLINE IN THE LAND OF THE YIK YAK

The director of the tediously stupid *The Perils of Gwendoline in the Land of the Yik Yak*, Just Jaeckin, once made better erotic X-rated feature films. In trying to make a movie where everyone sort of keeps their clothing on, however, Jaeckin has a lot to learn. The story is based upon a French comic strip and the movie in many ways is like *Barbarella*, but Jaeckin jumps so quickly from one set to the next that you never believe it is taking place outside of a soundstage, even during the outdoor scenes. Children sometimes find movies like this to be entertaining, but this film has too many incidents of blatant violence and carnage to be shown to little ones. It is too stupid to be shown to anyone else.

PERSISTENCE OF VISION VOLUME ONE: MONITORING THE MEDIA
PERSISTENCE OF VISION VOLUME TWO: OUTSIDE THE LINES
PERSISTENCE OF VISION VOLUME THREE: NEW NARRATIVE

An alternative to standard audio/video entertainment is available in the anthology series of video artworks entitled *Persistence of Vision. Volume One: Monitoring the Media* is a collection of nine works by seven different artists. The pieces share a common theme, examining the medium of television. *Volume Three: New Narrative* has eight works, each by a different artist. The disc emphasizes works in which narrative structure was a central concern of the artist.

The discs have chapter markers and are in CAV. The sound on the pieces varies between monaural and stereo, and the discs are not CX-encoded. The quality of the image also varies from piece to piece, with the newer work looking fresher than the older pieces. The still frame flicker is kept to a minimum when CAV functions are utilized.

Avoid reading the back of the jackets on either disc, at least until you have seen the works themselves. The first priority of video art is to entertain, to hold one's attention and sway one's emotions. The first priority in writing about video art, however, is to wax philosophically about the intentions of the artists, as if there were some sort of common handbook of rules, conventions, and metaphysical quandaries which the artists regularly and almost measurably address. For example, on *New Narrative*, the jacket description of William Wegman's enjoyable 'Dogs (Back and Forth)' goes as follows, "'Dogs (Back and Forth)' focuses on two dogs who obey an invisible guide which choreographs them in a synchronized unison. Wegman's humorous vignette at its heart is a story of loyalty." As is clear in the video itself, the gaze of the two dogs, who otherwise remain still, is following a hand holding an old tennis ball. It is amusing, and can probably serve as an example of curiosity, stupidity, or even loyalty, but ultimately, it is just a lengthy shot of a couple of dogs, and to say it is more than that is to admire an emperor's new wardrobe.

The video works on *New Narratives* are generally relaxing and enjoyable (the collection in *Monitoring the Media* is more challenging). There is a New Wave opera, 'Possibly in Michigan,' about a pair of women who are followed by a strange man, and an almost conventional tale, 'The Woman Who Went Too Far,' about a weathergirl who runs with the wrong crowd. There is also a documentary with a catchy musical score, 'L.A. Nickel,' about the goings on at a street corner in LA. The rest are more obscure in purpose, but contain images which leave a viewer with thoughts and emotions long after they have concluded. The simplest is 'Der Westen Lebt,' interposing shots of a speeding locomotive's wheels with split second shots of a couple embracing. 'Le Train,' 'Accidents in the Home,' and 'Chanoyu' manipulate the speed and placement of images to corrupt the reality of otherwise placid scenes. Each work has a few visual surprises that encourage multiple run throughs.

The standout work in *Monitoring the Media* is an amazing combination of self-control and bad taste entitled 'The Eternal Frame.' It is about a reenactment of the Kennedy assassination in Dallas, and maintains a constant balance between an awareness on the part of the filmmakers that what they are doing is pathetic (in effect, they make a movie about themselves) and the elaborate means by which they accomplish their goal. The piece does everything a modern work of art is supposed to do, rearranging the way a viewer thinks about the world. Because it is both disgusting and funny, both raw and elaborately processed, and both utterly vulgar and highly sophisticated, no one can watch it without being affected by its audacity.

Ronald Reagan was an easy target for video artists, not only because of the raw material he provided, but because he fairly obviously represented, through his own background in the broadcast and film industry, the victory of television in defining and guiding our society. Two pieces on *Monitoring the Media* utilize Reagan imagery. 'The President's World' takes the easy shot, interposing clips from his portrayal of the young George Armstrong Custer in *Santa Fe Trail* with his later public pronouncements and military adventures. 'Excerpts and Euphoria' has more complicated goals as it uses several screens within screens to show the Hinckley assassination attempt and the news fallout which continued for months after the event.

Three blackout sketches about television by Ilene Segalove are scattered through the disc. They might have been more effective if they had been presented together. Another piece, 'Composite News Composite,' is little more than an excuse to show off a gimmick, the 'averaging' of several faces to create a single, composite visage. 'Three Transitions' is also a gimmick work, as the artist manipulates his own image with the help of video technology.

The one other work on the disc, 'Television Delivers People' is simply a text scroll on a blue background, set to innocuous but sprightly background music. The text, however, is about the power of broadcast television, and although the arguments are diminished by the growth of cable TV and the weakening of the network monopoly, the central thesis, that television delivers consumers to advertisers and not vice versa, is thought provoking. It is the sort of thing that one wishes pirates would spike the airwaves with, since it can potentially rouse more rabble than porno clips.

By far the strongest of the three *Persistence of Vision* anthologies released by Voyager, *Volume Two: Outside the Lines* contains a number of short works which are highly entertaining and skillful. Unlike *Volume One* and *Volume Three*, none of the pieces on the hour-long CAV disc are of questionable value.

Most of the works successfully integrate the electronic manipulation of images and sounds with provocative subject matter. Among the most simple are 'postcards' by Cahen, Huter and Longuet which start to move as one stares at them. Other short pieces included 'East/ West,' by Su-Chen Hung, which depicts two halves of a mouth speaking two different languages (which can be subverted by isolating the audio channel – on the whole, however, the use of CAV and other user manipulations seems too much like cheating); 'Videoflashes,' by Michel Jaffrennou, depicting a woman boiling meat inside her television set; and 'Fetishistic Scopophilia,' by Alicia Nogueira, depicting a group of fish swimming outside of a fashion video.

'The Space Between the Teeth,' by Bill Viola, is a highly amusing portrait of a man sitting in a chair, screaming at random intervals. 'Ich Mache die Schmerz-Probe,' by Marcel Odenback, is less inspired, mixing images of weights being lifted with sounds of stress, music, and other miscellaneous footage. In 'Sunstone,' Ed Emshwiller coaxes faces and pieces of faces out of different materials. 'Arcade,' by Lyn Blumenthal and Carol Ann Klondarides with Ed Paschke, is an elaborate collage of contemporary images, some spruced up with an electronic paintbox, which moves to a fast paced rhythm. Rhythm is everything in 'Ear to the Ground,' the crowd-pleasing finale on the disc. The video, by John Sanborn and Kit Fitzgerald with David van Tiegham, shows Tiegham tapping a number of different structures in lower Manhattan with a pair of drumsticks. Some of the percussions he discovers during his exploration are surprising.

More so than its two companion volumes, the disc supplies the sort of program material which people normally envision when they hear the term, 'video art.' This is especially true of the finest piece on the disc, 'Sabda,' by Dan Reeves. 'Sabda' begins with breathtaking images of what appears to be India, and imposes electronic image manipulations to enhance the emotional impact of each vision. Text from Hindu poems scroll across the screen and incidental sounds fill the audio track. Unlike some of the other works on the disc, Reeves' initial footage would be stunning even if he had left it alone. The enhancements serve as accents and punctuations which organize and magnify the poverty, the spirituality, and the life in the things he has seen. His choices show that he understands not only the world around him, but, equally, his own psyche.

PERSONAL SERVICES

In the same way that athletes have not yet approached the limits of human capability in most sporting activities – which is why records continue to fall – movies have yet to come close to tapping the true dramatic and comic potential of sex. The funniest parts of *Personal Services*, a comedy about a bordello in London, occur when the characters talk about or display sex with limited euphemism. You realize that you hardly ever hear people talking like that on the screen and much of the humor is from the shock of hearing such language come out of your TV set.

The monaural film is difficult to understand at first because of the British accents, and the soundtrack, which is rough and noisy, doesn't help matters. The print clearly suffers from budgetary limitations all the way down the line, although some may argue that the display of sex still requires an environment like that to appear legitimate.

PETE TOWNSHEND WHITE CITY THE MUSIC MOVIE

We have sat through enough novella-length conceptual video programs by rock stars to expect the worst and thus we were pleasantly surprised by the intelligence of *Pete Townshend White City The Music Movie*. Townshend's bright concept is to appear as a narrator/observer and let someone else (Andrew Wilde) portray the put-upon central character, thus eliminating all the aspects of narcissism which plagued shows such as *The Wall*, *Jazzin' for Blue Jean*, et cetera.

Townshend's music sounds great. The quality of the picture is only fair (old film stock aside), but this seems to be more of a fault with the print than with the disc. The stereo is always good on productions like this since so many sound-oriented artists are involved with its creation. The single sided disc has no chapter markers.

'The Making of White City' is included at the end and once again we were surprised by the truly intelligent commentary Pete Townshend provided. His talk about how he came to make the video covers the same ground other rock stars have trod, but Townshend is able to explain his motivations in a way which shows that he understands the artistic process. He has put his understanding to good use.

PETER BROOK'S THE MAHABHARATA (Import)

Peter Brook's The Mahabharata is based on a key epic legend of the Indian subcontinent, compiled in its most common formation some 3500 years ago. Brook adapted a good chunk of it as a nine-hour stage work featuring an international cast. He then filmed the production on an enclosed soundstage for the movies and for television. The film version lasts three hours and the TV version runs six television hours which actually logs closer to five in real time. It is this TV version which has been released on the import disc, together with an hour long 'Making of' documentary, in a seven-sided four-platter set that comes in the classiest, sturdiest box jacket we have ever seen used for laser discs.

It is often the case that when mythological epics are adapted as dramatic works they tend to be superficial historical exercises, concentrating upon bullet-point events and overly god-like cut-out characters. *The Mahabharata* seems to begin in that manner, but once the show settles on the principal narrative – the story of five royal brothers outcast by their cousin – the work suddenly achieves both a scope and a pace conducive to exploring the deepest conflicts in human character. It is also a terrific soap opera, and is presented in a very Western manner, down to a suppression of the traditional toy-like Indian colors, which have been replaced by a multitude of muddy browns.

The documentary is a nice supplementary feature (a booklet also comes with the disc, but it is in Japanese) which details how Brook came to create the production and provides a few different ways in which a viewer can approach the work.

The picture transfer is spotless. The sound is mildly stereophonic and thoroughly supportive. The documentary is monaural and both the picture and the sound are in a slightly rougher state. The entire disc is in English and has Japanese subtitles which we rarely noticed. A viewer will be vaguely aware of the subplots dropped to shorten the work – there are a few loose ends – and it is a shame the full nine-hour presentation has not been preserved for the screen.

PETER PAN

Back when video was a much simpler concept NBC broadcast a modified version of the stage musical, *Peter Pan*, starring Mary Martin. Although certain to be imbedded as a black and white production in the heads of those old enough to have seen one of the original yearly broadcasts, someone had the prescience to videotape the show in color. The colors are really only hints of colors, as the equipment used was fairly primitive by today's standards, yet the image presented on the disc, colors aside, is probably the same image which is preserved in one's memory – soft edges, contrast levels set so high you can almost count the different tones on one hand, and Martin's beaming grin. The sound has been 'Stereo Enhanced,' but the effect never distorts what is already a somewhat rickety soundtrack and, instead, gives the audio a little more stability and fullness.

One will likely be tempted, and we would encourage it, to hit 'pause' at every blackout (signifying a commercial break). Not only are the performances, when taken in the right frame of mind, good fun, but the choreography is accomplished, the music is memorable, the lyrics are catchy, and the story has just the right mix of playful absurdity and veiled meaning. The musical is wonderful, but it revels in the artifice of the stage and in the delightful exuberance of exaggerated stage performances geared, to an extent, toward children. A mild breather between each act will assist in putting the program in perspective, and will stretch the pleasure it provides.

PETER TOSH – LIVE

Despite his flowing robes and dreadlocks, Peter Tosh has a fairly businesslike approach to his music. Fortunately, the other members of his band act a little looser. In the beginning of *Peter Tosh – Live* you can barely tell it is him singing. The sound comes out while his lips barely move. He plays ten songs on the 59-minute concert disc, including a reggae rendition of 'Johnny B. Goode' which sounds like a 45 being played at 33 1/3. The picture is grainy but the CX-encoded stereo is fine and there is so little reggae available on laser that we will take it any way we can get it.

PETER GUNN VOLUME 1

Blake Edwards directed three of the four episodes on *Peter Gunn Volume 1*. The half hour programs are by necessity short on plot, but they are filled with mood and character, and make good entertainment. The disc is gorgeous. There are two episodes on each side, marked by chapters, and a brief opening sequence. The full opening and closing credits for each episode are included. The black and white source material has a very sharp focus and an image which is free of blemishes. The sound is set a little low, making some of the dialog difficult to follow, but there is Henry Mancini's expressionistic musical score which, beyond the annoying opening theme (You've heard it: 'Daaaaaaa da, daaaaaaa di da,' etc.), is an important component of the drama.

The programs follow a fairly strict format, though by the same token they are also quite varied. It was probably the only television show to come out of the fifties where the characters look like they are fondling one another just out of camera range. There is a quick murder before the opening credits. Gunn, played a little too woodenly by Craig Stevens, is called in and conducts an investigation which plays loop-de-loop with a police inquiry. The combination of both efforts is required to solve the case, usually with Gunn acting as a catalyst, and there is a quick fight/action sequence before the finale.

In 'Rough Buck' a prize fighter is murdered and Gunn interviews his way to the solution. The narrative has little forward movement and too many two shots. 'The Chinese Hangman' is much better. A religious cult leader asks Gunn to track down a woman, and Gunn ends up going to Paris and Spain in order to find her. Edwards' sense of economy and his ability to tell a story visually – although there is substantial voice-over – pack a considerable amount of entertainment into a brief half hour fling. Another strong episode is 'Death House Testament,' in which Gunn is abducted and drugged for information he does not possess. His method of escape is clever and the episode even includes a brief dream sequence. In 'Skin Deep,' which was directed by Boris Sagal, Gunn tricks a murderer into revealing where the body has been hidden. The episode is brisk and well executed.

PHANTASM II

In *Phantasm II*, a pair of men chase after a mysterious being who is digging up graveyards and destroying small towns in eastern Oregon. The script is a bit abstract, but unlike the first *Phantasm*, which was abstract because of inept scripting, there is a deliberateness in the dream-like mood of the sequel. The film, however, is neither scary nor horrific enough to warrant much attention.

The disc has a few interesting stereo effects. The picture is slightly blurry, but passable. There is a gag in the fine print at the end of the credits if your video monitor is large enough to make it legible.

THE PHANTOM OF LIBERTY
(see **THE DISCREET CHARM OF THE BOURGEOISE**)

PHANTOM OF THE MALL: ERIC'S REVENGE

Eric was just about to get it on with his girlfriend when mall developers set fire to his house. Everyone thought he died, but now his girlfriend is working in the mall and a mysterious figure is crawling about in the rafters, watching over her in *Phantom of the Mall: Eric's Revenge*. The film lacks humor or ingenuity, but there are a couple of cute murders. The picture transfer is accurate, but the film is a low budget effort that was shot fuzzy. The sound lacks pizzazz. The movie was made in Promenade Mall in Woodland Hills, California and Sherman Oaks Galleria.

PHANTOM OF THE PARADISE

Phantom of the Paradise is a cult movie which is ideal for multiple viewings and perfect disc material. Unfortunately, the picture transfer is only fair, with blurry colors which often excede their boundaries. The sound is digitally enocded, but the analog track comes across more sharply. The disc is also insufficiently chapter encoded.

The film is both a celebration and a parody of pop music, epitomized by the charming comical performance of Paul Williams. Directed by Brian DePalma, it mixes both *The Phantom of the Opera* and 'Faust,' with allusions to dozens of films and other errata thrown in for good measure. The story is intentionally comical and, admittedly, some of the jokes, about drugs and about flamboyant behavior, are dated. But DePalma's flashy visual storytelling is well suited for disc, as is the film's strongest component, the musical score. Williams's music is supposed to lampoon various genres of rock and roll, but in lowering his defenses against cliché he freed the shackles on his creativity, which had always been affixed to cliché, anyway. Although the songs have different styles and tempos, they all reinforce the 'Faust' theme, and the repeated phrases (both lyrical and musical) come to the fore in the three love ballads. These songs are not intended to be humorous (although the manner in which the cast performs them is often blatantly amusing) and add the soul which romance adds to comedy.

PHANTOM OF THE OPERA

Our favorite part of the LumiVision George Eastman House release of the 1925 *Phantom of the Opera* is the copious chapter listing on the back of the jacket, which uses Roman numerals. The packaging of the disc is exemplary. It comes in a gatefold jacket, which contains an excellent essay by Scott

MacQueen on the history of the film.

The audio presentation contains not only a Wurlitzer organ score and a few sound effects, but an overly eager collection of audience reaction sounds, which tend to undercut, instead of enhance, the fun the movie has to offer. The sound is digitally encoded and stereophonic, but it is best left at a low volume, not because of its quality but because of its content.

The narrative is jumbled, particularly in the beginning, but when the drama finally settles down it is enjoyable, and the Phantom's demise is a classic gag which has never been duplicated. The source material swings wildly in quality, as the various notations on its history attest. Some scenes are nearly opaque, while others are vivid and brilliantly detailed. Side two is in CAV, with some unsteady still frames during the first minutes and none thereafter.

PHANTOM OF THE OPERA

Those who enjoy gorgeous Technicolor prints, no matter what the movie is, will want to gobble up the 1943 *Phantom of the Opera*. We thought the color looked great, until we saw the trailer at the end of side two, which is even more stunning. With Technicolor, the pleasure doesn't just come from the vivid colors. It is the way that the colors are separated. There is no bleeding or blending between a hue and the hue which borders it. Every variation stands by itself on the screen.

It all looks so good that, in the case of *Phantom*, the whole movie seems inspired. This remake, with Claude Rains in the title role, is not well scripted. The characters have only superficial relationships with one another and little motivation for their actions. But the disc is so well done that the story never becomes tedious. You're on edge the whole time, not so much wondering where the Phantom will strike next as what the set and costumes will look like when he arrives. Or how it all will sound. The disc has been digitally encoded and for a WWII era film, the sound is superb.

PHENOMENA (Import)

Dario Argento's *Phenomena*, available on disc in Japan, was released theatrically in the United States some 20 minutes shorter under the title, 'Creepers.' The story, about a girl who has a strong empathy with insects and is being shadowed by a psychotic killer, is full of dizzying plot twists and gruesome murders. Lots of rotting flesh and lots of maggots appear, so it is best not to watch the film after a big dinner. Argento also includes a tribute to *Friday the 13th*, but his efforts so outclass the latter that it is a wonder why he bothered.

The movie is in English. The image is scanned and cropped, and Japanese subtitles hang down both the left and right of the screen, depending upon where they are least distracting. We didn't notice them too often, since most of the time we were hiding under our couch. When we did peek, we noted the picture quality was okay, but not pristine.

The analog stereo sound is marvelous. In some cases the footsteps and the voices are so realistic we had to cover both our eyes and our ears. Argento's editing is merciless. He never lets you relax or feel assured about a character's surroundings. Some horror movies have dream sequences which provide an excuse to show a little more gore. The dream sequences in *Phenomena* turn out to be real.

PHIL COLLINS

The 8-inch *Phil Collins* improves with multiple viewings. His music is very intelligent and the videos are thought-provoking. The last number, a schizophrenic version of the Supremes' 'You Can't Hurry Love,' may even induce home viewers to stand and applaud. The picture and sound are fine.

PHIL COLLINS – LIVE AT PERKINS PALACE

We have intentionally defamed Phil Collins on several occasions and have no interest in repeating ourselves while reviewing *Phil Collins – Live at Perkins Palace*, except to mention that the stubble on his cheeks and chin grow noticeable during the course of his 55-minute concert. In the first shot of him, his face is pale and smooth. By the last shot his face is a dirty gray and you could probably strike matches on it if there wasn't so much sweat.

Collins uses a great amount of energy in his concert performance, on the drums, on the keyboard, and singing. The disc has a clean picture and good sound. The camera work brings the viewer as close to Collins as one would wish to go. The performance is boisterous and live while still being intimate. 'Through These Walls' sounds especially impressive, though he had to put on a bathrobe and lie down on the stage to get into the mood. If method acting helps a rock star get inside his material, so be it.

THE PHILADELPHIA STORY

Jimmy Stewart explained some of the advantages of working under the studio system in the talk he gave on *Winchester '73*, but direct evidence is available in *The Philadelphia Story*. Stewart's role is secondary, although he seems to have as much screen time as Katharine Hepburn and maybe even more than Cary Grant, and his personality does not completely fit that of his character's, so much so that if he had not been under contract with the studio it is doubtful he would have had the part. The result, however, is that you don't become impatient waiting for Grant to come back on the screen. There is a lengthy, inebriated scene between Hepburn and Stewart which could have become very tiresome if a lesser talent were filling the role.

The black-and-white source material has a few scratches, at least one splice, and speckles here and there, but it will do. The CX-encoded monaural sound is pleasing in the way that it seems to accurately preserve the recording capabilities of the era.

For those who are unfamiliar with the work, allow us to say that it is based on a very witty play and has an elaborate construction which generates one amusing moment after another. Hepburn has rarely seemed as radiantly romantic and Grant is in top form. Stewart is a bonus, and all the more reason to get the disc.

PHILIP PEARLSTEIN DRAWS THE ARTIST'S MODEL

Philip Pearlstein Draws the Artist's Model clarifies what an interactive program should provide to a consumer because it functions on more than just one knowledge or entertainment level. The program can be shaped to one's interests and can be approached for alternate uses if one's mood or needs should change.

Pearlstein is a major contemporary artist who paints what appears to be a singular subject – nudes on furniture in unusual but realistic perspectives. He also teaches life drawing at Brooklyn College. The video portions of the disc, which have a well employed dual audio soundtrack, observe and listen to Pearlstein in both the studio and the classroom. Lessons in technique, and a thorough collection of the works he has created, appear on still frames to punctuate the different video chapters (there are 43 chapter markers).

In summary, the disc serves as a succinct history in the concepts of art across the last 2000 years; a full-fledged lesson in creating perspective; a whole collection of lessons in life drawing (obliquely erotic nudity is present throughout the disc) including models who can be still-stepped on a rotating turntable so that the rendering angle is your choice; an excellent summary of impressionist and cubist theory; and a complete, if guarded, look at the maturation of a single contemporary artist, Pearlstein.

The colors are perfect, but still frame video sequences of the models occasionally quivered.

PHYSICAL EVIDENCE

The crime thriller, *Physical Evidence*, is easy-going and enjoyable. Burt Reynolds stars as a cop framed for a murder and Theresa Russell is a public defender who doesn't completely believe he's innocent. Without sacrificing the drama, the script contains a number of lightly humorous touches. Russell is especially enjoyable. Glamorous and professional in the courtroom, her entire composure goes soggy when she's at home and out of the public eye. Less advantage is taken of Reynolds' character. He appears to know exactly what ought to be done, but the plot never calls him on it. The final struggle, however, is perfectly conceived and upsets what one realizes is a tremendously imbedded cliché.

The skin tones are a little pink, but the picture looks sharp. The film's sound editing is dopey. Russell's character lives in a fancy high tech apartment, yet there's a ticking clock on the soundtrack in one of the night scenes. Not likely, from the looks of the all-electronic decor. Over all, the stereo sound is not elaborate.

PHYSICS OF SPORTS

The first physics-oriented educational discs took stabs at utilizing the CAV format's constant of 30 frames per second to enable students to measure the time and distance of moving objects. Videodiscovery's *Physics of Sports*, however, uses that concept in dozens of demonstrations. A student with a piece of acetate to place over the video screen can trace and calculate the speed and efficiency of the human body in activities as varied as shot putting and wheelchair racing.

Data collection, however, is not the only function of the disc. Divided into chapters such as 'Linear Motion in Sports,' 'Projectiles in Sports,' 'Energy Transformations, 'Momentum,' 'Forces in Sports,' and 'Modelling Human Motion,' the disc provides material and guidance for investigating such concepts as center of mass, work and energy, acceleration, and the conservation of energy. The efficiency of different bow designs can be accurately measured in an archery demonstration. By using acetate to trace stick figures, students can scientifically compare the techniques of trained and untrained athletes in the acts of jumping, putting, etc., and provide suggestions for improving the performances of the untrained athletes, based purely on the physical laws governing the body's movements. By measuring the distance covered from one frame to the next, the acceleration and deceleration of hurdlers can be carefully tracked.

The disc is great fun. Although students would eventually have to shovel through the mathematical formulas to fully appreciate the lessons, the basic concepts are taught and reinforced with clarity. For example, the center of mass of an axe is marked with a bright piece of tape. The axe is then thrown at a target. Although it spins wildly in the air, using still step on the throw reveals that the axe's center of mass followed a perfect arc to the bull's eye.

The sound is decent and the picture is accurate enough to facilitate on-screen measurements. A student guide and a teacher's guide accompany the disc and provide a satisfying amount of supplementary information. The disc is priced for the educational market.

PICASSO (Import)
An 85-minute documentary about the development of Pablo Picasso's painting styles has been released in Japan on laser disc in CAV. It is called *Picasso*. Although the text on the outer jacket cover is in English, the dual audio disc is in Japanese and French. The documentary was made by the French filmmaker, Didier Baussy, utilizing the collection placed on display for the opening of the Musee Picasso in Paris, including 'Guernica.'

The film moves in relatively chronological order, examining paintings two or three at a time, from each of Picasso's periods. The narration talks about the paintings and the periods while the film intercuts closeups of the paintings with the images which led to their development. In other words, there is a lot of bullfighting footage.

The disc is digitally encoded and the dual audio feature does not work correctly on the digital track. The Japanese narration can be effectively isolated, but when playing the French narration is attempted, the Japanese remains louder. The analog tracks work correctly.

The way to really understand Picasso's later works is to follow the train of thought which travels through his career. When you view his works in succession it is easy to comprehend the motives behind his experimentation and the brilliance with which he executed his new ideas. The disc is not a definitive survey of his work, but if the narration is ever made available in English, it will be a useful starting point.

THE PICK-UP ARTIST
James Toback started out by making laughable thrillers, but he finally got smart and made a comedy thriller, instead. *The Pick-Up Artist* is his most tolerable movie to date, though it still has a few rough edges and may turn off those who are not totally enamored of its star, Molly Ringwald.

Ringwald portrays a girl whose father owes money to a mobster. She is pestered and ultimately rescued by a shallow but earnest make-out artist, played by Robert Downey. Unlike some teen stars, Ringwald has not lost the timing in her delivery as she matures. Working with Toback usually separates real actors from imposters, sometimes painfully, but she slides through the project as if it were just another formula vehicle to display her charms. The movie isn't great, but it has one or two sweet moments. The disc is in an acceptable condition. Nothing is overtly wrong with the picture, and the stereo sound has a nice atmosphere.

PICNIC AT HANGING ROCK (Import)
We first saw *Picnic at Hanging Rock* in London a couple of years before it opened in the United States and came away feeling that we had just been through one of the most unusual and different movies we had ever seen.

The Japanese disc of *Picnic at Hanging Rock* runs 115 minutes. The American film version ran 110. We still remember two scenes which were missing from the American version and are missing here. In one, the young rich boy and the young chauffeur, fairly drunk, tell each other that they know what happened to the missing girls. It was a cumulatively ambiguous scene which seemed to capture the essence of the whole film. The other was the ending, which had the Rock disappear in the mist the way it appears in the opening, *High Plains Drifter*-style. What is present on the disc but missing from the American version we cannot say, except to state that the disappointment we felt when we rushed to the movie again after it opened here is abated. The disc gives us the complex rush of emotional confusion from which the American film release had cheated us.

Except for the bright, white Japanese subtitles, the transfer is gorgeous. The complexions on the cheeks of the schoolgirls tell everything the dialog later reveals about their personalities.

Like the rest of the movie, the soundtrack has many subtle effects and the level of noise interferes with attempts to push the volume.

Weir uses many quotations from literature during the film, but they succeed because the atmosphere he creates is mysterious enough to accommodate putting on airs. One of the teenaged schoolgirls, in the sleepy aftermath of a picnic lunch, reads from a book, "Shall I compare thee to a summer's day..." while visually, her innocence and beauty have no equal. Weir opens the film with lines from Edgar Allan Poe in voiceover, "Is all we see or seem, but a dream within a dream?" It is immensely clear that, probably from the day he was old enough to read, Weir's favorite poem is likely another offering from Poe, 'Ulalume.'

THE PICTURE OF DORIAN GRAY
Oscar Wilde threw many veils over Dorian's immoral immortality and the 1945 film, *The Picture of Dorian Gray*, adds even more. It becomes difficult to track each character's suicide or despondency. The text on the jacket cover gets it wrong when it says that the movie is "one film that, like its hero, looks better with each passing year." It isn't that he looks better, it is that he doesn't change at all and the movie, with its dated sexual innuendo, still looks like a 1940s film.

The show is in black-and-white except for the portrait which, though not consistently, is shown in color. The print is fresh. The sound has no problems, either. We shall wait to see if the disc, like Dorian, retains its freshness through the passage of time.

PIERROT LE FOU
Typical of Jean-Luc Godard's work in the sixties, *Pierrot le Fou* is playful and irreverent, as the actors, Jean-Paul Belmondo and Anna Karina, pretend, on and off, to be gangsters, while the world around them generally pays no attention. There are constant digressions, in which the pair read literary quotations or comment philosophically on modern life, and there is also running commentary on the US involvement in Vietnam. The gangster play-acting, which sometimes includes a corpse or two, is parodistic enough that the humor generated from it provides the film with its cohesion. The quotations and philosophical treatises are so well chosen that the passages retain their relevancy as time passes, providing a stronger counterbalance to the humor than the sophomoric gags used to fill the gaps in most parodies.

The disc has been letterboxed, with an aspect ratio of about 2.1:1. The widescreen is constantly utilized in many imaginative ways and the film would be helpless without it. White English subtitles appear on the image and are sometimes difficult to follow, especially on a smaller monitor. The color transfer is slightly pale, but the source material seems to be in usable shape. The monaural sound is worth amplifying because Godard's sound editing is as tricky as his film editing. For those unfamiliar with the movie, the volume dropouts are deliberate.

PIN
A mad ventriloquist movie which makes *Magic* look like Shari Lewis and Lambchop, *Pin* has been done a disservice by its jacket art. The artwork and copy imply that the film is a horror effects effort, when in fact the violence in the psychological thriller is minimal, and a need for effects is non-existent.

The first half hour is especially good. A young boy growing up in a strict household develops a fixation on a mannequin in his father's office. When he becomes an adult, the fixation turns into schizophrenia. Even when the story settles into its primary exposition, the clichés of other such movies are avoided. The characters who come into contact with the protagonist know that he is mad, they just don't realize that he is dangerous.

The jacket cover does even more disservice by indicating that the film is monaural when in fact it is in digital stereo surround. The soundtrack is not elaborate, but it contributes to the film's unnerving atmosphere. The picture transfer is good, too, though the film's look never exceeds its budget.

THE PIN-UP GIRL/DOWN ARGENTINE WAY
The films may seem like trifles, but CBS/Fox has gussied up two Betty Grable movies, *The Pin-Up Girl/Down Argentine Way*, putting them together on a three sided 'Betty Grable

Double Feature' disc package which is difficult to resist. The color transfers are gorgeous, and the original monaural soundtracks have been manipulated to create a passable stereo surround. The movies strengthen each other's appeal as well, since the viewer will likely not have had enough by the time either one is ended.

The color transfer of 'Down Argentine Way' is fantastic. The fleshtones are rich, the costumes are luscious, and even the outdoor stock footage is incredibly vivid. The colors look great on 'The Pin-Up Girl' as well, although, at least partially because of the cinematography, the quality is less consistent. The color highpoint of the disc, however, is the musical number in 'The Pin-Up Girl,' 'Red Robins, Bob Whites and Bluebirds.'

The sound on both films is a Chace Surround Stereo effort, the process which was also used on *Bambi*. Sometimes the separations get a little too carried away, but the soundtrack can always be played back monaurally if the viewer is bothered by the effects. The music takes on a dimensionality, the bass has more strength, and the essence of the original soundtrack is preserved and clarified.

The movies are both musicals in which the plot is a minor inconvenience strung between the song and dance numbers. In 'Pin-Up Girl' Grable is a stenographer who becomes a popular nightclub singer after she meets a war hero and lies to him about her profession. In 'Argentine Way' she portrays a rich horse fancier chasing after the son (played by Don Ameche) of an Argentine rancher who hates her father. Carmen Miranda sings a couple of numbers in the latter, but it couldn't have taken more than a day to film her set – or two days, one to put on her costume and one to film. ('Down Argentine Way' also contains worse than average negative stereotyping of Hispanic characters.) The legendary Nicolas Brothers appear in 'Argentine Way,' a spectacular skating group, the Skating Vanities, show up in 'Pin-Up Girl,' and throughout both films the dancers and singers are terrific. In both films as well, Grable is wonderful. Her personality carries her through different costumes, different hair styles and different looks without ever losing intimacy with the viewer. Even when the Nicholas Brothers are on, you can't wait for the movie to get back to her.

PINK CADILLAC

Having lowered our expectations suitably, we found that we rather enjoyed the Clint Eastwood movie *Pink Cadillac*. Critics are programmed to dislike such films, but audiences didn't respond to it either, probably because Eastwood's presence in the movie is almost secondary to Bernadette Peters. Even when he is in a scene, he is sort of standing on the side. However, he does give a relaxed and funny performance which seems more realistic than his appearances in a couple of dopier, more popular movies. He tells jokes in character and clowns a bit, but he's smooth when it comes to dispatching the admittedly caricatured bad guys. The picture transfer is okay, though some intense colors look grainy. The stereo sound has intermittent surround effects, but the gunshots sound terrific. The film runs a minute over two hours (gaps in the narrative indicate substantial trimming, especially in the beginning) and is spread evenly to three sides. The plot concerns a skip tracer who falls for his charge and helps her retrieve her kidnapped child.

PINK FLOYD IN CONCERT DELICATE SOUND OF THUNDER

Mark Isham directed *Pink Floyd in Concert Delicate Sound of Thunder* and created a remarkably compelling concert video from a performance by a rock group noted for their somnambulistic orchestrations. Amazingly, Isham remains true to the music. The images, a mixture of performance shots, stage lightshow displays (Pink Floyd bends over backwards in their concerts to prevent their fans from falling asleep, no matter how deep and molassistic their chords), and conceptual imagery (dogs with glowing eyes and the like), are edited to the rhythm of the music and yet are varied sufficiently to hold a viewer's curiosity and attention. There is none of the distortion on the stereo disc which one would normally expect from a live recoring. The show, recorded at the Nassau Coliseum on Long Island, lasts 100 minutes. The picture transfer is decent, and the many smokey lighting effects survive without distortion.

PINK FLOYD LIVE AT POMPEII (Image)
PINK FLOYD LIVE AT POMPEII (Polygram)

One of the better single-group rock films, *Pink Floyd Live at Pompeii*, depicts the group not only in the studio, but set up in an ancient amphitheater, which does little to boost the resonance of their recording, but makes them look impressive. The film, which was made by French and Belgian television interests, is intelligently edited, mixing footage of the musicians with footage of ancient frescoes and bubbling hot springs. The tone is always stimulating and the film never becomes tiresome, although we could have done without the few interviews scattered between each number.

The movie is over fifteen years old and looks a little weary, though not enough to cause problems. The colors on the Polygram disc are more confident and the source material has fewer rough edges. The sound is the same on both discs – good, but unmistakenly fifteen years old.

In one of the interviews, the group members take pains to differentiate themselves from amateurs, and they almost had us convinced that it takes special training and professional musicianship to produce their one-chord-change-in-every-ten-measures style of rock. That was, until near the end, when they incorporate the wailing of a pet dog into one of their songs. Sure, the dog sounds terrific, but we highly doubt that he graduated from Julliard.

PINK NIGHTS

A monaural, CX-encoded, analog, and blurry disc, *Pink Nights* is nevertheless worthy of consideration. The Chicago production is independent in spirit and goes very much against the Hollywood grain. The young cast is inexperienced but delightfully refreshing in appearance. They look like the kids next door instead of like the kids in the slick teen films. The script, which, like the rest of the movie, seems awkward at first, is about a young man in high school who eventually acquires three young ladies as roommates. It is innocent, guilt-free fun and gets its humor from concepts and characters instead of pranks and gags.

PINOCCHIO
(see **FAERIE TALE THEATRE**)

PINOCCHIO
PINOCCHIO (CAV)

We couldn't keep our hands off the still frame function when we started to watch the CAV release of Walt Disney's *Pinocchio*. No frame contains a disruptive jitter.

One of the most interesting effects which has escaped anthologization is the amount of detail and color the artists show or do not show when a figure is moving quickly. They draw the figure fully, and then add colored streaks to indicate the direction of the movement and provide a subliminal illusion of real movement. When the moths flit about Jiminy Cricket, they really do flit, jumping from one side of the screen to the other in each frame.

The animation in *Pinocchio* is so good that you forget you are watching a cartoon. The incredibly accurate depth of field lulls your resistance to the drawings. Although some of the episodes stir feelings of anxiety (or horror for the young), the story is not overly moralistic. The part where Pinocchio's nose reacts to his lies is pushed through quickly and never mentioned again.

The movie is 87 minutes long, but the disc is spread to four sides and the break between the first and second platter is the same as the break between side one and side two on the CLV disc. The quality of the picture and the sound is indistinguishable between the two discs. The only time scratches are in evidence is when they appear on the individual animation cels. The sound on both discs is CX-encoded. The CAV release has 11 chapter markers, which averages to less than three a side. We would have preferred a few more, particularly among the clock displays and the thrills of Pleasure Island.

If your kids seem uninterested in the property, have a party and watch it yourself. Maybe if they see grownups enjoying it they'll be more tempted to check it out.

PINOCCHIO AND THE EMPEROR OFTHE NIGHT

The ad art claims that *Pinocchio and the Emperor of the Night* is a 'continuation of the family classic.' 'Recapitulation' would be more like it. Although the characters are different, the plot devices, moral problems, and anxieties are all the same.

The transfer is nice. The solid, obnoxious colors are well defined, and the image has no difficulties with intense reds or blues. The stereo sound, which includes songs by Rickie Lee Jones, is garish, but is in keeping with the style of the film. The disc also has chapter markers.

The running time is endless for a children's animated feature – 91 minutes. The main problem with the script is that the balance between the bad things which happen and the good or cute things which happen is all wrong, so the movie not only looks awful and sounds awful, but it makes you feel awful, without respite. Neither adults nor kids will enjoy it.

THE PIRATE
The cornucopiately colored Gene Kelly and Judy Garland movie, *The Pirate*, has been released in full splendor. Directed by Vincent Minnelli, every shot in the film is overflowing with bright, energetic hues. The disc handles them well, never destabilizing when a particularly intense shading comes along.

The sound is monaural and has been digitally encoded, although it remains flat and uninspired. The music is by Cole Porter, and his athletic wordplay is the ideal supplement to Gene Kelly's dancing. The disc has only seven chapter markers.

The story, set on a Caribbean island in the Nineteenth Century, involves an unhappy betrothal, a troupe of travelling performers, and an infamous pirate. The narrative is cute enough to provide an excuse for the dancing, as well as for the costumes and set design. Maybe the only reason we hadn't liked the movie was that we had just never seen it on disc before.

THE PIRATES OF PENZANCE
(see **YEOMAN OF THE GUARD**)

PLACES IN THE HEART
(see **THE RIVER**)

PLACIDO DOMINGO – HOMMAGE A SEVILLA
In the hour-long collection of passages from operas localed in Seville, *Placido Domingo – Hommage a Sevilla*, Jean-Pierre Ponnelle uses the location to recreate the drama as well as providing a mood for the music, as if the program consisted of excerpts from a half dozen opera movies he wished he could have made. The collaboration of Domingo and of James Levine, conducting the Vienna Symphony Orchestra, gives the presentation the highest level of quality, but the three never lose sight of their prime motivating factor, the fun they are having. The epitome of this is a duet from 'Barber of Seville,' in which Domingo plays and sings not only Figaro, but Count Almaviva as well, giving himself, at one point, a shave.

The picture quality of the disc is okay, though some of the images are blurred. The sound is excellent and is effectively surround encoded. The songs are not translated on screen, but a libretto is provided on an insert, along with an uninteresting review of the program.

THE PLAINSMAN
We love westerns, but Cecil B. DeMille's *The Plainsman* is too pushy. The black-and-white film is a concoction which is surprisingly short on action or spectacle. In an attempt to create a 'big' story, DeMille calls his characters 'Wild Bill Hickok' and 'Buffalo Bill.' The result, when played by Gary Cooper and James Ellison, is endless exchanges of dialog such as the following: "No, Bill. It's too bad they had to send you. I'm sorry." "But they did, Bill."

The print is rough in places, but looks acceptable. The sound is never a problem. The high point of the disc is an original theatrical trailer at the end of side two. It is a little worse for wear, but greatly entertaining, and ought to be played before the movie, so the viewer will not see through its contrivances.

PLAN NINE FROM OUTER SPACE
Before World War II, there was a group of poets who called themselves 'Surrealists.' They would write down words, drop them into a hat, pull them out randomly, write them down in the order the words came out, and call the works 'poems.' And yet, some of the works, and the way the words fell out with one another, are poems. Thus it is with the random pieces of film which were spliced together to make *Plan Nine from Outer Space*, the best awful, the grandest worst, or the most marvelously stupid movie ever made.

Although it is left unmentioned on the jacket cover, side two is in CAV. You don't get to freeze the scene where an actor, positioned behind a box, reads his lines directly from a script, but you do get to slow down an already lethargic fist fight and examine, at leisure, the paper plate flying saucer catching on fire and exploding.

When taken into consideration that no one knew at the time they were creating what is now recognized as a milestone in cinematic accomplishment, the black-and-white print looks great and the sound isn't too bad. The acting is real bad and the continuity is worse. The dialog is so pathetic it sounds like the way people really talk: "This is the most fantastic story I've ever heard." "And every word of it is true, too." "That's the fantastic part of it."

Constructed from brief footage of Bela Lugosi stalking about in a vampire outfit, made right before he died, and a confused flying saucer zombie story, which was filmed several years afterward, the show lurches from one ineptly staged moment to the next, acquiring, as it moves along, the elegance of an inebriated soul who, for a brief moment, can be mistaken for a dancer. The actor playing a grave digger, for example, drops his shovel the first time he grabs for it, and never seems to be able to hold it properly. When he finally manages to get a little dirt on it, he tosses the few pebbles away from the open grave, rather than on top of the coffin. Incompetence? Perhaps, but does not this inability to bury the dead foreshadow the zombie aspect of the plot as well as Lugosi's contrived presence? *Plan Nine from Outer Space* is a necessary addition to anyone's movie collection, because, in comparison, all the other movies collected will seem like masterpieces.

PLANES, TRAINS, AND AUTOMOBILES
Don't be taken in by the appeal of the two stars, Steve Martin and John Candy, and seriously consider acquiring *Planes, Trains, and Automobiles*. The movie is more painful than humorous, and the script has long gaps in it where nothing works at all. Like the trip depicted, the film just goes on and on and on. (There is even a pointless gag after the end credits have finished scrolling.) The transfer is okay. The picture has a little grain to it, but not much. The sound is fairly effective.

PLANETARY IMAGE VIDEODISC VOL. 1
NASA and the United States Government have produced the *Planetary Image Videodisc Vol. 1*. The images are all black-and-white and the only descriptions provided are the sometimes cryptic code numbers barely discernible along the edges of the photos. The disc contains minimally enhanced images from the Mariner, Viking, and Voyager missions. A few SEASAT images are included at the very end, depicting geological formations on Earth to facilitate comparisons.

Side one has about 50,000 Mariner photographs of the surface of Mars. It is both wonderful and frustrating because the clearer an image is, the more you wish you knew what you were looking at. The disc does contain addresses where one can write for further information. The Mars material, including the thousands of views taken from the Viking Lander which appear on side two, is the most impressive. The Voyager data has been well processed on other discs, so that seeing blurry black-and-white images of the Jovian atmosphere (Saturn is not included) is anticlimactic, especially when there are some 20,000 of them to sift through. Mariner images of Mercury and unphotogenic Venus round out the disc.

PLANETARY IMAGE VIDEODISC – VOLUME II
JPL PUBLIC INFORMATION ARCHIVE
We were put off by the repetitive banality of the first *Planetary Image Videodisc*. Thus we were surprised to find ourselves enjoying *The Planetary Image Videodisc – Volume II*. Like its predecessor, *Volume II*, which is provided by NASA and the US Government, contains 100,000 photographs obtained from various US manned and unmanned space expeditions. This time, however, close to 10% of them are in color. Only one dull, endless stretch of black-and-white Voyager images from Saturn (close to 30,000 of them, many just showing a crescent of white) is reminiscent of the first disc.

More than 7000 color photos taken by the Apollo astronauts are featured. Anyone who has ever taken a camera along on vacation knows that you can usually only get about one decent picture out of two dozen snapshots and a trip to the moon is no exception.

A thousand images from the Surveyor mission and another thousand from Ranger are shown, along with seven thousand more from other lunar orbiters. These not only offer an historical perspective but show material which is rarely used now that more sophisticated images are available. When the Ranger photos are played at normal speed they turn into a harrowing landing.

Along with the photos of Saturn and a couple of Saturn's moons, 400 rarely-seen Pioneer photos of Jupiter and 400 more of Venus have been included. Rounding out the disc is a museum exhibit about Mars designed around the material transmitted from the Viking lander. Explanatory text accompanies some of the Martian pictures although it is usually out of focus and difficult to read.

One more NASA disc, the *JPL Public Information Archive*, a one-sided CLV collection of NASA/JPL promotional and educational films, opens with an excellent William Conrad-narrated examination of the mid-60 Ranger landings. The same photos which were included on the *Planetary Image, Vol. II* disc are oriented to the moon's total geography. An equally informative short on Mariner's Mercury approach also appears, without the photos. Alas, most of the disc is silent and features the computer-generated speculative animation – Voyager's exploration of Jupiter and Saturn and elapsed-time photography of Jupiter's atmosphere – which has appeared on other discs in a more useable manner. The 50-minute program ends on a bright note, however. There is a marvelous silent film clip of an engineer type experimenting with a rock-grabbing robot vehicle in what looks like a JPL parking lot. He is so proud when the machine finds and grabs the correct rock, he stops just short of giving the equipment a biscuit as a reward.

PLATOON (Image)
PLATOON (HBO)
Home video can sometimes trivialize the intensity of a program even if the owner/viewer has disciplined viewing habits. *Platoon* is one of those movies that you walk away from, the first time you see it, not talking for another hour or for the rest of the evening. Buying the disc gives one the opportunity to watch the movie many, many times, until every last piece of tension is turned into camera angles and editing. Even then, it remains a powerful piece of entertainment.

The disc was released initially by HBO and then reissued with digital sound by Image. The sound transfer on the Image disc is clearly better than HBO's. It not only has sharper, better defined components, but it does not seem to be pushed as hard (the analog and digital tracks are almost identical). The picture quality of the two discs are closer in similarity. In some night scenes, however, there is a noticeable gain in color and sharpness on the Image disc.

PLATOON LEADER
Bringing the Vietnam genre up to date, Michael Dudikoff stars in *Platoon Leader*, a terrific action film which embraces the new Vietnam clichés in an efficient and entertaining manner. Dudikoff portrays a green lieutenant who learns the ropes from two almost mystical sergeants while guarding a village against the VC.

The film has a glossy picture and a full blown stereo surround soundtrack. The transfer is great. There are some white speckles near the beginning, but even they are vivid and sharply focussed. The night scenes remain undistorted. The sound editing is consistent and sensible, contributing significantly to the entertainment.

PLAYBOY PLAYMATE OF THE YEAR 1989 KIMBERLEY CONRAD
"When I did my centerfold they had me stay at the Playboy Mansion in LA. It was absolutely beautiful. The redwood trees, quiet water – it was a little piece of the country in the middle of the big city. Oh, and the animals! I loved all of them." So says Kimberley Conrad, a.k.a. Mrs. Hugh Hefner, on *Playboy Playmate of the Year 1989 Kimberley Conrad.* The picture is mildly grainy. The sound is mildly stereophonic and clean. When asked what she and Hefner had in common, Conrad cites "love for animals" as a significant shared interest.

PLAYBOY VIDEO CENTERFOLD: INDIA ALLEN
One of the better Playmate profiles, *Playboy Video Centerfold: India Allen* runs a half-hour and is in CLV. Allen has a free spirited but no-nonsense personality, and so does her mother and her dog, both of whom are featured. The segments are brisk and varied, and the program never settles down long enough to become tiresome. The sound has a stereo music track. The picture looks good, with only the strongest colors taking on a slight blur.

PLAYBOY VIDEO COLLECTOR'S EDITION VOLUME 2
FIRST ANNUAL PLAYMATE REVIEW
PLAYMATE REVIEW 2
PLAYMATE REVIEW 3
PLAYBOY VIDEO MAGAZINE VOLUME FIVE
PLAYBOY VIDEO MAGAZINE, VOLUME 6
PLAYBOY VIDEO CENTERFOLD LYNNE AUSTIN
PLAYBOY VIDEO CENTERFOLD DONNA EDMONDSON
PLAYBOY VIDEO CENTERFOLD – REBEKKA ARMSTRONG
PLAYBOY VIDEO CENTERFOLD – LUANN LEE
PLAYBOY VIDEO CENTERFOLD – TERI WEIGEL
The following has been transcribed, with careful accuracy, from the discs identified.

Playboy Video Collector's Edition Volume 2 :
(Lynda Wiesmeier)
"Freedom, to me, means that I can do anything I want to do."

"The only responsibility that I have other than myself is my dog and I love my dog...We have a lot of fun, she goes almost everywhere with me."

"I love to roller skate. I like to roller skate at the beach. It's kind of, uh, a way of being free. You can go real fast."

Playmate Review 2 :
(Ruth Guerri)
"Well I think I stayed in St. Louis because my family is here. When I work for people that I work for year after year they become close to you, they're like family. I think St. Louis is known for the Arch, among other things. But the Arch is an amazing thing. It was built when I was very small and I don't think I appreciated it until I was older. And I don't know how it was built. I'm not sure. And it's amazing to stand below it and be so tiny and look up at that great big thing."

"I wanted to be a boy when I was little. I used to carry a wallet."
(Marlene Janssen)
"Rock Island is called Rock Island because it is between Rock River and the Mississippi River and it's somewhat of an island. It has some connecting parts."

"I like the antiquity of the Quad Cities."

"Ballooning was one experience that I never really thought I'd be able to do."
(Carina Persson)
"The city is man-made but nature is part of what we all are."

"It reminds me of Denmark. It reminds me of home. I lived close to Denmark...and went to Denmark a few times every week."

"I had the opportunity to go out on a fishing boat...They told me a little about how the fishing works and how the boat works and I didn't know that whales come into the nets and they have to fix the nets pretty often because the big fish that goes into it and destroys it."
(Marianne Gravatte)
"I grew up in Arcadia. That's a small town in southern California. My father was a produce buyer for a grocery store and he got me my first job bagging groceries. I liked it. Every day was different. You never knew what to expect."

Playmate Review 3 :
(Melinda Mays)
"In Atlanta the history plays a major part of the city. Everything kind of revolves around the Old South. It's a wonderful city and it wouldn't be what it is without the past. Nobody really lived in the past, but we all remember the past."

"There's a club in Atlanta called The Limelight. To me, it's the best club in town. They have a great dance floor and the lighting, the whole thing is just great. It's really an unusual place that I don't think most cities have. It's current."
(Lonny Chin)
"Vancouver to me is really like the California of Canada because you have the ocean except we even have a little bit more because we have the mountains."

"I daydream of living like a little princess and having everything I want but to me that's a fantasy. My biggest fantasy is to be a sex symbol. A famous, famous sex symbol – not just a little sex symbol – but that's just a fantasy."

Playboy Video Magazine Volume Five :
(Penny Baker)
"I think being a Playmate is going to open a lot of doors to me in New York. Anyone will want to work with me now, or a lot more people will. Also, I can get a lot more notoriety. I can get a boyfriend if I want a boyfriend."
(Photographer Richard Fegley)
"There's a question that a lot of people ask, are you a people photographer or are you a place photographer? The other category of photographer is shooting people in places. That's the best combination."

"I think the part of photography that I really care about is lighting. I love lighting."

Playboy Video Magazine, Volume 6 :
(Tricia Lange)
"When I have a day off I like to stay in bed almost all day."

"I love meeting new people. I treat people all the same no matter who they are, whether they're a big celebrity or if they're a construction worker or a teacher or a teller in a bank. It doesn't matter. You can learn a lot of things from different people that you meet and the different cities that I travel to. People, although they may be raised in different places, are all virtually the same."

"It's really exciting to ride the dune buggy all over the sand dunes...but it's even more special just to know that a few sand dunes away you can have your own world. There are no footsteps. The sand dunes seem to go on forever. The dunes have such a tranquil effect on me. You can really be at peace with yourself there. So beautiful and so untouched, and so beautiful. Life has been so wonderful to me in the last few months. I don't know for sure what's going to happen to me in the future."

Playboy Video Centerfold Lynne Austin :

"Just outside of Clearwater there's a charming little Greek fishing community called Tarpin Springs. Brenda Lee – my best friend – and I spent the day there taking in the sights. And the food is not to be missed. One of the biggest attractions of Tarpin Springs are the sponge diving expeditions. That's where they actually go down and dive for natural sponges."

"I've always thought Playboy had the classiest, the most tasteful pictures. That's the only reason I would ever do nudes, period, is with Playboy. The top of the line. I was treated like a queen, you know. I didn't want for anything."

Playboy Video Centerfold Donna Edmondson:

"I first started noticing boys when I was about four years old and I was in nursery school. There was like this really cute little kid and he had like red hair that stuck straight up on his head and I thought he was just great. So. Anyway, I don't think he liked me as much as I liked him because we were outside in a playground and we were up on a sliding board and he pushed me off the side of it. Right down smack on my chin. It was like right here. It has thirteen stitches there from that day. So. Anyway, I just wanted to say that people think that Playmates are perfect and we're really not."

"I got my real estate license because I love houses. I love being at home. It's the place where you can really get away from everything and be yourself."

Playboy Video Centerfold – Rebekka Armstrong :

"I love being a part of Playboy. I can't believe it, it's like everything I ever wanted in life. It has matured me so much. All the pictures they took of me are so – they're unbelievable."

Playboy Video Centerfold – Luann Lee :

"I come from a large family. I have three brothers and one sister and my parents are still married."

"I love California. There's so much to do."

Playboy Video Centerfold – Teri Weigel :

"I love sports, especially gymnastics and aerobics. At one point in my life I considered competing professionally."

"I still try to do a little bit of my routine now and then. I'm definitely not as good as I used to be. One always needs a spotter when you're doing gymnastics."

"I've modelled a lot of clothing. I would have to say that lingerie is my favorite. When I'm in a lingerie store, I wish that I could try on all the garments."

"In California it seems like everyone is trying to keep in shape, and the best way, I've found, is to workout with a couple of Playmates."

"The kneebends give us the most trouble, because we have to hold to a count of 'ten.'"

"When I was a kid I never dreamed that I'd live in California or see my pictures in magazines. Playboy has helped me to do that."

PLAYBOY VIDEO PARTY JOKES

The 50-minute *Playboy Video Party Jokes* is a bland and sometimes desperate array of fey one liners and predictable burlesque routines. Jokes told by actors in staged bar or party settings alternate with doctor and adultery skits. It is not stupid enough to be funny when you're stoned and it is not bright enough to be funny when you're straight. Euphemisms abound. Playboy may have stopped airbrushing their photos, but their humor remains too polite to really prick up your ears. Different viewers will respond to different punch lines, but unless your viewing room is packed full of attentive gigglers, the disc becomes tiresome quickly. The monaural sound is difficult to hear and must be played at a higher than normal volume. The picture is a bit fuzzy.

PLAYBOY'S WET AND WILD
(see **SPORTS ILLUSTRATED 25TH ANNIVERSARY SWIMSUIT VIDEO**)

PLAYING FOR KEEPS

Although *Playing for Keeps* opens with one of Pete Townshend's operatic rock songs, which sounds super, the show quickly dissolves into a youth oriented entertainment which will mostly be of interest to those who are too young to buy their own laser discs. The film is about a trio of high school kids who purchase a hotel in the middle of nowhere and try to fix it up, to the consternation of the local chemical company that had other plans for the property. The acting is broad and obvious, and the script is predictable. The picture is grainy in places. The sound is consistently well done, but it isn't enough.

POETRY IN MOTION

If you like people you will enjoy *Poetry in Motion*. The 90-minute documentary film depicts poets discussing and reading their works, with an emphasis on the performance aspects of reading. The poets range in both fame and quality, but you have never seen a more eccentric collection of characters assembled for one purpose. The movie contains no great revelations about poetry or poets, but in showing people who are obsessed with sharing their discoveries about thoughts and sounds, it reveals humanity's nobler side. The enlightenment comes not from the words, but from the faces. There is a tendency for the viewer to feel very protective of the artists depicted on the disc, to feel that they have an inalienable right to continue their activities however strange and unfounded the results may appear.

The program is organized in a sequential manner, and was filmed primarily in New York and Toronto, in the early eighties. Some performers are seen in front of a live audience and others are seen on a set designed especially for the film. Popping up throughout the show, like a nasty bookmark, is Charles Bukowski, who exercises his inalienable right by badmouthing everything. While we can't agree with Bukowski – and he doesn't want anyone agreeing with him anyway – we did find that the format prevents one from making a fair assessment of the abilities of the poets, since most are on and off too quickly. However, most of the poets clearly have an urban orientation and, in our opinion, tend to be too topical, which will make the poems seem dated fairly rapidly, though the film's concept will remain valid.

Shot in 16mm, the picture has a worn down appearance and institutional monaural sound. Some of the material is scatological, limiting the disc's educational potential to the upper grades.

THE POINT

The picture quality of the made-for-television animated feature on *The Point* could not be better. The colors are bright and solid, and small details are easy to make out. The sound is monaural and, despite digital encoding, shows its age a little. It is no worse than it would have sounded on broadcast TV, but it is not much better.

The caroon has several sequences which will encourage children to repeatedly play the disc, but the program also has an adult appeal. Ostensibly concerning a young boy with a round head in an otherwise pointed head society, the underlying moral has little to do with the obvious lessons on prejudice and tolerance. Instead, the narrative is a thinly veiled trip through psychotherapy, at the end of which the hero discovers that his life, too, has a point. Harry Nilsson's overtly phallic 'Me and My Arrow' ('Arrow' is the boy's dog) is only one of several songs, all marked by chapter encoding, which reinforce this theme.

The drawings are terrific and Nilsson's music is engaging. (The back of the jacket cover also lists Nilsson as the show's director, while the front of the jacket cover correctly identifies Fred Wolf as having performed those duties.) Side two of the disc is in CAV, with two unsteady still frames out of every five. Speed manipulations are generally uninteresting, but freezing the frames which do not wiggle gives one a chance to examine even more closely the cheerful, good humored artwork.

THE POINTER SISTERS: LIVE IN AFRICA

You'd think that if the Pointer Sisters went all the way to Africa they'd sing for more than a half hour, but they don't last much longer than that on *The Pointer Sisters: Live in Africa*. The concert emphasizes the group's jazz talents as opposed to their more popular dance numbers, and they come across sounding – and acting – like Manhattan Transfer. Still, their set (which, to be fair, was just one act in a festival program) is more melodic than many outdoor concert recordings are, and several of the numbers, which include 'Salt Peanuts,' 'Steam Heat,' and 'All Night Long,' are both smooth and lively. The sound is fine. The picture is a little grainy, but, under the circumstances, it is acceptable.

POINTER SISTERS – SO EXCITED

The picture on the 8-inch, *Pointer Sisters – So Excited*, is noticeably grainy, which is disappointing, because the Pointer Sisters ought to look as sharp as possible. There are seven music videos on the two-sided CLV disc. The best is 'Jump,' which alternates images of the singers with images of athletes in competition. Another, 'Twist My Arm,' is partially animated and quite colorful.

THE POINTSMAN

Some movies are boring, but others are so stupid that incredulity will hold a viewer's attention. Such is the case with the ridiculous Dutch film, *The Pointsman*. Although the movie is in Dutch with English subtitles, it is almost dialog-less. The stereo surround sound is unusually elaborate and may attract sound fanatics. The picture is deliberately grainy and accurately transferred.

A woman gets off a train (by accident? fate? stupidity?) at a remote point station, inhabited by a gaunt, grisly young man of few words whose only job is to come out of the station once in a while and shift the tracks to route oncoming trains. The man and woman stare at each other for a half hour, set up house for a half hour, and then have inadequate sex and split up for a half hour. Apparently the filmmakers thought that since the movie's title has a point in it, nothing else had to.

POLICE ACADEMY
POLICE ACADEMY 2: THEIR FIRST ASSIGNMENT

Both *Police Academy* and *Police Academy 2: Their First Assignment* are monaural. Both have been transferred to disc using adequate but unremarkable masters. The second film, having been made after the first was a success, has more spectacular, expensive gags and higher priced comedians filling in the bit roles. Neither movie is as grossly hysterical as it must have seemed in a crowded movie theater, but neither movie is a failure, either. The two work well as a double bill and amount to three hours of adolescent pranks and anxieties. One wonders what the Three Stooges might have done had they been able to use sex as viciously as it is employed here.

POLICE ACADEMY 3: BACK IN TRAINING

The clever inspiration for *Police Academy 3: Back in Training* was to take the various comics who had portrayed citizens (and bad guys) in *Police Academy 2* and have their characters sign up to become cops. The movie, which is 83 minutes long with padding, is too self assured to tolerate criticism. Enough of the gags work to keep one from falling asleep during the routines that don't.

POLICE ACADEMY 4: CITIZENS ON PATROL

The fourth installment in the *Police Academy* series, *Police Academy 4: Citizens on Patrol*, is a scaled down effort. The plot has 'normal citizens' going through a ribald police training program, but the producers did not spend the money to cast real comics as the citizens. There is an impressive segment involving skateboard stunts, but that pretty much identifies who the program is intended for. Impatient adults had best avoid it.

Although the movie is monaural, the sound has been digitally encoded and possesses all the subtleties of a police whistle. The skateboard crowd will not complain. The print has an errant mark or two on it, but the picture looks brand new.

POLICE ACADEMY 5: ASSIGNMENT MIAMI BEACH

Police Academy 5: Assignment Miami Beach has a sharp picture transfer and good sound. The 90 minute episode has a steady litany of low brow gags, and even if only one in every five amuses you, there are still plenty to provide dependable entertainment.

THE POLICE – EVERY BREATH YOU TAKE – THE VIDEOS

Fourteen music videos are collected on *The Police – Every Breath You Take – The Videos*. The two most established videos, 'Every Breath You Take' and 'Wrapped Around Your Finger,' are visually striking and artistically effective, but the other numbers are less inspired. All the videos are variations on the format of showing the band members performing the song. The locations, outfits, and settings change, but the concept is consistent. Outside of the two numbers mentioned above, however, the imagery is either nondescript or overwrought. And Sting often comes across as an actor trying to be a singer, instead of the other way around. The sound transfer lacks a fresh demeanor and the picture is very grainy, particularly in the poorer videos.

POLICE SQUAD! – HELP WANTED
TOP SECRET!

"*Police Squad!* was the type of television show people who never watch television wanted to watch. As people watched the first episode they told two friends and they told two friends and so on and so on, but the show was cancelled before the geometric progression of viewers had a chance to affect Nielson."

"You mean Nielsens, the television popularity rating system."

"No, I mean Leslie Nielson, the popular television star of *Police Squad! – Help Wanted*, the 75-minute three-episode (two on side one, one on side two) laser disc from Paramount Home Video. Old Swamp Fox himself. His performance alone is worth the price of the disc, but there is so much more. All the different comical bits and throwaway jokes in the background. The creators of *Airplane!*, Jim Abrahams, David Zucker, and Jerry Zucker, proved they could be just as funny with television as with motion pictures, even with the smaller budget and the lower quality of the print and sound. The flat mono is actually a comic plus with the awful background music. The poetry of it all is enough to make Dante proud."

"You mean the great Italian poet?"

"No, Joe Dante, who directed the second episode."

"Gee, those guys, Abrahams, Zucker, and Zucker. They should make another movie."

"That would be *Top Secret!*"

"I was just guessing. When will it be released?"

"It has. On laser disc, from Paramount."

"Well, why won't they tell anybody what it's called?"

"It's *Top Secret!* The print is sharp and is in stereo. The music is by Maurice Jarre."

"Well, if you can't tell me what it's called, at least tell me what it is about."

"I told you, it's *Top Secret!* No one ever believes it could be funny when they hear what it is about, but it is. A popular American rock star (Val Kilmer) is invited to play at a music festival by the East German government as a diversion from the government's plan for destroying NATO's naval fleet. The rock star meets and falls in love with a girl (Lucy Gutteridge) working for the Resistance and helps foil the German scheme."

"What does that have to do with the laser disc you were telling me about by the *Police Squad!* guys."

"That's *Top Secret!* Along the way there are parodies of Elvis movies, surprise cameos, and the usual collection of oddball sight gags and mixed-up verbal humor. They get a lot of mileage from taking the German language literally."

"If the disc is top secret, how can I find it?"

"There's no secret about *If....* Paramount released that disc as well."

"Well, I don't care. I'm going to get a concert disc by a famous British rock group."

"Who?"

"No. Yes."

POLTERGEIST
POLTERGEIST (Letterboxed)
POLTERGEIST (Import)

The original MGM/UA release of *Poltergeist* was mastered specifically for the laser presentation (it is CX-encoded without automatic tripping) and has held up well for an early transfer. MGM/UA then released the title again, letterboxed with an aspect ratio of about 2:1. In both cases the picture is superb, and starts to blur only during scenes involving strong red lights. The amount of blur is indistinguishable between the discs. The sound has more impact on the digitally encoded letterboxed disc.

The letterboxing presents an interesting comparison to the cropped disc. It is well known that Steven Spielberg was at least as heavily involved with the filming of the movie as was the nominal director, Tobe Hooper. Without any evidence beyond what is in front of us, we speculate that the scenes in which Spielberg asserted himself work better on the widescreen whereas the scenes which were left to Hooper's guidance work better when cropped. The house 'implosion' is lost on the letterboxed picture and the hallucinations have more shock when scanned. On the other hand, we've seen the cropped disc many times, yet in watching the letterboxed version, the scene where the toy clown attacks the boy made us scream. On the blown up cropped image, the shot is too tight and you do not get a sense of how unprotected the boy is. The import, which uses the same source material as the American letterboxed version, is in CAV.

POLTERGEIST II

Competence is not enough. *Poltergeist II* is well constructed and follows a logical plot line. It has some exciting special effects and a couple of good screams. But it should never have been made and is not worth watching. It perverts the accomplishments of the first *Poltergeist* without adding anything to an understanding of its themes and explorations. The picture is faintly grainy but unharmed.

POLTERGEIST III

The first sequel to *Poltergeist* was strenuously unsatisfying, but the sequel to the sequel, *Poltergeist III*, is reasonably entertaining. The narrative takes place in a downtown Chicago high-rise, and the interior decoration is loaded with mirrors, which the filmmakers do an excellent job in utilizing without showing themselves. Instead of grotesque special effects, the film relies heavily on surprises in the mirrors to scare the viewer, and it succeeds as well as the average genre effort.

The stereo surround sound is expensively

produced and good for a thrill or two. Except for Heather O'Rourke's bright red pajamas, the picture is stable and decently transferred. The break between side one and side two is perfectly chosen.

POP GOES THE COMIC

If you want to see an early and largely unheralded comic masterpiece, put on side two of *Pop Goes the Comic*, a collection of several films by Max Linder. Linder was a French silent film comedian whose brilliant work was mostly destroyed during the Great Wars. He made a few films in Hollywood, however, and several of these efforts are condensed and combined on the two part Pop program. Side one melds together 'That's My Wife' and 'Seven Years Bad Luck,' and includes many inspired gags, including the best 'missing mirror' routine of them all. But side two contains a complete film, 'The Three-Must-Get-Theres,' which lampoons the story of D'Artagnan as if it were quoting from years of film adaptations preceding it. Set in costume, but not above throwing in an automobile or a typewriter at an opportune moment, the comedy is a unique mixture of slapstick and abstract jokes, and provides enough evidence to establish Linder as one of the greatest of the silent film comedians.

The black-and-white source material is in rough but workable shape. The framing is difficult, especially during 'Wife,' where heads tend to appear at the very top of the screen. The monaural sound contains a mildly comical musical score with a slight continental flavor and a number of jokey sound effects.

THE POPE OF GREENWICH VILLAGE

Mickey Rourke and Eric Roberts have been bad actors for their entire careers and show no signs of mellowing. They appear together as third cousins in *The Pope of Greenwich Village*, a poor man's *Mean Streets*. The picture is not too faded and has no serious flaws. Since the film runs a couple minutes over two hours, side three is in CAV, with two unsteady still frames out of every five. The sound is digitally encoded monaural and provides a nice, full rendition of Frank Sinatra's recording, 'Summer Wind,' over the end credits. The movie is fortunate to be graced with two fine performances, by Geraldine Page and Kenneth McMillan, and the impact they have, without screaming, without breaking dishes, and without mumbling, demonstrates the potential power of their craft. When the movie is over, you remember every word they have said. Beyond that, however, the only thing you can remember is Roberts screaming about his thumb getting cut off. Would that it had been his tongue.

PORK CHOP HILL

Like its meaty successor, *Hamburger Hill*, *Pork Chop Hill* is a rewarding depiction of a futile battle. Set in the final days of the Korean War and decorated with only a minimum of patriotic justification, the film depicts a Pyrrhic effort on the part of an American army company to seize and hold a useless hill in support of a negotiations bluff. Practically the whole film is the battle and it has a constant ring of authenticity. Written by the commander who led the charge, the narrative makes clear that battle strategies are fuzzy wish lists, that in the heat of it no one has even the faintest idea of what is going on, and that the winner is usually the side lucky enough to have made the fewest rampant mistakes. However haphazard the efforts of the armies which clash may be, the script is meticulous in capturing the events within the battle which led to victory, so that even though the soldiers have no idea what is occurring, the viewer is never left in a similar quandary. Although restricted by a fifties depiction of violence, the horror and randomness of the slaughter are effectively communicated. *Pork Chop Hill* was directed by Lewis Milestone.

Sam Leavitt's stunning black-and-white cinematography has been transferred without a single imposed blemish. The elaborate night photography is undistorted and pitch black remains pitch black. The sound is in standard condition for the era, and the disc is thoroughly chapter encoded.

PORKY'S REVENGE

An old joke pops up early on in *Porky's Revenge*, about a female who looks appealing from a distance but is less attractive in close quarters. It is told well, visually, so that it made us laugh and decide that the disc was not a total waste. This installment lacks the cujones of Bob Clark's brilliantly hysterical original, but it tries to mix the same formula of sexually oriented practical jokes and life-imperiling revenge. When you realize that the movie is never going to seriously challenge its R rating, boredom sets in. It is also a bit grainy.

PORTRAIT OF AFRICA

Dan Moss conceived and directed *Portrait of Africa*. The hour long stereo program contains sharp looking images taken exclusively in Kenya and Tanzania, set to the music of Vangelis, Ladysmith Black Mambazo, and Miriam Makeba. Why the generic dribbles of Vangelis have been mixed with the other two is beyond us. The disc obtains a jaunty earnestness when the other musicians are featured, and seems to be stalling for time when the Vangelis numbers are used. Nevertheless, the video images are lovely, depicting both landscapes and indigenous peoples, and the disc will not disappoint those who are partial to Moss's format.

PORTRAIT OF ENGLAND

An hour of baroque chamber music featuring the classical trumpeter, Wynton Marsalis, is accompanied by images of British architecture and landscapes in *Portrait of England*. The stereo music has clear, sharp sounds and a nice atmosphere. Marsalis' performance is often forceful and his interpretation of the pieces, while not varying from the norm, is innovative and lively. The images, however, are dry and lifeless. There are no people. There is no rain, which is intrinsic to why the gardens look so green and why the buildings look so swelled. The picture is also slightly hazy and the colors are a bit muddy. There is a nice jacket insert which contains a map of England so that a viewer with a rudimentary familiarity of the countryside can follow the path of the camera.

THE POSTMAN ALWAYS RINGS TWICE
THE POSTMAN ALWAYS RINGS TWICE (Remake)

By suppressing all the sex, the older version of *The Postman Always Rings Twice* became a nasty little parable, where the subtle resentments and disappointments of marriage were exaggerated to the point of violence and murder. The black-and-white film stars John Garfield and Lana Turner. The source material is in good condition, and there is no aspect of the disc which hinders one's appreciation of the film. The film runs under two hours and has been released on a single platter.

The Jack Nicholson and Jessica Lange remake is an older disc. The picture, which was stylized in oranges and browns, is heavy in grain and distortion. The basic transfer is okay, however, and the image and sound will be tolerable to most viewers. In contrast to the first film, the second *Postman Always Rings Twice* is all sex, giving the movie less thematic strength but making the watching of it a lot more fun.

POT O'GOLD

Whoever wrote the brief jacket copy for the 3M Collectible Classic, *Pot O'Gold*, did not watch the movie, because they got the plot summary all wrong. "James Stewart brings *Pot O'Gold* to life as the Horace Heidt Band sounds off on a radio quiz show." The radio show in question is most emphatically *not* a quiz show, and the plot ends up revolving around the fact that it isn't.

The film is an honest-to-goodness musical where Stewart and Paulette Goddard break into song as they walk down the street and solve all their problems by getting a big break on a radio show. Anyone who is a fan of Jimmy Stewart will want the disc since the movie is a showcase for his amenable and energetic personality.

The black-and-white print is a bit muddy. The sound wobbles in places and is inconsistent in volume.

POWER

Movies about politics are few and far between. One seeks out entertainment to escape the realities of the world, not to grovel in them. *Power* is about a political consultant assisting a half-dozen candidates during an off-year election. To make things interesting, the script writers included some genuine bad guys, a crime, and the silly title, but the movie would have been just as engaging without them. There is enough gloss and humor to support repeated viewings.

The colors are rich and brassy. The sound is monaural and not CX-encoded, but it has the sophistication of a contemporary recording. A lengthy trailer for *Sting – Bring on the Night* appears at the end.

A PRAYER FOR THE DYING

The choices director Michael Hodges made in *A Prayer for the Dying* are significantly accommodating to the advantages of stereo surround sound. Throughout the movie, scenes are set in quiet, cavernous rooms, and during the gaps in the dialog the atmosphere is deadly still. The analog track is noisy, but the digital track, unless you push the volume to its uppermost reaches, is absolutely silent. You can play it loud enough that conversations take on movie theater echoes, and Bill Conti's superb score swells symphonically, without the slightest distortion.

But that is the only reason to get the disc. The picture is grainy and the story is a necessity only for those who enjoy giggling at religious imagery. It is replete with a blind girl who sees souls, and a statue of the Crucifix which the hero, a terrorist played by Mickey Rourke, clings to in desperation before falling to his death. Another character is crucified in a more literal fashion, and there is a priest with a violent past whose church is next door to a carnival. The circumstances under which these individuals cross paths are either improbable or plain silly, and only Alan Bates, who treats the whole project as a joke, has an attitude which matches the material.

PREDATOR

You could make a case that the creature which massacres the US reconnaissance commandos in *Predator* represents the evils of war or covert activity, but the movie is too much fun to bother. You could also make a case that the CBS/Fox disc is a disappointment because it is not digitally encoded and because the contrast levels are set for video cassette, but the disc is too much fun as well, and there is no point in analyzing it too closely. The picture is decent – not perfect, but comparable to the quality of most major releases. The lack of digital encoding is the only thing which is wrong with the sound, since the stereo mix is terrific and the musical score is as entertaining as the sound effects.

You can also make a case that the filmmakers fudged the ending, which by all rights ought to have been an atomic explosion. Otherwise, the script is a marvelously witty bait and switch which will be especially enjoyable to future generations less aware from publicity campaigns and word of mouth as to what the story is actually about. Violent and exciting, the movie is great home video, something which will keep you tense and thrilled for at least the first three or four dozen viewings, and it makes a wonderful, exciting disc for Saturday afternoons while Mom is out shopping.

THE PRESIDIO

The narrative of the *Presidio* is difficult to accept. The plot mechanics continually rely on characters who should know better doing something conveniently stupid. It is a murder mystery and the details are kept at a superficial level to prevent interference with a subplot involving romantic and family complications. Sean Connery, Mark Harmon, and Meg Ryan star. Harmon has a real difficulty projecting a personality for the length of a feature film. He needs a false nose.

The break between side one and side two is perfectly chosen to emphasize an amusing punchline. The picture quality is okay, but the edges get blurry from time to time. The sound is fun and contains a few satisfying rumbles.

PRETTY IN PINK

Molly Ringwald is appealing in *Pretty in Pink*, but the film has little else going for it. It is about a romance between a rich boy and a poor girl in a high school where students seem to walk around with their parents' income sewn to their epaulets. *Pink* also has a washed out color scheme, and the picture looks pale although the transfer is clearly accurate. The stereo is clean and has severe shifts in volume – loud rock songs to quiet romantic moments – without disrupting one's concentration.

PRETTY KILL

Yaphet Koto plays a chief of detectives with a Brando-like swaggering mumble in *Pretty Kill* and he's marvelous, but then the whole cast is very good. Susannah York has a bit part which she treats as if it were the center of the film, and Suzanne Snyder, portraying a young woman with a split personality, is scary as all get out. The script could have used a little more doctoring to create a photo finish ending, but the film is quite entertaining. The sound is a bit overbearing although the digital track is cleaner than the monaural track. The picture is grainy in the darker scenes, but not unduly so. The mangled syntax of the title turns out to mean nothing and is just one more indication that, had a little more thought and money gone into the production, the movie could have been even better than it is.

PRICK UP YOUR EARS

Although the devilishly-titled biography, *Prick Up Your Ears*, has some material, such as the public restroom cruising scenes, which viewers may find discomforting, the film is literate, witty, and refreshingly intelligent. The movie was made with sober boxoffice expectations in mind, so the film stock is second rate and the stereo, although pleasing (the music soundtrack, by Stanley Meyers, is good), cannot be raised above a sensible volume.

Prick is the biography of Joe Orton which was written by John Lahr and adapted to the screen by Alan Bennett. Lahr is portrayed in the film by Wallace Shawn, who probably looks more Lahr-ish than Lahr himself. The film cuts between Lahr's research efforts and Orton's life. Orton, a teddy boy playwright, was killed in the late sixties by his lover. The movie concentrates on relationships, but it does not make a mystery of Orton's creative process. Enough information is given about his background and his lifestyle so that his capabilities, although never explicitly demonstrated, are implied. He lived in a grungy apartment and had nothing to do day or night but read, type, and solicit sex from strangers.

PRIME CUTS – JAZZ & BEYOND

A startling reverse action shot of a woman dropping into a pool of water opens side two of the 8-inch *Prime Cuts – Jazz & Beyond.* The image is part of a music video by Andreas Vollenweider and is only one of several impressive visual displays presented on the disc. The various artists featured include Miles Davis, Herbie Hancock (whose videos are always dependably inventive), Chuck Mangione (in a clever piece where a woman arranges his image in blocks), Al DiMeola, Hiroshima, Weather Report and Clarke/Duke Project.

PRIME EVIL

The transfer of the cheaply produced but engaging devil worship thriller, *Prime Evil*, looks accurate, although the original film stock is second rate. The sound has no noticeable flaws. The film follows all the rules of the genre and is in some ways a textbook example of what a decent devil worship movie should offer. It may be difficult to tell some of the cast members apart, or to tolerate their unprofessional line readings, but the basic appeal – the paranoia, the seductiveness of evil, the gross murders – is carefully preserved. The disc runs under 90 minutes and is in CLV.

PRINCE AND THE REVOLUTION LIVE

The two-hour concert disc *Prince and the Revolution Live* is dark and blurry. Prince is only clear and in focus when the house lights come on. The one spectacular exception to this is a kaleidoscopic Rorschach depiction of'When Doves Cry.'

The sound is undoctored and full of the mistakes which make a live recording unique. Nothing wrong with that, but the live track plays to a severe disadvantage because of Prince's habit of letting the audience sing his lyrics for him. It is not that he is being lazy. He puts on quite an acrobatic performance and is probably too pooped to belt out a chorus even if he wanted to. Besides, the audience knows the words, which, because of their collective apparent age, is the part that makes us cringe. If you have children, it would be best to keep this disc locked in a cabinet when not in use.

PRINCE OF DARKNESS

John Carpenter's *Prince of Darkness* is an undergraduate mixture of physics and metaphysics which postulates that Christ was an alien from outer space. It contains conceptual elements from many of Carpenter's other films, as well as his experienced command of mood and tension. The ending cops out by not finding a true science fiction resolution, but Carpenter has never been strong on endings anyway. He usually prefers an unnerving sleight of hand over a definitive show stopper.

The sound was done in Ultra-Stereo. The analog track has a little hiss, but the digital track is remarkably clean. The music, Carpenter's never ending electronic duh-da, gets to you after a while, but that is what it is supposed to do. The color scheme is antichromatic in places. The transfer is fine, but the cinematography is not impressive.

THE PRINCE OF PENNSYLVANIA

The cast in *The Prince of Pennsylvania*, which includes Bonnie Bedelia, Amy Madigan, and Fred Ward, doesn't help. The film is one more misunderstood teenager tale, set in Pennsylvania mining country. The script provides a couple of strong dramatic moments in which the actors and actresses can earn their pay, but it also has comic aspirations. Fred Ward may have many talents, but clowning is not among them. Madigan fares the best, but only because she isn't the center of attention (her funniest bit occurs while she's wearing a Freddy Kruger-type mask). The sound is isn't bad. The fleshtones have a faint pinkishness, and the print has a couple of marks.

THE PRINCE'S TRUST ALL-STAR ROCK CONCERT

The songs featured on *The Prince's Trust All-Star Rock Concert* are listed on the back of the jacket with numbers next to them, but there are no chapter markers encoded on the disc. The concert was a benefit effort which takes on the mood of a rock and roll old-timer's day, with Elton John, Rod Stewart, Paul McCartney, Tina Turner and a few others playing an hour's worth of hits for an enthusiastic audience. The show only runs about a half-hour a side, but the louder you turn the volume up the better it sounds. The disc has one comical moment as well, when the camera cuts to a shot of Prince Charles, attempting to boogie to 'Long Tall Sally.' He needs to practice more with his wife.

THE PRINCESS AND THE PEA
(see **FAERIE TALE THEATRE**)

THE PRINCESS AND THE PIRATE
(see **THE LITTLE FOXES**)

THE PRINCESS BRIDE (Voyager CLV)
THE PRINCESS BRIDE (Voyager CAV)
THE PRINCESS BRIDE (Nelson)

We expected the Voyager Criterion Collection version of *The Princess Bride* to look better than Nelson's version, but what surprised us was that it sounded so much better. The sound on Nelson's release seemed perfectly acceptable to us until we put the Voyager version on. It was like taking ear muffs off. Suddenly the treble was sharply defined, almost piercing, and the bass had 'oomph' with personality. A comparison of the analog tracks of the two discs displayed similar discrepancies. Indeed it will ultimately be the sound, and not the mild letterboxing, which will win converts to Voyager's version.

Although the negative for *The Princess Bride* has an aspect ratio of 1.33:1, which is essentially how it appears on the Nelson release, the director, Rob Reiner, set up his shots using a 1.66:1 viewfinder, which is essentially how it appears on the Voyager discs. The Nelson image has more picture information, but it is not the composition which Reiner intended. Voyager's CLV and CAV versions are identical, and the CAV presentation contains no special features. The picture on Nelson's version is grainier than the bright, colorful Voyager effort, although it still looks okay.

The film remains enjoyable on multiple viewings and some performances become even more comical the more often one is exposed to them. The film is a creative and humorous fairy tale, about lovers who overcome great odds to be together. There is only one sequence which doesn't work, a torture scene that stops the movie dead and should at least have been shorter, if not eliminated altogether. Whether the film meets Voyager's Criterion Collection definition to the letter is debatable, but the film is great fun, and so is the disc.

THE PRINCIPAL

James Belushi is great in *The Principal*, whether he is giving a speech, throwing out a one-liner, or just raising an eyebrow. He's in total control on the screen, and so the minor improvements which his character achieves with the discipline in a low-income neighborhood high school (in Oakland) is believable. Sometimes in movies like this the kids clean up their act as if they had been sprinkled with faerie dust, but not here.

The transfer receives passing marks. The picture quality has no flaws of any substance, and the digitally encoded sound gives the music more substance than its supposed source – boom boxes in the hallways – could possibly achieve.

PRISON

A haunted prison – we love the concept. *Prison* is a formula horror concoction which follows the rules right down to the plot inconsistencies and untied loose ends. It is appealing because the victims are not sweet, innocent teenagers cut down in the prime of their lives. They are tough, no good criminals, and you can't wait to see them get wasted. The disc is in fairly decent shape. The picture has trouble with orange lights and dark corridors, but is no worse than most other low budget efforts. The Ultra-Stereo sound fluctuates occasionally in the right channel, but also provides some nice stereo effects, including incidental conversations and murmurs during crowd scenes.

THE PRISONER VOLUME 1
THE PRISONER VOLUME 2
THE PRISONER VOLUME 3
THE PRISONER VOLUME 4
THE PRISONER VOLUME 5
THE PRISONER VOLUME 6
THE PRISONER VOLUME 7
THE PRISONER VOLUME 8
THE PRISONER VOLUME 9
THE PRISONER VOLUME 10
THE PRISONER VOLUME 11
THE PRISONER VOLUME 12
THE PRISONER VOLUME 13
THE PRISONER VOLUME 14
THE PRISONER VOLUME 15
THE PRISONER VOLUME 16
THE PRISONER VOLUME 17

Beginning with *Episode 7*, the picture quality of *The Prisoner* television series improves considerably. The first couple offerings are particularly weak – ill-colored and grainy. They begin to improve a little after that, and by *Episode 7* the fleshtones are very sharp and the image looks bright and solid. There continue to be minor glitches throughout the collection – a scratch here and there, a bad splice or momentary image jiggle – and on some discs the second half of the program has a noticeably better color transfer than the first half, but there are no faults which will prevent collectors from deeming the presentations acceptable. The digital monaural sound is fairly consistent throughout the series. It is a little rough, but still worth amplifying.

Each single-sided disc has been released separately in CLV. The chapter encoding is consistent throughout the collection in being coordinated with the commercial insert points, and every one of the seventeen episodes runs 50 minutes.

The Prisoner is about a secret agent who resigns from his job and awakens the next day in a curiously good natured seaside spa from which there is no escape. The series is resolutely finite and has a distinctive beginning, middle and end, yet each episode can exist independently of the others. There are minor links, however, which tighten the work when it is seen as a single entity. The program is ideal source material for those who wish to ponder such subjects as 'the relationship between the individual and the state' or 'Free Will vs. Determinism,' etc. Single episodes also contain highly satirical representations of various institutions, such as education, politics, the courts, and so forth. The shows are also fun on a simple will-the-good-guy-beat-the-bad-guys level.

It is clear, however, that the filmmakers were using psychoanalysis as a guide for both the over all structure of the program. When a person resigns from life and enters a state which can vary in degrees but is commonly referred to by doctors as 'depression,' the cure is an extended series of self-examining emotional probes, known as 'psychoanalysis.' To look at the process from the outside, it can seem very intellectualized, but to the patient going through it, it is an emotional battle in which conscious thought is a barrier to the cure. The purpose of the doctor in the process is to allow the patient a chance to step outside of himself. The doctor guides the healing process by asking pertinent questions and exploring emotional truths, until the patient can again function and take over his own healing process. At first, the patient is entirely rebellious, perhaps even denying that there is a problem. Then, there is a tacit cooperation with the doctor, playing along, but the patient is always looking for a quick out. As the patient becomes more comfortable with the process, amidst digressions, a genuine desire to follow the doctor's suggestions develops. But only after the patient comes to complete grips with the trauma which caused the depression, and realizes that a balanced emotional state can exist independently of the traumatized state, can the cure be realized.

Volume 1 is the obligatory opening setup, 'The Arrival.' Within, the viewer is given a basic tour of the 'Village' compound and its primary rules. A brief piece of complexity, involving another prisoner and an escape plot, is worked into the second half. In *Volume 2*, 'The Chimes of Big Ben,' Patrick McGoohan, who was Executive Producer of the series and its principal instigator, as well as the star, gives a deft explanation of his intentions, while ostensibly describing a piece of abstract art, "It represents freedom, or a barrier, depending how you look at it." 'Chimes' is about a more elaborate escape plot, which incorporates the abstract art mentioned above and, in one of the many examples of the meanings upon meanings which the program offers, demonstrates that the artwork is not in the slightest way abstract.

Volume 3 contains the episode, 'A. B. and C.' misidentified on the jacket cover as 'A, B, & C.' The episode is quite entertaining, since it involves the manipulation of dreams. Number Six is stimulated through his subconscious to reveal, with the help of a machine that projects his dreams onto a screen, his plans and his contacts. The dream sequences are especially well done within the confines of the TV format. Since escape is not an issue, and the hero makes progress, 'winning' a confrontation with his captors.

Volume 4, 'Free for All,' is a memorable episode about an election in The Village, in which Number Six 'runs' for the 'Two' position. The program contains a number of satirical references to the political process. The viewer is more distanced from the emotions of the characters than in other episodes, making the pleasures of the plot device appear superficial, but the piece is an excellent variation on the format and a good example of why the program remains so stimulating. As for the hero, he cooperates too willingly with his captors and suffers a setback. 'The Schizoid Man,' on *Volume 5*, is great fun. Number Six meets a doppleganger who attempts to steal his identity. The special split screen effects are well done, and the plot twists are enjoyable. It is at this point that the hero begins the a true self-recognition process.

Volume 6 'The General' is about a speed education course to which the Village is subjected, and ends with a major victory for the Prisoner, as he causes a master computer to completely self-destruct by entering a query with four simple characters. *Volume 7* 'Many Happy Returns' demonstrates a major shift in the Prisoner's relationship with his surroundings, as he wakes up to find the Village empty. He escapes, returns to London, but ends up back in the Village all the same. *Volume 8* 'Dance of the Dead' is probably the least satisfying episode, although any show in which the antagonist is dressed in a Peter Pan costume cannot be all that bad. A costume party is satirically mixed with a courtroom scene, but the program reveals what is probably the weakest component in the whole series, its inability to present a viable female character. Things get wild in *Volume 9* '"Do Not Forsake Me Oh My Darling"' as the Prisoner's mind is transplanted to the body of another and then sent on a mission to retrieve a scientist hiding in the Austrian Alps. The ending is clever. The Prisoner's collaboration with his captors becomes even more advanced as he saves Number Two from an assassination attempt in *Volume 10* 'It's Your Funeral.' He then has a relapse in *Volume 11* '"Checkmate,"' as an escape with the assistance of other Villagers, including a man he meets during a live chess game, fails due to a false mistrust among the members of the group escaping. It is his last defeat.

With *Volume 12* '"Living in Harmony,"' the tone and the attitude of the series enters its final phase. The Prisoner takes a continually stronger command of events in each of the remaining episodes. The enjoyable 'Harmony' is a wonderful exercise in displacement, as the essential aspects of the Prisoner series are re-enacted in a Western setting. As much as it is the most different of all the episodes, it is also the most representative and, arguably, the best.

The stills on the jacket cover for *Volume 13* 'Change of Mind' are from other episodes and are terribly misleading. The Prisoner foils an attempt to drug him and survives being ostracized by the other Villagers. In *Volume 14* 'Hammer into Anvil' he completely takes the upper hand and plays a series of tricks on Number Two, forcing the latter to go mad. Like 'Harmony,' *Volume 15* 'The Girl Who Was Death' is another digression, a fantasy story about a resourceful secret agent who saves London from a missile disguised as a lighthouse. A discussion of sex and the 'death wish' would be valid for term papers, but the episode is primarily enjoyable for its elaborate action sequences.

The final two episodes, *Volume 16* 'Once Upon a Time' and *Volume 17* 'Fallout,' comprise a single entity, and 'Time' ends on such a cliffhanging hook that it was sheer torture the first time we saw the series and had to wait an entire week for the conclusion. We had dreams about it every night in the interim. Both were directed by the star, Patrick McGoohan. The locale moves from the Village to some barely decorated soundstage sets and Leo McKern is hauled in for a challenging acting task as Number Two. The episodes are the most blatantly psychoanalytical, as methods of therapy are even discussed among the characters. Locked into the production values of the late sixties, both episodes can seem awfully silly to an impartial viewer. In 'Time' the Prisoner reverts to his childhood and then regains his composure by killing Number Two while both are locked in an underground shelter. In 'Fallout' Number Two is resuscitated and the Prisoner is hailed by a forum of hooded figures as having achieved ultimate power as an individual. It is also revealed that the Prisoner, or 'I,' is Number '1.' The whole place then collapses into a mess of cheap props and steam, and the Prisoner drives off to London with a dwarf. The absence of women in the finale is telling, but the two hour sequence is so absurd as to be ideally resolute, and for the time and conditions under which it was made, it is hard to fault the filmmakers for their choices.

PRISONERS OF THE LOST UNIVERSE

Made on a budget which makes the *Star Trek* episodes look like epic extravaganzas, *Prisoners of the Lost Universe* is a slow-witted fantasy. The story is about three people from contemporary Los Angeles who fall into a space warp and find themselves in an alternate world where only criminals have guns and everyone likes red meat. When you see that the ghouls who want to eat the slave girl are actually actors wrapped in mounds of muddy toilet paper you realize that someone lost this universe on purpose and whoever found it was not doing the rest of us any great favor.

THE PRIVATE LIFE OF HENRY VIII

The running time cited in reference publications for *The Private Life of Henry VIII* is 97 minutes and the running time on the disc is 93 minutes, although the jacket cover says 96. The film was tremendously risque for its day and this may have been the cut which was released theatrically. The print is a bit ill-used as well, with scratches and fuzzy edges. The sound is early thirties, but it is clear enough so that the dialog can be understood, something which is not always the case with old British films. Charles Laughton portrays Henry as a foolish imbecile barely aware of what is happening around him.

PRIVATE RESORT

The makers of *Private Resort* act like they are the ones who discovered the bikini. Now the bikini was a wonderful discovery, or invention, or stepping stone for civilization, but you essentially get the same thrill flipping through the Sears catalog that you do watching this movie. The transfer is grainy and the monaural sound is weak and scratchy. The film is supposed to be a comedy, but when you get right down to it, the Sears catalog is funnier.

PRIZZI'S HONOR

If the ending of *Prizzi's Honor* disappointed you on the first viewing, don't let that hinder your purchase. The finale is more inevitable and more amusing the second and subsequent times through. The script maintains a nice balance between the the Machiavellian plot twists and laid-back characterizations. Concerning a group of powerful but slightly inept gangsters who seem to spend most of their efforts stealing from themselves, *Prizzi's Honor* is a comical and romantic view of life in the mob.

The picture is mildly grainy but the Alex North score and incidental opera themes are in full stereo. Digital encoding gives the disc the class it deserves.

THE PRODUCERS (Voyager)
THE PRODUCERS (Nelson)

You can take your pick between Voyager's version of *The Producers* and Nelson's version. Both discs are in CLV. Voyager's version is matted and includes the theatrical trailer. The film was also available at one time on the old Magnetic Video label. (We've never seen the Magnetic Video version, but friends who have inform us that it is not a pretty sight.)

The prints used by both Nelson and Voyager vary between very good and excellent. On one or two reels of Voyager's version the skin tones of the actors look pinkish, there is some red and blue shifting, and there is some momentary speckling. Most of the time the color is exact and marvelously garish. Nelson's rendition occasionally looks paler and has a little more speckling, but on the best reels the two discs are equal in visual pleasures. On either disc you can read the fine print in the end credits and see the sweat boiling in every crease in Zero Mostel's face.

The monaural sound on the Voyager *Producers* has been CX-encoded without automatic tripping. Surprisingly, even with the CX-encoding off, the track sounds better than Nelson's soundtrack, which is automatically CX-encoded. In general, however, this hardly matters since the film has a roughness that is in keeping with the era in which it was made, magnifying the rude antics of the principal characters.

The theatrical trailer included on the Criterion Collection release is classically constructed (one of the last not to look like a television commercial), and is so effective that the scenes one remembers from the film if one hasn't seen the movie in a while are only the scenes which appear in the trailer. Voyager's disc also has 16 chapter markers, but it is not enough. Two out of the three main musical numbers do not have unique markings.

THE PROFESSIONALS

RCA/Columbia has redone the titles for *The Professionals* so that they will fit on a cropped and scanned television screen. They even had the tenacity to do the title which says, "Filmed in Panavision." The number of times in which an important point of drama is lost because one of the characters is dropped from the screen is too great to mention and the transfer quality is below average.

The Professionals came out in 1967, back before neighborhood theaters were equipped with muscular Dolby systems, so the stereo track comes as something of a surprise. Maurice Jarre's music is best served by it, with castanets hanging in mid air, timpany booming through the floor, and everything except the balalaika swelling and splashing throughout one's video room. The sound effects, particularly some barking dogs, have an eerie sense of immediacy.

Lee Marvin, Burt Lancaster, Woody Strode, and Robert Ryan play the four heroes. As if that weren't enough, Jack Palance, Ralph Bellamy, and Claudia Cardinale are also present. The director, Richard Brooks, manages to include intelligent conversation and even some philosophy amid the action. The film is 117 minutes long, but was spread to three sides to avoid breaking up an important scene. Whether you collect westerns or not, this one is worth having, blurry and mangled as it is.

PROFILES IN AMERICAN ART JOHN CLYMER

American Technology Resources issued a series of twelve laser discs, each of which profiles a different American artist. The one-sided discs are in CAV, but contain no still file feature or any segment which is specifically designed for interactive use. The discs are priced for the educational market.

The series is called *Profiles in American Art*. The one disc which we had an opportunity to view, *John Clymer*, was an informative and well executed documentary about Clymer and the research he conducts to create illustrations of the Old West. In an interview near the beginning, Clymer says that he became an artist because he didn't want to work hard, but he actually goes through many meticulous efforts to assure the verisimilitude of his paintings.

As with the other discs in the *Profiles* series, *John Clymer* is narrated by the *National Geographic Series* veteran, Alexander Scoby. The background music is in stereo and the disc has been CX-encoded without automatic tripping. Still frames depicting motion jiggle two out of every five, but the closeups of Clymer's paintings can be captured clearly.

The other 11 artists covered in the series are Eric Sloan, Donald Teague, Edward Fraughton, Glenna Goodacre, William Whitaker, Conrad Schwiering, Sergei Bongart, George Carlson, Wilson Hurley, John Stobart, and Bob Kuhn.

PROJECT X

If you like monkey movies don't miss *Project X*, an engaging effort in anthropomorphism which pushes only a little beyond reality. Horror stories abound of projects which have lost funding and of chimps, having achieved glimmers of mastering human language, packed off to cancer research. *Project X* takes the situation two steps further. It gives the chimps a slightly higher level of intelligence than they actually have, and it gives their fate a happy ending. Would that it were true. Obviously, not even the movie makers believed in their subject, or they would have come up with a better title.

The disc is of below average quality. The sound is analog stereo and is acceptable, but the picture is very grainy. If you don't like monkey movies, avoid the disc.

PROMISED LAND

Meg Ryan gives a giddy, engaging performance in *Promised Land*, a Sundance Institute production filmed in Utah. The movie, which has the feel of some scriptwriter's revenge upon his past, is about four kids a couple of years out of high school and how they are settling in or not settling in to the next phase of their lives. Ryan, who portrays something of a loose cannon, accomplishes the difficult task of seeming like she is always almost drunk. The others, Kiefer Sutherland, Jason Gedrick and Tracy Pollan, play their parts well, but they remain serious, so it is up to Ryan to bring life to the picture, and she does. The disc is grainy and pale. The Private Music music track is in stereo, but the other sounds stay in the center. The disc is digitally encoded and has chapter markers for the music cues. The screenplay has a few weaknesses, but the four characters are sufficiently developed to make the time one spends with them rewarding.

THE PROTECTOR

In *The Protector*, Jackie Chan portrays a New York cop who travels to Hong Kong with his partner (Danny Aiello) to retrieve a mobster's abducted daughter. The plot is full of holes, but the film is firmly constructed. In the first incident, it appears that the story is being dragged out, but by the fourth time, you realize that Chan's persistence is an important personality trait. Chan's charisma outside of his athletics, however, is limited. Aiello is the only real actor in the movie, and he gets all the good lines. Our favorite: "I never go anywhere in Southeast Asia without an Uzi."

The disc is a bit grainy, but not enough to spoil the fun. The program has plenty of violence and some hysterical nudity – stark naked women are employed by the bad guy to glue heroin/cocaine inside melons. They report to work in the buff.

The disc also has a cheesy stereo soundtrack which could not be better. Full of echoes and atmosphere, the mix reminds one of cavernous neighborhood theaters in the days before they were plexed into noisy kennels.

THE PSYCHEDELIC FURS – ALL OF THIS AND NOTHING

The golden days of music videos are on display in *The Psychedelic Furs – All of This and Nothing*. The band has a mushy new wave sound which was all the rage in the early eighties, and most of the eight videos come from the heyday of MTV. The videos are standard stuff, but several efforts are worth a look. The color experimentation on the seemingly black and white 'Love My Way' is exceptional, as are the video art effects in 'Sleep Comes Down.' Finally, there is a number which shows the group performing in a downpour, 'Heaven.' It is the kind of let's-try-it-once gag which music videos were so good at until the format exhausted itself. The oldest videos have a slightly worn picture quality and the sound is a little fuzzy. The chapter encoded collection is a half hour long and has no interruptions between the numbers.

PSYCHO

PSYCHO (DiscoVision)

The day we bought our first laser disc player, we spent close to two hours stepping through the shower scene of *Psycho*, frame by frame. This was back in the days of DiscoVision, when all discs were in CAV, and it was also back in the days when owning your own copy of a favorite film was still a little inconceivable. Thus, the emotional release was several fold, not only did we thrill to the scene, not only did we get to examine shot by shot how it was constructed, but we got to do it in our own living room, for as long as we wanted. It was a turning point in the whole concept of entertainment.

These days everyone can watch *Psycho* as much as they wish. MCA has put out several iterations of CLV releases, and if one owns a high-end player, one can even step through the shower scene a frame at a time. We had heard discouraging things about the CLV versions, however, and had avoided them in favor of our aging CAV copy. The disparaging opinions were apparently communicated to high places, because MCA has remastered *Psycho* one more time, and has finally produced a CLV version worth bringing home to Mother.

There are still about a half dozen things wrong with the disc, but these are minor complaints which we will dispense with quickly. It is silly that MCA should go through the effort they have to produce a superb monaural soundtrack and then leave it in CX-encoded analog. The break between side one and side two, although closing in on the hour mark, could still have occurred a minute later, when there is a natural fade to black and a change in scene and mood. In the film, the lower portion of the screen is masked during the shower scene. Hitchcock claims this was done on purpose, to hide nudity, though he might be lying. In any case, earlier transfers have kept the masking, but the new version just fills the screen up with picture, so that it is never present.

The picture quality of the transfer, however, is gorgeous, and looks better than the CAV version played at triple speed. The detail is so clear that you can get distracted by the set decorations; every tiny object and shadow is discernible. The original theatrical trailer for *Psycho* was included in a group of trailers at the end of *The Birds*. At the end of *Psycho* are six re-release trailers, all of them claiming that the broadcast version of the movie is not as earthy as the theatrical version, and, more appropriately, from a film history standpoint than any ratings board could have imagined, that the film is rated 'M.'

Psycho is a thriller which is rich in psychological trickery. Some of Hitchcock's personal themes, such as the association between birds and parents (and note that the film opens in Phoenix), will probably have little effect on viewers, except to strengthen subconsciously the clues which link the entire film together (Norman performs taxidermy on more than just birds, and uses bird imagery in his speech). Other themes viewers will refuse to acknowledge, even when the evidence is plain as the nose on one's face. The license plate on the heroine's automobile is ANL-709, and we have friends who will insist and insist to us that it is purely a coincidence and that Hitchcock was not sending out a squirmy message, despite the many other toilets, drains, and swamps in the film. Finally there are the eyes, which are used, perhaps, as a sort of alternative drain. It is the emphasis on peeping, viewing, and 'not blinking' which pulls the viewer into the emotions of the film. Whether it is the pleasing closeups of the stars, perfectly centered on the screen, or the horrific reversal on the face of the corpse at the end, Hitchcock strove to get as close as he could to his audience without actually reaching out and touching them, by taunting the most sensitive, exposed organ on their faces, the one being used to touch him.

PSYCHO III

The second *Psycho* sequel, *Psycho III*, turns out to be just as reverential and clever as the first. It has an opening scene which will have Hitchcock fans standing and applauding in their living rooms. Like *Psycho II*, *Psycho III* retains snippets of dialog from the original, bent to ironic echoes; and scattered, gloriously choice camera angles reprised and replayed in living, wicked color.

Color, however, is a problem for the disc. The film, conceptually, uses the flat, basic colors which Hitchcock liked to work with. The delicately lit skin tones go off the deep end, looking more purplish than tan. The picture is also a little grainy.

There is nothing overtly innovative about the digital soundtrack, but subtle use of the electronic effects from *The Birds* occurs at a key moment. Tony Perkins does a terrific job picking up on his character 25 years after the first jaunt, and, of course, Mother looks like she hasn't aged a day.

PSYCHOLOGY ENCYCLOPEDIA VIDEO DISK

The single-sided CAV educational disc, *Psychology Encyclopedia Video Disk*, has a mixture of still frame sections and motion sequences. It is divided into chapters by subject as follows: 'Intro/Methods,' 'Biological Bases,' 'Sensation/Perception,' 'Developmental,' 'Intelligence – Cognition,' 'Learning & Memory,' 'Testing,' 'Motivation and Emotion,' 'Social,' and 'Human Sexuality.' The still frame material, more illustrative than textual, could easily be reproduced in a book format and is included on the disc to facilitate computer operated lessons, presumably designed by an instructor using the disc, correlated with the motion footage and computer generated text.

The disc is priced for the educational market. It may be of interest to non-academic consumers, however, not only for the nice little survey of Psych 101 which the still frames provide, but for the motion footage. Specifically, there are two moving optical illusions which take advantage of the flat television screen, a cube which appears to be turning clockwise or counterclockwise depending upon when the viewer blinks an eye, and a trapezoid which doesn't seem to be turning at all, though a pencil attached to it certainly is. It is the sort of sequence which one can quickly throw on one's player to astound guests, and would assuredly become part of one's demonstration repertoire.

Other motion sequences include original films from Pavlov's lab (with horrifying footage of a dog being given electric shocks during a behavior study), films taken by John B. Watson of an infant conditioned to fear bunny rabbits and fur blankets, another infant being lifted by a pencil, a sequential CAT scan of the human brain, a bio-feedback demonstration, a rat learning how to obtain food, an explanation of the rat-teaching mechanism, and color cognition demonstrations.

PUBLIC ENEMY

James Cagney is just a kid in *Public Enemy*, but his presence is totally captivating. The film is very old and much of it was directed as if it were a silent picture, but when Cagney is not encumbered by such archaic devices as closeups without backdrops, he uses both his body and his voice to dominate the screen in a manner which few other actors or actresses have ever achieved. It may be wonderful when he smashes a grapefruit into a companion's face in anger, but he is thrilling to watch even when he is portraying a corpse. In *Public Enemy* he doesn't fall for the Mother-complex or the male bonding trips the script tries to lay on him, and the movie's simple psychology is effective entirely because he ignores it.

Some of the rougher edges on the soundtrack are smoothed out, but there are several lengthy dropouts. The print, which opens with a re-release prolog essay that attempts to excuse the glorification of gangsters before getting on with the regular prolog essay that also tries to do the same thing, looks ancient and has many scratches.

PUBLIC ENEMY: FIGHT THE POWER LIVE

One gets the sense that a lot of what the rap group, Public Enemy, does is wishful thinking. They create a context which prevents one from taking their more untoward lyrics seriously, and it is easy to dismiss their numbers, even the good ones, as juvenile whining. Which is not to say that *Public Enemy: Fight the Power Live* is not a compelling program. Were it not for the chapter markers, it would be difficult to tell where the songs end or what is part of the music and what is a separator. The hour program is crammed with images and ideas.

With the same forceful rhythm that spurs on the music, the pictures shift from views of concerts to news footage and to all other sorts of images, usually involving the group's attempts to emulate those who have left mainstream society. Most of the songs are performed live and as a result the lyrics are drowned out by the cacophony, but the disc will be of primary interest to those who are already familiar with the words in any case. Spike Lee's Public Enemy music video, 'Fight the Power,' comes through loud and clear, and it is the centerpiece of the disc, as if the other music videos leading up to it and trailing after it were designed to perform that very function. The picture transfer and the digital stereo are acceptable, though the bass in the live numbers doesn't pack the punch which a studio recording would provide. One comes away from the disc thinking that if Public Enemy is seriously presenting the strongest arguments available for rebelling against the Establishment, then the Establishment must be doing something right.

PUCCINI MADAMA BUTTERFLY

Jean-Pierre Ponnelle filmed the *Madama Butterfly* on a soundstage with a bright white backdrop, signifying a constant fog beyond the bluff upon which Cio-cio-san's modest dwelling sits, and allowed the coccoonish whiteness to take up much of the screen much of the time. The picture is uniformly hazy and often fog bound. For those with projection monitors or other large, sensitive television screens, unless you are an opera fanatic, the disc is not worth it.

This was an early Ponnelle effort, and, with the exception of some well-executed dream sequences, it is not very good. Mirella Freni, afforded the luxury of recording Cio-cio-san in a studio, does not take the singing to the heights one would expect (only the chorus seems to truly benefit from the audio environment).

Placido Domingo, as Pinkerton, had little screen experience when the film was made and does not project his character as well as he does elsewhere. His singing, however, is satisfactory as is the overall sound quality on the disc. The opera, performed by the Vienna Philharmonic and conducted by Herbert von Karajan, is in Italian and has English subtitles.

PUCCINI TOSCA

Puccini Tosca is a real movie, with stereophonic birds atwittering, actual cannon fire, and cuts to shots of the shepherd boy singing offstage at the opening of Act III. None of the program was filmed in a soundstage. Instead, the church and salon interiors are legitimate, and the execution at the end takes place on a roof with all of Rome (and fortunately no television antennas) in the background.

Directed by Gianfranco de Bosio, the film smooths out details in a way which stage performances cannot accomplish. Not only is the painting of Mary Magdalene, which the artist Cavaradossi (played by Placido Domingo) works on as the opera opens, scrumptious, but the viewer is privy to a miniature of Tosca (played by Raina Kabaivanska) that Cavaradossi carries next to his heart, and it, too, is enrapturing. After Tosca kills Scarpia (Sherril Milnes), she flees his office down a long stairwell, the trail of her gown flowing behind her. The film can't cure the basic shortcomings of Puccini's score, but it comes a long way toward making the work fluent and dramatic.

The singing is fine. Domingo gave a more charged performance on the 'Live at the Met' Pioneer release, but there is nothing inadequate about his presence and he has a natural, accommodating acting style which works well in front of a camera. Kabaivanska's vocals are more energetic and, appropriately, she is the center of attention in any scene where she appears.

The sound effects are more stereophonic than the music, but the recording, made in 1976, should not cause any problems. The picture is mildly grainy and there is a vertical white line which appears for a while on side three. The opera is in Italian and the program has English subtitles. Each Act appears on a separate side (including Act III, which is 27 minutes long and is in CLV) and the disc comes in a box jacket, accompanied by a brochure styled insert which contains a full history of the opera's origins and a complete plot synopsis. There is no coordination, however, between the synopsis and the chapter encoding.

PULLING GS
An artistic profile of several different aviation subjects, *Pulling Gs*, includes some terrific footage of the sleek SR-71 Blackbird, a nice pictorial of various helicopters in action, a good computer animated depiction of a jet in flight, and the expected amount of cameras positioned on different planes as they take off, twist or spin, and pierce the sky.

The jacket cover is a little misleading as to the content of the sound program which accompanies the visuals. You hear one jet once at the very beginning, get one brief lecture on some cockpit controls at the start of chapter three, and are otherwise left with a leisurely paced electronically oriented music score. The music was recorded and transferred in digital all the way through (much of it was even created digitally), so it arrives without contamination on the digital track, although it certainly doesn't exercise the limits of one's sound system. The analog track is less powerful, but it is still very clean.

The 56-minute disc is in CAV format. Most of the time the frames do not jiggle, but since a variety of visual sources were utilized, there is an occasional still-frame flicker. The footage varies in quality, with the promotional material from the manufacturers being in much better condition than the Department of Defense films. There are 8 chapters, 4 to a side, each of which has a theme of some sort. An enthusiastic set of notes is included on a four-page booklet. Frame numbers where specific maneuvers or other points of interest occur are identified in the notes.

PUMPING IRON
Arnold Schwarzenegger's uncannily well crafted career began with a mock-documentary about bodybuilding entitled *Pumping Iron*. The movie, which also stars Lou Ferrigno, is well paced and is an appealing film even to those who are not enthusiastic about its subject.

Apportioned in thirds, the film legitimately documents a couple of 'World Championship' contests and the preparations taken by the competitors. The contrivance is Arnold's participation. The camera catches him so differently than the others that the only explanation for his smooth and forceful presence can be that he is acting, probably with substantial rehearsal before many of the shots. No matter, the movie is entertaining and has a touch of reality to it, and the award Arnold wins is real and apparently deserved.

The film has a documentary appearance. The lighting is rough and the edges are soft. The disc transfer looks good, taking these facets into consideration. Some of the music is stereophonic, but the sound is no better than the picture. Side one is in CAV, with two unsteady still frames out of every five, but plenty of opportunities to freeze bodybuilding portraits.

PUMPING IRON II – THE WOMEN
The quasi-documentary, *Pumping Iron II – The Women*, fills a niche no movie before ever attempted to fill. Not only does the story follow the participants at a 1983 Women's Body Building Championship, it gets into the center of the sport's personality conflict. A woman who has emphasized musculature over feminine physique enters the contest and so a controversy arises concerning how the women should be judged and what the standards for Women's Bodybuilding are. The movie was shot in 16mm and blown up to 35mm, so it looks pretty grainy. The disc suffers the transition adequately and is in stereo, although not much more than the music appears to have separations.

PUMPKINHEAD
The horror concoction, *Pumpkinhead*, has an American Gothic atmosphere and an elaborately constructed monster which bears more than a passing resemblance to Ronald Reagan. The Ultra-Stereo separations are limited. Much of the movie takes place under difficult lighting effects, which look especially grainy. The monster is summoned when a group of bratty college kids cause an accident. The results are predictable, but the disc is passable entertainment if it is a cold, stormy night outside and there is a warm fire on the hearth.

PUNCHLINE
Near the end of side one on *Punchline* the script takes a turn downwards which is so sudden and sharp that the viewer never fully recovers an affection for the film, which had been going pretty good up until that point. The movie is about two budding comedians, played by Tom Hanks and Sally Field, who cross paths long enough to help one another. Although it is never specifically indicated, the character played by Hanks has the personality and dynamism of a cocaine addict. It is no wonder that the film failed at the boxoffice, because once his character's darker side appears, the movie stops being fun and not even Field and John Goodman (typecast as Field's long-suffering husband) can rescue it.

The movie runs a couple minutes over two hours (another mistake) and is spread to three sides, in CLV. The picture looks orange and strong colors often appear grainy. The analog stereo surround sound is limited in special effects, but acceptable.

THE PUPPETOON MOVIE
An excellent compilation of George Pal 'Puppetoon' featurettes, is humorously introduced by Gumby and a dinosaur, *The Puppetoon Movie*. The 1987 program has clearly been constructed for video and not theatrical presentation, but it is the perfect format to present the sometimes unappetizing stop motion animation. The figurines do not seem threatening or abstract, and the short films blend together well. The only reservation some viewers may have would be for the numerous black puppets, which are often presented with exaggerated lips and bulging eyes (though a straight interpretation of the 'John Henry' tale is the disc's strongest cartoon).

The integrity of the short Pal films are respected and presented with their original monaural sound. The introduction, however, has been done in Ultra-Stereo, and starts the disc off with a bang. Most of the shorts were filmed in Technicolor, and all have been excellently preserved and transferred. Several are marked by more than one chapter marker, a listing of which can be found on the back of the jacket Side two of the disc is in CAV, with two unsteady still frames out of every five. The best utilization of the CAV format is to speed image and make the figures look even more realistic than they already appear.

PURGATORY
Tanya Roberts stars in *Purgatory*, a women's prison movie which is tainted by racial overtones. Roberts portrays a Peace Corps worker falsely accused of carrying heroin in an African country and thrown into a prison where the inmates are used for prostitution. The filmmakers try to include enough white villains to give the semblance of equal opportunity exploitation, but the leering sequence in which Roberts' companion is gang raped by black prison guards is difficult to shake off after the disc is over.

The picture is grainy, but the digitally encoded monaural sound has some body to it and is best amplified. The movie isn't worth the trouble, however. It is the sort where characters shoot when they ought to run and run when they ought to shoot. Let the title, then, be its own final destination.

PURPLE PEOPLE EATER
Adults will have little patience with *Purple People Eater*, a mindless children's film involving a phony looking shaggy purple creature, a young musician, and the elderly residents of a small apartment complex facing eviction. You can say 'let's put on a show!' several times before they finally get around to doing it. The disc is not in stereo surround as the jacket cover proclaims but is instead a reasonably strong digitally encoded monaural. The picture transfer is bright, but Image did not bother to give all the songs chapter markers. Little Richard and Chubby Checker make brief performance appearances and Neil Patrick Harris stars.

PURPLE RAIN
Movies like *Flashdance* and *Footloose* were designed with the idea that segments from the movie could be put together as music videos for promotional purposes. *Purple Rain* is the first movie to be put together from music videos. It is also the first time in the history of cinema that the boy professes his affection for the girl by giving her his favorite earring.

The star of the film, Prince, once hit the jackpot with disco songs which went beyond euphemism and actually started naming the portions of the human anatomy and bodily functions which are normally associated with romance. One song representative of that period surfaces in *Purple Rain*, but the other numbers are more suitable for air play and the film is certifiably commercial.

Prince portrays a singer whose stint at a local club is jeopardized by his messed-up home life, his messed-up love life, and his general immaturity. No wonder young people all across America identified with it.

Purple Rain has a glossy look and is sharply edited. The picture is fairly good and the stereo is overpowering in all the right ways. The disc sorely misses chapter markers. Those who are looking for a two-hour music video with a coherent story will not be disappointed.

THE PURPLE ROSE OF CAIRO
Usually, good films with downbeat endings are better the second time because you know what is going to happen. Woody Allen's *The Purple Rose of Cairo* is less magical the second time you watch it and the ending doesn't work any better than it did the first time.

The sound on a Woody Allen film is usually its least accomplished technical aspect, but it is represented adequately on the disc. The color, however, is grainy. The daytime 'real world' scenes are lit more brightly than they should have been, but that was probably a conceptual choice by Allen in coordination with the life-is-tough ending.

The story, ending aside, is brilliant. It is the perfect movie to spring on people who know nothing about the plot, because it has the ultimate in verisimilitudenous twists, right near the beginning. Allen, who stayed behind the camera to write and direct, follows through on his initial premise in a pleasingly logical fashion. *The Purple Rose of Cairo* is witty, amusing, charming, nostalgic, thought-provoking, and intelligent. Someone should take up a collection to give it a decent conclusion.

THE PUZZLE OF THE TACOMA NARROWS BRIDGE COLLAPSE

The educational laser disc, *The Puzzle of the Tacoma Narrows Bridge Collapse*, has been available for some time, but it is likely that few laser disc consumers have heard of it. The Tacoma Narrows is a tidally active passage of water at the south end of Puget Sound. On the east side of its steep banks is the city of Tacoma, Washington, and on the west bank, in the late 1930s, there was a lot of pristine woodland which developers and city planners could only stand on the bluffs and stare at, longingly. It is such an apt spot for a bridge that after the first one fell down, a second was put in its place.

The first Tacoma Narrows Bridge began wiggling as soon as it was built. On a breezy, but not unusually stormy November day (though it likely was the strongest wind the bridge had been submitted to) six months after the bridge opened, the vibration increased to a gallop. The roadway twisted like a piece of licorice, snapped away from the suspension cables, and went crashing into the whitecapped waters of the Sound.

This has all been captured on the first part of *The Puzzle of the Tacoma Narrows Bridge Collapse* with excellent documentorial clarity. The 27-minute CAV disc is intended to be an introduction to a specific concept in Physics, 'Simple Harmonic Motion,' but the subject is approached so thoroughly that the disc has real educational value for first graders (watching the collapse), college undergraduates, and all those in between.

When the concept of waves is introduced, footage of the whitecaps beneath the bridge is rerun, revealing a sense of poetry. The disc is also entertaining as home video, though the educational market price may be prohibitive for that kind of application.

Although the disc has been designed to interface with a computer, a linear run-though of the program is not the least confusing. The poor sound quality is the disc's only unattractive feature. When the puzzle is solved and those old enough to follow the physics understand why the bridge failed, they may be amazed that things like this don't happen more often.

PYGMALION
MY FAIR LADY

The print used for *Pygmalion* is as fractured as Eliza Doolittle's English and Henry Higgins' manners. Not that we have ever seen a print which looked better than this one; we haven't. But prospective owners should be aware that this is not a well-preserved film. In one reel, the lower right corner is out of focus. In another, the volume drops significantly. At every reel change there are scratches, splices, and other odd markings. The film has been preserved on laser disc, but not restored.

Still, it is nice to have this incarnation, with Leslie Howard as Higgins and the similar-looking Wendy Hiller as Eliza. With the exception of the volume drop-off, Voyager has done an excellent job transferring the film to disc. No precious line of dialog is ever mangled by a splice. Besides, don't some movies work better if they actually look old? Here it makes the lines seem more risque, and hides the flaws in Howard's performance (he can't help being too nice for the part, and if the film were smoother it would be more noticeable).

The sound has not been CX-encoded. The dialog is usually clear and the constant hiss can be contained by keeping the volume at reasonable levels. The disc is in CLV and has chapter markers.

We enjoyed the disc, and after it was over we had several hours to kill, so we decided to put on *My Fair Lady*. The essay on the back of the *Pygmalion* jacket notes that it is difficult to watch the earlier film without humming the later one. The reason, however, is not elaborated upon and it is worth noting. The tunes pester the back of one's mind during *Pygmalion* not because *Lady* was so popular, but because George Bernard Shaw's prose is so perfectly scanned that it could often be adapted as lyric, without modification.

The primary advantage which *Lady* has to offer is the expansion of Eliza's part. Her transition is made more believable. Unfortunately, one has trouble believing Audrey Hepburn to be anything short of a Duchess to begin with, so her performance is not as effective as Heller's. Rex Harrison, however, demonstrates that he had far greater stage experience with the part than Howard had, and delivers every syllable of dialog with a purposeful energy.

The colors are beautiful, but the sharpness of the picture is tentative, and deteriorates rapidly on larger screens. There is some color shifting, some fuzziness, and more than an acceptable amount of marks and scratches. The image is also scanned. Poor Colonel Pickering is forever being cropped.

The sound is stereophonic and CX-encoded. The sound transfer is fairly decent, but the recording is from an older technology than the methods employed in contemporary films, and this may bother some viewers. The disc has no chapter markers, and the intermission break is suppressed. The exit music is retained, however, and, with a smart-alecky deliberateness, the FBI Warning appears during its crescendo.

PYTHON WOLF
STALKING DANGER

In an attempt to imitate the success of Michael Mann and other Hollywood directors who have dabbled in television, William Friedkin put together a couple of pilot episodes for a series entitled 'C.A.T. Squad.' The programs, *Python Wolf* and *Stalking Danger*, have been released as separate discs. Whereas other Hollywood directors turn to television to explore dramatic situations that are beyond the economic feasibility of theatrical film, Friedkin, on the other hand, displays nothing but utter contempt for his audience and the medium. The films are such an insulting grind of violence and phony high tech gimmicks that it is gratifying the networks had better sense than to pick up the series.

The disc jacket art for *Python Wolf* is misleading, including a drawing of four characters who look nothing like the characters in the program. The title is actually the name of an illegal intelligence unit which the Squad locks horns with, although the jacket copy implies that 'Python Wolf' is the organization to which the heroes belong. The R rating on the jacket is a joke. The plot, something about a group of right wing South Africans who are so radical their own government wants to eliminate them, is a tangled mess of mislaid logic and cynical social consciousness.

The plot for *Stalking Danger* is less complicated, about chasing down an international assassin. The assassin kills many innocent characters before getting his, and the team tracks him down by obtaining key pieces of information offscreen, with a character invariably walking into a room and announcing the next lead. Because of the violence, the episode is so aggressively mean to a viewer's sympathy that one can't even relax and enjoy the show for its stupidity.

The picture transfer is very good on *Python Wolf* and almost as sharp on *Stalking Danger*. The monaural sound is passable on both discs and Danger uses the worst of Ennio Morricone for a musical score.

QUADROPHENIA (see THE BRIDE)

QUARTET (Import)

James Ivory's film adaptation of the Jean Rhys novel, *Quartet*, is available on disc in Japan. The movie stars Maggie Smith and Alan Bates, who portray a rich couple that live in Paris in the late twenties and offer lodgings to a young woman, played by Isabelle Adjani, whose husband has been sent to jail. The joys in the film are mostly in the tightly controlled but exquisitely comical performances of Smith and Bates. The movie is a drama, but their every little nuance is so deliberately coy that one can't help but laugh at each arched eyebrow and every disguised mutter. There isn't anything significantly wrong with the story or with Ivory's execution, but, like a stage vehicle which is really just an excuse to see a star in the flesh, the film's value is the chance it gives Smith and Bates to strut, and they do so with a marvelously retentive abandon.

The film is in English, with some passages in French (only one scene is consequential and it can be understood well enough), and has Japanese subtitles. There is a very thin black band at the top of the screen. The picture quality leaves something to be desired. The film is in color and was made with filters which give everything a brownish cast. On disc, however, most scenes simply look too orange, and the image is very grainy. The sound is indistinctive and causes some of the dialog to be obscured. The jacket cover art is wonderful (a life sized closeup of Adjani, who has silver-blue eyes).

QUARTET SCHUBERT STRING QUARTET "ROSAMUNDE"
Good, basic filmmaking is at work in *Quartet*, subtitled *Schubert String Quartet "Rosamunde,"* which has deservedly won awards for its conception and execution. Set to Franz Schubert's String Quartet D. 804, traditionally referred to as the "Rosamunde" Quartet because it was originally composed for the entr'acte of a play by the same name, the film, conceived by Anton van Munster, depicts both the construction of the instruments and the playing of the piece. Combining footage of mastercraftsman Jaap Bolink and his wife, Annelies Steinhauser, building violins and cellos by hand, with a depiction of a quartet, dressed informally, playing the piece, and adding peripheral contributions, such as the felling of a tree which would yield the wood for the violins, the etching and printing of the score, and the horses (who are only shown running free) that will eventually give up their tails for the sake of fine music, the movie provides both a documentary look at the execution of a craft and an evocative interpretation of Schubert's music. The images are edited to the flow and emotions of the score.

The half-hour disc appears to have been recorded separately from the scenes depicting the musicians, but the sound is well formed despite its studio acoustics. Stringed instruments have the hardest time with digital encoding, but each comes through separately and clearly on the soundtrack. The picture is not as good. The print is fresh, but the image is grainy. An excellent insert comes with the disc, containing an interview with van Munster and an essay discussing the gestation of Schubert's quartet.

QUATERMASS II
The egg hatching sequence in *Alien* was spawned in *Quatermass II*, a black-and-white British science fiction film featuring the astrophysicist hero, Professor Quatermass. The first couple minutes of night photography look awful, but the remainder of the film is in passable condition. The sound is quite noisy. The volume on the analog track is set lower, but when raised it is equally noisy.

The 'Quatermass' films are rare accomplishments in that they manage to be truly scary despite the use of inexpensive special effects. The thrill is not in the vision, but in the idea behind it and how that idea is communicated. In *Quatermass II*, thermos-sized meteorites sprinkle the countryside and are gathered by mysterious workers from a large chemical complex. The meteorites contain a surprise for anyone who gets too close. By the end Quatermass has battled monsters, zombies, and angry townspeople, and has saved rural England, as well as the world, from certain destruction.

Side one is in CAV although the conclusion has the most elaborate special effects. The source material may look a little worn down, but if *The Crawling Eye* is in your collection, *Quatermass II* belongs next to it.

QUEEN CHRISTINA
MGM's costume romance starring Greta Garbo, *Queen Christina*, looks sharp, but tattered. The film itself is a choppy effort which plays best during its middle third, when the Queen sneaks away from her court and falls in love, incognito. The whole tone of the film shifts during this sequence, taking on a cozy, snow-bound atmosphere which it cannot possibly sustain when the characters return to officialdom. The 1934 black-and-white production definitely looks its age, though the presentation is generally acceptable. The sound is fuzzy and has a couple of bad surges. The volume is set higher for the original theatrical trailer which comes on after the film is ended, and you may have to go running to your amplifier to readjust for it. The trailer is a fascinating attempt to hide the historical aspects of the narrative and to capitalize on Garbo's own notoriety. The disc has also been decently chapter encoded.

THE QUEEN OF SPADES
(see **EUGENE ONEGIN**)

QUEENSRYCHE – LIVE IN TOKYO
(Import)
Back when we were in high school there was a youngster living in our neighborhood who owned a go-cart. He drove it down the streets with a fierce, satisfied look in his eye and was adept at eluding the County police through a knowledge of the hidden links between several extended driveways. We assumed that he couldn't elude the police forever and would eventually end up in jail or, at best, become a garage mechanic. Life being what it is, he is now a member of the heavy metal rock group, Queensryche.

When the group first played in New York we called his mother and demanded that she arrange an opportunity for us to visit him backstage. We had no trouble getting in, because the bouncers took one look at us and knew we weren't there to smash windows or steal guitar stands. It was an exciting moment, but to tell the truth, we really weren't surprised to discover that the band, despite their authoritarian title and tough-guy images, are the sweetest kids who ever got together to have a good time. That's the secret of all the heavy metal bands. They are really sort of the pro wrestlers of rock and they treat their fans better than performers of any other pop genre.

They appear to be having fun performing in front of a Japanese audience in *Queensryche – Live in Tokyo*. Half the time they forget they are supposed to be looking like tough Americans. They grin and wail away on their instruments and it is clear that one of them, at least, has turned his go-cart into a guitar.

The imported disc is superbly transferred, but the program suffers from poor production standards. The picture is victimized by the stage lighting and in the long shots the musicians are nothing more than colored blurs. The sound recording is barely in stereo and has no sense of freshness. Each of the ten numbers the group performs has a chapter marker. The lyrics are included on a jacket insert, in English. The disc has no subtitles.

QUICKSILVER
The plot of *Quicksilver* could fit on a short telegram: Boy loses millions. Stop. Boy becomes bike messenger. Stop. Boy makes millions for friends he met at messenger service and meets nice girl he saves from bad driver. Stop. Unfortunately, the movie is longer than that, and there are not enough acrobatic bicycle tricks to fill in the pauses. The stereo sound is okay, especially if you like the noise of traffic. The picture, however, is a bit grainy. Mercurial, it isn't.

QUIET COOL
It is a well known tenet that actors who are heroes on TV shows make good movie villains, and actors who have established themselves as villains in the movies are great as good guys on the TV. One of our favorite movie baddies, James Remar, plays a good guy in *Quiet Cool*. He shuffles his feet and mumbles too much for the big screen, but the movie is enjoyable home video. He plays a New York cop who cleans out a battalion of marijuana growers in the California Redwoods as a favor to a dead friend. Some of the smaller details are a bit obnoxious, but the big action scenes are well executed and Remar is at his best when he forgets that he is supposed to be good – there's no compassion in his eyes as he massacres the enemy. The movie also has a Western-style showdown at the end, a touch which is usually disastrous in contemporary films, but works surprisingly well here.

The picture is below average. Major objects are silhouetted by a red glow. The sound is monaural and has not been CX-encoded, though the quality of the sound is better than average.

THE QUIET EARTH
The New Zealand film, *The Quiet Earth*, is based on an original novel but smacks suspiciously of 'The World, the Flesh, and the Devil.' It starts off like a 'Twilight Zone' episode, about a man who awakens to discover that everyone else in the world has disappeared. The script is not carefully blocked out, and too much time is spent on the opening part, but if the viewer sticks with the film long enough, rewards eventually come. The science fiction aspects are stimulating, and the drama, though limited, is respectable.

The gorgeous ad art of Saturn on the horizon, which CBS/Fox has wisely employed for the jacket, is a cheat, since the scene using the graphics appears only briefly and most of the film has no special visual effects at all.

The analog surround stereo sound is less accomplished than the digital sound, but except for a let's-make-'em-nervous bass, the sound editing is not an elaborate effort. On some copies the digital track is missing on side one. The picture transfer looks okay, so long as strong, glowing colors are not present.

THE QUINTESSENTIAL PEGGY LEE
It is exiting to have Peggy Lee's articulate voice on *The Quintessential Peggy Lee*. You can turn up 'Fever' as loud as you want without distortion. The hour-long concert, split fairly evenly to two sides, was filmed in Atlantic City in a modest-sized cabaret at one of the casinos. Lee wears an orange outfit which blurs during the long shots, but, during closeups and when the stage lights aren't red, the picture is sharp. What can you say about a star who can perform 'When You're Smiling' as if it were a serious love song and get away with it? We thought 'Is That All There Is?' was finished after *After Hours*, but she revives it effortlessly. And movie fans will not want to miss her closing number, 'Johnny Guitar.'

THE RACCOONS COLLECTION
If you obtain a copy of *The Raccoons Collection* cartoons, watch side two first. Side two is a full-length cartoon called 'The Raccoons and the Lost Star.' Side one is a compilation of several different Raccoon cartoons set to music, called 'The Raccoons Let's Dance!' and contains lengthy clips from 'Lost Star.'

The cartoons are in stereo, though only the music and a few sound effects are actually given a boost. Some padding of material is inevitable. 'Let's Dance' is all padding, stuffed with forgettable songs by Rita Coolidge, Leo Sayer, and others. The cartoonists deftly exploit a group of comical villains who are even more clutzy than the bumbling heroes. The point of view angles and visual style are up-to-date but the humor and excitement are dependably old-fashioned.

RAD
Hal Needham's *Rad* is about an underdog stunt bike (BMX) racer who beats a bunch of seasoned professionals and earns the respect of his hometown. You always have to stay with a Needham movie through to the end before dismissing it because just as the comedy or the drama is becoming strained he comes up with another spectacular stunt to grab your attention. Bicycles fly through the air up, down, and backwards. If only the dialog had the same freedom from gravity. The disc is just blurry enough so that you can't read the red letters in the credit roll which tell you not to try this sort of daredevil pedaling in your living room.

RADIO BIKINI
Some of the commentators broadcasting on location in the footage contained on *Radio Bikini*, a documentary about the first atomic tests to be conducted after the end of World War II, complain that they are unimpressed by the blasts. However, the images which are shown on the screen, recorded by a battalion of photographic equipment, are humbling, even when viewed on a small TV. The scale of the mushroom cloud is readily apparent. It is a canker in heaven, a self-inflicted scar which man has set upon his womb.

The documentary, unfortunately, has a chip on its shoulder. The 56-minute film tells the story of two victims: The chief of the Melanesian tribe which was relocated to depopulate the Bikini Atoll, and a sailor who became sick, clearly because of radiation exposure, before the exercises were over and struggled for the next thirty years with deformity and cancer. That is good reporting, but by confining the other side of the story to the promotional films and live broadcasts from the era, the documentary is not balanced enough to be convincing. Surely some former military or government official, after thirty years have passed, would be willing to talk about what the project intended to accomplish and what data were gathered from it. Was it worth disrupting lives and the environment? The snide implications one draws from the government's propaganda efforts diminish the power of the film as a fair document of the incident.

The footage is pretty amazing. Color films have been restored with excellent clarity and the black and white material is also fascinating. The sound is digitally encoded, although the source material is naturally scratchy. There is one last item which no one in the film comments upon, but its implications are telling. Sheep were tied to the decks of empty vessels deliberately anchored in the blast zone. Cameras accompanying the first crew to explore the damage caused by the explosion discover the carcasses of the sheep. The animals are burnt, but they are already surrounded by a flurry of very active, healthy flies.

RADIO DAYS
Woody Allen's nostalgic musings about childhood in Far Rockaway, New York, *Radio Days*, has made it onto disc in reasonably nice condition. The picture quality maintains Allen's low-key colors with a minimum of corruption. The sound is fine.

The title probably throws a lot of viewers off the track of what the film is really about. The script creates the narrative equivalent of twisting the dial on a radio, picking up pieces of different stories, moving on to others, and then coming back to earlier ones as events have inexplicably advanced. One or two of the stories tribute the efforts of those behind the microphones, and the first time you see the film you may be disappointed that more of the movie hasn't been allocated to these characters, but the soul of *Radio Days* is in Far Rockaway, and on subsequent viewings you will realize that is exactly where it belongs. The movie is good home video, because it is more effective after you comprehend the rules under which it is operating. The radio stuff is a little fantastic, more like what one would imagine was going on in a studio than what really went on. Despite a token number of deliberate gags, the best moments in the movie are the simple, believable portrayals of families surviving the New Deal and growing, sometimes in spite of themselves, into the future.

RAFFI A YOUNG CHILDREN'S CONCERT WITH RAFFI
RAFFI RAFFI IN CONCERT WITH THE RISE AND SMILE BAND
SHARON, LOIS, & BRAM SHARON, LOIS, & BRAM'S ELEPHANT SHOW – SLEEP OVER
SHARON, LOIS, & BRAM SHARON, LOIS, & BRAM'S ELEPHANT SHOW – LIVE IN YOUR LIVING ROOM
If you have an ongoing relationship with a person who has yet to lose a tooth or tie a shoelace, chances are you have heard of Raffi, or are perhaps even plotting ways to accidentally drop a brick on his records. Well, put your hand in the air and stop, because now there are some Raffi laser discs. Actually, Raffi is a smooth performer, and you can listen to his music, a combination of traditional tunes a few mildly nonsensical ones he wrote himself, hundreds of times without getting irritated or bored. The problem is that kids will want to listen to him thousands of times. His voice has a sweet softness and an enthusiastic pitch, and watching kids listen to him is like watching kittens with catnip.

The stereo on *RAFFI A Young Children's Concert with RAFFI* and *RAFFI Raffi in Concert with The Rise and Smile Band* is good, adeptly preserving Raffi's vocals and capturing the responses of the audience with clarity. The picture quality is also good, with stage lighting causing no significant distortion. The songs have chapter markers. No listing is provided on either jacket cover, but an insert, with song lyrics, accompanying *Young Children's Concert*, presents the songs on that disc in order. Both programs run about three quarters of an hour.

Both concerts are similar in presentation and the backup band on *Raffi in Concert* remains in the background. A few songs are repeated on the two discs, but most of the material is different. The camera work and editing on both discs are impressive. Raffi's audience tends to participate in each song whether encouraged to do so or not, and the program cuts constantly between the singer and the kids. Finding a new face almost every time, the cameras always land on a picturesque child who is completely absorbed in what is going on. Obviously, from the reaction of his audience, Raffi would be appealing on video anyway, but the construction of the two programs heighten his appeal even more, and encourage both children and dubious adults to start singing and quacking and jumping around.

Those who fill the description at the beginning of this review and have access to the cable channel, Nickelodeon, are undoubtedly familiar with Sharon, Lois & Bram as well. They sing the same songs Raffi does, and have the same appeal, though in comparing them, Raffi would be the Picasso and Sharon, Lois, & Bram would be the Braque. A&M has released two discs of their programs, as well, *SHARON, LOIS, & BRAM Sharon, Lois, & Bram's Elephant Show – Sleep Over* and *SHARON, LOIS, & BRAM Sharon, Lois, & Bram's Elephant Show – Live in Your Living Room.* Each program runs a half hour and is presented in CLV. *Sleep Over* is monaural and *Living Room* is stereo.

Living Room is in the same format as the two *Raffi* discs, a live concert, though comparing it to the *Raffi* programs can be an amusing experience for the discerning viewer. Unlike the slick *Raffi* production, the cameras in *Living Room* are forever capturing kids who are not paying attention to the singers, kids who are fighting with the kids behind them, and kids who are throwing temper tantrums and actively being subdued by their parents. And with Raffi fresh in one's mind, Sharon, Lois, & Bram do not seem quite so ethereal or charismatic. Still, they get the job done, and the target group will surely be pleased.

Sleep Over has a different format. The three singers and a group of children use a slumber party skit as an excuse to sing some songs and play some games. The program puts the singers in their best light and is immediately captivating, particularly to young viewers. Some of the most energetically choreographed songs are awkwardly lip synched, but otherwise the set runs smoothly and is a nice change of pace from a straight concert.

The picture quality on both discs tends to be a little more grainy and fuzzy than on the *Raffi* discs. The discs are chapter marked, and the song listings on the back of the jacket, although not accompanied by numerals, represent the proper order of presentation. The labels on all four offerings are too similar in appearance for young fans to differentiate.

THE RAILRODDER/BUSTER KEATON RIDES AGAIN

A twenty-minute color film which Buster Keaton made in Canada in 1964, 'The Railrodder,' is presented in CAV on *The Railrodder/Buster Keaton Rides Again*. The dialog-less movie, in which Keaton travels across Canada on a two-seat motorized open air 'railrodder,' is not only charming, but has many heart-stopping stunts, stunts that the elderly Keaton executes with the same grace and simplicity that he demonstrated 40 years earlier when he was at the pinnacle of his profession.

Side 2, 'Buster Keaton Rides Again,' is a 'making of' feature, filmed behind the scenes during the shooting of 'Railrodder,' and incorporating an objective portrait of Keaton's life and career. Although 'making of' movies are never to be trusted, there is evidence, supported by the completed film, to suggest that the visionary director of 'Railrodder,' Gerald Potterton, is rather inexperienced, and that Keaton's own creativity and filmmaking knowledge played a large part in the movie's success. Having been lulled by veiled portraits in *The Comic* and *Sunset Boulevard*, we were stunned by the vitality and brilliant intuition which Keaton displays in 'Rides Again.' It is immediately clear that it was his own business judgements and sloppiness which led to his career slide, and not the advent of the talkies which, had he the self control he shows here, he could have mastered with the same ease that he balances on moving railroad vehicles. And what a face the years gave him!

The color on 'Railrodder' is faded and the image quality is only fair. The CAV encoding has two unsteady still frames out of every five. 'Rides Again' is in CLV and is black and white, with no significant flaws. The monaural sound on 'Railrodder' has many cute effects and is worth amplifying. Contrary to the tag on the jacket cover, neither side of the disc has been chapter encoded.

RAIN MAN
MIDNIGHT COWBOY

The curiously emotionless ending of *Rain Man* obviously did not hurt its impact as an entertainment, though it does leave one feeling that the movie could have been better than it was. As it stands the film could be turned into a great TV series. Except for the two stars in the cast, the movie has the feel of a good TV pilot – an involving establishment of character with no forthright conclusion.

Although the fleshtones are a little too pink at times, the disc package is scrumptious. It comes in a handsome, milk white gatefold jacket, nicely illustrated, with 40 encoded chapter markers listed on the inner spread. The film's sound editing is average for a major film, and some of Dustin Hoffman's mumbles are difficult to make out, but the disc's soundtrack is superbly transferred and presents the audio better than all but the classiest first run theatrical exhibitions. Except for the pinkish flesh in some scenes, and an instability in some of the most intense colors, the picture transfer looks fine.

Another Oscar-winning film which starred Dustin Hoffman, *Midnight Cowboy*, comes from a less elegant time. The monaural sound is actually in decent condition, since it has no exceptional distortion. The picture, however, looks its age, especially in night or dark interior scenes. The worst scenes have globs of unmanageable colors vying for control of the screen. The daylight footage is passable, though the fleshtones often look too orange.

Hoffman's performance in *Midnight Cowboy* is perhaps even more amazing than his performance in *Rain Man*. In *Rain Man* he expertly follows a certain set of psychological quirks and confinements, but in *Cowboy* his whole appearance changes, as if his face were two inches longer. (And the last shot seems to be a deliberately dark variation of *The Graduate*.) *Cowboy* originally received an X rating, and was re-rated to R after advancing social standards left the brief glimpses of nudity and suggestive sexual acts less threatening. Nevertheless, there are important passages, particularly during the obscured flashbacks, which inevitably disappear when the film is shown on broadcast television. The movie is locked into a sixties stylistic approach which can feel dated, but Hoffman's performance can prevent one from ever tiring of the film. That will surely be the case with *Rain Man* as well, as Hoffman's voice seems to have a subliminally comic rhythm no matter what manner of character he embodies.

THE RAINBOW

The most normal movie Ken Russell made in a very long time, *The Rainbow* has a good looking picture. The stereo surround sound is a little too loud and enthusiastically separated, but not beyond manageable limits. A cagey but interesting interview with Russell appears on a jacket insert. The film is based upon a story by D.H. Lawrence and has its share of free spirited passion and overwrought symbolism. Still, it is essentially a simple and relaxing tale about a young woman coming of age in the late 1800s. The ending is anti-climatic.

RAINBOW BRIDGE FEATURING JIMI HENDRIX

The transfer of *Rainbow Bridge Featuring Jimi Hendrix* is very good although the movie was made inexpensively and has monaural sound. The source material is clearly the freshest available and the disc preserves it as well as can be expected.

The 74-minute film ends with a 30-minute Hendrix concert which Image has isolated on side two. The first part of the film is a fictional concoction which follows a woman as she travels to Hawaii and visits the concert site. Along the way she interacts with a number of young people. The film was made in the late sixties and purposefully represents the most extreme aspects of the sixties culture, inadvertently depicting the antecedents of the New Age movement. The film becomes more valuable as a historical tool – even if much of it is a put-on, because it is like that which was not – the further time withdraws from the era. There are better Hendrix concerts around – though this one is okay – and there are certainly better sounding Hendrix records, but few films captured the sixties so unselfconsciously and look so silly in retrospect.

RAINBOW BRITE – THE MIGHTY MONSTROMURK MENACE

The picture on *Rainbow Brite – The Mighty Monstromurk Menace* is tentative and solid colors are often broken with lines of interference. The show contains a brief summary of what was apparently an earlier episode, although no such episode is available on disc. The Hallmark-inspired characters exude color with their every breath. Their 'Rainbow Land' is threatened by some black-and-white meanies who, after 40 minutes of being pounded by rainbows and cuteness, beat a wise retreat.

THE RAINMAKER

Katharine Hepburn is miscast in *The Rainmaker*. She is captivating in some scenes, but her accent doesn't match the accents of the characters who are supposed to be her family and neighbors. The film is an adaptation of a very stagey play, one which is more removed from narrative reality than a movie can normally accommodate. The story – about a family whose lives are changed for the better by the intrusion of a charismatic confidence artist – would be so difficult to convert to a true movie world that the filmmakers don't bother to try. Burt Lancaster does exactly what a good actor on a stage would do in his performance of the con man, and he is completely captivating despite the artificial nature of his presence. One is tempted to stop the movie and replay his scenes with Hepburn, in order to watch each performer, and it says as much about the movie that repeating parts of it are a pleasure as it does that interrupting it is not a bother.

Paramount doesn't think interrupting it is a bother. They've placed the side breaks with seeming deliberateness at key dramatic moments, encouraging the viewer to flip the disc quickly. The film runs a couple minutes over two hours and side three runs less than twenty, in CLV. As can be viewed in the opening credit sequence, which is windowboxed, very little of the original image is lost to cropping. In this case, the presentation seems effective. The original Technicolor colors look good, although the picture looks too dark in some places and too blue in others – a horse's mane ends up with blue highlights which were likely not the intention of the original color consultants. The focus looks sharp and the sound is worth amplifying.

RAISING ARIZONA

The visionary satire, *Raising Arizona* is a radically amusing look at real living, slicing up life in the way Cubist paintings slice up real forms. Since the film was made by the Coen brothers, who also made *Blood Simple*, it has the same sort of stylized intensity, and they get away with it because of their sense of humor. The ending, best of all, is a dream sequence in which the hero sees what would happen if the story were extended to include his whole life. It is a daring device, normally utilized in the telling of a myth, and it provides a final legitimacy to the car chases, baby gags, explosions, and lower income vernacular which precede it.

The bright, almost surreal lighting looks terrific on a TV set. The stereo sound is wonderful, with a few effects which are as original and inspired as the plot itself. The break between side one and side two is also perfect, occurring immediately after a hapless villain walks face first into a telephone pole.

RALPH BAKSHI'S STREETFIGHT
Ralph Bakshi's brilliant, unreleasable 'Coonskin' makes a surprise appearance with a Here-we-all-work-on-the-Mississippi-ized title, *Ralph Bakshi's Streetfight.* The film mixes live action and cartoons. Two convicts, waiting to escape from prison, tell one another stories they have heard about Harlem. The animated sequences, for a while at least, really attempt to evoke contemporary folk tales.

The disc, however, is not for the squeamish. The source material looks worn down even though the movie mostly sat on a shelf after it was made. There are scratches and pale colors in the live sequences. During the animation, most of the solid reds or oranges lack stability. The sound is scratchy. To all of this, one must add warnings about the cartoon itself. Gore and sex are plentiful and cartoonishly exaggerated. The 'n' word is used a lot, and although it always seems appropriate – the folk vernacular is legitimate – not enough time has passed to prevent it from grating upon the ears.

RAMBO, FIRST BLOOD PART II (HBO)
RAMBO, FIRST BLOOD PART II (Image)
Since Sylvester Stallone doesn't talk too much in *Rambo, First Blood Part II*, it is an entertaining feature. The combination of fights, explosions, and Jerry Goldsmith's uplifting score makes the movie an ideal home video item. It's only 96 minutes long and boredom never becomes an issue.

Two American versions were released, an analog disc from HBO and a digital release from Image. Despite the slight boost given to the sound by digital encoding, the differences in picture quality are slight, and there is no point in trading one for the other. Both are grainy and pale. The side break is significantly better on the Image disc, however.

RAMBO III
One reason that *Rambo III* proved to be less popular in the US than the first two installments was the lack of any 'bad' Americans. The hero is never trapped in a moral quandary and the audience never has an opportunity to feel sorry for him. The film is just straight white hats and black hats, and it is as enjoyable as any Saturday afternoon adventure.

The cropped image affects only one scene at the beginning when Rambo is seen cavorting with the heavens, working on the roof of a monastery on the top of a mountain. The view is gone. The picture transfer, however, is good, and none of the many night scenes are disturbed by impurities. The digital sound is also a lot of fun. Although ultimately a bit murky, the surround sound is in keeping with the rest of the movie's budget. The disc has a single chapter marker, for the closing song and credit scroll. Our favorite component, as with the first two *Rambo* films, is Jerry Goldsmith's score. We recommend the first attack on the Afghan camp – the sharps kick in just as Rambo decides to take action. We love it, and so long as Goldsmith continues to score the movies, we will continue to look forward to the discs.

RAN
When you hear crickets on a movie soundtrack, it is usually meant to invoke the feeling of a hot summer's day. Akira Kurosawa uses the constant chirping of crickets in *Ran* as mocking laughter to belittle the foolishness of the aging lord who has misjudged the loyalties and affections of his three sons. Kurosawa uses every blade of grass and every breath of wind to tell his story. As the drama darkens, so do the clouds.

Even though every word of dialog is different, the sexes of many of the characters have been changed, the settings, costumes, and social etiquette are foreign, and details of the plot are changed or switched around, *Ran* is unmistakably 'King Lear.' This says much about the power of Shakespeare's writing, that the drama can be changed so extensively without losing the central themes; and it says much about the power of Kurosawa's direction, that he could change so much and still produce the most cogent and engaging interpretation of *Lear* yet put to film.

The 160-minute movie, in Japanese with English subtitles, has gorgeous color and rich stereophonic sound. Since anyone who buys the disc would have preferred to see it in widescreen, the scanning and cropping is a silly waste. Otherwise it is an excellent production.

RANCHO NOTORIOUS
The colors are a bit too dark on Fritz Lang's *Rancho Notorious*, but the details are captivating and the fleshtones are appealing. The source material has a few splices and looks a bit soft in places, but the presentation is better than most copies one sees of the film. The sound is fine.

Arthur Kennedy portrays a man searching for his fiancee's killer, a search which leads him to a sort of safe house for bandits, run by Marlene Dietrich. Lang's direction is inspired. He maintains a dramatic tension and an erotic subtext, and manages to include some unusual political satire as well. The film is terrific fun when taken at face value, and is highly repeatable entertainment, but it can also support extensive analysis.

RANDY NEWMAN AT THE ODEON
The atmosphere in the Odeon where Randy Newman is playing on *Randy Newman at the Odeon* is intimate and it imparts the feeling that he is at a bar somewhere playing the piano rather than in a fancy nightclub which charges a ransom to get in and even more for the drinks. Newman's music is accomplished but his lyrics require too much concentration and sitting through twenty numbers is taxing. Linda Rondstadt and Ry Cooder conveniently step up from the audience to do a couple of numbers with Newman and their participation is the high point of the show. The sound and visual quality on the Pioneer Artists disc is excellent, as usual.

RAPUNZEL
(see **FAERIE TALE THEATRE**)

RAQUEL – TOTAL BEAUTY AND FITNESS
The following narrative excerpts have been transcribed with careful accuracy from the 86-minute stereophonic *Raquel – Total Beauty and Fitness*, which has a sharp-looking video tape source but no chapter markers or alternate channel sound:

"Keep pulling your forehead to your shins."

"On the inhale air will automatically come through your nose so do concentrate especially on making it vibrate off the back of your throat."

"Use me as your mirror image so even if I say go to the left you'll be going to your right."

"In the beginning, if all you can do is pick up your foot and balance, that's all you need. It took me six weeks to get my leg up this high."

"Balance and concentration. Two things you won't get in any other exercise program."

RASCAL DAZZLE
Embassy's *Rascal Dazzle* is a compilation of Little Rascal routines, narrated by Jerry Lewis. After a scattered opening, the sequences become long enough to tell a story, but anyone who is familiar with the material is bound to feel frustrated by the jumps from segment to segment. Purists, who buy a laser disc because of its archival qualities, will not be satisfied.

The sound is fairly strong and the picture is no worse than what one has seen before, although it varies from one gag to the next. Because of the way *Rascal Dazzle* has been constructed, you don't get a good handle on the personalities of more than one or two of the kids (Alfalfa seems to stand out).

RASHOMON
One can acknowledge that a movie makes a significant contribution to the cinematic arts without really enjoying it all that much, and that is where we stand on *Rashomon.* The film is too basic for our tastes, and too clever for its own good. It presents a rape and a murder from four different viewpoints, and frames the tale with a heavy dose of symbolism. The director, Akira Kurosawa, went on to make films of much greater subtlety, emotional impact, and fun. If Kurosawa had to get this one out of his system in order to do that, very well, but there is really no reason to dwell on *Rashomon* much outside of film school.

The black-and-white film was made in Japan in 1950, so one can expect a few scratches and soft edges. The Criterion Collection presentation, however, is reliable, as usual. The monaural sound is also a little scratchy, but no more so than one would expect. The original Japanese dialog appears on the digital track, and English language subtitles, which are always readable, appear on the screen. One channel of the analog track also has the Japanese dialog, and the other channel has a soundtrack with dubbed English dialog. We only sampled bits and pieces of the English track, but it didn't seem bad.

THE RATINGS GAME
Danny DeVito directed *The Ratings Game* for cable TV before he went on to more successful endeavors. He also stars. The film is about a successful trucker from New Jersey who becomes the producer and star of the nation's number one television show by locating and kidnapping the two hundred or so sample families who have rating meters on their TV sets. Hysterical premise, right? The picture is unharmed by wear. DeVito sings 'Volare,' wins the 'TV Digest Popularity Award,' and goes to prison.

RATT: THE VIDEO
Devoted fans are the only potential purchasers of *RATT: The Video*, a two-sided CLV 8-inch. The program is a combination of five music videos separated by extensive interviews. If a poster of RATT isn't pinned up in your bedroom then the interviews are more than you will want to sit through. Their music is accomplished, with no glaring flaws. Their videos are earnest and suitably insolent. Their disc has a picture of varying quality and a sound which is devoid of subtlety. In sum, RATT looks like they are having a great time and making a lot of money in the process. The rest of us should have it so good.

THE RAVEN/THE BLACK CAT
Stealthily creeping past the shadow of the words 'electronically time compressed' for a moment, we would like to drop on your doorstep and meow that MCA has released two Halloween movies on one disc, *The Raven/The Black Cat*. Although the prints of the early '30s films look their age, the sound has none of the serious distortions which occasionally mar old, cheap movies. *Raven* is in slightly better condition than *Cat*, but both blur around the edges and suffer from an errant scratch or two up the middle.

Both movies star Bela Lugosi and Boris Karloff and provide a better opportunity to savor their performances than the more established horror classics do. Lugosi, not strung-out and less encumbered by make-up, is a particular joy to observe as he hams up every line of mad doctor dialog (he's a disgrace to the medical profession in both films). Karloff, a more competent actor, gives the small scenes to Lugosi and then steals each movie in the cumulative finale.

As for the disclaimer on the jacket, "These films have been electronically time compressed in order to bring you this unique double feature. No editing has been done," we found the formerly 61-minute *Raven*, which had a distinctly staccato clip to the dialog, to appear more speeded-up than the formerly 65-minute *Cat*. Neither presented the problem we found in *That's Entertainment* where Frank Sinatra sounded like Liza Minelli. This is a good, economical way to get a couple of cheap old movies onto disc, and it is probably the only way to do it in the current market.

RAW COURAGE
ALVIN RIDES AGAIN
NIGHT PATROL
A two-day, re-creational jog across the New Mexican desert turns into a *Deliverance*-type ordeal in *Raw Courage*. It is entertaining, but hasn't got enough style to support more than one sit-through.

The three joggers are terrorized by a paramilitary group using the desert for war games. The group gets around on motorcycles and why the joggers don't just grab a couple of the bikes and take off when the trouble starts is never sufficiently explained. The joggers are heading toward a town called 'Glory,' and this gives them the excuse to say things like, "We've come too far to turn back now. We have to make it to Glory."

The picture looks dusty and the sound is rough. The disc has an amusing trailer for *Night Patrol* and is generally better than the cover would lead one to believe.

Alvin Rides Again, an Australian film, starts out like a soft-core porn comedy but ends up being an unfunny slapstick and vaudeville piece about Australian gangsters. The picture is blurry and the sound is mediocre. The disc also has the *Night Patrol* trailer, but even it didn't seem as funny here.

The credits for *Night Patrol* are in French ('un film de Jackie Kong') and throughout the disc there is every so often a joke or pun sophisticated enough to indicate that the people who made the thing are actually intelligent. Near the end, in fact, there is a perfect little parody of *The Good, the Bad, and the Ugly*, but most of the film's humor is flatulent. With a decent looking picture and a nice soundtrack, the disc will be funny for the first five minutes, no matter which five minutes it is that you watch. After that, restlessness will likely occur. At least it is more entertaining than *Alvin Rides Again*, a useless trailer for which can be seen at the end.

RAW DEAL
RAW DEAL (Import)
The Japanese version of *Raw Deal* is preferable to the version released by HBO. Not only is it slightly letterboxed (Japanese subtitles still appear on the picture), but the picture is sharper, the colors are stronger, and the digital stereo sound is more clear. HBO's version is cropped, grainy, bleeds reds, and is CX-encoded analog. The movie, however, is entertaining in either format, and works well enough on the domestic disc to be an acceptable presentation.

Raw Deal got curiously good reviews when it first came out, although a close look at the plot will reveal that the hero, played by Arnold Schwarzenegger, doesn't accomplish much. He goes undercover to join a Chicago mob operation, hangs out for a while, and then kills everybody. Not that this isn't an ideal subject for a relaxing, rainy afternoon, but why was *Raw Deal* singled out as superior to Arnold's other efforts? Overcompensation is the only answer which comes to mind.

RAWHEAD REX
Rawhead Rex is a Celtic demon terrorizing rural Ireland in *Rawhead Rex*. Clive Barker wrote the screenplay, which is nothing more than a monster-in-the-woods tale, but it is presented with more respect for clarity and purpose than most of its ilk can muster. Directed by George Pavlou, the film never has a slow moment or a false move.

We wish we could say the same about the disc. The film was originally in stereo, as witnessed by an end title card that Image would have been better off masking, since the disc is monaural. Despite digital encoding, the sound is rough and suitable only for low volume playback, although there are some bass frequency effects which might have had potential if the source had been better. The picture is grainy. The demise of one major character must be inferred from the dialog, but the 87 minute print is apparently complete. The disc is in CLV.

RAY BRADBURY THEATRE
Ray Bradbury's short stories are usually more atmospheric than solidly plotted. While his most famous works have clearly delineated concepts, the bulk of his writing is foggier and more concerned with mood than with action or drama. Bradbury's name appears as the sole writing credit on each of the four episodes contained in *Ray Bradbury Theatre*, which unofficially precedes its title with 'The Best of.' The multi-national television anthology series is typical Bradbury material, memorably moody but a little less than dramatically riveting. Except that the 'Golden Era' TV shows often did it very well, the half-hour time slot is usually too limited for serious fiction, a fact which one is reminded of four times during the course of the disc.

The episodes are listed incorrectly on the jacket cover. 'The Fruit at the Bottom of the Bowl,' a Poe-styled tale starring Michael Ironside and Robert Vaughn, about a murderer who becomes obsessed with removing his fingerprints from the scene of the crime, and 'Gotcha,' about a man who meets a woman who seems like the ideal mate until the night they play an unnerving game, are paired on side one. 'The Emissary,' the most Bradburian and best piece, about a dog who brings things to his bedridden master, and 'Skeleton,' about a hypochondriac who visits a creepy doctor, appear on side two.

Two chapter markers are encoded on each side, circumventing the opening credits and marking the actual beginning of each episode. The digitally encoded monaural sound is reasonably strong, but the picture is often blurry.

RAY DAVIES – RETURN TO WATERLOO
Ray Davies, of the Kinks, made an hour-long concept video for British television called 'Return to Waterloo.' which has been released on a single sided disc. The title refers to a round-trip commuter ticket and the narrative involves the daydreams and nightmares of a middle-aged businessman going to work on the train one morning. Eight songs accentuate the forays into fantasy. Use of a cheap film stock limits the clarity of the picture. Davies does not provide enough stylistic visual flair to encourage full multiple viewings, but his sense of narrative is good – the ending is just right – and the songs will have one scanning and sampling a couple of times through at a sitting.

THE RAZOR'S EDGE
Comedians are excellent actors because they can usually find a comic hook in their character on which they can bait and snare an audience. But when there is no comedy in a piece they are left to flounder and that is what everyone expected or saw in Bill Murray's performance in *The Razor's Edge*. We saw more.

Released by RCA/Columbia in a picture which remains dead center even when the characters are cut off on the sides and in flourishing stereo, the film was based on a novel by W. Somerset Maugham. Maugham is not considered a great novelist and *The Razor's Edge* is by no means a great film, but it has the right-sized doses of philosophy, love affairs, and adventure. Murray portrays an American whose experiences in World War I change his values and goals and prevent him from settling down after the war is over. He lets loose with a funny voice or wild quirk just often enough to keep a viewer concentrating and waiting for the next snippet of humor. He found his hook.

The movie is a unique combination of genres and talents and for that reason alone it is worth acquiring on disc. There will be evenings when it could be the only disc in your collection that you will really feel like watching. For the same reason, people keep on reading Maugham's books.

RAZORBACK (Import)
Available on import, *Razorback* was directed by Russell Mulcahy, who made some of the best music videos, and it is both visually and audibly obnoxious. The story is about a huge killer pig terrorizing the Australian outback. It is sort of like falling asleep with MTV after eating a dish of spicy sausages. Mulcahy goes wild with the smoke machine and with spotlights and silhouettes and with music video-type imagery such as having old cars in the branches of dead trees. He's got to do something to get your mind off the fact that the phony killer pig looks like it is rolling on wooden wheels, and he half succeeds.

So why get the disc? The film never had a US theatrical playoff and can be considered relatively rare. This always impresses know-it-alls examining one's collection. Secondly, the presentation is letterboxed, with most of the subtitles appearing below the picture, in the black stripe. Third, the surround sound is a showoff feature, and occasionally you are truly apt to cringe when the bacon attacks. Finally the sound and the picture are laser perfect. It is still so rare to see productions take full advantage of the laser disc medium that we can't resist the ones which do. Even the ones about huge, deadly pork chops.

RE-ANIMATOR
One reviewer said the music in *Re-Animator* was 'evocative' of *Psycho*. 'Note for note' would be a more accurate description. It is a real shame that the gruesome finale is not available in CAV. The picture, however, is very grainy. The film is a cheap horror classic about doctors who murder each other over the secret of life. The disc is fun for those who have strong stomachs, but it would have been more enjoyable if better care had gone into the production.

READY STEADY GO! SPECIAL EDITION – THE BEATLES
Pioneer released the 20-minute *Ready Steady Go! Special Edition – The Beatles* as a single-sided 8-inch disc. It is monaural and was recorded on the television studio/with live audience set used in most of the 'Ready Steady Go!' programs. How much of the singing is synched and how much is live is hard to say. Each member of the Fab Four performs a single number. They then do a medley of hits, and finish by taking turns going softer and louder with 'Shout.' 'All You Need Is Love' plays over the end credits.

The black-and-white concert, uninterrupted, gives the viewer a good assessment of the frenzy which surrounded the group when they first got started, and provides a clear understanding of the richness of talent which was feeding that frenzy. The disc is great fun, but it is also a reference work, a quick and easy depiction of four youths who managed to get their fingers on the pulse of the whole world.

READY STEADY GO! – VOLUME ONE
READY STEADY GO! – VOLUME TWO
Ready, Steady, Go – Volume One is a must acquisition for anyone who is a fan of old British rock and roll. The hour-long, black-and-white disc is not in stereo, but you get used to the quality of the sound fast enough. These excerpts from the British TV show 'Ready, Steady, Go!' feature full, *uninterrupted* performances by the Beatles ('You Can't Do That' and 'Can't Buy Me Love'), the Rolling Stones ('Under My Thumb' and 'Paint It Black'), and twelve other famous/semi-famous singing stars from the sixties. Included are the young Van Morrison singing 'Baby Please Don't Go' with Them, The Animals, who had been together seven months at the time of the recording, 15-year-old Lulu performing 'Shout,' Dusty Springfield looking and lip synching like a female impersonator, and Gerry and the Pacemakers fighting off frantic fans to get through 'Ferry Across the Mersey.' Peter Cook and Dudley Moore also pop up for a comedy number that leaves the studio audience totally bewildered.

In contrast to the cream on *Volume One*, the clips on *Ready Steady Go! – Volume Two* are just crop. The disc will still be of interest to dedicated fans, but selective viewers can afford to pass it by. As promised by the jacket cover, for example, the Rolling Stones do appear, but they perform a pantomime while Sonny and Cher's 'I Got You Babe' plays on the soundtrack. It's bizarre, but hardly of historical interest. The high point of the disc comes early on, when John Lennon asks Dusty Springfield if he can see her scabs. There is also a captivating performance by Jerry Lee Lewis, who looks like an escapee from a James Whale film, but beyond that, the entertainment is better exemplified by the moment when Gene Pitney misses his camera cue. He sings bars and bars before he realizes he should turn.

The black-and-white images vary from clip to clip, but are generally weaker than those in the first collection. Both discs contain extra material of The Dave Clark Five, culled from another source (Clark produced the collections), which tend to interrupt the flow of the programs..

THE REAL BUDDY HOLLY STORY
Paul McCartney produced and hosts a 90-minute documentary, *The Real Buddy Holly Story*. The disc is no substitute for a decent CD anthology, but Holly fans will appreciate the thoroughness of the material. It seems as if every last faded snapshot or roll of film which contains an impression of Holly is included in the program. Audio outtakes can also be heard. The people who used to work with Holly are hauled to their old haunts to reminisce and play the songs they used to play. Details as to how, specifically, Holly's recordings were constructed, are among the most valuable pieces of information the show has to offer. A demonstration of the drum beat, for example, is provided for a number of the songs. One hears more music played by strangers (or McCartney) than by Holly, however, and songs are sometimes cut short. McCartney does contribute some interesting comments about Holly's influence on his and John Lennon's music. The most fascinating interviewee, however, is Keith Richard of the Rolling Stones. Flopping his arms around and looking at the camera as if it were moving in a circle, Richard gives the impression that you could not trust what he said if he looked at his watch and reported to you the time, yet every statement he makes about Holly is insightful and contemplative. The disc's picture and sound quality vary depending upon the condition of the source material, but the transfer looks and sounds adequate. Side two is in CAV with two unsteady still frames in every five but plenty of opportunities to freeze home movies and other rare glimpses of Holly.

REAL GENIUS
Val Kilmer and Michelle Meyrink give entertaining performances in *Real Genius*, but the unbalanced plot drops the humor to tell the story just as things really start to get funny. The film's stereo mix is erratic. This is one of those teen science movies that everyone gets confused with all the other teen science movies.

REAL MEN
Jim Belushi, portraying an overly resourceful secret agent, and John Ritter, portraying an innocent milquetoast, are teamed together to save the world in *Real Men*. It is an old fashioned movie, and is daffy enough to turn some viewers off, but it has its comical moments. The stereo mix is also amusing, and adds to the entertainment. The picture, however, is a bit too orange.

REBECCA (see **ALFRED HITCHCOCK'S REBECCA**)

REBECCA OF SUNNYBROOK FARM/THE LITTLE COLONEL
The three-sided disc package, *Rebecca of Sunnybrook Farm/The Little Colonel*, has been reprocessed for stereo, but the enhancement is minimal and the digitally encoded sound is fairly clean.

Temple is a marvel. Even today, with hundreds of youngsters appearing on the television in commercials and sit-coms, no one has so magnetic a command of the screen. She is always on. When she blows a line she gets by anyway by tilting her head at a weird angle and finding just the right facial expression to re-establish her authority. Although it is clear from the editing that her ability to retain instructions is limited by her age, her ability to execute the instructions is unnerving.

The print for 'Rebecca of Sunnybrook Farm' is in very good condition. There are a couple of burps, but the black and white images are sharp and the contrasts are rich. The film, in which Temple, as the title character, becomes a radio star when a producer moves next door to her farm, has a terrific cast, including William Demarest, Randolph Scott, and Jack Haley. Haley's talent for physical comedy is particularly well exhibited and one wishes he had been more widely employed (or found his way into more memorable films).

'Little Colonel,' however, may be the definitive Temple film. It has one of the tightest narratives, a contrivance about three bickering generations on a Southern plantation after Reconstruction (or as if Reconstruction, and the War itself, had never taken place). Those who are sensitive to the stereotyped portrayal of black characters in the movies will have difficulty accepting the film, though the stereotyping is more of a condescending than a bigoted nature. A scene, for example, where two servants mangle an attempt to spell words within their conversation so Temple will not know what they are talking about is demeaning, but it is also genuinely amusing.

On the plus side, Bill Robinson and Temple make a great dance team. Robinson is a spectacular tap dancer, but forcing him to dance with Temple slows him down and gives the viewer a unique opportunity to obtain a clear view of his basic footwork.

The black-and-white print looks nice. There is one major splice and a few scattered patches, but the contrast levels and picture clarity are admirable. The final minute and a half is in a milky Technicolor, one of the earliest utilizations of the process, and it is a grand finale to an entertaining disc.

REBEL
The Matt Dillon movie *Rebel* is actually a musical although, don't worry, Dillon never sings. That task is left to Debbie Byrne, who plays a cabaret hostess. The movie is Australian and takes place during World War II. Dillon, who has a strange, coated-tongue accent, portrays a soldier from Georgia who is AWOL in Sydney. His presence weakens the film, but everything going on around him is terrific. As the credit sequence reveals, the film was shot in wide screen, so the cropping makes the picture seem very cramped and close. The sound is in stereo. Had the transfer been better and the original aspect been maintained, the disc would have been wonderful. As it is, it isn't bad.

REBELLION (see **YOJIMBO**)

RECRUITS
The prospect of viewing a movie which tries to be a cheap rip-off of the *Police Academy* series fascinated us. Would it be the film equivalent of a poor imitation of a Cracker Jacks diamond ring? The movie is *Recruits*, and the answer is that it is worse. The commitment which Vestron makes to the disc clearly indicates their belief in the quality of the property. They get the name of the town wrong in the jacket copy. The picture is grainy. The sound is a flat monaural and is absent of CX-encoding.

There is one amusing gag, a take off on Dirty Harry's "Did I fire all six rounds or only five," where an innocent bystander enthusiastically pops up with, "It was six. You fired all six shots. It sounded like five because two were so close together." But there are so many gags which are unamusing and ineptly executed that by the time you get to the good one you'll have forgotten what laughter is for.

THE RED BALLOON/WHITE MANE
The jacket cover for the Criterion release *The Red Balloon/White Mane* is absolutely gorgeous. The CLV disc contains two Albert Lamorisse films from the 1950s. ('Balloon' was made in 1956, not 1952 as the jacket notes claim.) The sound is CX-encoded, but we recommend that volume levels not be turned up too high. Part of the charm is what Lamorisse managed to accomplish on a limited budget, and the disc replicates the errors as well as the magic.

The red of 'The Red Balloon' is vivid. The dialogue-less story, about a boy who has a balloon for a pet, should continue to captivate audiences for decades to come.

'White Mane,' about a boy who has a wild horse for a pet, is narrated in English – that is, an English soundtrack has been laid over the French without displacing it. A still on the back of the jacket is a good example of the black-and-white print's condition in some of its weaker moments.

Watching both films, one cringes at the stunts Lamorisse had his young actors perform for the camera. The results made exciting, memorable cinema, but could just as easily have turned into disaster. There seems to be no escaping the darker side of innocence.

RED DAWN
Red Dawn is an antidisestablishmentarianistic fantasy about a Russian/Cuban invasion of the midwestern United States. A group of high school kids who seem to have been the only ones who hightailed it to the mountains when the Russians landed spend close to two hours of movie time cleverly disrupting the invasion with guerrilla tactics. Then, because no other ending could be found for the story, they stop playing hide and seek to stand and shoot it out with their enemy.

The picture is a little grainy. The stereo has a macho shove to it, and the explosions and gunfire sound terrific in the living room. Thank goodness it's only a movie, right?

THE RED DESERT
Carlo di Palma's color cinematography in Michelangelo Antonioni's *The Red Desert* is generally considered to be one of the finest accomplishments within the artform. Unfortunately, you will have a difficult time discerning why this is so from the disc. A quick comparison will show that the colors in the picture transfer look nothing like the colors in the still on the jacket cover. The colors on the disc are faded, and fleshtones tend to drift from yellow to chalk white. Otherwise, the picture transfer is meticulous, and if this were *Cousin, Cousine* or something like it, the effort would be quite acceptable. *The Red Desert*, however, demands perfection, and this it did not get.

The sound is fine, but the analog track, although noisier, is livelier. The film is in Italian and has yellow English subtitles designed for video. The picture has a slight matting and, even though a character is sometimes dropped from the frame, the essence of the composition is maintained.

Some collectors will still want the disc, for as stunning as the photography is, the movie has other attributes as well. *The Red Desert* was remarkably prescient, and therefore remains both relevant and satisfying with the passage of time. The environmental issues which it examines are issues that have become even more vital and focussed today than they were when the film was made. Although it was probably not noticed in the spaced-out sixties, everybody in the movie seems to suffer from some level of mercury poisoning. A woman wanders aimlessly around the industrial dumping grounds that surround her apartment. A child loses feeling in his legs. The film contains Antonioni's usual roundup of psychic maladies, but for once he's got a physical cause – pollution – and it is such a perfect symbol that his characters can literally tramp through it.

RED HEADED STRANGER
The opening credits of *Red Headed Stranger* state that the film was produced, 'in association with Wrangler Jeans.' It has the format which the successful TV movie westerns have had, using an established country/western tune and wrapping a drama around it. Unlike most TV films, however, the program is stereophonic, and has a nice mix.

The script is fairly simple, but it has some interesting moral turns as Nelson, the hero, shoots his first wife. He also shoots a few other people, sometimes on fairly flimsy excuses. But that is what westerns are all about, morality and violence. Katherine Ross and Morgan Fairchild also star, the latter having a wet bodice scene which has been airbrushed on the jacket cover. The disc has chapter markers not just for Nelson's songs, but for the film's dramatic highlights as well. The picture quality is excellent, save for a spurious speckle or two.

RED HEAT
All women's prison films are comedies, but *Red Heat*, which stars Linda Blair, has the demeanor of a serious film. As serious, at least, as a film can be which takes place in an East German prison where everybody, guards, prisoners, and maintenance people, converse unfailingly in English. Blair is an American who is kidnapped when she sees something she shouldn't have. She manages to avoid the broom handle this time, but she gets licked by Sylvia Kristel, which appears to be as loathsome a fate. The picture is blurry and looks like it was produced in an East German prison itself. The sound is digitally encoded and is supposedly in stereo.

RED HEAT
Arnold Schwarzenegger makes great home video, Walter Hill makes great home video, and Jim Belushi makes great home video, so who can resist getting *Red Heat* ? The disc has a decent surround soundtrack. The picture leaves room for improvement, but as long as the movie stays away from moody lighting, the image looks okay. The disc opens with 5 minutes worth of trailers, but a chapter marker denotes the beginning of the film itself.

There is a lot wrong with the movie, which is why it was a disappointment in the boxoffice. Arnold is given so little character he's more like a 'Terminator' than a Russian cop; Belushi's Eastern European ethnicity ought to be emphasized to contrast Arnold's 'Aryan' dullness, but it isn't; and the scriptwriters did very little thinking about how a Russian detective would actually react to a place so alien as Chicago. None of this matters, however, when you're cuddled up to your TV set looking for some fast fun. There are enough oneliners, enough gunshots (the film is less graphically violent than most contemporary thrillers), and enough flexed muscles to satisfy any viewer in search of familiar territory.

THE RED PONY
Aaron Copeland's grand orchestral score for *The Red Pony* sounds wonderful on the digital monaural disc. The picture is also in good

shape, with the rich Technicolor hues looking well preserved in most sequences.

The film is a fine adaptation of a John Steinbeck story about a boy living on a ranch. The script often refuses to conform to the conventions of family classic horse stories. The boy's parents are barely on speaking terms and treat him with a realistic impatience. There are daydream sequences which are effective because the rest of the movie isn't sugary. The scene near the end in which the boy's pony dies may be too intense for youngsters, and adults may note the Hollywoodized lack of an afterbirth when a colt is born, unfortunate because the film up until then has been so realistic. In general, however, the drama will make viewers of all ages think, feel and form value judgements, without insulting anyone's intelligence. Like Copeland's score, the film has a Steinbeckian sense of self-importance, and lives up to it.

RED RIVER (CBS/Fox)
RED RIVER (MGM/UA)

Filmed with more cattle than anyone could ever hope to assemble today, *Red River* is a perfect mixture of huge, exciting action sequences and entertaining characterizations. The transfer is sharp and nearly flawless. The monaural sound fades away at times, but not often enough to spoil one's entertainment.

John Wayne and Montgomery Clift play Captain Bligh and Fletcher Christian-type roles on a 1000-mile cattle drive in the old west. Wayne's performance is so good as he gradually shifts from a resourceful leader to a vengeful paranoid that you are disappointed when he snaps out of it at the end. There are gun fights and storms and fist fights and rescues and the greatest stampede ever. There are even girls and kissing, and since the movie was directed by Howard Hawks, you can bet the heroine doesn't blink when an arrow goes through her shoulder.

MGM/UA's source is in ragged condition, and the picture on the CBS/Fox disc remains more satisfying. The greytones are significantly sharper on the CBS/Fox disc, and a number of scenes on the MGM/UA effort look outright blurry. MGM/UA has digitally encoded monaural sound, but it is not a significant improvement over the CBS/Fox effort. The MGM/UA disc comes in a gatefold jacket and is promoted as containing the director's cut, which runs 132 minutes. The CBS/Fox version runs exactly the same length of time, although its jacket cover says otherwise.

RED SCORPION

The surround sound on *Red Scorpion* is super, making the disc an enjoyable choice for action fans. The movie slows down a little at the beginning of the second act, but there are enough explosions, gun fights, and body contact violence to please viewers amenable to such goings on. The film has a moderately original premise, since the hero is a Russian mercenary fighting in Southwest Africa who undergoes a change of heart when he sees the destruction his government is inflicting upon the local population. He also has lots of muscles.

The picture is grainy in some places and is not quite as inspired as the sound.

THE RED SHOES

Someone with admirable intelligence at Paramount decided that side two of the 136-minute disc, *The Red Shoes*, should be done in CAV. This is the dramatic midpoint of the film, and it features the complete performance of a ballet called 'The Red Shoes,' an effort which brings all the characters together in the first half of the film and then splits them apart in the second.

The ballet, which is seen in its entirety on side two, has different pleasures and revelations to offer when it is run at different speeds. In still-step one can see the cinematic tricks which are used to expand the fantasy portions of the ballet, particularly a pair of wires which pull the straps of the shoes off the dancer's feet and give the illusion, since the footage is run backwards, that the straps are wrapping around her legs. In the slower slow motion speeds, one can see the physiological demands of the dancing. The male dancer grimaces momentarily as he strains to lift his partner, and then retrieves his stage smile as soon as his exertion is under control. Most interesting of all is a closeup of a ballerina's feet as she moves forward on her toes. You watch her weight shift from one leg to the other and realize that if she held still for one more frame, her whole foot would snap.

In the faster slow motions, the artifice begins to disappear and the lyrical beauty of bodies in motion takes over. Even though you cannot hear the music, which would be distorted if the sound were activated, you can feel every note of the orchestration in the way the ballerina arches her back and extends her arms. The fast speeds intensify the quality of the picture and clarify the choreographical design. Speeding up the dancers does not belittle their efforts, but it allows one to summarize their interplay and fully recognize their accomplishments.

At the reel change points there is a little fading, and here and there the edges look fuzzy, but in general the disc is another tribute to the glories of three-strip Technicolor. We got especially excited about the appearance of the color orange. Late on side one, some oranges in a dish caught our eye, since they appeared so separate from the rest of the image that we were tempted to grab for one and take a bite. Then, at the opening of side two, there is a glass of orange juice which is even more vivid, more correct and enticing than any of the dozens of orange juice commercials appearing on broadcast TV.

The sound on the disc is a little more troublesome. It is analog monaural and has been CX-encoded, but since the film was a post-War British production, the quality of the recording was limited. The disc starts out very scratchy, but calms down after a while (the reel change points, again, seem to be the worst). If one does not press the volume hard, however, the result is not distracting, and one should not let such a fault disrupt the entertainment.

To best appreciate *The Red Shoes*, especially if you have not seen it before, you should avoid following any single character too closely. The director, Michael Powell, is a master at creating point of view, and he shifts steadily between a half dozen characters. If you commit yourself emotionally to any one of them, you miss much of what the movie intends to communicate about the world of ballet companies and artistic conflict. Powell's inventive camera tricks seem to be the cinematic equivalent of the British lack of idiom. His maturity allows him to do tricks such as showing the blurred strands of thread twinkle in the image as we see what a character is supposedly seeing as he peeks through the curtain at the audience. What would be blatantly obvious in the hands of a lesser artist is stated to perfection by Powell. Like listening to an intelligent lecturer who begins with simple concepts and then builds upon them quickly so that his subject, although understandable, becomes supremely sophisticated and complex, watching Powell's film technique is disarming. Suddenly the themes are unusually elaborate and the emotional conflicts are intricately linked.

A final word is appropriate concerning the 'Red Shoes' ballet, which illustrates Powell's talents. Viewers may find the ballet to be misleading since they are expecting, dramatically, to see the heroine give it her all in front of the audience. Instead, the dance expands from the confines of the stage in the manner of a Busby Berkeley effort. In Berkeley musicals, this effect was utilized simply to show that movies could do what stage shows could not. In *Red Shoes* clues are placed so that one realizes, perhaps on subsequent viewings, that the impressionistic ballet is actually a representation of the ballerina's concentration as she performs. This is brought to a crescendo by the final image of the piece, an ocean surf which appears to be breaking against the edge of the stage. It is, in fact, applause.

RED SONJA

"Sonja, you must learn to like men a little better," the Master with Sticks Coming from His Head tells Brigitte Nielsen in *Red Sonja*, "Hatred of men in a lovely young woman, it could be your downfall."

Red Sonja is one of those movies where you can only enjoy it if you appreciate the aesthetics of ineptness. It has been a long time since we have seen opening and closing credits, for example, which are squeezed as awkwardly as they are here, turning Nielsen's horse into a giraffe and her sword into a vaulting pole. Even though the cropping destroys a nice dinosaur skeleton bridge, it is probably saving the movie more embarrassment than it is causing and is therefore tolerable. The picture transfer on the disc is extremely grainy in some shots, but is in decent condition for the most part.

Despite enough chopped heads and severed limbs to open up a mannequin repair outfit, the movie will be appealing to children or anyone with a Saturday afternoon to spare. Nielsen doesn't have enough freckles to be a true redhead, and she doesn't have enough muscles to hold her heavy sword for very long (her entire body, following Newton's laws, sort of swings in an opposite motion to the weapon).

THE RED TENT

A fairly interesting adventure drama, *The Red Tent*, based upon a true incident, is about an attempt to fly a dirigible to the North Pole that ends in disaster. The Soviet/Italian production had an enormous budget and an international cast. Sean Connery, who receives top billing, has a cameo part. The real stars are Peter Finch, as the Italian general who leads the expedition, and Hardy Kruger, as the unscrupulous pilot who rescues him.

Some of the effects, particularly during the dirigible scenes, are excellent, and are not harmed by the video presentation. The source material has a number of speckles and other impurities, but is generally acceptable. The monaural sound is less successful, sporting a garish Ennio Morricone musical score as well as audio noise and a quiver here and there.

The narrative is successful in concentrating more on process than on character. It is framed with an awkward stage device in which the elderly general, reminiscing, discusses the incident with figmentary manifestations of the other characters. The film plays very successfully in a viewer's memory, however, where the framing device completely vanishes while an in-depth understanding of the personalities involved, the organizational flaws that led to the disaster, and the precarious nature of an explorer's life remain.

REFORM SCHOOL GIRLS

If you ever want to throw an improv group for a loop: When they ask the audience for a movie genre, shout, "Women's prison films!" before somebody else shouts 'western' or something. Inevitably, it is a genre which the group has not practiced, but it has rich potential, and they usually come up with their best inspirations attempting to deal with it. Unfortunately, the makers of *Reform School Girls* were not similarly inspired. The movie is a tightly constructed reiteration of every women's prison cliché one can think of. The problem is that a cliché can be charming in innocence, but is monotonous if repeated deliberately without embellishment.

The movie seems to have been made for home video. It has a bright, squared picture with solid colors and lurid camera angles. The print has only a hint of graininess.

REGARD FOR THE PLANET 50,000 PHOTOGRAPHS BY MARC GARANGER

The first commercially released disc to make full use of the CAV storage capabilities and present some 53,000 individual photographs is *Regard for the Planet 50,000 Photographs by Marc Garanger*. It took us several days to get through the single-sided disc, and even then we felt we could have spent longer looking at the photos. Only a handful of still frames were disrupted by lines of distortion. If you want to see how bad the color on your television set is, compare the photo on the jacket cover with the copy on frame 46285, and weep. Nevertheless, the picture transfer is clearly an elaborate and exhaustive effort, and does justice to the project.

Marc Garanger, alas. The best we can say about the majority of photographs on the disc is that they are nice. There are a few photos which are so blurry or pointless that one wonders why they were included, and there are a few photos so stunning that one's eyes are riveted to them. Tens of thousands of the pictures, however, are just pictures, competently taken, purposely composed, and nice.

Although the disc attempts to use the collection to provide a view of life around the globe, most of the images actually come from France and the Soviet Union, with only a token representation of other locales (and when Garanger visits the Caribbean, he visits the French Caribbean). The photographs chosen for the disc were culled from a collection of about a million and a half. Since the pictures are said to be representational of Garanger's work, we shall refer to them as such. Garanger photographs landscapes with an eye for large topographical forms and patterns. His interest in architecture is also one of patterns and repetition. There are a number of photographs depicting rooftops or small buildings bunched together. He is attracted to signs, advertising posters, and graffiti, and to the ornamental detail decorating both old and new buildings. When he visits a museum, he photographs the works individually instead of recording the museum's arrangement and display. He takes portraits head-on, and appears to get permission from most of his subjects beforehand. Hence, he captures a lot of grins. When he visits some place exotic he acts just like a tourist, taking pictures of the local inhabitants at work, of the unusual clothing or cultural accoutrements, and of the front door of any French establishment which happens to have a branch office there.

Snow and horse racing seem to bring out the best in him. Cock fighting and unplanned occurrences, the worst. His abilities as a news photographer are limited, as he appears to do better when he has time to set up a shot. The disc contains an excellent series of pictures on wine making and on cheese making. A worthwhile depiction of the Chartres Cathedral investigates the Cathedral's design from a wide range of viewpoints. A selection of black-and-white photographs taken during a stint in the Army in Algeria establishes his credentials and are the most powerful stills on the disc. Although nothing else comes close to capturing the drama of those photos, a segment covering a trip to Ecuador epitomizes Garanger at his best, capturing the people, the land, and the compromises of civilization. The sequence is one of the few where Garanger manages to evoke a genuine sense of spontaneous texture, and does not flinch from the tensions of poverty. Also of interest is the extensive collection of photographs from the hinterlands of the Soviet Union, not so much for the bland compositions as for the thoroughness with which both the old and the new (the ethnic heritage and the central bureaucracy) are depicted in an uneasy collaboration. Educators should be warned that there is a complete series of polite but frank photos depicting a Lamaze birth.

The collections are deliberately shuffled to downplay the concentration on French locations and subject matter. Some photographs which were clearly taken in sequence are separated by dozens of others. At other times the order of sequence is carefully preserved. To hold a viewer's interest during such a marathon slide show, however, variations in format are a necessity. The collection exhausts the maximum limit of chapter markers (78 to a side), but it is a shame that the jacket listing could not provide frame identification for the subdivisions which are identified but not chapter marked.

The disc utilizes all three audio channels, to mixed results. A collection of folk tunes played on folk instruments by the Everest Recording Group can be found on the digital audio track, and it is so clear and so pleasant that the disc qualifies as an easy-listening CD. A recreation of an interview with Garanger running a little over a half hour is split onto the two analog tracks. Taken from a shaky translation of the actual interview, one speaker voices the questions and another voices Garanger's answers. The questions are leading, and the answers are non-committal or accommodating. It is best avoided.

We don't know anyone who would not have an interesting face if caught by the right photographer in the right light, but after absorbing Garanger's scattered collection of portraits, an odd duplicity caused by the craft of photography began to make itself clear. Every day, in billboards and magazine advertisements, one sees photos of youthful, unblemished faces. Yet when photographers are exploring humanity, instead of trying to sell it something, they are invariably attracted to faces with wrinkles, to weathered appearances, to faces which have been bumped around by life or pricked by time. It is reassuring to know that as one ages one ceases to be a commodity and becomes, instead, a work of art.

REILLY: THE ACE OF SPIES

Television doesn't get much better than *Reilly: The Ace of Spies*, a British series about foreign intrigue at the turn of the century which stars Sam Neill. The pilot episode, 'An Affair with a Married Woman,' has been released on disc, and it is marvelous.

The picture transfer is fair. Some of the scenes look nice and others have a mildly worn look. On the whole, the image is grainy. The sound is a little better. There is a really good musical score, by Harry Rabinowitz, which for the most part is well served by the disc's audio presentation, although too much amplification will also bring out weakness in the music's more delicate passages. Side two of the 78-minute program is in CAV, with blurred movement in many still frames and some brief nudity.

Reilly is the antithesis of the typical American spy show. Action sequences often happen off-screen, while the drama itself concentrates on the resultant emotional ramifications. The historical allusions are great fun. The episode on the disc plays around Reilly's discovery that the Russians have uncovered large oil deposits in the 'Persian Basin.' In order to get the information into the right hands, the hero must compromise the virtue of one woman and, inadvertently, cause the death of another. The use of Maltese locations for the Russian scenes is terrific, and the leaps between exotic situations and intimate drama cleverly widen the scope of the fiction. The program is a complete entertainment, although Reilly is off on another assignment at its close.

RELAX WITH DENIS WEAVER

The hour-long *Relax with Dennis Weaver* has three parts, with the same three segments repeated within each part. In the first part, Weaver introduces each segment. A different narrator advises the viewer to calm down while the segment is actually running. In the second part, Weaver is gone and the segments play through with the narration retained. In the third part, the narration is dropped and the segments play through with only their evocative visuals and generic music. You certainly don't get tense wondering what is going to happen next.

If people can use this disc – instead of, say, *Lethal Weapon 2* – to help them relax, so be it, but usually the appeal of such programs is not so much in their content but in the quality of their transfer, and here the offering is distinctly disappointing. The evocative visuals have an extra level of moody blurriness. Intense colors are littered with errant lines and speckles. The music seems to survive without much harm, but Weaver's voice is unaccountably distorted by the stereo processing, and the narration doesn't do that much better. It is enough to give you a nervous twitch.

RELENTLESS

The surround sound on *Relentless* had us jumping out of our seat. It is actively and effectively used, and increases the film's level of entertainment. The picture is a bit grainy but passable. Leo Rossi and Robert Loggia portray detectives hunting down a serial killer. The killer takes their investigation personally. Rossi is a rookie, anxious to use all the latest methods to catch the killer, and Loggia is a veteran, who just wants to put in his eight hours and go home. The film covers no new ground, but it travels smoothly over familiar paths.

REMEMBERING MARILYN

We were minding our own business, watching *The Asphalt Jungle* one afternoon, when a woman appeared on the screen of our TV which brought the movie to a dead halt. Thanks to the magic of home video, we played the scene several times over before continuing with the rest of the film. It wasn't until a few scenes later that we realized the actress was Marilyn Monroe, and the resonance of her eroticism lingered long after the disc was over. Her ability to please the camera comes from more than the contours of her face or her body, it is a craft which no one ever mastered as thoroughly, or, to the abandonment of all else, so tragically. That she was on intimate terms with the greatest artists, athletes, politicians and scientists of her age only served to verify that she was too talented, too unable to rein in a drive to overachieve. She was the essence of movie stardom. No matter how well she assumed a character's personality, her own presence dominated her roles.

Fans of Marilyn Monroe who enjoy looking at amateur footage to search for the light behind the star will be pleased with *Remembering Marilyn*. The 48-minute documentary is crammed with behind-the-scenes and in-the-backyard shots of Monroe, along with news footage, scenes from the movie she never finished, and even shots of her doing cartwheels on the beach when she was an adolescent. The highpoint shows Monroe in a marvelous gasoline commercial: "This is the first car I ever owned. I call her Cynthia. She's going to have the best care a car ever had. Put Royal Triton in Cynthia's little tummy." "Right, Lady."

The documentary, narrated by Lee Remick, attempts to give a full biography and a little insight. Since one's reaction to Monroe is emotional and cannot accurately be described in words, most of the interviewees have difficulty explaining her appeal (the best explanation is always the films and photographs themselves), but after three quarters of an hour viewers will at least be able to surmise the essentials, and form some strong opinions of their own. The picture quality varies with the clips, but the transfer is accurate and the digital monaural sound is fine.

REMO WILLIAMS

Remo Williams is a movie which one can take or one can leave, and on disc it is best left alone. As the grainy, in-and-out-of-focus picture grinds on and on, it just begins to wear you out, and you stop rooting for the film. Even Joel Grey, who gets pulled back into the script at the end because the screenwriters get desperate, can't save the disc. The sound is in stereo with CX-encoding and no pizzazz. The movie is 121 minutes long according to the jacket cover, and it fits on one platter. If you believe that, perhaps you'll believe all the secret agent stuff in the plot. If seeing is believing, however, the disc is in big trouble.

RENDEZ-VOUS

The jacket cover gives no indication, but *Rendez-Vous* has been letterboxed, with an aspect ratio of about 1.9:1. The film is in French and has English subtitles. When the subtitles fit on a single line, they appear beneath the image, but when they run to two lines, one line appears on the image and the second appears beneath it. The sound is fine.

Unfortunately, that is about all the disc has going for it. The picture is a muddy brown and is consistently soft. Side two is in CAV, but the image is so blurry that it is difficult to differentiate steady and unsteady still frames. The film is not very good, either. The jacket copy on the disc, which praises the movie as a 'masterful examination of obsessive passion,' is at best wishful thinking. The story is about a young aspiring actress who has just moved to Paris. Her capacity for affection is limited and is not encouraged by the various men she meets. If the movie were in English it would be ridiculous, but because the characters are speaking French they can hit one another as a prelude to kissing and get away with it. But not for too long, however. It is a *Rendez-Vous* which need not be kept.

RENEGADES

In *Renegades* the bad guy, in the middle of a frantic getaway from a diamond robbery, pauses to smash a museum display and steal a spear, an act which makes no logical sense whatsoever but does provide motivation to Lou Diamond Phillips' character, an American Indian, to join forces with Keifer Sutherland's character, an undercover cop involved in the diamond heist, in order to bring the spear grabbing, diamond guzzling villain to justice. It doesn't get any better, though some viewers may be pleased with the tacked on ending, in which Sutherland invites Phillips to his motel room at the fade out. The disc is full of the sort of loud, heavy ordnance sounds which are adeptly rendered in digital stereo surround. The picture is about average.

RENT-A-COP

Whose idea was it to team Burt Reynolds and Liza Minnelli in *Rent-A-Cop* ? Since both performers are box office poison (this is not a criticism of their abilities, merely a financial reality based on their track records over the past 10 years) was it thought that they would cancel out each other's bad karma? The movie is enjoyable. Minnelli's portrayal of a hooker is poorly written and difficult to accept, but everything else in the plot flows comfortably. Reynolds has his role down pat, and it is a shame his movies keep failing because he really has a handle on how to shift between action and comedy. The picture is okay but not stunning. The stereo surround sound is workmanlike.

RENTED LIPS

Martin Mull stars in *Rented Lips* and the scenes he appears in are often humorous, but when he is not present, the movie is as bad as they come. Mull portrays a documentary filmmaker who is hired to complete a porno film. There are a number of 'in' film business jokes, and a number of bad bathroom gags. The picture quality is passable. The Ultra-Stereo sound is competently executed. There are chapter markers, since Mull's character eventually turns the movie into a musical.

REPENTANCE

The two-and-a-half hour Soviet comedy, *Repentance*, about a dead leader who will not stay buried, comes in a gatefold jacket containing an essay. Unfortunately, it amounts to little more than an elaborate plot summary. The sound is digitally encoded and subject to the restraints of Russian recording equipment. The film is in Russian and has pale yellow subtitles.

The script is a superb and complex satire with obvious allegorical overtones to contemporary Russian history and less obvious explorations of the delicate and confusing relationship between the Church and the Soviet state, suggesting that the hypocrisies of the government and the hypocrisies in the Church are indistinguishable, except that the Church is nicer these days. The film, with many surreal images and plot twists, is dense in lessons and multiple intentions.

As stimulating as the story may be, however, the movie is something of a hardship upon the eyes. The transfer is a little grainy, but it is the visual scheme of the movie itself which causes strain. The camera rarely moves, the sets and costumes are variations on the dullest colors imaginable, and the lighting is inexperienced, casting shadows where there ought to be shades and glare where there ought to be illumination. Like a Five Year Plan, you have to suffer through the film and realize its rewards later.

REPO MAN

Although the sound is monaural, *Repo Man* has been CX-encoded – a wise move because the soundtrack is important, not only for the New Wave score, but for the precious dialog. It is the conversations, as an assortment of lowlifes repossess cars and chase after UFO's, which make the disc worth watching more than a single time. The individual scenes look like no one bothered to yell 'Action!' or 'Cut!' but the result is more carefully planned than it first appears since some very loose strands of plot all end up winding around each other.

RETRIBUTION

A better than average horror film, *Retribution* is about a man who has visions of violent crimes. Close scrutiny will reveal as many faults as any typical horror film is burdened with, but the plot is constructed to keep the viewer guessing, and the gross stuff is parceled out for much the same purpose. You could do worse.

The picture quality in the opening scenes is quite good, but it deteriorates as the film goes along, though part of the fault is with the filmmakers, who seem to shift their scenes between two different budgets. The sound is in stereo surround, but except for one eerie scene in a meat packing establishment, the separations are limited to the complacent musical score.

THE RETURN OF FRANK JAMES
(see **JESSE JAMES**)

RETURN OF THE JEDI
(see **STAR WARS**)

RETURN OF THE KILLER TOMATOES
Return of the Killer Tomatoes is in stereo, though the separation effects are limited and not of great interest. At least the dialog is audible. The picture transfer also looks accurate and the picture is cheap but glossy.

The center of the film is about a mad scientist who creates an army of men from tomatoes and toxic waste. Obviously a comedy and obviously insulated from most critical analysis, the narrative continually steps away from itself to make jokes about the movie's production. There are enough gags and enough sex to discourage one from turning it off, but repeated viewings will be limited. If you're looking for something really silly, there are better choices available.

THE RETURN OF THE LIVING DEAD
Gross and occasionally amusing, the horror comedy *The Return of the Living Dead*, which has nothing to do with George Romero but everything to do with the sort of films that he spawned, has been given a nice transfer. The picture is grainy in some of the night scenes, but the colors look solid and accurate, and in light the image has a nice shine. The sound is acceptable. The story, about a chemical which seeps into a graveyard and brings about a mass resurrection, gives the filmmakers a chance to exaggerate for laughs while remaining true to their genre. The cast includes the reliably bad James Karen and Clu Gulager and a group of teenage types. The corpses have personalities, and there is a half of a dog, mounted as a medical display, who starts barking after the gas hits him.

RETURN OF THE LIVING DEAD PART II
The original *Return fo the Living Dead* was a subversively funny interpretation of the zombie concept, and ought to have signalled the end of the genre in that it was a parody, but zombies never die. Although *Return of the Living Dead Part II* contains sequences which are deliberately slapstick, it is not aggressively humorous. *Part II* is mildly amusing and mildly entertaining. Except for its portrayal of women (they all screech too much), there really isn't anything wrong with the movie, but it is going over ground already trodden to death and to death again. The Ultra-Stereo sound, which has been digitally encoded, includes some nice separations. The picture quality is acceptable. The 89-minute film is in CLV.

RETURN OF THE SWAMP THING
Return of the Swamp Thing is a little closer to the spirit of the comic than the first *Swamp Thing* movie was, but it still stops short of its promise. The script has some good lines, but Heather Locklear, who plays the heroine, has no sense of comic delivery, and the whole movie seems to take its cues from her. Louis Jordan has a couple of amusing moments, talking to a parrot named 'Gigi,' but Swamp Thing isn't much of a super hero – he just beats up villains – and *Return of the Swamp Thing* isn't much of a film. The Ultra-Stereo soundtrack on the is in analog and separations are reserved primarily for the musical score. The picture is grainy in places, but passable.

THE RETURN OF THE VAMPIRE
Fans of old black-and-white horror movies will not have a complete collection unless they obtain *The Return of the Vampire*, from RCA/Columbia and Image. Bela Lugosi stars as the title character, terrorizing a family in London during the war. The script covers no new ground, but reworks the standard plot devices with reasonable efficiency.

The film was made in 1943 but looks ten years older. The source material has a number of speckles, but its condition is passable. In places the sound suffers from audio crosstalk, but the show should not be amplified too greatly in any case. Side two of the 69-minute effort is in CAV with two unsteady still frames out of every five.

RETURN TO OZ
Except for the cheap candy-colored orange label and equally unappetizing jacket cover art, *Return to Oz* is excellent. The stereo is so good that even the non-fantasy stuff in the beginning is thrilling. While we would liked to have been able to see the widerscreen, the tight compositions enhance the psychological peculiarities of the plot.

"Portions of this material may not be suitable for small children," says the jacket. They aren't kidding. Electric shock therapy, indeed. The doctor doesn't even stick anything in Dorothy's mouth to stop her from biting her tongue off before he throws the switch. A lightning bolt hits the clinic in the nick of time, however, and Dorothy escapes, falls into a river, and wakes up next to her chicken, in Oz. 'Oz' backward is 'Zo' – 'life.' The backward reality of Oz is often threatening – any object at any moment can come alive and bite. The movie is not for children. It is for adults who have a little patience, fancy video monitors, and great stereo equipment.

RETURN TO SNOWY RIVER
(see **THE MAN FROM SNOWY RIVER**)

REVENGE
Nowhere on the jacket cover does it mention it, but *Revenge* has been letterboxed, with an aspect ratio of about 2.3:1. The movie, which was directed by Tony Scott, opens with a jet fighter buzzing mesas in the Southwest. Now, as a movie, this is sort of a dumb and superfluous opening, since the hero, played by Kevin Costner, never flies again after the credits are ended, but as a laser disc, letterboxed and tagged with a Scott-style stereo surround soundtrack, it is a great sequence which is collectible in and of itself, regardless of the two hours which follow.

Scott's wide array of visual enthusiasms are effectively presented with the letterboxing. The image quality is inconsistent, although it is generally very good. Parts of the film are intentionally foggy, but the disc tends to amplify the negative aspects of Scott's filter tricks. The break between side two and three is perfectly chosen, and serves to emphasize a passage of time more effectively than if the film had been allowed to play straight through.

The film is based upon a Jim Harrison story and Harrison contributed to the screenplay. Taken literally, the story is silly – about a man seeking vengeance after sleeping with his rich friend's wife and being beaten for it, but both Harrison and Scott are stylists who often successfully substitute an attractive form for a hollow content. They fail in *Revenge* only in that they fool no one, but if a viewer *wants* to enjoy a Sun Belt melodrama about adultery and endurance, the movie, and the disc, are there to be had.

REVENGE OF THE NERDS
The color on *Revenge of the Nerds* is all washed out and the soundtrack is flat. The disc has not been cut with preservation in mind, but then the property is hardly worth preserving. A good idea for an exploitation film, *Revenge of the Nerds* gets a few laughs out of its collection of misfit college students who are dumped on by everyone else at campus. Those who are hesitant are advised to trust their instincts and avoid the disc.

REVENGE OF THE NERDS II: NERDS IN PARADISE
Any self-respecting nerd will be outraged at some of the dialog in *Revenge of the Nerds II: Nerds in Paradise*. Consider this line about the placement of Ft. Lauderdale, Florida: "It's located 26 degrees 4 minutes north longitude 80 degrees 9 minutes west latitude." And they had a .500 chance of getting it right, too. The sound is in stereo, but is uninteresting. The picture is acceptable, but will not stand up to close scrutiny. Nothing in the movie or the disc stands up to close scrutiny, except, maybe, some of the jokes.

REVOLUTION
Revolution is not as silly as critics would lead one to believe – Al Pacino's accent, for example, sounds linguistically legitimate – but it plods and leaps from one unlikely historical re-creation to the next, relentlessly. The sound is great. It is the cinematography which doesn't work, and the flaws are accurately rendered on disc (as are a couple of splices at the very end). Phony rainstorms, phony smoke, phony fog, phony snow and phony sunshine prevent you from being transported to the time and the place on a sustained basis. Add to that a tendency for the longer scenes to be filmed in the dark. Either you can't see what's happening at all, or you see all the artifice that is contributing to the attempt at illusion.

RHINESTONE
Directed by Bob Clark, *Rhinestone* might have been a minor hit if it hadn't been burdened by a stellar cast and over-expectations. It is a tossup as to whether Dolly Parton's original songs or Sylvester Stallone's original

dialog is closer in essence to fingernails being drawn across a slate blackboard.

The disc is in surround sound. The really funny sequences are evenly spaced out so you'll have to sit through the whole disc and listen to Stallone sing to catch them all. The hard of hearing may enjoy it.

RICH LITTLE: ONE'S A CROWD

We suppose that Rich Little is talented. In five-minute appearances he can be entertaining. 86 minutes of Little, however, is a little too much. His imitations are embarrassing, whatever their technical attributes, and his humor, completely subjugated by the other aspects of his act, is sporadic and trifling. Taken from a number of live performances, *Rich Little: One's a Crowd* is excruciating. To give one example: He does a take-off of Bogart's extended summary of the crimes at the end of *The Maltese Falcon*. In the background, the orchestra plays 'As Time Goes By.'

The picture has difficulty with intense colors, particularly when images are superimposed behind Little. The sound is digitally encoded stereo and is in fine shape. There are chapter markers for major skits, but not for every different voice. The disc is in CLV.

RICHARD PRYOR – LIVE AND SMOKIN'

Recorded in 1971 before his film career began, the material on *Richard Pryor – Live and Smokin'* is raw and daring. Indeed, there are some segments which Pryor himself would not touch today with a symbolic ten-foot pole, particularly material dealing with his own sexual identity. We can't recommend this disc – it's only 45 minutes long and the print is grainy and poorly recorded – but it is compelling.

RICHARD STRAUSS – SALOME – KARL BOHM
(see **SALOME'S LAST DANCE**

RICHARD THOMPSON – ACROSS A CROWDED ROOM

The jacket art on *Richard Thompson – Across a Crowded Room* is cluttered with interesting images, but the program is just a straight concert. The picture is very blurry, having been filmed on a poorly-lit stage. The sound is much better. Thompson's guitar playing is delivered with much greater clarity than live recordings usually accomplish and it is quite tempting to forego turning on the television at all when listening to the disc.

RICHARD WAGNER DER RING DES NIBELUNGEN DAS RHEINGOLD
RICHARD WAGNER DER RING DES NIBELUNGEN DIE WALKURE
RICHARD WAGNER DER RING DES NIBELUNGEN SIEGFRIED
RICHARD WAGNER DER RING DES NIBELUNGEN GOTTER DAMMERUNG
THE MAKING OF THE RING – CHEREAU – BOULEZ

Several generations have grown up approaching opera the wrong way, hearing a work before they ever, if at all, see it. That is not what was originally intended by the creators of the artform and, thanks to video, eyes can once again wrest equality with ears. *Richard Wagner Der Ring des Nibelungen* has more plot per measure than any operatic work we know of, but listening to a record and following a libretto won't give you the thrill when the lovers first clutch one another, discovering they are brother and sister. Not even the music gives that to you, it only undulates the emotion. You have to see the performers and believe the lust in their expressions.

Philips has released Wagner's entire four-opera cycle in four separate disc packages, along with a fifth disc, *The Making of Der Ring des Niebelungen*, which summarizes the program. Disc owners can watch the whole 'Ring Cycle' in a single day, and with a little timing the finale could begin just as twilight is settling in. Such a marathon viewing, however, would be something of a strain upon the eyes, because none of the discs have a strong picture transfer.

A resurgence of interest in mythology, however, makes the Bayreuth Centenary production, conceived and directed by Patrice Chereau, somewhat ill-timed. The production is one which does away with the typical Saxon costumes and natural settings, replacing them with Wagnerian era fashions and industrial scenic designs. The first scene of the first opera, *Das Rheingold*, opens not in the swirling waters of the Rhine, but at the base of a hydro-electric dam. The irony is obvious – man has indeed turned secrets of the Rhine into limitless power – but a preference for a clear presentation of the myth itself would be preferred. The production also takes on the appearance of a stage run-through, though no audience is present. The orchestra is unseen, but the recording is live, and picks up the thuds of moving props.

The hour-long single-sided *Wagner – The Making of The Ring – Chereau – Boulez* tells far more about the operas and the centennial production than any of the jacket inserts do. It is a good cheerleading piece which could convince some potential purchasers to go all the way, and it also provides rare footage from earlier Bayreuth 'Ring' productions, as well as Wagner family home movies. The picture quality is even poorer than the operas themselves, and the sound is only stereophonic during the excerpts.

Whatever insights Chereau may provide to the narrative by undercutting Wagner's original vision, he is cramping the music, and in doing so, diminishes its impact. Pierre Boulez, conducting the work, came from another direction with the same purpose, cutting the orchestra down in size so that the music would not overpower everything, a further attempt to take from the ears and give to the eyes. Chereau and Boulez were reacting against the Teutonic exaggerations which had set into previous productions, and in a way they over-reacted. As you watch the program, you look through the sets and costumes to imagine the Viking outfits of yore, but the story is humanized, and it grabs you with the same beguiling force that it grabbed those who heard variations of it while sitting around the hearth hundreds of years ago.

A booklet which accompanies each disc contains two plot summaries, one in a confusing matrix summarizing every chapter marker in four different languages, and a second, which mixes synopsis material with scattered commentary. The music flows continuously from one scene to the next and the breaks between the three sides happen without warning. The lyrics are in German and have English subtitles.

The picture on *Das Rheingold* is weak, as if the source material had missed a dose or two of golden apples. The sound is in better shape. With all the brass Wagner uses, one really needs an elaborate audio system to do the disc justice. The digital track is noticeably clearer than the analog track. None of the performers, including Donald McIntyre as Wotan and Hermann Becht as Alberich, achieve more than competency in their performances. Boulez's conducting, however, is vigorous and fresh. Chereau's staging is well-executed technically and has plenty to offer.

Die Walkure, the second installment, has the same drawbacks as *Das Rheingold*. The disc, nevertheless, is immensely entertaining, and verifies that anyone who liked *Lord of the Rings* or *Excalibur*, and can afford the investment, should not let the *Ring* slip from their fingers. The image is grainy and foggy. The sound is better, and has no noticeable faults. Every act comes on a separate platter. The side divisions are consistently well chosen. Although the stage and costume design is, on the whole, obnoxious, the Valhalla set which opens Act II is stunning, containing a huge Foucault pendulum that rocks back and forth through most of the Act. Although the camera does not always capture it – thereby changing the experience from that of the audience members who probably never took their eyes off it – one is always aware of its presence.

Essentially an eight-character opera with no chorus appearances, the presentation of *Siegfried* is less effective on television than *Die Walkure* or *Das Rheingold*. The spectacular stage piece in each act – the revelation of a forge in Act I, the appearance of a dragon in Act II, and the fire-encircled shrine in Act III – is not approached with a sense of wonder by the video director, Brian Large. The production is reprieved only by a rousing performance from Manfred Jung in the title role and by the inherent pleasures of Wagner's creation. The sound is in keeping with the quality of the first two discs. Unfortunately, so is the picture transfer. The image looks green around the edges and is often grainy.

With the release of *Gotterdammerung*, *Der Ring des Nibelungen* comes to its conclusion and Valhalla goes up in flames. The image is particularly weak. It is both grainy and blurry, with gold and fire forever leaking into the surrounding colors. The sound is acceptable, as it has been in the other installments. The recording is weakest in capturing the voices of the female singers (Gwyneth Jones, however, is much better in *Gotterdammerung* than she was in *Siegfried*), but is surprisingly grand when the chorus joins in during Act II.

In *The Making of the Ring*, it is let slip that Chereau was brought in somewhat late and had to rush to put things together. It is evident throughout the collection that his more radical conceptual ideas were not fully realized. Chereau worked hardest, however, at telling the story, and the emotions of the story come through on the video presentation almost as strongly as the emotions of the music. It is magnificent. You want to boo and throw tomatoes at the end, not because of Chereau's challenging tableau, but because he fully realizes Wagner's teasing 'Life is tough and then you die' message – 16 hours to get back to where you started from? The Earth at least takes 24.

RICK SPRINGFIELD – PLATINUM VIDEOS

Rick Springfield – Platinum Videos is a one-sided CAV collection of six Springfield music videos. The picture is speckled and slightly blurry from beginning to end. We were not impressed with the sound, either. The first three videos share a motif of voyeurism. The last three are more interesting, conceptually, veering into fantasy, science fiction, and spiritualism. Springfield's lyrics might have flunked out of a law school poetry class ("You know I feel so dirty, When they start talking cute, I want to tell her that I love her, But the point is probably moot."), but his music is frustratingly catchy.

RICK SPRINGFIELD – THE BEAT OF THE LIVE DRUM

Rick Springfield still acts like he learned how to play rock and roll by reading GQ, but *Rick Springfield – The Beat of the Live Drum* is very impressive. The 70-minute program is a filmed concert, but the music has been dubbed in a studio. Unlike some shows, the producers don't try to hide the post-synching. Instead, it is played up. At the same time, video effects have been added judiciously to give the impression that vehicles out of *Blade Runner* are cruising over the auditorium. The disc's picture has a live concert lighting blur, but the act is more effective if you don't examine it too closely.

RICK'S YOUR PLACE FOR FANTASY

Rick's – Your Place for Fantasy is a blatant rip-off, consisting entirely of material re-edited from several other topless dancing programs. It has a very blurry and grainy picture, and fuzzy sound which only household pets will be able to discern as stereo. The jacket's running time listing of 45 minutes is pure wishful thinking, because the disc actually lasts only 37.

RICOCHET RABBIT

There are probably more physical gags in a single Chuck Jones cartoon than there are in all 88 minutes of *Ricochet Rabbit*. Still, when a good, surrealistically violent gag does appear, it is genuinely amusing, making the disc, which is best not viewed entirely in one sitting (or multiple times, as the episodes begin to grate after a bit), worthwhile for animation enthusiasts. The transfer is beautiful. The colors are bright and the image is sharp. The sound is a bit harsh and is best left without amplification.

Ricochet Rabbit contains 13 shorts. They are listed on the back of the jacket in order, with succinct descriptions for those who wish to assess the program's contents. The anthropomorphic hero is a sheriff who moves so quickly he can play ping pong with himself. In each cartoon he corrals an inept bad guy.

RIDERS OF THE STORM

The best one can say about *Riders of the Storm* is that it is an interesting failure, although most viewers will probably not be as generous. The narrative concerns a pirate television station being operated out of a retro-fitted B-29 which never lands (how it gets fuel is not explained, how the crew gets food is), and the efforts by those running the station to spoil the chances of an arch-conservative presidential candidate. The special effects are negligible.

The disc has been released by Nelson, which is so desperate to sell it that they have allowed the jacket copy to reveal the plot's one big, though obvious, secret. The sound is a little rough but passable. The picture is blurry in places. The film stars Dennis Hopper and Michael J. Pollard. Both are confined to a small, cramped set, and it often appears that footage, particularly of Pollard, has been utilized which was taken after the director yelled 'Cut.' That is, if anybody connected with this film ever had the sense to yell 'Cut.'

RIKKY AND PETE

A theatrical trailer for *Rikky and Pete* appears after the film is ended, which should please both movie enthusiasts and those wishing to quickly relive the comedy's best moments. Although the disc has chapter encoding, there is not a marker for the trailer.

The stereo mix is very good, full of fun little sound effects coming from all over, and the disc has digital encoding and a clean transfer. The picture also looks good. The film was made by the team responsible for *Malcolm* and *Rikky and Pete* is to *Malcolm* what a first novel is to a graduate thesis. Like the earlier work, the plot involves a socially maladjusted young man with a penchant for constructing elaborate contraptions. In this film, he travels to the outback with his sister to achieve financial independence and maturity by mining in the desert. The plot moves a little aimlessly, and some of the dialog is so Australian that subtitles would be helpful, but there are a couple of great gags and the disc is generally enjoyable.

RIO LOBO
THE SONS OF KATIE ELDER

Howard Hawks directed *Rio Lobo*, which was first released in 1970 – not the best of times for westerns or John Wayne-style heroics. The movie, however, is good entertainment and makes an enjoyable disc. It is an action film, opening with a train robbery and then advancing to a tale about a town with a corrupt establishment, which Wayne's character is obliged to straighten out. Except for the veterans, the acting is terrible, but the film moves so quickly you don't have time to think about the performances.

The transfer is satisfying. The film was not a widescreen effort, so little is lost in its presentation on the small screen. The colors are a little pale and there are a few speckles, but the source material is in good shape otherwise. The sound is digitally encoded stereo and while there are no surround enhancements, the stereo effects rescue Jerry Goldsmith's otherwise cluttered score and do justice to everything from steam whistles to spurs.

Paramount has done a less impressive job with *The Sons of Katie Elder*. The colors have the same paleness as *Rio Lobo* but the third side, inexplicably, looks more washed out than sides one or two. As is evidenced in the opening credits, *Elder* is a widescreen movie and it is scanned and cropped. More atmosphere than action is lost in the process, but the cropping will still bother many viewers. The sound is digitally encoded monaural. It is in good shape, with few distortions, and there are some explosions which have a real kick. The music, by Elmer Bernstein, makes a satisfying complement to Goldsmith's effort in *Rio Lobo* and strengthens the viability of watching the titles as a double bill.

The film, directed by Henry Hathaway, concerns the reunion of four brothers at their mother's funeral. Inevitably, they sniff out the wrongdoings which in part led to her death. Dean Martin, who is used effectively, stars with Wayne. The narrative has less forward movement than the Hawks film, and should go first if a double bill is planned, but it is an old fashioned sort of entertainment, about good guys, bad guys, family and land, and its pleasures will prove as durable as Wayne's image.

RIO REVISITED

Rio Revisited, with Antonio Carlos Jobim and Gal Costa, is a satisfying Brazilian music concert. It features Jobim's sea breeze sambas and Costa's tropical vocals. The band also has five extremely attractive backup vocalists, and the video director wisely pans across them again and again during the course of the program. The impressively produced disc truly looks as good as it sounds.

THE RISE OF CATHERINE THE GREAT

A film which is unsuccessful at invoking a romantic sympathy for royalty, *The Rise of Catherine the Great*, stars Elizabeth Bergner and Douglas Fairbanks, Jr. It is as erratic as Catherine's husband, lurching between an attempt to make historical figures human and an inability to comprehend their motivations. The sound is fuzzy, and the black-and-white picture has a worn and soft appearance.

RIT/SPECIAL LEE RITENOUR LIVE

Under the standards of normal discs, *RIT/Special Lee Ritenour Live* would be considered an excellent effort, both in production and content, but it is not perfect. The applause, for example, sounds like it is muted, as does some of the talking between numbers. When Ritenour's band plays, however, the recording is perfectly satisfactory. Ritenour's electric guitar instrumentals are integrated with Phil Perry's full-winded vocals to create a program which sustains one's attention. It is nice to know that the population of jazz discs has risen so far that we can feel blase about dismissing a well-made entry.

RITA, SUE & BOB TOO

The marvelously bawdy *Rita, Sue & Bob Too* is one of those low-budget British efforts where the source material looks as if it crossed the Atlantic behind the boat, but the film itself is rich in wit and life. To get the bad part out of the way first, the picture quality falls apart whenever the lights go down, and even in the sunshine the image has a cheap look to it. The sound is scratchy, and requires careful adjustment to obtain the right compromise between being loud enough so that one can understand the accents and soft enough so one can avoid overt distortion.

The movie is about two babysitters who break up a marriage and move in with the husband. One of the most difficult dramatic tasks is to make infidelity look appealing, but here it is totally excusable. There isn't much nudity, but the dialog is randy enough to make a sailor blush – another advantage for having it on home video, and another reason not to turn the volume up too high.

THE RIVER

The essay on the back of the Voyager release, *The River*, delicately avoids suggesting that the English language film, by the accomplished French director, Jean Renoir, was a failure, but details the many problems Renoir encountered putting it together. The film, however, is a classic example of the failure of a great artist which is more worthy than the successes of others. In spite of all the problems and changes which Renoir had to confront while making the movie, the result remains a rewarding and memorable experience.

The River tells the story of an English family living near Calcutta. Based upon the memories of one family member, the film is intentionally a western view of Indian life and culture. It relies heavily on voice-over narration and features a cast which by and large cannot act. Renoir's sensibilities rescue the footage by preventing any aspect of the story – the travelog, the romances, the coming-of-age indulgences – from taking control. Even the one tragic sequence is subdued on subsequent viewings. This approach gives *The River* a little mystery, something it sorely needs to maintain appeal.

The CLV disc has no special features except for chapter markers. An early Technicolor effort, the film does not have the glitter of a Hollywood studio production, but the picture quality is satisfying. Intensely colored blossoms and fabrics tend to blur a little and the image never looks as good as the still on the jacket cover. The mildly aged monaural sound is digitally encoded. The movie was the first Western film to use a completely Indian musical score.

THE RIVER
COUNTRY
PLACES IN THE HEART

It was something of a scandal that three movies about farming were all released at roughly the same time. Now that they have been issued on disc, it is even possible to hold a plight-of-the-farmer triple-bill party. The worst movie of the three is *The River*. Starring Sissy Spacek and Mel Gibson and directed by Mark Rydell, the film has a falseness that it just can't shake. For one thing, the real star of the movie is cinematographer Vilmos Zsigmond, but the camera work is so lovely and so perfect that it magnifies every error. Particularly the wardrobes. All the clothing looks too new; muddy, and torn in strategic places, but by no means lived-in.

Country does everything right that *The River* does wrong, but it still fails. The couple portrayed by Sam Shepard and Jessica Lange are not threatened by an overflowing river. Instead it is a storm of debt which is bringing them to the brink. As is carefully explained in the film, government policy provoked the farmers into stretching themselves on what appeared to be guaranteed credit, and then changes in policy snapped the last of their financial security. The portrayal is so well accomplished that side one seems brilliant, and it is only the embarrassingly relentless pessimism on side two which will dull a viewer's appreciation.

The picture on the disc looks good and the sound is impressive. We were particularly astonished by a cat pictured in a transitional insert and the fidelity of his contented purring.

The Robert Benton film, *Places in the Heart*, is about a thousand other things besides farming. A woman (Sally Field) struggles to bring in the cotton crop and pay her mortgage. But where that was the be-all and the end-all of the other two films, it is only the spine of Benton's story. Taking place in the '30s in Texas, *Places in the Heart* also touches upon adultery, race relations, vision, and the location of the human spirit. The film's remarkable ending is a cleverly crafted conceit which rescues the picture from meandering into nothingness. The photography of Nestor Almendros is full of the glowing beiges that have become his trademark. The sound sometimes feels as dry and scratchy as the cotton fields.

RIVER OF DEATH

A very silly but utterly enjoyable Alistair MacLean adventure film, *River of Death* features one of our favorite B-movie actors, Michael Dudikoff, along with a gaggle of second-rate stars, including Robert Vaughn, Donald Pleasance, and Herbert Lom. Set in the Amazon jungle, Dudikoff portrays a guide who stumbles upon a 'lost city' and barely returns to tell about it. Several shady individuals then hire him to go back again, for reasons which are shrouded from the hero but plainly obvious to the viewer. No matter, there are enough gunfights, explosions, and wild natives to distract cooperative viewers from such minor considerations as logic and reality. The movie is a cockeyed takeoff on 'Heart of Darkness' directed by someone who clearly sat through *Apocalypse Now* more than once.

The disc opens with a rousing trailer for *Crack House*. The Ultra-Stereo surround sound is too loud and a bit clunky, but it does its job. The picture transfer is good, although the original production looks a little grainy and the night scenes are a bit murky.

RIVER OF NO RETURN

The stills on the back of *River of No Return* are squeezed. It is another reminder that the Cinemascope film is not a Cinemascope disc. The opening and closing credits are letterboxed, providing a tantalizing peak at how discs like this may someday appear. The cropping spoils some gorgeous vistas, but it also hides some embarrassing rear projections, so it is almost a wash. The color is a little pale, but the costumes and props are anything but, and provide a continuous array of chromatic surprises. One salivates at the thought of what the film might have looked like if material closer to the original negative had been used for the transfer.

The story has Monroe and Robert Mitchum riding down a river in a raft, fighting Indians and falling in love. The stereophonic sound is super when it is coordinated, and the combination of trombones and smoke signals makes one totally forget about racial defamation. When the dialog is sent to a side channel, however, the volume is lower than when it comes from the middle, which may bother some viewers. The sound encoding is analog, and the recording is more than 30 years old, so a certain amount of audio clutter is inevitable.

Monroe is wonderful, even though this is one of her weaker acting efforts. She concentrates too hard on diction and articulation, which can be downright humorous when she tries to be emotional but still manages to get out every last consonant. When she's holding onto the oar of the raft, however, getting splashed and struggling to keep her balance, her body is articulate with a perfection that her voice could never achieve.

THE RIVER RAT

The River Rat starts out like a Martin Ritt-type childhood-on-the-river picture but twists itself into a rousing murder and greed suspense film as soon as your defenses are down. Martha Plimpton gives a no-nonsense performance as a young girl whose father (Tommy Lee Jones) is released from prison. The movie will please both kids and adults, though some may feel the language is suitable only for maturer audiences. When the girl first tries to strike up a conversation with her stoic father, she cheerfully asks him about the mechanics of prison rape.

The picture is grainy, but the sound has some dimensionality despite its being monaural. Clearly filmed on a minor budget, every angle and mood is rich with surprise and emotion. At one point there is a spectacular special effect about which we will say no more except that it is wonderfully unexpected, as is the disc.

RIVER'S EDGE

When compared to *River's Edge*, most other movies about kids seem patronizing or pompous. The amazing thing about the plot is that it manages its overly metaphorical title, its thematic alienation, and an arcade of other symbols, without ever interfering with the characters even slightly. No actress or actor does or says anything which doesn't seem utterly true. It is a movie taking place in a non-movie world, the plot pushed just hard enough by two murders to keep emotions and interests flowing.

Everybody who has been to high school in the last 30 years knows these kids. They are the ones who, no matter how they later matured, were, at that point, on the edge of life instead of in the mainstream. Whether it was because of a disintegration in their families or an unevenness in their biochemistry, they didn't know why they were alive or what they should do about it. Their actions ranged from entropy to chaos.

The picture is a mildly grainy in the night scenes but displays no other major flaws. The sound is monaural, but it has a stronger impact than many stereo soundtracks, and is reasonably free of noise.

ROAD HOUSE

The contemporary story in *Road House* is structured like a western, but instead of having a sheriff come to clean up the town, the hero is a bouncer hired by a local roadhouse tavern. The film so deliberately casts the good guy, played by Patrick Swayze, as a mythic protagonist that some viewers may find the situations mildly absurd. Those who enjoy martial arts movies and those who just like to see a good brawl should have a great time watching Swayze do his thing.

The picture's aspect ratio is a pleasing 2.3:1. The movie would not be as enjoyable if the sides were cropped, if only for the atmosphere which would escape as a result. The color transfer is less satisfying. Oranges and reds look grainy and darker scenes sometimes look too blue. The sound is okay, although the surround mix isn't very interesting.

ROAD TO UTOPIA

If you're in a hurry you can pretty much dispense with side one of *Road to Utopia* and just start right off with side two. All the best gags seem to be in the latter half of the film. If you have more time, however, by all means don't miss side one, since playing the whole movie stretches out the pleasure. The Bob Hope and Bing Crosby Yukon adventure is not the best *Road* picture, but it is the only one, so far, to make it to disc, and so it serves as a pipeline to memories of all the others.

The black-and-white print is not in mint condition, but it will do. An original theatrical trailer appears at the end, mildly framed so that the whole image can be seen, and it is in beautiful condition. The disc has chapter markers for the songs, few of which have aged very well. The monaural sound is in decent shape. Some people find that because of the inept scripting, rushed takes, and slapdash production in these films, the entertainment is strained. They've forgotten what it is to be young.

THE ROAD WARRIOR (see MAD MAX)

THE ROBE

Some viewers may find the inconsistent picture quality in the CBS/Fox Special Wide Screen Edition of *The Robe* too distracting to enjoy the film. The accuracy of the color shifts from very good to less than fair, and the stronger the colors are, the more blurred they become. In some sequences there are red halos, which have nothing to do with the film's religious theme, hovering around the characters. The source material which was used is also damaged. A couple of reels are marred by a white horizontal bar running across the lower portion of the screen. There are one or two splices, as well, and a few speckles spread about. Night scenes also tend to appear fuzzy.

The letterboxing pulls back the curtain on a production which is always consciously making use of the widescreen. The filmmakers felt compelled to divide the screen in half as much as possible. There is always a column, a shading, or something, usually in the background, running up and down the exact center of the image.

The movie is great fun, transporting the viewer to Ancient Rome (Hollywood-style) and then providing alternating doses of the teachings of Jesus and of good old fashioned Christian violence. Richard Burton accomplishes the impossible by retaining his dignity in a number of silly, playacting situations. It is also a joy just listening to him.

The movie served as a showcase for overproduced stereophonic sound, and the disc is full of enjoyable ping-pong conversations. That said, the sound also has some drawbacks. The music tends to go off pitch in places and the separations could be stronger and more distinctive than they are.

After the film is ended, there are two pleasing newsreel segments, depicting the New York and Los Angeles premiers of the film. A trailer for the film's sequel, 'Demetrius and the Gladiators,' follows the newsreels. It has a squeezed, full screen image.

ROBERT KLEIN ON BROADWAY

Robert Klein's humor in *Robert Klein on Broadway*, is intelligent, and the sophisticated audience responds accordingly. The last quarter of the hour-long show, however, is given over to a song and dance parody which is a little bit of a letdown after his funny jokes. He should open with the piece instead. Both the picture and the sound are very nice. The image is of cable quality. The sound is in stereo, which gives the audio track a solid and immediate atmosphere. The uninhibited stereophonic laughter makes Klein's humor seem even funnier.

ROBIN HOOD
SNOOPY COME HOME
THE ADVENTURES OF THE LITTLE PRINCE

The human mind perceives by registering unexpected sensory responses and ignoring the expected responses, according to recently published studies. If this is so, then younger children cannot see or understand what is around them as well as older children or adults because too much of it is still new. They cannot concentrate because they have yet to acquire the experiences which will fill the expectation portion of their neurology.

While a live action picture contains an almost infinite amount of information to register, a drawing contains a decidedly finite amount and is ideal for a child who is exercising powers of concentration.

Cartoons from the Walt Disney organization are the prettiest, richest, most visually rewarding cartoons there are. They have depth and constant action and color and inventive perspectives and a whole kingdom of personality.

Children are sure to be enraptured by the Walt Disney disc, *Robin Hood.* It is an 80-minute animated re-working of the Robin Hood legend with various animals used to characterize the participants. Robin is a dashing fox and Maid Marion is a svelte vixen. Little John is a variation of the same bear Phil Harris voiced in 'The Jungle Book.' The sound is fine and the picture looks superb.

Snoopy Come Home is closer to the average animated feature. There is less movement and the characters are almost always kept in the foreground. Adults will find the Peanuts characters to be intelligent and charming the first time the disc is viewed and children will want to watch it more than once.

The Adventures of the Little Prince, has even less movement than *Snoopy Come Home*. The plots claim to be based only on "conceptions of Antoine de Saint-Exupery," but remain very faithful to the spirit of his writing. The sound on the disc is a tinny monaural and the picture is slightly blurry. The disc is comprised of two half-hour features, 'Somewhere in Space' and 'A Small Alien.' The Little Prince is the ruler of a planet which is about as big as nine school buses stacked in rows of three. He heats his morning tea on a small volcano and spends his day tending to the maintenance of his principality. In the first episode, a small red rose blossoms in the soil and turns out to have a rather thorny personality. In the second, the Prince hitches a ride to Earth and meets the typical Saint-Exupery aviator, who is stranded in the desert and tinkering with the engine of his flying machine. Is the Little Prince actually a manifestation of the aviator's parched and deluded brain? We wish we could see more episodes, but we also feel that only really small children will share our appreciation of the material.

ROBIN WILLIAMS LIVE!

We found ourselves laughing so hard during *Robin Williams Live!* that we kept on backing up to play a funny part over again. Thus it took us more than two hours to get through the 65-minute disc. Williams appears in the cavernous Metropolitan Opera House, which is a stunt in itself, since he clearly manages to hold the attention of the furthest balcony as he moves through his energetic routine. Much of his humor is topical, so it is difficult to say if viewers will catch all the references several years from now, but when he starts aiming at the age-old targets of sex and family life, his bulls-eyes will always be relevant. The picture on the disc is a little speckled, but you will probably be laughing too much to notice.

ROBINSON CRUSOE OF CLIPPER ISLAND

One of the least satisfying of the Republic serials released on disc is *Robinson Crusoe of Clipper Island.* The serial is 14 chapters long and Republic has time-compressed the program by close to twenty minutes to fit it onto the four-hour disc. The worst aspect, however, is the cheating the filmmakers do on the cliffhangers. Almost every chapter beginning changes footage supposedly being replayed from the chapter before. To site just one example, at the end of one chapter an airplane is seen crashing into the sea, while at the beginning of the next it pulls out of the dive and continues to fly.

The plot, which, despite the program's original promotional come-ons, has nothing to do with Daniel Defoe, is about spies who use a South Pacific island for unclear, but unquestionably evil purposes. A dirigible company (the film's most intriguing component) uses the island as a fueling stop for its trans-Pacific flights, and when a maiden voyage is sabotaged, a Polynesian American agent, played by Ray Mala, is sent to investigate. The acting is poor, footage is repeated far too often, and the show is too long for its own good. It can still be enjoyed, but should not be anyone's first choice.

The picture throughout looks soft and fuzzy. There are also the standard number of scratches and splices. The analog track is cleaner and more stable than the digital track, especially on side four, where the digital track suffers from a number of drop outs. A theatrical trailer opens the disc.

ROBOCOP

The sound on *Robocop* will knock your arms and legs off. The disc has been digitally encoded and was mastered from separate audio tapes (as opposed to the usual process mastering both the sound and the picture from one video tape source). The result has an awesome dynamic range and is unencumbered by distortion, Miranda rulings, or fuzz of any sort. The thumping bass will be everybody's favorite effect, but there is a lot to be said for the high pitched whirring and clicks, as well as the music, sound editing and stereo separations. The sound is so vivid that, upon playing the disc, you will think you have awakened with bionic ears.

The picture also looks decent. The dark areas of the screen have no distracting flaws and the colors, which are purposely rusty and somber, look accurate. We wish the screen might have been even slightly wider, but none of the action is inhibited by the presentation. The director was used to making movies for the cost of Robocop's teflon shoe strings, and he keeps the peripheral imagery simple.

In many ways, the movie provides a very believable vision of the future. We love the television news broadcasts – Acapulco under siege, artificial heart commercials (Ever see the health oriented commercials which saturate current news broadcasts? These would fit right in.) – and the de facto replacement of local government by corporations. The action and the violence will be why most people buy the disc, but the film is as rich in solid ideas as it is in mashed metal and flying flesh.

ROBOT MONSTER

The really good bad movies have to have something special about them, something which prevents them from simply being dull wastes of time and celluloid, and *Robot Monster* is one of the best of the worst. The movie, which runs just a little bit over an hour, attempts to excuse its most flagrant shortcomings with a narrative framing device that makes most of the plot a little boy's dream. The filmmakers fool no one, however, since it is doubtful that even little boys dream of 'space platforms' which look exactly like plastic jet planes being twirled with a stick held, at one point clearly, by a hand. The title character is a notorious concoction involving a metal helmet with antennas attached to a gorilla suit.

The picture transfer is largely irrelevant, since it is readily apparent that the movie makers got not only their props but their film stock at a garage sale. There is a game musical score by Elmer Bernstein, who was either starving or doing somebody a big favor. Side two is in CAV with perfect still frames. Best of all, at the end of side two, there is a sublime theatrical trailer for the film. It is at chapter four and should really be watched first. Actually, once you've seen the movie a couple of times, it is the only thing you need to watch.

ROCK AND ROLL: THE EARLY DAYS

Although the narrator, John Heard, often interrupts the songs on *Rock and Roll: The Early Days*, it is not as much of an interference as it has been in other rock and roll documentaries. Some songs are played all the way through, and when Heard's voice does come on, it doesn't completely displace the music.

As a text, the documentary provides an excellent analysis of the origins and central thrusts (including Elvis's midsection) of pop music in the 1950s. The single-sided disc is brief, but manages to fully illustrate the major transitions from swing and rhythm and blues to rock and roll. The program has much to teach, but one item which we found to be especially interesting was the way in which the record companies continually attempted to promote bland mediocrity on the heels of innovation. The example used is Fabian's 'Turn Me Loose,' but it could just as easily apply to the music which opened the fifties, as it could apply to the music of the mid-seventises and mid-eighties.

The performance clips, most of which are in black-and-white, are in exceptional condition. One gets to see Buddy Holly perform 'Peggy Sue' from beginning to end, Fats Domino play with 'Ain't That A Shame,' Elvis grind out an interesting version of 'Hound Dog,' and numerous others. The program also includes the best clip we have seen yet of Jerry Lee Lewis and his 13-year-old bride, she chewing on her sunglasses while he sweats out some very pointed questions from reporters.

The sound is CX-encoded although most of the songs are monaural. The disc has 19 chapter markers, representing the numbers which come closest to being played in their entirety.

ROCK AND RULE

In Japan there are dozens of adult-themed animated features on disc but in America there are very few, which makes *Rock and Rule* more valuable than it deserves to be. The cartoon, about an evil rock and roll star in a post-apocalyptic world who schemes to raise the Devil through technology and music, gets by on some limp numbers by Debbie Harry, Cheap Trick and Iggy Pop (and one brief but decent song by Lou Reed). If there were more movies like this on disc, *Rock and Rule* could be easily dismissed. Since it is virtually the only one of its kind, intelligent animation fans should grab it and count their blessings.

The sound is a bit noisy. The picture looks a little out of focus in places. The animation is minimal and there are no color schemes or detailed drawings which really challenge the capabilities of laser playback or the imagination.

ROCK 'N ROLL MELTDOWN

A forty minute compilation of heavy metal music videos, *Rock 'n Roll Meltdown*, is available on a single sided CLV disc. The stereo sound has clarity and force. The quality of the transfer varies from one video to the next, but is never more than mildly blurry.

The collection represents some of the best heavy metal videos in the Polygram library, although a few are also available elsewhere. There is the *Blade Runner* inspired 'Rhythm of Love' from the Scorpions, an amusing piece about rock musicians having the run of a Catholic girls' boarding school, 'Prime Mover' from Zodiac Mindwarp and the Love Reaction, a traffic jam which turns explosive in 'All We Are' from Warlock, and the only offering to which one could provide the adjective 'class' without placing one's tongue in one's cheek, 'Sex Action' from the L.A. Guns. A number of concert videos are also included, for a total of nine selections.

ROCKETS (Import)

Space tech enthusiasts will be interested in the Japanese release, *Rockets*. It's a two-CAV disc package about the history of rockets from Day One until now. The drawback is that the whole thing is in Japanese, so the good historical footage is separated by a confusing and boring array of talking heads.

Ironically, nearly half the show is narrated by Neil Armstrong, a person we don't see enough of these days. We get to see enough of him here, but the Japanese voice synchronized with his lips is not his own.

The documentary has a refreshingly different perspective from the space shows we see in America. The amount of Soviet footage included on the disc is so evenly matched to the American footage that you would never guess there are differences in public domain access within the two cultures. There is also a hard look at the lives which were lost in the Apollo fire.

ROCKETSHIP X-M

The difference between a good disc and a bad disc can really come down to just the quality of the print. *Rocketship X-M* is a silly, engaging tale of interplanetary travel which only succeeds because Image has done such an admirable job with the disc.

The black-and-white print is in good shape. When the crew lands on Mars the entire film stock shifts to a red tint! (The jacket says that this is the Special Edition of the film, with special effects which were added in 1978.) The picture jiggles in a few places, but not to the point of distraction. Side two, which begins with the Mars landing, is in CAV, all the better to examine the ancient matte drawings. The CX-encoded monaural sound has some surprising moments, such as a loudspeaker, early on, which truly sounds separated from the rest of the dialog. The music is by Ferde Grofe, who also wrote the 'Grand Canyon Suite.'

Dig this. The spaceship, man's first, is supposed to go to the moon, but the wrong amount of fuel is used and it ends up at Mars instead. The CAV has two wiggling still frames out of every five. The disc label incorrectly states that side two is in CLV.

ROCKY IV

Despite all the dark scenes and dark corners (to hide the lack of extras), you cannot see a single line, ghost, or wiggle on the screen in *Rocky IV*. The sound is also in good shape and the disc is chapter encoded.

From all reports, they even love Sylvester Stallone in Russia, which may or may not be a good thing. We hope they aren't lulled into thinking all Americans are as slow-witted. After plastering his Russian/Nazi antagonist he somehow manages to pull together some thoughts in front of a microphone and even the Soviet Premier has to stifle a tear. Perhaps in 'Rocky V,' or, more appropriately, 'Rocky VI VI VI,' he'll take on the Devil himself.

THE ROD STEWART CONCERT VIDEOS

We like Rod Stewart better when he slows down a little so we can hear the words he is singing. On *The Rod Stewart Concert Video* side one contains many of his later fast/incoherent efforts and side two contains the slower/articulate pop hits from the seventies. It is an 80-minute program, so everyone is bound to see and hear something which they enjoy. In very fine print, the jacket states that the program contains material, "never before seen or heard on home video or pay TV." If they mean it, we're impressed.

RODNEY DANGERFIELD: NOTHIN' GOES RIGHT
The format of *Rodney Dangerfield: Nothin' Goes Right*, is the same as *It's Not Easy Being Me*. Both discs were filmed in Dangerfield's comedy cabaret, featuring the routines of a number of standup comedians, with Dangerfield serving as M.C. and providing filler material. *Nothin' Goes Right* lasts 83 minutes and showcases seven, generally unknown comedians. The material is usually racist or scatological, and the more racist or scatological it is, unfortunately, the funnier it is. Some of it is quite disgusting and quite funny. The picture quality is okay and the sound is acceptable. The stereo effects occasionally isolate laughter in the audience to a single channel. The disc is chapter encoded, although there is no listing on the jacket cover of the order in which the comics appear. Side two is even in CAV, but there are only two uses for it so far as we could see – speeding up the shots of Dangerfield blowing up a plastic doll, and slowing down the unusually speedy end credit roll.

ROGER AND ME
One of the things they teach you on the first day of Film Appreciation class is that there are two types of documentaries, those which record actual occurrences in a straightforward manner and those which manipulate reality in search of a greater truth. *Roger and Me* is clearly one of the latter. It opens not with a brief history of the Indian settlements and what have you that led to the establishment of the municipality of Flint, Michigan, not with a summary of the auto industry fortunes in the post-World War II heydays, and not with any attempt to put forth a hypothesis on labor and capitalism. Instead, it opens on snapshots from the childhood of the filmmaker, Michael Moore, and proceeds as egocentrically as possible to make a fun and even inspiring movie out of a sad and uninspiring subject, mass industrial layoffs.

The 'Roger' of *Roger and Me* is Roger Smith, Chairman of General Motors during most of the layoffs depicted in the film (which, in case you haven't heard, plays fast and loose with things like chronology). If Smith were Hollywood typecast, say bald and cigar crunching, or perfectly groomed and expressionless, the movie would be too didactic to be enjoyable. Smith, however, has a charismatic camera presence and a kindly demeanor, and the nasty things Moore implies about him are often set in perfect contrast to the image presented. This is documentary cinema at its best, because the image is real – Smith is a decent human being – just as the disastrous results of his executive decisions are real. As the title of the movie suggests, *Roger and Me* is about the unbridgeable gap between the forces of economics and the effects of economics, and Moore, earnestly pretending to be unable to meet Smith in the flesh, provides the ideal set of metaphors to make that gap understandable and, perhaps, to bridge it a little bit, after all.

The film was made in 16mm and blown up to 35, so it has an inherent graininess, but it is clear that Warner's picture transfer is satisfactory. The sound is cleaner than it deserves to be, although it lacks dynamic range. Warner has enthusiastically chapter encoded the disc, and while we would quibble with some of the descriptions provided, the chapter placements are perfect.

ROGER RAMJET
For those who may vaguely recall the series *Roger Ramjet* the cartoons are each about five minutes long, and Gary Owens supplied the voice for the hero, who encounters bad guys and does good deeds. The animation is almost limited to single-line-per-cel movements, but the jokes are almost ceaseless. (Ramjet announces that he retrieved a sheik's daughter, who had been kidnapped. "You mean you went to kidnap her back?" Someone asks. "No, I went to kidnap all of her.")

The condition of the cartoons is fair, though it is doubtful that under pristine circumstances they would appear very colorful or smooth. A dark smudge appears on the screen for most of side one, which will have you running to your TV with the Windex until you realize the flaw is on the disc. The sound is digital monaural and is deliberately abrasive. Each cartoon has a chapter marking. The disc runs 78 minutes and contains three half-hour collections.

ROGER WATERS RADIO KAOS
A twenty-minute compilation of four Roger Waters music videos, linked with a vague narrative, has been released on a single-sided CAV disc, *Roger Waters Radio Kaos*. The still frames tend to appear blurry, but the CAV is useful in breaking down the packed imagery of the videos. Waters' music is reminiscent of his contributions to Pink Floyd, combining an amplified beat with a soft melody line and vocal. The sound is digitally encoded stereo and the picture looks acceptable. The four songs are 'Radio Waves,' 'Sunset Strip,' 'Four Minutes,' and 'The Tide is Turning.'

ROLLERBALL
Rollerball has stereo sound and a mildly speckled picture. The colors look a bit aged, but the picture remains presentable. None of the action sequences are harmed by the cropping. The movie runs a couple minutes over two hours and the disc runs to three sides, in CLV. The stereo effects are minimal and the soundtrack, like the colors, lacks freshness.

Like all bad science fiction movies, the messages of *Rollerball* are immediately accessible, and like most bad science fiction movies, the film is entertaining anyway, because there are so few features like it which are better. The movie depicts a society, which is referred to but never adequately depicted, that is ruled by large corporations. The companies stage a nasty version of roller derby to assuage the masses, but become uptight when an athlete, played by James Caan, begins to achieve individual recognition and popularity. The movie makes a weird action picture, because outside of the three violent roller matches, it is all subdued conversation and arched eyebrows. We would not want to dissuade anyone from obtaining the disc, but we recommend that they be familiar with the work beforehand.

ROLLING IN THE SKY F/A-18 BLUE ANGELS
Rolling in the Sky F/A-18 Blue Angels, is about America's precision flying squad. The picture is flawless from beginning to end and the camera angles are such that you can make out the faces of the pilots in mid-air. The sound is in stereo surround, and when the sound effects from the jet planes pass through an audio system, it is thrilling. However, much of the disc is given over to an innocuous, dance rhythm music score, so you will never mistake the disc for living under a flight pattern. *Blue Angels* has two sides, both in CAV. Different sequences have different frame rates, but most of the still frames are perfect and a desire to manipulate the images is high, especially when the music is playing.

ROLLING IN THE SKY/SNOWBIRDS
The Canadian precision flying group, Snowbirds, is featured on the digital CAV disc, *Rolling in the Sky/Snowbirds*. The picture quality is good, but the bright red undersides of the jet planes do not have the same tone on the disc that they do on the jacket photos.

Side one features an air show, with cameras on the ground, in the air, and in the cockpit. There is a musical number at the beginning and the end, but otherwise the sounds are of the jets and whatever can be heard above their roar. Every still frame which contains movement flickers. An insert accompanying the disc lists, in English, the frame numbers for the specific maneuvers the planes perform. The disc also has 15 chapter markers.

Side two is all music – the typical quasi-jazz sounds one normally associates with import discs. The images are a mixture of the airshow footage and scenic vistas of the Canadian Rockies and tundra, captured from the cockpit. Sometimes it is right side up and sometimes it is upside down.

ROMEO AND JULIET
(see **THE TAMING OF THE SHREW**)

ROMEO & JULIET
In essence, the Soviet ballet production *Romeo & Juliet* is a silent film, played to the Sergei Prokofiev score. It looks and feels like a Soviet silent, with rhythmic editing, screen compositions that gage light and dark areas to the music, and well framed closeups. As a ballet, the film's pleasures are intermittent. Part of a dancer's appeal is generated by the dancer's stamina – the viewer's velocity of concentration becomes tied to the dancer's movement. When a ballet film is edited, and cuts away from the dancer's performance, you not only lose the connection, you lose the emotional acceleration. In *Romeo & Juliet*, it is difficult to follow the dancing in many of the scenes for a sustained period of time.

As a film, however, the disc is a stunning discovery. The movie is in color, and was made in 1954 on elaborate and impressive outdoor sets. During its previous theatrical releases in the US, the program is periodically interrupted by a silly explanation of what is happening, as if no one who would be inclined to watch the program was familiar with the story. The disc, however, omits these intrusions, and presents the ballet straight through, with a single, logical break to change sides. Thus it becomes a decent 'silent movie' presentation of the Shakespeare play, as well as a memorable record of Leonid Lavrovsky's choreography (the ballroom scene is spectacular) and of Galina Ulanova's interpretation of Juliet. The editing may fragment her performance, but it certainly can't suppress it. Ulanova has an exceptional sense of balance, and this is clearly captured and highlighted every time she is lifted in the air by her partner. Her arm movements are slightly awkward, and this, too, is magnified by the film, but one gets the sense while watching the disc that the production is a unique and priceless accomplishment.

The color transfer is also impressive. One is constantly aware that the movie is no Hollywood production – at times it looks as rickety as a silent film, too – but the picture is fresh, and only a mild softness prevents the colors from sparkling. The opening titles are mildly matted, but the film itself is not, and occasionally characters on the far edges of the screen get chopped off. The sound is monaural, and the music wobbles in a couple of places. There is also an everpresent 'whir' in the background.

ROMERO

Raul Julia's performance in *Romero*, as the Archbishop in El Salvador who was assassinated for urging that his countrymen stop killing and torturing one another, is exemplary. He conveys not the character's martyrdom, but his befuddled comprehension of the moral lawlessness encircling him. Romero, the film suggests, was chosen by the Church hierarchy as a safe leader, one who was bookish and not inclined to get involved in El Salvador's politics. What they did not anticipate, however, is that the man would apply the same passion and concentration to his new position that he once applied to reading, and when government forces begin abusing the Church's sanctuary, he reacts improperly precisely because he has no background in political relations. Julia takes risks with his performance – he shouts at the top of his lungs, or remains totally impassive in the face of despair – but he never falls into histrionics. His presence is so attractive as to make the film's political posturing readily digestible.

The picture transfer is acceptable, though the film's original image lacked gloss, and the stereo surround sound has a number of well chosen effects. The musical score draws from classical and traditional pieces, some unusually placed but oddly appropriate.

RONNIE MILSAP – GOLDEN VIDEO HITS

A collection of seven music videos, three concert performances and four conceptual exercises can be had on *Ronnie Milsap – Golden Video Hits*. The disc is analog, runs a half hour on a single side, and is in CAV.

There isn't too much to do with the CAV except to freeze a few artistic shots here and there. Milsap's music is reasonably fresh and straightforward, and the disc provides a nice selection which ends before his limitations become too apparent.

The stereo is subdued and the sound is too many times removed from its original source. So is the picture, for that matter, but the quality of laser playback still makes the program effective.

Two of the conceptual videos are worth a brief notation. 'Any Day Now,' which is also Milsap's biggest hit, has the strongest imagery, including an enchanting paper moon, and tightens the entire disc by renewing one's flagging attentions. The opening video, 'She Loves My Car,' will make car lovers cringe, as the performers drive a lovely little coupe through a corrosive ocean surf and then allow a woman in spike heels to recline on its hood. It is probably a more apt analogy to real relationships, however, than was intended.

ROOFTOPS

If this old world starts bringing you down, don't count on *Rooftops* for an escape. The Robert Wise film was widely and deservedly panned. Although it is not as bad as some low-budget portrayals of urban life created by novice directors, it is pretty silly stuff for a veteran director with an elaborate budget. The plot vaguely turns around a Brazilian martial arts dance, the Capoeira. Every once in a while there is a sequence of shots or movement which evokes better days, but most of the time there is a silly story about kids living on the roofs of abandoned buildings and battling drug dealers who are too stupid to use guns in the face of flying feet. The picture is murky and grainy. The digital stereo surround sound is active, but unremarkable.

ROOM SERVICE

We had seen one of the worst Marx Brothers movies, *Room Service,* on late night television a couple of times before and could never stay awake through to the end. We stayed awake for the disc, but at 78 minutes and without commercials, it was still a challenge. The sound was so distorted that we had to turn off our stereo system and use the TV. The print has numerous scratches and splices. The property was a non-Marx Brothers stage play which could only be partially adapted to their talents. Virtually all of the action takes place in one dingy, unstimulating hotel room. Groucho portrays a theatrical producer who is trying to connive backers for a play and avoid eviction. Lucille Ball and Ann Miller have speaking parts, but don't let that fool you.

A ROOM WITH A VIEW

The stereo on A *Room with a View* has a raw, unprocessed sound, but it provides an accurate ambience for the various locations in the film and enhances the pleasure of the disc. The sound design is by no means sloppy; the filmmakers take extra care to increase the volume during closeups and lower it for medium and long shots. The occasional internal monologues, in fact, are the loudest of all and can make one jump from one's seat.

It is a pity that *Room* is not in letterboxed format because every shot in the movie is abundant in decoration and posture. The daylight scenes are sharp, the photography is beautiful, and the story is an absolute joy. The movie is a comedy in that it is lighthearted. We did not laugh until Maggie Smith returned on side two, but once we started, we had to stop the disc to recover.

ROOSTER COGBURN

John Wayne maintained essentially the same personality through most of his films in the sixties and seventies, so something like *Rooster Cogburn*, where he has put on an eye patch and combed his hair like Tip O'Neill, is a real treat, because he is *acting*. He hams it up and it is a joy to watch him not because of any great command of craft, but because he is someone very familiar who is letting loose a little.

This movie, which also stars Katharine Hepburn, bored us to tears when we saw it at the drive-in and when we saw it on broadcast TV, but we found ourselves thoroughly captivated and entertained by the disc. If you do obtain the disc, you should spend one viewing making a conscious effort to watch whoever is not at the center of attention, because both Hepburn (who is not as awkward as Wayne, but is still clearly enjoying herself) and Wayne are performing for the camera even when it isn't pointing straight at them. And if that weren't enough, the movie has a wonderful second-rate TV ham, Anthony Zerbe, chewing up scenery with bits of business of his own as the bad guy.

The scenery itself is captivating and is also a bit overplayed. Most of the movie was shot in Oregon and has a National Forest look to it. The picture is a bit on the pink side and contains many sloppy day-for-night transfers. Laurence Rosenthal's score has trouble when the notes go off the staff in either direction, but the dialog, gunshots, and explosions are acceptable. A trailer appears at the end. It is squeezed, but still cannot completely fit on the TV screen, and it is out of focus.

ROPE

MCA missed a terrific opportunity to press side two of *Rope* in CAV. The film is only 81 minutes long and the second side runs for 28, but the whole disc is in extended play and it is too late to do anything about it.

Alfred Hitchcock's first color film was an exploration of technique utilizing the fewest number of cuts possible for a feature length movie. His unfamiliarity with the color process led to the necessity of refilming much of the movie after it was discovered that the views of twilight outside the window of the single set location did not look convincing. Thus his one intention, economy, was lost, but it is clear, particularly on multiple viewings, that the technique he employed was the only way to film the material successfully.

Rope is an unambitious play about a pair of murderers hiding their deed from guests at a dinner party. Sometimes bad plays can be made into better movies because actors who must stand still and pretend to listen on stage are simply out of view with tight camera angles. That is what happens here. Hitchcock's concept, to have the movie flow without interruption (except for a couple of key moments), prevents the tension from ever letting up. The viewer goes into the one room with the murderers and stays there, as the suspicions build and build. In subsequent viewings, when one becomes familiar with the plot and concentrates upon the atmosphere instead, the tension and the emotion of the work seem even heavier. This makes the disc ideal for ownership.

The transfer is disappointing. While viewers with the latest in television technology will probably be able to make out the details of Hitchcock's cute little neon cameo, on our TV it is little more than a round blur.

ROSANNE CASH RETROSPECTIVE

The music videos on *Rosanne Cash Retrospective* are separated by brief, friendly commentary, but Image has meticulously chapter encoded the numbers and the interludes so that it can be gotten around if one wishes to do so. A listing of the chapters appears on the back of the jacket. The stereo sound has full, rich tones and is quite nice. The collection of videos span a number of years and styles, but the picture transfer looks acceptable, with only the most intense colors causing a mild graininess.

Nine songs are featured on the 40-minute disc. Cash says that a video is not the ultimate interpretation of a song, but the better songs on the disc, including 'I Don't Know Why You Don't Want Me,' and 'It's Such a Small World,' are also the best videos. Cash's music is more mainstream than country-western and her sense of melody is usually better than her lyrics.

THE ROSARY MURDERS

You have to suspend your normal critical facilities to truly appreciate *The Rosary Murders* – accept it on faith so to speak – but you don't have to wait for the disc to be over to reap the rewards. There are several exciting murders, some good puzzles, devious performances by Donald Sutherland and Charles Durning, and engaging moral quandaries. There is even an error – a character who has committed suicide is buried in a Catholic cemetery – and some overly elaborate scheming on the part of the killer, but if you enjoy reading or watching mysteries, you will enjoy this.

The disc is in digitally encoded stereo, but the mix on the film is not interesting. The print is also a little dreary looking.

ROSE MARIE

Jeanette MacDonald and Nelson Eddy star in *Rose Marie*. This is the one where they are Mounties, wandering around in the Rocky Mountains of Quebec. The print looks clean. At minute 39 on side two there's a dropout on the left track. MacDonald plays a famous singer searching for her brother, an escaped convict. Eddy is a Mounted Policeman, out to get his man. Naturally, they end up in a canoe warbling 'Indian Love Call' to one another.

ROSSINI IL BARBIERE DI SIVIGLIA

A chance to enjoy a true double bill in the epic life of Figaro, the impish barber-cum-servant, is now possible because Deutsche Grammophon has released *Rossini Il Barbiere Di Siviglia* with Hermann Prey in the title role. Prey filled the same shoes in the Deutsche Grammophon release, *Mozart Le Nozze Di Figaro*. Both films were directed by Jean-Pierre Ponnelle, and both use the same soundstage sets (dressed differently).

Barbiere is less captivating than *Nozze* because Prey's supporting cast, including Teresa Berganza and Luigi Alva, is weaker, but the program, all 2 1/2 hours of it, would be an excellent warmup for the second feature. Rossini's music is invigorating, and Ponnelle's direction increases one's awareness of the music's structure. As in *Nozze*, Ponnelle never forgets that his first purpose is to entertain, though the editing and camera placement is less self-assured in *Barbiere*.

The picture is grainy and a little faded. The stereo sound is clean and is in good synchronization with the image. The disc runs to three sides. An insert is provided in the box jacket which contains a chapter listing plot synopsis, and a questionable essay that tries too hard to link *Barbiere* with the rise of the Industrial Age. We would also take issue with a common fallacy which is repeated in the essay, the suggestion that Figaro's advice does the Count no good whatsoever in the latter's attempt to gain access to the Doctor's house. This is not true, for the Count could not, later, have conceived his successful guise of the music teacher had he not assessed the situation during his first visit in the Figaro-inspired guise of a drunken soldier. In real life, success often appears in innocuous increments which can only be accurately valued when the whole endeavor is completed.

ROSSINI – STRAUSS – SMETANA – LISZT

Two distinct programs are contained on *Rossini – Strauss – Smetana – Liszt*, which is identified on the jacket cover, but not the spine, as 'Solti in Concert.' On side one, George Solti conducts the Chicago Symphony Orchestra in six Gioacchino Rossini overtures (but not 'William Tell'). On side two, Solti conducts the Bavarian Radio Symphony Orchestra in a program of three pieces, 'Don Juan' by Richard Strauss, 'Vetava' ('The Moldau') by Bedrich Smetana, and 'Les Preludes' by Franz Liszt. Although the Rossini overtures are a lot of fun, the technical qualities of the Bavarian effort are superior to those of the Chicago program. Both concerts are performed in front of a live audience. The Bavarian Orchestra gives a sharper interpretation of the pieces, has been recorded more clearly, and is better photographed. Side two also has a clearer transfer. A jacket insert contains an interesting essay explaining how Rossini came to write each overture, and how the other composers put together their representative works.

ROUND MIDNIGHT

Among other things, the tenor saxophone seems particularly will positioned for digitally encoded playback. Unlike musical instruments which explore the edges of the spectrum, the tenor sax fills the middle, totally and brilliantly.

Few movies and few discs have as accomplished soundtracks as *Round Midnight* does. To begin with, there are the twenty or so jazz numbers, which sound better than live or studio recordings because, in the interests of drama, the volume levels shift depending upon how close the camera is to the musicians. As the angle of view increases, the volume fades, and, if only briefly, your mind believes you are in the tavern with them. The quality in the sound carries over to the dialog and the sound effects. If the engineers have worked so hard on the music, they are not going to spoil things by giving footsteps the wrong echo.

The picture quality is slightly blurry, even in the daylight scenes, but the visuals which really matter, the closeups of the musicians handling their instruments, are fine.

Dexter Gordon portrays a saxophonist living in Paris whose lifestyle is bettered when he is befriended by an impish admirer. It doesn't last, but nothing except the music ever does, or so the movie wishes to say.

ROXANNE

Steve Martin's adaptation of 'Cyrano de Bergerac,' *Roxanne*, is wonderful. When classic stories are modified for contemporary settings, the result is often more clever than it is engaging. That is not the case with *Roxanne*, as Martin knows exactly when he ought to digress and when he should not. Like its source, the movie is a romance, and if the entertainment is extended by the nose, so much the better. The stereo effects in the big scenes are pleasing. The picture looks new and only slightly ripe. Cropping and scanning harms the pretty scenery, but does not affect the story or the makeup.

ROXY MUSIC – THE HIGH ROAD

Roxy Music – The High Road has a bad picture and weak sound. The visuals are grainy, and the camera angles tend to break the group into parts. The music is interesting enough, with scattered rock beats, an off-key lead vocal, and some jazz accompaniment. The audience responds well, so they can obviously hear it better than we can. Some fireworks go off near the end. Before that, we didn't even realize the concert was out-of-doors.

ROY ORBISON AND FRIENDS

The hour long *Roy Orbison and Friends* was recorded in a very stylish black and white which looks terrific on disc. The sound is stereo and the disc has 15 chapter markers which are listed on the back of the jacket.

Bruce Springsteen, Elvis Costello, Jackson Browne and others appear with Orbison on the stage, and look like they are having a great time performing as his back up band. Bonnie Raitt is even there, doing background vocals. They all apparently rehearsed, at least a little bit, though ultimately the songs are not as sharp as Orbison's original singles.

THE ROYAL BALLET – THE NUTCRACKER – TCHAIKOVSKY

Ever since Tiny Tim died, Britain has known how to celebrate Christmas. *Royal Ballet – The Nutcracker – Tchaikovsky*, with choreography by Lev Ivanob and Peter Wright, is traditional to the max, and far more satisfying than the American Ballet Theatre interpretation. The principal dancers, Lesley Collier, Anthony Dowell, Julie Rose, and Guy Niblett, are adequate to their roles and, except for the mouse battle, the camera usually captures the essence of the choreography.

The picture quality is very good and the digitally encoded sound has less hiss than the analog track. Pioneer has provided an insert with the cast listing to compensate for the lack of a double jacket. Our only complaint about the disc is that the chapter encoding is totally inadequate. It has been coordinated to scenes instead of to dances and the stocking's worth of interludes involving Sugar Plum faeries, dancing flowers, etc., are lumped together with a single, useless marker.

THE ROYAL BALLET – SWAN LAKE
MIKHAIL BARYSHNIKOV'S DON QUIXOTE
THE NUTCRACKER SUITE
LA FILLE MAL GARDEE
MANON
THE KIROV BALLET – SLEEPING BEAUTY
SERAPHIC DIALOG (DiscoVision)
CORTEGE OF EAGLES (DiscoVision)
ACROBATS OF GOD (DiscoVision)
BALLET ESPANOL – CARMEN DE YASUKO NAGAMINE (Import)

Ballet has never made as close a relationship with the camera as the other performing arts have. When a choreographer designs a dance he is creating a symphony of movement. The tendency of the camera to isolate dancers upsets this vision.

Swan Lake is probably the best ballet ever conceived. It has one of Tchaikovsky's most carefully constructed scores. The story contributes to the drama and merges emotionally with the dancing and the music, a situation which is rare indeed. The pinnacle moment in *Swan Lake* comes at the end of Act II. The swan, transformed through enchantment into a lovely ballerina, dances in the woods with a dashing, earnest young prince and the two fall hopelessly in love. Suddenly, an evil sorcerer appears. He waves his arms and the ballerina/swan, while straining to break free, is pulled backwards. Where is the camera pointing while the ballerina (Natalia Makarova) is performing this incredible lean one way/move the other step? Why at the Prince's face, of course. May the editor of this production someday find his own neck stretched out upon his splicer....

Nonetheless, *Swan Lake* is a beautiful disc. The orchestra, recorded live, has a fresh and spirited sound. Makarova and Anthony Dowell (as the Prince) make an attractive couple. For the most part the camera is drawn back, taking in the whole stage as it should.

Mikhail Baryshnikov dances with such restrained precision that it comes as an extra shock when he suddenly leaps higher and farther than anyone would think possible. What a shame side two of the 90-minute *Mikhail Baryshnikov's Don Quixote* is not in CAV. Baryshnikov's finale throws the audience into a frenzy.

Composer Ludwig Minkus is not exactly a household name and the music for *Don Quixote*, while adequately Spanish-sounding and functional, is not memorable. Quixote is only an incidental character in the ballet, which has the subheading of 'Kiri's Wedding.' Baryshnikov portrays a dashing young playboy who likes to dance and strum the guitar. The camera does its share of intruding, but never spoils the big moments. As with *Swan Lake*, the sound is very clear.

The lack of a live recording is the first troublesome problem one notices in Mikhail Baryshnikov's version of *The Nutcracker Suite*. The orchestra comes over the sound system, but you can't hear anything associated with the dancers themselves. It is as if you are watching them through a large window and the music you are hearing just happens to coincide with their movements. The sound is CX-encoded and the picture is acceptable, but we recommend you keep this disc away from your tree.

British choreography is about as appetizing as British cuisine and Frederick Ashton and Kenneth MacMillan are sort of the meat and kidney pies of British dance. *La Fille Mal Gardee* is widely known because it was the first real ballet to become available on disc in the US and a lot of people, desperate for anything, bought it. The ballet, though mediocre, has a few nice moments in it, particularly a dance with ribbons in the first act. The sound and picture are both nice.

Kenneth MacMillan's *Manon*, on the other hand, is an embarrassment. The dancers spend so much time running back and forth in an attempt to act out the story of 'Manon Lescaut' that there is precious little space left for more than a few pas de deux. The sound and picture quality is similar to *Gardee*. Fortunately, Russian ballet has more going for it than Russian cuisine. *The Kirov Ballet – Sleeping Beauty* is good, particularly the last two acts. It is 164 minutes long – though some of that is applause – and is spread to four sides. Precise, conservative dancing makes the disc appealing in parts, but taking in the whole performance in one sitting is a little exhausting.

On the old and defunct DiscoVision label, three Martha Graham discs comprised what was actually a single television show, '3 by Martha Graham.' Here, the dances were blocked, in part, to suit the camera. Narrated by John Houseman, each of the discs has poorly-recorded sound and a picture quality greatly inferior to what was standard even then. The color has a copper green tint on all three CAV discs and any subtleties which might once have existed in the contrasts or shadings are no longer discernible.

Seraphic Dialog is the rarest, but the least satisfactory, of the three discs. A brief enactment of the life of Joan of Arc, the dancers interact with one another very little and we are left with a series of confusing solos. *Cortege of Eagles*, a complicated retelling of the politics in ancient Troy, is more interesting. Graham, who is not exactly young, has a central role, and thus the disc is a valuable preservation of her technique. The music, by Eugine Leste, is more developed than Norman Joio's score in *Seraphic Dialog*. Cortege is also the only one of the three discs to fill more than one side. The best of the three is a circus-like comical piece called *Acrobats of God*. A spoof on the importance placed upon athletics in dance, the dancers perform very unusual stunts in a sprightly and distracted manner as Graham (appearing again) moves them about with a bull whip. Carlos Surinach's score is suitably playful.

Finally, there is the Japanese release, *Ballet Espanol – Carmen de Yasuko Nagamine*, an excellent candidate for Dan Ackroyd's old 'Bad Ballet' shtick. The live production is so pathetic that ballet fans may actually be interested in picking it up – you can't watch the thing without breaking into the giggles. The disc is CX-encoded and the picture is fair. The poor woman who plays Carmen gets so tired by the second act that she is given high heels so she doesn't have to go through the pretense of trying to stay on her toes. In the end, the parallels between Carmen and the bull in the ring take on an unfortunate appropriateness. Like a bird which cannot fly, this project should have never, never left the ground.

THE ROYAL DUTCH BALLET – NAPOLI

The Royal Dutch Ballet is one of the better international ballet troupes, but caution should prevail on purchasing *The Royal Dutch Ballet – Napoli. Napoli* is a narrative ballet, using music from five different composers and choreography from a nineteenth century master, August Bournonville. It has very little dancing in it, until the last twenty minutes, and even that segment is subdued. It is primarily prancing and mime, to music, and as talented as the performers are, contemporary viewers are apt to feel restless.

The three-sided CLV disc is separated on an act-per-side basis, although the entire program is only 98 minutes long. The live performance was apparently recorded in 1986, but the picture already has a slight video ripeness to it. It lacks the perfection of other dance titles, but is certainly in passable condition. While the camera moves back for the dances in the finale, it spends much of the time in close when the narrative is going, destroying whatever choreography there is by isolating performers.

The digital track comes across as a little more lively than the analog track. The disc is also encoded with chapter markers.

RUDE AWAKENING

The comedy *Rude Awakening* has one central flaw – it is not funny – but other than that, the concept is witty and the plot has a touch of insight and intelligence.

Two sixties hippies, played by Cheech Marin and Eric Roberts, are isolated for a couple of decades and return to New York in the eighties, aghast at what they find. Although the idea is great, none of the gags work as well as one would hope. If the film does entertain viewers, it is on the strength of the performances alone, particularly Julie Haggerty, who gets to exercise a wide range of attitudes and emotions as the girl they left behind. The disc has a fuzzy picture but an active stereo surround track.

THE RULES OF THE GAME

Somehow you should see Jean Renoir's *The Rules of the Game* if you have never seen it before, because it is one of the few films which, by its existence, enriches all other movies. Whether you want the Voyager Criterion Collection edition, the only way to obtain the movie on disc, may be another matter. As with the Criterion Collection version of Renoir's *Grand Illusion*, the best available source material is not in the greatest condition and the disc has no single frame programming material to justify its CAV formatting. More so than *Grand Illusion, Rules of the Game* is worth studying on a frame-by-frame basis, but few disc consumers may feel the format, coupled with the condition of the print, justifies the expense.

The movie, which withstands endless repeated viewings, has the structure of a classic farce, but is set in France in the late thirties. Its messages about the French ruling class on the eve of war may be of interest only to historians, but the complex weaving of love affairs among the gentry and their servants has a far reaching appeal which transcends both time and locale. It is a sober comedy, with slapstick applied like a rare perfume, yet the viewer will likely find the humor of the characters and the irony of their plights to be intoxicating.

Undoubtedly Voyager has done an excellent job transferring the film to disc. The print is certainly watchable, and the white English subtitles make hearing it no problem. The disc is confidently chapter encoded, and after the movie there is a brief, informative conversation between Renoir and one of the actors from the film, Marcel Dalio. The disc has four sides and comes in a gatefold jacket.

A formulaic lecture which was written by Alexander Sesonske and is read without emotion by Peter Bogdanovich can be found on one of the disc's analog audio tracks. It will enhance one's understanding of the film, though *The Rules of the Game* may be best appreciated without others telling one how to interpret it, at least until a strong familiarity is established. One advantage to the lecture is the elaboration it provides for significant portions of the dialog which were obscured by the simplistic subtitle translations. A separate and more worthwhile portion of the lecture, dealing specifically with the history of the film's production, subsequent destruction, and restoration, can be found on the second audio track after the film is ended.

THE RULING CLASS

The presentation of *The Ruling Class* is in less than pristine shape. The colors are faded, the picture is soft, and splices even cause the image to slip at one point. The movie is about an insane English lord and the jockeying going on within his family to have him committed. The film has a cult following owing to a few choice pieces of dialog and an exhausting performance by Peter O'Toole. It is spiced with several memorable and well-timed scenes (which are less effective on multiple viewings), but, owing to its stage source material, it also contains a number of wild exaggerations. It has too much undergraduate humor and drama to hold the patience of the average viewer (first the hero thinks he's Jesus, later on he thinks he's Jack the Ripper), particularly when hindered by the disc's transfer. The material may have political and social symbolisms, but the literal level is too unpleasant to invite deeper analysis. The monaural sound lacks clarity, but the film's sound editing, like everything else in the production, is sporadically inspired.

RUMPELSTILTSKIN
(see **FAERIE TALE THEATRE**)

RUNAWAY TRAIN

'That which does not kill you with boredom makes you sleep stronger,' to paraphrase Jon Voight's paraphrasing of Nietszche at the opening of *Runaway Train*. The picture is all right, although the original film was severely grainy in places, as if the editor had been required to scrape together and blow up long shot outtakes for closeup reaction shots. The sound is in digital and the train is constantly rattling through your viewing area as if it were actually going somewhere. It is the story which doesn't go anywhere except downhill.

THE RUNNING MAN

We were amused by the jacket copy on the back of the *The Running Man*: "The year is 2019. Television is now ruling people's lives." Do they mean that it doesn't at the moment? Suitably enslaved, we put the disc on and found it to be the typical Arnold Schwarzenegger property that we have come to know and love. Brisk, well scripted, mildly humorous, and reasonably exciting.

The picture is grainy and not as slick as it ought to look. The sound has a little more going for it, particularly a rollercoaster bullet ride which sounds as if it is taking your entire viewing room along for the fun. The filmmakers know a good thing when they hear it, and so they send Richard Dawson (who gives a terrific, self-kidding performance; the kind to excuse all his other sins) down the same tube at the end. The thrill is enough to get you past Arnold kissing the heroine and walking into a fluorescent sunset with her.

RUNNING ON EMPTY

Although the plot uses the radical underground concept to set the stage, *Running on Empty* is actually about a boy, played by River Phoenix, who must cope with the unusual, transient lifestyle his fugitive parents have adopted.

The picture is mildly grainy, but passable. The audio, which is CX-encoded analog monaural, has phase distortions, most noticeable on side one during a scene in a girl's bedroom, creating an occasional electronic twang.

The movie strains credibility, but never ceases to be thoroughly involving. It asks viewers to believe that a pair of socially maladjusted criminals would be in every other way the model of harmonious domesticity, but uses that premise to create an intriguing dilemma for the boy. The script writers even had the audacity to stir rich grandparents into the plot convolutions. Everything in *Running on Empty* is false, but it is the sort of falsity which makes people fall in love with the movies and helps them run away, at least for a while, from the problems that are dogging them.

RUNNING SCARED

Peter Hyams is often guilty of sacrificing the internal logic in his films for the sake of a few thrills, but there are worse crimes a director could commit. The big moments in *Running Scared*, such as the car chase on the 'El,' pay for the better moments, such as the repartee between Billy Crystal and Gregory Hines. The disc has a slightly blurry picture, but the story is so involving that you have to concentrate to notice the photography at all, let alone the transfer. Because of the cropping, however, you often lose either one or the other's reaction expression. The voices are a bit too piercing when the volume is pushed. *Running Scared* falls into the popular sub-genre of 'comedians cast as detectives,' where the wisecracks, no matter how smoothly they are told, come not from the situation within the plot but from the opportunity to score a laugh.

RUSH – A SHOW OF HANDS

A projection screen behind the group in *Rush – A Show of Hands* displays a number of animated images which are often intercut on the video program, encouraging one to keep one's eyes on the screen. The group's music is a generic rock and they need all the help they can get. Although the strongest colors blur, the band members are well lit, and the cameras capture their performance as seen from the audience as well as from the stage. The 90-minute program has about 15 numbers which are listed in order on the back of the jacket although the encoded chapter markers start at zero again on side two. The sound is adequate for the concert recording.

RUSH – GRACE UNDER PRESSURE TOUR

When the music video, 'The Big Money,' appears at the end of *Rush – Grace Under Pressure Tour*, the stereo mix demonstrates how cacophonous the rest of the program, a live concert in Toronto, is. The concert is not lit for film and the picture is at the mercy of the spotlights. The sound on the live performance is not distinctive, and so Rush, a synthesizer and guitar group which quotes Franklin D. Roosevelt in one of their songs, is not presented in a flattering manner, until the end video. The disc is 70 minutes long.

RUSH – THROUGH THE CAMERA EYE

A set of pleasant music videos has been collected on *Rush – Through the Camera Eye*, a 40-minute digital CLV disc. The rock group, Rush, makes the mistake in one of the videos of including an oscilloscope readout of their music. The fearful symmetry of the group's sound is proof that their compositions lack imagination, but they apparently have had substantial success with their risk-free rock.

The videos vary in subject efficiently and the program never seems to repeat itself. The picture has more than the usual trouble with red lights but is otherwise acceptable.

RUSSKIES

We're too old for *Russkies*. Only those who spend their money on comic books rather than laser discs will fully appreciate the movie's charms. The story is about a Russian sailor separated from his companions during an espionage mission at Key West, and befriended by a trio of youngsters who assume the worst. You have to completely suspend disbelief, forget about Alan Arkin and the other movie, and let the film dictate its rules as well as its rewards. All of that is a lot easier if adult sensibilities don't get in the way.

The picture is grainy and has, excuse us, a red shift. The music and a smattering of sound effects are stereophonic and well served by the digital encoding, lending an illusion of sophistication to the proceedings.

THE RUSSIANS ARE COMING, THE RUSSIANS ARE COMING

The Russians Are Coming, The Russians Are Coming is about a Russian submarine which has run ashore on a small island off New England and the panic this instills in the island's citizenry. Alan Arkin, Carl Reiner, Paul Ford, and other members of the large cast interact in an ensemble fashion which rarely works when more than a few comics are competing for screen time. Arkin seems particularly under-appreciated today for his resourcefulness and the range of his abilities. Fifty percent of his dialog here is in Russian.

The color and sound are adequate, but the print has scratches, dots, and vertical lines which are preserved by the transfer. The scanning manages to capture most of the peripheral gags.

RUST NEVER SLEEPS
One of the poorer single-group rock films, *Rust Never Sleeps*, is a tedious record of a 111-minute Neil Young concert. The concert is so ill-lit that it is a wonder the audience at San Francisco's Cow Palace can see what is going on. For the camera and the disc image, most of the stage is a hazy blur, and we wouldn't be surprised if footage turned up in the next *Nova* UFO expose. The show has not been edited, and an immense amount of time is spent adjusting amplifiers and moving equipment, in the dark, between numbers. The sound is equally bad. Young is out of key and his instruments shriek when they should twang. The prolific Young has done good work in the recording studio, but there is something about a live audience which brings out the worst in him. Old timers will note with interest that the chapter encoded disc opens with a logo for RCA's Selectavision System. If all their source material was like this it is no wonder they went belly up.

RUSTLER'S RHAPSODY
The gunfire in *Rustler's Rhapsody* sounds like a jet plane. Unfortunately, the movie has little else going for it. It is not a musical although it has been billed as such, contains a running commentary about the rules of the genre. The show is a combination of film criticism and slapstick. To be effective, the filmmakers should think of absolutely everything and hit you from every angle without letting up. It doesn't happen.

While a lot of attention is paid to costumes, landscapes and other visual clichés pass unnoticed. The hero does ride off into the sunset at the end, but nothing is made of it.

RUTHLESS PEOPLE
The bright, mod-colored credit sequence which opens *Ruthless People* looks better than most discs. The sound has a loud rock score and some cute left/right separations as well. The plot, about a woman who is kidnapped and whose husband hasn't the slightest intention of paying the ransom, has been done several times in the past, but rarely has the story been so well thought out and the humor so easily generated.

SABOTAGE
(see **YOUNG AND INNOCENT**)

SABOTEUR
Alfred Hitchcock's *Saboteur* begins with a fire in an airplane factory in California and ends on the torch of the Statue of Liberty. Images of fire may haunt the protagonist from beginning to end (even the saboteur's name is "Frye"), but Hitchcock's real message is about the Masonic goodwill which America offers to strangers. The hero takes on the name of "Mason" at one point and mentions that he once "played the triangle" in his high school band. The base of the Statue of Liberty is also Masonic in design. Using a plot with a few too many coincidences manipulating the suspense, Hitchcock provides a perverse milieu of Americana to help the wrongly-accused hero, but the sincerity of the samaritans is never mocked. Even on multiple viewings, you can see nothing undercutting them, whereas the villains – whether it is the spy talking about how he wants his son to grow long, blond hair, or the midget who looks and acts like Hitler – are dryly buffooned throughout.

The print is very sharp looking and virtually flawless. There are some beautiful color stills on the back of the jacket (the film is in black-and-white) and a rarely-seen theatrical trailer at the end of the disc.

Robert Cummings stars, and his presence is often belittled by those who dislike the film. Don't listen. Try picturing Cary Grant giving an impassioned speech about the meaning of America and liberty. Cummings is perfect. Hitchcock only used Grant when he wanted to play around.

SABRINA
Sabrina is a romance, directed with some underhandedness by Billy Wilder. By the same *joie de vivre* with which the characters overcome their differences to be together at the end, however, so too can a viewer overcome the cynicism and odd casting to fall head over heels with the film.

Audrey Hepburn portrays the daughter of a chauffeur who distracts the younger son of her father's employers on the eve of the son's business-inspired marriage. The son's elder brother steps in to romance the chauffeur's daughter and save the deal. Sounds harmless, but the brothers are played by William Holden and Humphrey Bogart, hardly one's idea of siblings or romantic rivals. Bogart looks both short and sickly, especially in his scenes with Hepburn, who is lanky and radiant. Some critics even go so far as to say that Bogart is wrong for the part, but we don't think so. If the film is taken at face value, it depicts the sort of odd but genuine pairings which occur in real life. Bogart often relied upon his having been cast well to give a good performance, but Wilder manipulates him perfectly, getting comedy out of him and a few tugs of the heart as well.

But it is Hepburn's film and she is glorious, passing convincingly from adolescence to adulthood, taking innocuous lines and absorbing them into her character, and melting a viewer's heart every time she opens or closes her mouth. A typical example of Hepburn's exceptional abilities can be heard when she says to Bogart, "I know why you didn't tell me. Because you think it's wrong. They'll say I'm too young for you. There'll be an awful scandal and the market will go down." She pronounces the word 'scandal' with authority and the word 'market' with deferential fascination. How could anyone not fall in love with that kind of subliminally acquiescent seduction?

The black-and-white picture is mildly grainy and the grey levels are indistinctive. Shadows tend to run together. The monaural soundtrack has been digitally encoded, but the music sounds wobbly in key places. The side break denotes the film's dramatic turning point.

THE SACRIFICE
Image has given an exceptional transfer to *The Sacrifice*, a properly ambiguous and nurtured tale directed by Andrei Tarkovsky and photographed by Sven Nykvist. The disc runs 145 minutes and is in Swedish with bright white English subtitles which are highlighted, when necessary, to remain totally legible throughout the film. The picture is slightly letterboxed with an aspect ratio of about 1.66:1 (the subtitles appear partially on the picture and partially on the black band beneath it). The sound is satisfying. The three-sided disc also has chapter markers, and Image's one error is in the break between side one and side two, which comes at a too logical moment and disrupts the rhythm of the drama. A break five minutes later would have been more appropriate.

Nykvist's cinematography is a consummate and definitive accomplishment which ought to have received every award handed out. As the mood of the movie changes, so does the look of the film. It scales from color to black and white and from light to dark, and Image keeps up with it every step of the way. The brightest scenes look vivid and the darkest scenes escape distortion. The picture remains sharply focussed and free from any impurities. The transfer is an appropriate and deserving effort.

It is advisable that the viewer consume a decent quantity of caffeine before tackling the film. Opening with a single, compelling, ten minute camera shot, Tarkovsky advances the enigmatic narrative slowly. Without spoiling the plot, it can be noted that the story takes place in a remote, multiple level beach house on the Baltic coast. Two couples, a local postman, servants, and a child are visiting the house when a global disaster takes place. The characters are then given a reprieve, for a price. Conversation is sparse and deliberately cryptic, as are the relationships and even the existence of a few of the characters. The film is pointedly vague, but by the end Tarkovsky balances every cipher and overly intellectual interlude, making the final shot as satisfying as the first. Other movies are designed to make a viewer think or feel, but *The Sacrifice* is constructed to squeeze emotion out of contemplation – the more one thinks about the film, the more one feels about life.

SADE – DIAMOND LIFE VIDEOS
The one-sided 8-inch, *Sade – Diamond Life Videos*, contains four music videos. On the back of the jacket, there is a note saying that the sound was digitally mastered, but no one bothered to follow through and digitally encode the disc. The analog sound is good, but you can hear enough noise to know how much better it would have been. The picture looks a little grainy.
The four video clips are interspersed with an interview in which Sade explains that we are all still mispronouncing her name (there isn't really an 'r' sound between the 'a' and the 'd,' it is more of a 'half r'), and gives some profound insights into her lifestyle. "Everything I do completely dominates my life," she says, leading one to suppose that everything she doesn't do does not dominate it.

The biggest hit on the disc is 'Smooth Operator,' but the best music video is a number about playing cards called 'Your Love is King.'

SAGEBRUSH TRAIL & RANDY RIDES ALONE (see **MAN FROM UTAH & BLUE STEEL**)

SAHARA
One of our favorite late night or weekend afternoon relax-and-escape features is *Sahara*, with Humphrey Bogart. This is the one where Bogart portrays a tank commander

who, with about a dozen fellow soldiers, holds out in the only oasis for miles and keeps a whole battalion of thirsty Nazis at bay. Without ever seeing the film before you could probably recite the dialog, but the story moves quickly, the cinematography is good, and Bogart is Bogart. We couldn't ask for more from a film.

But we could ask for more from a disc. We have no idea if there exists a better print for the black-and-white feature or not, but the one which has been used for this release is spliced, speckled, and looks like it spent some time in a dusty tank itself. The monaural sound has not been CX-encoded and crackles even when it is run through a TV speaker.

SAIGON COMMANDOS

The premise for *Saigon Commandos*, about Army MPs in Saigon, would make an interesting television series. They solve crimes and generally seem to have the run of the place. The movie, unfortunately, needed a lot of work that it did not get. There is a voice-over narrative which would make Michael Herr bury his face in his hands, and one can find more emotion in plastic GI Joe action figures than in the members of the cast. An Asian rock band opens with a sultry rendition of 'House of the Rising Sun,' and nothing but ruin follows. The picture quality on the disc is also tarnished whenever the heroes enter the red light district, which is often enough. The whole picture washes out, but even in the bright daylight, the film looks cheap. The sound levels vary depending upon how far away an actor is standing from a mike, and even digital encoding cannot rescue the half-hearted monaural soundtrack. Side two of the disc is only 28 minutes long, but it is in CLV.

SALAAM BOMBAY!

A young boy's life on the streets is the subject of *Salaam Bombay!*, a movie which follows a tradition of films that depict children trapped by poverty. Like all such films, it was made on a low budget but appears seamless in its exposure of the city's dark side. Like all such films, it ends bleakly, but communicates the strength of the human spirit through the small victories that the protagonist does achieve as he matures. And like all such films, it is difficult to dislike, since the locale is both simple and exotic, and the narrative consistently avoids the easiest manipulations.

The picture has a mild matting which provides an aspect ratio of about 1.66:1. The movie is in Hindi with English subtitles which appear on the picture. The image is consistently grainy, but the colors look fresh and the movie wouldn't be as effective if it gleamed with a Hollywood shine. The sound is on par with the picture.

SALAMANDRE CHATEAUX OF THE LOIRE

Lovers of architecture, art, and history can all gather around the interactive video disc from Voyager, *Salamandre Chateaux of the Loire*. The disc provides a day trip tour of 18 Royal chateaux strung along the River Loire in central France. It is 30 minutes long and is in CAV on a single side.

The picture on the disc is meticulously clear. The images are brightly colored and highly detailed. An aerial view of each chateau opens the disc, accompanied by a quiet baroque score which soothes and focuses one's concentration. The three segments which follow provide lectures on the interiors of selected chateaux, the construction history of every chateaux (illustrated with computer graphics), and the crests and emblems associated with the houses. The lectures are in English on one audio track and French on the other. The sound is not CX-encoded. The last section is a still frame combination of text and photos which gives a generalized history of the region and then a specific history/analysis of each chateau.

Many of the chateaux contain collections of paintings and other works of art, and these are adequately displayed on the disc. The history of the French nobility is also given a thorough run-though, and we, at least, began to get a handle on it for the first time. The disc's real strength, however, is in the exposition of architecture. One chateau, an abbey for women called 'Fontevraud,' is a stunning piece of design. It is a fully integrated grouping of towers and hallways, budding out from an interior courtyard, and yet, from every side, the design looks entirely different – in some places square, or round, or triangular. The spare lines on the hallways, both interior and exterior, provide a strong perspective and act as a controlling link between functionality and decoration. The building is one of those rare architectural masterpieces in which clutter is stimulating without seeming busy. You could be cloistered there for a decade without feeling confined or bored.

The chateaux are a tableaux of architectural style, in fact, since every Dauphin or Royal Mistress felt the need to remodel. This is where the clever computer animation segment becomes quite useful, since it shows sequentially the additions and the demolitions at every site. If you go back to the areal tour at the beginning of the disc after studying the other sections a bit, Catherine Medici's homesickness for Italy suddenly becomes glaringly clear.

SALOME'S LAST DANCE
RICHARD STRAUSS – SALOME – KARL BOHM

One daren't blink while watching Ken Russell's *Salome's Last Dance* for fear of missing something. The film is a clever concoction in which Russell finds the perfect excuse for doing his worst. By setting a fully recreated performance of Oscar Wilde's play within a house of ill-repute before the turn of the century, and taking some minor liberties with the dimensions of the stage, Russell can be as weird or disgusting as he wishes, without alienating a viewer's sensibilities. Unlike the awful dialog in some of his other films, the verbal component is mostly Oscar Wilde's poetry and prose. No matter how degenerated everything looks, the soul of the film will always be young.

Strong reds and scenes lit in red tend to go fuzzy, but otherwise the picture looks decent. The sound has some interesting bass effects and is generally enjoyable. The disc has some chapter markers, but more of them wouldn't have hurt.

Only slightly less decadent is *Richard Strauss – Salome – Karl Bohm*, a soundstage recording of the Strauss opera (in German with English subtitles) which was also based on Wilde's text. Teresa Stratas is fully captivating in the difficult title role. Hans Beirer, Astrid Varnay and Bernd Weikl also star.

Gotz Friedrich directed the film, and Karl Bohm conducted the music. The stage is larger than the space Russell had to work in, and while one can't expect the same delirious intensity from the opera, the format allows for tight closeups and liberal crosscutting at crucial moments. The sound is a little fuzzy during some of the vocals and the picture is consistently grainy. An insert accompanies the disc which contains a great deal of informative material about the opera and the production depicted.

THE SALT OF THE EARTH

Visually, *The Salt of the Earth* is an impressive film, and the first three quarters of an hour would probably work better if all the dialog and narration were replaced with a few well chosen title cards. The drama is redeemed on side two, as the nitty-gritty strategies by both parties in a mine worker strike really start to unfold. The movie was made by blacklisted filmmakers at the height of the post-war Red scare.

The original production budget was limited, to say the least, and so the print inevitably has a few scratches on it. The monaural sound, which is also of varying quality, has not been CX-encoded. Like someone who has worked in the mines all his life, the movie appears older than it is, but that does not diminish its strength.

Many of the actors were amateurs, real miners from New Mexico, where the film takes place. Their line readings continually bring the pace of the film to a halt, but the photography always gives the viewer stimulating input, and the whole cast perks up when they stop their contrived suffering and begin to relive the actual year and a half they spent on strike. The politics are elaborate, as the wives of the miners win gains not only from the mining company, but from their husbands. The story has also a happy ending, which helps immeasurably in movies like this.

In addition to the feature film, there is a short on side two which was made by the 'Hollywood Ten,' (several of whom contributed to *Salt*) right before they were sent to prison. The short, 'The Hollywood Ten,' explains the unfair circumstances under which they were incarcerated. However, including it on the disc inadvertently presents an awkward juxtaposition – the eternal contrast between those who are sympathetic to a movement and those who need the movement to survive. Each 'Ten' victim is shown with his family and children and you ascertain immediately that, unlike the families in *Salt*, they are not wanting for hot water.

SALVADOR

A grainy picture and rough, monaural sound (not CX-encoded) seems to be how *Salvador ought* to be presented. The disc may not look slick or sound all that pure, but the movie is about the grime of reality and the condition of the disc becomes part of the theme.

James Woods portrays a second-rate photographer covering El Salvador during the end of the Carter Administration. The film only becomes preachy in one extended and tedious scene where Woods lectures CIA representatives. The director, Oliver Stone, does find it incredible that the more severely-positioned spokespeople actually believe the things they are saying, but he resists the temptation to posture them as hypocrites. Jim Belushi also has a major part which was created to give the film comic relief.

Between the revolutionary folksongs and rock and roll hits on the music soundtrack, there is a very exciting score by Georges Delerue. One is so used to hearing his work in cheap, monaural movies that no other composer could have suited the film as well.

SALVADOR DALI: A SOFT SELF-PORTRAIT

The 60 minute *Salvador Dali: A Soft Self-Portrait*, made for European television a couple of decades before the release of the disc, is as surreal, dense, and kitschy as its subject. Contrary to the jacket copy, the disc is in CLV. Considering the source and age of the material, the transfer looks fairly good. It is a bit ragged, but conveys its essential elements. Dali's deliberately obscure accent and the antique equipment used to record it necessitate the replay of several passages. Orson Welles performs the voice-over narration.

The show is entertaining and informative, but only in a roundabout fashion. Many of the film's images are Dali's images, come to life. A little history of his progress as a painter is recorded, as is his own interpretation of some of his recurring symbols. The documentary is also a worthy record of the atmosphere in Port Ligat, Spain, when Dali was its primary tourist attraction.

SAME TIME NEXT YEAR

Ellen Burstyn appeared in the stage production of *Same Time Next Year* for more than a year before doing the film. Alan Alda did not. Alda is effective at times, but there are also scenes where it is obvious that he should have spent more time rehearsing. He's not obnoxious enough, the way he might have become after a year of responding to the laughter of an audience. Burstyn, on the other hand, has subtle ticks and mannerisms which she developed previous to starring in the film. She's alert, amusing, and not distracting, so that the movie rises and sinks on whether Alda has mastered a scene or not. The movie is about a couple who only meet once a year for a weekend tryst, with the scenes taking place in five year increments.

We were surprised to find ourselves enjoying the program, but it is a typical example of the ability of a well produced disc to improve the tolerability of a movie. The print is nice, the sound is okay, and side three is in CAV.

SAMMY AND ROSIE GET LAID

There are speckles on the image throughout *Sammy and Rosie Get Laid* and a tendency for colors to blur together as well. Faces appear a little on the orange side, but the picture is mildly glossy. The digital sound still doesn't help one decode the heaviest accents – the sound wasn't recorded clearly enough – but it is noticeably cleaner than the analog track and less noisy than the speckled image would lead one to anticipate.

Other than the implication that sex is the only escape from poverty, the film is insightful and stimulating. The dialog is titillating to the point where one *wants* to replay passages and try to decode the accents. It takes place in London's East End, in the middle of a riot, but is actually about a former Pakistani official visiting his son. The film's power comes from its examination of the guilt felt by the father, who was responsible for acts of violent repression in his own country, and the guilt felt by those he comes into contact with, socially, during the visit. The sex stuff is just the sugar coating to make the medicine go down easier, but the film is potent in moral ambiguities.

SAN FRANCISCO NAUGHTY MARIETTA

If Jeanette MacDonald were acting today, she wouldn't have to sing to be a star. She has an '80s face – a sharp, angular jaw, a square chin, and jeweled business-before-pleasure eyes. In *San Francisco* she plays opposite Clark Gable and sings enough that the film would have qualified as a musical had anyone sung with her. It has a conclusion (the 1906 earthquake and fire) which is so spectacular that if you haven't seen the movie in a while, it is probably the only thing you remember about it. Gable has charisma with virtually everybody, but MacDonald's barely-repressed desire for him is magnetic. MacDonald's singing is also one of the movie's main entertainments, especially when she lets loose on her final music hall rendition of 'San Francisco.'

The picture is sharp, but has an odd-looking texture. The print also appeared to freeze at odd moments. One explanation we have heard for this phenomenon, which seems to happen on many MGM discs, is that breaks or damages in the film have been compensated by repeating good frames.

Victor Herbert's *Naughty Marietta* is a more typical Jeanette MacDonald vehicle. Here she is teamed with Nelson Eddy, whose body language is saying that he is only touching her for as long as he has to. The operetta format is an entertaining adaptation of *Manon Lescaut*, with MacDonald playing a woman of French royalty who hightails it to wild New Orleans when marriage threatens her. In a supporting part as the wife of the Louisiana governor, Elsa Lanchester is outrageously good, strutting through the entire production and practically demanding that all eyes focus on her.

The print is torn or scratched at regular intervals. For those who are unfamiliar with the property, it is from this work that Western Civilization was blessed with Mr. Herbert's 'Ah, Sweet Mystery of Life,' and one wonders where earthquakes are when you need them.

SAN FRANCISCO BLUES FESTIVAL

A pleasant afternoon blues concert in a San Francisco park is excerpted on *San Francisco Blues Festival*. The digitally encoded stereo sound has a nice, airy quality to it. The picture is not as strong, since many solid colors tend to appear unstable.

Eight artists are featured sequentially on the single sided CLV disc, performing 16 numbers. Included are Clifton Chenenier, John Hammond, Albert Collins, Clarence Brown, and Robert Cray. Brief interviews separate each session, but the disc is still manageable as a musical program, and provides a relaxing hour of foot stomping, harmonica wailing, and guitar picking.

SANDS OF IWO JIMA

Documentary footage from the actual invasion of Iwo Jima was incorporated into the John Wayne WWII film, *Sands of Iwo Jima* (misidentified on the jacket spine as just 'Iwo Jima'). The black-and-white film mixes home made action footage with the real stuff, and the last hour of the 109-minute film is reasonably entertaining, but the opening, in which the stereotypical unit is introduced, is dull and even embarrassing. It is best to start watching the disc at chapter 6, when the action starts.

The sound is in fair condition. Except for the documentary footage, the reel change points and the night scenes, the picture looks quite good. Forrest Tucker co-stars, and *Sands of Iwo Jima* is one of those rare instances where John Wayne's character meets his maker. The dialog contains derogatory descriptions of Asians.

SANJURO (see **YOJIMBO**)

SANTA CLAUS THE MOVIE

Sometimes the break between side one and side two on a laser disc can reveal structural flaws within the the movie featured on the disc. John Lithgow does not appear in *Santa Claus The Movie* until the disc is turned over, and 'The Movie' isn't really a movie until he shows up. The first half is just a string of holiday scenes showing how Santa got started and imagining what a large-scale toy production run by elves would look like. The Image release is in CX-encoded stereo and has a slightly blurry picture. On side two, Lithgow portrays a greedy toy manufacturer who has conned a wayward elf, played by Dudley Moore. The concoction does not seem strong enough to earn a spot in a crowded holiday viewing schedule and the disc has nothing special to recommend.

SANTA FE TRAIL

Has anyone ever portrayed more famous people on the screen than Errol Flynn? You can come away thinking every historical figure in America was brash, good looking, and athletic. *Santa Fe Trail* is not about the Santa Fe Trail, it is about that great American terrorist, John Brown. No, Flynn does not portray Brown, he portrays J.E.B. Stuart who, along with West Point '54 classmate and romantic rival, George Armstrong Custer (Ronald Reagan, very young), battles Brown in Kansas and eventually captures him at Harper's Ferry, Pennsylvania. The movie gives a fairly balanced view of Brown, whose exploits make textbook writers cringe, even today, but the script tries to make Stuart into a Friend of the Slaves and it just doesn't cut it. The portrayal of blacks will have some viewers throwing bricks at their TV screens.

SAPS AT SEA/OLIVER THE EIGHTH (see **THE BOHEMIAN GIRL/THE MUSIC BOX**)

SATISFACTION

In *Satisfaction*, Justine Bateman's character belongs to a female rock group which spends the summer playing in a tavern at an unidentified ocean beach community. The film is pleasant, though the specter of Bateman mangling the title song may be enough to scare away fans, if not members of her immediate family. The picture looks dark, muddy, grainy, and generally second rate. The analog Ultra-Stereo soundtrack has little to offer.

SATOMI HAKKEN-DEN (see **YOJIMBO**)

SAVAGE STREETS
Linda Blair has a nude scene in *Savage Streets* and her belly clearly has a couple of rolls and a distinct fold. She is still sexy, and, not having the sheared, glossy, interchangeable starlet build, she is sexier than all the other naked women in the movie, by default. The film is a prurient exploitation of sadism and revenge. There is a rape scene which probably is in violation of the child pornography laws in at least a few states. The plot has a beginning, a middle, and an end, but nothing else in it is logical, understandable, or all that thrilling. The rock score comes through well while the dialog and incidental sounds are under-supported. The picture is passable.

SAVING GRACE
Tom Conti is a wonderful actor who brings redemptive qualities into every role he plays. How many actors could portray a Pope who sneaks out of the Vatican to help a despondent mountain town? In *Saving Grace* he achieves a careful balance between authority, naivety, and gall and upholds a suspension of disbelief throughout the story. Two other fine actors, Edward James Olmos and Giancarlo Giannini, also contribute to the quality of the presentation. Only when the movie itself is out of focus is the picture less than perfect.

SAWDUST AND TINSEL
(See **AUTUMN SONATA**)

SAY ANYTHING
We hesitate to state that *Say Anything* is about two young people who have just graduated from high school, in fear that those who are turned off by teen comedies will avoid the disc. The film is a wonderful romance involving two finely constructed characters (and a third, the girl's father). Although set in the usual teen milieu, the movie stands apart in many ways. The boy's friends may provide some good comedy lines and a couple of amusing highjinks, but they are framed and utilized by the filmmakers as a classical dramatic chorus, to echo his thoughts. The device is perfectly executed, so that the viewer is not put off – and may not even be aware – of the detached nature of their commentary. The performances are all outstanding. The plot concerns the romance and the choices the couple must make about their future. There is also a melodramatic subplot, but it is lightly and effectively executed.

The stereo surround sound is forceful and solid, and makes a good impression. As with the rest of the film, the rock score is effectively applied and not the least bit alienating. The picture is slightly grainy, particularly when solid reds are involved, but is passable. The make-up, however, is ill-applied upon the cast and stands out more so than in the average film. On early copies the digital audio track would not play on some players.

SAY YES
Was Jonathan Winters ever funny? It is difficult to remember. There are some brief flashes of invention within his top-billed cameo in *Say Yes*, but there is also too much desperation in his manner. He plays a billionaire who expires forthwith and leaves an inheritance to his grandson provided the grandson be married inside of a short time period. Once Winters is out of the way, the movie shapes into a pleasant enough romantic comedy. It is not well made – you can see the film crew in the reflections – and the director does not encourage or trust his cast of unknowns, relying primarily on the elaborate plot mechanisms to carry the story. Vertical streaks, blurry oranges, and other imperfections adversely affect the quality of the picture.

SCANDAL
The picture quality of *Scandal* is disappointing. The film is grainy throughout, and the color is flat in places. The sound is in digitally encoded stereo, but only the music and an occasional crowd murmur make use of the surround channel. The many early sixties pop hits which show up on the musical score sound great, however.

The film, based upon a true story, is about a woman who has affairs with a government official and a Soviet spy, in Britain. This is the unrated version, though the material that did not appear in the American theatrical version and has been added to the video presentation is more conceptual and dramatically oriented than explicitly sexual. There are a couple of shots in an orgy scene which have been restored, but the two major sequences that have been added back have no nudity at all. One sequence reveals the age of the woman (she is a minor at the time) and removes an aura of naivete present in the American theatrical release. The other addition is more inexplicable, showing the woman wheedling rent money for a friend out of an elderly companion. This latter sequence is referred to later during the trial scenes.

Whether the movie, as it appears on disc, is close to the truth or not, it is entertaining and also a little subversive. The filmmakes fun of older men who chase after younger women in a way to which those who fit the description will be oblivious. The performances are satisfying and the narrative's depiction of life among the elite would be rewarding even if history had not provided it with a pat conclusion. The disc would make an interesting double bill with *Darling*.

SCARAMOUCHE
SCARAMOUCHE (CAV)
The color on *Scaramouche* is gorgeous. Our favorite part is when Eleanor Parker's blended purple-and-blue eye shadow changes consistency between the medium shot and the closeup. If the colors were any less vivid, you wouldn't notice the mistake. But even the air is colorful in *Scaramouche*, especially a billowy, silver morning mist over Golden Gate Park – which doubles as the French countryside during several outdoor scenes. Every still frame is a full color portrait.

Scaramouche is one of those free-spirited MGM classics which it is virtually impossible to begrudge. It has an exhausting sword duel at the finale and the right mix of action, humor, and drama building up to it. Stewart Granger, who plays the vengeful revolutionary disguised as a theater clown, is ideal for the role of the hero, because his thoughtfulness makes his actions more believable and his accomplishments less fantastic. He performs his comical scenes with the same panache, never exaggerating his efforts.

A CAV and a CLV version are available. The picture quality is the same on both versions. The CLV presentation has digital sound, while the CAV disc, which has alternate audio track programs, is analog only. The supplementary track on the CAV disc is one of Voyager's better efforts. An hour long discussion by Dick Dinman focuses very closely on the production history of the film. Admirably, his essay for the back of the jacket cover adds even more information and does not simply reiterate his talk. Furthermore, Dinman is not the only one to give a talk on the disc. Granger gives a relaxed and good humored half hour interview, his comments ranging from the perils he suffered during the filming to barbed remarks about Sean Penn. The film's director, George Sidney, also has a half-hour talk, providing further technical insights.

SCARFACE
One of the first MCA Encore Edition releases was the 1932 Howard Hawks film, *Scarface*, staring Paul Muni as a gangster who winds up controlling racketeering in an unnamed city by killing all of his competitors. The film is still effective today because of the way Hawks packs action into every scene and visual excitement into every shot.

Censor disapproval of the first ending Hawks filmed led to the filming of a second, where the hero's crimes are clearly articulated and condemned before he is dispatched. The movie with this ending was called, 'Scarface, Shame of the Nation.' That version was retired as soon as restrictions were relaxed and *Scarface*, with the original Hawks finale, is the commonly exhibited version. MCA included both endings on side two, delineating them with chapter markers.

THE SCARLET PIMPERNEL
The black-and-white classic about a British aristocrat who rescues members of the French aristocracy from the guillotine, *The Scarlet Pimpernel* has very little action and quite a bit of talk, but it has romantic appeal (the Pimpernel's wife doesn't realize her husband is a dashing hero) and a fair amount of intrigue. The source material is soft looking but has no major errors and the sound is fuzzy but tolerable. Leslie Howard, in whom heroic demeanor is a near impossibility, nevertheless stars.

SCAVENGERS
Scavengers is an adventure film which appears to have arrived at home video with only a limited theatrical run. It has some interesting stunts – for some reason parachutists jump out of the back of an airplane on motorcycles – and a pleasing amount of slapstick humor. The sound is in stereo but is very scratchy if the volume is raised beyond normal. The picture looks fresh, but is also quite grainy.

SCHOOL DAZE
Outside of the context of Spike Lee's other films, most of which are even better, *School Daze* is a work of brilliant and satisfying originality. The movie, employing the structural base of a musical comedy, uses an all-

black college as a metaphor for black American culture. It opens with a linguistically powerful "Yo!" and spends two hours exploring the strengths, the betrayals, and the assimilation of Black culture before ending with the admonition, "Wake up!" In terms of filmmaking alone, the movie is worth studying on a frame-by-frame basis – among the cleverest of Lee's cinematic tricks are a football game which the viewer never actually sees, the use of the soundtrack to blend music and language (both of which often appear on the back channel of the surround track), and a hysterically gross love scene juxtaposed with a sensuous love scene, both of which studiously avoid the normal clichés. The movie so steadfastly avoids clichés that some viewers may be completely mystified as to what is going on. What is going on is that Spike Lee is establishing himself as one of the finest filmmakers of our day using rich and previously unskimmed reference resources for his source material.

The disc is terribly sloppy and unappealing. The picture is grainy, blurry, and too orange. Anytime Lee makes use of special lighting techniques, the image completely deteriorates. The sound is analog and the bass is fuzzy. No chapter markers have been encoded. About the only right thing RCA/Columbia did was to stretch the 114-minute film to three sides.

SCENES FROM THE CLASS STRUGGLE IN BEVERLY HILLS

Scenes from the Class Struggle in Beverly Hills is a truly wicked and quite funny comedy about the raunchy lives of the rich. The title is probably a bad marketing choice, since the 'Beverly Hills' moniker usually gets thrown onto cheap, unsophisticated exploitation efforts. *Class Struggle*, directed by Paul Bartel, is something completely different. The script writers are listed as Bartel and Bruce Wagner, but some of the dialog and situations sound like they have come from the hand of the actor/playwright, Wallace Shawn, who has a major role in the film.

Jacqueline Bisset, who is given one the best parts she has had in a very long time, portrays a successful television actress whose husband has recently passed away. A daft selection of characters staying at her mansion for the wake leads to uninhibited desires and botched liaisons. One of the clever aspects to the script is the way in which lines of dialog, for very logical reasons, are repeated in different situations. Somehow, too, the sex gags manage to be outrageous without seeming juvenile. It is rare that adults can sustain themselves on such subjects without reverting to childishness.

Bartel's films have limited budgets, and the film stock is second rate, but that noted, the picture transfer looks good. The separation effects are limited on the Ultra-Stereo surround sound, and the ambience is dulled.

SCOOBY-DOO

On the jacket cover and in the live Hanna and Barbera interludes between the episodes, *Scooby-Doo* is praised as a cartoon which has had a lasting appeal. The appeal should not be examined too closely, however, because the cartoon has gotten by for so long on mediocrity and conformity. It is the program kids turn to when nothing better is on and a program the networks could rely upon to bridge more dynamic and interesting shows.

Scooby-Doo contains 4 episodes that demonstrate clearly how adaptable the cartoon, which usually depicts apparent supernatural events that turn out to have logical explanations, has been. The first episode, 'What a Night for a Knight,' runs about 20 minutes and concerns mysterious goings on in an art museum. It is an older episode and has a laugh track. The second episode, 'The New Scooby-Doo Movies Starring Sonny and Cher,' runs a full 40 minutes and stretches into side two. The narrative concerns mysterious goings on in a desolate beach resort. Mr. and Mrs. Bono contribute their voices to the episode, but Cher's reading has a bored resonance. Following that is a 7-minute 'Scooby and Scrapy-Doo' short, 'Scooby Gumbo,' which concerns goings on in a New Orleans restaurant. Finally, there is a 13-minute piece, 'Wizards and Warlocks,' a reasonably inventive effort about a gamester's contest.

The colors are mildly faded and not very pleasing to begin with. The monaural sound is clear enough to discern Cher's displeasure with the proceedings and is otherwise passable.

SCORPION

Ostensibly a martial arts action picture starring Tonny Tulleners, *Scorpion* turns out to be, after an extensive prolog, a ripoff of the Steve McQueen movie, *Bullitt*. Not only is the plot the same, but significant lengths of dialog have been lifted word for word from Alan Trustman and Harry Kleiner's script for the McQueen film.

The plagiarism doesn't stop with the script, either. Many camera angles are the same and the actors are made up and dressed to look like their counterparts in the other movie. The writer/producer/director of *Scorpion*, William Riead, even has the audacity to name the two heroes 'Steve' and 'Gordon,' after McQueen and actor Don Gordon. The stupidity of the situation had us tied to our seat waiting (it seemed like forever, although the movie is only 98 minutes long) to see what they would do with the car chase. First, however, it is amusing to note that Riead lifted the bad along with the good, taking an item from the plot of *Bullitt* (a hit victim unlocks the door for his murderers) which made no sense whatsoever in the first film and continues to make no sense in this one. Riead also utilizes camera setups which supported a subplot between Bullitt and his girlfriend, and transfers them to *Scorpion* even though he has dropped the subplot itself. The transfer is cheap looking. There are speckles on the print and polluted colors around the edge of the picture. The sound is noisy. We waited and waited and it finally came. The car chase turns out to be on foot. It figures, since the entire effort is pedestrian.

SCORPIONS – TO RUSSIA WITH LOVE AND OTHER SAVAGE AMUSEMENTS

Scorpions – To Russia with Love and Other Savage Amusements is a 45-minute documentary with song interludes about the band's visit to the Soviet Union. The German group's imitation of American hard rock is always bouncy and listenable in a loud sort of way. Several music videos, which were constructed using footage from the Russian trip, are included. The disc has digital sound and delivers the bass with a decent boom. The picture has a little grain from the 16mm source material and stronger colors blur together, but the show is generally so enjoyable that it doesn't matter.

SCORPIONS – WORLD WIDE LIVE

If you have a daughter who wears t-shirts promoting the heavy metal rock group, Scorpions, it is best you not watch *Scorpions – World Wide Live* lest she turns out to be one of the youngsters getting a bare breast autographed by the lead guitarist. The disc jacket cover says, "parental discretion advised," but it looks to us like they are a little too late.

The hour-long program contains eleven numbers from various concerts in the US, Rio, Japan, and Europe. Between each number are images of publicity appearances and the frantic enthusiasm of Scorpions fans.

Although the Scorpions sing in English, the band members are German, so the edge is off their delivery because they don't understand that the lyrics, however simpleminded, aren't supposed to be understood. The music has a steady, non-irritating beat. The disc is only in analog although the music had been mastered using digital equipment. The picture is excessively grainy.

SCREAM GREATS VOLUME ONE

If blood and entrails are your cup of tea then you will want to spend time with the hour-long CAV horror documentary *Scream Greats Volume One* featuring make up/effect artist Tom Savini. The disc has oodles of spraying guts and splattering flesh, all of which can be sped up, slowed down, or examined on a frame-by-frame basis. The footage (mainly from George Romero's features and Paramount's *Friday the 13th* series) is a generation or two further away from the original than one would prefer with this kind of access. Savini talks about his experiences in Vietnam and it is clear that he has come to terms with his own horrors by passing them along to everyone else.

The documentary, sponsored by Fangoria Magazine, provides a strong sense of Savini's personality (and of his family, his wife clearly enjoying and suffering the strains of their partnership). The sound on the disc is stated to be in stereo, but only one or two passages actually come across that way. The disc is also encoded with 17 chapter markers, so you can find the most gruesome scenes immediately in order to disturb older relatives.

SCREAM GREATS VOLUME TWO – SATANISM AND WITCHCRAFT

The CAV functions are useful on the 58-minute documentary about Satanic worship, *Scream Greats Volume Two – Satanism and Witchcraft*, to freeze the frames in popular sequences from several Devil-oriented films. Movies have a subsidiary role on the program, however, which is primarily about the nutsy, never-borrow-a-cup-of-sugar-after-eight world of next-door neighbor devil worshipers. The filmmakers, taking great delight in conflicts of opinion, interview devil worshipers who do it for fun, devil worshipers who do it for money, devil worshipers who do it because the priests in Catholic high school couldn't answer every picky question, people who fight the devil spiritually, people who investigate rumors of devil worship sacrificial practices, and people who claim to have been victims of devil worshiper tortures when they were children.

The picture varies in quality, but is usually pretty good. The clips from old silent films about the devil are in excellent condition, while the scenes from *The Omen*, *Rosemary's Baby*, 'The Entity,' 'The Wicker Man,' and others are several generations away from their source. In still-frame mode the action usually jiggles, but it is easy enough to make out the wire guiding the lightning rod into David Warner or to examine the superimposed flash of Rosemary's baby's baby reds. Intriguing footage of a real exorcism is also included, as are scenes from an elaborate devil worship orgy. Some people seem to go through a lot of hocus-pocus just to have a little fun.

SCREEN TEST
Four college kids decide that the best way to meet girls is to hold auditions for an X-rated movie in *Screen Test*. There is a plethora of bare breasts, but no organized wit and nothing which could be considered cute, erotic, or passable entertainment. The picture and the monaural sound are unblemished.

SCROOGE
"You don't look like a ghost," trembles Albert Finney's Ebeneezer Scrooge.

"Thank you," pipes Dame Edith Evans's Spirit of Christmas Past.

The 1970 musical version of Charles Dickens's 'A Christmas Carol,' *Scrooge*, is available from CBS/Fox. The performances of Finney, Evans, and Alec Guinness (as Jacob Marley's piquant ghost) and the natural appeal of the source material makes the disc well worth acquiring, even if it is not in wide screen and will only be viewed once or twice a year. The picture is generally reliable, although the disc has trouble handling some of the lighting in the fantasy sequences.

CBS/Fox is to be commended for retaining the film's opening and closing overture and accompanying the music with a blank screen. The stereo is wonderful, particularly when the bells peal on Christmas Day.

To quibble with some of the movie's production values would be a bit of a humbug. Sure you can occasionally see the wires when the characters are floating in air, and certainly, it is a mistake when Scrooge never recognizes that 'Thank You Very Much' is about his own demise, but this is a version more entertaining than not. Reading Dickens's tale aloud is still the best way to share the story with those you love, but showing them the movie can be just as cozy and jolly.

SCROOGED
In *Scrooged*, the contemporary re-working of 'A Christmas Carol,' Bill Murray, as a TV network executive, doesn't even bother to get his hair cut for his part, but his exposure to real television executives gives his interpretation a viciously sublime edge. The script is a mess, and almost everything in it is only half complete, but Murray forces his character through every shift of mood and attitude. He makes it work – without him, you couldn't enjoy the gags that succeed, the marvelous cameos, or the hyperdriven special effects, because you wouldn't have a reason to stick with them. The film is dense enough with ideas, however, that repeat viewings are also satisfying.

The special effects and accompanying surround sound effects will be what draws most fans to the disc. The many night scenes look solid and the focus on the picture is very sharp. Flesh tones, which sometimes come across a shade too orange, present the only noticeable distortion. The film was rated PG-13 for a reason, so caution is advised before putting it on after the family's holiday meal.

THE SEA CHASE
John Wayne plays a 'good' German in a World War II movie, *The Sea Chase*. The jacket cover makes excellent use of the film's original advertising artwork. The movie fits on one platter, but runs a full two hours, so that by the time it is over you really feel like you have sat through a minor epic.

The Cinemascope picture has been letterboxed with an aspect ratio of about 2.25:1. At times the image looks squeezed and at other times so much of the top and the bottom of the picture are on view that flaws on the sides of the image flash by at regular intervals. The color transfer is rich, though the image has some speckling and scattered lapses in intensity. If *The Sea Chase* were a highly regarded classic, the transfer might seem sloppy, but for a film of little renown, the disc is gorgeous.

The stereo surround track is also imperfect, but super. Although there are volume dropouts and other minor flaws, the movie has an old-fashioned sound mix that is full of enjoyable separation effects, well worth amplifying past the point of distortion. The disc also features Warner's reliable chapter encoding.

The movie is as strange as they come. Wayne portrays the captain of a German merchant marine vessel caught in an Australian harbor at the outbreak of World War II. He sneaks out, and is dogged all the way back to Germany by British destroyers. Also aboard is a spy fleeing the British, played by Lana Turner, and although the captain dislikes her immensely, they're making out before the side break. There is enough suspense in the concept to pull the viewer along, and the cast, which also includes Tab Hunter and James Arness, increases the entertainment. The letterboxed images are attractively composed, particularly during the action montages. The whole disc is a pleasure, and it almost compensates for the say-it-ain't-so vision of the Duke collaborating with the Nazis.

THE SEA HAWK
Fifteen minutes are missing from *The Sea Hawk*, but before we get to the spilled milk we must say that the film, as it stands, is reasonably entertaining. Errol Flynn portrays a privateer, robbing Spanish galleons with the quiet approval of Queen Elizabeth I. The sea battle which opens the picture is especially spectacular. The version on the CBS/Fox disc is one which Warners edited for their 1949 theatrical rerelease. The picture and sound transfers are passible.

SEA OF LOVE
SEA OF LOVE (Letterboxed)
Because the producers opted for a crowd-pleasing mystery solution instead of concentrating on the vulnerabilities of the victims and the suspects, *Sea of Love* is only really good as a one night stand. The film is great for one viewing, but lacks the substance to support multiple viewings.

Al Pacino stars as a police detective investigating a serial killing and dating a woman who is, if nothing else, a prime suspect. The detective's anger toward his ex-wife's husband cleverly foreshadows events later in the film, but the movie's highpoint is a group of interviews the detective conducts in a restaurant with different women who think they have answered a personal ad to go on a date. The sequence is an excellent example of using a public locale to intensify the emotional suspense of a scene.

The picture is a little grainy, mainly because most of the movie takes place at night. The stereo surround sound is okay, but it becomes too accurate in places, making the dialog loops easy to spot. Two versions were released, a standard version and a slightly matted letterbox edition. There is very little difference between the two. For every shot where there is a little too much wall behind a character, there is a shot where an interesting hairstyle or curious object is lopped off. The width of the image is unchanged.

THE SEARCHERS
The picture quality on John Ford's *The Searchers*, is only average, with scratches and faded colors in places, but the sound is terrific for a movie which is not in stereo. Gunshots have an extra echo and approaching horses can be heard well before they come into view.

Many consider *The Searchers* to be John Wayne's best movie. It is certainly one of his best performances. He laughs and cries and has genuine changes of heart. The story is more problematic. Wayne portrays Ethan Edwards, a Confederate war vet who returns to his brother's homestead which, after a moment's grace, is burned to the ground by an Indian raiding party. His niece is kidnapped and most of the story covers the years Edwards and Martin Pawley (Jeffrey Hunter), an adopted member of the family, spend trying to locate her.

And the first time they find her, Edwards tries to shoot her, for she is grown, nubile, and clearly knows her way around a teepee. *The Searchers* is controversial because of the attitudes expressed by the characters, in all likelihood quite natural for their time and setting. Indian men are usually referred to as 'bucks.' Women who have been retrieved from their clutches are insane or catatonic. Yet it is this attitude, far more than director Ford's penchant for loving details of the Old West, that gives the film its edgy power. Edwards, personified by Wayne, is no better than the Native American terrorists he is chasing, and everyone in the film knows this.

SECOND SIGHT
As stupid as *Second Sight* is, it is also fairly funny. The film, starring Bronson Pinchot and John Larroquette, is about a private detective agency which uses a psychic (Pinchot) to solve cases. The movie is such a mess that there are embarrassing gaps in the narrative where it is obvious that inept sequences were removed during the editing and not replaced. Still, if one tolerates the silliest discretions, both Pinchot and Larroquette have moments of adept comic inspiration.

The colors are accurate, but the source material is speckled. The stereo surround mix is not too interesting.

SECRET AGENT
(see **YOUNG AND INNOCENT**)

THE SECRET LIFE OF WALTER MITTY
HANS CHRISTIAN ANDERSON
THE COURT JESTER

The color in *The Secret Life of Walter Mitty* isn't quite as good as other Technicolor Embassy discs have been, but the presentation is adequate. The sound preserves the shrillness of an early 1950s recording with embarrassing accuracy.

Danny Kaye portrays a chronic daydreamer who becomes involved in real intrigue. The movie shows the daydreams, and some are clever because of the subtle ways they include details from the outside.

The color in *Hans Christian Anderson* is much better. The back of the disc jacket says that the film was nominated for six Academy Awards, but it is impossible to imagine which six. Kaye portrays a stylized version of Anderson. He sits around his small town telling stories to children, leaves for Copenhagen when the town parents discover their children are going to him instead of to school, falls in love with a married ballerina in Copenhagen, writes down his stories to become a local celebrity, and then returns to the small town when he realizes the ballerina doesn't love him. The rest is songs and some extended dance/ballet numbers.

Some of Kaye's films are building a serious cult following. By all means check out *The Court Jester* if you see it at a bargain price or feel like taking a chance. Kaye portrays a minstrel cavorting with a Robin Hood-type band. He takes on the guise of a court jester in order to save his kingdom. Kaye's sprighty dancing and his joyful, tounge-twisting dialog reading allow him to slip in and out of character without spoiling the film's mood. The color is sharp and the disc has chapter markers for all the musical numbers.

THE SECRET OF MY SUCCESS

Any bright young actor would have been great in *The Secret of My Success*. Michael J. Fox was just lucky that he landed the part. The real secret to the success of the film was in the contribution of the generally underappreciated director, Herbert Ross. Ross took the script, an updating of *How to Succeed in Business Without Really Trying*, and made it into a sophisticated, well disciplined comedy. The elements of farce which run freely through the story are never allowed to go so wild that the pace deteriorates. Fox is just along for the ride, and by doing his job correctly, he reaped great benefits. But then that is what the movie is about, the art of being in the right place at the right time. The picture is excellent and the stereo surround sound is accomplished. The rock score is supportive instead of being overbearing. Early in the film, Fox's character discovers an inefficiency in lower levels of the corporation's division of departmental responsibilities. You keep expecting him to bring it up after he amasses some power, but the movie is true to life. He forgets about it.

THE SECRET OF THE NIMH
THE SECRET OF THE NIMH (Digital)

The stereo and surround effects are mildly improved on MGM/UA's digital reissue of Don Bluth's *The Secret of the NIMH* in comparison to the older analog disc, though it should be noted that the surround encoding, especially as it applies to Jerry Goldsmith's score, is very impressive. The color transfer on MGM/UA's older version tended to oversaturate. The color on the new version compensates a little too much in the other direction, taking some richness out of the hues, but in general it is a more solid and sharper picture. The older disc looked too blurry in places, which diminished its effectiveness. The new version heightens the animation and gives the viewer a better chance to enjoy the movie. Both discs are in CLV.

NIMH is a complicated and satisfying animated feature which is mis-represented in almost every summary that we have read. It was Bluth's first major independent effort, and has fewer compromises than his subsequent films have displayed. The story is probably too complicated for children, at least on an initial viewing, but essentially concerns the political struggles within a group of intelligent rats and mice, as they debate the need to move further away from humans. It is no *Animal Farm*, however, and contains many charming and attractively drawn sequences.

THE SECRET POLICEMAN'S PRIVATE PARTS

The concert material composing *The Secret Policeman's Private Parts* is barely viewable. The sound has no range on the comedy segments and minimum enhancement on the four legitimate musical interludes. The picture looks like it was filmed in Super-8 by someone in the audience. It is grainy, dim, and requires a lot of patience. The 77-minute CLV program consists of highlights from Amnesty International fund raisers. Most of the sketches being performed involve members of the Monty Python comedy group. Many of the bits appear elsewhere, such as the 'dead parrot' routine, and the 'singing lumberjacks' routine. Although the jacket lists the disc as being in stereo, little of it is. Pete Townshend performs a pleasant, acoustical guitar version of 'Drowned,' which is the nicest moment on the program. There are 28 chapter markers.

SEE NO EVIL

A largely untapped potential exists for murder thrillers involving handicapped heroes. *See No Evil*, however, never quite lives up to its promise. Richard Fleischer's film, made in the early seventies and starring Mia Farrow, is about a blind woman who is the only survivor of a mass murder in the mansion she is visiting. Can she get help before the murderer, who has left an identifying valuable, returns? The monaural sound is digitally encoded and the sound effects are often emphasized, accentuating the viewer's identification with the heroine's point of view. In the climatic finale, however, as the murderer is attempting to drown the heroine in a bathtub, the camera angle shifts to an underwater shot of the bad guy, arms extended, as if he were choking the lens. Standard stuff, but that's not what the heroine is seeing, and the effect disassociates one's sympathies, right as one ought to be panting for a last minute rescue. The pace of the film is also alienating, slowing down to a crawl whenever the situation ought to become quick and desperate.

The picture looks good. The colors are not faded and the focus is sharp. Intense colors have only a slight instability. An above average number of white speckles are scattered through the print, but that is the only age-related flaw. The film's score is an unusually over-enthusiastic effort by Elmer Bernstein.

SEE NO EVIL, HEAR NO EVIL

The murder comedy in which Richard Pryor portrays a blind man and Gene Wilder portrays a deaf man, *See No Evil, Hear No Evil*, is inevitably enjoyable. We wish that the filmmakers could have made the plot tighter and the movie funnier than they did, but the movie is good enough to be entertaining. The picture is fine and the sound is passable.

SEE YOU IN THE MORNING

Halfway through *See You in the Morning* you still don't know what it is about. What finally materializes is a tale of remarriage doubly tangled in the vulnerabilities the couple brings from their previous unions and the new problems they confront in settling down together. The film is edited for encryption, perhaps because the plot would be too bland if it were presented in a straightforward manner. Jeff Bridges and Alice Krige are the couple. The movie is more friendly than romantic. The characters become too detailed and familiar for you to identify with them; instead, you root for them as you would root for any couple with whom you are intimately acquainted.

The picture transfer is unusual. It looks quite good, except for red fabric, which looks inept. Krige has several red outfits and at times she looks so blurry it seems as if she's been electronically superimposed upon the image. The sound is stereo surround, but the separation effects are minimal and little is stereophonic.

SEIZE THE DAY

The intense and emotionally downhill adaptation of Saul Bellow's *Seize the Day*, starring Robin Williams, is as depressing as it is well-made. Stylistically, the film has many tight closeups, as much to facilitate the fifties New York setting (though it comes across as a very Chicagoish New York) as to accommodate the telefilm screen compositions. Williams portrays a man who has lost his job, his family, and his sense of initiative. He completely forsakes the comical inventiveness which he allows his other dramatic characters to affect, but it is his performance which makes the film so captivating. He's revved up, but, in character, he can't do anything but spin his wheels. The viewer is blinded by his energy until it is too late to escape the trap his character is in.

The picture is a little worn down and is grainy. The sound editing is adept, but the digital monaural sound has a limited range.

SELF DEFENSE

A movie made with low grade film stock and sound recording equipment, Self Defense is set and filmed in Halifax, Nova Scotia. The transfer can't do much to improve the blurry picture because the story takes place on a single evening after the sun goes down and darkness permeates the screen from beginning to end. The picture is so awkward that at times it is difficult to tell whether it was a good guy or a bad guy who got shot. The sound is flat and fuzzy. About an all-night siege on a mostly empty tenement in an empty part of town, the plot is fairly engaging once the premise is established. Action fans who can tolerate aesthetic compromises should enjoy the disc.

THE SENSUAL WORLD KATE BUSH THE VIDEOS

The source material for *The Sensual World Kate Bush The Videos* is mildly grainy, the sound is clear and the presentation is sufficiently effective. Each number on the 8-inch disc is preceded by an interview, but the interruption is low key and not a real problem. The videos, 'Love and Anger,' 'The Sensual World,' and 'This Woman's Work,' are well crafted, compelling the viewer to pay attention without a bombardment of conflicting images. The title number is the best, adeptly evoking Technicolor chromatic designs to depict Bush tripping freely through a studio set forest.

SEPTEMBER

Woody Allen's Bergmanish *September* is a sequel to Harold Robbins' 'Where Love Has Gone.' We're kidding, of course, about it being a sequel, but the film does draw its central plot manipulation from Lana Turner's biography, and it is set (though it was filmed entirely on soundstages and never goes outside) in Vermont, halfway between Hollywood and Sweden.

The movie has undergone a decent transfer to disc. The lighting in the film, although not pleasing, is difficult, and it survives with only a mild addition of grain. The monaural soundtrack is digitally encoded and provides an effective presentation for the many jazz numbers, ostensibly playing on the record player in the summer house where the story takes place. There are also chapter markers for the music. More importantly, side one of the 82-minute feature is in CAV. Running through the movie at triple speed, one can see that Allen's choice of camera angles and movement just doesn't have the power or the insight the drama demands. There is nothing which locks a viewer's eyes to the screen.

Allen depends too much upon his cast to bring off the material, and while each actor or actress has one or two scenes in which they are fully in control and entertaining, there are many more times when the lines are too stiff, too much like the belabored written word instead of the improvised spoken word. There once was a time when people in story conferences would be clutching their stomachs in hysterics over dialog passages such as the following: "My husband's a wonderful man. He's bewildered because I wanted this summer apart. He's a radiologist. He takes x-rays but I never let him take them of me because if he looked inside he'd see things that he wouldn't understand. He'd be terribly hurt." What did she do? Swallow his Rolex?

SEPTEMBER AFFAIR

Even though it isn't nearly as good of a film, *September Affair*, will make a terrific double bill with *Dodsworth*. About an industrialist and a pianist who take advantage of a plane crash to have a secretly extended sabbatical in Italy, the film even contains a cameo appearance of sorts by Walter Huston, who sings Kurt Weil's 'September Song' on a phonograph record. The film stars Joseph Cotten and Joan Fontaine and is a bit of a fantasy (nobody ever gets on anybody's nerves), so the script ought not to be scrutinized too closely. Being in black-and-white makes the movie easier to accept, but the film works best when it doesn't have to stand alone as entertainment.

The print has a few rough spots but no severe problems. The sound is also in passable condition.

SERAPHIC DIALOG (see THE ROYAL BALLET – SWAN LAKE)

THE SERPRENT AND THE RAINBOW

Because *The Serpent and the Rainbow* was the first horror film since the *Amityville* fiasco to derive its narrative, at least partially, from documented occurrences, it received better than average notices when it was released. Unfortunately, Wes Craven's tale of voodoo rituals and Haitian corruption never becomes as special as it seems to promise. It is a standard fantasy film and takes as many wrong turns as right ones. What ought to have been an intriguing battle between the white scientist who combines his Western education with a knowledge of voodoo basics and the black magician who has all the powers of evil at his command instead becomes a zap-me-zap-you effects exercise. Much is made in the film of a jaguar totem, but when its function really ought to be utilized, guiding the hero during the climax, it is nowhere to be seen.

The film has many intense colors and some are rarely stable. The stereo surround sound has been digitally encoded and the music – tropical drumbeats and wood instruments – is the strongest component.

SESAME STREET PRESENTS: FOLLOW THAT BIRD

What *Sesame Street Presents: Follow That Bird* ends up being is a *Muppet Movie* with Big Bird instead of Kermit, and its failure can be blamed on the vapid personality of the large feathered title character. What the movie should have been was a 90-minute zap pow like the 30-minute TV show is, hitting you with the differences between up and down, in and out, and what it means to be the number 4. There's much too little of that and much too much of singing stupid songs to twinkling stars that even two-year-olds will not sit still for. They can't. They've been trained by 'Sesame Street' the TV show to expect gratification on a subsecond timetable. The disc makes Mister Rogers seem fast-paced.

SEVEN BRIDES FOR SEVEN BROTHERS
SEVEN BRIDES FOR SEVEN BROTHERS (Letterboxed)

There seems to be a jinx on *Seven Brides for Seven Brothers.* MGM/UA mastered and remastered a scanned and cropped version and both times failed to achieve a satisfying color transfer. With the Deluxe Letter-Box Edition, the color transfer is still inconsistent (at one point near a reel change the image goes totally brown and white), but it is improved to the point of acceptability. The colors remain slightly pale, but outdoor images look rich and strong hues never bleed. The focus is soft, but with the letterboxing shrinking the image, it never becomes much of a problem.

The letterboxing, however, presents the screen composition off center. On the right, there is often empty space between the last character and the edge of the screen. On the left, there is often a character partially cut off or completely missing. Because the letterboxing increases a viewer's awareness of the image's consistent symmetry, the off balance presentation is almost constantly distracting. (MGM/UA's source material was designed for the generation of optical prints. The actual camera negatives, we understand, are in worse shape.)

The digital stereo surround sound on the letterboxed disc is very good, considering the age of the recording, and is a good improvement over the audio on the cropped version. The songs are chapter encoded, though without sufficient lead in. MGM/UA has also included an enjoyable musical short to open the letterboxed disc, a Cinemascope view of a studio orchestra doing a poorly orchestrated medley of MGM song hits. The sound on the right channel in the short is slightly distorted and the image is reddish, but the clip's historical and camp value make it well worth while.

One of seven brothers (Howard Keel) comes down from a mountain homestead to find a bride (Jane Powell). When he brings her home the other brothers decide that they want wives also, and end up kidnapping six for the winter. Their endeavors are suitably chaste and by spring everyone is in love. The more times we see the film, the better it gets. The plot is advanced with great economy – one camera angle on Jane Powell's eyes, for example, says more than a page of 'meet cute' dialog – leaving plenty of space for the magnificent dance numbers.

As for the letterboxing, which has an aspect ratio of about 2.25:1, there is more than enough of the choreography on view to demonstrate how much more lyrical and sweeping it is when the dancers are not cramped by the cropping. Cropped, the film is energetic, but in widescreen, the movie achieves an elegance of which the energy is only one sustaining factor. Only in widescreen can the atmosphere and the technique of the film be legitimately appreciated.

SEVEN HOURS TO JUDGEMENT

A bereaved husband forces the judge who let his wife's killers go free to face the seamy side of the city's night life in *Seven Hours to Judgement*. The disc's picture is grainy and the Ultra-Stereo sound (the Dolby logo incorrectly appears on the back of the jacket) is fuzzy, with few stereo and fewer surround effects. The film is contrived and forgettable.

THE SEVEN-PER-CENT SOLUTION

If you have any friends who enjoy life and literature but, because of some sort of cultural isolation, are not familiar with *The Seven-Per-Cent Solution*, you can delight them by putting on the disc and scanning directly to the point where Sherlock Holmes and Dr. Watson arrive in Austria. From there you can let the film play out for about ten minutes and they will see everything through the eyes of Holmes instead of the eyes of Watson, who has tricked Holmes into traveling to Vienna to cure the detective of a drug addiction. As Holmes reaches the final destination, charges up the stairs to grapple with the evil Dr. Moriarty, and is confronted, instead, by Dr. Sigmund Freud, the effect is marvelous even when you know everything which is going to happen and is totally magical for those who were unprepared for the surprise.

The movie works so well at this point because of the quality of the acting. Nicol Williamson, while he might not embody a traditional image of Holmes, is an excellent choice to embody Holmes beset by cocaine. He is rude. The reaction of many people when they learn that Robert Duvall is playing Dr. Watson – 'but why?' – is answered in the seriousness of his portrayal. Duvall presents a Watson who is more believable than most others have been, one who is Holmes' equal, perhaps even his superior in emotional stability, but one who recognizes the supremacy of the detective's intellectual abilities and willingly accommodates Holmes's need of an assistant. Finally, there is Alan Arkin as Freud. His performance is the rare sort which increases one's appreciation of the craft of acting. He penetrates no inner psyche. Instead, in the best tradition of performers who give pleasure to their audiences, he puts on the beard and the accent, lifts his eyebrow every time Holmes drops a clue about the source of his addiction, and generally shows with his hands and his body that he is a young but serious man who thinks. His cooperative sparring with Williamson is all that a movie needs to make a viewer happy.

The title was once available in CAV on the DiscoVision label and was re-released by MCA in CLV with digitally encoded monaural sound. It is a difficult film to transfer to disc, because the photography contains some very poor attempts to invoke nostalgia through deliberately blurred images and overly browned indoor lighting. No matter how sharp the transfer is, the disc image appears flawed. MCA, however, has probably not done as good a job as they could have, as there is an occasional, errant white line moving upwards through the picture.

The digital track is sharper and cleaner than the analog track. Some of the music has been rescored for home video. The film's musical score is by John Addison and it is one of the best he has done. The music is jaunty and catchy, enhancing the drama while, without undercutting anything, reminding the viewer that this is Sherlock Holmes, Dr. Watson, and Sigmund Freud, running after criminals.

SEVEN SAMURAI
SEVEN SAMURAI (CAV)

The CAV presentation of Voyager's Criterion Collection edition of Akira Kurosawa's *Seven Samurai* comes on eight sides of four platters. Do consumers want a 203-minute film in CAV? That remains to be seen, but those who do will know that they have acquired a treasure. As Michael Jeck's narration on the second audio track makes clear, the film has virtually no superfluous footage (you don't feel like you've used an entire day watching it the way you do with most epics), and every frame of every shot is worth freezing and studying. Kurosawa's incredibly consistent telephoto shots, putting innumerable activities and faces into sharp focus, the constant awareness of position and relational direction, the clear personalities and ticks of every player, and the environment are all worth drowning in, studying and staring at for days on end. Voyager has also released a CLV version which retains Jeck's talk.

If, that is, one can resist playing the disc without interruption. The film, like the best classic movies, is marvelous fun. It is an adventure with heroic deeds and precisely executed excitement, and it is difficult to stop watching once the story is underway.

Seven Samurai is in black-and-white and was made in Japan in the early fifties. Inevitably the source material appears a bit worn, but the print has no significant faults and is generally inviting. New subtitles have been struck, so that sexual innuendo and off-color curses, so abhorrent to art house patrons in the fifties, can now be savored in the privacy of the home. The subtitles are white, but are always legible. The picture on both versions is the same.

The sound on the CAV disc is monaural and has not been CX-encoded. The CLV disc is digitally encoded, with the lecture on the analog track. The volume may need to be raised a bit for the film, but that is because Kurosawa has utilized many subtle sound effects which can easily slip out of range.

Because of the film's length, Jeck has time to talk about everything. Contrary to the assertion on the jacket insert, Jeck's commentary is continuous. His knowledge is thorough and he is as at ease discussing Kurosawa's camera technique as he is at discussing the economics of the Japanese film industry. If Jeck is remiss at anything, it is perhaps in the concentration on the mechanical elements of the narrative, particularly when the environment is involved. He points out that Kurosawa's use of wind and rain is deliberate, and tells how these occurrences affect the rhythm of the story, but he fails to note that these and other components have specific spiritual meanings that remain consistent throughout Kurosawa's films (e.g., rain is the cleansing of the soul).

THE SEVEN YEAR ITCH

The copy on the jacket of *The Seven Year Itch* describes some tantalizing cuts which were made after the film first opened in New York. If Fox had really been with it, they would have restored those scenes for the disc, but they did not. The film was done in Cinemascope, so you lose close to half of it with cropping, but the colors are genuine and, as with most Billy Wilder films, it has aged well even if the subject material is dated.

The sound is in stereo and contains a few little surprises. The soundtrack is old, but it doesn't sound bad if you don't push it. The movie must have been very inexpensive to make, since it never ventures far from the single set of its stage source material. The story, about a man tempted by his new, free-spirited neighbor, is a Hollywood staple, and it moves briskly and humorously. The famous shot of Monroe's skirt being raised by the burst of air from a subway grating, however, just doesn't work on the TV. And we were disappointed that Fox didn't include that still on the back of the jacket.

1776

No one apparently saw the need to put the simulated stereo sound of *1776* in CX-encoding, but then, when the film first came out, few people saw the need to its having been produced at all. Sort of a cross between 'The Missiles of October' and 'Carousel,' *1776* is a musical about the debate which went into the composition and signing of the Declaration of Independence and about the supposedly frustrating link between creativity and sexual desire. It is rated G.

The film is odd enough to be a cult favorite. It is an adaptation of a Broadway musical and includes more of its origin, such as jokes about New York and New Jersey, than it should have. William Daniels is probably a little more pushy than the real John Adams was, but the authors chose to make him, instead of Thomas Jefferson (Ken Howard), the central protagonist. Much of the action takes place on the edges of the screen, which have been dutifully cropped. The breaks between each of the three sides do not occur at natural pauses.

THE SEVENTH SEAL
THE SEVENTH SEAL (CAV)

Every Fourth of July in the town where we grew up, there is a parade, sponsored by the Junior Chamber of Commerce. When we were very young we despised it, thinking it trite and contrived. As we grew older we developed a cynical appreciation for it, and looked forward to its stupidity – which third-rate TV star would be this year's 'Grand Marshall?' – and amusing incompetence. It was only when we became much older and made peace with ourselves did we accept and enjoy the parade for what it was, a well-intentioned holiday celebration.

We used to have the same trouble with allegory. Like a psalm or a bawdy limerick, the message of an allegory is so obvious that it appears as an assault to a mind which is more appreciative of subtle interpretations and nuance. The trick is to accept such a work without passing judgement, and to appreciate the tale – or any work of art – on the terms with which it has been offered.

Peter Cowie, in his lecture on the second audio track of Voyager's *The Seventh Seal*, says that Ingmar Bergman considered the movie to be nothing more than "a little film I and my friends made one summer." Would that it were true! If that was the spirit in which it was made then it does deserve the praise which has been heaped upon it in subsequent decades. Yet to praise almost any component of *The Seventh Seal* is to invite condemnation from the cynics.

Keeping in mind that the film was made back in the 1950s on a small rocky island in southern Sweden, the print is in very good condition. There are no blemishes or interruptions. The black and white picture is not always perfectly crisp, but one would be hard pressed to identify a specific flaw. The sound is rough. The practice of lowering the volume to remove the hiss when silence occurs on the film – which other disc producers have also employed – is more annoying and distracting than if the soundtrack were just allowed to crackle and pop on its own accord. The rickety noises do not seem out of place with the Middle Ages story locale, and the soundtrack quality is what one has come to expect from movies made by theater groups on small Swedish islands. There are no differences in picture or sound quality on the CAV and CLV presentations.

The film is in Swedish and has English subtitles. The subtitles give one a general summary of the dialog, but do not catch every subtlety, and this can become annoying the more often one watches the movie.

The CAV disc ends with a brief, still frame summary of Bergman's film career (including clips from a couple films). The information about Bergman's movies and career is sparse and superficial. Some production stills are included, identifying the activities which went on behind the camera, but the material is constructed to provide more of an introduction to Bergman's work than a useable reference. Cowie's lecture, which is retained on both versions, is also a bit too introductory for our tastes. Cowie does provide a lot of valuable background information concerning the movie's production and the personalities involved, but he often falls into the trap of describing, in awestruck tones, what one is looking at on the screen.

THE SEVENTH SIGN

'Revelations' has provided the fodder for a number of bad movies. *The Seventh Sign*, with Demi Moore, is one of the better attempts at realizing the Second Coming, maintaining the right balance between the personal and the all-knowing. Thanks to Moore's nervy performance, the movie is also fairly creepy, especially if the house is quiet while you're watching the disc.

The disc has a meticulous stereo surround soundtrack which adds greatly to the entertainment. The picture quality is also good, although the color scheme of the film itself is subdued and uninspiring.

THE SEVENTH VICTIM

Some films refuse to age and one good example is *The Seventh Victim*. Even though the Greenwich Village apartment where the destitute poet is living goes for about $1500 a month these days, the story's mystery and morality have not lost their values to an inflation of graphically depicted eroticism and violence.

There is a shower scene which predates (and probably influenced) *Psycho*. Although the threatening figure on the outside is a woman wearing a hat, the shadow she casts on the shower curtain makes her look like a devil. The ending of the movie is a stunning piece of editing and script writing. In about a minute, a half-dozen subplots are brought to sudden, but totally logical, conclusions.

Despite one or two scratches and a dropout on side one at minute 32, the print is lovely. It will make an admirable addition to any collection and will beckon a viewer often on dark and lonely nights.

THE 7TH VOYAGE OF SINBAD

A typical Ray Harryhausen production, *The 7th Voyage of Sinbad* has a vaguely logical plot which provides an excuse for the animation of a half-dozen imaginative creatures. The score is by Bernard Herrmann and unfortunately RCA/Columbia chose not to have the monaural disc CX-encoded. Scratches on the print mar the opening credits, but otherwise the presentation looks acceptable.

The pace is brisk and although a couple of the creatures were put into the movie by Harryhausen to show off, most, like the cyclops, are well blended into the story. Children, especially, should enjoy it. One situation which has always bothered us, though: How can Bagdad be Sinbad's home port when it is some 300 miles from the nearest ocean?

SEX, LIES AND VIDEOTAPE
(Voyager CAV)
SEX, LIES AND VIDEOTAPE
(Voyager CLV)
SEX, LIES AND VIDEOTAPE
(RCA/Columbia)

If you have a liberal discretionary income, we would have to recommend Voyager's CAV Criterion Collection release of *sex, lies and videotape* over the Voyager CLV Criterion version or the CLV version, which has been released by RCA/Columbia. The supplementary section of the CAV disc adds an extra dimension to the film by focussing on its brilliant but essentially novice creator, Steven Soderbergh.

The Criterion transfer is gorgeous. Closely supervised by the filmmakers, the picture is probably in better condition than any theatrical print which has had more than one play. In comparison, the RCA/Columbia color transfer is good, but it is too dark, and a bit over-saturated. In late afternoon scenes the fleshtones of the characters become slightly too orange on the RCA/Columbia disc, but retain the precise color of sunlight on skin in the Criterion versions.

The Criterion version is mildly letterboxed and the RCA/Columbia version is not. RCA/Columbia crops a little off the sides of the image, but Voyager, to achieve its theatrical rendition, has masked the top and the bottom. Generally, the addition of objects and colors on the sides of the image improves the film, but once you have watched the RCA/Columbia version you become very aware on the Criterion version when the crown of one of the performers is lopped off. Voyager's aspect ratio is about 1.7:1.

The stereo surround sound on the Criterion disc, which was also supervised by the filmmakers, is so close to perfection that it can be used in a query on the differences between digital and analog sound. The digital track is absolutely silent, containing no noise other than what has been placed upon it intentionally. The analog track however, which does have mild background hiss, seems to achieve a greater ambience and sharpness, as if it were producing a more realistic audio than the digital soundtrack. RCA/Columbia's soundtrack is not quite as clearly defined as the Criterion version, but it is adequate, and the analog and digital tracks are fairly similar. Those who don't anticipate how much fun the audio on the film can be, incidentally, are advised to check out the 'tape smashing' scene at the end.

sex, lies and videotape is an enjoyable film about two sisters with opposing personalities, the husband of one having an affair with the other, and a stranger whose video camera hobby upsets the domestic balance in the lives of both sisters. Materials in the supplementary section of the CAV disc demonstrate that the sex talk and sex activity in the story is determinedly trimmed back and subdued. The film is a romance, but its addictive appeal is partially due to the camera setups and cinematography. There is one scene in one of the sisters' apartments where one character – the earthy one – is in a wood brown room and is dressed in warm tones, while the other – the prissy one – is dressed in white and is in a white outer room. The camera frames them so that the brown room is in the center of the image, with the white room enveloping it, and the composition shows not only the dichotomy between the two women, but the 'inner' drive and 'outer' veneer that the characters must cope with.

The supplementary section contains an interview with Soderbergh, a 14-minute short Soderbergh made to upgrade his portfolio previous to doing the film, two trailers, a scene dropped after the first cut, the final shooting script, and a diary kept by Soderbergh during the course of the production. The information in the diary and the script can be obtained in book form, but the other material is exclusive to the CAV disc.

The short film, 'Winston,' is in black-and-white, and concerns a young man whose imagination works against him when he thinks he has a rival for his girlfriend's affections. It is visually stimulating, but nowhere near as relaxed or confident as *sex, lies*. Soderbergh's interviews and his diary will not only help the viewer understand how the film came to exist – and how much of its success can be attributed to the talented cast – the material also brings the viewer, as a confidant, into the creative process. There is a tendency, after listening to or reading some of Soderbergh's commentary, to go running back and relive the scenes, if not the entire film, again. The supplementary section gives you the motivations beneath the narrative, and it fleshes out the characters, their actions, and the consequences. Spending time with the CAV disc will improve the film's pleasures significantly.

SEXY LINGERIE

Attractive underwear is the supposed subject of *Sexy Lingerie*. The video tape footage consists primarily of silent romantic sketches set to music. The picture and sound are passable. The music is mildly stereophonic.

SFX MUSEUM VOL. 1 – TO THE YEAR 2010 RICHARD EDLUND, ASC
(Import)
SFX MUSEUM VOL. 2 – APOGEE & DREAM QUEST: MOTION CONTROL
(Import)
SFX SPECIAL – SPECIAL EFFECTS
(Import)

The *SFX Museum* series, from Japan, is a set of discs that profile different special effects experts and how these technicians work movie magic. *SFX Museum Vol. 2 – Apogee & Dream Quest: Motion Control* highlights the work of two special effects houses (Apogee and Dream Quest).

The discs are in CAV, include still frame segments, and are bilingual, allowing the effects experts to explain what they are doing in English as the Japanese on the second channel is suppressed. Captions used on still frames, unfortunately, are in Japanese only.

The CAV can be put to good use on lengthy clips from such films as *Star Wars*, *Never Say Never Again*, *Battlestar Galactica*,

Starflight One, *Firefox*, *Escape From New York*, *One From the Heart* (the opening credits), *Blue Thunder*, *Buckaroo Banzai*, and many others. With the CAV functions, a viewer can step through the complicated matte process and see how each piece eventually fits into the whole. The clips are shown letterboxed, but not in stereo.

SFX Museum Vol. 1 – To the Year 2010 Richard Edlund, ASC is in much the same format. There are fewer clips on the disc, but the narration (in English, with Japanese subtitles) is informative and thorough. Edlund spends too much time proclaiming that his special effects house is the best – he's welcome to his opinion – but the individual technicians hold up the gizmos they use and give fascinating talks about how each component contributes to what we see on the screen. A still step section features storyboards for *Ghostbusters*, some depicting scenes which were left out of the final film. All the film clips, including a complete trailer for *2010*, are shown in full aspect.

Another volume is identified on the jacket cover as *SFX Special* and on the spine as *Special Effects*. The hour-long disc is unlike the others. It is a dual channel bilingual presentation without a single Japanese subtitle in sight. None of the clips are presented in letterboxed format and the quality of them varies from crisp (*The Empire Strikes Back* and *Blade Runner*) to dark and blurry (*Return of the Jedi*). Instead of being about a single special effects house, the disc summarizes the history of special effects and the scope of current effect techniques. The disc is loaded with chapter markers.

The program opens with clips from the works of the Melies brothers and then goes on to excerpts from *King Kong* before cutting to *The Empire Strikes Back* and today's technologies. The most fascinating sequence reveals how many of the realistic effects in *The Right Stuff* were accomplished. To imitate an out-of-control F-14, the filmmakers tossed a model out of a second story window, like a frisbee.

The last two sections of the program demonstrate sound effects and computer graphics. A sound effects expert takes a 3-second sound clip of a whirring helicopter and, through looping and distortion, turns it into an entire helicopter ride.

SGT. PEPPER'S LONELY HEARTS CLUB BAND

In celebration of the 20th anniversary of the Beatles LP, *Sgt. Pepper's Lonely Hearts Club Band*, MCA released the movie, *Sgt. Pepper's Lonely Hearts Club Band*, on disc. They would have done the world a greater favor and the original work more honor had they fixed themselves a hole and buried every last copy, work print and negative, and then thrown away the shovel.

The Blue Meanie of the piece was the music coordinator, George Martin. Instead of trying to fit the famous songs to the styles of the rock stars who were interpreting them, Martin imposed the same orchestrations he'd used with the Beatles. The disc has 24 chapter markers which cover most of the songs and manage to mark all the low points. Sandy Farina singing 'Here Comes the Sun?' And we always thought the walrus was Paul.

The sound is surround encoded, so there is no escaping it. The picture, although colorful, has enough scratches to indicate that apathy is guiding its preservation. The trailer is included after the movie , but we recommend that when Paul Nicholas intones early on, "I don't really want to stop the show...," you reply, 'No problem,' and hit the eject key.

SHADOW DANCING

About a third of *Shadow Dancing* is taken up with modern dance sequences – ostensibly rehearsals, but dancing nonetheless – choreographed by Tim Spain. The dancing, led by Gregory Osborne of the National Ballet of Canada, is lumpy but satisfying, particularly in the quantity with which it is offered. The drama, however, is a tale of possession which can't get a grip on itself. The filmmakers cheat a little, exaggerating sequences to make situations appear more threatening than they turn out to be. The picture quality is passable and the stereo sound is okay. The plot concerns a young woman who gets a shot at a lead part in a dance program which is premiering in a refurbished theater. Lust and revenge, involving a ballerina, took place in the same location many years ago. Has the dead ballerina come back? Is the vaguely menacing parrot evil or just cantankerous? Don't expect the answers to be as clear or as satisfying as the jetes.

SHADOW OF A DOUBT

Alfred Hitchcock's *Shadow of a Doubt* has little of the show-off type thrills or single-minded manipulations that define most of his work. With a script by Thornton Wilder, the film is one of the few in which Hitchcock is more interested in mood than in plot. By utilizing a relatively large family as characters, the pre-existing emotional dynamics are already in place and do not have to be created as the film unfolds. (Most families in Hitchcock films have very few children – one or two, and if two, they are often separated widely by age. In *Shadow* there are three, fairly evenly spaced.) The film's strength comes from the interplay within the family and the tension that often lurks beneath their cheerful, distracted ennui.

Hitchcock creates a turn-of-the-century mood in what is supposed to be Santa Rosa in the early forties, creating kind of a cross between *Meet Me in St. Louis* and *Blue Velvet*. When one real adult, an uncle predisposed to violence, enters the household, the evil which he represents affects a viewer's attitudes toward the other characters more than the evil he actually commits. There is also one perfectly conceived minor character, a young waitress in a seedy bar, whose entire story is completely drawn with a handful of lines, and who also represents the meeting point between goodness and evil – life as it really is.

The black-and-white picture looks very nice. A re-release trailer has been included after the film is ended, and the difference in the contrast levels on the trailer and on the film is telling. In the trailer, faces are lost in the shadows, but in the movie there is never a doubt about what can be seen. The sound has very little background noise. The print has one major splice and the soundtrack has a couple minor twinges, but everything is just about perfect.

SHAG THE MOVIE

Set in Myrtle Beach, South Carolina, during the early sixties, *Shag The Movie* is a pleasant summer teen film, told, refreshingly, from a female point of view. The four heroines, played by Bridget Fonda, Phoebe Cates, Annabeth Gish, and Page Hannah, sneak off to the beach resort for a final fling in the face of marriage and college, and the adventure rearranges their life priorities. The characterizations are distinctive and the romances are charming. A dance contest figures into the plot peripherally, but the film is essentially much simpler and much better than the ad art implies.

Only the music is in stereo, but the soundtrack contains a number of good, uncommon oldies, and they all sound vibrant. The picture has some grain, particularly when intense colors are involved, but it is passable.

SHAKEDOWN

There are actually some nice touches in *Shakedown*. The stunts are so wild the producers had to put an admonishment at the end warning viewers that the stunts were performed by professionals and should not be attempted at home. Darn – we were just going to run out, get into a Porsche, drive to the airport as a jet plane is warming up, identify immediately the plane we want when we spot it on the runway and race to it during takeoff, climb onto the wheels, set off an explosion to destroy the jet in mid air, and escape unscathed. Well, it looks easy enough when you see Sam Elliott doing it. Elliott's presence, by the way, is another one of the film's advantages. Usually his long flowing locks and gruff appearance prevent him from becoming a believable character, but here, as a cop who has probably been undercover for too long, he fits right in. The film is about police corruption and drug lords and also stars Peter Weller, who portrays that most popular character these days – a distracted public defense attorney who believes his client in spite of himself. But enough of the film is contrived and weakly scripted so that the disc should not be considered unless you have a weakness for this kind of thing. The picture and sound transfers are impeccable.

SHAKER RUN

Even though the star is Cliff Robertson, *Shaker Run* takes place in New Zealand, as the dialog tends to emphasize for about half the movie. The film stock was probably sitting around in New Zealand a while before it got used and it probably got processed there as well. The transfer isn't much better, adding a slight blur which is particularly evident in poorly filmed night scenes. There are some good car stunts, all filmed in an agonizingly disorienting slow motion. The plot has a spectacular finish, but not a true conclusion. Whenever the camera points to the speedometer to show how fast the car is going, the odometer always has the same mileage on it.

SHAMPOO

Although it is usually thought of as a sex comedy, *Shampoo* is actually a frothy, lathered look at the kinks and complications of lives which are in bad need of a trim, set, and perm. It is a midsummer lover's frolic gone astray in a Los Angeles November. One of the most common misconceptions about the movie is that it is some sort of Casanova ego trip for its star, Warren Beatty. If you watch the film closely, or often enough, you will realize that Beatty's character, the amorous hairdresser, is never able to consummate his trysts. He is either interrupted or (by vague implication) impotent every time. So much for prowess. He appears either dense or distracted through most of the story, but each time you start to write him off as an insensitive lout, he comes up with a remark or an expression that shows he is desperately trying to figure out what life is supposed to mean.

The color does not look as if it has faded at all and scratches are kept to a minimum. Those responsible for putting the show together, Hal Ashby, Robert Towne, and even Beatty, later began acting like they'd lost their concepts. The job they did on *Shampoo*, however, will never go out of style.

SHAMUS
As the bid to make Burt Reynolds a star was just getting revved up in the early seventies, he made a detective movie called *Shamus*. It is distinctly a period piece, with loud, gross outfits, free-spirited sexuality, and hip, monaural music, but it does have some redeeming values. For one thing, the hip monaural music by Jerry Goldsmith is constantly squirting out of the edges of its molding. Reynolds' humor is relaxed enough to survive the passage of time unscathed. He doesn't give one of his wink-at-the-audience performances, but he doesn't take his situation too seriously either. His one-liners are still funny even though the plot creaks with age. Dyan Cannon also appears. Although she is wearing the most godawful outfits (Who was dictating our fashions then? Upholstery companies?), she has that wonderful cackling laugh and a relaxed presence which is in perfect synch with Reynolds. Their first 'meet cute' scene is timelessly slick.

The picture is dark and drab, with a seventies realist color scheme that also seems upholstery-inspired. The print appears to be in good condition and more a victim of its time than of the passage of time. The sound is best kept at a reasonable volume. There are a few chapter markers. The plot, which lifts a couple of scenes from *The Big Sleep*, has Reynolds portraying a private detective hired by a wealthy man to retrieve some stolen goods. This is the sort of mystery where a succession of characters tells the detective who, where and how it happened. No intellectual strain, but with Reynolds as the hero, the viewer would never believe it if he thought his way to the conclusion anyway.

SHANGHAI SURPRISE
Madonna portrays a missionary in *Shanghai Surprise*, but this role is more positional than vocational. She meets Sean Penn, an alcoholic tie salesman/adventurer who shouts, "Now I know why cannibals like to barbecue missionaries!" They team up to retrieve opium and jewels from warlord gangsters. As an inspiration to children throughout America, the pair fail in their quest to land the jewels but get away, in the end, with all the opium. Hey, something's going to have to hold their relationship together. "Guns cause pain; opium eases pain," Madonna elucidates at one point.

The picture looks great, but the stereo sound is very hissy. Immortal quotes from bad movies are more valuable than either opium or jewels, and it is almost worth buying the disc to hear her offer Penn dinner, "We can't have you leaving Shanghai without tasting the duck."

SHARON, LOIS, & BRAM (see **RAFFI A YOUNG CHILDREN'S CONCERT WITH RAFFI**)

SHE-DEVIL
Roseanne Barr's performance in *She-Devil* is a failure. It is not that Barr is bad, she's just dull. Her role, that of a victimized wife who wreaks revenge on her estranged husband and his mistress, is so full of potential that it is frustrating to watch her not do anything with it. The picture transfer is fine and the sound is okay.

SHE WORE A YELLOW RIBBON (VidAmerica)
SHE WORE A YELLOW RIBBON (Image)
Originally released by VidAmerica with a, to say the least, tepid print, *She Wore a Yellow Ribbon* was released in much better condition by Image. For some reason Image chose to give the disc an especially ugly jacket cover, but don't let that scare you. The Technicolor print is lovely. Every strata on the pillars in Monument Valley and every shade in the crease of the cavalry uniforms is separately defined. The print is spotless, and is never soft or hazy. The colors are a little light, as are the flesh tones, but the hues are consistently and distinctively defined, and, unlike the VidAmerica disc or most versions of the movie that we catch on TV, the picture enhances the film's entertainment instead of distracting from it. The digital monaural sound is also in decent shape.

The film, directed by John Ford and starring John Wayne, is a recognized classic of the Western genre, for good reason. It tells the story of the final cavalry patrol for a captain, played by Wayne, who is about to retire. The events of the patrol, however, are unimportant, even though it takes up a good portion of the film. The movie shifts gracefully from the concerns of the soldiers to the significance of the indigenous uprisings, and with a little action and a little blarney, places historical perspective, like the strata in the monuments, on a human scale. Although the narrative moves at a decent pace – especially for Ford – it has no extended action sequence. Viewers who have not seen a decent print of the film are not as likely to be seduced by its complacencies. When you can see the richness of the land, then you can better understand why the characters fight so hard to hold what they have taken.

SHEENA
Sometimes parts of a movie can justify the purchase of a whole disc. In *Sheena*, there is one thrilling stereophonic sequence near the end where the evil princess-elect drops Sheena (Tanya Roberts) onto a waterfall from a helicopter. It ends with Sheena slithering down a vine and announcing to her adopted tribe, her hands still bound, "See! Even in chains we can defeat them!"
Sheena, orphaned in the jungle as a child, is an apprentice shaman who communicates to animals telepathically and to humans in curt phrases. Except for a poorly made-up horse who is supposed to be a trained zebra, everyone in the cast gives believable performances and the action is logical and well paced. Behind the phony Vangelis-type score, the film's soundtrack is filled with the requisite chirps and cackles of the jungle and is ideal for disc quality exposition. The movie also makes a big thing out of the hero and the heroine kissing, a lost pleasure which we wouldn't mind seeing more of in today's life-is-like-the-jungle cinema.

SHEENA EASTON
'Telefone,' the first video on the 8-inch *Sheena Easton* disc, makes use of popular horror film characters to represent the anxieties of a woman whose lover will not answer her phone calls. It was a fairly popular video, and rightly so. The last song is a concert rendition of Easton's biggest hit, 'Morning Train.' The cut also appeared on Pioneer' 12-inch, *Sheena Easton – Live at the Palace*.

SHEER HEAVEN
In *Sheer Heaven*, models put on a lingerie show, though the program quickly turns into a topless dancing exercise. The disc runs over an hour and side one is 27 minutes long in CLV. The picture is grainy but tolerable and the monaural sound is okay.

SHENANDOAH
The Technicolor print used for *Shenandoah* is in very nice condition. You can even make out colors in the night scenes. The movie is a passable Civil War effort, if you like Jimmy Stewart. There are a couple of impressive battle sequences and a few moments of high drama amidst the homey, too-cute-to-be-true family scenes. Stewart portrays a farmer who tries to remain neutral as the War rages about his spread. The sound has a decent range for its age. The trailer for *Shenandoah* ("Glenn Corbett, colorful star of 'Route 66'...") appears at the end of the disc, with its own chapter marker.

SHERLOCK HOLMES AND TERROR BY NIGHT
SHERLOCK HOLMES AND THE WOMAN IN GREEN
The 3M Collectible Classics release of *Sherlock Holmes and Terror by Night* has a still from a different movie on the back of the jacket and runs only 30 minutes on each CLV side, but it is a wonderful Sherlock Holmes effort which should not be missed. Basil Rathbone and Nigel Bruce portray Holmes and Watson, on a train from London to Edinburgh to protect a valuable jewel which gets stolen despite their vigilance.

What a joy it is to watch Rathbone fool everyone in the movie and no one in the audience by palming the jewel and replacing it with an imitation. And what a thrill to see the murderer shove Holmes outside the speeding train and lock the door, assuming that one need do no more to dispose of the great detective. It gets better every time you play it.

Also available and almost as entertaining is *Sherlock Holmes and the Woman in Green*. A series of murders plague London and in each instance the victim's little finger has been removed. Is a psychotic on the loose, or is this the fiendish work of someone far more calculating and diabolical? The most delightful moment comes when Holmes confronts an arch nemesis. Wasteful introductory conversation is avoided with the curt acknowledgment that each knows exactly what is on the other's mind. Unfortunately, 3M has allowed the print to contain several disruptive breaks.

SHERLOCK HOLMES AND THE SECRET WEAPON
(see **DRESSED TO KILL**)

SHE'S HAVING A BABY
Both Elizabeth McGovern and Kevin Bacon show a flair for comedy in *She's Having a Baby*, a misleadingly titled John Hughes film about the early phases of marriage. The movie is inconsistent. There is not enough drama in the uneventful plot to support the running time, so a number of gags are thrown in to stretch things out. McGovern and Bacon handle the shifts in mood with surprising adeptness, but the movie never settles on a single path of emotional development, and most viewers will be alienated by its changes in feeling.

The picture is mildly grainy and on some reels the flesh tones look too orange. The stereo mix is wonderful. If you play the disc, don't miss the sequence where coins drop out of Bacon's pocket and roll in a circle on the floor. They pass through every speaker you have, even the ones that aren't connected.

SHIP OF FOOLS
You'll have to turn the volume up if you want to hear *Ship of Fools*. The levels are set unusually low, but it is probably the fault of the film, because Ernest Gold's music and Oscar Werner's big tantrum blasted through our speakers while the rest of the time the cast mumbled intolerably. One of the last big budget dramas to be filmed (appropriately) in black-and-white, *Fools* is a shipboard soap opera about a pre-World War II Atlantic crossing. Although the subplots are meant, through their variety, to have meanings beyond the level of who-is-sleeping-with-whom, a typical episode of 'Love Boat' will have just as much to say on hypocrisy in the human spirit. Of the cast, only Elizabeth Ashley transcends the material. The picture is nearly flawless and the cinematography is striking. You may find yourself content to just look at it even if you can't hear what's going on.

SHIRLEY MACLAINE'S INNER WORK-OUT
We like the idea of exercising with Shirley MacLaine a lot better than exercising with Jane Fonda. You see, with Shirley, you only exercise imaginary parts of your body with imaginary exercises. You don't get sweaty and no nineteen year old can do it better than you.

Shirley MacLaine's Inner Workout is a 70-minute imaginary workout, designed to improve your 'chakra,' imaginary colored marbles near your spine which are always in need of alignment and attentive contemplation. MacLaine, in her best professional-making-a-fast-buck lecture voice, shows where the seven make-believe chakra are located on a mannequin, and which real organs each one is in cahoots with. She then crosses her legs and breathes deeply as the video animation unit takes over, showing successively colored circles pulsating to New Age music.

We can't wait to tell you about side two, but first we should say that the colors are even more blurry than Shirley's factual base and the stereo sound is best kept low, especially so that your neighbors won't hear Shirley advising you about the chakra which controls your private parts.

On side two, MacLaine does another exercise, in which she sits perfectly still for a very long period of time. In this exercise the screen is not interrupted by animation. Virtually the entire side contains one single image, of Shirley sitting there. Now get this. Side two is in CAV! Wow, think of the imaginary interactive possibilities! You have only to contemplate the still frame function and zap, Shirley doesn't move. Or use the triple speed function, and watch her remain perfectly still very quickly. Random access can usurp the entire space/time continuum by arriving at the same Shirley, still still, at any frame. And when it is all over, you can go back to whatever else you were doing, content in the knowledge that these imaginary exercises have made the imaginary portion of your own health as fit as an imaginary fiddle.

SHIRLEY VALENTINE
Some of the jokes in *Shirley Valentine* have been dubbed over with American gags, only the music is in surround and it is louder than anything else though sometimes that is on purpose, some of the characterizations are simplistic, and its exaggerated profile of typical tourists is a cliché, but these complaints are minor and *Shirley Valentine* , is a funny and good feeling movie about a woman who finally breaks out of her shell at forty and decides she prefers living in Greece to being a housewife in London. The script has a number of surprises, and even though after a while one can begin to anticipate them, it is in the same way that one anticipates having a good time. The movie is also very pleasingly sexy. The picture on the disc is mildly grainy, but perfectly acceptable.

SHOCK CORRIDOR
Sam Fuller's *Shock Corridor* is a sober but deeply satirical depiction of a modern asylum, in which the patients are clearly intended to remind one of various American political and social philosophies. The narrative concerns a reporter who has himself committed in order to solve a murder. The closer he comes to the truth, however, the closer he comes to going insane himself. Filmed in Fuller's cigar-in-your-face style, the movie is an intense and memorable experience, and one well worth having on video disc even if repeat viewings are best separated by long periods of distraction.

The CLV disc has digital monaural sound with no significant audio flaws. The black-and-white picture transfer looks terrific. The print has a couple of splices, but the focus is razor sharp and the contrasts are rich. Voyager has dredged up some rarely seen color sequences (travelog-style clips depicting the fantasies of some of the inmates) and has letterboxed the image with a 1.85:1 aspect ratio.

SHOCKER
The side break on *Shocker* pretty much divides the film into two different movies. Side one is vintage Wes Craven, as a young man foresees the crimes of a psychopathic killer in his dreams and then attempts to help the police stop the murders. Side two is more experimental – the spirit of the killer starts jumping from body to body and then through television monitors – and it is much less successful on a visceral level, though one has to admire the risks Craven is taking by expanding his narrative in that manner. The picture transfer is very sharp, though some of the special effects work is shoddy. The Ultra Stereo surround sound has only a few interesting effects and the rock music that pops up on the soundtrack is usually annoying.

SHOGUN ASSASSIN
FUGITIVE SAMURAI
Quite a while ago, MCA released *Shogun Assassin* on disc. The film was a reconstituted and dubbed compilation of the first two or three Japanese 'Sword of Vengeance' films, also known as the 'Baby Cart' pictures because the hero, a banished samurai, pushes his son around the countryside in a makeshift, and rather deadly, wooden pram. We've never seen a copy that didn't have a few speckles, but that never stopped us from enjoying the show. The sound is strong and the picture, although not in widescreen, is bright and colorful. Because of the intelligence behind the original films and the care which went into their bastardization, it is one of our favorite discs.

Fugitive Samurai is a reconstituted and dubbed compilation of a Japanese television remake of the first two or three 'Sword of Vengeance' films. Different actors fill the roles. Many of the shots are exact duplicates of the shots in the original movies, though other camera setups are slightly changed. The violence is a little more subdued, though there is still plenty of blood. The central narrative deals with the story which is summarized briefly during a couple of flashbacks in *Shogun Assassin* – how the samurai, who is known as 'Wolf' or 'Lone Wolf,' lost his position as chief executioner and escaped with his baby son after his wife was assassinated.

The *Fugitive Samurai* disc makes *Shogun Assassin* look like a Criterion Collection offering. The source material used for the movie itself was faded and dull, so the disc never had a chance. The colors are greenish or brownish, and the picture looks fuzzy. The dubbing on *Shogun Assassin* was adept, but the soundtrack concocted for *Fugitive Samurai* is awkward and unfulfilling. The irritating musical score is slightly stereophonic and the digitally encoded sound is no worse than everything else.

The plot mixes complex Machiavellian conspiracies with some good old fashioned stare and slash sword fights. Even in this format, a reworking of a remake, the details which gave the original films such elegance – for example, the association between the little boy and water and between his father and the wind – still trickle through. While not recommended for those who are just getting started with the genre, the disc is a reasonable morsel for those who are starved for the samurai experience.

THE SHOP ON MAIN STREET

The 1965 Czechoslovakian black-and-white film *The Shop on Main Street* tells the story of a man assigned by his brother-in-law to be the 'Aryan Controller' of a sewing shop run by a little old Jewish lady during the Nazi era. The conflict in the man's heart between his desire to protect his own interests and the affection he develops for the old woman leads to tragedy.

The film's strength is in the portrayal of its characters, and it is often humorous. However, when the woman, who has been oblivious to evil throughout the film, finally understands what is happening and uses, for the first time, the word 'pogrom' you can feel the link of horror to previous generations which the word expresses. Even subtitled, it is a chilling moment.

The print is in rough shape, with scratches and other lines evident throughout. The image is soft and even the subtitles are sometimes blurry. The sound is in line with the picture. The film runs a little over two hours and is spread to three sides in CLV.

SHOOT TO KILL

The picture quality of *Shoot To Kill* is so good that every light in a night shot of the Vancouver skyline looks like a glowing bead. The image is consistently sharp and free of blur or grain. The digital stereo sound is also in good condition. There is almost no background noise, and the separations are clear and entertaining.

The film, a thriller, is marvelously exciting and great fun. It stars Sidney Poitier and Tom Berenger, who track a murderer through the North Cascade wilderness. There are a few dramatic freedoms taken – the bad guy doesn't kill the heroine when he ought to – but the plot grabs you with a perfect, crime novel opening, and never lets go.

SHOOT THE PIANO PLAYER

We were surprised to discover that *Shoot the Piano Player* no longer seems out of the ordinary. It is still a strong, entertaining film, which mixes giddy humor with a downbeat tale of romantic disappointment and murder. But it doesn't seem daring in its juxtaposition of emotions, or out of the ordinary in its detachment from its characters. Perhaps that helps to clear the air, because without the distraction which these components once caused, the movie can be recognized as a tight, clearly expressed escapade in the bittersweet alleys of life.

The original black-and-white DyaliScope has been letterboxed, and is raised so that subtitles can appear beneath the picture. A dubbed English soundtrack appears on the second audio channel, while the original French dialog is contained on the primary channel.

Keeping in mind that the film was made in France in 1960, the transfer looks satisfactory. Occasionally the image has a little too much grain, and the vivid contrasts are soft in places. The sound, which has a lot of music, is not CX-encoded or otherwise protected, but it meets expectations. Apathy prevented us from listening to more than a couple of sentences on the English language channel, but the track appeared no worse for wear.

The 84-minute film has been encoded with plenty of chapters and is followed by a trailer for a post-award American release. The disc is CLV throughout. The trailer, which is not letterboxed (and demonstrates how much more fulfilling the wider image can be), is amusing, and it provides a telling lesson on how movies which did not come from Hollywood were once sold. The narrator uses many big words to describe the relatively simple and straightforward plot, emphasizing and praising the movie's sophisticated emotional contrasts. No wonder people used to be intimidated by foreign films. It seems from the trailer that the distributors didn't have the faintest idea what the true affability of the movie was for an audience.

SHORT CIRCUIT

Short Circuit only runs 98 minutes, and the stereo mix has some nice touches. The print appears to have been processed one too many times. As soon as things get a little dark, it looks as if the Pacific fog rolled onto the set. This was the second hit movie in as many years, by the way, to be filmed in Astoria, Oregon (the other was *Goonies*). They make enough of a to-do about the location in the dialog that they ought to be ashamed of themselves for trying to pass a sunset off as a sunrise. The movie has so many jokes that its premise, the protection of a robot who has accidentally achieved consciousness, will live a long time on home video.

SHORT CIRCUIT 2

In *Short Circuit 2* the animated robot arrives in a large US metropolis which is so obviously Toronto, right down to the Ontario license plates, that you wonder why they bother pretending otherwise. A subplot concerning the acquisition of citizenship only makes matters worse. The film is a good 20 minutes too long, but some of the dialog is entertaining. The transfer looks sharp, and the nice stereo sound fares well with digital encoding.

SHOUT AT THE DEVIL

The opening of *Shout at the Devil* looks used and the film is cropped, but after the first twenty minutes or so, the picture improves and is very good. Beyond the opening markings, there are no scratches or other impurities. The colors are bright and vivid, and the focus is sharp. The monaural sound is okay.

The formula adventure film, which stars Roger Moore and Lee Marvin, is designed to appeal to an international audience, which means that it will seem simplistic and vaguely artificial to American viewers. Set during the beginning of World War I in East Africa, it is about two unscrupulous ivory hunters whose pleasure in tormenting the nearby German border outpost backfires when war is declared in Europe. Marvin overacts shamelessly and Moore is hopelessly reserved, but the film has a number of pleasing action sequences and captivating cinematography which is only partially obscured by the cropping. And, if you are in a forgiving mood, even Marvin's antics are appreciable. Side three is in CAV with alternating steady and unsteady still frames. Barbara Parkins also stars.

SHOW BOAT (CAV)
SHOW BOAT (CLV)

James Whale's captivating 1936 interpretation of *Show Boat* has been given the Criterion Collection treatment. Voyager has released two disc versions, a straight forward single platter CLV edition and a CAV edition which is three platters long and includes, among other things, just about all of the 1929 quasi-silent version anyone needs to see.

An alternate audio track lecture has been included on both the CLV and CAV discs. The lecture is given by Miles Krueger, a 'Show Boat' scholar who approaches the film as a component of the stage musical's ongoing history. Krueger is also responsible for the supplemental materials on the CAV disc. He gives Whale a short shift, which is emphasized further in a grouchy interview on the CAV disc with Allan Jones, one of the actors from the film. However, Whale's expressionistic camera work, his control of the background and foreground activities, and, complaints aside, his molding of the largely stage-experienced cast performances for the cinema, makes the film a stunning and memorable piece of entertainment. The other curiosity is Krueger's silence on Paul Robeson. While he gives complete sketches of all the other players, and even goes into great detail when citing the accomplishments of an actor portraying a servant who is seen for less than a minute, he avoids elaborating on Robeson's fascinating career. The odd thing about this is that it is the involvement of Whale and Robeson which makes the film a suitable entry in the Criterion Collection and not simply an asterisk in the history of stage or movie musicals.

Krueger's contribution to both discs, however, cannot be belittled. He provides a very complete summary of the musical's gestation and realization. Although his audio talk tends to slip into superlatives at times, and to state the obvious, he also provides information on everything from the history of show boats and minstrel shows to the qualifications of the cast members. He discusses the changes in the narrative from both the original stage production and from Edna Ferber's novel upon which the stage production was based. His organization of the supplementary section on the CAV disc is refreshing, and a lot of fun to step through.

The source material comes from '35 mm black and white master fine grain composite film elements,' the key word being 'composite.' It shifts in quality with some sequences appearing grainier than others. Although the difference is slight, the image on the CAV disc is a little brighter than the image on the CLV disc. Overall, the black and white film looks and sounds okay, but there is no mistaking its age.

The 110-minute film fits onto two platters on the CAV version, with the third platter dedicated to the supplemental material. The high points of side five, which is in CAV, are the motion sequences. There are extensive excerpts from a 1929 silent film version adapted directly from Ferber's novel and then hastily re-adapted to the suddenly popular stage musical and 'talking film' medium. The best part is the opening sequences in which a real show boat and tow boat, constructed on the Sacramento River, reveal the grandeur Hollywood could create back in the days when labor was cheap. Rare movies of the 1932 stage revival, shot by someone who snuck a home movie camera into the theater, give valuable glimpses of the stage production in action. There is also a choice color documentary, made in the thirties, depicting a real show boat.

Side six is in CLV and has no picture. It does have two and a half hours of audio material – two radio programs and a couple of interviews conducted by Krueger. One radio program is an Orson Welles 'Campbell Soup Hour' compression of Ferber's novel, with Ferber herself reading one of the parts and closing the program with a warning against Fascism. The script is awkwardly put together, but the cast, which includes Margaret Sullavan, Ray Collins, and Helen Morgan, is interesting. A 'Radio Hall of Fame' adaptation of the musical which has much of the film's cast, is more enjoyable. Neither program should be listened to without a healthy break in time from a screening of the film, nor should the two be played back to back. Krueger's principal interview is with Hazel Dawn and Norma Terris, who talk about their experiences in the stage productions. There is, however, a separate five-minute telephone interview with Jones, about the movie and about Whale, which is unusually negative and ends on a particularly nasty remark, followed, without notation, by silence.

SHOWBOAT

The editing in *Showboat* is marvelous. There is the opening number, where the camera, after a lengthy build-up, cuts to the chorus dancing in unison at the front of the boat on a cymbal crash. There are the time passage montages, of a couple falling in love while they kiss during a succession of stage performances and of objects used by a gambler and toys used by the daughter he doesn't know he has which progress in symbolism until they conclude with the gambler's cane, now in the daughter's possession. The narrative, with its great leaps in time, is tricky to hold together without alienating a viewer, and the editing is what makes it succeed.

The bright colors of *Showboat* are preserved on the disc without substantial degradation. The most intense colors quiver a little, and from shot to shot the skin tones change some (the picture is also marked in a few places by a blue stripe one associates with imperfect Technicolor prints), but viewers will have so many colors to absorb they won't miss the ones that got away. The sound transfer is a bit weak, but the songs are adequately chapter encoded.

SHY PEOPLE

Jill Clayburgh is unappealing in *Shy People.* It may be the way her part has been written, as a pushy, naïve New York magazine reporter visiting the Louisiana bayou, but it is also the way she presents it. Good actors and actresses can take unsympathetic parts and still hold an audience under their spell. Clayburgh fails, and the movie sinks with her.

The picture quality and the digitally encoded sound are both good. The 119-minute disc has chapter markers and is spread to three sides. It stars Barbra Hershey, who does a much better job even though her role, as the impoverished subject of the reporter's article, is almost as difficult. The film was directed by Andrei Konchalovsky, who also directed *Runaway Train*, and although *Shy People* is more domestic in structure, it has the same bull-headed emotions and the same disregard for a viewer's sophistication.

THE SICILIAN

We love watching Michael Cimino's movies even though we can't stand them. *The Sicilian* has the same contradictions, though it is better behaved than most. The plot is excellent, but the script is awful. The sound editing is terrific, but sound effects and incidental background conversations are silly. The photography is lovely, but it leaves the actors standing awkwardly in scenes blocked more for photographic effect than for human nature. The stars are appealing, but they can't act worth a damn, though how they could with the script, the camera, the sound, and the direction all working against them is beyond us.

The producers of *The Sicilian* kept Cimino from going over budget, but discovered, to their horror, that he had constructed a movie which ran for longer than two hours. Now this may not seem like such a sin to you or to us, but for people who are trying to sell movies they don't understand, it is an outrage, so they took the film and cut it the way one would cut a pizza one wished to place in a smaller box. Fortunately, home video is not as dependent upon running times for income, so Cimino's original cut has been restored, scraps and all, for home video release. The plot is a stimulating mixture of politics, history, and gangsters – the thesis that an outlaw is a microcosm of the law and that organized crime is no different, conceptually or morally, from other big businesses, is an excellent subject for an action film, since it can tolerate the combination of all the blood, sex, and philosophy an artist can dish out. *The Sicilian* has nowhere near the class of *Once Upon a Time in America* or *The Godfather* pictures, but it shares in the essentials of their appeal.

The picture has been cropped, to the detriment of all involved. The image is usually too grainy, which can be alienating as well. The digital sound is terrific in the lower ranges, but the analog track, although noisier, is also brighter on the upper end.

SID & NANCY

The two lovers in *Sid & Nancy* beat one another, flop around on heroin, and talk nonsense, and yet there is the shadow of truth in every action they have. The music of the Sex Pistols was an illumination, outshining the half-decade of arthritic mush which masqueraded as pop music in the middle seventies. The movie is about the spark and the afterglow, beginning when the Pistols established themselves in England and Nancy met the group's bass player, Sid Vicious, and ending when Sid stabbed Nancy, apparently on request, in a decrepit hotel room in New York. They loved each other, and he made great, never-to-be-repeated music.

The picture is blurry. Several of the songs are not performed by the original artists and they lack the raw power of the originals, as if the movie recordings had been done *too* well. The movie lets you see Sid through Nancy's eyes and Nancy through Sid's eyes and even though you (presumably) aren't as strung out as they are, you can still make out the silhouette of their anarchy.

THE SIEGE OF FIREBASE GLORIA

Some parts of *The Siege of Firebase Gloria* are tiresome and strained – most of the death scenes are stupefying – but other aspects of the film are compelling. About a US military encampment which is almost overrun during the Tet Offensive, the film is saved by the same savvy soldiers who manage to save the base. When they are snapping out orders and making quick, instinctive decisions, they hold your attention. When they have to unwind so the film can break its pace, the entertainment unravels. The disc has a decent picture, flat, monaural sound, and chapter markers. The script offers an interpretation on history, suggesting that the Tet Offensive was intended by the North Vietnamese government not only to throw the US for a loop, but to waste enough VC that thereafter no one would question who was running the show.

SIESTA

Siesta never lets you relax. If you watch the disc, not matter how bad you think the script is, you have to keep watching until the end, or until you figure out that the script is not nearly as bad as it appears. By the end, the film does not become brilliant or anything, just cute, but its cleverness is appreciated. We can't say any more about the Sunbelt romantic thriller without spoiling things.

The Marcus Miller and Miles Davis music sounds terrific on the Ultra Stereo digitally encoded audio track. The picture looks accurate, in heat or in shadows. The quality of the presentation encourages the viewer to stay with the movie through to the end.

SIGNS OF LIFE

A simple drama about several people living in a New England seaport, *Signs of Life*, stars an elderly Arthur Kennedy and Beau Bridges. Specific plot devices include the closing of a boat yard and the near drowning of a retarded boy. The dramatic situations are obvious and the film is only sporadically interesting, but there are some extended night sequences which are beautifully photographed, and the disc's picture transfer renders them admirably. The picture is sharp and colorful. The sound is satisfactory.

SILENT MOVIE

The only full-color silent feature film ever made, Mel Brooks's *Silent Movie* is a one-joke idea, but it's a good joke. Brooks's background in comedy is verbal, not visual, and he misses an easy gag right off by not having Sid Caesar light his double cigars with a double-flame lighter. However, the comical bits and the physical abilities of Marty Feldman and Dom DeLuise are enough to satisfy any demands for light entertainment and good humor.

The analog stereo soundtrack supports John Morris's lengthy, thankless score. The colors are bright and cheap and have survived the video transfer well.

SILENT RUNNING

Now that it has been surpassed by cuter robots and heavier iron, is there still a need for *Silent Running*? Sort of. With Douglas Trumbull's special effects – even the silly stuff such as the passage through 'Saturn's outer ring' – there will always be something which is stimulating to the mind and the imagination. We were surprised to see in the credits that 'Mike Cimino' had a hand in the script, but perhaps that explains why the story seems more sympathetic towards the people who want to destroy the last remnants of Earth's foliage, which has been housed on several gigantic spacecraft, than to the maniac hero who wants to preserve it when the final jettison order comes through. The plot may be silly, but it is science fiction and, what the movie lacks in logic, it compensates with fantasy. The picture looks aged but solid. The monaural sound is passable and there are several low rumbles which shake one's shelving with a satisfying thrust.

SILK STOCKINGS
Nice looking colors, letterboxing with an aspect ratio of about 2.3:1, and occasional separation effects is how Silk Stockings is really presented, contrary to the marvelous film collector anthem, stereophonic sound, which Fred Astaire and Janis Page sing therein ("Glorious Technicolor, breathtaking Cinemascope, and 'Stereophonic Sound.'") Nevertheless, the movie, which is an MGM/UA Deluxe Letter-Box Edition release, is improved significantly by the fine transfer. The musical is short on plot and long on song and dance numbers which don't advance the narrative, but the disc looks so sharp that the viewer is not alienated by the slower moments. The show is also a barely disguised stage vehicle. Letterboxing makes that aspect more forthright and easier to accept.

The film has a subdued color scheme. Even the Paris sets are contrasted to the Moscow sets with improved texture instead of brightness. The colors look solid on the disc, with only the faintest haze hovering around strong blues. The sound, as we indicated, has limited stereophonic effects, but distortion is minimal and the songs, to use Astaire's vernacular, sound swell. Because of the near to two hour running time, the side break is forced to interrupt a gag.

The songs are by Cole Porter and most are intoxicating. The story, adapted from *Ninotchka*, is about Russians sent to Paris on a trade mission and seduced by the perks of capitalism. Astaire and Cyd Charisse tend not to dance together (they even appear to have separate choreographers, according to the screen credits), but they are heavenly when in motion, even if they are dancing with chairs or undergarments. After you get to know the movie, the jokes work even when they don't work, and the film becomes one more cherished MGM musical of the sort which is not made any more. The disc, at least, assures that it will not be forgotten.

SILVERADO
The joy of *Silverado* is that it is probably the only time this cast of contemporary actors is ever going to appear in a Western. It's fun to see them in their beards, playing cowboys, and if the plot seems to take all of side one just to get started (it's a three-sided disc), it hardly seems to matter. The RCA/Columbia release has a terrific stereo soundtrack. When dogs start barking faintly in the background, your neighbor's pets may pitch in as well. The picture is also nice looking but it is not in widescreen.

SINBAD OF THE SEVEN SEAS
Lou Ferrigno's dialog is dubbed in *Sinbad of the Seven Seas* but then again, so is everyone else's. The inexpensive looking film uses voice over narration to zip the plot from one situation to the next. The picture is mildly grainy, but the film is actually too glossy – the sets might have been more convincing if the image weren't so vivid. The sound is irritating and best left unamplified.

The story has the hero retrieving several jewels to break an evil spell, but the nature of the cheap sets and contrived special effects prevent all but the very young from feeling any sense of adventure or chivalry. The filmmakers have the audacity to claim that the movie is based upon Edgar Allan Poe's 'The Thousand-and-Second Tale of Scheherazade,' although they fail to provide even a single allusion to that delightful stylistic exercise. May their fate be the same as Poe's Scheherazade, who, at the end, is finally and permanently dispatched by her fed-up husband.

SINBAD THE SAILOR
The glories of Technicolor are in full display on *Sinbad the Sailor*. The picture transfer is gorgeous, and the colors of the film itself are exquisite. The film was made almost entirely in a studio, but the waters in the 'sea' tank change shades of blue just as they would on a real ocean. Some of the brightest reds and purples look a bit soft, but otherwise the image is sharp and free of distortion.

Sinbad is an extremely talky and stage-bound adventure film from the late Forties, starring Douglas Fairbanks, Jr., Anthony Quinn, and Maureen O'Hara. There are a number of fight and chase stunts, but fthe dialog never uses one sentence when three longer ones will do, and the action scenes are too broken apart by conversations to achieve any momentum. The sets are dressed no more elaborately than the average *Star Trek* episode, but the costumes have some flourish, and every object which is included, foreground or background, is enlivened by the color. The monaural sound also has luster, and is worth over-amplifying, despite its age.

SINCERELY CHARLOTTE
Isabelle Huppert portrays a woman on the lam from a murder she may or may not have committed in *Sincerely Charlotte*. (You find out near the end, but it has little to do with the plot.) She enlists the assistance of a former lover and they rekindle their romance in the freedom of the French countryside. The film is in French with pale yellow English subtitles. The transfer is very good, with only a few, nearly invisible scratches on the picture, and the sound is fine.

SING
An amalgamated throwback of every decade imaginable, *Sing* has music video dreams from the eighties, disco-style dancing from the seventies, gooey social concerns from the sixties, street toughs from the fifties, let's-put-on-a-show enthusiasms from the forties, replacing-the-star-at-the-last-minute heroics from the thirties, and a weaving of Black and Jewish cultures into a single musical idiom, a la the twenties. When they all come together in the finale it is entertaining, but in the bits and pieces leading up to it, the film is somewhat juvenile. The plot concerns a final concert given by the student body at an inner city high school which is being closed, and how a teacher, by holding his parole over his head, inspires a near-dropout to become an ace musical director.

The picture transfer looks sharp and the colors are solid. The stereo surround sound is nicely executed, particularly during makeshift choral passages.

SINGIN' IN THE RAIN (Voyager CLV)
SINGIN' IN THE RAIN (Voyager CAV)
SINGIN' IN THE RAIN (MGM/UA)
Voyager's Criterion Collection *Singin' in the Rain* was transferred from 'MGM's 35mm archival negative,' an Eastmancolor iteration of the original Technicolor source. The same negative was used to master MGM/UA's CLV disc, and problems remain with the skin tones, which seem to change hue from one reel to the next. The difference in the quality of the picture between the Voyager disc and MGM/UA's disc is worth noting. Voyager's disc has a sharper image and a superior consistency in tone which is commensurate with the effort that goes into a Criterion title. The sound is also cleaner. But the image on the Criterion disc has been made to appear very light, so that every background detail is clearly apparent. There are no picture or sound quality differences between the two Voyager presentations.

Ron Haver's alternate audio track lecture, which is present only on the Voyager CAV disc, is relaxed and informative. Haver provides tidbits about the film's production and how the script compares to the actual experience it depicts – Hollywood's transition from silent to sound motion pictures. We were happy to hear him settle once and for all the controversy surrounding the note-for-note similarity of 'Make 'Em Laugh' and its antecedent, 'Be a Clown,' and, in a corollary, provide perfect capsule descriptions of the personalities of Irving Berlin (who got very upset even though it wasn't his song) and Cole Porter (who couldn't have cared less). The biggest gap in Haver's information is a clear delineation of how the directorial chores were spread between Gene Kelly and Stanley Donen, who shared the screen credit.

Because of the way the CAV disc is laid out, the big 'Broadway Melody' production number is interrupted by the end of side three, but it has sensibly been interrupted at a reel change point, so the distraction is kept to a minimum. Every viewer will have different preferences with the CAV functions, but Haver identifies one utilization that will tempt everyone, capturing a surprise appearance by Lana Turner.

The supplementary material on the CAV disc is enjoyable, but limited in scope. Three excerpts from other MGM musicals, which used songs from the score previous to their inclusion in *Singin' in the Rain*, are shown, along with a quick replay of the appropriate number in *Rain*. It is a shame they didn't have room to show every movie – there must be at least a dozen, from *Babes in Arms* to *Alien* – which has ever used 'You Are My Lucky Star.' There is also a 1926 'talking picture' demonstration, and one outtake, really, showing a stunt man flubbing a couple of attempts to leap from a trolley into a convertible. The most frustrating inclusion is the original theatrical trailer – frustrating, because of MGM's stupidity in their initial handling of the film. The lengthy discussion of the need to put sound into movies is shown almost in its entirety, and then Jean Hagen's hysterical punchline, which would have doubled the audience for the picture, is left out.

By the way, if for some reason you have never seen *Singin' in the Rain* before, you ought to. There is so little in life that is so irresponsibly fun.

SIOUXSIE AND THE BANSHEES

Siouxsie and the Banshees is our idea of a rock group. Their unique sound, with a hard, yet laconic rhythm, is part pressure cooker and part burnout. What other group could turn 'Helter Skelter' into a slow dance song?

How could the managers of the delicate Royal Albert Hall ever let such riff-raff have the run of the place? It makes one cringe, but that is where Siouxsie's hour-long concert video was filmed. The picture is a little hazy and thin horizontal lines occasionally appear on the source material, but it is well within the realm of acceptability. The group uses a number of interesting stage lighting effects which are captured effectively on the disc. One in particular, a dark emerald light, we do not recall ever having seen before. The stereo sound is also good, and captures the concert performance without losing the music's essentials.

SIOUXSIE AND THE BANSHEES – ONCE UPON A TIME (Import)

The Japanese 8-inch, *Siouxsie and the Banshees – Once Upon a Time*, contains 31 minutes of music – nine numbers. The videos all have different styles, though none wander too far from depicting a performance using distorting video effects. The lead singer, Siouxsie-Sioux, dances as if one foot were nailed to the stage, and has chalkboard hair. They give themselves away in 'Playground Twist' when a group of children playfully tackle Miss Sioux. She may pretend that she is a screaming tough from another planet but it is clear that she is actually a nice person. The disc also features 'Hong Kong Garden,' 'The Staircase,' 'Happy House,' 'Christine,' 'Red Light,' 'Israel,' 'Spellbound,' and 'Arabian Knights.' A lyric sheet, in English, is included with the disc.

SIROCCO

Humphrey Bogart runs around the Middle East in a trench coat again in *Sirocco*, but it doesn't do him much good. The script not only casts him as an arms dealer, but fails to create a single morally defensible character. Set in Syria, the French occupying forces are oppressive, the Syrians are all terrorists, and Bogart's character, in the middle, is just there to make a profit from the situation. The film is not sophisticated enough to search for truths in the milieu it has constructed, but it is not entertaining enough to do anything else. The only viewers we would recommend *Sirocco* to are Bogart fans in need of feeding a strong depression.

The disc has a sharp looking black-and-white picture that is shiny and generally undamaged. The sound is also acceptable.

SISTER, SISTER

Sister Sister, is what we would call 'Neo Southern Gothic.' Set on a mansion in the Louisiana bayou (conveniently cut off from civilization by a flood), the plot has more twists than a cypress root. It is a murder thriller, and is well executed by an inspired cast which includes Judith Ivey and Eric Stoltz. One character, however, is subject to hallucinations, so how much of the narrative is just a figment of her imagination is impossible to say.

The Ultra-Stereo soundtrack is digitally encoded and quite entertaining. The picture is bright, but the cropped image spoils more than one scary moment, and takes the edge off the tension.

THE SISTERHOOD

The actresses in *The Sisterhood* are supposed to be playing fierce Amazon warriors, but they are so inept at swordplay that the stunt men they are fighting have to pause to give the women enough time to lift their swords and swing. It is a good thing they have magical powers, or they'd never get anywhere.

Lynn-Holly Johnson stars in the post-apocalyptic tale in which all women, except the aforementioned, are the property of men. Everybody rides through the dusty landscape in used cars and fights with swords. The movie is only 75 minutes long and the ending has the financial smell of a script's finale being tossed away for a two-page clean up, but most of it is good fun.

The sound recording is pretty bad (and the music score is worse), making the sound difficult to hear at times. The picture transfer, however, is decent, even though the print has scratches on it. Side two is less than thirty minutes long, but the disc is in CLV.

SIXTEEN CANDLES

If you turned off your television and just listened to the soundtrack, *Sixteen Candles* would still be funny. The dialog is letter perfect and delivered with instinctive naturalness. "I just thought that turning 16 would be so major that I'd wake up with an improved mental state that would show on my face," announces Molly Ringwald's character in the beginning. Instead, her family forgets that it is her birthday and her only suitor is a blond-headed waif with an ego the size of a school bus.

Sixteen Candles has a few of the crazy-teenagers-coming-of-age elements, but it is more like *Risky Business* in its approach, undercutting the frivolity with a cynical view of the values held by the young. Unlike *Risky Business* though, the cynicism in *Sixteen Candles* is light and natural and disappears in a puff when the right boy comes along.

The picture and sound are fine.

16 DAYS OF GLORY

Every four years somebody makes a movie about the Olympics. Usually the movies are well-produced, providing established film-makers with a chance to test their skills at recording sporting events.

The record of the 1984 Los Angeles Olympics, *16 Days of Glory*, focuses on a few oddball competitions, emphasizes the personality of the athletes, and contains some of the most overwrought narration since the *Victory at Sea* discs. They open the section on Michel 'The Albatross' Gross with footage of an albatross and a description of the bird's massive wingspan. The movie does not even cover all sixteen days and its presentation of women athletes is an abomination. They don't show up on the 145-minute disc until side three.

The music is in stereo. The narration is one voice which stays in the middle. The picture is a little foggy. The film has some redeeming moments, such as when the over-the-hill swimmer beats a younger rival in a sprint, out of sheer force of experience. It also has endless footage of the opening and closing ceremonies and chapter markers delineating the competitions. All eight of them.

'68

'68 is about an Hungarian family struggling to keep a restaurant going in San Francisco during the watershed year that began in idealistic euphoria and ended in reticent sobriety. The film looks like it was financed with tips, and the disc is also in pretty bad shape, with the colors and image details sometimes being harder to make out than the fine print on a faded psychedelic poster. The sound is monaural and is in analog with CX-encoding. Despite a number of era hits, the soundtrack is on the level with the rest of the film's production budget. The disc has been encoded with a single chapter marker throughout. Yet, despite the film's faults, the characters (including a cameo appearance by Neil Young as a cycle shop owner) are more believable than in many big budgeted movies and the plot, although easygoing, is difficult to put down. You're not only interested in what is going to happen next to the characters, you're also wondering what will happen next to the nation.

SKIN DEEP

Skin Deep has one outrageous idea (though it might work even better on the stage) – glow-in-the-dark condoms. That is good for a few laughs, but the rest of the story, about a drunk middle-aged man who worries about his sex drive, it can't sustain all 100 minutes. The sound is in stereo, but the surround effects are minimal. The print is extremely grainy and is cropped.

SLAMMER GIRLS

Parts of *Slammer Girls* are reminiscent of Woody Allen's *Take the Money and Run*, while other parts are direct steals. The movie, a women's prison comedy, has a few clever gags (the Governor of the state is campaigning for the Death Penalty because he secretly owns an electric chair company) and many, many dumb gags (we won't go into it).

The monaural sound has a reasonably decent mix. Several seconds of footage which ended the first side are repeated at the opening of the second side. Side two runs less than 30 minutes, but is in CLV. The picture transfer is well done and the print has obviously not had much use.

SLAPSTICK OF ANOTHER KIND

For an author with a reputation of being whimsical, Kurt Vonnegut can be awfully cruel to his characters and, by extension, to the general public. *Slapstick of Another Kind*, Steven Paul's adaptation of Vonnegut's *Slapstick*, is an ugly, unfunny comedy that is painful to watch. Starring Jerry Lewis and Madeline Kahn in double roles, and featuring Marty Feldman, children might find the antics amusing, but few others will have the patience for it. Lewis and Kahn portray the parents of twins who were actually conceived by beings from outer space. They also portray the twins, with bulbous noses, large foreheads, and nasal voices. The picture is grainy and the sound is weak.

SLAUGHTERHOUSE-FIVE

Slaughterhouse-Five disguises a meanspirited contempt for humanity with the imposition of coy whimsy. We can't understand why Holly Near, who plays the hero's wife, would cooperate with such an unsympathetic, or how Kurt Vonnegut could get away with such an artificial narrative, but Vonnegut's story and George Roy Hill's film adaptation continue to be considered classics by many.

The picture on the disc is in good condition and the plot is jumbled around enough (and edited by Dede Allen) to prevent one's concentration from wandering. The music is by Glenn Gould! Even in monaural, it floats out of one's speakers like one of Vonnegut's ethereal spheres. The film's trailer has been included at disc's end, and it is an interesting example of how tough selling a movie can sometimes get. "He survived the deadliest day on Earth to enjoy the sexiest night in outer space," says the jacket cover. The story is actually about a man who has had a nervous breakdown, mixing gobs of memory and wish fulfillment in his own head. Try selling that to a potential audience and you, too, would opt for war, sex, and outer space.

SLAVES OF NEW YORK

Thirty seconds into *Slaves of New York*, as the heroine struggles with two grocery bags and a dog, it is obvious that the Merchant/Ivory production is not a significant accomplishment. The film, based upon a group of open ended short stories, is lackadaisical and numbing. *Slaves* stars Bernadette Peters and is about the avant garde art scene in New York City, and about how monogamous relationships are so hard to come by. It is never clear when the filmmakers are making fun of the milieu and when they are glamorizing it, though even in reality it is often difficult to separate the two. It is possible to enjoy the movie – we did – but you have to be completely prepared for its mediocrity at the outset.

The disc is not exceptional, either. The stereo sound has only a few significant surround effects. The picture is passable, but mildly grainy at times. Side three of the 121-minute disc is in CAV with two unsteady still frames out of every five. The movie's one acknowledgement to the avant garde, occasional split screen sequences, fit well on the TV image and are coordinated with dialog channel separations.

SLEEPER (CBS/Fox)
SLEEPER (MGM/UA)

MGM/UA has put a chapter marker on *Sleeper* for practically every gag. It's great, and we wish all the home video companies could be so enthusiastic. The picture transfer is passable, but the disc does not look as nice as the CBS/Fox version. Although the CBS/Fox disc has a few speckles, the colors are solid and the fleshtones are accurate. The colors are blurry on the MGM/UA disc and the fleshtones often look too pink. The CX-encoded monaural sound is better on the MGM/UA disc, but the difference is minor (the CBS/Fox version has manual CX-encoding which is best left off). The side break on the CBS/Fox disc is ideal, occurring immediately after a punchline. The side break on the MGM/UA disc does not enhance a joke and contains a curiosity – a closeup shot of a video communications screen has been removed, and the sound for the shot and the shot after it is extended into an artificial fade-to-black. As for Woody Allen's movie, about a health food store owner who wakes up 200 years into the future, the topical humor is already fading away, but his slapstick will last forever.

SLEEPING BEAUTY
(see **FAERIE TALE THEATRE**)

SLEEPING BEAUTY
SLEEPING BEAUTY (CAV)

Walt Disney's *Sleeping Beauty* has a rich dynamic range of sounds which would lose both power and delicacy if it were not stereophonic. You are apt to notice the playful separation effects, but since the program is a cartoon, you don't mind. It is fun to listen to the Tchaikovsky score, because it gets the same treatment as the characters and special effects. The first clarinet and second clarinet come out of the left and right speakers separately, a mixing trick no self-respecting symphonic recording would dare attempt.

Sleeping Beauty was filmed in Technirama, which has a more rectangular aspect ratio than one's TV set. Many of the shots show the characters dwarfed by their environment, a composition which is most stunning on a larger canvas than television. The scanning and cropping is harmful to the cartoon because there are so few moving cels. Anything which subtracts from the overall impact of the image makes the production look that much less expensive.

The colors on the disc are wonderful. Sleeping Beauty's rose red lips never appear smeared. The tiniest touches and the broadest swathes of color are never distorted. The transfers on the CLV and CAV presentations are identical. The break between sides on the CLV disc upsets a running gag about the color of a gown and should have occurred two minutes later. Although the breaks on the CAV disc come in different places, they, too, are ill chosen. Both breaks interrupt the narrative in the middle of a beat and could easily have occurred a few minutes earlier or later at a less disruptive moment. Only the CAV disc has been chapter encoded.

As with the other CAV cartoons, the faster speeds increase the intensity of the images and collate storyboarding techniques. Since the film is a product of the Disney factory, and one can spend hours savoring every still (all of the frames are steady). The disc has 18 chapter markers. The colors, conveyed accurately by the disc, are rich, and the drawings project a fairytale feeling. In still frame mode you can examine the artistic compromises which the budget enforced. In some shots of the forest, the trees in the background are left with square tops in place of rounded ones.

THE SLEEPING CAR

Two attractive performers, James Naughton and Judi Aronson, make *The Sleeping Car* slightly more enjoyable than the average cheap horror effort. Kevin McCarthy also gets into the act. The story is about a haunted railroad car that has been converted to a living space for unsuspecting college students. The couch eats most of them. The premise may be dumb, but the filmmakers execute it reasonably well. The source material has a couple scratches, but the color transfer looks okay. The monaural sound also gets by.

SLEUTH

Side three of the 139-minute *Sleuth* is in CAV, and the advantage, after savoring the film itself, is to replay at fast speed the final scene where Laurence Olivier frantically searches the manor for incriminating clues as Michael Caine stands about, gloating. The rapid movement magnifies Olivier's arched eyebrow and Caine's wicked grin. With Olivier, particularly, you can begin to separate his artifice – all the little tricks he pulls while stealing a scene – from his acting.

The still frames on side three are steady three out of every five. Every reel change brings a flurry of scratches and dots. In two places the dialog is disrupted by splices. The sound is CX-encoded, but the film was made way back in the primitive 1970s, before hi-fidelity recording was standard operating procedure. John Addison seems to have a knack for scoring crime adventures with lighthearted patter, and his music in *Sleuth* adds enjoyment to the film.

SLIPPING INTO DARKNESS

'More Than Skin Deep' was the working title of *Slipping into Darkness*, and it is an appropriate description of the film. The movie is a murder and revenge exploitation thriller, but the director, Eleanor Gaver, studiously avoids the normal clichés. The script consistently waits for the very last minute to give the viewer information necessary for understanding what is going on.

A young boy is killed in a quasi-accident. His brother and two friends pick up the three college girls they think are responsible and take them for a joy ride which inevitably leads to murder. The six, however, remain on remarkably friendly terms, even after things get rough. Gaver proves that formula films can accommodate real explorations of character and use shallow emotions to examine complicated value judgements. The emotional make-up of the six principal characters and the performances of the cast members are more complex than the vegetables filmmakers usually plant in such roles. The film tricks the viewer into remaining attentive, because the action continually shifts focus and characters continually shift moral positions.

Except for the music the sound is flat and lacks energy. The picture transfer is nice, and has no major faults.

SLIPSTREAM
SLIPSTREAM (Import)

Slipstream has been released in Japan in letterboxed format with an aspect ratio of about 1.66:1. However, the cropped picture transfer on the Image disc is far superior to the orange and yellow Japanese version, and the movie is, ultimately, not important enough to be concerned about its edges.

Which is not to say that the film, a post-holocaust science fiction piece about a land where gliders are a primary form of transportation due to an eternal wind and where an android is being hunted by a vicious law officer, does not have value. Sitting through it twice in succession, we were impressed by the number of ideas the script writers managed to slip into the narrative, by the film's romantic aspects, and by several action sequences which have a big budget look to them. The stereo surround musical score, by Elmer Bernstein, also has some flourish.

The import has Japanese subtitles on the picture. The image is truly letterboxed, because the sound boom still appears at the top of the screen in one shot, and the sides provide just enough extra space to prevent characters from talking off screen. The most rapidly edited sequences are also easier to follow. Image's presentation, however, is legitimate, even though the film's own production standards waver from time to time. The running times on both discs are identical. Early copies of the domestic version had difficulty playing on some players, though the problem was later corrected.

SLUGGER'S WIFE

A cute little visual pun opens up Hal Ashby's *The Slugger's Wife*. A professional baseball player, Michael O'Keefe, tries to pick up an attractive singer over the course of several evenings and the film cuts to his slump in the batter's box to show that he's striking out. But then, it turns out that this is what the *whole movie* is about. He even marries the woman, but their relationship remains as shaky as his ball playing. In the end he breaks a (baseball) record and she cuts a record (album).

The cinematography, which comes out very grainy on the disc, is exciting. The CX-encoded sound is full of very nice touches, including a baseball that bounces off to the left. A good hitter is successful a little more than once in every three tries and a bad hitter is successful a little less than once in three. This movie falls somewhere in between.

SLUGS

The sound quality on *Slugs* is so poor that any hope of relaxing and enjoying the film, however gross and silly it may be, is defeated. (There is one marvelously icky sequence where a young naked couple arise from their bed of lust and begin slipping and sliding...) The audio track has no upper range at all, so dialog can only be heard if the volume is raised to abnormal levels. But when the volume is raised, the intermittent music track blasts through. One is forever lowering the volume after the music is finished, and then raising it again, right before it plays. The picture is grainy and has a streaking which looks as if the title characters had crawled across the screen.

SLUMBER PARTY MASSACRE II

Proof that the slasher genre has run its course – if any were needed – is readily available in *Slumber Party Massacre II*. The killer talks to the audience, wields an electric guitar/drill, and dances to rock music as he chases his nubile victims. The filmmakers do not care what is a dream sequence and what is not. In fact, they don't seem to care about much at all except for making sure that the products for which the filmmakers received payment to promote are in the shots and that no one misses the parallel between the drill and a phallus. It is supposed to be funny, but viewers will require patience, not a sense of humor, to stay with it to the end. Those who do are rewarded with the end credit scroll (not a minute to soon) and the fine print on the Copyright notice which threatens anyone duplicating the program with 'a midnight visit from the Driller Killer.' Ha ha ha.

The sound and the picture indicate that the movie was not made with a lot of money – Black & Decker must have turned them down – but it evidently has been transferred to disc as well as can be expected.

SMITHEREENS

Susan Seidelman's first film, *Smithereens*, is more slapdash than her later work, but it displays the same confidence in characterization which makes all her movies so enjoyable. The image may be grainier than hidden police cameras and the sound may be on the rough side, but the people are so real and so funny that all is easily forgiven. The story is about a young woman bouncing aimlessly between two men in lower Manhattan. One of the men is a musician, staying at a friend's loft. The other lives in a van on an empty lot. The film has the same class of furniture one keeps in one's garage, but it also has the same funk.

Because of the shoestring nature of the production, it is difficult to judge the transfer as an inhibiting factor, but we did spot the tail end of the leader at the beginning of the second reel. The sound is monaural and is digitally encoded. Image has included chapter markers for some of the music cues, but has ignored others.

SMITHSONIAN LASERDISC COLLECTION:
INSECTS
DINOSAURS
GEMS AND MINERALS
THE NATIONAL ZOO
THE FLYING MACHINES
FIRST LADIES

Lumivision has released a selection of short documentaries produced by the Smithsonian Institution, which use the Smithsonian collections as subject material. The documentaries work surprisingly well. At first, one is put off by the glossy video image and the seemingly limited scope of the production, but the programs are crammed with information and tempered by pleasant, neighborly interviews with museum staff members and scientists. The knowledge provided ranges from basic scientific concepts to intriguing trivia.

The six discs in the *Smithsonian Laserdisc Collection* are all formatted in CAV. The utility of the standard play encoding is questionable. Because of the video tape source material, still images involving movement are blurry. The picture transfers range from super sharp (*National Zoo* and *Insects*) to mildly blurry (*Gems and Minerals*). Generally they are fine and support the viewing of minute details on a number of varied objects. The sound is in decent shape, and there is usually a pleasant background score. Most of the programs last about an hour and all have been chapter encoded.

It is also worth noting that the programs seem to contain a hidden agenda, emphasizing and selling the Smithsonian as an active participant in world research programs, combatting the Institution's common image as 'the nation's attic.'

Insects, subtitled 'The Little Things That Run the World,' explains the various services which the Smithsonian Institution provides with its huge bug collection, and also discusses the evolution of insects and the standard, but fascinating, details on various insect functions. Footage of insects eating trees, eating each other, and participating in social activities are included. Like most of the programs, the show touches lightly on a number of different topics, but manages to communicate a lot of information in a short period of time.

What *Insects* does for insects, *Dinosaurs*, subtitled 'Fantastic Creatures That Ruled the Earth,' does for dinosaurs. In the place of live footage, there are artistic renderings of the beasts, and there is also a sequence on fossil hunting in the field, but the format of the two programs is surprisingly similar. The latest theories and counter theories on how the dinosaurs expired are explained simply and clearly, and the program is an excellent starting point for anyone who wants to separate dinosaur fact from dinosaur fiction.

Although a bit disorganized, *Gems and Minerals*, subtitled 'The Ultimate Rock Video,' manages to cover a lot of territory in 45 minutes. The subject material ranges from the appeal of finely cut jewelry to hunting for meteors in Antarctica. Some of the visuals are hokey – actors dressed in costumes model the jewelry at one point – but the narrator continuously reels off a mixture of data and stories about the gems, and you can't help but absorb a good portion of it. Minerals are treated in a more serious fashion, though what a 'mineral' is never is adequately explained.

The voiceover narration in *The National Zoo*, which is subtitled 'The Zoo Behind the Zoo,' is constructed as a conversation between a child and an adult. The program is more designed for children's viewing than the others are, although it still covers the preservation and research programs which seem to guide the Zoo's organization. The program mixes exotic animals with a look behind the scenes. It not only covers tasks such as keeping certain animals fed, but shows how the Zoo intends to prevent them from becoming extinct as a species. In terms of raw information, however, the program has less to offer than the others do.

The producers do an exceptional job of labeling all the aircraft appearing in old film clips on *The Flying Machines*, subtitled 'Preserving the Machines That Enabled Us to Fly.' The program gives a rich, thumbnail history of flight, and also details how the Smithsonian is actively preserving aircraft. The show is loaded with great photos and clips, making the presence of the CAV encoding the most advantageous in the series.

Finally, there is *First Ladies*, subtitled 'Symbols for a Nation.' First Ladies, according to the program, fall into three different categories, the 'Martha Washington' type, the 'Abigail Adams' type, and the 'Dolly Madison' type. Jackie Kennedy was a 'Dolly Madison.' Rosalyn Carter was an 'Abigail Adams.' Barbara Bush is a 'Martha Washington.' Anyway, some famous First Ladies of the past are adeptly profiled, and those still living are gracefully puffed. A few are even interviewed. To assure us that the Smithsonian is on top of things, the science of preserving 'Inaugural Ball' gowns is intricately detailed.

SMOOTH TALK

The soundtrack in *Smooth Talk* is not in stereo, but it comes off the disc as being the next best thing. You hear the summer crickets and the cars zooming past on the highway and the James Taylor music and it all seems to be proportioned correctly to what you are seeing on the screen.

The picture is a bit grainy, but the movie was filmed in a sort of lyrical blur, so the faults of the disc are well-disguised. About a summer in Sebastapol/Santa Rosa when a young girl looses her virginity, the plot is so well-structured that you can admire the quality of the acting without losing your belief in the characters. It is the acting that you remember – Laura Dern's constant fluctuations, Treat Williams's heavy monologue near the end – and it is the acting that will encourage multiple viewings.

SNOOPY COME HOME
(See **ROBIN HOOD**)

SNOW WHITE
(see **FAERIE TALE THEATRE**)

SO WELL REMEMBERED

The source material varies on *So Well Remembered* in quality, shifting in levels of sharpness, cleanliness, and contrast. The sound also crackles a bit. Side one runs several seconds over an hour, but the break creates the ideal intermission point.

Avoid reading the jacket text as it gives away several plot points without telling what the movie is really about. The film, based upon a James Hilton novel (and narrated in a somewhat unprofessional manner by Hilton) is set in a small English town before and during World War II. The central story is about a newspaper editor and the woman he marries, but the plot also reaches out in a soap opera manner to involve the romantic lives of several other characters. The film is about love, politics, and sincerity, and it uses a wide time frame to make the characters represent greater social truths. Like most of Hilton's creations, it is earnest and sappy, but it is the soap opera trappings which you remember later on, while the messages work on your subconscious.

SOLARBABIES

Filmed in a gravel pit somewhere, *Solarbabies* is a post-apocalyptic fable which is best suited for those whose age is in the upper ranges of the single digits. The story is clearly fragmented to hold the running time to 95 minutes, but even if it had been allowed to play out, there is little it would have to offer: Kids on roller skates with ray guns, a glowing orb with personality, and some interesting architecture involving tires and scrap iron. PG-13.

The sound is terrific. It is digitally encoded, and the volume is jacked up whenever the bad guys appear. The loudspeaker announcements are particularly endearing. Neighbors who had previously suspected that you ran your abode as if it were a police state will now be thoroughly convinced.

The picture is acceptable. It is noticeably scanned, but since the seven heroes are often posed in group shots, the cropping helps get rid of one or two of them.

SOLDIER OF ORANGE

The colors in the Dutch World War II epic *Soldier of Orange* were drab to begin with, but the picture has been adequately transferred to disc. The monaural sound is also drab. The 144-minute movie is principally in Dutch, and has English subtitles. It comes in a gatefold jacket which features interesting interviews with the director, Paul Verhoeven, and the star, Rutger Hauer.

Like the fate of The Netherlands itself during World War II, the story is a downer. Although the film intends to follow the variety of paths open to Dutch citizens during the war, by using a group of students as a microcosm, the plot concentrates upon a few inept attempts at resistance, all of which end in failure. The personalities of the characters and the pacing of the action, however, prevent a viewer's interest from flagging. In depicting the will to survive, it also imparts the spirit.

A SOLDIER'S STORY

Race is intrinsic to *A Soldier's Story*, but the plot is a mystery first, last, and foremost. Howard Rollings, Jr., portrays an Army officer, back in 1944 when there were precious few black officers, who has been sent to investigate the murder of a sergeant in a 'Colored Unit' stationed in the South. As his character interviews the suspects and strips away the lies and the conceits which surround the murder, the viewer delights in watching the actors hide their true character feelings behind false feelings.

The film, taking place primarily in a barracks environment, has a color design which emphasizes shades of light brown and pale yellow mixed with bright, white light (see the disc's jacket cover). The result may initially appear to be faded, but the print is quite fresh and the colors are not even slightly off. The sound is fine.

THE SOLDIER'S TALE

Projects like *The Soldier's Tale* ought to be encouraged. The show is a combination of animation and Igor Stravinsky's music. The animation encourages just enough concentration to give the score a framework.

The cartoon is an extended folk tale, with a lurching plot and, ultimately, a sad ending. The narration, while it retains Slavic rhythms, is extensive and compromising. If you want to listen to the Stravinsky, you'd rather there were less talk. If you want to enjoy the story, you'd rather there were more. There is a quick little how-they-made-the-show documentary after the end credit roll.

SOME KIND OF WONDERFUL

The kissing looks pleasantly real in *Some Kind of Wonderful* and the youngsters talk with more intelligence than most screenwriters are willing to give them. The movie has got some faults, though. We are getting tired of movies which break the social milieu of a high school down strict economic lines, since in reality money doesn't actually contribute to one's status until much later in life. Emotional maturity, the lack of parental supervision, and the status of one's older siblings are just a few factors which have a much greater impact on one's social standing at that age. The last half hour of *Some Kind of Wonderful*, however, redeems its errors, since the whole film turns out to be one long set-up for several nice, soft-spoken romantic interludes, the kind which waft through your own memory and mingle with your own special moments. There is nothing wrong with the picture, and the digital sound has a good beat. We kept on waiting for the Drifters song, though, and it never came.

SOMEONE TO WATCH OVER ME

Ridley Scott's *Someone to Watch Over Me* opens with a view of present day New York which makes the city look like the Los Angeles of *Blade Runner*. The only things missing are the flames and the flying cars. It is Scott's first 'normal' movie, with a contemporary setting and an assembly line script, but as you are watching it visions of *Legend* and the Nostromo and the Napoleonic Wars keep popping into your head. He goes for the kill with every camera set up.

Now don't get us wrong, because this is great news for disc owners. The movie may be silly and the acting may be pathetic, but that is because the creative artists involved care more about surround sound processing than they do about silly details like emotions and logic. You don't have time to giggle or grimace because you never know where the next noise is coming from.

The transfer could have been better than it is. The picture is super glossy. However, it has a slight orange haze. If ever a movie begged to be digitally encoded it is this one and it is not. There are dropouts here and there on some of the higher frequencies, but it is more of a bother than anything else. Too many enjoyable things are happening on the sound mix to complain.

Once you master the disc you will know what scenes to show your friends and what ones to avoid. You would never want to show anyone the whole movie, which is about the joys and guilts of infidelity, anyway. It works better if you think there is more to it than there is.

SOMETHING WILD

The enjoyable *Something Wild* is a comedy about the troubles which impulsive sex can cause if the parties involved turn out to like one another. There are several violent scenes which some viewers will feel are out of synch with the rest of the proceedings. Since the movie is, in part, about the limits of acceptable behavior, and since violence often lurks immediately beyond those limits, the rougher passages are not improper and raise the level of seriousness and concentration with which one approaches the entertainment. The picture is not sharp enough to read the song credits on the end title scroll, but it is generally in better condition than many other HBO discs have been. The stereo is nice, and the movie has one of the better popular song scores.

SON OF DRACULA

If you look at the trailer on side two of *Son of Dracula*, the movie looks scratched and worn down just like a normal Universal horror film. But the main feature looks so new and unblemished that it seems like a fake movie, something made recently and just processed in black-and-white as a gag. The film is a staid effort, lacking the breathtaking set designs or lighting innovations which the best horror movies possess. The plot, which has

Dracula coming to America as 'Count Alucard' in hopes of taking a bride and gorging on fresh American beverages, has a well executed conclusion but little else going for it. Lon Chaney, Jr., is the Count, and the more we listen to him the more he reminds us of Claude Akins. The sound is not in quite as good shape as the picture and is best left without excess amplification. Side two is in CAV. In the spirit of Dracula's alias, you can run the picture in reverse and watch how the smoke effects are accomplished. After the trailer there is a nice collection of publicity stills.

THE SON OF FRANKENSTEIN

The third Frankenstein movie, *The Son of Frankenstein*, has a knockout cast, with Boris Karloff portraying the monster, Basil Rathbone as the doctor, and Bela Lugosi as Ygor. The plot lacks the metaphysical and spiritual impact of the first two films, but it moves efficiently through a series of murders and a number of well crafted characterizations. The print looks spotless and the sound is strong. The film runs 99 minutes, and the disc has no special features.

SON OF MONTE CRISTO

At minute 16 on side one of *Son of Monte Cristo* there is a rousing sword fight and from that point forward, no matter how badly produced the film is, you can't put it down. A swashbuckler which was made in 1940, the plot allows the shadows of 20th century politics to darken an imaginary 19th century Balkan duchy (misidentified on the jacket copy as Liechtenstein). George Sanders portrays the villain and he has a crewcut you could putt across. Clayton Moore also shows up, in a small role, and it is a rare opportunity to see his eyebrows. Louis Hayward is the hero and Joan Bennett is the heroine. He tells her, "You know, you're even more beautiful when you're angry."

Somewhere between the original print and the final product an extra layer of haze found its way to the screen. The sound is fairly noisy and the volume levels have a tendency to rise and fall randomly.

SON OF PALEFACE

Roy Rogers and Trigger join Bob Hope and Jane Russell in *Son of Paleface*. Hope sleeps with Trigger, but has to settle for Russell in the end. The source material has nice colors, but it also has a few splices and scratches, and looks soft in places. The sound is passable. The musical numbers slow things down a little, but the lampooning is enjoyable and all of the performers, including Trigger, have a good time making fun of themselves.

THE SONG REMAINS THE SAME

Even though the quality of the original film is poor in the concert segments, the transfer of *The Song Remains the Same* is the most impressive not in the Middle Earth conceptual segments, but in the poorly filmed Madison Square Garden performance material. The colors are bland and unseparated, but the image is tremendously fresh and immediate.

The 137-minute Led Zeppelin movie played in theaters, but it doesn't really have the sophistication of a well made rock film. To break up the monotony of the concert (hey, we like Zeppelin as much as the next person, but there are only 12 chapters/songs on the entire disc, which averages to more than two digits a song), extraneous music-video-styled skits appear at random moments.

The disc has also been encoded with digital sound, which would be another plus except that the music is the concert recording and lacks the polish of the group's studio efforts. Sometimes when a band plays live, there is an excitement and a sense of exploration when the musicians respond to the audience. But Led Zeppelin can't seem to get excited about much of anything beyond Stonehenge, and they play like Druids. The disc ends up sounding like a well produced bootleg album. Warners is to be praised, however, because they have done a good job with the disc and even let 'Stairway to Heaven' play out after the credit roll is finished, to a blank screen. Since it was the studio recorded version, the number, blank screen and all, held our attention more than any other passage on the disc.

A SONG TO REMEMBER

The print used for *A Song to Remember* doesn't have the shine of the best Technicolor transfers, but the scratches are few and far between. The sound, unfortunately, is not CX-encoded. Poor planning for a film about the life and music of Chopin.

Biographies of Chopin often seem to cast George Sand as a bad influence in the composer's life and biographies of Sand often seem to cast Chopin as a bad influence on Sand's life. If that's not proof that they loved each other, we don't know what is.

Song is sporadic with insight. You suddenly become very aware of the Polish folk melodies swirling around within 'The Polonaise,' but the brooding melancholy of 'Nocturn' is passed off as a result of Sand's taste in haberdashery. The piano music sounds good, even in monaural and even with the extra noise in the background. Fans of Chopin will be pleased, but fans of Sand had best look elsewhere if they wish to find their sunrise.

SONGWRITER

The films of Alan Rudolph have never set the world aflame, but every work has managed to develop a cult following. *Songwriter* had such a small budget that the filmmakers couldn't afford to show a building burning or match the dialog to the lip movements in the long shots. It stars Willie Nelson and Kris Kristofferson as a pair of reasonably successful country-western songwriters who wish to extricate themselves from a tightly bound music contract. The way in which they do so provides enough of a plot to prevent those who are impartial to the many songs on the film's soundtrack from getting restless. The best aspect of the movie, though, is Lesley Ann Warren's performance as a mixed-up singer pulled into stardom by Nelson's schemes. The picture is grainy, but the sound is okay.

SONNY ROLLINS – FESTIVAL INTERNATIONAL DE JAZZ DE MONTREAL
(see **THE JAZZ LIFE VOL. 1**)

SONS OF THE DESERT/BLOTTO
(see **THE BOHEMIAN GIRL/THE MUSIC BOX**)

SOPHISTICATED LADIES

The revue of Duke Ellington numbers, *Sophisticated Ladies*, is typical of a Broadway production. The show is stronger in the dancing department than in the singing department, but stage productions are still so rare on video that virtually any record of one is worth collecting, if only because the disc is cheaper than a ticket. The picture is soft, but passable, and the stereo sound is fair, subduing some of the live ambience in the recording. At the intermission, a cast biography is provided, an especially nice touch since one usually tends to examine the playbill most closely at that point, after a familhiarity with the performers has been established. It conveniently occurs right before the end of side one.

As for the show, the choreography is marvelous, the costumes are cheesy but fun, and the performers appear comfortable working with one another. The music, of course, is sublime, although the orchestra does its best to bring it back to earth.

SOUL MAN

It isn't until about halfway through side two that there is finally a scene funny enough to redeem *Soul Man* from being totally useless. The plot is a dull effort about a boy who masquerades as a black student in order to maintain a scholarship at law school. Most of the jokes are not funny and the characters are more erratic than sympathetic. Maybe, in the not-too-distant future, the movie won't make any sense at all. The picture and sound are passable.

THE SOUND OF MUSIC

The Special Wide Screen Edition of *The Sound of Music* is a high-profile title. Since the transfer is not perfect some viewers will probably be dissatisfied with it. Chief among the disc's disadvantages is the 'Color by De Luxe' source material. It is slightly faded, and on some reels it is faded even more, creating a distinctive red shift. The sky often an uncloudy white and is never a deep blue. Characters are dogged by pink halos. The curtains, which are made into the children's outfits, change shades in every shot. The interior scenes and the night scenes look rich, and the film's essential elegance, as communicated by the disc, can still be inferred. The 171-minute film has been forced onto three sides interupting a song for one of the side breaks.

How all of this will affect a viewer's emotional response to the film will clearly vary from user to user. We loved the disc so much that we didn't mind the pale colors. Scanning randomly through the disc reveals that parts of it look awful, but when we watched it through from beginning to end, we were beguiled by the presentation's more positive attributes and, of course, by the movie itself. The detail on the image, which has been letterboxed with an aspect ratio of about 2:1, is so sharp that the texture of every object in focus is clearly conveyed. The only time the image looks fuzzy is when the filmmakers themselves apply the gauze.

Although we prefer to see discs side separated in a comfortable manner, we had no real complaints with the disc layout. The problematic break, which comes in the middle of 'Do Re Mi,' occurs at one of those protracted Rodgers and Hammerstein pauses, where the characters stop to chat for a moment before taking up the song again. Since you go get your Oreos and milk singing the tune to yourself anyway, the interruption does not seem bothersome.

The stereo surround is superb. Surround effects are limited, and some of the dialog has an extremely delicate touch, but the disc audio transfer is without fault. The music is fluid and smooth, never reaching the distortion levels which other older recordings have bumped up against. CBS/Fox was unable to locate the overture, but they did find the intermission music which plays, refreshingly, to a dark screen in the middle of side two.

The restored screen composition is thrilling. The scanned and cropped version of *The Sound of Music* loses much of the subtle emotional details that give the film the depth which attracted theater audiences. The cropped version is crass, covering the film's highlights, but missing its visual richness and emotional legitimacy. When Julie Andrews and Christopher Plumber first meet, for example, the director, Robert Wise, keeps them at the far opposite sides of the screen, a balance which is only broken when Andrews speaks about the children. In many of the songs it is necessary to see all of the children at once, since they are arranged like the keys on a xylophone and their movements provide a sweet, visual interpretation of the music. Smaller details are also harmed by cropping, such as the sense of a cross on the altar at the end of the wedding scene which, through a beautifully edited montage, turns into a swastika.

The script for *The Sound of Music* takes a gamble by having the biggest emotional payoff – the father's reconcilement with his children – occur shortly after the first hour. That's the climax, and the rest of the film is one long coast, with just enough tension, humor and music to hold a viewer's attention. You don't just leave the movie feeling good, you start feeling good before the film is halfway over, and you just never stop.

SOUTH PACIFIC

The thought of transferring *South Pacific* must be a video engineer's nightmare. Those awful color washes that the filmmakers utilized to evoke mood and compensate for a lack of screen activity look as bad on the theatrical prints of *South Pacific* that we have seen as they did on the first scanned and cropped CBS/Fox disc. As soon as the color on the print goes, details in the tinted sequences disappear completely. So we were plenty surprised to see that not only is the color on the CBS/Fox Special Wide Screen Edition in terrific shape, but the sequences with the color washes are so well restored that the effect is no longer annoying – it actually evokes the romantic, dreamlike moods which the filmmakers wanted to convey.

The picture has some mild fluctuations in sharpness, the blue washes cause some grain, and ultimately it would have looked better in Technicolor, but the presentation is very satisfying. The image has an aspect ratio of about 2.4:1 and encompasses all the significant characters and artwork. The washes and gauze irises make even less sense when the image is cropped, but the letterboxing can be justified simply because of the character blocking. In the cropped version you lose the awareness that some characters are present in certain scenes. Even when the scanning includes them, the dramatic tension evaporates when a character disappears from view. The key scene in which this is particularly important is the scene in which Nellie, played by Mitzi Gaynor, learns that Emile, played by Rossano Brazzi, once had a Polynesian wife. It is a scene which doesn't work well anyway, because Gaynor really isn't playing the Arkansas belle it is buried in the script that she is supposed to be. She's too movie musical cheerful, and when she acts aghast, her prejudices aren't in synch with the character she's been playing. Scanned, the focus is entirely on her, and you don't believe her emotions for a moment. Letterboxed, there is Brazzi, the wine, and the midnight sky – enough visual input to soften the blow from her change of heart. She still isn't convincing, but she doesn't seem as ridiculous.

The surround sound is wonderful. In the songs, whenever there is a chorus, the voices fill up your viewing room. Although the recording is aged, it has a fullness and an adept utilization of the stereo channels. The three sided disc comes in a gatefold jacket, and there is a beautiful color still blown up on the inner sleeve, compensating for the awkward picture on the jacket cover. The disc has an overture, entr'acte and exit music. After the movie is ended, there is a marvelously bad black and white promotional film about the movie and about Todd-AO. This is the 158 minute version of the film.

South Pacific is the one movie musical we would love to rewrite and remake. From the opening, which cuts straight from a plane flying towards an island to a musical number on the island without a helicopter style zoom to bridge the two shots, to the ending, in which the main character, who could easily have been manipulated to show that he had paid his dues, is killed instead of sneaking off to live on Bali Ha'i (the character to help him do it, Ray Walston's, is already in place), it just seems like the movie makers were too close to the stage production to think the property through as a film. The songs are great, the material is rich and has plenty of potential – so why did the director resort to colored washes to keep the audience interested during the love numbers? The film's vitality is restored on the disc by the beautiful job CBS/Fox has done with the transfer but, as with Bali Ha'i, we can't help thinking that there could be an even better movie out there, waiting for the right tropical wind to help it materialize through the mist.

SPACE ARCHIVE VOLUME 1 – SPACE SHUTTLE: MISSION REPORTS STS 5, 6, & 7
SPACE ARCHIVE VOLUME 2 – APOLLO 17: MISSION TO TAURUS LITTROW
SPACE ARCHIVE COLLECTOR'S EDITION – SHUTTLE DOWNLINK: THE REPAIR OF SOLAR MAX

The *Space Archive* series, released by Optical Data Corporation (also called Video Vision Associates in the early days), has been a consistently exciting and rewarding enterprise. *Volume 1*, entitled *Space Shuttle: Mission Reports STS 5, 6, & 7*, features photographs and video recordings from three Space Shuttle flights. *Volume 2*, *Apollo 17: Mission to Taurus Littrow*, is a record of the last manned moon flight. A *Collector's Edition*, *Shuttle Downlink: The Repair of Solar Max* includes material from the Shuttle missions, STS 8, 9, 41B, & 41C. 41C, the flight during which the Solar Max satellite was repaired, took place just five months before the disc was pressed.

The value of owning one or both of the Space Shuttle discs depends upon one's interest in the Shuttle project. The Apollo disc, however, belongs in every library. It is a unique presentation that cannot be duplicated in any other medium. Even a full scale exhibit of the same material at the National Air and Space Museum in Washington DC does not convey as strong a feeling for what the adventure was like. Included in the package are the disc, a booklet providing a history of Apollo 17, an identification of the stills displayed on the disc, and a beautiful two-foot square map/photograph of the area in Taurus Littrow explored during the moonwalks.

Each of the CAV *Space Archive* discs contains video highlights of the various space missions, usually about 50 minutes' worth, and around a thousand still images – which normally take another hour to traverse using the laser player's still/step or slow motion functions.

The disc is educational, but it is also a lot of fun. Gene Cernan and Jack Schmitt act and sound as if they are digging in a backyard instead of on an alien landscape 230,000 miles away.

A popular feature in the first volume was the view of Earth's land masses from space. An even better collection has been put together for *Shuttle Downlink* but, because the disc was rushed into production for the sake of timeliness, identification was withheld from more than a hundred of the most interesting stills. (The curious dots in the middle of what looks like desert are, according to a spokesperson for Optical Data, "irrigation projects in Libya and Saudi Arabia.") The accompanying text promised that the stills would be identified in a sheet available on request, but the lapse seems pointless and harms the educational value of the product. An experiment with bees on the same flight is also given a short shrift.

The most valuable segment in *Space Shuttle* is a gyroscope demonstration given by 'Mission Specialist' Joseph Allen. All the explanations one has heard about how gyroscopes assist the navigational abilities of space craft cannot match the simple image of the spinning top remaining perfectly stationary in mid-cabin (this demonstration is also repeated in a later *Space Archive* disc, *Encounters*). Much of *Space Shuttle* is given over to the space walk in STS 6. But by the time one gets to *Shuttle Downlink* and STS 41C, the astronauts are comfortably buzzing back and forth as if they strolled in space every day.

SPACE ARCHIVE VOLUME 3: MARS AND BEYOND – SIGHTSEEING IN THE OUTER PLANETS
SPACEWATCH (Import)

The concept of the *Mars and Beyond* disc is almost as exciting as its subject. *Space Archive Volume 3: Mars and Beyond – Sightseeing in the Outer Planets* has a good-sized collection of still photos and several films featuring animated sequences, historical footage, and composite shots of the Voyager and Viking missions. The most spectacular feature of the CAV disc, however, is its use of 3-D to bring Mars out of your television screen and into your living room.

The literature enclosed with the disc (which also comes with two pairs of glasses made of cardboard and cellophane) recommends that the viewer use a high resolution monitor for best results. Great. Buy us one and we'll use it. Turning off all the lights helps to enhance the effect as does doubling up the glasses. The first sequence is the most thrilling, as an arm on the Viking lander comes reaching out to grab your nose.

The chapters devoted to Viking are very thorough, with lots of stills, explanations, and motion sequences. The section on Voyager does not teach as much as it should and there aren't nearly enough stills. Side two is a straightforward (linear) NASA film on the Voyager mission which is even more unbalanced, passing from gee-whiz non-explanations to detailed analysis of eccentric subjects like Jupiter's magnetic fields. The tone of the narration is also condescending.

A Japanese disc called *Spacewatch* is a bilingual (English on one channel, Japanese on the other) tour of the planets and the stars much in the format of the NASA film on side two of *Mars and Beyond*, but much more cohesively organized. The CAV disc contains material from both the Soviet and American space programs and manages to nutshell pretty much everything we know about each planet up to Saturn. The disc goes on to give an excellent tour of the stars in the northern sky during each of the seasons and a quick summary of manned space explorations. The captions on many of the pictures are in both Japanese and English. The CAV can be put to good use in dozens of places and *Spacewatch* is an excellent disc for both the home and the educational environment.

SPACE ARCHIVE VOLUME 5 – GREETINGS FROM EARTH

The pleasure of owning several thousand photographs on a single disc is not shared by all, but the beauty of *Space Archive Volume 5 – Greetings from Earth* should win a few more believers.

Even the introductory titles at the beginning of the one-sided CAV disc are pleasing. As soft piano music plays and different scenes from the disc appear, the various title cards flicker onto the screen in calm, unhurried fades. After the titles, the subdued, bubbly music of Tangerine Dream accompanies video material shot on a Space Shuttle flight. Edited for artistic instead of scientific merit, the sequence helps to relax one's mind and prepare one for the rush of information that will follow.

Although the focus of *Greetings from Earth* is the still frame collection, other features add to the value of the disc. There is a segment of Cray-generated animation, including a rotated Earth. There are computer-assisted radar maps of the Earth's true topography, and satellite photos of storms and turbulence which, when run as motion pictures, give one a global view of how weather systems undulate.

The main feature, some 2000 Landsat photos of the US, is not intended for viewing in sequential order. The viewer is supposed to browse, to pick a hometown or a favorite vacation spot and see what it looks like from above. The array of stills depicts almost the entire continental United States on a scale in which football stadiums and shopping centers are clearly visible. The photos have false, coded colors, but interpreting the information on them is easy enough once one gets the hang of it.

Like all the *Space Archive* discs, a booklet has been included to assist one in identifying the stills. The information included several errors which we noticed immediately. Staten Island is called 'Richmond, LI.' Olympia, Washington is identified as 'Tacoma, WA' and Tacoma, Washington is identified as 'Seattle, WA.' There is no telling how many other mistakes the text contains. In an adept marketing move, a thorough Landsat view of Japan is also provided, along with cursory glances at the rest of the world. A wonderful segment on 'Seasons' shows how various locales look in summer, winter, and spring.

SPACE ARCHIVE VOLUME 6 – ENCOUNTERS

Side one of *Space Archive Volume 6 – Encounters* contains stills from the Voyager/Uranus flyby and numerous observations of Halley's comet. The disc opens with a music video combining excerpts from the various computer images in the later programs and a simple electronic score.

There are fewer still photo sections on the Optical Data CAV release than on the other *Space Archive* discs. Less than 40 photos comprise the Uranian segment. The notes in the accompanying six-page booklet adequately detail the surface features of the moons, but we miss the volume of observations which previous discs provided. Some of the computer animation is hyper-realistic, whereas some of the rarer NASA films on side two are by nature faded and grainy.

Side two contains a study of zero gravity. We were surprised that footage such as the Skylab astronauts jogging *2001*-style has not been more widely disseminated. Perhaps it has been suppressed to avoid the impression that our tax dollars are being spent in play. More interesting are closeups of liquid in zero-g and a study of how magnets react to the earth and each other. Experiments with real toys, such as a Slinky and a paddleball, are also shown, as part of a special educational promotion which, we are assured, the astronauts participated in during their "free time." The demonstrations are informative and manage, with the assistance of the visuals, to explain complicated laws of physics in a simple and understandable manner.

Concluding the disc is a brief memorial to the Space Shuttle Challenger, with footage from one of Challenger's successful flights. Since the sequence is promoted on the jacket cover without descriptive detail, we feel that it is necessary to mention that no depiction of the final flight is included.

SPACE CAMP

Don't even bother watching side one of *Space Camp*. Side two is where the kids are up in the Space Shuttle trying to get back down, and no matter how unlikely the process which got them up there, getting down is exciting and a lot of fun. There aren't many decent sound effects, however. The bass when they take off is a joke and the John Williams score is too brassy. The picture is fuzzy.

SPACE CRUISER YAMATO – NEW VOYAGE (see MY YOUTH IN ARCADIA)

SPACE DISC 1 VOYAGER
SPACE DISC 2 APOLLO
SPACE DISC 4 THE SUN
SPACE DISC 5 ASTRONOMY
SPACE DISC 6 EARTH SCIENCE

Optical Data Corporation, producer of the *Space Archive* series, has also put out a series of educational discs identified as their *Space Disc* collection. The CAV discs are priced for the educational market, but one can occasionally come across them discounted or second-hand.

Although a *Space Disc* disc lacks the gloss of a *Space Archive* production, it also has many advantages over the consumer series and the acquisition of these titles is well worth considering if you have more than a passing interest in aerospace entertainment. Each disc comes with a bound 'Image Directory' providing a description of every still frame and the source for that frame, should you wish to obtain it as a slide or print.

The first, *Space Disc 1 Voyager*, does not justify its price until the end of side one. Both sides begin with a 'Program Overview,' a still and motion summary of what the Voyager space probes accomplished during their Jupiter and Saturn passes.

After the overview, side two proceeds with NASA pre-encounter movies of Jupiter and Saturn. These speculative computer-generated films actually contain misinformation, such as a laughable suggestion that the haze around Io, soon to be identified as volcanic emissions, is caused by "intense radiation bombardment of the surface material." The movies provide a this-is-what-we-expect-to-find hypothesis which is answered on side one with 'this is what we found.'

Side one has three parts. The overview, mission profiles of how the two Voyager probes passed the two planets, and what the probes found. There is some repetition between the profile segment and the final segment. There are some interesting time lapse sequences involving Jupiter's rotation. The sounds of Jupiter and Saturn have also been provided. The narrative passages on side two, however, reveal that the non CX-encoded audio leaves much to be desired.

The one problem with *Space Disc 2 Apollo* is that too much is attempted on a single disc. All six Apollo moon landings are depicted through stills and motion segments. The Image Directory booklet accompanying the disc is close to 200 pages long.

Despite having a good ten years to analyze the data, the information gleaned from the Apollo missions and specifically from the images included on the disc is not adequately disseminated. The booklet contains a nice EVA map of each landing except the first (where the astronauts stayed very close to the lander), and a short summary and explanation of the mission. At the very end there is an 'Apollo Scientific Summary' which is dated 1973. Almost no insights gleaned since this date have been included.

Space Disc 4 The Sun is primarily about

the star at the center of our solar system, but several other features have been jammed into the two-sided CAV disc, including 60 Landsat photos of Canada.

The program covers everything – sunspots, flares, coronas, photogenic eclipses – thoroughly, on one side of the disc. About 3000 still photos are supplemented by a substantial collection of time-lapse motion sequences. Each sequence is introduced with a title frame which identifies the speed at which the sequence should be played. A few of the sequences are accompanied by a voice-over lecture, but most are silent.

Side two has a 30-minute educational film on 'The Universe,' narrated with sleepy calmness by William Shatner. At the end of both sides is a still collection apparently intended as a slide show to be accompanied by a computer diskette which is not included.

Although every disc has a unique thrust, a lot of material is repeated from one disc to the next. A 13,400 still collection, in fact, is repeated on both sides of *Space Disc 5 Astronomy*. The stills provide a thorough mapping of the night sky, which translates into endless sequences of white pinpoints.

After the stills, there is a collection of short motion sequences. Most of the films are computer-generated demonstrations depicting astrophysical principles on a galactic scale. Some are accompanied by narration and all are adequately explained in the booklet. Other shorts, in a repeat of other discs, survey the topologies of the various planets, again with computer-generated animation. Twenty-six of these movies have chapter markers on side one and 36 appear on side two.

The most useful and entertaining of all the *Space Disc* discs we have viewed is *Space Disc 6 Earth Science*. A portion of *Earth Science* was used in the gorgeous *Greetings from Earth* disc and the accompanying booklet contains the same geographical misidentifications which we noted in that package. The 8000-still collection is repeated on both sides, while a collection of motion sequences is spread over the remainder of the disc.

Most of the photographs collected in *Earth Science* are grouped as photo essays or slide lessons covering different aspects of geology and atmospheric science. Included are stills of glaciers and their effects, volcanoes going off or laying dormant, unique land forms, fossils, a cloud catalogue, rivers and erosion, and spreads on Mt. St. Helens, Antarctica, and Hawaiian volcanoes. The still section also contains a segment on minerals which combines text with photos to imitate a museum display and an 'Earth Science Glossary.' Along with all that, there are Landsat photos of the entire United States, including Alaska and Hawaii.

The motion sequences are a vast improvement over the somewhat confused jumble which were squeezed onto the other *Space* discs. The sound is still of institutional quality, but every sequence is narrated. A computer-generated depiction of continental drift over the past billion years is followed by another computer-generated speculation on the evolution of North America.

The knowledge presented on *Earth Science* is cleverly organized so that you can spend hours browsing or exploring. Raw data is there for those who wish to study geology in depth, but an overview is always present for those who just want to pick up a little more about the world around them.

SPACE GHOST AND DINO BOY

Space Ghost and Dino Boy combines two video cassette collections and contains 14 seven minute cartoons. Both sides open and close with the original title sequences, and side one contains a lengthy home video promotion at the end.

The cartoons are in fairly good condition and the sound is okay. 'Space Ghost,' about an astronaut who wears a hood and fights bad aliens with his power glove, features the voices of Gary Owens and Tim Matheson. 'Dino (rhymes with wino) Boy' is about a contemporary youth who crashes in a 'Lost World' and befriends a cave man. The time limit prevents elaborate plotting, but the formula allows for mild exercises in imagination. Although episodes for the two cartoons have been mixed together on the disc, the mindlessly enjoyable adventures can start seeming repetitive fairly rapidly. It is best not to watch both sides in the same sitting. And those who have invested a lot of time in explaining to their youngsters how Jupiter is a gaseous planet with no discernable surface will find their best intentions demolished as Space Ghost battles a Jovian crater creature in the opening episode.

SPACEWATCH (see SPACE ARCHIVE VOLUME 3: MARS AND BEYOND – SIGHTSEEING IN THE OUTER PLANETS)

SPANDAU BALLET OVER BRITAIN

The picture on *Spandau Ballet over Britain* is so grainy and foggy it looks as if the camera itself was smoking. Playing the disc will make you think you are actually at the rock concert, with wax paper wrapped around your head. The group performs eleven numbers on the 50 minute program. The recording is live and overly miked on the vocals. Although the music of Spandau Ballet is pleasant, the disc is for fans only.

SPANISH MAIN

The print used for the Technicolor *Spanish Main* is inconsistent in quality, but it always remains within acceptable levels. The sound has no significant problems. In places the picture is a little fuzzy, a little blurry, and contains some speckles. The colors never look stunning, or, for that matter, totally accurate, but the presentation is generally enjoyable, as is the film itself. Paul Henreid portrays a pirate, a sort of Victor Laszlo with a bandana, who steals the fiancee of a Spanish bigwig in the Caribbean. Few pirate movies were able to transcend the genre to become genuine film classics and this isn't one of them, but as a boisterous romance with some yardarms thrown in, the movie isn't bad.

SPARTACUS

As soon as the Overture begins you realize that the disc presentation of *Spartacus* is quite probably the best version anyone has heard in a long time. The sides of the picture are cropped to fit the television screen, but the print is fresh and the sound seems to come from everywhere.

Stanley Kubrick's film was a successful epic which proved that movies about ancient Rome did not have to draw from the Bible to impart spiritual strength. Kirk Douglas portrays a slave whose rebellion gives a Roman general (Laurence Olivier) the opportunity to consolidate his power. By using classically trained British actors as the Roman upper crust (including Charles Laughton and Peter Ustinov) and scruffy untrained American actors as the slaves (Tony Curtis, and Douglas), Kubrick is able to blend the stories of the higher and lower classes without disturbing the complicated rhythm that must be sustained to keep both parts interesting.

SPEED ZONE

A weak willed *Cannonball Run* sequel, *Speed Zone* has one or two interesting car stunts but much more footage of cars zigzagging down highways, going nowhere in particular and not very rapidly. The stars compiled for the event, John Candy, the Smothers Brothers, Jamey Farr, and others, hardly make one's pulse quicken in recognition, save for a charming cameo by Lee Van Cleef. The picture looks very good and the sound is okay.

SPIDER-MAN

Four episodes of the live action television program, 'The Amazing Spider-Man,' have been released in a single disc package, *Spider-Man*. Although the credits have been combined for video cassette releases, which pasted two episodes together, each hour show runs closer to 45 minutes and is relegated to a single side on the disc. The source material is in sort of raunchy condition, but then the program was no Michael Mann production to begin with. There are splices, blotches, and other sporadic contaminations, as well as the show's own dull color scheme. The monaural sound is also a bit warped and should not be too heavily amplified.

For those who are unfamiliar with the program, it is reasonably faithful to the spirit of the comic, except for a toning down of the fantasy elements that generate the dramatic conflicts. It is not great television, but some of the stunts are witty or reasonably elaborate, and the scripts are versatile. Morgan Fairchild appears in 'Night of the Clones,' in which the duplicate that a scientist has made of himself becomes an evil twin, and tries to generate an evil Spider-Man. In 'Escort to Danger,' directed by Fernando Lamas, Spider-Man foils a kidnap plot tied to a coup d'etat, and in 'Con Caper' he stops a burglary master-minded by escaped convicts. The most entertaining episode, 'The Curse of Rava,' pits the hero against an Eastern mystic with psychokinetic powers.

SPIDERS

Fritz Lang's adventure thriller, *Spiders*, was made in 1919. The movie was intended to be an episodic spectacle, about an evil organization, The Spiders, and a playboy hero who continually disrupts their schemes. The roots of the Indiana Jones films can be seen in the feature which, as it exists today, lasts 138 minutes and is comprised of what was originally two separate films (more were planned but not produced). The first part is contained on side one of the disc and the second part is on side two and three, with side two presented in CAV. The musical score, organ accompaniment by Gaylord Carter, is monaural and remains unobtrusive.

The image is usually dark. Details are also taken away by the tinting, although the colored shadings are otherwise quite effective. The picture is mildly framed and well presented, though the condition of the original material is no better than average.

The movie is not wholly satisfying. It seems as if many of the best parts are still missing. For example, the hero is being chased on horseback by a group of bad guys. In the distance, his friend is getting ready to sail in a hot air balloon. The friend, unaware of the hero's predicament, sets sail. Suddenly the hero is dangling from one of the ropes of the balloon. How he actually got there is left to the imagination. The narrative has many cliffhanging situations and a pleasing sense of exploration. It also has the usual silliness, such as when a homing pigeon returns to his roost to deliver a message to the bad guys, on a boat travelling in the middle of the ocean.

SPIES LIKE US

Spies Like Us is just as incoherent and disjointed as the Crosby/Hope pictures it wishes to invoke. It is also almost as funny. Perfect for home viewing, actually, because it will become more stupid and more amusing the more times you watch it. The director, John Landis, steals the picture from Chevy Chase and Dan Ackroyd, getting more laughs from business which he has placed on the edges of the screen, like the Soviet Highway Patrol insignia of a bear and a reindeer embracing, than from the two stars. Ackroyd and Chase have the same cool screen presence. It is more suited for TV and they are usually funnier on film when they are teamed with stronger personalities. The disc is probably most effective when played in a room full of crying babies, barking dogs, et cetera. The picture transfer is weak and the soundtrack is a little noisy.

SPIKE OF BENSONHURST

We can't get excited about *Spike of Bensonhurst*, a Paul Morrissey film which has his typical conglomeration of bad acting, ill chosen accents, and unlikely narrative events. The film is too ethnically exaggerated to appeal as a nice comedy and too unprovocative to qualify as dark humor (though the hero's indifferent attitude toward the two women he impregnates is inspired). In the midst of it, Ernest Borgnine gives an unusually well tempered and appealing performance as a Mafia chief attempting without much success to control his wife and daughter. Most viewers, however, will be impatient with the film's pace and absurdities.

The disc is not so hot, either. It is 'stereo enhanced' although you could have fooled us since most of the time the sound just falls with a thud. The picture is soft on the edges and a little grainy.

SPITTING IMAGE (Import)

Excerpts from the British satrical program, *Spitting Image* are available on disc in Japan. The hour-long, single-sided disc contains a multitude of short blackout sketches, with a chapter marker appearing, for no apparent reason, after, approximately, every sixth sketch.

The disc is bilingual, with English on one track and Japanese on the other, but the songs are solely in English and are accompanied by subtitles. The picture quality on the disc is generally good and the sound is adequate though, because of the dual tracks, it is not CX-encoded.

In case you haven't seen the show or read about it, *Spitting Image* is populated entirely by grotesque puppets which nevertheless bear uncanny likenesses to important figures in the worlds of politics and entertainment. The disc, for example, opens with Ronald Reagan, one of the program's most recurring and scathing presences, pulling out a wad of nose hairs, dipping them in Grecian Formula hair color, and then plugging them back in. After a couple nights of the real network newscasts, it doesn't seem so gross.

The funniest material, however, has little to do with politics. There are wicked, wicked sendups of Paul McCartney ('War is horrible, I love Linda'), Madonna ('Wearing underwear on the outside of my clothes'), Bruce Springsteen ('Born to teach shop'), Bob Dylan ('I don't know which cheeeeese to chooooose'), Prince ('wishing for a real mustache'), Barbra Streisand (taking her vocal inflections several steps too far), Wham, and even a 'We Are the World' takeoff where they all reappear together. There is Prince William, plotting to do in his grandmother, an imaginary look at the knockabout domestic life of John McEnroe and Tatum O'Neal, Leonard Nimoy attempting 'Hamlet' ('To be or not to be, that is not logical, Captain'), and a 'before' and 'after' Moonie. Our favorite skit was a parody of an LP commercial, offering song hits, from rock to opera, which praise RS-232 communication interfaces. Irreverence is like a compass, and in the brambles of modern culture, not to mention politics, shows such as Spitting Image are essential for keeping a straight path.

THE SPOILERS

The outfits Marlene Dietrich wears in *The Spoilers* are gorgeous and, towards the second half of the movie, she starts wearing them over again. Side two of the black-and-white feature is in CAV. Every frame freezes into a perfect photo. *The Spoilers* is an adventure film, taking place in the Yukon during the turn-of-the-century gold rush, about miners and swindlers, cheap romance and true love.

SPOOKIES

The script, the direction, and the acting in *Spookies* are all on the level of a bad student film. The plot, involving demons that terrorize humans in a large abandoned mansion, is incomprehensible. What the humans are doing there, how many survive, where the demons came from and what they want are all questions left unanswered at the none-too-soon end of the film. The picture transfer is decent although the source material is not. The sound preserves the poorly written and ineptly read dialog, as well as the awful one-note-at-a-time-or-all-the-notes-together score.

SPORTS ILLUSTRATED 25TH ANNIVERSARY SWIMSUIT VIDEO
SWIMWEAR ILLUSTRATED ON LOCATION
PLAYBOY'S WET AND WILD

There was once a time when an Albert Maysles film about the Sports Illustrated 'Swimsuit Issue' would have been full of biting irony, a behind-the-scenes look at the real motivation for producing a survey of the kind of summer wear no one could buy even if they wanted to. Times change, however, and Maysles, like everyone else, has to pay the bills. *Sports Illustrated 25th Anniversary Swimsuit Video*, a film by Maysles and Susan Froemke, is, instead, a slick and captivating view of the photo sessions in which the models, rather than the garments, are the focus of attention.

The film is an hour long and is expertly edited to hold a viewer's interest. The locale shifts from one exotic address to the next, as the world's most famous models endure the indulgences of make-up men, photographers, and creative directors while they get a little tan.

The disc opens and closes with two Dodge commercials which sound great going through the hi-fi. The monaural sound has a full range and is quite satisfying. The picture also looks sharp.

In contrast, *Swimwear Illustrated on Location* is so fuzzy that sometimes the tummies of the models blend right into their bikinis. The 45-minute program is a cheap, boring imitation of the Sports Illustrated film – and to think Sports Illustrated only does it once a year while Swimwear Illustrated does it every month. The setting never leaves Miami, the conversations between the photographers and the creative directors sound staged, and long passages are devoted to showing the models standing in their outfits while music plays. Supposedly the disc is in stereo, but it didn't sound nearly as good as the *Sports Illustrated* disc.

Trust Playboy to get into the act as well, though the poor models who work for them must not get paid much since they apparently can't afford bathing suits. Someone must have told them that they were going to model water and they fell for it. *Playboy's Wet and Wild*, which runs an hour, combines water-oriented excerpts from other Playboy videos with some new and similarly damp material.

The picture is mildly grainy, but shifts in quality depending upon the source of the clip and how many times it has been used in other Playboy video efforts. The sound is in stereo and although again it does not sound as good as the *Sports Illustrated* disc, it is a significant improvement over *Swimwear Illustrated.*

THE SPY WHO CAME IN FROM THE COLD

The densely plotted espionage classic *The Spy Who Came in from the Cold* was directed by Martin Ritt, and is in black-and-white. The print has no more than an occasional speckle, and many scenes sparkle. The monaural sound is passable, but the complicated dialog may call for higher than normal amplification.

If you get the disc, be sure to pay attention to Sol Kaplan's musical score. There is a nightclub sequence in which his music, for a striptease, deliberately borrows from Monty Norman's 'James Bond Theme.' At the time of its release the film was seen as a realistic alternative to the excesses of the Bond features, though in hindsight John LeCarre's tour-de-force plot twists are simply an intellectual variation on the rollicking action sequences and gadgetry of the more popular spy extravaganzas. The sympathy LeCarre's character, George Smiley, has obtained from subsequent novels puts the ending of the film in a new light, since the Smiley character is used as something of a heavy. The movie, however, remains an entertainingly bleak and bitter look at the amorality of government and at the limited choices available to those who want to retain their humanity while crossing moral boundaries.

THE SPY WHO LOVED ME (CBS/Fox)
THE SPY WHO LOVED ME (MGM/UA)
THE SPY WHO LOVED ME (MGM/UA Letterboxed)

After a couple of missed tries, *The Spy Who Loved Me* was finally done right on disc. It has been letterboxed with an aspect ratio of about 2.1:1, and thus the previous scanned and cropped versions were not done half as good (well, almost). The Deluxe Letter-Box Edition from MGM/UA is the best.

To recap briefly, CBS/Fox Video released an awful, scanned, mono, time-compressed version and then MGM/UA released a passable, scanned, analog stereo version. Improvements on the second MGM/UA release, besides the letterboxing, include digital encoding, an improved stereo mix, a more careful picture transfer, the formatting of side three in CAV, the addition of a theatrical trailer, and a gatefold jacket. (Similarities in jacket design to the first MGM/UA version, however, have been giving retailers fits.)

Not only has information been added to the sides of the image, but the top and bottom have also been expanded on the letterboxed version, as can be calibrated on the through-the-periscope shots. The additional picture content significantly improves the impact of the film's elaborate soundstage sets, and also adds to the emotional impact of the action. Although there are still sequences in the film which look grainy, the picture is sharper than MGM/UA's earlier version. It also looks less washed out. The contrasts are stronger and the colors are slightly richer. The near-impossible red light sequences in the submarine have been handled as well as apparently they could be, and no longer seem distracting.

Both the analog and digital tracks on the letterboxed disc have an airiness which is missing from the previous MGM/UA version (because of the time-compression, the CBS/Fox soundtrack was noticeably out of pitch). There is much more detail to the separations, and less thrust in the center. The surround track may be under-utilized, but the sound is finally the treat that it ought to be.

Because of the use of CAV and the trailer, the side breaks are awkward. The final battle can be broken down in Standard Play, and with the trailer, a number of other stunts can also be examined.

The Spy Who Loved Me still has a polyester feel to it, with some jokes, as well as the whole Giza sequence, seeming quite dated. The elimination of the villain is also uncomfortably cold-blooded. With the disc presentation, however, the film is definitely a pleasure to view, as the disc finally captures the full spirit of original theatrical presentation. We've seen the movie a number of times now, and as dopey as Barbara Bach appears raising her hand to plant a karate chop, the Airhead Award has to go to Roger Moore for his line, "Where there's an ocean, a marine biologist is never on holiday." Don't get us wrong, we look forward to the line every time we watch the movie.

SPY IN BLACK

Michael Powell's terrific espionage thriller, *Spy in Black*, which concerns German agents infiltrating England in World War I, was made just before World War II started to get dicey. It is patriotic, but it also depicts German characters in a more sympathetic light than they would receive again for quite a while. The story is set on a remote Scottish island and has a fairly simple set of plot twists, but sprinkled throughout it are Powell's heavenly special effect shots. The combination of a little intrigue and an occasional near-magic shot of boats bobbing in a fog-bound harbor is all a movie really needs to capture a viewer's attention for a while.

The black-and-white source material is inevitably worn down, but we weren't put off by it. It is soft and grainy in places, looking even worse when stock footage is employed. The sound is acceptable.

SQUARE DANCE

A coming of age story (literally, since the heroine gets her first menstrual flow) about the summer a girl spends with her mother in Fort Worth, *Square Dance*, will only interest those who can tolerate middle American drama. The sound is okay. The picture could have been more distinctive, but it gets by. The narrative is relatively involving, and the cast does include Jason Robards, Jane Alexander, and Rob Lowe, but the goals of the film are limited and so is the film's appeal. Lowe's performance, in particular, as a young man with developmental problems, will drive some viewers nuts. The movie has an emphasis of realism, but it only goes so far. The heroine is supposed to be handy in the kitchen, but in an extended dramatic scene where, to keep her busy, she is absent-mindedly preparing a cake, she puts vanilla in the bowl first and only later starts to crack and beat the eggs.

THE SQUEEZE

Michael Keaton and Rae Dawn Chong star in *The Squeeze*, an uninteresting comedy/mystery involving a couple of murders and a lottery fix. The stars are personable, but the script is not. The disc is in stereo, and the music track is nicely separated from the dialog and sound effects. The picture is blurry, but it is fresh and looks unused.

ST. ELMO'S FIRE

It looks like *St. Elmo's Fire* was designed for young people who dream about someday getting their own apartments. The story certainly has little to do with the real world, since these kids have somehow landed pads in Georgetown which would make some highly paid lobbyists envious. The colors look a little too unsteady, with the disc unable to handle all the neon and tavern lighting. There is a scene where a couple breaking up argues over who gets what records, which was done much better with books in *Annie Hall.*

STACKING

Filmed in Billings and Lavonia, Montana, the scenery in *Stacking* is spectacular. The colors are rich and the image is crisp. The monaural sound is CX-encoded and does no harm. The story is about a young girl who rises to responsibility when her father is hurt in an accident. The script does not follow a focus. Individual scenes go on for a very long time, and significant information is withheld from the viewer for no reason other than it can't be worked into the conversations naturally. Many viewers will lose patience with it, but what the film lacks in drama it makes up in an evocation of everyday life that is as striking as the Big Sky vistas.

STAKEOUT

The picture transfer on *Stakeout* is fair. Anything within the film which has been lit with red light comes out blurry, and there are speckles in a few places. The stereo sound has no errors, but it doesn't have much gusto. The 117-minute film is spread to three sides, all in CLV.

The disc is enjoyable despite minor flaws because the movie is so entertaining. It is about a cop who falls in love with the woman he's been assigned to spy upon, and was understandably a big hit. The casting of Richard Dreyfuss and Emilio Estevez, as the cop and his partner, was particularly inspired. In Estevez's case, it takes him out of the teen idol genre and he has an opportunity to be dry and spunky. For Dreyfuss, it is a relief to see him playing someone normal. In the past when he was cast as a detective, he had to represent disillusionment and futility. Here he is just a fool in love.

STALKING DANGER
(see **PYTHON WOLF**)

STAND AND DELIVER

To our mind Edward James Olmos can do no wrong, and he certainly verifies this in *Stand and Deliver*, by making calculus look appealing. The film is a great math movie, one which nerds and toughs can enjoy together. The picture looks so good one will forget one is not in the classroom with the cast. The sound, although monaural, is so fresh that stereo effects are not missed.

STAND BY ME

The thing we like most about *Stand By Me*, other than that they built the treehouse in a madrona, is the confident, free-form use of flashbacks within flashbacks. It gives the impression that the filmmakers have total control over the story and lowers one's resistance to the proceedings. The two-day hike that the four boys take to search for the body of an accident victim has all the trappings of being a metaphor of Our Journey Through Life, but it always manages to be just witty enough so that you don't feel like you have to sit down and write an essay about it.

The disc has an acceptable soundtrack and a picture which is slightly grainy, but unharmed by the resultant blur, which adds to the nostalgic feel of the late '50s time period when the story takes place.

The movie has gained well-deserved praise for depicting young boys as they really talk and think. Although the publicity efforts bent over backwards to downplay the source material for the film, the tale demonstrates that Stephen King has genuine talent buried beneath the candy wrappers. If King has sold his soul for fame and fortune, the adventure depicted in *Stand By Me* retrieves a little of it.

STAND BY ME – A PORTRAIT OF JULIAN LENNON

When *Stand By Me – A Portrait of Julian Lennon* was made, Lennon barely had enough material to fill up half of the hour-long video program. As is in clear evidence on the disc, Lennon's musical abilities, while promising, are fairly limited. His compositions are not distinctive, his lyrics are juvenile, and his singing is unremarkable. He does have one thing going for him – enough charisma to captivate an auditorium.

The 59-minute show is a one-sided CLV CX-encoded stereo disc. The songs were recorded during Lennon's first tour, but most of the numbers are broken up with interviews so that you rarely get to hear something all the way through.

STANDARDS – KEITH JARRETT, GARY PEACOCK, JACK DeJOHNETTE

Standards – Keith Jarrett, Gary Peacock, Jack DeJohnette runs close to two hours. It is filmed in soft lights so that the picture has none of the harsh clarity one associates with boisterous pop performances. The sound recording picks up all of the humming and huffing which is suppressed in a studio work. Jarrett, in particular, accompanies his every solo with a 'nya, nya-nya' working itself out of his clenched teeth. Jarrett's proficiency at the keyboard more than makes up for his impromptu vocals.

STANDARDS II – KEITH JARRETT, GARY PEACOCK, JACK DEJOHNETTE

Like the first *Standards*, *Standards II – Keith Jarrett, Gary Peacock, Jack DeJohnette* depicts just the three musicians, playing the piano, bass, and drums. The program lasts 90 minutes and has an intermission which comes at the side break. Except for Jarrett's frustrating habit of humming to himself as he's playing, the music is exquisite, beautifully formed and delicately executed. The camera runs out of things to point at after a while, but the listener will be undaunted, even after repeated play. The picture and sound are excellent. *Standards* was released by Pioneer, but *Standards II* comes from Home Vision.

STANLEY & IRIS

In *Jacknife* Robert DeNiro portrayed a man who overcomes emotional barriers to find romance and a sense of self worth. His performance was believable and charming, but in *Stanley & Iris* he has the same sort of role and it doesn't work at all. The film's continuity is strange, as if scenes were re-shuffled during the editing, and while a scene here or there is engaging, neither he nor Jane Fonda fully embody their characters. They're stars, play acting about adult illiteracy, and watching the movie is like having to go to a class you don't enjoy.

The picture has been letterboxed, with an aspect ratio of about 2.35:1. The letterboxing provides a legitimate presentation of the theatrical image, which is gratifying. The colors are accurate, but the picture is grainy and mildly unappealing. The stereo surround soundtrack has a few subtle separation effects and is pleasing. There is a good theatrical trailer after the film is ended which tries its best to make the movie look like fun.

THE STAR CHAMBER

It has been our experience, after viewing a great many discs, that a movie usually reaches its stride somewhere around the twenty minute marker. That is the point where the introductions are over and the essence of the film has begun, the point where, if the viewer is not hooked, the film is in real trouble. A half hour into Peter Hyams' *The Star Chamber* it is still a series of seemingly unconnected incidents involving the arrests and failed prosecutions of street criminals. Michael Douglas, the film's star, has appeared only briefly, as the presiding judge in two of the trials. That the incidents seem to be leading nowhere, and that, while the movie is set in LA, the rules of justice appear exaggerated to the point where the film seems to be taking place in a different country, doesn't really matter. It would be great fun just to put up your feet and watch Hyams do this stuff all afternoon. Eventually, however, a real plot materializes, with the mistaken casting of Hal Holbrook reinforcing its conceptual similarities to the plot of *Magnum Force*. Whatever – the less concerned one is with the details, the more one will enjoy the show.

Hyams used a number of innovative camera techniques, and some come out on the disc a little foggy, although generally the picture is in decent shape. The sound is in stereo surround and has a few nice, but limited effects.

A STAR IS BORN

Image's release of *A Star Is Born* is the 1937 version of the Hollywood dirty laundry story, starring Janet Gaynor as the innocent, successful newcomer and Fredric March as the alcoholic has-been. The first pressing was in extremely bad condition, although a subsequent run was much cleaner. The film is in Technicolor, but the colors are weak and the picture is too dark. The sound levels on side two are lower than side one.

STAR OF MIDNIGHT

Bad performances by everyone in the cast except William Powell do not prevent *Star of Midnight* from giving a viewer a good time. Technically, the lighthearted murder mystery is an embarrassingly misguided ripoff of 'The Thin Man' series. Powell's character, a rich lawyer who solves crimes, drinks heavily but never gets tipsy. Ginger Roger's character, his quasi-spouse, is nosey, but lacks self-absorption. It is awkwardly made, but the movie has enough humorous moments, enough red herrings, and enough star appeal to get by. The transfer gets by as well. The picture is bright, but not in perfect condition. The sound is scratchy and best left without amplification.

STAR STRUCK

When Cyndi Lauper's music video, 'Girls Just Want to Have Fun,' first hit the air waves, part of its popularity came from its being different than all the other music videos – a free-spirited romp which implied that not feeling guilty is a lot more fun than innocence. But the video did have a precedent. Two years earlier an Australian movie came out which was 90 minutes of the same thing: *Star Struck*.

Jo Kennedy portrays a young singer who wants to be famous. Working in her mother's tavern and chasing around Sydney with her blue-haired cousin, she has a few crazy adventures and eventually becomes famous. The songs, her wardrobe, and the carefree attitude which director Gillian Armstrong stamps upon everything makes *Star Struck* a relaxing, exuberant experience. The stereo musical score is pleasing, but it is the appeal of the personalities which give the songs life. The picture is a little blurry.

STAR TREK TELEVISION SERIES

EPISODE 6 – THE MAN TRAP & EPISODE 8 – CHARLIE X
EPISODE 2 – WHERE NO MAN HAS GONE BEFORE & EPISODE 7 – THE NAKED TIME
EPISODE 5 – THE ENEMY WITHIN & EPISODE 4 – MUDD'S WOMEN
EPISODE 10 – WHAT ARE LITTLE GIRLS MADE OF? & EPISODE 12 – MIRI
EPISODE 11 – DAGGER OF THE MIND & EPISODE 3 – THE CORBOMITE MANEUVER
THE MENAGERIE PART I & II
EPISODE 1 – THE CAGE
EPISODE 13 – THE CONSCIENCE OF THE KING & EPISODE 9 – BALANCE OF TERROR
EPISODE 17 – SHORE LEAVE & EPISODE 14 – THE GALILEO SEVEN
EPISODE 18 – THE SQUIRE OF GOTHOS & EPISODE 19 – ARENA
EPISODE 21 – TOMORROW IS YESTERDAY & EPISODE 15 – COURT-MARTIAL
EPISODE 22 – THE RETURN OF THE ARCHONS & EPISODE 24 – SPACE SEED
EPISODE 23 – A TASTE OF ARMAGEDDON & EPISODE 25 – THIS SIDE OF PARADISE
EPISODE 26 – THE DEVIL IN THE DARK & EPISODE 27 – ERRAND OF MERCY
EPISODE 20 – THE ALTERNATIVE FACTOR & EPISODE 28 – THE CITY ON THE EDGE OF FOREVER
EPISODE 29 – OPERATION – ANNIHI LATE! & EPISODE 34 – AMOK TIME
EPISODE 33 – WHO MOURNS FOR ADONAIS & EPISODE 37 – THE CHANGELING
EPISODE 38 – THE APPLE & EPISODE 39 – MIRROR, MIRROR
EPISODE 30 – CATSPAW & EPISODE 35 – THE DOOMSDAY MACHINE
EPISODE 31 – METAMORPHOSIS & EPISODE 41 – I, MUDD
EPISODE 32 – FRIDAY'S CHILD & EPISODE 44 – JOURNEY TO BABEL
EPISODE 40 – THE DEADLY YEARS & EPISODE 47 – OBSESSION
EPISODE 36 – THE WOLF IN THE FOLD & EPISODE 42 – THE TROUBLE WITH TRIBBLES
EPISODE 46 – THE GAMESTERS OF TRISKELION & EPISODE 49 – A PIECE OF THE ACTION
EPISODE 48 – THE IMMUNITY SYNDROME & EPISODE 45 – A PRIVATE LITTLE WAR
EPISODE 51 – RETURN TO TOMORROW & EPISODE 52 – PATTERNS OF FORCE

EPISODE 50 – BY ANY OTHER NAME & EPISODE 54 – THE OMEGA GLORY
EPISODE 53 – THE ULTIMATE COMPUTER & EPISODE 43 – BREAD AND CIRCUSES
EPISODE 55 – ASSIGNMENT: EARTH & EPISODE 61 – SPOCK'S BRAIN
EPISODE 59 – THE ENTERPRISE INCIDENT & EPISODE 58 – THE PARADISE SYNDROME
EPISODE 60 – AND THE CHILDREN SHALL LEAD & EPISODE 62 – IS THERE IN TRUTH NO BEAUTY?
EPISODE 56 – SPECTRE OF THE GUN & – EPISODE 66 – DAY OF THE DOVE
EPISODE 65 – FOR THE WORLD IS HOLLOW AND I HAVE TOUCHED THE SKY & EPISODE 64 – THE THOLIAN WEB
EPISODE 67 – PLATO'S STEP-CHILDREN & EPISODE 68 – WINK OF AN EYE
EPISODE 63 – THE EMPATH & EPISODE 57 – ELAAN OF TROYIUS
EPISODE 71 – WHOM THE GODS DESTROY & EPISODE 70 – LET THAT BE YOUR LAST BATTLEFIELD
EPISODE 72 – THE MARK OF GIDEON & EPISODE 69 – THAT WHICH SURVIVES
EPISODE 73 – THE LIGHTS OF ZETAR & EPISODE 76 – REQUIEM FOR METHUSELAH
EPISODE 75 – THE WAY TO EDEN & EPISODE 74 – THE CLOUD MINDERS
EPISODE 77 – THE SAVAGE CURTAIN & EPISODE 78 – ALL OUR YESTERDAYS
EPISODE 79 – TURNABOUT INTRUDER

Even the name 'Star Trek' has a certain uniqueness to it. 'Trek' is practically the only word in the English language which ends with a 'k' unsupported by another consonant. The concept of *Star Trek* was also unique. The 'transporter,' for example, eliminated the need to have boring stock footage of shuttle craft taking off and landing and turned a writing problem (How do we get the characters down there?) into one of the high points of each show ('Beam me up, Scotty!').

Paramount systematically released the episodes in the order they were originally broadcast, two to a disc (a single episode on each side). The 41 disc collection is 7 inches thick and weighs 25 pounds. The shows are grouped in release order (the original air date is printed on the jacket cover) although they are identified (as *Episode 6*, *Episode 8*, et cetera) in the order of actual production. With the exception of the first three episodes the format (and the angle of Spock's eyebrows) is fairly well settled and the actual production sequence is not too significant. The jacket covers of the discs are very similar, which may frustrate consumers who are searching for a specific release.

The episodes are reasonably consistent in picture and sound quality. (with scratches only appearing on stock footage) and sound. Most look quite good. The colors are fresh, and the skin tones are accurate. CX-encoding was inconsistently applied to the analog audio tracks, but in general the monaural audio does not sound as shrill as other television shows transferred to disc have sounded.

At the end of every episode, there is a trailer for another episode, usually the next in the disc series. Early copies of many of the discs had severe problems with warping, no pun intended, a problem which was corrected in subsequent manufacturing runs.

Episode 6 – The Man Trap & Episode 8 – Charlie X were the first two episodes broadcast. 'Man Trap' has a bug-eyed monster, which is why it was probably the first telecast, as monsters are always popular. The highlight of 'Charlie X,' about a passenger (played by Robert Walker, Jr.) who cannot control the special powers he has acquired or his own emotional state, is an opportunity to hear Nichelle Nichols (Uhura) sing, and she sounds so good you wish they'd have used her that way more often.

The first show on *Episode 2 – Where No Man Has Gone Before & Episode 7 – The Naked Time* stars a very young Sally Kellerman, whose icy and enigmatic performance is perfectly suited for the tale of 'mutating ESP abilities.' 'The Naked Time' is about a disease which causes the Enterprise crew members to act out their impulses.

Episode 10 – What Are Little Girls Made Of? & Episode 12 – Miri is one of the least desirable discs. The first show is an overly complicated story about a mad scientist building androids. 'Miri' is a real mistake. The crew discovers that old favorite, a planet identical to Earth, and beams down to find a world similar to the American sixties, where everyone over puberty has died of a disease and everyone under lives for hundreds of years.

All four episodes in *Episode 5 – The Enemy Within & Episode 4 – Mudd's Women* and *Episode 11 – Dagger of the Mind & Episode 3 – The Corbomite Maneuver* are terrific. 'Enemy Within' is about a transporter accident which splits Captain Kirk (William Shatner) into two people, one 'good' but hopelessly passive and one 'bad' and aggressive. 'Mudd's Women' is about a space pimp, Harvey Mudd (Roger Carmel), whose character is so blatantly unethical that he became a popular occasional guest on the series. In 'Dagger of the Mind,' the Enterprise makes a delivery to a penal colony. There is an escape, but the stowaway turns out to be the assistant director of the colony. One of the best examples of pure *Star Trek* can be found in 'The Corbomite Maneuver,' in which the crew must outwit an apparently malicious alien space ship with a little logic and a lot of bluffing. Even the cheap special effects are explained by the time the story is over.

Star Trek: The Menagerie Part I & II, which was released previous to the other episodes (with a different jacket cover style, and no trailer), was a deft integration of the *Star Trek* pilot episode, *The Cage*, and the regular series format. It was first shown as a two-parter during the November sweeps in 1966 (not 1967 as is erroneously indicated on the jacket cover). Spock hijacks the Enterprise to return the paraplegic Captain Pike (Jeffrey Hunter) to a taboo planet where something mysterious happened on a mission years earlier.

"Airdate: Never aired on television," it says on the back of *Star Trek Television Series Episode 1 – The Cage*. This is a shame, because the pilot episode, which according to the jacket copy was rejected by the TV networks as 'too cerebral,' is exactly that, a tight science fiction-based story taking full advantage of the pathways provided by imagination.

Familiarity with *The Menagerie* does not prepare one for the impact which *The Cage* has. The trick in the later story was to present the original footage as evidence in a court martial of Spock. The show's producer, Gene Roddenberry, utilized the original color negative from 'The Cage' in cutting and pasting 'The Menagerie,' but he retained a black-and-white work print of the pilot. To reconstruct *The Cage*, he combined the color *Menagerie* material with footage from the black-and-white work print (which is a bit worn and scratchy). The result is complete and the shifts from color to black-and-white often pass unnoticed. *The Cage* turns out to have a surprise ending which was disguised in the *Menagerie* reworking.

Episode 13 – The Conscience of the King & Episode 9 – Balance of Terror opens with an unlikely amateurish production of 'Macbeth.' One of the actors in the troupe may be a retired mass murderer and it is up to Captain Kirk to pass judgement on the man's actions. 'Balance of Terror,' like 'The Corbomite Maneuver,' is a battle of stategy and wits between the Enterprise and an invisible alien craft. The complicated second guessing which goes on between Kirk and the alien commander makes the episode a favorite for repeated viewings.

Theodore Sturgeon wrote the script for 'Shore Leave' on *Episode 17 – Shore Leave & Episode 14 – The Galileo Seven*. About a planet-sized amusement park where every fantasy comes true, the audience is hooked from the beginning, when McCoy (DeForest Kelley) sees a large white rabbit holding a pocket watch. The intention of 'Galileo Seven' is to explore the tensions caused when emotionless Spock must display his leadership abilities.

Two standard, entertaining episodes are available on *Episode 18 – The Squire of Gothos & Episode 19 – Arena*. 'Gothos' is a typical *Star Trek* plot about an alien being who turns out to be a child after the crew of the Enterprise all but exhaust themselves trying to defeat it. 'Arena' is an action-laden tale about Kirk and a lizard in a tank-top who have been placed on a planet to solve their civilization's differences through hand-to-hand combat. The removal of commercial breaks, however, damages the continuity. At one exciting moment, Kirk's legs are trapped by a boulder and the lizard is bending over to shove a knife into the Captain's chest. The show cuts away to the brief darkness that indicates a sponsor's pause and then returns all too quickly. Does the lizard plunge the dagger into poor, defenseless Jim? No, he *moves the boulder* to get a better angle, and of course Kirk scurries away. No wonder dinosaurs are extinct.

Entertainment of a more cerebral nature is available on *Episode 21 – Tomorrow is Yesterday & Episode 15 – Court-Martial*. 'Tomorrow' is a predictable but well thought-out time warp exercise where the Enterprise is mistaken in the late 1960s for a UFO. In one quaint scene, Kirk, at a Nebraska Air

Force Base, is attempting to retrieve a computer tape which contains records of the Enterprise sighting. He remarks at how primitive the computers look, and indeed, to viewers today, they do. Elisha Cook stars as Kirk's defense attorney in 'Court-Martial.' A point of law is part of the issue here. Is a computer a reliable or acceptable witness?

Finally, everyone who owns *The Wrath of Khan* will want to obtain *Episode 22 – The Return of the Archons & Episode 24 – Space Seed.* 'Space Seed' is, as all good Trekkies know, the episode upon which *Wrath of Khan* was based. Ricardo Montalban portrays the leader of a group of genetically advanced humans who were expelled from Earth two hundred years earlier and have been adrift in a frozen state since that time, until the Enterprise provides a thaw. Those interested in trivia will note that Chekov, who discovers Khan's spaceship in the feature film, is not yet a member of the crew in this episode. 'Return of the Archons' is another standard, well-executed story about mysterious occurrences on a planet where everyone is friendly or hostile depending upon the time of day.

'The City on the Edge of Forever' is considered by many to be the best *Star Trek* episode. We have other favorites, but screenwriter Harlan Ellison and director Joseph Pevney created a nearly perfect moment of fantasy and feeling in the story about a woman who must die to prevent a time paradox. The episode is part of *Episode 20 – The Alternative Factor & Episode 28 – The City on the Edge of Forever*. 'Forever' has been given a stereo music track which is mildly distracting (the rights to the original music could not be secured). 'Factor' has some extremely cheap-looking effects, but still manages to be a moderately entertaining tale about a man battling his double in an alternate universe. The one flaw in the episode is that Kirk acts as if he had never heard of antimatter, which elsewhere is identified as the primary fuel source for the Enterprise.

One of our favorite episodes appears on *Episode 23 – A Taste of Armageddon & Episode 25 – This Side of Paradise*. In 'Armageddon,' the Enterprise visits a planet which has bureaucracized war – computers randomly identify victims who must then report to disintegration chambers. The flip side, 'This Side of Paradise,' gives Leonard Nimoy a chance to break a little out of character when Spock is exposed to spores which enable him to fall in love (with Jill Ireland).

Both episodes on *Episode 26 – The Devil in the Dark & Episode 27 – Errand of Mercy* are terrific. 'Devil' is a monster story about a creature whose evolution has a silicon, rather than a carbon, base. 'Errand' was the first episode to present the Klingons and the greed for career advancement in the eyes of one Klingon, played by John Coucos, when he realizes he has captured a Starship Commander, is a wonderfully subtle comic moment.

Episode 29 – Operation – Annihilate! & Episode 34 – Amok Time marks the end of the first season of episodes (in April, 1967) and the beginning (broadcast in September, 1967) of the second. 'Annihilate!' is a mildly interesting medical mystery about a flying platelet which is impervious to destruction. The second season got off to a rousing start with 'Amok Time,' which was also written by Sturgeon. This is the episode where Spock must return to Vulcan and mate and it provided the inspiration and tone for much of *The Search for Spock*.

The second season episodes have a spruced-up title sequence and a more sophisticated look in general. The effects are often more expensive and the closeups of the stars have more texture. Shatner's hair, for example, is no longer oiled down flat.

Episode 33 – Who Mourns for Adonais? & Episode 37 – The Changeling includes the episode which was the primary inspiration for *Star Trek – The Motion Picture*. 'Changeling' is able to summarize the whole of *Star Trek-TMP* in the first ten minutes and spends the remaining forty dwelling upon an Oedipal struggle between the errant space probe and Kirk – who the space probe sees as 'The Creator.' 'Adonais' is a less effective episode which suggests that the 'Gods' of Greek Mythology were actually visitors from another world. The episode also contains a flagrant error: Spock refers to the name of the being tormenting Kirk on the planet below even though they had no communication after Kirk learned the being's name.

One of the best pairings in the disc series is *Episode 32 – Friday's Child & Episode 44 – Journey to Babel*. 'Journey' is the episode where Spock's father and mother (Jane Wyatt!) become involved in a murder and espionage plot while travelling aboard the Enterprise on a diplomatic mission. 'Friday's Child' presents an unusual civilization where aggression and honesty are held in equal regard. Predictably, the fool Klingon who turns the planet against Captain Kirk can't help but be dishonest and do himself in. Julie Newmar guest stars as a pregnant warrior.

The Harvey Mudd character is the center of attention in 'I, Mudd,' part of *Episode 31 – Metamorphosis & Episode 41 – I, Mudd*. The comical nature of the episode makes it an amusing change of pace. 'Metamorphosis' is a standard but well-executed tale about a hermit who has a sustaining and perhaps romantic relationship with a cloud-creature. 'Mirror, Mirror' makes dandy use of the old alternate universe trick to put Kirk and three others on a replica of the Enterprise in *Episode 38 – The Apple & Episode 39 – Mirror, Mirror*. Aboard the alternate Enterprise, the crew is a band of cutthroats and Kirk must pretend to be the baddest of them all until he can find a way out. 'The Apple,' unfortunately, is a weakly constructed episode about a group of dullards, including David Soul, serving a machine in a sort of paradise.

Episode 30 – Catspaw & Episode 35 – The Doomsday Machine has an overly clever Halloween piece and a standard, but fairly exciting, variation on the not under-used 'Moby Dick' story device. 'Moby Dick' surfaces again in 'Obsession,' part of *Episode 40 – The Deadly Years & Episode 47 – Obsession*. In 'Doomsday Machine,' another commander endangers the Enterprise to destroy a planet-gobbling worm (and there is a sound dropout on the disc at minute 8). In 'Obsession,' Kirk becomes a bit of Ahab himself as he starts chasing after a sweet smelling gas cloud with a notorious past. 'Deadly Years' is a slower moving episode in which Kirk and several other crew members age precipitously.

Of strongest interest to both fans and newcomers is *Episode 36 – The Wolf in the Fold & Episode 42 – The Trouble with Tribbles.* 'Tribbles,' which first played during the Christmas/New Years holidays in 1967, is, deservedly, one of the most popular episodes in the series. 'Wolf' opens with a closeup on the pulsating chest of a belly dancer. The dancer is subsequently murdered and Scotty is accused of the crime. We recommend this disc for those who are interested in obtaining just one *Star Trek Television Series* offering.

'The Immunity Syndrome,' of *Episode 48 – The Immunity Syndrome & Episode 45 – A Private Little War*, is about a gigantic amoeba floating in space which eats the Enterprise. The way in which they extract themselves is never completely clear, but it is not as important to the story as what happens between Spock, McCoy, and Kirk as they reason their way out of their dilemma. 'War' also concentrates so heavily on characterizations that the Klingon, who started all the trouble on a planet with a peaceful, primitive civilization, is allowed to slip out of the story unnoticed after the damage has started.

'By Any Other Name' and 'Return to Tomorrow' in *Episode 50 – By Any Other Name & Episode 54 – The Omega Glory* and *Episode 51 – Return to Tomorrow & Episode 52 – Patterns of Force* both deal with alien forms who get off on inhabiting human bodies. Coincidentally, both 'Omega Glory' and 'Patterns of Force' are about worlds which are similar to Earth at different points in history. There is a logical explanation for the world imitating Nazi Germany in 'Patterns' and it is enjoyable to see Spock decked out in an SS uniform. No logical reason is given for the Earth imitation in 'Glory,' but its ending, about post-holocaust inhabitants discovering the meaning of documents like the United States Constitution, is inspirational and justifies its context.

A logical explanation is also given for the world which has taken on the appearance of Chicago gangster territories in the 1920s in 'A Piece of the Action,' part of *Episode 46 – The Gamesters of Triskelion & Episode 49 – A Piece of the Action*. In fact, it is almost the same logical explanation which was used for 'Patterns,' and it provides an excuse to have some fun with the anachronisms and show Spock decked out in a wide-brimmed hat and spats. 'Gamesters' is a familiar plot, with Kirk and two crew members forced to become interplanetary gladiators, but the approach is different and concentrates on the meanings of love and freedom.

Episode 53 – The Ultimate Computer & Episode 43 – Bread and Circuses represents the end of the second season. 'Computer' is about a machine being tested aboard the Enterprise and Kirk spends most of the show trying to outthink the thing in order to save mankind. 'Bread and Circuses' has the world-similar-to-Earth plot device again — and this time the writers even come up with a catchall excuse, 'Hodgkin's Law of Parallel Planet Development.' The episode postulates the extension of Roman society into the Twentieth Century and gets in some terrific digs at television networks during a bright satire on the broadcasting of gladiator battles.

The first episode of *Episode 55 – Assignment: Earth & Episode 61 – Spock's Brain* was the last episode of the second season and it was also a pilot for another television series which, unfortunately, never received a green light. Robert Lansing and Terri Garr are featured, and that would have been quite enough to keep us glued to our screen. Taken as an episode, 'Earth' is stimulating, because there are many bits of business, such as an intelligent cat, which are not elaborated upon, under the assumption that they would be expanded later on. The premise has a vague resemblance to *2001* and the result is television which does not insult your intelligence by explaining every last quirk.

With the beginning of the notorious third season, Roddenberry abandoned his direct involvement with the show's production. 'Spock's Brain' opened the season. Most of the cast have haircuts, but no other major changes are noticeable. In the episode an alien woman steals Spock's brain, and Nimoy must walk about like a zombie until it is returned. The story has the right mixture of fantasy and tension and is satisfying.

The third season really gets underway with *Episode 59 – The Enterprise Incident & Episode 58 – The Paradise Syndrome* and the disc is good evidence that the much maligned effort has more going for it than one would expect. 'Paradise' is a certifiable cult favorite in which Kirk, suffering from amnesia, falls for a luscious Indian maiden, Sabrina Scharf, in an Arcadian utopia. The emphasis on romance and the total silliness of the whole exercise makes it a strong favorite among those who have become overly familiar with the normal plot formulas. 'The Enterprise Incident' is also quite enjoyable, as Spock romances a Romulan commander to assist in the absconding of a cloaking device.

All four episodes on *Episode 60 – And the Children Shall Lead & Episode 62 – Is There in Truth No Beauty?* and *Episode 56 – Spectre of the Gun & Episode 66 – Day of the Dove* are equally engaging. Melvin Belli shows up as the bad guy on 'Children,' manipulating the minds of the Enterprise crew until Kirk figures out his scheme. 'Truth' is a clever concoction about an entity, being transported on the Enterprise, which only Spock can look at without being driven insane.

'Spectre' is a pleasant tale in which Kirk and his staff are forced by aliens to reenact the gunfight at O.K. Corral, and 'Day of the Dove' is about a being which thrives off the hatred felt when the Enterprise captures a group of Klingons. The Klingon leader is Michael Ansara, a star so forgotten that he isn't even listed in the jacket credits.

Both episodes on *Episode 65 – For the World Is Hollow and I Have Touched the Sky & Episode 64 – The Tholian Web* are entertaining, and both possess plot gimmicks which are dispensed with too quickly (even with the running time constraints) once a conclusion is required. In 'World is Hollow' the crew discovers a spacecraft so gigantic that its inhabitant believe they live on a planet. The gimmick is an incurable disease foisted onto Dr. McCoy and then removed without flourish. 'Tholian Web' utilizes memorable graphics when the Enterprise is trapped by two smaller craft which weave an energy field around it. The main plot, however, concerns Kirk's entrapment in an alternate universe and how his secondaries must cope without him. The web disappears with hardly a comment when the plot moves elsewhere. The picture quality on the entire disc is okay, but not as good as other episodes have been. There is an extended 'red light' sequence in 'World is Hollow' which looks awful.

Michael Dunn appears in 'Plato's Stepchildren' on *Episode 67 – Plato's Stepchildren & Episode 68 – Wink of an Eye*. He is the jester to a group of immortals inspired by Earth's famous philosopher, and has been under their telekinetic subjugation for 2500 years. Except for a handful of token inserts, none of the episode takes place on the Enterprise. The telekinesis enables Shatner, Nimoy (who even gets to sing!) and Kelley to do crazy things with their limbs, an activity which is always enjoyable to observe. The print is in excellent condition, one of the nicest we have seen.

The print and picture quality of 'Wink of an Eye,' however, is less satisfying, and solid colors tend to bleed. In 'Wink' the Enterprise is captured by a group of people who exist in hyper-time, where a second to normal folks is the same as an hour to them. This gives the cast an opportunity to Stand Perfectly Still as Kirk, who has entered the realm of the invaders, comes up with a plan to retrieve control of his ship. The timing is all messed up, but the fantasy is pleasing.

One of the rare episodes in the third season that is both entertaining and intelligent is 'Let That Be Your Last Battlefield,' on *Episode 71 – Whom the Gods Destroy & Episode 70 Let That Be Your Last Battlefield*. The plot concerns two aliens who hold irreconcilably opposing points of view – one authoritarian and one libertarian – and the havoc they cause when their argument is brought onto the Enterprise. 'Gods' is a more ordinary episode, concerning a master criminal on a prison planet ('Elba II') who can change shapes at will, and provides an opportunity, once again, for both Shatner and Nimoy to break out of their standard characters, with the usual hoary results.

Contrary to standard procedures on most television programs, one person, John Meredith Lucas, both wrote and directed 'Elaan of Troyius,' part of *Episode 63 – The Empath & Episode 57 Elaan of Troyius*. The show is tight, elaborate, and very entertaining. In fact, we had not planned to watch it right away, after viewing 'The Empath,' but upon seeing the trailer for it, we couldn't resist putting it on. The plot concerns a diplomatic mission in which the Enterprise has been assigned to transport a reluctant bride to her wedding, an arrangement that will bring peace between two warring planets. The woman is a cross between Shakespeare's Kate and Homer's Helen, and she is played to perfection by France Nuyen. Klingons are also lurking about, hoping to spoil the wedding, and the program was the first time the standard design for the Klingon spacecraft was employed.

'Empath' takes place on an unusually empty soundstage, where Kirk, McCoy, Spock and a mysterious woman who cannot talk are being held against their will. Unraveling the reasons for their confinement is the primary thrust of the plot, but the acting is magnified by the lack of props, and the personalities of the characters sustain one's interests.

Spock is given an unusually harsh personality in 'That Which Survives' on *Episode 72 – The Mark of Gideon & Episode 69 – That Which Survives*, for no apparent reason. He is in command of the Enterprise while Captain Kirk is investigating an unusually young planet, and continually criticizes or corrects the information given to him by the crew members on the Command Deck. The plot concerns a mysterious woman who appears out of nowhere and kills people by touching them. The plot construction is contrived, but a viewer is kept in suspense until the end, and the script offers a couple of original touches. 'The Mark of Gideon' has nothing original to offer and is loaded with illogical situations. Kirk is beamed to a planet to perform diplomatic duties, but never arrives at his destination. The planet turns out to be overpopulated, and its inhabitants hunger for his diseases. No matter how much leeway one tries to give it, the episode is embarrassing and stupid. Both programs exhibit an unusual amount of graininess, with intense colors appearing blurry and unstable. By this time the stock footage was getting severely speckled as well.

Strong colors fare better on *Episode 73 – The Lights of Zetar & Episode 76 – Requiem for Methuselah*. There are only a few instances when the blurs and grain are noticeable. 'Zetar' has a strong opening, giving Scotty a romantic interest, but the plot deteriorates in the second half, when it is revealed that a group of colored lights, which have killed all the inhabitants of a library/research center, don't really know what they want. The episode does have an elaborately edited soundtrack. 'Requiem for Methuselah' is the opposite. It has an uninteresting opening but grows on the viewer as it progresses. Dispensing with the rest of the cast, the show features the three leads only, visiting a planet which has just two inhabitants and a robot. There is more than a passing resemblance to *Forbidden Planet*. Spock's final activity and line of dialog is an unusual alternative to the happy talk which normally concludes the show.

There is more than a passing resemblance to *Metropolis* in 'The Cloud Minders,' which also may have inspired the cloud city in *The Empire Strikes Back*. In an unusual narrative device, Nimoy performs an elaborate voiceover to establish the situation. The inhabitants of the city subjugate an 'inferior' race which lives on the planet below, mining valuable minerals. Kirk must negotiate what in essence is a labor strike in order to obtain some of the minerals in an emergency. The special effects are simple, but engaging. Shatner, however, wears a futuristic gas mask at one point, and he couldn't induce more giggles if he were to put on glasses and a false nose. In 'The Way to Eden,' the other episode on *Episode 75 – The Way to Eden & Episode 74 – The Cloud Minders*, futuristic hippies hijack the Enterprise in search of an idyllic planet. The hijackers are intended to be comical and are effectively so.

Roddenberry devised the story and contributed to the script of 'The Savage Curtain,' and the entire episode is energized. For once, Spock's jokes are funny, the crew members do things which are in character but outside of their normal rote mannerisms, and the premise, though preposterous, has legitimate science fiction underpinnings. The story begins with Abraham Lincoln inviting Kirk and Spock to a calm spot on the surface of a molten planet. The basic plot is common to other episodes – beings are pitting Kirk against gladiators with alternate moral philosophies to see which is superior. The approach, however, is fresh, and the actor playing Lincoln, Lee Bergere, does a great job. The episode is quite enjoyable.

Mariette Hartley shows up in the companion program on *Episode 77 – The Savage Curtain & Episode 78 – All Our Yesterdays*, wearing a halter top and trying to make out with Spock. The episode is another one in which only the three leads are featured. The plot has an interesting premise. The people of a planet doomed by a supernova escape through a passage to the era of their choice in the planet's past. Unfortunately, the script is feeble and takes little advantage of the concept's potential. Both programs are mildly grainy. The print used for 'All Our Yesterdays' tends to vary in color quality, not only from scene to scene, but from shot to shot. A mild background noise is present on 'Curtain' whenever the musical score appears.

The final disc, *Episode 79 – Turnabout Intruder*, is also a good one. Roddenberry again had a hand in writing the script, which is a combination of (in order) *Fatal Attraction*, *18 Again*, *Tootsie*, and *The Caine Mutiny*. A jealous woman from Captain Kirk's past exchanges bodies with him. Shatner has a terrific time mincing around and doing his nails while giving orders. The script is well-executed, but must cheat at the end to meet the running time.

A final word on owning the complete *Star Trek Television Series* collection. Although we occasionally seek out a specific episode in our collection, we most often find ourselves just diving into the group and picking out a show at random to play, intriguingly similar to the pot luck one has when one catches the program on broadcast television. Because of the limitations involved with the fantasy, a viewer requires a certain amount of discipline to accept the proceedings. It may be that even though one is familiar with many of the episodes, one still requires a mystery – Which episode is it going to be? – to establish the initial bond, until one's imagination can mindmeld with the fantasies and the entertaining indulgences of the filmmakers.

STAR TREK III – THE SEARCH FOR SPOCK

Star Trek III – The Search For Spock, was the first non-music oriented digitally encoded laser disc released anywhere. Whether it helps the film or not is another matter, for the picture is grainy and the story is very loosely organized.

If you accept the far-fetched premise that Spock's corpse regenerates at the exact pace by which the rest of a planet is moving from Silurian to post-Holocene, then you will undoubtedly find the film entertaining. Directed by Leonard Nimoy, parts of the movie are actually more effective on a television screen than in a theater. This is because the characters often get grouped in the center of the picture and with fewer empty spaces on a smaller screen, the set looks less like a soundstage.

Star Trek III is intended to be about the strength of friendship. The characters ought to be surprised at themselves, at how much they have broken the rules to retrieve Spock. With the exception of the Lt. Savick character, who may or may not be pregnant with Spock's child (will we ever know?), not one of them looks unsure about the future. Nimoy has removed the awe of the universe and the awe of man's capabilities which the crew would usually discover within themselves by the end of an episode. If it weren't for the sound, the disc would be completely uninspiring.

STAR TREK IV: THE VOYAGE HOME

There is so much pleasure and good nature in *Star Trek IV: The Voyage Home* that the movie needs no improvement. If you wanted to get technical you could find a hundred things wrong with it, but nothing spoils the simple, comical execution of the entertainment.

The movie, which is scanned and cropped, often feels cramped. There is less tension in the big dramatic moments (Will Spock make the right calculations to return the ship?) because the balance isn't right between the faces and the funny displays, but there is also less tension between the viewer and the story, because on home video the movie loses all pretensions of being any more than a grand piece of television. In stereo.

The sound is terrific and has been digitally encoded. The movie benefits from a large, assured budget, so plenty of money went into getting the sound effects just right.

The film runs 119 minutes, but has been split to three sides. The quality of the picture, unfortunately, leaves something to be desired. It is more blurry than the stills on the back of the jacket, and you can even see scratches on the print in a couple of places. Like the movie itself, however, the quality of the picture on the disc will not stop one from wanting to watch the show again.

STAR TREK V – THE FINAL FRONTIER

A few saving graces will make *Star Trek V – The Final Frontier* worthwhile for at least some laser disc fans. The digital surround sound mix is fantastic. Jerry Goldsmith's score, easily the best in the series, is superbly mixed by Bruce Botnick, whose name often shows up in the credits of a film or a music concert when the audio has been unusually impressive. The music is marvelously separated, easily turning one's viewing room into a symphonic concert hall, with or without a surround processor. Added to that are the many special sound effects and the secondary dialog, which are not only directionally located but are as clearly executed as the main dialog track. A few of the special visual effects also look nice.

But then there is the movie, a meandering disaster (at least on disc one can scan past the campfire scene instead of suffering through it in real time) which neither its heritage nor its audio track can rescue. The filmmakers have apparently used *Star Trek The Motion Picture* as their guiding format, flying in shuttles instead of using transportation beams, and searching for the meaning of the universe instead of just dealing with a local problem or two. The fault runs on two levels. Not only is the plot silly, but individual scenes are too long and too poorly constructed to stop the viewer from recognizing that the plot is silly.

The disc's picture quality varies from good to poor. Some of the special effects look just fine – the model work in particular, and that is what laser disc viewers want to see. Other scenes, however, are hopelessly fuzzy, and since the special effects are rationed, the disc is blurry more often than it is not.

STAR WARS
THE EMPIRE STRIKES BACK
RETURN OF THE JEDI
STAR WARS (CAV)
THE EMPIRE STRIKES BACK (CAV)

The first batch of *Star Wars* discs was pressed at Pioneer's plant in Japan and rushed by airplane to the US, to be followed, belatedly, by the rest of the press run. It is difficult to impart the thrill which was felt by those who managed to obtain one of the first CBS/Fox discs. *Star Wars* had been theatrically released before home video was an established cultural phenomenon; it was the sort of movie one went to see in a theater more than twice. To have it on disc meant not only that you could play it whenever you felt like, it meant that the video disc player had been a legitimate investment. Tears streamed out of our eyes the first time we saw the cruiser come (and keep coming and coming) across the top of our television screen.

At the time we didn't notice that the single-plattered CLV disc had a running time of 118 minutes or that the loss of the screen's edges had made the fight in the cantina incomprehensible. We already had the segment memorized.

When the single-plattered CLV release of *The Empire Strikes Back* came out, the excitement had subsided somewhat. That film, however, survived cropping much better than *Star Wars* had, and finally there was an opportunity to watch the two in tandem. (*Star Wars* has a subheading identifying it as 'Episode IV, A New Hope,' though no one we know calls it by that name. *Empire* is identified as 'Episode V.')

We were not at all excited about the release of *Star Wars* and *The Empire Strikes Back* in CAV, particularly after we saw the jacket layouts, which were duplicates of the CLV jackets, right down to the running times. Clocking the films with a stopwatch, however, revealed that the jackets were in error. Unlike the CLV versions, the CAV *Star Wars* and *The Empire Strikes Back* run 121 and 124 minutes, respectively, the true, original running times of the films.

The picture on the original *Star Wars* discs is a bit weak on the first two sides and improves considerably in the latter half of the film. There is a splice on side three at frame 14486. *The Empire Strikes Back* is gorgeous, with a crisp print and barely a speckle. Using the CAV, in *Star Wars* we were finally able to examine the architecture of the building between the parked beast and the cantina entrance. As we had always suspected, it changes form from the long shot to the medium shot. In slow motion, we were able to discern the mirror which makes Luke's hover car appear wheel-less. At one point, it passes in front of a rock which disappears as the craft goes by.

The digitally encoded *Return of the Jedi* has the best sound of all five intitial *Star Wars* discs. When the sand barges explode, all your shelf knickknacks tumble, but when

Yoda dies, the stillness is equally deafening. Unfortunately, the picture quality is the weakest. The colors are blurry and merge together too often. The indoor scenes and special effects look especially fuzzy. (No CAV version of *Jedi* was released in the US.) The scanning and cropping make it a different movie. In a shot early on which had a double sun on the far right and a creature gobbling another creature on the left, the scanning zeroes in on the puppets at the expense of the suns. It figures.

Believe it or not, there are a few people who have not seen any of the *Star Wars* films, and more are born every day. One of the joys of owning the three movies is the ability it will give you to share the magic with others. This way, even after satiation sets in, you will still be able to feel the thrills you felt during your own first viewing.

STAR WARS (Letterboxed)
STAR WARS (Import)
THE EMPIRE STRIKES BACK (Letterboxed)
THE EMPIRE STRIKES BACK (Import)
RETURN OF THE JEDI (Letterboxed)
RETURN OF THE JEDI (Import)

As an enthusiasm for letterboxing took hold, CBS/Fox released the *Star Wars* trilogy in CLV once again, as Deluxe Widescreen Edition offerings. In Japan, the trio were also released as exquisite Special Collection editions. Both versions have their strengths. The Japanese releases are in CAV. The aspect ratios of the import versions measure about 2.3:1, as opposed to 2.4:1 on the domestic efforts, but the width on both is exactly the same. While this implies that the image is wider than the Japanese version, it actually is not. The Japanese screen composition has more picture at the bottom of the image. For that matter, there is also a little more picture information on the bottom of the old cropped CLV version than on the domestic letterboxed version (though the letterboxed version has more at the top). The Japanese framing tends to look the most correct and balanced.

The image transfer of *Star Wars* is richer on the American release. The differences are minor, but colors on the American version look more confident. In the cantina sequence on the Japanese version, for example, there is a slight haze which is gone from the American version. The sound on the domestic letterboxed rendition is also superior. On the earlier American release, the surround echo, when Luke and Leia are trapped above a chasm, was overdone and sounded forced. On the Japanese release, the compensation was too great and the echo was weakened almost to the point of losing the effect. The domestic letterboxed version gets it just right, so that it sounds like an echo, but encourages the viewer to believe that the chasm is real.

On both the domestic and foreign letterboxed discs, the contrast is set for disc resolution and space is really black. The matted squares and triangles which surround every spaceship model on the older discs are invisible on the letterboxed efforts.

Viewing *Star Wars* in widescreen is more than just being able to see the whole worm skeleton in the sand. From the opening prolog to the medal ceremony at the end, almost every shot has a vanishing point in the middle of the screen. When you view the cropped version there is very little scanning, but the reinforcement of the central image is gone. The whole drama becomes less involving and less vital. It is more like a television entertainment and less like a movie.

The ice cave sequence in the Japanese Special Collection edition of *The Empire Strikes Back* is startling, and the CBS/Fox rendition is almost as good. What appears on the older disc versions as a simple mix of bright white and dark grey obtains a tingling array of gradient shadows. The Japanese effort rates as one of the very best color film transfers to disc, and the CBS/Fox version follows it closely.

The scanned and cropped version of *Empire* has never bothered us. Only the major battles and Luke's fight with Darth Vader are seriously harmed by the dropping of the screen's edges. There is too much detail revealed in the blown up version to lament the removal of the edges. The *Star Wars* films are significant for the amount of detail which is crammed into a shot, particularly during spaceship interiors, so the miniaturization of the image necessitated by the letterboxing does prevent one from making out dials, readouts, and other minor mechanisms visible on the cropped versions. However, space cruisers colliding, attack ships whizzing through an asteroid belt, and a city floating in the clouds are just a few of the visions enhanced when the width of the viewing area is doubled.

The three-sided CBS/Fox *Empire* comes in a gatefold jacket. The disc has a few chapter markers, but they are inadequately placed. The listing identifies a highlight of the chapter, but after you call the chapter up you still have to scan a while to get to the incident listed. (The packaging on the Japanese Collector's Item discs is lovely, and the chapter encoding is thorough.) The movie, with Leigh Bracket's dialog and all those bankable special effects, gets more entertaining with every viewing, and at the end, you want to jump right into *Return of the Jedi*.

Of the three *Star Wars* films, the video transfer for *Return of the Jedi* has always been the most problematic. The film's picture is often excessively grainy, even in shots which contain no special effects. Such is the case with both the CBS/Fox Special Wide Screen Edition version and the import Special Collection presentation.

CBS/Fox's scanned and cropped version was over saturated, and bright colors tended to bleed, making it the least satisfying of the three. Although CBS/Fox's letterboxed version is different from the Japanese version, it is about the same in levels of picture quality, and the colors are more confident. A good example of how the improved color quality on the letterboxed discs helps the film comes near the end. The Emperor's throne room on the Death Star is illuminated by bright, turquoise lights, which are washed into a pale blue on the cropped disc. On the letterboxed presentations, the lights are distinctive and presage the Emperor's fiery blue demise. More shots on the Japanese version look better, but some on the CBS/Fox letterboxed version are stronger and less pale. The picture on the letterboxed versions still looks soft and is very grainy in places, but the action scenes are so pleasing that most viewers will not mind. The first hour is the weakest.

The letterboxing on the CBS/Fox disc has the same aspect ratio as the Japanese disc, about 2.3:1. The framing, however, is set slightly lower, cutting off a little too much at the top. The subtitles for alien-speak appear beneath the picture, in the black (and are in Japanese on the import version). Although some sequences are enjoyable on the cropped version – and the closeups are satisfying – other scenes are incomprehensible without the sides, at least until you've watched the movie a dozen times or so.

The most significant improvement offered by the CBS/Fox letterboxed disc is not the picture, but the sound. The cropped disc has a clearer and more atmospheric audio track than the curiously subdued Japanese version, but the domestic letterboxed presentation is better still. The bass is incredible. Not only does it boom enthusiastically, but it is fully defined and articulate as it booms. The surround channels offer not only directional sound effects, but a stronger sense of environment. The best demonstration comes right at the beginning – Jabba the Hutt may be grotesque (although he could have used a little slime), but his voice will reach right into your heart.

It was the still frame function which we found ourselves utilizing most often on the Japanese CAV *Jedi*, to savor the phantasmagoria. Anybody who has been inundated with the Walt Disney *Sleeping Beauty* disc will undoubtedly grab for the still frame command as soon as the pig guards ('Gamorrean Guards') appear in Jabba's den. They are not so much siblings to the Evil Witch's pig guards in *Sleeping Beauty* as they are genetic twins. The triple speed function is also effective in enhancing the illusions and disguising the mirrors and wires. A feature unique to the Japanese *Jedi* has been included at the end of the disc, a Special Collection Scrapbook. The scrapbook contains still photos and (silent) motion footage comparing the letterboxed compositions to the scanned and cropped compositions on all three *Star Wars* films.

Side three of the domestic letterboxed disc is also encoded in CAV, giving viewers an opportunity to step through the finale of the forest battle, the fight between Luke and the Emperor (subliminal flashes of a skeleton appear on Darth Vader), and the destruction of the Death Star. The disc is chapter encoded, though timidly, and comes in a gatefold jacket.

Having seen all three films now in letterboxed format, we have a firm sense of the different visual strategy each one possesses (we always sat too close to the screen in movie theaters to notice it before). *Star Wars* had a classically symmetrical composition, which would be audacious and embarrassing if the film were any less perfect than it is, and which is completely lost, removing the subconscious portion of the film's strength, when the movie is cropped and scanned for video. *The Empire Strikes Back* has a much more integrated picture composition and is the most comprehensible when cropped and scanned. The widescreen adds more special effects and more extraneous details, enriching the picture, but provides less support, thematically, to the obsession-and-quest plot thrust. Many scenes in *Return of the Jedi*, the fight on the sand barge in particular, are incomprehensible when cropped and scanned. After the dark, single-mindedness of *Empire*, *Jedi* is intended to be playful, to be a release. The film plays like a Saturday afternoon adventure, from the comedy of the natives mistaking the robot for a god to the melodrama of Luke's reconciliation with his father. The compositions are also playful, and often contain conflicting images. An effect or gag will occur on one side of the screen while something serious is happening on the other side.

From an economic point of view, *Star Wars* opened an infinite world to the film marketplace (something a more complex narrative could not have achieved). Before *Star Wars*, science fiction was a cinematic side show. Now special effects films are recognized as containing the greatest potential for seizing the imagination and the discretionary income of audiences. For that same reason, and because of the quality of the format, the best selling laser discs are all special effects oriented. More so even than the films which have outsold it, home video owes its raison d'etre to *Star Wars*, and discs, which have thrived so far as an ownership medium, owe it most of all.

STARCHASER: THE LEGEND OF ORIN
(see **VOLTRON, DEFENDER OF THE UNIVERSE**)

STARMAN
Our favorite shot in *Starman*, where Jeff Bridges remains in character as the camera pulls away from the truck he and Karen Allen are riding in the back of, gets lost on the small screen. You can't see him bob his head on the long, long shot because the image is too small and the resolution just isn't good enough.

Starman is a noble effort to show that love is more than physical attraction. Bridges, playing an alien who duplicates the body of a woman's dead husband, makes his mannerisms look twice removed, as if someone inside his head were pulling switches and levers to make the body function. Like the limits of memory, the alien is not a perfect copy, but again, like memory, the truth of the emotional bond between the two of them supersedes the flaws. Such a bond can also be found in the relationship between a viewer and a movie, and the filmmakers emphasize this in the beginning by having the woman watch the flickering images of her late husband. So, too, it represents the way that movies can be great and lousy at the same time; and the way that imperfect discs can still be worth having.

STARS & BARS
A comedy with a growing cult reputation among videophiles, *Stars & Bars* is about an Englishman working for a New York auction house who travels to Georgia to represent the owner of a valuable painting. The film has elements of farce, wonderful performances, and consistently avoids the standard comic clichés. The cast includes Daniel Day Lewis, Harry Dean Stanton, Martha Plimpton, Keith David, and others. Even those cast in the most outlandish parts, such as Maury Chaykin who portrays a redneck that dresses like Elvis, deftly underplay their roles so that the comedy accumulates during multiple viewings. The film is sophisticated, but it also contains basic slapstick gags, including an amusing sequence in which Lewis is trapped out of doors, stark naked. The disc looks good, with strong colors appearing distorted in only a few scenes. It is in stereo and the mild surround track is used mainly for the musical score. There are audio glitches at one point, but it is not enough to spoil the entertainment.

STARSHIP – KNEE DEEP IN THE HOOPLA
Starship – Knee Deep in the Hoopla is a 51-minute 12-inch CLV digital disc containing the complete audio program of the rock group's LP, *Knee Deep in the Hoopla*, and two music videos based on cuts from the same album. The music videos open the disc. After that, while the LP portion plays, a single photo of the album cover fills the screen. The idea here is that the disc contains everything a regular CD contains, plus the two music videos.

Hoopla opens with a 30-second 'Table of Contents' listing the chapter markers for every song. The picture quality on the two videos, 'We Built this City' and 'Sara,' is superb. These two songs are then repeated on the CD portion of the program, since they are the first two songs on the album. Seven other numbers follow.

STATE OF THE ART OF COMPUTER ANIMATION
By far the best of the computer animation anthologies available on disc, *State of the Art of Computer Animation* is an excellent starting point for those who are just getting into the artform, and an imperative addition to the collections of those who already have a passion for pixels. The program is superbly edited, so that none of the more than forty pieces featured will make the viewer feel impatient or fatigued.

The animation is as pleasing to children as it is to adults, and is amazing not just because of the way in which it was produced, but because of its power to stimulate new perspectives of thought. There are cartoons, excerpts from commercials, and plain experimental efforts, mixed together to flow from one to the next with no more than a blackout pause between each (the credit scrolls for each short are saved until the end). Every work is a highlight, but the best can probably be identified as a Lucasfilm piece ('The Adventures of Andre and Wally B.'), about a man and a bee in an incredibly natural looking forest; a transformation of a Landsat photo of Los Angeles into a three dimensional topographical landscape; and a piece about a toy penguin wandering through a hyper-realistic living room.

The program has undergone an excellent transfer to disc. The images are consistently sharp, and the digitally encoded sound takes full advantage of the shorts which were produced in stereo ('Wally B.' again). There are chapter markers for every segment and side two of the 80 minute show is in CAV. Only two of the shorts on side two seem to have a difficulty with shaky still frames, as the rest are consistently steady and open to the many possibilities which disc playback has to offer.

STATE OF THE UNION
State of the Union is a Frank Capra film based on a play about a man running for President and the conflict which arises between his wife and the woman who is running his campaign. It is a talky feature, and loaded with 1948 references which will become obscurer and obscurer with each passing election. The performances of Spencer Tracy, Katharine Hepburn, Angela Lansbury, and Van Johnson, on the other hand, are timeless. The plot seems to mistake pragmatism for evil and idealism for good, but that is what movies are for.

The black-and-white print looks crisp and has no more than a couple of jumps. The movie runs 123 minutes, and side three is in CAV. A trailer is also included, with its own chapter marker.

THE STATE OF THINGS
The black-and-white feature, *The State of Things*, belongs to what could probably be called a genre of European films about film crews waiting to make movies. Like *Contempt* and 'Beware of a Holy Whore,' the cast and cast-within-the-cast sit around talking and waiting and talking and waiting. For some reason, we love these movies. Usually when characters are bored, the viewer is not far behind, but placing forced boredom onto a cluster of talented and creative characters provides just enough stimulation to make things continually interesting. Directed by Wim Wenders, the black-and-white images and the vaguely trivial, vaguely profound dialog are enough to keep a viewer's attention from wandering. Wenders wanted to have fun making the movie, and he communicates that without having to show his hand.

The cinematographer, Henry Alekan, had substantial experience working in black-and-white, unlike a number of American cinematographers who come to such an assignment having only toyed with filters and shadows. As we indicated above, if the dialog doesn't hold you, the image will. The picture is a bit soft, but the transfer is acceptable. Contrary to the statement on the jacket cover, the film is in English, with some incidental French which is left untranslated. No subtitles appear.

The sound is passable. The two hour movie is stretched to three sides, the last one (not photographed by Alekan – side two was the best candidate for standard play) in CAV. The disc comes in a gatefold jacket and the innerspread text provides good background information on how *The State of Things* came into existence.

THE STATUE OF LIBERTY
An hour-long documentary about the Statue and what it represents, *The Statue of Liberty* is not CX-encoded and consists mostly of pans across still pictures accompanied by narration. It is the story of an artist with a vision wilder than anything Christo has ever come up with; of what the newspapers, like Pulitzer's, could accomplish when they lent their circulation to a good cause; and of the French and the Norman origination of 'liberty.' Some interviews and a few film clips are also provided and the show even manages to get in the ending from *Planet of the Apes*. The content is intelligent and informative and not given to a particular point of view. James Baldwin, for example, has some pretty strong things to say, questioning the concept of liberty in America.

STEAL THE SKY
Don't be mislead by the jacket cover for *Steal the Sky*, which suggests that the film is a *Top Gun* rip-off. The movie is actually a terrific espionage and romance story, about an Israeli plot to steal an Iraqi MIG. Mariel Hemingway, portraying an American who lives in Bagdad, does some of her best work in the film. She is more relaxed and believable than she has been in the past. The movie has the pace and budget of a typical Israeli action picture, but the patriotism is often undercut by irony, and the script's first priority is always the emotions of the characters. There is humor (an Iraqi band playing Beatle songs), methodical excitement, and an admirable tendency to avoid supplying the viewer with extraneous information. The picture is sharp, and some of the flight scenes are great fun. The stereo sound is not elaborately produced, but has no significant flaws.

STEALING HEAVEN
The director's cut of *Stealing Heaven*, which has been restored for home video, gives the film integrity, but it is not enough. *Heaven* is a muddy costume romance, set in the twelfth century, based upon a legend about a monk and a nun whose love for each other exemplified the endurance of passion. The best romantic movies have scenes in which a viewer's identification with the protagonists is near total, in which shifts in emotions are completely understood, or even shared. *Stealing Heaven* has a curiously neutral point of view – even the erotic scenes are in long or medium shots – causing neutrality in a viewer's feelings for the lovers as well. The picture is soft and flesh tends to look too red. The sound is stereo surround, but the effects are intermittent and uninspired.

STEALING HOME
A meandering story of nostalgia, *Stealing Home* is ultimately satisfying and romantic. The picture is grainy and there is an uninteresting digitally encoded stereo surround soundtrack, save for a few choice oldies. A man returns to his hometown to collect the ashes of a friend, and his thoughts, in flashback, move through the major events in his life. Mark Harmon and Jodie Foster star.

STEEL DAWN
Patrick Swayze is seen standing on his head in the middle of a desert at the opening of *Steel Dawn*, and so you surmise fairly rapidly that the film is not about early rising blue collar workers, as the title implies. And if your TV isn't working and you can only play the sound through your stereo system, you would hear that the story is a struggle between simple farmers and a powerful landowner who wants their water, and that Swayze is a stranger who helps to protect them, and you would think that the movie is a western. Well, it is, except that it takes place in the future, where guns have been superseded by a new and more powerful weapon, the sword.

The picture is grainy. The sound is so good, on the other hand, that you can hear the actors talking with an indoor echo when they are supposed to be standing outside.

STEEL MAGNOLIAS
Gussied up as an ensemble comedy centered around a beauty parlor, *Steel Magnolias* is actually about a diabetic who decides to have a child and then dies from kidney failure about a year after the baby is born. The film conveys the emotions of sorrow to the viewer and also generates a few laughs to alleviate the tension. The cast includes Shirley MacLaine, Julia Roberts, Sally Field, Olympia Dukakis, Daryl Hannah, and Dolly Parton, and they are often all in the same shot together, so you have to watch some scenes seven times to absorb them completely. On the whole, though, the script seems to shift between being contrived and being inconsequential. The picture transfer is acceptable. Stereo separations are limited to the music and a few key sound effects.

STEELE JUSTICE
An action picture with weak performances but a steady flow of fights and other violent activities, *Steele Justice*, was withdrawn from the market shortly after release. The plot, about a Vietnam vet/ex-cop avenging the murder of his former buddy/partner, is outlandishly improbable, but carries the movie effectively. The actors are less effective, but so long as they keep their mouths shut and talk with their knives, guns, fists, etc., nobody is going to argue with them. The sound is and has no major problems. The picture transfer is fine, though the production lacks gloss. The camera crew can be seen in a reflection on a car window at one point.

STEEP AND DEEP
Sometimes nothing advances with technology. A long time ago, adventure photographers would put together their most thrilling footage and travel the lecture circuit, running the film and providing ongoing commentary at the podium while it unreeled. Well, that is essentially what happens on *Steep and Deep*. The filmmaker, Warren Miller, babbles on and on, telling weak joke after weak joke as skiers on the screen soar, crash, and loop the loop. It even has an intermission (!) after the first 45-minute reel is ended. Wisely, that is where Image breaks the side.

The sound quality and musical score are unmemorable. The disc is 90 minutes long and looks okay when one takes the inevitably faded condition of the source material into account. Miller and his crew tour the country and the world, giving capsule descriptions of major resorts and always making the athletics interesting enough to keep a viewer's attention from wandering. Some of Miller's comments are humorous ("Real snow falls out of the sky...The snow grooming machine operators stay up all night and they pack it down so you still won't have any powder snow to ski on.") and the footage is entertaining. Like the lectures of the past, the disc is something of a con where you know you've been taken, but you don't really mind.

STELLA DALLAS (see **BALL OF FIRE**)

THE STEPFATHER
Side one of *The Stepfather* has the feel of an inept cable TV movie with a little too much violence, but side two is terrific, and even the gore turns out to have been a set up to increase a bevy of power-of-suggestion thrills. The story makes use of a classic fairy tale device – the false parent – but it turns out to have a powerful effect upon one's involvement with the characters. Whether one is feeling protective or antagonistic towards other family members while watching the disc, the story manipulates and agitates those feelings. When it turns out, in the end, to be a stop-the-psycho hair-raiser, it catches you by surprise because you've been distracted.

The picture is faintly grainy, but the movie is unharmed by this since its production standards were not all that ritzy to begin with. The Ultra-Stereo sound has some nice attic echoes, a tense, bass heartbeat, and an undistinguished but ever present musictrack. If any of it had the fuller sound of a more sophisticated processing system, it would be out of place.

STEPHEN KING'S PET SEMATARY
Although one gets the feeling that the title came first and the plot second, *Stephen King's Pet Sematary* is an enjoyable tall tale about the messy trouble caused by bringing the dead back to life. The plot has something of a downward spiral, but that never seems to bother King fans, and there are sequences within the story which are legitimately touching and eerie.

The picture transfer is very good and the surround sound is fantastic. The film is about a family who moves into a house by a busy highway and large trucks are forever passing from one speaker to another. The sound has atmosphere, plenty of directional effects, and contributes significantly to assaulting a viewer's defenses.

STEPHEN KING'S SILVER BULLET
It doesn't appear that *Stephen King's Silver Bullet* was filmed with very expensive materials, so one can't expect too much from the disc. It is not in stereo and has not been CX-encoded. The picture is mildy hazy. Fortunately, the performances of Gary Busey and his two young co-stars are quite good and Stephen King's basic formula for mixing equal amounts of 'normal' psychological problems and horror keeps the plot moving.

STEPPENWOLF
Fred Haines' 1974 interpretation of Herman Hesse's *Steppenwolf* bypassed its potential audience by about five years. Viewed today, the movie does not seem nearly as stupid or pointless as it did rolling off the deservedly brief peak of interest in Hesse's literature which raged during the heyday of the counterculture.

Max Von Sydow stars, embodying the central character, Harry, and narrating several segments which utilize Monty Python-style animation to illustrate Hesse's densest meanderings. The cast's English matches their lip movements, though often with a visible delay. The film's most howling failure is the casting of Dominique Sanda as Hermine. She can barely make it through the phonetics of an English sentence, let alone deliver a translation of Hesse's obtuse prose convincingly. Still, viewers with a sense of nostalgia may be intrigued by what Haines has put together. On the other hand, those who wish to know more up front about the disc's narrative content had best just avoid the whole thing.

The picture on the disc is a reasonably accurate transcription of the film, which looked worn down to begin with. Some sections are okay, but others are very dark or are saddled with unstable colors. The monaural sound is more successful. The film's credits contain the Dolby logo and there is a strong jazz score by George Guntz, but to our knowledge the film was not stereophonic.

STEVE MARTIN LIVE!

The material in *Steve Martin Live!* comes from around 1979, just as the comedian's first set of routines was starting to go stale. The show, which is contained on a one-sided disc, is a record of a live performance in which Martin, with a dozen or so props, energetically runs through his stuff. There are also two filmed skits which open the disc. Martin, dressed in white, works on a darkened stage, so that herringbone patterns, ghosts, et cetera, are easy to spot in the background. The sound is passable.

STEVEN WRIGHT LIVE

The drama in *Steven Wright Live* comes from seeing if he can last the whole 50 minutes on stage without cracking a smile. The stand up comedian's routine is to deliver a constant stream of one liners (Example: "For my birthday I got a humidifier and a dehumidifier. I put them in the same room and let them fight it out.") in a calm, deadpan voice. There are times when his lips start to curl, and he has to grip the microphone stand real hard until the urge to giggle passes, but he makes it, and it is a remarkable display of self control.

The picture is acceptable and the stereo sound makes the audience's laughter come from everywhere. Despite the quality of the disc and the amazing effort put forth by Wright, however, 50 minutes of one liners is 50 minutes of one liners. After you've heard them once or twice, you will be apt to watch the disc with the same straight-faced expression Wright has.

STEVIE NICKS
STEVIE NICKS – I CAN'T WAIT

In the 12-inch concert disc, *Stevie Nicks*, you could barely tell it was her because she spent almost the whole time hunched over the microphone, her face hidden by her hairdo, her gowns, and the stage lighting. There is a lot more of her to see on the 8-inch, *Stevie Nicks – I Can't Wait* – plenty of closeups and plenty of decolletage. The six music videos on the two-sided 26-minute disc have no narratives. The picture quality varies, but the stereo is consistently good. The numbers, 'Stop Draggin' My Heart Around,' 'Stand Back,' 'Leather and Lace,' 'If Anyone Falls,' 'Talk to Me,' and 'I Can't Wait,' will give one a better feeling for Nicks' talent than the 12-inch concert disc without taking up as much time, space, or money to get the point across.

STEVIE NICKS – LIVE AT RED ROCKS

The program contained in *Stevie Nicks – Live at Red Rocks* is actually entitled, 'Stevie Nicks – Rock a Little.' Even though the sound has been over-engineered to make it conform to the expected standards of pop recordings, the acoustics of the setting still sneak through – particularly a trembling bass which is probably, to this day, bouncing off the stone faced cliffs on either side of the stage.

Simple division will indicate that a 57-minute performance disc which has 9 chapter markers also has some padding. Nicks may have been around rock and roll for a long time, but her stage repertoire appears limited. The program has not been edited very well and the stage isn't lit to accommodate the filming. There are enough, clear closeups to satisfy fans, but the disruptive flow of images prevents one from obtaining a sense of the command Nicks has on the stage, or of the emotion she wants to communicate. The credits claim that Mick Fleetwood and Peter Frampton are also present, but they don't get in the way, which is just as well. A few optical effects create the impression that lightning is flashing during 'Dreams,' but, in general, the material could have used more natural elements and fewer manufactured ones.

STEWARDESS SCHOOL

The jacket cover for RCA/Columbia's *Stewardess School* shows a girl in a white dress sitting on a motorcycle. Interpretation: Instead of trying to sell the movie's nonexistent humor, RCA/Columbia is trying to sell the movie's nonexistent sex. The story is about a wacky crew of air service trainees. Many plot ends are left dangling in the finale, including a bomb which never goes off. The picture is grainy and the sound is weak.

STICK

The stereo surround in *Stick* is impressive. The Elmore Leonard story is the sort one picks up to read on a short airplane trip. The movie, which was directed by its star, Burt Reynolds, is not really suitable for an evening at the theater – and it flopped at the box office – but it is perfect for a lazy afternoon at home. The cast, including Charles Durning, Candice Bergen, and George Segal, gives the movie the glitz it needs to succeed.

Problems during the shooting resulted in some bad cover shots and poorly edited sequences. There is an occasional glare or double image on the camera lens. The angles are disorienting the first time Bergen is seen. A scorpion is placed on a man's arm and we never find out if the man gets stung or not. *Stick*, however, is not intended to be about the problems of humanity. It is just about some dirty goings on in Ft. Lauderdale and so it doesn't have to be perfect to give satisfaction. Corruption is its own reward.

STICKY FINGERS

Two roommates find a bag of illegal money. Criminals want it back and the police want the criminals. It is a fairly standard plot device, but it has been given one amusing variation in *Sticky Fingers* to suit the gender of the two leads, Helen Slater and Melanie Mayron. They start shopping with the money – they just can't help themselves. The disc was made with inexpensive film stock and monaural sound. The audio is digitally encoded and sounds okay. The picture could probably look better, but it is difficult to tell which problems are the fault of the cinematography and which are the fault of the transfer. The 89-minute disc is in CLV throughout. Slow pacing and a limited number of inspired ideas prevent *Sticky Fingers* from being overly successful, but the movie leaves its mark.

THE STING

MCA has issued several versions of *The Sting*. The most recent has digital sound, side three in CAV and a theatrical trailer. The sound is monaural, but it has a crispness which makes listening to the film a pleasurable experience. The anachronistic score is so familiar now that to hear it accompany the film on a decent sound system increases one's pleasure and anticipation for the familiar events which follow. The picture also looks good, although there is a splice or two. The color scheme of the film is heavily into browns and yellows and a manufactured old-fashioned look, but the colors on the disc are clearly original and unblemished by the passing years.

We were unsure what to do with the CAV functions on side three, except to freeze our own portraits of the stars. The disc has chapter markers to coincided with the on screen chapter title cards. The trailer has a post-Oscar header attached to it, but appears to contain the original promotion strategy and contains a few clips which did not make it to the final cut. Selling the film was not exactly a tough assignment. All they had to do was prove that Robert Redford and Paul Newman appear in the same shots.

STING – BRING ON THE NIGHT

The disc label for *Sting – Bring on the Night* is misleading. Chapter markers are listed on both sides of the label whereas the actual chapter encoding occurs entirely on side two. The film, a documentary of interviews and musical performance, was directed by Michael Apted. The sound is impressive and clean. The picture is on the grainy side, so that the visuals are not as remarkable as the music.

The movie is supposed to serve as an introduction and promotion of Sting's venture away from a rock sound and into a jazz sound. Like Barbra Streisand, Sting is apparently risking his entire life and career with this change in style and will end up wandering the streets looking for returnable empties or discarded cigarettes if he fails.

Unlike the cheerier record company concoctions, Apted gets away with including footage showing arguments and venal road managers. As one member of the band puts it, the combination of musicianship and stardom makes him "want to barf." In what must be a milestone for crass showmanship, the camera is also privy to the birth of Sting's son. Sting stands, without a surgical mask, looking cool and holding his hand over the mother's belly. The mother, having no emotional defenses left, looks exhausted and a bit scared. After the baby emerges, Sting's facade drops, but the tension in the room from being on camera is clearly stronger than the joy of the event. What a way to start a life.

STING THE MUSIC VIDEOS PART 1 &...NOTHING LIKE THE SUN THE VIDEOS

A super collection of Sting music videos is available on *Sting The Videos Part 1 &... Nothing Like the Sun The Videos*. The stereo soundtrack has no perceptible flaws.

The music videos, a combination of two video cassette programs, are beautifully produced and vary nicely in style and subject matter. Some are straight performance videos, some are more abstract, and some have mild narratives. The picture quality varies a little from one to the next, but in general the disc looks terrific. There are about an equal number of black-and-white and color videos, mixed together. No extraneous material interrupts the flow of the songs.

Sting's music is competent and pleasant. The studio recordings for the videos tend to soften his weaknesses and establish a continuity in his careening search for a suitable style. With one or two exceptions, the videos manage to avoid the major music video clichés and provide images which keep the viewer attentive to the music.

THE STONE KILLER

Michael Winner's *The Stone Killer* was a 1973 effort funded by Dino De Laurentiis. Winner is one of our least favorite directors, and here the acting, or just the attempt by the cast to move their lips without falling out of character, is not a pretty sight. The action sequences are better, or perhaps they are simply a relief, since no one talks. The film was based on a legitimate crime novel, by John Gardner, and it has an elaborate plot in which Charles Bronson, as a cop, finds himself in the middle of a mob war. The print looks like it went through a mob war as well, and has numerous splices. Winner's basic sense of color also leaves much to be desired, as do the racial epithets which are viciously sprinkled through the hip dialog. The monaural sound is uneventful.

STOP MAKING SENSE (Import)

No Japanese subtitles appear on the *Stop Making Sense* import. It is a beautiful disc. Much of the screen composition in the film (of a Talking Heads concert) is half black or partially black. The members of the group are lit by key lights and darkness surrounds them, or the camera faces the back of their heads and looks out into the dark auditorium. All of this blackness appears on the screen without a single squiggle, speckle, or artificial pattern. The film is somewhat grainy, because of the necessity of filming on a partially dark stage. It is digitally encoded, and the sound is as clear as the picture.

STORMY MONDAY

A refreshingly pleasant thriller, *Stormy Monday* is set in Newcastle, England. The story concerns a jazz club owner and a drifter who stand up to an American developer. The script is beautifully crafted, spinning off one believable coincidence after the next until all of them eventually twist round each other. Thread through each scene is a marvelous jazz score, constantly changing in style and tempo, to match the shifts in drama. The movie stars Tommy Lee Jones, Melanie Griffith, and Sting, and all three, even Sting, are greatly entertaining.

The disc looks good, too, with only a mild graininess in the most intense reds and oranges disrupting the image. The soundtrack is not digitally encoded, contrary to the jacket cover, but the stereo surround has wonderful depth and it is doubtful digital encoding could have improved much on it.

STORMY WEATHER

If the apartheid nature of all-black musicals does not disturb you, CBS/Fox has released the wonderful all-black revue *Stormy Weather*. The film has a narrative of sorts, but since it stars Bill Robinson, whose dancing abilities were significantly more accomplished than his acting abilities, the plot – his reminiscences – remains no more than a linking device. The acts, which include Fats Waller, Cab Calloway, the Nicholas Brothers, Katherine Dunham, Lena Horne, and Robinson, are wonderful, and CBS/Fox's chapter markers consistently change every three minutes, though there is no listing of them on the jacket cover.

The transfer is nice. The digital sound has been enhanced with rechanneled stereo, which causes no significant distortion and gives the music a little extra body. The black and white picture has no major problems and the focus looks crisp. The program runs about 80 minutes but CBS/Fox has left the disc in CLV, a particular shame since it is the dynamic Nicholas Brothers stairwell dance which concludes the film.

THE STORY OF IRENE AND VERNON CASTLE

The last film that Fred Astaire and Ginger Rogers made at RKO, *The Story of Irene and Vernon Castle*, has been released on laser disc by Turner and Image. The death of Astaire's character at the end of the film and the ghostly fade-out of the two of them, double exposed, dancing into the vanishing point, made for a fitting finale to a group of films which were so unique and similar as to constitute a single work of art. The final film, the last time they would appear in black-and-white, is considered by many to be a disappointment – the dance sequences are not distinctive and the ending is a downer. However, the ending is easier to take on multiple viewings and the early part of the film is fresh and enjoyable, especially the 'meeting' scene, which is set with the two of them swimming in Long Island Sound. The plot is also refreshingly free of the breakup and makeup spirals which most of the stories in the series spring from. Although there is no one musical number which stands out, there are moments of wonderful grace and beauty, particularly a dance move in which Rogers wraps herself backwards around Astaire as he spins a half dozen times.

The print looks fine. The blacks are a little purplish, but that can be compensated with color controls if it seems annoying. The images are solid and show no deterioration. There is an occasional scratch, but it is not enough to disrupt the proceedings. The sound is fine and the chapter markers cover the musical sequences as well as the significant dramatic moments.

THE STORY OF O PART II

The roughness of the sound presentation *The Story of O Part II* is probably intended to arouse one's passion, the assumption being that the anger one inevitably directs toward one's sound system will be rechannelled by the narrative. Certainly that is the intention of the mock-Anton Weber score and the dubbed dialog. It may also be the intention of the cheap film stock, though in terms of the picture quality, the transfer does not appear to diminish that which was lousy to begin with. There may be some slight blurring, but the bad lighting and the inept colors were there before anyone involved with the disc got a hold of the film. The image has also been cropped, though it has not been scanned. Whatever is in the middle of the picture is what you get, even if everyone is standing on the sides.

Visually, the unrated program never surpasses an 'R' sensibility, but it is gung-ho in the idea department and inevitably more stimulating than a show-it-all-up-front hardcore feature. The story is about a letter who looks like a woman and bosses everyone around. There is some corporate intrigue, since the letter is hired to corrupt a financier and his family. She does so, down to and including the family's pet canine. Perhaps the producers intended to spin off a sequel in the lower case.

STRANDED

Maureen O'Sullivan is one of the stars in *Stranded*, which is about an elderly woman and her grand daughter who receive visitors from another world. O'Sullivan's presence is representative of the film as a whole – good natured and reasonably professional. The bulk of the plot concerns the police approach to an assumed hostage crisis, yet the title appears to be a misnomer, because the aliens have no difficulty leaving when it comes time to go. The picture has an overly orange tint, but is otherwise stable. The sound is okay.

THE STRANGER AND THE GUNFIGHTER

Here is a cute, if tasteless idea, which has been used more than once: Portions of a treasure map are tattooed on the behinds of four ladies of the evening and it is up to the hero to record the bare facts before the bad guys can. *The Stranger and the Gunfighter* is a combined chop suey and spaghetti western. The Chinese played an integral part in the building of the old West, so there is no reason why they shouldn't be a part of the myth, as well.

Lo Leigh portrays a martially talented youth who is sent to America to find his deceased uncle's fortune. Lee Van Cleef is a gunfighter who befriends him, grudgingly. There are many elements of comedy – Van Cleef even sings – but it takes about twenty minutes to get used to the dubbing before the combination of action and farce start to work for you.

Most of the violence is imaginary, though some blood is displayed near the end. The sound is flat and the print is rugged in places, but one doesn't expect perfection in a property like this.

STRANGER THAN PARADISE

If someone at CBS/Fox had been smart, the disc version of *Stranger Than Paradise* would have had a chapter encoded for every blackout. Unfortunately, that is not the case, but we suppose we should be thankful that the movie made it to disc at all, since the title is what is commonly referred to as being outside of mainstream cinema.

In a sense, too, the movie may require the discipline of paying an admission fee and sitting in a theater to be appreciated. You have to be committed to it to enjoy it, and in the home environment one can easily grow impatient. The black-and-white movie is constructed without closeups or alternate camera angles. Every scene is a single take from a single camera, separated from the next by a blank screen. The film is about a trio of lowlife characters on an odyssey to nowhere. They think and talk in halting phrases and have simple personalities. The movie can be excruciating or it can be quite enjoyable depending upon how much one enjoys the company of the characters.

The picture on the disc is in satisfactory condition, and the monaural sound is fine. Since the movie was constructed in something of a makeshift manner, it transfers well to video. Convincing friends to sit still for it, however, may be a challenge.

STRANGERS ON A TRAIN

The black-and-white contrasts in Alfred Hitchcock's *Strangers on a Train* are vivid. The print has a few scratches here and there, but it nevertheless looks fresh and helps one submerge in the drama. The sound is fine.

We still can't get over how well Hitchcock constructed the tennis match which precedes the grand finale. Because the drama is tense (the hero must win quickly to leave the stadium and stop the murderer) one is naturally involved, but Hitchcock, by putting the camera everywhere and then constructing the match in the editing room, gets you involved in the game itself. If the matches one sees on television were done half as well, ratings would soar. The movie is one of Hitchcock's most free spirited, a carnival of action, tension, and murder. And it will make you think twice about striking up conversations with strangers.

STRATEGIC AIR COMMAND

Like the stills on the back of the jacket, the Technicolor source used for *Strategic Air Command* is gorgeous. We wish we could feel as excited about the movie, but the Jimmy Stewart effort is closer to a recruitment film than an action picture. It is more often boring or embarrassing than it is thrilling, and the plot leaves specific dramatic points – such as the results of an investigation concerning a major crash – dangling.

Although it is monaural, the filmmakers really tried to give the airplane sounds some punch. With the full cooperation of SAC, cameras were placed every which way on the pre-B-52 contraptions which are the real stars of the show. In cropped VistaVision, you sit on the wing and on the landing gear and in the cockpit and just about everywhere but the tail. After a while, there is nothing to do but look for interesting formations in the clouds.

STRAUSS ELEKTRA

The marathon, single act *Strauss Elektra*,by Richard Strauss, was filmed on a soundstage. The two hour work fares differently in recording conditions where the singers can take breaks than it does on the stage, where the title character, almost always present, must carry on with little interruption. Thus the disc has many advantages, because it allows you to see as well as to hear Leonie Rysanek energetically work her way through the role. The digital track noticeably cleaner than the analog track, and carries every note to its fullest potential. Some critics find the Strauss work to be a little too shrill, but the disc presents the fully satisfying performance with complete accuracy, so viewers and listeners can decide for themselves.

The film retells the story of Elektra and her vengeance against her mother, Clytemnestra, on a single, mud and pillars set which would not have been out of place in *The Running Man*. Why do set designers always think that since ancient Greece is in ruins now it was in ruins when people lived there? The picture is often deliberately monochomatic and is faintly grainy. There is a rainstorm, lots of blood and slime, and nobody is ever completely dry.

The disc is three-sided and comes in a box jacket. The breaks between the sides are awkward, since there are few natural pauses in the work. The opera is in German and has English subtitles. There are two essays and a plot synopsis (linked to the chapter markers). One essay is almost too narrowly focused, on the gestation of *Elektra*,while the other, which examines the psychoanalytical underpinnings of the legend, is disappointingly vague.

STRAW DOGS
STRAW DOGS (Import)

The 'letterboxing' on the Japanese import of *Straw Dogs* amounts to the thinnest of black lines at the top and bottom of the screen. The effect is so mild that some viewers might not notice its presence at all. Any viewer who has suffered through the sloppy domestic CBS/Fox version, which was released in the early days, will nevertheless appreciate the improvements which the Japanese version has to offer. The CBS/Fox print was faded and out of focus most of the time, and the sound was completely lacking in ambience. The import version, which is in English and has Japanese subtitles, looks very sharp, and the colors are much improved, although there is probably room for further enhancement. The print also has one or two splices. The monaural sound is still not CX-encoded, but it is much better than the CBS-Fox copy, and presents no problems when the volume is kept at a reasonable level.

We were afraid that the Japanese version would be censored, but what we discovered instead was that the American version is missing footage – or, rather, frames – present on the import disc during the rape scene. From the looks of the editing, however, there may still be more which belongs there. Both discs have side breaks right before the rape begins, and it is interesting, because that scene then defines the theme for all of side two.

Straw Dogs works best as an intense satire on marriage. From the beginning, when two women are shown lugging a 'man trap' to a car, to the end, when Dustin Hoffman is driving in the same car, unaware that his passenger is a child murderer, the movie blasts away at the problems of domestic relationships and intimacy. Because the director is Sam Peckinpah and the ending is dutifully violent, much can be presented which, under ordinary circumstances, would drive an audience to distractions. The episodes during which the husband (Hoffman) and the wife (Susan George) pick at each other take up more of their time than the moments when they are on good terms. Their ability to make decisions, or to 'act' (which has always been promoted as the film's ostensible purpose, though its real lessons are far more complicated), is hopelessly inept. But somehow they manage to survive, and, more pragmatically than heroically, to endure.

STRAY CATS

Stray Cats burst forth with a look and a bass guitar sound which had not seen the light of day in thirty years. All four music videos on the 8-inch disc are terrific, with the right blend of humor, energy, and glamor. 'Stray Cat Strut' is an excellent example of how a simple, straightforward video of a group playing their hit song can contain enough visual pizzazz to make viewers want to watch it again and again. The picture and sound are decent.

STREAMERS

After a progressive slackening of structured narratives in his films during the late seventies, it is probably very wise that Robert Altman chose to go through a phase of filming works intended for the stage. The discipline of an imposed beginning, middle, and end forced him to concentrate on camera angles, something he had seemed to care about less and less in his multi-casted episodic epics. In *Streamers*, the set and the actors are low budgeted, and the movie has to be as tight as possible or else it would fizzle into nothing.

The story is about four men waiting to be sent to Vietnam, but it is also, in the typical fashion of modern drama, about stripping away pretense and about who is and who isn't homosexual. The cast has no stars, but the performers fit into the parts well, especially Michael Wright, whose black street talk plays like a first violin's main melody to the rest of the quartet's middle class American English.

The picture on the disc is a little weak. This is exemplified by the red colored credits which bleed pretty badly in the beginning and end, but it is also in evidence whenever the lights are lowered. The sound is monaural, though the background noises – rainstorms outside the barracks, and crickets when it isn't raining – give an illusion of dimension.

STREET SMART (see **MEAN SEASON**)

A STREETCAR NAMED DESIRE (CBS/Fox)
A STREETCAR NAMED DESIRE (Warner)

If you own the CBS/Fox version of *A Streetcar Named Desire*, you ought to just throw it away and get the Warner version. Although the latter is not in perfect condition, it is so far superior to the former that to watch the CBS/Fox version is to do yourself and the film a disservice. The situation is not comparable to owning nicer pearls or a fancier dress. The picture quality and the sound quality on the Warner release of *Streetcar* are so much better that your concentration encounters fewer obstacles. You spend less brain power watching the movie and more in feeling or even living the drama. Time and your own environment are suspended.

The picture on the Warner version is as clear as the illumination of a bare light bulb. The picture on the CBS/Fox disc is as foggy and inconsistent as a paper lantern. On the Fox disc, the intensity of the black-and-white print changes from scene to scene whereas the Warner print is sharply focussed and carries the same contrast levels throughout the film. The Warner's print does have a few scratches and one or two splices, but the CBS/Fox print is no better in this regard. The sound on the Warner disc has been CX-encoded. It is still noisy, but it possesses a level of fidelity which the CBS/Fox disc, which is not CX-encoded, lacks.

The jacket cover for the CBS/Fox release claims that the film is 120 minutes long, but that is no more honest than the 25 candles on Blanche's cake. The disc runs 118 minutes, and if the theme music sounds a little rushed, or if the opening credits jiggle a little, it is because the disc has been time compressed. Warner has put the movie straight, and allowed it to run the full 122 minutes it is supposed to run, onto three sides. It is here, however, that Warner has made its one bad judgement with the disc. The break between side two and side three, for no discernible reason, appears in the middle of an important scene, with the interruption causing an unwelcome interference with the building tension. The break between side one and side two is not as bad, but it could easily have occurred nine minutes later, when a long passage of time is marked in the narrative.

STREETS OF FIRE

Streets of Fire is largely a reunion for the makers of *The Warriors*. Directed by Walter Hill and starring Michael Pare, the story is about an enigmatic drifter who rescues a singer (Diane Lane) kidnapped by a motorcycle gang. It is one of the dopey movies one is apt to buy in the place of something better, the way one eats candy instead of fruit. Everything from the sets to the emotions is false and glossy, but this is intentional. The loud music and the leather and the chrome and the minimalist dialogue and all the wonderful violence and PG sex are not without charms. Pare is too talented to be restrained by enigma and Hill is too resourceful to not be entertaining. The picture and sound are pleasingly glossy.

STREETS OF GOLD

If you like boxing movies don't miss *Streets of Gold*. Klaus Maria Brandauer gives a light-footed performance as a Soviet emigrant who establishes himself as a boxing coach. The movie is cheap, with lousy photography and single-track monaural sound. The disc transfer makes matters worse whenever a scene is not lit with bright sunlight. The opening is slow and burdened with awkwardly constructed scenes intended to introduce the characters and the neighborhood, but once the show gets underway, you won't want to stop it.

STREETWISE

The best documentaries are more amenable to repeated viewing than most fictional films, because they create just the right balance between reality and staging. Enough staging to give pacing and coherence, and enough reality to give the viewer a taste of an alternate world. Such is the case with *Streetwise*, a documentary about kids hustling on the streets of Seattle.

Contrary to the stylistic black-and-white promotional materials, the film is actually in color, and while parts of it naturally have a verite grain, you can tell that little was lost moving the source to the disc. The monaural sound is digitally encoded and has a level of quality which is equal to the picture.

Seattle is not exactly the most destitute town in the world. All the bums have shoes and socks, matching shoes and socks for that matter, but then you wonder if there is any other town in the country where teenage prostitutes, pimps, and scroungers would have been so hospitable to documentary filmmakers.

The film is not sensationalist. Although the disc ends with a brief commercial for the 'Runaway Hotline,' the whole point of the program is that almost nobody can really do much for these kids. They are the ones who are inevitably going to fall irretrievably through the statistical cracks. Hearing them talk about the things they want out of life and how they ended up doing what they are doing is the core of the movie, because the filmmakers get close enough to reveal the outlines of the emotions the kids are hiding.

STRIKE UP THE BAND

Strike Up the Band is a Mickey Rooney/Judy Garland vehicle which was directed by Busby Berkeley. The one jarring mistake is a scene which starts out as if it is a dream sequence, but then turns out to be the real thing. (The original film seems to have been significantly trimmed, although it still has a lengthy running time.) The sound is fine and the black-and-white print is nearly flawless.

STRIP TEASERS
STRIP TEASERS II

The stage show in *Strip Teasers* is a no-nonsense presentation of more than a dozen topless strippers, and there are no elaborate promotional gags to disrupt the presentation. Within the confines of their vocation, the dancers are talented. The picture is only mildly grainy and the monaural sound is strong. The program lasts an hour.

A sequel, *Strip Teasers II* is five minutes shorter and, despite the addition of special video image effects, not quite as satisfying. Although the sound is listed as stereo, its quality is impossible to differentiate from the disc above. The picture is grainy, but passable.

THE STRONG MAN

Frank Capra's *The Strong Man* is the kind of silent film that most people picture in their head when the subject of silent films comes up. There is a blind girl, a well meaning but sort of weakling hero wearing a tad too much makeup, a plot with simplistic moralities, and an unsophisticated, though refreshingly straightforward, cinematic style (the saving grace for many silent films with today's audiences may be that the movies rarely waste one's time with artistic elaborations).

The film stars Harry Langdon, a comedian who was popular in his day but whose child-like demeanor has prevented his fame from passing to successive generations of viewers. *The Strong Man* is his best known film, and a large part of that is because of Capra's involvement with it. Still, the major sequences, though drawn out, are amusing, and how can one be grumpy about a movie which has a blind heroine?

The picture is softer than it has been on some of Image's other Silent Classic offerings. Most of the movie is in kind of a brown wash which is not all that pleasant. The image also has a few scratches. The Carl Davis score is a bit too jokey for our liking, but the stereo sound has no major flaws. Side two of the program is in CAV, with movement appearing blurry in a little more than half of the still frames.

A STUDY IN TERROR

Robert Morley plays Mycroft Holmes in *A Study in Terror*,and he is so unlike John Neville's Sherlock as to place doubts upon the detective's true parentage. The film is a British effort from the mid-sixties with some fairly graphic violence and a little, teasing amount of sex. Holmes, once again, is after Jack the Ripper, and viewers can instigate a pool when it comes time to turn the disc over to pick out which of the many likely suspects is actually Saucy Jack. Neville's Holmes looks like an escapee from Madame Tussaud's, but the script has a steady supply of Holmesian touches – he even chases the killer through a soupy fog – and will satisfy those who are attracted to the material in the first place.

The print looks very nice. It has a few scratches and loses the edges of actors to cropping, but the Eastmancolor source is surprisingly colorful and rich in Victorian reds. The sound has no significant flaws.

THE STUNT MAN

From the opening Rube Goldberg mise-en-scene to the closing aerial waltz, *The Stunt Man* is a frothy, magical movie. The script is set in odd angles, catching sight of the characters in moments and actions which don't make any sense until the story is over. Only when viewed several times do the motivations of the characters cease to appear fanciful and instead take on impeccable logic.

Peter O'Toole is the star, often dropping in from the top of the screen like Jupiter, descending from the Heavens for a day trip. He portrays a film director shooting a World War I picture outside of San Diego. A series of complications bring an escaped criminal (Steve Railsback) onto the set as a substitute stunt man. The director and the convict are cut from the same cloth, and they search each other's personalities to find what is missing inside themselves.

The picture on the 130-minute 3-sided disc is adequate but the monaural sound is noisy.

THE STYLE COUNCIL FAR EAST & FAR OUT

The all-Japanese film crew on *The Style Council Far East & Far Out*, subtitled 'Council Meeting in Japan,' provides such a clear picture that you can make out details on all the band members even when the stage is completely dark. The picture is great and the stereo sound is effective. The group mixes big band, rock, and soul, searching for a lowest common denominator which is only intermittently satisfying. The multiple piece group does provide for an interesting hour's concert, however, because of the variety in musical activity.

SUBWAY

Usually if a movie doesn't have a plot it can still get by on high style, but of a movie doesn't have a plot or a style it has nothing. *Subway* is a French film which has been dubbed in English. Trust the French – it is a chic film about the homeless. They live in garrets throughout the Paris Metro and continually outwit the security forces attempting to impose society upon them. If it sounds like fun, you're out of luck, because it is not. The characters speak in symbols which make less sense than most subway maps. They are rude and unsympathetic, yet the film approaches them as if they were the cutest group of misfits ever to panhandle a public thruway. Characters perform major actions on impulse because the filmmakers can't think of any other reason or motivation for their activity.

The picture is adequately rendered, although the movie really only has a handful of glossy, show-off shots. The sound is in stereo, sporadically, and the dubbing is not.

SUDDEN DEATH

Sudden Death is not as merciful as the title implies. It is 90 minutes of tediously constructed misogynic violence. The transfer accurately re-creates the film's cheap production values. What it needs is a sudden burial.

SUDDENLY, LAST SUMMER

The only disappointment in *Suddenly, Last Summer* is that Elizabeth Taylor's character escapes the lobotomy Katharine Hepburn's character is trying to force on her with the unwitting assistance of a young doctor (Montgomery Clift). The story, which was penned by Tennessee Williams and Gore Vidal, is the sort where you *want* to see the characters do their worst to one another.

Joseph Mankiewicz's semi-stagey production is lively. All dialog and little action, the thrill comes from watching the performers maneuver their moods and accents though the gradual revelation of what happened suddenly, last summer. The black-and-white transfer is gorgeous, although the sound is unprotected and a bit noisy.

SUGAR CANE ALLEY

Coming of age in an impoverished rural environment, and escaping by means of an education, has been the subject of many successful films, novels, and plays, but that never seems to diminish the impact when the story is told again. *Sugar Cane Alley* ('Rue Cases Negres,' which is translated in the film's subtitles as 'Black Shack Alley') is about a boy growing up on a sugar plantation on the Caribbean island of Martinique shortly after the turn of the Century. The boy is bright, not just because he does so well at school that his teacher accuses him of cheating, but because he listens to the people in the shantytown. He acts as a witness to the transference of culture from Africa to America, and you can see in his brow and his smile that he understands. The movie is funny and inspiring, and it will bring any viewer closer to life and humanity.

The print is not as rich in color as one wishes it could be. The monaural sound, on the other hand, is nice, and the ever-chirping crickets feel stereophonic. The film is in French and has English subtitles. The subtitles disappear during a couple of conversations, however, one of which is clearly risque.

SULLIVAN'S TRAVELS

Preston Sturges' *Sullivan's Travels* is probably too perfect a film. Except for Eric Blore's first scene, there is nothing in the movie which will leave the viewer in a fetal position, laughing uncontrollably, but the script has a concentrated narrative drive and a firm emotional command. It is easy to put the comedy on a pedestal, for it has no false moves and is as relevant today as it was in 1941. Joel McCrea portrays a popular film director who sets out to make a movie about human suffering and discovers that it is his mission in life to relieve the pain of poverty and despair, not document it. The film is about the way movies can lift your spirit, and its power is all-encompassing, because it accomplishes that very task itself.

The focus is sharp and the black-and-white source material is clean. The sound has no significant problems. The theatrical trailer has been provided at the end of disc. The clip is an interesting record of how the film was marketed, since the feature's few, basic physical gags are all collected and emphasized.

SUMMER

Eric Rohmer's 'Le Rayon Vert' – 'The Green Flash' – was entitled *Summer* for American audiences. The slightly grainy transfer is good enough that you can actually see the flash in the sunset at the end, though probably not without backing up to it a couple of times with the remote. It's there.

The print is in acceptable condition. The subtitles will drive some viewers to distraction, for they are in white, and appear against white backgrounds for great lengths of time. A title card in the film says, 'samedi, 4 aout,' and the subtitle underneath reads, 'Saturday, August 9.' We're surprised the film didn't end up getting called 'Winter.'

The jacket copy summarizes only side two. On the whole, the film is about a young woman attempting to enjoy her vacation time without much success. She continually takes trips out of town and then decides to cut them short and return. The pleasure one receives from the film is in how close one comes to understanding the woman's personality, as if the viewer were a travelling companion. You even get angry at her sometimes, but that's part of it.

SUMMER CAMP NIGHTMARE

Those who will soon – or have just recently – added the suffix, 'teen,' to the number of years in their age may enjoy *Summer Camp Nightmare*. It is about youths who take over a summer camp and go wild for a week or two, an enjoyable fantasy for viewers who still have strict bedtimes. The movie's film stock looks inexpensive, but the transfer to disc is faithful and unflawed.

SUMMER HEAT

Lori Singer is miscast as the wife of a tobacco farmer during the thirties who has an affair with a hired hand in *Summer Heat*, a disc which was released briefly and then withdrawn from the market. Singer's improbably coiffed character has no personality and leaves an empty center in what is otherwise a brisk and enjoyable melodrama. The picture transfer is good, disrupted only by a few stray speckles. The sound is fine. Side two is in CAV, with two unsteady still frames out of every five. The film was made on location in North Carolina.

A SUMMER PLACE

We love *A Summer Place* more every time we see it. The film is ideal for a rainy summer afternoon or evening. It runs a few minutes over two hours and has a soap opera plot, probably closest in similarity to 'Peyton Place,' though there is less melodrama. The plot has two tiers. It is about young lovers, portrayed without embarrassment by Troy Donahue and Sandra Dee, and it is about an illicit romance between his mother (Dorothy McGuire) and her father (Richard Eagan). Arthur Kennedy and Constance Ford (who makes a wonderful villainess) also star. Like any antique, *A Summer Place* is old enough that even though it lacks artistic refinement, it can be appreciated for its craftsmanship.

On side one, there is a five minute sequence which is badly speckled, and there are other speckles which pop up here and there, but the Technicolor source material is rich and the fleshtones and blue seas look wonderful. The film was not a widescreen effort and the presentation is unharmed by the video framing. The monaural sound is acceptable and Max Steiner's score has more memorable themes than you might realize. As for the popular title tune, it may show up everywhere else, but this was where it came from and where it belongs. It also has a much more melancholic orchestration than the common elevator rendition.

SUMMER RENTAL

The John Candy vehicle, *Summer Rental*, doesn't even have a plot until side two. Some of the summer vacation gags are fun and the picture quality seems fairly good, but the movie isn't the sort to encourage close scrutiny.

SUMMER STOCK

The Gene Kelly and Judy Garland frolic, *Summer Stock*, is not one of MGM's best known musicals, but it has several interesting features and is enjoyable despite the aged appearance of the two stars. Garland's character owns a farm which is invaded by Kelly and a theater group. In one number, the group is rehearsing a 'South Seas' duet, using the farm equipment as temporary props. A viewer will tend to dismiss the piece as a rehearsal, but, of course, it is a complete segment for the movie, and invokes both the romance of the tropics and the humor of the barn setting, an intriguing accomplishment. There is also an opportunity to see Eddie Bracken and Phil Silvers in the same shot, doing some business with their eyeglasses which is quite precious. The film manages to be both energetic and casual, and it epitomizes the MGM 'factory' musical, a structure of entertainment that has sadly fallen from economic viability.

The colors look lighter than they do on the best MGM/UA discs, but the composition of the film itself is so color-conscious that watching the disc is still a treat. The sound is CX-encoded monaural and one should be prepared for the early fifties quality of its recording. The disc has been given an intelligent set of chapter markers, including one for the film's most memorable number, Garland's black hat and black mini-skirt rendition of 'Get Happy.'

SUMMERTIME

It is symptomatic of the weak material that no one has ever come up with a decent title for the Arthur Laurents play, 'The Time of the Cuckoo.' Adapted as a stage musical, it was called *Do I Hear A Waltz?* and for David

Lean's film version of the play, it was given the generic title *Summertime*. The story is about a spinsterish administrative assistant who finally finds romance in the labyrinthine alleys and piazzas of Venice. The moral – that girls should not wait so long to fall in love – is embarrassing, but at least the film retains some dignity through the combined talents of Lean and Katharine Hepburn.

The colors are as bright as Venice on a summer morning, but the print did have a few rough spots. The twangy monaural sound is best left at a low volume.

SUN CITY

The one-sided disc, *Sun City*, features the music video, 'Sun City,' followed by a documentary on how and why the video was made. The picture quality is deliberately varied, but the transfer looks acceptable and the sound has a nice beat.

SUNDAY IN THE PARK WITH GEORGE

Not too long ago it was thought that the world and all upon it were made up of dots. Now it is understood that these components are not dots but simply strings which have a high probability of appearing as dots. Dots, however, are everywhere. Dots of just three colors are combined to form pictures on your television screen. Dots are imbedded upon the surface of a laser disc, to be reinterpreted as electronic signals which determine the order of the three colors. The mathematical equivalent of dots, bits, are also encoded on the disc, to serve in the creation of digital sound. You start thinking about all of this and more as you watch *Sunday in the Park with George*, a video recording of the Broadway stage musical about the French pointillist painter Georges Seurat. It is a largely fictional portrayal of Seurat, but the fictions allow the writers to examine the tensions in Seurat's most famous work, 'A Sunday Afternoon on the Island of Grand Jatte,' and to examine the propagation of art and life. The story is placed in perspective by the second act, which is set in present day and postulates that Seurat has a great-grandson living in America. The grandson is also an artist, a sculptor, and is working at the forefront of artistic technology. He uses lasers.

We get goose pimples because the drama is as much about pride for one's family as it is about artistic creation. We also get goose pimples because the music is pointillist, full of quick, individual notes, which the singers must strain to breath and pronounce without missing a beat. We got goose pimples from the disc immediately, because the pings and pizzicati start coming from everywhere as soon as the curtain rises.

The sound on *Sunday* is not like the studio recorded CD, but it doesn't have to be. It is a live recording, and the hiss is as welcome as the coughing and the missed notes (the audio noise is noticeably stronger on the analog track). It could always be miked better than it is, but the stereo is strong enough to make you feel like the dots are everywhere and the music is everywhere.

The 147-minute program runs across three sides. There are a few chapter markers for the major numbers. The picture is fuzzy and the first group manufactured contained heavy speckling. Many of the objects and actors followed by faint ghosts, but if you stand far enough away, the distortions disappear. If you stand too close to your TV, the picture is all dots anyway.

SUNNY SIDE UP

The 45-minute CLV *Sunny Side Up*, highlights a car trip from Sausalito to Malibu. The picture is as sharp and clear as any laser disc we have ever seen. The sound, which is in digital, is also exemplary. The subject matter – what one sees from the car window or at various stops – is mundane and of little interest to those who do not live in the neighborhood. The accompanying music (there is no other sound) features the instrumental group, Casiopea, and would not be out of place in the Starlight Room at the local Holiday Inn.

SUNSET

The principal detriment to the otherwise fine presentation of the enjoyable Blake Edwards film, *Sunset*,is that it has been scanned and cropped. The picture, except for a few night scenes which look too grainy, is bright and sharp, and the digital stereo sound is wonderful. Edwards is a champion of the widescreen format and his films are severely hurt when the edges are sliced. You lose some of the fun.

The movie probably works better on home video, cropping aside, than it does in a theater, because it stars two actors, James Garner and Bruce Willis, who have personalities that have been successful on the small screen. They portray the Wyatt Earp and the Tom Mix, who meet while Mix is filming a western, and solve a murder in their spare time. The film is easy to criticize. Neither star embodies his character, and the mystery is all too contrived. No matter, there is Henry Mancini's score, Edwards' visual style, delightful sets and costumes, and Willis and Garner trying to out-relax each other.

THE SUPER FIGHT

Just five weeks after the Middleweight Championship fight between Marvin Hagler and Sugar Ray Leonard in April, 1987, Image released the entire extravaganza on *The Super Fight*. They lucked out, because the fight is terrific and so the disc is too.

Fight shows all twelve rounds in their entirety, and, instead of cutting to Gillette commercials, shows what went on in each fighter's corner between the rounds, as well. Thus, a viewer wishing to see a good fight can come back to the disc after sufficient time has passed and relive the match again. (The poster promised on the jacket cover is not packed with the disc and was supposed to have been distributed by dealers with every copy purchased.)

With one unfortunate exception, Image has done a beautiful job with *The Super Fight*. Every round has its own chapter marker, and the last four, which are on side two, are in CAV. Image's luck being what it is, those final rounds were the best and most furious of the whole bout. The images are bright and sharply detailed. The sound is in CX-encoded stereo. The real time ringside commentary is informative without being obtrusive.

The disc's only flaw is that every still frame on the CAV side quivers when depicting motion. The glove on Leonard's chin or in Hagler's belly is inevitably blurred, disrupting any real evaluation of contact. The lower slow motion speeds are also affected, although the upper slow motion speeds reveal the beauty of the thrust and parry between the two boxers without spoiling the images. The fast speeds are also instructive, revealing the patterns of encroachment and wary dodging.

SUPERGIRL

The concept of 'Superman' comes from an awkward translation of a German philosophical concept in the 1800s which searched for moral perfection. Taking the concept literally for the comics, 'Superman' was not only morally strong, he was physically strong as well.

Supergirl is an equal opportunity spin-off. She travels into hell to find moral guidance and is stronger for having taken the trip. The movie was a flop because the special effects were *Barbarella*-level tacky, everyone was tired of Superperson films, and the director didn't believe in the script. Except for the brief scenes with Peter O'Toole, the movie has no tension and no magic.

The picture has lines and scratches. The sound is strong and the stereo mix is sort of cute, but it is also noisy and overbearing. The worst fault of this presentation is that the picture remains in dead center, even when the only action is on the edges.

SUPERMAN
SUPERMAN (Letterboxed)

The letterboxed version of the first Superman movie has an aspect ratio of about 2.4:1. Although the presentation is a significant improvement over the earlier scanned and cropped release, the picture and the sound are still below average in quality. The picture is often very grainy or hazy, and even when it is not, it lacks the shine which the film had in its original theatrical play. The colors are off slightly, and lack the sharpness which is vital in making some of the sets and production models look convincing. The digital stereo surround sound is also inconsistent and lacks sharpness. Some separations suffer from significant volume drop outs, and the music kicks in on the surround only during crescendos or at random moments. For the film's best sequences, the letterboxing is gratifying, but the movie, which had five writers and panic stricken producers, also has a number of weakly conceived sequences and these, too, are magnified by the letterboxing, which reveals a paucity of inspiration just as readily as it liberates the best special effects work. At least with Warner's enthusiastic chapter encoding you can leap through the worst of it with a single bound.

SUPERMAN II
SUPERMAN II (Digital)

Warner remastered *Superman II* with digital sound and side two in CAV. The disc is not letterboxed, which is surely a disappointment to fans though it is hardly the end of the world. The film functions well as a scanned and cropped effort, and the details lost on the sides are minor.

The picture is glossier and sharper than the earlier version. The digital surround sound is less improved, but the film has a number of entertaining sound effects and they are well executed. The CAV segment, primarily depicting the three bad guys destroying an attack force in a rural town, is good fun. The earlier disc just filled up the first two sides, leaving much of side three, in CLV, for the end credit scroll. The movie's Clark Kent material is ill-considered and out-of-synch with the tone that the series should have, but the special effects are super and so is the disc.

THE SUPERMAN CARTOONS OF MAX & DAVE FLEISCHER

Comprising a complete collection, all seventeen animated shorts have been included on *The Superman Cartoons of Max & Dave Fleischer*, and an eighteenth, 'Snafuperman,' has been thrown in as an added bonus. The 148-minute program fits on three sides. Each short has a chapter marker, and a listing with plot descriptions of each cartoon is provided on the back of the jacket. The shorts are presented in the order they were first released.

The cartoons are special, and are the sort of material which collectors become very passionate about. We think the transfers look good, and it is probably the best produced Fleischer *Superman* anthology available on home video. But a number of friends have contacted us saying they have seen better looking versions of this or that cartoon. Hence, casual collectors may be more interested in the disc than dedicated fans.

There is nothing outrageously wrong with any of the cartoons. Some look a little softer than others, and on the softer ones the colors tend to bleed more. The best looking episodes have sharply delineated images, with rich colors that look, well, un-buffed. The sound is fine and worth amplifying.

As for content, the cartoons contain a wide mix of subjects and situations, and most are good fun. Created with quasi-rotoscoping, they have an adult point of view, combining pleasing imaginative fantasies with a serious, detective-film atmosphere and a futuristic/art deco setting. In some, Superman battles prehistoric monsters and in others he just subdues Nazi thugs (the cartoons were made during the war years and a couple have strongly negative stereotyping of Asians). There is a distinct lack of characterization, but this is compensated by the dark emotional mood and by the consistently unique images.

The black and white 'Snafuperman' is a war cartoon of little importance or interest. The source material is fair.

SUPERMAN IV: THE QUEST FOR PEACE

The most comic bookish of the four 'Superman' movies is *Superman IV: The Quest for Peace*. This is not necessarily a bad thing, since comics are often imbued with wisdom as well as simpler pleasures. In *IV*, for example, Superman is given a sagely warning early on that he could harm society by helping it too much, advice which he appears to understand, but then blithely ignores and pays the consequences. The idea is complex, and even though the rest of the movie is mindless, pre-school level fun, one idea is more than many movies possess.

The disc has an unremarkable soundtrack and looks fairly decent. It runs for only 90 minutes, but has Warner's liberal distribution of chapter markers. If you can get past the opening, where Superman saves a Soyez space station while his cape flutters in the breezy vacuum of outer space, you'll probably get through the rest of it.

SUPERTRAMP BROTHER WHERE YOU BOUND

The 18-minute extended music video, 'Brother Where You Bound,' has a full credit roll at the end, like a real movie. It is featured on side one of the 8-inch *Supertramp Brother Where You Bound*. The cut is spectacular, and is just convoluted enough so that you can never pin it into a single category. There is a wild selection of video camera effects and an intriguing paranoid narrative about a man running away from everybody and everything.

Two other cuts, on the flip side of the CLV disc, are less impressive. 'Cannonball' is about a cave man who has a nasty dream and 'Better Days' is a visually stimulating evocation of time travel.

THE SURE THING

Although it would be easy to find fault with *The Sure Thing*, it is such a nice movie that there isn't any point in picking it apart. There is nothing special about the sound or the picture. The story concerns a boy and girl who fall in love as they hitchhike across the US. It relies on the personalities of the two leads, John Cusack and Daphne Zuniga, and they play off each other very well. While it is difficult to imagine that one could watch the disc too often, it may be worth keeping around for a pick-me-up.

SURRENDER

Steve Guttenberg appears in the ad artwork on the jacket cover of *Surrender* without a mustache, although his character retains one throughout the film. He has the 'Ralph Bellamy role' in the rich people romantic comedy, and he plays his part perfectly. Except for his salary, however, we can think of no reason for his being in the film, since the part is secondary to the narrative and unsympathetic. The script has many amusing moments, so that one does not mind the way in which the final third drags on. The running time is only 95 minutes, anyway. It seems to be the fault of the movie that not all the shots are in focus, because otherwise the transfer looks fine. In the many closeups of Michael Caine and Sally Field, their tans always look properly shaded. The Ultra-Stereo sound is also fun, and the disc is loaded with chapter markers.

SURVIVOR

Survivor has a number of dark indoor/night scenes which remain completely stable. The picture looks a little soft and the most intense colors blur a bit, but on the whole it is satisfactory.

The post-Apocalyptic plot has the hero wandering around in a desert. He meets a girl, the girl is kidnapped, he goes to find her and uncovers a large underground colony run by a nasty bad guy. The film has an unusual amount of voice over narration, as compensation for an almost complete lack of dialog until the final half hour. The sound is loud and a bit unmanageable.

SUSPECT

Those who have any familiarity with the American justice system will cringe at the central conceit in *Suspect*, that a juror (Dennis Quaid) surreptitiously begins investigating the case he is sitting on, and then collaborates with the defense attorney (Cher). The defense attorney's immediate action ought to have been to have the juror removed. That's why there are alternate jurors, and he could have been freer to help her after he stepped down. But instead they go on, and it makes for some marvelously tense moments – we started screaming at Quaid in one instance – and ends up being, if unlikely, at least vaguely conceivable and definitely exciting.

The transfer is good, but early copies were subject to widespread manufacturing flaws. The stereo sound editing on the film is accomplished, and the digitally encoded track comes across more smoothly than the analog track. The 122-minute film has been released in a gatefold jacket, with an essay, about the filming of *Suspect*, in the centerspread. True, the essayist misspells the title of one of the director's other films, but the article is informative, and coming upon it was a pleasant surprise.

SUSPICION

Alfred Hitchcock used to enjoy telling interviewers that he had wanted to make Cary Grant a murderer in *Suspicion*, and that his producers had prevented him. It was balderdash, however, because the film's ending has just the right mix of sentiment and ambiguity as it stands and was clearly the ending intended all along. The film, about a marriage with some definite communication problems, improves with multiple viewings, because, like Hitchcock's own pronouncements, there is never a reference point to tell the viewer what is a lie and what is the truth. Is Grant's character scheming or just error-prone? Each viewer's psychology will likely impose a different interpretation.

The disc has a sharply detailed black-and-white picture which contains a number of splices and speckles. The monaural soundtrack accompanies the picture flaws with pops and clicks. The volume is set low, and swings even lower near the middle of side two.

Suspicion is one of many classic Hitchcock films which a decent movie library must contain. Although the action is limited, the film is gripping both emotionally and stylistically. The viewer follows the maturation of the heroine as she is threatened by an ever-increasing shadow of webs. Grant's performance appears carefully controlled by the director, but his presence as 'Cary Grant' is as deliberate a factor in the film's construction as are the personality quirks of his character. And watch for the glass of milk he carries up the stairs. It had a light bulb inside to make the milk glow, ominously.

SUSPIRIA

With an aspect ratio of about 2.4:1 and a good looking color transfer Image's release of *Suspiria* gives the film its best opportunity to attract potential fans. The film's color washes are so intense that inevitably grain will appear during some sequences, but the beautiful set designs and superb cinematography are on display in shot after shot. The movie was one of the last significant films to be made with the Technicolor color matrix, and the filmmakers deliberately manipulated the process to create one or two toned washes for enhancing the mood in certain scenes.

Unless you are a fan of Jessica Harper's, the film's appeal rests entirely on its technical accomplishments and stylistic presentation, but this is enough to make the disc a pleasing experience.

Although the denouement has elements of fantasy, the script is structured as most Dario Argento stories are structured, as a murder mystery with an accent on terror. We were struck, during this viewing, by the scene in which a young woman in a flimsy nightgown, trying to escape a figure chasing her with a knife, crawls through a window and falls into a thick matting of loosely coiled razor wire. Ouch.

Image has included two original theatrical trailers at the end of the movie, one from the American release and one from the European release. It should be noted that the tag line on the disc's jacket cover reads, "The only thing more terrifying than the last 10 minutes of this film are the first 90!" while the announcer in one of the trailers says that the only thing more terrifying than the "last 12 minutes" are the "first 92." The disc's running time is 98 minutes. (Argento's films seem to get as hacked up as his characters.)

The disc has digital stereo surround sound which tends, deliberately, to lack the elegance of the camera set ups. The sound editing is loud and irritating, but the post synchronized dialog isn't disconcerting, and the audio track is intended to undo one's nerves.

Letterboxing improves the presentation of *Suspiria* considerably, giving a symmetry to every shot and revealing how truly elaborate the color experiments are. Cropped, a character will appear to be bathed in a blue light for a single shot. Letterboxed, it is revealed that another portion of the screen is bathed in red (the effect having been accomplished by lowering the intensity of the third color in the matrix).

SUSPIRIA, PART 2 (Import)
'Deep Red' has been given the ridiculous title, *Suspiria, Part 2*, even though its namesake, Dario Argento's biggest hit, was made after 'Red' had been released. Both titles appear in the opening credits of the program, but it is *Suspiria, Part 2* which is smashed onto the jacket cover and the label, so that is the name of the import disc. The English language film is in letterboxed format, with Japanese subtitles appearing beneath the picture. The sound is monaural and is passible. The picture looks a little used, but is not severely damaged.

David Hemmings stars as a pianist who is shadowed by a psychotic killer after he witnesses a murder. The identity of the murderer is revealed at that time, if you can focus on an insignificant portion of the screen for a 30th of a second. Otherwise, you have to bear the twists and turns and red herrings until the thrilling conclusion. Although Argento sometimes advances the plot with awkwardly staged dialog, and does not tie together all the loose ends, the film is another celebration of nervous tension and relentless unease. The combination of stylish camera angles, thick plotting, and uninhibited death fulfills the worst fears of anyone who ever avoided walking through an empty house in the dark.

SWEDENHIELMS (see **INTERMEZZO**)

SWEENEY TODD
For some reason Image left the stereo indicator off the jacket cover of *Sweeney Todd* (subtitled, 'The Demon Barber of Fleet Street'). The audio is indeed stereophonic, and although the live recording has some odd attributes, it is most satisfying. The picture transfer, too, though not always razor sharp, is pleasing. The program is a video recording of a stage production, which took place in an inflated auditorium and was in sore need of the sort of intimacy that the cameras at least partially provide. The sound recording has a different ambience from a live opera recording – a fresher, more immediate replication which compensates in realism what it loses in purity. The picture is sometimes fuzzy or off-color, but it is usually very satisfying. Because of the way the production is staged, very little is lost in isolating the primary action. George Hearn and Angela Lansbury star.

In many ways the highly acclaimed Stephen Sondheim musical, about a murderous barber whose victims become the primary ingredient in a hot-selling pot pie, is an innovative and remarkable work. Sondheim's lyrics are breathlessly ingenious. Directed by Harold Prince, the balance between plot and music, between comedy and horror, between cheerfulness and bitterness, and between the believable and the abstract is always successful but never predictable. If the show has any flaws at all, it is in the music itself, which is too much a reiteration of Sondheim's earlier works, and Lansbury, whose comedy is sharp, but whose singing is a weak link. Anyone who obtains the disc, however, will hardly be concerned about splitting hairs, except upon Todd's shaving utensils.

SWEET CHARITY
While we would not recommend the film *Sweet Charity* to our lowest enemies, we enthusiastically recommend the disc to everyone. The sound is a bit old, but it was remixed for surround, and gives the boom, boom boom boom, boom, boom of 'Big Spender' the audio equivalent of pelvic thrust. The overture, entre'acte and walkout music are also featured. The major dance numbers, along with the opening and closing credits, are in letterboxed format. Since the movie is not even remotely a sacred work of art, the extra zooms don't hurt a bit. We are far more grateful that MCA has put what it has in widescreen than we are annoyed with the parts which are scanned and cropped. The marvelously naive trailer for the roadshow engagement, which comes at the very end of the disc, is not in wide screen, and that is disappointing. It would also have been nice if they could have dredged up a trailer from the revised ad campaign, for contrast.

The quality of the picture itself is good. None of the darker scenes look distorted, and the daylight shots appear solid. The 148-minute feature is spread to four sides, so the intermission break could be placed between the platters. This allowed MCA to leave both side two and side four in CAV. Side four hasn't got much to offer, but side two has a major dance number with Shirley MacLaine, Chita Rivera, and Paula Kelly, which is wonderful in slow motion and fascinating (which of the three can kick the highest?) in still step. None of the still frames quiver.

The disc has a spectacular finale which the movie itself does not have, two endings. The original roadshow downer version, and the panicked already-lost-their-shirts smiley version. The movie itself was a multi-million dollar training ground for Bob Fosse so that he could go on and make profitable films for other companies. The first ending would have been artistic, except that the movie is not art. The second ending contains a howling mistake by including the only scene in the whole film where Charity is not present, making the effort an obvious afterthought. But it is a happy ending, and it does come at the very end, after the walkout music from the first ending. It makes one wish that the decision points in real life were but a chapter marker away.

SWEET DREAMS
Patsy Cline's original recordings are dubbed over Jessica Lange's lip-synching on *Sweet Dreams* and the resulting sound is remarkably clean and clear on the disc's digital track. The analog soundtrack is noisier and not as well defined. The picture is passable, though dark scenes contain distortions.

Directed by Karl Reisz, the film is always understated in its depiction of Cline's rise to fame. The bigger house she buys when she gets rich looks like a modest suburban unit in the center of a development track. The dramatic movement of the story is driven by Cline's off again/on again relationship with her husband. The rapport Lange has with Ed Harris and the music is enough to make the film a repeatable entertainment.

SWEET HEARTS DANCE
If the jacket cover of *Sweet Hearts Dance* appeals to you, then the disc will, too. The movie, which stars Don Johnson, Susan Sarandon, Jeff Daniels and Elizabeth Perkins, is about two couples in a small Vermont town going through early mid-life crises one winter. Not only is the cast terrific, but there is a conscious attempt to evoke the feel of the season. The characters may be trying to recapture old memories, but it is obvious to the viewer that they are making new ones at the same time.

The picture has an occasional speckle and a few weak colors, but not enough to harm the presentation. The sound is passable, but only the musical score and a few sound effects are in stereo surround.

People tend to put down Don Johnson, but he can have an entertaining screen presence. The lengthy experience he's had in front of the camera gives him the confidence to know what he can do and the wisdom to get around the things he has problems with. As usual, however, Susan Sarandon steals the movie. Of the four characters, her's is the most poorly conceived in the script, yet she adds so much to the part in the way that she curses, gazes, or holds her posture that she ends up with the richest, most fully developed personality in the film.

SWEET LIBERTY
We don't wish to insult any readers, and we know they have a variety of tastes, but can you really imagine anyone who buys *Sweet Liberty* watching it more than once or twice in five years time? What is it that would excite them? The scene where Michael Caine

and Alan Alda exchange places on the roller coaster? (A resounding metaphor which captures the predicament of their characters within the plot, to be sure.) Or the scene where Alda, in bed with his girlfriend, rolls over onto a pin cushion? (Again, symbolic both of the trouble he is about to find himself in and of his personality in general.) The movie is about a movie crew which invades a small town to film a British invasion of its colonies. Parallels abound, but laughs do not. The disc has a good picture and decent CX-encoded monaural sound. We would prefer, however, to leave the defense of *Liberty* to others.

SWEET SMELL OF SUCCESS

Although a print would have to wear down severely to spoil James Wong Howe's shiny, street-wet black-and-white cinematography, the source material MGM/UA has used for *Sweet Smell of Success* looks almost new, with only a scattering of scratches to reveal its true age. There are also some great stills on the back of the jacket. The second martini-ish Elmer Bernstein/Chico Hamilton score sounds refreshing though the audio track could be crisper.

The 97-minute film is quick entertainment, tracing the steps of an aggressive press agent (Tony Curtis) over two nights and a day as he struggles to please a powerful gossip columnist (Burt Lancaster). It is all about manipulating personalities, the night life of New York City, and the in-fighting which goes on to achieve a single sentence blurb in an influential column. The script has wit, the acting is engaging, the photography and music tie it all together, and the disc presents it as if it were hot off the press.

THE SWIMMER

The ambiguities in *The Swimmer* have withstood the passage of time well. It helps that the director, Frank Perry, did not make the parties or fashions too trendy. Except for a concern that the hero, who walks through backyards and acreage to take a dip in the swimming pools of his neighbors, is exposing himself to Lyme disease, the story has hardly aged. The style of the narrative is to tell the viewer very little, but to imply a great many things. Thus, the details of what has happened to the hero over the preceding two mysterious years are never revealed, but the emotions are made very clear. The age and status of a number of characters are deliberately vague, forcing the viewer to concentrate on the mood of the conversations instead of on what is said. The film is highly re-watchable, because knowledge of the plot specifics does not spoil the emotional structure.

The print does show its age a little, and many of the fleshtones look too pink. The musical score is set louder than the dialog, so one may find oneself constantly readjusting the playback volume.

SWIMMING TO CAMBODIA

Spalding Gray had a secondary role in *The Killing Fields* which he parlayed into an hour-and-a-half monolog at a bleachers-for-seats performance space. The monolog, an adept contemporary history of Cambodia interspersed with predictable but amusing anecdotes about shooting a movie in a foreign locale, was filmed by Jonathon Demme as a motion picture entitled *Swimming to Cambodia*. Those who are searching for a companion piece to *The Killing Fields*, or for 90 minutes of intelligent conversation, will find the disc to be a worthy investment.

The area around Gray not illuminated by stage lighting remains solid black, without a squiggle in sight. The digital monaural sound is in excellent condition, with significantly less noise than the CX-encoded analog track.

SWIMWEAR ILLUSTRATED ON LOCATION

(see **SPORTS ILLUSTRATED 25TH ANNIVERSARY SWIMSUIT ISSUE**)

SWING OUT SISTER...AND WHY NOT

The four numbers on *Swing Out Sister...and why not*, 'Breakout,' 'Surrender,' 'Twilight World,' and 'Fooled by a Smile,' are catchy and are supported by visually busy music videos which withstand numerous viewings.

Swing Out Sister is a three-person group with a multiple band sound. The vocalist, Corrine Drewery, can hold her own against a wall of brass, though who is actually playing all those instruments is never made clear by the videos. The 8-inch disc has a decent picture, though some colors have a slight blur around the edges. The sound is good.

SWING: THE BEST OF THE BIG BANDS VOLUME 1
SWING: THE BEST OF THE BIG BANDS VOLUME 2

Our favorite part in *Dark Passage* is when Humphrey Bogart, examining Lauren Bacall's record collection, says, "I see you like swing music," and Bacall replies, "Yes, legitimate swing." How that conversation is replayed with each new popular music genre – tacit acceptance, but only with the understanding that baser elements are not to be included. We don't know if Bacall's character would have found every act on the *Swing: The Best of the Big Bands* discs to be legitimate, but time has enshrined them all and their musical offspring have more than justified their musical parentage.

MCA has done a marvelous job scrounging through its archives of rarely distributed musical short features to resurrect these clips. All are complete numbers from the big band era, usually staged in a nightclub setting. The black and white picture transfer is, without an exception, fantastic, so that one would think the pieces had been filmed just yesterday were it not for the life or youth in the performers.

The monaural sound has also been touched with magic, though singers do not always appear to be mouthing the words as perfectly as one hears them. The bands all have a solid, mono impact which compares honorably with the best studio recordings of the era.

The programs, which were released as 45-minute video cassettes, have been combined on single 90-minute laser discs. Each side ends in a credit roll, and, disconcertingly, *Volume 2* contains programs identified as 'Volume 3' and 'Volume 4.' The discs are chapter encoded to performers (who sometimes perform more than one song).

Volume 1 includes Billy Holiday, Gene Krupa, Tommy Dorsey, Woody Herman, Sarah Vaughan, Nat King Cole, Lionel Hampton, the Hi-Los, Rosemary Clooney, and others. It would be impossible to pick a favorite, but the efforts seem to fall into two categories: Great (Holiday, Dorsey, etc.) or pleasingly weird (the Hi-Los, Sugar Chile Robinson, and several others). Playing the disc more than once, and playing it for friends, is a likely activity.

Teresa Brewer, on *Volume 2*, probably comes closest to embodying Bacall's worst fears, by performing a blanched rendition of 'Old Man Mose.' But with the Ink Spots, Mills Brothers, Skylarks, Count Basie, Duke Ellington, and so much more, *Volume 2* has as much going for it as *Volume 1*. The best piece is Ellington's 3-minute musical summary of the 'History of Jazz.'

SWING TIME
SWING TIME (CAV)

A friend suggested that we watch *Swing Time* on our older player, so we could take advantage of the 'sliding scale' slow motion. Later generation laser players offer but a limited number of slow motion speeds, clumsily compensated by the jog/shuttle function, while older players have a greater incremental range, especially as the speed approaches normal. This was wise advice, because the best way to watch the dance numbers is to view them at just slightly less than full speed. You can still make out the rhythm of movement, but you can also see the dancers responding to each other's prompts and cues. And yet this sort of deconstruction does nothing to harm the empathy between Ginger Rogers and Fred Astaire. Their duets become more erotic. You can see that they are responding to each other on a micro level, every touch greeted with an enthusiastic acknowledgement.

The print has a few scratches and some other glitches, but all you will notice is the remarkable clarity and freshness of the picture. The CAV presentation has a brighter and slightly more detailed image than the CLV disc. The CLV version has digital sound, but the analog sound on the CAV presentation isn't bad.

The plot for an Astaire/Rogers film often imitates a dance number. They go together, break apart, get together again. When Eric Blore disappears in the first half of *Swing Time*, a good deal of the humor disappears with him. But the film survives.

Voyager has provided a second audio track lecture on the CAV disc only, given by Astaire scholar John Mueller. His talk is selectively informative. He has a lot to say about how the Jerome Kern music and the big dance numbers came about, but he says nothing on the contributions of the movie's director, George Stevens. The CAV disc also has 50 behind-the-scenes productions stills, and a lengthy excerpt from a 1935 musical, 'Hooray for Love,' depicting a musical and tap dance performance by Bojangles Robinson and Fats Waller.

SWITCHING CHANNELS

When the source material is as funny as 'The Front Page,' it is unusually difficult in an adaptation to eradicate all of the laughs, but *Switching Channels* comes pretty close. Adapted, via 'His Girl Friday,' to a television all-news 'Satellite Network,' which seems unduly wrapped up in local Chicago politics, the film stars Kathleen Turner, Burt Reynolds, and Chistopher Reeve. None of them are helped by the script or the direction, and none of them can sustain a presence of wit longer than a scene or two.

The picture looks new, but the flesh tones are consistently too red, and intense colors tend to exceed their boundaries. The sound is dull and insignificant.

THE SWORD IN THE STONE

Walt Disney's *The Sword in the Stone*, a 79-minute animation feature, covers the period between Arthur's first meeting with Merlin to the removal of the Sword from the Stone. Although the characters are human, they become fish, squirrels, birds, et cetera, thanks to Merlin's magic. The drawings have a pleasing sketchiness which make them easier to relax with than the economically solid figures in today's cartoons. The picture and sound transfers are fine.

SYLVESTER

Horse movies seem to come along every two years or so, even though few of them since *National Velvet* have ever made any money. *Sylvester* is typical of the genre, with moments of anxiety in the beginning and triumph at the end as an unfettered young lady and her horse come from nowhere to win a major competition.

Other than giving the horse the name 'Sylvester Stallone,' the script is intelligent. The presence of Richard Farnsworth helps considerably. The picture is a little pale and the sound is acceptable.

SYLVIA SCARLET (see BRINGING UP BABY/SYLVIA SCARLETT)

T.V.'S GREATEST BITS

The one-sided 53-minute program *T.V.'s Greatest Bits*, is a condescending but satisfying compilation of commercials, clips, and TV show introductions geared to a specific year, 1964. This implies that other episodes could become available depicting other years, and we would be quite happy to plunk down money each for four decades' worth. Whether or not this is the only version in existence, however, Lorimar should have noted on the front of the jacket that the collection covers one year, and not buried that information in the text on the back.

The program is hosted by Gary Owens and guest hosted by Bob Denver, who provide short introductions to various passages. The most annoying aspect to the show is that Owens is often superimposed, *Zelig*-style, into the old clips. When he replaces the girl grabbing the fourth undergarment from the wall of the watertower in the opening of 'Petticoat Junction,' it is clear that the producers don't understand who their audience really is. The impositions, however, are less severe in the second half, and the show comes a good way to redeeming itself with a series of cartoon theme songs. Listening to them on a record is one thing, but the theme to 'The Jetsons,' for example, feels more zippy when you can actually see Jane grab George's billfold in time to the music. None of the clips are in great condition, but that is to be expected, and there are a few surprises, such as the rich color in the opening of 'The Beverly Hillbillies' (real black 'black gold'). The sound has been CX-encoded, for what it is worth.

If a visitor from 1964 were to wake up with today's broadcast TV, he would think the commercials obscure and confusing. The commercials of 1964 are surprisingly direct and expository, with men smoking their pipes and driving their luxury automobiles, and the women hiding hygiene secrets from everyone but their hairdressers. One huckster complains to those in his audience who have not bought his product, "What are you waiting for?" But there was quality in 1964, as well. The dynamic editing and sophisticated production design in the opening credits of 'Perry Mason' is fantastic, and Glen Yarborough singing 'Things Go Better with Coca-Cola' encapsulates the clash between Madison Avenue and folkrock in just a few short bars.

TAFFIN

Taffin will satisfy those who enjoy crime thrillers with enigmatic heroes. Played by Pierce Brosnan, Taffin is a bill collector in a small Irish village with more in his past than meets the eye (the untrained eye – his dashing downscale wardrobe and ever present five-day stubble spell hero even in long distance establishing shots). The townspeople ask him to help stop a chemical plant and faster than one can say 'The Man That Corrupted Hadleyburg' things get rough and everyone turns on him. The movie is good escapist entertainment and Brosnan fulfills his role without missing a beat.

The disc has a passable picture which lacks the gloss of a big budget production. The sound is monaural with no embellishments.

THE TAILOR OF GLOUCESTER (see PECOS BILL)

TAKA IIMURA AYERS ROCK

Some viewers may feel that 38 minutes is a little too long to be looking at a rock. *Taka Iimura Ayers Rock* combines clear, stationary video camera images of Ayers Rock in Australia with a one-sound-at-a-time digital jazz score. Some of the passages – the dissolves, the angles, the light captured – are very good, while other stretches of footage remind one of the nice calendars they have at Woolworth's.

THE TALE OF MR. JEREMY FISHER AND THE TALE OF PETER RABBIT (see PECOS BILL)

THE TALE OF THE FROG PRINCE (see FAERIE TALE THEATRE)

A TALE OF TWO CHIPMUNKS/THE UNSINKABLE DONALD DUCK MICKEY KNOWS BEST/THE IMPORTANCE OF BEING DONALD

Six cartoons and some makeshift linking material appear on *A Tale of Two Chipmunks/The Unsinkable Donald Duck*, from Walt Disney. The disc has two 24-minute home video programs on one side. Each cartoon, 'Chicken in the Rough,' 'Chips Ahoy,' 'The Lone Chipmunk,' 'Donald's Day Off,' 'Lion Around,' and 'Sea Scouts,' has its own chapter marker. The sound, which is a little weak, is monaural and not CX-encoded. The picture is bright and colorful, with the pastels, setting the tone in the post-war Donald Duck cartoons, being especially pleasant. A couple of the cartoons have appeared in other laser disc anthologies.

Mickey Knows Best/The Importance of Being Donald is even better. The connective material between the six cartoons is slighter, and less confusing. They are all from the late thirties, sporting vivid colors and elaborate, complex animation. They also contain more of the raw violence which makes older cartoons so endearing. Donald gets mad at an Amateur Show audience which is ridiculing him, so he sprays them with a machine gun. The cartoons are 'Moving Day,' 'Mickey's Amateurs,' 'Mickey's Elephant,' 'Donald's Better Self,' 'Polar Trappers,' and 'Timber.' A young friend of ours was disappointed that the choo-choo train on the cover never appears on the disc, but otherwise found as much delight in the program as we did.

TALES FROM THE CRYPT

Side one of *Tales from the Crypt* is in CAV, with two unsteady still frames out of every five and a chance to closely examine the seamless opening sequence, which appears to depict the camera diving down a stairwell and twisting through catacombs. The disc is in beautiful shape, with a sharp, glossy picture and entertaining digital stereo surround sound. The program is an anthology, featuring three short films by well known directors.

The best of the group is an amusing and irreverent piece, 'And All Through the House,' about a woman who murders her husband on Christmas Eve and is then terrorized by an escaped mental patient in a Santa suit as she tries to get rid of the body. It was directed by Robert Zemeckis and has just the right mixture of humor and fright. (There is at least one good scream in it.) The Christmas songs playing in the background on the surround channel add atmosphere as well as comedy. The CAV episode, 'The Man Who Was Death,' was directed by Walter Hill and is about a state executioner laid off from his job but unable to give up his vocation. The zap of the electric chair also sounds terrific on the surround channel, and Ry Cooder's electric guitars kicking in just as zap is finishing provides another amusing and engaging effect. The final episode, 'Dig That Cat...He's Real Gone!,' directed by Richard Donner, is about a man given an operation which enables him to die nine times. What a shame he can't keep count. The piece is directed in a very experimental manner which some might legitimately suggest verges on sloppiness.

THE TALES OF HOFFMAN (Import)

One of the first operas to reach movie screens in relatively complete condition was Michael Powell and Emeric Pressburger's *The Tales of Hoffman*. It has been released on disc in Japan in a version lasting 109 minutes, some 20 minutes or so shorter than how it was originally conceived. The color looks like a Persian carpet which has been in the sun too long, and the monaural sound, which is not CX-encoded, has many crackles and dropouts. The movie is valuable, however, in almost any condition, and looks no worse than it does during its rare appearances on broadcast TV.

The Tales of Hoffman is not just an opera. It is also presented as a ballet, in the same way which one would mix cake and ice cream – a little of one, then a little of the other. Jacques Offenbach's score seems to accommodate these variations without difficulty. The lyrics are sung in English, and special attention appears to have been made in the recording to keep it comprehensible (Japanese subtitles are also present, but they rarely interfere). Although held in setting to the opera's four locales, the film, in the hands of Powell and Pressburger, is never stagebound. It leaps everywhere, from one fantastic or moody conceptualization to the next. Puppets become ballerinas, devils vault through mirrors, and drawings are transformed to live figures. Some critics complain that the movie is too peripatetic, but that is Offenbach's fault. Powell and Pressburger were just following his lead.

THE TALK OF THE TOWN

Jean Arthur runs around in Ronald Colman's pajamas for the first twenty minutes or so of *The Talk of the Town*, and she's gorgeous. It is a drag when she finally gets dressed and puts her hair up. The whole movie clams up. Cary Grant portrays a radical, accused of arson, who hides in the summer home of a Supreme Court nominee, played, with a beard, by Colman. Anything can happen in the movies.

RCA/Columbia has chosen to include a fairly notorious promotional still on the back of the jacket, which adds a little more value to the disc. The print has its share of scratches and fuzzy images. The film is close to two hours long because the filmmakers couldn't decide which guy Arthur would get in the end.

TALK RADIO

The on-air phone conversations in *Talk Radio* don't sound right. The film is about a Dallas radio announcer who takes his evening talk show and his own mental stability to the edge of sanity (the film's claim to be based on the experiences of the assassinated Colorado deejay, Alan Berg, seems somewhat contrived). The movie concentrates on the announcer's psychology and creates an interesting profile of an artist harnessing his own burnout. The callers, however, sound nothing like the callers one hears on real late night talk shows, or, at best, they all sound like the one worst crank call to slip through the screening. The common man/woman just isn't as monotonous as the voices in the film are portrayed, and it impacts the film's credibility, severely.

The surround effects are curiously limited, as if the film's sound editors had included the separations as an afterthought. There is a nice, bassy 'whompf' whenever the door to the studio opens or closes. The picture is passable, with some intense colors appearing mildly grainy, but the many night scenes surviving without distortion.

TALL, DARK AND HANDSOME

The picture on *Tall, Dark and Handsome* is below average. The 70-minute CLV program, about the all-male floor show at Chippendale's, converges real footage with staged and fantasy sequences. There are dance numbers, vaguely focussed (in more ways than one, considering the blurry picture) skits, and a lot of desperate innuendo. The sound is in stereo, but has no oomph.

TALL IN THE SADDLE

Free of the intellectual baggage and higher meanings which most westerns available on video disc possess, *Tall in the Saddle*, is a good, old fashioned John Wayne western, period. Like many in the genre, the plot is fueled by a mystery (who killed the rancher?) and depicts corruption in a small town. Wayne, the stranger, enters and cleans everything up. The movie embraces every cliché so joyously that it is nearly impossible to dislike. There is a rousing stagecoach ride, a 'good' girl and a 'bad' girl competing for Wayne's affections, a lip-smacking drunk played by Gabby Hayes who pronounces 'poison' 'pisen,' and the usual collection of gun and fist fights. Wayne is terrific, particularly in a scene in which his character, while nervous, must pretend to ignore threatening gunfire.

The black-and-white print has a few splices but the picture is sharp and we can't possibly imagine its flaws upsetting anybody. The film runs under 90 minutes and lasts close to an hour on side one, but remains in CLV. A decent set of chapter markers have been encoded. The sound is subject to a fluctuation or two and is best kept at a low volume, though amplification clearly captures the atmosphere of the original recording (the phony stagecoach sound effects and studio-recorded dialog perfectly matches the phony stagecoach rear projection and soundstage setting).

THE TAMING OF THE SHREW
ROMEO AND JULIET

Franco Zeffirelli's adaptation of *The Taming of the Shrew* was released on disc by RCA/Columbia and his phenomenally successful version of *Romeo and Juliet* was put out by Paramount. Both discs are worthy additions to one's library.

Shrew is the sloppier transfer of the two. It looks luscious enough, as any Zeffirelli endeavor does, and it sounds very sharp for a monaural film, but the flashes of nudity are missing and the print is speckled in places. The movie is a joyous vehicle for Elizabeth Taylor and Richard Burton, celebrating the comic poetry and the devious power games of the principal characters.

In order for *The Taming of the Shrew* to work today, it has to be seen as an exaggerated satire of courtship and marriage. Zeffirelli pulls this off, and his embellishments, such as a wonderfully disastrous wedding scene which is only hinted at in the text, add to the humor without taking away the thrust of the story.

Zeffirelli's *Romeo and Juliet* was condemned by critics because he substantially altered the text (Paris doesn't fight Romeo at the end) and because the movie was such a huge hit. Yet the film ought to be praised for its popularity. Zeffirelli took a rather silly story which even Shakespeare occasionally made fun of (See Act V of 'A Midsummer Night's Dream') and made it alive and relevant 400 years after it was written.

Using genuine teenagers (Olivia Hussey and Leonard Whiting), Zeffirelli made their language, such as the lovely sonnet which they share before their first kiss, a natural part of their adolescent hesitation. The chatter is full of poetic flourish because the characters are working up their nerve behind their words. The original film was in scope, and with Zeffirelli's eye, you feel like you've lost half the richness when you are only viewing half the screen. The picture is mildly blurry and faded.

TAMMY WYNETTE IN CONCERT

Tammy Wynette in Concert includes some classic songs, such as 'Stand by Your Man,' 'Will the Circle be Unbroken,' 'D I V O R C E,' 'You Light Up My Life,' 'Makin' Love,' 'I Don't Want to Play House,' and others. The stereo sound has a clear, clean delivery and Wynette's voice is not inhibited by the live environment.

Unfortunately, Wynette is. Although the picture is very bright and clear, Wynette has a limited amount of charisma on stage. Even in her open-your-heart-to-the-audience piece, 'Turn Around,' her emotional delivery is guarded and unfeeling, as if she expected the words which she has memorized to do the job for her.

TAMPOPO

The charming Japanese comedy *Tampopo* is about a woman who upgrades her luncheonette with the help of two men who are rivals for her affection and a couple others who are experts in preparing food. The narrative, however, is laced with Bunuellean blackout sketches that are also food related, and it is the abstract and amusing nature of these sequences, which tend not to involve the main characters, that probably propelled the film onto so many ten-best lists.

The disc is in Japanese and has English subtitles which apparently work because we were rarely aware of them. The image has a slight matting, but not enough to qualify as a true letterbox. The picture transfer looks fine. The film stock does not provide a slick image, but the colors look fresh and the dark scenes have no distortion. The sound is also in good shape.

TANGO AND CASH

Whoever really edited *Tango and Cash* deserves a healthy percentage of the film's profits. The movie is paced like an old-time serial and never gives the viewer a chance to get restless. The images and the sounds bombard you. It's a knockout, particularly on laser disc. When we put the Warner release on, we had to leap up and lower the volume on our amplifier. We thought our speakers were going to blow up.

The film was directed by Andrei Konchalovsky, whose movies we usually dislike, but his imprint on the film is over-ridden by the pacing. The picture is incredibly sharp and the colors are perfect. The surround sound has a killer bass and is generally boisterous and fulsome. The picture has been letterboxed, with an aspect ratio of about 2.3:1. In most cases, the image composition looks legitimately rectangular, although there is a binocular shot which shows the top and bottom of the lenses lopped off.

The editing has turned the film, about a drug lord (Jack Palance) attempting to frame and exterminate two cops (Sylvester Stallone and Kurt Russell), into a constant cliffhanger. If you stop to think about the story it is unbelievable and silly, but there's no stopping and thinking. Even the courtroom scene is a marvel of rushed one-liners, and should be studied for its efficiency and clever execution.

The ending is wild, as the filmmakers pull out a James Bond-style van and pit it against an army of construction vehicles. *Tango and Cash* is a movie of the future, the type people would be watching in *Clockwork Orange*-land, and while the thought of mindless violence as entertainment used to sound boring, we're finally beginning to see what the prognosticators are getting at.

TANNHAUSER

Even though the whole night is still ahead of them, the orchestra for the Metropolitan Opera under conductor James Levine does a smashing job with the overture to *Tannhauser*. Richard Wagner's overture is longer than many symphonic pieces, but the group attacks it as if it were the concluding number for the evening. Despite the elaborate sets, nothing in the program is as impressive visually as the overture in Act I and the introduction to Act III. Not even the wild 'Bacchanal' ballet.

The picture is spotless. The sound recording allows the orchestra to overpower the singers a little in Act I, but is adjusted properly for the remaining program. The disc is 176 minutes long on four sides, but the sessions of lengthy applause can be scanned to cut it down a little. The break between side one and side two is daring. It marks the transition in Act 1 from Scene 1 to Scene 2, in which the locale is supposed to change from a supernatural environment to a natural one. The transition is important, so it is shown on side one immediately before the break, rather than using the break to mark the change in scenes.

Richard Cassilly, who portrays the title character, is on stage through almost the entire opera and paces himself accordingly. The plot is about the conflict between paganism and Catholicism, rendered in a typically Germanic Presbyterian style. The presentation has English subtitles, and a libretto, in German and English, is included in the box jacket, along with an excellent essay on the opera's production history.

TAP

One of the Nicholas Brothers, Harold, appears in *Tap*, a contemporary film starring Gregory Hines which carries on the tradition of the black musical in a less restrictive atmosphere. Nicholas may not quite have the stamina he once had, but he still could probably leave an entire aerobics class panting for breath.

The film's cinematography is a weak link, and although the picture transfer is very good, shots and scenes still look murky or grainy. The digitally encoded stereo surround sound is less problematic. It sounds terrific. The musical score is fully separated and the taps echo all over the place. There is a full fade to black which marks the center of the film, but Image ignored it when chosing the side break, which instead feels abrupt.

The narrative is meant to be a loosely constructed drama, in the manner of the inconsequential plots of the older movies, but the actors are all better than the script gives them a chance to be. Hines portrays a paroled convict who sharpened his dancing skills while in solitary confinement and, upon release, attempts to rekindle a romance with a dancing partner he had once forsaken. Particularly wasted is Sammy Davis, Jr., who appears ready to give one of those gritty, serious performances that old troupers win Oscars for, but gets stuck with such a flimsy, repetitive part that he can be praised only for making it through the film without embarrassing himself. The dancing is wonderful, and for home video that is all a viewer requires, but there is a lot of potential talent within the film which is left untapped.

TAPEHEADS

The people who made *Tapeheads* need to take drugs or something. The comedy is too sober. It tries very hard to be outrageous, but it also tries to be sensible, and it can't be both. The film, about a pair of misfits who want to break into the music video business, has some inspired moments when barbs are directed specifically at the music industry, but overall it is a bit ho-hum. It stars John Cusack and Tim Robbins.

The Ultra-Stereo sound is digitally encoded. The sound engineers were hip enough to throw a little dialog onto the back channel along with the simplistic sound effects and jokey rock music score. The picture has trouble with reds, which tend to blur, but remains reasonably presentable.

TARGET

The wonderful spy adventure, *Target,* loses something in the post-production work. The relationship between Gene Hackman and Matt Dillon isn't completely fleshed out – they're missing a level of familiarity – and the action scenes are often missing the most exciting points of view. The movie also has several different musical scores, all credited to Michael Small. Some of it sounds like good old-fashioned European mystery music from the '60s, but there is also a boring synthesizer beat which dulls the color of the proceedings.

The transfer has an orange tint which turns long shots of faces into small golden blurs. The pressing is a disappointment, but the movie survives it. You don't always have to hit the bull's-eye in order to win.

TAXI DRIVER
TAXI DRIVER (CAV)

Voyager has succeeded in transferring Martin Scorsese's *Taxi Driver* to disc and retaining the full impact which the movie had as a theatrical film. The mild letterboxing frames the image perfectly, while the colors retain the precise mixture of grain and gloss which gave the movie its humid atmosphere. The freshness of the image is so fulfilling that it compensates for the dated fashions that might otherwise alienate the viewer from some of the characters. (The story is about a lonely individual who almost becomes an assassin.) The film style is so powerful, the psychology so fascinating (and, as later events proved, instinctively accurate), and the narrative so involving that the movie is a highly intelligent and intense form of entertainment.

Voyager has released a CLV version and a CAV version. The picture on both looks the same, and the digital monaural sound on the two discs, which seems to capture the slightly dull pitch of the original soundtrack perfectly, is also the same. Voyager has provided a marvelous feature on the analog track of both discs as well. The musical score has been isolated on a single analog channel and chapter markers have been placed at every music insert. With some deft chapter programming, the viewer can recreate the movie's soundtrack album, without the intrusion of the Robert DeNiro monologs that made the LP an awkward choice for romantically somber background music.

The CLV disc has no other special features. The other analog track on the CAV disc is given over to commentary by Scorsese, with inserted comments from the scriptwriter, Paul Schrader. Scorsese's breathless observations are reactive, but he keeps piling on information as it pops into his head and by the end of the disc the viewer thoroughly understands the forces and ideas which contributed not only to the creation of *Taxi Driver*, but to the filmmaking experience in general. His words on the construction of the controversial and violent finale are especially enlightening. (He wanted to emulate tabloid photos.) Schrader, who is a little less reserved than he was during the extensive interviews that he gave at the time of the film's initial release, also has some insightful remarks about the film, and about himself.

The CAV disc, which comes in a gatefold jacket, has a minor still frame supplementary section squeezed onto the end of side four. The section includes the recreation of an early draft of Schrader's script – demonstrating, as Scorsese emphasizes, how fully realized Schrader's work was from its inception – a brief essay about Bernard Herrmann's work on the score, a listing of Scorsese's film work, 107 production and publicity photos, and an interesting compilation of about 200 of Scorsese's storyboard sketches.

A TAXING WOMAN

The Japanese film about a demure tax investigator who is always a step ahead of the cheats she is auditing, *A Taxing Woman* is a delight, depicting the step by step process government agents use to snare unreported income, in a way which makes bookkeeping look as fun as searching for treasure. The film also has a superbly executed matter-of-fact style, capturing, for example, the multiple introductions and confusion which can happen during a first day on the job, and the messy hygiene which follows lovemaking. Following a normal dramatic pattern, the film opens with a number of short scores and then settles into depicting the big one, but at 127 minutes it ends much too quickly and leaves one wishing for more.

The disc runs to three sides and comes in a single sleeve jacket. Side three is in CAV with perfect still frames. The final bust is elaborately edited and some viewers will be interested in using the Standard Play functions to break it down. The adequately recorded monaural sound is digitally encoded and the musical score, like the heroine, is deliberately appealing. The picture is soft and has a definite low budget foreign appearance. The dialog is in Japanese and small English subtitles, which are sometimes difficult to read, appear on the screen.

TCHAIKOVSKY – SWAN LAKE – NUREYEV – FONTEYN

The famous 1966 recording of Rudolf Nureyev and Margot Fonteyn performing 'Swan Lake' is available on *Tchaikovsky – Swan Lake – Nureyev – Fonteyn*. It wasn't until we watched about fifteen minutes and several solos that we realized there is no audience present at the performance. The Vienna State Ballet Orchestra remains unseen, as well. The dancers don't seem to know what to do with themselves after completing their athletic efforts; there is no applause for them to catch their breath with. Nevertheless, the program is valuable and much of the dancing is stunning. Fonteyn has such precise control of her body that it looks as if the air around her had frozen in exact geometrical patterns. Nureyev's dancing is also magnificent, although even the most devoted fans may find themselves chuckling at his closeups. Too much eye shadow.

The ballet was also choreographed by Nureyev, who builds up his own part up and probably does not showcase Fonteyn as well as she deserves. His concepts are inconsistent, but there are some very nice touches, including the dance of the four cygnets, and the entire fourth Act.

Although the dancers are alone, the cameras never get in among them. Except for one overhead shot, the look of the performance is no different from a live recording. There are a few scratches on the print, but it is in satisfactory condition when one considers its age. The sound is fine, but the musical performance is a little tired. The disc is loaded with chapter markers and breaks the side during a pause in Act II. A single sheet French/English insert comes with the disc, containing a comprehensive history of the ballet's origins.

TCHAIKOVSKY: SYMPHONY NO.6/PIANO CONCERTO NO.1/ WEISSENBERG/BERLINER PHILHARMONIKER/KARAJAN

Two of Peter Tchaikovsky's crowd pleasers have been combined on a crowd pleasing disc, *Tchaikovsky: Symphony No. 6/Piano Concerto No. 1/ Weissenberg/Berliner Philharmoniker/Karajan*. The recordings, by the Berliner Philharmoniker, conducted by Herbert von Karajan, were shot in 1967. The visual approach to the pieces, particularly 'Piano Concerto,' is innovative, making the disc a viable video offering. Karajan's rendition of Symphony No. 6 ('Pathetique') is rousing. His presentation of 'Piano Concerto,' which features Alexis Weissenberg on the piano, is not exceptional, but it is good enough to serve the program.

The age of the recordings is evident, but never detrimental. The picture quality is acceptable, though some portions look a little more faded and grainy than others.

Directed by Ake Falck, 'Piano Concerto,' under the guise of being a standard orchestral performance (it is filmed in a concert hall without an audience), is loaded with oddball POV shots. There is a shot of a clarinetist whose playing is seemingly unaffected even though the camera appears to be standing in substitute for his nose. There are fingering shots which are taken with such closeups that you can make out the fingerprints of the musicians. And there is a wild head-on POV shot of Weissenberg's hands on the piano keyboard, sort of a 'sheet music point-of-view' angle. If Falck's style can be faulted, it is that he tends to segment the orchestra too much.

'Pathetique' was directed by Karajan and, visually, is a little calmer overall, though there are strong similarities between the two programs. Karajan fails to pull back and encompass the entire orchestra for the crescendo in the third movement, and generally lets the music lead the visuals without anticipation. On the whole, though, the disc takes two musical works which, in terms of audio, are overplayed, and, with an enjoyable video presentation and competent performance, breathes life back into them.

TCHAIKOVSKY – VIOLIN CONCERTO – 'ROMEO & JULIET' – PERLMAN – ORMANDY

Itzhak Perlman's solos, on *Tchaikovsky – Violin Concerto – 'Romeo & Juliet' – Perlman – Ormandy*, are spellbinding. He draws the music from his instrument with such a smooth confidence that watching him play is as pleasurable as listening.

Although the running time on the back of the jacket is listed as 58 minutes in CLV. Perlman appears in a live performance with Eugene Ormandy and the Philadelphia Orchestra on side one, performing Tchaikovsky's 'Violin Concerto' at Philadelphia's Academy of Music. On side two, Ormandy and the Orchestra perform Tchaikovsky's 'Romeo and Juliet' overture in the same concert hall. The program, which appears to have a videotape source, is ten years old, but is in excellent condition. The picture is flawless, and the stereo sound is excellent. Both pieces are superbly recorded (the 'Romeo and Juliet' overture has a fullness which encourages one to raise the volume on one's sound system to the maximum), and although the visual format is similar to the *Mozart Violin Concertos* disc, the combination of better camera angles and finer picture quality make the program far more captivating. An insert is included with the disc, containing an excellent essay about Ormandy's career and overviews of the Tchaikovsky pieces.

TEACHERS

For 28 minutes the stereo on *Teachers* is nil, and then suddenly a rock song comes blasting out. Only the songs and false fire alarms will move the volume level indicators on all but the most sensitive audio equipment. The regular sound is flat and often difficult to hear.

Since most of the colors blend with the drab, institutional green of the high school hallways, the movie is visually uninspiring. Nick Nolte portrays a high school teacher whose values are tested when a lawsuit is brought against the district by a student who never learned to read. Sold as a comedy, the film is actually trying to make a statement about something, but it is less in touch than the typical 'Lucas Tanner' episode. C+

TEARS FOR FEARS

A few scratches are in evidence on the 8-inch *Tears for Fears*. The sound is on par with other 8-inch music discs. The group, Tears for Fears, has committed itself to producing songs linked to a single theme: The way childhood anxieties affect later life. The three videos included on the disc, 'Mad World,' 'Change,' and 'Pale Shelter,' are well designed and appealing to watch. The images are rarely predictable.

TEARS FOR FEARS IN MY MIND'S EYE

The concert environment puts a decent bite in the overly gummy music of Tears for Fears. The hour long stereo performance in *Tears for Fears In My Mind's Eye* is effectively recorded, bringing out both the tension and the melodic essence of the group's songs. The picture is clear, and is subject to a constant barrage of repetitive video effects.

TEARS FOR FEARS – SCENES FROM THE BIG CHAIR

The 8-inch from Tears for Fears was cute but inconsequential. We were therefore pleased to discover that the digital 12-inch from the group, *Tears for Fears – Scenes from the Big Chair*, is quite a significant production. The program is an effective blend of music videos, concert footage, and self-critical interviews. By the end you have a capsulized understanding of the band and what their concerns are.

The picture is a little grainy, but the digital sound is superb. The group's music combines a heartbeat rhythmic bass with as many as six vocal harmonies and a few other instruments jiggling sounds around. The group's songs are usually about mending and upsetting deeply-seated anxieties. The digital encoding enables one to delineate the way the music is depicting that same psychology.

TEEN WOLF

Michael J. Fox takes on a Lincolnthropic countenance in *Teen Wolf*, a movie which depicts the stresses of puberty rather graphically without resorting to violence. It doggedly wanders from one situation to the next and nips at the fleas of inspiration, missing as many as it finds. The disc is not in stereo, but the teen-oriented soundtrack is nice and loud. The picture is passable.

TEENAGE MUTANT NINJA TURTLES "THE EPIC BEGINS"
TEENAGE MUTANT NINJA TURTLES SUPER ROCKSTEADY/HEROES IN A HALFSHELL
TEENAGE MUTANT NINJA TURTLES T HE SHREDDER IS SPLINTERED/ HOT RODDING TEENAGERS

The deliberately and amusingly contrived cartoon series, *Teenage Mutant Ninja Turtles*, first appeared on disc with an introductory 72-minute episode entitled *"The Epic Begins."* The disc has "For Ages 5 and Up" plastered on the jacket, although the material is no more heady than any cartoon this side of *Rainbow Brite*. The limitations of the animation compel the viewer's imagination to fill in much of the action, but the jokes are good and the series has always lived up to its title.

The plot has the *Turtles* battling a fiendish mastermind who wants to open a door to another dimension so an army can march through. Flashbacks concerning the Turtles' origins are also included. The animation is reasonably colorful, though not stunning, and the disc weakens when intense solid colors are used. The sound is monaural and workmanlike. Side two is in CAV. Due to the nature of the animation, the still frame pattern has one unsteady frame followed by a steady frame which is repeated, followed by a new steady frame, and repeating the pattern from there.

Two other collections of *Teenage Mutant Ninja Turtles* cartoons, *Super Rocksteady and Mighty Bebop/Heroes in a Halfshell* and *The Shredder Is Splintered/Hot Rodding Teenagers*, contain the source material which had been condensed in *"The Epic Begins."*

Both discs combine two video cassette programs, each program containing two TV half hour episodes. Both open with a trailer for the film. Both have decent monaural sound and chapter encoding which identifies only the start of each episode and not the commercial breaks. The picture on *Shredder* is good, but *Super Rocksteady* looks a little pale.

We have to say that we are tremendously disappointed with the way the cartoons have been organized. The initial Turtle cartoon episodes followed an extended but distinctive narrative line – sort of like the earliest episodes of 'Dallas' – but the collections on the disc pay no attention to the narrative order. The earliest two episodes, represented in 'Heroes in a Halfshell,' appear on side two after two episodes from much later in the series are shown on side one, 'Super Rocksteady and Mighty Bebop' and 'The Mutagen Monster.' Since the latter two were not used in 'Epic Begins,' and since both are quite amusing ('Super Rocksteady' is about robotic versions of the bumbling bad guys; 'Mutagen Monster' is about a giant bull and contains many cow puns), the collection is at least viable. The second disc, which could have been even more entertaining, is a narrative disaster. The 'Shredder Is Splintered' and 'The Return of Shredder' appear on side one, when they ought to be seen after the episodes on side two, 'Hot Rodding Teenagers from Dimension X' and 'A Thing About Rats.' What's more, 'Rats' which appears second on side two, is supposed to precede 'Hot Rodding Teenagers,' as there are direct references in the latter to the former. Except for 'Return of Shredder,' it was these episodes which were cleverly combined into the remainder of *"The Epic Begins."*

TEENAGED MUTANT NINJA TURTLES THE MOVIE

Made on a small movie company's budget, *Teenage Mutant Ninja Turtles The Movie* was a grainy affair to begin with, and the disc looks fairly muddy whenever night scenes or effects work are involved. The digital surround sound also lacks the sophistication of a big budget effort, though there is compensation in a number of cute sound effects. The highpoint on the audio track is the initial appearance of the heroes. The screen goes dark and their first fight is presented entirely with sound.

Turtles could muster no more than a PG rating, but it is a lot of fun if the adult who is watching it is in the right frame of mind. We would not recommend it to those who are not prepared to enjoy it at the onset, as the movie has several slow passages and often fails to make full use of an action or dramatic situation. The one-liners are not as witty as the one-liners in the cartoons, either. There is, however, a gratifying sense of light silliness to the whole affair.

THE TELEPHONE

There's an explanatory plot twist at the very end of the stagey Whoopi Goldberg film *The Telephone*, but we practically had to chain ourselves down to stop from turning the disc off before we got to it. The script, by Harry Nilsson and Terry Southern, is exasperating, and, twist or no twist, it is a strain on a viewer's patience. Goldberg portrays an actress who spends an evening in her apartment hustling friends and holding off creditors over the telephone. Fine, but the dialog written for her is plain stupid, and she's unable to bring any life to it, let alone capture the imagination of others.

The picture is blurry and the digital Ultra Stereo sound is better off when played back in mono. Side two of the CLV disc runs less than 30 minutes, so the 96-minute running time listed on the back of the jacket is off by about a quarter of an hour. Thank goodness.

THE TEMPEST

A videotaped, soundstage-bound performance of William Shakespeare's *The Tempest* stars Efrem Zimbalist, Jr. Zimbalist gets his lines right (well, most of them – we caught him substituting 'third' for 'thread' in "For I have given you a thread of mine own life...") but he has all the imagination and talent of a semi-retired ham getting his kicks in summer stock. The rest of the cast is less deadly, but bringing out the poetry in the dialog is beyond them. They have enough troubles just moving their arms and legs at the right time and making their cues.

The source material is grainy and pale. The sound, which has an occasionally stereophonic background score, is laugh inducing at first, as the volume rises and falls considerably when the actors move about on the soundstage. The problems decrease after a while, but first impressions are the strongest. The program runs a couple minutes over two hours and is spread for three sides. There are chapters, one for an act, which means that they are only of use on side two, which contains two of the four acts. The only thing the disc will be good for is helping those who are as yet still burdened with having to analyze the play for homework visualize the material.

THE TEMPTATIONS & THE FOUR TOPS

The hour-long *The Temptations & Four Tops* is a collection of footage from the two Motown singing groups, vaguely tracing their accomplishments from the mid-sixties to the present day. Although the stereo sound leaves something to be desired and the picture is always a little on the blurry side, the show has a lot to offer both fans and passing acquaintances. Highlights include a delightful jam session with the Four Tops and Aretha Franklin, a color clip from the Ed Sullivan Show featuring The Temptations and The Supremes, and all that cute coordinated waving the two groups do with their hands while they sing. On the downside, the show is never focussed enough to give a true history of either group, or to even approach a summary of their musical style. Those who are used to listening to the songs on the radio under conditions of distraction, however, will feel at home with the disc.

TEN FROM YOUR SHOW OF SHOWS

Kinescoped skits from 'Your Show of Shows,' released as a feature film in the early seventies, are available in *Ten from Your Show of Shows* with digital sound and ten logical chapter markers. The program is 92 minutes long. A faint black band appears at the top and bottom of the screen. This is disappointing, since it inhibits the illusion that one is watching an old TV program, even if it adds, minutely, to the fidelity of the picture. Otherwise, the picture and sound quality are consistent with one's expectations based on the source of the material.

It is interesting that every new artform must go through a period of juvenilia before reaching maturity. Nobody today could get away with the kind of comedy Sid Caesar, Imogene Coca, and Carl Reiner perpetrate. It is too basic, too physical, and too silly. Yet it was obviously hysterical, and probably generated a higher decibel level of laughter in America than any television show today produces. Life just isn't that funny anymore.

TEN LITTLE INDIANS

Those who take special delight in Agatha Christie stories may wish to indulge in the Cannon release, *Ten Little Indians*, the corollary being that those who are not partial to Christie films had best avoid it. The stars are of a decidedly short magnitude, the filmmakers having rounded up Donald Pleasance, Brenda Vaccaro, Herbert Lom, and, for a hero, Frank Stallone. But, the movie follows the rules well enough that once you've spotted the murderer, you'll wonder what's going on when he is so obviously killed.

The disc is enjoyable because the presentation adds to the entertainment. There is a haze on the picture from time to time, but the image is essentially bright and the colors are fresh. Christie's 'Indians' plot is a genre unto itself, having been remade so many times and in so many ways. The movie is set in period, between the wars, and in Africa. As with the other Christie movies getting to the ending is more fun that the ending itself. The break between side one and two on the disc is haphazard. The Ultra-Stereo surround sound has some great directional effects, and there is a beautiful remastered recording of Noel Coward singing 'Mad Dogs and Englishmen' which plays over the final credit scroll.

10 RILLINGTON PLACE

The final 40 minutes of *10 Rillington Place* are captivating, but the first hour and change are a strain. The film is a docudrama about a man convicted for another's crimes. Depicting the British mass murderer, John Christie, the film is based so closely on real events that it takes on the dreary dullness of life. Richard Attenborough portrays Christie and John Hurt, who looks very young, portrays a man accused of one of Christie's crimes. The film's colors and sets are drab and depressing, though the disc makes them look even worse. The print is faded and the actors are often etched in pink. The sound is passable.

TEN WANTED MEN

A young looking Richard Boone gives a marvelously scummy performance as the jealous, bad rancher in the Randolph Scott western, *Ten Wanted Men*. The film was made in Technicolor, and has an average transfer. The flesh is often too orange, bright reds look grainy, darker sequences look fuzzy, and some shots look faded, but most of the time the colors look nice and the focus is sharp.

The film was not a widescreen effort, so the image retains most of the original screen composition. The transfer, however, has an annoying tendency causing frames within the movie to freeze momentarily before a cut. The sound has no significant flaws. The film lasts under 90 minutes, but brevity works in its favor. Both Boone and Scott project much more of their personalities than what has been written for them, and the movie, which is essentially an extended series of conflicts between them, delivers exactly what it promises.

TENDER MERCIES
Tender Mercies takes place in the Texas Outback and outdoor scenes are brightly lit. These look real sharp. It is the indoor scenes which appear murky. There is also some dirt on the print early on. The disc does not have CX-encoding, despite the musical orientation of the program material. Robert Duvall portrays a washed-up singer who moves in with a woman (Tess Harper) and her kid. Harper was a revelation although she has since done little but play the same role again and again. The kid can neither act nor kick a football. It is Duvall's film and he does his job well, but this isn't the sort of disc one wishes were in CAV.

TENEBRAE (Import)
One of Dario Argento's best mystery thrillers *Tenebrae*, is available on disc in Japan. Theatrically released in truncated form in America with the title, 'Unsane,' the movie is full of dizzying plot twists and gruesome murders. Tony Franciosa portrays a mystery writer shadowed by a psychotic killer who stuffs the pages of the writer's latest novel into the severed throat of a victim. Every time you think you know who the murderer is, the suspect is dispatched. There are outrageous coincidences in the plot, utilized to keep the story moving, but Argento is not the sort of director you want to pick an argument with. You may be next.

The disc is in letterboxed format with the Japanese subtitles appearing over the picture. The sound is monaural and has not been CX-encoded. It is flat, but it has no rough spots. The film is dubbed in English, and the dubbing serves only to disorient one further, particularly when it comes to the voice and gender of the killer. The picture quality is not stunning, but lacks any noticeable flaws. The blood is red enough. Argento has several show-off moments. In one scene early on, he follows a victim from the other side of a perfume rack in a department store and always manages to frame her head so that the perfume labels comment on the woman's presence. In the movie's most elaborate scene, the camera crawls up and down the side of a building to establish the location of characters for a murder. The camera is omniscient, and appears to go in and out of windows, and turn totally upside down, without a splice.

TEQUILA SUNRISE
The signature sequence in *Tequila Sunrise*, a conversation in silhouette against a golden setting sun, is blurry and unstable on the disc. The picture is tolerable, but strong reds tend to go fuzzy, and the fleshtones often look pink. The sound, on the other hand, is quite nice. The musical score often fills the surround track with solos from Lee Ritenour or David Sanborn. (No Eagles are to be heard.) Warner's usual array of chapter markers are also well chosen.

The film is a step above the normal crime thriller. It has its share of outlandish coincidences, but these are employed by the writer/director, Robert Towne, to construct emotional truths. The important thing in most crime dramas anyway is to sit back and let the artists entertain you. Mel Gibson and Kurt Russell portray old friends who are not so far on opposite sides of the law as it first appears. They are both attracted to a woman, played by Michelle Pfeiffer, and the central gag in the story is that the woman has nothing to do with the crimes the Gibson character may or may not be committing. The love story and the crime story are perfectly entwined so that advancement in the one serves as commentary on the other.

TERENCE TRENT D'ARBY INTRODUCING THE HARD LINE...LIVE
The music is good, the picture is grainy and the interviews are weird in *Terence Trent D'Arby Introducing the Hardline...Live.* D'Arby, who has an energetic stage presence, and his band perform vaguely reggae riffs which are adequately transferred on the disc. The analog track is noticeably weaker than the digital track. The picture quality is only fair. The footage is not elaborately lighted, but the transfer has also weakened the image. Between the songs, which are performed live in Munich, pieces of a hotel room interview and similar footage are used to let the viewer get to know D'Arby better. He should have kept to singing, because his comments are unprofessional and immature. The disc is 65 minutes long. Side two runs 17 minutes and is in CLV.

TERMINAL EXPOSURE
Two young men discover they have photographed a murder on an LA beach in *Terminal Exposure*. The film is riddled with humor which is offensive to women, blacks, gays, and just about everyone, and the plot is closer to a farce – there is even an ice cream fight – than a thriller. The surround sound is quite good, and the editors were not afraid of throwing dialog onto the back channel. The picture is okay so long as it stays in the sun, but every time things get dark, they get blurry. The film also has a number of gags in the end credit scroll.

TERMINAL FORCE
A sophomoric action film with bad acting, bad sound recording, bad editing, and bad just about everything else, *Terminal Force* is about a suspended police detective assigned, because he is expendable, to rescue the daughter of a witness against the mob. The sound editing is really bad, with conversations swinging in and out of microphone range. The cinematography and picture quality are poor.

Side two is in CAV, with two unsteady still frames out of every five, allowing the viewer to manipulate an extended but amazingly limp car chase and the no-two-people-in-the-same-shot (one actor could play all the parts) final shoot out.

THE TERMINATOR (Image)
THE TERMINATOR (HBO)
Both versions of *The Terminator* on disc have gone out of print. Image's transfer is significantly superior to the HBO transfer. There is still a little grain in some sequences and the digital sound is monaural, but the fog and the fuzz have been cleaned up and when the picture is not grainy it is very sharp. Image has also added chapter markers.

Even though the film has what is commonly referred to as non-stop action, it is also a powerful romance, about a man who crosses time to meet the woman he has idealized. It is interesting to note that Linda Hamilton's subsequent role in 'Beauty and the Beast' resonates through her presence in *The Terminator*. The movie is as wonderful for home video as it was for dating. It is a rare chance for those who are seeking thrills and those who are seeking tenderness to share a pleasurable evening on the sofa.

TERROR IN THE AISLES
(see **THAT'S SHOCK**)

TERROR TRAIN
The first revenge-for-a-prank slasher movie, *Terror Train* was also the first effort from Jamie Lee Curtis to be free of the John Carpenter influence, though you'd never guess it from the film itself. The movie is a murder mystery in a contained environment, a train excursion, and the identity of the killer is withheld until the ending, which goes 'pffft' shortly thereafter. The violence is tame by home video standards, but a potential for repeated viewings does exist if one's defenses are down. The picture is weak and on the blurry side. The music and a few background effects are in stereo although there is no stereo processing listed in the film's credits.

TESTAMENT
Paced more slowly than *The Day After*, *Testament* is a disorganized series of emotional sketches and incidents centered in a Northern California town quietly dying of fallout after a nuclear war. No skin blotches or hair loss in this one, characters just, "crawl into a ball," and die. The problem with *Testament* is the romantic tone it eventually establishes, where death is trivialized in favor of grief and pity.

Jane Alexander portrays the central character, a mother coping with the sudden loss of civilization and the absence of her husband. The best scene in the film has nothing to do with nuclear war. Responding to a question from her character's daughter, Alexander provides a beautifully spoken soliloquy on what it feels like to make love.

The ponderous pace and low budget design wear one down. As a subject, post-World War III America might be well suited for a *M*A*S*H*-type situation comedy, but the childhood reminiscences and the dream death pallor that *Testament* offers is boring. The last thing people who are truly concerned with the subject can afford to do is put others to sleep.

TEX AVERY'S SCREWBALL CLASSICS
A solid two hours of MGM Tex Avery cartoons are available on *Tex Avery's Screwball Classics*. Avery's animation recipe contains

equal measures of surrealism and violence, and seem like the sort of dreams one might have after eating too many banana splits. However, the disc is terrific and anybody who is partial at all to cartoons is bound to be pleased with the collection.

The first cartoon, 'Swing Shift Cinderella' contains so many gags which resurfaced in *Who Framed Roger Rabbit* that the filmmakers were clearly using it as a primary source of inspiration. Visual puns abound, as forks in the road always turn out to be utensils. In general, the cartoons feature protagonists who suffer wildly conceived ills at the hands of other characters. To pick just one sequence that typifies the squirmy pleasures of Avery's work: In 'Slaphappy Lion,' a lion swallows a mouse who has been pestering him. Inside, the mouse starts playing the lion's ribs, like a xylophone. The lion, angered, swallows a lit bomb to rid himself of the mouse, and the mouse, upon seeing the bomb, panics. He runs back up the lion's throat and out of his mouth. The bomb, still lit, remains.

The cartoons have chapter markers and are listed on the jacket. They contain a number of racist gags which a viewer is obliged to accept as a document of the social atmosphere in another era. The sound is in decent shape . The volume is set low, however, which will cause the next program you put on to blast away, unless you remember to readjust the audio when the *Avery* disc has ended.

TEXAS CHAINSAW MASSACRE PART 2

We accepted the first murder in *The Texas Chainsaw Massacre Part 2*, anticipating that the director could then hold back for the rest of the movie and maintain a level of fear based upon imagined horrors. But no, the second murder was even worse, and that was it for us, which is a shame, because the movie up to that point contained two very promising performances, by Dennis Hopper and Caroline Williams. The picture is a little grainy, but the CX-encoded sound won't disappoint those whose stereo systems are as strong as their stomachs.

TEXAS SHOWDOWN – BATTLING BEAUTIES

The format of *Texas Showdown – Battling Beauties* is similar to *Blondes vs. Brunettes*, but the material is fresh. Viewers are invited to vote at the end of the disc for the team they prefer, by mailing their choice to a Celebrity address. Ladies from the two teams dance in pairs, first in bathing suits, which stay on, then lingerie, which come off, and then on top of customers who eagerly ply them with loose cash. The narration sounds like it is coming across a string from a tin can, and the music on the digital stereo soundtrack isn't much better. Chapter encoding is reserved for major sequential shifts instead of individual acts. The picture remains grainy throughout the hour long program.

THAT HAMILTON WOMAN

The fully restored *That Hamilton Woman* has a fairly delicate sound mix, considering its age and the print has a fair amount of scratches. The movie is about Admiral Nelson (the man on the huge pillar in London's Trafalgar Square) and his affair with the wife of an Ambassador, Lady Hamilton. A vehicle for Laurence Olivier and Vivien Leigh, the movie was made in 1941 and was intended to be one of Olivier's flag-waving 'Save Britannia' efforts. Napoleon is presented so often as the Hitler of his day that they almost had us believing it. In the end, the Hamilton Woman allows her man to go off and die for his country, realizing that she is saving the world in the process.

THAT WAS ROCK

If the volume on *That Was Rock* is turned up too loud, heavy distortion occurs, but if the levels are held to reasonable settings, then the disc sounds terrific. *That Was Rock* is a cut and paste of 'The T.A.M.I/T.N.T. Show,' introduced by Chuck Berry. It is 90 minutes long and depicts a concert (*no* lip synching) by some of the great pop stars of the mid sixties, including The Supremes, Smokey Robinson, Lesley Gore, Jan & Dean, James Brown, and The Rolling Stones. Many of them appear on stage together for the finale.

It is in black-and-white and is broken up by color inserts of Berry, introducing the different performers. As much as we like Berry, we would have preferred to watch the show unwrap as it was originally intended, without someone trying to convince us that we are going to like what we already know we are going to like. There are no chapter markers.

Our favorite passage is Lesley Gore's set. She can't decide whether she should smile for the camera – clearly her natural inclination – or look serious because she is singing about the nasty ways men have treated her. So she twists the edges of her mouth up and down depending upon the stanza, and it seems a better representation of an adolescent female's plight than any lyric could capture.

The original picture is in let's-make-a-buck-on-a-fad cheap black-and-white. It looks aged, but certainly wasn't harmed while being transferred to disc. Part of turning the extravaganza into *That Was Rock* was to turn the monaural recording into 'rechannelled stereo.' It has been executed so conservatively that one would be hard pressed to identify a sound not coming from dead center, but the attention given the soundtrack is clearly one of the reasons why the disc succeeds. That is, along with Dean on his skateboard and the closeup of Diana Ross's mascara.

THAT WAS THEN...THIS IS NOW

Not only does *That Was Then...This Is Now* have a good stereo soundtrack, the picture is a little clearer and sharper than average.

That Was Then was filmed in a contemporary setting, but the mood it creates has a nostalgic feel, from the thrills of teenaged love to the dangers of unrestricted nocturnal prowling. Like all the movies based on S.E. Hinton novels, the words and actions of the teenaged characters seem genuine. Unlike the other Hinton movies though, the melodrama here isn't dripping over the edges like an overused condiment. The big dramatic turns in the plot are filmed from lean, neutral angles, under the assumption that emotions are sufficiently filling. Emilio Estevez stars.

THAT'S ENTERTAINMENT
(Time-compressed)
THAT'S ENTERTAINMENT

The most blatant and disgusting use of time-compression, the removal of individual frames of film to create an overall drop of running time, occurred on the first MGM/UA release of *That's Entertainment*. The 130-minute film was squeezed onto a single CLV platter. Not only did the narrators sound like they were talking in fast forward, but the songs sounded like 3/4 time being played at 6/8. It was awful, and the disc's condition suppressed any possibility of enjoying the film.

MGM/UA made amends, however, by releasing a revised version of the disc (though it has the same catalog number). It runs 134 minutes including overture and exit music, has digital sound, chapter encoding, and is in CAV format for more than half its running time. The image transfer is also improved. The disc is four sides long. The first side, containing the introductory material and less energetic musical numbers, is in CLV. Sides two, three, and four are in CAV and contain seemingly all of the greatest movie musical numbers ever filmed.

The CAV is good fun. Who can resist slowing down Fred Astaire as he dances with Gene Kelly, Cyd Charisse, a hat rack, or on the ceiling? Or still framing Gene Kelly's acrobatics, or his brilliant duet with Jerry the Mouse? (Watch Jerry slip his leg on either side of Kelly's before he gets spun around.) How about Esther Williams in triple speed reverse, being sucked out of the water? Donald O'Conner doing 'Make 'Em Laugh?' The barn raising dance in *Seven Brides for Seven Brothers*? There are many opportunities to freeze beautiful portraits of Judy Garland, and a chance to catch Frank Sinatra and Bing Crosby walking arm-in-arm. Even the scan function has its advantages, such as the summary of images it provides during the *American in Paris* ballet.

The stereophonic digital sound also puts the earlier disc to shame. The picture image is cropped during the widescreen clips, and the source material displays a few flaws during the narrator sequences, but the clips, both black and white and color, look great.

The movie, MGM's valedictory, is unusually entertaining considering its length and format. Only once, in overstating the appeal of Fernando Lamas, does the narration really get carried away. With the advent of home video, many of the sequences which one rarely had an opportunity to view in their original context are now readily available. Yet the collection, which was made by people who did see these films all the time, never becomes tiresome. The pace (when not time-compressed!) is right, the respect and gushy memories are right, and the talent, pictured in action, is overwhelming. *That's Entertainment* is not just a collection of great movie moments, it is a great movie on its own, with the most incredible cast one will ever see and hear.

THAT'S ENTERTAINMENT, PART II
THAT'S DANCING!

The compilation extravaganza, *That's Entertainment, Part II*, was released on disc by MGM/UA before the company started getting its act together. The Fred Astaire and Ginger Rogers dance number from *Barkleys of Broadway* which lacked a chapter marker on the *Barkleys* disc, for example, lacks a chapter marker on *That's Entertainment, Part II* also. The program is analog only and the three sided disc is CLV throughout. The clips involving fresh Technicolor transfers or black-and-white source material look fine, but other color sequences look ripe and intense colors tend to appear unsteady. The CX-encoded stereo sound lacks the thrust and clarity which other MGM/UA discs have sported.

The film clips in *That's Entertainment, Part II* are wonderful. Many are rare and intriguing. There are snippets from Technicolor travelogs which, no matter how corny, look scrumptious. There are the Jimmy Durante segments, which make one wish MGM had teamed him at least once with Spencer Tracy. And there are the musicals, so many that it is doubtful more than a handful of people have seen them all.

The organization of the clips, however, is less accomplished, and the narration is downright useless. Unlike the first *That's Entertainment* film, there is no unifying theme or point to what is being presented. There are segments – Frank Sinatra movies, comedy pieces, etc. – but nothing beyond the umbrella entertainment term to link them. The narration provides no insight, only straight identifications and dubious statements such as the suggestion that Arthur Freed's bringing Frank Sinatra to Hollywood to sing 'Ole Man River' was inevitable.

A much stronger narrative line is provided in *That's Dancing!* Although not scholarly, the film gives a nice survey of the presentation of dance in the movies and includes a healthy selection of non-MGM material. The picture and sound transfers are as good as *That's Entertainment, Part II*, and the disc is actually better in one regard, because the widescreen film clips are letterboxed. The two sided disc, however, lacks chapter markers.

Included among the film clips is the ridiculous (but wonderful) audition finale from *Flashdance*, and that piece really defines what dance in movies is all about – the glorious tension between high art and popular taste. The film seems to cover everything, from the first nickelodeon frolics to Michael Jackson's music videos, and the narration aptly justifies the inclusion and the significance of each piece. There is Busby Berkeley and Ruby Keeler, Gene Kelly and Judy Garland, Eleanor Powell, *The Red Shoes*, and even *Sweet Charity*. Also included is the alternate 'If I Only Had a Brain' cut from *The Wizard of Oz*. *That's Dancing!* is less exhausting than the *That's Entertainment* films, but it has all of the spirit and all of the best moves.

THAT'S LIFE

There are numerous closeups of both Jack Lemmon and Julie Andrews in *That's Life* and the fleshtones never become pink or orange. The only real fault in the transfer of the film to disc is that Blake Edwards shot the original in Panavision and it suffers from having been cropped. The sound is a little noisy.

The script doesn't quite have the right balance. It is the story of an architect who his turning sixty and feeling bad about it, and the problems the other members of his family are having. Although Lemmon is playing the architect, he is in the movie too much, and the difficulties which burden the sons and daughters are not presented extensively enough to provide dramatic or comic balance. It could have been a well rounded entertainment, but instead it is eccentric and difficult to sympathize with.

THAT'S SHOCK (TERROR IN THE AISLES) (Import)

The horror film compilation and documentary, *Terror in the Aisles*, has been released in CAV format in Japan under the title of *That's Shock*. The program stretches for three sides and is letterboxed even when the film clips are from movies which were not in widescreen. The subtitles hang discreetly on the right. The quality of the picture is uniformly excellent. Even the older color films look new. The sound is flat and has not been CX-encoded. Not all of the original music is retained with the clips.

Surely most everything one ever wanted to see in slow motion is available here. The exploding head in *Scanners*, for example. Or the pop-goes-the-weasel chest in *Alien*. Major sequences from *Psycho*, *The Birds*, *The Thing* remake, *Halloween*, *Jaws*, and lots more are in there. You get the wolf transformation from *An American Werewolf in London* and the merry-go-round accident from *The Fury*.

It is narrated by Donald Pleasence and Nancy Allen, who pretend they are in a theater audience and make generalized statements about how horror films can be so scary. There's something on the disc to disgust every member of the family.

THAT'S SINGING – THE BEST OF BROADWAY

The American Dance Machine is a dance company which specializes in resurrecting the choreographic highlights from defunct Broadway shows. They are featured in *That's Singing – The Best of Broadway* at a gala which takes the concept one step further by bringing in the original stage stars to sing the songs that made the musicals hits. Filmed in a theater in California, *That's Singing* nevertheless captures the true spirit of Broadway – even though the show stars Debbie Reynolds, Tony Perkins, Diahann Carroll and more than a dozen others, it is New York stars Chita Rivera and Ethel Merman who get the biggest hand.

There are about twenty numbers, all of which have been marked with chapters. Some of the dance numbers performed by the Dance Machine concentrate on recreating the original choreography, while most of the star turns are just that, the star singing the hit in a faint approximation of the original vocal intensity. The costumes generally attempt to recall the original look of the shows, while the set is a single, odd jumble of plywood, stairs, and big Al Hirschfeld drawings. The program's editing interferes with the larger production numbers, but is great when one star is singing in closeup. Some of the shots are out of focus, and the music is not always recorded perfectly. The digital sound and picture transfer, however, are exemplary.

Even at its worst – Tony Perkins sweating through a number he probably had trouble with 30 years earlier when he sang it in a show – the program is intriguing. At its best, with songs from Stephen Sondheim shows, 'Ain't Misbehavin',' 'Bye Bye Birdie,' 'Grease' (a chance to see how Barry Bostwick first made a name for himself), 'How to Succeed in Business,' 'Over Here,' and others, the show is a musical lover's pastry tray of goodies. And while we usually avoid mentioning such things, we can't resist adding that Donna McKechnie wears a sweater which sent our heart jumping out of our throat.

THE THE: INFECTED

The The is a British band which is represented by 8 striking music videos on *The The: Infected*. Some of the videos were filmed in South America and have a third-world-as-degradation theme which is distasteful. Others, however, particularly the ones directed by Tim Pope, are riveting, with hot-blooded, fully clothed sex which makes the viewer completely oblivious to the group's music. The music is suitably mature and free of the sweet vocals which infect a number of British bands, but none of the songs stand out. The picture transfer is fine and the stereo sound is clear. The disc lasts 47 minutes.

THEATER OF BLOOD

Vincent Price is such a bad actor that he would have made a wonderful Richard III. In the enjoyably hoary murder thriller which also features Diana Rigg and a number of British character actors, *Theater of Blood*, Price portrays a Shakespearean actor who is offing the critics responsible for his bad notices. He gets to do snippets from a number of Shakespeare's plays and he is as bad as his character is supposed to be, but then comes his Richard III and for the few moments that he's dressed up and reading the lines he's perfect.

Now we don't normally take to the idea that someone should go around murdering critics, since more than one disc producer is after our own head, but the movie is always a treat when it shows up on late night TV, and the disc is in great shape. The print is surprisingly colorful for an early seventies film, and the sound has no significant flaws. The movie has plenty of gore, but it comes from a time when gore was still fun. The plot is not as strong as the concept, but the cast more than makes up for it. Our only disappointment is with the jacket cover, which seems intent upon limiting sales.

THEATRE OF THE IMAGINATION RADIO STORIES BY ORSON WELLES & THE MERCURY THEATRE

Close your eyes and you can almost see how the movie of 'Heart of Darkness,' which Orson Welles never made, would have looked: It opens with Marlowe, gazing through a store front window at a map of Africa, when the reflection of a woman, who has approached and is standing behind him, appears, superimposed over the tangle of river that he will eventually navigate. She is Kurtz's wife.

Welles produced a radio drama of Joseph Conrad's story shortly after he abandoned work on the film script, and it is available on *Theatre of the Imagination*, subtitled *Radio Stories by Orson Welles & The Mercury Theatre*.

The single-plattered disc has no video. The two analog tracks and the single digital track on each side of the CLV disc comprise six hours of programing material. It is best to listen to the disc an hour or so at a time, and to stretch it out over a week or longer.

The disc is most emphatically not like the audio cassettes one sees on metal racks in chain book stores. The impetus for the disc came when copies of the recordings were discovered in a Rosebudish box in a garage. To produce the disc, the original acetate plates were tracked down (These are all live broadcasts. Occasionally the actors make mistakes and must recover gracefully; and occasionally one hears interference from other broadcasts on the airwaves, transporting the listener further into the past and the spirit of the disc. There are also plenty of commercials and pleas for buying War Bonds.) and transferred using sophisticated digital technology.

The analog tracks have not been CX-encoded. None of the segments, except a contemporary documentary at the end of the program, sound fresh, but most are clear and subject only to a slight static. Chapter markers have been scattered to note the beginning of each segment.

Students and enthusiasts of sound in films cannot miss this disc, for it provides an understanding of how cinema's greatest sound editing was compiled and nurtured. Today's filmmakers often get their start in television, where sound is treated as a necessary evil or bastard child. When a contemporary film is praised for the quality of its soundtrack, the people working on it often have a background in music – but the problem with music is that the goal there is to blend everything together. The goal of a film's soundtrack ought to be to keep the sounds separate, so that every addition to the track advances the story in some way.

To hear how it should be done, listen to the disc, where the artists had to tell a drama with sound alone. There are two ways of doing so, and both are represented by the disc's longest features, 'Rebecca' and 'A Tale of Two Cities,' each running about an hour on the digital track. 'Rebecca' is the poorest offering on the disc, but its failure serves to illustrate the successes of the other works. Following the book's first person narrative, most of the story is told with the dialog provided where quotations would appear in print. It is dull, and totally superseded by Alfred Hitchcock and David Selznick's vivid film. 'Cities,' on the other hand, seems like it must have been recorded in a gymnasium. There are crowd scenes and courtroom scenes, hoof beats, carriages, and the guillotine. The narrator sets the scene – London in this year, Paris in that – and then dialog and background noises tell the rest. It is fully captivating and provides insight to the manner of Dickens while taking complete advantage of his rousing, almost chilling plot. What a shame Welles didn't try making a film of that one, too.

The other narratives appearing on the disc run about a half hour apiece. There is the well-executed 'Heart of Darkness,' a nice, melancholy romance entitled 'The Apple Tree,' a curious, slightly ironic variation on the children-grow-up-too-fast shtick entitled, 'My Little Boy,' a spooky highway ghost story called, 'The Hitchhiker,' a cute little fable about a man who exchanges places with a monkey, 'Wilbur Brown, Habitat Brooklyn,' and an episode from 'The Shadow,' entitled 'The White Legion.' We grew up well into the age of television, but even we know about 'The Shadow,' a cult radio program if there ever was one, and an almost perfect utilization of the medium. The hero, played by Welles, uses hypnosis to become invisible and eavesdrop on criminals (though no explanation of this is provided by the jacket notes). When invisible, Welles' voice is altered (through a megaphone and dropping an octave, it sounds like). To hear his 'Shadow' voice is as much of a thrill as seeing the Millennium Falcon hit light speed.

Although the jacket notes gloss over the piece, there is one segment where Welles gets in over his head, interviewing the father of a Black serviceman killed in WWII. Welles crosses the fine line which limits his abilities to artistic endeavors, as he attempts to get the father to agree that the War had improved the opportunities for equality. The father, obviously aware of the widespread segregation which still existed at the time, refuses to comply, leaving Welles stuttering. The remainder of the disc is filled with short features. You haven't heard the weather until you've heard it read by Orson Welles. There is a documentary, produced recently, in which John Houseman and others talk about running between the radio studios and Broadway. A rich, rich pre-*Citizen Kane*, post-'War of the Worlds' interview with Welles and H.G. Wells ends with the latter Wells, uncannily prophetic as usual, speculating that *Kane* would undoubtedly contain, "a lot of jolly good, new noises."

THERE'S NO BUSINESS LIKE SHOW BUSINESS

The aspect ratio on the letterboxed image of *There's No Business Like Show Business* is about 2.25:1. Oranges – unfortunately a popular color with the film's art director – are blurry, and some reds have mild halos, but everything else looks sharp and compact. The colors are bright and appear well defined.

There's No Business Like Show Business opens with an extended sequence of musical interludes which end up lasting more than a half hour. Then, when one has given up hoping for a plot, a story materializes, about two generations of stage performers. The movie does not blend the magic of music, dance, and emotion in the way which the best musicals do. Even when the song numbers work out, the presentation could have been smoother than it is. Ethel Merman, whose voice was never as amenable to recording equipment as it was to fresh air, is just one of the movie's problems. Donald O'Conner and Marilyn Monroe have better luck, but their non-musical scenes are deadening. The film is for die-hard movie musical fans, and those who are just dabbling in the genre would be better off dabbling elsewhere.

The songs are by Irving Berlin. The disc is in digitally encoded stereo surround sound, with some noticeable separation effects. It is best, however, to keep the volume at a reasonable level, since the movie is older and was not designed to withstand modern amplification. Both Merman and Monroe, whose singing styles are just about as opposite as one can get, sound best when the decibels are reined in.

THESE THREE

Lillian Hellman's attitude toward children, as expressed in *These Three*, makes W.C. Fields look like Mister Rogers. The film, adapted by Hellman from her play *The Children's Hour*, stops just short of urging that more quicksand be put in public playgrounds. As the little girls start screaming, or lying, or making pacts with Satan, the camera zooms in to distort their innocent countenances even further.

The film was directed by William Wyler and shot by Gregg Toland. The story is about two women who run a boarding school and how their lives are destroyed by a brat they make the mistake of punishing too often. As it was made in 1936, the little girl's lie, which shuts the boarding school down, involves a relationship between one of the women and the other's fiance, rather than between the two women as the original play and later remake had it. The sound is strong.The print looks sharp for most of the film, but it is speckled in places.

THEY CALL ME TRINITY
TRINITY IS STILL MY NAME

The two Trinity films, *They Call Me Trinity* and *Trinity Is Still My Name*, make for a good four hours of down home entertainment. Starring Terence Hill and Bud Spencer, the movies have a lot of gunplay and fist fights but absolutely no blood. Hill, a good-looking actor whose popularity in Europe never carried over to the States, portrays Trinity, a wandering wastrel with more than a few hidden talents. Spencer portrays Trinity's rotund and ambitious half-brother. He has a tendency to quiet those who are pestering him by conking them on the crown of the head with his massive fist.

They Call Me Trinity is a regular spaghetti western. Trinity and his brother protect a group of farmers from horse ranchers who need land for grazing. *Trinity Is Still My Name* pads comedy onto the story of the two brothers mucking up a gun smuggling operation. None of the humor is sophisticated – there is a good share of gags devoted to belching – but we never found ourselves growing impatient with the proceedings.

Both films were made a little over ten years before the discs were produced and the picture looks slightly faded and scratchy in places.

THEY CAME TO CORDURA

The scanning and cropping on the Cinemascope film, *They Came to Cordura*, doesn't hurt the presentation too much until the very end. At the finale, the image remains on the hero as a minor character makes an important discovery and starts yelling, off screen. Because of the cropping it seems to come out of nowhere and undercuts the emotional impact of the scene.

The colors are mildly faded and the image is a little grainy. The monaural sound is passable. Side three is in CAV with two unsteady still frames out of every five.

The film stars Gary Cooper and Rita Hayworth, and has several recognizable supporting players. It is about a cavalry major leading several soldiers back to America from Pershing's excursion into Mexico. The major is taking them back to give them awards for heroism – something the army needs for its PR effort – but each man he has chosen has a reason for not wishing to go, and the film settles into an exploration of human nature. The performances are enjoyable and stop the script, which is too soul-searching and illogical, from seeming silly or overbearing.

THEY GOT ME COVERED
In *They Got Me Covered*, Bob Hope portrays a newspaperman who chases down a Nazi spy ring in D.C., despite his chickenhearted instincts. There is a gag with a knife near the opening of side two which is perfect to call up quickly when you want to make visitors laugh. The black-and-white picture looks sharp and new, without too many splices.

THEY LIVE
John Carpenter's amusingly paranoid *They Live* is an efficient science fiction thriller. Carpenter made a series of 'B' films, forsaking big budget epics for inexpensive and mildly experimental ventures. The script for *They Live* is in some ways quite good – there are some great one-liners, logical plot twists, a stunning basic concept (aliens are subliminally pacifying our society, but their manipulations can be seen when one wears special glasses) and an ending, for once, which is not disappointing – but the movie also has the feel of a low budget work, with the characters sneaking around alleys and empty lots while the city goes about its business behind them. And it stars Roddy Piper.

The picture quality is passable, though in some scenes the fleshtones look too pink. The sound is in stereo surround, but the dialog track is weak and sometimes difficult to understand.

THEY LIVE BY NIGHT
The jacket cover for Nicholas Ray's *They Live By Night* is gorgeous. The graphic is a beautiful black-and-white still of Farley Granger and Cathy O'Donnell. The black-and-white source material which has been used for the disc can't possibly compare. Most viewers will find the presentation to be passable, but it does have scratches, mild amounts of graininess and other small distractions. The stunning, innovative bird's-eye overhead shots, for example, would make a stronger impression if their integration with the rest of the film were smoother. The sound is also a little rough and should not be amplified too greatly. The 1948 movie, a classic about a young man on the run after a bank robbery who finds momentary peace when he elopes with a young woman, is visually arresting – which is why one wishes for a print with fewer imperfections – and dramatically astute. The narrative is relaxed and subtle. The law doesn't close in around the characters, they wrap themselves up in fear and guilt and then deliver themselves to justice.

THEY WON'T BELIEVE ME
Alfred Hitchcock's longtime assistant and collaborator, Joan Harrison, produced *They Won't Believe Me*, a soapy drama about infidelity and guilt which stars Robert Young and Susan Hayward and was directed by Irving Pichel. Harrison's influence can be seen in the relative economy by which the story advances, and in the odd but effectively lighthearted tone which the heavy-handed drama manages to maintain. The plot, fairly undisturbed by the censors, is about a man unhappy with his marriage and the two affairs he conducts. Eventually there is violence, but the incidents are secondary to the unhappiness and tension which cause them. Hayward is very good and the rest of the cast is effective. The black-and-white source material is in reasonably good condition and the presentation is acceptable. The sound is fine.

THIEF
Michael Mann's debut film, *Thief*, set the tone for the eighties, since Mann transposed most of the stylistic ideas he developed with the movie onto his hit television production, *Miami Vice*. Because *Thief* was a theatrical film, the look is enhanced considerably by the budget. He has the time and the money to get every shot right, to burrow his camera into a drilled lock or send it sweeping across an elaborately illuminated street. Movie makers have been spraying water on blacktop for years, but Mann was the first to make it bead, as if the blacktop were waxed.

It wasn't just a look, though, it was also a sound. In *Thief*, the score, by Tangerine Dream, buzzes like a slow motion alarm. Its precise emotional equivalent is the alertness one has at night while driving without drowsiness – a focussed, attentive, enveloping sound which recedes just enough to accommodate dialog or sound effects.

Other than cropping and an occasional speckle, the picture never taints the film's original sheen. Even the colors in neon signs stay tight and solid. The stereo surround sound has been executed effectively. There are chapter markers, and side three, which contains a number of pyrotechnics, is in CAV, with two unsteady still frames out of every five. Much of the finale is fascinating with any sort of manipulation, from simply suppressing the sound to running the main sequences at alternate speeds. The editing and cinematography are as lyrical and intense as the music.

The film is about a burglar whose success gets him into trouble. His attempt to find happiness and start a family is spoiled by the greed of the mobsters he works for. Running over two hours, however, the movie is as strong on character as it is on heists, violence, and sleek cinematography. James Caan gives an excellent performance in the title role, often seeming as if he were about to explode. There are scenes to establish character which run on for unusual lengths in time. Mann is as daring with the patience of his viewers as he is with their eyes and ears.

THE THIEF OF BAGDAD
If you can stand two and a half hours of Rimsky-Korsakov being played over and over – don't get us wrong, we rather enjoyed it – then turn up the sound on *The Thief of Bagdad*, a Thames Video Image Silent Classics release. The Carl Davis orchestration is in scrumptious digital stereo, and the 'Scheherazade' tunes are only obnoxious if you lose sight of the film's spirit.

The Douglas Fairbanks classic runs 153 minutes and would have been better if it had been trimmed a little before its initial release. The plot, about a thief who falls in love with a princess and then faces numerous challenges to beat rivals in retrieving a treasure that will earn her hand, takes a long time to get revved up. The film is spectacular, but the filmmakers apparently felt that they had to justify the expense by stretching out the narrative. The movie was directed by Raoul Walsh but was conceived and produced by Fairbanks. There are many terrific special effects, including an underwater sequence that we can't imagine how they pulled off, and some appropriately huge crowd scenes. The movie requires patience and commitment to be enjoyed, but the rewards are plenty.

The picture transfer looks good. Many segments have been monochromatically tinted, and we are undecided as to whether the effect, which was done recently, is valid. The source material has some spotting and scratches, and it is a little softer, but with all the special effects that is to be expected. The image is solid enough and clear enough to tell the story without distractions. Movement is smooth and realistic.

THE THIEF OF BAGDAD
The Technicolor print on *The Thief of Bagdad* is as fresh as the day the movie was released and the CX-encoded sound probably sounds better than it ever has sounded before. Shades of red, of brown, of blue, and of gold are so captivating that you will probably want to watch the movie twice right off: The first time just to admire the production values and the second time to pay attention to the story. The transfer, with the exception of a few glowing reds and some curious, scattered single frame jumps, is superb.

The story is a pastiche of legends and fantasy in which a handsome, naive king finds his true love, with the aid of a thief. One of the joys of seeing *The Thief of Bagdad* in a theater is the participation it encourages. The audience enthusiastically hisses Conrad Veidt and cheers when Sabu saves the day. Therefore, when you get your copy of the disc and bring it home, be sure to invite plenty of friends over before you put it on.

THIEF OF HEARTS
An attractive film with a strong cult following, *Thief of Hearts* is about a burglar with a lot of spare time between jobs. He gets to reading a set of diaries he burgled and decides to pick up the woman who wrote them, fulfilling her fantasies, as it were. The show has a Michael Mannish look to it and a Moroder score. It also depicts the sort of heavy petting which feature filmmakers like to pretend is the ultimate in passionate intimacy. Some of this footage did not appear in the theatrical release. None of it is going to get anyone arrested.

The sound is full and the music has a good beat. The picture is on the grainy side, but some of that is conceptual. The plot remains true to its unusually original premise and repeated viewings are a definite possibility. If it had been done with stars, the movie would have been great.

THE THIN BLUE LINE
A cross between *Koyaanisqatsi* and 'America's Most Wanted,' *The Thin Blue Line* proves that even tabloid moviemaking can become a simmering cauldron for the cinematic arts. On paper the documentary is a simple combination of interviews with the individuals involved in a Texas murder case and a staged re-enactment of the crime, which draws a conclusion that the wrong man was convicted. But, on film, with the music of Philip Glass playing on the stereo surround soundtrack, with the interviewees illuminated by the sort of lighting Steven Spielberg uses when he wants to make humans look like aliens, and with the editing set to a rhythm

that Glass can't even keep pace with at times, the movie is more than a simple assimilation of information, it is an attempt to derive stylized poetry from the banal language of standard news reporting. In an academic environment it would be easy to pick the film apart, but for home video it is refreshingly different and repeatable.

The picture transfer is generally good, although there are some passages in which strong colors look a bit blurry. Even the slightest cropping, however, damages the footage depicting documents and headlines. Early on, for example, key dates are cut off the right edge of the screen, and it isn't until later in the film that the disc viewer can verify the chronology of events.

The chapter marking is insufficient and fails to take advantage of every fade-out. Only the music is in stereo, but Glass's score contains some strong low frequency explorations which will test the limits of your audio system.

THE THIN MAN

The dapper and inebriated Nick and Nora Charles do not embarrass themselves on *The Thin Man*. The print looks very sharp except when the film itself is out of focus and the sound is acceptable. In case the stories blur together in your head, this is the one about the scientist who disappears after his mistress is murdered. Not every actor and actress could sustain the sympathy Myrna Loy and William Powell show for each other. It's not so much the witty dialog supplied by scenarists as it is the way they are able to hit each other without getting hurt.

THE THING

The appeal of *The Thing* is not in the science fiction elements of the story but in the non-stop overlapping dialog, which almost has the rhythm and structure of early avant-garde music. James Arness is listed on the jacket cover as the star, but his performance is of little interest. Kenneth Tobey, during a brief moment in his career when he could get away with being the leading man, portrays the Arctic Air Force commander who must prevent the dug-up alien from destroying an isolated science station. The movie is actually titled 'The Thing from Another World,' but a truncated name is the least of the disc's problems. The transfer is abominably poor, with scratches, splices and poor framing. *The Thing* should be avoided unless you absolutely must have it.

THE THING
THE THING (Letterboxed)

The great modern horror films often appear repulsive the first or second time you view them. Sometimes they have to be that strong to leave an impression within the genre. No matter how gross they seem, however, you keep coming back for another peek, drawn in, maybe even on a subconscious level, by the quality of the execution. Such is undoubtedly the case for many viewers with John Carpenter's superb adaptation of *The Thing*, which has been reissued as a letterboxed edition title.

The picture has an aspect ratio of about 1:2.33. A scanned and cropped version of the film has been available for a very long time, and except for the relatively primitive transfer techniques that contributed to its inception, the disc was quite satisfying. The improvements on the new edition, however, demonstrate how far laser discs have come. The picture is exquisite. The movie takes place mostly at night in the Antarctic winter, and there isn't a single flaw in evidence on the solid black or white portions of the image. The colors are sharp, and the picture is so clear that there is a tendency to pay no attention to it at all, to become completely enveloped by the drama.

And what a drama. An alien organism digests and imitates members of the crew at an Antarctic science station. Whenever an imitation is discovered, it freaks out and tries to escape in several directions at once, splitting up its human form into gobs of gruesome tentacles, spidery, crab-like legs, and fierce incisors. The tension which mounts as the real humans try to determine who is on their side is palpable. (On the artistic level, the film is about how to make decisions on the fly.) The lack of an optimistic ending (it is sort of a draw) probably contributed to the film's failure at the boxoffice, but it only disappoints on the initial viewing, since afterwards you are prepared. The best sequences are so cluttered with frights that you can never completely anticipate every surprise, even after dozens of viewings.

The older disc did not have automatic CX-encoding, much less digital encoding. The volume is slightly higher on the older disc, and the sound is functional, but the surround separations are more clearly defined on the newer presentation and the whole audio track seems sharper. The musical track has been slightly modified for home video, although Ennio Morricone's John Carpenterish score is still in place. The new disc also has an excellent theatrical trailer tacked onto the end. The trailer should be seen after the movie is over, because it changes the plot in subtle but distinctive ways. One advantage that must be accorded the older disc – the jacket copy included a complete cast list.

The movie worked just fine in cropped format, but the return to the original Panavision compositions adds a stately grandeur to the outdoor scenes and a wicked efficiency to the tight action sequences. *The Thing* is a movie that can disgust people with its imagery alone, so a return to the balanced symmetries and clever character blocking can help to justify its legitimacy.

THE THIRD MAN
(see **THE LADY VANISHES**)

38 VIENNA BEFORE THE FALL

38 Vienna Before the Fall is about the rise of Nazism and the persecution of the Jewish population in Austria. The movie, which somehow garnered an Oscar nomination, is considered significant because it is Austrian. It is of little value, though, as international cinema. The filmmakers are willing to show the desperation which the victims of the Nazis felt, but the movie tends to imply that Austria was like any other country conquered by Germany, and consciously avoids showing Austrians in positions of malignant authority. The narrative specifically follows the fortunes of an actress and her husband who, like everyone else, are slow to recognize the seriousness of the Nazi threat. The actress portraying the actress has no charisma and provides no evidence to support the claims that her character is popular or accomplished on the stage. The camera angles are pedestrian and the sound editing is predictable. The picture is a blur, but it probably isn't Lumivision's fault, since the movie looks like it was made deliberately fuzzy (don't be fooled by the still on the jacket cover – not a single shot on the disc looks that clear). The film is in color, with mostly orange, gold, and brown tones. The monaural sound is adequate. The film is in German and has white English subtitles.

THE 39 STEPS
(see **THE LADY VANISHES**)

THE THIRTY NINE STEPS

Don't let your aversion to remakes of famous films inhibit you from purchasing *The Thirty Nine Steps*, a perfectly made adventure thriller which is based not on Alfred Hitchcock's *The 39 Steps*, but on the John Buchan novel that Hitchcock vaguely followed. The 1979 rendition, which stars an absolutely dashing Robert Powell, is ideal home and family entertainment, free of severe violence (and no sex), yet full of action, intelligence, and clever plotting.

The picture transfer is very good, with no noticeable flaws beyond a speckle or two. The monaural sound is digitally encoded and is fully acceptable. There is also a marvelous, grandly executed musical score, by Ed Welch. The movie is good, escapist fun, which can be watched many times without losing its charms.

THIS GUN FOR HIRE

It is rare that the trailer for a movie will be in better condition than the movie itself, but that is the situation on *This Gun for Hire*. The movie isn't in bad shape, but the edges are a little soft on the black-and-white print. The picture on the trailer, which appears after the film, is more sharply defined. The sound on the trailer has a rawness which makes the dialog and the sound effects more distinctive than their counterparts in the feature.

The movie is an excellent thriller from the early forties, starring Veronica Lake, Robert Preston, and Alan Ladd. Ladd portrays the 'villain,' a hired killer, but since the people who hired him turn out to be selling nerve gas to the Japanese, the ambiguity of his moral position is what gives the story its staying power. Ladd's performance is engrossing. He shifts effortlessly between a sensitive awareness of his surroundings and a cold-blooded heartlessness for those he has been hired to kill. The movie is fast paced, and even though the plot hinges on a series of outrageous coincidences, the emotional resolutions are satisfying. Side two is in CAV. Two frames out of every five quiver, but enough are left over to create some nice portraits of Veronica Lake.

THIS IS SPINAL TAP

If you can find someone who has never heard of *This Is Spinal Tap*, play the disc and see how long it takes for them to realize that it is a put-on. This 'rockumentary,' as Rob Reiner so seriously intones at the beginning, about an inept heavy metal group called Spinal Tap, is actually a carefully scripted comedy.

Directed by Reiner and starring

Christopher Guest, Michael McKean, and Harry Shearer (they all worked on the script as well), the inexpensive documentary look keeps the comedy under control. There are few overt gags. Instead, humor creeps in through the personalities of the band members and the situations they find themselves in. They go to a record store to sign autographs (on a totally black album jacket) and no customers enter the store. To open one of their numbers on stage, they step out of seven-foot pods, except for one band member who gets locked in.

The music (also written by Guest and McKean) attacks the clichés of rock so subtly that the soundtrack album (also totally black) might be mistaken for one from a legitimate group. (The CX-encoded stereo is only fair, but that, like the spotty picture, may be intentional.) One of the band members explains to an interviewer that he admires both Mozart and Bach – he says he is a "Mach." Sure enough, during one of his solos he manages to destroy a Mozart melody as only a heavy metal rocker can.

This Is Spinal Tap is good-natured entertainment. The story – the girlfriend of one of the band members nearly causes the group to break up – is enough to keep the loose ends in place. Footage which was added to the video cassette release is not inluded on the disc.

THIS IS VIDEO CLASH

The 30-minute *This is Video Clash* has chapter markers and is digitally encoded. Unidentified on the jacket, the sound is apparently in stereo, although it is several steps away from the original song recordings and comes across with a slight dullness. The videos are primitive by today's music video standards, but are edited effectively to the rhythm of the music. The images are often very grainy or otherwise out of kilter, but that is an intentional effect, part of the group's bad boy image, and must be tolerated. Their music is easier to take, and the louder and rougher, the better.

THIS ISLAND EARTH

This Island Earth may be a hokey movie, but it is a fun disc. The monaural sound thunders with neighborhood theater strength. The Technicolor print, for all its green washes and phony day-for-night filters, is beautiful. Side two is in CAV. It not only contains the exciting conclusion, but the theatrical trailer and 62 black-and-white promotional stills as well.

Is the movie worth this fuss? "Ruth, don't tell me that, as a woman, you're not curious about our destination." "Where are we going?" Ruth is portrayed by Faith Domergue, a Howard Hughes protege, and her breasts are always crooked in her space flight outfits, even in the stills. The story is about a group of scientists who are coerced into assisting aliens who wish to change lead into uranium to save the besieged planet, Metaluna. Had they left uranium alone, they probably wouldn't have had their problems to begin with, but that's alien logic for you. The story never pauses long enough to cause restlessness and the matte paintings of Metaluna are beautiful.

THOMPSON TWINS – INTO THE GAP LIVE

Thompson Twins – Into the Gap Live is an 83-minute concert. The analog program, a Pioneer 'Official Import,' has a somewhat grainy picture. The lights are blurry and the darker shots look speckled. Fortunately, Thompson Twins's musical ability and stage presence make an entertaining program. It opens with an interview (with Japanese subtitles) in which one of the band members begins to cry as she talks about the pressures of being on the road. The scene sensitizes you to the performance which follows. Their stage show is not elaborate, but the members of the band trade the spotlight back and forth to keep the viewer's focus attentive. The only thing we can't figure out is which two are the twins.

THOMPSON TWINS – SINGLE VISION

The music video collection on *Thompson Twins – Single Vision*, is one of the best we have seen. Their music is harmonious and the one-sided CLV disc contains the group's most accomplished efforts. Each of the 12 cuts has something special to it, and all have inventive, subtle imagery, uncommon special effects, and add illumination to the songs without mirroring the lyrics.

The analog sound is okay, but the picture is grainy. The disc jacket has an insert which contains the lyrics for each number.

THOROUGHLY MODERN MILLIE

Listening to *Thoroughly Modern Millie* reminded us of crushed velvet upholstery and tickets with seat numbers on them. Julie Andrews stars in the flapper-era farce about white slavery and careerism, along with Mary Tyler Moore, Carol Channing, and John Gavin. It has an Overture and an Intermission and what sounds like a full-piece orchestra playing right in your living room. The production values of the disc obliterate the inanities of the film. An Oscar-winning score of dull, forgettable tunes becomes vibrant and catchy with this presentation. Even the incidental music, full of oddball instrumental sounds, is captivating because you are suddenly aware of every contributing honk and shuffle. The colors look new and unblemished. The disc has 12 chapter markers to match the big musical numbers and runs for 138 minutes across three sides.

THORNTON WILDER'S OUR TOWN

The soundstage interpretation *Thornton Wilder's Our Town* was originally broadcast on NBC and has a TV-chic cast, including Barbara Bel Geddes, Ned Beatty, and Hal Holbrook (as the stage manager). The play, which evokes both the beauty and sadness of peace, is adeptly executed in this production, retaining an acknowledgement of its stage trappings but allowing the intimacy which a video or film interpretation can provide. Holbrook seems to have a handle on every gag Wilder implanted in the narrator's spiel (listen to him flutter his voice slightly before mentioning that the Baptist Church is located near the river), and the rest of the cast, even Robby Benson, is more resourceful and professional than most casts one sees performing the piece.

Though the picture is not crisp, the video tape source material survives the transfer well enough to prevent any viewer distractions. The sound is monaural and is not CX-encoded, but it has no severe problems. A couple of chapters have been encoded to mark the major scene changes. The disc runs up to the edge of the time limit on both sides, and must break several seconds after a natural pause on side one to accommodate a lengthy title promotion at the end of side two.

THOSE MAGNIFICENT MEN IN THEIR FLYING MACHINES

Despite a few blurry spots, *Those Magnificent Men in Their Flying Machines* looks beautiful, with the blue, blue skies and the white cliffs of Dover being especially striking. The film was initially presented in Todd-AO and has been alternately squeezed and cropped to get on the small screen. But the original stereo soundtrack is retained as is the wonderful Entr'Acte which conveniently appears at the very end of side two (the show is 138 minutes long).

The 1965 movie is not as funny as one fondly remembers. There is a large cast so that the plot can jump from character to character often enough to stave off boredom. Once the planes are in the air by whatever means, their uniqueness also holds a viewer's attention. You can tell by the way the story advances that much was left out of the final cut. The incidents seem arbitrary and the characters aren't clownish enough to fulfill their comic potential. The number of times the disc would be replayed is probably dependent upon the number of children in one's household.

THREE AMIGOS

Three Amigos, which stars Steve Martin, Chevy Chase, and Martin Short, is about three very dumb actors who end up defending a real Mexican town against real bad guys. If you take the movie just seriously enough to care about the characters, who are never offensive and always earnest in their own manner, you can't help but giggle at their foibles. It may be difficult to stay with them for the whole 105 minutes, but that is where the disc comes in. Once the premise is established, you can jump to just about anywhere in the film and find amusement.

The disc is in fairly good shape. If the movie does suffer from a distortion here or there, the flaw is not critical, it is just one more piece of irreverence. The sound is in stereo, and the same situation applies. The awful songs which the characters occasionally break into are enhanced rather than harmed by failures in the dynamic range.

THE THREE BILLY GOATS GRUFF AND THE THREE LITTLE PIGS

(see **PECOS BILL**)

THE THREE CABALLEROS
THE THREE CABALLEROS (CAV)

Walt Disney has released the theatrical, Latin American-themed animated fiesta, *The Three Caballeros*, in two laser disc versions, a CAV and a CLV rendition. There is virtually no difference in the quality of the picture or sound within the two versions, so one's choice will be entirely dependent upon one's preference for the playing format.

The 71-minute film opens with several cartoons, likely inserted to capture the attention of younger audience members, and then moves on to an assemblage of more esoteric animation and innovative sequences which combine cartoons with live action. The narrative is vaguely travelog oriented, with Donald Duck flitting from country to country, sampling cultural pleasures along the way. There are plenty of songs and lots of confetti colors.

The CAV still frames make impressive frozen images of the masterful Disney factory animation. On both discs, the picture is in good shape, although strong colors, especially reds, tend to become a bit blurry. The film is not one which the Disney organization has seen fit to remaster in stereo, and so it is an analog monaural disc, with CX-encoding. The CAV disc has been chapter encoded, though inadequately.

THREE FOR THE ROAD

B.W.L. Norton directed *Three for the Road*, a standard tale about a young Congressional aide (Charlie Sheen) transporting the daughter of a Senator to a juvenile reform institution. They fall in love, the Senator's a jerk, and nothing out of the ordinary occurs. The film has more moments of anxiety than of good feeling, but there is a happy ending. The picture is a little grainy, but passable. The sound has limited stereophonic effects and is of little interest.

THREE FUGITIVES

The picture quality of *Three Fugitives* is impressive. The image is slick and glossy, and there are only a couple of shots where grain is visible at all. The digitally encoded stereo surround sound is also transferred well, and the sound editing is full of directional effects.

The comedy is sharper because the picture is sharp – you laugh at the timing of the actors and at bits of business which would seem extraneous under other conditions because your senses are more alert to what is happening on the screen. The elaborate story is primarily about an ex-convict, played by Nick Nolte, who is taken hostage in a holdup. The police assume he is in on the job and soon he is on the lam with the hapless robber, played by Martin Short, and the robber's young daughter. If there were a single noticeable flaw in the disc it would blow the mood and the film would seem trivial, but that never happens and the movie ends up being as much fun as the filmmakers seem to have intended it to be.

THREE MEN AND A BABY

Both the sound and the picture on *Three Men and a Baby*, are very good. The stereo effects are enjoyable and well defined, and the colors never leave their boundaries. The script is an improvement over its antecedent, *3 Men and a Cradle*, and it imposes only a token amount of ineptitude upon its three leads. Although the domestic situation seems unlikely or not thoroughly developed, accepting it is the only strenuous act a viewer must perform. The casting, of Tom Selleck, Steve Guttenberg and Ted Danson, was brilliant, and the choice of the director, Leonard Nimoy, was equally inspired. The film is pure sit-com, and needed a director who was more comfortable with the dimensions of television. The concept is so obvious that the presentation has to avoid grand designs.

3 MEN AND A CRADLE

It is hard to believe that Vestron could not have come up with a nicer print for *3 Men and a Cradle*. The movie was made in France and is by nature less perfect than big-budgeted American films, and much of it was shot in a soft light to be easier on the infant, but the picture on the disc is always blurry and often lacking in any color other than tones of faded brown.

The movie is about three bachelors taking care of a baby, but actually there is so little plot that the story is split into two episodes – one about drug dealers and one about what happens when mom returns. Predictably the men fall in love with the little tyke, but they don't really seem to take an interest in the baby's intellectual development, which is normally the most satisfying aspect to raising a child.

Vestron has been sensible enough to retain the French dialog and English subtitles. The sound is monaural and not CX-encoded, and playback is best kept at a low volume.

THE THREE MUSKETEERS

Every generation gets a new version of 'The Three Musketeers.' In 1948, MGM made *The Three Musketeers* with Gene Kelly as D'Artagnan, along with Van Heflin and Gig Young as Musketeers, Vincent Price as Richelieu, and June Allyson and Lana Turner as the good and bad love interests, respectively. The film is no better and no worse than any other version of the tale, and it makes for rousing, reliable entertainment. The only glaring problems with the work are the use of California for the French locations and the substitution of some monotonously repetitive Tschaikovsky pieces for whatever score it was that didn't get delivered on time.

The color is rich and the efforts of the MGM costume department are shown to great advantage. Some consider this to be the finest Technicolor transfer available on disc. The print is scratchy in places, however, and this carries over to the monaural soundtrack.

THREE O'CLOCK HIGH

The visual style of *Three O'Clock High*, reeks of graduate filmmaking, but the result provides a nice looking disc. The comedy itself – about a boy in high school who has been told he's going to be pounded at the end of the day – isn't as strong, but it has a few clever moments (the topic in every class the boy attends has something to do with violence) and an ending which quotes from *It's a Wonderful Life* with just the right spirit. Other than a rhythmic ticking, the sound effects aren't as showy as the glossy visual effects. The movie was filmed in Ogden, Utah.

THE 3 PENNY OPERA

One of the advantages to the fact that *The 3 Penny Opera* was written in German is that there are so many wonderful English translations slinking about. When a musical is written in English, that's it, but we know of at least six different versions of 'Mack the Knife,' and they all sound great in the shower. The show itself is magnificent, and any familiarity with it can have you walking down the street whistling happily about Mankind and Starvation without thinking twice. It is a comedy about gangsters, so it can be as philosophical as it wants, because nobody is going to snicker at a gangster with a sense of humor. The original G.W. Pabst film, made by many of the artists who were involved with the original German stage production, has been released by Voyager.

The Nazis were none too happy with the anarchy of *3 Penny Opera*, so the print which survives has been pieced together from stray cans of film that somehow eluded a concentrated effort to extinguish the movie's existence. This is especially ironic since the film ends with Bertolt Brecht's famous admonition that 'those in darkness cannot be seen.' The print is not in great shape, and Voyager is charging more than a thousand times three pennies, but when the first rickety strains of music billow out of your sound system you're hooked, just like you would be if you heard a great singer whose only recordings could be played upon a Victorola. (Because of a dual audio soundtrack, the disc is not CX-encoded.) The picture quality matches that of the sound and reminds one, endearingly, of antique pornographic postcards.

On the second audio track is an utterly Brechtian translation of the dialog by Anneliese Varaldiev. The film is in German and has English subtitles. The reason given for the presence of the translation is that the subtitles are inadequate, but listening to Varaldiev one quickly ascertains that the subtitles are actually quite thorough. Made in 1931, *3 Penny Opera* was a very early sound film, and so the only action on the soundtrack, other than the music, some gunshots, and the scratches, is the immediate dialog. No background conversations or group chatter are present, and the subtitles cover almost every word, spoken or sung. No matter, Varaldiev's throaty interpretation is a pleasure to hear and is simply another enjoyable version of *3 Penny Opera* to be added to the roster.

The CLV disc has 22 chapters, but several important music cues are missed, and a couple of the songs are not identified by their proper titles on the jacket cover chapter listing. This should not discourage you, however, from obtaining the disc, enjoying the music and the aphorisms, and thumbing your nose at the Third Reich.

THE THREE STOOGES VIDEODISC VOLUME 1
THE THREE STOOGES VOL. III
THE THREE STOOGES VOL. VI
THE THREE STOOGES VOL. VII
THE THREE STOOGES VOL. VIII
THE THREE STOOGES VOL. IX

When we were little we despised the Three Stooges, but now we think they are hysterical, which just goes to show that maturity is not necessarily synonymous with emotional and intellectual advancement.

RCA/Columbia, through Pioneer, released *The Three Stooges Videodisc Volume 1* and *Volume 2*. The discs contained two video cassette programs, or six 17 minute featurettes. Image, having obtained a collaboration of their own with RCA/Columbia, started putting out more *Three Stooges* programs. However, Image is following RCA/Columbia's video cassette programming format of three featurettes per compilation, encasing them on a single sided disc. Furthermore, Image is following the video cassette naming convention, so that in releasing *Vol. III*, they are actually putting out half of *Videodisc Volume 2*. Now far be it from us to suggest that any of these companies are being run by Larry, Moe, and Curly.

Videodisc Volume 1 has a solid black-and-white picture and an acceptable non-CX monaural soundtrack. There is one bad splice in one of the shorts, but otherwise the source material looks like it is in good condition and the picture resolution is strong. The disc is not chapter encoded and contains three shorts per side. Most of the shorts are quite amusing. The opener, 'Dizzy Pilots,' has some of the funniest slapstick, as the three torture one another while building an airplane. 'A Bird in the Head' is a mad-scientist-and-gorilla skit which they have done better elsewhere, but it still has its moments. In 'Three Sappy People' the Stooges pose as psychiatrists and end up curing their patient with a marvelous pie fight. 'Uncivil Warriors' doesn't accomplish much with its Civil War locale, but 'Three Missing Links' places the trio as actors on location in Africa to predictable and amusing results. The finale, 'Micro-Phonies,' revolves around lip-synching songs and has too much plot for its own good

None of the three films on Image's disc, *The Three Stooges Vol. III*, is as amusing as the better films on *Videodisc Volume 1*. The shorts include 'An Ache in Every Stake,' in which the Stooges, as ice delivery men, take over a kitchen to bake a birthday meal in repetition of the gags in a number of their other films; 'Calling All Curs,' a tale about a dog-napping which has some funny moments; and 'Pop Goes the Easel,' in which the Stooges hide out in an art school and which ends with a clay fight that is a pale imitation of the food fight on *Videodisc Volume 1*.

The sound on Image's effort is digitally encoded and a little stronger than the older disc. Image has also provided welcome chapter markers, and even lists them on the back of the jacket. The picture quality is average. The shorts look good, but there are a few scratches and, at one point, a momentary 'rolling bar' passes through the frenetic hijinks.

The three shorts on *The Three Stooges Volume VI* are all unusual and include one, 'Punch Drunks' which was written by the trio. 'Violent Is the Word for Curly' begins in a gas station, as the Stooges destroy just about every vehicle which pulls up. It ends at an all girls school, where the three are mistaken for professors and there is an honest to goodness musical number, about the alphabet, in the middle. 'A Plumbing We Will Go' is an enjoyable mixture of hijinks and crazy pipe connections. 'Drunks' begins with the three not knowing one another. They team up to make Curly a prize fighter. The picture transfer is very nice on all three shorts and the sound is fine.

In 'Dutiful but Dumb,' on *Three Stooges Volume VII*, the three are photographers trying to take pictures in an Eastern European country where such activity is punishable by death. It also contains an amusing sequence in which Curly attempts to have oyster stew while a live oyster snaps at his croutons, but the short ends without a resolution. The picture quality looks fine. The picture is softer and more washed out on 'Movie Maniacs,' in which the three are mistaken, understandably, for motion picture executives. 'Oily to Bed, Oily to Rise,' which is in good condition, is one of the best shorts in any of the collections we have seen thus far. It has a plot with a beginning, middle, and happy ending, as the trio save a widow with three lovely daughters from land swindlers. In one frightening but amazing stunt, Curly appears to fall 20 feet flat onto his back, off an oil gusher. And he kisses Moe at the end.

The Three Stooges Volume VIII opens with the clip montage music video, 'The Curly Shuffle,' in stereo. Following that are three weaker shorts, though they still have some inspired moments. 'Cash and Carry' lands the trio in an empty house, which they come close to destroying while searching for treasure. They eventually dig their way into a US Treasury vault which happens to be next door. The picture looks a little washed out. The best part of 'No Census, No Feeling,' in which the three become census takers (at 4 cents a name), is set in a mansion, as they interrupt the daily activities with their usual vigor. 'Some More of Samoa' casts them as tree surgeons and then sends them to a tropical island to obtain a rare tree from a tribe of cannibals. The last two shorts have sharp pictures, although 'Census' has a couple of splices.

Even though 'We Want Our Mummy,' on *The Three Stooges Volume IX*, can't possibly live up to its potential, it is one of those classic situational comedies where simply contemplating the set-up can cause you to chuckle. They're searching for an archaeologist. They're in a tomb. You fill in the blanks from there. The same goes for 'Yes, We Have No Bonanza,' in which they are prospectors, out west. Unfortunately, none of the gags click in 'Restless Knights,' an uninspired 'Three Musketeers' take off. 'Bonanza' has the best looking print. 'Mummy' is okay. It is a little washed out, looks damaged in a couple of places, and varies from sharp to fuzzy. 'Knights' has the poorest source material of the three. It is soft, looks too dark, and has a sound drop out.

3:10 TO YUMA

Anyone partial to Westerns will enjoy *3:10 to Yuma*. The black-and-white feature is in fairly good condition and the opening song, by Frankie Laine, comes through just fine. Glenn Ford portrays a smooth-talking bandit who pulls every trick he can think of to psyche out Van Johnson before the 3:10 train to Yuma Prison arrives. There is plenty of action and tension, but the real entertainment comes from watching Ford oil his way through every conversation and predicament. The screen writer actually writes himself into a corner in the end, and has to cheat a little to get out of it, but the movie is so enjoyable that most viewers will forgive the happy ending.

THE THREE WORLDS OF GULLIVER
(Import)

In only one instance do the subtitles get in the way of the special effects on the Japanese release of *The Three Worlds of Gulliver*. That is when the Lilliputans are seen walking through Gulliver's legs. For most of the disc, particularly with all the ground-level camera angles, one is never looking at the bottom of the screen.

The colors are strong, but the print has a 'rounded edges' look to it, commensurate with its age. The sound is monaural and has not been CX-encoded, but the timbre in the voices of the giants is effective on a hi-fi, and Bernard Herrmann's score is always endearing.

The movie is more faithful to Swift than other adaptations have been, particularly in the first half where much is made of the Lilliputan king's attempt to start a war over a disagreement about how to open an egg. Gulliver puts out the fire by spitting, but what can you expect from a film made in 1960? Ray Harryhausen did many of the special effects and they are delightful. The disc has ten chapter markers.

THROW MOMMA FROM THE TRAIN

The one-joke movie, *Throw Momma from the Train*, not only has a great punchline, it also has a wonderful surround stereo track. The sound is as delightful as the comedy itself. The picture quality is fine, but is not as impressive, since some of the darker scenes lack purity. The 88-minute film is in CLV.

THUMBELINA
(see **FAERIE TALE THEATRE**)

THUMBELINA (see **PECOS BILL**)

THUNDERBALL (CBS/Fox)
THUNDERBALL (MGM/UA)
YOU ONLY LIVE TWICE (CBS/Fox)
YOU ONLY LIVE TWICE (MGM/UA)

MGM/UA has released Deluxe Letter-Box Editions of two widescreen James Bond movies, *Thunderball* and *You Only Live Twice*. The films look gorgeous. The colors are crisp and the strongest, brightest reds have no more than a faint haze. Night scenes are jet black and the fleshtones look like fleshtones. The sound on both discs is digitally encoded monaural, but the audio is virtually noise-free. The letterboxing, to echo the ad campaigns when the films were reissued as a double feature, gives you twice the excitement you normally get on a James Bond disc.

The *Thunderball* disc opens with a grungy copy of the beginning 007 iris, but – surprise – it is part of the original theatrical trailer. The disc has two trailers at the beginning, for *Thunderball* and for *You Only Live Twice* (the *Twice* trailer could not fit on the *Twice* disc because of running time constraints). Then the real iris appears, with an aspect ratio of 2.4:1, and it looks thrilling.

At 133 minutes, MGM/UA's *Thunderball* runs 4 minutes longer than the scanned and cropped CBS/Fox version. The source material was reportedly in more pieces than the *Thunderball* jigsaw puzzle we once owned as a child, so the restoration MGM/UA has performed is marvelous. There are one or two cuts which still appear awkward, but their effect is insignificant. The print's one flagrant and damaging splice comes at the very end, but we'll get to that in a moment.

Everybody has their favorite James Bond movie and ours is *Thunderball*. It seems less farfetched than the films which followed it, but more elaborate than the films which preceded it. Bond's many romances are logical and pleasing, and he actually solves a mystery instead of simply visiting the bad guy and being told the answer before escaping. The action and the stunts are clever. Perhaps it is just the freshness of the Bahamian locations. The film is the entertainment equivalent of a light tropical breeze – inconsequential, but perfect.

The disc has no chapter markers, but side three is in CAV with perfect still frames. The final underwater battle, in all its letterboxed glory, is in CAV, as well as the fight on the hydrofoil. And so is the disc's most glaring flaw, an obvious splice which has eliminated – just as it eliminated on the CBS/Fox disc – the 'James Bond will return in *You Only Live Twice* ' message. It left us in a funk, but not for long.

You Only Live Twice has an aspect ratio of 2.3:1. It is the big stunt sequences which benefit the most from the widescreen – the helicopter fight, the grand final battle, and the chase through the shipyard – but the lyrical travel shots of the Japanese countryside take the best advantage of the combined improvement to the screen composition and the color. The film runs just under two hours and the disc comes on a single platter with a comfortable side break.

The title was also released by CBS/Fox. Except for some speckling which was generated during the manufacturing process on the earliest batches of the disc, the CBS/Fox version, which was scanned and cropped, looked decent. To be sure the opening title sequence was squeezed and many of the widescreen stunts were rendered partially incomprehensible, but the colors were stable and there were some great closeups of Connery. The MGM/UA version, though, has such crisp colors and sharply focussed details that the CBS/Fox version looks silly in comparison, as if one were peeking at a part of the film through a dirty window.

The CBS/Fox disc had electronically rechanneled stereo sound, which didn't do much. The MGM/UA disc is content to be monaural, and sounds quite good. The film's age barely inhibits the soundtrack's potential for atmosphere. John Barry's film score is the most consciously symphonic and the most highly regarded in the series.

The film was the one which burned everybody out of the James Bond series and caused its first serious hiatus. In an attempt to out-do its predecessors, the sets are larger and the perils are more presumptuous. The movie might have gotten away with it, too, except that in one serious category, pacing, it does not keep up with its kin. For a while it tries, but then everyone runs out of steam. Connery appears impatient, and by the time the film gets to the Japanese wedding ceremony, which seems to be re-created in full, many viewers start to get a little itchy as well.

Still, *You Only Live Twice* is a James Bond movie, one with Connery no less, and anybody who has enjoyed the series will want the Deluxe Letter-Box Edition for their collection. It is good fun, and it looks super. MGM/UA has done such a good job that it is difficult to obtain either *Twice* or *Thunderball* without being tempted to obtain the other.

THUNDERBIRDS COUNTDOWN TO DISASTER

Although it is unlikely that many of you will ever take the time to watch the disc, we're going to be mean and not tell you the joke which appears at 2 minutes 13 seconds on side one of *Thunderbirds Countdown to Disaster*. The program is a combination of two 'Thunderbird' episodes from the old animated puppet TV series. As with *Thunderbirds in Outer Space*, the episodes have been given new opening and closing credits under the pretense that one film is being presented instead of two separate stories. As with the other disc, Image fails to divide the sides at the story break, but a few more chapter markers have been encoded. The audio sounds okay. The print has a few scratches on it, but the transfer looks decent. The two episodes, one involving a rescue beneath the collapsed Empire State Building and another involving explosions near a deep sea oil rig, are notably stronger than the two which appeared on the *Outer Space* disc, so adults who happen to watch the program will not spend quite as much time counting how many of Newton's laws are broken every 45 seconds by the wired and wooden heroes ("The automatic camera detector! Someone is photographing the ship!"). The opening credit sequence is also better than the opening sequence on the first disc, but it is here that the obviously disrespectful video artists designing the updated titles have slipped several gags, unobtrusively, onto a mock computer readout which is, theoretically, passing by too quickly behind the credits to be seen without laser video system freeze frame capabilities. The joke which we noted, concerning one of the Thunderbird puppet heroes and his relationship to a famous television puppet from the nineteen fifties, is the most wicked.

THUNDERBIRDS IN OUTER SPACE

Watching the puppet-animated *Thunderbirds in Outer Space* is as exciting as moving a little plastic jet plane in front of your face and going, "Zoom, zoom!" We recall that at a particular age the programs were enjoyable, but that was several exponents ago. It is not the puppet animation itself which is a turnoff, since you go into it knowing that the heros are going to be a bunch of stiffs, but there are long gaps in conversations, as if it were the puppets who were actually thinking about and delivering the dialog, and there is endless repetition in the action sequences. The episodes included deal with outer space rescues.

The disc program takes two forty-minute ('hour' time slot) episodes and combines them, adding title sequences to the beginning and end which are newer than the episodes themselves. The whole thing runs just under 90 minutes and is in CLV. The monaural sound is okay, and the picture looks pretty good, although intense colors look blurry.

THUNDERBOLT AND LIGHTFOOT

Since *Thunderbolt and Lightfoot* was Michael Cimino's first directorial effort, there is a tendency now to watch it with an eye for disasters yet to come. The beautiful photography and strong soundtrack are there, along with the tedious storyline and dithering dialog.

The movie is sort of a caper picture – Clint Eastwood, Jeff Bridges, and George Kennedy rob an armory – but it is mostly a meandering macho buddy story where Bridges, at the very end, turns into jello and dies. Symbolically, Eastwood breaks a cigar in half and drives on.

The print is lovely with the exception of some splices near the opening of side two. The Montana locations are used with great effectiveness and one sorely misses the full Panavision effect, since cropping cuts away at the film's only real asset. The sound, not stereo (contrary to the claim of the label) and not CX-encoded, still has some oomph to it.

THX-1138 (Import)

Some catalogs of Japanese discs list *THX-1138* as having a digital track, but in reality the disc hasn't even been CX-encoded. The print which was used for the monaural film looks a little aged, although the most important colors – fleshtones and white – look accurate. The sound is a little fuzzy, but the Japanese subtitles help identify character names. A brief nude scene has been masked. George Lucas's debut has held up well and actually seems gutsy from an investment standpoint. It is oblique enough to withstand repeated viewings.

TIGER WARSAW

Filmed in Shenango Valley, Pennsylvania, *Tiger Warsaw*, an uninteresting 'Prodigal Son' tale, stars Patrick Swayze. The film has something of a show-off style, which tends to draw too much attention to its construction. If the thought of watching Swayze's character hug his parents is your idea of an emotional climax, then you may enjoy the movie. Only one performance really stands out. Barbara Williams portrays a divorced mother who hasn't let her economic and romantic restrictions suppress her spirit. It is a shame the rest of the movie didn't have her spunk. The disc's picture is blurry and too orange, and the sound is flat.

TILL THE CLOUDS ROLL BY
(see **WORDS AND MUSIC**)

TILL THE END OF TIME

It is odd how a film such as *Till the End of Time* can have so greater an emotional impact than more contemporary features. The movie, made immediately after the War, is about World War II veterans coping with civilian life and coming to terms with peace. It is very much a drama of the era, when movies could show mothers cooking warm meals without intending to be satirical, yet the film manages to really tug on the heartstrings of most viewers. In comparison, a film such as *Coming Home* may have a couple of sexy sequences, but the emotions of the characters are never transferred to the audience. There is something to be said for a little exaggeration, though when filmmakers today, such as Steven Spielberg, try it, they get jumped on from all quarters.

The black-and-white print looks quite good, both sharp and intact, with clear contrasts. The sound is also in decent shape, except for one brief quiver near the beginning.

The movie stars Guy Madison, Dorothy McGuire, and Robert Mitchum, with McGuire, as a wistful but pragmatic war widow, delivering the most memorable performance. The film also has that awful adaptation of Chopin's 'Polonaise,' the title song, which plays over and over in every imaginable style and beat. By the end, the lyrics seem to refer to the song itself.

TIME AFTER TIME

A movie such as *Time after Time* works best on home video. You are compelled to watch it, and after several viewings you can come to terms with its deficiencies. It works best after it has become a bit worn in your memory, and the rougher edges have smoothed out. From the failure of the hero to use the time machine properly to catch the villain, to the insistence of a character that a dime be used to call 911, the flaws in the plot become flaws in the characters. The hero is presented as being a poor strategist and it is quite plausible that he couldn't come up with a solution to his troubles which virtually anyone who watches the movie could come up with. He's distracted. And most people, unfortunately, don't realize that a dime is not needed to call 911, so it is conceivable that the heroine wouldn't know, either.

Time after Time is in good, but not perfect shape, as it seems to fall in a window which a lot of seventies films fall into – too new to be restored, but too old to look sparkling new. The credit sequences are letterboxed but the rest of the movie isn't, and the picture often feels cramped. The film was originally in stereo, and the disc has been digitally encoded. The sound is quite polished although the stereo effects are limited. The musical score was written by Miklos Rosza. The score is true perfection, since his music belongs to another age and, like the hero, adapts to new technology with an inscrutable panache.

THE TIME GUARDIANS

Dean Stockwell and Carrie Fisher star in *The Time Guardians*, an enjoyable science fiction thriller with a reasonable budget. The special effects are satisfying and the story, about good guys and bad guys who chase and battle one another through time, keeps the viewer alert. The image composition is cropped for the disc, which is a shame because the model work is affected, but the picture transfer looks fine and the stereo surround sound is intermittently pleasing.

A TIME OF DESTINY

Old world passions inflict tragedy upon the lives of a young married couple in *A Time of Destiny*. The transfer is gorgeous. The film's cinematography and sound editing are impressive and lose nothing in the transition to laser. The picture is bright, spotless, and correctly colored. The stereo sound, although analog, is fantastic. Not only is a typical Ennio Morricone score ever present, but there is always some background sound effect which is so real it seems disconnected from the film. There is a whopper of a rainstorm as well.

Destiny takes place during World War II and concerns a mad brother (William Hurt, playing a bad guy for once) bent upon revenge against his sister's husband after an elopement causes his father's death. The emotions are less than subtle, but the overplaying is excused by the plot, so if you can stand it, you will enjoy it.

TIMERIDER: THE ADVENTURES OF LYLE SWAN
THE TIME MACHINE

Time travel stories rarely do well at the box office, but those lucky enough to catch a movie like *Timerider* or *The Time Machine* will find pleasant memories of the plot twists lingering in their day dreams. The films often contain gaps in logic or realism far greater than the span of their fantasy, but the idea is so intriguing that no matter how poorly it is presented technically, your imagination starts stretching to accept it and doesn't stop, even when the film has ended.

Timerider: The Adventures of Lyle Swan (and if you know the Spanish word for 'swan' you'll figure out the goose pimple conclusion as soon as the characters are introduced) is about a motorcross contestant who passes through an experiment in a remote area of Mexico and is zapped, motorcycle and all, into the Wild West.

The picture quality and the stereo on the disc are superior. The movie has about a half hour's worth of plot and is padded with scenic shots of motorcycles running about in the desert. It doesn't matter. While you're listening to the roar of the cycle and enjoying the scenery, your own mind is doing the screenwriter's work for him.

George Pal's *The Time Machine* is silly. The hero (Rod Taylor) travels 800,000 years into the future and meets people who speak perfect, unvowel-shifted English because they have some talking rings. The rings are more convincing than any of the other performers. People are bred, like cattle, for a society of white-haired ogres who live underground and eat everybody who turns 21. It is even less believable when you see it on the screen.

Yet, *The Time Machine* has one 20-minute sequence which is perfectly conceived. To travel in time the hero sits in a plush red chair attached to a sled and a large disc. As he moves the controls, the world around him begins to speed up and soon he is watching advances in architecture, fashion, and war whiz by him. It is something you can do at home, just by closing your eyes.

The picture is well preserved, though the cinematography is a little washed out and the sets are fairly bland in the scenes set in the future. The sound quality on the MGM/UA disc is curious. The dialog is muted, as if the volume had been lowered, but the sound effects blast out of one's speakers. That's Pal for you.

THE TIMES OF HARVEY MILK

The most fascinating aspect of *The Times of Harvey Milk* is the glimpse one gets of Milk's assassin, Dan White. The award-winning documentary, appropriately titled, tells the complete story of Harvey Milk's promising rise in the San Francisco establishment. It is a profile of a political activist who is just getting started, but who clearly has an instinct and the talent for politics that ought to have taken him a long way. But at the same time that Milk is elected to a newly created city 'Board of Supervisors,' so too is Dan White. White comes across, even if one ignores his political and social opinions, as a Travis Bickle who used his outward persona to achieve the first rung of public office. The interviews with him are far more fascinating than the interviews with Milk, just as evil is far more complex and beguiling than good, and in all the footage taken of him, even months before the shooting, he looks like he could go over the edge at any moment. (The video presentation ends the film with an added title card, noting White's suicide a year after being released from prison.)

The documentary footage is understandably rough, and is never as clear as the stills on the back of the jacket. The sound is solid, and even verges on hi-fidelity during a clip from a Sylvester concert. Side two is less than 30 minutes long, but the disc is in CLV throughout.

TIN MEN

One of Barry Levinson's seemingly endless combinations of nostalgia and comedy, *Tin Men*, has a bright, solid picture with few flaws. The stereo sound is digitally encoded and is also of good quality. The mix is sophisticated and understated. The movie is about aluminum siding salesmen in the early sixties and two in particular, played by Danny DeVito and Richard Dreyfuss, who start feuding over an auto accident. DeVito's ability to generate laughs does not disguise the limited aspirations of the film itself. The idea that these two are supposed to get hearts by the end, or that they've always had them, is muffed. Although events happen to each character, nothing useful comes from the lessons experienced. When a change in personality occurs, it is abrupt and almost unrelated to a character's experiences.

TINA TURNER LIVE – PRIVATE DANCER TOUR

A 55-minute concert is contained on one side of the CLV disc, *Tina Turner Live – Private Dancer Tour*. The photography, along with its other faults, is slightly grainy. Her rendition of 'Private Dancer' is much better than the music video version, both musically and visually. Turner sings her hits and is joined in the end by Bryan Adams for one number, and then David Bowie for two. When she and Bowie start going at it from opposite ends of the stage the cameras get lost, but the music comes through loud and clear.

TINA TURNER – QUEEN OF ROCK AND ROLL
TINA TURNER – PRIVATE DANCER

The Disc Factory, the video company that brought us a 75-minute disc (see *The Big Trees*) and claimed that it was 89 minutes long, now brings us *Tina Turner – Queen of Rock and Roll* in (as per the jacket) CX-encoded stereo – only it is not CX-encoded.

The picture quality is acceptable. You can make out the beads of perspiration on Tina's neck even when she's dancing. The sound, though not utilizing its full potential, is clear and really very good. According to the jacket, the concert was filmed, "at Harlem's legendary Apollo Theater." According to the credit roll at the end of the show, the performance was, "videotaped live on stage in London," a stop on the A Train we are unfamiliar with.

The hour-long concert, in CAV, does not include Turner's later hits but that does not matter. She can't do anything wrong. The more she sweats, the sexier she looks. The more her voice cracks, the closer she gets to the heart of a lyric. Four of her later hit singles are available on the 8-inch, *Tina Turner – Private Dancer*. This disc really is CX-encoded and it makes an excellent coda to the *Queen of Rock and Roll*. The videos are well conceived. 'What's Love Got to Do With It,' a song of anxiety, is sung as Turner strolls happily down the streets of New York in an effective contrast. 'Better Be Good to Me' and 'Let's Stay Together' are make-believe concert performances which give her a glamourous image. 'Private Dancer' is a clever miniature film depicting a dance hall girl who fantasizes about other types of dancing.

TINA TURNER – RIO '88

Tina Turner fills an entire soccer stadium for *Tina Turner – Rio '88*. When her songs move into a lower octave the notes don't float away before they get to the microphone. Turner's act runs about 75 minutes, but only manages to accommodate thirteen songs. The high point is an interesting and soulful interpretation of Lennon/McCartney's 'Help,' and it is one of the few numbers not harmed by the acoustics. The picture is a little blurry and the sound is at the mercy of the recording. The chapter markers do not coincide with those listed on the jacket cover, but the order is the same.

TO HAVE AND HAVE NOT

The ever-popular revival house favorite, *To Have and Have Not* is a supremely relaxing World War II adventure yarn which lacks what one normally thinks of as a plot, substituting in its stead a few incidents of action and intrigue on an island in the French Caribbean, and a dynamo romance between Humphrey Bogart and Lauren Bacall which carries over into their characters on the screen for the world and its generations to share. Though short on plot, the script is written to the gills, and is loaded with memorable dialog. Besides, the movie is entertaining precisely because it doesn't have a plot – it doesn't have anything that makes a viewer think or ponder or moralize; there is nothing to distract one from the romance and the few flying bullets.

The black-and-white picture has speckles in places, and even a splice, but the contrasts look rich and the presentation is satisfying. At its best, everything looks smooth and glossy. The sound is on par with its age. The disc is not chapter encoded, but at the end of side two after the movie has ended, MGM/UA has included a cartoon, 'Bacall to Arms,' which is a 'Looney Tunes' look at the experience of seeing *To Have and Have Not* in a theater. There is also a terrific theatrical trailer which squeezes every last bit of action to be had out of the film.

TO KILL A MOCKINGBIRD

The beautiful opening credit montage of *To Kill a Mockingbird* is letterboxed, and even though the rest of the movie is not, the effect is enough to put one in the right mood. The courtroom sequence looks better with the tight television closeups than it does with a rectangular composition, anyway. The movie is in black-and-white, but there are a couple of gorgeous color stills on the jacket cover. The disc is 11 minutes longer than two hours but is CLV throughout.

The print is in terrific condition, and that may be another reason why the opening is so stunning. Also contributing to the effect is Elmer Bernstein's score, which is rendered quite adequately in CX-encoded monaural. It is clear that he worked longer and harder on that score than anyone, including him, works on any movie music today. The music is daring. At one point, for example, the orchestration retains its tempo from one scene to the next even though the cut is supposed to represent a lengthy passage of time.

With one or two minor exceptions, showing the entire story from the point of view of the lawyer's children is a perfect narrative device. The movie is an effective and timeless evocation of growing up in a small, humid Southern town during the Depression. The screenplay is by Horton Foote, a playwright, and even though the movie is based on a novel, it is anchored very strongly to just three locations, so that by the end of the film you feel as if you have lived there yourself. The clearest testament we can give to how well the film is constructed is that when, as a child, we first saw the movie, we thought the ending was quite ambiguous. Now that we are older the ambiguities are gone, but twenty years from now, who knows.

TO LIVE AND DIE IN LA

William Friedkin has a bad ear for street dialog. His actors use the correct lingo, but their diction is so practiced that it reminds one of Eliza Doolittle's first tea party. "What are you doing in my crib?" a character in *To Live and Die in LA* asks with such careful phrasing that you think he's talking about a playpen instead of a pad. In fact, Friedkin seems to have a bad ear for everything. He obviously didn't hear anybody warning him during the story conferences that the plot, about counterfeiters, is as bogus as a three-dollar bill. Nor were his ears perky during the sound editing. Characters standing slightly to the left have voices coming from beyond the foul line, as if one's left stereo speaker had suddenly tiptoed over another 15 feet. The high point in laughs comes when a character is making a phone call from a bar. The patrons of the bar are watching a boxing match on television and the *sounds from the match are in stereo*, as if the character were phoning from the middle of the ring. To die.

The picture is grainy and none of Friedkin's gaga widescreen compositions survive cropping. This is one of those movies where red lights are supposed to be indicative of sin, but the disc can't hold the glows.

TO NEW HORIZONS: EPHEMERAL FILMS 1931-1945
YOU CAN'T GET THERE FROM HERE: EPHEMERAL FILMS 1946-1960

While you might not recognize the specific clips included on the *Ephemeral Films* discs, you will certainly recognize, perhaps even fondly, the style and subject matter of the pieces. They are educational and corporate sponsored efforts which presented a dated and narrow viewpoint when they were made, so much so that there is humor in them now. The discs, *To New Horizons: Ephemeral Films 1931-1945* and *You Can't Get There from Here: Ephemeral Films 1946-1960*, are each an hour long and are presented in CAV format. The sound is CX-encoded with manual tripping. Both the sound and the picture quality on the discs are at the mercy of the condition of each clip, but the quality of the transfer is excellent, every still frame is perfect, the colors, when employed, are terrific, and the material has clearly been chosen and handled with the greatest care. Few of the films look their age.

The linking theme of *Horizons* is the creation of a utopia, or just a very happy place, through technology. This is epitomized by the famous 1939 New York World's Fair, which is covered extensively on side two. Along with some early examples of filmed commercials ('Snap, Crackle, and Pop' have been around a very long time) and stop motion photography, side one contains a fascinating documentary showing a pre-robot Detroit (well, Flint) assembly line, as insignificant pieces, prodded, zapped, and crunched by men on the line, gradually turn into automobiles. The scope and the atmosphere of the assembly plant are communicated, but its value today is its historical significance. At one point this was the most efficient, most successful method for manufacturing automobiles. Today it no longer is.

Side one of *Horizons* also contains some outrageous traffic safety guides and a weird economics lesson performed by stop motion puppets. Along with the World's Fair material, a wild hard sell for advertising on billboards, some daydreaming about television, and an imaginary robot in action, side two also contains a benign peek at how they made sound effects on the old radio programs. As with much of the disc, you'll find yourself giggling while you watch it.

You Can't Get There From Here focuses on social guidelines and the dawn of the television family. The irony here is that while many of these pieces glorify the position of the housewife and promise her more freedom with advanced technology, while reinforcing the concept that she must remain married to her house, the washers and dryers and other electronic appliances on display were in fact responsible for breaking down the social and economic restrictions confronting women at the time. Hence, in one short where a teenage girl mocks her friends for suggesting that Universal Suffrage is an apt topic for a paper on women's emancipation and chooses instead to praise Whirlpool appliances, she has more of a point than she realizes.

The other subject of *You Can't Get There from Here* is teenage morals. Many of the film clips look and play like 'Reefer Madness' at its most amusing, but there is also a certain poignancy in the world they depict. One in particular, 'A Date with Your Family' (great title), which is identified in the jacket notes as 'a dark look at suburban family life,' actually left us feeling winsome. It creates an unbelievable picture of what a family dinner should be like, but its message – that dinner should be special and provide a respite from the pressures of the day – is stronger than its cartoon aspects.

The wonderful still on the jacket cover, unfortunately, does not represent a sequence appearing on the disc. Along with some elaborate production numbers from GM and Ford (all this for a Falcon?), there is an amusing piece about how cold germs are passed, an effort praising tranquilizers and an animated TV spot for Eisenhower's first Presidential campaign. On both discs the clips progress chronologically.

TO RUSSIA WITH ELTON

A decade old concert tour of the Soviet Union serves as a reminder of how far things have come in *To Russia with Elton*. The musicians act, probably with good reason, as if they are performing a major contribution to detente, and they show a real paranoia about encouraging the audience to boogie. The concert is the same old set Elton John has been doing for years, and it is available with better audio and better images elsewhere. The songs, which are chapter encoded, are separated by interludes, which are not, showing John getting the – if one sees enough of these 'in Russia' video programs – typical western rock star treatment. The sound has stereo separations but a limited dynamic range and side two is in CAV with perfect still frames. The picture is old looking and grainy, though the camera angles on the stone-faced crowd during the concert sequences are unique and grabbing.

TO SIR WITH LOVE (Import)
Director James Clavell captured the 'mod' look of the teenagers in *To Sir with Love* without braying to it, so that their style of dress and attitude does not throw the whole movie into another era. The concerns of the kids, the parents, and the teachers are universal. The success which one teacher, played by Sidney Poitier, has in making a real connection with the students in his class will never cease to be inspiring.

The one aspect of the plot which is obvious now but passed us completely by in our youth is that Poitier's character has no intention of being a teacher (converts are the greatest believers). He takes the position to hold him over and then gets so annoyed when the kids won't respond to him that his emotions take over and he starts teaching on instinct. His performance is so wonderful that no matter how old you are, you feel like one of the students and hold your breath just as they do when he ceremoniously drops the school books in the waste basket and starts talking about life and being an adult.

The print used for the Japanese release has probably been in existence as long as the film itself. The sound is scratchy (the title song is played no less than three times) and the color so faded that only bright colors, such as Lulu's big red earrings, come through. The subtitles are not distracting because one's attention never wanders long enough to look at them.

THE TOAST OF NEW YORK
Frances Farmer stars in *The Toast of New York*. The black-and-white classic, about the New York financial scene in the late 1800s, is a very good movie for several reasons, not the least of which is Farmer's unsettling but captivating performance. The film also stars Cary Grant, and recreates the atmosphere of old New York brilliantly. The plot leans heavily on complex financial maneuvers and is all the better for it. The sound shows its age. The picture is a little soft and has a few discrepancies, but the presentation is satisfying and the movie is intriguing.

TOBY MCTEAGUE
Dog sledding is the subject of *Toby McTeague*. It is filled with clichés which still work and clichés which don't work anymore, as son must earn the respect of scornful father to win the dog sled race save the dog farm. The big race is entertaining and the rest of the movie isn't bad, though it has good intentions and Canadian Broadcasting Corporation written all over it. The sound is monaural, but it feels stereophonic, and the picture is only grainy when the filmmakers themselves start pushing their f-stops.

TOKYO POP
Warner has not digitally encoded the stereophonic *Tokyo Pop*, which may indicate the faith they have in the program. It is about a punk singer who decides moving from New York to Tokyo would be good for her career. She ends up making it big in Japan with syrupy renditions of 'Do You Believe in Magic?' and 'Natural Woman,' and falls in love with the leader of her backup band. True laser disc fanatics, however, may recognize the film as something else – an attempt to adapt a Japanese film genre to attract international audiences. The plot has the same vacant coincidences and hand-holding lust which many Japanese making-it-to-the-top-of-the-charts teen movies are constructed with, and the format is as corny in English as it is in Japanese.

The picture and sound on the disc are acceptable but not exceptional. There are chapter markers, proving that Warners at least looked at the film before releasing it, but unless 'Do You Believe in Magic?' gives you goosebumps, don't expect much.

TOM JONES
Tom Jones disc was a very early release on the Magnetic Video. The colors are so horribly faded in some places that the night scenes are often an impenetrable blur. The sound is equivalently noisy.

The boisterous adaptation of Henry Fielding's 18th-century comic novel has several amusing supporting performances (Albert Finney plays the title character), not the least of which are the antics of Hugh Griffith and Edith Evans. Supporting roles have a tendency to magnify during repeated viewings in the home video environment. Perhaps a whole movie of Evans and Griffith would be more than one could bear, but as it stands, every frame they are in is precious. The break between side one and two helps emphasize a gag.

TOM PETTY: A BUNCH OF VIDEOS AND SOME OTHER STUFF
A bunch of old fashioned music videos and a bunch of amateur rock star filler material are combined in *Tom Petty: A Bunch of Videos and Some Other Stuff.* Stevie Nicks does a duet with Petty in one number and Ringo Starr can be seen pounding on the drums in another, but most of the videos are the sort MTV started out with, mildly conceptual, mildly slick, and easy rolling music with just enough rocking to keep you awake and tapping. The clips vary in picture quality, but the digital stereo sound is consistently strong. The chapter encoding is detailed on the back of the jacket. Side two is in CAV with steady and unsteady still frames dependent upon the type of source material used. The disc runs a few minutes over an hour.

TOO MANY GIRLS
There is a running gag about the beanies which adorn the heads of most of the sorority girls in *Too Many Girls*, a Rodgers and Hart musical set in a college in New Mexico. They can't come out and say it, but they hint loudly enough the girls wearing the beanies are the ones who are still virgins, and when Lucille Ball's character dons one, it is almost in defiance of her true nature. There is a self confidence and a self awareness which runs through all of her pre-TV film roles, and it was a trait which she should have reclaimed when she wanted to revive her career in the seventies.

Desi Arnaz also appears in *Girls*, although after an amusing opening piece the two never interact. Ann Miller appears as well, but only for dancing sequences, in which she is spectacular, as usual. If that isn't enough, the movie also stars Eddie Bracken. Paced by Miller, the dancing scenes are terrific, and the songs aren't bad, either. Ball is too smooth to be funny, but she has an arresting presence and, like the college boys in the movie, you pant longingly every time she's out of a shot and feverishly every time she's in one.

The black-and-white print has a few scattered markings and some shots look worn down, but it generally sharp and free of any significant flaws. The sound is in keeping with recordings of the era and is reasonably clear.

TONY BENNETT SINGS
The picture on *Tony Bennett Sings* comes from a videotape source but it is still blurry and green looking. Bennett's set lasts 50 minutes and takes place before an Edmonton, Alberta audience. He sings songs which we like very much, but he seems to be singing by rote and he never takes command of the tunes. Coming from him, the songs sound bland and uninteresting. He must have left his heart somewhere, because it certainly isn't in his music.

TOP GUN
Some of the impact is lost watching *Top Gun* on a screen which is smaller than the airplanes; you don't quite have that feeling that you're in the air running wingman for the lead jet the way you would in the front row of a big theater. Since the film was not a widescreen production, however, it fits well in the video frame. The picture transfer is spotless, however, and the stereo surround sound is free of distortion. The result has a lot of pizzazz and the disc is a popular demonstrations piece. We found ourselves stopping in the middle of the movie to replay the air sequences two or three times. While this certainly indicates that the film is impressive, it also indicates that the suspense is only fleeting and the ties between one segment and the next are weak.

The disc doesn't have the Pepsi commercial.

TOP HAT
Audiences still applaud and cheer the dance numbers when *Top Hat* plays in revival theaters but a home viewer is not quite as likely to be so demonstratively aroused. Even less arousing is the quality of the master used to press the VidAmerica Classic Series disc release of the Fred Astaire/Ginger Rogers classic. There are probably fewer than a thousand frames in the entire print which do not have some sort of unnatural mark on them. The sound, too, is in poor condition, as if it were emanating from a Victrola instead of a laser player.

The movie is widely considered to be the pair's best effort. It is a sharp mixture of comedy and dance assisted immeasurably by a wacky cast of supporting players.
Rogers gives a performance which has

retained its passion and lust through half a century of changing moral standards.

TOP SECRET! (See **POLICE SQUAD! – HELP WANTED**)

TOPAZ
Alfred Hitchcock filmed three endings for his troubled production of the Leon Uris novel, *Topaz*, and all three appear on the disc. No books written about Alfred Hitchcock go into any detail concerning the alternate endings, and most dismiss the movie entirely, so scholars analyzing the disc will be covering new material. It is the third ending, referred to as the 'European ending' since it is how the film was shown theatrically in Europe, which is the true and most appropriate ending for the film and closest in spirit to the rest of the picture.

The print used for the transfer to disc is in excellent condition and the monaural sound, which has some strength to it during Maurice Jarre's score and also during gunshots, has been CX-encoded.

Hitchcock did not do as bad a job adapting the novel to film as he liked to claim he did. The novel was a breezy best seller which was capitalizing on some inside information about Soviet spies in the French government, taking the easy way out by presenting it in a fictional context.

Hitchcock embellished the drama with dry, dry humor ("Work on this Cross will you – and don't brighten it up too much.") and experiments in storytelling style (a lengthy conversation is shown but, drowned out by street sounds, not heard). At some point he may have realized the movie wasn't working and rushed the completion, but enough of his point of view is present to hold a viewer's imagination, especially on the sobered expectations of multiple viewings.

Side three is in CAV. The trailer has also been included and it contains several shots which did not make the final cut of the film. It is a masterpiece of false hope, shuffling the ponderous 127-minute drama into two minutes of vital excitement.

The standard ending is the second constructed ending and completes the movie on the disc with only the denotation of a change in chapters to identify it. The disc is encoded with markers for the other two endings and for the trailer. The 'preview ending,' which was the first ending Hitchcock tried, is pretty crazy, and is best left as a wacky surprise for those who purchase the disc. The final ending on the disc is the final ending Hitchcock came up with, showing the bad guy (Michel Picolli – the movie has far more good French actors than it has even mediocre American actors) happily flying off to Moscow instead of committing suicide as he does on the standard finale.

TOPLESS DANCING TEXAS STYLE (see **BLONDES VS. BRUNETTES TEXAS STRIP-OFF**)

TOPPER
The first colorization of an old black-and-white movie to be released on laser disc, 3M's Collectible Classic, *Topper*, looked awful. Colorized movies have been moderately popular on video tape, but then video tape has such lousy color, who can tell the difference? Apologists claim that you can turn the color off on your television, but we say keep it till it grows up. Someday, for better or for worse, the process may improve. For now, the system is effective only when the actors remain perfectly still. Perhaps one of the films of Robert Bresson would make a better demo. Here, whenever anything moves, the colors forget for a moment that they are supposed to follow. They aren't the sort of colors you would want to have following you anyway. Flesh isn't an issue. The color people had to work that out before they could start. It is the cars, clothing, and furniture which have been rendered in pastelish olive greens and egg yellows. The sort of colors one expects to find in a sink if one hasn't done the dishes for a while.

TOPPER RETURNS
The Kirbys are nowhere to be seen in *Topper Returns* and we're not just being funny. The ghost in this iteration of the popular series/concept is Joan Blondell, who is 'murdered' early on and then makes Topper (Roland Young) find her murderer. Most of the movie takes place in a mansion with secret passages. It is an entertainment as airy as Blondell's character and well served by a nice transfer. The black-and-white print is in good condition and the sound is CX-encoded. Eddie 'Rochester' Anderson has a substantial part wherein he is called upon to roll his eyes a lot, but if you can stand that, the rest of the movie falls right into place behind it.

TORCH SONG
Torch Song is a very dumb Joan Crawford movie that has been turned into a smart and highly entertaining disc. How did MGM/UA do it? Well, they've utilized nice looking Technicolor source material which has only one major flaw – the blue streaking that is common on a lot of old Technicolor prints. They've given the movie a chapter marker for every camp howler (example: Crawford, in black face, removes her wig with disgust when she sees Michael Wilding's character leaving the theater – Chapter 40) and practically every scene change in the film. For the first half hour the chapter encoding seems to be in a neck-and-neck race with the time code. In all likelihood, the chapter listing on the back of the jacket will help you catch howlers which might otherwise have slipped by unappreciated. They've digitally encoded the monaural sound and preserved for posterity all the really bad songs on the soundtrack (You think 'Tenderly' is a classic? Don't listen too closely to the lyrics – "The trembling trees, embraced the breeze, tenderly..."). And, they've included a fascinating theatrical trailer at the end of the disc, which, while attempting to sell the movie and show the major dramatic moments, steadfastly avoids the central plot device – that Wilding's character is blind.

TORCH SONG TRIOLOGY
When a performer from a stage play has the opportunity to re-create the role from the play on film, it is usually a reliable and entertaining performance, since the subtle pauses and shifts in tone or eyebrow levels have been honed in front of and confirmed by live audiences, sometimes for months on end. Such is the case with Harvey Fierstein in *Torch Song Trilogy*, an episodic drama about the love life of a female impersonator. Fierstein also wrote the piece, which is so refreshingly literate and cleverly constructed that for a while it can seem to do no wrong. The third act sags, perhaps because Fierstein drops the device of shifting between his character's public and private life, but even as one becomes impatient for the film to end, it is a benign impatience.

The picture is too pink, and a bit grainy here and there. The stereo surround sound has been digitally encoded and is the disc's strongest attribute. The musical score is also a lot of fun. The side breaks are an embarrassment. The film runs over two hours and is spread to three sides. The natural blackouts which denote the separations of the 'Trilogy' are ignored, and instead the film is crammed into the first two sides with indiscriminate break points. Side three runs under twenty minutes.

TORCHLIGHT
The topical, well-meaning *Torchlight* is a ragged, whimpering film about marriage, success, and drugs. Drugs, according to the narrative, are not good. The poor, defenseless rich get pulled from the primrose path by associating with that phony upper class pretender, the drug dealer. The badly-transferred disc is a bore and won't be funny, like 'Reefer Madness,' until thirty or forty years from now, when the lifestyles of the characters become as silly as their addictions. The color on the disc constantly washes out and the sound is flat and scratchy. The text on the jacket cover evocatively claims, 'What once was a happy home deteriorates into Lillian's fight to salvage the ruins of her life.' Translated: She tries to get her husband to go to a couple of clinics and when he won't, she leaves him.

TORN CURTAIN
Although the strongest colors tend to blur slightly, the picture transfer of *Torn Curtain* is so compelling that it improves the entire film. There is a scene in which Paul Newman and Julie Andrews are having a tense discussion in a soundstage hotel room with huge ceilings, and on most versions of the film we have viewed, the set looks washed out and phony. On the disc, the walls are richly colored and suddenly Newman and Andrews, instead of being alienated, are dwarfed by their surroundings. The effect gives a dramatic point of view that adds a pawns-in-the-game universality to their predicament. Nothing can solve the script problems in the film's second half, during which the characters run but, despite their experiences, do not develop. The first half, however, is improved considerably, and the moral quandaries really start to take hold.

The sound has no significant problems. Side three of the 129-minute disc is in CAV, with perfect still frames providing a number of opportunities to examine the technical aspects of Alfred Hitchcock's direction. Following the film, an original theatrical trailer appears. Hitchcock is not present in it, but the ad is still a fascinating concoction, blatantly misleading potential viewers into thinking that the film is more exciting and complex than it turns out to be.

TOSCA

The Metropolitan Opera production of *Tosca* is terrific. Giacomo Puccini's rendition of the story about a woman who mistakenly betrays her lover and then murders to protect him is essentially a four-character composition. The principal singers, Placido Domingo, Hildegard Behrens, and Cornell MacNeil, pierce the air with their voices, each distinctly separated and clearly defined. The only fault which is occasionally distracting occurs when a cut brings up a camera angle placing a singer on one side of the screen while the singer's voice is coming from the other side. The picture is unblemished, even when the stage is bathed in orange light.

The stage production was put together by Franco Zeffirelli. It is not as luscious as some of his work, but it has been masterly dramatized without undercutting the musical presentation. Puccini is not a complex composer, and he often goes for the easy payoff instead of exploring a theme for subtler riches. With this production of *Tosca*, it doesn't matter. There is so much talent involved, including the talents of the laser technology, that asking for more would be gluttonous.

The three-act, 127-minute opera fits perfectly on three sides, with every act on a side of its own. The subtitled presentation has been pieced together from two performances at the Met in March of 1985. A booklet which comes with the discs includes the complete libretto in Italian and English, and is printed on *glossy* paper. We are hard-pressed to think of anything they could do to improve the package.

TOTAL RECALL

The marvelously inspired turning point in *Total Recall* – the confrontation with the Rekall psychiatrist – occurs a couple minutes into side two, yet another instance where the side break on a disc presentation reveals the intentions of the filmmakers by making the viewer aware of the scene which has been relegated to the exact middle of a film. The film, most of which takes place on Mars, has many difficult lighting and color effects, and all look stable and free from severe grain. The picture is accurate enough that the best special effects – the crane shots which move from a window of real people, seamlessly, to an unreal landscape panorama – are as striking on the disc as they were in the theater.

There is room for improvement with the stereo surround sound transfer, but for most enthusiasts, the audio will be sufficient. The film has a big budget soundtrack with loads of loud sound effects and a musical score which has been constructed by composer Jerry Goldsmith and mixer Bruce Botnick. On the disc, the separations could be clearer and the explosions could pack even more punch than they do, but it is probably safer to leave it as it is.

The movie was not filmed in a widescreen format. What cropping there is on the video presentation drops no more than a few cute 'future product' background details. The disc has been chapter encoded and there is a listing of the chapters on the back of the jacket, cued to quotations from the film which are really too short to spur one's memory properly.

Keeping in mind that there have only been a handful of great science fiction films, *Total Recall* is a very good science fiction film. It is also a fairly decent action picture, although the chase scenes are less effective on multiple viewings. The much vaunted violence is less gratuitous than it has been made out to be, and is well integrated with the narrative. In this respect, Arnold Schwarzenegger's performance is also a lot more satisfying than was generally acknowledged. He had to combine a very physical role with a shifting personality, while holding onto the audience's sympathies.

TOUCH OF EVIL

The lengthy, clever, complex opening shot in *Touch of Evil* is the kind of spellbinding cinematic moment which makes you want to go out, buy a motion picture camera and a crane, and start filming things. A hand puts a bomb in the trunk of a car, the car starts driving, the car crosses the paths of two pedestrians who are played by famous stars (Charlton Heston and Janet Leigh). Your eyes and your attention race backwards and forwards. Do you follow the stars or the bomb? And there's not a single cut to break your confusion until, boom, the bomb explodes.

Directed by Orson Welles, the film is one moment of high style and scrumptious ingenuity after the next. His blocking of the characters and the camera, so that all circle around one another, creates a visual and thematic macrame of knotted morals and twisted, even lurid, motivations. This is the restored version which runs 108 minutes. The monaural sound comes across like a stiff-plattered LP from the fifties in good condition – clear and crackling.

Finally, the disc contains the theatrical trailer, which is also in good shape. It shows what Universal thought, or didn't think, about the property, in that it emphasizes the heavy sex and violence in the plot. But it has aged well, and shows that even if the company buried the movie when they first released it in 1958, somebody liked it.

TOUCHE ROSS VIDEO TAX GUIDE 1987

The ninety minute *Touche Ross Video Tax Guide 1987*, which comes from a video tape source, has a business world look to it, with accountants who lack strong fashion sense speaking about aspects of tax preparation while their eyes remain glued to a spot significantly left of the camera. The disc is not CX-encoded, but both the picture and the sound can stand up against the average training film without embarrassment.

The *Guide* gives a general summary of the various pathways created by the bureaucratic necessity of paying income taxes. Although some details are dated the show has been designed so that general concepts will remain valid through the passage of time. It is easy to digest, and exposes one to the parameters set by Uncle Sam and the IRS. If there is some aspect to the 1040 form that you have never studied but want to understand better, the program explains things well enough that afterwards you can read the details without getting lost. The most important concept the narrators try to impart is that one should plan ahead. The disc is also tax deductible, unless the IRS catches you showing it at parties.

TOUGH GUYS

The rapport between Burt Lancaster and Kirk Douglas in *Tough Guys* is genuine. It carries the script, which is a slight effort otherwise, and it carries the video disc, despite the screen cropping which turns the film from a Burt Lancaster *and* Kirk Douglas movie into a Burt Lancaster *or* Kirk Douglas movie. Fortunately, the disc has a nice picture and a subdued, but enjoyable, stereo soundtrack.

Lancaster and Douglas portray two hoodlums who have been released from prison after thirty years behind bars. The anachronism jokes are amusing, but the personalities of the pair, who never fit with society to begin with, provide the strongest humor.

TOUGH GUYS DON'T DANCE

Ever sit around a fire and listen to someone spin a tall tale? Watching Norman Mailer's *Tough Guys Don't Dance* is the next best thing. Mailer directed and wrote the screenplay from his novel (though Robert Towne's name appears on the 'thank you's' at the end, and you can bet it wasn't because he loaned the producers a beach house) and he has demonstrated a true fidelity to the breathless plot, bright characterizations and devious humor he concocted for the book. Mailer wrote the book in a rush, to satisfy a contract, and the result is so entertaining one wishes he'd sign a dozen more commitments. He starts with a premise – a man finds two severed heads with his marijuana stash – and then just starts explaining why it happened, as the bodies stack up. Like the menus Gaughin did for the restaurant in Tahiti, or the school song Cole Porter wrote, Mailer doesn't so much lower his standards, he raises the whole genre by dabbling in it.

The film takes place on the tip of Cape Cod and the picture is full of fog, screen doors, and wood grain. It has an inviting warmth, and the transfer is only grainy when the original material is grainy. Mailer uses the whole screen, and so even though the movie has a limited aspect ratio, bodies still get cut off on the edges from time to time. The sound is in stereo and has been digitally encoded, but the mix is not as witty as the rest of the movie.

TOUR OF DUTY
BRAVO COMPANY – TOUR OF DUTY II
THE HILL

What with the violence and the lack of any strong linkage between the beginning, middle, and ending, *Tour of Duty* does not come off like a typical television pilot. Instead, it works quite well as a Vietnam *movie*, not as intense as *Hamburger Hill*, but more mature and sophisticated than the Chuck Norris efforts. It fills in a gap, because you don't have to commit your full concentration to enjoy it and you're not a basket of nerves when it is over, yet it is tightly paced so that there are emotional payoffs at regular intervals. There are transgressions – the bad guys let a good guy escape, allowing him to warn his company about an ambush in the nick of time – but they are carefully rationed.

The disc is 93 minutes long, with a perfect freeze frame break between sides one and two, and could easily have been broken into two separate episodes, the first being an introduction and the second dramatizing the discovery of an enemy tunnel network. The picture transfer is excellent. It has vivid colors and no flaws in the darkness of the night scenes or the tunnel scenes. The sound is digitally encoded, but it is monaural, taking the impact out of the many original rock songs included on the music soundtrack.

Bravo Company – Tour of Duty II is formatted in the guise of a feature for video casettes, but re-divided to an episode a side for the disc. The two episodes, 'Pushin' Too Hard' and 'Under Siege,' are even stronger than the episodes contained in the first *Tour of Duty* disc. In 'Pushin' Too Hard,' a female television reporter joins the troop on recon, to predictable but lively results. 'Under Siege' is superb, concerning a desperate attempt to hold down a base which is about to be overrun by a division of NVA.

The picture image is a little grainy, but passable. The sound, which includes a number of sixties hits ('I'm Your Puppet' is played as the soldiers pose for the TV news camera), is monaural, but verges on the fidelity of a stereo presentation.

The poorly designed jacket cover does not make it clear, but *The Hill*, is actually 'Tour of Duty III,' a combination of two more episodes from the captivating dramatic television series about the war in Vietnam. The two episodes on the new disc, 'Angel of Mercy' and 'The Hill,' are split by the side break, although there is no other denotation to mark where one ends and the next begins. The credits for the two episodes are combined at the end of the program.

'Angel of Mercy' is set in a hospital and mixes intrigue involving a wounded VC colonel with a romance between the lieutenant and a nurse. 'The Hill,' a stronger episode, concerns a pointless mission to take and retake a hill. In a superbly crafted throwaway moment, the entire platoon is exposed to Agent Orange.

As with the earlier discs, the picture is on the grainy side but the monaural sound, which includes a couple of decent oldies elbowing between the pan flutes on the music track, is worth amplifying.

THE TOWERING INFERNO

The all-star, all-spectacle disaster film, *The Towering Inferno*, is available from CBS/Fox as part of the Special Wide Screen Edition series. We don't envy the job which the scenarist had to perform – making the characters interesting enough to suit the billing, keeping the action at a high level, and deciding, very much like God, whom to kill and whom to save. However, in what is physically the middle of the film and dramatically ought to be a major turning point, the script spends an inordinate amount of time with Paul Newman, Jennifer Jones, and two children in a staircase – a drawn out sequence which ends with all four of them essentially back where they started from, and no nearer to safety.

The real test of an actor or actress, however, is not whether they can do 'Hamlet,' but whether they can step into a part such as those offered in *The Towering Inferno* and make an audience care for them (or despise them, in the case of Richard Chamberlain's engagingly spineless villain). The scenes with Newman and Steve McQueen are all too brief, but they are as thrilling as any of the explosions, because the two are true movie stars who need only a high concept to get them started. Thank goodness for the letterboxing, which lets the viewer verify that they were both really on the set at the same time.

The fleshtones sometimes look a half-step too orange and sometimes look a half-step too pale, but never vary enough to make a viewer uncomfortable. More importantly, the orange lighting in the many scenes lit by raging fire never looks distorted or unsteady. The image has an aspect ratio of 2.1:1.

Surround effects are limited primarily to the musical score (which, all things considered, would make great elevator music), sirens and explosions. The film's age also adds a bit of noise to the soundtrack. Still, the big set pieces pack the expected audio punch and certainly will not disappoint those who have turned the volume up.

THE TOXIC AVENGER
THE TOXIC AVENGER (Import)

The R-rated version of *The Toxic Avenger*, available domestically on disc, undercuts much of the film's essential, gory appeal. The title character is a super hero who has been given strength and rendered ugly by chemical wastes. He rips limbs and organs from criminals, but in this version he's grabbing at air. All the good stuff is off screen. Remaining are the sophomoric production values and pre-pubescent humor, neither of which can sustain the entertainment.

The Japanese release is 92 minutes long and restores scenes of graphic violence missing from the 85-minute American disc. It contains more than that, however, since comedy scenes of a low nature which were intended as a substitution for the violence when the film was released in prissy foreign countries have also been tossed in. Hence, the version on the disc is even more complete than the original US theatrical release.

Several of the film's grossest shots are replicated in a negative image on the Japanese disc, but other than that the picture transfer is excellent. The colors are bright and the image is sharp. The monaural sound was in pretty bad shape on the movie and this carries over to both discs, neither of which has been CX-encoded.

TOY SOLDIERS

During a vacation cruise down the coast of Central America, several rich American college kids are captured by Death Squads masquerading as leftist guerrillas in *Toy Soldiers*. The kids who escape put together a commando team and come back to free their friends. Jason Miller and Cleavon Little give the project what little class it has, but the disc is definitely a title best rented and not purchased. In fact, the only reason you may want to pick it up is that after the 85-minute show is over, there is a wonderful, theatrical trailer for another Image release, *Angels Die Hard*. As trailers like this are inevitably better than the actual films, it is almost like getting two shows in one.

TRAFFIC LIVE IN SANTA MONICA

The sound in *Traffic Live at Santa Monica* is monaural and it is a bit tinny – since the recording is live, key riffs are even disrupted by feedback. No matter, the music is relaxed and pleasant. The group's style often ventured away from rock to a sort of improvisational folk/jazz fusion and every number seems stretched a little to make the concert last an hour. The video was directed by Taylor Hackford. There are some primitively colorful distortion effects during one number, but otherwise the cameras remain on the musicians as they play. The picture quality looks aged and blurry, but it is passable.

THE TRAGEDY OF ANTONY & CLEOPATRA (see **JULIUS CAESAR**)

TRAINS JAPAN (Import)

A number of train documentaries are available in Japan. The only one with which we have any direct familiarity is *Trains Japan*. The CAV disc consists of two Japanese passenger train trips, viewed from every imaginable angle. By the end of the disc, almost every aspect of the ride has been captured. Side two, narrated in Japanese, depicts a C61-2. Side one, depicting a C57-135, has no narration.

The disc is older and has a video tape source with an occasionally fuzzy image and a slight greening around the edges. The monaural sound is not CX-encoded but it has a vivid realism. The CAV still frames blur whenever fast movement is involved.

TRANCERS

Trancers is an unintentionally hysterical takeoff on *Blade Runner* and *The Terminator* which has developed something of a cult following among home video enthusiasts. The movie has everything that makes cheap science fiction so enjoyable. It opens with a voiceover, "Last January I finally synged Martin Whistler out in one of the rim planets..." and never lets up. After the budget is sufficiently strained depicting the future, the hero is transported into present-day Los Angeles. The movie is coherent and contains a full-length punk rendition of 'Jingle Bells.'

TRANQUILITY

The 47-minute single-sided CLV disc, *Tranquility* contains three video segments which are each shown three times. The segments: a timelapse record of activity in the sky, a real time view of ocean waves breaking against the shore, and another time-lapse view, of plants growing and flowers blossoming. They are first shown as they were recorded, then they are shown with the colors modified slightly, and then again, with the colors modified greatly. While all this is going on, a digitally recorded digitally encoded synthesizer and light instrumental score plays on the audio. The intention, apparently, is for the viewer to 'hear' the music without hearing it, and to 'see' the video without seeing it, an impetus to keep the TV on at dinner parties.

TRANSMUTATIONS

The Clive Barker/George Pavlou effort, *Transmutations*, has a strong opening. A popular lady of the night is kidnapped by deformed creatures and a tough private detective is hired by a rich industrialist to find her. Like Barker's other efforts, the plot unravels effectively, and if it doesn't quite live up to its promise, it is difficult to imagine how it really could. We never screamed while watching it, but the director kept us on edge most of the time, which is just as unnerving. The stereo effects are limited to the musical score, and the soundtrack has the amount of hiss one would expect from a low budget

British thriller. The quality of the picture is also second rate, but, like the denouement, it doesn't interfere with the spirit of the entertainment.

TREASURE: IN SEARCH OF THE GOLDEN HORSE

The interactive discs available to consumers have so far not amounted to much, but *Treasure: In Search of the Golden Horse* is one of the best examples of how entertaining interactive discs can be. You really do 'play' with the disc, freezing frames for clues, suppressing one audio channel to examine the emphasis of certain narrative passages, jumping backward and forward with random access to put clues together, or speeding up the picture to see images more clearly. You may even find yourself adjusting the color controls of your television set to flush out camouflaged forms.

'Treasure' is the name of a horse owned by a girl whose father makes a golden statuette, also of a horse, called 'Somewhere.' The statuette and the horse disappear on a dark, threatening night and the girl spends a good portion of her life searching for Treasure, somewhere. A golden horse with a guaranteed $500,000 attached to it is buried somewhere in the United States, et cetera, and clues revealed on the disc are supposed to lead you to it.

Although the prize was found, belatedly, the disc's appeal remains. There are clues in practically every frame. You have to listen for homonyms (sea/see/C, tea/T, et cetera), look for polynyms (letter/letter, degree/degree), and be on the alert for the slightest multiplicity of meaning. There is also the recurring appearance of a black bird. At one point the bird can be glimpsed in a trunk at the house to the Keeper of the Maps. The Keeper of the Maps is played by Elisha Cook, Jr., who had a major role in *The Maltese Falcon*. This is the, uh, stuff dreams are made of.

THE TREASURE OF THE SIERRA MADRE

We have never seen the CBS/Fox version of *The Treasure of the Sierra Madre*, but it cannot have been all that good because the 126-minute film was released on a single platter. Not so with the MGM/UA release which properly separates the movie onto three sides. The disc looks great, with no flaws to speak of save for a slight jitter in the picture near the end of side one. The sound is of standard quality for its age.

The black-and-white film, about prospectors who suffer a change in disposition when they discover gold, is an uncompromising classic. Because of its downbeat theme, it is more enjoyable on multiple viewings than on the first run through, but that is all the more reason to install it in your library. Walter Huston's performance is ceaselessly pleasing, and his presence is the primary factor which will draw viewers back to the movie again and again. As the spunky geezer who leads his two partners to riches, he is comical, biting, and compellingly wise. Tim Holt's personality transition is subtle and intriguing. Only Humphrey Bogart seems to take his mood changes as terraces instead of inclines, and only because he is a star does one tolerate it so readily. The film has a wonderful sense of adventure, of sending the heroes out to a conceivably remote geographical location and then grinding down their facades as they return. Also worth noting is Max Steiner's memorable score, which almost seems out of place in the dust and the grit, but its sweetness continually cues the viewer to maintain sympathy for the heroes.

A TREE GROWS IN BROOKLYN

The print used for *A Tree Grows in Brooklyn* is not pristine, but the scratches and age marks seem to evoke the mood of the film. The black-and-white picture always looks a little washed out, and always has a spot or a speckle somewhere, but none of the flaws overwhelm the presentation. As with a number of Elia Kazan's films, the narrative is more important than the image anyway. There are almost no closeups on objects or other attempts to tell the story in visual terms. It is all dialog and character blocking.

The story, however, is a guaranteed tear-jerker, and advances smoothly from giving details about life in the days when a dime could buy ten things to creating a complex interplay between a number of memorable and touching personalities. The film runs more than two hours and the disc is extended to three sides. The time works emotionally on the viewer, giving the goals and concerns of the characters a real chance to take root. The disc has a decent number of chapter markers, and digital sound which should be held to minimum amplification.

TREMORS

The witty and ingenious *Tremors* makes wonderful home video. It is about monster worm things which terrorize an isolated community in the Southwest. The picture is a little pale, but acceptable, and the sound is great fun. With enjoyable characters, monsters which have logical flaws that the heroes can take advantage of, and sufficient special effects to get the point across, the PG-13 movie is full of amusing thrills and attentive scares.

THE TRIAL/MR. ARKADIN (Import)

Two films by Orson Welles which were made in Europe under shoestring conditions have been released as a double bill on disc in Japan, *The Trial/Mr. Arkadin*. The movies ought to show up domestically someday, but we couldn't wait that long. Welles is a magician, and he can create spellbinding entertainment on miniscule budgets while other filmmakers expend far more and achieve much less.

The disc comes in a gatefold jacket with each film on its own platter. They are monaural and not CX-encoded. The films are in English, and Japanese subtitles sometimes get in the way of the visuals. Both prints are in pretty bad condition, with splices and crackles throughout, but then it is our understanding that both movies were in almost that condition when they were made.

The disc presentation intends that they be watched in the order identified by the title, since the second platter is marked as 'side 3' and 'side 4,' but having seen both films before, we preferred to watch them in reverse sequence, since the ending of 'The Trial' is meant to be savored and not superseded by more entertainment.

It is said that Orson Welles' *Touch of Evil* is the ultimate 'B movie,' and if that is the case, then 'Mr. Arkadin' is the ultimate 'C movie.' Cinematically, it is fully captivating, with indulgent, eye-popping camera angles and fantastic sound editing. (Paul Misraki's score is also super.) The story, written by Welles, is legitimate, a twisting crime thriller involving a multi-millionaire, his daughter, and a Wellesian vagabond. The film had various running times, and this version logs in at 92 minutes.

The film often appears to be held together, however, by broken strings. When you see it in a theater, you expect the film to slip its sprockets and start burning at any moment. When you see it on disc, you keep expecting it to freeze or skip. There will be a brilliantly conceived sequence, then a horrible, jarring cut and some quick dialog advancing the story six months, and then another brilliant sequence. Welles's laziness, or his inability to see a project through to completion, is most evident in a film like this, yet we would have been quite happy if he had only made a dozen more, equally squalid and equally inspired.

'The Trial,' which Welles made in 1962 with Tony Perkins as Joseph K., is also a piecemeal effort. Sadly, Welles' mastery of sound had also fallen to the wayside by then, and the actors don't even seem to interrupt each other as much.

The movie, however, is still a masterpiece, since its condition works in its favor – after all, if it's Cinemascope and stereophonic sound, it isn't going to be Kafka. Welles keeps Perkins remarkably calm throughout the film, and he interprets the story properly, letting it ravel and unravel without a crescendo. Again, there are some brilliant sequences, including a vision of a gigantic office which puts the multi-million dollar *Brazil* to shame. On the whole, the film works because its subject is so accommodating to gaps in logic. The more you have to strain to understand what is happening to K., the more you are on his side.

TRIBUTE TO JOHN COLTRANE

Subtitled, 'Select Live Under the Sky '87 10th Special,' *Tribute to John Coltrane* features Wayne Shorter and Dave Liebman on saxophone, Richie Beirach on piano, Eddie Gomez on bass and Jack DeJohnette on drums. Their evocation of Coltrane's music is nicely executed, and the digital recording captures clear, airy tones which are well suited for digitally encoded stereo playback. The stage is very dark, and some colored lighting effects look grainy, but the picture is usually sharply detailed when illuminated. The video director, Kaname Kawachi, has a good eye, and uses the camera angles to enhance the essence of the performers and their music. The hour long concert was taped in Japan in 1987.

TRINITY IS STILL MY NAME
(see **THEY CALL ME TRINITY**)

THE TRIP TO BOUNTIFUL

Geraldine Page's consummate performance in *The Trip to Bountiful* is certainly the main attraction of the laser disc, but there is another advantage to the film which has not been as widely promoted. The narrative is based on a play about an elderly woman who sneaks away from her son and daughter-in-law to take a bus trip (she pays in pennies) to the house where she grew up. Unlike the majority of contemporary plays, there are no shocking revelations about any of the major characters to move the story along. No hidden secrets or perverse revelations about small town life. That is what makes it such a pleasant movie to watch.

In opening up the play, the filmmakers have done an enchanting job of capturing the topography of the Texan Gulf coast. In the final shot, as a car drives away from the dilapidated homestead, it dips up and down as it crosses the rolling fields. You realize that thousands of years earlier, the land was beach and dunes.

TROLL
The stereo sound in *Troll* has no surprises, but it isn't bad. Neither is the movie, which wastes no time in getting started and mixes comedy, horror, and special model effects in moderate doses. It is about a sorceress and a boy battling a troll who has taken the boy's sister and is spawning baby trolls all over the place. All of the action takes place within an apartment building. The picture is cheap looking, but unaffected by the laser presentation.

TRON (Import)
TRON
Anyone who has ever worked in data processing will appreciate *Tron*, a Walt Disney film which combines live action and computer animation to depict an anthropomorphic journey through the logic circuits of a computer. And anyone who has ever seen *Tron* on home video will appreciate the Japanese release, which is letterboxed and digitally encoded.

The domestic Disney release is in stereo, but has CX-encoding with manual tripping. The movie has some tough picture transfer problems – glowing red and blue lights which are deliberately fuzzy. The domestic transfer was adequate in handling the problems and looked impressive during sequences involving solid colors.

Tron, however, is significantly damaged when the sides of the image are cropped. The Japanese release has an aspect ratio of about 2:1, and the additional picture information consistently adds to the film's appeal. One of our favorite matte shots, of a vast labyrinth of office cubicles, is completely lost on the domestic version, and we were excited to see it restored on the Japanese.

The picture transfer on the Japanese release is stronger, but the fuzzy parts are still fuzzy. The print also has a few speckles on it. Japanese subtitles appear beneath the letterboxed image, and the disc has 20 chapter markers. The digitally encoded stereo surround sound is also improved over the domestic release.

The film's visual metaphors are beautifully executed – shots of the 'real world' are made to look like silicon chip patterns, and the world inside the computer, depicted with computer animation, is visualized using the descriptive metaphors that programmers and technicians often employ when speaking about hardware or software components. The easiest way to describe the interaction of computer programs is to use the terms of human interaction. The filmmakers take this a step further and depict the programs as humans, adding metaphysics by having the programs speak of their users as 'gods.' Since the basic suspense adventure plot is successful, the film is both entertaining and thought provoking. (In the real world, however, a much lower opinion of users is the norm.)

TROUBLE IN MIND
Although *Trouble in Mind* has some cult popularity, it is a lousy movie, where every offbeat narrative step leaves one feeling either bad or indifferent. The disc has a quality stereo soundtrack which includes several Marianne Faithful numbers and a mild, jazzy score. Director Alan Rudolph has collected a fairly interesting cast, but the script is a jumble of deliberately impressionistic ideas which never coagulate into a feasible concept. The picture, deliberately foggy because it's taking place near the water, is foggier still because of the transfer.

THE TROUBLE WITH ANGELS
What a shame Hayley Mills doesn't work any more. It is always nice when you can see an actor or an actress, like a friend, grow from childhood to maturity. *The Trouble with Angels* was a typical Mills vehicle from the early sixties. Although it is about girls in a Catholic boarding school and falls just short of being a recruiting film for cloisterhood, it enjoyed great popularity and spawned a couple of sequels.

The print is worn and faded. The musical score, by Jerry Goldsmith, contains flashes of the brilliance which radiates steadily from his later work. Had Mills stuck around, the same might have happened with her.

THE TROUBLE WITH HARRY
A comic parable about impotence, *The Trouble With Harry* is a relaxed and charming Alfred Hitchcock film concerning a corpse repeatedly uncovered by those who are trying to bury it. The disc is in perfect condition and the sound, although primitive by today's standards, is captured with such clarity that whispers never intended for the audience's ears come through loud and clear (fortunately, the actors remain in character).

Jerry Mathers, in his one other claim to fame, portrays the four-year-old who discovers the body. Shirley MacLaine, in her first film role, portrays the boy's mother. Edmund Gwenn, as a retired sea captain, believes the corpse was murdered and John Forsythe (looking very much like Bogart, his character's name is Sam Marlow) portrays an artist who helps everyone cover and uncover Harry.

Filmed in the New England autumn, the movie is as light as a fallen leaf, but if Hitchcock had not maintained the correct balance between humor, romance, and black comedy, the entertainment could have deteriorated rapidly. Movies where characters do not respond directly to what is in front of them always disturb audiences a little. Less troublesome is Bernard Herrmann's whimsical score, and airy touches such as a closet door that won't stay still.

Hitchcock is best known for his suspense films, but that was not the limit to his talents. He made several comedies and one, *Rich and Strange*, was similar in tone to *The Trouble with Harry*. In both, he may have been looking towards Shakespeare's 'The Tempest' for inspiration, searching for a view of old age which reconciles the disappointments of life with the magical beauty of living. A character in *Harry* reads from a Shakespeare sonnet as he trips over the corpse, "Let me not to the marriage of true minds admit impediments." It was the first time we realized that 'admit' not only means 'to allow in,' it also means 'to tell the truth.'

TRUE BELIEVER
James Woods plays a liberal lawyer who wears his hair like Tom Paine (and whose office is in the same building where Paine died) in an enjoyable courtroom drama, *True Believer*. It is amusing to note that in both the artwork and the publicity stills on the jacket cover, the full extent of Woods' coiffure is hidden. Woods' performances are erratic. In some films he is quite good, but in others he is too out of control and becomes a parody of his better self. As the burnt-out lawyer who comes alive again when he takes on the retrial of a decade old case, his courtroom scenes are too exaggerated, even for his supposedly fiery character, but away from the docket he gets a much better handle on the personality he is inhabiting. The denouement is also reasonably clever, so much so that we wish more time had been allocated to unraveling the mystery.

Most of the fleshtones and a lot of other objects are too orange on the disc, though the intensity of the error changes from scene to scene. The picture only becomes grainy where there is strong illumination. The stereo surround sound is effective and has no significant problems. The side change needlessly breaks up a scene, but it works better than it ought to.

TRUE BLOOD
The colors are pale and the sound is weak on *True Blood*, but the fault is more with the original production than with the source material or transfer. The narrative moves at an admirable pace. The story is about a young man who returns to his neighborhood after an absence of ten years and tries to retrieve his younger brother from the influence of nasty gang leader. Although scar makeup has been applied a little too liberally, the characterizations are fresh and entertaining. In addition, the action sequences are uncomplicated, but effective.

TRUE LOVE
There are two kinds of weddings in America, normal weddings and New York weddings. For those who have never had the privilege of attending the latter, its essence is captured in full flower on *True Love*. The movie, directed by Nancy Savoca, is as much a cultural document as it is a clever little comedy. The humor is subtle and bittersweet, and at the end the young groom's budding alcoholism is as strong as his budding sense of responsibility. The film is not for everyone, because it is so close to reality that some viewers will feel there are not enough barriers between the fiction and themselves. It is wildly humorous, but only in its juxtaposition of the absurdities which dog all weddings ("...And this is for the ushers. Some nice Christ heads.") Some people will watch the disc without ever cracking a smile.

The film was made on a low budget and the production standards are commensurate with the investment. The stereo surround sound is great fun, but it has a lot of hiss, so it is best when the hiss is part of the environment, such as during the awful reception band's rendition of 'Celebration.' The picture transfer is fine.

TRUE STORIES
We kept on expecting David Byrne to break into a chorus of 'Won't You Be My Neighbor' during *True Stories*, his musical look at real life (as he imagines it) in a smallish Texas community. This is one of those movies where friends glancing at it over your shoulder will comment that it is stupid and you will be hard pressed to explain why it is not, even though you may be enjoying it. The music is by Byrne's group, The Talking Heads, and this helps the film immeasurably. There is a tendency while watching it to wait patiently for the next song, abiding the comical vignettes without taking them too seriously. One's speakers go limp during these interludes and only stand up straight again when the next musical number starts. The picture transfer is acceptable, although the darker scenes are slightly grainy.

Byrne's visual approach is more noticeable on a compact TV screen than it would be in a theater. The vanishing point is always in the exact middle of the screen, and the horizon on his outdoor shots always cuts the screen in a perfect half. This concept is an adequate representation of his filmmaking efforts since it is impossible to tell whether he is being simplisiticly obvious or subtly subversive.

TRUE WEST
The transfer of *True West* looks okay. Recorded on video tape, it arrives on disc without too many impurities. The stereo sound is still a little noisy, and the image could have been sharper, but there is nothing in the presentation to distract one from enjoying the program. We have a soft spot for plays recorded for video. Usually the disc costs less than the price of two tickets, and the presentation always shows the performance in its best light. Uninhibited by an audience, the actors get a break between takes and can chance things they could never master consistently.

As one marvelous, circular, dizzy camera shot in the last act shows, *True West* was filmed on a four-wall set. It is not a good play and confirms the adage that writers should not write about writing. It is about two brothers trying to write a movie script, and how they smash up the furniture and each other instead. This is an amusing symbol for the angst of the creative process, but it doesn't stop the psychology of the characters from appearing empty and the dialog from seeming forced. Nevertheless, even bad plays are fun to watch when decent actors are involved, and that is the case here. Both John Malkovich and Gary Sinise have a great time with the material, and their earnest pleasure will infect the viewer.

TUCKER: THE MAN AND HIS DREAM
TUCKER: THE MAN AND HIS DREAM (Import)
Francis Coppola's movie for people who love World's Fairs, *Tucker: The Man and His Dream*, is available as a scanned and cropped domestic disc and as a letterboxed import.

On Paramount's domestic renditon, Vittorio Storaro's complex cinematography, with subtle orange and blue washes and enthusiastically tricky lighting, has been transferred carefully, but excessive graininess in the image, particularly during the second half of the film, deflates the value of the disc. The stereo sound is more consistent, and, as with every Coppola picture, it is a work of art on its own.

The Japanese version is letterboxed, at about 2:1, still a little cropped from the original Technovision aspect ratio. Japanese subtitles appear beneath the picture. Comparing the two discs reveals that Paramount did more than just scan and crop the presentation. In instances where graphics or text appeared on the screen, the image is judiciously squeezed to take it all in.

The picture quality of the Japanese print, however, is clearly inferior to the American effort. Storaro's most exaggerated effects, which came out a bit murky on Paramount's version, don't stand a chance on the Japanese disc, where even scenes which take place in the bright daylight without any filter effects at all look pale and mis-colored. The sound quality is the same on both discs.

There is a wonderful scene in *Tucker*, the sort one remembers forever even if one sees the movie only once, of a boy and his father meeting Howard Hughes in a dark echoey hanger which is holding the Spruce Goose. Although the movie is about the father, the brilliance of it, along with Dean Stockwell's marvelous cameo turn as Hughes, was to include the boy. His presence encourages the viewer to approach the entire scene with a juvenile awe which might have been lost had just the two men played it alone.

Unfortunately, Coppola didn't have enough ideas like that to sustain the film. Stylistically, the story-telling is brilliant. Coppola uses blocking and transition techniques, which he has been developing over the past couple of decades, that no other filmmaker has even thought to copy. The film is about a maverick businessman who attempts to construct and sell an automobile, but is ultimately defeated by a conspiracy involving the established car manufacturers and the politicians they support. The parallels to the plight of Coppola's own filmmaking ventures are obvious, and the filmmakers, including George Lucas who served as Executive Producer, made a mistake by using the material to make a message instead of a movie. The movie remains a systematically depressing experience, and the joys it has to offer diminish significantly with every viewing.

After the Japanese disc is ended, there is a seven minute interview with Coppola and Lucas, as well as shots of the film in production, in ultra-vivid video which makes the colors, especially after the Japanese transfer, startling. Coppola and Lucas have fascinating things to say about the roots of the film and about their relationship with one another, but all you will remember afterwards is how shiny all the cars looked.

TUFF TURF
The first pressing of *Tuff Turf* was in extremely bad condition, although a subsequent run was much cleaner. The story is a formula concoction with the requisite amount of fights, flash, and flesh. A 'new kid' gets beat up a couple of times, but ends up winning the girl and wasting the heavy. The details lack the rudiments of logic, but the movie is as entertaining as could be expected. *Tuff Turf* opens with a trailer for *Lust in the Dust*.

TUNE-UP A.V. (Import)
The Japanese import *Tune-Up A.V.* begins with elaborate but understandable diagrams to adjust the picture and sound on one's audio-video system. The ideal settings for images such as color bars are shown in photographs on the disc jacket. Included with the disc is a blue filter one can hold up to one's eyes to fine tune the color separations and intensities even more.

After all that business is dispensed with, the half hour single sided disc takes one on a trip by land, sea and air, to the thrill of surround sound and a the-window-pane-is-missing picture. There is a steam train, replete with a whistle, fireworks which seem to burst inside you, a hair-raising motor boat ride up a river gorge, a slightly calmer interlude with waterfalls, and then a landing-the-Sony-Company-jet finale. The disc is so perfectly mastered that you can turn the volume up as loud as you dare without distorting the playback. Let the neighbors think someone has placed railroad tracks in their backyard.

THE TUNNEL
The Spanish production, *The Tunnel*, is a ridiculous romance, about a painter who gets upset because his girlfriend won't give him straight answers. The stars, Jane Seymour and Peter Weller, speak ineptly-written English dialog, while many others are dubbed. The picture is grainy and pale. The Ultra-Stereo sound is fuzzy and muted. The film ends with Weller's insipid voice-over narration stating, "In the time that I have been locked away I have often tried to reason why the blind man's last cry was, 'Senseless!' but a great fatigue or maybe a dark instinct always prevents me from pursuing it." We'll pursue it for him. The blind man was referring to the movie itself.

TURANDOT
Giacomo Puccini's finest accomplishment, *Turandot*, is performed in the gargantuan Arena di Verona. The opera, Puccini's last effort, is perhaps the only work in which he successfully utilizes his infectious melodies to build a complex and sweeping musical structure. It is made all the more powerful by the fact that Puccini had not finished the opera when he died; 'potential' becomes one more of the many attributes one can assign to its strength.

The Arena adds problems to the sound recording which some may find disturbing. The outdoor amphitheater does not have the acoustics amenable to technological perfection. The way to enjoy the performance on Turandot is to accept the spirit of the presentation. If Ghena Dimitrova's high notes get lost in the night air and masonry, one can readily imagine how it would have sounded in an enclosed, polished wood and velvet opera house. The weakness of Ivo Vinco's Timur, however, is also compromised, and therefore enhanced, by the public address nature of the acoustics. The orchestra, which must have been closest to the microphones, sounds just fine.

The other problem with the Arena is that, although it makes for a scrumptious center still in Pioneer's double sleeved jacket, it is impossible to film effectively for video. Either the shots have such a wide angle that the players are dots themselves, or the angle is so close that you lose all sense of the theatrics surrounding the principal characters. The quality of the image is very good when the camera is close enough that you can see something. The 115-minute show has been spread to three sides so each act can be resident on a separate side. A plot synopsis and Italian/English libretto, graced with a pair of equally scrumptious black and white stills, is included with the disc.

TURANDOT
The spectacle of Giacomo Puccini's *Turandot*, as interpreted by Franco Zeffirelli and the Metropolitan Opera, is almost too much to squeeze onto a TV screen. Usually, opera programs can get away with one establishing shot to let the viewer ogle the set and then proceed with closeups and group shots of the singers as they go about their business. But this version of *Turandot* is so elaborate that no camera angle can do it justice – the long shots lose too much detail and the closer shots crop too much. Nevertheless, the image transfer, from a video tape source, is excellent. A scene which most discs would botch, where the stage is bathed in blue lighting and three singers are illuminated by subtle white key lights, hasn't even a hint of distortion. Black backgrounds remain solid black and every sequin on every costume is in clear, colorful focus.

Zeffirelli's set designs are more Cantonese than Mandarin, but such are the pleasures of operatic license. The sets and costumes are so opulent that the disc would be worth watching even if the audio did not work, though with noise-free digital stereo sound, the audio works quite well. As is often the case in a live performance, the orchestra is miked better and balanced better than the singers. Placido Domingo's performance loses the most in this environment, though the audience is still quite pleased with his work. Eva Marton and Leona Mitchell survive the transfer better and give exceptional performances. The program is in every way superior to the Arena di Verona rendition.

The three-sided disc, broken up an act to a side, comes in a box. The opera is in Italian and has English subtitles. The disc has chapter markers which are coordinated with an extensive plot synopsis, to be found on a printed insert. A lengthy essay also appearing on the insert provides an excellent summary of the creation and structure of the opera.

THE TURN OF THE SCREW
'The Innocents' it isn't, but Petr Weigl's film of Benjamin Britten's opera, *The Turn of the Screw*, has several positive aspects. Britten's fascinating score (everybody, appropriately, likes to refer to it as 'haunting') is effectively presented by the studio recording. Close attention to the piano passages will reveal the limitations of the soundtrack, but the full impact in the most dramatic moments is moving and adds to the emotions of the music. The major parts are sung (in English) by one set of performers (including Helen Donath, who leaves room for improvement, and Robert Tear, who is very effective) and acted by another set (they appear to be Hungarian). Tight-lip synchronization is dispensed with, but the voices never seem out of place with the faces, only out of time.

The print has a few speckles, but is in passable condition. The opera, clearly, would be more effective on the stage, where the director would be forced to use other tricks besides editing to facilitate the appearances and disappearances of the ghosts. But Weigl is appropriately conscious of matching his camera shots to Britten's musical ideas, and simply observing the images enhances one's awareness of the music.

Although the program runs less than two hours, it has been spread to three sides and released in a box jacket. This would enable logical side breaks, but Britten's tightly woven (almost literally, since his music follows a 'screw' motif) score is difficult to interrupt at any point. A plot synopsis effectively describes Britten's overriding structure as well as the details of Myfanwy Piper's libretto. The synopsis is included on a jacket insert, along with an essay which goes into good detail about the opera's creation and strategies. The essay also explains that Britten ingeniously emphasized a gay subtext in the story, which adds to the drama's tension. Weigl magnifies this further, and it works well, but his failure to provide the governess with an equally clear turmoil leaves the disc more compelling as a musical program than as a cinematic accomplishment.

TURN OF THE SCREW/CARMILLA
Two of Shelley Duvall's hour-long Nightmare Classics, originally produced for the Showtime cable network, have been issued on a single disc, *Turn of the Screw/Carmilla*, conveniently positioning one episode on each side. The programs are mildly stereophonic, primarily on the music tracks. The picture on 'Carmilla' (which is actually on side one) is a little over-saturated, and reds tend to look fuzzy. 'Turn of the Screw' (on side two) is in better shape, with no major irregularities.

Both episodes are rather enjoyable. 'Carmilla' is an erotic vampire story, based on a tale by Sheridan Le Fanu. Set in the Old South, the feature's one failing is a lack of dialect or accents in the dialog. Meg Tilly is a vampire who seduces the daughter of a lonely plantation owner. There is just the right amount of flesh, blood, and moody romanticism, and Roddy McDowall (the only one who manages an accent) even pops up as a vampire fighter.

Amy Irving is pleasantly unnerving as the uptight governess in 'Turn of the Screw.' The script tends to be less ambiguous than it might have been, but the execution is effective even though the resolution is anticlimactic.

TURNER AND HOOCH
About one quarter of *Turner and Hooch* is taken up with the murder mystery and about three quarters of it is taken up by the domestic situation comedy depicting the fastidiously neat Turner, played by Tom Hanks, trying to cope with having inherited Hooch, a jumpy, slobbering de Bordeaux. The film's marketing was clever, selling the movie as a cross between *K-9* and *Big*, but it was also misleading since the film is nothing like that at all. It is more like *The Odd Couple* with growling and woofing in the place of witty repartee.

The picture is crisp and the colors are accurate from beginning to end. The stereo surround sound is also in good shape, although the sound editing it not very creative.

TURTLE DIARY
From a story by Russell Hoban, script by Harold Pinter, and direction by John Irvin, *Turtle Diary* is a quiet, intelligently funny, felt sketch of life. If you describe the narrative, which is incidental to becoming friends with the characters for 90 minutes, then your real friends' eyes will glaze over as you start to tell them it is about kidnapping turtles from the London Zoo. It isn't really.

The transfer is sloppy. The picture is speckled and the sound crackles with steady intensity. The stereo mix is earnest and charming, as is the movie if you aren't expecting much.

12 ANGRY MEN
If *12 Angry Men* hadn't been released by Voyager as part of their Criterion Collection, we probably wouldn't have paid much attention to the break in continuity which comes near the end of the film on side two. Other than that flaw, the transfer is excellent and the rich contrasts within each image are captivating. But the question which arises is, if this is a Criterion Collection title, why didn't someone find an alternate source to fill the break in the film, which interrupts the coherence of a significant dramatic speech?

12 Angry Men makes a wonderful home video experience not just because the plot is amenable to multiple viewings, but because the acting is so thoroughly involving. The casting is magnificent. Almost every one of the minor names in the group went on to establish an admirable career. Audiences which saw the film when it first opened could not possibly appreciate the presence of Martin Balsam, Jack Klugman, Robert Webber, or Jack Warden the way viewers do today. Their established personalities enrich the unspoken parts of their characters. Perhaps the best is Lee J. Cobb, who looks like a Rambo doll which has melted in the sun.

The disc has been given chapter markers. The black-and-white picture is bright and for the most part unblemished. The sound has not been CX-encoded, but is reasonably free of noise. The volume levels, however, fluctuate considerably in a couple of places.

THE TWELVE CHAIRS
Mel Brooks's Jewish folk tale exercise, *The Twelve Chairs*, was a significant confidence-builder in his career, although in retrospect one wishes he had concentrated more on the folk precedents within the story and less on the silly tomfoolery which later became the emphasis of his films. The colors are much better than in the stills on the back of the jacket.

TWELVE O'CLOCK HIGH
In reality, *Twelve O'Clock High* has very little to do with airplanes. It is about management, about the steps a base commander, played by Gregory Peck, takes to restore dis-

cipline in his bombing squadrons. Lip service is given in the beginning to the horror and mutilation caused by warfare, and viewers starved for action are treated to real footage of American and German aircraft engaging in battle near the end, but the bulk of the 134-minute film is a step by step lesson in exercising command. It is so entertaining that the film would make a good stage play.

The three-sided disc is in CLV. The black and white print seems to change tone from time to time, even when documentary footage is not involved. Otherwise, it is in good shape, as is the sound.

25X5 THE CONTINUING ADVENTURES OF THE ROLLING STONES

Our entire life passed before our ears as we watched *25x5 The Continuing Adventures of the Rolling Stones*. The 130-minute three-sided program is a documentary which traces the history of the Stones' successes, and as it moved from year to year with clips and music bites, so too did our own memories. It is likely that anyone who has owned a radio for the past 25 years will probably have the same experience watching the disc.

As is indicated in the title, the group has more than a century and a quarter of rock and roll between them. There are often voiceover interruptions during the songs, but it quickly becomes apparent that the songs are so familiar you can listen to them elsewhere if you have to hear them. The show, which was made with the cooperation of most of the band members, has no real focus. Some albums and tours are described in detail, others are ignored. Some scandals are broached, others are forgotten. Although the narrative is linear, the chronology is sometimes jumbled for the sake of the story. The overall impact of the program, however, is favorable and informative, showing the development of both the group and the major pop music fads.

Some clips are shown in full, the most impressive of which are incredibly fresh and vivid color shots from 'The Ed Sullivan Show' in 1966. Keith Richards gives the best interviews. As we have noted on other programs, Richards' demeanor is sometimes a bit flaky, but his comments are always wise and insightful. His description of the events which led to writing 'Sympathy for the Devil' is marvelous.

Because the disc is broken into three sides, it is easy to mark the chronology and see that the Stones greatest glories came early on, however long they have lingered in the rock 'n' roll spotlight. The source material varies in quality but it is often very good and the transfer looks fine. The stereo sound is at the mercy of the original recordings and never has too great a punch.

2010 (see **2001: A SPACE ODYSSEY**)

TWENTY THOUSAND LEAGUES UNDER THE SEA
TWENTY THOUSAND LEAGUES UNDER THE SEA (Remastered)
TWENTY THOUSAND LEAGUES UNDER THE SEA (Import)

Walt Disney's interpretation of the Jules Verne classic, *Twenty Thousand Leagues under the Sea*, a popular title among laser disc owners, has been released in letterboxed format and digitally encoded sound in Japan.

The disc looks terrific and is a thrilling accomplishment. Like so many widescreen adventure films, *Twenty Thousand Leagues under the Sea* has, in the past, seemed boring and trivial when shown on television. The reason for that is 1) only half the screen was available to the television viewer, and 2) the tricky lighting in the underwater sequences disintegrates in home video.

The Japanese disc solves both these problems. The aspect ratio of the picture is about 2.2:1, bringing most of the Cinemascope image into view. The director, Richard Fleischer, and the cinematographer, Franz Planer, always utilize the full screen in their shot compositions. Sometimes objects will be placed in the foreground on one side of the screen, to enhance the appearance of depth. Many times the actors in the cast will be grouped in three's, and even when they are not, some kind of activity or object always seems to be present in a far corner of the screen. In addition, both the submarine and the giant squid are seen in shots where their horizontal figures are fully boxed by the rectangular screen. How threatening can the squid be if you don't see his head and his arms at the same time?

Twenty Thousand Leagues under the Sea was released twice in the US by Walt Disney. The first version of the 127-minute film was time-compressed onto a single platter and was a pathetic disc. The second version, currently in release though often difficult to come by, was substantially improved. The colors, though not as accurate as those on the new Japanese version, look good. The print has a number of speckles and the sound is analog bound, but it is a passable presentation for those who can tolerate the cropping.

On the letterboxed version, the tighter picture image adds to its sharpness, but even without that factor the basic picture transfer is excellent. The most intense colors never become blurry, and the underwater scenes never become a problem. The fleshtones, and the brass and velvet of the submarine's interior, all look accurate.

There is not much difference between the analog and digital audio tracks. The stereo and surround separations on the film itself are intermittent, though occasionally a voice will come from the far starboard or port. The sound recording is from 1954, and has the impurities which one would associate with its age. On the whole, it could stand to have more thrust, but it gets the job done without upsetting things.

The three-sided disc comes in a gatefold jacket. Side three only runs a quarter of an hour, but is in CLV. The jacket art is marvelous, full of great stills. A two foot by two foot pinup of the Nautilus blueprints comes with the disc, making the package an exciting treat even before one puts the first platter in a player.

The program is in English. Japanese subtitles appear in the black band beneath the letterboxed image and can easily be blocked from sight. The disc also has a number of chapter markers.

It is interesting to compare the performances of Kirk Douglas, Peter Lorre, and James Mason. Douglas gives a Disney-styled, exaggerated performance, while Mason refuses to, creating a contrast between them which is advantageous to their roles in the film. Lorre, who was rarely in top form during the fifties, plays himself instead of his character, and while, technically this may be faulty, his presence provides the kind of balance to Douglas that Mason cannot give. Lorre's scenes are consistently entertaining and, in a way, he rescues the film.

Like most fifties science fiction efforts, *Twenty Thousand Leagues under the Sea* has a number of flaws, but like all the best laser disc transfers, the flaws in the film don't matter – in watching the disc you can understand what first attracted fans to the movie. And fans continue to be attracted. Disney liked to open and close his adaptations of classic stories with the image of a book, opening to the first page at the beginning, and shutting on the words, 'The End.' Some people may worry about the effect home video is having on today's youth, but we are unconcerned. When a very young friend who watched the disc with us saw that final shot of the novel's cover being closed, and even though he knew he could replay the disc and watch the giant squid and the volcano as often as his heart desired, the first words out of his mouth were, "I want to get that book!"

TWICE IN A LIFETIME

Our favorite performance in *Twice in a Lifetime* is by Amy Madigan, as the frustrated, high-strung daughter who isn't afraid to shoot off her mouth, but Gene Hackman, Ellen Burstyn, Ann-Margret, and the rest of the cast make their characters attractively believable. It is, however, a movie without fireworks. Hackman plays a steelworker who leaves his wife and moves in with a woman he met in a bar because his wife would never go to the bar with him. The stereo mix is not flamboyant until the Paul McCartney (?!) theme song is played at the end. The picture looks good, but the photography is a mishmash of lights and moods which only conveys the impression that the movie is a jumble of disunified ideas.

TWILIGHT ZONE
TWILIGHT ZONE – THE MOVIE (digital)

Although the disc retains the same catalog number, Warner's originally mis-titled *Twilight Zone* has been digitally remastered and reissued with the correct title, *Twilight Zone – The Movie*. Digital encoding cleans up the surround sound somewhat, but more noticeably, the picture has also been improved. The colors are more confident and the details are brighter. Warner has added chapter codes and has tried to improve the side break although, because of music overlaps, they could not break off exactly on a shift between stories. The only part of the movie which we can stand is George Miller's *pièce de résistance* at the end, about a man who sees a gremlin tearing up the engines of the passenger plane he is riding, but that is, as they say, enough to make the disc worthwhile, especially now that with the chapter codes, one doesn't have to scan through Joe Dante's jaded exercise in kiddie horror to get to it.

TWILIGHT'S LAST GLEAMING

The colors in *Twilight's Last Gleaming*, are actually a little sharper than the faded still on the jacket cover, but the still of the White House alternates between a pale yellow and a mild pink. Many of the characters are a little orange around the edges as well. The film has a number of adeptly employed split screen sequences, and these have been letterboxed, although the position of the letterboxed image on the screen shifts curiously from sequence to sequence. The rest of the movie is cropped, but not severely. The sound is best kept at a reasonable volume.

The film is taut and suspenseful, clear up to the last scene. The finale seems almost deliberately chosen to disappoint audiences, and is no easier to take on subsequent viewings than it is the first time through. Burt Lancaster portrays a mad general who takes command of a missile silo in Montana and threatens to launch Armageddon if his demands are not met. Directed by Robert Aldrich, the film has a pre-Tom Clancy authenticity and some inauthentic preaching about the causes of the Vietnam War. If only the script writers and Aldrich had come up with a more clever or heroic ending, the film's other problems wouldn't matter, but the movie, which goes on for 144 minutes, leaves one with a bad taste and a sense of wasted time.

TWINKLE SQUARE

Twinkle Square, is a video trip through Southern California, emphasizing signs, window designs, and roadside architecture. The music, by Hiroshi Satoh, is not irritating. There are four numbers which have vocals, but you don't even register whether the singing is in English or Japanese. The sound and the picture are exquisitely clear. The one-sided CLV disc lasts 29 minutes.

TWINS

The picture is in soft focus throughout *Twins*, and is often excessively blurry. Fortunately most of the movie takes place during the day, but the few scenes involving dark backgrounds or foregrounds are inevitably grainy. The stereo surround sound is also a questionable accomplishment. The dialog lacks clarity and the musical score surges and subsides without relation to any identifiable cues. The disc has so many impediments that it could very well hamper one's enjoyment of the film. The 'can't lose' script, casting Arnold Schwarzenegger and Danny DeVito as twins sidestepping some crooked goings-on to search for their mother, has lengthy stretches, particularly in the first half, which rely more on the concept than the plot, and a poorly produced disc can lower a viewer's tolerance for such scenes. It is a shame, for no matter how calculated the film may be, the performers deserve a better venue.

TWISTER

The surround sound is as wild and off-the-wall as the rest of *Twister*, a funny portrait of a very eccentric family living in a mansion in the Midwest. There are all sorts of oddball sounds which shift in direction whenever the camera angle changes. Dialog also gets tossed to the back channel, and everywhere else imaginable.

The characters in the movie are all extremely self-centered and seem to talk more to themselves than to those around them. Once you get onto their wavelength, however, the movie can be quite amusing, and enough absurd events are thrown into the plot to keep it rolling for 90 minutes. The picture is less satisfying. The colors are sickly and the edges are soft. The tone of the movie, however, is accommodating to the picture quality, and if a viewer can give the audio delivery free reign, the disc will not be disappointing.

TWISTED SISTER – STAY HUNGRY

Quite by accident we once wandered into a concert by the heavy metal rock group, Twisted Sister, and immediately saw our life pass before our eyes. Fortunately we escaped unscathed, and you can well imagine our excitement when we learned of the laser disc, *Twisted Sister – Stay Hungry*, from Pioneer Artists. Here was an opportunity to observe Twisted Sister from the safety of our own home!

Barricaded behind barbed wire and bravely facing a mass of frenzied adolescents, the group explores the subtleties of amplification by occasionally pausing between numbers. What they call the 'lead vocalist' is one Dee Snider. He looks like a large blond poodle who got his tail caught in a paper shredder and he sings the way most people announce that their houses are on fire. He has a charming propensity for using the 'f' word, not only as a verb and a noun, but as an adjective, an adverb, an article, a preposition, and a gerund.

While songs like 'The Beast,' 'Burn in Hell,' and 'Under the Blade' will never become Twyla Tharp ballets, there is a certain riotous good feeling that gets generated when Twisted Sister performs, the same sort which we are sure was felt in Nuremberg in 1932. We wonder, watching Sister twist, what Nero would have done during the burning of Rome had there been electric bass guitars.

TWO FOR THE ROAD (Import)

Almost every plot summary we have read for *Two for the Road* gets the key point wrong, although the back of the jacket on the disc, which is an import in English with Japanese subtitles, gets it right. The car trips the couple take during the first decade of their marriage are not across Europe, the trips are across *France*. All except the final one are shown in flashback. The movie opens in England at the beginning of their final trip (as they are boarding an air ferry) and ends as they finally cross the border into Italy.

The film is intolerably confusing for those who have never seen it before and are attempting to watch it casually. The many flash-backwards and forwards, keyed to locations in the French countryside in the half-dozen or so trips which the couple (Audrey Hepburn and Albert Finney) make, are shuffled so that there seems to be almost no relation between chronology and narrative. But if one gives the movie the full attention it deserves, one is rewarded with an amusing, glamorous look at the many stages of love and adult life. The film changes a little every time you watch and is a completely different movie depending upon the age and experience of the viewer. When we were very young and naive, we thought the film was romantic and sweet. As we got older and more idealistic, our opinion of the movie changed; we found it to be cynical and cold-hearted. Now that we have had some experience with maturity ourselves, we find the movie to be wise and, again, a little romantic. But it has never not been amusing, particularly the infamous sequences involving William Daniels, Eleanor Bron and a monstrously spoiled child (Gabrielle Middleton).

The colors look okay, but the print has the sporadic one or two frame freezes (usually imposed to hide splices) which one normally associates with older American MGM titles. The subtitles spoil one or two long shot vistas, but are otherwise not too annoying and are better than not having the movie on disc at all. Henri Mancini's score is mangled by the poor frequency ranges, but the dialog is unaffected. And unlike broadcast television, Hepburn and Finney's little name-calling exchange is left intact.

TWO IDIOTS IN HOLLYWOOD

Self mockery is employed in *Two Idiots in Hollywood*, a disc which unequivocally lives up to its title. Although drawn from experimental theater sources, the film is unappealing and the two stars lack charisma. Still, the movie is so exasperating that surely some viewers will find it useful, or, in a perverse sort of way, entertaining. The plot sends the title characters, roommates who lead slovenly and somewhat isolated lives, from a midwestern town to Los Angeles. Eventually one is accused of murder and the other creates a Pac-Man TV show. Every occurrence is laced with absurdity, and there is just enough of a hint that the artists involved are intellectuals to feel ashamed for them.

The stereo surround sound is very scratchy and not worth amplifying beyond sensible levels. The picture quality is often intentionally poor, but the transfer looks adequate. For what it is worth, there are chapter markers and side two is in CAV, with two unsteady still frames out of every five.

TWO MOON JULY

The only justification we can make for *Two Moon July* is that, in being an anthology of the avant-garde, it is also an avant-garde anthology. The program is a presentation of 'The Kitchen,' a performance space dedicated to showing an eclectic mix of innovative artists and performers. The single-sided disc, however, has 23 chapter markers in the space of 57 minutes – an indication that no performer is represented with the kind of breadth necessary for assessing the value or integrity of a creative effort. The one segment which comes the closest is an excerpt from Dana Birnbaum's 'Damnation of Faust,' a straightforward record of kids hanging out in a playground which takes on several layers of universal meanings and messages simply because Birnbaum has an uncanny camera sense.

The presentation, dubbed by the jacket cover as a "Lyric collage that reflects the interdisciplinary mix of The Kitchen," includes snippits of dance and music performances, along with excerpts from experimental films and experimental videos. Most of the pieces, including performances by Laurie Anderson, David Byrne, and Philip Glass, are intriguing, but before one can truly assess whether the artist is on to something or bluffing, the program is on to the next act.

With the exception of the film excerpts, the program was recorded on video tape, and the picture quality is acceptably glossy. The sound, which incorporates an elaborate stereo mix in a couple of the segments, has some hiss, and is not as clean as discs which have been derived from program material produced by the mainstream music industry.

TWO MOON JUNCTION

An over-stylized and under-scripted romance, *Two Moon Junction* has been carefully photographed and edited, and some of the camera angles are pleasingly original, but the filmmakers are showing off a little, and they don't really have a plot strong enough to justify it. The film concerns a young, rich woman who takes up with a carnival roustabout several weeks before she is to be married. She means it to be a fling, but then starts to realize that the affair may have more to offer than the life which has been mapped out for her. The ending is a coin toss by the scriptwriters which comes down on the happy side, but a desire to turn the film into an analysis of passion and power leaves a feeling of emptiness. It looks terrific and the sex is great, but the movie has no personality.

Strong reds look blurry and the picture has a mild grain, but it is passable. It is surprising that the film, which has such intense camerawork and an elaborate sound mix, is not stereophonic, but such is the case.

TWO RODE TOGETHER

The source material used for John Ford's *Two Rode Together* is in beautiful condition. There is only one splice and one poorly transferred day for night sequence (which looks haunting, but out of place). The monaural sound is also in solid condition.

The rich and accurate colors on the disc help the movie enormously. Contrary to the deceitful text on the back of the jacket ("Directed by the undisputed master of action films, John Ford.") the film is a moral exploration which involves a lot of talking and very little violence or excitement. The story is about two men sent by the army to halfheartedly negotiate the return of individuals who had been captured as children by Indians. Because of the cast, which includes Jimmy Stewart and Richard Widmark, the cinematography, and the crumbling convictions that marked Ford's films of the sixties, the movie is both dramatic and enlightening. Because of the pleasurable quality of the disc, it is also entertaining.

2001: A SPACE ODYSSEY (Voyager)
2001: A SPACE ODYSSEY (MGM/UA)
2010
2010 (Letterboxed)
2010 (Import)

Transferred from a '35mm intermediate negative to a video digital format master tape,' under the watchful eye of Stanley Kubrick himself, the clarity and the color of the image on Voyager's *2001: A Space Odyssey* are virtually perfect. The sound has been transferred from a 'six-track surround stereo magnetic soundtrack,' and has been digitally encoded (the analog track is CX-encoded with automatic tripping, as is the dual audio material at the end of the disc). The ambience within the uncluttered corridors, the utter silence of space, and the sudden, piercing alarms on various control panels are all incredibly vivid. The music sounds good, too.

Some viewers may have one potential reservation about the presentation. The film, which was originally released to theaters in single strip Cinerama and/or SuperPanavision, is letterboxed on the Voyager release with an aspect ratio of about 2:1. The original theatrical formats were as much as 15% wider. A simple comparison of the beginnings of side one on the Voyager version and the original scanned and cropped MGM/UA version show how vastly superior the letterboxed version is. You need go no further than the 'Thus Spake Zarathustra' opening credits. The credit typography on the original print is gaunt and spacious, indicative of the movie's overriding style. The credits on the American home video (CLV) release are pathetic. They are fat and squeezed together, and the picture behind them is frozen into a cheap-looking still. The 'b' and 'r' of 'Kubrick' are even crooked!

In every way, Voyager's presentation is fantastic. It is in CAV format and has been spread to six sides. Entrance music, exit music, and the Intermission music have all been included. After the exit music, there is a wealth of supplementary material on the disc about the film and about space.

The improved color and sharpness is most striking of all in the 'Star Gate' sequence. No longer do the forms and shapes appear to blur together. Each is separate, and passes by just slow enough for the viewer's eyes to register the image. One of the inclusions in the appendix is a short film by John Whitney which was the inspiration for Kubrick and the effects people working on the sequence, and it, too, looks perfect. Every shot in the movie and on the disc is fabulous.

The 'Supplementary Section' contains excerpts from various publications which have detailed the construction and meaning of the film (*2001* is an examination of the true maturity of contemporary mankind, observed against a scale which ranges from the beginning of human beings to their potential evolutionary manifestations), as well as a wonderful collection of memorandums that passed between the filmmakers and their science advisors during the film's production, and transcripts of interviews with scientists in the late sixties who speculated upon the scientific underpinnings of some of the film's technological and thematic speculations. At first, the inclusion of passages from Arthur Clarke's books and similar material may seem like overkill – most of it is still available in bookstores – but reading it will reveal that the disc's producers have selected the right passages from each work to truly convey the background and intention of *2001: A Space Odyssey*. There is also a superb essay on the back of the jacket box, by Howard Suber, which summarizes the film's essential attributes. If you don't believe the film is one of the most brilliant cinematic and science fiction achievements before you read the anthology on the disc, you certainly will after you read it.

Many people wanted to know what happened at the end of *2001* and for a long time, one theory was as valid as the next. What was left open in the film and in Clarke's novelization is the fate of the Earth and mankind when the astronaut/Ulysses returns from his voyage. To cash in a sequel, Clarke chose one of many possible scenarios, but even though the rendition is his and the film adaptation follows Clarke's novel closely, it can't be the definitive follow-up to *2001*. He had to step on his paint to get out of his corner.

There is plenty of tension to serve the drama, even on multiple viewings, as the American and Russian crew travel in the Russian ship to investigate the American craft abandoned at the end of *2001*. The mystery of HAL's nervous breakdown is given a pat explanation, but HAL's heroics at the end are to be cheered. The Earth scenes which begin *2010* are often belittled, but they are not totally without merit. The most powerful moment comes when Dr. Heywood Floyd (Roy Scheider) returns to Hawaii from Washington DC, a trip which in another era took many months. His wife (Madolyn Smith) is blasé about it ("How was Washington?") but is stunned when he announces a few moments later that he is going to Jupiter and will be away for more than two years. The world which had gotten so small has become large again and sailors are once more leaving their families to voyage far from home.

Mistrust in the writer/producer/director Peter Hyams is raised in the transition scene from Earth to space. Floyd and his wife make love, and there ought to be a cut right there to the Russian spaceship, but instead there are a couple of other shots – Floyd checking out his sleeping son, sunrise on the beach – before the switch is made. In making the sequel to *2001*, one would think the director would be mindful of the most well known cut in the entire picture and pay tribute to it.

MGM/UA released both a scanned version and a letterboxed version. There is also a Japanese MGM/UA Collector's Item Series widescreen CAV version which was made from the same master as the domestic letterboxed effort. The image on the domestic release has an aspect ratio of about 2.25:1, and is a hair shorter than the Japanese disc which has the same image width but a greater height and an aspect ratio of about 2.2:1. Because of the Hyams' aesthetic priorities, the difference in composition and visual impact in any of the three versions is negligible.

All three versions are grainy and have difficulties coralling glowing reds and oranges. In general, the letterboxed image is sharper than the scanned and cropped effort. The audio is impressive and one wishes the picture looked as good as it sounds.

Like the novel, *2010* is not a legitimate sequel to *2001*. Rather than expanding upon the themes and ideas of the first film, it contracts them. Clarke made a valiant effort at the sequel, using 'Aeneid' as his model, but we prefer to think of the end of the original *Odyssey* as the true conclusion, the Star Child regarding Earth as a universe of open possibilities.

U2: UNDER A BLOOD RED SKY

One of the better rock concert programs, *U2: Under a Blood Red Sky*, actually took place during overcast conditions. It was filmed at the outdoor grotto auditorium, Red Rocks, in Colorado. The stage is well lit and the disc's picture quality is impressive.

Side one of the 55-minute disc is in CAV, with every still frame having a little blur, and side two is in CLV. We could not see any practical application for the CAV format, but that is not to say the band isn't interesting to watch. Sometimes groups become so stiff on the stage, even if the vocalist is sliding around and the drummer is doing somersaults, that their music becomes a telegram summary of their studio work. U2, however, moves their studio to odd locations to begin with, and their stage performance, while less melodic, has a confidence which makes them sound both forceful and graceful. The digitally encoded stereo sound picks all this up (it is a good transfer), but the music sounds even better when a viewer watches the images, because the musicians are in full command of their craft. They aren't trying to catch up to an impossibility (recreating the studio on stage) and they aren't playing by rote (yet). When you see it and hear it, you understand why the audience is so excited.

U2: THE UNFORGETTABLE FIRE COLLECTION

We are always on the lookout for laser discs which can double as record albums and we thought we'd found one with *U2: The Unforgettable Fire Collection*, but the last number – the title song – is preceded by a lengthy documentary about its production. The hour-long disc has just four songs, though 'Unforgettable Fire,' is played through twice, with different visuals each time. The videos have the sophistication and simplicity which one associates with the group itself. They concentrate on the performance of the song, and add outside images sparingly but adeptly.

The quality of the picture is limited. It is not bad, but it isn't as glossy as it could have been. The sound is digitally encoded, though the group, searching for the right ambience, sometimes pushes a little too much clutter onto the music tracks.

UB40 UB40 CCCP THE VIDEO MIX

"I wish see again," says a young Russian fan at the end of the concert depicted, in segments, on *UB40 UB40 CCCP The Video Mix*. The hour-long program is a mixture of vacation and concert footage, cut to create individual music videos out of the concert numbers. The reggae band plays many of their biggest hits, which are enjoyable, but the group looks more relaxed playing tourist. Their concert performance is adequate, but the feedback they get from the audience is uninformed (or even hostile, as ushers are constantly attempting to quell excessive dancing among the audience members) and takes away some of their spark. Neither the picture nor the sound recording is exceptional. The source material is mildly fuzzy and the transfer adds a little more blur.

ULTRA Q VOLUME 5 (Import)

A black-and-white Japanese version of 'Outer Limits,' *Ultra Q*, is available on disc in Japan in collections of four, sequenced in the same manner that the episodes were first broadcast on Japanese TV. We had the opportunity to sample one disc, *Ultra Q Volume 5*, and enjoyed it quite a bit. If you are the sort who buys Japanese monster movies with no care for the language impediment, then you may wish to consider the disc. The special effects are low budget but have an inevitable humanity which cheap America bug-eyed monsters never quite achieve. A lot of miniature work is also utilized and the scales are often gratifyingly meticulous.

The protagonists are a young female newspaper photographer and her two male gofers. They fly in helicopters and use other means to track down unexplained occurrences and record them. Because each episode runs less than a half hour, the plots are easy enough to figure out and long passages of conversation bereft of other activity are rare. The first episode is an adeptly executed dream tale in which the heroine is shrunk in size and then beset upon by nuns, bald prison convicts, and others. It has the real feel of a dream and was a fascinating introduction to the series. In the second episode a Barugan-type monster tears up the countryside and threatens a group of children. In the third episode a monster quite unique and impossible to describe in a short space employs blob-like creatures to make humans disappear. The monster in the final episode is a variation on *The Creature from the Black Lagoon*, who goes on a rampage when his baby is stolen. You gotta see the baby.

A brief snippet of a fifth episode appears at the end, dubbed in English for some reason. The black and white prints sometimes appear a bit weary and the CX-encoded monaural sound is nothing special. The episodes are marked by chapters and a gorgeous booklet containing sketches of some of the effects comes with the disc.

UMBERTO D.

The black-and-white print used for *Umberto D.* has an Italian Neo-Realist look to it, with a number of scratches, splices, and a quiver or two. The contrasts are sharp, however, and the image is generally satisfying. The condition of the sound is in keeping with the rest, and is passable.

Directed by Vittorio De Sica, *Umberto D.* is beautifully, perhaps perfectly, photographed, and a succession of shots during any sequence in the film, when analyzed, will provide a lesson on how black and white photography can be employed to illustrate the corporeal and the spiritual simultaneously. The narrative, however, is about an elderly man facing eviction (it has a flagrantly similar dramatic structure to De Sica's *Bicycle Thief*), and it is such a calculated downer that sitting through it is like visiting a distant relative in the hospital. You do it more out of duty than out of pleasure.

THE UMBRELLAS OF CHERBOURG (see **LES PARAPLUIES DE CHERBOURG**)

THE UNBEARABLE LIGHTNESS OF BEING

A three-hour souffle about the unplanned courses of love and politics, *The Unbearable Lightness of Being*, is set during the fall of Prague Spring but concerning a doctor who pays little attention to events beyond his immediate concern. The film is based upon a refreshingly concise novel by Milan Kundera, although it has been directed by the normally mystical and foggy Philip Kaufman. The film was a flop theatrically, but the respect it has received by those who have seen it in the theater or on home video renews our faith in the spread of intelligence through the general population. The story intends to show that even superficial lives have vitality, and also creates a complex political allegory to suggest that the Dubcek regime, like the doctor, had neither the pragmatism nor the extremism it required for survival.

The picture on the disc is a little too grainy, enough to bother those with especially sensitive video systems. The stereo sound is limited but effective. Kaufman saves the strongest sonic impact for the Russian invasion, but those who watch the disc should listen to how the fatal storm sneaks onto the soundtrack in the finale. The CLV disc is spread to four sides and has a few chapter markers. The disc jacket emphasizes the program's sexual content, and, intelligence or no, that is probably why most viewers stick with the film and enjoy it.

UNCLE BUCK

We have to say that the side break on *Uncle Buck* is perfect. A character gets hit in the nose, with a shot of a fist coming straight toward the camera, and kapow, the side is over. The picture transfer is in good shape. The surround sound is marvelous, and there is a repeating gag concerning a car's backfire which will kick you across the viewing room. The movie, however, is something of a disappointment, considering its boxoffice gross. John Candy is a bachelor uncle, asked to watch the kids for a week in an emergency and inevitably providing them with a different and better rounded outlook on life by the time his stay is ended. The bad guys – school administrators, randy boyfriends – are easy targets for Buck's wrath, and there are no really bright or unanticipated sequences to liven up the plot. Candy's performance is admirable, but the movie, sound effects aside, is dull.

UNDER THE BANNER OF THE SAMURAI (see **YOJIMBO**)

UNDER THE BOARDWALK

The title *Under the Boardwalk* is misleading, because the song is an East Coast beach tune, but the movie is about surfers in LA. The film's most unique aspect is its dialog, which employs an exaggerated amount of surfing vernacular. The story has the format of a standard beach film, mildly humorous, involving status rivalries, romance, and a surfing contest. It is adequately executed, but the surfing is unexciting and the script, dialog aside, is uninspired.

Since most of the story is set in the sun, the picture looks okay. Only the music is really in surround and only a couple of the tunes, such as the title song, are well produced. Image's chapter encoding is half hearted, ignoring the music numbers.

UNDER THE CHERRY MOON

It may take a few years for people to realize how truly bad *Under the Cherry Moon* is. Some things are obvious right away, like the pajamas which are being passed off as evening wear and the black-and-white photography which in this day and age is associated with high art (the movie would have been just boring if it had been in color). You first have to examine the film to see where Prince (who directed as well as starred) was intent on being serious (or, in the comical scenes, was seriously trying for a laugh) before you realize that every attempt is a failure. Is one supposed to laugh because he has discovered he has been downing bat droppings with his soup? Are we supposed to believe that his dry, rubber kisses are passionate? And is it meant to be dramatic, rather than comical, that the rifle shot which kills his character causes him to twist like a pretzel in mid-air as his eyes pop out? The only reliable aspect of his art is his music, and in *Cherry Moon* even that is a tad bit repetitive and desperate.

The disc is exquisite. The picture is sharp and bright. The sound is digitally encoded and was laid down with the sort of care which music people, when they make movies, pay attention to. The common sound effects, such as answering machine beepers and ringing phones, are indistinguishable from the real thing. If only Prince had been a special effect, he might have been more believable.

UNDER THE GUN
The bad guys chase the good guys through LA traffic with a bazooka in *Under the Gun*, an enjoyable second-rate action picture. The story, about a St. Louis cop who travels to Los Angeles when his brother is murdered by black market gun dealers, has its share of gaping holes, but the filmmakers are adept at lulling the viewer into complacency and then pulling out a surprise, such as the bazooka. Sam Jones and Vanessa Williams star. Williams has difficulty repeating even the simplest lines of dialog convincingly. The picture looks fine and the Ultra Stereo sound is simplistic but clean.

UNDER THE VOLCANO
On many movies you can hear occasional discrepancies in the soundtrack indicating the last minute overlay of a voice or an effect. In John Huston's *Under the Volcano* you can hear everything but the shuffling of the stools in the recording room. The sound has been recreated with great clarity and precision.

The book from which *Under the Volcano* was adapted was written by a poet, Malcolm Lowry, and the film will work a lot better for a viewer if it is approached as a poem instead of as a novel. Albert Finney portrays a retired British consul in Mexico who is never not drunk. His mind and his mouth lurch from one subject to the next and the reasons why his wife (Jacqueline Bisset) has returned to him are tenuous. The film never officially implies that her presence is a figment of his imagination, but that is the only believable explanation for her motives. If drunks bore you, then so will this disc. Like so many of Huston's commercial failures, however, the movie has a certain cultish appeal in the way it sticks so reverently to its source.

UNDERSEA KINGDOM
The highpoint of the Republic serial *Undersea Kingdom* is when Sharad, the High Priest of Atlantis, raises the 'Ceremonial Sword' and you can see the big round underarm perspiration stains on his robes. The movie stars Ray 'Crash' Corrigan, who portrays a naval officer accompanying a professor and a few others on a submarine trip which leads them to Atlantis. Most of the program then concerns an evil ruler in Atlantis who wishes to defeat the good ruler and destroy the 'world above.' The acting is really bad, but the dopey special effects are fun and the narrative has at least some elaboration and forward movement to it, as well as a large scale battle scene (footage of which is used twice).

The picture is usually grainy and a bit soft. The sound is rickety, but workable, and some of the explosions give off a pleasing, dull 'boom.' Republic opens the disc with a re-release trailer.

THE UNDERSEA WORLD OF JACQUES COUSTEAU: THE DESERT WHALES (see **THE UNDERSEA WORLD OF JACQUES COUSTEAU: THE SINGING WHALES**)

THE UNDERSEA WORLD OF JACQUES COUSTEAU – THE DRAGONS OF GALAPAGOS
In *The Dragons of Galapagos*, Cousteau's crew pester a few iguanas who have re-adapted to the sea after living on a remote island for generations. The team measures the physiological capabilities of the animals, but the narration draws few conclusions from the data. Frisky fur seals dancing in the sea are also used to pad the hour. At the end, the documentary tries to make fun of tourists who have come to visit the island, but after all the poking and prodding the scientists did to the wildlife, the animals are probably quite relieved to see the Kodak cameras and Bermuda shorts. The color is fair and the sound is passable.

THE UNDERSEA WORLD OF JACQUES COUSEAU: THE FLIGHT OF THE PENGUINS
If you fancy penguins then you will probably want *The Undersea World of Jacques Cousteau: The Flight of the Penguins*. We have our reservations about the *Cousteau* format, but there is certainly enough footage of the wobbly little headwaiters to hold one's attention for an hour. The monaural sound is digitally encoded and since not even penguins can tell themselves apart and have to identify one another by voice, there is plenty of midrange squawking. The picture is a little old and Antarctica is usually overcast, but the transfer is acceptable.

Cousteau's film unit captures most of the phases in a penguin's life effectively. There are times, however, when they promise more than they deliver. How do penguins catch and swallow their food? How do the youngsters, abandoned by their vacationing parents, leave the rocks when winter comes? In both cases, there is an elaborate build-up to these questions and then a sudden cut to a different subject in the place of an answer.

THE UNDERSEA WORLD OF JACQUES COUSTEAU: THE FORGOTTEN MERMAIDS
Did you know the manatee's closest relative is the elephant? Jacques Cousteau has a whole hour of manatee material on *The Forgotten Mermaids*. Sea cow fanciers may rejoice at the attention the lumbering, cute-as-William-Howard-Taft inland Florida water mammal receives. Cousteau's anti-civilian polemic, however, spoils some of the fun. He acts like he is the only one in the world who appreciates the big, stupid, living buoys. At one point he rants about outboard motorists, endangering the manatee for the sake of the thrill of using their outboards. Yet, a couple of scenes later, he himself is at the helm of a skiff, giving who knows how many manatees mohawks as he cruises up river. The picture and sound are acceptable, with the source material possessing the standard, aged demeanor.

THE UNDERSEA WORLD OF JACQUES COUSTEAU: OCTOPUS-OCTOPUS
Octopus-Octopus travels from the Mediterranean to Puget Sound to provide an informative hour about the eight-legged mollusk. The program has fewer severe tangents than many of the *Cousteau* episodes and will leave a viewer with a basic understanding of the creature's habits. The print is more worn down than most and the sound is passable.

THE UNDERSEA WORLD OF JACQUES COUSTEAU: THE SINGING WHALES
THE UNDERSEA WORLD OF JACQUES COUSTEAU: THE DESERT WHALES
In *The Undersea World of Jacques Cousteau: The Singing Whale*, Cousteau goes to great length to describe the gentleness of whales and to assert that they are not at all like *Moby Dick*. But in the beginning of the other *Cousteau* program, *The Desert Whale*, the narrator informs the viewer that whales often break apart boats and are dangerous subjects. We never believe anything Jacques Cousteau tells us anyway.

Both discs are digitally encoded monaural. Since *Singing Whales* includes a substantial amount of whale song, it is worth running through the hi-fi, though neither disc should be turned up very loud. The picture on both is grainy and rough-looking, but well preserved. Each runs an hour on a single sided platter.

The scientists have one seemingly simple goal in *Singing Whales*, to film the Atlantic humpback whale head on. Camera shy or confrontationally reluctant, the whales refuse to cooperate, and the crew of the Calypso is reduced to pestering one poor mother and her new calf, until even she becomes so stressed out by the intrusion that she exhibits anger at her tormentors. To hear Cousteau describe this interlude, however, you would think it is an inter-species love feast.

Desert Whales is slightly more interesting. Here, Cousteau has the whales trapped in the lagoons of Baja California, and he can pester them to his heart's content. Almost deliberately, Cousteau seeks out a beached whale, so that he and his crew can attempt to 'save' it. They fail, but the closeups they obtain make the effort worthwhile.

THE UNDERSEA WORLD OF JACQUES COUSTEAU: THE SMILE OF THE WALRUS
The viewer learns little about the life cycle of the walrus in *The Smile of the Walrus*, but the program has a number of appealing sequences – frogmen diving in frigid Arctic water, scientists taking care of an orphaned baby walrus, eskimos practicing folk art – and is entertaining. The walrus pack which the crew seeks to study remains elusive, and legitimate science goes with it, but that has never stopped Cousteau in the past, and under wildly adverse conditions he puts on a surprisingly good show.

THE UNDERSEA WORLD OF JACQUES COUSTEAU: A SOUND OF DOLPHINS
Only Jacques Cousteau fanatics will be interested in *A Sound of Dolphins*, an uninformative mishmash of dolphin shots which somehow managed to cop an Emmy. The picture and sound are passable. The only interesting segment comes at the end, with a well-photographed display of dolphins leading fish into the nets of an African tribe which has been taking advantage of the unsolicited herding for as long as anyone can remember. The low point comes when the crew almost murders a dolphin they have captured for study and Cousteau, instead of apologizing, excuses his behavior by saying that whale hunters kill dolphins for pet food, while he is hand feeding this poor animal and nursing it back to health. His subjects are probably still whistling and clicking about that one.

THE UNDERSEA WORLD OF JACQUES COUSTEAU – THE UNSINKABLE SEA OTTER
Who can resist the jacket cover for *The Unsinkable Sea Otter*? The disc features an hour of little, soggy Wilford Brimleys, relaxing on their backs in the water and eating shell food with more dexterity than most restaurant patrons. The program is one of the more compelling in the Cousteau series, not because of any great insights to the biology of water mammals but because the subjects are so inexhaustibly photogenic. The color is faded and the sound is fuzzy.

THE UNDERSTUDY: GRAVEYARD SHIFT II
All things considered, *Graveyard Shift* was an okay vampire-themed horror disc. Its sequel, *The Understudy: Graveyard Shift II*, is also an interesting exercise. It is set almost entirely on a movie soundstage, with the vampire from the first film, Silvio Oliviero, resurfacing to prey upon the actresses in a horror film. It has less eroticism than the first movie, but is not without a fair amount of passion. The filmmakers have a good time with the subject of movie making, and the film-within-the-film is also elaborate (it's a demonic take-off on *The Hustler*).

As with the first film, the production is inexpensive but admirable. Since the picture is already malformed, the transfer can do no more than prevent it from looking too blurry, which it does. The sound is passable. The disc runs under 90 minutes, in CLV.

UNDERWATER!
The color is inconsistent on *Underwater!* When it isn't perfect it looks slightly washed out. When it is perfect, the Technicolor is gorgeous, and enough reels are spotless to make the disc worthwhile for Technicolor buffs or for those who are sufficiently undemanding to enjoy the film.

Directed by John Sturges, *Underwater!* is slow paced and inconsequential, about a dive for sunken treasure which is only partially successful. The elaborate underwater photography and the vivid colors will stimulate a viewer's imagination. Unfortunately, the actor portraying the hero, Gilbert Roland, is so untalented that he can't even smile convincingly, and Jane Russell, the nominal star, is often treated as scenery.

The picture transfer does nothing to impede the quality of the source material. The sound has its ups and downs, but under the circumstances viewers will probably not be too concerned about the audio.

UNFAITHFULLY YOURS
The second half of *Unfaithfully Yours* is the part which usually gets summarized in capsule descriptions of the film, as an orchestra conductor, played by Rex Harrison, envisions a plot to do in his wife while he is conducting a concert, and the emotions of the music (Rossini, Wagner, and Tchaikovsky) guide his inventions. From beginning to end, however, the Preston Sturges film is wonderfully comical and entertaining. Sturges' dialog is fast paced and elegantly intelligent, causing Harrison's line readings to approach the cadence and pitch of his singing in *My Fair Lady*. Harrison also has a terrific kissing scene with Linda Darnell which rivals Cary Grant and Ingrid Bergman in *Notorious*. The script busily sets up the Othello-esque misunderstanding and its denouement, but Sturges does not simply place characters and scenes together to advance a story. Every situation is a miniature gem of inspired humor and every character and object are designed to generate giggles whenever they appear.

The film is ideal for viewing dozens of times, since different aspects of it become funny as familiarity sets in. CBS/Fox has released the disc with a decent black and white source which has a minimum of scratches. The image lacks the vividness of the best black and white transfers, but it does nothing to impair one's appreciation of the film.

The sound editing on *Unfaithfully Yours* is exceptional for a medium budget monaural film from the forties. Not only must the orchestral playback rise and fall to incorporate dialog during the dream sequences, but Sturges uses odd noises and sounds throughout the film for humor, just as he uses the odd knickknacks and characters. The digitally encoded sound on the disc is in good shape and delivers the soundtrack without distortion. The film's original theatrical poster, with three detail shots, has been placed at the end of the disc.

THE UNHEARD MUSIC
A movie which was made ten years after it should have been, *The Unheard Music*, about the punk rock group, X. X's music is wonderful – raw and uninhibited. The movie is also good fun, mixing selections from their repertoire with amusing archive clips and a profile of the band. There is a great interview with a record company executive which completely epitomizes what seems to go wrong with pop music in regular cycles.

The stereo sound makes some use of the surround codes during the music sequences, but not to any level of significance. The sound transfer preserves, for better or for worse, the original recording. The picture is deliberately raunchy. The film runs a little short of 90 minutes, but is presented in CLV.

THE UNHOLY
A decent array of low budget special effects makes *The Unholy* interesting enough to hold one's attention. The picture is hazy, but the stereo soundtrack isn't bad. The story is about a priest who must do battle with Satan's henchmen in a church. Fortunately, he's got You Know Who on his side, so everything comes out okay in the end.

UNINVITED
The guests aboard a luxury yacht on a Caribbean cruise are terrorized by a pussycat which turns into a ravenous hand puppet at regular intervals in *Uninvited*. Although the cast includes George Kennedy, Alex Cord, and Clu Gulager, the movie is hardly a stellar accomplishment and induces a dozen yawns for every scream. The picture is grainy and the monaural sound, though digitally encoded, is as cheap as the toy boat which sinks in the watering can storm.

UNION CITY
The cheaply made curiosity staring Deborah Harry, *Union City*, is better than most bad movies in that it maintains a consistency of emotion. It is feasible, even, that some very tolerant individuals would enjoy it. Loosely based on a crime short story from the thirties by Cornell Woolrich, the characters stumble around in a stupor and mumble their dialog to one another. Most of the movie takes place on the fourth floor of a tenement, and the interactions of the characters, including a murder, keep the plot moving for 90 minutes while establishing an off-kilter atmosphere. The sound recording, however, is awful, and digital encoding cannot breathe life into the monaural tracks. The picture, which has been transferred about as well as could be imagined, also has a few marks on it and was poorly lit to begin with. The deadening effect of the film's technical components prevent one from taking the movie seriously as an entertainment.

THE UNNAMABLE
The writings of H.P. Lovecraft used to scare the hell out of us. It was his dense, Miltonic prose which did it. He forces you to concentrate and read every word, imposing a deliberately slow pace which, like the dream where you can't move your legs fast, leaves you unable to avoid the terrors he throws at you. Movies which use Lovecraft as a source, however, are usually anything but dense. It would take a skilled stylist to adapt one of his stories successfully, and usually skilled stylists have better things to do.

Thus we are stuck with *The Unnamable*, which wants very much to be true to the spirit of Lovecraft but lacks any style whatsoever. It is about a house, apparently unmolested for 300 years, which suddenly becomes the object of curiosity for several students at a nearby college. There is a thing, still alive, in the attic, and it dispatches the rudest jocks as soon as they start poking around. It is up to the wimpy intellectuals to save the heroine. Standard stuff, and there are only a couple of potential screams to be had. The picture is muddy and the sound is victimized by the production budget.

UNNATURAL CAUSES
John Sayles wrote and Lamont Johnson directed *Unnatural Causes*, a made-for-television effort about Agent Orange which manages to avoid being just another disease of the week by concentrating upon the efforts of a Veterans Administration counselor, played by

Alfre Woodard, to research and verify links between the use of defoliants and the failing health of Vietnam vets. John Ritter also stars. The film is a tribute to the individuals within the Federal service bureaucracies who care about the citizens they assist. With Johnson's confident visual style and Sayles' thorough, well-paced script, the film is always engrossing and never depressing, more of a detective story than a soap opera.

The picture quality of the disc is okay. The film has an institutional look, but the colors are not faded. The sound is also acceptable.

THE UNSINKABLE MOLLY BROWN
THE UNSINKABLE MOLLY BROWN
(letterboxed)
The *joie de vivre* in *The Unsinkable Molly Brown* has always felt a bit strained to us, and the feeling is enhanced when the edges of the screen are missing. MGM/UA has two versions of the Colorado gold rush musical available, a standard scanned and cropped version, and a letterboxed version.

On the cropped disc, deeper colors are rarely stable, something which creates a real problem when Molly leaves her log cabin for a life in red velvet. The volume levels on the dialog are inconsistent. A handful of the musical numbers have been marked with chapters, sometimes after the songs begin.

The color transfer on the letterboxed version is a tremendous improvement over the scanned and cropped rendition. Not only are the reds stable, they are carefully shaded and delineated. The letterboxing, which has an aspect ratio of about 2:1, is important, opening up vistas and adding splendor. MGM/UA also dug up an Overture and exit music, which was missing from the scanned disc, and the chapter encoding has been improved. The audio channels on the digital stereo soundtrack of the letterboxed version have been reversed, though on subsequent pressings the problem is to be corrected.

THE UNTOUCHABLES
The eager display of ventilated brain tissue during much of *The Untouchables* is a grotesque but nevertheless apt symbol for the enthusiastic intelligence which radiates throughout the film. There is a love for the English language present in the dialog. There is a love for filmmaking in the way that every scene is not just another camera set-up; it is another concept, so that the editing brings vertical and horizontal pans together with odd stationary angles and other curious points of view, rendered with such confidence that by the end one feels one has lived through the film inside and out. And there is a love for music in Ennio Morricone's score, which is where the disc becomes particularly effective.

The sound editing is fantastic, but nowhere more so than in Morricone's music. Listening to it, one hears each piece of the orchestration as a separate entity, floating about the room like a balloon. The sound on the disc is sharp and well produced and the title is destined to be a favorite for laser disc owners who want to show off for their friends. It is a demo disc with guts.

The picture is also superb, but the image is cropped and to lose even a sliver of the film's guiding vision is to lose its soul. The scanning is done with competence, but it remains obvious that the film has tensions which the home video rendition does not have.

The Untouchables runs 119 minutes, but has been spread to three sides on the disc, all in CLV. There is hardly a minute of it which is not spellbinding, if one can tolerate the blood. And it is nice to see a gangster movie where the cops are the heroes.

UP YOUR ALLEY
Linda Blair keeps her clothing on and doesn't get beat up in *Up Your Alley*. The film is a comedy about a reporter who puts on an old coat and hangs out with some homeless people for a story. To keep things interesting, a murderer is lurking in the shadows, but it is all fairly tame. The performances are contrived and unconvincing, but a few of the lines are genuinely funny. The picture is cheap and blurry, and the sound, though forceful, goes fuzzy here and there.

URUSEI YATSURA – ONLY YOU
(see **MY YOUTH IN ARCADIA**)

UTILITIES
Robert Hays and Brooke Adams star in *Utilities*, a comedy of sorts about a social worker (Hays) who rebels against the unfair practices of a large public utility. Adams is the cop who arrests him and they fall in love as his protest grows to folk-hero proportions. Filmed in Toronto, it is poorly put together and neither hysterical nor inspiring, although Hays and Adams are accomplished enough to lend it some amount of charm. The sound boom makes an appearance, but the sound on the disc is monaural and uninteresting. The picture looks grainy.

V (Import)
V2 (Import)
The elaborate two-part mini-series about an alien takeover of Earth, *V* has been released in Japan in a single 5-platter boxed set. The mini-series was originally broadcast in two different segments several months apart. The first segment, directed by the series creator, Kenneth Johnson, ran for two nights in two-hour slots on each night (an 'hour' actually represents a little less than 45 minutes of broadcast time without commercials, and every 'hour' section appears on a separate disc side). The second segment, a follow-up in which Johnson was not directly involved and which was significantly inferior to the first part, ran for three nights of two-hour slots and concluded the story begun in the first segment. Enough open ends were left to establish a regular television series, which is also available in its entirety in Japan as a boxed set, called *V2*.

The programs in both packages are presented bi-lingually, with the original English dialog available on one sound channel and a dubbed Japanese rendition available on the other channel. In support of the English version, however, Japanese subtitles still appear on the screen, though we barely noticed them at any time during the entire 474 minutes of *V* and 943 minutes of *V2*. There is no CX-encoding.

On side ten of *V*, after the epic is ended, a 15-minute documentary appears, in English, showing how some of the spaceship models were made. Each platter begins and ends with a credit scroll. A lovely brochure comes in the opera-style box with the discs, depicting, with lines and photos as well as Japanese script, the relationships between the various characters. Each side has a couple of chapter markers.

The first two platters, representing Johnson's original effort, are in every way superior to the last three. Even the picture transfer looks better, as the later discs tend to appear less stable when strong reds are utilized. The first film has super, exciting special effects, and a few action sequences which would be sufficient to turn a feature film into a boxoffice hit.

There is rarely a slow moment. Johnson not only moves the plot at a speedy clip, but he varies the point of view styles, telling parts of the story through TV broadcasts and other devices, so the viewer, over the long haul, will continually be stimulated by the presentation. He has a solid theme, comparing the alien conquest of Earth to the Nazi takeover of Germany. He effectively captures and holds the viewer's imagination by creating unique characters (the leader of the underground is a female med student), by offering an easy lesson on totalitarian rule, and by including a little humor ("Ray Bradbury was just on with Arthur Clarke," says a character referring to a news broadcast when the UFOs first appear in the sky) with the action and the special effects.

The second segment is more tolerable in repeat viewings, since the worst plot twists no longer come as a shock, but it manages to undue just about everything Johnson accomplished. The budget is clearly smaller, so there are fewer special effects and more bad takes. Every sequence is presented in the same manner, creating a monotony which is particularly telling when the entire show is viewed in one sitting. Attempts to explore themes are sacrificed for the plot at hand. Leadership of the underground is shifted de facto to two male heroes. The orchestra which performed the music for the first film (robbing the theme for *North by Northwest*, but so what) is replaced by a single dopey dance beat synthesizer. And the humor completely disappears. Seen in one day, however, the program is fairly entertaining and, since the worst of it comes on the last platter, it is generally a rewarding experience.

The television series presented on 19 sides in *V2* was constructed similar to a soap opera, with plot strands running from one episode to the next while the conflict between the humans and the aliens advances measurably in each hour. Its conclusion is resolute, making the disc package a single logical entity, although some open ended twists were initiated in the final episode to facilitate a series renewal, however unlikely that may be.

The first episode is a two-parter, which begins with a lengthy recapitulation of the mini-series and then sets the stage for the revised format by having Los Angeles declared an open city. The third episode is a false start and contains several plot elements which are re-introduced in the fourth episode with significant changes. The fifth through the thirteenth episodes are set in LA and use an unusually large number of cast regulars. In the final six episodes the cast is trimmed as, apparently, is the budget, and the focus shifts from the earth heroes to the alien villains.

The humor returns in the television series, and that will be its primary appeal to those crazy enough to obtain the disc package. Each of the first thirteen episodes opens with a 'newscast' by Howard Smith which must have thrown one or two viewers for a loop when the program was first broadcast. There is a takeoff on the *Casablanca* 'anthem' scene and other bemused touches. Robert Englund, a series regular, is given a steady stream of malapropisms. As the series advances, the conflict between the main villain, played by Jane Badler, and her arch rival, played by June Chadwick, becomes the soul of the show. Like two parallel lines converging, each is forever trying to outdo the other, to no avail.

Inevitably, no major special effects were struck for the series, so stock footage from the mini-series is used again and again, and the aliens are more apt to chase the heroes on dirt bikes than in space shuttles. For the convenience of the series, some devices, such as the modulated voices of the aliens, are dropped or simplified. The plot of each episode is fairly similar (the heroes must destroy an alien device of some sort), but in support of the larger plot machinations the repetition of ideas is rarely tiresome. More admirably, a motif of parent and child relationships also runs through most of the episodes.

The program comes on ten platters in a beautifully designed if slightly fragile box, which includes, once again, a nice looking glossy brochure. The picture quality on the disc is generally acceptable, though a shot here and there looks a bit fuzzy, when strong reds are involved. The camera crew can also be spotted in reflections every once in a while. The sound is stronger than on *V*, and the music is of a canned television variety which is usually unnoticeable. On side 20, a twenty-minute profile of Badler appears, combining footage from a press conference in Japan tied to the release of *V* on cassette with clips from many of her best moments in the series. The voice-over narration is in Japanese, but the clips and the conference interview are in English.

As we indicated above, Badler makes the disc worthwhile. In no way is the program on the artistic level of the excellent *Crime Story* package but, like the live mice the aliens are always swallowing, it is difficult to put down. Take for example, the following exchange, as Chadwick and Badler, both vamping for the camera, are preparing a formal duel to the death: "I've never been defeated in mortal combat," Chadwick says. "Idiot," replies Badler, "If you had, you'd be dead."

VAGABOND

Directed by Agnes Varda, *Vagabond* is an excellent, meandering piece of entertainment. The film is about a young woman who drifts through a few farms and small towns in the French countryside during one winter. The heroine doesn't live long enough to become crazy, she's just uninterested in society, and her adventures seem to magnify the needs and desires of ordinary life.

The movie is in French and has English subtitles. There are faint black bands at the top and bottom of the screen, giving the picture a very slight addition in width. The picture is clean and bright. The monaural sound has also undergone a decent transfer. This is especially helpful to the musical score, a mixture of broken piano chords and French pop tunes. It is also worth noting that the descriptions of the characters and cast in the end credit roll is quite delightful.

VALENTINO RETURNS

The concluding act of *Valentino Returns*, a comedy about growing up in Stockton, California in the fifties, is highly enjoyable. The events leading up to it, however, are less promising. The story is basically about a boy who buys a Cadillac and tries to meet women with an obnoxious friend. Frederic Forest portrays the boy's father and Veronica Cartwright portrays the boy's mother. The relationship between the two of them is a lot more fun than anything in the central narrative. The picture and the sound are passable. The title is the name of the car.

VALET GIRLS

Nominally about a group of female parking attendants, *Valet Girls* drops the premise fairly rapidly and concentrates instead upon Hollywood parties and loose morals. One of the valets wants to become a singer, and a few of the musical interludes aren't bad, although her two big numbers are awful. The colors tend to bleed and the sound is undeveloped.

VAMP

Sandy Baron does a pretty good Cybill Shepherd imitation as the heroine in *Vamp*. The film is a passable effort about vampires chasing college kids around a night club strip joint. There are a few scary scenes and the expected amount of flesh and blood. Grace Jones appears briefly, but her subordinates and their prey take up most of the screen time. The sound is passable and the picture is a bit on the grainy side.

VAMPIRE'S KISS

Nicolas Cage, who talks through his sinuses whenever he gets excited, portrays a yuppie who thinks he's a vampire in an excruciatingly pointless exercise, *Vampire's Kiss*. The picture is slightly pale and the surround sound is unimpressive.

VAN GOGH REVISITED

(see **VINCENT VAN GOGH: A PORTRAIT IN TWO PARTS**)

VAN MORRISON – THE CONCERT

Have you seen Van Morrison lately? He looks like Robert Morley. Morrison appears in *Van Morrison – The Concert*. The picture on the 90-minute concert program, recorded at the Beacon Theater in New York, looks good. The black spaces behind the band members are solid, and only strong red lighting causes a mild attack of grain. The digitally encoded sound is okay, and the separations are good for a live show. Morrison's voice wears out after his first two numbers, but his band, playing a combination of blues and Irish folk rock, fills in the gaps.

THE VANCOUVER DISC

Voyager has retrieved a heretofore rare video program, *The Vancouver Disc*, and has repressed it for distribution to the growing number of collectors who are interested in unusual laser disc treats. The one-sided CAV disc combines 18,000 still images with a wide ranging collection of short time-lapse motion sequences. The intention is to give the user a sense of the city in a historical and cultural context. Voyager is emphatic in the accompanying four-page index and on the jacket cover to point out that *The Vancouver Disc* was an early (1982), experimental effort. Many of the photos, especially the slides, are blurry and none are identified with decent title cards. We even caught one, at 14029, which was reversed. There is no on-disc index, awkward stretches of blank or introductory space which take forever to step through, and no stop marks at the beginning of different subject sections. The disc has charm, however, and a lot of pleasurable experiences to share.

A stereo music soundtrack plays throughout the disc accompanying not only the time-lapse material, but the still collection as well. A female announcer introduces each chapter with minimum fanfare. For several sequences a camera gets put on a car, a boat, and a train to go zooming through the city and around the countryside.

A terrific gathering of postcards, posters, and neon signs follow the photo archive. A substantial look at Canadian artists and at the collections of several Vancouver museums mix well with the historical stills. You can witness the once and continuing influence of indigenous natives upon the present civic culture. It is a natural choice for artistic expression, since the native art is an expression of the same atmospheric and biological environment which still surrounds the city. The residents continue to construct totem poles because they are responding to an interpretation of their own nativity.

Less expansive, but equally intriguing, are stills from various regional theater productions. These give one a great opportunity to look at various stage sets ranging from good ideas ('A Doll's House' in a doll's house) to bad ('Macbeth' in and around a rope Jungle gym). There is a short collection of business logos on trucks during the twenties and thirties, a lovely collection of stained glass pieces within a nice sequence of British Columbian contemporary craft works, a mime show which we could live without and a time-lapsed look at how Pacific storms spin around in the Gulf of Alaska and then come banging down into the Pacific Northwest coast. One wonders if the whole coast line itself is not curved by the same forces which guide the winds.

VANISHING POINT

The filmmakers provided just enough ambiguity so that *Vanishing Point* could withstand the passage of time. The movie is a bit dated – the suicidal hero uses drugs without remorse – but its essential appeal, as an existential car chase which never stops, has survived. The filmmakers were smart – a shot of a surfboard washing up by itself indicates a drowning aside. By keeping the psychology of the characters hidden, the movie encourages a viewer to return for repeat viewings, not just to sample the driving thrills, but to ferret out the meaning of it all.

The soundtrack is a little flat but usable. Most of the movie is set in the Nevada desert, which is somewhat lacking in color. The later reels seem stronger than the early reels, and the movie looked pale when it first came out, but the disc presentation, on the whole, is mildly faded.

THE VELVET VAMPIRE

The perversities of *The Velvet Vampire* have aged since the film was produced in 1971, lowering its impact and appeal. The disc still has nudity and blood, but not in quantities which give today's viewers a thrill. The acting in the movie is so wretched that the film is a numbing, rather than stimulating, experience. The picture is inevitably pale and worn looking, though one also gets the sense that it is probably an exquisite transfer of a movie that was likely filmed through the bottom of a Coke bottle. The sound is also stupefyingly flat and low in volume. Side two is in CAV with perfect still frames. The narrative concerns a couple invited for a desert weekend by a provocatively dressed woman who turns out to have unusual habits. The script pays more attention to plot than similar movies bother to, but the characters are more immortal than the film ever will be, and they all die.

VENGEANCE IS MINE

The print which Voyager has used for *Vengeance Is Mine* is in excellent condition and the colors are vivid, but it lacks a Hollywood gloss and may look a little grainy when compared to Voyager's other efforts. The 1979 Japanese color film has English subtitles. The monaural sound has not been CX-encoded, not even with the manual tripping option. The sound is in as good a condition as the print, but once again, it is not Hollywood.

Vengeance Is Mine is a docudrama about a murderer who avoids capture for several months by taking on a business-like demeanor and pretending to be a respectable citizen. His true nature, however, cannot stay suppressed. The script has been constructed to build up to the most dramatic events by utilizing flashbacks to shuffle the chronology. Despite the subtitles, the Japanese dialog prevents one from following the jump cuts as smoothly as one ought to, though, of course, the advantage to home video is that one can always return to a passage one does not understand.

The film, which was directed by Shohei Imamura and stars Ken Ogata, is a comprehensive character study and provides a compelling look at the grimy side of life. Imamura has a consummate awareness of the immediate vicinity in a location. The sex is steamy because it starts raining on the would-be lovers and the violence is tempered when the murderer, drenched in blood, takes a bite out of a sour pomegranate. The eroticism is deliberately sloppy, as is the violence (be warned that there is murder, involving a hammer, which requires several blows to complete), and one only recognizes the film's elegance after it is ended and its scope is fully revealed.

The film runs 139 minutes. Voyager has released the disc in CAV on five sides. Except when we needed more time to read a subtitle, however, we never felt compelled to take advantage of the standard play functions. *Vengeance Is Mine* is best savored at normal speed, where the director and the natural environment can corrupt one's sympathies using the pretense of normality.

VERDI – AIDA
BEETHOVEN – SYMPHONY NO. 9

The sound on the 'Arturo Toscanini Collection' discs, 'Volume 5' *Verdi – Aida* and 'Volume 2' *Beethoven – Symphony No. 9*, is digitally encoded monaural, but the audio has been meticulously engineered to coax the purest sounds available from the source material. The concerts not only sound legitimate, the recordings are more full and deliver more detailed tones than on many stereophonic discs. The lack of a real vibrating bass and a fuzziness created when a number of high pitched sounds are bunched together are the only real drawbacks, and the significance of the performances more than compensate for the audio limitations.

The images on the discs come from kinescope film recordings of the television broadcasts, achieved by filming a TV screen during the broadcast. The quality of the black and white picture is remarkable. Even when the contrast is out of synch or the shot itself is out of focus, the picture remains stable. Closeups of the performers are vivid, and the harsh lighting (many audience members wear dark glasses) needed for the television cameras accentuates a roughness in facial features which, perhaps, came to be imitated by horn rimmed glasses and the other exaggerated styles that were popular around the same era.

Aida runs to four sides (it was actually compiled from two separate broadcasts, Acts 1 and 2 were presented the first night and are contained on the first platter; Acts 3 and 4 were broadcast a week later and are contained on the second) and *Symphony No. 9* is a single platter. The discs are chapter encoded.

An essay called 'Watching Toscanini,' by Harvey Sachs, appears on the back of each disc and is worth reading in the video store even if you don't plan to buy any of the titles. Sachs not only explains why Toscanini's work is so respected, he also draws away the mystique from what a conductor does (or ought to do). In essence – the conductor's true labors occur during rehearsal and his guidance of the orchestra on stage should be no more than mild traffic directions, maneuvering the musicians through the most difficult intros, issuing minor corrections, and keeping time.

The complexity of such endeavors are readily observable in *Aida*. Since it is a concert performance of the opera there is no need for subtitles, although a lengthy synopsis is included on the jacket. The presentation is interesting in that the singers are centered, with the orchestra spread around them, and the recording is monaural. Rather than separating the musical parts, there is an emphasis upon hearing Verdi's work as a whole entity. The female leads, Herva Nelli and Eva Gustavson, make a stronger impression than the male leads, Richard Tucker and Giuseppe Valdengo, but in general the voices tend to merge more with the instruments and give the listener a chance to appreciate the unity in Verdi's composition. The duets are also enhanced under these conditions. The singers provide visual drama, as well, because the physical effort of standing and singing tends to captivate the viewer – and, apparently, the original video director – more than the activities of the other musicians. In summary, this is probably not the best 'Aida' Toscanini ever conducted, but it is a valuable glimpse at his conceptualization, and is the only complete opera to be offered in the series.

Toscanini's interpretation of Beethoven's *Symphony No. 9* is the Beethoven's 'Ninth Symphony' that plays in your dreams. He keeps the orchestra on a precipice for the entire 67 minutes, seeming to exaggerate but always holding back, so that Beethoven's glories are magnified but never distorted. It helps that the orchestra is relatively small, particularly in the string section. Many contemporary renditions of the piece tend to sound mushy, as resonance from one note played by too many instruments drowns out the beginning of the next. The soloists are also superb, especially the bass, Robert Scott, who seems invigorated by Toscanini's direction. The video presentation is playful, exploring the orchestra and cutting too knowingly on some of the most familiar passages. Near the end, Toscanini's profile is superimposed upon the chorus, a thematic and dramatic image which sums up the power the performance has generated. It is a wonderful hour of music and certainly the disc to consider if you only wish to sample one from the series.

VERDI FALSTAFF

Verdi Falstaff has been filmed on a soundstage. Gotz Friedrich's direction maintains a theatrical stage blocking, but the camera moves freely among the players, and the locales and acts blend from one to the next without awkward interruptions. It is a nice rendition of the opera, in Italian with English subtitles, and manages to be steadily amusing without overpowering Giuseppe Verdi's remarkable score. The picture quality is all right, though it never glimmers. The singing sometimes appears to be mildly out of synch. The sound is a little noisy and has at least one loud 'pop.'

Gabriel Bacquier portrays Falstaff and Karan Armstrong, who has a brief nude scene, appears as Mrs. Ford. The music is played by the Vienna Philharmonic under the conducting of Georg Solti, who instills a liveliness in the orchestra and the cast.

The two-hour show is separated neatly onto three sides, an act per side, and comes in a box. A thorough essay about the creation of the opera, a plot synopsis with chapter cross references, and a chapter listing appear on an insert which comes with the disc.

VERDI REQUIEM

The 96-minute performance *Verdi Requiem* is contained on a single two-sided disc, with the break occurring between the second and third movements. The four soloists are Margaret Price, Jessye Norman, Jose Carreras, and Ruggero Raimondi. The performance was part of the Edinburgh International Festival in 1982 and features the Edinburgh Festival Chorus and the London Symphony Orchestra, conducted by Michael Davis, in Edinburgh's Usher Hall. The sound is digitally encoded (the digital track has less hiss than the analog) and competently recorded. The picture is very crisp, but the direction and editing could have used a little more forethought. We found the camera was not always pointing at the performers we wanted to be watching. The soloists are superb, and the presentation is fine, although it doesn't quite have the kick which a more daring interpretation would produce.

VERDI: REQUIEM (Karajan)
(see **MOZART: REQUIEM**)

VERDI RIGOLETTO

In *Verdi Rigoletto,* directed by JeanPierre Ponnelle, the opening debauchery looks like something out of a Fellini movie. The style is deliberately arresting, but even though the remainder of the program is approached in a more traditional manner, the freedom of performing for the camera, instead of for an audience, is fully utilized. Luciano Pavarotti's acting, for example, can sometimes evaporate for the sake of his singing when he performs on stage. Here, Ponnelle keeps him fully in character (as the Duke), while his singing, which is almost invisibly post-synched, takes full advantage of a studio environment. You want to stop the disc to applaud.

Ingvay Wixel and Edita Gruberova are also featured, along with the Vienna State Opera chorus and Vienna Philharmonic. The disc runs three sides, an act to a side, and the opera is in Italian with English subtitles. The sound is exceptionally clear. The picture is average in quality, but improves in the Third Act. The disc has plenty of chapter markers, which are also cross referenced in a lengthy synopsis that is included, along with a cast list and a very good essay about the opera's beginnings, in an eight-page insert.

VERDI'S RIGOLETTO AT VERONA

The jacket of MasterVision's *Verdi's Rigoletto at Verona* would not be out of place in the generic section of the local grocery store, right up there with the marshmallows and potato chips. The lettering is white on black and black on white, without any frivolous design elements or iconic representations of the program within. The disc is cheaper than the London Records *Rigoletto.* Like other generic products, it isn't that much cheaper and you lose more than just the colored ink on the jacket. What you don't lose, however, is the essence of the opera itself.

The bad stuff first: No libretto accompanies the disc, nor is the program subtitled. A reasonable plot synopsis appears on the back of the jacket, along with a chapter listing, but that is it. The picture transfer is awful. Not only does the original production pass in and out of focus as often as the Duke's heart, but it has since aged to the point where even if the camera is in focus the lines are soft, and green has won a victory over its peers in the battle for color continuity. The sound has all the hiss and flutter one would expect when looking at the picture. The single plattered disc runs a full 120 minutes and breaks between side one and side two in the middle of an aria, in the middle of a note.

Before you put the disc back on the shelf, however, you should consider the good as well: The performances (Garbis Boyagian as Rigoletto, Alida Ferrarina as Gilda, Vincenzo Bello as the Duke, and, notably, Antonio Zerbini as Sparafucile) are very good. The opera is performed in the gargantuan Arena di Verona, but it has been filmed and recorded differently from the Pioneer Artist programs that have taken place there. Except for the establishing shots, the full stage is dispensed with and the camera stays acceptably close to the important players. The recording captures every foot shuffle and sheathed sword, but it also catches the voices of the singers before the sound becomes lost in the night air. It has the vibrant, immediate sound of a real performance, and the cast is full of energy and adrenaline. Since the singing is the essential part of the program in any case, the disc delivers everything its packaging appears to promise.

VERTIGO
THE LADY EVE

Like most enthusiasts of the cinema, we often fantasized about owning a revival house when we were younger. We would daydream of the inventive double bills which would grace our marquee, and we lit upon one pairing in particular which we felt would be ideal, two pieces of entertainment which would complement each other exquisitely. To our knowledge, no real revival house ever had the brains to run them together, but now you can play this dream double bill at home and treat your friends to an evening of two perfect, and perfectly matched, movie masterpieces. *Vertigo* and *The Lady* ("Positively the same dame!") *Eve*.

In that one should have dinner before dessert, one should watch Alfred Hitchcock's *Vertigo* first. *Vertigo* is film with a very precise color plan, and some viewers may not be satisfied unless the original Technicolor hues are perfectly replicated. They are not, but the disc's presentation is managable. The fleshtones look rich and solid colors are stable. The sound is not CX-encoded. The three sided disc has 14 chapter markers.

Many people profess the opinion that *Vertigo* is Hitchcock's best film, while others remain unimpressed. We become more tempted to concur with the former group the more often we watch the film. Multiple viewings definitely diminish the problems one may have with the course of the plot, and can heighten one's appreciation of the chilly emotional fog enveloping each character. Numerous viewings can also give one a chance to appreciate the subtleties in Hitchcock's style, such as the editing while Jimmy Stewart is following Kim Novak's car down the streets of San Francisco. The cut to Novak's car is always as it is just turning a corner, which leaves one, almost subconsciously, with a feeling of unfulfilled desire.

Vertigo is about a man who falls in love with the same woman twice without realizing it. So is *The Lady Eve*, but to a much happier conclusion. The Preston Sturges film was released by MCA, as part of their 'Gene Shalit's Critic's Choice' series. The black and white print is nice looking, with only a scattering of scratches, although there is a point on side two where, momentarily, the full screen image contorts. The sound is CX-encoded. A beautiful, original trailer for the movie appears at the end of the disc, and there are some great color stills on the jacket.

The film is such a fine comedy because, even after one has memorized all the witty one-liners, the performances of Henry Fonda, Barbara Stanwyck and the supporting cast, especially Eric Blore and William Demarest, continue to be amusing. The script is tight. The comedy ranges from slapstick pratfalls to sophisticated jokes about operas. In the best tradition of old black and white movies, sexual innuendo is everywhere, as is the Fonda character's pet snake.

As a double bill, *Eve* has the class to follow *Vertigo* without diminishing its impact. For those who become too emotionally involved with the Hitchcock work, the Sturges film can lift one gently back to reality. No decent library should be without either disc in any case, and if one has friends who are by chance unfamiliar with the films, having the discs will give a collector the opportunity to become a grand showman.

VICE ACADEMY

The silly burlesque, *Vice Academy*, has a few amusing gags about voluptuous vice squad trainees. The picture quality is above average and the colors are bright. The sound is so accurate you can hear the shifts in ambience during the overdubs.

VICE VERSA

The body switching comedy, *Vice Versa*, which stars Judd Nelson and Fred Savage, isn't as painfully bad as some other genre offerings have been. Savage, the younger one, is perfect as the adult, but Nelson's child doesn't seem to match the character he's supposed to have inherited. The movie is sporadically amusing and pleasant.

The picture is often too red, and tends to look a bit grainy, which is a shame because the cinematography is above average. The stereo effects are negligible. The sound boom makes an appearance on the lower edge of the screen near the end of side one.

VICTOR/VICTORIA
VICTOR/VICTORIA (Letterboxed)

There is a scene in *Victor/Victoria* in which an acrobat, trying to see a talent agent, starts balancing on a wine bottle on the desk of the agent's receptionist. During this distraction, the heroine sneaks into the agent's private office and can soon be heard emitting her glass-shattering B-flat. The camera, in a long shot which is something of a cheat since the reception area can't possibly be that big, remains stationary, with the acrobat on the far left and the open office door on the far right. The wine bottle shatters, the heroine gets the job, and the acrobat comes crashing to the floor. The gag is nowhere near as effective on a scanned and cropped video presentation because the viewer is not frantically glancing back and forth, trying to take everything in. *Victor/Victoria*, directed by Blake Edwards, is filled with visual humor which has been designed to make use of the full rectangular Panavision image. Until MGM/UA released their Deluxe Letter-Box Edition disc, the only function the title could serve on home video was to provide stimulus in assisting the recollection of how funny the movie was in the theater.

The revised MGM/UA version (a scanned and cropped version from MGM/UA had been available for some time; it enhances only one shot – Lesley Ann Warren's farewell at the train station) has an aspect ratio of 2.1:1. The many red interiors are unable to escape a certain amount of grain, but it is not enough to hamper the impact of the presentation. The digital surround sound is wonderful, particularly during the song numbers, which seem to have been cranked up by the film's sound editors. The movie, which is spread to three sides and comes in a gatefold jacket, has 54 chapter markers, enough to capture all the best moments.

Victor/Victoria has a lot going for it – a clever script, wonderful performances, great musical numbers, etc. – but one aspect contributing strongly to the movie's success is the decision to film it entirely on studio stage sets. The cozy artificiality of the phony Parisian setting not only reverberates the theme of the narrative, it also calls to mind the atmosphere of past musicals. The sets create the sort of world where anything goes and, to the delight of the viewer, the movie follows right along.

VICTORY AT SEA – VOLUMES I-III
VICTORY AT SEA – VOLUMES IV-VI
VICTORY AT SEA – VOLUMES VII-IX
VICTORY AT SEA – VOLUMES X-XII
VICTORY AT SEA – VOLUMES XIII-XV
VICTORY AT SEA – VOLUMES XVI-XVIII
VICTORY AT SEA – VOLUMES XIX-XXI
VICTORY AT SEA – VOLUMES XXII-XXIV
VICTORY AT SEA – VOLUMES XXV-XXVI

The *Victory at Sea* series has aged nearly to the point of uselessness. Embassy's *Victory at Sea – Volumes I-III*, *Volumes IV-VI*, *Volumes VII-IX*, and *Volumes X-XII* offer little more than sailors running frantically back and forth and hardware exploding under the gaze of shaky cameras. The 1955 television series was made with the assumption that World War II was fresh in everyone's memory and thus the narrator has only to say, "Corregidor," and the audience will know what he is talking about.

In fact, the discs might be far more watchable if the narrator, Leonard Graves, would just shut up. The episodes do not contain interviews or explanations or reasons or anything about the Second World War except genuine Allied and Axis footage, dramatic but phony-looking inserts, Richard Rodgers's clichéd score, and Graves's narrative. His words ("The face of Fascism shows the first furrows of defeat.") are used, like the music, to evoke an emotional response to the pictures, but facts are few and far between. And pity the poor school child who uses these discs to study his homework. Q: What happened on December 7, 1941? A: The Japanese raped Pearl Harbor.

Two episodes are featured on side one of each disc and one episode is on side two. There is no mention of it on the jacket cover or the disc label, but the second side of each disc is in CAV. The transfers are good though much of the original footage is naturally rough. *Volumes I-III* concern the North Atlantic convoys before America entered the war, Pearl Harbor, and the North Atlantic convoys after America's entry. *Volumes IV-VI* feature the Battle of Midway, the confusing situation in the Mediterranean, and Guadalcanal. *Volumes VII-IX* cover the beachheads in the Solomon Islands, the Italian effort in the Mediterranean, and the Allied invasion of North Africa (and includes two spectacular pieces of footage – a bomb falling through the wing of a plane and a ship exploding after it has turned over in the water). *Volumes X-XII* summarize the course of conflict in the South Atlantic and above the Arctic Circle, and carrier battles in Micronesia.

The CAV is best utilized on this last disc, as there are several spectacular battle sequences and a whole montage of bad aircraft carrier landings. If you want one disc, it is hard to choose the least offensive. *Volumes X-XII* is the most informative, if only because it is dealing with less well-known aspects of the war. There is a good explanation of what happened in the Aleutians and a closer attention to details than was exhibited on the earlier shows. You cringe though, when the narration compares the German efforts in the Atlantic to 'the days of skulls and crossbones,' and then praises similar British efforts in the next episode as being 'in the spirit of Drake and Essex.' Thank goodness the Allies were victorious. If the Nazis had won, we'd still be listening to this stuff every night.

Leonard Graves really starts getting into it on the final *Victory at Sea* episodes. "Andnowww: Deeeeee-Dayyy." He still sounds like someone who would enjoy pulling the wings off of flies and mosquitoes, particularly if they were Japanese mosquitoes and Nazi flies. Like the first four discs, the second four are in CAV mode on side two. Each holds three episodes. The fifth and final disc has two episodes to round out the series and is in CAV all the way through.

Volumes XIII-XV contains an episode about the battles for New Guinea, 'Melanesian Campaign,' an episode about the liberation of Italy, 'Roman Renaissance,' and 'D-Day,' which is the CAV episode. "The New Guinea natives are primitive and warlike. Head hunting and sorcery are part of their lives, but an enlightened colonial administration has won their loyalty." Just don't put too many of them in the boat with one missionary.

The next disc, *Volumes XVI-XVIII*, has one episode about the waning submarine warfare in the Atlantic, 'Killers and the Killed' and two episodes about activity in the South Pacific, 'The Turkey Shoot' and 'Two if by Sea.' "The Japanese resist, the Japanese die, the Japanese do not surrender." The most amusing trick on this one is the way the school children of Guam are shown lackadaisically playing baseball under American rule and then performing militaristic calisthenics after the Japanese take over. The CAV episode, about Pelelia and Angaur, is slow-moving and contains very little in the way of interesting footage.

Another typical offering is *Volumes XIX-XXI*. Two of the episodes are about tactical maneuvers in the South Pacific, 'The Battle for Leyte Gulf' and 'Return of the Allies.' The CAV episode, 'Full Fathom Five,' is about the United States submarine program and how it differs, morally, from German submarine warfare.

Fortunately, the last two discs are upbeat and are worth sampling if you are loathe to invest in the entire set. *Volumes XXII-XXIV* covers the end of the war in Europe, 'The Fate of Europe,' a nice half-hour explanation of what happened on Iwo Jima and why it was important, 'Target Suribachi,' and comprehensive coverage, with maps, of what happened in China and South East Asia, 'The Road to Mandalay.' The European episode also contains interesting footage of the Russians and Germans battling in Crimea.

The CAV is best utilized on the final disc, *Volumes XXV-XXVI*, in an episode about Japan's Kamikaze program, 'Suicide for Glory.' A nuclear explosion is the opening image on 'Design for Peace,' the final episode. Half of the show is used to tie together all the loose ends and then the second half is given over to footage of soldiers and sailors coming home.

The sound is an accurate re-creation of 1950 television standards, holding a lid on Richard Rodgers's blasts and swells. At one point, Graves says, "The real war will never be known to any, other than those who fought it." That appears to be the theme of the entire documentary, because after ten hours and 26 episodes you know virtually nothing about World War II or how a contemporary Navy operates that you didn't already know. If it weren't for all the rare, valuable footage which is never going to appear anywhere else, the show and the discs would be a total waste of time.

VIDEO A GO-GO – VOLUME 1

For music groups without enough videos to fill an 8-inch, Pioneer has released *Video A Go-Go – Volume 1*, a two-sided collection of videos from six different performers. The disc is like striking it lucky on MTV for a whole half-hour. The quality of the picture varies, but the stereo sounds great.

The first cut is one of those bawdy rock songs that they're trying to get banned from 7-11 stores or something, 'Obsession,' from Animotion. Following that is a perfectly abridged Cinderella tale, 'Fresh,' from Kool & the Gang. Rounding out side one is the wacky 'Look My Way' from The Vels and Stephanie Mills's 'The Medicine Song,' which ought to make people start talking about nurses again. Side two features the carefree female trio, Bananarama, singing and bouncing to 'Cruel Summer' and then a funky finale from the Bar Kays with 'Freak Show on the Dance Floor.' The Mills number appeared on a previous 8-inch, but the rest of the material is new to laser.

VIDEO A GO-GO – VOLUME 2

The dance-oriented *Video A Go-Go – Volume 2* features 'Solid' by Ashford & Simpson and 'Party Train,' an inferior Gap Band number, both of which can be seen on other discs. Another music video, 'Cold Dresses,' hasn't been seen before, but is not worth seeing. To further frustration, however, the remaining three cuts are excellent and justify obtaining the disc. Kool & the Gang's elaborate and creepy 'Misled' has a narrative which would support a feature-length film. The Bar Kays effort, 'Your Place or Mine,' is a little more simple, about a girl deciding who she is going to pick up at a disco. The only video on the disc which does not look grainy and which sounds strong and clear is Kurtis Blow's energetic 'Basketball' rap.

VIDEO LOVE SONGS

A compilation of music clips entitled *Video Love Songs* includes clips that have appeared on other discs. The only number on the disc which comes close to honest feelings is Diana Ross's tribute to Marvin Gaye, 'Missing You,' that also appeared on *Visions of Diana*. The others are more in line with John Denver singing 'Don't Close Your Eyes Tonight.' If you were her, wouldn't you?

There are seven songs on the 12-inch disc, each marked by a chapter. The sound is analog and the picture looks once too often removed from its source.

VIDEO PLAYMATE CALENDAR 1989

Below is a month-by-month selection of precisely transcribed comments to be found in *Video Playmate Calendar 1989*, a 50-minute release with a decent stereophonic musical score and a picture which looks mildly blurry in places.

January: "I like sleeping. I love sleeping. It's my favorite thing. I love to sleep."

February: "One thing I like about dance is that you use your body to do your job."

March: "I love being happy – dancing, playing – and most of all, I love life."

April: "Usually I don't buy an outfit and then go buy shoes. I buy shoes and then buy about five outfits. Huh hee!"

May: "Sensuality for me is a mood, an atmosphere – kind of those, those magical feelin's that you have all in your mind. There's nothing like a hot, summer Florida night to bring out the sensuality in me."

June: "I believe in falling in love."

July: "A lot of people think I'm from Chicago. I'm not, I'm from North Dakota."

August: "Everybody always says, 'Susie, you don't look like a nurse.' I used to wonder what they meant by that. And there was a time, believe me, that I was not so pretty. I used to give so much of my time taking care of other people that I forgot about myself. Cause I always wanted to be a nurse, you see. I used to bring home stray dogs – now I just mess with stray people. Why do I like long hair? Well, one time I went and saw this movie called *Romeo and Juliet* and she had the most beautiful hair I'd ever seen and after that I wanted long hair. It grew and it grew, and I got it."

September: "As for the photographers, well, I've worked with some real jerks. But they all have different personalities. But the photographers at Playboy are special."

October: "I love sleeping."

November: "I learned early on about the pursuit of happiness."

December: "You know when I started gettin' into film it was just eh, it was a great way to express myself and then other people can enjoy it. Hopefully. Maybe not, but then again that's a part of acting. Maybe I can make 'em sad. Or, I don't know."

VIDEO REWIND: THE ROLLING STONES GREAT VIDEO HITS

The disappointing menagerie of Rolling Stones music videos on *Video Rewind: The Rolling Stones Great Video Hits* makes one appreciate the concept of 8-inch discs. There are only three videos on this 12-inch from Vestron that are worth having, and the effectiveness of these is harmed by the haranguing barrage of attempted outrageousness that runs through the rest of the program.

No chapter markers are provided. The 'Neighbors' video is a cute concept. The Stones are playing their song in one apartment and the camera moves from peeking at them through a window to peeking at the activities in the windows surrounding them. 'Angie' is a straight-faced stare-into-the-camera-and-sing-your-haunting-ballad number. The pleasurable effect of this video causes one to suspect that if the group took their material more seriously the disc would have been much better. 'Undercover of the Night' is a big-budget production which gets lost in the clutter of the other clips. Viewed separately, it is a thoughtful look at war and politics in the Americas.

A VIDEO STANDARD

A company which specializes in audio benchmark and quality music software, Reference Recordings, has produced a laser video disc which they claim, "is probably the finest ever made," *A Video Standard*. The single-sided CAV disc has a multitude of potential uses revolving about the testing and teaching of audio video component functionality.

The claim that the disc is the 'finest' comes from the way it was constructed. Normal standards for the limitations of information contained on a disc were ignored during the pre-mastering and mastering process, so that the disc contains and delivers more information than present hardware components can process. The result is simple enough. Whatever flaw you may see or hear when you play *A Video Standard* is probably a flaw in your own video or sound system. Nevertheless, the title has been subject to some manufacturing difficulties.

The program material is presented in a disorganized, engineerish manner. Although some stop points have been encoded, other still-frame sections whiz by, and you have to be quick on the draw with your remote to catch them. There are also too few chapter markers encoded.

A booklet has been provided, which contains an extensive frame number index. Once one is familiar with the disc, it is not too difficult to find where a specific test pattern is hiding. The booklet also contains a wealth of explanatory and supplementary material, though the text is no better organized than the disc.

Briefly, the disc contains the following video sequences: A video recording studio being prepared for a shoot; a letterboxed helicopter ride across a river gorge in Northern California (constructed with two video cameras, which create side-by-side images); an intriguing collection of film footage transferred first to video from a print source, and then again, from the negative source to demonstrate the different results from the two methods; video calibration test patterns and explanations (including still frames); a still sequence showing how laser discs are produced; an extensive graphics sequence supporting stereo and surround audio tests; another set of video calibrations still frames (and instructions for void-your-warranty type monitor adjustments); and disc credits including photographs of the personnel involved in the production.

In addition, the audio sequences, when not putting out beeps and hums (example: '100 to 10 KHz @ -20dB'), contain a set of musical recordings, with jazz on the digital track and classical music on the analog track. The pieces serve as a promotional sampler for Reference Recording's music labels. It should be noted that although the analog track has a little hiss in the background, the digital track is completely free of distortion or impurities.

The disc is intended for viewers who like to tinker with their television sets. The range of tests is wide enough and sophisticated enough that the disc will be of use to audio/video professionals, but we also found it useful in guiding – but not dictating – the improvement of the picture on one of our sets. Packed with the booklet is a classy-looking blue filter, which can be used to adjust the color on one's set against reference color bars on the disc. Although it took us a while to sort through the materials and figure out the steps involved, we finally got the color bars looking as close to the way they are supposed to look as we possibly could. We then put on a disc which we knew looked terrific, and it looked awful – but – with a couple of quick and minor adjustments (the human factor) we suddenly had the most precise and satisfying picture we had ever been able to achieve.

Many of the video and audio tests require professional testing equipment to utilize effectively. Some of the tests, however, require only that one fool with brightness and hue on one's TV. We felt that the audio tests did not include enough surround material (the music is in surround, but is more difficult to calibrate). Unlike the video tests, the audio testing is primarily a fact and figure sequence, and the booklet has little to say about what practical applications can result from the exercises.

VIDEODISC MUSIC SERIES

The University of Delaware *Videodisc Music Series* is priced more for institutions than for individual consumers, but the four-disc set is well worth considering if you have any inclination toward the study or appreciation of classical music.

In proof, perhaps, that interactive discs are intended to supplement, rather than replace, other educational materials, the program is accompanied by texts which stack two-and-a-half inches high.

The discs, which are in CAV and have CX-encoded stereo sound, examine 12 well-known works by a variety of 18th and 19th century composers. Musicians are seen performing the pieces, which are then replayed with the visual accompaniment of a horizontally scrolling musical score. Above the score is placed an umbrella diagram, representing the total thematic ascensions and declinations within the work, in a series of colored domes, where a repetition of color indicates a repetition of theme. Occasionally, the piece is replayed a second time, with more detailed, color-coded analysis scrolling in tandem with, or in place of, the printed score.

Making use of the stop-and-go video disc functions, demonstrations of antique instruments, analysis of how instruments work, nuances of musical technique, and similar types of details are highlighted. If the music requires special efforts from more than a single performer, split screens are used to reveal the coordination of the musicians.

The 12 pieces, spanning 8 sides, include Haydn's 'Surprise Symphony,' Mozart's Quintet for Clarinet and Strings K. 581 First Movement and Piano Concerto in G Major K. 453 First Movement, Berlioz's 'Symphonie Fantastique,' a Gregorian chant from which Berlioz drew his inspiration, 'Dies Irae,' Debussy's 'Prelude in the Afternoon of a Faun,' Brahm's 'Schaffe in Mir Gott,' excerpts from the Zeffirelli *La Boheme* without subtitles (and, unfortunately, without the scrolling scores), Carl Bach's Fantasia in G Minor, Beethoven's 'Pathetique' piano sonata, and Chopin's 'Polonaise.' The most interesting segment contains three adaptations of Goethe's poem, 'Erhkonig,' by Carl

Loewe, Johann Reichardt, and Franz Schubert. The supporting analysis concentrates on Schubert's version.

There are dozens of chapter stops on every disc. Although the recordings sometimes have an institutional feel, they are generally pleasing enough that one could play the discs for background music were it not for all the imbedded stops. The picture is acceptable, although our every attempt to freeze a piano hammer resulted in a jittery blur.

At the end of every side there is a still-frame database of close to 1800 slides. As is the manner with interactive educational video discs, the same collection is repeated on every side, but that does not diminish its value. Portraits of the composers featured on the disc are included, as are depictions of the houses where the composers lived, their best friends, original handwritten compositions, posters, evocations of their era, et cetera. Pictures of music halls and instruments follow, as do 150 paintings from artists, from Delacroix to Degas, who were working in the same locations and time frames, as well as authors, royal patrons, and the cities which have inspired musical accomplishment. Also featured is a complete still-frame synopsis of *La Boheme* and a terrific collection of costume drawings.

Despite the presence of a semester's worth of knowledge, the four discs and accompanying texts have something else, very special, to offer. Real music appreciation. The package is constructed so that a sixth grader can obtain a sense of how music is put together and so that a graduate student can analyze Mozart's tonal developments in the sonata-allegro form.

VIENNA IN MUSIC/WIEN NACH NOTEN

A friend of ours whose career has been devoted to the study of experimental film was given a copy of *Vienna in Music/Wien nach Noten* and reacted, after having viewed it, with the same disgust one would suppose an art museum curator might feel upon having received, with some enthusiasm on the part of the giver, a painting purchased at Woolworth's. We sympathize, but negative comments from someone so cinematically oriented alerted us to an important difference between discs and films. *Vienna in Music* is a 90-minute anthology of Nineteenth Century Viennese music (mostly, but not exclusively, from the Strauss boys), with pictures added as a secondary attraction. The point of the disc is the music, and regardless of one's opinion of the musical quality of the pieces, enough are collected (and well played, by the Vienna Philharmonic under Will Boskovsky) to let the disc serve as a catalog summary of an era and a style.

The images chosen to go with the pictures provide a tour of Vienna's surroundings and heritage. Every chapter has a different theme – from the Lippizans to the Prater – and is sometimes presented in period dress, although they fool no one. The low point comes when 'The Blue Danube' opens with a shot of a tour boat breaking through the tranquil and by now oil slicked river.

The disc's picture quality is fair. It has a video tape source, but the strongest colors tend to blur. The sound is passable and a brief essay concerning the 22 pieces can be found on an insert accompanying the disc.

VIETNAM, THE TEN THOUSAND DAY WAR VOL. 1
VIETNAM, THE TEN THOUSAND DAY WAR VOL. 2
VIETNAM, THE TEN THOUSAND DAY WAR VOL. 3
VIETNAM, THE TEN THOUSAND DAY WAR VOL. 4
VIETNAM, THE TEN THOUSAND DAY WAR VOL. 5
VIETNAM, THE TEN THOUSAND DAY WAR VOL. 6

Embassy has released a six-and-a-half-disc documentary, *Vietnam, The Ten Thousand Day War*. Derived from a 13-part television series, every 48-minute episode of the show is on a separate side (*Vol. 6* contains two discs, but has the same list price as the others). Despite the inherent quality of news footage, the picture on all the discs is superb. The sound has been excellently mastered throughout.

Vol. 1 contains a summary of the following twelve episodes, 'America in Vietnam,' and we recommend that if you obtain the whole set, you not watch this side until another time as it contains nothing but highlights from the pictures and narration of the other episodes and so spoils, a little bit, the fresh, informative impact which the other episodes contain. Side two, 'Dien Bien Phu,' is about everything leading up to America's involvement in Vietnam. It has some fascinating footage from the French Southeast Asian campaign and an adequate explanation of what was happening in the minds of both the French and the Vietnamese at the time.

The series has a leftish, but for the most part objective, viewpoint. Action scenes are interspersed with talking heads to pace Richard Basehart's narration. By presenting the opinions of all the parties involved, the show refrains from taking a stand of its own. If the Communists interviewed come off sounding at least a little more sensible than the Americans, it is not enough to raise anyone's ire. By the end, everyone interviewed is given plenty of opportunities to present their viewpoints.

The politics of South Vietnam and America's gradually growing political involvement are depicted in *Vol. 2*, 'Days of Decision' and 'Uneasy Allies.'

The war is shown on *Vol. 3*. The Communist efforts are described in 'The Trail,' and the American response is shown in 'Firepower.' We found the depiction of civilian deaths as a result of Nixon's Hanoi bombing to be disturbing. An interview with a member of one of the bombing crews who found humor in his actions did not help matters. Arguments that atrocities occurred on both sides cannot excuse the slaughter of children by anyone.

On *Vol. 4*, 'Siege' depicts the Tet Offensive and the prolonged attack on Khe Sahn. The affects of the fighting on American public opinion are shown in 'Frontline America,' which is about the anti-war protests. 'Soldiering On' and 'The Village War' on *Vol. 5* are more confused in their focus, perhaps echoing the deteriorating conditions during the later stages of the war. 'Soldiering' is about American troop morale, including the POWs. 'Village War' recaps South Vietnam's military strategies and shows the final American efforts to force a stalemate in the fighting.

The last set, *Vol. 6*, 'Peace,' 'Surrender,' and 'The Unsung Soldiers,' is a complete look at the American withdrawal and South Vietnamese capitulation from every military, political, and social angle imaginable. The problem which Vietnam vets faced upon their return is also covered. In the show's one glaring error, an attempt is made to tell the story of a group of boys from a small Kentucky town who were sent to the war in the same National Guard unit and were killed on the same night during an artillery attack. Later in the episode, the grave of one of the boys is shown and his stone indicates that he was killed two years before the others left for duty. A little narrative license, however, is not going to spoil the accuracy or usefulness of this ten-hour documentary. Enough is presented to provide an excellent reference base for anyone wishing to research the war or to understand it.

A VIEW TO A KILL (CBS/Fox)
A VIEW TO A KILL (MGM/UA)

The wider image on MGM/UA's letterboxed version of *A View to a Kill* makes the James Bond movie easier to digest than the CBS/Fox scanned and cropped version, though the fire truck sequence is still too absurd to accept. The letterboxing has an apsect ratio of about 2.2:1. The picture transfer looks reasonably fresh on both discs though cropping on the CBS/Fox disc tends to magnify some of the grain.

The stereo surround sound on the MGM/UA disc is sharper and more clearly separated than the analog sound on the CBS/Fox version. The movie's sound editing is reasonably entertaining. Side three of MGM/UA's disc is in CAV for the grand finale. There is also a trailer for the film on the CAV side. It includes footage and dialog designed specifically for the promo but also encompasses many of the action highlights.

VINCENT, FRANCOIS, PAUL AND THE OTHERS

The subtitles on *Vincent, Francois, Paul and the Others* are bright and crisp, so you know your monitor is in focus. The movie behind the subtitles, however, is foggy as all get out, and it is a strain to watch. The director, Claude Sautet, adds to the problem by shooting through windows and, near the beginning, through thick smoke, but even when the smoke clears the image remains drenched in a thick haze. The colors look okay, but not consistently. At one point, the headlights from a car shine in green instead of yellow. The sound is a little shrill, but passable. Although the 'Letterbox' tag appears on the jacket cover, the French-language film has been given so slight a matting that it may not even show up on some monitors.

The film is difficult to appreciate under the best of conditions and nearly impossible to enjoy as a disc. For the record, it features a gaggle of France's best actors and actresses, including Yves Montand, Michel Piccoli, Gerard Depardieu, and Stephane Audran. The performances are engaging, but the story is an oft-repeated tale about men suffering with their fifties and sympathy for the characters, until the very end, is hard to come by.

VINCENT VAN GOGH: A PORTRAIT IN TWO PARTS
VAN GOGH REVISITED
Vincent Van Gogh will never be everybody's favorite artist. His intense, swirling palettes, outspoken compositions, and numerous self-portraits aggravate calmer sensibilities. As a disc however, *Vincent Van Gogh: A Portrait in Two Parts*, is an excellent example of how to use art for archival and entertainment applications in one program.

One side, in CLV, is a 50-minute one-man theater presentation about the life of Van Gogh, starring Leonard Nimoy. This is not as bad as it sounds, since the dialog is extracted from the famous correspondence between the artist and his brother, Theo. Nimoy gives Van Gogh's words emotion and while it may not always be the correct emotion, Van Gogh had such a crazy life that a broad-stroke portrayal is bound to be at least partially accurate.

The other side, in CAV, is a thorough (though not complete as some advertisements claim) collection of Van Gogh's works, separated by short text essays delineating the major phases of his career. On one audio track, Nimoy gives a no-nonsense summary of Van Gogh's life and work. On the other audio track, he reads more from Van Gogh's letters. The material alternates between current day location shots of Van Gogh's former haunts and lingering closeups of his works. The documentary, however, is divided into sections, and at every division point there is a still file collection with a much larger survey of the appropriate artworks. A insert lists each piece and the frame number where it is located. It is difficult to see how a painter and his work could be better served than by what has been accomplished with this disc. The education it offers is perpetual.

Rights to Nimoy's stage show expired, however, so the interactive material was reissued as a single-sided CAV disc called *Van Gogh Revisited*. Now we are not for a moment going to compare the disc to the painter's own physiognomy after he decided he no longer needed to hear things in stereo. Nimoy's hour-long performance was entertaining, but it was superfluous to the utility of the disc. Nimoy's analytical audio track is retained, but the letter excerpts on the alternate track are read by an unidentified speaker. What remains is a summary of the major phases in Van Gogh's biography and a rich collection of still frames.

THE VINEYARD
The Vineyard is a blend of zombies, prosthetics, martial arts, nudity, violence and dopey goings-on. The plot concerns an immortality formula which uses nubile airheads, both male and female, as an active ingredient, stirred with liquid in a large vat. The movie is something of an ego trip for James Hong, who co-wrote and co-directed the film and is also the star, portraying the guy who gets, until he is dispatched, all the nubile flesh he desires. The picture is sharp but never leaves the confines of the film's budget. The Ultra-Stereo surround sound is loud, but appropriate.

VIOLETS ARE BLUE
The dialog which explains the title probably got dropped in the editing somewhere. *Violets Are Blue* is about two lovers who are reunited briefly after a fifteen-year separation and feel gushy for a week or two before going their separate ways again.

Fans of Sissy Spacek and/or Kevin Kline may find the disc to be worthwhile. There is one exciting scene, but it is near the middle of side two, so you have to watch most of the movie before you get to it.

THE VIRGIN QUEEN OF ST. FRANCIS HIGH
The producers list "God" first in their acknowledgements on the end credit roll of *The Virgin Queen of St. Francis High* and they ought to, because if we were He we would have smote the whole production on the first day of filming. The movie is an excruciating tale of chaste, adolescent sexual frustration which the world would be better off without. The sound recording is amateurish, so digital encoding and the inclusion of a few stereophonic rock songs does nothing for the disc. The picture is grainy and ill-lit. There is an alarm clock in the movie with a little hand that does not point to the hour when the big hand points to the 12, which no one appears to notice. And even though all these kids supposedly go to St. Francis High, not one of them is wearing a medallion or a crucifix.

VISIBLE RESULTS. LIZA MINNELLI.
The 8-inch disc, *Visible Results. Liza Minnelli.* is grotesque and ludicrous. From her grating destruction of the lovely ballad, 'Losing My Mind,' to her silly analogy of a broken relationship with a nuclear war, 'Don't Drop Bombs,' the songs are distasteful and the videos are childish. The picture transfer, however, is spotless and vivid.

A VISION SHARED A TRIBUTE TO WOODY GUTHRIE AND LEADBELLY
(see **BOUND FOR GLORY**)

VISION QUEST
Of interest only to residents of Spokane, Washington or those who participated in wrestling during high school, *Vision Quest* is an excessively uninteresting drama about a boy who wants to beat the state champ in his weight class. He does.

The disc has an overly grainy picture and a top-ten rock score which includes a brief glimpse of Madonna performing in a Spokane tavern.

THE VISIONS OF DIANA ROSS
The 8-inch *The Visions of Diana Ross* has six songs on it, three to a side, and most of the videos have at least something going for them. In an updated version of 'Why Do Fools Fall in Love' Ross dances and skips down the streets of Las Vegas, unencumbered by any story line. 'All of You' is her duet with Julio Iglesias. The best number is 'Missing You.' The song is clearly articulated and the video includes footage of a stage performance with Marvin Gaye. The quality of the picture on the disc is excellent, although the cameramen have a tendency to keep Ross heavily gauzed.

THE VISITORS
A Swedish horror film which has been dubbed into English, *The Visitors* has a slightly different tone than the standard American horror cheapie, but it doesn't generate any extra thrills. The story is about a family which moves into a house in the country that has an unseemly past. Not too long after they settle in, things start going bump in the attic. There are several effectively created sequences (in one, the hero is hanging and spinning upside down, and something is coming to get him), but a lot of standard family-troubles stuff in between, and the dubbing tends to distance the viewer. The picture is cheap looking but competently transferred. The digital sound is more out of phase than it is in stereo.

VISUAL PATHFINDERS: FILMS BY NORMAN McCLAREN (Import)
Eleven films the Canadian filmmaker, Norman McClaren, whose short animated works helped to expand the boundaries of picture and sound coordination, are available on a two-sided CAV disc from Japan, *Visual Pathfinders: Films by Norman McClaren.* It has been designed and produced especially for disc and contains a still frame photo section at the end which charts McClaren's career. In a short opening segment, McClaren gives an introduction, in English, which is accompanied by Japanese subtitles. No other subtitles appear in the program, however, and the title cards which accompany the still frames are in English.

The short features include 'Begone Dull Care,' 'Hen Hop,' 'C'est l'aviron,' 'Blinkity Blank,' 'Neighbors,' 'Dots,' 'Mail Early for Christmas,' 'Lines Horizontal,' 'Canon,' 'Mosaic,' and 'Synchromy.' They are arranged chronologically and give an excellent sense of McClaren's growth as an artist, since the final pieces are the most complex and self-assured.

McClaren has two basic styles. One is an animation of forms and shapes set to music, such as with the Oscar Peterson scored 'Begone Dull Care,' which McClaren illustrated by marking up the negative itself. The other style is a manipulation of real images through stop action, represented here by 'Neighbors,' in which two men fight over a flower which sprouts on their property line. The most unusual piece is an early effort, 'C'est l'aviron,' which depicts a boat floating past woodsy scenery. It is both crude and haunting, and leaves a strong impression. It is also very Canadian.

The sound has been CX-encoded, but it is monaural and retains some of its rugged beginnings. The prints are all in good shape, and it is sometimes difficult to tell whether the scratches are from age or from McClaren. Utilizing the CAV features of the disc turned us off, since the works suffered immeasurably from the loss of the soundtrack. The still-frame section, however, is excellent, and contains several photo essays concerning McClaren's techniques.

VISUAL PATHFINDERS: THE WORLD OF ALEXANDER ALEXEIEFF AND CLAIRE PARKER
Imagine a canvas meticulously imbedded with more than a million straight pins. An artist, poking or running a roller on either side, could create intriguing bas reliefs with adjustable shadows. Imagine, then, such a canvas animated, a frame at a time. The artists, unable to view their previous shots,

rearrange the pins and lighting to create unusual, textured images – not quite sculptures or puppets, yet much more dimensional than cel animation. That is the medium on display in *The World of Alexander Alexeieff and Claire Parker*, a Pioneer Special Interests *Visual Pathfinders* disc.

The disc contains five shorts which Alexeieff and Parker made by animating their 'pin screen,' including an adaptation of Gogol's 'The Nose' and representations of Mussorgsky's 'Night on Bald Mountain,' and 'Pictures at an Exhibition.' There are also seven commercials, intended for movie theaters, which present a concise summary of how the two filmmakers earned their rent over the years. Each piece involves an innovative utilization of stop motion photography and the results are as captivating as the pin screen pieces. Rounding out the CAV disc is a brief documentary of Alexeieff and Parker at work on a pin screen composition, and a still frame segment, showing examples of book illustrations by the artists and scrapbook photos.

The theater commercials appear to be cropped slightly and this seems shortsighted, considering the intentions of the *Pathfinder* series. The CAV functions can often be used to break down the animation, though one should try to keep one's remote control unit out of one's hands on the first run through. The sound, especially on the older shorts, is weak, and the presence of CX-encoding on the disc may be to its detriment, since the process inevitably blocks out the most ragged and, hence, delicate portions of the recording.

As with all of the *Visual Pathfinder* discs, a sharp-looking booklet comes with the disc which provides both biographical details and production/intention analysis of each short. The conclusion of the biographical essay, written by Cecile Starr, captures our feelings perfectly: "In 1956 Alexeieff wrote that the time would come when his films would be available to the general public for repeated viewings, as they read poems and listen to music over and over again. This video laser disc, *The World of Alexander Alexeieff and Claire Parker*, which contains all their pin-screen films and a sampling of advertising films and engravings, encompasses even more than he imagined."

VISUAL PATHFINDERS: THE WORLD OF BOB ABEL (Import)

One *Visual Pathfinders* offering which is available in Japan, *The World of Bob Abel*, will probably not show up in America because of difficulties in obtaining copyright waivers. Abel makes commercials, and the disc contains many standout efforts, particularly from the campaigns for Levis, 7-Up, and AT&T. Other notable selections include the Transamerica 'King Kong' spot, the amazing ITT 'Growing Cities' sleight of hand, and a clever Japanese ad for batteries involving a light sword fight in which the loser wasn't using a long lasting power source. Abel's computer generated graphics have also been used in films such as *The Black Hole* and *Tron*, and segments from both are shown on the disc, though without their original soundtracks. Other notable pieces include a computer animated view of Chicago which explores the flexibility of perspective as it moves in and around the cityscape, and a short animated film set to the music of Gershwin, featuring geometric shapes that know how to party.

The still-frame section contains many production photos showing how the elaborate model work in pieces such as the 'King Kong' spot was accomplished. The CAV functions are useful to break down interesting works which have always whizzed by on broadcast TV. The commercials, which include some European ads, are presented in their original language, without subtitles. We discovered a curious phenomena as we were watching the disc, however, and that was the tendency to tune out the material. Years of training, we suppose.

VISUAL PATHFINDERS THE WORLD OF CHARLES AND RAY EAMES

The most compelling of the CAV *Visual Pathfinders* series, *The World of Charles and Ray Eames*, leaves one wishing passionately for more. Not only are the six films contained on the two-sided disc superb, but the picture transfer is especially sharp.

The sound is CX-encoded monaural. The narrative dialog which is present on some of the selections is weak, but the music is stronger and the score for almost every piece was written by Elmer Bernstein, making the disc, among other things, an important and jaunty addition to the libraries of those who collect his recordings.

The importance of the disc can be narrowed to the presence of two distinctly different but equally stimulating films which are to be found on side two, 'Toccata for Toy Trains' and 'Powers of Ten.'

Each has its proponents, but our own favorite is the 'Toy Trains' piece. The film, which has no narration after an introduction, is set in a scaled point of view that makes the many toy trains and toy backdrops appear to be adult-sized. The trains employed in the film are not Lionel-styled models, but wind-up trains, tin trains, carved trains, paper trains and even candy trains. Since the point of view is maintained throughout the film, the viewer can acknowledge the components of the make-believe without being distracted by the artificiality of the setting. You get so wrapped up in the journey, which begins at one station, crosses countryside, and ends at another, that you forget how simplistic the toys are. The high point of the film is a stunning shot in which a train appears to travel through the camera. The camera leaps into the engine and barrels down the coal car and successive passenger cars before popping out of the caboose. If you recall ever looking at a toy and imagining what it would be like to exist in the toy's world, and especially if you *still* do that sort of thing, 'Toccata for Toy Trains' is for you.

In comparison, 'Powers of Ten' may seem a bit too purposeful, but it is still great fun. The film begins at a picnic scene and then zooms outward exponentially, so that in a matter of a few minutes the entire known universe is in view. The exponent is then reversed, and the view is miniaturized until a swirling unknown of flavored quarks can be seen within a proton. Every step is carefully labeled on screen, so that the scope of the universe and the mathematics needed to understand the scope are easily accessible. A narrator provides even more explanation for the various checkpoints, but the piece is a natural for the triple-speed CAV function. The third film on side two, which precedes 'Powers of Ten,' is an early draft entitled 'A Rough Sketch for a Proposed Film Dealing with the Powers of Ten and the Relative Size of Things in the Universe.' Since the entire concept is worthy of an encore and since the two films have some distinct differences, it is not a bad thing that the disc includes both.

The biographical information on Charles and Ray Eames provided in an insert which comes with the disc is sketchy in places (the insert also contains a lengthy essay by Paul Schrader and is generally informative). The Eameses invented the stiff plastic chairs one has to sit on when one visits the library, and we assume it was the economic freedom this act provided which allowed them to ponder and create their so frivolous and intellectually rewarding films.

The opening film on side one is also a toy-oriented piece, 'Tops.' The narrative structure is similar to 'Tocatta for Toy Trains.' A multitude of tops are seen being wound up, being spun, spinning, slowing, and stopping. Bernstein's score is also remarkable, as he seems to grab a new sound within his melody for every top. The tops progress and digress in simplicity, and the film, like 'Trains,' is almost impervious to satiation.

The least satisfying film on the disc, 'House,' is included more for what it represents than for the rewards it provides. The movie is a series of elegantly edited still photographs which examine the house that the Eameses designed and resided in, considered by many to be a major architectural milestone. The movie is included to provide at least vaguely biographical material (unlike the other *Visual Pathfinders* discs, *Eames* has no still photo collection) and to acknowledge the pioneering work which the couple achieved with multi-media and slide presentations. As an entertainment, it is slow going.

The final film on side one is perhaps the most challenging piece included on the disc. 'National Fisheries Center and Aquarium' is a filmed proposal for a museum in Washington, DC which was never built. Although an initial response to the piece is to wish that more toy films had been included instead, multiple viewings can increase respect for the movie's efficiency and intelligence. By mixing graphics with models (some noticeably and invitingly toy-scaled) and stock footage of real fish, the film not only gives a succinct and clearly defined vision of how the Aquarium would look and function, it also teaches the viewer about museums, about fish, and about the necessity of knowledge. Because it is on the disc, it can furthermore be used to teach the art of film-making, and exemplifies what the entire *Visual Pathfinders* collection has achieved.

VISUAL PATHFINDERS: THE WORLD OF JOHN WHITNEY

John Whitney is a computer graphics specialist who searches for harmonics within geometry and uses mathematics to create art. Hovering at the fulcrum between the science of numbers and the creativity of spirit, his creations possess a balance which can be surpassed only by Nature itself.

The six pieces on *Visual Pathfinders: The World of John Whitney*, 'Arabesque,' 'Matrix

III,' 'Matrix I,' 'Hex Domo,' 'Permutations,' and 'Catalog,' are similar in concept. A common geometric figure – a triangle, for example – is repeated and moved with variations based upon unit measurements which were set by the initial figure. The variations alternately appear as a random scattering of lines and a concise symmetrical design. Using the capacity of the computer to modify color in exact increments, Whitney varies the hue of the figures as well. He also applies appropriate music, and although in some cases the sound seems more of an afterthought, it often contains the same deliberate symmetries which evolve in the visual material. (The disc is CX-encoded. Some of the segments are monaural and some are in stereo.)

Whitney's efforts with analog computers (number-crunching, geared monsters which created complex spirographs) and optical printers in the fifties pioneered the graphic lettering on film which we now take for granted. Whitney worked with Saul Bass on the credit sequence in *Vertigo*, and designed the process which was utilized in the 'Star Gate' sequence of *2001: A Space Odyssey*. His training in music, however, tempered his engineering zeal. He is both an inventor and an artist, an Edison who not only designs the phonograph but also cuts singles. His artworks are songs for the eyes.

The two-sided disc has several special features. It is in CAV, although a frame for frame calibration with Whitney's films is not possible since they were done at 24 frames a second (video runs at 30). The 'Still Step' command does allow one to break down the permutations, and triple speed places a different context on their exhibition. Whitney appears at the opening of side two, and his comments are as much fun to replay as the films themselves. At the end there is a still file section, containing photos of Whitney in various stages of his life and career.

A stylish looking booklet has also been included with the disc, providing more details of Whitney's biography and explaining the technical steps Whitney executed to create each piece (using frame numbers to cite specific effects). One wishes only that more of Whitney's own words could have been incorporated, since he is clearly one of those rare and valuable geniuses who likes both to tinker and to talk.

VISUAL PATHFINDERS: THE WORLD OF OSKAR FISCHINGER

The fourteen works represented on *Visual Pathfinders: The World of Oskar Fischinger* are principally animated pieces set to music, but they represent Fischinger's lifelong search in the elements of music – harmony, rhythm, and melody – within animated images.

Fischinger began his career in pre-Nazi Germany. Like many of the artists in the *Pathfinders* series, he had a wide and technical background in the arts, and felt compelled to express synthesis of his knowledge through the medium of film. He moved to Hollywood in the late thirties and stayed there, though he met with limited commercial success. Among the works featured on the disc are charcoal doodles shot in negative and coordinated to music such as Brahms' 'Hungarian Dances;' a short film made with large, colored two-dimensional figures which Fischinger did for MGM (and which opens with MGM's logo); an impressive effort in which Fischinger painted upon a series of plexiglass cels as the cameras kept on rolling, albeit a frame a time; and an animated work in color which has no soundtrack whatsoever and was intended, by the artist, to kindle music within the viewer's mind. Also included are several theater commercials and a short film compiled from still photos which Fischinger snapped during a multiple week stroll from Munich to Berlin.

The is well executed. Many of the recordings are old, but sturdy. One effort, however, had to be replaced. The soundtrack on the plexiglass painting short was unusable, so a newer recording of Bach's 'Brandenburg Concerto No. 3' has been supplied in its stead. The spirit of the work is unharmed by the substitution.

The disc is in CAV, and it is fun to play with. For one thing, practically every still frame is a work of art in itself. For another, Fischinger's essential intentions are retained even if the pieces are speeded up, slowed down, or run backwards. The power of the colors and figures, moving and changing, provides aesthetic pleasures at any speed.

In the still frame section there are numerous biographical photos and depictions of the equipment he used to create his films. There is also a collection of 100 paintings. These are as arresting as Fischinger's motion pictures, and their presence is further proof that video discs are a unique, flexible, and powerful medium for the exhibition of an artist's work.

VITAL IDOL

Despite his efforts to the contrary, which include a conscious attempt in training the left side of his lip to curl like Elvis, Billy Idol's hands will never be the Devil's playground. His persona is too deliberate, and his voice, although acceptably deep, lacks a true control. The music videos collected on *Vital Idol* demonstrate a satisfying vitality. Idol has plastered himself on each of the nine video credits as having responsibility for the concept. Every video is similar in style, even when the subject matter varies. Lots of people dancing around in post-apocalyptic rags. For 41 minutes, however, it is entertaining, and even if you do not worship Idol, you may enjoy the disc. The colors are worn down. The sound is not as clear as a straight recording, but only the most critical fans will fail to find the disc idyllic.

VIVA LAS VEGAS

Elvis movies comprise some of the most frustrating attempts at entertainment in existence. You want to like them, but most are so poorly written and edited that nothing happens between the songs. You wear yourself out, emotionally, chasing what scraps of narrative there are. *Viva Las Vegas* is an MGM/UA Deluxe Letter-Box Edition offering, with an aspect ratio of about 2.5:1, and the letterboxing retrieves the only two assets that make the film worthwhile, the car race during the last fifteen minutes that saves the movie, and the Ann-Margret dance numbers, which make it worth preserving.

When you see the car race cropped, it is no different from any gratuitous cut-and-paste effort, with barely discernible continuity and confused suspense. With the full widescreen image, however, the sequence is terrific, especially on a larger monitor. The track rises and dips and your stomach goes right with it. The placement of the cars is easy to keep track of, and the scene, unlike most of the film, is completely involving.

The dance scenes are not as harmed when the picture is cropped, but the numbers are still much more satisfying when all the chorus dancers can be viewed moving in unison behind the stars. The Metrocolor source material is mildly indistinctive, but the focus is very sharp. The monaural sound is also in good shape. There is a nifty theatrical trailer after the movie is over which contains one line that we particularly enjoyed, "Hear Elvis on his new RCA-Victor extended-play record!"

VIVA SANTANA

An unusually structured 80-minute documentary about Carlos Santana, *Viva Santana* includes clips of everything, from 'The Ed Sullivan Show' to *Woodstock*. The picture varies in quality depending upon the clip. Between numbers, Santana speaks in voiceover about his experiences and musical influences. Although he sometimes mumbles and is difficult to hear, his comments are informative and uninhibited. The song performances are often pieced together from different sources and deliberately swing from monaural to stereo to stereo surround within a single number, to match the clip source. Some listeners may find the fluctuations annoying, but others may be impressed by the innovation which, among other things, is in keeping with the mixture of musical styles Santana is famous for. So long as it doesn't happen on every disc it is an interesting effect.

VIVA ZAPATA!

The sound on Elia Kazan's only stab at an action picture, *Viva Zapata!*, is digital monaural. The analog track is a little noisy but the digital track is very clean, although in general the soundtrack lacks strength. The black and white print has only a small number of breaks and scratches, and the image looks sharp.

Marlon Brando mumbles his way through the title role. He is supposed to be an inarticulate man of the people, but his downcast puppy dog expressions sometimes do more harm than good. If John Steinbeck's script was not overly symbolic and preachy when the film was first released, it certainly comes across that way now. Yet most viewers tolerate the film and even look forward to the sort of multiple viewings that laser discs so graciously facilitate. The movie is entertaining because of Brando, because there is gunfire and explosions at regular intervals, and because the cinematography is trying to be as fancy as Steinbeck's writing and, in failing, does a better job of it. That could be Zapata's epitaph.

VIVALDI: THE FOUR SEASONS

Overcome the stigma of turning off the television when playing music programs on video and, with *Vivaldi: The Four Seasons*, one will be treated to a lovely, intelligent analog stereo performance of Vivaldi's work. The sound is full and the bass is particularly effective.

Turn the television on and one is bombarded with an extremely tacky collection of travel photography. There is a theme – Paris in spring, New York in summer, Venice in the fall, and Moscow in winter. One reviewer pointed out that Venice is nicer in the summer and New York is more pleasant in the autumn and felt the two should have been switched, but by all reports Moscow isn't exactly amiable in the winter, either.

VLADIMIR HOROWITZ THE LAST ROMANTIC

The world is invited into the living room of Vladimir Horowitz to watch him play on his own piano in *Vladimir Horowitz The Last Romantic*, a film by the Maysles brothers. It is an 88-minute program and has been digitally encoded. The sound is better than studio quality because, despite the hiss, Horowitz sounds like he is playing in a living room, complete with oddball acoustics and wall to wall plush carpeting. Owning the disc is the next best thing to having him play in your living room, and his piano is in better tune.

Horowitz plays ten numbers (an eleventh plays over the end credits). Between each piece, Horowitz and his wife discuss the music with the filmmakers. He offers insights which only a veteran pianist could provide, such as explaining that Chopin wrote better piano music than Tchaikovsky because he understood the piano better. Wisely, chapter markers have been encoded for both the musical numbers and the conversations.

A good-sized essay printed on an insert accompanying the disc explains how the filming and recording were accomplished. The picture is slightly grainy, but the closeups of Horowitz's fingers are unhindered.

VOLTRON, DEFENDER OF THE UNIVERSE: CASTLE OF LIONS
VOLTRON, DEFENDER OF THE UNIVERSE: PLANET DOOM
STARCHASER: THE LEGEND OF ORIN

The two *Voltron, Defender of the Universe* discs are not alike. *Castle of the Lions* appears to be an 83-minute pilot episode/episodes which has an involving story, some rip-'em-to-shreds violence, and a few well-constructed vistas. It has the minimum allowable movement, but for those who are partial to such efforts, *Lions* is worth considering.

Planet Doom is not. *Doom* is simply a collection of four regular Saturday morning shows. The credits and titles have been removed to give the vague impression of a single feature, but unlike *Lions*, the delineations between one episode and the next are clear and the slots where one would normally stick candy and toy commercials are easy to spot.

'Voltron' is a group of five buddies who tool around in lion-shaped space ships which form a single, badassed robot when the going gets tough. They don't so much defend the universe as they defend one wimpy castle in the middle of nowhere, but there seems to be no end to the number of bad guys who try to waste the place. The animation is Japanese and the characters look exactly like the characters in all other Japanese cartoons.

Planet Doom and *Castle of Lions* are both in stereo. The sound has an equivalency to the limited range and detail of the drawings, but the loud music, echo-hall villains, and various fight effects are a lot of fun and are worth pumping through a fancy stereo system.

The animated feature film, *Starchaser: The Legend of Orin*, is a little more sophisticated than the typical Saturday morning fare; there is enough movement in each shot to encourage concentration on the story instead of the artwork. The plot is a little more sophisticated as well, and quite violent. Although it was originally issued to theaters in 3-D, it offers sufficient fantasy with just two dimensions.

Watching *Starchaser* on disc, however, is like looking through a muddy window. The transfer does not do the material justice and often looks smeared, faded, or speckled. Although the title is in CX-encoded stereo, the sound on the *Voltron* discs was better.

VOLUNTEERS

Nicholas Meyer directed *Volunteers*, but the comedy is surprisingly flat. He does manage to quote camera angles from *Bridge on the River Kwai*, but there isn't enough comic inspiration like that to sustain the story of Peace Corps misfits building a bridge in the jungles of Thailand. The other properties he has directed have seemed more special than this. Why did he bother?

The video transfer is ridiculous. Some scenes are so grainy you can see the insides of your television set between the pieces of picture. The sound is stereophonic, with a few cute separation effects, an interesting score by James Horner, and limited fidelity.

VOYAGER GALLERY

Side one of *Voyager Gallery* is organized as follows: A summary of the Jupiter, Saturn, and Uranus flybys includes initial, composite 'encounter' movies and a demonstration of the sounds caused by planetary radiation/wave activity; a quick explanation of how image processing works; detailed 'movies' (sequential photos) and summary material for each of the three planets, including atlases of the moons which possess surface features and a fantastic computer animated journey across the topography of the Uranian moon, Miranda; the meat of the disc, 1100 still frames containing selected photos and detailed (sometimes three frame's worth) notes identifying the subject of each photo and providing the best guess as to how that subject came into existence; and, an up-close motion picture of Halley's Comet in flight.

The movies are narrated to identify the objects under observation, but elucidation is saved for the still frames and text. The text is difficult to read, but that is the price one pays. We caught only one still frame which jiggled.

Even if you could fit four color photographs on a page and still squeeze in the text, the material on Voyager Gallery would need at least 500 pages if it were in book form and would be prohibitively expensive. Thus the disc is justified from an economic standpoint. Whether you are interested in Saturn's 'kinky' ring, or the curious gas which is spewing out of the volcanos of Io in the way that water vapor is expelled from volcanos on Earth, the disc is rich in analysis of the data which the Voyagers provided.

The movie of Halley's comet was obtained from photos taken by the Giotto satellite and depicts the comet moving at 10 times normal speed. Utilizing CAV functions, one can increase its speed even further and obtain an eerie vision of the remnants of Creation.

All of side two is taken up by an electronic composition created by William S. Weisbach, entitled 'Sound Portraits of the Planets.' Digitally recorded and digitally encoded, the sound on side two is as clean as your ears. (Side one is analog without CX-encoding.) Two entertaining essays are included on the inner jacket spread in which Weisbach explains what he is up to. While his essay looks like it belongs on the bulletin board in the local yoga store ("Earth plays Mi, Fa, Mi...symbolizing 'miseria, fames, miseria,' or the misery, famine, misery of our planet..." He thinks it's bad here – they haven't had a decent harvest on Mars in 825,000 years.), the music itself is a super workout for one's sound system. It is guaranteed to blow the dust out of your amplifiers and knock down every tree within 500 meters of your house. The visual material is drawn primarily from computer animated interpretations of the Voyager paths, but it is expertly edited and quite sympathetic to the music. The result is entertaining no matter what astral plane you are observing it from.

THE VOYAGER ODYSSEY

The Voyager space probe images of Neptune and its moons, the highlight of which is a computerized topological sketch of Titan, are available on *The Voyager Odyssey*. The hour program is presented, broken comfortably to two sides, in CAV. There is no narration, and a good part of the disc's promotion is an emphasis on its digital stereo surround soundtrack, which features anonymously performed classical music pieces, from the ubiquitous 'Also Spach Zarathrusta' and 'The Blue Danube Waltz' to fresher offerings such as Ralph Vaugn Williams' Symphony No. 7, Alan Hovhaness' 'Mysterious Mountain,' selections from Aram Khatchaturian's 'Gayna,' Liszt's 'Preludes,' and Respighi's 'Pines of Rome.' The music has an interesting dimensionality and is as clean and comprehensive as the jacket notes claim. It is not lively enough to be our first choice as a demonstration piece, but others may find it useful in that regard.

The video footage mixes photos from the two Voyager probes of the four outer planet systems with computer animation depictions of the probes in action. Title cards are employed to explain the images. The still frames are steady and the transfer is decent.

W.C. FIELDS/STRAIGHT UP

Clips from the films of W.C. Fields can be entertaining in a different way from the films themselves. When a scene is viewed in its original context, the brilliance of its composition and of Fields' performance may slip past unnoticed, at least during the first dozen viewings or so, because the viewer is distracted by the meaning of the scene and by the rest of the film. When set apart in a compilation piece, such as the documentary *W.C. Fields/Straight Up*, the magnification caused by drawing total attention to the execution of the individual scene makes it that much more funny and satisfying.

Straight Up is a well researched and adeptly presented portrait of Fields' life and films. It combines contemporary interviews with film clips and a narration, nicely read by

Dudley Moore. Although some of the clips are not of pristine quality, the transfer of the documentary is clearly well done and the sound is good. The movie lasts 100 minutes, and the disc's only real fault is its chapter encoding, which is practically non-existent.

THE WACKIEST SHIP IN THE ARMY
The awkward but enjoyable 1960 comedy, *The Wackiest Ship in the Army* is about a yachtsman with an officer's commission who is assigned command of a small schooner during World War II. The script, apparently pared down from something considerably longer, leaves characters in unresolved fixes and plot motivations in a dense fog. The basic premise, and the spy mission to which the schooner is assigned, work so well that the viewer can afford to ignore what isn't fully explained. Whoever trimmed the script knew what they were doing.

The opening credits of the Cinemascope production are presented in letterboxed format, but the rest is scanned and cropped. Skin tones often look too orange, and the colors shift in quality while never quite seeming to achieve accuracy. Whether a symptom of the panning or something else, there is an annoying tendency for frames to freeze immediately before cuts. The sound is satisfactory.

WAGNER
The four-hour TV mini-series, *Wagner*, starring Richard Burton, has been released in Japan. The program is quite a disappointment. The script was written for the incorporation of quotations and bullet-point biographical details, not drama. Even a rudimentary or trivia-oriented analysis of Wagner's music is nowhere to be found. Burton is slumming and the distinguished cast is ill-used. There is a scrumptious three-head shot of Ralph Richardson, Laurence Olivier, and John Gielgud, but nothing comes of it. Olivier, in fact, has just one speech, which he delivers with a discomforting wheeze.

The show is broken into four episodes, one to a side. The two platters each have opening and closing credits, the closing credits applying only to the second episode on the platter. Donald Moffat provides an extensive voiceover narration to fill in the historical gaps, but we would rather have tried to figure it out for ourselves. The second episode is the strongest, and almost worth watching independently if you should happen to come across the disc, but the full effect of the program belittles the subject and tests the viewer's stamina.

The disc itself is in fairly good condition. Vittorio Storaro's cinematography survives well enough, considering the oranges he is so fond of shading things with. The image is slightly soft, but passable. The sound is in stereo with mild surround effects. The only selling point the disc really has is its amalgam of Wagner's scores, which, conducted by Georg Solti, make the bridges livelier and more compelling than the conversations.

WAGNER
Volume 1 of the 'Arturo Toscanini Collection,' *Wagner*, represents the very first telecast concert given by Toscanini. According to the jacket notes, the camera setups were not rehearsed ahead of time in fear of disturbing 'the Maestro.' Nevertheless, the mix of camera angles is more varied and more satisfying than it is on several of the other programs. The picture is clear and many different musicians make it into the shots.

The program features the Act III Prelude to 'Lohengrin,' the overture and Bacchanale from 'Tannhauser,' 'Forest Murmurs' from 'Siegfried,' 'Dawn' and 'Siegfried's Rhine Journey' from 'Gotterdammerung,' and 'Ride of the Valkyries' from 'Die Walkure.' In the early passages the music seems more removed from the images than it does on the other Toscanini discs, as if the sound engineers got a little too carried away cleaning up the track. The opposite problem is at hand in 'Valkyries.' Although Toscanini puts on quite a show, the recording is not airy enough and his punches are turned into dull thuds. The passages from 'Siegfried' and 'Gotterdammerung,' however, are superbly executed and, with the cameras capturing a number of the musicians who appear in synch with the music, a pleasure to view.

WAGNER: OVERTURES/BERLIOZ: ROMEO AND JULIET
The picture quality on side one of *Wagner: Overtures/Berlioz: Romeo and Juliet* is outstanding, but side two is a little grainy and not quite as good. The disc features Sir Georg Solti conducting the Chicago Symphony Orchestra at the Orchestra Hall in Chicago. The disc has chapter markers and a single page insert which contains a pair of cryptic essays about the featured pieces.

The picture on side one is so clear that you can see the grain in the wood of the violins and flaws in the brass on the trumpets. Although the performance is live, the cameras achieve tight closeups on many of the instruments. What you don't see directly is the faces of the performers. The disc is all fingering. The overtures are to 'Flying Dutchman,' 'Tannhauser,' and 'Tristan and Isolde.' The sound lacks crispness.

WAGONMASTER
The second half of John Ford's *Wagonmaster* is quite entertaining, as the logistics of getting the covered wagons across rough territory mix well with the carefully constructed personality conflicts. The movie takes a long time before it hits its stride though, and viewers may be apprehensive seeing it through. Visually, the film is one of Ford's best. At several points in the action he simply pauses and provides head and shoulder portraits of each cast member, the psychology of the dramatic situation being powerful enough that the actors don't have to do a thing to look like they are doing a lot.

The single platter disc comes in an impressive gatefold jacket and there is a lengthy essay about the making of the movie on the innerspread. The picture looks very good during the movie's best moments, but appears softer during some less important passages. The monaural soundtrack has a number of Ford-style folk songs and is best held to a reasonable volume.

WALKING TALL
PART 2 – WALKING TALL
FINAL CHAPTER – WALKING TALL
The sound boom or its shadow is so prominently displayed in *Walking Tall* that it ought to be considered a supporting character; a deity, perhaps, listening to Buford Pusser's prayers or bobbing down from the top of the screen to test his resolve and faith. The movie certainly tests one's faith in filmmaking. The shots rarely match and are poorly edited for drama, the acting of the secondary characters, boom excluded, is self-conscious and loud. The colors look wrong. The sound is either fuzzy or (when the boom is in real close) glaring. In the middle of everything is Joe Don Baker, whose performance as Sheriff Pusser is outstanding and surely the one reason why the otherwise amateur effort became a major hit. In a movie where every other actor and actress thinks that shaking and screaming is the way to show emotion, his tranquility is attractive.

The sound boom which played such an integral role in the first *Walking Tall* is completely absent from *Part 2 – Walking Tall.* In fact, it doesn't look like a boom was used at all since the entire movie has post-synchronized sound. The dubbing is sometimes so far off it appears as if the actors were really speaking Italian or something when the camera was going.

Joe Don Baker, who made a good impression as Buford Pusser in the first film, was replaced in the sequels by Bo Svenson. Svenson's approach is less sensitive and more comic book heroic, but the movie is closer to the typical exploitation formula, so his presence is not incongruous. The technical aspects of the movie look as bad as the first film's, if not worse. A child's red sweater becomes a floating rouge cloud. The sound is mediocre.

Anyone familiar with police procedurals will cringe at how bad Buford the Cop is at day-to-day law enforcement. It takes about half of the movie before he suddenly realizes that if he arrests people instead of hitting them, he can use them as informers. The ending is hysterical. A crazed killer is holed up in the upper room of a boarding house. He has a machine gun, a couple of handguns, and who knows what else, all clearly unregistered. Buford, standing on the staircase with his deputy, shouts through the door of the room, telling the killer to throw his gun through the window. The killer, muttering 'hee, hee, hee,' under his breath, puts one of the handguns in his back pocket and drops the other one out onto the lawn. He tells Buford that he did what he was told and Buford breaks the door down. The killer grabs the gun from his back pocket and shoots Buford. Buford, on the floor, shoots the killer three times. The killer grabs his machine gun and shoots the ceiling a whole mess. There is a long pause as the killer flops dead on the bed and then Buford's alert deputy, who was only two steps below him on the stairs, leaps into the doorway, gun drawn, as if he had run the entire distance.

Bo Svenson is also Buford in *Final Chapter – Walking Tall.* This episode has the most professional looking production values and the least exciting plot. Buford cleans up the county and then loses the next sheriff election because people have short memories. Put out to pasture, he mopes around until – get this – a Hollywood producer comes and offers to film his life's story. Certainly one of the most profound metaphysical twists ever put in a drive-in movie, one introspective scene has Buford in a theater, watching the enactment of his wife's death and his own disfigurement. The films ends with Buford's fatal automobile crash, filmed in total darkness until the car explodes.

The disc has just as many speckles as *Part 2*, but the colors appear more confident and the sound, although still dull and monaural, really looks like it comes from the people doing the speaking.

WALL STREET

Oliver Stone's *Wall Street* was heavily criticized when it was first released, but then, a curious thing happened. Writers and others continued to refer to the film long after its play should have concluded. The reason is evident on the disc. The world depicted in the film is like one's day dreams. Plush, luxurious, and very much at ease during the 126-minute playing time, the film allows the viewer to linger in the realm of the rich and powerful. The plot and dialog do not ring entirely true, but there is enough cerebral action to make the story an enjoyable, re-playable drama; and the acting is uniformly grand. The stereo sound is great, and the mix is wonderful, but the disc has only an analog rendering. The picture transfer is less successful, and takes a little of the gloss off the fancy interior decorations. But it is neither the disc's flaws nor the film's moral which one remembers when the movie is ended. Rather, it is the premise of what life could be like if one could have it all.

WALT DISNEY MINI-CLASSICS: BEN AND ME/BONGO

The two features on *Walt Disney Mini-Classics: Ben and Me/Bongo*, each of which is about a half-hour long, were originally created for theatrical presentation and then modified, with added material, for television broadcast. 'Ben and Me' began as an independent theatrical short. 'Bongo,' which tells the tale of a circus bear who finds romance in the woods, was a component of the feature, *Fun and Fancy Free*. Since the same art department was twiddling with the cartoons, the added material is as rich as the original. In 'Ben and Me,' for example, a 'family history' of the mouse, who eventually meets and inspires Benjamin Franklin, was added to expand the cartoon for TV. While the sequence is a diversion from the central narrative, it is great fun and deserves to be included. Although a title card at the end of both cartoons states that footage is missing, the sequences which have been dropped involve no more than a few seconds of introductory framing. The essence of both cartoons is preserved.

The picture transfer is fine. 'Ben and Me' has generally soft colors which survive without distortion. 'Bongo' has stronger reds and oranges which tend to blur slightly. The monaural sound is not CX-encoded, but it's no big deal.

WANTED DEAD OR ALIVE

The jacket cover for *Wanted Dead or Alive* looks great, with an almost pinup-sized photo of Rutger Hauer, scratching a cootie on the back of his shoulder and demonstrating the safe handling of a firearm. Hauer is good in the movie, too. He's a little more human than usual and a little more sympathetic, though you don't for a moment believe that his character is actually the grandson of Steve McQueen's character from the old TV series. Not unless his grandmother was Dutch.

We caught a glimpse, once, of a vertical white line, and thought we noticed one or two speckles elsewhere, but otherwise the picture is perfect. Much of the movie takes place at night (Hauer looks like a bum in the daylight), but only when the filmmakers themselves push the capacity of their film does the image become grainy. When it is solid on the movie it is solid on the disc. The title has Ultra-Stereo Sound, one of our favorite processes for non-serious films. The plot is about a group of terrorists who want to blow up a chemical plant in El Segundo to poison the rest of LA.

WAR AND PEACE

We usually enjoy sprawling epic stories, but the 208-minute Dino De Laurentiis *War and Peace* from Paramount is not a thrilling investment. De Laurentiis has been trashing great film properties for years. This 1956 release has an international cast whose dialog is universally post-synched – fortunately, in the case of Anita Ekberg, but unfortunately in the case of Henry Fonda, whose lip movements rarely match his speeches.

The film is not totally without merit. Audrey Hepburn has a substantial role and there is not a false note in her performance. The second huge battle scene is spectacular. But why are these people waltzing five years before the waltz was invented? Why is Herbert Lom playing Napoleon Bonaparte as if he were Chief Inspector Dreyfus? How does Fonda injure his dueling opponent by shooting at the ground? Did the bullet bounce off the snow? And why does one get a sense from this movie that *War and Peace* is, above all else, about bad marriages? Is that a theme filmmakers everywhere respond to in earnest?

Except for the reel-change points, the color looks well-preserved and the breaks, splices, and speckles are kept to a minimum. This is Nina Rota's worst score and it sounds like it is being played through a PA system.

THE WAR LOVER

Steve McQueen plays a creep in *The War Lover*, a movie about WWII bombing pilots. His character is uniquely drawn, so you have to figure that someone involved with the script actually knew somebody who had the same personality flaws. McQueen is a pilot, and Robert Wagner, who ends up with the girl, plays his goody-goody co-pilot. The bombing run sequences are well put together, and there is some terrific stunt flying, but the better the flight scenes are, the more impatient a viewer becomes when the characters are on the ground.

The transfer has a few splices, but the black and white print looks passable when it isn't utilizing stock footage. The monaural sound is worth amplifying, even if the rumble of the flak sounds muffled.

THE WAR WAGON

John Wayne and Kirk Douglas talk directly to the audience in the theatrical trailer for *The War Wagon*, which appears on the disc. It doesn't seem to completely capture the spirit of the film, which is a satisfying action picture with nothing to offer except uninterrupted entertainment, but it is a welcome addition to the program, especially since, once the movie itself is ended, one wishes there were more.

The credit sequence is letterboxed but the rest of the film and the trailer are not, and the credits leave one wishing for the day when movies like this, which rarely appear in theaters, can be seen in their original aspect ratio. You are supposed to see Douglas's grin and Wayne's scowl in parallel. Seeing them sequentially tells a different story.

The print is excellent. There are a few moments where Wayne and his horse both appear a little more orange than necessary, but through most of the movie the pines are a rich green, the water is sky blue, and the wagon is a scruffy chalkboard black.

The plot goes through some convolutions so that Wayne and Douglas can rob thousands of dollars in gold without offending Western-hero standards and practices laws. The 1967 film was made at a time when the counterculture was beginning to make inroads in the motion picture business. That it remains engaging when so many movies from that era have become dated and difficult to tolerate is proof that the Establishment could do some things very right.

WARLORDS

The helicopters buzzing David Carradine on the jacket cover of *Warlords*, never appear in the movie, which is a filmed-in-a-gravel-pit post-apocalypse action picture. The script shows some promise, but there is not enough substance to support the 85-minute film and the padding is both obvious and boring. The picture transfer looks spotless, though the film stock is uneven and the movie's colors are uniformly dull. The sound is best left without amplification.

WARM NIGHTS ON A SLOW MOVING TRAIN

A prostitute working out of a sleeper car on a dreary overnight express is the subject of *Warm Nights on a Slow Moving Train*, a slow moving film which goes nowhere. The film stock in the Australian production creates muddy looking colors, but otherwise the picture transfer is passable, as is the monaural sound. There is a murder in the final quarter hour, but it is of little consequence to the narrative, which essentially depicts the various johns with whom the heroine interacts. They have all the personality and pizzazz of johns in real life, and the movie is as thrilling as a lengthy commute.

WARRANT: DIRTY ROTTEN FILTHY STINKING RICH

Musically uncreative, the Heavy Metal rock band, Warrant, performs songs about weakness in women and about their own prowess on *Warrant: Dirty Rotten Filthy Stinking Rich*. They use many four letter words and have a cluttered, unchoreographed stage act which takes undue advantage of the gullibility of the young. The songs are mostly performed in a live environment, in St. Petersburg, Florida, though they are edited as videos. A running skit about a man in a grotesque mask intrudes between each song. The picture is mildly grainy and the stereo sound is unexceptional.

THE WARRIOR AND THE SORCERESS

We spotted the plot for *The Warrior and the Sorceress*, before the first line of dialog was spoken. A lone man enters a rough-looking town. Sure enough, one of the first questions he asks is which of the two houses controlling the town is the stronger. Although the credits say, 'Story by John Broderick and William Stout,' the plot comes straight from *A Fistful of Dollars* and *Yojimbo*, which, so it is said, came from Dashiell Hammett's 'Red Harvest,' and came close to popping up again in *Mad Max Beyond Thunderdome*. With all this good company, one would think the film had possibilities, but if it really did, do you think it would have been called *The Warrior and the Sorceress*?

On a world where there are twice as many suns and mammary glands as Earth, David Carradine portrays the stranger who plays the two powerful houses against each other for cash, for the fun of it, and to free the oppressed. The show's scariest monster is a set of lips, white teeth, and tentacles which look about as threatening as a beanbag chair. Needless to say, the disc is scratchy, noisy, and uninspiring.

WATCHERS

Based on a legitimate science fiction thriller by Dean R. Kootz, *Watchers* is about a nasty biogenetic experiment who has a telepathic link with an affable golden retriever. The monster gruesomely murders everyone the dog comes in contact with. The film stars the teenage actor, Corey Haim, and the redoubtable Michael Ironside. Although the movie follows a standard format, its viewpoint is fresh and it never insults a viewer's intelligence. It is also reasonably exciting.

The film stock is cheap, but the transfer does nothing further to downgrade the picture. The sound is also in acceptable shape.

WATERMELON MAN

Made during a brief transitional period when films about contemporary racial prejudice could attract film companies and audiences, *Watermelon Man* is about a white insurance salesman who wakes up one morning black. Richard Pryor could probably do this sort of thing very well, but the star, Godfrey Cambridge, assumes that his makeup, for his 'white' phase, is enough for the joke and proceeds to create an uninteresting, improbable character. The off-kilter music soundtrack is deliberately played at the wrong times and, less deliberately, the script lurches from one idea to the next, sometimes contradicting its own logic. The disc, released by RCA/Columbia, has a green label.

WAXWORK

When we saw a piece of *Waxwork* in a video store we were very impressed. The segment was a recreation of *The Mummy*, with seductive colors and the 'Swan Lake' theme rendered in stereo. We were anxious to get a hold of the disc, but when we finally put it on we discovered, before the opening credits were finished, that *The Mummy* bit was a lucky cinematic punch and the rest of film was a standard horror effects workout. The movie is probably harmed and not helped by the 'uncensored' gore footage added for the home video release, since the material tends to squelch a viewer's imagination.

The film is about a waxwork exhibit which transports visitors into genuine re-creations of the scenes depicted. The plot allows the film-makers the freedom of allusion, but except for *The Mummy* and a *Night of the Living Dead* black-and-white segment, they don't try hard enough. The film may be an above average genre effort, but one can't help seeing that it could have been better still.

The stereo sound is decent. The picture transfer, however, looks sloppy. The original print appears to be sharp and intense, but the disc image is often broken up with speckles, and there is burp on side two. The chapter encoding is also inadequate, as it should have been more closely associated with the display sequences.

WAY OUT WEST/BRATS

The quality of the print and sound on *Way Out West/Brats* is no better than the age of the two Laurel and Hardy movies contained on the disc. The first, running a little over an hour, has the two comics attempting to retrieve the deed to a gold mine from the clutches of an evil saloon keeper. The second, running about 20 minutes, is a surreal vision of havoc in a child-sized world. *West* has many long stretches of unrehearsed improvisation punctuated by brief moments of manic destruction. *Brats* features Laurel and Hardy as both the baby-sitters and the youngsters they are watching. Huge props are used to make the comics look like small children. The premise and length are ideal for the material and the result will easily attract repeat viewings.

WE ALL LOVED EACH OTHER SO MUCH

Ettore Scola's *We All Loved Each Other So Much* is a film about four friends who suffer through the political and economic swings of post-War Italy. One of the friends is a film buff, and the most memorable sequences in the film are devoted to Italian movie trivia, such as a visit to the set of *La Dolce Vita* and lengthy discussions about the filming of *The Bicycle Thief*. The film runs a few minutes over two hours (the third side of the disc is less than 30 minutes long, in CLV), but covers several decades, so that it never seems to do any era or interlude complete justice.

The movie is half in black and white and half in color. The color on the disc is faded and sick-looking. The focus is continuously soft, so that not even in the black and white sequences can the viewer relax and enjoy the show. The image is also squeezed in a number of places, making faces look gaunt or pear-shaped. The sound is fair and the disc has no chapter markers.

WE ARE THE WORLD USA FOR AFRICA

The 8-inch *We Are the World USA for Africa* is a bargain, a contribution, a record of an event, and a lovely present from the singing stars of America to their fans. We would have preferred the music video to be at the front of the disc, followed by the documentary about the song's recording, but the chapter encoding prevents the format from being awkward.

The documentary, narrated by Jane Fonda, is really an expansion of the music video. The singers gather, practice, sing their harmonies and solos, and appear on the screen in amazing candid group shots. They're in the same recording studio at the same time. All of them.

The root of all American pop music is in the culture brought to our shores from Africa. By saying, "We are the children...," the singers are acknowledging that debt. Responsibility in America for hunger and starvation is not the responsibility of a parent who feeds a child, it is the responsibility of a child who honors a parent. It is an obligation which comes with the privilege of having one's own place in the world.

WE THE LIVING

Lumivision has released a three-hour, black and white, 1936 Italian production of Ayn Rand's *We the Living*, from Angelika Films. The movie fits comfortably on three sides (the first side break is a real cliffhanger, the second is more awkward but manageable).

Although the first hour is a little slow going, the story, about a love triangle, eventually digs its soap opera hooks in deeply. The viewer is trapped by the fates guiding the characters. To be sure, the early Soviet Russia setting is littered with Rand's fish-in-a-barrel pot shots, but it is the romance and not the politics or wispy philosophical themes which will attract viewers. Rand's rape fantasy couplings are also subdued, with just enough of a hint left to give the movie a little spice.

The disc comes in an elegant gatefold jacket, with chapter markers and background essays on the innerspread. A quick intermission occurs in the middle of side two. The film itself is old, was banned by Mussolini, etc., and has been restored to a workable, but still ragged condition. Some of the dialog has clearly been re-dubbed, but it is all in Italian and is best kept at a reasonable volume. The English subtitles are white and tiny, and reading them may be strenuous for some viewers, although others prefer the style to subtitles which have bigger letters and less translation. Once you get used to it, the condition of the movie is not much of a bother. Lumivision, as a joke or just to get you into the mood, has made their opening logo all scratchy and speckled to match the print.

WEATHER REPORT LIVE IN TOKYO – JAPAN DOMINO THEORY

(see **THE JAZZ LIFE VOL. 1**)

WEEDS

An amusing satire about a group of ex-convicts who form a theater troupe and travel the country performing in a play based upon their experiences in prison, *Weeds* is a careful mixture of serious and funny which is worth watching once. Nick Nolte stars, and gives an inspired, comical performance. The movie makers are so careful not to overstate their cause that it takes ten minutes before one can figure out what is going on at all, but they prevent the film, which has close to a two-hour running time, from getting stale. Most viewers, however, will get all there is to get from a single viewing, so multiple screenings are questionable.

The surround sound has well executed effects and is an admirable accomplishment. The picture is passable.

WEEKEND AT BERNIE'S

The evening we went to see *Ghostbusters II* at our local movie theater, the audience laughed harder and longer at a trailer for *Weekend at Bernie's* than they did at anything in the main feature. The trailer was brilliant, and the movie itself is sufficiently amusing. The premise concerns two young men invited to their boss's beach house for the weekend. They arrive to find the man murdered, but, because of an escalating set of circumstances, they are compelled to maintain the impression that the man is still alive, even manipulating his arms and legs like that of a puppet as they drive around town in order to sustain the deception. The movie isn't perfect. It stars Andrew McCarthy and Jonathan Silverman, and two practiced comedians could probably have done even more with the material. But it is good enough to give the viewer some great belly laughs and provide some pleasing escapist entertainment.

The picture looks okay, though at times the image seems slightly pale. The roar of the surf is ever present on the surround channel during the beach scenes, and the sound editing is consistently witty and satisfying.

WEEKEND PASS

Weekend Pass is about four sailors who have just completed basic training and are visiting LA before leaving on their first assignments. The likeable movie has plenty of energy and plenty of bare breasts, but hardly seems worth the price of a laser disc. The picture and sound transfers are unremarkable.

WEIRD CARTOONS VOL. 1

There are plenty of non-racial cartoons included in *Weird Cartoons Vol. 1*, leaving one to believe that the cartoons which depict grotesquely exaggerated racial stereotypes have been included gratuitously, or even underhandedly, as if the presence of Betty Boop and Daffy Duck could excuse them. It doesn't. The inclusion of the racially oriented shorts compromises the value of the other cartoons and spoils the disc.

The shorts, all public domain items, are in pretty bad condition, but many are valuable and fascinating exercises in early animation. Each side of the disc opens with one of Walt Disney's pre-Mickey Mouse creations, 'Alice,' a little girl whose filmed actions were combined with animated surroundings. One concerns an egg-laying assembly line and the other is about a 'bull tossing' contest. Both are fascinating depictions of Disney's earliest animated explorations. Each side also contains a Betty Boop cartoon, one a visit to a surrealistic world where things tend to happen in opposition to reality – the barber's razor plants hair on his customer's head – and the other about an inventors convention.

Beside the Boop cartoons, the Fleischers are represented by 'Small Fry,' a cartoon which appeared in a more complete and colorful condition on *The Fabulous Fleischer Folio Volume One*, and 'The Cobweb Hotel,' an unnervingly gruesome but fascinating tale about a grotesque, hairy spider who keeps his victims in bondage in various hotel rooms until they are liberated by the heroes. Also appearing on the disc is a black-and-white Daffy Duck wartime cartoon about recycling, a fun collection of intermission teasers, and messy but fascinating efforts in early stop-motion animation.

The quality of all the cartoons is fairly poor, and the sound retains all the scratches and crackles the shorts obtained as they were passed reel to reel through the ages.

WEIRD SCIENCE

There is a certain point in a young man's life – roughly the six months between being 14 and a half and being 15 – when he will appreciate *Weird Science*. The movie was directed by John Hughes, who has made a name for himself by being in touch with the youth culture in movies such as *Sixteen Candles*, *The Breakfast Club*, and *Pretty in Pink*. With *Weird Science* though, his intimacy with the mind-set of today's young people is too exclusive. The movie is about a pair of fifteen-year-old boys who, through a bit of magic, create a cover girl who will perform their every wish, the joke being that they don't know what to do with her once they create her.

The disc, listed as a Home Video Version because some of the music differs from the theatrical release, has been encoded with digital sound. The soundtrack is constantly loud and overused – hey, we're trying to connect with fifteen-year-olds here – but the difference between the digital track and the analog is distinct.

WELL DEVELOPED
(see **PARAMOUNT COMEDY THEATER**)

WEST SIDE STORY (Voyager CAV)
WEST SIDE STORY (Voyager CLV)
WEST SIDE STORY (CBS/Fox)

The transfer of Voyager's *West Side Story* was supervised by the film's co-director, Robert Wise, whose knowledge adds considerably to the veracity of the project. Much of the film takes place during sunset or at night, and the movie is filled with the sort of color problems – impressionistic reds and oranges – which normally give video presentations fits. The picture is letterboxed with an aspect ratio of about 2.2:1 and the disc presents every shot with vivid accuracy, adding a richness which was missing even from the 1968 theatrical re-release. The result is one stunning sequence after another.

The title was released on laser disc previously, initially on the Magnetic Video label without CX-encoding and then reissued with CX-encoding by CBS/Fox itself. To be fair, when that disc first appeared, few movies were available in stereo on home video and it was, for its time, an exciting release, the sort which convinced people to buy laser players. However, those versions are now completely useless – how can you enjoy the choreography when half the dancers are missing from the shot? The first time Maria and Tony spot each other they are at the opposing edges of the screen, an emotional visual which cannot be translated to video without letterboxing.

The sound on the Voyager discs is digitally encoded with some surround effects. It is worth noting that the sound transfer is very good. Every singing voice is delivered from the discs in a fully rounded and defined tone. The orchestral passages also have a grandness which rarely materializes on a film soundtrack.

The film runs 150 minutes. Wise claims that the film was not supposed to have an intermission, and Voyager has obliged by leaving it out, but there is an unusually long fade to black at the traditional intermission point of the stage show. The CLV disc is three-sided and comes in a gatefold jacket with an uninteresting innerspread. The CAV disc has six sides, including a superb supplemental section, and comes in a flimsy box. The chapter placement on the discs is inconsistent. The quality of the presentation on the two formats is indistinguishable. The CLV has no extra features.

In the supplementary section of the CAV disc, the 'Tonight' sequence is broken up with text. The viewer reads two or three brief paragraphs explaining both the how and the why of the way in which a passage in the song is paced and blocked, then, by pressing 'play,' the viewer sees the passage which was discussed. The sections are just long enough so that the essence of the text can remain in the viewer's memory while that section of the song is playing. Also featured on the CAV disc is a half hour interview with Wise. He provides a practical summary of how the Broadway hit was brought to the screen. Production memos and notes are re-created in still frame, as are the set sketches and storyboards which are interspersed with still photos from the finished film. A wonderful collection of snapshots which were taken by the filmmakers on New York's West Side in preparation for the production are also included, as are two theatrical trailers.

Everybody, when they're walking down the street, has, at one time or another, lifted an arm or a leg to pirouette instead of trudge. The film is popular for many reasons but it is perhaps most popular because it encourages feelings of grace inside the viewer. Most street punks are rude, belligerent and selfish, but you don't walk down the street wishing they could dance, you walk down the street wishing you could. For three hours or four hours (you can't watch the disc without going back and replaying sections) *West Side Story* lets you feel what it would be like to float past the grime.

WESTERNER (see **THE LITTLE FOXES**)

WESTWORLD
WESTWORLD (Import)

The MGM/UA Deluxe Letter-Box Edition of *Westworld* utilizes the same master which was used for the Japanese CAV MGM/UA Collector's Item Series offering. The image has an aspect ratio of about 2:1, but the picture is hopelessly grainy and pale. This is frustrating, because the movie is an ideal home video selection. It is 88 minutes long and basically puts forward its premise – a vacation resort where androids cater to the fantasies of the guests – twists the plot – the androids get sick and start killing the guests – and then ends before the concepts become exhausted.

The quality of the picture consistently prevented us from fully relaxing and enjoying the disc. There are many instances where the full screen is used, not to place characters in a surrounding or comment on the irony of existence, but simply to soak up the concept of the vacation resort and of bio-electronic flesh. The picture is so grainy that in the darkest scenes, the corners turn green and even start to become light again. The versions which show up on broadcast TV, however, aren't any better.

The CAV functions on the import disc allow one to manipulate barroom brawls and freeze computer terminal displays. The CAV disc runs to four sides, although the last is only 8000 frames long, end credit roll included. There are also 21 chapter markers.

The sound on both discs is fine. The film's music is in stereo, along with scattered sound effects. The soundtrack is a good cross between high tech peeps and rowdy rumblings.

WET WATER T'S OUTRAGEOUS STRIP REVIEW

What was left of the T-shirts to begin with disappears very quickly in *Wet Water T's.* The program, filmed in a Ft. Lauderdale saloon where even the beers look watered down, features a dozen ladies competing for wolf whistles before a relatively dull, all-male crowd. The emcee's favorite line is, "All the way," and in the course of his spiel, forgetting that he is already there, he introduces one of the girls as having come "All the way from Ft. Lauderdale!" It's that type of show. The girls have phony names, and one even forgets who she is and must be tapped by her neighbor when she is called. The woman with the most pronounced hairdo and make-up wins, which says something about nudity and fetishes, or about the eyesight of most of the bar patrons.

Side two of the disc is in CAV and contains an entirely different program, a boxing match of which the emcee here says, probably deliberately, "They gave us a fight you will never remember." How right he is. Every still frame is blurry, but the picture on both programs looks sharp. The sound is digitally encoded monaural, but has a decent resonance. The same song, however, is played over and over during the T-shirt contest, and it is not an impressionable tune. Trailers for similar programs also appear in CAV on side two.

A better program is contained on *Outrageous Strip Review*, which has the on-screen title 'Outrageous! The Strip Review.' Here the women are seasoned professionals, and their cynical efficiency (one can be seen quickly whispering instructions to an audience member as she pulls him onto the stage) is more believably erotic than the naive amateurism of the T-shirt contestants.

The single-sided disc lasts an hour. The picture quality is decent, but the camera angle is usually ill chosen, and the monaural sound is weaker than *Wet Water T's.*

WHALES

Packing far more into a half-hour interactive program than the consumer-oriented *National Geographic Video – The Great Whales* could manage in an hour, The National Geographic Society has an educational laser disc, entitled *Whales*, which is not available through standard retail sources. Made in coordination with the Nebraska Videodisc Design/Production Group, the disc has four main chapters, depicting whale characteristics, the varieties of whales, whale behavior, and whale interaction with Man. Following this, there is a mixed still-frame and live-action section which uses the format of an appendix, a glossary, and 'Follow-up Activities,' supplying even more information.

The CAV disc manages to provide just about every piece of knowledge about whales one could expect to absorb in 30 minutes. The footage is pleasing, showing whales going about their business and dwarfing everything around them except the ocean itself. We've seen many whale programs before, but this was the first time it really sunk in that a humpback whale's song can be heard a *thousand* miles away from its source. The information presented is intended to be introductory in nature and is more appropriate for lower grades than for upper, but it is an excellent beginning point for anyone who wishes to know what it means to be a whale.

The transfer is decent, although not every still frame forms a steady image. The monaural sound is not CX-encoded, but it isn't in bad shape. The voice-over narration was recorded specifically for the disc, and has been merged with splashing and 'song' sound effects. There are stops imbedded at the beginning of each chapter, so one cannot relax with the disc unless one has a remote in hand. A brief Teacher's Manual comes with the disc, explaining more about video discs than it does about whales.

THE WHALES OF AUGUST

The neat thing about *The Whales of August* was the chance to see Lillian Gish's name blazing on first-run theater marquees in 1988. It proves that movies are still very young.

The transfer leaves something to be desired. The image is often grainy and the colors wander. The sound is a little noisy, too.

As a drama, *The Whales of August* just scrapes by. It is an opportunity for a half dozen elderly actors and actresses to be active. They don't have to do much, since the editing and the many shots pointing away from the speaker conceal any lack of stamina. They probably didn't even have to remember all of their lines, since the plot has few revelations or grand speeches. The whole project seems contrived while one is watching it, but it fares better in memory – the errors recede while the forcefulness and endurance of the personalities in the cast remain.

WHAM! IN CHINA: FOREIGN SKIES

The rock group Wham!, musically, does not deserve their exclamation point, but the disc, *Wham! in China: Foreign Skies* does. Despite the bright red jacket and rock-oriented promotion, the program is actually a documentary called *Foreign Skies* which was made by the accomplished British film director, Lindsay Anderson. Anderson has a dry, refined sense of humor, and so does the disc. It is an excellent portrayal of two cultures coming into brief, confused contact and so well-made we would recommend it for anyone who has never heard of Wham! before.

There are eight chapter markers on the 61-minute digital disc, and seven songs are played in full, although the bulk of the concert material does not appear until the very end, when one is finally ready to relax and listen to it. During most of *Foreign Skies*, Anderson follows the two lead singers of Wham! as they tour Peking and Canton and make promotional, touristy type appearances. More often than not, Anderson is pointing his cameras at the populace rather than the rock stars. Whether it is the British Consul talking about cricket matches or the street vendors who wouldn't know a Wham! from a what-have-you, it is so fascinating you don't want to take your eyes from the screen.

The disc is well produced, but both the picture and the sound, except for the concert overlays, are of documentary quality. The picture has been put on the screen in original aspect, even though this means there is just a small black ribbon at the top and the bottom.

WHAT COMES AROUND

Chapter indicators appear on the jacket of *What Comes Around.* They just don't appear on the disc. The chapters were supposed to have denoted the numbers Jerry Reed sings during the film, but we're not going to miss them. The movie was filmed in Tennessee and they seem to be using the same cabin that was used in *Evil Dead*, though don't let that get your hopes up. The disc is monaural and has been CX-encoded, but nothing can really help the imperfect sound recording.

If the characters happen to walk in front of something noisy while they are talking, the noise is heard instead of the talk. Reed apparently had something to do with making the movie, because his name appears 13 times on the jacket cover and nearly that much in the opening and closing credits. He portrays a singer, hooked on drugs, who is pulled out of his addiction by his younger brother. The movie is a comedy. It actually has a certain unrefined combination of humor and car crashes which can stay one's eject-button finger. The picture is excessively grainy and we hope they don't make a sequel.

WHAT HAPPENED TO KEROUAC

An oral biography of Jack Kerouac, *What Happened to Kerouac* runs into the same problem most oral biographies run into – acquaintances of a famous person don't really know that person very well and the better they know him the less willing they are to talk. It takes a skilled biographer to organize such material in a way which will provide a legitimate portrait of the subject, and that is never really accomplished in the *Kerouac* film. We would still recommend the disc for anybody who is planning on studying the writer in depth, and for those whose hobby is the Beat milieu, but it is not a movie which will hold the interest of the casual viewer. Highlights of the 97-minute effort include an all too brief interview with Carolyn Cassady, who speaks with a twinkle in her eye about the menage a trois with her husband and Jack, and a devastating clip from William Buckley's 'Firing Line' interview show in the late sixties in which Kerouac, totally zonked, still gets the best of Buckley. The picture and sound quality are typical of a scraped together documentary, and the disc transfer appears to have done the material no further harm.

WHAT HAVE I DONE TO DESERVE THIS!

Pedro Almodovar's *What Have I Done to Deserve This!* is a comedy about a family living in a crowded apartment, scraping up an income through odd jobs and drug sales. The film revels in Almodovar's peripatetic sexuality, diving into many different comical situations and character interactions. The heroine is a housewife who lives on amphetamines to stretch out her working day so she can do her own chores and still have time to earn money housekeeping for others. Her young sons, barely out of grade school, casually sell both drugs and themselves. The husband, a taxi driver, is a jerk who complains about the state of things at all the wrong moments. His mother also lives in the apartment, and brings home a stray lizard to keep as a pet. The film exaggerates reality in all the right ways, and Almodovar even draws from Alfred Hitchcock's 'Lamb to the Slaughter' to pull everything together. The humor is often unexpected. As the situations become more and more absurd, the characters become more and more amusing simply by remaining so nonchalant about everything.

The film was made with inexpensive color stock and the image is a bit soft, but there are no severe flaws in the picture transfer. A thin black band is present at the top and bottom of the screen. The movie is in Spanish and has white English subtitles which appear over the image. The subtitles are easy enough to read, but contain many annoying typographical errors. The digitally encoded monaural sound is fine.

WHEELS OF FIRE

Wheels of Fire is a sub-90-minute CLV stock-car version of *The Road Warrior*. The disc is not CX-encoded and it is a bit on the scratchy side, but to the credit of the laser medium, it must be noted that even viewers who are not listening closely will be able to hear every sound overlay and every post-synchronized addition to the dialog.

The camera set-ups were so poorly thought out that the movie looks as if it had been edited on a bus driving down a bumpy road. The picture is not bad, although side two on the copy we viewed had a few speckles. The post-holocaust world depicted is one where people trade leather for water, but seem to have an endless supply of bullets and gasoline. There are many explosions, but none are convincing and besides, we're getting tired of seeing any car which runs off the road in a movie ignite in flames.

WHEN HARRY MET SALLY

The performances in *When Harry Met Sally* are so much fun that the script could be much more annoying than it is and you would still have a great time watching it. The film is a romantic comedy which spans a couple of decades and concerns two people who take a very long time to realize they were meant for each other. Billy Crystal and Meg Ryan star, and they do a wonderful job mixing a sharp sense of timing with a subtle set of staged maturations.

The picture looks fine. The stereo surround sound does not have much in the way of rear channel separations, but there is an active 'Rodgers and Hart, etc.' musical score which sounds luscious, and directional dialog in the split screen sequences. The side break, which comes at the end of the cafeteria scene, is perfect.

WHEN NATURE CALLS

The title isn't the half of it. *When Nature Calls* is a pastiche of movie parodies, some of which are funny and some of which are not, depending upon how stoned you are. The film opens with some poorly conceived 'Coming Attractions' trailers, along with a beautifully scratched and worn down 'Coming Attractions' teaser. This establishes a precedent so that during the intermission, the filmmakers can present an hysterical take-off on the marching hot dogs concession cartoons we all know and love. The wieners turn ribald, and the butter in the popcorn is a hot dog's answer to the movie's title. Just as we always suspected.

The disc is CX-encoded, but there are no other special features and it is in monaural. About 60 out of the 76 minutes of film depicts a city family who have moved to the great outdoors. There is a theme song, 'The Outdoorster's,' and a family pet who begs to be shot with tranquilizer darts. Would that they all had been.

WHEN THE WIND BLOWS

Children may be captivated by side one of *When the Wind Blows*, an animated 80-minute feature, but side two gets pretty heavy and most younger viewers will protect themselves by losing interest. The film is about the effects of nuclear war, and the jacket cover is accompanied by an admonishment that parental guidance is suggested.

Although it is more of a lesson than a relaxation, the cartoon is superb. The story, adapted from a novel by Raymond Briggs, concerns an elderly couple living in a cottage in the country, remote enough that after the bomb hits they lose all contact with whatever was left of civilization. The narrative is leisurely, and perhaps a little too coy (the man prepares himself by judiciously following government brochures), but it has emotional power (by conveying strength through melancholy) and its point of view is unique.

The picture transfer is very good. The colors are almost consistently solid and the boundaries are sharply defined. The stereo sound is also well done. The disc is in CLV throughout and has a handful of chapter markers.

WHERE EAGLES DARE

The picture on *Where Eagles Dare* has a few inconsistencies. Sometimes, especially when trick photography or special filters are involved, the image is grainy and blurry, but for well-lit indoor shots, or shots in the snow during the day, the picture looks as precise as Clint Eastwood's aim and Richard Burton's enunciation. The colors are close to accurate and the fleshtones are satisfying.

It was a relief to see that the disc looked as nice as it does, because we would hate to see the letterboxing go to waste. The image has an aspect ratio of about 2:1. It allows the viewer to take in more scenery, more atmospheric set design, and more explosions than would be possible in a cropped rendition of the film.

The disc also has a marvelous stereophonic surround mix. Explosions, gun shots, scratchy radio messages, the wind, footsteps, and Burton's fabulous voice all sail from one's speakers and burst above one's head. Our favorite line in the film, Burton's campy, Gertrude Steinish, "But what the hell – a hole is a hole is a hole..." bounces through the air. The aged recording contains a fair amount of noise, but the sounds are well defined and the mix is a whole lot of fun.

The film runs 158 minutes, and has an Intermission, replete with Entr'Acte music, separating side two and side three. As an adventure thriller, the film cannot withstand hundreds of repeated viewings, but it can certainly withstand dozens. It is a great show to watch when you are snowed in for the night, or if you feel like waking a few neighbors by replaying World War II.

WHERE THE WILD THINGS ARE AND HIGGLETY PIGGLETY POP! – GLYNDEBOURNE FESTIVAL OPERA

Where The Wild Things Are and Higglety Pigglety Pop! – Glyndebourne Festival Opera is a disc of which the desire to like is much stronger than the actual liking. Eccentric children may find it enjoyable. For adults, however, it is a test of patience.

The digitally encoded release features a pair of short works – each runs about three quarters of an hour and is consigned to a side – based upon Maurice Sendak's picture books. Sendak did the stage and costume design, and also provided the libretto. Oliver Knudsen wrote the music and conducts the performances showcased on the disc. The presentation is confined to a stage, but is not performed in front of an audience. Dissolves are used in some situations to speed the change of scene. The music is atonal and does not contain the sort of ditties children are apt to hum while playing on a swing. The combination of the lyrics and the singing gives one the same chance of picking out a recognizable word that one has when one listens to an Italian or German opera. Fortunately, a libretto comes with the disc, though it serves to emphasize that lyricism, or even simple word play, is not Sendak's forte. Anyone familiar with his stories will also know that the subject matter is usually more disturbing than whimsical.

The most fabulous and compelling aspect to the program is the costumes (and to a lesser extent, the sets). The monsters in 'Wild Things' are captivating and the Sealyham Terrier costume in 'Higglety Pigglety' is uncanny in its realism. The picture quality on the disc, however, is imperfect. The colors are not sharply defined and the image is soft.

The music playback is excellent. The singing is not, since the costumes apparently get in the way. The two shows do give adults a legitimate look at a child's view of the world, one where many things are lumbering, threatening, and make sounds which are only partially recognizable or patternable. Kids generally look to entertainment as an escape from this kind of thing. Adults, having already been through it, have no wish to go back.

A WHISPER TO A SCREAM

A strong third act and an enjoyable turn by Yaphet Kotto as an incredulous police detective are almost enough to save *A Whisper to a Scream*, about a woman who works as a phone-sex operator and is threatened by a psychotic killer. Much of the plot is irrational, and some viewers may be put off by the exploitive nature of the material (although the film's heroine is an independent woman, the murders have a strongly voyeuristic point of view). The film stock is second rate and the picture has a slight grain. The sound is digitally encoded stereo, with the separation effects limited to the musical score.

THE WHISTLE BLOWER
If you like Michael Caine you won't want to miss *The Whistle Blower*. He gives one of his best performances portraying an ordinary man whose son has died under questionable circumstances. The film has much to say about power and morality, and its lessons linger thanks to the convincing change of heart which Caine's character experiences. The music is in stereo, but the sound is generally uninteresting. The lighting in the picture occasionally reveals a limited budget, and while the transfer is well done, the disc's strength is in the film itself, not the presentation.

WHITE CHRISTMAS
We were disappointed with the digital sound in the opening of *White Christmas*. But after the noisy credit scroll overture and the GI number, we were distracted from the disc by what we thought was a set of chimes which began to play somewhere in our viewing room. At first we thought that a young friend of ours had a new toy, and only as Bing Crosby's relaxed and gentle phrasing of the title number filled the air around us did we realize that the chimes had been a gift from the disc. The sound is listed as "Stereo Enhanced," a condition which is described on the jacket as being, "monaural audio digitally remixed to stereo with surround channel." Anyone who has watched the movie year after year on a TV is likely to be stunned by the improved audio.

The movie was made in VistaVision, but most people are used to watching it on television, so the lost edges will probably not be an issue. The chapter listings on the jacket cover start over at "Chapter 1" on each of the three sides, whereas the actual encoding keeps numbers advancing as you turn the discs over. Time to get the calculators out.

Under restraint because he is paired with Crosby, Danny Kaye puts in one of his better performances in the holiday classic. He does a good parody of Martha Graham in one number but is often most appealing when he is not the center of attention.

The print is in fine shape. Parts of the screen are blurry at times, but the color looks brand new and it is clear that Paramount made an extra effort to do a good job. May all their disc transfers be so bright.

WHITE HEAT
"I told you to keep away from that radio. If that battery is dead, it will have company." *White Heat* is a rousing, Warner Brothers action picture, released on disc by CBS/Fox. James Cagney portrays a psychotic hoodlum who outsmarts the law until he befriends an undercover cop. The director, Raoul Walsh, likes to end his films with fights in high places, and he does so here with spectacular results. The print is scratched in numerous places, but the sound is CX-encoded and isn't bad.

WHITE LINE FEVER
The picture transfer on *White Line Fever* is surprisingly nice. The movie was not a widescreen effort, so nothing is lost moving it to video. The colors are accurate, and even though the 1975 movie was a low budget effort with washed out cinematography, the picture looks fresh and new. The sound is passable, and side two is in CAV with two unsteady still frames out of every five. Jan-Michael Vincent portrays an independent trucker who hesitates when asked to haul illegal goods and is immediately bullied and blackballed. The film lacks a wholly satisfying conclusion, but it has some decent stunts and follows a comfortable, middle-of-the-road formula.

WHITE MISCHIEF
There is nothing like a murder to pull the sheets away from a facade. *White Mischief* is based upon a true story, about adultery, murder, and other tomfoolery in Kenya near the outbreak of World War II. If there hadn't been a murder, no one would be the wiser today about the rich colonials and their kinks. The movie, however, suffers from the lack of dramatic structure which often plagues real life events. Furthermore, the sex is all posed and passionless (for the tropics, no less) and Joss Ackland, who has a central role as the wronged husband, is stoic beyond interest. Would that Trevor Howard, who has a brief but captivating supporting appearance, had been given the bigger part – he might have turned the whole film into something worth watching more than once.

The picture transfer is acceptable. The sound is also in decent condition, though the film's stereo mix is intermittent in effect.

WHITE NIGHTS
Nothing in *White Nights* is quite as good as the opening Roland Petit ballet. RCA/Columbia has released the 136-minute feature as a three-sided disc, but one wishes that the opening number had been put into standard play and that the rest of the show was in digital. The picture is often washed out, gauzy, or both.

Love the title. It refers not only to the midsummer Arctic twilight, but also to good guys vs. bad guys, the chess-like strategies which the ballet dancer employs to get himself out of Russia, and his teaming with a black expatriate. There is not enough dancing and not enough plot to justify the time the story takes up. It is best saved for a long winter evening. The stereo surround sound is good.

WHITE WATER SUMMER
The picture transfer of *White Water Summer* is fairly good, with only the more intense colors turning blurry or grainy. The stereo surround track also seems to be in decent shape when the obnoxious pop-hit musical score isn't blasting away, and contains some pleasant outdoor atmospheric effects.

The film is about a young boy from the city who is sent, against his better judgement, on a camping expedition. There are actually three different movies mixed together. One, which may have been added afterwards, has the boy speaking directly to the camera and making snide comments about his adventure. It is intended to generate laughs. Another concerns the boy's conflict with the expedition leader, a pushy return-to-nature type, well played up to a point by Kevin Bacon, who goes through something of a severe personality change in the film's second half. It is intended to generate drama. Finally, there is the best part, showing the details of the expedition, which isn't intended to do anything and is often sabotaged by the filmmakers afraid that audiences won't tolerate pastoral inactivity. The film does such a good job at showing the camping adventures from the boy's point of view that you feel every bit of wonder or anxiety that he feels as he is exposed, for the first time, to the process of living outdoors. It is so adept at evoking simple pleasures that dramatics, scattered by the filmmakers like litter, spoil everything.

WHITE WILDERNESS (Import)
The old Walt Disney nature documentaries are available on laser disc in Japan with dual-channel sound which features the original English narration on one track and the Japanese equivalent on the other. The colors on *White Wilderness* look suspicious in places – the sea looks too blue and the land too brown. The sound is a bit weak from having been relegated to one channel.

Adults will probably spot many of the imposed artifices or note when the narrator slyly avoids the question of mating. The images, though, are fascinating, and the narrator's voice is soothing. Whether it is the polar bear cub pushing a snowball onto his sibling or the wolverine leaping to snap at a raven, watching the disc more than once will be like hiking down the same forest path again and again. Mating isn't everything; when we were much younger we used to look forward to seeing these shows with great anticipation because of the scenes where the animals kill and eat other animals. Viewing *White Wilderness*, we were satisfied to discover that the blood and violence is still there in living, Disney color.

WHITESNAKE – FOURPLAY (Import)
The Japanese 8-inch, *Whitesnake – Fourplay*, is a 17-minute concert disc and thank goodness it isn't any longer. The group is about as subtle as the pun in the disc's title, and how they made it from taverns to a stage concert and 8-inch disc is beyond our comprehension. The lead singer grits his teeth and grovels, "Don't break my heart again, like you did before, don't break my heart again, I couldn't take it anymore..." and you think, 'who's he kidding?' We hope Whitesnake goes back under whatever rock it was they crawled out from and leaves laser discs for musicians with talent.

WHITNEY HOUSTON – THE NO. 1 VIDEO HITS
Whitney Houston's songs are conservatively recorded, which is usually an indication that the sound engineers are making a heavy contribution. It is difficult to be upset with the 8-inch *Whitney Houston – The No. 1 Video Hits*, however, because it lasts just long enough to please a viewer and then stops. The picture quality is acceptable, and the four videos are fun to watch. Each one, 'You Give Good Love,' 'Saving All My Love for You,' 'How Will I Know,' and 'The Greatest Love of All,' was done by a different director. Houston is attractive, and the camera gets in so close that you can see her fillings. It would be easy to make fun of 'The Greatest Love of All,' drawing attention to what Woody Allen has to say about loving one's self, but the whole disc is over before temptation sets in.

WHO AM I THIS TIME?
Susan Sarandon is so enchanting in *Who Am I This Time?* that the disc is worth obtaining for her performance alone. The hour-long romantic comedy is about a woman who joins an amateur theatrical group and becomes enamored with her leading man (played by Christopher Walken) although his personality offstage is a complete cipher.

The picture is grainy and unattractive, and the sound is uninteresting. Sarandon, however, embodies her part so accurately and so seductively that while you are watching the show nothing else matters. She makes you root for her character, and then passes along the happiness when her character succeeds. Written by Kurt Vonnegut and directed by Jonathan Demme, *Who Am I This Time?* is a blissful hour of entertainment which puts many longer programs to shame. It was filmed in Evanston and Hinckley, Illinois.

WHO FRAMED ROGER RABBIT
WHO FRAMED ROGER RABBIT(CAV)
If ever there were an argument for the continued existence of CAV feature film laser discs, it is Touchstone's dazzling presentation of *Who Framed Roger Rabbit.* The picture transfer is perfect. The colors are true and the focus is precise. At triple speed the images look as real and as three dimensional as a scene in a View Master. In slow motion, the film's pleasures are stretched like Silly Putty. And, like a conga line of Cracker Jacks, every still frame holds a surprise. The CAV is as much fun to manipulate as it is to play straight through.

Touchstone has also released a CLV edition, but its charms are cheaper and less satisfying. The CAV disc has mild letterboxing, while the CLV disc is full screen, with just enough of the sides cropped off to make the image feel cramped and the inventiveness seem suppressed. The colors on the CLV disc are not as pure, either. Roger Rabbit's red outfit is blurry in CLV and solid in CAV. The CLV disc loses the subtleties in shading and hue, becoming a bland imitation of the original. The CAV disc is genuine progeny.

The digitally encoded stereo surround mix is wonderful, and exhibits a full range of inspired sounds. There seemed to be little difference in sound quality on the two discs.

The movie is a remarkable accomplishment which cannot be deprecated by citing earlier combinations of animation and live action. The scope and technical excellence of *Who Framed Roger Rabbit* is unmatched. The narrative approach has a fresh sense of self-awareness which is as benevolent and impish as the title character (in contrast, recall Joe Dante's segment in *Twilight Zone*, the more typical path which literate homages to illiterate pleasures tend to take). Most important of all, there is the performance of Bob Hoskins. It is more rare than acknowledged that a performer brings a quality to a role which no substituted performer could have provided, but Hoskins consistently proves to be more flexible and animated than the cartoon characters surrounding him. He's a cross between Bert Lahr and Spencer Tracy, but there is something else inside giving him energy that is entirely unique.

Watching Hoskins' reactions is just one of the many pleasures the CAV disc, which has been given a moderate number of chapter markers, has to offer. Other than an early reflection of the film crew in the window of a trolley car, the movie seems to have no errors. Any randomly frozen frame catches Hoskins completely in character responding to the animated figures around him. Other amazing special effects that are worth examining closely include the sight of the audience through the fabric in Jessica Rabbit's skirt, the continual appearance of realistic shadows for the cartoon characters and the absence of shadows for the models that were used as stand-ins during the live shots, the constant weaving of real and animated arms and legs, and the manipulation to Hoskins' figure during his Toontown elevator ride.

The CAV disc can also be used to enhance the clever kinescopic tribute created when Roger begins rapidly flipping photos of Jessica playing patty-cake. The sequence doesn't work properly in the movie itself, but a viewer quickly manipulating the forward and reverse controls on the laser player can better the filmmakers and keep the effect going indefinitely, or until the desire to play with some other part of the movie sends the viewer to the next tempting frame.

THE WHO LIVE: FEATURING THE ROCK OPERA TOMMY
The complete 70-minute or so presentation of 'Tommy' at the beginning of the 135-minute, *The Who Live: Featuring the Rock Opera Tommy* is both a good and a bad conception. It is good in that the music sounds terrific and is supported by a group of guest stars who help maintain the adrenalin throughout the piece. It is bad, however, in that the rest of the concert becomes anticlimactic and, as a selective anthology of The Who's past hits, disjointed, because the 'Tommy' parts are missing.

The video tape source material is in good shape. The picture is brightly lit, although one camera angle faces directly into the lights and produces an image dominated by a large yellow blob. The stereo sound is fine and begs to be amplified beyond reasonable limits. Side three is in CAV with movement blurring in the still frames.

THE WHO – WHO'S BETTER, WHO'S BEST
The Who – Who's Better, Who's Best is a decent anthology of music and video. Side one, which is in black and white, runs under a half hour in CLV. Side two is in color and runs closer to a full hour. Some video clips depict old concert recordings, while others simply compile miscellaneous footage and are set to the standard studio recordings. The disc compilation contains several extra numbers and is in much better condition. Title cards introduce each number and bend over backward to apologize for slight deteriorations in the older recordings. The chapter markers listed on the back of the jacket do not coincide with the chapter encoding, which starts over at zero on side two. Apologies notwithstanding, the clips look terrific and the music sounds great. The volume is set high, so be prepared to run to your amplifier when the bass from 'My Generation' first rolls in. The Who are as accomplished at posing for the camera as they are at writing and playing rock'n'roll, so videos of their performances tend to reinforce the strength of their songs.

WHO'LL STOP THE RAIN
Who'll Stop the Rain is one of the great contemporary adventure films. A description of the plot can not do justice to the emotional impact that the film can give to a viewer. Parts of the script are pretentious and far-fetched, but these lapses are minor and excusable within the context the plot creates. At the heart of it, *Who'll Stop the Rain* is a triangular romance. The hero is hired by his best friend to transport two kilos of heroin from Vietnam to the States. Eventually the hero is forced to go on the run with his friend's wife, and to facilitate a reconcilement during a showdown on a Southwestern mesa. Side three, which contains the shootout, is in CAV, with two unsteady still frames out of every five.

The print is passable, but it is not in perfect condition – the edges look soft – and the monaural sound is an unfortunate product of the times when the movie was made, before stereo presentations were standard procedure. The film longs for greater audio fidelity. The disc is chapter encoded.

The audacity of allowing the hero to move heroin is just one of the uncompromising dares which the plot takes with a viewer's sympathies. By the end one is so committed to the protagonists that their emotional responses have true resonance. The stars, Nick Nolte, Tuesday Weld, and Michael Moriarty, never come across like movie heroes, so the nobility their characters achieve is hard fought and lasting. When Nolte's character does relinquish Weld to Moriarity, Nolte's response is as moving as Rick's parting from Ilsa, though all he does is mutter, "She didn't even say goodbye." It is the first time you know how he really feels about her.

WHOOPI GOLDBERG
A valuable recording of Whoopi Goldberg's Broadway show is available in stereo, but her voice is not miked for TV and it sounds slightly muted. The picture on *Whoopi Goldberg* is fine and we were too busy laughing to pay close attention to the quality, anyhow. Unlike comedians who smash watermelons with hammers for humor, Goldberg's material has real punch. She presents what in essence are five short stories, narrated in different vernaculars. The stories resonate beyond the percussion of the one-liners. In one routine, a junkie gets on an airplane and flies to Amsterdam, ending up in the Anne Frank House, contemplating the plights of minorities. In another, an empty-headed Valley Girl cheerfully describes the way she destroyed her reproductive system while performing a self-abortion with a hanger from the cleaners. Heavy stuff, but you have to laugh that much harder to get it through your system.

WHO'S AFRAID OF VIRGINIA WOOLF?
A whirring noise appears on the last reel of *Who's Afraid of Virginia Woolf?*, as if someone had left a lid off on the recording equipment. Until that point, the disc is nearly perfect. The monaural sound is digitally encoded and enhances Richard Burton's voice in the way that polishing enhances silverware (the analog track is not nearly as much fun). The black-and-white print is beautiful to look at, to the point of softening Elizabeth Taylor's

raunch. The contrasts are very distinctive, and even the shadows have lighter and darker shadings. The concluding sound problem will bother some viewers and not others.

In his jacket notes for *The Graduate*, Howard Suber makes the cryptic comment that *Woolf* "had not done much to prove that [Director Mike Nichols] had any particular aptitude for the medium." Could have fooled us. *Who's Afraid of Virginia Woolf* can be very silly material – about adults playing odd psychological games when they are far too drunk to actually have their wits about them – if it is not presented with the exact amount of distractions. Nichols does just that, moving into characters and moving away from characters in counter rhythm to the material. The overabundance of key lights and other stage habits can be excused, particularly when they produce such a lovely image on the screen.

The three-sided *Woolf* has chapter markers, and the description of each chapter on the jacket is enough to get anyone into the mood for the show. The material takes a rather nasty view of life and love, but that is the essence of its popularity. Dirty laundry has rarely seemed so appealing.

WHO'S HARRY CRUMB?

The John Candy comedy, *Who's Harry Crumb?*, never lives up to its potential, which was limited to begin with. The second half, in which the plot, about an inept private detective trying to solve a kidnapping, finally begins to thicken, is more entertaining than the first, which is primarily a collection of unsuccessful skits.

The picture is fine although intense colors are a bit blurry. The stereo surround sound is a big budget production. The intriguing photo on the jacket cover depicts a scene which did not make the final cut.

WHO'S THAT GIRL

Although the comic pace disintegrates at the end, *Who's That Girl* is amusing and wants to please. The opening credit sequence is especially commendable. It is animated, which is a rarity these days, and turns out to be the prolog for the story. Madonna is on her best behavior, but she can't hold a scene for more than a couple of minutes – a music video's worth. She runs out of presence and has to change her outfits again.

The transfer is impeccable. Much of the film's sound is not all that interesting, but there are the cross-selling singles and a cougar who sounds like he's loose in your viewing room. The picture is bright and colorful, and Madonna's lipstick does not smear. The disc also has chapter markers.

THE WILD BUNCH

Anarchy is the prevalent theme in Sam Peckinpah's rule-breaking *The Wild Bunch*. Although overly symbolic (the anarchy of aging, of childhood, of technology, of dying, et cetera), the film has a couple of outrageous gunfights and lengthy passages of sleepy, poignant character development. This is the restored version, at 145 minutes, at least two minutes longer than the initial general release and longer still than several truncated versions Warner has experimented with. It is easy to see why they tried to trim it, because the action is compartmentalized and even in the complete version it is difficult to understand the motivation behind the violence.

William Holden portrays the leader of an aging band of criminals, including Ernest Borgnine, Warren Oates, and Ben Johnson, who are pursued by an even grimier gang of bounty hunters, led by Robert Ryan. The added footage is primarily of flashback scenes depicting the relationship between Ryan and Holden which are out of rhythm with the rest of the film. The decision does not seem as political as it was made out to be at the time because the scenes have a phony feel and disrupt the rhythm of the narrative. The picture is good, but the sound is noisy and the image is cropped.

THE WILD GEESE

The color transfer on *The Wild Geese* is good, but the source material has some scratches and a splice or two. There is also a variation in tone which shifts from reel to reel. The sound has some enjoyable surround separation effects, but is also quite noisy in places, which may be distracting to some viewers.

The action adventure film is a dubious concoction which unfortunately has a half dozen wonderful British movie stars to attract an unsuspecting public. The thought of Richard Burton, Richard Harris, Roger Moore, Stewart Granger, Barry Foster and Hardy Kruger in the same movie, which also has its share of decent action scenes, is too much for many viewers to resist. But the South African production can leave a very bad taste. The lasting image from the film is of a sickly black politician who is carried across the bush on Kruger's back, and the symbolism is as deliberate as it is patronizing. The real failure of the film, however, has nothing to do with politics. The scriptwriters kill off the most sympathetic heroes and leave the more ambiguous ones alive. Lacking a moral compass, the movie loses not only its ethical values but its common sense judgement as well.

THE WILD LIFE

Usually youth-prank and sexual-awareness movies have some kind of point which allows them to draw the comedy through the story and weave together a riotous, fun-filled, and profitable 90 minutes of entertainment. In *The Wild Life*, the filmmakers forgot to worry about what their point ought to be and the movie becomes an uninspiring collection of loose ends.

The stereo is good. The opening song isn't loud enough or full enough and for a moment you worry that the master is off, but soon discover that the song isn't the soundtrack of the film but an accurate re-creation of the sound from a portable tape deck one of the characters is lugging around. Christopher Penn gives a wonderful performance as an uninhibited high school wrestler. There is also a parrot who knows how to dance to acid rock.

THE WILD ONE

Today the gang looks about as threatening as a summer stock version of the Sharks and the Jets, but Marlon Brando's presence makes *The Wild One* worthwhile. The movie, which runs less than 90 minutes, is ideal for the repeated plays of home video ownership. Despite the out-of-date slang and an amusingly phallic second-place trophy, it is possible to still take the movie seriously, largely because of Brando's steady swagger.

Part of the black-and-white picture seems to be blurry for lengthy stretches, but that may be a fault with the original print. There is a break in the continuity on the fourth minute of side one, but otherwise the feature appeared to be intact.

THE WILD PAIR

Bubba Smith's performances are improving; not that he's ready to do Chekhov or anything, but he's following direction and talking as if it were coming from impulse instead of memory. He's paired with Beau Bridges in *The Wild Pair*, which has also been directed by Bridges. The cast also features Lloyd Bridges, as the main bad guy, and a cute little moppet, two years of age at the most, named Dylan Bridges (who has gorgeous blond hair and a promising career ahead of him). The movie is about a cop and an FBI agent who bust a drug ring run by a paramilitary group. Beau can't get into perfect synch with Smith, so the humor isn't as strong as it could have been, but Bridges the director doesn't make fun of his co-star and, as a result, Smith makes an intelligent, attractive hero. One who can break the necks of people he doesn't like with a single 'whack.'

The disc has a simple but engaging stereo surround track. The picture is acceptable, although visually, the movie itself is not too stimulating. The CLV program runs 89 minutes. Much of the drama is padded, however, and hardly any of the padding is fun, except for the scenes of Dylan playing with Grandpa.

WILDCATS

In *Wildcats*, Goldie Hawn is a football coach, and it opens with a wonderful montage of home movies showing a little girl who loves football (she gets a helmet for Christmas when her sister gets a doll). Nothing else in the film is quite that inspired, but most of it is fun. The movie was directed by Michael Ritchie, who has achieved most of his success with sport films and comedies. Only the music appears to be truly stereophonic. The transfer is a little grainy.

WILL PENNY

Praised for its realism, *Will Penny* is a western which ends with the title character, played by Charlton Heston, pouring a bag of sulfur down a chimney onto a fire to smoke bad guys out of a cabin so he can shoot them, and then five minutes later entering the cabin to have a touching love scene with the heroine. Those must have been the days when men and women had noses of steel.

Since it is at the end, that is the part of *Will Penny* we always remember, but actually the film is pretty good. Heston gives an unusually fine performance, completely free of his standard mannerisms and wooden line reading. There are parts to the film, particularly in the beginning, which differ from the normal portrayals of cowboys and have a ring of authenticity. The plot has very little linear movement, but just enough keeps on happening to prevent the viewer from becoming bored.

The color tones are rich and generally free of grain. In some night sequences flesh looks a bit on the orange side, but most of the time the image looks accurate. The sound is acceptable, though the musical score, by David Raksin, is a bit sappy.

WILLARD
The rodent-infested *Willard* still works well as entertainment, even though screen gore has come a long way since it was made. The print is in good condition and you can see the rats in the darker scenes. The film's flat, strained monaural sound tests one's patience at times.

WILLIE NELSON GREATEST HITS LIVE
Willie Nelson has gathered a large crossover following by concentrating on the folk elements in his music. His hour long concert on *Willie Nelson Greatest Hits Live*, filmed in Austin, is relaxed and inviting. The concert recording has definite limitations, particularly on the higher end, but the stereo sound is adequate. The picture also tends to blur unless Nelson is in one of his many tight, brightly lit closeups. The atmosphere of the entire production, however, seems to accommodate a certain amount of sloppiness.

WILLOW
Twenty-five years from now, or sooner, someone will make a big budget fantasy action picture with familiar character types, and someone else will complain that it is just a rip-off of *Willow*. So what. As long as a film like *Willow*, which was harshly criticized for being like other popular movies, can stand on its own, it makes no difference what its sources are. The movie is lengthy in a good way, has special effects which look incredible on a television screen, and has plenty of action. It has good guys, bad guys, magic and romance. We hope someone does make more movies like it.

Running 130 minutes, the movie, which is about a dwarf's efforts to protect a baby from being killed by an evil queen, is broken almost too evenly onto three sides of the disc. The stereo sound mix is commensurate with the rest of the film's budget. Neither the picture nor the sound quality of the disc is outstanding, but both are very good and do nothing to hamper one's enjoyment of the film. Cropping hurts the fighting scenes and some of the deliberate spectacle shots.

WINCHESTER '73
The black-and-white picture on *Winchester '73* looks incredibly fresh. The sound has been consigned to one channel on the analog disc and a 90-minute interview with James Stewart is on the other.

The 1950 movie is terrific. An Anthony Mann western which follows the ownership of a rifle amongst murderers and thieves, it has a cast which only begins and ends with Stewart. Dan Duryea, who has next-to-top billing, doesn't appear until the film is almost over, but his brief performance is hotter than a lit stick of dynamite. The film is well-paced, has plenty of action sequences, and is majestically photographed.

We usually don't like the lectures we have heard on disc, because they either make us feel like we should be taking notes or are as forgettable as an interesting article one chooses not to clip from a newspaper. Jimmy Stewart's talk, which is regularly prompted by Paul Lindenschmid, is an entirely different case. It is very easy to pour yourself a glass of something, prop your feet up, watch the pretty photography, and listen to Stewart ramble through his anecdotes. It is easy to anticipate that there will be evenings when we will want to listen to them again.

WINDHAM HILL – AUTUMN PORTRAIT
WINDHAM HILL – WINTER
The October colors of Windham County, Vermont, are the subject of *Windham Hill – Autumn Portrait*. The disc features the interchangeable music of nine Windham Hill recording artists, which, with the exception of Bill Quist's rushed interpretation of Eric Satie, makes for a pleasant and relaxing hour of articulate music.

Color is the main attraction. In one segment, green, yellow and red leaves of all shades float on a pond of bright light-blue water. The disc program, however, is foliage, foliage, and more foliage. At the beginning you feel like you are going for a country drive, but by the end it is more like raking the yard.

We have seen *Windham Hill – Winter* numerous times and every viewing has sent a chill across our shoulders. The picture is so perfect that smudges and fingerprints on the TV screen get in the way.

The shot which gives us goose pimples is of a steam locomotive chugging into a snowbank. Steam billows through snow-weighted branches as the engine plows across a puffy white carpet to the music of Shadowfax. Additional artists include William Ackerman, Darol Anger, Mark Isham, Liz Story and seven others. You see frozen branches and melting snow banks, icicles dripping and the wind blowing a fog of snow along a mountain ridge. It is the same feeling one has reading a page or two of Thoreau about winter at Walden; not so much an insight to the workings of nature as a natural moment so perfectly described that it will never be forgotten.

WINDHAM HILL – CHINA
Selections from the usual array of Windham Hill performers can be found on the single-sided CLV disc, *Windham Hill – China*. Every piece chosen has vague references to the Chinese musical idiom, but none are deliberately Oriental. As usual, the music is superbly recorded and transferred. The accompanying visual material is a mixture of landscapes and people shots from southeastern China. Edited to the music, the images are noticeably grainy, making the disc more effective on a small TV screen than on a large one.

WINDHAM HILL – TIBET
So few travelogs are available on disc that even a wordless program such as *Windham Hill – Tibet* has appeal. The disc's strongest component is its music recording and sound (the score is by Mark Isham), but the subject is interesting enough that it could draw disc owners who have no intention of playing the music.

The picture is mildly blurry throughout, but the sound is clean and pure. The music is vaguely Oriental and Himalayan. It has strength, but is lightheaded. The images on the single-sided CLV program are fascinating. Although Tibet is portrayed as stereotypically mystical, the architecture and the untechnological activities of the inhabitants are worth studying. The show makes us wonder, however, what the filmmakers have left out. Has Tibet no plumbers? No taxis? No teenagers? The credits give thanks to the assistance of TTV, Tibetan Television. Now that would be interesting – "Cow blocks stairwell. Details at eleven."

WINDHAM HILL – WATER'S PATH
WINDHAM HILL – WESTERN LIGHT
The concept behind *Water's Path* was a cliché a hundred years ago when Smetana did it and is still a cliché today. The video starts with clouds forming in the sky, dropping rain which forms into a tiny stream which, 50 minutes or so later, evaporates from the ocean into the clouds again. The images are accompanied by cuts from various Windham Hill artists (including Shadowfax, George Winston, Ira Stein, William Ackerman, and others). Most bothersome to us was Bill Quist's rendition of several Eric Satie tunes. Every note in a Satie piece ought to have its own breath. Quist rushes though them, to visions of calm water yet, as if he were in a hurry to finish the gig and get home.

A lack of narrative weakens *Western Light* although overall it is a better program than *Water's Path*. The music, by Ackerman again, along with Alex de Grassi, Mark Isham, and Liz Story, is oriented toward the acoustical guitar and after an overly sweeping introduction it is quite pleasant. The video, which is grainy in places, was shot primarily in Glen Canyon National Recreation Area and Mesa Verde National Park. You could call up the chapter markers randomly and not notice they were out of order. Much of it was filmed from an airplane, swooping in and around geological features of all sizes and shapes. Also included are visions of the deserted cliff dwellings once inhabited by indigenous, architecturally ingenious Americans.

WINDHAM HILL IN CONCERT
LIVE AT THE VILLAGE VANGUARD
Both *Windham Hill in Concert* and *Live at the Village Vanguard* have soundtracks with so few errors that you can probably count the hisses and buzzes on the two discs on one hand. In both programs the camera is often, visually, inches away from the performers' hands and lips.

Windham Hill in Concert really isn't. Most of it was filmed in a studio under very controlled lighting conditions, with only the intros and the applause swinging over to the outdoor concert amphitheater. There is no telling how much of the recording is studio and how much is live, because both are flawless. As with other *Windham Hill* discs, the equipment which was used to produce the program is listed on the back of the jacket. Bill Ackerman opens with several numbers. Michael Hedges, whose wildly-intricate guitar playing is the highlight of the disc, follows with several more. Scott Cossu does one piano piece and the group, Shadowfax, finishes with five numbers. The one problem with the disc is that it runs for a total of 68 minutes so that the running time on each side is only around a half hour.

Live at the Village Vanguard runs 53 minutes and fits entirely on one side. The disc features John Abercrombie on guitar, Michael Brecker on tenor sax, Marc Johnson on bass, and Peter Erskine on drums. During one number there are some 16mm clips of Japan, but other than that the disc is simply a record of the concert. On some of the other Vanguard-localed discs, the musicians often launch into elaborate improvisational solos. Here, Abercrombie & Co. stay low-key and keep the atmosphere relaxed.

WINDY CITY

The script for *Windy City* is so pathetically bad that the quality of the picture and sound only helps to emphasize how awful it is. The ridiculous voice-over narration floats out of one's speakers like a lead brick. The pretty Chicago locations inevitably look more realistic than the actors who pretend they live there. About a writer whose friend dies and whose girlfriend marries someone else, the show has no special surprises and no insight. Avoid the disc.

WINGS

Wings, a silent film released by Paramount, was, ironically, the first digitally encoded laser disc to actually reach video stores in America. As film critic and scholar Andrew Sarris often enjoys pointing out, silent films were never intended to be viewed silently. The film, which won the first Academy Award for Best Picture (they weren't even called Oscars then), has an old-fashioned Wurlitzer soundtrack (performed by Gary Carter) which has been digitally recorded and encoded. Suffice to say it sounds terrific, even on analog playback.

There are many excellent, relevant silent movies which deserve to be seen by today's audiences and pressed onto laser disc. Unfortunately, *Wings* is not one of them. A typical 'Best Picture,' it is over-produced, unthreatening and ever so slightly dull. Made just when sound was about to burst forth from the screen, it is a showcase of technical accomplishments tied into a simplistic story about two rivals who become buddies and heroic aces in the Great War. Clara Bow is the most attractive principal player – she even has a nude scene – but Gary Cooper, who appears all of a minute and a half near the beginning, is riveting. His lanky performance conveys the weary nervousness of combat and after he is gone you could care less what happens to the two nebbishes who are supposed to be the stars.

WINGS OF DESIRE

Wim Wenders' fascinating slice through the layers of the human psyche, *Wings of Desire,* has a wonderful stereo surround soundtrack – angels wander about Berlin while the inner voices of the people they pass fill every corner of the viewing room. Too bad most of it is in German, because the yellow English subtitles can't begin to itemize the output.

The script was written by Wenders and playwright Peter Handke. It is deliberately opaque, edging onto pieces of short stories as the angels peek into the private lives of different individuals, and then veering elsewhere. It is probably the only way the filmmakers could present the material without succumbing to recognizable silliness. A linking story eventually materializes, as one of the angels becomes attracted to a trapeze artist and mutates into a human in order to meet her. The essence of *Wings of Desire,* however, is not in its vague magic or quasi romance, it is the evocative posturing represented most distinctly by a movie set within the film (Peter Falk, speaking English, has a major role in *Wings*, playing himself. It is an enjoyable touch.) which is comprised of several cut-away levels of floors, all in disrepair. In the same way that Picasso would present an entire head on a flat surface, so do Wenders and Handke present all the layers of a person's consciousness in single swathes of sound and image.

The movie is mostly in black-and-white, although there are extended color sequences. The picture is consistently good, though it is mildly cropped. The film runs 130 minutes and is spread to three sides in CLV.

WINNERS TAKE ALL

Winners Take All has a promotional quote from 'Motorcycle Industry' on the jacket cover. Well, one really wouldn't expect 'Film Comment' to have glowing words for it, right? The racing scenes are better than documentaries about real races, since they have been staged and edited for excitement. Motorcycles fly all over the place, and they don't always land right side up. The story is engaging, but it finishes a half hour before the movie does. The disc has an acceptable picture and sound. The darker scenes are a bit grainy and the monaural sound doesn't really capture the dizzy whine of the bikes, but 'Motorcycle Industry' enthusiasts should be pleased.

WINNIE THE POOH AND THE BLUSTERY DAY/WINNIE THE POOH AND A DAY FOR EEYORE

After a constant barrage of Donald Duck's jabbering, Pluto's barking, and Goofy's fumbling injuries, the peacefulness of the Winnie the Pooh cartoons are as relaxing as words on a printed page. The two episodes *Winnie the Pooh and the Blustery Day/Winnie the Pooh and a Day for Eeyore* are on a single side of a CLV disc and are not marked by chapter encoding. They are monaural and have not been CX-encoded.

The charm of the series is sustained because the source material is followed so closely. The animation, both foreground and background, is so true to its source that it often appears to be taking place in the book itself, with letters being blown across the screen in the blustery wind. Even when the Disney animators digress, they do it in style, such as the decent 'Pink Elephants' imitation which is used as a bridging sequence in 'Blustery Day.'

The transfer is very nice and makes the artwork look lovelier still. 'Eeyore' has appeared in a previous Disney anthology, but works better as part of this double bill. By obtaining both this disc and *Winnie the Pooh and the Honey Tree/Winnie the Pooh and Tigger Too*, one would have a decent, feature length collection of Pooh adventures. For the drawings alone, it is worth it.

WINNIE THE POOH AND THE HONEY TREE/WINNIE THE POOH AND TIGGER TOO

The nice thing about Walt Disney's Winnie the Pooh cartoons is their fidelity to the original drawings. Two 25-minute features appear together on the single sided *Winnie the Pooh and the Honey Tree/Winnie the Pooh and Tigger Too*. In both features, the backgrounds retain the wispy, bent-ear simplicity of the book illustrations, with the addition of soft, almost invisible colors.

In 'Honey Tree,' Pooh gets stuck in Rabbit's front door and later has a run-in with some bees. In 'Tigger,' which takes place in the fog and the snow, Tigger bounces on everyone's nerves until they realize that they should accept him for what he is. We detected marks on the negative in only one spot, and otherwise the picture is in excellent condition. The sound, which is monaural and not CX-encoded, is strong and re-creates the voices with a pleasing fullness. The cartoons have appeared elsewhere with alternate running times.

WINTER KILLS

You have to watch the cult film, *Winter Kills*, a couple of times to understand its oddball humor and intelligence. On the first viewing the show seems ridiculous. It is a 'comedy' about the Kennedy assassination (the names are changed) and the various conspiracy theories surrounding it. Unlike most exaggerated satires, although the incidents in *Winter Kills* are absurd, the humor, for the most part, is very dry and subdued. It is ultimately an appealing combination, and the movie has a large cast, including Jeff Bridges, John Huston, Richard Boone, Anthony Perkins, and others. Even Elizabeth Taylor shows up in a shot or two.

The disc, unfortunately, is awful. The film was made in Panavision and the Nelson release is squeezed from beginning to end. On top of that the colors are horribly faded and the image looks grungy. The sound also has its share of distortions.

WINTER PEOPLE

Winter People is a Depression-era backwoods tale about a clockmaker who stumbles into a clan feud and falls in love. Starring Kurt Russell, in a different type of role from the sort he normally plays, and Kelly McGillis, the drama has its pleasures, but the setting does not stop the film from seeming slightly absurd. It is not as dreary as the generic title implies, but it is not uplifting, either.

The picture is soft and grainy, and the film's colors tend to emphasize browns. The stereo surround sound has a few scattered effects.

WIRED

Wired is a movie which should never have been made, a stupid idea which never rises above being a stupid idea. Bob Woodward's book was fascinating, accurate, and a legitimate effort. The film does provide insight on how Woodward came to write it, but the biography is of John Belushi, and the filmmakers, realizing that not much of the comic's offstage life was all that funny, desperately try to add laughs by having Belushi's soul/corpse argue with an angel about whether he has died or not. The skits from 'Saturday Night Live' are imitated (poorly), rather than re-created, and nothing about the development of Belushi's talent is presented with clarity or understanding. The portrait of a self-destructive millionaire is reasonably accurate, but it could be any old slob. The harder the movie tries to show that Belushi was special – and he was – the more confused it becomes. The disc has a passable picture and stereo surround sound with limited separation effects.

WISDOM
You can't really get much dumber than *Wisdom*, a fantasy film written and directed by Emilio Estevez. It turns out to be a dream, but while it is going Estevez portrays a kid who can't get a job and decides to invade banks and burn up mortgages. Disregarding that banks keep those kinds of things on computers and that the police have a make on his car from the beginning but they don't catch him until right before he wakes up, the movie is still hard to swallow. Who daydreams about becoming a hero by burning up other people's mortgages? The laws of inverse proportion being at work again, the print is gorgeous and the sound is super. The second unit director is more talented than Estevez, so there are several car crashes on side two which are legitimately thrilling. The sound has a couple of cute moments, including a you-are-there go-cart ride. The digital sound also adds to the clarity of Estevez's voice-over narration, making it even more hysterical than it looks on paper: "So, I decided I was going to become exactly what the world had expected me to become. Something our society had left me no choice but to become. A criminal. I only had one small problem. I was a criminal without a crime."

WISH YOU WERE HERE
Emily Lloyd's performance as a brazen, foul-mouthed teenager in *Wish You Were Here* is an enjoyable tease. Lloyd portrays a girl growing up in a small English town who feels compelled to shock the adults around her with off-color remarks. Then she discovers sex for real, and it takes some of the spunk out of her. The early scenes cause one to recall the movie fondly, though the story doesn't really amount to much. The 90-minute feature ends just as the characters develop enough to become interesting. The picture is grainy and rough in a few places, but the colors are in good shape and the sound is acceptable.

WITCHBOARD
WITCHTRAP
Two films created and directed by Kevin S. Tenney are available on two separate discs, *Witchboard* and *Witchtrap*. The films have nothing in common except that they are both good examples of economically created thrillers. The scripts are tight, the scares – even when it is just the hero tapping the heroine on the shoulder at the wrong moment – are legitimate, and the entertainment is catchy.

Witchboard has a slightly noisy monaural soundtrack (though the sound editing, like everything else, is admirable) and a consistently grainy picture. The film, about a couple who pull out a Ouija Board at a party and accidentally call up the spirit of an axe murderer, does everything right to keep the viewer intrigued and on edge. From beginning to end the plot follows a legitimate internal logic, while Tenney, who has a competent sense of style, induces one good scream after another.

Witchtrap is not as rewarding, but it is still fairly entertaining. The plot has a number of similarities to *The Legend of Hell House*, and is about a team sent to exorcise a haunted mansion. The dialog is delivered more awkwardly and there are fewer screams than in *Witchboard*, but it is clear that the film was constructed with imagination. The picture is a little stronger as well, but the stereo soundtrack has few separation effects and never lives up to its potential.

THE WITCHES OF EASTWICK
Warner has summoned up a dazzling transfer for *The Witches of Eastwick*. The sound is particularly impish and full of sly, stereophonic surprises. The picture is always in confident possession of its faculties, and flesh never turns orange no matter how weird the lighting gets. The demons of pan and scan will sometimes nip a full Cher off screen, but some evils can never be tamed.

At last, there is a movie about Satanic possession which is not about Satanic possession. Three suburban women, all artists, manifest the Devil and proceed to give him Hell. The witty script, based upon a novel by John Updike, leans heavily on the ironies and tensions of suburban living. Part of its popularity probably rests in the cloudiness of its message; each viewer gazing upon it will have a singular interpretation of good and bad in the actions of the characters. It must have been a very dynamic date movie, since it starts out being kind of anti-male, but then ends up being kind of anti-female. Everyone who watches it will squirm at some point. Despite all the special effects, however, the story is basically true to life. Whenever men and women get together, there will always be sorcery and witchcraft, in abundance.

WITCHTRAP (see WITCHBOARD)

WITHNAIL AND I
Technically, *Withnail and I* is a comedy. It even says so on the jacket cover. The film is so excruciatingly literal and the camera angles are so unmotivatedly neutral, however, that it isn't the least bit funny, even when you spot an intended gag (the two heroes fishing in a stream with a shotgun, for example).

The film is about two male roommates who are not gay but still hang onto each other like a pair of old maid sisters. A holiday in a Welsh cottage brings their relationship to a crisis point. The film ends with them breaking up in the rain and one reciting Shakespeare to a wet fence. Visits to the dentist are more entertaining.

There are a couple of Jimi Hendrix numbers which come blasting out of the soundtrack, but the dialog is exceedingly British and difficult to hear. The film is so uninteresting that when one does comprehend a line, one forgets it immediately anyway. The picture was filmed dark. Perhaps the movie was made during one of the many Welsh brownouts. In any case, it is as difficult to see as it is to hear and why one would want to do either is beyond us.

WITHOUT A CLUE
A revisionist Sherlock Holmes tale, *Without a Clue* stars Ben Kingsley as the genius Watson and Michael Caine as the actor he hires to portray his fictional Holmes. Before going any further, it is important to make clear that, despite the ribbing given to the sacred Sherlockian cow, there is not a single false note in the entire film. Both actors give wonderfully comical performances, and the script maintains just the right balance between plot, cerebral wit, and slapstick. The mystery, concerning Professor Moriarty and a counterfeiting scheme, has traditional airs that the filmmakers are careful to respect. The entire film is a joy, and so is the disc, which has a beautiful, crisp picture and a dandy, stereo surround soundtrack.

WITHOUT RESERVATIONS
In *Without Reservations*, Claudette Colbert is a famous author, travelling from New York to Hollywood on a train, who gets bumped from her first class booking and has to ride coach. For various reasons she keeps her identity a secret when she meets and quickly falls in love with a service man, played by John Wayne. We're surprised variations of that plot device don't show up more often. The movie is an enjoyable romantic comedy, a little slow in the third act, but filled with memorable characters and easy charm. The sound is fine and the source material looks good, though there are a few speckles here and there. The last shot in the film is of an empty bed, with the implication being that it is not going to be empty for long.

WITNESS
The picture on *Witness* is a little on the blurry side. The glowing Amish oil lamps make many of the indoor scenes look orange/brown and the disc carries the brownout a step further. The stereo is well-managed, however, and the movie is less harmed by the quality of the transfer than it ought to be.

Witness is a beautifully directed film. The moment when Harrison Ford realizes that the Amish boy has recognized a photo of the murderer is done with a pleasing economy, as is the romance between Ford and the boy's widowed mother. What you don't realize until you see the movie a couple of times is that Ford's character is actually kind of slow-witted. He doesn't call the FBI, he lets his partner get killed, he doesn't know his boss is corrupt, and he lets the girl go in the end.

THE WIZARD
Those who could care less about *The Wizard*, and that would be about 99 and a hefty fraction percent of the populace, may wish to check out the disc anyway. The picture transfer is as good as the movie is bad, and that is saying a lot. The disc has to have one of the best picture transfers ever, and it is a shame that the movie bearing it has to be so useless. The colors are crisp, the image is minutely detailed, and the presentation is flawless. The stereo surround sound also packs a punch.

The movie is excruciating, littered with plugs for products from Twinkies to the Universal Studio Tour, not to mention the dozen or so video games on display (the heroes cross Nevada to enter a contest in LA). It is meant to be for the high single digit and beginning double digit crowd, but its value even on that level is questionable. There is a comically drawn bad guy, and the heroine escapes his grasp at one point by announcing that he had molested her. Whatever his bad points, he had not, and her falsehood – which is played as a gag to heap more trouble on him – is the wrong sort of behavior to condone or encourage.

THE WIZARD OF LONELINESS
The Wizard of Loneliness has a number of witty performances, some by children not even old enough to know any better. The film is about a boy staying at his grandparents' house in Vermont during the final year of World War II. There is a gothic subplot concerning a stranger who figures significantly in the lives of several characters, but that is just a device to keep the story moving. The film's charm is in the naturalistic poutiness of the kids and the passive grumpiness of the adults. The whole movie has character.

The picture looks fresh, with no more than a mild graininess in a few sequences. The sound has no noticeable problems.

THE WIZARD OF OZ (Voyager)
THE WIZARD OF OZ (MGM/UA)
For three decades American families gathered around their television sets every year to watch a tale of a young girl who journeys into a fantasy land and, from her experiences, realizes there's no place like home. *The Wizard of Oz* was, in a way, one of the first and most significantly re-watchable home video hits, and is probably more effective as family entertainment on television, where its threatening, 'camp' imagery is held in check, than it is on a big screen.

The Criterion transfer is significantly better than the CLV disc which was released a while back from MGM/UA (without CX-encoding). The best example of the improvement which the Criterion disc offers can be found at the scene involving the gatekeeper at the door to the Emerald City. On the first MGM/UA disc, his two-toned outfit is pale grey-blue and flat olive green. On the Criterion disc, the grey-blue parts are olive green, and what was olive-green becomes a fluorescent lime. The difference is amazing.

The Criterion disc also includes the use of a sepia wash on the black and white sequences which bookend the picture (though sepia remains on the footage which shows the door opening to the first view of Oz on the first MGM/UA version). When compared, the sepia provides a more pleasant image than harsh blacks and greys, and, interestingly, it makes the approaching tornado look more dramatic and exciting.

Besides the improved picture quality, the other advantage to acquiring the Criterion disc is the presence of a wonderful collection of film clips and photographs on side four in the 'Supplementary Section.' Unlike other Criterion discs, the text is kept to a minimum. There are a vast array of photographs, however, most of which are sufficiently identified, showing publicity poses, ad art, marquee designs, behind-the-scenes pictures, art from a Broadway stage hit production of 1903, and even *Wizard of Oz* Christmas ornaments.

Motion footage includes some interesting segments from a 1925 silent film which deviated significantly from the original plot; a promotional film made before Buddy Ebsen was poisoned by his Tin Man make-up and had to be replaced by Jack Haley; a fabulous, well preserved segment showing the first staging of the 'If I Only Had a Brain' number (it had to be shortened); a 1956 re-release trailer (which is intelligently introduced by a title card discussing the structure of its predecessors); and 'home movies' shot behind the scenes by songwriter Harold Arlen, which also show a dance number dropped from the final cut. There is some supplementary audio material as well.

Ron Haver's talk on the second analog track is a disappointment. It is not coordinated with the Supplementary material nor with the concept of CAV functions. Most frustrating is his failure to identify where, exactly, the 'Jitterbug' sequence was to have gone. He has a few interesting pieces of trivia, and explains the major technical tricks, but spends too much time discussing the structure of the widely read L. Frank Baum book and how it was ingeniously adapted to the screenplay.

THE WIZARD OF OZ
('50th Anniversary Edition')
At a lower price than the CAV Criterion Collection rendition, MGM/UA has released a super 50th Anniversary CLV presentation of *The Wizard of Oz*. The disc has a different and for the most part better color transfer than the Criterion effort and a more satisfying supplementary addendum. There is also an intriguing alternate audio track and sixty chapter markers, almost twice as many as the Criterion Collection version provided.

The sound encoding may be confusing to those who do not study the fine print on the back of the jacket cover. *Both* the analog and the digital track have the same separated audio program, so whether you play the analog or the digital soundtrack, you have to identify a single audio channel for playback. When both audio channels are played together the sound is distorted. One channel contains the film's soundtrack. The other channel contains just the music and sound effects, obtained from a 'nitrate music and effects track' originally used for dubbing foreign releases. It has less hiss than the full soundtrack and contains all the major songs except the Scarecrow's number, which was restaged at the last minute. Now, only nutcases such as ourselves are going to want to sit through the entire film listening to the incidental orchestration and the constant clinks of the Tin Man, but even casual users will benefit from sampling the track. Our recommendations: Check out the scene in which Professor Marvel 'reads' Dorothy's mind – the music is lovely and contains a hint of what is to come – and the melting of the Wicked Witch. The analog track is not CX-encoded.

The picture is not perfect, leaving room for yet another version to appear someday, but it is much nearer to a definitive interpretation of the original Technicolor hues than was the Criterion Collection version. The picture is often too orange and the reds bleed a little. The Horse of a Different Color is unstable. However, the superiority of the colors can be seen the instant Dorothy lands in Oz. On the Criterion version the Yellow Brick Road is sort of a jaundice peach. On MGM/UA's version it is a golden yellow, and though one supposes, ideally, that it ought to be a bright lemon, its intensity, clarity, and richness is matched by every color which follows. (Some viewers prefer the sedate but solid Criterion colors.) Both discs utilize a sepia tone for the beginning and ending black and white sequences and we could discern no significant difference between them.

The supplementary material collected on the MGM/UA disc is coherently introduced and admirably presented. The theatrical trailer which appeared on the Criterion Collection'version is included, as is the extended 'If I Only Had a Brain' number and the MGM Studios 'visit.' The 'home movie' presentation of 'The Jitterbug' number is repeated, but the song's intro is presented for the first time, over carefully edited still photos. A well preserved clip from the 1939 Academy Awards, in which Mickey Rooney hands Judy Garland a 'Special Oscar,' is shown. Still photos of Buddy Ebsen's initial Tin Man portrayal are exhibited, as a recording of him singing 'If I Only Had a Heart' plays on the soundtrack. It is just as well that Ebsen lost the part, because his singing is a bit loopy and his Tin Man interpretation would probably have been too close in spirit to the Scarecrow, too full of hayseed.

The unique realization of *The Wizard of Oz* on film is an accomplishment which seems utterly cinematic (the sets change too often for the film to feel stagey) and utterly American (in no other culture are such silly, buffoonish characters – i.e., 'Yankee Doodle' – so dogmatically heroic). The second soundtrack offers the viewer a chance to watch the ensemble play without the distraction of dialog, but there is so much to look at that you can never take it all in. If you own any version of *The Wizard of Oz*, take it out and watch it on a periodic basis. It can easily be stashed away like a collector's item because it exists so vividly in most viewers' memories. No matter how well one can recite the dialog, however, the performances and the colors are too vivacious to stay jailed in one's head. That's why there are laser discs.

THE WIZARD OF SPEED AND TIME
The scatterbrained *The Wizard of Speed and Time* consists of almost nothing but in-jokes about special effects production. The comic narrative concerns a young man hired by an unscrupulous producer to do a stop motion animation sequence for a TV special. *Wizard* is a cluttered film which attempts to use forced cutes as a substitute for charm. It will only be of interest to viewers who believe that F/X is everything and context is a bother.

The picture is transferred accurately to disc, but the original production is so overly manipulated that the image automatically looks a little worn down. The film contains a number of single-frame inserts, including messages such as, "The surest way for evil to prevail is for good people to do nothing," and "Question authority." Since CLV still frame functions do not access every frame, the 92-minute disc ought to be in CAV to be presented properly. The digitally encoded stereo sound is adequate. A trailer appears after the film is ended, but by then you already know that the movie doesn't live up to it.

WIZARDS
The disc presentation of one of Ralph Bakshi's more commercial animated efforts, *Wizards*, is commendable. Although the most intense colors quiver a bit, the picture looks sharp and the source material appears decently preserved. The stereo sound is digitally encoded and side two of the disc is in CAV. Stereo effects are limited primarily to the intemperate musical score. Because of the method of animation, the CAV side has a single jittery still frame after every two steady ones.

The plot concerns two rival wizards, one good and one evil, who rule over a post-apocalyptic world. Bakshi skimps on background illustrations and uses still pictures for lengthy transition scenes, but the comic book appearance of the cartoon and the uncomplicated story accommodates these transgressions. At its best, the colors are inventive, the characterizations are amusing and the plot is thought-provoking. Some viewers, however, will find the film more entertaining on the first viewing than on subsequent viewings, since a limited depth of field is not exclusive of the artwork.

THE WOLF MAN

The sound on *The Wolf Man* is monaural and is quite acceptable. The black-and-white print is in terrific condition and side two, which is in CAV, is especially appealing because of the increased clarity of the picture when the disc is operated at triple speed. Looking at the individual frames is also gratifying, and this satisfaction is increased with a collection of more than 80 publicity photos which appear after the disc has ended. The original theatrical trailer is included for good measure, and it has some nice, hoary looking graphics. There are also three pleasing color stills on the jacket cover.

The Wolf Man is one of Universal's better horror offerings. It moves at a speedy clip and has a pack of stars, including Claude Rains (as Chaney's father, though they act like they'd never met before), Bela Lugosi, and Ralph Bellamy. The publicity stills have staged shots of the various players scowling at one another. Even if one's library is filled with old horror discs, one ought to make room for this offering. It is a disc which one can look forward to pulling out whenever the autumn moon is full.

THE WOMAN IN RED

The stereo on *The Woman in Red* is very good. The Stevie Wonder score, the dialog, and the sound effects come across crisply and effectively. The movie, written and directed by the star, Gene Wilder, is one more painful attempt to find humor in the foibles of attempted infidelity.

In order to enjoy stories about spouses trying to cheat, you have to hate the characters. That way, if they mess up you can laugh at them. Wilder is an effective comedian and he gets some mileage out of various slapstick routines, but he is too nice and when he starts acting stupid, sympathy for him elicits the wrong emotions from an audience. More suitable is Gilda Radner's Lotte Lenya routine and, in fact, if Wilder had started chasing after her instead of Kelly Le Brock, the movie might have had a chance.

A WOMAN OF DISTINCTION

A minor film from the early fifties, *A Woman of Distinction* is about a college dean, Rosiland Russell, who sees the light and ends up quitting her job to get serious and get married. The plot may make a few feminists cringe, but it is a lighthearted feature and has some amusing gags stuffed into the plot inconsistencies. The black-and-white picture looks good, and there is nothing wrong with the monaural sound except that it has not been CX-encoded.

WOMAN OF THE YEAR

The romantic purity of the Spencer Tracy and Katharine Hepburn film, *Woman of the Year*, is a refreshing change from the distractions of contemporary films. The black-and-white picture is soft in places, but it is in pretty decent shape and the monaural sound is fine. The film is about the adjustments a couple must make to be married and to maintain the affections which brought them together to begin with. Like most of the Tracy/Hepburn films, it avoids the normal male/female stereotypes while embracing the genders of the two stars. If you want to know how movies could be sexy back when they weren't allowed to be, or if you just want an enjoyable two hours of romantic comedy, *Woman of the Year* is an excellent choice.

WOMEN ON THE VERGE OF A NERVOUS BREAKDOWN

The bright, primary colors of Pedro Almodovar *Women on the Verge of a Nervous Breakdown* survive the disc transfer without the slightest drop in solidity or intensity. The fleshtones are rich and the focus is precise. The movie is a delight to look at, and so is the disc. The image has been letterboxed with an aspect ratio of about 1.8:1. The letterboxing effect adds significantly to the entertainment. The picture is set very high – it will be flush with the top of most TV screens – and large yellow English subtitles appear beneath the image, in the black band (the film is in Spanish). The monaural sound is also in good shape.

The plot has elements of a farce, but the movie, about a woman whose lover has left her and incidents involving their mutual acquaintances, aims for and achieves bigger things. The farcical incidents – characters just missing each other, items tossed from a penthouse always landing in an appropriate spot – are treated like random events. Once the heroine understands that the randomness is universal, she learns to cope with the events that affect her life.

The bright colors and vivid picture contribute to the vitality of the film's atmosphere. The sets are inspired, and shift teasingly between soundstage concoctions and real Madrid locales. The performances are all very witty and the characters are adeptly drawn, so that one's memory of the film's population lingers pleasantly for quite a while after the film is ended.

WONDERLAND

After beginning as a look at Liverpool's male hustler scene, *Wonderland* then becomes a thriller, when, after a half hour, two boys witness a mob rubout. The film ends, however, as an animal rights drama, since one of the boys, while in hiding, takes a fancy to some dolphins. The movie is more dopey than it is tantalizing and we doubt even dolphins would enjoy it much. The picture is blurry, especially when red lighting is involved. The surround sound lacks delicacy, but has a few punchy separation effects.

WOODSTOCK

We couldn't help smiling to ourselves when John Sebastian stepped out in *Woodstock* and began singing about the way younger generations tend to discount the values of their parents. Ahh, but could even he have guessed that in so short a time those cute little naked tots banging on the drumset would choose 'Ronald Ray Guns' (as a voice on the soundtrack album called him) as their leader and embrace investment banking with the same passion that their parents embraced flowers and hashish pipes?

Warner has done a very good job on what must have been an extremely difficult film to transfer. Shot in 16mm, blown up and taped together every which way, blur and grain are essential components in many of the concert sequences. (On the disc, intense colors tend to destabilize slightly and some skin tones are too pink.) The theatrical presentation would change height and width when split-screen sequences were utilized. The disc presentation maintains a constant width but changes height, shifting between an aspect ratio of about 1.7:1 and 2.55:1. As is evident during the split-screen sequences involving three equal-sized images, and there is still a little more on the edge which could have been included, but the essential material is accessible. The presentation is commendable.

The disc also takes the stereo sound up to the limitations of the original recording equipment. Many of the musical numbers lack the clarity which are available on today's concert videos, but that's the new generation for you. The disc sounds the same way the film first did in a cavernous theater, and the PA announcements, in surround, are indistinguishable from the real thing.

Woodstock runs a few minutes over 3 hours (it always seems to go very fast, however) and is spread to four sides. Some of the chapter indentifications are listed incorrectly.

The disc was released on the 20th Anniversary of the weekend-long rock festival. The astutely constructed film (which is actually titled 'Woodstock 3 Days & Peace & Music') combined some of the festival's best acts with pertinent and mostly unrehearsed interviews covering every aspect of the event. Some of the music has since been so overplayed and is so flatly recorded as to seem stale, even when combined with the images of the musicians. Most of the songs, however, continue to strike an inner chord. The interviews are fascinating, capturing an on-site oral history of what turned out to be more of a momentary wish-come-true than a social cornerstone.

THE WORD

Irving Wallace was a talented practitioner in the art of cliffhanging narrative, and he achieved great success by applying his style to high-concept situations and then padding the structure with extensive, but shallow, research. One of his most inspired novels, *The Word*, was adapted as a two-part television mini-series, starring David Janssen. The adaptation has been released as a four-sided, 188-minute disc. The story concerns the discovery of a post-script to the New Testament, and Wallace's clever touch was to show that, ultimately, it did not matter if the document was forged or not. The program, however, is still too short to do more than rush through a bare outline of the plot. The ending, which ought to be a revelation, comes across instead like a cheap way out of a painted corner.

Although John Huston's name and image appear all over the jacket cover, he has less than a half minute of screen time. Artistically blurred opening credit sequence aside, the picture transfer is very good, and there are some beautiful, full screen closeups of Janssen and of James Whitmore. The fleshtones look terrific. The monaural sound, on the other hand, is poorly executed, and Alex North's score sounds wobbly more often than it does not. The lack of commercial breaks is also a detriment, since the filmmakers use those points to imply passage of time.

WORDS AND MUSIC
TILL THE CLOUDS ROLL BY

MGM's revue-style biographies of famous composers, *Words and Music* and *Till the Clouds Roll By*, run a little over two hours apiece. While watching them in a theater can be a bit of a strain, particularly when they are paired together, watching them at home is more manageable and more rewarding.

The Technicolor color transfers in both programs are beautiful, though *Words and Music* is more consistently alluring. Some reels in *Till the Clouds Roll By* look soft, and there is a greater chance to spot an errant scratch or speckle. The sound is also stronger on *Words and Music*. *Clouds* is a little scratchy and has one or two bad 'pops.' Neither movie was a widescreen effort so both are well framed. Both discs come in nice gatefold jackets with lots of artwork on the innerspreads, and on both discs, side three, which contains the cumulative musical numbers, is in CAV.

Technically, the style of musical represented by the two films can be said to imitate the many pre-'Oklahoma' musicals which the composers themselves were involved in, most having a bare narrative that served as no more than an excuse to string along some songs. The movies are loaded with cameo appearances by MGM stars singing the songs the composers have written. Both films are so wildly ambiguous when it comes to the private lives of the composers that the filmmakers would have been better off not bringing up certain subjects at all instead of taunting viewers with the curious maladies and foggy anxieties from which the artists apparently suffer.

Words and Music is about Richard Rodgers and Lorenz Hart, with Mickey Rooney's Hart being the center of attention. Rooney's performance is embarrassingly contrived, though under the circumstances it is doubtful another actor could have done any better. The image on the jacket cover of Rooney and Judy Garland is misleading, as Garland only appears near the end to sing a couple of numbers. The movie does feature many wonderful Rodgers and Hart songs. Side three has Gene Kelly and Vera-Ellen dancing 'Slaughter on Tenth Avenue' in CAV. A mild slow motion can stretch out the beauty of the ballet and in still frame, a viewer can observe how precisely coordinated Kelly and Ellen are, even when separated by half a stage.

Robert Walker's relaxed performance of Jerome Kern in *Till the Clouds Roll By* helps to cue the viewer that one's concentration should be on the music instead of the person. The movie has several other things going for it as well. It opens with a twenty minute synopsis of 'Showboat,' giving Lena Horne a chance to at least sample the role which should have been hers. Later on, Judy Garland has two elaborate production numbers which Vincente Minnelli stepped in to direct. Finally, there is the movie's grand finale (in CAV), a medley of Kern tunes performed by different artists and concluding with Frank Sinatra, in a white tuxedo, singing 'Old Man River.' Now, some folks are understandably put off by this spectacle, but we think the Sinatra piece is terrific and a wonderful way to end the movie. It was the only method the filmmakers could use to present the song stripped of its literalness, to convey the message to the viewer that 'Old Man River,' which has many meanings, is also about music itself.

WORKING GIRL

The Cinderella power meeting story, *Working Girl*, is mildly grainy. The surround sound is pleasurable, however, and the disc has been chapter encoded.

The movie is a wonderful romance with a terrific closing act. We have some minor quibbles with the script – Sigourney Weaver's character could have been more cleverly constructed, the heroine has a friend whose functions in the office are unclear, and some of the stereotyping is a bit unfair – but like all wonderful movies, none of that matters when everything starts fitting into place. Since the two actresses in the film, Weaver and Melanie Griffith, received all the praise, it seems worth noting that Harrison Ford gives a marvelous performance as well. He provides his white collar character a blue collar soul, and he doesn't have to push himself to be charming.

WORKING STIFFS

Whereas a successful TV series is usually picked up for syndication after its run is over, a series which gets cancelled after a couple of episodes, regardless of quality, heretofore was condemned to oblivion. But if many episodes are ideal for a television station which wants to run something every night or every week, a handful of episodes are perfect for a home video collection. Such is the case with *Working Stiffs* (identified on the jacket front, but not the spine, as 'Vol. 1' though no others ever appeared) which Paramount released on a 75-minute CLV disc. The show stars Jim Belushi and Michael Keaton as two brothers who work as maintenance men in their uncle's building in Chicago. The situation comedy relies heavily on the rapport established between the two leads, but the humor owes much to the improvisational style of Chicago's Second City group. The jokes vary in levels of sophistication, but most importantly, there is little in the show which is *not* funny.

The sound and picture are surprisingly sharp considering that the source was abandoned to the sitcom graveyard six years earlier. The program was shot in front of a live audience, and occasionally you can hear laughter about a gag that the camera or editor has missed. Paul Reubens appears in one of the episodes.

A WORLD APART

Set in South Africa in 1963, *A World Apart* is also about whites standing more or less on the sidelines and witnessing the exploitation of blacks. Unlike the embarrassing *Cry Freedom*, however, the protagonists are committed to anti-apartheid from the very start. Based upon a real story about a white family torn apart by the implementation of South Africa's 'Emergency Laws,' the movie is a valid drama up to a point. The tale is told primarily through the eyes of a teenage girl whose mother, played by Barbara Hershey, has been sent to jail. The drama avoids clichés and is an interesting examination of how a police state could conceivably function in a modern society, showing both the methods of implementing totalitarianism and the resultant emotional repercussions. Only at the end, when an attempt is made to widen the scope, and to imply a shared experience with the direct victims of apartheid, does the film falter. Not only does it remind the viewer of how insignificant the sufferings of the heroine have been, it is a boring sequence which the filmmakers tried too hard to make uplifting.

The disc has a nice stereo surround soundtrack. The film's colors are brownish, but the picture looks a little blurry in places. Image has included an excellent interview with the film's director, Chris Menges, on an insert which comes with the disc.

WORLD GONE WILD

The future is the setting for *World Gone Wild*, a low budget fantasy with the plot being an umpteenth uncredited adaptation of *The Seven Samurai* (the heroine even has a photo of Steve McQueen in her trailer). The film stars Bruce Dern, Michael Pare and, as the bad guy, Adam Ant. The stars and the gun fights are entertaining, but the movie fails to stimulate the imagination. The picture quality is fine. The sound is a little flat, though it is clearly not the fault of the transfer.

THE WORLD OF dBASE

A 74-minute training videotape for offices which just happen to have a laser disc player in the back room, *The World of dBASE* is of little practical value to home viewers. The disc is intended for use by those who are just beginning to familiarize themselves with a specific piece of personal computer software, dBASE III.

No semblance of interactivity or other special disc features are utilized. If you are familiar with office environment training tapes, you will recognize the style. The acting is about par with lousy soap operas or good X-rated films; the narration is repetitive and overly articulate; and the world's troubles can be solved by a few, simple, memorized commands. Constructing a database is a creative act, equal to writing a poem or planting a garden. The beauty of choosing fields with just the right sizes and attributes so that information can be manipulated speedily without running out of disc space is an elegance which is beyond the grasp of the characters in *dBASE*.

THE WORLD OF SUZIE WONG

The picture on *The World of Suzie Wong* looks a little soft, but the colors are rich and the image is generally pleasurable. The musical score is distorted briefly, near the end, but otherwise the audio is tolerable. The film runs a few minutes over two hours and is spread to three sides, in CLV.

The film is a romance from the early sixties, about an artist who falls in love with a prostitute in Hong Kong. The artist is portrayed by William Holden with his typical stiff collar, once-an-executive-always-an-executive approach. Today's realities make some of the material seem unlikely, but as an exploration of emotion and motivation the film remains a satisfying experience.

THE WORLD WET T-SHIRT FINALS BEST BUNS ON THE BEACH

The format of *The World Wet T-Shirt Finals* is identical to *Wet Water T's*. The wet T-shirts are discarded quickly, and the contest is a subdued sequence of dripping topless dancers. The producers really ought to pass more liquor out in the audience to make things interesting. The narration is set at normal levels, but the music score is horribly muted. The picture is okay. Robbi wins.

Having nothing to do with bakeries or the seashore, the format of *Best Buns on the Beach* is identical to the *Wet T-Shirt* disc, except that the emphasis is on rear ends and the dancers appear to have more experience. The picture and sound transfer are good. Blondi wins.

THE WRAITH

It is invigorating when a cheap exploitation film doesn't insult your intelligence. That is the key to the success of *The Wraith*, a teen hot rod version of *High Plains Drifter* with a script which is wise enough to let the viewer fill in the explanation. There can be only one sensible answer (it would involve an extraterrestrial emergency room), but by leaving that piece to the viewer and providing other emotional resolutions in its place, the movie keeps one involved clear to the end credit roll. The dialog is also intelligent throughout the script, and although the cast generally overplay their parts, the result is a satisfying entertainment that subtly leaves one wishing for more.

Most of the movie takes place in the bright Tucson sun, and the picture is rarely flawed. The stereo sound hasn't got the qualities of a big budget effort, but it is also in acceptable condition.

WRESTLEMANIA

(see **THE BEST OF THE WWF VOL. 1**)

WRESTLING'S – BLOOPERS, BLEEPS AND BODYSLAMS

(see **THE BEST OF THE WWF VOL. 1**)

THE WRONG GUYS

The dialog in *The Wrong Guys* is difficult to hear no matter how high you push the volume and even though the disc has some sort of surround encoding. The soundtrack is inept, and weak in the upper ranges. The picture has distortion during night scenes, but is passable at other times.

The movie is a juvenile effort, not very funny, about a group of men who reunite their old Cub Scout pack to go camping. A murderer is hiding out near the camping grounds. There are some gags with a squirrel which are amusing, but most of the jokes, even when you can hear them, do not inspire laughter. There is also a gag after the end credits.

WRONG IS RIGHT

The opening and closing credits for *Wrong Is Right* are in French. Apparently the source material for the film was the best Image could find, though they didn't take the trouble to grab an English credit sequence from somewhere else. No matter, the less effort spent on the disc the better, since the film is a near-useless political satire about a television reporter, Arab terrorists, and the American government. What Sean Connery is doing in it is beyond us, but at least he didn't make a habit of such appearances. The script is a mess, the satire is unfocussed, and the actors make themselves and their subjects appear silly. What's worse, the film goes on for almost two unbearable hours.

The picture is still a little old and faded. The sound has no problems. An interview with the director, Richard Brooks, is included on an insert, but it is a reiteration of the interview which appeared in *Dollars* and, perhaps wisely, makes no mention of *Wrong Is Right*.

THE WRONG MAN (Import)

One of Alfred Hitchcock's few miscalculations, *The Wrong Man* is available on disc in Japan. He made the film immediately after completing the first season of 'Alfred Hitchcock Presents' in the mid-fifties. Hitchcock may have been lulled into thinking that a story which really would be best suited for TV – in this case a docudrama based on a true incident about a man who was arrested for crimes committed by someone identical to him – would work as a theatrical motion picture. Wishing to emphasize realism, Hitchcock chose to film as much of the movie as possible on the locations where events had actually taken place. To his surprise, the sets were mobbed, because in a few short months he himself had become a media celebrity, thanks to the television series. The distraction may also have led him to believe that anything he made would be a hit.

The movie wasn't, and it is a depressing experience to attend in a theater, despite the happy epilog which scrolls by after the film is completed. The man who is falsely arrested (Henry Fonda) sees his bills pile up as he tries to prove his innocence. His wife (Vera Miles) has a nervous breakdown and must be committed to a hospital at a point when his own emotional strength is the most strained.

But it is great television. The black-and-white print has few rough spots but is also rich in contrasts and sharply defined. The subtitles are a bother in a few scenes but do not upset the presentation overall. The subject matter is clearly more tolerable on television and much easier to appreciate when one's own emotional flexibility can be synchronized with the show's presentation. The high point of the film remains Anthony Quayle's performance as an incompetent lawyer who actually prevents a jail sentence through ineptitude – his court strategy is so confused that a juror becomes impatient and causes a mistrial.

The compelling jazz score is one of Bernard Herrmann's least-anthologized Hitchcock efforts and it has interesting similarities to the score for *Taxi Driver*, a later Herrmann evocation of the 'real' New York.

WUTHERING HEIGHTS

Rarely do classic, perfectly written novels become classic, perfectly made films, but such is the case with *Wuthering Heights*. The emotional bonds between Heathcliff (Laurence Olivier) and Cathy (Merle Oberon) pull at the audience too, and every event which keeps the lovers apart draws the viewer closer to the both of them. Olivier's performance is the film's strongest point. The portrayal of Heathcliff could easily be comical, the brooding, mysterious moodiness supplanting every other character trait. Olivier's achievement was to retain the mystery but also make Heathcliff human. His eyes never stop moving as he watches and measures his surroundings. Oberon's stare is vacant, but she somehow manages to puff her face when her character is content and look gaunt when in despair. Their eternal romance has thrilled viewers for almost fifty years and it shows no signs of abating.

The quality of the disc is disappointing. The print had many scratches and the sound had more distortion than should be allowed.

THE X FROM OUTER SPACE/YONGARY MONSTER FROM THE DEEP

Two monster movies which are pretty bad even for the genre have been combined onto one three-sided laser disc, *The X from Outer Space/Yongary Monster from the Deep*. 'Yongary' begins on side two at chapter 4.

Since viewers are likely to be familiar with such films from television broadcast rather than theatrical play, the condition of the movies is of less importance than it is on other programs. Both movies are filled with scratches and splices. The color on 'X' is okay, but 'Yongary' looks murky. The digital monaural sound is passable, although the music on 'Yongary' tends to wiggle. If there is cropping on 'X,' it doesn't hurt too much, but the cropping on 'Yongary' – it hasn't been scanned – is often distracting, preventing one from viewing critical activities.

'X' is a Japanese film with one blond American actress included, for marketplace variety. 'Yongary' is Korean, and one of the few values the double bill has to offer is to allow western audiences a chance to absorb the subtle differences between the two cultures, particularly in the activities and attitudes of the female characters.

'Yongary' has very cheap, very obvious special effects, and is a simple Godzilla rip-off, with a large bath of ammonia doing him in at the end. This cleanliness theme is supported throughout the narrative and could be taken, seriously, as political symbolism with the monster representing the forces of communism. That's its only hope, at least, because the special effects and the drama aren't going to win any converts.

Compared to 'Yongary,' the narrative of 'X' is more elaborate and better paced. Astronauts bring back that ultimate piece of contraband, the mysterious space egg, and sure enough, it cracks into a rubber monster faster than you can say something before your lips move. The special effects are almost as bad as on 'Yongary,' and the monster, Guilala, looks like he has a huge pencil stuck inside his cheeks. They get him with shaving cream, or some sort of outer space atomic chemical that looks suspiciously similar to shaving cream.

THE YEAR MY VOICE BROKE

The Australian film, *The Year My Voice Broke*, is a drama about coming of age in a small town in New South Wales. The story is a common one, but the performances are affecting – particularly Ben Mendelsohn, as a 'hyperactive' delinquent – and the scenery is pretty. The picture is a little grainy, but poses no significant problems. The sound is mildly stereophonic, and the disc has chapter markers.

THE YEAR OF THE DRAGON

Michael Cimino's godawful *The Year of the Dragon* has been released in digital sound by MGM/UA and we wouldn't have missed it for all the celluloid in North Carolina. We have friends who feel truly indignant about this film, but it is intentionally offensive and getting your ire up over it is as productive as getting mad at MSG.

The print looks a little washy, and the movie loses a little of its colorful demeanor. It does not seem as gratuitous when confined to a television screen, although the stereo surround sound is suitably boistrous.

As for the celebrated director, he has shown an incredible ability to convince wealthy producers that they should play Charlie Brown to his Lucy-holding-the-football style of filmmaking. The jacket cover quotes one critic as saying, "Michael Cimino has talent to burn." Please, oh please, may we light the first match?

A YEAR OF THE QUIET SUN
DIE EHE DER MARIA BRAUN
(THE MARRIAGE OF MARIA BRAUN)

(Import)

We find it intriguing that the American hero in the Polish film, *A Year of the Quiet Sun* is more benevolent than the American soldiers in the similarly themed *Marriage of Maria Braun*. Both films are about women struggling to survive in the months immediately following the end of World War II. Both films also use the heroines to represent their respective countries, Poland and Germany, and, if the artists are editorialzing, the opinion held of the United States is clearly warmer behind the Iron Curtain than in front of it.

Sun is mostly in Polish and has English subtitles, though there are, without subtitles, passages of English dialog. The picture is faintly letterboxed, with a tiny black band at the top and bottom of the screen, and the subtitles appear on the picture itself. The picture, artistically, is sometimes very brown or very blue, but the quality of the film stock is never impressive, and one gets the feeling that all the brown scenes are that way because of the film and not the vision of the filmmakers. It has clearly gone through several generations to reach American home video, but its condition matches the feelings the film itself is trying to impart. The digital encoding stabilizes what is left of the soundtrack.

Ranier Werner Fassbinder's *Die Ehe der Maria Braun* (*The Marriage of Maria Bruan*) is letterboxed in the same way that *Sun* is, just barely. It is in German, with some incidental conversation in English, and has Japanese subtitles on the picture itself. Fassbinder had access to capitalist film stock and so the picture is more attractive, though it still appears to have gone through several generations before arriving in Japan and looks grainy. The monaural sound is not CX-encoded and is inevitably scratchy. The centerspread of the gatefold jacket is loaded with information about the film's history and construction, but, unfortunately, it is all in Japanese. And, of course, a familiarity with either the film or the German language is a prerequisite for watching the disc.

When viewed in tandem, *Sun* is clearly more naturalistic and real than the stilted, theatrical *Braun*, yet the talent which composed *Braun* is overwhelming and the latter is unquestionably the stronger, more memorable film. It is also more entertaining. *Sun*'s narrative is straightforward, and the theme of the visual composition is to show a character and his or her surroundings, with an emphasis on squalor. *Braun* is far more ambitious in the narrative, sound editing, and, especially, the screen compositions. What it lacks in compassion or onscreen emotion, it compensates for in a passion for the medium. It is addictive. With *The Marriage of Maria Braun*, you love the movie, or the disc, and want to watch it again and again. With *A Year of the Quiet Sun*, you have affection for the characters, and recollect them fondly, but avoid sharing their hardships more than the one time that you had to.

THE YEARLING

The problematic swamp and flesh colors in *The Yearling* survive the transfer to disc as well as can be expected. The sound gets powerful scratchy in places, to use the film's way of speaking. The story, about a family struggling to maintain a farm in the Florida hinterlands during the post-Civil War era, has a number of exciting and well handled dramatic sequences. It is maturely told, enough to withstand the rising level of sophistication among viewers.

The colors are rich and sometimes they look overripe or they get fuzzy, but the film runs long enough that the impression it leaves, of the deep green grass and the stunning azure sky, lingers with the desire that the story would continue for several hours more.

YEHUDI MEMUHIN

The presentation of *Yehudi Memuhin*, subtitled 'Tribute to J.S. Bach Live from the Barbican in London,' is equal in quality to the best classical releases. The picture is soft, but that is the disc's only flaw. The music, performed before a live audience on a somewhat bare stage, is airy and clean on the digital stereo soundtrack. Memuhin performs one solo, the 'E Major Partita,' plays the 'A Minor Violin Concerto' with the English Chamber Orchestra, and then conducts the orchestra in the 'Peasant Cantata' and 'Coffee Contata' with the singers Nicolas Rivenc, Alison Hargen, and Jean-Luc Viala. The 90-minute program is a nice mixture of Bach's works. Memuhin's solos are smooth, and the singing of both Rivenc and Hargen is impressive.

YELLOW SUBMARINE

From the three different shades of yellow on the submarine itself to the uncategorizable hues which spew forth in the finale, only laser playback could support the palette of fresh, pizzazzy colors utilized in *Yellow Submarine*. The 87-minute extravaganza of Beatle tunes, pop art, horrid puns, and good triumphing over evil looks fantastic, and has digital sound to boot.

The stereo mix is overly deliberate, so that the voice of a character walking across a hill on the screen in a 'long shot' will pass from the left speaker to the right speaker in almost the same arc. In a movie like this, however, that sort of thing is fun, and it matches the 'one channel for the instruments and one for the vocals' separation of the songs themselves. The music sounds terrific, too, even the worst song the Beatles ever wrote, 'All Together Now.'

The disc is in CLV and the songs have chapter markers. The source material has a few scratches, but nothing serious or diminishing. For those of you who slept through the Sixties or weren't born yet, the film is a cartoon representation of the Beatles and their adventures in several lands of fantasy as depicted by popular artists and animators of the day. The movie holds up remarkably well and has not been harmed by the passage of years or fads. We were surprised, in fact, at how new and fresh it seemed, and are quite sure that we will still like the disc and that we will still play the disc when we're sixty-four.

YENTL (CBS/Fox)
YENTL (MGM/UA)

After a tantalizing trailer which is matted in a near proper 1.66:1 aspect ratio, MGM/UA's presentation of *Yentl* then deflates to fill the viewing screen for the film itself. Comparison of the images in the trailer to images in the film show how much the mildly expanded sides add to each sequence's impact. One scene, which is not in the trailer, is impacted most of all. In the beginning of the cumulative sequence in which Barbra Streisand, as the title character, reveals her gender to Mandy Patinkin, Patinkin is laying supine on a bed in a hotel room. He is on the far left and Streisand is on the far right and when they are both in the shot his body remains in the image but his head is cropped off, even while he delivers dialog. How can the scene, which is the emotional climax of the film, not be affected by the absence of Patinkin's expressions?

The color transfer is improved significantly from the earlier CBS/Fox version. The cinematography has the kind of impossible lighting and color schemes which are difficult to translate to video successfully. It is all browns and oranges, heavily filtered, but whereas the CBS/Fox version looked washed out and too yellow, the MGM/UA version looks reasonably confident.

The CX-encoded analog stereo sound on the CBS/Fox version was something of a disaster. The music was often distorted and sometimes outright wobbly. The digitally encoded audio on the MGM/UA version solves that problem, but replaces it with others. The basic impact of the stereo and surround separations are much stronger on the CBS/Fox version, and sound practically muted on the MGM/UA disc when a direct comparison is made.

Although the songs are listed with time codes on the back of the CBS/Fox jacket, that disc is actually chapter encoded. MGM/UA's disc comes in a gatefold jacket and is also chapter encoded, with a listing appearing on the innerspread.

The format of the film, in which Streisand sings soliloquies to bridge segments of the narrative, seems to turn off some people, as does the tidiness of the plotting. *Yentl*, however, is a tribute to spirited argument, and ultimately it doesn't matter if Streisand, who also directed and collaborated on the screenplay, is right or wrong in her execution. Her effort is sufficient justification for the film's existence and is sufficiently constructed to provide entertainment and a bit more.

YEOMAN OF THE GUARD
THE MIKADO
H.M.S. PINAFORE
THE PIRATES OF PENZANCE (Pioneer)
THE PIRATES OF PENZANCE (MCA)

The English language is considered to be the most precise language in existence. Most major discussions in the major scientific fields are conducted in English for that reason. And for that reason there has yet to be a truly great English opera. We simply get too hung up on what the words *mean* to go blithely singing them up and down the scales. When it comes to music, English-speaking composers have excelled in only one category, the *song*, where an idea is put forth quickly and exactly.

In the latter half of the nineteenth century, when opera was the cultural and creative musical rage, Arthur Sullivan and William Gilbert tried their hand at it and discovered they could not approach the format seriously. In the middle of *Yeoman of the Guard*, which was about as serious as Gilbert and Sullivan ever got, Gilbert seizes on one of the character's names, 'Phoebe,' and he can't let go of it, toying with three and four syllable 'ee' rhymes. You realize that opera was not made for the English language; musical comedy was made for the English language.

The 'operettas' of Gilbert and Sullivan, a whole series of which showed up on PBS and was subsequently released on disc by Pioneer, are the direct ancestors to musical comedy and the American musical theater. The discs run between ninety minutes and two hours. The picture transfers are older, but in good shape, and the stereo generally dependable.

Yeoman was conceived as a 'serious' piece, but comes across, at least in this production, as an Elizabethan farce with an artificially downer ending. Joel Grey portrays a clown who loses his girl friend to a brave soldier. The thrust of the show, however, concerns the soldier's attempt to avoid execution in the Tower of London. The soldier is successful and the clown's bad luck seems unimportant. The sound on the disc is too accurate. You can tell that the singing voices were recorded in a studio instead of on the set and although this allows the orchestra to come through clearly it hurts the continuity of the presentation. The lighting is also odd, at times too dark to show an actor's face and at other times so bright that features are washed out in a glare.

The best disc in the series is the show which most people consider to be Gilbert & Sullivan's finest achievement. *The Mikado* is a wonderful burlesque of Far Eastern culture with nearly a dozen memorable tunes to support the comedy. Played in a broad, music-hall fashion, the cast members are happy and relaxed as they milk the material for all it is worth with wagging, bovine grace.

William Conrad appears near the end as the title character and, unfortunately, his singing is not up to the standards set by the rest of the cast. The orchestra and the voices are evenly balanced and the transfer is immaculate.

Attempting to do to the Royal Navy what they did to Japan, *H.M.S. Pinafore* is not quite as good as *The Mikado* and while Gilbert does a good satirical turn with the story of *Pinafore*, Sullivan misses an opportunity to bring his special touch to maritime folk tunes and writes palatial ballads where he ought to be composing subversive shanties.

The voices here are stronger than the orchestra, but the choreography, which is undistinguished on the other discs, is quite comical (the dancers are constantly avoiding a mast in the middle of the stage) and the cast, with the exception of Frankie Howard who makes the presence of the Admiral too weak, is energetic, melodic, and not afraid of having fun.

Rich in parodies of different operatic styles and poses, *The Pirates of Penzance* is an accomplished and highly musical comic work. The disc has quite a few pleasurable and amusing passages, and a worthy cast including Peter Allen, as the Pirate King, and Keith Mitchel as the Major General. *Pirates* is a clever, artificial story about a lad who was sent to serve as an apprentice 'pilot' and was accidentally signed into service as an apprentice 'pirate' by a confused nursemaid. His loyalty to his pirate comrades is tested when he meets a young woman.

The story's most intriguing achievement probably passed over the heads of many at the time, but is much more obvious today. The fall of the British empire is encapsulated in the idea that Queen Victoria is a parody of Queen Elizabeth I.

There is another version of *The Pirates of Penzance* available on disc, and it is even better. From MCA, the Joseph Papp production, directed by Wilford Leach, stars Linda Rondstadt, Angela Lansbury, Kevin Kline, and Rex Smith. It runs 18 minutes longer than Pioneer's version. One of the disc's few faults is that the limited width of the screen prevents one from catching all the gags. The disc's other fault is that the lovely stereophonic audio channels have been reversed.

As the Pirate King, Kline is almost too good for the movie. His performance is so busy and so solid that his presence inevitably detracts from the rest of the ensemble. The many months the group spent performing together allows even Rondstadt and Smith to come across like veterans, though Smith can be caught a couple of times losing his expression and breaking into a grin. Kids will enjoy the disc unless they are old enough to think they know better.

YESSONGS
YESSONGS (Digital)

It is hard to say how relevant the '1973 world tour' of the rock group, Yes, will be for today's video audiences. *Yessongs* is a concert film with a grainy, blue picture. Yes was known for their precise, electronic compositions and while their work was attractive when it came from a studio session, it is utter cacophony in cavernous auditoriums.

There are a few, short inserts of biological/nature footage which help the pace. The filmmakers err, however, when they include the sound of frantic whistles and clapping on a shot of a bored and immobile audience hardly moving in their seats. The most popular portion of the concert is a Rick Wakeman medley of Christmas tunes (we're not kidding) which today's listeners will probably find a bit schmaltzy. Well, what can you expect from such an old-fashioned group?

The disc was reissued with a digital soundtrack. Both the picture and the sound appeared more stable on the later disc.

YNGWIE MALMSTEEN – TRIAL BY FIRE LIVE IN LENINGRAD

Yngwie Malmsteen is an enthusiastic guitarist who appears to have chosen heavy metal as a genre more out of whim than compulsion. Malmsteen is Scandinavian, but his songs are in English, at least when one can hear the words. He entertains an auditorium of amenable but perplexed Soviet teenagers in *Yngwie Malmsteen – Trial by Fire Live in Leningrad*. Sometimes he does the old trick of playing an acoustical guitar solo to give his drummer and amplifiers a rest, and it is the dexterity with which he attacks these passages which leads one to think that he is only into hard rock because he thinks that's where the money is.

The disc runs 90 minutes and presents the live concert with no interruptions. The disc has no chapter markers and the image is grainy but tolerable. The sound is victimized by the quality of the live recording, which mutes most of the instruments and causes the instrument tracks to run together. You really cannot make out the words on many songs because the vocals aren't miked sufficiently and do little more than provide a cackling backup for the guitars.

YOGI BEAR
THE FLINTSTONES
HUCKLEBERRY HOUND AND FRIENDS
JONNY QUEST

Image and Hanna-Barbera released collections of cartoon 'greatest hits' under the series title, 'Hanna-Barbera's Personal Favorites.' On all the discs the two venerable animation industrialists, William Hanna and Joseph Barbera, introduce the programs and provide some interruption between many of the cartoons. Each disc runs over 90 minutes because it is loaded with promos for other H-B videos. Collectors will be disappointed to find that the opening theme song sequence for the featured cartoon is missing on most of the programs, and the closing theme song sequence is never seen. Image has provided chapter markers for the beginning of each cartoon, as well as for a few other choice moments, such as an Ann-Margret number on *The Flintstones* disc. The picture quality is generally okay, but the discs tend to emphasize the limitations and paleness of the animation. The monaural sound is fine.

The best collection, superior to the others in both wit and scholarship (the episodes truly reflect the high points of the series) is *Yogi Bear*. Yogi's Brooklyn Italian accent is timeless and the gags are humorous enough to compensate for the cramped character movements. The cartoons also have some great puns. "We're in the honey," Yogi says when he discovers a bee hive, and, in reference to a makeshift catapult he has constructed, "It don't mean a thing if you don't pull that string."

Eleven six-and-a-half-minute episodes are included. The first, 'Yogi Bear's Big Break,' is, appropriately, the first produced, and serves as sort of an introduction to the characters, showing Yogi attempt, without success, to escape from the park. 'Slumber Party' features a baby duck who, in seeming innocence, continuously interrupts Yogi's hibernation. In 'Queen Bee for a Day,' another amusing episode, Boo Boo, dressed in a bee outfit to steal honey for Yogi, is mistaken by an entomologist for a rare insect. 'Ice Box Raider' and 'Spy Guy' are typical episodes in which Ranger Smith sets traps to prevent Yogi from stealing food. The brightest point on the disc is the collection of three cartoons which lampoon famous fairy tales, 'Oinks and Boinks,' a takeoff on the 'Three Little Pigs,' 'Hoodwinked Bear,' a takeoff on 'Little Red Riding Hood' and 'Snow White Bear.' The final three offerings represent the series at its most creative. In 'Droop-A-Long Yogi,' a movie company comes to the Park to film a western, and both Yogi and Ranger Smith are hired as extras. 'A Bear Pair' is the memorable episode in which Boo Boo and Yogi win a trip to Paris and Yogi causes an international incident when he insists upon flavoring his filet mignon with ketchup. 'Rah Rah Bear' is also choice, as Yogi travels to Chicago to help the Bears beat the Giants. Accentuating every third syllable, he approaches a cop: "Pardon me city ranger. Where are the Bears battlin' the Giants?" The cop answers nonchalantly and only does a double take after Yogi walks away.

There are 12 cartoons on *Huckleberry Hound and Friends*. The best remembered of the 'Huckleberry' episodes, 'Spud Dud,' about a giant marauding potato, is included, as is 'Huckleberry Hound Meets Wee Willie,' the premiere episode, in which Huckleberry is a cop and Wee Willie is a large gorilla, 'Science Friction,' in which Huckleberry is a 'Scotland Backyard' detective investigating a mad scientist, 'Knight School,' in which Huckleberry joins the Round Table and fights a dragon, and 'Legion Bound Hound.' A cartoon series, 'Pixie and Dixie,' about two mice at odds with a cat named Jinx, who refers to the rodents as 'meeces,' is represented by three cartoons on the disc. In 'Cousin Tex,' the mice send for a cousin, from the state where everything is bigger, to beat up the cat. In 'Pied Piper Pipe,' the cat hypnotizes them with a flute until they stuff a dog whistle in it. In 'Plutocratic Cat,' they move into a house which has a more sophisticated feline, but get bored and decide to go back. A cartoon series about a polar bear and a seal, 'Breezly and Sneezly,' who pester an Arctic air base, is represented by 'Freezing Fleas,' which are employed by the bear to get past a guard dog, and 'Stars and Gripes,' an amusing takeoff on 'Cinderella.' We wish some of these could have been left out, however, in favor of more 'Quick Draw McGraw' episodes. The two 'McGraw' cartoons which are included, 'El Kabong,' a takeoff on 'Zorro,' and 'Dynamite Fright,' which has the dog that goes into ecstasy whenever he is given a dog biscuit, are both more original and more amusing than the derivative cat, mice, or bear.

The Ann-Margret episode, 'Ann Margrock Presents,' is the high point of *The Flintstones* collection, as she arrives in Bedrock to do a concert and ends up babysitting Pebbles to get away from it all. There are a couple of musical numbers. The elaborate creativity in depicting contemporary devices with prehistoric components was the hallmark of *The Flintstones* series. The only pre-Pebbles episode, 'The Split Personality,' shortchanges those effects for a concentration on character – Fred is hit on the head and becomes urbane – which is not what one is looking for in a definitive four-episode collection. 'The Blessed Event,' about the birth of Pebbles, is appropriate and amusing. The last episode 'The Stone-Figure Caper' features a magical character, The Great Gazoo, which the writers started turning to when they ran out of standard plot devices, a cop-out break with the format's internal logic which nevertheless, from the episode at hand, provides a few good gags. The disc also contains the opening theme song sequence, which is shown once. Although the time limits prevent as many *Flintstone* episodes from being shown – and thank goodness they are shown in their entirety – the anthology doesn't really seem to capture the essence of the series or convey the charms it had to offer.

Neither Hanna nor Barbera seem all that excited about introducing *Jonny Quest*, the half-hour adventure series with imaginative locales and limited character movement. Adults will feel impatient with the dramatic series, which has weak, illogical plots and an endless line of demeaning Third World stereotypes functioning as villains. 'Skull and Double Crossbones' concerns underwater treasure. 'Calcutta Adventure' involves an improbably constructed poison gas complex in the Himalayas. 'The Robot Spy' is about a spider-like eyeball which invades the Quest laboratories but is easily dispatched. The only episode of any real accomplishment is the last one, 'The Devil's Tower,' which manages to create a well paced sequence in which the Quest party must make their way down the side of a tall escarpment as a mad Nazi in a bi-plane throws grenades at them. The sound on the disc is more distorted than on the other offerings, and the quality of the colors sometimes shift in intensity from shot to shot within an episode. For the record, Tim Matheson provided the voice of Jonny.

YOICHI AOYAGI LADIES IN ALASKA

When not covered in snow, Alaska is a land of mud and flies. The mud is in limited evidence on *Yoichi Aoyagi Ladies in Alaska*, but the flies are all over the place. The 83-minute program, which we prefer to think of as 'Seward's Follies,' is a scenic tour of the 49th State, as viewed from the eyes of four young girls who go everywhere without clothing. The snow and the icy rivers in which they pretend to whoop it up are the least of their problems. As they sit in the grass and make believe they are on the road to utopia, you can see the bugs flitting around them. And, since video can't be airbrushed and since the disc transfer makes the picture clearer than a window with the glass missing, you can see the bug bites on their shoulders, their backs, their thighs, and even on their bare bottoms. It is a Kafkaesque wet dream.

The stereo soundtrack, which is as clean and vivid as the picture, features the uninteresting and eventually invisible music of a trumpets and synthesizer group called MEDIA. No dialog or natural sounds are included.

The disc jacket is sealed twice. It is covered by an amusing hold-this-up-to-the-phone-book-and-read-the-secret-message cardboard cover with holes cut out so the title and a few arms can be seen. Presumably, this is an imposition required so the disc can be displayed in 7-11 stores, since the part of the jacket obscured by the cardboard shows the women in their natural lack of attire, swatting at flies and memorizing the many Eskimo words for snow.

Aoyagi photographs the girls and the scenery from every R-rated position imaginable. The angles range from super long shots, where the girls are just little shivering dots on the horizon, to super closeups, where a single nipple towers above a breast like Mt. McKinley. The disc jacket lists the chapters for highlights of the tour, which is great except that the disc program itself lacks chapter encoding. The jacket also claims that the disc is in CLV, but side two is actually in CAV. The picture quivers whenever a figure is in motion, but the uses of CAV here are limited anyway. After all, it goes on for 83 minutes, and how much more of Alaska can a person be expected to look at?

YOJIMBO (Embassy)
YOJIMBO (Voyager)
SANJURO
REBELLION (Import)
UNDER THE BANNER OF THE SAMURAI (Import)
SATOMI HAKKEN-DEN (Import)

We must admit we are samurai addicts. When no one is looking we practice with our umbrella, grunt 'Ho!' at the suit of armor in the window of a local antique shop, and mutter 'domo' when the butter or salt is passed. Fortunately, there is a good selection of samurai films available on disc, not the least of which is Akira Kurosawa's *Yojimbo*, which has been released both by Embassy and, later, though in CLV only, by Voyager.

Embassy's version was scanned and cropped, and the source material was a murky and rough-sounding print. A good quarter of Toshiro Mifune's performance is lost because he is often positioned on the cropped edge of the screen, observing rather than participating in the action.

Voyager's version is letterboxed, but the credit sequence is windowboxed and when the image enlarges for the film itself, the effect is disparaging. The viewer quickly realizes that although Voyager's presentation is a signficant and welcome improvement over the Embassy version, the movie's director, Akira Kurosawa, uses such complete screen compositions that to lose even a sliver of the image is to lose a good deal of its emotional impact.

Otherwise, the black-and-white source material which Voyager has used has a number of scratches and similar markings, but it is sharp and has an effective range of grey levels. Voyager's disc has digital monaural sound, which seems to be in good shape, and plenty of chapter markers. The English subtitles, which seem more sophisticated than Embassy's, appear beneath the picture.

The differences between this *Yojimbo* and *A Fistful of Dollars* are really more interesting than the similarities. The latter was not a quicky rip-off but a carefully considered remake. Look at the differences between the American cowboy, who has a Cadillac-sized horse, a leather saddle, a saddlebag full of goodies, and a whole armory of pistols and rifles. The samurai, on the other hand, has but his sandals, his robe (the inspiration for the Clint Eastwood parka?), and his sword. What Sergio Leone avoided is what Kurosawa and, later, Eastwood himself, couldn't resist – the suggestion that the vagrant hero is actually some sort of deity or moral force who has come into the town to clean it up.

Embassy found a much nicer print to use for *Sanjuro* and they re-did the subtitles. Unfortunately, the film credits mention 'stereophonic sound' while the jacket cover states 'hi-fi mono' (not CX-encoded). No widescreen here, either, and it is sorely missed.

Yojimbo was intended to be tongue-in-cheek, but it had its serious moments. Kurosawa's sequel, *Sanjuro*, is much more playful. This is the only Kurosawa film we know of which does not have a rainstorm, a symbol the director uses to show the soul of the protagonist being cleansed. Everyone's soul here is just as dirty at the end as at the beginning. Mifune, playing the same character he did in *Yojimbo*, wakes up in an abandoned shack to overhear a conspiracy against a corrupt district superintendent. He assists the bumbling conspirators although they constantly trip him up just as he is about to solve their dilemmas. There are plenty of sword fights, but no blood until after you've given up expecting it.

One samurai disc available in Japan is *Rebellion*, which was directed by Masaki Kubayashi and often appears on a double bill in American revival houses with the slightly better-known Kubayashi film, *Hara-kiri*. If one sees it once with English subtitles, it is enough to follow the plot on the Japanese dialog disc, although details inevitably pass one by. *Rebellion*, in black-and-white, is about a family torn by politics and desire. The print is scratchy and the disc is not CX-encoded. There are some terrific sword fights at the end, but the 128-minute movie is not for those who want quick thrills.

Another samurai import is *Under the Banner of the Samurai*, also referred to as 'Samurai Banners.' The 166-minute historical epic attempts to depict several decades of battles and political maneuverings. The print is not sparkling new, but the colors are impressive. There is a chase on foot through the snow which is breathtaking, and the director never fails to include scenic panoramas to locate his characters in space and time. In the end, Mifune (who also stars in *Rebellion*) gets shot in the eye with an arrow. The film is typical of epics like 'Chushingura' and if you're that familiar with the genre, you'll probably want the disc.

Discs derived from the films of producer Haruki Kadokawa, the Roger Corman of Japan, are in a genre by themselves, but one, *Satomi Hakken-den* (the title can be translated as "Eight Dogs' Story of Satomi"), deserves mention here. The picture is one of the most impressive we have seen. The sound is CX-encoded stereo, but the sound editing is not nearly as creative as the art direction. The 136-minute disc is in moderately wide format, with bands at the top and bottom. It is about a group of misfits who are joined by little glowing marbles to fight an evil sorceress. The story is no problem at all to follow because the details of the plot are repeated over and over, both verbally and visually. The quality of the disc is so good that you can even make out colors when the filmmakers use lousy day-for-night filters. There is a fight in a blizzard of cherry blossoms, which is stunning. An old woman turns into a centipede on camera, the surprise of the metamorphosis more than compensating for the papier-mache appearance of the monster. After the movie, there is a colorful trailer for an animated jungle picture.

This *is* a disc for action fans, especially those who want to be a little daring. It may not be as contemplative about man's position in the universe as the 'serious' samurai films, but it has so many unusually colorful sets and costumes and enough wild stunts that you end up appreciating your own position in the universe a little more when it is over. As long as existence includes samurai movies and laser discs, life can't be all that bad.

YOKO ONO – THEN AND NOW

The jacket cover of *Yoko Ono – Then and Now* states that the documentary narrative "features numerous songs by both John and Yoko." What it doesn't say is that every song is drowned out or truncated by the narration. The program excerpts frustrating snippets from what is clearly great material and then tediously reiterates the Lennon/Ono saga. Give us a biographical film about Yoko Ono's life (and it is a fascinating life) or give us a collection of music videos, but don't give us a biography and pretend that it is a collection of music videos.

The CX-encoded sound is a mixture of stereo and mono material. The footage, from many different sources, is of varying quality, but the disc itself looks and sounds flawless.

We found it frustrating that there wasn't more music. Parts of Ono's post-assassination videos, the last videos she and Lennon made together, the 'Imagine' video, the 'Give Peace a Chance' group-sing, and their early avant-garde explorations are offered up and then whipped away as soon as the requisite 30 seconds has passed. The most fascinating clip is an all-too-brief jam during the *Let it Be* recording when all four Beatles and Ono dive headfirst into avant-garde wails and screams. Doesn't anyone realize that fans are interested in this stuff?

YONGARY MONSTER FROM THE DEEP (see **THE X FROM OUTER SPACE/YONGARY MONSTER FROM THE DEEP**)

YOU CAN'T HURRY LOVE

Other than some nice comic turns by David Leisure, Charles Grodin and Kristy McNichol, *You Can't Hurry Love* has nothing going for it. The script is unreal, about a young man in Los Angeles who tries to meet girls through a dating service, and the film, with the exceptions identified above, is not very funny. The music is in stereo, but nothing else is or aspires to be, and the picture is more often blurry than not blurry.

YOU NEVER WERE LOVELIER

The print used for *You Never Were Lovelier* is riddled with scratches, holes, and crackles. All have been faithfully preserved on the disc along with a soundtrack, which is equally scratchy.

The film, starring Fred Astaire and Rita Hayworth, is unremarkable. Each shot is always three or four beats too long and most of the movie appears to have been put together from one stationary cover angle and little else. Even the Jerome Kern score is unimaginative.

Astaire portrays a dancer who becomes involved with the daughter of a hotel owner. To give everything an exotic flavor, the location is said to be 'Buenos Aires.'

YOU ONLY LIVE TWICE

(see **THUNDERBALL**)

YOU'LL NEVER GET RICH

An early variation on the standard credit scroll – the credits appear on billboards and road signs – opens the pre-War Fred Astaire and Rita Hayworth barracks musical, *You'll Never Get Rich*. The 88-minute program, presented in CLV, has Cole Porter songs and plenty of Astaire's captivating dance numbers (though he also starts shuffling in the stockade, when the black inmates, the only blacks in the film, haul out their harmonicas and banjos). Hayworth is especially lanky and becoming, though her romantic attraction to Astaire is unconvincing. The print has a break, and speckles near the reel changes, but it is in passable shape and the transfer looks sharp. The sound has no significant problems. There are plenty of chapter markers.

YOUNG AND INNOCENT
SECRET AGENT
SABOTAGE

Few artists can communicate ideas as efficiently as Alfred Hitchcock. He always knows exactly what he should be pointing his camera at. His enthusiasm for sharing his control of the medium is the most evident in his early British films. Despite his cameo appearances, he is not saying, 'look at me, look at me,' with his inventive camera angles and movement. Rather, he is saying, 'look at what is possible.'

Voyager has released three of Alfred Hitchcock's suspense films from the mid 1930s, *Young and Innocent*, *Secret Agent*, and *Sabotage*, under the banner of 'The Criterion Collection.' Each disc is in CLV.

Except for chapter encoding, unfortunately, no special features accompany the programs. It seems a shame, especially, that, although each of the films runs under 90 minutes and all have rousing finales, none were pressed with side two in CAV. None of the three have been CX-encoded, either. The source material used for two of the three discs is only average. The continuity is coherent and the images are reasonably sharp, but, like prints one is apt to see at a revival house, there are scratches, splices, and foggy moments on both *Young and Innocent* and *Secret Agent*. *Sabotage* is in better condition, but even it lacks the richness of Voyager's best efforts.

This is no cause to avoid the titles, however, since all are engaging and play well on the TV. The most entertaining of the three is probably *Young and Innocent*, a rousing tale about a man wrongly accused of murder who must avoid the police until he proves his innocence. This is a basic story format which is present in several of Hitchcock's most popular films. One cannot belittle the movie by saying it is entertaining from start to finish, however, since the artistry behind the presentation of each scene is as thrilling as the drama itself. The opening shots, of a domestic argument and the subsequent discovery of the victim washed up on a beach, are a stunning mixture of emotional texture (a closeup of a seagull screaming, the limp body rolling in the sand) and concise storytelling (the hero, seen running for help, is presumed to be running away).

The heroine in the story is the daughter of the police chief. She meets the hero while visiting Daddy and, instinctively believing his innocence, is compelled to help him. While the text of the plot is concerned with capturing the real murderer, the not too disguised subtext concerns the girl's coming of age. The film holds up well to multiple viewings, since the plot is logical, often amusing, and contains numerous opportunities for Hitchcock to exercise his enthusiasm. It is worth noting, incidentally, that although Hitchcock often professed that the key to keeping an audience in suspense was to give them enough information so they can fret for the characters on the screen, the most thrilling moment in *Young and Innocent* works precisely because their is no prelude to it. And if you haven't seen the movie before or if you've forgotten, you'll have to find out for yourself what that moment is.

The biggest surprise for us, among the three releases, was *Secret Agent*. We have always despised the film and so we were shocked to discover, as we watched the disc, that we had been looking at it the wrong way. The film is definitely an acquired taste, but the key to enjoying it is to disregard the title most emphatically, and to remember that it is based upon a story by W. Somerset Maugham. In basic terms, although the plot is superficially about espionage, the movie is actually about sex. The hero and the heroine are teamed on a mission as husband and wife. After a while, they actually fall in love. Sounds like the material for a typical Hitchcock picture, but the manner in which it is presented discards the simple pleasures of watching the two (played by Madeleine Carroll and John Gielgud) bicker and gush. Instead, they act like real adults and sleep with other people, possibly even other sexes, until they get around to going with each other. As a suspense film, the movie, in which the hero has an innocent man murdered, is a disappointment. But as a drama about the ambiguities of adult relationships, about failure, and about compromising, it is a revelation, and one of Hitchcock's finest achievements.

Sabotage also takes a while to get used to, but it is a simpler and clearer morality play than *Secret Agent*. Hitchcock has a young boy killed in the course of the plot and the elaborate build-up to the death can leave one with ill feelings (these days the entire sequence would have been removed after previews). At its best, however, *Sabotage* is another demonstration of the art of conveying emotion through the combination of pictures and sound. Good and evil are clearly defined and the suspense when they clash, thanks to Hitchcock's techniques, is nerve-wracking.

YOUNG EINSTEIN

A comedy which will bore some and delight others, *Young Einstein* seems ideally suited for the laser medium, having a wonderful stereo surround soundtrack and a bright, squared picture which has at least a few nice special effects. The plot is sort of a farcical, tie-died *Ragtime*, and the less emphasis placed upon it the better, since the funniest moments involve side gags and small details which have little to do with the central narrative (eg., after some establishing shots to show that it is morning and with birds atwittering in the trees, the hero's mother steps through a doorway of their rustic homestead to heave the washwater out of a bin, but she hooks it and dumps the water onto herself).

The hero is played by someone named Yahoo Serious whose talent for writing (he collaborated on the screenplay) appears to exceed his talent for clowning, though in the environment he has created he can get away with almost anything. More impressive is Odile Le Clezio, the heroine, who gives a beautiful, delicately comical performance in the middle of utter madness. The picture looks sharp but takes on grain when strong reds or browns are involved. Music and special effects are heavily employed on the surround channels. The audio has extra clarity and detail, and there are some terrific explosions. The disc is good fun, but you have to release both your inhibitions and your intelligence to enjoy it.

YOUNG GUNS

We were glad to see that the Western is alive and kicking in *Young Guns*. The film was a surprise hit, the first Western to earn a profit since *Butch Cassidy and the Sundance Kid*, and the first unself-conscious Western since who knows when. Loaded with a full barrel of young 'brat pack' actors – Charlie Sheen, Emilio Estevez, Keifer Sutherland, Lou Diamond Phillips – the film blazes away with action and simple dramatics. Ostensibly concerned with the early escapades of Billy the Kid, the movie mixes gunfights with just enough personality interludes to justify its existence. It is by no means a great film, but it is such a welcome and legitimate rejuvenation that it deserves a round of rowdy cheers.

Young Guns makes only one attempt to explore the already fully-mapped genre, by maintaining a burnt color scheme which often makes the images look like tinted daguerreotypes. Throughout the entire picture, no color escapes subjugation, and long stretches of footage are completely brown and white. The effect works nicely, and is replicated on the disc without difficulty. The picture transfer is acceptable. There are a few speckles, but not enough to get in the way. The surround sound is marvelous, as the many gun battles zing bullets liberally around one's viewing area. The musical score, however, has a souped-up dance beat which sounds ridiculous. A couple of chapters are encoded on the disc, but not enough to be useful.

YOUNG LADY CHATTERLEY II

Adam West has a small role in *Young Lady Chatterley II* and he is by default the most talented performer in the film. Like many softcore movies, *Chatterley* is a comedy, but only West has the talent to do more than recite barely-memorized lines.

The jacket claims the disc is in stereo although the results are enough to make sound fanatics cringe. The picture is unblemished but overly gauzy. The characters jump out of their clothing so quickly that there is little eroticism, and since the display remains above the waist, it becomes very repetitive very early on. It can only be recommended for situations where one is not anxious for time to pass, because it is the longest 87 minutes we have suffered through in quite a while.

THE YOUNG LIONS

The still on the jacket cover of *The Young Lions* is a cheat, since the three stars never appear in the same shot together in the movie as live characters, but it is a legitimate cheat, since that was how the film was sold originally. Based upon a typically soapy Irwin Shaw story about American and German soldiers in World War II, the movie stars Marlon Brando (vis un aczent), Montgomery Clift, and Dean Martin. As the topical significance of the cast fades, the film becomes less important than it once seemed. It is not very good – the moral lessons are more obvious than in Shaw's better efforts – but it is watchable and even addictive, because the drama provides a series of emotional cliff hangers as it jumps from one character to the next. It is also fun, because even though the stars are no longer topical, their screen personas remain well established and popular.

The black-and-white film is presented with an aspect ratio of about 2.3:1. The black-and-white transfer is sharp, and the few flaws which do appear are inconsequential. The digital stereo surround sound is not as elaborately mixed as it is in other films of the era. The stereo effects are subdued and may require a little extra tuning to achieve the correct mood.

The Young Lions has always seemed perfectly acceptable as a scanned and cropped television presentation. However, the letterboxing does help the movie a lot, since the screen compositions are often subtly balanced and one responds to the emotions of a scene more instinctively when the full image is available. The film runs a little short of three hours and is presented on three sides.

YOUNG NURSES IN LOVE

A Chuck Vincent burlesque set in a hospital, *Young Nurses in Love* is grainy and the stereo sound has few separations but plenty of distortion. Ribald gags take precedence over nudity in the 76-minute feature, but few of the antics are sufficiently amusing to make the film worthwhile. Side two is in CAV, with two unsteady still frames out of every five.

YOUNG SHERLOCK HOLMES

Inconsistencies of plot to which one paid no notice during the first rousing viewing of *Young Sherlock Holmes* prevent subsequent run-throughs from manifesting the same thrills. How does Holmes know who makes the paraffin found, conveniently, on the torn piece of cloth? How does he get onto the chandelier? To take part in the fun, you are supposed to give a movie like this a little leeway, but the script abuses its privileges.

The sound effects are spectacular – especially simple sounds like the swish of the swords – but the heightened clarity of the music and dialogue just emphasize the limitations of each. The picture is a little grainy. The special effects are not as impressive as on a large screen, and that includes the one scene which almost makes purchasing the disc worthwhile: Watson's anthropomorphic pastry hallucination.

THE YOUNG STRANGER

Rescued by an uninhibited happy ending, *The Young Stranger*, is an almost unbearably corny drama about adolescent angst. The story is about a teenage boy who is presumed guilty after a skirmish at a movie theater and his frustrations in trying to convince his family that he is innocent. Everybody wears ties and acts as if they've stepped out of an episode of 'Father Knows Best,' at least up to a point. The black-and-white picture transfer is a little soft on side one, but very sharp on side two, which is in CAV with two unsteady still frames out of every five. The sound is fine. The film was John Frankenheimer's first directorial effort, and an interview with him is included on an insert with the disc.

YOUNGBLOOD

Hockey is the subject of *Youngblood*, which stars Rob Lowe and Patrick Swayze. For those who have worn out their copy of *Slapshot*, this is a good companion piece. Both Lowe and Swayze are believable enough as farm team hockey players trying to make it into the big leagues. There is plenty of nicely shot skating footage and a passable drama. Ed Lauter, the poor man's Robert Duvall, plays the coach. The colors often blur together and the edges are hazy. The stereo mix is enjoyable.

YOURS, MINE AND OURS

Both Lucille Ball and Henry Fonda give admirable performances in *Yours, Mine and Ours*, a naturally awkward story about a widow and a widower who bring eighteen children into their marriage. Rather than examining the true joys and horrors which the situation would likely create, the late sixties film maintains a superficial and even blind approach to subject. However, Ball indulges in a few antic mannerisms without falling out of character, and Fonda provides a steady and attractive balance while still managing a little straight-faced comedy of his own.

The disc runs almost a full two hours, so the side break, though carefully executed, interrupts the film's dramatic turning point. The picture is reasonably colorful and the transfer is fine, though not exceptional. The sound is also acceptable.

ZABRISKIE POINT

A few campus rebellion films in the '60s and early '70s were sincere and entertaining. Most were boring and insincere (capitalists have a difficult time making anti-capitalist films, it's against their nature). None of the movies were good, but one film was so unique that MGM/UA felt justified in releasing it on disc, Michelangelo Antonioni's *Zabriskie Point*. The colors are faded and the sound is scratchy, but that is the least of the disc's problems.

"Prepare yourself for a challenging experience," the jacket cover says.

On one very long afternoon a young man is involved in a campus riot, rides a bus to the end of the line after maybe shooting a policeman, walks to an airport and steals a private plane, flies over a desert and buzzes a girl who is driving to Phoenix, lands the plane and goes driving with the girl, stops in the middle of the desert to talk to the girl and make love and do a lot of walking, walks back to the car, drives back to the airplane, paints the airplane all sorts of colors and flies it back to the airport where he stole it. He is then shot, but the afternoon isn't, as the girl still has time to drive the rest of the way to Phoenix, hear the report of the boy being shot over the radio, and dynamite her boss's house as the sun is (finally) setting over the horizon. It must be the middle of summer for the days to be so long, but then, no, if it was the middle of summer, school wouldn't have been in session and the students would have been at home with their summer jobs instead of occupying the dean's office and reprogramming the computer to "make all the engineers take art courses."

"You know I don't have to prove my revolutionary credentials with you," one young coed tells a council. "You know there's a lot of white students who are already out on the streets fightin' just, just like you guys do in the ghetto and you know there's a lot of unhappy, dissatisfied white people who are potential revolutionaries." The movie is apparently supposed to be about them.

When the girl in the car (Daria Halprin) goes for a stroll with the boy from the airplane (Mark Frechette – the characters are also called Daria and Mark, probably so that the actors could remember who they were supposed to be), the filmmakes a point of showing that they are way out in the desert, miles of hot, penetrating miles from civilization. So while they are having their tryst in the dust, a camper pulls up and, to represent bourgeois decadence, the couple in the camper are dressed in polyester tourist clothes and their child has an ice cream cone. An ice cream cone? In the middle of Death Valley? Perhaps it is a mirage.

The dialog could not possibly have been written by Sam Shepard, who was one of the screenwriters. It must have been done by one of the foreigners also listed in the writing credits. How else can one explain a sequential conversation like:

"It was nice of you to come with a guy who doesn't turn on." (Mark didn't want to share Daria's 'smoke.')

"I'm pretty tolerant."

"What are you doing out here? Phoenix – was that for real?"

"My boss wants me there. Some conference."

"You are pretty tolerant."

"Pretend your thoughts are like plants."

"Okay."

"What do you see? Neat rows, like a garden? Or wild things like ferns and weeds and vines."

"I see sort of a jungle."

"It would be nice if they could plant thoughts in our head. So nobody would have bad memories. We could plant, you know, wonderful things instead. Like a happy childhood. Real groovy parents. Only good things."

"Yeah, to make you forget how terrible it really was."

"That's the point. Nothing's terrible."

"Far out."

They disrobe and roll around some, and images of other naked figures cavorting in the sand are used to comment on the eroticism of wastelands and what some people will do for a paycheck. A little while after the two get their clothes back on, Mark pulls out a gun and Daria is shocked. She ought to be if her eyes are so bad she missed noticing the firearm when they were naked.

We have loved *Zabriskie Point* since we were younger than the characters, and we still enjoy it. Some bad movies you only want to see once, but this one you may want to keep in your library, embarrassing as it is. The picture is faded and rough in places. The music, by Pink Floyd, is rousing, but the sound is often poorly reproduced, to the point where pieces of conversation cannot be followed.

ZARDOZ

Before John Boorman was allowed to make *Excalibur* he had to come up with his own myths, so he put Sean Connery in a ponytail and bikini and had him scampering about the hills of Ireland in *Zardoz*, a silly Seventies science fiction film which has been released as a 'Special Wide Screen Edition' offering by CBS/Fox. Connery is intended to represent virility with a capital 'I,' as he crashes a nest of immortal but infertile flowers-and-beads types. Boorman is reasonably serious about it, and, divorcing the script from the movie, one can see that he was analyzing the development of civilization in a symbolic, mythic sort of way, but time has been far more cruel to the movie than it is to any of the characters therein. If it weren't for Connery, whose willingness to be a good sport redeems his performance, the film would be a disaster.

The disc has an aspect ratio of about 1.85:1, and the visuals are so cluttered that every little bit helps. The picture quality is okay, as the original production budget prevents it from being any better.

We will give CBS/Fox the benefit of the doubt and say that the disc is in 'stereo.' Perhaps it is 'stereo' without audio channel separations. In any case, the important thing is that CBS/Fox has dug up the best audio source available. Although it is a little scratchy, the depth and atmosphere of the film's soundtrack are clearly at an optimum.

ZATO ICHI MONOGATARI (Import)
ZATO ICHI (Import)

Picture a blind man entering a room where a rowdy collection of thugs are playing dice. The blind man asks if he can have a turn and, having indicated that his pocketbook is ample, is given the cup. He shakes it and flips it onto the table, but the dice escape and are exposed. The men around him greedily wager and he loses some of his money. He asks for another chance. Again he shakes and puts down the cup. This time even more money is wagered, but this time, as he reaches down to lift the cup, he 'discovers' the exposed dice and claims they must have slipped out of his sleeve. He then lifts the cup to expose the true pair, and collects a fortune. The thugs, upset at having been induced to part with their winnings, follow him into the woods. Ah, but this is no ordinary blind man who happened to be lucky at dice. This is Zato Ichi, the blind swordsman, and woe be to the thug who thinks that sight is a necessity for victorious swordplay. In the closeups of Zato Ichi's ear, one can see a sinus opening on the upper crest, and one starts to believe it is emitting some kind of sonar signal. Zato Ichi never misses.

Zato Ichi Monogatari ('The Life and Opinion of Masseur Ichi') has been released in Japan. The 1962 black-and-white film was the first in the popular series. It has a fairly straightforward plot which is easy enough to follow after a couple of viewings, even if the nuances are lost.

The disc is letterboxed at a rousing 2.1:1, and the cinematography is compelling enough to hold a viewer's attention through the lengthier Japanese conversations. The print is spotless, and although it lacks the shiny contrasts of most American transfers the image is pleasing. Some of the night shots have a peculiar grey shading which is haunting. The monaural sound is not CX-encoded and is less accomplished.

Only one other film from the popular series has been released on disc in Japan. *Zato Ichi* is in color, and the cinematography is often stunning. Inevitably there are a number of conversation scenes which will make English speaking viewers restless, but if some of the character motivations are unclear, the plot and the sequence of events is understandable enough to bridge one's interest between the bloody sword fights. The narrative in fact seems to rely heavily upon the standard Zato Ichi set pieces – his gambling trick, his gentleness, his run-in and socializing with an affable rival who has been hired to eliminate him, his ability to drop 50 swordsmen without suffering a scratch, and his sadness over the violence that surrounds him.

The sound is good, and the musical score even features an English language theme song, 'The Loner.' The picture transfer is okay. Some of the strongest oranges and golds blur a little, but the fleshtones are accurate and often look quite sharp. The program is letterboxed, with an aspect ratio of about 1.66:1, and the addition to the sides of the picture is gratifying. It is because the cinematography looks so nice that the disc can be recommended. The language of the images require no translation.

ZAZIE DANS LE METRO (Import)

Louis Malle's cartoon-inspired interpretation of the Raymond Queneau novel, *Zazie dans le Metro*, is available in Japan. The quality of the picture on the disc surprised us, because the faded prints we were familiar with in revival houses did not prepare us for the bright and humorous colors Malle employed in the film. The transfer is very good. Since the movie was made in the early Sixties, the edges are a bit ragged, but the essential parts are fresh and vivid. The sound is monaural without CX-encoding, though it sounds okay on a hifi system. The movie is in French with Japanese subtitles.

The movie is intended to function on two levels, one for adults and one for children. The adult level is obscured without a dialog translation, but much of the movie's appeal to youngsters, or to adults who don't mind a little fun, remains even when the dialog is incomprehensible. *Zazie* is about a young girl visiting her uncle in Paris and often running off by herself to explore the streets. Her uncle works nights, and though it is not clear without a translation, he is a female impersonator.

Several years before Richard Lester, Malle used jump cuts, speeded up film, and similar manipulations to enhance the comic material. The film has many visual gags. Malle's intention was to create a movie which appealed to both young and old without insult, and since modern cinema is hardly inundated with the tricks Malle pulled, we find the sequences refreshing, enough so to justify owning and watching the disc even if the dialog is inaccessible. The disc's additional surprise – Malle's amusing experiments with color – makes it that much more worthwhile.

ZELLY & ME

Zelly & Me is an excruciating drama about a young girl and her overly strict grandmother. The film is not poorly made – David Lynch even has a small role in it – but the subject is not entertaining, and not enlightening enough to get away with not being entertaining. The disc has a very grainy, orange picture, and unremarkable sound.

ZIEGFELD GIRL
(see **BABES ON BROADWAY**)

ZIEGFELD FOLLIES

Thanks to the Chapter Skip function, a movie which was pure torture to sit through in a theater, *Ziegfeld Follies*, becomes a tolerable and even entertaining laser video disc. The film intends to mimic a real 'Follies' production, but some things are best left to their own medium. A series of short, unconnected sequences, the movie is fine when presenting musical numbers but intolerable when presenting, without realistic sets or props, 'comical' skits. It is best to concentrate upon the good. Included among the musical numbers is an Esther Williams water ballet, the Fred Astaire and Gene Kelly dance collaboration which *That's Entertainment* did not do justice to, a notoriously strange Judy Garland effort in which she attempts, only half successfully, to vamp, and satisfying appearances from Kathryn Grayson, Lena Horne, and Astaire again. And to quote from the marvelously thorough chapter descriptions on the back of the jacket, there is also "Lucy and Her Whip."

The color is a little faded, but the film is often so colorful that even when the image looks worn down it can still be captivating. The picture on the disc also has a mild shift around the most intense colors and reds look somewhat unstable. The sound is fine.

ZIGGY STARDUST AND THE SPIDERS FROM MARS: THE MOTION PICTURE

We thought one or more components of our audio video system had failed as we got into *Ziggy Stardust and the Spiders from Mars: The Motion Picture*, but experimentations quickly proved that it was the film itself and not our equipment, or even the disc, really, that was at fault. The movie is a record of a David Bowie concert which looks and sounds like it was recorded by someone in the audience using cameras and tape machines they purchased at a 7-11 before going into the concert. The film, when you can actually make out an image in the blur, has almost no variation in color. The erratic stereo sound has the dynamic range of a long distance call.

ZOMBIE

Zombie is a derivative of George Romero's *Dead* films, except that it lacks Romero's sense of social satire. The grainy, cheap-looking effort is set on an island in the Caribbean and stars Tisa Farrow. The gore is suitably icky, but the endeavor feels mechanical. The original production had a poor picture and weak sound, so one cannot expect the disc to improve upon it. There are a couple of volume dropouts, but the presentation is generally as coherent as the film itself.

ZORRO'S FIGHTING LEGION
ZORRO'S BLACK WHIP

Set in Mexico before the revolver was invented, the Republic serial *Zorro's Fighting Legion* is a classic Zorro offering. He burns a 'Z' on the hillside to call his Legion together, and scratches another on the forehead of a bad guy. As Don Diego he swishes with the same enthusiasm that, as Zorro, he crosses swords. There is a bad guy, who, disguising himself as an Indian god, 'Don Del Oro,' is decked out in a suit which would not be out of place in an outer space robot thriller. The stunts are super, the cliffhangers satisfying, and the acting is engaging.

The source material is in fairly good condition. Only at the end is there a string of noticeable splices. Elsewhere the flaws are intermittent and the image looks sharp and clean. The sound is fair, but there is an enjoyable theme song and Republic has printed the lyrics on the back of the jacket. Contrary to the jacket cover, no theatrical trailer is included on the disc.

Another Republic serial, *Zorro's Black Whip*, is set 70 years later in Idaho. Is Zorro a doddering old codger who can barely scribble the first letter of his name in the dirt with his cane? Who can say – Zorro isn't in the program. Oh, there is some sort of reference in the first episode, but the person riding around in a costume similar to Zorro's and wielding a black whip is more intent upon helping Idaho gain statehood than in teaching anyone their alphabet. No matter, *Zorro's Black Whip* is another terrific effort. The solutions to the cliffhangers are especially clever (you'll love the one where the bad guy jabs a pitchfork into the heroine's mid-section). The twelve-chapter effort runs just two minutes over three hours, but there is only one sequence of events, the identification of the bad guy at the very end, which seems rushed.

The picture looks terrific. There are a few splices and a couple of bad looking scratches, but more often than not the image looks clean and sharp. The sound is passable. Although the jacket cover claims that a theatrical trailer opens the program, there is none.

ZULU

The well-transferred, letterboxed, digitally encoded, three sided CLV epic *Zulu*, is ideally suited for wet Saturday afternoons. The 138-minute movie is the sort of cult entertainment which one would hardly hope to find on disc, much less in such fine condition.

Most impressive of all is the sound. The film was made in 1964 and has an old fashioned stereo mix with extensive separations (even the music is over-separated), all of which are great fun. Adding to that, however, is the audio set piece, the Zulu war chants, which, coming on top of John Barry's rousing score, swell the acoustics in your viewing room until every outside sound is muffled – even the rain hitting the window. There is some hiss associated with the age of the recording, but in the excitement of it all, one hardly notices the problem.

The film is about a short-handed group of British soldiers who hold off a massive force of native attackers. The disc's image has a 2:1 aspect ratio, which is absolutely necessary for taking in the scope of the battle. The story has a minimum of subplots and is primarily an exposition of tactics, which are explained clearly and executed with a sense of realism. The dramas, involving minor squabbles among the men in the encampment, are just enough relief to pace the battle scenes and keep one interested in the outcome.

The image looks terrific, maybe a little washed out in one or two places, but otherwise as fresh as a recent release. Voyager has enclosed an incomprehensible map on a jacket insert. Some have complained that Voyager failed to include the film's overture and other extraneous music on the disc. Although it would have been nice if the disc's producers had been able to dig it up, the restoration of the film itself is a magnificent effort, and the lack of some 'walk in' music is no reason to avoid obtaining the disc.

Voyager has also printed an apology for the subject matter on the inside of the jacket, and utilized most of the innerspread to state the Zulu point of view. Few viewers, however, should have a problem with the film's morals, since the horror of war is the subject. It is made clear that the victory is both hollow and tenuous, thrilling only to those who are observing the action from a place which is safe and cozy.

ZULU DAWN

The entire 117 minutes of *Zulu Dawn* is dedicated to depicting the events leading up to the famous African battle, and to the battle itself, where thousands of Zulu warriors defeated a misguided British battalion in the late 1800s. No bothersome romantic subplots and very little camaraderie get in the way of showing the inept British movement across the African topography and how, even with their superior firepower, they could not save themselves from being slaughtered. This is the movie's redeeming characteristic. The acting is weak, despite such stellar presences as Peter O'Toole and Burt Lancaster, and there is no story, just chronology. Strategy and battle techniques, however, are depicted clearly.

The colors look reliable, but the print is old and has a few marks on it. The picture is squeezed during the opening credits and then cropped for the film itself, removing a digit from the cast of thousands and inhibiting not only the pretty scenery, but many of the shots intended to orient location. The Zulu leaders speak in their native tongue, and this dialog has been subtitled. But, it was also subtitled on the print which Image obtained to make the disc, and so those subtitles have been blocked out by a colored band and the subtitles intended for the video presentation have been superimposed across the band.

Although the Dolby logo appears in the credit scroll the disc is in monaural. The sound is a little flat, as is the uninteresting Elmer Bernstein score.

X-RATED TITLES

"AND I DO WINDOWS...TOO"

There are only four erotic interludes in *"And I Do Windows...Too."* The narrative concerns a man wishing to meet a woman who will wash windows. The videotape source is a little soft but passable and the sound is fine. One of the interludes includes an unusual activity involving three people, but otherwise the program has little to offer.

ANGEL'S REVENGE

The sound is amusing on *Angel's Revenge*. The CX-encoded monaural track is very clear and the original recording is inept. Either you can hear the film crew whispering instructions to the performers, or the mike is under the sheets and all you hear are horribly magnified scraping and shuffling noises. The video tape source provides a very good picture, but the camera crew isn't any more accomplished than the sound crew, and key lights are forever being moved in the middle of the action. The narrative, which is more deliberately misogynic than most, depicts several men who seek out women not predisposed to seduction. Due to the content, side one is in CAV, with moving figures appearing blurry in every still frame. Among the more actively utilized props is a large feather duster.

BLAME IT ON GINGER

The narrative style of *Blame It on Ginger* is commendable for the genre. The story involves a weekend outing, but features commentary by the characters to the camera, punctuating their activities. It is mildly humorous as well. The picture comes from a video tape source and looks fuzzy. The sound is all right. Side two is in CAV, with blurred movement in the still frames.

BLONDE FIRE
THE JADE PUSSYCAT
CHINA CAT

Although Seka is promoted as the star of the X-rated *Blonde Fire* she only appears in a two short sequences, at the beginning and end of the film. The other star, John C. Holmes, appears throughout the movie. The narrative, concerning a double-cross in a diamond sale, is executed with coherence but not urgency. The filmed image is aged considerably and looks both faded and blurry. The analog sound is CX-encoded and about standard in quality. Side two, which has an unusual amount of speckling, is in CAV, with two unsteady still frames out of every five. Among the more actively utilized props is a pair of handcuffs.

Holmes also appears, with Georgina Spelvin, in another older film, *The Jade Pussycat*. Although faded, the condition of the source material is otherwise passable. The CX-encoded sound has a limited dynamic range, however, which has a dulling effect upon the viewer. The narrative is an elaborate and occasionally effective take off on *The Maltese Falcon*. The disc is CLV throughout, and the feature is followed by three explicit trailers. Among the more actively utilized props is a battery-operated device.

The direct sequel to *Jade Pussycat*, *China Cat* stars Holmes as well. The narrative in the sequel is less inspired than the script for the earlier film, though the picture and sound quality are similar. Side two out in CAV, with two unsteady still frames out of every five. Contrary to the jacket cover art, the appearance of cast members with Asian heritage is extremely limited. Another cast member barely disguises her reading a lengthy monolog from cue cards on her lap. Among the more actively utilized props are some deftly applied knockout drops.

BORN TO BE BAD

Born to Be Bad, about female bikers raising trouble in a tavern, has a video tape source which is in fairly good shape. The brightly colored title also has a sharp monaural soundtrack, and side two is in CAV, with movement appearing blurry in the still frames.

CHINA CAT (see BLONDE FIRE)

CLUB GINGER

Collectors who are looking for an X-rated film which attempts to provide camera angles and activities that vary from the standard X-rated disc may wish to obtain *Club Ginger*. The picture, which has a video tape source, looks very good, and the sound is fine. Although there is no narrative per se, the incidents depicted are photographed and edited in such a way as to hold a viewer's attention better than most.

DEBBIE DOES EM ALL

The monaural sound on *Debbie Does Em All* is CX-encoded, but one wouldn't want to raise the volume too high even if the neighbors aren't around. The transfer of the picture is quite good, though the picture itself is typically cheap looking. *Debbie* has a limited narrative (about a stewardess who has quick adventures in several different cities) and limited humor. There is one moment of good camp, however. For a scene in an airplane cockpit, the instrument panel has been rear-projected. The pilot even pretends to reach up and flick switches. Side two is in CAV, with two unsteady still frames out of every five.

DEVIL IN MISS JONES PART 3 A NEW BEGINNING
DEVIL IN MISS JONES PART 4: THE FINAL OUTRAGE

Hell makes such a good subject for X-rated adult films because the movies and the location have so much in common. An extended two-part tale about a Dantesque journey through the uninhibited netherworld, *Devil in Miss Jones Part 3 A New Beginning* and *Devil in Miss Jones 4: The Final Outrage*, is available as two separate discs. The films have an unusual level of negative black stereotyping, but those who turn their cheek to the racism will find that the narrative, however limited, taps on a suppressed portion of the collective unconscious. *Part 3* has a more accomplished narrative than *Part 4*. The latter depicts the completion of the heroine's journey, but provides less character and background exploration.

Both movies have filmed source materials and have been transferred competently, with *Part 4* looking a little stronger than *Part 3*. Side two of *Part 3* is in CAV, with two unsteady still frames out of every five. *Part 4* runs just a little more than an hour, but remains in CLV. The sound on *Part 3* is CX-encoded monaural and is of standard quality. The sound on *Part 4* is also CX-encoded, but the music track is in stereo and sounds pleasant. The score on both films contains a deliberately wide variety of styles, and is reasonably creative.

DOLL FACE

The narrative of *Doll Face* has the format of a 'serious drama,' and concerns a disturbed young girl who moves in with her benign stepfather. Some San Francisco locations are used as filler. The transfer is satisfactory, although, as with most X-rated efforts, the edges look a little soft. The sound is CX-encoded monaural and is also free of severe impairments. Side two is in CAV format, with two unsteady still frames out of every five.

FULL METAL BIKINI

The only claim to fame for *Full Metal Bikini* is that it was made entirely out of doors. There is no narrative. The video tape source is fresh and the scenes are well-lit, but the colors are mildly saturated. The film's sound recording is inept, and much of the dialog is incomprehensible, not that it matters.

THE GIRL WITH THE MILLION DOLLAR LEGS

Discriminating enthusiasts might be interested obtaining *The Girl with the Million Dollar Legs*. It has a fresh video tape source and an extremely sharp picture. Like many of the newer productions, the narrative is sporadic, about a woman employed in a night club where a talent search contest is to take place, but it is executed with an assured manner and a strong sense of pacing. The film is supposedly set in 'Paris' and many of the cast members have legitimately heavy French accents. They also tend to sigh in French during moments of passion. The sound is CX-encoded monaural. The audio recording has fewer errors than the films above, though it would never be mistaken for a real film soundtrack. The musical score, including a song which goes on for six minutes over the opening credits, is surprisingly pleasant.

THE GREATEST LITTLE CATHOUSE IN LAS VEGAS

A comedy which at least tries to be funny, *The Greatest Little Cathouse in Las Vegas*, is about an IRS agent who visits a bordello on a field audit. The film source material is in good shape and the picture isn't bad. The CX-encoded monaural sound is passable, but the musical score is irritating at times. Among the more actively utilized props is a sort of dog collar and leash.

HAVING IT ALL

The picture quality in *Having It All* is near perfect. Generated from a video tape source, the picture is sharp and vivid. The CX-encoded monaural sound is probably too accurate, since the sound recording is inept and swings in volume are common. Side two is in CAV, with moving images appearing blurry but stationary images remaining in focus on still frame. The narrative is no more than a loose collection of events involving a weekend in the country. Among the more actively utilized props is a carrot.

THE JADE PUSSYCAT
(see **BLONDE FIRE**)

LA BIMBO
La Bimbo, was recorded on videotape. The picture is extremely vivid, similar in quality to the better concert discs. The CX-encoded monaural sound lacks ambience, but it accurately re-creates the original recording hiss and occasional instructions whispered by the film crew off screen. Despite the title, the narrative is demure and concerns a housewife who attempts to regain the attention of her distracted husband. Side two is in CAV with movement blurring in still frame.

THE LAST CONDOM
One of the 'neo-hardcore' X-rated films, created for the video market and designed more for viewing by couples than by onanists, *The Last Condom* consists of four independent skits which are set in the same motel room, bridged with a silly linking device which is best ignored. The skits depict four different relationships and are very well written and acted, sometimes probing real human emotions from an angle which is normally relegated to experimental theater or not seen at all. It isn't art, but it is a brush stroke in the right direction. The picture transfer, from a video tape source, is crisp. The monaural sound is either too vivid, making the sheets crunch, or so generalized that the activities of the film crew can easily be distinguished – particularly a still photographer who starts clicking his shutter at the height of the action.

LEGENDS OF PORN
LEGENDS OF PORN II
Most X-rated discs run about 80 minutes, but *Legends of Porn*, lasts a full two hours. The program has the veneer of a legitimate documentary, as the narrator gives repetitive superlatives and brief employment backgrounds for the actors and actresses who appear in a wide selection of pornographic film clips. Padding is kept to a minimum until the end. The footage is primarily from the mid-Seventies and is both faded and blurry. The sound is also in rough shape.

Legends of Porn II runs the standard 80 minutes. The narrator states that feedback from the first film was used in designing the second, but *II* seems less like an attempt at establishing a compendium and more like a collection of promotional clips for other videos. The source material varies from old and fuzzy to recent and sharp. The sound is relatively consistent.

LUST ON THE ORIENT EXPRESS
The plot of *Lust on the Orient Express* mildly lampoons both the Sidney Lumet film and the Nick & Nora Charles features. The transfer is reasonably good. The print is fresh, but clearly originates from the sort of substandard film stock one associates with such productions, as does the CX-encoded monaural sound. Both sides are in CLV, although the label for side two is mistakenly listed as CAV.

MARILYN CHAMBERS' PRIVATE FANTASIES #2
MARILYN CHAMBERS' PRIVATE FANTASIES #3
MARILYN CHAMBERS' PRIVATE FANTASIES #6
The *Marilyn Chambers' Private Fantasies* discs are single-sided hour-long collections of four or five X-rated vignettes. The discs come from a film source which is slightly pale and grainy but in passable condition. There is no significant difference in quality between *Private Fantasies #2*, *Private Fantasies #3*, and *Private Fantasies #6*. All have monaural sound with dialog shifting in and out of range during the recording. The *#2* and *#6* discs have a similar mix of narratives and are pedestrian efforts, but *#3* is a little more innovative and the recommended sampling in the group. Because the discs are single-sided, they have a mildly lower sticker price than the average X-rated title.

MIAMI SPICE
Miami Spice is about female vice agents who land a big drug bust after performing elaborate undercover work. Actual Miami locations are extensively utilized. The picture quality varies in levels of graininess and the colors have no luster. The monaural sound is CX-encoded and has a bit of hiss. Conversations in scenes which take place on a boat are obscured by the sounds of the boat's engines. Side two is in CAV, with two shaky still frames out of every five, and includes trailers for 'Miami Spice II' and *Traci I Love You.*

MISCHIEF IN THE MANSION
(see **ON YOUR HONOR**)

NEW WAVE HOOKERS
A production with many similarities to the *Devil in Miss Jones Part 3/4* films, *New Wave Hookers* is about two sleeping men who dream of running an out-call service for prostitution. The disc comes from a filmed source with stale colors and an indistinct focus. The sound is tolerable. Side two is in CAV, with two unsteady still frames out of every five.

NOTHING TO HIDE
The jacket cover on *Nothing to Hide* is littered with quotations indicating that the film won awards for its erotic content. Although it follows the conventions of a regular hardcore feature, the narrative, a variation on 'Of Mice and Men,' is extensive, the emotional range of the acting is elaborate, and the editors, for once, don't feel they have to utilize every last frame of footage. The disc is in CLV format on both sides and has a passable CX-encoded monaural soundtrack (it is weakest at the beginning). The colors are bright, and the picture, though not glossy, is okay, despite a few speckles and splices.

ON YOUR HONOR
MISCHIEF IN THE MANSION
Nominally concerning a judge who employs a parolee as her houseboy, *On Your Honor* is actually comprised of five erotic interludes, each bridged with a couple minutes of narrative. The video tape source material is often blurry and the colors are faded (or wrong, a dress which is blue in one scene looks green later on). The sound is set a little low. The back of the jacket cover contains the complete credit scroll, though one wonders why they bothered since it is largely pseudonymous.

Another release, *Mischief in the Mansion*, is suspiciously similar to *On Your Honor* in almost every category. Again there are five erotic interludes, the final two interlaced through editing. The video tape source is of low quality. The sound is audible. Some of the cast members are different, but viewers seeing the two films together will have difficulty recalling which was which.

PEEPING TOM
Peeping Tom (most emphatically not the Michael Powell slasher classic) is mildly surreal, as it is about an overworked businessman suffering from exhaustion who hallucinates various hardcore interludes. Nothing truly out of the ordinary occurs, however. The print is in good condition and the monaural CX-encoded sound is tolerable. Side two is in CAV, with three steady still frames out of every five.

PUMPING ETHEL
Much of *Pumping Ethel* was video taped out of doors, so the sound recording, which is in CX-encoded monaural on the disc, is wildly inconsistent. The picture quality is good, particularly when the bright sun is assisting with the lighting. The narrative concerns a man and a woman who rob a gas station but dawdle afterwards, and fail to get away. Side two is in CAV with movement appearing as a blur in the still frames.

ROCKEY X
ROCKEY "X" – THE FINAL ROUND
Rockey X and *Rockey "X" – The Final Round* have moderately complete narratives involving boxing ring rivals, and actually have staged fight scenes, unusual in a genre which is generally devoted to love. Without overlaid sound effects, the actors do not do an entirely convincing job of wasting one another, but it is refreshing just to see them try. In *Rockey X* the rivals meet for the first time. For some reason it has a Christmas setting, which involves romantic interludes near fixtures that impart a spirit of the holidays. *Final Round* appears to be a sequel to another sequel, but it is easy enough to fill the blanks in the narrative, as the two rivals, whose fortunes have changed since the first film, meet in the ring for the last time.

Both films have video tape sources. *Rockey X* looks mildly grainy, with shots taken at one location appearing significantly blurrier than shots taken elsewhere. The sound is acceptable. The picture and sound quality of *Final Round* are slightly stronger and more consistent.

THE SEVEN SEDUCTIONS OF MADAME LAU
The film source material on *The Seven Seductions of Madame Lau* looks soft and a bit worn, but it is functional. The sound has a few obvious dropouts and is a bit noisy, but there is a catchy musical score. The film is actually called 'The Seven Seductions,' and no cast members of Asian extraction appear, although Carol Doda and Georgina Spelvin show up. The narrative is thicker than most, cutting back on the erotic sequences slightly

in order to include more dialog. The story concerns an adventurer who seeks help from the title character to cure a dissatisfaction with his lifestyle.

SWEAT

Sweat has a standard narrative format and a fuzzy picture. The video tape source has a semblance of the freshness one associates with video productions, but it is also grainy and fuzzy looking. Side two is in CAV and due to the nature of the source material movement blurs in every frame. The monaural sound is CX-encoded and the instructions to the cast being issued by the film crew can be heard on the soundtrack. The story, vaguely humorous, concerns a woman searching for an erotic workout extensive enough to make her perspire.

SWEET DREAMS SUZAN

The copyright on the jacket cover for *Sweet Dreams Suzan* is dated 1973, although the copyright on the film itself is dated 1979. In any case, it is an older film, in some ways less explicit than more recent productions, though the content is essentially the same. The filmed source material is grainy and has dull colors. The sound is dubbed and not always in synchronization with lip movements. The narrative depicts several dreams a woman relates to her psychiatrist, and ends with a violent rape. The disc runs just slightly more than an hour and side two is in CAV with two unsteady still frames out of every five.

TRACI I LOVE YOU

Tracy Lords stars in *Traci I Love You*, portraying a model being shadowed by a photographer. The narrative is advanced primarily through voice-over dialog which serves to emphasize that 1) the program is simply a series of interludes filmed on a soundstage and 2) Lords is an inept actress even by the relaxed standards of porn stardom. The source material was recorded on videotape, but the picture lacks brightness or consistency. The jacket's claim of 'Stereo' here means that someone was eagerly twiddling with the reverb during post production. Side two is in CAV and produces a sharp still image so long as nothing is in motion. The break between side one and side two occurs in the middle of a conversation, but who cares, right?

UNTAMED PASSIONS

Riding crops and the like are the primary subject of *Untamed Passions*, about goings-on in a mansion. The video tape source has been transferred to disc in fairly good condition and strong colors are only mildly fuzzy. The sound is clear, but too much amplification brings out a number of clearly spoken directions from the film crew in the middle of several scenes. Side two is in CAV with still frames which are less blurry than most when video tape source material is involved.

WHITE CHOCOLATE

Side one of *White Chocolate* is in CAV, while side two is CLV, for no apparent reason, since the standard material is evenly distributed throughout the program. The source material was recorded on video tape, but the lighting is faulty, so the image rarely looks as distinct as it ought to, and the edges are often fuzzy. The narrative concerns nothing more than a series of interludes at a weekend cabin. The sound is CX-encoded and is clear enough to pick up camera crew conversations in one or two places. Two of the actresses are black. Another has numerous dime-sized bruises on her arms and legs. Some of the improvisational conversations, included to break the interludes apart, have a pleasant, engaging tone.

WPINK-TV

Nominally set in a television studio, *WPINK-TV* is a 'comedy' which spoofs different broadcast activities. The narrative style is refreshingly jumbled and although the movie is not funny, it could be categorized as raucous. The sound is fine. The picture, which includes a couple out-of-the-ordinary close-ups, has a video tape source and is mildly fuzzy but acceptable. Side two is in CAV with action blurring in still frame.

Appendix A: American Releases

The titles listed in this Appendix were released in America between 1981, when DiscoVision abandoned the CAV format and Pioneer assumed most of the responsibility for marketing the technology, and the end of 1990, when this book was compiled. Some CLV discs in the early Eighties retained the DiscoVision jacket designs but properly belong in this listing and have been included.

The formula for determining a what constitutes a disc's title is explained in the introduction. Some titles have been abridged in this listing for space purposes. In the past, titles have appeared in catalogs but have never actually materialized as discs, such as 'King of the Gypsies,' and these have not been included. Additionally, catalog entries for disc formatting have been erroneous and this has been rectified whenever possible. If a title is no longer 'in print' an 'O' code precedes the catalog number. If a program has been issued more than once with different catalog numbers, each listing is separate, with the exception of Walt Disney titles which tend to be reissued without knowledge of past releases and are dealt with accordingly. If a disc retains the same catalog number but has been remastered with significant improvements, these are detailed in chronological fashion within the title's data.

The codes accompanying the titles of the discs can be interpreted as follows:

An asterisk (*) appears if the title has been reviewed in **The Laser Video Disc Companion**.

The 'Catalog Number,' usually printed on the jacket of the disc, is listed in parenthesis after the title and (if present) special descriptive information. An 'O' precedes the parenthesis if the disc is no longer in print.

The company responsible for the release of the disc is indicated using a two or three letter code:

Acd	Academy Home Video
A&M	A&M Video
BMG	BMG Classics
Col	RCA/Columbia Pictures Home Video
CV	Coliseum Video
DF	The Disc Factory
Dis	Walt Disney Home Video/Touchstone Home Video/Buena Vista Home Video
Fox	CBS/Fox Video
Grl	Grollier Publishers
HBO	HBO Video/Thorn/EMI/HBO Home Video
HHT	Hollywood Home Theater
HV	Home Vision
IE	Image Entertainment/X-rated discs
J2	J2
KL	Karl-Lorimar Home Video
LVA	LVA Film Classics/Laservision Associates/'Michael Agee'
MCA	MCA Home Video
MGM	MGM/UA Home Video
MPI	MPI Home Video
MV	MasterVision
NAP	North American Phillips
Nel	Nelson Entertainment/Embassy Entertainment/Blay
NFL	NFL Home Video
ODC	Opttical Data Corporation/Video Vision Associates
OPA	Optical Programming Associates
PA	Pioneer Artists/Pioneer Artists Signature/Pioneer Imports/Pioneer Special Interests
Pac	Pacific Arts Video
Par	Paramount Home Video
PGM	PolyGram Music Video/Philip Classics/Deutsche Gramaphon/London
Rep	Republic Pictures Home Video
RR	Reference Recordings, Inc.
Son	Sony Video/Sony Classics
SZ	Saul Zaentz Company
3M	3M
UE	United Entertainment
VA	VidAmerica
Ves	Vestron Home Video/Vestron MusicVideo/LightningVideo/Children's Video Library
VMx	VidMax
Voy	Voyager Company/Voyager Press/Criterion Collection
VPI	Videodisc Publishers, Inc.
WB	Warner Home Video/Cannon Video/Elektra

The year the title first appeared in retail stores is indicated as 1981-84,or 1985, 1986, etc.

Codes indicating the sound status of a title are listed as 'AM' for analog monaural, 'AS' for analog stereo, 'DM' for digital monaural and 'DS' for digital stereo. If a program is both monaural and stereophonic, the stereo indicator is used. If a disc has independent audio programs on two or more tracks for more than 50% of the program, 'DC' precedes the sound codes.

If the title has been formatted in CAV, the code, 'CAV' appears. If no marking appears, the disc is in CLV. If one or more sides of the title is in CLV and one or more sides of the title is in CAV, 'CLV/CAV' appears.

If a title has been remastered with significant improvements, information about the upgrade is listed following the 'U' code.

The 'lb' code indicates the presence of letterboxing and is used solely to differentiate multiple versions of a title.

The titles have been divided into three categories, indicative of the primary content of the program. 'Movies' includes films, television shows, cartoons, narrative shorts, and musical works which have a narrative and have not been filmed in a live format. 'Music' includes concert performances, music-oriented narratives which have been filmed in a live format, and musically oriented thematic or experimental exercises. 'Miscellaneous' covers documentaries, interactive discs, comedy performances filmed in front of a live audience, exercise discs, and anything else which is otherwise uncategorizable.

*Abbott & Costello Meet Frankenstein (22008)MCA/86 AM CLV/CAV
*The Abominable Dr. Phibes/Dr. Phibes Rises Again (ID6902VE)IE/90 DM
*About Last Night (30735)Col/87 AS
*Above the Law (11786)WB/88 DS
Absence of Malice O(VLD1015)Col/81-84 AM
The Absent Minded Professor (28AS)Dis/81-84 AM
*Absolute Beginners (ID5148)IE/87 DS
*Absolution (ID6124TW)IE/88 DM
*The Abyss (156180)Fox/90 DS
*Action Jackson (ID5288LO)IE/88 DS
*The Accidental Tourist (11825A/B)WB/89 DS
*The Accused (LV1760)Par/89 DS
*Adam — Giselle — Fracci — Brun (0702021)PGM/88 DS
*Adam's Rib (CC1147L)Voy/88 AM
*Adventures in Babysitting (595AS)Dis/88 DS
*The Adventures of Baron Munchausen (50156)Col/90 DS
*The Adventures of Buckaroo Banzai (VL5056)Ves/85 AS
*The Adventures of Captain Marvel (LV25001)Rep/89 DM
The Adventures Of Chip 'N Dale With Donald Duck O(46AS)Dis/81-84 AM
*The Adventures of Eliza Fraser O(I5008)IE/85 AM
*The Adventures of Mark Twain O(LV2376)Par/87 AM
*The Adventures of Robin Hood O(454080)Fox/81-84 AM
*The Adventures of Robin Hood (CC1166L)Voy/89 DCAM CAV
*The Adventures of Robin Hood (24160)Voy/90 DCDM
*The Adventures of Sherlock Holmes/Voice of Terror (217880)Fox/89 DM
*Adventures of the American Rabbit O(ID6741KV)IE/89 DM
Adventures of the Galaxy Rangers (30983)Col/89 AS
*The Adventures of the Little Prince O(CL1508)Ves/85 AM
*Affair in Trinidad (32008)Col/89 AM
*Africa Screams (I5128)IE/87 AM CLV/CAV
The African Queen (2025-80)Fox/81-84 AM
*After Hours (11528LV)WB/86 AM
*Against All Flags (40636)MCA/88 AM CAV
*Against All Odds (30077)Col/81-84 AS
*Agatha Christie's Partners in Crime The Secret Adversary (PAV12595)Pac/86 AM
*Agatha Christie's The Ambassador's Boots/The Man in the Mist (ID7474PA)IE/90 DM
*Agatha Christie's The Clergyman's Daughter/The Sunningdale Mystery (ID7473PA)IE/90 DM
*Agnes of God O(30563)Col/86 AS
*The Agony and the Ecstasy (100780)Fox/89 DS
Airplane! (LV1305)Par/81-84 AM
Airplane! II: The Sequel (LV1489)Par/81-84 AM
*Aiport '77 (ID5118)MCA/87 AM
*Airport (10005)MCA/87 DS CLV/CAV
*The Alamo (101813)MGM/90 DS
*Alamo Bay (VLD30561)Col/86 AM
*Alexander Nevsky (ID6228CO)IE/89 DM
*Alfred Hitchcock Presents (orig.) (40009)MCA/87 AM
*Alfred Hitchcock's Rebecca (CC1999L)Voy/90 DCDM
*Alfred Hitchcock's Rebecca (CC1998L)Voy/90 DCDM CAV
Alice (ID7863TT)IE/90 DM
*Alice Adams (ID6453TU)IE/89 DM
Alice In Wonderland (36AS)Dis/81-84 AM
*Alien (1090-80)Fox/81-84 AS
*Alien from L.A. (ID6150ME)IE/89 DS
*Alien Nation (158580)Fox/89 DS
*Aliens (1504-80)Fox/87 AS
*All About Eve (107680)Fox/89 DS
*All Dogs Go to Heaven (ML102043)MGM/90 DS CAV
*All Dogs Go to Heaven (ML101868)MGM/90 DS
*All of Me (2715)HBO/86 AM
*All Quiet on the Western Front (21005)MCA/87 DM CLV/CAV
All That Jazz (1095-80)Fox/81-84 AS
*All the King's Men (30588)Col/86 AM
All the Right Moves (129980)Fox/81-84 AM
*All's Fair (ID6560ME)IE/89 DS
*Allegheny Uprising (ID6540TU)IE/89 DM
*Aloha Summer (ID6032LO)IE/89 DM
*Alpine Fire (ID6521VE)IE/89 DM
Alsino and the Condor (ID7476PA)IE/90 DM
Altered States (11076LV)WB/81-84 AS
*Alvin Rides Again O(I5020)IE/85 AM
*Always (Jaglom) (V5161)Ves/86 AM
*Always (Spielberg) (40967)MCA/90 DS
*Amadeus (LV1791)SZ/87 DS
*Amazing Grace and Chuck (TVL0029)HBO/88 AS
*Amazon Women on the Moon (40684)MCA/88 AM CLV/CAV
*The Ambushers (30736)Col/87 AM
*American Anthem (LV386)KL/87 AS
*The American Friend (ID5342PA)IE/89 DM CLV/CAV
*American Flyers (11520LV)MCA/86 AS
American Gigolo (LV8989)Par/81-84 AM
*American Gothic (ID6700VK)IE/89 DM
American Graffiti O(16001)MCA/81-84 AS
*An American In Paris (ML100006)MGM/81-84 AM U/89 DM
*American Ninja 2 (ID5161)IE/87 DS
American Ninja III Blood Hunt (31108)WB/89 DS
American Roulette (ID7131VK)IE/90 DM
*An American Tail (40536)MCA/87 DS CAV
*An American Werewolf In London O(40017)MCA/81-84 AM
*An American Werewolf in London (ID5239VE)IE/88 DM
The Amityville Horror (VL4022)Ves/81-84 AM
Amityville II The Possession O(17095)Nel/81-84 AM
*Amityville 3-D (VL5034)Ves/81-84 AS
*Amsterdamned (ID6375VE)IE/89 DS
*Anatomy of a Murder (30701)Col/86 AM
*Anchors Aweigh (ML100309)MGM/88 AM
*And God Created Woman (Bardot) O(VL3002)Ves/81-84 AM
*And God Created Woman (1987) (ID6094VE)IE/88 DS
*And I Do Windows...Too (X-rated) (Z0083)IE/89 AM
And Justice for All O(VLD1020)Col/81-84 AM
The Anderson Tapes O(VLD1025)Col/81-84 AM
*Android (I5077)IE/87 AM CLV/CAV
Andy and the Airwave Rangers (90246)Col/90 AM
*Andy Warhol's Bad (ID7563NL)IE/90 DM
*Angel and the Badman O(DFI3)DF/81-84 AM
*Angel and the Badman (ID7269NE)IE/90 DM
*Angel and the Badman (LV20107)Rep/90 DM
*Angel Heart (ID6127IV)IE/88 DS
Angel Of H.E.A.T. (VL4009)Ves/81-84 AM
*Angel III: The Final Chapter (ID6092NW)IE/89 DM
*Angel's Revenge (X-rated) (Z0061)IE/89 AM CLV/CAV
Angelo My Love (VLD1026)Col/81-84 AM
*Angels Die Hard (I5013)IE/85 AM
*Angels over Broadway (30688)Col/86 AM
Angels with Dirty Faces O(458480)Fox/85 AM
*Anguish (514580)Fox/88 AS
*Animal Behavior (ID7228HB)IE/90 DS
*Animal Crackers (22005)MCA/85 AM CLV/CAV
*Animal Farm (VL4418)Ves/86 AM
*Animal Follies (ID6613HA)IE/90 DM
*Animal House (16007)MCA/81-84 AM
*The Animated Adventures of Gene Rodenberry's Star Trek (LV60754)Par/89 AM
*Anna (ID6095VE)IE/89 DM

Anne of Avonlea (650AS)Dis/90 DM
Anne of Green Gables (642AS)Dis/90 DM
*Annie O(VLD1030)Col/81-84 AS
*Annie (lb) (30127)Col/90 DS
*Annie Hall O(451880)Fox/81-84 AM
*Annie Hall (ML100251)MGM/88 AM
*Another Country (75585)Nel/85 AM
*Another Woman (ID6502OR)IE/89 DM
Any Which Way You Can (11077LV)WB/81-84 AM
*The Apartment (ML101685)MGM/89 DS
*Aphrodite (ID6903VE)IE/90 DM
*The Appaloosa (ID5119)MCA/87 AM
Apocalpyse Now (LV2306)Par/81-84 AS
*Appointment with Death (37211)WB/88 DM
*Apprentice to Murder (ID5269NW)IE/88 DM
*April Fool's Day (LV1832)Par/87 DS
*Armed and Dangerous (30724)Col/87 AS
*Armed Response (30758)Col/87 AM
Around the World in 80 Ways (902296)Nel/89 AS
*Around the World in Eighty Days (11321A/B)WB/87 DS
Arrowhead (LV5227)Par/90 AM
Arsenic and Old Lace O(460380)Fox/81-84 AM
Arthur (22020LV)WB/81-84 AM
Arthur 2: On the Rocks (11811)WB/89 DS
*The Asphalt Jungle (CC1126L)Voy/88 AM
*The Assassin (ID7225HB)IE/90 DS
*Assassination (ID5138)IE/87 AS
*Asylum (ID7124FL)IE/90 DM
*At Close Range (V5170)Ves/86 AS
Atlantic City (LV1460)Par/81-84 AM
*Au Revoir Les Enfants (ID6395OR)IE/89 DS
*Auntie Mame (11152)WB/90 DM
*Autumn Sonata (902180)Fox/81-84 AM
Avenging Angel O(I5021)IE/85 AM
*Avenging Force (ID5066)IE/87 AS AM
*The Awful Truth (30625)Col/86 AM
*Babes in Arms (ML100585)MGM/85 AM
*Babes on Broadway (101677)MGM/90 AM
*Babette's Feast (ID6396OR)IE/89 DS
*Baby Boom (474480)Fox/88 AS
Baby, It's You (LV1538)Par/90 DM
*Baby, The Rain Must Fall (ID6495RC)IE/89 DM
*Baby: Secret of the Lost Legend (269AS)Dis/87 AS
*The Babysitter (TVL3388)HBO/88 AM
*The Bachelor and the Bobby-Soxer (ID6837TU)IE/90 DM
*Bachelor Mother (ID6888TU)IE/90 DM
Bachelor Party (144080)Fox/85 AS AM
*Back to Bataan (ID6541TU)IE/89 DM
*Back to School (TVL2988)HBO/87 AS
*Back to the Beach (LV31980)Par/88 DS
*Back to the Future (1135LV)MCA/86 AS
*Back to the Future Part II (40914)MCA/90 DS
*Back to the Future Part II (lb) (40965)MCA/90 DS
*Backfire (ID6931VK)IE/90 DM
*The Bad and the Beautiful (ML100959)MGM/89 AM
*Bad Dreams (165980)Fox/88 AS
Bad Girls (X-rated) (I0011)IE/81-84 AM
Bad Influence (59236)Col/90 DS
Bad Jim (77046)Col/90 AM
The Bad News Bears (LV8863)Par/81-84 AM
The Bad News Bears Go to Japan (LV1114)Par/90 AM
The Bad News Bears in Breaking Training (LV8965)Par/90 AM
*Badge of the Assassin (ID6929VK)IE/90 DM
Badlands (11135LV)WB/81-84 AM
*Bail Out (ID7284VE)IE/90 DM
*Baja Oklahoma (ID5324LO)IE/88 DS
*Ball of Fire (30275)Nel/85 AM
*The Ballad of Cable Hogue (11298A/B)WB/87 AM
The Ballad Of Gregorio Cortez (20625)Nel/81-84 AM
*Bambi (942AS)Dis/90 DS
*Bambi (942CS)Dis/90 DS CAV
Bananas O(4555-80)Fox/81-84 AM
*The Band of the Hand (30709)Col/86 AS
*The Band Wagon (ML100113)MGM/87 AM
Bang The Drum Slowly (LV8732)WB/81-84 AM
*The Bank Dick (22014)MCA/86 AM CLV/CAV
Barbara Dare's Rome Adventure (X-rated) (Z0115)IE/90 AM
Barbarella (LV6812)Par/81-84 AM
*The Barbarians (ID5314ME)IE/88 AS
Barbarosa (J26035)J2/90 DM
*Barbary Coast (30285)Nel/85 AM
Barefoot In The Park (LV8027)Par/81-84 AM
*Barfly (37212)WB/88 DM
*The Barklays of Broadway (ML100321)MGM/88 AM
*Barry Lyndon (11178A/B)WB/87 AM
Bartleby (ID6844CO)IE/90 DM
*Bat 21 (ID6388ME)IE/89 DS
*Batman (1966) (147080)Fox/90 DM
*Batman (1989) (12000)WB/90 DS
**Batteries Not Included (40770)MCA/88 DS
*Battle of Algiers (ID6786AX)IE/89 DM
*Battleship Potemkin (ID6229CO)IE/89 DM CLV/CAV
Battlestar Galactica (19007)MCA/81-84 AM
*The Bay Boy (ID6687OR)IE/89 DM
*BC Holiday Happenings O(75075)Nel/81-84 AM CAV
*Beach Blanket Bingo (TVL3349)HBO/88 AM
Beach Girls (LV2314)Par/81-84 AM
*Beaches (797AS)Dis/89 DS
*Beany and Cecil (ID6223RC)IE/89 DM
*The Bear (70216)Col/90 DS
*The Beast Must Die (ID7126FL)IE/90 DM
Beastmaster (ML100226)MGM/81-84 AS
*The Beat (ID6524VE)IE/89 DS
*Beat Street (VL5047)Ves/81-84 AS
*Beat the Devil (ID6020RC)IE/88 DM
Beatlemania, The Movie (IG5006)IE/81-84 AS
*Beauty and the Beast (Cocteau) O(60385)Nel/86 AM
*Beauty And The Beast (Faerie Tale Theatre) (639580)Fox/81-84 AM
*Becket (ID6199MP)IE/90 DS
Bedknobs & Broomsticks (16AS)Dis/81-84 AM
*Bedroom Eyes II (ID7100VK)IE/90 DM
*Bedroom Window (VL5209)Ves/87 AM
*Beethoven's Nephew (ID6186NW)IE/89 DM
*Beetlejuice (11785)WB/88 DS
*Being There O(702680)Fox/81-84 AM
*Being There (938)WB/90 DM
*The Believers (TVL0034)HBO/88 AS
*Bell, Book and Candle (ID6109RC)IE/88 DM
*Bells Are Ringing (ML00063)MGM/86 DS
*The Bells of St. Mary's (ID6231RE)IE/89 DM
Ben (I5052)IE/86 AM
*Ben-Hur (ML100004)MGM/81-84 AS
*Ben-Hur (lb) (ML101525)MGM/88 DS
*Ben-Hur A Tale of the Christ (ML101474)MGM/89 AS
*Benji the Hunted (594AS)Dis/88 AS
*A Berenstein Bears Celebration O(75085)Nel/81-84 AM CAV
*Berlin Blues (31072)WB/90 DM
*Bert Rigby, You're a Fool (656)WB/89 DS
*Best Defense (LV1587)Par/85 AS
Best Friends (11265LV)WB/81-84 AM
Best Little Whorehouse in Hong Kong (X-rated) (Z0102)IE/90 AM
Best Little Whorehouse in San Francisco (X-rated) (Z0087)IE/90 AM
The Best Little Whorehouse In Texas O(17008)MCA/81-84 AM
*The Best of Mary Hartman, Mary Hartman Volume I O(25005)Nel/81-84 AM
*The Best of Mary Hartman, Mary Hartman, Volume II O(25015)Nel/85 AM
*The Best of the Little Rascals (LV27019)Rep/89 DM
*Best of the Ray Bradbury Theatre (ID6596VS)IE/89 DM
Best of the Ray Bradbury Theatre Volume 2 (ID7122FL)IE/90 DM
The Best of the Ray Bradbury Theatre Volume 3 (ID7128FL)IE/90 DM
*Best Seller (ID6025VE)IE/88 DM
*The Best of Times (13075)Nel/86 AM
*The Best Years of Our Lives (30315)Nel/85 AM
*Betrayed (ML101553)MGM/89 AS
*Betty Blue (390780)Fox/89 DS
*Betty Boop: 50th Anniversary (LV27065)Rep/90 DM
*Beverly Hills Bodysnatchers (ID6751SG)IE/89 DS
*Beverly Hills Cop (LV1134)Par/85 DS
*Beverly Hills Cop II (LV1860)Par/88 DS
*Beverly Hills Madam (ID6691OR)IE/89 DS
Beverly Hills Wives (X-rated) (Z0110)IE/90 AM
Beyond Taboo (X-rated) (Z0120)IE/90 AM
Beyond the Stars (ID7315IV)IE/90 DS
*The Bicycle Thief (ID6256CO)IE/89 DM
*Big (165880)Fox/89 DS
*The Big Blue (31026)Col/89 DS
*Big Business (605AS)Dis/89 DS
The Big Chill (VLD2018)Col/81-84 AM
*The Big Easy (TVL0052)HBO/88 AM
*The Big Heat (ID6384RC)IE/89 DM
The Big Picture (50266)Col/90 AS
*The Big Red One O(705280)Fox/87 AM
*Big Shots (ID5218LO)IE/88 DS
The Big Sleep O(453280)Fox/81-84 AM
*The Big Trees O(DFI2)DF/85 AM
*Big Top Pee-Wee (LV32076)Par/89 DS
*The Big Town (ID5209VE)IE/88 DM
*Big Trouble (30627)Col/81-84 AM
*Big Trouble in Little China (150280)Fox/87 AS
*Biggles (ID5318NW)IE/88 DS
*Bill & Ted's Excellent Adventure (87416)Nel/89 AS
*Billy Rose's Jumbo (ML101819)MGM/90 DS
*Biloxi Blues (40799)MCA/89 DS
*Bird (11820A/B)WB/89 DS
*The Bird with the Crystal Plumage (ID6593VC)IE/90 DM
*The Birds (11017)MCA/86 AM
*Birdy (VLD30457)Col/85 AM
*The Bishop's Wife (30305)Nel/85 AS AM
Bite The Bullet O(VLD2008)Col/81-84 AM
*Bizet's Carmen (VLD30487)Col/85 AS
*Black and White in Color (ID5256LO)IE/88 DM
Black Beauty (LV8079)Par/90 DM
*Black Caesar (ID5310OR)IE/88 DM
The Black Hole (11AS)Dis/81-84 AS
*Black Moon Rising (I5057)IE/86 AM
*Black Narcissus (CC1138L)Voy/88 DCAM
*Black Orpheus (CC1172L)Voy/89 DM
*Black Orpheus O(2002L)Voy/87 AM CAV
*Black Rain (LV32220)Par/90 DS
*Black Rain (lb) (LV322202L)Par/90 DS
*The Black Room (ID6714RC)IE/89 DM
*The Black Stallion O(450380)Fox/81-84 AS
*The Black Stallion (ML101604)MGM/89 DS
The Black Stallion Returns O(471280)Fox/81-84 AS
Black Sunday (LV88552)Par/81-84 AM
*Black Widow (503380)Fox/87 AS
*Blacula (TVL3242)HBO/88 AM
*Blade Runner (13805)Nel/81-84 AS
*Blade Runner (CC1169L)Voy/89 DS
*Blade Runner (CC1120L)Voy/87 DS CAV
*Blame It on Ginger (X-rated) (Z0062)IE/89 AM CLV/CAV
*Blame It On Rio (VL5040)Ves/81-84 AM
*Blaze (915AS)Dis/90 DS
Blazing Saddles (1001LV)WB/81-84 AM
*Blind Date (30822)Col/87 AS
*Blindside (902376)Nel/88 AM
*Bliss (ID5315NW)IE/88 DM
*The Blob (1958) (CC1165L)Voy/89 DS
*The Blob (1988) (ID6270TS)IE/89 DS
*Blonde Fire (X-rated) (Z0064)IE/89 AM CLV/CAV
*Blood Feast O(HHT001)HHT/85 AM
Blood Money (J26034)J2/89 DS
Blood on the Sun (LV20344)Rep/90 DM
Blood Red (7738)Nel/90 AM
Blood Relations (77406)Nel/90 AM
*Blood Simple (40180)MCA/85 AS
*Blood Wedding (ID5351ME)IE/88 DM
*Bloodhounds of Broadway (50276)Col/90 AS
*Bloodsport (37062)WB/89 DS
Bloody Mama (ID7522VE)IE/90 DM
Blow Out (VL4023)Ves/81-84 AS
*Blow-Up (CC1148L)Voy/88 AM CAV
*Blow-Up (ML100015)MGM/88 AM
*Blue City (LV1649)Par/87 AM
*Blue Collar (ID5120)MCA/87 AM
Blue Hawaii (200180)Fox/81-84 AS
The Blue Iguana (LV32148)Par/89 AS
Blue Lagoon O(VLD2990)Col/81-84 AS
*The Blue Max (106280)Fox/89 DS
*Blue Steel (ML101885)MGM/90 DS
*Blue Velvet O(LV399)KL/87 DS
*Blue Velvet (lb) (692)WB/90 DS
Blue Thunder (VLD2991)Col/81-84 AS
*The Blues Brothers (16020)MCA/81-84 AS U90 DS CLV/CAV
The Boat (Das Boot) (VLD2293)Col/81-84 AS
*Bob & Carol & Ted & Alice (ID6022RC)IE/88 DM
Bob Fosse's Star 80 (20013LV)WB/81-84 AM
*Bob Le Flambeur (Bob the Gambler) (ID6492RC)IE/89 DM
*Body and Soul (ID6235RE)IE/89 DM
Body Chemistry (90756)Col/90 AM
*Body Double (VLD30160)Col/85 AS
Body Heat (20005LV)WB/81-84 AM
*The Body Snatcher (I6004)IE/86 AM
Body Talk (X-rated) (I0019)IE/81-84 AM
*Bohemian Girl/Music Box O(DFI11)3M/86 AM
*Bolero (Derek) (I5009)IE/85 AS
Bon Apetit (X-rated) (X216)IE/81-84 AM
Bon Voyage Charlie Brown (LV1158)Par/81-84 AM
Bonnie And Clyde (1026LV)WB/81-84 AM
*The Boost (ID6579HB)IE/89 DS
Bootsie (X-rated) (Z0116)IE/90 AM
The Border (10033)MCA/81-84 AM
*Boris Godunov (ID6841CO)IE/90 DM
*Born Free (ID6166RC)IE/89 DM
*Born in East L.A. (40727)MCA/88 AM CAV
*Born of Fire (ID7134VK)IE/90 DM
*Born on the Fourth of July (40901)MCA/90 DS

*Born on the Fourth of July (lb) (41009)MCA/90 DS
*Born to Be Bad (X-rated) (Z0076)IE/89 AM CLV/CAV
*Born Yesterday (30143)Col/88 AM
*The Bostonians (VL5067)Nel/85 AM
*Bound for Glory (ID6512MG)IE/89 DS
The Bounty (VLD5044)Ves/85 AS
*Boxcar Bertha (ID7521VE)IE/90 DM
*Boy and His Dog (I5071)IE/87 AM
Boy Named Charlie Brown (712780)Fox/81-84 AM
*The Boy Who Could Fly (LV351)HBO/87 AS
*Boy Who Left Home To Find Out About The Shivers (639380)Fox/81-84 AM
*Boyfriends and Girlfriends (ID6685OR)IE/90 DM
Boys From Brazil (900280)Fox/81-84 AS
*The Boys in Company C (ID6299RC)IE/89 DM
*The Boys in the Band (701780)Fox/89 DM
*The Boys Next Door (INW5194)IE/88 DM
*Braddock: Missing in Action III (ID5400ME)IE/88 DS
*Brady's Escape (VL7021)Nel/85 AM
The Brain (ID6272IV)IE/89 DM
*Brainstorm (ML100314)MGM/81-84 AS
*Branded (LV5009)Par/90 AM
*Brass (ID6361OR)IE/89 DM
*Brass Target (ML100199)MGM/81-84 AM
*Brazil (40171)MCA/86 DS
Breaker Morant O(19405)Nel/81-84 AM
Breakfast At Tiffany's (LV6505)Par/81-84 AM
The Breakfast Club (40167)MCA/85 AS
*Breakheart Pass (ID6514MG)IE/89 DM
*Breakin' (ML100447)MGM/81-84 AS
Breaking Away (108180)Fox/81-84 AM
*Breaking In (ID7319HB)IE/90 DS
Breaking Up Is Hard to Do (ID7264VK)IE/90 DM
*Breakout (ID6298RC)IE/89 DM
Breathless (VL5017)Ves/81-84 AM
*Brewster's Millions (490194)MCA/85 AS
*Brian's Song (ID6108RC)IE/89 DM
*Bride of Frankenstein (23003)MCA/85 AM CLV/CAV
*The Bride (30569)Col/86 AS
The Bridge On The River Kwai (VLD2010)Col/81-84 AM
*A Bridge Too Far (ML101859)MGM/90 DS
*The Bridges at Toko-Ri (LV5906)Par/88 AM
*Brigadoon (ML100040)MGM/81-84 AS U/88 DS
*Brigadoon (lb) (ML101817)MGM/90 DS
*Bright Lights, Big City (ML101436)MGM/88 DS
*Brighton Beach Memoirs (40476)MCA/87 DM
*Britten Turn of the Screw (0705001)PGM/88 DS
*Broadcast News (165480)Fox/88 AS
Broadway Danny Rose (VL5041)Ves/81-84 AM
*Broadway Melody of 1940 (ML101111)MGM/89 AM
Broken Blossoms (ID6861HB)IE/90 DS
*Bronco Billy (11104)WB/89 DS
*Bronson Death Wish 4: The Crackdown (ID5219ME)IE/88 DS
*The Brood (ID7562NL)IE/90 DM
Brubaker (109880S)Fox/81-84 AM
*Buck Privates (22007)MCA/86 AM CLV/CAV
Buck Rogers in the 25th Century O(13002)MCA/81-84 AS
Bud and Lou (J26045)J2/90 DM
*The Buddy Holly Story (30801)Col/88 AS
*Buffet Froid (ID7432IN)IE/90 DM
*Bugs & Daffy: The Wartime Cartoons (ML101494)MGM/89 AM
*Bugs Bunny Classics (101476)MGM/90 AM
*Bugs! & Elmer! (ML101610)MGM/89 AM
Bugsy Malone (LV8898)Par/81-84 AM
*Bull Durham (ID6312OR)IE/89 DS
*Bulletproof (30932)Col/89 AS
*Bullies (40431)MCA/87 AM
*Bullitt (1029)WB/87 DS
*The 'Burbs (40878)MCA/89 DS
*Burglar (11705)WB/87 DS
*Burke and Wills (902146)Nel/87 AS
Burndown (ID7326VV)IE/90 DS
Burning Rage (J26039)J2/90 DM
*Burning Secret (ID6461VE)IE/89 DS
*Burns and Allen, Vol. 1 (VLD30537)Col/86 AM
Bury Me an Angel O(I5018)IE/85 AM
Bus Stop (103180)Fox/85 AM
*Buster (ID6569HB)IE/89 DS
Bustin'Loose O(16026)MCA/81-84 AM
Butch Cassidy & The Sundance Kid (106080)Fox/81-84 AS
Butterfly (VL6007)Ves/81-84 AM
*Buy and Cell (ID6185NW)IE/89 DS
*Bye Bye Brazil (ID7130FL)IE/90 DM
*Bye Bye Birdie (VLD30150)Col/85 AS
*C.H.U.D. (I5044)IE/86 AM
Cabaret (703580)Fox/81-84 AM
*Cabin in the Sky (100558)MGM/90 AM
Cactus Flower O(VLD3011)Col/81-84 AM
Caddyshack (2005LV)WB/81-84 AM
Caddyshack II (11791)WB/89 DS
Cafe Flesh (X-rated) (Z0093)IE/90 AM
*Cage (ID7348OR)IE/90 DS
Caged Fury (77036)Col/90 AM
Caged in Paradiso (ID7216VK)IE/90 DM
*The Caine Mutiny (VLD39245)Col/85 AM
California Suite O(VLD3010)Col/81-84 AM
*Caligula O(PL5032)Ves/81-84 AM
*Caligula (X-rated) (ID5249VE)IE/88 DM
*Call Me (ID6172VE)IE/89 DM
Call to Glory (LV40150)Par/85 AM
Camelot (11084LV)WB/81-84 AS
Campus Man (LV1867)Par/88 AM
*Can-Can (101680)Fox/89 DS
Candy Goes to Hollywood (X-rated) (I0028)IE/85 AM
Cannonball Run (VL6001)Ves/81-84 AM
Canonball Run II (1377LV)WB/81-84 AM
*Can't Buy Me Love (597AS)Dis/88 AM
Capricorn One (900780)Fox/81-84 AS
Caravaggio (ID7258CV)IE/90 DM
Carbon Copy (16095)Nel/81-84 AM
*The Cardinal (ID5230VT)IE/89 DS
*Caribe (ID6246VE)IE/89 DM
*Carmen (I5069)IE/87 AM
*Carmilla/Turn of the Screw (31156)WB/90 DM
Carnal Knowledge (400380)Fox/81-84 AM
Carnal Knowledge (20306)Nel/89 AM
Carrie O(451580)Fox/81-84 AM
*Cartoon Classics: Here's Donald/Here's Goofy (396AS)Dis/88 AM
*Cartoon Classics: Here's Mickey/Here's Pluto (395AS)Dis/88 AM
*Cartoon Classics: Mickey & Minnie/Chip 'N' Dale (868AS)Dis/88 AM
*Cartoon Classics: Mickey & the Gang/Nuts About Chip 'N' Dale (798AS)Dis/89 AM
*Cartoon Classics: Silly Symphonies/Animals Two by Two (670AS)Dis/88 AM
*Cartoon Classics Silly Symphonies Vol. 13: Fanciful Fables O(365AS)Dis/86 AM
*Cartoon Classics Silly Symphonies Vol. 14: Animal Tales O(366AS)Dis/86 AM
Cartoon Classics Volume 2 O(145AS)Dis/81-84 AM
Cartoon Classics Volume 3 O(164AS)Dis/81-84 AM
*Casablanca O(451580)Fox/81-84 AM
*Casablanca (ML101264)MGM/89 AM
*Casablanca (CC1179L)Voy/89 DCDM CAV
*Casino Royale (30630)Col/86 AM
*Casonova's Big Night (LV5316)Par/87 AM
*Cassandra (ID5175)IE/88 DS
*Casual Sex? (40788)MCA/89 DS
*Casualties of War (50186)Col/90 DS
Cat on a Hot Tin Roof (ML100060)MGM/81-84 AM
*Cat on a Hot Tin Roof (remake) (VL4213)Ves/86 AM
*The Cat People (original) (I6005)IE/86 AM
Cat People (remake) (11014)MCA/81-84 AS
*Cat's Eye O(473180)Fox/85 AS
Catch Me If You Can (ID7427VV)IE/90 DS
Catch-22 (LV6924)Par/81-84 AM
*Cattle Queen of Montana O(781AS)Dis/85 AM
*Cavegirl (VLD30529)Col/86 AS
*Cellar Dweller (ID6064NW)IE/89 DS CLV/CAV
Centerspread Girls (X-rated) (I0016)IE/81-84 AM
*Certain Fury (I5040)IE/85 AS
Cesar and Rosalie (ID7759AX)IE/90 DM
Chained Heat (ID7529VE)IE/90 DM
*Chain Reaction O(90035)Nel/85 AM
The Champ (ML100034)MGM/81-84 AM
Champions (20865)Nel/81-84 AS
*Chances Are (ID6621TS)IE/89 DS
The Changeling (VL6006)Ves/81-84 AS
*Chaplin Lost and Found: ESSANAY I (ID6048ME)IE/89 DM CLV/CAV
*Chaplin Lost and Found: ESSANAY II (ID6049ME)IE/89 DM CLV/CAV
*Chaplin Lost and Found: Kesytone (ID6047ME)IE/89 DM
*Chaplin Lost and Found: Mutual I (ID6050ME)IE/89 DM
*Chaplin Lost and Found: Mutual II (ID6051ME)IE/89 DM
*Chaplin Lost and Found: Mutual III (ID6052ME)IE/89 DM
Chapter Two O(VLD3040)Col/81-84 AM
*The Charge of the Light Brigade O(460280)Fox/81-84 AM
Chariots of Fire (2004LV)WB/81-84 AS
*Charlie Chan at the Wax Museum/Charlie Chan in Rio (171480)Fox/89 DM
Charlotte's Webb (LV8099)Par/81-84 AM
Charly O(802080)Fox/81-84 AM
*The Chase O(30617)Col/86 AM
*Checking Out (ID6759VV)IE/89 DS
Cheech & Chong's Next Movie (16021)MCA/81-84 AM
Cheech & Chong's Nice Dreams (VLD3355)Col/81-84 AM
*Cheech & Chong's The Corsican Brothers (LC9900)Ves/85 AS
*The Cheerleaders (ID7129FL)IE/90 DM CLV/CAV
Cheetah (912AS)Dis/90 DS
*Cherry 2000 (ID6242OR)IE/89 DS
*Children of a Lesser God (LV1839)Par/87 AM
Children of the Corn O(40395)Nel/81-84 AM
*Child's Play (ML101593)MGM/89 DS
*China Cat (X-rated) (Z0057)IE/89 AM CLV/CAV
*China Girl (ID5208VE)IE/88 DS
The China Syndrome O(VLD3060)Col/81-84 AM
Chinatown (LV8674)Par/81-84 AM
*The Chipmunk Adventure (ID5262LO)IE/88 DS CLV/CAV
Chocolat (ID9505OR)IE/90 DM
Chocolate Kisses (X-rated) (I0047)IE/88 AM
The Chocolate War (ID7201VV)IE/90 DM
*Choose Me (I5045)IE/86 AM
*A Chorus Line (21835)Nel/86 DS
Christine (VLD3065)Col/81-84 AS
*A Christmas Carol (UEI1119)UE/88 AM
*A Christmas Story (ML100446)MGM/81-84 AM
*CHUD II (ID6654VE)IE/89 DS
*A Chump at Oxford/Men O'War O(N/A)3M/86 AM
Ciao! Manhattan (ID7464PA)IE/90 DM
The Cincinnati Kid (ML100135)MGM/81-84 AS
*Cinderella (animated) O(410AS)Dis/88 DS
*Cinderella (animated) O(410CS)Dis/88 DS CAV
*Cinderella (Rodgers & Hammerstein) (611180)Fox/87 AS
*Citizen Kane (I6002)IE/85 DCAM
*Citizen Kane (CC1115L)Voy/88 AM
*Citizen Kane (CC101)Voy/85 AM CAV
City Heat (1433LV)WB/85 AS
*Claire's Knee (ID5353ME)IE/88 DM
*The Clan of the Cave Bear (679580)Fox/86 AS
*Clara's Heart (11823)WB/89 DS
*Clash of the Titans (ML100074)MGM/81-84 AS
Class (VL5026)Ves/81-84 AM
Class of 1984 (VL5022)Ves/81-84 AM
Class Reunion (VL5021)Ves/81-84 AS
*Clean and Sober (1182A/B)WB/89 DS
*Cleopatra (40644)MCA/88 AM
*The Climb (ID5321VV)IE/88 DM
*Cloak and Dagger (40124)MCA/85 AS
A Clockwork Orange O(1031LV)WB/81-84 AM
Close Encounters of the Third Kind O(VLD3095)Col/81-84 AS
*Closely Watched Trains (ID6167RC)IE/89 DM
Clown House (59106)Col/90 AM
*Club Ginger (X-rated) (Z0078)IE/90 AM
*Club Paradise (11600LV)WB/87 DS
*Clue (LV1840)Par/86 AM
Coalminer's Daughter (15005)MCA/81-84 AM
Coast to Coast (LV1342)Par/81-84 AM
*Cobra (11594LV)WB/86 DS
*The Coca-Cola Kid (VL5099)Ves/86 AM
*Cocktail (606AS)Dis/89 DS
*Cocoon (147680)Fox/86 AS
*Cocoon The Return (171080)Fox/89 DS
*Code Name: Emerald (473480)Fox/86 AM
*Code of Silence (TVL2985)HBO/87 AM
*Coffy (ID6081OR)IE/88 DM
Cohen & Tate (77276)Nel/89 AS
*Cold Feet (ID7347IV)IE/90 DM
Cold Front (ID7379HB)IE/90 DS
*The Collector (ID6077RC)IE/89 DM
*The Color of Money (22037)Dis/87 DS
*The Color Purple (11534A/B)WB/87 DS
*The Color Purple (11745)WB/87 DS CAV
*Colors (ID6241OR)IE/89 DS
*Combat Academy (ID6184NW)IE/89 DM
Coma (ML100013)MGM/81-84 AM
Come Back to the 5 And Dime Jimmy Dean, Jimmy Dean O(13335)Nel/81-84 AM
*The Comedy of Terrors/The Oblong Box (ID7496HB)IE/90 DM
*The Comic (ID6268RC)IE/89 DM
Coming Home O(451680)Fox/81-84 AM
*Coming to America (LV32157)Par/89 DS
*Commando (148480)Fox/86 AS
Communion (ID7306VV)IE/90 DS
*The Company of Wolves (VL5092)Ves/85 AS
The Competition (VLD3100)Col/81-84 AS
*Compromising Positions (LV1928)Par/86 AM
Conan, The Barbarian (13008)MCA/81-84 AM
Conan, The Destroyer (40079)MCA/85 AM
*The Conformist (LV8121)Par/81-84 AM

*A Connecticut Yankee in King Arthur's Court (40601)MCA/87 DM
*Consuming Passions (ID6017VV)IE/88 DS
*Contempt (ID7675NL)IE/90 DM
Continental Divide (40020)MCA/81-84 AM
The Conversation (LV2307)Par/81-84 AM
*"Coogan's Bluff" (40867)MCA/89 AM
*Cookie (00660)WB/90 DS
Cool Blue (59016)Col/90 AM
Cool Hand Luke (11037LV)WB/81-84 AM
Cool Sheets (X-rated) (Z0126)IE/90 AM
*Cop (LV12659)Par/89 AM
*The Cotton Club (17145)Nel/85 DS
*The Couch Trip (ID6010OR)IE/88 DM
*Counterforce (ID6766IV)IE/89 DS
Coupe de Ville (40932)MCA/90 DM
Courage Mountain (59166)Col/90 AS
*The Courier (ID6650VE)IE/89 DM
*The Court-Martial of Billy Mitchell (LV20770)Rep/89 DM
*Cousin, Cousine (ID6782AX)IE/90 DM
*Cousins (LV32181)Par/89 DS
*Country (241AS)Dis/85 AS
*The Court Jester (LV5512)Par/81-84 AM
*The Covered Wagon (LV2501)Par/90 DS
*Crackhouse (31135)WB/90 DS
Crackers O(40043)MCA/81-84 AM
*The Crawling Eye (ID5113)IE/87 AM CLV/CAV
*Crazy Moon (76846)Nel/88 AM
Crazy People (LV32299)Par/90 DS
*Creator (ID6872HB)IE/90 DM
*Creature (I5076)IE/87 AS
*The Creeping Flesh (ID6712RC)IE/90 DM
*Creepshow 2 (INW5185)IE/88 DM
Cria Cuervos (ID7454IN)IE/90 DM
*Crime Story (INW5195)IE/88 DM
*Crimes and Misdemeanors (ID7361OR)IE/90 DM
*Crimes of Passion O(15015)IE/85 AM
*Crimes of Passion (unrated) (15026)IE/85 AM
*Crimes of the Heart (ID5141)IE/87 AM
*The Crimson Pirate (11269)WB/87 DM
*Critical Condition (LV1879)Par/87 AM
*Critters (32666)Col/87 AM
*Critters 2 (32773)Col/89 AS
*Crocodile Dundee (LV32029)Par/87 DS
*"Crocodile" Dundee II (LV32147)Par/89 DS
*Cromwell (30639)Col/87 AM
*Cross Country O(40205)Nel/81-84 AM
Cross Fire (77436)Nel/90 AM
Crossfire (ID6889TU)IE/90 DM
*Crossing Delancey (11826)WB/89 DS
Crossing the Line (59226)Col/90 AS
*Crossroads (30665)Col/86 AS
*Cry Baby (40958)MCA/90 DS
*Cry Freedom (40763)MCA/88 DS
*A Cry in the Dark (11868A/B)WB/89 DS
Cujo (11331LV)WB/81-84 AM
*Curfew (ID6329NW)IE/89 DM
*The Curse (ID5207ME)IE/88 DS
*Curse of the Cat People (I6006)IE/86 AM
*Curse of the Demon (ID6078RC)IE/88 DM
*Cutter's Way (ID6472MG)IE/89 DM
*Cyborg (31030)WB/89 DS
*Cyclone (30792)Col/87 AM
*Cyrano de Bergerac (Ferrer) (ID7115NE)IE/90 DM
*Cyrano de Bergerac (Jacobi) (ID6991TU)IE/90 DM
*D.A.R.Y.L. (LV1810)Par/86 AS
D.C. Cab O(40061)MCA/81-84 AS
*D.O.A. (1949) (ID6880NE)IE/90 DM
*D.O.A. (1988) (698AS)Dis/88 DS
*Da (ID6111VV)IE/88 DS
*Dad (40933)MCA/90 DS
Daddy's Boys (90236)Col/90 AM
*Daffy Duck's Movie: Fantastic Island (11324LV)WB/81-84 AM
*Daffy Duck's Quackbusters (11807)WB/89 AM
*Daffy! & Porky! (ML101611)MGM/89 AM
*Dakota (ID6577HB)IE/89 DM
*Damien Omen II (108780)Fox/90 DM
*Damn the Defiant! (ID6877RC)IE/90 DM
*Damn Yankees (35109)WB/90 DM
*Dance, Girl, Dance (ID6771TU)IE/89 DM
*Dance of the Damned (Id6426VV)IE/89 DM
*Dance with a Stranger (VL5137)Ves/86 AM
*Dancers (37066)WB/88 DS
*Dangerous Liaisons (11872A/B)WB/89 DS
Darby O'Gill and the Little People (38AS)Dis/81-84 AM
Dark Age (902186)Nel/90 AS
*Dark Before Dawn (ID6655VE)IE/89 DM
*The Dark Crystal (ID6850HB)IE/90 DS
*Dark Passage O(464380)Fox/87 AM
*Dark Tower (ID7200VV)IE/90 DM
*Dark Victory (ML101312)MGM/89 AM
*Darling (CC1155L)Voy/89 DCAM
*Darling (20116)Nel/89 AM
*Date with an Angel (ID6586HB)IE/89 DS
*A Date with Judy (ML101460)MGM/90 AM
*David and Lisa (30761)Col/87 AM
*David Copperfield (ML100649)MGM/88 AM
Davy Crockett & the River Pirates (27AS)Dis/81-84 AM
*Dawn of the Dead (ID6683HB)IE/89 DM CLV/CAV
*The Day After O(13755)Nel/81-84 AM
A Day at the Races (ML100064)MGM/81-84 AM
*Day of the Dead (I5048)IE/86 AM
Day of the Dolphin O(400480)Fox/81-84 AM
Day of the Locust (LV86792)Par/81-84 AM
*The Day of the Triffids (ID7638JO)IE/90 DM
*The Day the Earth Stood Still (101180)Fox/88 DS
Days of Heaven (LV8942)Par/81-84 AS
*The Dead (ID6135VE)IE/88 DS CLV/CAV
*Dead Aim (ID6563VE)IE/89 DS
*Dead-Bang (658)WB/89 DS
*Dead Calm (11870)WB/89 DS
*Dead End (30385)Nel/85 AM
*Dead Heat (ID6090NW)IE/88 DS
*Dead Man Out (ID6873HB)IE/90 DS
Dead Men Don't Wear Plaid O(16028)MCA/81-84 AM
*Dead of Night (ID6853HB)IE/90 DM
*Dead of Winter (514780)Fox/87 AS
*Dead Poets Society (947AS)Dis/90 DS
*The Dead Pool (11810)WB/89 DS
*Dead Reckoning (30641)Col/88 AM
*Dead Ringers (ID6387ME)IE/89 DS
The Dead Zone (LV1646)Par/81-84 AS
*Deadline (ID5158)IE/88 DM
*Deadly Companions (ID6911NW)IE/90 DM
*Deadly Dreams (ID6112VV)IE/89 DS
*Deadly Friend (11601LV)WB/87 AM
*Deadly Illusion (30879)Col/88 AS
*Deadly Possession (ID6661VE)IE/90 DM
Deal of the Century (11339LV)WB/81-84 AS
*Death Before Dishonor (ID5203NW)IE/88 DS
Death Hunt (112580)Fox/81-84 AS
*Death of an Angel (ID6056NS)IE/88 DM
*Death of a Salesman (Hoffman) (LV380)KL/87 AM
*Death on the Nile (ID6919HB)IE/90 DM
*Death Watch O(19555)Nel/81-84 AM
Death Wish (LV8774)Par/81-84 AM
Death Wish II (VL4017)Ves/81-84 AM
*Death Wish III (ML100821)MGM/86 AM
*Deathrow Gameshow (ID5402ME)IE/88 DM
*Deathstalker (VL5048)Ves/85 AM
*Deathstalker II (ID6522VE)IE/89 DM
*Deathstalker III The Warriors from Hell (ID6523VE)IE/89 DM
*Debajo del Mundo (ID6315NW)IE/89 DM
Debbie Does Dallas (X-rated) (I0006)IE/81-84 AM
Debbie Does Dallas II (X-rated) (I0032)IE/85 AM
*Debbie Does 'Em All (X-rated) (I0041)IE/88 AM CLV/CAV
Debbie Goes to College (X-rated) (Z0104)IE/90 AM
*The Deceivers (11767)WB/89 DS
The Deep O(VDL3120)Col/81-84 AM
Deep Throat (I0030)IE/81-84 AS CLV/CAV
*Deepstar Six (ID6346IV)IE/89 DS
The Deer Hunter (10026)MCA/81-84 AS
*Defense of the Realm (76896)Nel/87 AM
Deliverance (1004LV)WB/81-84 AM
*Delta Force (I5049)IE/86 AS CLV/CAV AM
Demon Seed (ML100129)MGM/85 AM
*Demons (ID5200NW)IE/88 DM
*Demonstone (ID7565FR)IE/90 DM
*Desert Bloom (30689)Ves/86 AM
*The Desert Fox (101480)Fox/89 DM
*Desert Hearts (VL5120)Ves/87 AM
*The Desperate Hours (LV5509)Par/90 AM
*Desperately Seeking Susan (2991)HBO/86 AM
*Destination Moon (ID5110)IE/87 AM
*Destroyer (ID6183VV)IE/89 DM
*Detour (ID7644NE)IE/90 DM
*Devil and Daniel Webster O(60515)Nel/85 AM
The Devil in Miss Jones I (X-rated) (I0005)IE/81-84 AM
The Devil in Miss Jones II (X-rated) (I0033)IE/81-84 AM
*The Devil in Miss Jones III (X-rated) (Z0058)IE/89 AM CLV/CAV
*The Devil in Miss Jones IV (X-rated) (Z0066)IE/89 AS
*Devil in the Flesh (ID6684OR)IE/89 DM
*The Devil's Rain (ID6594VC)IE/89 DS
*Diamond Head (30548)Col/87 AM
Diamond Run (ID7604VV)IE/90 DS
*Diamonds Are Forever O(460580)Fox/81-84 AS
*Diamonds Are Forever (lb) (101741)MGM/90 DM CLV/CAV
*Diary of a Chambermaid (ID5354ME)IE/88 DM
*The Diary of Anne Frank (107480)Fox/90 DS CLV/CAV
*Die Hard (166680)Fox/89 DS
Dillinger (ID7524VE)IE/90 DM
*Dim Sum (ID5333PA)IE/88 DM
Diner (ML100164)MGM/81-84 AM
*Dinner at Eight (ML100533)MGM/85 AM
*Diplomaniacs (ID7013TU)IE/90 DM CLV/CAV
*The Dirt Bike Kid (901086)Nel/86 AM
*Dirty Dancing (ID5172)IE/88 DS
*The Dirty Dozen (ML100008)MGM/81-84 AS
*Dirty Harry (1019LV)WB/81-84 AM U/90 DS
*Dirty Rotten Scoundrels (ID6481OR)IE/89 DS
*The Discreet Charm of the Bourgeoise (ID5352ME)IE/88 DM
A Disney Christmas Gift (224AS)Dis/81-84 AM
*Disney Mini-Classics: Ben and Me/Bongo (939AS)Dis/89 AM
*Disney's Chip 'N' Dale Rescue Rangers: Crime Busters/Double Trouble (618AS)Dis/89 DM
*Disney Dream Factory 1933-1938 O(257AS)Dis/85 AM
Disney's Best of 1931-1948 O(167AS)Dis/81-84 AM
*Disney's DuckTales: Accidental Adventurers/Seafaring Sailors (616AS)Dis/89 AM
*Disney's DuckTales: Daredevil Ducks/High-Flying Hero (934AS)Dis/89 AM
*Disney's DuckTales: Lost World Wanderers/Duck to the Future (799AS)Dis/89 AM
*Disney's Ducktales: Masked Marauders/Fearless Fortune Hunters (607AS)Dis/88 AM
*Disorderlies (11752)WB/88 DM
*Disorganized Crime (951AS)Dis/89 DS
*Distant Thunder (LV1855)Par/89 DS
*Distant Voices, Still Lives (ID7221IV)IE/90 DS
Diva O(ML100183)MGM/81-84 AM
Dixie Ray, Hollywood Star (X-rated) (N/A)IE/86 AM
*Do the Right Thing (40894)MCA/90 DS
Doctor Detroit (40-001)MCA/81-84 AM
Doctor Ginger (X-rated) (Z0127)IE/90 AM
*Doctor Zhivago (ML100003)MGM/81-84 AS
*Doctor Zhivago (lb) (ML101526)MGM/88 DS
Dodge City O(462580)Fox/81-84 AM
*Dodsworth (30405)Nel/85 AM
*The Dogs of War (ID6469MG)IE/89 DS
*Doll Face (X-rated) (I0051)IE/88 AM CLV/CAV
*Dollars (ID6107RC)IE/89 DM
*Dolls (ID5178)IE/88 DS
*Dominick & Eugene (ID6428OR)IE/89 DS
*Domino (ID6626IV)IE/89 DM
Don't Look Now (LV8704)Par/81-84 AM
*Don't Mess with My Sister! (ID7302VA)IE/90 DM
*Dona Flor and Her Two Husbands (ID7121FL)IE/90 DM
*Donald's Bee Pictures O(255AS)Dis/85 AM
*Donovan's Brain (ID6411MG)IE/89 DM CLV/CAV
Donavan's Reef (LV6220)Par/81-84 AM
*The Doors Live in Europe 1968 (ID6581HB)IE/89 DM
*Double Indemnity (21004)MCA/88 AM
*Down Among the "Z" Men (ID7477PA)IE/90 DM
Down and Dirty in Beverly Hills (X-rated) (Z0077)IE/89 AM
*Down and Out in Beverly Hills (473AS)Dis/87 DS
Down the Drain (59096)Col/90 AS
Downhill Racer (LV6910)Par/81-84 AM
*Dr. Alien! (LV12722)Par/89 AS
*Dr. Jekyll & Mr. Hyde (ML100651)MGM/86 AM
Dr. Jekyll and Mr. Hyde (Kirk Douglas) (ID7178SO)IE/90 DM
*Dr. No O(4525-80)Fox/81-84 AM
*Dr. No (ML101401)MGM/88 AM
*Dr. Seuss Video Festival (ML100176)MGM/81-84 AM
Dr. Strangelove (VLD3134)Col/81-84 AM
Dracula (11011)MCA/81-84 AS
*Dracula (1931) The Restored Version (23001)MCA/88 AM CLV/CAV
*Dragonslayer (LV1367)Par/81-84 AS
*Dragnet (40685)MCA/88 AS
*Dream a Little Dream (ID6631VE)IE/89 DS
*The Dream Team (40882)MCA/89 DS
*Dressed to Kill (Sherlock Holmes) O(N/A)3M/86 AM
Dressed to Kill (DePalma) (VL4050)Ves/81-84 AM
The Dresser O(30111)Col/81-84 AM
*Driving Miss Daisy (11931)WB/90 DS
*Drugstore Cowboy (ID7354IV)IE/90 DS
*Drums Along the Mohawk (138280)Fox/90 DM
*Duck Soup (22004)MCA/86 AM CLV/CAV
*Dudes (ID6125IV)IE/88 DS
The Duellists (LV8975)Par/81-84 AM

Dumbo (24AS)Dis/81-84 AM
Dunder Klumpen (VL3012)Ves/81-84 AM
*Dune (40161)MCA/85 AS
*The Dungeonmaster (9907)Ves/85 AM
*E.T. The Extra-Terrestrial (13009)MCA/88 DS
*E.T. The Extraterrestrial (40925)MCA/89 DS CAV
*The Eagle (ID6864HB)IE/90 DS
*An Early Frost (30760)Col/87 AM
*Earth Girls Are Easy (ID6656VE)IE/89 DS
*Earth Vs. The Flying Saucers (ID6042RC)IE/88 DM CLV/CAV
*Earthquake (10002)MCA/87 DS CLV/CAV
*East of Eden (1005)WB/85 AS
*The Easter Bunny Is Coming to Town (ID7421VE)IE/90 DM
*Easter Parade (ML100256)MGM/88 DS
Easy Money (VL5029)Ves/81-84 AM
Easy Rider (VLD3140)Col/81-84 AM
Eat a Bowl of Tea (50246)Col/90 AM
*Echo Park O(LV2391)Par/87 AM
Ecstasy Girls (X-rated) (I0009)IE/81-84 AM
*Eddie and the Cruisers (20665)Nel/81-84 AS
*Eddie and the Cruisers II (ID6955IV)IE/90 DS
Eddie Macon's Run O(12025)MCA/81-84 AM
*Edge of Sanity (ID6760VV)IE/89 DS
Educating Rita O(VLD3142)Col/81-84 AM
*The Egg and I (40317)MCA/88 AM
*The Eiger Sanction (12002)MCA/87 DM CLV/CAV
*81/2 (CC1177L)Voy/89 DM
*Eight Men Out (ID6429OR)IE/89 DM
*8 Million Ways to Die (611880)Fox/86 AM
*18 Again (ID6030NW)IE/88 DM
84 Charlie Mopic (09946)Col/90 AS
*84 Charring Cross Road (ID6040RC)IE/88 DM
*El Amor Brujo (ID5345PA)IE/89 DM
El Cid O(VL3014)Ves/81-84 AM
*El Dorado (LV66252)Par/90 AM
*Electra Glide in Blue (ID6410MG)IE/89 DS
*Electric Boogaloo Breakin' 2 (ML100580)MGM/85 AS
*Electric Dreams (ML100487)MGM/85 AS
The Electric Horseman O(10025)MCA/81-84 AM
*Eleni (76095)Nel/86 AS
The Elephant Man (LV1347)Par/81-84 AS
Elephant Man (stage) (J26030)J2/90 DM
*Elmer Gantry O(458280)Fox/85 AM
*Elvira Madigan (LVD8908)Lum/89 DS
*Elvira, Mistress of the Dark (ID6289NW)IE/89 DS
*The Emerald Forest (21795)Nel/85 AS
*The Emissary (ID6648VV)IE/90 DS
Emmanuelle (VLD3146)Col/81-84 AM
Emmanuelle in the Country (ID7718MN)IE/90 DM
Emmanuelle, The Joys of a Woman (LV8890)Par/81-84 AM
*The Emperor and the Nightengale (ID6282SO)IE/89 DS
*Empire of the Sun (11844)WB/89 DS CAV
*Empire of the Sun/The China Odyssey (11753A/B)WB/89 DS
*The Empire Strikes Back (142580)Fox/81-84 AS
*The Empire Strikes Back (142584)Fox/85 AS CAV
*The Empire Strikes Back (lb) (142585)Fox/90 DS
The Enchanted Cottage (ID6779TU)IE/90 DM
The End O(460780)Fox/81-84 AM
*End of the Line (ID5407LO)IE/88 DS
Endless Love O(40018)MCA/81-84 AM
Endless Summer (PA12530)Pac/81-84 AM
*Enemies, A Love Story (ID7776ME)IE/90 DS
*Enemy Mine (149280)Fox/86 AS
*The Enforcer (Bogart) (LV21173)Rep/90 DM
*The Enforcer (Eastwood) (11082)WB/87 DS
Enigma O(20505)Nel/81-84 AM
Enter the Dragon (61006LV)WB/81-84 AM
Equus (ID7403MG)IE/90 DM
*Eraserhead O(30176)Col/81-84 AM
Ernest Saves Christmas (953AS)Dis/89 DS
The Erotic Adventures of Pinocchio (ID7293PO)IE/90 DM
Escape from Alcatraz (LV1256)Par/81-84 AM
Escape from New York (16025)Nel/81-84 AS
Escape to Witch Mountain (13AS)Dis/81-84 AM
*Eternal Evil (ID5194VE)IE/88 DM
*Eugine Onegin (ID6843CO)IE/90 DM
*Every Girl Should Be Married (ID6988TU)IE/90 DM
*Every Time We Say Goodbye (LL9951)Ves/87 AM
*Every Which Way but Loose (1028)WB/89 DS
*Everybody's All-American (11827A/B)WB/89 DS
Everything You Always Wanted to Know About Sex but Were Afraid to Ask O(459880)Fox/81-84 AM
*Evil Dead 2 (IDVL5212)IE/88 AM
*The Evil That Men Do O(VLD30407)Col/85 AM
*Evil under the Sun (ID6918HB)IE/90 DM
*Ewoks The Battle for Endor (ML101425)MGM/90 DS
*Excalibur (22018A/B)WB/87 DM

Exhausted (X-rated) (Z0052)IE/89 AM
Exodus O(454480)Fox/81-84 AM
*The Exorcist O(1007LV)WB/81-84 AM
*The Exorcist (1007A/B)WB/90 DS CLV/CAV
*The Expendables (ID6510ME)IE/89 DM
*Experiment in Terror (ID6076RC)IE/89 DM
The Experts (LV1941)Par/89 DS
*Explorers (LV1676)Par/86 DS
The Exterminator (20026)Nel/89 AM
*Extreme Prejudice (ID6128IV)IE/88 DS
*Extremities O(LV12511)Par/87 AM
*Eyes of Fire (VL5205)Ves/87 AM
The Eyes of Laura Mars O(VLD3149)Col/81-84 AM
*Eyes without a Face (ID7429IN)IE/90 DM
*Eyewitness (111680)Fox/88 AS
*F.I.S.T. (ID6413MG)IE/89 DM
*F/X (TVL3769)HBO/87 AS
*The Fabulous Baker Boys (ID7353IV)IE/90 DS
*Fabulous Fleischer Folio Volume One O(852AS)Dis/85 AM
*Fabulous Fleischer Folio Volume Two O(853AS)Dis/85 AM
*Fahrenheit 451 (40199)MCA/87 AM
Fail Safe O(VLD3152)Col/81-84 AM
*Falcon and the Snowman (VL5073)Ves/85 AS
Falling in Love (LV1628)Par/85 AM
*Fame (ML100027)MGM/81-84 AS U/90 DS
*The Family (ID6294VE)IE/89 DM
*Family Business (70236)Col/90 DS
*Family Plot (11005)MCA/88 AM CLV/CAV
Family Thighs (X-rated) (Z0095)IE/90 AM
The Fan (LV1469)Par/81-84 AM
*Fanny and Alexander (21755)Nel/81-84 DCAM
*Far from Home (ID6649VE)IE/89 DM
*Far from the Madding Crowd (101820)MGM/90 DS
Far North (77256)Nel/89 AS
Far Out Man (90626)Col/90 DS
*A Farwell to Arms O(N/A)3M/86 AM
*Farewell to the King (ID6688OR)IE/89 DS
Fascination (X-rated) (X113)IE/81-84 AM
*Fast Food (ID6705FR)IE/89 DM
*Fast Forward (VLD30478)Col/85 AS
Fast Times at Ridgemont High O(16029)MCA/81-84 AM
*Fat Man and Little Boy (LV322522)Par/90 DS
*Fatal Attraction (LV1762)Par/88 DS
*Fatal Beauty (ML101134)MGM/88 AS
*Fatal Vision (N/A)Col/87 AM
*Father (ID7388CS)IE/90 DM
*Father's Little Dividend (LVA1012)LVA/90 AM
*Fear (ID6156VV)IE/89 DM
Fear City (ID7649HB)IE/90 DM
Feds (11828)WB/89 DS
*Fellini Satyricon (CC1135L)Voy/88 AM CAV
*Ferris Bueller's Day Off (LV1890)Par/87 DS
Fiddler on the Roof O(452480)Fox/81-84 AS
*Fiddler on the Roof (lb) (ML101744)MGM/90 DS
*Field of Dreams (40884)MCA/90 DS
*Field of Honor (ID6954OR)IE/90 DM
*50th Anniversary Gone with the Wind (ML10678)MGM/89 DM
*52 Pick Up (ID5068)IE/87 AS
*Fight for Us (31138)WB/90 DM
*Final Chapter Walking Tall (LL9911)Ves/85 AM
*The Final Conflict (111580)Fox/90 DS
*The Final Countdown (ID5238VE)IE/89 DS
*A Fine Mess (30723)Col/87 AM
Finian's Rainbow (11208LV)WB/81-84 AS
*Fire and Ice (76826)Nel/88 AS
*Fire and Ice (anim.) (30184)Col/86 AS
Firefox (11219LV)WB/81-84 AS
*Firesign Theatre Hot Shorts (PA85144)PA/85 AS
*Firestarter (40075)MCA/85 AM
*Firewalker (ID5137)IE/87 AS
*First Blood (1573)HBO/86 AS
*First Born (LV1755)Par/85 AM
First Monday in October (LV1408)Par/81-84 AM
*First Name: Carmen (ID6781CS)IE/89 DM
*A Fish Called Wanda (475280)Fox/89 DS
*The Fisherman and His Wife (ID7168SO)IE/90 DS CAV
*Fist Fighter (ID6812IV)IE/90 DS
*A Fistfull of Dollars O(455680)Fox/85 AM
*A Fistful of Dollars (lb) (ML101796)MGM/90 DM
*Five Easy Pieces (CC1196L)Voy/90 DM
*The Flame and the Arrow (11681)WB/87 AM
*The Flamingo Kid (VL5072)Ves/85 AM
Flash Gordon (13006)MCA/81-84 AS
Flashback (LV32110)Par/90 DS
Flashdance (LV1454)Par/81-84 AS
*Flashpoint (ID5147)IE/87 AM
*Flesh and Blood (ID5247VE)IE/88 DS

Flesh Gordon (R-rated) (ID7575ME)IE/90 DM
*Fletch (40190)MCA/86 AS
*Fletch Lives (40881)MCA/89 DS
The Flight (ID7393VK)IE/90 DM
*The Flight of the Navigator (499AS)Dis/87 AS
*The Flight of the Phoenix (122180)Fox/85 AM
*The Flintstones (ID6614HA)IE/90 DM
*Floating Weeds (CC1183L)Voy/89 DM
*Florida Straits (ID52229OR)IE/88 DS
*Flowers in the Attic (ID5202NW)IE/88 DM
*The Fly (remake) (150380)Fox/87 AS
*The Fly II (158680)Fox/90 DS
*The Fly/Return of the Fly (171580)Fox/89 DS
The Flying Deuces (VL2009)Ves/81-84 AM
*Flying Leathernecks O(934)VA/86 AM
The Fog O(406780)Fox/81-84 AM
The Fog (20036)Nel/89 AM
*Food for the Gods, Part 2 (ID6482IV)IE/89 DM
*Footlight Parade (101676)MGM/90 DM
Footloose (LV1589)Par/81-84 AS
For a Few Dollars More O(467580)Fox/81-84 AM
*For Keeps (ID6053TS)IE/88 DS
*For Me and My Gal (ML101379)MGM/89 AM
*For Your Eyes Only O(456880)Fox/81-84 AS
*For Your Eyes Only (lb) (101725)MGM/90 DS CLV/CAV
The Forbidden Dance (77106)Col/90 AS
*Forbidden Games (CC1130L)Voy/88 DCAM
*Forbidden Planet (ML100041)MGM/81-84 AS
*Forbidden Planet (CC1153L)Voy/89 DS CAV
Forbidden World (ID7561NL)IE/90 DM
*Force of Evil (LV21362)Rep/90 DM
Force 10 from Navarone (VL4051)Ves/81-84 AM
Forever Emmanuelle (ID7579RU)IE/90 DM
*Forever, Lulu (ID6074TS)IE/88 DS
A Forgotten Tune for the Flute (ID7194FR)IE/90 DM
*Fort Apache O(703)VA/86 AM
*Fort Apache (ID6545TU)IE/89 DM
Fort Apache, The Bronx (VL6000)Ves/81-84 AM
48 Hours (LV1139)Par/81-84 AS
*42nd Street O(450280)Fox/81-84 AM
*42nd Street (101745)MGM/90 DM
*The 400 Blows (668080)Fox/86 AM
The Four Seasons O(16025)MCA/81-84 AM
*The Fourth Man (ID5357ME)IE/89 DM
*The Fourth Protocol (ID5170)IE/88 DS
*Foul Play (LV1116)Par/81-84 AM
*Frank Capra's "It's a Wonderful Life" (LVA1001)LVA/88 AM
*Frank Capra's Meet John Doe (LVA1005)LVA/89 AM CLV/CAV
*Frankenstein General Hospital (ID6083NS)IE/88 DM
*Frankenstein Meets the Wolfman (40422)MCA/87 AM CLV/CAV
*Frankenstein, The Restored Version (23002)MCA/86 AM CLV/CAV
*Frantic (11787)WB/88 DS
Fraternity Vacation O(I5037)IE/85 AM
*Freaks (ML100843)MGM/86 DM
*Freeway (ID6125NW)IE/89 DM
The French Connection (100980)Fox/81-84 AS
The French Lieutenant's Woman O(458680)Fox/81-84 AM
*Frenzy (11006)MCA/89 AM
*Fresh Horses (31027)Col/89 AS
Frida (ID6801CS)IE/90 DM
Friday The 13th (LV1395)Par/81-84 AM
Friday The 13th Part II (LV1457)Par/81-84 AM
Friday The 13th, Part III (LV1539)Par/81-84 AM
Friday the 13th The Final Chapter (LV1765)Par/81-84 AM
*Friday the 13th Part V A New Beginning AM (LV1823)Par/85
*Friday the 13th, Part VI Jason Lives AM (LV31982)Par/87 DS
*Friday the 13th Part VII: The New Blood (LV32209)Par/88 DS
*Friday the 13th Part VIII Jason Takes Manhattan (LV32298)Par/90 DS
*Friendly Persuasion (731880)Fox/89 DM
Friends, Lovers & Lunatics (ID7193FR)IE/90 DM
*Fright Night (30562)Col/86 AS
*Fright Night 2 (ID6813IV)IE/89 DS
The Fringe Dwellers (ID7177SO)IE/90 DM
*Frog (ID5276OR)IE/88 DS
Frog Prince O(805AS)Dis/81-84 AM
*From Beyond (VL5117)Ves/87 AS
*From Here to Eternity (30762)Col/87 AM
*From Pluto with Love O(261AS)Dis/85 AM
*From Russia with Love O(456680)Fox/81-84 AM
*From Russia with Love (ML101402)MGM/88 AM
*From the Earth to the Moon (ID6945TU)IE/90 DM
*From the Hip (ID5155)IE/88 DM
*The Front (ID6019RC)IE/88 DM
*Fugitive Samurai (ID7179SO)IE/90 DM
*Full Metal Bikini (X-rated) (Z0053)IE/89 AM

*Full Metal Jacket (11760)IE/88 DM
*Full Moon in Blue Water (ID6475ME)IE/89 DM
*Funeral in Berlin (LV6609)Par/90 AM
*Funland (ID6665VE)IE/90 DS
*Funny Face (LV5608)Par/85 AM
Funny Girl (VLD3155)Col/81-84 AS
*Funny Lady (30685)Col/86 AS
*Funny Farm (11809)WB/88 DS
A Funny Thing Happened on the Way to the Forum O(461880)Fox/81-84 AM
*The Further Adventures of Tennessee Buck (ID5401ME)IE/88 DS
*Future Hunters (ID6349VE)IE/89 DM
*G-Men Vs. The Black Dragon (LV21455)Rep/90 DM
*Gaby (ID5289TS)IE/88 DM
Galaxina O(13007)MCA/81-84 AM
Galaxy of Terror (23940)Nel/89 AM
Gallipoli (LV1504)Par/81-84 AM
The Gambler (LV8678)Par/81-84 AM
*Gamera/Gamera Vs Guiron (ID7580CE)IE/90 DM
*Gamera Vs Gaos/Gamera Vs Zigra (ID7581CE)IE/90 DM
Gandhi (VLD6161)Col/81-84 AS
*The Garden of the Finzi-Continis (ID5260LO)IE/88 DM
*Gardens of Stone (373180)Fox/88 DS
Gas Pump Girls (VL5502)Ves/81-84 AM
*Gaslight (ML100473)MGM/85 AM
*The Gate (IDVL5208)IE/88 AS
Gator Bait II (LV12597)Par/89 AM
*The Gauntlet (11083)WB/89 DS
*The General (ID6862HB)IE/90 DS
*Gentleman Jim O(452780)Fox/86 AM
*Gentlemen Prefer Blondes (101980)Fox/88 AM
*George Jones the Living Legend in Concert (ID6367ME)IE/89 AS
*Georgy Girl (ID6351RC)IE/89 DM
Getting It Right (ID7196VV)IE/90 DS
*Ghost Chase (ID7288VV)IE/90 DS
Ghost Fever (902096)Nel/87 AM
Ghost Story O(11013)MCA/81-84 AM
*Ghost Town (ID6154NW)IE/89 DS CLV/CAV
*Ghostbusters (30413)Col/85 AS U/(lb) 90 DS
*Ghostbusters (305802)Col/86 AS CAV
*Ghostbusters (lb) (CC1182L)Voy/89 DS
*Ghostbusters (lb) (CC1181L)Voy/89 DS CAV
*Ghostbusters II (50166)Col/89 DS
*Ghoulies II (ID6069VE)IE/89 DS
*Giant (11414)WB/85 AS
*Gidget (VLD30740)Col/85 AM
*Gigi (ML100050)MGM/81-84 AS
*Gigi (lb) (ML101709)MGM/89 DS
*Gilda (30194)Col/88 AM
Gimme Shelter (VLD3163)Col/81-84 AS
*Girl Crazy (ML100567)MGM/90 DM
The Girl from S.E.X (X-rated) (I0012)IE/81-84 AM
Girl in a Swing (ID7409HB)IE/90 DS
A Girl in Every Port (ID7015TU)IE/90 DM
Girl on the Run (X-rated) (Z0117)IE/90 AM
A Girl to Kill For (59116)Col/90 AM
Girl with the Hungry Eyes (X-rated) (Z0123)IE/90 AM
*The Girl with the Million Dollar Legs (X-rated) (Z0072)IE/89 AM
*Girls Just Want to Have Fun O(I5038)IE/85 AS
Girls of the Night (X-rated) (I0024)IE/86 AM
*Girlfriend from Hell (ID7375IV)IE/90 DS
*Give My Regards to Broad Street (144880)Fox/85 AS
*The Gladiator (ID6031NW)IE/88 DM
*The Glass Menagerie (40787)MCA/88 AM
*Gleaming the Cube (ID6630VE)IE/89 DS
*Glen and Randa (ID6592VC)IE/90 DM
*Glenn Miller Story (17009)MCA/86 AS
Gloria (VLD3160)Col/81-84 AM
*Glory (70286)Col/90 DS
*Go Johnny Go O(N/A)3M/86 AM
Go Tell The Spartans (VL5000)Ves/81-84 AM
*God Told Me To (ID7560NL)IE/90 DM
*The Goddess (30728)Col/87 AM
The Godfather (LV8049)Par/81-84 AM U/90 DM
The Godfather, Part II (LV8459)Par/81-84 AM U/90 DM
*The Gods Must Be Crazy (145080)Fox/87 AM
Godzilla (VL3010)Ves/81-84 AM
*Godzilla 1985 (I5042)IE/86 AM
*Godzilla Vs. Gigan/Godzilla Vs. Mechagodzilla (ID6507NW)IE/89 DM
*Godzilla Vs. The Smog Monster/Monster from a Prehistoric Planet (ID6923OR)IE/90 DM
Goin' South (LV1133)Par/81-84 AM
Going Berserk O(40012)MCA/81-84 AM
*Going My Way (21017)MCA/86 AM CLV/CAV
*Going Undercover (ID7132VK)IE/90 DS
*The Gold and the Glory (ID6347IV)IE/89 DS
Gold Diggers (X-rated) (Z0094)IE/90 AM
*Gold Diggers of 1933 (ML101673)MGM/90 DM
*Golden Boy (ID6265RC)IE/89 DM
*The Golden Child (LV1930)Par/87 DS
The Golden Seal (30225)Nel/81-84 AM
*The Golden Voyage of Sinbad (30199)Col/86 AM
*Goldfinger O(459580)Fox/81-84 AM
*Goldfinger (ML101403)MGM/88 AM
*Goldilocks and the Theree Bears (636880)Fox/81-84 AM
*Gone with the Wind (ML100284)MGM/85 AS
Good Guys Wear Black (VL6002)Ves/81-84 AM
*Good Morning Babylon (ID5180)IE/88 DM
*Good Morning, Vietnam (660AS)Dis/88 DS
*The Good Mother (610AS)Dis/89 DS
*Good News (ML100877)MGM/89 AM
*The Good, the Bad and the Ugly O(454580)Fox/81-84 AM
*The Good, the Bad and the Ugly (lb) (101739)MGM/90 DM
Goodbye Columbus (LV4572)Par/81-84 AM
The Goodbye Girl (ML100069)MGM/81-84 AM
*Goodbye New York O(VL5105)Ves/85 AM
*Goodbye My Lady (11842)WB/90 DM
*Goodbye People (20705)Nel/86 AM
*The Goonies (11474LV)WB/86 AS
*Gorgo (ID6590VC)IE/89 DM
*The Gorgon (ID6079RC)IE/88 DM
The Gorilla (ID7242NE)IE/90 DM
*Gorillas in the Mist (40851)MCA/89 DS
Gorky Park (VL5035)Ves/81-84 AM
*Gotcha! (40188)MCA/85 AM
Gotham (31011)WB/89 AS
*Gothic (IDVL5215)IE/88 AS
*The Graduate O(400680)Fox/81-84 AS
*The Graduate (CC1115L)Voy/87 DCDS CAV
*The Graduate (CC1168L)Voy/89 DCDS
The Graduate (20716)Nel/89 DS
*Grand Hotel (ML100564)MGM/85 AM
*Grand Illusion (CC1114L)Voy/88 AM CAV
Grand Opening (X-rated) (Z0128)IE/90 AM
*The Grapes of Wrath (102480)Fox/89 AM
*Graveyard Shift (ID5176)IE/88 DM
Grease (LV1108)Par/81-84 AS
Grease 2 (LV1193)Par/81-84 AS
*Great Balls of Fire (ID6953OR)IE/90 DS
The Great Escape O(455880)Fox/81-84 AM
The Great Gatsby (LV8469)Par/81-84 AM
*The Great McGinty (40595)MCA/89 AM CLV/CAV
The Great Muppet Caper (903580)Fox/81-84 AS
*The Great Outdoors (40811)MCA/89 DS
The Great Train Robbery O(453180)Fox/81-84 AS
*The Great Waldo Pepper (10004)MCA/87 AM
*A Great Wall (ID5300PA)IE/88 DM
*Greatest Little Cat House in Vegas (X-rated) (Z0055)IE/89 AM
The Greatest Show On Earth (LV6617)Par/81-84 AM
*Greed (101360)MGM/90 DM
*Green Ice (J26038)J2/89 DS
Greetings (ID6935VK)IE/90 DM
*Gremlins (11388LV)WB/85 DS
*Grey Fox (15035)IE/85 AS
*Greystoke Legend of Tarzan Lord of the Apes (13375LV)WB/81-84 AS
*Gross Anatomy (961AS)Dis/90 DS
*Grotesque (ID6116ME)IE/89 DM CLV/CAV
*Ground Zero (ID6344IV)IE/89 DS
*Guess Who's Coming to Dinner (30541)Col/86 AM
Gulliver's Travels O(VL2011)Ves/81-84 AM
*Gulliver's Travels (LVA1003)LVA/88 AM CLV/CAV
*Gulliver's Travels (ID7408NE)IE/90 DM CLV/CAV
*Gulliver's Travels (LV21650)Rep/90 DM
*Gun Fury (30687)Col/87 AM
Gunfight at the O.K. Corral (LV6218)Par/81-84 AM
*The Gunfighters (ID7103VK)IE/90 DM
*Gung Ho (LV1751)Par/86 AS
*Gunga Din O(911)VA/85 AM
*The Gunrunner (ID6458NW)IE/89 DM
The Guns of Navarone (VLD3170)Col/81-84 AM
Gus (29AS)Dis/81-84 AM
*Guys And Dolls (703980)Fox/81-84 AS U89 DS
*H.M.S. Pinafore (PA84067)PA/81-84 AS
*Hail Mary (ID7532VE)IE/90 DM
Hair O(459380)Fox/81-84 AS
*Hairspray (32822)Col/89 AS
*Half Moon Street (1328)Nel/87 AM
*Halloween (15033)IE/85 AM
Halloween II O(11019)MCA/81-84 AS
Halloween III, Season of the Witch O(11020)MCA/81-84 AM
*Halloween 4: The Return of Michael Myers (210080)Fox/89 DS
*Hamburger Hill (ID5190)IE/88 DS
*Hamburger The Movie (I5082)IE/87 AM
*Hamlet (LV125692)Par/88 AM
*Hammered: The Best of Sledge (ID6393NW)IE/89 DM
Hang 'em High O(462880)Fox/81-84 AM
Hanky Panky (VLD3171)Col/81-84 AM
*Hanna's War (ID6478ME)IE/89 DS
*Hannah and Her Sisters (ID5144)IE/87 AM
*The Hanoi Hilton (37068A/B)WB/87 DS
*Hanover Street (ID6170RC)IE/90 DM
*Hans Christian Anderson (30445)Nel/85 AM
*Hansel and Gretel (Faerie Tale Theatre) (640980)Fox/81-84 AM
Hanussen (50296)Col/90 AM
Happy Birthday to Me (VLD3175)Col/81-84 AM
The Happy Hooker O(WL5503)Ves/81-84 AM
The Happy Hooker Goes Hollywood O(28009)MCA/81-84 AM
Happy Together (ID6803IV)IE/90 DM
Hard Country (J26037)J2/90 DM
*A Hard Day's Night O(MP1064D)/81-84 AS
*A Hard Day's Night (CC1175L)Voy/89 DM
*A Hard Day's Night (CC1113L)Voy/87 DS CAV
Hard Times O(VLD3176)Col/81-84 AM
Hard to Hold (40073)MCA/81-84 AS
*Hard to Kill (11914)WB/90 DS
Hardbodies (30366)Col/85 AM
*Hardbodies II (30706)Col/87 AM
Hardcore O(VLD3177)Col/81-84 AM
*Harem (VL5201)Ves/87 AS
*Harlem Nights (LV32316)Par/90 DS
*Harlem Nights (lb) (LV32316L)Par/90 DS
Harold and Maude (LV8042)Par/81-84 AM
Harry and Son (VL5037)Ves/81-84 AM
*Harry and the Hendersons (40677)MCA/87 DS
*Harvey (40321)MCA/90 DM
*The Harvey Girls (ML101003)MGM/89 AM
Hatari! (LV66292)Par/81-84 AM
*Haunted Honeymoon (TVL3911)HBO/87 AS
*Haunted Summer (ID6509ME)IE/89 DS
*The Haunting (ML100903)MGM/86 AM
*Having It All (X-rated) (Z0070)IE/89 AM CLV/CAV
*Hawaii (ML101860)MGM/90 DS
*Hawk the Slayer (ID6925IV)IE/90 DM
*Hawkin's Breed (ID7263VK)IE/90 DM
He Man and the Masters of the Universe (VLD3181)Col/81-84 AM
*He Man & The Masters of the Universe, Volume 2 (VLD30320)Col/85 AM
*Head (30702)Col/86 AM
Heart Condition (75036)Col/90 AS
Heart Like a Wheel (130080)Fox/81-84 AM
*Heart of Dixie (ID6692OR)IE/90 DS
*Heart of Midnight (ID6500VV)IE/89 DS
Heart of the Stag O(I5014)IE/85 AM
Heartaches (VL4024)Ves/81-84 AM
*Heartbreak Hotel (609AS)Dis/89 DS
*The Heartbreak Kid (I5075)IE/87 AM
*Heartbreak Ridge (11701A/B)WB/87 DS
Heartbreaker (X-rated) (Z0099)IE/90 AM
*Heartburn (LV1688)Par/87 AM
Hearts of Fire (ID5252LO)IE/90 DS
*Heat (LV12584)Par/87 AM
*Heat of Desire (ID6220RC)IE/89 DM
*Heathers (ID6547NW)IE/89 DM
*Heaven Can Wait (Lubitsch) (177180)Fox/90 DCDM
*Heaven Can Wait (Beatty) (LV1109)Par/81-84 AM
Heaven Help Us (ID7652HB)IE/90 DM
*Heidi/The Poor Little Rich Girl (173180)Fox/89 DS
*Hell Comes to Frog Town (ID5317NW)IE/89 AM
*Hellbound Hellraiser II (ID6291NW)IE/89 DS
*Hellhole (VLD30495)Col/86 AM
*Hello Again (656AS)Dis/88 DS
Hello Dolly (100180)Fox/81-84 AS
*Hello Mary Lou Prom Night II (ID5221VE)IE/88 DM
*Hellraiser (INW5186)IE/88 DS
*Help! (C2003L)Voy/87 DS CAV
*Help! (C2004L)Voy/87 DS
*Her Alibi (11835)WB/89 DS
Herbie Rides Again (42AS)Dis/81-84 AM
Hercules (Ferrigno) (ML100319)MGM/81-84 AS
*Hercules (Schwarzenegger) O(DFI1)DF/81-84 AM
*Hercules Unchained (20745)Nel/86 AM
*Here Comes Mr. Jordan (30015)Col/88 AM
*Hero and the Terror (ID6290ME)IE/89 DS
*Hey Babu Riba (ID6686OR)IE/90 DM
Hey Cinderella! O(806AS)Dis/81-84 AM
*Hide and Go Shriek (ID6082NS)IE/88 DM
*The Hidden (ID5206ME)IE/88 DM
*The Hidden Fortress (CC1111L)Voy/87 AM CAV
High Anxiety (110780)Fox/81-84 AS

*High and Low (ID5334PA)IE/88 DM
*High Noon (CC1173L)Voy/89 DCDM
*High Noon (CC1107L)Voy/86 DCAM CAV
A High Road to China (11309LV)WB/81-84 AM
High Season (77146)Nel/89 AM
High Sierra O(462980)Fox/81-84 AM
*High Society (ML100292)MGM/85 AM
*High Spirits (ID6476ME)IE/89 DS
High Stakes (ID7215VK)IE/90 DM
High Tide (77226)Nel/89 AM
*Higher and Higher (ID6895TU)IE/90 DM
*Highest Honor (40345)Nel/85 AS
Highlander (ID6679HB)IE/89 DS
*Highpoint O(40365)Nel/85 AS
*The Hill (Tour of Duty) (ID6755NW)IE/89 DM
*The Hills Have Eyes (ID6695MN)IE/89 DM
*History is Made at Night (LL9005)Ves/86 AM
The History of the World, Part I (111480)Fox/81-84 AS
*The Hit (75995)Nel/85 AM
*Hit List (09926)Col/89 AS
*Hit the Deck (ML100441)MGM/89 DS
*The Hitcher (TVL3756)HBO/88 AS
*The Hitchhiker Volume 1 (ID5263LO)IE/89 DM CLV/CAV
*The Hitchhiker Volume 2 (ID5264LO)IE/88 DM CLV/CAV
*The Hitchhiker Volume 3 (ID5408LO)IE/89 DM CLV/CAV
*The Hitchhiker Volume 4 (ID5405LO)IE/89 DM CLV/CAV
*Hobson's Choice (60535)Nel/86 AM
*The Holcroft Covenant (31022)WB/89 AS
*Holiday (30784)Col/87 AM
*Holiday Inn (40288)MCA/85 AM
Hollywood Hot Tubs 2: Educating Crystal (ID7355IV)IE/90 DS
*Hollywood on Trial (ID6311CO)IE/89 DM
*Hollywood Shuffle (ID5167)IE/88 DS CLV/CAV
*Hombre (101280)Fox/90 DM
*Home Is Where the Hart Is O(ID6733KV)IE/89 DM
*Homeboy (ID6817IV)IE/90 DS
Homework O(16030)MCA/81-84 AM
*Honey, I Shrunk the Kids (909AS)Dis/90 DS
The Honeymoon Killers (ID7545VE)IE/90 DM
Honeysuckle Rose (1043LV)WB/81-84 AS
*Honkeytonk Man (11305A/B)WB/89 DS
*Hoosiers O(TVL0041)HBO/88 AS
*Hoosiers (ID6085VE)IE/88 DS
*Hope and Glory (77136)Nel/88 AM
*Hoppity Goes to Town (LV21866)Rep/90 DM
Hopscotch (20756)Nel/89 AM
*Horror Planet (ID7559NL)IE/90 DM
*Horse Feathers (40777)MCA/89 AM CLV/CAV
*The Horse's Mouth (CC1171L)Voy/89 DM
*The Horse's Mouth/Tunes of Glory O(N/A)Voy/87 AM
Hostage Tower (19045)Nel/81-84 AM
Hostile Guns (LV6715)Par/90 AM
*Hostile Takeover (ID7220IV)IE/90 DM
Hot Blooded (X-rated) (I0023)IE/86 AM
Hot Girls in Love (X-rated) (Z0122)IE/90 AM
*Hot Pursuit (LV32082)Par/88 DS
Hot Stuff (VLD3180)Col/81-84 AM
*Hot to Trot (11788)WB/89 DS
*Hotel Colonial (77236)Nel/89 AS
The Hotel New Hampshire (VL5037) Ves/81-84 AS
*The Hound of the Baskervilles/Sherlock Holmes Faces Death (220680)Fox/89 DM
*House (I5058)IE/86 AM
*House II (INW5184)IE/88 DM
House Calls (16006)MCA/81-84 AM
*House of Games (ID6588HB)IE/89 DM
*The House on Carroll Street (ID6921HB)IE/90 DM
*House on Haunted Hill/Attack of the 50 Foot Woman (217980)Fox/89 DM
House On Sorority Row (VL4059)Ves/81-84 AM
*House Party (75036)Col/90 DS
*Houseboat (LV5806)Par/87 AM
*The Housekeeper (ID5166)IE/88 DM
*How the Best Was Won O(259AS)Dis/85 AM
*How the West Was Won (ML100356)MGM/86 DS
How I Got into College (172880)Fox/90 DS
*How I Won the War (ID6471MG)IE/89 DM
*How the Leopard Got His Spots (ID7167SO)IE/90 DS CAV
*How the Rhino Got His Skin/How the Camel Got His Hump (ID6285SO)IE/89 DS
*How to Get Ahead in Advertising (ID6896VV)IE/90 DS
*How to Marry a Millionaire (102380)Fox/88 AS
*How to Succeed in Business without Really Trying (101705)MGM/90 DM
*Howard the Duck (40511)MCA/87 AS
*The Howling (16155)Nel/81-84 AM
*Howling III (ID6123IV)IE/89 DS
*Howling IV (ID6239IV)IE/89 DM
*Howling V: Rebirth (ID6815IV)IE/90 DM
*Huckleberry Hound and Friends (ID6618HA)IE/90 DM
Hud (LV6630)Par/81-84 AM
*Humperdink: Hansel und Gretel (0712021)PGM/89 DS
*The Hunchback of Notre Dame O(I5034)IE/85 DCAM
*The Hunchback of Notre Dame (ID6402TU)IE/90 DCDM
*Hunger (ML100281)MGM/81-84 AM
*Hunk (30813)Col/87 AS
*The Hunt for Red October (LV320202)Par/90 DS
*The Hunt for Red October (lb) (LV320202L)Par/90 DS
*Hunter (LV1192)Par/81-84 AM
*Hunter's Blood (75656)Nel/87 AM
*Hurricane (3045)Nel/86 AM
*Hyper Sapiens: People from Another Star (35202)WB/90 DM
*I Am the Law (31001A)Col/89 AM
*I Could Go on Singing (ML101578)MGM/89 DM
I Like to Watch (X-rated) (I0014)IE/81-84 AM
*I Love Lucy Vol. 1 (232480)Fox/90 DM
*I Love Lucy Vol. 2 (232580)Fox/90 DM
*I Love Lucy Volume 3 (242980)Fox/90 DM
*I Love Lucy Volume 4 (243080)Fox/90 DM
*I, Madman (ID7232ME)IE/90 DS
*I Married a Witch (LL9004)Ves/86 AM
*I Never Sang for My Father (ID6493RC)IE/89 DM
*I Spit on Your Grave O(ZL016)Ves/81-84 AM
*I Spit on Your Grave (ID7300VA)IE/90 DM
*I Vitelloni (ID6255CO)IE/89 DM
*I Walked with a Zombie (ID6400TU)IE/89 DM
*I Wanna Hold Your Hand (35066)WB/89 AM
*I Was a Teenage Zombie O(902166)Nel/88 AM
*I'll Cry Tomorrow (ML101484)MGM/90 DM
I'm Dancing As Fast As I Can (LV1295) Par/81-84 AM
*Ice Pirates (ML100427)MGM/81-84 AM
*Ice Station Zebra (ML101888)MGM/90 DS
*Iceman (40074)MCA/81-84 AS
*Idolmaker (ML100370)MGM/81-84 AS
*If... (LV6838)Par/81-84 AM
If You Could See What I Hear (5014)Ves/81-84 AM
*Il Barbiere di Siviglia (La Scala) (0725041)PGM/88 DS
Il Bidone (ID6795CS)IE/90 DM
*Ilsa Harem Keeper of the Oil Sheiks (ID6601PO)IE/90 DM
*Ilsa She Wolf of the SS (ID6600PO)IE/89 DM
*Ilsa the Wicked Warden (ID6602PO)IE/89 DM
Immediate Family (50196)Col/90 DS
The Immortalizer (59216)Col/90 AS
Improper Channels (VL5011)Ves/81-84 AM
*Impulse (bad milk) (VL5066)Ves/85 AM
*Impulse (bad cop) (11887)WB/90 DS
In Cold Blood O(VLD3108)Col/81-84 AM
*In Country (11888)WB/90 DS
*The In Crowd (ID6148OR)IE/89 DS
In Name Only (ID6998TU)IE/90 DM
*In the Heat of the Night (ML101265)MGM/89 AM
*In Like Flint (176180)Fox/90 DM
*In the Mood (ID5221LO)IE/88 DM
*The Incredible Hulk, Vol. 1 (anim.) O(I5061)IE/86 AM AM
*The Incredible Hulk Returns (ID6421NW)IE/89 DS
*The Incredible Mr. Limpet (11808)WB/90 DM
The Incredible Shrinking Woman (16023)MCA/81-84 AM
*Incredible Storydisc O(37610)OPA/85 DCAM CAV
The Incredible Voyage of Stingray (ID7583IV)IE/90 DM
Incubus O(VL4016)Ves/81-84 AM
*Indiana Jones and the Last Crusade (LV31859)Par/90 DS
*Indiana Jones and the Last Crusade (lb) (LV31859L)Par/90 DS
*Indiana Jones and the Temple of Doom (LV1643)Par/86 DS
*Indiana Jones and the Temple of Doom (LV16432)Par/86 DS CAV
*The Informer (ID6401TU)IE/89 DM
*Ingmar Bergman's The Magic Flute (LV23512)Par/86 DS
*Inherit the Wind O(465180)Fox/85 AM
*Innerspace (11754LV)WB/88 DS
*An Innocent Man (910AS)Dis/90 DS
Insatiable (edited) (X-rated) O(I0001)IE/81-84 AM
Insatiable (X-rated) (I0007)IE/81-84 AM
Insatiable II (X-rated) (I0031)IE/81-84 AS
Inside Desiree Cousteau (X-rated) (I0018)IE/81-84 AM
Inside Moves (J26036)J2/89 DM
*Insignificance (ID5143)IE/87 AM
*Intermezzo (Swedish) (LVD8906)Lum/89 DS CLV/CAV
*Intermezzo (remake) (803680)Fox/86 AM
*Internal Affairs (LV32245)Par/90 DS
*International House (40512)MCA/87 AM CLV/CAV
*The Interns (ID6553RC)IE/89 DM
*Into the Fire (ID6376VE)IE/89 DM
*Into the Homeland (ID5358LO)IE/88 DS
Into the Night (40170)MCA/85 AM
*Into Thin Air (ID6058NS)IE/88 DM
Introducing Barbii (X-rated) (Z0079)IE/89 AM
Intruder (LV12723)Par/90 AM
*Invaders from Mars (I5064)IE/87 AS
Invaders from the Deep (ID7584IV)IE/90 DM
*Invasion of the Body Snatchers (1956) (CC1174L)Voy/89 DM
*Invasion of the Body Snatchers (1956) (CC1108L)Voy/86 DCAM CAV
Invasion of the Body Snatchers (remake) (ML100297)MGM/81-84 AS
*Invasion USA (ML100764)Par/86 DS
*The Invisible Kid (ID6138ME)IE/89 DS
*The Invisible Man (23007)MCA/87 DM CLV/CAV
*Irezumi (ID7478PA)IE/90 DM
*Iron Eagle (616080)Fox/87 AS
*Iron Eagle II (ID6288IV)IE/89 DS
*The Iron Triangle (ID6345IV)IE/89 DS
*Ironweed (ID5248VE)IE/88 DS
Irreconcilable Differences (VL5057)Ves/85 AM
*Ishtar (30849)Col/87 AM
*The Island (ID5122)MCA/87 DS
*It Came from Beneath the Sea O(30491)Col/86 AM
It Happened One Night (30382)Col/81-84 AM
*It Should Happen to You (ID6707RC)IE/90 DM
It's A Mad, Mad, Mad, Mad World O(453480)Fox/81-84 AM
*It's a Gift (ID5088)MCA/87 AM CLV/CAV
It's a Wonderful Life (colorized) O(N/A)3M/86 AM
*It's a Wonderful Life (CC1112L)Voy/87 DCAM CAV
*It's a Wonderful Life (LV22060)Rep/89 DM
It's My Turn (VLD3190)Col/81-84 AM
*Ivan the Terrible Part I (ID6254CO)IE/89 DM
*Ivan the Terrible Part II (ID6309CO)IE/89 DM
*I've Heard the Mermaids Singing (90234)Nel/88 AS
*J. Edgar Hoover (ID7202VV)IE/90 DM
Jabberwocky O(VLD3189)Col/81-84 AM
*Jack and the Beanstalk (Faerie Tale Theatre) (636980)Fox/81-84 AM
*Jack and the Beanstalk (Gene Kelly) (ID6612HA)IE/89 DM
*Jack's Back (LV12669)Par/89 AM
*Jacknife (ID6793HB)IE/90 DS
*The Jade Pussycat (X-rated) (Z0071)IE/89 AM
*Jagged Edge (30591)Col/86 AS
*Jailhouse Rock (ML10011)MGM/85 AM
Jakarta (ID7207VV)IE/90 DS
*Jake Speed (I5060)IE/86 AS
*James Clavell's Tai-Pan (VL5180)Ves/87 AS
*The January Man (475980)Fox/90 DS
Jason and the Argonauts (VLD3191)Col/81-84 AM
Jaws (12001)MCA/81-84 AM
Jaws 3 (40044)MCA/81-84 AM
*Jaws The Revenge (40723)MCA/88 AS
*Jayce and the Wheeled Warriors (30975)Col/89 AM
The Jazz Singer (LV2305)Par/81-84 AS
*Jean de Florette (ID6136OR)IE/88 DS
Jeremiah Johnson (1106LV)WB/81-84 AM
The Jerk (16015)MCA/81-84 AM
*Jesse James (148580)Fox/90 DM
*Jesus Christ Superstar (17002)MCA/87 DS
The Jetsons Meet the Flintstones (ID6611HA)IE/89 DM
*Jewel of the Nile (149180)Fox/86 DS
*Jezebel O(462680)Fox/85 AM
*Jezebel (ML101313)MGM/89 AM
The Jigsaw Man (ID7497HB)IE/90 DM
*Joan of Arc O(889)VA/85 AM
Joe O(VL6005)Ves/81-84 AM
*Johhny Got His Gun (ID5275ME)IE/89 DM
*Johnny Be Good (ID6149OR)IE/88 DS
*Johnny Guitar (ID6117RE)IE/89 DM
*Johnny Handsome (ID7313IV)IE/90 DS
*Jojo Dancer Your Life Is Calling (30683)Col/87 AS
*Jolson Sings Again (30766)Col/87 AM
*The Jolson Story (30683)Col/87 AS
*Jonny Quest (ID6610HA)IE/90 DM
*Jonny Quest Volume 2 (ID6620HA)IE/90 DM
*Journey into Fear (ID6403TU)IE/89 DM CLV/CAV
*The Journey of Natty Gann (400AS)Dis/87 DS
*Journey to the Center of the Earth (124880)Fox/85 AS
*Journey to the Seventh Planet/Angry Red Planet (ID7491HB)IE/90 DM
*Joy of Living (ID6891TU)IE/90 DM
The Judge and the Assassin (ID7322CS)IE/90 DM
*Judgement at Nuremberg (ML101536)MGM/89 AM
*Judgement in Berlin (32774)Col/89 AM
*Jules and Jim (667980)Fox/87 AM
*Julia (109180)Fox/90 DS
*Julia and Julia (503480)Fox/88 AS
*Julius Caesar (ID6259RE)IE/90 DM

*Jumpin' Jack Flash (1508-80)Fox/87 DS
*June Night (LVD8904)Lum/89 DS CLV/CAV
*The Jungle Book (Sabu) O(13255)Nel/81-84 AM
*Just a Gigolo (LVD8915)Lum/90 DS
*Just One of the Guys (VLD30493) Col/86 AM
*K-9 (40880)MCA/89 DS
*Kandyland (ID5231NW)IE/88 DM
*Kansas (ID6250ME)IE/89 DS
*The Karate Kid (VLD30406)Col/85 AS
*The Karate Kid, Part 2 (30717)Col/87 AS
*The Karate Kid III (23972)Col/90 DS
*Keaton's Cop (31151)WB/90 AS
The Keep (LV1563)Par/81-84 AS
*Keeping Track (902006)Nel/87 AM
*Keetje Tippel (ID6799CS)IE/90 DM
*Kelly's Heroes (ML100168)MGM/81-84 AS
*Kentucky Kernels (ID6985TU)IE/90 DM
*The Key (32006)Col/89 AM
Key Largo O(459480)Fox/81-84 AM
*Kickboxer (ID7320HB)IE/90 DS
*The Kid from Brooklyn (30475)Nel/86 AM
*Kidnapped (David Naughton) (ID5291VV)IE/88 DS
The Kill Reflex (59096)Col/90 AS
Kill Slade (77656)Nel/89 AM
*The Killer Elite (ID6412MG)IE/89 DM CLV/CAV
*Killer Klowns from Outer Space (ID6251ME)IE/89 DS
*The Killing (CC1146L)Voy/88 AM
*A Killing Affair (ID6758FL)IE/89 DM
*The Killing Fields (11419)WB/85 AS
The Killing Floor (77696)Nel/89 AM
*The Killing Time (ID5268NW)IE/88 DM
*Killpoint (VL5046)Nel/85 AM
*Kind Hearts and Coronets/The Captain's Paradise (ID6867HB)IE/90 DM
*The Kindred (IDVL5210)IE/87 AM
The King & I O(100480)Fox/81-84 AS
*King David (LV126)Par/85 AS
*King Kong (16003)IE/85 DCAM
*King Kong (CC1116L)Voy/88 DCAM
*King Kong (CC102)Voy/85 DCAM CAV
King Kong (remake) (LV8872)Par/81-84 AM
*King Kong Lives (ID5154)IE/87 DM
King of Comedy (VLD3192)Col/81-84 AM
*The King of Hearts (CC1225L)Voy/90 DM
*King of Kings (ML100326)MGM/88 AS
Kinjite: Forbidden Subjects (31036)WB/89 DS
*The Kiss (ID6394TS)IE/89 DS
*Kiss Me Kate (ML100307)MGM/86 DS
*Kiss of the Spider Woman (900016)Nel/86 AM
*Kiss Tomorrow Goodbye (LV22205)Rep/90 DM
*The Kitchen Toto (37069)WB/89 DM
Klute (1027LV)WB/81-84 AM
*Knights of the Round Table (ML100399)MGM/88 AS
*Knock on Any Door O(30029)Col/81-84 AM
Kramer Vs Kramer (VLD3205)Col/81-84 AM
*Kronos (I5084)IE/87 AM CLV/CAV
Krull O(VLD3207)Col/81-84 AM
*Krush Groove (11529LV)WB/86 DS
*L.A. Bounty (ID6624IV)IE/89 DS
*La Bamba (30854)Col/88 AS
*La Bimbo (X-rated) (I0050)IE/88 AM CLV/CAV
La Cage Aux Folles O(450680)Fox/81-84 AM
*La Cage Aux Folles 3 (30645)Col/86 AM
*La Chienne (ID7453IN)IE/90 DM
*La Clemenza Di Tito (0725071)PGM/89 DS
*La Dolce Vita (ID6262RE)IE/89 DM
*La Lectrice (ID6952OR)IE/90 DM
La Passante (ID7484PA)IE/90 DM
*La Strada O(CC1129L)Voy/88 DCAM
*La Traviata (40048)MCA/81-84 AS
*Labyrinth (76665)Nel/87 DS
*The Lacemaker (CC1222L)Voy/90 DM
*The Ladies Man (LV6015)Par/90 AM
*Lady and the Tramp O(582AS)Dis/87 DS
*Lady and the Tramp O(582CS)Dis/87 DS CAV
*Lady Beware (ID6179IV)IE/89 DS
Lady Chatterley's Lover (ML100184)MGM/81-84 AM
*The Lady Eve (40353)MCA/88 AM
*Lady from Shanghai (VLD30451)Col/85 AM
The Lady in Question (32025)Col/89 AM
*The Lady Vanishes (1979) (ID6103ME)IE/89 DM
*Lady in White (ID6018VV)IE/88 DS
*Lady Jane (LV17052)Par/87 DS
Lady Sings the Blues (LV8374)Par/81-84 AM
*The Lady Vanishes (1104L)Voy/85 AM
*Ladyhawke (1464LV)WB/85 DS
*Laguna Heat (ID5323LO)IE/88 DM
*The Lair of the White Worm (ID6430VE)IE/89 DS
*Lassie Come Home (ML101866)MGM/90 DM
Lassiter (11372LV)WB/81-84 AM
Lambada (31193)WB/90 DS
*The Land Before Time (40924)MCA/89 DS CAV
*The Land Before Time (40864)MCA/89 DS
*The Last Condom (X-rated) (Z0068)IE/89 AM
*Last Days of Man on Earth (ID7558NL)IE/90 DM
The Last Detail (VLD3252)Col/81-84 AM
*The Last Emperor (77156)Nel/88 DS
*The Last Emperor (77506)Nel/89 DS CAV
*Last House on the Left (VL5096)Ves/86 AM
*The Last Hurrah (30922)Col/88 AM
The Last of the Red Hot Lovers (LV8094)Par/81-84 AM
Last Resort (5177)Ves/87 AM
Last Rites (475780)Fox/90 DS
*The Last Starfighter (40078)MCA/81-84 AS
Last Tango in Paris O(450780)Fox/81-84 AM
*The Last Temptation of Christ (40842)MCA/89 DS
The Last Unicorn (J26032)J2/90 DS
*Latino (350480)Fox/86 AS
*Laura (109480)Fox/90 DM
*The Lavender Hill Mob/The Man in the White Suit (ID6866HB)IE/90 DM
*L'avventura (CC1162L)Voy/90 DCDM CAV
*Law of Desire (ID7399CV)IE/90 DM
*Lawrence of Arabia O(VLD3250)Col/81-84 AS
*Lawrence of Arabia (50136)Col/89 DS
*Lawrence of Arabia (CC1197L)Voy/89 DS
*Lawrence of Arabia (CC1185L)Voy/89 DS CAV
*Le Grand Chemin (ID6151PA)IE/89 DM
*Lean on Me (11875)WB/89 DS
Leatherface: Texas Chainsaw Massacre 3 (75016)Col/90 AS
*Legal Eagles (40479)MCA/87 AS
*Legend (40193)MCA/86 DS
*The Legend of Hell House (146580)Fox/90 DM
*The Legend of Sleepy Hollow (Rabbit Ears) (ID6284SO)IE/89 DS
Legend of Sleepy Hollow (X-rated) (Z0097)IE/90 AM
Legion of Iron (59246)Col/90 DS
Lenny O(456380)Fox/81-84 AM
*Leonard Part 6 (30896)Col/88 AS
*Leoncavallo — Pagliacci — Pretre (0702041)PGM/88 DS
*Les Miserables (126880)Fox/89 DM
*Less than Zero (164980)Fox/88 AS
Let It Ride (LV32200)Par/90 DS
*Let's Dance (LV5006)Par/90 DM
Let's Get Harry (TVL9953)HBO/88 AS
Let's Talk Sex (X-rated) (I0015)IE/81-84 AM
*Lethal Weapon (11709)WB/87 DS
*Lethal Weapon 2 (11876)WB/90 DS
*Lethal Woman (ID7298VA)IE/90 DM
*The Letter O(468480)Fox/87 AM
*Letter to Brezhnev (ID5142)IE/87 AS
*Leviathan (ML101707)MGM/89 DS
*Licence to Kill (475580)Fox/90 DS
*License to Drive (166780)Fox/89 DS
*The Life and Death of Colonel Blimp (CC1137L)Voy/88 DCAM
*Life with Mickey O(260AS)Dis/85 AM
*Lifeboat (139380)Fox/90 DM
*Lifeforce (VL5097)Ves/86 AS
*The Lift (I5079)IE/87 AM
*Light of Day (IDVL5200)IE/87 AS
*Light Years (ID6704VK)IE/89 DS
Like a Virgin (X-rated) (Z0107)IE/90 AM
*Like Father, Like Son (ID5287TS)IE/88 DS
*Lily in Love (VL5159)Ves/86 AM
Limit Up (ID7309VV)IE/90 DM
*Lion in Winter (20575)Nel/86 AM
*Lionheart (35203)WB/90 DS
Lipstick O(LV8882)Par/81-84 AM
*Liquid Sky (I5078)IE/87 AM
Listen to Me (10326)Col/90 AS
Little Big Man (713080)Fox/81-84 AM
Little Darlings (LV1301)Par/81-84 AM
*Little Dorrit (37222)WB/90 DS
The Little Drummer Girl (11416LV)WB/85 AM
*The Little Foxes (30505)Nel/85 AM
The Little Girl Who Lives Down the Lane (ID7527VE)IE/90 DM
*The Little Mermaid (913AS)Dis/90 DS
*The Little Mermaid (913CS)Dis/90 DS CAV
*A Little Night Music (ID7557NL)IE/90 DM
*Little Nikita (35000)Col/89 AS
The Little Prince (LV8017)Par/81-84 AS
*The Little Prince and Friends O(ID5330PA)IE/88 DM CLV/CAV
*The Little Princess O(DFI10)3M/86 AM
*Little Red Riding Hood (Faerie Tale Theatre) (638980)Fox/81-84 AM
*Little Shop of Horrors (11702)WB/87 DS
Little Sweetheart (7691)Nel/90 AM
Little Thief (ID7230HB)IE/90 DM
*Little Treasure (VLD30560)Col/86 AM
*Little Vera (LVD8907)Lum/89 DS
Live and Let Die O(463380)Fox/81-84 AM
*The Living Daylights (527780)Fox/88 AS
*Lock Up (ID6814IV)IE/90 DS
Logan's Run (Ml100082)MGM/81-84 AS
*Lola Montes O(2001L)Voy/86 AM CAV
*Lola Montes (CC1213L)Voy/90 DM
*The Lone Ranger Volume 1 (ID6913RH)IE/90 DM
*A Long Day's Journey into Night (ID5243VE)IE/88 DM
*The Long Riders (ML100454)MGM/88 AM
*Lone Runner (ID5255ME)IE/88 DS CLV/CAV
Lone Wolf McQuade (VL5019)Ves/81-84 AM
The Lonely Guy O(40014)MCA/81-84 AM
Lonely Lady O(40055)MCA/81-84 AM
*Long Gone (ID6060LO)IE/89 DS
*The Long Voyage Home (LL9007)Ves/86 AM
*The Longest Day (102180)Fox/89 DS
The Longest Yard (LV8708)Par/81-84 AM
*Look Who's Laughing (ID6775TU)IE/90 DM
*Look Who's Talking (70186)Col/90 DS
Looking For Mr. Goodbar (LV8874)Par/81-84 AM
Lord of the Flies (1989) (77466)Nel/90 DS
Lords of Discipline (LV1433)Par/81-84 AM
*The Lords of Flatbush (30479)Col/86 AM
Lorelei (X-rated) (Z0085)IE/90 AM
Losin' It (20165)Nel/81-84 AM
*Lost Angels (ID6689OR)IE/90 DS
*The Lost Boys (11748)WB/88 DS
*The Lost Boys (lb) (12007)WB/90 DS
*Lost Horizon (30763)Col/87 AM
The Lost Idol (ID7391SG)IE/90 DM
*The Lost Squadron (ID6890TU)IE/90 DM
*The Lost Weekend (21001)MCA/89 AM
*Love Among the Ruins (803880)Fox/90 DM
Love and Death O(458580)Fox/81-84 AM
Love at First Bite (VL4052)Ves/81-84 AM
Love at Stake (77166)Nel/89 AM
The Love Bug (12AS)Dis/81-84 AM
*The Love Goddesses (V1024L)Voy/90 DM
*Love Happy (ID6234RE)IE/89 DM
*Love Is a Many-Splendored Thing (103980)Fox/87 AM
*Love Me or Leave Me (ML100755)MGM/89 DS
Love Story (LV8006)Par/81-84 AM
*Love with the Proper Stranger (LV6312)Par/89 DM
Loverboy (70206)Col/89 AS
*Loves of a Blonde (ID6168RC)IE/89 DM
Loving You: Elvis Presley (PA89241)PA/90 DS
Lucky Stiff (32827)Col/89 AM
*Lust for Life (ML101869)MGM/90 DS
*Lust in the Dust O(I5029)IE/85 AS
*Lust on the Orient Express (X-rated) (I0036)IE/87 AM
*The Lusty Men (7023TU)IE/90 DM
*Luv (ID6549RC)IE/89 DM
*M O(60615)Nel/86 AM
M*A*S*H (103880)Fox/81-84 AS
M*A*S*H, Farewell, Goodbye, Amen O(121580)Fox/81-84 AM
*Mac and Me (ID6397OR)IE/89 DS
*Macao (ID7003TU)IE/90 DM CLV/CAV
*Macaroni (LV1937)MCA/86 AM
*MacArthur (15003)MCA/87 DS CLV/CAV
*Macbeth (Polanski) (30622)Col/86 AM
*Macbeth (Welles) (ID6088RE)IE/89 DM
*Mack the Knife (77006)Col/90 AS
MacKenna's Gold (ID6352RC)IE/90 DM
*Mad Max (VL4030)Ves/81-84 AM
*Mad Max Beyond Thunderdome (11519LV)WB/86 AS
*Madame Sousatzka (40840)MCA/89 DS CLV/CAV
*Made in Heaven (ID6011LOR)IE/88 DS
*Made in USA (77306)Nel/89 AM
Magic (150150)/81-84 AM
*The Magic Balad: Tadanari Okamoto (PSI88017)PA/88 AM CAV
*The Magic Christian (ID6233RE)IE/89 DM
Magic Pony (VL3011)Ves/81-84 AM
*The Magician O(60125)Nel/81-84 AM
*The Magnificent Ambersons (CC1109L)Voy/86 DCAM CAV
The Magnificent Seven O(455380)Fox/81-84 AM
*Magnum Force (1039A/B)WB/87 DS
Mahogany (LV8835)Par/81-84 AM
*Maid to Order (ID6180IV)IE/89 DS
*Major League (LV32270)Par/89 DS
*Making Mr. Right (TVL0016)HBO/88 AS
Malarek (ID7159SO)IE/90 DS
*Malcolm (VL5183)Ves/87 AM

*Malone (ID5169)IE/88 DS
*The Maltese Falcon O(453080)Fox/81-84 AM
*The Maltese Falcon (ML101546)MGM/89 AM
Mame (111000LV)WB/81-84 AM
*Man Facing Southeast (ID5204NW)IE/88 DM
Man for All Seasons (VLD3332)Col/81-84 AM
*The Man from Snowy River (123380)Fox/81-84 AS
*The Man from Utah/Blue Steel (I5055)IE/86 AM
*A Man in Love (77116)Nel/88 AS
*Man of La Mancha O(457580)MGM/87 AS
*Man Outside (ID5322VV)IE/88 DS
The Man Who Could Work Miracles (ID7682NL)IE/90 DM
The Man Who Fell to Earth (VLD3333)Col/81-84 AM
*The Man Who Knew Too Much (original) O(M15)3M/86 AM
The Man Who Knew Too Much (original) (ID7462FP)IE/90 DM
*The Man Who Knew Too Much (remake) (40129)MCA/85 AM
The Man Who Loved Women (VLD3334)Col/81-84 AM
The Man Who Shot Liberty Valance (LV6114)Par/81-84 AM
*The Man Who Would Be King (743580)Fox/90 DM
*The Man with the Golden Gun O(460680)Fox/81-84 AM
*The Man with the Golden Gun (ML101419)MGM/90 DM CLV/CAV
The Man with Two Brains (11319LV)WB/81-84 AM
*The Manchurian Candidate (ML101369)MGM/88 AM
Mandingo (LV8771)Par/81-84 AM
*Manhattan (ML100469)MGM/85 AM
*The Manhattan Project (ID6681HB)IE/90 DS
*Manhunter (LV411)KL/87 AS
*The Maniac Age: Yuji Kuri (PS188-004)PA/88 AM CAV
The Manitou (900546)Nel/89 AM
*Mannequin (ID5149)IE/87 DS
*Manon of the Spring (ID6137OR)IE/88 DS
The Many Adventures of Winnie The Pooh O(25AS)Dis/81-84 AM
*Marat/Sade (LVD8914)Lum/90 DS
Marathon Man (LV8789)Par/81-84 AM
*Marilyn Chambers Private Fantasies #2 (X-rated) (I0035)IE/85 AM
*Marilyn Chambers Private Fantasies #3 (X-rated) (I0040)IE/86 AM
Marilyn Chambers' Private Fantasies #5 (X-rated) (I0046)IE/89 AM
*Marilyn Chambers' Private Fantasies #6 (X-rated) (Z0059)IE/89 AM
*Mark Twain's A Connecticut Yankee (713)MV/88 AM
Marked for Murder (ID7383VK)IE/90 DM
*Marked Woman (ML101309)MGM/89 AM
*Marnie (40156)MCA/87 AM
*Married to the Mob (ID6287OR)IE/89 DS
*The Martian Chronicles (ID6370FR)IE/89 DM
*Martin (ID6852HB)IE/90 DM
*Marty O(463480)Fox/86 AM
*Mary of Scotland (ID6452TU)IE/89 DM
Mary Poppins (023AS)Dis/81-84 AS
*Mascagni Cavalleria Rusticana (0702031)PGM/88 DS
*Mask (40173)MCA/86 AM
*The Mask (3D) (ID6910RH)IE/90 DM CLV/CAV
*The Masks of Death (ID5267LO)IE/88 DM
*Masque of the Red Death/The Premature Burial (ID5246VE)IE/88 DM
*Masquerade (474980)Fox/88 AS
*Mass Appeal (40168)MCA/85 AM
*Masters of the Universe (37073)WB/88 DS
*Matador (ID7252CV)IE/90 DM
*Matewan (ID5217LO)IE/88 DM
*Maurice (ID5253LO)IE/88 DM
Mausoleum (ID7683NL)IE/90 DM
Max Dugan Returns (123680)Fox/81-84 AM
*Max Headroom The Original Story (LV367)KL/87 AS
*Maximum Overdrive (LV395)KL/87 AS
Maximum Security (ID7265NW)IE/90 DM
McVicar (ID7525VE)IE/90 DM
Me and Him (50236)Col/90 DS
*The Mean Season (ID5146)IE/87 AM
*Mean Streets (11081)WB/87 DM
*Meatballs (VL6009)Ves/81-84 AM
*Meatballs II (VLD30405)Col/85 AM
*Meet Me in St. Louis O(ML100005)MGM/81-84 AM
*Meet Me in St. Louis (remaster) (ML101827)MGM/90 DM
*Mel Brooks' Spaceballs (ML101179)MCA/88 DS
Melvin And Howard O(10031)MCA/81-84 AM
Memorial Valley Massacre (77676)Nel/90 AS
*Memories of Me (475480)Fox/89 DS
*The Men's Club O(LV12512)Par/87 AM
*Men Don't Leave (11897)WB/90 DS
*Mercenary Fighters (ID6044ME)IE/88 DM
*Mesmerized (ID6883VE)IE/90 DM
*Messenger of Death (ID6292ME)IE/89 DS
Metalstorm — The Destruction of Jared-Syd O(40045)MCA/81-84 AS
*Metropolis (VL5090)Ves/85 DS
*Miami Spice (X-rated) (I0044)IE/88 AM CLV/CAV
*Miami Vice (80133)MCA/86 DS
*Miami Vice II The Prodigal Son (40349)MCA/86 DS
*Mickey Knows Best/The Importance of Being Donald O(534AS)Dis/87 AM
Mickey Mouse & Donald Duck Cartoons Collection One O(69AS)Dis/81-84 AM
Mickey Mouse & Donald Duck Cartoons Collection Two O(70AS)Dis/81-84 AM
Mickey Mouse & Donald Duck Cartoons Collection Three O(34AS)Dis/81-84 AM
Mickey's Christmas Carol (225AS)Dis/81-84 AS
*Micki & Maude O(VLD30456)Col/85 AM
Midnight (ID7163SO)IE/90 DM
*Midnight Cowboy (ML100193)MGM/88 AM
*Midnight Crossing (ID6187VE)IE/89 DS
Midnight Express O(VLD3275)Col/81-84 AM
*Midnight Run (40810)MCA/89 DS
*A Midsummer Night's Dream (PS188015)PA/89 AM CAV
*Mighty Joe Young O(I5032)IE/86 DCAM
*Mighty Joe Young (tinted) (ID7008TU)IE/90 DS
*The Mighty Quinn (476180)Fox/90 DS
*The Mikado (PA83061)PA/81-84 AS
*The Milagro Beanfield War (40796)MCA/88 DS
*Mildred Pierce O(457980)Fox/81-84 AM
*Mildred Pierce (10742)MGM/90 AM
*Miles from Home (766)WB/89 DS
*The Milky Way (Lloyd) (ID5356ME)IE/88 DM
*The Milky Way (Lloyd) (LVA1013)LVA/90 AM
*The Milky Way (Bunuel) (ID5356ME)IE/90 DM
*Millennium (ID7223IV)IE/90 DS
Milli Vanilli: In Motion (PA90019)PA/90 AS
Million Dollar Mystery (TVL0045)HBO/88 AS
*Mindfield (ID7723MN)IE/90 DM
A Minor Miracle...A Major Success (55005)Nel/81-84 AM
*Miracle Mile (ID6912HB)IE/90 DS
*Miracle on 34th Street (107280)Fox/87 AM
The Mirror Crack'd (ID7494HB)IE/90 DM
*Mischief (145980)Fox/85 AM
*Mischief in the Mansion (X-rated) (Z0101)IE/90 AM
*The Misfits (ML101650)MGM/90 AM
*Miss Firecracker (ID6808HB)IE/89 DS
Miss Right (ID7172SO)IE/90 DM
*Miss Sadie Thompson (ID6638RC)IE/90 DM
Missing (10034)MCA/81-84 AM
*Missing in Action (ML100557)MGM/85 AM
*Missing in Action 2 The Beginning (ML100658)MGM/85 AM
*The Mission (11639A/B)WB/87 DS
*Mission Batangus (I5010)IE/85 AM
Mission Galactica: The Cylon Attack (13003)MCA81-84 AM
*Mission Manila (ID7304VV)IE/90 DS
*Mississippi Burning (ID6566OR)IE/89 DS
Mister Magoo in Sherwood Forest (LV2320A)Par/81-84 AM
The Mistress (X-rated) (I0017)IE/81-84 AM
Mob War (ID7197VV)IE/90 DM
*Moby Dick O(463580)Fox/81-84 AM
*Modern Romance (ID6110RC)IE/88 DM
*The Moderns (77126)Nel/89 DS
Mommie Dearest (LV12633)Par/81-84 AM
*Mon Oncle (61385)Nel/86 AM
*Mon Oncle (CC1205L)Voy/90 DM
*Mona Lisa (ID6846HB)IE/90 DM
*The Money Pit (40287)MCA/86 DS
*The Monkees (ID6267RC)IE/89 DM
*The Monkees Volume 2 (ID6353RC)IE/89 DM
*Monkey Business (Marx Bros.) (40172)MCA/87 AM CLV/CAV
*Monkey Business (Rogers & Grant) (514080)Fox/88 AM
*Monkey Shines (ID6258OR)IE/89 DS
The Monster Club (ID7287IV)IE/90 DM
*The Monster Squad (IVE5187)IE/88 DS
*Monteverdi L'Orfeo (0712031)PGM/88 DS
*A Month in the Country (ID6033LO)IE/88 DM
Monty Python and the Holy Grail O(VLD3337)Col/81-84 AM
Monty Python's The Meaning of Life O(16031)MCA/81-84 AS
The Moon Is Blue (610280)Fox/81-84 AM
*Moon over Parador (40802)MCA/89 DS
Moonlighting O(10035)MCA/81-84 AM
*Moonraker O(463680)Fox/81-84 AS
*Moonraker (lb) (ML101710)MGM/90 DS
*Moonstruck (ML101135)MGM/88 DS
*Moontrap (ID6752SG)IE/89 DM
More Sport Goofy O(168AS)Dis/81-84 AM
*More! Police Squad! (LV60630/02)Par/85 AM
*Morgan Stewart's Coming Home (TVL0025)HBO/88 AM
*Morgan the Pirate (ID7684NL)IE/90 DM
*The Morning After (ID5140)IE/87 AM
*Morocco (ID5123)MCA/87 AM
Moscow on the Hudson (VLD30309)Col/85 AS
*The Mosquito Coast (11711A/B)WB/87 DS
*Motel Hell (ML100901)MGM/86 DS
*Mother (ID6308CO)IE/89 DM
The Mountain Men (VLD3340)Col/81-84 AM
*Moving (11789)WB/88 DS
*Moving Violations (146280)Fox/85 AM
*Mozart Le Nozze Di Figaro (0725031)PGM/88 DS
*Mr. & Mrs. Smith (ID6405TU)IE/89 DM
Mr. Ace (ID7162SO)IE/90 DM
*Mr. Blandings Builds a Dream House (ID6450TU)IE/89 DM
*Mr. Hulot's Holiday (CC1119L)Voy/88 AM CAV
*Mr. Lucky (ID6449TU)IE/89 DM
Mr. Magoo: Columbia Pictures Cartoons Volume 12 (30997)Col/89 AM
Mr. Mom (VL5025)Ves/81-84 AM
*Mr. North (ID6249VV)IE/89 DS
*Mr. Skeffington (ML101310)MGM/88 AM
*Mr. Smith Goes to Washington (VLD30064)Col/85 AM
*Ms.45 (ID6329RO)IE/89 DM
*The Mummy (40030)MCA/86 AM CLV/CAV
*The Muppet Movie (900180)Fox/81-84 AS
Muppet Musicians of Bremen O(807AS)Dis/81-84 AM
*The Muppets Take Manhattan (673180)Fox/85 AS
Murder by Death (VLD3348)Col/81-84 AM
Murder By Decree O(405980)Fox/81-84 AM
Murder by Numbers (ID7707MN)IE/90 DM
Murder on the Orient Express (LV87902)Par/81-84 AM
Murder One (77346)Nel/89 AS
Murmur of the Heart (ID9502OR)IE/90 DM
Murphy's Law (LV1239)IE/86 AM
*Murphy's Romance (30649)Col/81-84 AM
*Muscle Beach Party (TVL9945)HBO/88 AM
Music Box (ID7362IV)IE/90 DM
*The Music Man (11473LV)WB/86 AS
*The Mutant (VL5062)Ves/85 AS
*Mutilator (VL5102)Ves/86 AM
Mutiny on the Bounty (orig.) (ML100450)MGM/85 AM
*Mutiny on the Bounty (1962) (ML100031)MGM/88 AS
*Mutiny on the Bounty (1962 lb) (ML102030)MGM/90 DS
*My American Cousin (ID5067)IE/87 AM
*My Beautiful Launderette (LV385)KL/87 AS
My Bloody Valentine (LV5431?) (LV1447)Par/81-84 AM
*My Chauffer (VL5135)Ves/86 AM
*My Darling Clementine (139880)Fox/90 DM
*My Demon Lover (32821)Col/87 AM
*My Dinner with Andre (ID5307PA)IE/89 DM
*My Fair Lady (703880)Fox/81-84 AS
*My Favorite Brunette (ID6882NE)IE/90 DM CLV/CAV
My Favorite Year (ML100188)MGM/81-84 AM
My Left Foot (ID7370HB)IE/90 DM
*My Life As a Dog (LV12651)Par/88 AM
My Little Girl (ID7127FL)IE/90 DM
*My Mom's a Werewolf (ID7119FL)IE/90 DM
*My Science Project (360)Dis/86 AS
*My Stepmother is an Alien (31028)Col/89 AS
My Tutor O(40022)MCA/81-84 AM
My Wonderful Life (70326)Col/90 AS
*Mysterious Island (VLD3349)Col/81-84 AM
*Mystic Pizza (ID6398VV)IE/89 DS
*Nadine (384180)Fox/88 AM
*The Naked Gun (LV32100)Par/89 DM
*The Naked Jungle (LV6012)Par/90 AM
*The Naked Kiss (CC1184L)Voy/89 DM
*The Naked Prey (LV6525)Par/90 AM
*The Name of the Rose (1342)Nel/87 AS
*Napoleon (40086)MCA/86 AS CLV/CAV
*The Narrow Margin (ID6947TU)IE/90 DM CLV/CAV
Nashville (LV8821)Par/81-84 AS
Nasty Hero (09646)Col/90 AM
Nate & Hayes (LV1549)Par/81-84 AS
*National Geographic Man-Eaters of India (VL1077)Ves/87 AM
*National Lampoon's Christmas Vacation (11889)WB/90 DS
*National Lampoon's European Vacation (11521LV)WB/86 AM
National Lampoon's Vacation (11315LV)WB/81-84 AM
*National Velvet (ML100480)MGM/89 AM
*Native Son (LL9963)Ves/88 AM
Natural (VLD30380)Col/85 AS
*Naughty Marietta (ML100371)MGM/85 AM
*Nazarin (ID6802CS)IE/90 DM
*Near Dark (ID6585HB)IE/89 DS
*Necromancer (ID7199VV)IE/90 DS
Neighbors O(VLD3352)Col/81-84 AM
Network (ML100012)MGM/81-84 AM

*Nevada Smith (LV65322)Par/90 AM
*Never a Dull Moment (ID6995TU)IE/90 DM
Never Cry Wolf (182AS)Dis/81-84 AS
*Never Give a Sucker an Even Break (22015)MCA/87 AM CLV/CAV
Never on Tuesday (LV12731)Par/89 AM
Never Say Never Again (11337LV)WB/81-84 AS
*Never Too Young to Die (900466)Nel/87 AS
*The NeverEnding Story (11399LV)WB/85 AS
*The New Adventures of Pippi Longstocking (35008)Col/89 AS
*New Adventures of Winnie the Pooh: Newfound Friends/Great Honey Pot Robbery (617AS)Dis/89 DM
*The New Centurions (ID6380RC)IE/89 DM
*The New Kids (VLD30409)Col/85 AS
A New Life (LV32160)Par/89 AM
The New Three Stooges, Vol. I & II (75225)Nel/85 AM
*New Wave Hookers (X-rated) (Z0056)IE/89 AM CLV/CAV
*New York Stories (952AS)Dis/90 DM
*New York, New York O(459680)Fox/81-84 AS
*"New York, New York" (ML10321)MGM/89 DS
Newsfront (90025)Nel/85 AM
*Next of Kin (670)WB/90 DS
*Niagra (513880)Fox/88 AM
*Nicholas and Alexandra (30072)Col/86 AM
*A Night at the Opera (CC1131L)Voy/88 DCAM CAV
*A Night at the Opera (CC1202L)Voy/90 DM
*A Night in the Life of Jimmy Reardon (385580)Fox/88 AS
*'night Mother (40542)MCA/87 AM
*Night of the Creeps (TVL9959)HBO/88 AS
Night of the Demons (LV23019)Rep/89 DS
*The Night of the Generals O(VLD30430)Col/85 AM
*The Night of the Hunter (CC1128L)Voy/88 AM
*Night of the Living Dead O(DF18)3M/85 AM
*Night of the Living Dead (16000)IE/85 AM
Night of the Living Dead (LV27460)Rep/90 DM
*Night Patrol (I5025)IE/85 AM
Night Porter (150250)Nel/81-84 AM
Night Shift (20006LV)WB/81-84 AS
*A Night to Remember (Loretta Young) (32000)Col/89 AM
The Night Train to Kathmandu (LV12605)Par/90 AM
*Night Zoo (ID6155NW)IE/89 DS
The Nightcomers (ID7685NL)IE/90 DM
Nighthawks O(12021)MCA/81-84 AM
*The Nightingale (Faerie Tale Theatre) (639280)Fox/81-84 AM
*A Nightmare on Elm Street (15035)IE/85 AM
*A Nightmare on Elm Street 2 Freddy's Revenge (I5047)IE/86 AM
*A Nightmare on Elm Street 3 The Dream Warriors (ID5053)IE/87 DS
*A Nightmare on Elm Street 4: The Dream Master (ID6218ME)IE/89 DS
*A Nightmare on Elms Street 5 The Dream Child (ID7189ME)IE/90 DS
*91/2 Weeks (ML100973)MGM/87 DS
*976-EVIL (09876)Col/89 AS
Nine To Five (109980)MCA/81-84 AS
*1900 (LV88043)Par/90 AM
1941 O(16014)MCA/81-84 AM
*1969 (ID6750ME)IE/89 DS
*1984 (ID6236IV)IE/89 DM
*Ninja Turf (30648)Col/86 AM
*Ninotchka (ML100115)MGM/85 AM
*The Ninth Configuration (ID5199NW)IE/88 DM
No Holds Barred (90206)Col/89 AS
*No Man of Her Own (40391)MCA/87 AM CLV/CAV
*No Man's Land (ID5254OR)IE/88 DS
*No Mercy (30791)Col/87 AS
*No Retreat, No Surrender (ID6506NW)IE/89 DM
*No Small Affair (30429)Col/85 AS
*No Way Out (TVL0051)HBO/88 AS
*Nobody's Fool (ID5164)IE/88 DM
Norma Rae (108280)Fox/81-84 AS
*North By Northwest (ML100104) MGM/81-84 AM
*North by Northwest (CC1145L)Voy/88 AM CAV
*North by Northwest (lb) (CC1226L)Voy/90 DM
North Dallas Forty (LV8773)Par/81-84 AM
*North to Alaska (121280)Fox/90 DS
*Nothing in Common (TVL9960)HBO/88 AM
Nothing Sacred O(N/A)3M/86 AM
*Nothing to Hide (X-rated) (I0048)IE/88 AM
*Notorious O(801180)Fox/81-84 AM
*Notorious (CC1204L)Voy/90 DCDM
*Notorious (CC1203L)Voy/90 DCDM CAV
Now & Forever O(11021)MCA/81-84 AS
*Now Voyager O(457280)Fox/85 AM
*Now Voyager (ML101316)MGM/88 AM
Nudo Di Donna (ID7485PA)IE/90 DM
Nurses of the 407th (X-rated) (I0003)IE/81-84 AM CLV/CAV

*Nuts (11756)WB/88 DS
The Nutty Professor (LV6712)Par/81-84 AM
Obsession O(VLD3357)Col/81-84 AM
*The Octagon (ID6045ME)IE/88 DM
*October (ID6253CO)IE/89 DM
*Octopussy O(471580)Fox/81-84 AS
*Octopussy (ML100294)MGM/81-84 AS
*Octopussy (lb) (ML101640)WB/90 DS
Odd Couple (LV8026)Par/81-84 AM
*Odd Man Out (LV12575)Par/88 AM
The Odessa File O(VLD30317)Col/85 AM
*Of Human Bondage O(N/A)3M/86 AM
*Off Limits (165780)Fox/89 AS
*Offbeat (455AS)Dis/87 AM
*An Officer and a Duck O(258AS)Dis/85 AM
An Officer And A Gentlemen (LV14672)Par/81-84 AM
*The Official Story (ID5344PA)IE/89 DM
*Oh God! You Devil (11418LV)WB/85 AM
Oklahoma! (702080)Fox/81-84 AS
*Oklahoma! (lb) (702085)Fox/90 DS
Old Boyfriends (20086)Nel/89 AM
*Old Gringo (50206)Col/90 DS
Old Yeller (37AS)Dis/81-84 AM
*Oliver! (LVD30526)Col/86 AS
*Oliver Twist (LV12571)Par/88 AM
The Omen (107980)Fox/81-84 AS
On a Clear Day You Can See Forever (LV69272)Par/81-84 AM
On Dangerous Ground (ID6978TU)IE/90 DM
On Golden Pond O(903780)Fox/81-84 AM
On Golden Pond (J26031)J2/90 DM
On Her Majesty's Secret Service O(460480)Fox/81-84 AM
*On the Town (ML100057)MGM/81-84 AM
On the Waterfront (30354)Col/81-84 AM
*On Your Honor (X-rated) (Z0074)IE/89 AM
*Once Bitten (VL5115)Ves/86 AM
*Once Upon a Honeymoon (ID6451TU)IE/89 DM
*Once Upon a Time in America (20017)WB/85 AM
*Once Upon a Time in the West (LV6830)Par/85 AM
The One & Only, Genuine Original Family Band (42017AS)Dis/81-84 AM (30AS)/86
*One Crazy Summer (11602LV)WB/87 AM
*One Day in the Life of Ivan Denisovich (ID6276SO)IE/89 DM
*One Eyed Jacks (LV65372)Par/90 AM
*One Flew over the Cuckoo's Nest (LV4531)SZ/88 DS
*One from the Heart (VLD3360)Col/81-84 AS
*One Magic Christmas (475AS)Dis/87 AS
*One Million Years BC O(N/A)3M/86 AM
*One More Saturday Night (30703)Col/86 AS
*Only the Valiant (LV23062)Rep/90 DM
Only When I Laugh (VLD3362)Col/81-84 AM
Orca, The Killer Whale (LV8935)Par/81-84 AM
*Ordeal by Innocence (ML100057)MGM/86 AM
Ordinary People (LV8964)Par/81-84 AM
*The Original Adventures of Baron Munchasusen (Baron Prasil) (ID7294PO)IE/90 DM
*Opera Do Malandro (ID6157VV)IE/89 DS
*Operation Petticoat (ID6089RE)IE/89 DM
*Opportunity Knocks (40964)MCA/90 DM
*Options (ID6484VE)IE/89 DS
*Orphans (ID5261LO)IE/88 DM
*Otello (Zefferelli) (ID5152)IE/87 DS CLV/CAV
The Other Side of Julie (X-rated) (I0021)IE/81-84 AM
Our Daily Bread (ID7507DS)IE/90 DM
*Our Hospitality (ID6863HB)IE/90 DS CLV/CAV
*Our Man Flint (113180)Fox/90 DM
*Our Relations/Murder Case O(M18)3M/86 AM
*Our Town (111)MV/87 AM
*Out Cold (ID6794HB)IE/90 DM
*Out of Africa (40350)MCA/86 DS
*Out of Bounds (30722)Col/87 AS
*Out of the Dark (09896)Col/89 AS
*Out of the Darkness (ID6928VK)IE/90 DM
The Out-Of-Towners (LV6914)Par/81-84 AM
Outland (20002LV)WB/81-84 AS
*The Outlaw O(N/A)3M/86 AM
*The Outlaw Josey Wales (11125A/B)WB/87 DS
Outlaw Ladies (X-rated) (I0013)IE/81-84 AM
*Outrageous Fortune (569AS)Dis/88 DS
*The Outsiders (11310)WB/87 DS
*Over the Top (11713)WB/87 DS
*Overboard (474680)Fox/88 AS
*The Owl and the Pussycat (ID6106RC)IE/88 DM
*The Ox-Bow Incident (113180)Fox/90 DM
*Oxford Blues O(472580)Fox/87 AS
*P.K. and the Kid (ID5156)IE/88 DM
*P.O.W. The Escape (I5059)IE/86 AS
*The Package (ID9504OR)IE/90 DS

*Paint It Black (ID7332VE)IE/90 DS
Paint Your Wagon (LV6933)Par/81-84 AS
*Painted Stallion (LV25038)Rep/90 DM
*The Pajama Game (35085)WB/90 DM
*Pale Rider (11475LV)WB/85 AS
*The Paleface (40106)MCA/86 AM
*The Palm Beach Story (40380)MCA/87 AM CLV/CAV
*Palm Springs Weekend (12008)WB/90 DM
*The Paper Chase (104680)Fox/90 DM
Paper Moon (LV8465)Par/81-84 AM
Paperhouse (ID6660VE)IE/90 DS
Papillon (709080)Fox/81-84 AM
*Paradise Alley (ID5116)MCA/87 AM
*Paramedics (ID6188VE)IE/89 DS
*Pardon Us/The Chimp O(N/A)3M/87 AM
Pardone Mon Affaire O(30125)Nel/81-84 AM
The Parent Trap (107AS)Dis/81-84 AM
*Parenthood (40921)MCA/90 DS
*Parents (ID6485VE)IE/89 DS
*Paris, Texas (145780)Fox/90 DM CLV/CAV
*Parsifal (ID6420CO)IE/89 DS
*Part 2 Walking Tall (LL9910)Ves/85 AM
*Party Incorporated (ID6548NW)IE/89 DM CLV/CAV
*Pascali's Island (ID6320IV)IE/89 DM
*Pass the Ammo (ID6126IV)IE/88 DS
*A Passage to India (VLD30485)Col/85 AS
*The Passion of Beatrice (ID6225VV)IE/89 DM
Paternity (LV1401)Par/81-84 AM
*Paths of Glory (CC1157L)Voy/89 DM
*The Patriot (VL5193)Ves/87 AM
Patton (100580)Fox/81-84 AS
*Patton (lb) (100585)Fox/89 DS
*Patty Hearst (ID7191ME)IE/90 DM
*Patty Rocks (ID6014VV)IE/88 DM
Pauline at the Beach (ID7188ME)IE/90 DM
*The Pawnbroker (ID6261RE)IE/89 DM
Peacemaker (ID7674FR)IE/90 DS
*Pecos Bill (ID6283SO)IE/89 DS CAV
*Pee-Wee's Big Adventure (11523LV)WB/86 AS
*Peeping Tom (X-rated) (Z0065)IE/88 AM CLV/CAV
*Peggy Sue Got Married (380080)Fox/87 AM
*Pendulum (ID6300RC)IE/89 DM
*Penn & Teller Get Killed (672)WB/90 DS
*Pennies from Heaven (ML100191)MGM/89 AM
Penny Serenade (LV23173)Rep/90 DM
The Penthouse (X-rated) (Z0100)IE/90 AM
*Perfect (VLD30494)Col/86 AS
*Perfect Witness (ID7488HB)IE/90 DS
Performance (11131LV)WB/81-84 AM
*Perils of Gwendoline (VL5071)Ves/85 AS
Permanent Record (LV32039)Par/89 DS
*Personal Services (VL5221)Ves/88 AM
*Pet Sematary (LV1949)Par/89 DS
*Peter Gunn Vol. 1 (ID6914RH)IE/90 DM
*Peter Pan (ID7810GT)IE/90 DS
Pete's Dragon (10AS)Dis/81-84 AS
Phantasm O(406680)Ves/81-84 AS
Phantasm (20056)Nel/89 AM
*Phantasm II (40839)MCA/89 DS
*The Phantom of Liberty (ID5349ME)IE/88 DM
*Phantom of the Mall: Eric's Revenge (ID7195FR)IE/90 DM
*Phantom of the Opera (LVD9008)Lum/90 DS
*Phantom of the Opera (1943) (21011)MCA/87 DM CLV/CAV
Phantom of the Opera (Englund) (77016)Col/90 DS
*Phantom of the Paradise (147380)Fox/88 AS
Phase IV (LV8470)Par/81-84 AM
*The Philadelphia Story (ML100059)MGM/87 AM
*Physical Evidence (ID6537VE)IE/89 DS
*The Pick-Up Artist (152980)Fox/88 AS
*The Picture of Dorian Gray (ML100566)MGM/85 AM
*Pierrot le Fou (ID7455IN)IE/90 DM
*Pin (ID6450NW)IE/89 DM
*Pin Up Girl/Down Argentine Way (174180)Fox/90 DS
Pink and Pretty (X-rated) (I0037)IE/81-84 AM
*Pink Cadillac (23771)WB/90 DS
Pink Floyd The Wall (ML100268)MGM/81-84 AS
*Pink Nights (ID6015NW)IE/88 AM
The Pink Panther O(450980)Fox/81-84 AM
The Pink Panther Strikes Again O(456480)Fox/81-84 AM
*Pinocchio (anim.) O(239AS)Dis/85 AM
*Pinnochio (anim.) O(239CS)Dis/87 AM CAV
*Pinocchio (Faerie Tale Theatre) (639080)Fox/81-84 AM
*Pinocchio and the Emperor of the Night (ID5316NW)IE/88 AS
Pirahna II The Spawning (13895)Nel/81-84 AM
*The Pirate (ML100101)MGM/89 DM
*Pirates of Penzance (Ronstadt) (17011)MCA/81-84 AS
*The Pirates of Penzance (PA83059)PA/81-84 AS

A Place In The Sun (LV5815)Par/81-84 AM
*Places in the Heart (683880)Fox/85 AM
*The Plainsman (24001)MCA/88 AM
*Plan Nine from Outer Space (I5070)IE/87 AM CLV/CAV
*Planes, Trains and Automobiles (LV32036)Par/88 DS
*Platoon (TVL0040)HBO/88 AS
*Platoon (ID6084VE)IE/88 DS
*Platoon Leader (ID6356ME)IE/89 DS
Play It Again Sam (LV8112)Par/81-84 AM
Play Misty For Me (12024)MCA/81-84 AM
Playing Away (902366)Nel/89 AM
*Playing for Keeps (40563)MCA/87 DS
Plaza Suite (LV8046)Par/81-84 AM
*The Point (ID5240VE)IE/88 DM CLV/CAV
*The Pointsman (ID6189VE)IE/89 DS
*Police Academy (200016LV)WB/85 AM
*Police Academy 2 Their First Assignment (20020LV)WB/85 AM
*Police Academy 3 Back in Training (20022LV)WB/86 AM
*Police Academy 4: Citizens on Patrol (20025)WB/87 DM
*Police Academy 5: Assignment Miami Beach (20025)WB/88 DM
Police Academy 6: City Under Siege (11873)WB/89 DM
*Police Squad! Help Wanted (LV60630)Par/85 AM
Pollyanna (45AS)Dis/81-84 AM
*Poltergeist (ML100165)MGM/81-84 AS
*Poltergeist (lb) (ML101639)MGM/89 DS
*Poltergeist II (ML100940)MGM/86 DS
*Poltergeist III (ML101250)MGM/89 DS
*Pop Goes the Comic (ID7508DS)IE/90 DM
*The Pope of Greenwich Village (ID6473MG)IE/89 DM
Popeye (LV1171)Par/81-84 AS
*Pork Chop Hill (ID6513MG)IE/89 DM
Porky's (114980)Fox/81-84 AM
Porky's II: The Next Day (129480)Fox/81-84 AM
*Porky's Revenge (146380)Fox/86 AM
Porsche, The Girl, The Car (X-rated) (Z0112)IE/90 AM
Posse (LB8316)Par/90 AM
*The Postman Always Rings Twice (1946) (ML101001)MGM/89 AM
*The Postman Always Rings Twice (remake) O(707780)Fox/81-84 AM
*Pot O'Gold O(M20)3M/86 AM
*Power (LV401)KL/86 AM
PRAY-TV (ID7526VE)IE/90 DM
*A Prayer for the Dying (ID5177)IE/88 DS
*Predator (151580)Fox/88 AS
*The Presidio (LV31978)Par/89 DS
Pretty Baby (LV8940)Par/81-84 AM
*Pretty in Pink (LV1858)Par/87 DS
*Pretty Kill (ID5165)IE/88 DM
*Prick Up Your Ears (ID5520VV)IE/88 DS
The Pride of the Yankees O(714580)Fox/81-84 AM
*Prime Evil (ID6252NW)IE/89 DM
*Prince of Darkness (40761)MCA/88 DS
*The Prince of Pennsylvania (32828)Col/89 AM
Prince of the City (22021LV)WB/81-84 AM
*Princess and the Pea (Faerie Tale Theatre) (639780)Fox/81-84 AM
*The Princess and the Pirate (30575)Nel/85 AM
*The Princess Bride (CC1140L)Voy/88 DS CAV
*The Princess Bride (77096)Nel/88 DS
*The Princess Bride (CC1194L)Voy/89 DS
*The Principal (ID5286TS)IE/88 DS
*Prison (ID5270NW)IE/88 DS
*The Prisoner Volume 1 (ID6201MP)IE/89 DM
*The Prisoner Volume 2 (ID6202MP)IE/89 DM
*The Prisoner Volume 3 (ID6203MP)IE/89 DM
*The Prisoner Volume 4 (ID6204MP)IE/89 DM
*The Prisoner Volume 5 (ID6205MP)IE/89 DM
*The Prisoner Volume 6 (ID6206MP)IE/89 DM
*The Prisoner Volume 7 (ID6207MP)IE/89 DM
*The Prisoner Volume 8 (ID6208MP)IE/89 DM
*The Prisoner Volume 9 (ID6209MP)IE/89 DM
*The Prisoner Volume 10 (ID6210MP)IE/90 DM
*The Prisoner Volume 11 (ID6211MP)IE/90 DM
*The Prisoner Volume 12 (ID6212MP)IE/90 DM
*The Prisoner Volume 13 (ID6213MP)IE/90 DM
*The Prisoner Volume 14 (ID6214MP)IE/90 DM
*The Prisoner Volume 15 (ID6215MP)IE/90 DM
*The Prisoner Volume 16 (ID6216MP)IE/90 DM
*The Prisoner Volume 17 (ID6217MP)IE/90 DM
*Prisoners of the Lost Universe O(N/A)DF/85 AM
Private Benjamin (11075LV)WB/81-84 AM
Private Eyes (VL5001)Ves/81-84 AM
Private Lessons O(16027)MCA/81-84 AM
*The Private Life of Henry VIII (31005)Nel/86 AM
*Private Resort (VLD30539)Col/86 AM
Private School (40032)MCA/81-84 AM
*Prizzi's Honor (VL5106)Ves/86 DS

The Producers O(405880)Fox/81-84 AM
*The Producers (CC1136L)Voy/88 AM
*The Producers (20516)Nel/88 AM
*The Professionals (30390)Col/87 AS
*Project X (519280)Fox/87 AS
Prom Night (12022)MCA/81-84 AM
Prom Night III The Last Kiss (ID7364IV)IE/90 DS
*Promised Land (ID6024VE)IE/88 DS
*The Protector (11538LV)WB/86 AS
Protocol (11434LV)WB/85 AS
Psycho (11003)MCA/81-84 AM
Psycho II O(40008)MCA/81-84 AS
*Psycho III (40359)MCA/87 DS
*Public Enemy O(458980)Fox/87 AM
*Puccini Madama Butterfly (0715041)PGM/89 DS
*Puccini Tosca (0715021)PGM/88 DS
Pulse (35004)Col/89 AS
*Pumping Ethel (X-rated) (Z0065)IE/89 AM CLV/CAV
*Pumpkinhead (ML101605)MGM/89 AS
*Punch Line (35010)Col/89 AS
Puppetmaster (LV12733)Par/90 DS
*The Puppetoon Movie (ID6122IV)IE/89 DM CLV/CAV
*Purgatory (ID6565NS)IE/89 DM
*Purple People Eater (ID6389ME)IE/89 DM
*Purple Rain (11398)WB/81-84 AS
*The Purple Rose of Cairo (VL5068)Ves/85 AM
*Pygmalion (CC1133L)Voy/88 AM
*Python Wolf (ID7262VK)IE/90 DM
Quackser Fortune Has a Cousin in the Bronx (ID6595VC)IE/90 DM
*Quadrophenia (VLD3368)Col/81-84 AS
*Quatermass II (ID6230CO)IE/89 DM CLV/CAV
*Queen Christina (ML100531)MGM/90 DM
*Queen of Spades (ID6842CO)IE/90 DM
Quest For Fire (114880)Fox/81-84 AS
Quest for the Mighty Sword (59256)Col/90 DM
*Quicksilver (30644)Col/86 AS
*Quiet Cool (32768)Col/87 AM
*The Quiet Earth (304280)Fox/89 DS
Rabbit Test (900036)Nel/89 AM
Race For Your Life Charlie Brown (LV8850)Par/81-84 AM
Racing with the Moon (LV1668)Par/81-84 AM
*The Racoon's Collection O(13555)Nel/81-84 AS
*RAD (13085)Nel/86 AS
*Radio Days (TVL0014)HBO/88 AM
Raggedy Man O(10032)MCA/81-84 AM
Raging Bull O(452380)Fox/81-84 AS
Ragtime (LV1486)Par/81-84 AM
Raiders of the Lost Ark (LV1376)Par/81-84 AS
Raiders of the Lost Ark (LV12762)/81-84 AS CAV
*Rain Man (ML101648)MGM/89 AM
*The Rainbow (ID6664VE)IE/90 DS
*Rainbow Brite Vol. 2 (CL1510)Ves/85 AM
*The Rainmaker (LV56062)Par/90 AM
Raise The Titanic (902380)Fox/81-84 AM
*Raising Arizona (519180)Fox/87 DS
*Ralph Bakshi's Street Fight (1093)Acd/88 AM
*Rambo O(3002)HBO/86 AS
*Rambo First Blood Part II (ID6119IV)IE/89 DS
*Rambo III (ID6170IV)IE/88 DS
*Ran (373280)Fox/87 AS
*Rancho Notorious (ID7017TU)IE/90 DM
*Rapunzel (Faerie Tale Theatre) (637080)Fox/81-84 AM
*Rascal Dazzle O(13245)Nel/85 AM
*Rashomon (CC1149L)Voy/89 DS
*The Rating's Game (LV2385)Par/86 AM
The Raven (VL4021)Ves/81-84 AM
*The Raven/The Black Cat (40386)PA/85 AM
*Raw Courage O(I5019)IE/85 AM
*Raw Deal (TVL9982)HBO/88 AM
*Rawhead Rex (ID5233VE)IE/88 DM
*The Razor's Edge (30410)Col/85 AS
*Re-Animator (VL5114)Ves/86 AM
Real Bullets (ID7317VK)IE/90 DM
*Real Genius (VLD30568)Col/86 AS
*Real Men (474380)Fox/88 AS
Rear Window (40081)MCA/81-84 AM
*Rebecca of Sunnybrook Farm/The Little Colonel (170280)Fox/89 DS
*Rebel (VL5184)Ves/87 AS
Rebel Without A Cause (1011LV)WB/81-84 AM
Reckless (ML100421)MGM/81-84 AS
*Recruits (VL5179)Ves/87 AM
*The Red Balloon/White Mane (C2000L)Voy/86 AM
*Red Dawn (ML100499)MGM/85 AS
*Red Desert (ID6792CS)IE/90 DM
*Red Headed Stranger (901536)Nel/87 AS
*Red Heat (Arnold) (ID6244IV)IE/89 DS

*Red Heat (Linda) (IVE5189)IE/88 DS
*The Red Pony (ID6232RE)IE/89 DM
*Red River O(465580)Fox/85 AM
*Red River (101724)MGM/90 DM
*Red Scorpion (ID6693SG)IE/89 DS
*The Red Shoes (LV1252-2)Par/88 DM CLV/CAV
*Red Sonja O(473380)Fox/87 AS
*The Red Tent (LV80412)Par/90 AM
Reds (LV1331)Par/81-84 AM
*Reform School Girls (I5083)IE/87 AM
*Reilly: The Ace of Spies (ID6901HB)IE/90 DM
The Rejuvenator (ID7181SO)IE/90 DS
*Relentless (90496)Col/90 DS
*Remo Williams (TVL3676)HBO/88 AS
*Rendez-Vous (ID7389CS)IE/90 DM
*Renegades (40895)MCA/89 DS
*Rent-A-Cop (ID6580HB)IE/89 DS
*Rented Lips (ID6178IV)IE/89 DS
*Repentance (ID5406ME)PA/88 DM
*Repo Man (40071)MCA/85 AM
The Rescue (869AS)Dis/89 DS
*Retribution (ID6456VV)IE/89 DS
*The Return of Frank James (132880)Fox/90 DM
Return of Indiana Joan (X-rated) (Z0096)IE/90 AM
Return of Johnny Wadd (X-rated) (Z0063)IE/90 AM
*Return of the Killer Tomatoes (ID6153NW)IE/89 DS
*Return of the Living Dead (ID6851HB)IE/90 DM
*Return of the Living Dead Part II (ID5272LO)IE/88 DS
The Return of Martin Guerre (13045)Nel/81-84 AM
*Return of the Jedi (147880)Fox/86 DS
*Return of the Jedi lb (147885)Fox/90 DS CLV/CAV
Return of the Pink Panther O(903180)Fox/81-84 AM
Return of the Pink Panther (J26064)J2/90 DM
*Return of the Swamp Thing (90176)Col/89 AS
*Return of the Vampire (ID6711RC)IE/90 DM
*Return to Oz (341AS)Dis/86 AS
*Return to Snowy River (699AS)Dis/88 DS
*Revenge (50216)Col/90 DS
*Revenge of the Nerds (143980)Fox/85 AS
*Revenge of the Nerds II (151480)Fox/88 AS
Revenge of the Pink Panther (461080)Fox/81-84 AM
*Revolution (11532LV)WB/86 DS
*Rhinestone (143880)Fox/85 AS
Rich and Famous (ML100111)MGM/81-84 AM
Rich and Strange (ID7407NE)IE/90 DM
*Ricochet Rabbit (ID6616HA)IE/90 DM
*Riders of the Storm (76816)Nel/88 AM
The Right Stuff (20014LV)WB/81-84 AS
*Rikky and Pete (475080)Fox/89 DS
*Rio Lobo (701680)Fox/90 DS
*The Rise of Catherine the Great (ID7687NL)IE/90 DM
Risky Business (11323LV)WB/81-84 AS
*Rita, Sue & Bob Too (ID5251LO)IE/88 DM
*The River (Renoir) (CC1176L)Voy/89 DM
*The River (40160)MCA/85 AS
*River of Death (31128)WB/90 DS
*River of No Return (513980)Fox/88 AS
*The River Rat (LV1642)Par/85 AM
*River's Edge (76906)Nel/87 AM
*Road House (ML101776)MGM/89 DS
*Road to Utopia (40109)MCA/88 AM
*Road Warrior (11181LV)WB/81-84 AS
*The Robe (102280)Fox/89 DS
*Robin Hood O(228AS)Dis/81-84 AM
*Robinson Crusoe of Clipper Island (LV25045)Rep/90 DM
*Robocop (ID5168)IE/88 DS
*Robot Monster (ID7164SO)IE/90 DM CLV/CAV
*Rock and Rule (ML100728) MGM/81-84 DS
*Rocketship X-M (ID5109)IE/87 AM CLV/CAV
*Rockey X (X-rated) (Z0054)IE/89 AM
*Rockey X The Final Round (X-rated) (Z0067)IE/89 AM
Rockin' with Seka (X-rated) (I0010)IE/81-84 AM
Rocky O(454680)Fox/81-84 AS
Rocky II O(456580)Fox/81-84 AS
Rocky III O(470880)Fox/81-84 AS
*Rocky IV (473580)Fox/86 DS
Rodan (VL3013)Ves/81-84 AM
*Roger Ramjet (ID6728RH)IE/89 DM
*Rollerball (ID6765MG)IE/89 DS
Rolling Thunder (ID6904VE)IE/90 DM
Roman Holiday (LV6204)Par/81-84 AM
Romance with a Double Bass (ID7479PA)IE/90 DM
Romancing The Stone (135880) Fox/81-84 AS
*Romeo and Juliet (Zefirelli) (LV6809)Par/81-84 AM
*Romeo & Juliet (ballet) (ID6839CO)IE/90 DM
*Romero (ID7217VK)IE/90 DM
*Rooftops (ID6633IV)IE/89 DS

*Room Service O(LL936)VA/85 AM
*A Room with a View (691580)Fox/87 AS
Roomates (X-rated) (N/A)IE/81-84 AM
*Rooster Cogburn (ID5117)IE/87 AM
*Rope (40110)MCA/85 AM
*The Rosary Murders (ID5183)IE/88 DS
The Rose Garden (31142)WB/90 AM
*Rose Marie (ML100374)MGM/86 AM
The Rose (109280)Fox/81-84 AS
Rosemary's Baby (LV6831)Par/81-84 AM
*Rossini La Cenerentola (0725021)PGM/88 DS
Rough Cut (LV1213)Par/81-84 AM
*Round Midnight (11603A/B)WB/87 DS
*Roxanne (30853)Col/87 AS
RSVP (VL4159)Ves/85 AM
*Rude Awakening (ID7114HB)IE/90 DS
*The Rules of the Game (CC1150L)Voy/89 DCDM CAV
*The Ruling Class (ID7556NL)IE/90 DM
Rumblefish O(40056)MCA/81-84 AS
*Rumpelstiltskin (Faerie Tale Theatre) (639180)Fox/81-84 AM
Runaway (VLD30469)Col/85 AS
*Runaway Train (ML100867)MGM/86 DS
Running Brave (183AS)Dis/81-84 AS
*The Running Man (ID5234VE)IE/88 DS
*Running on Empty (11843)WB/89 AM
*Running Scared (ML101008)MGM/87 DS
*Russkies (ID5260LO)IE/88 DS
*The Russians Are Coming, the Russians Are Coming, O(4573-80)Fox/81-84 AM
*Rustler's Rhapsody (LV1781)Par/86 DS
*Ruthless People (485)Dis/87 DS
Rx for Sex (X-rated) (Z0129)IE/90 AM
*Sabotage (CC1117L)Voy/88 AM
*Saboteur (40111)MCA/86 AM
*Sabrina (LV5402)Par/90 AM
*The Sacrifice (ID5343PA)IE/89 DM
*Sagebrush Trail/Randy Rides Alone (I5056)IE/86 AS
*Sahara O(30098)Col/88 AM
*Saigon Commandos (ID5274ME)IE/88 DM
*Salaam Bombay! (ID6761VV)IE/89 DS
*Salome (0722091)PGM/89 DS
*Salome's Last Dance (ID6247VE)IE/89 DS
Salsa (31001)WB/88 DS
*Salt of the Earth (VP1005L)Voy/88 AM
*Salvador (VL5167)Ves/86 AM
*Same Time, Next Year (ID5124)MCA/87 AM CLV/CAV
*Sammy and Rosie Get Laid (ID5216LO)IE/88 DM
Samson & Delilah (LV67262)Par/81-84 AM
*San Francisco (ML100474)MGM/85 AM
*Sands of Iwo Jima (ID6087RE)IE/89 DM
*Sanjuro O(60635)Nel/86 AM
*Santa Claus The Movie (I5054)IE/86 AS
*Santa Fe Trail O(N/A)3M/85 AM
*Saps at Sea/Ollie the Eighth O(N/A)3M/86 AM
*Satisfaction (165580)Fox/88 AS
Saturday Night Fever (PG-rated) (LV1113)Par/81-84 AS U/(R-rated)
Saturn III (9004-80)Fox/81-84 AS
Savage Beach (90706)Col/90 AM
*Savage Streets (VK5058)Ves/85 AM
Savannah Smiles (20585)Nel/81-84 AM
Save the Tiger (LV8479)Par/81-84 AM
*Saving Grace (21895)Nel/86 AM
*Sawdust and Tinsel O(60305)Nel/81-84 AM
*Say Anything (170180)Fox/90 DS
*Say Yes (30629)Col/86 AM
*Scandal (ID6809HB)IE/89 DS
Scandal in a Small Town (ID7101VK)IE/90 DM
Scandalous (VL5038)Ves/81-84 AM
Scanners (20805)Nel/81-84 AM
*Scaramouche (CC1132L)Voy/88 DCAM CAV
*Scaramouche (CC1193L)Voy/89 DM
*Scarface (21020)MCA/85 AM
Scarface (40047)MCA/81-84 AS
*The Scarlet Pimpernel (ID7688NL)IE/90 DM
*Scavengers (1119)Acd/88 AM
*Scenes from the Class Struggle in Beverly Hills (ID6762VV)IE/90 DS
*School Daze (35006)Col/89 AS
*Scooby-Doo (ID6615HA)IE/90 DM
*Scorpion (30814)Col/87 AM
*Screen Test (30578)Col/86 AM
*Scrooge! (712680)Fox/81-84 AS
*Scrooged (LV32054)Par/89 DS
*The Sea Chase (11374)WB/90 DS
*The Sea Hawk O(469580)Fox/85 AM
*Sea of Love (40883)MCA/90 DS
*Sea of Love (lb) (41007)MCA/90 DS
Search and Destroy (ID7205VK)IE/90 DM
*The Searchers (1012LV)WB/81-84 AM
*Second Sight (659)WB/90 DS
Secret Admirer (ID7499HB)IE/90 DS
*Secret Agent (CC1118L)Voy/88 AM
*The Secret Life of Walter Mitty (30625)Nel/85 AM
*The Secret of N.I.M.H (ML100211)MGM/81-84 AS U/90 DS
The Seduction of Joe Tynan O(10024)MCA/81-84 AM
*The Secret of My Success (40637)MCA/87 DS
*See No Evil (ID6444RC)IE/89 DM
*See No Evil, Hear No Evil (70226)Col/90 DS
*See You in the Morning (657)WB/90 DS
Seems Like Old Times (VLD5545)Col/81-84 AM
*Seize the Day (ID6849HB)IE/90 DM
*Self Defense (ID6561ME)IE/89 DM
Semi-Tough O(451780)Fox/81-84 AM
The Sender (LV1537)Par/81-84 AS
Sensuous Moments (X-rated) (Z0113)IE/90 AM
*September (ID6059OR)IE/88 DM
*September Affair (LV5012)Par/89 DM
Serial (LV1191)Par/81-84 AM
*The Serpent and the Rainbow (40772)MCA/88 DS
Serpico (LV8689)Par/81-84 AM
*Sesame Street Presents Follow That Bird (11522LV)WB/86 AS
*Seven Brides for Seven Brothers (ML100091)MGM/85 AS U/88 DS
*Seven Brides for Seven Brothers (lb) (101708)MGM/90 DS
Seven Days In May O(LV6313)Par/81-84 AM
*Seven Hours to Judgement (ID6390ME)IE/89 DS
*The Seven-Per-Cent Solution (11008)MCA/87 DM
*Seven Samurai (CC1167L)Voy/89 DCAM CAV
*Seven Samurai (CC1236L)Voy/90 DCDM
*Seven Seductions of Madame Lau (X-rated) (Z0080)IE/89 AM
*The Seven Year Itch (104380)Fox/88 AS
*1776 (VLD30204)Col/85 AS
*The Seventh Seal (CC1212L)Voy/90 DM
*The Seventh Seal (CC1110L)Voy/87 DCAM CAV
*The Seventh Sign (ID6100TS)IE/88 DS
*The Seventh Victim (I6007)IE/86 AM
*The Seventh Voyage of Sinbad (VLD300114)Col/85 AM
Sex Life of a Porn Star (X-rated) (Z0103)IE/90 AM
*Sex, Lies & Videotape (90486)Col/90 DS
*Sex, Lies and Videotape (lb) (CC1216L)Voy/90 DS CAV
*Sex, Lies and Videotape (lb) (CC1217L)Voy/90 DS
Sex On The Run (WL5501)Ves/81-84 AM
Sex World (X-rated) (I0027)IE/85 AM
*Sgt. Pepper's Lonely Hearts Club Band (17004)MCA/87 AS
*Shadow Dancing (ID6753SG)IE/90 DS
*Shadow of a Doubt (40112)MCA/89 AM
Shadows in the Storm (ID7318VK)IE/90 DM
*Shag (ID6943HB)IE/90 DS
The Shaggy Dog (43AS)Dis/81-84 AM
*Shakedown (40820)MCA/88 DS
*Shaker Run (30845)Par/86 AM
*Shampoo O(VLD30582)Col/86
*Shamus (ID6297RC)IE/89 DM
Shane (LV6522)Par/81-84 AM
*Shanghai Surprise (ML5141)Ves/87 AS
*She-Devil (ID7369OR)IE/90 DS
*She Wore a Yellow Ribbon O(933)VA/86 AM
*She Wore a Yellow Ribbon (ID6543TU)IE/89 DM
*She's Having a Baby (LV32027)Par/88 DS
She's Out of Control (10306)Col/89 AS
She's So Fine (X-rated) (Z0089)IE/90 AM
*Sheena O(VLD30404)Col/85 AM
*Shenandoah (ID5125)IE/87 AM
*Sherlock Holmes and Terror by Night O(N/A)3M/86 AM
*Sherlock Holmes and the Secret Weapon O(N/A)3M/86 AM
*Sherlock Holmes and the Woman in Green O(N/A)3M/86 AM
*Ship of Fools (30542)Col/86 AM
*Shirley MacLaine's Inner Workout (ID6296VE)IE/89 DS CLV/CAV
*Shirley Valentine (LV32248)Par/90 DS
*Shock Corridor (CC1189L)Voy/89 DM
*Shocker (40931)MCA/90 DS
Shogun (LV1423)Par/81-84 AM
*Shogun Assassin (12023)MCA/81-84 AM
*Shoot the Piano Player (CC1143L)Voy/88 AM
*Shoot to Kill (697AS)Dis/88 DS
The Shootist (LV8904)Par/81-84 AM
*The Shop on Main Street (ID6169RC)IE/89 DM
*Short Circuit (372480)Fox/87 AS
*Short Circuit 2 (ID6164TS)IE/88 DM
A Shot In The Dark O(452880)Fox/81-84 AM
*Shout at the Devil (ID7528VE)IE/90 DM
*Show Boat (1936) (CC1144L)Voy/89 DCDM CAV
*Show Boat (1936) (CC1191L)Voy/89 DCDM
*Show Boat (1951) (ML100167)MGM/89 AM
Show Business (ID6983TU)IE/90 DM
*Shy People (37076)WB/88 DS
*The Sicilian (ID5245VE)IE/88 DS
*Sid & Nancy (13096)Nel/87 DS
*The Siege of Firebase Gloria (ID6414FR)IE/89 DM
*Siesta (ID5215LO)IE/88 DS
*Signs of Life (ID7219IV)IE/90 DM
*Silent Movie (143780)Fox/85 AS
Silent Night, Deadly Night (ID6909IV)IE/90 DM
Silent Night, Deadly Night Part 2 (ID6908IV)IE/90 DM
Silent Night, Deadly Night Part 3 (ID6816IV)IE/90 DM
The Silent Partner (VL5007)Ves/81-84 AM
Silent Rage (VLD5549)Col/81-84 AM
*Silent Running (40483)MCA/87 DM
*Silk Stockings (101738)MGM/90 DS
Silkwood O(13775)Nel/81-84 AM
Silver Streak (108080)Fox/81-84 AM
*Silverado (VLD30567)Col/86 AS
Sinbad and the Eye of the Tiger (VLD5550)Col/81-84 AM
*Sinbad of the Seven Seas (31130)WB/90 DM
*Sinbad the Sailor (ID6406TU)IE/89 DM
*Sincerely Charlotte (30771)Col/87 AM
A Sinful Life (90256)Col/90 AS
*Sing (ID6725TS)IE/89 DS
*Singin' in the Rain (ML100185)MGM/81-84 AM
*Singin' in the Rain (CC1152L)Voy/88 DCAM CAV
*Singin' in the Rain (CC1210L)Voy/90 DM
*Sirocco (ID6494RC)IE/90 DM
*Sister, Sister (ID5271NW)IE/88 DS
*The Sisterhood (ID5403ME)IE/89 DM
Six Weeks O(VLD3375)Col/81-84 AM
*Sixteen Candles (I5012)MCA/81-84 AS
*'68 (ID5313NW)IE/89 AM
Sizzle Beach (ID7135VK)IE/90 DM
Skeleton Coast (77446)Nel/89 AM
Ski Patrol (59086)Col/90 AS
*Skin Deep (ID6632ME)IE/89 DS
*Slammer Girls (ID5179)IE/88 DM
Slap Shot O(16004)MCA/81-84 AM
*Slapstick of Another Kind (VL5031)Ves/81-84 AM
*Slaughterhouse-Five (ID5092)MCA/87 AM
*Slaves of New York (ID6622TS)IE/89 DS
Sleepaway Camp III: Teenage Wasteland (77586)Nel/89 AM
*Sleeper O(452280)Fox/81-84 AM
*Sleeper (ML101463)MGM/89 AM
*Sleeping Beauty (22004)Dis/87 AS
*Sleeping Beauty (476CS)Dis/87 DS CAV
*Sleeping Beauty (Faerie Tale Theatre) (637180)Fox/81-84 AM
*The Sleeping Car (ID7218VK)IE/90 DM
Sleepless Nights (X-rated) (Z0125)IE/90 AM
Sleepwalk (77686)Nel/89 AM
*Sleuth (I5072)IE/87 AM CLV/CAV
*Slipping into Darkness (ID6355VV)IE/89 DM
*Slipstream (ID6764VV)IE/90 DS
*The Slugger's Wife (VLD30486)Col/85 AS
*Slugs (ID5193NW)IE/88 AM
Slumber Party '57 (VL4007)Ves/81-84 AM
*Slumber Party Massacre II (76886)Nel/87 AM
Small Sacrifices (ID7502FR)IE/90 DM
Small Town Girls (X-rated) (I0020)IE/86 AM
*Smithereens (ID6054ME)IE/88 DM
Smokey and the Bandit O(12004)MCA/81-84 AM
Smokey and the Bandit II O(12012)MCA/81-84 AM
Smokey and the Bandit Part III O(40013)MCA/81-84 AM
*Smooth Talk (VL5143)Ves/86 AM
Smurfs and the Magic Flute (CL2509)Ves/81-84 AM
*Snoopy Come Home (712580)Fox/85 AM
*Snow White and the Seven Dwarfs (Faerie Tale Theatre) (639480)Fox/81-84 AM
So Deep, So Good (X-rated) (Z0111)IE/90 AM
*So Well Remembered (ID7009TU)IE/90 DM
*Solarbabies (ML101027)MGM/87 DS
*Soldier of Orange (ID5350ME)IE/88 DM
*A Soldier's Story (VLD30408)Col/85 AS
*Soldier's Tale (ML1000376)MGM/81-84 AS
Some Kind of Hero (LV1118)Par/81-84 AM
*Some Kind of Wonderful (LV31979)Par/87 DS
Some Like It Hot O(457780)Fox/81-84 AM
*Some Like It Hot (ML103848)MGM/88 AM
*Some Like It Hot (CC1180L)Voy/89 DCDM CAV
Someone Behind the Door (I5041)IE/86 AM
Someone to Love (LV12673)Par/90 AM
*Someone to Watch over Me (30877)Col/88 AS
Something Special (ID7712MN)IE/90 DM
*Something to Sing About (LVA1004)LVA/90 AM

Something Wicked This Way Comes (166AS)Dis/81-84 AS
*Something Wild (TVL0001)HBO/87 AS
Somewhere in Time (13005)MCA/81-84 AM
*Son of Dracula (40766)MCA/89 AM CLV/CAV
*Son of Frankenstein (40764)MCA/89 AM
*The Son of Monte Cristo (M21)3M/86 AM
*Son of Paleface (ID6709RC)IE/90 DM
*The Song of Bernadette (103480)Fox/90 DM
*The Sons of Katie Elder (LV67292)Par/90 DM
*A Song to Remember (30456)Col/86 AM
*Songwriter O(VLD30437)Col/85 AS
*Sons of the Desert/Blotto O(M16)3M/86 AM
Sophie's Choice (704580)Fox/81-84 AM
*Sophisticated Ladies (ID6371J2)IE/89 DS
*SOS Coast Guard (LV23826)Rep/90 DM
*Soul Man (ID5100)IE/87 AS
*The Sound of Music (105180)Fox/81-84 AS U87 DS
*The Sound of Music (lb) (105185)Fox/89 DS
Souunder (LV2324)Par/81-84 AM
South Pacific (704580)Fox/81-84 AS
*South Pacific (lb) (704585)Fox/90 DS
Southern Comfort O(30155)Nel/81-84 AM
Souvenir (LV12732)Par/90 AM
Soylent Green (ML100070)MGM/81-84 AM
*Space Camp (VL5174)Ves/86 DS
Space Hunter-Adventures in the Forbidden Zone O(VLD3381)Col/81-84 AS
Space 1999 (J26050)J2/90 DM
*Space Ghost and Dino Boy (ID6619HA)IE/90 DM
*Spanish Main (ID6407TU)IE/89 DM
*Spartacus (40002)MCA/85 AS
Spectreman O(IG5005)IE/81-84 AM
*Speed Zone (ID7192ME)IE/90 DS
*Spider-Man (ID7763PR)IE/90 DM
*Spiders (ID7503DS)IE/90 DM
*Spies Like Us (11533LV)WB/86 AM
*Spike of Bensonhurst (ID6286VV)IE/89 DS
Splash (213AS)Dis/81-84 AS
Split Decisions (764)WB/89 DS
*The Spoilers (40015)MCA/86 AM CLV/CAV
*Spookies (ID6277SO)IE/89 DM
Sport Goofy O(165AS)Dis/81-84 AM
Spring Break (VLD3378)Col/81-84 AM
Spy (LV83403)Par/90 AM
*Spy in Black (ID7689NL)IE/90 DM
*The Spy Who Came in from the Cold (LV6509)Par/89 AM
*The Spy Who Loved Me O(463880)Fox/81-84 AM
*The Spy Who Loved Me (ML101421)MGM/88 AS
*The Spy Who Loved Me (lb) (101743)MGM/90 DS CLV/CAV
*Square Dance (ID5305PA)IE/88 DS
*The Squeeze (TVL0053)HBO/88 AS
*St. Elmo's Fire (VLD30559)Col/86 AS
*Stacking (902276)Nel/88 AM
*Stakeout (596AS)Dis/88 DS
Stalag 17 (LV5816)Par/81-84 AM
*Stalking Danger (ID6934VK)IE/90 DM
*Stand and Deliver (11805)WB/88 DM
*Stand By Me (30736)Col/87 AM
*Stanley & Iris (ML102044)MGM/90 DS
A Star Is Born (Judy Garland) (11335LV)WB/81-84 AS
*A Star is Born (1936) (I6001)IE/85 AM
*The Star Chamber (129580)Fox/89 DS
*Star of Midnight (ID6835TU)IE/90 DM
*Star Struck (90015)Nel/81-84 AS
*Star Trek: Menagerie Pts. I & II (LV60041)Par/81-84 AM
Star Trek The Motion Picture O(LV8858)Par/81-84 AS
Star Trek The Motion Picture (Longer Version) (LV88582S)Par/81-84 AS
Star Trek II The Wrath of Khan (LV1180)Par/81-84 AS
*Star Trek III The Search for Spock (LV1621)Par/85 DS
*Star Trek IV: The Voyage Home (LV17972)Par/87 DS
*Star Trek V: The Final Frontier (LV32044)Par/89 DS
*Star Trek Television Series The Cage (LV60040106)Par/87 AM
*Star Trek TV: A Taste of Armageddon/This Side of Paradise (LV6004091)Par/85 AM
*Star Trek TV: And the Children Shall Lead/Is There In Truth No Beauty? (LV60040110)Par/87 AM
*Star Trek TV: Assignment: Earth/Spock's Brain (LV60040108)Par/87 AM
*Star Trek TV: By Any Other Name/The Omega Glory (LV60040105)Par/86 AM
*Star Trek TV: Catspaw/The Doomsday Machine (LV6004097)Par/86 AM
*Star Trek TV: Dagger of the Mind/The Corbomite Maneuver (LV6004085)Par/85 AM
*Star Trek TV: Devil in the Dark/Errand of Mercy (LV6004092)Par/85 AM
*Star Trek TV: For the World is Hollow/The Tholian Web (LV60040112)Par/88 AM
*Star Trek TV: Friday's Child/Journey to Babel (LV6004099)Par/86 AM
*Star Trek TV: Metamorphosis/I, Mudd (LV6004098)Par/86 AM
*Star Trek TV: Operation: Annihilate!/Amok Time (LV6004094) Par/85 AM
*Star Trek TV: Plato's Stepchildren/Wink of an Eye (LV60040113)Par/88 AM
*Star Trek TV: Return of the Archons/Space Seed (LV6004090) Par/85 AM
*Star Trek TV: Return to Tomorrow/Patterns of Force (LV60040104) Par/86 AM
*Star Trek TV: Shore Leave/The Galileo Seven (LV6004087)Par/85 AM
*Star Trek TV: Spectre of the Gun/Day of the Dove (LV60040111)Par/87 AM
*Star Trek TV: The Alternative Factor/City on the Edge of Forever (LV6004093) Par/85 AM
*Star Trek TV: The Apple/Mirror, Mirror (LV6004096)Par/86 AM
*Star Trek TV: The Cage (LV60040106) Par/87 AM
*Star Trek TV: The Conscience of the King/Balance of Terror (LV6004086) Par/85 AM
*Star Trek TV: The Deadly Years/Obsession (LV60040100) Par/86 AM
*Star Trek TV: The Empath/Elaan of Troylus (LV60040114)Par/88 AM
*Star Trek TV: The Enemy Within/Mudd's Women (LV6004083) Par/85 AM
*Star Trek TV: The Enterprise Incident/The Paradise Syndrome (LV60040109)Par/87 AM
*Star Trek TV: The Gamesters of Triskelion/A Piece of the Action (LV60040102)Par/86 AM
*Star Trek TV: The Immunity Syndrome/A Private Little War (LV60040103)Par/86 AM
*Star Trek TV: The Lights of Zeltar/Requiem for Methuselah (LV60040117)Par/89 AM
*Star Trek TV: The Man Trap/Charlie X (LV6004081)Par/85 AM
*Star Trek TV: The Mark of Gideon/That Which Survives (LV60040116)Par/89 AM
*Star Trek TV: The Savage Curtain/All Our Yesterdays (LV60040119)Par/89 AM
*Star Trek TV: The Squire of Gothos/ Arena (LV6004088) Par/85 AM
*Star Trek TV: Tomorrow is Yesterday/Court-Martial (LV6004089) Par/85 AM
*Star Trek TV: The Ultimate Computer/Bread and Circuses (LV60040107)Par/87 AM
*Star Trek TV: The Way to Eden/The Cloud Minders (LV60040118)Par/89 AM
*Star Trek TV: Turnabout Intruder (LV60040120)Par/89 AM
*Star Trek TV: What Are Little Girls Made Of/Miri (LV6004084)Par/85 AM
*Star Trek TV: Where No Man Has Gone Before/The Naked Time (LV6004082)Par/85 AM
*Star Trek TV: Who Mourns for Adonais?/The Changeling (LV6004095) Par/85 AM
*Star Trek TV: Whom the Gods Destroy/Let That Be Your Last Battlefield (LV60040115)Par/88 AM
*Star Trek TV: Wolf in the Fold/The Trouble with Tribbles (LV60040101) Par/86 AM
*Star Wars (113080)Fox/81-84 AS
*Star Wars (113084)Fox/85 AS CAV
*Star Wars (lb) (113085)Fox/89 DS
*Starchaser The Legend of Orin O(LV2347)Par/86 AS
Stardust Memories O(455480)Fox/81-84 AM
*Starman O(VLD30412)Col/85 AS
*Stars and Bars (35005)Col/89 AS
Starting Over (LV1239)Par/81-84 AM
*State of the Union (40579)MCA/87 AM CLV/CAV
*The State of Things (ID5340PA)IE/89 DM
The Stay Awake (77666)Nel/89 AM
Staying Alive (LV1302)Par/81-84 AS
Staying Together (ID7227HB)IE/90 DS
*Steal the Sky (ID6567HB)IE/89 DS
*Stealing Heaven (ID6457VV)IE/89 DS
*Stealing Home (11818)WB/89 DS
*Steel Dawn (ID5214VE)IE/88 DS
*Steel Magnolias (70246)Col/90 DS
*Steele Justice O(ID6746KV)IE/89 DM
*Stella Dallas (3066)Nel/85 AM
*The Stepfather (75676)Nel/87 AS
Stepfather II (ID7226HB)IE/90 DS
*Stephen King's Silver Bullet (LV1827)Par/86 AM
*Steppenwolf (ID6699VK)IE/90 DM
The Sterile Cuckoo (LV6904)Par/81-84 AM
*Stewardess School (30769)Col/87 AM
*Stick (40139)MCA/85 AS
*Sticky Fingers (ID6134ME)IE/89 DM
Stiff Competition (X-rated) (I0038)IE/85 AM
Still of the Night O(471180)Fox/81-84 AM
Still Smokin (LV2315)Par/81-84 AM
*The Sting (11001)MCA/81-84 AM U/90 DM CLV/CAV
The Sting II O(11017)MCA/81-84 AM
Stir Crazy (VLD3380)Col/81-84 AM
*The Stone Killer (ID6023RC)IE/88 DM
*Stormy Monday (LV12674)Par/89 DS
*Stormy Weather (116880)Fox/89 DM
The Story of O (ML100202)MGM/81-84 AM
*The Story of O Part II (ID5235VE)IE/88 AM
*The Story of Vernon and Irene Castle (ID6780TU)IE/90 DM
*Stranded (32771)Col/88 AM
Strange Invaders (VL5030)Ves/81-84 AM
*The Stranger and the Gunfighter O(VLD30355)Col/85 AM
*Stranger than Paradise (689680)Fox/87 AM
*Strangers on a Train (11062)WB/87 AM
*Strategic Air Command (LV5426)Par/87 AM
*Strauss Elektra (Vienna) (0715001)PGM/88 DS
Straw Dogs (800580)Fox/81-84 AM
*Streamers (I5080)IE/87 AM
*Street Smart (ID5157)IE/87 DS
*A Streetcar Named Desire O(457180)Fox/81-84 AM
*A Streetcar Named Desire (34019A/B)WB/87 AM
*Streets of Fire (40085)MCA/85 AS
*Streets of Gold (VL5199)Ves/87 AM
*Strike Up the Band (ML100565)MGM/85 AM
Stripes (VLD5557)Col/81-84 AM
*The Strong Man (ID6865HB)IE/90 DS CLV/CAV
*A Study in Terror (ID6080RC)IE/88 DM
Student Bodies (LV1476)Par/81-84 AM
*Stunt Man (111080)Fox/81-84 AM
*Subway (696980)Fox/87 AS
*Sudden Death (VL5117)Ves/86 AM
Sudden Impact (11341LV)WB/81-84 AM
*Suddenly Last Summer (VLD5560)Col/81-84 AM
*Sugar Cane Alley (ID5348ME)IE/88 DM
*Sullivan's Travels (40551)MCA/90 DM
*Summer (ID5331PA)IE/88 DM
*Summer Camp Nightmare (75666)Nel/87 AM
Summer Heat (ID7301VA)IE/90 DM
*Summer Heat (Lori Singer) (ID6747KV)IE/89 DM
Summer Lovers (17045)Nel/81-84 AS
*Summer Rental (LV1785)Par/86 AM
*A Summer Place (11593)WB/90 DM
Summer School (LV1518)Par/88 AM
*Summer Stock (ML100851)MGM/88 AM
*Summertime O(6019)Nel/85 AM
*Sunday in the Park with George (ID5151)IE/87 DS
*Sunset (ID6133TS)IE/89 DS
Sunset Boulevard (LV4927)Par/81-84 AM
*Supergirl (I5024)IE/85 AS
Superman (1013LV)WB/81-84 AS
*Superman (lb) (12030)WB/90 DS
*Superman II (11120LV)WB/81-84 AS U/90 DS CLV/CAV
Superman III (11321LV)WB/81-84 AS
*Superman IV: The Quest for Peace (11757)WB/88 AS
*The Superman Cartoons of Max and Dave Fleischer (ID7325BR)IE/90 DM
*The Sure Thing (2178)Nel/85 AM
*Surrender (37077)WB/88 DS
*Survivor (ID5195VE)IE/88 AM
Survivors O(VLD3382)Col/81-84 AM
*Suspect (ID5292TS)IE/88 DS
*Suspicion (ID6404TU)IE/89 DM
*Suspiria (ID6900MN)IE/90 DS
Swamp Thing (16055)Nel/81-84 AM
*Sweat (X-rated) (Z0060)IE/89 AM CLV/CAV
*Swedenhielms (LVD8905)Lum/89 DS CLV/CAV
Swedish Erotica #39 (X-rated) (I0022)IE/85 AM
Swedish Erotica #52 (X-rated) (I0025)IE/85 AM
*Sweet Charity (17003)MCA/87 DS CLV/CAV
*Sweet Dreams (ID5145)IE/88 DS
*Sweet Dreams Suzan (X-rated) (Z0086)IE/89 AM CLV/CAV
*Sweet Hearts Dance (ID6075TS)IE/89 DS
*Sweet Liberty (40434)MCA/87 AM
*Sweet Smell of Success (ML101434)MGM/89 AM
Sweetie (ID7605IV)IE/90 DM
Swept Away (VLD5568)Col/81-84 AM
*The Swimmer (ID6386RC)IE/89 DM
Swing Shift (11376LV)WB/81-84 AM
*Swing Time (1106L)Voy/86 DCAM CAV
*Swing Time (CC1200L)Voy/90 DM
Swiss Family Robinson (53AS)Dis/81-84 AM
*Switching Channels (ID6073TS)IE/88 DM

The Sword and the Sorcerer O(13010)MCA/81-84 AS
*The Sword in the Stone (229AS)Dis/86 AM
*Sylvester (VLD30476)Col/86 AS
*Sylvia Scarlett (ID6834TU)IE/90 DM
Table for Five (704380)Fox/81-84 AM
Taboo (X-rated) (I0034)IE/85 AM
*Taffin (ID6409MG)IE/89 DM
*The Tailor of Gloucester (ID6279SO)IE/89 DS
Take Off (X-rated) (X213)IE/81-84 AM
Take the Money and Run (800780)Fox/81-84 AM
*Tales from the Crypt (ID6807HB)IE/90 DS CLV/CAV
Tales from the Darkside Volume 1 (ID6906IV)IE/90 DM
Tales from the Darkside Volume 2 (ID6940IV)IE/90 DM
Tales from the Darkside Volume 3 (ID6941IV)IE/90 DM
Tales from the Darkside Volume 4 (ID6942IV)IE/90 DM
*The Tale of Jeremy Fisher/The Tale of Peter Rabbit (ID6281SO)IE/89 DS
*The Tale of the Frog Prince (Faerie Tale Theatre) (637280)Fox/81-84 AM
*A Tale of Two Chipmunks/Unsinkable Donald Duck O(523AS)Dis/87 AM
Talk Dirty To Me Part 6 (X-rated) (Z0082)IE/90 AM
*The Talk of the Town (30780)Col/87 AM
*Talk Radio (40841)MCA/89 DS
*Tall in the Saddle (ID6544TU)IE/89 DM
*The Taming of the Shrew (30110)Col/81-84 AM
*Tampopo (LV24050)Rep/89 DM
*Tango and Cash (11892)WB/90 DS
Tank (40072)MCA/81-84 AM
*Tap (ID6623TS)IE/89 DS
*Tape Heads (ID6516PA)IE/89 DS
*Target (709780)Fox/86 AS
Tarzan, The Ape Man (Bo Derek) (ML100109)MGM/81-84 AS
Tarzan, The Apeman (1932) (ML100043)MGM/85 AM
Taste of Money (X-rated) (Z0105)IE/90 AM
Taxi Driver O(VLD5920)Col/81-84 AM
*Taxi Driver (C1218L)Voy/90 DCDM
*Taxi Dirver (C1219L)Voy/90 DCDM CAV
*A Taxing Woman (LVD8903)Lum/89 DM CLV/CAV
The Teacher (ID7299VA)IE/90 DM
*Teachers O(472880)Fox/85 AS
*Teen Wolf O(LV2350)Par/86 AM
*Teenage Mutant Ninja Turtles: Super Rocksteady/Heroes on a Halfshell (ID7643IV)IE/90 DM
*Teenage Mutant Ninja Turtles: The Epic Begins (ID6448IV)IE/89 DM CLV/CAV
*Teenage Mutant Ninja Turtles The Movie (ID7609IV)IE/90 DS
*Teenage Mutant Ninja Turtles: The Shredder Is Splintered/Hot Rodding (ID7642IV)IE/90 DM
*The Telephone (ID6016NW)IE/89 AS
*The Tempest (ID6606CN)IE/90 DS
10 (2002LV)WB/81-84 AM
The Ten Commandments (LV6524)Par/81-84 AS
*Ten from Your Show of Shows (ID6055ME)IE/88 DM
*Ten Little Indians (31134)WB/90 DM
Ten to Midnight (ML100282)MGM/81-84 AM
*10 Rillington Place (ID6433RC)IE/89 DM
*Ten Wanted Men (31000)Col/89 AM
*Tender Mercies (1640)HBO/86 AM
*Tequila Sunrise (11821)WB/89 DS
*Terminal Exposure (ID6562VE)IE/89 DS
*Terminal Force (ID6637NW)IE/90 DM
*The Terminator O(2535)HBO/86O AM
*The Terminator O(ID6677HB)IE/89 DM
Terms of Endearment (LV1407)Par/81-84 AM
Terror in the Swamp O(I5023)IE/85 AM
*Terror Train (166580)Fox/88 DS
Tess (VLD5945)Col/81-84 AS
*Testament (LV1739)Par/81-84 AM
Tex (142AS)Dis/81-84 AM
*Tex Avery's Screwball Classics (101736)MGM/90 AM
The Texas Chainsaw Massacre O(ZL034)Ves/81-84 AM
*The Texas Chainsaw Massacre, Part 2 (I5065)IE/87 AS
*That Hamilton Woman (31075)Nel/85 AM
*That Was Then...This Is Now (LV1954)Par/86 AS
That's Entertainment (ML00007)MGM/81-84 AS
*That's Life (VL5203)Ves/87 AM
*Theater of Blood (ID6408MG)IE/89 DM
*There's No Business Like Show Business (108680)Fox/89 DS
*These Three (3068)Nel/85 AM
They All Laughed (VL5005)Ves/81-84 AM
*They Came to Cordura (ID6642RC)IE/90 DM
*They Call Trinity O(20205)Nel/85 AM
*They Got Me Covered O(30695)Nel/86 AM
*They Live (40843)MCA/89 DS
*They Live By Night (ID6979TU)IE/90 DM
They Made Me a Criminal (ID7567NE)IE/90 DM
They Shoot Horses, Don't They? O(800480)Fox/81-84 AM
They Won't Believe Me (ID7005TU)IE/90 DM
*Thief (ID6468MG)IE/89 DS CLV/CAV
*The Thief of Bagdad (silent) (ID6860HB)IE/90 DS
*The Thief of Bagdad (Korda) (31085)Nel/85 AM
*Thief of Hearts (LV1660)Par/85 AS
*The Thin Man (ML100608)MGM/86 AM
*The Thing (original) O(944)VA/85 AM
*The Thing (remake) (11015)MCA/81-84 AS
*The Thing (remake lb) (40946)MCA/90 DS
Things Are Tough All Over O(VLD5948)Col/81-84 AM
Things Change (35011)Col/89 AM
Third Degree Burn (LV12760)Par/90 AM
*The Third Man (1105L)Voy/86 AM
The Third Solution (70136)Col/90 AM
*38 Vienna Before the Fall (LVD8913)Lum/90 DM
*The 39 Steps (1103L)Voy/85 AM
*The Thirty Nine Steps (ID5309ME)IE/88 DM
*This Gun for Hire (ID5126)IE/87 AM CLV/CAV
*This Is Spinal Tap (20815)Nel/81-84 AS
*This Island Earth (40327)MCA/86 AM CLV/CAV
This Land Is Mine (ID7628TU)IE/90 DM
*Thoroughly Modern Millie (17001)MCA/86 DS
*Those Magnificant Men and Their Flying Machines (103380)Fox/86 AS
*The Three Amigos (TVL0007)HBO/87 AS
*The Three Caballeros (91AS)Dis/88 AM
*The Three Caballeros (91CS)Dis/88 AM CAV
Three Days of the Condor (LV8803)Par/81-84 AM
*Three for the Road (ID6238IV)IE/89 DS
*The Three Fugitives (950AS)Dis/90 DS
*Three Men and a Baby (658AS)Dis/88 DS
*3 Men and a Cradle (VL5192)Ves/87 AM
*The Three Musketeers (MGM) (ML100652)MGM/86 AM
*Three O'Clock High (40686)MCA/88 DS
*The 3 Penny Opera (CC1139L)Voy/88 AM
The Three Stooges, Volume 1 (VLD5947)Col/81-84 AM
The Three Stooges, Volume 2 (VLD39235)Col/85 AM
*The Three Stooges Vol. III (ID6171RC)IE/89 DM
*The Three Stooges Vol. VI (ID6447RC)IE/89 DM
*The Three Stooges Vol. VII (ID6489RC)IE/89 DM
*The Three Stooges Vol. VIII (ID6639RC)IE/89 DM
*The Three Stooges Vol. IX (ID6716RC)IE/90 DM
The Three Stooges Volumes 26 & 28 (90766)Col/90 DM
The Three Stooges Volumes 27 & 29 (90776)Col/90 DM
*3:10 to Yuma O(VLD30444)Col/85 AM
*Throw Momma from the Train (ID5231OR)IE/88 DS
*Thumbelina (Faerie Tale Theatre) (639680)Fox/81-84 AM
Thunder and Mud (90596)Col/90 DS
*Thunderball O(461180)Fox/81-84 AM
*Thunderball (lb) (ML101564)MGM/89 DM
*Thunderbirds in Outer Space (ID6499IV)IE/89 DM
*Thunderbirds: Countdown to Disaster (ID6555IV)IE/89 DM
*Thunderbolt and Lightfoot O(454780)Fox/85 AM
Thunderground (ID7208SG)IE/90 DM
Thursday's Game (ID7133VK)IE/90 DM
*Tiger Warsaw (ID7155SO)IE/90 DM
Tightrope (11400LV)WB/85 AM
Till Marriage Do Us Part (VL3005)Ves/81-84 AM
Till Marriage Do Us Part (subtitled) (ID7755AX)IE/90 DM
*Till the Clouds Roll By (ML100094)MGM/90 DM
*Till the End of Time (ID6455TU)IE/89 DM
*Time after Time (22017)WB/87 DS
The Time Bandits O(LV2301)Par/81-84 AS
*The Time Guardians (77366)Nel/90 AS
*The Time Machine (ML100152)MGM/81-84 AM
*A Time of Destiny (75706)Nel/89 AS
Time of the Gypsies (50306)Col/90 DS
*Timerider The Adventures of Lyle Swan O(PA12528)Pac/81-84 AS
*Tin Men (571AS)Dis/88 DS
To Be Or Not To Be (133680)Fox/81-84 AS
To Catch A Thief (LV6308)Par/81-84 AM
*To Have and Have Not (ML100747)MGM/90 DM
*To Kill a Mockingbird (10009)MCA/87 AM
*To Live and Die in LA (VL5123)Ves/86 AS
*Toast of New York (ID6886TU)IE/90 DM
*Toby McTeague (902116)Nel/87 AM
Tokyo Joe (32007)Col/89 AM
*Tokyo Pop (812)WB/88 AS
Tom & Jerry Cartoon Festival Vol. I (ML100019)MGM/81-84 AM
Tom and Jerry Cartoons No. 2 (ML100146)MGM/81-84 AM
*Tom Jones O(451180)Fox/81-84 AM
Tommy (VLD5951)Col/81-84 AS
*Too Many Girls (ID6774TU)IE/90 DM
Tootsie (VLD5955)Col/81-84 AM
*Top Gun (LV1692)Par/87 DS U/90
*Top Hat O(LL929)VA/86 AM
*Top Secret! (LV1567)Par/85 AS
*Topaz (40473)MCA/87 AM CLV/CAV
*Topper O(M14)3M/86 AM
*Topper Returns O(M19)3M/86 AM
Tora! Tora! Tora! (101780)Fox/81-84 AS
*Torch Song (ML101552)MGM/90 DM
*Torch Song Trilogy (32829)Col/89 AS
*Torchlight (75905)Nel/85 AM
*Torn Curtain (40472)MCA/89 AM CLV/CAV
Torrents of Spring (ID7617HB)IE/90 DM
*Total Recall (ID7779IV)IE/90 DS
*Touch of Evil (21010)MCA/87 AM
*Tough Guys (511AS)Dis/87 AS
*Tough Guys Don't Dance (ID5205ME)IE/88 DS
*Tour of Duty (ID5250NW)IE/88 DM
*Tour of Duty 2: Bravo Company (ID6093NW)IE/89 DM
*The Towering Inferno (107180)Fox/89 DS
*The Toxic Avenger (LL9953)Ves/87 AM
The Toxic Avenger Part II (860)WB/89 DM
Toy (VLD5975)Col/81-84 AM
*Toy Soldier O(I5016)IE/85 AM
*Traci I Love You (X-rated) (I0043)IE/88 AM CLV/CAV
Trading Places (LV1551)Par/81-84 AM
*The Tragedy of Antony & Cleopatra (ID6607CN)IE/90 DS
Trail of the Pink Panther O(471080)Fox/81-84 AM
*Trancers (VL5086)Ves/85 AM
*Transmutations (ID5196VE)IE/88 DS
Treasure Island (41AS)Dis/81-84 AM
Treasure Island (musical) (PA83062)PA/81-84 AS
Treasure of Sierra Madre O(463980)Fox/81-84 AM
*Treasure of the Sierra Madre (ML101587)MGM/89 AM
*A Tree Grows in Brooklyn (151780)Fox/90 DM
*Tremors (40957)MCA/90 DS
Tribute (VL6003)Ves/81-84 AM
*Trinity Is Still My Name O(20215)Nel/85 AM
*The Trip to Bountiful (13415)Nel/86 AM
Tripwire (90746)Col/90 DM
*Troll (VL5121)Ves/86 AS
*Tron (122AS)Dis/81-84 AS
Troop Beverly Hills (10296)Col/89 AS
*Trouble in Mind (901096)MCA/86 AS
*Trouble with Angels (VLD30250)Col/85 AM
*The Trouble with Harry (40103)MCA/85 AM
*True Believer (35012)Col/89 DS
*True Blood (ID651FR)IE/89 DM
True Confessions (ML100145)MGM/81-84 AM
True Grit (LV6833)Par/81-84 AM
*True Love (ML101763)MGM/90 DS
*True Stories (11654)WB/87 DS
*True West (1084)Acd/88 AM
*Tucker: The Man and His Dream (LV32144)Par/89 DS
*Tuff Turf O(I5027)IE/85 AM
*Tunes of Glory (CC1170L)Voy/89 DM
*The Tunnel (ID6564VE)IE/89 DS
*Turner and Hooch (911AS)Dis/90 DS
*Turtle Diary (VL5173)Ves/86 AS
*12 Angry Men (CC1127L)Voy/88 AM
*Twelve Chairs (I5073)IE/87 AM
*12 O'Clock High (107580)Fox/89 DM
*Twenty Thousand Leagues Under the Sea (015AS)Dis/81-84 U/81-84
Twice Dead (77456)Nel/89 AM
*Twice in a Lifetime (VL5119)Ves/86 AS
*The Twilight Zone The Movie (11314LV)WB/81-84 AS U/90 DS
*Twilight's Last Gleaming (765380)Fox/89 DS
*Twins (40873)MCA/89 DS
*Twister (ID7108VE)IE/90 DS
*Two Idiots in Hollywood (ID6558NW)IE/89 DS
*Two Moon Junction (30966)Col/89 AM
Two of a Kind O(139980)Fox/81-84 AS
*Two Rode Together (ID6644RC)IE/89 DM
*2001: A Space Odyssey (ML100002)MGM/81-84 AS
*2001: A Space Odyssey (CC1160L)Voy/88 DS CAV
*2010 (ML100591)MGM/85 AS
*2010 (lb) (ML101661)MGM/89 DS
UFO Volume 1 (ID7246TY)IE/90 DM
UFO Volume 2 (ID7247TY)IE/90 DM
UFO Volume 4 (ID7249TY)IE/90 DM
UHF (ID9501OR)IE/90 DS
*Umberto D (CC1214L)Voy/90 DM
*The Unbearable Lightness of Being (ID6257OR)IE/89 DS
*Uncle Buck (40900)MCA/90 DS
Uncommon Valor (LV1657)Par/81-84 AS
Under Fire (VL5033)Ves/81-84 AS
Under the Biltmore Clock (77706)Nel/90 AM
*Under the Boardwalk (ID6559NW)IE/89 DS

*Under the Cherry Moon (11605LV)WB/87 DS
*Under the Gun (ID6696MN)IE/89 DS
*Under the Volcano (401254)MCA/85 AM
*Undersea Kingdom (LV25050)Rep@/90 DM
*The Understudy: Graveyard Shift II (ID6646VV)IE/89 DM
*Underwater! (ID6454TU)IE/89 DM
*Unfaithfully Yours (124980)Fox/90 DM
Unfaithfully Yours (remake) (134080)Fox/81-84 AS
*The Unholy (ID6068VE)IE/89 DS
*Uninvited (ID6086NS)IE/88 DM
*Union City (ID6037RC)IE/88 DM
*The Unnamable (ID6703VK)IE/90 DM
*Unnatural Causes (ID6057NS)IE/89 DM
Unsettled Land (77496)Nel/89 AS
*The Unsinkable Molly Brown (ML100578)MGM/88 DS
*The Unsinkable Molly Brown (lb) (ML101876)MGM/90 DS
*Untamed Passions (X-rated) (Z0081)IE/89 AM CLV/CAV
*The Untouchables (LV1886)Par/88 DS
Up 'n Coming O(X-rated) (N/A)IE/81-84 AM
Up 'n Coming (uncut X-rated) (I0002)IE/81-84 AM CLV/CAV
Up In Smoke (LV8966)Par/81-84 AM
Up the Creek (VL5043)Ves/81-84 AM
*Up Your Alley (ID6625IV)IE/90 DM
Urban Cowboy O(LV1285)Par/81-84 AM
Urban Cowgirls (X-rated) (I0004)IE/81-84 AM
Used Cars O(VLD6000)Col/81-84 AM
*Utilities (VL5059)Ves/85 AM
*Vagabond (ID5301PA)IE/88 AM
*Valentino Returns (ID6938VK)IE/90 DM
*Valet Girls (VL5175)Ves/87 AM
Valley Girl (VL5016)Ves/81-84 AM
*Vamp (I5063)IE/86 AM
*Vampire's Kiss (ID6810HB)IE/90 DS
*Vanishing Point (102880)Fox/90 DM
*The Velvet Vampire (ID7555NL)IE/90 DM
The Velveteen Rabbit O(I5011)IE/85 AM
*Vengeance Is Mine (CC1134L)Voy/88 AM
*Verdi Falstaff (Vienna) (0715031)PGM/88 DS
*Verdi Otello (La Scala) (0725011)PGM/88 DS
*Verdi Rigoletto (0715011)PGM/88 DS
The Verdict (118880)Fox/81-84 AM
Verne Miller (77316)Nel/89 AM
*Vertigo (40082)MCA/81-84 AM
*Vice Academy (ID6757FL)IE/89 DM
Vice Squad (20155)Nel/81-84 AM
*Vice Versa (35007)Col/89 AS
*Victor/Victoria (ML100151)MGM/81-84 AS
*Victor/Victoria (lb) (101737)MGM/90 DS
Videodrome O(11018)MCA/81-84 AM
Vietnam, Texas (59196)Col/90 AM
*View to a Kill O(473080)Fox/85 AS
*A View to a Kill (lb) (ML101726)MGM/90 DS CLV/CAV
*Vincent, Paul, Francoise and the Others (ID6798CS)IE/90 DM
*The Vineyard (ID6636NW)IE/89 DS
*Violets Are Blue (30690)Col/86 AM
*The Virgin Queen of St. Francis High (ID5273ME)IE/88 DS
Virginia (X-rated) (I0020)IE/85 AM
*VisionQuest (11459)WB/85 AS
*The Visitors (ID6930VK)IE/90 DM
*Viva Las Vegas (ML101993)MGM/90 DS
*Viva Zapata! (135280)Fox/89 AM
*Voltron Castle of the Lions (I5051)IE/86 AS
*Voltron Planet of Doom (I5050)IE/86 AS
*Volunteers (TVL2983)HBO/88 AS
*The Wackiest Ship in the Army (ID6551RC)IE/89 DM
Wacko (ID7530VE)IE/90 DM
*Wagonmaster (ID7001TU)IE/90 DM
*Walking Tall (LC9500)Ves/85 AM
*Wall Street (165380)Fox/88 AS
Walt Disney Mini Classics Mickey and the Beanstalk The Reluctant Dragon (394AS)Dis/88 AM
*Wanted Dead or Alive (ID5201NW)IE/88 DS
*War and Peace (LV56262)Par/85 AM
*The War Lover (ID6645RC)IE/90 DM
War Party (ID7113HB)IE/90 DS
The War of the Worlds (LV5303)Par/81-84 AM
*The War Wagon (40016)MCA/87 AM
Wargames O(471480)Fox/81-84 AS
Wargames (ML100293)MGM/81-84 AS
*Warlords (ID6932VK)IE/90 DM
*Warm Nights on a Slow Moving Train (ID7118FL)IE/90 DM
Warm Summer Rain (90676)Col/90 AM
*The Warrior and the Sorceress (VL5060)Ves/85 AM
The Warriors (LV1122)Par/81-84 AM
*Watchers (ID6343IV)IE/89 DM
*Watermelon Man (VLD30463)Col/85 AM
Wavelength (40185)Nel/81-84 AM
*Waxwork (ID6293VE)IE/89 DS
*Way Out West/Brats O(N/A)3M/85 AM
The Way We Were (VLD6040)Col/81-84 AM
*We All Loved Each Other So Much (ID6264RC)IE/89 DM
*We the Living (LVD8902)Lum/89 AM
We Think the World of You (77376)Nel/89 AM
We're No Angels (orig.) (LV5414)Par/81-84 AM
We're No Angels (1989) (LV32154)Par/90 DS
Wedding Band (90506)Col/90 DS
Wedding in Galilee (ID7334KN)IE/90 DM
*Weeds (ID6576HB)IE/89 DS
*Weekend at Bernie's (ID6818IV)IE/90 DS
*Weekend Pass (VL5045)Ves/85 AM
*Weird Science (40200)MCA/86 DS
*West Side Story O(451980)Fox/81-84O AS
*West Side Story (CC1192L)Voy/89 DS
*West Side Story (CC1178L)Voy/89 DS CAV
*The Westerner (30755)Nel/85 AM
*Westworld (ML100097)MGM/89 DS
*The Whales of August (76006)Nel/88 AM
*What Comes Around (8258)Nel/86 AM
*What Have I Done to Deserve This? (ID7256CV)IE/90 DM
What's Up Tiger Lily (VL4018)Ves/81-84 AM
*Wheels of Fire (VL5088)Ves/86 AM
When a Stranger Calls (VLD6050)Col/81-84 AM
*When Harry Met Sally (77326)Nel/89 DS
*When Nature Calls (I5081)IE/87 AM
*When the Wind Blows (ID6237IV)IE/89 DS
When Worlds Collide (LV5106)Par/81-84 AM
*Where Eagles Dare (ML100137)MGM/89 DS
*A Whisper to a Scream (ID6647VV)IE/89 DS
*The Whistle Blower (76656)Nel/87 AS
*White Chocolate (X-rated) (I0049)IE/88 AM CLV/CAV
*White Christmas (LV61042)Par/86 DS
White Dawn (LV8724)Par/81-84 AM
*White Heat O(464280)Fox/87 AM
*White Line Fever (ID6643RC)IE/90 DM
*White Mischief (77246)Nel/89 AS
*White Nights (30611)Col/86 AS
*White Water Summer (30858)Col/88 AS
*Who Am I This Time? (ID7571ME)IE/90 DM
*Who Framed Roger Rabbit (940AS)Dis/90 DS
*Who Framed Roger Rabbit (940CS)Dis/90 DS CAV
*Who'll Stop the Rain (ID6470MG)IE/89 DM
Wholly Moses! O(VLD6060)Col/81-84 AM
*Who's Afraid of Virginia Woolf? (11056A/B)WB/87 DM
*Who's Harry Crumb? (ID6556TS)IE/89 DS
*Who's That Girl (11758)WB/87 DS
*The Wild Bunch (1014LV)WB/81-84 AM
*The Wild Geese (769180)Fox/89 DS
*The Wild Life (40145)MCA/85 AS
*The Wild One (30623)Col/86 AM
*The Wild Pair (ID5188ME)IE/88 DS
Wild Zone (59126)Col/90 AM
*Wildcats (11583LV)WB/86 AS
*Will Penny (LV6723)Par/89 AM
*Willard (I5053)IE/86 AM
*Willow (30936)Col/89 DS
*Winchester '73 (40325)MCA/87 DCAM
*Windy City (708080)Fox/85 AM
*Wings (LV2851)Par/85 DS
*Wings of Desire (ID6635OR)IE/90 DS
*Winners Take All (13276)Nel/87 AM
*Winnie the Pooh A Day for Eeyore/Winnie the Pooh and the Blustery Day (598AS)Dis/87 AM
Winnie the Pooh and Friends O(226AS)Dis/85 AM
*Winnie the Pooh and the Honey Tree/Winnie the Pooh and Tigger, Too (521AS)Dis/87 AM
*Winter Kills (20566)Nel/90 AM
*Winter People (77266)Nel/90 DS
*Wired (ID7222IV)IE/90 DS
*Wisdom (37081)WB/87 DS
*Wish You Were Here (ID6273FR)IE/89 DM
*Witchboard (ID7709MN)IE/90 DM
*The Witches of Eastwick (11741LV)WB/88 DS
*Witchtrap (ID7703MN)IE/90 DS
*Withnail and I (ID6131ME)IE/88 DM
*Without a Clue (ID6501OR)IE/89 DS
*Without Reservations (ID6944TU)IE/90 DM
*Witness (LV1738)Par/86 AS
Witness for the Prosecution O(466580)Fox/85 AM
The Wiz O(17005)MCA/81-84 AS
*The Wizard (40934)MCA/90 DS
*The Wizard of Loneliness (ID6302VV)IE/89 DM
*The Wizard of Oz O(ML100001)MGM/81-84 AM
*The Wizard of Oz (50th Anniversary) (ML101656)MGM/89 DM
*The Wizard of Oz (CC1159L)Voy/88 DCAM CAV
The Wizard of Oz (anim.) (LV2322)/81-84 AS
*The Wizard of Speed and Time (ID7209SG)IE/90 DS
*Wizards (134280)Fox/89 DS
*The Wolf Man (40031)MCA/88 AM CLV/CAV
*The Woman in Red (VL5055)Ves/81-84 AS
*Woman of the Year (ML100093)MGM/88 AM
The Women (ML100506)MGM/85 AM
*Women on the Verge of a Nervous Breakdown (ID6951OR)IE/90 DM
*Wonderland (ID7147VE)IE/90 DM
Woody Woodpecker and His Friends O(61008)MCA/81-84 AM
*The Word (ID7487FR)IE/90 DM
*Words and Music (ML100861)MGM/90 DM
Words of Love (X-rated) (Z0098)IE/90 AM
*Working Girl (170980)Fox/90 DS
*Working Stiffs (LV60940)Par/85 AM
*World According to Goofy O(256AS)Dis/85 AM
*A World Apart (ID7190ME)IE/90 DS
*World Gone Wild (ID6132ME)IE/88 AM
*The World of Suzie Wong (LV66082)Par/89 AM
*WPINK TV (X-rated) (Z0088)IE/89 AM CLV/CAV
*The Wraith (ID5232VE)IE/88 DS
*The Wrong Guys (ID6063NW)IE/88 DS
*Wrong is Right (ID6381RC)IE/89 DM
*Wuthering Heights (30795)Nel/85 AM
*The X from Outer Space/Yongary, Monster from the Deep (ID6922OR)IE/90 DM
Xanadu (17006)MCA/81-84 AS
Yankee Doodle Dandy O(451380)Fox/81-84 AM
*The Year My Voice Broke (ID6342IV)IE/89 DS
The Year of Living Dangerously (ML100243)MGM/81-84 AM
*Year of the Dragon (ML100713)MGM/86 DS
*A Year of the Quiet Sun (ID5284LO)IE/88 DM
*The Yearling (ML100500)MGM/89 DM
*Yellow Submarine (ML101170)MGM/87 DS
Yellowbeard (VL5024)Ves/81-84 AM
*Yentl O(472480)Fox/81-84 AS
*Yentl (101747)MGM/90 DS
*Yeoman of the Guard (PA84074)PA/85 AS
Yes, Giorgio (ML100208)MGM/81-84 AS
*Yogi Bear (ID6617HA)IE/90 DM
*Yojimbo O(61435)Nel/86 AM
*Yojimbo (CC1211L)Voy/90 DM
Yor The Hunter from the Future (VLD6070)Col/81-84 AM
*You Can't Hurry Love (ID5257VE)IE/88 DS
*You Never Were Lovlier (VLD30401)Col/85 AM
*You Only Live Twice O(452680)Fox/81-84 AM
*You Only Live Twice (lb) (ML101565)MGM/89 DS
*You'll Never Get Rich (ID6354RC)IE/89 DM
*Young and Innocent (CC1116L)Voy/88 AM
Young and the Restless (X-rated) (Z0118)IE/90 AM
Young Doctors in Love (VL5012)Ves/81-84 AM
*Young Einstein (11759)WB/90 DS
Young Frankenstein (110380)Fox/81-84 AS
*Young Guns (ID6245VE)IE/89 DS
*Young Lady Chatterly II O(VL9926)Ves/86 AS
The Young Like It Hot (X-rated) (I0026)IE/85 AM
*The Young Lions (105780)Fox/90 DS
Young Mr. Lincoln (142080)Fox/90 DM
*Young Nurses in Love (ID6460VE)IE/89 DM
*Young Sherlock Holmes (LV1670)Par/87 DS
*The Young Stranger (ID6989TU)IE/90 DM
*Youngblood (ML100966)MGM/89 DS
The Younger the Better (X-rated) (I0008)IE/81-84 AM
*Yours, Mine & Ours (ML101702)MGM/90 DM
The Yum-Yum Girls O(28010)MCA/81-84 AM
Z (dubbed) (VLD6100)Col/81-84 AM
Z (subtitled) (ID7570AX)IE/90 DM
*Zabriskie Point (ML100196)MGM/85 AM
Zapped! (16045)Nel/81-84 AM
Zapped Again (77756)Nel/90 AS
*Zardoz (120880)Fox/90 DS
Zelig (22027LV)WB/81-84 AM
*Zelly and Me (35003)Col/89 AM
*Ziegfeld Follies (100173)MGM/90 DM
*Ziegfeld Girl (101585)MGM/90 DM
*Zombie (ID6697MN)IE/89 DM
*Zorro's Black Whip (LV25054)Rep/90 DM
*Zorro's Fighting Legion (LV25055)Rep/90 DM
*Zulu (CC1154L)Voy/89 DS
*Zulu Dawn (ID5173)IE/88 DM

*A-Ha Hunting High and Low (CLD86004)PA/86 DS
Abba O(74006)MCA/81-84 AS CAV
Abba in Concert (MP066US)PA/81-84 AS
ABC Mantrap (PA84080)PA/81-84 AS

*Academy of Ancient Music The Messiah (PA86174)PA/86 DS
*Aerosmith Live: Texxas Jam '78 (ID6487CB)IE/89 DS
Aerosmith Video Scrapbook (522980)Fox/90 DS
Aerosmith: Things That Go Pump in the Night (PA90301)PA/90 DS
*Aida Arena di Verona (PA82017)PA/81-84 AS
*Aida Teatro Alla Scala (PA88210)PA/88 DS
Air Supply in Hawaii (PA83058)PA/81-84 AS
*Al Jarreau in London (PA85125)PA/85 DS
*Alabama's Greatest Video Hits (PA87185)PA/87 DS
Albert Herring (PA88222)PA/88 DS
*Alchemy Dire Straits Live (ID6305ME)IE/89 DS
*Alice Cooper Trashes the World (ID7578CB)IE/90 DS
*Alice Cooper Video Trash (8") (ID7292CB)IE/90 DS
*All Soul's Day Concert 1984 — Berliner Philharmoniker — Karajan (SLV45984)Son/90 DS
*All Star Swing Festival (ML1048)Ves/86 AS
All Strings Attached (0813411)PGM/90 DS
*Allman Brothers Band Brothers on the Road (PA84087)PA/81-84 AS
Alvin Ailey (PA89244)PA/90 DS
America Live in Central Park O(PA82013)PA/81-84 AS CAV
*American Ballet Theatre in San Francisco (PA86166)PA/87 AS
*American Ballet Theatre Live at the Met (PA85111)PA/85 AS
*Amy Grant Find a Way (8") (PA86M038)PA/86 AS
Amy Grant in Concert (LV38400)A&M/89 DS
Andre Watts in Concert (LV12708)Par/89 DS
*Andrea Chenier (PA87187)PA/87 DS
*Anita Baker One Night of Rapture (40105)WB/88 DS
Anna Karenia (Bolshoi) (ID6840CO)IE/90 DM
April Wine Live in London (PA82025)PA/81-84 AS
*Argerich/Freire (SM0583059)PA/87 DS
*Aria (1113)Acd/88 AS
*Ariadne Auf Naxos (0725111)PGM/89 DS
*Art Blakey & the Jazz Mesengers (ID7166SO)IE/90 DS
Ashford & Simpson (PA83041)PA/81-84 AS
Ashford & Simpson (8") (PA85M012)PA/85 AS
Asia in Asia (PA84092)PA/81-84 AS
*Atlantic Starr (8") (PA87M050)PA/87 AS
*B.B. King and Friends (ID6871HB)IE/90 DS
*B.B. King Live at Nick's (RO194DL)Son/86 AS
*B.B. King Live in Africa (ID7240HB)IE/90 DS
*Babyface Tender Lover The Videos (8") (ID7577CB)IE/90 DS
*Bananrama The Greatest Hits Collection (0806311)PGM/89 DS
*Band is Back, The (PA85120)PA/85 AS
*Barbra Streisand A Happening in Central Park (PA88205)IE/88 DM
*Barbra Streisand One Voice (PA87204)PA/87 DS
*Barbra Streisand Putting It All Together (710180)Fox/86 DS
The Barber of Seville (NY Opera) (LV127072)Par/90 DS
Barry Manilow in Concert at the Greek Theatre (PA84065)PA/81-84 AS
*Barry Manilow Live at Blenheim Palace (PA87181)PA/87 DS
Barry Manilow On Broadway (PA90022)PA/90 DS
*Beach Boys An American Band (VL1011)Ves/85 AS
*Beethoven Symphony No. 9 (Bernstein in Vienna) (0722081)PGM/88 DS
*Beethoven — Symphonies Nos. 4 & 7 — Carlos Kleiber (0702001)PGM/88 DS
*Beethoven — Symphony No. 3 — Bruggen (0702071)PGM/89 DS
*Beethoven — Symphony No. 9 (603326RG)BMG/90 DM
Beethoven: Concerto No. 3/Brahms: Concerto No. 1 (Rubenstein) (0712091)PGM/89 DM
The Beethoven Cycle: Guarneri Quartet (PA89243)PA/90 DS
*Beethoven: Symphonies Nos. 3 & 7 (0722111)PGM/89 DS
*Beethoven: Symphonies Nos. 5 & 6 (0722011)PGM/88 DS
Belinda Carlisle: Runaway Videos (PA90023)PA/90 DS
Ben Sidran On the Live Side (PS87017)PA/87 DS
*Benatar (PA85112)PA/85 AS
*Berlin (PA85122)PA/85 AS
Bernadette Peters in Concert O(74008)MCA/81-84 AS
*Bernstein: West Side Story — The Making of the Recording (0722061)PGM/88 DS
*The Best of Blondie (ID5302PA)IE/88 DS
*The Best of Elvis Costello (709280)Fox/89 DS
*The Best of Pat Benatar (VL1073)Ves/87 AS
*The Best of Spike Jones Vol. 1 (LV12538)Par/87 AM
*The Best of Spike Jones Vol. 2 (LV12539)Par/87 AM
*Bette Midler Art or Bust! (VL3080)Ves/85 AS
The Bette Midler Show O(12515)Nel/81-84 AS
Bette Midler's Mondo Beyondo (ID7493HB)IE/90 DM
*Big Bands at Disneyland Cab Calloway O(251AS)Dis/85 AS
*Big Bands at Disneyland Lionel Hampton O(252AS)Dis/85 AS
*Big Bands at Disneyland Woody Herman O(253AS)Dis/85 AS
*Big Brother and the Holding Company Ball and Chain (ID6731RH)IE/89 DM
*Big Country Live (ID6357ME)IE/89 DS
Billy Budd (PA90298)PA/90 DS
*Billy Joel: Eye of the Storm (ID7631CB)IE/90 DS CAV
Billy Joel Live from Long Island (629780)Fox/81-84 AS
*Billy Joel The Video Album Volume I (619880)Fox/86 DS
*Billy Joel The Video Album Volume II (356980)Fox/87 DS
Billy Squire Live in the Dark (PA83036)PA/81-84 AS
Blancmange (8") (PA84M018)PA/85 AS
*Blues Alive (PA85143)PA/85 AS
*Bob Dylan Don't Look Back (LV2382)Par/86 AM
Bob Marley and the Wailers Live from the Santa Barbara Bowl (PA82020) PA/81-84 AS
*Bob Marley Legend (ID6038RC)IE/88 DS
Bobby Brown: My Prerogative (PA89247)PA/90 DS
*Bobby McFerrin Spontaneous Invention (PS87015)PA/87 DS
Bobby Short at the Cafe Carlyle (ID7271VW)IE/90 DS
*Bobby Short Live at the Carlyle (ML100589)MGM/86 DS
Body Music (PA84085)PA/81-84 AS
*Bolshoi Ballet Live: Divertissements (PA87200)PA/88 DS
*Bolshoi Ballet Spartacus (PA84098)PA/85 AS
*Bon Jovi Breakout (8") (PA86M035)PA/86 AS
*Bon Jovi New Jersey the Videos (0812971)PGM/89 DS
*Bon Jovi: Slippery When Wet (0802971)PGM/88 DS
*Boris Gudunov (PA88207)PA/88 DS
The Boys: Video Messages (PA89249)PA/90 DS
*Brahms Piano Concertos Nos. 1 & 2 (0722071)PGM/88 DS
*Brahms: Violin Concerto/Double Concerto (0722031)PGM/88 DS
*Branford Marsalis: Steep (ID6961CB)IE/90 DS
Brazilian Knights and a Lady (0813431)PGM/90 DS
*Britny Fox Year of the Fox (ID6959CB)IE/90 DS
*Bruce Springsteen Video Anthology 1978-88 (ID6325CB)IE/89 DS
*Bruckner Symphony No. 7 (0712051)PGM/88 DS
*Bryan Adams Reckless (PA85115)PA/85 AS
Caledonian Dreams O(ME060US)PA/81-84 AS CAV
*Cameo (PA85105)PA/85 AS
*Camilo Sesto Madrid Con Amor (SM0580039)PA/87 AS
*Canteloube: Chants D'Auvergne (0712121)PGM/89 DS
*Canyon Consort (PS87018)PA/87 DS
*Carl Perkins: Blue Suede Shoes (PA87194)PA/88 DS
*Carly Simon Live from Martha's Vineyard (ID6572HB)IE/89 DS CAV/CLV
*Carmen (0725091)PGM/89 DS
Carmen (Bolshoi) (ID6838CO)IE/90 DM
*Carmen McCrae Live (MCR01LD)HV/90 DS
Carole King One to One (PA83051)PA/81-84 AS
*Carols for Christmas (PA86178)PA/86 AS
*Carpenters Yesterday Once More (PA85123)PA/85 AS
*The Cars Heartbeat City (PA85108)PA/85 AS
*Casey Kasem's Rock 'N Roll Goldmine: The British Invasion (ID6190VE)IE/89 DM
*Casey Kasem's Rock 'N Roll Goldmine: The San Francisco Sound (ID6191VE)IE/89 DM
*Casey Kasem's Rock 'N Roll Goldmine: The Soul Years (ID5182)IE/88 DM
*Casey Kasem's The Sixties (ID5181)IE/88 DS
Casiopea: Perfect Live (SM0683140)PA/89 DS
Celebrating a Jazz Master: Thelonious Sphere Monk (PA89234)PA/89 DS
*Celebrating Bird: The Triumph of Charlie Parker (PS87022)PA/88 DS
*Chaka Khan (8") (PA86M031)PA/86 AS
*Chaka Khan This Is My Night (PA85129)PA/85 DS
Charlie Daniels Band (710580)Fox/81-84 AS
*Chicago 17 (CLD86005)PA/86 DS
Chick Corea Gary Burton Live in Tokyo (PA83037)PA/81-84 AS
Chick Corea Inside Out (PA90006)PA/90 DS
Christine McVie (PA84084)PA/81-84 AS
*Christmas at Rippon Cathedral (RIP01LD)HV/89 DS
*Cinderella Tales from the Gypsy Road (0821631)PGM/90 DS
Claude Bolling Concerto for Classical Guitar and Jazz Piano (PA82022)PA/81-84 AS
Cocker (CLD87007)PA/89 DS
Colonel Abrams (CLD86006)PA/89 DS
*Color Me Barbra (351880)Fox/86 AM
The Compleat Beatles (ML100166)MGM/81-84 AS
Coney Hatch (8") (PA86M030)PA/86 AS
Cool Cats 25 Years of Rock 'N Roll Style (ML100317)MGM/81-84 AS
Crosby, Stills & Nash Daylight Again O(74020)MCA/81-84 AS
*The Cure In Orange (40107)WB/88 DS
*The Cure Staring at the Sea (40101)WB/88 DS
*Cyndi Lauper in Paris (357080)Fox/88 DS
Daryl Hall and John Oates Rock 'N Soul Live (PA84077)PA/81-84 AS
*Daryl Hall and John Oates Video Collection (8") (PA86M034)PA/86 AS
Dave Mason Live at Perkins Palace (PA82021)PA/81-84 AS
*David Bowie (8") (PA84M002)PA/81-84 AS CAV
*David Bowie Glass Spider (ID6198MP)IE/89 DS
*David Bowie Jazzin' for Blue Jean (PA85112)PA/85 AS CAV
*David Bowie Love You Till Tuesday (ID6307ME)IE/89 DS
David Bowie Serious Moonlight (PA84097)PA/85 AS
*David Sanborn Love & Happiness (PS87019)PA/87 DS
*Davidsbundlertanze New York City Ballet (PA88214)PA/88 DS
*Dead or Alive: Rip It Up Live (ID6963CB)IE/90 DS
Debbie Gibson The Out of the Blue Tour (PA89244)PA/90 DS
*Debussy/Ravel (0722381)PGM/90 DS
*The Decline of Western Civilization (ID6046ME)IE/88 DM
*Def Leppard Historia (0803591)PGM/89 DS
*Deja View (LV025)KL/87 DS
Deja Vu (VAL3804)PA/89 DS
*Dennis De Young 3 Piece Suite (8") (PA87M051)PA/87 AS
*Der Fliegende Hollander (0705061)PGM/89 DS
*Der Rosenkavalier (PA86172)PA/87 DS
Diana Ross in Concert (PA84070)PA/81-84 AS
*Diane Schuur The Count Basie Orchestra (PS88023)PA/88 DS
*Dick Clark's Best of Bandstand (VL1028)Ves/86 AS
*Dick Clark's Best of Bandstand The Superstars (ML1081)Ves/87 AS
*Die Fledermaus (PA84099)MCA/85 AS
*Die Zauberflote (0705051)PGM/89 DS
Dirt Band Tonight O(PA83034)PA/81-84 AS
*Dirty Dancing Live in Concert (ID6248VE)IE/89 DS
*Disney Sing Along Songs: The Bare Necessities/You Can Fly (393AS)Dis/88 AM
*Disney Sing Along Songs: Zip-A-Dee-Doo-Dah/Heigh Ho (588AS)Dis/88 AM
*Distant Harmony Pavrotti in China (ID6226PA)IE/89 DS CAV/CLV
Dizzy Gillespie All Star Tribute (PA89254)PA/90 DS
*Dokken: Unchain the Night (40102)WB/88 DS
Dolly in London (PA83068)PA/81-84 AS
*Don Carlo (PA84075)PA/81-84 AS
*Don Johnson Heartbreak (399180)Fox/87 DS
*Doobie Brothers Listen to the Music (ID6791VE)IE/89 DS
*Doors Dance on Fire (PA85126)PA/85 AS
*The Doors Live at the Hollywood Bowl (40592)MCA/87 DS CAV/CLV
*Dream Academy (CLD86003)PA/86 DS
*DTV Golden Oldies O(707AS)Dis/81-84 AS
DTV Pop & Rock O(705AS)Dis/85 AS
DTV Rock, Rhythm, and Blues O(706AS)Dis/85 AS
*Duran Duran (PA83044)PA/81-84 AS CAV
*Duran Duran Dancing on the Valentine (8") (PA84M013)PA/85 AS
*Duran Duran Sing Blue Silver (I5031)IE/85 DS
Dvorak's Slavik Dance (MC037US)PA/81-84 AS
Earth Dreaming (LVD9009)Lum/90 DS
Earth, Wind & Fire in Concert (PA83039)PA/81-84 AS
*Echoes of Ellington Vol. 1 (0813351)PGM/89 DS
Echoes of Ellington Volume 2 (0813351)PGM/90 DS
*Eddie Money Pictures of Money (ID6967CB)IE/90 DS
*The 80th Birthday Recital: Arrau (0702111)PGM/89 DS
Elektra (PA88221)PA/88 DS
*Elton John Breaking Hearts Tour (ML1024)Ves/86 AS
Elton John in Central Park New York (PA83057)PA/81-84 AS
*Elton John Live in Australia (IJ5198)IE/88 DS
Elton John Visions (120150)Nel/81-84 AS
*Elvis Aloha from Hawaii (PA85145)PA/85 AS
*Elvis '56 (ID5174)IE/88 DM
*Elvis His 1968 Comeback Special (PA85146)PA/85 AS
*Elvis Memories (ML1054)Ves/87 AM
*Elvis on Tour (ML100153)MGM/81-84 AS
*Elvis: One Night with You (ID5319LY)IE/88 DS
*Emerson, Lake & Palmer Pictures at an Exhibition (ID6694MN)IE/90 DS
*Eric Clapton and Friends (ID5213VE)PA/88 DS
*Eric Clapton Live Now (ML1027)Ves/86 AS
*Eric Clapton the Cream of Eric Clapton (0811891)PGM/90 DS
Ernani Teatro All Scala (PA83060)PA/81-84 AS
*Europe (ID6336CB)IE/89 DS
*Eurythmics Live (0802211)PGM/88 DS
Eurythmics Sweet Dreams (PA84078)PA/81-84 AS
The Eve Bingo Miki and Inner Galazy Orchestra O(MJ001)PA/81-84 AS CAV
An Evening with Danny Kaye (LV12704)Par/89 DS
*An Evening with Kiri Te Kanawa (0712081)PGM/89 DS
*Evening with Paul Anka (PA85149)PA/86 DS
An Evening with Placido Domingo (PA90013)PA/90 DS
An Evening with Ray Charles (74612)MCA/81-84 AS CAV
*Exile in Concert (ID6368ME)IE/89 DS
*Fairport Convention It All Comes 'Round Again (ID5355FA)IE/88 DS

Falstaff Royal Opera (PA84064)PA/81-84 AS
*Fine Young Cannibals Live at the Paramount (0819331)PGM/90 DS
The First Barry Manilow Special O(ML100148)MGM/81-84 AS
Fleetwood Mac O(74001)MCA/81-84 AS CAV
Fleetwood Mac in Concert Mirage Tour '82 (PA83048)PA/81-84 AS
Fleetwood Mac Tango in the Night (PA89236)PA/89 DS
*Folk City 25th Anniversary Concert (ID6756FL)IE/90 DS
*Follies in Concert (ID6322FR)IE/89 DS
Four Tops Live O(IG5003)IE/81-84 AS
Fraggle Songs Volume One O(810AS)Dis/81-84 AS
*Francesca Da Rimini (PA87180)PA/87 DS
*Frank Sinatra Portrait of an Album (ML100648)MGM/86 DS
*Frankie Goes To Hollywood From a Wastland to an Artificial Paradise (PA87189)PA/87 AS CAV
*Freddie Hubbard Live at the Village Vanguard (PS86008)PA/86 DS
*Freedom Beat (ID5303PA)IE/89 DS CAV/CLV
*The Gadd Gang Live on Digital Video (GAD01LD)HV/90 DS
*Gap Band Video Train (8") (PA86M042)PA/86 AS CAV
*George Michael: Faith (ID63330CB)IE/89 DS
*Giacomo Puccini — La Boheme — Herbert Von Karajan (0722051)PGM/88 DS
*Girls of Rock and Roll O(680780)Fox/85 AS
Giselle (ABT) (LV12702)Par/90 DS
Gloria Estefan & the Miami Sound Machine: Evolution (ID6972CB)IE/90 DS
*Gloria Estefan and the Miami Sound Machine (ID6488CB)IE/89 DS
Go-Gos Wild at the Greek O(I5022)IE/85 AS
*The Golden Age (PA87199)PA/87 DS
*Golden Earring Live from the Twilight Zone (PA85139)PA/85 AS
Golden Earring Notorious Videos (8") (PA85M005)PA/85 AS
Golden Earring Something Heavy Going Down (8") (PA85M027)PA/85 AS
*Gospel According to Al Green (ID6698MN)IE/89 DS
*Grace Jones: State of Grace (ID6104RC)IE/88 DS
Grateful Dead Dead Ahead (PA82010)PA/81-84 AS
Grateful Dead So Far (PA89238)PA/89 DS
*Greenpeace Non Toxic Video Hits (VL1032)PA/86 AS
*Grieg/Chopin/Saint-Saens: Piano Concertos (0712001)PGM/88 DS
Grover Washington, Jr. in Concert (PA82011)PA/81-84 AS CAV
*GRP All Stars Live from the Record Plant (PS86012)PA/87 DS
A GRP Christmas Collection (PA89235)PA/89 DS
GRP Superlive (PA89237)PA/89 DS
*Guess Who Together Again (PA85130)PA/85 AS
*Hank Williams A Star Spangled Country Spectacular (PAV12599)Pac/86 AS
*Hansel and Gretel (Met) (PA85136)PA/85 AS
*Hard to Handle Bob Dylan with Tom Petty and the Heartbreakers (350280)Fox/86 DS
Harry Chapin The Final Concert O(709680) Fox/81-84 AS
*Harvest Jazz Festival: Stan Gets and Richie Cole (ID6278SO)IE/89 DS
*Haydn Concertos Nos. 1 & 2 (0702081)PGM/89 DS
*Haydn — Die Schopfung — Bernstein (0725061)PGM/89 DS
*Heart (8") (PA86M046)PA/86 AS
*Heartland Reggae (ID7760AX)IE/90 DM
Helix (8") (PA85M029)PA/85 AS
Herbie Hancock and the Rockit Band (661980)Fox/81-84 AS
History Mix Godley and Creme (8") (ML0753)Ves/87 DS
*Hommage A Sevilla (0722101)PGM/89 DS
*Horowitz in Moscow (PA87179)PA/87 DS
*Horowitz Plays Mozart (0722151)PGM/89 DS
*Hot Rock Videos Volume 1 (8") (PA86M032)PA/86 AS
*Hot Rock Videos Volume 2 (8") (PA86M045)PA/87 AS
*A Hot Summer Night with Donna (PA84083)PA/81-84 AS
Huberman Festival Vol. 1 (PA84073)PA/81-84 AS
*Huey Lewis and the News The Heart of Rock 'N' Roll (PA86161)PA/86 DS
*Huey Lewis and the News Video Hits (694180)Fox/86 DS
*I Lombardi (PA86156)PA/86 AS
*Idomeneo (PA85134)PA/85 DS
*Il Barbier di Siviglia The Barber of Seville: Glyndebourne Festival Opera (PA88211)PA/88 DS
*Il Trittico Teatro Alla Scala (PA88219)PA/88 DS
*Imagine (11819)WB/89 DS
*Imagine the Sound (VP1022L)Voy/90 DS
In the Big Dream (PA90021)PA/90 DS
*Incident at Channel Q (PA87186)PA/87 DS
*Indigo Girls Live at the Uptown Lounge (ID6970CB)IE/90 DS
*INXS: In Search of Excellence (0811991)PGM/89 DS
Issac Stern, Itzhak Perlman, Pinchas Zuckerman (LV12703)Par/89 DS
*Iron Maiden Video Pieces (8") (PA84M006)PA/81-84 AS CAV
Itzhak Perlman Beethoven Violin Concerto in D, Op. 61 (PA83042)PA/81-84 AS
*J. Geils Band (8") (PA84M003)PA/81-84 AS CAV
*J.S. Bach: Six Brandenburg Concertos (0712041)PGM/88 DS
*The Jam: Video Snap (ID6306ME)IE/89 DS
James Galway Plays Mostly Mozart (LV12679)Par/89 DS
James Taylor in Concert O(702380)Fox/81-84 AS
Janet Jackson Control the Videos (PA87195)PA/87 DS
*Janet Jackson's Rhythm Nation 1814 (LV38408)A&M/89 DS
*Jazz Life 7 (b5) Chico Hamilton (J0067DL)Son/86 AS
*Jazz Life 7 (b5) Johnny Griffin (J0068DL)Son/86 AS
*Jazz Life 7 (b5) Mike Mainieri (J0073DL)Son/86 AS
*Jazzvisons: Latina Familia (0813391)PGM/90 DS
*Je Te Veux (SM0583012)PA/86 DS
*Jefferson Starship (PA84088)PA/81-84 AS
*Jermaine Jackson Dynamite Videos (8") (PA86M033)PA/86 AS
*Jessye Norman (0702141)PGM/89 DS
*Jessye Norman Christmastide (0702121)PGM/88 DS
Jessye Norman Sings Carmen (0702181)PGM/90 DS
*Jethro Tull Slipstream (ID7467PA)IE/90 DS
The Jets: Airplay (PA89251)PA/90 DS
*Jimi Hendrix Live at Monterey (ID6573HB)IE/89 DS
*Jimi Hendrix: Johnny B. Goode (ID6316SO)IE/89 DS
*Jimi Plays Berkeley (ID5360VE)IE/88 DS
*Joe Cocker Mad Dogs and Englishmen (PA85133)PA/85 AS
*Joe Cool Live (JOE01LD)HV/90 DS
*Joe Jackson Big World Sessions (8") (PA86M049)PA/87 AS
*Joe Jackson Live in Tokyo (LV38406)A&M/89 DS
*John Cougar Mellencamp Ain't That America (PA86124)PA/85 DS
*John Lennon and the Plastic Ono Band Live (ID6582HB)IE/89 DS
*John Lennon Imagine (PA86164)PA/86 AS
*John Lennon Live in New York City (PA86163)PA/86 DS
*John Waite No Brakes Live (PA85110)PA/85 AS
*Johnny Winter Live (PA85121)PA/85 AS
Joni Mitchel Refuge of the Road (PA84100)PA/85 AS
Joni Mitchel Shadows and Light (PA81003)PA/81-84 AS
Judas Priest Fuel for Life (710480)Fox/90 DS
Judas Priest Live (513480)Fox/90 DS
The Judds Across the Heartland (PA89240)PA/89 DS
Judy Garland in Concert (PA83040)PA/81-84 AS
*Judy's Favorites (I5043)IE/86 AM
*Julio Iglesias in Spain (ID6964CB)IE/90 DS
*Jump the Blues Away (0813331)PGM/90 DS
*Kajagoogoo (8") (PA84M004)PA/81-84 AS CAV
*Kaoma World Beat: The Lambada Videos (8") (ID7398CB)IE/90 DS
Karajan in Salzburg (0722141)PGM/90 DS
*Kazumi Watanabe The Spice of Life Concert (SM0683184)PA/88 DS
*Kenneth MacMillan's Romeo and Juliet The Royal Ballet (PA86170)PA/87 DS
*Kenny and Dolly Real Love (PA86175)PA/87 DS
Kenny G Live (PA90003)PA/90 DS
Kenny Loggins Alive O(PA82019)PA/81-84 AS
Kevin Rowland Dexy's Midnight Runners (PA84081)PA/81-84 AS
The Kids from Fame Live at the Royal Albert Hall (ML100205)MGM/81-84 AS
Kim Carnes (8") (PA84M010)PA/85 AS
*Kirov Ballet Giselle (PA85103)PA/85 AS
*Kirov Ballet The Sleeping Beauty (PA83055)PA/81-84 AS
*KISS Animalize Live Uncensored (PA85141)PA/86 DS
*KISS Crazy Nights (8-inch) (0803739)PGM/89 DS
*KISS: Exposed (0801011)PGM/88 DS
*Kitaro: The Light of the Spirit (SM0583194)PA/88 DS
The Knack Live at Carnegie Hall (PA82016)PA/81-84 AS
*Kool and the Gang Tonight (PA85107)PA/85 DS
*Krokus Video Blitz (PA85118)PA/85 AS
*Kyoto Vivaldi (ID5098)IE/88 DS
L'Africaine (PA90297)PA/90 DS
*L'Amour des Trois Oranges The Love of Three Oranges (PA88218)PA/89 DS
*La Boheme (Met Opera) (PA85135)PA/85 DS
La Boheme (SF Opera) (PA89253)PA/90 DS
La Boheme Royal Opera (PA82028)PA/81-84 AS
La Cerentola (PA90024)PA/90 DS
La Fanciulla Del West (PA83056)PA/81-84 AS
*La Fille Mal Gardee (Royal Ballet) (PA81007)PA/81-84 AS
*La Fille Mal Gardee (Basler Ballet) (0702151)PGM/89 DS
La Florza Del Destino (PA88227)PA/89 DS
La Gioconda (PA90002)PA/90 DS
La Melodie D'Amour Le Grand Orchestra De Paul Mauriat (MP-092)PA/81-84 AS
La Sylphide (PA89229)PA/89 DS
The Ladies Sing the Blues (ID7273VW)IE/90 DM
Larry Carlton Live (PA89231)PA/89 DS
*The Last Radio Station (PA87183)PA/87 AS
The Last Waltz (ML100482)MGM/85 AS
*Laura Branigan (PA85101)PA/85 AS
*L'Elisir D'Amore (PA86169)PA/87 DS
Les Paul & Friends (ID7236HB)IE/90 DS
*Les Troyens (PA85137)PA/86 AS
Let It Be O(450880)Fox/81-84 AM
L'Heure Espagnole & L'Enfant Et Les Sortileges (PA88223)PA/89 DS
*Linda Rondstadt in Concert with Nelson Riddle What's New (ML1012)Ves/81-84 AS
*Lionel Ritchie All Night Long (PA85109)PA/85 AS
*Lionel Ritchie The Making of Dancing on the Ceiling (LV394)KL/87 AS
Lita: Lita Ford (PA89239)PA/89 DS
Little River Band Live Exposure (PA83038)PA/81-84 AS
*Live at the Village Vanguard (PS86009)PA/87 DS
Live from the Met: Highlights Volume 1 (PA88220)PA/88 DS
*Living Colour: Primer (ID6958CB)IE/90 DS
Liza in Concert (PA81002)PA/81-84 AS CAV
Lohengrin (PA88224)PA/89 DS
Loretta O(74004)MCA/81-84 AS CAV
*Lou Reed Coney Island Baby Live in Jersey (ID5241VE)IE/88 DS
Love and Rockets The Haunted Fish Tank (PA89242)PA/89 DS
Loverboy Live (PA84071)PA/81-84 AS
*Lucia de Lammermoor (PA84076)PA/81-84 AS
*Luther Vandross Live at Wembley (ID6966CB)IE/90 DS
Ma Vlast (MC034)PA/81-84 AS
*Madama Butterfly (La Scala) (PA87203)PA/88 DS
*Madonna (8") (PA85M019)PA/85 AS
*Madonna Live from Italy Ciao Italia (PA89228)PA/89 DS
*Madonna Live The Virgin Tour (PA86160)PA/86 DS
*Magical Mystery Tour (ID6197MP)IE/88 DS
*Mahler Symphony No. 8 (0722161)PGM/89 DS
*Mahler: Symphony No. 2 (0722001)PGM/88 DS
*Makoto Ozone Crystal Love (SM0580095)PA/86 DS
Manhattan Transfer in Concert (PA83029)PA/81-84 AS
*Manhattan Transfer "Vocalease" (PS85003)PA/86 DS
*The Manhattan Transfer: Vocalease Live 1986 (PS87020)PA/87 DS
*Manon (PA83047)PA/81-84 AS
Manon (City Opera) (LV127012)Par/90 DS
Manon Lescaut (Met) (PA88215)PA/88 DS
Manon Lescaut Royal Opera (PA84072)PA/81-84 AS
*The Many Faces of Bird (0813291)PGM/89 DS
*Maria Callas Concerts 1959, 1962 (PA85150)PA/86 AM
*Martin Briley Dangerous Moments (8") (PA85M026)PA/85 AS CAV
*Marvin Gaye (ID6415FR)IE/89 DS
Maze (PA82023)PA/81-84 AS
Mel Torme & Della Reese in Concert O(74009)MCA/81-84 AS CAV?
The Merry Widow (National Ballet of Canada) (PA89245)PA/90 DS
*Metalica $24.98 Home Vid Cliff 'Em All (40106)WB/88 DS
*Metropolitan Opera 100th Anniversary Gala (PA84095)PA/85 AS
*Michel Petrucciani Live at the Village Vanguard (PS87016)PA/87 DS
*Mick Jagger Running Out of Luck O(350380)Fox/86 DS
A Midsummer Night's Dream (Glyndebourne) (PA89232)PA/90 DS
*Mikhail Baryshnikov's Don Quixote (PA84082)PA/81-84 AS
Minor Detail (8") (PA84M014)PA/85 AS
*Missing Persons Surrender Your Heart (8") (PA84M015)PA/85 AS
*The Monkees Heart and Soul (ID6729RH)IE/89 DM
*Monterey Pop (CC1164)Voy/89 DM
*The Motels (8") O(PA84M001)PA/81-84 AS CAV
*Motley Crue: Uncensored (40104)WB/88 DS
*Motor Fantasy (SS0786011)PA/86 DS CAV
*Motorhead Another Perfect Day (8") (PA87M052)PA/87 AS
*Motown 25 Yesterday Today Forever (ML100302)MGM/86 DS
*Motown Time Capsule The 60's (PA86173)PA/86 AS
*Motown Time Capsule The 70's (PA86176)PA/87 AS
*Motown's Mustang (PA86168)PA/86 AS
Mozart/Beethoven Quintets for Piano & Wind (0722131)PGM/90 DS
*Mozart: Piano Concertos Nos. 19 & 23 (0722021)PGM/88 DS
*Mozart: Requiem (Bernstein) (0722431)PGM/90 DS
*Mozart Violin Concertos Nos. 1-3 Etc. (0722121)PGM/89 DS
*Mozart Violin Concertos Nos. 4 & 5 (0721191)PGM/90 DS
*Mr. Drums Buddy Rich and His Band (PA85132)PA/86 DS
*Mr. Mister Welcome to the Real World (CLD86002)PA/86 DS
*MTV Closet Classics (ML1043)Ves/86 AS
MUSE Concert No Nukes O(706580)Fox/81-84 AS
Music of Melissa Manchester O(PA82015)PA/81-84 AS
*My Elegy (SM0680031)PA/89 DS
*My Name is Barbra (351080)Fox/86 AM

*Nabucco (PA87157)PA/87 DS
*Naked Eyes (8") O(PA84M009)PA/81-84 AS CAV
Nanci Griffith Live (PA90025)PA/90 DS
*Napoli (PA87206)PA/88 DS
*Natasha (PA87184)PA/87 DS
*Nazareth Live (ID7775EM)IE/90 DS
*Neil Diamond Greatest Hits Live (ID6425CB)IE/89 DS
*Neil Diamond I'm Glad You're Here (ML1062)Ves/86 AS
Neil Diamond Love at the Greek (ML1005)Ves/81-84 AS
Neil Sedaka in Concert (74007)MCA/81-84 AS CAV
*Neil Young in Berlin O(VL7077)Ves/86 DS
*Neil Young Rust Never Sleeps (ID5236VE)IE/88 DS
*Neil Young Solo Trans (PA85131)PA/85 DS
*Nelson Mandela 70th Birthday Tribute (ID6337CB)IE/89 DS
Neville Brothers and Friends Tell It Like It Is (ID6939HB)IE/90 DS
New Edition Past & Present (PA89252)PA/90 DS
New Kids on the Block Hangin' Tough (ID6960CB)IE/90 DS
New Kids on the Block Hangin' Tough Live (ID6969CB)IE/90 DS
New Kids on the Block Step by Step (ID7725CB)IE/90 DS
*New Year's Concert in Vienna (0722461)PGM/89 DS
*New Year's Concert 1987 — Wiener Philharmoniker — Karajan (SLV45985)Son/90 DS
*New Year's Eve Concert 1984 — A.-S. Mutter — Herbert Von Karajan (SLV45983)Son/90 DS
*New Year's Eve Concert 1988 — Kissin — Herbert Von Karajan (SLV45986)Son/90 DS
New York, 25 Hours: The Last Avenue (PI88003)PA/88 DS
*Nezmusic (ID6338PA)IE/89 DS
A Night with Lou Reed (PA85114)PA/85 AS
*Nightsongs (SM0583066)PA/86 DS
The Nutcracker (Bolshoi) (ID7241SP)IE/90 DS
The Nutcracker (Royal Ballet) (PA87202)PA/87 DS
*The Nutcracker Suite (PA82032)PA/81-84 AS
Ode to Freedom (0722501)PGM/90 DS
Olivia O(74005)MCA/81-84 AM CAV
Olivia in Concert O(74021)MCA/81-84 AS CAV
Olivia Physical O(74017)MCA/81-84 AS CAV
One Night Stand (704480)Fox/81-84 AS
*One Night with Blue Note Volume 1 (PS86006)PA/86 DS
*One Night with Blue Note Volume 2 (PS86007)PA/86 DS
Orfeo Ed Euridice (PA89233)PA/89 DS
Otello Arena di Verona (PA83054)PA/81-84 AS
*The Other Side of Nashville O(ML100351)MGM/81-84 AS
Ozzy Osborne: The Ultimate Ozzy (619980)Fox/90 DS
*Ozzy Osborne: Wicked Videos (ID6335CB)IE/89 DS CAV
*Pale Moon Tenmei & Carioca (ME18115KT)PA/86 DS
The Paris Opera Ballet: Six Ballets (ID7517VW)IE/90 DS
Pastel Color (MP046)PA/81-84 AS CAV
*Pat Benatar Hit Videos (8") (PA85M028)PA/85 AS
*Pat Benatar The Visual Music Collection (ML1073)Ves/85 AS
*Pat Travers Just Another Killer Day (PA85104)PA/85 AS
*Patti LaBelle Look to the Rainbow Tour (PA86167)PA/86 DS
*Paul McCartney Put It There (0816491)PGM/90 DS
*Paul Mauriat Classical Elegance (VAL3015)PA/86 DS
*Paul McCartney and Wings Rockshow O(PA82027)PA/81-84 AS
*Paul McCartney Rupert and the Frog Song (8") (PA86M037)PA/86 AS CAV
*The Paul McCartney Special (ID6318SO)IE/89 DM
Paul Simon (PA81001)PA/81-84 AS CAV
Pavrotti in London (PA83043)PA/81-84 AS
*Pete Townshend White City The Music Movie (VL1025)Ves/86 AS
Peter Allen & the Rockettes at Radio City Music Hall O(74016)MCA/81-84 AS
Peter Grimes The Royal Opera (PA82008)PA/81-84 AS
*Peter Tosh Live (PA87152)PA/87 AS
*Phil Collins (8") (PA84M007)PA/81-84 AS CAV
*Phil Collins Live at Perkins Palace (PA84094)PA/85 AS
Phil Collins Singles (PA90005)PA/90 DS
Picture Music (PA84063)PA/81-84 AS
*Pink Floyd at Pompeii (ID5237VE)IE/88 DS
*Pink Floyd in Concert: Delicate Sound of Thunder (ID6486CB)IE/89 DS
*Pink Floyd Live at Pompeii (0807311)PGM/89 DS
Pippin O(PA82009)PA/81-84 AS
*Pointer Sisters Live in Africa (ID7239HB)IE/90 DS
*The Pointer Sisters So Excited (8") (PA86M047)PA/86 AS
Police Around the World (IG5007)IE/81-84 AS
*The Police: Every Breath You Take (PA87196)PA/87 DS
Police Synchronicity Concert O(PA84096)PA/81-84 AS
*Portrait of Africa (ID6768TA)IE/89 DS
*Portrait of England (ID6769TA)IE/90 DS
Portrait of Ireland (ID6899TA)IE/90 DS
*Prime Cuts Jazz and Beyond (711480)Fox/85 AS
*Prince and the Revolution Live (PA86163)PA/86 AS
*Prince's Trust All Star Rock Concert (ML101089)MGM/87 DS
*Psychedelic Furs All of This and Nothing (ID6962CB)IE/90 DS
*Public Enemy Fight the Power Live (ID6957CB)IE/90 DS
*Quartet — Shubert: Rosamunde (07020621)PGM/88 DS
Queen Greatest Flix (PA82026)PA/81-84 AS
Queen The Works (8") (I801)IE/85 AS
Quiet Riot Bang Thy Head (354180)Fox/90 DS
*Quintessential Peggy Lee (PA86153)PA/87 DS
R.E.M. Succumbs (LV38403)A&M/89 DS
Rachmaninov Piano Concerto No.2/Strauss Don Quixote (0722041)PGM/89 DS
*RAFFI A Young Children's Concert with Raffi (LV38401)A&M/89 AS
*RAFFI Raffi in Concert with the Rise and Smile Band (LV38402)A&M/89 AS
Rainbow Goblins Story (MP023)PA/81-84 AS CAV
Rainbow, Live Between the Eyes (PA83052)PA/81-84 AS
*Randy Newman at the Odeon (PA85102)PA/85 AS
*RATT The Video (8") (PA86M043) PA/86 AS
*Ray Davies Return to Waterloo (PA86171)PA/86 AS
*Ready Steady Go! Special Edition The Beatles (8") (PA87M053)PA/87 AM U/DM
*Ready Steady Go! Volume One (PA88198)PA/88 AM
Reba McIntire (PA89250)PA/90 DS
REO Speedwagon in Concert Live Infidelity (706180S)Fox/81-84 AS
*Richard Thompson Across a Crowded Room (PA86151)PA/86 DS
*Richard Wagner Der Ring des Nibelungen Das Rheingold (0705011)PGM/88 DS
*Richard Wagner Der Ring des Nibelungen Die Walkure (0705021)PGM/88 DS
*Richard Wagner Der Ring des Nibelungen Siegfried (0705031)PGM/88 DS
*Richard Wagner Der Ring des Nibelungen Gotterdammerung (0705041)PGM/88 DS
Rick Derringer Rock Spectacular (PA85091)PA/86 AS
*Rick Springfield Platinum Videos (PA85128)PA/85 AS
*Rick Springfield The Beat of the Live Drum (PA86155)PA/86 DS
Ringo Starr and His All-Star Band (PA90005)PA/90 DS
*Rio Revisited (0813311)PGM/89 DS
*The Rise and Fall of Ziggy Stardust (ID5320LY)IE/88 DS
*RIT Special Lee Riteneur Live (PS86013)PA/87 DS
Rock Adventure (MS009)PA/81-84 AS CAV
*Rock and Roll The Early Days (PA87190)PA/87 AM
*Rock N Roll Meltdown (0805511)PGM/89 DS
*Rod Stewart Concert Video O(LV099)KL/87 DS
Rod Stewart Tonight He's Yours O(121150)Nel/81-84 AS
*Roger Waters: Radio Kaos (ID6334CB)IE/89 DS
Rolling Stones Let's Spend the Night Together (12315)Nel/81-84 AS
*Roseanne Cash Retrospective (ID6976CB)IE/90 DS
Rostropovich Dvorak Cello Concerto Saint-Saens Cello Concerto No. 1 (PA82024)PA/81-84 AS
*Roxy Music The High Road (PA84079)PA/81-84 AS
*Roy Orbison and Friends (ID6571HB)IE/89 DS
*Royal Ballet Swan Lake (PA82018)PA/81-84 AS
Rubber Rodeo Scenic Views (8") (PA84M016)PA/85 AS
*Rubinstein in Concert (0712001)PGM/89 DS
*Rush A Show of Hands (0805751)PGM/89 DS
Rush Exit Stage Left (PA83035)PA/81-84 AS
*Rush: Grace Under Pressure Tour (0801031)PGM/88 DS
*Rush Through the Camera Eye (PA85112)PA/86 AS
*Sade Diamond Life Videos (8") (7091-84)Fox/85 AS
Samson et Delilah (SF Opera) (PA90296)PA/90 DS
Samson et Dalila The Royal Opera (PA82014)PA/81-84 AS
*San Francisco Blues Festival (ID6374SO)IE/89 DS
Scorpions First Sting (8") (PA85M023)PA/85 AS
*Scorpions: To Russia with Love (0806151)PGM/89 DS
*Scorpions World Wide Live (PA87191)PA/87 AS
Secret Policeman's Other Ball O(ML100175)MGM/81-84 AS
*The Sensual World Kate Bush The Videos (8") (ID7291CB)IE/90 DS
Sexy Shorts (I5030)IE/85 AS
*Sharon, Lois, & Bram's Elephant Show Live in Your Living Room (LV38103)A&M/89 AS
*Sharon, Lois, & Bram's Elephant Show Sleep Over (LV38102)A&M/89 AS
*Sheena Easton (8") (PA84M005)PA/81-84 AS CAV
Sheena Easton A Private Heaven (8") (PA85M012)PA/85 AS
Sheena Easton Live at the Palace, Hollywood (PA83045)PA/81-84 AS
Simon & Garfunkel The Concert in Central Park (713380)Fox/81-84 AS
Simon Boccanegra (PA88225)PA/89 DS
*Siouxsie and the Banshees: Nocturne (ID6358ME)IE/89 DS
Sleeping Beauty (Bolshoi) (ID7279SP)IE/90 DS
*Solo Tribute: Keith Jarrett (JAR01LD)HV/90 DS
*Solti in Concert: Rossini/Strauss/Smetana/Liszt (0712071)PGM/88 DS
Sonezaki Shinju O(MP005)PA/81-84 AS
*The Song Remains the Same (11389A/B)WB/87 DS
*Spandau Ballet (ML1072)Ves/87 AS
Squeeze: Squeeze Play (LV38407)A&M/89 DS
*Stand By Me A Portrait of Julian Lennon (PA86165)PA/86 DS
*Standards Keith Jarret, Gary Peacock, Jack DeJohnette O(PS86010)PA/86 DS
*Standards II: Keith Jarrett, Gary Peacock, Jack DeJohnette (STA03LD)HV/90 DS
Stars of the Russian Ballet (ID7700CO)IE/90 DM
Stars on 45 (40064)MCA/81-84 AS
*Starship Kneedeep in the Hoopla (CLD86001)PA/86 DS
Stephanie Mills Television Medicine (8") (PA85M024)PA/85 AS
Steve Miller Band Live (PA83053)PA/81-84 AS
*Stevie Live at Red Rocks (PA88209)PA/88 DS
*Stevie Nicks (PA83033)PA/81-84 AS
*Stevie Nicks I Can't Wait (8") (PA86M039)PA/86 AS
*Sting Bring on the Night (LV344)KL/86 DS
*Sting The Videos Part 1 &...Nothing Like the Sun The Videos (LV38405)A&M/89 DS
*Strauss Der Rosenkavalier (Bavarian State) (0725051)PGM/88 DS
*Strauss Die Fledermaus (Bavarian State) (0725001)PGM/88 DS
*Stray Cats (8") (PA84M008)PA/81-84 AS CAV
*The Style Council: Far East and Far Out (ID6360ME)IE/89 DS
Styx Caught in the Act Live (PA84086)PA/81-84 AS
*Sun City (ID5150)IE/87 DS
*Sunny Side Up (SM0580086)PA/86 DS
*Supertramp Brother Where You Bound (PA86M040)PA/86 AS
Swan Lake (ABT) (LV126782)Par/90 DS
*Sweeney Todd (ID6423TU)IE/90 DS
*Swing Out Sister "And Why Not" (8-inch) (0801979)PGM/89 DS
*Swing: The Best of the Big Bands Volume 1 (40800)MCA/88 AM
*Swing: The Best of the Big Bands Volume 2 (40801)MCA/88 AM
Symfonie c 9 e moll Anton Dvorak (From the New World) (MC036)PA/81-84 AS
*Taka Iimura Ayers Rock (SM0580062)PA/86 DS
Takanaka World (MP020)PA/81-84 AS CAV
Tales of Hoffmann The Royal Opera (PA81006)PA/81-84 AS
*Tammy Wynette in Concert (M1061)Ves/86 AS
*Tannhauser (PA86159)PA/86 DS
*Tchaikovsky Violin Concerto (0702101)PGM/89 DS
*Tchaikovsky — Swan Lake — Nureyev — Fonteyn (0702011)PGM/88 DS
*Tchaikovsky Symphony No.6/Piano Concerto No. 1/Wessen/Karajan (0722411)PGM/90 DS
*Tears for Fears (8") (PA84M019)PA/85 AS
*Tears for Fears: In My Mind's Eye (ID6359ME)IE/89 DS
*Tears for Fears Scenes from the Big Chair (PA86147)PA/86 DS
*The Temptations and The Four Tops (ID6416FR)IE/89 DS
*Terrence Trent D'Arby: Introducing the Hard Line...Live (ID6331CB)IE/89 DS
*That Was Rock (I5074)IE/87 AS
*That's Entertainment (ML100007)MGM/88 DM CAV/CLV
*That's Singing (ID5259LO)IE/88 DS
*The The Infected (ID6965CB)IE/90 DS
There's a Meetin' Here Tonight (PA81004)PA/81-84 AS
38 Special Wild Eyed and Alive (PA85119)PA/85 AS
*This Is Video Clash (709870)Fox/88 AS
Thomas Dolby (8") (PA84M011)PA/85 AS
Thomas Dolby LIve Wireless (PA84066)PA/81-84 AS
*Thompson Twins into the Gap Live (SM0680138)PA/87 AS
*Thompson Twins Single Vision (SM0583051)PA/87 AS
*Tina Turner Break Every Rule (PA87197)PA/87 DS
*Tina Turner Live Private Dancer Tour (PA85140)PA/85 DS
*Tina Turner Private Dancer (8") (PA85M017)PA/85 AS
*Tina Turner Queen of Rock and Roll O(N/A)DF/85 AS
*Tina Turner Rio '88 (0803491)PGM/89 DS
*To Russia with Elton (904080)Fox/90 DS
*Tom Petty A Bunch of Videos and Other Stuff (ID6832TP)IE/90 DS
*Tosca (PA86158)PA/86 AS CAV
*Traffic Live at Santa Monica (ID6043RC)IE/89 DM
*Tribute to John Coltrane Select Under the Sky '87 (COL02LD)HV/90 DS
Tropical High Noon (ME104U)PA/81-84 AS
The Tubes Video (PA82012)PA/81-84 AS CAV
*Turandot (Arena di Verona) (PA87201)PA/87 DS
*Turandot (Met) (0725101)PGM/89 DS
*25X5 The Continuing Adventures of the Rolling Stones (ID6975CB)IE/90 DS
*Twinkle Square (SM0480097)PA/86 DS
Twist of Fate O(40066)MCA/81-84 AS
*Twisted Sister Stay Hungry (PA84093)PA/81-84 AS
*UB40 UB40 CCCP The Video Mix (LV38404)A&M/89 DS
Un Ballo in Maschera (PA84089)PA/85 AS
*U2: Rattle and Hum (LV32228)Par/89 DS
*U2: The Unforgettable Fire Collection (ID6021RC)IE/88 DS

*U2: Under a Blood Red Sky (ID6039RC)IE/88 DS
*Van Morrison The Concert (0819751)PGM/90 DS
*Verdi Requiem (PA88213)PA/88 DS
*Verdi Requiem (Karajan) (0722421)PGM/90 DS
*Verdi — Aida (Toscanini) (603316RG)BMG/90 DM
*Verdi's Rigoletto at Verona (371VLD)MV/87 AS
*Video A Go-Go Vol. 1 (8") (PA86M036)PA/86 AS
*Video A Go-Go Vol. 2 (8") (PA86M041)PA/86 AS
*Video Love Songs (PA87192)PA/87 DS
*Video Rewind The Rolling Stones Great Video Hits (ML1016)Ves/81-84 AS
*Vienna in Music (0712061)PGM/89 DS
*Visible Results. Liza Minnelli. (8") (ID7397CB)IE/90 DS
*Visions of Diana Ross (8") (PA86M048)PA/87 AS
*Vital Idol (VL1204)Ves/87 AS
*Viva Santana (ID6333CB)IE/89 DS
Vivaldi: Le Quattro Stagioni (0702351)PGM/90 DS
*Vivaldi: The Four Seasons (ML100372)MGM/81-84 AS
Vladimir Horowitz in London (PA82031)PA/81-84 AS
*Vladimir Horowitz The Last Romantic (PA87-193)PA/87 DS
*Wagner: Overtures/Berloiz: Romeo and Juliet (0712011)PGM/88 DS
Warrant: Dirty Rotten Filthy Stinking Rich Live! (ID6971CB)IE/90 DS
*We Are the World USA for Africa (8") O(PA84M025)PA/85 AS
We're All Devo (PA84069)PA/81-84 AS
Weather Report Evolutionary Spiral (8") (JOO30DL)Son/86 AS
Wham! (8")(304888)Fox/85 AM
*Wham! in China Foreign Skies (714280)Fox/87 DS
*Where the Wild Things Are & Higglety Pigglety Pop! (PA88212)PA/88 DS
White Music (MS008)PA/81-84 AS CAV
*Whitney Houston The No. 1 Video Hits (8") (PA86M044)PA/86 AS
*The Who Live Featuring the Rock Opera Tommy (ID6968CB)IE/90 DS
The Who Rocks America O(623480)Fox/81-84 AS
*The Who: Who's Better, Who's Best (0803459)PGM/88 DS
Willie Nelson and Family in Concert (662380)Fox/81-84 AS
*Willie Nelson's Greatest Hits Live (ID6527VE)IE/89 DS
*Windham Hill Autumn Portrait (PS85005)PA/85 DS
*Windham Hill China (PS87021)PA/87 DS
*Windham Hill in Concert (PS87014)PA/87 DS
*Windham Hill Tibet (PS88024)PA/88 DS
*Windham Hill Water's Path (PS85001)PA/85 DS
*Windham Hill Western Light (PS85002)PA/85 DS
*Windham Hill Winter (PS85004)PA/85 DS
*Woodstock (11762A/B)WB/89 DS
Wozzeck (PA90001)PA/90 DS
Wynton Marsalis Blues and Swing (PA89230)PA/89 DS
*X: The Unheard Music (620080)Fox/89 DS
*Yehudi Menuhin: Tribute to J.S. Bach (ID7142VW)IE/90 DS
*YesSongs (VL7033)Ves/85 AS U/90 DS
*Yngwie Malmsteen Trial By Fire (0809991)PGM/89 DS
*Yoko Ono Then and Now (PA85116)PA/85 AS
*Ziggy Stardust and the Spiders from Mars (ID5320LY)IE/88 DS
Zubin Mehta Leontyne Price (LV12705)Par/89 DS

Adult Party Games O(37608)OPA/81-84 CAV AM
Aerobicise The Beautiful Workout O(LV2308)Par/81-84 AS
Aerobicise The Beginning Workout O(LV2312)Par/81-84 AS
Aerobicise The Ultimate Workout O(LV2313)Par/81-84 AS
*The Ages of Humankind: The Hubley Studios (761AS)Dis/87 AM
*Airshow (ID7171SO)IE/90 DS
*All the Best, Steve Allen (ID6477ME)IE/89 DM
*Allegro Non Troppo (ID6266RC)IE/89 DS
*American Visions: Arcadia (LVD9013)Lum/90 DS
*American Visions: Great Smokey Mountains (LVD9012)Lum/90 DS
*American Visions: Olympic (LVD9014)Lum/90 DS
*Andrew Dice Clay Live! The Dice Man Cometh (ID6885VE)IE/90 DS
*Andrew Wyeth The Helga Pictures (VP187)VPI/88 AS CAV
*Ansel Adams: Photographer (ID53339PA)IE/88 DM
*Aretha Franklin The Queen of Soul (ID6726PA)IE/89 DS
*Audubon Society's VideoGuide to the Birds of America (2511VLD)MV/86 AM
*Autumn Whispers (ID6520MT)IE/89 DS
*Bachdisc (V1013L)Voy/88 DM CAV
*Backstage at the Kirov (ID7465PA)IE/90 DS
Bagunca (VAL3006)PA/89 AS
*Basic French by Video (2314)MV/88 AM
*Basic Spanish by Video (2311)MV/87 AM
*Beat of the Festival of Claymation (ID5298PA)IE/88 DS CAV
Belly Dancing O(37602)OPA/81-84 DCAM CAV
*Benjamin Britten — War Requiem — Derek Jarmin (0712151)PGM/89 DS

*Best Buns on the Beach (ID6422NS)IE/89 DM
*The Best of Chevy Chase (ID5162)IE/88 DM
*The Best of Comic Relief (ID5265LO)IE/88 DM
The Best of Eddie Murphy (LV2323)Par/89 DM
Best Of 60 Minutes Vol. One (7050-80)Fox/81-84 AM
*The Best of the Cutting Edge (ID6730RH)IE/89 DS
*Best of the WWF Vol. 1 O(LV003)CV/86 CLV/CAV AM
Beverly Hills Knockouts (ID7261CE)IE/90 DM
*Big City Comedy (VL3137)Ves/86 AM
*Bill Cosby, Himself (1456-80)Fox/85 AM
*Bill Viola I Do Not Know What It Is I Am Like (1004L)Voy/87 AS CAV
*Bill Viola Selected Works (10003L)Voy/87 CAV AM
*Billy Crystal A Comic's Line (LV2329)Par/85 AS
*Billy Crystal Don't Get Me Started (VL3140)Ves/86 AS
*Blondes Vs. Brunettes Texas Strip-Off (ID6364CE)IE/89 DS
*Boy's Night Out (ID6465CE)IE/89 DM
*The Boys of Summer O(VL7017)VA/86 AM
Buddy Hackett: Live and Uncensored (PA87106)PA/88 AS
*Bugs Bunny Superstar (ML101323)MGM/88 AM
*Bujones: In His Image (PA90014)PA/90 DS
*Buster Keaton A Hard Act to Follow (ID6898HB)IE/90 DM
California Bikini Classics (ID7260CE)IE/90 DM
*Canyon Dreams (ID5171)IE/88 DS
Carlin At Carnegie (VL2017)Ves/81-84 AM
*Carlin on Campus (VL3061)Ves/85 AM
*Carrozzeria Michelotti (PI88005)PA/88 DS CAV
Carrozzeria: Bertone (P188002)PA/88 DS CAV
*Chariots of the Gods? (ID6855VC)IE/90 DM
*Catch a Rising Star (PA85142)PA/85 AS
*Comedy Videos (VL3120)Ves/85 AM
*Comic Relief III (ID6735KV)IE/89 DS
*The Compleat Al (708480)Fox/85 AS
*Computer Magic (ID7648CP)IE/90 DM CAV
Creative Camera O(HP019)PA/81-84 DCAM CAV
*Crystal Vista (LVD8911)Lum/89 DS CAV
*Dance of Darkness (V1023L)Voy/90 DS
*Dario Argento's World of Horror (ID6701VK)IE/89 DM
*The Death Trap Videodisc (DEATRA01LS)ViD/89 AM
Dick Cavett's Hocus Pocus (VL3006)Ves/81-84 AM
*Dojoji Temple, House of Flame Kihachiro Kawamoto (PS188016)PA/89 AM CAV
*Dorf on Golf (ID6373J2)IE/89 DM
Dr. Duck's Super Secret All-Purpose Sauce (ID7483PA)IE/90 DM
*Dream Machine An Anthology of Computer Graphics (V1001L)Voy/87 DM CAV
*Dream Machine Volume Two Computer Dreams (V1012L)Voy/89 DM CAV
*Ducks Unlimited Guide to Waterfowl and Game Birds (2611LVD)MV/88 AM
*Eadweard Muybridge: Motion Studies (V1028L)Voy/90 DS CAV
The Eagle Has Landed (ID7482PA)IE/90 DM
Eddie Murphy Delirious (LV2323)Par/81-84 AS
Eddie Murphy Raw (LV32037)Par/88 DS
*The Eighth Van Cliburn International Piano Competition (605556RG)BMG/90 DS
*The Electric V. Thomas Wilbrandt (0712171)PGM/90 DS
*Elvis: The Great Performances Volume One: Center Stage (1032AS)Dis/90 DS
*Elvis: The Great Performances Volume One: The Man and His Music (1033AS)Dis/90 DS
*Encyclopedia of Animals Volume 1 Mammals 1 (PS188001)PA/88 AM CAV
*Encyclopedia of Animals Volume 2 Mammals 2 (PS188007)PA/88 AM CAV
*Encyclopedia of Animals Volume 3 Mammals 3 (PS188008)PA/88 AM CAV
*Encyclopedia of Animals Volume 4 Birds 1 (PS188006)PA/88 DCAM CAV
*Encyclopedia of Animals Volume 5 Birds 2 (PS188009)PA/88 DCAM CAV
*Encyclopedia of Animals Volume 6 Reptiles and Amphibians (PS188002)PA/88 DCAM CAV
*Encyclopedia of Animals Volume 7 Insects and Spiders (PS188010)PA/88 DCAM CAV
*Encyclopedia of Animals Volume 8 Fish and Invertebrates (PS188011)PA/88 DCAM CAV
Entertaining the Troops (ID7514SO)IE/90 DM
An Evening at La Cage (IG5004)IE/81-84 AM
An Evening with Robin Williams (PA83050)PA/81-84 AS
*The Eye Hears the Ear Sees (ID6788ML)IE/90 DM
*The Fantasy Film Worlds of George Pal (INW5197)IE/88 DM
*Female Impersonator Pageant (I5002)IE/85 AM
*First Annual Playmate Review (625580)Fox/81-84 AM
The First National Kidisc (64619)OPA/81-84 DCAM CAV
*Fonteyn & Nureyev: The Perfect Partnership (PA90017)PA/90 DM
Football Follies and Sensational Sixties (LV001)NFL/81-84 AM

*Footsteps of Giants (ID5338PA)IE/88 DM
*For All Mankind (V1019L)Voy/89 DS CAV
*For All Mankind (V1018L)Voy/89 DS
*45/85 America and the World Since World War II Volume I 1945-52 (VL1044)Ves/86 AM
*45/85 America and the World Since World War II Volume I 1953-60 (VL1045)Ves/86 AM
*45/85 America and the World Since World War II Volume I 1961-75 (VL1046)Ves/86 AM
*45/85 America and the World Since World War II Volume I 1976-85 (VL1047)Ves/86 AM
Free Fall (SS0586019)PA/88 DM CAV
*From Mao to Mozart (ID5277LO)IE/88 DS
Fun & Games (37601)OPA/81-84 DCAM CAV
*Gabe Kaplan As Groucho (ID6372J2)IE/89 DS
*Galapagos My Fragile World (ID6525VE)IE/89 DS
Gallagher Mellon Crazy (LV2339)Par/85 AS
*Gallagher Some Uncensored Evening (PA83046)PA/81-84 AM
*Gallagher Stuck in the 60s (LV02332)Par/85 AM
*Gallagher The Maddest (LV02333)Par/85 AS
Gardening at Home O(11110)OPA/81-84 DCAM CAV
*Gary Shandling 25th Anniversary Special (LV2390)Par/87 AS
*George Carlin Playing with Your Head (VL3154)Ves/87 AS
*George Gershwin Remembered (0712111)PGM/89 DM
*Gift of the Whales (ID7097MM)IE/90 DM CAV
Girl Groups The Story of A Sound (ML00194)MGM/81-84 AM
The Girls of Penthouse (VL3047)Ves/85 AM
Girls of the Crazy Horse Too (ID7231IC)IE/90 DM
Glamour Through Your Lens (ID7396HO)IE/90 DS
Golden Decade of College Football, 1970-1979 (370180)Fox/81-84 AM
Great Adventurers and Their Quests: Indiana Jones and the Last Crusade (LV83064)Par/90 DM
Great American Centerfold Search (ID6326CE)IE/90 DM
*Great National Parks Yosemite/Grand Canyon/Yellowstone (LVD8901)Lum/89 DS
*The Great Quake of '89 (ABCCD1)Voy/89 DS CAV
The Greatest Adventure (VI2005)Ves/81-84 AM
Greg Norman The Complete Golfer Part I (LV126832)Par/89 AM CAV
Greg Norman The Complete Golfer Part II (LV12685)Par/89 AM CAV
*Hawaiian Paradise (LVD9011)Lum/90 DS
The Hardbody Workout (ID6466CE)IE/89 DM
Hearts & Minds (LV2250)Par/81-84 AM
*Heaven (ID5308PA)IE/88 DS
Here It Is, Burlesque (VL3004)Ves/81-84 AM
History Disquiz (37069)OPA/81-84 DCAM CAV
*Hollywood Out-takes and Rare Footage (VLD30432)Col/85 AM
Hotel Terminus (ID6763VV)IE/90 DM
How to Watch Pro Football (86515)OPA/81-84 DCAM CAV
*Howie Mandel Watusi Tour (LV12546)Par/87 AS
*Hulkmania (LV002)CV/86 AM CLV/CAV
I Like to Hurt People (I9515)IE/86O AM
*Illumination (LVD8909)Lum/89 DS CAV
In Search of Historic Jesus (ID7112VE)IE/90 DM
*Invasion Earth (ID6028NW)IE/88 DM CAV/CLV
*Island Breeze (MS16222LD)PA/87 AS CAV
It Came from Hollywood (LV1421)Par/81-84 AM
*It's Howdy Doody Time (ID6369FR)IE/89 DM
*It's Not Easy Being Me (ID5224OR)IE/88 DS
*Jack Nicklaus Shows You the Greatest 18 Holes of Major Championship Golf (547980)Fox/89 DM CAV/CLV
*The James Dean Story (ID5306PA)IE/88 DM CAV/CLV
*Jane Fonda Workout (PA85117)PA/85 AS
*Jane Fonda's New Workout (PA87177)PA/87 AS
*Jane Fonda's Prime Time Workout (PA85127)PA/85 AS
*Jane Fonda's Workout Challenge (PA85138)MCA/85 AS
*Jay Leno An American Dream (12547)Par/87 AS
Jazzercise (32068)OPA/81-84 DCAM CAV
*Jets and Classics (IVE2)ODC/89 DS CAV
*Jimi Hendrix Rainbow Bridge (ID6727RH)IE/89 DM
*John Fitzgerald Kennedy (LVD9007)Lum/90 DM
*Joseph Campbell and the Power of the Myth with Bill Moyers (V1014L)Voy/89 AM
Jim Fixx on Running (32007)MCA/81-84 AM
Joy of Relaxation (37604)OPA/81-84 AM CAV
Joy of Stocks Forbes Guide to the Stock Market (ML100332)MGM/81-84 AM
Kanako (ME-064US)PA/81-84 AS CAV
*King: Montgomery to Memphis (ID5335PA)IE/88 DM
*Knowledgedisc (GEP85010)Grl/85 CAV
*Koyaanisqatsi O(PA12539)Pac/85 DS
*Koyaanisqatsi Life out of Balance (ID5304PA)IE/89 DS CAV/CLV
*Lamaze Method Techniques for Childbirth Preparation O(11105)Nel/81-84 AM

*Last of the Blue Devils (ID7289RF)IE/90 DM
*Legends of Porn (X-rated) (I0039)IE/88 AM
*Legends of Porn II (X-rated) (Z0069)IE/89 AM
*Les Miserable: Stage by Stage (0806471)PGM/89 DS
*Lightning Over Water (ID5341PA)IE/89 DM
*The Lily Tomlin Special Volume 1 (ID5258LO)IE/89 DM
Lords of the Ring Superstars and Super Bouts (N/A)IE/86O AM
*The Lost Pharaoh: The Search for Akenhaten (ID6790ML)IE/90 DM
*The Louvre 1 Paintings and Drawings (VO120L)Voy/90 AM CAV
*The Louvre 2 Sculpture and Objects d'Art (VO121L)Voy/90 AM CAV
*The Louvre 3 Antiquities (VO122L)Voy/90 AM CAV
*The Making of a Legend: Gone with the Wind (ML101527)MGM/89 DS
*The Making of Der Ring des Nibelungen (0702051)PGM/88 DS
Making Michael Jackson's Thriller (VL1000)Ves/81-84 AS
Making of Raiders of the Lost Ark (LV83049)Par/81-84 AM
Making of Star Wars and the Empire Strikes Back (105280)Fox/81-84 AS
*The Mamas and the Papas: Straight Shooter (ID6754RH)IE/89 DS
*Man on the Moon (230084)Fox/89 DM CAV
*Marlene (13446)Nel/87 AM
The Marx Brothers in a Nutshell (ID6662VE)IE/90 DM
Master Cooking Course (31615)OPA/81-84 AM CAV
*Masterpieces of the Met (MAS01LD)HV/90 AM CAV/CLV
Maze Mania O(37603)OPA/81-84 AM CAV
*The Meier Chronicles (ID7640IT)IE/90 DM CAV/CLV
*Mein Kampf (75555)Nel/85 AM
*Mercedes Benz The First 100 Years (SM0783105)PA/87 DS CAV
*Michael Jackson Moonwalker (ID6324CB)IE/89 DS
*Michael Jackson The Legend Continues (ID6767VE)IE/89 DS
*Michael Jordan: Come Fly with Me (217380)Fox/89 DS
Michael Nesmith in Elephant Parts O(PA81005)PA/81-84 AS CAV
Milton Berle's Mad World of Comedy (ID6915RH)IE/90 DM
*Mingus (Charlie Mingus 1968) (ID7290RF)IE/90 DM
Mondo Cane (IG5001)IE/81-84 AM
*Monty Python's Flying Circus Volume One (LV12543)Par/87 AM
*Monty Python's Flying Circus Volume Two (LV12544)Par/87 AM
*Monty Python's Flying Circus Volume Three (LV12545)Par/88 AM
*Monty Python's Flying Circus Volume Four (LV12560)Par/89 AM
*Mousercize (703AS)Dis/85 AM
Muscle Motion Featuring the Men of Chippendales (PA83049)PA/81-84 AS CAV
*Mystery of Picasso (ML4486)Ves/87 AM
MysteryDisc Many Roads to Murder (VMD83002)VMx/81-84 DCAM CAV
MysteryDisc Murder, Anyone? (VMD83001)VMx/81-84 DCAM CAV
*National Gallery of Art (VPINGA84)/81-84 AS CAV
*Nat. Geographic African Wildlife (VL1050)Ves/86 AM
*Nat. Geographic Africa's Stolen River (ID6531VE)IE/89 DM
*Nat. Geographic Among the Wild Chimpanzees (IDVL1083)IE/88 AM
*Nat. Geographic Atocha, Quest for Treasure (VL1052)Ves/86 AM
*Nat. Geographic Australia's Aborigines (ID6667VE)IE/90 DM
*Nat. Geographic Australia's Animals (ID5280VE)IE/88 DM
*Nat. Geographic Ballad of the Irish Horse (IVE5193)IE/88 DM
*Nat. Geographic Battleship Bismark (ID6884VE)IE/90 DM
*Nat. Geographic Born of Fire (ML1057)Ves/87 AM
*Nat. Geographic Cameramen Who Dared (ID6668VE)IE/90 DM
*Nat. Geographic Creatures of the Nambib Desert (VL1070)Ves/87 AM
*Nat. Geographic Egypt Quest for Eternity (VL1076)Ves/87 AM
*Nat. Geographic Gorilla (VL1039)Ves/86 AM
*Nat. Geographic Great Whales (ML1055)Ves/87 AM
*Nat. Geographic Grizzlies (IVE5192)IE/88 DM
*Nat. Geographic Himalayan River Run (IVE5191)IE/88 DM
*Nat. Geographic Iceland River Challenge (VL1031)Ves/86 AM
*Nat. Geographic Jerusalem: Within These Walls (IDVL1084)IE/88 AM
*Nat. Geographic Land of the Tiger (VL1030)Ves/86 AM
*Nat. Geographic Minature Miracle (ML1068)Ves/87 AM
*Nat. Geographic Polar Bear Alert (ML1069)Ves/87 AM
*Nat. Geographic Rain Forest (ML1056)Ves/87 AM
*Nat. Geographic Realm of the Alligator (IDVL1082)IE/88 AM
*Nat. Geographic Save the Panda (VL1051)Ves/86 AM
*Nat. Geographic Secrets of the Titanic (ML1063)Ves/87 AS
*Nat. Geographic The Explorers (ID6115VE)IE/88 DM
*Nat. Geographic The Incredible Human Machine (VL1040)Ves/86 AM
*Nat. Geographic The Sharks (VL1029)Ves/86 AM
*Nat. Geographic Tropical Kingdom of Belize (VL1078)Ves/87 AM
*Nat. Geographic Yukon Passage (VL1041)Ves/86 AM
*National Geographic Video: In the Shadow of Vesuvius (ID6532VE)IE/89 DM
*National Geographic Video: Lions of the African Night (ID5278VE)IE/88 DM
*National Geographic Video: Living Treasures of Japan (ID6028VE)IE/89 DM
*National Geographic Video: Love Those Trains (ID6669VE)IE/90 DM
*National Geographic Video: Mysteries of Mankind (ID6463VE)IE/89 DM
*National Geographic Video: Return to Everest (ID6652VE)IE/89 DM
*National Geographic Video: Rhino War (ID6027VE)IE/89 DM
*National Geographic Video: Rocky Mountain Beaver Pond (ID6176VE)IE/89 DM
*National Geographic Video: Search for Great Apes (ID6533VE)IE/89 DM
*National Geographic Video: Strange Creatures of the Night (ID6651VE)IE/89 DM
*National Geographic Video: The Invisible World (ID5279VE)IE/88 DM
*National Geographic Video: The Secret Leopard (ID6175VE)IE/89 DM
*National Geographic Video: The Soviet Circus (ID6530VE)IE/89 DM
*National Geographic Video: The Superliners (ID6177VE)IE/89 DM
*National Geographic Video: The Wilds of Madagascar (ID6653VE)IE/89 DM
*National Geographic: Creatures of the Mangrove (ID6026VE)IE/89 DM
*National Geographic: The White Wolf (ID6295VE)IE/89 DM
*Natural Light: Windance (LVD8910)Lum/89 DS CAV
NFL Symfunny and Legends of the Fall (LV003)NFL/81-84 AM CAV
*1986 World Series Highlights (30717)Col/87 AS CAV
*Nova Video Library: Saving the Sistine Chapel (ID6377VE)IE/89 DM
*Nova Video Library: Signs of the Apes, Songs of the Whales (ID5282VE)IE/88 DM
*Nova Video Library: The Bermuda Triangle (ID5281VE)IE/88 DM
*Nova Video Library: The Science of Murder (ID6071VE)IE/88 DM
*Nova Video Library: The Shape of Things (ID6070VE)IE/88 DM
*Nova: All American Bear (ID6535VE)IE/89 DM
*Nova: Animal Olympians (ID6072VE)IE/89 DM
*Nova: Back to Chernobyl (ID6657VE)IE/90 DM
*Nova: Cities of Coral (ID6658VE)IE/90 DM
Nova: Echoes of War (ID7105VE)IE/90 DM
*Nova: Einstein (ID5211VE)IE/88 DM
*Nova: Fat Chance in a Thin World (ID5283VE)IE/88 DM
*Nova: Hitler's Secret Weapon (ID6194VE)IE/89 DM
*Nova: One Small Step (ID6534VE)IE/89 DM
*Nova: Predictable Disaster (ID6536VE)IE/89 DM
*Nova: The Secret of the Sexes (ID6192VE)IE/89 DM
*Nova: UFO's: Are We Alone (ID5210VE)IE/88 DM
*Nova: Visions of the Deep (ID5212VE)IE/88 DM
*Nova: War from the Air (ID6659VE)IE/90 DM
*Nova: Whale Watch (ID6193VE)IE/90 DM
Nova: Yellowstone's Burning Question (ID7106VE)IE/90 DM
The Occult Experience (ID7185SO)IE/90 DM
*O'Keefe (OKE01LD)HV/90 AM CAV/CLV
Oriental Dreams (ME003)PA/81-84 AS CAV
*Outrageous Strip Review (ID6328CE)IE/89 DM
*Painting with Light (ID6165PA)IE/89 DM
*Paramount Comedy Theater Volume 2 Decent Exposures (LV12532)Par/87 AS
*Paramount Comedy Theater Volume Three Hanging Party (LV12533)Par/88 AS
*Paramount Comedy Theater Volume Four Delivery Men (LV12534)Par/88 AS
*Paramount Comedy Theater Volume 5 Cutting Up (LV12531)Par/88 AS
Party Games For Adults Only (37608)MCA/81-84 AM
*Pee-Wee's Playhouse Christmas Special (ID7233ME)IE/90 DS
*Pee-Wee's Playhouse Fun-O-Rama (ID6304ME)IE/89 DM
*Pee-Wee's Playhouse Potpourri (ID6366ME)IE/89 DM
*Penthouse Video Love Stories (ID5242VE)IE/88 AM
*Penthouse Video On the Wild Side (ID6097VE)IE/88 DM
*People Places Things No. 1 Flight of the Dream Team (LV8801)Lum/88 DS CAV
*The Perfect Body Contest (ID5361VE)IE/89 DM
*The Persistance of Vision Volume 2 Outside the Lines (VP1009L)Voy/89 AM CAV
*The Persistence of Vision Volume 1 Monitoring the Media (V1008L)Voy/88 AM CAV
*The Persistence of Vision Volume 3 New Narrative (V1010L)Voy/88 AM CAV
*Philip Pearlstein Draws the Artist's Model (N/A)/86 AM
Playboy 1990 Calendar (ID6870HB)IE/90 DS
Playboy 35th Anniversary Playmate (ID6587HB)IE/90 DS
*Playboy Party Jokes (ID6584HB)IE/89 DM
*Playboy Playmate of the Year 1989 Kimberley Conrad (ID6575HB)IE/89 DS
*Playboy Playmate Review No. 3 (680980)Fox/85 AS
Playboy Playmate Workout O(637380)Fox/81-84 AS
Playboy Playmates at Play (ID7238HB)IE/90 DS
Playboy Playmates of the Year The 80s (ID6676HB)IE/90 DM
*Playboy Sexy Lingerie (ID6770HB)IE/89 DS
Playboy Sexy Lingerie II (ID7489HB)IE/90 DS
*Playboy Video Centerfold Donna Edmundson (LV515)KL/88 DS CAV
Playboy Video Centerfold Dutch Twins (ID6675HB)IE/90 DS
*Playboy Video Centerfold India Allen Playmate of 1988 (ID6785HB)IE/89 DS CAV
*Playboy Video Centerfold Luann Lee (LV513)KV/88 DS CAV
*Playboy Video Centerfold Lynne Austin (ID5133)IE/87 DS CAV
Playboy Video Centerfold Peggy Sands (ID6870HB)IE/90 DM
*Playboy Video Centerfold Rebekka Armstrong (LV509)KV/88 DS CAV
Playboy Video Centerfold Susan Arnett (ID7235LO)IE/90 DM
*Playboy Video Centerfold Teri Weigel (LV503)KV/88 DS CAV
Playboy Video Centerfold: Karen Foster/Deborah Driggs (ID7237HB)IE/90 DS
*Playboy Video Magazine, Volume 6 O(620680)Fox/85 AS
Playboy Video Vol. 1 O(620180)Fox/81-84 AS
*Playboy Video, Vol. II O(620280) Fox/81-84 AS
*Playboy Video Vol. III O(620380) Fox/81-84 AS
Playboy Video Vol. IV O(620480) Fox/81-84 AS
*Playboy Video Vol. V O(620580) Fox/81-84 AS
*Playboy Wet and Wild (ID6583HB)IE/89 DS
*Poetry in Motion (VP1020L)Voy/89 DM
Private Collection (ID7266CE)IE/90 DM
*Pulling Gs (IVE1)ODC/87 DS CAV
*Pumping Iron (ID6224RC)IE/89 DM CAV/CLV
*Pumping Iron II The Women (VL5093) Ves/85 AS
*Radio Bikini (ID5336PA)IE/88 DM
*The Railrodder/Buster Keaton Rides Again (ID6789ML)IE/90 DM CAV/CLV
*Raquel Total Beauty and Fitness (2651)HBO/86 AS
*The Real Buddy Holly Story (ID6317SO)IE/89 DM
Red Foxx Video In A Plain Brown Wrapper (VL2008)Ves/81-84 AS
*Regard for the Planet 50,000 Photographs by Marc Garanger (V1017L)Voy/89 DCDS CAV
*Relax with Dennis Weaver (LVD8912)Lum/90 DS
*Remembering Marilyn (ID6526VE)IE/89 DM
*Rich Little: One's a Crowd (ID6182OR)IE/89 DM
Richard Pryor Here & Now (VLD3376)Col/81-84 AS
*Richard Pryor Alive and Smokin' (VL3075)Ves/85
Richard Pryor, Live on the Sunset Strip O(VLD3375)Col/81-84 AM
*Ricks Your Place for Fantasy (ID6418CE)IE/89 DM
*Robert Klein on Broadway (VL3151)Ves/87 AS
*Robert Longo: Arena Brains (40108)WB/88 DS
*Robin Williams Live! (3147)Ves/87 AS
*Rodney Dangerfield: Nothin' Goes Right (ID6181OR)IE/89 DS
*Roger and Me (11978)WB/90 DM
*Rolling in the Sky F/A-18 Blue Angels (PI88001)PA/88 DS CAV
*Rolling in the Sky Snowbirds (SM0583098)PA/87 DS CAV
*Salamandre Chateaux of the Loire (VP1006L)Voy/88 AM CAV
*Salvadore Dali: A Soft Self-Portrait (ID5337PA)IE/88 DM
*Scream Greats Volume One (LV2368)Par/86 AS CAV
*Scream Greats Vol. 2 Satanism and Witchcraft (LV2378)Par/87 AS CAV
*Sea is a Lady Toshiki Kadomatsu (PI88004)PA/88 DS
*Secret Policeman's Private Parts (PA87188)PA/87 AS
Sex Search (ID7671MI)IE/90 DM
*Sheer Heaven (ID6464CE)IE/89 DM
*16 Days of Glory (LV83712)Par/86 DS
*Smithsonian Laserdisc Collection: Dinosaurs (LVD9003)Lum/90 DM CAV
*Smithsonian Laserdisc Collection: First Ladies (LVD9006)Lum/90 DM CAV
*Smithsonian Laserdisc Collection: Gems and Minerals (LVD9005)Lum/90 DM CAV
*Smithsonian Laserdisc Collection: Insects (LVD9004)Lum/90 DM CAV
*Smithsonian Laserdisc Collection: The Flying Machines (LVD9001)Lum/90 DM CAV

*Smithsonian Laserdisc Collection: The National Zoo (LVD9002)Lum/90 DM CAV
Snow Motion (76926)Nel/89 AS
Solid Gold 5-Day Workout (LV85039)Par/81-84 AS
*Space Archive 6 Encounters O(SA06)ODC/86 AM
*Space Archive Collector's Edition Shuttle Downlink O(SACE)ODC/81-84 AM CAV
*Space Archive Volume 1 Space Shuttle O(SA01)ODC/81-84 AM CAV
*Space Archive Volume 2 Apollo 17 O(SA02)ODC/81-84 AM CAV
*Space Archive Volume 3 Mars and Beyond O(11418LV)ODC/85 AM CAV
*Space Archive Volume 5 Greetings from Earth O(SA05)ODC/85 AS
*Sports Illustrated 25th Anniversary Swimsuit Video (ID6574HB)IE/89 DM
*Statue of Liberty (VL1049)Ves/86 AM
*State of the Art of Computer Animation (ID5332PA)IE/88 DS CAV/CLV
*Steep and Deep (ID5266LO)IE/88 DM
*Steve Martin Live! (VL3134)Ves/86 AM
*Steven Wright Live (3146)Ves/87 AS
*Streetwise (ID6761VV)IE/88 DM
*Strip Teasers (ID6467CE)IE/89 DM
*Strip Teasers II (ID6511CE)IE/89 DS
Strong Kids, Safe Kids (LV85037)Par/85 AM
*Super Fight (ID5139)IE/87 AS CLV/CAV
Super Memories of the Super Bowls (LV005)NFL/81-84 AM CAV
Super Seventies (LV004)NFL/81-84 AM CAV
*Swimming to Cambodia (ID5163)IE/88 DM
*Swimwear Illustrated (ID6529VE)IE/89 DS
*Tall, Dark and Handsome (ID6327CE)IE/89 DS
*Texas Showdown: The Battling Beauties (ID6417CE)IE/89 DS
That's Dancing (ML100603)MGM/85 AS
*That's Entertainment Part II (ML100007)MGM/88 AS
*Theater of the Imagination: Radio Stories by Orson Welles/Mercury Theatre (V1012L)Voy/88 DCDS
*The Thin Blue Line (ID6568HB)IE/89 DS
*The Three Billy Goats Gruff/The Three Little Pigs (ID7170SO)IE/90 DS
*The Three Caballeros (91CS)Dis/89 AM CAV
*Thumbelina (Rabbit Ears) (ID7169SO)IE/90 DS
*The Times of Harvey Milk (ID5299PA)IE/88 DM
*To New Horizons: Ephemeral Films 1931-1945 (VP1010L)Voy/88 AM CAV
Toast to Lenny Bruce (PA85148)PA/86 AS
*Topless Dancing Texas Style (ID6365CE)IE/90 DS
Touch of Love...Massage (30001)OPA/81-84 AS CAV
Touch Ross Video Tax Guide 1987 (2811)MV/87 AM
*Tranquility (ID6243MT)IE/89 DS
*Treasure: In Search of the Golden Horse (VL2023)PA/81-84 AS CAV
*TV's Greatest Bits (LV412)KL/87 AM
*24 Heures du Mans (MS18222BT)PA/86 DS CAV
*Two Moon July (ID5404PA)IE/88 DS
*The Undersea World of Cousteau: A Sound of Dolphins (ID5295PA)IE/89 DM
*The Undersea World of Cousteau: Dragons of the Galapagos (ID5325PA)IE/88 DM
*The Undersea World of Cousteau: Octopus-Octopus (ID5293PA)IE/89 DM
*The Undersea World of Cousteau: Smile of the Walrus (ID5294PA)IE/89 DM
*The Undersea World of Cousteau: The Desert Whale (ID5326PA)IE/89 DM
*The Undersea World of Cousteau: The Flight of the Penguins (ID5327PA)IE/89 DM
*The Undersea World of Cousteau: The Forgotten Mermaids (ID5328PA)IE/89 DM
*The Undersea World of Cousteau: The Singing Whale (ID5296PA)IE/89 DM
*The Undersea World of Cousteau: The Unsinkable Sea Otter (ID5297PA)IE/88 DM
*The Undersea World of Cousteau: Whales (ID5329PA)IE/88 DM
*Van Gogh Revisited (V1016)Voy/89 AM CAV
*The Vancouver Disc (N/A)Voy/86 AS CAV
*Victory at Sea, Volumes I-III (75725)Nel/85 CLV/CAV AM
*Victory at Sea, Volumes IV-VI (75735)Nel/85 CLV/CAV AM
*Victory at Sea, Volumes VII-IX (75745)Nel/85 CLV/CAV AM
*Victory at Sea, Volumes X-XII (75755)Nel/85 CLV/CAV AM
*Victory at Sea, Volumes XIII-XV (75765)Nel/85 CLV/CAV AM
*Victory at Sea, Volumes XVI-XVIII (75775)Nel/85 CLV/CAV AM
*Victory at Sea, Volumes IXX-XXI (75785)Nel/85 CLV/CAV AM
*Victory at Sea, Volumes XXII-XXIV (75795)Nel/85 CLV/CAV AM
*Victory at Sea, Volumes XXV & XXVI (75705)Nel/85 AM CAV
*Video Playmate Calendar 1989 (ID6584HB)IE/89 DS
*A Video Standard (LD101)RR/89 DS CAV
*Vietnam, The Ten Thousand Day War, Vol. 1 (76345)Nel/85 AM
*Vietnam, The Ten Thousand Day War, Vol. 2 (76355)Nel/85 AM
*Vietnam, The Ten Thousand Day War, Vol. 3 (76365)Nel/85 AM
*Vietnam, The Ten Thousand Day War, Vol. 4 (76375)Nel/85 AM
*Vietnam, The Ten Thousand Day War, Vol. 5 (76385)Nel/85 AM
*Vietnam, The Ten Thousand Day War, Vol. 6 (76395)Nel/85 AM
*Vincent Van Gogh A Portrait in Two Parts (N/A)NAP/81-84 DCAM CLV/CAV
*A Vision Shared: A Tribute to Woody Guthrie and Leadbelly (ID6332CB)IE/89 DS
*Visual Pathfinders The World Of Alexeieff and Parker (PS188005)PA/88 AM
*Visual Pathfinders The World of Charles and Ray Eames (PS188013)PA/89 AM CAV
*Visual Pathfinders The World of John Whitney (PS188003)PA/88 AS CAV
*Visual Pathfinders: The World of Oskar Fischinger (PS188012)PA/88 AM
*Voyager Gallery (SD1)ODC/88 DS CAV
*The Voyager Odyssey (LVD9018)Lum/90 DS
*W.C. Fields Straight Up (ID6663VE)IE/90 DM
*Weird Cartoons (ID6732RH)IE/90 DM
*Well Developed (LV12548)Par/87 AS
*Wet Water T's (ID6363CE)IE/89 DM
*What Happened to Kerouac? (ID6702VK)IE/89 DM
*Whoopi Goldberg (VL3112)Ves/86 AS
*The World of dBase (61008)Col/85
World of Martial Arts (37605)OPA/81-84 DCAM CAV
*World Wet T-Shirt Finals (ID6419CE)IE/89 DM
*Wrestlemania O(LV004)CV/86 AM
*Wrestling's Bloopers, Bleeps, and Bodyslams O(LV001)CV/86 AM CLV/CAV
Yesterday's Witness (ID7470PA)IE/90 DM
Yoga Moves with Alan Finger (30002)MCA/81-84 AS
*Yoichi Aoyagi: Ladies in Alaska (ID5098)IE/88 DS CAV/CLV
Yosemite: The Fate of Heaven (ID7520IV)IE/90 DM
*You Can't Get There from Here (VP1011L)Voy/88 AM CAV

Appendix B: DiscoVision Titles

The DiscoVision titles were released between 1979 and 1981. Although no longer in print, they are often offered for trade by collectors and may still be gathering dust in the back room of a Magnavox dealer or two. At times, some titles have been considered to be valuable and worth several multiples of their original list prices.

Because titles were often released to stores and then immediately recalled because of production errors, some which exist in extremely limited numbers have not been listed. The titles below had at least a moderate circulation and are most apt to be those which collectors will be offering for trade.

An asterisk (*) indicates that the disc has been reviewed in *The Laser Video Disc Companion*. Descriptive information and catalog numbers appear in parenthesis. Titles which were released in CLV format are indicated. All others were released in CAV.

The titles have been separated in two categories, 'Movies' and 'Miscellaneous.' The division is similar to the division in Appendix A, except that all music titles have been bundled in the 'Miscellaneous' listing.

MOVIES

Abbott & Costello Meet Frankenstein (22-008)
The Adventures of Chip 'N' Dale (D61-506)
Airport '77 (10-010)
American Graffiti (16-001)
Animal Crackers (22-005)
At Home with Donald Duck (D61-505)
Battlestar Galactica (19-007)
Bingo Long Traveling All-Stars & Motor Co., The (16-011)
Bionic Woman (20-001)
The Birds (11-007)
Blue Collar (10-017)
The Blues Brothers (16-020)
The Bride of Frankenstein (23-003)
Buck Privates (22-007)
Car Wash (16-003)
The Choirboys (12-011)
Coalminer's Daughter (15-005)
The Coyote's Lament (D61-507)
The Day of the Jackal (11-004)
Deliverance (W10-519)CLV
Diary of a Mad Housewife (10-006)
Dracula (orig.) (23-001)
Duel (19-002)
Earthquake (10-002)
The Eiger Sanction (12-002)
The Electric Horseman (10-025)
Family Plot (11-005)
*Fellini's Casanova (15-004)
Francis, The Talking Mule (22-003)
Frankenstein (23-002)
*Frenzy (11-006)
Going My Way (21-017)
Gray Lady Down (12-005)
Great Waldo Pepper, The (10-004)
The Greek Tycoon (10-011)
Hardy Boys Mystery of the Haunted House (19-008)
Heroes (10-012)
High Plains Drifter (14-002)
Hindenburg (11-002)
House Calls (16-006)CLV
If I Had a Million (21-003)
Incredible Shrinking Man, The (23-004)
Jaws (12-001)
Jaws 2 (12-010)
The Jerk (16-015)
Jesus Christ Superstar (17-002)
Joe Kidd (14-004)
Kidnapped (D18-506)
Kids Is Kids (D61-504)
The Last Married Couple in America (16-017)
Last Remake of Beau Geste (16-005)
Lives of a Bengal Lancer (21-002)
Lonely Are the Brave (12-008)
Looking for Mr. Goodbar (P10-520)
The Lost Weekend (21-001)
Love Story (P10-523)
Luther (American Film Theatre) (10-016)
Ma and Pa Kettle (22-002)
MacArthur (15-003)
The Marcus-Nelson Murders (19-006)
Midway (12-003)
National Lampoon's Animal House (16-007)
1941 (16-014)
On Vacation with Mickey Mouse & Friends (D61-503)
The Other Side of the Mountain (10-003)
*Psycho (11-003)
The Railway Children (18-002)
Rollercoaster (11-009)
Rooster Cogburn (14-003)
Ruggles of Red Gap (21-018)
Saturday Night Fever (P10-521)
The Seven Per-Cent Solution (11-008)
Sgt. Pepper's Lonely Hearts Club Band (17-004)
Shenandoah (14-001)
Six Million Dollar Man Cyborg (19-003)
Six Million Dollar Man Secret of Bigfoot (20-002)
Slap Shot (16-004)
Slaughterhouse-Five (10-007)
The Slipper and the Rose (18-001)
Smokey and the Bandit (12-004)
Smokey and the Bandit 2 (12-012)
The Sting (11-001)
Thoroughly Modern Millie (17-001)
Three Days of the Condor (P11-510)
To Kill a Mockingbird (10-009)
Tom Sawyer (TV) (19-001)
Which Way Is Up? (16-009)
The World of Abbott & Costello (22-006)

MISCELLANEOUS

*Acrobats of God (Martha Graham) (72-004)
Archeological Dating/The Big Dig (64-016)
The Art Conservator (71-001)
Baboons of Gombe (Jane Goodall) (51-001)
Better Tennis in Thirty Minutes (32-004)
Big Fights Ali vs. Folley and Williams (87-001)
The Bolero (73-001)

Catch as Catch Can (NFL) (86-005)
Coral Divers of Corsica (J. Cousteau) (51-013)
*Cortege of Eagles (Martha Graham) (72-003)
CPR/Choking (64-001)
Ecology Barry Commoner's View (64-009)
Elton John at Edinburgh (74-001)
Forgive and Forget/Thank You, Thank You (94-002)
Gamebreakers, The (NFL) (86-006)
Gene Littler's Golf (32-001)
Greek Cooking with Theonie Baklava/Orange Sweets (31-002)
Greek Cooking with Theonie Moussaka/Spaghetti (31-003)
Greek Cooking with Theonie Spinach Pie/Dolmathes (31-001)
The Guide (religious) (92-001)
Hyena Story (Jane Goodall) (51-003)
If You Can Walk/Listen to the Mountains (32-006)
In Pursuit of Number One (86-012)
Julia Child Quiche Lorraine & Co. (31-009)
Julia Child The Omlet Show (31-007)
Julia Child To Roast a Chicken (31-008)
Le Corbusier (71-002)
Lions of the Serengheti (Jane Goodall) (51-004)
Louis vs. Conn 1st and 2nd Fights (87-002)
Magic Rolling Board/Skateboard Safety (86-013)
Making of a Torah/Portrait of a Jewish Marriage (93-001)
Mammoth Mountain Adventure (86-010)
Marciano vs. Wolcott and Moore (87-004)
Math That Counts (64-010)
The Moebus Flip (86-007)
Money in the Marketplace/Choosing What to Buy (64-013)
*National Gallery Art Awareness Collection (71-003)
Needlecraft with Erica Satin Stitch Chains (35-002)
Octopus, Octopus (J. Cousteau) (51-011)
Robinson vs. Graziano and La Motta (87-005)
Romagnolis' Table A Roman Family Dinner (31-011)
Romagnolis' Table Abruzzi Specialities (31-012)
Romagnolis' Table Made in Milan (31-013)
The Runners (NFL) (86-003)
Sentinel The West Face (86-014)
*Seraphic Dialog (Martha Graham) (72-005)
Silent Safari (64-008)
The Singing Whales (J. Cousteau) (51-007)
Ski Racer (86-008)
Sleeping Sharks of the Yukatan (J. Cousteau) (51-006)
Smile of the Walrus (J. Cousteau) (51-012)
Smoking How to Stop (52-003)
Solar System/The Universe (64-002)
Sound of the Dolphins (J. Cousteau) (51-008)
Swimming Breast Stroke and Butterfly (32-003)
Swimming Freestyle and Backstroke (32-002)
They Call It Pro Football (NFL) (86-001)
Total Fitness in Thirty Minutes a Week (52-001)
Tragedy of the Red Salmon (J. Cousteau) (51-009)
Trials and Triumphs (NFL) (86-004)
Unsinkable Sea Otter (J. Cousteau) (51-010)
VD The Hidden Epidemic (64-018)
Way Home, The (91-001)
What Makes Rain?/Storms (64-006)
Who Is God? Where Is God?/God's World, Our World (94-001)
Wild Dogs of Africa (Jane Goodall) (51-002)
Winterwings (86-009)
World at War Bonzai (55-002)
World at War Genocide (55-004)
World at War Morning (D-Day) (55-001)
World at War The Bomb (55-003)
Young, Old, and Bold (NFL) (86-002)

Appendix C: Japanese Titles

The Japanese titles listed below represent a coherent survey of the Japanese market. Titles common to both America and Japan have not been listed unless the Japanese version has a special feature such as letterboxing. Numerous Japanese films, Japanese music programs, karaoke discs, and discs where the subject matter could not be readily translated have also not been included.

The generic disc is assumed to be in English and in CLV format.

The codes accompanying the titles of the discs can be interpreted asfollows:

1. An asterisk (*) appears if the title has been reviewed in **The Laser Video Disc Companion**.
2. The 'Catalog Number,' usually printed on the jacket of the disc, is listed in parenthesis after the title and (if present) special descriptive information.
3. If the title has been pressed in CAV format, the code, 'CAV' appears. If one or more sides of the title is in CLV and one or more sides of the title is in CAV, 'CLV/CAV' appears.
4. The 'lb' code indicates letterboxing.
5. Sound codes are the same as those used for the American titles.
6. If the program is not in English, the code 'NE' appears. If the language format of the program could not be determined, but an educated guess suggests that it is probably not in English, 'E?' appears. Titles in English may have Japanese subtitles or may have Japanese dialogue on the second audio track.
7. Because the Japanese catalogs conveniently print the running times for all discs, that information has been passed along at the end of most listings.

The titles have been divided into the same three categories which separated the American titles, with the execption of 'Animation,' which has been split from the 'Film' section.

MOVIES

A Bout de Souffle (Breathless) (SF0781281) AMNE 90m
A Couer Joie (A78L7019) AMNE
A Nous Deux (SF0785150) AMNE 105m
The Abominable Dr. Phibes (G88F5356) AM 95m
*Absolute Beginners (lb) (SF0785123) DS 107m
The Accidental Tourist (scanned) (NJL11825) DS 122m
Aces High (K88L5022) AM 110m
Adieu L'Ami (Bronson & Delon) (C596273) AMNE 110m
The Adventures of Don Juan (Flynn) (NJL99414) AM 111m
African Story (Jimmy Stewart) (RV0601001) NE 112m
The Agony and the Ecstacy (scanned) (FY589) AM 129m
Airport '79 The Concorde (SF0781380) AM 113m
Airwolf (SF0780117) AM 87m
Airwolf 2 — Mission Airwolf (SF0781098) AM 97m
Airwolf III Flight into Danger! (SF0781275) AM 87m
Aladdin and His Lamp/The Snow Queen (Tim Burton) (SV0801036) DM 97m
Alfie (SF0731599) AM 113m
*Alfred Hitchcock Presents (remake) (SF0781217) AM 95m
Alice's Restaurant (NJL99423) AM 107m
Aliens (SF0981282) CLV/CAV DS 137m
All the President's Men (NJL01018) AM 139m
Allan Quartermain and the Lost City of Gold (lb) (SF0785501) AS 100m
Alphaville (SF0785126) AMNE 100m
Amazing Stories I (SF0781407) DS 111m
Amazing Stories II (SF0781450) DS 74m
Amazing Stories III (SF0781475) DS 75m
Amazing Stories IV (SF0781484) DS 74m
Amazing Stories V (SF0781506) DS 72m
Amazing Stories VI (SF0781512) DS 74m
Amazing Stories VII (SF0781543) DS 71m
Amazing Stories VIII (SF0781562) DS 95m
Amazones (FY048) AME? 108m
Amazones and Supermen (lb) (SF0785212) AME? 94m
Anastasia (PILF1058) AS 105m
Andrei Rublev (PILF1118) DMNE 182m
Anna Karina (Leigh) (G98F2633) AM 110m
*Anna Pavlova (SF0985008) ASCX 135m
Annie (scanned) (SF0705275) AS 127m
Another Country (lb) (SF0475513) DM 92m
The Apartment (scanned) (NJL99483) AM 121m
The April Fools (SF0781363) AM 95m
Arabian Nights (Pasolini in English) (NJL99466) DM 126m
Arch of Triumph (PILF7033) DM 133m
*Armageddon (Genma Taisen) (AH009) ASNE 131m
Armour of God (lb) (G98F0138) AM 98m
Ascenseur Pour L'Echafaud (HCL0012) AMNE
Autumn Sonata (lb) (SF0781025) AME? 92m
Avanti! (NJL99369) AM 139m
The Aviator (NJL99551) AS 98m
*The Awakening (K88L5027) AS 101m
Back to the Future (SF0981168) DS 116m
Bad Boys (K88L5047) AM 106m
Badge 373 (SF0781467) AM 116m
Bagdad Cafe (SF0475366) AM 115m
Barabbas (SF0985028) AM 133m
The Barefoot Contessa (NJL99262) DM 132m
Basket Case (7001688) AM 93m
Bataille du Rail (HCL1061) AMNE
Battle Beyond the Stars (08JL72023) AM 98m
Battle Creek Brawl (G88F0077) AME? 96m
The Battle of Britain (scanned) (NJEL99292) AM 127m
Battle of the Bulge (NJEL11086) AM 141m
Battle of the River Platte (LVB1005) AM 119m
Battletruck (G88F0105) AS 93m
Beach Red (NJL99559) AM 100m
Belissimo Novembre (HCL2028) NE 93m
*Belle de Jour (W78L2057) AMNE 100m
Beneath the Planet of the Apes (SF0781254) AM 95m
Benji (G88F5308) AM 87m
The Bible (scanned) (SF0981162) AM 171m
Big Boss (kung fu) (G88F0061) AME? 100m
The Big Sleep (remake) (SF0785001) AM 100m
*Big Wednesday (NJEL11182) AS 115m
The Bird with the Crystal Plummage (lb) (88C596154) AM 97m
Birdman of Alcatraz (NJL99258) DM 149m
Bizet's Carmen (SF1081033) DSNE 149m
*Blakes 7 (G88F0131) AMNE 120m
*Blakes 7 I (G88F0143) AMNE 120m
Blind Fury (PILF7040) DS 88m
Blood Feud (Wertmuller) (PILF1112) DMNE 96m
Blood for Dracula (lb) (G88F0048) AS 94m
Bloodline (SF0781536) AM 117m
Blow Up (SF0785036) AM 111m
The Blue Max (scanned) (FY559) AM 153m
*Blue Velvet (lb) (SF0985208) AS 122m
Boccacio '70 (lb) (SF1081391) AMNE 204m
Bonjour Tristese (SF0785102) AM 90m
Borsalino (SF0981079) AMNE 124m
Borsalino & Co. (98C596056) AMNE 106m
Boulevard de Rhum (lb) (SF0501413) AMNE 119m
The Boys from Brazil (FY545) AM 124m
Braddock Missing in Action III (lb) (SF0785265) AS 103m
*Brainstorm (lb) (G128F5516) CAV DS 106m
Branigan (NJL99427) AM 112m
The Bridge at Remagen (NJL99545) AM 117m
A Bridge Too Far (scanned) (LVB1001) AS 178m
Brief Encounter (K88L5046) AM 86m
Bring Me the Head of Alfredo Garcia (NJL99376) AM 108m
*Bringing Up Baby/Sylvia Scarlet (SF0981256) AM 196m
The Brinks Job (lb) (88C596169) AM 103m
The Bronte Sisters (W98L6014) AMNE
Brother from Another Planet (ML780001) DM 109m
Brother Sun, Sister Moon (SF0981197) AM 121m
Bug (SF0781542) AM 99m
A Bullet for the General (lb) (SF0471772) AME? 117m
The Burglars (SF0785221) AME? 109m
Butterflies Are Free (SF0785158) AM 109m
Cactus Flower (SF0785220) AM 104m
The California Dolls (All the Marbles) (PCLM00011) 112m
California Dreaming (G88F5353) AM 92m
Cannibal Holocaust (SF0781337) AM 96m
Cannonball Adderly (L0801099) DM 53m
Can't Stop the Music (K88L5021) AS 120m
The Canterbury Tales (Pasolini in English) (NJL99616) DM 112m
Capricorn One (FY533) AM 124m
Captain Kronos Vampire Hunter (NDH005) AM 90m
Captain Scarlet Revenge of the Mysterons from Mars (BELL14) ASNE 105m
Captain Scarlet The Mysterons (BELL12) ASNE 105m
*Carmen (TED036) AMNE 101m
Carrie (NJEL99223) AM 98m
Cartouche (HCL1053) AMNE
*Casanova (Chamberlain) (NJL35023) AM 155m
Casque d'Or (FY028) AMNE 99m
The Cassandra Crossing (FY554) AM 122m
Casualties of War (scanned) (PILF7028) DS 104m
Cat Ballou (SF0785162) AM 96m
The Cat O'Nine Tails (lb) (88C596150) AM 115m
Champions (FY117) ASE? 114m
*Charade (SF0471631) AM 113m
Charley Varrick (SF0781325) AM 111m
The Charterhouse of Parma (1947) (W98L2067/8) AMNE
*Children Shouldn't Play with Dead Things (NDH008) AM 85m
*Clash of the Titans (G128F5529) CAV DS 118m
*Class of Nuke 'Em High (SF0785217) AM 96m
*Combat! 1 (SF0501491) AM 100m
*Combat! 2 (SF0501492) AM 100m
*Combat! 3 (SF0501493) AM 100m
*Combat! 4 (SF0501494) AM 100m
*Combat! 5 (SF0501495) AM 100m
*Combat! 6 (SF0501496) AM 100m

*Combat! 7 (SF0501497) AM 100m
*Combat! 8 (SF0501498) AM 100m
*Combat! 9 (SF0501499) AM 100m
*Combat! 10 (SF0501500) AM 100m
*Combat! 11 (SF0501501) AM 100m
*Combat! 12 (SF0501502) AM 100m
Commando (SF0781191) DS 90m
Conquest (lb) (G88F0125) AM 83m
Conquest of the Earth (1980) (SF0781310) AM 99m
*Convoy (K88L5006) AM 106m
The Corruption (lb) (SF0785203) ASE? 85m
The Country Girl (SF0781401) AM 104m
The Crazies (L0985020) AM 103m
Creature from the Black Lagoon (SF0781119) AM 76m
Creepshow (G98F5025) AS 120m
*Crime Story The Complete Works (L520702030) AM 974m
*Cross of Iron (K64L5009/10) AM 128m
Cruising (FY587) AM 102m
Curse of the Pink Panther (08JL99429) AM 110m
Daimajin (DLVD101) AMNE 84m
Daimajin's Revenge (DLVD102) AMNE 84m
Daimajin Collection (lb) (PILD7001)CLV/CAV DMNE 260m
The Dain Curse (EHL1019) AM 108m
Damien Omen II (scanned) (SF0781300) AM 107m
The Damned (NJL11059) AM 155m
Damsel in Distress (A78L7008) AM
Dance with a Stranger (lb) (EHL1077) AM 104m
The Dark Crystal (scanned) (PILF1011) DS 93m
Dark Star (G88F0154) AM 83m
Das Boot (FY059)W ASNE 135m
Date with an Angel (lb) (SF0785326) DS 105m
Dawn of the Dead (SF0980076) AS 127m
Day for Night (NJL11134) AME? 117m
The Day of the Jackal (PILF1107) DM 142m
Days of Vengence (lb) (98C596064) AM 102m
The Days of Wine and Roses (NJL11161) AM 118m
The Dead (lb) (SF0475400) AM 83m
Dead & Buried (G88F5035) AM 94m
The Decameron (Pasolini in English) (NJL99366) DM 108m
Dedee D'Anvers (HCL1048) AMNE
Deepstar Six (lb) (PILF1012) DS 99m
Defiance (G98F5366) AM 103m
The Defiant Ones (NJL99412) DM 97m
Demons 2 (lb) (88C596223) AS 91m
Der Veriorene Der Ehre Katharinia Blum (Lost Honor...) (W78L2060)
Derzu Uzala (lb) (FY041) AMNE
Des Gens sans Importance (HCL0025) AMNE
Destroy All Monsters (lb) (TLL2058) AMNE 89m
Destroy All Planets (lb) (DLZ0122) AMNE 90m
Detective (Godard) (MRLC90002) DMNE 98m
Detective Story (Wyler) (SF0731641) AM 103m
The Devil's Rain (scanned) (NDH009) AM 86m
Diabolica (lb) (88C596159) AM 107m
*Dial M for Murder (08JL61046) AM 105m
The Diary of Anne Frank (scanned) (FY576) AM 150m
*Die Ehe der Maria Braun (The Marriage of Maria Braun) (lb) (SF098-0089) AMNE 120m
Die Hard (scanned) (SF0931670) DS 132m
Dillinger (G88F5326) AM 96m
*The Dirty Dozen (lb) (G128F5534) DS 150m
Dirty Mary Crazy Larry (FY528)O AM 92m
Diva (lb) (SF0780038) AMNE 118m
Divorzio All'Italian (NALA10010) AMNE 107m
Django (lb) (98C596066) AME? 92m
Doctor Butcher (lb) (NDH111) AM 82m
Dog Day Afternoon (NJL01024) AM 125m
The Domino Principle (SF0780012)O AM 102m
Don Giovanni (00LC101/2) ASNE 168m
Doors of Hell (OOLS3435) ASE? 194m
Doucement Les Basses (98C596059) AMNE 85m
Down by Law (SF0781236) AM 107m
Dr. Dolittle (SF0981193) AS 144m
Dr. Phibes Rises Again (G98F5373) AM 89m
*Dragonslayer (lb) (LA09814046) DS
Dream Lover (PCLM00012) 104m
The Driver (K88L5035) AM 88m
Drowning By Numbers (PCLP00063)
Drunken Master (Jackie Chan) (98C596011) AME? 111m
Duel (SF0471787) AM 90m
Dun-Huang (lb) (DLZ152) DSNE 143m
Dunkirk (W78L2053) AME? 120m
E.T. The Extra-Terrestrial (scanned) (SF0781555) DS 115m
Each Dawn I Die (NJL99636) DM 92m
*Eclipse (lb) (FY023) AMNE 123m
Edipo Re (OOLS8) AMNE 106m
El Cid (lb) (SF1080004) AS 186m
El Sur (00LS80017) AMNE 95m
El Topo (NDH104) AM 123m
Ela Nave Va (And the Ship Sails On) (lb) (SF0981049) AMNE 130m
Electric Boogaloo Breakin' 2 (lb) (SF0785030) AS 94m
11 Harrowhouse (FY584) AM
*The Empire Strikes Back (lb) (SF1481242) CAV DS 124m
The End of the Affair (SF0475314) AM 110m
Enter the Ninja (G78F5527) AM 100m
Erik the Viking (lb) (PILF7046) DS 94m
Escalier C (lb) (SF0501488) AME? 97m
The Escape Artist (SF0781056) AS 94m
Escape to Victory (Victory) (LVB1012) AM 116m
Estate Violenta (SF0785160) AMNE 98m
Et Dieu...Crea le Femme (HCL0017) AMNE
Etat de Siege (State of Siege) (lb) (PILF1026) AMNE 121m
Eva (FY064)W AMNE 112m
The Evictors (G98F5367) AME? 88m
*Evil Dead (SF0785044) AM 86m
*The Ewok Adventure (SF0781184) AS 95m
Executive Action (NJL01025) AM 91m
Exorcist Part 2 The Heretic (NJL01023) AM 103m
Extreme Prejudice (lb) (SF0781358) DS 105m
*Eye of the Dragon (3D) (98SX1) AMNE 93m
*Eye of the Needle (08JL99275) AS 112m
The Fabulous Dorseys (FY020) AM 91m
The Fall of the House of Usher (G88F5343) AM 80m
Fall of the Roman Empire (lb) (SF0980024) AS 180m
Falstaff — Chimes at Midnight (lb) (00LS80121/2) AM 116m
*Fandango (G88F0105) AS 90m
Fanfan la Tulipe (HCL0027) AMNE
Fanny and Alexander (lb) (SF1381412) AMNE 311m
Fantastic Voyage (scanned) (SF0781178) AM 101m
Far from Vietnam (anth.) (A65L7039) AMNE 116m
Far North (SHLY2) DS 90m
Farewell, My Lovely (Mitchum) (SF0781348) AM 96m
Fatal Attraction (SF0981511) DS 120m
The FBI Story (NJL11285) AM 143m
Fear No Evil (EHL1021) (AM) 99m
Fellini Intervesta (78LS65) AMNE 106m
*Fellini's Casanova (lb) (SF0980031) AMNE 154m
55 Days at Peking (lb) (SF0980003) AS 160m
The Final Conflict (scanned) (FY555) AS 109m
Final Exam (EHL1031) AM 93m
Fire and Ice (skiing) (lb) (88C596240) AS 81m
*First Blood (lb) (SF0501558) DS 94m
First Men in the Moon (SF0781386) AM 99m
First Mission (Jackie Chan) (SF078-5089) AME? 98m
Fist of Fury (lb) (G88F0071) AME? 100m
Fitzcarraldo (lb) (FY060) AME? 157m
The Five Pennies (SF0471789) AM 117m
*Flesh for Frankenstein (Andy Warhol's Frankenstein) (lb) (G88F0045) AM 97m
Flight of Dragons (anim.) (K88L5045) AMNE 96m
The Flying Ghost Ship (VOLD1004) ASE? 59m
Fool for Love (lb) (SF0781192) AM 107m
Footloose (SF0780055) DS 107m
For Pete's Sake (SF0785146) AM 90m
For the Love of Benji (G88F5310) AM 84m
For Whom the Bell Tolls (SF0571620) AM 130m
Foreign Correspondent (FY022) AM 120m
The Formula (SF0785024) AM 117m
The Fortune Cookie (NJL99387) AM 121m
Frankenstein and the Monster from Hell (G88F5314) AM 89m
French Connection II (FY560) AM 119m
Frogs (G88F5332) AM 90m
*The Fugitive 1 (SF0471761) AM 90m
*The Fugitive 2 (SF0471762) AM 93m
*The Fugitive 3 (SF0471763) AM 93m
*The Fugitive 4 (SF0471764) AM 86m
*The Fugitive 5 (SF0471765) AM 93m
*The Fugitive: Volume 6 (last episode) (SF0471766) AM 93m
Full Moon High (G98F5372) AM 96m
Funhouse (SF0780116) AS 95m
The Fury (FY572) AM 118m
Futureworld (G88F5335) 76m
Game of Death (G88F0107)W AME? 100m
Gamera (DLVD103) AMNE 79m
*Gamera vs. Barugon (DLVD104) AMNE 101m
Gamera vs. Byros (lb) (DLZ0122) AMNE 90m
Gamera vs. Gaiga (lb) (DLZ0127) AMNE 83m
Gamera vs. Gaos (lb) (DLZ0121) AMNE 87m
Gamera vs. Guiron (lb) (DLZ0123) AMNE 82m
Gamera vs. Zigra (lb) (DLZ0128) AMNE 88m
Gamera vs. Gaiga (lb) (DLZ0127) AMNE 83m
Gentleman's Agreement (SF0471770) AM 119m
Gentlemen Prefer Blondes (SF0781301) AM 91m
Gervaise (G58F0272) AMNE
Get Crazy (EHL1024) AM 92m
The Getaway (NJL11122) AM 123m
Ghostbusters (scanned) (SF0785115) DS 105m
Ghoulies (G88F5334) AM 81m
Ginger e Fred (SF0985170) AMNE 128m
Giulietta Delgi Spiriti (SF0981365) AMNE 136m
Give My Regards to Broad Street (SF0781305) DS 109m
*The Go-Between (SF0781385) AM 111m
The Gods Must Be Crazy (lb) (FY083) AME? 109m
Godzilla (original) (TLL2002) AMNE 98m
Godzilla 1985 (TLL2027) ASNE 103
Godzilla Vs. Ghidrah (lb) (TLL2107) AMNE 92m
Godzilla Vs. Gigan (lb) (TLL2107) AMNE 89m
Godzilla Vs. Hedorah (lb) (TLL2068) AMNE 85m
Godzilla Vs. Ibira (lb) (TLL2049) AMNE 87m
Godzilla Vs. King Kong (lb) (TLL2064) AMNE 89m
Godzilla Vs. Megalon (lb) (TLL2147) AMNE 82m
Godzilla Vs. Monster Zero (lb) (TLL2042) AMNE 94m
Godzilla vs. Mothra (lb) (TLL2021) AMNE 89m
Godzilla's Revenge (lb) (TLL2109) AMNE 70m
Going Steady (FY058) AM 90m
The Gold Rush/Circus (SF0981266) AM 144m
Golden Boy (stage musical) (98L68011/2) DS 120m
Golden Needle (G98F5365) AM 92m
The Good Wife (lb) (SF0785505) ASE? 97m
Goodbye, Mr. Chips (scanned) (PCLM00007) 155m
Goonies (10JL-11474) DS 114m
The Gospel According to St. Matthew (OOLS67) amne 137m
Grand Prix (scanned) (G138F5543) AS 176m
The Great Dictator (SF0881295) AM 125m
Greed (anim.) (G88F0032) CAV ASNE 57m
The Green Berets (NJL01002) AM 133m
Grizzly (SF0785011) AM 87m
Hambone (G88F0139) ASE? 90m
Hammett (SF0781055) AS 97m
*Hangmen Also Die! (SF0501455) AM 120m
Happy Birthday Donald (Duck) (SF0781170) AM 97m
Hard Times (SF0785111) AM 89m
The Harder They Come (lb) (TED063) AME? 104m
Harry and Tonto (PILF1073) DM 116m
Haunted Palace (Poe) (G98F5370) AM 88m
Heaven's Gate (scanned) (NJL99284) DS 219m
Hecate (lb) (FY056) AME? 108m
*Henry V (LVB1004) AM 136m
High Spirits (lb) (PILF1055) DS 98m
The Hills Have Eyes, Part 2 (K88L5054) AS 86m
Hiroshima Mon Amour (SF0785133) AMNE 91m
*Histoires Extraordinaires (Spirits of the Dead) (lb) (SF0980069) AMNE 121m
Hitch-Hike (lb) (98C596124) AM 103m
The Holy Mountain (lb) (NDH108) AME? 116m
Hot Dog (lb) (SF0780002) AM 97m
The Hound of the Baskervilles (1983) (EHL1032) AM 100m
House (lb) (SF0781158) AM 92m
Housekeeping (SF0505285) DS 111m
Humongous (EHL1049) AM 93m
The Hunchback of Notre Dame (Anthony Quinn/Gina Lolabrigida) (W78L2051) AM 120m
Hundra (98C596100) AS 95m
*The Hunger (lb) (G128F5533) CAV DM 96m
The Hustler (scanned) (FY577) AM 150m
*I Confess (08JL61063) AM 95m
I Married a Monster from Outer Space (SF0781102) AM 78m
I, the Jury (08JL61294) AM 107m
Ieri, Oggi, Domani (lb) (SF0985128) AMNE 119m
Il Camorrista (SF0981387) AMNE 172m
Il Momento Della Verita (lb) (SF0471782) AMNE 107m
Il Passagir De La Pluie (Rider on the Rain) (G128F5007) AME? 121m
Immoral Tales (L0985023) AMNE 105m
The In-Laws (08JL01009) AM 103m
The Incredible Journey (SF0780072) AM 80m
The Informer/The Lost Patrol (SF0981507) AM 160m
The Inn of Sixth Happiness (PILF1059) AS 157m
The Insect Woman (lb) (NDS2020) AMNE 123m
Inseminoid (G78F5015) AM 93m
Inspector Clouseau (08JL99536) AM 92m
Investigation of a Citizen Above Suspicion (SF0781384) AME? 109m
Irma La Douce (scanned) (NJL99509) AM 137m
Iron Eagle (SF078-1313) DS 116m
Iron Eagle II (w/supplementary) (SF0731672) DS 100m
Island at the Top of the World (LA88L06015)
*Island of Dr. Moreau (G88F5327) AM 99m
Ivan the Terrible, Parts 1 & 2 (inc. footage from 'Part 3') (PILF1100) DMNE

James Clavell's Shogun (SF0931601) AME? 160m
Jim Henson Storyteller Series 1 (50LS80159) AS 48m
Jim Henson Storyteller Series 2 (50LS80160) AS 48m
Jim Henson Storyteller Series 3 (50LS80161) AS 48m
Jim Henson Storyteller Series 4 (50LS80162) AS 48m
Jim Henson Storyteller Series 5 (50LS80163)CAV AS 24m
Joe Kidd (SF0735330) AM 88m
Johnny Got His Gun (FY043) AM 112m
Jonathon Livingston Seagull (DLZ0124) AS 99m
Joyeuses Paques (lb) (SF0785059) AMNE 99m
Juggernaut (NJL99455) AM 111m
Jungfrukallan (SF0785163) AMNE 90m
Junior Bonner (lb) (SF0501426) AM 100m
Junk Man (L0985025) AM 96m
*Kelly's Heroes (lb) (G128F5522) DS 144m
Kid Creole (08JL99335) AM 94m
The Kid/A Dog's Life/Shoulder Arms/The Pilgrim (SF0981294) AM 176m
The Killers (1964) (SF0781485) AM 95m
King Kong vs. Godzilla (lb) (TLL2064) AMNE 97m
King Kong/Son of Kong (SF0981202) AM 170m
*King Solomon's Mines (remake) (lb) (SF0785138) AS 100m
Knight Rider (SF0781249) AM 96m
Knight Rider Knight of the Juggernaut (SF0781250) AM 97m
Knockabout (lb) (G88F0111) AME? 92m
Kuragejima: Legends from a Southern Island (lb) (NDS2019) AMNE 175m
L'Adolescente (lb) (SF0785156) AMNE 94m
L'Affaire Maurizius (HCL1062) AMNE
L'Amour en Douce (lb) (PILF1013) AMNE 91m
L'Annee Derniere a Marienbad (Last Year at Marienbad) (lb) (SF0785135) AMNE 94m
L'Avenir D'Emily (lb) (SF0785211) AMNE 107m
L'Empire De La Passion (lb) (SF0681230) AMNE 107m
L'Empire des Sens (lb) (SF0681229) AMNE 105m
L'Idiot (1944) (HCL0018) AMNE
L'Innocente (lb) (Visconti) (FY100) AMNE 129m
L'Une Chante, l'Autre Pas (One Sings, the Other Does Not) (lb) (SF0780113) AMNE 107m
La Balance (SF0781283) AMNE 102m
La Beaute du Diable (HCL1057) AMNE
La Belle Equipe (HCL0015) AMNE
La Boum (SF0785056) AMNE 111m
La Boum 2 (SF0785057) AMNE 108m
La Curee (HCL0021) AMNE
La Guerre Est Fin (lb) (SF0785143) AMNE 123m
La Kermesse Heroique (HCL0033) AMNE
La Marie du Port (HCL0013) AMNE
La Morte A Venezia (Death in Venice) (NJL11060) AMNE 150m
La Polizia Ringrazia (lb) (PILF1005) AMNE 98m
La Prima Notte di Quiete (lb) (SF0985169) AMNE 131m
La Ragazza con la Valigia (lb) (SF0985164) AMNE 122m
La Ragazza Di Bube (lb) (SF0781388) AMNE 111m
*La Ronde (lb) (1950) (HCL0037) AMNE
La Symphonie Pastorale (G58F0267) AMNE
La Tulipe Noire (98C506055) AME? 98m
La Vie Est Un Long Fleuve Tranquille (EV0603025) DMNE 91m
Laserblast (NDH004) AM 85m
Last Days of Frank and Jesse James (G98F5374) AM 97m
*The Last Emperor (lb) (SF1031567) DS 219m
*The Last Starfighter (lb) (G128F0083) CAV DS 101m
The Last Time I Saw Paris (SF0471784) AM 116m
The Last Wave (G98F0140) AM 106m
Le Bal (NJL34018) AM 113m
Le Ble en Herbe (HCL1050) AMNE
Le Capitaux (HCL1063) AMNE
Le Caporal Epingle (The Elusive Corporal) (PILF1004) AMNE 106m
Le Corbeau (A65L7040) AMNE 95m
Le Corniaud (G58F0274) AMNE
Le Dernier Metro (SF0985082) AMNE 133m
Le Dernier Millionaire (HCL0023) AMNE
Le Feu Follet (HCL0019) AMNE
Le Gitan (98C596057) AMNE 103m
Le Lecon Particuliere (HCL1058) AMNE
Le Mans (SF0781362) AM 109m
Le Million (HCL0029) AMNE
Le Paquebot Tenacity (A65L7035) AM 74m
Le Passager De La Pluie (Rider on the Rain) (C596274) NE 120m
Le Quai des Brumes (SF0781118) AMNE 91m
Le Rideau Cramoisi (HCL1060) AMNE 44m
Le Roi it L'Oiseau (G88F0108) AMNE 85m
Le Rouge et Le Noir (1954) (HCL0030) AMNE
Le Salaire de la Peur (Wages of Fear) (SF0985147) AMNE 149m
Le Samourai (G78F5021) AMNE 105m
Le Serpent (Yul Brenner) (A98L7016) AME? 140m
Le Silence est d'Or (HCL0014) AMNE
Le Tigre Aime La Chair Frache (Chabrol) (MRLC90003) DMNE 84m
Le Tigre Se Parfume A La Dynamite (Chabrol) (MRLC90004) DMNE 85m
Le Trio Infernal (lb) (SF0785194)W AMNE 100m
Le Vieux Fusil (lb) (SF0781374) AMNE 101m
Le Voyage en Ballon (HCL0035) AMNE
Legend (NJL38528) DS 91m
Leri, Oggi, Domani (SF0985128) AMNE 119m
Les Amants (HCL0012) AMNE
Les Amants de Montparnesse (HCL0009) AMNE
Les Aventuriers O(FY052) AMNE 112m
Les Belles de Nuit (HCL0022) AMNE
Les Bijoutier du Claire de Lune (L0805047) AMNE
Les Carabiniers (SF073144) AMNE 80m
Les Cousins (HCL1045) AMNE
Les Fruits De La Passion (lb) (SF0781453) AM 88m
Les Grandes Manouevres (HCL0038) AMNE
Les Jeux Sont Faits (G58F0268) AMNE
Les Liaisons Dangerluses 1960 (HCL0011) AMNE
Les Maudits (HCL0034) AMNE
Les Petroleuses (Bardot/Cardinale) (A78L7018) AME?
Les Portes de la Nuit (HCL1059) AMNE
Les Possedes (Wajda) (lb) (SF0475510) AM 116m
Les Quatre Cents Coups (400 Blows)/Les Mistons (lb) (SF0985064) AMNE 117m
Les Ripoux (lb) (SF0781040) AMNE 107m
Les Seins de Glace (98C596058) AMNE 106m
*Les Uns et Les Autres (FY042) ASNE 184m
Les Visiteurs du Soir (HCL1052) AMNE
Let Sleeping Corpses Lie (NDH010) AM 94m
Let's Get Lost (C596291) AM 119m
Let's Make Love (PILF1046) AS 119m
Lethal Weapon 2 (scanned) (NJL11876) DS 115m
*Letter from an Unknown Woman (FY019) AM 85m
Liberation: The Battle for Moscow Part 1 (lb) (NDH112) AMNE 170m
Liberation: The Battle for Moscow Part 2 (lb) (NDH113) AMNE 180m
Licence to Kill (scanned) (NJL35137) DS 133m
Life and Opinion of Masseur Ichi (lb) (DLZ0144) AMNE
Lifeforce (lb) (SF0785063) AS 102m
Lili (G88F5531) AM 81m
Lili Marlene (W78L2059) AME? 120m
Limelight (SF0881267) 137m
Liquid Sky (lb) (TED113) AM 114m
Little Red Riding Hood/Rip Van Winkle (Coppola) (SV0801037) 50m
A Little Romance (NJL02001) AM 110m
Little Shop of Horrors (1960) (SF0501360) AM 73m
Living Free (SF0785090) AM 92m
*Lolita (PCLM00017) AM 153m
The Long Gray Line (SF0575308) AM 131m
The Longest Day (scanned) (SF088-140) AM 178m
Looker (08JL70003) AS 93m
Lost Command (SF0981451) AS 124m
The Loudest Whisper (The Children's Hour) (NJL99584) DM 109m
Love at First Bite (lb) (TED134) AM 96m
Love in the Afternoon (lb) (SF0575380) AM 134m
Love Me Tender (SF0781164) AM 89m
Lucas (SF0731626) DS 100m
Lucky Luciano (lb) (G88F0089) AME? 111m
*Ludwig (lb) (FY088) AMNE 184m
Mac and Me (lb) (SF0735339) DS 97m
Madame Claude (L0985024) AMNE 110m
Madame Sousatzka (lb) (CSLF11834) DS 121m
*Mahler (G98F0217)
The Main Event (08JL1021) AM 105m
Maison sous le Arbres (G58F0276) AMNE
A Man and a Woman (NJEL71655) AMNE 104m
A Man and a Woman: 20 Years Later (NJEL71634) DSNE 113m
The Man from Laramie (SF0475313) AM 98m
Maniac (NDH007) AS 86m
Major Dundee (SF0505248) AM 117m
Maria's Lovers (SF0781066) AM 109m
Marie October (HCL1044) AMNE
Marooned (SF0985137) AS 129m
Martin (SF0780075) AM 95m
Mary Poppins (lb) (PILF1051) DS 140m
Masculin Feminin (SF0785159) AMNE 103m
Masque of Red Death (G98F5371) AM 89m
Massacre Time (lb) (98C596067) AM 92m
Masters of the Universe (lb) (PILF1056) DS 107m
*Max Headroom 1 (SF0505251) DM 96m
*Max Headroom 2 (SF0505252) DM 96m
*Max Headroom 3 (SF0505253) DM 96m
Max Mon Amour (lb) (SF0781454) AM 97m
Maximum Overdrive (lb) (SF0785210) AS 98m
McQ (NJL11140) AM 112m
Me, Natalie (SF0731769) AM 111m
Medea (SF0781232)W AMNE 111m
Mega Force (G88F0097) AS 103m
Melody (To Love Somebody) (FY027)O AM
Merry Christmas Mr. Lawrence (lb) (FY055) AS 123m
Message from Space (lb) (TED080) AME? 105m
Mickey Spillane's Mike Hammer (Keach) (C596287) AM 96m
Micky Spillane's Mike Hammer: More Than Murder (Keach) (C596296) AM 96m
Midway (SF0571663) AM 131m
Mighty Jack (BELL34) AMNE 100m
Million Dollar Mermaid (G98F5555)
Miracle (Jackie Chan) (lb) (PILF1040) DME? 118m
The Miracle Worker (NJL99355) AM 103m
Miracolo A Milano (SF0680023) AMNE
Missing Link (SF0731696) DS 92m
*The Mission (lb) (SF0985191) DS 126m
Modern Times (SF0681258) AM 87m
The Moderns (lb) (SF0575512) DS 126m
Monsieur Verdoux (SF0881296) AM 124m
Monsignor (SF0931622) AM 121m
Monster in the Closet (lb) (SF0785233) AM 90m
The Monster Squad (SF0785242)CLV/CAV DS 82m
Morning Glory/Hepburn & Tracy doc. (SF0881432) AM 118m
Mortelle Randonnee (lb) (SF0571655) AMNE 120m
Mothra (lb) (TLL2007) AMNE 101m
Movie Movie (SF0781539) AS 106m
Mozart (1976 German) (TES145) AMNE 120m
Mr. Boo The Private Eyes (lb) (G88F0070) AME? 100m
Mr. Vampire Saga 4 (PILF1054) DME? 93m
Mrs. Soffel (G98F5571)
Murder in the Rue Morgue (1971) (G88F5347) AM 87m
Murphy's War (K88L5040) AM 100m
My Tutor (lb) (EHL1030) AM 97m
The Name of the Rose (lb) (SF0985503) DS 132m
Necropolis (G98F5405)
Nemuri Kyoshiro 1 (lb) (PILD7007) DMNE 82m
Nemuri Kyoshiro 2 (lb) (PILD7008) DMNE 83m
Nemuri Kyoshiro 3 (lb) (PILD7010) DMNE 85m
Nemuri Kyoshiro 4 (lb) (PILD7011) DMNE 81m
Neptune's Daughter (G98F5554)
Never on Sunday (NJL99538) AMNE 93m
Never Say Never Again (lb) (FY084) AS 134m
NeverEnding Story (lb) (SF0780039) ASE? 95m
Night Gallery (SF0781382) AM 98m
A Night to Remember (Titanic) (K64L50801) AM 123m
Nightcap Movies 1 (international short films) (MRLC90007) DMNE 97m
Nightmares (SF0781061) AM 100m
*1984 (L0985012) AM 113m
1941 (SF0471693) DS 118m
99 44/100% Dead (FY578)O AM 97m
Ninja III The Domination (K88L5038) AM 92m
Nomads (SF0781527) AM 92m
The Norsemen (G98F5365) AM 90m
*North by Northwest (lb) (G128F5528) CLV/CAV AM 137m
North Shore (SF0731624) DS 96m
Nosferatu The Vampyre (1979) (SF0781302) AM 96m
Not As a Stranger (NJL99645) DM 136m
Notti Blanche (SF0781351) AM 107m
The Nun's Story (NJL11171) AM 152m
O Thiassos (SF1080096) AMNE 232m
The Oblong Box (G88F5359) AM 94m
The Odessa File (SF0985094) AM 129m
Oh! (lb) (W78L2056) AMNE 107m
Oh Heavenly Dog (FY563) AM 103m
The Old Gringo (scanned) (PILF7047) DS 114m
The Old Man and the Sea (Quinn) (SF0471795) AM 97m
On the Beach (NJL99684) DM 135m
Once Upon a Time in America (lb) (SF1080007) AM 204m
*One from the Heart (SF0780126) AS 107m
The Only Game in Town (PILF1074) DM 114m
Operation Thunderbolt (SF0985207) AM 126m
Operazione San Genraro (lb) (SF0471783) AMNE 102m
Orca (lb) (88C596168) AM 92m
Ordeal By Innocence (lb) (SF0785031) AM 95m
*The Osterman Weekend (K88L5016) AM 102m
Our Man in Rio (W78L2054) AME? 113m
Out on a Limb (mini-series) (OOLS82/4) AM 236m
*The Outsiders (lb) (SF0780130) AS 91m
Over the Top (SF0781297) DS 94m
The Owl and the Pussycat (SF0785157) AM 93m
Oxford Blues (lb) (SF0785181) AS 98m
Paisan (FY037) AMNE 119m

Pal Joey (SF0475311) AM 109m
Pane Amore e Fantasia (HCL2031) AMNE 91m
Panic in Needle Park (FY566) AM 110m
Paper Chase (FY562) AM 111m
Paradigm (lb) (SF0781477) ASE? 103m
Paradine Case (SF0781298) AM 114m
Paradise (EHL10084) AS 96m
The Parallax View (SF0781504) AM 102m
Parasite (EHL1067) AM 86m
Paris, Texas (lb) (SF0981010) AM 146m
Paris When It Sizzles (SF0731676) AM 110m
The Party (NJL99505) AM 99m
Pavra E Amore (lb) (PILF7042) DMNE 113m
Pensions Mismosas (HCL0032) AMNE
Pepe le Moko (W78L2058) AMNE 94m
Per Pochi Dollari Ancora (98C596068) AME? 100m
Per Un Pugno Di Dollari (Fistful of Dollars) (SF0471771) AMNE 97m
Perfect Strangers (EHL-1081) AM 92m
*Peter Brook's Mahabarata (PILF1025) DS 420m
Phenomena (98C596099) AS 111m
The Philadelphia Experiment (LVB1007) AM 102m
Picnic (scanned) (SF0475388) AM 108m
*Picnic at Hanging Rock (SF0781152) AM 116m
Pieces (G88F5314) AM 89m
The Pied Piper (lb) (FY026) AM 90m
The Pied Piper of Hamelin/The Dancing Princess (Meyer/Medak) (SV0801035) AM 99m
Pink Flamingos (NL881004) DM 93m
The Pit and the Pendulum (G88F5344) AM 81m
Planet of the Apes (SF0781176) AM 112m
Playtime (HCL1049) AMNE 120m
Plein Soleil (FY029) AM 117m
Pocketful of Miracles (scanned) (NJL99705) AM 137m
Poil de Carotte (HCL0010) AMNE
Poirot Series Vol. 1 (David Suchet) (HBLT60091) AM 105m
Poirot Series Vol. 2 (David Suchet) (HBLT60092) AM 105m
Police Story (lb) (G88F0088) AME? 103m
*Poltergeist (lb) (G128F5524) CAV DS 115m
Poltergeist II (lb) (PCLM00009) DS 91m
Polyester (PFF86001) AM 86m
The Poppie Is Also a Flower (EHL1041) AM 86m
Porte des Lilas (HCL0026) AMNE
The Poseidon Adventure (SF0781226) AS 117m
The Poseiden Adventure Part 2 (NJL11103) AM 115m
Possession (lb) (DLZ0151) NE 123m
Pot Bouille (FY025) AMNE 116m
The Premature Burial (G88F5348) AM 81m
The Prince and the Pauper (Crossed Swords) (lb) (SF0981424) AS 121m
The Prince and the Showgirl (NJL11154) AM 117m
Private Lessons (lb) (88C596208) AMNE 117m
Private Music (SM0483085) CAV DS 30m
The Prize (PCLM00021) 135m
Prizzi's Honor (lb) (SF0985077) AS 129m
Project A (lb) (Jackie Chan) (FY103) AME? 105m
The Punisher (lb) (PILF7027) DS 90m
Quartet (W73L2072) AM 100m
Quatorze Juillet (1932) (HCL0007) AMNE
Rambo First Blood II (lb) (SF0501559) DS 96m
Rambo III (lb) (SF0781560) DS 101m
Ran (lb) (G128F0060) ASNE 162m
The Raven (1963) (G88F5345) AM 86m
*Raw Deal (lb) (SF0785155) DS 105m
*Razorback (lb) (K88L5008) AS 95m
Real Life (EHL1082) AME? 94m
Rebecca (SF0981247) AM 131m
*Rebellion (FH014) AMNE 128m
Remo Williams (SF0785187) DS 116m
Return from the River Kwai (SF0475397) DS 102m
*Return of the Jedi (lb) (SF1481343)CAV DS 132m
Return of the Secaucus Seven (NL881002) DM 106m
The Return to Oz (lb) (SF0881180) AS 110m
Revenge of Godzilla (TLL2024) AMNE
Revolver (lb) (NDS2016) ASNE 115m
Richard III (EHL1029) 139m
The Right Stuff (11JL70014) DS 193m
Rio Bravo (NJL11050) AM 135m
Road House (scanned) (NJL99704) DS 114m
The Robe (scanned) (FY525) AM 133m
Robin and Marian (SF0475384) AM 107m
Robin and the Seven Hoods (NJL11369) AM 118m
Rocco E Suoi Fratelli (lb) (Visconti) (SF1085153) AMNE 176m
Rockers (lb) (TED079) AM 99m
Roctober Blood (G88F5355) AM 92m
Rodan (TLL2011) AMNE 83m
Rolling Thunder (G88F5341) AM 99m
Roots (ML1) DM 565m
Rosa Luxemburg (SF0781531) AME? 118m
Rosalie Goes Shopping (C596338) AS 94m
The Royal Flash (FY583) AM 101m
Royal Wedding (G98F5556)
Run Silent, Run Deep (NJL99543) DM 93m
Runaway Train (SF0785144)W AS 110m
Ryan's Daughter (PCLM00004) AS 194m
Sacco E Vanzetti (lb) (SF0981306) AME? 125m
Sahara (1983) (SF0475363) DS 106m
Sailer Who Fell from Grace with the Sea (FY035) AM 105m
Saint-Tropez Blues (HCL0028) AMNE
Salome (1953) (SF0475312) AM 103m
The Salute of the Jugger (PILF1102) DS 104m
The Sand Pebbles (FY556) AM 179m
*Satomi Hakken-Den (lb) (FH016) ASNE 136m
Saturday the 14th (TED117)W AS 76m
Say Amen, Somebody (LL880102) DS 100m
Scarecrow (NJL11098) AM 112m
Schizoid (G78F5520) AM 89m
Sciusucia (Shoeshine) (SF0685038) AMNE 90m
Scream Blacula, Scream (G98F5361) AM 96m
Senso (FY046) AMNE 119m
Separate Tables (NJL99593) AM 100m
Seven Year Itch (SF0781179) AM 104m
Shaolin Drunken Monk (88C596142) AMNE 83m
Shaolin Temple (FY085)W AMNE 100m
Shaolin Temple The Bronzemen (GF78F5001) AMNE 95m
Shaolin Wooden Man (lb) (TLL2008) AME? 106m
Sharky's Machine (10JL72024) AS 122m
*The Shining (NJEL11079) AM 143m
Shock Treatment (SF0781273) AS 95m
The Sicilian (lb) (SF0785324) DS 115m
The Sicilian Clan (SF0731593) AME? 118m
The Silence (00LS3) AMNE 95m
Sincerely, Charlotte (lb) (NDH114) AMNE 95m
Sisters (SF0501414) AM 92m
Sky Pirates (lb) (SF0785202) AS 88m
Sky Riders (FY567) AM 91m
Sky's the Limit (Astaire) (A78L7012) AM
Slamdance (lb) (SF0785387) AS 100m
Slipstream (lb) (SF0471653) DS 103m
Snake in the Eagle's Shadow (Jackie Chan) (98C596012) AME? 98m
The Snows of Kilimanjaro (SF0471778) AM 117m
Snuff (LVB1013) AM 82m
Solaris (TLL2334)W AMNE 165m
The Solid Gold Cadillac (PILF7020) AS 99m
Soldier Blue (EHL1020) AM 116m
Soleil Rouge (Red Sun) (G88F0044) AME? 115m
Somebody Killed Her Husband (lb) (TED131) AM98m
Somebody Up There Likes Me (PCLM0020) 114m
Son of Godzilla (lb) (TLL2077) AMNE
Song of the South (PILF1096) DM 94m
Soul Man (lb) (SF0785188) DS 105m
Sous Les Toits de Paris (HCL0003) AMNE
Space 1999 1 Alien Attack (BELL18) AM 115m
Space 1999 2 (BELL20) AM 105m
Spartan X (lb) (Jackie Chan) (SF0780019) AME? 108m
Special Effects (EHL1078) AM 106m
Spencer's Mountain (NJL11635) AM 120m
Spiderman (1976 live action) (SF0785085) AM 89m
Spiderman (1978 live action) (SF0785093) AM 89m
Spiderman (1980 live action) (SF0785100) AM 92m
The Spirit of St. Louis (NJL11048) AM 135m
Splendor in the Grass (NJL11164) AM 124m
Squeeze Play (88C596190) AM 90m
St. Valentine's Day Massacre (FY574) AM 100m
*Star Wars (lb) (SF1481196) CAV DS 121m
Starflight One (G88F5336) AS 120m
Stay As You Are (English dubbed) (SF0475375) DM 100m
The Steamroller and the Violin (Tarkovsky) (PILF1117) DMNE 45m
The Stolen Airship (SF0501479) AME? 88m
Straw Dogs (lb) (SF0501410) AM 118m
Strawberry Statement (G78F5506) 101m
Street Trash (SF0785199) AM 102m
Submersion of Japan (Tidal Wave) (lb) (TLL2314) AMNE 144m
The Sugarland Express (SF0781372) AM 110m
Summer Lovers (G88F5354) DM 99m
Summer of '42 (NJEL01033) DM 102m
Sunday, Bloody Sunday (NJL99515) AM 111m
Sunflower (lb) (FY044) AMNE 107m
Supercarrier 1 (TV series) (KILF5001) AM 91m
Supercarrier 2 (TV series) (KILF5002) AM 95m
Supercarrier 3 (TV series) (KILF5003) AM 94m
Supercarrier 4 (TV series) (KILF5004) AM 93m
Supergirl (G118F5005) AS 125m
Suspiria (FY082) AS 99m
Suspiria 2 (lb) (98C596112) AM 106m
Take Me Out to the Ball Game (G98F5560)
The Taking of Pelham One, Two, Three (NJL99243) AM 101m
Tales of Hoffman (1951) (K88L5028) AM 110m
Tall in the Saddle/John Wayne: The Duke Lives On (SF0881411) AM 135m
Taps (FY571) AS 126m
A Taxing Woman's Return (TLL2367) ASNE
Tempest (Mazursky) (SF0985247) DS 142m
The Tenant (SF0931577) AM 126m
*Tenebrae (lb) (88C596149) AM 101m
The 10th Victim (EHL10124) AS 99m
Terror at the Opera (Argento) (SF0475368) DS 95m
Terror of Mechagodzilla (lb) (TLL2089) AMNE
Texas (1941) (SF0475317) AM 93m
Thank God It's Friday (SF0785134) AS 89m
That Darn Cat (SF0780125) AM 116m
Theorem (L0985018) AMNE 99m
Therese Raquin (FY024) AMNE 106m
There Must Be a Pony (C596279) AM 96m
There's No Business Like Show Business (scanned) (PILF1001) AM 117m
They Live (lb) (SF0731669) DS 96m
The Thomas Crown Affair (NJEL01029) AM 114m
The Three Musketeers/The Four Musketeers (Lester) (SF0981423) AM 209m
*The Three Worlds of Gulliver (SF0475373) AM 94m
Thunder Run (EHL1088) 91m
*THX-1138 (08JL61162) AM 86m
Tierra Brava (lb) (98C596065) AME? 104m
Times Square (K88L5024) AS 106m
The Tin Drum (lb) (SF0980037) AMNE 142m
*To Sir, with Love (SF0505277) AM 105m
Top Gun Collector's Edition (SF1201480) DS 118m
Top Hat/Flying Down to Rio (SF0981134) AM 187m
Town without Pity (NJL99688) DM 104m
*The Toxic Avenger (SF0785184) AM 92m
The Trip (G98F5377) AM 85m
Trois Hommes et Un Couffin (lb) (SF0501434) AM 107m
Trop Belle Pour Toi! (NALA10001) ASNE 91m
The Towering Inferno (scanned) (NJL11253) AS 158m
The Train (NJL99704) DM 134m
The Trial/Mr. Arkadin (SF0981364) AM 217m
The Trip to Bountiful (SF0785201) AM 108m
The Trojan Women (SF0785295) AM 112m
Truck Turner (G98F5378) AM 91m
*Tucker: The Man and His Dream (lb) (SF0731630) DS 111m
Tulips (EHL-1038) AM 92m
The Turning Point (SF0981278) AM 119m
Twelve Angry Men (NJL99408) AM 96m
Twilight of the Cockroaches (KF0989001) DSNE 105m
The Twilight Zone 1 (TV remake) (SF0471605) AM 96m
The Twilight Zone 2 (TV remake) (SF0471623) AM 96m
The Twilight Zone 3 (TV remake) (SF0471628) AM 96m
The Twilight Zone 4 (TV remake) (SF0471643) AM 96m
The Twilight Zone 5 (TV remake) (SF0471651) AM 95m
The Twilight Zone 6 (TV remake) (SF0471664) AM 105m
The Twilight Zone 7 (TV remake) (SF0471781) AM 97m
The Twilight Zone 8 (TV remake) (PILF1003) AM 95m
The Twilight Zone 9 (TV remake) (PILF1038) AM 95m
The Twilight Zone 10 (TV remake) (PILF1048) AM 95m
The Twilight Zone 11 (TV remake) (PILF1060) AM 96m
The Twilight Zone 12 (TV remake) (PILF1072) AM 96m
Twin Peaks (NJL35205) DS 114m
Twist and Shout (lb) (PILF1022) ASNE 102m
*Two for the Road (FY565) AM 111m
Two Girls and a Sailor (G98F5557)
2 ou 3 Choses Que Je Sais D'Elle (lb) (Godard) (SF0785152) AMNE 87m
2000 Maniacs (NDH006) AM 88m
2001: A Space Odyssey/2010 Collector's Set (scanned) (PCLM20001) DS 255m
*2010 (lb) (G128F5508) CAV DS 116m
UFO (BBC TV) (BELL24) AM 105m
Ultra Q 1 (BELL56) AMNE 108m
Ultra Q 2 (BELL58) AMNE 108m
Ultra Q 3 (BELL60) AMNE 113m
Ultra Q 4 (BELL62) AMNE 113m
*Ultra Q 5 (BELL64) AMNE 100m
Ultra Q 6 (BELL66) AMNE 100m
Ultra Q 7 (BELL68) AMNE 100m
Ultraseven (BELL48) AME? 100m
Ultraseven 1 (Bell40) AMNE 107m
Ultraseven 2 (Bell42) AMNE 105m
Ultraseven 3 (BELL44) AMNE 105m

Ultraseven 4 (BELL46) AMNE 103m
Ultraman 6 (78C596157) AMNE 82m
Ultraman Kids (58C596025) CAV AMNE 25m
*Umbrellas of Cherbourg (Les Parapluies de Cherbourg) (lb) (00LF3) AMNE 91m
Un Carnet du Bal (HCL0020) AMNE
Un Flic (lb) (G88F0119) AMNE 100m
The Undefeated (FY564) AM 118m
*Under the Banner of the Samurai (FH013) AMNE 166m
Une Aussi Longue Absence (HCL0024) AMNE
Une Belle Fille Comme Moi (SF0785083) AMNE 99m
The Unforgiven (NJL99523) AM 117m
An Unmarried Woman (FY553) AM 117m
The Untouchables TV Series: The Scarface Mob (SF0781509) 99m
*V (NJL11443) AM 458m
*V2 (NJL11576) AM 999m
Valachi Cosa Nostra (LVB1010) AME? 119m
Valley of the Gwangi (08JL61385) AM 92m
Vampire Lovers (G98F5360) AM 89m
Vera Cruz (NJL99485) AM 94m
Vibes (PILF7044) DS 99m
Vivre Sa Vie (FY053) AMNE 83m
Von Ryan's Express (FY540) AM 117m
Voulez Vous Danser Avec Moi? (L0805048) AMNE
Voyage to the Bottom of the Sea (FY552) AM 105m
Voyage of the Damned (SF1081549) AM 182m
*Wagner (HCL6001) DS 215m
Wagonmaster/The Fugitive (SF0981218) AM 184m
Wait Until Dark (NJEL11080) AM 108m
The Wall (G98F5539) DS 95m
Walker (SF0731658) AM 94m
Way of the Dragon (lb) (G88F0084) AME? 100m
*Westworld (lb) (G128F5530) CAV DS 88m
Wet Gold (K80L5052) AS 96m
What's Up Doc? (NJL01041) AM 90m
When Eight Bells Toll (A75L7034) 95m
When Harry Met Sally (lb) (PILF7025) DS 96m
Wild Strawberries (00LS2) AMNE 89m
The Wind and the Lion (PILF7023) DS 113m
Wings of Desire (CSLF1152/3) DSNE 128m
A Winner Never Quits (C596288) AM 96m
Winning Run (FY048) AM 95m
Winter Kills (EHL10144) AS 96m
Wish You Were Here (lb) (SF0785235) AM 91m
Wolfen (08JL72019) AS 115m
A Woman of Paris/Sunnyside/The Idle Class/A Day's Pleasure/Pay Day (SF0981320) AM 183
The World According to Garp (NJEL11261) DM 137m
*The Wrong Man (08JL61065) AM 105m
Xtro (NDH102) AM 85m
The XYZ Murders (EHL1085) AM 86m
The Yakuza (NJL11397) AM 112m
Yol (SF0781027) AMNE 115m
Young Love Lemon Popsicle 7 (SF0785224) AME? 91m
Young Master (lb) (kung fu) (G88F0063) AM 106m
Young Toscanini (lb) (SF0475509) DS 110m
Zardoz (scanned) (SF0781240) AM 106m
*Zato Ichi (lb) (SF0471654) DMNE 103m
*Zato Ichi Monogatari (lb) (DLZ0144) AMNE
*Zazie Dans le Metro (HCL0036) AMNE
Zig Zig (HCL2027) AMNE 82m

ANIMATION

Ace O Nerae! Final Stage 1 (BEAL305) CAV DSNE 50m
Ace O Nerae! Final Stage 2 (BEAL306) CAV DSNE 50m
Ace O Nerae! Final Stage 3 (BEAL307) CAV DSNE 50m
Ace O Nerae! Final Stage 4 (BEAL308) CAV DSNE 50m
Ace O Nerae! Final Stage 5 (BEAL309) CAV DSNE 50m
Ace O Nerae! Final Stage 6 (BEAL310) CAV DSNE 50m
AD Police File-1 (NRLL1021) NE 40m
Adieu, Galaxy Express 999 (TD00013) AMNE 130m
Adventure! Iczar 3 Vol. 2 (POLH2001) NE 80m
The Adventures of Horus (lb) (TD00045) AMNE 82m
Akira (lb) (SF0701550) DSNE 124m
Alien Zone-X from A-Zone (BEAL128) CAV AMNE 45m
Angel (HBLA60050) ASNE 45m
The Angel's Egg (88LX6) ASNE 75m
Animal Treasure Island (BELL373) AMNE 78m
Ankoku Shinwa (PILA1018) ASNE 100m
Anne of Green Gables 1 (BELL77) AMNE 100m
Anne of Green Gables 2 (BELL79) AMNE 100m
Anne of Green Gables 3 (BELL81) AMNE 100m
Anne of Green Gables 4 (BELL83) AMNE 100m
Anne of Green Gables 5 (BELL85) AMNE 100m
Anne of Green Gables 6 (BELL87) AMNE 100m
Anne of Green Gables 7 (BELL89) AMNE 100m
Anne of Green Gables 8 (BELL91) AMNE 100m
Anne of Green Gables 9 (BELL93) AMNE 100m
Anne of Green Gables 10 (BELL95) AMNE 100m
Anne of Green Gables 11 (BELL97) AMNE 100m
Anne of Green Gables 12 (BELL99) AMNE 100m
Anne of Green Gables 13 (BELL173) CAV AMNE 50m
Antique Heart (L0985052) DSNE 40m
Aoki Honoo (C596339) NE 50m
Area 88 1 & 2 (K28L10001) AMNE 98m
Area 88 3 (K98L1009) ASNE 96m
Ariel Visual 1 (G48F0333) CAV ASNE 30m
Ariel Visual 2 (G48F0335) CAV DSNE 30m
Arion (98LX7) ASNE 119m
Armored Trooper Votoms Perfect Collection (ATX1) DMNE 1500m
Ashita No Joe 2 (C59626170) AMNE 1124m
Ashita No Joe Memorial Collection Part 1 (NDL1001) AMNE 1000m
Ashita No Joe Memorial Collection Part 2 (NDL1002) AMNE 1000m
Assemble Insert Part 1 (50L68057) CAV DSNE 30m
Assemble Insert Part 2 of 2 (50L68058) DSNE 30m
Asuka of Flowers (TD00151) ASNE 48m
Aura Battler Dunbine 1 (BELL177) CLV/CAV ASNE 75m
Aura Battler Dunbine 2 (BELL179) CLV/CAV ASNE 75m
Aura Battler Dunbine 3 (BELL181) CLV/CAV ASNE 75m
B.B. 1 A Boy Meets a Boy (BELL331) NE 45m
B.B. 2 Enter the Ring (BELL332) NE 45m
Baoh: Armed Phenomenon (TLL2150) DSNE 48m
Batoreiba Vol. 6 (48L68006) CAV DSNE 30m
Battle Royal High School (98SX16) CAV ASNE 60m
Bavi Stock I (anim.) (NDL501) CAV ASNE 48m
Best of Lolita (WL98001) ASNE 60m
Best of Will Vinton (PILA1036) DM 50m
Betty Boop (DLZ0126) AM 81m
Black Magic Marionette M-66 (BEAL109) CAV ASNE 48m
Borgman Last Battle (TLL2143) ASNE 60m
Botchan (TOLA1061) DSNE 50m
Brutus (69FLD01) CAV DSNE 30m
Bubblegum Crisis (LO985036) DSNE 53m
Bubblegum Crisis 2 Born to Kill (LO685042) CAV DSNE 30m
Bubblegum Crisis 3 Blow Up (LO685042) CAV DSNE 30m
Bubblegum Crisis 4 Revenge Road (L0805053) DSNE 40m
Bubblegum Crisis 5 Moonlight Rambler (AV0981021) DSNE 45m
Bubblegum Crisis 6 Balance of Terror (AV0981054) DSNE 45m
Bubblegum Crisis 7 Double Vision (TOLA1066) ASNE 50m
Bubblegum Crisis Hurricane Live 2033 (TOLA3047) CAV DSNE 30m
Bubblegum Crisis: Hurricane Live 2033 (TOLA1070) NE 30m
Bubblegum Crisis Music Video (LO495049) CAV DSNE 30m
Butchigiri 2 (C596351) NE 50m
Call Me Tonight (adult sf anim.) (NRLL1003) ASNE 40m
Carol (CSLW1234) DSNE 60m
Cartoon Festival I (Disney) (SF0780042) AM 79m
*Cartoon Festival II (Disney) (SF0780047) AM 74m
Cartoon Festival III (Disney) (SF0780067) AM 73m
Chaning Monster's Night Train: Garala (TOLA1063) ASNE 80m
Children of the Wind Monster 1 (38LS4027) CAV ASNE 30m
Children of the Wind Monster 2 (38LS4027) CAV ASNE 30m
Children of the Wind Monster 3 (38LS4028) CAV ASNE 30m
Children of the Wind Monster 4 (38LS4029) CAV ASNE 30m
Children of the Wind Monster 5 (38LS4030) CAV ASNE 30m
Children of the Wind Monster 6 (38LS4031) CAV ASNE 30m
The Chocalate Panic Picture Show (68LF13) CAV ASNE 30m
Christmas Animation (TOLA1006) DSNE 50m
Cinderella Explorers (C596300) ASNE 50m
City Hunter Vol. 1 (HCL3002) AMNE 98m
City Hunter Vol. 2 (HCL3003) AMNE 98m
City Hunter Vol. 3 (HCL3004) AMNE 98m
City Hunter Vol. 4 (HCL3005) AMNE 98m
City Hunter 2 Vol. 1 Good Days (PILA1002) DMNE 96m
City Hunter 2 Vol. 3 Good Girls (PILA1003) DMNE 96m
City Hunter 2 Vol. 3 Good Rival (PILA1004) DMNE 96m
City Hunter 2 Vol. 4 Good Target (PILA1005) DMNE 96m
City Hunter 2 Vol. 5 Good Business (PILA1006) DMNE 93m
City Hunter 2 Vol. 6 Good Partner (PILA1007) DMNE 96m
City Hunter 2 Vol. 7 Good Angel (PILA1008) DMNE 96m
City Hunter the Movie (PILA7003) DSNE 87m
Cleopatra D.C. (LSTD175) ASNE 60m
Cleopatra Sex Goddess (lb) (G73F0321) AMNE 113m
Conan, The Boy in Future (BELL33) AMNE 119m
Conan, The Boy in Future I (BELL5) AMNE 120m
Conan, The Boy in Future II (BELL7) AMNE 120m
Conan, The Boy in Future III (BELL9) AMNE 112m
Conan, The Boy in Future IV (BELL11) AMNE 113m
Conan, The Boy in Future V (BELL13) AMNE 112m
Conan, The Boy in Future VI (BELL15) AMNE 115m
Conan, The Boy in Future VII (BELL17) CAV AMNE 60m
Conan, The Boy in Future Memorial Box (BELL328) CLV/CAV DMNE 754m
Cream Lemon (PCLP00011) NE 40m
Cream Lemon 1/2 (G98F0053) CAV AMNE 52m
Cream Lemon 3/4 (G98F0054) CAV ASNE 55m
Cream Lemon 5/6 (G98F0067) CAV ASNE 50m
Cream Lemon 7/8 (G98F0085) CAV ASNE 50m
Cream Lemon 9/10 (G98F0098) CAV ASNE 50m
Cream Lemon 11/12 (G98F0120) CAV ASNE 50m
Cream Lemon 13/14 (G98F0147) CAV ASNE 50m
Cream Lemon Ami Sore Kara 1 (G68F0337) ASNE 40m
Cream Lemon Ami Sore Kara 2 (G68F0338) ASNE 40m
Cream Lemon Ami Sore Kara 3 (PCLP00003) ASNE 40m
Cream Lemon Graduation Album (G98F0237) CAV ASNE 60m
Cream Lemon New Vol. 1 (G98F0202) CAV ASNE 50m
Cream Lemon New Vol. 2 (G98F0213) CAV ASNE 50m
Cream Lemon New Vol. 1 (G98F0225) CAV ASNE 50m
Cream Lemon New Vol. 1 (G98F0241) CAV ASNE 50m
Cream Lemon New Vol. 1 (G98F0250) CAV ASNE 50m
Cream Lemon Special (78AX5) ASNE 45m
Crusher Joe (7008298) ASNE 132m
Crying Freeman 1 and 2 (LSTD00180) NE 100m
The Crystal Triangle (OOLS4008) DSNE 80m
Curtain Call (anim.) (BEAL103) CAV ASNE 45m
Cyber City Oedo 808 Data 1 Inishie No Memory (LKL204) ASNE 40m
Cybernetics Guardian "Cyguard" (A780003) ASNE 45m
Cyborg 009 (lb) (TD00083) AMNE 64m
Cyborg 009: Monster War (lb) (TD00088) AMNE 60m
Dabide No Hoshi 1 (APLD4001) ASNE 90m
Dabide No Hoshi 2 (APLD4002) ASNE 90m
The Dagger of Kamui (SF0880077) ASNE 132m
Daisy Duck (Disney) (SF0681087) CAV AM 55m
Dallos Act 1 (BEAL1) CAV AMNE 60m
Dallos Act 2 (BEAL13 CAV AMNE 60m
Dallos Special (BELL43) ASNE 90min
Dancougar 1 (BEAL301) CAV DSNE 30m
Dancougar 2 (BEAL302) CAV DSNE 30m
Dancougar 3 (BEAL303) CAV DSNE 30m
Dancougar 4 (BEAL304) CAV DSNE 30m
Dancougar Requiem for Victims (96LS84001) ASNE 90m
Dancougar Songs Special (70LS840002) CAV DSNE 27m
Dangaioh (BEAL155) CAV DSNE 45m
Dangaioh 2 (BEAL189) CLV ASNE 40m
Dangaioh 3 (BEAL247) CAV DSNE 40m
A Day of Lemon Angel (G68F0266) DSNE 60m
Demon Hunter (NRAL1016) CAV DSNE 30m
Devilman (BEAL235) CAV DSNE 51m
Devilman 2 (BEAL237) CAV DSNE 60m
Dirty Pair 1 (7004678) CAV AMNE 50m
Dirty Pair 2 (7004778) CAV AMNE 50m
Dirty Pair 3 (7004878) CAV AMNE 50m
Dirty Pair 4 (7004978) CAV AMNE 50m
Dirty Pair 5 (7005078) CAV AMNE 50m
Dirty Pair Affair of Nolandia (BEAL101) CAV ASNE 55m
Dirty Pair Complete Collection (7004078) AMNE 70m
Dirty Pair Eden Project (BELL135) AMNE 80min
Dirty Pair Flight 005 Conspiracy (BEAL299) CAV DSNE 60m
Dirty Pair From Lovely Angel with Love (7003078) CAV AMNE 47m
Dirty Pair Great Search Collection (7003878) AMNE 70m
Dirty Pair Masterpiece Collection (7001778) AMNE 70m
Dirty Pair Mystery Collection (7002878) AMNE 70m
Dirty Pair Special Edition Collection (7002378) AMNE 85m
Dirty Pair Wink Collection (7003978) AMNE 70m
Dog Soldier (CSLW1133) ASNE 45m
Dokushin Apartment Dokudami So (C596289) ASNE 50m
Dokushin Apartment Dokudami So II (C596294) ASNE 47m
Dokushin Apartment Dokudami So III (C596340) ASNE 45m
Dominion (SF0481521) DSNE 40m
Dominion 2 (SF0481522) DSNE 40m
Dominion 3 (SF0481523) DSNE 40m
Dominion 4 (SF0481524) DSNE 40m
Donald Duck and His Duckling Gang (SF0471703) CAV DM 28m
Donald's Golden Jubilee (SF0781181) AMNE 97m
Dragon Fist (TOLA1071) DSNE 40m
Dragon's Century AD 1990 (GV0881001) ASNE 30m
Dragon's Century RC 297 (GV0881002) ASNE 30m
Dragon's Heaven (L0985046) CAV DSNE 45m
Dream Hunter II (K98L1010) ASNE 60m
Dream Hunter III (K98L1011) ASNE 60m
Earthian II (TOLA1077) DSNE 45m
Egyptian King's Cartouche (N48L1) ASNE 44m
Eiji (PCLP0067) NE 45m
Etranger (78LX5) ASNE 90m
Famous Guard of Slaves (98LX12) ASNE 60m

Fire and Ice (Bakshi) (SF0981068) CAV DS 95m
Firefly's Grave (lb) (SF0981540) CAV DSE? 90m
Five Star Stories (TLL2153) NE 65m
Frederick Park (SF0981422) CAV DME? 87m
Fuma No Kojiro War of the Sacred Sword 1 (CSLW1305) NE 30m
Fuma No Kojiro War of the Sacred Sword 2 (CSLW1306) NE 30m
Fuma No Kojiro War of the Sacred Sword 3 (CSLW1307) NE 30m
Fuma No Kojiro War of the Sacred Sword 4 (CSLW1308) NE 30m
*Fun and Fancy Free (SF0780043) AM 73m
Future War 198X (TED014) ASNE 125m
Galactic Hero Legend Complete Series (588SX30) DSNE 650m
Galactic Patrol Lensman LD Special (PCLP2001) NE 210m
Galaxy Express 999 #1 (TED001) AMNE 128m
Galaxy Express 999 #2 (TED013) AMNE 130m
Gall Force 1 Eternal Story (CSLW1265) DSNE 86m
Gall Force 2 Destruction (90LS4009) DSNE 45m
Gall Force 3 Stardust War (90LS4022) DSNE 60m
Gall Force Earth Chapter 1 (WOOL5005) DSNE 45m
Gall Force: Earth Chapter 2 (WOOL5008) DSNE 65m
Garfield (D0783002) AM 50m
Garfield II (D0783003) 50m
Gatchaman: TV Series Part 1 Perfect Collection (POLV900127) CLV/CAV DMNE 2520m
Giant Gogu (SF4501656) DMNE 780m
Golgo 13 (G78F001) AMNE 94m
Gosenzo Sama Ban Ban Zai! 1 (BELL273) CAV ASNE 30m
Gosenzo Sama Ban Ban Zai! 2 (BELL275) DSNE 30m
Gosenzo Sama Ban Ban Zai! 3 (BELL277) DSNE 30m
Gosenzo Sama Ban Ban Zai! 4 (BELL279) DSNE 30m
Gosenzo Sama Ban Ban Zai! 5 (BELL281) DSNE 30m
Gosenzo Sama Ban Ban Zai! 6 (BELL283) DSNE 30m
Goshogun (TKLA50003) DMNE 740m
Grave of the Firefly (SF0501508) DSNE 90m
Grave of the Firefly (SF0981540) CAV DSNE 90m
Great Detective Holmes (TKLO50023) AME? 630m
Gunbuster 1 (BEAL207) CAV ASNE 55m
Gunbuster 2 (BEAL209) CAV DSNE 60m
Gunbuster 3 (BEAL211) CAV DSNE 60m
Gundam (BEAL185) DSNE 534m
Gundam 0800 Vol. 1 (BEAL221) CAV DSNE 30m
Gundam 0800 Vol. 2 (BEAL223) CAV DSNE 30m
Gundam 0800 Vol. 3 (BEAL225) CAV DSNE 30m
Gundam 0800 Vol. 4 (BEAL227) CAV DSNE 30m
Gundam 0800 Vol. 5 (BEAL229) CAV DSNE 30m
Gundam 0800 Vol. 6 (BEAL231) CAV DSNE 30m
Guy (ULF04) DSNE 40m
The Guyver 1 (BEAL261) CAV DSNE 30m
The Guyver 2 (BEAL263) CAV DSNE 30m
The Guyver 3 (BEAL265) CAV DSNE 30m
The Guyver 4 (BEAL267) CAV DSNE 30m
The Guyver 5 (BEAL269) CAV DSNE 30m
The Guyver 6 (BEAL271) CAV DSNE 30m
The Guyver Out of Standardized (BEAL119) CAV DSNE 60m
Hades Project Zeorymer 1 (AV0981007) DSNE 30m
Hades Project Zeorymer 2 (AV0981052) DSNE 30m
Hades Project Zeorymer 3 (TOLA1062) DSNE 30m
Hades Project Zeorymer 4 (TOLA1064) DSNE 30m
The Hakkenden Part 1 (AL480008) CAV ASNE 30m
The Hakkenden Part 2 (AL480009) CAV ASNE 30m
Hanna-Barbera HBTV Vol. 1 Old Time Rock and Roll (VAL3027) CAV DS 30m
*Hanna-Barbera Presents Top Rock (HBTV Vol. 2) (VAL3028) DS 32m
Hanna-Barbera HBTV Vol. 3 Motown Sounds (VAL3029) CAV DS 30m
Hanna-Barbera HBTV Vol. 4 Rock (VAL3030) CAV DS 30m
*Heartcocktail (8") (30PL2005) DS 19m
Heartcocktail 1 (07PL24) DSNE 45m
Heartcocktail 2 (07PL29) DSNE 45m
Heartcocktail 3 (08PL31) DSNE 45m
Heartcocktail 4 (08PL36) DSNE 45m
Heartcocktail 5 (08PL43) DSNE 45m
Heavy (PILA1017) ASNE 50m
Hegentaimayakou (TOLA1063) ASNE 80m
Heidi (48C596251) AMNE 107m
Heidi 1 (BELL111) AMNE 100m
Heidi 2 (BELL113) AMNE 100m
Heidi 3 (BELL115) AMNE 100m
Heidi 4 (BELL121) AMNE 100m
Heidi 5 (BELL125) AMNE 100m
Heidi 6 (BELL133) AMNE 100m
Heidi 7 (BELL139) AMNE 100m
Heidi 8 (BELL141) AMNE 100m
Heidi 9 (BELL143) AMNE 100m
Heidi 10 (BELL145) AMNE 100m
Heidi 11 (BELL147) AMNE 100m
Heidi 12 (BELL149) AMNE 100m
Heidi 13 (BELL151) AMNE 100m
Hello Kitty Galaxy Express All Character's Summer Holiday (TOLA1075) NE
Hengen Taima Yakou Karula May Part 1 of 3 (VLSA5001) CAV DSNE 50m
Hi-Speed Jecy 1,2 (70105) CAV AMNE 60m
Hi-Speed Jecy 3,4 (70106) CAV AMNE 60m
Hi-Speed Jecy 5,6 (70107) CAV AMNE 60m
Hi-Speed Jecy 7,8 (70108) CAV DSNE 60m
Hi-Speed Jecy 9,10 (VPLV70109) CAV DSNE 60m
Hi-Speed Jecy 11,12 (VPLV70110) CAV DSNE 60m
History of Riyon Part 1 & 2 (ULF05) CAV DSNE 30m
Honneamise Memorial Box (BEAL367) NE 200m
Hyper-Psychic Geo "Garaga" (AL980004) ASNE 100m
Itoshiki Special: Impressions of Europe (PCLP00020) ASNE 30m
Jack and the Beanstalk (G98F0169) AME? 98m
Jumping — Osamu Tezuka (SF1281171) CAV AMNE 120m
Jungle Emperor Perfect Collection (NDL1003) AMNE 1300m
Kazama No Kojiro Vol. 1 (38LS4027) CAV ASNE 30m
Kazama No Kojiro Vol. 2 (38LS4028) CAV ASNE 30m
Ketsudan Vol. 1 (NDL101) AMNE 100m
Ketsudan Vol. 2 (NDL102) AMNE 100m
Ketsudan Vol. 3 (NDL103) AMNE 100m
Ketsudan Vol. 4 (NDL104) AMNE 100m
Ketsudan Vol. 5 (NDL105) CLV/CAV AMNE 75m
Ketsudan Vol. 6 (NDL106) CLV/CAV AMNE 75m
Ketsudan Vol. 7 (NDL107) CLV/CAV AMNE 75m
Kiki & Lala's Blue Bird (TOLA1074) DM 65m
Kiki's Delivery Service (TKLO50001) DSNE 103m
Kiti and Mimi's Happy Birthday (AV0501057) DSNE 50m
Kizuoibito (NRLL1002) ASNE 40m
Kizuoibito 2 (NRLL1007) ASNE 35m
Kizuoibito 3 (NRLL1008) ASNE 30m
Kizuoibito 4 (NRLL1009) ASNE 30m
Kosani the Cellist (K78L1001) AMNE 63m
La Planete Sauvage (BELL41) AM 75m
La Port a l'Ete (lb) (TED053) AMNE 59m
Laputa: Castle in the Sky (128LX89) ASNE 124m
Leda: The Fantasy War (TLL2012) ASNE 72m
Ledius: Fantasy History of Love (TLL2119) ASNE 48m
Legend of Heavenly Sphere "Shurato" Vol. 5 (PILA1025) DMNE 98m
Legend of Heavenly Sphere "Shurato" Vol. 6 (PILA1026) DMNE 98m
The Legend of Lemnear (AL780002) ASNE 45m
Legend of Syrius (L1005030) DSNE 108m
Legend of Lyon "Flare" (ULF06) NE 60m
Legend of Lyon "Flare" 2 Forbidden Planet (ULF07) CAV DSNE 30m
Legend of the Galaxy Hero (588SX30) DSNE 650m
Lemon Angel 1 (G88F0232) CAV ASNE 60m
Lemon Angel 2 (G88F0238) CAV ASNE 60m
Lensman (G78F0020) ASNE 108m
Les Trois Mousquetaires (BELL253) DMNE 45m
Lightning Trap: Leina & Laika (TOLA1067) CAV DSNE 30m
Lilliput Put (anim) (SF0681108) CAV AME? 50m
Living Forest (AY004) CAV AM 49m
Locke the Superman 1 (BEAL239) CAV DSNE 30m
Locke the Superman 2 (BEAL241) CAV DSNE 30m
Locke the Superman 3 (BEAL243) CAV DSNE 30m
Lolita 1 (WL0001) CAV AMNE 30m
Lolita 2 (WL0002) CAV AMNE 30m
Lolita 3 (WL0003) CAV ASNE 25m
Lolita 5 (WL0009) CAV ASNE 30m
Lolita Special (NDL001) CAV AMNE 60 m
Longshot Vol. 2 (O5PL50) CAV DMNE 30m
Lord of the Rings (SF0985061) AS 133m
Lupin the 3rd 1 (BELL153) AMNE 100m
Lupin the 3rd 2 (BELL161) AMNE 100m
Lupin the 3rd 3 (BELL163) AMNE 100m
Lupin the 3rd 4 (BELL167) AMNE 100m
Lupin the 3rd 5 (BELL169) AMNE 103m
Lupin the 3rd 6 (BELL171) CLV/CAV AMNE 75m
Lupin the 3rd Bye Bye Liberty Crisis (70104) AMNE 96m
Lupin the 3rd Castle Cagliostro (lb) (TLL2023) AMNE 100m
Lupin the 3rd Legend of Babylon (TLL2031) AMNE 100m
Lupin the 3rd Monkey Punch 1 (BELL199) ASNE 100m
Lupin the 3rd Monkey Punch 2 (BELL201) ASNE 100m
Lupin the 3rd Monkey Punch 3 (BELL203) ASNE 100m
Lupin the 3rd Monkey Punch 4 (BELL205) ASNE 100m
Lupin the 3rd Monkey Punch 5 (BELL219) ASNE 100m
Lupin the 3rd Mystery of Mamo (TLL2005) AMNE 90m
Lupin the 3rd The Plotters (TLL2120) ASNE 73m
Lupin the 3rd TV Special 2 (VPLY70130) ASNE 97m
Machine Robo Revenge of Cronos Best Selection II (TOLA1060) DMNE 110m
Machine Robo: Revenge of Cronos Complete Edition (TOLA1068) DMNE 75m
Macross The Movie: English Edition (TLL2084) AM 118m
Maison Ikkoku Vol. 1: In the Season (G98F5064) AMNE 90m
Maison Ikkoku Final Battle (G100F5056) AMNE 70m
*Make Mine Music (Disney) (SF0780110) AM 74m
The Man Who Planted Trees (PILA1019) DS 30m
Manxmouse (98SX19) AMNE 70m
Maps: Legendary Heros (BELL285) ASNE 52m
Masked Rider #1 (TED054) AMNE 100m
Masked Rider #2 (TED093) AMNE 100m
Masu Sensen Part 1 (TKLA50009) DSNE 45m
Masu Sensen Part 2 (TKLA50010) DSNE 45m
Masu Sensen Part 3 (TKLA50011) DSNE 45m
Masu Sensen Limited Edition (TKLA50012) DSNE 135m
*Megazone 23 Part II: English Edition (W78L1004) DS 95m
Meet the Raisins! (PILA1031) DM 24m
Melody Time (Disney) (SF0781214) AM 76m
Memory of a Hat (TD00120) ASNE 100m
Metalskin Panic (G98F0233) CAV DSNE 45m
Mickey and the Gang (SF0471702) CAV DM 28m
Midnight Eye Goku II (LSTD174) NE 50m
Midoriyama High School at the Koshien (PILA1020) DSNE 82m
Mindscape Vol. 2 (SF1281392) CAV AME? 117m
Miracle World 3 (SF0585189) DSNE 50m
Miroku (78SC21) CAV DSNE 60m
Miroku 2 (78SX22) ASNE 30m
Miroku 3 (78SX23) CAV DSNE 60m
Mobil Suit Gundam The Movie 1 (BELL391) NE 144m
Moonbird (SF0681213) CAV AM 60m
The Mouse and His Child (AV0601056) AMNE 81m
Mumin 1 (BELL285) AMNE 100m
Mumin 3 (BELL289) AMNE 106m
Mumin 4 (BELL291) AMNE 106m
Mumin 5 (BELL293) AMNE 106m
Mumin 6 (BELL295) AMNE 106m
My Melody Red Riding Hood (TOLA1072) DMNE 30m
*My Youth in Arcadia (TED002) AMNE 130m
Nausicaa of the Valley of the Winds (98LX1) AMNE 116m
New Captain Tsubasa 3 (35LS4035) CAV ASNE 30m
New Captain Tsubasa 4 (CSLW1113) ASNE 30m
New Captain Tsubasa 6 (CSLW1115) CAV ASNE 30m
New Captain Tsubasa 7 (CSLW1116) CAV ASNE 30m
New Captain Tsubasa 8 (CSLW1117) CAV ASNE 30m
New Captain Tsubasa 9 (CSLW1118) CAV ASNE 30m
New Captain Tsubasa 10 (CSLW1119) CAV ASNE 30m
New Captain Tsubasa 11 (CSLW1120) CAV ASNE 30m
New Captain Tsubasa 12 (CSLW1121) CAV DSNE 30m
New Captain Tsubasa 13 (CSLW1122) CAV DSNE 30m
Night on the Galactic Railroad (G95F5017) ASNE 107m
Noroi (C596293) ASNE 43m
Ogami Matsugoro (C596336) NE 50m
Once Upon a Mouse and other Mousetime Stories (Disney) (SF0781126) AMNE 75m
Orange Road 1 (7006178) AMNE 100m
Orange Road 2 (7006278) AMNE 100m
Orange Road 3 (7006378) AMNE 98m
Orange Road 4 (7006478) AMNE 98m
Orange Road 5 (7006578) AMNE 98m
Orange Road 6 (7006678) AMNE 98m
Orange Road 7 (7006778) AMNE 100m
Orange Road 8 (7006878) AMNE 100m
Orange Road 9 (7006978) AMNE 100m
Orange Road 10 (7007078) AMNE 100m
Orange Road 11 (7007178) AMNE 100m
Orange Road 12 (7007278) AMNE 100m
Orange Road The Movie (TLL2134) ASNE 69m
Orguss 1 Special/Dream of Mooma (BELL39) CAV ASNE 45m
Orguss 2 Memoria/4th Dimension Arena (BEAL45) CAV ASNE 50m
Parasol Henbei (TOLA1081) AMNE 100m
Parasol Henbei 2 (TOLA1082) DMNE 90m
Parasol Henbei 5 (TOLA1085) NE 80m
Parosel Henbei 4 (TOLA1084) NE 80m
Pat Labor Mobile Police 1 (05PL42) CAV DSNE 30m
Pat Labor Mobile Police 2 (05PL50) CAV DSNE 30m
Pat Labor Mobile Police 3 (05PL51) CAV DSNE 30m
Pat Labor Mobile Police 4 (45L68004) CAV DSNE 30m
Pat Labor Mobile Police 5 (45L68005) CAV DSNE 30m
Pat Labor Mobile Police 6 (45L68006) CAV DSNE 30m
Pat Labor Mobile Police 7 (45L68028) CAV DSNE 30m
Patlabor The Mobile Police The Movie (BELL300) DSNE 120m
Pluto's Tales (SF0471704) CAV DM 28m
Polar Bear (70LS4012) CAV ASNE 30m
Popeye 1 (50LH8035) AM 60m
Popeye 2 (50LH8036) AM 60m
Popeye 3 (50LH8037) AM 60m
Popeye 4 (50LH8038) AM 60m

Popeye 5 (50LH8039) AM 60m
Popeye II Vol. 1 (HBLA60071) AS 80m
Popeye II Vol. 2 (HBLA60072) AS 80m
Popeye II Vol. 3 (HBLA60073) AS 80m
Popeye II Vol. 4 (HBLA60074) AS 80m
Popeye II Vol. 5 (HBLA60075) AS 80m
Prince of the Sun (BEAL372) NE 82m
Prince Who Chases Serpents (lb) (TD00061) AMNE 86m
Prism Season (G55X0310) CAV DMNE 30m
Project A-KO (PCLP00006) CAV DSNE 116m
Project A-KO 2 (PCLP00007) CAV DSNE 55m
Project A-KO 3 (PCLP00008) CAV DSNE 55m
Project A-KO 4 (PCLP00005) CAV DSNE 60m
Purple Eyes in the Dark (AV0681002) CAV DSNE 30m
Puss in Boots (lb) (TD00068) AMNE 80m
Queen Millenia (G128F0004) AMNE 121m
Revenge of Cronos (AV0781055) AMNE 120m
Riki-Oh 2 (NALL10002) NE 45m
Rumic World 1: Fire Tripper (SF0585154) ASNE 48m
Rumic World 2: The Supergal (SF0585171) ASNE 48m
Rumic World 3: Smiling Target (SF0585189) DSNE 50m
Rumic World 5: One Pound Gospel (SF0481551) DSNE 50m
The Samurai (78LG106) ASNE 45m
Samurai Troopers 1 (38LS4025) CAV AMNE 30m
Samurai Troopers 2 (38LS4026) CAV AMNE 30m
Sanrio Character Series (TOLA1069) 40m
Santabear's First Christmas (VAL3701) CAV DM 23m
The Satisfaction (ZA602) ASNE 50m
Seishun Fufu Monogatari: Koiku No Mainichi (C596292) ASNE 50m
Shiawase No Katachi 1 (MRLA90001) CAV DMNE 30m
Shonan Bakusozoku (TED133) ASNE 52m
Shonan Motorcycle Gang 6: GT-380 History (LSTD00179) NE 50m
Shooting Master "Zillion" 1 (7008578) AMNE 100m
Shooting Master "Zillion" 2 (7008678) AMNE 100m
Shooting Master "Zillion" 3 (7008778) AMNE 100m
Shooting Master "Zillion" 4 (70088) AMNE 100m
Shooting Master "Zillion" 5 (70089) AMNE 100m
Shooting Master "Zillion" 6 (70090) AMNE 100m
Shooting Master "Zillion" 7 (70091) AMNE 100m
Shooting Master "Zillion" 8 (70092) AMNE 100m
Shooting Master "Zillion" Burning Night (K78L1028) DSNE 47m
Shooting Master "Zillion" Fantastic Memories (70005978) AMNE 45m
Shooting Master "Zillion" JJ Reseiks (70005878) AMNE 45m
Silk Road O Tobu! (AV0501001) DMNE 90m
Silver Kamen Perfect Final (TLL2155) NE 660m
The Snowman (David Bowie) (CLSW1150) CAV AS 26m
Sonic Soldier Borgman 1 (70095) AMNE 90m
Sonic Soldier Borgman 2 (70096) AMNE 90m
Sonic Soldier Borgman 3 (70097) AMNE 88m
Sonic Soldier Borgman 4 (70098) AMNE 88m
Sonic Soldier Borgman 5 (70099) AMNE 88m
Sonic Soldier Borgman 6 (70100) AMNE 88m
Sonic Soldier Borgman 7 (70101) AMNE 88m
Sonic Soldier Borgman 8 (70102) AMNE 88m
Sonic Soldier Borgman 9 (VPLY70103) AMNE 83m
Sonic Soldier Borgman Madnight Gigs! (AV0681023) CAV DSNE 30m
Sora Tobu Yureisen (lb) (BEL1371) NE 60m
Spacecruiser Yamato #2 (128C596015/16) ASNE 165m
Spacecruiser Yamato Music Symphony (78C596041) ASNE 55m
Spacecruiser Yamato MV No. 1 (128C596022) ASNE 60m
*Spacecruiser Yamato New Voyage (128C596014) AMNE 95m
Spacecruiser Yamato Perfect Collection (BELL315) DSNE 710m
Spacecruiser Yamoto Pefect Collection (BELL316) NE 650m
Space Runner "Ideon" (SF5805349) AMNE 890m
Space Runner "Ideon" (SF5805291) AMNE 910m
Sport Goofy's Vacation (SF0471705) CAV DM 28m
SPT Layzner Act I (LVB5001) ASNE 56m
SPT Layzner Act II (LVB5002) ASNE 55m
SPT Layzner Act III (LVB5003) ASNE 55m
Standing Earth Protection Army (L0805039) ASNE 49m
Starship Troopers 1 (BELL213) ASNE 50m
Starship Troopers 2 (BELL215) ASNE 50m
Starship Troopers 3 (BELL217) ASNE 50m
Steel Ghost: Big Monster Fight (98LX11) CAV ASNE 60m
Stingray (BELL8) ASNE 105m
Stripy (SF0681265) CAV AMNE 52m
Supernatural Beast City (LKL201) ASNE 85m
Sugato Sanshiro: Appearance of 34 Sons (TOLA1030) DSNE 70m
Suntory Animation Series (AV0501048) DMNE 48m
Super Beast-God Dancougar Act 4 (BEAL304) NE 30m
Super Darius: Perfection (NALG10001) DSNE 107m
Super Fortress 'Macross' Memorial Box (BELL245) CLV/CAV DSNE 1000m
Take the 'X' Train (G78F0287) ASNE 50m
Tales from Grimm and Anderson (AY008) CAV AME? 50m
Technopolice 21st Century (TLL2009) AMNE 88m
Ten Little Gall Force (50LS4013) ASNE 30m
Tetsuwan Atom (Astro Boy) Collection (SF2201700) AMNE 5580m
Thousand and One Nights (lb) (G128M0150) AMNE 128m
Three Little Pigs (Disney) (SF0780070) AM 80m
Three Sexy Magic Girls (BEAL105) CAV AMNE 30m
3000 Miles in Search of Mother 1 (BELL360) NE 200m
3000 Miles in Search of Mother 2 (BELL361) NE 200m
3000 Miles in Search of Mother 3 (BELL362) NE 200m
3000 Miles in Search of Mother 4 (BELL363) NE 200m
Thunderbirds 1 (BELL4) ASE? 105m
Thunderbirds 2 (BELL5) ASE? 105m
Thunderbirds 3 (BELL6) ASE? 105m
Time Stranger (TLL2075) ASNE 91m
Tokyo Vice (W78L1011) CAV DSNE 60m
Touch (lb) (TLL2056) ASNE 93m
Touch 2 (lb) (TLL2079) ASNE 79m
Touch 3 (lb) (TLL2103) ASNE 85m
Transformers The Movie (HCL7001) AS 90m
Treasure Island (lb) (TD00060) AMNE 78m
TV Animation Theme Collection Vol. 4 (45LH8012) CAV E? 30m
Twinkle NORA Rock Me! (G88F0078) CAV ASNE 45m
Unicorn (AV0601049) DMNE 90m
Unicorn to the Magic Island (AV0601050) DMNE 90m
Urban Square (BEAL123) CAV ASNE 55m
*Uresei Yatsura 1 Only You (W98L6013) AMNE 90m
Uresei Yatsura 2 Beautiful Dreamer (TLL2001) AMNE 98m
Uresei Yatsura 3 Remember My Love (G98F5011) AMNE 93m
Uresei Yatsura 4 Lum the Forever (G98F5031) AMNE 94m
Uresei Yatsura 5 Final Battle (G100F5057) AMNE 90m
Uresei Yatsura Dreams Come True (G98F5046) CAV AMNE 60m
Uresei Yatsura Memorial Album I'm the Syu Cha (G78F5039) DSNE 30m
Uresei Yatsura Ryoko's September Tea Party (G78F5033) CAV AMNE 60m
Uresei Yatsura TV Series 1 (G78F8005) AMNE 100m
Uresei Yatsura TV Series 2 (G78F8006) AMNE 100m
Uresei Yatsura TV Series 3 (G78F8007) AMNE 100m
Uresei Yatsura TV Trailers (G68X5059) AMNE 72m
Uresei Yatsura - Original Video (PCLA00001) NE 30m
Urotsukidoji (JVLB35015) DSNE 108m
Utsunomiko 1 (BEAL351) NE 30m
Utsunomiko 2 (BEAL352) NE 30m
Vampire Hunter D (CSLW1268) DSNE 80m
Vampire Princess Miyu 1 (G55F0259) CAV DSNE 30m
Vampire Princess Miyu 2 (G55F0277) CAV DSNE 30m
Vampire Princess Miyu 3 (G55F0298) CAV DSNE 30m
Vampire Princess Miyu 4 (G55F0309) CAV DSNE 30m
Venus Wars (BELL255) DSNE 102m
Violence Jack: Evil Town (LKL203) CAV AMNE 60m
Votoms 1 ASNE (L0885015) ASNE 55m
Votoms 2 ASNE (L0885016) ASNE 55m
Votoms Battle of Hegroedits (LVB5005) ASNE 56m
Votoms the Unknown Red Shoulder (L0885017) ASNE 53m
Wandering Kid Part 1 (JVLB35003) ASNE 40m
Wandering Kid Part 2 (JVLB35013) ASNE 45m
Wandering Kid Part 3 (JVLB350143) ASNE 40m
Wanna Be's (90LS4002) CAV DSNE 45m
Watership Down (SF0475399) AMNE 93m
What's Michael? (513320) ASNE 53m
What's Michael? 2 (W78L6016) ASNE 45m
White Prince (TLL2151) ASNE 82m
Winnie the Pooh and the Honey Tree (SF0471706) CAV DM 28m
Yagami Gun No Katei No Jijo 1 (KVLA1001) NE 30m
Yagami Gun No Katei No Jijo 2 (KVLA1002) NE 30m
Yagami Gun No Katei No Jijo 3 (KVLA1003) NE 30m
Yoroiden Samurai Troopers 1 (CSLW1134) CAV DSNE 30m
Yoroiden Samurai Troopers 2 (CSLW1135) CAV DSMNE 30m
Yoroiden Samurai Troopers 3 (CSLW1136) CAV DSNE 30m
Yoroiden Samurai Troopers 4 (CSLW4137) CAV DSNE 30m
Yoroiden Samurai Troopers Trooper Video Collection (CSLF121120) DMNE 600m
Yotoden (SF1205389) DSNE 126m
Youju Kyoshitsu Complete Edition (DLZ0156) ASNE 100m
Youma (TLL2132) ASNE 38min
Youma Part 2 (TLL2133) ASNE 40m
Zoffy (anim.) (88C596019) AMNE 85m

MUSIC

ABC: Greatest Video Hits (VALP3160) DS 57m
AC-DC Fly on the Wall (05JL50102) DS 27m
Aerosmith: 3X5 Permanent Vacation (35P69006)CAV DS 26m
After Midnight Nat King Cole (L0801123) DM 42m
Al Hirt A History of Jazz (LVD529) DS 53m
Alan Holdsworth in Japan (TED041) AS 82m
Alarm Spirit of '86 (88LP101) AS 74m
Albeniz (KIMM21) DS 20m
Alcatraz Metalic Live '86 (TED026) AS 77m
Alexander O'Neal: The Voice (CSLM756) DS 23m
Alexis Wasenberg: Chopin (LO701108) DS 54m
All Star Country Fair (SM0683165) DS 72m
The Allman Brothers Band: Brothers of the Road (SM0373429) DS 112m
Amalia Rodriguez (L1001061) DS 90m
American Dreams Stage New York 60's (WL68004) DS 55m
Anarchy Movie 85 (TED103) DS 78m
Annie's Mix Anne Lewis (SM0483256) DS 56m
Anton Carlos Jobim Live in Japan (LVD531) DS 45m
Antonio Gaudi (98LF5) AS 72m
The Arms Concert (TED048) AS 114m
Art Blakey with Wynton Marsalis (MJ073) CAV AS 54m
Ashkenazy in Moscow Vol. 1 (TOLW3528) DS 100m
Ashkenazy in Moscow Vol. 2 (TOLW3529) DS 100m
Aswad Live (G68M0052) AS 60m
Atlantic Starr (SM0483128) CAV DS 16m
Australia Now (MP158) AS 61m
Bach 1 (KIMM4) DS 20m
Bach 2 (KIMM17) DS 20m
*Ballet Espagnol Carmen de Yasuko Nagamine (LNK502) AS 89m
Bananarama (W48L3007) CAV DS 16m
Bananarama And That's Not All (8") (JM0380030) AS 30m
The Band Japan Tour 1983 (SM0373341) DS 110m
*Barbara a Patin (96LM21) AS 100m
Barenboim Plays Beethoven (WPLP9705) DS 54m
Barenboim Plays Mozart Vol. 1 (WPLP9703) DS 53m
Barenboim Plays Mozart Vol. 2 (WPLP9704) DS 52m
*Barry Gibb Now Voyager (SM0680047) DS 82m
Barry White and the Love Unlimited Orchestra (VAL3520) DS 50m
The Bartered Bride (148C576198/9) DSNE 137m
Bauhaus Best Collection In the Flat Field (TED108) AS 80m
Bayreuth Set II (CDV509517) DS 1406m
The Beach Boys: 25 Years Together (TOLW3035) DM 85m
The Beach Boys: The Real Story (TOLE3064) DS 95m
Beastie Boys Compilation Reel (68LP109) DS
Beat Club 1 (SM0483221) DM 48m
Beat Club 2 (SM0483222) DM 40m
Beat Club 3 (SM0483223) DM 51m
Beat Club 4 (SM0483224) DM 33m
Beat Club 5 (SM0483225) DS 49m
Beat Club 6 (SM0483226) DS 41m
Beat Club 9 (SM0453481) DM
Beat Club 10 (SM0453482) DM
Beat Club 11 British Invasion 3 (SM0453483) DM 52m
Beat Club 12 British Invasion 4 (SM0453484) DM 56m
Beat Club 13 Jazz Rock (SM0453485) DM
Beat Club 14 American Rock (SM0453486) DM
The Bee Gees: Greatest Hits LIve (VALJ3123) DS 100m
Beethoven (KIMM19) DS 20m
Beethoven: "Emperor" (Munich Orch. c/Gulda) (PHLP4804) DS 40m
*Beethoven Ninth Symphony (MC035) AS 71m
Beethoven 1 (KIMM9) DS 20m
Beethoven Piano Sonatas (Serkin) (WOOZ24045)
Beethoven Symphony No. 3 Eroica (MC051) AS 52m
Beethoven Symphony No. 3 Eroica (68C596105) DS 51m
Beethoven: Symphony No. 5 (NHK Orch. c/Suitner) (TOLW3585) DS 65m
Beethoven Symphony No. 5/Mozart Symphony No. 35 (MC044) AS 69m
Beethoven Symphony No. 6 Pastorale (MC053) CAV AS 47m
Beethoven Symphony No. 6/No. 7 (NHK Orch. c/Sawallisch) (TOLW3581) DS 80m
Ben Webster: C-Jam Blues Jazz from Studio 61 (VPLR70123) 27m
Berlin Live in Japan (SM0583170) DS 53m
Berlioz: Symphonie Fantastique (TOLW3532)
Best of Jack Teagarden (TE0069) AM 47m
Best of KISS (SM0683171) DS 90m
*Best of Kool & the Gang (78LM50) AS 59m
Big Band & Combo Special (TED073) AM 59m
Big Country Live (SM0680078) AS 77m
Bill Wyman (8") (JM0380024) AS 21m
Billy Eckstine with Bobby Tucker (LVD545) 53m
Billy Vaughn Orchestra (SM0653379) DS 53m
Bitetti: Aranjuez Recital (TOLW3527) 62m
Bizet: Cantata (TOLW3539) DS 80m
Black Vocal Varieties (TED070) AM 60m
Blancmange Hello Good Evening (SM0583026) AS 57m
Blood Sweat & Tears in Little Club (MP027) CAV AS 55m
Blue World of Diving (PILW1004) DS 60m
Bob Welch and Friends (SM0680082) AS 81m

Bohemian Concert, The (78LC1005) DS 55m
Bon Jovi Tokyo Road (L0981055) AS 75m
Boy George: Sold (L0307029) DS 20m
Brahms 1 (KIMM5) DS 20m
Brahms 2 (KIMM15) DS 20m
Brahms Symphony No. 4 in E Minor (N. German Orch c/Wand) (SKL1014) DS 46m
Brahms: Symphony No. 1 (NHK Orch. c/Sawallisch) (TOLW3582) DS 90m
Brenda Lee in Concert (CRLR80008) DS 45m
Brian Eno Thursday Afternoon (96LM19) AS 82m
British Rock Hits Now 13 (TOLW3032) DS 60m
British Rock The First Wave (SM0583072) AS 60m
*Bronski Beat The First Chapter (8") (JM0388002) AS 21m
Bros When Will I Be Famous (434P109)CAV DS 30m
Brothers: Top of Black Music Vol. 1 (SM0580123) AS 60m
Bruce Willis: The Return of Bruno (SM0453400) DS 60m
Bruckner Symphony No. 4 (W64L1021) DS 50m
Bruckner Symphony No. 8 (Israel Philharmonic c/Mehta) (SM0653359) DS 87m
Brutus Gallery (image music) (68LS3001) CAV DS 25m
Bunin in Italy (TOLW3538) DS 80m
Burt Bacharach in Concert (HCL6002) DS 48m
Buzzcocks: Buzzcocks Live (VALC3185) DS 50m
Cabaret Voltaire (SM0683020) AS 82m
The Cars Live (VAL3814) DS 63m
Carla Brey Live (SM0680020) AS 85m
Cassiopea Live (SM0580110) DS 52m
Celibidache: Bruckner (CSLM911) DS 84m
Charles Aznavour: Chanson D'Azunavour (SKL24) AS 50m
Charley Pride in Concert (CRLR80012) DS 49m
Cheap Trick Concert (NDS5001) AS 60m
Cheap Trick: Every Trick in the Book (ESLU81) DS
Chicago Symphony Orchestra (00LS82006) DS 95m
Chick Corea Band A Very Special Concert (G78M0006) AS 57m
The Chick Corea Elektric Band: Live in Madrid (POLV1702) DS 56m
Chico Hamilton Live at the Village Vanguard (SM0580064) AS 54m
China Crisis Showbiz Absurd (8") (JM0388010) AS 22m
Chopin 1 (KIMM10) DS 20m
Chopin 2 (KIMM20) DS 20m
Chopin: Piano Concerto No. 2 (TOLW3534) DS 33m
Christmas with Herman Prey (LSZS179) DS 48m
Classic Highlight Vol. 1 Opera (SM0103394) DS 120m
Cliff & Shadows 1984 Together (SM0680092) AS 81m
Cliff Richard (MP172) AS 55m
*Collaboration George Kawaguchi Meets Shelly Mann (MJ041) CAV AS 47m
Commercial Fiat Flux Breakdown (SM0583007) AS 44m
Concert in the Park King Sunny Age (LVD513) DS 77m
Coney Hatch (SM0483103) CAV DS 17m
Count Basie Orchestra (LVD515) DS 80m
The Cream Farewell Concert (VPLR70119) 50m
Crusaders Live in Tokyo (G88M2011) AS 60m
Culture Club A Kiss Across the Ocean (MP151) AS 60m
Cutting Crew (MLV8) AS 41m
The Damned Live (TELP48001) 85m
Daryl Hall and John Oates: The Liberty Concert (G47M0319) DS 73m
Daryl Hall & John Oates Live at the Apollo (TED109) AS 56m
Dave Brubeck A Musical Portrait (G88M0029) AM 79m
David Bowie (NDS5002) AS 99m
David Bowie in Ziggy Stardust (TED029) AS 90m
David Bowie Jazzin' for Blue Jean (8") (JM0380018) CAV AS 21m
David Lee Roth (35P69023)CAV DS 30m
Davy Jones Live (MP040)O CAV AS 48m
Dead Or Alive Live in Japan (684P108)CAV DS 30m
Dead or Alive Live It Up (424P113) DS 40m
Debussy (KIMM22) DS 20m
Dedicated to Mozart: Complete Sonatas for Violin and Piano (CRLB55001) DS 413m
Deep Purple (TED062) AM 54m
Deep Purple: Doing Their Thing (CRLR80001) AM 23m
Deep Purple Rock Flashback (TED007) AS 77m
Dennis De Young Three Piece Suite (VAL3025) CAV DS 20m
Depeche Mode Live in Hamburg (SM0683005) AS 83m
Depeche Mode Some Great Videos (SM0583062) AS 46m
Der Freischitts (MC043) ASNE 135m
Der Rosenkavalier (1961) (K94L5031/2) AMNE 193m
Diane Schurr with Count Basie (VAL-3041) DS 55m
Die Estfarang Aus Dem Serail (Mozart) (TES144) ASNE 120m
Die Zauberflote (Magic Flute) (TES140) AS 118m
Dionne Warwick in Concert (HCL6003) DS 47m
Dionne Warwick in London (SM0605605) DS 120m
Dionne Warwick Live at the Forum (SKL32) AS 50m
Dire Straits — Alchemy Live (SM0680091) DS 50m
Dire Straits Brothers in Arms (W48L3002) CAV DS 20m
Dizzy & All-Star Dreamland (TED006) AS 90m
*Dizzy Gillespie Live at Concerts by the Sea (MJ126) AS 59m
Dizzy Gillespie Special Birthday Concert (SM0653403) AS 120m
Do They Know It's Christmas? (8") (JM0380028) AS 30m
Don Giovanni (K84L5055/6) ASNE 170m
Don't Watch That Watch This! 1 (SM0680114) AS 89m
Don't Watch That Watch This! 2 (SM0680119) AS 76m
Don't Watch That Watch This! 3 (SM0583031) AS 47m
Don't Watch That Watch This! 4 (SM0583034) AS 51m
Doobie Brothers Collection (MP072) CAV AS 56m
Dream Night Special (78LM38) DS 60m
Dream The Best of Vocal Groups (TED074) AM 80m
Duke and Ella at the Cote D'Azure (SM0683261) AM 66m
Duran Duran Arena (LO881037) AS 60m
Duran Duran: Decade (TOLW3047) DS 70m
Duran Duran 6 X 3 (TOLW3034) DS 30m
Dvorak (KIMM13) DS 20m
Dvorak: Cello Concerto (WV0453522) DM 45m
Dvorak: Symphony No. 9 (NHK Orch. c/Sawallisch) (TOLW3583) DS 60m
Dvorak Symphony No. 9 From the New World (MC052) CAV AS 46m
Dvorak Vionlicello Concerto (MC038) CAV AS 40m
Easy Livin' A History of Uriah Heep (SM0683070) AS 74m
*Eat to the Beat Blondie (MP028) CAV AS 44m
Eddie Money Live at the Kabuki (SM0580028) AS 58m
Edgar Winter & Rick Dillinger Live in Japan (TELP45002) 70m
The '86 MTV Video Music Awards Collection (35P69011) DS 41m
Eizin Suzuki California Wind (LVB3001) AS 60m
El Nido (image) (68C596077) CAV AS 30m
Ella Fitzgerald and the Paul Smith Trio (SM0483237) DS 59m
ELO (LVB2001) AM 58m
ELO: Live at Wembly (VALC3176) DS 66m
Elton John (8") (JM0340033) AS 17m
Emerson Lake & Palmer (TED005) CAV AS 45m
Englebert Humperdink Spectacular (G78M5350) AS 60m
Eurythmics: Savage (WV0483019) DS 52m
Evening with Michel Legrand (SM0583074) DS 56m
Everly Brothers Album Flash (8") (JM0380051) AS 27m
Fariground Attraction: M's Box Neo Standards (MELP45002) DS 44m
Fats Domino Blueberry Hill (CRLR80006) DS 42m
Fine Young Cannibals The Video (VAL3121) DS 31m
Fixx Concert in St. Petersburg (SM0583053) AS 57m
Foreigner Super Rock in Japan (LVB2007) AS 57m
Four Tops (MP068) CAV AS 52m
*Frank Sinatra Live in Japan (SM0680096) DS 76m
Free: Greatest Video Collection (VALJ3174) DS 46m
Gallois Versailles Concert (SM0580113) DS 55m
Gary Moore Live in Ireland (TED114) AS 87m
Genesis Live (SM0883095) DS 102m
Genesis Three Sides Live (K78L5014) AS 83m
Genesis: Visible Touch (TOLW3054) DS 48m
George Benson and Earl Klugh (O7WL55) DS 60m
George Shearing at Ambassador Auditorium (MJ016) CAV AS 50m
*Gerry Mulligan Live at Eric (MJ129) AS 59m
The Giants of Rock 'N' Roll (C596299) DS 100m
Gil Evans and his Orchestra (NDJ02) CAV AS 57m
Gil Scott-Heron: Live (VALC3178) DS 63m
Girlschool Play Dirty Live (SM0583091) AS 58m
Glam Rock (WV0403026) DS 51m
Glenn Gould Plays Beethoven (CRL501) DS 59m
Glenn Miller Orchestra Live in Japan (LSP2063) DS 53m
Go-Go's Prime Time (8") (EHL6002) AS 26m
Godley and Creme History Mix (JM0348012) DS 18m
Golden Earring The Video Singles (8") (JM0380044) AS 30m
Good Time Rock 'N' Roll (CRLR80013) DS 28m
Gospel An Unforgettable Music Experience (LL880103) DS 92m
Grace Jones (MP117) AS 45m
Grand Funk Live The American Band (DLZ0112) AS 55m
Great Rock and Roll Swindle (MP141) AM 104m
Grieg (KIMM8) DS 20m
The Gypsy Kings Concert at the Royal Albert Hall (424P124) DS 55m
Hall & Oates Seven Big Ones (SM0483143) CAV DS 29m
Harry Connick Jr.: Singin' & Swingin' (CSLM779) DS 45m
Harry James Orchestra (L0801081) AM 50m
Hawkwind Live (VALC3191) DS 60m
Heart (8") (L0607004) DS 18m
Heavan 17's Industrial Revolution (8") (JM0380002) AS 23m
Heavy Pettin (SM0583059) AS
Heifetz & Piatigorsky (WV0553513) DM 75m
Heifetz 70th Anniversary (TOLW3531) DM 64m
Helen Merrill: Sings for You (SM0653374) 54m
Henry Mancini and Friends (SM0580034) AS 48m
Henryk Szeryng: Violin on Stage (PILC1014) DM 46m
Herbie Hancock Rockit Band Live in Japan (G98M2003) AS 90m
Hip-Hop A Street History (SM0580057) AS 60m
The Hooters Live Nervous Nights (CSLM139) DS 42m
Hot Street Top of Black Music Vol. 2 (SM0583011) AS 60m
Hothouse Flowers in Concert (VALP3167) DS 60m
Howard Jones: Like to Get to Know You Better (35P69012) AS 58m
Howard Keel: Live at the Royal Albert Hall (CRLR80011) DS 46m
Huey Lewis Fore! and More! (LO501105) DS 49m
I Love Mozart (jazz) (LVD518) DS 46m
I Musici (TES143) AS 100mn.
Ian Hunter in Concert (VALP3150) DS 59m
Ice Ballet (LVD557) DS 54m
Icicle Works Seven Horses Deep (SM058306) AS 58m
The Ike & Tina Turner Show (G58M5349) AM 21m
Ian Hunter in Concert (VALP3150) DS 59m
INXS: Kick the Video Flick (35P69025) DS 30m
Iron Maiden — Behind the Iron Curtain (L0681020) AS 30m
Iron Maiden: Life After Death (CSLM773) DS 90m
Isaac Stern (EV0803009) DS 84m
J.S. Bach Die Orgel Meisterwerke (69C596119) DS 42m
J.S. Bach Four Overtures (MC065) AM 85m
Jaco Pastorius Live in Montreal (SM0580006) AS 58m
Jacqueline du Pre Elgar: Cello Concerto (WPLP9701) DS 75m
Jacqueline du Pre Schubert "Trout" Quintet (WPLP9702) DS 56m
Jacques Loussier Plays Bach (VAL3092) DS 60m
The Jam — Trans Global Unity Express (8") (JM0380047) DS 30m
James Brown Live in Berlin (VAL3102) DS 60m
James Brown in Japan Cold Sweat (SM0683064) DS 80m
James Last Berlin Concert (VALP3181) DS 95m
Janet Jackson Control (SM0483142) CAV DS 24m
*Jazz Life Vol. 1 Richie Cole (MJ062) CAV AS 51m
Jazz Life Vol. 2 Johnny Griffin (MJ067) CAV AS 47m
*Jazz Life Vol. 3 Nat Adderley (MJ069) CAV AS 55m
Jazz on a Summer's Day (00LF2) AM 82m
Jazz Vocal Collection 1 I Only Have Eyes for You (TED049) AM 84m
Jazz Vocal Collection 2 Route 66 (TED072) AM 60m
Jazz Vocal Special (TED017) AM 40m
Jermaine Jackson (SM0583135) DS 31m
Jerry Lee Lewis: I Am What I Am (SM0553412) DS 77m
Jerry Lee Lewis The Killer Performance (SM0580083) AM 50m
Jimi Hendrix Alive on Live (TED094) AM 42m
Jimi Hendrix, Otis Redding Live at Monterey (SM0373426) AM 68m
Joan Sutherland Recital (WV0453517) DS 50m
Joe Cocker Spirit of Live Concert (MP031) CAV AS 54m
Joe Jackson Big World Sessions (SM0583127) DS 33m
Johann Strauss (KIMM7) DS 20m
John Coltrane The Coltrane Legacy (TED121) AM 62m
John McLaughlin Paco De Lucia Larry Coryell (LVB2002) AM 55m
John Waite (8") (JM0340050) AS 19m
Jose Carreras in Berlin (A78L3003) AS 90m
Journey American Tour '83 (TED037) AS 110m
Judas Priest Live (96.4M-6) AS 84m
Judy Collins: Live at the Forum (SKL28) AS 50m
*Julian Lennon Live at Yomuri Land East (L0901066) DS 55m
Julius Ceasar (opera) (TES142) ASNE 118m
Kajagoogoo (MP136) AS 60m
*Kate Bush Live at Hammersmith Odeon (MP102) AS 52m
Kate Bush Story (L1001076) AS 55m
Kate Bush The Hair of the Hound (SM0483111) CAV DS 20m
*Kate Bush The Single File (SM0580019) AS 47m
Kathleen Battle: Diva (SKL1001)CAV DS 30m
Keith Jarret Vermont Solo (G88M0013) AS 90m
Keith Jarrett Last Solo (VAL3001) AS 92m
Kerbang Video Kompilation 20 Rock Monsters (SM0683042) AS 89m
*Kid Creole and the Coconuts Live in New York (G78M0011) AS 48m
Kim Wilde (SM0483058) DS 23m
Kim Wilde (07WL55140) DS 40m
Kim Wilde: Keep Me Hangin' On (35P69018) DS 32m
*King Crimson Two of a Perfect Pair (SM0373322) DS 100m
King of Swing Benny Goodman Special Live (L0781053) DS 48m
Kinks: One for the Road (G78M5306) AM 60m
L'Elisir D'Amore (TES141) AS 85m
La Fanciulla del West (SM1580104) DS 140m
La Toya Jackson: A Sizzling Spectacular (PILP1005) DS 52m
Latin Special Babalu (TED071) AM 58m
Laurie Anderson Talk Normal (SC0476105) AM 90m
Led Zepplin Super Show (TOLW3057) AM 78m
Lee Konitz Live at the Village Vanguard (SM0580046) AS 55m
Lee Ritenour (SM0783150) CAV DS 55m

Leonid Kogan (WV0453518) DM 55m
Level 42 Greatest Video Hits (VALP3138) DS 67m
Level 42: Fait Acompli (VAL3101) DS 90m
Level 42 Video Singles (W48L3003) CAV DS 21m
Lionel Richie All Night Long (8") (JM0380038) AS 34m
Lionel Richie Super Live (VAL3050) DS 60m
Liszt (KIMM18) DS 20m
Living INXS (SM0353321) DS 47m
Lloyd Cole and the Commotions Rock and Roll with the Commotions (SM0580067) AS 38m
London Rock and Roll Show (TED107) AS 90m
Loretta Lynn in Concert (CRLR80016) DS 40m
Lou Rawls in Concert (CRLR80007) DS 47m
Lou Reed & John Cale: Songs for Drella (WPLP9039) DS 55m
Lou Reed The New York Album (WPLL9037) DS 76m
Louie Bellson and his Big Band (NDJ03) CAV AS 55m
Madonna (8") (JM0340036) DS 18m
Madonna Mitsubishi Special Live in Japan (08WL35) SDI 90m
*Madonna Who's That Girl Live in Japan (45P69017) DS 90m
Mahler Symphony No. 1 "Titan" (w/Audrey Hepburn) (NALC1003) DS 91m
Mahler: Symphony No. 3 (Amsterdam c/Haitink) (SM0653461) DS 96m
Mahler: Symphony No. 4 (Amsterdam c/Haitink) (SM0653462) DS 64m
Making of Arena, The (L0781048) AS 50m
Mal Waldron & Jackie McLean (SM0583120) DS 55m
Mal Waldron Quintet (SM0680038) AS 63m
Malolm McLaren Duck Duck (SM0583052) AS 48m
Manhattan Jazz Quintet (K98L1007) DS 88m
The Manhattan Project (PILJ1009) DS 59m
*Manhattan Transfer Vocalease Live 1986 (VAL3017) DS 90m
Marc Bolan (SM0580073) AM 58m
Marc Bolan on Video (SM0353342) DS 58m
Marc Laforte Piano Recital (WV0453512) DS 60m
Maria Callas (L1481032) AM 106m
Marine Fantasia (L0881030) DS 40m
Marlene Dietrich (L100-1062) AM 50m
Martha Argerich (SKL1012) DS 45m
Martha Argerich Concert (78LC1002) DS 55m
Marvin Gaye: Greatest Hits Live (VALJ3187) DS 55m
Max Roach Live at Blues Alley (MJ134) AS 59m
McCoy Tyner Harvest Jazz (G78M0034) AS 32m
McCoy Tyner in Montreal (SM0580077) AS 58m
Melikov: Legend of Love (KRLC1013/4) 113m
Memories of The Duke (NDJ01) AM 81m
Mendelssohn (KIMM6) DS 20m
Mendelsson Violin Concerto (68C596122) DS 51m
Menuhin in Moscow (LSZS00192) DM 110m
The Metal Years (anth.) (SM0473395) DS 92m
Metaledge (TED098) AS 70m
Metallica: 2 of One (8") (25LP135) DS 20m
Michael Schekner Group (78C586091) AS 59m
Michael Schenkler Group (TED27) AS 75m
The Michael Schenker Group: Live at Hammersmith Odeon (VALP3149) 52m
Midnight Session (LVD501) DS 85m
Mike Mainieri Manhattan AME?press (MJ061) CAV AS 50m
Mike Oldfield Tubular Bells (MP140) AS 70m
Miles Davis Live in Montreal (SM0583046) DS 59m
Minnie the Moocher and Many Many More (NL781001) AM
Minor Detail Canvas of Live (8") (JM034-0031) AS 12m
Misty BGV by Big Band Jazz (LVD502) DS 47m
Modern Dance Premiere (A65L3006) 100m
Modern Jazz Quartet: Again (MJ042) AS 79m
*Montand International (96LM20) AS 96m
Monteverdi: Il Ritorno d'Ulisse In Patria (Salzburg) (PILC1003) DS 190m
Montreux Jazz Festival Vol. 1 J.A.T.P. Concert (SM0653311) DS 103m
Montreux Jazz Festival Vol. 2 The Piano Masters (SM0653312) DS 100m
Montreux Jazz Festival Vol. 3 Solo & Trio (SM0653313) DS 80m
Montreux Jazz Festival Vol. 4 The Essence of Jazz (Basie) (SM0653314) DS 100m
Montreux Jazz Festival Vol. 5 The Trumpet Masters (SM0653315) DS 100m
Montreux Jazz Festival Vol. 6 Two Saxs (SM0653316) DS 100m
Montreux Jazz Festival Vol. 8 The Jazz Guitar/Joe Pass (SM0553318) DS 50m
Morgenrot (image music) (LVD516) DS 47m
Motorhead Deaf Rot Blind (SM0580071) AS 51m
Motorhead: Live in Toronto (VALC3177) DS 56m
Motown Returns to the Apollo (SM0883087) AS 145m
Mozart 1 (KIMM1) DS 20m
Mozart 2 (KIMM11) DS 20m
Mozart 3 (KIMM25) DS 20m
Mozart Concert (78LC1003) DS 55m
Mozart: Cosi Fan Tutte (Straatsoper Dresden) (LSZS00193) DS 158m
Mozart: Idomeneo (TOLW3567/8) DM 130m
Mozart: Mass in C Minor (Stuttgart) (PLLC5006) 57m
Mozart/Saint-Saens: Piano Concertos (SKL1015) DS 56m
Mozart: Symphony No. 40 (NHK Orch. c/Suitner) (TOLW3584) DS 85m
Mr. Mister Videos from the Real World (SM0483102) CAV DS 14m
Mt. Fuji Jazz Vol. 1 (L0801087) DS 55m
Mt. Fuji Jazz Vol. 2 (L0801088) DS 55m
Mousgorsky Pictures at an Exhibition (58LM4) CAV AS 33m
Muddy Waters Live at the Forum (SKL26) AS 50m
MUSE (Musicians United for Safe Energy) (VALJ3158) DS 103m
Music in Monk Time (78LM22) AS 60m
Nancy Wilson with Chick Corea Band (G78M0005) AS 47m
Natalie Cole: Miss You Like Crazy (WV0303029) DS 25m
The National Symphony Orchestra Plays George Gershwin (CRLB40003) DS 57m
Neil Sedaka: Live at the Forum (SKL27) AS 50m
Neil Young: Freedom A Live Acoustic Concert (WPLL9038) DS 31m
Nena: Starportrait Nena (784M7) AS 60m
Netherlands Dance Theatre (PILC1004) DS 90m
*New Edition The Videosingles (8") (JM0340043) AS 16m
New Order Pumped Full of Drugs (78C586098) AS 54m
New Stars on Blue Note (SM0553391) DS 55m
NHK 1 (short classical pieces) (ME010) CAV AS 52m
NHK 2 (short classical pieces) (ME011) CAV AS 52m
NHK 3 (short classical pieces) (ME012) CAV AS 52m
NHK 4 (short classical pieces) (ME013) CAV AS 52m
Niagra Fall of Sound Orchestra Niagra Song Book (ME110) AS 40m
Nick Heyward Part 1 (SM0583123) DS 53m
Night Ranger 7 Wishes Tour (SM0683092) DS 80m
Night Ranger Japan Tour (96LM17) AS 90m
Nini Rosso (VAL3023) DS 70m
Nini Rosso: Thanks to Dear Friends (VAL3823) DS 54m
Northern Lights: Tears Are Not Enough (7002078) DS 84m
Now Music 6 (SM0683061) AS 75m
Now Music 8 (SM0683145) DS 78m
*Now That's What I Call Music Video (MP139) AS 49m
Now That's What I Call Music Video 2 (SM0583035) AS 56m
Now That's What I Call Music Video 3 (SM0683036) AS 78m
Now That's What I Call Music Video 4 (SM0683037) AS 81m
Now That's What I Call Music Video 5 (SM0683038) AS 76m
Nylons in Tokyo Lion Sleeps Tonight (SM0583001) DS 51m
Oistrach & Richter (TOLW3537) DS 100m
Oistrach Remembers (WV0453521) DM 51m
Olaf Baer Recital (TOLW3526) DS 59m
Olivia in Australia (VAL3087) DS 60m
Olivia Newton John Twist of Fate (8") (JM0380001) AS 24m
Olivia Physical (SM0353492) DS 54m
Olivia Soul Kiss (51129) CAV AS 24m
On the Beach (image music) (SM0580087) DS 42m
One More Time The Big Band! (CRLR80015) DS 50m
One World Todd Rundgron & Utopia Live '83 (TED078) AS 60m
Orange Juice dAdA with Juice (SM0583027) DS 47m
Orchestral Maneuvers in the Dark Crush (SM0683010) AS 66m
Orchestral Maneuvers in the Dark Live (MP147) AS 52m
Orff: Carmina Burana (Battle, Allen) (PHLP6804) DS 65m
Oscar Peterson (VAL3038) DS 80m
Oscar Peterson Big 4 (MJ143) AS 56m
Oscar Peterson The Quintet Live (VAL3838) DS 88m
Oscar Peterson: Grand Piano (PILJ1001) DS 58m
Ozzy Osborne: Speak of the Devil (VPLR70117) 80m
Ozzy Osbourne Bark at the Moon (SM0683040) DS 74m
Paul McCartney Flowers in the Dirt Special (WV0603030) DS 75m
Paul Simon Graceland The African Concert (45P69010) DS 90m
Pat Benatar Hit Videos (SM0483110) CAV AS 26m
Pears/Anderson/Segovia (WV0453514) AM 52m
Pet Shop Boys (EV0783010) DS 90m
Peter Paul and Mary 25th Anniversary Concert (VAL3821) DS 90m
Peter Paul and Mary Holiday Concert (VAL3118) DS 90m
Phil Collins: No Jacket Required (35P69013) DS 28m
Phil Collins: No Ticket Required (35P69014) DS 90m
Playboy Jazz Festival Vol. 1 (G88M0014) AS 90m
Playboy Jazz Festival Vol. 2 (G88M0015) AS 90m
Pointer Sisters So Excited (SF0483109) CAV DS 30m
Police Around the World (K78L5015) AS 75m
Police Every Breath You Take The Videos (VAL3031) AS 59m
Pop Music Now Volume 9 (SM0583193) DS 60m
Power of Three (SM0553448) DS 60m
Power Station Live (L0681052) CAV AS 26m
Pressure Points Camel Live in Concert (SM0680121) DS 79m
Prince: Sign O' the Times (SM0473360) DS 84m
The Prince's Trust All-Star Rock Concert 1986 (VAL3126) DS 90m
The Prince's Trust All-Star Rock Concert II 1987 (VAL3127) DS 90m
The Prince's Trust All-Star Rock Concert III 1988 (VAL3128) DS 90m
The Prince's Trust All-Star Rock Concert IV 1989 (VAL3125) DS 100m
Prokofiev: Romeo and Juliet (Komische Oper Berlin) (LSZS00194) DS 105m
Public Enemy: PE TV Mega Live (CSLM138) DS 59m
Quarterflash Live at the Palace! (SM0580102) AS 55m
The Queen Elizabeth Foundation Pop Concert (MELP45001) DS 59m
Queen Live in Japan (68AL1002) AS 58m
Queen Live in Rio (L0781025) AS 60m
Queen: Magic Tour Live (CSLM774) DS 88m
Queen The Works (8") (L0497001) AS 17m
Queen We Will Rock You (TED047) AS 95m
*Queensryche Live in Tokyo (L0981019) AS 50m
Quincy Jones Reflections Live at Budokan (VAL3003) AS 60m
R. Strauss: Intermezzo (ANF3506) DS 155m
R.E.M. Pop Screen (WPLL9036) DS 33m
Rachmaninoff (78LM59) DS 50m
Rachmaninov Piano Concerto No. 2 (Nakamura Hiroko) (CSLM902) DS 46m
Rainbow Japan Tour '84 (TED030) AS 115m
Rainbow The Final Concert (SM0583049) AS 57m
Ramsey Lewis Quartet in Montreal (SM0580061) AS 58m
Randy Newman Live at the Forum (SKL29) AS 50m
RATT The Video (05JL50101) DS 37m
Raymond Lefevre Grand Orchestra (PILP1001) DS 54m
Ready Steady Go: Sounds of Motown (L0781042) AM 48m
Ready Steady Go Special Edition Otis Redding (L0681041) AM 25m
Ready Steady Go The Beatles Live (LO581022) AM 18m
Ready Steady Go Volume Three (SM0583071) AM 57m
Reggae Xmas (G68M0066) AS 45m
REO Speedwagon (LVB2008) AS 80m
Rhythmstick (PILJ1007) DS 59m
Richard Wagner: Der Ring des Nibelungen (TOLW3601) DS 960m
Ricoched The Private Film of David Bowie (78C586121) AS 60m
Rising Force Live '85 (51128) AS 85m
Robert Palmer (8") (WV0257002) DS 20m
Roberta Flack in Concert (HCL6004) DS 48m
Roberta Flack Live at the Forum (SKL31) AS 50m
Rock Adventure II Rock and Sports in Summer (SM05803173) DS 40m
Rock Around the Dock: The Wind of Liverpool (CRLR80004) AS 45m
Rock 'N' Roll The Greatest Years The 50's 1 (VALJ3129) 55m
Rock 'N' Roll The Greatest Years The 50's 2 (VALJ3130) 55m
Rock 'N' Roll The Greatest Years '63 (VAL3106) DS 42m
Rock 'N' Roll The Greatest Years '64 1 (VAL3107) DS 47m
Rock 'N' Roll The Greatest Years '64 2 (VAL3108) DS 58m
Rock 'N' Roll The Greatest Years '65 (VAL3109) DS 44m
Rock 'N' Roll The Greatest Years '66 (VAL3110) DS 46m
Rock 'N' Roll The Greatest Years '67 1 (VAL3111) DS 43m
Rock 'N' Roll The Greatest Years '67 2 (VAL3112) DS 45m
Rock 'N' Roll The Greatest Years '68 (VAL3113) DS 50m
Rock 'N' Roll The Greatest Years '69 (VAL3114) DS 50m
Rock 'N' Roll The Greatest Years '70 (VAL3115) DS 50m
Rock 'N' Roll The Greatest Years '71 (VAL3116) DS 50m
Rock 'N' Roll The Greatest Years '72 (VAL3117) DS 50m
Rock 'N' Roll The Greatest Years '73 (VALJ3192) DS 60m
Rock 'N' Roll The Greatest Years '74 (VALJ3193) DS 60m
Rock 'N' Roll The Greatest Years '75 (VALJ3194) DS 60m
Rock Revolution (TED090) AS 57m
Rockin' the Night Away (CRLR80014) DS 48m
Rod Stewart and Faces: Video Biography 1969-74 (VAL3884) DS 58m
Rod Stewart: Tonight He's Yours (SM0373343) DS 90m
The Rolling Stones: The Stones in the Park (CRL301) DM 53m
Roman Holiday Live in Tokyo (96LM47) AS 76m
Ron Carter Live Double Bass (VAL3020) DS 55m
Rostropovich Conducts Shostakovich on Stage at Wolf Trap (CRLB40001) AM 55m
Roy Orbison: Live! In Taxas (CRLR80005) DS 32m
Run DMC The Video (VAL3058) DS 20m
Samantha Fox: Sam 1986-1989 (ALLB6) DS 52m
Sammy Davis, Jr. Memories of the Golden Years (G88M0027) AS 60m
Satsujin Kippu Wa Heart Iro (C596350) NE 50m
Saxon Live (TED056) AS 57m
Saxon Live Innocence! (SM0583108) AS 60m
Schubert 1 (KIMM2) DS 20m
Schubert 2 (KIMM14) DS 20m

Schubert Symphony No. 8/Bruckner Symphony No. 4 (MC045) AS 93m
Schumann (KIMM12) DS 20m
Scott Hamilton Live in Tokyo (LVD535) DS 52m
Secret Policeman's Other Ball Music (TED038) AS 60m
Sheena Easton Act 1 (L0981012) AS 47m
Shelia E: Romance 1600 (G78M0116) CAV DS 57m
Shirley Bassey Live (VAL3043) DS 52m
Shostakovich (LSZS172) DM 60m
Sinead O'Conner Live: The Value of Ignorance (VALP3169) DS 37m
Siouxsie and the Banshees (SM0580079) AS 60m
*Siouxsie and the Banshees Once Upon a Time (8") (JM0380049) AS 31m
Sisters of Mercy in Concert at the Royal Albert Hall (SM0583008) DS 57m
SK (SM0580105) DS 38m
Sky (G88F0033) AS 85m
Smetana (KIMM16) DS 20m
Smetana String Quartet: Farewell Concert (WV0553516) DS 85m
Soft Cell Non-stop Exotic Video Show (G78M0022) AS 55m
Sonny Rollins: Jazz Colossus (VAL3837) DS 101m
*Sonny Rollins Festival International de Jazz de Montreal (MJ169) AS 58m
Sound of Jazz (12/8/57 TV) (VPLR70120) 57m
Sound of Miles Davis (VPLR70121) CAV 27m
The Sounds from Montego Bay (LVB2005) AS 120m
South Side Johnny — Having a Party (SM0583106) AS 59m
Spandau Ballet Live (VALP3141) AS 53m
Special AKA On Film (8") (JM0380034) AS 38m
Square — Adventures (58LM16) AS 33m
Square — Resort (68LM43) AS 35m
Square Live, The (78LM62) DS 53m
Stansilav Bunin Munich Recital (A78L3005) DS 90m
Stanislav Brunin, Piano Chopin (68LC103) AS 43m
Stardust BGV by Piano Tough (LVD508) DS 48m
Stephanie Mills Television Medicine (8") (JM0340046) DS 14m
Steve Ray Vaugn (SM0680088) DS 86m
Steve Winwood LIve (WV0383025) DS 60m
Stevie Nicks I Can't Wait (SM0483094) CAV DS 26m
Stevie Ray Vaughn and Double Trouble (SM0373454) DS 60m
Stewart Copeland The Rhythmatist (VAL83513) DS 58m
*Stop Making Sense (SM0373323) DS 99m
Stray Cats: Stray Tracks (SM0353432) DS 52m
The Style Council: Greatest Video Hits (VAL3099) DS 60m
Style Council Jerusalem (W68L3008) AS 35m
The Style Council: Our Favorite Songs (SM0353363) DS 29m
Style Council Post Modern (TED033) AS 80m
The Style Council "Showbiz" Live! (POLV1701) DS 53m
Style Council What We Did on Our Holidays (8") (JM0340027) AS 16m
Style Council, The (8") (JM0388011) DS 29m
Super Groups (SM0580131) AS 59m
Super Keyboard (MJ142) AS 77m
Super Live Special 1: B.B. King (SKL21) AS 50m
Super Live Special 2: Rita Coolidge (SKL22) AS 50m
Super Rock Aid Vol. 1 The Columbian Volcano Appeal Concert (SFXL12) DS 60m
Super Rock Aid Vol. 2 Stand By Me (SFXL13) DS 60m
Super Rock '84 in Japan (78C586090) AS 55m
Super Rock '84 in Japan Special Digest (78C586089) AS 58m
Superstar Collection ABBA Story (SM0453353) DS 56m
Superstar Collection James Brown Story (SM0453354) DS 58m
Superstar Collection Marc Bolan Story 1 (SM0453351) DS 45m
Superstar Collection Marc Bolan Story 2 (SM0453352) DS 48m
Supertramp Brother Where Are You Bound (SM0483118) CAV DS 29m
Swans Way — History and Image (SM0580091) DS 50m
Sweet Soul Music Featuring Otis Redding (L0881054) AM 49m
Swing Out Sister: Kaleidoscope World the Video (VAL3120) DS 25m
Swingtime Video 1 Meet the Band Leaders (SKL1) AM 49m
Swingtime Video 2 Meet the Band Leaders (SKL2) AM 53m
Swingtime Video 3 Meet the Band Leaders (SKL3) AM 47m
Swingtime Video 4 Meet the Singers Volume 1 (SKL4) AM 49m
Swingtime Video 5 Meet the Band Leaders (SKL5) AM 53m
Swingtime Video 6 Meet the Band Leaders (SKL6) AM 47m
Swingtime Video 7 Meet the Band Leaders (SKL7) AM 52m
Swingtime Video 8 Meet the Band Leaders (SKL8) AM 56m
Swingtime Video 9 Meet the Singers Volume 2 (SKL9) AM 56m
Swingtime Video 10 Unforgettable Performances 1950-52 (SKL10) AM 47m
Swingtime Video 11 Meet the Band Leaders (SKL11) AM 55m
Swingtime Video 12 Meet the Band Leaders (SKL12) AM 52m
Swingtime Video 13 Meet the Band Leaders (SKL13) AM 58m
Swingtime Video 14 Meet the Band Leaders (SKL14) AM 45m
Swingtime Video 15 Meet the Band Leaders (SKL15) AM 54m
Swingtime Video 16 Meet the Band Leaders (SKL16) AM 54m
Swingtime Video 17 Meet the Band Leaders (SKL17) AM 51m
Swingtime Video 18 Meet the Dixieland Band Volume 1 (SKL18) AM 55m
Swingtime Video 19 Meet the Band Leaders (SKL19) AM 44m
Swingtime Video 20 Meet the Dixieland Band Volume 1 (SKL20) AM 53m
Swingtime Video Special Collection (SKL501) AM 57m
Sylvie Live from Paris (MP056) CAV AS 55m
Sylvie Vartan Live in Las Vegas (G88M0003) AS 60m
T-Rex Laser Love (8") (JM0348001) AS 12m
Takanaka — Jumping Take Off (wind surfing) (W68L6001) DS 44m
Takanaka Go on (513314) AS 44m
Talk Talk (8") (JM0340035) AS 17m
Talking Heads (L0501122) DS 52m
Tchaikovsky (KIMM3) DS 20m
Tchaikovsky "To the Memory of a Great Artist" (Richter) (WV0453520) DM 86m
Tchaikovsky: Violin Concerto (Mullova) (NALC10001) 85m
Tears For Fears In My Mindseye (SM0580098) DS 58m
Tears for Fears: Seas of Love the Video (VALP3124) DS 21m
Tears of a Clown The Great RC Succession (L1001069) DS 55m
10CC and Godley & Creme: Changing Faces (VAL3870) DS 60m
10CC Live in London (VAL3018) DS 55m
Ten Years After (VPLR70125) 52m
Terence Trent D'Arby (MLV7) AS 41m
Test Dept. Program for Progress (SM0580135) AS 42m
Theolonious Monk (L0801080) AM 42m
This Is Tom Jones (MP015) CAV AS 49m
This Is Video Clash (684P101) AS 32m
Thompson Twins Live in Liverpool (G78M0012) AS 60m
Tiffany Live in Japan (55P69032) 55m
Tin Toy Club (image) (SM0580132) CAV AS 49m
Todd Rundgren Nearly Human Live at the Sun Plaza (WPLP9041) DS 95m
Tom Jones In Concert (ALLB2) DS 63m
Tom Waits: Big Time (SM0475608) DS 87m
Top of the Pops (G78M0023) S 53m
Trumpet Kings The Greatest Jazz Vol. 1 (TED095) AM 72m
20 Great Conductors (TES162) AM 55m
UB40 Labour of Love (8") (JM0380023) AM 31m
UB40 Live (MP144) AS 60m
UFO The Misdemeanor Tour (SM0583104) DS 60m
Ultravox (68C586006) CAV AS 30m
Ultravox The Collection (SM0580050) AS 55m
Unicorn: Early Unicorn Movement (38LH211) DS 30m
Uriah Heep Live (VALC3190) DS 62m
Utopia (8") (JM0380025) AS 24m
Value of Entertainment (SM0583082) AS 47m
Van Halen: Live without a Net (45P69022) DS 93m
Vandenberg Live in Japan (SM0680005) AS 91m
Venon Live The Seventh Date of Hell (SM0583079) AS 57m
Ventures: Original Members (G78M2007) AS 56m
The Ventures Live in LA (SM0353433) DS 50m
Venus Odyssey (sf image) (88AX2) AS 60m
Verdi (KIMM23) DS 20m
Verdi: Macbeth (TOLW3559) DM 149m
Very Best of British Film & Music (SF0781076) AS 73m
Video A Go-Go Vol. 2 (8") (JM0388007) DS 27m
Video Aid (SM0680032) AS 90m
Video Rock Attack (SM0580136) AS 58m
Video Waves (SM068-0032) AS 93m
Vienna Boys Choir: The Beautiful Blue Danube (WV0453515) DS 60m
Vintage Rock of the 70's and 80's Vol. 7 (SM0483227) 52m
Vintage Rock of the 70's and 80's Vol. 8 (SM0483228) 39m
Visage (SM058-3019) AS 52m
Vivaldi (jazz guitars) (SM058-0022) DS 43m
Vow Wow: U.K. Tour Live (FV0481025) DS 60m
Wagner (KIMM24) DS 20m
Wagner Festival (TOLW3523) DS 95m
Wagner: Die Meistersinger Von Nurnberg (Sydney) (ANF3517) DS 264m
WASP Live at the Lyceum, London (L078-1026) AS 60m
We Are the World USA for Africa (G58M0050) AS 54m
*Weather Report Live in Tokyo Japanese Domino Theory (42LP126) DS 61m
Weber: Konzerstuck/Liszt: Piano Concerto No. 2 (Brendel) (SKL1011) DS 42m
West Coast Rock Vol. 1 (VAL3134) 60m
West Coast Rock Vol. 2 (VAL3135) 60m
West Coast Rock Vol. 3 (VAL3136) 60m
Wet Wet Wet Video Hits (VAL3088)CAV DS 25m
When the Music's Over (deceased musicians) (78LM49) AM 55m
Whitesnake (78C586092) AS 60m
Whitesnake Commandos (L0781005) AS 55m
*Whitesnake Fourplay (8") (JM0340006) AS 17m
Whitesnake: Trilogy (35P69021) DS 22m
Whitney Houston The #1 Video Hits (SM0483101) CAV DS 19m
Wien Music: Austrian Radio Symphony Orchestra (TOLW3525) DS 60m
Willie Nelson Live at the Budokan (96LM13) AS 82m
Wishbone Ash Live (VPLR70132) DS 55m
Women in Rock (SM0583139) AS 57m
Wonder Kids America View California (image) (WL0007) AS 60m
Word Vol. 1 Rap Video Compilation (ALLB3) DS 40m
X: Visual Shock 2.5 (CSLM192) DS 30m
X: Visual Shock Vol. 2 (CSLM143) DS 60m
XTC Look Look (MP145) AS 45m
Yanagi George Sound Location (98SX8) CAV AS 60m
Yes 9012 Live (VAL3013) DS 69m
Youthquake Dead or Alive (684M16) CAV AS 22m
Zebra One (SM0583018) DS 43m
Zimerman Piano Recital (WOOZ24039) 104m
Zoot Sims In a Sentimental Mood (K98L1008) AS 52m

MISCELLANEOUS

Above Los Angeles Day and Night (68C596237) DSE? 38m
Ace the Pace (auto racing) (G78X0017) ASNE 80m
The Action 2 (action film clips) (HCL2020) 45m
Adventures in Paradise (78LW4) AMNE 80m
Aegean Sea (POLV1001) DS 45m
African Lion (Disney) (SF0780086) AM 72m
The Air-Show (90LS5007) CAV DS 57m
Air Surround 2 (8-inch) (LC0248126) DS 19m
Air Surround Aerobatic Teams Catalogue (8") (LC0258110) DS 19m
Airplanes Biplanes (DW022) CAV AMNE 50m
Airplanes Breaking the Sound Barrier (DW027) CAV AMNE 50m
Airplanes Lindberg (DW024) CAV AMNE 50m
Airplanes Race for Speed (DW025) CAV AMNE 50m
Airplanes Summary (DW038) CAV AME? 103m
Airplanes World War I (DW023) CAV AMNE 50m
Airplanes World War II (DW026) CAV AMNE 50m
Akira/Production Report (SF0481465) AS 45m
Alaskan Brown Bear (DA001) CAV AMNE 50m
*Aliens, Monsters, Dragons & Me Ray Harryhausen (SF058-1054) CAV 46m
Alps Town Series 1 (ALLA29) 45m
Alps Town Series 2 (ALLA30) 45m
American Amusement Park (ALLA21) DS 45m
American Video Art Anthology Vol.1 (SC0786063)CAV DME? 51m
American Video Art Anthology Vol.2 (SC0786064)CAV DME? 51m
America's Cup (90LS85003) DI 53m
America's Cup (G88F0040) ASE? 75m
Amtrak (CSLW1278) DSE? 50m
Andre Tarkovsky (PILF1119) DMNE 98m
Antique Cars (DW035) CAV AMNE 97m
Archi-File (35,000 pictures, 10 times normal disc price) (CICAF8601) CAV SNE
The Arctic (VOLD1001) ASE? 50m
*Art Film Gallery 1 Matisse (SC0986091)CAV AMNE 60m
Art Film Gallery 2 Degas (SC0986092)CAV AMNE 60m
Art Film Gallery 3 Rene Magritte (SC0986093)CAV AME? 54m
Art Film Gallery 4 Picasso (SC0986100)CAV DSE? 85m
Art Film Gallery 5 Kadinsky (SC0986094)CAV AME? 60m
Art Film Gallery 6 Vermeer (SC0986095)CAV AME? 45m
Art Film Gallery 8: Pierre Bonnard Aventures du Nerf Optique (SC0986097)CAV AMNE 53m
Art Film Gallery 9: Les Silences de Manet (SC0986098)CAV DSNE 54m
Art Film Gallery 10: Raphael (SC1286099)CAV AM 180m
*Art Pepper Notes from a Jazz Survivor (VPLR70124) AS 48m
Astron Belt (game disc) (PG001) CAV SNE
Audi Quattro The World Rally Championship (SS0580021) CAV ASNE 26m
Badlands (game disc) (PG004) CAV SNE
The Bahamas (68C596227)CAV DS 30m
Bali High (surfing) (G68X0100) ASE? 28m
Band on the Run (G88F0047) ASE? 86m
Battle in the Sky Vol. 1 European Combat Aircraft (SC0486061)CAV DSE? 27m
Battle in the Sky Vol. 2 American Combat Aircraft (SC0486062)CAV DSE? 27m
Beat Comic No Sense (JF0980007) ASE? 60m
Behind the Scenes at Walt Disney Studio (SF0781149) AM 73m
Best Golf Swing (VOLD1005) NE 50m
Best Golf Swing (VOLD1006) NE 50m
Best Ski Stemm Turn Technic (VOLD1007) AME? 40m
Best Ski Step Turn Technic (VOLD1008) AME? 40m

Best Water 100 (Mozart) (ALLA22) DS 50m
Big Wave (FY113) ASE? 93m
Billie Holiday: 1915-1959 The Long Night of Lady Day (VPLR70122) 67m
Birds of the Seychelles (DA003) CAV AMNE 50m
Blazing Boards (surfing) (G88F0099) DSE? 92m
Blue Angels (SS0586036) CAV DS 40m
Blue Danube (POLV1007) DS 45m
Break It (dancing) (78LM44) CAV AS 60m
Brighton Run (antique cars) (LVB6002) ASE? 48m
British Open Golf Championship '88 Ballestelos Vs. Price (68LS5051) AM 55m
British Open Golf Championship '89 (CSLW1155) AME? 110m
Calypso Island (LVD514) DS 47m
Canadian Rockies (image music) (68C596207) DS 32m
Canadian Rockies: Banff National Park (CSLW1199) DS 44m
Car Crashes Part 1 (68C596115) CAV ASNE 30m
Cat Time (SS0680024) CAV ASE? 30m
Chuo Horse Race GI Series (PCLP00075) E? 160m
Circus Circus (auto racing) (G78X0016) ASNE 60m
Circus Circus GP'86 (motorcycle racing) (G88X0137) ASNE 90m
Circus Circus II GP '85 World Championship Road Race 500 (G88X0086) ASNE 90m
Classic Creatures: Return of the Jedi (7001078) AM 48m
*Coming Soon (SF0780118) CAV AS 54m
Computer Graphics (SS0986021) CAV ASNE 55m
Concord (CSLW1154) 40m
Contrail ANA Boeing 767 (image music) (G68X2005) CAV AS 24m
Cosmos Circuit (game disc) (SS0980011) CAV ASNE
Cote D'Azure (BV0351008) DS 28m
Crystal Eyes (windsurfing) (G88F0002) AS 103m
A Day in the Wave (image) (58LW3) AS 41m
A Day on the Savannah (DA002) CAV AMNE 50m
Dear America Letters Home from Vietnam (lb) (SF0731637) AM 86m
Die Romantische Strasse (POLV1004) DS 45m
Dog's Fantasy Vol. 1 (58C596128) DS 44m
Dog's Fantasy Vol. 2 (58C596137) DS 31m
Dog's Feeling (HBLT60110) DM 60m
Don Quixote on Skis (in Antarctica) (DS007) CAV AS 40m
Driver's Eyes 2 "In Car Manx Rally" (PILW1019) DM 50m
Early Filmmaking 1893-1917 Vol. 1 (78VC100) AS
Early Filmmaking 1893-1917 Vol. 2 (78VC101) AS
Early Filmmaking 1893-1917 Vol. 3 (78VC103) AS
East Germany (POLV1017) E? 50m
'85-'86 Suzuka 8-hours (Motorcycle racing) (88C596166) ASNE 120m
'85 Japan Grand Prix Road Race (68C596113) ASNE 55m
'85 Japan Grand Prix Trial (motorcycles) (68C596126) ASNE 50m
'85 Japan Motorcross Grand Prix (68C596116) ASNE 50m
'84 WEC in Japan (auto racing) (68C596052) CAV ASNE 30m
'86 Japan Grand Prix Road Race (motorcycle) (68C596173) ASNE 60m
'83 Suzuka 8 Hours Wold AME?durance Championship Race (G78Q0002) ASNE 50m
English Castle (POLV1009) DS 45m
Enjoy Diving Skin & Scuba (88C596139) CAV ASNE 60m
European Garden (POLV1008) DS 45m
*F for Fake (SF0781075) AM 89m
F-1 Grand Prix '87 1 (SC0586049)CAV AME? 60m
F-1 Grand Prix '87 2 (SC0586050)CAV AME? 60m
F-1 Grand Prix '87 3 (SC0586051)CAV AME? 60m
F-1 Grand Prix '87 4 (SC0586052)CAV AME? 60m
F-1 Grand Prix '87 5 (SC0586053)CAV AME? 60m
F-1 Grand Prix '88 1 Brazil (SC0486081) AME? 52m
F-1 Grand Prix '88 2 Monaco/Mexico (SC0486082) AME? 58m
F-1 Grand Prix '88 3 Canada/Detroit (SC0486083) AME? 54m
F-1 Grand Prix '88 4 France/Great Britain (SC0486084) AME? 50m
F-1 Grand Prix '88 5 W. Germany Hungary (SC0486085) AME? 50m
F-1 Grand Prix '88 6 Belgium/Italy (SC0486086) AME? 58m
F-1 Grand Prix '88 7 Portugal/Spain (SC0486087) AME? 55m
F-1 Grand Prix '88 8 Japan GP (Suzuka) (SC0486088) DMNE 55m
F-1 Grand Prix '88 9 Australia & Digest (SC0486089) AME? 55m
F-1 Grand Prix '88 10 World Champion Special (SC0486090) AME? 55m
F-1 Grand Prix '89 Part 1 (SC0656121) AME? 116m
F-1 Grand Prix '89 Part 2 (SC0656122) AME? 120m
F-1 Grand Prix '89 Part 3 (SC0656123) AME? 120m
F-1 Grand Prix '89 Part 4 (SC0656124) DSE? 120m
F-1 Grand Prix '89 Part 5 (SC0656125) AME? 120m
F-1 Grand Prix '89 Special: Honda (SC0456120) AME? 60m
F-1 Grand Prix '90 Part 1 (PILW1009) DME? 120m
F-1 Grand Prix '90 Part 2 (PILW1010) DME? 120m
F-1 Grand Prix Circuit (PILW1001) DSE? 40m
Fashion Quartet '86 (L0983003) ASE? 90m
Finlandia (image music) (L0781047) DS 50m
Fireworks (50LS5015)CAV DS 30m
Flower Fantasy (TOLB1012) 80m
Follow the Sun (surfing) (51137) AME? 78m
Follow the Sun II (surfing) (511319) AME? 90m
France (101 Strings) (TELD45005) DS 30m
Free Ride (surfing) (G88F0007) ASE? 90m
Free Ride Maui Wave Beat (78LS5001) ASE? 50m
Freefall Skydiving (SS0586019) CAV DS 28m
*From Star Wars to Jedi The Making of a Saga (7001178) AM 66m
From the Windows of the World's Trains (MJL1044) DS 60m
*Godzilla Fantasia (lb) (TLL2055) DS 90m
Golf with Isao Aoki 1 (7000568) CAV AMNE 30m
Golf with Isao Aoki 2 (7000668) CAV AMNE 30m
Golf with Isao Aoki 3 (7000768) CAV AMNE 30m
Golf with Isao Aoki 4 (7000868) CAV AMNE 30m
The Grand Canyon (G78X5330) CAV AS 60m
Grand Prix Motorcross '84 21st Japan Motorcross Grand Prix (68C596062) ASNE 45m
Grand Prix Road Race '84 21st Japan Grand Prix Road Race (68C596062) ASNE 45m
The Great American Roller Coaster 1 (ALLA15) DS 60m
The Great American Roller Coaster 2 (ALLA20) DS 45m
Great Barrier Reef (69C596076) CAV AS 30m
Great Circuses of the World (SS058009) CAV AMNE 60m
Guiana Highlands 1 "The Lost World" (SV0601051) DS 60m
Guiana Highlands 2 (SV0601052) DS 60m
Guitar Bible (55P69035) DS 43m
H.R. Giger (78LS14) ANE? 42m
H.R. Giger (78LS13) AME? 34m
H.R. Giger (78LS37) AME? 50m
Halley's Comet, The (78TX5) CAV ASE? 44m
Hawaiian Sunset (TOLB1016) DS 45m
Heli-Skiing (NDE01) ASNE 60m
Hokaido Foxes (L1005031) ASNE 117m
Hollywood Legends 1 Marilyn Monroe (HCL5001) E?
Hollywood Legends 2 Grace Kelley (HCL5002) E?
Hollywood Legends 3 Steve McQueen (HCL5003) E?
Hollywood Legends 5 Gregory Peck (HCL5006) E?
Howzit Bradda! (surfing) (NDS3002) ASE? 70m
Hungary (TOLB1013) 40m
*I Clowns (lb) (OOLS80147) AM 91m
Image Pops 1 Comedy (no audio) (SC0306111) CAV 30m
Image Pops 2 Sport (no audio) (SC0306112) CAV 30m
Image Pops 3 Science Fiction (no audio) (SC0306113) CAV 30m
Image Pops 4 Dance (no audio) (SC0306114) CAV 30m
Image Pops 5 '50's (no audio) (SC0306115) CAV 30m
Image Pops 6 '60's (no audio) (SC0306116) CAV 30m
Infinite Escher: The Work of M.C. Escher (CSLW1219) DS 40m
Ingrid (SF0501565) AME? 70m
Inter Stellar (game disc) (SS0980008) CAV SNE
International Airports in Europe (KKL2) E?
Irish Horses (G98K2826) CAV ASE? 57m
Island Breeze (windsurfing) (MS162) CAV AS 60m
Italian Museum (101 Strings) (TELD45006) 30m
Italian Ski Beat Vol. 1 (ALLA16) DSE? 60m
Italian Ski Beat Vol. 2 (ALLA17) DSE? 60m
Italian Ski Beat Vol. 3 (ALLA18) DSE? 45m
Italian Ski Beat Vol. 4 (ALLA19) DSE? 45m
*Invitation to a Little 'Orgel Museum' (LVD510) DS 50m
Jacky ICKX (auto racing) (68C596125) AME? 55m
Jamaica (68C596229)CAV DSE? 30m
James Bond Happy Anniversary 007 (NJL35041) AM 60m
Japan's Defense Force: The Air Armaments (SV0331042) NE
Japan's Defense Force: The Ground Armaments (SV0331040) NE
Japan's Defense Force: The Maritime Armaments (SV0331041) NE
Jet Stream (JAC1) DS 51m
Jet Stream B-747 & DC-10 Duo First Flight (78LS82003) CAV DS 25m
Jet Stream B-747 Cockpit (L0789013) DS 29m
Jet Stream B-747 Cruising (W78L8001) DS 29m
Jet Stream B-747 Super Flight (88LS82001) DS 50m
Jet Stream Hawaii (0789013) DS 29m
Jet Stream Orient Express (L0789015) DS 29m
Jet Stream South Pacific (JALC101) DS 27m
Jet Stream West Coast (78LS82002) CAV DS 25m
Joe Piscopo (G88X5311) AS 55m
John McEnroe/Ivan Lendl (G68X5337) ASE? 45m
John Sanborn (video art) (SS0786012) CAV AS 60m
K2 (DW033) ASNE 118m
Kenwood Dennard Drums Seminar (78C586031) ASE? 60m
*Kitties & Puppies (78SX2) AS 116m
Lake Baikal (DW003) CAV AMNE 50m
Lambada Dance Party (ESLU83) DSE? 35m
Last Paradise "Bali" (64C596249) DS 30m
Let's Dance (instructional) (SS1480023) CAV ASNE 180m
Li Kiang River (DW040) CAV AMNE 50m
Life of Birds Fall & Winter (SS005) CAV AMNE 113m
Life of Birds Spring & Summer (SS004) CAV AMNE 104m
Life Underwater (SS002) CAV AMNE 120m
Little Kyoto I (ALLA12) DSNE 60m
Little Kyoto II (ALLA13) DSNE 60m
Little League Baseball 1 (HS003) CAV AMNE 50m
Little League Baseball 2 (HS004) CAV AMNE 50m
Living Desert (SF0780108) AM 69m
Los Angeles: Starlight City (CSLW1269) DSE? 42m
*Louvre (G128Q0005) CAV AMNE 120m
Luchino Visconti (SF0471566) AME? 71m
Macross SF Challenge Game (L0989001) CAV ASNE
The Magic Mountain (amusement park) (ALLA14) DS 60m
*Making of Godzilla (lb) (TLL2038) AMNE 104m
Making of Labyrinth (EHL8001) DI 57m
Making of Ran (GF785012) AMNE 77m
Making of Superman (G88X0042) AM 98m
Maldives (image) (68C596074) CAV AS 30m
Margot Fonteyn Story (PILC1013) DS 90m
Marine Fantasia (TOLB1022) DS 40m
Marine Flower (SS0986014) CAV DS 52m
Mauritius: Elegant Resort (POLV1014) DSE? 41m
Memories of Japan Grand Prix (78LW1) ASNE 59m
*Men Who Made the Movies: Alfred Hitchcock (SS0580046) CAV AM 58m
Modern Combat Aircraft 1 Combat Helicopters (68C596245)CAV AME? 57m
Modern Combat Aircraft 2 West's Land-Based Fighters/Bombers (68C596246)CAV AME? 60m
Modern Combat Aircraft 3 F-18 Carrier Borne (68C596247)CAV AME? 60m
Modern Combat Aircraft 4 F-4 Phantom II (68C596248)CAV AME? 60m
More Kitties & Puppies (68SX12) AS 60m
*Motorcycle Crashes Vol. 2 (68C596177) CAV AS 30m
Mt. Fuji Travelog (BV0601004) DSNE 45m
MTB Touring (Mountain Bike) (TSMB67001) DS 41m
Mysterious Mammals of Australia (G98K2802) CAV AS 58m
National Geographic 2500 Metres Underwater (G98K2820) CAV AS 58m
National Geographic Among the Wild Chimpanzees (G98K2801) CAV AS 58m
National Geographic Atocha (G98K2817) CAV AS 58m
National Geographic Creatures of the Nambib (G98K2810) CAV AS 58m
National Geographic Crocodiles (G98K2820) CAV AS 58m
National Geographic Egypt Gods of Eternity (G98K2805) CAV AS 58m
National Geographic Insects (G98K2814) CAV AS 58m
National Geographic Land of the Tiger (G98K2807) CAV AS 58m
National Geographic Nocturnal Animals (G98K2823) CAV AS 58m
National Geographic Place of Dry Water (African Wildlife) (G98K2805) CAV AS 58m
National Geographic Polar Bear Alert (G98K2818) CAV AS 58m
National Geographic Rain Forest (G98K2811) CAV AS 58m
National Geographic Save the Panda (G98K2819) CAV AS 58m
National Geographic Secrets of the Titanic (G98K2823) CAV AS 58m
National Geographic The Great Whales (G98K2809) CAV AS 58m
National Geographic The Invisible World (G98K2804) CAV AS 58m
National Geographic The Sharks (G98K2813) CAV AS 58m
National Geographic The Violent AME?rth (Born of Fire) (G98K2806) CAV AS 58m
National Geographic Trains (G98K2812) CAV AS 58m
National Geographic Wonderous Actions in Nature (G98K2822) CAV AS 58m
National Ski Method of Japan (HS023) CAV AMNE 57m
Natural States (68C596206) DS 45m
Naturing Special 1 Kishi Keiko's River Nile 6700 Kilos (MJL1046) DSE? 120m
Naturing Special 2 Andes (MJL1037) DSE? 120m
Naturing Special 3 Nishida Toshiyuki 365 Days of Alaska (MJL1038) DSE? 120m
New York Cosmos 1977-1980 (NJL34011) AME? 116m
NHK Audio Graphic Caribbean Sea Paradise Island (W48L1019) DS 50m
NHK Great Barrier Reef (W48L1020) DS 45m
NHK Louvre Art Museum Vol. 1 (SV1001043) DSE? 103m
NHK Louvre Art Museum Vol. 2 (SV1001044) DSE? 103m
NHK Louvre Art Museum Vol. 3 (SV1001045) DME? 100m
NHK Louvre Art Museum Vol. 4 (SV1001046) DME? 100m
NHK Louvre Art Museum Vol. 5 (SV1001047) DME? 100m
NHK Louvre Art Museum Vol. 6 (SV1001048) DME? 100m
NHK Louvre Art Museum Vol. 7 (SV1001049) DME? 100m

NHK Special The Imperial Palace (GV1161004) AMNE 100m
NHK Summer in Hokaido (W48L1018) DS 50m
Niagra Canadian Color (68C596226) DS 41m
1984 Olympics: Gymnastics (98C596042) AME? 120m
1984 Olympics: Swimming (98C596046) AME? 60m
1984 Olympics: Track & Field (98C596045) AME? 60m
1984 Olympics: Volleyball (98C596049) AME? 60m
1984 Olympics: Weight Lifting (98C596048) AME? 60m
1984 Olympics: Wrestling (98C59047) AME? 60m
1990 Safari Rally Kenya (PCLP00057) E? 45m
"Ocean Wind" Wind of Hawaii (101 Strings) (TELD45004) DS 30m
Old Trains (78C596211) AMNE 58m
On Any Sunday II (NDS3001) AM 90m
100 Years of U.S. Golf 1888-1988 (CSLW1299) AMNE 90m
1000 Miglia (101 Strings) (TELD45007) 30m
Orient Express (CSLW1224) DS 45m
Palau Majuro (image) (68C596141) CAV AS 30m
Paris Dakar (motorcycle) (78C596028) AMNE 40m
Paris Dakar Rally (SC0786066) AME? 115m
The Pentagon B-2 Stealth (PCLP00014) 30m
*Picasso (SS0986039) CAV AMNE 85m
Poem of Light and Wind (64C596244) DS 32m
Porche 24 Heures Du Mans (L0783001) ASE? 50m
Post Modern in USA (architecture) (TBS004L) CAV ASE? 60m
Propeller Power WWII Aiprlane Catalog (CSLW1181) DS 40m
Rail Travel in Europe (L1002074) ASNE 56m
Rallye Monte Carlo 1984 (68C596036) CAV ASNE 27m
Red Arrows (HBLD60102) AS 30m
Rembrandt (TOLE3026) AME? 110m
Reptiles (G98K2815) CAV ASE? 50m
Rhine River (DW002) CAV AMNE 50m
Ride on Wind (windsurfing) (SM0683047) DS 70m
The Riders: Barry Sheene (G78F5009) ASE? 91m
Ringmasters The Great American Bash (wrestling) (G78X346) ASE? 60m
Road Racing Special (59C506069) CAV ASNE 30m
Road Racing World Championship 500cc (TLL2060) ASNE 60m
The Road Warriors (wrestling) (TLL025) AME? 88m
Rock Guitar Guide Michael Shanker Ron Wood (TED004) CAV AS 60m
*Rockets (DW037) CAV AMNE 108m
Rolling Blaster (game disc) (SS0980044) CAV SNE
Rolling in the Sky Patrol du France (SC0586068) CAV DS 50m
Rolling in the Sky: Blue Impulse (SC0656103) CAV DS 51m
Safari Rally 1984 (68C596037) CAV ASNE 30m
Samba in Rio (LVD526) DS 47m
San Francisco (68C596233) DS 32m
Say Goodbye to the President (PILF1053) AM 71m
Scenes Ski World Cup (DS045) CAV ASNE 30m
Scotland's Grand Slam 1984/Ireland's Triple Crown 1982 (G128S0039) AME? 186m
Seven Days in Space (Discovery Shuttle) (SC0786059) AME? 87m
The 7th Fleet (40LH8043) AS 50m
Seychelles (68C596075) CAV AS 30m
*SFX Museum Vol. 1 Richard Englund, ASC (SS0980005) CAV AM 57m
*SFX Museum Vol. 2 Motion Control (SS0980010) CAV AM 60m
SFX Museum Vol. 3 C.G.I. in SFX (SS0980018) CAV AM 60m
SFX Museum Vol. 4 (SS0986020) CAV AM 60m
SFX Museum Vol. 5 (SS0986034) CAV AM 60m
*SFX Special (SS0980022) CAV AM 57m
Ships (DW036) CAV AMNE 108m
Ships (DW043) AMNE 256m
Silk Road #1 Chang An (DW008) CAV AMNE 50m
Silk Road #2 Across the Yellow River (DW009) CAV AMNE 50m
Silk Road #3 Tung Huang (DW010) CAV AMNE 50m
Silk Road #4 Hei Shui Chen (DW011) CAV AMNE 50m
Silk Road #5 Lo Lan (DW012) CAV AMNE 50m
Silk Road #6 Turkestan (DW014) CAV AMNE 50m
Silk Road #7 Khotan, Uigor Oasis (DW014) CAV AMNE 50m
Silk Road #8 Turfan (DW015) CAV AMNE 50m
Silk Road #9 Tien Shan Pass (DW016) CAV AMNE 50m
Silk Road #10 Tien Shan Northern Route (DW018) CAV AMNE 50m
Silk Road #11 Tien Shan Southern Route (DW017) CAV AMNE 50m
Silk Road #12 From Kashgar to the Pamirs (DW019) CAV AMNE 50m
Silk Road Volumes 1 - 12 (SC4006054) ASNE 600m
Silk Road at Sea 1 (SC0986071) DSNE 110m
Silk Road at Sea 2 Arabia (SC0986072) DSNE 100m
Silk Road at Sea 3 India (SC0986073) DSNE 98m
Silk Road at Sea 5 China/Vietnam (SC0986075) DSNE 98m
Silk Road at Sea 6 (SC0986076) DSNE 98m
Silk Road Series Athens & Istanbul (SS0586009) CAV ASNE 50m
The Silk Road of the Sea/Sens (SM0483299) DSNE 55m
Silk Road Rome to China (SC0486070) DSNE 58m
Silk Road Collection 2 (SC4006055) ASNE 900m
Ski Progress Instruction (TLL2062) CAV AMNE 60m
Ski Super Technic (SS0680049) CAV ASNE 30m
Sky Walking in Hawaii (68C596238) DS 30m
The Sounds of Tubular Swells (surfing) (G88F0118) AME? 82m
*Spacewatch (SW071) CAV AM 60m
Star Fighters (game disc) (SS0980002) CAV ASNE
Stealth (animals) (HBLD60101) ASE? 60m
Steam Engines (VOLD1010) AM 52m
Storm Riders (lb) (L0985006) AME? 76m
Strike Mission (game disc) (PG002) CAV ASNE
Submarine Feelings (underwater image) (68C596144) CAV AS 30m
Sunsets from Hotels around the World (image music) (68C5962042) DS 44m
Super Ski White Jet Alps (G78Q0003) CAV ASNE 50m
Suzuka Race (HBLS60103) DS 90m
Swiss Alps (511320) AS 31m
Swiss Mountain Railway Vol.1 (ALLA26) DS 50m
Swiss Mountain Railway Vol.2 (ALLA27) DS 50m
Switzerland The Alps (C596170) CAV AS 35m
T.G.V. 270km (68LS5035) DSNE 40m
Tadanori Yokoo Mirror Myth (96LW7) AS 54m
Takazumi Katayama (mortorcycle racing) (G68F5008) ASNE 42m
Tall Ships (TOLB1021) DSE? 44m
Terra (image) (58LM15) AS 40m
Terror on Tape (78C596147) AM 84m
*That's Shock (Terror in the Aisles) (lb) (SF0985066) CAV AM 93m
13 Jours En France (C596272) AMNE 109m
This Is Dolby Pro Logic (CSLW1182) DS 30m
Time Capsule '60 Vol. 1 1960-1965 (SM0353459) DS 41m
Time Capsule '60 Vol. 2 1966-1970 (SM0353460) DS 36m
Tomosuke Noda: Canoe Touring (CT67000) DS 55m
Tournament of Wimbledon 1971-1980 (DS041) CAV 58m
Trade Wind (TOLB1017) DS 55m
Trade Wind Windsurfing Watersailing Sufsailing (L0883002) ASNE 55m
Trains Africa (DW031) CAV AMNE 50m
Trains France (DW030) CAV AMNE 50m
Trains Great Britain (DW029) CAV AMNE 50m
*Trains Japan C62 (DW020) CAV AMNE 55m
Trains Orient Express (DW032) CAV AMNE 55m
Trains Summary of Steam Engines (DW039) CAV AMNE 97m
*Tune Up AV (50LS5023)CAV DS 30m
Tune Up AV II (CSLW1172) CAV DS
*TV Fetish (SS0486013) CAV AS 29m
27 Years of DC-8's (W78L1010)CAV DSE? 28m
U.S. Army (48LH8042) AS 50m
U.S. Marine (40LH8040) 50m
U.S. Modern Jet Fighters (40LH8041) 50m
U.S. Special Forces (40LH8045) AS 50m
U.S.Army Weapons (40LH8044) 50m
U.W.F. Best Bout '88 (PILW1002) AME? 110m
U.W.F. Best Bout '89 (PILW1003) DME? 170m
U.W.F. Official Rule Video (SC0486104) ASE? 60m
Uluwatu Super Session (surfing) (78KX7) ASNE 50m
The Universe Within 1 (N75L5) DSE? 50m
The Universe Within 2 The Heart (N75L6) DSE? 50m
The Universe Within 3 The Digestive System (N75L7) DSE? 50m
The Universe Within 4 The Liver (N75L8) DSE? 50m
The Universe Within 5 Bones and Muscles (N75L9) DSE? 50m
The Universe Within 6 The Lymphatic System (N75L10) DSE? 50m
The Universe Within: CG Special (N28L12)CAV DSE? 14m
USA SL Trains (OL602037) DMNE 50m
Venetian Romance (SM0653376) DS 45m
Views of Mt. Fuji (L090-2009) DS 50m
Vincent: The Life and Death of Vincent Van Gogh (NALA10012) 99m
Vintage Speed Race (antique cars) (LVD522) DSNE 47m
*Visual Pathfinders Bob Abel (SS0980050) CAV AM 57m
Visual Pathfinders Leni Reifenstal (SS0980050) CAV AME? 57m
*Visual Pathfinders Norman McClaren (SS0980051) CAV AM 60m
Viva Ice World (skating) (78C596044) ASE? 74m
Waterfall Symphony (ALLA23) DS 50m
Wavesailing Gals (78LW6) AME? 50m
We Are the World: The Story Behind the Song (G38M0317) DM 54m
West Coast Bike Touring SF-LA (AC200012) 20m
Wet Lips (TED039) AMNE 60m
White Wilderness (SF0780124) AM 72m
Win One's Way: Sky World Cup 1990 (C596348) E? 30m
Wind Riders (58LW2) AMNE 43m
Windy People '90 Camel Supercross (PCLP00083) E? 120m
The Wonderful "Visual Gallery" (8") (LC0248121)CAV DS 14m
World Big Star Golf (CSLW1300) AMNE 90m
The World's Greatest Stunts: A Tribute to Hollywood Stunts (HCL2007) E? 48m
World Endurance Championship in Japan (auto racing) (68C596004) CAV ASNE 30m
World Figure Skating Championships (88TX1) AME? 55m
World GP '83 (DS046) CAV ASNE 81m
World GP '84 (SS0880012) CAV ASNE 88m
World GP '85 (SS0880052) CAV ASNE 90m
World of Bees (SS003) CAV AMNE 60m
World of Birds (G98K2816) CAV ASE? 50m
WSPC Fuji Film Cup '90 (VOLD1009) AS 58m
Yacht Race: Kenwood Cup (W68L1016) DSE? 45m
Yellow River (W98L1002) DSNE 80m
Yoron Paradise on Earth (68C596191) CAV AS 30m

Appendix D: Non-Retail Discs

Sources for titles, which were reviewed in **The Laser Video Disc Companion** but are not available through normal retail outlets, are listed below. Both the price and the source may be subject to change and some of the titles may no longer be 'in print.'

Bio Sci Video Disc
The Death Trap Videodisc
Physics of Sports
VideoDiscovery, PO Box 85878, Seattle WA 98145. $495.

Discursions — Voyager Press, 2139 Manning, Los Angeles CA 90025. $75.

Energy Transformation Using the Bicycle — University of Nebraska-Lincoln, PO Box 80669, Lincoln NE 68501. $125.

Exotic Plants: A Videodisc Compendium — Videotunes, PO Box 339, Soquel CA 95073. $230.

Frame Up 14 Contre 1 — Imedia International, PO Box 347, MIT Branch Post Office, Cambridge MA 02139

Helen L. Allen Textile Collection — Helen L. Allen Textile Collection, 1300 Linden Drive, University of Wisconsin-Madison WI 53706. $250.

The Image Disc — American Association of Physics Teachers, Suite 101, 5110 Roanoke Place, College Park MD 20740. $45.

Images of Antiquity — Rev. Joseph Ponessa, PO Box 70, Malta MT 59538. $57.

Interactive Catalog 1 — George Eastman House, 900 East Avenue, Rochester NY 14607

JPL Public Information Archive (see *The Planetary Image Videodisc Vol. 1*)

National Air & Space Museum Videodisc Series — Smithsonian Institution Press Books, PO Box 1579, Washington DC 20013. $40 each.

The Ninety-Six: A Cattle Ranch in Northern Nevada — American Folklife Center, Library of Congress, Washington DC 20540. $150.

The Planetary Image Videodisc Vol. 1 (PB85-144756)

The Planetary Image Videodisc Vol. 2 (PB85-144764)

Psychology Encyclopedia Video Disc — Scott, Foresman & Co., College Customer Service, (312)729-300. $99.95. Catalog #038610.

JPL Public Information Archive (PB84-191162) — National Technical Information Service, US Department of Commerce, Springfield VA 22161. $50 each.

The Puzzle of the Tacoma Narrows Bridge Collapse — John Wiley & Sons, Inc., 605 Third Avenue, New York NY 10158. $150.

Space Disc Series Optical Data Corporation, PO Box 4919, Warren NJ 07060-4919. Write for price and availability.

Videodisc Music Series — University of Delaware, Office of Computer-Based Instruction, Newark DE 19716. $295.

Whales — National Geographic Society, 17th and M Street NW, Washington DC 20036. $97.50.

NOTE: 'Shared Discs,' in which program material from private sources are combined onto a collective disc, are produced by Comsell Inc., 500 Tech Parkway, Atlanta GA 30313.

Appendix E: Karaoke Titles

'Karaoke' discs are all 8-inch releases, usually containig between three and five songs. The instrumental track to the song plays on the soundtrack, while the lyrics and a simplistic 'video,' some of which are animated, appear on the screen. Special players are equiped with microphones so that a viewer's own voice can be amplified along with the music. No units designed specifically for shower stalls are available at this time.

Laser Karaoke — Video Sing Along Christmas Vol. 1 (WKCH001)PA/88 DS
Laser Karaoke — Video Sing Along Christmas Vol. 2 (WKCH002)PA/89 DS
Laser Karaoke — Video Sing Along Christmas Vol. 3 (WKCH003)PA/89 DS
Laser Karaoke — Video Sing Along Country Vol. 1 (WKCO001)PA/89 DS
Laser Karaoke — Video Sing Along Country Vol. 2 (WKCO002)PA/89 DS
Laser Karaoke — Video Sing Along Country Vol. 3 (WKCO003)PA/89 DS
Laser Karaoke — Video Sing Along Country Vol. 4 (WKCO004)PA/89 DS
Laser Karaoke — Video Sing Along Country Vol. 5 (WKCO005)PA/89 DS
Laser Karaoke — Video Sing Along Country Vol. 6 (WKCO006)PA/89 DS
Laser Karaoke — Video Sing Along Country Vol. 7 (WKCO007)PA/90 DS
Laser Karaoke — Video Sing Along Country Vol. 8 (WKCO008)PA/90 DS
Laser Karaoke — Video Sing Along Country Vol. 9 (WKCO009)PA/90 DS
Laser Karaoke — Video Sing Along 50's Hits Vol. 1 (WK50001)PA/89 DS
Laser Karaoke — Video Sing Along 50's Hits Vol. 2 (WK50002)PA/89 DS
Laser Karaoke — Video Sing Along 50's Hits Vol. 3 (WK50003)PA/89 DS
Laser Karaoke — Video Sing Along 50's Hits Vol. 4 (WK50004)PA/89 DS
Laser Karaoke — Video Sing Along 50's Hits Vol. 5 (WK50005)PA/89 DS
Laser Karaoke — Video Sing Along 50's Hits Vol. 6 (WK50006)PA/89 DS
Laser Karaoke — Video Sing Along 50's Hits Vol. 7 (WK50007)PA/89 DS
Laser Karaoke — Video Sing Along 50's Hits Vol. 8 (WK50008)PA/90 DS
Laser Karaoke — Video Sing Along 80's Hits Vol. 1 (WK80001)PA/89 DS
Laser Karaoke — Video Sing Along 80's Hits Vol. 2 (WK80002)PA/89 DS
Laser Karaoke — Video Sing Along 80's Hits Vol. 3 (WK80003)PA/89 DS
Laser Karaoke — Video Sing Along 80's Hits Vol. 4 (WK80004)PA/89 DS
Laser Karaoke — Video Sing Along 80's Hits Vol. 5 (WK80005)PA/89 DS
Laser Karaoke — Video Sing Along 80's Hits Vol. 6 (WK80006)PA/89 DS
Laser Karaoke — Video Sing Along 80's Hits Vol. 7 (WK80007)PA/89 DS
Laser Karaoke — Video Sing Along 80's Hits Vol. 8 (WK80008)PA/89 DS
Laser Karaoke — Video Sing Along 80's Hits Vol. 9 (WK80009)PA/90 DS
Laser Karaoke — Video Sing Along 80's Hits Vol. 10 (WK80010)PA/90 DS
Laser Karaoke — Video Sing Along 80's Hits Vol. 11 (WK80011)PA/90 DS
Laser Karaoke — Video Sing Along 80's Hits Vol. 12 (WK80012)PA/90 DS
Laser Karaoke — Video Sing Along 80's Hits Vol. 13 (WK80013)PA/90 DS
Laser Karaoke — Video Sing Along 80's Hits Vol. 14 (WK80014)PA/90 DS
Laser Karaoke — Video Sing Along 80's Hits Vol. 15 (WK80015)PA/90 DS
Laser Karaoke — Video Sing Along Nursery Vol. 1 (WKNU001)PA/89 DS
Laser Karaoke — Video Sing Along 70's Hits Vol. 1 (WK70001)PA/89 DS
Laser Karaoke — Video Sing Along 70's Hits Vol. 2 (WK70002)PA/89 DS
Laser Karaoke — Video Sing Along 70's Hits Vol. 3 (WK70003)PA/89 DS
Laser Karaoke — Video Sing Along 70's Hits Vol. 4 (WK70004)PA/89 DS
Laser Karaoke — Video Sing Along 70's Hits Vol. 5 (WK70005)PA/89 DS
Laser Karaoke — Video Sing Along 70's Hits Vol. 6 (WK70006)PA/89 DS
Laser Karaoke — Video Sing Along 70's Hits Vol. 7 (WK70007)PA/89 DS
Laser Karaoke — Video Sing Along 70's Hits Vol. 8 (WK70008)PA/89 DS
Laser Karaoke — Video Sing Along 70's Hits Vol. 9 (WK70009)PA/89 DS
Laser Karaoke — Video Sing Along 70's Hits Vol. 10 (WK70010)PA/89 DS
Laser Karaoke — Video Sing Along 70's Hits Vol. 11 (WK70011)PA/89 DS
Laser Karaoke — Video Sing Along 70's Hits Vol. 12 (WK70012)PA/90 DS
Laser Karaoke — Video Sing Along 70's Hits Vol. 13 (WK70013)PA/90 DS
Laser Karaoke — Video Sing Along 70's Hits Vol. 14 (WK70014)PA/90 DS
Laser Karaoke — Video Sing Along 70's Hits Vol. 15 (WK70015)PA/90 DS
Laser Karaoke — Video Sing Along 70's Hits Vol. 16 (WK70016)PA/90 DS
Laser Karaoke — Video Sing Along 70's Hits Vol. 17 (WK70017)PA/90 DS
Laser Karaoke — Video Sing Along 60's Hits Vol. 1 (WK60001)PA/89 DS
Laser Karaoke — Video Sing Along 60's Hits Vol. 2 (WK60002)PA/89 DS
Laser Karaoke — Video Sing Along 60's Hits Vol. 3 (WK60003)PA/89 DS
Laser Karaoke — Video Sing Along 60's Hits Vol. 4 (WK60004)PA/89 DS
Laser Karaoke — Video Sing Along 60's Hits Vol. 5 (WK60005)PA/89 DS
Laser Karaoke — Video Sing Along 60's Hits Vol. 6 (WK60006)PA/89 DS
Laser Karaoke — Video Sing Along 60's Hits Vol. 7 (WK60007)PA/89 DS
Laser Karaoke — Video Sing Along 60's Hits Vol. 8 (WK60008)PA/89 DS
Laser Karaoke — Video Sing Along 60's Hits Vol. 9 (WK60009)PA/89 DS
Laser Karaoke — Video Sing Along 60's Hits Vol. 10 (WK60010)PA/89 DS
Laser Karaoke — Video Sing Along 60's Hits Vol. 11 (WK60011)PA/89 DS
Laser Karaoke — Video Sing Along 60's Hits Vol. 12 (WK60012)PA/89 DS
Laser Karaoke — Video Sing Along 60's Hits Vol. 13 (WK60013)PA/90 DS
Laser Karaoke — Video Sing Along 60's Hits Vol. 14 (WK60014)PA/90 DS
Laser Karaoke — Video Sing Along 60's Hits Vol. 15 (WK60015)PA/90 DS
Laser Karaoke — Video Sing Along 60's Hits Vol. 16 (WK60016)PA/90 DS
Laser Karaoke — Video Sing Along 60's Hits Vol. 17 (WK60017)PA/90 DS
Laser Karaoke — Video Sing Along Standards Vol. 1 (WKST001)PA/89 DS
Laser Karaoke — Video Sing Along Standards Vol. 2 (WKST002)PA/89 DS
Laser Karaoke — Video Sing Along Standards Vol. 3 (WKST003)PA/89 DS
Laser Karaoke — Video Sing Along Standards Vol. 4 (WKST004)PA/89 DS
Laser Karaoke — Video Sing Along Standards Vol. 5 (WKST005)PA/89 DS
Laser Karaoke — Video Sing Along Standards Vol. 6 (WKST006)PA/89 DS
Laser Karaoke — Video Sing Along Standards Vol. 7 (WKST007)PA/89 DS
Laser Karaoke — Video Sing Along Standards Vol. 8 (WKST008)PA/89 DS
Laser Karaoke — Video Sing Along Standards Vol. 9 (WKST009)PA/89 DS
Laser Karaoke — Video Sing Along Standards Vol. 10 (WKST010)PA/90 DS
Laser Karaoke — Video Sing Along Standards Vol. 11 (WKST011)PA/90 DS
Laser Karaoke — Video Sing Along Standards Vol. 12 (WKST012)PA/90 DS
Laser Karaoke Video Sing Along Vol. 1 O(PA84K001)PA/81-84 AS
Laser Karaoke Video Sing Along Vol. 2 O(PA84K002)PA/81-84 AS
Laser Karaoke Video Sing Along Vol. 3 O(PA84K003)PA/81-84 AS
Laser Karaoke Video Sing Along Vol. 4 O(PA84K004)PA/81-84 AS
Laser Karaoke Video Sing Along Vol. 5 O(PA84K005)PA/85 AS

Appendix F: CD-Video

5-inch 'CD Videos' are the size of standard CDs and contain one music video followed by three or four audio cuts which have no supporting video material. Not all combi players are equiped to handle them, and the marketing effort supporting their release has not been too successful. All are in digital stereo. Company abbreviations are listed at the beginning of the 'American Releases.'

Angela Winbush: Angel (8707002)PGM/89
Anita Baker: Sweet Love (64001)WB/89
Bon Jovi: Wanted Dead or Alive (8707212)PGM/89
Bon Jovi: Livin' on a Prayer (8707012)PGM/89

Bon Jovi: Never Say Goodbye (8707022)PGM/89
Bon Jovi: You Give Your Love a Bad Name (8707372)PGM/89
Cameo: Candy (8707222)PGM/89
Cameo: Word Up (8707032)PGM/89
Cinderella: The Last Mile (8707482)PGM/89
Cinderella: Nobody's Fool (8707042)PGM/89
Cinderella: Don't Know What You've Got (8707342)PGM/89
Cinderella: Gypsy Road (8707252)PGM/89
Cinderella: Somebody Save Me (8707052)PGM/89
The Cure: Just Like Heaven (64002)WB/89
Dan Reed Network: Get to You (8707302)PGM/89
Dire Straits: Brothers in Arms (25812)WB/89
Dire Straits: Money for Nothing (25813)WB/89
Dire Straits: Sultans of Swing (25814)WB/89
Dire Straits: Twisting by the Fool (25810)WB/89
Dire Straits: Walk of Life (25811)WB/89
Donald Fagen: New Frontier (25679)WB/89
Fat Boys: The Twist (8707422)PGM/89
Fat Boys: Wipeout (8707062)PGM/89
Flight of the Dream Team (CDV8801)Lum/89
Hothouse Flowers: Don't Go (8707492)WB/89
John Cougar Mellencamp: Check It Out (8707292)PGM/89
John Cougar Mellencamp: Lonely Ol' Night (8707082)PGM/89
John Cougar Mellencamp: Paper in Fire (8707072)PGM/89
Kingdom Come: Get It On (8707202)PGM/89
Kingdom Come: What Love Can Be (8707232)PGM/89
KISS: Crazy Crazy Nights (8707092)PGM/89
KISS: Let's Put the X in Sex (8707502)PGM/89
KISS: Tears Are Falling (8707102)PGM/89
KISS: Turn on the Night (8707242)PGM/89
Kool & The Gang: Rags to Riches (8707382)PGM/89
Kool & The Gang: Stone Love (8707112)PGM/89
L.A. Guns: Sex Action (8707282)PGM/89
Level 42: Something About You (8707122)PGM/89
Levert: Casanova (81830)WB/89
Madame X: Just That Kind of Girl (81831)WB/89
Madonna: Papa Don't Preach (25680)WB/89
Men Without Hats: Pop Goes the World (8707182)PGM/89
Moody Blues: I Know You're Out There Somewhere (8707262)PGM/89
Moody Blues: No More Lies (8707262)PGM/89
Moody Blues: Your Wildest Dreams (8707132)PGM/89
New Frontier: Under Fire (8707402)PGM/89
The Rainmakers: Downstream (8707192)PGM/89
Randy Newman: I Love L.A. (25680)WB/89
The Robert Cray Band: Right Next Door (8707142)PGM/89
The Robert Cray Band: Don't Be Afraid of the Dark (8707412)PGM/89
The Robert Cray Band: Smoking Gun (8707152)PGM/89
Rush: The Big Money (8707172)PGM/89
Sa-Fire: Boy, I've Been Told (8707432)PGM/89
Scorpions: Believe in Love (8707352)PGM/89
Scorpions: Big City Nights (8707162)PGM/89
Scorpions: Rhythm of Love (8707272)PGM/89
Tears For Fears: Everybody Wants to Rule the World (8707452)PGM/89
Tony!, Toni!, Tone!: Born Not to Know (8707362)PGM/89
Vanessa Williams: The Right Stuff (8707332)PGM/89
Yngwie Malmsteen: Heaven Tonight (8707312)PGM/89

Appendix G: Video Disc Producers

The following companies, which have licensed titles for replication on laser video disc for the consumer market or have marketed laser video related products, can be contacted at the addresses identified:

Academy Home Entertainment
Box 788 Pinehaven Shore Road
Shelburne VT 05482

CBS/Fox Home Video
P.O. Box 900
Los Angeles CA 90035

Coliseum Video
430 West 54 Street
New York NY 10019

Grollier Electronic Publishers
95 Madison Avenue
New York NY 10003

Image Entertainment
9333 Oso Avenue
Chatsworth CA 91311

Lumivision Corporation
1490 Lafayette Street
Suite 305
Denver CO 80218

LVA Film Classics
Laservision Associates
Michael Agee
PO Box 5023
Garden Grove CA 92645

MasterVision
969 Park Avenue
New York NY 10028

MCA/Universal Home Video
70 Universal City Plaza
Universal City CA 91608

MGM/UA Home Video
10000 Washington Boulevard
Culver City CA 90232

MPI Home Video
15825 Rob Roy Drive
Oak Forest IL 60452

Optical Data Corporation
PO Box 4919
Warren NJ 07060-4919

Pacific Arts Video
50 North La Cienega Boulevard
Beverly Hills CA 90211

Paramount Home Video
5555 Melrose Avenue
Los Angeles CA 90038-3197

Pioneer Electronics Coporation
4-1, Meguro 1-Chome, Meguro-ku
Tokyo 153 JAPAN

Pioneer LDCA
2265 East 220 Street
PO Box 22782
Long Beach CA 90801-5782

Polygram Music Video
A&M Video
Deutshche Grammaphon
London Records
Philips Video Classics
825 8th Avenue
New York NY 10019

RCA/Columbia Home Video
2901 West Alameda Avenue
Burbank CA 91505

Reference Recordings
PO Box 77225X
San Francisco CA 94107

Republic Pictures Home Video
PO Box 66930
Los Angeles CA 90066-0930

Sony Video
1700 Broadway
New York NY 10019

3M/Optical Recording Project
223-5S-01 3M Center
St. Paul MN 55144

VidAmerica
235 East 55 Street
New York NY 10022

Vestron Video
PO Box 4000
Stamford CT 06907

The Voyager Company
1351 Pacific Coast Highway
Santa Monica CA 90401

The Voyager Company (Janus Films)
888 Seventh Avenue
Fourth Floor
New York NY 10106

Walt Disney Home Video
Touchstone Home Video
Buena Vista Home Video
Hollywood Pictures Home Video
500 South Buena Vista Street
Burbank CA 91521

Warner Elektra/Asylum
75 Rockefeller Plaza
21st Floor
New York NY 10019

Warner Home Video
4000 Warner Boulevard
Burbank CA 91522

Appendix H: Bibliography

Much of **The Laser Video Disc Companion** originally appeared in **The Laser Disc Newsletter**. The **Newsletter** is published monthly and is devoted solely to laser video discs. A free sample can be obtained by writing Suite 428-B, 496A Hudson Street, New York NY 10014.

Two other monthly periodicals which emphasize laser video discs and maintain a steady publication schedule are **The Laser Disc Gazette** (Road 2, Box 654, Harpers Ferry WV 25425), published by Rad Bennett, and **LASERSCENE** (formerly **LASERviews**, 386 Noe Street, San Francisco CA 94114), published by Scott A. Hughes.

Other laser video disc publications still actively publishing include **Laser** (420 4th Avenue, Bethlehem PA 18018) published by Steve McGouldrick and notable for its amazing collection of entertainment-related trivia, and **Pond Scum** (19126-6 Haynes Street, Reseda CA 91335). **MusDisc News** (Department of Music, University of Delaware, Newark DE 19716) covers both educational and consumer music discs. Two British publications that give decent coverage of NTSC discs are **Laser Disc Review** (PO Box 526, London, SW10 9AB, Great Britain), and Stars and Sripes Laser News (5 Sedgemead, Netley Abbey, SO3 5EY Hampshire, Great Britain), which is devoted entirely to NTSC discs.

Laser Video File is a catalog of in-print disc titles which is published semi-annually by New Visions, Inc. (PO Box 828, Westwood NJ 07675). Some Appendix data in **The Laser Video Disc Companion** was verified using this source. The retailer, Sight and Sound (1275 Main Street, Waltham MA 02154), publishes a yearly **Import Catalog**. Some Appendix Import data was obtained or verified using this source. Other import data was obtained from Japanese catalogs, and we are grateful for the translations provided privately to us by Marc Comfort and Tony Tsang. Individual laser video disc and home video companies also publish catalogs and information sheets promoting their products, as do most mail order houses. Notable mail order catalogs that can be used for research include those published by Laser Island (1810 Voorhies Avenue, Brooklyn NY 11235), Barr Digital (2567 152nd Avenue NE Redmond WA 98052), and Starship Audio-Industries (605 Utterback Store Road, Great Falls VA 22066).

The Perfect Vision (PO Box L, Sea Cliff NY 11579) is a glossy quarterly which devoted to high-end home entertainment products, and includes extensive and elaborate coverage of laser video discs. **Video Theater** (1215 Ravenwood, Boulder CO 80303) also covers discs extensively.

Mainstream monthly video publications, such as **Video** (460 West 34 Street, New York NY 10001) and **Video Review** (902 Broadway, New York NY 10010) cover the disc market in a generalized manner. **Billboard** (1 Astor Place, New York NY 10036) includes a regular collumn devoted to discs. Home Electronics industry publications, such as **TWICE** (902 Broadway, New York NY 10010) also provide laser video disc information.

Publications geared and priced for the industrial/professional market, which carry news about educational discs and hardware advancments include **The Videodisc Monitor** (PO Box 26, Falls Church VA 22046), **Optical Memory News** (256 Laguna Honda Boulevard, San Francisco CA 94116), and a variety of publications from Meckler Publishing, 11 Ferry Lane West, Westport CT 06880. Emerging Technology Consultants (PO Box 12444, St. Paul MN 55112) publishes a listing of educational discs, with regular updates. A catalog of educational titles is available from Aimes Media (6901 Woodley Avenue, Van Nuys CA 91406-4878). The International Interactive Communications Society (IICS) is a consortium of video disc professionals, has chapters in every major US city. Many of these groups publish local bullitens. To find out more information, contact the National Headquarters at 2120 Steiner Street, San Francisco CA 94115.

Some publications have gone out of print, but may still be available from collectors. **Laser Works** (1984-85) was a general interest laser video disc publication. **The Laser Trader** (1985-86) emphasized the DiscoVision collector's market. **LaserNews** (1987) concentrated on hardware and peripherals, and was a precurser to **Video Theater**. **Disc Deals** (1985-87) was a general interest laser video disc publication which emphasized reader *participation*. **The Laser Collector** (1988-89) also encouraged reader participation and was oriented towards disc reviews. **Disc Disciple** (1987) was also review oriented, as were **Laser Video Magazine** (1989), and **Straight Laser** (1989). **Videofax** (1988), a glossy high-end home entertainment quarterly, was eventually merged with **The Perfect Vision**.

Books about laser video discs have been few and far, far between. All cover either the industrial market or the market as it existed during the DiscoVision eras. **Video Discs The Technology, The Applications, and The Future** by Efrem Sigel, Mark Schubin, Paul F. Merrill, with Kenneth Christie, John Rusche, and Alan Horder (Van Nostrand Reinhold Company, 135 West 50 Street, New York NY 10020) contains a history of the video disc, extensive details on how video discs are produced, and dated market projections. **The Videodisc Book A Guide and Directory 1984 Edition** by Rodney Daynes and Beverly Butler (John Wiley & Sons, Inc. 305 THird Avenue, New York NY 10158) contains essays on vide disc 'authoring' and production tips, along with another history of the technology and an attempted listing of every video disc, consumer and industrial, which had been produced up to 1984. Much of the material in The Laser Video Disc Companion concerning the history of the laser video disc, and some concerning its technology, was culled from both of these sources.

Optical Recording Project/3M (223-5S 3M Center, St. Paul MN 55144) has a manual/brochure entitled **Premastering/Post Production Procedures for Scotch Videodiscs** which provides a very thorough explanation of the process required to take a movie and turn it inteo a laser disc. We relied on this publication for some technical details, and also drew valuable information from the Pioneer demo disc, *Laserdisc What It Is & How It Works* (USP-001), which was sent to us, gratis, when we bought our first player. The disc stars Mr. Wizard, who leaps from explaining the beavior of photons on a sub-atmomic level to rubbing chocolate ice cream across a disc, and is still a favorite way to explain the technology to visitors.

The Educator's Handbook to Interactive Videodisc by Ed Scwartz (Association for Educational Communications & Technology, 1126 16th Street NW, Washington DC 20036) and **Should Schools Use Videodiscs?**, an ITTE Technology Leadership Network Special Report (National School Boards Association, 1680 Duke Street, Alexandria VA 22314) survey the utilization of interactive video discs in the classroom environment. James Lardner has written an excellent chronicle of the birth of the entire home video industry, **Fast Forward**, published by W.W. Norton & Co. (500 Fifth Avenue, New York NY 10017).

A more complete bibliography is available from The Laser Library, a department of the Nashua Public Library at 2 Court Street, Nashua NH 03060. They also have most of the material on file and would be an excellent startion point for research on the technology and the industry of laser video discs.

The previous edition of **The Laser Video Disc Companion** was published by New York Zoetrope in 1988 and has undergone some revision for its inclusion in this the **Updated Edition**.

ONE HUNDRED GREAT DISCS

The following is a suggested collection of 100 excellent discs which would not only form an ideal 'core' for any enthusiast's library, but would provide entertainment for virtually any private temperment or social gathering. The listing is restricted to domestic discs (if there were one import disc that we could recommend, it would have to be the 'Restored Version' of *The Last Emperor*) and an attept has been made to limit the choices to discs which are still 'in print.' Quality of the transfer and quality of the content have both been taken into account. We have also attempted to keep the titles with high price tags to a minimum.

The Adventures of Captain Marvel
Adventures of Robin Hood (Voyager CLV)
Airport
Bach Six Brandenburg Concertos
Back to the Future
Bambi (CLV)
The Barkleys of Broadway
Beethoven — Symphony No. 9 (Auturo Toscanini Collection)
Beethoven Symphony No. 3 — Brugen
Ben-Hur (Letterboxed)
Ben-Hur A Tale of the Christ
Black Narcisus
Blade Runner (Voyager CLV)
The Bolshoi Ballet Divertissments
Bugs Bunny Classics
Cartoon Classics: Starring Mickey & Minnie/ Starring Chip 'N' Dale
Chaplin Lost and Found: Mutual III
Christmas at Rippon Cathederal
Citizen Kane (Voyager CAV)
Contempt
Daffy! & Porky!
The Dead
Die Hard
Doctor Zhivago (Letterboxed)
Dumbo
El Amor Brujo
El Dorado
Elvis — His 1968 Comeback Special
The Empire Strikes Back (Letterboxed)
Excalibur
The Eye Hears The Ear Sees
Far from the Madding Crowd
50th Anniversary Gone with the Wind
Footlight Parade
For All Mankind (CLV)
Force of Evil
Frankenstein: The Restored Version
The General
Ghostbusters (RCA/Columbia Letterboxed)
The Godfather
The Godfather, Part II
GRP All-Stars Live from the Record Plant
A Hard Day's Night (Voyager CLV)
The Harvey Girls
Hoppity Goes to Town
The Horse's Mouth
The Hound of the Baskervilles/Sherlock Holmes Faces Death
Il Barbiere Di Siviglia (Glyndebourne)
The Invisible Man
It's a Wonderful Life (Republic)
Journey into Fear
King Kong (CLV Voyager)
The King of Hearts
Koyaanisqatsi: Life Out of Balance
La Dolce Vita
The Lady Eve
Laura
Lawrence of Arabia (RCA/Columbia Letterboxed)
Lethal Weapon 2
The Magnificent Ambersons
Mon Oncle (Voyager)
Mozart Le Nozze de Figaro
National Geographic Video — Land of the Tiger
New Year's Concert 1987 — Wiener Philharmoniker — Karajan
A Night at the Opera (CLV)
North by Northwest (MGM/UA)
Notorious (Voyager CLV)
Our Hospitality
Patton
Psycho
Raiders of the Lost Ark
The Red Shoes
Return of the Jedi (Letterboxed)
Seven Samurai (CLV)
Singin' in the Rain (Voyager CLV)
Star Trek Television Series Trouble with Tribles/ Wolf in the Fold
Star Wars (Letterboxed)
State of the Art of Computer Animation
Strangers on a Train
A Streetcar Named Desire
Swing Time (CLV)
That's Entertainment
The Thief of Bagdad (Korda)
The Third Man
The Three Musketeers
Thunderball (Letterboxed)
To Have and Have Not
Touch of Evil
2001: A Space Odyssey (Voyager)
Vertigo
Visual Pathfinders: The World of Charles and Ray Eames
The Voyager Odyssey
West Side Story (Voyager CLV)
Where Eagles Dare
Who Framed Roger Rabbit (CAV)
Windham Hill — Winter
Without a Clue
The Wizard of Oz (50th Anniversary)
Women on the Verge of a Nervous Breakdown
Yojimbo (Voyager)

GUILTY PLEASURES

We could not in all good conscience include the following in the previous list though we sorely wanted to:

Bill Viola Selected Works
Bizet's Carmen
Blue Velvet
Carly Simon Live from Martha's Vineyard
The Crawling Eye
The Doors Dance on Fire
Dragonslayer
Empire of the Sun/A China Odyssey
A Fistful of Dollars (Letterboxed)
Gorky Park
Joseph Campbell and the Power of the Myth
A Nightmare on Elm Street
The Painted Stallion
Predator
sex, lies and videotape (CAV)
The Thing (Letterboxed)
The Thirty Nine Steps (remake)
The Three Stooges Volume VII
Total Recall
Weekend at Bernie's

About BASELINE

BASELINE was founded in 1983 to provide online databases and other information services to the film and TV industries. The world's largest source of information about film and TV, the company now has professional clients around the world in more than thirty countries. More than 25 separate databases list information on hundreds of thousands of film and TV cast and crew members; more than 100,000 films, TV series, specials, movies, and episodes; more than 5,000 film and TV shows currently in production; and more than 15,000 companies active in the industry. Additional services include online news, financial information and communications.

More information about BASELINE is available by calling 1.800.CHAPLIN or writing to us at 838 Broadway, New York, NY 10003 or 8929 Wilshire, Beverly Hills, CA 90211. Many BASELINE services are also available on Mead Data Central's *Nexis* service.

Try FLIKS

FLIKS is BASELINE's online service for film fans. If you have a computer and modem, you can get insider details on films scheduled for release in the upcoming months; reviews of thousands of films, with new releases added weekly; industry standbys such as opening-night audience film evaluations; lists of top current and historical hits, box office successes and bombs; and popularity ratings that don't always agree with the critics. Additional services include topical discussion forums, chat and electronic mail with fellow fans, and classified and personal ads.

For information on how to get FLIKS on your PC or Mac, call BASELINE at 212.254.8235, 310.659.3830, or 1.800.CHAPLIN.